.25

The United Nations and Economic and Social Co-operation

By

ROBERT E. ASHER, WALTER M. KOTSCHNIG,
WILLIAM ADAMS BROWN, JR., AND ASSOCIATES

THE BROOKINGS INSTITUTION
WASHINGTON, D.C.

Published April 1957

Library of Congress Catalogue Card Number 57–9377

Printed in the United States of America
The George Banta Company, Inc.
Menasha, Wisconsin

Preface

In the summer of 1951, the Brookings Institution began a series of studies on the United Nations. The series was initiated by the late Dr. Leo Pasvolsky who, until his death in 1953, was Director of the International Studies Group at the Institution. The general plan for the research was formulated in the winter of 1949–50 when many proposals for changes in the United Nations system were being widely discussed in the United States. Much of the public discussion indicated the need for a systematic analysis of the issues arising from the experience with the United Nations system and for a careful evaluation of the immediate and ultimate implications of the various courses of action being proposed. To assist in meeting this need became, therefore, the central purpose of the Brookings studies.

While this research has been under way, new developments have further affected the attitude of many Americans toward the United Nations, and some American pressures for changes in the United Nations system have been increasing. Now that the General Assembly and the Security Council have agreed in principle that a General Conference should be called at "an appropriate time" for the purpose of reviewing the Charter, it is hoped that the Brookings studies will be of special value in contributing to better public understanding of the problems that will be involved.

The studies are being published in seven volumes, of which some have already appeared. Although these volumes form a related series, each of them constitutes a separate study of a major feature of the United Nations system. The order given below is not the actual order of publication, but it represents the logical arrangement of the series.

One volume is entitled *A History of the United Nations Charter*. It will present, from the American point of view, the evolution and negotiation of the Charter as part of the developing United Nations system during the period from 1940 to 1945. A major purpose of the volume will be to show the principal ideas and proposals considered by the United States Government in reaching its final position on the specific provisions of the Charter.

Three volumes will analyze and appraise the principal activities and organizational problems of the United Nations and its related agencies since January 1946 when the Organization came into being.

One of these, entitled *The Organization and Procedures of the United Nations*, will cover the general organizational development of the United Nations. It will be concerned both with particular organizational problems in each of the principal organs—the General Assembly, the Security Council, the Economic and Social Council, the Trusteeship Council, the International Court of Justice, and the Secretariat—and with some of the general problems encountered, such as the interpretation of the Charter, the definition of domestic jurisdiction, and the admission of new Members.

The second of these, which has already been published, is entitled *The United Nations and the Maintenance of International Peace and Security*. It deals with methods and processes for maintaining peace and security through the United Nations. It covers the procedures that have been developed under the Charter for the peaceful settlement or adjustment of disputes and situations, the use of collective measures in threats to or breaches of the peace, and the regulation of armaments, and seeks to evaluate these methods and processes in light of the conditions in which the United Nations has had to function.

The third, entitled *The United Nations and Promotion of the General Welfare*, will cover the major activities undertaken by the United Nations in response to the insistent pressures that, during the postwar period, have brought to the fore issues in the field of general welfare. The work of the Organization and its related agencies in dealing with problems of international co-operation in economic and social affairs, in the promotion of human rights, and in the advancement of dependent peoples will be analyzed, and the efforts made to harmonize conflicting national views in solving these problems will be appraised. The chapters dealing with human rights, which will comprise Part Three of this volume, and with dependent peoples, which will comprise Part Four, have already been published as separate monographs under the titles of *The United Nations and Human Rights* and *The United Nations and Dependent Peoples*, respectively.

Another volume in the series will deal with *Regional Security and the United Nations*. It will analyze and appraise the history and activities of the principal regional security, collective defense, and similar arrangements that have developed within the framework of the United Nations Charter. The volume will describe how and why the arrangements came into existence and the manner in which they have functioned, and will analyze some of the problems raised by their establishment and operation, both within the scope of the individual groupings and in relation to the broader United Nations system.

A sixth volume, which has already been published, is entitled *Proposals for Changes in the United Nations.* It presents a description and analysis of the principal proposals advanced by governments and by private groups and individuals for changes in the United Nations system. The analysis includes a review of the major arguments advanced both for and against particular proposals, the impact of the proposals on the United Nations, and their implications for United States policy.

The final volume, entitled *The United States and the Future of the United Nations*, will attempt an over-all appraisal of the United Nations system from the American point of view. This volume, which will be based primarily on the studies in the other six volumes, will present general conclusions and recommendations regarding such changes as may appear to be desirable in the United Nations Charter or in the organization and functioning of the system.

The present publication includes the chapters that will comprise Part Two of the volume on *The United Nations and Promotion of the General Welfare.* Separate publication of these chapters in advance of the full volume has been undertaken because of current interest in the subjects they cover. An appropriate index for these materials will be provided in the full volume when it appears later this year.

The preparation of the manuscript for this monograph was a co-operative undertaking. Robert E. Asher was responsible for the preparation of the Introduction and Chapters II, IV, V, X, and XI, and undertook the task of co-ordinating the manuscripts for the other chapters. William Adams Brown, Jr. prepared Chapters I and III, and collaborated with Wilfred Owen and the late Priscilla St. Denis in the preparation of Chapter VI. Walter M. Kotschnig prepared Chapters VII, VIII, and IX. Louis Lazaroff provided materials on which portions of Chapters II and X are based, and Edward G. Posniak provided certain materials for Chapters V and X. A. Evelyn Breck, with the aid of Medora Richardson, edited the final manuscript.

It should be noted that although Mr. Kotschnig was Director of the Office of International Economic and Social Affairs, Department of State, when he wrote the chapters for which he is responsible, he wrote them in his personal capacity. His comments and conclusions do not, therefore, necessarily reflect the official views of the Department of State.

The conclusions in the present study are those of the individual authors. The general conclusions and recommendations that will be made in the final volume on *The United States and the Future of the United Nations* will take into account the conclusions reached in this and the other studies in the series, but they will be formulated from the point of view of the United Nations system as a whole and of United States policy with respect to it.

The authors and the Institution acknowledge with gratitude the many thoughtful comments and constructive suggestions made by a number of present and former officials in both government and international organizations who responded to inquiries or read drafts of the manuscript. Their courtesy and willingness in making their expert knowledge and experience available have aided in clarifying many difficult points and issues. The individual assistance of each of them is greatly appreciated.

After Dr. Pasvolsky's death, Robert W. Hartley was given the responsibility for bringing to completion this series of studies on the United Nations, and the manuscript for the present publication has been prepared under his direction. The Institution has had the benefit of continuing consultation with Ernest A. Gross, James N. Hyde, Joseph E. Johnson, C. Easton Rothwell, and Willard L. Thorp, who comprise an informal group, organized during the summer of 1953, to advise on the direction of the project, and to whom the Institution is heavily indebted for many helpful suggestions.

Finally, on behalf of the Institution, I wish to express grateful appreciation to the A. W. Mellon Educational and Charitable Trust of Pittsburgh for the generous grants that have made possible this series of studies on the United Nations system. The conclusions and recommendations of these studies have been reached, however, wholly independently of the Mellon Trust, which is not to be understood as approving or disapproving the views expressed in this and the other volumes in the series.

ROBERT D. CALKINS
President

February 15, 1957

Contents

THE UNITED NATIONS AND ECONOMIC AND SOCIAL CO-OPERATION

*Introduction**

FOR more than ten years, the United Nations and a group of related specialized agencies have been engaged in a momentous effort to promote orderly economic and social progress in a disorderly world. The fostering of economic growth, social change, and essential cultural adjustment—without sacrificing valued cultural assets or jeopardizing such economic and political stability as may have been achieved—is inherently difficult. The intrinsic complexity of this task has been increased by the political tensions and cleavages that have exacerbated international relations since the close of the Second World War.

When the General Assembly and the Economic and Social Council of the United Nations met for their respective first sessions in January 1946, the world economy was in a critical state and cracks had begun to appear in the wartime alliance. The dominant mood was nevertheless one of hope and confidence. The most devastating war of all time had at long last been brought to an end, and people could again devote their energies to productive undertakings. "Seldom before in human history," said the representative of the United States at the first meeting of the Council, "has an organization been created with greater opportunity to save mankind than has been given to the Economic and Social Council under the Charter of the United Nations."[1]

Bread, milk, meat, sugar, and fats and oils were being rationed in many countries. There were also severe shortages of other essential foodstuffs. The demand for coal, steel, timber, and electric power far exceeded the available supply. Countless homes in Europe and Asia had been destroyed or made uninhabitable, and the remaining dwellings—inadequate before the war—had become dangerously overcrowded in most of the larger cities. Vast numbers of refugees were unable to return to their homelands. Railways, highways, bridges, ports, and factories awaited repair and reconstruction. The prewar network of international trade and payments was disrupted. A welter of problems, long-term and short-term, needed attention.

* By Robert E. Asher.

[1] U.N. Economic and Social Council, First Session, *Official Records*, First Meeting (Jan. 23, 1946), p. 14.

It was recognized that many formidable obstacles would have to be surmounted before international co-operation could contribute significantly to the solution of the outstanding economic and social problems of the day. Some well-informed persons were frankly skeptical and quick to caution against exaggerating the potentialities of the new agencies. In the mood of the time, however, the obstacles to effective collaboration were for the most part viewed through a golden haze, and few appeared insuperable. The United Nations and the specialized agencies, it was assumed by the general public, would play a major role in repairing the ravages of war, in preventing depressions, and in promoting the "conditions of stability and well-being which are necessary for peaceful and friendly relations among nations."[2]

Ten years later the golden haze had been dissipated, and the barriers to international co-operation through global associations of sovereign states had become all too evident. At the same time, underlying conditions had improved tremendously. Both industrial and agricultural production at the end of the first postwar decade were at record levels. So, too, was international trade. Widespread depression had been avoided. Illiteracy had been reduced drastically. Life expectancy had been increased.

How much, if any, of this remarkable improvement in economic and social conditions should be attributed to the efforts of the United Nations and its affiliated agencies? What have been the major accomplishments of the United Nations system in each of the principal fields of activity? Have the organizational and constitutional arrangements impeded or facilitated the various endeavors? Have peaceful and friendly relations among nations been strengthened or strained? Answers to these questions could provide a basis for more realistic expectations regarding the second decade of the United Nations than those of the immediate postwar period.

The close relationship between the maintenance of international peace and security and the promotion of economic and social progress was clearly seen by the United States Secretary of State at a time when plans for the United Nations were still in an embryonic stage. Speaking in the late summer of 1943, he pointed out that:

> The success of an organized system of international cooperation with the maintenance of peace as its paramount objective depends, to an important degree, upon what happens within as well as among nations. We know that political controversies and economic strife among nations are fruitful causes

[2] Charter of the United Nations, Art. 55. For the text of the Charter, see Appendix A.

of hostility and conflict. But we also know that economic stagnation and distress, cultural backwardness, and social unrest within nations, wherever they exist, may undermine all efforts for stable peace.

The primary responsibility for dealing with these conditions rests on each and every nation concerned. But each nation will be greatly helped in this task by the establishment of sound trade and other economic relations with other nations, based on a comprehensive system of mutually beneficial international cooperation, not alone in these respects, but also in furthering educational advancement and in promoting observance of basic human rights.[3]

Thus, from the beginning, the broad purposes of the United Nations have been twofold. There have, however, been important differences in the ways in which these purposes have been fulfilled. The Charter provided in some detail for the methods and processes to be used in the maintenance of international peace and security.[4] But in the solution of problems of an economic, social, cultural, and humanitarian character, the Charter specified only the general objectives to be achieved and authorized the use of a variety of methods and processes to attain those objectives. Much time since 1946, therefore, has been devoted to clarifying concepts, defining functions, and establishing machinery. Because of the very nature of the problems confronting the United Nations in the economic and social field, the Organization and the specialized agencies affiliated with it have become involved in a wide range of complex and controversial undertakings.

Emergency responsibilities of great magnitude have been assumed in connection with relief and rehabilitation in war-devastated areas, and with the care and resettlement of refugees. Noteworthy steps have been taken to deal with such long-range problems as the re-establishment of a functioning network of international trade and financial relationships, the maintenance of full employment, the improvement of social welfare services, and the economic and social development of underdeveloped countries. Serious differences of view have arisen regarding proposals for the promotion and protection of private foreign investment, for mitigating fluctuations in the prices of internationally traded primary commodities, and for supplementing loans to underdeveloped countries with grants-in-aid from an international fund. On the other hand, campaigns against communicable diseases, regulation of the traffic in

[3] "Our Foreign Policy in the Framework of Our National Interests," Radio Address of Sept. 12, 1943, U.S. Department of State *Bulletin*, Vol. 9 (Sept. 18, 1943), p. 177.

[4] See the volume in this Brookings series, *The United Nations and the Maintenance of International Peace and Security*.

STRUCTURE OF THE ECONOMIC AND SOCIAL COUNCIL

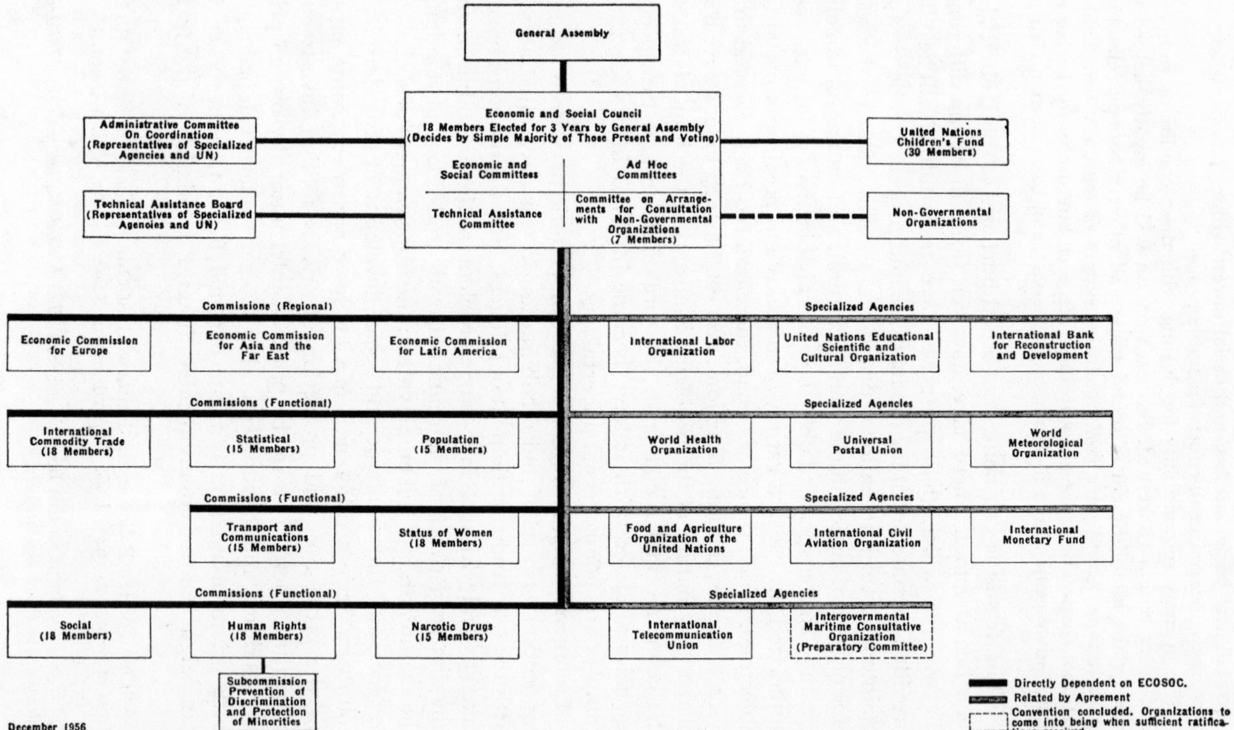

December 1956
Courtesy of U.S. Department of State.

narcotic drugs, and diffusion of agricultural technology have proved relatively noncontroversial.

The Economic and Social Council has been involved to some extent in all of these activities, in ways that have changed significantly over time. Designated by the Charter as a principal organ of the United Nations, it was, by a further provision of the same instrument, placed under the authority of another principal organ—the General Assembly. Moreover, the Council originally consisted of more than one third of the membership of the United Nations. Now that the membership of the Organization has increased to eighty while the membership of the Council remains fixed by the Charter at eighteen, the Council provides a place for fewer than one fourth of the members. This change has also had an effect on relations between the Council and the Assembly.

Under the Council, commissions have been established to deal with regional economic problems, demographic matters, transportation and communication, statistics, narcotic drugs, and other matters. The organizational network also includes—as the accompanying chart shows—ten specialized agencies dealing with labor, health, education, food and agriculture, civil aviation, telecommunications, postal services, meteorology, international investment, and monetary policy.[5]

Some contend that the United Nations has assumed responsibilities for matters that are beyond its proper scope and should be left to the domestic jurisdiction of its Member states. Others argue that, despite the wide range of its activities, the United Nations has not yet really begun to cope with the problems with which it should deal if it is to achieve the broad purposes set forth in its Charter. More co-ordination and consolidation of the organs and agencies have been claimed by some to be a vital need, whereas others have urged continuation of the present arrangements or the granting of even greater autonomy to the component parts of the system.

To aid in a better understanding of these and similar issues, this study seeks to analyze and appraise the major attempts to promote international economic, social, and cultural co-operation through the United Nations system, *i.e.*, through the United Nations Organization and the cluster of specialized agencies that have been brought into relationship with it. The study reviews the more fruitful approaches to international co-operation, indicates where obstacles have been encountered that

[5] For summary information on specialized agencies, see Appendix B; for membership of the United Nations and the specialized agencies, see Appendix C; for membership of the regional economic commissions, see Appendix D.

set limits on such co-operation, and explores the nature of the existing limitations. It deals primarily with work undertaken during the ten years beginning on January 10, 1946, when the first session of the General Assembly was called to order. Where appropriate, however, important developments that occurred during the year 1956 have also been taken into account.

To provide perspective and background, the legacy of relevant experience inherited by the United Nations is described first. The provision of short-term aid in a variety of emergency situations is then discussed. The successes and failures of the United Nations system in dealing with some of the longer-range economic problems are analyzed next, specifically those problems connected with the expansion of international trade and the improvement of payments arrangements, the stimulation of production and investment, the maintenance of full employment and economic stability, and the development of transportation and communication. Reviewed thereafter are diverse programs in the social and cultural fields, including various types of social action to improve levels of living, measures in the interests of welfare and social defense, and international co-operation in educational, scientific, and cultural matters.

The pressing problems of the vast areas no longer resigned to grinding poverty and subordinate status—which are alluded to throughout the volume—are recapitulated and analyzed from a somewhat different point of view in a discussion devoted exclusively to the problems of underdeveloped countries. The endeavors of the United Nations system to cope with these problems are illustrative of a growing fusion of the international economic, social, and cultural programs designed to encourage more rapid growth in the least privileged areas of the world.

The study closes with a summary and appraisal of the record made. Some of the criteria for making this appraisal grow out of the Charter—the objectives it initially stated, the lines of action it laid down. Others derive from the conditions in which the United Nations has had to operate and the unanticipated situations with which it has had to deal. Still others result from the expectations of the peoples in its Member states—their demands, their illusions and disillusions, their fears, and their hopes.

CHAPTER I

*The Inheritance of the United Nations**

THE depression of the 1930's, the Second World War, and the major lines of cleavage between developed countries, underdeveloped countries, and Communist-controlled countries that had become apparent even before the Charter entered into force left a lasting imprint on the economic and social work of the United Nations. In addition, there was in each of the major fields a legacy of specific experience and achievement. In some areas, the new organization was in a position to continue and expand prewar forms of co-operation that had met with general, if not universal, approval. In others, it had to decide whether it should or could supplement or expand emergency measures designed to ease the transition from war to peace. In still others, it had to adjust itself to new forms of long-range international co-operation devised during the war and still untested. Some account of the specific inheritance of the United Nations from the interwar and war years is therefore an essential preliminary to a survey of its economic and social activities.

League of Nations and the Interwar Years

International co-operation on economic and social problems was both intensive and experimental during the interwar period. There was a rich experience, particularly through the League of Nations, in the application of many of the methods and procedures now utilized by the United Nations system.[1] The League, however, did not during these years attempt to bring within its own orbit as wide a range of international activity as the United Nations has done. A history of its economic and social work from 1919 to 1939 would not contain chapters on "Full Employment and Economic Stability" and on "The Problems of the Underdeveloped Countries." The pressures that made these matters a central preoccupation of the United Nations were to a large

* By William Adams Brown, Jr.

[1] See the volume in this Brookings series, *The United Nations and Promotion of the General Welfare*, Part One.

extent the product of events during the depression of the 1930's and the Second World War, and it was only after 1939 that the League became intensively concerned with them.

As has been true in the postwar years, the initiative for certain major efforts of international co-operation during the interwar years came from sources outside the framework of any international organization. The onset of the depression of the 1930's, for example, called forth the greatest mobilization of financial resources to achieve an international objective that had ever been seen up to that time.[2] The League of Nations, not being endowed with vast and readily mobilized resources, was not able to play an important role in this remarkable, if unsuccessful, demonstration of international solidarity at a time of major crisis. Similarly, with the beginnings of recovery, when an effort was made to restore some measure of international collaboration in trade and payments, it was made in large part outside the League of Nations.

Co-operation through international organizations between the wars, nevertheless, deeply influenced the United Nations. Its failures led directly to a wartime search for new methods of organizing international action that would be more effective. Its successes, especially in social co-operation in which the work of the League underwent something of a renaissance after the onset of the depression, led to a search for methods of reviving and expanding types of collaboration that had proved effective.

The major fields of economic and social collaboration during the interwar years were international trade and payments, production and investment, transport and communications, and social and intellectual co-operation. In addition, an attempt was made to improve international co-operation in meeting the needs of individual countries requiring emergency assistance. The first step in tracing the evolution of the concrete problems confronting the United Nations when the Charter entered into force is to indicate the successes and failures recorded in each of these fields.

Co-operation to Meet Disaster Situations

In the special field of emergency aid, the League sponsored an international organization that had the objective of giving first aid and co-

[2] Roger Auboin, *The Bank for International Settlements, 1930–1955*, Essays in International Finance, International Finance Section, Department of Economics and Sociology, Princeton University (1955), p. 10.

ordinating international action in the event of a "major disaster due to *force majeure*."[3] The convention and statutes of this organization, the International Relief Union, were drawn up by a conference convened by the Council of the League in 1927 and came into effect in December 1932. Eventually thirty governments ratified or acceded to the convention, but the United States was not among them.

Between 1932 and the beginning of the Second World War, when its activities were interrupted, the General Council of the Union met only twice. It contributed £1,000 to assist earthquake victims in two Indian districts in 1934, and sent some relief to earthquake victims in Baluchistan a year later. The bulk of its work was devoted to research on preventive measures that could be taken against disaster.

This effort, though well intended, could not be regarded as successful, and the International Relief Union was eventually liquidated by the United Nations.[4]

International Trade and Payments

Between the end of the First World War and the onset of the depression, no less than five important international conferences were called in an effort to reach agreement on general principles of conduct in the field of trade and payments. In these conferences, a large measure of agreement was reached on the desirability of incorporating, in commercial agreements, a most-favored-nation clause under which all supplying countries would be given equal treatment in the application of tariff rates to a given product. There was also general agreement on the necessity of checking competitive increases in tariffs, eliminating exchange controls and other nontariff barriers to trade, and returning to stable exchange rates. In an effort to give effect to these agreed principles, many methods were used, including protocols, conventions, and internationally agreed standards and models. Among these were a draft Convention on Prohibitions, a treaty for the Protection of Foreign Nationals and Enterprises, a draft treaty on the Protection of Industrial Property, a Model Convention for the Simplification of Customs Formalities, and a standard classification of customs nomenclature.

A great part of the work of drawing up these instruments was done

[3] U.N. Economic and Social Council, Tenth Session, *Relations with Inter-Governmental Organizations: Report by the Secretary-General*, Annex III, Doc. E/1574/Add. 1 (Jan. 23, 1950), p. 2

[4] See below, Chap. II.

by experts of the League of Nations. Much of it was enduring, for it was later drawn upon heavily in all the technical aspects of postwar co-operation in this field. With one exception, however, this work did not go to the heart of the central problems raised by the high-sounding resolutions of the major conferences. The exception was the draft Convention on Prohibitions, which contained definite commitments against the use of quantitative restrictions on trade and exchange controls except under certain specified conditions. The draft Convention on Prohibitions, which would have come into force if only one additional country had adhered to it, was the high-water mark in the effort to translate agreed principles into action prior to the depression. The next stage was a series of desperate actions in 1930 to stem a world-wide upward trend of tariffs. Among these were an International Conference for a Tariff Truce called by the League of Nations, the drafting of a Commercial Convention and a protocol for future negotiations, and the calling of an international conference to put the protocol into effect.

A final effort to check these trends was made at the London Economic Conference of 1933. Until then, most of the actions described above were either wholly or mainly European. It became clear, however, that regional collaboration could not cope with world-wide economic forces in a time of major crisis. It was also made clear that, once a chain reaction of economic defense and counterdefense is set in motion, the battle for international collaboration to uphold agreed principles by conventions, protocols, and conferences is already three quarters lost. The failure of the London Conference proved that this battle is wholly lost if great trading powers all give priority to domestic considerations or operate on different sets of priorities when domestic and international policies come into conflict.

The stated objectives of the London Economic Conference were in consonance with the principles laid down by the earlier conferences, but no agreement was reached on how domestic and international measures should be combined to give effect to these principles. The conference broke down because countries imposing direct trade and exchange controls would not relax them until currency stabilization was assured; countries on the gold standard (with bitter experience in inflation) would not adopt price-raising policies for fear of inflation; Great Britain would not adopt price-raising policies and a large public works program at the risk of unbalancing its budget; and the United States would not allow a domestic price-raising program to be interfered with by currency stabilization.

After the failure of the London Conference, the retreat from liberal trading principles became a rout. A large part of the trade in Central Europe and almost all of the trade of Europe with Latin America became bilateral. New philosophies of trade were developed that were hostile to multilateralism and to the most-favored-nation treatment, and these led to the growth of government-controlled trade, the planning of international trade, and the acceptance of autarchy as an objective of economic policy. Under German leadership and example, trade in a large part of Europe was made an instrument for increasing war potential and a weapon to achieve political aims. New administrative techniques of trade, both for offense and defense, were perfected, including clearing payments and compensation agreements, the control of trade and capital movements by exchange regulations, and the use of multiple exchange rates.

Although the League of Nations was opposed to these divisive tendencies, it made no further attempt to convene general conferences on international trade and exchange problems. Instead, meetings were organized "limited to certain groups of states which had the same kind of problems to face, either because of geographical propinquity or some other common feature, or attended by officials, groups or individuals interested in trade in particular commodities."[5] The League of Nations also drew up model conventions on double taxation, which became the basis of some two hundred agreements, and made a number of major economic reports.

These activities of the League kept the banner of liberal trading principles flying, but the two major attempts to revive them in practice, after the failure of the London Conference, were initiated by the United States. The first was the Trade Agreements Act of 1934, which, by giving the President authority—for a limited period of time—to enter into trade agreements without obtaining congressional approval for each agreement, made the reciprocal lowering of barriers a more feasible undertaking. Agreements negotiated under this program incorporated the unconditional most-favored-nation principle and also contained general clauses relating to nontariff barriers to trade that were in harmony with the recommendations of these conferences and of the experts of the League of Nations.

The second attempt was the Tripartite Declaration of 1936 dealing with foreign exchange policy. This declaration, signed by France, the United States, and the United Kingdom, contained a pledge that the

[5] F. P. Walters, *A History of the League of Nations*, Vol. 2 (1952), pp. 749–52.

adhering governments would maintain the greatest possible equilibrium in the system of international exchanges and would support a general policy of relaxing progressively the existing system of quotas and exchange controls with a view to their abolition. This fresh affirmation of principles previously accepted was accompanied by a statement that the signatories would pursue a policy that would tend to promote prosperity in the world and improve the standard of living. The new emphasis on the standard of living, which had been lacking in earlier declarations and agreements, was from this time carried forward into all future negotiations and debates on the general problems of trade and payments.

This new approach was due in large measure to the acceleration during the depression of four basic trends in the formulation of commercial policy—trends that have widened the area of international conflict on many issues. They are: (1) special treatment of agricultural products in international trade; (2) the growth of international cartels; (3) the growth of regional and preferential arrangements; and (4) the subordination of commercial policy to employment and development policy. Even during the interwar period the first three of these trends posed the twin problems that have hampered postwar efforts to achieve a harmony of national views both within the United Nations and outside it: namely, conflicting approaches by a single country to different trade problems, and conflicting approaches of different countries to a single such problem.

The earlier failures of the League of Nations to obtain observance by its members of general principles governing international trade and monetary policies also demonstrated the inherent weakness of international action that goes no further than resolutions and recommendations. The alternative was to induce countries to undertake specific commitments—for example, by becoming members of new international agencies of a more specialized type. Firmly held attitudes, however, toward currency stabilization, the maintenance of employment in domestic industry and agriculture, and other matters affecting international trade and payments, were largely responsible for the insistence of many countries that these new agencies should not be given authority to interfere with the domestic policies of their members. Yet the same experience that increased the sensitiveness of countries to any outside interference in their domestic policies also increased their awareness of the basic need for harmonizing domestic and foreign policies with respect to trade and payments if a workable world trading system were to be reconstituted. This experience also proved that the problem of operating such a system effectively cannot be separated from that of preventing the international spread of depressions.

Production and Investment

During the interwar period, the concern of international agencies with production and investment problems took three principal forms. The first was encouragement of co-operation between labor and management for increased production and productivity, with a view to improved labor standards. This was an integral part of the work of the International Labour Organisation (ILO). The second was the assembly of information relating to world production and the analysis of influences affecting its fluctuations. This was an important part of the work of the Secretariat of the League of Nations, which regularly collected and published production statistics and, in its annual *World Economic Survey* and in special studies, analyzed the factors currently affecting production.[6] Third, there was the mobilization of credits and loans to meet the emergency problems of individual countries. This last was the major concern of the Financial Committee of the League.

The activities of the Financial Committee passed through four distinct phases, the first of which involved an attempt to put into effect an International Credits Scheme, the essence of which was the creation of a new type of security to be placed in the private financial market. Although this scheme was a failure, it laid the groundwork for the next phase. The second phase involved the development of reconstruction schemes for particular countries obtaining loans with the help of the League of Nations. It required no basic change in the principles of the International Credits Scheme, but considerable modification in its techniques as applied to individual countries. In particular, it involved the appointment of commissioners of the League with extensive powers. The two great successes of this phase were the reconstruction of Austria and Hungary in 1921 and 1924, but loans were also granted by the League to Esthonia and Danzig, and similar plans were considered for Albania, Portugal, and Rumania. The granting of extensive control over internal domestic economic and financial policies to an international agency in return for financial assistance was a feature of all these operations.

[6] See League of Nations, *Memorandum on Production and Trade, 1925 to 1929/30* (1931), and *World Production and Prices, 1938/39* (1939).

The third phase involved the application of the same principles and techniques to assist Greece and Bulgaria in connection with their serious refugee problems. The purpose of the League of Nations was to aid in absorbing these refugees into the economies of the receiving countries, and to do this, it had to be concerned with the whole range of their economic and financial problems. The fourth phase, which disclosed some of the basic weaknesses of the techniques employed by the League, was characterized by a second appeal for help from Austria, Hungary, Greece, and Bulgaria in the early stages of the depression of the 1930's. For many reasons, it proved impossible for the League to provide financial resources and to do more than offer advice and make general recommendations.

The work of the Financial Committee was a pioneering effort to meet problems that reappeared under another guise after the war and later had to be dealt with by different methods. The International Credits Scheme, for example, was the first serious attempt to develop the idea of mobilizing private financial resources with the aid of a guarantee by an international agency. The reconstruction loans of the League represented a harsh solution of an issue that arises whenever an international agency extends financial assistance to a sovereign country—namely the terms and conditions on which such assistance shall be granted. In the United Nations, this issue has been debated in the context not of reconstruction but of economic development, and the solutions that have been proposed are a far cry from the sterner ones adopted by the League.[7] The experience of the Financial Committee in dealing with refugee problems demonstrated that an international organization dealing with a major problem of resettlement must concern itself with many aspects of the internal affairs of the countries of resettlement. Finally, the failure of the Financial Committee to bring effective help to individual countries at the onset of depression, like the failures of the League in the trade and payments field after 1930, demonstrated that the real solution to problems of this kind lies in reducing the severity of the depression itself.

Transport and Communications

The beginning of the interwar period found a number of nineteenth century forms of international co-operation in the field of transport and communications still being actively carried on. Among these were the

[7] See below, Chap. IV.

Universal Postal Union, an International Meteorological Organization, international conventions regulating traffic on the Danube and Rhine, the Berne Convention regulating railway freight traffic in Europe, and rate conferences of private shipping companies.[8] Before the turn of the century, a nongovernmental International Maritime Committee was organized to establish rules and practices to govern international ocean commerce.

There were also co-operative organizations in the field of communications. An International Telegraphic Conference was held in Paris as early as 1865, and a treaty signed at that time established the International Telegraph Union. It was amended in 1885 to include provisions concerning international telephone service. In 1903, the first International Radio Conference was held in Berlin establishing the International Radio Telegraph Union. The resultant protocol embodies principles that are still the basic law of international radio regulations.[9] In 1927, the first International Table of Radio Frequency Allocation was adopted, and in 1932, the consolidation of principles and regulations governing radio, telephone, and telegraph operations was accomplished by a Madrid Telecommunications Convention. At that time, the International Telegraph Union and the International Radio Telegraph Union were merged into the International Telecommunication Union. It was commissioned to revise and keep up-to-date the regulations governing international telegraph, telephone, and radio communications. But the functions of the Union, although widened, did not undergo any radical change until after the Second World War.

A major step in filling the obvious gaps in this system of international collaboration was taken by the Aeronautical Commission of the Paris Peace Conference, which initiated, in 1919, an International Air Convention Relating to the Regulation of Aerial Navigation, which in turn established an International Commission for Air Navigation (ICAN). A further step was taken by the Assembly of the League of Nations, which in 1921 convoked an International Conference on Communications.

This conference drafted a Convention on Freedom of Transit and a Convention on the Regime of International Waterways, both of which were ratified by a large number of countries and were in effect until 1939. It also prepared for two other conventions: one on the Interna-

[8] These are discussed later in this study. See below, Chap. VI.

[9] Richard T. Black, "Telecommunications Policy and the Department of State," U.S. Department of State *Bulletin*, Vol. 30 (Jan. 8, 1954), pp. 83–87.

tional Regime of Maritime Ports, which provided that every contracting state would grant to the vessels of every other contracting state equal treatment with its own vessels in its various maritime ports, and one on the International Regime of Railways, both of which were completed in 1923 by a conference called by the Communications and Transit Organization of the League.[10]

These four conventions dealt with long-familiar problems, mostly technical in nature. Neither the United States nor the Soviet Union was a signatory, and much of the co-operation achieved under them proved to be the working out of orderly arrangements governing internal transport in Europe.[11]

In contrast, the International Commission for Air Navigation, whose membership included all the major powers except the United States, was confronted with problems that could be solved effectively only on a nearly world-wide basis. During the period of its operations, which began in 1922 and continued until 1939, the main function of ICAN was to ensure the application of the air convention, but its activities were in practice limited largely to technical matters—due to the early incorporation into national and international law of the principle that every state has the sole and exclusive sovereignty over its own air space.

This principle meant that although all states had the right to fly over the high seas, every state had the full right, except as it might limit itself by treaty or other international agreements, to determine the methods by which it would allow the entry of foreign aircraft into its territory. International co-operation on civil aviation, aside from technical matters, therefore meant co-operation on such major questions as transit rights, routes, frequency of landings, and the pickup and discharge of cargo within the territory of a country by foreign planes. In the interwar period, these problems were further complicated by questions concerning the relation of civil aviation to disarmament. During the Second World War, the activities of ICAN were much reduced, but the institution did not disappear, and after the liberation of Paris, plans were made for the revival of its work.

None of the great economic and political problems in civil aviation were dealt with by ICAN nor could much be accomplished about them by the Communications and Transit Organization of the League, because Germany, the United States, and the Soviet Union were not ready to join in international agreements on such matters. This was

[10] Walters, *op. cit.*, Vol. 1 (1952), pp. 143, 178–79.
[11] See below, Chap. VI.

also true of emerging problems in the field of radio communication, and only a small advance was made in the rest of the telecommunications field.[12]

Although the Communications and Transit Organization was frustrated in dealing with basic economic and political issues in civil aviation, it carried on one of the most fruitful operations of the League. Its activity was concentrated primarily on technical problems related to railway transport, inland navigation, ports and maritime navigation, road traffic, and power transmission in Europe. In these fields, it accomplished much useful work.[13] The failure of the great powers to employ it for consultation and co-operation on the emerging issues of aviation and radio communication as well as on technical problems illustrated, however, the fact that international organization as such could be no substitute for the willingness on the part of the major powers to use it.

Although the Communications and Transit Organization of the League met for the last time in 1939, its work was, as far as possible, carried forward thereafter by the Secretariat of the League. Consequently, the Economic and Social Council of the United Nations did not have to make a fresh start in the collection of data and the analysis of problems in the field of transport and communications.

Social and Cultural Co-operation

International co-operation during the interwar years on trade and payments and transport and communications was concerned mainly with the relations of governments in their day-to-day economic intercourse. In the field of investment, the emphasis was heavily on the special problems of individual countries in time of emergency. In the field of social co-operation, however, the emphasis was primarily on "the cares and anxieties of the individual and his family."[14] But these distinctions cannot be made too sharply. The objective of raising the standard of living was implicit in many forms of interwar "economic" co-operation, and the development of "social" co-operation, especially in the fields of health and labor, showed that the cares and anxieties of the individual cannot be separated from the problems of more effective utilization of resources, expansion of trade, and other economic problems.

[12] Walters, *op. cit.*, Vol. 1, p. 180.
[13] *Ibid.*
[14] *Ibid.*, Vol. 2, p. 750.

The interests of the ILO in conditions of labor were continually broadened. They were dealt with by international conventions and recommendations, studies, and co-operation with individual countries. The first interests of the ILO included the shortening of hours of work, the setting up of employment services, the improvement of conditions of work of children, young women, and prospective mothers. The reduction of industrial injuries and occupational diseases, and vocational training and placement of the handicapped, also became fruitful areas of work. To these were soon added leadership in the promotion of social security, in particular, social insurance, the improvement of techniques of discussion and negotiation between employers and workers, and more generally, the promotion of a fair share in the fruits of progress for workers and employers. The concern of the ILO with the problem of effective uses of resources in production and distribution was implicit between the wars, and its concern in general economic problems was destined during the war to become more explicit. This was also true of the work of the Health Committee of the League of Nations.

The first job of the Health Committee—an undertaking in which it was highly successful—was the control of epidemics immediately after the First World War. The second was to ensure in so far as possible that public health services would be guided by the principles of preventive medicine. These activities were supplemented by the conclusion of two sanitary conventions—the International Sanitary Convention of 1925 (Maritime) and the International Sanitary Convention on Aerial Navigation (1933).

It was a third phase of the work of the Health Committee that took it directly into the arena of economic policy and raised problems of co-ordination with the activities of other organs and agencies. This was the promotion of national action in combating some of the general social and economic conditions adversely affecting health, such as bad housing and malnutrition. The impetus to this broadening of the whole field of social co-operation was derived from studies of nutrition by the League of Nations begun in 1935 under Australian leadership. These studies culminated in the publication by the League in 1937 of a *Report on New Technical Efforts towards a Better Nutrition.* The ILO, the International Institute for Agriculture (not a League of Nations organization), and the committees of the League on Intellectual Cooperation and on Child Welfare were associated with these studies. The nutrition study emphasized the need for expansion of consumption so as to improve the health and physique of populations, and this emphasis led to a basic analysis of the relation of nutrition not only to health but to agricultural and economic policy. Other studies carried on by the Health Committee of the League on housing, slum clearance, and town-and-country planning, were regarded by the committee as of an importance equal to or even greater than that of the nutrition studies. Here again close co-operation with the ILO was developed, and a Housing Committee of the League was created.

The League also made pioneering and invaluable contributions to social co-operation in less controversial fields, such as narcotics control and the suppression of traffic in women and children. The League, moreover, was active in the field of intellectual co-operation. In 1921, it established a Committee on Intellectual Cooperation, and in 1925, an International Institute of Intellectual Cooperation. The committee had three major aims—to improve the material conditions of intellectual workers; to build up international relations and contacts between teachers, artists, scientists, and actors, and members of the intellectual professions; and to strengthen the influence of the League for peace.[15] National committees on intellectual co-operation were also established under the auspices of the League. The effectiveness of this work was modest, but one enterprise, the *Index Translationum*, survived the war.[16]

One major line of cleavage cut across the whole field of social co-operation. It has been described by the historian of the League as follows:

> None of the authoritarian States would participate, although it was always open to them to do so. Germany, Italy, and Japan were hostile to every form of international institution. The Russian attitude was different. They were particularly well disposed toward the Health Committee [of the League] . . . but they took no part in any of the studies or meetings concerned with the general raising of the standards of living. In many aspects, these activities were based on ideas which found no place in a Communist economy. And, above all, the Russians desired to discourage any suggestion that all this could be placed on a level with the essential duties of the League.[17]

In one form or another, most of the activities of the League in international social co-operation survived the war. Many of them became part of the inheritance of the United Nations in the form of well-organized work that needed only to be carried forward along established lines. The energy and enthusiasm that went into the work of the League on nutrition and related problems carried over into the war period, and

[15] *Ibid.*, Vol. 1, pp. 190–91.
[16] See below, Chap. IX.
[17] Walters, *op. cit.*, Vol. 2, p. 757.

were important factors in the creation of a new international agency—the Food and Agriculture Organization of the United Nations. Moreover, because the most acute problems in this area were in Africa, Asia, and Latin America, the nutrition work of the League of Nations was a forerunner of the preoccupation of the United Nations system with the special problems of the underdeveloped countries.

Although the failures of the League in the field of trade and payments seemed to call for the creation of new agencies, the successes of the League in focusing attention on neglected areas of international social co-operation gave impetus to the creation of such agencies in these fields. These successes depended in large measure on the willingness of states to take action either under international auspices or in accordance with international recommendations on many matters falling within their domestic jurisdiction, and on their willingness to join in making studies and recommendations on such matters.

Studies and Recommendations of the League (1939–45)

Both the Economic, Financial and Transit Department of the League of Nations Secretariat, after its removal to Princeton, New Jersey, and the Delegation on Economic Depressions of the League undertook extensive analyses of the problems involved in easing the transition from war to peace. These problems were also dealt with in studies and recommendations by the International Labour Office, especially at the ILO conferences of 1941 and 1944.

The work of the Secretariat took the form of a series of special studies on the handling of relief and reconstruction problems after the First World War; and that of the delegation took the form of a report on postwar economic policy, the first volume of which was published in 1943.[18]

The general theme of the report of the delegation was that no government would be able to overcome its transitional problems by acting alone. The most notable feature of the report was its insistence that the solution of transitional problems involving international co-operation should be directly correlated with measures for long-range collaboration. It placed great emphasis on employment, improved standards of

[18] The report was entitled *The Transition from War to Peace Economy.* For full references on this and other publications of the League that are mentioned below, see Hans Aufricht, *Guide to League of Nations Publications*, 1951.

living, and other objectives with strong social and humanitarian content, and recommended action during the transition, both by governments and international agencies, on a wide range of interrelated problems. To meet these needs, the delegation suggested the creation of several new international agencies, some of which were already being planned, although not entirely on the lines it recommended. Among them were an agency to deal with questions of commercial policy, an advisory agency for co-ordinating policies on full employment, an international reconstruction and development corporation, and a clearing or equalization fund along the lines finally agreed upon in establishing the International Monetary Fund. The delegation also emphasized the responsibility of creditor nations for taking radical and unilateral action for the reduction of trade barriers, a recommendation that was to be repeated in the debates of the United Nations organs and in the reports of United Nations experts.

The League also made general studies bearing on long-range problems, including the continuation of basic demographic studies, work on double taxation, and statistical work of several kinds. The main emphasis, however, was on trade and payments, economic stability, and the conditions of private investment.[19]

The mechanism by which a major economic depression may spread from one country to another and finally throughout the world had been laid bare in a famous report to the League of Nations Assembly in 1931, *The Course and Phases of the World Economic Depression*, and this had been followed in 1941 by a theoretical analysis of *Prosperity and Depression*. During the war, these themes recurred and, in addition, the special aspects of economic stability of particular interest to underdeveloped countries were analyzed.[20] Late in 1945, a special Joint Committee on Private Investment, which met in Princeton, was appointed and published its findings and recommendations early in 1946.

This body of work gave intellectual expression to currents of thought and concepts of national interest that influenced the practical work of

[19] In the field of trade and payments, the major publications were: *Commerical Policy in the Interwar Period: International Proposals and National Policies* (1942); *International Currency Experience: Lessons of the Interwar Period* (1944); *Europe's Trade: A Study of the Trade of European Countries with Each Other and with the Rest of the World* (1941); *The Network of World Trade* (1942); *Quantitative Trade Controls: Their Causes and Nature* (1943); *Trade Relations between Free Market and Controlled Economies* (1943); *Customs Unions* (1947); *International Cartels* (1948); *Industrialization and Foreign Trade* (1945); and *Commercial Policy in the Postwar World* (1945).

[20] See *The Course and Control of Inflation* (1946); *Economic Stability in the Postwar World* (1945); and *Raw Material Problems and Policies* (1946).

preparing postwar programs of international economic co-operation. This is shown first by the range of topics considered to be parts of "commercial policy"; second, by the emphasis placed on the idea that national import policies are fundamentally dependent on the state of domestic economic activity, particularly employment, and that no stable and liberal system of trade relationships can be attained in conditions of economic insecurity; third, by the firm conclusion that no liberal trading system is likely to survive a major world economic depression; fourth, by the recognition given to new currents stirring in the underdeveloped countries; and fifth, by a fresh stress on the interdependence of developed and underdeveloped countries.

The generally high quality of the analytical studies of the League of Nations provides an invaluable guide to an understanding of the substantive differences that divided the nations in their approach to the emergency problems of the transition and the long-range problems of co-operation in major economic and social fields after the Second World War. It was unfortunate, however, that what should have been among the first tasks of the new organization that was being born was in fact the last task of the dying organization that preceded it.

Emergency Action to Ease the Transition from War to Peace

In contrast to the situation prevailing during the First World War, many active steps were taken during the Second World War to prepare for the transition from war to peace. The major forms of emergency action planned during the war to meet transitional problems were the relief and rehabilitation of liberated and occupied territories, the handling of the refugee problem, attempts to meet an impending shortage of materials, especially food, and European co-operation to meet urgent transitional problems through regional co-operation.

Relief and Rehabilitation

The two major programs set in motion toward the end of the Second World War to meet the most urgent transitional problems of liberated and occupied territories were the civilian supply programs of the American and British military authorities and the program of the United Nations Relief and Rehabilitation Administration (UNRRA). Neither of these was concerned with long-range reconstruction, and at the time when the United Nations Preparatory Commission met in London in the winter of 1945–46, UNRRA—under a decision of its Council of the preceding August—was already making plans for its own liquidation.

Although UNRRA bore the name of the United Nations and carried on its major operations after the United Nations Charter was signed, it never became a part of the United Nations system. But its influence on the economic and social work of the new world organization was greater than that of any other predecessor organization except the League of Nations.

As an incident to its efforts to provide the greatest possible amount of relief and rehabilitation, UNRRA became involved in attempts to alleviate a world food shortage, in the problem of refugees, in the special needs of children, nursing mothers, and pregnant women, and in the broader fields of public health and education. Many of its workers in central, southern, and eastern Europe found themselves dealing with situations both in rural and urban areas that were characteristic of some of the long-range problems of underdeveloped countries. In most of its activities, moreover, it was found that there was need for technical assistance, including training programs, which the agency provided.

The experience of UNRRA in its main work of relief and rehabilitation also provided precedents that were important for the United Nations. Among the most useful were some of the principles developed by the UNRRA Council governing the granting of assistance and its use by those countries lacking the foreign exchange to pay for essential supplies. Foremost among these was the principle that the UNRRA program be designed to help people help themselves. Two other major principles were that in the distribution of relief no distinction should be made among recipients on the basis of race, creed, or political belief; and that receiving governments should be responsible for seeing that supplies were distributed in accordance with UNRRA principles. Both of these were later applied in all United Nations emergency operations, as was the requirement that such supplies should be exempt from export and import taxes. Still another principle was that the proceeds of sales of UNRRA goods, after payment of administrative expenses, should be used for further relief. This was a direct forerunner of the use of counterpart funds in United States assistance programs and such United Nations programs as that of the Korean Reconstruction Agency.

Another principle governing the use of UNRRA funds was that they should not be used for "reconstruction." The estimates of reconstruction needs far exceeded any sums that the agency could be reasonably expected to provide, and the use of such funds for this purpose ran counter to the American conviction that the main reliance for reconstruction after the war should be placed on private investment. However justifiable in the prevailing circumstances, this restriction on UNRRA activities had some unfortunate consequences. The difficulty of making a precise distinction between reconstruction and rehabilitation was demonstrated throughout its entire history, and the attempt to preserve it limited the scope, the variety, and the depth of the program that was followed.

The methods by which UNRRA acquired its very substantial resources not only set precedents for the United Nations but also provided some warnings. The agency was financed by voluntary and periodical contributions from national governments, and all subsequent United Nations emergency programs, with some variations, inherited this method of financing the bulk, if not all, of their operations. In the case of UNRRA, however, governments contributing to the program were not left free to contribute as much or as little as they chose. Administrative expenses were allotted by the UNRRA Council, and a formula was adopted for dividing, among contributing countries, the total burden of furnishing supplies and services on an equitable basis. It proved impractical to develop any formula that would adequately reflect the capacity to pay of the various contributing countries, and a rough-and-ready solution was found by obtaining from countries whose territory had not been occupied by the enemy a commitment to contribute 1 per cent of their national incomes as computed by them for this purpose. At the request of the council, two such contributions were solicited. UNRRA was, nevertheless, always in financial difficulties, and at one time had drastically to curtail its operations because of delays by the United States Congress in appropriating funds for the second American contribution.

There were other aspects of the experience of UNRRA that raised warning signals of trouble ahead for the United Nations. The United States provided about 70 per cent of the resources of the agency, each of its directors-general was an American, and Americans tended to expect it to behave as if it were a United States governmental agency. UNRRA therefore exemplified, in high degree, a problem that is bound to arise when an international agency carries out multilateral operations and a single country provides most of the funds.

Finally, the experience of UNRRA demonstrated once again the reluctance of the Soviet Union to allow important powers to be exercised by an international agency. This was manifest in the insistence of the Soviet Union on some form of veto power over decisions that might otherwise be taken by the policy-making organs of UNRRA, by its attitude on the details of agreements between the agency and recipient countries, and by the reluctance of Byelorussia and the Ukraine to furnish information required of all UNRRA "clients." Although these Soviet attitudes did not prove to be insuperable impediments to the work of the agency, and the intransigence of Eastern European countries on the matter of information has often been exaggerated, they were indicative of a problem that has been carried over into the United Nations. The first serious breach between the Soviet Union and other members of the UNRRA Council was on another issue, which also had important repercussions on the early work of the United Nations—the treatment of displaced persons and refugees.

Refugees and Displaced Persons

At the close of the Second World War, various voluntary organizations, the military authorities, and three international organizations were concerned with the problem of refugees and displaced persons. Although thirty governments contributed to the work of one of the international organizations—the Intergovernmental Committee on Refugees—its operational expenses were jointly underwritten by the United Kingdom and the United States. It accomplished some useful work, but the care of millions of displaced persons was wholly beyond its resources. Only a minor contribution to the refugee problem could be made by the Office of the High Commissioner of Refugees under the League of Nations, which was still caring for refugees from the First World War. The major responsibilities therefore devolved on UNRRA and the military authorities, who encountered considerable difficulty in defining their respective functions and responsibilities.

The number of displaced persons and refugees found by the Allied armies in their zones of occupation at the time of the German surrender, in May 1945, was about 8 millions.[21] In the months immediately preceding and following the surrender, approximately 5 to 6 millions were returned to their countries of nationality—a prodigious achievement on the part of the military authorities—but a new stream of refugees from Eastern Europe soon began to pour into the occupied zones,

[21] U.S. Displaced Persons Commission, *The Displaced Persons Commission: First Semi-Annual Report to the President and the Congress, Feb. 1, 1949* (1949), p. 2.

especially Western Germany and Austria. The role of UNRRA, unlike that of the Intergovernmental Committee on Refugees, was originally conceived in terms of providing temporary relief to displaced persons while assisting them in the process of repatriation. More than 750,000 were repatriated under its auspices, most of them before November 1945. There were many, however, who refused repatriation. When it became clear that the numbers of such persons would be substantial, the United States, British, and French governments agreed that, with the exception of traitors and war criminals, individuals who did not want to return to their country of origin should not be forced to do so and should be eligible for UNRRA assistance. The Soviet Government, however, insisted that all displaced persons and refugees should be repatriated, and interpreted the refusal of any such person to return voluntarily to his country of origin as clear evidence of guilt by reason of collaboration with the enemy. Such persons, it held, were subject to extradition.

On this issue, UNRRA was forced to take a stand, and it did so in a resolution passed by its council in August 1945. In the face of strenuous Soviet objection, the council decided that the agency would care for displaced persons without the agreement of their countries of origin, but, as a concession to the Soviet Union, required the administration to make every effort to encourage repatriation and to consult with the governments concerned. Until then all major decisions of the council, in spite of disagreements, had been made unanimously. This decision was the first open breach between East and West within UNRRA.

As early as 1944, it had become clear to UNRRA that there would still be a problem of dealing with displaced persons and refugees after its own work had come to an end. It therefore worked vigorously for the establishment of an effective United Nations refugee organization and made a considerable effort to have the organization ready in time. In its efforts to establish such an organization, the United Nations fell heir to all the bitterness that had arisen in UNRRA over the question of involuntary repatriation. It also fell heir to a serious problem of resettlement with which neither UNRRA nor the Intergovernmental Committee on Refugees had been able to cope.[22]

Shortages of Materials

One of the most difficult problems for UNRRA at the beginning of its operations was to obtain the supplies needed for its program in

[22] See below, Chap. II.

competition with the pressing demands arising from the conduct of the war. UNRRA frequently had difficulty in making out its case before the combined boards through which the United Kingdom and the United States handled the general problem of wartime allocations in behalf of the Allied powers.[23] As the war came to a close, this system of allocation suffered two kinds of pressure. One was from private interests anxious to be relieved of the check on their activities imposed by governmentally controlled allocations. The other was from countries in the United Nations alliance that were anxious to have a greater voice in the allocation process. The justice of this claim was recognized by Prime Minister Churchill and President Roosevelt when, in late 1944, they directed the combined boards to collaborate increasingly with the representatives of other members of the wartime coalition. Considerable progress was made before the end of the war in carrying out this directive.

Just before the end of the war, an American policy statement was developed dealing with the termination of the combined boards and the setting up of various international commodity committees additional to those already in being. This statement recognized that the continuation of some wartime controls was essential to an orderly transition from war to peace, and it strongly emphasized the need for a distribution of supplies during that transition that would be equitable in terms of the reconversion and rehabilitation of the world economy.

The recognition by the United Kingdom and the United States of the need for an equitable international distribution of supplies during the transition was in harmony with the recommendations of the Report of the League of Nations Delegation on Economic Depressions. The concept of equitable distribution in times of shortage later found frequent echoes in debates of the United Nations. The combined boards, however, did not really set a lasting precedent for the new world organization, although their international commodity committees did provide for continuity of policy and were utilized by the United Nations in efforts to combat the world food shortage.

Regional Co-operation in Europe

One other form of wartime emergency action that had important consequences for the United Nations was the attempt made in Europe

[23] S. McKee Rosen, *The Combined Boards of the Second World War—An Experiment in International Organization* (1951), *passim.* Canada alone among the other Allied powers was a member of one of the boards—the Combined Food Board.

to solve some of its most urgent transitional problems on a regional basis.

From 1940 to 1944, many suggestions had been put forward for postwar regional co-operation in Europe on a more or less permanent basis.[24] The general trend of thought, however, was toward a global approach, and the United Nations Charter made no specific provision for, although it did not rule out, regional organizations in the economic field. Nevertheless, there was a strong impulse to meet certain European problems on a regional basis. This expressed itself within the framework of UNRRA in the tendency of its Committee of the Council for Europe and the UNRRA European Regional Office (ERO), to act as if they were autonomous bodies; and in the establishment of three technical regional organizations known as the E organizations.

When the war ended, the intricate transport network on which the entire European economy depended was virtually paralyzed. To overcome this situation, a large measure of regional co-operation was needed, and to provide this, the European Central Inland Transport Organization (ECITO) was created. It was designed to serve as a co-ordinating and consultative organ to study the technical and economic conditions of international traffic in Europe and to give advice and make recommendations to the member governments on means of restoring and co-ordinating the transport capacity of the European system. These functions were divided into two categories: the first concerned with the problems of the transitional emergency period; and the second with long-range problems of European transport.

Another urgent economic problem was the restoration of coal production. In July 1945, the combined production of Belgium, Czechoslovakia, France, Germany, the Netherlands, Poland, and the United Kingdom was only 57 per cent of the aggregate prewar production of these countries.[25] The second of the E organizations, the European Coal Organization (ECO), was consequently established to promote the supply and equitable distribution of coal and scarce items of coal-mining supplies and equipment, and to safeguard as far as possible the interests of both producers and consumers.

The third E organization, the Emergency Economic Committee for

[24] See U.S. Department of State, *Postwar Foreign Policy Preparations, 1939–1946*, Publication 3580 (February 1950), pp. 25, 127, 138, 146, 148, 197–98, 228, 372, 394, 472, 482, 656.

[25] U.N. General Assembly, First Session, Second Part, *Official Records*, Supplement No. 3, "Preliminary Report of the Temporary Sub-Commission on Economic Reconstruction of Devastated Areas" (1947), p. 19.

Europe (EECE), was designed to consider a broad range of problems. It was an advisory body on economic questions relating to production, supply, and distribution during the final stages of the European war and the immediate transitional period, and on questions of reconstruction policy.

The E organizations were essentially emergency bodies. When, however, the United Nations took its first step toward the creation of a regional economic commission for Europe by appointing a Temporary Subcommission on the Economic Reconstruction of Devastated Areas, a possibility was opened up for the continuation of some of their activities under United Nations auspices.

The E organizations were an experiment in the selection of those areas of international co-operation that are suitable for a regional approach. The greater effectiveness of ECITO and ECO as compared with EECE showed that the more concrete and localized are the problems selected for regional treatment, the greater is the likelihood that they will be solved successfully on a regional basis. The experience of the E organizations also demonstrated once again the difficulties of obtaining Soviet membership in international economic organs of a specialized character, and in obtaining cordial co-operation from the Soviet Union once it had agreed to participate.[26]

Continuity and Innovation in Social and Cultural Co-operation

The inheritance of the United Nations from the emergency measures taken or planned during the latter part of the war was in part a demonstration of new methods of collaboration to meet a situation of economic and social crisis, in part an object lesson in some of the potentialities and limitations of regional economic collaboration, and in part the preservation and enrichment of international social collaboration, especially in the field of health.

Through its activities in education, in the introduction of social and child welfare activities, and in the revival and introduction of health programs, UNRRA became a link between the pioneer international collaborative efforts in these fields that existed before the war and those that followed after. As part of its public health program, UNRRA

[26] The Soviet Union joined neither ECO nor EECE. Efforts to obtain Soviet participation in the Provisional Organization for European Inland Transport formed in April 1945 were unavailing, and it was not until this organization was reorganized as ECITO in September 1945 that the Soviet Union accepted membership.

assumed responsibilities for administering certain international sanitary conventions that were revised by the UNRRA Council to meet wartime needs. It also assumed the duty of collecting and disseminating information on the appearance and movement of all communicable diseases that, in its opinion, constituted a menace to other countries. It became responsible for delineating yellow-fever areas of the world and establishing standards of yellow-fever vaccine. Its medical and sanitation supply programs as a whole were planned to fulfill four main functions: rehabilitation of hospitals, clinics, and laboratories; prevention of epidemic diseases; restoration of the drug industry; and provision of specialized supplies for war victims.

On such matters, the Health Committee of the League of Nations co-operated closely with it. This committee endeavored to maintain as far as possible its work on such subjects as epidemiological intelligence, malaria, nutrition, and biological standardization, and added to this the task of encouraging effective use of the international nomenclature on blood groups that had been worked out earlier.

Continuity of effort was also preserved in the field of narcotics control by measures to safeguard this control during the war, to adapt it to special wartime conditions, and to prepare for the early resumption in full of the prewar system. In contrast, aside from the collection of data and the publication of one important study, most of the work of the League for the protection of women and children lapsed during the war.[27]

Prior to the first meetings of the General Assembly and the Economic and Social Council of the United Nations, steps were taken to ensure that this work would be continued and expanded. The establishment of a World Health Organization had been proposed by several nations at the San Francisco Conference, and a draft constitution was developed by the United States Department of State and the United States Public Health Service in 1945 and early 1946 for this purpose. An advisory group of national health and civic leaders had urged the creation of such an organization in October 1945, and in December 1945, Congress formally requested the President to convoke a conference to establish it.

A great deal of thought was given to postwar educational co-operation by the Allied Ministers of Education, by the governments of the United States and the United Kingdom, and by many nongovern-

[27] See League of Nations, *Report on the Work of the League During the War, Submitted to the Assembly by the Acting Secretary-General* (October 1945), pp. 80–109, where all this work is described in detail.

mental organizations. A conference of Allied Ministers of Education was convened in 1944 to make plans for educational and cultural reconstruction and for a United Nations organization for educational co-operation. This suggestion was backed by the United States and other nations at the San Francisco Conference, and as a result, the commitments under Article 55 concerning educational and cultural co-operation were included in the Charter. Some of the major issues for a proposed international organization were settled in the earlier wartime discussions—for example, whether the organization should be temporary for educational reconstruction or a permanent body, and whether the emphasis should be shifted from the League of Nations idea of concentrating on contacts between intellectuals to a broader movement affecting all people. It was therefore possible to reach formal agreement on a constitution for the United Nations Educational, Scientific and Cultural Organization in two weeks in November 1945.

In 1944 also, a major step was taken by the International Labour Organisation, which had been moved temporarily to Montreal during the war, in preparation for its future work. The twenty-sixth session of the International Labour Conference, held in Philadelphia in the spring of 1944, laid down major objectives and actions suitable for various countries for progress toward social security and made important recommendations on employment policies during the transition from war to peace. Its most significant action, however, was the adoption of a Declaration of Aims and Purposes (the Philadelphia Charter), which was incorporated in the ILO constitution as an amendment. This declaration marked a definite rejection of a narrow conception of the functions of this organization and was, in fact, a bid on the part of the ILO for responsibilities of the type later assigned to the Economic and Social Council. It affirmed that "all human beings, irrespective of race, creed or sex, have the right to pursue both their material well-being and their spiritual development in conditions of freedom and dignity, of economic security and equal opportunity," and that the "attainment of the conditions in which this shall be possible must constitute the central aim of national and international policy."[28] The declaration further maintained that it was the responsibility of the ILO to examine all economic and financial policies and measures in the light of this fundamental objective, thus illustrating once again the tendency of international agencies concerned with any one major aspect of human

[28] "The Twenty-sixth Session of the International Labour Conference, Philadelphia, April–May 1944," *International Labour Review*, Vol. L (July 1944), p. 38.

relations to recognize the interdependence of all social and economic problems, and to stake out a claim to be heard in connection with all such problems.

Atlantic Charter and Article VII as Guidelines

The main lines of Anglo-American agreement on the course that should be followed in reconstructing international economic relations after the war were first laid down in the Atlantic Charter and in Article VII of the Mutual Aid Agreement between the United States and the United Kingdom of February 1942.[29] Both were in complete harmony with many conference resolutions and other international pronouncements of the interwar period.

The Atlantic Charter declared that the United States and the United Kingdom would endeavor, with due regard to their existing obligations, to further the enjoyment by all states of access on equal terms to the trade and raw materials of the world; that they desired to bring about the fullest collaboration among nations in obtaining for all improved labor standards, economic advancement, and social security; and that they hoped to establish a peace that would enable all men to live out their lives in freedom from fear and want.[30] These principles and objectives were incorporated in the Declaration by United Nations, which before the end of the war was adhered to by forty-seven countries;[31] and also in the famous Article VII of the Mutual Aid Agreement.

This article began by stating that in determining the benefits to be provided to the United States in return for lend-lease, the terms and conditions should "be such as not to burden commerce between the two countries, but to promote mutually advantageous economic relations between them and the betterment of world-wide economic relations." This most general aim was to be achieved by "agreed action . . . open to participation by all other countries of like mind, directed to the expansion, by appropriate international and domestic measures, of production, employment, and the exchange and consumption of goods . . . to the elimination of all forms of discriminatory treatment in

[29] Hereinafter referred to also as the Mutual Aid Agreement. For text of this agreement see U.S. Department of State *Bulletin*, Vol. 6 (Feb. 28, 1942), pp. 190–92.

[30] For text of the Atlantic Charter see U.S. Department of State *Bulletin*, Vol. 5 (Aug. 16, 1941), pp. 125–26.

[31] U.S. Department of State, *Toward the Peace, Documents*, Publication 2298 (1945), p. 2.

international commerce, and to the reduction of tariffs and other trade barriers." The principles of this article were, in one way or another, formally accepted by sixteen other governments before the end of the war, including the Soviet Union, China, and all the British Dominions except India.

The emphasis on employment and better standards of living in Article VII, and on improved labor standards, economic advancement, social security, and freedom from want in the Atlantic Charter, struck a note that was responsive to new currents of political and economic thought and feeling that had grown strong during the depression and war years. In simple language, it was carried forward in Article 55 of the United Nations Charter. But the word "development," which appears in Article 55 and which had so many implications for the work of the United Nations, is not to be found either in the Atlantic Charter or in Article VII. This is understandable, for both documents were the product of Anglo-American agreement and incorporated essentially the long-range economic objectives of the most highly developed of all nations, the United States.

These long-range objectives were stated most clearly in the references to nondiscrimination and reduction of trade barriers in Article VII and in the reference to "equal access" (a term never defined and impossible of precise definition) in the Atlantic Charter. But even here the interpretation to be put on the principle was obscured by the phrase "with due respect to existing obligations" in the Atlantic Charter (a phrase intended to safeguard imperial preference), and by the insistence of Great Britain that Article VII did not imply unilateral abandonment of the preference system. The failure of India to sign a mutual aid agreement containing Article VII was a warning that underdeveloped countries would not accept a policy of trade-barrier reduction that might interfere with their development programs. The acceptance of the article by the Soviet Union, whose economic system and policy were quite unsuited to any meaningful application of it, showed that the larger the number of nations, the more difficult it is to reach meaningful agreement on objectives in the field of trade and payments policy.

Because the establishment of a general world organization was completely speculative at the time Article VII was negotiated, the article did not look toward action by such an organization but toward agreed action by all countries "of like mind." The methods chosen were first, agreement between the United States and the United Kingdom and a few other major countries on principles and objectives; and second, agreement among a much larger number of countries at international conferences convened to draw up the basic instruments of new international organizations.

With the maturing of plans for the United Nations, a means was provided for shifting the sponsorship of such conferences from a small group of leading powers to a general international organization. But even before the United Nations was ready to assume this responsibility, a series of such conferences held under the aegis of Article VII demonstrated that the concept of agreed action by "like-minded countries" (another term extremely difficult to define) is quite different from the concept of agreed action by a world conference or, for that matter, by a regional conference. For in global and regional conferences the differences that have to be harmonized are not only differences on matters of secondary importance arising within a framework of common agreement on the general road to be traveled, but are the deep-seated cleavages on fundamental issues that arise among countries differently organized and in different stages of economic development.

Creation of New Agencies Under Article VII

Two months after the signature of the Mutual Aid Agreement between the United States and the United Kingdom in February 1942, a comprehensive proposal for postwar action in the fields of currency stabilization, international investment, food and agriculture, and all the various aspects of commercial policy was developed in the United States Treasury Department. This "single-package" approach emphasized the close interrelationships and mutual dependence of successful co-operation in all these fields. It did not prove practical, however, to include all of them in a single series of international negotiations. This would have required the solution of serious conflicts of jurisdiction between the various departments and agencies of the United States Government. These were not resolved, and the United States did not propose a "single-package" negotiation. Had it done so, there is little reason to suppose that similar conflicts of jurisdiction within other governments would not have arisen to complicate, if not to frustrate, negotiations of such an all-embracing character.

As a result, negotiations on commercial policy under Article VII on the one hand, and currency stabilization and international investment on the other, were carried on separately, and neither was closely related to negotiations in the field of food and agriculture. Although the principles of Article VII were also taken as a point of departure for negotiations in the fields of civil aviation and telecommunications, it was not until the autumn of 1945 that the United States sought to include these subjects in conversations that would parallel those on commercial policy. It was an oddity of Anglo-American leadership on postwar economic problems that this initiative was taken after, rather than before, an international conference on civil aviation. The actual approach to agreed action under Article VII was in fact not well co-ordinated in leadership, timing, or procedures. This was well illustrated at the outset by the selection of food and agriculture as the subject of the first major conference to be called under the aegis of this article.

Hot Springs Conference

During the Second World War, a group of men closely associated with the activities on nutrition of the League of Nations was actively preparing for an early revival of international co-operation in this field. Their plans and hopes made a strong appeal to President Roosevelt, who saw in them an opportunity to launch postwar economic and social co-operation among the United Nations in an area in which conflicts of view, at least as far as aims were concerned, would be less sharp than in the presumably more difficult fields of trade and finance. It was on his initiative that an international conference on food and agriculture, which led to the establishment of the Food and Agriculture Organization of the United Nations, was convened at Hot Springs, Virginia, in May 1943. This conference, therefore, became a sort of trial run in co-operation among the United Nations, and the selection of the subject of this trial run came as a surprise to most participants.[32]

The Hot Springs Conference was confronted both with a prospective short-run emergency food problem after the war and with the long-range problem of international co-operation to improve prewar standards of nutrition and food distribution throughout the world. The purport of its resolutions on the short-term problem was that governments should act in co-operation to increase production, to allocate supplies, and to prevent violent fluctuations in the prices of food, of instruments of production, and of other necessities including industrial goods, that might arise from unrestrained competition for inadequate supplies. On long-range policy, it made a comprehensive series of recommendations dealing not only with production policy as such, but with agricultural credit, co-operative movements, land tenure and farm labor, education and research, conservation of land and water resources, land settle-

[32] See the volume in this Brookings series, *A History of the United Nations Charter.*

ments for food production, occupational adjustments in rural population, and international commodity arrangements. It also made recommendations on the international distribution of food and on the organization of marketing.[33]

A fundamental question was raised in connection with proposed resolutions on special international measures for wider food distribution. In debating these resolutions the conference was in fact exploring not only some of the practical limits of international collaboration between sovereign states, but the moral and ethical basis of such collaboration as well. Evidence showed that considerable numbers of people in certain areas of the world were far from being able to meet minimum energy needs and that the physical development of some of these people appeared to be retarded by insufficient food, while at the same time some of the large food-exporting countries were unable to dispose of their exportable supplies and were taking restrictive measures to reduce these "surpluses." The continuation of such a situation was felt by some participants to be not only inconsistent with mutually advantageous international relations but also intolerable from a humanitarian and moral point of view. Although the conference did not take decisive action on this issue, it called upon the future Food and Agriculture Organization to study the whole problem.

The resolutions and recommendations of the Hot Springs Conference read very much like a check-list of the problems that later confronted not only the Food and Agriculture Organization but also the other economic and social organs of the United Nations. Frequent references will be made to them at later points in this study, and it will be shown that two of the most fundamental problems have not yet found any generally acceptable solution. The stability of raw-material prices was an issue that had become acute during the depression and continues to raise extremely difficult technical as well as political issues. The international distribution of food supplies involved a question that was as much ethical as it was economic: whether the existence of gross inequalities in available food supplies imposes a moral obligation on the more favored nations to come to the aid of the less favored.

Bretton Woods Conference

The calling of the Hot Springs Conference was considered by important British officials to be a diversion from the main stream of ne-

[33] Ernest F. Penrose, *Economic Planning for the Peace* (1953), p. 125.

gotiation under Article VII of the Mutual Aid Agreement, which was concerned with commercial and foreign exchange policy and international investment. But even the main stream of these negotiations had been diverted into two channels: the Article VII conversations on commercial policy; and the negotiations for new agencies in the field of foreign exchange and investment, which were both started and concluded earlier than the commercial policy conversations.

Before the entry of the United States into the war, plans were being made for an inter-American stabilization fund, and plans for an inter-American bank had reached the stage at which a convention for such a bank had been submitted to the Congress for ratification. When the global postwar foreign economic objectives of the United States were formulated in Article VII, these two inter-American projects were dropped in favor of plans for a fund and a bank whose operations would be world-wide. These plans were the subject of intensive negotiations, lasting more than two years, before the convening of a conference at Bretton Woods to draw up articles of agreement for the two institutions. The negotiations were largely taken up by attempts to reconcile an American plan for a fund and a British proposal for an international clearing union. During these negotiations and at the conference itself, a large number of important issues, particularly between the United States and the United Kingdom, were compromised, and the compromises were incorporated in the Articles of Agreement of the International Monetary Fund.

For example, a preliminary issue that had to be decided before substantial progress could be made in drawing up the Articles of Agreement was whether the resources of the International Monetary Fund should be used to assist in solving the economic problems of the transition, or be reserved to assist member countries in stabilizing their exchange rates after reconstruction problems were solved. The United Kingdom took the position that they should be used for both purposes, whereas the United States wished them to be used for the second only, because it assumed that the transition would be short and that, except in times of seasonal and cyclical disturbance, resources to maintain exchange stability would soon be available from other sources. On this issue, the view of the United States prevailed, and one consequence of this was that the International Monetary Fund (IMF) was actually designed to meet a set of conditions that have not, up to the time of writing, been characteristic of international economic relations.

Another important issue settled at Bretton Woods had to do with foreign exchange rates. Although several of the smaller countries argued in favor of flexibility in exchange rates, there was general agreement that the promotion of exchange stability in a free market should be a major objective of the IMF. At Bretton Woods, there was, however, a serious Anglo-American disagreement regarding the concept of stability that should be applied, even though both countries agreed that it should not be identified with rigidly fixed rates. The United States position was that exchange rates should be altered only if there was a fundamental disequilibrium and only by a four-fifths vote of the Fund. This would, under weighted voting, have given a veto power over most proposed exchange-rate changes to the United States. To many British critics, this seemed too much like a return to the gold standard, even though prior international agreement on exchange rates was a radical departure from gold-standard principles. The United Kingdom wished to avoid any commitments that seemed to bind it in advance to fixed rates, and it was unwilling to give any international organization veto powers on such a vital matter as the sterling-dollar rate. A compromise was worked out that preserved the principle of international agreement on proposed changes, yet left the initiative and considerable freedom of action to vary rates within wide limits to the members of the Fund.

In its proposal for a clearing union and indeed throughout the negotiations, the British, with support from other countries, laid great stress on the responsibilities of creditor countries, the United States in particular, to correct their international creditor position by appropriate commercial and investment policy, and on their obligations pending such correction to supply the world markets with their own currency in sufficient amounts to relieve the heavy pressures on debtor countries. The United States resented the implication that the principal creditor country was to be held primarily—even solely—responsible for the balance-of-payments difficulties of all the other members of the Fund, and successfully insisted on safeguards that restricted access to the resources of the Fund and limited the obligations of the United States.

Closely related to the issue of creditor as well as debtor responsibilities for correcting balance-of-payments difficulties was the question how far the Fund should be allowed to go in making recommendations with respect to the internal policies of its members affecting their balances of payments. Although the original British plan had made some provision for such recommendations when the resources of the proposed clearing union had been heavily drawn upon, the British, Australian, and many other delegations were not willing to accept any commitments under the Fund that would require them to change their domestic economic and social policies in order to put their balances of payments in order. They held that if the principal creditor, the United States, did not take the necessary steps to correct its own imbalance on the credit side, the debtor countries were fully justified in maintaining or resorting to exchange controls or in altering their exchange rates if this were necessary to avoid deflationary measures that might lead to unemployment.

The vigor with which this point of view was pressed is to be explained largely in terms of the basic national attitudes developed as a result of the experience of the depression years. Although the United States was reluctant to accept this view, at least in the extreme form in which it was sometimes presented, it was agreed at Bretton Woods that the Fund should not refuse a request from a member for a change in its exchange rates if such a change were necessitated by the social and economic policies of that member.

The issue of domestic jurisdiction was one of several major problems that complicated negotiations with the Soviet Union, both for the Fund and the International Bank for Reconstruction and Development (IBRD). Soviet experts doubted whether the Soviet Union, in view of its totally different economic organization, could be fitted into the proposed agencies, and they sought exemptions from many of the suggested commitments. They also pressed for numerous exceptions in their favor on the ground that special treatment should be accorded to countries that had been invaded by the enemy. They strongly resisted any commitment to supply information of the kind usually regarded as appropriate and indeed essential before the resources of lending agencies, international or otherwise, are made available to borrowers.

Aside from these special difficulties with the Soviet Union, the negotiators of the Bank at Bretton Woods had to reconcile several other cleavages in national viewpoints. The British viewed the operations of the Bank as almost entirely in the form of guarantees, with only a limited role for direct loans from paid-in subscriptions. As a result, paid-in subscriptions were restricted to 20 per cent of total subscriptions, of which 18 per cent was to be in local currency, which could not be utilized for loans except with the consent of the member whose currency was involved. The remaining 2 per cent was to be paid in gold or dollars.

At the Bretton Woods Conference, the Latin American participants attempted to have half of the resources of the IBRD earmarked for development, and although they failed in this, they succeeded in having development added to the name of the Bank and having equal emphasis put on reconstruction and development in its Articles of Agreement. Another cleavage of opinion arose from the desire of the United States to confine the lending operations of the Bank to specific projects that directly increase the productivity of the borrowing country. The wish of many other delegations to have the Bank given authority to make restocking and stabilization loans was, however, met to the extent of allowing the Bank to make loans other than project loans "in special circumstances."[34] Moreover, the loans of the Bank, in accordance with the statement of purpose of the Bank in Article I of its Articles of Agreement, were to be made only when private capital was unavailable on reasonable terms; also, under Article V, Section 8, the Bank was to co-operate with any general international organization and with public international organizations having responsibility in related fields, and to give consideration to the views and recommendations of such organizations in making loans and guarantees relating to matters falling directly within their competence. These two provisions were a potential source of conflict with organs and agencies of the United Nations in which the underdeveloped countries were numerous and united in purpose.

Both the Hot Springs and Bretton Woods conferences recognized that their work was incomplete without international agreement on principles of commercial policy. Both passed resolutions urging governments to seek early agreement on ways and means to reduce obstacles to international trade, and in the resolutions adopted at Bretton Woods stress was also laid on co-operation to maintain high levels of employment and to bring about the orderly marketing of staple commodities at prices fair to the producer and consumer alike.

These resolutions pointed up a problem of co-ordination that had been rendered doubly acute by the very conferences that passed them. By bringing the Food and Agriculture Organization, the Fund, and the Bank into existence before the charter of an international trade organization had been drawn up, they foreclosed any possibility of a truly integrated approach to closely related problems. Commodity policy, with which the Food and Agriculture Organization was much concerned, was an integral part of the Article VII conversations on commercial policy, and in many ways commercial policy and foreign

[34] Art. III, Sec. 4 (vii), U.S. Department of State, *United Nations Monetary and Financial Conference, Bretton Woods, N.H., July 1 to July 22, 1944: Final Act and Related Documents*, Publication 2187 (1944), p. 73.

exchange policy are more intimately related to each other than investment policy is to either. Exchange controls and direct trade controls, for example, are often alternative means of achieving the same objectives, and there is a close relationship between the inconvertibility of currencies and discrimination in trade. It is doubtful, however, whether —as a practical matter—this problem could have been solved when the new agencies were being created, by entrusting responsibility for international co-operation in both fields to a single international body, inasmuch as co-operation in the field of currency stabilization required contributions of large resources that would not have been forthcoming without a system of weighted voting such as that provided for in the Fund.

Conversations on Commercial Policy

When the Bretton Woods Conference passed a resolution urging governments to agree on principles of commercial policy, the conversations on commercial policy under Article VII had just begun. For a period of eighteen months after the signature of the Anglo-American Mutual Aid Agreement, the United States and United Kingdom had been engaged in an effort to resolve conflicts of opinion within their respective countries sufficiently to justify the opening of these conversations. The first of them took place in October 1943 between American and British experts, and in the early months of 1944, between American and Canadian experts. Although contact was maintained among the experts of the three governments, these conversations were not formally renewed until the summer of 1945.

In the interval, the United States Government prepared a draft of a multilateral convention, including a draft charter for an international trade organization, which incorporated a code of conduct on the main subjects dealt with in the conversations—commercial policy, cartel policy, commodity policy, and employment. This code was modified in the second part of the conversations in the summer of 1945, and the whole negotiation was concluded in the autumn of 1945 when the British agreed in principle to the main points of the "Proposals for Consideration by an International Conference on Trade and Employment."[35]

[35] U.S. Department of State, *Proposals for Expansion of World Trade and Employment*, Publication 2411 (November 1945), pp. 8–28.

The history of these conversations provides an excellent illustration of the point made elsewhere in this study that there cannot be a co-ordinated approach to economic co-operation through international agencies unless there is a co-ordinated approach within the governmental structure of major countries. Of the total period of three and one-half years from the signature of the Mutual Aid Agreement to an accord in principle on the proposals, about three years were spent mainly in efforts to compromise domestic differences of opinion on the issues involved.

The proposals provided for a separate undertaking on the part of governments to seek full employment, under which each of the signatory nations would agree to take action "designed to achieve and maintain full employment within its own jurisdiction." They would also agree to refrain from seeking to "maintain employment through measures which are likely to create unemployment in other countries or which are incompatible with international undertakings designed to promote an expanding volume of international trade and investment in accordance with the comparative efficiencies of production." They further specified that nations signatory to the full-employment undertaking should make "arrangements," both individually and collectively, under the general sponsorship of the Economic and Social Council of the United Nations Organization, "for the collection, analysis, and exchange of information on employment problems, trends, and policies," and that they should "under the general sponsorship of the Economic and Social Council, consult regularly on employment problems and hold special conferences in case of a threat of widespread unemployment."[36]

A separate agency in the field of commodity policy was strongly supported by both British and American spokesmen for agriculture, and it was not until late in the negotiations that commodity policy was included in the scope of the proposed international trade organization. In the Article VII conversations, there was concurrence from the start that the prewar experience with commodity agreements largely dominated by producer interests should not be repeated, and that there was need for entrusting the responsibilities in this field to some international agency. It was much more difficult, however, to reach a basic solution on one important substantive question that cut across national lines. This question was whether the regulation of production and exports

[36] *Ibid.*, pp. 9–10.

should be regarded as a normal, permanent feature of commodity agreements or an exceptional and temporary expedient to tide over special difficulties and be discarded as soon as possible. The latter conception was finally incorporated in the statement of principles governing commodity agreements that appeared in the proposals. In its essentials, this was carried over into the Havana Charter. The United Nations, therefore, was able to take Chapter VI of the Havana Charter as a point of reference in its discussions of commodity agreements.

A similar point of reference for United Nations discussions was provided in Chapter V of the Havana Charter, which dealt with restrictive business practices. The basic content of this chapter was also determined in the Article VII conversations, but it did not represent any real meeting of minds between the United States and the United Kingdom, whose views in this respect were shared by most European governments. The feasible limits of international co-operation in dealing with restrictive business practices affecting international trade were found to be not the acceptance of detailed commitments, as in commercial policy, nor agreement to act on a formal set of principles as in commodity policy, but merely agreement to follow certain procedures. What was really agreed to was the idea that the proposed international trade organization should in this area receive complaints, make recommendations, and request information on measures taken to carry out these recommendations. These were all procedures capable of being applied and later frequently applied (as in the Trusteeship Council) by some of the principal organs of the United Nations.

The proposals affirmed the principle of unconditional most-favored-nation treatment—a principle that the Economic Intelligence Service of the League of Nations had previously upheld. They laid down rules of conduct in technical matters, and they linked together much more closely than had the interwar conferences the related problems of tariff reduction and the elimination of preferences. Like the League of Nations Prohibitions and Restrictions Convention of 1927, they contained a general prohibition on quantitative restrictions, but with exceptions not contained in that convention, the two most important of which were the balance-of-payments exception, a major concern of the United Kingdom, and an agricultural exception directly related to the commitments made by the United States Government to American agricultural producers.

Agreement was also reached in the conversations on one major question of procedure in tariff matters. This was the question whether tariff reductions should be sought by some type of horizontal percentage cut agreed to in a single multilateral negotiation, or whether they should be sought through negotiations between pairs of countries. The former position was strongly maintained by the United Kingdom representatives, whereas the latter was the traditional method under the Trade Agreements Program of the United States and probably the only method acceptable to the United States Congress. Mainly for this reason, the horizontal reduction method was not accepted, but certain multilateral features were introduced through proposed negotiations for mutual concessions by groups of countries acting simultaneously.

It was the intention of the United States and the United Kingdom to hold the door open for eventual participation by the Soviet Union in the proposed trade organization. For this purpose, a state-trading formula was devised, which required state-trading countries to carry out their international trade on commercial principles, and to observe special rules, appropriate to their form of economic organization, which would have an effect equivalent to that of the commitments undertaken by other countries on the reduction of trade barriers and the elimination of discrimination.

Although the Soviet Union had accepted Article VII in its Mutual Aid Agreement with the United States, its representatives abroad made no secret of their suspicion of its basic aims. Even while the conversations were in progress, they left no doubt that, in their view, the real object of the advanced industrialized countries in advocating freer trade was to hold the market for manufactured goods in less developed countries and to check the industrialization of these countries.[37]

In the Article VII conversations, the interests of countries dependent mainly on raw material production were taken seriously into account in the exploration of buffer stocks and other devices to damp down fluctuations in the prices of primary commodities. The exclusion of this subject from the proposals was due more to the inherent difficulties that surround the practical operation of all such devices than to a lack of understanding of the importance attached to it by such countries. The viewpoint of the underdeveloped countries was also considered in another way, but with equally negative results. These countries were then, and have since remained, strong advocates of the traditional argument for high protection for infant industries. It was therefore suggested that this point of view might be met halfway by proposing fresh

[37] Penrose, *op. cit.*, p. 112.

exceptions, in the interest of economic development, to the ban on quantitative restrictions; but it was finally decided to postpone this issue until the Conference on Trade and Employment.

Civil Aviation and Telecommunications

The drive for the creation of new agencies under the general principles laid down in Article VII of the various mutual aid agreements was also a feature of wartime preparations for postwar co-operation in the field of transportation and communication. The major initiative was taken by the United States, which convened an international conference on civil aviation in Chicago in November 1944. This cut short efforts then being made to revive the work of the International Commission on Air Navigation.

At the conference in Chicago four basic documents were drawn up: an Interim Agreement on International Civil Aviation establishing a Provisional International Civil Aviation Organization; a permanent Convention on International Civil Aviation establishing a permanent International Civil Aviation Organization to which were attached twelve technical annexes; and two agreements relating to what came to be known as the Five Air Freedoms, which were to be administered in accordance with the principles of the interim agreement and the convention.

The first two of these freedoms were nontraffic freedoms. They provided for the privileges of flying across the territory of another nation and of landing for nontraffic purposes only. The third and fourth freedoms provided for the privileges of discharging and loading passengers, mail, and cargo coming from or destined for the home nation of an aircraft. The fifth freedom permitted the loading and discharging of passengers and cargo destined for and coming from any other nation. Thus, for example, an airline of country A would be permitted to load and discharge traffic between countries B and C in both of these countries.

Canada proposed an agreement on the first four freedoms, but the United Kingdom was unwilling to accept the third and the fourth, and the United States, whose aviation industry was certain to be in a strong competitive position after the war, insisted on the fifth freedom. The fifth freedom was also opposed even more strongly by the United Kingdom and by many other countries. This difference among nations was responsible for the drafting of the two air agreements for submission to prospective members of the international organization, one of which included only the first two freedoms, the International Air Services Transit Agreement, and one which included all five, the International Air Transport Agreement.[38]

The participants in the conference were also sharply divided on the question whether an international agency should be given authority to fix rates, capacities, and frequencies. The United Kingdom and some other countries favored such an agency, and Canada went even further by proposing that it should be given authority also to fix routes. To all this, the United States was strongly opposed. No agreement could be reached on these issues, and the convention consequently concerned itself mainly with technical matters, although it gave the new organization the function of studying and making recommendations on unsettled issues and provided a recourse to advisory and recommendatory powers assigned to the new international organization in regard, for example, to such matters as disputes over charges imposed for the use of airports and other disputes concerning these two agreements.

The period immediately following the Chicago conference was one in which a great number of very complex international civil aviation problems were under constant negotiation. Among these were the revival of air transport in Europe, the rights of passage over and entry into countries of Eastern Europe under Soviet influence, rights of entry of foreign aircraft into the Soviet Union itself, the disposition of the vast system of air bases and air arrangements of a military kind that had been built up by the United States during the war, and other similar problems. Many countries, including Britain, were reluctant to assume long-range international commitments on civil aviation until solutions of these problems had been worked out.

At the same time, countries, particularly in Europe where a chaotic condition prevailed, were being confronted with very urgent problems concerning radio frequencies. A conference on civil radio frequencies of liberated countries was held in London in September 1945, while at the same time an Inter-American telecommunication conference was being held in Rio de Janeiro. Suggestions were made for dealing with the frequency problem in Europe through a single agency on an interim basis, pending a permanent solution of the problem of international priority at a conference of the International Telecommunication Union or otherwise.[39]

[38] On the fate of these two agreements, see below, Chap. VI.

[39] On these conferences, see below, Chap. VI.

Inter-American Conference at Mexico City

At various points in the foregoing survey of wartime preparations for postwar collaboration, it has been necessary to stress the special viewpoint of the underdeveloped countries. The general attitude of these countries on commercial policy and other economic questions was brought to sharp focus in the Inter-American Conference on Problems of War and Peace held in Mexico City in February–March 1945.

Although this conference was concerned mainly with political and security questions, there were two important economic items on its agenda: economic co-operation during the war and transition period, and consideration of methods to develop such co-operation for the improvement of the economic and social conditions of the people of the Americas.

The most urgent economic concerns of the Latin American countries at the time were that: (1) a sudden termination of huge wartime procurement contracts from the United States would precipitate social and economic disturbances; (2) the resumption of trade after the war on prewar patterns would compel the Latin American countries to relinquish much that had been gained in the field of industrialization since 1940; (3) the dollar balances accumulated during the war by Latin American nations would lose part of their purchasing power or be spent for imports not essential for economic development; (4) the Latin American countries would not receive an "equitable" share of available capital goods after the end of the war as compared to other areas; and (5) a decline in raw material prices would menace the stability of their economies.

The first of these fears was the product of the special economic relations between Latin America and the United States during the war, and did not have general significance for the United Nations. This was not true of the others. Although not all underdeveloped countries had made the same progress toward industrialization as had some Latin American countries, many of them attached primary importance to industrialization as the key to economic development and stability. They therefore shared the Latin American concern regarding the possible effects on their development plans of a resumption of prewar patterns of trade, and this point of view was repeatedly expounded in United Nations debates. The idea that underdeveloped countries had a right in times of scarcity to an "equitable" share of capital goods, and in times of inflation to safeguards against any fall in the purchasing power of their foreign exchange holdings—and that the advanced countries had an obligation to do something about this—also recurred regularly in United Nations debates in times of strain or crisis. The importance attached to measures for stabilizing primary commodities was, as has been already noted, a recurrent theme in other wartime negotiations and continued to be so under the United Nations.

Although the United States met these viewpoints halfway at the Inter-American Conference on Problems of War and Peace, there was no real harmony of views on certain basic long-run policies. The United States attempted at the conference to incorporate in the Economic Charter of the Americas the principle of free enterprise and the general commercial policy principles that were under discussion in the Article VII conversations. It was not successful, however, in including in this charter a declaration against the establishment of state enterprises for the conduct of trade, or a declaration that the reduction of trade barriers was an unequivocal aim of policy. The Latin American countries were not even willing to include in the charter a paragraph condemning the evils of economic nationalism, but only the evils of "excessive nationalism."[40] On trade policy, the lines of cleavage were very clearly drawn.

On the other hand, there was agreement on many forms of economic and social co-operation. The United States, for example, declared its intention to propose and support measures for closer co-operation among the American countries in public health, nutrition and food supply, labor, education, science, freedom of information, transportation, and economic development, including industrialization and the modernization of agriculture. These were all areas of co-operation that were soon to gain prominence in the efforts of the United Nations system to promote the welfare of underdeveloped countries.

The Legacy in Brief

Had the United Nations been content merely to continue or expand prewar forms of collaboration and new forms that emerged during the war, its task would have been definite and its objectives clear. The United Nations, however, was from the outset confronted with national

[40] U.S. Department of State, *Report of the Delegation of the United States of America to the Inter-American Conference on Problems of War and Peace, Mexico City, February 21–March 8, 1945*, Publication 2497 (1946), p. 123.

attitudes and aspirations that had never before occupied the center of the stage under traditional forms of international collaboration, in particular the preoccupation of its Members with full employment, economic development, and economic stability.

The preparations made during the war for new approaches to international co-operation on long-range economic and social problems were in striking contrast to the almost complete neglect of postwar economic problems during the First World War. They were significant for the United Nations in two principal ways. In the first place, they demonstrated that the lines of cleavage among the industrialized countries and between them and underdeveloped countries that had been intensified by the depression of the 1930's were not transitory. In the second place, they posed important organizational problems for the United Nations by creating new agencies that were already in being before the United Nations itself was organized. The United Nations was consequently, at the outset, confronted with the difficult problem of determining how meaningful the relations between its own organs and these agencies could be made. Were they to be purely formal? Were the organs of the United Nations to be confined to the fringes of the problems that were the special province of these new agencies; or were they to become an active force in harmonizing views and solving problems in the areas of their concern?

In recommending policies and selecting methods for promoting the economic and social objectives specified in the Charter, the members of the United Nations were confronted with a situation of almost infinite complexity. They had in the first place to provide the specialization necessary for effective action. Second, they had to consolidate the component parts into an over-all effort to achieve common objectives, and as a result to embark on an almost constant search for means of achieving co-ordination. Third, they had to harmonize, as far as possible, national viewpoints within each of the specialized fields in such a way that they would contribute to the pursuit of over-all objectives. The new organization therefore had to analyze economic and social problems and their interrelationships, to increase mutual understanding of national aims and aspirations, and to promote forms of political accommodation that would make it possible to deal with acutely controversial economic and social issues.

This formidable task was begun at a time when the true dimensions of the postwar reconstruction problem had not yet been disclosed. The time and resources needed to solve this problem were generally underestimated, and wartime preparations for an orderly transition to peacetime conditions were generally thought to be adequate. The extent to which the fledgling United Nations system would be called upon to deal with emergency problems for which it was not prepared was not foreseen. This led to unexpected difficulties in harmonizing national attitudes toward some forms of long-range co-operation, because countries preoccupied with urgent short-run problems would not, and often could not, commit themselves in advance to follow policies that were desirable and appropriate in normal times. This would not in all probability have been a major obstacle to the advancement of the economic objectives of the Charter if there had been a sufficient measure of international agreement on what was desirable and appropriate in the long run. Unfortunately, despite the compromises reached at the Hot Springs, Bretton Woods, and Chicago conferences, and during the Anglo-American discussions on commercial policy under Article VII of the Mutual Aid Agreement, the prospective members of the United Nations remained divided on many important economic and social issues.

Economic Issues

One of the most important of these issues was the extent to which liberal commercial and foreign exchange policies should be subordinated to full-employment policies. Absolute priority for full employment was being insisted on by Australia, and the position of the United Kingdom on this question was almost, if not quite, as strong. The United States was taking the more traditional and more long-range view that employment policy should not stand in the way of desirable economic adjustments brought about by the reduction of trade barriers and the elimination of trade discrimination, which would make a solid contribution to higher standards of living. The United States was not without supporters, but the countries inclined toward the British and Australian views were in the majority.

This conflict was closely related to, and in part responsible for, the raising of another issue on which there was an equally sharp clash of national viewpoints. During the negotiations leading up to the Bretton Woods Conference, Great Britain had fought for the principle of making creditor countries assume heavy international responsibilities for correcting their favorable balances of payments so that debtor countries would not have to carry the whole burden of making the economic adjustments required to restore or maintain international equilibrium. The United States, on the other hand, insisted that, as in the past, countries in balance-of-payments difficulties were responsible for putting their balances of payments in order.

Although shortly after the end of the war a large measure of agreement on commercial policy had been reached in principle by the United States and the United Kingdom, the issues that divided the various nations in this field were still numerous. The underdeveloped countries had made it clear that they did not accept the reduction of trade barriers as an unequivocal aim of policy, because they believed that the protection of new industries was indispensable for the carrying out of their development plans. Many of these countries saw positive advantages in the use of quantitative import restrictions in the interests of development, while the United States and Great Britain had agreed that such restrictions should be condemned in principle, even though this principle was diluted by major exceptions.

The attention of the underdeveloped countries was concentrated on the removal of all possible obstacles to the early fulfillment of their development plans. Among these were the possible loss of purchasing power of their foreign exchange reserves in times of inflation, and the instability of the prices of the primary commodities that were their principal exports. It was already clear that on questions of commodity policy, the underdeveloped countries would probably not see eye-to-eye with the major industrialized countries.

Another issue on which there was no common international approach at the end of the war was that of cartels. Most countries were agreed that cartels should not be allowed to have harmful effects on international trade, but the question whether cartels were contributing to orderly trade and to general economic stability, or had harmful effects was a bone of contention between the United States and many European countries. In addition, there was no real agreement on the principles that should govern international aviation and shipping. At the end of the war, the United States, because of the strong competitive position of its aviation industry, took a free-trade attitude (a stand it later reversed) toward international aviation, and on this, it was opposed by nearly all other countries. In the field of shipping, however, in which the American competitive position was not strong, both the American position and that of the principal maritime powers were exactly the opposite of the positions taken with respect to aviation.

In many cases in which the United States found itself ranged against other countries on specific issues of commercial, monetary, commodity, and transport policy, the main reason was its greater commitment to and belief in the virtues of free competitive enterprise. Confronted with immense problems of reconstruction and deeply committed to the principles of a welfare state, countries such as the United Kingdom felt compelled to rely heavily on economic planning and on a system of economic controls. Most underdeveloped countries believed that the allocation of resources to carry out development programs, including the resources derived from foreign investment, had to be guided by the state. Very few countries therefore shared the American conviction that reconstruction and development should be financed mainly by private capital investment.

Social and Political Issues

At the end of the war, opinion seemed much more united on proposals for collaboration to promote humanitarian, cultural, and social objectives than they were on basic economic issues. American initiative played a major role in the establishment of the Food and Agriculture Organization, partly because the prospects of expanding the work of the League of Nations for better nutrition and improved standards of living for masses of people living on near-subsistence levels had stirred the imagination of the President. American support for the far-reaching economic measures required to make this program effective, however, was much more reserved. Humanitarian considerations widely shared by all nontotalitarian countries also played a role in the establishment of the International Refugee Organization, the World Health Organization, and the United Nations Educational, Scientific and Cultural Organization, and in the adoption of the Declaration of Philadelphia by the International Labour Organisation. Even in these areas, however, there were some major differences in national attitude. These differences were well illustrated by the debates on the functions of UNESCO.[41]

At the time the United Nations Charter was signed, there were already many indications that fruitful co-operation with the Soviet Union on economic and social questions might be extremely difficult. The Soviet Union had made no secret of its suspicion that the liberal trade objectives of Article VII of the mutual aid agreements cloaked a design on the part of industrialized countries to preserve their export markets for manufactured goods at the expense of the development of

[41] See below, Chap. IX.

underdeveloped countries. Patient efforts to adjust the Articles of Agreement of the Fund and those of the Bank so as to meet the special requirements of the Soviet Union had not led that government to accept membership in these institutions. The Soviet Union refused to participate in the Chicago Aviation Conference of 1944, and at the end of the war, it was clear that the aircraft of other countries for some time to come would not be allowed to fly over Soviet territory. On the question of repatriation of refugees, which was to be a major concern of the IRO, there was an irreconcilable breach between the Soviet Union and the members of the UNRRA Council. Many important problems that were being actively canvassed by other countries were of no interest to the Soviet Union—for example, the relationships that should prevail between foreign trade and employment policies and the measures that might be taken to prevent the spread of depressions internationally. The Soviet Union was hostile to the ILO and considered its tripartite representation of government, employers, and workers as a major impediment to Soviet participation.

Despite the wide range of international disagreement on fundamental economic and social problems that existed at the time the Charter of the United Nations was signed, the general atmosphere that surrounded the drafters of the Charter was one of hope, even of enthusiasm, for a new era of international economic and social collaboration. There was a determination not to fall back into the economic anarchy of the depression years and to make new advances toward ameliorating the lot of masses of people through international collaboration on problems of health, education, and social welfare. In such an atmosphere, the lions in the path did not look excessively fierce or dangerous, and the path to be traveled seemed smoother and straighter than it really was.

CHAPTER II

*Action in Emergency Situations**

ALTHOUGH it was recognized at the end of the Second World War that a welter of relief and reconstruction problems required the immediate attention of the United Nations, it was assumed that the new international organization would soon be able to concentrate exclusively on other matters. There was little realization of the extent to which the United Nations would continue during its first decade to be concerned with programs for meeting emergencies.

For the most part, the programs considered below were designed to provide short-term aid in connection with special problems arising in the wake of wars, floods, droughts, earthquakes, epidemics, and similar disasters not directly attributable to the functioning of the economic system. Some of these programs were intended to carry on activities initiated by the United Nations Relief and Rehabilitation Administration (UNRRA) after the liquidation of that agency, and all profited from the experience gained by it.[1] Of the four major United Nations programs to provide relief in the wake of war, two—the program of emergency assistance to needy children, and the program for the care and resettlement of the remaining refugees of the Second World War—are lineal descendants of UNRRA programs.

While the United Nations was still wrestling with the problem of refugees of the Second World War, it was compelled to assume a measure of responsibility for the refugees of two later wars. A new agency was created within the United Nations for the purpose of aiding the Arab refugees displaced from Palestine by the Arab-Israeli conflict. Refugee assistance required by the homeless as a result of the Korean war, however, was administered as part of the general relief and reconstruction program for the area rather than through a special refugee organization.

Concurrently with the operation of its emergency relief and rehabilitation programs, the United Nations system engaged in various actions

* By Robert E. Asher. Portions of this chapter are based on materials prepared by Louis Lazaroff.

[1] For information on the legacy bequeathed by UNRRA, see above, Chap. I, and the volume in this Brookings series, *The United Nations and Promotion of the General Welfare*, Part One.

to relieve the acute food shortage that characterized the immediate postwar period and to develop machinery for handling future famines. The allocation functions of the wartime Combined Food Board were continued by successor agencies until 1949; *ad hoc* assistance was organized in a few disaster situations; and much thought was given to proposals, first for a World Food Board, later, for an International Commodity Clearing House, and still later, for a Famine Reserve. These proposals, developed primarily in the Food and Agriculture Organization (FAO), would have required the assumption by international agencies of more comprehensive responsibilities than key governments were prepared to vest in them. By 1952, measures for mobilizing famine relief had been divorced from other more controversial aspects of agricultural policy. No new international machinery was established to provide foodstuffs in future famine emergencies, but agreement was reached on arrangements for spotting potential famines and co-ordinating the voluntary efforts of nations to relieve them. Relatively little attention was devoted to the related problems involved in meeting potential emergency requirements for clothing, shelter, and other nonfood items.

During 1951 and 1952, another arm of the United Nations—the Collective Measures Committee of the General Assembly—undertook a study of the measures that might be invoked in the gravest emergency with which an international agency can be confronted—a threat to or a breach of the peace. The committee considered not only the political and military measures but also the economic and financial measures that might be invoked to deter or weaken an aggressor nation, to aid the victims of aggression, and to permit an equitable sharing of the cost of collective action among co-operating countries. Although the entire range of United Nations preparations to meet aggression is analyzed and appraised elsewhere in this series,[2] the economic and financial measures are reviewed here, in the context of emergency actions of an economic and social character.

Relief and Rehabilitation in the Wake of War

UNRRA financed a broad range of relief and rehabilitation services to war-devastated areas in two continents. After the termination of

[2] See the volume in this Brookings series, *The United Nations and the Maintenance of International Peace and Security.*

the program the United States financed a bilateral Post-UNRRA Relief Program and an Interim Aid Program to provide further grant assistance to Austria, China, Greece, Italy, and certain other countries. These were followed in 1948 by the European Recovery Program, which was also initiated by the United States and was also operated outside the United Nations framework.

The United Nations inherited from UNRRA, however, certain residual relief problems of the Second World War. It met these and the new relief problems of two later wars by establishing four temporary operating agencies: the United Nations International Children's Emergency Fund to help meet the needs of children; the International Refugee Organization to care for and help resettle the remaining refugees of the Second World War; the United Nations Relief and Works Agency for Palestine Refugees in the Near East, to aid Arab refugees of the Arab-Israeli War; and the United Nations Korean Reconstruction Agency to bring succor to the victims of aggression in Korea.

Aid to Needy Children

The United Nations International Children's Emergency Fund (UNICEF) was established by the General Assembly in December 1946 to utilize some of the residual funds of UNRRA for work that, with the anticipated termination of the agency, threatened to come to a stop.[3] In countries devastated by war, UNICEF was to aid needy children, nursing mothers, and pregnant women. It was to provide food, clothing, and medical supplies, which were to be distributed, in accordance with UNRRA principles, on the basis of need and without regard to race, creed, nationality status, or political belief. Work was to be carried out in co-operation with permanent international agencies such as the World Health Organization, and only with the consent of the governments of the countries aided.

Total pledges and contributions to UNICEF from all sources during its first three and one half years, from 1947 to mid-1950, amounted to nearly $150 million, exclusive of the "internal matching" contributions made by countries receiving UNICEF aid to meet locally incurred expenses and to make the program a properly co-operative undertaking. Of the $150 million, approximately $32 million came from the residual assets of UNRRA. Government contributions, mostly from the United

[3] Res. 57(I), Dec. 11, 1946.

States, accounted for $105 million. The balance of nearly $13 million came from voluntary private contributions and included the share of UNICEF of the funds raised by the world-wide United Nations Appeals for Children.

The aid was used to furnish: (1) dried skim milk, fats, fishliver oils, and some meat, for supplementing the diets of 4 to 8 million children per year; (2) cotton, wool, and leather for processing in the receiving countries into clothing, blankets, layettes, and shoes for 6 million children; (3) transport, medical equipment and supplies—and salaries for some professional personnel—for one of the largest mass immunization programs ever undertaken: the testing of 17 million children for tuberculosis and the giving of BCG vaccinations to 9 million; (4) imported equipment for milk-drying and milk-pasteurizing plants; (5) aid in building national child health and welfare services; and (6) insecticides, penicillin, and vaccines for the control of communicable children's diseases.[4]

Initially, the work of the Children's Fund was confined overwhelmingly to Europe, but as war-created needs began to be met and as impediments to freedom of operations in Eastern Europe increased, the focus shifted from Europe to the underdeveloped countries. By mid-1950, UNICEF had become a world-wide operation functioning in Asia, Latin America, the Middle East, and North Africa as well as in Europe. The General Assembly late in 1950 recognized that the initial emergency assignment of UNICEF had been substantially completed and, in effect, placed it on a trial basis as a permanent agency. On December 1, it extended the life of the organization for another three years, and officially ratified the shift in emphasis from meeting short-range requirements in Europe to meeting long-range child health and welfare needs in the underdeveloped countries.[5]

The action of the General Assembly was a defeat for the United States delegation, which had tried in the Social Commission, the Economic and Social Council, and the General Assembly to obtain support for reducing drastically the scope and operations of the agency. Member states from Asia and the Middle East argued vigorously and effectively against curtailment merely because "the emergency was over in

[4] U.N. General Assembly, Fifth Session, *Official Records*, Supplement No. 3, "Report of the Economic and Social Council Covering the Period from 16 August 1949 to 16 August 1950" (1950), pp. 89–90.

[5] Res. 417(V), Dec. 1, 1950.

Europe." Children in other regions, they said, had been for centuries, and still were, in a "state of emergency."[6]

For the next three years UNICEF concentrated on a long-range program, primarily in the underdeveloped countries, involving the strengthening of maternal and child welfare services, mass health campaigns, and child-feeding programs. During this period also, however, it provided emergency aid to children, pregnant women, and nursing mothers when they were victims of floods, earthquakes, and similar disasters; and supplies to such emergency programs as the United Nations Relief and Works Agency for Palestine Refugees and the United Nations Korean Reconstruction Agency. By the end of 1953, its three-year trial period over, UNICEF was established by the General Assembly as a permanent agency with no change in function. It continues to be financed, however, by voluntary annual contributions from governments, nongovernmental organizations, and private individuals.

UNICEF represented the first sizable operational responsibility to be assumed directly by the United Nations. In a comparatively brief period of time, it was transformed from a short-range emergency activity into a permanent vehicle of United Nations social policy. It illustrates the shift of United Nations focus from the restoration of prewar standards in Europe to raising the level of living in the underdeveloped countries. Many of the activities that UNICEF has helped to finance since 1950 could have been fully paid for by recipient governments without severely taxing their resources, had they attached sufficient importance to child welfare services. UNICEF helped demonstrate the permanent value of such services and, by making its aid conditional, offered governments an incentive for allocating local resources to programs benefiting needy children.

UNICEF was promptly and widely acclaimed one of the most successful undertakings of the United Nations, both in terms of services rendered and public support obtained.[7] Its popularity may be attributed partly to sentimental enthusiasm for such obviously humani-

[6] U.S. Department of State, *United States Participation in the United Nations: Report by the President to the Congress for the Year 1950*, Publication 4178 (1951), pp. 177–78. See also U.N. General Assembly, Fifth Session, Third Committee, *Official Records*, 278th–87th Meetings (Oct. 6–18, 1950), pp. 46–105. The statement that a "permanent state of emergency persisted in the underdeveloped countries" was made by the representative of France and subsequently echoed by spokesmen for the Philippines, Iraq, and other governments.

[7] See, for example, the discussions in U.N. Economic and Social Council, Thirteenth Session, *Official Records*, 481st–564th Meetings (July 30–Sept. 21, 1951).

tarian work as aiding needy, helpless children, and partly to the invidious role in which critics would inevitably be placed. More important is the fact that the problems tackled by UNICEF have been clearly defined; the remedies are known and accepted; and dramatic results are obtainable at modest cost.[8]

Refugees and Displaced Persons

As noted earlier in this study, it was clear in 1946 that there would still be a large problem of refugee care after the termination of UNRRA. The agency consequently urged the United Nations to establish a successor organization equipped to carry on a program of relief, repatriation, and resettlement.[9] In February 1946, the General Assembly took the first steps toward setting up such an agency, and in December of that year—six months before the proposed ending of UNRRA operations in Europe—the Assembly approved the constitution of a new, temporary specialized agency, the International Refugee Organization (IRO).[10]

The IRO was given a broader mandate than UNRRA. In addition to the displaced persons in Austria, Germany, and Italy inherited from UNRRA (including unaccompanied children outside their countries of origin), the IRO was made responsible for Jewish refugees who had fled the Nazis before the war, who had survived concentration camps, or who had been in hiding; for non-Germans in Germany and Austria expelled by the Nazis but who had returned and were unable to reestablish themselves; for Spanish Republicans and other refugees of the Spanish regime; and for racial, religious, national, or political refugees from the interwar period. The IRO was thus given responsibility for refugees formerly under the protection of the League of Nations High Commissioner for Refugees and the Intergovernmental Committee for Refugees as well as those inherited from UNRRA.

At the General Assembly, the debates over the status of children were particularly bitter. The Soviet Union demanded that children be returned immediately to their countries of origin. In reply, it was pointed out that this might be contrary to the interests of the child and that it was often impossible to determine the country of origin. It was decided

[8] For a review of UNICEF as a continuing program of the United Nations, after completion of its "emergency" phase, see below, Chap. VIII.

[9] See above, Chap. I.

[10] Res. 62(I), Dec. 14, 1946.

that, if possible, children and parents should be reunited, wherever the latter might be. Orphans or unaccompanied children about whose nationality there was no doubt whatsoever were to be returned to their country, provided, however, that the best interests of the individual child would be served thereby. In the final analysis, therefore, it was left to the discretion of IRO to decide the future of such orphans or unaccompanied children as well as the future of those whose nationality was in doubt.

Differences of view concerning the treatment of political dissidents were equally sharp. The Soviet bloc sought to deny them assistance from the international community, to force refugees from Communist regimes to return to their countries of origin, to limit resettlement to those persons who had left their homes before the end of the war, and to prohibit resettlement in other lands if the country of origin—for example, the Soviet Union—refused its consent. Led by the United States, the United Kingdom, and France, the majority supported the position that refugees who were not war criminals, ordinary criminals, or traitors, yet had valid reasons for refusing repatriation, were entitled to the protection of IRO. However, to meet the objections of Arab nations fearful of possible mass Jewish resettlement in Palestine, the IRO was obliged to avoid sponsoring any scheme that would create political difficulties in the countries of resettlement or in neighboring countries, to avoid imposing resettlement of refugees on sovereign nations, and to avoid policies of resettlement that might run counter to the desires of the majority of the indigenous populations of non-self-governing regions or territories.

Although the IRO was financed by voluntary contributions, strenuous efforts were made by the United States and the United Kingdom to secure widespread participation. The majority agreed that "to the extent practicable," expenditures for persons displaced as a result of action by Germany and Japan should be charged to those countries, but the Soviet proposal that no provision for such refugees be made in the budget of the IRO was defeated. Similarly, the majority defeated Soviet proposals to the effect that all countries receiving refugees should pay the costs involved; that the paying capacity of the countries devastated by war should be taken into account in assessing member governments for support of the International Refugee Organization; and that the assessment of ability to pay should be left to the individual governments.

The scale of contributions adopted by the IRO was based initially on the assumption that all or most of the Members of the United Nations would participate in the work of the organization. As it turned out, however, only sixteen Members and two nations not Members—Italy and Switzerland—did so, and contributions constantly fell short of real requirements. No nation in the Soviet bloc became a party to the constitution of the International Refugee Organization.

The Preparatory Commission for an International Refugee Organization began to function on July 1, 1947, when more than 700,000 persons became dependent on that agency for food and shelter. By the end of 1948, the IRO itself came into being. It operated until February 1952. During its life, over 1,619,000 persons registered with the IRO and came under its mandate. Unlike UNRRA, the IRO had responsibility for arranging both the repatriation and the resettlement of refugees. Approximately 73,000 persons were repatriated; over 1 million were resettled in forty-eight countries, most of them in the United States, Australia, Israel, and Canada. Both UNRRA and the IRO had early identified the so-called "hard-core" group of refugees consisting mainly of the aged, the infirm, and the sick, for whom resettlement was especially difficult. Despite the obvious obstacles, the IRO made arrangements for settling almost 32,000 such individuals.

Engaged as it was in helping people re-establish their lives, the IRO was obliged to carry on a broad and complex program of social welfare in the international sphere. The work of assisting refugees in returning to their former homes or going to new ones involved the identification, registration, and classification of persons; reuniting scattered families or what remained of them; the provision of food, clothing, housing; health services; vocational training, including special training for the handicapped; unearthing opportunities for resettlement and employment; arranging for the institutional care of persons who would require it for most or possibly all of their lives; the operation of a transport fleet for moving refugees under its mandate; and the provision of political protection for refugees. Gradually refugees dispersed throughout the world were registered with the Organization. Although the greatest number were concentrated in Germany, applicants for assistance appeared in more than twenty countries in Africa, the Americas, and Asia, as well as in Europe.

The IRO did not solve the refugee problem, but it did succeed, in the face of continued Soviet intransigence at the General Assembly and the Economic and Social Council, in arranging for the repatriation or resettlement of the bulk of the refugees under its mandate. It rapidly recruited an able international staff. In general, the member governments, although preoccupied during the latter part of the existence of the IRO with arrangements for successor agencies, assumed the necessary financial obligations, provided stable delegations to sessions of the IRO Council, co-operated in attempting to resolve problems of policy and administration, and accepted a share of the "hard-core" refugees expected to be permanent public charges. Of its over-all budget of nearly $400 million, the United States contributed more than half. The next largest contributions were made by the United Kingdom, France, and Canada in that order.

The IRO was assisted by more than one hundred voluntary agencies that could, through case work, help reach the individuals whose special problems would otherwise receive scant attention in a mass program. The voluntary agencies were especially valuable in helping to solve the problems of "hard-core" refugees, in helping refugees become established in the countries of resettlement, and in formulating programs for aid to refugees after the termination of the International Refugee Organization.

The IRO stressed the problems that would remain after its liquidation in February 1952. No provision had been made for the future care of thousands of persons in tragic circumstances. These included "hard-core" refugees and others inside and outside institutions in Germany and Austria; refugees in the Middle East, Greece, and Trieste; and Europeans who had been transferred from Shanghai to the Philippines by the IRO. More and more persons were slipping secretly into Western Europe from behind the Iron Curtain. For refugees who had been settled locally, there remained—especially in Germany—the complex question of their integration into the national community, with some assurance of material security and legal and political protection. Finally, as the IRO reminded the United Nations, there were over nine million homeless and uprooted people outside the IRO mandate whose problems had never been assumed as a responsibility of the United Nations: among them, Germans who had been transferred to Germany from other countries or who had fled the Allied armies; Chinese refugees in Asia and the Far East; and refugees on the Indian subcontinent.

With the liquidation of the IRO, United Nations policy on refugees shifted from emphasis on relief, repatriation, and resettlement to problems connected with the assimilation of refugees in the countries of settlement, and the legal and political protection due them. In establishing the new Office of United Nations High Commissioner for Refugees, the United Nations completed a circle and returned to the more limited role played by the League of Nations.[11]

Refugees of the Arab-Israeli Conflict

The relief program for Palestine refugees that the United Nations began late in 1948 with the hope of terminating in mid-1949 is still in operation. After eight difficult years, more refugees were in need of relief than at the beginning, and no early reduction in requirements was expected.

More than half of the 922,000 refugees under care in June 1956 were concentrated in Jordan, a small country, poor in resources, where they represented one third of the total population of the nation. The remaining refugees were to be found in the Egyptian-controlled Gaza Strip, and in Lebanon and Syria. Through June 30, 1956, the equivalent of $266 million had been contributed for their care, employment, and resettlement. Of this total, voluntary agencies had contributed the equivalent of approximately $16 million. About half the total number of refugees registered on June 30, 1956, were children fifteen years of age or under.

The international approach to the Palestine refugee problem has not been characterized by rigidity or reluctance to experiment. The program has passed through at least three major phases. For the first year, it was a straight relief operation. There was then a year during which the emphasis was on public works rather than direct relief. After mid-1951, the theme became "reintegration," *i.e.*, re-establishment of refugees, without prejudice to their claims to eventual repatriation or compensation, where they could be self-supporting rather than dependent on public works projects for employment. Each of these phases is described briefly below.

For some days before the proclamation of the State of Israel on May 15, 1948, Palestinian Arabs had been leaving Palestine, either in fear of the future or in the hope of returning to the area as conquerors. On the day after the proclamation, the Arab League—Egypt, Iraq, Jordan, Lebanon, Saudi Arabia, Syria, and Yemen—instituted armed action.

[11] For information concerning the work of the Office of the High Commissioner for Refugees, see below, Chap. VIII. For a comprehensive history of IRO, see Louise W. Holborn, *The International Refugee Organization* (1956).

Additional tens of thousands of Palestinian Arabs who lived on the Israeli side of the present armistice lines then fled, leaving behind them their houses, fields, shops, and careers. By November 1948, there were estimated to be three quarters of a million Arab refugees. Professional men as well as those who had been farmers or shopkeepers were reduced, almost without exception, to starvation levels. In the countries of refuge, they depressed even further the existing low level of wages, they increased the vulnerability of their havens to epidemics, and they became charges on economies that could not support them.

On November 19, 1948, the General Assembly identified aid to Palestine refugees as "one of the minimum conditions for the success of the efforts of the United Nations to bring peace to that land," and requested the Secretary-General to appoint a Director of United Nations Relief for Palestine Refugees, with appropriate responsibility for planning and implementing a relief program. Member and nonmember nations were urged to contribute approximately $32 million for relief from December 1, 1948 to August 31, 1949.[12] A month later, on December 11, 1948, the General Assembly resolved that:

> . . . refugees wishing to return to their homes and live at peace with their neighbours should be permitted to do so at the earliest practicable date, and that compensation should be paid for the property of those choosing not to return and for loss of or damage to property which, under principles of international law or in equity, should be made good by the Governments or authorities responsible.[13]

The relief program was to have ended in August 1949. There being no improvement of the situation in Palestine by then, the Secretary-General extended the program pending a decision by the General Assembly.

When the General Assembly met, it had before it the report of a distinguished Economic Survey Mission, endorsed by the Director of Relief, recommending a drastic reduction in direct relief with emphasis instead on helping the Arab governments initiate and support public works programs in the countries where refugees were located. In December 1949, one year after the General Assembly had created the United Nations Relief for Palestine Refugees, it created a successor agency—the United Nations Relief and Works Agency for Palestine Refugees in the Near East (UNRWA)—to carry out the relief and works programs recommended by the Economic Survey Mission.[14]

[12] Res. 212(III), Nov. 19, 1948.
[13] Res. 194(III), Dec. 11, 1948.
[14] Res. 302(IV), Dec. 8, 1949.

The efforts of the new agency to set in motion a program of public works were impeded by delays in collecting contributions, sharp increases in prices following the outbreak of the Korean war, unexpected opposition from the refugees themselves, and limited co-operation from the governments in the area. A few road-building and afforestation projects were undertaken in Lebanon, Syria, and Jordan, but they proved five times as costly to finance as direct relief. Moreover, when the roadways were built or the forestry jobs done, the refugees found themselves with no alternative but to return to the relief rolls. Consequently, although direct relief was to have ended by December 1950, the General Assembly authorized UNRWA to continue such relief on a diminishing scale to June 30, 1952, and meanwhile to concentrate on projects that would lead to "reintegration" of the refugees.

By "reintegration projects," the General Assembly meant projects developed in collaboration with Middle Eastern governments to make the refugees permanently self-supporting, without prejudice to their right to return to their homes or to secure compensation. Reintegration was to be accomplished through assisting refugees in finding employment; training them for occupations in which there was a shortage of workers; making loans and grants to refugees for small enterprises; building homes in areas where jobs were available; developing agricultural opportunities through well-drilling, irrigation, and construction of access roads; and financing general economic development. It was recognized that the funds provided for this purpose would not be sufficient to solve the refugee problem, but it was hoped that the host countries would inaugurate parallel schemes for economic development.[15]

From July 1951 on, UNRWA sought to negotiate projects with the host governments. When the eighth session of the General Assembly convened in September 1953, the high hopes for the reintegration program had suffered the same fate as those for the earlier program of public works. There had been practically no change in the number of refugees requiring United Nations aid.[16] Despite denials by UNRWA

[15] U.N. General Assembly, Seventh Session, *Official Records*, Supplement No. 13, "Annual Report of the Director of the United Nations Relief and Works Agency for Palestine Refugees in the Near East, Covering the Period 1 July 1951 to 30 June 1952" (1952), pp. 7–8.

[16] Indeed the number of refugees on relief would have been greater than the 872,000 that it was, the Director stated, had not Israel in July 1952 assumed responsibility for some 19,000 Arab refugees within its borders. Moreover, the refugee movement at the outbreak of hostilities was a two-way flow, and Israel had promptly assumed responsibility for the 17,000 Jewish refugees who fled from Arab lands into Israel. It has since then taken in very many more Jewish refugees from Arab lands,

and the United Nations itself, the refugees continued to suspect that reintegration was designed to wean them from their goal of repatriation, and they remained reluctant to participate in the program. The members of the Arab League charged that the reintegration program meant in effect that the possibility of repatriation had been abandoned and that the refugees were being condemned to permanent exile. On the other hand, it should have been fairly obvious that the prospects for repatriation were growing dimmer as the years went by without any reduction in Arab-Israeli tensions.

Only a few reintegration projects were agreed on between UNRWA and the Middle Eastern governments. During 1953, at the request of UNRWA, a plan was drafted by an American firm, employed under the direction of the Tennessee Valley Authority, for using the Jordan Valley water resources for irrigation and hydroelectric power. The President of the United States appointed a personal representative with the rank of ambassador to explore the possibilities of the project with the governments of the region. Although progress has been made, no consensus has been reached. If and when large numbers of jobs are created through economic development projects, the refugees will inevitably have to compete for them with the almost equally destitute general population. In this competition, they are more than likely to be by-passed in favor of the indigenous population.

Meanwhile, the contributing governments have grown increasingly reluctant to continue supplying funds, and the host countries remain about as ill-equipped as ever to bear the burden unaided. In these circumstances, the eighth session of the General Assembly in late 1953—with the Soviet bloc abstaining, as it had throughout the controversy, but with no negative votes—decided to continue UNRWA until June 30, 1955, hopeful that it could negotiate a transfer of its continued heavy responsibility for direct relief to the Arab governments. No progress in this direction having been made, the ninth session of the General Assembly in December 1954 extended the life of the agency to June 30, 1960.[17]

The great accomplishment of the United Nations is that, because of the perseverance and unquenchable optimism of the free world, it has at least kept the refugees alive. It has supplied nearly a million persons with food rations of 1,500 to 1,600 calories per day. It has sheltered

repatriated a substantial number of Arab refugees, and released some of the funds held in blocked accounts of refugees in Lebanon.

[17] Res. 818(IX), Dec. 4, 1954.

about a third of this number in camps. It has prevented serious epidemics and has provided some schooling for children and some training for adults.

The political friction that has blocked and interfered with the operations of UNRWA at almost every stage in its history has manifested itself in a number of ways. Israel has contended that the Arab refugees are the responsibility of the Arab states, not of the United Nations; that the condition of the refugees is the direct result of the attack by the Arab states on Israel; that their return in large numbers would threaten Israeli internal security; and that the best solution is to settle the bulk of the refugees in the Arab states. In an attempt to make a package deal on the entire matter, Israel at one time offered to repatriate 100,000 Arab refugees provided this agreement were made part of a general political settlement. The offer was rejected by the Arab states, which contended that the policy of the United Nations was repatriation for all refugees who desired it. Nevertheless, a number of refugees have infiltrated back into Israel and have been accepted as citizens. The Arab states have charged that the condition of the refugees was worse than pictured by the director of the agency in his reports to the United Nations (although these reports have been notably frank); that the relief assistance given was desperately inadequate; that there was much sickness and few doctors; that the salaries of the international staff were too high; and that refugees should replace the many foreign nontechnical employees of UNRWA.

As the director stated, now that the "period of acute emergency is past, when the efforts of the international community were gladly accepted . . . the Agency is becoming something of an embarrassment to the host governments."[18] Despite some bans on their employment, refugees continue to glut the markets of their hosts with cheaper labor. In Jordan, every third person is on the ration list. In the Gaza Strip, where refugees constitute two thirds of the population, the Egyptian Government has been required to extend relief to its citizens as well. Host governments have ignored the international status of the agency and have interfered seriously with its operations. They have refused entry to some personnel of the agency and forced others to leave without explanation. They have attempted to impose income taxes on per-

[18] U.N. General Assembly, Eighth Session, *Official Records*, Supplement No. 12, "Annual Report of the Director of the United Nations Relief and Works Agency for Palestine Refugees in the Near East, Covering the Period 1 July 1952 to 30 June 1953" (1953), p. 3.

sonnel of the agency; landing charges on United Nations planes; excise taxes on supplies required by the agency; and taxes on interest earned by its bank deposits.

The United Nations for too long saw the Palestine refugee problem as a source of friction between the hostile states, which, if removed, would make peaceful settlement possible. It misgauged the bitterness of the conflict and underestimated vastly the difficulty of solving it through economic measures. In the present unhappy situation, there is much to be said for a United Nations policy that would place heavier responsibilities on the Arab governments to accept the bulk of the refugees, on the refugees to re-establish their lives in Arab lands, and on Israel to accept a small proportion and compensate the remainder.[19] The United Nations could then concentrate on assisting in the settlement of claims for compensation, removing the restrictions on mobility, which severely limit the ability of qualified refugees to take advantage of economic opportunities in different Middle Eastern countries, providing technical assistance and financial aid for projects that would raise the level of economic life generally in the region, and maintaining international peace in the area.[20]

Victims of Aggression in Korea

Within a few days of the outbreak of war in Korea on June 25, 1950, the United Nations appealed to Member governments for relief assistance as well as military aid for the victims of aggression. On July 31, the Security Council followed up its earlier broadside appeal with a resolution requesting the Unified Command to assume responsibility for the relief and support of the civilian population in Korea, and to establish, in the field, procedures for distributing emergency aid. The resolution went on to request the Secretary-General, the Economic and Social Council and other United Nations organs, and the specialized agencies to provide relief assistance to the Unified Command.[21] The

[19] The U.S. Secretary of State reported to the Senate Committee on Foreign Relations on February 24, 1956, that the United States stood ready to join with others in putting up the funds that would enable Israel to reimburse such refugees for their losses.

[20] See James Baster, "Economic Aspects of the Settlement of Palestine Refugees," *The Middle East Journal* (Winter 1954), pp. 58–68.

[21] Res. S/1657, July 31, 1950. The appeal to the Economic and Social Council, which elicited a prompt, favorable response, was made in accordance with Article 65 of the Charter, requiring the Economic and Social Council to assist the Security Council on the request of the latter.

United States Department of the Army assumed responsibility for estimating requirements on behalf of the Unified Command.

By October, when the General Assembly considered Korean relief, it was also confronted with the question of post-hostilities aid. The Assembly gave the Economic and Social Council two jobs. First, the Council was asked to develop plans in consultation with the specialized agencies for the relief and rehabilitation of Korea on termination of hostilities and—indicative of the hopes held by the Assembly for an early end to the war—to report on this problem within three weeks. Second—indicative of the desire that Korea should endure as a monument to the collective effort of the United Nations—the Council was asked to expedite a study of long-term measures for promoting economic development and social progress in Korea.[22]

The Economic and Social Council estimated that at least $250 million would be required between January 1, 1951, and early 1952, and made some organizational recommendations that were approved by the Assembly in December 1950. By a vote of 51 to 0, the General Assembly established the United Nations Korean Reconstruction Agency (UNKRA), to operate under the general guidance of the United Nations Commission for the Unification and Rehabilitation of Korea (UNCURK), and to be headed by an Agent-General appointed by the United Nations Secretary-General after consultation with UNCURK.[23]

A two-pronged policy thus emerged: the provision of emergency relief under the direction of the Unified Command (United States) during hostilities, and the provision of longer-term, post-hostilities aid through UNKRA. The purpose of the emergency program was to prevent disease and unrest behind the lines. Relief for the million or more homeless refugees, many of whom had moved south in order to get into the area controlled by the Unified Command, was but one aspect of the general problem of caring for the civilian victims of the war. As of the close of 1954, the Unified Command had received or had been promised for its emergency relief program the equivalent of more than $471 million from twenty-seven Member states and four states not members of the United Nations, from nongovernmental organizations, specialized agencies, the League of Red Cross Societies, and individuals. More than 95 per cent of this total, however, came from American sources. Nearly

[22] Res. 376(V), Oct. 7, 1950.

[23] U.N. General Assembly, Fifth Session, Plenary, *Official Records*, 314th Meeting (Dec. 1, 1950), p. 525. Res. 410(V), Dec. 1, 1950.

$420 million was contributed by the United States Government and $28 million by American private agencies.

Through the UNKRA program, the United Nations wished not only to provide subsistence but, in addition, to lay the groundwork for a model democratic economy that would adequately reflect the highest principles of the United Nations. Much of the policy set forth in the General Assembly resolution establishing UNKRA was a restatement of UNRRA policy, but there were also differences. The United Nations now stated that a program of relief and rehabilitation was necessary to provide the economic basis for a "unified, independent, and democratic government in Korea" and should be consistent with "the pattern of long-term economic development in Korea."[24]

Relief supplies were to be sold only in justified cases, and local currency proceeds so derived, or amounts equal to the value of the items supplied, were to be paid into an account under the control of the Agent-General. The funds were then to be used for additional relief and rehabilitation activity, to meet local currency expenses of the agency, or to combat inflation. Supplies were to be distributed equitably without discrimination as to race, creed, or political belief, and made available as appropriate through public and co-operative organizations, voluntary agencies, and "normal channels of private trade."[25]

The Korean Government was to take economic and financial action to ensure the effective use of United Nations and Korean resources, particularly action to combat inflation. It was to exempt supplies received under the program from import taxes, permit personnel of the United Nations to supervise distribution, and accord them the necessary privileges, immunities, and facilities.

The Agent-General of UNKRA was required to consult with and be guided generally by the United Nations Commission for the Unification and Rehabilitation of Korea on questions of policy concerning program and activities, and was to begin the relief and rehabilitation program after he, the Unified Command, and UNCURK had agreed the time was propitious.

On February 7, 1951, UNKRA was "activated." Until the negotiation of the cease-fire on July 27, 1953, however, the activities of the military in administering the United Nations emergency relief and short-term aid program dwarfed other efforts. UNKRA was confined to negotiating agreements with the Unified Command covering areas of responsibility; to organizational activities and planning schedules;

[24] *Ibid.*, Pt. B.
[25] *Ibid.*

and to carrying on a few minor projects complementing and supplementing the relief programs administered by the United Nations Civil Assistance Command, Korea (UNCACK). In January 1952, the Agent-General of UNKRA became responsible for recruiting a large share of the specialized civilian personnel needed in Korea. Personnel provided by the specialized agencies, nongovernmental organizations, and voluntary agencies were transferred to the United Nations Korean Reconstruction Agency, which in turn seconded them to the United Nations Civil Assistance Command. By 1953, more than half of the civilian personnel of the latter agency had been so provided.

The most important UNKRA activity during this period, however, was its development, together with the Unified Command and the Republic of Korea, of the first comprehensive long-range rehabilitation program. This program was designed to go into effect even before hostilities had come to an end. It envisaged the spending of $70 million for the period ending June 30, 1953, in the hope of helping the Korean Government halt the rapid economic deterioration in the country. The program, however, was late getting started and was not completed by its original target date.

With the cease-fire in July 1953, UNKRA entered a new and larger phase of activity. A $130 million reconstruction program for the year ending June 30, 1954, to supplement the earlier $70 million program, was approved a month after the cease-fire. Additional commitments authorized by the eighth session of the General Assembly would have brought the total program commitments by UNKRA, as of June 30, 1955, to $266 million. The necessary contributions were not forthcoming, however, and the program again fell considerably short of the goals set by the General Assembly.

Meanwhile the United States Government, having given aid to South Korea through the Economic Cooperation Administration before the outbreak of the war, having carried the main burden of Korean defense and relief during the war, and having been willing to pay a financial price for a truce,[26] made available an additional $200 million as the

[26] As Congressman Walter H. Judd said during the hearings on the Mutal Security Act of 1954, "A further fact is that the President of the United States promised them if they would agree to the truce we would give them up to one billion dollars of assistance in rehabilitating the country. We didn't say we would give it to the United Nations. This was one of the prices we paid for getting our boys out of the war there." The Minnesota Congressman's explanation was confirmed by a representative of the Department of State. *Mutual Security Act of 1954*, Hearings before the House Committee on Foreign Affairs, 83 Cong. 2 sess. (1954), pp. 450, 455–56.

first installment on a bilateral post-armistice program of economic rehabilitation in Korea. This further deflated UNKRA and gave the Government of Korea, whose leaders were expert in the politics of maneuver, additional opportunities for playing off one program against another.

The Korean Government had long been distrustful of the United Nations and at odds with UNKRA on basic issues. It wanted to decide what contracts would be let and to whom, whereas UNKRA was prepared to consult with the Korean Government on specifications but insisted that the Agent-General award contracts in accordance with a competitive bidding procedure. The Korean Government wanted exclusive control of the local currency proceeds derived from the sale of UNKRA supplies, although the General Assembly resolution that established the agency clearly gave the Agent-General control of the counterpart account. And like the governments of other underdeveloped countries, the Korean Government favored a program heavily weighted on the side of investment in capital facilities, including the inevitable steel mill. Fearful of the inflationary impact of a program that would put wages in the hands of workers without simultaneously increasing the available supply of consumer goods, UNKRA and the Unified Command urged less emphasis on investment and more on consumer goods. Thus, differences of opinion on program content were added to differences regarding financial and administrative procedures.

While these issues, as well as others, were postponing the signature of any over-all agreement between UNKRA and the Government of the Republic of Korea, the relations of the agency with the military command were also far from smooth. The military authorities were not averse to an agency that would provide funds and personnel for use under military direction but, even in this relationship, difficulties arose in connection with security clearances for civilian personnel and the provision of facilities enabling them to eat, work, travel, and obtain information necessary to the discharge of their duties. UNKRA, however, was intended to be more than an incidental aid to the achievement of military objectives, and the agency inevitably had views on economic and social objectives—and methods of attaining them—that were at variance with those of the military command.

Various arrangements were made to facilitate joint programing, coordinated operations, and orderly transfers of responsibility from one program to another, but the effect of the arrangements was to keep UNKRA in a subordinate role. An American civilian Economic Coordinator of Relief and Rehabilitation Operations, not an UNKRA official, became responsible for the establishment of over-all economic and financial policies, and the agency became responsible primarily for a series of long-range rehabilitation projects.

By the time a reasonably clear-cut role had been negotiated for UNKRA, and relationships with the military had grown more harmonious—as was the case after agreement early in 1953 on the $70 million UNKRA program—the enthusiasm of the governments that launched the agency had largely evaporated. The unexpected length of the Korean War and the retention of primary responsibility for relief operations by the military authorities during this period meant mounting administrative expenses, declining morale within the administrative staff, and extreme difficulty collecting pledges and contributions from Member governments. Although UNKRA had hoped that—with the termination of hostilities and the beginning, in 1953, of larger-scale, longer-range programing for relief and reconstruction—the promised contributions would be forthcoming more promptly, the reverse was the case.

The UNKRA program included projects to help rehabilitate agriculture, manufacturing, electric-power production, transportation, mining, housing, education, and health, sanitation, and welfare. Considerable quantities of various types of supplies were imported, including seeds, hatching eggs, fertilizer, irrigation equipment, spindles for the textile industry, dies for wire manufacture, briquetting presses to reduce the requirements for bituminous imports, railroad ties and trucks for the transportation system, rock-drilling equipment for mining, machines for fabricating earth blocks for the housing industry, educational materials ranging from books to supplies for vocational training, and medical supplies. In addition, UNKRA established a Small Industries Loan Fund with dollars and *hwan* resources to make loans to small, privately owned enterprises. By the end of 1954, these and related activities were beginning to bear fruit. Larger stocks of Korean-made goods, increased harvests, and greater fish catches by a more modern fishing fleet improved the prospects for eventual economic stability. Relations of the agency with the Government of Korea became more harmonious after the replacement of the first Agent-General in mid-1953, but at the cost of concessions to the views of the Government of Korea on program priorities.

The experience of this agency is proof that the specialized agencies, despite their autonomy, can be mobilized in response to resolutions of the

Security Council, the General Assembly, and the Economic and Social Council. The World Health Organization, Food and Agriculture Organization, International Refugee Organization, and United Nations Educational, Scientific and Cultural Organization all supplied teams of specialized personnel to help survey Korean requirements, to make recommendations within their own special fields of competence, and to provide technical services.

The experience of the agency illustrates also the fruitfulness of the relationships that the United Nations fosters with nongovernmental national and international voluntary agencies. Over and above the $28 million in supplies that these nongovernmental organizations contributed to the emergency program in response to the resolution of the Economic and Social Council, the voluntary agencies contributed approximately $8 million in relief supplies in support of their own programs in Korea. The United Nations agency, UNKRA, was able to systematize the efforts of private groups to provide material assistance to the Korean people, to encourage the establishment or continuation of specific programs in health, welfare, and other fields, and to support the voluntary agencies through the provision of ocean freight and direct program grants. Joint planning and programing in the social field between UNKRA and these voluntary agencies was achieved through the Korean Association of Voluntary Agencies.

In the first flush of enthusiasm, there had been hopes that Korea could be helped by UNKRA to rise from its ashes to heights it had never before attained. Despite the very substantial volume of economic aid obtained through multilateral and bilateral programs, however, it has become clear that South Korea will not emerge within the foreseeable future as a model of creative international relief efforts. The inadequate per-capita consumption levels of the prewar period had not been restored by the end of 1955, and interest in the area was clearly waning.

Emergency Action to Meet World Food Shortages

During the past ten years, the concern of the United Nations with world food problems has been focused on four main objectives: raising low levels of food production and consumption, and fighting chronic malnutrition; counteracting excessive fluctuations in the prices of agricultural products; promoting the rational disposal of intermittent agricultural surpluses; and relieving famine and other emergency situations.[27] The promotion of each of these objectives has presented special problems and called for special types of United Nations activity. The first three are treated later in this volume[28] and only the last is considered here, even though all four problems are closely interrelated.

Proposals for a World Food Board

In February 1946, during the first part of its first session, the General Assembly adopted a resolution, submitted by the major powers, that urged all governments and peoples to take prompt and drastic action separately and jointly through the new Food and Agriculture Organization to conserve supplies and to bring about the maximum production of grains.[29] This resolution also requested both the governments and the FAO to provide as much information as possible on the current world food situation and future outlook. At this time, it was generally expected that the period of postwar stringency would be brief and that it would soon be succeeded by one of agricultural surpluses. But when the General Assembly reconvened for the second part of its first session in October 1946, the situation had already taken a turn for the worse. The severe winter of 1946–47 in Europe, followed by an unprecedented drought in central and southeastern Europe, helped to convert a situation of temporary stringency into a world food crisis.[30]

While the first session of the General Assembly was in recess, the FAO responded to the resolution of February 1946 by calling a "Special Meeting on Urgent Food Problems," which was attended by the representatives of six international organizations and of twenty-one countries. After analyzing current food problems, this special meeting concluded that the existing machinery for meeting emergency food needs was inadequate.

Within a month after the special meeting, and in accordance with its recommendations, a new emergency agency was established—the International Emergency Food Council. This was in effect a successor to the Combined Food Board,[31] and like that board, it functioned through

[27] Food and Agriculture Organization, *Functions of a World Food Reserve—Scope and Limitations*, FAO Commodity Policy Studies No. 10 (1956), p. 3. (Hereinafter cited as *Functions of a World Food Reserve.*)

[28] See below, Chaps. III, IV, V, and VII.

[29] Res. 27(I), Feb. 14, 1946.

[30] For a vivid account of the serious view of the situation taken by the United States, see Harry S. Truman, *Memoirs: Year of Decisions* (1955), pp. 464–80.

[31] See above, Chap. I.

commodity committees and allocated food supplies to UNRRA and other claimants. Nineteen governments were represented on it; the Director-General of the FAO was a member of its Central Committee; and the FAO itself acted as secretariat.

At the same time, the Director-General of the FAO was, at the request of the special meeting, preparing suggestions for dealing with long-term problems of production, distribution, and consumption of agricultural products for submission to the September 1946 conference of the FAO. These took the form of proposals for a World Food Board acting through commodity committees and performing the following functions:

1. To stabilize prices of agricultural commodities on the world markets, including provision of the necessary funds for stabilizing operations.
2. To establish a world food reserve adequate for any emergency that might arise through failure of crops in any part of the world.
3. To provide funds for financing the disposal of surplus agricultural products on special terms to countries where the need for them is most urgent.
4. To co-operate with organizations concerned with international credits for industrial and agricultural development, and with trade and commodity policy, in order that their common ends might be more quickly and effectively achieved.[32]

For the purpose of stabilizing prices, the World Food Board, operating through its commodity committees, was to be given powers to hold stocks of each of the most important commodities, and to release or add to these stocks with a view to counteracting excessive market fluctuations.[33]

The proposed World Food Board, in brief, would be occupied with all the major problems relating to food and other agricultural products that have continued to concern the United Nations up to the present time. In September 1946, the FAO Conference accepted the general objectives of the proposed World Food Board, but did not agree to recommend its establishment. The conference decided instead to convene a Preparatory Commission for further study of the proposals. In addition, the FAO endorsed a resolution of the UNRRA Council on the need for special action to finance future imports of food for nations receiving UNRRA aid.

In October 1946, the Economic and Social Council, with the report of the Special Meeting on Urgent Food Problems in hand, requested the Secretary-General of the United Nations to assist the FAO in preparing proposals for long-term international machinery to deal with

[32] *Functions of a World Food Reserve*, p. 46.
[33] *Ibid.*

these problems, and directed the President of the Economic and Social Council or his alternate to participate in the meetings of the Preparatory Commission.

When the General Assembly reconvened, it had all this as background. It also had a *World Food Appraisal for 1946–47* issued by the FAO in September 1946 and the reports of the Secretary-General on the measures taken by United Nations organs and specialized agencies in response to the General Assembly resolution of the preceding February. In addition, it heard from the Secretary-General of the International Emergency Food Council. The Second (Economic and Financial) Committee of the General Assembly, to which these matters were referred, was less concerned with long-range problems than with the methods of meeting the more immediate relief problems, which would remain after UNRRA ceased activities on December 31, 1946.

On relief matters, the delegations were sharply divided in their conceptions of the scope and gravity of the problem, in their views on the need for international action, and in their ideas of methods to be employed. On the one hand there were nations, such as Denmark, that felt that drastic international action was required. On the other hand, there were those nations that followed the lead of the United States in questioning the need for new international relief machinery. Various compromises were suggested in an attempt to bring these two groups together. These compromises were rejected and the resolution that was finally adopted by the General Assembly, in December 1946, was confined largely to urging continued efforts by governments and international agencies to overcome the expected food deficit in 1947.[34] Having disposed in this hortative fashion of the immediate problem, the General Assembly was willing to look to the FAO and the Preparatory Commission on World Food Proposals to make concrete plans for long-range attacks on the food supply problem.

The Preparatory Commission met in 1946–47 and brought forward a series of recommendations for sales of foodstuffs, at special prices, for the improvement of nutrition and for a network of commodity stabilization methods of different kinds. Among the latter was the accumulation of three different kinds of reserves—working stocks, famine reserves, and price stabilization reserves—to be administered partly by international agreement. It was proposed that the famine reserves be held nationally by exporting and importing countries for use nationally and internationally under agreed conditions, and that the amount to be carried by

[34] Res. 45(I), Dec. 11, 1946.

each country should be decided for each commodity by international agreement.

In linking its famine-reserve proposal with a general stabilization program, the Preparatory Commission of government representatives was in agreement with the suggestions of the Director-General of the FAO, but it did not accept his proposal for a World Food Board.

Partly because of United States opposition, which reflected, among other things, awareness of congressional objections to international control of American food reserves, fear of compromising domestic freedom of action on price supports and other matters, dissatisfaction with the financial implications of the proposal, and the growing American interest in the contemplated International Trade Organization, the commission discarded the plan for a World Food Board in favor of a proposed World Food Council. The council was not to be a separate operating agency, but an integral part of the FAO with responsibility for consultation, review, and some types of action between the annual sessions of the FAO Conference. It was to examine current developments in intergovernmental commodity arrangements, particularly as they affected adequacy of the food supply, the use of food reserves, famine relief, and special food programs for the undernourished; to promote consistency and co-ordination of national and international agricultural commodity policies; to initiate study and investigation of critical agricultural commodity situations; and to advise on such emergency measures as would affect the export and import of supplies required under national programs of agricultural production.[35]

A World Food Council along these lines, although a come-down from the World Food Board, still seemed to the United States and some other countries too great a threat to their freedom of action in the politically sensitive area of agricultural policy. The third session of the FAO Conference in 1947 therefore established instead the FAO Council to act as the main FAO organ on world food questions in the intervals between sessions of the conference and assigned the following emergency functions to the new council:

1. Continuation of the allocation activities of the International Emergency Food Council through its commodity committees although the council itself was dissolved and incorporated into the new FAO Council as the International Emergency Food Committee.

2. Supervision and promotion of studies of continual commodity shortages.

[35] Food and Agriculture Organization, *Report of the FAO Preparatory Commission on World Food Proposals* (February 1947), pp. iii–vii, 11–14, 21–30, 52–55.

3. Advice on emergency measures to be taken regarding the import and export of agricultural products.

The functions and responsibilities of the new International Emergency Food Committee were similar to those of the Central Committee of the predecessor council. Eleven countries were elected to membership on the International Emergency Food Committee, and the ten commodity committees of the council on beans and peas, cereals, cocoa, fats and oils, feeds, fertilizers, meat and meat products, rice, seeds, and sugar were retained. During the eighteen months of its life, the International Emergency Food Council had been responsible for equitable international distribution of a massive volume of foodstuffs, and had stimulated the convening of a special cereals conference in Paris to consider the serious world grain situation.

During the months immediately following the establishment of the International Emergency Food Committee within the FAO Council, world conditions in food and agriculture continued to deteriorate. Reports of poor crops, a predicted serious world shortage of bread grains, and existing shortages of pesticides, farm machinery, and draft animals all pointed toward imminent famine in many countries. In 1948, however, the situation began to improve, and the need for allocating commodities became less urgent. In June 1949, the FAO Council terminated its International Emergency Food Committee. The world food situation was by that time characterized by surpluses of certain commodities, particularly in the dollar area, although supplies in other parts of the world were insufficient or barely sufficient. This situation prompted the FAO to convene a group of experts to propose measures for promoting the balanced expansion of world trade in agricultural products.

Proposals for an International Commodity Clearing House

The report of the experts recommended the establishment of a new international agency, the International Commodity Clearing House, to operate with a capital fund equivalent to \$5 billion to carry on, with the consent of the countries concerned, a wide variety of commodity transactions.[36] In the short run—*i.e.*, during the period of trade disequilib-

[36] Food and Agriculture Organization, Fifth Session of FAO Conference, *Report on World Commodity Problems*, Doc. C 49/10 (Nov. 21, 1949). The experts were: John B. Condliffe (United States), Colin Clark (Australia), J. K. Galbraith (United States), D. Ghosh (India), Gustavo Polit (Chile), and A. Radomysler (United Kingdom).

rium and currency inconvertibility—the purpose of these transactions would be generally to keep commodity trade moving and, in particular, to forestall the accumulation of surpluses in hard-currency countries in the face of need in soft-currency countries. In the long run, their purpose would be to moderate the effects on prices of short-run changes in commodity demand and supply.[37]

The capital fund was to be provided initially by national quotas, based on national incomes of member countries and payable in their own currencies. Of the quota of each nation, 20 per cent would be due when the country joined the organization and would become part of the general fund of the Clearing House. The other 80 per cent was to be available on call for use in the purchase of surplus commodities in the country in question.

Two main types of short-term transactions were envisaged. The first involved use of the 80 per cent for the acquisition of surpluses, presumably in hard-currency areas, at commercial prices. These were to be resold, for soft currencies, to countries that could not otherwise buy them. Pending convertibility, the Clearing House would hold the soft currencies of receiving countries, which would be guaranteed by those countries against losses from currency depreciation, in accounts for the supplying countries. The second type of short-run trading operation was to be financed by the Clearing House, using its own general fund (the 20 per cent of the national quotas) as a revolving fund, to purchase surpluses at less than commercial prices for resale outside the general channels of commerce, *e.g.*, for relief purposes.

The proposals for an International Commodity Clearing House were not accepted by the FAO Conference. Had they been accepted, the bulk of the resources of the Clearing House probably would soon have been frozen in inconvertible currencies, for convertibility has not yet been achieved. Having rejected two well-intended but over-ambitious plans for the stabilization and better distribution of world food supplies under international auspices, the FAO Conference in 1949 contented itself with appointing a purely advisory Committee on Commodity Problems to analyze and interpret the international commodity situation and advise the council on suitable action.

Proposals for an Emergency Famine Reserve

The next effort of the United Nations to address itself to the problem of emergency rather than chronic food shortages began in August 1951

[37] *Functions of a World Food Reserve*, p. 51.

with the introduction jointly by Chile and the United States of a draft resolution at the thirteenth session of the Economic and Social Council. This resolution, which was subsequently adopted, in effect supported the existing pattern of bilateral assistance in times of emergency, and called on the FAO to keep "existing or emerging food shortages in individual countries under continuous surveillance," to continue its periodic studies of the problem, and—in case of pending shortages—to make emergency reports to the FAO Council, the FAO Conference, and the United Nations Secretary-General for transmission to the Economic and Social Council.[38]

At the next conference of the FAO, in November–December 1951, two important follow-up resolutions were passed. One of these directed the Director-General to initiate investigations of existing or potential food shortages or famine once he had learned of them, and to report the extent of need to the United Nations and appropriate specialized agencies; also to convene a special meeting of the FAO Council and interested governments for the purpose of working out a program of action if relief were deemed necessary. This resolution proved to embody the main approach of FAO to the problem of emergency food shortage from then on, and was reaffirmed in November 1953 after sustained effort to develop proposals for an emergency famine reserve had proved fruitless. These latter efforts were authorized in another resolution of the 1951 conference, which asked the FAO Council to study and explore suitable ways and means whereby an emergency food reserve could be established and made available promptly to member states threatened or affected by serious food shortage or famine.[39]

With this background of prior action by the Economic and Social Council and by the Conference of the Food and Agriculture Organization, the General Assembly, in January 1952, for the first time expressed a formal interest in setting up procedures for dealing with future famine emergencies resulting from natural causes.[40] The resolution of the Assembly was passed after extensive debate in which the United States, emphasizing the potentialities of private organizations, took the position that bilateral or voluntary action continued to be the best means of meeting famine emergencies, but that such voluntary efforts should be facilitated and co-ordinated through the United Nations. In contrast, India sought to have the General Assembly take a more favorable

[38] Res. 405(XIII), Aug. 31, 1951.

[39] For the text of these resolutions (Nos. 15 and 16), see Food and Agriculture Organization, *Report of the Sixth Session of the Conference, 19 November–6 December 1951* (March 1952), pp. 47–48.

[40] Res. 525(VI), Jan. 26, 1952.

stand on the question of establishing a famine reserve, and the Soviet Union proposed that world resources then being employed in the manufacture of armaments be used instead to increase food production. The resolution as passed endorsed the recommendation of the Economic and Social Council for reports by FAO in cases of emergency, and requested the Secretary-General, in consultation with the heads of FAO, WHO, and other agencies, to prepare recommendations for the fourteenth session of the Economic and Social Council on ways of bringing about concerted action by governments, intergovernmental organizations, and voluntary agencies in time of famine resulting from crop failure.

In the report to the Economic and Social Council called for by this resolution, the Secretary-General recommended a set of procedures to be followed by governments, intergovernmental organizations, and voluntary agencies in the event of a famine emergency. He stressed the importance of prior standing arrangements to facilitate the immediate provision of funds and supplies in the event of an emergency. In dealing with questions of finance, he referred to the studies the FAO was making on the possibility of setting up a famine reserve, and suggested that such a reserve would probably not meet all needs. Additional funds might be required to meet "the initial impact of a disaster, when suffering is likely to be most severe and when the danger of panic, hoarding, and inflation is most threatening."[41] Inasmuch as neither the specialized agencies nor the voluntary organizations could be expected to have on hand the funds required, the report suggested four other possible sources: advance voluntary pledges or contributions by governments to a special fund; budgeted contributions by governments to such a fund; use of the Secretary-General's authority to make special disbursements from the United Nations Working Capital Fund; and advances by United Nations agencies to be reimbursed from the responses to an appeal by the Secretary-General.

At its fourteenth session in mid-1952, the Economic and Social Council endorsed the Secretary-General's concept of the roles of the Food and Agriculture Organization, the United Nations, and the voluntary agencies. But, except for a reference to the pending studies by the FAO of ways and means of establishing an emergency famine reserve, the Council remained discreetly silent on the subject of financing famine relief.[42]

[41] U.N. Economic and Social Council, Fourteenth Session, *Food and Famine, Procedures for International Action in the Event of Emergency Famines Arising from Natural Causes*, Doc. E/2220 (May 14, 1952), p. 11.

[42] Res. 425(XIV), June 30, 1952.

The FAO famine-reserve studies were carried on by working parties of experts who elaborated a series of plans, of which the most practicable appeared to them to be the establishment of an internationally owned emergency relief fund equipped with the necessary organization and finance for drawing on nationally owned stocks as needed. As a working tool for the purpose of their calculations, the experts developed a kind of yardstick unit, the Emergency Food Reserve Unit, which was defined as the quantity of food required for supplementing the diet of one million people at the rate of 1,200 calories per person per day for one month. The total calorie intake assumed by the FAO for an emergency subsistence period was 1,900, but some 700 calories would presumably be available locally.[43] As a minimum, the experts advocated a reserve of twenty units, which would cost approximately $32 million and would be sufficient to maintain 5 million people for four months.

Upon receiving the report of the experts, the FAO Council decided that all the facts were available and that it was time for the governments to determine what they would do. At the FAO Conference of 1953, the governments declined to adopt the recommendations of the expert group. It was clear that, despite all preparatory work, the political decision to provide either funds or pledges under any of the alternate plans submitted would not be forthcoming. The President of the United States had just announced that $100 million in surplus American farm products were to be made available on a bilateral basis when needed to meet emergency famines abroad. Most of the surplus-producing nations, particularly those whose financial resources would be called on to maintain any form of international reserve, refused to support the suggestions of the FAO. On the other hand, with the exception of Pakistan, which had just benefited from American famine aid, the majority of the nations likely to be subject to famine urged adoption of an international reserve plan.

The discussion was vigorous. In general, the United States, Canada, and the countries favoring the unorganized, *ad hoc* approach called for under Resolution 15 of 1951, claimed that this approach had worked well in practice, and that the FAO experts had failed to demonstrate that it would not continue to work well. They asserted that governments would respond voluntarily and promptly in time of need, that it was questionable whether international action as contemplated under a reserve plan would be sufficiently speedy, and that it was also questionable whether famine needs were sufficiently great to warrant setting up new machinery. Those in favor of some form of reserve argued

[43] *Functions of a World Food Reserve*, p. 55.

variously that a reserve was necessary from the humanitarian point of view; that it would not be a substitute for national action, but a supplement to it; that purely *ad hoc* assistance would not allay the fears of the people subject to famine nor provide them with the necessary security; that, on the contrary, *ad hoc* assistance would always be uncertain and never assured or speedy.

The resolution of the conference as finally adopted stated that, although there was a difference of opinion regarding whether a reserve was necessary, in a sense this was academic, because Member nations evidently would not support it either by funds or stocks.[44] The 1953 resolution reaffirmed Resolution 15 of 1951, and supported *ad hoc* measures to relieve famine conditions as "useful and necessary." It warmly approved the $100 million aid proffered by the United States, urged other nations to aid also, and recommended that the FAO be prepared to co-ordinate such action. Finally, the resolution suggested that countries belonging to the International Monetary Fund should apply to it for additional foreign exchange to finance food imports during emergencies.

With the passage of this resolution, the whole structure of the FAO preparatory work for the establishment of an international reserve to meet emergency food shortages collapsed. Yet something remained as a result of all the effort. The FAO has assumed definite responsibilities for keeping under review situations in which there is danger of famine, for ascertaining the type and scope and for estimating the possible duration of imminent crises, and for mobilizing voluntary support in time of need. This has been made possible by separating the problem of famine relief from the problem of price stability for agricultural commodities. Until 1952, the two problems had often been considered together and had become confused in the process.

Emergency Aid for Other Purposes

International emergency relief requirements most frequently take the form of sharply increased needs for food (principally grains) from abroad. However, floods, fires, earthquakes, epidemics, and other disasters may require pumping equipment, tents and temporary shelters, clothing, blankets, and medical supplies in greater volume than a hard-hit country can supply. During the course of its life, the United Nations has on several occasions assisted nations having emergency require-

[44] Food and Agriculture Organization, *Report of the Seventh Session of the Conference, 23 November–11 December* 1953 (1954), Res. 21.

ments of this type. When such situations have been brought to the attention of Member governments, the response has been voluntary, prompt, and generous, but no regular procedures have been established for meeting these emergencies.

Except for its interest in providing famine aid, the United Nations has never looked with favor on the establishment of such procedures. From the League of Nations, it inherited the International Relief Union, which had been brought into being by convention in 1932 for the purpose of giving aid and co-ordinating international action in the event of a "major disaster due to *force majeure*."[45] After the formation of the United Nations, the Union urged its member governments to support a plan to bring it into some kind of relationship with the new organization. Attempts to obtain funds from the United Nations Educational, Scientific, and Cultural Organization to continue its research activities were unsuccessful, as was its approach to the Economic and Social Council for a permanent relationship with the United Nations. With the support of the President of the International Red Cross Committee and some of its member governments, the International Relief Union sought to have its convention revised so as to enable it to coordinate the work of various temporary United Nations relief organizations and to "provide a centre for regular meetings of the representatives of the States interested in the establishment of an international relief programme."[46] Other member governments favored its termination, and the Economic and Social Council recommended in 1950 that United Nations Members belonging to the International Relief Union take steps to terminate it.[47]

Under the United Nations, the pattern of action in cases other than those involving serious shortages of food has included notification to United Nations organs and agencies concerned with social welfare, particularly the Children's Fund and the World Health Organization, and the transmittal of official appeals to Member nations for assistance. The Children's Fund has definite responsibilities for helping to meet the relief needs of women and children, and the World Health Organization has an obligation to assist in times of epidemic. None of the other agencies has been set up or financed to meet emergency relief requirements wherever they happen to arise.

There is no regular channel in the United Nations through which

[45] See above, Chap. I.

[46] U.N. Economic and Social Council, Tenth Session, *Relations with Inter-Governmental Organizations*, Doc. E/1574/Add. 2 (Jan. 30, 1950), p. 4.

[47] U.N. Economic and Social Council, Fourteenth Session, *Food and Famine, Procedures for International Action in the Event of Emergency Famines . . .*, p. 3, note 2.

appeals for aid are initiated. The General Assembly was in session when northern Italy was inundated by severe floods late in 1951, and its Third (Social, Humanitarian, and Cultural) Committee adopted a resolution proposed by Uruguay requesting the President of the General Assembly and the Secretary-General to advise all United Nations organizations having social welfare responsibilities of Italian needs, and urging these agencies to provide immediate assistance. On other occasions, the initiative has been taken by the Economic and Social Council, by the FAO, or by UNICEF.

In a report to the Economic and Social Council on procedures for dealing with famine emergencies, the Secretary-General suggested that the procedures for meeting emergencies arising from crop failures could be applied to other disaster situations.[48] The resolution of the Economic and Social Council, which followed consideration of the Secretary-General's report, however, confined itself to United Nations action in times of famine emergency. Nevertheless, it is conceivable that in the future, the Secretary-General will, with the acquiescence of the General Assembly and the Economic and Social Council, invoke the procedures applicable to famine situations when other emergency situations are brought to his attention. The pattern may in this manner become accepted practice long before it is embodied in a formal resolution.

Collective Measures Against Future Aggression

Of a quite different order and character than the efforts of the United Nations to prepare for crises due to natural disasters were the efforts to prepare collective measures to meet the man-made disaster of aggression.

Only fortuitous circumstances had enabled the United Nations to take swift action against the North Korean aggression: there was a United Nations Commission on Korea present to report the facts of the attack, the Soviet delegate had boycotted the Security Council and therefore was not able to veto its action recommendations, and American forces were available in Japan to rush to Korea with desperately needed assistance to help check the initial onslaught. The United Nations, taking advantage of these circumstances, created and organized a cooperative military enterprise which was unique in history and which offered considerable promise for the future.

The Korean experience revealed the need for further planning to realize the potentialities of collective action through the United Nations and to

[48] *Ibid.*, p. 3.

strengthen the United Nations as an instrument of collective security in the future.[49]

The "Uniting for Peace" resolution adopted by the General Assembly, in November 1950, represented an important step in this direction. The resolution provided, among other things, for the establishment of a Collective Measures Committee of fourteen members to study and report on methods that might be used to strengthen international peace and security under the Charter.[50]

During 1951 and 1952, the committee considered political, military, and economic measures and embodied its conclusions in two major reports to the General Assembly.[51] The present discussion deals only with what the committee called "measures of an economic and financial character," a field which it analyzed with outstanding skill.[52]

Although the analysis of the committee was notably lucid and well-reasoned, it appears to have had little effect on the actions of Member governments. The elaboration of measures to be used at some unknown future date against a hypothetical aggressor that might have at its disposal resources as vast as those of the Soviet bloc, or as modest as those of Jordan, was inevitably a somewhat theoretical exercise. Enthusiasm for the project was generated primarily by the United States. It was carrying the brunt of the Korean burden, was alert to the possibilities of similar attacks on other vulnerable areas, and was determined that the United Nations should be better prepared to resist future aggression than it had been in Korea. At the same time, however, the United States was carrying on delicate negotiations with its North Atlantic Treaty partners regarding methods of sharing the cost of rearmament. The United States was eager to have Members of the world organization committed to effective resistance to aggression,

[49] U.S. Department of State, *United States Participation in the United Nations: Report by the President to the Congress for the Year 1951*, Publication 4583 (July 1952), p. 49.

[50] The fourteen members were: Australia, Belgium, Brazil, Burma, Canada, Egypt, France, Mexico, Philippines, Turkey, the United Kingdom, the United States, Venezuela, and Yugoslavia.

[51] U.N. General Assembly, Sixth Session, *Official Records*, Supplement No. 13, "Report of the Collective Measures Committee," (hereinafter cited as "First Report of the Collective Measures Committee"); U.N. General Assembly, Seventh Session, *Official Records*, Supplement No. 17, "Report of the Collective Measures Committee," (hereinafter cited as "Second Report of the Collective Measures Committee.")

[52] For a comprehensive discussion of United Nations activities in the preparation of collective measures against future aggression, see the volume in this Brookings series, *The United Nations and the Maintenance of International Peace and Security*, Chaps. XVI–XIX, particularly Chaps. XVI and XVIII.

but it was not at all eager for the United Nations to develop formulae for burden-sharing that might complicate the concurrent discussions of the subject in the North Atlantic Treaty Organization.

The underdeveloped countries were reluctant to undertake any commitments that might interfere with the realization of their development plans. It is worth noting, for example, that the "Uniting for Peace" resolution ends not with a recommendation that governments increase their readiness to take collective action against military aggression, but that they "intensify individual and collective efforts to achieve conditions of economic stability and social progress, *particularly through the development of under-developed countries and areas.*"[53] The underdeveloped countries were eager for the United Nations to develop detailed blueprints for a World Food Board or for utilizing a hypothetical fund to make grants-in-aid for economic development—projects that the United States considered academic—but they were hesitant to blueprint measures for repelling future aggression—an undertaking that the United States considered urgent. The closer the Korean situation moved toward an armistice, the more vocal became the fears of other nations that the studies of the Collective Measures Committee reflected a bellicose, and hence wrong, philosophy on the part of the United Nations.

The Soviet bloc, of course, was fundamentally opposed to the work of the Collective Measures Committee. Its representatives argued repeatedly that the committee was illegal, that its activities reflected the aggressive aims of imperialist powers, and that it should be abolished.

Weakening the Aggressor

Among the recent practical experiences on which the Collective Measures Committee could draw were the panoply of economic warfare measures employed in conjunction with military measures against the Axis Powers during the Second World War; the arms embargo invoked by the United Nations as part of the Palestine truce; the hastily-improvised machinery for repelling the attack on South Korea; and the ban on shipments of items of strategic importance to Communist China following its intervention in Korea. In addition, the United States, from 1948 on, had been negotiating with friendly nations, outside the United Nations framework, for withholding items of strategic importance from countries of the Soviet bloc. There were

[53] Res. 377 A (V), Nov. 3, 1950, para. 15. (Italics supplied.)

many lessons to be drawn from these experiences. Plans must be ready in advance or disastrous delays would occur at the crucial moment. The application of agreed measures should be prompt, thorough, and universal. Nevertheless, relatively few countries could be brought to terms by economic measures alone. The cost of applying sanctions, unless pro-rated in some manner, would fall very unevenly on co-operating countries. The employment of sanctions against nations breaching or threatening the peace was but one side of the coin, and the more questionable side at that; mobilizing assistance for the victim was the other side. In this field of emergency relief, there was likewise a legacy of practical experience on which to draw.

The Collective Measures Committee therefore considered both measures to weaken the economy of an aggressor and to strengthen the economy of the victim. It reminded Member governments that political, economic and financial, and military measures could be applied singly or in combination, according to the circumstances giving rise to the threat to, or breach of, the peace, the geographical location of the offending state, its economic self-sufficiency, and its sensitivity to moral pressure.[54] Some countries remain virtually immune to the effects of economic measures. Moreover, the efficiency of sanctions against states capable of economic endurance would diminish over time, both because of defections among the states participating in the sanctions and because of the ability of the states subjected to sanctions to adapt their economies to the changed situation. The countries most vulnerable to economic measures would be those that are highly developed and, at the same time, significantly dependent on international trade, particularly on imports of foodstuffs.[55]

> Collective measures are not without cost to those employing them, ... The damage which is done to the economy of an aggressor by such measures is matched, in the aggregate, by a corresponding loss distributed over the economies of the countries applying the measures. The economic basis for the action lies in the assumption that each of the cooperating countries will suffer a small and bearable loss, while the counterpart effect will be concentrated on the single economy of the aggressor and will be much more damaging.[56]

In practice, the costs will fall unevenly on co-operating nations and tend to be greatest for those having special supply or market relationships with the transgressor. In the view of the committee, the central importance of measures to equalize the burden had not in the past been

[54] "First Report of the Collective Measures Committee," para. 22.
[55] *Ibid.*, paras. 44 and 50.
[56] *Ibid.*, para. 52.

sufficiently appreciated. The committee made a few general suggestions concerning such measures, including the provision of alternative markets, raw materials, loans, and grants, but concluded rather lamely that no rules for sharing the cost of economic measures could be laid down in advance.[57]

The committee discussed in turn each of the economic and financial measures available for use against a potential aggressor: a total or a selective embargo on its commodity trade, the banning of some or all financial transactions with the government or nationals of the aggressor, the severing of physical communications, and the blocking or vesting of funds or property abroad. The total embargo was recommended as the basic and most effective sanction; the arms embargo as the most obvious form of selective embargo. To guard against loss of time in debating which armaments to ban, the Collective Measures Committee in 1952 compiled a list of arms, ammunition, and implements of war designed for application *in toto* the moment an arms embargo was declared. Two additional lists were prepared. The first, designed as a logical supplement to an arms embargo, comprised items virtually as vital as armaments themselves, namely, items of primary strategic importance such as transport materials and equipment, petroleum and petroleum products, communications and electronic equipment, and air-field or road construction equipment. The second was a reference list of strategic items such as power-generating equipment that might be of major importance in particular instances of aggression.[58]

Strengthening the Victim of Aggression

The selection and continuation of measures to deter aggression depend, unfortunately, on imperfect knowledge of the requirements, inventories, and ability of the aggressor to find substitutes for anything that is being withheld. In theory, at least, rendering effective assistance to the victim is simpler because the needs of the victim can be ascertained directly. When hostilities occur, relief and refugee assistance must be regarded as essential features of the program, along with loans, grants, supplies, and the more traditional forms of aid.[59]

With the Korean experience fresh in mind, the committee concluded that during the period of hostilities, relief assistance must be the responsibility of the armed forces. Only after hostilities have ceased

[57] *Ibid.*, paras. 52–56.
[58] "Second Report of the Collective Measures Committee," App. H and I.
[59] "First Report of the Collective Measures Committee," paras. 57–59.

in the area to be assisted can the job be undertaken by civilian agencies.[60] Several extremely pertinent questions concerning this conclusion have been raised:

> . . . Does it also follow that during a period of prolonged armistice negotiations, when hostilities still technically exist but when the military line is stabilized, that responsibility for relief and rehabilitation should rest with the armed forces? What is meant by the term "in the area"—the area immediately adjacent to the fighting, or the whole country in the case of Korea? Even though the military command must assume immediate responsibility for relief and rehabilitation, is it not possible to bring the military command under some over-all international civilian direction that will give better assurance that nonmilitary considerations will receive due attention?[61]

An investigation of the readiness of the specialized agencies to co-operate, within the limits of their constitutions, in the application of collective measures brought forth expressions of willingness to do so. It became clear, however, that these agencies could commit themselves in advance to make only marginal contributions.

Although national governments could be expected to operate the basic economic and financial controls, international machinery would be needed to co-ordinate the undertaking. The Collective Measures Committee, therefore, recommended that a co-ordinating committee, whose membership should depend on the circumstances of the case, be established by the Security Council or the General Assembly immediately on the finding of a threat to or breach of the peace.[62]

Since 1952, the United Nations has done little to extend or refine its earlier studies of collective economic measures. This very fact jeopardizes the value of the work that has already been done, for in an era of rapid technical progress, sanction procedures and embargo lists tend to become useless unless they are continuously revised in the light of the most recent information. In the age of the hydrogen bomb, the framework developed by the Collective Measures Committee in the shadow of the Korean aggression can quickly become irrelevant.

As matters stand, the United Nations has compiled some useful source material for reference in the event of further threats to the peace. The suggested framework is itself incomplete and lacks the formal approval of the General Assembly. Despite the efforts of the United States and certain other countries to have the Assembly at its

[60] *Ibid.*, para. 144.

[61] See the volume in this Brookings series, *The United Nations and the Maintenance of International Peace and Security*, pp. 488–89.

[62] The major functions of this co-ordinating committee are described in the "First Report of the Collective Measures Committee," para. 114.

sixth session go on record as "approving" the first report of the Collective Measures Committee, the Assembly in the end "noted" rather than "approved" it. At the seventh session, China called for prompt negotiations among Member states to secure ratified agreements relating to their participation in collective measures, but its initiative evoked little favorable response.

Pattern Established by Practice

The efforts of the United Nations to solve economic and social problems that, initially at least, seemed to be of an emergency character, have met with only limited success. Each of the organs and agencies established to meet such situations was given complex assignments. Some had their terms of reference changed repeatedly during the course of their activity and were confronted with almost insuperable operational difficulties.

The operating programs have been dependent on periodic voluntary contributions. Because some of the programs have required substantial sums, and because all have required broad participation and a continued high level of sympathy, they have been seriously handicapped by inadequate financing and declining interest. Advance planning for more than a few months ahead has been impossible; pledges have not met requirements, and actual contributions have fallen short of pledges; contributions in inconvertible currencies and in kind have further complicated the problem. Most of the burden has tended to fall on a few of the richer, hard-currency nations, principally the United States, and these in turn have become restive under their burden.

To difficulties inherent in the system of financing must be added the difficulties resulting from major political differences among Member states. Thus far the United Nations has not succeeded in solving the problem of Palestine refugees and is still confronted with a tragic situation that seems destined to continue until there is greater Arab-Israeli agreement in the area.

The persistent attacks by the Soviet bloc on the work of the International Refugee Organization doubtless hampered its work. Nevertheless, the IRO was probably second only to UNICEF as the most successful of the major United Nations efforts in the emergency field, namely UNICEF, IRO, UNRWA, and UNKRA. Re-establishment of the Palestine refugees on a self-sufficient basis and the reconstruction of Korea are essentially long-range undertakings requiring substantially more resources than are likely to be contributed voluntarily to international emergency agencies. The relative success of UNICEF has been due not so much to the management or character of the machinery as to the fact that the objectives of UNICEF are universally supported, the concept is simple, and the cost is low.

In planning or carrying out relief programs, it has become the established practice of the United Nations to lean on private voluntary agencies for important specialized services.

None of the attempts of the United Nations to establish stand-by machinery to meet future disasters can be regarded as successful. Only a few remnants of the elaborate proposals for famine reserves have been adopted, and no formal arrangements have been made for meeting disaster requirements for non-food items.

The lack of adequate stand-by arrangements is unquestionably a deficiency but should not obscure the fact that, when face to face with an emergency, the international community has invariably accepted a share of the responsibility for relieving the emergency, either through *ad hoc* co-operation among established agencies, or through newly-created temporary bodies. The willingness of the international community to provide help in the event of sudden need, most dramatically illustrated in 1944–46 by UNRRA, is therefore firmly rooted in practice, although not clearly proclaimed in principle.

The absence of approved machinery for co-ordinating the application of collective economic and financial measures against an aggressor, and of arrangements for sharing equitably the cost of applying them, is also a deficiency. It is easy, however, to overestimate the potential value of economic sanctions because decisions concerning their employment are inevitably made without adequate knowledge of the aggressor's requirements, inventories, intentions, or willingness to suffer deprivation. It is open to question, therefore, whether the war-making capacity of the aggressor will be damaged severely enough to justify the superstructure engaged in administering the sanctions and the strains among governments applying them. On the other hand, supplies, loans, grants, and refugee aid for the victim are indubitably helpful. For this more traditional form of action in an emergency situation, the United Nations has ample precedents.

CHAPTER III

International Trade and Payments*

DURING the ten years since the first meetings of the principal organs of the United Nations, all efforts to harmonize national viewpoints and to solve long-range problems of international trade and payments, whether through the United Nations system or outside it, have been strongly influenced by the basic differences of national attitude described earlier in this study. As previously shown, however, the lines of cleavage that came to the surface in the international negotiations prior to the entry into force of the United Nations Charter were, except in the case of the Soviet Union, not such as to preclude fruitful and friendly negotiation. They were often the product, not of deep-seated differences in social organization or political philosophy, but of judgment regarding the policies that would best promote objectives that, although held in common, appeared to come into conflict in particular situations.

Questions of timing, priorities, and methods have been the staple of international discussion between the major trading countries, particularly between the United States and the countries of Western Europe and of the British Commonwealth. To some extent, this has also been true of the differences between the industrialized and the underdeveloped countries, although the tendency of the latter to make common cause in the United Nations against the industrialized countries on issues affecting trade and payments has frequently underscored the more fundamental character of these differences.

The case has been different with the Soviet Union and its Eastern European satellites. The relatively small fraction of international trade carried on by these countries and the basic differences between their forms of economic organization and those of other members of the United Nations have made it difficult for them to participate constructively in international co-operation in the field of trade and payments.[1]

* By William Adams Brown, Jr.

[1] In 1948 this group of countries accounted for about 7 per cent of total world trade, and in 1953 for about 9 per cent. This slight increase in their share of an expanding volume of world trade was due almost entirely to an expansion of trade among themselves and with mainland China. *Cf.* U.N. Economic Commission for Europe, *Economic Survey of Europe in 1954* (1955), pp. 112–13.

In the debates of the General Assembly and the Economic and Social Council, the Soviet bloc has actively sought to exploit the differences existing between the underdeveloped and the industrialized countries, but in the main, the impact of the Soviet Union on the trade and payments activities of the United Nations has been indirect. The tensions created by its political and military policies, which have divided the world into contending blocs, have had a pervasive effect on all forms of postwar international economic co-operation both within and outside the United Nations. It is these policies, rather than differences in economic organization, that have excluded the Soviet bloc from sustained and constructive participation in international negotiations and debates on the central problems of international trade and payments.

The work of the United Nations system in the field of international trade and payments has been influenced in an extremely complex way by the national attitudes of Member governments, by the actual progress made in improving the situation in world trade and payments, and by the international co-operation achieved outside the system. Until recently, the work has had to be carried on in circumstances that were not propitious for the achievement of common objectives through international agencies with nearly world-wide membership. It has been complicated further by the failure to develop an integrated approach to international trade and related problems through the proposed International Trade Organization, and by the multiplicity of agencies, both within and outside the United Nations system, concerned with one or another aspect of these problems.

During the period preceding the invasion of South Korea in June 1950, the work of the United Nations and related agencies was gradually taking form. The International Monetary Fund (IMF) had to make basic decisions concerning its functions and principles of operation in a period of fundamental international disequilibrium in world trade. The Economic and Social Council was called upon to sponsor negotiations for an International Trade Organization (ITO) and to wrestle with the problem of which functions to allocate to that organization. Hopes that the ITO would come into existence were finally extinguished about the time of the invasion of South Korea, but a related trade agreement—the General Agreement on Tariffs and Trade (GATT)—had in the meantime come into being and, under it, the first steps toward a reduction of trade barriers had been taken.

These activities were greatly influenced by the launching of the

European Recovery Program outside the framework of the United Nations. The need arose for reconciling a regional approach to trade and payments in Europe with the global principles to which the Fund and the GATT were committed. At this time also, the work of the regional economic commissions of the United Nations was beginning to take form and some consideration was given in their meetings to trade problems from the regional point of view. During this period, moreover, the interest of the Food and Agriculture Organization (FAO) in trade problems was developing. Meanwhile the Economic and Social Council was largely concerned to emphasize the interests of underdeveloped countries in trade policies and to discuss the general trade problem largely in terms of employment.

The influence of the Korean War in promoting rearmament and two years of extreme fluctuation in world prices had very significant repercussions on the whole approach of the international community to trade and payments problems. The period following the invasion of South Korea may therefore be considered separately. When progress toward international equilibrium was resumed in 1953–54, the IMF developed a new lending policy, which might be available as conditions favorable to convertibility emerged. At the same time, the GATT was confronted with difficult problems connected with regional activities in Europe, with its own relationships to underdeveloped countries, and with questions regarding its methods of negotiation.

From the End of the War to the Invasion of South Korea

The outstanding economic characteristics of the period preceding the invasion of South Korea were the gradual disclosure of the true dimensions of the recovery and reconstruction problem, the general readjustment of foreign exchange rates, and the progress made during the first two years of the European Recovery Program toward international equilibrium.

Emergency Action and the Fundamental Disequilibrium in Trade

At the end of the Second World War, it was widely assumed, especially in the United States, that after a short period of transition the International Bank for Reconstruction and Development (IBRD) would become the principal source of intergovernmental lending, that the operations of the International Monetary Fund would assure the orderly functioning of a system of multilateral payments, and that the proposed International Trade Organization would be able to play an important role in providing the international economic environment necessary for the maintenance of high levels of world trade. These hopes with regard to the Bank and the Fund, which formally became specialized agencies of the United Nations when agreements were reached on November 15, 1947, were not fulfilled because of the fundamental disequilibrium in trade. The disequilibrium in trade also greatly influenced the commitments that countries in balance-of-payments difficulties were willing to assume in the ITO negotiations.

The sponsorship of these negotiations raised several important problems for the Economic and Social Council with which it was not ready to deal effectively because it was still engaged in developing its own organization and in dealing with emergency economic problems such as the arrangements for the allocation of materials in short supply, the continuation of certain activities of the United Nations Relief and Rehabilitation Administration (UNRRA), and the economic reconstruction of devastated areas.[2] Although the Articles of Agreement of the Fund stated specifically that the Fund was "not intended to provide facilities for relief or reconstruction or to deal with international indebtedness arising out of the war," they did provide for transactions with members even during the postwar transitional period.[3] In judging requests for such assistance, the Fund was obligated to give its members "the benefit of any reasonable doubt,"[4] and it did so by selling to members $606 million in dollar exchange between March 1947 and April 1948. Of these sales $526 million were to European members.

The executive directors of the Fund acknowledged that in making these advances, the Fund was running the risk that its resources would be used for purposes other than temporary assistance, but stated that they were anxious to have the Fund "make a contribution to the maintenance of national economies and of exchange stability during

[2] United Nations, *Report of the Secretary-General on the Work of the Organization*, Doc. A/65 (June 30, 1946), p. 14. For a discussion of these activities, see Chaps. II and IV of this volume.

[3] United Nations Monetary and Financial Conference, Bretton Woods, N.H., July 1 to 22, 1944, *Articles of Agreement, International Monetary Fund and International Bank for Reconstruction and Development* (1945), Art. XIV, Sec. 1, p. 29. (Hereinafter cited as *Articles of Agreement.*)

[4] *Ibid.*, Sec. 5, p. 30.

the transitional period."[5] This was clearly an understatement inasmuch as the Fund was operating in a crisis situation in which France was living from hand to mouth as far as dollar reserves were concerned, and Britain was struggling with an exchange crisis, with no reasonable expectation that either country would soon be able to restore balance-of-payments equilibrium.[6] In 1947, the Bank made its contribution by extending four general-purpose loans to European members, amounting in all to nearly $500 million.[7] Of the combined total of $1,099 million made available, $979 million went to the Benelux countries, France, and Great Britain.

The main co-operative efforts to help countries in balance-of-payments difficulties to meet their essential import requirements, however, were made outside the United Nations system. They included very large grants and credits by the United States to individual countries; substantial credits within the British Commonwealth; the accumulation of European currencies by other countries, including Latin American countries; the extension of large credits in bilateral trade and payments agreements, particularly in Europe but also with Latin American countries; the major operations of the UNRRA program and the civilian supply programs of the American and British military authorities in occupied and liberated areas; and, in addition, substantial private grants mainly from the United States.[8]

This vast mobilization of resources financed a flow of essential imports into countries that had suffered extensive war damage or whose economies had been seriously weakened by the war. Although these imports were on a scale sufficient to maintain minimum standards of living during the first critical stages of reconversion and reconstruction, they were far from sufficient to meet the potential demands of many of the importing countries. These demands were restrained by numerous forms of government action. Aside from the brief period of sterling convertibility in 1947, almost every country in the world except the

[5] International Monetary Fund, *Annual Report of the Executive Directors for the Fiscal Year Ended April 30, 1948* (1948), p. 46.

[6] Of the British drawings on the Fund, $250 million was in September, October, and November 1947, immediately following the suspension of convertibility, and the remaining $60 million was drawn in March 1948. *The Economist* (Dec. 6, 1947), p. 933, and (Apr. 3, 1948), p. 563.

[7] See below, Chap. IV.

[8] International Monetary Fund, *Annual Report of the Executive Directors for the Fiscal Year Ending June 30, 1947* (1947), pp. 10–13. For a review of American loans and grants during this period, amounting to $14.5 billion, see also William Adams Brown, Jr. and Redvers Opie, *American Foreign Assistance* (1953), Chap. III, *passim*.

United States was carrying on its trade under severe exchange and direct trade controls or other forms of government regulation.

The period as a whole was marked by an impressive improvement in production, especially in war-devastated countries.[9] For a time, this improvement tended to obscure the true gravity of the prevailing economic dislocations. Unlike the First World War, the Second World War had seriously impaired the capacity of many countries producing raw materials. At the same time, almost all such countries were intent on diversifying their economies and reducing their dependence on the production of primary commodities. The situation was further complicated by the political obstacles that hindered an expansion of trade between Eastern and Western Europe, and by the virtual elimination of Germany and Japan from world markets. In the case of the Netherlands, France, and the United Kingdom, the balance-of-payments problem was further aggravated by the loss of very large sources of invisible income, which increased their dependence on exports of goods and services to meet their import requirements.

Although the volume of imports in 1946 of most countries outside the dollar area failed by substantial margins to reach prewar levels, largely because of difficulties in obtaining supplies from customary sources, most of these countries were in serious balance-of-payments difficulties. Their import demand was heavily concentrated on the Western Hemisphere, and especially on the United States. In 1946, exports from the United States exceeded those of 1938 by 90 per cent in volume, and exports from Canada surpassed the Canadian level of 1938 by 45 per cent. In both countries imports were about 40 per cent above prewar. The export surplus of the United States was no less than $7.7 billion, of which $4.9 billion was financed by United States government grants and credits, and $1.9 billion by the liquidation of gold and short-term dollar assets of other nations.[10]

These figures, of course, do not fully describe the disorganized pattern of world trade and payments that prevailed when the Fund and the Bank were completing their organizational work and were preparing to begin operations. This pattern was influenced by the availability of reserves of individual countries and the extent to which they could obtain loans and credits, as well as by supply factors. It was also influenced by restrictions imposed on trade and payments, by

[9] International Monetary Fund, *Annual Report . . . April 30, 1948*, pp. 2–3.

[10] For detailed comparisons between the situation in 1946 and that in 1938, see International Monetary Fund, *Annual Report . . . June 30, 1947*, pp. 4–10.

major changes in shipping, and by many other factors. The figures do, however, disclose the general characteristics of the "fundamental disequilibrium" that existed at that time and the dimensions of the problem still to be solved. Because the United States had an export surplus on current account with almost every other geographical area of the world, this problem was universally described as the dollar problem.

In order to meet their current account deficits with the United States in 1947, other countries had to liquidate $4.4 billion in gold and short-term dollar assets. The dollar deficit of Europe with the United States was by far the largest of any major geographical area, and in 1947, European gold and short-term dollar assets declined by $2 billion. The weakness of the British position was fully disclosed in the sterling convertibility crisis of 1947, while in the three major continental countries of Europe—France, Italy, and Germany—a state of economic and political crisis prevailed. The situation in the Eastern European countries, where Soviet influence was a major political factor, was economically and financially even more precarious.[11]

At this critical juncture, plans were formulated for a new large-scale program of international co-operation—the four-year European Recovery Program—which it was hoped would solve the main problems of European recovery. During the first half of this program, there was substantial progress toward general balance-of-payments equilibrium although this encouraging trend was temporarily reversed during the mild recession in the United States in the first half of 1949. The position of the United Kingdom in particular was adversely affected. The severe drain on British gold and dollar reserves was not due primarily to British trade relations with the United States but was the result mainly of increased gold and dollar payments to nondollar countries and to certain capital movements and other financial transactions motivated by rumors of impending sterling devaluation.[12] This outflow of capital was reversed when, on September 21, 1949, the sterling-dollar rate was lowered from $4.03 to $2.80 per pound. Two months before the devaluation of sterling, which was followed by a world-wide readjustment of exchange rates, United Kingdom import quotas had been reduced sufficiently to cut dollar imports by 25 per cent, and

[11] Brown and Opie, *op. cit.*, pp. 119–23.

[12] U.S. Department of Commerce, *Balance of Payments of the United States, 1949–1951*, A Supplement to the *Survey of Current Business* (1952), p. 6.

similar restrictions had been imposed by other Commonwealth countries.

Before the effects of sterling devaluation and the increased quantitative restrictions of the Commonwealth could be reflected in the figures of international trade, the trend of economic activity in the United States had again turned sharply upward and American imports from almost all major geographical areas began to increase. By the end of the third quarter of 1950, the United States export surplus on current account with the rest of the world almost disappeared. This was also true of the export surpluses of Canada with nondollar areas.

In most European countries, inflation was being brought under control, although there was still no assurance that its basic causes had been eliminated. European industrial production, Germany excepted, was above prewar levels by a considerable margin, and even agricultural production was slightly above prewar. Intra-European trade was steadily expanding. Merchandise imports from the United States were substantially reduced, and exports to the United States slightly increased. European exports to the rest of the world were rapidly expanded. The dollar deficit of the members of the Organization for European Economic Cooperation (OEEC), which in 1947 had been $7.5 billion, had been reduced in the first half of 1950 to an annual rate of $2 billion, and American aid was beginning to contribute to reserves.

There was also some improvement in Latin American and Far Eastern countries, but this was not comparable to that of Europe. The balance-of-payments position of many of these countries had been weakened by the decline in the prices of raw materials in the first half of 1949. This decline continued at irregular intervals immediately after the September devaluation, the fall of prices of metals and petroleum being especially serious for some Latin American countries. However, late in 1949 and in the first half of 1950, the prices of raw materials began to rise again, and this was the most general cause of such improvement as took place. In most of these countries, inflation continued to be a factor working against the restoration of balance-of-payments equilibrium, and in only a few—notably Japan where, as in Germany, there had been a radical change in occupation policy—was the improvement attributable to increased production.[13]

[13] For the major developments in international payments during this period see International Monetary Fund, *Annual Report of the Executive Directors for the Fiscal Year Ended April 30, 1950* (1950), pp. 16–21; *Annual Report of the Executive Directors for the Fiscal Year Ended April 30, 1951* (1951), pp. 1–13; and U.S. Department of Commerce, *Balance of Payments of the United States, 1949–1951*, pp. 1–3.

Marshall Plan and Work of the United Nations

One of the first effects of the launching of the European Recovery Program was to relieve the Fund of pressure to use its resources in ways that were really inconsistent with its basic purposes. On April 20, 1948, the Executive Directors of the Fund decided that the members of the Fund that were also participants in the European Recovery Program could negotiate with the Fund for dollars only in exceptional and unforeseen circumstances. The purpose of this action was to conserve the resources of the Fund so that at the end of the recovery period, these members might have unencumbered access to them.[14] More important, from the long-range point of view, were the problems raised for the United Nations by the appearance on the scene of the Organization for European Economic Cooperation, entirely outside the jurisdiction of the United Nations, through which its Western European members were to co-operate to solve many of their monetary and trade problems on a regional basis.

The terms of reference of the OEEC on commercial policy required co-operation toward the objectives of reducing trade barriers between the participating countries and of establishing the world multilateral trading system contemplated in the Havana Charter for an International Trade Organization.[15] Inasmuch as nondiscrimination was a basic principle of the Havana Charter, these two objectives were, in the short run at least, potentially contradictory,[16] and this contradiction was not removed by the inclusion in the Charter of some ingenious devices for reconciling certain types of preferential trade arrangements with a world-wide effort to promote nondiscriminatory trade. It was almost inevitable, therefore, that as a result of the work of the OEEC, the difficulty of reconciling regional and world objectives in the field of trade, as in the monetary field, would assume serious proportions.

The OEEC had the advantage of being able to deal with European monetary and trade problems together on a regional basis, but the United Nations system was not in a position to do so on a world basis. It was handicapped from the outset by the dispersion of responsibility

[14] International Monetary Fund, *Annual Report . . . April 30, 1948*, App. IV, pp. 74–75.

[15] Great Britain, *Convention for European Economic Co-operation, Paris, 16 April 1948*, Cmd. 7388 (1948), Arts. 5 and 6.

[16] On this point see William Adams Brown, Jr., *The United States and the Restoration of World Trade* (1950), pp. 308–10.

for international co-operation on trade and payments among different international bodies. These handicaps were expected to be overcome in considerable measure by the creation of the ITO as a specialized agency. The responsibilities envisaged for this agency were considerably expanded during the course of the long negotiations for the ITO Charter, and one of the many ways in which the European Recovery Program influenced the future work of the United Nations was its important, although indirect, contribution to the success of these negotiations. Had there not seemed to be good prospects that the European Recovery Program would put Europe as a whole on a self-sustaining basis, the charter might have been so weakened as to prove unacceptable to the American negotiators. This was not a matter of transitory significance, ending with the abandonment of the ITO itself. Many provisions of the charter continued to influence international co-operation on trade and related problems, including co-operation through the United Nations, long after the ITO had been abandoned.

Sponsorship of ITO Negotiations

In making public the Anglo-American *Proposals for Expansion of World Trade and Employment* in November 1945, the United States Secretary of State announced that the United States representatives in the appropriate United Nations organs would urge that an International Conference on Trade and Employment meet under the sponsorship of the United Nations. It was proposed at the Preparatory Commission of the United Nations that the question of achieving "an equitable adjustment of prices in the world markets" be included in the scope of the conference.[17] It is significant that the very first issue thus raised in the United Nations concerning the proposed International Trade Organization was one of special interest to the underdeveloped countries. This issue was raised again when, at its first session (January–February 1946), the Economic and Social Council considered and adopted a resolution calling for the establishment of a Preparatory Committee of nineteen members. As introduced by the United States, this resolution proposed an agenda confined to matters dealt with in the proposals, but it was amended in the Council by requesting the Preparatory Committee to "take into account the special conditions which prevailed in countries whose manufacturing industry is still in its initial stages of

[17] U.N. Preparatory Commission, *Report of the Preparatory Commission of the United Nations*, Doc. PC/20 (Dec. 23, 1945), p. 22.

development, and the questions that arise in connection with commodities which are subject to special problems of adjustment in international markets."[18]

The resolution also reserved the right of the Council to make suggestions to the Preparatory Committee and so involved it in taking positions on substantive as well as procedural questions. The subsequent communications between the Preparatory Committee and the Council illustrated an important segment of a much broader problem confronting the United Nations, the appropriate allocation among all its agencies and organs of functions relating directly or indirectly to international trade and payments.

Allocation of Functions Within the United Nations System

In a *Report on Commercial Policy in the Post-War World*, published in 1945, the Economic and Financial Committees of the League of Nations had dealt with the relationship between commercial policy, production, and employment as follows:

> We are strongly of the opinion that the direct association of commercial policies with policies designed to secure an expansion of production and consumption and the maintenance of high and stable levels of employment is an essential prerequisite to progress towards international economic co-operation. The failure in the interwar years to emphasize the essential interdependence of these issues was indeed one of the reasons for the lack of success that was then experienced. We believe that . . . the most hopeful method of securing progress would be a general conference to deal *jointly* with commercial policy and the international aspects of employment policy.[19]

The thesis that an expanding economy and a high level of domestic employment are *prerequisites* for international economic co-operation has had a strong appeal to many Members of the United Nations. Nevertheless, it is open to question. When, however, the Secretary-General of the United Nations in his report to the second session of the General Assembly in 1947, quoted this view of the League of Nations commit-

[18] The nineteen members selected were Australia, Belgium, Brazil, Canada, Chile, China, Cuba, Czechoslovakia, France, India, Lebanon, Luxembourg, the Netherlands, New Zealand, Norway, South Africa, the Soviet Union, the United States, and the United Kingdom. Only the Soviet Union refused to serve. For the text of the resolution see United Nations, *Report of the First Session of the Preparatory Committee of the United Nations Conference on Trade and Employment* (October 1946), Annexure 1, p. 42.

[19] League of Nations, *Commercial Policy in the Post-War World: Report of the Economic and Financial Committees* (April 1945), p. 64. Italics supplied.

tees, he did so uncritically and without qualification. The advice of the League committees that a joint approach be made to commercial and employment policies had already been followed when the Economic and Social Council approved the agenda of the Preparatory Committee, but the Secretary-General was not content merely to emphasize the interdependence of commercial and employment policies. He took a position on the priorities that should be assigned to them by declaring that: "Unemployment in advanced industrial countries, and the underdevelopment of many areas of the world are much more serious and fundamental in their effect on the volume of world trade than the restrictive practices which are often merely the secondary phenomena of profound economic instability."[20] He thus gave his support to a body of opinion within the United Nations system that tended to minimize the positive contributions of a liberal commercial policy to high levels of employment and to economic development, even though these had been strongly emphasized in the basic instruments both of the Fund and the GATT.[21]

The Preparatory Committee found it difficult to reach agreement on what functions in the field of employment and economic development should be assigned to a trade organization, and what functions should be reserved for the Economic and Social Council, and how the two should be related. With respect to employment, the Preparatory Committee was confronted with the following dilemma. It recognized that preventing the international spread of depressions was beyond the capacities of an international trade organization. At the same time, it was made clear that some governments might not accept the commitments on commercial policy of the proposed ITO Charter unless there were firm assurances that some such continuing effort would be made either through the ITO or through the Economic and Social Council. To solve this problem, the Preparatory Committee decided that the future members of the ITO should be under obligation to co-operate with the Council on such matters as the assembling and dissemination of infor-

[20] U.N. General Assembly, Second Session, *Official Records*, Supplement No. 1, "Annual Report of the Secretary-General on the Work of the Organization" (1947), p. 26.

[21] See *Articles of Agreement*, Art. I(ii), p. 1; also, The Contracting Parties to the General Agreement on Tariffs and Trade, *General Agreement on Tariffs and Trade: Basic Instruments and Selected Documents*, Vol. I (May 1952), p. 13. The General Agreement was amended in 1955. With certain minor changes in the text, the preamble, which recognized explicitly the contribution of a liberal commercial policy to better standards of living, became Article I (Objectives). See *ibid.*, Vol. I (Revised, April 1955), p. 7.

mation relevant to the problem, and the initiation of various forms of consultation with intergovernmental agencies. Responsibilities for international co-operation to prevent the spread of depressions and to maintain full employment were left to the Council itself.

Another difficult problem before the Preparatory Committee was to determine what the functions of an international trade organization should be in the field of economic development, and how its responsibilities in that field should be related to those of the Economic and Social Council and of the many international agencies already concerned with economic development. At its first session (October 1946), the committee recognized the existence of a special relationship between economic development and the other objectives of the proposed charter, especially the expansion of trade, and in the final text of the charter, elaborate provision was made for co-operation within the organization and with the Economic and Social Council and other agencies to promote such development. This was in addition to many concessions made to underdeveloped countries in the commercial policy provisions of the charter—in particular, concessions regarding the use of quantitative restrictions for economic development purposes.[22]

In the field of commodity trade, the problem of allocating functions within the United Nations system was complicated by the fact that the Food and Agriculture Organization had a strong interest in any form of co-operation affecting trade in agricultural products. It was proposed, for example, early in the discussions of the Preparatory Committee, that commodity agreements on agricultural products should be placed under the FAO and not the ITO. In general, the representatives of FAO looked on commodity agreements as a desirable and constructive device for helping to solve the problems of primary commodities. In the Preparatory Committee and in the debates at the Havana Conference, therefore, the FAO often found itself in opposition to those who wished to treat international commodity agreements as necessary but essentially emergency exceptions to general rules of commercial policy. The United States supported the latter viewpoint, and it prevailed in the final drafting of the commodity chapter of the Charter.

At the time the Preparatory Committee first met, a number of international commodity discussions were already under way and the committee recommended that the Economic and Social Council establish

[22] For texts of the Charter and the resolutions of the Havana Conference, see United Nations Conference on Trade and Employment held at Havana, Cuba from Nov. 21, 1947 to Mar. 24, 1948, *Final Act and Related Documents* (March 1948).

an interim body to keep in touch with these developments. In March 1947, the Economic and Social Council adopted a resolution establishing the new agency under the resounding name of the Interim Co-ordinating Committee for International Commodity Arrangements.[23] This resolution recommended to governments that they adopt as a general guide in international consultations or actions with respect to commodity problems the principles laid down in the draft ITO Charter, and it directed the new interim committee to keep informed of, to facilitate, and to co-ordinate, such consultations or actions.[24]

Finally, the entire ITO negotiation was an attempt to allocate functions within the United Nations system in such a way as to provide a world-wide approach to many interrelated fields in accordance with certain agreed principles. To achieve this, it was necessary to compose conflicting viewpoints both among and within governments, some of which had been well developed in the interwar years and some of which were brought to the surface by the dislocations of the war itself. The United States negotiators, for example, while striving to assert general principles of multilateralism and nondiscrimination and to keep the use of restrictions other than tariffs to a minimum, also found it necessary to insist on provisions that would safeguard the subsidies and import quotas required by American domestic agricultural policy. A large group of the underdeveloped countries strongly urged that they be given special rights to introduce new preferential arrangements and import quotas in the interests of economic development.

The European countries, in general more susceptible than the United States to balance-of-payments difficulties and more accustomed to governmental controls and to the regulation of foreign trade, insisted that provision should be made for enabling them to deal with their balance-of-payments difficulties through the use of such methods. In addition, rules had to be devised governing trade carried on partly or—as in the case of the Soviet Union—wholly by the state, and trade carried on by international cartels.

The final text of the Havana Charter therefore contained many escape clauses, reserved rights, and transitional arrangements. It reflected the dislocations not only of the Second World War but also of a whole generation. Nevertheless, it contained specific commitments in eight different fields as well as many undertakings for consultation.

[23] Res. 30(IV), Mar. 28, 1947.

[24] U.N. Interim Coordinating Committee for International Commodity Arrangements, *Review of International Commodity Arrangements* (1947), pp. 7–9.

The charter recognized that the employment policies of its members were of vital concern to other members and contained certain broad commitments in regard to such policies. It also recognized economic development as a vital factor in the expansion of trade and in raising standards of living, and provided for co-operation in this field. It committed its members to negotiate for reductions in the general level of tariffs and for the elimination of preferences and the avoidance of other forms of trade restrictions and discriminatory trade practices except in agreed circumstances or conditions. It obligated its state-trading members to conduct their operations on commercial principles and to negotiate their margins between cost and selling price in the way other members negotiated duties. It permitted countries in balance-of-payments difficulties or in process of economic development to use quantitative restrictions but specified the conditions under which they could be used. It committed its members also to reduce the harmful international effects of restrictive business practices through a procedure of complaint investigation and recommendation, to eliminate export subsidies if possible, and to refrain from using any form of subsidy to increase their shares in world markets. Intergovernmental commodity agreements in primary and related commodities were to be used only for defined objectives and under specified conditions.

Many compromises had been made concerning all these commitments, but the basic principles of the charter as a whole were those set forth in Article VII of the mutual aid agreements. The charter was an attempt to achieve co-ordinated action on a number of interrelated and extremely complex problems through a single international agency, at a time when the world was still struggling with the problems of basic reconstruction. It was criticized in the United States on three main grounds: that it was too strong, that it was too weak, and that it dealt unsatisfactorily with employment and investment policies. It was criticized also, even by its drafters, because of its extreme length and complexity, which were due both to the scope of the subjects covered and the compromises required by the special interests of the large number of countries represented.

Although the ITO failed to come into existence, in the field of commercial policy most of the provisions intended for the ITO were applied through the GATT.[25] The Economic and Social Council became the residuary legatee of responsibilities for international co-operation in-

[25] See William Diebold, *The End of the ITO*, International Financial Section, Department of Economics and Social Institutions, Princeton University (1952).

cluded in the ITO Charter with which no other agency was competent to deal. At the same time, the Council fell heir to the tentative and hard-won solutions worked out in the draft charter on a great many problems, of which restrictive business practices affecting international trade and international commodity agreements were the most notable. These were fairly substantial offsets to the fragmentation of the work of the United Nations in the field of trade and related problems that was one of the consequences of the failure to bring the ITO into existence. To some extent the provisions of the Havana Charter on co-operation between the Fund and the proposed ITO, which were carried over into the GATT, compensated for difficulties caused by wartime decisions to assign international responsibilities in the field of foreign exchange and in the field of trade to different agencies.

GATT Negotiations

The Fund and the GATT have considered many problems relating to trade and payments restrictions together, and the GATT to some extent has filled the gap left by the failure of the ITO to come into existence as a specialized agency of the United Nations. For these reasons, and because the United Nations Secretariat has continued up to the present to render certain administrative services to the secretariat of GATT on a reimbursable basis, it has become customary to speak of the GATT loosely as if it were part of the United Nations system.

The General Agreement on Tariffs and Trade was negotiated in 1947 at a meeting of the members of the Preparatory Committee of the United Nations Conference on Trade and Employment. Although this meeting was held in Geneva, Switzerland under the sponsorship of the Preparatory Committee in connection with and as part of its second session, it was the United States and not the Preparatory Committee that invited the participants to attend and negotiate multilaterally for the reduction of tariffs. The Agreement was, and remains a multilateral tariff agreement among sovereign states. The obligations it imposed were all related to the tariff concessions contained in it, and it was completely independent of the proposed ITO, which contained many obligations of quite a different kind. Had this not been the legal status of the GATT, it would have been impossible for the United States to become a contracting party under the Trade Agreements Act of 1934 without special legislation by Congress.

The seven-month long tariff negotiations carried on at Geneva were conducted under the bilateral-multilateral procedure worked out in the

Anglo-American trade and financial negotiations and elaborated by the Preparatory Committee. The multilateral part of this procedure required a pooling of information among all participants, which many countries found hard to accept. There was a strong tendency therefore to fall back on straight bilateral bargaining. Fortunately, this was successfully resisted.[26] The bilateral-multilateral method prevailed with only minor modifications, and mutual tariff concessions covering some 45,000 tariff items relating to about half of world trade were negotiated.

The General Agreement was signed on October 10, 1947, by the representatives of the twenty-three countries participating in the negotiations. It was given provisional application on January 1, 1948, by nine of these countries under a Protocol of Provisional Application, and by September 1948, all the original signatories had, by adhering to this protocol or in other ways, become contracting parties.[27] The tariff schedules negotiated at Geneva were made an integral part of the Agreement (Part I, Article II) and became effective with respect to each country as soon as it became a contracting party. When acting collectively under the Agreement, these countries were known as the Contracting Parties.[28]

Like other tariff agreements, the General Agreement contained general clauses dealing with nontariff barriers to trade and trade discrimination. Most of these were adaptations of draft provisions of the proposed ITO Charter, and the decision on how much of the charter should be incorporated in the Agreement was a difficult one. The final selection was restricted to provisions designed to protect the value of the tariff concessions included in the Agreement, mainly because the United States delegation did not have congressional authority to go beyond this. The Agreement was, however, sufficiently liberal to con-

[26] See William Adams Brown, Jr., *The United States and the Restoration of World Trade* (1950), pp. 131–33. Another important technical problem, that of preventing governments from attempting to improve their bargaining position by new tariff and other restrictive measures in preparation for the negotiations, was also successfully overcome.

[27] Australia, Belgium, Brazil, Burma, Canada, Ceylon, Chile, China, Cuba, Czechoslovakia, France, India, Lebanon, Luxembourg, Netherlands, New Zealand, Norway, Pakistan, South Africa, Southern Rhodesia, Syria, United Kingdom, United States.

[28] Technically, GATT is an agreement, not an agency. Correct usage requires that the contracting parties, when acting collectively under the Agreement, be identified as the CONTRACTING PARTIES. In the interests of readability, however, Contracting Parties (initial capitals only) is used in this study to mean the adherents acting in their collective capacity. Moreover, at times the term GATT will be employed in this study not only as an abbreviation for the Agreement but also in an organizational sense.

stitute a comprehensive international code of conduct in the field of commercial policy.[29]

Under this code, the contracting parties are obligated to observe two basic rules of conduct: (1) to accord to each other most-favored-nation treatment on tariffs, and national treatment on internal taxation and charges, and, as a corollary of this, not to introduce new or increase existing preferences; and (2) not to initiate or maintain prohibitions or restrictions other than duties, whether made effective by quotas, import or export licenses, or other measures, on imports from or exports to each other. Aside from the rule against new or increased preferences, these obligations are subject to numerous but carefully defined exceptions, including the formation of customs unions or free-trade areas, and the use of quantitative restrictions in connection with agricultural stabilization schemes, for economic development, and for balance-of-payments reasons. The Agreement also includes many so-called technical articles covering a wide range of practices affecting imports and exports. If any contracting party believes the benefits accruing to it under the Agreement have been nullified or impaired by the action of another, it has rights of complaint, and remedies are provided.

The negotiation of mutual tariff concessions, the settlement of differences, and the application to particular cases of the rules governing quantitative restrictions under the balance-of-payments exception were from the beginning the three principal activities of the Contracting Parties. The last of these required the active co-operation of the Fund.

In the words of Article XV of the General Agreement, it was necessary to ensure that the contracting parties would not "by exchange action frustrate the intent of the provisions of [the] Agreement, nor by trade action, the intent of the provisions of the Articles of Agreement of the International Monetary Fund." This was difficult because the Articles of Agreement of the IMF gave considerable freedom to its members to use exchange restrictions, both discriminatory and nondiscriminatory, during a transitional period, while the General Agreement laid down specific substantive standards and rules governing the conduct of its members in the application of quantitative trade restrictions. To meet this problem, an elaborate formula was included in the GATT, which, it was hoped, would prevent frustrations of this kind. Both instruments also contained detailed provisions for consultation with members looking toward the relaxation of restrictions in their own fields, and these also had in some way to be dovetailed. The General

[29] Brown, *op. cit.*, pp. 234–59.

Agreement therefore provided for co-operation between the Fund and the Contracting Parties in co-ordinating their policies, and it further provided that on all matters concerning monetary reserves, balance-of-payments or foreign exchange arrangements, the Contracting Parties would consult with the Fund and accept all findings or other facts presented by the Fund relating to such matters.

Role of the Fund

While the ITO Charter was being negotiated, the Fund arrived at a number of basic policy decisions in addition to those affecting the use of its resources that have already been mentioned. Under the Articles of Agreement of the Fund, members are permitted, during a transitional period to maintain restrictions on transfers and payments for current international transactions and to adapt their restrictions to changing circumstances. Even during this period, however, a small degree of initiative is given to the Fund: it is authorized in exceptional circumstances to make representations to any member that conditions are favorable for the withdrawal of restrictions. The Articles of Agreement did not set a fixed date for the end of the transitional period, but they required members to consult with the Fund annually, beginning in March 1952, concerning the further retention of those restrictions still being applied on the basis of the transitional provisions.

So long as most members of the Fund continued to run heavy current account deficits with the United States, the Fund did not feel justified in exercising even the small amount of initiative concerning exchange restrictions reserved to it, although it suggested technical improvements. These limitations, however, did not apply to its responsibilities concerning par values, which were not limited by any transitional provisions.

One of the main purposes and obligations of the Fund is "to promote exchange stability, to maintain orderly exchange arrangements among members, and to avoid competitive exchange depreciation."[30] The Fund is not authorized formally to propose to any member a change in its par value, but its concurrence is required both for the establishment of "initial par values," and for subsequent changes (beyond a 10-percent limit) proposed to it by members.[31] The executive directors made it clear that the Fund would not resist justifiable proposals for changes

[30] *Articles of Agreement,* Art. I(iii), p. 1.
[31] *Ibid.,* Art. XX, Sec. 4, pp. 38–41, and Art. IV, Sec. 5, pp. 5–6.

in par values, that it considered stability and rigidity as two different concepts, and that stability implied that when changes in par values were necessary, they should be made in an orderly manner.[32]

The exchange arrangements existing among its members were far from orderly at the time the Fund began operations. The first problem presented to the Fund was, therefore, whether it should use the authority given to it in connection with the establishment of initial par values to bring about a general adjustment. On this question, the decision of the Fund was that the time was not yet ripe for such action. The Fund had the right to reject initial par values proposed to it by members if it thought they could not be maintained without causing excessive recourse to the Fund, but it accepted in December 1946 initial par values based on existing exchange rates proposed to it by thirty-two of its members. Consideration of initial par values for eight other member countries was postponed at their request. Whether any proposed initial par values were rejected has not been made known.

In almost all cases, the rates accepted by the Fund overvalued the currency of the member in terms of dollars and were being maintained under the protection of restrictive mechanisms. The Fund recognized that many of these rates would later have to be adjusted,[33] and in the summer of 1949 developed, for the first time, an argument in favor of a general adjustment of exchange rates accompanied, both in deficit and surplus countries, by policies necessary to make the new rates effective. The Fund held that inflated prices in countries that did not customarily settle their international transactions in dollars were one of the major reasons for the failure of exporters in Europe, the Middle East, and the Far East to offer their exports in larger part to the Western Hemisphere countries, and that this difficulty could be removed only as the general pattern of exchange rates was adjusted to relative prices and demands.[34] At this time, American official opinion was strongly in favor of early devaluations of most European currencies, especially sterling, and this view must have been expressed in the Fund by the American executive director. There is, however, in the nature of the case no direct evidence that the Fund pressed its members on this issue prior to the devaluations of September 1949.

[32] International Monetary Fund, *Annual Report . . . April 30, 1948*, p. 21.

[33] International Monetary Fund, *Annual Report . . . June 30, 1947*, App. X, Statement Concerning Initial Par Values, pp. 70–71.

[34] International Monetary Fund, *Annual Report of the Executive Directors for the Fiscal Year Ended April 30, 1949*, (1949), pp. 15–16, 29. This report took account of developments up to July 1949.

The following conclusions, made public in 1950, concerning the role of the Fund in these devaluations appear to be well-grounded:

> Because of the confidential nature of the Fund's operations, an outsider cannot know whether the September devaluations were taken with no more than perfunctory references to the International Monetary Fund. The Fund officially stated at the time that the devaluations were taken through its machinery, but the statements of officials of several governments—especially the French and the British—strongly suggest that consultations with the Fund were no more than token and that the crucial devaluation, that of sterling, was sprung on it without observing more than a semblance of consultation. And to many outsiders it appears that other devaluations sprang in considerable measure out of efforts, after Britain had acted, to adjust to a *fait accompli*. At the same time it must be recorded that its Fourth Annual Report showed the Fund was alert to the possibility and was not taken by surprise. It should also be recognized that, of necessity, devaluations must be handled quickly; it is, therefore, the Fund's responsibility to be fully prepared to consider proposals on short notice. Further, it is possible that the Fund's staff may have held confidential discussions with individual member governments and exerted some influence on their final action, but there is no evidence that such was the case. The Fund did state that the devaluations were in conformity with its views, but this can be true even though the decisions were taken unilaterally.[35]

Within the space of four days, from September 18 to 21, 1949, the Fund had considered and concurred in proposals for changes in the par value of thirteen of its member countries and of some of their dependent territories, and had also approved exchange rates for several other member countries that had no agreed par values.[36] In no case did it withhold its approval. The devaluation of sterling was the key to the almost world-wide readjustment of rates, and it was not to be expected that the United Kingdom would relinquish to the Fund its freedom of action on such a vital matter as the sterling-dollar rate, or that other important trading nations would do so.

The basic conception of exchange stability under the Fund agreement was that of fixed exchange rates adjusted from time to time by international consultation and agreement. The Fund was therefore opposed in principle to freely fluctuating exchange rates and to any practices that tended to move the actual exchange rates of its members away from their declared par values. This was the basis of its opposition in principle to the multiple exchange rate practices of many of its Latin American and some of its other members; and although, on this issue, it pursued a

[35] International Finance Section, Department of Economics and Social Institutions, Princeton University, *Survey of United States International Finance, 1949* (1950), pp. 115–16.

[36] International Monetary Fund, *Annual Report . . . April 30, 1950*, p. 28.

liberal policy, its influence was exerted toward a simplification and integration of multiple exchange rate systems.[37]

While the Fund was thus developing its basic policies, two very important questions concerning its role became the subject of extensive international discussion: (1) How could the Fund help prevent the international spread of economic depressions? (2) How should it be related to the European Payments Union? The first of these questions was raised in an important report on full employment made in December 1949 by a group of experts appointed by the Secretary-General of the United Nations, and is discussed at a later point in this study.[38] The second was raised by the turn of events in Europe and required the Fund to give immediate consideration to the formulation of its own position.

When improvements in intra-European payments arrangements were first under discussion by the countries participating in the European Recovery Program, the Fund was consulted concerning these arrangements. Although sympathetic to the aim of multilateralization of European payments, the Fund was also concerned with the possibility that "prolonged dependence on restrictions and discriminations would be likely to divide the world economy into economic blocs, each with its own price structure, each tending increasingly to insulate itself from the rest of the world by the necessity of protecting its own inconvertible currency system by trade restrictions and exchange controls."[39] The fear that the European Payments Union contemplated by the OEEC countries might contribute to the formation of a permanent soft-currency area in Europe was shared by the National Advisory Council on International Economic and Financial Problems of the United States, the body from which the American executive director of the Fund received his instructions. These apprehensions, together with the opposition of some important OEEC members to close relationships between the Fund and the European Payments Union, made it difficult to find a basis for co-operation between them. Although some highly technical proposals were put forward to place their relationships on a formal basis, none was accepted, and it was not until June 1952 that any of the resources of the Fund were used to facilitate the operation of the Union.

[37] An elaborate statement of IMF policy on multiple exchange rates was communicated to members on June 18, 1947. International Monetary Fund, *Annual Report . . . April 30, 1948*, pp. 65–72.

[38] See below, Chap. V.

[39] International Monetary Fund, *Annual Report . . . April 30, 1949*, p. 19.

Role of the GATT

Inasmuch as the European Payments Union (EPU) combined a program of intra-European currency convertibility with a program of intra-European trade liberalization, the issue raised by establishment of the EPU was fundamental not only for the Fund but also for the GATT. The EPU was widely regarded, especially in the United States, as being at one and the same time a step toward European economic integration and a transitional arrangement through which European countries could move away from bilateralism and toward general convertibility of currencies and nondiscrimination in trade. If these two aims could not be reconciled, there would be a clear conflict between the regional objectives of the EPU and the world-wide objectives to which the United Nations system was committed through the Fund and the GATT.

So far as the GATT was concerned, the EPU was welcomed as an important step toward convertibility and toward the realization of one of the basic principles of the GATT—namely that tariffs should resume their traditional role as the principal instrument of commercial policy.[40] For countries entitled to use discriminatory quantitative restrictions under the balance-of-payments exception, the relaxation of such restrictions in intra-European trade while they were maintained against dollar imports did not constitute a violation of the Agreement. Members of the EPU in over-all international balance, however, would be violating the GATT by discriminating in this way against dollar imports.

A more serious problem of conflicting obligations was raised by other plans for European integration that were proposed and discussed during the summer of 1950, of which the Schuman plan for a European Coal and Steel Community was the most important. All such proposals, whether for a large European preference area or for open-market "communities" for particular sectors of the European economy, were incompatible with obligations assumed under the General Agreement. If any of these proposals matured, as the Schuman proposal did, the Contracting Parties would, in the words of their third annual report, "have to steer a difficult course between the rigid application of the rules of the Agreement, with the risk of frustrating what might be a promising initiative for the recovery and strengthening of the European economy and acceptance of regional arrangements, which would weaken the basic principle of equality of treatment."[41]

[40] Interim Commission for the International Trade Organization, *GATT in Action*, Third Report on the Operation of the General Agreement on Tariffs and Trade (1952), p. 24.

[41] *Ibid.*, p. 28.

While the GATT was being confronted with ticklish problems of reconciling its world-wide objectives with European economic regionalism, it was expanding its own membership by new multilateral tariff negotiations at Annecy, France in 1949, which resulted in the accession of Denmark, the Dominican Republic, Finland, Greece, Haiti, Italy, Liberia, Nicaragua, and Sweden. Italy thus became the first ex-enemy to take its place in the GATT family, but active consideration was being given also to the future accession of Germany and Japan.

In September 1948, a protocol, entirely separate from the General Agreement, had been drawn up by the Contracting Parties on the initiative of the United States, providing most-favored-nation treatment for Germany by the countries acceding to it, and by August 1949, fourteen countries had assumed this obligation. The next step was to include Germany in the list of countries to take part in the next round of tariff negotiations to be held at Torquay, England, in 1950. In the case of Japan, similar action was much longer delayed. The United States had proposed extension of most-favored-nation treatment to Japan, but encountered such strong opposition that it withdrew the suggestion. The root causes of this opposition had by no means been removed when, in July 1952, Japan made a formal request to enter into tariff negotiations with a view to accession.

It is not necessary to labor the point that the new emphasis on European regionalism and the new economic relations being established with former enemy states were matters heavily charged with political implications. Yet the Contracting Parties dealt with them primarily, if not exclusively, as economic problems. There was one area, however, in which such an approach was not possible—East-West trade. American controls on exports to communist countries had been under attack in various organs of the United Nations, and during the Annecy negotiations, Czechoslovakia charged that the United States was violating the General Agreement by imposing export restrictions on Czechoslovak trade.[42] Two years later, on September 27, 1951, the Contracting Parties officially declared that the United States and Czechoslovakia would be free to suspend the obligations of the Agreement with respect to each other on the purely political ground that, as the United States contended, the general deterioration of relations between the two countries made it impossible to fulfill them.[43]

[42] Interim Commission for the International Trade Organization, *The Attack on Trade Barriers* (1949), p. 19.

[43] "Actions Taken on Strengthening Administration of GATT," U.S. Department of State *Bulletin*, Vol. 25 (Nov. 19, 1951), p. 830.

Concern of FAO and Regional Economic Commissions

The inherent difficulties of international economic co-operation through many agencies are further illustrated by the general work of the FAO and the United Nations regional commissions in the field of trade and payments. In his early reports to the Council and the Conference of FAO, the Director-General of that agency placed great stress on such problems as the effect of hard and soft currencies on commodity trade; the decline in the volume of world trade in food as compared to prewar; and the difficulty of finding a basis whereby the surplus foodstuffs of North America could be exchanged for other commodities—the last being a euphemistic way of expressing the interest of the FAO in American tariff and price-support policies. The fifth Conference of the FAO asked the Director-General to make a selective study of measures taken by governments to maintain or achieve certain price relationships between commodities, especially import and export commodities,[44] and the organization has since continued to place great emphasis in its research program on studies of international trade in food and agriculture.

It has tended, however, to overestimate the practical possibilities of effective co-operation in the control and distribution of agricultural products. Such overestimates had been made when proposals were advanced for a World Food Board and an International Commodity Clearing House.[45] After these were rejected, the FAO appointed a Committee on Commodity Problems to operate in a much narrower field. Initially, the main function of this committee was to deal with surplus commodity situations in food and agriculture arising from balance-of-payments difficulties. After attempting unsuccessfully to interest other governments in the purchase of certain surplus commodities held by the United States, it tried to lay down the general principles that should govern the distribution of food on special terms for the development of nutrition programs.[46]

The FAO continued to be a strong advocate of the type of international commodity arrangements it had supported during the ITO negotiations. It did not, however, become the major link between the

[44] Food and Agriculture Organization, *Report of the Fifth Session of the Conference, 21 November–6 December 1949* (March 1950), p. 10.

[45] See above, Chap. II.

[46] Food and Agriculture Organization, *Work of FAO, 1949/50: Report of the Director-General* (October 1950), p. 40. See also Chaps. V and VII below.

United Nations and the various international commodity councils and committees such as the International Sugar Council, the International Wheat Council, the International Wool Study Group, and the Rubber Study Group. The main instrument of co-operation between the United Nations and these groups was the Interim Coordinating Committee for International Commodity Arrangements, which, as noted above, was established in 1947 to carry out the procedures laid down in the Havana Charter concerning international study groups and conferences in anticipation of the ITO. The continued functioning of this "interim" body served to fill a gap in international co-operation that would otherwise have been left by the demise of the ITO.

The interest of the FAO in international trade problems was also shown by the co-operation between its secretariat and the secretariats of the regional economic commissions of the United Nations. The commissions for Latin America and the Far East, in particular, became important forums for the discussion of regional aspects of world trade and payments problems. Before the regional commissions could devise methods of effective co-operation in the field of trade and payments, however, certain preliminary questions had to be answered. What was the economic basis for regional co-operation in these fields? What were its potentialities and limits? What forms should it take?

The first of these was the most fundamental. The economies of the Latin American countries were not, like those of Europe, closely bound together by an intricate network of trade, communications, and payments. Most of them were relatively insensitive to economic and financial developments in other Latin American economies. Almost all of them were dependent on world markets for the sale of a relatively few products. All shared a common desire for economic development leading to an intensive demand for imported capital goods and frequently to differential treatment of imports according to a judgment of essentiality. In many of these countries inflation was endemic, with resultant adverse effects on their balances of payments. Intra-Latin American trade was much smaller than Latin American trade with other areas and in order to overcome the exchange controls extensively used in the area, a substantial part of it was carried on by barter arrangements.

Most of these generalizations are applicable, although with some qualifications, to many countries in Asia and the Far East. In the Far East, as in Latin America, the exchange of primary products for capital goods with other areas was far more important than intraregional trade. Many Far Eastern countries continued to maintain close financial links with Europe—India, Pakistan, Burma, Ceylon, Hong Kong, and Malaya with the sterling area; the Associated States of Indo-China with France; and Indonesia with the Netherlands.[47]

In both regions there was a strong feeling that their trade patterns were of a colonial type, and that much could and should be done to change them. This was especially true of Far Eastern countries whose independence had been but recently achieved, and for whom the expansion of trade with their neighbors was for the first time an important objective of economic policy. Consequently, the United Nations commissions, like the regional meetings of the FAO, emphasized intraregional trade expansion. But trade with other areas, which was part of the world problem being dealt with by other agencies, continued by force of circumstances to be their major concern.

During the period under consideration, the work of the Economic Commission for Latin America (ECLA) with respect to international trade and payments was almost entirely exploratory. An analysis of the possibilities of multilateral compensations of Latin-American trade and payments was prepared by the Fund and considered by the commission at its second session (May–June 1949), but conditions were deemed not favorable to such a project. At its third session (June 1950) the commission was still of this opinion, but with the example of the European Payments Union before it, it asked the Fund to explore the possibilities of partial multilateral clearings within the region. The commission also asked its executive secretary to undertake, with the executive secretary of the Economic Commission for Europe (ECE), a study of ways and means of expanding Latin American trade with Europe, and to study the possibilities of expanding intra-Latin American trade. It is noteworthy that the latter subject was a late arrival on the agenda of the commission, which gave priority to the Latin American role in the network of world trade.

The emphasis of the Economic Commission for Asia and the Far East (ECAFE) on intraregional trade and payments was, from the beginning, stronger than that of the ECLA, but ECAFE was far from neglecting trade with nations outside the Asian region. At its third session (June 1948), the commission considered a report from its secretariat outlining the possibilities for developing intraregional trade and urging the establishment of a permanent trade promotion branch in the secretariat. The recommendation was approved, and the commission soon became very active in this field.

[47] Even after it became independent, Indonesia continued to make its European settlements through the European Payments Union via the Netherlands.

At the fifth session of the commission (October 1949), the Fund presented an extensive study, which it had been requested to make on intraregional trade. It had also been asked to consider the desirability of a regional multilateral clearing arrangement, a matter on which it reserved its position. ECAFE itself concluded, however, as ECLA had done a few months before, that the time was not propitious for such a project.[48] Thereafter, the Fund co-operated actively with the ECAFE secretariat in joint studies on the financing of trade and the mobilization of domestic capital—a subject that was given top priority at the sixth session of the commission in May 1950.

Although the Economic Commission for Europe was no less interested in the trade and payments problems of its members than the other two commissions, its work in this field was of quite a different order. In view of the fact that the major intra-European trade and payments problems were dealt with by OEEC, of which the Soviet Union and its satellites were not members, it was almost inevitable that the interests of the ECE, in which the Eastern countries were participants, would be concentrated on East-West trade.

The commission was from the beginning engaged in three operations that directly affected the flow of trade within Europe—the allocation of solid fuels among European consuming countries, the allocation of scrap produced in Europe, and the establishment of "buying limits" for timber-importing countries. These allocations were part of an extensive program of co-operation in increasing availabilities and improving productive methods, but with the restoration of better balance in supply and demand in 1949, they were terminated. The commission also touched on many matters directly affecting the international flow of European goods through its Inland Transport Committee, which dealt with such matters as international highways, customs formalities, road and rail transport, and inland waterways and seaports.

At its third session (April–May 1948), the commission, after prolonged East-West debate, set up an Ad Hoc Committee on Industrial Development and Trade to examine the functions it might appropriately undertake in order to promote the industrial reconstruction and development of war-devastated and underdeveloped countries and to expand international trade between the countries of Europe and also

[48] U.N. Economic and Social Council, Ninth Session, *Official Records*, Supplement No. 13, "Report of the Economic Commission for Asia and the Far East," p. 18; and U.N. Economic and Social Council, Eleventh Session, *Official Records*, Supplement No. 8, "Report of the Economic Commission for Asia and the Far East," pp 16–17.

between European countries and countries outside Europe.[49] In September 1948, this committee recommended that a Committee for the Development of Trade be established, but agreement on its terms of reference was reached only over vigorous opposition of the countries in the Soviet bloc. In the debate, the Eastern European nations took the position that a satisfactory increase in East-West trade was dependent on the development of production in their countries, and they clearly implied that this development should in large measure be financed by the West. The Committee on the Development of Trade, thus brought into being in an atmosphere of strife between East and West, met in May 1949 primarily to consider ways and means of expanding East-West trade. It was completely deadlocked, however, and rendered no report to the commission.

In November 1949, the Executive-Secretary sent an *Aide Memoire* to participating governments suggesting an entirely new approach involving (1) relatively long-term purchase commitments by Western European nations, formed on the model of the International Wheat Agreement, for cereals and other supplies from Eastern European nations, and (2) use of the proceeds by the Eastern European nations for purchases from an agreed list of Western products.[50] This initiative was followed by a long series of negotiations between the secretariat and interested governments, which culminated in an *ad hoc* meeting of these governments in Geneva in November 1950 and annual trade consultations thereafter.

These efforts were characteristic of the ECE secretariat. It was not content merely to analyze, but it also made strenuous efforts to achieve practical results through facilitating and encouraging international negotiation on concrete problems. General analysis of European trade and payments problems in all their aspects was, moreover, provided in the annual *Economic Survey of Europe* begun in 1948, and in the *Quarterly Bulletin* of the commission, which first appeared in 1949.

Economic and Social Council and General Assembly

Prior to the Korean crisis, questions of international trade and finance were discussed in the Economic and Social Council and its Economic

[49] U.N. Economic and Social Council, Seventh Session, *Official Records*, Supplement No. 10, Annex 1.

[50] U.N. Economic Commission for Europe, *Report to the Fifth Session of the Economic Commission for Europe, by the Executive Secretary, on the Future Work of the Commission*, Doc. E/ECE/114/Rev. 1 (April 1950), p. 57, and App. IV

and Employment Commission in connection with the annual economic surveys and special economic reports submitted by the Secretariat. In these documents attention was increasingly devoted to current international relationships in the field of commerce and finance, especially in the report on *Major Economic Changes in 1948*.[51] The Council discussions on them were, however, often diffuse and desultory, ranging over such topics as the general obstacles to trade, the desirability of long-term agreements on trade in essential products, the dollar problem, and suggested revisions of the Articles of Agreement of the International Monetary Fund to make it more effective in helping other countries to deal with balance-of-payments fluctuations without resort to deflationary measures or trade restrictions.

In the General Assembly in November 1948, Poland attacked the United States for using export controls to deny a broad range of items to communist countries on security grounds, for according priority to countries participating in the Marshall Plan for goods in short supply, and for including provisions covering East-West trade in the bilateral agreements between the United States and the Marshall Plan countries. A Polish resolution, strongly supported by the Soviet Union, Czechoslovakia, and Yugoslavia, launched a debate that was carried on in the Second (Economic and Financial) Committee and in the plenary meetings.[52]

American practices were vigorously defended by the United States, with support from many other countries. Discrimination was defended on two grounds: first, that it was necessary to assure the rapid recovery of Western Europe by giving the co-operating countries priority for commodities in short supply, and second, that the United States could not furnish materials for building up the military potentials of Eastern European countries in view of their aggressive tendencies. Western nations also pointed out that the nations in the Soviet bloc could and regularly did engage in trade discrimination on political grounds under their system of bilateral agreements. They challenged the communist bloc to accept the most-favored-nation principle with the exceptions so painfully agreed upon in the ITO negotiations.

The differences of view between East and West were irreconcilable,

[51] U.N. Secretariat, Department of Economic Affairs, *Major Economic Changes in 1948* (January 1949), pp. 20–31.

[52] U.N. General Assembly, Third Session, Second Committee, *Official Records*, 69th Meeting (Nov. 2, 1948), pp. 154–60, and 71st–76th Meetings (Nov. 4–12, 1948), pp. 185–278. For text of Polish resolution, see p. 159. See also U.N. General Assembly, Third Session, Plenary, *Official Records*, 164th–65th Meetings (Nov. 26, 1948), pp. 592–609.

and the Polish resolution was finally rejected in the General Assembly.

In its annual summary of economic changes during the 1949–50 period, the Secretariat reached the conclusion that the trade and payments setback of 1949 demonstrated anew that progress in solving the difficult and long-run structural problems underlying the imbalance in international transactions could be made only in a context of full employment in more highly industrialized countries and progressive economic expansion in underdeveloped areas.[53] It was in this context that international trade and payments policies were most intensively canvassed in debates of the General Assembly and the Council.

Following the receipt of the report of a group of experts on full employment in December 1949,[54] the Council debated international trade policies as part of its general discussions on employment. The recommendations of the experts affecting international trade, the reception given to their report at the tenth and eleventh sessions of the Council in 1950, and the lengthy resolution on full employment, which was adopted by the Council and which included sections dealing with trade and payments, are all discussed later in this volume.[55] It should be noted here, however, that in this major resolution, the basic commercial policy principles and objectives of the Havana Charter were reasserted in substance, although not by direct reference.[56]

The work of these experts was to be supplemented by further studies on trade and payments questions of particular concern to underdeveloped countries under a resolution of the Council of August 1950. This resolution requested the Fund and the Bank to assemble data on the absorption of foreign exchange resources of such countries by the service of foreign investment, and it requested the Secretary-General to study "the relation of fluctuations in the prices of primary products to the ability of underdeveloped countries to obtain foreign exchange."[57] The new study of price relationships was begun at a time when the terms of trade were turning strongly in favor of the underdeveloped countries under the impact of the crisis in Korea. In many ways, this crisis represented a turning-point in the consideration of trade and payments problems by the Council and the Assembly, and it had significant effects on the work of all other parts of the United Nations system in this area.

[53] U.N. Secretariat, Department of Economic Affairs, *World Economic Report, 1949–50* (March 1951), pp. 5–10.

[54] U.N. Department of Economic Affairs, *National and International Measures for Full Employment* (the Kaldor Report), Doc. E/1584 (December 1949).

[55] See below, Chap. V.

[56] Res. 290(XI), Aug. 15, 1950, para. 9(a).

[57] Res. 294B(XI), Aug. 12, 1950.

After the Invasion of South Korea

The dislocation of the world price structure during the two years immediately following the invasion of a small country whose independence had been recognized by the United Nations appears in retrospect as a temporary interruption in world progress toward a better international equilibrium. It accentuated, however, many of the interests of special concern to the underdeveloped countries and had a great effect on the approach of the Economic and Social Council and of the regional commissions. The resumption of progress toward international equilibrium that followed also raised certain major long-range problems for the Fund and the GATT.

Economic Impact of Invasion of South Korea

The most lasting economic consequence of the reaction to Communist aggression in Korea was the large-scale diversion of additional material and man-power resources to rearmament, but the effects of this increased diversion were felt only gradually. In contrast, the price effects were immediate and spectacular as a result of the intensive demand for industrial raw materials and other primary commodities, both from governmental and private sources. There was a world-wide speculative effort, first in the United States and later elsewhere, to build up inventories of such commodities far beyond current requirements as a protection against future shortages.

The general upward movement of commodity prices reached its peak in February 1951 when raw material prices were on the average 45 per cent above the level of June 1950.[58] The balance-of-payments position of the countries producing raw materials was greatly eased, and their gold and dollar reserves, particularly those of Latin American countries, were increased. Despite the deterioration in the terms of trade of European countries, which imposed a severe burden on them estimated by the International Monetary Fund to be at an annual rate of $2 billion, almost all the countries belonging to the OEEC were also able to improve their reserve position.

Late in 1950, American consumer demand began to decline, and the United States Government took various steps to reduce the prices paid for certain important raw material imports. The course of the Korean

[58] Bank for International Settlements, *Twenty-Second Annual Report* (1952), p. 72. A comprehensive survey of the price developments of 1950–52 is given on pages 68–89 of this report.

war also took a turn favorable to the United Nations forces, and it became clear that the level of raw material prices was fast becoming untenable. The International Index of Raw Material Prices fell from the February 1951 level of 145 (June 1950 being taken as 100) to 108 in February 1952, and in May 1952 it returned to the June 1950 level.[59]

For the underdeveloped countries, especially of Southeast Asia, the sharp fall in export prices disappointed many hopes and raised many new difficulties. The imports of these countries continued to expand after the raw material boom had subsided, with the result that their reserves were rapidly depleted. At the beginning of 1952, many countries producing raw materials were in serious balance-of-payments difficulties and had to adjust their development programs to a lower level of imports.

In the first part of 1952, the countries of the outer sterling area began to draw heavily on their sterling balances. This added to the difficulties of the United Kingdom. Sterling area reserves suffered their third and most serious contraction since the war, falling from $3.8 billion in June 1951 to a low point of $1.7 billion in June 1952. On three occasions, November 1951, January 1952, and March 1952, the United Kingdom imposed a series of new import restrictions, mainly against dollar trade but also against the trade of the continental members of the European Payments Union.

France was also in balance-of-payments difficulties in the winter of 1951–52, due mainly to continued inflation, and restrictive measures taken by France and the United Kingdom together constituted a serious setback to the trade liberalization program of the OEEC.

Industrial production in Europe in 1952 failed for the first time since 1945 to rise above the level of the preceding year, and in the first part of that year the exports of continental Europe, like those of the United States and the United Kingdom, declined substantially. After taking into account private capital movements and remittances, the world dollar deficit with the United States rose from $0.3 billion in 1950 to $3.2 billion in 1951. The "dollar shortage" again appeared to be as formidable as ever.

In the latter part of 1952, the situation began to change for the better. Industrial production in Europe began to rise again, and in most European countries, there was a revival of monetary policy as a major

[59] *Ibid.* For a comprehensive discussion of the readjustment period following the boom, see The Contracting Parties to the General Agreement on Tariffs and Trade, *International Trade 1952* (1953), Pt. I, pp. 1–54.

weapon of internal stabilization. This was true also of the United Kingdom.

At the end of the year, sterling reserves had begun a slow but steady rise. Although still substantial, the deficits of continental Western Europe vis-à-vis Canada and the United States were being reduced. The improvement was sufficient to permit some of the European countries, including the United Kingdom, to relax their trade restrictions somewhat, although a notable exception was France, which continued to intensify them. There was also an improvement in the position of the countries producing raw materials, although there were some important exceptions, such as Brazil. Moreover, the declining trend in United States "commercial" exports, which had been a feature of the American balance of payments since the beginning of the European Recovery Program, was resumed, while imports continued to increase gradually. The current account deficit of the rest of the world with the United States declined in 1952 to $1.8 billion. The trend in the latter part of the year was sharply downward, and at the end of the year the deficit had disappeared entirely.

The generally favorable development of international trade toward a more balanced position in 1953 was summarized by the United Nations Secretariat as follows:

> International trade reached a high point in 1953; the value of world exports (excluding those of eastern Europe and mainland China), measured in constant prices, rose above the preceding peak in 1951. In the first nine months of 1953 the export quantum was 15 per cent above the average for 1950, or about 40 per cent above 1948 or 1937. In the same time a substantial improvement was attained in the regional pattern of world exports. United States foreign aid was not only significantly reduced, but there was in fact a flow of gold and dollars of a similar magnitude from the United States to the rest of the world. An important factor contributing to this change was the rise in exports of the rest of the world while commercial exports of the United States fell sharply from 1952 to 1953.[60]

This did not mean, of course, that all transitional problems had been solved. Nevertheless, from 1953 on, the United Nations system as a whole was less influenced than at any previous time by emergency situations left by the Second World War. Reconstruction in the physical sense was approaching completion; prices of internationally traded goods were relatively stable; and the extreme dependence of other countries on dollar sources of supply was being gradually reduced. The

[60] U.N. Secretariat, Department of Economic Affairs, *World Economic Report, 1952–53* (1954), p. 75.

abnormal inventories built up after the Korean crisis had been worked off, and it became possible to regard the price dislocations of 1950–51 merely as a historical episode. Nevertheless, these dislocations left their mark on almost every aspect of the work of the United Nations system in the field of international trade and payments.

Responses of the Economic and Social Council and the Assembly

When the Economic and Social Council at its twelfth session in February-March 1951 reviewed the world economic situation, plans for large-scale rearmament were being pushed forward, the boom in commodity prices had about reached its peak, and inflationary forces were still strong. In making its recommendations to governments on policies to be followed in these circumstances, it gave priority to three matters of primary concern to the underdeveloped countries. These countries tended to look on Western rearmament as a threat to their development programs. They were concerned lest exceptional demands for capital goods in the industrialized countries deprive them of what they regarded as an equitable share in the international distribution of such goods. They were also afraid that their command over such goods would be diminished if inflation continued unchecked in industrialized countries, with a consequent fall in the purchasing power of their rapidly rising reserves. Both fears had been expressed by the Latin American countries at the Inter-American Conference on War and Peace held in Mexico City in 1945, and were ingrained in the thinking of many representatives of underdeveloped countries. At the same time, these countries wished to preserve the advantages of the favorable terms of trade that were the consequence partly of demand created by rearmament and partly of inflation.

It is somewhat of an understatement to say that these views, even though not wholly consistent, were reflected in the resolution adopted by the Council on March 20, 1951, on the world economic situation. This resolution was, in turn, a reflection of concerns that were being expressed by underdeveloped countries also at meetings of two of the regional economic commissions, the Economic Commission for Asia and the Far East, and the Economic Commission for Latin America.[61]

[61] See, for example, U.N. Economic and Social Council, Thirteenth Session, *Official Records*, Supplement No. 7, "Report of the Economic Commission for Asia and the Far East," p. 48; U.N. Economic and Social Council, *Annual Report of the Economic Commission for Latin America*, Doc. E/2021. E/CN 12/266 (June 15, 1951), pp. 20, 110–14, and 147.

Although the concept of rearmament as a common effort to safeguard international peace and security was incorporated in the resolution of the Council, at least by implication, its wording left no doubt that the primary purpose of the resolution was to safeguard the economic interests of the underdeveloped countries. All members of the United Nations were called upon: first, to take special measures—during the period of general shortage of goods—to bring about adequate production and equitable international distribution of capital and essential consumer goods and raw materials especially needed for the maintenance of international peace and security, the preservation of standards of living, and the furtherance of economic development; second, to take measures, direct or indirect, to regulate at equitable levels and relationships the prices of essential goods moving in international trade; third, to maintain this equitable regulation of distribution and prices as long as strong inflationary pressures persisted, in order to minimize changes in the purchasing power, in terms of imports, of current earnings from exports as well as of monetary assets. There was a fourth recommendation that was not open to the charge of special pleading, that all members take all steps in their power to prevent the development of inflationary pressures, thereby preventing speculative profits and maintaining the purchasing power of the poorer sections of the population.[62]

The recommendation of the Council on equitable allocation did not differentiate between the types of allocation that might be feasible for capital goods and for raw materials. Nor did it assign responsibility for taking action to any United Nations agency. So far as capital goods were concerned, it was essentially a plea to the industrialized countries not to allow their defense programs to interfere with the plans of the underdeveloped countries. Although the recommendation that steps be taken to increase the production of goods especially needed for the maintenance of international peace and security might be interpreted to imply that the underdeveloped countries should give greater emphasis to the production of strategic materials, this was not the spirit of the resolution. The underdeveloped countries strongly insisted on their right to determine their development programs without interference, and they were inclined to argue that economic development as such, without any emergency deviations from long-range plans, was their best contribution to peace and security.

The anxieties of the underdeveloped countries about the availability of capital goods were probably somewhat exaggerated. At the time they were given formal expression in the resolution of March 20, 1951, many

[62] Res. 341 (XII), Mar. 20, 1951.

special measures were being taken by the industrialized countries to increase the production of capital goods to meet the combined demands of their domestic economies, their export markets, and their rearmament. Indeed, the whole concept of the equitable distribution of capital goods once produced was extremely vague, and it is difficult to visualize what general measures could have been taken to ensure it. The nub of the problem was the scarcity of raw materials entering into the production both of capital and consumer goods, and it was to the conservation and effective utilization of such raw materials that the export controls and domestic allocation machinery of the industrialized countries were directed.

These measures did raise problems of equitable international allocation capable of being dealt with through an international agency. On these problems also, the United Nations could take no effective action, because the intensification of the East-West conflict made it impossible to entrust international allocation functions to a United Nations agency as had been done immediately after the war when the Food and Agriculture Organization, a specialized agency of which the Soviet Union was not a member, fell heir to certain functions of the wartime Combined Food Board.[63]

In January 1951, when the allocation problem was being discussed in the Economic and Social Council, the United States, Great Britain, and France agreed that international action should be taken entirely outside the United Nations to deal with the world scramble for raw materials. The method chosen was the creation of a new agency called the International Materials Conference, comprised essentially of commodity groups representing the producing and consuming countries of the free world having a substantial interest in the commodities involved. Quarterly allocations for a number of raw materials in short supply, particularly metals, were worked out and accepted through these commodity groups, and the position in cotton and wool was kept under review by them. Some major commodities, such as tin and natural rubber, however, of interest especially to underdeveloped countries, remained outside the jurisdiction of the conference.

Many of the contracting parties to the GATT participated in the International Materials Conference. In accordance with recommendations of the conference, they introduced new controls over trade in materials for industry, and the conflict between these measures and the basic principles and objectives of GATT was underlined by the Contracting Parties in the following terms:

[63] See above, Chap. II.

. . . these [measures] may be but the forerunners of further controls on an international scale stemming from other factors such as the economic and financial plans of the North Atlantic Treaty Organization. These new controls will almost inevitably run counter to the progressive removal of controls on international trade which is one of the principal aims of the General Agreement. But the Agreement recognizes the possible need for such exceptional measures, and lays down the condition of equality of treatment for the international distribution of scarce products. While progress towards the early attainment of the objectives of the Agreement will thus be interrupted, the very existence of its principles and the pursuit of its objectives become all the more important in the long run, because in the absence of limitations these temporary distortions would be even more harmful to trade. Governments will also be able more easily to withdraw emergency measures if these measures are regarded from the beginning as agreed departures from normal rules.[64]

This reaction to the International Materials Conference was in strong contrast to that of many underdeveloped countries in the principal organs of the United Nations. In their view, the work of the conference did not constitute an adequate response to the resolution adopted by the Economic and Social Council on March 20, 1951, because it dealt neither with the problem of equitable distribution of capital goods nor with that of long-range price stabilization at equitable levels and relationships. This was made clear by a resolution of the General Assembly of January 12, 1952, which urged all members to continue to make every effort to carry out the four recommendations of the resolution adopted by the Council in March 1951.[65]

The drastic decline in the prices of raw materials in 1951 greatly intensified the concern of the principal organs of the United Naions with the second major theme of the resolution of the Council of March 20, 1951—the regulation of the prices of essential goods moving in international trade at equitable levels and relationships. So great was this concern that from this time onward it dominated the approach of the Council and the Assembly to problems of commodity trade and became a central feature of their efforts to promote greater stability in the world economy.[66] As will be shown later in this study, the United Nations continued to issue reports and pass resolutions that contained a measure of good advice with respect to their trade and commodity policies not only for the industrialized countries but also for the underdeveloped

[64] Interim Commission for the International Trade Organization, *GATT in Action, Third Report on the Operation of the General Agreement on Tariffs and Trade* (January 1952), p. 25.

[65] Res. 523(VI), Jan. 12, 1952.

[66] For this reason, further consideration of this aspect of United Nations activities in the field of trade is discussed in this study in the general context of full employment and stability. See below, Chap. V.

countries. The advice to the former, however, was concerned mainly with their duty to take account of the special problems of the latter. This set the general tone, but the balance was to some extent redressed by the revival of the cartel issue at the thirteenth session of the Council (July–September 1951).

Revival of the Cartel Issue in the Economic and Social Council

The problem of restrictive business practices having harmful effects on international trade was of primary interest to the industrialized countries. As pointed out earlier, the United States and the Western European countries were divided on this question during the interwar years. Their viewpoints were compromised in Chapter V of the Havana Charter, and it was the principles of that chapter that were incorporated in a resolution of the Economic and Social Council adopted in September 1951.[67]

The initiative on this matter was taken by the United States delegation. Commitments to follow the principles of the Havana Charter on restrictive business practices had been included in the bilateral agreements negotiated by the United States with countries in the European Recovery Program, and at this time the so-called Benton Amendment to the Mutual Security Act of 1951 requiring that American aid be used to promote private competitive enterprise in the participating countries was under active debate in Congress.[68] The United States delegation felt that it would be desirable to generalize these principles through action by the Council, and at the same time to fill an obvious gap in international economic co-operation by reviving a part of the Havana Charter that had never been severely criticized in the United States.

The resolution passed by the Council was in harmony with these views. It recommended that Member states should take appropriate measures and co-operate with one another to prevent business practices affecting international trade that restrain competition, limit access to markets, or foster monopolistic control, when such practices have harmful effects on the expansion of production or trade, on the development of underdeveloped countries, or on standards of living. This was a repetition of the language of the Havana Charter, except that the reference to economic development was made more explicit.

[67] Res. 375(XIII), Sept. 13, 1951.
[68] *Congressional Record*, Vol. 97, Pt. 8, 82 Cong. 1 sess., pp. 10943–52.

An *Ad Hoc* Committee on Restrictive Business Practices was established to report on methods of giving effect to this recommendation.[69] Early in 1953, this committee agreed on a final report that contained twenty draft articles of agreement covering international co-operation in this field. These were based on Chapter V of the Havana Charter, with only minor changes. The report also outlined the structure and internal procedures of an agency that might implement these substantive proposals.

At its sixteenth session (June–August 1953), the Council received the report of the committee and remanded it for further study by Member governments, nongovernmental organizations, and the Secretariat. This action is to be explained mainly by a change in the attitude of the United States, which both surprised and disappointed many other countries. It was taken at a time when the United States Government was greatly influenced by a strong movement in favor of a constitutional amendment (the Bricker amendment) to limit the treaty powers of the President. There is some ground also for supposing that under a new administration, the United States Government had become more sensitive to the views of a few strong opponents of action in this field, and the most active supporters of the recommendation were no longer in its service. The government was beginning to feel that the kind of international obligations that the United Nations was tending to impose were those that would be enforced more strictly by the United States than by other governments, and that no real changes in the cartel practices of foreign countries would in fact result from giving effect to the recommendation. Whatever the reasons for the waning of American enthusiasm, the subject was for all practical purposes removed for some time to come from further consideration by the principal organs of the United Nations.

Fund and GATT: Operations, Policies, and Problems

One of the consequences of the Korean crisis was to accentuate certain differences between the views of the Economic and Social Council, the General Assembly, and the regional commissions on the one hand, and the GATT and the Fund on the other. For example, the concept of "equitable" international distribution of capital goods according to

[69] U.N. General Assembly, Seventh Session, *Official Records*, Supplement No. 1, "Annual Report of the Secretary-General on the Work of the Organization, 1 July 1951–30 June 1952" (1952), p. 69.

some criterion of need, which was upheld by many underdeveloped countries in the Assembly, the Council, and the regional commissions for Latin America and for Asia and the Far East, was different from the concept of equal (nondiscriminatory) treatment in the market place to which the GATT was committed. An example of a different kind is a difference of opinion that developed between the Fund and the secretariat of the Economic Commission for Europe on the proper foreign exchange policy to be followed during the period of inflation after the invasion of South Korea.

In 1951, the secretariat of the Economic Commission for Europe presented an elaborate argument in favor of a general appreciation of European exchange rates in terms of dollars as a means of checking inflation in Europe, the principal cause of which—in its opinion—was the rise of import prices.[70] This argument for exchange appreciation as an anti-inflationary device was considered and rejected by the Fund, which reached the conclusion that "widespread appreciation would be as ineffective for solving [the problem of inflation] as widespread depreciation was for solving the problem of deflation in the thirties."[71]

Whatever the merits of these views, the point to be stressed is that they were in conflict and were not "co-ordinated" in advance of publication. In view of the fact that the initiative on exchange rates rests in any case with the governments, a service was probably rendered by the raising and analysis of this entire issue by competent international civil servants.

During the post-Korea inflation, the Fund received no proposals for the appreciation of the exchange rate of a member, but on the closely related issue of fluctuating or "floating" rates, it had to take action. On September 30, 1950, Canada, with the approval of the Fund, suspended its fixed par value in order to counteract a speculative inflow of capital from the United States. Because the purpose of this suspension was not to improve the Canadian balance-of-payments position, the Fund chose to regard this as an exceptional case. In giving its approval, it was careful to take note of the Canadian intention to remain in consultation with the Fund and to re-establish an effective par value as soon as circumstances warranted.[72] The Fund strongly maintained its general

[70] U.N. Department of Economic Affairs, Economic Commission for Europe, *Economic Survey of Europe, 1950* (1951), pp. 157–64.

[71] International Monetary Fund, *Annual Report . . . April 30, 1951*, p. 36.

[72] International Monetary Fund, Press Release No. 145 (Sept. 30, 1950).

position that "a system of fluctuating exchange rates is not a satisfactory alternative to the par value system."[73]

There were in fact few changes in par values in 1950–51, and the Fund held that the new structure of rates established in the earlier devaluations had largely eliminated disparities in price levels.[74] In other respects, progress toward "orderly" exchange arrangements, as these were conceived by the Fund, was very slight. There was no pronounced trend toward reducing multiple exchange rate practices, although the Fund was able to report some desirable modifications in a few countries during the upward swing of prices. This slight improvement was counterbalanced by the development, especially by European countries, of "new competitive exchange policies involving the use of retention quotas or special facilities for the acquisition of import rights." These were designed to stimulate exports to the dollar area mainly, but the Fund believed that they had much in common with multiple currency practices and that if extensively used they could readily be employed as weapons of economic aggression.[75]

During this period also, the Fund became engaged in the development of a new lending policy. As early as September 1946, the authority of the Fund to use its resources had been interpreted by a decision of its Board as being restricted to "temporary assistance in financing balance of payments deficits on current account for monetary stabilization operations."[76] This principle called for further elaboration, and procedures announced in 1951 and 1952 were designed to give confidence to member countries undertaking practical programs of action to help achieve the purposes of the Fund—especially those members willing to run graver risks because of the availability of assistance from the Fund. Members whose programs were found acceptable were to be assured that the resources of the Fund would be available, if required, to carry out such programs under a stand-by credit arrangement. This policy was approved and put into effect by a series of decisions in May

[73] International Monetary Fund, *Annual Report . . . April 30, 1951*, p. 39. For the economic considerations accepted by the Fund as justification for its action in making the exception in the Canadian case, which are of major importance in the development of the policy of the Fund, see *ibid.*, pp. 44–45.

[74] *Ibid.*, p. 33.

[75] International Monetary Fund, *Annual Report of the Executive Directors for the Fiscal Year Ended April 30, 1952* (1952), p. 62.

[76] On this question see International Monetary Fund, *First Annual Meeting of the Board of Governors: Report of the Executive Directors and Summary Proceedings, Sept. 27 to Oct. 3, 1946* (November 1946), pp. 23–27, 106.

1951 and in February and October 1952. Although these decisions provided for a more liberal lending policy, they also stressed the importance of preserving the revolving character of the resources of the Fund. The exchange purchased from the Fund was not to be outstanding beyond the period reasonably related to the payments problem for which it was purchased—a period falling within the outside range of three to five years.[77]

At the end of 1952, therefore, the Fund was prepared to consider requests by members for stand-by credit arrangements designed to give assurance that, during a fixed period of time, transactions up to a fixed amount would be made whenever a member requested, and without further consideration of its position.[78] The size of stand-by credits available under this policy was still limited by the restrictive provisions of the Articles of Agreement, and this was quite different from the large-scale stabilization credits that might be required for a collective return to convertibility.

During the fiscal year ended April 30, 1954, only four stand-by credits, amounting in all to $90 million, were arranged, of which only $25.5 million was utilized. One such credit amounting to $35 million was granted in the fiscal year ending April 30, 1956, but no drawings were made under any stand-by credit during the fiscal years 1955 or 1956. This record reflected the general improvement in the balance-of-payments positions of the members, which was reflected also in the substantial amount by which repurchases from the Fund exceeded new drawings in these two fiscal years. Of the total of $1,236.4 million drawn from the Fund from the beginning of its operations to April 30, 1956 only $187.3 million had not been repurchased or otherwise offset. This moderate use of the revolving fund provided for by the IMF was reversed in late 1956. In October 1956, France made a stand-by arrangement permitting it to purchase, with French francs, up to $262.5 million in foreign currencies from the Fund during the ensuing twelve months. This was followed in December 1956 by an arrangement under which the United Kingdom was authorized to purchase foreign currencies with sterling up to the full amount of its quota, $1,300 million. Of this,

[77] International Monetary Fund, *Annual Report . . . April 30, 1952*, pp. 40–51, and App. IV, pp. 87–90.

[78] International Monetary Fund, *Annual Report of the Executive Directors for the Fiscal Year Ended April 30, 1953*, pp. 50–51 and 95–96. The time limit for stand-by credits was fixed at six months with the possibility of renewal for another six months by a decision of the Executive Board. In a later decision of December 23, 1953, the Fund declared itself willing to give sympathetic consideration to stand-by arrangements of more than six months "in the light of the problems facing the member and the measures being taken to deal with them." *Annual Report . . . April 30, 1954*, p. 131.

$561.5 million was added directly to the United Kingdom monetary reserves, and $738.5 million was in the form of a twelve-month stand-by credit which required a waiver of the standing rules of the Fund.[79]

The new lending policy did not mean that the Fund was willing to extend its concept of temporary assistance to include very large-scale advances in periods of widespread recession or depression. The Fund did not support the recommendation of the report of the experts to the Economic and Social Council on *Measures for International Economic Stability* for an enlargement of its resources so as to increase the effectiveness of its activities in such circumstances.[80] The Fund was, in fact, no more willing than the Bank to support the more exuberant proposals for anticyclical action put forward in the Council and General Assembly by those who had little or no responsibility for their execution. Such differences of approach have an important bearing on the question of co-ordination and the autonomy of specialized agencies within the United Nations system, and in this context the reasons for the unwillingness of the Fund are especially significant. These were stated by the Fund in a published report:

> The basic problem of depression cannot . . . be overcome by the availability of international short-term credit to be repaid in the next boom. The cure for a depression will require national measures to stimulate effective demand, especially in the great industrial countries. It may take time, however, before these measures bring recovery. The Fund can assist members which in the meantime may be faced with serious balance-of-payments difficulties, and by so doing reduce the deflationary pressure on the world economy as a whole. . . . The Fund has for some time had under consideration the question of increasing the members' quotas, having in mind such factors as the magnitude of possible balance-of-payments deficits in a depression and the fall in the purchasing power of money since 1946. It has, however, concluded that an increase in its resources is not a question for action at the present time. Its existing resources are by no means small as a source to finance cyclical balance-of-payments deficits. The Fund's resources, moreover, are secondary reserves, and the ability of countries to maintain import demand in a depression will depend also on the size of their reserves. It is important, therefore, that countries follow policies that will enable them to build up reserves in periods of prosperity which would provide a first cushion to absorb the shock of a recession.[81]

While the Fund was preparing itself for the time when it could fulfill one of the major functions for which it had been established, the GATT was also giving consideration to some basic long-range problems. A

[79] International Monetary Fund, *Annual Report . . . April 30, 1954*, pp. 106–08; *Annual Report of the Executive Directors for the Fiscal Year Ended April 30, 1956* (1956); pp. 120–25, and International Monetary Fund Press Release, Dec. 10, 1956.

[80] See below, Chap. V.

[81] International Monetary Fund, *Annual Report . . . April 30, 1952*, pp. 45–46.

third series of multilateral-bilateral tariff negotiations was completed at Torquay in April 1951. The resulting concessions were bound for three years, and the earlier Geneva and Annecy concessions were rebound for the same period. As a result, more than 58,000 tariff rates covering a large part of world trade were stabilized till the end of 1953.[82] This was a great accomplishment, but it was an open question whether a further extension after 1953 would be possible.[83] One of the reasons for this was a growing conviction that the negotiating procedures thus far followed might have outlived their usefulness.

The results of the Torquay tariff negotiations were not as extensive as had been hoped, partly because the negotiations coincided almost exactly with the great upsurge of prices after Korea, and partly because of special bargaining difficulties that had not been present to the same degree at Geneva and Annecy. The United Kingdom, Australia, and New Zealand were not willing to reduce margins of preference in return for tariff reductions or bindings by the United States, and as a result no concessions were exchanged between these important countries. More important for the whole bargaining technique of the GATT were the difficulties caused by the disparities in European tariff levels.

Under the GATT rules, the binding of a low tariff was treated as equivalent to the reduction of a high one. The low tariff countries of Europe, having used up their bargaining power in the earlier negotiations urged that this principle be stretched to make the mere prolongation of a low tariff binding the equivalent of a reduction in a high tariff. The high tariff countries felt that this would require them to give unrequited concessions and refused to agree. This put the low tariff countries at a disadvantage. The reduction of quantitative restrictions under the trade liberalization program of the OEEC was at this time increasing the importance of tariffs, and this made the disadvantage of the low tariff countries even greater.

Two remedies were suggested: one by the Benelux countries that the disparity in tariff levels should be reduced by unilateral action by the high tariff countries; and one by France that all participating countries should, over a period of three years, reduce their tariffs by 30 per cent. Both were carefully examined by the Contracting Parties, and the French proposal underwent many refinements, including the incorpora-

[82] Interim Commission for the International Trade Organization, *GATT in Action*, p. 8.

[83] The Contracting Parties to the General Agreement on Tariffs and Trade, *International Trade 1952* (June 1953), p. 100.

tion in it of some features of the Benelux plan. By the end of 1952, however, there was no agreement except that more study was required.[84]

There was one serious obstacle to the progressive reduction of tariffs through the GATT procedures that was not squarely met by either the Benelux or the French proposals. This was the difficulty of applying to underdeveloped countries the basic principle of GATT that such reductions should take place on the basis of an exchange of roughly equivalent concessions. The exports of many such countries were predominantly primary products that were admitted free of duty by highly industrialized countries. The latter were consequently not in a good position to offer equivalent tariff concessions in exchange for the reduction of the often highly protective duties applied by the underdeveloped countries to the processed or manufactured goods of which they were heavy exporters. This difficulty was compounded by the drive for industrialization in the underdeveloped countries, which had become convinced exponents of the infant-industry argument. The search for some method of making membership in the GATT more attractive to underdeveloped countries without a complete surrender of basic principles had become a major preoccupation of the Contracting Parties by the time of the Torquay meeting. Subsequent annual reports of the Contracting Parties show that almost complete liberty of action in imposing quantitative restrictions in the interests of economic development was retained by underdeveloped countries despite membership in the GATT.[85]

In addition to the long-range problems of stabilizing tariff rates and devising new negotiating procedures, the Contracting Parties were at the time of the Torquay meeting also confronted with the difficult question of Japanese adherence to the Agreement. The problem was how to provide safeguards against the revival of certain prewar Japanese trade practices and against a flood of extremely low-cost Japanese goods without attaching conditions to Japanese adherence that would discriminate against Japan. In July 1952, Japan formally requested an opportunity to enter into tariff negotiations with a view to adherence, but the Contracting Parties remained divided on this issue and only a provisional solution was reached in 1953.[86] It was not until the summer of 1955 that these negotiations were held. In September 1955,

[84] *Ibid.*, p. 99.

[85] The Contracting Parties to the General Agreement on Tariffs and Trade, *International Trade 1953* (June 1954), pp. 105–06.

[86] *Ibid.*, pp. 122–23.

Japan became a contracting party, but fourteen of the thirty-four contracting parties, including the United Kingdom, withheld application of the Agreement to their relations with Japan.[87] The problem basically remained unsolved.

Meanwhile precedents for the application of the General Agreement to a great variety of concrete situations were being established.[88] Many of the problems were settled by diplomatic action, but many others were brought formally before the Contracting Parties. Some complaints were rejected; others were sustained and some form of remedial action taken. Other differences were mediated and thereafter settled directly by the parties, as in the notable case of the India-Pakistan dispute over the license fee imposed by Pakistan on raw jute. Still others were carried forward from session to session in the hope that the countries complained of would sooner or later change their practices. A case in point was the vigorous complaint of many countries against import quotas imposed by the United States under Section 104 of the Defense Production Act.[89]

The basis of all these complaints was that one or more contracting parties felt they had been deprived of benefits under the Agreement by the action of another. On certain issues involving the general clauses of the Agreement this basis was not available. The most important of these was the application of quantitative restrictions for balance-of-payments reasons, an issue in which the Fund was also deeply involved.

As noted earlier, the United Kingdom and other Commonwealth countries agreed in July 1949 to intensify their import restrictions in order to halt a severe drain on sterling area reserves. The Contracting Parties, however, did not call them immediately into consultation, preferring to wait until they could appraise the economic effects of the currency devaluations of September 1949. Consequently, the first full-dress consultations were held at the Torquay meeting of GATT with Australia, Ceylon, India, New Zealand, Pakistan, Southern Rhodesia, and the United Kingdom, and also with Chile, which had imposed new

[87] Article XXXV of the General Agreement permits a contracting party to withhold application of the Agreement from another contracting party with which it has not entered into tariff negotiations.

[88] The third annual report of the Interim Commission for the International Trade Organization listed ten different kinds of disputes that had come before the Contracting Parties. *Gatt in Action* (January 1952), pp. 13–14.

[89] For an evaluation of the record of the Contracting Parties in the settlement of differences, see Raymond Vernon, *America's Foreign Trade Policy and the GATT*, Essays in International Finance, No. 21, Princeton University, Department of Economics and Sociology (October 1954), pp. 15–18.

restrictions. Several hard-currency countries (Belgium, Cuba, Canada, and the United States) contended that the time had come when the Commonwealth countries other than India and Pakistan might begin a cautious but progressive relaxation of restrictions. This was also the view of the Fund, which submitted a report and background paper on each of the consulting countries, and participated actively in the consultations.

The respresentatives of Australia, Ceylon, New Zealand, Southern Rhodesia, and the United Kingdom argued that the Fund had not taken account of certain adverse factors already operating, including rearmament, the full force of which would not be felt until 1951. They strongly opposed any relaxation in spite of the improvement in their reserves during the post-Korean price rise.[90]

The consultations therefore had no visible result, except that all were agreed that no relaxation was feasible for India, Pakistan, and Chile. This outcome was perhaps fortunate in view of the serious fall in sterling area reserves a few months later when commodity prices began to decline drastically. The Fund can be fairly criticized, without having recourse to hindsight, for not having taken this possibility sufficiently into account in tendering its official advice. A miscalculation of this magnitude was in fact very likely to give aid and comfort to those who favored a rigid application of the principle of noninterference by international bodies in matters of domestic jurisdiction.

To check the drain on sterling reserves, the United Kingdom, in November 1951, imposed the first of a series of new restrictions, but again the Contracting Parties took no immediate action. On this occasion, an important reason for postponement was that the restrictions affected principally the countries with which the United Kingdom was in regular consultation in the OEEC. The United Kingdom was not alone in intensifying old and imposing new restrictions on balance-of-payments grounds, and in October 1952, after the effects of the Korean crisis had worked themselves out, the Contracting Parties in co-operation with the Fund consulted with Australia, Ceylon, France, Italy, the Netherlands, Pakistan, and the United Kingdom. In these consultations, more attention was paid to the protective effects of the restrictions, and all the consulting countries acknowledged the importance of applying them in such a manner as to avoid unnecessary

[90] For the text of the communiqué on these consultations issued by the Contracting Parties on December 13, 1950, see International Monetary Fund, *Staff Papers*, Vol. 1 (April 1951), p. 442.

damage to the commercial and economic interests of other contracting parties.[91]

In 1952, general consultations were begun by the Fund on the need of its members for continued exchange restrictions, and by the Contracting Parties on the need for discriminatory application of restrictions on trade. Because most of the GATT adherents were permitted under the General Agreement to discriminate in trade in a manner having equivalent effect to exchange restrictions they might apply as members of the Fund, the GATT had a major interest in the outcome of the Fund consultations. During the first year of consultations, this outcome was disappointing, and the Fund had to report that "although some countries were applying policies designed to produce favorable conditions for the removal of restrictions, most countries were so preoccupied with their immediate problems that any substantial withdrawal of restrictions was impracticable."

These annual and other less formal consultations kept the Fund in contact with all of its members except Czechoslovakia. They were for the most part confidential, but they were one of the most important contributions of the Fund during the period when little use was being made of its resources. For example, in the year ending April 30, 1953, forty-three members of its staff were sent to meet officials and technicians of member countries, often on narrow technical problems, but sometimes on more fundamental problems involving a reform or a reorganization of the exchange system of the member. In the spring of 1954, the second series of annual consultations with Fund members on exchange restrictions was completed, and it became evident to the Fund that a considerable number of major trading countries regarded as possible both relaxation of restrictions and progress toward convertibility. There had been, in fact, a considerable relaxation of exchange restrictions, notably against the dollar area, while these consultations were in progress. The Fund expected this trend to continue and was able to report in the spring of 1956, after the fourth series of consultations, that very few countries had intensified their restrictions and a large number had found it possible to reduce them. With wider transferability of currencies in international payments, there had been a corresponding lessening of emphasis on discrimination and strict bilateralism and some simplification and decline in the use of multiple currency practices.[92]

[91] The Contracting Parties to the General Agreement on Tariffs and Trade, *International Trade 1952*, p. 106.

[92] International Monetary Fund, *Fifth Annual Report on Exchange Restrictions* (1954), p. 2; and *Seventh Annual Report on Exchange Restrictions* (1956), p. 2.

As in the case of the consultations with the Fund on the exchange adjustments of 1949, there is no direct evidence to show whether, or in what degree, these consultations influenced the action of the countries concerned. In the nature of the case, national consultations with international agencies could not bring about the abolition of restrictions that were symptoms of basic structural disequilibrium. The frequent warnings in the reports of the Fund against inflationary practices of all kinds suggest that this institution may have placed too much reliance on the elimination of international price disequilibria as the main, if not the sole, prerequisite for the elimination of restrictions. Nor could it be expected that sovereign states would follow a course recommended by an international institution unless they were convinced that it would serve their national interest as well as the interest of the world community.

Still the Fund was in a position, after reviewing the situation and policies of many of its members, not only to make constructive technical suggestions but to point out ways in which unnecessary and often unintended damage to other members could be avoided without sacrifice of national interests and objectives. There is reason to think that advice of this kind was frequently accepted, especially after 1952 when the basic causes of chronic disequilibrium were being gradually overcome and when sterling convertibility became an objective of practical policy to be achieved by gradual but persistent relaxation of controls.

One of the most perplexing aspects of the sterling convertibility problem was the working out of a smooth transition from the regime established in Europe under the European Payments Union to a regime in which some, but not all, European currencies would become convertible. The consultations of the Fund and the GATT on exchange and trade restrictions, the policies of the Fund on the use of its resources, the complaint procedures of the GATT and its techniques of tariff negotiation, were all affected in one way or another by the fact that some Fund members and contracting parties were also members of this Union. The postponement by the Contracting Parties of action on the trade restrictions of the United Kingdom of November 1951, pending their discussion in the more suitable forum of the OEEC, and the relation of the GATT tariff negotiations to the trade liberalization program of the OEEC have already been referred to. Other aspects of the problem may be illustrated by the growing creditor position of Belgium in the European Payments Union.

In September 1951, the Belgian Government introduced several measures to deal with this problem. In accordance with suggestions from the EPU, Belgium restricted dollar imports on the theory that reduced purchases from the United States would mean increased purchases from European countries and better balanced accounts with them. The United States and the Canadian governments lodged a complaint with the Contracting Parties on the ground that this violated the obligations assumed by Belgium under the GATT, and requested authorization to take compensatory action. The Contracting Parties did not pursue the question immediately "in view of the many serious problems" it presented for governments and the prospects for early removal of the restrictions.[93]

While this complaint was pending, Belgium asked the Fund for a stand-by credit. This was the first such request, and in granting it, the Fund was influenced by the fact that the payments position of Belgium in the European Payments Union "was the key to a significant part of the payments problem of a number of other Fund members." It was in fact the key to the continued existence of the Union. As a result of its large surpluses with other EPU countries, Belgium had extended to the Union more than twice the amount of credit it had originally agreed to. This exposed the Belgian economy to inflationary pressures, and the price of Belgian consent to the extension of the Union for another year was a settlement of the excess credit. As part of this settlement, it was agreed to request the Fund to give Belgium a stand-by credit of $50 million, while the European Payments Union would make five annual payments of $10 million to Belgium to put that country in a position to repay the Fund. This was an effective form of co-operation between the Fund and the European Payments Union, despite the fact that no continuing formal relationship between the two bodies had been worked out. In the reports of the Fund, it was treated as if it were an entirely independent transaction between the Fund and one of its members.[94]

In October 1952, the American-Canadian complaint against Belgium was again reviewed by the Contracting Parties, but action was again deferred pending the outcome of the forthcoming consultations of Belgium with the Fund. After these consultations, the Fund found that relaxations of the discriminatory restrictions might be feasible and requested Belgium to reconsider the necessity of such restrictions. The

[93] Interim Commission for the International Trade Organization, *GATT in Action*, pp. 17–18.

[94] International Monetary Fund, *Annual Report . . . April 30, 1952*, pp. 43–44. In this report the Fund stated that it was still considering the problem of how to develop closer relations with the European Payments Union (*ibid.*, p. 80).

complaint was not pressed, and the restrictions were modified early in 1953.[95]

This was a happy outcome, but it was due to a fortunate change in the Belgian position in the European Payments Union coinciding with an improvement in its dollar position. For a year and a half, Belgian necessities as a member of a regional organization and its obligations as a member of a world organization were reconciled only by recourse to the rights of Belgium to impose discriminatory restrictions under Article XIV (transitional arrangements) of the Fund Agreement. This temporary expedient did not represent any real solution to the problem of reconciling regional and world-wide obligations.

The question of possibly conflicting regional and general international obligations was posed even more sharply for the GATT by the European Coal and Steel Community. There was nothing in the GATT that expressly covered this case, but in November 1952, the Contracting Parties examined the treaty establishing the Coal and Steel Community, found that its objectives were broadly consistent with those of the GATT, and granted a waiver of GATT obligations to the six countries in the Community. This waiver allowed them to act as if they were a single country as far as coal and steel were concerned, and stipulated that their barriers to imports should not be more restrictive than when the waiver was granted. The members of the European Coal and Steel Community also agreed that they would seek to avoid unreasonable barriers to exports to nonmembers and would abide by the decisions of the Contracting Parties in disputes that might arise over commercial policy matters within the jurisdiction of the GATT. This was the middle course that the Contracting Parties felt impelled to follow, but it did not relieve them of difficulties. At subsequent sessions, serious questions were raised about the precise obligations imposed by the waiver, the binding nature of the assurance given by the High Authority, and the extent to which the interests of third countries had, as required by the waiver, been protected and taken into account.

Although, as the foregoing review has shown, the work of the Fund and the GATT was considerably influenced by the economic repercussions of the Korean crisis, their principal concern during this troubled period was with the continuing long-range problems of co-operation in their respective fields, the major problem of the Fund being related to the use of its resources, and the major problems of the GATT centering

[95] The Contracting Parties to the General Agreement on Tariffs and Trade, *International Trade* (1952), p. 94.

around its negotiating procedures, the wide scope of the exceptions to its general rules, and its provisional status.

It was only with difficulty that the consent of all but one (Brazil) of the contracting parties was obtained in 1953 for extending the validity of the assured life of the GATT tariff schedules from January 1954 to July 1955. This gave the Contracting Parties an eighteen-month respite for a further examination of the new methods of tariff reduction that had been proposed. When, however, a fourth round of tariff negotiations was carried on at Geneva from January to May 1956, the established procedures were adhered to. These negotiations were entered into in a generally pessimistic mood by the twenty-two contracting parties participating, chiefly because of the very limited negotiating authority of the Americans.[96] Although the results were considerably better than were expected, they were by no means spectacular.

Before these tariff negotiations were held, there was a general review of the Agreement as a whole in accordance with a decision reached by the Contracting Parties at their eighth session (September–October 1953). This review was completed on March 7, 1955, and protocols were opened for acceptance by the contracting parties covering revisions to the Agreement and the creation of a new body, the Organization for Trade Cooperation (OTC), to administer the revised agreement.[97]

The principal results of this review were a reaffirmation of the basic objectives and obligations of the General Agreement; an extension of the firm validity of the tariffs bound under it indefinitely, subject to their withdrawal at three year intervals or with the consent of the OTC;

[96] The major provision of the Trade Agreements Extension Act of 1955 authorized tariff reductions to a maximum of 15 per cent from rates existing January 1, 1955 and no more than 5 per cent in any one year.

[97] The possibility that the OTC, if it comes into being, will become a specialized agency of the United Nations appears at present to be ruled out by the provisions of the draft legislation authorizing the membership of the United States in the OTC. Section 351(e) of H.R. 5550, as submitted to the Congress by the Administration in early 1956, read as follows:

"In adopting this Section, the Congress does so with the understanding

"1. that the functions of the Organization for Trade Cooperation will be limited to (a) the administration of the General Agreement on Tariffs and Trade and (b) facilitating intergovernmental cooperation solely in the field of trade, and

"2. that, therefore, the Organization for Trade Cooperation will not be an intergovernmental organization having wide international responsibilities in the economic field as described in Article 57 of the Charter of the United Nations (relating to specialized agencies).

"Accordingly, it is the sense of the Congress that the Organization for Trade Cooperation shall not be brought into a specialized agency relationship with the United Nations under the permissive language of Article 11(b) of the Agreement on the Organization for Trade Cooperation."

a new procedure for the review of quantitative restrictions for balance-of-payments purposes; and a fresh set of rules giving underdeveloped countries greater freedom to impose quantitative restrictions for the establishment of new industries, subject to a new review and consultation procedure. At the same time, by separate action, the Contracting Parties granted waivers on matters of vital importance to the United Kingdom, Germany, and the United States.

The establishment of the OTC would not, however, resolve the still unanswered question whether more effective methods of continuous collaboration between the Fund and the GATT could be devised. This question has been intensively discussed in the OEEC, in the annual meetings of the Fund and the Bank, and in the GATT itself. It is a difficult one because of the basic differences in the nature of the two agencies, which have been brought out in the preceding discussion. Although the provisions of the General Agreement requiring consultation with the Fund were intended to bring the two agencies together, these differences of objective and procedure have made effective co-ordination of effort between them extremely difficult. There has therefore developed in some quarters a strong desire to strengthen the liaison arrangements, so as to bring the objectives of both the GATT and the Fund to bear when a country consults with either.

Fund, GATT, and Commissions of the Council

As has been indicated earlier, the decentralization of the United Nations system led to a considerable amount of co-operation and consultation between the specialized agencies and the commissions of the Council in the field of trade and payments, as in other fields. Much of this was due to the efforts of the three regional commissions to fulfill their mandate to strengthen the economic relations of countries in their areas with each other and with other countries of the world. The two parts of this mandate—the stimulation of trade with the rest of the world, and the stimulation of intraregional trade—could not be entirely separated, and both were of direct concern to the Fund, the GATT, and the FAO. Although the approach of the three regional commissions to this part of their mandate had certain common features, there were some significant differences both on priorities assigned to different parts of the problem and on action taken.

At its fifth session in April 1953, the Economic Commission for Latin America considered an analysis by its own secretariat of the characteristics of the intraregional trade of seven important Latin American countries. The difficulties of reconciling commercial policies that would help Latin American countries to sustain their raw material exports to the world market and restrict the import of certain kinds of manufactured products to protect their nascent industries, with commercial policies that would promote intraregional trade, were explored in connection with this report. Further studies were requested.[98] At the same time the commission considered two other important studies on trade and payments. One was a study undertaken jointly by the secretariats of ECLA, FAO and ECE on trade between Latin America and Europe, a subject on which the commission also requested further studies. The other was a report prepared by a member of the staff of the Fund, acting as a consultant, on the problem of effecting multilateral compensatory settlements between Latin American countries through the European Payments Union. No action on the clearing proposal was taken by the commission at this time, but further studies were requested on this matter also.[99]

The problems and prospects of expanding trade between Europe and Asia and the Far East were explored in a joint ECAFE/ECE/FAO report considered in February 1954 by the Committee on Industry and Trade of the Economic Commission for Asia and the Far East. The committee commended its suggestions for consideration by the governments concerned, and at the same time took a number of positions on the foreign trade problems of the area that were both moderate in tone and constructive in content.[100] The committee acknowledged that the apprehensions of the commission concerning the supply of capital goods had not been fully justified and dropped further work on the subject. It emphasized the importance of intraregional trade, but stated that this should not prejudice the trade of the countries concerned with the rest of the world. It made a number of constructive suggestions for the expansion of trade between Asia and Europe, which it felt was entirely consistent with a general expansion of international trade.

The Economic Commission for Asia and the Far East was not content with studies and reports, but engaged actively in trade promotion. Its secretariat became a clearing-house for trade information, and the

[98] U.N. Economic and Social Council, Sixteenth Session, *Official Records*, Supplement No. 3, "Economic Commission for Latin America, Annual Report (15 February 1952–23 April 1953)," pp. 22–23.

[99] *Ibid.*, pp. 12, 18, and 26.

[100] U.N. Economic and Social Council, Seventeenth Session, *Official Records*, Supplement No. 3, "Annual Report of the Economic Commission for Asia and the Far East," pp. 6 and 7.

commission held regular trade promotion conferences, which increasingly included business representatives in their membership. It also developed training programs for personnel in trade promotion. All of these activities concerned both intraregional trade and trade with the rest of the world, and in carrying them out, the co-operation of the secretariat of the Economic Commission for Europe was enlisted.

In its efforts to expand trade between Eastern and Western Europe, the Economic Commission for Europe was, as already noted, also not content with studies and reports. The executive secretary continued to convene East-West Trade Consultations and some trading opportunities were undoubtedly disclosed in the annual consultations. Until the death of Stalin, the continued participation and interest of Western European countries in these talks, however, was probably due mainly to a feeling that they were a means of somewhat diminishing international tension. They continued to look to the OEEC and to the European Coal and Steel Community, and more recently to a proposed "common market," as the principal instrumentalities for expanding intra-European trade. The ECE, however, was able to be helpful in working out some of the trade problems that followed the expulsion of Yugoslavia from the Cominform.

In regulating the arrangements between the GATT and the Commission on International Commodity Trade established by the Economic and Social Council in 1954, obstacles were encountered.[101] The Contracting Parties were given an opportunity by the Economic and Social Council to consider to what extent the problem of instability in primary commodity prices should be worked out under the auspices of the GATT, but no firm stand on the question could be taken by them, due largely to the opposition of the United States to the assumption of any price stability functions by the GATT.

The Parts and the Whole

Up to the present time, the structure of the United Nations system of specialized agencies has been incomplete because of the absence of an agency or agencies in the field of trade, including in that term commercial policy, cartel policy, and commodity policy. Within the United Nations system, primary responsibilities for foreign exchange policy, which is intimately related to trade policy, have been assigned to an agency with no direct responsibilities for trade policy—a circumstance for which the United Nations Organization cannot be held responsible.

[101] See below, Chap. V.

Within the system, responsibilities in the field of commodity policy have been divided between an interim organization with very limited authority (the Interim Coordinating Committee for International Commodity Arrangements), the FAO as an incident to its major activities, and—more recently—a new Commission on International Commodity Trade established by the Economic and Social Council.

The Fund, the interim committee, the new commission, and—to a lesser extent—the FAO, all have a legitimate concern with commercial policy, or at least with the results of commercial policy, and therefore with the work of the GATT, the main international instrumentality operating in this field. The GATT is a multilateral trade agreement and not an organization, although it may soon be administered by the Organization for Trade Cooperation which, it now seems, is not destined to become a specialized agency of the United Nations. The accomplishments of the GATT cannot be put to the credit of the United Nations, but the accomplishments of the United Nations system as a whole in the field of trade and payments cannot be evaluated without reference to the record thus far made under the GATT, which, like the Fund, was designed to contribute to the primary and global economic objectives laid down in the United Nations Charter.

The Fund

The Fund has been true to the basic concepts written into its charter. It has agreed to most, but not all, of the changes in par values proposed to it by members. It has opposed in principle freely fluctuating rates, multiple exchange rates, broken cross-rates, and gold sales at prices involving deviations from agreed par values. It has resisted pressures for the use of its resources for purposes for which they were not intended in order to conserve them for purposes for which they were intended. For the seasonal or cyclical difficulties that the Fund was intended to meet, its contribution to international liquidity has, by force of circumstances, been modest. The capacity of the Fund to respond to a balance-of-payments crisis of quite a different kind has been demonstrated by its response during the closing of the Suez Canal after November 1956.

The Fund has tried to hasten the return to currency convertibility by emphasizing the inherent disadvantages of exchange controls and the possibilities of relaxing them at a faster rate than member governments have been inclined to adopt. In contrast to the Economic and Social Council and the General Assembly, the Fund has emphasized the need for domestic monetary and fiscal policies that would promote a return to international equilibrium, even though it has been prevented by its Articles of Agreement from withholding its consent to proposed changes in par values on the ground that a change in domestic policies of the member states might render them unnecessary. The Fund has regularly reviewed the exchange policies of its members in consultation with them; has made constructive technical suggestions; and has pointed out ways in which unnecessary damage to other members might be avoided without sacrifice of national interests and objectives.

The Fund has co-operated actively with the GATT, and although in one instance at least it appears to have given bad advice, it has endeavored to see that the work of the GATT has not been "frustrated" by exchange restrictions permitted under the Articles of Agreement of the Fund. This co-operation, however, still leaves much to be desired, and its improvement is at present a matter under active discussion.

The Fund has preserved the revolving character of its assets in order to remain at all times in a position to fulfill the function of extending temporary assistance in financing balance-of-payments difficulties on current account for monetary stabilization purposes, despite the fact that this, prior to the Suez crisis, meant that only a small portion of its resources was made available to members. Between 1952 and 1956, it prepared itself for a more liberal use of its resources in conditions that for the first time approximate those under which it was supposed to function, by introducing a system of stand-by credits and using its waiver powers to overcome some of the rigidities surrounding access to its resources. These policies enabled the Fund to act boldly during the Suez crisis.

The record of the Fund has been severely criticized on several scores. It has been criticized by economists and public officials who are in basic disagreement with the concept, held by the Fund, of orderly exchange arrangements. To many who believe that flexible exchange rates are a prerequisite for the full convertibility of sterling and other major currencies, the Fund has appeared outdated, old-fashioned, and unrealistic. The Fund has been criticized on the other hand by those who believe its principal defect has been its ineffectiveness in persuading member governments to put its basic tenets into action.

When countries such as Canada and Peru felt that flexible exchange rates were in their interest, the Fund has found reasons for going along with them. These were such good reasons that the Fund has not been greatly reproached on this account. Many critics feel, however, that the Fund has been far too complacent in the matter of multiple exchange rates. This "complacency" has been due in part to a realistic recognition of the fact that multiple exchange rates have been used frequently to accomplish domestic objectives by countries that did not have the monetary and fiscal equipment and the administrative competence of the major trading countries of the world.

The Fund has been unfavorably compared to the European Payments Union on the ground that the EPU has been able, by the close and continuous consultation of its members, to influence greatly their monetary and other internal policies in the interests of Europe as a whole; whereas the Fund, partly because of its cumbersome organization and partly because of its world-wide membership, has no similar record to boast of.

Perhaps more fundamental than any of these criticisms are the three following: (1) Major changes in exchange rates have not been made since the war by international agreement in any real sense; the world is not ready to accept this principle, and the Fund therefore has become an artificial construction through which changes in par values are recorded but not decided upon. (2) The Fund has not adjusted its thinking to the realities of a world that has forever turned its back on nineteenth century methods of reaching international equilibrium. (3) The Fund has not been able to perform the role intended for it and has not to date been able to discover any other role.

It is not the function of this study to pass judgment on the validity of these criticisms, especially those that rest on doctrinal grounds, such as the relative merits of fixed and flexible exchange rates. It is rather to reach some general conclusions whether the record of the Fund thus far has made a contribution to the objectives of the United Nations Charter.

International agreement on "orderly exchange arrangements" is clearly in accordance with these objectives because the disorganization or disruption of foreign exchange relationships can, as the experience of the depression showed, have disastrous effects on almost any other form of international co-operation. Opinions may and do differ on what should constitute orderly exchange arrangements, but on this question, the burden of proof must rest on those who believe that the Fund has been mistaken in its basic concepts, inasmuch as it has for a decade been a forum for international consultation and discussion on this problem. There can be no doubt, however, that the Fund has not been and is not likely to be a forum in which the crucial decisions on changes in par values, especially those of major currencies, are made.

The objectives of the United Nations are global objectives, and the Fund has been a force working against their undue subordination to regional ones. The moderation of cyclical disturbances and the prevention of the international spread of economic depressions have become major objectives of the United Nations in which the Fund has been expected to play a significant role. It has resisted pressures to play this role in a manner favored by majorities in the Council and by some of the expert advisers to the Council. It is preparing to act with greater boldness in the use of its resources whenever conditions become ripe for the fulfillment of its stabilization functions.

The GATT

Like the Fund, the GATT was in the first instance designed to promote the objectives of Article VII of the mutual aid agreements, in this case by making a contribution to the elimination of all forms of discriminatory treatment in world commerce and to the reduction of tariffs and other trade barriers. In the system of priorities developed in the Council and the General Assembly, the reduction of trade barriers and the removal of discriminations in trade did not occupy a very prominent place and were in fact subordinated to other values. This may have been due in part to the very success of the GATT, as well as the lack of interest of the Soviet Union in tariffs and related trade problems. For those who attach great importance to trade barrier reduction, it may appear fortunate that the Contracting Parties were not obliged to make reports to the Council and the Assembly and to submit to pressures of the kind to which the Fund and the Bank were subject. The pressures to which the GATT has recently been subjected are of a different kind. Since about 1952, its work has had to be carried out against the resistance of mushrooming protectionist demands. The impression has been growing that little further progress in reducing tariff levels is likely to be made by the use of its special methods of negotiation.

Like the Fund, the GATT has been a force tending to prevent an undue emphasis on regional at the expense of global objectives. Furthermore, the Contracting Parties have, like the executive directors of the Fund, although on a more extensive scale, met some of the special problems of individual members or groups of members by the use of waiver provisions in the Agreement. The most important of these have been the waiver granted in 1952 to members of the European Coal and Steel Community to act as one country in the application of tariffs and a group of waivers granted during the renegotiation of the Agreement in 1954 and 1955. Among the latter were two which, although surrounded by administrative safeguards, allowed the United Kingdom to introduce new preferences that were justified on technical grounds.[102] Another was the waiver granted to countries no longer able to justify quantitative restrictions on balance-of-payments grounds, which allowed them to continue such restrictions for a time in order to provide a period of adjustment for certain interests that had been protected by them as an incident to their main function. Far the most important was the waiver granted to the United States, which permitted it to apply quotas under Section 22 of the Agricultural Adjustment Act. This flexibility must be counted among the accomplishments of the GATT, for no international agency dealing with economic matters can accomplish very much if it attempts to bind its members to courses of action that they regard as contrary to their vital interests. It has not resulted in a retreat from the basic objectives of the Agreement, but rather has marked out the area in which these objectives can be pursued with maximum prospects of success.

While the GATT provides for the sponsorship of negotiations for tariff reductions and recognizes that the success of such negotiations, if multilateral in character, will depend on the participation of all major trading countries, no contracting party is specifically obligated to participate in such negotiations. All are, however, obligated to accord to each other most-favored-nation treatment on tariffs, and national treatment on internal taxation and charges, and as a corollary of this, not to introduce new or increase existing preferences. The rehabilitation of the most-favored-nation clause, which was an important objective of the efforts of the League of Nations in the interwar period, could hardly be more complete as a general rule of international conduct. Deviations from this rule by the principal trading countries now have to be justified and accepted as in the general interest by an international body.

Moreover, the GATT has provided an element of stability in tariff rates that was lacking in the interwar years by binding these rates for successive three-year periods. At present, they are bound until December 31, 1957, and there is provision for automatic extension for further three-year periods subject to the renegotiation of individual items.

The principle that, when benefits under the Agreement have been impaired or nullified by the action of a contracting party, remedies must be found by the withdrawal of the measures complained of, the

[102] See George Bronz, "An International Trade Organization: The Second Attempt," *Harvard Law Review*, Vol. 69 (January 1956), p. 449.

granting of compensatory benefits, or equivalent retaliatory action by the injured country has been applied successfully in most cases. Even though some of these disputes have remained unsettled and some of the practices complained of have not been altered, the Contracting Parties have felt increasingly that retaliation is not an adequate remedy, because it merely increases the number of restrictions and works against the central purpose of the Agreement. They have therefore placed increasing reliance on consultation, discussion, advice, and persuasion. As a result, the GATT has become an international forum for the adjustment of disputes on commercial matters for which there is no previous parallel.

It must be admitted that the exceptions to the rules governing the conduct of contracting parties leave a wide area for the use of quantitative restrictions and other nontariff barriers to trade and that the good will of underdeveloped countries toward the GATT has recently been purchased at the price of making it much easier for them to follow a policy of protection. On this score, the GATT has been severely criticized, especially in the United States. There has also been a considerable amount of criticism emphasizing not the weakness of the GATT but its strength. This has come chiefly from supporters of the Commonwealth preference system and from those who fear that through the GATT other countries will be able to dictate the foreign trade policy of the United States. This latter argument, although politically powerful, is based on a misunderstanding of the Agreement itself.

To all this there is a major offset—the agreement of countries, however powerful, to take account of the effects of their trade policies on other countries and to justify them before an international body. To this must be added one further consideration. The contribution of the GATT to the expansion of trade has been as much what it has prevented as what it has positively achieved. In a recent study of the GATT, this point has been effectively made as follows:

> There is nothing rash in the conclusion that the General Agreement and its enforcement methods have helped measurably in the development of rules of the game among trading nations. This does not mean that the Agreement has necessarily brought peace to areas where economic warfare was consciously desired. GATT or no GATT, nations which had the desire to engage in economic warfare with one another during the period would have done so; witness the deterioration of our [United States] trade relations with Czechoslovakia, one of the original signers. But the converse is equally true; nations with a reasonable desire to avoid trade warfare with their neighbors might none-

theless have been at each other's throats in the absence of standards of international behavior such as the GATT. For governments are under constant pressure from their domestic interests to take measures which injure the trade of their neighbors. Where there is no code for distinguishing the actions that are justified from those that are not, a lapse from grace is easy. And once the cycle of recrimination and counterretaliation begins, no self-imposed standard of reasonable conduct can long be maintained.[103]

United Nations System as a Whole

The United Nations system as a whole has been attempting to deal with several major issues in the field of trade and payments: the relation of commercial policy to employment and development policy; the potential conflicts between global and regional approaches to trade and payments policies; the relation of commodity trade to economic stability; and the role of short-term credit from international sources in preventing the international spread of depressions.

Although such a formulation of major issues greatly oversimplifies the over-all picture of United Nations activities in this area, it serves as a basis for drawing some general conclusions.

1. The failure of key governments to ratify the proposed Charter for an International Trade Organization demonstrated that an interlocking series of commitments by a large number of countries in so vast a field is not, and is not likely to be, within the feasible limits of co-operation through any international agency.

2. The overwhelming importance attached to employment and development and the subordination of commercial policy to these objectives by majorities in the Council and the Assembly have led these organs to underestimate, and at times to ignore, the contributions that the reduction of trade barriers can make to the raising of standards of living, and the dangers involved in the failure of Member governments to adopt domestic policies that will promote international equilibrium.

3. The conflict between regional and global approaches to trade and payments problems has been dealt with by the United Nations system as a whole and by the GATT with flexibility and moderation and without sacrifice of global objectives. There has been good co-operation between the Fund and the regional commissions in the study of both the intraregional and the world trading problems of their respective areas, and two of the commissions have engaged in active trade promotion (the ECE on east-west trade, and the ECAFE on

[103] Vernon, *op. cit.*, p. 18.

trade within its area); but there has not been any substantial change in the pattern of world trade as a result of these efforts. Schemes for regional payments arrangements that might have strengthened existing tendencies to divide the world into regional groupings have been explored and rejected. The relationship between the Fund and the GATT and regional organizations outside the United Nations—the EPU and the European Coal and Steel Community—has been such that neither agency has impeded constructive solutions (in the case of EPU, transitional ones) of European problems; but both have continued to exert their influence against regional as opposed to world-wide solutions of international trade and payments problems.

4. There has been a tug-of-war between the Economic and Social Council and the Fund on the amount and use of its resources. This has not been due to any difference of opinion regarding the need for adequate international reserves and the functions of the Fund as a source of secondary reserves needed to provide international liquidity. It has been due to much more fundamental questions, such as the responsibilities of creditor countries for helping debtor countries to solve their balance-of-payments difficulties by providing through the Fund or otherwise the credits necessary to sustain the volume of their imports; the extent to which monetary and fiscal policy should be relied on to correct balance-of-payments difficulties of a cyclical character without undue recourse to international short-term credit; and the question whether the Fund has been unduly zealous in guarding against the use of its funds by countries that are in need not of short-term accommodation but of long-range assistance.

It is a good thing that these issues have been raised and debated within the United Nations system, and that the boldness of the majority of the members of the Council and some of the experts reporting to the Council has been matched by the caution of the Fund. With the completion of the major work of reconstruction, the rediscovery of the role of monetary policy, the steady increase in the transferability of major non-dollar currencies, and their *de facto* convertibility at a modest cost, the tide is now running in favor of the general principles upheld by the Fund.

If the record of the United Nations system as a whole is judged in the light of the extraordinary complexity of international trade and payments relationships and of the long list of international disagreements and conflicts inherited by the United Nations, it is a record of progress on all but the most intractable problems.

CHAPTER IV

*Production and Investment**

A NUMBER of the problems in the field of trade and payments that have come before the United Nations during its first ten years are fundamentally production problems. At the end of the Second World War, the productive capacity and other economic resources of the world were heavily concentrated in the United States. Unless a better pattern of world production evolved, other nations, it was feared, might be confronted not with a temporary but with a chronic dollar shortage, regularly tending to spend more dollars for purchases in the United States than they could earn in sales to the United States or in third markets. Recent events, in particular the experience of 1953–54 when an American recession coincided with a vigorous expansion of production in Europe, have cast doubt on whether the underlying structural disequilibrium is as acute or as permanent as it seemed to be during the early postwar years. Whether the adjustments already made in terms of production and trade, however, are sufficient to banish the prospect of a chronic dollar shortage is still an open question.

The efforts the United Nations has made to expand industrial and agricultural output and to mobilize investment for productive undertakings, like the work in trade and payments, may be divided for purposes of analysis into two time periods: a "formative period" lasting from 1946 to mid-1950, and an "operating period" extending from mid-1950 to date. During the formative period, the reconstruction of war-devastated areas had top priority, and the spotlight was on Europe. By the end of the period, the raising of standards of living in the underdeveloped areas of Asia, Africa, and Latin America had become the central economic aim of the United Nations. Activities during the operating period were consequently world-wide in scope.

The International Bank for Reconstruction and Development during the formative period mobilized sizable resources, developed its loan principles and procedures, completed the reconstruction phase of its work, and made a start on the long-term job of helping underdeveloped countries prepare and realize programs of development. The formative

* By Robert E. Asher.

period in the life of the International Bank was paralleled by exploratory work in the field of production and investment by other agencies of the United Nations, most notably the Food and Agriculture Organization, the Economic and Social Council, the Economic and Employment Commission of the Council, and the regional economic commissions. Shortages of food, fuel, and capital equipment characterized the period, and much attention was given to methods of overcoming temporary deficits. Various types of inter-agency collaboration were developed, although none was as formal as the procedures employed after 1950 for carrying out the Expanded Programme of Technical Assistance.

The realization that important increases in production could be obtained through exchanges of know-how, with comparatively insignificant expenditures of capital, lay at the heart of the technical assistance program. Although the program as a whole is analyzed and appraised at a later point in this study,[1] certain aspects of the work intimately affecting output in industry and agriculture are discussed below.

The inauguration of the Expanded Programme of Technical Assistance was recognized by both developed and underdeveloped countries as a landmark in international economic co-operation under United Nations auspices, but the underdeveloped countries continued to feel that shortage of capital was the main obstacle to a more rapid improvement in their living standards. Many heated discussions arose in United Nations forums regarding the scale and terms on which loan capital should be provided, the measures required to increase the flow of private international investment, the methods of mobilizing domestic capital in underdeveloped countries, and the need for public grants-in-aid from abroad to supplement other sources of development funds. Solution of these problems was made more difficult by conflicting national attitudes concerning intergovernmental versus private lending and investment, and the respective rights and obligations of the receivers and providers of international investment. Some of these same conflicts of attitude arose during the complex negotiations to implement an American proposal for promoting the peaceful uses of atomic energy through the establishment of a world bank for fissionable materials.

The dissatisfaction of many underdeveloped countries with their share in the expansion of world production, and their passionate desire for rapid economic development, inevitably involved the United

[1] See below, Chap. X.

Nations in the removal of obstacles to economic development within the underdeveloped countries themselves. Among these were lack of technically trained man power, chronic underemployment in agriculture, immobility of labor force, lack of knowledge of potential resources, lack of administrative organization and skills, traditional systems of land tenure, lack of adequate domestic savings and of means of directing them into productive channels, inadequate communications, and shortage of social capital generally.

The attention given to underdeveloped areas in the present discussion of production and investment issues, as elsewhere in this study, is necessitated both by the intrinsic importance of their problems and by the increasing emphasis given to them in the work of the United Nations. It should be borne in mind, however, that the objectives of the Charter in the field of production and investment, as in other fields, were originally conceived of as world-wide objectives, and that the economic, social, political, and cultural aspirations dependent for realization on an expansion of production are not confined to any particular group of countries.

Formative Period: 1946–50

The idea that the international community as a whole and, more specifically, the inhabitants of the wealthier nations, have a responsibility for the welfare of their fellow men in remote, poorer nations is relatively new in international affairs. Although it has gained ground during the postwar years, especially since 1950, it remains far from a self-evident truth. The idea that the members of a victorious wartime coalition have a collective responsibility for helping to repair war damage to the worst-devastated areas within the alliance is also new, but has won much wider acceptance. Even before the Charter of the United Nations had been ratified, the wartime coalition had assumed a responsibility in connection with relief, rehabilitation, and reconstruction by establishing the United Nations Relief and Rehabilitation Administration (UNRRA) and approving the Articles of Agreement of the International Bank for Reconstruction and Development (IBRD).

Development of Loan Principles and Procedures by the International Bank

Whereas UNRRA was an emergency organization dominated by humanitarian considerations, the International Bank was envisaged as a permanent organization operating more or less on business principles. UNRRA, already in being at the time of the Bretton Woods Conference, was to meet immediate relief and rehabilitation requirements—primarily through grants. Once emergency needs were met, countries would presumably be in a position to borrow. Loans for the medium-term job of reconstruction and the long-term job of economic development, if not obtainable in the private capital market on reasonable terms, would be available through the Bank.[2]

Subscriptions to the capital fund of the Bank were to be made by all of the members, roughly in accordance with their economic capacities. Under the Articles of Agreement, the capital subscription required of each member is divided into three parts. A small fraction, 2 per cent, is paid in gold or United States dollars, and may be used freely by the International Bank for any of its activities. Another 18 per cent is payable in the currency of the subscribing country—in pounds, francs, guilders, etc.—and may be used for lending only with the consent of the subscriber. The remaining 80 per cent is, in fact, only a guarantee fund. It is not available for direct lending, but is subject to call if and when it is required to meet obligations of the Bank arising out of its borrowing or guarantees.

The capital structure of the Bank was thus designed to provide it with some loan resources of its own (the 20 per cent of their capital subscriptions that members would pay in), and a guarantee fund four times as great (the other 80 per cent) to enable the Bank to mobilize private capital, either through the sale of its obligations to private investors or by guaranteeing international credits privately financed. The emphasis in the Articles of Agreement was on facilitating investment by others, not on investment by the Bank itself. When private capital was unavailable on reasonable terms, however, the Bank was "to supplement private investment by providing, on suitable conditions, finance for productive purposes out of its own capital, funds raised by it and its other resources."[3]

The Secretary of the United States Treasury who was President of the Bretton Woods Conference, described the central aim of the Bank in his closing address to the conference:

[2] For a useful history of the Bank, from which this analysis has borrowed liberally, see *The International Bank for Reconstruction and Development, 1946–1953*, prepared by the Staff of the Bank (1954). (Hereinafter cited as *The International Bank, 1946–1953*.)

[3] United Nations Monetary and Financial Conference, Bretton Woods, N.H., July 1 to 22, 1944, *Articles of Agreement, International Monetary Fund and International Bank for Reconstruction and Development* (1945), Art. I(ii), p. 51. (Hereinafter cited as *Articles of Agreement*.)

. . . The chief purpose of the International Bank for Reconstruction and Development is to guarantee private loans made through the usual investment channels. It would make loans only when these could not be floated through the normal investment channels at reasonable rates. The effect would be to provide capital for those who need it at lower interest rates than in the past, and to drive only the usurious money lenders from the temple of international finance.[4]

Before the resources of the Bank could be put to effective use, a number of policy issues concerning the scope and character of its operations had to be settled. To raise funds in the private capital market, the Bank would have to win the confidence of the investing community. To win the confidence of the investing community, it would have to hew closely to the line of standard banking practices. Yet if it were really to assist as expected in "raising productivity, the standard of living and conditions of labor,"[5] it would inevitably have to take certain risks that private enterprise would not take. Which risks should these be?

The desperate need for reconstruction funds in Europe and the rising demand in other areas for more rapid economic development called for speedy action. These strong external pressures had to be reconciled with the injunctions in the Articles of Agreement that the Bank act "prudently" and "pay due regard" to the prospects that the borrower would repay the loan. An "equitable" division of limited resources had to be made between the vast but probably finite claims of reconstruction and the vaster and almost infinite need for development funds.

The promotion of a climate favorable to private foreign investment had to be reconciled with the national sensitivities of countries that were in fact hostile to private foreign investment. The Bank had to refrain from interference in the political affairs of any member, but it was expected to satisfy itself that its loans would be put to productive use and that the economic house of the borrower was in reasonably good order.

Knowledge that the authorized capital of the Bank was $10 billion, of which more than $8 billion had been subscribed by mid-1947, could give a misleading impression of the resources at its disposal. The 20 per cent represented by paid-in capital amounted to $1.6 billion. Only

[4] Closing address to the United Nations Monetary and Financial Conference by Henry Morgenthau, Jr., July 22, 1944, U.S. Department of State *Bulletin*, Vol. 2 (July 30, 1944), p. 113.

[5] *Articles of Agreement*, Art. I(iii).

$727 million was in gold or United States dollars, and the balance was in the currencies of other member countries. For all practical purposes, the resources of the Bank for direct loans were limited initially to the $727 million, for its clients needed supplies obtainable in 1947 only in the United States market, with gold or United States dollars.[6]

The founders of the Bank, as noted earlier, assumed that the guarantee provisions, behind which stood the other 80 per cent of the American subscription and that of other members, would enable the Bank to mobilize private capital without great difficulty. Just as the founders underestimated the magnitude of European reconstruction requirements, they underestimated the damage wrought by depression and war on the pattern of international trade and payments and on the psychology of private investors. Private investors, mindful of earlier experiences with defaulted foreign loans and distrustful of governmental and intergovernmental institutions, were not interested in lending money to foreign borrowers, even with the safeguard of a guarantee by the Bank. Marketing the bonds of European, Latin American, and Asian borrowers, backed by the guarantee of an institution whose credit was not yet established, therefore could not be adopted as a major fund-raising technique.

The Bank, on the advice of its management and without objection from its membership, decided instead to sell its own bonds and to devote the proceeds to project loans. This, too, proved more difficult than anticipated. The psychological barriers of investors' reluctance to engage in foreign lending, ignorance concerning the Bank and the resources behind it, and opportunities for profitable investment in the domestic market, were reinforced by a major legal barrier. The most likely purchasers of Bank securities at the time—institutional investors in the United States—were subject to state and federal laws that did not authorize investment in the Bank type of security. An extensive tour of state capitals by representatives of the Bank and a publicity campaign, which continued to the summer of 1949, were necessary to obtain legislation and rulings in the various states that would qualify bonds of the International Bank as appropriate investments for national banks, commercial and savings banks, and insurance companies.

In July 1947, the Bank made the first public offering of its own bonds: $100 million in ten-year, 2¼ per cent bonds, and $150 million

[6] International Bank for Reconstruction and Development, *Second Annual Report, 1946–1947*, p. 15.

in twenty-five-year, 3 per cent bonds. Both issues were substantially oversubscribed, and the bonds immediately sold at a premium over the public offering price. This was, of course, gratifying to the management of the Bank. On the other hand, making such bonds eligible and attractive to the most conservative American investors, however important to the longer-run operations of the International Bank, reinforced the pressures toward caution inherent in any organization dominated by officials of treasuries and central banks. Procedural safeguards that delayed the granting of loans, or limited the purposes for which they could be granted, or required ancillary domestic reforms as the price of their approval, could all be justified as essential in order to gain and hold the confidence of private investors. The alleged dependence of the Bank on "Wall Street" consequently became the target of much criticism.

In material terms, what the world outside of North America needed and wanted at the close of the war was the largest possible increase in output, telescoped into the shortest possible period of time. The Bank was certain to be judged in the light of the contribution it could make to this objective. It was therefore under great pressure to give prompt approval to meritorious projects, provided it could satisfy itself on what constituted a meritorious project.

The project approach was intended to avoid the kind of unproductive loans for ill-defined purposes that had been made at high rates of interest during the 1920's and followed by wholesale defaults. If applications were tied to the financing of specific power plants, railroad lines, and irrigation facilities, there would be a better opportunity to judge the amounts needed, the goods and services for which the sums would be expended, and the prospects of repayment. Hence the requirement limiting loans to specific projects except in unusual circumstances.[7]

Proper evaluation of proposals for specific projects, however, required information regarding the over-all prospects and policies of the borrowing country. Regardless of the caliber of the technical designs and specifications, a power plant proposed to the Bank as a specific project would represent a waste of valuable resources if its initial capacity were greatly in excess of foreseeable requirements for electricity. Scaled down to its proper proportions, the plant might appear as an unqualified boon to industrial and agricultural production in the area, but the benefits could be reduced by tax and credit

[7] *Articles of Agreement,* Art. III, Sec. 4 (vii).

policies that discouraged enterprise. To assure the most productive use of the total resources of a nation, the Bank at an early stage began encouraging member governments to formulate long-term investment programs within the framework of which individual project proposals could be more intelligently assessed.

Under its Articles of Agreement, the Bank was expected to finance only those productive projects for which other financing was not available on reasonable terms. Surveying the field during its formative period, the Bank assumed that private capital would be most readily available for the development of export products such as tin, rubber, and petroleum. It hoped that light manufacturing industries such as textiles, which required smaller amounts of capital and which were traditionally private enterprise activities, would continue to be financed privately. On the other hand, large amounts of capital would be required for basic facilities—transportation, communications, and power projects—no longer attractive to private capital, but prerequisites for the attraction of private capital to other fields.

Public utilities had attracted private foreign capital to underdeveloped countries in prewar days, but it would have been unrealistic to expect them to continue doing so after the war on any appreciable scale. The investment was too large, the return too small, the prospect of government intervention too great. Projects to develop electric power and transport facilities were accordingly judged appropriate for Bank financing, although not without some audible expressions of misgiving on the part of the American financial community.

At the same time, and not without equally audible expressions of concern in some other parts of the world, the Bank was led to eschew a field traditionally reserved for public investment even in the highly developed, free enterprise economies: namely, investment in sanitation, education, and health work. These so-called "social overhead investments" were widely recognized as fundamental to other development work. Their contribution to increased production was less measurable and direct, however, than that of a railroad or power plant, and they could be completed without large expenditures of scarce foreign currencies. It therefore seemed logical to consider projects for eliminating malaria, wiping out illiteracy, building elementary schools, or establishing clinics, as unsuitable, in normal circumstances, for financing by the International Bank. Still, the crying need for such projects, and the paucity of domestic resources to finance them, helped in later years to fan the flames for grant-aid programs to supplement loan aid.

Affecting somewhat more subtly the types of projects for which loans would be desired, was the government-guarantee requirement. The Bank could make loans only to governments or in cases where repayment of both principal and interest were fully guaranteed by the government of the area in which the project was to be located. Yet the group most likely to invigorate the climate for private enterprise in underdeveloped countries, the persons desirous of establishing privately owned manufacturing or processing plants, would be least likely to seek Bank financing for fear that the government guarantee demanded by the Bank would subject them to closer government scrutiny and interference than would otherwise be the case. Governments, for their part, would be reluctant to criticize this hesitancy because lack of proposals from the private sector would relieve the government of charges of favoritism for having placed its guarantee behind the borrowings of particular private groups within its borders. Moreover, the governments would then be freer to submit proposals of their own for government-owned facilities that would enhance the prestige of the state. It was the government-guarantee requirement, and the inability of the Bank to supply equity capital, that prompted later proposals for an International Finance Corporation.

So long as currencies remained inconvertible, the requirement of the Bank that repayment must be made in the currency that was borrowed operated as a further barrier. It meant that a project financed by a dollar loan normally had to contribute directly or indirectly to the dollar earnings of the borrowing nation. The availability of Bank financing only for the foreign exchange costs of approved projects was intended to limit to the minimum the future foreign exchange burden of servicing the debt. It meant, moreover, that borrowers would have to meet their own local currency costs, *i.e.*, the funds required for the payment of local labor and domestically produced supplies as contrasted with the currencies needed to pay for the capital equipment obtainable only from abroad. This arrangement, it was believed, would test the sincerity of the interest of a nation in more rapid development and give it an incentive to mobilize its own resources. To many, who were troubled by the relative absence of local savings to mobilize, it seemed an arbitrary limitation. Supporters of the view that IBRD loans should cover the total costs of development projects argued that if British investors in the nineteenth century had limited their investments in Argentina or British Dominion railway projects to the value of the imported equipment required for building the railways, the projects would have remained dead letters.[8]

As reported earlier, the Bank was clearly intended, when making loans to cover the foreign exchange costs of proposed projects, to assume some risks that private banks would not assume, but at the same time to limit itself to investments that were reasonably likely to be repaid. The special risks that it was willing to assume included world war and widespread depression. In other respects, it was determined to make a conscientious assessment of the prospects of repayment. The scope of its conscience is revealed in the following quotation:

> . . . The assessment of repayment prospects involves an exercise of judgment after consideration of a multitude of factors. The availability of natural resources and the existing productive plant within the country are the obvious starting points, but equally important is the capacity of the country concerned to exploit its resources and operate its productive facilities effectively. This involves, among other things, an evaluation of the effectiveness both of the government administration and of the important private enterprises operating within the country, the availability of managerial, supervisory, and technical skills, the types of investment which are proposed to be undertaken both with domestic resources and with funds borrowed from the Bank, and the economic and financial policies which are likely to be followed, particularly insofar as they affect the levels of consumption and of domestic savings and the flow of foreign private capital. The probable impact of all these factors upon the country's future balance of payments position must then be assessed in the light of such considerations as the likely course of prices for the country's principal exports and imports, the stability of export markets, the essentiality of imports, and the effect of population increases. Moreover, in a world of inconvertible currencies, it is not sufficient simply to consider how much over-all foreign debt the borrower can service, it must also be determined in what currencies such a service obligation can be met.
>
> Complicating judgment in every case is the fact that credit-worthiness is not determined by economic forces alone; within fairly wide limits it is determined, too, by the intangible factor of the country's traditional attitude towards its foreign debts. A country which shows a willingness to maintain debt service at the expense, if necessary, of short-term domestic interests is plainly a better credit risk than a country, even with a potentially somewhat stronger economy, which does not treat its foreign obligations with equal seriousness and which may therefore be unwilling, in times of stringency, to make sacrifices in consumption standards to maintain debt service. In this connection, the past debt record of the country is significant.[9]

[8] This was said, for example, by Nicholas Kaldor, a principal author of the report of the experts on "National and International Measures for Full Employment." U.N. Economic and Social Council, Eleventh Session, *Official Records*, 385th Meeting (July 12, 1950), pp. 78–79.

[9] *The International Bank, 1946–1953*, pp. 42–43.

The breadth of the concern of the Bank with the affairs of its borrowers precluded prompt conclusion of loan negotiations. Instability in a borrowing country would jeopardize the prospects for repayment of loans made by the Bank, would alarm purchasers of Bank securities, and would frighten away the private investors for whom the Bank was supposed to prepare the road. A demand for the correction of unsound financial practices as a condition for the granting of a loan consequently seemed to the Bank management to be entirely justifiable. The difficulty was that what was unsound in the eyes of the Bank was not universally recognized as such. Moreover, where it was recognized, correction was not always politically practicable. The delays of the Bank, its stress on "fair and equitable settlements of outstanding debts," "balanced budgets," "sound tax systems," "sound monetary systems," "avoidance of inflation," etc., gave rise to much debate when the representatives of underdeveloped countries became more vocal in international forums.

The determination of a reasonable rate of interest on Bank loans was likewise a controversial issue. Prewar loans were believed to have been made at exorbitant rates. To members in need of credit, "reasonable" at the close of the Second World War meant rates appreciably lower than those charged at the close of the First World War. The appropriate rate, in the view of the Bank, was the estimated cost to the Bank of a comparable borrowing in the United States market, plus a margin to cover operating expenses and build up a reserve. The resultant 4 per cent or more seemed high to many prospective borrowers, influenced by the knowledge that the American Export-Import Bank was making loans at interest rates of $2\frac{1}{4}$ to $3\frac{1}{2}$ per cent and that large-scale intergovernmental grants were still being made for reconstruction purposes. Their dissatisfaction with the rates charged by the International Bank gave rise to a persistent clamor for additional United Nations machinery to provide "low-interest" loans for "low-yielding, slow-yielding" projects.[10]

There were other issues concerning the scope and character of operations of the Bank that had to be resolved, temporarily at least, before actual loans could be made, but they were minor in comparison with the problems of mobilizing loanable resources, determining the types of projects for which loans would be made, and fixing appropriate terms. All of the loan principles and procedures of the Bank could be

[10] In 1956, the interest rate on loans of more than fifteen years was raised to 5 per cent (including the controversial commission of 1 per cent required by the Articles of Agreement during the first ten years of the life of the Bank).

justified as logical outgrowths of one or more requirements of its Articles of Agreement. They were intended to enable the Bank to borrow successfully in the private market, to pave the way for a revival of private international lending, to limit the use of public funds to public purposes, and to break with the Lend-Lease and UNRRA concepts by re-establishing the old-fashioned notion that international finance is business, that a borrower should be a good risk, and that he should not only be capable of repaying the funds he borrows, but also be of a mind to do so. In total, they constituted a fairly formidable set of hurdles to be cleared before a loan could be obtained. It remained to be seen whether the erection of such a set of hurdles to meet specific provisions in the Articles of Agreement could be reconciled with the larger objectives implicit in the Articles as a whole: the speedy reconstruction of war-devastated areas and the triggering of the longer-term process of satisfying in some measure the pent-up aspirations of the peoples in underdeveloped countries.

The dual purpose of the Bank—reconstruction and development—is clear from its name. Thanks to the work of the Leith-Ross committees in London and to the operations of UNRRA, more was known at the Bretton Woods Conference about the reconstruction needs of war-devastated Europe than about the capital requirements of underdeveloped countries, although in both cases the knowledge was pitifully deficient. The underdeveloped countries, particularly in Latin America, were fearful that the Bank "would allocate too large a share of its resources to reconstruction and that not enough would be left for development."[11] Discussion of the relative emphasis to be placed on reconstruction and development was heated. The kind of compromise language that has so frequently enabled international meetings to surmount difficulties without resolving them was finally adopted. "The resources and the facilities of the Bank shall be used," said the Articles of Agreement, "with equitable consideration to projects for development and projects for reconstruction alike."[12]

[11] Antonin Basch, "International Bank for Reconstruction and Development, 1944–49: A Review," *International Conciliation*, No. 455 (November 1949), p. 794.

[12] Art. III, Sec. 1 (a). The word "equitable," brimming with high moral connotations and never defined, later performed similar service in Article XX(II) of the General Agreement on Tariffs and Trade (countries "are entitled to an equitable share of the international supply" of scarce products); in the Economic and Social Council (the regulation "at equitable levels and relationships" of the prices of essential goods, Res. 341 (XII), Mar. 20, 1951); and in the General Assembly ("the establishment of fair and equitable international prices for primary commodities," Res. 623(VII), Dec. 21, 1952). It seemed to afford at least as much satisfaction to the underdeveloped countries as the term "sound," in "sound" projects and "sound" financial policies, gave to representatives from the more advanced free-enterprise economies.

In practice, "equitable consideration" meant reconstruction first, then development. The requirements for European reconstruction—urgent, visible, basic to the re-establishment of a functioning world economy—turned out to be far in excess of the ability of the Bank to meet them. They claimed not only the first $500 million loaned by the Bank and sales by its companion institution, the International Monetary Fund (IMF), of more than $500 million in dollar exchange to European members of the Fund, but also many billions from the United States in the form of post-UNRRA relief, credits connected with the settlement of lend-lease obligations, loans from the Export-Import Bank of Washington, and grant assistance under the European Recovery Program. Not until after Marshall Plan funds began flowing to the countries in the Organization for European Economic Cooperation (OEEC) did the IBRD begin making loans to other areas for economic development purposes. In this uncharted, post-reconstruction field, however, the Bank did its trail-blazing at a more dignified pace.

It opened its doors on June 25, 1946. Within a few months, applications for more than $2.5 billion in dollar loans had been received from nine countries. The first loan was made in May 1947 to France—$250 million to the *Crédit National*, guaranteed by the French Government. The original application was for $500 million, but the Bank decided to limit its commitment to the immediate future, saying it would be willing to consider a further application later in the year.[13] Fortunately, the United States Secretary of State in June 1947, in a speech at Harvard University, introduced what became known as the Marshall Plan or—more formally, the European Recovery Program—thereby enabling France to look elsewhere than to the IBRD for help in meeting its reconstruction requirements.[14]

The Netherlands had applied to the IBRD for an even larger sum than France—$535 million—to help cover its reconstruction requirements for 1947–49. The Bank, limiting its commitment to the 1947 portion of the program, approved a loan of $195 million in August 1947. These were followed promptly by loans of $40 million to Denmark and $12 million to Luxemburg.

[13] International Bank for Reconstruction and Development, *Second Annual Report, 1946–1947*, p. 18.

[14] Only eight months earlier, U.S. Secretary of the Treasury Snyder had said to the First Annual Meeting of the Board of Governors, of which he was chairman: "As we all know, the International Bank must now assume responsibility for underwriting reconstruction loans to countries otherwise unable to borrow on reasonable terms." International Bank for Reconstruction and Development, *Proceedings and Related Documents* (Oct. 29, 1946), p. 6.

The plight of Western Europe in 1947 was desperate. The Bank courageously cast its resources into the breach. It functioned as one of the lifelines to a sinking Europe until Marshall Plan grants were mobilized. Its first four loans were not for specific productive projects but for the "general purpose" of financing a variety of essential dollar imports. It then withdrew from the reconstruction field although Czechoslovakia and Poland, prevented by the Kremlin from participating in the European Recovery Program, still had loan applications totaling $1 billion before the Bank.

The factors militating against approval of the Czech and Polish loan applications were, of course, political. But intergovernmental agencies are not supposed to discriminate on political grounds. The economic justification for the position of the Bank was set forth in its annual report for 1948:

> It is unfortunate but nonetheless true that the existing political difficulties and uncertainties in Europe present special problems which have thus far prevented the Bank from making loans in those countries. The Bank is fully cognizant of the injunction in its Articles of Agreement that its decisions shall be based only on economic considerations. Political tensions and uncertainties in or among its member countries, however, have a direct effect on economic and financial conditions in those countries and upon their credit position.[15]

Unable to obtain a loan and not in a position to participate constructively in the work of the Bank, Poland withdrew in 1950. Czechoslovakia, also unable to obtain a loan, and unsuccessful in its quest for a further period of grace in which to pay that part of its capital subscription due in gold or United States dollars, was suspended from membership as of December 31, 1953, and membership was formally terminated at the close of 1954.

In addition to the unapproved applications from Poland and Czechoslovakia, the Bank had applications on file from Chile, Iran, and Mexico. The first development lending—$16 million to Chile, of which $13.5 million was for hydroelectric development and $2.5 million for the production of agricultural machinery—was not undertaken until March 1948.

The record of approximately $500 million loaned for reconstruction as compared with $16 million for development purposes during its first two years in business made the Bank vulnerable to the charge of insensitivity to the urgency of raising living standards in underdeveloped

[15] International Bank for Reconstruction and Development, *Third Annual Report, 1947–1948*, p. 14.

countries. The desire of these countries for capital, however, was not matched by any corresponding ability to prepare properly documented, technically sound project applications. The underdeveloped countries were underdeveloped as respects administrators and technicians, as well as natural resources. Before they could absorb large amounts of capital, they needed technical assistance.

Although technical assistance was subsequently to become one of the most important activities of the Bank, nothing is said in the Articles of Agreement about this form of aid. Nevertheless, in its first annual report, the Bank indicated its willingness to consider furnishing technical assistance in the preparation of loan applications. Gradually, the technical assistance concept was broadened, from helping a prospective borrower find competent technicians to prepare necessary engineering and financial data for specific projects, to full-scale surveys of economic conditions in member countries. By mid-1948, such surveys had been made or were in process in a number of areas, chiefly in Latin America, in response to requests from governments. The job of missions organized by the Bank was to survey the potentialities and problems of the countries to which the missions went and to help the countries formulate realistic, long-term development programs.

Meanwhile the granting of Bank loans for development purposes was necessarily slow. In the Latin American region, Mexico and Brazil obtained loans in early 1949. The first loans to Asia, $44 million to India for railway rehabilitation and the improvement of agricultural production, were approved during the second half of 1949. The first loans to the Middle East and Africa (to Iraq and Ethiopia, respectively) were not approved until 1950. Despite growing pressure for greater assistance to underdeveloped areas, total Bank loans to non-European nations as of mid-1950 amounted to only about a quarter of a billion dollars. Of this sum, less than $100 million had actually been disbursed.

An important broadening of the principle that loans would be made only for specific projects took place in 1950, however, with the approval of a dollar loan to Australia to finance the purchase of assorted capital goods and equipment "needed for development projects, both private and governmental."[16] The specific project concept was further broadened by the approval in October 1950 of a loan to a new Turkish Industrial

[16] International Bank for Reconstruction and Development, Press Release No. 205 (Aug. 22, 1950), p. 1. The extensive investment requirements of Australia arose in part from its acceptance during the postwar period of large numbers of immigrants n relation to its population.

Development Bank. Prior to this, the International Bank had not been equipped to assist small- and medium-sized private undertakings, partly because of the government-guarantee requirement, partly because of the inability of the Bank to make equity investments, and partly because of the impracticability of employing the resources of a large international agency to investigate applications for small loans. The establishment of a local institution that could carry out the necessary financial and technical investigations, and make either loans to or equity investments in private domestic enterprises provided an answer to these difficulties. Private Turkish interests subscribed equity capital for the Industrial Bank, the Central Bank of Turkey furnished additional capital on a loan basis, and the International Bank provided a dollar loan as well as technical assistance in bringing the new institution into being.

The inability of potential borrowers in underdeveloped countries to submit approvable loan applications during the early years of the Bank or, as those borrowers sometimes viewed it, the slowness of the Bank in approving applications, made it unnecessary for the Bank to expand its own public borrowing at a rapid rate. The first borrowing in a currency other than United States dollars occurred in 1948 when the Bank sold about $4 million worth of 2½ per cent Swiss Franc Serial Bonds. A second issue, somewhat larger than the first, was sold in 1950.[17]

The development of a broader market outside the United States was hampered by obstacles analogous to those previously encountered by the Bank within the United States. The status of Bank obligations under the investment laws of different countries was unclear. Legislation was required in order to classify Bank securities as eligible investments for banks, insurance companies, and similar institutions within member countries. Action was also required before dollar bonds could be traded on local stock exchanges. Some progress had been made as of mid-1950, however, in Chile, Cuba, Mexico, and the Netherlands.

Meanwhile, the Bank management continued its attempts to acquire interest-free funds by persuading member governments to release additional portions of their capital subscriptions. In March 1947, the United States had released unconditionally the 18 per cent payable in the currency of the subscribing country and employable only with the consent of that country. Canada had rather promptly released Canadian dol-

[17] A second public offering of bonds in the United States market was made in 1950. The purpose was not to obtain additional capital but rather to redeem an earlier $100 million issue of 2¼ per cent bonds and effect a savings in interest payments. It was notable as the first issue of the Bank bonds sold by competitive bidding to underwriters.

lars for purchases in Canada but not for purchases anywhere in the world. Efforts to secure the consent of other members were comparatively unsuccessful though partial releases had been obtained by mid-1950 from a handful of European and Latin American nations for goods and services to be purchased within the territory of the lender. With this qualification, the funds were of little use so long as borrowers wanted capital goods obtainable only in North America.

By mid-1950, the formative period of the Bank may be regarded as having ended and the main lines of its work as fairly well defined. Until 1947, attention had been devoted to problems that had to be resolved, at least in a preliminary way, before any borrowing or lending could be undertaken. The period from mid-1947 to mid-1950 included these major developments: (1) completion of the reconstruction phase of the work of the Bank, *i.e.*, the extension of loans to help four Western European nations carry on until the European Recovery Program came to their rescue; (2) the approval of one or more development loans to other major regions of the non-Communist world; (3) the emergence of technical assistance as an important aspect of IBRD activity, and survey missions as effective devices for focusing expert analysis on the problems of particular countries; (4) a broadening of the specific project provision to the point where the requirement meant no more than there should be advance agreement on the manner in which loan proceeds would be expended; (5) successful small-scale efforts to obtain capital, public and private, outside of the United States; (6) the solidifying of the credit position of the Bank and general satisfaction on the part of the private investment community with the "soundness" of its management; and (7) growing impatience in many other circles with the rate and volume of its lending.

Concern of Other Agencies with Production and Investment

While the International Bank was developing its operating techniques, other agencies within the United Nations system concerned with production and investment issues were undergoing a similar evolution. But the Food and Agriculture Organization (FAO), the Economic and Social Council, the Economic and Employment Commission and the three regional economic commissions of the Council were not equipped, as was the Bank, with funds for large-scale investment in productive projects and were not confined within pre-established frameworks as detailed as the Articles of Agreement of the Bank. For the agencies lacking capital endowments, "operating techniques" tended to mean the compilation of reports and analyses and, through subsequent discussion of their implications at intergovernmental meetings, the stimulation of appropriate action by national governments.

Pending the completion of studies that would outline the main problems in need of attention at the international level—and the consent of governments to a concerted attack on such problems—these United Nations agencies were feeling their way, probing for vacuums to fill, groping for methods of being useful. In this spirit, they embarked on a series of projects, seeking to overcome specific shortages in the supply of food, fuel, power, and transportation, while gathering the facts required for an analysis of the more intractable longer-term problems. "Breaking bottlenecks," it was called in the literature of the day, although this now sounds curiously unconstructive for such nobly conceived agencies. But even in the earliest dealings with shortages, there were undercurrents of fear regarding future surpluses. If the longer-range analyses and forecasts revealed potential surpluses, however, such reports usually went on to explain that the excess related only to "effective demand," to what people could afford to buy, not to what they needed. To meet real needs and provide twentieth century standards of decency, it was rightly reported, would require levels of production far higher than any that were likely to be achieved.

Another feature of the early work in production and investment was that the agencies began spilling over into each other's fields of interest and working out various forms of interagency co-operation on an *ad hoc* basis. The FAO, for example, would encounter obstacles that could not be overcome without the collaboration of other international agencies. It found that the biggest impediment to increased rice production in Thailand was the prevalence of malaria, and it called the attention of the World Health Organization to the situation. The key to greater food production in the Near East lay in large-scale investments in irrigation and reclamation projects of a kind that might be eligible for IBRD financing.

To the Economic Commission for Europe (ECE), the FAO recommended certain steps to increase the availability of timber for European reconstruction. The ECE, in helping to implement these recommendations, established a pattern of co-operation with the FAO that served as a model for FAO collaboration with the other regional commissions. The ECE and the FAO together then went on, with the International

Bank, to work out the main lines of a complicated short-term loan by the Bank to help Finland and Yugoslavia increase their timber exports to Belgium, Denmark, France, Italy, the Netherlands, and the United Kingdom.[18]

Although the General Assembly and the Economic and Social Council were concerned at an early date with such production problems as the reconstruction of war-devastated areas and the attainment of an increase in the world's food supply, they imposed relatively little co-ordination from above, and merely ratified the practical forms of inter-agency co-operation worked out at the regional and country levels by agencies with overlapping interests. Gradually, however, the Council and the Assembly became more assertive in the establishment of priorities on a global basis and concerned with the form and substance of agency efforts to attack problems in the order of their importance.

The main directions of the early explorations of the United Nations in the field of production and investment appear to have been the following:

1. The provision, on a limited basis, of a wide variety of technical services. The early United Nations activities thus laid the foundations for the expanded and co-ordinated program of technical assistance initiated in 1950.

2. The development of regional approaches to economic problems. Although the number of economic problems suitable for handling on a regional rather than on a global or national basis is fairly limited, the regional approach, tried initially as an experiment in Europe, took firm root during the 1947–49 period in other regions where it had much less chance of flowering than in Europe. For better or for worse, it became a permanent feature of the United Nations landscape.

3. At the country level, further impetus was given to the formulation of national development programs establishing investment targets and priorities. The formulation of such programs seemed essential to the rendering of intelligent decisions concerning the relative merits of urgent, competitive claims on limited investment resources. Yet international encouragement of national planning inevitably tended to strengthen national governments, both *vis à vis* private and local interests within their boundaries and *vis à vis* the emerging international machinery for co-ordinating the economic activities of member states.[19]

[18] For details, see International Bank for Reconstruction and Development, Press Release No. 171 (Feb. 8, 1950).

[19] For an interesting elaboration of this point, see Gunnar Myrdal, *An International Economy: Problems and Prospects* (1956), Chap. 4. "National political machin-

4. On a global basis, the investment problem was gradually broken into functional segments that lent themselves to more intensive analysis: the mobilization of domestic capital in underdeveloped countries; the stimulation of private foreign investment; the role of public loan capital from abroad; and the need for grant aid.

Initially, however, the food crisis was virtually at the top of the list of urgent economic problems. Supplies of cereals, meats, fats and oils, and sugar were woefully inadequate and ill-distributed among nations. Rationing schemes were in operation in all the industrialized countries. There they succeeded, by and large, in preventing starvation or wholesale undernourishment and, in some cases, in providing a better balanced diet for low-income groups than had been available in prewar days. The plight of the underdeveloped countries where starvation, undernourishment, and incredibly monotonous diets had been the lot of the people for generations, was more critical. It was in these areas, least able to feed their prewar inhabitants, that population was thought to be increasing at the most rapid rates. The world was unanimous in desiring a greater output of food.

Among the international agencies, primary responsibility for increasing the production of foodstuffs, fibers, and forest products rests with the Food and Agriculture Organization. The efforts of the FAO to alleviate the postwar world food shortage, first by continuation of wartime allocation arrangements and then by more imaginative schemes for building up reserves against future famines and stabilizing trade in foodstuffs, have been described earlier.[20] Although the ups and downs of agricultural output during the period were noted, the emphasis in that discussion was largely on courses of action to be pursued during periods of crisis. To round out the earlier picture, some indication should be given of the development of international co-operation between the FAO and other parts of the United Nations system for the purpose of obtaining long-term increases in supply.

The General Assembly at its first session, it will be recalled, had urged

---

ery . . . has a firm basis in people's attitudes of allegiance and solidarity; this machinery is getting stronger and its psychological basis firmer every year. It is used in the service of interests that are felt to be commonly shared within the nation. Machinery for international cooperation is, by contrast, weak and ineffective, and it lacks a solid basis in people's valuations and expectations. Even without any real inherent conflict between the two goals, this tremendous and steadily increasing preponderance of national political machinery has deflected—and, if a radical change of the trend is not induced, will continue to deflect—the development of practical policy towards economic nationalism." (Pp. 33–34.)

[20] See above, Chap. II.

all governments and peoples to take immediate and drastic action, both directly and through the international organizations, to secure an adequate collection of crops from producers, to avoid waste, to reserve grain supplies for direct human consumption, and to secure increased production.[21] The FAO was requested to publish full information on the world food position and outlook. According to the FAO, no such survey on a country-by-country basis had ever been made before.[22] The appraisal of the world food situation in 1946 indicated that shortages of certain essential foodstuffs would continue for another three or four years. It also warned that unmarketable surpluses of farm products might suddenly appear.

The Conference of the FAO that year recommended a series of measures for the best use of the 1946 harvest and the attainment of maximum output in 1947. The FAO emphasis on the scarcity of fertilizers as a limiting factor in raising output foreshadowed some of its later technical services to increase the availability and expand the use of fertilizers. Similarly, the FAO stressed the enormous waste, running into millions of tons per year, caused by insects, rodents, and fungi. The introduction of relatively simple precautions, not requiring large capital investments, could reduce this damage substantially. The FAO therefore began promoting the adoption of such measures.

The limited output of chemical fertilizers in Europe was due not to the ignorance or the perversity of manufacturers but to inadequate allocations of coal, which was also very scarce. Low production of farm machinery was due to the steel shortage. The movement of food from farm to market was hampered by lack of transport. The responsibility of the FAO for stimulating an increase in world food production could not be met without the co-operation of other international agencies.

Accordingly, the Economic and Social Council, in early 1948, considered an agenda item proposed by the FAO concerning co-ordinated action to meet the world food crisis. The Council invited the specialized agencies and the regional economic commissions, in consultation with the FAO, to study ways and means of increasing food production by eliminating shortages of oil, coal, steel, and power that were directly or indirectly affecting the production of fertilizers and agricultural machinery, and the availability of transport.[23]

[21] Res. 27(I), Feb. 14, 1946.

[22] Food and Agriculture Organization, *First Annual Report of the Director-General to the FAO Conference* (July 5, 1946), p. 10.

[23] Res. 103(VI), Mar. 2, 1948.

The FAO, having solicited and obtained a broad "hunting-license" from the Council, then tried to concentrate on a limited number of the most essential production and supply problems in each region. In the Far East, a Working Party on Agricultural Requisites serving both the FAO and the Economic Commission for Asia and the Far East (ECAFE) had been formed to consider short-term needs for chemical fertilizers, pesticides, irrigation and drainage equipment for small projects, and other requisites. Nothing very concrete seems to have resulted from this initiative, and the 1948–49 report of the Director-General of the FAO records a decision of the working party to the effect that "at the present time no scope for international action is apparent from the recommendations on fertilizers and agricultural requisites."[24] This did not, of course, mean satisfaction with the situation, but rather that technical assistance at the country level might be more effective than further intergovernmental consultation at the regional level. Food production in the Far East continued to lag. Restoration of at least prewar per-capita levels of consumption continued to be a main preoccupation of the region and to introduce a depressing note of realism into the ambitious plans for industrialization.

The most serious food deficit in the Far East was in rice. The negotiations that ultimately led to the establishment of the International Rice Commission in Bangkok in 1949 began with the convocation of an FAO study group in India in 1947. The study group surveyed the rice situation and predicted a continued grave shortage for another five years. Many of its recommendations for increasing production involved costly, long-term investments, which the FAO was in no position to implement. In addition to irrigation and drainage programs, rehabilitation of the transport system, and the like, for which the extension of international credits was recommended, there were suggestions for other, more immediate measures—in particular an active campaign to reduce the estimated 12 million tons of rice per year lost as waste. Here the FAO could and did provide technical assistance.

The permanent International Rice Commission set up in 1949 was given the assignment of formulating a world rice policy based on human needs, and of promoting a program of rice production, distribution, conservation, and consumption that would utilize fully advanced research and technology.[25] Meanwhile, however, the nature of the deficit

[24] Food and Agriculture Organization, *Report of the Director-General: Work of FAO, 1948–49* (October 1949), p. 15.
[25] *Ibid.*, pp. 9–10.

had changed. In 1947, Far Eastern nations were prepared to buy more rice than was available on the world market and foresaw a continuation of this situation for another five years. By 1949, the region was nearly self-sufficient again "so far as effective demand for rice was concerned,"[26] although the extent to which technical aid from the FAO contributed to the attainment of this new equilibrium is not clear. In any event, the FAO felt that further increases in rice production were needed, but that agricultural development must be accompanied by simultaneous industrial development in order to provide the purchasing power that would render them marketable.

In Africa, as well as in the Far East, livestock production was unnecessarily low because of the prevalence of rinderpest, a cattle disease the spread of which could be checked by a virus vaccine developed in Canada during the war. Here was an ideal field for technical assistance, an area in which dramatic results could be obtained in short order at low cost. Since 1946, therefore, FAO experts have initiated or participated in immunization campaigns and given advisory assistance to underdeveloped countries in the production of vaccines for reducing the ravages of rinderpest.

The general experience of the FAO in the Far East and Africa was duplicated in the Near and Middle East. Large-scale, long-term investments in agriculture would be needed if food production were to keep pace with population growth, but the techniques employed in the area were so primitive that low-cost, simple improvements could make an important immediate difference. In the arid regions, the crying need for large investment was in irrigation facilities.

In Latin America, as in Asia, FAO personnel worked with the secretariat of the regional economic commission in developing programs and recommendations in the fields of agriculture, fisheries, and forestry. A Joint Working Party of the FAO and the Economic Commission for Latin America (ECLA) made recommendations for increased food production in each of the Latin American countries. FAO forestry experts helped actively to focus the attention of Latin American governments on the potentialities of their own vast forest resources. In all of the underdeveloped regions, discussions and reports sponsored by the FAO publicized the institutional barriers to increased production, which reinforced the technical barriers. Antiquated systems of land tenure, exorbitant interest rates, the absence of agricultural extension services

[26] *Ibid.*, p. 16.

to speed the diffusion of know-how, the lack of marketing facilities—these were obstacles as formidable as ignorance concerning the use of steel-tipped plows, disease-resistant seeds, or nitrogenous fertilizers.

In Europe, technical advice from the FAO on how to increase food output was less necessary than in the underdeveloped regions, and more attention could be given to increasing the availability of timber for housing and reconstruction purposes. At the time the Economic Commission for Europe was holding its first organizational session in Geneva, the FAO was sponsoring a timber conference in Marianske Lazne, Czechoslovakia. The data assembled for this conference forecast a deficit in 1948 large enough to reduce housing programs in European timber-importing countries by 600,000–750,000 dwelling units. The conference recommended modification of established conservation practices to permit an increase of 10 per cent in cuttings of saw timber and thus to reduce the anticipated deficit by a third.

The Marianske Lazne conference recognized that some countries would need foreign aid in order to increase their timber output. Pursuing this question, the ECE Timber Committee was able to obtain a commitment from Sweden to increase its timber exports in exchange for an increased coke allocation, which, in turn, was arranged by the ECE Coal Committee. Later the ECE and the FAO laid the groundwork for the timber loan to which reference has already been made—the short-term loan of the International Bank to Finland and Yugoslavia.

Decentralization of certain United Nations work to the regional level undoubtedly had great advantages. The measures agreed upon tended to be more concrete than those discussed at world-wide gatherings. Global forums were relieved of burdensome details, and a series of training schools was provided in which extreme nationalist views might be toned down in the common interest. Opponents of any kind of autarky, however, might find reason to be disturbed by the flavor of regional autarky in some of the early United Nations actions. European self-sufficiency in timber and coal was frequently cited as a desirable goal without serious reference to cost or efficiency of production. Asia strove in similar fashion for self-sufficiency in rice. The FAO Latin American Commission for Forestry and Forest Products called various "principles" to the attention of ECLA, including the principle that, in procuring equipment for modernizing their forest industries, the countries of the region should give preference first to Latin American nations, second to countries offering favorable rates of exchange, and third to countries requiring payment in dollars.[27] These developments, coupled with current investigations of regional payments schemes,[28] could hardly fail to arouse some uneasiness and fears of discrimination in Canada and the United States.

The decentralization of FAO activities did not stop at the regional level. Technical assistance was provided directly to national governments at a very early stage. An FAO mission that went to Greece in 1946 produced a long-term development plan and called it to the attention of the Economic and Social Council and the International Bank.[29] More specialized FAO missions went to Thailand to see what could be done to expand the production of rice and forest products and improve the management of livestock; to Poland to advise on problems connected with the rehabilitation and improvement of agriculture, forestry, and related industries; and to Venezuela to advise on the production of edible oils. Joint missions of the FAO and IBRD also went to several other Latin American countries.

Although the reconstruction of devastated areas had immediately been recognized by the General Assembly as a matter of vital importance, no United Nations agency was concerned with industrial rehabilitation in the broad manner in which the FAO was concerned with agricultural rehabilitation. A Temporary Subcommission on the Economic Reconstruction of Devastated Areas was, however, established in 1946 under the Economic and Employment Commission of the Economic and Social Council. The "devastators," as the subcommission members were familiarly known, subdivided into two working groups: one for Europe and Africa, and one for Asia and the Far East.

Their bulky report on Europe described the extent of war devastation, the progress of recovery, and the nature of the short-term and long-term problems confronting European industry and agriculture. Discussion of it led the Economic and Social Council to request the Secretary-General to undertake forthwith special studies of the needs of devastated areas for long-term and short-term financing of their urgent reconstruction requirements, on favorable terms; to review the means for meeting these needs; and to call attention to cases where the existing means were inadequate. The reference to "favorable conditions" of financing occurs frequently in later United Nations resolutions, and

[27] *Ibid.*, p. 35.
[28] See above, Chap. III.
[29] See below, Chap. X.

always means terms favorable to the borrower. Sometimes it means loans at rates of interest lower than those of the IBRD, or at longer maturities; sometimes it means loans with waiver provisions suspending repayments when conditions are "unfavorable"; sometimes it is merely a euphemism for grants.

More importantly, the report of the "devastators" led to the establishment in 1947 and 1948 of the regional economic commissions whose collaboration with the FAO has already been mentioned. In the industrial as in the agricultural field, the early work of these commissions—the ECE in Europe, ECAFE in Asia and the Far East, and ECLA in Latin America—consisted in part of breaking bottlenecks and in part of studies and discussions devoted to longer-term problems. For example, the Steel Committee of the ECE, in co-operation with the Coal Committee, arranged for an allocation of metallurgical coke that is reported to have permitted a 400,000-ton increase in European steel production in the second quarter of 1948. ECLA, with the help of the IBRD, surveyed the cotton textile industry of Latin America and found that the backwardness "which was usually attributed solely to the existing equipment" was "due to a great extent to inefficient organization and management of the factories."[30] ECLA also began studies of the legal and economic factors affecting investment, public and private, foreign and domestic, in Latin America. ECAFE, with the help of the International Bank, studied the need for long-term and short-term capital for rehabilitating the economies of Far Eastern countries and for developing new industries there, as well as the regulations affecting foreign investments in the region. Both ECAFE and ECLA, particularly the former, began studying the possibilities of mobilizing domestic capital through savings banks, savings bonds, improved tax collections, agricultural banks, and other institutional arrangements.

At Lake Success, then the headquarters of the United Nations Organization, the possibilities of increased production through the more efficient use of existing resources were discussed at a unique United Nations Scientific Conference on the Conservation and Utilization of Resources, suggested by the United States, and held in 1949. Although no Soviet scientists participated, seven hundred experts from fifty other nations joined the discussion groups in their individual capacities, not as government representatives. They met at a time of widely publicized,

[30] U.N. Secretariat, Department of Public Information, *The Economic Growth of Twenty Republics, The Work of the Economic Commission for Latin America* (1954), pp. 11–12.

gloomy predictions concerning the ability of the world to support a growing population on a shrinking base of natural resources. They discussed techniques susceptible of more widespread use in the fields of minerals, fuels and energy, water, forest, land, and fish and wildlife resources.

According to the postmeeting report of the Secretary-General, the experts tried to address themselves to such questions as: "What are the costs of applying these techniques measured in terms of money or human effort?" and "What returns can be expected from a given method, either in the form of increased yields, reduced expenditures per unit of production, or in the elimination of waste?"[31] Their papers made clear that it was technically possible for the world to achieve substantially higher standards of living, provided that institutional and other obstacles to the use of better techniques could be overcome, and provided that war could be avoided. Again and again, they brought out the interdependence of different resources and the need for integrated development. The effect of the exchange of know-how at the conference was to provide a kind of preview of the range of projects that might later be undertaken on a country basis under the Expanded Programme of Technical Assistance of the United Nations.[32]

The conference was a discussion session with no attempt made to reach agreement on resolutions and recommendations. Although the Secretary-General believed, and was not alone in his view, that this approach resulted in a more fruitful conference, five years were to pass before another large group of experts was brought together under United Nations auspices solely for an exchange of views.[33] Meanwhile, the art of moving from one agenda item to the next without pausing for intervening resolutions was almost forgotten.

Increasingly, the development of underdeveloped countries became the major economic preoccupation of the United Nations agencies. The

[31] U.N. Economic and Social Council, Tenth Session, *United Nations Scientific Conference on Conservation and Utilization of Resources, Report by the Secretary-General to Tenth Session of ECOSOC*, Doc. E/1579 (Dec. 28, 1949), p. 4.

[32] As the United States Representative reported at the tenth session of the Economic and Social Council in a comprehensive review of the conference, "The United Nations Scientific Conference on the Conservation and Utilization of Resources had constituted a prologue to the expanded programme of technical assistance, presenting its problems and its possibilities." U.N. Economic and Social Council, Tenth Session, *Official Records*, 349th Meeting (Feb. 13, 1950), p. 28.

[33] In August 1954, a World Population Conference was held in Rome and in August 1955, an International Conference on the Peaceful Uses of Atomic Energy was held in Geneva.

problems of Europe faded into the background as economic activity there returned to or surpassed prewar levels. The Marshall Plan, to be sure, was much discussed at United Nations meetings. Long and vitriolic attacks were launched on it by delegates from the Soviet bloc, largely for the purpose of creating friction and division between the United States and its Western European allies, partly for the purpose of misrepresenting the program to the nonparticipating nations, and occasionally—in the case of spokesmen from the Soviet satellites—for the purpose of demonstrating to watchful delegates from the Soviet Union their devotion to the party line. Underdeveloped countries at times expressed a sense of grievance as a result of the large-scale aid given to Europe on a priority basis under the European Recovery Program. Western delegates defended the Marshall Plan, and made counterattacks on various aspects of the Soviet economy. Nevertheless, the entire battle was a propaganda side-show, not expected by any of the major participants to affect directly the levels of production and investment in Europe.

There was, however, real hope that the concerted attention of the United Nations to the problem of economic development could affect the production and investment levels in underdeveloped countries. Accordingly, the Economic and Social Council, in 1949, asked the Secretary-General to prepare a report on "methods of financing the economic development of underdeveloped countries, including methods of stimulating the international flow of capital for this purpose."[34]

The Secretary-General's report illustrated the confusion, the lack of co-ordination, and the deep cleavages of opinion prevalent at the time in this field.[35] It was a symposium containing the report of the third session of the Subcommission on Economic Development; critical comments on the report of the subcommission by the parent body, the Economic and Employment Commission, in terms amounting almost to a repudiation of the work of the subcommission; and memoranda of varying quality from the FAO, the IBRD, the IMF, and the International Labour Organisation (ILO). The contribution of the Department of Economic Affairs of the United Nations Secretariat consisted primarily of comments on the contributions of the other agencies.

All the interrelated issues that continued to divide the delegates in later discussions were foreshadowed in this report. Included among

[34] Res. 179(VIII), Mar. 4, 1949.

[35] U.N. Secretariat, Department of Economic Affairs, *Methods of Financing Economic Development in Under-developed Countries* (1949).

them were: (1) the role of national versus international action in mobilizing capital for economic development; (2) the importance of applying available capital to industry versus agriculture or, within the industrial sector, to heavy versus light industry; (3) whether the basic obstacle to more rapid development was lack of capital or whether other factors were even more fundamental; (4) whether loan capital should be provided on terms more liberal than those offered by the International Bank; (5) whether large-scale, grant aid should be made available through the United Nations to finance non-self-liquidating projects; (6) what inducements could and should be offered to private investors.

There was general agreement that domestic finance would have to cover the bulk of investment requirements. There was also agreement that domestic savings in underdeveloped countries were very low, very unevenly distributed, and frequently employed for very unproductive purposes from the point of view of the underdeveloped country—hoarded in the form of gold chains and bars, invested in urban real estate and high-rental apartment buildings, devoted to the construction of monumental government edifices, or exported to safe havens in the more developed countries. There was agreement that by reorganizing their domestic banking and investment machinery and tax systems, underdeveloped countries could do more to finance their own development programs, but there were differences of view about how much more.

The extent to which nations would put their domestic houses in order would itself affect the volume of foreign capital that they could attract. Most of the agency reports recognized that, to enlarge the flow of private investment, substantially greater incentives would have to be offered, but as the Secretary-General's summary stated it, divergent conclusions were drawn from this common premise.[36] The International Bank and the spokesmen for developed, private-enterprise economies stressed the methods by which existing deterrents to private investments might be overcome. Spokesmen for underdeveloped countries, dubious about the likelihood of attracting private capital on an adequate scale for investments essential to their national development programs and in some cases not greatly interested in doing so, emphasized alternative methods of financing. These included the extension of loans on better terms than those offered by the Bank and the provision of grant aid.

The symposium also contained a brief summary of postwar attempts

[36] *Ibid.*, p. 24.

to clarify the private investment picture through the development of a multilateral code of fair treatment for foreign investors. The critical issues, as summarized by the Secretary-General, had been: (1) the treatment to be accorded to foreign investors with respect to taxation, the repatriation of their earnings, the participation of domestic nationals and domestic capital in their enterprises, and similar matters, and (2) the methods of determining the compensation due to foreign investors in the event of expropriation or nationalization.[37]

The drafters of the Havana Charter for an International Trade Organization had already foundered on these issues. According to United States standards, the investment provisions were perhaps the weakest feature of the proposed charter put forward in April 1948, and one of the major reasons for the failure of the United States to ratify the document. The Economic Agreement signed in May 1948 at the Conference of American States in Bogota seemed to represent an improvement by providing for "prompt, adequate and effective" compensation in the event of nationalization or expropriation, but the provision was virtually nullified by reservations, which, as the Secretary-General of the United Nations reported, rejected any notion that "fair" compensation should be determined by courts or agencies other than those of the capital-importing nation.

Given this background, it is understandable that the United Nations Subcommission on Economic Development was unable to suggest acceptable formulae for the nondiscriminatory treatment of foreign investors. Reviewing the postwar record of private international investment early in 1950, the subcommission, in the only session it held after publication of *Methods of Financing Economic Development in Under-developed Countries*, was pessimistic. The United States was the only important exporter of private capital. Dollarwise, its net outflow of private capital in the highest postwar year, 1948, was hardly more than the corresponding figure in 1928, and, in terms of actual purchasing power, was probably little more than half the value in the peak year of the 1920's. The 1949 outflow was below that in 1948. Portfolio investments, which were substantial in the 1920's, were no longer viewed with favor by private investors. Direct investments in underdeveloped countries were overwhelmingly concentrated in a few oil-producing areas.[38] The

[37] *Ibid.*, p. 29.

[38] U.N. Economic and Social Council, Economic and Employment Commission, *Report of the Fourth Session of the Subcommission on Economic Development*, Doc. E/CN.1/80 (May 19, 1950), pp. 10–11.

prospect for a broadly-distributed, substantial increase in private foreign investment was, in the opinion of the subcommission, dim.

The subcommission concluded that codes and treaties would not substantially promote the flow of private foreign investment because what was really needed was good faith and confidence. If there were mutual confidence, the code would be superfluous; in the absence of such confidence, the code would not lead to greater investment.[39] The truth seemed to be that multilateral negotiation of an investment code would succeed only in codifying the lowest common denominator; interested governments felt that they could obtain better deals for their nationals through unilateral declarations or bilateral negotiations.

The result of the discussion of private foreign investment in the subcommission was the disassociation of the Indian chairman and the Mexican vice chairman from the rather moderate, formal proposals for stimulating private investment offered to the Economic and Social Council by the subcommission.

With no disagreement however, the subcommission asserted, in more positive fashion that any earlier United Nations organ, that the United Nations and the specialized agencies had a responsibility to go out and help underdeveloped countries prepare economic development programs. Such programs, said the subcommission, would necessarily contain a proportion of "low-yielding and slow-yielding projects" in which capital would have to be invested before other projects would appear attractive. These low-yielding and slow-yielding projects constituted essential "social and economic overhead capital." Investments for the promotion of health, education, and housing were classifiable as "social overhead," and those for the improvement of transport, communications, and power as "economic overhead."[40] Because it was difficult for underdeveloped countries to finance these projects from their own meager resources, it was important that foreign capital be available for the purpose. Investment in overhead projects would broaden the base for later investment in more directly productive undertakings. Because of the non-self-liquidating character of the social overhead projects, a strong case could be made for grants, or loans at nominal rates of interest, to finance them.

Given the limited prospects for an enlarged flow of private investment, the trickle of public loans at the interest rates charged by the International Bank, the scarcity of domestic resources to tap, and the

[39] *Ibid.*, p. 14.
[40] *Ibid.*, p. 21.

political necessity for raising living standards in underdeveloped areas, the creation of a United Nations Economic Development Administration (UNEDA) to provide long-term loans at nominal rates of interest was again suggested.[41] In view of the fact that the main burden of financing UNEDA would clearly fall on the United States, and that an agency financed by a single nation could not be truly international, the subcommission did not recommend its creation. It did, however, urge the Council to consider the problem.

The May 1950 report was the swan song of the Subcommission on Economic Development, whose members were expected to serve in their individual capacities instead of as government representatives. The pretense that the financing of economic development could be regarded primarily as a technical economic issue was abandoned. It quickly became a burning political issue in the Economic and Social Council and in the General Assembly.

Work of the United Nations System Since 1950

So far as production and investment are concerned, the United Nations system since 1950 has continued to function as a somewhat inconsistent fount of policy guidance; as an increasingly effective instrument of co-operation in the solution of technical problems; and as a modest source of capital funds. The main areas of activity have been the following: (1) the provision of technical assistance to underdeveloped countries on an augmented basis within the framework of the Regular and the Expanded Programmes of Technical Assistance of the United Nations (2) outside of this specialized framework, the focusing of international attention on, and the development of international co-operation with respect to, a host of technical problems affecting production and investment in both developed and underdeveloped countries; (3) the loan, through the International Bank, of about $2.2 billion during the period January 1, 1950–December 31, 1956; (4) continued debate concerning the measures needed to expand and stabilize the international flow of private investment; (5) the elaboration of schemes and the effort to mobilize support for new international financing agencies to supplement the loans of the International Bank: specifically, for (a) an International Finance Corporation to invest in private enter-

[41] It had first been put before the subcommission by its chairman, the Indian expert, in 1949 at the third session.

prise without governmental guarantees, and (b) a Special United Nations Fund for Economic Development to make long-term, low-interest loans and grants-in-aid to underdeveloped countries; (6) negotiations—conducted primarily in the political and security framework rather than in the economic and social framework of the United Nations—to establish a new agency of vast potential economic significance: the International Atomic Energy Agency.

There was a narrowing of activities at the top and a broadening at the base. At the sessions of the General Assembly and of the Economic and Social Council—the more political forums—the economic debates tended increasingly to concentrate around the drive of the underdeveloped countries for a grant-aid agency within the United Nations framework. The developed countries, unwilling to establish costly, new operational arms of the United Nations, resisted this drive. They compromised on resolutions calling for more studies and reports concerning the role and operations of such an agency when circumstances would permit its establishment. Almost imperceptibly, the issue became not whether a grant-aid agency should be established but when. The developed countries also tried to deflect the drive for capital by highlighting the institutional obstacles to development. They advocated productivity programs, land reform, and similar activities that could be stepped up by the underdeveloped countries themselves, with relatively little capital from abroad. It was much easier, however, for the underdeveloped countries to say that the General Assembly and the Economic and Social Council should establish a grant-aid agency than for the developed countries to say what the General Assembly and the Economic and Social Council should do about land reform. Antiquated systems of land tenure, low industrial productivity, lack of esteem for private initiative and enterprise are the product of long-standing cultural, economic, political, and social conditions that cannot be changed by resolutions adopted at lofty levels.

The almost exclusive preoccupation with the grant-aid issue, which characterized the discussion of economic development in the Assembly and the Council, was not reflected in the debates of the regional forums. The Latin Americans, the most persistent proponents of grant-aid at United Nations headquarters, displayed more interest at the regional commissions of the United Nations, as did the Asians, in discussions of technical aspects of forestry and fishery development, exploration of mineral resources, improvement of transport facilities, expansion of electric power production, and the establishment of manufacturing industries. However, the precise role of regional co-operation in the solution of production and investment problems was not greatly clarified during the period.

At the country level, the variety of activities was immense. It was limited only by the imagination of governments in submitting technical assistance proposals, the availability of experts to implement the proposals, and—more recently—the availability of funds to finance eligible projects.

Technical Assistance and Technical Co-operation

In listing above six main areas of United Nations activity since 1950 in the field of production and investment, a distinction was made between technical assistance offered under either the Regular Programme or the Expanded Programme of Technical Assistance of the United Nations and other technical co-operation developed within the United Nations system. Although the distinction has organizational validity, it is artificial in other respects. Both technical assistance and technical co-operation have as their objective the more efficient employment of the human and material resources of the world. Illustrative of the work of the United Nations in this field during the period are the activities of the system with respect to the conservation and use of mineral resources, the control and utilization of water resources, the release of technical data concerning the peaceful uses of atomic energy, and the provision of technical assistance to stimulate agricultural output.

The successful conference of 1949 on the Conservation and Utilization of Resources seemed for a brief period to presage further action on a global scale to facilitate the efficient use of mineral resources. The Secretary-General, pursuant to a request by the Economic and Social Council, studied the conference proceedings and proposed to the Council in 1950 an international program, the main elements of which were to be the systematic survey and inventory of nonagricultural resources on the one hand and, on the other, international conferences on particular resource problems. Authorized to go ahead,[42] the Secretary-General selected iron ore as the first subject for a particular resource survey. He appointed a committee of experts and, in 1954, issued a report under the impressive title, *Survey of World Iron Ore Resources: Occurrence, Appraisal, and Use*. This was to have been followed by similar

[42] Res. 345(XII), Mar. 9, 1951.

reports on coal and lignite, and other important nonagricultural resources. No such reports were issued, however. The world as a whole might benefit from up-to-date information on the location, extent, and quality of its major mineral deposits, but the value of the global surveys to any individual country was marginal compared to the value of surveys of the resources within its own territorial borders.

Interest consequently shifted to regional and country studies. The Economic Commission for Asia and the Far East published a report on the coal and iron resources of the region,[43] sponsored a regional Conference on Mineral Resources in Tokyo in 1953 (the first United Nations meeting in Japan), and issued documents concerning the utilization of lignite in ten Asian countries. The Economic Commission for Europe gathered data on the energy resources of Austria and Yugoslavia and the feasibility of exporting power across international boundaries to Italy, Germany, and Switzerland. The Economic Commission for Latin America ran an Iron and Steel Seminar in Bogota at which experts from North America and Europe joined Latin Americans in frank analyses of the problems involved in establishing an efficient steel industry in Latin America.

At the country level, technical assistance was obtained both for general purposes such as exploring the mineral resources of Tanganyika, and for specific purposes such as exploiting marble quarries in the Philippines, advising on the cutting of quartz crystals in India, and reorganizing the salt industry in Ceylon. Given international acceptance of the authority of the United Nations system to furnish technical assistance on a retail basis, the chief policy problem raised by projects of the types mentioned is to ensure that they fit logically into the long-term economic development program of the requesting country, that they cannot be completed without external aid, and that they consequently represent a valid claim on the resources of the international community.

In the case of mineral resources, the top organs of the United Nations stimulated interest by the summoning of a large international conference that helped launch a variety of projects at the regional and country levels. Within the complicated structure of the United Nations, however, the flow of activity and interest is a two-way affair. Discussion of an issue at the top levels stirs up activity at lower levels; conversely, activity initiated at lower levels frequently points to the need for policy pronouncement or for program co-ordination at the top.

[43] U.N. Economic Commission for Asia and the Far East, *Coal and Iron Resources of Asia and the Far East* (1952).

The Conference on the Conservation and Utilization of Resources stimulated interest in water development as well as in mineral development. At the same time, the variety of regional and country responses to pressures to control floods, irrigate crops, develop hydroelectric sites, deepen river channels, eliminate stream pollution, and discover new sources of water in arid lands underscored the need for greater co-ordination and more integrated planning. The consequence was a resurgence of concern at the top.

One of the first acts of ECAFE had been the establishment of a Bureau of Flood Control. The United States, in commenting on the work of the bureau at meetings of ECAFE and of the Economic and Social Council, consistently stressed the need for viewing the problem not solely in terms of flood control but also in terms of multiple-purpose river basin development. While ECAFE was concerned with flood control, the United Nations Educational, Scientific, and Cultural Organization (UNESCO) developed a lively interest in the special problems of arid zones. The FAO was interested in irrigation and in fisheries; the IBRD in hydroelectric power development, navigation, and irrigation projects; the World Health Organization (WHO) in stream pollution.

The United States, as a nation aware of the potential benefits of the multipurpose approach to river valley development and as the Member of the United Nations most concerned with procedural and organizational issues, circulated a note to the Economic and Social Council in early 1951 pointing out that segments of the water resource problem came within the competence of various agencies but that no single agency had a co-ordinating responsibility in this field. The note suggested a survey by the Secretary-General and the specialized agencies that could serve as the basis for a better organized effort to promote efficient use of the world's water resources.

The United States suggestion was adopted, and the Secretary-General prepared a report summarizing the activities of some thirty international organizations concerned with one phase or another of water control. After consideration of his report in 1952, a resolution endorsing the multipurpose approach to water resource development was adopted by the Council.[44] More importantly, the resolution vested the Secretary-General with co-ordinating responsibility; asked him to promote the development of basic water resource data and the international exchange of information and experience; and invited him to make recommendations for further international activity in this field.

[44] Res. 417(XIV), June 2, 1952.

To date, however, little co-ordination or stimulation appears to have been provided by United Nations headquarters. The interest of the United States Government in giving the Secretary-General a more active role in connection with water resource development declined with the change in domestic administration, and the support and resources required from Member governments for effective discharge of the Secretary-General's new responsibilities were not forthcoming.

On the other hand, it was the initiative of the United States that led the United Nations during the period 1954–56 to assume new roles in promoting the peaceful uses of atomic energy. American initiative was responsible for two related lines of action. One—the complex negotiations arising out of President Eisenhower's suggestion that the United Nations establish a kind of world bank for fissionable materials—is discussed later. The second—the convening of a technical conference on the peaceful uses of the atom—is mentioned here because it is comparable in character to the Conference on the Conservation and Utilization of Resources.

The suggestion for a major scientific conference to consider the development of atomic energy through international co-operation was put forward by the United States Secretary of State in his address to the General Assembly on September 23, 1954.[45] It was referred to the First (Political and Security) Committee, where there was extensive and inconclusive discussion concerning the functions and structure of the proposed International Atomic Energy Agency but general approval of the holding of a conference in 1955 for the exchange of scientific information. Upon emergence from the First Committee, the proposal was unanimously endorsed by the Assembly.[46]

Held in Geneva, Switzerland, during August 1955, the ensuing International Conference on the Peaceful Uses of Atomic Energy was the largest and probably the most important international technical gathering under United Nations auspices during the entire postwar period. In the diplomatic terminology of the Secretary-General, "a great deal of important data hitherto restricted for reasons of security was made public for the first time at this Conference."[47] In the American press it was said that "so much information had been dammed up on that topic [atomic power] for ten years that the resulting flood turned Geneva

[45] U.N. General Assembly, Ninth Session, Plenary, *Official Records*, 475th Meeting (Sept. 23, 1954).

[46] Res. 810(IX), Dec. 4, 1954.

[47] U.N. General Assembly, Eleventh Session, *Official Records*, Supplement No. 1, "Annual Report of the Secretary-General on the Work of the Organization, 16 June 1955–15 June 1956," p. 3.

into the greatest scientific irrigation project of modern times . . . the competition generated a friendliness that had been unknown between East and West since wartime days."[48]

Seventy-three nations sent delegations. In addition to more than 1,400 delegates, there were 1,350 observers, principally from academic institutions and industrial enterprises, and 900 representatives of public information media. In contrast to the many meetings of the United Nations of benefit primarily to the underdeveloped countries, this conference had relevance for the production and investment plans of developed and underdeveloped countries alike. It covered economic as well as technical aspects of nuclear energy, and among other things, helped make plain that atomic power was as yet no panacea for the ailments of underdeveloped nations.

The conference began with general sessions. These were followed by three parallel sets of specialized sessions dealing broadly with (1) physics and reactors; (2) chemistry, metallurgy, and technology; and (3) medicine, biology, and radioactive isotopes.[49] The 1,050 papers submitted at the conference, the text of the oral presentations, and the record of the discussions have been published by the United Nations in sixteen printed volumes, which constitute the greatest single collection of information yet made available on the peaceful uses of atomic energy.[50] The "impressive results" of the conference were noted at the tenth session of the General Assembly, and a decision was made that a second scientific conference on atomic energy should be held in two to three years time.[51]

The more prosaic job of keeping agricultural output in line with demand, a task that had required a massive production drive during the initial postwar years, assumed new dimensions in the 1950's when surpluses again made their appearance. To date, both national governments and international agencies have been more successful in dealing with acute shortages than with unsalable surpluses. The shortages have occurred in wartime or as a result of other catastrophes and crises during which the spirit of sacrifice and compassion has remained strong. The shortage is invariably expected to be temporary. Meanwhile, consumers are asked to endure for a time a rationing scheme based on need rather

[48] John Lear, "Ike and the Peaceful Atom," *The Reporter* (Jan. 12, 1956), p. 21.

[49] U.N. General Assembly, Eleventh Session, *Official Records*, "Annual Report of the Secretary-General on the Work of the Organization, 16 June 1955–15 June 1956," p. 3.

[50] United Nations, *Peaceful Uses of Atomic Energy—Proceedings of the International Conference in Geneva, August 1955*, Vols. 1–16 (1956).

[51] Res. 912(X), Dec. 3, 1955.

than ability to pay. Producers are exhorted to increase supply and are frequently aided by governments in doing so.

Surpluses emerge in a very different psychological setting. The existence of a surplus is evidence of a soft spot in the economy. The situation may grow worse before it grows better. The remedies are far from self-evident. Allowing prices to fall means hardship for producers. Buying up the surplus and holding it off the market requires large sums of money. Disposing of accumulated supplies without disrupting normal marketing arrangements is exceedingly difficult. Stepping up consumption is a gradual process.

So long as the FAO could campaign for greater production, it was superficially on safe ground. In 1951, it could still report that food production was about 9 per cent above the 1934–38 average, but population was up more than 12 per cent. The increases in food production, moreover, were concentrated largely in the developed areas, particularly in North America. The FAO Conference in Rome, in late 1951, decided that the whole effort of the FAO should be directed toward obtaining a greater output of food. A goal was set and publicized: food production should increase by at least 1 or 2 per cent more than the annual population increase. Agricultural development plans should be drafted, and technical assistance should be sought in executing agreed plans.

The production target first set by FAO was warmly endorsed by the Economic and Social Council in 1952.[52] By 1953, it was clear that the world as a whole had overshot the mark. Per-capita consumption in important areas was still below prewar levels, but in a number of commodities embarrassing surpluses were being accumulated. As the London *Economist* stated: "What began as a straightforward crusade for higher production everywhere of practically everything eatable has turned, with the reappearance of agricultural surpluses, into a somewhat bewildered search for a 'selective' policy of expansion—which FAO is much less well fitted either to devise or encourage."[53]

The FAO has been unable to prevent surpluses from being accumulated, to police their distribution, or, in pursuit of its policy of "selective expansion," to obtain in food-deficit areas the desired increases in output of products needed for nutritional purposes. More technical assistance, however, has been devoted to agriculture than to any other sector of the economy, and the FAO has unquestionably made effective use of the funds available.

[52] Res. 424(XIV), June 19, 1952.
[53] *The Economist*, Vol. 170 (Jan. 2, 1954), p. 31.

In the early days of the United Nations, "industrialization," symbolized by the desire for a steel mill regardless of the accessibility of iron ore or metallurgical coke, was the aim of almost every underdeveloped country. After 1950, however, "balanced development" became the watchword, and the importance of modernizing agriculture began to be more widely appreciated. With FAO aid, new tools and implements have been introduced, better seeds developed and supplied, crop rotation taught, pastures improved, irrigation programs developed, locust control projects initiated, reforestation undertaken, and forestry and fishery services strengthened.

Rice-breeding and rice-processing experiments organized by the International Rice Commission are conducted by national experiment stations in a number of Far Eastern countries. Great progress is being made in rendering rice cultivation less laborious and more efficient. Ironically, however, the volume produced by the cumbersome methods currently employed seems to be more than consumers in the low-income areas of the Far East can afford to buy. Stocks in 1953 reached a point that found Thailand and Burma facing real difficulty in disposing profitably of their crops and making no secret of their concern about American surplus-disposal programs.

Although stressed by FAO, the vast potentialities of the oceans, lakes, and streams as sources of food supply have hardly begun to be tapped. The problem is a two-fold one of educating the public that fish is a nutritious food on the one hand and, on the other, improving the methods of catching, chilling, transporting, and distributing fish. UNESCO is assisting in the educational program. The technical assistance projects of the FAO include simple undertakings such as the establishment of hatcheries, the stocking of canals and rice paddies with fish, and the improvement of primitive fishing vessels and equipment. They also include advanced undertakings such as demonstrations of the latest electronic devices for locating schools of fish.

Provision of Public Loan Capital

The disclosure, through productivity campaigns and other technical assistance measures, of ways to increase output without important new capital investment has in no way blunted the desire for fresh loan capital as a means of stepping up production and productivity. This desire, moreover, was satisfied only to a modest extent by the scale of IBRD lending during the period 1950–56.

In May 1951, an international group of experts appointed by the United Nations Secretary-General in response to an invitation from the

Economic and Social Council issued a provocative and widely-discussed report on economic development.[54] The pages on "Government Lending" were more flattering to the United States Export-Import Bank than to the International Bank for Reconstruction and Development, although no details concerning the work of the former institution were supplied. The experts merely said that they were "impressed by the job which the [Export-Import] Bank is doing, and wish to recommend that other developed countries might well establish similar institutions."[55]

The International Bank, according to the experts,

> . . . has not adequately realized that it is an agency charged by the United Nations with the duty of promoting economic development. It should do everything that lies in its power to break down the obstacles to sound investment in the under-developed countries. The Bank should set itself to reach, within five years, some such target as an annual rate of lending of not less than $1 billion to the under-developed countries. If it shows no signs of approaching this target, the whole question of the proper international organization for the provision of adequate amounts of loan capital to the under-developed countries should be reviewed by the United Nations.[56]

The International Bank at the time was lending to the underdeveloped countries at a rate below $200 million annually. The authors of *Measures for the Economic Development of Underdeveloped Countries* were not unmindful of the difficulties confronting the Bank and the progress made since 1946 in overcoming these difficulties. Throughout their report, however, they appear to have grossly overestimated the capacity of the underdeveloped countries to absorb capital rapidly. They tended to assume that the majority of countries were either on the threshold, or could readily be brought to the threshold, of a vast new era. Only a minority, in their view, were unprepared for more rapid development, unable to put forward adequate plans, or utterly lacking the nucleus of trained workers necessary to put approved plans into operation.

The Economic, Employment and Development Commission, the first organ in the United Nations to consider the report of the experts, decided, at the urging of the representatives of the industrialized nations, that no useful purpose would be served by reference to the lending target of $1 billion per year. The Economic and Social Council agreed.

[54] U.N. Department of Economic Affairs, *Measures for the Economic Development of Underdeveloped Countries*, Report by a Group of Experts Appointed by the Secretary-General of the United Nations, Doc. E/1986 (May 3, 1951). (Hereinafter cited as *Measures for Economic Development.*)

[55] *Ibid.*, p. 82.

[56] *Ibid.*, pp. 83–84.

Its resolution on the report simply recommended that the existing lending agencies continue to expand their operations.[57]

The expansion hoped for had not occurred by the end of 1954, although more favorable terms of trade provided the underdeveloped countries with the equivalent of several billion dollars in purchasing power during the raw material boom that followed the outbreak of war in Korea. For the period 1950 through 1954, no clear trend is discernible, either in total lending by the Bank or in its lending to underdeveloped countries. Total lending fluctuated between $200 million and $300 million per year; loans to underdeveloped countries, between $150 million and $212 million. The figures for 1955 and 1956 indicate that the corner may have been turned. The rate of lending rose sharply, but much of the increase went to Europe and Australia.

INTERNATIONAL BANK LOANS BY CALENDAR YEARS, 1950–56[a]

Year (1)	Number of Loans (2)	Number of Countries Obtaining Loans (3)	Total Loans (In thousands) (4)	Loans to Underdeveloped Countries[b] (In thousands) (5)
1950	17	10	$ 279,230	$ 179,230
1951	17	11	208,408	158,408
1952	16	12	292,483	212,004
1953	22	13	256,900	156,700
1954	16	15	282,700	171,700
1955	27	20	406,500	204,500
1956	24	17	507,408	270,150
1950–56	139	41[c]	$2,233,629	$1,352,692

[a] Compiled from "Chronological List of Loans," unnumbered, undated press release from International Bank for Reconstruction and Development; *Eleventh Annual Report*, 1955–56, pp. 28–37; and Memorandum of Dec. 20, 1956 from Office of Information of International Bank.

[b] The Bank does not attempt to segregate loans to underdeveloped countries. The figures in column 5 have been derived by subtracting from the official totals in column 4 amounts indicated below for loans to countries that, because of their per-capita income levels, are not usually regarded as underdeveloped:

1950: $100 million (to Australia)
1951: 50 million (to South Africa)
1952: 80.5 million (to Australia, Finland, and the Netherlands)
1953: 100.2 million (to Japan and South Africa)
1954: 111 million (to Australia, Austria, Belgium, and Norway)
1955: 202 million (to Australia, Austria, Finland, Italy, Japan, Norway, and South Africa)
1956: 237.25 million (to Australia, Austria, Finland, Italy, Japan, and Norway)

[c] Because some of the same countries obtained loans in different years, this total is less than the sum of the figures in the column.

From its inception through December 31, 1956, the Bank has made loans totaling nearly $3 billion to more than forty different countries. More than 35 per cent of this total has gone to Europe, with Finland

[57] Res. 368C(XIII), Aug. 22, 1951.

and Yugoslavia the only European recipients that were not participants in the Marshall Plan. About 25 per cent has gone to Latin America, with Brazil, Colombia, and Mexico together accounting for nearly two-thirds of the Latin American total. South Africa and Australia account for about 15 per cent. The remaining 25 per cent has gone to Asia and to African areas other than the Union of South Africa; among these, India has been by far the heaviest borrower.

The classification of loans by purpose is necessarily somewhat arbitrary. The Bank has, however, made such a classification, and the resultant distribution is shown in the accompanying table. Excluding the early reconstruction loans, about two thirds of the $2.9 billion loaned as of December 13, 1956, has been allocated to electric power and transportation projects.[58]

Reconstruction	$ 497,000,000
Electric Power	886,000,000
Transportation	686,000,000
Communications	26,000,000
Agriculture and Forestry	274,000,000
Industry	369,000,000
General Development	140,000,000
Total	$2,878,000,000

To date, all service charges and principal repayments have been met. As yet they remain modest offsets against new lending, but they will increase steadily. Whether the burden of the service charges on the operations of the Bank will become large enough to constitute a serious drain on the foreign exchange resources of the underdeveloped countries depends in part on the relationship between the amount of new lending and the size of the service charges, and, more importantly, on the cumulative and indirect effects of the loans by the Bank on the general economies of underdeveloped countries. The loans of the Bank can contribute to capital formation in the underdeveloped countries, irrespective of the increase in charges they give rise to, so long as lending continues. Nevertheless, the contribution of the Bank is unlikely to be great enough to reduce the pressure for additional sources of development funds.

The improvement in general economic conditions during the postwar period has spared international institutions the added strain of having to operate in bad times. In the United Nations discussions concerning

[58] Source: International Bank for Reconstruction and Development, *Facts About World Bank Lending* (Dec. 13, 1956).

the role of the Bank in promoting international economic stability, three types of action have been suggested:

1. It has been proposed that targets, considerably above present levels, be set in advance for the total outflow of long-term capital from developed to underdeveloped countries. As private investment will fall off sharply in periods of depression, public lending should be increased reciprocally in order to maintain a stable total flow. The Bank should be reorganized to enable it to make up the shortfall and ensure stability.[59]

2. In a more flexible fashion than mechanically maintaining some target level, the Bank should reach advance agreements with countries on their development programs and be prepared to expand promptly its rate of lending in times of recession or depression. In other words, there should be a shelf of public works ready for prompt execution.[60]

3. More modest than either of the above, the Bank, if it cannot vastly increase its lending during periods of recession, should at least ease the burdens of borrowers at such times by declaring a moratorium or a partial moratorium on repayments of outstanding loans.

The first form of activity has generally been regarded as overly ambitious, impractical, and because of the assurance of increased public funds to compensate for any decrease in the private flow, likely to reduce the incentives of borrowers to attract private capital. The second runs afoul of political realities in assuming, as does the first, that the Bank can defer the financing of desirable projects in good times merely in order to have them ready for execution when times are less good. Times are perpetually hard in the underdeveloped countries, and they would be the first to balk at the prospect of temporarily shelving mature and well-conceived development projects.[61] The Bank, for its part, has steadfastly maintained that the modest level of its lending has been due to the lack of appropriate projects and the limited capacity of potential borrowers to service additional loans, not to a desire to conserve resources for times of increased need.

[59] See U.N. Department of Economic Affairs, *National and International Measures for Full Employment*, Report by a Group of Experts Appointed by the Secretary-General, Doc. E/1584 (Dec. 22, 1949), pp. 54–58, 90–92.

[60] See U.N. Department of Economic Affairs, *Measures for International Economic Stability*, Report by a Group of Experts Appointed by the Secretary-General, Doc. E/2156 (Nov. 27, 1951), pp. 28–30.

[61] In depression periods, however, the Bank might help finance the completion of projects that had been started without recourse to the Bank but could not be finished during a period of declining export proceeds without outside aid.

It seems plain that the Bank is not at present equipped or prepared to act as a countercyclical lending agency. Neither has it yet indicated the extent to which it might, in a period of deflation, mitigate the burden of servicing existing loans. Under the Articles of Agreement, a member suffering "from an acute exchange stringency," may ask for a relaxation of the conditions of payment.[62] In these circumstances, the Bank may accept service payments in the currency of the borrowing nation (rather than the currency in which the loan was made) for a period of not more than three years, or the life of the loan may be extended, or the amortization terms modified. The Bank, having struggled to establish the concept that loans are business, not charity, and that repayments are expected to be made as scheduled, has been reluctant to indicate in advance how liberal it might be during a depression. If it is to function as a bank, it must, in so far as it can, behave like a bank.

Although the volume of Bank lending has been slow to rise, the Bank has nevertheless become a more influential factor in the field of investment. Further broadening of the specific project concept has permitted funds to be advanced for a greater variety of activities. Additional survey missions have uncovered investment opportunities in areas about which little was previously known.

The loan by the Bank in 1950 to the Turkish Industrial Development Bank was mentioned earlier as an example of the broadening of the specific project concept with which the Bank commenced its operations. A second loan was made to the Turkish Industrial Development Bank in 1953, after which that institution successfully marketed a new issue of its own stock. However, despite the fact that the IBRD made a total of six loans to Turkey between 1950 and 1954 and stationed a high-level representative there, relations between the IBRD and the Turkish Government were not always harmonious. As time went on, IBRD officials became increasingly critical of the accumulation of short-term debt by Turkey and of its failure to curb the inflationary pressures that made it a chronic debtor to the European Payments Union. The Turkish Government claimed the Bank was overly orthodox: as the investments of the postwar period began to bear fruit, more goods would become available both for domestic consumption and for export; inflationary pressures and balance-of-payments deficits would then be overcome. Meanwhile, said the government, the delay of the Bank in granting further credits to Turkey was inexcusable, and its representative in Turkey—a former Finance Minister of the Netherlands—had no business discussing the financial problems of Turkey with the officers

[62] *Articles of Agreement*, Art. IV, Sec. 4(c).

of the European Payments Union. In a formal letter, the Premier demanded withdrawal of the representative, throwing in for good measure a complaint illustrative of a long-standing grievance of the underdeveloped countries: the Bank had loaned more than $225 million to the Netherlands, a developed country, and only $63 million to Turkey, an underdeveloped country.

The dispute is indicative of the differences of view in different parts of the world concerning the economic policies appropriate for nations promoting more rapid economic development, specifically the strictness with which inflation should be controlled. It is also a wholesome reminder that international agencies as well as individual foreign governments can be accused of intervening in the domestic affairs of a country.

On the theory that local institutions like the Turkish Industrial Development Bank are better equipped than the International Bank to investigate the credit-worthiness of and to extend credit to small domestic enterprises, development financing institutions have been established, with the aid of the Bank, in Ethiopia and, more recently, in India. The Industrial Credit and Investment Corporation of India is a complex financial partnership. The initial capital consists of $10.5 million of equity money subscribed by private investors, British and American as well as Indian, and $25.75 million in loan capital subscribed by the International Bank and the Government of India. The loan of the Indian Government is in rupees derived from the sale of a grant of steel by the United States Foreign Operations Administration. The International Bank loan is a fifteen-year loan of $10 million at $4\frac{5}{8}$ per cent interest, with amortization to begin after a five-year period of grace. The representatives of the $10.5 million of share capital will manage the Bank and arrange its loans to and equity investments in private Indian undertakings.

The original policy of the International Bank, it will be recalled, was to limit developmental loans to the foreign exchange costs of equipment imported for specific productive projects. This policy was frequently criticized in the Economic and Social Council and elsewhere both because it failed to cover the full cost of capital equipment even for specific projects and because it appeared to prohibit lending for general developmental purposes. Roads, schools, hospitals, and other social and economic overhead investments may require large local currency expenditures, which in turn may increase the demand for imported goods, but they do not themselves require foreign equipment nor do they earn foreign exchange. In at least a few cases, the Bank has been willing to make general-purpose loans to finance undertakings of this kind, confident that the over-all improvement in the economy of the borrower would make repayment possible. Thus the Bank has made several loans to a development corporation in Italy, the *Cassa per il Mezzogiorno*, to meet the increased demand for dollar imports generated by the development program for southern Italy. In Iran, the Bank, having reached agreement with the government on the over-all magnitude of a development program for the years 1955–62, is financing the anticipated deficit during the first three years of the program.

The first loan entirely in a currency other than United States dollars was a very small one in sterling and three other European currencies made to Iceland in 1951. Pakistan obtained one in 1954. Again, the amount was small—£5 million—to help finance the foreign exchange costs of a natural-gas pipeline to be constructed in Pakistan, but the arrangements are interesting. The borrower was a new company, the Sui Gas Transmission Company, three quarters of whose shares were held by private investors in Pakistan and the United Kingdom and one quarter by the Pakistan Industrial Development Corporation. The Transmission Company was to be operated by the Pakistan subsidiary of the Burmah Oil Company. Six British Banks participated in the loan, in small amounts, without a guarantee by the Bank.[63]

As the free world economy has improved, more of the loan capital of the Bank has been raised in the private market outside the United States; more of its disbursements have been made for purchases outside the United States; and a progressive internationalization of its resources has occurred. Bank disbursements, of course, lag well behind loan commitments and by June 30, 1956, less than $2 billion of the $2.7 billion loaned as of that date had been expended. Of this amount, however, nearly 40 per cent had been expended for purchases outside the United States in nations able to supply, on a competitive basis, the equipment and other items needed by borrowers.[64]

Mobilization of Private Capital for Investment Purposes

Classification of the International Bank as a public lending institution tends to understate its role as a promoter of private investment. More and more, the Bank has become a kind of international invest-

[63] International Bank for Reconstruction and Development, *Ninth Annual Report, 1953–1954*, p. 17.

[64] International Bank for Reconstruction and Development, *Eleventh Annual Report, 1955–1956*, p. 17.

ment fund, raising money in the private capital markets of the United States, Canada, and Western Europe for investment in underdeveloped countries. The projects in which it invests, primarily electric power and transportation facilities, are prerequisites for the attraction of private capital to underdeveloped areas. The specific techniques used by the Bank to promote private foreign investment, however, can best be understood in the light of certain general developments in this field since 1946.

Much of the essential background for understanding the approach of the United Nations toward international investment problems is contained in a report of the Secretariat on the international flow of private capital during the period 1946 to 1952.[65] In this report, the main trends in the international movement of private capital are summarized as follows:

> The floating in international capital markets of foreign government bonds, once so important in international financing, is now limited to special cases of loans between countries maintaining close commercial or political relations with each other.
>
> Similar floating of shares and debentures of business enterprises, and trade in outstanding securities, have also declined to minor importance, except when the transactions are related to so-called direct investments, involving managerial control through enterprises in the investing country. Such investments accordingly account for the great bulk of private long-term capital moving between countries.
>
> The growth of direct investments does not result principally from the transfer of fresh funds from the capital exporting countries, but from the reinvestment of a large proportion of the profits earned.
>
> Under-developed countries in Latin America derive most of their inflow of foreign private capital from the United States, and dependent territories from their respective metropolitan countries in western Europe. (This does not apply to investments in the petroleum industry.) Relatively little capital is flowing to the independent countries in South-eastern Asia.
>
> There is no flow of private capital to countries with centrally planned economies in eastern Europe and Asia.
>
> New private foreign investments in public utilities have been more than offset by the liquidation of such investments, particularly in railway properties; the outstanding amount of such investment has accordingly tended to decline.
>
> The petroleum industry accounts for a large proportion of foreign direct investments in recent years.
>
> In other extractive industries, foreign direct investment has expanded, particularly in the dependent territories of western European countries.

[65] U.N. Secretariat, Department of Economic Affairs, *The International Flow of Private Capital, 1946–1952*, Doc. E/2531 (Jan. 18, 1954).

Most of the foreign direct investment in manufacturing has been made, not in under-developed, but in economically advanced countries. Nevertheless, certain Latin American countries have received considerable amounts of United States capital for investment in manufacturing.[66]

The report points out that the volume of private capital exports during the period under review corresponded in real terms to about half of the volume during the 1920's. Because populations have increased in both capital-importing and capital-exporting countries, the decline in capital movement per capita has been still greater. Basic to any significant increase in the flow of private capital to underdeveloped countries, however, is the creation of a climate more hospitable to economic growth.

Climates in which custom and tradition are the prime regulators of human behavior are hostile to economic growth. For growth to occur, the climate must be receptive to change, hospitable to innovations that increase productivity and enlarge total output. It must be capable of generating further innovations. For the growth to be balanced, the desire for continuous improvement must permeate all sectors of the economy and the whole of society.

The creation of such a climate is a complex and subtle process. It involves more than the negative function of removing obstacles. Enterprise in underdeveloped countries is not just chafing under restrictions; it is frequently nonexistent. Many members of the United Nations have tended to assume that the positive key to the process is finance. Financing has been thought of in terms of (1) mobilizing domestic capital in underdeveloped countries; and (2) increasing the flow of international capital from the more developed to the less developed nations by means of private loans and equity investments, public loans, and public grants.

The rate of domestic capital formation in underdeveloped countries is painfully low. Except for a few rich citizens, the inhabitants cannot reduce consumption in order to release resources for investment. The underdeveloped countries, it has been observed before, cannot save because they are so poor, and remain so poor because they cannot save. The inability of the masses to reduce consumption, however, does not completely close the circle.

The surplus income of the favored few can be tapped for public investment by tax systems that are more progressive than at present, but not so progressive as to discourage savings and investment. Better op-

[66] *Ibid.*, pp. 27–28. Since the above-cited report was published, there has been some revival of the floating of foreign government bonds in international capital markets, but the totals remain small.

portunities for investment in local enterprises can be provided through the establishment of development banks, savings institutions, and stock markets. Surplus labor, more plentiful in underdeveloped countries than surplus capital, can be employed in community development programs to increase the capital stock of the community. Although present consumption levels, by and large, cannot be reduced, increases in output can, to a considerable extent, be channeled into investment rather than into consumption.

Foreign capital is necessary, both to stimulate the process of domestic capital formation and to add to the available supply of capital in underdeveloped countries. Where national income is low, small amounts of outside capital can make a great difference in the local capital supply.[67] The risks to private foreign investors, however, are so much greater today than before the First World War, and the rewards so much smaller, that such investors remain cautious. At the receiving end, nationalist ambitions and vivid memories of past exploitation keep the welcome cool.

The factors limiting the flow of private investment have been summarized in various United Nations reports.[68] Underdevelopment is itself a major obstacle. The lack of skilled labor, public utilities, and transportation systems limits the field for investment, and low per-capita income limits the market for goods and services. International tension, persistent inflation, and political instability seal off large areas. In industrialized countries such as the United States and Canada, domestic investment continues to be highly profitable. Moreover, in the event of difficulties, investors are more confident of their ability to obtain relief from their own governments than from the governments of foreign countries. In the so-called capital-importing countries, the following specific obstacles have been noted:[69]

1. Legal restrictions on the entry of foreign capital and the control

[67] See Eugene Staley, *The Future of Underdeveloped Countries* (1954), pp. 260–62.

[68] See, for example, U.N. Secretariat, Economic and Social Council, *Survey of Policies Affecting Private Foreign Investment*, Doc. E/1614/Rev. 1 (Mar. 8, 1950); International Bank for Reconstruction and Development, *Report on the Proposal for an International Finance Corporation*, Doc. 2215 (April 1952); U.N. Secretary-General, *International Flow of Private Capital for the Economic Development of Underdeveloped Countries*, Doc. E/2546 (Feb. 19, 1954); U.N. Secretariat, Department of Economic Affairs, *The International Flow of Private Capital, 1946–1952.*

[69] The listing is virtually verbatim from U.N. Secretary-General, *International Flow of Private Capital for the Economic Development of Underdeveloped Countries*, Doc. E/2546. As pointed out in the Secretary-General's memorandum, some of these restrictions are "symptoms of underlying economic conditions rather than the expression of policy towards foreign capital as such." P. 46.

and operation of foreign-owned enterprises. Among such restrictions are: exclusion of foreign capital from particular industries or types of economic activity; restriction of entry of foreign capital on a case-by-case basis; requirements for minimum financial or other participation by nationals of the capital-importing country in all business enterprises or in selected types of economic activity; stipulations regarding participation by nationals in the labor force of enterprises established within the country; regulations governing the exploitation of minerals and natural resources; official fixing of prices and rates, particularly in the public utility industry; and official regulation of labor relations.

2. Exchange restrictions, quantitative restrictions on imports and exports, and other types of control over international transactions.

3. Fiscal measures such as the imposition of taxes that may be nondiscriminatory in form but are discriminatory in substance.

4. Policies concerning nationalization, expropriation, and public ownership of industry.

Reduction of these obstacles by resolutions of either the Economic and Social Council or the General Assembly has proved just as impractical as reduction by multilateral investment treaties. At the Council and the Assembly, the United States has taken the lead in keeping the private investment issue alive, partly as an offset to the mounting pressure for public funds and partly to express its own deeply felt convictions about the role of private enterprise in the development process. In most of the rest of the world, enthusiasm for free private enterprise is clearly more restrained than in the United States and in some of the free world nations there is considerable distrust, not just of private foreign investments but of private enterprise generally. Nevertheless, all nations outside the Soviet bloc and Yugoslavia reiterate in the United Nations their desire for private foreign capital and their interest in giving adequate assurances to potential investors. Still, there remains a gap between the maximum that it is politically possible for most of them to offer by way of assurances and the minimum that is necessary to attract capital on a significant scale.

The resolutions of the principal organs of the United Nations are, on the whole, confined to generalities. In them, governments commit themselves, not to eliminate, but rather to *try* to eliminate certain obstacles or establish certain facilities. Each remains judge of the adequacy of its efforts.

Even if the resolutions were to be more concrete—if, for example a firm twenty-five-year moratorium on further nationalization of industrial enterprises were negotiated—the effects on the flow of private international capital would be uncertain. Individual investors might or might not be moved to invest larger sums in distant places. Whereas the decisions of governments regarding the provision of grant and loan aid can be affected directly and immediately by debates at intergovernmental forums, the decisions of private investors can only be indirectly influenced.

Nevertheless, the debates reveal a growing sophistication on the part of both capital-importers and capital-exporters about the role of private investment, and the resolutions include numerous recommendations regarding the kinds of action that should be taken to promote its flow. The improved climate that resolutions, such as the one adopted by the Council in August 1951,[70] both create and reflect, is from time to time worsened by a resolution like the one on "the right of economic self-determination" introduced by Chile and accepted by the Commission on Human Rights in 1952,[71] or the one adopted by the General Assembly in late 1952 on the "Right to Exploit Freely Natural Wealth and Resources."[72] The latter resolution, widely publicized in American business and financial circles, arose out of an attempt by Uruguay and Bolivia to have the United Nations recognize anew the right of Members to nationalize their domestic resources. As introduced, it was conspicuously one-sided in emphasizing the rights but not the obligations of governments that nationalize industries. Strongly opposed by the United States as a deterrent to private investment, it was ultimately amended into less offensive form and adopted by a vote of 36 to 4 with

[70] Res. 368B(XIII), Aug. 22, 1951—opposed by the Soviet Union and Poland as a one-sided interference in the domestic affairs of Member nations but accepted, after negotiation, by the rest of the Council—recommended that capital-exporting nations provide potential investors with the fullest possible information on foreign investment opportunities; undertake measures for the avoidance of double taxation; be prepared to negotiate treaties to ensure conditions favorable to the investment of private foreign capital; provide, to the extent desirable and feasible, guarantees to potential investors against certain nonbusiness risks affecting foreign enterprise; impress on investors the importance of serving the economic and social welfare of the capital-receiving countries. Parallel recommendations were made to capital-importing nations. The latter were urged specifically to provide adequate assurances, through treaties or otherwise, regarding the treatment to be accorded to foreign investors in the operation, management, and control of their enterprises; in the remittance of earnings and the withdrawal of capital; in the protection of their persons and property; and in the matter of compensation in the event of expropriation.

[71] See the monograph in this Brookings series, *The United Nations and Human Rights*, Chap. I.

[72] Res. 626(VII), Dec. 21, 1952.

20 abstentions.[73] The negative votes, due more to the legislative history of the resolution than to its final provisions, were cast by the United States, the United Kingdom, South Africa, and New Zealand, whereas Canada and most of the countries of Western Europe abstained.

It is obvious that nationalization is an extremely sensitive subject. No underdeveloped country will go on record against it in a United Nations forum. On the other hand, the action of the Assembly in 1952 in response to the Uruguayan-Bolivian initiative marked no real shift in policy or emphasis on the part of United Nations Members. Better balanced and more comprehensive resolutions on private investment issues, clearly more indicative of the considered views of the Members, were passed both before and after the 1952 session.[74]

The blunting of extreme views that has become evident in debates and resolutions is in part due to plainer speaking in United Nations publications. The following quotation from a 1955 report is a far cry from the tone of some of the earlier reports issued by the United Nations:

> . . . Under-developed countries in other words, are competitors for foreign capital, and in so far as market forces prevail, investment is likely to be made in that field and in that country which, comparative risk being taken into account, appear to offer the highest prospective rate of return over a reasonable period of time. The under-developed country is in effect entering a competitive market as a buyer; it cannot dictate both the volume of capital and entrepreneurial ability it is proposing to absorb and the price and conditions it is prepared to offer. Difference in potential reward is one of the principal reasons why in the international movement of private capital, most of the industrial investment has taken place in more advanced countries while investment in under-developed countries has been very largely in primary activities producing raw materials and foodstuffs for markets abroad.[75]

At the same time, spokesmen for the more developed countries have come to recognize that private investment in underdeveloped countries cannot be a substitute for public investment and is more likely to follow it than to occur without it. Consequently, the gap between the views of capital exporters and capital importers—a gap that has defied bridging by multilateral treaties and codes—is being bridged repeatedly in bi-

[73] U.N. General Assembly, Seventh Session, Plenary, *Official Records*, 411th Meeting (Dec. 21, 1952), p. 495.

[74] See, especially, Economic and Social Council Res. 512B(XVII), Apr. 30, 1954, "International Flow of Private Capital for the Economic Development of Underdeveloped Countries," the recommendations of which were endorsed by the General Assembly in Res. 824(IX), Dec. 11, 1954.

[75] U.N. Department of Economic and Social Affairs, *Processes and Problems of Industrialization in Under-developed Countries*, Doc. E/2670 (December 1955), p. 86.

lateral negotiations.[76] In a number of countries, mutually satisfactory arrangements have been made, and the International Bank, as well as other informed sources, has noted a distinct improvement in the private investment climate.

The International Bank, in addition, has contributed directly to this improvement. The regular long-term loans of the Bank are financed, to an increasing extent, from capital raised in the private markets of member countries. The total of outstanding bonds of the Bank as of mid-1956 amounted to $850 million, and of this total, an estimated $380 million—or 45 per cent—was held by investors outside the United States.[77] The President of the Bank has stressed that it also offers a vehicle for short-term capital in the form of loan participations and sales of securities of borrowers from its portfolio.[78] Loan participations are being arranged whereby private investors take short-term and medium-term maturities, without an IBRD guarantee but with the protection inherent in retention of the longer maturities by the international agency. This development is still insignificant in terms of the total flow of international investment, but is nevertheless encouraging. In the year ending June 30, 1955, the Bank for the first time raised nearly $100 million, or more money from the sale of the obligations of borrowers than from the sale of its own bonds.[79]

In addition to sales to private investors of its bonds and sales of the securities of its borrowers, the International Bank has been instrumental in a further move to re-establish private portfolio investment. Combined operations have been arranged under which loans by the Bank have been made at the same time that foreign dollar bonds of the borrowing governments were offered to the public through groups of American underwriters. In this manner, for example, $50 million was obtained by Belgium, $20 million as a loan from the Bank, and $30 million by a simultaneous offer of Belgian bonds on the New York investment market.

[76] See U.N. Economic and Social Council, Twentieth Session, *Recent Governmental Measures Affecting the International Flow of Private Capital, A Report Prepared by the Secretary-General in Accordance with General Assembly Res. 824(IX)*, Doc. E/2766 (June 2, 1955).

[77] International Bank for Reconstruction and Development, *Eleventh Annual Report, 1955–1956*, p. 16.

[78] International Bank for Reconstruction and Development, *Summary Proceedings*, Ninth Annual Meeting of the Board of Governors, Washington, D.C. (1954), p. 9.

[79] Address of Eugene R. Black, President to the Boards of Governors of the International Bank for Reconstruction and Development and the International Monetary Fund, Sept. 12, 1955, *International Financial News Survey* (Sept. 23, 1955), pp. 99–103.

In the receiving countries, as has been noted earlier, the Bank has been instrumental in the establishment of national development banks equipped to finance local private undertakings; has made country surveys that have brought to light new opportunities for private investment; has itself financed the foreign exchange costs of public utility and transportation services needed by private industry and agriculture in underdeveloped countries; has stimulated the mobilization of local capital by requiring the other-than-foreign-exchange costs of approved projects to be raised domestically; and has strongly advocated orthodox policies designed to improve the climate for private capital.

The experience of the postwar years in promoting the flow of private international investment indicates that a good deal of time was wasted in premature efforts to develop multilateral codes and treaties in forums in which a handful of capital-exporting nations were negotiating with a very much larger number of capital-importers. Such codes are more likely to reflect the climate already in existence than to create a different one and consequently could not be developed when views were as polarized as they were during the early postwar years. Opinions have mellowed since then, mutual understanding has grown, and techniques have been found for associating public and private funds and management in ways that make the earlier one-or-the-other approach obsolete. Private investment alone will rarely suffice to stimulate economic growth in areas that have long been stagnant. Recent history suggests, however, that as public projects for the development of power and transportation facilities are completed, as production for the local market becomes feasible and attractive—in short, as development itself occurs—a broad field for domestic and foreign private investment in manufacturing, distribution, and extractive industries opens up.[80]

Establishment of the International Finance Corporation

United States concurrence, after more than three years of fence-sitting, has made possible the establishment of an International Finance Corporation (IFC). In the field of public-versus-private financing of economic development, the proposed corporation is another half-way house. Its initial capital consists of funds subscribed by member governments. These are public funds, but they will be used for financing—in association with private investors and without the requirement of a

[80] For a brief, readily understandable analysis of the major legal, political, and economic issues currently involved in the promotion and protection of private foreign investment, see Seymour J. Rubin, *Private Foreign Investment* (1956).

governmental guarantee—the establishment and expansion of private undertakings, particularly industrial enterprises in underdeveloped countries. Sales of IFC holdings in successful ventures are expected to provide a revolving fund for reinvestment.

The merits of the IFC were never a subject of real controversy in the United Nations. Developed countries did not publicly oppose the idea, but insisted that more study was necessary before conclusions regarding its practicability could be reached. The consistent support of the underdeveloped countries seems to have been due less to convictions about this particular technique for stimulating development than to enthusiasm for anything that would give them access to more capital without jeopardizing their independence. There is no evidence, therefore, that creation of an International Finance Corporation will reduce the pressure for a grant-aid agency.

An International Finance Corporation with a capital fund of $400 million was first publicly suggested in March 1951 in a report to the President of the United States by the International Development Advisory Board, of which Nelson A. Rockefeller was chairman.[81] The Board recommended that "the United States take the initiative in creating an International Finance Corporation, as an affiliate of the International Bank, with authority to make loans in local and foreign currencies to private enterprise without the requirement of government guaranties and also to make nonvoting equity investments in local currencies in participation with private investors."[82] Within a few weeks international status was given to this idea by the group of experts appointed by the United Nations Secretary-General to prepare *Measures for the Economic Development of Underdeveloped Countries*. Their report, issued in May 1951, commended the proposal to the United Nations for study.[83] No detailed consideration was given to this recommendation at the ensuing session of the Economic and Social Council although in its omnibus resolution on financing economic development, the Council requested the International Bank to prepare a report on the contribution that an international finance corporation could make.[84]

The report by the International Bank concluded that an international finance corporation could fill an important gap in the existing ma-

[81] The proposal actually originated with the staff of the International Bank for Reconstruction and Development and was publicized by the Board after consultation with the Bank.

[82] U.S. International Development Advisory Board, *Partners in Progress: A Report to the President* (March 1951), p. 84.

[83] *Measures for Economic Development*, p. 82.

[84] Res. 368(XIII), Aug. 22, 1951.

chinery for economic development, but went to great pains to make clear that the views being expressed were those of the staff of the Bank, not of its Executive Directors or member governments.[85] The report stressed the importance of private investment, particularly equity capital, in the development field and noted reasons for the low level of the postwar flow of private capital. It mentioned as two major limitations on the ability of the Bank to contribute directly to the growth of private investment: (1) the requirement that loans made by the Bank be guaranteed by the government of the country in which the project to be financed is located; and (2) the fact that the Bank does not engage in equity financing. It did not suggest modifying the Articles of Agreement of the Bank in order to overcome these difficulties, for this would have required resubmitting the Articles to the parliaments of Member countries for ratification.

The International Bank reported that an international finance corporation could make three important contributions. First, it could provide funds to enable private investors, both domestic and foreign, to undertake promising projects otherwise held back for lack of sufficient capital. Second, it could direct the attention of private investors to profitable opportunities abroad and induce them to enter the foreign investment field by an offer of financial participation in sound proposals. Third, it could encourage investors to embark on projects from which they might be deterred by lack of confidence rather than lack of capital.

The report was discussed by the Economic and Social Council in 1952. At that time, several Member states indicated their willingness to participate in the proposed corporation, but the key country—the United States—was cool to the proposal and reluctant to discuss it in detail. The year 1952 was a presidential election year; the initial reaction in some American business circles had been hostile; the precise outlines of the proposal were still somewhat hazy; and the International Bank was in any event better qualified technically to clarify the outline than was the Council. Moreover, the United States voice in the Bank, where weighted voting prevailed, was a great deal more powerful than its voice in the Economic and Social Council.

Consequently, in deference to the United States view, the Council merely noted that the Bank was continuing its study of the proposal and asked that the Council be kept informed of the results of such further

[85] International Bank for Reconstruction and Development, *Report on the Proposal for an International Finance Corporation* (April 1952).

explorations.[86] There was actually little to study; the real issue was always the willingness of the United States to participate. Despite evidence of increasing support for the proposal on the part of the American business community, the United States Government remained uncommitted until November 1954 when the Secretary of the Treasury announced the willingness of the Government to solicit congressional approval for United States participation to the extent of $35 million in an International Finance Corporation having an authorized capital of $100 million.[87] The ninth session of the General Assembly then approved without dissent a resolution initiated by the United States requesting the International Bank to prepare draft statutes (articles of agreement) for the new corporation.[88]

In April 1955, the Bank submitted to its member governments proposed articles of agreement for the new International Finance Corporation, to become effective after formal acceptance by at least thirty governments whose combined subscriptions amounted to not less than $75 million.[89] In the space of a little more than a year, the necessary acceptances were obtained. The IFC which came into being in mid-1956, however, differs in some important respects from the organization envisaged in 1951. The authorized capital is $100 million, not $400 million. The entire subscription, however, is payable in gold and United

[86] Res. 416(XIV), June 23, 1952. The seventh session of the General Assembly, n Res. 622(VII), Dec. 21, 1952, endorsed the action of the Council. For information on the situation in 1953 and 1954, see U.N. Economic and Social Council, Sixteenth Session, *Report of the International Bank for Reconstruction and Development on the Question of Creating an International Finance Corporation*, Doc. E/2441 (May 25, 1953); and International Bank for Reconstruction and Development, *A Second Report on the Status of the Proposal for an International Finance Corporation* (June 1954).

[87] Inter-American politics undoubtedly played a role in the timing of the United States announcement. It was made on the eve of the departure of a high-level American delegation to a special economic meeting in Rio de Janeiro at which the United States might otherwise have appeared singularly empty-handed.

[88] Res. 823(IX), Dec. 11, 1954, adopted by a vote of 50 in favor, none against, and 5 abstentions (Soviet bloc). See U.N. General Assembly, Ninth Session, Plenary, *Official Records*, 510th Meeting (Dec. 11, 1954), p. 479.

[89] For the text of the Articles of Agreement, see *Message from the President of the United States Urging Enactment of Legislation Permitting the United States to Join With the Other Free Nations in Organizing the International Finance Corporation*, H. Doc. 152, 84 Cong. 1 sess. (1955). For summary and explanatory information, see International Bank for Reconstruction and Development, Press Release No. 397 (Apr. 15, 1955); International Bank for Reconstruction and Development, *The Proposed International Finance Corporation* (May 1955); and Statement on the International Finance Corporation, by Robert L. Garner, Vice-President, International Bank for Reconstruction and Development, at the Tenth Annual Meeting of the Board of Governors, Istanbul, Sept. 15, 1955.

States dollars (and therefore fully convertible), and the corporation is empowered to raise additional funds.

More puzzling, in view of the desire to provide a mechanism that could supply equity financing to private industrial undertakings, is the absolute prohibition against the best-known form of equity financing, the holding of common or preferred stock. This prohibition apparently grew out of the belief of certain officials of the United States Government that the possession of capital stock, even nonvoting shares, in private enterprises would somehow involve the IFC in ownership or management responsibilities inconsistent with the private character of the enterprises it would assist. Despite the prohibition against holding either common or preferred stock, the IFC will be able to supply venture capital without offending American sensitivities. "It may, for instance, buy securities which give it the right to participate in the profits of an enterprise and which, when sold, can be converted by the purchasers into capital stock."[90]

Even assuming that the IFC gets under way more rapidly and more smoothly than any predecessor international agency, its contribution within the foreseeable future cannot possibly be substantial enough to dampen the drive for grant aid.

The vigorous and as yet unsuccessful campaign of the underdeveloped countries for the establishment of international machinery to provide additional investment assistance in the form of grants and very long-term, low-interest loans has continued unabated since 1951. That campaign, however, is analyzed at a later point in this study, in connection with the special problems of the underdeveloped countries, because it is in the latter context that the issue has been debated in the Economic and Social Council and the General Assembly.[91]

A World Bank for Fissionable Materials?

A new kind of international bank—dealing not in dollars, pounds, and francs but in fissionable materials—was suggested to the United Nations in a dramatic address by President Eisenhower on December 8, 1953. He proposed that governments possessing the secret of atomic development (the Soviet Union, Great Britain, and Canada as well as the United States)

> . . . to the extent permitted by elementary prudence, should begin now and

[90] International Bank for Reconstruction and Development, *Tenth Annual Report, 1954–1955*, p. 27.

[91] See below, Chap. X.

continue to make joint contributions from their stockpiles of normal uranium and fissionable materials to an international atomic energy agency. We would expect that such an agency would be set up under the aegis of the United Nations.

The more important responsibility of this atomic energy agency would be to devise methods whereby this fissionable material would be allocated to serve the peaceful pursuits of mankind. Experts would be mobilized to apply atomic energy to the needs of agriculture, medicine and other peaceful activities. A special purpose would be to provide abundant electrical energy in the power-starved areas of the world.

Thus the contributing Powers would be dedicating some of their strength to serve the needs rather than the fears of mankind.[92]

At the time of the President's proposal, it was legally impossible for the United States, under the Atomic Energy Act of 1946, to release fissionable material to a foreign government. Consequently, new domestic legislation as well as protracted and difficult international negotiations extending over a period of nearly three years were required before the proposal could be translated into a convention likely to be ratified by a significant number of governments. The issues raised during these negotiations transcend economic and social policy and extend deeply into the realm of political and security policy. Analysis of these issues in a discussion of production and investment would therefore be inappropriate.

Necessary amendments to the Atomic Energy Act of 1946 were obtained in 1954, and a bilateral program of assistance to foreign governments was initiated by the United States in 1955. The negotiations for a multilateral agency began inauspiciously with private discussions between the United States and the Soviet Union. When these bogged down because of Soviet unwillingness to discuss the American proposal unless the United States would first agree to an unconditional ban on the use of nuclear weapons, the United States proceeded to discuss with seven other nations plans for an international atomic energy agency of considerably more modest scope than the atomic bank outlined by the President in 1953.

The proposed scope of the agency was enlarged again, however, as a result of thorough discussion at the ninth session of the General Assembly in 1954; circulation, in August 1955, of the draft statute prepared by the United States and seven other nations to the eighty-four states Members of the United Nations or of a related specialized agency; further debate of the tenth session of the General Assembly in 1955;

[92] U.N. General Assembly, Eighth Session, Plenary, *Official Records*, 470th Meeting (Dec. 8, 1953), p. 452.

the deliberations of a committee of twelve nations in February–April 1956, and a major international conference in September–October 1956. Finally, on October 23, 1956, eighty-two nations, including the Soviet Union, voted unanimously to approve the twenty-three articles of the statute (constitution), which will come into force as soon as instruments of ratification have been deposited by eighteen nations, including at least three of the following five: Canada, France, the Soviet Union, the United Kingdom, and the United States.[93]

The statute of the agency provides authority for an extremely broad program. The International Atomic Energy Agency can become not only a medium of substantial economic and technical assistance to member nations in building atomic power plants, but also a control organ administering world-wide safeguards on the use of nuclear energy. It is empowered to receive and store fissionable materials in different regions of the world and to make them available to nations whose atomic energy projects have been approved.

The terms on which materials will be sold or leased to members will depend on the cost of the materials to the agency. In a message to the final meeting of the conference of eighty-two nations in New York in October 1956, the President of the United States promised to make available,

> . . . on terms to be agreed with the Agency, 5,000 kilograms of the nuclear fuel uranium 235 from the 20,000 kilograms of such material allocated . . . by the United States for peaceful uses by friendly nations. . . . In addition to the above mentioned 5,000 kilograms of uranium 235, the United States will continue to make available to the International Atomic Energy Agency nuclear materials that will match in amount the sum of all quantities of such materials made similarly available by all other members of the International Agency,

[93] See U.N. General Assembly, Ninth Session, Plenary, *Official Records*, 475th–76th, 479th, 481st–92nd, 498th, 503rd Meetings (Sept. 23–Dec. 4, 1954); U.N. General Assembly, Ninth Session, First Committee, *Official Records*, 684th–85th, 687th, 690th, 707th–25th Meetings (Oct. 8–Nov. 23, 1954); U.N. General Assembly, Ninth Session, *Official Records*, Annexes, Agenda item 67: "International Co-operation in Developing the Peaceful Uses of Atomic Energy," Res. 810(IX), Dec. 4, 1954; U.N. General Assembly, Tenth Session, First Committee, *Official Records*, 757th–72nd Meetings (Oct. 7–28, 1955); U.N. General Assembly, Tenth Session, Plenary, *Official Records*, 550th Meeting (Dec. 3, 1955); U.N. General Assembly, Tenth Session, *Official Records*, Annexes, Agenda item 18: Peaceful Uses of Atomic Energy; and Res. 912(X), Dec. 3, 1955. See also U.N. General Assembly, Eleventh Session, *Official Records*, Supplement No. 1, "Annual Report of the Secretary General on the Work of the Organization, 16 June 1955–15 June 1956," pp. 3–6. For text of statute of the International Atomic Energy Agency, see U.S. Department of State *Bulletin*, Vol. 35 (Nov. 19, 1956), pp. 820–27.

and on comparable terms, for the period between the establishment of the Agency and July 1, 1960.[94]

Small pledges of fissionable materials have been made also by the Soviet Union and the United Kingdom.

"The cost of fuel is only one part, and a comparatively small part, of the investment involved in an atomic energy program. Reactors, processing plants, and installations to house them are the expensive items."[95] Despite the efforts of certain underdeveloped countries, the role of the new agency in helping members to acquire these items is strictly limited. It may assist any member or group of members to make arrangements to secure necessary financing from outside sources, but it may not provide financial guarantees or assume financial responsibility itself.[96]

The precise role to be played by the new agency thus remains to be seen. Negotiations among the members of the European Community for Coal and Steel for establishment of a supra-national atomic energy agency, EURATOM, are well advanced. The United States program of bilateral agreements includes arrangements with thirty-seven other nations. The bilateral programs of other atomic powers provide further competition for the new agency. Even if the sale and lease of fissionable materials continues to be handled primarily on a bilateral basis and the banking role of the global agency is minimized, it can make a major contribution to the general welfare through fostering the exchange of scientific and technical information, encouraging the training of experts, developing health and safety standards, and administering safeguards against the military use of fissionable materials.

The Balance Sheet

The most striking feature of the United Nations attack on production and investment problems has been diversity. This applies to the general approach, to specific projects undertaken, and to practical results obtained. A multitude of organs and agencies have given attention to fundamental issues such as the mobilization of domestic capital for pro-

[94] "Letter and Statement by President Eisenhower," U.S. Department of State *Bulletin*, Vol. 35 (Nov. 19, 1956), pp. 814–15. The value of 5,000 kilograms—11,000 pounds—at the price of $16 per gram currently charged by the United States Government for U-235 is $80 million.

[95] William R. Frye, "The UN and the Atomic Revolution," *Foreign Policy Bulletin* (Sept. 1, 1956), p. 190.

[96] Statute of the International Atomic Energy Agency, Art. XIB.

ductive purposes, the stimulation of private foreign investment, the use of public funds so that they will have maximum impact, and the creation of a climate in which experimentation and initiative will flourish. Factors inhibiting and stimulating productivity in agriculture, mining, and manufacturing have been debated *in extenso*. At the same time, the special investment requirements, production potentials, and market outlooks for a host of particular industries, particular enterprises, and particular localities have been analyzed. The variety of activities undertaken in local communities and national capitals, in regional forums, and in the more rarified atmosphere of the General Assembly, tends to obscure the pattern of this intricate mosaic.

Initially, the reconstruction of war-devastated areas had top priority. The United Nations Relief and Rehabilitation Administration operated between 1945 and 1947, primarily in eastern and southern Europe, but also in some of the war-devastated areas of Asia. In 1947, the International Bank for Reconstruction and Development made a series of reconstruction loans to certain nations in western and northern Europe. The reconstruction job, however, soon proved to be beyond the resources—and probably beyond the capacity—of the United Nations. After the Soviet Union rejected the Anglo-French invitation to join in working out a new European Recovery Program, European reconstruction went forward with Marshall Plan aid, almost entirely outside the framework of the United Nations.

Within the United Nations, the economic and social development of underdeveloped countries—the raising of standards of living in Asia, Africa, and Latin America—became the central economic aim of the system. There was agreement that lack of know-how was a formidable obstacle to progress in these regions, and that important increases in production could be obtained with comparatively insignificant expenditures of capital. In recognition of this fact, the Expanded Programme of Technical Assistance was established by the United Nations, largely on the initiative of the United States. The underdeveloped countries recognized the inauguration of the program in 1950 as a landmark in international economic relations, but continued to feel that shortage of capital was the main obstacle to their more rapid development. By providing some of the *expertise* necessary for translating grandiose schemes into concrete projects, and by steadily uncovering new opportunities for capital investment, the technical assistance program reinforced these feelings.

Governments of underdeveloped countries were eager for public loan capital on a more liberal scale and on better terms than could be obtained from the International Bank. They exerted unending pressure for more activity and greater flexibility on the part of that institution. The Bank responded by a fairly rapid expansion of its technical services and a much more gradual stepping-up of its lending and spending. The total of IBRD loans to underdeveloped countries, $150-to-$270 million per year during the period 1950–56, has seemed modest in the eyes of developed as well as underdeveloped countries.

On private investment, the underdeveloped countries have been ambivalent, stressing their desire and need for it but unable or unwilling to offer incentives sufficient to attract capital in significant volume. The International Bank has been ingenious in developing techniques for associating private with public capital and paving the way for a revival of private international investment. The lengthy debates and many reports of the United Nations on the private foreign investment problem have shed a good deal of light on the issue and have helped to narrow the differences separating capital importers from potential exporters. The improved climate, noticeable since about mid-1952, has not yet, however, significantly enlarged the flow of funds.

As the underdeveloped nations have seen it, their problems are almost insoluble without additional government aid from abroad, particularly for non-self-liquidating projects like schools, hospitals, and roads, that are nevertheless basic to development. Since 1951, the establishment of a United Nations fund to make grants-in-aid has become the primary economic objective of the underdeveloped countries in the United Nations. Spokesmen for the Soviet bloc until recently have repeatedly claimed that foreign funds from capitalist sources, whether public or private, would bring exploitation and enslavement, but the drive for greater aid has continued.

The United States, which would be the main contributor to a grant-aid fund, first opposed and lately has sought to postpone its establishment.[97] American representatives have emphasized instead what the underdeveloped countries could do with their own resources and by using established forms of international assistance. The preparation of national development plans has been encouraged, and excessive concentration on industrialization at the expense of agriculture has been discouraged. The possibilities of utilizing the spare time of villagers on community improvement projects of their own choosing have been publicized. Antiquated systems of land tenure have been criticized and a wholesome impetus given to broad, democratically-conceived, land

[97] See below, Chap. X.

reform programs. Better machinery for mobilizing domestic capital has been advocated, along with the removal of obvious barriers to foreign private investment. Agreement has been reached on the statute of an agency to promote the development of atomic energy for peaceful purposes.

Ten years of running debate on production and investment problems has highlighted and perhaps intensified differences between countries on a few issues. Grant aid for economic development is the outstanding case. On many other matters agreement has been reached, and concrete programs of action have been initiated. The mutual education of delegates in developed, underdeveloped, and intermediate countries has been furthered by a long series of reports and studies. The technical assistance program has captured the imagination of millions. The Food and Agriculture Organization has operated effectively in a sector of the economy in which small investments can make large differences in output and in which the increased output can provide an important offset to the inflationary pressures generated before longer-term investments pay off. To the growth of industrial establishments in underdeveloped countries an additional fillip may now be supplied by the International Finance Corporation, an affiliate of the International Bank.

The direct contribution of the United Nations system to the impressive increase in world output that has occurred since the end of the war has necessarily been modest. The broad economic objectives of the United Nations have at the same time, of course, been the objectives of Member governments, many of which have vigorously pursued programs of their own—frequently drafted with assistance from agencies of the United Nations—for enlarging agricultural and industrial output. Within each nation, innumerable nongovernmental groups have worked toward these same ends. Moreover, on the international side, United Nations activities have been paralleled, and in some cases dwarfed, by programs conducted outside the framework of the United Nations, most notably the foreign economic programs of the United States Government. Nor should the contribution of completely unplanned and unprogramed factors be forgotten.

In these circumstances, it becomes almost impossible to isolate and measure separately the effect of United Nations activities. The combined result of the United Nations and other influences, national and international, has not only been the attainment of record levels of output during the first postwar decade, but the establishment of a foundation for a much larger and better-balanced growth during the second decade.

CHAPTER V

*Full Employment and Economic Stability**

THE various United Nations programs designed to help repair the ravages of war, to promote the development of underdeveloped countries, and to stimulate production, investment, and trade have had a common purpose—to foster conditions of full employment and steadily rising standards of living. The counterpart of the efforts to attain higher levels of productive employment and economic activity has been the consideration of measures for avoiding reverses involving mass unemployment and cumulative deflation. Noteworthy attempts have been made to build into the United Nations system additional anti-depression safeguards and comprehensive arrangements for the co-ordination of national full-employment policies.

The attainment and maintenance of full employment—important as it has come to be—is not an end in itself and is by no means the sole economic objective of governments. Apparent and, in the short run at least, frequent real conflicts between full employment and other objectives of economic policy have arisen, and the need for reconciling these conflicts both domestically and internationally has had to be faced. Accordingly, the analysis below, after tracing briefly the origins of today's preoccupation with full employment, mentions the related aims with which full employment has had to be reconciled and the general approach of Members of the United Nations to this task. Identified next are the interests of certain specialized agencies: of the International Monetary Fund and the International Bank in economic stability, of the International Labour Organisation in full employment, and of the Food and Agriculture Organization in more stable commodity prices and in the constructive use of agricultural surpluses. For the most part, attention in this analysis is focused on the consideration of problems of full employment and economic stability in the United Nations itself, where the evolution of postwar thinking on these matters is vividly illustrated.

The analysis is divided into two time periods, with a dividing line drawn at the close of 1949. By that time, the accumulated inflationary

* By Robert E. Asher.

pressures of the Second World War had worn off, pockets of unemployment had begun to appear, and a reversion to the nationalistic policies of the 1930's was feared. In December 1949, far-reaching proposals for strengthening the ability of the international economy to resist depression were put forward by a group of experts appointed by the Secretary-General of the United Nations. By the time their recommendations reached the Economic and Social Council, however, the American economy was again surging forward. Governments rejected the major innovations suggested by the experts. Nevertheless, the discussion of their proposals at the 1950 session of the Council represented a high-water mark in United Nations consideration of full employment and economic stability.

Thereafter, other groups of experts were commissioned by the Council and the General Assembly to prepare further reports, both on the general problem of stabilizing the international economy and on the more specific problem of stabilizing the prices of primary commodities moving in international trade. Although these reports, too, became subjects of intense discussion at United Nations meetings, they did not bring about international co-ordination of national full-employment policies, the provision of new sources of credit for meeting temporary setbacks, the completion of a network of commodity agreements, or adequate measures to prevent surplus agricultural products from being utilized in a destabilizing fashion.

Despite much talk and many studies, the international community therefore remains almost entirely dependent on nationally devised and nationally executed safeguards against recession. The ability of the major industrial nations to avoid deep and prolonged depression has, of course, increased greatly during the past two decades. Nevertheless, if a serious depression should begin, it would be rash to assume that the United Nations would make any greater contribution to checking its spread than did the League of Nations.

General Background

The abiding fear of large-scale unemployment and deflation, which characterized the 1930's and to which the "freedom from want" clause of the Atlantic Charter was a response, shaped the postwar aims, aspirations, and programs of peoples and governments everywhere. At the same time,

> . . . a great transformation was taking place in economic thought. The economy was no longer regarded as being fundamentally self-directing and

capable of maintaining continuous full employment except for periodic crises. Instead, the possibility of an equilibrium at a low level of employment for an indefinite period of time had been recognized. Economic analysis had now become engaged in critical enquiry into the determinants of the general level of employment.[1]

This critical inquiry was epitomized in John Maynard Keynes' *General Theory of Employment, Interest and Money*, published in 1936, which was in large measure responsible for the "great transformation" in economic thought.

Because depression anywhere threatens prosperity everywhere, and because national antidepression policies also have international repercussions (the "export of unemployment" is a tempting form of foreign trade in a depression), international discussions during the war inevitably became concerned with questions of employment and stability in the postwar world.[2] These discussions culminated at the San Francisco Conference in the inclusion in the United Nations Charter of Article 55 explicitly requiring the new Organization, "with a view to the creation of conditions of stability and well-being," to promote "higher standards of living, full employment, and conditions of economic and social progress and development."

A similar policy declaration is contained in the United States Employment Act of 1946, although it speaks of "maximum" rather than "full" employment. The Canadian White Paper on *Employment and Income* presented to Parliament in 1945, the several declarations by the British Government on the subject, the postwar French Constitution, and other national undertakings following the close of the Second World War make similar references to "full employment" or high and stable levels of employment.

Basic National Attitudes

Although the great depression that began in 1929 made the elimination of unemployment the paramount social problem and the maintenance of full employment the dominant economic objective of governments, the need for reconciling this objective with other objectives of economic policy has posed numerous dilemmas. Like any individual nation, the United Nations has had to recognize that promotion of the general welfare involves a delicate reconciliation of aims that are not wholly consistent. Within the United Nations, moreover, national

[1] International Labour Organisation, *Fourth Report of the International Labour Organisation to the United Nations* (1950), pp. 25–26.

[2] See above, Chap. I.

governments, reflecting divergent social and economic philosophies, have differed importantly in their approach to the full-employment problem. Broadly speaking, four basic national attitudes toward full employment have been reflected in United Nations debates. The United States, Canada, and a few European countries have held that high and stable levels of employment can best be achieved through market forces and free enterprise, with the role of government more or less limited to compensatory action in the event of recession or excessive boom, mainly through monetary and fiscal policy, but also through building into the economy various "stabilizers" such as unemployment compensation, progressive taxation, bank deposit and mortgage insurance, and agricultural price supports. The viewpoint presented by the United Kingdom and shared by many other countries has been that government should at all times play a more positive role in maintaining full employment. For the underdeveloped countries, the main problem has not been unemployment, but underemployment, and its chief cure rapid economic development. The position of the Soviet Union and its satellites has been that unemployment is an insoluble problem under capitalism and a nonexistent problem under communism. The differences between the first two groups are matters of degree; reconciliation with the third viewpoint presents far greater difficulties but is by no means impossible; the introduction of the fourth point of view makes for propaganda instead of economic analysis and cacophany instead of harmony.

Effective reconciliation of full employment, economic stability, and other objectives of the United Nations Charter has inevitably required extensive consideration of methods of achieving agreed goals, in particular the respective spheres for national and for international action. This line is, however, difficult to draw. Basically, the maintenance of total demand at a level sufficient to absorb a growing labor force in productive employment has been accepted as a national responsibility, and the principle was early established that there should be no interference by international organs, in the interest of other objectives, with the discharge by a member country of this responsibility.

A ruling of the executive directors of the International Monetary Fund at their first meeting made it clear that if, while pursuing a full-employment policy, a country found itself in balance-of-payments difficulties that threatened the success of this policy, it could—without interference by the Fund—relieve the external pressure by a change in its exchange rate, even though the Fund might hold that a change in the internal policy could in the long run prove a more constructive solution.[3] Similarly, it was provided in the draft charter for an International Trade Organization that no member should be required to withdraw or modify restrictions that it was applying under the article dealing with balance-of-payments restrictions on the ground that a change in its domestic policies devoted to maintaining full employment and development would render these restrictions unnecessary. Yet there can be no doubt that employment and stability in other countries might be affected by the consequences of the policies thus protected against interference by specialized agencies.

Major International Problems

The question regarding international economic stability that has been of constant concern to Members of the United Nations other than the United States has been what to do in order to prevent balance-of-payments crises and other disastrous effects from occurring because of temporary failure on the part of a major industrialized nation like the United States to maintain full employment and a high level of effective demand at home. Assume, for example, as the European nations have been wont to do, that the American economy should suffer a substantial setback. In the ensuing recession, United States imports would fall, and exports, in theory at least, would tend to be pushed more vigorously. What courses of action would then be open to a nation whose exports to the United States would decline, whose marketings in third countries might encounter heavier competition from United States exports, and whose reduced foreign exchange earnings would threaten such balance-of-payments equilibrium as it might have attained?

If the nation had ample reserves, or adequate sources of credit, it might survive the strain without reducing its imports. If not, and if demand were sufficiently elastic, it might depreciate its currency in order to improve its export prospects and discourage imports. Or it might impose direct controls on its imports and foreign exchange transactions in order to conserve funds for the purposes it regarded as most essential. Finally, it might accept wage cuts and unemployment in its export industries, and deflation generally until its import re-

[3] For the text of this ruling made pursuant to a request from the United Kingdom for an interpretation of Article IV, 5(f) of the Articles of Agreement, see International Monetary Fund, *First Annual Meeting of the Board of Governors, Report of the Executive Directors and Summary Proceedings, September 27 to October 3, 1946* (1946), pp. 105–06.

quirements were reduced to a level that could be financed from current export earnings.

The underdeveloped countries, even more than the countries of Western Europe, have emphasized their vulnerability to external forces. Possessed of undiversified economies, they have felt excessively dependent on the vicissitudes of world demand for a few export products such as tin, copper, coffee, rubber, or sugar. In 1952, there were thirty-two nations in which two commodities accounted for over 50 per cent of total export earnings. There are at least six countries that regularly earn from 50 to 90 per cent of their dollars from coffee exports to the United States. Such nations are unable to obtain whatever stability benefits may be obtainable from averaging the price movements of a number of different exports; yet the orderly execution of their development programs depends heavily on greater regularity in current export earnings.[4]

The range of short-term fluctuations in the prices of most internationally traded primary products is wider than that of prices in general. The downturns are, therefore, more disastrous for primary producers than for others. At the same time, primary producers in underdeveloped countries appear to benefit less from an upswing of export prices than they lose during comparable downswings. Because the economies of underdeveloped countries have very limited absorptive capacities, the advantages accruing from sudden increases in export earnings are likely to be partially dissipated in inflation or else lost in the initiation of development projects that the country is unable to complete or maintain when the boom is over.

Some of these difficulties might be avoided if increased earnings could be sterilized during boom periods and released during downswings, but such action requires greater political maturity and administrative skill than is usually available in an underdeveloped nation. The impact on the economies of underdeveloped countries of short-term fluctuations in demand for raw materials in the industrialized nations could also be made less severe by international commodity agreements, if these would limit the range of fluctuations, and by programs of economic diversification, which would reduce the vulnerability of underdeveloped countries to particular fluctuations. Diversification requires considerable capital, takes long years to accomplish,

[4] U.N. Department of Economic Affairs, *Commodity Trade and Economic Development*, Report by a Committee Appointed by the United Nations Secretary-General, Doc. E/2519 (Nov. 25, 1953), para. 24.

and in some cases, would be an uneconomic expedient because the area is uniquely equipped to continue as a highly specialized producer. The demand for international commodity agreements consequently cannot be regarded as transitory.

From this brief statement of the problem and catalog of alternatives open to developed and underdeveloped countries, it should be clear why United Nations discussions of full-employment and stability inevitably became concerned with the adequacy of domestic full-employment programs in major trading nations; the degree to which failure to maintain full employment at home should carry a responsibility for making good the foreign trade losses caused elsewhere; the adequacy of national and international monetary reserves; the use of trade restrictions and exchange controls; the mitigation of fluctuations in primary commodity markets; and the regularization of the flow of long-term investment capital. Although the inability of labor to cross frontiers because of immigration barriers has added to the instability of the international economy, it has, by and large, been accepted in United Nations economic discussions as a fact of contemporary life. Migration from lands of lesser opportunity to lands of greater opportunity has been given relatively little emphasis as an equilibrator in the international economy.

Concern of the Specialized Agencies

The concentration of attention in this study on discussions of full employment and economic stability in the Economic and Social Council and other organs of the United Nations tends to obscure the continuing concern of a number of specialized agencies in this area. It is desirable at the outset, therefore, to give some indication of the interests of the International Monetary Fund (IMF), the International Bank for Reconstruction and Development (IBRD), the International Labour Organisation (ILO), and the Food and Agriculture Organization (FAO).

Fund and Bank

The International Monetary Fund, as conceived at Bretton Woods in 1944, was to be concerned primarily with problems of exchange stability and related questions arising out of international trade and payments. Its first and third purposes, according to its Articles of

Agreement, were "to promote international monetary cooperation" and "to promote exchange stability." Its second purpose was "to facilitate the expansion and balanced growth of international trade, and to contribute thereby to the promotion and maintenance of high levels of employment and real income and to the development of the productive resources of all members as primary objectives of economic policy."[5] The emphasis at the Bretton Woods Conference, as distinct from the emphasis at the San Francisco Conference, was not on full employment *per se*, but on the expansion and growth of international trade; not on economic stability, but on the development of productive resources as "primary objectives of economic policy." These are significant distinctions. Moreover, the Articles of Agreement of the International Monetary Fund speak of "high levels of employment," not "full employment."

These differences in terms of reference help to explain the divergent policies at times recommended by the Fund and the United Nations Organization. There is, moreover, a fairly sharp distinction between the generally conservative outlook of central bank presidents and monetary experts, comprising the Board of Governors and Staff of the Fund, and the more pragmatic viewpoints of the delegates to the principal organs of the United Nations and of the experts commissioned to prepare special reports for their consideration. As has been pointed out,

> . . . One cannot believe in full employment or free trade as desirable economic objectives exclusively on economic grounds. . . . Emphasis on employment, and even more on unemployment, conveys the idea that there is an urgent social problem to be solved, whereas emphasis on monetary factors may create a very different impression—as it did during the nineteenth century.[6]

Perhaps the differing economic philosophies of the Fund and the United Nations Organization, although they tend to complicate harmonious co-operation between the agencies, are not altogether lamentable. The more conservative approach of the Fund and its emphasis on monetary factors help to keep certain indispensable objectives of economic policy—the expansion of international trade, the development of productive resources, and the importance of a relatively

[5] United Nations Monetary and Financial Conference, Bretton Woods, N.H., July 1 to 22, 1944, *Articles of Agreement, International Monetary Fund and International Bank for Reconstruction and Development* (1945), Art. I(ii), p.1.

[6] Arthur Smithies, "Economic Welfare and Policy," *Economics and Public Policy* (1955), pp. 1–2.

stable price level—from being subordinated in the United Nations to full employment as an objective. Vice versa, the concentration of the United Nations on full employment and the maintenance of effective demand provides a counterweight to the preoccupation of the Fund with monetary factors and exchange and budgetary policies.

Whereas the International Monetary Fund was intended to serve as a source of credit for members in temporary balance-of-payments difficulties, the International Bank for Reconstruction and Development has been concerned with stability from a longer-range point of view. Article I(iii) of the charter of the Bank charged it with promoting "the long-range balanced growth of international trade and the maintenance of equilibrium in balances of payments by encouraging international investment for the development of the productive resources of members, thereby assisting in raising productivity, the standard of living, and conditions of labor." As pointed out earlier in this volume, the Bank has inevitably become deeply concerned with the prospects for stability, avoidance of inflation, and attainment of balance-of-payments equilibrium on the part of potential borrowers.[7] It has been less concerned with stability problems from the global, theoretical point of view.

ILO and FAO

The International Labour Organisation antedates the Bank and Fund by twenty-five years. Its views on the unemployment problem illustrate the profound changes in economic thinking that have occurred since 1919. When the ILO was founded, the prevailing view was that the economy was basically self-directing through the operation of the natural forces of supply and demand. Governmental activity was looked upon mainly as interference with natural forces, and the sphere within which it was expected to operate was confined primarily to a compensatory public works policy. The ILO Constitution consequently provided simply that "the prevention of unemployment" should be one of the major objectives of the agency.[8]

A quarter of a century later, the emphasis had shifted, and the 1944 Declaration of Philadelphia recognized "the solemn obligation of the International Labour Organisation to further among the nations of the

[7] See above, Chap. IV.

[8] International Labour Organisation, *Fourth Report . . . to the United Nations*, pp. 22–23.

world programmes which will achieve full employment and the raising of standards of living." The statements on full-employment policy approved by the International Labour Conference in 1944 and 1945 contrast sharply with the more limited view taken after the First World War, and opened the doors to a far wider range of activities.[9]

The ILO in recent years has given consideration to the statistical and institutional requirements for carrying out a policy of full employment. It has consistently emphasized that modern economic analysis distinguishes three major types of unemployment: (1) frictional and seasonal unemployment—inevitable in any economy where consumers are free to change their tastes, producers are free to improve their methods of production, and workers may move from one job or industry to another; (2) unemployment arising from shortages of raw materials and capital—either from short-run shortages as an aftermath of war destruction and disorganization, or from more persistent capital shortages, as in the underdeveloped countries; and (3) general unemployment arising from a deficiency in aggregate demand.[10] Discussions in the United Nations have emphasized the third type of unemployment, characteristic of the major industrial countries in the 1930's, although the underdeveloped countries have been concerned primarily with the second kind. The ILO has made modest but useful contributions to the diagnosis and treatment of all three types of unemployment.

Apart from its general policy statements on full employment, the ILO has pioneered in the adoption of concrete measures, which, although subsidiary, can contribute to the maintenance of employment at a high level. These relate to the organization of the labor market and include such questions as the organization of employment services, vocational training, vocational guidance, and migration. In each of these fields the International Labour Conference has adopted international conventions, recommendations, or resolutions that have facilitated the spread of successful techniques from the more advanced to the less advanced countries.[11]

The particular concern of the Food and Agriculture Organization with problems of economic stability, apart from its general concern with the attainment of a proper balance between agricultural and

[9] *Ibid.*, pp. 22 and 26.

[10] *Ibid.*, p. 29.

[11] For a full description of these ILO activities, see the ILO reply to the United Nations questionnaire on "National and International Action to Achieve or Maintain Full Employment and Economic Stability," Doc. E/1111/Add. 1 (Feb. 16, 1949). Also, see below, Chap. VII.

industrial development, arises from "excessive" fluctuations in the availabilities and prices of agricultural commodities. Mitigation of these fluctuations involves consideration of such measures as buffer-stock maintenance, production and consumption controls, surplus disposal schemes, and other commodity control arrangements.

At the discussions of the Preparatory Committee for an International Trade Organization, consideration was given to proposals for vesting in the FAO the responsibility for commodity agreements on agricultural products. The decision of the committee, however, was that commodity agreements should be handled in the context of general commercial policy and allocated to the prospective ITO. Pending establishment of the ITO, the interim arrangements described elsewhere in this study were made, and the FAO was brought into the picture through its authority to nominate one of the members of the Interim Coordinating Committee for International Commodity Arrangements.[12] More recently, the FAO interest in international economic stability has taken the form of a lively concern with surplus disposal arrangements, both from the point of view of the threat to stability posed by ill-considered schemes and the opportunity to promote the general welfare by a constructive disposition of accumulated surpluses.

Although a number of agencies have thus been concerned with aspects of the stability problem, over-all responsibility for developing recommendations to prevent the international spread of recessions has been left to the United Nations Economic and Social Council.

Consideration of Employment and Stability Problems in the United Nations, 1946–49

Eager to implement the full-employment provision of the Charter, the United Nations Economic and Social Council, at its first session in January–February 1946, established an oddly named subsidiary, the Economic and Employment Commission. At its second session in mid-1946, the Council made the new, fifteen-man commission responsible for advising it on "the prevention of wide fluctuations in economic activity and the promotion of full employment by the coordination of national full-employment policies and by international action."[13]

[12] See above, Chap. III.

[13] U.N. General Assembly, First Session, Second Part, *Official Records*, Supplement No. 2, "Report by the Economic and Social Council to the General Assembly," p. 8.

Subcommission on Employment and Economic Stability

The Economic and Employment Commission, in turn, was directed by the Council to establish a Subcommission on Employment and Economic Stability. After some difficulty, it was decided that the subcommission should have seven members, and that they should serve as "individual experts." The instructions that the commission gave them merit quoting in full:

1. To report to the Commission as early as possible on current world economic conditions and trends, giving particular attention to any factors that are preventing, or are likely to prevent in the near future, the maintenance of full employment and economic stability, together with analyses indicating causal factors involved and recommendations as to desirable action.

2. To report to the Commission at its early convenience on:

(a) The preliminary views of the Sub-commission concerning the kinds of international action which are likely to be feasible and of assistance in maintaining economic stability and full employment. In this connexion the Subcommission should bear in mind important links between stability and development and should examine such proposals as:

(i) The concerted timing, to the extent which might be appropriate and practicable in the interests of employment policy, of national and international measures to influence credit conditions and the terms of borrowing;

(ii) National or international arrangements, in suitable cases, to promote due stability in the real incomes of producers of primary products, taking account both of the interests of consumers and producers regardless of country;

(iii) The timing, to the extent appropriate and practicable in the interests of employment policy, of capital expenditures on projects that are either of an international character or are internationally financed; as well as the expansion of investments in less developed countries as measures designed to maintain stability of employment during periods of depression in more highly industrialized countries.[14]

Noteworthy in these instructions are several themes that recur, with variations, throughout the life of the commission and its subcommission, as well as in the Council and the General Assembly. One is the importance of international action, the assumption that new kinds of international action would be desirable and feasible in maintaining economic stability and full employment. Another is the stress on "important links between stability and development." That the economic development of underdeveloped areas can contribute to the maintenance of stability and full employment in the industrialized areas is

[14] U.N. General Assembly, Second Session, *Official Records*, Supplement No. 3, "Report by the Economic and Social Council to the General Assembly," p. 9.

usually conceded. It may reasonably be doubted, however, whether the two are as inseparably linked, from a strictly economic point of view, as they are made to appear in United Nations reports and debates.

Illustrative of the overlapping interests of different international agencies and the compromises of national viewpoints that result in ambiguous, if not meaningless, language is paragraph 2(a)(ii) giving the subcommission a role in the commodity agreement field. Atypical in United Nations literature, it should be added, is the apparent taking for granted in paragraph 2(a)(iii) of "periods of depression in more highly industrialized countries." Although delegates fully expected a recurrence of depression, they preferred in their resolutions to speak of "recession," "decline in effective demand," or "undue fluctuations."

Most of the first formal report of the Subcommission on Employment and Economic Stability to the commission and the Council was devoted, not to the long-term problem of maintaining effective demand, but to the more immediate problem of inflation. In the years 1946–48, the control of accumulated inflationary pressures and the restoration of wartime devastation were the most pressing issues. Although the report of the subcommission contributed but little to either the economic analysis of inflation or the knowledge of techniques for dealing with it, the report did help to focus the attention of the United Nations on the problem.

By 1948–49, the inflationary threat was beginning to subside, and pockets of unemployment were appearing in various countries. Enthusiasm for international action was likewise waning in some of the key areas. The report drafted by the subcommission in April 1949 was pessimistic about both the psychological climate and the economic outlook. It recalled the magnificent efforts made before the end of the war to establish effective machinery for international economic collaboration and concluded on the nostalgic note that such movements are likely to occur "only on rare occasions such as the union of nations in a war for all they hold dear."[15]

The subcommission was troubled by certain evidences of disillusion and return to nationalistic policies. First, the replies to an employment questionnaire circulated by the Secretary-General convinced the subcommission that "few nations now put their main reliance on international cooperation in the event of serious depression." Second, most

[15] U.N. Subcommission on Employment and Economic Stability, *Report of the Third Session*, Doc. E/CN.1/66 (Apr. 26, 1949), para. 27.

nations at that time envisaged a resort to import restrictions, although outlawry of this form of beggar-my-neighbor policy had been a basic objective of postwar planners. Third, despite wartime efforts to assure that remedial measures would be of an expansionist character serving to increase demand rather than restrict supply, other parts of the world could be expected to parallel American agricultural restrictions should the oversupply of primary products become general.[16] Discussions on the problem of primary products had been "disappointing." The International Bank seemed to the subcommission "a useful but a minor addition to existing financial machinery at a time when world uncertainty makes venture capital extremely unventuresome."[17]

To correct the situation, the subcommission recommended vigorous efforts to negotiate commodity agreements, reconsideration of the Articles of Agreement of both the Bank and Fund, and new international consultations at the highest level to review the activities and policies of all the organizations involved in maintaining full employment.

Economic and Employment Commission and the Council

The Economic and Employment Commission, more sensitive to jurisdictional issues than the experts on the subcommission, commented to the Economic and Social Council that the desirability of revising the Articles of Agreement of the Bank and of the Fund was, in its view, a question to be dealt with only by those specialized agencies. The Economic and Employment Commission also rejected the proposal for early high-level consultations, and suggested instead that the Council consider convening special sessions of the commission should the world economic situation warrant it.[18]

The employment situation was on the agenda of the Council in 1949, not only via the reports of its subsidiaries, but also because the Communist-controlled World Federation of Trade Unions (WFTU) had proposed as an agenda item "Unemployment and Full Employment." The motivation behind the action of the WFTU was obvious, and the opportunity was fully exploited by the spokesmen of the Soviet bloc.

[16] *Ibid.*, para. 31.
[17] *Ibid.*, para. 32.
[18] U.N. General Assembly, Fourth Session, *Official Records*, Supplement No. 3, "Report of the Economic and Social Council Covering the Period from 30 August 1948 to 15 August 1949," pp. 24–25.

All members of the Council agreed that there had been some increase in unemployment, but there was considerable difference of opinion regarding the importance and the causes of the increase. The majority, led by the United Kingdom, felt that although the decline in employment might be of a temporary character, countries should be prepared to deal with it promptly if the necessity for action arose; at the first sign of a recession the United Nations should be prepared to review the situation. Some members, including the United States, stressed that unemployment in their countries reflected a healthy readjustment to peacetime conditions and was purely temporary. Others, led by the Soviet Union, considered that unemployment was already critical and that concrete measures should be taken immediately by the Council to restore full employment and "to protect workers from the effects of unemployment."[19]

Following this inconclusive debate, the Council adopted a noncommittal resolution recommending to the General Assembly the inclusion on the agenda of its next session of an item on measures for promoting full employment and economic stability.[20] More important, the Council invited the Secretary-General to appoint a small group of experts to prepare a report on national and international measures required to achieve full employment.[21] This was to result in the significant and controversial document discussed below. The Council also adopted a resolution urging governments to give any anticyclical measures they might adopt a form that would promote the economic development of underdeveloped countries—once again linking full employment with economic development, primarily to satisfy the demands of the underdeveloped countries.[22]

In addition, the Council considered recommendations from the Economic and Employment Commission on organizational matters. The commission recommended that the Subcommission on Employment and Economic Stability, as well as the Subcommission on Economic Development, be abolished. Instead, the Secretariat should assist the commission directly and should be strengthened by *ad hoc* groups of experts and by individual experts selected by the Secretary-General. The commission complained that it had been handicapped by inadequate contact with current developments and concrete prob-

[19] *Ibid.*, p. 25.

[20] Res. 221F(IX), Aug. 11, 1949.

[21] Res. 221E(IX), Aug. 11, 1949.

[22] Res. 221D(IX), Aug. 10, 1949. A similar resolution was adopted by the General Assembly at its fourth session, Res. 308(IV), Nov. 25, 1949.

lems. The recommendation for abolition of the laboriously created subcommissions was tabled for a year, but was accepted by the Council in 1950.

The dissatisfaction of the commission with the work of its subcommission stemmed in part from the original illusion that members nominated by governments would act as "experts" rather than as representatives of governments. In fact, of course, many of them did not—and perhaps could not—act in such fashion, and even their *expertise* was dubious in some cases. The decision to substitute *ad hoc* groups of bona fide experts selected by the Secretary-General raised the possibility that the experts would reflect the biases, if any, of the secretariat, but nevertheless was a move to obtain reports of a higher order of economic analysis, relatively unmarred by the intrusion of political considerations. At the same time, the disappointment of the commission with its subcommission was to some extent a function of its own naiveté. The commission, for example, had directed its subcommission to give particular attention to the problem of recognizing incipient downturns in economic activity, and had been annoyed by the inability of the subcommission to prepare promptly a significant report on the subject. Yet economists have long been baffled and continue to be baffled by the difficulty of determining which are the key economic indicators, when changes in those indicators presage a downturn, and whether the downturn, if it occurs, will be long and deep, short and sharp, or long and mild.

Regional Commissions

The complaint of the commission about its own "inadequate contact with current developments and concrete problems" touched upon a real weakness of the world-wide functional commissions.[23] Their deliberations too often appeared to take place in a vacuum, where they dealt with abstract conceptions, divorced from firm connections with the pressing issues in specific countries or regions. While the Economic and Employment Commission and its subcommissions were withering on the vine, the United Nations regional commissions, with their larger and more active secretariats, were deepening their roots and flourishing.

In fact, some of the most concrete and specific contributions to the discussions of full employment and economic stability were prepared by the secretariats of the Economic Commission for Europe (ECE)

[23] U.N. General Assembly, Fourth Session, *Official Records*, Supplement No. 3, p. 26.

and the Economic Commission for Latin America (ECLA). Their annual economic surveys quickly became authoritative source books, rich in data, penetrating in analysis, provocative, sometimes irritating, and usually more influential than the *World Economic Report* issued by the headquarters office. Although the *World Economic Report* also provided information on employment and unemployment, prices and wages, trade and balances of payments, it concentrated more on description than analysis, tended to accept official statistics at their face value somewhat more readily than did the regional surveys, eschewed forecasts, and avoided evaluations of the efficacy of economic policies being pursued by governments.

The *Economic Survey of Europe in 1949*, compiled by the ECE secretariat, brought to light a formidable array of data, analyzed in stimulating fashion, on the situation and prospects of the European economy. Characteristically pessimistic in tone was the lengthy chapter entitled "The Continuing Problem of International Equilibrium," bearing the main message of the volume. Looking ahead to 1952 and the scheduled end of United States aid under the European Recovery Program, the authors foresaw trouble for the rest of the world. Achievement of equilibrium at a high and expanding level required more foresight and planning than was likely to be forthcoming. Balance at a lower level would jeopardize living standards and probably require trade and payments restrictions on a sizable scale. This view was both challenged and supported in plenary meetings of the commission.

The *Economic Survey of Latin America, 1949*, similarly brought together information dealing with employment and unemployment in Latin America, and the relations of fluctuations in production and exports of Latin American nations to recessions elsewhere. The main thesis of the survey was that the exports of Latin American countries were not in 1949, and were not likely to become, great enough to provide for the expected increases in population and to pay for the imports needed for economic development. The conclusion drawn from this thesis was that there would continue to be a persistent tendency toward disequilibrium in Latin America, a generalization that the survey found it necessary to qualify when it came to analyze economic conditions in specific Latin American countries. Moreover, as the United States delegation pointed out when the survey was under discussion at the Economic and Social Council, it tended to postulate a rapid rate of economic development in Latin America and to take for granted a high rate of population growth instead of investigating what the rates might be if economic development in Latin America were to proceed in a fashion more analogous to that of Western Europe and the United States.[24]

The situation with respect to full employment and economic stability problems in the United Nations as of the close of 1949 may be summarized briefly as follows:

1. The architects of the postwar international structure, working in the long shadow of the 1929–32 depression, had been preoccupied with the avoidance of cumulative deflation, but the initial postwar years were in fact characterized mainly by persistent inflationary pressures.

2. The subsidiary structure created by the Economic and Social Council to advise it on employment and stability questions—an Economic and Employment Commission of government representatives and a smaller "expert" Subcommission on Employment and Economic Stability—was proving unsatisfactory and destined soon to die.

3. By way of replacement, provision had been made for an *ad hoc* group of experts appointed by the Secretary-General to prepare a special report on *National and International Measures for Full Employment*, the first of a distinguished series of United Nations reports to be issued by such groups.

4. Basic information on economic conditions throughout the world was being provided by the regular Secretariat, most notably in the annual economic surveys of the regional commissions and in the *World Economic Report*.

5. By 1949, inflationary pressures were subsiding and signs of deflation were appearing. There was little confidence in the ability of the international economy to withstand even minor shocks and great pessimism abroad about the ability of the United States to avoid depression. Between June 1948 and June 1949, industrial production in the United States fell 12 per cent, and unemployment increased by 1.5 million. Between the fourth quarter of 1948 and the second quarter of 1949, the value of United States imports fell by 15 per cent, thus substantially reducing the dollar earnings of a dollar-short world.[25]

[24] U.N. Economic and Social Council, Eleventh Session, *Official Records*, 401st Meeting (Aug. 7, 1950), pp. 230–32.

[25] U.N. Department of Economic Affairs, *National and International Measures for Full Employment*, Report by a Group of Experts Appointed by the Secretary-General, Doc. E/1584 (Dec. 22, 1949), pp. 8, 9. (Hereinafter cited as *Measures for Full Employment.*) Shortly after publication of these figures, a less disquieting and better-balanced review of 1948–49 developments in the United States economy was given to United Nations Members by the United States representative to the tenth session

This gave rise to demands in the United Nations for improved international machinery to help nations withstand cyclical fluctuations and, in the absence of any steps to meet those demands, to the threat of a return to more narrowly nationalist policies.

6. In retrospect, the skepticism of the United States delegates concerning the need for immediate measures to strengthen the international institutional framework was vindicated by the course of events. The United States recession was short-lived, and the economy had regained its momentum even before the added stimulation of the Korean boom took effect. The pockets of unemployment in member countries vanished as well, and the Soviet announcement of a new and worse capitalist depression turned out, once more, to be premature.

Consideration of Employment and Stability Problems Since 1950

In the consideration of full employment and economic stability problems by organs of the United Nations, a high-water mark was registered in 1950 in terms of comprehensiveness of proposals considered, eminence of the group that put forward the proposals, and level of the debate concerning them. In the end, governments rejected the specific innovations that were suggested, but enlarged the area of consultation and raised their sights in the process.

The discussions during 1950 were based on a report prepared by five distinguished economists appointed by the United Nations Secretary-General pursuant to a resolution adopted by the Economic and Social Council during the preceding summer.[26] This report, which was entitled *National and International Measures for Full Employment*, soon became known as the Kaldor Report. Its recommendations were discussed with more than customary frankness in the United Nations because of the absence of delegates from states in the Soviet bloc, which were protesting the continued recognition of the National Government of

---

of the Economic and Social Council. In his statement on the World Economic Situation, he included data on total United States production as well as industrial production and on exports and aid as well as imports. See United States Mission to the United Nations, Press Release No. 812 (Feb. 21, 1950), p. 4.

[26] Res. 221E(IX), Aug. 11, 1949. The five economists were: John Maurice Clark, Professor of Economics at Columbia University, who worked in association with Arthur Smithies, Professor of Economics at Harvard; Nicholas Kaldor, Fellow of King's College, Cambridge; Pierre Uri, Economic and Financial Adviser to the *Commissariat Général du Plan*, Paris; and E. Ronald Walker, Economic Adviser to the Australian Department of External Affairs.

China. This made it feasible for representatives of the free nations to air differences of view that they would have been reluctant to expose to Soviet exploitation. Moreover, these representatives at the 1950 sessions of the Economic and Employment Commission and the Economic and Social Council were themselves more competent in the field of economics than their colleagues at other sessions. The Soviet boycott of the United Nations had ended, however, when the Economic and Social Council held its debates on full-employment during the years 1951–54. For this and other reasons brought out later, the debates of the Council on the subject never resulted in the systematic international review of national policies and programs for which a groundwork had been established in 1950.

After the rejection of the bold recommendations of the Kaldor Report, alternative measures for cushioning the international impact of recessions were proposed, and the report of a second group of experts was published in late 1951. This second report, which was entitled *Measures for International Economic Stability*, became known as the Angell Report and was considered by the Economic and Social Council in 1952.[27] The report proposed international action to complete a series of long-term commodity agreements, to enlarge the flow of international capital, and to increase the monetary reserves of countries other than the United States.

The recommendation for renewed efforts to negotiate multilateral commodity agreements coincided with the collapse of the post-Korean boom in raw material prices and precipitated a comprehensive discussion of general commodity problems. The quest for greater stability in primary commodity trade continued to occupy a prominent place on the international agenda from 1952 on, but the problem remains unsolved.

National and International Measures for Full Employment

The authors of the Kaldor Report painted with broad strokes and avoided qualifying details. They placed primary reliance on quantita-

[27] U.N. Department of Economic Affairs, *Measures for International Economic Stability*, Report by a Group of Experts Appointed by the Secretary-General, Doc. E/2156, ST/ECA/13 (Nov. 27, 1951). (Hereafter cited as *Measures for Economic Stability.*) The experts were: James W. Angell of Columbia University; G. D. A. MacDougall of Oxford University; Javier Marquez, Alternate Executive Director, International Monetary Fund, and formerly Professor at the National School of Economics, Mexico; Hla Myint, of Oxford University, and formerly of the University of Rangoon; Trevor W. Swan, Australian National University.

tive indicators. Their great fear was that action to correct unemployment would be delayed disastrously if it were not triggered automatically. Their aim, accordingly, was to identify the signals for automatic corrective action and the type of action to follow once the alarms were sounded. They were far more concrete regarding measures to avoid deflation than they were regarding measures to avoid inflation. The effect of their recommendations was to place on the United States chief responsibility for the maintenance and underwriting of stability.

The experts included recommendations for domestic and for international action, with primary emphasis on the former. As a first line of defense against unemployment, they recommended that each government establish and announce a full-employment target and a program to maintain employment at the target level. The second line of defense was to be a set of automatic countermeasures for application if the maintenance program failed. The third was an elaborate international scheme to sustain foreign trade and investment if the domestic countermeasures did not succeed in doing so.

It was urged that in industrialized countries the full-employment target be stated in terms of the smallest percentage of unemployment among wage-earners that the country could reasonably hope to maintain in the light of seasonal movements and structural changes in the economy. If the full-employment program of a government failed to prevent unemployment from exceeding the target percentage by a predetermined amount for three successive months, compensatory measures should be applied automatically. The measures should be capable of raising effective demand promptly and throughout the economy. The case the experts made for automatic action was that government officials would otherwise wait too long and do too little. Furthermore, the guarantee of countermeasures would promote confidence, which, in turn, would contribute to stability.

The international recommendations of the experts were conceptually more novel. They were designed to eliminate the "structural disequilibrium in world trade"; to establish a stable flow of international investment to underdeveloped countries; and to stabilize the flow of international trade.

The Kaldor Report did not explain what it meant by the establishment of a new equilibrium in world trade. What it advocated was a more orderly arrangement, through international meetings of an Expert Advisory Commission under the Economic and Social Council, for harmonizing the import and export, and the lending and borrowing, plans of governments. Deficit countries (*i.e.*, countries that were unable to finance imports from export earnings) would declare the amounts by which they desired to raise their earnings from exports or reduce their expenditures for imports. Surplus countries (*e.g.*, the United States, which was then enjoying a substantial excess of exports over imports) would declare the amounts by which they would raise their disbursements for imports, the extent to which they would curtail their exports, and the amount of long-term lending they would undertake. By an undefined process of mutual adjustment, a new balance at a high level of trade would be negotiated.

The program for stabilizing the flow of long-term lending would require the lending countries to fix annual targets for their long-term international investments for five years ahead. Shortfalls on the part of private investors would be offset by contributions of public funds. Unless loaned directly by governments, those public funds would be placed at the disposal of the International Bank. The Bank would set up a new department for lending them to underdeveloped countries.

International trade would be stabilized in somewhat similar fashion. If, in any given year, the imports of a particular country fell because of a decline in effective demand within its borders, and this fall were not fully offset by a decline in the value of its current exports of goods and services, it would deposit with the International Monetary Fund an amount equal to the fall in its imports less the fall in its exports in the given year as compared with a reference year, which would normally be the preceding year. The Fund would lend these deposits to the affected countries in appropriate amounts so that the latter would not be forced willy-nilly to curtail their imports. This would prevent the cumulative contraction that occurs when country A, because of failure to maintain full employment at home, reduces its imports, thereby reducing the export earnings of countries B, C, and D, which might in turn be forced to contract their own imports and thus add to the difficulties of country A.

The Economic and Employment Commission, meeting only a month after publication of the Kaldor Report, reviewed it in a preliminary way and, without making substantive recommendations to the Economic and Social Council, posed a number of searching questions. The Council, at its tenth session in February–March 1950, heard some additional comments and urged governments to study the report further so that they would be ready to express their considered views at the eleventh session in the summer of 1950. By that time, the Council had before it a 225-page report from the ILO, which was designed to complement the Kaldor Report.[28] Whereas the recommendations of the Kaldor Report dealt mainly with measures to stimulate effective demand, the ILO report reminded the Council that "full employment is likely to intensify certain economic problems, notably how to maintain flexibility and efficiency in production and how to avoid inflation."[29] It also included advice on the reduction of seasonal unemployment, the transfer of workers to new jobs, and the special employment problems of underdeveloped countries.

The proposals of the Kaldor Report were hotly debated from the point of view of technical adequacy, economic desirability, and political feasibility. Among the major issues raised were the following:

1. Automaticity versus discretion. Is it possible to rely on formulae to the extent that the experts did? Is the advantage of a precisely formulated series of commitments regarding steps to be taken illusory and, in the words of a leading American economist, likely to be offset by the disadvantage of "substantial uncertainty as to the economic consequences of these steps in relation to the fundamental objective of preventing serious unemployment"?[30]

2. Freedom versus controls. Would the network of regulations required to implement the plan of the experts discourage initiative and sacrifice important freedoms? Would countries make adequate efforts to export if trade deficits were covered semi-automatically? Would countries in need of foreign investment try to attract private funds if the governments of creditor nations were committed to make up with public funds any shortfalls in private foreign investment?

3. Relationship between full employment and other United Nations objectives. The United Nations Charter grouped three related objectives: "higher standards of living, full employment, and conditions of economic and social progress and development."[31] Did the experts give primacy to full employment to the detriment of other objectives, such as economic expansion, economic efficiency, and the establishment of a multilateral trading system? Was too little attention given to the dangers of inflation, particularly suppressed inflation, and to the relations between wages, prices, and profits?

4. Allocation of responsibility to the United States and the rest of

[28] International Labour Organisation, *Action Against Unemployment*, Studies and Reports, New Series, No. 20 (1950).

[29] *Ibid.*, p. 3.

[30] Jacob Viner, "Full Employment at Whatever Cost," *Quarterly Journal of Economics*, Vol. 64 (August 1950), p. 395.

[31] Art. 55(a).

the world. Was solution of the dollar problem primarily the job of the United States? Was it realistic to expect the United States, if it proved unable to stabilize its own economy, nevertheless to provide other countries with the sizable sums they might in more prosperous years have earned from sales to the United States?

The representatives of the United States, the United Kingdom, and Canada were most prominent in the debates. Important roles were played also by the representatives of Denmark and France; by the representative of Australia who had served as one of the five experts; by another of the experts, Nicholas Kaldor, who, although lacking any authorization to speak on behalf of the experts as a group, was invited by the Council to participate in a personal capacity; and by representatives of the Bank and the Fund. The underdeveloped countries, some of which had also discussed the experts' report at the Economic Commission for Latin America, considered the key recommendations inapplicable to them, and this point was conceded by the United States, the United Kingdom, and Canada.

In so far as recommendations for domestic action were concerned, the United Kingdom delegation fully accepted the report of the experts. The representatives of the British Labour Government declared that: "The maintenance of full employment was not just a desirable aim; it was the cornerstone of its [Britain's] whole economic policy, a top priority objective which it must achieve by every means consistent with the preservation of the country's freedoms."[32]

The Canadians were more cautious, on both philosophic and technical grounds. They said they were unwilling to overemphasize full employment at the expense of stability and other objectives of the Charter. Moreover, they could not accept the recommendation for establishing a maximum percentage of unemployment as the triggering device for a host of compensatory measures because they could not put it into effect. In similar vein, the Danish representative suggested that the experts might advantageously have paid greater attention to the pursuit of full employment as a means of securing maximum production and income rather than as a goal in itself. In his opinion, the strong influence of Keynes had led the experts to overemphasize the need for expansion and confine themselves too exclusively to the negative question of how to avoid unemployment. He praised the ILO report for having placed greater stress than did the United Nations experts

[32] U.N. Economic and Social Council, Eleventh Session, *Official Records*, 390th Meeting (July 17, 1950), p. 113.

on the profit expectation and, therefore, on wage-price relationships as a main factor in determining private investment. He stated that he had received the impression that the experts at times had been less concerned with correcting the disequilibrium of which unemployment was a symptom "than with the suppression of that symptom alone, and indeed in such a manner that real adjustment of the underlying factors or of the structure of production was unlikely to take place."[33]

The mechanical nature of the proposed compensatory arrangement was criticized by the United States on the ground that every economic crisis has its own characteristics. "In . . . a complex economy, where unemployment can arise from a multiplicity of causes, simple mechanical devices, however ingenious, are not likely to do the job. Rather than solve the problem by a formula, we propose to place our major reliance upon the preparation of a variety of programs for adoption in appropriate combination in the case of threatening recession or depression."[34]

Although official representatives of the Soviet nations were not present during the 1950 discussions, their viewpoint was expressed by the representative of the World Federation of Trade Unions. According to the WFTU, the Charter required the United Nations to promote full employment, meaning zero unemployment. Therefore, when the experts recognized an unemployment rate of some 2 to 5 per cent of the labor force as a reasonable minimum, they were in effect advocating a violation of the Charter. The problem of full employment, according to the WFTU, had been solved only "in the Soviet Union and the people's democracies, where the harmonious development of planned economy was accompanied by a constant rise in income, productivity, and employment."[35] In stark contrast to this idyllic condition stood the worsening situation under capitalism.

This was the line consistently taken by delegates of the Soviet bloc in United Nations discussions of full employment and economic stability, and it was one of the reasons later discussions proved so frustrating.

The international measures proposed by the experts, involving novel

[33] U.N. Economic and Social Council, Tenth Session, *Official Records*, 357th Meeting (Feb. 20, 1950), pp. 85–86.

[34] Statement by United States Representative on the U.N. Experts Report on Full Employment, U.S. Delegation, U.N. Economic and Social Council, Eleventh Session, Press Release No. 2 (July 17, 1950), p. 11.

[35] U.N. Economic and Social Council, Eleventh Session, *Official Records*, 391st Meeting (July 18, 1950), p. 143.

and intricate arrangements for stabilizing the flow of investment and trade, were also vigorously debated. By stressing technical difficulties in implementing these proposals, speakers kept the debate on a high, nonpartisan plane. Equally apparent, however, was the fact that the nations on which the main financial burdens would fall (primarily the United States) were not prepared to underwrite what seemed to them questionable and costly schemes for maintaining international stability.

By far the most important feature of the international program advocated by the experts was the proposal for stabilizing the flow of international trade. The United States delegation said it was unable to accept the proposal that countries suffering depression be obliged automatically to deposit with the International Monetary Fund currency to which others would have automatic drawing rights. In its view, there was no simple method by which the Fund would be able to determine to what extent a reduction in imports in any one country was the result of a decline in effective demand and to what extent it might be due to changes in technology, inappropriate exchange rates, or restrictive policies abroad. Early introduction of a trade stabilization plan might merely aggravate the existing disequilibrium by enabling deficit countries with inconvertible currencies to continue to import goods without making the readjustments necessary for balancing their economies and trading levels. Even the Australian Government, the delegate of which to the Economic and Social Council had served as one of the experts, found that the particular scheme he had helped to draft raised "a number of practical difficulties."[36]

The United Kingdom preferred measures whereby a country suffering from a fall in effective demand would take special steps to stimulate imports, thus maintaining employment levels in the export industries of other countries. However, it was prepared to support a scheme along the lines of the experts' proposal whereby the depression country would enable other countries to maintain their imports despite declines in their export earnings.

The proposal for stabilizing foreign lending by stepping up the public contribution to offset any decline in private lending ran into numerous objections from potential lenders, although it was naturally approved by the underdeveloped countries. The remaining international recommendation of the experts was for the creation of an advisory commission to establish a new structural equilibrium in world trade. This recommendation came at a moment when the Council was determined to

[36] *Ibid.*, p. 137.

reduce and consolidate its subsidiary structure, and neither among the underdeveloped countries nor among the industrialized nations was there active support for the proposed commission.[37]

In the lengthy, four-part resolution finally adopted by the Council, earlier American-British-Canadian differences were compromised, and none of the rigidity of the recommendations of the experts was incorporated.[38] The first two parts of the resolution, dealing with domestic full-employment standards, however, broke new ground in formalizing the obligations of Member governments to subject their domestic policies to international scrutiny. An American proposal for the annual consideration by the Council of the problem of achieving and maintaining full employment and balance-of-payments equilibrium was adopted, effective in 1951. Each government was urged: (1) to publish annually a statement of its economic objectives, accompanied wherever practicable, by a statement of quantitative goals or forecasts relating to employment, production, consumption, investment, and other pertinent measurable, economic factors; (2) to publish its full-employment standard; (3) to formulate, announce, and periodically review the policies, programs, and techniques that it intended to pursue for the purpose of achieving its objectives. The Secretary-General was asked to obtain by questionnaire full information concerning the above matters, and to assemble and analyze the information for the consideration of the Economic, Employment and Development Commission and the Council. The International Labour Organisation was encouraged to continue its efforts to facilitate international comparability of employment and unemployment data.

The international provisions in the third and fourth parts of the resolution included a series of general exhortations to governments to achieve and maintain equilibrium in their balances of payments, at high levels of trade and investment, and with minimum restrictions; to avoid actions adversely affecting the economies of other countries; to provide statistical information to the Secretary-General; to co-operate in investigating ways and means of preventing domestic recessions from

[37] At its eleventh session, the Economic and Social Council abolished the Subcommission on Employment and Economic Stability and the Subcommission on Economic Development, and renamed the Economic and Employment Commission the Economic, Employment and Development Commission. Res. 295(XI), Aug. 12 and 16, 1950.

[38] At the outset of the discussion at the eleventh session of the Council, separate draft full-employment resolutions had been introduced by the representatives of the United States, the United Kingdom, and Canada. Res. 290(XI), adopted Aug. 15, 1950, borrowed from all three drafts.

spreading internationally; and to facilitate migration and the international mobility of labor. At the same time, the International Bank was urged to achieve and maintain a high and stable rate of lending in ordinary circumstances and, if possible, to expand the volume of its lending in periods of recession. The International Monetary Fund was urged to make its resources available to members to meet needs arising from economic recessions "as fully and readily as its Articles of Agreement permit."

These two parts of the resolution also opened employment opportunities for three new groups of "independent experts": one to prepare a special report on unemployment and underemployment in underdeveloped countries; another to analyze government replies to a special balance-of-payments questionnaire called for in the resolution but, by later action of the Council, postponed indefinitely; and a third to formulate and analyze "alternative practical ways of dealing with the problem of reducing the international impact of recessions."[39]

The resolution adopted by the Council in 1950 was believed at the time to represent a significant step toward fulfillment of the full-employment pledge in Article 55 of the Charter. The Secretary-General was accordingly asked to give wide publicity to this resolution. It should be noted, however, that the chief obligation that it placed on Members was the obligation to provide information for review and comment by the Secretariat, by independent experts, and by delegates of other governments. The success of the exercise would depend both on the degree to which nations filed meaningful data and on the degree to which common standards of value, common objectives, and homogeneity of outlook in other respects were shared by the parties engaged in the collective review.

Measures for International Economic Stability

The 1950 resolution on full employment provided no real guidance for the new group of experts commissioned to devise alternative practical measures for cushioning the international impact of domestic recessions. An amendment to that resolution adopted at the twelfth session of the Economic and Social Council proved no remedy for this deficiency. It asked the new group to include in its report recommendations for establishing and maintaining "appropriate relations between

[39] Res. 290(XI), Aug. 15, 1950, para. 19.

prices of raw materials, on the one hand, and essential manufactured goods on the other, and thus to ensure greater economic stability."[40] This reflected the deep concern of underdeveloped countries on account of declining raw material prices, their desire for an international parity scheme, and their growing power in United Nations forums. In view of the known opposition of industrialized countries to any parity scheme, however, the amendment could hardly be regarded as pointing the way to feasible and acceptable methods for mitigating the international impact of recessions.

Although the new report—the Angell Report—which was published in late 1951, was favorably received by many who were sharply critical of the Kaldor Report, its specific recommendations cannot be said to have fared with notably greater success. The document opened with a timely summary of the problem:

> It is now generally accepted that the major countries have both the will and the means to avoid deep and prolonged depressions. The full employment pledges embodied in the United Nations Charter, and in other national and international instruments, reflect the fact that in one decade the world has taken a long step forward in social attitudes and economic techniques. But we are still living in the shadow of the great depressions of the past. Full employment commitments cannot wipe out overnight the ingrained distrust of dependence upon a many-sided international system, and do not themselves create the complex institutional and economic framework which such a system requires for its working.[41]

The experts recommended international action of three types: the negotiation of multilateral long-term commodity agreements; an expansion of the flow of international capital; and an increase in the monetary reserves of countries other than the United States. Their recommendations in the financial field indicate that the experts shared the dissatisfaction of the Kaldor group with the roles that the Bank and the Fund were then playing, but were less concerned than their predecessors with ensuring absolute stability in the flow of international payments.

As summarized by the Angell Report, the upshot of the recommendations of the Kaldor Report on foreign investment and trade would have been to ensure the availability of a steady flow of foreign exchange on both current account and long-term capital account, the former being protected by supplementary deposits against recessions of effective demand that would reduce the flow of foreign exchange

[40] Res. 341A(XII), Mar. 20, 1951, para. 5.
[41] *Measures for Economic Stability*, para. 1.

below its previous annual peak, and the latter against fluctuations within five-year periods. The Angell group were convinced that some new international provisions working in this general direction were essential.[42]

With respect to the flow of long-term capital, the experts provided fresh support for the advocates of low-interest loans and grants, by stating that a strong case could be made for loans to some of the under-developed countries on especially easy terms as well as for grants. Rigid stabilization of the total flow of long-term capital, however, was neither practicable nor desirable. Nevertheless, the International Bank should be prepared to expand greatly its rate of lending in the event of recession. To be able to do so and to help, as recommended by the experts, in financing buffer stocks set up pursuant to international commodity agreements, the International Bank would need a more reliable source of loan funds than the private investment community. To this end, the experts suggested: (1) increasing, above the 20 per cent authorized by its Articles of Agreement, the portion of the subscribed capital of the Bank actually available for making loans; (2) increasing the total capital itself; or (3) setting up arrangements under which governments or central banks could purchase the securities of the Bank if the need arose. Effective use of the additional capital would, of course, require projects that could be initiated or expanded at the onset of recession. The Bank, it will be recalled, consistently shunned the role of anticyclical safeguard and maintained that it had no business deferring the financing of desirable projects in prosperity in order to execute them in adversity.[43]

The proposal in the Angell Report for helping countries overcome temporary declines in foreign trade earnings,

> . . . unlike the scheme recommended in *National and International Measures for Full Employment*, is basically the equivalent of a once-for-all increase in its members' foreign exchange reserves, which can do no more than enable them to smooth out temporary fluctuations in the availability of foreign exchange. It cannot repeatedly make good the full losses of recession years, and so will not permit any country's payments for imports to exceed in the long run its actual exchange earnings on current and capital account. . . .[44]

The group analyzed in a stimulating and constructive manner the need for reserves in terms of current trade levels and probable swings.

[42] *Ibid.*, paras. 20 and 21.
[43] See above, Chap. IV.
[44] *Measures for Economic Stability*, para. 36.

It concluded that in 1951 the gold and dollar reserves of most countries, together with the "comparatively trivial" supplements available through the International Monetary Fund, were totally inadequate to meet the kind of decline in dollar earnings that could occur during a recession in the United States. Price rises since the creation of the Fund had greatly diminished the real value of its resources. Access to those resources in the event of recession should be greatly liberalized, especially by waiving the rule limiting annual drawings to 25 per cent of the quota of a member, and the resources themselves should be increased. Practical, *i.e.*, political, difficulties might prevent an over-all increase in Fund subscriptions, in which case the Fund ought to be able to rely on borrowing from the country experiencing the major recession, *e.g.*, the United States.

> That country might well take a liberal view of lending its currency to the Fund as a means of preventing unemployment in its export industries, of reducing the need for other countries to take new discriminatory measures against its exports, and of giving effect to the spirit of its international full employment commitments.[45]

In 1952, during consideration of the Angell Report by the Economic and Social Council, there was a large measure of agreement that existing monetary reserves were seriously inadequate. There was agreement that a larger volume of resources and a greater willingness on the part of both governments and the International Monetary Fund to use them freely could help offset the international repercussions of recessions. But the United States, for example, pointed out that the mere availability of additional resources offered no guarantee that a disequilibrium would be corrected. "In the absence of domestic monetary and international trade policies designed to correct the disequilibrium, such additional resources could be very rapidly dissipated."[46] The representative of the Fund reported that the existing resources of the IMF, if regarded as secondary reserves, were not small; that the question of increasing government quotas had been considered but was regarded as premature; and that the Fund believed it could operate with sufficient flexibility to be helpful in a depression with no change in its Articles of Agreement.

Although it is doubtful whether the view presented by the Fund

[45] *Ibid.*, para. 34.

[46] Statement by U.S. Representative in the Economic and Social Council on Agenda Item 4—Report of the Experts on International Stability, U.S. Mission to the United Nations, Press Release No. 1508 (June 30, 1952).

representative was widely shared, the resolution of the Economic and Social Council on the Angell Report,[47] in so far as the Fund and the Bank were concerned, was not essentially different from what the Council had already recommended two years earlier, following its discussion of the Kaldor Report. The Fund was urged to apply its rules flexibly, to give careful consideration to the suggestions made in the Angell Report, to use its resources as promptly and fully as consistent with its Articles of Agreement, to keep under continuing review the question of adequacy of reserves, and to furnish the Economic and Social Council an analysis of this question in 1953.

Although the preamble of the 1952 resolution seemed to support the case for stronger international facilities to mitigate the repercussions of depression, the operative portions foreshadowed no early strengthening. The net effect, therefore, of United Nations consideration of the second report by experts was to leave countries as dependent as before on domestic resources and nationally devised safeguards against depression.

Annual Full-Employment Review

The annual full-employment review, regarded in 1950 as perhaps the most constructive provision of the resolution of the Council on full-employment, appears to have had very little direct influence on policy making at the national or international level. Since 1954, full employment has been dropped as a separate item on the agenda of the Council, although the secretariat has continued to collect information on the subject by questionnaire and to use the replies both for circulation to other governments and for preparation of the annual *World Economic Report.*

During the period 1951 to 1954, the full-employment questionnaire required the submission of narrative as well as statistical information in forms not easy to summarize and evaluate. Governments were slow to respond and on the ground that statements of economic objectives, summaries of plans for preventing undue increases in unemployment, and explanations of inflationary pressures do not change significantly from year to year, merely referred in later years to their early replies to certain questions. The Secretariat's analysis was seldom available soon enough to be of use during the full-employment debate in the Council. The debate took place at the height of the cold war in a public,

[47] Res. 427(XIV), July 10, 1952.

political forum. A similar annual economic review undertaken outside the United Nations framework by a more homogeneous group of nations—the member countries of the Organization for European Economic Cooperation—has been much more fruitful.

At the Economic and Social Council, delegates from the Soviet bloc consistently used the full-employment discussion to exaggerate grossly the levels of unemployment in free-world nations; to predict further worsening of the situation, culminating in collapse at an early date; to charge that rearmament represented a vain attempt to stave off inevitable depression; and to attack, as causes of instability, unemployment, and lower standards of living, the export controls adopted by the West for security reasons. In this atmosphere, hindsight proved as hard to exercise as foresight, and other delegates found themselves fully occupied setting the record straight or redressing it in their favor. They stressed auspicious developments within their domestic economies, minimized weaknesses, and publicized the current economic difficulties of nations in the Soviet bloc. There was no systematic and sympathetic review of the employment problems of different Member governments; no effort to ascertain, through orderly discussion, the pros and cons of alternative solutions; no serious attempt, within the United Nations, to synchronize national employment policies.

To date, the United Kingdom remains the only nation having a specific full-employment standard in strict accord with the recommendations of the Council in 1950. A number of other industrialized nations have fulfilled the recommendation in spirit, if not in letter, but almost certainly in response to domestic rather than international pressures. The United States, for example, explained that although it could fix no definite and unalterable percentage of the labor force as its maximum unemployment level, it made (up to and including 1953) annual announcements of employment goals that served as guides for economic policy. Australia, Canada, Belgium, Denmark, France, New Zealand, and Sweden also advised the Secretariat that they had not adopted fixed, quantitative, full-employment standards, in some cases because of the manner in which their external payments situation had conditioned their ability to maintain high levels of employment at home.

In 1953, the non-Communist, pro-Western International Confederation of Free Trade Unions (ICFTU), fearful that reductions in rearmament expenditures might result in unnecessary unemployment and hardship, asked the Council to give special consideration to "reconversion after the rearmament period." The ICFTU fears were echoed by many delegates to the Council, and there was some sentiment for discussing reconversion policies as a special aspect of the full-employment problem. The United States and the United Kingdom, however, viewed the reconversion problem as basically no different from the problems caused by changes in demand in other sectors of the economy. Consequently, the techniques available for maintaining employment at high levels could be used in the event of reconversion difficulties in the same manner as in the event of difficulties arising from other causes. This view was ultimately accepted by the Council.[48]

In 1953, at the same time that the specter of deflation was being raised by the ICFTU, the Swedish Government was reviving a plea made a year earlier that the Council consider concrete measures for dealing with the inflationary threat implicit in full-employment programs. Sweden had proposed the appointment of a committee of experts to make recommendations for national and international measures designed to reconcile the attainment and maintenance of full employment with the avoidance of inflation. The Council, in 1952, had preferred to turn the job over to the Secretary-General,[49] who presented the 1953 session with an inconclusive paper. The Council then decided to solicit further information from governments.[50] No new measures have been proposed although over the course of the years, the United Nations in its global and regional surveys, country studies, and quarterly bulletins has circulated a number of analyses of inflation. The maintenance of full employment admittedly carries risks of inflation and the techniques for eliminating these risks have not been mastered.

From the foregoing review of the full-employment discussions in the Economic and Social Council after 1950, it is clear that the delegates ranged over a wide field without coming firmly to grips with the problems touched upon. Conscious of this deficiency and of "the need for more constructive discussion of important questions," the Council decided, in 1954, to eliminate full employment as a separate agenda item and to discuss it as part of the regular review of the world economic situation. The United Nations Secretary-General, "assisted by appropriate officials of the Secretariat, including the executive secretaries of the regional economic commissions," has been made responsible for introducing the discussion of the world economic situation. The execu-

[48] See Res. 483B(XVI), Aug. 4, 1953, and Res. 531B(XVIII), Aug. 4, 1954.
[49] Res. 426B(XIV), July 10, 1952.
[50] Res. 483A(XVI), Aug. 4, 1953.

tive heads of the interested specialized agencies have been invited to participate actively.[51] These procedural modifications are serving at least to start the discussion on a higher plane, but it remains to be seen whether they will succeed in making the discussion as a whole more rewarding.

International Commodity Arrangements

The drastic decline in the prices of raw materials during 1951, after their sharp rise following the outbreak of the Korean war, intensified the long-standing desires of most Members of the United Nations for assurances of greater stability in primary commodity trade. This limited objective assumed increased importance as more ambitious schemes for stabilizing total international trade, for increasing monetary reserves through planned international transfers, or for greatly expanding the flow of investment funds were rejected one by one. The high priority assigned to the regulation of the prices of essential goods moving in international trade at equitable levels and relationships was manifested in two principal ways. One was the multiplication of studies and reports on international price relationships. The other was a growing emphasis on the price objectives of intergovernmental commodity agreements.

Before the post-Korean price rise, the primary impetus for the negotiation of commodity agreements had been the fear that burdensome surpluses would develop, and it was to deal with this problem that provision was made for commodity "control" agreements in the Havana Charter for an International Trade Organization. As early as March 1947, the Economic and Social Council had endorsed the principle that such agreements were justified only when a burdensome surplus had developed or was expected to develop, by recommending to governments that they be guided by the principles and objectives of this part of the draft Havana Charter.[52] The first suggestions by a United Nations agency that these principles should be modified were made on procedural rather than substantive grounds. In its review of international commodity problems for 1949, the Interim Coordinating Committee on International Commodity Arrangements (ICCICA) reached the conclusion that in some cases it would not be either necessary or desirable to delay discussion about the basis for an agreement until the

[51] Res. 557B(XVIII), Aug. 5, 1954.
[52] See above, Chap. III.

stage when burdensome surpluses were present.[53] Its chairman consequently urged the Council to lay down procedures under which the committee might convene commodity conferences without undue delay. This suggestion was, with a minor modification limiting the initiative of the committee, adopted by the Council in August 1950.[54]

These principles were again recommended as a guide to governments in a resolution approved by the Council in September 1951, but by that time a change was in the making.[55] The authors of the Angell Report, as noted earlier, had had their terms of reference modified by the Council in 1951 to include the preparation of recommendations

> . . . concerning the appropriate national and international measures required to mitigate the vulnerability of the economies of underdeveloped countries to fluctuations in international markets, including measures to adjust, establish, and maintain appropriate relations between prices of raw materials on the one hand, and essential manufactured goods on the other.[56]

A major portion of their report, which was submitted to the fourteenth session of the Council (May–August 1952), was devoted to proposals for international commodity arrangements. It precipitated "the first major international discussion of general commodity problems . . . held since the drafting of the Havana Charter."[57]

According to the experts, the growing belief in the likelihood of an expanding world economy had removed one fundamental obstacle to commodity agreements. They noted that when the Havana Charter was negotiated, such agreements were considered almost wholly in the context of burdensome surpluses, but felt that it was now possible to view them in quite a new light. They therefore considered the potentialities of such agreements in the general context of long-range price stabilization. The serious disadvantages of violent price fluctuations for countries dependent mainly on exports of primary commodities were analyzed sympathetically along familiar lines and, in addition, a somewhat new note was struck by a thorough examination of the problems created for industrialized countries by such fluctuations. From this, the experts concluded that the time was ripe for governments "to reconsider the case for a series of commodity arrangements of various types

[53] U.N. Interim Coordinating Committee on International Commodity Arrangements, *Review of International Commodity Problems, 1949* (1950), p. 16.

[54] Res. 296(XI), Aug. 2, 1950.

[55] Res. 373(XIII), Sept. 13, 1951.

[56] Res. 341A(XII), Mar. 20, 1951.

[57] U.N. Interim Coordinating Committee on International Commodity Arrangements, *Review of International Commodity Problems, 1952* (1953), p. 3.

as a means of keeping short-run movements of primary product prices, both upward and downward within reasonable bounds, and of helping to stabilize the international flow of currencies."[58]

This sharp break with concepts that had been vigorously advocated by the United States in the negotiation of the Havana Charter found wide support in the Council itself, in the Economic Commission for Latin America, in the FAO, in the Interim Coordinating Committee, and in the General Assembly. There were, however, some notable differences between the attitudes of the principal organs and the subordinate agencies.

The Interim Coordinating Committee for International Commodity Arrangements strongly emphasized that the difficulties envisaged in the Havana Charter might come either from a condition of surplus or from one of shortage, and that commodity agreements should aim at price stability—but not price rigidity—in both situations. It also pointed out, however, that the practical obstacles to the conclusion of commodity control agreements were such that in recent years only one—the International Wheat Agreement—had entered into force. It concluded therefore that it was "too much to expect a series of commodity agreements which might achieve a measure of price stability substantially throughout the field of primary commodities."[59]

The principal organs of the United Nations were more ambitious and less restrained in their approach to the whole question of price instability. It was, in fact, a characteristic of the economic work of the United Nations that the closer a United Nations agency was to operations and to concrete, day-to-day problems, the less inclined it was to underestimate practical difficulties and encourage extravagant hopes. The further it was removed from operations, the greater the tendency to multiply resolutions and reports analyzing a given problem in very general terms or emphasizing those aspects of special interest to a numerically strong group of Members.

The aspect of the problem that especially interested the underdeveloped countries—fluctuations in the terms of trade—was dealt with in a special report submitted by the Secretariat to the Council.[60] This

[58] *Measures for Economic Stability*, pp. 17–26, quotation from p. 25.

[59] U.N. Interim Coordinating Committee for International Commodity Arrangements, *Review of International Commodity Problems, 1952*, pp. 1, 6.

[60] U.N. Department of Economic Affairs, *Instability in Export Markets of Under-Developed Countries in Relation to their Ability to Obtain Foreign Exchange from Exports of Primary Commodities 1901–1950*, Doc. E/2047/Rev. 1, prepared in response to Res. 294 (XI), Aug. 12, 1950.

report was concerned with the long-term problem of the relation between fluctuations in the prices of primary commodities and the ability of the underdeveloped countries to obtain foreign exchange. It pointed out that the instability caused by fluctuations in raw material prices was accentuated rather than modified by the behavior of other items in the balances of payments of raw-material producing countries, and that "the interaction of these destabilizing factors produces extreme instability in the capacity of underdeveloped countries to finance imports of necessary commodities by means of their own exports, and in general to finance their economic development."[61]

This special study was completed before the major break in prices in 1951, and the underdeveloped countries, whose terms of trade were improving while it was in preparation, were not satisfied with its broad generalizations. Consequently, under pressure from these countries, the Council, in July 1952, requested that the Secretary-General prepare a new study of the relative movements of prices of various classes of goods moving in international trade.[62] This request was symptomatic of a view widely held in many countries producing raw materials—that over the years such countries had suffered not only from price instability but had also been systematically exploited by the industrialized countries through having to accept adverse terms of trade. This view had been expressed, for example, in the 1950 survey of the Economic Commission for Latin America, which included a theoretical explanation of the allegedly inevitable deterioration of the terms of trade of primary producing countries.[63] Its argument was countered in the Angell Report.[64] Although both sides of the question were thus presented in United Nations reports, the notion of exploitation of underdeveloped countries as a result of unfavorable terms of trade has persisted and demands for more favorable terms continue to be made in the Economic and Social Council and the General Assembly.

It was, in fact, in the Assembly that the concern of the underdeveloped countries with the terms of trade found its most robust expression, and that the conflict of views between them and the industrialized

[61] U.N. General Assembly, Sixth Session, *Official Records*, Supplement No. 1, "Annual Report of the Secretary-General on the Work of the Organization, 1 July 1950 to 30 June 1951" (1951), pp. 90–91.

[62] Res. 427(XIV), July 10, 1952.

[63] U.N. Department of Economic Affairs, *The Economic Development of Latin America and Its Principal Problems*, Economic Commission for Latin America, Doc. E.CN. 12/89/Rev. 1 (1950), pp. 8–14.

[64] *Measures for Economic Stability*, paras. 42–47.

countries was most irreconcilable. Stabilization of commodity prices was discussed as one of the principal means of financing economic development, and it was quite clear that this "means of financing" was to be provided by the industrialized countries. The general approach of a majority of the Assembly is shown by the title of a resolution adopted in 1952, namely, "Financing of Economic Development Through the Establishment of Fair and Equitable International Prices for Primary Commodities and Through the Execution of National Programmes of Integrated Economic Development."[65]

When this resolution was drafted, international price relationships had once more become approximately those prevailing before the invasion of South Korea, and the Members of the United Nations were just emerging from the shock of a major dislocation in the world price structure. Yet the terms of the resolution suggested that existing price relationships were neither just nor equitable and that the industrialized countries should revise their policies to remedy the situation. As originally proposed by Argentina in the Second Committee of the Assembly, the resolution made drastic suggestions for changes in these policies, in the form of a recommendation to all Member states that:

(a) Whenever governments adopt measures affecting the price of primary commodities entering international trade, they should duly consider the effect of such measures on the terms of trade of countries in the process of development in order to ensure that the prices of primary commodities *remain* in an adequate, just and equitable relation to the prices of capital goods and other manufactured articles so as to permit the more satisfactory formation of domestic savings in the countries in process of development and to facilitate the establishment of just wage levels for the working population of these countries with a view to reducing the existing disparity between their standards of living and those in the highly industrialized countries;

(b) Their governments should refrain, unless unavoidably required by national security in times of war and without prejudice to technological research and progress, from encouraging the production of any synthetic or substitute materials that unnecessarily affect the international demand for natural primary commodities;

(c) Their governments should intensify their efforts to reduce restrictions on imports of primary commodities.[66]

The first two of these proposed recommendations were strongly opposed by the industrialized countries. The second did not command the solid support of the underdeveloped countries and was replaced in

[65] Res. 623(VII), Dec. 21, 1952.

[66] U.N. Department of Public Information, *Yearbook of the United Nations, 1952* (1953), p. 374. Italics added.

committee by an Indian amendment for further study of the synthetics problem. All the underdeveloped countries, however, supported the first recommendation, which was the heart of the resolution, and all attempts by the industrialized countries to amend it were voted down. Indeed, the only amendment accepted was an inconsequential one replacing the word "remain" by the phrase "are kept."

The grounds on which the strong opposition of the industrialized countries was based have been summarized as follows:

> . . . (1) that a system of international parity prices such as that implied in the draft could not be instituted unless foreign trade were controlled by the State; (2) that such a system would make the economic structure more rigid and would not be conducive to increased productivity; (3) that there were no objective criteria for determining an "adequate, just and equitable" relationship between prices of primary commodities and those of capital and other manufactured goods; and (4) that it would be better to deal with the problem through individual commodity agreements as the need arose.[67]

As finally passed by the General Assembly, the resolution did contain a recommendation on commodity agreements, which was the result of several amendments by underdeveloped countries, but it bore little resemblance to the proposals of the Havana Charter and was closely tied in with the main price objectives of the resolution as a whole. It was recommended that governments co-operate in establishing multilateral as well as bilateral international agreements or arrangements relating to individual primary commodities as well as to groups of primary commodities and manufactured goods, for the purpose of achieving appropriate relationships. In the light of obstacles to commodity agreements but recently reported on by ICCICA, this was indeed optimistic.

The resolution also asked the Secretary-General to prepare a report on the financial repercussions that changes in the terms of trade between primary commodities and capital goods produced on the national incomes of countries in the process of development, and to appoint a small group of experts to report on practical means to ensure stable and equitable price relationships in international trade. It was characteristic of the attitude of the majority that the Secretary-General was not asked to examine the financial effects of adverse terms of trade on industrialized countries even though these countries had had to bear heavy burdens from this cause only a year and a half before.

The resolution was adopted by the General Assembly by a vote of 35

[67] *Ibid.*, p. 375.

to 15 with 9 abstentions.[68] It did not command the support of a single industrialized country and thus represented a signal failure of the United Nations in harmonizing national viewpoints on a matter of vital importance. The long struggle about commodity policy continued thereafter with some clarification and improved understanding of the separable issues that had become confused in the 1952 debates but without satisfactory reconciliation of the views of the United States, as the nation most cool to the commodity-agreement approach to stability, and its Latin American neighbors, as the nations most vocal in their advocacy of agreements.

At its fifteenth session, March–April 1953, for example, the Council recommended that the membership of ICCICA be strengthened by the addition of a person of wide experience in the problems of underdeveloped countries. This appointment was duly made, and the ICCICA continued to take part in intergovernmental commodity negotiations, which resulted in 1953 in a renewal of the International Wheat Agreement and the preparation of new agreements in tin and sugar. But the headway being made through the commodity-by-commodity approach was regarded by the underdeveloped countries as inadequate and their dissatisfaction was reflected in the decision of the General Assembly, in late December 1952, to appoint a new group of experts to report on the international measures that would be feasible to achieve stable and equitable price relationships in international trade.[69]

The report of this group of experts was submitted in November 1953.[70] Although it was a document of high quality, it received less attention from the Council and the Assembly than the Kaldor and Angell reports, in part because of its more specialized subject matter, and in part because the publication of reports prepared by outside experts for organs of the United Nations was no longer a novelty. The report stressed the benefits to be derived from greater stabilization of commodity markets and recommended a flexible "multiple approach" combining over-all stabilization policies with specific measures for individual commodities. It examined existing evidence on long-term trends

[68] U.N. General Assembly, Seventh Session, Plenary, *Official Records*, 411th Meeting (Dec. 21, 1952), p. 490.

[69] Res. 623(VII), Dec. 21, 1952.

[70] U.N. Department of Economic Affairs, *Commodity Trade and Economic Development*, Submitted by a Committee appointed by the Secretary-General, Doc. E/2519 (Nov. 25, 1953). The experts were Charles F. Carter of the Queens University, Belfast; Sumitro Djojohadikusumo of the Djakarta School of Economics, University of Indonesia; J. Goudriaan of Pretoria University; Klaus Knorr of Princeton University; and Francisco Garcia Olano, *Escuela Superior de Economica*, Buenos Aires.

in terms of trade and decided that the evidence of the past offered no help in predicting future movements of a secular character. It opposed stabilizing the terms of trade. It was forthright on the problem of synthetics and came out firmly against retarding technological progress for the sake of avoiding the pains of adjustment that inevitably attend progress. It analyzed alternative stabilizing devices, with particular sympathy for international buffer-stock arrangements.

It concluded that there was no ground for confidence that agreements for single commodities would be made in sufficient number to meet the more general demands of underdeveloped countries for stability of earnings, and that there was no effective international procedure for discussing and proposing action on the general problem of stabilization—a matter that transcended the problems of particular commodities. The experts suggested, therefore, that the Economic and Social Council establish an intergovernmental commission, advisory in nature, the main tasks of which would be to consider and make recommendations to the Council on general proposals for stabilization and, when the stability of the markets of the world appeared threatened, to make prompt recommendations to the Council for appropriate intergovernmental action.[71]

The Council at its seventeenth session decided by a vote of 12 in favor, 5 against, and 1 abstention to establish a Commission on International Commodity Trade, but postponed activating the commission until the eighteenth session (July–August 1954).[72] At that session, over the strenuous opposition of the United States and the United Kingdom, an Argentine resolution launching the commission was adopted by a vote of 12 to 3, with 3 abstentions.[73]

The main function of the new commission as set forth in its terms of reference was "to examine measures designed to avoid excessive fluctuations in the prices of and the volume of trade in primary commodities including measures aiming at a just and equitable relationship between the prices of primary commodities and the prices of manufactured goods in international trade, and to make recommendations."[74] The commission was to maintain relations with all international organizations having anything to do with international trade. Inasmuch as there

[71] *Ibid.*, pp. 81–84.

[72] Res. 512A(XVII), Apr. 30, 1954. U.N. Economic and Social Council, Seventeenth Session, *Official Records*, 791st Meeting (Apr. 30, 1954), p. 234. In opposition were Belgium, France, Norway, the United States, and the United Kingdom. Australia abstained.

[73] Res. 557F(XVIII), Aug. 5, 1954; U.N. Economic and Social Council, Eighteenth Session, *Official Records*, 829th Meeting (Aug. 5, 1954), p. 257.

[74] Res. 512A(XVII), Apr. 30, 1954, and Res. 557F(XVIII), Aug. 5, 1954.

were a number of agencies having such an interest, a new problem of overlapping jurisdiction was raised for the United Nations system. This was recognized in the resolution quoted above, which instructed the commission to consult with the FAO Committee on Commodity Problems and indicated the willingness of the Economic and Social Council to take into account the views of the contracting parties to the General Agreement on Tariffs and Trade (GATT) regarding the extent to which the problem of instability in primary commodities should be dealt with under that Agreement.

Accordingly, at the 1954–55 negotiations for the revision of the GATT, a working party considered proposals for international action to overcome problems in primary commodity trade and submitted for governmental review the draft of a new International Agreement on Commodity Arrangements. The proposed agreement was intended to provide the main co-ordinating mechanism for all commodity arrangements and to be allied in appropriate fashion to the GATT. In November 1956, however, the Contracting Parties decided to abandon the project,[75] largely because skepticism concerning the value of international commodity agreements had grown more pronounced than ever in official United States circles.

Meanwhile, the Commission on International Commodity Trade of the Economic and Social Council, in which the United States has refused to participate, has held lengthy meetings and laid out a program of work. Any effort to dissolve it is likely to be strongly opposed by countries like Argentina that are not contracting parties to the GATT and that prefer to see commodity problems considered in the context of economic development instead of in the framework of commercial policy.

International action in the field of commodity arrangements has, in the words of a perceptive writer on trade problems, been "haphazard, opportunistic, and lacking in any apparent systematic framework." The major improvement in principle introduced during the postwar period, equal representation for consumers (*i.e.*, importing countries) in the negotiation of individual commodity agreements, has vastly complicated the completion of agreements but has not ensured adequate representation of the public interest. The delegations of both importing and exporting nations have commonly been dominated by wheat, sugar, and tin specialists

[75] General Agreement on Tariffs and Trade, Press Release GATT/324, Nov. 21, 1956, p. 13.

. . . skilled in the problem of producing and marketing their particular products and responsible in their respective governments for these commodities alone. As officials whose responsibilities are confined to specific commodities, these representatives have naturally been more concerned with rendering a good account of developments in those commodities than with worrying about such larger issues as the optimum use of the nation's total resources, or the precedent-making implications of any particular arrangements. From the nature of their position, the problems of their particular commodities have had to be considered by these officials as unique situations, entitled to any solution which empirically seemed to fit.[76]

On the other hand, the officials at the Economic and Social Council or General Assembly level, theoretically equipped with the necessary breadth of view, have persistently underestimated the politico-economic and technical difficulties that invariably arise when the discussions move from broad principles to concrete commodity negotiations.

Surplus Disposal Problems

The absence of international arrangements to ensure greater stability in primary commodity prices increased the anxiety of United Nations Members over the possible destabilizing effects of programs for the disposal of agricultural surpluses—surpluses accumulated, in large measure, as a result of domestic stabilization policies. These anxieties related primarily to the intentions of the United States, possessor of the most gargantuan stocks in the world.

The surplus disposal drive of the United States began to gather force in 1953–54. Of total United States exports of agricultural commodities amounting to \$3.14 billion in 1954–55, 43 per cent, or \$1.34 billion, were aided by government programs of one kind or another.[77] All of the sales, subsidies, grants, and barter arrangements were subject to the principle that they would not be allowed to disrupt normal trade, but this did not quiet the fears of other United Nations Members dependent on the export of primary products.

These fears were expressed in various United Nations forums, nowhere more vigorously than in the address of the spokesman for Australia before the annual meeting of the International Monetary Fund in September 1954:

From the viewpoint of Australia and other primary producers of foodstuffs and raw materials there is a[n] . . . immediate and dangerous threat. It is of

[76] Raymond Vernon, "Organizing for World Trade," *International Conciliation*, No. 505 (November 1955), p. 180.

[77] Interagency Committee on Agricultural Surplus Disposal, *Prospects of Foreign Disposal of Domestic Agricultural Surpluses* (1956), pp. iii–iv.

course the growing surplus of agricultural products in the Western world, many of them stimulated by uneconomic subsidies in the large producing countries. In compiling their Annual Report the Executive Directors appear to have paid scant attention to this critical factor. Subsequently, Congress has, however, provided funds and taken other steps which revive in our minds the ugly specter of subsidized exports to other countries. No words, no lip service to the commercial interests of allied countries, however genuine and well meant, can obscure the actual threat to the livelihood of thousands of agricultural producers in other parts of the world. As one who is responsible to a great number of these producers, I say earnestly, but without rancor, that such policies may do the world a great disservice. We, in common with many others, lack the power and the long purse with which to withstand such overwhelming competition—at least within the framework of the liberal, nondiscriminatory, world trading system which it is our common purpose to attain. We cannot compete on equal terms if U.S. domestic surpluses are to be sold abroad from the bargain basement.[78]

In the Fund, delegates could do little about the surplus problem except give vent to their emotions. The FAO, however, had for several years been actively involved in the development of constructive solutions.[79] Its Committee on Commodity Problems, first established in 1949 after rejection of the proposals for an International Commodity Clearing House, proved to be a useful forum for consultation on commodity matters and in 1954 drafted a statement of FAO Principles of Surplus Disposal[80] that has been formally accepted by the United States and a majority of FAO members as a code of international behavior. The principles are necessarily general, however, and difficult to enforce.

At the request of its Committee on Commodity Problems, the FAO staff began making pilot field surveys in the underdeveloped countries likely to receive surplus supplies. A potentially important study of the manner in which surplus farm products might be used in India to finance additional development, without competing with sales of domestic Indian agriculture and without displacing the normal marketings of other nations, was published in 1955.[81] The study reported that

[78] International Monetary Fund, *Summary Proceedings of the Ninth Annual Meeting of the Board of Governors, September 1954* (1954), pp. 72–73.

[79] See above, Chaps. II and III.

[80] Food and Agriculture Organization, *Report of the Twenty-fifth Session of the FAO Committee on Commodity Problems*, Doc. C/55/22 (July 1955), App. A. The Committee also established in 1954 a Consultative Subcommittee on Surplus Disposal, which has met periodically in Washington, D.C.

[81] Food and Agriculture Organization, *Uses of Agricultural Surpluses to Finance Economic Development in Under-developed Countries—A Pilot Study in India*, Commodity Policy Studies No. 6 (June 1955).

to meet the standards for surplus disposal suggested at international conferences, surpluses should be used for financing development only if they meet two basic conditions. First, the country must already be doing all that it can without the surpluses to carry out economic development, so that the surpluses make possible additional development. Second, the new projects using the surpluses must expand domestic consumption of the surplus products to the full extent of the surpluses added to the supply. Introducing an element of specificity that had previously been lacking, the study went on to calculate the proportion of the wage payments to extra labor that could be expected to reappear as increased demand for surplus products, to examine how the rest of the cost of the additional projects might be met, and what effect that decision, in turn, would have on the consumption of surplus foods.[82]

While FAO was engaged in probing the feasibility of utilizing surplus commodities to improve nutritional standards, relieve famine, and promote economic development, the contracting parties to the GATT continued to be concerned from the viewpoint of possible harmful effects on the trade of third countries. In March 1955, at the ninth GATT session, the Contracting Parties passed a resolution recommending that countries, when disposing of surplus agricultural products, undertake to consult with the principal suppliers in other interested countries, with a view to an orderly liquidation of the surplus and the avoidance of prejudice to the interests of other countries. At the tenth session, in December 1955, a number of countries reported that the consultation procedures under the resolution had helped to reduce the disruption of international trade, but most delegations "also expressed the view that consultations had not been as effective as they would have wished."[83] The surplus disposal problem, it would appear, must be added to the list of difficult problems for which the United Nations has not yet found a satisfactory solution.

The Record in Review

The determination of every major government to attain and maintain full employment and to avoid depression became plainly apparent during the 1945–55 decade. For the achievement of these common pur-

[82] In this connection, see also Food and Agriculture Organization, *Functions of a World Food Reserve—Scope and Limitations*, FAO Commodity Policy Studies No. 10 (1956), pp. 29–41.

[83] General Agreement on Tariffs and Trade, Press Release 266 (Dec. 6, 1955), p. 15.

poses, however, the international economy remains almost wholly dependent on domestic efforts, domestic resources, and domestic stabilizers—some of which have introduced new rigidities into the economy and increased the danger that countries will either run into balance-of-payments difficulties themselves or create such difficulties for others.

The many United Nations activities of aid to specific sectors of the economy or to specific geographic areas do not add up to a co-ordinated international program for maintaining an expanding world economy or for preventing the international spread of deflationary pressures should they make their appearance in a major industrial nation. The development, through the General Agreement on Tariffs and Trade, of a code of conduct in the trade field represents an important net gain, but in most other respects international machinery for preventing the spread of unemployment has not been notably strengthened since the Bretton Woods Conference of 1944.

> The experts at Bretton Woods were deceived in more than the scale of the problem. Its essential nature was not clearly foreseen. Preparation was made to cover a brief reconstruction period, mainly by loans of the [International] Bank, and then to face the deep-seated problems of development on the one hand and of recurring trade dislocation on the other. The development problems were handed to the Bank. For the cyclical crises, the [International Monetary] Fund's articles laid down certain rules: . . . Provision was made for a five-year period of transition which was to elapse before the rules took effect. Thereafter, however, the long-run problem of development and the cyclical problem of temporary dislocation were regarded as separate and distinct. . . . No provision was made for the contingency that the business cycles were organically related to the deep-seated developmental forces, and that most cycles would operate in the same direction.[84]

The successive groups of experts commissioned by the Economic and Social Council and the General Assembly to make proposals for strengthening the international system have recognized the relationship. Their proposals have been designed both to establish a better long-term equilibrium and to reduce the amplitude of periodic departures from the equilibrium position. Although much of their analysis of the problem has been accepted, and a number of their prescriptions for domestic action have been endorsed, their most important recommendations for international action have been rejected. The international community has not been willing to guarantee the maintenance of a given level of international trade or flow of investment funds, to

[84] Charles P. Kindleberger, "Bretton Woods Reappraised," *International Organization*, Vol. V (February 1951), pp. 34–35.

increase vastly the volume of international reserves available for meeting short-term requirements, to negotiate a series of commodity agreements to stabilize the prices of internationally traded raw materials, or to set up international machinery for disposing of surplus agricultural products without disrupting normal trade.

The United States has been instrumental in bringing about this situation. It has contributed massive sums to the reconstruction of the world economy but the contributions, for the most part, have been direct rather than through international agencies. The United States has been reluctant to entrust sizable additional resources to international management for use as antidepression insurance, especially when existing resources have not been seriously taxed. Noting the freedom of sovereign nations to pursue domestic policies that keep them in or on the verge of balance-of-payments difficulties—and the persistence of a number of countries in following such policies—the United States has suspected that the insurance might be dissipated without correcting the maladjustments for which it was intended.

Recently, the international economy has shown itself to be better disciplined, less fragile, and more resilient than many believed possible. In 1949, when the world was still quite vulnerable, a minor recession in the United States precipitated a payments crisis in a number of foreign countries. In 1953–54, during an American recession of comparable magnitude, Europe enjoyed outstanding prosperity. Fortuitous factors unquestionably played a role, but there is also no doubt that nearly all countries in 1956—at least until the Suez Canal crisis—were in a stronger position than at almost any time since the end of the Second World War.[85]

In 1954, the volume of world trade was about 65 per cent larger than prewar. At the same time, the abnormally large proportion of world exports supplied by the United States and Canada declined from 30 per cent of the total in 1948 to 25 per cent of the much larger total in 1954. The rest of the world added about $2.5 billion to its gold and dollar reserves in 1953 and $1.7 billion in 1954.[86] Commodity prices, on the average, remained relatively stable. Employment levels remained high during the first half of the 1950's, and there has consequently been little pressure on nations to "coordinate" their employment policies—

[85] International Monetary Fund, *International Financial News Survey* (Sept. 13, 1955), pp. 103–07.

[86] *Ibid.* In 1955, however, while foreign countries were adding another $1.7 billion to their gold and dollar reserves, British reserves declined by about $640 million.

an undertaking that is inherently much more difficult than it was assumed to be in the early postwar years.

Despite the encouraging progress toward equilibrium, the world at large is not confident of its ability to withstand the impact of fluctuations in the American economy or of the ability of the United States to maintain prosperity. The American economy, because of its sheer size, is far and away the most important single element in the world picture.

Rich in resources, immensely diversified, comparatively self-sufficient, the United States is able to take in stride shocks that would paralyze less hardy victims. It has performed remarkably well during the postwar period. It has weathered demobilization and disarmament, the Korean conflict and the rearmament build-up, and, more recently, substantial cutbacks in the defense program. Consumer demand has remained high. United States foreign trade has been concentrated more heavily than before the Second World War on Canada and Latin America with the result that Europe, comparatively speaking, has become less vulnerable to fluctuations in United States import demand. The import demand itself has grown more stable because food has become a larger element in the import total.

A battery of stabilizers has been built into the economy since 1932. These built-in stabilizers can be depended upon to retard deflation, but they are not capable of preventing a depression or reversing it once it gets under way. Positive antirecession measures would doubtless be invoked, however, regardless of the party in power.

Would they be invoked promptly enough to avoid difficulties for the more precariously balanced economies of other nations, and would other large nations likewise manage their affairs with the necessary skill and dispatch? This is the current dilemma of the United Nations system. If the major industrial nations, and above all the United States, can be trusted to maintain relatively full employment at home, the need for elaborate international antidepression safeguards will be greatly reduced. If they cannot be relied upon to protect their home fronts, they will hardly be foresighted enough to commit themselves to appropriate international defenses. But if the international community waits until the emergency is upon it to strengthen its defenses, it may find it has waited too long.

CHAPTER VI

*Transportation and Communications**

IN DEALING with economic problems of the type discussed earlier in this study, the United Nations has had to improvise machinery, to test it on unfamiliar terrain, to raise sizable sums of money, and to face many controversial political and social issues. Its work in the field of transportation and communications—confined on the whole to the provision of long-range, well-recognized, technical services through genuinely specialized agencies and organs—has proceeded more tranquilly than its other economic activities.

International co-operation to facilitate postal deliveries, weather observations, and telegraphic communication has a long history. It antedates by many years the establishment of both the League of Nations and the United Nations. Since ratification of the United Nations Charter, however, the older, world-wide, technical agencies (as well as the newer International Civil Aviation Organization) have been brought officially into the United Nations system as specialized agencies. The bulk of their work has continued to be based on reciprocal exchanges of a technical, non-controversial character, which it has not been thought necessary to analyze in detail for purposes of this study.

In one notable respect, however, intergovernmental activity in transport and communications during the postwar period has differed from work during earlier periods. Through the International Bank for Reconstruction and Development and the Expanded Programme of Technical Assistance, the United Nations and its related agencies have been able to help nations directly in planning and building the railroad lines, highways, airports, telephone systems, port improvements, and other concomitants of the higher standards of living to which the peoples of the less developed areas so ardently aspire.

In recent years, innovations in transportation and communications have greatly accelerated the pace at which men have been able to overcome barriers of space and time that during most of the world's history have kept nations apart. Further developments already on the horizon promise to make the world still smaller as aeronautical science and

* By Wilfred Owen, William Adams Brown, Jr., and Priscilla St. Denis.

telecommunications accelerate the rate of innovation and make the air, rather than earth and water, the medium through which international relations are effectuated.

Modern transport and communications also serve to promote economic development and the general welfare by making it possible in many areas of the world to use resources that until now have remained either undiscovered or that have been deemed useless because the cost of making them available has been prohibitive. Undertakings now technologically possible in these areas can bring about improved social and economic conditions by facilitating internal trade and travel and by promoting international trade and cultural relations.

Unfortunately, however, the role of transport and communications has not been confined to what is favorable to the general welfare. On the contrary, these instrumentalities have also helped to create some of the conditions leading to international friction and to provide the vehicles and weapons of international conflict. To prevent the use of these tools for warfare and to direct their use wisely in the interest of social and economic objectives, is a major challenge to international organization today.

Nature of the Problem

Adequate transportation and communication are essential ingredients of economic growth and development. The improvement of agricultural yields, for example, presupposes the means to permit effective distribution of perishables and the movement of surplus foods to areas of short supply. Utilization of mineral resources involves the ability to haul bulk materials at costs that make mining operations economically feasible. Improvements in health, education, and government operations all depend on communications and access to remote areas. The conduct of private business and trade likewise relies to an important degree on the availability of rapid and low-cost transport and communications. These objectives require the construction of all-weather roads, waterways, railroads, airways and airports, the installation of communications facilities, the provision of needed equipment, and the training of personnel. Technically and financially such objectives are difficult to meet, but they are essential first steps in the improvement of the general welfare.

In much of the world today, the isolation resulting from primitive methods of transportation and communications is a principal factor in the retarded development of areas that might otherwise be sources of substantial wealth. This is illustrated by the problem of transport modernization in Africa.

In southern Africa, railroad lines extending far into the interior carry out copper, wood, and other raw materials to the coastal ports. The financial strength of the rail system and the cost of transport out of the interior are dependent on the availability of traffic in the reverse direction, but the poverty and primitive levels of living among the interior population create little demand for the manufactured goods that might be exchanged. Vast distances, widely separate cities, and scarcity of fuel combine to create transport difficulties of great magnitude. In other parts of Africa, the large number of small autonomous political units reduces efforts to solve national transportation and communication problems to a local and un-co-ordinated basis. Finally, low levels of national income make impossible the domestic supply of capital required to develop facilities that can break the interrelation of underdevelopment and lack of adequate transport and communication. Without substantial foreign capital, the possibilities of opening up this vast continent and applying the wealth of its forests and minerals to the improvement of levels of living seem remote.

Even in those countries that have been able to develop substantial transport services, the available facilities have frequently been geared to strategic rather than economic objectives. Railroads, for example, often provide no direct connections between economically important points, and where economic factors have influenced transport development, primary emphasis has been given to serving major heavy industries rather than agriculture. One of the reasons for the relatively slow progress of many countries has been the lack of a balanced transportation system.

The world transportation and communications setting in which the United Nations operates is predominantly one of growth and change, but is also one of startling contrast. Rising population, expanding consumer requirements, and higher levels of production in many parts of the world have been both cause and effect of a steadily increasing volume of passenger travel and goods movement both within national boundaries and internationally. Along with growth in volume, there has been a shift in the geographical patterns of transportation as a result of changing postwar political ties and shifting material sources and markets. Changes in method of movement have also altered the picture as the volume of motor transport has multiplied, and as air transport has accounted for a major share of international passenger traffic. Another factor has been the increasingly vital role of communications for both private and official purposes as radio and television have made possible a volume and excellence of communications hardly dreamed of a few years ago.

Some $75 billion of goods move annually in international trade, and the world tonnage of ocean-going vessels is 45 per cent above the prewar total. On the world's 10 million miles of highways, there are now 100 million motor vehicles, more than double the 1940 figure, and the air-lines of the world are carrying 85 million passengers a year.

But the growth, change, and technical progress of transport and communications that have been so spectacular in the western world are in sharp contrast to the scientific lag typical of the less developed areas. Asia, with more than 50 per cent of the population of the world, has less than 9 per cent of the highways of the world, 22 per cent of its railway mileage, and 3 per cent of its motor vehicles. In contrast to North America, where there is one motor vehicle for every four people, in Asia there is only one motor vehicle for every 689 inhabitants. In India, the figure is one vehicle for every 1,194 people. The population of India is more than twice that of the United States; yet it operates only 90,000 trucks compared with 10 million trucks serving the United States.

In the United States, a powerful railroad locomotive is capable of hauling a ton of materials one mile with the energy from two teaspoonsful of diesel oil, but in vast areas of the world, it is still the human back along with the pack animal, the bullock cart, and the crude hand-propelled water craft, that support the commerce of nations. One modern jetliner passing overhead may utilize more power than all the mechanical energy available for transportation in vast areas of the earth below.

In these circumstances, many of the economic and social goals toward which the underdeveloped countries are working cannot be realized without substantially greater advancement than has been made to date in the provision of transport facilities. The question what the United Nations is doing to help make such facilities available has broad significance because success in this field may affect the results of other activities designed to promote the general welfare.

International machinery and agreement are necessary if international transportation or communication is to be possible. International movement and message transmission tend to be contemptuous of national boundaries, whereas national sovereignty imposes conditions that must be dealt with realistically and patiently if the possibilities of transport and communications are to be realized at all. The nature of these problems has been undergoing rapid change with advancing technology. The United Nations has been concerned with the changing character of these problems, and also with problems relating to the lack of technological progress in the underdeveloped areas and the close interrelation between the conditions of transportation and communications and the conditions of economic progress and general welfare. In many parts of the world, the United Nations has been called on to assist in developing needed facilities, domestic and international, in areas where the problem is not one of co-ordinating facilities that already exist but rather of laying the groundwork for the minimum levels of transport and communications essential to social and economic progress. The United Nations has had to face these two aspects of the problem in almost all the fields of transportation and communications.

Impact of Communications Developments

Among the international problems deriving from modern technology, those having to do with modern methods of message transmission introduce many new and challenging difficulties. Electromagnetic waves travel great distances and in doing so, cross national boundaries. There is a limit to the number of electromagnetic waves that can be received without interference, and the limited radio spectrum must be shared by all the nations of the world. Inasmuch as the medium through which these waves travel is the public domain, the rapidly growing demand for radio services must be adjusted to the limited capacity of the spectrum through common consent.

Today, the achievement of satisfactory working relations in the field of telecommunications under conditions of rapidly changing technology requires continual international adjustments. The international aspect of radio has developed to the point where "almost no major frequency allocation can be made without considering world-wide usage."[1] Foreign merchant ships entering New York harbor, for example, cannot use the same bands for radar as New Yorkers use for television, and because certain parts of the radio spectrum are best adapted to aviation radio purposes and to radiotelephone and radiotelegraph, these limited

[1] U.S. Federal Communications Commission, *Sixteenth Annual Report, Fiscal Year Ended June 30, 1950*, p. 163.

bands must be shared by all nations to preserve equity and to achieve effective use of available frequencies with a minimum of congestion. International treaties and agreements are necessary to allocate frequencies and to settle equipment and interference problems. In addition, there must be agreement on telephone and telegraph rates and other matters.

Special Problems of Aviation

In the field of aviation, the problem is essentially that each of the nations of the world has sovereign control over the air space above its territory. This principle was established before it was imagined that mechanical contrivances might travel beyond the atmosphere of the earth. International agreement may soon be needed on the use of the outer space by the nations of the world. But leaving aside this emerging problem, the principle of air sovereignty means that international flights are possible only through bargaining among nations regarding the reciprocal rights for air carriers. No world-wide agreement has been possible on the kinds of commercial air transport rights that should be exchanged multilaterally, so that a great number of bilateral agreements provide the basis on which international air traffic rests. These bilateral treaties represent varying degrees of departure from the goal of providing the world with the most efficient and low-cost air transport service.

International agreement has to be reached on many other aspects of aviation, of course, to make flying from one country to another possible. Because the air space and available airport facilities must be used jointly by the aircraft of all participating nations, there must be general agreements on types of navigation and landing aids, competence of personnel, emergency procedures, certification of aircraft, and other standards. And the desirability of preventing unfair or destructive competition has led to agreement on matters involving both service and rates.

Technical and economic problems are complicated, however, by factors that underlie the whole question of freedom of the air. Participation in air operations is not conditioned merely by the desire to provide air services, but by considerations of national security and prestige that have impelled nearly every nation to seek a place in the world air transport system regardless of economic justification. This has frequently resulted in excess capacity, duplicating services, and resort to competing subsidies to preserve uneconomic operations. The problem has been to arrive at an acceptable compromise between the goal of meeting world needs economically and the objective of respecting the rights of all nations wishing to participate in the provision of air services.

Water and Land Transport
Problems

Merchant shipping involves many of the same problems encountered in the air, for in this sphere, too, the role of commercial transportation is closely related to national defense and national prestige. The resultant dimensions of merchant marine operation by the various maritime nations frequently lead to an oversupply of shipping capacity, the intensification of competition on shipping routes of the world, and the necessity of arriving at international agreement on discriminatory practices.

Problems associated with rail, inland water, and road transport, while less spectacular, are equally vexing. In rail transport, international operations are complicated by the need for standardization of track gauge and equipment, the need for arrangements to permit the interchange of cars moving from one country to another, and the question of through routes and rates. Waterway transport requires agreement on freedom of movement and maintenance of facilities, while international road transport raises issues regarding type and size of equipment, permissible weights, payments for use of the road system, operating standards, insurance provisions, and the like. The problem of establishing international agreement on standards and procedures for road transport has encountered many obstacles stemming from the relative newness of motor transport, the many separate operating units involved, and the competitive struggle between road and rail.[2]

In all fields of transport, there is the problem of establishing rules and regulations for commercial transport, and of minimizing international barriers to the movement of people and goods through the simplification of customs and immigration formalities, visa requirements, health and police procedures, and monetary transactions.

[2] Even in the United States, without the complication of international boundaries, problems of motor transport regulation and the relation between road and rail transport have not been satisfactorily resolved. Differences in allowable loads and in methods of paying for the use of the highways of the several states through which interstate shipments pass have not been eliminated by interstate agreement. In the matters of driver licensing, rules of the road, and signs and signals, there is still little uniformity among the several states, and in matters of road design and financial policy, wide variations continue to exist.

As indicated in the foregoing discussion of the nature of the problems of international transport and communications, those created by national boundaries are not only technical and economic but are also problems affected to an important degree by political and security considerations that often overshadow other obstacles to the realization of satisfactory transportation services.

Organizational Arrangements of the United Nations

The continuity of international work initiated before the end of the Second World War in the field of transportation and communication was assured when the Preparatory Commission of the United Nations suggested that the Economic and Social Council establish a Temporary Transport and Communications Commission to advise the Council in its relations with the intergovernmental organizations already operating in the field.[3] The Temporary Commission met in 1946 and set up the framework of the future permanent Transport and Communications Commission.

The Transport and Communications Commission, which came into being the following year, is the transport advisor to the Council. Its task is to promote the study and solution of international transport and communications problems and to co-ordinate the activities of the various international organizations dealing with these matters.

The commission deals in addition, on a world-wide basis and for all means of transport, with the problems of passport and frontier formalities and barriers to the international transport of goods, and as noted below, with certain relatively minor features of international road transport and shipping relations.

Significant contributions to the study of transportation problems are made through the efforts of the United Nations to collect, standardize, and make available statistics on transportation and communications as a basis for research and policy determination. Today much more is known about the problems encountered in these areas because extensive data have been made available through international organizations.

Co-ordination of activities in various fields is provided to some extent through relations of the commission with nongovernmental organizations having consultative status in the field of transport and communica-

[3] U.N. Preparatory Commission, *Report of the Preparatory Commission of the United Nations*, Doc. PC/20 (Dec. 23, 1945), pp. 28, 38.

tions.[4] Contacts have also been maintained with certain intergovernmental organizations outside the United Nations framework, for example, the Central Office for International Transport by Rail and the Central Commission for the Navigation of the Rhine.

The commission, however, maintains its contacts with major fields (aviation, telecommunication, postal and weather services) mainly through international organizations that were already in existence before the commission was itself established. These agencies are the International Civil Aviation Organization (ICAO), the International Telecommunication Union (ITU), the Universal Postal Union (UPU), and the World Meteorological Organization (WMO), all of which have been brought into relationship with the United Nations as specialized agencies.

The United Nations has recognized the competence of each of these agencies in its own field, but whenever a problem is the concern of two or more specialized agencies, there is a need for co-ordination. This is one of the functions of the Transport and Communications Commission. In the case of safety at sea and in the air, for example, it is necessary to bring together ICAO, the ITU, the WMO, and maritime authorities. In the transportation of explosives and other dangerous goods, the organizations involved also include the International Labour Organisation (ILO), the Universal Postal Union, and a number of interested intergovernmental and nongovernmental organizations.

The scope of transport and communications problems considered by the United Nations system is indicated by the fact that four of the ten specialized agencies deal with these matters. Establishment of the Intergovernmental Maritime Consultative Organization, not yet operative, will raise the total to five. In addition, both the International Labour Organisation and the International Bank for Reconstruction and Development are active in the transport and communications field. The ILO is concerned with wages, hours, occupational hazards, and other conditions of work, and with the training of skilled personnel in the underdeveloped countries. The Bank has directed a large part of its resources to the financing of transportation facilities and has made a number of comprehensive country studies for the development of long-range transportation plans.

[4] Among the nongovernmental organizations which have made useful contributions to the work of the United Nations are the International Chamber of Commerce, International Road Federation, International Air Transport Association, International Chamber of Shipping, International Transport Workers Federation, International Union of Official Travel Organizations, and International Union of Railways.

The Transport and Communications Commission could rely on no specialized agencies, however, to deal with problems of inland transport. A survey of these problems led to the early conclusion that circumstances governing railroad, inland water, and highway transport were so different in different parts of the world that these methods of transport should be dealt with regionally. The commission, however, reserved to itself certain functions in this field.

On its initiative, a Road and Motor Transport Conference was convened at Geneva in 1949 to deal with technical matters governing road transport, including standards for driver licensing, traffic regulations, vehicle registration, and signs and signals. The conference concluded a new world-wide convention on road and motor transport, which provides for the international recognition of operators' licenses issued by any contracting state to persons over eighteen years of age who have given proof of driving competence. This action has since been followed by recommendations for minimum requirements for the licensing of motor vehicle drivers, so that all countries can ultimately have the assurance that foreign drivers on their highways have met reasonable standards of training and competence. Out of the 1949 meeting also came a study of signs and signals that may eventually lead to a single standard incorporating the best elements of existing practices.[5]

The commission also took the initiative on one other road transport problem. Although it was decided, on the one hand, that the problem of customs formalities for commercial road vehicles and for the transport of goods by road should be dealt with on a regional basis, on the other hand, problems of customs formalities for the temporary importation of private motor vehicles and their equipment and for the personal effects of tourists traveling by all methods of transport were considered to be world-wide in scope. A special United Nations conference in New York in 1954 prepared and opened for signature two conventions, one concerning customs facilities for touring and the other on the temporary importation of private road vehicles.

These were minor exceptions to the principle recommended by the commission that the problems of inland transport be dealt with through the regional commissions, and the latter were organized to discharge this function. The Economic Commission for Asia and the Far East established an Inland Transport Committee. Although some of its member countries had participated in the transportation work of the League

[5] H. H. Kelly and W. G. Eliot, "The Growing Structure of International Motor Traffic Agreements," U.S. Department of State *Bulletin*, Vol. 30 (Jan. 25, 1954), pp. 117–20.

of Nations, there were in this area few existing organizations operating in this field.[6] The special function of the Inland Transport Committee was to provide technical assistance and to plan and develop transport facilities, rather than to co-ordinate existing facilities. The Economic Commission for Latin America was confronted with a situation somewhat comparable to that in Asia, but there were some existing Pan-American technical organs concerned with rail and road transport, and the establishment of a separate transport committee under the regional commission was not deemed necessary.

The problems to be met in Europe were rather different, and arrangements were made to deal with them through an Inland Transport Committee within the framework of the Economic Commission for Europe (ECE).[7]

European Inland Transport

The field of inland transport has been the subject of extensive international co-operation in Europe for many years, through both governmental and commercial organizations. The idea of freedom of navigation of the international rivers was formulated as early as 1792, and by the middle of the nineteenth century binding agreements had been made by interested European nations. The Danube was placed under international administration one hundred years ago, and the Rhine was regulated by the Mannheim Convention a dozen years later. These conventions provided for freedom of navigation to vessels of all nations and promoted uniformity of maintenance and policing of waterways. After the First World War, commissions were established for the Danube, the Elbe, and the Oder.[8]

International arrangements governing railroad freight transportation were established by the Berne Convention of 1890. In 1924, this convention was revised to include passenger traffic, and further revisions have produced the conventions in effect today. The Central Office for International Railway Transport, which was set up by the Berne Convention, has been concerned with the conditions under which goods and passengers are carried in international railway transport and has established relations with a number of railroad organizations dealing with

[6] U.N. Economic and Social Council, Fourth Session, *Official Records*, Supplement No. 8, "Report of the Transport and Communications Commission" (1947), pp. 56–60.

[7] *Ibid.*

[8] H. Osborne Mance, *International River and Canal Transport* (1945), pp. 1–79.

international transport law, commercial and technical matters, and conditions governing operation and exchange of rolling stock.[9]

Highway transportation activities on an international scale were of much more limited scope. A European Convention on Motor Transport was signed, however, as early as 1909, and the question was later studied by the Transit Committee of the League of Nations.[10]

In the prewar period of international co-operation on transport questions, the only activity ostensibly on a world level consisted of the Organization for Communications and Transit of the League of Nations and a number of rail, road, and navigation associations, but their work was concentrated on European inland transport and closely related problems.

During the war, discussions took place on the problem of meeting postwar European transport requirements, and to deal with this situation, the European Central Inland Transport Organization was established in 1945 to aid in reconstruction work.[11] When this emergency organization was terminated in 1947, the transport systems in Europe had to a large degree been restored to fair working order, and its unfinished business was left to the Inland Transport Committee of the ECE.[12]

Difficult problems still stood in the way of a satisfactory rehabilitation of European inland transport. Many of them were posed by the international character of the boundaries, and by the great need for husbanding resources while achieving an integrated system of transportation that makes economic sense. Moreover, there was no organization dealing with international road transport, and this part of the transport system, badly needed to supplement the disorganized rail system, was suffering from retarded highway development and a variety of obstacles to free movement. The problem of standardizing railroad rolling stock had assumed major proportions, and better utilization of rail cars serving in international traffic was a compelling requirement. The need for prompt action to support the general program of European economic

[9] Hans Hunziker, "The Berne Conventions and the Central Office for International Railway Transport," *Transport and Communications Review*, Vol. 2 (January–March 1949), pp. 10–15.

[10] H. Osborne Mance, "International Inland Transport in Europe: Recent Developments in Organization," *Journal of the Institute of Transport*, Vol. 25 (March 1954), pp. 337–42.

[11] For further information on prewar and wartime co-operation, see above, Chap. I.

[12] "European Inland Transport Since the End of the War," *Transport and Communications Review*, Vol. 1 (October–December 1948), pp. 14–26.

recovery was obvious, and measures aimed at this goal were needed.

The ECE Inland Transport Committee prepared draft conventions for the simplification of European frontier formalities for rail transportation of passengers and of goods, both of which have been adopted. On the recommendation of the committee, an agreement was concluded between international agencies and nongovernmental railway organizations aimed at avoiding duplication of functions; and the committee has also dealt with tariff and monetary problems and the possibilities of a uniform system of accounts for main railway lines. Improvement in commercial transport by roads was accomplished under the ECE through agreements in 1947, which lifted restrictions on the freedom of the road, and an agreement in 1954, relating to economic regulation of road carriers.

United Nations activity in Europe has met with special difficulties, partly because of the East-West split and partly because of the dominance of state railway administrations in the European transport field. Solutions have also been sought outside the framework of the United Nations. The Council of Europe, for example, has suggested a supranational European Transport Authority with powers similar to those of the European Coal and Steel Community. In the special field of rail transportation of coal and steel, three major problems have been faced by the High Authority of the European Coal and Steel Community: elimination of discrimination in rates between domestic and foreign shippers; the establishment of international through rates; and the harmonization of national structures of rail rates. The first two problems have been fully met, and some progress has been made on the third. Other organizations have adopted different approaches to the tasks first attempted by the European Central Inland Transport Organization.[13] Among these was the formation of a European Conference of Ministers of Transport, in October 1953, by the countries belonging to the Organization for European Economic Cooperation (other than Iceland and Ireland), and Spain.[14]

[13] E. R. Hondelink, "Transport and Communications Problems in Development Programmes," *Transport and Communications Review*, Vol. 6 (July–September 1953), pp. 11–20. See also L. A. Lewis, "Coordination of European Inland Transport," U.S. Department of State *Documents, State Papers*, Vol. I (October 1948), pp. 451–99, and "Transport in the Common Market," *Bulletin from the European Community for Coal and Steel* (February–March 1955), pp. 1–4.

[14] For the background and work of this Conference, see *The Present State of Economic Integration in Western Europe*, Report by the Research Directorate of the Secretariat-General of the Council of Europe, Strasbourg, Doc. SG/R(55)3/Rev. (July 1955), pp. 31–35.

International Civil Aviation Organization

Although technical co-operation in the field of aviation was initiated as early as 1919 by the Paris Peace Conference, the first attempt to take international action on such questions as transit rights, international routes, and air transport services was not made until the International Civil Aviation Conference met in Chicago in 1944. This conference sought to fill one of the major gaps in the structure of international co-operation as it had developed during the interwar years.[15] It laid the groundwork for most of the principles that still apply to international civil aviation, except of course for the basic principle that each nation has sovereignty over its own air space. This principle has long been generally accepted and was explicitly reaffirmed in the convention drafted at the Chicago conference, which provided that no scheduled air services may be operated over the territory of a contracting party without the permission of that state.[16]

The permanent international organization, which was planned at this conference to promote the application of these principles, was the International Civil Aviation Organization. It came into existence in 1947 and became the first of the specialized agencies in the field of transport and communications to become associated with the United Nations.

The objectives of ICAO are to develop the principles and techniques of international air navigation and to foster the planning and development of international air transport to ensure the safety and orderly growth of international civil aviation. This includes the improvement of aircraft design and operation for peaceful purposes; the development of airways and facilities; the provision of efficient and economical air transport; the prevention of waste caused by unreasonable competition; the assurance that nations have a fair opportunity to operate international airlines without discrimination; and the promotion of safety of flight and the general development of all aspects of international civil aeronautics.

[15] See above, Chap. I.

[16] U.S. Department of State, *International Civil Aviation Conference, Chicago, Illinois, November 1 to December 7, 1944: Final Act and Related Documents*, Publication 2282 (1945), Art. 6, p. 60. Article 5 of the Convention, however, required a contracting party to allow the entry of private and nonscheduled flights of foreign aircraft of other contracting parties, subject to such regulations, conditions, and limitations as it might unilaterally impose.

As was expected, ICAO has been concerned with the continuation of prewar co-operation in such matters as airways systems, aeronautical communications, rules of the air and air traffic control, licensing of aeronautical personnel, log book requirements, air-worthiness, aircraft registration and identification, aeronautical meteorology, aeronautical maps and charts, customs procedures, search and rescue, and accident investigation. It has been, however, confronted with broader problems, including that of striking a balance between subsidies, on the one hand, and restrictions of commercial rights, on the other, in order to ensure a trend toward lower costs, better service, and further development of air transport. In these matters, it has co-operated with a nongovernmental organization, the International Air Transport Association, to which all the largest international airlines belong. The International Air Transport Association has as one of its principal functions the development of agreement on international tariffs.

One of the earliest tasks of ICAO was to attempt to draw up a multilateral agreement to regulate commercial rights and to replace the multiplicity of bilateral agreements. The hope that such an agreement would be provided by the International Air Transport Agreement (Five Freedoms Agreement) drawn up at the Chicago conference was dashed by the failure of the principal carrier nations other than the United States to accept this agreement.[17] Consequently, it was renounced by the United States in July 1946, but the foundations for a new approach had been laid by the Bermuda Agreement between the United States and the United Kingdom signed on February 11, 1946. Up to that time, the United Kingdom had negotiated bilateral agreements based on the economic principles that it had supported in the Chicago conference. These provided for a definite division of frequencies of landing, plus control of rates, while the United States negotiated agreements in which there was no control of frequency, capacity, or rates.

The Bermuda Agreement provided for reciprocal United States-United Kingdom air services, fixed the routes to be operated by the respective services, adopted certain principles to govern capacity, and set up machinery for intergovernmental agreement on rates. It represented a shift in United States policy to the extent of the United States

[17] For a discussion of the five freedoms and the instruments in which they were incorporated, see above, Chap. I. The first two freedoms permitted flying across the territory of another nation and landing there for nontraffic purposes only; the third and fourth freedoms permitted the discharging and loading of passengers, mail and cargo coming from or destined for the home nation of an aircraft; the fifth freedom permitted the discharging or loading of passengers and cargo destined for and coming from any other nation.

concurring that if the rates charged were not agreeable to both governments, the question could be referred to ICAO. Each government would then use its best efforts to put into effect any advisory rate decisions made by ICAO. The agreement also set up certain principles to cover traffic capacity that involved a shift in the British position, particularly by including the amount of fifth freedom traffic, which each country could pick up in the other country while en route to foreign destinations. But the agreement did not seek any specific division of frequency or capacity.

Subsequent to the Bermuda Agreement, the United States negotiated other bilateral agreements in some of which it went even further than in the Bermuda Agreement in deferring to international authority. It expressed a willingness to use its best efforts to make effective the advisory opinions rendered by ICAO in disputes concerning frequency, capacity, and other economic problems as well as in disputes concerning rates. The United States then joined with other members of ICAO in urging the adoption of a multilateral agreement, and ICAO convened a conference at Geneva, in 1947, for this purpose. This project appeared promising owing to the Anglo-American compromise developed at Bermuda, but agreement was not reached.

With respect to the third and fourth freedom rights, there were differences of view at Geneva over what constituted an adequate provision against destructive competition. The main reason for the failure, however, was inability to reach agreement on the fifth freedom. The states with highly developed transport systems debated violently with the smaller states on the issue whether and to what extent limitations should be placed on the number of passengers and amount of freight an airplane should be allowed to carry between two points neither of which was in the country of the airline operating the plane. The smaller countries insisted that principles governing such fifth freedom traffic under the general Bermuda type of agreement were insufficient to protect local services and that any country had the right to refuse fifth freedom traffic to foreign air services. Twelve countries supported a Mexican resolution to this effect, while the United States, Great Britain, France, the Netherlands, and certain other countries insisted that whenever a route is negotiated, the countries on the route must allow fifth freedom traffic. There was a complete deadlock on this issue.

This was not the only issue. The United States indicated its willingness to agree to principles along the lines of the Bermuda Agreement regarding capacity, frequency, and rates and to accept decisions of the International Court of Justice under Article 36(2) of the Statute of the

Court or, alternatively, on specific agreement of both parties, to accept binding arbitral decisions in case of dispute. The United States was unwilling, however, to agree that routes should be fixed under multilateral agreement or that the granting or refusal of a route or any matter in connection therewith should be the subject of international decision or of arbitral awards, as desired by a number of other countries.

As a result of these basic differences, the conference decided that it was unjustifiable to submit an agreement for signature, with the result that routes for international flying and commercial rights exercised on the routes continued to be determined by bilateral agreements.[18]

These problems, however, remained on the agenda of ICAO, and at its fourth session in the summer of 1950, the ICAO Assembly requested member nations to place at the disposal of the organization the full benefit of their knowledge and experience in international air transport in order to make possible a satisfactory multilateral agreement that would define the exchange of commercial rights in international civil aviation.

These matters were debated at length by the assembly in June 1953, but it was concluded that the time had not yet arrived when it would be possible to obtain world-wide agreement concerning exchange of commercial rights in international air services. It was noted that at that time there existed over three hundred agreements between different pairs of governments on this question. It was agreed, however, that the ICAO Council should study what might be achieved by partial solutions, and a suggestion by the Council of Europe that a regional agreement on the question might be evolved was approved by the ICAO Assembly. Special attention was given to the needs of non-scheduled international air services, but the assembly felt it was too early to expect universal freedom for this type of transportation. The ICAO Council was requested, however, to study the question further to see how charter operations could be distinguished from regular services, and which charter operations could be given general freedom to operate internationally without encroaching on the traffic of regular services.

It was not until a year later that the ICAO Council decided to call the first meeting of a European Air Transport Conference and to co-operate in the drafting of multilateral agreements dealing with (1) the establishment of conditions leading to progressive liberalization of air transport on scheduled carriers undertaken by European operators in

[18] George P. Baker, "The Bermuda Plan as a Basis for Multilateral Agreement," McGill University (mimeo. speech, Apr. 18, 1947).

European regions, and (2) the establishment of parallel conditions for nonscheduled air service.

By that time, most of the countries belonging to ICAO were freely exchanging the rights of nonstop passage and the stopping for refueling or other noncommercial purposes, and some forty countries had accepted the International Air Services Transit Agreement. It was, however, on the issue of violation of the commitments under this agreement and of the convention itself, that the first dispute between members was submitted to ICAO. The complaint was made by India against Pakistan in the summer of 1952, and in January 1953, the ICAO Council was able to announce amicable settlement of the dispute by an agreement permitting Indian civil aircraft to fly over Pakistan territory to Kabul through two twenty-mile-wide corridors without having to follow the lengthy detours that had previously been required by Pakistan.

Efforts of the International Civil Aviation Organization in the technical field of air navigation have been more successful than in the economic field. Differences in languages, technical, economic, and social developments, operational experience, and educational standards among the nations operating aircraft necessitate uniform international standards to make international air operations practical. Among the accomplishments of ICAO has been the addition to the 1944 Chicago convention of fifteen international standards and recommended practices, which are designated as "annexes." Of this number, fourteen are concerned with standards and recommended practices for technical matters such as personnel licensing, rules of the air, meteorological codes, aeronautical charts, operations of aircraft, aeronautical telecommunications, and search and rescue. Only one is concerned with economics.[19]

These annexes were subject to continuous amendment and improvement. In June 1953, however, the ICAO Assembly, feeling that the basic text of the various international standards and procedures had reached a sufficient state of stability, decided that more emphasis should be placed on implementation. In the case of international standards for air-worthiness, however, the assembly felt that more work should be done to develop comprehensive international standards. Great emphasis has also been laid on the development of the five regional offices

[19] Annex 9, "Standards and Recommended Practices—Facilitation of International Air Transport." In January 1949, the Director of ICAO reported that the most significant achievement of the organization during 1948 was the adoption of standards controlling six different technical aspects of international flight. See U.S. Department of State, *International Civil Aviation, 1949–1950*, Publication 3915 (1950), pp. 4–7.

of ICAO (in Paris, Cairo, Bangkok, Lima, and Montreal) to enable regional representatives to assist national administrations more effectively, and in order to plan the provision of air navigation services for international civil aviation. Regional air navigation meetings are convened periodically by ICAO in each of eight regions.

The relation of civil aviation to peace and security, which had been raised at the Chicago conference, was again debated at the fifth assembly of ICAO.[20] The United States then proposed that in the light of the resolution of the United Nations General Assembly on "Uniting for Peace" and subsequent recommendations by the Economic and Social Council, the agreement between the United Nations Organization and ICAO be revised. This proposal was rejected by the Executive Committee of the ICAO Assembly on the ground that revision of the basic agreement was undesirable. Instead, the executive committee approved for submission to the assembly a revised United States proposal constituting a declaration of support of the "Uniting for Peace" resolution. This declaration was interpreted as meaning that ICAO would render all possible assistance within its competence to the principal organs of the United Nations on matters directly affecting world security.

International Telecommunication Union

During the war, rapid technological improvements and the increase in aeronautical, navigational, and broadcasting activities made the structure of the existing International Telecommunication Union clearly inadequate to deal with emerging problems, particularly in the field of radio.[21] Among these, were the allocation of radio frequencies and the bringing of radio regulations into line with recent technical developments. To meet this situation and to alter the structure of the Telecommunication Union so that it could be more readily brought into formal relation with the United Nations, were matters of urgent concern to the Economic and Social Council.

Accordingly the Council suggested the convening of international telecommunication conferences, which met in 1947 at Atlantic City. An agreement establishing the relationship between the International Telecommunication Union and the United Nations was approved at that time. The conferences completely reorganized the structure of the outdated International Telecommunication Union and achieved gen-

[20] See above, Chap. I.
[21] *Ibid.*

eral acceptance of a new frequency allocation table. This was to correct the situation that had developed under the old regulations adopted at a Cairo Conference in 1938, under which each country could simply decide on the wave lengths it wished to use, and inform the Union. The consequence of the Cairo regulations had been that many countries used the same frequencies, disregarded the separation of the frequencies, and reserved frequencies without using them. The frequency spectrum had become too crowded, and steadily growing interference increasingly endangered the reliability of telecommunications.

In view of the complexity of the problem of implementing the new frequency allocation table, the conferences provided for a series of special meetings in several regions of the world, an International Conference on High-Frequency Broadcasting, an International Administrative Aeronautical Radio Conference, and others. Originally, it was planned that the frequency lists resulting from these conferences would be incorporated with the master list prepared by a Provisional Frequency Board for final approval by an Extraordinary Administrative Radio Conference. However, the task of the Provisional Frequency Board was much more difficult than had been expected at the Atlantic City conferences.

For example, the International High Frequency Broadcasting Conference in Mexico City lasted over five months, from October 22, 1948 to April 10, 1949, in an attempt to put an end to the anarchy prevalent in high-frequency broadcasting. A majority voted down a proposal to complete the allocation plan at a later date, and only fifty of the sixty-nine countries participating signed the agreement reached. The United States and the Soviet Union were among those that did not sign.

In general, countries submitted frequency requirements far in excess of foreseeable needs, and total requests went well beyond the capacity of the frequency spectrum. As a result, the Extraordinary Administrative Radio Conference, which was scheduled for 1950, was postponed, for it became obvious that the objectives of the conference could not be achieved or any substantial agreement reached. The United States urged that the work accomplished at the Atlantic City conferences not be scrapped and the conference be held when conditions had become more favorable. It was subsequently held successfully in 1951.

The task of this conference—the fitting into the radio frequency spectrum of all radio stations of the world—was extraordinarily complex. It included broadcasting stations, airplane, ship, telegraph and telephone systems, land mobile stations, coastal stations, and radio location, direction-finding, navigation, beacon, experimental and amateur stations. The agreement signed by sixty-three members of the ITU represented a major step toward implementing a new table of frequency allocations. The conference adopted frequency allocation plans designed ultimately to provide for some 80,000 frequency assignments to specified stations. Although one of the most comprehensive agreements ever negotiated in the field of telecommunications, the agreement did not solve the difficulties inherent in the detailed assignments of the frequencies, and reliance was placed on a gradual implementation based on actual frequency use.

A Plenipotentiary Conference of ITU held in Buenos Aires in 1952 reaffirmed the decisions of the Extraordinary Administrative Radio Conference. It made a number of modifications in the convention designed to facilitate the working of the Union.

Although the most significant developments in communication technology have involved radio communications, there have been considerable advances in techniques in the fields of telephony and telegraphy and a greatly increased demand for international facilities as standards of living have risen. The International Consultative Committees of the International Telecommunication Union have done much work on the integration of the European telephone and telegraph systems and on the interconnection of the telephone and telegraph systems of Southern Asia and the Middle East with those of Europe and the Mediterranean basin.

Intergovernmental Maritime Consultative Organization

The concern of the United Nations in shipping problems has taken several forms. On the initiative of the International Labour Organisation, international conferences have been convened for the purpose of improving living conditions aboard ships and a Conference for the Revision of the Convention on Safety of Life at Sea was convened in London in 1948 by the United Kingdom. The Transport and Communications Commission has been concerning itself with the immediate tasks of arriving at the unification of maritime tonnage measurement and controlling the perennial problems of sea water pollution. But the major United Nations interest has been the attempt to reach agreement for the first time on a world-wide public agency in the field of shipping.

World shipping problems have over a long period been handled by rate conferences of organizations of private shipowners. These international cartels, designed to control competition by regulation of schedules, pooling of cargo, and control over rates, had their origin in the compelling need for self-regulation in an industry the financial position of which was frequently imperiled by cut-throat competition. The shipping conferences are mainly conferences of liner operators, and one of their purposes is to protect the services of liners—which due to their regularity may have to bear higher costs—against competition from outsiders, who may take the cream of the traffic when it suits them.[22]

The importance of merchant fleets to national defense has also introduced a wide variety of subsidy policies and practices among the maritime nations, which have intensified shipping rivalries. Despite some more general forms of co-operation referred to earlier in this study,[23] and the postwar proposals for an Intergovernmental Maritime Consultative Organization, the shipping conferences have remained the principal basis of international co-operation.[24]

During the war, centralized control of allied shipping was provided by the Allied Shipping Adjustment Board (1942–45). It was recognized that for some time ahead centralized control for at least part of the shipping of the world would be needed to provide necessary tonnage during the demobilization and early rehabilitation period. To this end and to pave the way for an orderly return of shipping to normal commercial operations, a United Maritime Authority was set up, including the representatives of nine maritime nations. This body was succeeded by a United Maritime Consultative Council in 1946 to draft recommendations for a permanent peacetime organization in the shipping field.

In the meantime, a number of nations that had never possessed merchant marines of any size undertook to build and operate their own fleets. Countries with adequate financial reserves at the end of the war were offering to place substantial orders with European nations on condition that at least half of the traffic would move in national vessels. Countries that had changed from colonial or dominion status to independence announced their intention to create their own national fleets. States that had no fleets but were dependent to a large extent on shipping, saw in the United Nations framework opportunities to appeal against what they considered to be oppressive practices on the part of the shipping lines that served them.

[22] Daniel Marx, Jr., "Shipping Conferences," *Transport and Communications Review*, Vol. 6 (October–December 1953), pp. 14–24.

[23] See above, Chap. I.

[24] Louis Delanney, "The United Nations Maritime Conference," *Transport and Communications Review*, Vol. 1 (July–September 1948), pp. 17–21.

There was growing sentiment consequently for a permanent governmental maritime agency at the time that the United Nations Transport and Communications Commission was organized in 1947. The commission was confronted with the existence of a great number of international conventions and agreements in the field of ocean shipping and several international organizations were dealing with aspects of the problem. The absence of a central organization meant that there was no intergovernmental agency comparable to the ITU or ICAO to represent shipping interests, as telecommunication and aviation were represented, in the discussions of problems of common interest. Examples of such problems are safety at sea and in the air and the application of radio aids in navigation.

In May 1946, the Transport and Communications Commission recommended that an intergovernmental body be established to fill this gap, but that it be limited to dealing with technical matters. In October 1946, the United Maritime Consultative Council completed a draft for a permanent organization that went far beyond technical co-operation. Its proposed functions included encouragement of the removal of all forms of discriminatory action and unnecessary restrictions affecting shipping engaged in international trade. The purpose was to promote the availability of shipping services to the commerce of the world without discrimination and permit the consideration by the organization of shipping problems of an international character. Pending the establishment of a permanent organization, a Provisional Maritime Consultative Council was established.

These developments were duly noted by the Transport and Communications Commission and by the Economic and Social Council. The latter convoked a United Nations Maritime Conference, which was given, as a basis of discussion, the draft completed by the United Maritime Consultative Council. This conference, which met in Geneva in 1948, adopted a Convention on the Intergovernmental Maritime Consultative Organization (IMCO). It also adopted a resolution establishing a preparatory committee to prepare for the first session of the new organization when the necessary support was achieved. The intended role of this organization was to provide for consultation on technical matters affecting international shipping, to promote safety and navigation standards, and to encourage the removal of discrimination and unfair restrictive practices by shipping concerns and governments.

It was over the inclusion of the economic problems of the industry that serious international differences developed. In the deliberations in Washington in 1946 on the draft of the United Maritime Consultative

Council, the Scandinavian countries had agreed to the inclusion of these matters, but at the Geneva conference, they favored restricting the new organization to technical matters alone. The United States was in a delicate position on the inclusion of provisions relating to unfair or discriminatory practices. It was using government-owned ships in private operations, operating government-owned vessels as a government project, subsidizing both construction and operation of private vessels, and even controlling allocation of cargoes in certain cases. In these circumstances, the United States proposed that in matters of unfair practices, the proposed IMCO should recommend that those matters capable of settlement by the normal processes of international shipping should be so settled. It proposed that matters concerning unfair restrictive practices of private shipping concerns be considered by IMCO only after the parties themselves had failed to reach an adjustment. Furthermore, the United States view was that if and when IMCO did take jurisdiction, such matters should be considered in the light of the applicable principles and precedents established by the specialized agencies having responsibility in the field of restrictive practices (*i.e.*, the proposed International Trade Organization). There was a clear danger that in this area of restrictive practices a body of doctrine might be developed in the shipping industry that would differ from that to be developed by the International Trade Organization.

The withdrawal of its proposals by the United States led to the adoption of a compromise proposed by the United Kingdom providing for the consideration by the maritime organization of matters concerning unfair restrictive practices by shipping concerns and of any matters concerning shipping that might be referred to it by any organ or specialized agency of the United Nations.

The British proposal, however, included two major limitations affecting the consultative and advisory functions of the organization on these economic matters. One of these was a provision that assistance and encouragement given by a government for the development of its national shipping and for purposes of security do not in themselves constitute discrimination, provided that such assistance is not designed to restrict the freedom of shipping of all flags to take part in international trade. All efforts to expand the definition of discrimination and unfair practices were unsuccessful. The second major limitation was that, in those matters that appeared to the organization capable of settlement through normal processes of international shipping business, the organization should so recommend. When in the opinion of the organization any matter concerning unfair restrictive practices was incapable of settlement in this way, and after an attempt to negotiate directly had failed, the organization should, at the request of one of the disputants, consider the matter.

The provision of the final draft concerning the removal of discriminatory action and unnecessary restrictions by governments affecting shipping engaged in international trade was thus surrounded by severe limitations. The function of providing machinery for co-operation among governments in technical matters and the encouragement of the general adoption of the highest practical standards in matters concerning maritime safety and efficiency of navigation appear therefore to be the most important and generally acceptable provisions of the convention as a whole.

The Intergovernmental Maritime Consultative Organization will be activated as soon as twenty-one countries have ratified the convention, including seven with merchant fleets of over a million tons. To date, seventeen nations, including the United States and the United Kingdom, have taken this step, but in other areas opposition to ratification has persisted. The Scandinavian nations, with their maritime economies and powerful shipping interests, would like to confine the new agency to technical matters so that the shipping industry would be left to regulate economic matters itself. In contrast, emerging and underdeveloped nations, desirous of establishing themselves in world shipping operations, wish to be free to provide such government aids as their aspirations would—at least in the early stages—require, and they do not feel sufficiently safeguarded by the reservation in the text of the convention on subsidies for promoting national shipping and national security.

Universal Postal Union

A common meeting ground for the solution of postal problems was provided by the establishment of the Universal Postal Union eighty years ago. The first International Postal Treaty established the concept that all member countries comprised a single postal territory for the reciprocal exchange of mail. Previously each country had entered into bilateral agreements for sharing the cost of mail transportation, and an intermediate country that handled the mail in transit could charge whatever it could arrange through negotiation.[25]

When the Universal Postal Union was established, uniform rates were

[25] A. Muri, "The Origin, Development and Activities of the Universal Postal Union," *Transport and Communications Review*, Vol. 1 (July–September 1948), pp. 22–25.

made applicable throughout the Union, and it was agreed to abolish payments by a sending country to the receiving country on the theory that a letter dispatched would generally call for a letter in return. Costs of carriage and delivery incurred by the two countries would thus balance out. The problem of compensating intermediate countries led to the adoption of a system of weighing shipments and estimating the amount of payment necessary to compensate for transit costs.[26] Over the years, due to changes in postal service, rates, and transportation charges, the Universal Postal Convention was revised and brought up to date at the postal congresses normally held at intervals of approximately five years. Although the continuity of these meetings was broken by the two world wars, the Union itself survived and in 1947, was brought into relation with the United Nations as a specialized agency.

Since that time, the Union, in order to keep pace with changing conditions and the steady increase in international correspondence, has added new services and revised regulations in the light of changing needs. The Thirteenth Postal Congress of the Union in 1952, for example, adopted a uniform scale of transit rates. It also adopted a more detailed scale of distances, with the corresponding transit rates, both for land and sea carriage. Airmail rates, which had been the subject of extensive study between the Union, the International Civil Aviation Organization, and International Air Transport Association, were fixed.

The Union has adopted provisions regulating the transmission of all types of international mail and fixed maximum and minimum rates, weight limits, and dimensions. It not only provides for transmission of international mail but prohibits certain articles, such as opium and other narcotics, and explosives, from being moved by mail across international boundaries.

World Meteorological Organization

Another early beginning of international co-operation is found in endeavors to provide information about the weather. A century ago an international conference dealing with a program for collecting meteorological observations by ships at sea was held in Brussels. During the next quarter century, additional international meetings were held, and in 1878, the International Meteorological Organization was established. Its members were the directors of the meteorological services of the various countries throughout the world, and although it did not have

[26] Fulke Radice, "The Problem of the Payment for Mails in Transit: A Historical Survey," *Transport and Communications Review*, Vol. 4 (April–June 1951), p. 27.

the full official backing of governments, it nevertheless carried out significant programs of perfecting and standardizing meteorological activities, especially services to maritime navigation, agriculture, and more recently, to aviation. In 1947, the agency was reorganized as a formal intergovernmental organization known as the World Meteorological Organization, and its operation as a specialized agency of the United Nations began in 1951.[27]

The organization is concerned with establishing networks of stations for making meteorological observations and setting up meteorological centers throughout the world. It has prepared a set of technical regulations relating to meteorology to serve as a guide to meteorological services and has standardized meteorological observations. Weather information is gathered by 2,500 volunteer merchant ships representing thirty countries. The organization has worked to further the application of meteorology to aviation and shipping, and agreements with appropriate agencies in these fields have been negotiated. It has prepared thunderstorm frequency maps in different parts of the world. One of the most important observations reported from weather stations is the type of cloud. To ensure uniformity in methods of reporting clouds, it has prepared an International Cloud Atlas. The World Meterological Organization is also participating in the preparations for International Geophysical Year (1957–58), a period of intensified world-wide study of the earth and its upper atmosphere.

Technical and Financial Assistance

Many needs for technical assistance have arisen in the field of transport and communications. They include advice on the organization or reorganization of private transport companies, government administration, public regulatory policy, maintenance and repair of railroad and motor vehicle equipment, sanitary measures at ports and airports, the installation of railway signals and aids to aerial navigation, the design of inland water transport craft, the development of road and bridge construction techniques, and the construction, modernization, and operation of maritime ports. The United Nations Technical Assistance Administration provides assistance in fields not covered by the specialized agencies, including road, rail, inland water transport, and shipping, as well as problems of transportation in general.

[27] "The International Meteorological Organization," *Transport and Communications Review*, Vol. 3 (April–June 1950), pp. 1–14.

The World Meteorological Organization conducts a wide variety of studies aimed at improving weather knowledge and applying meteorology to the problems of underdeveloped areas. On the basis of requests received under the Expanded Programme of Technical Assistance, the WMO has given attention to the organization and development of national meteorological services, and training has been provided for local personnel in underdeveloped countries. Technical assistance projects in 1955 involved agricultural, maritime, and aeronautical applications of meteorology in twenty-three countries. The WMO has operated projects to provide advice in synoptic meteorology and on the technique of obtaining meteorological information from the upper air. It has dealt also with water resource problems, including the prevention of floods and the provision of water for irrigation, electrical energy, and industrial uses.

The International Telecommunication Union, in conjunction with the Technical Assistance Administration, has sent experts to aid in setting up a telecommunications training center for radio, telegraph, and telephone personnel in Ethiopia. It has operated projects to study problems and provide advice on reorganization of telecommunication services in Iran and aided Pakistan in telephone and short-wave radio communication problems. Experts were sent to Afghanistan to study problems arising out of the installation of a telecommunications network.

The primary importance of civil aviation to an underdeveloped area is to provide a means of transport that can surmount geographical barriers, provide travel for great distances over land and sea in a short time, and pioneer inaccessible land areas without the large initial investment required for surface transportation. Aviation is also of value to agriculture and public health programs through dusting and spraying operations, mapping, and surveying. A report of the Technical Assistance Board points out that although the International Civil Aviation Organization "has been able to render some small assistance" in helping nations to establish air services, lack of funds has held the level of help far below the volume of requests.[28]

The International Civil Aviation Organization has placed primary emphasis on the development of aviation ground services, particularly air traffic control, communications, and meteorological services. Fellow-

[28] U.N. Economic and Social Council, Eighteenth Session, *Official Records*, Supplement No. 4, "Sixth Report of the Technical Assistance Board," p. 75. The share of ICAO in the budget of the Expanded Programme of Technical Assistance averaged about $800,000 per year during the period 1953–55.

ships have been granted for this type of training and for commercial pilot training; experts have also been sent to the recipient countries to provide such training together with guidance in improving the techniques of the local personnel in such operations as the repair and maintenance of aircraft engines, airframes, and airborne equipment.

The technical assistance extended by the International Civil Aviation Organization has also provided advice on the organization of government departments of civil aviation and the preparation of air laws and regulations; the conduct of air transport surveys; the establishment of statistical and accounting systems; airline organization and operation; the location, construction, and improvement of airports; the installation and operation of air navigation facilities and services; and the opening, in co-operation with the Mexican, Egyptian, and other governments, of civil aviation training centers in their countries.

Technical assistance in the field of inland transport has been facilitated by the regional economic commissions. Recommendations by the Singapore conference on inland transport arranged by the Economic Commission for Asia and the Far East in 1949 led eventually to a series of studies on road, rail, and waterway problems; and arrangements were made for the collection and dissemination of transport statistics and the establishment of a technical library service. Experts from Burma, India, Indonesia, Pakistan, Thailand, and Viet Nam have visited Europe and the United States to study technological improvements in inland transport, and railway personnel from sixteen countries have visited Europe, North America, and Japan to study modern railway operations. One result has been the establishment in Pakistan of a regional training center for railway operating and signaling officials.

Highway transport problems that have received special attention from United Nations agencies include economical methods of constructing, repairing, and maintaining highways; improvements in the use of existing road transport equipment; design of wheels and axles for animal-drawn vehicles to minimize road damage by iron-tired wheels; the development of international highway connections; and preparation of simplified manuals of instruction for motor vehicle drivers.

Through the co-operation of the Technical Assistance Administration, the Economic Commission for Latin America has undertaken the study of such problems as development and integration of the transport systems of the Central American countries. A technical commission was sent to that area for an intensive survey of the transport situation, and its work has contributed to the creation of a regional conscience and a sense of urgency concerning the role of transport as a factor in the integrated development of the region.[29] A treaty recently negotiated by the Central American republics under the auspices of the commission greatly simplifies automobile travel in the area and if, as is confidently expected, the treaty is ratified, it should be a boon to users of the Inter-American Highway. Studies are also being carried out on the working conditions and mechanization of Latin American ports and their comparative operating costs.

Technical assistance activities in the field of transport and communications, as elsewhere, have been limited by lack of funds. The need for capital to carry out desirable programs of transport development poses even greater problems.

The International Bank has provided significant financial support for self-liquidating projects. Activities engaged in by the Bank have included general economic surveys that include analyses of transportation, and loans for transportation development. More than $650 million —or nearly one third of the total amount loaned by the Bank through June 30, 1956 for developmental work—has been for the improvement of transport services. Of this sum, about $350 million has been for railroads and $160 million for highways. Highway construction has been financed in Colombia, Ethiopia, Guatemala, Haiti, Honduras, Nicaragua, Panama, and Peru. Railroads have been rehabilitated in Australia, Brazil, Burma, India, Pakistan, Thailand, and the Union of South Africa. Port development projects have been undertaken in Burma, Pakistan, Peru, South Africa, Thailand, and Turkey.[30]

Results of United Nations Action

In the work of the United Nations, the promotion of satisfactory transportation and communication services has encountered two major difficulties that are frequently present in the provision of these services both domestically and internationally.

First is the tendency in the field of transportation to consider each form of transport separately, or, conversely, the failure to take a comprehensive view of transportation as a whole. This situation stems from the fact that developments in technology have appeared at different periods

[29] "Survey on Transport in Central America," *Transport and Communications Review*, Vol. 6 (October–December 1953), pp. 34–49.

[30] See above, Chap. IV, for further information on the work of the International Bank and the volume of loans made for the development of transportation and communication facilities.

of history, so that each new and competing invention has given rise to new policies and methods, new governmental machinery, and new private and quasi-public agencies and associations. The result has been a proliferation of organizations in and outside government that makes comprehensive plans and policies substantively and administratively hard to come by. Separate agencies of transport come to be looked upon as rivals rather than related parts of the whole. Scattered organization is often an obstacle to the careful weighing of alternative transport possibilities and the effective physical co-ordination of facilities. Desirable standards of economy and service, however, are often dependent on careful selection of alternatives, joint use of facilities, satisfactory physical co-ordination, and uniform policies and procedures.

The second problem is the tendency to consider transportation and communications as something apart from the social and economic goals they are intended to support. This weakness appears to result from the highly technical nature of transport and communications and the natural preoccupation of experts with operational problems. The fact that transportation is the means by which social and economic objectives may be accomplished is sometimes lost sight of in the complex of scientific and engineering problems and the intensity of interagency rivalries.

The framework in which the transport and communications work of the United Nations is accomplished provides an organizational basis for overcoming these two difficulties, but in practice the results have been limited. The establishment of a Transport and Communications Commission in the United Nations has provided a focal point where problems common to all methods of transportation could be given proper attention, and where points of impact or relationship among the several transportation and communications media could be recognized and dealt with. To date, however, the potential of the system has not been realized.

The fact that the Transport and Communications Commission is part of the Economic and Social Council has likewise been a salutary arrangement, providing machinery by which it would be possible to consider these programs in relation to broader objectives. Transport services and communication facilities have an indispensable role in the economic development of communities and nations, in the conduct of trade, and in the achievement of economic and cultural goals. But actually the provision of transportation and communication facilities is carried on without a close relationship to economic and social development. This means that the opportunity to use transportation to accomplish broader objectives of economic development is in constant danger of being lost.

The influence exerted by the world organization has differed widely with different kinds of transportation and communications and with differing geographical situations. In cases where the scope of operations is world-wide, and therefore where world-wide co-operation has been needed from the beginning, fairly effective devices to cope with these problems were already established before the United Nations Organization was formed. This has been true particularly of the postal and weather services. In more recent times, the solution of aviation problems has not been noticeably furthered by the inclusion of the International Civil Aviation Organization in the United Nations system. The negotiation of agreements making international bodies in these areas specialized agencies of the United Nations has merely ensured that the official agencies dealing with these problems are part of the world system, and—what may in the long run prove to be of considerable importance—provided the opportunity for them to share in the Expanded Programme of Technical Assistance. Affiliation with the United Nations to date has had only a minor impact in bringing related transport and communications agencies to bear on a single problem, in overcoming the duplications and overlappings of international organizations, or in focusing attention on the economic and social implications of transportation and communications policy.

It was never intended, of course, that the United Nations Organization would displace existing agencies, and bringing the specialized agencies into relation with the Organization has not altered the nature of the predominantly technical work they were already undertaking. But where the need for a unified approach has been manifested, the Transportation and Communication Commission has been somewhat disappointing in meeting the need.

On the positive side, the United Nations Organization has resulted in the sponsorship of the new Intergovernmental Maritime Consultative Organization, and in isolated cases the Transportation and Communications Commission has provided integrating machinery that has aided the specialized agencies in reaching the solution of common problems. The most active operations of the United Nations Organization, however, have been in the fields of road, rail, and inland waterways, where regional rather than world-wide problems predominate. It was in this area that the largest organizational vacuum existed at the time the United Nations was established. But even in the case of regional activity most of the attention has been directed to the problems of European inland transport, largely because of the need for restoration and realignment of European facilities at the end of the war.

The accomplishments of the Inland Transport Committee of the Economic Commission for Europe have been substantial, and it has served in addition as a forum for discussion, which foments ideas that have led to action by the railroads, truckers, and other transport interests outside the commission itself. Much remains to be done, however, to overcome the barriers to freedom of movement that still interfere with the European transport system.

In other regions of the world where transportation patterns have not been crystallized, as they have in Europe and North America, the regional commissions uncover areas requiring technical assistance and facilitate the obtaining of such assistance. As yet there are no regional arrangements, however, in either Africa or the Middle East. In the underdeveloped areas, the necessity of relating transportation to economic development is more apparent than elsewhere, yet difficulties have been encountered by the United Nations in the meager financial support for technical assistance relative to the need. Furthermore, the difficulties to date of obtaining the necessary capital to finance large-scale investment have meant that accomplishments have lagged far behind urgent need.

In addition to further financial aid, there is also a need—as well as an opportunity—for the Economic and Social Council, through its Transport and Communications Commission, to sponsor comprehensive studies of transport requirements in the various underdeveloped areas in order to provide the guidance for technical assistance and investment and to ensure the most practicable plans in the light of local conditions and modern technology. Despite an organizational setting that permits a broad approach to the planning of transport and communications developments by the United Nations, a piecemeal approach by individual projects is still the rule in the requesting countries.

The great economic potential of modern transportation development is being demonstrated in many parts of the world today as transportation and communications facilities open the way to new wealth and higher standards of living. The United Nations Organization has not yet seized on the opportunity that lies in a concerted attack on inadequate transportation and communications as a means of opening the door to economic growth and development.

CHAPTER VII

*Social Action to Improve Levels of Living**

IT IS an outstanding characteristic of the present age that for the first time in history human society has dared to think of the welfare of the entire human race not as a dream but as a practical objective. Modern science and engineering, it is widely believed, have provided the tools to eradicate from the face of this earth hunger, want, and disease.

For these purposes, the economic programs discussed earlier in this study are essential, but they are not enough. Social action on a broad front is also required to help bring the benefits of scientific advance and of modern technology to the largest number of people in the shortest time and at the lowest cost.

One broad group of social programs—the group discussed below—has as its central purpose the promotion of higher levels of living for the population as a whole. Another group—analyzed later—tends to be concerned with special categories of the population such as mothers and dependent children, the handicapped, the refugees and migrants.[1] The latter approach frequently, but not always, puts the emphasis on defense, on protection, and on remedial action.

The programs discussed here, however, place the accent on development, both economic and social. They represent a dynamic approach. Under the aegis of the United Nations and its affiliated agencies, this approach is being internationalized.

The present analysis of the process of internationalization begins with a discussion of the problem of defining and measuring an individual's level of living—of selecting the key components that together comprise the level of living, and of choosing appropriate indicators of progress with respect to each component. Certain landmarks in the evolution, within the United Nations system, of the social approach to the improvement of levels of living are then noted. With a chronological frame of reference thus established, it becomes possible to review in a more meaningful way the many specific activities of the United Na-

* By Walter M. Kotschnig.

[1] See below, Chap. VIII.

tions aimed at improving the health, nutrition, housing, employment arrangements, and working conditions of the people in Member states. These activities have involved the Social Commission of the United Nations, the World Health Organization (WHO), the Food and Agriculture Organization (FAO), the International Labour Organisation (ILO), as well as other organs and agencies.

Definition and Measurement of Levels of Living

A clear grasp of what is meant by standards or levels of living, and of methods by which they can be measured, is essential to the development of purposeful action programs to improve such standards. During recent years, international concern with the problem of definition and measurement has been reflected not only in the deliberations of the Economic and Social Council and its Social Commission, but also in the discussions of the Seventh International Conference of Labour Statisticians of the ILO (1949), and the Rural Welfare Panel of the General Conference of the FAO (1949). An important report on defining and measuring levels of living, published in 1954, reflects the thinking both of the United Nations experts who drafted it and of the personnel of the United Nations Educational, Scientific and Cultural Organization (UNESCO), the ILO, FAO, and WHO, which participated actively in its preparation.[2]

The report suggested a distinction between the terms "standard of living" and "level of living." It recommended that in future discussions the expression "level of living" be employed when referring to actual conditions of life, as contrasted with aspirations or ideas of what ought to be. The latter concept involves judgments on which it is difficult to reach international agreement. The report of the experts therefore confined its analysis to the problem of definition and measurement of actual levels of living.

General agreement was reached on certain major conclusions: (1)

[2] United Nations, *Report on International Definition and Measurement of Standards and Levels of Living*, Doc. E/CN.5/299 (1954). (Hereinafter cited as *Report on Standards and Levels of Living*.) See also U.N. Statistical Office, *Survey of Social Statistics*, Statistical Papers, Series K, No. 1 (December 1954). Chapter VI (pp. 16–19) gives a brief summary of the report together with the comments of the Statistical Commission, which reviewed it in April 1954. It also contains a comprehensive review of the statistical activities of the United Nations and the specialized agencies as they relate to levels of living, as well as to the more traditional social welfare activities.

No single index can be devised to measure differences in levels of living between countries. (2) No type of monetary index as a general international measure of levels of living can be recommended. (3) The problem of measuring levels of living should be approached by analyzing many "components" representing generally recognized values and by the use of various "indicators" for the many types of components. (4) The statistical analysis of "indicators" and "components" should be accompanied by background information of a descriptive nature. (5) In addition to current efforts in the field of economic and social statistics to improve the factual basis for intercountry comparisons, family-living studies should be undertaken for the purpose of obtaining more comprehensive information on the actual conditions of life and work of individuals and families.

Much of the report was devoted to a discussion of "components" and "indicators." Components, as defined by the experts, are clearly delimited aspects or parts of the total life situation such as health, nutrition, education, etc., that are amenable to quantification. Indicators measure some aspect of a component—in the sense in which, for example, calorie consumption measures an aspect of nutrition and literacy rate measures an aspect of education.

The report suggested the following classification of *components* as suitable for international reporting on levels of living: (1) health, including demographic conditions; (2) food and nutrition; (3) education, including literacy and skills; (4) conditions of work; (5) employment situation; (6) aggregate consumption and saving; (7) transportation; (8) housing, including household facilities; (9) clothing; (10) recreation and entertainment; (11) social security; (12) human freedom.

In addition, the report urged the use of certain macro-economic items to indicate available or potential means for better satisfaction of needs. Among recommended indicators were percentage of the national income spent on the basic needs of life (food, clothing, shelter, and fuel); output of electric power per 100,000 of population; output plus import of steel and coal per 100,000 of population.

The experts recognized that an international analysis of levels of living, in terms of the components and indicators proposed, would fall short of giving a complete and balanced picture. They stressed, therefore, the importance of descriptive materials and background information, particularly in the form of social and cultural analyses, *i.e.*, studies of the conditions of living of special groups, and of social and cultural patterns. The report concluded, moreover, that an adequate over-all picture of levels of living would not be obtainable except through a very considerable expansion of studies of family living, that is, studies of actual conditions of life of families as directly observed and recorded in surveys. It suggested that as a next step, international organizations should undertake an examination of the possibility of developing relatively uniform techniques and schedules for family living studies in different parts of the world.

In this area, the International Labour Organisation had already done pioneering work, in particular, in its surveys of urban wage earners' families. Revised and extended recommendations on the conduct of family living studies were adopted by the aforementioned Seventh International Conference of Labour Statisticians, on the basis of a study prepared by the International Labour Office.[3] In underdeveloped areas, a rather considerable number of studies had been completed, as shown by a survey undertaken by the United Nations.[4] This survey showed, however, that much remained to be done in these areas because, with a few exceptions, the studies undertaken were on a very small scale and lacked comparability with regard to definitions, classifications, and presentation.

In summary, important progress is being made in defining and measuring levels of living, thus helping to bring into clear focus the major elements to be taken into account in any practical program for the improvement of levels of living.[5]

Development of Program of Social Action

When the Economic and Social Council, in June 1946, adopted terms of reference for its Social Commission, it did not make the pro-

[3] International Labour Office, *Methods of Family Living Studies*, Studies and Reports, New Series, No. 17 (1949).

[4] U.N. Department of Social Affairs, *Enquiries into Household Standards of Living in Less Developed Areas*, A Survey of the Organization and Geographic Range of Field Investigations of the Income, Expenditure, and Food Consumption of Selected Households in Africa, Asia, the Caribbean, Latin America, and the Pacific, 1930–1950, Doc. ST/SOA/1 (July 6, 1950).

[5] For recent information on this problem, see U.N. Economic and Social Council, Statistical Commission, *Comments of Governments on the Report on International Definition and Measurement of Standards and Levels of Living* (*A Summary Prepared by the Secretary-General*), Doc. E/CN.3/213 (Jan. 20, 1956). Observations by the interested specialized agencies are contained in *addenda* to Doc. E/CN.3/213. The Secretary-General's *General Conclusions Concerning Statistical Aspects of International Definition and Measurement of Levels of Living* are given in Doc. E/CN.3/214 (Feb. 2, 1956). Re-

motion of higher levels of living a specific function of the commission.[6] In the introductory portion of the resolution establishing the commission, however, the Council did mention that "the raising of the standard of living and the welfare of the peoples of the countries of the United Nations, which should include not only wages and income but all kinds of social services, is an important task of the United Nations." The very vagueness of this statement is significant. It shows that the raising of standards of living was not considered essentially a social problem. At best, social action was to be secondary in the promotion of better standards of living.

This is borne out by the fact that on the same day, the Council approved the terms of reference of the Economic and Employment Commission, the first paragraph of which stipulated that "the Commission shall advise the Economic and Social Council on economic questions in order to promote higher standards of living." The underlying assumption was clearly that economic development *per se*—improved methods of production, industrialization, larger trade, increased national incomes—would result in improved standards of living. There is, of course, justification for this assumption, and it is certainly true that there can be no substantial improvement in general levels of living without economic development. History, however, abounds in examples showing that economic development does not automatically result in a general improvement in the level of individual welfare. Not infrequently, existing inequalities in the distribution of wealth are increased, at least for a time, and periods of social instability and strife precede the attainment of stability at a higher level of individual welfare.

Several factors help to explain the initial lack of focus on the promotion of higher levels of living as a function of the Social Commission. First, the momentum of the social welfare activities of the League of Nations carried over into the United Nations. The social welfare activities of the League (though not those of the ILO) were aimed more at the protection of vulnerable groups in the population than at the active promotion of higher living levels for the population as a whole. Second, in its early economic and social activities, the United

---

cent work of the ILO in the field of family studies is summarized in *Report on Family Living Studies*, Doc. E/CN.3/215 (Jan. 19, 1956). The conclusions of the Statistical Commission are contained in U.N. Economic and Social Council, Statistical Commission, *Report of the Ninth Session*, Docs. E/2876 and E/CN.3/225, pp. 19–21.

[6] Res. 10(1), June 21, 1946.

Nations gave primary attention to the problems of the war-devastated countries. In the social field, this meant an emphasis on social rehabilitation, the rebuilding of social services, child and family welfare programs, and similar matters. Third, there were in existence or in process of creation a number of specialized agencies with operational functions in the social field and their respective roles were not yet clear. The International Labour Organisation had long been concerned with the improvement of labor conditions, the development of social security systems, and related matters. In spite of the Declaration of Philadelphia, it was not clear at the time to what extent the ILO might assume the major responsibility for promoting social action to improve standards of living.[7] In the field of health, an important component in the level of living, plans were under way for the creation of the World Health Organization. The proposed United Nations Educational, Scientific and Cultural Organization was also expected to contribute to higher standards of living. In these circumstances, the Social Commission appeared to be left with a residuum of social problems.

In 1947, the Economic and Social Council formally requested the Secretary-General to report to a future session of the Social Commission on the extent to which questions within the terms of reference of the commission had been or were being studied by the specialized agencies and intergovernmental organizations, and to suggest measures enabling the commission effectively to carry out the tasks entrusted to it, in particular, the study of standards of living in underdeveloped countries and areas.[8] At its third session in April 1948, the Social Commission had before it a report of its Advisory Committee on Planning and Co-ordination.[9] This report marked an important step forward in emphasizing the indivisibility of the social and economic aspects of promoting better standards of living and the need for co-ordinating both aspects.

[7] This declaration, adopted by the International Labour Organisation in 1944 (see Chap. I, above), affirms that all human beings, irrespective of race, creed, or sex, have a right to pursue both their material well-being and their spiritual development in conditions of freedom and dignity, of economic security and equal opportunity. The declaration asserts the need for effective national and international action, including measures to expand production and consumption, to promote the economic and social advancement of the less developed regions of the world, and to improve the health, education, and well-being of all people.

[8] Res. 43(IV), Mar. 29, 1947.

[9] U.N. Economic and Social Council, Social Commission, Third Session, *Report of the Advisory Committee on Planning and Co-ordination*, Doc. E/CN.5/46 (Mar. 23, 1948).

In establishing its own program, however, the Social Commission at that time developed a list of priorities on which work on "standards of living" appeared sixth and last after such items as social welfare services, prevention of crime and of prostitution.

In 1948 and 1949, some field inquiries into the living conditions of selected social groups in various parts of the world, particularly the less developed areas, were undertaken. The year 1950 marked a more decisive step forward in the social approach to the improvement of levels of living. That year the Council, on the recommendation of the Social Commission, adopted a resolution by which it requested the Secretary-General to submit to the Social Commission and to the Council a report on the world social situation to parallel the *World Economic Report* published annually, since 1947, by the United Nations.[10] In spite of misgivings on the part of many members of the Council about the feasibility of such an undertaking, the report, first published in 1952, became a real landmark in the development of the social work of the United Nations. Also in 1950, the Population Commission paid special attention to the interrelationship between population and economic development. It suggested that technical assistance be rendered to governments for surveys of the demographic situation of their countries as a part of broader surveys of economic and social conditions affecting development plans. It also suggested special studies of such subjects as the effects of changing social and economic conditions on birth and death rates; the influence of migration on population trends and on economic development; the estimation of future changes in population size and composition; and the effects of such changes on labor supply, utilization of resources, capital formation, consumption, production, and the standard of living.

The most important decision in 1951, involving the recognition of social action, provided that additional technical assistance activities undertaken for the benefit of underdeveloped countries in the field of social welfare should be considered under the Expanded Programme of Technical Assistance (EPTA) in cases where such work could not be financed from the regular budget of the United Nations.[11] Ever since, substantial social activities have been carried on under EPTA. In 1951, moreover, the Social Commission considered two papers on community welfare centers as instruments for the promotion of eco-

[10] Res. 309F(XI), July 13, 1950.

[11] This was recommended by the Economic and Social Council in Res. 399(XIII), Sept. 20, 1951, approved by the General Assembly in Res. 518(VI), Jan. 12, 1952.

nomic and social progress.[12] These papers helped to open the way for the adoption at a later stage of a program of community development that is proving an increasingly effective means of advancing levels of living.[13]

Potentially more important than these papers was the publication in 1951 of the report of a group of experts appointed for the purpose of exploring unemployment and underemployment in the underdeveloped countries, and the national and international measures required to reduce such unemployment and underemployment. Their report not only offered an extensive set of recommendations regarding measures for economic development, but contained also an incisive discussion of "Pre-Conditions of Economic Development."[14] It brought out with admirable clarity that economic development cannot be considered as a purely economic phenomenon but must be viewed in the context of social, political, cultural, and religious ideas, facts, and institutions.

Four outstanding events characterized developments in 1952. First, was the publication of the *Preliminary Report on the World Social Situation*, which brought together in a concise and purposeful way world-wide data on living conditions in both the developed and the underdeveloped countries.[15] It brought order into a welter of facts and figures out of which emerged an impressive picture of needs and aspirations. Second, the Economic and Social Council, explicitly recognizing the essential interdependence between the improvement of social conditions and the raising of living standards, transmitted the report to the specialized agencies for appropriate action and invited their recommendations on the development of programs of practical action in the social field.[16] Third, the Council requested the Secretary-General, in co-operation with the specialized agencies and appropriate nongovernmental organizations, to prepare for publication in 1954 a companion volume to

[12] U.N. Economic and Social Council, Social Commission, *Use of Community Welfare Centres as Effective Instruments to Promote Economic and Social Progress throughout the World—Report by the Secretary-General*, Doc. E/CN.5/244 (Feb. 28, 1951), and *Use of Community Welfare Centres as Effective Instruments to Promote Economic and Social Progress throughout the World—Document Submitted for Information by the United States of America*, Doc. E/CN.5/L.118 (Mar. 22, 1951).

[13] See below, Chap. X.

[14] U.N. Department of Economic Affairs, *Measures for the Economic Development of Under-Developed Countries* (1951), Chap. II, pp. 13–16. For a discussion of this report, see below, Chap. X.

[15] U.N. Department of Social Affairs, *Preliminary Report on the World Social Situation*, Doc. E/CN.5/267/Rev. 1 (Sept. 8, 1952). (Hereinafter referred to as *Report on the World Social Situation*.)

[16] Res. 434A(XIV), July 28, 1952.

the *Report on the World Social Situation*, this companion volume to survey national and international measures taken to improve social conditions throughout the world. It also arranged for publication, in 1956, of a second edition of the *Report on the World Social Situation.* Finally, the Council requested the Secretary-General, in co-operation with the ILO and other appropriate specialized agencies, to convene a small group of experts to prepare a report on the most satisfactory methods of defining and measuring standards of living and changes therein in various countries.[17] This undertaking, to which reference has already been made, was to lay the foundations for a systematic approach to the problem.

A pioneering study on the *Determinants and Consequences of Population Trends* was published in 1953.[18] It brought into focus the impact of changes in the size and structure of population on economic development and standards of living. In 1953 also, the Economic and Social Council, on the recommendation of the Social Commission, adopted a resolution setting forth a Program of Concerted Practical Action in the Social Field covering both the promotion of higher levels of living and the more traditional programs of social welfare.[19] In the preparation of its recommendations, the Social Commission had at its disposal an analysis by the Secretariat of social problems lending themselves to international action, and of the development of policies and activities relating thereto.[20]

The program as approved by the Council set forth a number of general principles, the first of which was that "economic and social development should go hand in hand with a view to improving standards of living." It stipulated that primary emphasis should be given by the United Nations system to projects that: (a) improve health and nutrition by increasing food supply, improving food distribution and dietary practices; (b) strengthen national health services, improve

[17] Res. 434B(XIV), July 25, 1952.

[18] U.N. Department of Social Affairs, *Determinants and Consequences of Population Trends*, A Summary of the Findings of Studies on the Relationships between Population Changes and Economic and Social Conditions, Doc. ST/SOA/Ser.A/17 (1953). A brief summary was published in 1954; see U.N. Department of Social Affairs, *Population Growth and the Standard of Living in Under-Developed Countries*, Population Studies No. 20, Doc. ST/SOA/Ser. A/20 (1954).

[19] Res. 496(XVI), July 31, 1953.

[20] U.N. Economic and Social Council, Sixteenth Session, *Official Records*, Annexes, Agenda Item 10: "Program of Concerted Practical Action in the Social Field of the United Nations and the Specialized Agencies." (Hereinafter cited as "Concerted Practical Action in the Social Field.")

maternal and child health, and prevent and control major communicable diseases; (c) strengthen national family and child welfare services; (d) improve social security measures; (e) develop and extend services for the welfare of groups in need of special care; (f) promote fundamental education, introduce or develop free compulsory primary education for all, and encourage scientific training and research; (g) improve housing and community facilities; (h) increase employment opportunities and improve the social and economic status of workers.

The Council at the same time urged that, in carrying out this program, particular attention be given to the use of the following practical methods and techniques for assisting governments in executing their social programs: (a) promotion and implementation of community development projects; (b) development of programs and facilities for training both professional and technical personnel and auxiliary and community workers; (c) development and strengthening of national and local organizations necessary for administering social programs.

In March 1954, the results of the work of the above-mentioned committee of experts on the measurement of standards and levels of living appeared, and in March 1955, the Secretary-General published the survey of programs of social development that he had been asked in 1952 to undertake.[21] Because international measures in the social field had been outlined in the Program of Concerted Practical Action in the Social Field, the 1955 report was confined to national measures. It revealed an extraordinary range of programs and activities carried on by national governments, both with a view to raising levels of living and protecting or rehabilitating special groups of the population.

Thus, by the beginning of 1955, the attention of the United Nations had clearly been focused on the social aspects of improving levels of living. Studies had been undertaken to develop a better understanding of what is meant by standards and levels of living and methods for their measurement. The impact of changes in population had been investigated. A mass of relevant data on actual living conditions had been gathered and presented. A careful analysis of the development of international programs had been prepared. Agreement had been reached within the United Nations and with the specialized agencies on a concerted program of practical international action in the social field. In theory at least, the old dichotomy between economic and

[21] U.N. Secretariat, Bureau of Social Affairs, *International Survey of Programs of Social Development*, Doc. E/CN.5/301/Rev. 1 (Mar. 31, 1955). (Hereinafter cited as *Survey of Programs of Social Development.*)

social objectives was resolved. The combination of the Economic and and Social Departments of the Secretariat of the United Nations into one department at the end of 1954 was more than a symbolic gesture.

With this as background, a more detailed analysis may be made of the insights gained as a result of studies and research, of the specific action programs evolved, and of the achievements registered.

Health

The objective of the World Health Organization is "the attainment by all peoples of the highest possible level of health."[22] Its constitution defines health as "a state of complete physical, mental and social well-being and not merely the absence of disease or infirmity."[23] Other agencies directly interested in health as here defined are the FAO (particularly with respect to nutrition); UNESCO (health education); and the United Nations Children's Fund or UNICEF (health of children and expectant mothers).

So important is the health component and so great was the need for international action that the World Health Organization was compelled to assume important operational and other functions even before it was permanently established. The Final Acts of the International Health Conference, which were signed on July 22, 1946, included an arrangement establishing an Interim Commission, which performed certain essential international health functions until the permanent organization was established on September 1, 1948. The Interim Commission re-established the epidemiological reporting services of the League of Nations and revived the technical work of that organization in such fields as vital statistics, the standardization of drugs and biologicals, the fight against important epidemic diseases, the supervision of international quarantine measures, and the adaptation of international sanitary conventions to conform with modern scientific knowledge and to meet new needs. In the autumn of 1947, it was called upon to help the Egyptian Government combat a major cholera epidemic. In the discharge of this task, it succeeded in getting Soviet planes to fly serum from Moscow and United States army planes to fly serum from Shanghai.

Since then the work of the World Health Organization has been developing in three major areas: the provision of central services, the

[22] United Nations, *Final Acts of the International Health Conference*, Constitution of the World Health Organization, Doc. E/155 (October 1946), Art. I.

[23] *Ibid.*, Preamble.

campaign against communicable diseases, and the development and strengthening of national public health services.

Central Services

Basic to the entire work of WHO are the functions that may be grouped under the general title of "central services." These include the stimulation and co-ordination of research and the broadening of the statistical frontiers of medical knowledge. Much of this work is carried on with the help of some thirty expert advisory panels composed of specialists in subjects ranging from alcoholism to zoonoses. These specialists supply the organization with technical advice by correspondence and provide the membership for its expert committees on antibiotics, biological standardization, drugs liable to produce addiction, health statistics, international pharmacopoeia, mental health, midwifery training, nursing, and other major fields.

Epidemiological bulletins are broadcast daily from Geneva (on six wave lengths in English and two in French), weekly from Singapore, and twice weekly from Alexandria. Closely related to this activity is the formulation of health and sanitary regulations. The publication of *Regulation No. 1 Regarding Nomenclature with Respect to Diseases and Causes of Death*[24] was followed in 1952 by the adoption of *Regulation No. 2: International Sanitary Regulations.* The latter are particularly important for purposes of standardizing national and international quarantine measures while expediting travel and trade.

The establishment of international pharmaceutical standards that facilitate and encourage the manufacture of drug products of uniform strength and potency throughout the world is another current activity of WHO. The first volume of the first *International Pharmacopoeia* (*Pharmacopoeia Internationalis*) setting uniform standards for two hundred important drugs was published in 1951 and a second volume in 1955.

Communicable Diseases

Of more immediate importance for the raising of levels of living are the large-scale campaigns carried on by the World Health Organization, frequently in co-operation with the Children's Fund, against certain endemic and other communicable diseases. This drive has benefited both from the work of many predecessors and from four developments

[24] See the volume in this Brookings series, *The United Nations and Promotion of the General Welfare*, Part One.

of the last ten years.[25] First, the general efforts undertaken since the Second World War to improve social and economic conditions have had important consequences for disease control through improvements in housing, nutrition, personal hygiene, environmental sanitation, general education as well as health education, and better medical care and health services. The World Health Organization itself has had a large share in some of these developments. Second, laboratory facilities have improved as a consequence of the increased demand from medical practitioners and health officers, so that diagnosis has become more adequate, and preventive measures can be applied earlier. Third, active immunization against specific diseases, although not new, has been undertaken on a larger scale since the war. Vaccination against yellow fever has been widely used for two decades and more recently vaccination against typhus has become a practical proposition; immunization against diphtheria and pertussis has become in many countries as widely accepted as small pox vaccination. Fourth, the greatest change in communicable disease control has been brought about by the development of three new types of products that have revolutionized the public health approach to different diseases: chemotherapeutic drugs, antibiotics, and insecticides.

A few examples of successful programs against communicable diseases will illustrate the dramatic effectiveness of modern medical means and the remarkable results achieved by governments working in co-operation with WHO.

Malaria is chiefly a rural disease, which has a severe adverse influence on agricultural and food-producing activities, reduces family income, prevents exploitation of fertile areas, and jeopardizes labor on large construction projects. Fortunately, the application of insecticides such as DDT to the walls of houses has made the control of rural malaria an economically feasible task even for countries that can afford little for public health budgets. Until recently, there have been approximately 300 million cases of malaria each year, with 3 million deaths. As a result of anti-malaria campaigns inspired or aided by WHO, approximately 229 million people, particularly in Asia and Latin America, but also in European countries such as Greece and Italy, have been protected against that disease. Ceylon is a striking example of what can be done. In that country, where work had been conducted on a demonstration basis for many years, a national malaria campaign was

[25] *Survey of Programs of Social Development*, pp. 27–28.

started in 1946. Whereas in that year there were 413 cases of malaria per 1,000 inhabitants, the rate dropped to 5 per 1,000 in 1954. In Latin America, Venezuela, also in 1946, initiated an anti-malaria program involving DDT spraying; 3.8 million people were directly protected in 1956; and malaria mortality, which was 173 per 100,000 inhabitants during the period 1941–45, dropped to 19 deaths among the entire population during 1955.

Extensive use has been made by teams from WHO, and by national teams guided by WHO experts, of penicillin in the treatment of syphilis, yaws, and related infections. The cost per person examined has been approximately ten cents. In Thailand, a campaign for the control of yaws has been in operation since May 1950. Of the 10 million Thais living in affected areas, 7.6 millions had been examined by the end of 1955, and more than a million cases had been treated.

Wide-ranging campaigns against tuberculosis have blunted the threat of that disease. These campaigns have included assistance to and the development of tuberculosis clinics, case finding, X-ray programs, training of specialized personnel, and vaccination with BCG (anti-tuberculosis vaccine). Under the nation-wide BCG vaccination program in India, initiated with assistance from WHO and the Children's Fund, nearly a million and a half persons are now being tested every month, and one third of these are being vaccinated. In Japan, a carefully planned and thorough tuberculosis control program, involving compulsory examination, immunization, reporting and registering of cases, clinical care, and home treatment, has been associated with a drop in deaths caused by tuberculosis from 187.2 per 100,000 inhabitants in 1947 to 62.3 in 1954.

Similar campaigns involving vaccination, environmental sanitation, and other procedures are being carried on against smallpox, yellow fever, typhus, diphtheria, and trachoma.[26]

Public Health Services

The World Health Organization itself considers its work on behalf of the development of public health services its most important task. It has defined the term public health as follows:

> Public health is the science and the art of preventing disease, prolonging life, and promoting physical health and efficiency through organized com-

[26] Such campaigns not only save and enrich human life but bring tangible economic benefits as well. For information on the economic aspects of health programs, see C.-E. A. Winslow, *The Cost of Sickness and the Price of Health* (1951).

munity efforts for the sanitation of the environment, the control of community infections, the education of the individual in principles of personal hygiene, the organization of medical and nursing services for the early diagnosis and preventive treatment of disease, and the development of the social machinery which will ensure to every individual in the community a standard of living adequate for the maintenance of health.[27]

In approaching this objective, the first task is the strengthening of national health services, and the second is the establishment and integration of local health services. The activities of WHO and other organs and agencies in the United Nations system can be grouped as follows:

1. Assistance to governments in the preparation of long-term national plans for health;

2. The setting up of model local health services or health demonstration areas in which both international and national personnel participate;

3. Emphasis within these health services on the improvement of environmental sanitation;

4. Health education of the public.

In promoting these objectives, all the known methods of international assistance, including the provision of advisers and of expert field workers, have been employed. Among the most important activities has been the development of facilities for the training of medical and paramedical personnel. The shortage of such personnel has been the greatest handicap in the development of adequate medical services. While Austria and the United States in 1952 had one physician for 650 and 770 inhabitants respectively, India had one physician for 5,700 inhabitants; Haiti, one for 10,000; and Nigeria, one for 58,000. This situation cannot be remedied overnight, but WHO is rendering substantial assistance by helping in the planning of medical schools, the occasional provision of teachers, and the granting of scholarships and fellowships.

In view of the time required to train physicians, high priority has been given also to the training of auxiliary personnel such as assistant doctors, nurses and nurses aides, assistant midwives, and sanitary inspectors. The periods required for such training are more limited and much can be achieved through the organization of short-term courses and on-the-spot training, particularly in connection with the development of local health centers or the work of health teams in the campaign against specific diseases.

The international activities relating to communicable diseases and

[27] World Health Organization, *Health Is Wealth* (1953), p. 14.

the development of public health services are so manifold and varied, and extend over so many territories, that it is quite impossible within the available space to give an adequate impression of their scope. A few statistics, however, may be of help. Between 1947 and the end of 1955, WHO awarded 5,355 fellowships, of which 1,103 were given in 1955. The beneficiaries of these fellowships were not only from the under-developed countries but also from Canada, the United States, and most of the nations of Western Europe. The weight attached to the several fields of activity is to some extent revealed by the fact that of the 1,103 fellowships given in 1955, 129 were awarded for study and training in public health; 151 for sanitation; 202 for nursing, maternal and child health; 186 for other health services; 303 for the study of communicable diseases; and 132 for clinical medicine and health education.[28]

During 1954—a typical recent year—WHO engaged in 337 work projects, most of them in the field, including both developed and under-developed countries.[29] Assistance to governments offered through these projects included expert advice in the development of national health plans and the establishment of national and local health services; assistance of individuals and teams in health campaigns, vaccination operations, and application of insecticides; training assistants to nurses and midwives; and a multitude of other training activities at all levels. Such work is contributing greatly to human happiness and well-being, to hope and faith in the future, to the determination to build steadily and persistently the basis for a better life.

Food and Nutrition

In 1951, the Director-General of the Food and Agriculture Organization remarked about the food supply:

> Grim is still the word for the world food situation. . . . In spite of the dark facts I find myself with the feeling of hope and confidence. This is because nations seem at last to be preparing for a genuinely large-scale world war against want. . . . This is essentially a movement to wipe out mass hunger and lift the burden of hopeless poverty from men's shoulders by applying modern scientific knowledge to the development of the earth's resources.[30]

[28] U.N. Technical Assistance Committee, *Eighth Report of the Technical Assistance Board*, Doc. E/2842; E/TAC/REP/66 (Apr. 10, 1956), p. 104.

[29] World Health Organization, *Official Records*, "The Work of WHO, 1954: Annual Report of the Director-General" (1955), pp. 127–89.

[30] Food and Agriculture Organization, *The Work of the FAO, 1950/51, Report of the Director-General* (1951), pp. 3–4.

The cautious note of optimism reflected in this passage has been justified by substantial improvements in the international food situation.[31] Not only are more people getting enough food, but more and more of them are beginning to enjoy the right food; real advances have been made both in the volume of food production and the level of nutrition. Internationally, the leading role in this battle against want has been played by the FAO, working in co-operation with WHO, with UNICEF, and UNESCO, as well as with other specialized agencies and the United Nations itself.[32]

What has been done thus far is only a beginning. A study prepared by the FAO for the Rome Conference on World Population in 1954 concluded that world production of cereals and many other crops could be at least doubled without assuming anything like the full application of technical knowledge; or alternatively, current production could be obtained from half or less than half of the present area under cultivation. In the case of livestock, the study concluded that the resources and technical basis exist for a level of production of animal products not less than five times the present world output. Fish production could be increased two or threefold without using more than a fraction of the productivity of the seas and inland waters.[33]

Even if these estimates are overoptimistic, they hold out real hope that levels of food consumption may before long become much more adequate than they are now. Recent statistics from a large number of countries on daily supplies of calories per capita (January 1952 or 1952–53) place those countries in the following broad categories:[34]

3,000 calories or over: Argentina, Australia, Canada, Denmark, Finland, Iceland, Ireland, New Zealand, Norway, Sweden, Switzerland, United Kingdom, and United States.

2,800–2,999 calories: Belgium-Luxembourg, France, Germany, Netherlands, and Uruguay.

2,600–2,799 calories: Austria, Cuba (1948–49), Czechoslovakia (1948–49), Turkey, and Union of South Africa.

[31] See above, Chaps. II and IV.

[32] The best accounts of the work of the Food and Agriculture Organization are to be found in Gove Hambidge, *The Story of FAO* (1955), and in Food and Agriculture Organization, *So Bold An Aim, Ten Years of International Cooperation Toward Freedom from Want* (1955).

[33] W. H. Pawley, *et al.*, *Possibilities of Increasing the Supply of Food and Agricultural Products by Exploitation of New Areas and Increasing Yields* (August 1954), 27 pp. (mimeo.).

[34] U.N. Department of Economic Affairs, Statistical Office, *Statistical Yearbook 1954*, pp. 272–75.

2,400–2,599 calories: Cyprus (1948–49), Greece, Israel, Italy, and Southern Rhodesia.
2,200–2,399 calories: Brazil, Chile, Colombia (1948–49), Egypt, Japan, Mauritius (1948–49), Portugal, and Venezuela.
2,000–2,199 calories: Honduras and Pakistan (1948–49).
Under 2,000 calories: Burma (1947–48), Ceylon, and India.

The deficiencies in caloric intake are, by medical standards adjusted to the conditions of the various countries, close to 20 per cent of requirements in parts of Southeast Asia and of Africa. This makes it imperative that every effort be made to provide not only *enough* but the *right kind* of food. This, in turn, raises the problem of nutrition, and of what the United Nations system is doing by way of studies, surveys, and action programs to improve the level of nutrition.

The central objective in nutrition is to make food production and consumption yield the best return in terms of individual health and well-being. Pioneering work in this field was undertaken by the Health Section of the League of Nations.[35] These early activities, together with progress made in such countries as the United States, offered a firm basis, by the end of the Second World War, for further international action. The promotion of nutrition became particularly promising when in 1953, as a result of the general increase in food production, the FAO could turn to the selective expansion of agricultural production, stimulating the output of foods in short supply or of special nutritive value.

The FAO and WHO are collaborating closely in this type of work. A Joint FAO/WHO Expert Committee on Nutrition has been in existence since 1950 and has provided effective co-ordination. The two organizations have fostered extensive studies of food needs in terms of human requirements for calories and nutrients. They have compared estimates of requirements against estimates of consumption, to determine whether the food supplies of countries are sufficient for their needs and whether existing food habits are satisfactory. A continuing task of the Nutrition Division of the FAO is to help countries to improve and refine national food balance sheets, which show the quantities of different food groups and the calories, proteins, and other nutrients available per head of population.

In recent years, on-the-spot surveys of food consumption and habits have not only added new knowledge of deficiencies in rice and maize diets but have led also to more important insights into protein malnutri-

[35] See above, Chap. I.

tion, which appears to be even more serious, particularly for children, than malnutrition resulting from vitamin or mineral deficiencies. World attention was focused on the widespread incidence of protein malnutrition by a study prepared jointly by the FAO and WHO in 1952 on this condition in Central Africa, where it is known as kwashiorkor.[36] During recent years, reports from all parts of the world have told of the same disease taking its toll of children, but under a great many different names, which by their variety had previously obscured the common cause—protein malnutrition. Further extensive surveys were made in Latin America in 1953. Conferences on the subject were organized jointly by the Food and Agriculture Organization and the World Health Organization in 1952 and 1953 in Gambia, Africa, in Java for South and East Asia, and in Venezuela for Latin America. These activities helped prepare the way for effective measures to meet this threat to the health and well-being of millions of young people.

The most direct way of meeting food deficiencies is by supplementary feeding. Such feeding programs were started by the United Nations Relief and Rehabilitation Administration (UNRRA) and later continued by the Children's Fund in co-operation with WHO and the FAO. School feeding programs with emphasis on protein-rich skimmed milk have by now become accepted practice in a number of countries, and many of these programs can be traced directly to international initiative. Special feeding programs are also being developed for plantation and industrial workers with remarkable results in terms of increased productivity.

In countries where milk is in short supply, the FAO has not only assisted in the development of the dairy industry but, under its leadership, successful experiments have been made in developing substitutes for animal milk and other foods of high nutritive value. To provide a protein-rich food, soy milk has been produced for some years in a factory in Hong Kong. Active experiments with soy and peanut preparations are being carried on also in other parts of Asia, particularly in the Philippines, Indonesia, and India. Fish is another protein-rich food, and the FAO has played a considerable part in advising on methods of increasing world fish yields from both fresh and salt water. It has pioneered in the stocking of rice paddies with fish and has promoted the development of the manufacture of fish flour that has no objectionable flavor. Similarly, new processes in the milling of rice

[36] J. F. Brock and M. Autret, *Kwashiorkor in Africa*, FAO Nutrition Studies, No. 8 (March 1952), 78 pp.

have been inspired by FAO-sponsored activities and experiments aimed at avoiding the almost complete loss of thiamine (Vitamin B-1) that occurs in the traditional milling of rice and is the major cause of beri-beri. In the Philippines, rice is being "fortified" on a large scale by vitamin additives.

In addition to developing substitute foods that are rich in protein, the FAO has made an outstanding contribution to the well-being of millions of people in the Middle East and Southeast Asia by saving the "natural" producers of protein-rich foods, *i.e.*, livestock. As described earlier, the FAO since 1946 has co-operated with, and in many cases initiated, campaigns to immunize livestock against rinderpest, a disease that formerly killed millions of head of cattle per year.[37] It has also stimulated the production of other animal vaccines.

Next in importance to improving the production of nutritious food, is the preservation of perishable food of high nutritional value. Here again the FAO has engaged in extensive activities to improve storage facilities, canning, and the development of preserving additives. The Children's Fund has done outstanding work in the establishment of milk-processing plants.

Education in nutrition and the training of nutrition personnel are other subjects that hold a high priority in the FAO/WHO programs. One of the most important aspects of these educational campaigns is the attempt to modify food habits in order to make the best use of available foods. International assistance in the field of education in nutrition has included the publication of a guide that is being widely used in interested countries.[38] International aid also includes the provision of technical advisers to government departments to assist in the development of appropriate national education programs in the field of nutrition. Finally, direct assistance in furthering the supply of trained workers extends to the provision of fellowships, the conduct of regional and national nutrition training courses, in-service training, and the organization of workshops.

More and more of these activities are being carried on and co-ordinated by national nutrition organizations. The creation of such organizations was recommended as early as 1943 by the Hot Springs Conference, which established the Food and Agriculture Organization. At the end of the Second World War, actively functioning nutrition organ-

[37] See above, Chap. IV.

[38] Food and Agriculture Organization, *Teaching Better Nutrition—A Study of Approaches and Techniques*, FAO Nutritional Studies, No. 6.

izations existed in only a few countries, mainly in North America, northern Europe, and Oceania. By 1953, nutrition organizations had been established in India, Indonesia, Japan, Thailand, the Philippines, Malaya, and Singapore. An Institute of Nutrition for Central America and Panama, founded in 1946 under the sponsorship of the Pan American Sanitary Bureau, has been serving the entire Central American region.

Housing

The *Preliminary Report on the World Social Situation* concluded that there is no country without a housing problem.[39] It estimated that as many as 150 million families in the less developed areas required more adequate homes in better physical surroundings. In the industrially advanced countries, the housing deficit was estimated to be more than 30 million family dwelling units. Housing that was poor before the war has become worse as a result of rapid urbanization, population increases, war devastation, and economic dislocations. At the same time, standards for adequate housing have risen.

The socio-economic implications of the situation have become a matter of concern to the United Nations and several of its specialized agencies. The importance of the housing component in determining levels of living was clearly set forth in connection with proposals for an integrated program in the field of housing and town and country planning:

> Housing is a most important element in standards of living. On the quantity and quality of the housing available, on the environment in which such accommodation is set, on the cost of housing in relation to family needs, and on the collective amenities made available to the community in the form of facilities for health, education, cultural and recreational services, depends to a large extent the well-being of the community. It is thus clear that the provision of adequate and healthy housing in a suitable environment at the lowest possible cost should constitute an important element in the promotion of "... higher standards of living ... and conditions of economic and social progress and development," with which the United Nations is charged under Articles 55 and 56 of the Charter.[40]

In view of the vast destruction wrought by the Second World War it is understandable that as early as 1946 a resolution was presented by Australia to the Preparatory Commission of the United Nations in

[39] See Chap. V, "Housing," pp. 53–59.

[40] U.N. Economic and Social Council, *Housing and Town and Country Planning*, Report of the Secretary-General, Doc. E/1343 (June 8, 1949), p. 6.

London requesting the establishment of a commission to deal with questions of housing and town planning. The proposal, however, was considered premature. The problem of housing was taken up later in 1946 by the Temporary Subcommission of the Economic and Social Council on the Economic Reconstruction of Devastated Areas. It presented a survey of immediate housing needs in Europe and drew attention to the fact that the common obstacles to speedy reconstruction were shortages of timber and coal, of skilled labor, and, in some countries, of manufactured goods. The main objective, it indicated, should be to carry out reconstruction conforming to modern social and technical requirements. The subcommission also associated itself with the report of a special meeting on emergency housing problems held in Brussels, in July 1946, under the auspices of the Emergency Economic Committee for Europe, which recommended that the Economic and Social Council sponsor a permanent international housing organization.

No such organization has been created. The idea was abandoned because (1) several existing agencies already included within their functions various aspects of housing, and a new agency might have led to duplication; and (2) it was believed that housing problems could best be handled on a regional basis. Therefore, from 1946 onward, stress was laid on the development of co-ordinated rather than centralized action, and emphasis was placed on regional activities.

Between 1946 and 1952, the General Assembly and the Economic and Social Council passed a series of basic resolutions that gave form and direction to intergovernmental action in the field of housing.[41] As a result of these resolutions and of practical experience gained over the years, co-ordinating responsibility in the field of housing has been assigned to the Social Commission. The Population Commission, which has been interested in housing in so far as fluctuations in the density of population may affect housing conditions and vice versa, has been supplying interested organizations with the population figures required to permit a better evaluation of housing problems. The Commission on Human Rights has been concerned with adequate housing as a "right," while the Commission on the Status of Women has been concerned with those aspects of housing that make life easier for the housewife, improve the health of the family, and provide children with the opportunity for safe and full development.

[41] See U.N. General Assembly Resolutions: 53(I), Dec. 14, 1946; 537(VI), Feb. 2, 1952. U.N. Economic and Social Council Resolutions: 50(IV), Mar. 28, 1947; 122D(VI), Mar. 1, 1948; 155F(VII), Aug. 13, 1948; 243D(IX), July 23, 1949; 434I(XIV), July 28, 1952.

Co-operation between the interested specialized agencies and the United Nations has been facilitated through a "Technical Working Group on Housing and Town and Country Planning" set up by the Administrative Committee on Coordination. Among the participating agencies, the FAO has been concerned primarily with housing standards for rural areas. It has been interested in addition in standardizing construction methods and timber materials in order to economize on these items. The ILO has been concerned not only with the working conditions of labor in the building industry but also with the availability of good housing for all workers. The problem of reducing production costs in the building industry and of subsidies to the industry to facilitate the provision of cheaper housing, have been subjects of extended study by the International Labour Organisation. UNESCO has been concerned with the improvement of the technical education of architects and planners, the development of technical schools, and the popularization of better housing through literature, films, and exhibitions. WHO has, of course, been interested in the health aspects of housing and housing standards, and particularly in better sanitation.

Within the Secretariat of the United Nations a Housing, Building and Planning Branch, as well as a Housing Reference Center, have been functioning since the early days of the Organization. The Secretariat publishes a bulletin that contains a great deal of technical information on housing, although some of it is highly specialized and, at times, academic.[42] The United Nations Technical Assistance Administration is concerned with technical assistance projects in the field of housing.

The programs and activities set forth in a report by the Secretary-General in 1949,[43] as revised by the Economic and Social Council in 1952[44] and developed in subsequent practice, lend themselves to discussion under four headings: housing conditions and planning; building materials and the construction industry; financing; and self-help housing.

Housing Conditions and Planning

Housing conditions are kept under review by the several regional commissions, particularly the Economic Commission for Europe (ECE) and the Economic Commission for Asia and the Far East (ECAFE).

The ECE, building on preliminary work of the Emergency Economic Committee for Europe, concentrated from the start on housing needs

[42] *Bulletin on Housing and Town and Country Planning.*
[43] U.N. Economic and Social Council, *Housing and Town and Country Planning.*
[44] Res. 434I(XIV), July 25, 1952.

and programs in Europe for the years 1948–55, requirements for building materials, and measures to economize in the use of scarce materials. The secretariat of the ECE publishes annual reviews of the European housing situation, in addition to a *Quarterly Bulletin on European Housing Statistics*, started in 1953. A major achievement of the ECE in the field of housing has been the establishment of the International Council for Building Research and Documentation, a European regional council of national research centers, which is in no way dependent on the United Nations for financing.

Work in Asia and the Far East was stimulated by a mission of experts on tropical housing that visited South and Southeast Asia in 1950 and 1951.[45] The United Nations Regional Seminar on Housing and Community Improvement held in New Delhi in 1954 was a direct consequence of the work of that mission. Government officials, representatives of the United Nations and the specialized agencies, and housing and planning experts attended this seminar, as well as the Regional Conference of the International Federation for Housing and Town Planning organized in conjunction with it. The seminar was followed by a session of the ECAFE Working Party on Housing and Building Materials, which helped to translate the findings of the seminar into recommendations to governments of the area.

As a result of these and other activities, plans are maturing for the establishment of two regional housing centers under the guidance of ECAFE in co-operation with the governments concerned, and with the assistance of the United Nations and interested specialized agencies. A center in Indonesia is expected to deal with housing in humid tropical areas; while a second center in India studies similar problems in dry tropical countries. The main task of these centers will be the co-ordination of studies, research, and developmental work carried out in the region on the economic, social, technological, and administrative aspects of housing, building, and planning.

The Economic Commission for Latin America (ECLA) has paid less attention to housing problems because housing has been a matter of special concern to the Organization of American States and its Inter-American Council on Housing. Both ECLA and the United Nations headquarters, however, had a share in the establishment in 1951 of the Inter-American Housing Center in Bogotá, which serves all of Latin America. The major function of the Center is to offer a

[45] U.N. Secretariat, *Low Cost Housing in South and South-East Asia*, Doc. ST/SOA/3/Rev. 1 (July 16, 1951).

one-year graduate course in housing that emphasizes the interrelationship of architecture, engineering, and the economic and social aspects of the housing problem.

Building Materials and Industry

To be economical, building activity has to be based essentially on local building materials. The United Nations has been able to encourage research regarding such materials by the provision of experts and of fellowships, by demonstration projects, and by help in the establishment of research and training centers such as those mentioned above.

Related to this problem of building materials is the problem of standardization, which is, of course, of importance both to developed and underdeveloped countries. In the economically less developed countries, there is generally a serious lack of standardization of building materials and construction methods. In the postwar period, however, there has been increasing experimentation, fostered partly by the United Nations, with basic housing designs and with a better use of readily available local building materials. Some of the results of these efforts were illustrated at the International Exhibition of Low Cost Housing staged in 1954 by the Government of India with the help of the United Nations. Eighty houses for the lower-income groups, built with different materials and designed in several countries, were exhibited there.

With a view to reducing the cost of building in Europe, the ECE has been investigating on a continuing basis the rationalization of building methods. On an even broader basis the Secretariat of the United Nations has been encouraging general building research, some of the results of which have been reproduced in the *Bulletin on Housing and Town and Country Planning.*[46]

Financing

Attention was given to the financing of housing in 1952 by the General Assembly, the Economic and Social Council, and the Social Commission. Although local financing was emphasized as practically the exclusive source of capital for housing purposes, sufficient pressure was generated by the representatives of the underdeveloped countries for the General Assembly to include a request to the Economic and Social Council to give urgent attention to "assistance to governments in

[46] Bulletin 8 (1953).

developing practical methods for financing housing programs from domestic *or external sources*."[47] The Social Commission at its eighth session also urged an exploration of the possibilities of external financing.

In the course of these discussions, it was suggested that the International Bank for Reconstruction and Development ought to extend its loan activities to the financing of housing. The Bank gave little encouragement to this suggestion. It indicated that the basic test of any project to be financed by the Bank was its contribution to productivity and that the relation of housing to increased productivity was most apparent in cases where housing development was an integral part of a directly productive project—for example, workers' housing for an industrial plant. In other cases, the most effective and economic way of stimulating more housing was investment in basic industries such as steel, power, transportation, and the like, that support an active building industry. Another basic requirement was that Bank loans are normally made to cover only foreign exchange needs rather than local currency needs. In summary, the aid of the Bank to housing would most likely take the form in the future, as in the past, of investment in basic utilities and industries, thus helping to build economies in which housing industries could become progressively more efficient.[48]

While the underdeveloped countries frequently reiterated their desire for international financing for housing purposes, the work of the United Nations, in research and in technical assistance, has emphasized the development of domestic resources. Recent reports, for example, contain valuable data on government housing schemes and subsidies, and on the methods employed in different countries to overcome the discrepancy between the "social rent" (what the consumer can afford to pay for adequate housing) and the "economic rent" (what the consumer should be charged according to actual costs.)[49]

Self-help Housing

In view of the inadequacy of available capital, the promotion of "self-help housing" has assumed increasing importance. Such self-

[47] Res. 537(VI), Feb. 2, 1952. Italics supplied.

[48] U.N. Economic and Social Council, *Housing and Town and Country Planning*, Statement by the Representative of the International Bank for Reconstruction and Development on Financing of Housing, Doc. E/CN.5/284 (May 23, 1952).

[49] U.N. Economic and Social Council, *Financing of Housing and Community Improvement Programs*, Report by the Secretary-General, Doc. E/CN.5/307 (Mar. 7, 1955). See also *Survey of Programs of Social Development*, Chap. IV.

help housing makes maximum use of underemployed labor and of materials available locally. In 1953, a self-help housing workshop and seminar was convened in Puerto Rico, sponsored jointly by the Caribbean Commission, the United States Foreign Operations Administration and the United States Housing and Home Finance Agency, and assisted by the Technical Cooperation Office of Puerto Rico. The seminar suggested that aided self-help be employed as a basis for providing adequate housing and other community facilities for low-income groups, in view of the advantages to the families concerned and to the government that could be derived from this method. A seminar on housing through nonprofit associations was organized by the United Nations and the Danish Government in collaboration with the Organization of American States. The seminar, which was held in Denmark in 1954 with the participation of thirteen Latin American countries, was a good example of the contribution that one geographic region can make to another. A similar seminar, again in Denmark but for countries from Asia, was held in 1956.

It is difficult to gauge the results of the activities of the United Nations system in housing. Despite what has been said and done, the progress made has been small compared with existing needs. It should, however, not be forgotten that most of the programs are long-range programs, the effects of which will be felt only during the years to come. In many parts of the world, real progress in housing depends on over-all economic development. Headway in housing can undoubtedly be speeded, however, and this is being done by the mobilization of domestic resources, both material and human—a mobilization that, at least to some extent, is being inspired and guided by international agencies.

Home Economics

Home economics represents another of the social approaches to the raising of levels of living. It is concerned with numerous aspects of family life, including home management, child training and care, cleanliness and elementary sanitation, the choice of foods, the preparation of family meals, the domestic production, storage, and processing of foods, and the provision and care of clothing and household furnishings. The purpose of education in home economics is to funnel the advances of science and management into the service of the individual family, especially through the education of women in the better use of family resources. Home-making is the chief full-time occupation of women throughout the world and adequate education in this field can contribute importantly to the attainment of higher levels of living.

The scope of international programs in this field is indicated in the following passage:

In particular, assistance is being rendered to governments in the following ways: providing technical advisers to government departments to assist in promoting education in home economics at all levels and in establishing training centres for home economics teachers and rural leaders; participating in rural demonstration, production and training centres where the education of women is a significant part of the total programme; holding regional meetings for government officials and other leaders responsible for the promotion and development of home economics education and extension; participating in meetings of international nongovernmental women's organizations whose programme and activities centre around the problems of the rural family; providing a home economics information exchange for the use of member governments and country leaders in home economics education and extension.[50]

A few illustrations may be helpful. Home economics work by the FAO was initiated in the Caribbean area in 1949. A technical meeting on nutrition and home economics held in 1952 gave direction to the program and resulted in the establishment of an Advisory Council on Home Economics for the British West Indies, a three-months training course in home economics at the University of Puerto Rico, and the evaluation and further development of home economics curricula in public schools in the area. Another six-weeks training course on nutrition and home economics, sponsored jointly by the FAO, the Organization of American States, and the Government of Ecuador, was held in Quito in 1954. Home economics projects are under way also in Egypt, and an extension of this type of work to the Far East is planned by the FAO.

This work is not confined to underdeveloped countries. FAO is active in Working Group No. 10 on Rural Home Economics of the Food and Agriculture Committee of the Organization for European Economic Cooperation. It thus collaborates with OEEC in planning training programs and special home economics projects in countries that are members of the OEEC.

Employment and Working Conditions

High levels of employment and equitable working conditions, including adequate wages and reasonable hours of work, are basic to the

[50] "Concerted Practical Action in the Social Field," p. 28.

achievement and maintenance of satisfactory levels of living. Such adjectives as "equitable," "adequate," "reasonable," and "satisfactory," can be defined only in terms of evolving social concepts.

Various economic policies and measures to attain and maintain high levels of employment have already been discussed in this study.[51] The present discussion is concerned with action aimed at improving the working conditions of individual workers, at setting and achieving standards of wages and hours that will permit "satisfactory" levels of living. Among other things, this requires a discussion of measures for making optimum use of available labor resources, since improved levels of living are contingent on increased productivity. In this context, such matters have to be considered as: vocational guidance and training; employment services; occupational health and safety; the protection of young workers and of women; and industrial relations.[52]

Although the International Labour Organisation has made some outstanding contributions to economic research, it has in recent years concentrated on labor issues as such. Broad economic policy issues have been left to the United Nations, but the ILO has continued to be the major agency in setting labor standards through conventions and recommendations, while increasingly developing practical action programs aimed at assisting countries in attaining these standards.

Man-power Programs

Vocational guidance and training, and employment services, have the common objective of matching people and jobs. They thus contribute to the integration of the individual in society and help society to meet the needs for different types of labor. A prerequisite for these activitiee is adequate employment information.[53] The ILO therefore has been giving high priority to man-power surveys and the development of continuing machinery for obtaining current employment information. These matters were given special attention at the Asian Man-power Technical Conference in Bangkok in 1951 and at the Latin American Man-power Technical Conference in Lima in 1952.

[51] See above, Chap. V.

[52] For additional discussion see "Concerted Practical Action in the Social Field," Chap. 6, pp. 35–51; and *Survey of Programs of Social Development*, Chaps. VII and VIII. Especially helpful are the annual reports of the ILO submitted to the United Nations since 1947 in pursuance of Article V, paragraph 2(a), of the Agreement between the United Nations and the ILO. Even more comprehensive and authoritative information is to be found in the *International Labour Code 1951*, Vols. I and II.

[53] *Cf.* International Labour Organisation, *Seventh Report of the International Labour Organisation to the United Nations* (1953), pp. 27 ff.

In preparing and carrying out man-power studies and surveys, the ILO works with the three regional economic commissions of the United Nations. Surveys were made in collaboration with ECAFE in 1948 and with ECLA in 1949. A special ILO-UNESCO Working Party on Trained Personnel for Economic Development has for several years been working on a manual to assist Asian countries wishing to carry out man-power surveys.

In order to facilitate surveys and to render them internationally comparable—which is important for migration purposes—it is essential to establish common definitions and classifications of occupations. The most outstanding contribution of the ILO in this field has been the publication of an international classification, in which occupations are grouped according to similarities of skill requirements.[54] It is designed to facilitate the transfer of workers belonging to an occupation in one group to other occupations within the same group, with a minimum of retraining or adaptation and with a maximum of productive efficiency. Definitions of occupations are also included for each group and, in addition, tables of occupational comparability have been worked out, thus facilitating job comparisons between countries using different occupational terminologies.

The objective in vocational guidance has been to assist governments to establish and develop facilities for aiding individuals to choose occupations and to progress in these occupations, with due regard for the characteristics, aptitudes, and training of the individual on the one hand, and the available occupational opportunities on the other. One of the chief contributions of the ILO in this respect was the adoption, in 1949, of a Vocational Guidance Recommendation.[55] Its provisions are based on the experience and practice of the United States and Western Europe where up to 50 per cent of young persons ready to leave school are now receiving guidance offered either by special counselors attached to the schools or through employment offices. In many cases such offices or special guidance centers provide guidance on a continuing basis, irrespective of age.

The recommendation, coupled with expert advice to governments,

[54] International Labour Organisation *International Classification of Occupations for Migration and Employment Placement*, Vol. I, Occupational Titles, Codes and Definitions; Vol. II, Tables of Occupational Comparability (June 1952).

[55] For texts of this and other recommendations and conventions adopted by the International Labour Conference 1919–51, see International Labour Office, *International Labour Code 1951*. For texts adopted after 1951, see periodic issues of the ILO *Official Bulletin*.

fellowships, regional meetings, and vocational guidance "kits" prepared by the ILO and UNESCO, has in recent years stimulated and aided the development of guidance programs in all parts of the world, particularly in Asia and Latin America. According to the annual report of the Director-General of the ILO for 1954, growing interest in the use of vocational guidance services and the application of aptitude testing in relation to youth training and placement has recently been displayed in a number of countries in the process of industrialization, among them Brazil, Greece, Israel, and Indonesia.

Guidance has to be supplemented by training, and this has required assistance in the development of vocational schools, training centers, and facilities for in-service training to provide special skills. At the same time, it is essential that occupational training be so organized as to make for the adaptability of the individuals trained. Adaptability is important both for mobility of labor in the highly developed countries and for the integration of a growing industrial labor force in countries in the process of development. This is one aspect of the fundamental education programs developed by UNESCO, of which more will be said later.[56]

In training, the ILO has been active also in promulgating standards. It followed its Vocational Guidance Recommendation by a Recommendation, in 1950, on Vocational Training (Adults). Regional conferences such as the Asian Conference of Experts on Vocational Training in Singapore, 1949, have been organized to help governments apply such standards. Going beyond this, the ILO, particularly through its program of technical assistance, has set up regional field offices for manpower training, productivity centers, and apprenticeship institutes such as the Apprenticeship Training Institute for Asian Countries that was held at the end of 1952. The program of the institute provided for a study tour of national apprenticeship services by fifteen officials from nine Asian countries, to observe methods and techniques of proved value in France, the Netherlands, Switzerland, and the United Kingdom.

In addition, the ILO has helped individual countries carry out training programs. Most outstanding of these is the ILO vocational training project in Yugoslavia. In 1954, with the help of technical assistance funds, nearly four hundred Yugoslav worker-trainees had been or were at work in various industries all over Europe. Some thirty-five

[56] See below, Chap. IX.

instructor-foremen from ten different countries assisted in training activities in Yugoslavia itself. In addition, a course in management techniques was organized in France for a group of general and technical managers from some of the more important industries in Yugoslavia. Reports from factories, from instructor-foremen, and from trainees indicate that improvements of great economic value have been introduced by the trainees on their return and by the instructor-foremen in the course of their work in the Yugoslav industries.[57]

Another link in the chain of international activities for the rational use of man power is the promotion of employment services. As early as 1919, the Unemployment Convention—the second convention ever passed by the International Labour Organisation—provided for the setting-up of employment services assisted by advisory committees, including employers and workers. With the growing awareness of the importance of such services, more elaborate principles were adopted, first in 1944, particularly in the Employment (Transition from War to Peace) Recommendation, and then, in 1948, in the Employment Service Convention and Recommendation. These laid down basic principles to be followed in order that employment services might ensure the best possible organization of the employment market as an integral part of the national program for the achievement and maintenance of full employment and the development and use of productive resources. These general standards have since been further elaborated in Europe through the adoption by the Council of the OEEC, in July 1954, of a series of International Standards of Employment Service Organization, which was developed with the assistance of the ILO with a view to achieving general conformity in Europe over a five-year period.

The ILO is assisting less developed countries in establishing employment services, using mainly such devices as experts and fellowships. Efforts are being made to provide for clearance on a regional and national scale, through employment services, of job offers and applications for employment. This has proved of particular importance in such countries as Brazil, where a special placement service in the State of Sao Paulo is facilitating the large-scale movement of agricultural workers and their families from the overpopulated regions of the northeast to the south of the country.

In summary, man-power programs represent one of the important fields for technical assistance and technical co-operation in raising levels

[57] International Labour Organisation, *Eighth Report of the International Labour Organisation to the United Nations* (1954), p. 66.

of living. During the last few years, close to 60 per cent of all the technical assistance work of the ILO has been devoted to man-power problems.

Conditions of Work

International concern with conditions of work has been focused primarily on four areas: wages and earnings; hours of work and holidays with pay; occupational health and safety; and the protection of special categories of workers (*e.g.*, children).

The latest of the conventions and recommendations that have been adopted by the ILO concerning the protection of wages—and the only major convention concluded in this field since the end of the war—is the 1949 Convention on Protection of Wages. It provides that wages ordinarily be paid both regularly and in the legal tender of the country; defines permissible deductions from wages; and includes safeguards against exploitation in company stores.

Although the number of conventions and recommendations regarding wages is large, it goes without saying that the standards they set are less effective where trade unions are not in existence, are too weak to serve as real instruments of collective bargaining, or are exploited for ends other than those for which they were founded.

Many countries, therefore, including of late a number of underdeveloped countries, have found it necessary to establish statutory minimum wages. The Asian Regional Conference of the ILO in 1953 gave special attention to this problem. In the words of the Eighth Report of the ILO to the United Nations:

> The Conference unanimously agreed that collective agreements are normally the best means for the determination and adjustment of wages. But, while recognising that the rapid expansion of collective bargaining between adequately organised groups of employers and workers was the ultimate objective, the Conference recommended that, pending this development and as a preliminary step towards collective negotiation, statutory minimum wages should be fixed and regularly reviewed by tripartite machinery. The enforcement of statutory wage regulations should be the responsibility of an adequately staffed and equipped authority. Finally, the Conference recommended that the closest possible attention should be given to maintaining a relationship between wage regulation and the requirements of economic development.[58]

Thus, the conference recognized the pitfalls of wage policies that, inspired by a desire to improve wage levels rapidly, may result in in-

[58] *Ibid.*, p. 17.

flationary pressures and interfere with sound economic development. Similar reflections can be found in other ILO publications on wage policies in Asia and in Latin America.[59]

An increasing number of developed countries are confronted with a narrowing of wage differentials as a result of minimum wage fixing, full employment, technological change, social policies, and other factors. This raises a number of problems that are being given increasing attention by the ILO and, to some extent, by UNESCO. Some reduction in the gap between the wages of skilled and unskilled workers, and even professional workers, may be desirable. However, if wage differentials are narrowed too much by regulation, the result may be a loss of incentive to acquire or use socially needed skills. In this connection, the ILO has studied various aspects of the application of systems of payment by results. It has also shown a concern for the economic conditions of professional workers, their employment and income levels.

Another important issue in wage policy is the principle of equal pay for equal work. This has been a matter of interest to the Commission on the Status of Women, which has passed a series of resolutions on the subject. The principle that there should be "equal remuneration for men and women workers, for work of equal value," *i.e.*, rates of remuneration established without discrimination based on sex, is now contained in the 1951 Convention on Equal Remuneration for Work of Equal Value adopted by the ILO. The 1951 convention provides for gradual application of this principle in keeping with the gradualist approach that is characteristic of the ILO.

Not only wages, but hours of work as well, have been burning issues in labor relations ever since the industrial revolution, and one of the chief preoccupations of the ILO. In recent years, the problem has become much less acute as an international issue for reasons that are clearly set forth in the following quotation:

> The excessive length of the working day and its ill-effects upon the health of workers, family life and productivity, have been among the first preoccupations of national and international action. International action in this field taken soon after the First World War resulted in the adoption of international standards limiting hours of work in industrial undertakings and in commerce and offices to eight a day and forty-eight a week, and fixing a minimum rest period of twenty-four consecutive hours per week in all public and private industrial undertakings. A trend towards a further reduction from the eight-

[59] International Labour Office, *Problems of Wage Policies in Asian Countries*, Studies and Reports, New Series, No. 43 (1956); and *Minimum Wages in Latin America*, Studies and Reports, New Series, No. 34 (1954).

hour day and forty-eight hour week led to the adoption of international regulations concerning the reduction of hours of work in particular industries or occupations but was interrupted by the Second World War and has since been held in check in many countries by various considerations connected with reconstruction or production requirements.

In the present circumstances international action in this field consists primarily in providing information on the regulation of hours of work and in assisting countries, on request, in drawing up laws and regulations in accordance with existing international standards.[60]

By contrast, international interest in the problem of holidays with pay has recently been much more pronounced. As early as 1936, the ILO had formulated international instruments setting forth minimum standards with regard to lengths of holidays, qualifying periods of continuous service, and similar questions, with a view to encouraging the introduction of annual holidays with pay in industrial and commercial establishments. A convention of the ILO, adopted in 1952, was designed to extend these principles to agriculture. It was followed, in 1954, by a recommendation concerning holidays with pay, providing that every person should be entitled after one year of continuous service with the same employer to an annual holiday with pay of not less than two normal working weeks. As a corollary to these developments, both the ILO and UNESCO have engaged in studies regarding better use of leisure time and the development of leisure time facilities.

Occupational health and safety is another field that has been of concern to the ILO since its inception. The objective has been to prevent occupational injuries and to protect the health of the workers in their places of employment. Occupational hazards have greatly increased in an increasingly industrialized world. With the growing mechanization of agriculture, a new element of risk has been added even in underdeveloped countries unaccustomed to the use of machines.

In this field, the setting of health and safety standards is one of the most important lines of attack. International standards of industrial safety are contained in comprehensive recommendations passed by the ILO prior to and since the Second World War. For example, a recommendation in this field, adopted in 1953, concerns "the protection of health of workers in places of employment" and deals with the control of health hazards, medical examinations, notification of occupational disease, and the provision of first aid facilities. It deals also in some detail with the ways in which environmental hygiene may be main-

[60] "Concerted Practical Action in the Social Field," p. 42.

tained in work places, the technical measures to protect workers from harmful agents, the use of protective clothing and equipment, the obligation to keep workers informed of any dangers arising from the nature of their work, and the periodic testing of atmospheric conditions to which workers are exposed.

International agencies have furthermore provided information on the health hazards of industrial and business life, and guidance for dealing with particular occupational diseases. The ILO publishes a periodical, *Occupational Safety and Health*, and has started revision of an earlier encyclopedia on *Occupation and Health.* Through technical assistance, advice and guidance is being offered to countries in safety and health matters, either by sending field consultants, granting fellowships for training, or on the basis of special research undertaken at the request of governments, safety associations, trade unions, and other groups.

For purposes of co-ordination, there is a Joint ILO/WHO Committee on Occupational Health. Partly as a result of the work of this committee, more and more emphasis is being placed on the health protection of workers in their places of employment, utilizing the latter as an avenue of approach to general health problems. At the same time, there has been a decided shift from emphasis on compensation in cases of occupational injury to emphasis on the reduction of occupational hazards.

In the promotion of better conditions of work for young persons and for women, the long record of the International Labour Organisation has been extended during the postwar period. Even in some economically advanced countries, but especially in the less developed countries, young children are still found at work in small-scale enterprises, handicrafts, and nonindustrial activities, including street trading and domestic service. In particular, great numbers of children are still working in agriculture under conditions detrimental to their health and well-being.[61]

The basic objectives of international action to provide for the protection of young workers in all countries, and particularly in technically less advanced countries, are to assist governments:

(a) to limit progressively child labour in all fields of occupation as rapidly as educational facilities are made available;

(b) to promote vocational guidance, vocational training and apprenticeship and placement services;

(c) to promote the extension of the protection of young workers to all occupations including employment in small-scale industrial enterprises, nonin-

[61] *Preliminary Report on the World Social Situation*, pp. 111–12.

dustrial occupations (including street trading), seasonal employment, and agriculture;

(d) to provide for adequate means of enforcing the legal provisions protecting young workers in all occupations.[62]

The international program of action to realize the above objectives has included many features such as guidance and training that have already been mentioned in this discussion. In addition, there are in existence ILO conventions, recommendations, and studies regarding minimum ages for admission to employment in industry, agriculture, and nonindustrial occupations; medical examination of young persons for employment; employment of young persons at night; and employment of young persons in nonmetropolitan territories. Most of these instruments lay down minimum standards for legislative action to provide for the protection of young workers; some include programs of general social protection, educational opportunity, and regulation of admission to employment and conditions of work, or set forth general principles concerning the administration of protective measures for children and young persons and the collaboration required on a national and international basis.

However great the educational value of these standards may be, their application remains a difficult question, particularly in agriculture and in the underdeveloped countries generally. Nevertheless, some real progress has been made as a result of this work, especially in Asia and the Middle East. New legislation regarding the employment of young people has been passed in recent years in India, Iran, Israel, Japan, and the Philippines.

An essential corollary to the setting of minimum ages for work is the development of free compulsory education. To the extent possible, legislation in both areas should be synchronized. An indication of the growing awareness of this need can be found in the conclusions of the ILO Asian Regional Conference that met in Tokyo in 1953. One of the main items on its agenda was the question of measures for the protection of young workers in Asian countries. The resolution adopted by the conference dealt in detail with the development of free compulsory education, vocational training, vocational guidance and youth employment services, and the extension of regulations for the restriction of child labor and the protection of young workers in employment.

Activities on behalf of women workers also have been extensive. Women workers have benefited, during the last fifty years, from the

[62] "Concerted Practical Action in the Social Field," p. 45.

progress of workers in general. Nonetheless, the participation of women in economic life has raised two related series of specific problems: those concerning equal opportunity for men and women regarding occupation and income; and those deriving from the maternal function of women and their role in society. The Convention on Equality of Remuneration approved in 1951 was the most important recent attempt to assure women equality of opportunity. Earlier conventions and recommendations provided for equality of opportunity for vocational training and employment services. The current efforts of UNESCO to promote equal educational opportunities for women attack existing inequalities in employment and remuneration at their root.

Other standards in the form of conventions and recommendations afford women workers the protection required for their biological and social functions as mothers and home-makers. Noteworthy in this context is the revision, effected in 1952, of the Convention on Maternity Protection originally adopted in 1919. Other related conventions cover such subjects as limitation of night work and of employment in unhealthy and hazardous occupations.

As one way of furthering the application of these standards, the ILO has promoted, by the usual methods of advice, training, publications, and international meetings, the development of legislation, including the establishment of women's bureaus in government departments of labor.

Although the progress made in protecting women and assuring them equality of opportunity with due regard for their biological and social functions is encouraging, it has raised new problems. Legislation on equal pay or on the provision of special protection for women may result in narrowing their opportunities for work and may make it more difficult for them to find employment. An answer to this problem is being sought in the enlargement of opportunities for vocational training for women and in providing for part-time work. The latter subject has been considered by the Commission on the Status of Women. The issue is still in the study stage, and the chief result to date has been a report on part-time employment prepared by the ILO at the request of the Commission on the Status of Women.[63]

Other groups of special concern to the ILO include agricultural workers and seafarers. Particularly in its technical assistance activities in the underdeveloped countries, the ILO has given attention to prob-

[63] U.N. Economic and Social Council, *Part-Time Employment, Preliminary Report Prepared by the International Labour Office*, Doc. E/CN.6/222 (Feb. 12, 1953).

lems of agricultural labor and has attempted to extend its standards, as far as possible, to agricultural workers. Some measure of success has been obtained with regard to workers on plantations, where approved standards can be most readily enforced. Working conditions on the land are, of course, only one aspect of levels of living of the agricultural population. Equally important are health, housing, and related matters. Substantial improvements in levels of living are contingent, therefore, not so much on special measures promoted by particular agencies or organs in the United Nations system as on the balanced development of the country as a whole.

Maritime conferences have been held periodically to establish and revise standards of employment and working conditions for seafarers. The conventions and recommendations of the ILO in this field have done much to equalize competitive conditions in the shipping industry.

Industrial Relations

The development and maintenance of sound relations between employers and workers constitute another essential element in achieving those higher levels of productivity on which improved levels of living to a large extent depend. They are equally basic to the existence of a "climate" in which men and women at work can pursue "both their material well-being and their spiritual development in conditions of freedom and dignity, of economic security and equal opportunity."[64] This explains the international concern for the promotion of freedom of association and the protection of the right to organize and bargain collectively.

With the adoption, in 1947, of a resolution concerning freedom of association and protection of the right to organize and bargain collectively, the International Labour Conference broadened its program for the improvement of industrial relations.[65] Prior to this date, the work of the ILO in the field of industrial relations had consisted of the development of techniques for intergroup discussion and negotiation, of giving a stimulus to the development of effective organizations of employers and workers in many countries and to the growth of systematic co-operation between such organizations, and of issuing numerous publications relating to industrial relations and cognate questions. The organization was eminently fitted for these tasks because of its tripartite composition.

[64] "Concerted Practical Action in the Social Field," p. 49.
[65] International Labour Office, *International Labour Code 1951*, Vol. I, p. 675.

The adoption by the conference, in 1947, of the above-mentioned resolution was followed by the adoption, in 1948 and 1949, of two conventions dealing with freedom of association and the protection of the right to organize and to bargain collectively. Other recommendations on collective bargaining, voluntary conciliation of industrial disputes, and consultation and co-operation between employers and workers at the job site were adopted thereafter.

Since 1949, considerable attention has been given to the "enforcement" of trade union rights. This has involved study and discussion, in the Economic and Social Council and the Governing Body of the ILO and subsidiary bodies, of allegations of violations of trade union rights.[66]

Quite recently, the ILO has broadened its concern with employment and working conditions to include the field known as human relations in industry. In 1955, the Director-General called for an international discussion of ways and means to create a more effective relationship between workers and employers. "Industrial democracy," in the words of the Director-General, "can never be an abstraction—it must be a living thing. The practice of labor-management relations in every day life is the key to its vitality."[67] The United States and a few other highly developed countries have made much progress in this field. The stimulation of similar progress elsewhere through the ILO involves a departure from its traditional emphasis on the setting of standards for legislation. The Director-General's willingness to adopt a new approach is clear from the following additional statement in the above-quoted report:

> Good industrial relations cannot be obtained through legislation. Legislation and administrative services are a necessary basic framework, but the working out of common problems of labor-management relations lies, inevitably, in the hands of the two parties most directly concerned.
>
> The mere fact that employers and workers agree to bargain collectively is not sufficient to insure satisfactory relationships. Much depends on the state of mind in which they engage in negotiations.[68]

In pursuing his subject, the Director-General pointed to the importance of joint labor-management committees, often also called works councils or works committees, both in private industry and in undertakings owned and operated by the state. He concluded that "a great deal more emphasis might well be laid on developing an understanding of

[66] See the monograph in this Brookings series, *The United Nations and Human Rights*, Chap. IV.

[67] International Labour Organisation, *Report of the Director General, International Labour Conference, Thirty-eighth Session* (1955), p. 8.

[68] *Ibid.*, pp. 63–64.

the human factors which make up the industrial society at the work level." And "solutions for many problems hitherto regarded primarily as concerning technical points or welfare may now be conceived with more explicit recognition of the psychological factors which lie at their roots."[69]

This new, more flexible conception of relations between labor and management is unlikely to win rapid acceptance. Employers may object to "interference" with what they consider their prerogatives of management. Workers may be uneasy and afraid of "psychological paternalism." They may consider their hard won right to collective bargaining an end in itself and may not be eager to accept a shift "from collective bargaining to collective thinking."

Nevertheless, the discussion has been opened, and it is likely to occupy the ILO and other international bodies for some time to come. It is probably no accident that it arose only a year after the Soviet Union and other Communist-dominated countries joined the International Labour Organisation. The promotion of human relations in industry and the harmonizing of labor-management relations may well prove to be an effective answer to some of the claims of Soviet Communism

Social Security and Income Maintenance

Social security means the provision of proper and sufficient benefits in a series of contingencies during which an individual may be prevented from earning his living, temporarily or permanently. It may also provide benefits for dependents deprived of the support of their breadwinner, and for medical care. In a broader sense, it may include assistance in the discharge of continuing family responsibilities in respect of which community aid may be considered expedient. Social security is a major element in maintaining incomes in times of adversity and old age and, in the case of unemployment benefits, has the incidental effect of mitigating economic recessions and depressions. It thus contributes indirectly to economic stability as well as directly to social stability. Social security may be achieved through social insurance, public services, and social assistance.

Social Insurance

The International Labour Organisation throughout its history has played a significant role in the development of social security, particu-

[69] *Ibid.*, pp. 77, 80–81.

larly through the promotion of social insurance. Under social insurance, individuals are entitled to benefits on the basis of contributions to an insurance fund paid by the beneficiaries, or by their employers, or by both; the state may also contribute a share to the fund or guarantee payment.

The adoption by the ILO of the first social security conventions in the late 1920's gave marked impetus to the world movement in this field.[70] For the first time, many governments began to consider the institution of social insurance plans. In increasing numbers, they turned to the ILO for information and help. The experts there were familiar with the best national practices as developed in countries such as Germany and the United Kingdom. They knew the mistakes to be avoided. The social security systems of many countries, including the United States, bear evidence of the help rendered by the ILO. Much of this work was carried forward on a regional basis through such bodies as the Inter-American Conference on Social Security, which was founded in 1942 with the assistance of the ILO and of the Inter-American Committee on Social Security.

Toward the end of and after the Second World War, there was an expansion of activities, studies, regional conferences, and seminars in this field. The Income Security and Medical Care Recommendations, approved by the International Labour Conference in 1944, played an important role in stimulating progress in social security based on insurance by laying down acceptable minimum standards and objectives adapted to present-day requirements of countries in different stages of economic development. They were a forerunner of the Social Security (Minimum Standards) Convention of 1952.

The ILO itself considers this last-named convention as the culmination of thirty years of work in the field of social security.[71] The convention covers nine different aspects of social security to be met primarily through insurance, namely, medical care, sickness benefit, unemployment benefit, old-age benefit, employment injury benefit, family benefit, maternity benefit, invalidity benefit, and survivors' benefit. It is framed in the light of the widely varying conditions in different parts of the world. Earlier international conventions on social security dealt with particular branches of social insurance. Most of them prescribed

[70] *Cf.* International Labour Office, *Lasting Peace the I.L.O. Way, The Story of the International Labour Organisation*, Second Edition (Revised) (1953).

[71] *Seventh Report of the International Labour Organisation to the United Nations*, pp. 41–42.

minimum conditions of entitlement to, and duration of, benefit, but they did not fix any rate of benefit, and their essential function was to provide the general legal framework for a social insurance system. The new convention starts from the conception of comprehensive social security. One of its leading features is that it prescribes rates of benefit for standard beneficiaries, such rates to be calculated, broadly speaking, either as percentages of the previous earnings of the beneficiary or breadwinner or as percentages of the average earnings of unskilled labor.

The convention has been characterized as follows:

> In the nature of the case, the Convention is a compromise. It represents the standards arrived at by fully authorised representatives of Governments, employers and workers, through free and democratic discussion. Like any agreement reached in this manner, it is the outcome of give-and-take. Like every other international labour Convention, it binds no one until the appropriate constitutional authorities in each country decide to ratify it. It is, moreover, a flexible instrument; States may become parties to it without accepting its provisions in respect of all branches of social security; in respect of each branch various alternatives are permitted, and some of these alternatives would not be regarded as appropriate in certain countries; temporary exceptions to certain provisions are allowed for States whose economy and medical facilities are insufficiently developed for the full application of the provisions of the Convention. The Convention is not intended to, and does not, interfere with voluntary private insurance in any way. It provides for a bed-rock of protection on which voluntary private insurance can and should build.[72]

Since the conclusion of this convention, the International Labour Organisation has pursued its work in the field of social security primarily along two lines: the preparation of studies and the provision of technical assistance. One study, which should prove of considerable value to less developed countries, concerns the different processes involved in administering social insurance and the techniques that may be used for making them effective. Attention is being given also to the costs of protection, and statistics pertaining to the cost of social security in different countries continue to be collected and analyzed.

The countries that constitute the Council of Europe have collectively sought the help of the ILO in working out a special Code of Social Security that recognizes the level of achievement typical of these countries and, to some extent, expresses their aspirations for improvement. Particularly interesting in this connection are the attempts at international co-ordination of social security schemes in the interest of foreigners and

[72] *Ibid.*, p. 42.

of migrants generally. The Committee of Ministers of the Council of Europe signed, in December 1953, two interim agreements on the equality of treatment for all nationals of members of the Council; both agreements were based on drafts prepared by the ILO.

In the last few years, a score of countries in the Near, Middle, and Far East, and in Latin America, have also been assisted by social security experts provided by the ILO. The ILO has in fact been directly involved in the planning of virtually all the new general schemes of social security that the less developed countries have introduced since the war.

Public Services

The ILO has frequently emphasized that it is primarily concerned with the ends of social security, *i.e.*, income maintenance and assured care in cases of illness, accident, and similar needs, and that flexibility is desirable in the choice of means. If less stress has been put on the public-service approach, it is due in part, undoubtedly, to the fact that it is much more controversial than social insurance.

The term *public service* is used here to designate schemes under which title to benefit is conferred on the population generally, or on a category thereof, at the expense of the community and without prior contribution by the beneficiaries (except in the form of taxes). The same benefit becomes available automatically to all who qualify (aged persons, families with children, maternity cases, etc.), and the possession of private means does not affect eligibility. The "public service" approach is perhaps best illustrated by policies in the Scandinavian countries (*e.g.*, the family-allowance system in Sweden), the United Kingdom (*e.g.*, the British Health Service), and Canada (*e.g.*, the Canadian automatic old-age pension).

In the Communist-controlled countries, public service appears to be the key to social security. Representatives of the Soviet Union and other Communist nations claim that their system assures their people of complete economic and social security without contributions from the workers. Theoretically, the system is based on insurance, with contributions coming entirely from the employer. Since the state is the only employer, however, it is the state that provides all the contributions and hence all the benefits.[73] These contributions, of course, are ultimately

[73] Benefits, however, are not in all cases automatically provided for a given category of the population, *e.g.*, those above a given age. Entitlement may depend on previous employment, and payments frequently vary with the type of such employment.

paid for by direct or indirect taxation, or by its equivalent, because real income transferred to the recipients must come from some elements of the public.

At the other end of the scale, is the United States with its emphasis on insurance financed by contributions from the workers, the employers, or both. In certain areas—for example, medical care—the United States has not accepted the principle of public insurance, and safeguarding against the cost of illness has been left to private insurance, with minimum provisions for public aid in the form of limited public health services and social assistance in cases of need.

There have been many statements but few debates in the United Nations on these issues. The "middle" countries have shown a marked reluctance to be drawn into political discussions initiated by Communist representatives. The debate that occurred at the Economic and Social Council, in July 1952, on the occasion of the discussion of the *Preliminary Report on the World Social Situation* soon developed into a controversy between the United States on the one hand, and the Soviet Union and its followers on the other, over Communist social concepts and organization as contrasted with those of a free society.[74] The resolution that was adopted following this debate did not refer in any way to the differences in basic concept.[75]

In practice, the public-service approach has most frequently been adopted by individual countries in the form of flat-rate, family allowances, as an integral part of population policies; of maternity benefits and old-age pensions; and of the provision of free medical care. These measures have usually been combined, in the free world, with social security schemes based on social insurance. In other words, social insurance and public service are not mutually exclusive, but to some extent are definitely complementary. The ILO has produced extensive studies in both areas and continues to provide technical assistance to governments on request.

Social Assistance

Social assistance comprises those forms of social security under which benefits at the expense of the community and without prior contribution on the part of the beneficiary are paid to individuals who, in terms of defined minimum standards, are "in need." A "means test" may be required before an individual becomes eligible for benefits.

[74] U.N. Economic and Social Council, Fourteenth Session, *Official Records*, pp. 547–90.

[75] Res. 434(XIV), July 25, 28, and 29, 1952.

In most of the countries with advanced systems of social security, assistance schemes serve as supplementary measures to provide for needy persons who are not covered, or are not adequately covered, by other forms of social security. Frequently, they come into operation when benefits under social insurance systems end because statutory or contractual time limits for the provision of such benefits have been reached, *e.g.*, in the case of unemployment insurance.

In many of the less developed countries, social assistance to the needy is offered, too often rather sporadically, in view of the obvious inadequacy of other social security measures. Although state and local authorities may have a share in such assistance, it is more often left to private agencies. Family and relatives and religious and other private groups remain the dominant means of assistance to the needy. Considerable effort has been made under the auspices of the United Nations and the ILO to stimulate, improve, and systematize social assistance programs in the underdeveloped countries.

The Trend to Date

Both in the thinking of the United Nations and the specialized agencies, and in their action programs for the promotion of higher levels of living, a large measure of "fusion" of the economic and social approaches has been attained. It has been recognized that the basic objective of any measures for economic development is the improvement of levels of living. There has also been a growing realization of the fact that the various social components that enter into the determination of levels of living have a direct bearing on economic development, and that better health, housing, and working conditions—to mention only a few—are essential to any acceleration of economic development. As a result of this acknowledged interaction of the economic and the social, the entire work of the United Nations and the specialized agencies in these fields has gained in realism and effectiveness.

The work has been focused increasingly on underdeveloped countries. This is only natural, considering their needs and the political implications of despair in the underdeveloped regions of the world. Moreover, even highly developed countries stand to gain indirectly by social improvements in the underdeveloped parts of the world. Elimination or control of communicable diseases in Asia or Latin America constitutes a shield for the protection of the population in the most highly developed countries. Improvements in wage levels, working conditions, and social security systems in the underdeveloped countries make for larger and more stable markets.

It may well be asked, however, whether there has not been overemphasis on work in the underdeveloped regions of the world and a consequent neglect of some of the immediate needs of the more highly developed countries, particularly in health, nutrition, housing, and social security. The underdeveloped countries have a majority of votes, particularly in the General Assembly, but in an interdependent world in which the co-operation of all countries is essential, it would not appear to be in the best interests of the underdeveloped countries to limit the economic and social activities of the United Nations to their needs, to the detriment of international action to assist directly in improving levels of living in the more developed areas.

By and large, the activities of the United Nations and the specialized agencies designed to promote higher levels of living have been practical and down to earth. Efforts are being made to avoid vague generalities and to concentrate on concrete goals and ways and means of attaining them. Conventions and formal recommendations continue to set standards, but emphasis in recent years has shifted to the practical grass-roots approach in advising and otherwise helping governments improve the levels of living of their peoples. This requires patient, painstaking, arduous work on the part of those rendering and those receiving the advice and assistance. The progress that has been made during the past ten years, although limited and uneven, is nevertheless remarkable. The world is moving forward in improving the lot of the common man, and the United Nations and the specialized agencies are playing a vital part in the progress achieved.

CHAPTER VIII

*Welfare and Social Defense**

IN DEVELOPING a broad social approach to the promotion of the general welfare, the United Nations has gone beyond the programs designed to obtain improvements in levels of living through making the environment more healthful, the diet more nutritious, the housing more suitable, and the working conditions more conducive to higher output with greater security and dignity for the wage-earner. In addition, the United Nations and the specialized agencies have actively promoted social work and welfare programs on behalf of specific groups that require special attention or protection—among them mothers and children, migrants and refugees, the physically handicapped, the drug addicts, and the offenders against the laws of society.

Despite the fact that the term "social welfare" has no exact counterpart in other languages and that there is no internationally agreed definition of the term "social work," there is widespread agreement among Member states in the free world that the outstanding characteristic of social work is its concern with the individual and his physical, mental, and emotional well-being.[1] Economic, medical, or other forms of personal assistance may be prerequisites for the achievement of such well-being, or it may be necessary to strengthen the social unit and groups—particularly the family—within which the individual seeks security. Not only may people need help in overcoming handicaps that militate against their full integration into society, but they also may have to be protected against social evils destructive of personality. The concern of social work, in brief, is with the total individual and his integration in society.

There are obvious difficulties in utilizing international machinery

* By Walter M. Kotschnig.

[1] During the preparation of a United Nations report entitled *Training for Social Work, An International Survey* (Doc. E/CN.5/196/Rev. 1, Oct. 23, 1950), Member governments were invited to submit definitions of "social work." The "definitions" ranged from descriptions of unorganized personal "charity," through organized activities for aid to the needy, to the most advanced types of "case work" employing the latest scientific discoveries in sociology, physiology, psychiatry, and related fields. Social work was described both as a means of dealing with "the poor" and as a profession providing services to and potentially required by all.

for the promotion of this many-faceted, individual approach—difficulties that are not apparent from a study of voting records on social problems raised at meetings of the United Nations. Most of the basic resolutions in the social welfare field were adopted by comfortable majorities, and many of them with no negative votes. The United States frequently took the lead in initiating action by the United Nations and was supported by most of the countries of Western Europe and of the Commonwealth. The underdeveloped countries supported every move for international assistance in the development of social welfare programs within their territories to the point at which, in the social as in the economic field, attention became focused increasingly on the underdeveloped areas.

Even the Communist-controlled countries, although they exhibited little enthusiasm for the social work approach, seldom engaged in outright opposition. Instead, they made speeches and proposals implying that most of the social work programs were at best palliatives and that the United Nations should turn instead to ensuring full employment, improved conditions of labor, guaranteed health services, and state-financed, state-controlled education schemes.

Although the voting record appears to reveal a remarkable degree of unanimity, co-ordinated progress in the social welfare field has been slow and painful, largely due to the confusion of ideas and concepts, aggravated by the enthusiasms of special interest groups and their desires to obtain international sponsorship for particular projects. Not all of the clamor of contending voices has disappeared, although the programs have become better co-ordinated and the work more effective.

These programs may be considered in four main groups: those designed to help in the organization of adequate national and local social welfare departments and services; those for the welfare and protection of the family as a unit, of children, and of the physically handicapped; those facilitating international migration and the protection and resettlement of refugees; and finally, those concerned with drug-addiction, prostitution, and the prevention of crime or treatment of offenders.

Organization and Administration of Social Welfare Services

The havoc caused by the Second World War immeasurably increased the need for assistance on the part of millions of poeple who had lost their homes, whose families had been dispersed, and who found it difficult to adjust to the dire conditions of postwar life. As mentioned earlier in this study, one of the functions of the United Nations Relief and Rehabilitation Administration (UNRRA) was the re-establishment of social welfare services in devastated areas.[2] Requests for help, however, were not confined to war-devastated countries. Beginning right after the war, the governments of many of the underdeveloped countries, desirous of improving the lot of their people, sought assistance in establishing national machinery for administering programs of social welfare and above all, in the training of social welfare personnel. The United Nations was thus confronted in the very first months of its existence with calls for a wide range of action in the social welfare field.

Advisory Social Welfare Services

When it was decided in 1946 to liquidate UNRRA, the General Assembly on recommendation of the Economic and Social Council, authorized the transfer to the United Nations of the social welfare functions that UNRRA had developed to assist in the rehabilitation of social services disrupted by the war. By a resolution adopted unanimously, the General Assembly authorized the Secretary-General, in consultation with the Economic and Social Council and with the co-operation of the specialized agencies, to provide "for the continuance of the urgent and important advisory functions in the field of social welfare carried on by UNRRA."[3] The resolution envisaged the provision of social welfare experts to governments desiring advice in this field; a program of fellowships to enable qualified social welfare officials from such nations to observe, and familiarize themselves with, the experience of other countries administering social welfare programs; advice, demonstration, and instruction in the field of the rehabilitation and vocational training of the physically handicapped; and the furnishing of technical publications helpful in the training of social welfare workers.

This action of the Assembly marked the birth of the first program of technical assistance undertaken by the United Nations. It has been functioning ever since under the name "Advisory Social Welfare Services." As originally conceived by the General Assembly, the program was to be limited in space, purpose, and time.[4] Intended for the war devastated countries, it was, however, quickly extended to other parts

[2] See above, Chap. I.

[3] Res. 58(I), Dec. 14, 1946.

[4] U.N. Economic and Social Council, *Evaluation of the Program of Advisory Social Welfare Services, 1947–1951*, Doc. E/CN.5/266 (Mar. 26, 1952).

of the world, particularly to the underdeveloped countries. Its purpose widened over the years to the point where the program embraced virtually all the social services not already within the scope of a specialized agency. During the period 1947 to 1949, the program was operated on a year-to-year basis. This proved unsatisfactory and inadequate. Three arguments in favor of permanency were advanced with increasing force in sessions of the Social Commission and of the Economic and Social Council. It was said that the number of requests for assistance received from all over the world showed that the program filled a real and permanent need. It was stressed that the operation of a program of this scope on a year-to-year basis was extremely difficult. Finally, it was emphasized that the work, in order to be done well and to be of lasting value, had to be concerned not only with the acute needs of the day but tied in addition to long-range action in the field of social welfare.

In 1950, the Assembly consequently made the program permanent and enlarged it.[5] It explicitly approved the shift in emphasis to underdeveloped countries. In 1951, the Assembly decided to make additionl funds available for the program of advisory services by authorizing the use, where necessary, of funds at the disposal of the Expanded Programme of Technical Assistance (EPTA).

At the beginning, the program consisted principally of the provision of fellowships, scholarships, and experts. To this were added, somewhat later, the organization of seminars and various other types of training facilities.

Between 1947 and the early 1950's, the number of awards per year under the fellowship program increased from approximately one hundred to nearly two hundred. After that, the number of awards for study abroad began to level off, due largely to the development of training facilities within the various countries seeking assistance. More striking is the increase in the number of recipient countries, from twelve in 1947 to forty-six in 1955, exclusive of non-self-governing territories.

There has also been a notable increase in the number of countries serving as hosts to persons awarded fellowships. There were eight countries in 1947 and twenty-eight in 1955. In the early years of the program, most of the fellows went to North America, particularly the United States, or to Europe. Of late, recipients coming to the United States have actually decreased in number as compared with the first year of the program. There has been some increase of fellows in Europe.

[5] Res. 418(V), Dec. 1, 1950.

More significantly, however, an increasing number of fellows have elected to go to countries similar to, and frequently only slightly more developed than, their own countries—to India, for example. This has enabled the fellows to study social welfare developments in a setting more like the one in which they must operate when they return, and it also has been less costly than study in North America or Europe. The granting of fellowships has been supplemented by the provision of scholarships, and in Europe, an exchange program was set up in 1950 to promote the intra-European exchange of social welfare personnel.

In 1947, out of nine countries receiving foreign experts under the program of Advisory Social Welfare Services, seven were European and two Asian. In subsequent years, there was a steady decline in the number of European countries and a gradual increase in the number of recipient countries in other regions of the world.[6] Latin America joined the program in 1948, followed by the Middle East in 1949, and finally by Africa in 1951. Whereas in 1947–48, Europe received approximately half the total number of experts provided by the United Nations in the field of social welfare, by 1951, its share had decreased to approximately 6 per cent of the total, and the Far East and Latin America together absorbed nearly 65 per cent of the experts nominated by the United Nations in that year. Similarly, there was a sharp decline in the number of experts coming from the Western world, particularly from the United States. In the latter case, one of the reasons for the decline was the difficulty encountered by the United Nations in obtaining American experts because of delays in security checks requested by the United States Government for its nationals. More fundamental, however, was the realization by the underdeveloped countries that experts from other underdeveloped countries frequently had a better understanding of their needs and of the methods of meeting those needs than experts from the more highly developed countries. The Soviet Union in 1947–48 provided three expert advisers. Since then, no Soviet experts have been made available under the program of Advisory Social Welfare Services to any country outside the Soviet orbit.

The first seminars on social welfare questions were held in 1947 in Latin America, followed by seminars in the Middle East on general

[6] The decline in the number of participating European nations was due, in part, to the establishment of direct contacts between European countries, resulting in the provision of experts through bilateral negotiations, although frequently with the advice of the Secretariat of the United Nations.

social welfare and rural welfare in 1949 and 1951 respectively. During the two years 1953 and 1954 alone, twenty-two seminars of different types were organized.[7]

More revealing than these figures is the fact that there have been considerable changes over the last eight years in the areas of interest of fellowship holders, and in the subject fields of experts requested by governments. Among fellowship holders, the figures indicate a sustained interest in such activities as the rehabilitation of the handicapped and the prevention of crime and treatment of offenders; and an increased interest in social surveys and statistics, the organization and administration of social welfare services, and the training of social workers and auxiliary personnel. With regard to requests for experts, changes in interest have been more marked. Although in previous years a majority of the requests from governments was concerned with special social problems, a significant number of requests were received in 1953–54 for assistance in the organization and administration at the national level of comprehensive social welfare programs. Requests of this kind were received from Burma, Gambia, Israel, Pakistan, the Philippines, Somaliland, Thailand, Turkey, and Yugoslavia. There has also been an increase in the number of requests for assistance in community development.[8]

Organization and Development of National Services

In response to the growing emphasis on the development of comprehensive long-range programs of social welfare, the United Nations, in co-operation with the International Labour Organisation (ILO), the World Health Organization (WHO), and the Food and Agriculture Organization (FAO), has assisted governments in strengthening or improving the organization and administration of their social services. The Economic and Social Council, as early as 1947, asked the Secretary-General to arrange for a study of methods of social welfare administration in use in different countries, and of methods of furnishing advice, information, and experts to countries requesting such assistance,

[7] For a complete list of these activities see U.N. Economic and Social Council, *Progress Made by the United Nations in the Field of Social Welfare During the Period 1 January 1953 to 31 December 1954 and Proposals for the Program of Work 1955–57*, Doc. E/CN.5/308 (Mar. 15, 1955), Annex B, pp. 1–2.

[8] See below, Chap. X.

with a view to helping them to organize the administration of their own social services.[9]

In response, the Secretary-General prepared a comprehensive survey covering thirty countries, which brought to light the great differences among them in social welfare methods and administration.[10] The introduction to the study mentioned that "in the light of the information here assembled, the Secretary-General feels that each country will be well advised to develop methods of social welfare administration in harmony with its own traditions and needs."[11] In 1952, the Secretary-General published a follow-up study of the situation in seven countries from five continents. This study covered the place of assistance to the needy within the social security structure; eligibility requirements; and the level of financing and administration of assistance.[12] References to problems of administration appear also in a large number of other publications.[13]

In addition to issuing publications that have served as guides and source material for governments and others interested in social welfare services, the United Nations has provided, as has already been noted, a large number of experts and fellowships in this area and organized various seminars and training centers. It has appointed regional advisers and established social welfare staffs in the major regions of the world in response to the growing preference both on the part of the Secretary-General and of the countries concerned for on-the-spot advice instead of studies prepared at headquarters.

There is evidence that progress is being made in practically all the underdeveloped parts of the world in the establishment of national welfare administrations. To what extent this is due to the stimulus and advice given by the United Nations is, of course, impossible to state with any certainty even though in some cases the tie-in is clear. The establishment of a Council of Social Service in Burma was a direct result of the work of several United Nations experts. Similarly, in Pakistan, a team of experts advised the government on the planning and organization of social welfare programs, including particularly the

[9] Res. 43(IV), Mar. 29, 1947. In this connection, see also Res. 390C(XIII), Aug. 9, 1951.

[10] U.N. Department of Social Affairs, *Methods of Social Welfare Administration*, Doc. E/CN.5/224 (Oct. 25, 1950).

[11] *Ibid.*, p. 2.

[12] U.N. Department of Social Affairs, *Methods of Administering Assistance to the Needy*, Doc. E/CN.5/273 (1952).

[13] U.N. Department of Public Information, *Ten Years of United Nations Publications, 1945–1955, A Complete Catalogue* (1955), pp. 7–8, 44–58.

the organization of social services at the national and local levels. Lebanon, Thailand, the Philippines, Turkey, Yugoslavia, and some countries in Latin America have also drawn heavily on the advice of experts from the United Nations in the organization and administration of their social services. The structure and working of the new social welfare administrations differ from country to country and frequently include in their scope not only social assistance of the type discussed below but also social security measures of the type described earlier in this study.[14] There appears to be, however, a fairly general recognition of the fact that too much centralization can militate against the achievement of the very purposes of personalized social assistance and can weigh too heavily on local drive and initiative. It is being realized that co-ordination and planning do not necessarily involve a high degree of centralized administration or exclusive governmental responsibility. A number of countries, including many that are less developed, are trying to reconcile effective co-ordination with maximum encouragement of local and voluntary initiative.[15]

Training of Welfare Personnel

The word "training" runs through every discussion of social work and social welfare. This is understandable. Public concern in these fields is of comparatively recent date, and many countries have few if any trained workers available. Moreover, social work by its very nature requires more than administrators and executives. It needs people capable of dealing on a person-to-person basis with the problems of individuals. This work normally has to be done in the local community and not from some national center. In other words, social welfare work requires a large number of people with special training, for the vital force is the trained individual rather than the system.

Although concerned from 1947 on with methods of assisting in the training of welfare personnel, it was not until 1951 that the Social Commission and the Economic and Social Council undertook to formulate principles for social work training.[16] These principles heavily empha-

[14] See above, Chap. VII.

[15] U.N. Bureau of Social Affairs, *International Survey of Programs of Social Development*, Doc. E/CN.5/301/Rev. 1 (Mar. 31, 1955), *passim.* (Hereinafter cited as *Survey of Programs of Social Development.*)

[16] Res. 43(IV), Mar. 29, 1947 and Res. 390B(XIII), Aug. 9, 1951 of the Council. See also U.N. General Assembly, Sixth Session, *Official Records*, Supplement No. 3, "Report of the Economic and Social Council Covering the Period 16 August 1950 to 21 September 1951," p. 83; and U.N. Department of Social Affairs, *Training for Social Work, An International Survey*, Doc. E/CN.5/196/Rev. 1 (Oct. 23, 1950).

sized that social work is a professional function to be performed by men and women who have received their professional training in recognized educational institutions. The stress on social work as a profession reflected primarily the views and aspirations of social workers in the United States, and the recommended standards proved too high for a large number of countries.

In 1952, the Council watered them down somewhat by recommending that training for social work take as many forms as appropriate to the needs of the various countries and that in-service training programs be regarded as essential for all categories of social welfare personnel, including persons who had not received formal training.[17] Subsequently, the emphasis shifted further—to the training of auxiliary personnel—because facilities for full professional and "on-the-job" training did not keep pace with needs. Moreover, at the local level, less than professional training was often all that the community could afford.

Currently, international assistance for the training of social welfare workers attempts to serve the following purposes:

(1) to make available information concerning the content and method or training key personnel and keeping such personnel up to date with new knowledge, and to promote expansion of facilities for such training;
(2) to assist governments in speeding up the recruitment and concentrated training of supplementary personnel, now called "auxiliary and community workers," by
  (a) examining and making known the variety of functions now being performed, or needed to carry social welfare programmes into practical effect in local communities;
  (b) making known the methods found most effective in attracting and preparing such persons for their duties;
  (c) assisting directly in the development of expanded training facilities;
  (d) co-operative efforts by the organizations belonging to the United Nations family in formulating basic principles for the training and use of social welfare personnel at all levels.[18]

To help realize these purposes, technical assistance is provided under both the program of Advisory Social Welfare Services and the Expanded Programme of Technical Assistance. Experts have been employed, field surveys made, scholarships and fellowships provided, regional seminars and technical groups organized, training equipment supplied

[17] Res. 434F(XIV), July 25, 1952.

[18] U.N. Economic and Social Council, Sixteenth Session, *Official Records*, Annexes, Agenda Item 10: "Program of Concerted Practical Action in the Social Field of the United Nations and the Specialized Agencies," p. 72. (Hereinafter cited as "Concerted Practical Action in the Social Field.")

(on a limited basis), and studies and reports on subjects pertaining to the training of social work personnel have been distributed. These activities have by no means been confined to underdeveloped countries. More seminars and expert meetings have been held in Europe on training than on any other social program of the United Nations.

The expansion of activities designed to increase the number of auxiliary workers has characterized much of the work in underdeveloped countries. A special *ad hoc* interagency meeting on the training of auxiliary workers was held in Geneva in July 1954, with representatives of the secretariats of the United Nations (including the United Nations Children's Fund, UNICEF), FAO, ILO, United Nations Scientific and Cultural Organization (UNESCO), and WHO participating. This meeting discussed the formulation of general principles concerning the training of auxiliary and community workers and the content and production of training materials, and selected a number of field projects suitable for joint demonstration purposes.[19] Prior to the Geneva meeting of experts, regional meetings of specialists in this subject had taken place in Gandhigram, India, for the Far Eastern region; in Beirut, Lebanon, for the Middle Eastern region; and in Bogota, Colombia, for the Caribbean and Central American region.[20]

Advances with respect to all levels of training have been made in many underdeveloped countries. In Asia, the number of professional schools or courses offering at least one year of training in social work increased from fifteen in 1949–50 to twenty-seven in 1953–54. The number of schools of social work in the Middle East increased during the same period from five to ten; in Latin America from forty-eight to sixty-four. In 1953–54 alone, experts to assist in training social welfare personnel were sent to fifteen countries and advice was given on surveys of existing training facilities; general questions of administration, curricula, field work, and selection of students for admission; and on the development of facilities for in-service training or for the training of auxiliary workers.[21]

In spite of these advances, the picture as a whole remains very un-

[19] See U.N. Economic and Social Council, *Seventeenth Report of the Administrative Committee on Co-ordination to the Economic and Social Council*, Doc. E/2659 (Oct. 15, 1954).

[20] A summary report on the training of auxiliary and community workers, including the discussions of the three regional meetings, can be found in U.N. Economic and Social Council, *Training of Welfare Personnel, Summary Report on the Training of Auxiliary and Community Workers*, Doc. E/CN.5/306 (Mar. 7, 1955).

[21] U.N. Economic and Social Council, *Training of Welfare Personnel, Training for Social Work: Second International Survey*, Doc. E/CN.5/305 (Apr. 8, 1955).

even. Not only are there still many countries without training facilities or with inadequate facilities, but there continue to be very wide divergencies in the content of training. In the United States and Canada, there is a full two- to three-year, post-graduate, professional course with emphasis on the "scientific approach." In the United Kingdom and many European countries, there are special "social science" courses, frequently with emphasis on nursing, as in France. In Asia, there is a growing emphasis on developing patterns of work and training in conformity with local conditions in the region. Finally, there is an attempt in Latin America to develop case work practices in a continent where cultural attitudes make for social work *for* rather than *with* people. In brief, social work practice and training continue on the whole to rest on a body of knowledge and skills less clearly defined and less generally agreed upon than that of the long established professions and occupational groups.

These variations indicate that not only methods of social welfare administration but also of training should be developed in harmony with the traditions and needs of each country. They do not diminish the importance of international consultations and mutual assistance, but they call for caution lest theory become the enemy of practical action.

Family and Child Welfare

From the early days of the United Nations, family and child welfare programs were linked together and given special attention. The United Nations International Children's Emergency Fund was established in 1946 to offer aid not only to children, but also to nursing mothers.[22] When the Economic and Social Council decided, in 1948, to resume publication of the Legislative and Administrative Series on child welfare begun by the League of Nations, it soon extended its coverage to include family welfare.[23] In 1952, the Economic and Social Council

[22] See above, Chap. II.

[23] Res. 122A(VI), Mar. 1, 1948. Following the practice of the League, the Legislative and Administrative Series was supplemented by another series of reports on child and youth welfare, summarizing existing legislation and including information on other measures taken by governments. The series was discontinued in 1954, on the understanding that governments would continue to report on family and child care measures, primarily to provide continuing information for inclusion in other publications such as the quadrennial *International Survey of Measures for Social Development*. The move represented more than a streamlining of the publications program. It reflected a conclusion that the publication of legislative texts and of other measures adopted by governments is not a very effective way of advancing practical action because the texts and measures may have very limited applicability abroad.

approved an integrated program for child welfare, which had been proposed by the Social Commission, and which stressed the need for specific measures essential to the social security of the family.[24]

The international program in the field of family and child welfare that emerged from these deliberations and resolutions is directed toward the following basic purposes:

(a) encouraging governmental and nongovernmental programs designed
  (i) to strengthen family life;
  (ii) to promote special programs for mothers and children;
(b) supplementing such national programs, in agreement with governments, by direct international assistance to mothers and children in devastated or underdeveloped areas where necessary.[25]

International efforts to strengthen the family have to date centered largely on income maintenance. The approach to that problem through social insurance, public services, and social assistance has already been described earlier in this study.[26] Unemployment and disability benefits, family allowances, and tax exemptions for large families all serve to strengthen the economic foundations of the family. Measures to protect women and young people in employment similarly affect the welfare of the family. In addition to these areas—of special concern to the ILO—home economics training offers another approach to the strengthening of the family.

On the subject of income maintenance, the United Nations published a comprehensive survey in 1952.[27] This was followed, in 1956, by a second study dealing with methods of administering assistance to the needy in less developed areas, with special emphasis on problems of income maintenance for families. It was based on a survey of existing approaches to public assistance and pensions in nine selected countries in the Middle and the Far East and Latin America.[28] In preparation is a study dealing with the factors governing formulation of a co-ordinated policy aimed at the maintenance of family levels of living, and the methods of giving such a policy practical effect.

In addition to promoting family welfare through publications of the foregoing character, the United Nations has encouraged the education of social workers, along lines that frequently include training in mar-

[24] Res. 434E(XIV), July 25, 1952.

[25] "Concerted Practical Action in the Social Field," p. 62.

[26] See above, Chap. VII.

[27] U.N. Department of Social Affairs, *Economic Measures in Favour of the Family*, Doc. ST/SOA/8 (Mar. 31, 1952).

[28] U.N. Department of Economic and Social Affairs, *Assistance to the Needy in Less-Developed Areas*, Doc. ST/SOA/28 (1956).

riage and family counseling. The question of family planning, relevant in this connection, is highly controversial. It has been raised obliquely on a few occasions in discussions of the Population Commission and in the Economic and Social Council. It took more concrete form in the 1952 discussions in WHO regarding the provision of expert assistance to the Indian Government in a sample population survey that extended to problems of birth control. For religious and other reasons, the great majority of governments either oppose policies designed to reduce birth rates or have no policies on the matter. Only a few—including Egypt, Japan, and India—are actively pursuing policies of this kind or have sought advice from the international community in this connection.

Also related to the protection of the family are several legal instruments prepared under the auspicies of the United Nations. The first is the Convention on the Declaration of Death of Missing Persons. In 1948, the Economic and Social Council recognized the urgency and importance of mitigating the legal difficulties arising from the disappearance of numerous victims of war and persecution and expressed the view that these difficulties might best be met by an international convention.[29] This was a matter of considerable interest to large numbers of families from which some member had disappeared but despite the assumption of death, there was no adequate machinery to permit a legal declaration of death that would allow for property settlements or for remarriage. It was an international problem because many of the missing persons could be assumed to have met their death in foreign lands to which they had been taken as soldiers, slave laborers, or victims of concentration camps. The proposal for an international convention met with general approval in the Economic and Social Council and the Assembly except for the Communist bloc states, which were evidently opposed to investigations extending into their territories. Finally, in 1950, the General Assembly convened a plenipotentiary conference that adopted a convention prepared in the first instance by the Secretary-General and revised by an *ad hoc* committee of experts.[30]

In addition to the Convention on the Declaration of Death of Missing Persons, the United Nations has prepared a Model Convention on the

[29] Res. 158(VII), Aug. 24, 1948; see also Res. 209(VIII), Mar. 2, 1949, and Res. 249(IX), Aug. 9, 1949; General Assembly Res. 369(IV), Dec. 3, 1949.

[30] An essential element in the system provided by the Convention on the Declaration of Death of Missing Persons was the establishment of an International Bureau for Declarations of Death. The creation of such a bureau within the framework of the United Nations was approved by the Assembly in Res. 493(V), Nov. 16, 1950. The Convention entered into force on Jan. 24, 1952.

Enforcement Abroad of Maintenance Obligations.[31] The need for action in this area arose from a sharp increase in the number of cases in which a family found itself abandoned by the bread winner, who, having moved or been moved to another country, enjoyed virtual immunity from maintenance obligations by reason of legal obstacles to effective prosecution. In addition to cases of willful abandonment, instances of involuntary failure to provide support had arisen, because the restrictions imposed in a number of countries on the transfer of funds made it difficult for immigrants to remit money to their families.

A committee of Experts on the Recognition and Enforcement Abroad of Maintenance Obligations was set up by the Council in 1951.[32] It produced as a guide to governments for the preparation of bilateral treaties or uniform legislation not only the Model Convention on the Enforcement Abroad of Maintenance Obligations, but also a draft multilateral Convention on the Recovery Abroad of Claims for Maintenance. The Economic and Social Council decided, in the spring of 1955, to call a plenipotentiary conference to complete the draft, which was strongly supported by such countries as Belgium, Cuba, France, the Netherlands, and the Scandinavian countries. A universal convention in this field is, however, opposed by the United States as well as by some other federal states. On June 20, 1956, the United Nations Conference on Maintenance Obligations adopted and opened for signature the completed Convention on the Recovery Abroad of Maintenance.

In the early years of its existence, the Social Commission gave repeated attention to the drafting of a Declaration of the Rights of the Child, which was to replace the so-called "Geneva Declaration," originally drawn up by the Save the Children International Union in 1920, and subsequently endorsed by the League of Nations in 1924. In 1950, a draft completed by the Social Commission was referred to the Commission on Human Rights, but to date no agreement has been reached on the final text. The difficulties reside largely in the lack of enthusiasm or outright opposition to such a declaration on the part of a substantial number of governments that consider it undesirable to have "declarations" for special groups in addition to the Universal Declaration of Human Rights adopted by the General Assembly in 1948. There is also

[31] See the volume in this Brookings series, *The United Nations and Promotion of the General Welfare*, Part One, for additional discussion of this convention.

[32] Res. 390H(XIII), Aug. 9, 1951.

a feeling that the procedure is not particularly productive in terms of the protection of the interests of children.

In addition to drafting the ill-fated Delcaration of the Rights of the Child, the Social Commission has taken the lead in arranging for studies about special aspects of child care and protection.[33] Although undoubtedly useful in themselves, there is question whether studies of this specialized character are the proper responsibility of the United Nations, and no additional studies of this type are envisaged.

Of more direct impact on the development of action programs are the assessments of services for children such as were carried out in 1953 at the request of the governments of Burma, El Salvador, and Syria. Experience has shown that such surveys do stimulate practical action on the part of the countries surveyed. Further assessments in this field are therefore planned if requested by governments.

All this work is overshadowed both in scope and importance by the work of the Children's Fund. The story of the establishment of UNICEF and its work until it was made permanent in 1953 has already been told.[34] It will be recalled that even before the Children's Fund was made permanent, the Economic and Social Council and the General Assembly had agreed, in 1950, to a reorientation of the work of UNICEF. Emphasis was placed on long-range activities for children rather than on emergency action. At the same time, the Executive Board of UNICEF was reconstituted to consist of the eighteen members of the Social Commission plus eight additional member states, selected for a period of three years. This decision was taken to ensure the closest possible co-ordination and integration of the work of the Social Commission on the one hand and of UNICEF on the other, in so far as children were concerned. It was modified, in 1956, to permit direct election by the Economic and Social Council of all members of the Executive Board, irrespective of their membership on the Social Commission, after experience had demonstrated that some members of the Social Commission had little interest in the work of UNICEF and that almost all members were represented by different individuals in the Social Commission and in UNICEF.[35]

UNICEF has continued to provide aid, mostly in the form of supplies, for four major programs: the strengthening of maternal and child

[33] Among such studies are *Children Deprived of a Normal Home Life*, *Adoption of Children*, *Care of Children in Institutions*, *Day Care of Children*, and *Home Help Services*.

[34] See above, Chap. II.

[35] Res. 610B(XXI), May 1, 1956, recommending that the General Assembly amend para. 6(a) of its Res. 417(V), Dec. 1, 1950.

welfare services; the control of communicable diseases affecting children; feeding and nutrition programs; and emergency relief in disaster situations.

During the period 1951 through 1955, nearly 25 per cent of the program funds of UNICEF were devoted to maternal and child welfare services, and more than 10,000 maternal and child welfare centers were planned, established, or assisted. More than 37 per cent of the program funds were expended on mass health campaigns with the result that the total number of mothers and children tested for tuberculosis from the beginning of the program through December 1955 rose to 154.5 millions, and 59.9 millions received BCG vaccinations (antituberculosis vaccine), 56.5 millions have been examined for yaws, bejel, and syphilis, and 9.8 millions have been treated for these diseases.[36]

UNICEF works closely with the competent specialized agencies. For the mass health campaigns, WHO provides technical guidance and technical personnel who, under the arrangement of UNICEF with WHO, are to some extent financed by the Children's Fund. The nutrition work is carried on in co-operation with the FAO, and certain educational programs in co-operation with UNESCO. Under the nutrition programs, nearly 118 million pounds of dried skimmed milk, obtained free at the port of exit from the United States, were shipped during 1955. Moreover, to ensure better use of milk available locally for children, UNICEF continued to provide milk-drying and milk-pasteurization plants.

The funds at the disposal of UNICEF, consisting of voluntary contributions from governments and—to a small extent—of contributions from private sources, amounted to $70 million for the period 1951 to 1955. This was considerably less than was available during the emergency period, 1947 to 1950, when expenditures were concentrated overwhelmingly in Europe. The shift to the underdeveloped countries since then has been striking. Between 1951 and 1955, only 8.4 per cent of UNICEF aid went to Europe; 8.5 per cent to Africa; 40.8 per cent to Asia; 18.8 per cent to the Eastern Mediterranean region; 21.0 per cent to Latin America; and 2.5 per cent to activities benefiting more than one region.

UNICEF sets great store by the "matching" principle. This principle

[36] For details, see U.N. General Assembly, Tenth Session, *Official Records,* Supplement No. 6A, "United Nations Children's Fund: Financial Report and Accounts for the Year Ended 31 December 1954 and Report of the Board of Auditors" (1955); U.N. Children's Fund, *General Progress Report of the Executive Director*, Docs. E/ICEF/309 and E/ICEF/309/Add. 1 (Feb. 15, 1956).

strengthens the efforts of officials and national groups who are most actively concerned with child care programs and helps them obtain budgetary and administrative provisions for such programs, which otherwise would probably not be forthcoming. The utility of the matching principle is evident in reports that, for every dollar spent by UNICEF to the end of 1954, the governments receiving aid provided $1.66 in internal expenditures and commitments. This means that of each dollar spent, UNICEF contributed thirty-eight cents while the government assisted by the Children's Fund spent sixty-two cents. There is some doubt whether these figures can be fully sustained, because the matching expenditures include not only cash contributions, but also the estimated value of services that are difficult to evaluate in monetary terms. The fact remains, however, that the whole operation is thoroughly co-operative in character.

UNICEF represents the second largest action program of the United Nations, and it shares with the Expanded Programme of Technical Assistance the honor of being the most popular program of the United Nations. Deliberations in the Executive Board of UNICEF are as a rule smooth and noncontroversial. The annual review of the report of UNICEF by the Economic and Social Council is usually an occasion for unstinting praise.

The emotional appeal on behalf of children is strong, and this is, of course, all to the good. There are times, however, when this emotional drive tends to lead UNICEF into questionable fields. Thus, it has in recent years not only helped to create training facilities for child welfare workers but has gone so far as to pay to some extent the local expenses of trainees recruited from the very country in which they are trained. Except in the case of impoverished countries in the earliest stages of economic development, this kind of international "pump priming" should be unnecessary. More fundamental is the question whether broad supply operations necessitated by mass health campaigns or capital investments in penicillin factories and milk-processing plants should be continued indefinitely with funds raised on the basis of an appeal for aid to children. These operations obviously benefit not only children but also others. Anti-malaria campaigns or campaigns to eliminate yaws cannot distinguish between children and adults. In these circumstances, it might be proper to consider whether the terms of reference of UNICEF should be clarified to make it evident that in much of its work it acts as a supply organization in the execution of highly important functions serving the population as a whole and not just children and nursing mothers. Provided public opinion is properly educated, such an explicit recognition of the broad scope of the work of UNICEF need not weaken its "appeal" or reduce public support for its programs.

Rehabilitation of the Handicapped

Activities on behalf of the handicapped have been undertaken by the United Nations as an integral part of the program of Advisory Social Welfare Services. Adequate statistics are not available concerning the number of people in the world prevented by physical disability or defects from leading a normal and unaided life in their respective communities. Less highly industrialized countries have a lower incidence of handicap from such sources as industrial and traffic accidents, but a much higher incidence from disease. From the few figures that are available, it appears that in many countries 4 per cent to 5 per cent of the total population suffer from serious handicaps. Certain handicaps, such as blindness, are particularly prevalent in some of the underdeveloped countries. It is estimated that in India approximately 500 persons per 100,000 inhabitants are either totally blind or blind to the point of interfering seriously with their employment. In Libya, it is estimated that between 500 and 1,000 persons per 100,000 population are in the same category. The proportion of the deaf or hard of hearing to the point of serious handicap in learning and employment in both countries is also in the neighborhood of 500 per 100,000.

Modern programs aim at the prevention of handicaps due to accidents or disease, and at the rehabilitation and integration of the handicapped into the normal life of the community. Up to 1950, the United Nations system provided various types of assistance to nations establishing or expanding services to lessen the incidence of physical disability and to aid the physically handicapped.[37] These efforts were largely un-co-ordinated. The ILO continued its long standing activities for the reduction of industrial injuries and occupational diseases, for the vocational training and placement of handicapped persons, and for the social security of disabled workers and their families. The World Health Organization, through its campaigns to improve health and to limit disabling diseases, contributed much to the prevention of physical handicaps. UNESCO helped to promote the education of the physically handicapped, particularly the blind, and provided facilities for the

[37] *Cf.* U.N. Department of Social Affairs, *Services for the Physically Handicapped* (November 1953), pp. 24–25.

circulation of Braille materials. The United Nations itself, under the program of the Advisory Social Welfare Services, provided expert help and training programs on behalf of the handicapped in many nations.

Although the Social Commission dealt with these programs at almost every one of its sessions from 1946 onward, it was not until 1950 that a serious attempt was made to arrive at a co-ordinated program. In that year, the Economic and Social Council asked the Secretary-General to plan jointly with the specialized agencies and in consultation with the interested nongovernmental organizations, a well co-ordinated international program for rehabilitation of physically handicapped persons.[38] A program was then worked out by an *ad hoc* working group of the Administrative Committee on Coordination and submitted to and approved by the Social Commission in 1952. The program called for a new approach toward disability by setting forth the following six "theses," which indicate clearly the spirit and direction of the entire program.

Firstly, that the handicapped person is an individual with full human rights, which he shares in common with the able-bodied, and that he is entitled to receive from his country every possible measure of protection, assistance and opportunity for rehabilitation.

Secondly, that by the very nature of his physical handicap he is exposed to the danger of emotional and psychological disturbance, resulting from a deep sense of deprivation and frustration, and that he therefore has a special claim on society for sympathy and constructive help.

Thirdly, that he is capable of developing his residual resources to an unexpected degree, if given the right opportunities of so doing, and of becoming in most instances an economic asset to the country instead of being a burden on himself, on his family, and on the State.

Fourthly, that handicapped persons have a responsibility to the community to contribute their services to the economic welfare of the nation in any way that becomes possible after rehabilitation and training.

Fifthly, that the chief longing of the physically handicapped person is to achieve independence within a normal community, instead of spending the rest of his life in a segregated institution, or within an environment of disability.

Sixthly, that the rehabilitation of the physically handicapped can only be successfully accomplished by a combination of medical, educational, social and vocational services, working together as a team.[39]

[38] Res. 309E(XI), July 13, 1950.

[39] U.N. Economic and Social Council, *Report of the Secretary General on an International Program for the Rehabilitation of the Physically Handicapped*, Doc. E/CN.5/229 (Jan. 28, 1952), pp. 8–9.

Much of the work of the United Nations in this area and of the co-operating specialized agencies has been dedicated to obtaining general acceptance throughout the world of this new conception of physical disability. Instead of stressing separate facilities for the handicapped, every effort has been made to assist in the development of the necessary facilities as an integral part of services furnished in the field of health, education, social welfare, and employment, and not as an extraneous service for a particular class of the community.

The actual programs have been modest but quietly effective. No attempt has been made to develop a large-scale publications program as in certain other areas of social welfare. Instead a rehabilitation unit in the United Nations Secretariat has made available selected bibliographies on the rehabilitation of the handicapped, including a bibliography of films that are particularly helpful in rehabilitation work.[40] Technical assistance has been provided to a number of countries. For the most part, the experts have given advice to the governments concerned on administrative, legislative, and technical problems; others, serving on a short-term basis, have assisted in the integration and expansion of existing services.

In 1954–55, for example, sixty-four fellowships and scholarships were awarded for study abroad. The establishment of demonstration centers for physical rehabilitation also has proved to be an effective means of assistance. Such centers were established with technical assistance from the United Nations in Egypt, Yugoslavia, and Venezuela. Finally, regional meetings have been organized on the education and welfare of the deaf, the rehabilitation of the adult disabled, and the use of prosthetic devices. A regional center has been established in Indonesia. The specialized agencies have continued to work within their respective fields with the difference that their activities are now planned and carried out so as to help in the development of integrated services for the handicapped within broader systems of social insurance, public services, and social assistance.

Nongovernmental organizations have played a very active role in these programs, chief among them the International Society for the Welfare of Cripples and the World Council for the Welfare of the Blind, the International Union for Child Welfare, the World Veterans' Federation, and the World Medical Association. In 1953, these and other organizations combined in a Conference of World Organizations Inter-

[40] *Cf.* U.N. Department of Social Affairs, *Rehabilitation of the Handicapped,* Doc. ST/SOA/Ser. F/11: 2 (1953), pp. 26–85.

ested in the Handicapped, the purpose of which is to co-operate with the United Nations and the specialized agencies, particularly with the *ad hoc* Working Party on the Rehabilitation of the Handicapped. The co-operation developed between these nongovernmental organizations and the secretariats of various intergovernmental agencies is a good example of the way in which even a small international program can greatly increase its effectiveness by using to the full the knowledge and enthusiasm of nongovernmental groups. The United Nations system has thus been able to make a real contribution to the pioneering of new ideas and concepts, the establishment of facilities for rehabilitation, and the integration of the handicapped into normal life, with resultant benefits to the individuals concerned and to the economies of many countries.

Migrants and Refugees

Any consideration of international migration poses, in addition to social problems, extremely complicated demographic, economic, political, and legal issues. Despite the broad economic and political implications of migration, national and international action relating to migration has of late been concerned largely with the individual migrant, his selection, preparation for emigration, transport, placement, and adjustment to new conditions, as well as his protection as a worker and an alien. These matters require measures of the type analyzed below.

The coupling of activities relating to migrants and to refugees is a natural one because most refugees by definition are international migrants confronted, however, with special problems beyond those faced by other migrants.

Migration

The story of migration is as old as man, but the nature and conditions of migration have changed through the ages. Present day migratory movements and the problems surrounding them have certain characteristics that have to be mentioned in order to facilitate understanding of the activities of the United Nations and the specialized agencies in connection with migration.

In recent decades, millions of men, women, and children have been on the move. A substantial proportion of them have been refugees and displaced persons. In Europe alone, there were about 8 million displaced persons and refugees at the end of the Second World War to which were soon added some 8 million "expellees" from Eastern Germany and other parts of Eastern Europe. The establishment of India and Pakistan as independent states resulted in a move of approximately 9 million refugees from India into Pakistan and of about 5 million from Pakistan into India. The war in Palestine resulted in the movement of about 1 million Arab refugees from Palestine, and the war in Korea produced, at least temporarily, 4.5 million refugees and displaced persons in South Korea. Emergency measures taken on behalf of several of these groups have been discussed elsewhere in this study.[41]

The stream of migrants has been further swelled by the overpopulated countries of Europe—Italy, Germany, Greece, and the Netherlands. It was estimated, in 1952 by the ILO that the surplus working population in Italy was about 3.7 million persons and that a large proportion of these were prepared to emigrate. In the Federal Republic of Germany, the number of persons ready to emigrate was then estimated by the government to be 1.2 million. Even in the Netherlands, it was estimated that an annual emigration of 25,000 workers was necessary to maintain the economic and social balance of the country. Actual emigration has not reached these totals. As a matter of fact, in no year since the war has European overseas emigration reached the levels of the early 1920's, when in some years more than 1 million migrants left that continent for overseas destinations. The postwar peak was reached between 1949 and 1952 when upwards of 600,000 migrants per year, a large proportion of them refugees and displaced persons, left Europe.

Despite pressure for emigration, it has become increasingly difficult to find places of settlement. There is general agreement that certain underdeveloped countries would benefit from additional immigration, but such immigration is impeded to some extent by the lack of agricultural migrants for which the underdeveloped countries are most frequently looking and partly by the fact that land settlement in the economically competitive society of today, calling for better and more expensive equipment, has become a very costly process. As a result of this situation and the broader opportunities offered by more diversified economies, a large proportion of modern migration is directed toward industrialized rather than underdeveloped countries. This, in turn, requires different types of selection and better preparation of migrants to enable them to adjust to the working processes and the kind of life in highly industrialized countries.

[41] See above, Chaps. I and II.

As a result of these difficulties, plus the legal restrictions imposed on migrants for political and economic reasons, migration as a pioneering venture on the part of individuals has been largely replaced by migration organized by governments. Both the governments of the countries of origin (except, of course, in the case of refugees) and governments of the countries of reception play a key role in the selection, preparation, admission, transportation, and placement of migrants.

Although some international agencies, including the United Nations and the ILO, have concerned themselves with internal migrations, international migration still remains the primary objective of international attention. More than ever, it has become a problem calling for intergovernmental action. In the late 1940's, the General Assembly and the Economic and Social Council repeatedly, and the Trusteeship Council occasionally, took up migration issues. The ILO exhibited a growing concern with migration as a way to make better use of man power and stepped up those of its activities designed to protect the working conditions of migrants. The FAO gave consideration to migration in relation to land reform and the problems of rural settlement. UNESCO expressed its concern with the cultural assimilation of migrants, as well as with vocational guidance and training for prospective migrants. WHO centered its attention on health qualifications and examinations of migrants and the availability of the kind of health services required by migrants in the receiving countries. Meanwhile, the International Refugee Organization (IRO), as has been reported earlier in this study, carried the major burden of settlement of refugees both in Europe and overseas between 1949 and 1952.[42]

This mushrooming of interest in migration was bound to result in conflicts of jurisdiction. Much of the United Nations effort up to 1950 was directed at bringing some order into the international work in this field.[43] After several earlier attempts, the Economic and Social Council, in 1948, attempted to lay down a permanent pattern of allocation of functions.[44] It assigned responsibility for research on migration problems to the Population Commission, asking it to deal not only with the demographic aspects of migration but with the relationships between demographic, economic, and social factors in migration, and to give special attention to the over-all co-ordination of research and study in

[42] See above, Chap. II.

[43] In this connection, see U.N. Economic and Social Council Res. 42(IV), Mar. 29, 1947; Res. 85(V), Aug. 13, 1947; Res. 104(VI), Mar. 3, 1948.

[44] Res. 156(VII), Aug. 10, 1948.

this field by the United Nations and specialized agencies. The Social Commission was asked to advise the Council on the social aspects of migration, particularly the rights and benefits of immigrants, including those of indigent immigrants; family and community relationships of immigrants; and advance planning by government authorities with a view to the provision of social services and facilities for health and education for immigrants and their families after arrival in a new community.

The same resolution laid the basis for future interagency consultations by inviting the specialized agencies and the United Nations to submit to the Administrative Committee on Coordination any migration problems that might arise within their areas of interest in such circumstances that overlapping with other organizations might occur or that important aspects of problems of migration might be neglected. At the same time, the Council noted with approval the division of responsibility between the United Nations and the ILO agreed to in consultation between the Secretary-General of the United Nations and the Director-General of the ILO. Under this arrangement, the ILO was to deal with migrants as *workers*, including policies governing their recruitment and selection, vocational training, care during transportation, employment and working conditions, social insurance, formalities in connection with departure from the country of residence and admission to the country of destination, and such general assistance and advice to governments on migration schemes as the ILO might be able to give from its experience. The United Nations, on the other hand, was to center its attention on the problems of the migrant as an alien, including conditions of residence, expulsion, deportation and repatriation, naturalization, relief in case of indigency, and recognition and enforcement of maintenance obligations. In addition, the United Nations was to maintain not only its responsibility regarding demographic aspects of migration but was to concern itself also with the broad economic, financial, social, and legal aspects.

This action on the part of the Economic and Social Council brought some clarification into a confused situation. It was followed by direct consultations on an organized basis through an *ad hoc* Working Group on Migration established under the Administrative Committee on Coordination.[45] Starting in 1949, this Working Group helped gradually

[45] A first meeting of the Working Group, in which representatives of the United Nations Secretariat, ILO, WHO, FAO, IRO, UNESCO, and the International Bank participated, was held in March 1949, and resulted in a more detailed delimitation of responsibilities as set forth in U.N. Economic and Social Council, *Coordination of Migration Activities*, Doc. E/1341 (May 31, 1949).

to reduce overlapping and conflicts of jurisdiction, although to this day, work on migration is not as closely co-ordinated as is the work in other fields of interest of the United Nations. To some extent, this is, of course, due to the extreme complexities of the issues involved.

These complexities became more evident in 1950 and 1951 when the ILO attempted as part of its man-power program to develop concerted international action for the movement, care, and protection of migrants. The ILO had just completed a major revision of its 1939 Convention on Migration for Employment, which had been prepared by its Permanent Migration Committee. It was felt in the ILO that its activities relating to migration could no longer be limited to the "traditional" activities of the organization, that is, research and studies, compilation of statistics and legislation, and the drafting of international instruments designed to set standards. The movement for additional action gained strength with the impending liquidation of the International Refugee Organization.

A Preliminary Migration Conference was convened by the ILO in the spring of 1950. The conclusions of this conference, which covered the entire field from selection to settlement, and which were later endorsed by the Governing Body of the ILO, constituted a veritable code of rules for international technical assistance in the field of European migration. The success of this conference led the Organization for European Economic Cooperation to arrange for the placement of a fund of nearly $1 million (mostly of American origin) at the disposal of the ILO for financing some of the new activities.

The ILO appointed experts to advise governments on various migration problems. Migration field missions were established at Bonn, Vienna, and Rome and a special migration unit was attached to the ILO Manpower Field Office for Latin America at Sao Paulo. A number of Latin American countries were given technical assistance (in some cases provided jointly by the ILO and the FAO) in the estimation of immigration capacity, the formulation of immigration programs, the examination of specific immigration projects, and the establishment of employment services. A guide to employment service organization was prepared as well as a guide to vocational training of migrants. A study was initiated to facilitate comparisons between the occupational classifications used in the countries of emigration and immigration. Guides to the principal immigration countries were prepared giving essential information on living and working conditions.

This hopeful start led the ILO to convene a migration conference to examine an over-all plan for handling European migration.[46] The conference was held in October 1951 in Naples and had before it a comprehensive plan for the establishment and financing of an ILO Migration Administration.

When the conference convened, serious differences of opinion developed almost immediately concerning the extent and nature of the international assistance required. The United States made clear that it was not prepared to make a financial contribution to the proposed agency. This opposition, shared by Australia and a few other countries, was largely based on the fact that the ILO plan appeared grandiose and impractical in many of its aspects. Reluctance, particularly on the part of the United States, to create such a migration administration within the ILO was prompted also by the fact that the proposed administration would have to deal with refugees from Communist countries, and that Communist states, specifically Poland and Czechoslovakia, were members of the ILO. The power of this particular argument became evident while the conference was still in session. When the Congress of the United States, in approving the Mutual Security Act of 1951, allocated an amount not in excess of $10 million for the continued operation of a number of vessels utilized by the International Refugee Organization for the transport of displaced persons, it stated as its intent that "none of the funds made available pursuant to the proviso should be allocated to any international organization which has in its membership any Communist, Communist-dominated or Communist-controlled country, to any subsidiary thereof or to any agency created by or stemming from such organization."[47]

This stipulation was clearly aimed at the ILO. It undoubtedly contributed to the failure of the Naples conference to achieve its major objective. The conference did adopt certain basic principles and criteria, worked out in co-operation with WHO, for the medical examina-

[46] The emphasis of the international community on European migration is significant. During the nineteenth and early twentieth centuries, organized migration was viewed by the western world primarily as a European problem and scant attention was paid to migratory movements in other parts of the world. This tradition left its imprint on the international organizations interested in migration and left them ill equipped to render effective assistance in meeting the problems of non-European migrants, particularly those from Asia and the Far East. In so far as any assistance, other than emergency aid, is being given to non-European migrants as migrants, it is taking the form of technical assistance to governments in the utilization and organization of man power.

[47] *Mutual Security Act of 1951*, H. Rept. 1090, 82 Cong. 1 sess. (Oct. 2, 1951), p. 21.

tion of migrants, and these have proved useful. It also proposed the setting up of a Consultative Council on European Migration, but this was largely a face-saving device, and the proposed council never came into existence.

Shortly after the Naples conference, and on United States initiative, another intergovernmental conference on migration was held. Convened in Brussels in November 1951, this conference—to which no Communist governments were invited—decided to set up a Provisional Inter-Governmental Committee for the Movement of Migrants from Europe. Its proposed terms of reference included the organization of land, sea, and air transport for refugees and the charter of ships formerly under the auspices of the IRO. This Provisional Inter-Governmental Committee later became the Inter-Governmental Committee for European Migration (ICEM), which, after the liquidation of the IRO, became the operating agency for the transport of European migrants and refugees. Twenty-six governments interested in migration belonged to the committee in early 1956. Its budget for 1956 was set at more than $43 million. A large part of the budget is met by reimbursements from sending and receiving governments for actual transportation costs. The ICEM moved more than 400,000 refugees during the period 1952 through 1955.

The Inter-Governmental Committee for European Migration has never been a part of the United Nations system. It maintains close working relationships, however, with various organs of the United Nations such as the Office of the High Commissioner for Refugees and the Economic Commission for Latin America, and it benefits from the work of the United Nations and the interested specialized agencies in the field of migration.

Research and studies continue to bulk large in this work. The list of publications by the United Nations and the ILO is lengthening steadily, with the latter concentrating on man-power studies and the protection of the migrant as a worker. The United Nations has published such practical aids as a *Handbook of International Measures for Protection of Migrants* and a report on research activities in the field of migration undertaken from 1946 to the beginning of 1953 by the United Nations and the specialized agencies.[48] In addition, the United Nations has

[48] U.N. Department of Social Affairs, *Handbook of International Measures for Protection of Migrants and General Conditions to be Observed in Their Settlement*, Doc. ST/SOA/15 (Jan. 15, 1953); U.N. Department of Social Affairs, *International Research on Migration*, Doc. ST/SOA/18 (September 1953).

prepared studies on more specialized subjects—for example, *Simplification of Formalities and Reduction of Costs for Migrants*, and *Expulsion of Immigrants*.[49] Field activities, so far as the United Nations itself is concerned, have been very limited, however; a few experts have been provided and some fellowships granted. By contrast, the ILO has continued to give active attention to migration problems as part of its technical assistance work in the man-power field.

Yeoman work in the reception and care of migrants has been performed by nongovernmental organizations, which, following a suggestion of the Economic and Social Council, combined in a Conference of Non-Governmental Organizations Interested in Migration. The fifth meeting of the conference was held in May 1955 under the joint sponsorship of the United Nations and the ILO.

In the light of the developments outlined above, it is possible to draw one major conclusion. The political difficulties and the economic complexities of large-scale migratory movements have proved too much for the protagonists of centralized or even closely co-ordinated action, under United Nations auspices, in the field of migration. To the extent that migration is a technical problem, valuable assistance is being offered by the ILO. Practical help to individual migrants is frequently extended by nongovernmental organizations, national and international. Beyond this, multilateral action is strictly limited, even as regards European migration. Political considerations and differing needs and absorptive capacities of individual countries remain the determining factors in the organization of international migration. Even where governments combine in common action as in the case of ICEM, they are only willing to provide for a minimum of international machinery to aid them in achieving their national economic and political ends. Thus international migration, which, at first sight, would appear to be a problem eminently fitted for joint international action, continues to be dealt with essentially by national governments. It is significant that no important resolution on migration has been adopted either by the General Assembly or the Economic and Social Council since 1952. One of the

[49] A discussion of "Economic and Social Factors Affecting Migration" was included in U.N. Department of Social Affairs, *Determinants and Consequences of Population Trends*, A Summary of the Findings of Studies on the Relationships between Population Changes and Economic and Social Conditions, Doc. ST/SOA/Ser.A/17 (1953), pp. 98–133. Two studies have been prepared for the United Nations by the International Institute for the Unification of Private Law: *A Compilation of Legislative Texts on the Legal Status of Aliens*, and a *Compilation of International Instruments on the Legal Status of Aliens*. A *Migration Digest*, of which thirty-nine issues had appeared by 1954, has been discontinued by the Secretary-General.

last such resolutions recommended to "Member States and non-Member States, classified variously as countries of emigration and immigration, to conclude bilateral or multilateral agreements with a view to the equipment, transfer and resettlement of groups of emigrants, without racial or religious discrimination, as part of their general economic development."[50] The emphasis on direct agreements between governments rather than on international machinery is significant.

Refugees

First slated for termination by June 30, 1950, the International Refugee Organization finally closed its books in early 1952.[51] This did not mean that the refugee problem had been solved. The General Council of the IRO itself stated, shortly before its termination, that "although the problems inherent in the situation . . . are clearly not of sufficient magnitude to justify the maintenance of the IRO, they are so grave in terms of human suffering that they call for urgent consideration by the United Nations."[52]

In anticipation of this situation, the Economic and Social Council, as early as 1949, had asked the Secretary-General to prepare for the consideration of the General Assembly a plan for continuing machinery, either in the form of a High Commissioner's Office or of a service within the United Nations Secretariat.[53] The Assembly decided to establish as of January 1, 1951 a High Commissioner's Office for Refugees and, at the same time, outlined certain principles to govern its functioning.[54] It also requested the Council to submit more detailed plans to the Assembly. The Council then transmitted a draft "Statute of the High Commissioner's Office for Refugees."[55] Final action on this statute, which was taken by the General Assembly in 1950, provided for the appointment of a United Nations High Commissioner for Refugees and laid out in considerable detail his functions and the organization and financing of his office.[56] The General Assembly at the same session elected the first High Commissioner.[57]

The discussions preceding the approval of these arrangements were

[50] U.N. General Assembly Res. 624(VII), Dec. 21, 1952.

[51] See above, Chap. II.

[52] U.N. General Assembly, Sixth Session, *Problems of Assistance to Refugees: Communication from the General Council of the International Refugee Organization*, Doc. A/1948 (Nov. 10, 1951), p. 6.

[53] Res. 248A(IX), Aug. 6, 1949.

[54] See Res. 319(IV), Dec. 3, 1949, and Annex thereto.

[55] Res. 319A(XI), Aug. 11, 1950.

[56] Res. 428(V), Dec. 14, 1950.

[57] G. J. van Heuven Goedhart, who died in July 1956.

prolonged and heated. Major differences of opinion arose over the definition of the "refugees" who were to be brought under the mandate of the High Commissioner. Most of the Asian and Middle Eastern countries, and a few European and Latin American countries, wanted a liberal definition that would have included millions of non-European refugees such as Pakistanis moving into India and Indians moving into Pakistan. The United States, supported by such countries as the United Kingdom and Australia, took a much more restricted view. The United States wanted to avoid any general definition and preferred an enumeration of clearly defined categories of refugees, specifically those who had been considered refugees under the various arrangements and conventions concluded under the League of Nations and the constitution of the IRO, and any persons who, as a result of events before January 1, 1951, had become refugees. To be specifically excluded were persons recognized by the competent authorities of the country in which they had taken residence as having the rights and obligations of nationals of that country. This excluded all the expellees from Eastern Germany and other *Volksdeutsche* who had found refuge in the Federal Republic of Germany, as well as Pakistanis, Indians, and Chinese, who could look to the protection of their own governments. The Communist bloc countries maintained the astonishing thesis they had put forward at the time of the creation of the International Refugee Organization: that only the victims or opponents of one particular form of government—Nazi, Fascist or Falangist—could be refugees. Opponents of any other form of government were traitors and criminals, whose immediate repatriation for summary punishment was an international obligation.[58]

In the end, the General Assembly agreed on a compromise. It enumerated certain categories of refugees along the lines suggested by the United States but included a further paragraph bringing under the mandate of the High Commissioner:

> . . . any other person who is outside the country of his nationality or, if he has no nationality, the country of his former habitual residence, because he has or had well-founded fear of persecution by reason of his race, religion, nationality or political opinion and is unable or, because of such fear, is unwilling to avail himself of the protection of the government of the country of his nationality, or, if he has no nationality, to return to the country of his former habitual residence.[59]

[58] Elfan Rees, "The Refugee and the United Nations," *International Conciliation* No. 492 (June 1953), p. 272. This is one of the best summary accounts of the refugee problem as dealt with by the United Nations.

[59] Statute of the Office of the United Nations High Commissioner for Refugees, Res. 428(V), Dec. 14, 1950, Annex, Chap. II, Art. 6B.

Under these provisions, the mandate of the High Commissioner extended to approximately two million people, almost exclusively of European origin.

An even sharper conflict developed over the definition of the functions of the High Commissioner. The United States took the lead in emphasizing as the primary and almost exclusive function of the High Commissioner the task of legal and administrative protection, such as assuring that governments issue identity and travel papers and work permits enabling refugees to move about and to obtain their livelihood. The United States position was prompted by the belief that the relief problems remaining after termination of the IRO were not of such a magnitude as to require international financing and that the countries of refuge should and could assume responsibility for relief and other material aid. By contrast, certain countries of first residence for refugees, particularly France, urged that the High Commissioner be entitled and equipped to continue to give material aid to individuals and groups of refugees.

In a number of close votes, the Assembly finally agreed that the High Commissioner should assume the function of "providing international protection" and "of seeking permanent solutions" for the problem of refugees by assisting governments and, subject to the approval of the governments concerned, private organizations to facilitate the voluntary repatriation of such refugees, or their assimilation within new national communities.[60] The High Commissioner was given the power to "administer any funds, public or private, which he receives for assistance to refugees," but at the same time was enjoined not to appeal to governments for funds or make a general appeal, without the prior approval of the General Assembly.[61] As a matter of fact, most of the residual funds of the IRO were not turned over to the High Commissioner but to voluntary organizations aiding refugees.

From 1950 to 1954 was a period of continuous struggle on the part of the High Commissioner to obtain the funds that he considered essential to the discharge of his functions. In 1952, he obtained authority to appeal for funds for purposes of emergency aid.[62] He then set up a United Nations Refugee Emergency Fund for which he hoped to obtain $3 million. During the two following years, less than $1 million was contributed. The United States did not contribute to the United Nations

[60] *Ibid.*, Chap. I, Art. I.
[61] *Ibid.*, Chap. II, Art. 10.
[62] U.N. General Assembly Res. 538B(VI), Feb. 2, 1952.

Refugee Emergency Fund, but channeled its material aid through ICEM and through the newly created United States Escapee Program, which began in March 1952 with an allocation of $4.3 million for aid to refugees in Western Europe who had escaped from countries behind the Iron Curtain after January 1, 1948. Thus, the United States continued to be the largest contributor to the cause of refugee aid but did not make its funds available through United Nations channels.

After a decision had been taken by the General Assembly to continue the Office of the High Commissioner for another five years, from January 1, 1954,[63] the High Commissioner redoubled his efforts to obtain additional funds not only for emergency aid but also to assist in the finding of permanent solutions. He was encouraged in this by a grant of $2.9 million from the Ford Foundation in 1952 and $200,000 in 1954 to assist in providing permanent solutions for the refugee problem. These were obtained through the efforts of four of the major voluntary agencies working on behalf of refugees, and the High Commissioner became the trustee and administrator of the fund. It was used to facilitate agricultural integration, housing, vocational training, education, employment counseling, youth and community centers, medical rehabilitation, and overseas resettlement. The results were sufficiently promising to give a new impetus to the High Commissioner's drive for additional funds from governments.

He attained his end when the General Assembly, in 1954, finally agreed to authorize use of the United Nations Refugee Emergency Fund for the purpose of facilitating permanent solutions as well as for emergency needs.[64] The High Commissioner was authorized also to obtain additional funds on the basis of a detailed program he had submitted. The plan provided for a four-year program at a cost of $16 million. For the first time since the liquidation of the IRO, the United States not only voted for the establishment of this enlarged United Nations Refugee Emergency Fund but promised to seek a contribution from the Congress of the United States. The budget for the first year's operation was set for $4.2 million, with approximately $3 million to be used for the attainment of permanent solutions. Subsequently, the United States Congress allocated $1.2 million for the year 1955, provided that the United States contribution did not exceed one third of the total contributions made. Contributions of other governments fell short of expectations. By the end of 1955, only $2 million had been made available by

[63] Res. 727(VIII), Oct. 23, 1953.
[64] Res. 832(IX), Oct. 21, 1954.

these other governments, and the United States contribution to that date, therefore, was limited to $1 million. In the administration of these funds, the High Commissioner is assisted by an advisory committee, set up originally in 1951, and reconstituted with executive powers by the Economic and Social Council in 1955, as the United Nations Refugee Fund (UNREF) Executive Committee.[65]

Parallel to these actions involving the appointment of a High Commissioner and the development of his functions, the United Nations attempted to provide standard legal protection by a convention embodying earlier refugee conventions concluded under the League of Nations but adjusted to contemporary conditions. In a series of resolutions, the Economic and Social Council with the help of an *ad hoc* committee and, finally, of the General Assembly, advanced the drafting of such a convention to the point where a plenipotentiary conference was held in Geneva in July 1951.[66]

The conference completed and opened for signature a convention on the status of refugees, which has come into force largely as a result of ratifications on the part of European nations.[67] In the drafting of this convention, the same difficulties arose in defining "refugees" as had arisen in the drafting of the statute of the High Commissioner's office. The definition in the convention did not include the generalized definition of refugees that was included in the statute and that was cited above. The convention selected "events occurring before 1 January 1951" as the *terminus ad quo* for a refugee situation and further limited even this by leaving it to individual governments to decide whether they wished to include only events "occurring in Europe" before that date or would also include events "occurring in Europe and elsewhere."

In substance, the convention provided for freedom from discrimination and dealt with the legal status of refugees and their rights with respect to work, housing, education, public relief, social security, free-

[65] Res. 565(XIX), Mar. 31, 1955. In November and December 1956, Soviet intervention to crush a revolt in Hungary resulted in a mass exodus from that country. The General Assembly requested the Secretary-General and the High Commissioner for Refugees to arrange for emergency assistance to refugees from Hungary, and urged governments and nongovernmental organizations to contribute to this work. As a result, these officers promptly issued a joint appeal for $10 million to help meet the minimum initial needs of the refugees.

[66] U.N. Economic and Social Council Res. 116D(VI), Mar. 1–2, 1948; Res. 248B(IX), Aug. 8, 1949; Res. 319BII(XI), Aug. 16, 1950; U.N. General Assembly Res. 429(V), Dec. 14, 1950.

[67] U.N. Conference of Plenipotentiaries on the Status of Refugees and Stateless Persons held at Geneva, Switzerland from July 2–25, 1951, *Final Act and Convention Relating to the Status of Refugees* (1951).

dom of movement, and access to the courts. These provisions, if accepted, go a long way in facilitating the assimilation of refugees within their countries of residence. The United States participated in the drafting of the convention, but made clear that it had no intention of signing or ratifying it, on the ground that noncitizens, including legally admitted refugees, in the United States have even greater privileges than those set forth in the convention. Except for a few specific rights such as the right to vote, their position is in effect that of United States citizens.

In international programs of refugee aid, the record of voluntary organizations during the postwar years is outstanding. They have concentrated in their work on welfare, spiritual care, emigration assistance, and experiments in integration. After the establishment of the High Commissioner's office, and while the High Commissioner was barred from operational functions, the voluntary agencies had to assume the major burden of material aid to refugees.

Under the new plan for permanent solutions developed by the High Commissioner and accepted by the General Assembly, the voluntary agencies continue to be the chief action bodies in the carrying out of the program. It has been repeatedly suggested that they can make a dollar go further than any intergovernmental organization. Moreover, they bring to their work the human approach, which means so much, particularly when funds are scarce. These agencies—nearly forty of them—have established a Standing Conference of Voluntary Agencies Working for Refugees that is in consultative relationship with the Economic and Social Council, with the UNREF Executive Committee, and with the Inter-Governmental Committee for European Migration.

It has been said that "the United Nations in its spasmodic consideration of the refugee problem has persistently displayed either incredibly naive optimism, or a willful blindness to reality, neither of which is consistent with statesmanship." This may be too harsh a judgment, although there is much truth in the further statement that "it is some time since so few have been asked to do so much for so many on so little."[68]

Even with the restricted means available, and thanks to the help of the voluntary organizations, large numbers of refugees have been given emergency aid. Signal success was achieved in the placing of hard core cases, *i.e.*, the old, the sick, and the maimed. Outstanding contributions

[68] Rees, *loc. cit.*, p. 309.

in this respect were made by Norway, which received many of the blind, by Sweden and Switzerland, which took in the tubercular, by France, which accepted many epileptics, and by Belgium, Ireland, the United Kingdom, the Netherlands, and Germany, which agreed to take care on a permanent basis of many of the aged. The problem of these hard core cases is not altogether solved but nears solution. Under arrangements made by ICEM, in co-operation with the High Commissioner, more than 83,000 refugees were moved overseas for permanent settlement between 1952 and 1955. Until May 1956, when the authorities on the Chinese mainland closed the branch office of the High Commissioner in Shanghai, the 15,000 White Russian refugees stranded in China after the First World War were gradually being moved out of Communist China, again with the help of ICEM. Above all, the High Commissioner has succeeded in keeping alive and awakening, when necessary, the conscience of the civilized nations on refugee questions.

Social Defense

The dark forces in human nature, greed or lust or simply weakness, can easily become destructive of human personality unless they are kept under control. Society has to defend itself against them. There are three major areas of social defense that for many years have been recognized as a legitimate concern of governments, acting separately and jointly: the control of the traffic in dangerous drugs; the suppression of prostitution and of obscene literature; and the prevention of crime and the treatment of offenders.[69]

Narcotic Drug Control

The United Nations inherited no less than six international conventions and agreements dealing with the control of narcotic drugs, chief among them the Geneva convention of February 19, 1925 instituting a system of import certificates and export permits without which no international transaction in narcotic drugs could be made legally, and the Convention for Limiting the Manufacture and Regulating the Dis-

[69] In the terminology of the United Nations and for purposes of internal organization of the Secretariat, the control of dangerous drugs is not considered within the area of social defense. The ultimate purpose of international control, however, is the protection of the individual against the dangers of drug addiction, and for that reason the control of narcotic drugs is discussed in this study as an aspect of social defense.

tribution of Narcotic Drugs signed at Geneva on July 13, 1931. The United Nations also inherited two control organs, the Permanent Central Opium Board set up under the 1925 convention to "continuously watch the course of international trade" in narcotic drugs;[70] and the Drug Supervisory Body established under the 1931 convention to examine the estimates furnished annually by governments of their requirements of narcotic drugs for medical and scientific purposes. This machinery had continued to function on a limited scale throughout the Second World War, in itself a striking sign of the importance that governments had come to attach to the international control of traffic in narcotics.

The Economic and Social Council, by unanimous action on February 16, 1946, established the Commission on Narcotic Drugs. It has since served as the focal point of intergovernmental consultation and action in the field of narcotics control, as did the Advisory Committee on the Traffic in Opium and other Dangerous Drugs set up by the League of Nations in 1920. Also in 1946, the General Assembly unanimously adopted a protocol approving the assumption by the United Nations of the functions and powers exercised by the League of Nations in respect to narcotic drugs.[71]

The Commission on Narcotic Drugs and the Permanent Central Opium Board each present an annual report on their work to the Council. These are published, as is the annual statement issued by the Drug Supervisory Body on *Estimated World Requirements of Narcotic Drugs*. Four further series of publications are produced.[72] Special studies on particular questions or problems are also issued. Publicity is one of the most effective means of enforcement of controls, and information on measures taken by national governments is essential to effective international action.

The varied activities of the Commission on Narcotic Drugs can be broken down into five major categories: suppression of illicit traffic in narcotic drugs; control of synthetic and newly discovered drugs; control of the production of natural raw materials; consolidation of international treaties and protocols; and prevention of addiction and rehabilitation of addicts. With respect to the first of these areas of activity, there

[70] International Opium Convention, signed at Geneva Feb. 19, 1925, Art. 24.

[71] Res. 54(I), Nov. 19, 1946.

[72] The *Annual Summary of Laws and Regulations Relating to the Control of Narcotic Drugs*, the *Annual Summary of Annual Reports of Governments*, monthly *Summaries of Illicit Transactions and Seizures* reported to the Secretariat of the United Nations, and the quarterly *Bulletin on Narcotics*.

was general apprehension among experts during the war that after the war the illicit traffic in narcotics might get out of hand. These expectations fortunately did not come true, but the illicit traffic did reach substantial proportions and continues at a high level. Much of that traffic is aimed at the United States market where a few pounds of narcotics can bring large monetary returns. Moreover, the long frontiers of the United States make control extremely difficult.

Public debate in the Commission on Narcotics Drugs, frequently based on specific seizure reports transmitted by governments, is an instance in which necessity often overrides diplomatic niceties. The reports of the commission are replete with discussions of specific situations, with the origin of illicit drugs frequently and publicly traced to named countries of origin. The reports of the Permanent Central Opium Board sometimes also refer to specific instances of failure to comply with provisions of the relevant conventions. These reports and discussions as a rule do not result in pious resolutions but in effective national action in the form of the closing of factories, or of police or even military action to destroy illegal poppy plantings.

With the endorsement of the Economic and Social Council, special control measures were taken in Germany and Japan during the allied occupation. Further, when it was found that much of the smuggling of narcotics, particularly into the United States, was attributable to merchant seafarers and civilian air crews, the Economic and Social Council requested the Secretary-General to establish lists of persons who had been convicted of offenses against narcotic laws and recommended that governments revoke certificates and licenses held by such personnel.[73]

Increasingly effective steps have been taken over the last ten years, largely by way of persuasion, resolution,[74] and publicity, to prohibit completely the use of certain narcotics, particularly the smoking of opium, and thus to establish a precondition for the application of international laws and machinery to the suppression of illicit traffic. Opium smoking remains legal only in one of the traditional opium smoking countries, although transitional arrangements are in force in a number of others.

Further progress in the international control of the traffic in opium is being made through scientific research. In 1949, the United States

[73] Res. 436D(XIV), May 27, 1952.

[74] U.N. Economic and Social Council Res. 49(IV), Mar. 28, 1947; Res. 159IIB (VII), Aug. 3, 1948; Res. 505B(XVI), July 28, 1953.

offered, and the Commission on Narcotic Drugs accepted, the use of United States laboratory facilities to develop methods for determining by chemical and physical means the geographical origin of seized opium. The Economic and Social Council requested governments to send for purposes of laboratory research, samples of all opium seized in the illicit traffic. This research has proved successful. Because of the work of a Canadian chemist, it has now become possible to ascertain the country of original production of seized opium, and this is bound to make control measures more effective. A permanent United Nations Narcotics Laboratory is now scheduled to be established in Geneva.

A second series of measures is aimed at the extension of controls to synthetic and other newly-discovered drugs. A fresh threat to the health and well-being of millions of persons and to the entire functioning of international campaigns against drug addiction arose with the development of synthetic, addiction-producing drugs that threatened to flood the illicit market. On the initiative of the United States, rapid action was taken against this threat. The move to bring these drugs under international control resulted, in 1948, in the conclusion of a new protocol "to bring under international control drugs outside the scope of the Convention of July 13, 1931 for limiting the manufacture and regulating the distribution of narcotic drugs."[75] The protocol applies to all drugs "liable to the same kind of harmful effects as the drugs specified in Article I, paragraph 2 of the [1931] Convention." Accordingly, it makes it possible to place under international control not only existing synthetic drugs but also any other addiction-forming drugs, as rapidly as they are discovered.

Under the convention, it is for the World Health Organization to ascertain whether a particular drug is addiction-forming. Pending such determination, the protocol allows the Commission on Narcotic Drugs to take interim measures to place under control a drug considered by a state party to the protocol as likely to produce addiction or capable of being transformed into such a drug. The list of drugs being brought under control in this way is lengthening steadily.

In a third field of activities, the United Nations has made extensive efforts to bring under control the *production* of "natural" raw materials. Earlier conventions aimed at the control of the international *traffic* in raw materials used in the manufacture of drugs (Geneva convention of 1925) and the *manufacture* of such drugs (Geneva convention of 1931).

[75] U.N. Economic and Social Council Res. 159I(VII), Aug. 3, 1948; U.N. General Assembly Res. 211A(III), Oct. 8, 1948.

Beginning with the first session of the Commission on Narcotics Drugs in 1946, attempts were made to go one step further and to limit the production of "natural" raw materials. Opium, by far the most important of the raw materials concerned, was the subject of a series of meetings under the sponsorship of the United Nations, first among the major producing countries (India, Iran, Turkey, and Yugoslavia), then of the principal manufacturing countries (France, the Netherlands, United Kingdom, United States and, as observers, Belgium, Italy, and Switzerland) and, finally, by a joint meeting of the two groups.[76]

The purpose of these meetings was to establish an international public drug enterprise in the form of a monopoly for buying and selling opium in the legal trade. The proposed agreement provided for estimates of annual opium requirements, the establishment of export quotas, and an international agency for purchasing and selling opium. Each country party to the agreement was to create a national opium monopoly to control all stages of production and purchase the crop for resale to the international agency. The international agency thereupon was to sell the crop at a fixed price to the drug manufacturing countries, according to "advance" orders based on requirements. Provisions were included in the plan for inspection and for the imposition of sanctions for violations of the agreement.

The discussion of these proposals, originally advanced by the Secretariat of the United Nations, led to one of the few major disagreements among members of the Commission on Narcotic Drugs. Negotiations finally broke down on two key issues. No agreement could be reached on the price to be fixed by the international agency. It was also impossible to reach agreement on the question of international inspection, largely because some of the producing countries declared themselves unwilling or unable to permit inspection in their territories except on the basis of specific consent for each international inspection. Beyond these specific difficulties, negotiations were complicated by an undercurrent of reluctance, not only on the part of the manufacturers but also of some of the producers, to depart from the free market approach and to accept control of prices and of purchasing by the establishment of a monopoly system.

When these negotiations collapsed, attention was transferred to an alternative plan suggested by the French Government. This plan, after

[76] Recently Iran, in a far-sighted move taken on its own volition, has banned the cultivation of the opium poppy and the Economic and Social Council in Res. 626E(XXII) of Aug. 2, 1956, authorized the use of technical assistance to help Iran in enforcing this ban and bringing about necessary adjustments in the Iranian economy.

consideration by the Commission on Narcotic Drugs and the United Nations Secretariat, resulted in a draft protocol for limiting and regulating the cultivation of the poppy plant, the production of, international and wholesale trade in, and the use of opium. This draft was submitted to and, with amendments, approved by the United Nations Opium Conference convened at New York in 1953.[77]

The protocol, which in the absence of the stipulated number of ratifications has not yet come into effect, calls for the continuance of a free order system in international trade in opium, within which the production of opium is to be limited with a view to reducing the amounts harvested to the amounts needed for medical and scientific purposes. Indirect means are to be adopted to achieve this aim. Countries producing opium are to submit full statistics, and also advance estimates, of their production to the United Nations. Consuming countries are required under the 1931 convention to estimate their needs. Stocks of producing countries are to be limited to the equivalent of their exports of any two and one-half years since 1947, and the stocks of manufacturing and consuming countries are also to be limited. Individual governments of countries in which opium is produced, whether for export or not, undertake to establish national agencies to be the only legal purchasers of opium, and to carry into effect stringent measures of internal control, including the licensing of each grower and the supervision of the area cultivated. The number of countries authorized to export is limited to those presently producing opium.

International control is exercised not through an international monopoly but through the Permanent Central Opium Board and the Drug Supervisory Body. If a country fails to submit estimates, exceeds maximum stock limits, threatens to become a center of the illicit traffic, or otherwise fails to implement the protocol, the board is authorized to take a series of steps. In addition to consultation with the government concerned, publication and publicity, and local inquiry (with the consent of the government), the board can recommend an import and/or export embargo of opium, this last step being subject to appeal to a body set up within the framework of the International Court of Justice.

Parallel efforts were made to establish controls over the production of other "natural" raw materials used in the production of narcotic drugs, specifically cannabis and the coca leaf.[78] In the case of cannabis,

[77] United Nations Opium Conference, *Protocol and Final Act*, Doc. E/NT/8 (Sept. 28, 1953).

[78] Indian hemp, marihuana, and hashish are forms of cannabis.

which plays an important role in the fibre industry of a number of countries and which grows wild over many regions of the world, practical solutions sought under the direction of the Food and Agriculture Organization include encouraging the breeding of narcotic-free strains of the plant and also investigating the possibilities of replacement by other fibre crops having comparable industrial uses. This is an interesting example of co-operation between different United Nations organs and agencies. Where there is no production of fibre for industrial purposes, the view of the Commission on Narcotic Drugs is that the abuse of the plant should be prevented by all available means including prohibition of cultivation. The commission has expressed its formal agreement with the World Health Organization that the medical use of cannabis products is no longer necessary and should generally be prohibited. An exception would be made for a stated period of years for countries in which the use of cannabis is traditional in indigenous (*e.g.*, Ayurvedic) medicine.

A series of studies on the coca leaf was initiated by the request of the Government of Peru that a special commission of experts be appointed to study, in certain regions of the Andes, the effects of the chewing of coca leaf, the factors engendering the habit, the social and economic implications of the habit, and the measures that should be taken if this habit were proved to be harmful. In 1954, the Economic and Social Council was able to record the agreement of the Commission on Narcotic Drugs, the World Health Organization, and the governments principally concerned, including Peru and Bolivia, that the practice constituted a form of harmful addiction and that measures should be taken for its gradual suppression.[79] It recognized that in several countries suppression required far-reaching social and economic measures and would take a considerable period of time. Moreover, it recommended that the technical assistance services of the United Nations and specialized agencies aid in developing appropriate administrative or social measures for the gradual suppression of the chewing habit and urged that the governments concerned gradually limit the cultivation and the export of coca leaf to medical, scientific, and other legitimate purposes. Since then, an extensive program of technical assistance, including assistance in the development of substitute crops, has been established in the Andean *Alto Plano*.

The consolidation of international treaties and protocols relating to

[79] Res. 548(XVIII), July 12, 1954.

the control of dangerous drugs represents a fourth area of activity. On recommendation of the Commission on Narcotic Drugs, the Economic and Social Council decided in 1948 that work should be begun on the drafting of a new single convention to replace the existing multilateral treaties on narcotics control, not only in order to simplify existing international law and administrative machinery concerned with the control of narcotic drugs, but also to make the system of control stronger and more flexible.[80] This task has been a major preoccupation of the Commission on Narcotic Drugs ever since. Certain countries such as Canada lean toward a codification of existing conventions and agreements, while others favor not only codification but new steps to bring under control the production of "natural" raw materials; to forbid the non-medical use of opium, coca, and cannabis; to prohibit altogether the production of particularly dangerous drugs such as heroin, for which less dangerous substitutes have been found; to institute a system of international inspection; and to simplify existing machinery. Many of these proposals raise extremely difficult and complicated technical issues.[81]

There is some danger that the single convention might turn into a convention of the "lowest common denominator." This tendency has been a matter of concern particularly to the United States, and in the Commission on Narcotic Drugs, the United States has been advocating a strengthened, flexible instrument. Considerable further discussion on the basis of observations to be made by governments will be necessary before the present draft single convention will be ready for final action. In view of the large number of questions that remain unsolved, there is considerable doubt whether the convention will be completed and submitted to an intergovernmental conference in 1957.

In a fifth area of activity, growing attention is being given to the prevention of addiction and the rehabilitation of addicts. The following interesting section on the treatment of drug addiction was adopted by the Commission on Narcotic Drugs in 1954, for inclusion in the single convention:

> The Parties are cognizant of the importance of creating means for the medical treatment, care and rehabilitation of drug addicts and undertake to use their best endeavours towards this effort, on a planned and compulsory basis, in properly conducted and duly authorized institutions in those States where

[80] Res. 159IID(VII), Aug. 3, 1948.

[81] For a thorough discussion of these technical issues, see Herbert L. May, "The Single Convention on Narcotic Drugs: Comments and Possibilities," *Bulletin on Narcotics* (January–April 1955), pp. 1–14.

the seriousness of the problem of drug addiction and their economic resources warrant such measures.[82]

This paragraph reflects the growing concern with a previously neglected aspect of the fight against drug addiction. It puts the emphasis on cure and rehabilitation, the idea being to help individual addicts and to weaken the market for illicit traffic. This emphasis on the medical and social aspects of the problem rather than on the "policing" of the traffic in drugs is reflected also in the action of the Economic and Social Council urging governments to consider setting up means for the treatment, care, and rehabilitation of drug addicts on a planned and compulsory basis in properly conducted institutions.[83]

In spite of continuing weaknesses in the system of control of the traffic in narcotic drugs, and even greater weaknesses in procedures for the cure and rehabilitation of addicts, the record of the United Nations in facilitating control of one of the most dangerous social evils is impressive. In the debates of the various organs concerned with drug control, political issues, generally speaking, are minimized.[84] By and large, the differences that developed have been technical in character although economic and political considerations at times have acted as a brake on attempts to establish firmer controls. The breakdown of the discussions aiming at the establishment of an opium monopoly is an example in point. It cannot yet be said that the production, distribution, and use of narcotic drugs has been effectively limited to medical and scientific purposes, but the United Nations is assuredly making an increasingly effective contribution toward relieving mankind from the scourge of drug addiction.

[82] U.N. Economic and Social Council, Eighteenth Session, *Official Records*, Supplement No. 8, "Commission on Narcotic Drugs: Report of the Ninth Session, 19 April to 14 May 1954," Annex D, Sec. 41.

[83] Res. 548I(XVIII), July 12, 1954.

[84] Exceptional in this respect were the bitter debates provoked by the revelation on the part of the United States representative on the Commission on Narcotic Drugs that Communist China had become a major source of the illicit traffic in narcotics and appeared to be making a deliberate attempt to flood certain parts of the world with illicit drugs. See, for example, U.N. Economic and Social Council, Eighteenth Session, *Official Records*, Supplement No. 8, paras. 184–92 and U.N. Economic and Social Council, Twentieth Session, *Official Records*, Supplement No. 8, "Commission on Narcotic Drugs: Report of the Tenth Session, 18 April to 12 May 1955," paras. 300–06.

Suppression of Prostitution and Obscene Publications

The activities of the United Nations in connection with the suppression of prostitution and of obscene publications follow a pattern in many ways similar to developments in the field of narcotics control. The United Nations decided, in 1947, to assume the functions formerly exercised by the League of Nations under the conventions of 1921 and 1933 relating to the suppression of the traffic in women and children, and the convention of 1923 relating to the suppression of the circulation of, and the traffic in, obscene publications. The General Assembly adopted protocols to that effect, which were signed on November 12, 1947.[85] The United Nations, in 1948, similarly assumed the functions formerly exercised by the French Government under the agreement of 1904 and the convention of 1910 for the suppression of the white slave traffic and the agreement of 1910 for the suppression of the circulation of obscene publications.[86] The prewar international instruments relating to prostitution provided for the establishment of national authorities for the co-ordination of information relative to the procuring of women or girls for immoral purposes abroad, and for annual reports by governments. They also dealt with such issues as the repatriation of foreign prostitutes and the extradition and punishment of traffickers. The functions taken over by the United Nations were largely reporting functions.

The United Nations, furthermore, inherited from the League of Nations a draft convention prepared, in 1937, by the Advisory Committee on Social Questions of the League, designed to secure the prosecution and punishment of any person keeping or managing a brothel, or exploiting the prostitution of another person. Due to the outbreak of the Second World War, however, this draft convention was not completed. The draft, together with the other instruments relating to prostitution, served as a basis for the elaboration of a new consolidated convention that was intended to replace all preceding instruments on the subject, and was finally approved by the General Assembly, in 1949, as the Convention for the Suppression of the Traffic in Persons and the Exploitation of the Prostitution of Others.[87]

Several of the articles of the convention were passed by close votes,

[85] U.N. General Assembly Res. 126(II), Oct. 20, 1947.

[86] U.N. Economic and Social Council Res. 155D(VII), Aug. 13, 1948; U.N. General Assembly Res. 256(III), Dec. 3, 1948.

[87] Res. 317(IV), Dec. 2, 1949.

and in some cases positions were reversed at different stages of the discussion. Difficulties arose over the question of medical inspection and registration of known prostitutes. These were finally settled by omitting any reference to such inspection, over very strong opposition, particularly on the part of France. Another point of concern to a substantial group of countries was the deletion from the convention of a clause recognizing that a signatory might require that the motive of gain be established in the prosecution of procurers. The omission of such reference was strongly urged by Brazil, France, and the Soviet Union. The United Kingdom and several of the Commonwealth countries were in the forefront of those insisting on inclusion of such a clause on the ground that it would make it easier to define an offense under the convention.

Considerable controversy arose also over the question of a limitative "territorial article" sought by various administering powers, particularly the United Kingdom, on the ground that the far-reaching requirements laid down in the convention could not immediately be applied by legislation to various non-self-governing territories. The General Assembly decided not to include a territorial clause but made it quite explicit that "for the purposes of the present Convention the word 'State' shall include all the colonies and trust territories of a State signatory or acceding to the Convention and all territories for which such State is internationally responsible" (Article 23). Finally, the Assembly, over strong opposition from the United States and other federal states, decided to omit any "Federal-State clause," despite the fact that the Sixth (Legal) Committee of the General Assembly had voted for such a clause.

The divergences of view were reflected in the final vote of the Assembly; thirty-five states voted for acceptance, two (France and the United Kingdom) were opposed, and fifteen abstained. The abstentions included many developed states such as the United States, Denmark, New Zealand, and Sweden, that were as determined as any other states to suppress the evil of prostitution but could not accept some of the provisions of the convention. Although this convention was adopted more than five years ago, only seventeen countries have deposited with the Secretary-General instruments of accession or ratification.[88]

Two other approaches to the problem of prostitution have also failed

[88] It is in effect for Bulgaria, Byelorussian Soviet Socialist Republic, Cuba, Haiti, Hungary, India, Iraq, Israel, Norway, Pakistan, Philippines, Rumania, Poland, Ukrainian Soviet Socialist Republic, Union of South Africa, Union of Soviet Socialist Republics, and Yugoslavia.

to obtain adequate support. First, plans for the establishment of a special Far Eastern Bureau for the Suppression of Traffic in Women and Children, originally proposed in 1937 in the League of Nations, were abandoned due to the unsettled conditions in the region and the fact that the newly established governments of that part of the world did not believe a bureau would be of real assistance in their efforts to suppress the traffic. Second, various projected studies and action programs with respect to the traffic in women and children and the rehabilitation of prostitutes did not come to fruition.

At first sight, it would therefore appear that the United Nations has failed to make any real contribution in an area in which the League of Nations had been highly active. Any such assumption would miss the real point. What has happened is that the traffic in women and children has practically ceased to exist as an international problem. The introduction of rigid passport and visa regulations throughout the world, although imposed for reasons unrelated to the traffic, has proved more effective than the special international instruments created for its suppression. The problem of prostitution has thus become essentially a domestic one, dealt with by the various countries in their own way, just as they deal with the problem of the abuse of alcohol according to their own conditions and needs. It is generally recognized that such problems as the prevention of prostitution and the rehabilitation of prostitutes raise broad social issues toward the solution of which the United Nations is contributing indirectly through its various programs of technical assistance in social planning and development, including community organization and development, improvement of the status of women, and the strengthening of family life.

Prevention of Crime and Treatment of Offenders

In contrast to the decline in activities of the United Nations relating to traffic in women and children, there has been a marked increase in activities concerning the treatment of offenders and the prevention of crime. This has been due not only to an increase in criminality in many parts of the world but to circumstances and considerations largely unrelated to matters of crime and punishment and rehabilitation. It goes back to the drive in the late 1940's to absorb or to integrate into the United Nations, for the sake of "simplification," "avoidance of overlaps," and "economy," intergovernmental organizations outside the

United Nations but working in areas within the scope of Article 55 of the Charter.[89]

One of these organizations was the International Penal and Penitentiary Commission (IPPC) which, after prolonged negotiations, was absorbed into the United Nations following an independent existence of some seventy-five years. The plan of integration was approved by the commission on August 12, 1950, and by the General Assembly in December 1950.[90] The agreement reached provided for:

1. The appointment of national expert correspondents by the governments of Members of the United Nations, by states not Members of the United Nations that were members of the IPPC, as well as by other governments designated by the Economic and Social Council. By March 1955, eighty-one such correspondents had been appointed by the governments of forty countries.

2. The convening, on a biennial basis, of regional consultative group meetings of the national correspondents and other qualified persons. By the end of 1956, six such meetings had been held (three in Europe, and one each in Latin America, the Middle East, and Asia and the Far East).

3. The establishment of an international *Ad hoc* Advisory Committee of Experts to meet from time to time, preferably annually, at the headquarters of the United Nations to advise the Secretary-General and the Social Commission "in devising and formulating programs for study on an international basis and policies for international action in the field of the prevention of crime and the treatment of offenders, and also to advise on the co-ordination of the work of the United Nations consultative groups."

4. The organization of quinquennial congresses composed of members officially appointed by their governments, representatives of specialized agencies and nongovernmental organizations, and individual participants having a direct interest in the subjects to be discussed. The first of these congresses met in Geneva in the summer of 1955.

5. The publication by the United Nations of an international review. In implementing this provision, the United Nations issues, twice yearly, the *International Review of Criminal Policy.*

As was to be expected, these arrangements resulted in a considerable extension of activities on the part of the United Nations and, inciden-

[89] See the volume in this Brookings series, *The United Nations and Promotion of the General Welfare,* Part One.

[90] Res. 415(V), Dec. 1, 1950.

tally, in additional expenditure. The Social Defense Section in the Secretariat was enlarged, and the United Nations assumed full financial responsibility for meetings of the *ad hoc* Advisory Committee of Experts, including the expenses of its members. Previously, such expenses had been carried by the IPPC and participating governments. The United Nations also provided an increasing number of fellowships in this field and made itself responsible for the financing of various regional meetings, but it did not pay the expenses of individual participants.[91]

The program of studies and publications was stepped up. In addition to the *International Review of Criminal Policy*, studies have either been issued or are in preparation on such subjects as juvenile delinquency, probation and related measures, the indeterminate sentence, parole and after-care, criminal statistics, standard rules for the treatment of offenders (a revision of rules originally worked out by the IPPC), open penal and correctional institutions, and prison labor. Broadly speaking, these were also the major subjects dealt with at the various regional meetings and seminars and at the First United Nations Congress on the Prevention of Crime and the Treatment of Offenders in 1955.

After six years of operation under the 1950 agreement, there is no doubt that international action in the field has been increased, and its geographic scope has been greatly extended. The IPPC was essentially limited to Europe and North America. Under the United Nations, the work has been extended to all the major regions of the world and has evoked considerable interest, particularly in Asia where industrialization is leading to growing urbanization, the breaking of old family and community ties, and concomitantly to a rising tide of delinquency and crime. The regional approach has permitted the adjustment of programs and activities to regional, national, and local conditions. Parallel to the extension of the geographical scope has gone an extension in the substantive scope of the work, with more emphasis being placed on the prevention of crime and the rehabilitation of offenders and less on punishment.

All this is to the good. On the other hand, it is evident that far from resulting in "economies," as had been hoped by the protagonists of

[91] The Economic and Social Council has established consultative relationships with the principal nongovernmental organizations operating in the field of crime prevention and the treatment of offenders, including the Howard League for Penal Reform, the International Criminal Police Commission, the International Law Association, the International Society of Criminology, the International Union for Child Welfare, and the Society of Comparative Legislation. Meetings involving these organizations are held periodically.

integration, the collective bill for governments is very much higher than it was at the time of the independent existence of the IPPC. In itself, this is defensible so long as the program and activities do not become too divorced from the central purposes of the United Nations. In this connection, it is interesting to note that under the plans of the Secretary-General, the highly specialized criminological studies are in the future to be "farmed out" to outside institutions and organizations rather than to be undertaken by the Secretariat.

It also appears that a literal interpretation of the 1950 agreement may result in overorganization. The frequency of regional meetings is at present under discussion, for there is much evidence that an undue burden is being placed both on the United Nations Secretariat and on the governments in the various regions. Proposals for reductions in the number of meetings and publications have, however, given rise to misgivings on the part of some of the experts who were formerly members of the IPPC.[92] Only future experience can show whether these misgivings are justified. One conclusion would appear noncontroversial: any further attempts to absorb into the United Nations the functions of intergovernmental organizations operating in highly specialized fields will require most careful scrutiny. There is only a slim dividing line between purposeful integration serving the ends of the United Nations and integration that might result in weakening the central programing and activities of the Organization.

The Lessons of Experience

A few concluding observations may help to draw together the heterogeneous activities dealt with in the foregoing discussion of welfare and social defense.

The common denominator of most of the programs and activities in the field of welfare and social defense is the emphasis on assistance to the individual. This emphasis makes for an almost infinite variety of possible programs and approaches, dependent on the special needs of the individual and the social and cultural pattern in which he lives. The temptation to engage in activities beyond the scope and powers of an intergovernmental organization such as the United Nations is, there-

[92] See U.N. Economic and Social Council, *Progress Made by the United Nations in the Field of Social Welfare During the Period 1 January 1953–31 December 1954 and Proposals for the Programme of Work 1955–57*, Report by the Secretary-General, Doc. E/CN.5/308/Corr. 1 (Apr. 5, 1955), p. 94.

fore, great. The trend toward the dispersal of energies and efforts is accentuated by well-meaning "interest groups," which attempt to use the United Nations as a vehicle for the attainment of their special purposes and for technical studies and activities of limited international applicability that might better be carried out by nongovernmental groups. Good will tends to outrun a realistic estimate of what can be accomplished by intergovernmental action.

Considering these pressures, the United Nations has, on the whole, been surprisingly successful in developing basic programs and adapting them to national and local needs. Major requirements, such as the need for trained welfare personnel, have been ascertained and programs to meet them have been initiated. Long-range programs are increasingly taking the place of earlier short-term activities. The emphasis now is on assistance to governments in the development of integrated programs of their own. Brakes are being applied to the preparation of studies that are not essential to the formulation of policy recommendations on the part of the United Nations or are of only limited value to national governments as they confront their major tasks in improving the lot of their people.

The recognition of differences in cultural patterns and stages of development has led to a shift of work from headquarters to the field. Less time is being spent on the setting of international norms of achievement, and more attention is being paid to adjusting international assistance to the needs of specific regions and countries. The co-operative nature of the programs has been enhanced by the growing use of experts from underdeveloped countries.

It may still be felt by some that the United Nations is spending too much time, energy, and money on "unessential activities" concerned not with major problems of state but with the needs of the individual. This question cannot be decided on points of principle or by easy generalization. So long as governments ask for assistance in this area, there will be United Nations programs of social welfare. For anyone believing in the dignity and worth of the individual, it would be doubtful wisdom to discourage such work.

CHAPTER IX

*Education, Science, and Culture**

PRACTICALLY all of the activities of the United Nations system that are designed to bring about economic and social advancement have educational, scientific, or cultural aspects. The stimulation of production and investment, the facilitation of transportation and communication, or the encouragement of social action to improve levels of living have usually involved educational programs, arrangements for the exchange of technical information, and efforts to introduce new methods and standards.

Within the United Nations system, however, general responsibility for promoting collaboration among nations through education, science, and culture has been vested in the United Nations Educational, Scientific and Cultural Organization (UNESCO). The drafting of its constitution in 1945 raised some difficult questions, but these were resolved with remarkable speed and without bitterness. The establishment of UNESCO, in fact, met with almost universal acclaim.

It proved easier, however, to agree on broad objectives than on methods to realize them. The debate on programs began at the first General Conference of UNESCO in 1946 and, save for minor lulls, has continued ever since. The constitution appeared to authorize programs in virtually every field of endeavor, and repeated efforts have been made to ensure that the limited resources of the agency would be concentrated on a manageable number of projects. The difficulties that UNESCO has encountered, the controversies it has engendered, its achievements and its failures, warrant considered analysis.

Establishment of UNESCO

The Conference for the Establishment of an Educational, Scientific and Cultural Organization met in London, November 1–16, 1945. The fact that it was able to draft the constitution of UNESCO in a little over two weeks is a tribute to the preparatory work of the Allied Ministers of Education, who had been meeting intermittently in London

* By Walter M. Kotschnig.

since 1942;[1] to extensive preparations made by the governments of France, the United Kingdom, and the United States; and to the work of many nongovernmental organizations and groups in these and other countries.[2]

The conference had to resolve a number of difficult issues.[3] One issue that might have proved troublesome had been settled prior to the conference by preliminary discussions among the Allied Ministers of Education and various foreign offices, including the United States Department of State. The question was whether the new agency should be a temporary organization to meet emergency needs arising out of the war or a permanent organization with long-term objectives. As a result of the preliminary conversations, an earlier proposal for the creation of a United Nations Organization for Educational and Cultural Reconstruction, made by the United States at a 1944 meeting of the Allied Ministers of Education, was abandoned in favor of the more permanent organization. It was understood, however, that the permanent agency would, in its early stages, pay special attention to reconstruction needs.

A more basic issue arose over the attempt to define the nature and character of the organization. One school of thought, led by the French delegation, held that the new organization should serve above all to facilitate contacts and co-operation among the intellectual leaders of the world.[4] It should bring together the intellectual elites of the various countries and assist them in their search for a peace based "upon the intellectual and moral solidarity of mankind," a phrase taken from the preamble of the constitution of UNESCO. Essentially, this was the concept that had led the League of Nations Assembly in 1921 to set up the International Committee on Intellectual Cooperation, a decision followed in 1925 by the creation of the International Institute of Intellectual Cooperation in Paris.

[1] U.N. Information Organization, *Allied Plans for Education—The Story of the Conference of Allied Ministers of Education* (1945).

[2] Walter M. Kotschnig, "Toward an IOECD: Some Major Issues Involved," *Educational Record* (July 1944), pp. 259–87.

[3] See U.N. Educational, Scientific and Cultural Organization, Preparatory Commission, *Conference for the Establishment of the United Nations Educational, Scientific and Cultural Organization*, Doc. ECO/Conf./29 (June 1946).

[4] In UNESCO, even more than in other international agencies, references to positions taken by particular delegations are likely to be oversimplifications. Delegations are as a rule composed of representatives of the educational, cultural, and scientific communities of Member countries, are frequently divided in their views, and may speak with different voices, although each delegation in the end has only one vote.

Neither the committee nor the institute had proved singularly successful. The committee, composed of such outstanding individuals as Henri Bergson, Madame Curie, Albert Einstein, Gilbert Murray, Rabindranath Tagore, and other leaders of thought, frequently operated at a level beyond the comprehension of the common man or lacked the background and experience to translate its conclusions into practical action. The institute accomplished useful work in such technical fields as co-operation among libraries and museums, the protection of copyrights, and the exchange and free entry of educational films. It attempted with some success to develop closer co-operation between the officials in charge of secondary and of higher education. Concern with elementary education was not considered appropriate for an organization interested in the promotion of intellectual co-operation. Efforts were also made to bring about bilateral agreements to eliminate chauvinistic and biased statements from history textbooks.

The protagonists of UNESCO as an organization for the promotion of intellectual co-operation admitted some of the weaknesses and failures of the prewar experience, but pointed out that, except for a few individuals, the English-speaking world had not actively participated in the intellectual co-operation activities of the League, and that with their participation and larger resources, past weaknesses could be overcome.

This view was not shared by the United States, which held that UNESCO should be concerned with all the people—not only the intellectual elites—and that there should be a direct approach to them through education, cultural exchanges, and the widest possible use of such mass media as the press, radio, and films. This approach met with substantial support in the conference, particularly from those who were concerned with the reconstruction of educational facilities destroyed by the war and the even more serious damage done by the perversion of education under the Nazi rule. The extent to which the American thesis prevailed is revealed in Article I (2) of the Constitution:

. . . The Organization will:

(a) collaborate in the work of advancing the mutual knowledge and understanding of peoples, through all means of mass communication and to that end recommend such international agreements as may be necessary to promote the free flow of ideas by word and image;

(b) give fresh impulse to popular education and to the spread of culture; by collaborating with Members, at their request, in the development of educational activites; by instituting collaboration among the nations to advance the ideal of equality of educational opportunity without regard to race, sex, or any distinctions, economic or social; by suggesting educational methods best suited to prepare the children of the world for the responsibilities of freedom;

(c) maintain, increase and diffuse knowledge; by assuring the conservation and protection of the world's inheritance of books, works of art and monuments of history and science, and recommending to the nations concerned the necessary international conventions; by encouraging co-operation among the nations in all branches of intellectual activity, including the international exchange of persons active in the fields of education, science and culture and the exchange of publications, objects of artistic and scientific interest and other materials of information; by initiating methods of international co-operation calculated to give the people of all countries access to the printed and published materials produced by any of them.[5]

At first sight, the language of this article appears to indicate an almost complete acceptance of the concept of UNESCO as an organization of the people and for the people. It stresses "mutual knowledge and understanding of peoples"; it speaks of "popular education" and of "equality of educational opportunity"; and it authorizes the use of "all means of mass communication." At the same time, however, it states that the organization will maintain, increase, and diffuse knowledge and to this end encourage co-operation "in all branches of intellectual activity" including science. To highlight this last addition to the subject matter to be dealt with by the organization, the word "science" was included in the name of the organization.[6]

The result of the compromise achieved—for a compromise it was—was an article of broad and ill-defined scope. It can be interpreted to cover almost any human interest or activity. The article appears to assume—and has been so interpreted—that any and all activities in the fields of education, science, and culture are equally apt to further "universal respect for justice, for the rule of law, and for human rights and fundamental freedoms," that any type of knowledge *per se* is bound to

[5] U.N. Educational, Scientific, and Cultural Organization, *Final Act, Constitution, Rules of Procedure of the General Conference* (1953). Article I(3) of the Constitution, prohibiting the organization from intervening in matters essentially domestic, was written into the constitution despite earlier suggestions, for instance by the Educational Policies Commission of the National Education Association in the United States, that the organization be given a role in appraising educational methods and materials in various countries and that it expose, through investigations and reports, countries using methods and materials that in their effect would be "aggressive, militaristic, or otherwise dangerous to the peace of the world." The stringent "domestic jurisdiction clause" in its constitution, however, did not protect UNESCO against later allegations of trying to take over and pervert the schools of its member states.

[6] The word was added to the name and functions of the organization on the initiative of the United Kingdom, warmly supported by scientists in many other delegations.

advance "the common welfare of mankind."[7] These are assumptions that have made it difficult for the organization to develop clear-cut, coordinated programs of work.

Closely related to the controversy over the character and focus of the organization, was the question to what extent representation in the directing organs of UNESCO should be determined by governments and to what extent by nongovernmental organizations and groups, primarily of intellectuals. There was general agreement that the organization should be intergovernmental in that it should be financed by governments. Regarding representation, however, the French Government proposed that the General Conference should consist of: (1) a maximum of three delegates of the government of each member state; (2) five delegates of each National Commission of Intellectual Cooperation (which had been established under the aegis of the Committee on Intellectual Cooperation of the League); and (3) a delegate of each intellectual association of a world-wide character admitted by the General Conference. This proposal was not accepted, and the constitution provides that: "The General Conference shall consist of the representatives of the States Members of the Organization. The Government of each Member State shall appoint not more than five delegates, who shall be selected after consultation with the National Commission, if established, or with educational, scientific and cultural bodies."[8] Elsewhere in the constitution much emphasis was placed on national commissions or other national co-operating bodies composed of representatives of the principal bodies in each country interested in educational, scientific, and cultural matters, together with representatives of government. Under Article VII, the organization can communicate directly with such national commissions or co-operating bodies, which "shall function as agencies of liaison in all matters of interest" to the organization. Thus, much was done to minimize the role of governments.

Most important, it was decided that the Executive Board of UNESCO, which acts on behalf of the General Conference between sessions, was not to be a board of government representatives but of individuals elected by the General Conference from among delegates to the conference to serve in their personal capacities. This decision led to considerable difficulty as time went on, because under the constitution, the Executive Board was charged with administrative duties and responsibilities that involved commitments on the part of governments.

[7] *Constitution*, Art. I(1) and Preamble.

[8] *Ibid.*, Art. IV, A.

The Soviet Union did not participate in the London conference. The generally negative attitude of the Soviet Union toward the specialized agencies was undoubtedly accentuated by the fact that the Government of the Soviet Union considered education and related matters to be of purely domestic concern, and had little sympathy for the individualistic and liberalistic approach of the protagonists of UNESCO to the problems of peace and human welfare. At the London conference, there was a strong undercurrent in favor of universality of membership, although the memory of the recent holocaust in education, science, and culture caused by Nazi and Fascist action prevented writing this principle into the constitution. There was widespread regret that the Soviet Union was not willing to assume membership. UNESCO, however, was among the first of the newly created international organizations to admit to membership such countries as Austria, the Federal Republic of Germany, Italy, Japan, and Spain.

Controversy Concerning Programs

Once created, UNESCO rapidly launched a vast number of projects. This action was fully understandable in the light of the broad statement of purposes and functions in the UNESCO constitution, and it was accentuated by the encyclopedic interests of its first Director-General, Julian Huxley. It is impossible to understand fully the development of UNESCO during the first four years of its existence without taking into account his drive and enthusiasm. His exceptional abilities, his catholicity of interests, and his knowledge opened up many new lines of action. In speaking at the first General Conference in 1946 about the cultural activities of UNESCO, he said: "We have to think about music and painting, about history and classical studies, about language and architecture, about theater and ballet, about libraries and museums, and art galleries and zoos, about the history of art and the world's different cultures, about creative writing and about philosophy."[9] Earlier, he had set forth his concept of UNESCO in an essay in which he defined a twofold aim for the organization: "In the first place, it is international, and must serve the ends and objects of the United Nations, which in the long perspective are world ends, ends for humanity as a whole. And secondly it must foster and promote all aspects of education, science,

[9] U. N. Educational, Scientific and Cultural Organization, First Session, Plenary, *Records of the General Conference*, Second Meeting (Nov. 20, 1946), p. 21.

and culture, in the widest sense of those words."[10] By promoting all aspects of education, science, and culture, Huxley then hoped that UNESCO would, as stated in the conclusions of his essay, help the "emergence of a single world culture."[11]

Under Huxley's leadership, UNESCO went through a period of rapid development, a pioneering period, with ever new projects taken up, developed, and—not infrequently—abandoned. They ranged from substantial efforts to aid in the reconstruction of schools and libraries to ventures in adult education and the teaching of the ideas and ideals of the United Nations; from the development of abstracts, catalogues, and bibliographies to proposals for the definition of high "C" in music and the study of biology at high altitude. This was the great period of the establishment of new learned councils and societies initiated and supported by UNESCO, a period of exhilarating creativeness, which did not, however, result in any cohesive, co-ordinated program.

A variety of requests from the United Nations to UNESCO did nothing to help solidify the program. UNESCO was asked by the General Assembly of the United Nations to consider engaging on a program of translation of the classics and did initiate work in this field.[12] At its second session, the General Assembly requested the agency to concern itself with the exchange of workers and, in another resolution, with the teaching of United Nations ideals.[13] At its third session, the General Assembly referred to UNESCO and to the Economic and Social Council a plan for establishing an international center for training in public administration.[14] A proposal raised in the Economic and Social Council as early as 1946 for the establishment of international scientific research laboratories was also transmitted to UNESCO for action.[15]

In response to this last request, UNESCO proposed the creation of

[10] U.N. Educational, Scientific and Cultural Organization, Preparatory Commission, *UNESCO, Its Purposes and its Philosophy* (1946), p. 5. The essay was so challenging, provocative, and controversial that the Executive Committee of the Preparatory Commission decided that it should be published as a separate signed document representing a statement of the personal attitudes and beliefs of the Director-General and should not be construed in any way as representing the views of the Preparatory Commission. The General Conference at its first session took the same stand.

[11] *Ibid.*, p. 61.

[12] Res. 60(I), Dec. 14, 1946.

[13] Res. 133(II), Nov. 17, 1947 and Res. 137(II), Nov. 17, 1947.

[14] U.N. General Assembly, Res. 246(III), Dec. 4, 1948. See also U.N. Economic and Social Council, Res. 123(VI), Mar. 2, 1948.

[15] Res. 22(III), Oct. 3, 1946.

such laboratories in the following fields: (1) chemistry and biology of self-reproducing substances, including cancer; (2) nutrition and food technology; (3) life and resources of humid tropic zones; (4) oceanography and fisheries; (5) antarctic research; and (6) ornithological research.[16] These proposals overlapped the interests of several other specialized agencies, and in 1949, UNESCO revised the list.[17] First priority was then given to the creation of an International Computation Center, an International Institute for Research on the Brain, and an International Institute of Social Science. It furthermore recommended a lower priority list providing for the establishment of an International Laboratory for Arid Zone Research, an International Astronomical Laboratory, an International Institute of the Chemistry of Living Matter, and an International Meteorological Institute.

The plethora of proposals and projects developed by UNESCO in its early years was baffling and irritating, especially to the governments of the major contributing countries, and moves were made repeatedly in the general conferences of UNESCO to bring about a concentration and co-ordination of effort.[18]

At the fifth conference of UNESCO in 1950, a serious attempt was made to bring about a limitation of activities and to reach agreement on a restricted number of major programs. The conference, largely under United States leadership, developed a "decalogue" to cover UNESCO activities under the following priority headings:

(1) To eliminate illiteracy and encourage fundamental education;
(2) To obtain for each person an education conforming to his aptitudes and to the needs of society, including technological training and higher education;
(3) To promote through education respect for human rights throughout all nations;
(4) To overcome the obstacles to the free flow of persons, ideas, and knowledge between the countries of the world;
(5) To promote the progress and utilization of science for mankind;
(6) To study the causes of tensions that may lead to war and to fight them through education;
(7) To demonstrate world cultural interdependence;
(8) To advance through the press, radio and motion pictures the cause of truth, freedom, and peace;

[16] U.N. Department of Public Information, *Yearbook of the United Nations, 1947–48*, pp. 556–58.

[17] U.N. Department of Public Information, *Yearbook of the United Nations, 1948–49*, p. 664.

[18] See Charles S. Ascher, *Program-Making in UNESCO, 1945–1951, A Study in the Processes of International Administration* (1951).

(9) To bring about better understanding among the peoples of the world and to convince them of the necessity of co-operating loyally with one another in the framework of the United Nations;

(10) To render clearing-house and exchange services in all its fields of action, together with services in reconstruction and relief assistance.[19]

This listing reflected a renewed emphasis on education, the development of mass media in greater freedom, and the promotion of international understanding.[20] At the same time, it covered the entire field of the sciences without any limitations, and the tenth point offered an escape clause that permitted an unlimited number of activities so long as they related to education, science, and culture. The 1950 program, therefore, proved little more than a way-station on the road to a greater concentration of effort and resources. After 1950, the funds at the disposal of UNESCO under the Expanded Programme of Technical Assistance tended to accentuate, within the over-all program of the organization, projects of assistance in the development of underdeveloped countries.

In 1954, the Executive Board submitted, and the General Conference approved, a new approach to program-making, which provided for a division of the program into "general" and "special" activities.[21] General activities were to represent the continuing functions of the organization and to include the collection and exchange of information; assistance to international collaboration among specialists; the preparation of international conventions and regulations; inquiries, research, and studies necessary as a basis for the special activities; and similar functions. Special activities meant field projects of limited duration and scope, designed to meet specific needs of member states. These special activities were to be developed in the light of priorities determined by the General Conference. At the same time, the General Conference selected as its priorities: free and compulsory education at the primary level; fundamental education; programs relating to racial, social, and international tensions; mutual appreciation of Eastern and Western cultural values; and scientific research for the improvement of living

[19] U.N. Educational, Scientific and Cultural Organization, Fifth Session, *Records of the General Conference* (1950), Resolutions, p. 16.

[20] The emphasis on education was due in part to the support given the educational programs by Jaime Torres Bodet, who succeeded Huxley as Director-General of UNESCO.

[21] U.N. Educational, Scientific and Cultural Organization, Eighth Session, *Records of the General Conference* (1954), Resolutions, pp. 49–50. By this time Luther Evans, a former Librarian of Congress, had succeeded Jaime Torres Bodet as Director-General of UNESCO.

conditions.[22] Without eliminating clearing-house and related functions, this new departure in programing shifted emphasis to the field, where the needs are greatest. It remains to be seen whether this new departure will increase the efficiency of the program; it does not become effective until the 1957–58 period.

Problems of Method and Organization

The secretariat of UNESCO is divided into separate departments, five of which were originally established to supervise the several major programs: education, natural sciences, social sciences, cultural activities, and mass communications. A Department of Technical Assistance was later added, and there is also within the secretariat an exchange of persons service, which does not, however, rank as a department.

In itself, a division into five major substantive areas would appear natural, although other patterns of organization might have been adopted, and indeed were suggested but were rejected. Because of the unique constituency of UNESCO and the all-inclusive character of its program, however, certain drawbacks have developed to the arrangement that was accepted.

There has been complaint that the department for each major substantive area has been an empire unto itself: that the natural scientists boost their own department; that the educators attempt to increase the budget and scope for educational programs; and that the librarians and museum experts, the musicians and artists urge an expansion of the cultural activities of the secretariat. This competition has been fostered not only by "constituents," *i.e.*, representatives of the various disciplines in national delegations at the General Conference and by members of the Executive Board serving in their individual capacities, but also by nongovernmental "interest" groups and by officials within the secretariat. The latter, frequently men of science or letters, or leaders in education, have considered it their mission to serve what they conceive to be the best interests of their own field—the advancement of their particular discipline. The secretariat lobbies thus, at an early date, became a major element at the UNESCO general conferences. Not infrequently, the pet project of some department head would reemerge, after rejection by the Director-General in planning his program and budget, as a proposal by one of the delegations on the conference floor.

[22] *Ibid.*, p. 50.

Clearly, the difficulties involved in developing a co-ordinated program are great in an organization whose parts in certain respects have less in common than the subdivisions of other organizations and whose personnel are probably less accustomed to organizational discipline. For these reasons, UNESCO, perhaps more than any other international organization, requires strong leadership by its director-general and effective co-ordinating machinery within the secretariat itself.

Closely related to this organizational problem, is another basic issue regarding the way in which UNESCO can best carry on its work. Somewhat fewer than half of the approximately nine hundred members of the secretariat are in the professional category. They are responsible for preparing the numerous periodicals and current publications issued by UNESCO, which as might be expected, is the most productive of the specialized agencies in terms of the written word. Many of these publications fall under the general heading of clearing-house activities. They include science and education abstracts, indexes, bibliographies, current information bulletins, and similar tools of primary interest to scholars and others engaged in research or to technical personnel in libraries and museums. In a world in which in the field of natural science alone nearly one million papers are written each year, these activities are obviously of importance.

At the same time, it is clear that no one international organization, even with a central staff as large as that of UNESCO, can possibly render such services in all the fields embraced by the constitution of the agency. Furthermore, in order to provide for cross-fertilization of thought and achievement even within a single discipline, it is necessary to establish direct contacts between the individuals working in a given field. From the beginning, therefore, UNESCO has attempted to establish close relations with and to assist professional societies and other organizations operating in areas of interest to the agency. When no such organizations existed, UNESCO started them or offered aid in their creation.

The International Council of Scientific Unions (ICSU) has been the major single beneficiary of UNESCO aid. With its eleven affiliated international societies in such fields as astronomy, pure and applied chemistry, the biological sciences (in turn subdivided into more specialized associations and congresses), pure and applied physics, crystallography, etc., the ICSU received a first subvention of $275,000 in 1947. The amount was reduced gradually to an annual subvention of approximately $200,000. To fill gaps in the pattern of international voluntary organizations in the natural sciences, UNESCO assisted in the foundation and assured, by way of substantial subventions, the existence of a Council of International Organizations of Medical Sciences, a Union of International Engineering Organizations, and an International Union for the Protection of Nature.

Because the social scientists were less organized nationally and internationally than the natural scientists, UNESCO made special efforts to sponsor and aid in the creation of international associations of social scientists. In 1949, it helped establish four such organizations: the International Sociological Association, the International Political Science Association, the International Economic Association, and the International Committee of Comparative Law. By 1953, under the impetus of UNESCO, these organizations were linked in an International Social Science Council. The agency also aided in establishing an International Union of Scientific Psychology. The financial aid given these organizations and a few institutes and associations such as the International Institute of Administrative Sciences, established before UNESCO, rose from $10,500 in 1950 to nearly $60,000 in 1953, and to more than $75,000 in 1955 and in 1956.

Support given to international education associations has been much more modest. This may in part be due to a continuing preoccupation with the needs and aspirations of the scientific elite rather than with mass organizations. It is significant that in the field of education, UNESCO centered its organizing work on the universities, establishing the International Association of Universities, which, since 1951, has continued to receive the heaviest subventions from UNESCO ($23,000 in 1951 and an annual grant of $14,000 since then). Total subventions in the field of education rose from a low of $5,000 in 1950 to $29,600 in 1953, and to a little over $40,000 in 1955 and in 1956.

The list of societies in the cultural field initiated or aided by UNESCO is long and comprehensive. It includes one "umbrella" organization, the International Council for Philosophy and Humanistic Studies, composed of twelve learned societies; and, in addition, the International Theater Institute and the International Music Council; the International Council of Museums and the International Council on Archives; the International Association of Plastic Arts and the International Society for Education through Art; and several others. Subventions to these and related organizations have been steadily increasing and in 1955, reached nearly $200,000, of which $100,000 was for the International Council for Philosophy and Humanistic Studies. During the International Conference of Artists in Venice in 1952, an attempt sponsored by UNESCO to create an international council of arts and letters did not gather sufficient support among the assembled artists and writers. Repeated attempts by UNESCO to create an international press institute or association also failed and were abandoned when an independent International Press Institute was established in Zurich.

Financial support from UNESCO for international voluntary organizations, mostly nongovernmental, is not confined to subventions. Payments are also made on a contractual basis for carrying out specific projects included in the work program. Most of these contracts are for research and special inquiries, or for the organization of symposia, seminars, or exhibitions. In 1953, for example, thirty-eight contracts were concluded with twenty-six international nongovernmental organizations for a total of more than $166,000.

In total, the funds made available as subventions or contract payments are considerable. Scholars, scientists, and others are helped thereby to help themselves in developing their international contacts and advancing their studies and research. As they are helped, they assist UNESCO "to maintain, increase, and diffuse knowledge."[23] But there are also serious drawbacks to this policy. A review in 1954 of the employment of subventions by beneficiaries shows that a substantial part of the funds goes toward administrative expenses: the payment of salaries of secretaries and their travel, the administrative cost of organizing conferences and congresses as well as meetings of the administrative organs of the various councils, institutes, and organizations.[24] Another large portion of the funds is used for the publication of the proceedings of such meetings, many of which would appear to be of interest to only a very limited audience.

Although much of this organizational activity and financial help serves to promote international co-operation in fields that are of interest to UNESCO, it would seem that, at least in some cases, organizing activities *per se* have become the major purpose rather than creative study and research, or direct contacts among a widening circle of scholars, scientists, and practitioners of the arts. Furthermore, the channeling of the subventions through the various umbrella organizations means that, by the time the subventions have been divided among the organi-

[23] *Constitution*, Art. I.

[24] U.N. Educational, Scientific and Cultural Organization, General Conference, *Quadrennial Review by the Executive Board of the Employment of Subventions Granted to International Non-Governmental Organizations*, Doc. 8C/ADM/20 (August 1954).

zations affiliated with them, minute grants are made available for specific projects of a most highly specialized type. To those who hold that one of the primary tasks of UNESCO is to promote research—any type of research—this situation may be satisfactory. On the other hand, it certainly does not make for a concentration of resources and effort on major projects and programs.

The most basic objection to the policy of subventions that has been made by the United States and others at conferences of UNESCO is that it may prevent the international scientific and professional bodies from developing the strength and self-reliance that is characteristic of the best type of professional organization. When UNESCO sponsored and financed a large number of these organizations, the assumption was that aid was necessary to get the organizations started, but that it would be reduced as they got under way. Subsequent events did not bear out this assumption. In most cases, the original annual subventions were maintained, and in a number, they were increased. In many cases, the UNESCO subvention continues to be practically the sole major source of income. The agency finds itself, therefore, surrounded by a network of organizations many of which would virtually collapse if support were withdrawn.

The United States has repeatedly suggested that one way of meeting the problem would be to shift the emphasis from general subventions to payments made under contract for specific projects undertaken by nongovernmental organizations. This would counteract the tendency toward a splintering of projects and a diffusion of funds and would lead to greater self-reliance and viability on the part of the organizations concerned. To date, the idea has not met with sufficient support to carry it in sessions of the UNESCO General Conference. Whether the latest departure in program-making, *i.e.* the division into "general" and "special" activities, will lend new strength to this idea remains to be seen. The greater emphasis on activities designed to meet specific needs of member states may bring these needs into sharper focus and result in the application of more rigid criteria in granting subventions and in extending the grants under contract.

The national commissions, of which more than sixty have been created in member states, constitute another channel for the promotion of the objectives of UNESCO. There are great variations in the composition and character of these commissions. In some cases, they are primarily governmental bodies attached to the ministries of foreign affairs or of education, with all members appointed by the government.

More often, they are of mixed composition and are more directly representative of the educational, scientific, and cultural life of their countries. Commissions of this type appear best suited to the purposes of UNESCO. They can offer representative advice to their governments; carry knowledge and understanding of UNESCO to their people; help implement programs of the agency through studies and publications and the organization of meetings, festivals, and exhibitions; and promote travel and other means of communication with commissions in other countries. In other words, they give body and meaning to the work of UNESCO within their countries.

The agency assists in the development of national commissions by lending to the countries the services of some of its officials, or by enabling the organizers of the commissions to spend short periods at UNESCO headquarters. Despite the fact that a number of the commissions are dormant and only a minority are truly active, the effectiveness of national commissions is increasing.

Another problem of organization—the composition of the Executive Board of UNESCO—came to a head in 1954 at the General Conference in Montevideo. The United States, Australia, Brazil, and the United Kingdom introduced a constitutional amendment to make the Executive Board representative of governments. The amendment provided that the General Conference would continue to elect individuals rather than governments, but these individuals, in order to qualify as candidates, would have to be nominated by their governments and, after election, would be subject to the instructions of their governments.[25] Similar amendments had failed in earlier sessions, and at Montevideo, the issue proved to be the most controversial question of the conference. Those strongly opposed to this amendment, particularly France, argued that the true spirit of UNESCO as an educational, scientific, and cultural body would be lost; that political considerations would dominate; and that the intellectual stature of the organization would suffer.

The sponsors of the measure stressed the key role the Executive Board played in UNESCO, and argued that the change would increase the confidence of governments in the organization and their sense of responsibility for it. At the same time, the view was advanced that responsible governments certainly would, in view of the nature of the organization, consult with their national commissions and propose for

[25] U.N. Educational, Scientific and Cultural Organization, Eighth Session, *Records of the General Conference* (1954), Resolutions, p. 12.

appointment individuals who were truly representative of the educational, scientific, and cultural life of their countries. Despite a last-minute effort to postpone consideration for two years, the constitutional amendment was finally adopted by a vote of 49 to 9.[26] It is hoped that this change will help make the program more responsive to the educational and cultural aspirations of the peoples of the world, without reducing the intellectual stature of the organization. Much will depend, of course, on the extent to which representative national commissions succeed in impressing their views on their governments.

At the same session in 1954, the Soviet Union and the Byelorussian and Ukrainian Soviet Socialist Republics were admitted to membership; Poland, Hungary, and Czechoslovakia—which had left the organization in 1952—returned as active participants. The applications of Bulgaria and Rumania for membership were postponed, largely on the ground that the two countries had been condemned by qualified international bodies for their failure to observe human rights and to live up to treaty obligations. The delegations from the Communist-controlled countries took little part in the work of the Montevideo conference, but the longer-term effect of the participation of Communist-controlled countries on the organization remains a matter of speculation. It may be that the inevitable confrontation within UNESCO of the views and ideas of the free world with those of the Communist-controlled countries will not only help clarify basic intellectual and cultural problems of contemporary society but will give new strength to those who helped to establish UNESCO as a means "to further universal respect for justice, for the rule of law and for the human rights and fundamental freedoms which are affirmed for the peoples of the world, without distinction of race, sex, language or religion by the Charter of the United Nations."[27]

Achievements

Notwithstanding the conflicts and difficulties that have beset UNESCO from the outset, much has been achieved that is positive, constructive, and conducive to better relations among the peoples of the world. In each of the major areas of interest—education, the natural sciences, the social sciences, cultural activities, and mass communications—progress can be reported.

[26] *Ibid.*, Proceedings, pp. 177–78.
[27] *Constitution*, Art. I(1).

Education

In the realm of education, there have been four areas of concentration: educational reconstruction; fundamental education; formal education; and education for living in a world community.

In the field of educational reconstruction, UNESCO has acted as a catalytic agent rather than as an operating agency. Following the war, it surveyed needs and made available limited funds from its budget ($400,000 in 1947–48, and $155,000 in 1949) to stimulate broader international action. The bulk of the work was carried on by voluntary international organizations, which were brought together by UNESCO in a Temporary International Council for Educational Reconstruction. About thirty agencies participated in the Council and made available nearly $160 million, most of which was spent in Europe and the Middle East.[28]

The European reconstruction phase was completed in 1950. Acute need for help continued among the Arab refugees from Palestine, including some 200,000 children of school age. Largely with funds provided by the United Nations Relief and Works Agency for Palestine Refugees, UNESCO helped in building schools for the refugee children, providing teaching materials, and training teachers. By June 30, 1956, 350 such schools had been established.

The end of the conflict in Korea found that country with half of its schools and 80 per cent of the instruction materials destroyed. UNESCO contributed to the reconstruction effort chiefly by sending an educational mission to Korea, which reported on existing needs and made recommendations for a long-term plan of rehabilitation and educational development. The report of this mission played a major role in the formulation of the educational reconstruction program carried on by the Government of the Republic of Korea and the United Nations Korean Reconstruction Agency.

UNESCO has at no time, however, acted as a major operating agency in the field of educational rehabilitation. Its function has been to provide limited services and to stimulate and guide reconstruction efforts.

By contrast, the promotion of fundamental education has emerged as a major program of the organization. With more than half of the population of the world illiterate, the fundamental education program has been attempting to cope with a problem that is basic to human welfare and vast in scope. It is concerned with more than mere literacy.

[28] U.N. Educational, Scientific and Cultural Organization, General Conference, Fifth Session, Doc. 5C/OXR/15 (Apr. 20, 1950).

In 1952, the Director-General defined fundamental education as "that kind of minimum and general education which aims to help children and adults, who do not have the advantages of formal education, to understand the problems of their immediate environment and their rights and duties as citizens and individuals, and to participate more effectively in the economic and social progress of their community."[29]

It is evident that fundamental education means more than rudimentary instruction in the "three R's." It calls for the development of attitudes receptive to change in societies that are moving forward economically and socially—in many cases after centuries of standstill. It means the teaching of elementary concepts of hygiene, nutrition, and home economics, of improved agricultural methods, and of basic skills essential in industrial development. The concept is intended to permeate formal schooling at the elementary level, but more often it finds expression in a variety of ways in training adults, particularly at the village level.

The methods of fundamental education are, to a great extent, still in the process of being worked out. International programs attempt to awaken public interest in the aims and methods of fundamental education through pilot projects, publications, and similar means; through the development of teaching materials, including audio-visual aids; and through the provision of specialized staff. UNESCO is taking the lead in furnishing such aid, although other specialized agencies, particularly the World Health Organization, the International Labour Organisation, and the Food and Agriculture Organization, are co-operating.

UNESCO, for example, has been issuing the quarterly *Fundamental and Adult Education Bulletin* and other publications reporting on experiments made in various parts of the world. It also has assisted in the development of a number of national fundamental educational centers, and has established two international training centers, which play a major role in the development of the program. The first was established in 1951 in Patzcuaro, Mexico, to serve Latin America; the second in 1953 in Sirs-el-Layyan, Egypt, to serve the Arab states. Trainees from these centers have, on return to their home countries, played major roles in national efforts to promote fundamental education. The centers themselves have made a signal contribution in the development of teaching materials.

Fellowships, scholarships, seminars, and field work have also been

[29] U.N. Educational, Scientific and Cultural Organization, *Report of the Director-General to the United Nations, 1951–52* (1952), p. 14. See also, Brenda H. Tripp, "UNESCO in Perspective," *International Conciliation*, No. 497 (March 1954), p. 356.

employed to provide training in fundamental education. Finally, UNESCO has assisted in the creation of national committees for the promotion of fundamental education, committees in which governmental and nongovernmental groups co-operate. By the end of 1955, thirty-three such committees existed.

Although still in its experimental stage, the fundamental education program of UNESCO is a pioneering project, full of promise. It is more than an emergency substitute for the absence of formal schools, and its impact on human welfare should prove substantial.

Fundamental education, however, cannot take the place of formal systems of education on all levels. The promotion of such systems is another field of primary importance for UNESCO and has gained prominence within the over-all program in recent years. Effective aid has become possible as a result of the participation of UNESCO in the Expanded Programme of Technical Assistance and the use by UNESCO of the established methods of that program.

In this area, results are attained slowly. UNESCO has assisted in developing far-reaching plans for education in many underdeveloped countries, but the governments concerned are handicapped by insufficient funds to implement the plans. This has prompted the underdeveloped countries to urge the establishment of an international education fund. There is little indication that such a fund will be created, but it is hoped that, with the growing awareness in the underdeveloped countries of the need for comprehensive systems of formal schooling, increasing funds will be made available nationally.

In the promotion of formal education, UNESCO is assisted by the International Bureau of Education, a quasi-official organization founded before the Second World War with headquarters in Geneva, in which nearly seventy countries participate. UNESCO and the International Bureau jointly sponsor each year an International Conference on Public Education, which brings together key personnel from the various ministries of education throughout the world. These conferences and the staff of the International Bureau deal with the technical aspects of education such as teaching mathematics at the primary level, the techniques of reading, and educational administration.

In the field of higher education, UNESCO has promoted the exchange of university professors and has helped provide teachers for universities in underdeveloped countries. Much of this work is being carried on in co-operation with the International Association of Universities, which itself is a creation of UNESCO. In adult education, the efforts of UNESCO have centered on education for workers. It helped establish an International Center for Workers' Education in France in 1951. In addition, it has organized seminars dealing with such subjects as the administration and organization of adult education, new methods in adult education, and the development of international understanding through workers' education.

In the educational programs of UNESCO, the great emphasis on education for living in a world community has proved controversial.[30] Over the years, various programs for promoting international understanding through education have been developed under titles such as "education for international understanding" or "education for international co-operation." The 1952 program included the misleading term, "education for world citizenship." This was interpreted in some quarters, particularly among some groups in the United States, to mean that UNESCO was attempting to impose a common educational pattern aimed at developing allegiance to some world order or government. This was never in any way intended by the organization, although some passages can be found, in the mass of literature published by the agency and its friends, that might support such an interpretation. UNESCO and the sovereign governments that are Members of it have been aiming simply at the promotion of better understanding among the peoples of the world. Their emphasis in the program has been on diversity rather than on uniformity; on a knowledge and understanding of the different mores, traditions, and attitudes of the various countries and their peoples, and of the variety of their cultural riches. As conceived by UNESCO, education for living in a world community means the promotion of respect for the fundamental rights of individuals and cultural groups. If the term "world community" is used, it does not mean the promotion of any form of world government but an appreciation of the interdependence of the countries of the world and an understanding of the international organizations that have become necessary as a result of this interdependence. Above all, education for living in a world community means the promotion of a better understanding of the United Nations.

In this context, textbooks, of course, play an important role. UNESCO does not in any way control what is published in textbooks, but it can stimulate consultation among the writers and can encourage voluntary

[30] This program (education for living in a world community) is not administered solely by the Education Department of UNESCO, but by that department in co-operation with other branches of the secretariat.

arrangements among countries in order to eliminate from textbooks material based on prejudice and faulty perspective instead of on fact. For example, after a seminar in Brussels in 1950, several committees were set up by professional groups and national commissions in Europe to improve history textbooks through bilateral consultation.[31] Other seminars have dealt with the improvement of syllabi in schools and with better methods of teaching.

UNESCO itself has published a number of pamphlets on race, human rights, and similar subjects. At the time of the Korean war, the agency published several pamphlets on collective security, as well as a more thorough-going study of the subject. These were prompted by the desire to demonstrate the meaning of collective security measures taken by the United Nations to ensure the national independence and integrity of Member states.

In addition to the material already mentioned, the organization produced other literature dealing with the activities of other specialized agencies; it assisted the World Federation of United Nations Associations in organizing regional seminars for teaching United Nations principles; and it organized meetings of youth leaders with a view to promoting international understanding. These efforts were useful, but in this area, a clearer definition of the tasks of UNESCO and of the methods of performing them is still needed. In its search for a more effective program, it established, in 1953, an Expert Committee to Study the Principles and Methods of Education for Living in a World Community. The committee made some recommendations on which the Director-General might base a program for 1955–56, but the recommendations were referred instead to the member states and the national commissions for their consideration. Thus, the search continues for a comprehensive program to promote education for living in a world community.

Natural Sciences

The natural science group in UNESCO is closely knit, comprising the Natural Science Department in the Secretariat, the natural scientists in the General Conference and the Executive Board, and the affiliated scientific councils, unions, and organizations—and it has effectively pursued its objectives. The clearing-house activities developed in this field, either within UNESCO or by nongovernmental organiza-

[31] Tripp, *loc. cit.*, p. 360.

tions with financial help from UNESCO, are more comprehensive than in any other area and are undoubtedly rendering important service to individual scientists and research institutions throughout the world.

Field science co-operation offices have been established in South Asia, Southeast Asia, in the Middle East, and in Latin America. Their purpose is to facilitate, among the scientists and technologists of these regions, the exchange of information, personnel, and material, as well as the co-ordination of research. The offices are staffed by two or three experts who travel extensively as liaison officers. Symposia are organized within the respective regions to consider problems of special importance to the scientific life and economic advancement of the countries within the region. The scope of these offices has been gradually enlarged to include the social sciences.

In recent years, particularly in the underdeveloped countries, the teaching and popularization of the sciences have been receiving increasing attention. To this end, teaching aids and expert advice have been made available. Science clubs have been established in a growing number of countries, and the formation of national associations of science writers has been encouraged. Traveling science exhibits have met with considerable success.

Beyond these services and projects designed to promote science on the broadest possible front, UNESCO has attempted to bring into focus specific fields pre-eminently fitted for international scientific inquiry. None of the proposed international laboratories and institutes is actually functioning. Plans for the establishment of a Hylean-Amazon Institute collapsed because the governments directly concerned were unable or unwilling to provide adequate funds. All the other projects on the priority list, prepared by UNESCO in 1949, of international research laboratories in the natural sciences were abandoned, except an International Computation Center. Such a center was approved by the General Conference in 1951, and a special convention provided for its establishment in Rome. The convention fell short of the required ten ratifications, and it is not now expected that the center will ever come into existence.

These failures did not deter the protagonists of international laboratories—a few scientists and a number of governments—from urging the creation of an international institute of oceanography and one for studying the growth of cells, the latter intended to assist in cancer research. The Montevideo Conference in 1954 authorized preliminary exploration into the research facilities in these fields, but past experience and present lack of enthusiasm among governments make early action to establish the laboratories improbable. The most potent argument against these ventures is that there are already in existence many national research centers in universities and elsewhere, which enjoy substantial financial support. In most cases, they are open to scientists from other countries, and their findings are made freely available.

An exception to the negative record on laboratory establishment was the creation, under UNESCO sponsorship, of a European Council for Nuclear Research, comprised of eleven European nations, which is building a European Center for Nuclear Research in Geneva, Switzerland. The progress made to date in the realization of this project is attributable to the intense interest in the development of nuclear research and the difficulties encountered by European countries in establishing their own facilities for such research.

That it may not be necessary to establish international laboratories or other new facilities for international collaboration on a research project was demonstrated by the successful initiative of UNESCO in stimulating and co-ordinating arid zone research, which is of great practical interest to the people living in the vast arid zones of the world, including parts of the United States. UNESCO appointed an Advisory Committee on Arid Zone Research, charged with the task of co-ordinating existing information and of formulating the precise problems in need of investigation. Under this program, a system of associated research centers has been established whereby institutes now working on arid zone problems are, in suitable cases, recommended by the Advisory Committee for inclusion in the program.[32] As a result, considerable headway has been made in research on such matters as underground water, plant ecology, and wind and solar energy. As part of this project, UNESCO has embarked on the production of homoclimatic maps of arid and semi-arid zones, and provided other research materials. These research activities have been supplemented by the application of tested findings through technical assistance provided by UNESCO and the Food and Agriculture Organization.

Social Sciences

In many ways, UNESCO activities in the social sciences are similar to those in the natural sciences. There is the same pattern of assistance to various learned councils and societies, many of which were created by

[32] See James Swarbrick, "The Arid Zone—An International Task," *Impact*, Vol. IV, No. 4 (1953).

UNESCO or with its help. There is also the same emphasis on clearing-house activities and technical services. Because most international organizations of social scientists are still in their infancy, UNESCO has, through its own publication services, provided abstracts, inventories, and repertories, as well as such quarterly publications as the *International Social Science Bulletin* and *Current Sociology*. It has produced publications designed to further the teaching of the social sciences and has organized seminars and missions to that end. An International Institute of Social Science has also been established at Cologne with the help of UNESCO.

In its efforts to stimulate research in the social sciences, UNESCO has been concentrating fairly consistently on major issues directly related to the improvement of human relations. Considerable time and effort have been expended on the study of tensions between individuals, groups, and countries, and their causes. This program has already produced a large number of reports and publications on such subjects as group tensions in India and in other parts of the world; the changing attitudes of Japanese youth following the war; social structure and personality in the city and in rural communities; and democracy in a world of tensions. In addition to the analysis of social tensions, research is being conducted on the application of scientific methods in influencing those factors that are known to have a bearing on the origin of conflicts.

Related to these tension studies are other research activities encouraged by UNESCO, such as research into the social impact of industrialization, particularly in underdeveloped countries. These studies have a direct bearing on the technical assistance activities of the United Nations.[33] They gain in authority by virtue of the fact that technical assistance experts of the United Nations and related organizations, speaking and writing from first-hand experience, have participated in their planning and execution. The present trend is to conduct further studies on a regional basis, to take full account of the peculiarities and special aspects of the problem in different parts of the world.[34]

Other research projects sponsored by UNESCO also relate to pro-

[33] Among the most important of these publications are Margaret Mead (ed.), *Cultural Patterns and Technical Change* (1953); and M. E. Opler, *Social Aspects of Technical Assistance in Operation* (1954). The volume edited by Mead was produced under a contract with the World Federation for Mental Health; the volume by Opler grew out of a Conference of Experts sponsored by the United Nations and UNESCO.

[34] For example, a Research Center on the Social Implications of Industrialization in Southern Asia was opened in Calcutta in 1955.

grams and activities of the United Nations. One example is a series of studies of the cultural assimilation of immigrants, including refugees, in Australia, Brazil, Israel, Belgium, and France. Further field studies are planned or are under way to ascertain the most suitable measures for facilitating the assimilation of immigrants. Related also to operating programs are projected studies regarding certain social aspects of land reform and some of the legal problems involved in the implementation of such reform. Most of these studies are delegated to nongovernmental organizations such as the International Cooperative Alliance and the International Association for Legal Science.

Much effort and energy has been expended on a series of reports and monographs on human rights, particularly racial discrimination, beginning with publications on the concept and scientific basis of race and racial differences. Dealing with issues that are highly sensitive in many parts of the world, some of these publications have proved not only stimulating but also controversial.

Cultural Activities

The term cultural activities, as used in UNESCO, covers an extraordinarily broad range of programs and projects. It includes the usual clearing-house activities and technical services as applied to the needs of museums and libraries—to bibliographical handbooks and inventories of documentation services; catalogues of recordings and color reproductions of paintings; the compilation, through co-operating organizations, of albums of reproductions and the organization of traveling exhibitions of such reproductions; and the publication of a multilingual dictionary of artistic and archaeological terms. UNESCO every year organizes or assists in the organization of large numbers of meetings, bringing together artists, painters, writers, philosophers, historians, and others representative of the cultural life of their nations. It extends technical assistance in the development of libraries and museums, and in the restoration of art treasures and ancient monuments and archaeological sites. All these activities, many of which go beyond the League of Nations concept of co-operation among intellectuals, help to raise the cultural level of the population. It is difficult, however, to avoid the impression that, in its desire to serve, UNESCO has engaged in too many projects to permit effective guidance toward common ends.

There are some achievements that deserve special mention. The conservation and protection of the inheritance of the world of books, works of art, and monuments of history and science is a task of UNESCO under its constitution. Modern warfare threatens that inheritance with total destruction. To meet that threat to the extent possible, UNESCO, at the initiative of the Netherlands, sponsored the drafting of a Convention for the Protection of Cultural Property in the Event of Armed Conflict.[35] The convention was completed in 1954 and signed by thirty-seven countries including France, the Federal Republic of Germany, Italy, the United States, and the Soviet Union. It provides for the establishment of an International Register of Cultural Property under Public Protection and a series of measures designed to protect such property in the event of military operations. An additional protocol stipulates that such cultural property shall never be retained as war reparations. This convention is not yet in effect because it has not been ratified by the required five parties.

Another important convention, drafted under UNESCO auspices, is designed to provide protection throughout the world to authors and other copyright proprietors of literary, scientific, and artistic works, including writings, musical and dramatic works, films, paintings, and sculpture. The Universal Copyright Convention was completed at an international conference held in Geneva, in September 1952, and signed by thirty-five countries.[36] It obtained the requisite number of ratifications, including that of the United States, and entered into force in September 1955. It ensures for foreign authors essentially the same protection and treatment that each signatory nation accords to its own authors.

UNESCO has made a further contribution to the dissemination of culture by assisting in the selection and financing of the translation of representative literary works. This proved a major and difficult enterprise, especially the selection of the books to be translated. For this purpose, the assistance of the national commissions of the appropriate member states and the Council for Philosophy and Humanistic Studies was enlisted. So far, four series of translations have been started: an Arabic series, a Latin American series, a Persian series, and an Italian series. An Asian series is envisaged. In addition, UNESCO is continuing the publication of the *Index Translationum*, first started by the Inter-

[35] U.N. Educational, Scientific and Cultural Organization, *Final Act of the Intergovernmental Conference on the Protection of Cultural Property in the Event of Armed Conflict* (1954).

[36] *Universal Copyright Convention, 1952,* U.S. Department of State Treaty Series 3324.

national Institute of Intellectual Cooperation under the League of Nations. The fifth volume of this index, for example, listed 16,130 translations published during 1952 in forty-nine countries.

Also in this area, UNESCO assumed responsibility for drafting two other international instruments. The first is the Agreement on Importation of Educational, Scientific and Cultural Materials; the second, the Agreement for Facilitating the International Circulation of Visual and Auditory Materials of an Educational, Scientific and Cultural Character. Both of these agreements, which are now in force, were intended to facilitate the movement of cultural materials across national frontiers.

A book coupon scheme was devised by UNESCO to help make books, films, and scientific materials actually available to countries that, because of currency difficulties, are handicapped in buying them from abroad. UNESCO serves as a clearing-house and provides coupons in convertible currency in exchange for local currency, which it can use in other parts of its program. By the end of 1955, $9 million worth of UNESCO coupons had been issued. As an extension of this undertaking, a travel coupon scheme, operating on the same principle, was added in 1954.

In its promotion of intercultural relations, UNESCO has in recent years given special attention to furthering mutual appreciation of Oriental and Occidental cultural values.[37] Through the organization of round-tables and through publications, UNESCO seeks to interpret the cultures of the East, particularly of the Indian subcontinent, to the West and vice versa. Two major publications have so far resulted from this effort.[38]

Finally, in an effort to demonstrate the interdependence of nations and cultures and their contributions to the common heritage of mankind, UNESCO is sponsoring the preparation and publication of a scientific and cultural history of mankind. An international commission of fifteen members has been entrusted with full responsibility in the name of UNESCO for the preparation and execution of the work. The commission in turn has appointed 112 corresponding members and twenty advisers from more than forty countries. This history is to be published in six volumes, but pending its completion individual contributions are published in the *Journal of World History*, a quarterly review, which

[37] U.N. Economic and Social Council, *Report of the United Nations Educational, Scientific and Cultural Organization*, Doc. E/2735 (May 17, 1955), pp. 28–43.

[38] U.N. Educational, Scientific and Cultural Organization, *Interrelations of Cultures* (1953); and *Humanism and Education in East and West* (1953).

also reproduces comments on and criticisms of such contributions. Whether this undertaking will result in a universally recognized and accepted history of man and his heritage, only the future will tell.

Mass Communications

For an organization concerned not only with co-operation among the intellectual and cultural elites but also with the promotion of understanding among the peoples of the world, the fullest possible development and unrestricted use of mass media for the transmission of information and ideas are basic needs. That is why the United States at the London conference in 1945 sought to ensure that relatively high priority would be assigned by UNESCO to the development of mass media and the promotion of the free flow of information.

Ambitious projects, such as a plan for the establishment of a world-wide broadcasting system suggested in the early days of UNESCO, were discarded without serious discussion, due partly to difficulties in financing and in reaching agreement on programs to be broadcast, and partly to a lack of understanding of the importance of mass media, or even a positive disdain for them on the part of intellectuals and governments in Europe and elsewhere. Instead, UNESCO has concentrated primarily on fact-finding and on studies relating to the special use of mass media in education and the dissemination of art and the sciences. By 1954, over forty publications had been produced by UNESCO, including general surveys of the availability of mass media in some 170 states and territories. Other special studies dealt with such matters as the production, distribution, and content of newsreels; with films on art, including catalogues of such films; with the structure and operation of existing national and international news agencies and with newsprint; with educational broadcasting and television. These were supplemented by publications on the professional training of film technicians, journalists, and radio program personnel in various countries.

Many of these studies revealed serious gaps in the availability of mass media and trained personnel and thus tended to stimulate action to fill the gaps. The studies have been basic to a developing program of technical assistance, first proposed by the United States and carried on jointly by the United Nations and UNESCO, to help countries in the development of their own press, news agencies, and radio facilities. Expert missions and grants of fellowships have been the tools most frequently used. In the program for 1955–56, the General Conference in

Montevideo provided for the direct award by UNESCO of fifteen fellowships in mass communication.

UNESCO has avoided undertaking studies of censorship practices that interfere with the free flow of news and ideas. It considers this problem a political matter to be left to the United Nations for exploration, study, and remedy.[39] This does not mean, however, that UNESCO has been unconcerned with measures to facilitate a free flow of news and ideas and various cultural materials. Mention has already been made of two international agreements, initiated by UNESCO, in this field.

Beyond this, one of its most interesting studies shows how the flow of news around the world is hampered by high or discrepant cost of communications, and by shortages of cable and radio facilities, and urges adoption of more uniform press rates and wider use of new methods of communication to overcome these obstacles.[40] Steps were taken jointly by the Economic and Social Council, UNESCO, and the International Telecommunication Union to transmit to governments recommendations for reductions in rates for ordinary press telegrams; for extended facilities and lower charges for radio-communications to several destinations; for the establishment of press telephone calls as a separate category, with reduced rates for such calls; and for the removal of apparent discrepancies in rates for leased teleprinter lines. In co-operation with the Universal Postal Union, recommendations were formulated to facilitate and to reduce the cost of transmission through the mails of books, newspapers, periodicals, and other publications, and to permit payment in national currency at local post offices for subscriptions to foreign newspapers and periodicals. By the end of 1954, twenty-nine states had taken some action on these proposals. The book-coupon scheme, mentioned earlier, and a gift-coupon scheme developed by UNESCO are further evidences of its concern for the free flow of ideas and information.

To complete the picture, it must be recalled that UNESCO itself is making a massive contribution to the wide dissemination of written and recorded materials. A great deal has already been said about the books and reports distributed by the organization. To these must be added a weekly *World Review* radio-script sent out in Arabic, English, French, and Spanish to 103 countries and territories, a number of films

[39] For an analysis of the efforts of the United Nations to promote freedom of information, see the monograph in this Brookings series, *The United Nations and Human Rights*, Chap. III.

[40] Francis Williams, *Transmitting World News* (1953).

and film strips about the work of the United Nations, the specialized agencies, and various educational, scientific, and cultural subjects; the *UNESCO Features*, a bulletin supplying educational, scientific, and cultural information to the press, sent to 1,500 editors; and several other periodicals and newsletters.

Unresolved Issues

There can be no doubt that UNESCO is fully aware of the scope of its responsibilities and opportunities. It considers itself at the heart of the postwar effort to build, through international co-operation, peace based not on force and armed strength but on mutual understanding and consent.

The range of possible activities in this area is almost unlimited, and UNESCO has found it difficult to select the most effective means for attaining its goals. If the various co-operating nongovernmental organizations, the scientific, cultural, and educational councils and congresses—many of which were started by UNESCO—should attain greater independence and self-reliance, UNESCO might find it possible to withdraw from certain of its current activities and to concentrate more on major programs. This could be achieved without totally abandoning the more specialized endeavors, and the specialized work of the related independent organizations could still be useful to the major programs of UNESCO. In other words, UNESCO does not and should not have a monopoly on the international promotion of the scientific method or of education. These are also the instruments of other agencies, including the Food and Agriculture Organization and the World Health Organization.

The major programs of UNESCO are still in the stage of development. The fundamental education program is a great pioneering venture, but the search continues for ways and means to progress beyond studies, pilot projects, and national and regional centers. Good foundations, however, are being laid, and it is perhaps only a question of time and greater concentration on the part of UNESCO, before this program becomes a living reality throughout the underdeveloped regions of the world. Encouraging headway is being made by the program of education for living in a world community, although this program still lacks a clear focus.

There has been no satisfactory solution to the conflict over UNESCO as an organization for co-operation among intellectuals, on the one hand, and on the other hand, as an organization for the promotion of international understanding and the utilization of the achievements of education, science, and culture for the advancement of the general welfare and the enrichment of all. Many well-meaning people distrust UNESCO and the big words and activities that are beyond their understanding. At the same time, there are signs that many of the leading intellectuals, writers, and artists are becoming indifferent to the organization and somewhat weary of the feverish activity of those they consider to be scientific and cultural bureaucrats. Persistence and patience may resolve that conflict. Moreover, a concentration on major programs might command the respect and support of both these groups. The scientists need the humanists lest the world become the victim of its own scientific progress; and both they and the educators are essential to the organization if the sights, the levels of living, and the cultural life of the common man are to be lifted beyond age-old drudgery, tension, and prejudice.

CHAPTER X

*Problems of the Underdeveloped Countries**

It was obvious before the end of the Second World War that the problems of the underdeveloped countries would require far more attention from the international community than they had received from the League of Nations. Nevertheless, for the first three or four years after the signing of the United Nations Charter, the problems of stricken Europe tended to dominate the economic and social scene. The international agencies, when they were not preoccupied with organizational issues, turned their main energies to the relief and rehabilitation of needy people in war-devastated countries, to overcoming shortages attributable to the war, to re-establishing essential social services, and to the development of appropriate long-term trade and payments arrangements. The problems of the underdeveloped countries were by no means ignored; in fact, they grew more prominent each year, but until the inauguration of the Expanded Programme of Technical Assistance, they were indeed special problems.

At about mid-point in the first decade of United Nations history, the special problems of the underdeveloped countries ceased being special problems and became the stock in trade of United Nations economic and social programs. The problems now occupying the center of the world stage are very different in character, however, from those that in preceding decades constituted the staple of international negotiation. The rising interest in the problems of underdeveloped countries has involved more than a shift of geographic focus away from Europe to other continents. It has tended to obliterate many of the traditional distinctions between matters of international concern and matters essentially domestic.

The economic and social machinery of the United Nations, although it provided also for co-operation on educational, cultural, and health matters, was designed primarily to facilitate the attainment of agreements on matters that were international in the sense that they affected directly the movement of goods, funds, or people across

* By Robert E. Asher. Portions of this chapter are based on materials prepared by Louis Lazaroff.

international boundaries. This machinery, with the consent of all concerned, has become inextricably enmeshed in matters formerly regarded as domestic. The pressing problems of the underdeveloped countries have been elevated to the international level, not because they involve international transactions, but because they are common to a large number of countries, because those countries individually and collectively lack the resources to solve them, and because failure to solve them—or at least to move energetically and perceptibly in the direction of solutions—is widely believed to threaten the peace and security of the world as a whole.

The degree to which the United Nations system has, since mid-1950, been engaged in promoting the welfare of the people in underdeveloped countries will already have become apparent from preceding portions of this volume. It is not intended at this point to re-analyze programs that have already been analyzed, but rather to tie together some threads that have become separated and to separate certain threads that have become entangled. The first step in this process is to trace the development, as it unfolded throughout the United Nations system during the period 1946–49, of techniques suitable for dealing with the problems of the underdeveloped countries. Both the United Nations Organization and certain of the specialized agencies experimented during this period with the provision of individual experts and teams of experts, fellowships and other opportunities for training, and some supplies and equipment for demonstration purposes.

Activities of the United Nations Organization, 1946–49

The Expanded Programme of Technical Assistance (EPTA), begun in 1950, was the first major program of an operational character undertaken on a long-term basis by the United Nations and its related agencies to meet the special needs of the underdeveloped countries. It was, as its name indicates, an expansion of services developed in the period 1946–49. During these years, the term "technical assistance" came into general use in United Nations circles to describe a variety of services available from or through international agencies. Moreover, the available services—offered initially to developed and underdeveloped countries alike—came to be identified more exclusively as aids to the underdeveloped countries.

The salient characteristics of the underdeveloped countries are well known.[1] Two thirds of the world, roughly 1.6 billion people, live in nations in which the average annual income in 1950 was less than $150 per person. They produced only 17 per cent of the income of the world. The area they occupy includes all of Asia except Japan, all of Africa except the Union of South Africa, the bulk of Latin America, and the southeastern corner of Europe. In this broad belt, "poverty is old, but the awareness of poverty and the conviction that something can be done about it are new."[2] With the end of the war and the achievement of independence by hundreds of millions of people, this conviction, this revolution of rising expectations, gained explosive force.

General Assembly and Economic and Social Council

Although not adopted to meet the special needs of the underdeveloped countries, several resolutions approved by the General Assembly, at its first session in late 1946, were of special interest to them. The first concerned the need for relief after the termination of the United Nations Relief and Rehabilitation Administration (UNRRA), which provided supplies and technical assistance to China, Greece, Korea, the Philippines, and Yugoslavia, as well as to economically more advanced nations that had suffered devastation during hostilities.[3] It raised the hope—subsequently dashed—that large-scale relief programs might soon be undertaken within the United Nations system. The second resolution, in which the United Nations assumed a responsibility for carrying on the advisory social welfare functions of UNRRA, was a more direct forerunner of technical assistance.[4] It authorized the Secretary-General to include in the budget for 1947 funds for the provision of experts to advise governments, on request, on welfare services; to provide fellowships for the training of officials in social welfare; to provide specialized advice on the rehabilitation and training of the physically handicapped; and to provide technical publications for social workers.

Acting on a recommendation of the Economic and Social Council, the General Assembly created the United Nations International Children's Emergency Fund (UNICEF) and authorized it to receive contributions and to use them in arranging or providing for "supplies,

[1] See the volume in this Brookings series, *The United Nations and Promotion of the General Welfare*, Part One.

[2] Eugene Staley, *The Future of the Underdeveloped Countries* (1954), p. 20.

[3] Res. 48(I), Dec. 11, 1946.

[4] Res. 58(I), Dec. 14, 1946.

material, services, and technical assistance."[5] The establishment of UNICEF as an operational arm of the United Nations, not financed from the regular budget of the Organization, provided further precedents for the arrangements later made in connection with the Expanded Programme of Technical Assistance.

In another of its decisions, the General Assembly at its first session, took direct note of a special problem of the underdeveloped countries. It observed that all Members of the United Nations were not equally developed and that some were in need of expert advice on methods of meeting the requirements connected with economic development.[6] It called upon the Economic and Social Council to study the means by which such advice in the economic, social, and cultural fields could be provided to Members desiring it.

Prior to this, the Council had already assigned to its Economic and Employment Commission responsibility for "the promotion of economic development and progress with special regard to the problems of the less developed areas."[7] Under the Economic and Employment Commission, a Subcommission on Economic Development had been established to "study and advise the Commission on the principles and problems of long-term economic development, with particular reference to the inadequately developed parts of the world."[8] In deference to the widespread identification of industrialization with progress and power, the terms of reference of the Subcommission on Economic Development included the function of "studying the effects of industrialization and changes of a technological order upon the world economic situation."[9]

By the time the Council met in 1947, it had before it the observations of three of its commissions (Economic and Employment, Social, and Population), as well as a note from the Secretary-General. Out of these came an instruction from the Council to the Secretary-General to establish machinery within the Secretariat for helping Member governments through experts, research facilities, and other resources that the United Nations and the specialized agencies might make available, including the dispatch of teams of experts to study specific problems of underdeveloped countries.[10] This action provided the

[5] Res. 57(I), Dec. 11, 1946.

[6] Res. 52(I), Dec. 14, 1946.

[7] U.N. Economic and Social Council, First Year, Second Session, *Official Records*, p. 392.

[8] Res. 1(III), Oct. 1, 1946.

[9] *Ibid.*

[10] Res. 51(IV), Mar. 28, 1947.

necessary legal authority for the mission to Haiti that the Secretary-General organized in 1948, and it served to put the United Nations actively into the business of providing technical assistance in the whole field of economic development rather than solely in respect of social welfare services.

Subcommission on Economic Development

During the remainder of 1947 and throughout 1948, United Nations organs continued to accumulate information on the economic and social situation of underdeveloped countries, the specific needs of those areas, and the manner in which the burgeoning international machinery might help meet such needs. Although the Social Commission in the summer of 1947 discussed the special needs of underdeveloped countries in the field of social welfare, the Subcommission on Economic Development continued to think of development in economic and political terms. Its first report was in harmony with sentiments then prevalent in underdeveloped countries.[11] It stressed the importance of political independence and of freedom from foreign interference. It expressed the view that economic development must be thought of largely in terms of industrialization. "While economic development cannot be treated as identical with industrialization and due importance should be attached to agriculture in national development, it is nevertheless true that industrialization forms the decisive element of economic development."[12] It called for diversified economies, including diversification of the export trade of raw material exporters.

Touching on a theme that was to become familiar, the subcommission reported that recent rises in the prices of capital goods and transport services had greatly complicated the task of economic development. It therefore recommended a careful study of relative trends in the prices of capital goods and of primary products.[13] It advocated greater financial assistance, the provision of technical assistance on a broader scale, and a series of domestic actions by the underdeveloped countries, including the establishment of machinery for surveying their resources,

[11] U.N. Economic and Employment Commission, Subcommission on Economic Development, *Report—First Session—17 November to 16 December 1947*, Doc. E/CN 1/47 (Dec. 18, 1947).

[12] *Ibid.*, p. 11. Reservations regarding the word "decisive" were later expressed at the Economic and Employment Commission by the representatives of Belgium, Canada, France, the United Kingdom, and the United States, but not by representatives of the less developed nations.

[13] *Ibid.*, p. 22.

the setting up of targets and goals of economic development, and the examination of specified economic obstacles to more rapid advancement.

At its next session (June 1948), the subcommission examined in detail the types of technical assistance available through the United Nations system. A majority of the members, moreover, emphasized the need for special budgetary appropriations enabling the Secretary-General to provide technical assistance in larger measure.[14]

Technical Assistance for Economic Development

At the regional level, the establishment in 1947 of the Economic Commission for Asia and the Far East (ECAFE) had provided the underdeveloped countries for the first time with a United Nations forum of their own. During its first two years, ECAFE issued its first economic survey of the region,[15] and gathered material for its second survey. Its reports helped to reveal the dearth of basic statistical data on the situation and progress of the Asian region.

In the Caribbean area, the Secretary-General responded, in the summer of 1948, to the request of the Government of Haiti for a team to assist in planning the economic development of the country. Teams of a more specialized character had been sent to other countries, most notably by the Food and Agriculture Organization (FAO), the International Labour Organisation (ILO), and the International Bank for Reconstruction and Development (IBRD). But the mission to Haiti was a more comprehensive undertaking involving the United Nations Organization, the World Health Organization (WHO), the United Nations Educational, Scientific and Cultural Organization (UNESCO), the International Monetary Fund (IMF), and the FAO in a joint effort that demonstrated both the feasibility and the utility of such interagency co-operation.[16]

Thus, by the time the General Assembly convened in late 1948, the the United Nations was engaged at all levels in furnishing technical assistance to underdeveloped countries, but without any specific budget

[14] U.N. Economic and Employment Commission, Subcommission on Economic Development, *Report—Second Session—14 June to 29 June 1948*, Doc. E/CN.1/61 (July 1, 1948), p. 17.

[15] U.N. Secretariat, Department of Economic Affairs, Economic Commission for Asia and the Far East, *Economic Survey of Asia and the Far East* (1947).

[16] U.N. Mission of Technical Assistance to the Republic of Haiti, *Mission to Haiti* (July 1949).

for the purpose. Principles and policies to govern the administration of technical assistance had been recommended by the Subcommission on Economic Development, an organ comprised of experts, but had not yet been reviewed by governmental representatives. Without waiting, however, for the reactions of intermediate levels, the General Assembly adopted a resolution introduced by Burma, Chile, Egypt, and Peru instituting a program of technical assistance for economic development, appropriating a small sum—$288,000—for the first year of the program, and making the Economic and Social Council responsible for reviewing the program at regular intervals.[17] The four types of assistance in which considerable experience had already been accumulated were, so to speak, legitimized. The Secretary-General, on the request of Member governments and in co-operation with the specialized agencies, was authorized to:

1. Arrange for the organization of international teams of experts to advise governments on their economic development programs;

2. Arrange for facilities for the training abroad through fellowships of experts from underdeveloped countries;

3. Arrange for the training of local technicians within the underdeveloped countries.

4. Provide facilities to assist governments in obtaining technical personnel, equipment, and supplies, and organize other services, such as seminars and exchanges of information, that would promote economic development.

In a separate resolution adopted on the same day, the Assembly—to help overcome the shortage of qualified officials in underdeveloped countries—authorized the Secretary-General to make arrangements for the establishment of an International Center for Training in Public Administration.[18] Moreover, the Assembly gave a rationale for the assumption by the United Nations of greater obligations on behalf of the underdeveloped nations.[19] It stated that the low standard of living in underdeveloped countries had "bad economic and social effects" on the world as a whole and created conditions of instability that could prejudice "peaceful and friendly relations among nations." It reminded Member governments that the Charter had bound them to promote higher standards of living. It therefore recommended "further and urgent consideration" by the Council and the specialized agencies

[17] Res. 200(III), Dec. 4, 1948.
[18] Res. 246(III), Dec. 4, 1948.
[19] Res. 198(III), Dec. 4, 1948.

of all aspects of the problem of economic development in underdeveloped countries.

Activities of the Specialized Agencies, 1946–49

In the specialized agencies during the years 1946–49, as in the United Nations Organization, the problems of the underdeveloped countries became matters to be reckoned with by the international community, and experimental efforts were made—largely through technical cooperation and technical assistance—to meet the needs that were daily becoming more apparent. Africa on the whole remained a dark continent, but the problems of Asia and Latin America began to assume more precise outlines.

Technical Missions and Surveys

In 1946, the most obvious need was for increased food supplies. The rendering of technical assistance in the field of agriculture was not controversial during the early postwar years, and the FAO could pioneer, at the international level, in this type of activity.[20]

> Both the acquisition and the dissemination of technical knowledge must be reckoned more difficult in agriculture than in industry. As to acquisition . . . , industry has got itself organized into units large enough and rich enough to sponsor research from its own resources, whereas there are few farmers operating on a scale enabling them to contemplate anything of the kind. . . . As to the dissemination of knowledge, this too is more difficult in agriculture. So much of industry is built in large units which either carry on their own research or have on their staffs men whose job it is to keep informed of technical developments in the relevant field and who have the training to apply them to the needs of their firm. Farms are quite different from firms.
>
> . . . The organization and financing of agricultural research has from the outset been a function of governments, supplemented of recent years by the useful research programmes of the industries manufacturing farm requisites. Governments, in countries where they can afford it, also have established extension or advisory services, whose staffs bring to farmers the practical application of the findings of the research workers. Expensive though this may be,

[20] In fact, the Constitution of the FAO, Art. 1(3) makes it a function of the Organization "to furnish such technical assistance as governments may request," and "to organize, in cooperation with the governments concerned, such missions as may be needed to assist them to fulfill the obligations arising from their acceptance of the recommendations of the United Nations Conference on Food and Agriculture" held in 1943 at Hot Springs, Virginia. Food and Agriculture Organization, *Constitution* (1945).

it has been found the most effective way of speeding technical progress among the hundreds of thousands of small-scale producers.[21]

The less fortunate nations were aided by the FAO in numerous ways. A mission of twelve experts was sent to Greece during 1946 to study agriculture, fisheries, and related activities. Illustrative of the catholic nature of the interests of the FAO as well as the inherent difficulty in segregating its work from other economic activities, the report emphasized that agricultural development could not occur without parallel developments in other sectors. Its eighty-nine recommendations therefore dealt with industrialization, taxation, and public administration, as well as with irrigation and more narrowly agricultural issues.[22] By the close of 1948, the FAO had sent missions also to Poland, Thailand, and Venezuela and individual experts to a number of other countries.[23]

The organization of field missions was likewise an important activity of other specialized agencies during this period. An official summary of measures devised by the United Nations and the specialized agencies for promoting the development of underdeveloped countries classified such measures in the following order: (1) technical missions and the provision of individual experts; (2) other technical advice and assistance, including research; (3) international conferences, committees, and seminars; (4) technical training and fellowships; (5) equipment and supplies; (6) loans; and (7) other financial assistance.[24]

The ILO, which had sent missions to a number of the Latin American countries between 1936 and 1946, greatly extended this work and in the process, accumulated information on conditions of employment, training problems, and training facilities in Asia and the Far East as well as in Latin America. It was also active in assisting governments in drafting social security plans appropriate to their different structures and stages of economic development.

In the field of health, the furnishing of technical assistance to governments was authorized by the constitution of the World Health Organi-

21 Food and Agriculture Organization, *So Bold An Aim—Ten Years of International Cooperation Toward Freedom From Want* (1955), pp. 20–21.

22 Food and Agriculture Organization, *Report of the FAO Mission for Greece* (March 1947).

23 For additional information on the efforts of the FAO to alleviate the postwar world food shortage, to obtain a better long-term balance between demand and supply, and to improve standards of nutrition, see above, Chaps. II, IV, V, and VII.

24 U.N. Secretary-General, *Measures Devised by the Economic and Social Council and the Specialized Agencies to Promote Economic Development and Raise Standards of Living of Underdeveloped Countries*, Doc. E/1345 (May 25, 1949), pp. 1–2.

zation. Pending the establishment of WHO, the advisory services of UNRRA were continued by the Interim Commission of the World Health Organization. With residual funds from UNRRA, a broad international program of medical missions, visiting lecturers, and fellowships was financed. Programs for strengthening national and local health services, and for controlling malaria, tuberculosis, and venereal diseases received major attention.[25]

The International Bank alone among the specialized agencies expressed skepticism about the value of technical aid. In reply to an inquiry from the Secretary-General of the United Nations, the Bank in mid-1947 reported that it had received no requests for technical assistance as such and, in any event, neither had nor expected to have the staff to provide technical advice and assistance on a wide scale. It opposed adoption by the Economic and Social Council of a comprehensive policy on the granting of technical advice on the ground that the Council had insufficient experience to determine either the type of assistance required or the manner in which it should be rendered.

The Bank felt that a technical mission to aid a government in taking a census, or technical assistance in combating a contagious disease, was quite different from a technical mission to prepare a comprehensive reconstruction or development program. The recommendations of a mission with respect to reconstruction or development would normally be regarded as having the official sponsorship of the international agency or agencies that sent the mission. If the recommendations were then approved by the government concerned, the sponsoring international agency and related agencies would be under some obligation to carry them out. Because most of the projects recommended by field missions were likely to require financial aid, the Bank would be the agency most likely to be embarrassed by the situation.[26]

In November and December 1948, however, the President of the International Bank himself visited a number of Latin American countries. Out of these visits, and other negotiations, came the arrangements for a series of missions to survey development potentialities and financial requirements, and a new appreciation by the Bank of the value of this form of aid. The nations in question were, of course, more eager for loans than surveys. Nevertheless, the series of country surveys

[25] See above, Chap. VII.

[26] U.N. Economic and Social Council, *Expert Assistance to Member Governments—Addendum to Interim Note by the Secretary-General*, Doc. E/471/Add. 2 (July 29, 1947), pp. 25–27.

begun by the Bank during this period helped to bring development planning out of the clouds and to translate ardent aspirations into integrated investment programs.

Other Forms of Aid

Like the country mission, the international conference, during the years from 1946 to 1949, became a popular technique for meeting special problems of underdeveloped countries. Europe and North America lost their monopoly as hosts for international conferences, and the convening of sessions in underdeveloped countries became common. Cairo, Istanbul, Kandy, Montevideo, Nairobi, and New Delhi joined London, Paris, Geneva, and New York as potential sites for international gatherings.

Supplementing missions, conferences, and fellowships were diverse other technical services of value to underdeveloped countries. The ILO established an Asian Field Office on Technical Training. UNESCO helped a group of governments conduct intensive campaigns in fundamental education. The International Civil Aviation Organization (ICAO) installed technical staffs at a series of regional offices to advise and assist member states in carrying out the standards and practices recommended by the organization to meet the needs of the rapidly growing aviation industry. The International Monetary Fund prepared a study of banking and financial institutions in Chile, Egypt, and Mexico for the consideration of those governments and of the Subcommission on Economic Development.[27]

Although there were numerous instances of informal collaboration among specialized agencies, and between the agencies and United Nations organs, each agency moved ahead, on the whole, in its own way, in its own field. There was as yet little co-ordinated effort directed toward the development and execution of balanced country programs.

The provision of equipment and supplies, a major activity under UNRRA, dwindled to almost nothing. Hybrid corn seed, as well as samples of other types of seed, were distributed by the FAO, some books and scientific apparatus by UNESCO, and a small amount of medical literature by WHO. UNICEF, then an emergency activity, and the International Refugee Organization were, to be sure, dispens-

[27] U.N. Secretary-General, *Measures Devised by the Economic and Social Council and the Specialized Agencies to Promote Economic Development and Raise Standards of Living of Underdeveloped Countries*, Doc. E/1345 (May 25, 1949), pp. 29–50.

ing relief in considerable volume but their activities were confined primarily to Europe.

The high hopes of underdeveloped countries for loans from the International Bank were not realized during the first three years of the operations of the Bank.[28] In contrast to its lending of nearly $500 million to European nations for reconstruction purposes before the close of 1948, the IBRD had by then loaned only $16 million for development. This sum, borrowed by Chile, in March 1948, for electric power and agricultural development, was to be increased, in January 1949, by a loan of $75 million to Brazil and $34.1 million to Mexico, both for electric power development. Nevertheless, to the underdeveloped countries, the Bank seemed overly interested in establishing its credit in the private investment market in New York and insufficiently sensitive to the requirements and potentialities of the underdeveloped countries. Their sense of frustration was plainly evident at the General Assembly in 1948, although transformed in the Assembly resolution on economic development to a polite hope that the IBRD would take "immediate steps to adopt all reasonable measures to facilitate the early realization of development loans, particularly in areas economically underdeveloped."[29]

The situation of the United Nations system, in so far as its handling of the problems of the underdeveloped countries was concerned, appeared at the end of 1948 to be as follows:

1. As the problems of war-devastated Europe were overcome or moved outside the framework of the United Nations, the special problems of the underdeveloped countries filled the incipient vacuum both in the United Nations itself and in the related world-wide agencies.

2. The most generally recognized problem was the need for expert advice, for demonstrations of new techniques, for scholarships and training facilities, for technical literature, and statistical data. Budgetary limitations precluded meeting this need on more than a token scale, but the potentialities of technical assistance were revealed and a "regular" program of technical assistance for economic development was inaugurated in 1948.

3. By and large, development was envisaged as an economic problem. The introduction of new seed strains and fertilizers, better equipment and machinery, power plants and transportation systems was expected to

[28] See above, Chap. IV.
[29] Res. 198(III), Dec. 4, 1948.

lead to higher trade and higher incomes. Campaigns to reduce disease and illiteracy were initiated, but there was little appreciation, particularly in the underdeveloped countries, of the extent to which advancement was impeded by other social obstacles—by antiquated systems of land tenure, immobility of the labor force, veneration of custom and tradition, inability of the individual to participate in decision-making, and absence of entrepreneurial talents.

4. There was a tendency to think of development as synonymous with industrialization. Disappointment was voiced because capital was not forthcoming in larger volume to build the steel mills and mammoth manufacturing plants that the underdeveloped countries hoped to establish.

5. The International Bank, lacking adequately prepared loan applications from underdeveloped countries, was unwilling to commit substantial resources to projects in those areas. It was, however, developing an appreciation of their problems, building a staff to cope with them, and acquiring a reputation for soundness among potential providers of capital in the industrialized nations.

Expanded Programme of Technical Assistance

On January 20, 1949, President Truman included in his Inaugural Address as Point IV, a call for a "bold new program" to assist the underdeveloped nations of the world. He urged that it be undertaken as "a co-operative enterprise in which all nations work together through the United Nations and its specialized agencies wherever practicable."[30]

The prospect of an expanded program of technical assistance fired the imagination and evoked the enthusiasm not only of government officials but of peoples as well. Part of this great enthusiasm, which was as widespread and genuine among would-be donors as among prospective recipients, may have been due to the fact that the program lacked precise definition and so carried the promise of bringing with it all desired things. Although apparently involving only the transfer of know-how, not supplies and equipment, it seemed to the underdeveloped countries to presage a marshaling for their benefit of the resources of the richest country in the world, with its unparalleled record of successful accomplishment. To the underdeveloped countries, it appeared that they might at last become the focus of an international effort

[30] *Congressional Record*, Vol. 95, Pt. 1, 81 Cong. 1 sess., p. 478.

destined to continue until their standards of living approached those of the more developed areas.

In preparation for the proposed larger role of the United Nations in the field of economic development, the Economic and Social Council early in 1949—on the initiative of the United States delegation—asked the Secretary-General, in consultation with the specialized agencies, to formulate "a comprehensive plan for an expanded co-operative programme of technical assistance for economic development through the United Nations and its specialized agencies, paying due attention to questions of a social nature which directly condition economic development."[31] Differences of opinion promptly arose between the United Nations Organization and the specialized agencies regarding the method of financing.[32] The desires of the agencies for autonomy ran counter to the desires of the Secretary-General for tighter co-ordination and more unified control. The compromise solutions to this problem of administrative co-ordination that were adopted by the Economic and Social Council and the General Assembly favored the specialized agencies during the early years of the program but later strengthened and clarified the role of the United Nations. These have been described elsewhere in this series.[33] In addition, technical assistance projects in various functional fields have been analyzed.[34] The scope, significance, and the limitations of the program as a whole, however, have not yet been dealt with, and are therefore analyzed below.

Secretary-General's Proposals

In his proposals for an expanded program of technical assistance, the Secretary-General reminded the Economic and Social Council that the concept of economic development was not subject to precise definition. Development was a continuing process nowhere complete and nowhere totally absent. It involved not only economic but also social change, and the two were closely related. The Secretary-General warned that

[31] Res. 180(VIII), Mar. 4, 1949.

[32] United Nations, *Technical Assistance for Economic Development: Plan for an Expanded Co-operative Programme through the United Nations and the Specialized Agencies*, Doc. E/1327/Add. 1 (May 1949), p. 40. See also letter of transmittal from Secretary-General to the President of the Council quoted in U.N. General Assembly, Fourth Session, *Official Records*, Supplement No. 3, "Report of the Economic and Social Council Covering the Period from 30 August 1948 to 15 August 1949," p. 16.

[33] See the volume in this Brookings series, *The United Nations and Promotion of the General Welfare*, Part One.

[34] See above, Chaps. IV–IX.

the character of the development of a country must be determined by the inhabitants of the country itself, that it could not be patterned solely on the experience of other more developed countries, and that development programs must be carried on primarily with local capital and resources, including human resources.

Social change would result from economic change, and social impediments would to some extent inhibit economic change. Difficult problems of personal adjustment would arise. The magnitude of the social problems was thus more clearly appreciated in this report from the Secretary-General than in any earlier studies prepared by the United Nations. In addition, proposals were made regarding sectors in which work might be undertaken, the forms that assistance might assume, and the methods of organizing and financing the program.

The cost of the expanded program proposed by the Secretary-General in 1949 would have approximated $36 million during the first year and $50 million during the second. In practice, the maximum amount obligated during any one of the first six years proved to be $26 million.

Action by Economic and Social Council

Following extensive discussion of the Secretary-General's report, the Economic and Social Council—in high hopes—adopted a monumental resolution on technical assistance.[35] The resolution recommended the organization of a Technical Assistance Board and a Technical Assistance Committee; called for a conference at which all Members of the United Nations and all other governments belonging to any specialized agency participating in the program could pledge contributions to the new, expanded program; proposed an allocation of funds among the participating organizations; and included basic observations and guiding principles to govern the program. These principles still rule. They fall into five major categories: those of a general nature; those governing standards of work and personnel; the participation of requesting governments; the co-ordination of effort; and the selection of projects.

The most important general principle was that the primary objective of participating organizations should be to help underdeveloped countries strengthen their national economies. This was to be accomplished

[35] Res. 222(IX), Aug. 14 and 15, 1949; subsequently approved unanimously by the General Assembly in Res. 304(IV), Nov. 16, 1949.

through the development of their industries and agriculture, with a view to promoting their economic and political independence in the spirit of the Charter of the United Nations, and to ensuring the attainment of higher levels of economic and social welfare for their entire populations. Distinctions arising from the political structure of the country requesting assistance, or from the race or religion of its population, were to be avoided. The kinds of services rendered to a country were to be decided by the government concerned, and aid was to be given only to or through governments. Although the strengthening of national economies was an objective that could conflict with, as well as contribute to, the development of a better-balanced and more integrated international economy, it was here assumed to be a prerequisite for world development along desirable lines.

The principles governing standards of work and personnel were designed to help obtain employees of the highest professional competence and personal integrity. It was recommended that, in addition, the experts be chosen "for their sympathetic understanding of the cultural backgrounds and specific needs of the countries to be assisted and for their capacity to adapt methods of work to local conditions."[36] The standards to be observed by participating governments were intended to ensure that such governments would provide essential information, would give proper consideration to advice received, would contribute at least those project costs payable in local currency, and would progressively assume greater financial responsibility for projects initiated with help from abroad.

In indicating criteria to govern the selection of projects, the Economic and Social Council followed the Secretary-General's advice in placing social objectives on a par with economic goals. "The services envisaged should aim at increased productivity of material and human resources and a wide and equitable distribution of the benefits of such increased productivity, so as to contribute to the realization of higher standards of living for the entire populations."[37]

Although technical assistance had been a feature of international co-operation from the beginning, the launching of the Expanded Programme gave it a new significance. The rendering of technical assistance now became a major operational activity, the first such function to be undertaken by the United Nations Organization as a long-term assign-

[36] Res. 222A(IX), Aug. 14 and 15, 1949, Annex I—Standards of Work and Personnel, para. 2.

[37] *Ibid.*, Selection of Projects, para. 1.

ment. Designed to help meet the most generally recognized special problem of the underdeveloped countries—the lack of knowledge permitting them to break through their circle of poverty, dependence, and stagnation—the program gave a fresh priority and importance to raising living standards where they were lowest. It added a new dimension to the work of the United Nations—the ability to get to the grass roots and to shape assistance to the specific needs of an area.

The inauguration of the Expanded Programme provided a unique opportunity for co-ordinating the activities of the United Nations and the specialized agencies. Similarly, it provided an opportunity to fuse the economic and social aims of the United Nations system, bringing both to bear in a co-ordinated manner on the problems of particular areas. Initially conceived as a method of imparting to the underdeveloped countries knowledge and experience gained in the highly developed countries, it soon revealed also the great possibilities of mutual aid among underdeveloped countries. Experts from intermediate and underdeveloped countries often proved better equipped to assist in other underdeveloped lands than their professional colleagues in the most advanced nations.

The Expanded Programme of Technical Assistance has to date passed through three main stages: an initial period of preparation, which lasted until the end of 1951; a period of acceleration, characteristic of 1952; and what might be termed a period of consolidation, from 1953 to the present. In a sense, of course, all such divisions are misleading, for the entire life of the program has been a period of "preparation," a planting of seeds whose fruits are yet to ripen.

Launching the Expanded Programme

As a result of the Technical Assistance Conference, which met in New York in June 1950, fifty-four nations subscribed approximately $20 million to cover operations for the eighteen-month period ending December 31, 1951. The United States pledged 60 per cent of the total. Although the amount thus obtained greatly disappointed those who had been inclined to think of a "bold new program" in terms of the magnitude of UNRRA or the European Recovery Program, the $20 million available for the Expanded Programme of Technical Assistance proved more than adequate for the first eighteen months.

The approval of projects and recruiting of experts progressed slowly. Nevertheless, during the period covered by the initial contribution, nearly eight hundred experts were recruited from sixty-one countries and sent to seventy-five different countries and territories. More than eight hundred recipients of fellowships, from eighty-six countries and territories, were sent to study in forty-five host countries.

A second technical assistance conference held in Paris in February 1952 resulted in pledges equivalent to approximately $19 million for the calendar year 1952. The third pledging conference set a precedent in that it was convened before the beginning of the financial year during which the contributions were to be used. This tended to ease programing considerably. For 1953, sixty-nine governments pledged the equivalent of $22.4 million. By the end of December 1953, however, the cumulative total of unpaid pledges amounted to over $4.5 million. Although these arrearages were to a large extent made good during 1954, the actual amount obtained during the first four years hardly exceeded the amount proposed by the Secretary-General for the initial twenty-four months, and the boundless hopes of the underdeveloped countries had to be scaled down sharply.

Whereas the underdeveloped countries had little question that a massive concentration of resources on their special problems was the most important economic and social function of the United Nations, the more restrained views of the developed countries were revealed by the modesty of their contributions. Nevertheless, in the absence of comparable achievements in other fields, the developed countries participated in inflating the significance of technical assistance, and in justifying the United Nations to the public in terms of this phase of its work. There was a tendency on the part of the more developed nations to feel that with technical assistance initiated and seemingly successful, they could in good conscience fend off mounting pressures for further aid to the underdeveloped countries.

In the first stages of EPTA, the lack of adequate planning on the part of many of the underdeveloped countries was reflected in a rash of ill-considered and ill-defined requests for assistance. Pressures for speedy action and dramatic results led to approval of a number of projects that, in retrospect, were not in accord with recognized needs and might well have been delayed until the receiving countries had reached a higher level of development—if not longer.

There was a struggle among specialized agencies, and between the specialized agencies and the United Nations Organization, for autonomy in programing, for the right to meet requests for project assistance, and for prestige within the program. The struggle extended beyond the confines of the United Nations system to include competing bilateral programs, particularly that of the United States, whose new bilateral Point IV Program was becoming embroiled in very similar difficulties.

In the absence of integrated national plans for economic development, the government agencies within a given country, which had established relationships with particular intergovernmental agencies, made requests to those agencies for assistance. Such requests, if not in conflict with requests being made from other local sources, were inadequately related to them. This, plus the desire to obtain the best possible bargain in an atmosphere of competition among the specialized agencies and between the United Nations and bilateral programs, resulted in the same or similar requests for assistance being made of different United Nations programs and of multilateral and bilateral programs alike.

Among the underdeveloped nations, there was considerable disappointment not only with the volume of aid offered and the slowness with which it was made available, but also with the kind of aid given. In the zeal of the receiving nations for rapid and wholesale industrialization, the appearance of an expert instead of an industrial plant was a blow in itself. To policy makers in underdeveloped countries not accustomed to the need for assembling all the available facts before taking action, and impatient to see final results, the arrival and departure of experts on assignments of three-to-six months and the subsequent receipt of assessments and recommendations—difficult to read and more difficult to understand—seemed a bitter anticlimax.

From the viewpoint of the United Nations, time had to be spent to set in motion the machinery of a technical assistance program, and too many of the projects submitted by requesting governments had to be rejected or delayed because of inability to locate experts, or because of the vagueness or even the absurdity of the request. Frequently, the United Nations agencies, nonplussed by what to do about an especially vague request, took the simplest course and sent an expert or two to make a survey.

Before the first eighteen months had ended, however, many of the more important problems were in process of solution. The competition among participating agencies—which threatened to atomize any efforts to establish integrated and well-rounded policies for national development within the receiving countries—had begun to yield to order. Information on requests received began to be exchanged within the United Nations system and between the United Nations and the bilateral programs. The requests received from the underdeveloped nations improved and were scrutinized more carefully under the aegis of the Technical Assistance Board.

Acceleration During 1952

Whereas the United Nations found it difficult, during the first year and a half of operations, to identify enough suitable projects to obligate the sums available for technical assistance purposes, the situation was reversed by the end of 1952. During 1952, the program moved forward at an increasingly high rate of speed. During most of 1952, however, the United Nations continued to allocate its funds on a functional basis, to agriculture, to health, to education, and so on, rather than on a country basis.

The United States, in connection with its own Point IV Program, had struggled earlier with similar efforts by government departments to exercise autonomous control of projects in their respective fields, and to program Point IV funds on a functional basis. The United States had early centralized responsibility for the major part of its program in the Technical Cooperation Administration, and by the middle of 1951, was programing its funds on an individual country basis, with financial and project targets set by the national programs of the host countries.

A similar evolution toward more centralized responsibility for program approval having occurred in the United Nations, its programing, during the latter half of 1952, also began to follow the more logical country-planning technique. To facilitate country programing, the United Nations Technical Assistance Board established, in the more important countries, the office of Resident Representative, with responsibility for co-ordinating the activities of the various participating agencies in the host country, stimulating necessary planning by local authorities, and assisting in the formulation of requests. Although co-ordination continued to be a problem, and the arrival of resident representatives in the field offered no guarantee of co-operative relations among the international agencies, the climate improved, and attention could be shifted from co-ordination within the family of the United Nations to co-ordination with parallel technical assistance programs.

The problem of relating multilateral and bilateral projects within an individual country was not too difficult. There was, however, keen competition for the limited number of experts available for overseas duty, and some competition for the right to meet requests. This problem was, for a time, especially troublesome in the relations between the programs of the United Nations and those of the United States, although the latter, by adopting, in 1953, the stringent rules and time-consuming security requirements governing United States nationals employed in both multilateral and bilateral activities, made the competition for available Americans distinctly less brisk.

More basic problems confronted the United Nations in carrying on its program during the period of "acceleration." One of the obstacles in this effort to promote and encourage long-range economic growth was the absence of a relevant theory and a body of reliable data on the co-operative process in promoting economic development. Experts knew only dimly the key factors to consider, how they must be interrelated, or the art of relating them to the peculiar economic, social, and political conditions prevailing in a particular nation at a given time. Whereas in the beginning it was the economist who was consulted for guidance in planning programs of technical assistance, the attempts to execute programs in relatively unknown societies had revealed complexities, rigidities, and unities that underscored the usefulness of the social scientist with broader training. In the evolution of a theory of economic growth, more attention began to be given particularly to the findings of the cultural anthropologists.

More adequate and more clearly-defined projects resulted in the selection of experts more likely to achieve success. Many requesting governments became less rigid in demanding the world's best malariologist, port engineer, and agronomist, and some became willing to accept less well-known and younger specialists. At the same time, however, the requesting governments remained prone to see, in the renown of the experts nominated to assist them, evidence of the esteem with which they were regarded by their fellow Members in the United Nations.

Consolidation of Activities

During the period of consolidation, which began in 1953, programing continued to be hampered because a number of pledges, including the all-important contribution of the United States, were paid late in the period for which they were intended, after the close of the period, or not at all. Those paid in inconvertible currencies were, of course, of limited usefulness. The result was that, despite the rising trend in total pledges, there was a slight drop in 1953 in obligations incurred, as compared with 1952, and a further fairly substantial decline in 1954 as compared with 1953.[38]

Some projects consequently had to be curtailed, postponed, or withdrawn entirely. For this purpose, an interim program review was undertaken and, in a number of cases, a better use of resources was achieved in 1953. This tightening up, however, came hard on the heels of a deterioration in the economic condition of many underdeveloped countries as a result of the collapse in raw material prices. In the year 1954, although the number of contributing governments and the amount of their pledges were greater than ever before, the timing of payments on pledges was such that "a considerable slowing down in the tempo of operation" occurred.[39] A sharp increase raised expenditures to record levels in 1955, however.

During the period 1953–54, the limits of technical assistance as a motivator of more rapid development were more clearly revealed, the gap between needs and resources seemed to be widening, and the demand for grant aid grew more insistent. From this point forward, the technical assistance program, in the thinking of participating governments, tended to fall into place as a highly desirable activity, of greatest importance during the earliest stages of economic development but of decidedly lesser significance thereafter in relation to requirements for capital and equipment. Even so, the program remained exceedingly popular. By mid-1953, it no longer seemed feasible to the Soviet Union to ignore it while at the same time professing an interest in the welfare of the peoples in underdeveloped countries. Therefore, the Soviet Union and Poland, with some fanfare, announced their intention to contribute to the program.

The decision of members of the Soviet bloc to share in the program did not materially increase the total resources available. The total amounts pledged, by the United States, and by all contributors combined, the total contributions paid, and the unpaid balances as of December 31, 1955, for the first five financial periods are shown in the accompanying table, in United States dollar equivalents. It should be borne in mind, of course, that contributions to the EPTA constitute a very incomplete measure of the total resources that the United

[38] Total obligations incurred were as follows: $6,436,251 (1950–51); $22,968,129 (1952); $22,810,400 (1953); $19,464,742 (1954). See U.N. Economic and Social Council, Twentieth Session, *Official Records*, Supplement No. 4, "Seventh Report of the Technical Assistance Board" (1955), p. 32. (Hereinafter cited as "Seventh Report of the Technical Assistance Board.")

[39] *Ibid.*, p. 1.

EXPANDED PROGRAMME OF TECHNICAL ASSISTANCE: PLEDGES AND CONTRIBUTIONS, 1950–55[a]
(U.S. dollar equivalents—in thousands)

	1950–51	1952	1953	1954	1955	Total 1950–55
Number of countries pledged	54	65	69	74	71	—
Amount pledged by the United States	$12,008	$11,400	$12,767	$13,862	$15,000	$ 65,037
Total amount pledged	20,036	18,797	22,321	25,021	27,883	114,058
Amount paid during period:						
July 1950–Dec. 1951	$17,354	$ 5	—	—	—	$ 17,359
Jan. 1952–Dec. 1952	2,381	16,206	—	—	—	18,587
Jan. 1953–Dec. 1953	151	1,581	$18,939	—	—	20,671
Jan. 1954–Dec. 1954	51	953	3,197	$24,416	$ 100	28,717
Jan. 1955–Dec. 1955	—	—	32	394	25,147	25,573
Total	$19,937	$18,745	$22,168	$24,810	$25,247	$110,907
Balance unpaid, Dec. 31, 1955	$ 99	$ 52	$ 153	$ 211	$ 2,636	$ 3,151

[a] Source: U.N. Economic and Social Council, Twenty-second Session, *Official Records*, Supplement No. 5, "Eighth Report of the Technical Assistance Board" (1956), pp. 75, 87; U.N. Economic and Social Council, Twentieth Session *Official Records*, Supplement No. 4, "Seventh Report of the Technical Assistance Board" (1955), p. 268.

Nations system devotes to technical assistance; much of the international co-operation financed under the regular budgets of the participating agencies is essentially technical assistance.

The technical assistance program that has emerged after several years of experimentation and trial and error contains at least a little of something for everyone. Among the participating agencies, FAO has received the most funds, with the United Nations, WHO, UNESCO, ILO, and ICAO following in the order mentioned.[40] The International Telecommunication Union (ITU) and the World Meteorological Organization (WMO) round out the list, but have received only small amounts. Regionally, Asia and the Far East regularly account for more than 30 per cent of so-called direct project costs, Latin America for more than 25 per cent, and the Middle East for more than 20 per cent.[41]

Regardless of the form in which technical assistance has been provided, its ultimate objective has been the same. Through a better utilization of human and material resources at all levels and stages, it has sought to obtain greater output from industry and agriculture; more adequate health, education, and welfare facilities; improved trans-

[40] Within the United Nations, the organizational unit receiving the funds has been the United Nations Technical Assistance Administration (UNTAA), established by the Secretary-General in July 1950.

[41] For details concerning direct project costs by region and by agency, see "Seventh Report of the Technical Assistance Board," p. 21.

portation and communication; more efficient public services; and a generally higher level of individual welfare. There has, however, been a shift away from survey and study to direct participation by the international expert in development projects, public administration, and training activities. Concurrently, there has been a movement away from *ad hoc* requests on the part of a country to a series of interrelated projects and a tendency to replace individual experts with teams of specialists, both at the survey and the active stage. The number of experts and fellowships in the field of public administration has risen steadily. In all of the technical assistance work, there has been a growing emphasis on training, and this is regarded by the United Nations as "perhaps the most important and, indeed, the most encouraging development in recent years."[42]

Among the noteworthy programs not previously analyzed in the present study are the efforts of the United Nations system to promote land reform along democratic lines, to develop "productivity-consciousness" in industry, to improve public administration locally and nationally, and to encourage programs of community development.

Land Reform

Land reform has been a controversial issue. It was not solely or even primarily for the purpose of enlarging agricultural output in underdeveloped areas that the United States introduced the land reform problem at top levels of the United Nations in 1950 and 1951. There were likewise compelling political and social reasons for bringing this issue to the fore. The effect of a democratically conceived and democratically executed program of land reform on the dignity, self-respect, and self-reliance of millions of individual farmers could, the United States believed, be even more electric than the effect on their productivity and output.

[42] These main trends are noted in: U.N. Technical Assistance Committee, *The Expanded Programme of Technical Assistance: A Forward Look*, Report of the Technical Assistance Board with the Comments thereon of the Administrative Committee on Coordination, Doc. E/2885, E/TAC/49 (May 11, 1956), pp. 16–19. As an example of a series of interrelated projects, the review cites the assistance provided by the FAO to Brazil for the development of the forest resources of the Amazon basin. The first year was spent largely on an aerial survey of the area. In the second and third years, help was given in the establishment of mechanical logging and sawmilling demonstration centers. With a number of Brazilians trained in methods of utilizing forest resources, collaboration in the establishment of a pulp and paper factory has become possible.

As far back as 1943, the United Nations Food and Agriculture Conference at Hot Springs had recommended that each nation study the land tenure system and other agricultural conditions within its boundaries and ascertain whether changes were needed to promote the productivity and efficiency of agriculture and the welfare of agricultural workers. The new permanent organization (FAO) was to give every assistance in such studies. In general, the governments of underdeveloped countries were slow to respond to this invitation.

The representatives of underdeveloped countries in United Nations forums were often themselves owners of large estates or allied with such owners. They preferred to use international machinery for ventilating their needs for external aid. So long as they were petitioning for grants and loans, they could be certain of backing from their home governments and support from other underdeveloped countries. On land reform, they might be on the defensive, compelled to explain why they had progressed so little.

Under the United States occupation authorities, far-reaching land reform programs had been introduced in Japan and South Korea. The United States Secretary of State could therefore speak with authority at the 1950 session of the General Assembly when he took the lead in urging the United Nations to adopt programs for aiding the landless to become land owners. He was in tune with the aspirations of the people in underdeveloped countries, although not in every case with the governments of the moment; he was resuming the initiative exercised by the United States in the early years of the United Nations; and he was addressing himself to a fundamental economic and social problem.

The General Assembly asked the Secretary-General, in co-operation with the FAO and other specialized agencies, to prepare, for the session of the Economic and Social Council to be held in the summer of 1951, an analysis of the degree to which unsatisfactory forms of agrarian structure, particularly systems of land tenure in underdeveloped areas, impeded development and depressed standards of living.[43] Accordingly, the Secretary-General presented to the thirteenth session of the Council a report, which—like many other documents published by the United Nations—had been given a deceptively ponderous title, *Defects in Agrarian Structure as Obstacles to Economic Development.* It discussed for different areas, conditions of tenancy, size of farms, access to credit facilities, and arrangements regarding legal title and water rights. It

[43] Res. 401 (V), Nov. 20, 1950.

showed that interest rates paid by those who worked the land ranged from 20 to 100 per cent per year; that rental charges ran as high as 80 per cent of the annual crops; that land reform was not necessarily a matter of breaking up large estates but frequently a problem of consolidating fragmentary holdings into economic units.

There was a lively contest between the delegates of the United States and Poland for the opportunity to speak first on land reform. Resolutions on the subject had been introduced by both delegations. Over strong protests from Poland, the President of the Council ruled in favor of the United States. The ensuing United States statement again firmly equated land reform with a wide range of measures for improving the social and economic institutions connected with farm life. Land reform, said the United States delegate, should mean either the redistribution or the consolidation of holdings into farms of an efficient size; the reduction of unreasonable rental charges; the provision of security of tenure for the tenant; the improvement of working conditions for farm laborers; the supplying of agricultural credit on reasonable terms; the formation of voluntary co-operative societies for purchasing and marketing purposes; and the establishment of rural industries. Land reform should be regarded as an instrument for ensuring human dignity and social justice, and for easing social and political tensions, which might otherwise give rise to destructive violence.

The Soviet bloc accused the United States of insincerity, and espoused its own brand of land reform. Underdeveloped countries explained what their governments were doing. The final resolution, adopted by the Council with no dissent but with abstentions by the Soviet bloc, recognized that no simple nostrum was applicable.[44] It requested the Secretary-General to keep the problem under review, to give it high priority in the technical assistance program, to obtain comprehensive data from governments at least once every three years on progress made, and to keep the United Nations informed.

The FAO Conference approved an implementation program including further studies and a series of regional seminars, as well as assistance to individual governments. At its sixth session in 1952, the General Assembly approved the program undertaken. The regional seminars were serious meetings, remarkably free of propaganda overtones. Some of the headway made by individual countries in the past few years has doubtless been due to the discussions in the United Nations and specialized agencies. The prestige of local groups favoring action has been

[44] Res. 370(XIII), Sept. 7, 1951.

enhanced, and some general guidelines have been given to them. In Italy, Iran, Egypt, India, the Philippines, Taiwan, and many other areas, programs have been initiated or speeded up.

Productivity and Industrialization

Like the land reform problem, the productivity issue was introduced at the General Assembly and the Economic and Social Council by the United States. In the case of land reform, however, the Americans were riding a wave that had been gathering force for many years. In the case of productivity, they were trying to expand a ripple into a wave. Both issues were raised at a time of mounting pressure for grant aid, and both pointed to courses of action whereby the less advanced countries could make significant progress via the self-help and technical assistance routes.

The word "productivity" had only recently become popular outside the United States. Following the publicity given to the reports of the Anglo-American Council on Productivity in the early postwar years, productivity teams from other European nations visited the United States. The Organization for European Economic Cooperation (OEEC) began backing productivity campaigns, sponsoring productivity centers, and trying, with some success, to make workers and management productivity conscious. The sponsors of similar activity by the United Nations wanted to extend the effort to other areas of the world.

A beginning in this direction had already been made by the International Labour Office whose Director-General had included in his annual report in 1950 an excellent discussion of the need for and the obstacles to more rapid improvements in the productivity of labor.[45] This was followed by additional discussion in the 1951 report, referral of the matter to the various industrial committees of the ILO, the issuance of a series of reports by the committees, and the devotion of technical assistance funds to productivity projects in a number of countries.[46]

Although measurements and comparisons of productivity are diffi-

[45] See International Labour Conference, Thirty-third Session, *Report of the Director-General* (1950), Chap. III, "The Productivity of Labour."

[46] International Labour Organisation, *Productivity in Coal Mines* (May 1951); *Factors Affecting Productivity in the Metal Trades* (1952); and International Labour Office, *Practical Methods of Increasing Productivity in Manufacturing Industries*, Conclusion of a Meeting of Experts Communicated to the International Labour Conference at its Thirty-sixth Session as a Supplement to the Report of the Director-General (1953).

cult, the underlying concept, as used in the United Nations, is simple enough: productivity means the output of goods and services for a given input of labor. The special twist given to the concept in the OEEC and the United Nations during the early 1950's was the emphasis on an equitable sharing of the fruits of increases in industrial productivity by the workers, the owners, and the consumers. The theory was that industrial workers would resist change if they felt that the only result would be greater profits for owners. On the other hand, they might welcome change and create a climate hospitable to continuous productivity improvements if they could expect to share in the benefits and look forward to owning more of the things they produced.

Following the pattern developed in connection with land reform, the General Assembly, in January 1952, asked the Economic and Social Council

> (a) To study the varying ways in which the productivity of peoples everywhere can be increased by the application of existing scientific and technological knowledge; (b) To recommend . . . methods by which the results of the studies undertaken . . . can be made available to the under-developed countries at their request; (c) To report to the General Assembly at its seventh [next] regular session on the progress made. . . .[47]

The Secretary-General furnished the Council a working paper, prepared by an American expert, describing briefly the various national campaigns to raise productivity and suggesting areas for further study. The International Labour Organisation presented an additional paper summarizing its activities in the field of productivity, particularly its concern with vocational training, industrial safety, the difficult problems involved in the measurement and international comparison of productivity, and the linking of productivity efforts with an equitable sharing of the gains.

The discussion at the Economic and Social Council was rather perfunctory. The Council recommended that governments consider problems of raising productivity, establish national productivity centers where appropriate, and employ technical assistance to further their efforts.[48] The emphasis on an equitable sharing of the benefits declined, and the productivity campaign became part of the general drive of the underdeveloped countries for more rapid industrialization.

The development of a more efficient agriculture requires the transfer of large numbers of people to other occupations. Some of these can be

[47] Res. 522(VI), Jan. 12, 1952.
[48] Res. 416E(XIV), July 10, 1952.

absorbed in service activities, but many should and will move into industry. Although the underdeveloped countries have been inclined to underestimate the obstacles to rapid industrialization and to overestimate the benefits of large-scale production where there is no mass market, a substantial increase in industrialization is inevitable if the hoped for increases in real income per capita are to be realized. The widespread belief that economically advanced nations oppose industrial development in hitherto underdeveloped areas because of fears of competition from the emerging societies is not substantiated by the records of the Expanded Programme. The percentage of aid devoted to industrial development has been small, but the United Nations has assisted in establishing plants for manufacturing DDT, penicillin, surgical instruments, fertilizers, and building materials; it has helped establish cooperatives, and it has provided numerous other services to industry. In Egypt, Israel, India, and Pakistan, productivity institutes have been set up, and throughout the world nearly 1,000 engineers, foremen, and skilled workers have been trained on projects conducted within the framework of EPTA.[49]

The relatively small proportion of technical assistance devoted to industrial development is probably a reflection of two conditions. In the first place, for countries in the preindustrial phase of development, there are other fields in which technical assistance is likely to be more urgent and of greater immediate benefit. In the second place, to the extent that industry in underdeveloped countries is in the hands of private entrepreneurs, it lies outside the direct range of aid provided to or through governments.[50]

The expansion of industrial output is, of course, heavily dependent on the development of basic facilities in power, transportation, and communications. In the development of these large-scale economic overhead projects, it is to the International Bank rather than the technical assistance program that the underdeveloped countries have turned for help. The technical assistance program has, however, made it possible to supply experts to help with initial surveys of land, water,

[49] U.N. Economic and Social Council, Twenty-second Session, *Official Records*, Supplement No. 5, "Eighth Report of the Technical Assistance Board" (1956), p. 2. See also U.N. Secretariat, Economic Commission for Latin America, *International Co-operation in a Latin American Development Policy*, Chap. III, "Increased Productivity and Technical Assistance Policy," Doc. E/CN.12/359 (September 1954).

[50] U.N. Secretariat, Department of Economic and Social Affairs, *Processes and Problems of Industrialization in Under-Developed Countries* (1955), p. 98. (Hereinafter cited as *Processes and Problems of Industrialization.*)

and mineral resources; with structural designs and layout; with installation and maintenance of hydroelectric and irrigation equipment; planning and management of low-cost housing; and with facilities and opportunities for training the lock operators, cablemen, hydrographic engineers, and area planners needed in programs that require financial support from elsewhere for completion.

Public Administration

Related to industrialization, to land reform, and to numerous other problems of the underdeveloped countries is the inadequacy of their governmental and administrative services.

> The public administration of most underdeveloped countries faces two major problems to which we ought constantly to address ourselves: (1) there is a historic distrust of governmental institutions despite a growing dependence upon government, and consequently there is a widespread evasion of administrative authority; (2) a great burden of governmental formalism often paralyzes administrative action.
>
> The first problem—the tendency toward popular evasion of administrative authority—arises, in part, from the regressive distribution of governmental benefits and burdens between the many poor and the few opulent which typifies underdeveloped societies. This distribution raises delicate internal questions which international public administration experts can approach only indirectly.
>
> The second difficulty of public administration in underdeveloped countries—the traditional emphasis on administrative formalities—can be dealt with more directly. The elaborate administrative formality of under-developed countries comes as a surprise to those who expect overly elaborate procedures to be a characteristic of mature rather than immature public administration. The fact is that underdeveloped countries often suffer from too much, not too little, of the "mechanics" of administration. . . .[51]

Although each of the specialized agencies has been concerned with improving the level of public service in its sector, the over-all improvement and development of public administration as such has been the concern of UNTAA. It has been estimated that some 10 per cent to 15 per cent of the experts assigned by the United Nations and the specialized agencies since 1952 have been working in the field of public administration, strictly defined.[52]

The program had its origin in discussions at the Economic and Social

[51] Albert Lepawsky, "Technical Assistance: A Challenge to Public Administration," *Public Administration Review*, Vol. XVI, No. 1 (Winter 1956), p. 22.

[52] *Ibid.*, p. 25. The estimate is based on a classification in terms of actual project content instead of formal project title.

Council in early 1948.[53] Later in the year, the creation of an international center for training in public administration was discussed at some length by the Fifth (Administrative and Budgetary) Committee of the General Assembly. Objections to the proposal were based primarily on financial grounds, but also on grounds that such a program might be outside the scope of the United Nations and that the training of civil servants was the responsibility of national governments. Supporters stressed the need to help underdeveloped countries overcome the shortage of trained civil servants.[54] Finally, the committee, by a narrow margin, decided to recommend a draft resolution, which the General Assembly then adopted without change. The resolution stated that "an International Centre for Training in Public Administration shall be established under the direction of the United Nations."[55]

The idea of a major International Centre in the sense of an institute or group of institutes was, however, gradually abandoned. The "Centre" became the name for a program of technical assistance in the field of public administration, including some financial support for the International Institute for Administrative Sciences in Brussels, for the preparation of documentation in various languages on different aspects of public administration. In 1950, the term "programme" replaced the term "international centre" and a resolution was adopted by the Economic and Social Council recommending that "additional activities undertaken in the field of training in public administration . . . should be considered under the Expanded Programme for Technical Assistance."[56]

Under UNTAA, several regional and national training centers have been established. Among them are a regional School of Public Administration in Rio de Janeiro; a Public Administration Institute for Turkey and the Middle East in Ankara; a National Institute of Public Administration in Cairo; an Advanced School of Public Administration for Central America in Costa Rica; and a training course for government accountants in Libya.[57] More unique, as an activity of the United Nations, is the public administration project undertaken in Bolivia.

[53] See Res. 132(VI), Feb. 24, 1948, "International Facilities for the Promotion of Training in Public Administration."

[54] U.N. Economic and Social Council, *International Facilities for the Promotion of Training in Public Administration*, Doc. E/1336 (May 18, 1949), pp. 4–5.

[55] Res. 246(III), Dec. 4, 1948.

[56] Res. 292(XI), July 5, 1950.

[57] U.N. Economic and Social Council, *Technical Assistance in Public Administration*, Report by the Secretary-General, Doc. E/2415 (May 1, 1953), p. 5.

An international team that surveyed Bolivia in 1950 made a number of recommendations for action on economic and social matters and, in addition, urged that high priority be given to the public administration of the country as a whole. From 1952 to 1953, six foreign experts were assigned to the Ministries of Agriculture, Finance, Labor, and Social Welfare, to the Central Bank, and to the Office of the Comptroller General, to serve as members of the Bolivian civil service in helping to improve the operations of the agencies in question. There cannot be many instances in which sovereign nations have invited and freely accepted from international agencies a comparable measure of intervention in their domestic affairs.

The arrangement had the advantage of placing United Nations experts in responsible working positions in key offices, but it had its disadvantages also. The responsibility of the foreign "civil servant" to the local supervisor was not sufficiently clear to protect the prestige or effectiveness of both or to ensure the adoption of the recommendations proposed. Nevertheless, this phase of the experiment was regarded as successful; the project was continued in 1954, but the foreign experts relinquished their administrative authority and began serving as technical consultants only.

Community Development

In the efforts of the United Nations to generate economic and social development along lines that correspond to the felt needs of the people and that tend to be cumulative and self-sustaining, community development programs—as they have come to be known—have grown increasingly important. They embrace the villages and rural areas in which 80 per cent of the people in underdeveloped countries dwell. In these areas, the presence of many more hands than are needed to reap the meager harvests, and the enforced idleness of all hands at certain seasons, combine to make underemployment chronic. The aim of community development programs is to release latent local leadership and to channel surplus local labor into projects considered urgent and useful by the local population, thus simultaneously strengthening the foundations of democracy and adding to the capital stock of underdeveloped countries.

The purpose is "not so much to remedy any particular situation or to promote public works for any immediate need as to start a chain reaction of discussion, organization, action, achievement and renewed discussion of the next phase in development. The connexion is close between community development and the evolution of democratic local government . . . once the emerging societies have reached a certain stage in their evolution towards self-expression and self-government, their activities, whether directed through government machinery, central or local, or through private societies, will cease to depend on persistent stimulation from without. They will tend to rely increasingly on the functioning of services established as a part of the framework of their local institutions."[58]

In the late 1940's, both the Social Commission and the Economic and Social Council attempted on various occasions to clarify the role that local communities might play in improving the welfare of their people. In 1951, the Council, acting on a recommendation of its Social Commission (which, in turn, had been prompted by the United States) asked the Secretary-General to compile "full documentation" on the varying objectives and scope of community welfare centers, the methods used in establishing and operating them, the success achieved, and the difficulties met.[59] The report was to be submitted to the Social Commission in order that the commission might, "if possible, determine some general principles which underlie successful techniques."[60]

This resulted in one of the most comprehensive fact-finding efforts undertaken by the United Nations. Before the close of 1954, thirty-four governments had submitted voluminous data on conditions in their territories. Missions, jointly staffed by the United Nations and the specialized agencies, made surveys of selected community development experiments in the Caribbean area, in the Middle East, and in South and Southeast Asia.[61] Fourteen country monographs were published and four study kits issued, all in a United Nations series on community organization and development.[62]

[58] U.N. General Assembly, Tenth Session, *Official Records*, Supplement No. 16, pp. 23–24. Quoted in Carnegie Endowment for International Peace, "Issues Before the Tenth General Assembly," *International Conciliation*, No. 504 (September 1955), pp. 84–85.

[59] Res. 390D(XIII), Aug. 9, 1951.

[60] *Ibid.*

[61] United Nations, *Report of the Mission on Rural Community Organization and Development in the Caribbean Area and Mexico*, Doc. ST/SOA/Ser.O/7, ST/TAA/Ser.D/7 (March 1953); United Nations, *Report of the Mission on Community Organization and Development in Selected Arab Countries of the Middle East*, Doc. ST/SOA/Ser.O/9, ST/TAA/Ser.D/9 (November 1953); United Nations, *Report of the Mission to Survey Community Development Projects in South and Southeast Asia*, Doc. ST/SOA/Ser. O/10, ST/TAA/Ser. D/10 (December 1953).

[62] For a list of publications in this series issued between Jan. 1, 1953 and July 15, 1955, see U.N. Secretariat, Bureau of Social Affairs, *Social Progress Through Community Development*, Doc. E/CN.5/303/Rev. 1 (1955), Annex II. (Hereinafter cited as *Progress Through Community Development.*)

The most recent report in the series makes it clear that the investigation went far beyond a study of "social welfare centers" as physical facilities. It included descriptive accounts of many types of community effort, including community schools and experiments in group living, and summaries of national community development programs. It reviewed the methods employed in various parts of the world at different stages of economic and social development; analyzed the interactions of self-help and external assistance, national and international; and concluded with a review of the need for and training of local leaders and auxiliary workers.

As part of the Secretary-General's inquiry, persistent efforts were made to arrive at a clearer definition of the subject under consideration. The earlier concept of "community centers"—with its connotation of buildings and grounds—was soon abandoned in favor of a broader definition intended to cover programs of rural reconstruction, village betterment, and mass education. Agreement was finally reached on the use of the terms "community organization" and/or "community development." More specifically:

> Community development can be tentatively defined as a process designed to create conditions of economic and social progress for the whole community with its active participation and the fullest possible reliance upon the community's initiative. "Community development" implies the integration of two sets of forces making for human welfare, neither of which can do the job alone: (i) The opportunity and capacity for cooperation, self-help, ability to assimilate and adapt new ways of living that is at least latent in every human group; and (ii) the fund of techniques and tools in every social and economic field, drawn from worldwide experience and now in use or available to national governments and agencies.[63]

Community development, in short, is a technique for obtaining popular participation in the planning and execution of local programs of improvement. The employees of national governments or international agencies may stimulate local action by providing knowledge of improved techniques and tools and by training village workers, but leadership from outside should not replace local initiative. Depending on the felt needs of the community, the starting point may be a health project or the digging of some irrigation ditches. This experience may lead to community action to establish a school, a rural co-operative, or a village industry. The order in which projects are undertaken is less im-

[63] *Ibid.*, p. 6.

portant than the creation of a community spirit that will induce sustained self-help.

In addition to a tentative definition, the Secretary-General provided a summary of community action programs in different countries.[64] He described community development via simple work projects of local significance in Greece; community development in connection with large irrigation projects, land reform and resettlement schemes in the Belgian Congo; community development built around agricultural extension services in Pakistan; the establishment of rural welfare centers in Egypt; the development of community education in Puerto Rico; and the work of the Mass Education Council in Burma.

The most ambitious programs have been developed in India.[65] They have their foundation in the evolution of the Gandhian philosophy and the concept of village life that the disciples of Gandhi attempted to implement in experiments dating back as much as thirty years. These early experiments were followed by other multipurpose projects organized on a larger territorial scale, and evolved into a national program under the first Five-Year Plan published in 1952. By 1956, under this plan, 120,000 villages and 74 million people, or about one quarter of the entire rural population of India, were to be brought gradually under the influence of the scheme. Under the second Five-Year Plan—*i.e.*, by 1961—the entire country is expected to be covered by the program.

The employment of technical assistance funds for the initiation and extension of community development programs has been encouraged by the principal organs of the United Nations. In 1953, as in 1952, the Economic and Social Council included in its program of concerted practical action in the social field the "promotion and implementation of community development projects."[66] At the same time, the Council authorized the Secretary-General

> . . . to convene one or more small groups of senior policy making representatives of governments having similar social and economic problems and of representatives of the Secretariats of the United Nations and the specialized agencies concerned, to plan concrete programs for expansion of community development projects, including training facilities and the strengthening of or-

[64] *Ibid.*, Chap. III.

[65] *Ibid.*, pp. 66–72. For an additional discussion of the program in India and its significance, see Chester Bowles, *Ambassador's Report* (1954), Chap. 14, "Community Development—A Key to Village India," pp. 195–214.

[66] Res. 496(XVI), July 31, 1953.

ganizations for administering social programs related to community development in their respective countries.[67]

The first such meeting was held in 1954 in the Philippines, a country with a good record in the use of schools as the focal point for community development. During 1953 and 1954, experts on community development were made available to Afghanistan, Haiti, Iraq, Pakistan, Paraguay, Peru, the Philippines, and Yugoslavia, with a number of the experts for other Asian countries drawn from India. Aid from foreign experts has been supplemented by the granting of fellowships and scholarships to local personnel for study abroad.

The possibility of making significant economic and social progress through local action at the village level appears to be catching the imagination of underdeveloped countries. Inasmuch as surplus labor is far more plentiful than surplus capital, and self-help must in any event be the foundation for continuing economic and social advances, the rapid spread of community development programs should be regarded as one of the most encouraging phenomena in the contemporary world. The unleashing of local initiative in all its diversity could prove to be among the strongest forces for the promotion of democracy.

General Appraisal

Considered as a whole, the complex, extensive United Nations program for fostering economic and social development through technical assistance has been beset with difficulties of programing and recruitment, administration, finance, and philosophy that are only slowly being overcome.

The most pervasive difficulty, perhaps, is the lack of adequate understanding of the general problem of economic growth and development, and of the specific problems of individual underdeveloped countries that have reached different stages of development. This deficiency, of which more will be said later, means that there is no satisfactory method of deciding which projects merit approval because they can contribute significantly to the development of an area, and which projects should be deferred or rejected because their contribution is unlikely to be significant. To date, technical assistance appears to have been more successful in propagating technology in the narrow sense—*e.g.*, knowledge concerning seeds, fertilizers, tractors, or textile produc-

[67] *Ibid.*

tion—than in introducing social or administrative change. Projects designed to institute land reform, to promote taxation in accordance with ability to pay, or to ensure that government contracts are let on the basis of competitive bidding, have been undertaken only on a modest scale by underdeveloped countries.

Most projects are planned for one, two, or three years in the hope that by the end of the period enough local personnel will have been trained to permit the withdrawal of foreign personnel and the take-over by nationals of the country aided. Whether this is a legitimate expectation obviously depends on the project and on the country; in many cases, it is patently over-optimistic. Moreover, there is the question whether supplying experts should permanently be separated from supplying equipment. The cost of foreign experts is, after all, one of the smallest costs in a development program. After the value of this type of service has been demonstrated for a few more years, it may not be unreasonable to ask the countries that want experts to assume the cost themselves, perhaps using the United Nations as the employment agency that would unearth and nominate qualified technicians for participating governments to hire. Moreover, if foreign financial assistance becomes available on a larger scale in the form of loans and grants and private investments, an increasing volume of technical assistance will be provided as an integral part of the larger package.

The resources of EPTA for the last several years have proved too limited to finance valid projects that could otherwise be undertaken. In addition, the program has suffered from other financial difficulties. The practice of obtaining contributions for only one year at a time makes it difficult to organize and staff many projects of longer duration. Annual programs have to be altered, curtailed, or canceled if the annual pledges are not fully paid, or are paid late in the period. During 1954, for example, only one third of the total amount pledged had been collected by June 30, and nearly half of the total was still outstanding at the beginning of the last quarter of the financial year.[68] In 1955, however, the Congress of the United States appropriated funds not only for the calendar year 1955 but also for 1956, thus putting the program on a more stable basis. Additional attempts have been made to ease some of the financial difficulties of the program—the establishment of a $12 million reserve fund is an example—but it is too early to report that the uncertainties of financing have been overcome.

[68] "Seventh Report of the Technical Assistance Board," p. 4.

The technical assistance effort has posed a number of other problems in the fields of personnel, programing, evaluation, and administration. As has been noted above, experts are recruited from all over the world, from the less developed as well as the more developed countries, and tensions have in some instances arisen because of the differing backgrounds of members of the same team of experts. Yet it is on the human beings associated with the field operations of the program that the success of the effort largely depends. Nominations are obtained on an unofficial basis from governments, from educational institutions, professional associations, charitable foundations, and other sources. They are not always made in the best interests of the program. There is the competing pressure of home requirements and interests, and a scarcity of qualified individuals willing or able to accept arduous foreign assignments. There is the tendency to release the man who can most easily be spared without handicapping the operation of the local laboratory or department. And there is a readiness to nominate the friend or relative of the minister or the university president. The great preponderance of experts, however, have been well qualified for their tasks. Moreover, the Technical Assistance Board has begun the practice of retaining on a long-term basis a few experts who have demonstrated their capacity and versatility in several assignments. This may presage the development of a career service within the United Nations for technical assistance personnel.

Perhaps the most important problem in programing is the formulation of criteria for evaluating results. This problem, like others in the field of technical assistance, is not confined to the multilateral programs. Results may be measured in simple quantitative terms where projects are intended to increase the area of land under cultivation or the output of refined sugar, bituminous coal, or rice; or to reduce the incidence of trachoma, industrial accidents, or illiteracy. But statistics concerning the number of persons engaged in village health work, the number of villages reached by community development programs, or the number of textbooks prepared locally are inadequate indicators of the effectiveness of projects having broad social objectives. Standards for measuring the value of the economist who helps frame a new tax law or the cultural anthropologist who helps draft a national development program that will properly respect the cultural heritage of the area are still more difficult to establish. It is significant that many activities initiated as technical assistance projects have been taken over on a permanent basis by host governments, that others have been continued as projects despite major changes in the complexion of the governments of the countries in which they have been located, and that governments in host countries have been willing to increase the value of their local contributions to the program.

Several international agencies, among them WHO, ILO, and UNESCO, have studied the problems of evaluating technical assistance. A seminar was organized by UNTAA at McGill University in Montreal to undertake a preliminary consideration of the problems involved in evaluating projects of UNTAA. The Technical Assistance Board (TAB) asked four economists who had had experience in various parts of the world to undertake a review of the activities proposed for 1953. After the program had been in operation for five years, the Administrative Committee on Coordination asked TAB to review the experience gained to date and to consider plans for the future development of the program. Completed by TAB in May 1956, this report provides valuable data on directions in which the program might grow if substantially greater resources become available.[69]

By an independent source, the Expanded Programme of Technical Assistance has been appraised succinctly, though necessarily inconclusively, as follows:

> Inevitably the strengths of the Programme are its very weakness. Because it embraces the nations of the world, it must operate in all fields and its work must spread, even if thinly, into the remotest corners. Because it is international, it can draw upon skills and experience everywhere, but the problems of selection are magnified by that very fact. Because the political import of its activities is great it cannot escape the consequences of political pressures. Because the needs are urgent and the scope unprecedented it must sometimes act by trial and error.
>
> Over and above the problems inherent in the form and content of its operations, there are financial questions. In terms of its objectives the Programme has had sorely inadequate funds and even these have not been guaranteed. At best it has only been able to be the "yeast in the dough" and for maximum effectiveness it has had to mesh its modest efforts into those of other foreign programs and of the recipient governments. "It would, therefore, be difficult to separate the results attributable to technical assistance from the total improvement made, even if the latter could be accurately measured."[70]

[69] U.N. Technical Assistance Committee, *The Expanded Programme of Technical Assistance: A Forward Look*, pp. 32–41.

[70] Carnegie Endowment for International Peace, "Issues Before the Tenth General Assembly," *International Conciliation*, No. 504 (September 1955), pp. 111–12. Quotations within the quotation are from "Seventh Report of the Technical Assistance Board," p. 7.

Beyond Technical Assistance

Technical assistance, in the view of the underdeveloped countries, is "not enough." Its major limitation, according to these countries, is that in the United Nations it is generally divorced from the provision of capital. Some capital needs are being met through the International Bank and other channels, but many are not. Where development is already being impeded by a shortage of capital, additional technical assistance may even aggravate the situation by enlarging the unsatisfied demand for improvements that are costly.

That technical assistance is a limited approach to the complex problem of stimulating economic growth has long been conceded by the Economic and Social Council. The lengthy resolution on technical assistance adopted by the Council in 1949 recognized the necessity also for "an expanded rate of international capital flow."[71] This formulation caused no difficulty because it did not specify whether the expansion should take the form of loans, grants, or private investment. Since the launching of the technical assistance program, the major drive of the underdeveloped countries at the Economic and Social Council and at the General Assembly has been to establish new international machinery for collecting and distributing aid in the form of grants and long-term, low-interest loans.

Over this proposal the nations of the world have been sharply divided. The underdeveloped countries, almost without exception, have believed that shortage of capital was the major impediment to their more rapid development, that such development would clearly serve the best interests of the international community as a whole, and that new avenues to capital for development purposes should therefore be opened. The developed countries have questioned whether shortage of capital was the barrier it was purported to be and whether, in any event, the remedy was to provide it in the form of internationally administered grant aid.

The more rigid positions initially assumed in the debates, largely on political grounds, have become somewhat less doctrinaire—partly in response to changes in the political climate, but partly, too, as deeper insights into the nature of the development process have been gained. Recent analysis seems to indicate that "pure" technical assistance is most valuable during the earliest stages of development. As primitive societies become ready for the installation of basic power, transporta-

[71] Res. 222D(IX), Aug. 14, 1949.

tion, health, and educational facilities, foreign loans and grants become increasingly important. Private investment is most likely to flow at the next stage of development, after completion of the so-called economic and social overhead projects. To this emerging understanding of the nature of the development process, the United Nations has made some noteworthy contributions.

Understanding the Process of Economic Growth

Perhaps the first major contribution from a United Nations source to an understanding of the institutional framework required for development came in 1951 with the publication of a highly controversial report, to which references have been made earlier in this volume, recommending national and international measures for the economic development of underdeveloped countries.[72] The experts responsible for the preparation of the report clearly saw the revolutionary implications of a sharp acceleration in the rate of development.

> There is a sense in which rapid economic progress is impossible without painful readjustments. Ancient philosophies have to be scrapped; old institutions have to disintegrate; bonds of caste, creed and race have to be burst; and large numbers of people who cannot keep up with progress have to have their expectations of a comfortable life frustrated. Very few communities are willing to pay the full price of rapid economic progress.
>
> In our judgment, there are a number of under-developed countries where the concentration of economic and political power in the hands of a small class, whose main interest is the preservation of its own wealth and privileges, rules out the prospect of much economic progress until a social revolution has effected a shift in the distribution of income and power.
>
> There cannot be rapid economic progress unless the leaders of a country at all levels—politicians, teachers, engineers, business leaders, trade unionists, priests, journalists—desire economic progress for the country, and are willing to pay its price, which is the creation of a society from which economic, political and social privileges have been eliminated. On the other hand, given leadership and the public will to advance, all problems of economic development are soluble.[73]

[72] U.N. Secretariat, Department of Economic Affairs, *Measures for the Economic Development of Under-Developed Countries*, Report by a Group of Experts appointed by the Secretary-General of the United Nations (May 1951). (Hereinafter cited as *Measures for Economic Development.*) The experts were Alberto Baltra Cortez of Chile, D. R. Gadgil of India, George Hakim of Lebanon, W. Arthur Lewis of the United Kingdom, and Theodore W. Schultz of the United States. For earlier references to this study, see above, Chaps. IV and VII.

[73] *Ibid.*, pp. 15–16. In the view of the French delegation, "the experts had compiled a document in which technical considerations played their part, but which

In their analysis of the "pre-conditions of economic development"—from which the above quotation is taken—the experts stressed that economic progress would not occur in the absence of an atmosphere favorable to it. An experimental and scientific attitude was, therefore, the first pre-condition they mentioned.

In underdeveloped societies, acceptance of the *status quo* might be due, in the opinion of the experts, to the prevalence of an other-worldly philosophy that discouraged material wants. Alternatively, people might be unwilling to make the effort to produce wealth if the social prestige they desired were more easily obtained in other ways—through the acquisition of military skill, or the skill of the lawyer or priest. Men, moreover, would be unwilling to strive for progress where they could not secure the fruits of their efforts. In some societies, the techniques and rituals of agriculture were prescribed by law, and an innovator would be committing sacrilege. In societies stratified by caste, color, or creed, whole sections of the population were being deprived by the social system of the opportunity to contribute to a rising national income. Rapid economic progress was seldom found in societies lacking vertical social mobility.[74]

Thus, at its outset, the report of the experts sought to focus attention on the critical social and political factors that tended to prevent or retard economic progress in the underdeveloped countries. This portion of the analysis, despite its trenchancy, was generally welcomed.[75] Since 1951, the literature on economic development—both inside and outside the United Nations—has devoted vastly more attention to the deeply rooted institutional obstacles to development.

The main body of the report of the experts was given over to a summary of measures, national and international, that might be taken to accelerate development. The numerous concrete recommendations for national action to promote development tended, however, to be lost sight of in the consideration of the report by the Economic and Social Council in 1951, when attention was focused almost exclusively on the proposal for an International Development Authority to make grants-

---

appeared, in more than one respect, to be little more than a manifesto. It seemed, indeed, like a sign of the times—men of science venturing to encroach on the field of political action." U.N. Economic and Social Council, Thirteenth Session, *Official Records*, 502nd Meeting (Aug. 15, 1951), p. 201.

[74] *Measures for Economic Development*, pp. 13–16.

[75] For a highly critical review, however, see S. Herbert Frankel, "United Nations Primer for Development," *The Quarterly Journal of Economics*, Vol. LXVI, No. 3 (August 1952).

in-aid and on the dubious estimates of the amounts of foreign capital required by the underdeveloped countries. In retrospect, it would appear nevertheless that the more permanent contribution of the report was its discussion of the nature of the development process and the domestic actions required to initiate and encourage it.

Following the clarion call of the experts, all levels of the United Nations became involved in more searching consideration of the factors that encourage and discourage economic growth. Although the debates at the Economic and Social Council and the General Assembly continued to center around the desire of the underdeveloped countries for new international institutions to step up the flow of foreign capital, many other problems were actively and usefully explored. Economic analysis of a high order, for example, was provided by the staff of the Economic Commission for Europe in its examination of the problems of the underdeveloped regions of southern Europe.[76] Similarly, the Economic Commission for Latin America (ECLA) provided valuable current data and theoretical analyses of the development process in Central and South America.[77] The problems of Asia and the Far East were analyzed maturely and incisively at a Working Party on Economic Development and Planning that met under the auspices of the ECAFE in November 1955.[78]

Drawing on such of the foregoing source material as was available at the time and many other sources as well, the Department of Economic and Social Affairs of the United Nations Secretariat, in late 1954, issued an analysis of the process of industrialization and economic growth generally in underdeveloped countries that represented another long step forward.[79] The report as a whole was written in the Economic Development Branch of the Bureau of Economic Affairs but was circulated to outside experts in a number of countries for comment and criti-

[76] U.N. Economic Commission for Europe, *Economic Survey of Europe in 1953*, Doc. E/ECE/174 (1954).

[77] *Cf.* U.N. Economic Commission for Latin America, *Economic Survey of Latin America, 1951–1952*, Doc. E/CN.12/291/Rev. 2 (1953); *Economic Survey of Latin America, 1953*, Doc. E/CN.12/358 (1954); *International Co-operation in a Latin-American Development Policy*, Doc.E/CN.12/359 (1954); *Analyses and Projections of Economic Development*, Doc.E/CN.12/363 (1955).

[78] United Nations, "Economic Development and Planning in Asia and the Far East," *Economic Bulletin for Asia and the Far East*, Vol. VI, No. 3 (November 1955).

[79] U.N. Secretariat, Department of Economic and Social Affairs, *Processes and Problems of Industrialization in Under-Developed Countries* (1955). Prepared in response to Res. 461(XV), Apr. 23, 1953, of the Economic and Social Council, which included in paragraph 3 authority for the Secretary-General to consult with experts in making the study.

cism before publication. This combination of reliance on permanent staff and *ad hoc* consultants proved fruitful: the result was a judicious, penetrating statement of the nature of the industrialization process, the obstacles to industrialization, the domestic and international measures conducive to it, and the implications of industrialization. By emphasizing and illustrating the interdependence of progress in industry, agriculture, transportation, and education, the report gave new content to the oft-used but ill-understood term "balanced" or "integrated" development.

Further insights are being gained through the establishment, within the framework of the United Nations, of centers for study and training in problems of economic development. One of the first such programs was initiated jointly by the Economic Commission for Latin America and the United Nations Technical Assistance Administration in 1952. It is designed primarily to train economists who will be capable of integrating the recommendations of technical specialists into realistic development programs. Each trainee spends approximately eight months in study and work at the site of the commission in Santiago, Chile. By July 1955, fifteen of the twenty Latin American republics had on duty one or more officials trained under the program. Despite some doubts whether governments were making full use of the trainees, the results to date are regarded as encouraging.[80]

Serving a wider geographic area than the Latin American program, and aimed at a more senior level of civil servants, is the Economic Development Institute organized in Washington, D.C. by the International Bank, with financial assistance from the Rockefeller and Ford Foundations. The Institute maintains a small, full-time staff to plan and lead discussions and seminars designed to increase "the number of trained administrators skilled in dealing with problems of economic policy and with the planning and administration of development programs."[81] The first group of government officials began their six-month course of studies in January 1956.

Institutes such as the two mentioned above, supplementing the practical experience being gained every day by policy makers and research personnel in underdeveloped countries, are resulting in more sophisti-

[80] See U.N. Economic Commission for Latin America, Sixth Session, *Report on ECLA/TAA Economic Development Training Programme*, Doc. E/CN.12/376 (July 30, 1955).

[81] International Bank for Reconstruction and Development, *Economic Development Institute, Prospectus* (September 1955), p. 3.

cated national development programs than the series issued during the early postwar years. The initial plans were often hardly more than announcements of goals. Certain of their features were intensely nationalistic and the content of industrialization proposals, in particular, tended to be determined more by notions of what would enhance the prestige of the government than by realistic analysis of resources and requirements.

The current national development programs, like their predecessors, start from the assumption that some governmental intervention in the economic process is necessary. Allowing natural forces to determine the pace of development will not produce a rate of progress that is politically tolerable, if indeed it results in any progress at all. Present plans differ considerably, however, both from their predecessors and from each other, in their views of the points at which governmental intervention is most appropriate, the nature of the intervention, and the timing most likely to induce in orderly fashion the myriad changes in social structure, motivation, and standards of value that lie at the heart of economic development.[82]

The transformation of a static, primitive society into a modern nation, it is now clear, is a slow, uneven process, which cannot be achieved merely by exhortation or the injection of capital.

> Economic development is a whole complex of interdependent changes manifested simultaneously in the physical environment (new roads, buildings, harbors, machines, implements, chemicals), in the forms of association by which men live and work (growth of cities, changes in government, factory organization, business corporations, banking, readjustments in land tenure, family practices, even religion), and in the skills, habits, and thought patterns of millions of individuals (literacy, technical specializations, respect for scientific methods, ambition, the idea of progress). To pick out any one aspect of this interdependent complex and center attention on it involves a considerable danger of wrong analysis, out of which ineffective or even harmful policies may spring. If we must simplify, we are least likely to go wrong when we think of economic development as a massive problem in human education and social readjustment and only secondarily a problem in equipment.[83]

Within the framework of the Colombo Plan, the programs of certain Asian nations are from time to time subjected to constructive outside scrutiny, and opportunities are provided for co-ordinating offers of foreign assistance. Within the United Nations system, there is no organ or

[82] *Cf.* U.N. Secretariat, Department of Economic and Social Affairs, *United Nations Studies of the Technique of Economic Planning in Underdeveloped Countries*, Doc. RS/Conf. 7/4 (Dec. 21, 1955).

[83] Staley, *op. cit.*, pp. 202–03.

agency responsible for receiving and analyzing national development plans as they are issued by governments; for maintaining current records regarding their fulfillment; or for co-ordinating domestic, bilateral, and multilateral efforts to stimulate growth in a given area.

Drive for Grant Aid

Despite a heightened awareness of the need for basic changes throughout the fabric of their societies, the underdeveloped countries, in the principal organs of the United Nations, have concentrated since 1950 on their need for capital from abroad. In the eyes of the majority of its Members, the United Nations system remains ill-equipped to stimulate development precisely where help is most needed: namely, financing the non-self-liquidating projects that constitute economic and social overhead capital. The missing component, in their view, is machinery for collecting and distributing assistance in the form of grants and long-term, low-interest loans. Since 1950, the major economic battles at the Economic and Social Council and the General Assembly have been fought on this issue.

The basic arguments have remained unchanged as the debates waged in the early years at the Subcommission on Economic Development and the Economic and Employment Commission have moved through the Economic Committee of the Economic and Social Council, the Council itself, the Economic and Financial Committee of the General Assembly, and the Assembly in plenary meeting. Each organ has tended to ignore the work of subsidiary organs and to confuse two separable issues: the volume of aid available or likely to become available, and the machinery for distributing such aid. The General Assembly, where emotions have been highest and where the underdeveloped countries have the strongest voice, has insisted on steady movement in the direction of establishing a grant agency under United Nations auspices, and has been most ingenious in devising means for keeping the issue in the foreground at successive sessions.

Chile, India, and Yugoslavia have been the leading proponents for the early establishment of a grant agency. They have had the solid support of underdeveloped countries, including some that are more likely to be net contributors to than beneficiaries of a grant program, plus support from a growing number of the more industrialized nations. The United States, on whom the major financial burden would fall, has led the opposition but has been increasingly isolated.

The arguments of the underdeveloped countries have been simple and moving. Living standards in two thirds of the world are intolerably low. Poverty, famine, and disease exact a fearful toll. The toll is unnecessary and can no longer be borne with resignation. People everywhere are demanding a real improvement in their standards of living and a greater share in the benefits of modern industrial society. Their rightful aspirations must be satisfied, or world peace and stability will be in constant jeopardy. Without a foundation of economic security, the superstructure of military pacts and armaments rests on quicksand.

The gap in living standards between the have and have-not nations is said to be widening rather than narrowing. Some of the underdeveloped countries argue that the gap must be closed, *i.e.*, that growth rates must be more rapid in the underdeveloped than in the more developed economies. The majority concede that the fundamental problem is progress at the lower end of the scale regardless of the rate of improvement at the upper end. The requisite progress, they say, cannot be achieved with the resources at present available or likely to become available. The best solution for the problem is to finance the construction of basic educational, health, highway, and other noncommercial facilities by grant aid or by loans on especially easy terms, administered by a United Nations agency, which will ensure that "conditions" are not unilaterally imposed by donors or lenders.[84]

Proponents of a grant agency, moreover, claim that the benefits to industrialized nations in terms of increased trade and better international relations would far outweigh the costs, which would be small, both in relation to what such nations can afford and what they are already spending for other activities that are no more urgent than economic development. To these economic and political reasons, they add humanitarian reasons. In an interdependent world, the more fortunate cannot isolate themselves from the less fortunate and, in fact, have an obligation to help them. Some representatives of underdeveloped countries have claimed that the obligation is more direct: industrialized countries have exploited the underdeveloped countries in the past and should now repay their accumulated debts.

The task of replying to the underdeveloped countries has fallen primarily on the United States. It has stressed the availability of substantial unutilized lending capacity in both the International Bank and the

[84] Such loans—repayable in local currencies, or obtainable at rates of interest lower than those charged by the established international lending agencies or on the basis of more liberal provisions concerning amortization—have been referred to by the developed countries as "soft loans."

Export-Import Bank, and the fact that loans have been and can be made for non-self-liquidating projects. It has not denied the case for grant aid on a temporary basis in isolated instances but has questioned the desirability, in present circumstances, of establishing new United Nations machinery for the purpose. Grants-in-aid, the United States has said, should not be regarded as a normal feature of international economic co-operation. To the argument that it has granted many billions to the relatively rich continent of Europe through UNRRA and the Marshall Plan and therefore should be willing to assist the infinitely needier nations in other areas, the United States has replied that there is a vast difference between reconstruction and development. The restoration of war damage involved a short-term commitment of measurable dimensions; the raising of living standards in underdeveloped countries implies a long-term commitment of unforeseeable magnitude.

Moreover, the United States declared, it has in fact been making substantial grants to underdeveloped areas without the prodding of a new international agency. The prewar members of the Commonwealth of Nations have referred in similar terms to the contributions they and others make through the Colombo Plan and in other ways. To step up the level of aid would be impractical in the face of the financial claims of rearmament and existing commitments. To channel the same amount through a United Nations agency would not alter the rate of development but might raise serious political problems in donor countries. If real disarmament were achieved and mutual trust increased, the situation might be altered. Meanwhile the difficulties encountered in financing such modest undertakings as the Expanded Programme of Technical Assistance should give pause to those advocating more ambitious ventures.

Proposals During 1950-52

In early 1950, at the Subcommission on Economic Development, the United States was able to fend off endorsement of a proposal by the Indian expert for a United Nations Economic Development Administration. The Indian expert recognized that the United States was the only likely source of funds, and the subcommission reported that an agency financed primarily by a single government could not be truly international. Nevertheless, it urged the Economic and Social Council to consider the grant-aid problem.

The Council considered the matter at great length as part of the question of financing economic development. It adopted a carefully worded compromise resolution that avoided any direct mention of grant aid but nevertheless strengthened the hands of those who were advocating it.[85] The resolution "recognized" that the domestic financial resources of underdeveloped countries, plus available international capital, had not been "sufficient to assure the desired rate of economic development," and that development at the desired rate required "not only a more effective and sustained mobilization of domestic savings, but also an expanded and more stable flow of foreign capital investment." The resolution of the Council further recognized that the initiation of non-self-liquidating as well as self-liquidating projects was "justified." Inasmuch as no one maintained that it was "unjustified," the only object of the reference was to direct public attention to the category of project for which funds were proving most difficult to obtain. In the operative portion of its resolution, the Council did not ask the General Assembly for guidance, but recommended that a subsidiary organ—the Economic, Employment and Development Commission[86]—keep under review the problems involved in financing economic development, and from time to time make recommendations to the Council.

The General Assembly missed the hint from the Council on procedure, and expressed itself more categorically and more impatiently than the Council. It was "convinced" that the "needs" of the underdeveloped countries could not be met without an increased flow of public funds. It recommended that the Economic and Social Council consider "practical methods . . . for achieving the adequate expansion and steadier flow of foreign capital, both private and public, and pay special attention to the financing of non-self-liquidating projects which are basic to economic development." It requested the Council to submit its recommendations to the next session of the General Assembly.[87]

Notwithstanding the warnings of United States delegates at United Nations meetings, the hopes of the underdeveloped countries for an internationally administered grant-aid program were fed from other sources in the United States. The first of a series of postwar reports on United States foreign economic policy, prepared under the direction of a Special Assistant to the President, Gordon Gray, appeared while the General Assembly was debating the resolution quoted above.[88] This so-called Gray Report recommended United States grants for both

[85] Res. 294(XI), Aug. 12, 1950.

[86] Successor to the Economic and Employment Commission after abolition of the Subcommission on Economic Development in 1950.

[87] Res. 400(V), Nov. 20, 1950.

[88] Gordon Gray and Others, *Report to the President on Foreign Economic Policies* (1950).

technical assistance and economic development. A few months later, in March 1951, the United States International Development Advisory Board, under the chairmanship of Nelson Rockefeller, reported the existence of

> . . . many projects of basic importance to the development of underdeveloped countries that cannot be financed entirely on a loan basis. Our considered judgment is that *such public works can be most effectively financed and developed through a well-managed international agency*. . . . The Advisory Board recommends the prompt creation of a new International Development Authority in which all free nations will be invited to participate.[89]

It suggested that the new development authority be set up with total initial funds not to exceed a half billion dollars.

The same group of United Nations experts that had picked up from this report the idea for an International Finance Corporation also commended the proposal for an International Development Authority. On the basis of a series of highly debatable assumptions, the five experts appointed by the United Nations Secretary-General to prepare proposals for the Economic and Social Council on the economic development of underdeveloped countries concluded that a 2 per cent increase in per-capita national income would require an annual capital import into the underdeveloped countries well in excess of $10 billion for investment in industry and agriculture alone. If social overhead investment were included, the total would be much greater. About 80 per cent of the $10 billion, said the experts, would be needed for South Asia and the Far East. They urged that the United Nations establish an International Development Authority capable of making grants-in-aid in amounts that would increase rapidly up to a level of about $3 billion per year.[90] The magnitudes in which they discoursed caused alarm in the areas expected to export the capital. Moreover, the experts submitted virtually no evidence concerning the ability of underdeveloped countries to put large amounts of imported grant capital to effective use.[91]

The recommendation for an International Development Authority was debated by various bodies of the United Nations. The Economic,

[89] U.S. International Development Advisory Board, *Partners in Progress* (1951), pp. 72–73.

[90] *Measures for Economic Development*, pp. 75–80, 84–85.

[91] For a brief critique of the experts' estimates (as well as a lucid analysis of the whole problem of development financing) see "Financing Economic Development" by Benjamin Higgins and Wilfred Malenbaum, *International Conciliation* (March, 1955), especially pp. 291–92.

Employment and Development Commission concluded once more that it was not feasible to establish the proposed international agency because few countries would make substantial contributions. A minority however, supported a resolution inviting the General Assembly to establish the agency and endow it with authority to make both grants and long-term, low-interest loans. From 1951 to 1955, advocacy of grant aid was coupled in the United Nations with advocacy of soft loans. It is not clear whether the underdeveloped countries were genuinely convinced that loans on special terms were widely needed, whether they preferred such loans to grants, whether some, whose eligibility for grants might be dubious, wanted to ensure their entree to the agency, or whether the less developed nations simply assumed that the United States would be more receptive to a combination loan-grant agency than to a straight grant agency. Within the developed countries, many felt that the combination of business and charity involved in soft loans was more likely to exacerbate than to improve international relations, and that loans that are not loans should not be called loans.[92]

When the Economic and Social Council met in the summer of 1951, the proposal for an International Development Authority was hotly debated in the Economic Committee and in the plenary meetings of the Council. Although all members of the Council are represented on the Economic Committee, and although the Economic Committee had agreed, with only three abstentions and no dissents, to a long resolution, the Council in plenary meeting considered amendments to every paragraph of the committee text. The Council rejected a Chilean amendment that would have required it to prepare a blueprint for the

[92] "But the very fact that these loans are made on especially easy terms and are still called loans should make us suspicious. . . . In the end, although some loans will turn out well and will be repaid, others will bring in their train, first, severe strain on the economy of the borrower and, finally, default. When this happens, there is likely to be ill will, rational and irrational, on both sides. The lender will resent the default on a loan made in good faith, the borrower will resent the years lost in abortive struggle to maintain payment on a debt, which he probably regarded in the first instance more as a promise of prosperity than as a serious financial obligation. The effect of such defaults is to destroy credit generally and to wither the integrity of all orthodox lending. In my opinion, when a country has a choice between making grants or quasi-loans of this kind, it pays in the long run to choose grants." International Bank for Reconstruction and Development, Press Release No. 237, address of Eugene R. Black, President, to twelfth session of the Economic and Social Council, Mar. 6, 1951, p. 7. President Black's expression of preference, in certain circumstances, for grants marked the beginning of a change in the attitude of the Bank, which was confirmed at the next session of the General Assembly when he more explicitly endorsed internationally administered grant aid.

establishment, as soon as circumstances permit, of a special fund for grants-in-aid and long-term, low-interest loans, but accepted other amendments that went further in this direction than the resolution approved by the Economic Committee.[93]

The Chilean amendment, which the Council rejected in August 1951 by a vote of 10 to 1, with 7 abstentions,[94] was accepted by the General Assembly in January 1952. A spokesman for the United States delegation stressed his conviction as a member of the Congress that "the United States was not prepared to pledge itself to make a financial contribution . . . immediately or in the near future."[95] Other potential contributors expressed similar views. Nevertheless, the Second (Economic and Financial) Committee of the General Assembly, by a vote of 28 to 20, with 9 abstentions, sent to the Assembly a resolution instructing the Council to submit to the next session of the Assembly a "detailed plan" for establishing the special fund "as soon as circumstances permit."[96] This was adopted in the plenary meeting of the Assembly by a vote of 30 in favor, 16 against, and 11 abstentions.[97]

Recognizing, after further reflection, that 1952 was an election year in the United States and a peculiarly unpropitious moment for obtaining long-term views about United Nations machinery, the underdeveloped countries took the initiative at the Economic and Social Council during the following summer in suggesting that the preparation of the "detailed plan" be delegated to an independent committee of nine to be appointed by the Secretary-General instead of being undertaken forthwith by the Council.[98] It was foreseen that this device would

[93] Res. 368(XIII), Aug. 21, 1951.

[94] U.N. Economic and Social Council, Thirteenth Session, *Official Records*, 511th Meeting (Aug. 21, 1951), p. 288.

[95] Representative Mike Mansfield, U.N. General Assembly, Sixth Session, Second Committee, *Official Records*, 164th Meeting (Dec. 11, 1951), p. 123. However, on the preceding day the President of the International Bank for Reconstruction and Development, Eugene R. Black, had advised the Assembly that grants were necessary to accelerate development programs. "The management of the Bank," he said, "believed that in some countries the rate of development could not be substantially accelerated if the only external capital they received was in the form of loans with a reasonable prospect of repayment. It strongly believed that any additional assistance given to those countries should be in the form of grants rather than of quasi-loans, that the grants should preferably be administered through international channels, and that, to the fullest extent practicable, the technical facilities of existing international agencies should be utilized for such administration." *Ibid.*, 163rd Meeting (Dec. 10, 1951), pp. 114–15.

[96] *Ibid.*, 166th Meeting (Dec. 13, 1951), p. 139.

[97] U.N. General Assembly, Sixth Session, Plenary, *Official Records*, 360th Meeting (Jan. 12, 1952); Res. 520A(VI), Jan. 12, 1952.

[98] Res. 416A(XIV), June 23, 1952.

delay consideration of the blueprint beyond the next session of the Assembly.

Focus on SUNFED

The report of the committee on a Special United Nations Fund for Economic Development (SUNFED) was issued in the spring of 1953.[99] It suggested that operations should not begin until the equivalent of $250 million had been pledged by at least thirty governments. Contributions should be voluntary but could be made in the currencies of the contributors. Control should be vested primarily in an Executive Board on which "major contributors" on the one hand, and "other members" on the other hand, would have equal representation and equal voting rights. In addition to these controversial recommendations concerning local currency contributions and the strong voice to be given to recipient governments in policy determination, the experts' criteria for the allocation of resources were fuzzy, both as between loans and grants, and as between competing projects. On loans, the committee of experts thought the Fund should not ask for interest or attempt to recover principal when this would jeopardize the economic development of a country. On the distribution of available funds, the committee referred repeatedly to "the maintenance of geographical balance."

Before the Economic and Social Council could meet to consider the report of the experts, President Eisenhower revived the hopes of the underdeveloped countries for United States participation in a grant-aid program by his speech on April 16, 1953, to the American Society of Newspaper Editors. He called first for a system of internationally supervised world-wide disarmament. Then, reviving a view expressed at the General Assembly a year and a half earlier by President Truman, President Eisenhower said:

> This Government is ready to ask its people to join with all nations in devoting a substantial percentage of the savings achieved by disarmament to a fund for world aid and reconstruction. The purposes of this great work would be to help other peoples to develop the underdeveloped areas of the world, to stimulate profitable and fair world trade, to assist all peoples to know the blessings of productive freedom. . . . We are ready, by these and all such actions, to make of the United Nations an institution that can effectively guard the peace and security of all peoples.[100]

[99] U.N. Department of Economic Affairs, *Report on a Special United Nations Fund for Economic Development, by a Committee Appointed by the Secretary-General*, Doc. E/2381 (Mar. 18, 1953).

[100] "The Chance for Peace," address by the President, Apr. 16, 1953, U.S. Department of State *Bulletin*, Vol. 28 (Apr. 27, 1953), p. 602.

The President, it will be noted, did not advocate a grant-aid agency nor in any way endorse SUNFED, but the spirit and timing of his address gave a lift to those who did. It was very much in the minds of the delegates to the Council when they assembled in Geneva in the summer of 1953. On the initiative of the United States, the Council recommended and the General Assembly overwhelmingly adopted a resolution declaring that when sufficient progress had been made toward internationally supervised, world-wide disarmament, Members would ask their peoples to devote a portion of the resources so saved to an international fund for economic development and reconstruction.[101] The underdeveloped countries were pleased to receive pledges that could lead to sizable contributions in the distant future but did not consider them adequate substitutes for lesser contributions at an earlier date. They refused to agree that rearmament deserved a priority of indefinite duration over development.

SUNFED is still in the blueprint stage. The Economic and Social Council in 1953 simply transmitted the report of the experts to the General Assembly, the organ that had first asked for the blueprints, with a request that the Assembly consider what other preparatory steps could usefully be undertaken. The Assembly proved its ingenuity by designating a roving ambassador to keep the subject alive. It appointed the Belgian President of the Economic and Social Council, Raymond Scheyven, to obtain and examine government comments on the experts' report and to submit his findings to the Council and the General Assembly in 1954.

Scheyven toured the major capitals and found industrialized countries divided in their views. The key countries—the United States, the United Kingdom, and Canada—as well as New Zealand, the Federal Republic of Germany, Sweden, and Switzerland, were still unprepared to contribute to a fund. Another group of economically advanced nations—Denmark, Italy, Norway, and the Netherlands—declared themselves, however, ready to give material support to the fund. A third group—Belgium, France, Japan, and Luxembourg—were prepared to do so under certain conditions. The underdeveloped countries, of course, wanted the fund established immediately. Scheyven did not confine his report to a summary of the reactions of potential contributors. He included a plea for early establishment of the fund with primary emphasis on what he termed "the moral imperative,"

[101] U.N. Economic and Social Council, Res. 482A(XVI), Aug. 4, 1953, and U.N. General Assembly, Res. 724A(VIII), Dec. 7, 1953.

and "the duty of nations to help one another on an adequate scale."[102]

In a resolution approved unanimously, the Economic and Social Council, in the summer of 1954, noted the "increasing moral" and "increased degree of material" support for the establishment of SUNFED and recommended another government review of positions as well as an extension of Scheyven's appointment.[103] This recommendation was accepted by the General Assembly,[104] another *ad hoc* group of experts was appointed, and a new plan for SUNFED was submitted to the Economic and Social Council and the General Assembly by Scheyven in 1955.[105] The new plan, the most modest and realistic in the series on this subject, goes a long way toward meeting objections raised to earlier versions.[106] Like its predecessors, it envisages grants-in-aid as the most important and preponderant method through which the Special Fund would commit its resources. It differs from earlier reports, however, in certain other respects.

1. It quietly buries the proposals for loans on indefinite, renegotiable terms and provides only for fixed-interest loans repayable in the currency of the borrowing country, thereby filling a gap left by the requirement of the International Bank that its loans must be repaid in the currency borrowed;

2. It provides for much closer administrative ties between the Special Fund and the International Bank so that grant aid may be closely co-ordinated with other forms of external financing;

3. On the question of policy formulation, it plainly hints that a controlling voice for major contributors can be arranged;

4. To overcome misgivings about the establishment of grant aid as a permanent feature of international economic co-operation, it suggests that the Special Fund be set up on a trial basis for a five-year period.

[102] U.N. General Assembly, Ninth Session, *Official Records*, Supplement No. 19, "Special United Nations Fund for Economic Development," Final Report by Raymond Scheyven, Prepared in Pursuance of U.N. General Assembly Resolution 724B(VIII), (1954), p. 4.

[103] Res. 532A(XVIII), Aug. 4, 1954.

[104] Res. 822(IX), Dec. 11, 1954.

[105] U.N. General Assembly, Tenth Session, *Official Records*, Supplement No. 17, "Special United Nations Fund for Economic Development," Report Prepared in Pursuance of U.N. General Assembly Resolution 822(IX), (1955).

[106] Paradoxically, the realism in terms of capital resources that makes SUNFED politically acceptable to potential contributors may render it unrealistic in terms of its capacity to affect the pace of development in recipient countries. The smaller the special fund, the more likely it is to meet with approval but the less likely it is to have a significant impact in underdeveloped countries.

None of the numerous special reports to the United Nations has yet provided adequate answers to two questions. How many underdeveloped countries are approaching the limits of their borrowing power but are nevertheless in a position to make productive use of additional funds? What would their annual requirements for grant aid from abroad amount to during the next five to ten years? While Latin American countries have been among the most persistent proponents of grant aid in the Economic and Social Council and the General Assembly, the secretariat of the Economic Commission for Latin America, which is highly respected in that region, has placed greater stress on the need for increased loans, more private investment, and better terms of trade. The Middle Eastern governments, likewise staunch supporters of grant aid, in some cases have treasuries bulging with oil royalties. Their development seems to be hampered by factors other than lack of capital, although additional capital applied to irrigation projects could unquestionably speed the process. It is in Asia, specifically in the Indian subcontinent, that the case for grant aid is best documented. If more searching examination reveals that only a handful of the underdeveloped countries in the United Nations are in a position to use grant aid effectively, would the United Nations be justified in creating international machinery to serve such a limited clientele? This question has never been faced squarely.

Nevertheless the United Nations appears to be inching toward the creation of a grant fund. Recent changes in the international situation, specifically the emergence of the Soviet Union as a potential supplier of aid to underdeveloped countries, could conceivably bring about an ironic shift in present positions. Underdeveloped countries that have hitherto been strong advocates of internationally administered grant aid may conclude that they can do better by jockeying individual foreign governments into outbidding each other in offering aid; developed countries, such as the United States, may be transformed into warm supporters of an internationally administered fund in order to avoid being whipsawed into an intolerable competition for the privilege of financing foreign development projects. Barring any such dramatic reversal of majority and minority positions, the campaign for grant aid will continue unabated.

Retrospect and Prospect

Viewed in the perspective of history, the long-gathering drive of the underdeveloped countries for a new status as peoples and nations may well constitute the major event of the second half of the twentieth century. The problems of underdeveloped countries are psychological and political as well as economic and social. Irrational factors loom large in the picture. It would be a gross oversimplification, therefore, to think of this vast awakening and turbulence solely as a demand for a better material standard of life. Where economic gain and national prestige have come into conflict, nationalism has frequently carried the day.

Nevertheless, the heart of the problem of the underdeveloped countries is how to lift themselves from stagnation at a bare subsistence level to a condition of cumulative, self-generating expansion. Must they lift themselves by their own bootstraps, or can they count on continued help from abroad? How great is the obligation of people in more fortunate areas to collaborate in raising the level of well-being of those in less fortunate lands? What forms, if any, should their help take? Conversely, what accommodation should the numerically strong but economically weak majority of underdeveloped countries make in the interests of greater international harmony with the more developed areas?

By every device at their disposal, the spokesmen for underdeveloped countries have sought to arouse the conscience of mankind to the plight of their peoples, and to gain universal acceptance of the view that the international community as a whole has a responsibility for the welfare of its poorest inhabitants. The issue they have posed is moral as well as economic.

Within the framework of the United Nations, moral issues, if they are resolved at all, are resolved in political terms and in political forums. Although there has been little disposition to dispute the paramount importance of satisfying in reasonable measure the revolution of rising expectations, there have been serious differences between developed and underdeveloped countries about the nature and extent of their respective obligations. Debates at the technical levels have been repeated, with added emotion, at the political levels. Appeals have been carried successively from subcommissions to commissions, to the Economic and Social Council itself, and finally to the General Assembly. The United Nations has become a major battleground in what has been described elsewhere as a "curious war in which everyone professes to be on the same side, marching under the same banner, toward the same goal."[107]

[107] Isador Lubin and Robert E. Asher, "The Struggle for a Better Life," Chap. IV of *The U.S. Stake in the U.N.*, The American Assembly (1954), p. 74.

In relation to the immensity of the problem of satisfying in adequate measure the revolution of rising expectations, the contribution of the United Nations must be regarded as modest. Broadly speaking, it falls into four main categories: the provision of technical assistance through both the United Nations and the specialized agencies; the extension of loans through the International Bank; the exploration of proposals for internationally administered grant aid and other devices for enlarging the flow of capital to underdeveloped countries; and the development of a better understanding of the process of economic growth.

The Expanded Programme of Technical Assistance has become the best known, most far-reaching, and—in some ways—most flexible instrument for helping to solve a major problem of countries in the earliest stages of development. Although an organized exchange of information can bring about significant improvements in economic and social well-being, without an accompanying flow of capital, it remains a limited approach. Given a firmer financial foundation and concentrated more heavily on community development and similar forms of social engineering, however, the technical assistance program of the United Nations could become even more effective than it has been.

Although the total volume of loans from the International Bank to underdeveloped countries—about $1.6 billion through December 31, 1956—remains well below the expectations of those countries, even the severest critics of the Bank agree that its loans have been generally well conceived and have made a distinct contribution to the economic development of the borrowing nations. In addition to loan assistance, primarily for the completion of basic power and transportation facilities, the Bank has made its influence felt in other ways, most notably in the creation of a better climate for private investment. It might be said, in fact, that the International Bank has made a place for itself as much for the principles it has espoused and the approaches it has explored as for the capital it has provided. In this connection, the reports of the survey missions of the Bank to underdeveloped countries occupy an important niche, both as contributions to investment planning in the areas in question, and to the general body of literature on economic development.

The contribution of the United Nations as a whole to economic analysis and to a better understanding of the process of development is impossible to assess with any degree of precision. It seems clear that the many reports published by the United Nations on problems and aspects of economic development have exercised a considerable intellectual influence. Studies prepared outside the framework of the United Nations but influenced by earlier publications of the United Nations, have in turn influenced later United Nations studies, which have steadily become more penetrating and more sophisticated. These maturer views are beginning to be reflected in decisions of policy makers in underdeveloped countries.

The drive of the underdeveloped countries to establish a United Nations fund from which they can obtain financing for schools, hospitals, highways, port facilities, and other non-self-liquidating undertakings continues strong. Partly to divert this drive and partly for other more fundamental reasons, the United States and the developed countries have stressed social and institutional barriers that hinder progress in underdeveloped countries and that can be reduced without injections of foreign capital. The result of this tug of war has been to bring into the international arena a host of problems once considered matters of exclusively domestic concern and to raise a number of searching questions about priorities for action, but not to still the demands for capital and equipment. For the last few years, the question has no longer been whether a capital fund would be set up within the framework of the United Nations, but when.

The test of the merits of proposals such as that for a Special United Nations Fund for Economic Development is in any event not the warmth of the initial official reactions of governments. The test is more likely to lie in the reception first by expert circles and later by segments of the general public. New ideas, especially if they involve expenditures of money, are bound to encounter resistance from those who would have to put up the funds. But if the ideas are good, they tend to survive the official frowns and gain ultimate acceptance.

Had there been no United Nations, the formation of a political bloc of underdeveloped countries might have been deferred. *Ad hoc* solutions for the problems of a few especially restive lands might have been negotiated—or imposed by force. The simmering sickness of other, seemingly more quiescent, lands might have been neglected for the time being. Without the United Nations, it is probable that the emphasis given to the special difficulties of the underdeveloped countries would have been less universal, the analysis less searching and objective, and the incentives to action less compelling. But the problems would nevertheless have worked their way to the center of the world stage, for their solution is by almost any standard the major economic and social challenge of the day.

CHAPTER XI

*Summary and Appraisal**

THE CHARTER of the United Nations emphasizes the responsibilities of the Organization for fostering economic and social progress, encouraging respect for human rights, and advancing the welfare of dependent peoples. To help realize these objectives, a broad range of activities has been undertaken since 1946 within the framework of the United Nations system. As the scope of activities to promote the general welfare has broadened, their structure has become more complex.

The scope has been enlarged primarily in response to new and insistent pressures connected with the emergence of 600 million people from colonial status, the addition of a score of nations to the international conference tables, the revolution of rising expectations that is sweeping across the underdeveloped areas, the determination of all nations to avoid depression and mass unemployment, and the inability of many nation states—despite the persistence of nationalism and xenophobia—to discharge effectively the functions they must perform to survive as sovereign entities. Expanded by these pressures, the efforts of the United Nations to promote the general welfare have been curtailed by continuous conflict over the extent to which international restraints on national freedom of action should be accepted, and by the wide gulf that has separated the Communist-controlled world from the free world. Within the free world, there have been stubborn differences concerning the priorities to be assigned to various goals, the methods to be employed in attaining them, and the pace best suited to a long forward march.

The structure of the activities has become complex not only because the problems themselves are complicated, but also because different methods are required to solve them; because different countries are interested in their solution; and because nations find it politically possible, technically desirable, or economically advantageous to co-operate in more thorough-going fashion in some fields than in others. Moreover,

* By Robert E. Asher. The contents of this chapter have been derived from preceding chapters of this monograph and from Part One of the forthcoming volume in this Brookings series, *The United Nations and Promotion of the General Welfare.*

some of the international machinery in the United Nations system antedates the United Nations and could be brought into the system only in the form of autonomous units that do not mesh well together.

Appraisals of the manifold activities undertaken to date could be made from many points of view. This appraisal is intended to review the direction that the work has taken, to evaluate certain procedures and methods, to note some of the areas in which international co-operation through the United Nations system has been fruitful, and to call attention to the major limitations encountered. Finally, it is intended to ascertain whether the organizational framework has facilitated the work and, if it has not, whether changes in constitutional and organizational arrangements are needed.

Perspective

The economic and social work of the United Nations is an operation in depth. It touches the daily lives of millions of people and carries employees of the United Nations and the specialized agencies, in their regular lines of duty, to the most isolated communities. Whatever the founders of the specialized agencies may have envisaged, it is indeed questionable whether the founders of the United Nations foresaw such a comprehensive operation.

The Charter authorized the Economic and Social Council to establish commissions in economic and social fields and for the promotion of human rights, but from the legislative history of the Charter, it would seem that its drafters were thinking in terms of functional rather than of regional commissions. Nor does it appear that extensive operations at the country level were foreseen, although the Economic and Social Council was authorized by the Charter to perform services at the request of governments. Nevertheless, before five years had elapsed, not only eight functional commissions but also three regional economic commissions were in active status. In addition, a series of operating programs involving the feeding of children, the provision of technical assistance, and the rendering of emergency aid to the needy were being carried on as separately financed services of the United Nations.

The major techniques to be followed by the Economic and Social Council in order to promote the objectives stated in Article 55 of the Charter—higher standards of living, full employment, and conditions of economic and social progress and development—were (1) fact-finding and the preparing of recommendations to the General Assembly and to

Member governments, and (2) influencing the work of the specialized agencies. In line with the former, the Economic and Social Council was authorized to make studies and reports; to call conferences and prepare draft conventions; and to make recommendations on international economic, social, cultural, educational, health, and related problems. In line with the latter, the Council was authorized to negotiate agreements bringing existing specialized intergovernmental agencies into relationship with the United Nations; to initiate negotiations leading to the creation of additional specialized agencies; and to co-ordinate the activities of specialized agencies through consultation and recommendation. Thus both specialization and co-ordination were provided for in the Charter, but how far each should be pressed, and how the function of harmonizing conflicting national viewpoints should be divided between the United Nations proper and the specialized agencies was left to the test of experience.

Although the specialized agencies are vital parts of the United Nations system, each has its own constitution, budget, membership, secretariat, and headquarters office. Changes in the United Nations Charter unaccompanied by parallel changes in the constitutions of the specialized agencies would not modify the constitutional responsibilities of those agencies.

Eight of the existing ten specialized agencies were established before the United Nations Charter entered into force.[1] Two specialized agencies—the World Health Organization (WHO) and the United Nations Educational, Scientific, and Cultural Organization (UNESCO)—although projected by governments before the Charter entered into force, were in a true sense created by the United Nations to carry on and expand forms of co-operation on which pioneer work had been done during the interwar period. A projected International Trade Organization was stillborn although many of its proposed provisions on commercial policy were incorporated in the General Agreement on Tariffs and Trade (GATT). An Intergovernmental Maritime Consultative Organization will come into being if the underlying convention is ratified

[1] This total includes the World Meteorological Organization (WMO), which in 1950 inherited the functions of the long-established International Meteorological Organization, and which entered into agreement with the United Nations in 1951. The other seven agencies in existence before the Charter of the United Nations entered into force are: the International Telecommunication Union (ITU), the Universal Postal Union (UPU), the International Labour Organisation (ILO), the Food and Agriculture Organization (FAO), the International Bank for Reconstruction and Development (IBRD or the Bank), the International Monetary Fund (IMF or the Fund), and the Provisional International Civil Aviation Organization (which ceased being provisional in 1947 and became ICAO).

by four more states, at least one of which has a merchant marine of one million tons or more. The statute for an International Atomic Energy Agency, approved at a major international conference in October 1956, will enter into force on ratification by eighteen nations including at least three from among the following five: Canada, France, the Soviet Union, the United Kingdom, and the United States.

The broad economic and social objectives of the United Nations system are at the same time the objectives of most national governments. The United Nations supplements national action; it recommends, stimulates, facilitates, and co-ordinates. Moreover, it has no monopoly on international action; numerous multilateral programs operate outside the framework of the United Nations. In addition, the programs of the United Nations have been paralleled and, in some cases, dwarfed by bilateral programs, most notably those of the United States Government.

The impressive improvement that has occurred since 1946 in the economic and social health of the world—spectacular in the case of Europe, and substantial in Latin America, but meager in much of Asia—is thus attributable only to a limited degree to the efforts of the United Nations system. Despite the continuance of trends toward the fragmentation and disintegration of the self-balancing world economy of the nineteenth century, industrial and agricultural output during the postwar period, both in total and on a per-capita basis, have increased significantly. International trade has expanded markedly in volume as well as value. Gold and dollar reserves in the possession of countries other than the United States are more nearly adequate. Employment levels in the industrialized nations have remained high. Social services almost everywhere have been improved, literacy is on the increase, and mortality rates are down. The dazzling possibilities of harnessing the atom for peaceful purposes are being revealed. Hope is replacing despair in a number of the underdeveloped countries.

As a pulse-taker of the universe, the United Nations has recorded and analyzed its ups and downs. In addition, it has proffered advice, comment, and some material assistance. Its direct contribution to the promotion of the general welfare, however, cannot be isolated from national and from other international efforts.

Methods and Processes

In recommending policies and selecting methods of work in the economic and social field, the Members of the United Nations were confronted with a situation of almost infinite complexity. They had in the first place to provide the specialization necessary for effective action. Second, they had to consolidate the specialized components into an over-all effort to achieve common objectives and as a result, to embark on an almost constant search for means of achieving co-ordination. Third, they had to harmonize as far as possible national viewpoints within each of the specialized fields in such a way that they would contribute to the pursuit of the over-all objectives. The new organization therefore had to analyze economic and social problems and their interrelationships, to increase mutual understanding of national aims and aspirations, and to promote forms of political accommodation that would make it possible to deal with some acutely controversial issues.

This formidable task was begun at a time when the true dimensions of the postwar reconstruction problem had not yet been disclosed. The time and resources needed to solve this problem were generally underestimated. The extent to which the fledgling United Nations system would be called upon to wrestle with emergency problems for which it was not prepared was likewise unforeseen. This led to unexpected difficulties in harmonizing national attitudes toward some forms of long-range co-operation, because countries preoccupied with urgent short-run problems would not, and often could not, commit themselves in advance to follow policies that were desirable and appropriate in normal times. This might not have been a major obstacle to the advancement of the objectives of the Charter if there had been a sufficient measure of international agreement on what was desirable and appropriate in the long run. Unfortunately, despite the compromises reached at the Hot Springs, Bretton Woods, Chicago, and San Francisco conferences, and during the commercial policy discussions under Article VII of the Anglo-American Mutual Aid Agreement, the Members of the United Nations remained divided on many important economic and social issues. Meanwhile, the drive of the underdeveloped countries for a new status as peoples and nations was gathering force with a speed that was unappreciated.

Evolution of Priority Programs

Within the United Nations system, the Economic and Social Council and the General Assembly, as the principal general policy-making bodies, were confronted first with the task of selecting, from the vast array of problems that were of concern to Member governments, those that were most significant and most suitable for consideration by a world organization. They had to establish some system of priorities. An attempt was made to do this in a formal way by the General Assembly in 1947, but the problem was not then susceptible to such treatment and has not yet become so. Gradually, a greater consensus has been reached regarding major problems in each functional area of work and in each geographic region. So-called priority lists have been adopted periodically as guides to a more effective concentration of effort and resources. To satisfy the varied and varying interests of three or four score countries, however, it has been necessary to couch these lists in such general terms as to limit their usefulness in specific situations. Working priorities were nevertheless established, partly in response to the pressure of events, and partly in response to the new forces stirring in the world, which were making full employment, economic stability, and economic development primary objectives of economic and social policy.

These working priorities were also influenced by the fact that some of the most urgent problems of the industrialized countries requiring international collaboration were, from 1948 on, tackled entirely outside the United Nations system. For this and other reasons, the industrialized countries—although they shared the common aspiration for full employment and economic stability—did not turn to the United Nations as a source of help and guidance to nearly the same extent as did the underdeveloped countries. There is evidence in the record, however, to show that the increasingly one-sided emphasis on the demands and interests of a numerically strong group of Member governments, those of the economically underdeveloped countries, was sometimes carried to extremes.

During the early years, the emphasis was overwhelmingly on reconstruction. The international community, operating largely with resources obtained from the United States, undertook to help materially in the repair of damage and the restoration of essential services in war-devastated areas. Geographically, Europe was the chief beneficiary. Between 1945 and 1947, the United Nations Relief and Rehabilitation Administration (UNRRA)—which, despite its name, was never formally brought within the United Nations framework as a specialized agency—devoted the major portion of its sizable resources to relief work in Europe. Anticipating the termination of UNRRA, the General Assembly in 1946 established two agencies, the United Nations International Children's Emergency Fund (UNICEF, or the Children's Fund) to continue certain services for needy children, and the International Refugee Organization (IRO) to carry on a program of care, repatriation, and resettlement of refugees. During its initial years, the Children's Fund functioned primarily as an aid program for Europe. The IRO, during its limited lifetime, performed a similar role although it incidentally enriched a number of non-European nations by providing them with settlers whose education, training, and skills had been acquired in Europe.

In 1947, the Bank made four important reconstruction loans to European nations. The Fund, although not intended to provide facilities for relief and reconstruction, did in fact do so by some important sales of dollar exchange to its European members. The magnitude of the reconstruction job, however, proved far beyond the resources of the United Nations system. After the Soviet Union, in 1947, rejected the Anglo-French invitation to join in working out a new European Recovery Program, European reconstruction went forward, with Marshall Plan aid, almost entirely outside the framework of the United Nations.

The incipient vacuum in the United Nations was quickly filled by the special problems of the underdeveloped countries. Their problems, although perhaps subordinated, had by no means been ignored during the early postwar years. The ILO had become concerned with labor standards and social security provisions in underdeveloped countries during the interwar period, and this concern was intensified after the Second World War. The world-wide food shortage that characterized the years 1945 to 1948 caused the FAO relatively early in its life to broaden its span of attention and to encompass in its activities numerous services to underdeveloped countries. With the inauguration of the Expanded Programme of Technical Assistance in 1950, the special problems of the underdeveloped countries became, so to speak, the stock in trade of United Nations economic and social programs.

The rising tide of concern with the problems of underdeveloped countries has not only submerged the problems of Europe and concentrated attention instead on those of Asia, Latin America, and—to a lesser extent—Africa, it has also involved changes in the scale, scope, and nature of the activities undertaken. Assistance in the form of expert advice and training facilities has become a major method of operation, although the mobilization of pressures for a larger measure of direct financial assistance has remained the chief preoccupation of the underdeveloped countries during economic debates since 1951 in the General Assembly and the Economic and Social Council. Deeply rooted social and institutional barriers to more rapid development have been explored and assistance in understanding and overcoming them has been given.

Interpretation of Domestic Jurisdiction

In the process described above, many of the traditional distinctions between matters of international concern and matters essentially domestic have been obliterated. The pressing problems of the underdeveloped countries have been elevated to the international level, not because of their direct effect on the movement of goods, funds, people, and messages across international boundaries, but because the problems in question are common to a large number of countries, because those countries individually and collectively lack sufficient resources to solve them, and because failure to solve them—or at least to make perceptible progress in the direction of solutions—is widely believed to threaten the peace and security of the world as a whole. That the United Nations has helped to bring the problems of the underdeveloped countries to the forefront and has become concerned with the reduction of domestic as well as international obstacles to more rapid progress may be viewed by some as a perversion of its purposes, but has been regarded by an overwhelming majority as an indication of the responsiveness of the machinery to political and economic realities.

Legal interpretations of authority have not been sought. Article 2(7) of the Charter, prohibiting intervention by the United Nations in matters essentially within the jurisdiction of Member states, has almost never been invoked in economic and social discussions, although it has played a role in the discussions of human rights and problems of dependent areas. Instead, the limits of fruitful international co-operation are being discovered by experiment. The underdeveloped countries, eager to enlist the co-operation of the international community in solving their problems and sensitive to their unfavorable position in bilateral dealings, have tended to regard the United Nations system as a kind of protection and projection of their sovereignty. The industrialized countries have more often viewed the system as a potential restriction on their freedom of action, but they, too, have been willing for the area of international co-operation to be determined pragmatically, by probing the limits of mutual consent and common interest.

Discussion and Debate

Discovering the limits of mutual consent has required a vast amount of discussion. The multiplicity of forums available for the consideration of economic and social issues results in endless repetition of arguments copiously developed at earlier sessions of any one of the forums in question. At the same time, however, it sometimes provides a welcome opportunity for shunting around proposals while governments slowly make up their minds what to do about them. Discussions at working committee levels have been repeated at functional and regional commissions, redebated in the Economic and the Social Committees of the Economic and Social Council, and aired again in plenary meetings of the Council.

Council debates are frequently reconducted in the more political atmosphere of the General Assembly. The fifty or more nations not represented on the Council have been unwilling to accept as final recommendations that they regard as unsatisfactory in fields in which they are deeply interested. Afghanistan, Saudi Arabia, and Uruguay are not satisfied to the point of silence because, for a given three-year period, India, Egypt, or Venezuela happens to be serving on the Council. Even countries that are members of the Council may feel that their views will be received more sympathetically and will in any event be better publicized if repeated in the Assembly where the underdeveloped countries, if they vote together, command an impressive majority.

Some of the major economic and social issues of the day have heavy political overtones in the sense of involving important national interests: for example, the provision of efficient, low-cost air transport service between nations, or the exploitation of petroleum reserves and other natural resources. Some problems are posed as moral issues. What is the responsibility of the international community as a whole, or—more specifically—the inhabitants of the wealthier nations, for the welfare of fellow men in remote, poorer nations? Do refugees unable to find employment in the countries of refuge and unwilling to return to their homelands deserve help from the international community? If so, should the countries from which the refugees have come be expected to contribute to their maintenance? Should an international convention on forced labor deal only with its use in the production of goods entering into international trade, or should such a convention outlaw forced labor completely on the ground that it is wrong and reprehensible?

Within the framework of the United Nations, moral as well as political issues are resolved in political forums—if indeed they are resolved at all. It was, therefore, almost inevitable that the central position of the General Assembly would be underscored by the trend of events in economic and social affairs, just as it has been in peace and security affairs. Initially, there may have been ambiguity between Article 7(1) of the Charter bracketing the Economic and Social Council and the General

Assembly as "principal organs" of the United Nations and Article 60 placing the Council "under the authority of the General Assembly." If so, the ambiguity has by now been resolved in favor of Article 60. Continued reliance on the Assembly for broad policy guidance is essential, and the more fundamental the issues tackled by the Economic and Social Council the greater the involvement of the General Assembly will be. In a number of cases, however, the Assembly has gone well beyond the provision of policy guidance and substituted—as it can if it so desires—its own judgment on technical issues for the judgment of the Council.

Frequent repetition of debates has not improved their quality. The decline in the number of outstanding speeches, however, has probably been matched by a corresponding decline in the number of irresponsible speeches as all rely more and more for their basic facts on the same set of notes: namely, the documentation prepared and circulated by the secretariats. Speeches continue to be made for the press and for the record rather than for the purpose of influencing delegates whose freedom of action is in any event severely circumscribed by the instructions they carry from their governments.

The trend toward instructed, official, government representation in lieu of representation by experts serving in their individual capacities has facilitated the efforts of each government to assume mutually consistent positions in the different agencies of the United Nations system in which it participates. In the United Nations proper, two "expert" subsidiaries of the Economic and Social Council, the Subcommission on Economic Development and the Subcommission on Employment and Economic Stability, were abolished in 1950. As early as 1947, the constitution of the FAO was amended to eliminate a clause that stipulated that the members of the Executive Committee should exercise the powers delegated to them by the FAO Conference on behalf of the whole conference and not as representatives of their respective governments. In 1954, a similar amendment to the constitution of UNESCO changed its Executive Board into a body of government representatives.

When functional representation continues to be a feature—*i.e.*, in the ILO, which provides for representation from labor and management as well as from government in policy-making—the participation of totalitarian states has presented a knotty problem. Can the employee and management representatives of such states speak with the independence of employee and management representatives in democratic societies? Because the answer is "no," the probable effect in the free world will be to cast further doubt on the practicality of anything but government representation in intergovernmental policy-forming or administrative organs.

In these tumultuous times, however, high-level government representatives cannot be away from their desks for very many days at a stretch. Within the United Nations system, top-level government representatives still find it possible and useful to attend the annual meetings of the Bank and Fund, which are simultaneous, last less than a week, and are largely ceremonial in character. Outside the United Nations system, they attend the frequent meetings of the Council of the Organization for European Economic Cooperation as well as the more infrequent sessions of the Organization of American States and the Consultative Committee on Economic Development in South and Southeast Asia (the Colombo Plan).

Ministerial-level representation either at the Economic and Social Council or at the Second (Economic and Financial) and Third (Social, Humanitarian and Cultural) Committees of the General Assembly, for at least part of the time, is highly desirable both for prestige reasons and in order that recommendations to governments may be adopted more readily by governments. It should be possible to rearrange the agendas of these organs so that the most important business is concentrated in the first or last week of a session and is such as to justify the attendance of higher-ranking officials of Member governments than is now the case. Major issues will not be settled within the United Nations framework if the people best qualified to settle them do not attend meetings, and such people will not attend except for discussions of major issues.

Multilateral discussions uncover problems and help reveal areas of agreement and disagreement regarding their handling. Whether or not remedial action is taken, this is part of the process of establishing an international community, an aspect of the development of common values and standards. Governments participating for the first time in a sector of the economic and social work of the United Nations are usually surprised at the extent to which they have until then been isolated from what suddenly appears to be a mainstream of international thinking—how much "history" they have to catch up with.[2]

[2] Although the Organization for European Economic Cooperation is the only international agency specifically mentioned in the following quotation, the comment made is equally applicable to participation in the United Nations system: "The Spanish economy . . . is a living and irrefutable answer to the common criticism that committees, councils, international secretariats, studies and reports are a

International discussion forces governments, or at least some of the officials of governments, to look at issues from the point of view of other nations as well as from the viewpoint of their fellow nationals. No government wants to be charged publicly with being unsympathetic to the problems of others or, worse still, of pursuing policies that aggravate those problems. "If the experience of defending bad and unneighbourly policies before an alert and militantly inquisitive conference were made sufficiently painful to national spokesmen, some at least of their embarrassment would be transferred to their home ministries."[3] Not infrequently international discussion suggests ways in which potentially injurious actions by national governments can be taken without injuring others and without sacrificing the basic economic or social objective of the nation instigating the action.

Reports and Statistics

The vast documentation prepared by the Secretariat and *ad hoc* committees of experts provides a common take-off point for United Nations discussion. This documentation is somewhat more extensive than it would be were it not for the bad habit (not unknown to national governments) of ending inconclusive debates by requiring further studies. The Council and the General Assembly also have developed a habit of tacking on to almost any resolution calling for a study a requirement that the interests of underdeveloped countries should be given special consideration. Despite this distortion of the international perspective, the provision of basic information on world economic and social conditions has been one of the outstanding services of the United Nations system, particularly helpful to the governments that lack the resources and facilities for independent investigation of matters of interest to them.

---

waste of time. The contrast with Italy, also a poor backward Mediterranean country that was flat on its back in 1945, is striking.

"Two examples among many are economic statistics and the application of modern production methods in industry. Had Spain been a member of the Organization for European Economic Cooperation for five years, national pride, if nothing else, would have fostered and produced reliable and reasonably comparable statistics about such basic economic factors as national product, the balance of payments, cost of living and so forth. . . . Greece and Italy now do it. Seven years ago their statistics were certainly no better than Spain's.

". . . The exchange of technical information and above all of technical personnel among industries is regarded by many European business men as the most important single legacy of the Marshall Plan." Michael L. Hoffman, "Spain's Isolated Economy," *New York Times* (Sept. 30, 1955).

[3] "Baffled by Food Surpluses," *The Economist* (Jan. 2, 1954), p. 31.

Moreover, the fact that the United Nations reports are for the most part scheduled for consideration at an early meeting compels governments to scrutinize them promptly, while equally informative reports, prepared at home, may remain for months on the desks of busy officials before being transferred, unread, to their bookshelves.

The services of the United Nations system in compiling statistics—particularly in the fields of international trade, finance, and population—the annual summaries by specialized agencies of major developments in their respective fields, and the numerous compilations of laws and technical data, are generally conceded to be very valuable. The analytical reports vary more widely in quality and in impact. Reports on the world economic situation and on the world agricultural outlook are important for the education and orientation of the international community, but they are less likely to stimulate concrete action by Member governments than more searching analyses of narrower problems such as the obstacles to private foreign investment in specific areas, the methods of utilizing low-grade coal resources, the long-term outlook for pulp and paper, or the problems and processes of industrialization in underdeveloped countries.

The pioneering *Report on the World Social Situation* and the penetrating regional economic surveys of Europe, Latin America, and Asia, prepared by the Secretariat of the United Nations; the high professional level of the articles published in the *Staff Papers* of the International Monetary Fund; the annual analyses of developments in international trade prepared for the Contracting Parties to the General Agreement on Tariffs and Trade: the country reports by missions of the International Bank; certain teaching materials developed by UNESCO; reports from WHO on nutrition in different regions of the world; a provocative series of economic reports by *ad hoc* groups of experts appointed by the Secretary-General of the United Nations—these and many other reports have been hailed repeatedly by delegates and experts for the contributions they have made to the understanding of complex problems.

While generally deserving of high marks, the economic reports of the United Nations have also been criticized for certain shortcomings, more frequently by American economists than by those of nations in which government is expected to play a more positive role in economic affairs.[4] Although a measure of governmental intervention in the eco-

[4] See, for example, Raymond F. Mikesell, "Economic Doctrines Reflected in United Nations Reports," *American Economic Review*, Vol. XLIV (May 1954), pp. 570–71.

nomic process appears to be necessary in order for the economy to function at a rate that is politically tolerable, there has perhaps been a tendency in the literature of the United Nations to shy away from suggesting traditional methods of adjustment through the operation of the price system. In particular, there has been a tendency, at least until recently, to attribute the "dollar shortage" to causes almost entirely outside the control of countries in balance-of-payments difficulties, and to place disproportionate responsibility for its elimination on the United States. The rediscovery of the role of monetary policy and its relation to the balance of payments owes little to the analysis of international economic problems provided by the United Nations proper (*i.e.*, excluding the analyses of specialized agencies such as the Fund and the Bank).

Resolutions

Just as the take-off point for United Nations discussion of a problem is usually a report, the immediate end-product is a resolution. In order to evaluate, in the most general terms, the contributions made by formal resolutions to the promotion of the economic and social objectives of the Charter, it is necessary to slash through a jungle in which even the largest trees are surrounded by a thick growth of underbrush. In embarking on this task, it is helpful to distinguish between two types of resolutions: those designed to expand the structure of the United Nations system—chiefly through the creation of new agencies and organs—and those designed to transmit general policy guidance to Member governments.

Three major questions may be asked in evaluating the series of important resolutions responsible for the growth of the system itself to its present proportions. Did they expand the scope of United Nations activities in such a way as to promote the objectives of the Charter? Did the Council and the Assembly, before passing these resolutions, succeed in getting sufficient agreement on controversial issues to permit the proposed work to be carried out effectively? Did the Council and the Assembly, in passing these resolutions, arrive at a satisfactory solution of the dual problem of permitting both the specialization and the co-ordination needed for effective action?

An affirmative answer can be given to all three questions in the case of most resolutions of the type that extended United Nations activities on emergency problems, in the field of social welfare, and in the provision of technical assistance for economic development. The distribution of the health and social welfare activities of the League and of

UNRRA between WHO and other agencies was not highly controversial. The extremely controversial issue of involuntary repatriation of refugees was fought out in the negotiation of the constitution of the IRO. The emergency work for women and children carried on by UNICEF commanded general approval, and this enterprise was not made permanent until there was a genuine consensus in the Assembly. The United Nations Relief and Works Agency for Palestine Refugees and the United Nations Korean Reconstruction Agency were established, also in response to such a consensus, to perform a manageable range of functions in specific localities. The two major resolutions on technical assistance did raise controversial issues, but these were much more in the realm of finance and administration than they were in the realm of objectives.

In the establishment of UNESCO, in contrast, the specialization for effective action was not provided. An almost unlimited range of activities was authorized, and many of its troubles stem from this source. Nor was adequate provision for specialization made in the case of the proposed International Trade Organization (ITO). The Economic and Social Council was partly responsible for this inasmuch as it was unable or unwilling to give firm advice to the Preparatory Committee of the ITO regarding those employment and development functions that should properly be assigned to a trade organization. The resultant Havana Charter, replete with provisions concerning employment, investment, restrictive business practices, and intergovernmental commodity agreements, as well as commercial policy, covered an excessively broad range of controversial functions and failed of ratification. Up to the present time, therefore, the structure of the United Nations system of specialized agencies remains incomplete because of the absence of an agency in the field of trade that could deal with problems of commercial policy, cartel policy, and commodity policy. Moreover, foreign exchange policy, which is intimately related to trade policy, remains the province of an agency—the IMF—that has no responsibilities for trade policy.

The decision to establish an Economic Commission for Europe was a natural outgrowth of the work of the Temporary Subcommission on the Reconstruction of Devastated Areas set up by the Economic and Social Council. Once made, it was inevitable that Member governments in other parts of the world should feel that what was good for Europe was good for them. Consequently, not only an Economic Commission for Asia and the Far East but also an Economic Commission for Latin America was established, despite the fact that the Inter-American Economic and Social Council of the Organization of American States was already in the field. Had it not been for the Arab-Israeli conflict, a regional commission in the Middle East would also have been established. Back of the drive for these commissions was the view that there are some economic problems that can be handled better on a regional than on a world basis. The Council, however, offered little guidance on what these problems were, nor—despite some prodding from the United States—did it think through the larger implications of economic regionalism and possible conflicts between a regional approach to economic policy and the global approach to which the United Nations appeared committed, especially through the Fund, the Bank, and the proposed ITO.

Despite numerous disagreements on points of detail and, in the case of the regional commissions, of a certain lack of understanding of the full implications of the action taken, this series of resolutions reflected a broad consensus within the Council and the Assembly. Also it opened up wide areas in which the system as a whole could effectively contribute to the promotion of the general welfare.

This cannot yet be said of the series of resolutions intended to equip the United Nations system for making grants-in-aid to underdeveloped countries, for maintaining an international parity price scheme, or for establishing stand-by machinery to meet famines and natural disasters. The thinking that gave rise to the proposals was unacceptable to a strong and powerful minority of industrially advanced nations. As yet, there is no real consensus on the respective roles of public and private investment for development, on the use of grants as a normal feature of international economic relations, or on the form, if any, that international action to reduce fluctuations in the prices of internationally traded primary commodities should take. Yet even here, the record is somewhat mixed.

There has been a long series of resolutions putting pressure on the Fund and the Bank to enlarge their resources, change their established practices, and conform their policies to the views recommended to them by the Council and the Assembly. Opinions will differ whether these pressures have been entirely without effect. The establishment of the International Finance Corporation, which was the subject of a series of resolutions of the Council and the Assembly, is at least partially attributable to them. This has been due, however, not merely to majority votes in these organs but also to a gradual recognition, particularly on the part of the United States, that the general interest could be promoted by such an institution. No such meeting of minds has yet occurred with respect to a proposed Special United Nations Fund for Economic Development. Even here, however, national differences have been softened. The principal, though not the only, opponent of an agency to provide grants for economic development—the United States—has been put on the defensive by the intensity and persistence of the drive for such an agency. Opposition on grounds of principle has been abandoned and the debate has shifted to when, how much, and under what conditions.

The chief lesson to be drawn from these resolutions expanding or seeking to expand the framework of the United Nations system is a simple one—that a prerequisite for effective co-operation among sovereign governments is not a preponderance of votes but a meeting of minds. This is not to say that the minds of the minority will be uninfluenced by the votes of the majority, but rather that until the conversion is genuine the co-operation will be minimal. The service that international agencies render is to bring to the foreground and to highlight problems before they assume explosive proportions, to give key countries some indication of the kinds of action desired, and then to ratify and generalize what the key countries have already accepted as the most appropriate solution to a pending problem. Occasionally, too, they succeed in catching and preserving that golden moment when the key governments themselves are willing to subscribe to a standard of behavior or a code of conduct that is not only better than any they were previously willing to subscribe to, but more exacting than what they would accept a few years later.

The resolutions looking toward the creation of new machinery are far outnumbered by the long series of resolutions containing recommendations to governments. Many of these have been compromises and makeshifts, battered about in debate, and laying down no firm policy. This defect, plus a penchant for sonorous preambles to introduce "operative" sections addressing a few pious platitudes to governments, have weakened the effect of United Nations resolutions. Practical solutions of such complex problems as the relative weights to be assigned to industrialization and agricultural expansion in development plans, or how best to promote the free exchange of information among nations, cannot reasonably be expected to flow from highly generalized compromise resolutions addressed to more than seventy governments. The spotlight can be focused on a problem like land reform or barriers to private investment. However, the ability of governments to prevent depressions is hardly strengthened by exhortations from the Council and the Assembly to maintain full employment.

The conclusion to be drawn is that resolutions, with some honorable exceptions such as the Universal Declaration of Human Rights, are comparatively unimportant as sources of policy guidance—less important than the published studies and extensive discussions that precede them, and much less important than the advice rendered on the spot by the experts and technicians from the United Nations who visit the different countries. In many cases, the debates, the studies, and the surveys by experts have led to second thoughts and more moderate opinions. To some extent, these have been reflected in the resolutions themselves.

Conventions and Legally-Binding Agreements

The drafting of international conventions and instruments that become legally binding on ratification by signatory states was originally conceived as a major function of the Economic and Social Council, but has not in fact proved to be one. Conventions continue to be considered appropriate where action by a single nation would be ineffective without corresponding or complementary action of a binding character by other nations. But acute doubts have arisen concerning the value of conventions designed to universalize standards that do not depend on multilateral acceptance in order to be meaningful within particular areas. Thus, for purposes such as controlling the traffic in narcotic drugs, obtaining uniform safety regulations on the high seas and in the airways, and extending copyright protection internationally, a multilateral convention may be an appropriate method of securing adherence to necessary standards. On the other hand, uniform social security provisions among nations are not essential, and education is the chief value of conventions such as the Social Security Convention of 1952, which the ILO regards as the culmination of thirty years of study and discussion. Given the present range of differences among nations in standards of living, patterns of behavior, and social values, it is questionable whether the drafting of conventions is the most fruitful technique where uniformity among nations and reciprocity are not essential features.

Within the United Nations system, the greatest devotee of the convention technique has been the ILO, which by the end of 1955 had adopted and opened for signature 104 conventions covering different aspects of employment and working conditions. The record of ratifications and of implementation after ratification suggests that the technique has very definite limits. The result is that there has been a decided shift within the ILO from conventions to recommendations, technical assistance, and education at the grass roots.

Operational Functions

To the extent that operational functions in the economic and social field were foreseen at the San Francisco Conference, they were envisaged as functions of the specialized agencies rather than of the United Nations Organization. The creation of operating agencies within the United Nations Organization to provide technical assistance, emergency relief for the needy, and other forms of direct aid represents a departure from the original approach in favor of an organizational arrangement that permits more centralized policy control.

The establishment of operating agencies within the United Nations itself, however, has not limited participation in such agencies to the Members of the United Nations; it has not burdened the Economic and Social Council with administrative details, for these usually have been delegated to an executive director or a board; and it has given the United Nations flexibility to meet emergency situations. Had it been necessary, for example, to establish a specialized agency to deal with Korean reconstruction problems, protracted negotiations to draft and ratify a constitution would have been inevitable.

With the exception of the work of the Technical Assistance Administration, the operational responsibilities assumed by the United Nations proper have been undertaken initially as short-term assignments. Generally, the assumption of such functions has represented a humanitarian response to a situation of peculiar urgency or need. The response, however, has implied a more sustained interest on the part of contributors in the welfare of children than in that of adults. The Children's Fund has become permanent, but in relief and refugee work of the kind undertaken by the United Nations Relief and Works Agency and the United Nations Korean Reconstruction Agency, the sums needed and the time required for doing the job have repeatedly been underestimated. The system of voluntary annual contributions by which these agencies have been financed has prohibited necessary forward planning and fostered perpetual crisis within the agencies. It has been the most glaring weakness of the emergency programs, and budgetary procedures will sooner or later have to be modified to provide more stable financing for activities of this kind. A start has already been made in connection with the technical assistance program.

Although the primary difficulty has been to obtain total resources sufficient to complete the job, there has been a second difficulty, intimately related to the first. This has been to make the participation broad enough to be truly international. The proportion contributed by the United States has been decreasing in several of the programs, but even so, it continues to represent more than half of the total budget. Any international operation that depends on a single contributor, however rich that contributor may be, for the major part of its budget is likely to be international in name only. This may prove tolerable and even advantageous for a brief period, but it is almost certain to be unwholesome in the long run.

The transformation of the Children's Fund from an emergency operation to a permanent service raises the question whether what is essentially a long-range child health program should be carried on indefinitely as a function of the United Nations proper, while major responsibility for promoting international co-operation in the health field rests with a specialized agency, the World Health Organization. As good administration implies the grouping of closely related programs under unified direction, it would seem desirable, but not urgent, at some stage to consider a transfer of the Children's Fund to the World Health Organization. The sole objective, however, should be to provide for permanent, professional supervision and effective co-ordination with other health programs. The objective should not be to comply with any theoretical principle that the United Nations Organization must disengage itself from long-term operational functions. In the first place, the distinction between operational functions and functions not regarded as operational is frequently as unclear as the distinction between short term and long term. Even if the dividing line could be firmly drawn, the advantages of observing a hard-and-fast principle concerning the assumption of operational functions would probably be more than offset by loss of flexibility and reduced capacity to meet the ever-changing requirements of governments.

Relations with Specialized Agencies

The presence of a group of specialized agencies within the United Nations system raises at least two important questions: (1) which functions should most appropriately be assigned to the United Nations proper and which to specialized agencies; and (2) how to co-ordinate the activities of the constituent parts of the system. In so far as functions are concerned, there clearly are areas of economic and social co-operation that require a high degree of specialization and will continue to demand attention at international levels for long years to come. It would be a misfortune if each such area were not made the primary field of interest of a competent international agency enjoying a substantial degree of independence. In a world of problems as complex as those with which the United Nations system is trying to deal, there is much to be said for a system that provides generously for technical specialization, for freedom from central political control, and for opportunities to experiment. The urgent problems in the fields of health, education, exchange stabilization, aviation, and communications require different types of programs to meet them, different personnel, and different organizational approaches.

These differences cause understandable concern in some quarters. Administrative co-ordination in the sense of comparable salary scales, vacation privileges, budget practices, and central statistical services is being brought about by present machinery; but substantive co-ordination of policies and program priorities through the Economic and Social Council is still fairly nominal. The need for such substantive co-ordination, however, is to an important extent a function of the magnitude of the programs to be co-ordinated, and of the ability of governments to co-ordinate their own policies at the national level. Were the FAO and WHO each spending or supervising the expenditure of several billion dollars per year, co-ordination of substantive programs to maintain some parity between food supply and population would be much more important than when each is dispensing less than $11 million annually, spreading it thinly across several continents, and influencing only marginally the expenditures of national and local agencies.

At present levels of expenditure, problems of overlapping, jurisdictional disputes, and unclear lines of authority can be, and have been, met to a large extent by the unspectacular method of mutual accommodation, experimentation, and learning by experience. From the start, the specialized agencies have recognized, indeed in some cases have exaggerated, the interrelations of problems in their respective fields. The international meeting at which fraternal delegates from other international agencies almost outnumbered the official delegates from governments was a familiar spectacle in the early days of the United Nations. Knowledge of each other's activities has led to more fruitful forms of co-operation—the co-operation, for example, of teams of specialists, each member of which can bring to a co-operative endeavor the experience of a different agency.

The General Assembly is entitled and determined to give central political guidance to the economic and social work of the United Nations proper. An extension of this authority to the specialized agencies might eliminate such absurdities as the repeated consideration by health officers, economists, and educationists of motions to seat representatives of Communist China. The advantages of central political direction for the entire United Nations system at its present stage of development, however, appear to be more than offset by the loss of freedom to the constituent agencies.

The inauguration of the Expanded Programme of Technical Assistance provided an opportunity to integrate the programs of the agencies that comprise the United Nations system. This opportunity was seized only gingerly at first, but subsequent progress toward effective coordination has been steady, and there is no reason to believe that the process will be interrupted. The existence, however, of international programs of technical assistance outside the United Nations system (the United States Technical Cooperation Program and the Colombo Plan) has added to the complications arising from the existence of a number of autonomous specialized agencies.

The creation of additional specialized agencies obviously should not be undertaken lightly. Short-term services like the provision of emergency relief in the wake of local wars can be provided directly by the United Nations without the complications of establishing and disestablishing a specialized agency, but a relief undertaking of the magnitude of UNRRA would probably require the establishment of an independent agency. When sizable expenditures are involved, the price of participation by major donors is likely to be a greater voice than they have in the United Nations proper, in which each nation has an equal vote. The alternative at present is an independent agency such as the International Bank or the International Monetary Fund, where voting is weighted. Thus, the International Finance Corporation has been established as an affiliate of the Bank, and the odds are good that if a grant agency comes into being, it too will operate either as another affiliate of the Bank or under a charter that gives donors a controlling voice in policy formulation. It would seem in the general interest to keep the path open for the establishment and maintenance of agencies governed by weighted voting, or agencies such as the ILO in which important interest groups have a recognized voice. Insistence on greater control of specialized agencies by the United Nations will tend to seal off these possibilities.

The problem of UNESCO, whose field of specialization may initially have been too broadly and too vaguely defined, has already been mentioned. The remedy would seem to lie neither in closer supervision by the Economic and Social Council or the General Assembly, whose mandates are even broader and vaguer, nor in "co-ordination" with such unrelated activities as those of the Universal Postal Union and the International Civil Aviation Organization. It would seem to lie instead in continued reform from within, through delegates from governments determined to develop an effective work program.

Co-operation with Nongovernmental Organizations

Nongovernmental organizations (NGO's) have played a smaller role in the councils of the United Nations than they foresaw for themselves at the close of the San Francisco Conference. Despite the misgivings of some delegates about the desirability of including Article 71 in the Charter, the question was not extensively debated at San Francisco. In the lobbying of the NGO's, however, and in such discussion as occurred, a recurrent theme was that:

> . . . NGO's with large international membership would bring to the deliberations of the UN a cross-section of world public opinion. A related hope was that on vital issues and by more or less direct means NGO's would represent constituencies of world-wide scope who were not fully vocal through member governments.
>
> The implication of these hopes was that, in effect, Article 71 opened a new channel of communication between groups of private citizens and an intergovernmental organization. It raised possibilities of functional as well as geographical representation in the UN . . . [Nine years later] there is no noticeable impulse to extend consultative arrangements to give more scope to NGO's to present their members' views. The hopes at San Francisco that NGO's might ultimately become a kind of Second Estate of the UN have been largely quenched by the experience of the last nine years. Member states . . . have narrowed and not increased the scope of these arrangements since 1946.[5]

Nevertheless, the NGO's have had an impact on the emergency relief work of the United Nations in Korea and the Near East; they have participated constructively in the refugee and migration programs, par-

[5] Edwin A. Bock, *Representation of Nongovernmental Organizations at the United Nations* (1955), pp. 15–17.

ticularly in arranging for the reception and early care of immigrants; and they have been active in the technical work of organs and agencies in the transport and communications fields.

Role of Secretariats

In practice, the secretariats have become the chief repositories of *expertise*. As they have amassed information about problems, they have naturally accumulated views on how those problems should be solved, and have devised ways and means of gaining acceptance for their views. Recommendations are implicit in many of the reports prepared for delegates and Member governments, and there are increasing opportunities for top secretariat officials to participate directly in intergovernmental deliberations. Often, where progress is deadlocked for political reasons, the secretariat is able, on its own responsibility, to put forward acceptable compromise proposals that would be rejected as suspect if presented by participants to the controversy. In other cases (including some in which the purpose of the secretariat is self-aggrandizement as much as the solution of a political deadlock), the secretariat works through national delegations. Both among the sincere and conscientious delegates and among those looking for a painless passage to statesmanship, there are always some ready and willing to serve as stalking-horses for secretariat proposals.

The influence of the international civil servants is enhanced by the instability of government representation. Secretariats are permanent, but government representation rotates. If an organization is to function at all, there must be enough of a hard-core of participants to furnish tradition, a sense of shared accomplishments, and respect within national ministries for the views of the international community. Governments too often tend to make representation of their interests in a given international agency the private province of one or two officials comparatively isolated from the mainstream of government policy making, or to regard nomination to the delegation for an international conference as a sinecure that should be widely shared. Either view is unhealthy.

Although the initiative of secretariats in suggesting new approaches to problems in the economic and social fields, and their ability to issue reports without prior government clearance are resented in some quarters, circumstances appear to favor a further relative growth in secretariat influence. The decision in 1954, for example, to begin the annual discussion of the world economic situation in the Economic and Social

Council with statements from the Secretary-General and the executive secretaries of the regional economic commissions provides new opportunities for officers of the Secretariat to affect the approach to one of the major items on the agenda. The periodic visits to national capitals by officers of the United Nations Organization and of the specialized agencies give them a further chance to outline their ideas for new work, to discover common features of divergent national views, and to enlarge their knowledge vis-à-vis that of the delegates. To date, they have—on the whole—performed with objectivity and with a view to serving the interests of the international community as a whole. They can create mischief and may on occasion have done so. But there is little danger that secretariats will become too powerful. More likely, they will be kept too circumscribed to make the full contribution of which they are capable.

> Generally speaking, whatever the constitutions say, the powers of the secretariat are never anything else than delegated and they are limited in time. In the final instance all the power belongs to the governments for the simple reason that the efforts of the secretariat cannot be directed toward anything else than the reaching of agreements between the governments, agreements which the governments can decline to make.[6]

Achievements and Frustrations

Constructive international co-operation requires a clear understanding of the problems to be attacked, a respect for the views of all countries that may be affected, and a down-to-earth appraisal of the obstacles to be overcome. It cannot be conjured into being by high-sounding phrases, unless these phrases really express widely-shared aspirations and unless promotion of the welfare of the world community is a positive element in prevailing concepts of national interest. It cannot be forced by majority vote.

The assumption that the economic and social objectives of the United Nations and its related agencies were in harmony with the concepts of national interest held by Member governments has now been tested by ten years of experience. The record shows that, except for the almost unbridgeable gulf that separates the Soviet bloc from the rest of the world, this assumption was valid.

The years of United Nations research, discussion, and negotiation

[6] Gunnar Myrdal, *Realities and Illusions in Regard to Inter-Governmental Organizations*, L. T. Hobhouse Memorial Trust Lecture No. 24 (1955), pp. 22–23.

have resulted in a large measure of agreement regarding which are the most urgent of the economic and social problems of the world. Unfortunately, the gap remains wide between recognition that something constitutes a problem and attainment of a consensus regarding the handling of that problem. The gap is smallest when the problem can be reduced to a technical issue, and greatest when the problem appears as a political or moral issue. There is a

> . . . clear inverse correlation between success in international co-operation and political importance. Indeed, the best method of reaching international agreement on an issue is most often to divest it so far as possible from political content by defining it closely and delimiting it narrowly, so that it becomes a question which has the appearance of being merely technical, and, in addition, to move it away from the public gaze.[7]

On technical issues the differences are likely to be differences of detail rather than principle. Political leaders are willing to defer to the experts, provided the experts can operate on a modest budget. The experts of the free world—if they are divided—tend to be divided along other than national lines. Within the United Nations, a number of matters that were initially political issues have become primarily technical matters, widely accepted as appropriate functions for the United Nations system; for example, the lending, but not the granting, of public funds for economic development, and the sponsorship of negotiations between Eastern and Western Europe for the promotion of trade in nonstrategic items. The more ingenious international secretariats have made conscious efforts to speed the evolution from political to technical. Thus, the maintenance of an independent secretariat, free to exercise a certain amount of initiative, is important. Greater opportunity for private sessions is likewise necessary. Open covenants secretly arrived at need not spell trouble. Public sessions tend to highlight divergent views, to lock negotiators into positions from which they cannot gracefully extricate themselves, and to put a premium on the scoring of debating points.

In the end, however, international agreement is possible only when governments and peoples decide that they have more to gain than to lose by co-operation. The area of potential co-operation therefore expands or contracts over time. It depends, too, on the kind of commitment involved and the extent to which action by national legislatures is required to implement it.

Commitments of funds are entered upon with understandable reluc-

[7] *Ibid.*, p. 18.

tance. Emergency assistance programs in a few specific areas or situations—such as Korea or Palestine refugees—in which the United Nations has assumed military or political responsibility, have been accepted as appropriate forms of United Nations activity. But the expenditure of large sums elsewhere has to date appeared to involve conflicting national interests that could not be ignored or reconciled. The establishment of an internationally administered fund to make grants-in-aid for economic development has been resisted and postponed, and the establishment of a similar revolving fund for the relief of future famines has been rejected. Proposals for preventing the international spread of depressions by stabilizing the flow of international trade, the level of international investment, or the prices of important internationally traded primary commodities likewise have proved unacceptable to the major creditor nation—the United States. In the only permanent organizations in the United Nations system endowed with substantial financial resources, the International Bank and the International Monetary Fund, the price of life has been continuous deference to the views of the United States.[8] Any other nation making a comparable subscription to the capital funds of these agencies, however, could command comparable deference to its views.

Binding commitments concerning behavior may also prove difficult to obtain. Treaties and formal agreements, even though not calling for any great expediture of funds, can involve knotty legal and administrative issues. In many cases, as already noted, action by one nation would be ineffective without corresponding or complementary action by other nations. This need for an agreed international framework has been the rationale for a series of international conventions in the economic and social field to limit or prohibit the passing across international frontiers of drugs, germs, locusts, slaves, obscene literature, or unsafe aircraft, ships, and motor vehicles. There are many other problems that lend themselves to solution within the framework of an international convention or agreement but remain unsolved because of sharp and stubborn clashes of interest. The assignment of radio frequencies is an example; unilateral action makes for mutual interference and confusion, but multilateral agreement has not been readily obtainable. In an era of widespread broadcasting for political ends, it is understandable that nations with competing political philosophies

[8] *Cf.* Raymond F. Mikesell, "Barriers to the Expansion of United Nations Economic Functions," *Annals of the American Academy of Political and Social Science*, Vol. 296 (November 1954), p. 45.

should be unable to agree on the division among them of a limited number of high frequencies. Finally, there have also been sharp differences of opinion regarding the need for conventions and covenants to generalize standards of behavior that do not need to be upheld by all civilized nations in order to be upheld by some.[9]

The major share of United Nations work in the economic and social field involves neither financial nor legal commitments, but at most a moral commitment. This is frequently expressed as an obligation to "take into account" the views expressed in debates, to make "every effort" to progress toward some stated objective, or to provide information "as appropriate" in response to requests.

Consultation, exchange of information and experience, and joint review of data provided by secretariats, by *ad hoc* experts, or by *rapporteurs* constitute the regular grist of the United Nations mill. The practice of convening periodically for serious consideration of common problems helps to establish standards, ethics, and patterns of performance that can be of the greatest importance for the future of democratic society. The larger the area in which suitable self-imposed standards of performance and behavior become prevalent—standards that have moral force—the smaller the area in which legal sanctions formally restraining individual liberty are likely to be required.

Opportunities offered by the United Nations system for the exchange of information among health officials, demographers, land reform experts, commodity specialists, housing administrators, statisticians, or fuel and power producers cost relatively little, often prove very beneficial, and are almost never harmful. Frequently, they accomplish more than the spread of know-how; real business is done in the corridors and hotel rooms, if not at the formal sessions, of timber, coal, steel, and electric power meetings. It is easy, however, for the convening of meetings and the issuance of conference papers to get out of hand. Little clubs whose members gain status at home because they attend international meetings, and are listened to at international meetings on the theory that they have status at home, continue to gather at public expense. Public funds get diverted to the support of what should be private professional or trade associations. Constant vigilance is therefore required to prevent the United Nations umbrella from being used to shelter a dubious array of gregarious, self-perpetuating societies.

[9] See the monograph in this Brookings series, *The United Nations and Human Rights*, especially pp. 37–68.

Economic Problems

In the ever-changing area that governments choose to consider within the scope of the United Nations system, what have been the major substantive problems dealt with to date, and with what degree of success?

In the economic field, the United Nations system as a whole has been attempting to deal with a long list of exceedingly complicated issues. Leading this list and cutting across many other issues, is the adoption of measures to speed the economic and social development of underdeveloped countries. In production and investment, the United Nations has been concerned with the revival and expansion of industrial and agricultural production in order to overcome the extreme dependence of most of the world on supplies from the dollar area during the immediate postwar period; with the restoration of an international capital market, the removal of obstacles to the international flow of private investment, and the determination of the functions and scale of operation of public international lending institutions. It has been concerned also with the desirability and feasibility of providing capital for development purposes by means of soft loans or grants.

In transportation and communications, the work of the United Nations system has been much less controversial. On the whole, it has been confined to the provision of well-recognized, long-range, technical services through genuinely specialized agencies and organs. In trade and payments, the United Nations has been concerned with the reestablishment of a functioning multilateral system of trade and payments; with the relation of commercial policy to employment and development policy; and with the potential conflicts between global and regional approaches to trade and payments problems. The obverse of the concern of the United Nations with the attainment and maintenance of high and stable levels of employment, trade, investment, and economic activity generally has been consideration of measures for the avoidance of depression and mass unemployment, the role of short-term credit in preventing the international spread of depressions, and the relation of commodity trade to economic stability.

This oversimplified summary of the major areas of United Nations economic interest provides a basis for some general conclusions.

The priority given to the whole subject of economic development has in itself been a constructive achievement because it has focused world attention on newly liberated, latent forces of explosive potentialities. The fundamentals of the problem of development in its manifold aspects have been exhaustively explored, although the whole process of economic growth needs further study and understanding. The advocates of massive investment in heavy industry as the key to development in all cases and in all circumstances have become less numerous than they used to be; the importance of investment in agriculture, education, health, and public administration is more widely appreciated; balanced growth has become the watchword. The attention of the General Assembly, the Economic and Social Council, and other interested organs and agencies has been directed increasingly to problems that are both more concrete and more manageable than the elaboration of general principles for the economic development of fifty countries in markedly different stages of underdevelopment and with great variations in resources and potentialities.

The debates in the United Nations, the documentation provided for them, and the work of the International Bank and the International Monetary Fund have led to a much better understanding of the conditions that must be present before the flow of private investment can be greatly increased. Attempts to develop a multilateral code of fair treatment for foreign investors have foundered, but mutually satisfactory arrangements have in a number of instances been worked out bilaterally. The net flow of private investment has not increased significantly, but the climate for such investment has improved considerably, notwithstanding one or two well-publicized United Nations resolutions that temporarily clouded the skies.

The International Bank has increasingly become a kind of publicly managed investment fund whereby money raised in the private capital markets of the United States, Canada, and Western Europe is invested for productive purposes in underdeveloped countries. The total volume of its lending to underdeveloped countries through December 31, 1956—some $1.6 billion, at an average rate of interest of 4 to 5 per cent—has been modest. Governments of underdeveloped countries have exerted unending pressure for loan capital on a more liberal scale and on better terms than offered by the Bank, while the Bank has stressed the lack of adequately planned, technically sound projects for financing.

To appraise the Bank on the basis of the volume of its lending would be an error. Its major contribution has been to re-establish the old-fashioned notion that international finance is business; that a borrower should be a good risk, that he should be capable of repaying the funds he borrows, and be of a mind to do so; that honest, competent management is essential in a business undertaking, and that similar standards are necessary in government. The International Bank, it may be said, has made a place for itself as much for the principles it has espoused and the approaches it has explored as for the capital it has provided.

The Expanded Programme of Technical Assistance has fired the imagination of millions, dramatized the improvements that can be made with comparatively insignificant expenditures of capital, and enabled the United Nations to help reduce social and institutional barriers to progress within the underdeveloped countries themselves. Among these barriers are lack of knowledge of potential resources; lack of technically trained man power; chronic underemployment; immobility of the labor force; antiquated, burdensome systems of land tenure; low rates of domestic capital formation and inadequate means for directing available capital into productive channels; poor transport and communications; and lack of educational and health facilities.

At first, technical assistance was concentrated rather heavily on the spread of technology in the narrow sense—knowledge concerning seeds, fertilizers, tractors, tube wells, or textile production. More recently, it has been devoted increasingly to so-called community development programs and other promising ways of generating a cumulative, self-sustaining expansion in keeping with the felt needs of the people in underdeveloped countries. At the same time, the crucial importance of improved public administration at all levels of government has received greater recognition.

Although the technical assistance program as a whole unquestionably represents one of the most successful undertakings of the United Nations, satisfactory criteria have not been devised for evaluating results project by project or country by country, or for determining the type of expert aid and training most suitable for provision by an international agency. The program, precariously financed and thinly spread, is at best a small-scale undertaking—the foreign funds involved have never exceeded $30 million per year. The payment of salaries and transportation for foreign experts is a minute fraction of the cost of a development program. After the value of this type of service has been demonstrated for another few years, it may not be unreasonable to ask countries desiring it to underwrite it themselves, perhaps using the United Nations as the employment agency that would unearth and nominate qualified technicians for participating governments to hire.

As the underdeveloped countries have seen it, their problems are insoluble without greater financial assistance from abroad, particularly for meeting the costs of non-self-liquidating projects such as schools, hospitals, and roads, which are nevertheless basic to development. The five-year-long campaign of the underdeveloped countries for the establishment of a United Nations fund to make grants-in-aid and loans at nominal rates of interest has to date been unsuccessful. An important by-product of the campaign, however, has been the establishment, as an affiliate of the International Bank, of an International Finance Corporation, equipped to invest risk capital in private enterprises in underdeveloped countries without the governmental guarantee required in connection with loans from the Bank. Although some of the draft proposals for a grant agency have given the preponderant voice in the setting of terms and conditions to recipients rather than donors, the alacrity with which Members of the United Nations accepted an International Finance Corporation in which policy control is weighted in the same fashion as in the International Bank indicates that egalitarian views will not be pushed to the point of checkmating practical action.

It is difficult in some ways to draw a clear line of distinction between discussions in the United Nations of economic development and of another international problem of prime importance—preventing the international spread of depressions—or, more generally, maintaining economic stability. Reducing sharp fluctuations in the prices of internationally traded primary commodities, for example, has been discussed on some occasions as a contribution to economic development and on other occasions as a contribution to economic stability. The unsolved problem of commodity price stabilization remains in the foreground of international discussion because unless practical solutions in the interest of industrialized and underdeveloped countries alike can be devised, an important cause of world economic instability in the past will continue to exist in the future. Intensive explorations of the means thus far adopted, available, or proposed have shown that no single area of international economic relations is more beset with technical, financial, and politico-economic difficulties.

The co-ordination of national full-employment policies for the purpose of maintaining international stability was one of the earliest objectives of the United Nations. The resolution adopted by the Economic and Social Council in 1950, after extensive discussion of the report of a group of experts on *National and International Measures for*

Full Employment put Member governments under obligation to provide information regarding their employment position and policies for review and comment by the Secretariat, by independent experts, and by the delegates of governments. The enthusiasm evoked by this rather mild resolution, which was regarded as having added real meaning to a key provision of the Charter, was one of the errors of optimism of the Council. Thc *co-ordination* of national employment policies has not become a feature of international life, although full employment and the elimination of unemployment continue to be almost universal objectives of national policy, as they would have been had there been no United Nations.

Although the problem has been discussed at length in the United Nations, there is as yet no agreement concerning contracyclical lending by creditor governments, and it would be rash to assume that, if a major depression gets under way, the United Nations will be more successful in checking its spread internationally than was the League of Nations. In this all-important matter, reliance must be placed on the antidepression measures that the governments of all economically important countries are now determined to take in their own interest, in response to new internal social and political forces, rather than in response to international agreements and recommendations.

The overwhelming importance attached to full employment and rapid economic development, and the subordination of commercial policy to these objectives by majorities in the Economic and Social Council and the General Assembly, have probably led these organs to underestimate both the dangers of inflation and the contribution that the reduction of trade barriers can make to the raising of standards of living. Substantial progress has been made through the GATT—which filled part of the gap left by the failure of ITO—in reducing trade barriers and obtaining observance of a code of trade rules, without sacrifice of employment and development objectives. The extension of the most-favored-nation treatment in international trade and the stabilization of tariff rates, objectives for which the League of Nations struggled in vain during the interwar period, have been realized to a large extent through the GATT.

Potential conflicts between regional and global approaches to trade and payments problems have been dealt with by the United Nations system as a whole and by the GATT with flexibility and moderation and without sacrifice of global objectives. There has been good co-operation between the Fund, the Bank, the FAO, and the regional economic commissions in the study of both intraregional and interregional trading problems. The regional commissions have engaged in active trade promotion, but the pattern of world trade has not been significantly affected by these efforts. Schemes for regional payments arrangements that might have strengthened existing tendencies to divide the world into regional groupings have been explored and rejected. The relationship between the Fund and the GATT on the one hand, and on the other, those regional organizations outside the United Nations—thc European Payments Union and the European Coal and Steel Community—has been such that neither body has impeded constructive attacks on European problems, but both have continued to exert their influence against regional as opposed to world-wide solutions of international trade and payments problems.

There has been a running conflict between the United Nations Organization and the International Monetary Fund on the amount and use of the resources of the Fund. This has been due to differences on such fundamental questions as: the responsibilities of creditor countries for helping debtor countries to solve their balance-of-payments difficulties by providing, through the Fund or otherwise, the credits necessary to sustain the volume of their imports; the extent to which monetary and fiscal policy should be relied on to correct balance-of-payments difficulties of a cyclical character without undue recourse to international short-term credit; and whether the Fund has been too zealous in protecting its resources. The boldness of many members of the Economic and Social Council and some of its *ad hoc* experts has been matched by the caution of the Fund.

The approach of the United Nations system as a whole to these problems has been largely in the realm of ideas and, until quite recently, it remained to be seen whether the Fund would make the contribution to international liquidity of which it is potentially capable. That the Fund may now be prepared to play its full role is indicated by the announcements in late 1956 of arrangements authorizing France to purchase, with French francs, up to $262.5 million in foreign currencies and authorizing the United Kingdom to purchase, with sterling, up to $1.3 billion from the Fund.

Social Problems

It is difficult and probably unnecessary, for purposes of this analysis, to draw a clear line between the economic approach and the social approach to the attainment of conditions of stability and well-being, because there must be a large measure of fusion between thc two approaches for either one to be fully effective.

A distinguishing feature of all social work, however, is its concern with the physical, mental, and emotional well-being of the individual citizen in his ever-changing environment. This focus makes for an infinite variety of programs and services. It has consequently been necessary for the United Nations to resist the temptation to embark on an unmanageable series of programs of insufficient impact and of questionable suitability for a large intergovernmental agency. This temptation, powerful in the atmosphere of good will that prevailed in the early postwar years, was aggravated by the pressures and enthusiasms of well-meaning special-interest groups and the unhappy political position in which critics of humanitarian undertakings are inevitably placed.

In addition to short-term relief services, a remarkable range of long-term social services has been provided. Just as some economic programs have been developed to promote higher levels of production, trade, and investment while other economic programs have had the negative purpose of preventing the spread of harmful practices or the occurrence of large-scale unemployment, so the social programs of the United Nations have had both positive and negative aspects. One broad group of social programs has had as its central purpose the promotion of higher levels of living for the individual members of the community. This range of work has involved the Social Commission of the United Nations, WHO, the FAO, the ILO, and other organs and agencies in both independent and concerted efforts to improve the health, nutrition, housing, employment arrangements, and working conditions of the inhabitants of Member states.

Another group of social programs has been oriented toward special categories such as mothers and dependent children, the physically handicapped, the migrants and refugees, and the delinquents and potential delinquents. This orientation often, but not always, has placed the emphasis on protection, defense, prevention, and remedial care. On the whole, both types of programs have been initiated and carried on without evoking serious controversy among Member governments, despite some inherent difficulties in determining the manner in which and the extent to which international machinery should be utilized for promoting social welfare.

If popularity may be used as an index of success, the Children's Fund probably has been the most successful single social program of the

United Nations. The underlying concept is simple, the humanitarian appeal is great, and the cost is low.

The care, movement, and protection of international refugees and migrants—at first appearance, an ideal field for intergovernmental co-operation—has been hampered and handicapped by political differences almost from the start. Despite persistent attacks by the Soviet bloc on its work, the International Refugee Organization was able to arrange for resettlement of the bulk of the refugees under its relatively narrow mandate. The Arab refugees from Palestine, on the other hand, have been kept alive by the United Nations but no noticeable progress toward their reintegration into society has been made or seems likely until there is greater mutual understanding among contending governments in the tense Middle East.

In the field of migration, much attention was given during the period 1946–50 to the allocation of functions among the organs and agencies that had a legitimate interest in facilitating international migration on an orderly basis. The substantial headway that was made in clarifying responsibilities turned out to be largely a labor of love. Because of American reluctance to give a voice in the process to any international agency in which Communist-controlled governments were participants, the United Nations system was never called on to play a major operational role in connection with migration. Outside the framework of the United Nations, assistance to European migrants has been provided by the Inter-Governmental Committee for European Migration.

In the field of education, science, and culture, the unlimited breadth of the constitution of UNESCO encouraged the initiation of an encyclopedic range of activities. The first result was an enthusiastic, disorderly "parade of hobby horses" ridden by scholars and educators, musicians and painters, librarians and museum experts. In the procession were some down-to-earth projects such as aiding the reconstruction of schools and libraries in devastated areas and encouraging scientific research on arid lands, but flanking them were many esoteric pursuits. There was, and still is, confusion over whether the primary efforts of UNESCO should be directed toward the promotion of co-operation among the intellectuals of the world or directed to grass-roots activities such as reducing illiteracy and promoting basic education. In reality the agency must do both, because the stimulation of international co-operation among intellectuals is needed in order to develop fresh ideas that can be introduced into mass education. The grass-roots approach, supported by the United States, has gained ground of late, and the effect has been to give increasing emphasis within UNESCO, as in other parts of the United Nations system, to work on behalf of underdeveloped countries.

In the social programs of the United Nations, a major long-range objective has been to facilitate the establishment of adequate health and welfare services, manned by trained personnel, at national and local levels. As in the shorter-range programs designed to combat specific diseases or increase the availability of specific commodities, the basic tools have been the temporary assignment of foreign experts; the operation of pilot projects, training centers, and seminars; the provision of scholarships and fellowships; and the preparation and distribution of documentation. Through an intensified use of these tools under the technical assistance program, areas hitherto isolated are becoming acquainted with techniques employed elsewhere and being encouraged to adapt them to local requirements.

When modern technology lends itself to fairly direct transfer—for example, spraying with DDT to reduce the incidence of malaria or vaccinating with BCG to protect against tuberculosis—spectacular results can often be achieved in short order at little cost. Enough opportunities of this type have been seized by WHO, UNICEF, and the FAO to justify the existence of these agencies many times over. Results are more difficult to appraise, however, when the objective is to improve vocational training and guidance, to focus attention on housing problems, or to strengthen civil service or social security systems.

As a result of the interest of international agencies in nutrition, important insights into the nature and extent of protein malnutrition have been gained, world-wide attention has been focused on the problem, and major remedial programs have been initiated. But it would be an exaggeration to report comparable achievements as a result of excursions by the United Nations into the fields of housing, town and country planning, and home economics. In these areas, it would appear that the role of international machinery has not yet been adequately clarified.

For the most part, the activities of the ILO represent an extension and intensification of types of work initiated during the interwar years. Recently, however, there has been a departure from its traditional emphasis on the setting of standards for legislation and a greater interest in the dynamics of labor-management relations, the improvement of productivity, and the promotion of a climate in which real income will grow. This is a salutary development.

To even the most casual reader of the daily newspaper, it will be clear that the production, distribution, and use of narcotic drugs have not yet been restricted to legitimate medical and scientific requirements. Nevertheless, the record of the United Nations in facilitating control of narcotic drugs is in most respects outstanding. In another area of social defense in which the League of Nations was also active—the suppression of prostitution and the international traffic in women and children—the discussions in the United Nations have contributed modestly, if at all, to the desired objective. The introduction of rigid passport and visa regulations, regrettable for many other reasons, has, however, had the incidental benefit of practically eliminating such traffic.

Among the least publicized and most useful activities of the United Nations and the specialized agencies in the social welfare field, have been the efforts to promote rehabilitation of the physically handicapped and to obtain general acceptance of a new and more wholesome attitude toward the disabled members of a community.

Collectively, the social programs of the United Nations system, like the economic programs, have become concentrated increasingly on the improvement of conditions in the underdeveloped areas of the world. In those areas, the interaction of the social and economic approaches has helped to modify the views of many who ten years ago regarded lack of capital as virtually the sole obstacle to more rapid development and who failed to appreciate the fundamental character of numerous social obstacles. Only as these obstacles, too, are overcome, can captial be productively employed and the potentialities of the individual citizens who comprise the nations of the world be fully realized.

Past as Prelude

In the promotion of the general welfare, the real job of the United Nations system is to nurture, through education and shared experience, the nascent sense of international community and to strengthen the responsible, forward-looking elements within each country. For this, community development programs and other forms of technical assistance, literacy and health campaigns, financial aid for specific projects, and all the other myriad activities that reach down into the community are more important than resounding pronunciamentos from the General Assembly of the United Nations or the comparable organs of the specialized agencies.

Insufficiently stressed perhaps, but not to be neglected in any appraisal, have been the innumerable occasions on which actions harmful to the general welfare may have been prevented. International agencies, by bringing additional data and differing viewpoints to the attention of member countries, modify assessments by members of their own national interests. The voice of the international community is weak and muffled in comparison with the powerful voices of domestic interests, but where it corresponds with conscience, it is nevertheless a formidable deterrent.

> Every nation must come to terms with the fact that, though the force of collective self-interest is so great that national policy must be based upon it; yet also the sensitive conscience recognizes that the moral obligation of the individual transcends his particular community. Loyalty to the community is therefore morally tolerable only if it includes values wider than those of the community.[10]

The most rewarding areas for international economic and social co-operation—and the limits of such co-operation—are being discovered by experience. A continuation of this pragmatic, evolutionary approach seems preferable to legislative action for the purpose of modifying charters, constitutions, articles of agreement, and terms of reference. The basic instruments provide institutional frameworks within which multilateral discussion and negotiation may take place. They do not require governments to pursue courses of action that are contrary to their national interests, nor do they prevent them from adopting courses in line with such interests.

This is not to say that, if one could start afresh today, no changes in framework would be made. Whether a new charter for the United Nations would establish an Economic and Social Council, would assign to it the heterogeneous functions it now has, or would fix its membership at the present level, is questionable. Remedies for most of the existing weaknesses can be found, however, without resorting to amendment of the Charter. The Charter does not require the Council to meet, and sessions could be temporarily suspended or differently scheduled if there were a general desire to experiment with alternative arrangements.

[10] Reinhold Niebuhr, *The Irony of American History* (1952), pp. 36–37.

The record of the Assembly provides no basis for believing that the situation would be improved without the Council as an intermediary. Meaningful agreements are hard to negotiate in the atmosphere of the Assembly. The Assembly, moreover, has readily approved most of the actions of the Council. Even when it has overridden the Council, its decisions have probably been sounder because of the prior deliberations of the Council than they would otherwise have been.

New constitutions for specialized agencies might establish a more effective concentration of effort within agencies and more formal channels for obtaining co-ordination among agencies. But here again, if governments desired a more closely co-ordinated approach or a different scale of operation, they could obtain them without all of the complications that are involved in drafting or amending constitutions.

Economic, and perhaps political, conditions more favorable than those prevailing heretofore may narrow the area of apparent conflict and open opportunities for lengthening, broadening, and deepening the channels of voluntary co-operation among nations. If the experience of the first ten years is any criterion, future growth will be in the direction of intensified efforts to speed the peaceful development of underdeveloped areas. This is by common consent the outstanding long-range economic and social problem of the day. To its solution, the United Nations system has already made important contributions, but much more remains to be done. There is a respectable body of evidence, however, to indicate that only in the face of imminent common danger will sovereign governments make significant concessions for the common good. A less tense atmosphere would not necessarily presage major changes in the character or pace of international co-operation to promote the general welfare through the United Nations system.

In summary, the record of the United Nations system in harmonizing conflicts of view among Member governments, achieving the specialization necessary for effective international action, and contributing to economic and social progress, leaves much to be desired. Nevertheless, given the extraordinary complexity of the issues, the brief period during which economic and social problems have shared the limelight with political and military problems, and the paralyzing effect—during much of that period—of strife between the free world and the Communist world, the sum total of concrete achievements during the first postwar decade should afford a basis for qualified optimism about the future.

APPENDIXES

APPENDIX A

Charter of the United Nations[1]

WE THE PEOPLES OF THE UNITED NATIONS DETERMINED

to save succeeding generations from the scourge of war, which twice in our life-time has brought untold sorrow to mankind, and

to reaffirm faith in fundamental human rights, in the dignity and worth of the human person, in the equal rights of men and women and of nations large and small, and

to establish conditions under which justice and respect for the obligations arising from treaties and other sources of international law can be maintained, and

to promote social progress and better standards of life in larger freedom,

AND FOR THESE ENDS

to practice tolerance and live together in peace with one another as good neighbors, and

to unite our strength to maintain international peace and security, and

to ensure, by the acceptance of principles and the institution of methods, that armed force shall not be used, save in the common interest, and

to employ international machinery for the promotion of the economic and social advancement of all peoples,

HAVE RESOLVED TO COMBINE OUR EFFORTS TO ACCOMPLISH THESE AIMS.

Accordingly, our respective Governments, through representatives assembled in the city of San Francisco, who have exhibited their full powers found to be in good and due form, have agreed to the present Charter of the United Nations and do hereby establish an international organization to be known as the United Nations.

[1] Source: Photographic reproduction of the text given in *Charter of the United Nations and Statute of the International Court of Justice*, U. S. Department of State Publication 2368 (1945), pp. 1–20, which is a facsimile of the printed Charter agreed to and signed at the San Francisco Conference.

CHAPTER I

PURPOSES AND PRINCIPLES

Article 1

The Purposes of the United Nations are:

1. To maintain international peace and security, and to that end: to take effective collective measures for the prevention and removal of threats to the peace, and for the suppression of acts of aggression or other breaches of the peace, and to bring about by peaceful means, and in conformity with the principles of justice and international law, adjustment or settlement of international disputes or situations which might lead to a breach of the peace;

2. To develop friendly relations among nations based on respect for the principle of equal rights and self-determination of peoples, and to take other appropriate measures to strengthen universal peace;

3. To achieve international cooperation in solving international problems of an economic, social, cultural, or humanitarian character, and in promoting and encouraging respect for human rights and for fundamental freedoms for all without distinction as to race, sex, language, or religion; and

4. To be a center for harmonizing the actions of nations in the attainment of these common ends.

Article 2

The Organization and its Members, in pursuit of the Purposes stated in Article 1, shall act in accordance with the following Principles.

1. The Organization is based on the principle of the sovereign equality of all its Members.

2. All Members, in order to ensure to all of them the rights and benefits resulting from membership, shall fulfil in good faith the obligations assumed by them in accordance with the present Charter.

3. All Members shall settle their international disputes by peaceful means in such a manner that international peace and security, and justice, are not endangered.

4. All Members shall refrain in their international relations from the threat or use of force against the territorial integrity or political independence of any state, or in any other manner inconsistent with the Purposes of the United Nations.

5. All Members shall give the United Nations every assistance in any action it takes in accordance with the present Charter, and shall refrain from giving assistance to any state against which the United Nations is taking preventive or enforcement action.

6. The Organization shall ensure that states which are not Members of the United Nations act in accordance with these Principles so far as may be necessary for the maintenance of international peace and security.

7. Nothing contained in the present Charter shall authorize the United Nations to intervene in matters which are essentially within the domestic jurisdiction of any state or shall require the Members to submit such matters to settlement under the present Charter; but this principle shall not prejudice the application of enforcement measures under Chapter VII.

CHAPTER II

MEMBERSHIP

Article 3

The original Members of the United Nations shall be the states which, having participated in the United Nations Conference on International Organization at San Francisco, or having previously signed the Declaration by United Nations of January 1, 1942, sign the present Charter and ratify it in accordance with Article 110.

Article 4

1. Membership in the United Nations is open to all other peace-loving states which accept the obligations contained in the present Charter and, in the judgment of the Organization, are able and willing to carry out these obligations.

2. The admission of any such state to membership in the United Nations will be effected by a decision of the General Assembly upon the recommendation of the Security Council.

Article 5

A Member of the United Nations against which preventive or enforcement action has been taken by the Security Council may be suspended from the exercise of the rights and privileges of membership by the General Assembly upon the recommendation of the Security Council. The exercise of these rights and privileges may be restored by the Security Council.

Article 6

A Member of the United Nations which has persistently violated the Principles contained in the present Charter may be expelled from the Organization by the General Assembly upon the recommendation of the Security Council.

CHAPTER III

ORGANS

Article 7

1. There are established as the principal organs of the United Nations: a General Assembly, a Security Council, an Economic and Social Council, a Trusteeship Council, an International Court of Justice, and a Secretariat.

2. Such subsidiary organs as may be found necessary may be established in accordance with the present Charter.

Article 8

The United Nations shall place no restrictions on the eligibility of men and women to participate in any capacity and under conditions of equality in its principal and subsidiary organs.

CHAPTER IV

THE GENERAL ASSEMBLY

Composition

Article 9

1. The General Assembly shall consist of all the Members of the United Nations.

2. Each Member shall have not more than five representatives in the General Assembly.

Functions and Powers

Article 10

The General Assembly may discuss any questions or any matters within the scope of the present Charter or relating to the powers and functions of any organs provided for in the present Charter, and, except as provided in Article 12, may make recommendations to the Members of the United Nations or to the Security Council or to both on any such questions or matters.

Article 11

1. The General Assembly may consider the general principles of cooperation in the maintenance of international peace and security, including the principles governing disarmament and the regulation of armaments, and may make recommendations with regard to such principles to the Members or to the Security Council or to both.

2. The General Assembly may discuss any questions relating to the maintenance of international peace and security brought before it by any Member of the United Nations, or by the Security Council, or by a state which is not a

Member of the United Nations in accordance with Article 35, paragraph 2, and, except as provided in Article 12, may make recommendations with regard to any such questions to the state or states concerned or to the Security Council or to both. Any such question on which action is necessary shall be referred to the Security Council by the General Assembly either before or after discussion.

3. The General Assembly may call the attention of the Security Council to situations which are likely to endanger international peace and security.

4. The powers of the General Assembly set forth in this Article shall not limit the general scope of Article 10.

Article 12

1. While the Security Council is exercising in respect of any dispute or situation the functions assigned to it in the present Charter, the General Assembly shall not make any recommendation with regard to that dispute or situation unless the Security Council so requests.

2. The Secretary-General, with the consent of the Security Council, shall notify the General Assembly at each session of any matters relative to the maintenance of international peace and security which are being dealt with by the Security Council and shall similarly notify the General Assembly, or the Members of the United Nations if the General Assembly is not in session, immediately the Security Council ceases to deal with such matters.

Article 13

1. The General Assembly shall initiate studies and make recommendations for the purpose of:

a. promoting international cooperation in the political field and encouraging the progressive development of international law and its codification;

b. promoting international cooperation in the economic, social, cultural, educational, and health fields, and assisting in the realization of human rights and fundamental freedoms for all without distinction as to race, sex, language, or religion.

2. The further responsibilities, functions, and powers of the General Assembly with respect to matters mentioned in paragraph 1(b) above are set forth in Chapters IX and X.

Article 14

Subject to the provisions of Article 12, the General Assembly may recommend measures for the peaceful adjustment of any situation, regardless of origin, which it deems likely to impair the general welfare or friendly relations among nations, including situations resulting from a violation of the provisions of the present Charter setting forth the Purposes and Principles of the United Nations.

Article 15

1. The General Assembly shall receive and consider annual and special reports from the Security Council; these reports shall include an account of the measures that the Security Council has decided upon or taken to maintain international peace and security.

2. The General Assembly shall receive and consider reports from the other organs of the United Nations.

Article 16

The General Assembly shall perform such functions with respect to the international trusteeship system as are assigned to it under Chapters XII and XIII, including the approval of the trusteeship agreements for areas not designated as strategic.

Article 17

1. The General Assembly shall consider and approve the budget of the Organization.

2. The expenses of the Organization shall be borne by the Members as apportioned by the General Assembly.

3. The General Assembly shall consider and approve any financial and budgetary arrangements with specialized agencies referred to in Article 57 and shall examine the administrative budgets of such specialized agencies with a view to making recommendations to the agencies concerned.

Voting

Article 18

1. Each member of the General Assembly shall have one vote.

2. Decisions of the General Assembly on important questions shall be made by a two-thirds majority of the members present and voting. These questions shall include: recommendations with respect to the maintenance of international peace and security, the election of the non-permanent members of the Security Council, the election of the members of the Economic and Social Council, the election of members of the Trusteeship Council in accordance with paragraph 1(c) of Article 86, the admission of new Members to the United Nations, the suspension of the rights and privileges of membership, the expulsion of Members, questions relating to the operation of the trusteeship system, and budgetary questions.

3. Decisions on other questions, including the determination of additional categories of questions to be decided by a two-thirds majority, shall be made by a majority of the members present and voting.

Article 19

A Member of the United Nations which is in arrears in the payment of its financial contributions to the Organization shall have no vote in the General Assembly if the amount of its arrears equals or exceeds the amount of the contributions due from it for the preceding two full years. The General Assembly may, nevertheless, permit such a Member to vote if it is satisfied that the failure to pay is due to conditions beyond the control of the Member.

Procedure

Article 20

The General Assembly shall meet in regular annual sessions and in such special sessions as occasion may require. Special sessions shall be convoked by the Secretary-General at the request of the Security Council or of a majority of the Members of the United Nations.

Article 21

The General Assembly shall adopt its own rules of procedure. It shall elect its President for each session.

Article 22

The General Assembly may establish such subsidiary organs as it deems necessary for the performance of its functions.

CHAPTER V

THE SECURITY COUNCIL

Composition

Article 23

1. The Security Council shall consist of eleven Members of the United Nations. The Republic of China, France, the Union of Soviet Socialist Republics, the United Kingdom of Great Britain and Northern Ireland, and the United States of America shall be permanent members of the Security Council. The General Assembly shall elect six other Members of the United Nations to be non-permanent members of the Security Council, due regard being specially paid, in the first instance to the contribution of Members of the

United Nations to the maintenance of international peace and security and to the other purposes of the Organization, and also to equitable geographical distribution.

2. The non-permanent members of the Security Council shall be elected for a term of two years. In the first election of the non-permanent members, however, three shall be chosen for a term of one year. A retiring member shall not be eligible for immediate re-election.

3. Each member of the Security Council shall have one representative.

Functions and Powers

Article 24

1. In order to ensure prompt and effective action by the United Nations, its Members confer on the Security Council primary responsibility for the maintenance of international peace and security, and agree that in carrying out its duties under this responsibility the Security Council acts on their behalf.

2. In discharging these duties the Security Council shall act in accordance with the Purposes and Principles of the United Nations. The specific powers granted to the Security Council for the discharge of these duties are laid down in Chapters VI, VII, VIII, and XII.

3. The Security Council shall submit annual and, when necessary, special reports to the General Assembly for its consideration.

Article 25

The Members of the United Nations agree to accept and carry out the decisions of the Security Council in accordance with the present Charter.

Article 26

In order to promote the establishment and maintenance of international peace and security with the least diversion for armaments of the world's human and economic resources, the Security Council shall be responsible for formulating, with the assistance of the Military Staff Committee referred to in Article 47, plans to be submitted to the Members of the United Nations for the establishment of a system for the regulation of armaments.

Voting

Article 27

1. Each member of the Security Council shall have one vote.

2. Decisions of the Security Council on procedural matters shall be made by an affirmative vote of seven members.

3. Decisions of the Security Council on all other matters shall be made by an affirmative vote of seven members including the concurring votes of the permanent members; provided that, in decisions under Chapter VI, and under paragraph 3 of Article 52, a party to a dispute shall abstain from voting.

Procedure

Article 28

1. The Security Council shall be so organized as to be able to function continuously. Each member of the Security Council shall for this purpose be represented at all times at the seat of the Organization.

2. The Security Council shall hold periodic meetings at which each of its members may, if it so desires, be represented by a member of the government or by some other specially designated representative.

3. The Security Council may hold meetings at such places other than the seat of the Organization as in its judgment will best facilitate its work.

Article 29

The Security Council may establish such subsidiary organs as it deems necessary for the performance of its functions.

Article 30

The Security Council shall adopt its own rules of procedure, including the method of selecting its President.

Article 31

Any Member of the United Nations which is not a member of the Security Council may participate, without vote, in the discussion of any question brought before the Security Council whenever the latter considers that the interests of that Member are specially affected.

Article 32

Any Member of the United Nations which is not a member of the Security Council or any state which is not a Member of the United Nations, if it is a party to a dispute under consideration by the Security Council, shall be invited to participate, without vote, in the discussion relating to the dispute. The Security Council shall lay down such conditions as it deems just for the participation of a state which is not a Member of the United Nations.

CHAPTER VI

PACIFIC SETTLEMENT OF DISPUTES

Article 33

1. The parties to any dispute, the continuance of which is likely to endanger the maintenance of international peace and security, shall, first of all, seek a solution by negotiation, enquiry, mediation, conciliation, arbitration, judicial settlement, resort to regional agencies or arrangements, or other peaceful means of their own choice.

2. The Security Council shall, when it deems necessary, call upon the parties to settle their dispute by such means.

Article 34

The Security Council may investigate any dispute, or any situation which might lead to international friction or give rise to a dispute, in order to determine whether the continuance of the dispute or situation is likely to endanger the maintenance of international peace and security.

Article 35

1. Any Member of the United Nations may bring any dispute, or any situation of the nature referred to in Article 34, to the attention of the Security Council or of the General Assembly.

2. A state which is not a Member of the United Nations may bring to the attention of the Security Council or of the General Assembly any dispute to which it is a party if it accepts in advance, for the purposes of the dispute, the obligations of pacific settlement provided in the present Charter.

3. The proceedings of the General Assembly in respect of matters brought to its attention under this Article will be subject to the provisions of Articles 11 and 12.

Article 36

1. The Security Council may, at any stage of a dispute of the nature referred to in Article 33 or of a situation of like nature, recommend appropriate procedures or methods of adjustment.

2. The Security Council should take into consideration any procedures for the settlement of the dispute which have already been adopted by the parties.

3. In making recommendations under this Article the Security Council should also take into consideration that legal disputes should as a general rule be referred by the parties to the International Court of Justice in accordance with the provisions of the Statute of the Court.

Article 37

1. Should the parties to a dispute of the nature referred to in Article 33 fail to settle it by the means indicated in that Article, they shall refer it to the Security Council.

2. If the Security Council deems that the continuance of the dispute is in fact likely to endanger the maintenance of international peace and security, it shall decide whether to take action under Article 36 or to recommend such terms of settlement as it may consider appropriate.

Article 38

Without prejudice to the provisions of Articles 33 to 37, the Security Council may, if all the parties to any dispute so request, make recommendations to the parties with a view to a pacific settlement of the dispute.

CHAPTER VII

ACTION WITH RESPECT TO THREATS TO THE PEACE, BREACHES OF THE PEACE, AND ACTS OF AGGRESSION

Article 39

The Security Council shall determine the existence of any threat to the peace, breach of the peace, or act of aggression and shall make recommendations, or decide what measures shall be taken in accordance with Articles 41 and 42, to maintain or restore international peace and security.

Article 40

In order to prevent an aggravation of the situation, the Security Council may, before making the recommendations or deciding upon the measures provided for in Article 39, call upon the parties concerned to comply with such provisional measures as it deems necessary or desirable. Such provisional measures shall be without prejudice to the rights, claims, or position of the parties concerned. The Security Council shall duly take account of failure to comply with such provisional measures.

Article 41

The Security Council may decide what measures not involving the use of armed force are to be employed to give effect to its decisions, and it may call upon the Members of the United Nations to apply such measures. These may include complete or partial interruption of economic relations and of rail, sea, air, postal, telegraphic, radio, and other means of communication, and the severance of diplomatic relations.

Article 42

Should the Security Council consider that measures provided for in Article 41 would be inadequate or have proved to be inadequate, it may take such action by air, sea, or land forces as may be necessary to maintain or restore international peace and security. Such action may include demonstrations, blockade, and other operations by air, sea, or land forces of Members of the United Nations.

Article 43

1. All Members of the United Nations, in order to contribute to the maintenance of international peace and security, undertake to make available to the Security Council, on its call and in accordance with a special agreement or agreements, armed forces, assistance, and facilities, including rights of passage, necessary for the purpose of maintaining international peace and security.

2. Such agreement or agreements shall govern the numbers and types of forces, their degree of readiness and general location, and the nature of the facilities and assistance to be provided.

3. The agreement or agreements shall be negotiated as soon as possible on the initiative of the Security Council. They shall be concluded between the Security Council and Members or between the Security Council and groups of Members and shall be subject to ratification by the signatory states in accordance with their respective constitutional processes.

Article 44

When the Security Council has decided to use force it shall, before calling upon a Member not represented on it to provide armed forces in fulfillment of the obligations assumed under Article 43, invite that Member, if the Member so desires, to participate in the decisions of the Security Council concerning the employment of contingents of that Member's armed forces.

Article 45

In order to enable the United Nations to take urgent military measures, Members shall hold immediately available national air-force contingents for combined international enforcement action. The strength and degree of readiness of these contingents and plans for their combined action shall be determined, within the limits laid down in the special agreement or agreements referred to in Article 43, by the Security Council with the assistance of the Military Staff Committee.

Article 46

Plans for the application of armed force shall be made by the Security Council with the assistance of the Military Staff Committee.

Article 47

1. There shall be established a Military Staff Committee to advise and assist the Security Council on all questions relating to the Security Council's military requirements for the maintenance of international peace and security, the employment and command of forces placed at its disposal, the regulation of armaments, and possible disarmament.

2. The Military Staff Committee shall consist of the Chiefs of Staff of the permanent members of the Security Council or their representatives. Any Member of the United Nations not permanently represented on the Committee shall be invited by the Committee to be associated with it when the efficient discharge of the Committee's responsibilities requires the participation of that Member in its work.

3. The Military Staff Committee shall be responsible under the Security Council for the strategic direction of any armed forces placed at the disposal of the Security Council. Questions relating to the command of such forces shall be worked out subsequently.

4. The Military Staff Committee, with the authorization of the Security Council and after consultation with appropriate regional agencies, may establish regional subcommittees.

Article 48

1. The action required to carry out the decisions of the Security Council for the maintenance of international peace and security shall be taken by all the Members of the United Nations or by some of them, as the Security Council may determine.

2. Such decisions shall be carried out by the Members of the United Nations directly and through their action in the appropriate international agencies of which they are members.

Article 49

The Members of the United Nations shall join in affording mutual assistance in carrying out the measures decided upon by the Security Council.

Article 50

If preventive or enforcement measures against any state are taken by the Security Council, any other state, whether a Member of the United Nations or not, which finds itself confronted with special economic problems arising from the carrying out of those measures shall have the right to consult the Security Council with regard to a solution of those problems.

Article 51

Nothing in the present Charter shall impair the inherent right of individual or collective self-defense if an armed attack occurs against a Member of the United Nations, until the Security Council has taken the measures necessary to maintain international peace and security. Measures taken by Members in the exercise of this right of self-defense shall be immediately reported to the Security Council and shall not in any way affect the authority and responsibility of the Security Council under the present Charter to take at any time such action as it deems necessary in order to maintain or restore international peace and security.

CHAPTER VIII

REGIONAL ARRANGEMENTS

Article 52

1. Nothing in the present Charter precludes the existence of regional arrangements or agencies for dealing with such matters relating to the maintenance of international peace and security as are appropriate for regional action, provided that such arrangements or agencies and their activities are consistent with the Purposes and Principles of the United Nations.

2. The Members of the United Nations entering into such arrangements or constituting such agencies shall make every effort to achieve pacific settlement of local disputes through such regional arrangements or by such regional agencies before referring them to the Security Council.

3. The Security Council shall encourage the development of pacific settlement of local disputes through such regional arrangements or by such regional agencies either on the initiative of the states concerned or by reference from the Security Council.

4. This Article in no way impairs the application of Articles 34 and 35.

Article 53

1. The Security Council shall, where appropriate, utilize such regional arrangements or agencies for enforcement action under its authority. But no enforcement action shall be taken under regional arrangements or by regional agencies without the authorization of the Security Council, with the exception of measures against any enemy state, as defined in paragraph 2 of this Article, provided for pursuant to Article 107 or in regional arrangements directed against renewal of aggressive policy on the part of any such state, until such time as the Organization may, on request of the Governments concerned, be charged with the responsibility for preventing further aggression by such a state.

2. The term enemy state as used in paragraph 1 of this Article applies to any state which during the Second World War has been an enemy of any signatory of the present Charter.

Article 54

The Security Council shall at all times be kept fully informed of activities undertaken or in contemplation under regional arrangements or by regional agencies for the maintenance of international peace and security.

CHAPTER IX

INTERNATIONAL ECONOMIC AND SOCIAL COOPERATION

Article 55

With a view to the creation of conditions of stability and well-being which are necessary for peaceful and friendly relations among nations based on respect for the principle of equal rights and self-determination of peoples, the United Nations shall promote:

a. higher standards of living, full employment, and conditions of economic and social progress and development;

b. solutions of international economic, social, health, and related problems; and international cultural and educational cooperation; and

c. universal respect for, and observance of, human rights and fundamental freedoms for all without distinction as to race, sex, language, or religion.

Article 56

All Members pledge themselves to take joint and separate action in cooperation with the Organization for the achievement of the purposes set forth in Article 55.

Article 57

1. The various specialized agencies, established by intergovernmental agreement and having wide international responsibilities, as defined in their basic instruments, in economic, social, cultural, educational, health, and related fields, shall be brought into relationship with the United Nations in accordance with the provisions of Article 63.

2. Such agencies thus brought into relationship with the United Nations are hereinafter referred to as specialized agencies.

Article 58

The Organization shall make recommendations for the coordination of the policies and activities of the specialized agencies.

Article 59

The Organization shall, where appropriate, initiate negotiations among the states concerned for the creation of any new specialized agencies required for the accomplishment of the purposes set forth in Article 55.

Article 60

Responsibility for the discharge of the functions of the Organization set forth in this Chapter shall be vested in the General Assembly and, under the authority of the General Assembly, in the Economic and Social Council, which shall have for this purpose the powers set forth in Chapter X.

CHAPTER X

THE ECONOMIC AND SOCIAL COUNCIL

Composition

Article 61

1. The Economic and Social Council shall consist of eighteen Members of the United Nations elected by the General Assembly.

2. Subject to the provisions of paragraph 3, six members of the Economic and Social Council shall be elected each year for a term of three years. A retiring member shall be eligible for immediate re-election.

3. At the first election, eighteen members of the Economic and Social Council shall be chosen. The term of office of six members so chosen shall expire at the end of one year, and of six other members at the end of two years, in accordance with arrangements made by the General Assembly.

4. Each member of the Economic and Social Council shall have one representative.

Functions and Powers

Article 62

1. The Economic and Social Council may make or initiate studies and reports with respect to international economic, social, cultural, educational, health, and related matters and may make recommendations with respect to any such matters to the General Assembly, to the Members of the United Nations, and to the specialized agencies concerned.

2. It may make recommendations for the purpose of promoting respect for, and observance of, human rights and fundamental freedoms for all.

3. It may prepare draft conventions for submission to the General Assembly, with respect to matters falling within its competence.

4. It may call, in accordance with the rules prescribed by the United Nations, international conferences on matters falling within its competence.

Article 63

1. The Economic and Social Council may enter into agreements with any of the agencies referred to in Article 57, defining the terms on which the agency concerned shall be brought into relationship with the United Nations. Such agreements shall be subject to approval by the General Assembly.

2. It may coordinate the activities of the specialized agencies through consultation with and recommendations to such agencies and through recommendations to the General Assembly and to the Members of the United Nations.

Article 64

1. The Economic and Social Council may take appropriate steps to obtain regular reports from the specialized agencies. It may make arrangements with the Members of the United Nations and with the specialized agencies to obtain reports on the steps taken to give effect to its own recommendations and to recommendations on matters falling within its competence made by the General Assembly.

2. It may communicate its observations on these reports to the General Assembly.

Article 65

The Economic and Social Council may furnish information to the Security Council and shall assist the Security Council upon its request.

Article 66

1. The Economic and Social Council shall perform such functions as fall within its competence in connection with the carrying out of the recommendations of the General Assembly.

2. It may, with the approval of the General Assembly, perform services at the request of Members of the United Nations and at the request of specialized agencies.

3. It shall perform such other functions as are specified elsewhere in the present Charter or as may be assigned to it by the General Assembly.

Voting

Article 67

1. Each member of the Economic and Social Council shall have one vote.

2. Decisions of the Economic and Social Council shall be made by a majority of the members present and voting.

Procedure

Article 68

The Economic and Social Council shall set up commissions in economic and social fields and for the promotion of human rights, and such other commissions as may be required for the performance of its functions.

Article 69

The Economic and Social Council shall invite any Member of the United Nations to participate, without vote, in its deliberations on any matter of particular concern to that Member.

Article 70

The Economic and Social Council may make arrangements for representatives of the specialized agencies to participate, without vote, in its deliberations and in those of the commissions established by it, and for its representatives to participate in the deliberations of the specialized agencies.

Article 71

The Economic and Social Council may make suitable arrangements for consultation with non-governmental organizations which are concerned with matters within its competence. Such arrangements may be made with international organizations and, where appropriate, with national organizations after consultation with the Member of the United Nations concerned.

Article 72

1. The Economic and Social Council shall adopt its own rules of procedure, including the method of selecting its President.

2. The Economic and Social Council shall meet as required in accordance with its rules, which shall include provision for the convening of meetings on the request of a majority of its members.

CHAPTER XI

DECLARATION REGARDING NON-SELF-GOVERNING TERRITORIES

Article 73

Members of the United Nations which have or assume responsibilities for the administration of territories whose peoples have not yet attained a full measure of self-government recognize the principle that the interests of the inhabitants of these territories are paramount, and accept as a sacred trust the obligation to promote to the utmost, within the system of international peace and security established by the present Charter, the well-being of the inhabitants of these territories, and, to this end:

a. to ensure, with due respect for the culture of the peoples concerned, their political, economic, social, and educational advancement, their just treatment, and their protection against abuses;

b. to develop self-government, to take due account of the political aspirations of the peoples, and to assist them in the progressive development of their free political institutions, according to the particular circumstances of each territory and its peoples and their varying stages of advancement;

c. to further international peace and security;

d. to promote constructive measures of development, to encourage research, and to cooperate with one another and, when and where appropriate, with specialized international bodies with a view to the practical achievement of the social, economic, and scientific purposes set forth in this Article; and

e. to transmit regularly to the Secretary-General for information purposes, subject to such limitation as security and constitutional considerations may require, statistical and other information of a technical nature relating to economic, social, and educational conditions in the territories for which they are respectively responsible other than those territories to which Chapters XII and XIII apply.

Article 74

Members of the United Nations also agree that their policy in respect of the territories to which this Chapter applies, no less than in respect of their metropolitan areas, must be based on the general principle of good-neighborliness, due account being taken of the interests and well-being of the rest of the world, in social, economic, and commercial matters.

CHAPTER XII

INTERNATIONAL TRUSTEESHIP SYSTEM

Article 75

The United Nations shall establish under its authority an international trusteeship system for the administration and supervision of such territories as may be placed thereunder by subsequent individual agreements. These territories are hereinafter referred to as trust territories.

Article 76

The basic objectives of the trusteeship system,

in accordance with the Purposes of the United Nations laid down in Article 1 of the present Charter, shall be:

a. to further international peace and security;

b. to promote the political, economic, social, and educational advancement of the inhabitants of the trust territories, and their progressive development towards self-government or independence as may be appropriate to the particular circumstances of each territory and its peoples and the freely expressed wishes of the peoples concerned, and as may be provided by the terms of each trusteeship agreement;

c. to encourage respect for human rights and for fundamental freedoms for all without distinction as to race, sex, language, or religion, and to encourage recognition of the interdependence of the peoples of the world; and

d. to ensure equal treatment in social, economic, and commercial matters for all Members of the United Nations and their nationals, and also equal treatment for the latter in the administration of justice, without prejudice to the attainment of the foregoing objectives and subject to the provisions of Article 80.

Article 77

1. The trusteeship system shall apply to such territories in the following categories as may be placed thereunder by means of trusteeship agreements:

a. territories now held under mandate;

b. territories which may be detached from enemy states as a result of the Second World War; and

c. territories voluntarily placed under the system by states responsible for their administration.

2. It will be a matter for subsequent agreement as to which territories in the foregoing categories will be brought under the trusteeship system and upon what terms.

Article 78

The trusteeship system shall not apply to territories which have become Members of the United Nations, relationship among which shall be based on respect for the principle of sovereign equality.

Article 79

The terms of trusteeship for each territory to be placed under the trusteeship system, including any alteration or amendment, shall be agreed upon by the states directly concerned, including the mandatory power in the case of territories held under mandate by a Member of the United Nations, and shall be approved as provided for in Articles 83 and 85.

Article 80

1. Except as may be agreed upon in individual trusteeship agreements, made under Articles 77, 79, and 81, placing each territory under the trusteeship system, and until such agreements have been concluded, nothing in this Chapter shall be construed in or of itself to alter in any manner the rights whatsoever of any states or any peoples or the terms of existing international instruments to which Members of the United Nations may respectively be parties.

2. Paragraph 1 of this Article shall not be interpreted as giving grounds for delay or postponement of the negotiation and conclusion of agreements for placing mandated and other territories under the trusteeship system as provided for in Article 77.

Article 81

The trusteeship agreement shall in each case include the terms under which the trust territory will be administered and designate the authority which will exercise the administration of the trust territory. Such authority, hereinafter called the administering authority, may be one or more states or the Organization itself.

Article 82

There may be designated, in any trusteeship agreement, a strategic area or areas which may include part or all of the trust territory to which the agreement applies, without prejudice to any special agreement or agreements made under Article 43.

Article 83

1. All functions of the United Nations relating to strategic areas, including the approval of the terms of the trusteeship agreements and of their alteration or amendment, shall be exercised by the Security Council.

2. The basic objectives set forth in Article 76 shall be applicable to the people of each strategic area.

3. The Security Council shall, subject to the provisions of the trusteeship agreements and without prejudice to security considerations, avail itself of the assistance of the Trusteeship Council to perform those functions of the United Nations under the trusteeship system relating to political, economic, social, and educational matters in the strategic areas.

Article 84

It shall be the duty of the administering authority to ensure that the trust territory shall play its part in the maintenance of international peace and security. To this end the administering authority may make use of volunteer forces, facilities, and assistance from the trust territory in carrying out the obligations towards the Security Council undertaken in this regard by the administering authority, as well as for local defense and the maintenance of law and order within the trust territory.

Article 85

1. The functions of the United Nations with regard to trusteeship agreements for all areas not designated as strategic, including the approval of the terms of the trusteeship agreements and of their alteration or amendment, shall be exercised by the General Assembly.

2. The Trusteeship Council, operating under the authority of the General Assembly, shall assist the General Assembly in carrying out these functions.

CHAPTER XIII

THE TRUSTEESHIP COUNCIL

Composition

Article 86

1. The Trusteeship Council shall consist of the following Members of the United Nations:

   a. those Members administering trust territories;

   b. such of those Members mentioned by name in Article 23 as are not administering trust territories; and

   c. as many other Members elected for three-year terms by the General Assembly as may be necessary to ensure that the total number of members of the Trusteeship Council is equally divided between those Members of the United Nations which administer trust territories and those which do not.

2. Each member of the Trusteeship Council shall designate one specially qualified person to represent it therein.

Functions and Powers

Article 87

The General Assembly and, under its authority, the Trusteeship Council, in carrying out their functions, may:

   a. consider reports submitted by the administering authority;

b. accept petitions and examine them in consultation with the administering authority;

c. provide for periodic visits to the respective trust territories at times agreed upon with the administering authority; and

d. take these and other actions in conformity with the terms of the trusteeship agreements.

Article 88

The Trusteeship Council shall formulate a questionnaire on the political, economic, social, and educational advancement of the inhabitants of each trust territory, and the administering authority for each trust territory within the competence of the General Assembly shall make an annual report to the General Assembly upon the basis of such questionnaire.

Voting

Article 89

1. Each member of the Trusteeship Council shall have one vote.

2. Decisions of the Trusteeship Council shall be made by a majority of the members present and voting.

Procedure

Article 90

1. The Trusteeship Council shall adopt its own rules of procedure, including the method of selecting its President.

2. The Trusteeship Council shall meet as required in accordance with its rules, which shall include provision for the convening of meetings on the request of a majority of its members.

Article 91

The Trusteeship Council shall, when appropriate, avail itself of the assistance of the Economic and Social Council and of the specialized agencies in regard to matters with which they are respectively concerned.

CHAPTER XIV

THE INTERNATIONAL COURT OF JUSTICE

Article 92

The International Court of Justice shall be the principal judicial organ of the United Nations. It shall function in accordance with the annexed Statute, which is based upon the Statute of the Permanent Court of International Justice and forms an integral part of the present Charter.

Article 93

1. All Members of the United Nations are *ipso facto* parties to the Statute of the International Court of Justice.

2. A state which is not a Member of the United Nations may become a party to the Statute of the International Court of Justice on conditions to be determined in each case by the General Assembly upon the recommendation of the Security Council.

Article 94

1. Each Member of the United Nations undertakes to comply with the decision of the International Court of Justice in any case to which it is a party.

2. If any party to a case fails to perform the obligations incumbent upon it under a judgment rendered by the Court, the other party may have recourse to the Security Council, which may, if it deems necessary, make recommendations or decide upon measures to be taken to give effect to the judgment.

Article 95

Nothing in the present Charter shall prevent Members of the United Nations from entrusting the solution of their differences to other tribunals by virtue of agreements already in existence or which may be concluded in the future.

Article 96

1. The General Assembly or the Security Council may request the International Court of Justice to give an advisory opinion on any legal question.

2. Other organs of the United Nations and specialized agencies, which may at any time be so authorized by the General Assembly, may also request advisory opinions of the Court on legal questions arising within the scope of their activities.

CHAPTER XV

THE SECRETARIAT

Article 97

The Secretariat shall comprise a Secretary-General and such staff as the Organization may require. The Secretary-General shall be appointed by the General Assembly upon the recommendation of the Security Council. He shall be the chief administrative officer of the Organization.

Article 98

The Secretary-General shall act in that capacity in all meetings of the General Assembly, of the Security Council, of the Economic and Social Council, and of the Trusteeship Council, and shall perform such other functions as are entrusted to him by these organs. The Secretary-General shall make an annual report to the General Assembly on the work of the Organization.

Article 99

The Secretary-General may bring to the attention of the Security Council any matter which in his opinion may threaten the maintenance of international peace and security.

Article 100

1. In the performance of their duties the Secretary-General and the staff shall not seek or receive instructions from any government or from any other authority external to the Organization. They shall refrain from any action which might reflect on their position as international officials responsible only to the Organization.

2. Each Member of the United Nations undertakes to respect the exclusively international character of the responsibilities of the Secretary-General and the staff and not to seek to influence them in the discharge of their responsibilities.

Article 101

1. The staff shall be appointed by the Secretary-General under regulations established by the General Assembly.

2. Appropriate staffs shall be permanently assigned to the Economic and Social Council, the Trusteeship Council, and, as required, to other organs of the United Nations. These staffs shall form a part of the Secretariat.

3. The paramount consideration in the employment of the staff and in the determination of the conditions of service shall be the necessity of securing the highest standards of efficiency, competence, and integrity. Due regard shall be paid to the importance of recruiting the staff on as wide a geographical basis as possible.

CHAPTER XVI

MISCELLANEOUS PROVISIONS

Article 102

1. Every treaty and every international agreement entered into by any Member of the United Nations after the present Charter comes into force shall as soon as possible be registered with the Secretariat and published by it.

2. No party to any such treaty or international agreement which has not been registered in accordance with the provisions of paragraph 1 of

this Article may invoke that treaty or agreement before any organ of the United Nations.

Article 103

In the event of a conflict between the obligations of the Members of the United Nations under the present Charter and their obligations under any other international agreement, their obligations under the present Charter shall prevail.

Article 104

The Organization shall enjoy in the territory of each of its Members such legal capacity as may be necessary for the exercise of its functions and the fulfillment of its purposes.

Article 105

1. The Organization shall enjoy in the territory of each of its Members such privileges and immunities as are necessary for the fulfillment of its purposes.

2. Representatives of the Members of the United Nations and officials of the Organization shall similarly enjoy such privileges and immunities as are necessary for the independent exercise of their functions in connection with the Organization.

3. The General Assembly may make recommendations with a view to determining the details of the application of paragraphs 1 and 2 of this Article or may propose conventions to the Members of the United Nations for this purpose.

CHAPTER XVII

TRANSITIONAL SECURITY ARRANGEMENTS

Article 106

Pending the coming into force of such special agreements referred to in Article 43 as in the opinion of the Security Council enable it to begin the exercise of its responsibilities under Article 42, the parties to the Four-Nation Declaration, signed at Moscow, October 30, 1943, and France, shall, in accordance with the provisions of paragraph 5 of that Declaration, consult with one another and as occasion requires with other Members of the United Nations with a view to such joint action on behalf of the Organization as may be necessary for the purpose of maintaining international peace and security.

Article 107

Nothing in the present Charter shall invalidate or preclude action, in relation to any state which during the Second World War has been an enemy of any signatory to the present Charter, taken or authorized as a result of that war by the Governments having responsibility for such action.

CHAPTER XVIII

AMENDMENTS

Article 108

Amendments to the present Charter shall come into force for all Members of the United Nations when they have been adopted by a vote of two thirds of the members of the General Assembly and ratified in accordance with their respective constitutional processes by two thirds of the Members of the United Nations, including all the permanent members of the Security Council.

Article 109

1. A General Conference of the Members of the United Nations for the purpose of reviewing the present Charter may be held at a date and place to be fixed by a two-thirds vote of the members of the General Assembly and by a vote of any seven members of the Security Council. Each Member of the United Nations shall have one vote in the conference.

2. Any alteration of the present Charter recommended by a two-thirds vote of the conference shall take effect when ratified in accordance with their respective constitutional processes by two thirds of the Members of the United Nations including all the permanent members of the Security Council.

3. If such a conference has not been held before the tenth annual session of the General Assembly following the coming into force of the present Charter, the proposal to call such a conference shall be placed on the agenda of that session of the General Assembly, and the conference shall be held if so decided by a majority vote of the members of the General Assembly and by a vote of any seven members of the Security Council.

CHAPTER XIX

RATIFICATION AND SIGNATURE

Article 110

1. The present Charter shall be ratified by the signatory states in accordance with their respective constitutional processes.

2. The ratifications shall be deposited with the Government of the United States of America, which shall notify all the signatory states of each deposit as well as the Secretary-General of the Organization when he has been appointed.

3. The present Charter shall come into force upon the deposit of ratifications by the Republic of China, France, the Union of Soviet Socialist Republics, the United Kingdom of Great Britain and Northern Ireland, and the United States of America, and by a majority of the other signatory states. A protocol of the ratifications deposited shall thereupon be drawn up by the Government of the United States of America which shall communicate copies thereof to all the signatory states.

4. The states signatory to the present Charter which ratify it after it has come into force will become original Members of the United Nations on the date of the deposit of their respective ratifications.

Article 111

The present Charter, of which the Chinese, French, Russian, English, and Spanish texts are equally authentic, shall remain deposited in the archives of the Government of the United States of America. Duly certified copies thereof shall be transmitted by that Government to the Governments of the other signatory states.

IN FAITH WHEREOF the representatives of the Governments of the United Nations have signed the present Charter.

DONE at the city of San Francisco the twenty-sixth day of June, one thousand nine hundred and forty-five.

APPENDIX B

Summary Information on Specialized Agencies

(As of Dec. 31, 1956)

Name of Agency and Location of Headquarters	Major Functions	Net Budget for 1957 (In thousands)	Name of Chief Officer	Date of Establishment[b]	Entry into Force of Agreement with United Nations
International Labour Organisation (ILO) Geneva, Switzerland	Brings together government, labor, management to consider industrial, manpower and related problems; establishes labor standards by international conventions; provides technical assistance for improvement of labor conditions and living standards and promotion of economic and social stability.	$ 7,618	David A. Morse (United States)	Apr. 11, 1919	Dec. 14, 1946
Food and Agriculture Organization of the United Nations (FAO) Rome, Italy	Seeks to increase production from farms, forests, and fisheries, and to improve distribution; provides expert assistance to governments in agricultural problems; works to improve nutrition.	$ 6,800	B. R. Sen (India)	Oct. 16, 1945	Dec. 14, 1946
United Nations Educational, Scientific and Cultural Organization (UNESCO) Paris, France	Seeks to broaden base of education throughout the world, to bring benefits of science to all countries, and to encourage cultural interchange in order to increase mutual understanding.	$10,796 (for 1956)	Luther H. Evans (United States)	Nov. 4, 1946	Dec. 14, 1946
International Civil Aviation Organization (ICAO) Montreal, Canada	Encourages use of safety measures, uniform regulations for operation, simpler procedures at borders; promotes use of new technical methods and equipment.	$ 3,568 (Canadian)	Carl Ljungberg (Sweden)	Apr. 4, 1947	Apr. 4, 1947

International Bank for Reconstruction and Development (IBRD) Washington, D.C.	Makes loans for productive projects, furnishes technical advice, and promotes private foreign investment.	\$ 7,615 (for 1955–56 fiscal year) met from income	Eugene R. Black (United States)	Dec. 27, 1945	Nov. 15, 1947
International Monetary Fund (IMF) Washington, D.C.	Promotes exchange stability, maintenance of orderly exchange arrangements among members, and international monetary co-operation; sells currency to members in temporary balance-of-payments difficulties and advises governments on financial problems.	\$ 5,342 (for 1955–56 fiscal year) met from earnings and capital	Per Jacobsson (Sweden)	Dec. 27, 1945	Nov. 15, 1947
World Health Organization (WHO) Geneva, Switzerland	Acts as clearinghouse for medical and scientific information; sets international standards for drugs and vaccines and administers international sanitary regulations; helps, on government request, to fight disease and improve health services.	\$10,700	M. G. Candau (Brazil)	Apr. 7, 1948	Apr. 7, 1948 (Approved by General Assembly Nov. 15, 1947)
Universal Postal Union (UPU) Berne, Switzerland	Unites members for reciprocal exchange of correspondence.	\$ 457 (for 1956)	Fritz Hess (Switzerland)	1874	Nov. 15, 1947
International Telecommunication Union (ITU) Geneva, Switzerland	Promotes international co-operation for improvement and rational use of telecommunications of all kinds.	\$ 1,498	Marco Aurelio Andrada (Argentina)	1865	Nov. 15, 1947
World Meteorological Organization (WMO) Geneva, Switzerland	Promotes international co-operation in field of meteorology, especially in establishment of world-wide networks of meteorological stations and rapid exchange of weather data.	\$ 425	D. A. Davies (United Kingdom)	Mar. 23, 1950	Dec. 20, 1951

[a] Source: U.N. Department of Public Information. Excluded are the International Refugee Organization, a temporary specialized agency established in 1946 and terminated in 1952; the Intergovernmental Maritime Consultative Organization, which will come into being on ratification of its convention by four additional states; and the International Atomic Energy Agency, the statute of which was opened for ratification on October 26, 1956.

[b] Acting through preparatory commissions or similar organs, FAO, UNESCO, ICAO, and WHO actually began functioning before their formal establishment. The Universal Postal Union was known until 1878 as the General Postal Union. The International Telecommunication Union was established as the International Telegraph Union and adopted its present title in 1932. A forerunner of the World Meteorological Organization was established in 1879 by agreement among meteorological officials of states. The intergovernmental agreement on which the present organization rests entered into force March 23, 1950.

APPENDIX C

Membership of United Nations and Specialized Agencies[a]

(As of Jan. 9, 1957)

Country or Territory	United Nations	Specialized Agencies									
		ILO	FAO	UNESCO[b]	ICAO	IBRD	IMF	WHO[c]	UPU[d]	ITU[e]	WMO[f]
Afghanistan	X	X	X	X	X	X	X	X	X	X	X
Albania	X	X	—	—	—	—	—	[g]	X	X	—
Argentina	X	X	X	X	X	X	X	X	X	X	X
Australia	X	X	X	X	X	X	X	X	X	X	X
Austria	X	X	X	X	X	X	X	X	X	X	X
Belgium	X	X	X	X	X	X	X	X	X	X	X
Bolivia	X	X	X	X	X	X	X	X	X	X	X
Brazil	X	X	X	X	X	X	X	X	X	X	X
Bulgaria	X	X	—	X	—	—	—	[g]	X	X	X
Burma	X	X	X	X	X	X	X	X	X	X	X
Byelorussian S.S.R.	X	X	—	X	—	—	—	[g]	X	X	X
Cambodia	X	—	X	X	X	—	—	X	X	X	X
Canada	X	X	X	X	X	X	X	X	X	X	X
Ceylon	X	X	X	X	X	X	X	X	X	X	X
Chile	X	X	X	X	X	X	X	X	X	X	—
China	X	X	—	X	X	X	X	X	X	X	X
Colombia	X	X	X	X	X	X	X	—	X	X	—
Costa Rica	X	X	X	X	—	X	X	X	X	X	—
Cuba	X	X	X	X	X	X	X	X	X	X	X
Czechoslovakia	X	X	—	X	X	—	—	[g]	X	X	X
Denmark	X	X	X	X	X	X	X	X	X	X	X
Dominican Republic	X	X	X	X	X	X	X	X	X	X	X
Ecuador	X	X	X	X	X	X	X	X	X	X	X
Egypt	X	X	X	X	X	X	X	X	X	X	X
El Salvador	X	X	X	X	X	X	X	X	X	X	X
Ethiopia	X	X	X	X	X	X	X	X	X	X	X
Finland	X	X	X	X	X	X	X	X	X	X	X
France	X	X	X	X	X	X	X	X	X	X	X
Germany, Federal Republic of	—	X	X	X	X	X	X	X	X	X	X
Greece	X	X	X	X	X	X	X	X	X	X	X
Guatemala	X	X	X	X	X	X	X	X	X	X	X
Haiti	X	X	X	X	X	X	X	X	X	X	X
Honduras	X	X	X	X	X	X	X	X	X	X	X
Hungary	X	X	—	X	—	—	—	[g]	X	X	X
Iceland	X	X	X	—	X	X	X	X	X	X	X
India	X	X	X	X	X	X	X	X	X	X	X
Indonesia	X	X	X	X	X	X	X	X	X	X	X
Iran	X	X	X	X	X	X	X	X	X	X	—
Iraq	X	X	X	X	X	X	X	X	X	X	X
Ireland	X	X	X	—	X	—	—	X	X	X	X
Israel	X	X	X	X	X	X	X	X	X	X	X
Italy	X	X	X	X	X	X	X	X	X	X	X
Japan	X	X	X	X	X	X	X	X	X	X	X
Jordan	X	X	X	X	X	X	X	X	X	X	X
Korea, Republic of	—	—	X	X	X	X	X	X	X	X	X
Laos	X	—	X	X	X	—	—	X	X	X	X
Lebanon	X	X	X	X	X	X	X	X	X	X	X
Liberia	X	X	X	X	X	—	—	X	X	X	—
Libya	X	X	X	X	X	—	—	X	X	X	X
Luxembourg	X	X	X	X	X	X	X	X	X	X	X
Mexico	X	X	X	X	X	X	X	X	X	X	X
Monaco	—	—	—	X	—	—	—	X	X	X	—
Morocco	X	X	X	X	X	—	—	X	X	[e]	[f]
Nepal	X	—	X	X	—	—	—	X	—	—	—

Country or Territory	United Nations	Specialized Agencies									
		ILO	FAO	UNESCO[b]	ICAO	IBRD	IMF	WHO[c]	UPU[d]	ITU[e]	WMO[f]
Netherlands	X	X	X	X	X	X	X	X	X	X[e]	X
New Zealand	X	X	X	X	X	—	—	X	X	X	X
Nicaragua	X	—	X	X	X	X	X	X	X	X	—
Norway	X	X	X	X	X	X	X	X	X	X	X
Pakistan	X	X	X	X	X	X	X	X	X	X	X
Panama	X	X	X	X	—	X	X	X	X	X	—
Paraguay	X	X	X	X	X	X	X	X	X	X	X
Peru	X	X	X	X	X	X	X	X	X	X	X
Philippines	X	X	X	X	X	X	X	X	X	X	X
Poland	X	X	—	X	X	—	—	[g]	X	X	X
Portugal	X	X	X	—	X	—	—	X	X	X	X
Rumania	X	X	—	X	—	—	—	[g]	X	X	X
San Marino	—	—	—	—	—	—	—	—	X	—	—
Saudi Arabia	X	—	X	X	—	—	—	X	X	X	—
Spain	X	X	X	X	X	—	—	X	X	X	X
Sudan	X	X	X	X	X	—	—	X	X	X	[f]
Sweden	X	X	X	X	X	X	X	X	X	X	X
Switzerland	—	X	X	X	X	—	—	X	X	X	X
Syria	X	X	X	X	X	X	X	X	X	X	X
Thailand	X	X	X	X	X	X	X	X	X	X	X
Tunisia	X	X	X	X	—	—	—	X	X	[e]	[f]
Turkey	X	X	X	X	X	X	X	X	X	X	X
Ukrainian S.S.R.	X	X	—	X	—	—	—	[g]	X	X	X
Union of South Africa	X	X	X	X	X	X	X	X	X	X[e]	X
Union of Soviet Socialist Republics	X	X	—	X	—	—	—	[g]	X	X	X
United Kingdom	X	X	X	X	X	X	X	X	X	X	X
United States	X	X	X	X	X	X	X	X	X	X	X
Uruguay	X	X	X	X	X	X	X	X	X	X	X
Vatican City	—	—	—	—	—	—	—	—	X	X	—
Venezuela	X	X	X	X	X	X	X	X	X	X	X
Vietnam	—	X	X	X	X	X	X	X	X	X	X
Yemen	X	—	X	—	—	—	—	X	X	X	—
Yugoslavia	X	X	X	X	—	X	X	X	X	X	X
Total Members	80	77	74	80	70	60	60	84	96	91	95

[a] Source: United Nations Washington Information.

[b] UNESCO also has four associate members: Gold Coast, Sierra Leone, British East Indies territories, and British West Indies territories.

[c] WHO also has four associate members: Federation of Rhodesia and Nyasaland, Gold Coast, Nigeria, and Sierra Leone.

[d] UPU members also include Algeria; Belgian Congo; French Overseas territories; Netherlands Antilles and Surinam; Portuguese Provinces of West Africa; Portuguese Provinces of East Africa, Asia, and Oceania; Morocco (Spanish Zone); Spanish Colonies; United Kingdom Overseas Territories; and United States Territories.

[e] In ITU, Netherlands membership includes Surinam, Netherlands Antilles, and New Guinea; Union of South Africa membership includes Territory of Southwest Africa. ITU members also include Belgian Congo and Territory of Ruanda-Urundi; former French Protectorates of Morroco and Tunisia (designation not yet officially changed), French Overseas Territories and Territories administered as such; Portuguese Overseas Provinces; Federation of Rhodesia and Nyasaland; Zone of Spanish Protectorate in Morocco and Spanish Possessions; United Kingdom colonies, protectorates, overseas territories and territories under mandate or trusteeship; and United States territories. ITU also has five associate members: British East Africa; British West Africa; Malaya-British Borneo Group; Trust Territory of Somaliland under Italian administration and Bermuda-British Caribbean Group.

[f] WMO members also include Belgian Congo; Bermuda; British Caribbean Territories; British East African Territories and Indian Ocean Islands; British Malaya-Borneo Territories; British West African Territories; Federation of Rhodesia and Nyasaland; French Cameroons; French Equatorial Africa; French Oceanic Colonies; French Somaliland; French Togoland; French West Africa; Hong Kong; Madagascar; French Protectorate of Morocco (designation not yet officially changed); Netherlands Antilles; Netherlands New Guinea; New Caledonia; Portuguese East Africa; Portuguese West Africa; Spanish Protectorate of Morocco; Spanish Guinea Territories; Sudan; Surinam; Tunisia. (Morocco, Sudan, and Tunisia still hold WMO membership as territories. Sudan has applied for membership as a state.)

[g] Have notified WHO of their withdrawal; Albania, Bulgaria, and the Soviet Union have announced their intention to resume participation.

APPENDIX D

Membership of Regional Economic Commissions

(As of Dec. 31, 1956)[a]

Economic Commission for Europe (ECE)[b]

Albania[c]
Austria[c]
Belgium
Bulgaria[c]
Byelorussian Soviet Socialist Republic
Czechoslovakia
Denmark
Finland[c]
France
Germany, Federal Republic of[d]
Greece
Hungary[c]
Iceland
Ireland[c]
Italy[c]
Luxembourg
Netherlands
Norway
Poland
Portugal[c]
Rumania[c]
Soviet Union
Spain[c]
Sweden
Turkey
Ukrainian Soviet Socialist Republic
United Kingdom
United States
Yugoslavia

Economic Commission for Asia and the Far East (ECAFE)

Afghanistan
Australia
Burma (Apr. 19, 1948)[e]
Cambodia (Aug. 20, 1954)[f]
Ceylon (Dec. 10, 1954)[f]
China
France
India
Indonesia (Sept. 28, 1950)[e]
Japan (June 24, 1954)[f]
Republic of Korea (Oct. 20, 1954)[f]
Laos (Feb. 16, 1955)[f]
Nepal (June 6, 1955)[f]
Netherlands
New Zealand
Pakistan
Philippines
Soviet Union
Thailand
United Kingdom
United States
Vietnam (Aug. 23, 1954)

Economic Commission for Latin America (ECLA)[g]

Argentina
Bolivia
Brazil
Chile
Colombia
Costa Rica
Cuba
Dominican Republic
Ecuador
El Salvador
France
Guatemala
Haiti
Honduras
Mexico
Netherlands
Nicaragua
Panama
Paraguay
Peru
United Kingdom
United States
Uruguay
Venezuela

[a] U.N. Department of Public Information *Structure of the United Nations (Ninth Revision)*, Doc. ST/DPI/10 (April 1956), pp. 23–25, and United Nations Washington Information Center.

[b] European states that are not Members of the United Nations may be admitted in a consultative capacity, and Switzerland participates in this way in the work of the commission. Experts from East Germany participate in the subsidiary bodies of the commission in a consultative capacity.

[c] In accordance with General Assembly Resolution 995(X), December 14, 1955, this country became a member of the United Nations. At the same time, it automatically became a member of the commission. Italy, however, had already been admitted to membership in the ECE on July 19, 1954 under Economic and Social Council Resolution 517B (XVII), April 22, 1954, and most of the others had participated in a consultative capacity in the work of the ECE.

[d] Became a member of ECE on February 21, 1956 pursuant to Economic and Social Council Resolution 594 (XX), December 15, 1955.

[e] Date of admission to United Nations, at which time country automatically became member of ECAFE.

[f] Was an associate member of ECAFE prior to date indicated. At present there are two associate members of the commission—Hong Kong, and Malaya and British Borneo—entitled to participate without vote in meetings of the commission and to vote and hold office in subordinate bodies of the commission.

[g] Prior to December 14, 1955 when they became Members of the United Nations, Italy had been authorized under Economic and Social Council Resolution 515B (XVII), April 30, 1954, and Spain under Resolution 581 (XX), August 4, 1955, to attend sessions of the commission on a basis similar to that provided for a Member of the United Nations not a member of the commission, *i.e.*, in a consultative capacity.

Fodor's 06

GERMANY

Where to Stay and Eat
for All Budgets

Must-See Sights
and Local Secrets

Ratings You Can Trust

Fodor's Travel Publications New York, Toronto, London, Sydney, Auckland
www.fodors.com

FODOR'S GERMANY 2006
Editors: Amanda Theunissen, Christina Knight

Editorial Production: David Downing
Editorial Contributors: Kerry Brady, Ruth Craig, Uli Ehrhardt, Christina Knight, Heather Phibbs, Marton Radkai, Jürgen Scheunemann, Ted Shoemaker, Kevin White
Maps: David Lindroth, *cartographer;* Bob Blake and Rebecca Baer, *map editors*
Design: Fabrizio La Rocca, *creative director*; Guido Caroti, *art director*; Moon Sun Kim, *cover designer*; Melanie Marin, *senior picture editor*
Production/Manufacturing: Angela L. McLean
Cover Photo (Dinkelsbuhl Annual Children's Festival): Robert Harding World Imagery

ISBN 1-4000-1562-6

ISSN 1525-5034

SPECIAL SALES
This book is available for special discounts for bulk purchases for sales promotions or premiums. Special editions, including personalized covers, excerpts of existing books, and corporate imprints, can be created in large quantities for special needs. For more information, write to Special Markets/Premium Sales, 1745 Broadway, MD 6-2, New York, New York 10019, or e-mail specialmarkets@randomhouse.com.

AN IMPORTANT TIP & AN INVITATION
Although all prices, opening times, and other details in this book are based on information supplied to us at press time, changes occur all the time in the travel world, and Fodor's cannot accept responsibility for facts that become outdated or for inadvertent errors or omissions. So **always confirm information when it matters,** especially if you're making a detour to visit a specific place. Your experiences—positive and negative—matter to us. If we have missed or misstated something, **please write to us.** We follow up on all suggestions. Contact the Germany editor at editors@fodors.com or c/o Fodor's at 1745 Broadway, New York, NY 10019.

PRINTED IN THE UNITED STATES OF AMERICA

10 9 8 7 6 5 4 3 2 1

Be a Fodor's Correspondent

Your opinion matters. It matters to us. It matters to your fellow Fodor's travelers, too. And we'd like to hear it. In fact, we *need* to hear it.

When you share your experiences and opinions, you become an active member of the Fodor's community. That means we'll not only use your feedback to make our books better, but we'll publish your names and comments whenever possible. Throughout our guides, look for "Word of Mouth," excerpts of your unvarnished feedback.

Here's how you can help improve Fodor's for all of us.

Tell us when we're right. We rely on local writers to give you an insider's perspective. But our writers and staff editors—who are the best in the business—depend on you. Your positive feedback is a vote to renew our recommendations for the next edition.

Tell us when we're wrong. We're proud that we update most of our guides every year. But we're not perfect. Things change. Hotels cut services. Museums change hours. Charming cafés lose charm. If our writer didn't quite capture the essence of a place, tell us how you'd do it differently. If any of our descriptions are inaccurate or inadequate, we'll incorporate your changes in the next edition and will correct factual errors at fodors.com *immediately.*

Tell us what to include. You probably have had fantastic travel experiences that aren't yet in Fodor's. Why not share them with a community of like-minded travelers? Maybe you chanced upon a beach or bistro or B&B that you don't want to keep to yourself. Tell us why we should include it. And share your discoveries and experiences with everyone directly at fodors.com. Your input may lead us to add a new listing or highlight a place we cover with a "Highly Recommended" star or with our highest rating, "Fodor's Choice."

Give us your opinion instantly at our feedback center at www.fodors.com/feedback. You may also e-mail editors@fodors.com with the subject line "Germany Editor." Or send your nominations, comments, and complaints by mail to Germany Editor, Fodor's, 1745 Broadway, New York, NY 10019.

You and travelers like you are the heart of the Fodor's community. Make our community richer by sharing your experiences. Be a Fodor's correspondent.

Happy Traveling!

Tim Jarrell

Tim Jarrell, Publisher

CONTENTS

UNDERSTANDING GERMANY

CLOSEUPS

MAPS

ABOUT THIS BOOK

Our Ratings

Sometimes you find terrific travel experiences and sometimes they just find you. But usually the burden is on you to select the right combination of experiences. That's where our ratings come in.

As travelers we've all discovered a place so wonderful that its worthiness is obvious. And sometimes that place is so experiential that superlatives don't do it justice: you just have to be there to know. These sights, properties, and experiences get our highest rating, **Fodor's Choice,** indicated by orange stars throughout this book.

Black stars highlight sights and properties we deem **Highly Recommended,** places that our writers, editors, and readers praise again and again for consistency and excellence.

By default, there's another category: any place we include in this book is by definition worth your time, unless we say otherwise. And we will.

Disagree with any of our choices? Care to nominate a place or suggest that we rate one more highly? Visit our feedback center at www.fodors.com/feedback.

Budget Well

Hotel and restaurant price categories from **¢ to $$$$** are defined in the opening pages of each chapter. For attractions, we always give standard adult admission fees; reductions are usually available for children, students, and senior citizens. Want to pay with plastic? **AE, D, DC, MC, V** following restaurant and hotel listings indicate if American Express, Discover, Diner's Club, MasterCard, and Visa are accepted.

Restaurants

Unless we state otherwise, restaurants are open for lunch and dinner daily. We mention dress only when there's a specific requirement and reservations only when they're essential or not accepted—it's always best to book ahead.

Hotels

Hotels have private bath, phone, TV, and air-conditioning and operate on the European Plan (a.k.a. EP, meaning without meals), unless we specify that they use the Continental Plan (CP, with a Continental breakfast), Breakfast Plan (BP, with a full breakfast), or Modified American Plan (MAP, with breakfast and dinner) or are all-inclusive (including all meals and most activities). We always list facilities but not whether you'll be charged an extra fee to use them, so when pricing accommodations, find out what's included.

Many Listings

- ★ Fodor's Choice
- ★ Highly recommended
- Physical address
- Directions
- Mailing address
- Telephone
- Fax
- On the Web
- E-mail
- Admission fee
- Open/closed times
- Start of walk/itinerary
- Metro stations
- Credit cards

Hotels & Restaurants

- Hotel
- Number of rooms
- Facilities
- Meal plans
- Restaurant
- Reservations
- Dress code
- Smoking
- BYOB
- Hotel with restaurant that warrants a visit

Outdoors

- Golf
- Camping

Other

- Family-friendly
- Contact information
- See also
- Branch address
- Take note

WHAT'S WHERE

MUNICH

If Germany has a second capital, it must be Munich. The southern capital of the Free State of Bavaria is a stubborn and proud adversary of Berlin and likes to top the federal capital in culture, sports, entertainment, society, and even politics. Despite being one of Germany's top tourist destinations, even for Germans, Munich never feels overwhelmed by cheerful tour bus groups like cities such as Heidelberg can. The historic part of the city is large enough to maintain its own identity even during the busiest seasons. The city has a wonderful opera, great theater, many historic museums, and precious churches, but the main appeal is the laid-back, almost Mediterranean flair found in the many parks, cafes, and beer gardens. Thanks to the mild Föhn winds blowing across the Bavarian Alps, the weather is usually very amicable, with a mild spring, cold winter, and picture-perfect summers.

THE BAVARIAN ALPS

Majestic peaks, lush green pastures, and frescoed houses brightened by window boxes of flowers make for Germany's most photogenic region. Quaint little towns like Mittenwald, Garmisch-Partenkirchen, Oberammergau, and Berchtesgaden have preserved their charming historic architecture. There's not much in the way of nightlife here; in summer and winter alike, the landscape provides the chief form of entertainment. You can find the country's finest skiing in Garmisch-Partenkirchen and take countless scenic hikes above mountain lakes such as Tegernsee, Schliersee, or the pristine Königsee.

THE ROMANTIC ROAD

Picturesque beyond words, the Romantische Strasse (Romantic Road) is more than 355 km (220 mi) of soaring castles, medieval villages, half-timber houses, and imposing churches all set in a pastoral backdrop of hills and greenery. Best explored by bicycle or train (though certainly accessible by car), the route winds its way from Würzburg to Füssen crossing a few top destinations such as Rothenburg-ob-der-Tauber and Schloss Neuschwanstein, King Ludwig II's fantastical castle, along the way. This area can get very busy during the summer, so if you're allergic to crowds, beware. You may prefer to visit in the fall when the grapes ripen on the vines around Würzburg, or in December when the Christmas markets bring a more authentic bustle to the town squares.

FRANCONIA & THE GERMAN DANUBE

An immensely affluent area, thanks to the centuries-old success of craftsmanship and trade, Franconia is a proud, independent-minded region in northern Bavaria. Dominated by the Fränkische Schweiz (Franconian Switzerland), an appealing, hilly, and rural triangle between Nürnberg, Bamberg, and Bayreuth, Franconia offers plenty of outdoor diversions including skiing, golfing, hiking, and cycling. If you prefer urban adventures, you will certainly like Nürnberg, the region's unofficial capital and an odd mix of high-tech industry and one of Europe's most enticing medieval settings. Nightlife, entertainment, and culture follow more traditional paths here, but the Christkindlmarkt in December is a once-in-a-lifetime experience (and the stands with mulled wine make up for the conservative nightlife).

THE BODENSEE

The region surrounding the Bodensee (Lake Constance) is the sunniest area in all of Germany and is populated by an equally sunny breed of good-humored people. Here, the *Welt ist noch in Ordnung,* "the world is still the way it used to be," as Germans like to say, and it's easy to see why: the region is surrounded by some of the most beautiful mountains Western Europe has to offer, and the dense natural surroundings offer an enchanting contrast to the picture-perfect little towns and manicured gardens. The main attraction, other than the university city of Konstanz (one of the most popular student cities in Germany) is the lake itself. Shoreline promenades offer enchanting views, ferries crisscross the waters, and bike routes circle the lake; pedal long enough and you'll cross into Switzerland or Austria. The *Blumeninsel* (flower island) of Mainau is a highlight. Owned by distant relatives of the Swedish royals, the island has been turned into a formal garden paradise of tulips, roses, hyacinths, and narcissi.

THE BLACK FOREST

The Black Forest is synonymous with cuckoo clocks and primeval woodland: certainly thousands of acres are cloaked in pines, and at least one entire town, little Triberg, goes all atwitter every hour. To many younger Germans, the Black Forest is nothing but a faded 1950's postcard. In the years following WWII, this was one of Germany's most popular tourist regions, but these days, the Black Forest has lost some of its appeal, even

though it has regained its status as an unspoiled, natural area thanks to vigorous environmental protection programs. Apart from walking, hiking, and (in winter) some modest skiing, Black Forest attractions include the historic university town of Freiburg in the far Southwest—one of the most colorful and hippest student cities in Germany—and proud and mercurial Baden-Baden, with its long tradition of spas and casinos. Baden-Baden provides a stark contrast to the secluded woodlands, and remains more worldly and chic than the rest of the German Southwest put together.

HEIDELBERG & THE NECKAR VALLEY

For many visitors, Heidelberg is quintessential Germany; for many Germans, Heidelberg is quintessential German tourism. The medieval town is full of cobblestone alleys, half-timber houses, vineyards, castles, wine pubs, and Germany's oldest university—all of which attract crowds of camera-carrying vacationers, particularly in the summer. Still, if you're looking for a fairy-tale town, Heidelberg is it, and the city is a good starting point for the driving tour known as the Castle Road. This route makes its way through the Neckar Valley, passing fortresses and villages all the way south to the Schwabenländle, the German nickname for the Swabian cities of Stuttgart, Heilbronn, and Tübingen. Once ill-reputed as Germany's most boring city, Stuttgart now deserves a second look thanks to its revitalized theaters, museums, and exhibition halls. The Swabians are famous for their pasta mania, so bring your appetite: everything here is served with curly egg noodles called *spätzle*.

FRANKFURT

Frankfurters likes to think of their city as the secret capital of Germany (and, yes, people in Munich believe the same of their city), partly because of its status as a financial center, but also because of its significance as a transportation hub, and its overall upscale appeal. Dubbed "Mainhattan"—a nickname owed to the fact that it's the only German city with appreciable skyscrapers—the city of 652,000 is undoubtedly one of the country's most advanced, modern, and clean places, with some Disneyland-style historic attractions such as the re-built Römerberg. Frankfurt also has a reputation for being somewhat dull. For nightlife, locals and visitors alike go "dribbedebach" (Hessian slang for "across the river"),

to Sachsenhausen on the southern bank of the Main River. A charming, historic town, Sachenhausen is *the* place to indulge in the essentials of Hessian *Gemütlichkeit*—apple cider, onion breads, and hearty meat dishes.

THE PFALZ & RHINE TERRACE

Wine reigns supreme here. Bacchanalian festivals pepper the calendar between May and October, and wineries welcome drop-ins for tastings year-round. The entire region has a down-to-earth spirit making the enjoyment of good food and wine seem more important than the dealings of the world. In between vineyards and fields, historic towns dot the region. Three great cathedrals are found in Worms, Speyer, and Mainz. The streets of Worms were ancient even when Charlemagne and Luther walked them; and Mainz is the town where Johannes Gutenberg printed the first Bible. The region's most famous son is former German chancellor Helmut Kohl, the longest-reigning German head of state in the 20th century.

THE RHINELAND

The mighty Rhine River has defined German history for centuries and today the Rhineland is one of the most dynamic regions in all of Europe. Fascinating cities such as Cologne, are steeped in Roman and medieval history, offering stunning symbols of Gothic architecture such as the world-famous Kölner Dom. At the same time, Cologne along with Düsseldorf, the capital of the state of Northrhine-Westphalia, offer a look into Europe's future with internet companies and high-tech software firms flourishing along the sleek autobahn routes. Throughout Germany, the region is famous for the Karneval in February, when Rhinelanders, never shy to strike up a conversation, become even more sociable and join in boisterous, street parades and week-long celebrations—this is certainly the best time to visit Cologne. Outside the big cities, the Rhineland offers magnificent boat trips on the Rhine River, as well as hiking paths along the river banks.

THE FAIRY-TALE ROAD

The Märchenstrasse (Fairy-Tale Road), stretching 370 mi between Hanau and Bremen, is most certainly the road less traveled—all the better for those who choose it. Misty woodlands, ancient castles, and small towns full of half-timber houses are the focus in this area, known as Brothers Grimm country. It

was here that the great compilers of folklore mined for their sometimes-dark tales of magic and miracles. The Grimms' imaginations were nourished during a childhood in Steinau an der Strasse, a medieval beauty of a town where their stories delight children today at the Steinauer Marionettentheater. Don't come to this region looking for nightlife or chic international scenes, this is a meandering route through the heart of Germany, perfect for travelers seeking a more intimate view of the country's many charms.

HAMBURG

Known for having the highest number of millionaires in Germany, Hamburg loves to be snobbish—and rather cool to its guests. It certainly takes time to make friends with the stiff Hanseaten, the proud offspring of the patriarchal leading families of the Free and Hanseatic City of Hamburg. But the city, dominated by lakes, canals, the river Elbe, and Germany's biggest harbor, is undeniably beautiful—a German Venice on the North Sea. Summer is, without question, the best time to visit. Fall, winter, and even spring can be unbearably rainy or misty. But Germany's second-largest city has much to offer, even if the weather isn't cooperating. World-class museums of modern art, the Reeperbahn (no longer a shabby red-light district, but a mix of top musical stages and a thriving, upscale nightlife), some of the most upscale shopping malls in Germany, and many Michelin-starred restaurants offer ample distraction from nature's gloom.

SCHLESWIG-HOLSTEIN & THE BALTIC COAST

The tiny Danish-influenced state of Schleswig-Holstein, and the little-known East German state of Mecklenburg-Vorpommern form the German coastline along the Baltic Coast and North Sea. The windswept landscape here is scattered with medieval towns, fishing villages, long white beaches, and summer resorts. Still shaped by the region's proud Hanseatic past, cities like Lübeck, Wismar, and Stralsund offer stunning examples of the redbrick Gothic architecture once found throughout Northern Europe. Small sea resorts and the quaint islands of Sylt (in the West), Rügen, and Usedom (in the East) attract a summer crowd in the few sunny weeks that come this way. This area is very much off the beaten track making it some

what of a haven for bikers, hikers, fishermen, and swimmers who don't mind chilly—okay, frigid—water.

BERLIN

Berlin is back. This city of contrasts, a capital of 3.2 million thrown together from two once-divided parts, is re-emerging as one of the world's hippest urban destinations. Compared to other German cities, Berlin has always been dirty, noisy, and overcrowded; but its intensity makes the city a unique laboratory for new trends and ideas. With the most international residents in Germany, Berlin is a true crossroads, not only of Western and Eastern Europe, but of the world. Cutting-edge art exhibits, stage dramas, musicals, and rock bands often get their start here. Two cities' worth of world-class museums compete for your daylight hours, as do the shops along 2-mi Kurfürstendamm, which ends at a sobering World War II memorial, the Kaiser-Wilhelm-Gedächtniskirche. Even as Berlin moves forward and redefines itself, modern history remains embedded in its landscape at landmarks such as the Brandenburger Tor, which stood alone in divided Berlin's no-man's-land, and the newly-opened Memorial to the Murdered Jews of Europe.

SAXONY, SAXONY-ANHALT & THURINGIA

Often overlooked, even by West Germans, this region in the Southeast of Germany is a treasure trove of European high culture. Cities like Dresden, Leipzig, Weimar, and Eisenach are linked to Schiller, Goethe, Bach, Luther, and the likes. Beautifully restored in recent years, great monuments such as the Frauenkirche and the Zwinger are once again open to the awe and admiration of the public. As the entire area was hidden behind the Iron Curtain for forty years, it is less "Americanized" than many of its Western counterparts and offers, what some would call, a more authentic version of German culture and life.

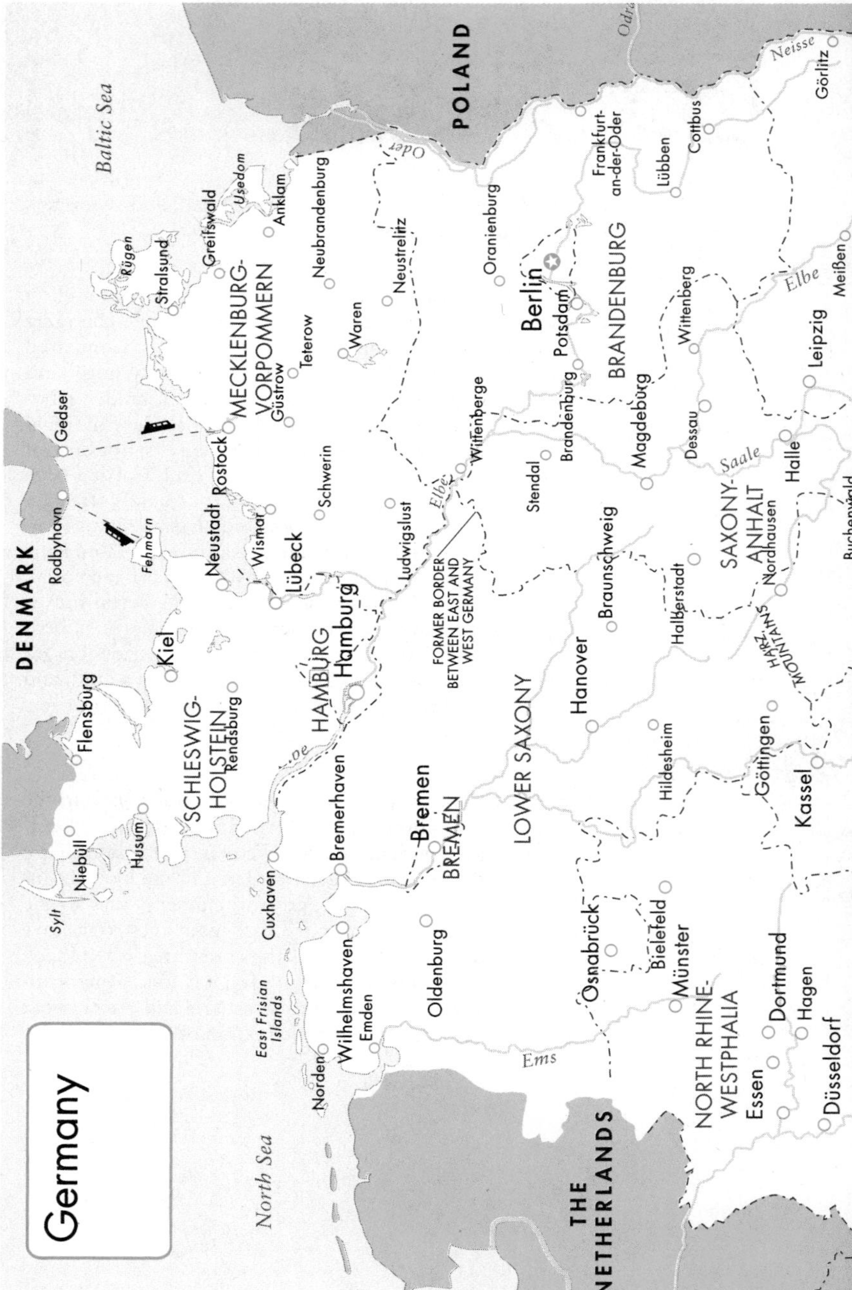
Germany
DENMARK
POLAND
THE NETHERLANDS
Baltic Sea
North Sea
Sylt
Niebüll
Husum
Flensburg
Kiel
Rendsburg
SCHLESWIG-HOLSTEIN
Rodbyhavn
Fehmarn
Gedser
Neustadt
Lübeck
Wismar
Rostock
Stralsund
Rügen
Greifswald
Usedom
Anklam
Neubrandenburg
MECKLENBURG-VORPOMMERN
Güstrow
Teterow
Waren
Neustrelitz
Schwerin
Ludwigslust
HAMBURG
Hamburg
Cuxhaven
Bremerhaven
Bremen
BREMEN
Wilhelmshaven
Emden
Norden
East Frisian Islands
Oldenburg
Ems
LOWER SAXONY
Osnabrück
Bielefeld
Münster
Hanover
Hildesheim
Göttingen
Braunschweig
Halberstadt
HARZ MOUNTAINS
Kassel
NORTH RHINE-WESTPHALIA
Essen
Dortmund
Hagen
Düsseldorf
FORMER BORDER BETWEEN EAST AND WEST GERMANY
Elbe
Wittenberge
Stendal
Brandenburg
Magdeburg
Oranienburg
Berlin
Potsdam
BRANDENBURG
Oder
Frankfurt-an-der-Oder
Lübben
Cottbus
Neisse
Görlitz
Wittenberg
Dessau
Saale
Halle
SAXONY-ANHALT
Nordhausen
Buchenwald
Leipzig
Elbe
Meißen

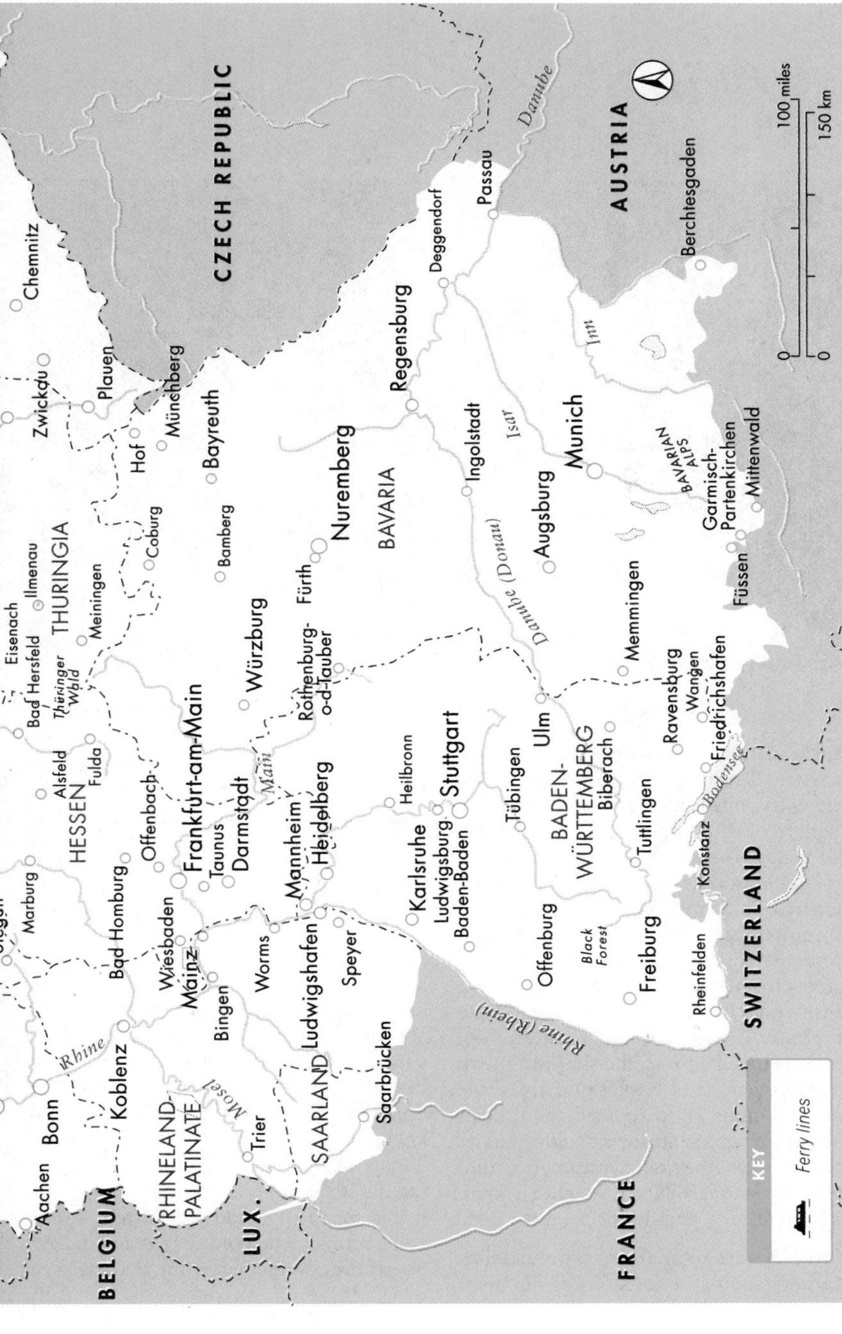
CZECH REPUBLIC
AUSTRIA
SWITZERLAND
FRANCE
BELGIUM
LUX.
Chemnitz
Zwickau
Plauen
Münchberg
Hof
Bayreuth
Regensburg
Deggendorf
Passau
Danube
Berchtesgaden
Inn
Isar
Munich
Ingolstadt
BAVARIA
Nuremberg
Fürth
Bamberg
Coburg
THURINGIA
Ilmenau
Meiningen
Eisenach
Bad Hersfeld
Thüringer Wald
Fulda
Alsfeld
HESSEN
Marburg
Siegen
Bad Homburg
Offenbach
Frankfurt-am-Main
Taunus
Darmstadt
Würzburg
Main
Rothenburg-o-d-Tauber
Mannheim
Heidelberg
Heilbronn
Stuttgart
Ludwigsburg
Karlsruhe
Baden-Baden
Tübingen
Ulm
BADEN-WÜRTTEMBERG
Biberach
Tuttlingen
Offenburg
Black Forest
Freiburg
Rheinfelden
Konstanz
Bodensee
Friedrichshafen
Ravensburg
Wangen
Memmingen
Danube (Donau)
Augsburg
Füssen
Garmisch-Partenkirchen
Mittenwald
BAVARIAN ALPS
Wiesbaden
Mainz
Bingen
Worms
Ludwigshafen
Speyer
Saarbrücken
SAARLAND
Rhine (Rhein)
Rhine
Koblenz
Bonn
Aachen
Trier
Mosel
RHINELAND-PALATINATE
100 miles
150 km
0
0
KEY
Ferry lines

QUINTESSENTIAL GERMANY

Meeting at the Market

The tradition of market shopping still thrives in Germany, especially in cities. On market day, often Saturday and/or mid-week, a square or small street is closed to traffic and vendors—from butchers to beekeepers—set up stands. You'll see fewer grandmothers and more fashionably dressed 30-somethings selecting from seven kinds of breads at the baker, organic (Bio) vegetables from the hippy farmer, or less-expensive ones from the Turkish seller. "Paper or plastic?" is out of the question. The goods get packed into the shopper's own large, woven, hand basket or canvas tote bag. Germans shop to feed themselves with fresh ingredients for a couple of days, not for a week (their refrigerators are a third the size of standard North American ones). The last stop is usually for fresh flowers.

Market Saturdays make a chore sociable. Markets smartly choose locations near sidewalk cafés, where young couples and families regroup for a coffee or beer. Throughout the morning, chairs are handed from one friend or acquaintance to the next as people come and go. After securing the necessities, shoppers might linger over the inexpensive third-world imports or expensive felt handbags on offer from one of the few "non-perishable" stands.

When it comes to Christmas time, German markets are world famous. Everything you need to celebrate the holiday is sold at the *Weihnachtsmarkt* (Christmas markets): handmade wooden ornaments from the Erzgebirge (Erz Mountains), Stollen (a bread-like fruit cake) from Dresden, and Lebkuchen (gingerbread) from Nürnberg. Artists and artisans set up stands decorated with green boughs and lights to sell wares made of wood, glass, felt, silver, and ceramic. The cold may come in, but big-store consumerism is out, making even

shopping for Christmas gifts an enjoyable fresh-air experience.

More Beer, Bitte

Nothing escapes the notice of German bureaucracy: the Federal Statistics Office reported that in the first quarter of 2005, sales of beer within Germany declined by 3.5%. The president of the German Brewers Association confirmed the news, saying "the classic number of beer drinkers between 35 and 45 is declining." This drop translates to 116 liters of beer per German being consumed annually instead of 118. Make some room on that bench, we'll help make up the difference.

The drinking age for beer and wine in Germany is 16 and drinking in public is permitted. Beer's fixture within the culture seems to abate its abuse. People might order a draft of Bitburger on their lunch break or a bottle of Becks to go with their popcorn at the cinema. In Köln and Bonn, the waiter will keep bringing small cylindrical glasses of Kölsch, a light ale made in the Rhineland, until you put a coaster on top of your empty one. There are hundreds of breweries in Germany, some strongly associated with a city, others available primarily within their state, and many which cross borders: while you won't find a Berlin pilsner in Bavaria, plenty of Bavarian Weissbiers (wheat beers) are available in the north. The ideal beer is simply one enjoyed in the fresh air of a Biergarten. A beer garden, such as the famous Chinese Pavilion in Munich's English Garden, might seat hundreds. Or, it could simply be a café's back garden of gravel and soaring chestnut trees, where nine picnic tables are shaded by three beer- or tobacco-sponsored umbrellas. You can enjoy a liquid lunch, or go to self-serve areas that might offer pastas or lamb in addition to grilled sausages and pretzels. While beer gardens exist all

If you want to get a sense of contemporary German culture, and indulge in some of its pleasures, start by familiarizing yourself with the rituals of daily life.

over Germany, the smoky beer hall experience—with dirndls and oompah bands—is unique to Bavaria.

Karneval

Every year on November 11, tradition dictates that women get to plant kisses upon the cheeks or lips of their choice—a fine start to the long Karneval season that ends the night before Ash Wednesday (in late February or early March). In Germany, the Rhineland celebrates this Catholic festival, also called Fasching, with the most traditions; and in the Rhineland, the epicenter of one last week of wild revelry is Köln, a city that's already considered one of the friendliest and most laid-back in the country.

The final days of the "fifth season" begin with Weiberfestnacht, a day when women doll themselves up and get into all sorts of mischief, including cutting off the ties of men caught wearing them. For the next four days and nights, business in Köln nearly grinds to a halt and copious amounts of the local brew, Kölsch, fuel evenings of masked balls and parties, sponsored by Köln Karneval societies. Formed by groups such as fire departments, churches, sports clubs, and choirs, the societies also prepare elaborate floats and marching bands for the main parade on Rosenmontag (the Monday before "Fat Tuesday").

In the Black Forest, many towns also have spontaneous street appearances of New Orleans-style bands. Their costume tradition is for men to dress up as a uniform gaggle of witches, wearing large, hand-carved masks. Karneval is a great time to experience Germany's wild side. If you're shy, pick up a mask, wig, or the ubiquitous red clown nose to lend the anonymity—or courage—you need to join in the fun.

WHEN TO GO

The tourist season in most of Germany runs from May through October, when the weather is at its best. Prices are generally higher in summer, so **consider visiting during the off-season to save money** (but be aware that the weather is often cold and some attractions are closed or have shorter hours in winter). Most resorts offer between-season (*Zwischensaison*) and edge-of-season (*Nebensaison*) rates, and tourist offices can provide lists of hotels that offer low-price inclusive weekly packages (*Pauschal-angebote*). It's wise to **avoid cities at times of major trade fairs,** when attendees commandeer all hotel rooms and prices soar. You can check trade fair schedules with the German National Tourist Office.

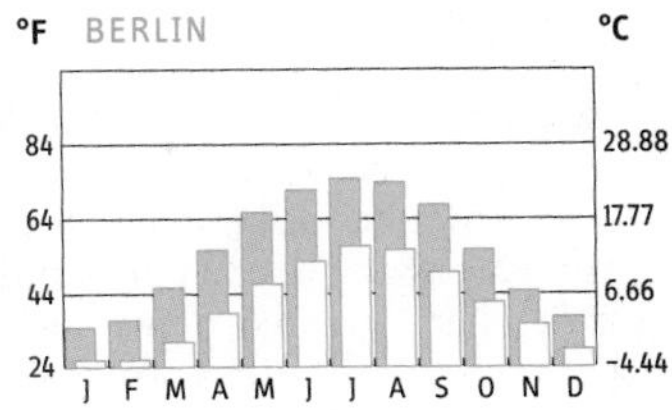

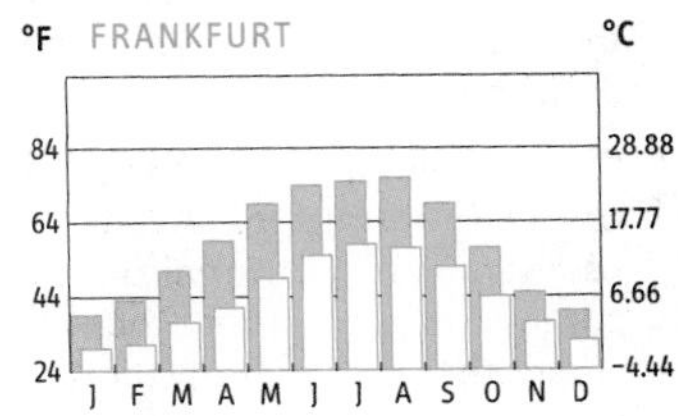

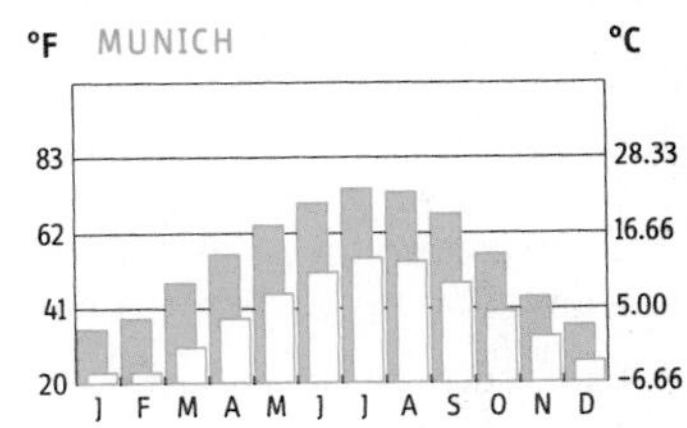

Climate

Germany's climate is temperate, although cold spells can drop temperatures well below freezing, particularly in the Alps, the Harz region of Lower Saxony and Saxony-Anhalt, the Black Forest, and the higher regions of northern Franconia. Summers are usually warm, though you should **be prepared for a few rainy days,** especially in the north. As you get nearer to the Alps, the summers get shorter, with warm weather often not beginning until the end of May. Fall can be spectacular in the south. Germans measure temperature in Celsius.

Forecasts **Weather.com** www.weather.com.

The adjacent charts show average daily maximum and minimum temperatures for Berlin, Frankfurt, and Munich.

IF YOU LIKE . . .

Being Outdoors

Germans have a long-standing love affair with mother nature and have designated large amounts of land as national recreation areas and urban parks and gardens. Cities have created many miles of bike paths, especially along waterways, and in places such as **Würzburg,** you can set off along the river and reach pure countryside within 30 minutes.

The most unusual landscape in the country is 19 mi south of Dresden in the **Sächsische Schweiz,** a national park of twisting gorges and sheer cliffs. Rock climbers fascinate those driving up the steep switchbacks to reach bald mesas. At a much higher altitude are the Bavarian Alps, where the Winter Olympics town **Garmisch-Partenkirchen** offers cable cars to ascend Germany's highest mountain. This is one of the country's best spots for skiing in the winter and hiking in the summer.

Lakes such as **Chiemsee** and **Bodensee** dot the area between the Alps and Munich and many hikers and bikers enjoy circling them. Boat rentals are possible, but you'll need a German-recognized license. On the island of **Rügen,** the turn-of-the-20th century resort town, **Binz,** fronts the gentle (and cold) waters of the Baltic Sea. Even on windy days, you can warm up on the beach in a sheltered beach chair for two. The Baltic Coast's most dramatic features are Rügen's white chalk cliffs in **Jasmund National Park** where you can hike, bike, or sign up for nature seminars and tours.

Medieval Towns

The trail of walled towns and half-timber houses known as the **Romantic Road** is a route long marketed by German tourism, and therefore the road more traveled. The towns are lovely, but if you'd prefer fewer group tours spilling into your photographs, venture into the **Harz Mountains** in the center of Germany.

Goslar, the unofficial capital of the Harz region, is one of Germany's oldest cities and is renowned for its Romanesque Kaiserpfalz, an imperial palace where emperors held diets. Goslar has been declared a UNESCO World Heritage site, as has the town of **Quedlinburg,** 30 mi to the southeast. With 1,600 half-timber houses, Quedlinburg has more of these historic, typically northern-German buildings than any other town in the country.

A mighty fortress south of the Harz Mountains is the **Wartburg** in the ancient, half-timber town of **Eisenach.** Frederick the Wise protected Martin Luther from papal proscription within these stout walls in the 16th century.

Options for exploring closer to Munich include **Regensburg** and **Nürnberg.** The former is a beautiful medieval city, relatively unknown even to Germans, and has a soaring French Gothic cathedral that can hold 6,000 people. Nürnberg dates to 1050 and is among the most historic cities in the country. Not only emperors but artists convened here, including the Renaissance genius Albrecht Dürer.

The Arts

Germany has a lively and centuries-old arts scene, though you will have to fling yourself to nearly every corner of the country to see all the important collections and great music venues located here. It's best to do advance research about what's happening when and where so you won't be disappointed by missing special performances or temporary exhibits.

If you're interested in buying works by German or international artists, **Köln** has the largest concentration of galleries—though most of the artists are working in affordable studios in **Berlin**.

The capital shows its art in small galleries and major museums such as Mies Van de Rohe's **New National Gallery**. The new **Berlinische Galerie** dedicates itself to art, photography, and architecture created in the city from 1870 to the present. The must-see and hear music venue in the city is the acoustically exceptional **Berlin Philharmonic**.

In summer, many orchestras and opera houses shut down for the season and outdoor music festivals substitute for arriving tourists. In **Bregnenz**, on the Bodensee, near Lindau, a dramatic floating stage supports orchestras and opera stars during the Bregenz Music Festival. In Beyreuth, the **Wagner Festival** is an important indoor exception.

Fans of old master painters must haunt the halls of the **Zwinger** in Dresden, where most works were collected in the first half of the 18th century, and the **Alte Pinakothek** in Munich, which has one of the world's largest collections of Rubens. Throughout the country, opera and concert tickets can be very inexpensive, but you must book tickets far in advance, as Germany is home to many music lovers.

GREAT ITINERARIES

GERMAN ABC's: ARCHITECTURE, BEER, AND CAPITAL CITIES

Day 1: Arrival Munich

Though a wealthy city with Wittelsbach palaces, great art collections, and a technology museum holding trains, planes, and even an imitation coal mine, what really distinguishes Munich from other state capitals are its beer halls, beer gardens, and proud identity: even designer-conscious Müncheners wear traditional dirndls and hunter green jackets for special occasions. Stroll the streets of the Altstadt (Old City), visit the Frauenkirche, choose a museum (the best ones will occupy you for at least three hours), and save the Hofbräuhaus or any other teeming brew house for last. Munich might be touristy, but hordes of German tourists love it as well. ⇨ *See Chapter 1,* Munich.

Logistics: Good for pairs or families, buy a €16 Partner Day Ticket for the 40-minute suburban rail trip from the airport into the city. Before boarding the train, stop by the airport's tourist office to begin getting your bearings. Most flights from North America to Bavaria's capital land before 10 AM; no matter how tired you may feel, try to stay on your feet to adjust to the new time zone.

Day 2: Neuschwanstein

From Munich, it's an easy day trip to Germany's fairy-tale castle in Schwangau. Though the 19th-century castle's fantastic silhouette has made it famous, this creation of King Ludwig II is more opera set than piece of history—the interior was never even completed. A tour reveals why the romantic king earned the nickname "Mad King Ludwig." Across the narrow wooded valley from Schloss Neuschwanstein is the ancient castle of the Bavarian Wittelsbach dynasty, Schloss Hohenschwangau, also open for tours. ⇨ *See Chapter 3,* The Romantic Road

Logistics: You can join an all-day bus trip or even a bike tour from Munich, or make the 2.5-hour journey on your own by rail (the best connection goes direct to Füssen and includes a bus transfer to the castle's village, Hohenschwangau). Call ahead (08362/930–830) to book your timed ticket entrance to the castles.

Day 3: Munich to Dresden

That Saxony's capital, Dresden, is the pinnacle of European baroque is obvious in its courtyards, newly rebuilt Frauenkirche, and terrace over the Elbe River. The city was largely shaped by Augustus the Strong, who in 1730, kindly invited the public to view the works crafted with precious stones in his Green Vault. Many of Dresden's art treasures lie within the Zwinger, a baroque showpiece. Spend the evening at the neo-Renaissance Semper Opera, where Wagner premiered his works, and drink Radeberger Pilsner at intermission. It's the country's oldest pilsner. ⇨ *See Chapter 15,* Saxony, Saxony-Anhalt & Thuringia

Logistics: It's nearly a 7-hour train trip from Munich to Dresden. The one-way, one-hour flight on dba can cost just €52 with advance booking on their website (www.flydba.com). Dresden's airport is 6 mi north of the city.

Day 4: Dresden and Berlin

Spend the morning touring some of the

rich museums of Dresden before boarding a train to Berlin. Germany's capital is not only unique for its division between 1949 and 1989, but is unlike any other German city in its physical expanse and diversity. Attractions that don't close until 10 PM or later are Sir Norman Foster's glass dome on the Reichstag, the TV tower at Alexanderplatz, and the Checkpoint Charlie museum. ⇨ *See chapters 15 and 16,* Saxony, Saxony-Anhalt & Thuringia and Berlin

Logistics: EC trains from Dresden to Berlin take just over two hours. Regional trains (RE) and ICE trains involve a transfer and take three hours. Don't worry about arriving at night: Berlin stays up late and has a low crime rate. Book a hotel in Mitte, the district that holds many museums and the most history.

Days 5 and 6: Berlin

Begin your first Berlin morning on a walk with one of the city's excellent tour companies. They'll connect the broadly-spaced dots for you and make the events of Berlin's turbulent 20th century clear. Berlin is a fascinating city in and of itself, so you don't have to feel guilty if you don't get to many museums. Since the mid-1990s, world-renowned architects have changed the city's face. You'll find the best nightlife in residential areas such as Prenzlauer Berg, Kreuzberg, or the northern part of Mitte. Berlin is a surprisingly inexpensive city, so you can treat yourself to more here than in Munich. ⇨ *See Chapter 16,* Berlin

Logistics: As it's likely that you'll use public transport at least three times a day in Berlin, use day passes for better value. If your week ends with an early flight out of Munich on Day 7, take a train back in the late afternoon of day 6. The journey takes 6.5 to 7 hours.

Day 7: Munich

On your last day, have breakfast with the morning shoppers at the open-air Viktualian Markt. Try to find Weisswurst (white sausage), a mild, boiled sausage normally eaten before noon with sweet mustard, a pretzel—and beer! ⇨ *See Chapter 1,* Munich

CASTLES IN WINE COUNTRY

Day 1: Arrival Koblenz / The Rhineland

Start your tour in Koblenz, at the confluence of the rivers Rhine and Mosel. Once you have arrived in the historic downtown area, head straight for the charming little Hotel Zum weissen Schwanen, a half-timber inn and mill since 1693. Explore the city on the west bank of the Rhine River and then head to Europe's biggest fortress, the impressive Festung Ehrenbreitstein on the opposite river bank. ⇨ *See Chapter 10,* The Rhineland

Logistics: If you're flying in, Koblenz can best be reached via the Cologne airport. Rent a car here and then enjoy the leisurely, scenic drive south on Autobahn 555, and later on Bundesstrasse 9 along the banks of the Rhine River.

Day 2: Koblenz & Surrounding Castles

Get up early and drive along the most spectacular and historic section of the "Vater Rhein." Stay on the left river banks and you'll pass many mysterious landmarks on the way, including Burg Stolzenfels, and later the Loreley rock, a 430-foot slate cliff named after a legendary, beautiful, blonde nymph. Stay the night at St. Goar or St. Goarhausen, both lovely river villages. ⇨ *See Chapter 10,* The Rhineland

Logistics: St. Goar is on the left river bank, St. Goarhausen is on the right; a ferry goes back and forth between them. On day three, you'll want to be on the right river bank to continue southeast by car on Bundesstrasse 42 to Eltville.

Day 3: Eltville & the Eberbach Monastery

The former Cistercian monastery Kloster Eberbach, in Eltville, is one of Europe's best preserved medieval cloisters. Parts of the film, *The Name of the Rose,* based on Umberto Eco's novel and starring Sean Connery, were filmed here. If you're interested in wine, spend the night at the historic wine estate, Schloss Reinhartshausen. This is a great opportunity to sample the fantastic wines of the region. ⇨ *See Chapter 10,* The Rhineland

Day 4: Heidelberg

On day four, start driving early so you can spend a full day in Heidelberg. No other city symbolizes German spirit and history better than this meticulously restored, historic town. Do not miss the impressive Schloss, one of Europe's greatest Gothic-Renaissance fortresses. Most of the many pubs and restaurants here are very touristy, overpriced, and of poor quality—so don't waste your time at them. Instead, head for the Romantik Hotel zum Ritter St. Georg, a charming 16th-century inn with a great traditional German restaurant. ⇨ *See Chapter 7,* Heidelberg & the Neckar Valley

Logistics: The drive from Eltville to Heidelberg takes about an hour.

Days 5 & 6: The Burgenstrasse & the Neckar Valley

Superb food and wine can be enjoyed in the quaint little villages in the Neckar Valley just east of Heidelberg—the predominant grapes here are Riesling (white) and

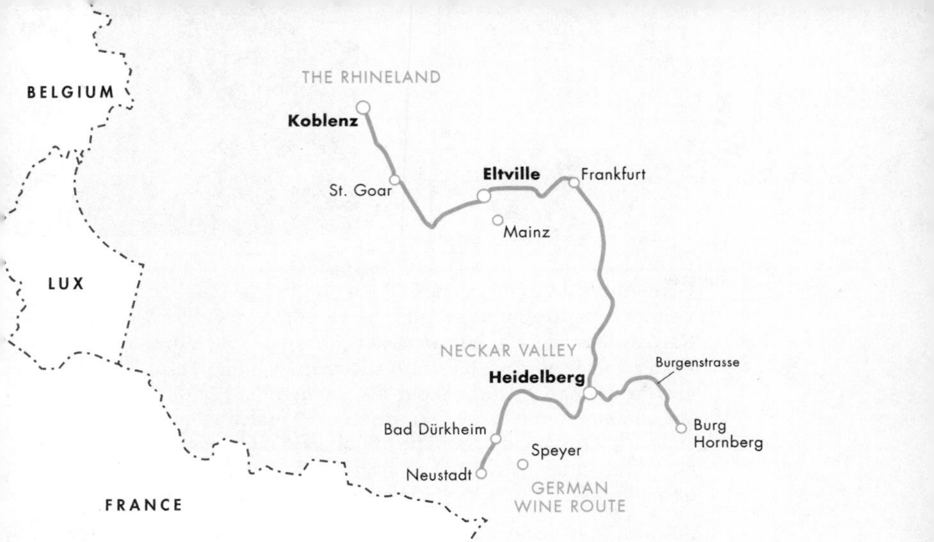

Spätburgunder (red). Try to sample wines from small, private wineries—they tend to have higher-quality vintages. Sightseeing is equally stunning, with a string of castles and ruins along the famous *Burgenstrasse* (Castle Road). Since you have two days for this area, take your time and follow B–37 to Eberbach and its romantic Zwingenberg castle, tucked away in the deep forest just outside the village. In the afternoon, continue on to Burg Hornberg at Neckarzimmern, the home to the legendary German knight Götz von Berlichingen. Stay the night here, at the former stables of the castle.

The next morning, continue further to Bad Wimpfen, the most charming valley town at the confluence of the Neckar and Jagst rivers. Spend half a day in the historic city center and tour the Staufer Pfalz (royal palace). Soaring high above the city, the palace was built in 1182 and emperor Barbarossa liked to stay here. ⇨ *See Chapter 7*, Heidelberg & the Neckar Valley

Logistics: Winding its way through the Neckar River valley, the historic Burgenstrasse loosely follows modern Bundesstrasse 37.

Day 7: German Wine Route

Devote your last day to the German Wine Route which winds its way through one of the most pleasant German landscapes, the gentle slopes and vineyards of the Pfalz. The starting point for the route is Bad Dürkheim, a spa town proud to have the world's largest wine cask, holding 1.7 million liters (450,000 gallons). You can enjoy wine with some lunch in the many Weinstuben here or wait until you reach Neustadt farther south, Germany's largest wine growing community. Thirty of the vintages grown here can be sampled (and purchased) at the downtown Haus des Weines. If time permits, try to visit one of the three major castles along the route in the afteroon: Burg Trifels near Annweiler is a magnificent Hohenzollern residence, perched dramatically on three sandstone cliffs—the very image of a medieval castle in wine country. ⇨ *See Chapter 9*, The Pfalz & Rhine Terrace

Logistics: Bad Dürkheim is only 1.5 hours from Bad Wimpfen via A–6 and A–61. Starting at Bad Dürckheim, the Wine Route mostly follows B–271 south. The drive back to Cologne (if you need to catch your return flight there) is a fast 2.5-hour trip on A–61 and A–565.

ON THE CALENDAR

ONGOING	Germany ranks number one in the world for the number of foreign visitors attending fairs and exhibitions. Top seasonal events include Karneval festivities in January and February, spring festivals around Easter and Pentecost, Bayreuth's Richard Wagner Festival in August, wine festivals throughout the southern half of the country in late summer and fall, the Oktoberfest in Munich in late September and early October, the Frankfurt Book Fair in October, and December's Christmas markets. For event listings, see the German National Tourist Office's Web site (🌐 www.germany-tourism.de). Between June 6 and July 9, 2006, Germany is hosting the **FIFA World Cup,** the championships of the world's most popular sport, soccer. Tournament matches will be held in 12 cities across the country: Berlin, Cologne, Dortmund, Frankfurt, Gelsenkirchen, Hamburg, Hannover, Kaiserslautern, Leipzig, Munich, Nürnberg, and Stuttgart. If you plan to visit any of these cities during the World Cup, book lodgings and reserve seats for train travel as far in advance as possible. For further information about the FIFA World Cup, log on to 🌐 www.fifaworldcup.com.
December	**Christmas Markets,** outdoor festivals of light, choral and trumpet music, handcrafted gift items, and mulled wine (*Gluhwein*), are held in just about every German city. Nürnberg's is the most famous.
	New Year's Eve is a noisy, colorful event in Berlin, where fireworks are set off from nearly every neighborhood street.
January	Ostensibly a 10-day farm show, **Internationale Grüne Woche** (Green Week) ☎ 030/30380 🌐 www.gruenewoche.com draws thousands to Berlin's convention center with its produce and fine edibles.
February	**Fasching season.** The Rhineland is Germany's capital of Karneval events. Some of the main Karneval cities are Koblenz, Köln, Mainz, Bonn, and Düsseldorf, although there's also plenty of activity in Munich and southern Germany. Festivities always run through February, finishing on Fasching Dienstag (Shrove or Fat Tuesday).
	Frankfurt International Fair is a major consumer-goods trade fair.
	International Filmfestspiele Berlin ☎ 030/259–200 is one of Europe's leading film festivals.
	The **International Toy Fair** takes place in Nürnberg.
March	**ITB** ☎ 030/30380, one of Europe's largest international tourism fairs, takes place in Berlin.

	Strong Beer Season in Munich brings out the bands and merrymaking in all the beer halls.
April	**Walpurgis** festivals. Towns in the Harz Mountains celebrate with spooky, Halloween-like goings-on the night before May Day.
May	**Medieval Festival.** By downing a huge tankard of wine in one gulp, a 17th-century mayor of Rothenburg-ob-der-Tauber saved the town from sacking. On Pentecost weekend his Meistertrunk is reenacted.
	Religious processions, featuring hundreds of horses, giant candles, and elaborate statues, are particularly spectacular in Catholic eastern Bavaria during Pentecost weekend. The best ones are at Bogen, Sankt Englmar, and Kötzting.
May–September	**Rhine in Flames** highlights the river with fireworks, floodlighted castles, and a fleet of illuminated boats; it's held around Bonn (May), Rüdesheim (July), Koblenz (August), and St. Goar (September).
June	**Kiel Week** is an international sailing regatta and cultural festival in the town of Kiel in Schleswig-Holstein.
June–September	**Castle Illuminations,** with spectacular fireworks, are presented in Heidelberg in June, July, and September.
	The **Schleswig-Holstein Music Festival** takes place over six weeks in July and August. World-famous and young musicians perform in cities and towns throughout Schleswig-Holstein.
	Several hundred **Wine Festivals** held throughout the 13 German wine-growing regions, celebrate local wine from early summer until the harvest in late autumn.
July	**Kinderzeche** is Dinkelsbühl's medieval pageant and festival. It reenacts an incident from the Thirty Years' War in which the children stood at the gate and pleaded with the conquerors to spare their homes.
August	**Kulmbach Beer Festival** takes place in Franconia.
	Richard Wagner Festival unfolds the Wagner operas in Bayreuth.
	The Student Prince, the noted Sigmund Romberg operetta set in Heidelberg, is performed in English in Heidelberg's castle courtyard.
September	**Berlin Festival Weeks** feature classical music concerts, exhibits, and many other special events.
	Folk and Beer Festival at Stuttgart/Bad Cannstatt is said to be just as big and raucous as Munich's Oktoberfest.

	Oktoberfest (late September–early October) in Munich draws millions of visitors to cavernous beer tents and fairgrounds.
	Wurstmarkt, the world's largest wine festival, is held next to a giant cask in Bad Dürkheim.
October	**Jazz Fest Berlin** is an international jazz festival held each autumn.
	Bremen Freimarkt is a centuries-old folk festival and procession in Bremen.
	Frankfurt Book Fair is a famous annual literary event and a browser's paradise.
November	**St. Martin's Festival** includes children's lantern processions and is celebrated throughout the Rhineland and Bavaria.

SMART TRAVEL TIPS

Finding out about your destination before you leave home means you won't spend time organizing everyday minutiae once you've arrived. You'll be more streetwise when you hit the ground as well, better prepared to explore the aspects of Germany that drew you here in the first place. The organizations in this section can provide information to supplement this guide; contact them for up-to-the-minute details, and consult the A to Z sections that end each chapter for facts on the various topics as they relate to the country's many regions. Happy landings!

ADDRESSES

In this book the words for street (*Strasse*) and alley (*Gasse*) are abbreviated as -str. or Str., and g. within italicized information. Brüdergasse will appear as Brüderg., for example.

AIR TRAVEL

BOOKING

When you book, look for nonstop flights and remember that "direct" flights stop at least once. Try to avoid connecting flights, which require a change of plane. Two airlines may operate a connecting flight jointly, so ask whether your airline operates every segment of the trip; you may find that the carrier you prefer flies you only part of the way. To find more booking tips and to check prices and make online flight reservations, log on to www.fodors.com.

CARRIERS

Lufthansa is Germany's leading carrier and has shared mileage plans and flights with Air Canada and United, among other airlines.

Germany's internal air network is excellent, with flights linking all major cities in little more than an hour. A handful of smaller airlines compete with low-fare flights within Germany and to other European cities. These companies are reliable, do most of their business over the Internet, and often beat the German rail fares. The earlier you book, the cheaper the fare.

To & From Germany **Air Canada** ☎ 888/247-2262. **American** ☎ 800/433-7300. **Continental**

☎ 800/525-0280. **Delta** ☎ 800/241-4141. **LTU** ☎ 866/266-5588. **Lufthansa** ☎ 800/645-3880. **Northwest** ☎ 800/225-2525. **United** ☎ 800/241-6522. **US Airways** ☎ 800/428-4322.

Within Germany **Air Berlin** ☎ 01801/737-800, 0870/738-8880 in the U.K. 🌐 www.airberlin.com. **Deutsche BA** ☎ 01805/932-322 🌐 www.flydba.com. **Germanwings** ☎ 01805/955-855 🌐 www.germanwings.com. **Hapag-Lloyd Express** ☎ 01805/093-509 🌐 www.hlx.com. **Lufthansa** ☎ 0180/380-3803 or 0180/5838-42672 🌐 www.lufthansa.com.

From the U.K. **British Airways** ☎ 0845/773-3377 🌐 www.britishairways.com. **EasyJet** ☎ 0871/244-2366, 01803/654321 in Germany 🌐 www.easyjet.com. **Lufthansa** ☎ 0345/737-747 🌐 www.lufthansa.com. **Ryanair** ☎ 0871/246-0000, in Germany 0190/170100 weekdays, 0190/811 773 weekends 🌐 www.ryanair.com.

CHECK-IN & BOARDING

Always **find out your carrier's check-in policy.** Plan to arrive at the airport about 2 hours before your scheduled departure time for domestic flights and 2½ to 3 hours before international flights. You may need to arrive earlier if you're flying from one of the busier airports or during peak air-traffic times. In Germany, be at your gate with boarding pass in hand 30 minutes before an internal flight. For international flights, check in at least 2 hours in advance. If the first leg of your flight is one within Europe, check in at least 1 hour in advance; allow an extra half-hour to claim V.A.T. taxes back at customs.

To avoid delays at airport-security checkpoints, try not to wear any metal. Jewelry, belt and other buckles, steel-toe shoes, barrettes, and underwire bras are among the items that can set off detectors.

Assuming that not everyone with a ticket will show up, airlines routinely overbook planes. When everyone does, airlines ask for volunteers to give up their seats. In return, these volunteers usually get a several-hundred-dollar flight voucher, which can be used toward the purchase of another ticket, and are rebooked on the next available flight out. If there are not enough volunteers, the airline must choose who will be denied boarding. The first to get bumped are passengers who checked in late and those flying on discounted tickets, so get to the gate and check in as early as possible, especially during peak periods.

Always **bring a government-issued photo I.D.** to the airport; even when it's not required, a passport is best.

CUTTING COSTS

The least expensive airfares to Germany are often priced for round-trip travel and usually must be purchased in advance. Airlines generally allow you to change your return date for a fee; most low-fare tickets, however, are nonrefundable. Fares between the British Isles and Germany through "no-frills" airlines such as Air Berlin, EasyJet, and Ryanair can range from €15 to €70.

It's smart to call a number of airlines and check the Internet; when you are quoted a good price, book it on the spot—the same fare may not be available the next day, or even the next hour. Always check different routings and look into using alternate airports. Also, price off-peak flights and red-eye, which may be significantly less expensive than others. Travel agents, especially low-fare specialists (⇨ Discounts & Deals), are helpful.

Consolidators are another good source. They buy tickets for scheduled flights at reduced rates from the airlines, then sell them at prices that beat the best fare available directly from the airlines. (Many also offer reduced car-rental and hotel rates.) Sometimes you can even get your money back if you need to return the ticket. Carefully read the fine print detailing penalties for changes and cancellations, purchase the ticket with a credit card, and confirm your consolidator reservation with the airline.

Consolidators **AirlineConsolidator.com** ☎ 888/468-5385 🌐 www.airlineconsolidator.com; for international tickets. **Best Fares** ☎ 800/880-1234 🌐 www.bestfares.com; $59.90 annual membership. **Cheap Tickets** ☎ 800/377-1000 or 800/652-4327 🌐 www.cheaptickets.com. **Expedia** ☎ 800/397-3342 or 404/728-8787 🌐 www.expedia.com. **Hotwire** ☎ 866/468-9473 or 920/330-9418 🌐 www.hotwire.com. **Now Voyager Travel** ✉ 1717 Ave. M, Brooklyn, NY 11230 ☎ 212/459-1616 🖷 718/504-4762 🌐 www.nowvoyagertravel.com. **Onetravel.com** 🌐 www.onetravel.com. **Orbitz** ☎ 888/

656-4546 🌐 www.orbitz.com. **Priceline.com** 🌐 www.priceline.com. **Travelocity** ☎ 888/709-5983, 877/282-2925 in Canada, 0870/111-7061 in the U.K. 🌐 www.travelocity.com.

ENJOYING THE FLIGHT

State your seat preference when purchasing your ticket, and then repeat it when you confirm and when you check in. For more legroom, you can request one of the few emergency-aisle seats at check-in, if you're capable of moving obstacles comparable in weight to an airplane exit door (usually between 35 pounds and 60 pounds)—a Federal Aviation Administration requirement of passengers in these seats. Seats behind a bulkhead also offer more legroom, but they don't have underseat storage. Don't sit in the row in front of the emergency aisle or in front of a bulkhead, where seats may not recline. SeatGuru.com has more information about specific seat configurations, which vary by aircraft.

Ask the airline whether a snack or meal is served on the flight. If you have dietary concerns, request special meals when booking. These can be vegetarian, low-cholesterol, or kosher, for example. It's a good idea to pack some healthful snacks and a small (plastic) bottle of water in your carry-on bag. On long flights, try to maintain a normal routine, to help fight jet lag. At night, get some sleep. By day, eat light meals, drink water (not alcohol), and **move around the cabin** to stretch your legs. For additional jet-lag tips consult *Fodor's FYI: Travel Fit & Healthy* (available at bookstores everywhere).

FLYING TIMES

Flying time to Frankfurt is 1½ hours from London, 7½ hours from New York, 10 hours from Chicago, and 12 hours from Los Angeles.

HOW TO COMPLAIN

If your baggage goes astray or your flight goes awry, complain right away. Most carriers require that you **file a claim immediately.** The Aviation Consumer Protection Division of the Department of Transportation publishes *Fly-Rights,* which discusses airlines and consumer issues and is available online. You can also find articles and information on mytravelrights.com, the Web site of the nonprofit Consumer Travel Rights Center.

i Airline Complaints **Aviation Consumer Protection Division** ✉ U.S. Department of Transportation, Office of Aviation Enforcement and Proceedings, C-75, Room 4107, 400 7th St. SW, Washington, DC 20590 ☎ 202/366-2220 🌐 airconsumer.ost.dot.gov. **Federal Aviation Administration Consumer Hotline** ✉ for inquiries: FAA, 800 Independence Ave. SW, Washington, DC 20591 ☎ 800/322-7873 🌐 www.faa.gov.

RECONFIRMING

Check the status of your flight before you leave for the airport. You can do this on your carrier's Web site, by linking to a flight-status checker (many Web booking services offer these), or by calling your carrier or travel agent. Always confirm international flights at least 72 hours ahead of the scheduled departure time.

AIRPORTS

Frankfurt is Germany's air hub. The large airport has the convenience of its own long-distance train station, but if you're transfering between flights, don't dawdle or you could miss your connection. In 2005, Delta and Continental began nonstop service between New York and Tegel airport in Berlin (there are three airports in Berlin). Continental also has nonstop service between New York and Hamburg. There are a few nonstop services from North America to Munich and Düsseldorf. Stuttgart is convenient to the Black Forest.

i Airport Information Berlin: **Flughafen Tegel** (TXL), **Tempelhof** (THF), **Schönefeld** (SXF) ☎ 01805/000-186, €.12 per minute 🌐 www.berlin-airport.de. Düsseldorf: **Flughafen Düsseldorf** (DUS) ☎ 0211/4210 🌐 www.duesseldorf-international.de. Frankfurt: **Flughafen Frankfurt Main** (FRA) ☎ 01805/372-4636, 069/6900 from outside Germany 🌐 www.frankfurt-airport.de. Hamburg: **Fuhlsbüttel International Airport** (HAM) ☎ 040/50750 🌐 www.ham.airport.de. Köln: **Flughafen Köln/Bonn** (CGN) ☎ 02203/404-001 🌐 www.airport-cgn.de. Munich: **Flughafen München** (MUC) ☎ 089/97500 🌐 www.munich-airport.de. Stuttgart: **Flughafen Stuttgart** (STR) ☎ 0711/948-2790 🌐 www.stuttgart-airport.de.

BIKES IN FLIGHT

Most airlines accommodate bikes as luggage, provided they are dismantled and boxed; check with individual airlines about packing requirements. Some airlines sell bike boxes, which are often free at bike shops, for about $20 (bike bags can be considerably more expensive). International travelers often can substitute a bike for a piece of checked luggage at no charge; otherwise, the cost is about $100. Most U.S. and Canadian airlines charge $40–$80 each way.

DUTY-FREE SHOPPING

You can purchase duty-free goods when traveling between any EU country, such as Germany, and a non-EU country. The big sellers at duty-free (also called tax-free) shops are perfumes and cosmetics, liquor, tobacco products, and chocolates.

BOAT & FERRY TRAVEL

Eurailpasses and German Rail Passes (⇨ Train Travel) are valid on all Rhine River services of the Köln-Düsseldorfer Deutsche Rheinschiffahrt (KD Rhine Line) and on the Mosel River between Trier and Koblenz (if you use the fast hydrofoil, a supplementary fee is required). The railroad follows the Rhine and Mosel rivers most of their length, meaning you can go one way by ship and return by train. Cruises generally operate between April and October (⇨ Cruise Travel).

The MS *Duchess of Scandinavia* carries passengers and cars three times a week for the 19½-hour run between Cuxhaven, Germany and Harwich, England.

Car Ferry **MS *Duchess of Scandinavia*** ☎ DFDS Seaways 08705/333-111 in the U.K. or 040/389-0371 in Germany 🌐 www.dfdsseaways.co.uk.

BUSINESS HOURS

Business hours are consistent throughout the country. Many smaller visitor information offices close by 4 during the week and might not be open on weekends. Catholic areas of the country, primarily Bavaria, have more closings for religious holidays than in other parts of Germany.

BANKS & OFFICES

Banks are generally open weekdays from 8:30 or 9 to 3 or 4 (5 or 6 on Thursday), sometimes with a lunch break of about an hour at smaller branches. Some banks close by 2:30 on Friday afternoon. Banks at airports and main train stations open as early as 6:30 AM and close as late as 10:30 PM. Some offices start picking up the phone as early as 8 AM and nearly all close by 5 PM. Automated telephone menus and even voice mail and answering machines are not a given in Germany, which means you shouldn't count on leaving a message after hours. *See* Mail & Shipping for post office hours.

GAS STATIONS

Along the autobahn and major highways as well as in major cities, gas stations and their small convenience shops are often open late, if not around the clock.

MUSEUMS & SIGHTS

Most museums are open from Tuesday to Sunday 10–6. Some close for an hour or more at lunch. Many stay open until 8 or later one day a week.

PHARMACIES

Most pharmacies are open 9–6 weekdays and 9–1 on Saturday. Those in more prominent locations often open an hour earlier and/or close an hour later. A list of pharmacies in the vicinity that are open late or on Sunday is posted on the door.

SHOPS

All stores are closed on Sunday, with the exception of those in or near train stations. Larger stores are generally open from 9:30 or 10 to 7 or 8 on weekdays and close between 6 and 8 on Saturday. Smaller shops and some department stores in smaller towns close at 6 or 6:30 on weekdays and as early as 4 on Saturday.

BUS TRAVEL

Germany has good local bus service but no nationwide network, other than the few cities served by BerlinLinien Bus. Deutsche Touring, a subsidiary of the Deutsche Bahn (German Rail) has offices and agents countrywide and travels from Germany to other European cities. For international travel, book your seat a week in advance. Its domestic service consists of one-day tours along the Castle Road and the

Romantic Road. The Romantic Road route is between Würzburg (with connections to and from Frankfurt) and Füssen (with connections to and from Munich, Augsburg, and Garmisch-Partenkirchen). With a regular Deutsche Bahn rail ticket, Eurailpass, or German Rail Pass you get a 60% discount on this route. Buses, with an attendant on board, travel in each direction between April and October.

All towns of any size have local buses, which often link up with trams (streetcars) and electric railway (S-bahn) and subway (U-bahn) services. Fares sometimes vary according to distance, but a ticket usually allows you to transfer freely between the various forms of transportation. Most cities issue day tickets at special rates.

Intercity Buses **BerlinLinien Bus** ✉ Masurenallee 4–6 Berlin ☎ 030/302–5361 or 030/3010–0175 🌐 www.berlinlinienbus.de. **Deutsche Touring** ✉ Am Römerhof 17, D-60486 Frankfurt am Main ☎ 069/790–350 📠 069/790–3219 🌐 www.deutsche-touring.de.

CAMERAS & PHOTOGRAPHY

The *Kodak Guide to Shooting Great Travel Pictures* (available at bookstores everywhere) is loaded with tips.

Photo Help **Kodak Information Center** ☎ 800/242–2424 🌐 www.kodak.com.

EQUIPMENT PRECAUTIONS

Don't pack film or equipment in checked luggage, where it is much more susceptible to damage. X-ray machines used to view checked luggage are extremely powerful and therefore are likely to ruin your film. Try to ask for hand inspection of film, which becomes clouded after repeated exposure to airport X-ray machines, and keep videotapes and computer disks away from metal detectors. Always keep film, tape, and computer disks out of the sun. Carry an extra supply of batteries, and be prepared to turn on your camera, camcorder, or laptop to prove to airport security personnel that the device is real.

VIDEOS

The German standard for video is VHS–PAL, which is not compatible with the U.S. VHS–NTSC standard.

CAR RENTAL

Rates with the major car-rental companies begin at about €55 per day and €300 per week, including value-added tax, for an economy car with a manual transmission and unlimited mileage. Volkswagen, Opel, and Mercedes are some standard brands of rentals; most rentals are manual, so if you want an automatic, be sure to **request one in advance.** If you're traveling with children, don't forget to **arrange for a car seat** when you reserve. The agency Sixt is affiliated with Lufthansa. Note that in some major cities, even automobile-producing Stuttgart, rental firms are prohibited from placing signs at major pickup, drop-off locations, such as the main train station. If dropping a car off in an unfamiliar city, you might have to guess your way to the station's underground parking garage and once there, look for a generic sign such as *Miet Wagen* (rental cars).

Major Agencies **Alamo** ☎ 800/522–9696 🌐 www.alamo.com. **Avis** ☎ 800/331–1084, 800/879–2847 in Canada, 0870/606–0100 in the U.K., 02/9353–9000 in Australia, 09/526–2847 in New Zealand 🌐 www.avis.com. **Budget** ☎ 800/527–0700 🌐 www.budget.com. **Dollar** ☎ 800/800–6000, 0800/085–4578 in the U.K. 🌐 www.dollar.com. **Hertz** ☎ 800/654–3001, 800/263–0600 in Canada, 0870/844–8844 in the U.K., 02/9669–2444 in Australia, 09/256–8690 in New Zealand 🌐 www.hertz.com. **National Car Rental** ☎ 800/227–7368 🌐 www.nationalcar.com.

CUTTING COSTS

For a good deal, book through a travel agent who will shop around. Do look into wholesalers, companies that do not own fleets but rent in bulk from those that do and often offer better rates than traditional car-rental operations. Prices are best during off-peak periods. Rentals booked through wholesalers often must be paid for before you leave home.

Local Agencies **Sixt** ☎ 01805/252–525, €.12 per minute 🌐 www.sixtusa.com.

Wholesalers **Auto Europe** ☎ 207/842–2000 or 800/223–5555 📠 207/842–2222 🌐 www.autoeurope.com. **Destination Europe Resources (DER)** ✉ 9501 W. Devon Ave., Rosemont, IL 60018 ☎ 800/782–2424 📠 800/282–7474. **Europe by Car** ☎ 212/581–3040 or 800/223–1516 📠 212/246–1458

🌐 www.europebycar.com. Kemwel ☎ 877/820-0668 or 800/678-0678 🖷 207/842-2124 or 866/726-6726 🌐 www.kemwel.com.

INSURANCE

When driving a rented car you are generally responsible for any damage to or loss of the vehicle. Collision policies that car-rental companies sell for European rentals typically do not cover stolen vehicles. Before you rent—and purchase collision or theft coverage—see what coverage you already have under the terms of your personal auto-insurance policy and credit cards.

REQUIREMENTS & RESTRICTIONS

In Germany your own driver's license is acceptable, but an International Driver's Permit is a good idea; it's available from the American or Canadian Automobile Association and, in the United Kingdom, from the Automobile Association and Royal Automobile Club. These international permits are universally recognized, and having one in your wallet may save you problems with the local authorities. In Germany you usually must be 21 to rent a car. Nearly all agencies allow you to drive into Germany's neighboring countries. It's frequently possible to return the car in another West European country, but not in Poland or the Czech Republic, for example.

SURCHARGES

Before you pick up a car in one city and leave it in another, ask about drop-off charges or one-way service fees, which can be substantial. Also inquire about early-return policies; some rental agencies charge extra if you return the car before the time specified in your contract while others give you a refund for the days not used. Most agencies note the tank's fuel level on your contract; to avoid a hefty refueling fee, return the car with the same tank level. If the tank was full, refill it just before you turn in the car, but be aware that gas stations near the rental outlet may overcharge. It's almost never a deal to buy a tank of gas with the car when you rent it; the understanding is that you'll return it empty, but some fuel usually remains.

CAR TRAVEL

Entry formalities for motorists are few: all you need is proof of insurance, an international car-registration document, and a U.S., Canadian, Australian, or New Zealand driver's license. If you or your car is from an EU country, Norway, or Switzerland, all you need is your domestic license and proof of insurance. *All* foreign cars must have a country sticker. There are no toll roads in Germany, except for a few Alpine mountain passes.

EMERGENCY SERVICES

The German automobile clubs ADAC and AvD operate tow trucks on all autobahns. NOTRUF signs every 2 km (1 mi) on autobahns (and country roads) indicate emergency telephones. By picking up the phone, you'll be connected to an operator who can determine your exact location and get you the services you need. The official road-side assistance number is ☎ 01802/222–222. If you have a mobile phone, just dial ☎ 222–222. Help is free (with the exception of materials).

GASOLINE

Gasoline (petrol) costs are around €1.10 per liter—which is higher than in the United States. Most German cars run on lead-free fuel. Some models use diesel fuel, so if you're renting a car, **find out which fuel the car takes.** Some older vehicles cannot take unleaded fuel. German filling stations are highly competitive, and bargains are often available if you shop around, but *not* at autobahn filling stations. Self-service, or *SB-Tanken,* stations are cheapest. Pumps marked *Bleifrei* contain unleaded gas.

PARKING

Daytime parking in cities and small, historic towns is difficult to find. Restrictions are not always clearly marked and can be hard to understand when they are. Rental cars come with a "time wheel," which you can leave on your dashboard when parking signs indicate free, limited-time allowances. Larger parking lots have parking meters (*Parkautomaten*). After depositing enough change in a meter, you will be issued a timed ticket to display on your dashboard. Parking-meter spaces are free at night. In German garages you must **pay immediately on returning to retrieve your car,** not when driving out. Put the ticket you got on arrival into the machine and pay the amount displayed. Retrieve the ticket, and upon exiting the garage, insert the ticket in a slot to raise the barrier.

ROAD CONDITIONS

Roads are generally excellent. *Bundesstrasse* are two-lane highways, abbreviated "B," as in B–38. Autobahns are high-speed thruways abbreviated with "A," as in A–7.

ROAD MAPS

The best-known road maps of Germany are put out by the automobile club ADAC, by Shell, and by the Falk Verlag. They're available at gas stations and bookstores.

RULES OF THE ROAD

Germans **drive on the right** and cars coming from the right have right-of-way at intersections. Road signs give distances in kilometers. There *are* posted speed limits on autobahns, and drivers are advised to keep below 130 kph (80 mph). Speed limits on country roads vary from 70 kph to 100 kph (43 mph to 62 mph) and are usually 50 kph (30 mph) through small towns. The blood-alcohol limit for driving in Germany is very low (.05%). Note that **seat belts must be worn at all times by front-** ***and*** **backseat passengers.** Passing is permitted on the left side only. Headlights, not parking lights, are required during inclement weather. Don't enter a street with a signpost bearing a red circle with a white horizontal stripe—it's a one-way street. Blue *EINBAHNSTRASSE* signs indicate you're headed the correct way down a one-way street. A right turn on a red light is permitted only if there's also a green arrow.

SCENIC ROUTES

Germany has many specially designated tourist roads which serve as promotional tools for towns along their routes. The longest is the Deutsche Ferienstrasse, the German Holiday Road, which runs from the Baltic Sea to the Alps, a distance of around 1,720 km (1,070 mi). The most famous, however, is the Romantische Strasse (Romantic Road; ⇨ Chapter 3), which runs from Würzburg to Füssen in the Alps, covering around 355 km (220 mi).

Among other notable touring routes are the Strasse der Kaiser und Könige (Route of Emperors and Kings), running from Frankfurt to Passau (and on to Vienna and Budapest); the Burgenstrasse (Castle Road), running from Mannheim to Bayreuth; the Deutsche Weinstrasse (German Wine Road; ⇨ Chapter 9), running through the Palatinate wine country; and the Deutsche Alpenstrasse (German Alpine Road; ⇨ Chapter 2), running the length of the country's Alpine southern border from near Berchtesgaden to Bodensee. Less well-known routes are the Märchenstrasse (Fairy-Tale Road; ⇨ Chapter 11), the Weser Renaissance Strasse, and the Deutsche Fachwerkstrasse (German Half-Timber Road).

CHILDREN IN GERMANY

Almost every city in Germany has its own children's theater, and the country's puppet theaters rank among the best in the world. Playgrounds are around virtually every corner, and there are about a half-dozen major theme parks around the country. Many tourist offices have booklets for younger visitors.

If you are renting a car, don't forget to arrange for a car seat when you reserve. For general advice about traveling with children, consult *Fodor's FYI: Travel with Your Baby* (available in bookstores everywhere).

BABYSITTING

For recommended local sitters, **check with your hotel desk.** Updated lists of well-screened babysitters are also available from most local tourist offices. Rates are usually between €8 and €13 per hour.

FLYING

If your children are two or older, ask about children's airfares. As a general rule, infants under two not occupying a seat fly at greatly reduced fares or even for free. But if you want to guarantee a seat for an infant, you have to pay full fare. Consider flying during off-peak days and times; most airlines will grant an infant a seat without a ticket if there are available seats.

When booking, confirm carry-on allowances if you're traveling with infants. In general, for babies charged 10% to 50% of the adult fare you are allowed one carry-on bag and a collapsible stroller; if the flight is full, the stroller may have to be checked or you may be limited to less.

Experts agree that it's a good idea to use safety seats aloft for children weighing less than 40 pounds. Airlines set their own policies: if you use a safety seat, U.S. carriers usually require that the child be ticketed, even if he or she is young enough to ride free, because the seats must be strapped into regular seats. And even if you pay the full adult fare for the seat, it may be worth it, especially on longer trips. Do **check your airline's policy about using safety seats during takeoff and landing.** Safety seats are not allowed everywhere in the plane, so get your seat assignments as early as possible.

When reserving, request children's meals or a freestanding bassinet (not available at all airlines) if you need them. But note that bulkhead seats, where you must sit to use the bassinet, may lack an overhead bin or storage space on the floor.

LODGING

Many hotels in Germany allow children under a certain age to stay in their parents' room at no extra charge. Beyond that age they may be charged half price or even be considered extra adults; be sure to find out if the cutoff age applies. If your room has a TV, be aware that sex-talk phone lines are advertised on television as early as 9 PM and that late-night pornographic programs are carried on non-cable networks.

SIGHTS & ATTRACTIONS

Places that are especially appealing to children are indicated by a rubber-duckie icon (🐤) in the margin.

SUPPLIES & EQUIPMENT

Supermarkets and drugstores (not pharmacies) carry disposable diapers (*Windeln*). Baby formula is available in powder form and comes in two types: *Anfangsmilch/nahrung* is labeled with a big number 1 and is suitable for infants ages 0–4 months; *Folgemilch/nahrung* is labeled with a big number 2 and is suitable for infants from 4 months. *Dauermilch/nahrung* is suitable for all ages. Coloring books (*Malbücher*) and crayons (*Buntstifte*) are widely available, as is modeling clay (*Knetmasse*).

COMPUTERS ON THE ROAD

Nearly all hotels in cities have in-room data ports, but you may have to purchase, or borrow from your hotel, a cable with an end that matches German phone jacks. Most notebooks with a modem or single modems will have a plug-in to match the German Telekom socket. If you're plugging into a phone line, you'll need a local access number for a connection. Wireless internet service in large hotels is becoming more and more common. Small pensions may not even have a phone in the room, or a jack that will match modem connections. Internet cafés are prevalent in German cities. Often they're smoky basement shops that sell a few soft drinks and snacks. In smaller towns, try the library for Internet use.

CONSUMER PROTECTION

Whether you're shopping for gifts or purchasing travel services, **pay with a major credit card** whenever possible, so you can cancel payment or get reimbursed if there's a problem (and you can provide documentation). If you're doing business with a particular company for the first time, contact your local Better Business Bureau and the attorney general's offices in your state and (for U.S. businesses) the company's home state as well. Have any complaints been filed? Finally, if you're buying a package or tour, always consider travel insurance that includes default coverage (⇨ Insurance).

BBBs Council of Better Business Bureaus ✉ 4200 Wilson Blvd., Suite 800, Arlington, VA 22203 ☎ 703/276-0100 🖷 703/525-8277 🌐 www.bbb.org.

CRUISE TRAVEL

The American-owned Viking River Cruises company tours the Rhine, Main, Elbe, and Danube rivers, with 4- to 8-day itineraries that include walking tours at ports of call.

The longer cruises (up to 18 days) on the Danube (Donau, in German), which go to the Black Sea and back, are in great demand, so **reserve six months in advance.** The company normally books American passengers on ships that cater exclusively to Americans. The ships are no-smoking, and English is the only language on board. If you prefer to travel on a European ship, specify so when booking. Köln–Düsseldorfer Deutsche Rheinschiffahrt (KD Rhine Line) offers trips of one day or less on the Rhine and Mosel. Between Easter and October there's Rhine service between Köln and Mainz, and between May and October, Mosel service between Koblenz and Cochem. Check the Web site for special winter tours. You'll get a free trip on your birthday, if you bring a document verifying your date of birth.

To learn how to plan, choose, and book a cruise-ship voyage, consult *Fodor's FYI: Plan & Enjoy Your Cruise* (available in bookstores everywhere).

Cruise Lines **KD Rhine Line** ✉ Frankenwerft 35, D-50667 Köln ☎ 0221/208-8318 📠 0221/208-8345 🌐 www.k-d.com. **Viking River Cruises** ✉ Hohe Str. 68-82, D-50667 Köln ☎ 0800/258-4666 toll-free or 0221/258-209 in Germany, 0207/752-0000 or 01372/742033 in U.K. 🌐 www.vikingrivercruises.com ✉ 21820 Burbank Blvd., Woodland Hills, CA 91367 ☎ 818/227-1234.

CUSTOMS & DUTIES

When shopping abroad, keep receipts for all purchases. Upon reentering the country, **be ready to show customs officials what you've bought.** Pack purchases together in an easily accessible place. If you think a duty is incorrect, appeal the assessment. If you object to the way your clearance was handled, note the inspector's badge number. In either case, first ask to see a supervisor. If the problem isn't resolved, write to the appropriate authorities, beginning with the port director at your point of entry.

IN AUSTRALIA

Australian residents who are 18 or older may bring home A$900 worth of souvenirs and gifts (including jewelry), 250 cigarettes or 250 grams of cigars or other tobacco products, and 2.25 liters of alcohol (including wine, beer, and spirits). Residents under 18 may bring back A$450 worth of goods. If any of these individual allowances are exceeded, you must pay duty for the entire amount (of the group of products in which the allowance was exceeded). Members of the same family traveling together may pool their allowances. Prohibited items include meat products. Seeds, plants, and fruits need to be declared upon arrival.

Australian Customs Service ✉ Locked Bag 3000, Sydney International Airport, Sydney, NSW 2020 ☎ 02/6275-6666 or 1300/363263, 02/8334-7444 or 1800/020-504 quarantine-inquiry line 📠 02/8339-6714 🌐 www.customs.gov.au.

IN CANADA

Canadian residents who have been out of Canada for at least seven days may bring in C$750 worth of goods duty-free. If you've been away fewer than seven days but more than 48 hours, the duty-free allowance drops to C$200. If your trip lasts 24 to 48 hours, the allowance is C$50; if the goods are worth more than C$50, you must pay full duty on all of the goods. You may not pool allowances with family members. Goods claimed under the C$750 exemption may follow you by mail; those claimed under the lesser exemptions must accompany you. Alcohol and tobacco products may be included in the seven-day and 48-hour exemptions but not in the 24-hour exemption. If you meet the age requirements of the province or territory through which you reenter Canada, you may bring in, duty-free, 1.5 liters of wine *or* 1.14 liters (40 imperial ounces) of liquor *or* 24 12-ounce cans or bottles of beer or ale. Also, if you meet the local age requirement for tobacco products, you may bring in, duty-free, 200 cigarettes, 50 cigars or cigarillos, and 200 grams of tobacco. You may have to pay a minimum duty on tobacco products, regardless of whether or not you exceed your personal exemption. Check ahead of time with the Canada Border Services Agency or the Department of Agriculture for policies regarding meat products, seeds, plants, and fruits.

You may send an unlimited number of gifts (only one gift per recipient, however) worth up to C$60 each duty-free to Canada. Label the package UNSOLICITED GIFT—VALUE UNDER $60. Alcohol and tobacco are excluded.

Canada Border Services Agency ✉ Customs Information Services, 191 Laurier Ave. W, 15th floor, Ottawa, Ontario K1A 0L5 ☎ 800/461-9999 in Canada, 204/983-3500, 506/636-5064 🌐 www.cbsa.gc.ca.

IN GERMANY

Since a single, unrestricted market took effect within the European Union (EU) early in 1993, there have no longer been restrictions for persons traveling among the 15 EU countries. However, there are restrictions on what can be brought in without declaration. For example, if you have more than 800 cigarettes, 90 liters of wine, or 10 liters of alcohol, it is considered a commercial shipment and is taxed and otherwise treated as such.

For anyone entering Germany from outside the EU, the following limitations apply: (1) 200 cigarettes or 100 cigarillos or 50 cigars or 250 grams of tobacco; (2) 2 liters of still table wine; (3) 1 liter of spirits over 22% volume or 2 liters of spirits under 22% volume (fortified and sparkling wines) or 2 more liters of table wine; (4) 50 grams of perfume and 250 milliliters of eau de toilette; (5) 500 grams of roasted coffee or 200 grams of instant coffee; (6) other goods to the value of €175.

Tobacco and alcohol allowances are for visitors age 17 and over. Other items intended for personal use can be imported and exported freely. If you bring in cash, checks, securities, precious metals, or jewelry with a value of more than €15,000, you must tell the customs people where you got it and what you intend to do with it.

If you have questions regarding customs or bringing a pet into the country, contact the Zoll-Infocenter, preferably by mail or e-mail.

Zoll-Infocenter ✉ Hansaallee 141, D-60320 Frankfurt am Main ☎ 069/4699-7600 📠 069/4699-7699 🌐 www.zoll.de ✉ info@zoll-infocenter.de.

IN NEW ZEALAND

All homeward-bound residents may bring back NZ$700 worth of souvenirs and gifts; passengers may not pool their allowances, and children can claim only the concession on goods intended for their own use. For those 17 or older, the duty-free allowance also includes 4.5 liters of wine or beer; one 1,125-ml bottle of spirits; and either 200 cigarettes, 250 grams of tobacco, 50 cigars, *or* a combination of the three up to 250 grams. Meat products, seeds, plants, and fruits must be declared upon arrival to the Agricultural Services Department.

New Zealand Customs ✉ Head office: The Customhouse, 17-21 Whitmore St., Box 2218, Wellington ☎ 09/300-5399 or 0800/428-786 🌐 www.customs.govt.nz.

IN THE U.K.

If you are a U.K. resident and your journey was wholly within the European Union, you probably won't have to pass through customs when you return to the United Kingdom. If you plan to bring back large quantities of alcohol or tobacco, check EU limits beforehand. In most cases, if you bring back more than 200 cigars, 3,200 cigarettes, 400 cigarillos, 3 kilograms of tobacco, 10 liters of spirits, 110 liters of beer, 20 liters of fortified wine, and/or 90 liters of wine, you have to declare the goods upon return.

HM Customs and Excise ✉ Portcullis House, 21 Cowbridge Rd. E, Cardiff CF11 9SS ☎ 0845/010-9000 or 0208/929-0152 advice service, 0208/929-6731 or 0208/910-3602 complaints 🌐 www.hmce.gov.uk.

IN THE U.S.

U.S. residents who have been out of the country for at least 48 hours may bring home, for personal use, $800 worth of foreign goods duty-free, as long as they haven't used the $800 allowance or any part of it in the past 30 days. This exemption may include 1 liter of alcohol (for travelers 21 and older), 200 cigarettes, and 100 non-Cuban cigars. Family members from the same household who are traveling together may pool their $800 personal exemptions. For fewer than 48 hours, the duty-free allowance drops to $200, which may include 50 cigarettes, 10 non-Cuban cigars, and 150 ml of alcohol (or 150 ml of perfume containing alcohol). The $200 allowance cannot be combined with other individuals' exemptions, and if you exceed it, the full value of all the goods will be taxed. Antiques, which U.S. Customs and Border Protection defines as objects more than 100 years old, enter duty-free, as do original works of art done entirely by hand, including paintings, drawings, and sculptures. This doesn't apply to folk art or handicrafts, which are in general dutiable.

You may also send packages home duty-free, with a limit of one parcel per addressee per day (except alcohol or tobacco products or perfume worth more than $5). You can mail up to $200 worth of goods for personal use; label the package PERSONAL USE and attach a list of its contents and their retail value. If the package contains your used personal belongings, mark it AMERICAN GOODS RETURNED to avoid paying duties. You may send up to $100 worth of goods as a gift; mark the package UNSOLICITED GIFT. Mailed items do not affect your duty-free allowance on your return.

To avoid paying duty on foreign-made high-ticket items you already own and will take on your trip, register them with a local customs office before you leave the country. Consider filing a Certificate of Registration for laptops, cameras, watches, and other digital devices identified with serial numbers or other permanent markings; you can keep the certificate for other trips. Otherwise, bring a sales receipt or insurance form to show that you owned the item before you left the United States.

For more about duties, restricted items, and other information about international travel, check out U.S. Customs and Border Protection's online brochure, *Know Before You Go*. You can also file complaints on the U.S. Customs and Border Protection Web site, listed below.

U.S. Customs and Border Protection ✉ for inquiries and complaints, 1300 Pennsylvania Ave. NW, Washington, DC 20229 🌐 www.cbp.gov ☎ 877/227-5551, 202/354-1000.

DISABILITIES & ACCESSIBILITY

Many cities and towns issue special guides for visitors with disabilities, which offer information, usually in German, about how to get around destinations and suggestions for places to visit.

LODGING

All the major hotel chains have special facilities for guests with disabilities. Some privately owned hotels also cater to travelers with disabilities; local tourist offices can provide lists of these hotels and additional information.

RESERVATIONS

When discussing accessibility with an operator or reservations agent, ask hard questions. Are there any stairs, inside *or* out? Are there grab bars next to the toilet *and* in the shower/tub? How wide is the doorway to the room? To the bathroom? For the most extensive facilities meeting the latest legal specifications, opt for newer accommodations. If you reserve through a toll-free number, consider also calling the hotel's local number to confirm the information from the central reservations office. Get confirmation in writing when you can.

TRAIN TRAVEL

The Deutsche Bahn (⇨ Train Travel) provides a complete range of services and facilities for travelers with disabilities. All InterCity Express (ICE), InterRegio, and DB Night trains and most EuroCity and InterCity trains have special areas and toilets for wheelchair users, and the larger stations have a portable device for lifting wheelchairs aboard. Reservations for wheelchair users and a travel companion are free of charge. A free service called the Bahnhofs-Mission (Railway Station Mission) has support facilities at all major and many smaller regional stations. It assists with boarding, leaving, and changing trains and also helps with reservations. Local trams and buses often have sections that can accommodate a wheelchair and entrances that are, if not flush with the platform, at least quite low to the ground.

Deutsche Bahn issues a booklet, with an English section, detailing its services. For access to train platforms that are not wheelchair accessible, to temporarily borrow a wheelchair, and for other services, **call Deutsche Bahn's mobility service line at least 24 hours before your trip.** You can order the same service online, one week in advance. Select "Internat. Guests" on the homepage and then "handicapped."

Deutsche Bahn **Mobility Service** ☎ 01805/512512 🌐 www.dbahn.de

TRANSPORTATION

The U.S. Department of Transportation Aviation Consumer Protection Division's online publication *New Horizons: Information for the Air Traveler with a Disability* offers advice for travelers with disabilities, and outlines basic rights. Visit DisabilityInfo.gov for general information.

Information and Complaints **Aviation Consumer Protection Division** (⇨ Air Travel) for airline-related problems; 🌐 www.airconsumer.ost.dot.gov/publications/horizons.htm for airline travel advice and rights. **Departmental Office of Civil Rights** ✉ for general inquiries, U.S. Department of Transportation, S-30, 400 7th St. SW, Room 10215, Washington, DC 20590 ☎ 202/366-4648, 202/366-8538 TTY 📠 202/366-9371 🌐 www.dotcr.ost.dot.gov. **Disability Rights Section** ✉ NYAV, U.S. Department of Justice, Civil Rights Division, 950 Pennsylvania Ave. NW, Washington, DC 20530 ☎ ADA information line 202/514-0301, 800/514-0301, 202/514-0383 TTY, 800/514-0383 TTY 🌐 www.ada.gov. **U.S. Department of Transportation Hotline** ☎ for disability-related air-travel problems, 800/778-4838 or 800/455-9880 TTY.

TRAVEL AGENCIES

In the United States, the Americans with Disabilities Act requires that travel firms serve the needs of all travelers. Some agencies specialize in working with people with disabilities.

Travelers with Mobility Problems **Access Adventures/B. Roberts Travel** ✉ 1876 East Ave., Rochester, NY 14610 ☎ 800/444-6540 🌐 www.brobertstravel.com, run by a former physical-rehabilitation counselor. **CareVacations** ✉ No. 5, 5110-50 Ave., Leduc, Alberta, Canada, T9E 6V4 ☎ 780/986-6404 or 877/478-7827 📠 780/986-8332 🌐 www.carevacations.com, for group tours and cruise vacations. **Flying Wheels Travel** ✉ 143 W. Bridge St., Box 382, Owatonna, MN 55060 ☎ 507/451-5005 📠 507/451-1685 🌐 www.flyingwheelstravel.com.

DISCOUNTS & DEALS

Several German cities sell discount passes that grant free or reduced admission to major attractions and discounts on public transportation. The passes are usually available at tourist offices or participating museums.

Be a smart shopper and compare all your options before making decisions. A plane ticket bought with a promotional coupon from travel clubs, coupon books, and direct-mail offers or purchased on the Internet may not be cheaper than the least expensive fare from a discount ticket agency. And always keep in mind that what you get is just as important as what you save.

DISCOUNT RESERVATIONS

To save money, look into discount reservations services with Web sites and toll-free numbers, which use their buying power to get a better price on hotels, airline tickets (⇨ Air Travel), even car rentals. When booking a room, always **call the hotel's local toll-free number** (if one is available) rather than the central reservations number—you'll often get a better price. Always ask about special packages or corporate rates.

When shopping for the best deal on hotels and car rentals, look for guaranteed exchange rates, which protect you against a falling dollar. With your rate locked in, you won't pay more, even if the price goes up in the local currency.

Hotel Rooms **Accommodations Express** ☎ 800/444-7666 or 800/277-1064. **Hotels.com** ☎ 800/246-8357 🌐 www.hotels.com. **International Marketing & Travel Concepts** ☎ 800/790-4682 🌐 www.imtc-travel.com. **Steigenberger Reservation Service** ☎ 800/223-5652 🌐 www.srs-worldhotels.com. **Turbotrip.com** ☎ 800/473-7829 🌐 w3.turbotrip.com.

PACKAGE DEALS

Don't confuse packages and guided tours. When you buy a package, you travel on your own, just as though you had planned the trip yourself. Fly/drive packages, which combine airfare and car rental, are often a good deal. In cities, ask the local visitor's bureau about hotel and local transportation packages that include tickets to major museum exhibits or other special events. If you **buy a rail/drive pass,** you may save on train tickets and car rentals. All Eurailpass holders get a discount on Eurostar fares through the Channel Tunnel and often receive reduced rates for buses, hotels, ferries, sightseeing cruises, and car rentals. A German Rail Pass is also good for travel aboard some KD German Rhine Line steamers and on certain ferries to Finland, Denmark, and Sweden (if the pass includes those countries). Discounts are available on some Deutsche Touring/ Europabus routes.

EATING & DRINKING

Almost every street in Germany has its *Gaststätte,* a sort of combination restaurant and pub, and every village its *Gasthof,* or inn. The emphasis in either is on simple food at reasonable prices. A *Bierstube* (pub) or *Weinstube* (wine cellar) may also serve light snacks or meals. Italian restaurants are about the most popular of all ethnic restaurants in Germany.

Service can be slow, but you'll never be rushed out of your seat. Something else that may seem jarring at first: people can, and do, join other parties at a table in a casual restaurant if seating is tight. It's common courtesy to ask first, though.

Regional specialties are given in the dining sections of individual chapters. The restaurants we list are the cream of the crop in each price category. Properties indicated by a ✕ are lodging establishments with worthwhile restaurants.

BUDGET EATING TIPS

Imbiss (snack) stands can be found in almost every busy shopping street, in parking lots, train stations, and near markets. They serve *Würste* (sausages), grilled, roasted, or boiled, and rolls filled with cheese, cold meat, or fish. Prices range from €1.50 to €2.50 per portion. It's acceptable to bring sandwich fixings to a beer garden and order a beer there.

Butcher shops, known as *Metzgerei,* often serve warm snacks or very good sandwiches. Try *Warmer Leberkäs mit Kartoffelsalat,* a typical Bavarian specialty, which is a sort of baked meat loaf with sweet mustard and potato salad. In northern Germany try *Bouletten,* small meatballs, or *Currywurst,* sausages in a piquant curry sauce.

Restaurants in department stores are especially recommended for appetizing and inexpensive lunches. Kaufhof, Karstadt, Wertheim, and Horton are names to note. Germany's vast selection of Turkish, Italian, Greek, Chinese, and Balkan restaurants are often inexpensive.

MEALS & SPECIALTIES

Most hotels serve a buffet-style breakfast (*Frühstück*) of rolls, cheese, cold cuts, eggs, cereals, yogurt, and spreads, which is often included in the price of a room. Cafés offer a similar choice, but coffee orders are not refillable here. By American standards, a cup (*Tasse*) of coffee in Germany is very petite. Order a *Pot* or *Kännchen* if you want a larger portion of the brew.

For lunch (*Mittagessen*), you can get sandwiches from most cafés and bakeries, and many fine restaurants have special lunch menus that make the gourmet experience much more affordable.

Dinner (*Abendessen*) is usually accompanied by a potato or Spätzle side dish. A salad sometimes comes with the main dish.

MEALTIMES

Gaststätte normally serve hot meals from 11:30 AM to 9 PM; many places stop serving hot meals between 2 PM and 6 PM, although you can still order cold dishes. Unless otherwise noted, the restaurants listed in this guide are open daily for lunch and dinner.

PAYING

Credit cards are generally accepted only in moderate to expensive restaurants, so check before sitting down. You will need to ask for the bill in order to get it from the waiter, the idea being that the table is yours for the evening. Round up the bill 5%–10% and pay the waiter directly rather than leave any money or tip on the table.

RESERVATIONS & DRESS

Reservations are always a good idea; we mention them only when they're essential or not accepted. Book as far ahead as you can, and reconfirm as soon as you arrive. (Large parties should always call ahead to check the reservations policy.) We mention dress only when men are required to wear a jacket or a jacket and tie.

Note, though, that even when Germans dress casually, their look is generally crisp and neat.

SMOKING

For such an otherwise health-conscious nation, Germans smoke a lot. When warm weather doesn't allow for open windows and terraces, bars can become uncomfortably smoky. No-smoking sections in restaurants are almost unheard of, although in summer, this problem is alleviated by outdoor seating. A smoker would find it intrusive if you requested him or her to refrain.

WINE, BEER & SPIRITS

Chapter 9, which follows the German Wine Road, and Chapter 10, which covers the Rhine and Mosel valleys, have the most information regarding wines and wine estates. The office "Wines of Germany" promotes the wines of all 13 German wine regions and can supply you with general background information and brochures such as the German wine-festivals schedule and *Vintners to Visit* (a roster of visitor-friendly wineries). It also arranges 6-day guided winery tours in spring and fall in conjunction with the German Wine Academy.

Germany holds its brewers to a "purity law" that dates back to 1516, and though there are cheaper brands and more expensive ones, across the board, German beer is good. It's legal to drink from open containers in public and having a beer at one's midday break is nothing to raise an eyebrow at.

Wine Information **German Wine Academy** ✉ Gutenbergpl. 3-5, 55116 Mainz ☎ 06131/282-942 🌐 www.germanwines.de. **Wines of Germany** ✉ 950 Third Ave. New York, NY 10022 ☎ 212/994-7523 📠 212/994-7596 🌐 www.germanwineusa.org.

ELECTRICITY

To use electric-powered equipment purchased in the U.S. or Canada, **bring a converter and adapter.** The electrical current in Germany is 220 volts, 50 cycles alternating current (AC); wall outlets take Continental-type plugs, with two round prongs.

If your appliances are dual-voltage, you'll need only an adapter. Don't use 110-volt outlets marked FOR SHAVERS ONLY for high-wattage appliances such as blow-dryers. Most laptops operate equally well on 110 and 220 volts and so require only an adapter.

EMBASSIES

Australia ✉ Wallstr. 76-79, D-10179 Berlin ☎ 030/880-0880 📠 030/8800-88210 🌐 www.australian-embassy.de

Canada ✉ Leipziger Pl. 17, D-10117 Berlin ☎ 030/203-120 📠 030/203-12121 🌐 www.canada.de

Ireland ✉ Friedrichstr. 200, D-10117 Berlin ☎ 030/220-720 📠 030/220-72299 🌐 www.botschaft-irland.de

New Zealand ✉ Friedrichstr. 60, D-10117 Berlin ☎ 030/206-2110 📠 030/206-21114 🌐 www.nzembassy.com

South Africa ✉ Tiergartenstr. 18, D-10785 Berlin ☎ 030/220-730 📠 030/2207-3190 🌐 www.suedafrika.org

United Kingdom ✉ Wilhelmstr. 70-71, D-10117 Berlin ☎ 030/204-570 🌐 www.britischebotschaft.de

United States ✉ Neustädtische Kirchstr. 4-5, D-10117 Berlin ✉ consular section Clayallee 170 ☎ 030/83050, 030/832-9233 for American citizens 📠 030/8305-1215 🌐 www.usembassy.de

EMERGENCIES

Throughout Germany call ☎ 110 for police, ☎ 112 for an ambulance or the fire department, and ☎ 11880 for medication needs.

ENGLISH-LANGUAGE MEDIA

NEWSPAPERS & MAGAZINES

The *International Herald Tribune* is widely available at newsstands. On Friday it includes a translated insert of the week's highlights as reported in the German daily *Frankfurter Allgemeiner Zeitung*. To find American publications such as *USA Today, Time,* or *Newsweek* and British publications such as the *Daily*

Mail, Daily Telegraph, or *Times,* go to a central newspaper shop, at a place such as a major train station.

RADIO & TELEVISION

In Frankfurt, the American Forces Network presents American news, sports, and music. Its AM broadcast (primarily talk) is at 873; the FM signal (primarily music) is at 98.7. You can pick up the BBC World Service in Berlin at 90.2 FM.

Most hotels have a range of American cable TV channels on offer, including CNN and MTV. BBC World broadcasts free.

ETIQUETTE & BEHAVIOR

Being on time for appointments, even casual social ones, is very important. Germans are more formal in addressing each other than Americans. Always address acquaintances as Herr (Mr.) or Frau (Mrs.) plus their last name; do not call them by their first name unless invited to do so. The German language has an informal and formal pronoun for "you": formal is "*Sie,*" and informal is "*du.*" Even if adults are on a first-name basis with one another, they may still keep the *Sie* form between them.

Germans are less formal when it comes to nudity: a sign that reads FREIKÖRPER or FKK indicates a park or beach that allows nude sunbathing.

GAY & LESBIAN TRAVEL

Though only a few of the German states have laws banning discrimination on the basis of sexual orientation, the German people are very tolerant. The law recognizes gay marriages and property rights, and it is unlikely that same-sex couples will have trouble at hotel front desks, even in rural areas.

Gay- & Lesbian-Friendly Travel Agencies **Different Roads Travel** ✉ 1017 N. LaCienega Blvd., Suite 308, West Hollywood, CA 90069 ☎ 310/289-6000 or 800/429-8747 (Ext. 14 for both) 🖷 310/855-0323 ✉ lgernert@tzell.com. **Kennedy Travel** ✉ 130 W. 42nd St., Suite 401, New York, NY 10036 ☎ 800/237-7433 or 212/840-8659 🖷 212/730-2269 🌐 www.kennedytravel.com. **Now, Voyager** ✉ 4406 18th St., San Francisco, CA 94114 ☎ 415/626-1169 or 800/255-6951 🖷 415/626-8626 🌐 www.nowvoyager.com. **Skylink Travel and Tour/Flying Dutchmen Travel** ✉ 1455 N. Dutton Ave., Suite A, Santa Rosa, CA 95401 ☎ 707/546-9888 or 800/225-5759 🖷 707/636-0951; serving lesbian travelers.

HOLIDAYS

The following national holidays are observed in Germany: January 1; January 6 (Epiphany—Bavaria, Saxony-Anhalt, and Baden-Württemberg only); Good Friday; Easter Monday; May 1 (Workers' Day); Ascension; Pentecost Monday; Corpus Christi (southern Germany only); Assumption Day—Bavaria and Saarland only; October 3 (German Unity Day); November 1 (All Saints' Day—Baden Württemberg, Bavaria, North Rhine-Westphalia, Rhineland-Pfalz, and Saarland); December 24–26 (Christmas).

Pre-Lenten celebrations in Cologne and the Rhineland are known as Carnival, and for several days before Ash Wednesday, work grinds to a halt as people celebrate with parades, banquets, and general debauchery. Farther south, in the state of Baden Württenburg, the festivities are called Fasching and tend to be more traditional. In either area, expect businesses to be closed both before and after "Fat Tuesday."

INSURANCE

The most useful travel-insurance plan is a comprehensive policy that includes coverage for trip cancellation and interruption, default, trip delay, and medical expenses (with a waiver for preexisting conditions).

Without insurance you'll lose all or most of your money if you cancel your trip, regardless of the reason. Default insurance covers you if your tour operator, airline, or cruise line goes out of business—the chances of which have been increasing. Trip-delay covers expenses that arise because of bad weather or mechanical delays. Study the fine print when comparing policies.

If you're traveling internationally, a key component of travel insurance is coverage for medical bills incurred if you get sick on the road. Such expenses aren't generally covered by Medicare or private policies. U.K. residents can buy a travel-insurance policy valid for most vacations taken during the year in which it's purchased (but check preexisting-condition coverage).

British and Australian citizens need extra medical coverage when traveling overseas.

Always **buy travel policies directly from the insurance company**; if you buy them from a cruise line, airline, or tour operator that goes out of business you probably won't be covered for the agency or operator's default, a major risk. Before making any purchase, review your existing health and home-owner's policies to find what they cover away from home.

Travel Insurers In the U.S.: **Access America** ✉ 2805 N. Parham Rd., Richmond, VA 23294 ☎ 800/284-8300 ℻ 804/673-1469 or 800/346-9265 🌐 www.accessamerica.com. **Travel Guard International** ✉ 1145 Clark St., Stevens Point, WI 54481 ☎ 800/826-1300 or 715/345-1041 ℻ 800/955-8785 or 715/345-1990 🌐 www.travelguard.com.
In the U.K.: **Association of British Insurers** ✉ 51 Gresham St., London EC2V 7HQ ☎ 020/7600-3333 ℻ 020/7696-8999 🌐 www.abi.org.uk. In Canada: **RBC Insurance** ✉ 6880 Financial Dr., Mississauga, Ontario L5N 7Y5 ☎ 800/387-4357 or 905/816-2559 ℻ 888/298-6458 🌐 www.rbcinsurance.com. In Australia: **Insurance Council of Australia** ✉ Level 3, 56 Pitt St. Sydney, NSW 2000 ☎ 02/9253-5100 ℻ 02/9253-5111 🌐 www.ica.com.au. In New Zealand: **Insurance Council of New Zealand** ✉ Level 7, 111-115 Customhouse Quay, Box 474, Wellington ☎ 04/472-5230 ℻ 04/473-3011 🌐 www.icnz.org.nz.

LANGUAGE

English is spoken in most hotels, restaurants, airports, museums, and other places of interest. However, English is not widely spoken in rural areas nor by people over 40; this is especially true of the eastern part of Germany.

Unless you speak fluent German, you may find some of the regional dialects hard to follow, particularly in Saxony and Bavaria. However, most Germans can speak "high," or standard, German.

LANGUAGES FOR TRAVELERS

A phrase book and language-tape set can help get you started. *Fodor's German for Travelers* (available at bookstores everywhere) is excellent.

LODGING

Assume that hotels operate on the European Plan (EP, with no meals) unless we specify that they use the Continental Plan (CP, with a Continental breakfast), Modified American Plan (MAP, with breakfast and dinner), or the Full American Plan (FAP, with all meals).

The standards of German hotels are very high, down to the humblest inn. You can nearly always **expect courteous and polite service and clean and comfortable rooms.** In addition to hotels proper, the country has numerous *Gasthöfe* or *Gasthäuser,* which are country inns that serve food and also have rooms, and pensions, or *Fremdenheime* (guesthouses). Most hotels have restaurants, but those listed as *Garni* provide breakfast only. At the lowest end of the scale are *Fremdenzimmer,* meaning simply "rooms," normally in private houses. (Look for the sign reading ZIMMER FREI or ZU VERMIETEN on a green background, meaning "to rent"; a red sign reading BESETZT means there are no vacancies.)

The hotels in our listings are divided by price into five categories: $$$$, $$$, $$, $, and ¢. The lodgings we list are the cream of the crop in each price category. Properties are assigned price categories based on the range from their least-expensive standard double room at high season to the most expensive. Properties marked ✕🏨 are lodging establishments whose restaurants are recommendable. We always list the facilities that are available—but we don't specify whether they cost extra. **Ask about breakfast and bathroom facilities** when booking. All hotels listed have a private bath or shower unless otherwise noted. A generous continental breakfast buffet is often included in the rate, but be careful to inquire, particularly in upscale city hotels. Breakfast spreads at some hotels can run between €9–€20 per person.

Room rates are by no means inflexible and depend very much on supply and demand. You can save money by inquiring about reductions: many resort hotels offer substantial discounts in winter, except in the Alps, where rates often rise then. Likewise, many $$$$ and $$$ hotels in cities cut their prices dramatically on weekends and when business is quiet. Prices can yo-yo from your steal to theirs. If you have booked and plan to arrive late, let the hotel know. And if you have to cancel a reservation, inform the hotel as soon as possible; otherwise you may be charged the full amount for the unused room.

Tourist offices will also make bookings for a nominal fee, but they may have difficulty doing so after 4 PM in high season and on weekends, so **don't wait until too late in the day to begin looking for your accommodations.** If you do get stuck, ask someone—like a mail carrier, police officer, or waiter, for example—for directions to a house renting a Fremdenzimmer or a Gasthof.

APARTMENT & VILLA [OR HOUSE] RENTALS

If you want a home base that's roomy enough for a family and comes with cooking facilities, consider a furnished rental. These can save you money, especially if you're traveling with a group. Home-exchange directories sometimes list rentals as well as exchanges.

International Agents **Drawbridge to Europe** ✉ 98 Granite St., Ashland, OR 97520 ☎ 541/482-7778 or 888/268-1148 📠 541/482-7779 🌐 www.drawbridgetoeurope.com. **Hideaways International** ✉ 767 Islington St., Portsmouth, NH 03801 ☎ 603/430-4433 or 800/843-4433 📠 603/430-4444 🌐 www.hideaways.com, annual membership $185. **Interhome** ✉ 1990 N.E. 163rd St., Suite 110, North Miami Beach, FL 33162 ☎ 305/940-2299 or 800/882-6864 📠 305/940-2911 🌐 www.interhome.us. **Villas International** ✉ 4340 Redwood Hwy., Suite D309, San Rafael, CA 94903 ☎ 415/499-9490 or 800/221-2260 📠 415/499-9491 🌐 www.villasintl.com.

CAMPING

Campsites are scattered across the length and breadth of Germany. Contact regional tourist offices for lists of sites. The majority of sites are open year-round, and most are crowded during high season. Prices at ordinary campsites range from around €10 to €25 for a car, tent, or trailer and two adults, though prices at fancier ones, with pools, sports facilities, and entertainment, can be considerably more. If you want to camp elsewhere, you must **get permission from the landowner beforehand;** ask the police if you can't track him or her down. Drivers of mobile homes may park for a limited time on roadsides and in autobahn parking-lot areas but may not set up camping equipment there.

CASTLE-HOTELS

Germany's historic castle-, or *Schloss*, hotels are all privately owned and run. The simpler ones may lack some amenities, but the majority combine four-star luxury with valuable antique furnishings, four-poster beds, stone passageways, and a baronial atmosphere. Some offer full resort facilities. Nearly all are in the countryside (⇨ Chapters 7 and 10, in particular, have several castle-hotel reviews). Euro-Connection can advise you on castle-hotel packages, including four- to six-night tours.

Euro-Connection ✉ 7500 212th St. SW, Suite 103, Edmonds, WA 98026 ☎ 800/645-3876 🌐 www.euro-connection.com.

FARM VACATIONS

Almost every regional tourist office has a brochure listing farms that offer bed-and-breakfasts, apartments, and entire farmhouses to rent (*Ferienhöfe*). The German Agricultural Association provides an illustrated brochure, *Urlaub auf dem Bauernhof* (Vacation Down on the Farm), that covers more than 2,000 inspected and graded farms, from the Alps to the North Sea. It costs €9.90 and is also sold in bookstores.

German Agricultural Association **DLG Reisedienst, Agratour** (German Agricultural Association) ✉ Eschborner Landstr. 122, D-60489 Frankfurt am Main ☎ 069/247-880 📠 069/2478-8110 🌐 www.landtourismus.de.

HOME EXCHANGES

If you would like to exchange your home for someone else's, join a home-exchange organization, which will send you its updated listings of available exchanges for a year and will include your own listing in at least one of them. It's up to you to make specific arrangements.

Exchange Clubs **HomeLink USA** ✉ 2937 NW 9th Terrace, Wilton Manors, FL 33311 ☎ 954/566-2687 or 800/638-3841 📠 954/566-2783 🌐 www.homelink.org; $75 yearly for a listing and online access; $45 additional to receive directories. **Intervac U.S.** ✉ 30 Corte San Fernando, Tiburon, CA 94920 ☎ 800/756-4663 📠 415/435-7440 🌐 www.intervacus.com; $128 yearly for a listing, online access, and a catalog; $68 without catalog.

HOSTELS

No matter what your age, you can save on lodging costs by staying at hostels—rates average €13.30 for people under 27 and €13.30–€22 for those older (breakfast included). Accommodations can range from single-sex, dorm-style beds to rooms for couples and families. Germany's more than 600 *Jugendherbergen* (youth hostels) are among the most efficient and up-to-date in Europe, and many are in castles. There's an age limit of 26 in Bavaria; elsewhere, there are no age restrictions, though those under 20 take preference if space is limited. The DJH Service GmbH provides a complete list of German hostels in its association, but note there are also scores of independent hostels with fine rates and standards. Hostels must be reserved well in advance for midsummer, especially in eastern Germany. To book a hostel, you can go on DJH's Web site or call a lodging directly; for DJH hostels it's helpful to be a member of a national hosteling association or Hostelling International (HI), the umbrella group for a number of national youth-hostel associations. Without membership, there's an extra charge, but with each overnight stay you receive a "welcome stamp." Six welcome stamps will grant you full membership in HI.

Membership in any HI national hostel association, open to travelers of all ages, allows you to stay in HI-affiliated hostels at member rates; one-year membership is about $28 for adults (C$35 for a two-year minimum membership in Canada, £15 in the U.K., A$52 in Australia, and NZ$40 in New Zealand); hostels charge about $10–$30 per night. Members have priority if the hostel is full; they're also eligible for discounts around the world, even on rail and bus travel in some countries.

In Germany **DJH Service GmbH** ✉ Bismarckstr. 8, D-32754 Detmold ☎ 05231/74010 📠 05231/740-149 🌐 www.jugendherberge.de.

Organizations **Hostelling International–USA** ✉ 8401 Colesville Rd., Suite 600, Silver Spring, MD 20910 ☎ 301/495-1240 📠 301/495-6697 🌐 www.hiusa.org. **Hostelling International–Canada** ✉ 205 Catherine St., Suite 400, Ottawa, Ontario K2P 1C3 ☎ 613/237-7884 or 800/663-5777 📠 613/237-7868 🌐 www.hihostels.ca. **YHA England and Wales** ✉ Trevelyan House, Dimple Rd., Matlock, Derbyshire DE4 3YH, U.K. ☎ 0870/870-8808, 0870/770-8868, 0162/959-2600 📠 0870/770-6127 🌐 www.yha.org.uk. **YHA Australia** ✉ 422 Kent St., Sydney, NSW 2001 ☎ 02/9261-1111 📠 02/9261-1969 🌐 www.yha.com.au. **YHA New Zealand** ✉ Level 1, Moorhouse City, 166 Moorhouse Ave., Box 436, Christchurch ☎ 03/379-9970 or 0800/278-299 📠 03/365-4476 🌐 www.yha.org.nz.

HOTELS

There are many European chain hotels in Germany. The Accor Hotel group is prevalent and includes the respectable chains Ibis, Mercure, Novotel, and Sofitel. Major American hotel chains—Hilton, Sheraton, Holiday Inn, Best Western, Marriott—are represented in cities.

Most hotels in Germany do not have air-conditioning, nor do they need it given the climate and the German style of building construction that uses thick walls and recessed windows to help keep the heat out. Smaller hotels do not provide much in terms of bathroom amenities. Except in four- and five star hotels, you won't find a washcloth. Hotels often have no-smoking rooms or even no-smoking floors, so it's always worth asking for one when you reserve. All hotels listed have private bath unless otherwise noted. Specify your preference for a shower or bathtub; though bathtubs come with a handheld shower nozzle, standing with free hands under a mounted spray is usually not possible. Beds in double rooms often consist of two twin mattresses placed side by side within a frame. When you arrive, if you don't like the room you're offered, ask to see another.

RESERVING A ROOM

Most hotels can process a letter or fax asking for a reservation in English, but here are sample phrases in German:

Sehr geehrte Damen und Herren! (Dear Sir/Madam).

Ich möchte ein Doppelzimmer/ Zweibettzimmer mit Bad reservieren (I would like to reserve a double/twin room with bath).

und zwar von. bis. (from. until.; dates are written day/month/year).

Ich hätte gern ein Zimmer auf der oberen Etage/auf der unteren Etage/mit Ausblick/ in ruhiger Lage (I would like a room on a high floor/a low floor/with a view/a quiet room).

Könnten Sie mir bitte weitere Informationen auf Englisch über Ihr Hotel zuschicken (Please send me more information in English about your hotel).

Mit freundlichen Grüssen (Kind regards).

Toll-Free Numbers **Best Western** ☎ 800/528-1234 🌐 www.bestwestern.com. **Choice** ☎ 800/424-6423 🌐 www.choicehotels.com. **Clarion** ☎ 800/424-6423 🌐 www.choicehotels.com. **Comfort Inn** ☎ 800/424-6423 🌐 www.choicehotels.com. **Four Seasons** ☎ 800/332-3442 🌐 www.fourseasons.com. **Hilton** ☎ 800/445-8667 🌐 www.hilton.com. **Holiday Inn** ☎ 800/465-4329 🌐 www.ichotelsgroup.com. **Hyatt Hotels & Resorts** ☎ 800/233-1234 🌐 www.hyatt.com. **Inter-Continental** ☎ 800/327-0200 🌐 www.ichotelsgroup.com. **Marriott** ☎ 800/228-9290 🌐 www.marriott.com. **Le Meridien** ☎ 800/543-4300 🌐 www.lemeridien.com. **Nikko Hotels International** ☎ 800/645-5687 🌐 www.nikkohotels.com. **Quality Inn** ☎ 800/424-6423 🌐 www.choicehotels.com. **Radisson** ☎ 800/333-3333 🌐 www.radisson.com. **Ramada** ☎ 800/228-2828, 800/854-7854 international reservations 🌐 www.ramada.com or www.ramadahotels.com. **Renaissance Hotels & Resorts** ☎ 800/468-3571 🌐 www.marriott.com. **Ritz-Carlton** ☎ 800/241-3333 🌐 www.ritzcarlton.com. **Sheraton** ☎ 800/325-3535 🌐 www.starwood.com/sheraton. **Westin Hotels & Resorts** ☎ 800/228-3000 🌐 www.starwood.com/westin.

ROMANTIK HOTELS

Among the most delightful places to stay—and eat—in Germany are the aptly named Romantik Hotels and Restaurants. The Romantik group has 185 establishments throughout Europe, with 86 in Germany. All are in atmospheric and historic buildings—a condition for membership—and are personally run by the owners, with the emphasis on excellent food and service. Prices vary considerably but in general represent good value, particularly the special weekend and short-holiday rates. Check the Web site for packages that include meals and spa options. A detailed brochure listing all Romantik Hotels and Restaurants is available by mail.

Romantik Hotels and Restaurants ✉ Lyoner Stern, Hahnstr. 70, D-60528 Frankfurt/Main ☎ 069/661-2340 📠 069/6612-3456 ✉ C/o tma target market america 505 Majorca Ave., Coral Gables FL 33134 ☎ 305/447-1222 or 800/650-8018 📠 305/574-7769 🌐 www.romantikhotels.com.

SPAS

Taking the waters in Germany, whether for curing the body or merely pampering it, has been popular since Roman times. More than 300 health resorts, mostly equipped for thermal or mineral water, mud, or brine treatments, are set within pleasant country areas or historic communities. The word *Bad* before or within the name of a town usually means it's a spa destination, where many patients reside in health clinics for two to three weeks of doctor-prescribed treatments.

There are four main groups of spas and health resorts: the mineral and moorland spas, where treatments are based on natural warm-water springs; those on the Baltic and North Sea coasts; hydropathic spas, which use an invigorating cold-water process developed during the 19th century; and climatic health resorts, usually in the mountains, which depend on their climates and fresh air for their health-giving properties.

Saunas, steam baths, and other hot-room facilities are often used "without textiles" in Germany—in other words, naked. Wearing a bathing suit is sometimes even prohibited in saunas, but sitting on a towel is always required (you may need to bring your own towels). The Deutsche Heilbäderverband has information in German only.

Deutsche Heilbäderverband (German Health Resort and Spa Association) ✉ Schumannstr. 111, D-53113 Bonn ☎ 0228/201-200 📠 0228/201-2041 🌐 www.deutscher-heilbaederverband.de.

MAIL & SHIPPING

Post offices (*Deutsche Post*) are recognizable by the postal symbol, a black bugle on a yellow background. Stamps (*Briefmarken*) can also be bought at some news agencies and souvenir shops. Letters take approximately 3–4 days to the United Kingdom, 5–7 days to the United States, and 7–10 days to Australia and New Zealand. Post offices are generally open weekdays 8–6, Saturday 8–noon.

OVERNIGHT SERVICES

The Deutsche Post has an express international service that will deliver your letter or package the next day to countries within the EU, within one to two days to the United States, and slightly longer to Australia. A letter or package to the United States weighing less than 200 grams costs €48.57. You can drop off your mail at any post office, or it can be picked up for an extra fee. Deutsche Post works in cooperation with DHL. International carriers tend to be slightly cheaper (€35–€45 for the same letter) and provide more services.

Major Services **Deutsche Post Express International** ☎ 08105/345-2255 🌐 www.deutschepost.de. **DHL** ☎ 0800/225-5345 🌐 www.dhl.de. **FedEx** ☎ 0800/123-0800 🌐 www.fedex.com. **UPS** ☎ 0800/882-6630 🌐 www.ups.com.

POSTAL RATES

Airmail letters to the United States, Canada, Australia, and New Zealand cost €1.55; postcards, €1. All letters to the United Kingdom and within Europe cost €.55; postcards, €.45.

RECEIVING MAIL

You can arrange to have mail (letters only) sent to you in care of any German post office; **have the envelope marked "Postlagernd."** This service is free, and the mail will be held for 7 days. Or you can have mail sent to any American Express office in Germany. There's no charge to cardholders, holders of American Express traveler's checks, or anyone who has booked a vacation with American Express.

SHIPPING PARCELS

Most major stores that cater to tourists will also ship your purchases home. You should check your insurance for coverage of possible damage. The companies listed under ⇨ Overnight Services also have international shipping services, although these are quite expensive.

MONEY MATTERS

Payment by credit card is not as frequent an option as in the United States, so be sure to have cash handy at all times. Prices throughout this guide are given for adults. Substantially reduced fees are almost always available for children, students, and senior citizens. For information on taxes, *see* Taxes.

Inquire if the region or city you're visiting offers a tourist card, which usually includes public transportation and discounts to attractions or tours.

ATMS

Twenty-four-hour ATMs (*Geldautomaten*) can be accessed with Plus or Cirrus credit and banking cards. Some German banks exact €3–€5 fees for use of their ATMs. Your PIN should be set for four digits; if it's longer, change it at your bank before the trip. Since some ATM keypads show no letters, know the numeric equivalent of your password.

CREDIT CARDS

All major U.S. credit cards are accepted in Germany. If you have a four-digit PIN for your card, you can use it at German ATMs.

Throughout this guide, the following abbreviations are used: **AE,** American Express; **DC,** Diners Club; **MC,** MasterCard; and **V,** Visa.

Reporting Lost Cards **American Express** ☎ 069/97970. **Diners Club** ☎ 069/6616-6123. **MasterCard** ☎ 0800/819-1040. **Visa** ☎ 0800/811-8440.

CURRENCY

Germany shares a common currency, the euro (€), with 11 other countries: Austria, Belgium, Finland, France, Greece, Ireland, Italy, Luxembourg, Netherlands, Portugal, and Spain. The euro is divided into 100 cents. There are bills of 5, 10, 20, 50, 100, and 500 euros and coins of €1 and €2, and 1, 2, 5, 10, 20, and 50 cents.

CURRENCY EXCHANGE

At press time, you could get €.77 for a U.S. dollar, €.62 for a Canadian dollar, €1.47 for a British pound, €.60 for an Australian dollar, €.56 for a New Zealand dollar, and €.12 for a South African rand.

For the most favorable rates, **change money through banks.** Although ATM transaction fees may be higher abroad than at home, ATM rates are excellent because they're based on wholesale rates offered only by major banks. You won't do as well at exchange booths in airports or rail and bus stations, in hotels, in restaurants, or in stores. To avoid lines at airport exchange booths, get a bit of local currency before you leave home.

Exchange Services **International Currency Express** ✉ 427 N. Camden Dr., Suite F, Beverly Hills, CA 90210 ☎ 888/278-6628 orders 🖷 310/278-6410 🌐 www.foreignmoney.com. **Travel Ex Currency Services** ☎ 800/287-7362 orders and retail locations 🌐 www.travelex.com.

TRAVELER'S CHECKS

Do you need traveler's checks? It depends on where you're headed. If you're going to rural areas and small towns, go with cash; traveler's checks are best used in cities. Lost or stolen checks can usually be replaced within 24 hours. To ensure a speedy refund, buy your own traveler's checks—don't let someone else pay for them: irregularities like this can cause delays. The person who bought the checks should make the call to request a refund.

PACKING

For cities, **pack as you would for an American city**: dressy outfits for formal restaurants and nightclubs, casual clothes elsewhere. Jeans are as popular in Germany as anywhere else and are perfectly acceptable for sightseeing and informal dining. In the evening men will probably feel more comfortable wearing a jacket in more expensive restaurants, although it's almost never required. Many German women wear stylish outfits to restaurants and the theater, especially in the larger cities.

Winters can be bitterly cold; summers are warm but with days that suddenly turn cool and rainy. In summer **take a warm jacket or heavy sweater** for the Bavarian Alps, where the nights can be chilly even after hot days. Germans rarely wear shorts other than when doing sports, particularly in cities.

To discourage purse snatchers and pickpockets, **carry a handbag with long straps** that you can sling across your body bandolier style and with a zippered compartment for money and other valuables.

For stays in budget hotels, **take your own soap.** Many provide no soap at all or only a small bar.

In your carry-on luggage, pack an extra pair of eyeglasses or contact lenses and enough of any medication you take to last a few days longer than the entire trip. You may also ask your doctor to write a spare prescription using the drug's generic name, as brand names may vary from country to country. In luggage to be checked, **never pack prescription drugs, valuables, or undeveloped film.** And don't forget to carry with you the addresses of offices that handle refunds of lost traveler's checks. Check *Fodor's How to Pack* (available at online retailers and bookstores everywhere) for more tips.

To avoid customs and security delays, carry medications in their original packaging. Don't pack any sharp objects in your carry-on luggage, including knives of any size or material, scissors, nail clippers, and corkscrews, or anything else that might arouse suspicion.

To avoid having your checked luggage chosen for hand inspection, don't cram bags full. The U.S. Transportation Security Administration suggests packing shoes on top and placing personal items you don't want touched in clear plastic bags.

CHECKING LUGGAGE

You're allowed to carry aboard one bag and one personal article, such as a purse or a laptop computer. Make sure what you carry on fits under your seat or in the overhead bin. Get to the gate early, so you can board as soon as possible, before the overhead bins fill up.

Baggage allowances vary by carrier, destination, and ticket class. On international flights, you're usually allowed to check two bags weighing up to 70 pounds (32 kilograms) each, although a few airlines allow checked bags of up to 88 pounds (40 kilograms) in first class. Some international carriers don't allow more than 66 pounds (30 kilograms) per bag in business class and 44 pounds (20 kilograms) in economy. If you're flying to or through the United Kingdom, your luggage cannot exceed 70 pounds (32 kilograms) per bag. On domestic flights, the limit is usually 50 to 70 pounds (23 to 32 kilograms) per bag. In general, carry-on bags shouldn't exceed 40 pounds (18 kilograms). Most airlines won't accept bags that weigh more than 100 pounds (45 kilograms) on domestic or international flights. Expect to pay a fee for baggage that exceeds weight limits. Check baggage restrictions with your carrier before you pack.

Airline liability for baggage is limited to $2,500 per person on flights within the United States. On international flights it amounts to $9.07 per pound or $20 per kilogram for checked baggage (roughly $640 per 70-pound bag), with a maximum of $634.90 per piece, and $400 per passenger for unchecked baggage. You can buy additional coverage at check-in for about $10 per $1,000 of coverage, but it often excludes a rather extensive list of items, shown on your airline ticket.

Before departure, itemize your bags' contents and their worth, and label the bags with your name, address, and phone number. (If you use your home address, cover it so potential thieves can't see it readily.) Include a label inside each bag and **pack a copy of your itinerary.** At check-in, make sure each bag is correctly tagged with the destination airport's three-letter code. Because some checked bags will be opened for hand inspection, the U.S. Transportation Security Administration recommends that you leave luggage unlocked or use the plastic locks offered at check-in. TSA screeners place an inspection notice inside searched bags, which are re-sealed with a special lock.

If your bag has been searched and contents are missing or damaged, file a claim with the TSA Consumer Response Center as soon as possible. If your bags arrive damaged or fail to arrive at all, file a written report with the airline before leaving the airport.

Complaints **U.S. Transportation Security Administration Contact Center** ☎ 866/289–9673 🌐 www.tsa.gov.

PASSPORTS & VISAS

When traveling internationally, carry your passport even if you don't need one (it's always the best form of I.D.) and **make two photocopies of the data page** (one for someone at home and another for you, carried separately from your passport). If you lose your passport, promptly call the nearest embassy or consulate and the local police.

U.S. passport applications for children under age 14 require consent from both parents or legal guardians; both parents must appear together to sign the application. If only one parent appears, he or she must submit a written statement from the other parent authorizing passport issuance for the child. A parent with sole authority must present evidence of it when applying; acceptable documentation includes the child's certified birth certificate listing only the applying parent, a court order specifically permitting this parent's travel with the child, or a death certificate for the nonapplying parent. Application forms and instructions are available on the Web site of the U.S. State Department's Bureau of Consular Affairs (🌐 travel.state.gov).

ENTERING GERMANY

U.S., Canadian, Australian, New Zealand, and British citizens need only a valid passport (even those that have been expired up to five years are considered valid) to enter Germany for stays of up to 90 days.

PASSPORT OFFICES

The best time to apply for a passport or to renew is in fall and winter. Before any trip, check your passport's expiration date, and, if necessary, renew it as soon as possible.

Australian Citizens **Passports Australia** Australian Department of Foreign Affairs and Trade ☎ 131–232 🌐 www.passports.gov.au.

Canadian Citizens Passport Office ✉ to mail in applications: 70 Cremazie St., Gatineau, Québec J8Y 3P2 ☎ 819/994-3500 or 800/567-6868 🌐 www.ppt.gc.ca.
New Zealand Citizens New Zealand Passports Office ☎ 0800/22-5050 or 04/474-8100 🌐 www.passports.govt.nz.
U.K. Citizens U.K. Passport Service ☎ 0870/521-0410 🌐 www.passport.gov.uk.
U.S. Citizens National Passport Information Center ☎ 877/487-2778, 888/874-7793 TDD/TTY 🌐 travel.state.gov.

RESTROOMS

It's customary to leave a €.20–€.30 gratuity in a restroom if it has an attendant.

SAFETY

Don't wear a money belt or a waist pack, both of which peg you as a tourist. Distribute your cash and any valuables (including your credit cards and passport) between a deep front pocket, an inside jacket or vest pocket, and a hidden money pouch. Do not reach for the money pouch once you're in public.

Germany has one of the lowest rates of violent crime in Europe. The best advice is to take normal precautions. Put valuables in the hotel safe. Don't carry a shoulder bag or purse in such a way that it can be easily snatched. Avoid remote areas late at night. And then, don't worry too much.

WOMEN IN GERMANY

If you carry a purse, choose one with a zipper and a thick strap that you can drape across your body; adjust the length so that the purse sits in front of you at or above hip level. (Don't wear a money belt or a waist pack.) Store only enough money in the purse to cover casual spending. Distribute the rest of your cash and any valuables between deep front pockets, inside jacket or vest pockets, and a concealed money pouch.

SENIOR-CITIZEN TRAVEL

Senior citizens qualify for some discounts in Germany, such as on the railways and in museums. For €11, the German Railroad's ReisePacket service (⇨ Train Travel) includes help boarding and getting off trains, transfer of luggage, and other small services.

To qualify for age-related discounts, mention your senior-citizen status up front when booking hotel reservations (not when checking out) and before you're seated in restaurants (not when paying the bill). Be sure to have identification on hand. When renting a car, ask about promotional car-rental discounts, which can be cheaper than senior-citizen rates.

Educational Programs Elderhostel ✉ 11 Ave. de Lafayette, Boston, MA 02111 ☎ 877/426-8056, 978/323-4141 international callers, 877/426-2167 TTY 📠 877/426-2166 🌐 www.elderhostel.org. **Interhostel** ✉ University of New Hampshire, 6 Garrison Ave., Durham, NH 03824 ☎ 603/862-1147 or 800/733-9753 📠 603/862-1113 🌐 www.learn.unh.edu.

SPORTS & OUTDOORS

Germans are very active and constantly organize themselves into sports teams and clubs. Hiking trails abound throughout the country, and city residents often use a bike to get around town. Germany is hosting the 2006 FIFA World Cup soccer matches in June and July, which will take place not only in 12 stadiums throughout the country, but virtually in any bar or restaurant with a TV screen. The German national tourism Web site and www.fifaworldcup.com have information about the venues and host cities.

BIKING

There are many long-distance bicycle routes in Germany. Among the best river bike paths are those along the Danube River (*Donau* in German), which you can join at Regensburg or Passau, and along the Weser River, which you can join at Hannoversch-Münden. The *Radfährerkarten,* issued by the Bielefelder Verlaganstalt and by Haupka Verlag, are good bike travel maps available at bookstores.

The Call-a-Bike rental service Deutsche Bahn is available in Berlin, Frankfurt, Köln, and Munich. Solidly built silver bikes cost €.07 per minute, not to exceed €15 for 24 hours. First register online or by phone (a credit card is necessary). The bikes are left electronically locked at major intersections. If a bike's lock's green light is blinking, it's free to use. Call the number on the lock to receive the code number to unlock it. When you're finished with the bike, lock it to a traffic sign or stand (but not to a traffic light) at a major intersection. Press a display button for the prompt: "Rückgabe Ja/Nein." Press "Ja" for the receipt code, which you'll need, along with the names of the crossroads, when calling to report you're finished. Most bike shops have rentals for €10–€20 per day.

Bikes cannot be transported on InterCity Express trains. Trains that do carry them have a little bicycle symbol on the timetable. Bike transportation costs €3 on local trains (RB, RE, IRE). On all other trains **you must make advance reservations** and pay €8. Bikes can usually be transported on municipal suburban trains, trams, and buses, but an extra ticket for your bike is often required.

Allgemeiner Deutscher Fahrrad-Club (German Cycle Club) Postfach 107747, D-28077 Bremen 0421/346-290 0421/346-2950 www.adfc.de. **Deutsche Bahn bicycle hotline** 01805/151-415 information, 0700/0522-5522 call-a-bike www.call-a-bike.de.

HIKING

Tourist offices in all Bavarian Alpine resorts have details on mountaineering schools offering weeklong courses. Most town tourist offices will have details on local hiking areas. The Deutscher Alpenverein maintains more than 50 mountain huts and about 15,000 km (9,300 mi) of Alpine paths. In addition, it can provide courses in mountaineering and route suggestions. The organization is not a tour-planner and does not make hut reservations. It can report on weather and trail conditions. Foreigners may become members.

Deutscher Alpenverein Haus der Alpinismus, Praterinsel 5, Munich 089/294-940 089/140-0312 www.alpenverein.de.

SKIING

The Black Forest has many marked and groomed cross-country ski trails (*Loipe*). Ask about ski and boot rentals in any town, as well as how to get to the local trail with the best snow conditions. Downhill (*Alpin*) is most popular in the Bavarian Alps, though you can do it in the Harz Mountains as well.

STUDENTS IN GERMANY

Most museums and performance venues and cinemas have reduced prices for students, so have your student ID card handy. Note that only local pupils qualify for "Ermässigung" (reduction) local public transportation tickets. EurAide offers help with travel plans at Munich's main train station and at Berlin's Zoologischer Garten train station. *See* Lodging for hosteling information.

I.D.s & Services **STA Travel** 10 Downing St., New York, NY 10014 212/627-3111, 800/777-0112 24-hr service center 212/627-3387 www.sta.com. **Travel Cuts** 187 College St., Toronto, Ontario M5T 1P7, Canada 800/592-2887 in the U.S., 416/979-2406 or 866/246-9762 in Canada 416/979-8167 www.travelcuts.com.

TAXES

VALUE-ADDED TAX

Most prices you see on items already have Germany's 16% value-added tax (V.A.T.) included. When traveling to a non-EU country, you are entitled to a refund of the V.A.T. you pay (multiply the price of an item by .138 to find out how much V.A.T. is embedded in the price). Some goods, such as books and antiquities, carry a 7% V.A.T. as a percentage of the purchase price. An item must cost at least €25 to qualify for a V.A.T. refund.

When making a purchase, **ask for a V.A.T. refund form** and find out whether the merchant gives refunds—not all stores do, nor are they required to. Have the form stamped like any customs form by customs officials when you leave the country or, if you're visiting several European Union countries, when you leave the EU. Be ready to show customs officials what you've bought (pack purchases together, in your carry-on luggage); budget extra time for this. After you're through passport control, take the form to a refund-service counter for an on-the-spot refund (which is usually the quickest and easiest option), or mail it to the address on the form (or the envelope with it) after you arrive home.

A service processes refunds for most shops. You receive the total refund stated on the form. Global Refund is a Europe-wide service with 210,000 affiliated stores and more than 700 refund counters—located at major airports and border crossings. Its refund form is called a Tax Free Check. The service issues refunds in the form of cash, check, or credit-card adjustment. If you don't have time to wait at the refund counter, you can mail the form to an office in Europe or Canada instead.

V.A.T. REFUNDS AT THE AIRPORT

If you're departing from Terminal 1 at Frankfurt Airport, where you bring your purchases to claim your tax back depends on how you've packed the goods. If the items are in your check-in luggage, check in as normal, but let the ticket counter know you have to claim your tax still. They will give you your luggage back to bring to the customs office in departure hall B, level 2. For goods you are carrying on the plane with you, go to the customs office on the way to your gate. After you pass through passport control, there is a Global Refund office.

If you're departing from Terminal 2, bring goods in luggage to be checked to the customs office in Hall D, Level 2 (opposite the Delta Airlines check-in counters). For goods you are carrying on the plane with you, see the customs office in Hall E, Level 3 (near security control).

At Munich's airport, the Terminal 2 customs area is on the same level as check-in. If your V.A.T. refund items are in your luggage, check in first, then bring your bags to the customs office on level 04. From here, your bags will be sent to your flight and you can go to the Global Refund counter around the corner. If your refund items are in your carry-on, go to the Global Refund office in the customs area on level 05 south. Terminal 1 has customs areas in modules C and D, levels 04.

V.A.T. Refunds **Global Refund Canada** Box 2020, Station Main Brampton, Ontario L6T 3S3 800/993-4313 905/791-9078 www.globalrefund.com.

TELEPHONES

AREA & COUNTRY CODES

The country code for Germany is 49. When dialing a German number from abroad, drop the initial "0" from the local area code. When dialing within a local area code, drop the "0" and the area code. To dial abroad from Germany, the country code is 001 for the United States and Canada, 0061 for Australia, 0064 for New Zealand, 0044 for the United Kingdom, 00353 for Ireland, and 0027 for South Africa.

Many companies have service lines beginning with 0180. The cost of these calls averages €.12 per minute. Numbers that begin with 0190 can cost €1.85 per minute and more.

DIRECTORY & OPERATOR ASSISTANCE

The German telephone system is fully automatic, and it's unlikely you'll have to employ the services of an operator unless you're seeking information. If you have difficulty reaching your number, call 0180/200–1033. You can book collect calls through this number to the United States but not to other countries. For information in English dial 11837 for numbers within Germany and 11834 for numbers elsewhere. But first **look for the number in the phone book or on the Web** (www.teleauskunft.de), because directory assistance is costly. Calls to 11837 and 11834 cost at least €.50, more if the call lasts more than 30 seconds.

INTERNATIONAL CALLS

International calls can be made from just about any telephone booth in Germany. It costs only €.13 per minute to call the United States, day or night, no matter how long the call lasts. Use a phone card. If you don't have a good deal with a calling card, there are many stores that offer international calls at rates well below what you will pay from a phone booth. At a hotel, rates will be at least double the regular charge, so **avoid making international calls from your room.**

LOCAL CALLS
A local call from a telephone booth costs €.10 per minute. You can drop the local area code.

LONG-DISTANCE CALLS
Dial the "0" before the area code when making a long-distance call within Germany. German newspapers often print a column with prefix telephone numbers that offer discounted rates at specific hours. Prefixes and rates at any given time are listed on www.billiger-telefonieren.de (German only). Dial the prefix, often five digits, before the phone number you wish to call. This prefix can save you as much as .08¢ per minute, with calls to the United States and Canada running under .02¢ per minute.

LONG-DISTANCE SERVICES
AT&T, MCI, and Sprint access codes make calling long-distance relatively convenient, but you may find the local access number blocked in many hotel rooms. First ask the hotel operator to connect you. If the hotel operator balks, ask for an international operator, or dial the international operator yourself. One way to improve your odds of getting connected to your long-distance carrier is to travel with more than one company's calling card (a hotel may block Sprint, for example, but not MCI). If all else fails, call from a pay phone. If you are traveling for a longer period of time, consider renting a cell phone from a local company.

Access Codes **AT&T Direct** ☎ 0800/225-5288. **Sprint International Access** ☎ 0800/888-0013. **MCI WorldPhone** ☎ 0800/888-8000.

MOBILE PHONES
The standard mobile phones used in the United States and Canada are *not* compatible with Germany's GSM digital mobile phone network. Because public phones are not nearly as ubiquitous as in North America, you should seriously consider renting a GSM cell phone (or a SIM card for Germany) if you intend to make and receive calls regularly. You can rent a cell phone at the Airport Communications Service at Frankfurt's airport. It's in the Frankfurt Airport Center 1 and near the Sheraton Hotel. They can also deliver to you at a prearranged meeting point. A base week rate is €40. At the Munich Airport Center, the Nokia Shop at Terminal 2 rents cell phones.

Phone Rentals **Airport Communications Service** ☎ 069/6959-1163 📠 069/6959-1165 🌐 www.aircom.de. **Nokia Shop** ☎ 089/9758-4550 🌐 www.rentacell.com.

PHONE CARDS
Post offices, newsstands, and exchange places sell cards with €5, €10, or €20 worth of credit to use at public pay phones (*Zelle*), and cards to use from home or mobile phones. An advantage of a card: it charges only what the call costs. A €5 card with a good rate for calls to the United States, United Kingdom, and Canada is EuroExtra.

PUBLIC PHONES
Telephone booths are not a common feature on the streets, so be prepared to walk out of your way to find one (most post offices have one). Most phone booths have instructions in English as well as German. Most telephone booths in Germany are card-operated, so **buy a phone card.** Coin-operated phones, which take €0.10, €0.20, €0.50, €1, and €2 coins, don't make change.

TIME
Germany is on Central European Time, which is six hours ahead of Eastern Standard Time and nine hours ahead of Pacific Standard Time. Germans use military time (1 PM is indicated as 13:00) and write the date before the month, so October 3 will appear as 03.10.

TIPPING
The service charges on bills are sufficient for most tips in your hotel, though you should **tip bellhops and porters**; €1 per bag or service is ample. It's also customary to leave a small tip (a euro or so per night) for the room-cleaning staff. Whether you tip the desk clerk depends on whether he or she has given you any special service.

Service charges are included in all restaurant checks (listed as *Bedienung*), as is tax (listed as *MWST*). Nonetheless, it is customary to **round up the bill to the nearest euro or to leave about 5–10%** (give it to the waiter or waitress as you pay the bill; don't leave it on the table, as that's considered rude). Bartenders don't expect, but appreciate tips. Those who bring drinks to your table do expect a small tip.

In taxis, **round up the fare about a euro** as a tip. Give more only if you have particularly cumbersome or heavy luggage.

TOURS & PACKAGES

Because everything is prearranged on a prepackaged tour or independent vacation, you spend less time planning—and often get it all at a good price.

BOOKING WITH AN AGENT

Travel agents are excellent resources. But it's a good idea to collect brochures from several agencies, as some agents' suggestions may be influenced by relationships with tour and package firms that reward them for volume sales. If you have a special interest, find an agent with expertise in that area. The American Society of Travel Agents (ASTA) has a database of specialists worldwide; you can log on to the group's Web site to find one near you.

Make sure your travel agent knows the accommodations and other services of the place being recommended. Ask about the hotel's location, room size, beds, and whether it has a pool, room service, or programs for children, if you care about these. Has your agent been there in person or sent others whom you can contact?

Do some homework on your own, too: local tourism boards can provide information about lesser-known and small-niche operators, some of which may sell only direct.

BUYER BEWARE

Each year consumers are stranded or lose their money when tour operators—even large ones with excellent reputations—go out of business. So check out the operator. Ask several travel agents about its reputation, and try to **book with a company that has a consumer-protection program.** (Look for information in the company's brochure.) In the United States, members of the United States Tour Operators Association are required to set aside funds (up to $1 million) to help eligible customers cover payments and travel arrangements in the event that the company defaults. It's also a good idea to choose a company that participates in the American Society of Travel Agents' Tour Operator Program; ASTA will act as mediator in any disputes between you and your tour operator.

Remember that the more your package or tour includes, the better you can predict the ultimate cost of your vacation. Make sure you know exactly what is covered, and beware of hidden costs. Are taxes, tips, and transfers included? Entertainment and excursions? These can add up.

Tour-Operator Recommendations **American Society of Travel Agents** (⇨ Travel Agencies). **CrossSphere-The Global Association for Packaged Travel** ✉ 546 E. Main St., Lexington, KY 40508 ☎ 859/226-4444 or 800/682-8886 📠 859/226-4414 🌐 www.CrossSphere.com. **United States Tour Operators Association** (USTOA) ✉ 275 Madison Ave., Suite 2014, New York, NY 10016 ☎ 212/599-6599 📠 212/599-6744 🌐 www.ustoa.com.

TRAIN TRAVEL

Deutsche Bahn (DB—German Rail) is a very efficient, privatized railway. Its high-speed InterCity Express (ICE), InterCity (IC), and EuroCity (EC) trains make journeys between the centers of many cities—Munich–Frankfurt, for example—faster by rail than by air. All InterCity and InterCity Express trains have restaurant cars and trolley service. RE, RB, and IRE trains are regional trains. Trains are usually punctual.

Once on your platform (*Gleis*), you can check the notice boards that give details of the layout of trains arriving on that track, showing the locations of first- and second-class cars and the restaurant car, as well as where they will stop along the platform. Large railroad stations have English-speaking staff handling information inquiries.

It's also possible to sleep on the train and save a day of your trip. CityNightLine (CNL) trains serving Austria and Switzerland and Nachtzug ("night train" or NZ) long distance trains have sleepers.

BAGGAGE SERVICE

Most major train stations have luggage lockers (in four sizes). By inserting exact change into a storage unit, you release the unit's key. Prices range from €1 for a small locker to €3 for a "jumbo" one. Smaller towns' train stations may not have any storage options.

Throughout Germany, Deutsche Bahn can deliver your baggage from a private residence or hotel to another or even to one of six airports: Berlin, Frankfurt, Leipzig-Halle, Munich, Hamburg, and Hannover. You must have a valid rail ticket. Buy a *Kuriergepäck* ticket at any DB ticket counter at which time you must schedule a pickup three workdays before your flight. The service costs €14.90 for each of the first two suitcases, and €15.80 for each suitcase thereafter.

German railway's ReisePacket service is for travelers who are inexperienced, elderly, disabled, or just appreciative of extra help. It costs €11 and provides, among other things, help boarding, disembarking, and transferring on certain selected trains that serve the major cities and vacation areas. It also includes a seat reservation and a voucher for an on-board snack. Purchase the service at least one day before travel; it is only for those traveling roundtrip and does include assistance on ICE Sprinters.

BUYING TICKETS

Tickets purchased through Deutsche Bahn's Web site can be retrieved from station vending machines. Always **check that your ticket is valid for the type of train you are planning to take, not just for the destination served.** If you have the wrong type of ticket, you will have to pay the difference on the train, in cash.

CLASSES

The difference between first- and second-class seats is that first-class passengers pay approximately 1.55% more for a bit more legroom and the convenience of having meals delivered directly to their seats. Most people find second class entirely adequate.

CUTTING COSTS

To save money, **look into rail passes.** But be aware that if you don't plan to cover many miles, you may come out ahead by buying individual tickets. If you plan to travel by train within a day after your flight arrives, **purchase a heavily discounted "Rail and Fly" ticket for DB trains at the same time you book your flight.** Trains connect with 14 German airports and two airports outside Germany (Basel and Amsterdam).

Deutsche Bahn offers many discount options with specific conditions, so do your homework on its Web site or ask about options at the counter before paying for a full-price ticket. For round-trip travel you can save 25% if you book at least three days in advance, and 50% if you stay over a Saturday night and book at least three to seven days in advance. However, there's a limited number of seats sold at any of these discount prices, so **book as early as possible,** at least a week in advance, to get the savings. A discounted rate is called a *SparPreis*. If you change your travel plans after booking, you will have to pay a fee. The surcharge for tickets bought on board is 10% of the ticket cost, or a minimum of €5.

The good news for families is that children under 15 travel free when accompanied by a parent or relative on normal, discounted, and some, but not all, special-fare tickets. However, you must indicate the number of children traveling with you when you puchase the ticket; to ride free, the child (or children) must be listed on the ticket. If you have a ticket with 25% or 50% off, a "Mitfahrer-Rabatt" allows a second person to travel with you for a 50% discount (minimum of €15 for a second-class ticket). The *Schönes Wochenend Ticket* (Happy Weekend Ticket) provides unlimited travel on regional trains on Saturday or Sunday for up to five persons for €32 (€30 if purchased online or at vending machine). Groups of six or more should inquire about "Gruppen & Spar" (group) savings.

Of all the German train classes, InterCity Express trains are the most expensive.

Deutsche Bahn Information Deutsche Bahn (German Rail) ✉ Stephanstr. 1, D-60313 Frankfurt am Main ☎ 0800/150-7090 for automated schedule information, 11861 for 24-hr hotline, roughly €0.80 per minute, 49/1805/996-633 from outside Germany, €0.12 per minute 🌐 www.dbahn.de. **German Rail Passenger Services** ☎ 08702/435-363 in U.K.

RAIL PASSES

If Germany is your only destination in Europe, **consider purchasing a German Rail Pass,** which allows 4–10 days of unlimited first- or second-class travel within a one-month period on any DB train, up to and including the ICE. A Twin Pass saves two people traveling together 50% off one person's fare. A Youth Pass, sold to those 12–25, is also much the same but for second-class travel only. You can also **use these passes aboard KD Rhine Line** (⇨ Cruise Travel) along certain sections of the Rhine and Mosel rivers. Prices begin at $180 for a single traveler in second class. Twin Passes begin at $270 in second class, and Youth Passes begin at $142. Additional days may be added to either pass.

Rail 'n Drive combines train travel and car rental. For instance, two people pay $159 each for two rail travel days and two car rental days within a month. You can add up to three more rail days, and each additional car rental day is $49.

Germany is one of 17 countries in which you can **use Eurailpasses,** which provide unlimited first-class rail travel in all participating countries for the duration of the pass. Two adults traveling together can pay either $498 each for 15 consecutive days of travel, or $592 each for 10 days of travel within two months. The Youth fare is $414 for 15 consecutive days and $488 for 10 days within two months.

Eurailpasses and some of the German Rail passes **must be purchased before you leave** for Europe. You can purchase a German Rail pass for 5 or 10 days of travel within one month at the Frankfurt airport and at some German train stations, but the cost will be higher (a youth ticket for 5 days of travel is just under €170). When you buy your pass, consider purchasing Railpass insurance in case you lose it during your travels.

In order to comply with the strict rules about validating tickets before you begin travel, **read the instructions carefully.** Some tickets require that a train official validate your pass, while others require you to write in the first date of travel.

Information & Passes DER Travel Services ✉ 9501 W. Devon Ave., Rosemont, IL 60018 ☎ 800/782-2424 🖷 800/860-9944 to request a brochure, 888/337-8687 fax-on-demand service 🌐 www.der.com. **Europe On Rail** ✉ 725 Day Ave., Suite 1, Ridgefield, NJ 07657 ☎ 201/255-2898 🖷 866/329-7245 🌐 www.europeonrail.com. **German Rail Passenger Services** ☎ 08702/435-363 in U.K.

FARES & SCHEDULES

Fare and schedule information on the Deutsche Bahn ☎ 11861 information line connects you to a live operator; you may have to wait a few moments before someone can help you in English. The automated number ☎ 0800/150–7090 is toll-free and gives schedule information. On the DB Web site, click on "Internat. Guests" and then "Timetable Information" to enter your departure and arrival points; the fare will be calculated next.

FROM THE U.K.

There are several ways to reach Germany from London on British Rail. Travelers coming from the United Kingdom should **take the Channel Tunnel to save time, the ferry to save money.** Fastest and most expensive is the route via the Channel Tunnel on Eurostar trains. They leave at two-hour intervals from Waterloo and require a change of trains in Brussels, from which ICE trains reach Köln in 2 ½ hours and Frankfurt in 3 ½ hours. Prices for one-way tickets from London to Köln begin at €100–€129. Cheapest and slowest are the 8–10 departures daily from Victoria using the Ramsgate–Ostend ferry, jetfoil, or SeaCat catamaran service.

Train & Pass Information Eurostar ☎ 0870/518-6186.

RESERVATIONS

Many travelers assume that rail passes guarantee them seats on the trains they wish to ride. Not so. You need to **book seats ahead even if you are using a rail pass**; seat reservations are required on some European trains, particularly high-speed trains, and are a good idea during summer and on popular routes. If you board the train without a reserved seat, you take the chance of having to stand. You'll also need a reservation if you purchase sleeping accommodations. Reservations are free if you make them online at the Deutsche Bahn Web site or at the time of ticket purchase at a vending machine. Otherwise, seat reservations on InterRegion Express and InterCity trains cost €3, and a reservation is absolutely necessary for the ICE-Sprinter trains (€10 for second class). There are no reservations on regional trains.

TRANSPORTATION AROUND GERMANY

The Deutsche Bahn, Germany's privatized railway, is an efficient way to travel around the country, though long-distance round-trip travel is often cheaper on discount airlines than by train. Day-of-travel train-ticket prices are not cheap, but an advance purchase can reduce a ticket price by as much as half. The carefully structured network of services—from the super-high-speed InterCity Express to regional trains—ensures fast connections between cities and good access to rural areas; very few towns are more than 10 km (6 mi) or so from a railroad station. Rural bus lines connect villages to the nearest train station.

The Deutsche Bahn "Sprinter" business special gets its passengers between Frankfurt and Munich or Berlin faster than a plane, by the time city-to-airport travel and check-in requirements are taken into account. The Frankfurt–Munich "Sprinter" stops only in Mannheim; the Frankfurt–Berlin one doesn't stop at all.

The only long-distance bus service in Germany is BerlinLinien Bus. Other buses that cross the country are either tourist services covering routes such as the Romantic Road or long-distance companies that pick up in German cities but sell tickets only to other European cities.

The autobahn network makes for good car travel, and though the recommended speed limit (130 kph [80 mph]) lets you cover distances quickly, school vacation times can jam the autobahn with traffic. All major German cities have multistructure urban transportation systems, incorporating subway (U-bahn) and metropolitan suburban (S-bahn) trains, trams, and buses. Public transportation in cities is invariably fast, clean, and efficient.

TRAVEL AGENCIES

A good travel agent puts your needs first. Look for an agency that has been in business at least five years, emphasizes customer service, and has someone on staff who specializes in your destination. In addition, **make sure the agency belongs to a professional trade organization.** The American Society of Travel Agents (ASTA) has more than 10,000 members in some 140 countries, enforces a strict code of ethics, and will step in to mediate agent-client disputes involving ASTA members. ASTA also maintains a directory of agents on its Web site; ASTA's TravelSense.org, a trip planning and travel advice site, can also help to locate a travel agent who caters to your needs. (If a travel agency is also acting as your tour operator, *see* Buyer Beware *in* Tours & Packages.)

Local Agent Referrals **American Society of Travel Agents** (ASTA) ✉ 1101 King St., Suite 200, Alexandria, VA 22314 ☎ 703/739-2782 or 800/965-2782 24-hr hotline 📠 703/684-8319 🌐 www.astanet.com and www.travelsense.org. **Association of British Travel Agents** ✉ 68-71 Newman St., London W1T 3AH ☎ 020/7637-2444 📠 020/7637-0713 🌐 www.abta.com. **Association of Canadian Travel Agencies** ✉ 130 Albert St., Suite 1705, Ottawa, Ontario K1P 5G4 ☎ 613/237-3657 📠 613/237-7052 🌐 www.acta.ca.**Australian Federation of Travel Agents** ✉ Level 3, 309 Pitt St., Sydney, NSW 2000 ☎ 02/9264-3299 or 1300/363-416 📠 02/9264-1085 🌐 www.afta.com.au. **Travel Agents' Association of New Zealand** ✉ Level 5, Tourism and Travel House, 79 Boulcott St., Box 1888, Wellington 6001 ☎ 04/499-0104 📠 04/499-0786 🌐 www.taanz.org.nz.

VISITOR INFORMATION

Learn more about foreign destinations by checking government-issued travel advisories and country information. For a broader picture, consider information from more than one country.

Local tourist offices are listed in the A to Z sections of the individual chapters. Staff at the smaller offices, especially in eastern Germany, might not speak English. Many offices keep shorter hours than normal businesses, and you can expect some to close during weekday lunch hours and as early as noon on Friday. The German National Tourist Office's Web site in the U.S. is www.cometogermany.com.

German National Tourist Office **U.S.** 122 E. 42nd St., 52nd fl., New York, NY 10168-0072 212/661-7200 or 800/651-7010 212/661-7174 gntonyc@d-z-t.com 8484 Wilshire Blvd., Suite 440, Los Angeles, CA 90211 323/655-6085 323/655-6086 gntolax@d-z-t.com www.cometogermany.com. **Canada** 480 University Ave., Suite 1410, Toronto, Ontario M5G 1V2, Canada 416/968-1685 416/968-0562 info@gnto.ca www.cometogermany.com. **U.K.** Box 2695, London W1A 3TN 020/7317-0908 020/7317-0917 gntolon@d-z-t.com www.germany-tourism.co.uk. **Australia** GPO Box 1461, Sydney, NSW 2001 02/8296-0488 2/8296-0487 gnto@germany.org.au. **Germany** Beethovenstr. 69, D-60325 Frankfurt 069/751-903 info@d-z-t.com www.germany-tourism.de.

Government Advisories **U.S. Department of State** Bureau of Consular Affairs, Overseas Citizens Services Office, 2201 C St. NW Washington, DC 20520 202/647-5225, 888/407-4747 or 317/472-2328 for interactive hotline www.travel.state.gov. **Consular Affairs Bureau of Canada** 800/267-6788 or 613/944-6788 www.voyage.gc.ca. **U.K. Foreign and Commonwealth Office** Travel Advice Unit, Consular Directorate, Old Admiralty Building, London SW1A 2PA 0870/606-0290 or 020/7008-1500 www.fco.gov.uk/travel. **Australian Department of Foreign Affairs and Trade** 300/139-281 travel advisories, 02/6261-1299 Consular Travel Advice www.smartraveller.gov.au or www.dfat.gov.au. **New Zealand Ministry of Foreign Affairs and Trade** 04/439-8000 www.mft.govt.nz.

WEB SITES

Do check out the World Wide Web when planning your trip. You'll find everything from weather forecasts to virtual tours of famous cities. Be sure to visit Fodors.com (www.fodors.com), a complete travel-planning site. You can research prices and book plane tickets, hotel rooms, rental cars, vacation packages, and more. In addition, you can post your pressing questions in the Travel Talk section. Other planning tools include a currency converter and weather reports, and there are loads of links to travel resources.

One site that goes in-depth regarding international telephone systems and modem hookup trouble-shooting is www.kropla.com.

Many German tourism-related Web sites have an English-language version, usually indicated by an icon of the American or British flag. For general information on Germany, visit www.cometogermany.com or www.germany-tourism.co.uk, which are the German National Tourist Office's sites. The first Web site is geared to Americans, the second to tourists from the United Kingdom. There are differences on these sites other than spelling.

CONVERSIONS

DISTANCE

KILOMETERS/MILES

To change kilometers (km) to miles (mi), multiply km by .621. To change mi to km, multiply mi by 1.61.

km to mi	mi to km
1 = .62	1 = 1.6
2 = 1.2	2 = 3.2
3 = 1.9	3 = 4.8
4 = 2.5	4 = 6.4
5 = 3.1	5 = 8.1
6 = 3.7	6 = 9.7
7 = 4.3	7 = 11.3
8 = 5.0	8 = 12.9

METERS/FEET

To change meters (m) to feet (ft), multiply m by 3.28. To change ft to m, multiply ft by .305.

m to ft	ft to m
1 = 3.3	1 = .30
2 = 6.6	2 = .61
3 = 9.8	3 = .92
4 = 13.1	4 = 1.2
5 = 16.4	5 = 1.5
6 = 19.7	6 = 1.8
7 = 23.0	7 = 2.1
8 = 26.2	8 = 2.4

TEMPERATURE

METRIC CONVERSIONS

To change centigrade or Celsius (C) to Fahrenheit (F), multiply C by 1.8 and add 32. To change F to C, subtract 32 from F and multiply by .555.

°F	°C
0	-17.8
10	-12.2
20	-6.7
30	-1.1
32	0
40	+4.4
50	10.0
60	15.5
70	21.1
80	26.6
90	32.2
98.6	37.0
100	37.7

WEIGHT

KILOGRAMS/POUNDS

To change kilograms (kg) to pounds (lb), multiply kg by 2.20. To change lb to kg, multiply lb by .455.

kg to lb	lb to kg
1 = 2.2	1 = .45
2 = 4.4	2 = .91
3 = 6.6	3 = 1.4
4 = 8.8	4 = 1.8
5 = 11.0	5 = 2.3
6 = 13.2	6 = 2.7
7 = 15.4	7 = 3.2
8 = 17.6	8 = 3.6

GRAMS/OUNCES

To change grams (g) to ounces (oz), multiply g by .035. To change oz to g, multiply oz by 28.4.

g to oz	oz to g
1 = .04	1 = 28
2 = .07	2 = 57
3 = .11	3 = 85
4 = .14	4 = 114
5 = .18	5 = 142
6 = .21	6 = 170
7 = .25	7 = 199
8 = .28	8 = 227

LIQUID VOLUME

LITERS/U.S. GALLONS

To change liters (L) to U.S. gallons (gal), multiply L by .264. To change U.S. gal to L, multiply gal by 3.79.

L to gal	gal to L
1 = .26	1 = 3.8
2 = .53	2 = 7.6
3 = .79	3 = 11.4
4 = 1.1	4 = 15.2
5 = 1.3	5 = 19.0
6 = 1.6	6 = 22.7
7 = 1.8	7 = 26.5
8 = 2.1	8 = 30.3

CLOTHING SIZE

WOMEN'S CLOTHING

US	UK	EUR
4	6	34
6	8	36
8	10	38
10	12	40
12	14	42

WOMEN'S SHOES

US	UK	EUR
5	3	36
6	4	37
7	5	38
8	6	39
9	7	40

MEN'S SUITS

US	UK	EUR
34	34	44
36	36	46
38	38	48
40	40	50
42	42	52
44	44	54
46	46	56

MEN'S SHIRTS

US	UK	EUR
14½	14½	37
15	15	38
15½	15½	39
16	16	41
16½	16½	42
17	17	43
17½	17½	44

MEN'S SHOES

US	UK	EUR
7	6	39½
8	7	41
9	8	42
10	9	43
11	10	44½
12	11	46

Munich

1

WORD OF MOUTH

"The market near the Marienplatz is wonderful. I had a great time stopping at one booth for an apple, another for cheese, yet a third for a beer, and a fourth for bread to assemble a fun lunch! It drove my husband mad, but I thoroughly enjoyed the process and the lunch!"

—bluecheesegirl

"I always seem to have the most fun with the Bavarians."

—mikemo

"I would definitely consider a visit to the Residenz where, among other things, there is a Ludwig, carved-carriage collection, the largest of which puts that gilded thing Queen Elizabeth occasionally rides in look absolutely cheap by comparison."

—TopMan

www.fodors.com/forums

Updated by
Kevin White

IN THE RELAXED AND SUNNIER SOUTHERN PARTY OF GERMANY, Munich (München) is the proud capital of the state of Bavaria. Even Germans come here to vacation, mixing the city's pleasures with those of the inviting and accessible natural surroundings—on clear days it's possible to see the Alps from town. The city bills itself as *Die Weltstadt mit Herz* ("the cosmopolitan city with heart"), but in rare bouts of self-deprecatory humor, friendly Bavarians will remind you that Munich isn't much more than a country town with a million people. It's the overall feeling of *Gemütlichkeit*—loosely translated as conviviality—that makes the place so special, with its open-air markets, numerous parks, and an impressive number of beer halls.

Munich was originally founded in the 12th century as a market town on the "salt road" between mighty Salzburg and Augsburg. Since then it has never lost its sense for business and trade. It continues to exist between two poles, tradition and high-tech, or as the locals say, "laptops and lederhosen." It's a city of ravishing baroque styling and smoky beer cellars, of grand 19th-century architecture and sleek steel-and-glass office buildings, of millionaires and farmers. The city is the stomping grounds for a host of media companies, from traditional publishing houses and top-notch digital postproduction companies to world-class film studios, and it has a concentration of electronics and computer firms—Siemens, Microsoft, SAP, for example—making the area a sort of Silicon Valley of Europe.

More importantly, however, Munich is the world capital of beer and beer culture. Between visits to the various high-caliber museums, you should definitely try some of the local brew, either in one of the larger, noisier beer halls or in a smaller *Kneipe,* a bar where all types of people get together for basic meals and beer. When the first spring rays of sun begin warming the air, Müncheners flock to their famous beer gardens, where tourists and locals alike gather in the shade of massive chestnut trees. The city's most famous festival, the beer-soaked Oktoberfest, started as an agricultural fair held on the occasion of a royal marriage and has now become one of the biggest public festivals in the world, spawning imitators around the globe.

The *other* Munich is one of refinement and sophistication, high-fashion boutiques and five-star restaurants. Various "all-nighter" events throughout the year celebrate museum-going, literature, and musical performances. The city's appreciation of the arts began under the kings and dukes of the Wittelsbach Dynasty, which ruled Bavaria for more than 750 years until 1918. The Wittelsbach legacy is alive and well in the city's fabulous museums, the Opera House, the Philharmonic, and much more.

Munich's cleanliness, safety, and comfortable pace give it an ever so slightly rustic feeling, despite the fact that it's a relatively large, prosperous city. This, combined with broad sidewalks, endless shops and eateries, views of the Alps, and a huge green park that easily gives Central Park a run for its money, the English Garden, makes Munich one of Germany's most enjoyable cities.

If you have
3 days

Visit the tourist information office at the Hauptbahnhof (main train station) and then head for one of the cafés at the nearby pedestrian shopping zone to get your bearings (try the cafeteria at the Hertie department store on the square opposite the train station or at the Mövenpick in the beautiful Künstlerhaus on Lenbachplatz). You can see the highlights of the city center and royal Munich in one day. Plan an eastward course across (or rather under) Karlsplatz and into Neuhauserstrasse and Kaufingerstrasse, plunging into this busy center of commerce. You can escape the crowds inside one of the three churches that punctuate the route: the Bürgersaal, the Michaelskirche, or the Frauenkirche, a soaring Gothic cathedral. Try to arrive in the city's central square, Marienplatz, in time for the 11 AM performance of the glockenspiel in the tower of the neo-Gothic Neues Rathaus (New Town Hall). Proceed to the city market, the Viktualienmarkt, for lunch, and then head a few blocks north for an afternoon visit to the Residenz, the rambling palace of the Wittelsbach rulers. End your first day with coffee at Munich's oldest café, the Tambosi, or sip an early-evening cocktail at Käfer's, both on Odeonsplatz.

On your second day, go on one of the guided bicycle tours which are nonstrenuous but will cover more ground than your first day. They're very educational, giving you a better feel for some specific museums or highlights you may want to go back to for a closer look. You'll be shown things like the Englischer Garden (where you stop for a beer), the Maximilianeum, the Peace Angel, and the Haus der Kunst. After the tour is over you can meander over the river at Isartor to the Deutsches Museum, an incredible collection of science and technology for all ages and personality types. On the third day take a closer look at some of the world-class museums. Simply walk north to Königsplatz, meandering past the Grecian-style pavilions there on your way to the Alte and Neue Pinakothek museums and the Pinakothek der Moderne. You may not be able to see all of them in one day. After the museums, you can walk east to Ludwigstrasse and make your way south back toward Odeonsplatz and Marienplatz.

If you have
5 days

For the first three days follow the itinerary described above. On the fourth day venture out to suburban Nymphenburg for a visit to Schloss Nymphenburg, the Wittelsbachs' summer residence. Allow a whole day to view the palace's buildings and its museums and to stroll through its lovely park, breaking for lunch at the restaurant in the botanical garden. On the fifth day, tour the Olympiapark in the morning. Ride to the top of the Olympic Tower for the best view of Munich and the surrounding countryside. Then either take a walk along the surprisingly quiet city banks of the Isar River or visit one of the two villa-museums, the Museum Villa Stuck or the Städtische Galerie im Lenbachhaus. The latter is huge and has a popular café.

EXPLORING MUNICH

Munich is a wealthy city—and it shows. Everything is extremely upscale and up-to-date. At times the aura of affluence may be all but overpowering. But that's what Munich is all about: a new city superimposed on the old; conspicuous consumption; a fresh coat of glitter along with the traditional rustic charms.

The City Center

Munich's Old Town has been rebuilt so often over the centuries that it no longer has the homogeneous look of so many other German towns. Postwar developments often separate clusters of buildings that date back to Munich's origins—and not always to harmonious effect. The outer perimeter of this tour is defined more by your stamina than by ancient city walls.

Numbers in the text correspond to numbers in the margin and on the Munich map.

a good walk

Begin your walk through the city center at the **Hauptbahnhof** 1, the main train station and site of the city tourist office (there is also an information center at Marienplatz). Cross Bahnhofplatz, the square in front of the station (or take the underpass), and walk toward Schützenstrasse, which marks the start of Munich's pedestrian shopping mall, the Fussgängerzone, 2 km (1 mi) of traffic-free streets. Running virtually the length of Schützenstrasse is Munich's largest department store, Hertie. At the end of the street, descend via the pedestrian underpass into a vast underground complex of boutiques, shops, and snack bars. Above you is the busy traffic intersection, **Karlsplatz** 2, always referred to as Stachus after an inn and beer garden that stood here back in the 19th century. Its fountain area is a favorite place to hang out. Just make sure your wallet is in a safe place.

Ahead stands one of the city's oldest gates, the Karlstor, first mentioned in local records in 1302. Beyond it lies Munich's main shopping thoroughfare, Neuhauserstrasse, and its extension, Kaufingerstrasse. On your left as you enter Neuhauserstrasse is another attractive fountain: a late-19th-century figure of Bacchus. This part of town was almost completely destroyed by bombing during World War II. Great efforts were made to ensure that the designs of the new buildings harmonized with the old city, although some of the modern structures are little more than functional. Though this may not be an architectural showplace, there are some redeeming features to the area, such as Haus Oberpollinger, on Neuhauserstrasse—a department store hiding behind an imposing 19th-century facade. Notice the weather vanes of old merchant ships on its high-gabled roof.

Shopping is not the only attraction on these streets. Worldly department stores rub shoulders with a remarkable church, the **Michaelskirche** 3. A Renaissance construction, the Michaelskirche was originally built in the 16th century and entirely redone after the war. The fountain in front of

Beer & Beer Gardens Munich has more than 100 beer gardens, ranging from huge establishments that seat several hundred to small terraces tucked behind neighborhood pubs and taverns. Beer gardens are such an integral part of Munich life that a council proposal to cut down their hours provoked a storm of protest in 1995, culminating in one of the largest mass demonstrations in the city's history. They open whenever the thermometer creeps above 10°C (50°F) and the sun filters through the chestnut trees that are a necessary part of beer-garden scenery. Most—but not all—allow you to bring your own food, but if you do, don't defile this hallowed territory with something so foreign as pizza or a burger from McDonald's.

Music & Opera Munich and music complement each other marvelously. The city has two world-renowned orchestras. The Philharmonic is now directed by Christian Thielemann, formerly of the Deutsche Oper in Berlin; the Bavarian State Opera Company is managed by an ingenious British director Peter Jonas. In addition there are wonderful choral ensembles, a rococo jewel of a court theater, and a modern Philharmonic concert hall of superb proportions and acoustics—and that's just for starters.

Shopping Munich has three of Germany's most exclusive shopping streets. At the other end of the scale, it has flea markets to rival those of any other European city. In between are department stores, where acute German-style competition assures reasonable prices and often produces outstanding bargains. Artisans and artists bring their wares of beauty and originality to the Christmas markets. Collect their business cards—in summer you're sure to want to order another of those little gold baubles that were on sale in December.

---

the church features Salome, in honor of the opera of the same name by Munich's famous son Richard Strauss. The massive building next to the Michaelskirche was once a 13th-century Augustine church. Today it houses the **Deutsches Jagd- und Fischereimuseum** (German Hunting and Fishing Museum) ❹. Opposite is one of Munich's famous brewery inns, the Augustiner Bierhalle. Behind its Renaissance and baroque facade—the establishment occupies two buildings—are vaulted ceilings and a delightful little courtyard decorated with frescoes.

Next on your tour is Munich's hallmark cathedral, the **Frauenkirche** ❺, whose twin onion domes can be seen from all over town (in a 2004 referendum, the citizens of Munich voted against the construction of any buildings taller than the Frauenkirche). To reach it, turn left at the museum onto the crescent-shaped Augustinerstrasse, which opens onto Frauenplatz, a quiet square with a shallow, sunken fountain. From the cathedral, follow any of the alleys heading east around the back and you'll reach the Marienhof, a small square behind the Marienplatz where the city's Jewish quarter once stood. To your right is **Marienplatz** ❻,

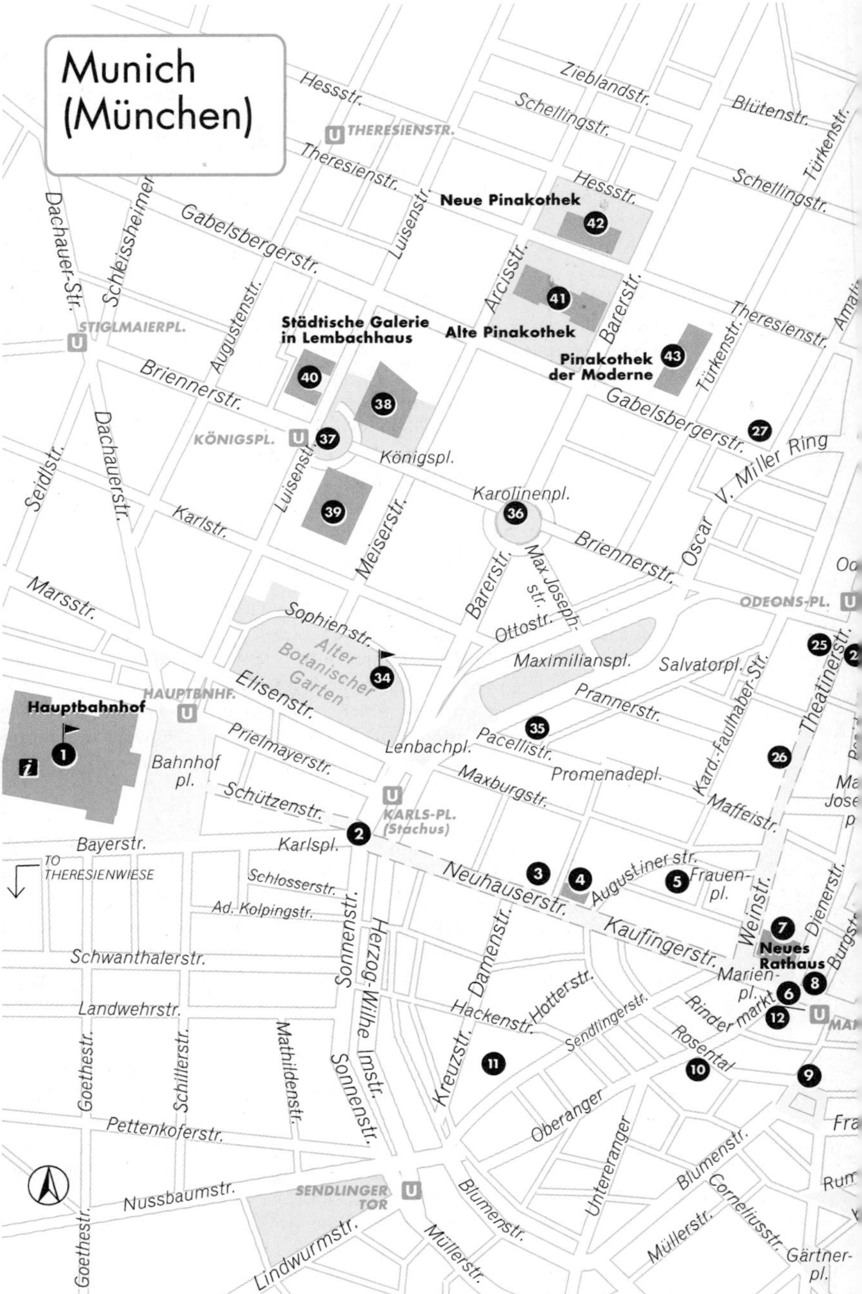
Munich (München)
Hessstr.
Zieblandstr.
Schellingstr.
Blütenstr.
Türkenstr.
THERESIENSTR.
Theresienstr.
Schellingstr.
Neue Pinakothek
Luisenstr.
Gabelsbergerstr.
Dachauer-Str.
Scheissheimer
Arcisstr.
Barerstr.
Theresienstr.
Städtische Galerie in Lembachhaus
Alte Pinakothek
STIGLMAIERPL.
Augustenstr.
Pinakothek der Moderne
Türkenstr.
Briennerstr.
Gabelsbergerstr.
KÖNIGSPL.
Königspl.
Dachauerstr.
Seidlstr.
Luisenstr.
Oscar V. Miller Ring
Karolinenpl.
Karlstr.
Meiserstr.
Briennerstr.
Max Joseph-str.
Barerstr.
Marsstr.
ODEONS-PL.
Sophienstr.
Ottostr.
Alter Botanischer Garten
Maximilianspl.
Salvatorpl.
Elisenstr.
Prannerstr.
HAUPTBNHF.
Hauptbahnhof
Theatinerstr.
Kard.-Faulhaber-Str.
Prielmayerstr.
Pacellistr.
Lenbachpl.
Promenadepl.
Bahnhof pl.
Maxburgstr.
Schützenstr.
KARLS-PL. (Stachus)
Maffeistr.
Bayerstr.
Karlspl.
TO THERESIENWIESE
Augustiner str.
Frauen-pl.
Schlosserstr.
Neuhauserstr.
Ad. Kolpingstr.
Sonnenstr.
Damenstr.
Weinstr.
Dienerstr.
Neues Rathaus
Kaufingerstr.
Schwanthalerstr.
Herzog-Wilhe lmstr.
Marien-pl.
Hotterstr.
Landwehrstr.
Hackenstr.
Sendlingerstr.
Rinder markt
Rosental
Goethestr.
Schillerstr.
Mathildenstr.
Sonnenstr.
Kreuzstr.
Oberanger
Pettenkoferstr.
Unterer anger
Blumenstr.
SENDLINGER TOR
Nussbaumstr.
Blumenstr.
Corneliusstr.
Goethestr.
Müllerstr.
Lindwurmstr.
Müllerstr.
Gärtner-pl.

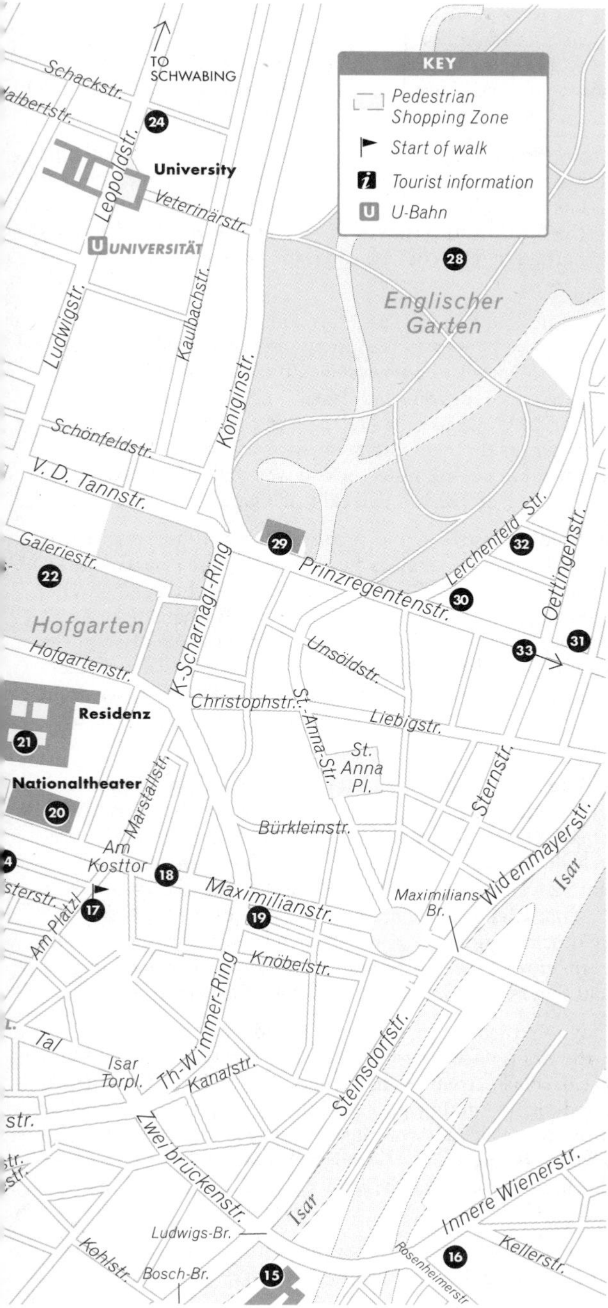
KEY
Pedestrian Shopping Zone
Start of walk
Tourist information
U-Bahn
TO SCHWABING
Schackstr.
University
Leopoldstr.
Veterinärstr.
UNIVERSITÄT
Ludwigstr.
Kaulbachstr.
Königinstr.
Englischer Garten
Schönfeldstr.
V. D. Tannstr.
Galeriestr.
Hofgarten
Hofgartenstr.
Residenz
Nationaltheater
K.-Scharnagl-Ring
Prinzregentenstr.
Lerchenfeld Str.
Oettingenstr.
Unsöldstr.
Christophstr.
St.-Anna-Str.
Liebigstr.
St. Anna Pl.
Sternstr.
Marstallstr.
Bürkleinstr.
Widenmayerstr.
Isar
Am Kosttor
Maximilianstr.
Maximilians-Br.
Am Platzl
Knöbelstr.
Th.-Wimmer-Ring
Steinsdorfstr.
Tal
Isar Torpl.
Kanalstr.
Zweibrückenstr.
Innere Wienerstr.
Ludwigs-Br.
Kohlstr.
Bosch-Br.
Rosenheimerstr.
Kellerstr.
24
28
29
32
22
30
31
33
21
20
18
17
19
16
15

which is surrounded by stores and dining spots and now hosts a tourist information center. Marienplatz, the true heart of Munich, is dominated by the 19th-century **Neues Rathaus** 7. The **Altes Rathaus** 8, a rebuilt medieval building of assured charm, sits more modestly at the eastern entrance of the square. Its pretty tower houses a toy museum.

Hungry? Thirsty? Help is only a few steps away. From the Altes Rathaus, cross the street, passing the Heiliggeistkirche, an early Munich church with a rococo interior added between 1724 and 1730. Heiliggeiststrasse brings you to the hustle and bustle of the **Viktualienmarkt** 9, the city's open-air food market, where you can eat a stand-up lunch at any of the many stalls.

From the market, follow Rosental and turn left onto Sendlingerstrasse, one of the city's most interesting shopping streets. On the way you'll pass the rear of the **Münchner Stadtmuseum** (City Museum) 10 at the corner of Oberangerstrasse. As you head down Sendlingerstrasse, on your right is the remarkable **Asamkirche** 11. The exterior fits so snugly into the street's housefronts that you might easily overlook the church were it not for the somewhat incongruous rocks it was built upon. At the end of the street is Sendlinger Tor, a medieval brick gate.

Backtrack up Sendlingerstrasse and turn right onto Rindermarkt (the former cattle market) to the single, square tower of the **Peterskirche** 12, the city's oldest and best-loved parish church. From the Peterskirche, reenter Marienplatz and pass in front of the Altes Rathaus once again to step into Burgstrasse. You'll soon find yourself in the **Alter Hof** 13, the inner courtyard of the original palace of Bavaria's Wittelsbach rulers (which is under renovation). A short distance beyond its northern archway, on the north side of Pfisterstrasse, stands the former royal mint, the **Münze** 14.

Return down Burgstrasse and make a left on Tal, once an important trading route that entered Munich at the Isartor, a massive brick gate with a tower attached. A frieze on the Isator depicts the 1322 battle of Ampfing, during which Munich was saved from an Austrian attack. Cross Isartorplatz into Zweibrückenstrasse, and you'll come to the Isar River. There, on Museum Island, is the massive building of the **Deutsches Museum** 15. A gigantic thermometer and barometer on its tower shows the way to the main entrance. This incredible museum has something for everyone, including budding scientists and young dreamers.

On a sunny day join the locals for ice cream and a stroll along the Isar River, where the more daring sunbathe nude on pebble islands. On a rainy day you can splash around in the Müllersches Volksbad, a restored art nouveau indoor swimming pool at Ludwigsbrücke, opposite the Deutsches Museum. The massive glass-and-brick facade on the hill above the Volksbad belongs to the **Gasteig Kulturzentrum** 16, home of the Munich Philharmonic Orchestra, the main city library, and multiple theaters, galleries, and cafés.

TIMING Set aside at least a whole day for this walk, hitting Marienplatz when the Glockenspiel plays at 11 AM or noon before a crowd of spectators.

Avoid shopping in the pedestrian zone between noon and 2, when workers on lunch break make for the department stores.

What to See

13 **Alter Hof** (Old Palace). This palace was the original medieval residence of the Wittelsbachs, the ruling dynasty established in 1180. The palace now serves as local government offices. Don't pass through without turning to admire the oriel (bay window) that hides on the south wall, just around the corner as you enter the courtyard. The west wing has become home to the **Vinorant Alter Hof,** a fine restaurant and wine cellar. ✉ *Burgstr., City Center* Ⓤ *Marienplatz (U-bahn and S-bahn).*

8 **Altes Rathaus** (Old Town Hall). Munich's first town hall was built in 1474. Its great hall—destroyed in 1944 but now fully restored—was the work of architect Jörg von Halspach. It's used for official receptions and is not normally open to the public. The tower provides a fairy-tale-like setting for the **Spielzeugmuseum** (Toy Museum), accessible via a winding staircase. Its toys and dolls are joined by quite a few Barbies visiting from the United States. ✉ *Marienpl., City Center* ☎ *089/294–001* *Museum €3* ⏲ *Daily 10–5:30* Ⓤ *Marienplatz (U-bahn and S-bahn).*

★ 11 **Asamkirche** (Asam Church). Munich's most unusual church has a suitably extraordinary entrance, framed by raw rock foundations. The insignificant door, crammed between its craggy shoulders, gives little idea of the opulence and lavish detailing within the small 18th-century church (there are only 12 rows of pews). Above the doorway St. Nepomuk, a 14th-century Bohemian monk who drowned in the Danube, is being led by angels from a rocky riverbank to heaven. The church's official name is Church of St. Johann Nepomuk, but it's known as the Asamkirche for its architects, the brothers Cosmas Damian and Egid Quirin Asam, who lived next door. The interior of the church is a prime example of true southern German late-baroque architecture. Frescoes by Cosmas Damian Asam and rosy marble cover the walls. The sheer wealth of statues and gilding is stunning—there's even a gilt skeleton at the sanctuary's portal. ✉ *Sendlingerstr., City Center* ⏲ *Daily 9–5:30* Ⓤ *Sendlingertor (U-bahn).*

4 **Deutsches Jagd- und Fischereimuseum** (German Museum of Hunting and Fishing). This museum contains the world's largest collection of fishhooks, some 500 stuffed animals (including a 6½-foot-tall North American grizzly bear), a 12,000-year-old skeleton of a deer found in Ireland, and a valuable collection of hunting weapons. You'll even find the elusive *Wolpertinger,* a legendary Bavarian animal. The museum also sells fine hunting equipment, from knives and rifles to sturdy clothing. ✉ *Neuhauserstr. 2, City Center* ☎ *089/220–522* *€3.50* ⏲ *Fri.–Sun., Tues., and Wed. 9:30–5, Thurs. 9:30–8* Ⓤ *Karlsplatz (U-bahn and S-bahn).*

15 **Deutsches Museum** (German Museum). Within a monumental building on an island in the Isar River, this museum of science and technology—filled with aircraft, vehicles, locomotives, and machinery—is an engineering student's dream. The immense collection is spread out over 19 km (12 mi) of corridors, six floors of exhibits, and 30 departments. Children now have their own area, the **Kinderreich,** where they can learn about modern technology and science through numerous interactive dis-

Fodor's Choice ★

plays (parents must accompany their child). The most technically advanced planetarium in Europe has up to six shows daily and includes a Laser Magic display. An IMAX theater—with a wraparound screen six stories high—shows nature and adventure films. The Internet café on the third floor is open daily 9–3. To arrange for a two-hour tour in English, call ☎ 089/217–9252 two weeks in advance. The **Center for Transportation** on the fairgrounds at the Theresienhöhe (where Oktoberfest is held) houses the museum's transportation exhibits and is open until 8 PM on Thursday. ✉ *Museumsinsel 1, City Center* ☎ *089/21790, 089/2112–5180 to reserve tickets at planetarium and IMAX* 🌐 *www.deutsches-museum.de* 🎫 *Museum €7.50, Planetarium €2 (extra for show), Center for Transportation €2.50 (€10 with museum plus shuttle)* ⏲ *Daily 9–5* Ⓤ *Isartor (S-bahn).*

off the beaten path

FRANZISKANERKLOSTERKIRCHE ST. ANNA (Franciscan Monastery Church of St. Anne) – This striking example of the two Asam brothers' work is in the Lehel district. Though less opulent than the Asamkirche, this small Franciscan monastery church, consecrated in 1737, impresses visitors with its sense of movement and its heroic scale. It was largely rebuilt after wartime bomb damage. The ceiling fresco by Cosmas Damian Asam glows in all its original vivid joyfulness. The ornate altar was also designed by the Asam brothers. Towering over the delicate little church, on the opposite side of the street, is the neo-Romanesque bulk of the 19th-century church of St. Anne. ✉ *St.-Anna-Str., Lehel* ☎ *089/212–1820* Ⓤ *Lehel (U-bahn).*

★ 5 **Frauenkirche** (Church of Our Lady). Munich's *Dom* (cathedral) is a distinctive late-Gothic brick structure with two towers that are the city's chief landmark. Each is more than 300 feet high, and both are capped by onion-shape domes. The towers are an indelible feature of the skyline and a Munich trademark—some say because they look like overflowing beer mugs.

The main body of the cathedral was completed in 20 years (1468–88)—a record time in those days. The onion domes on the towers were added, almost as an afterthought, in 1524–25. Jörg von Halspach, the Frauenkirche's original architect, apparently dropped dead after laying the last brick and is buried here. The building suffered severe damage during Allied bombing and was restored between 1947 and 1957. Inside, the church combines most of von Halspach's original features with a stark, clean modernity and simplicity of line, emphasized by slender, white octagonal pillars that sweep up through the nave to the tracery ceiling. As you enter the church, look on the stone floor for the dark imprint of a large foot—the *Teufelstritt* (Devil's Footprint). According to lore, the devil challenged von Halspach to build a nave without windows. The architect accepted the challenge. When he completed the job, he led the devil to the one spot in the well-lit church from which the 66-foot-high windows could not be seen. The devil stomped his foot in rage and left the Teufelstritt. The cathedral houses an elaborate 15th-century black-marble tomb guarded by four 16th-century armored knights. It's the final resting place of Duke Ludwig IV (1302–47), who became Holy

Roman Emperor Ludwig the Bavarian in 1328. The Frauenkirche's great treasure, however, is the collection of 24 carved wooden busts of the apostles, saints, and prophets above the choir, made by the 15th-century Munich sculptor Erasmus Grasser.

The observation platform high up in one of the towers offers a splendid view of the city. But beware—you must climb 86 steps to reach the tower elevator. ✉ *Frauenpl., City Center* ☎ *089/290–0820* 🎫 *Cathedral free, Tower €2* ⏲ *Tower elevator Apr.–Oct., Mon.–Sat. 10–5* Ⓤ *Marienplatz (U-bahn and S-bahn).*

16 **Gasteig Kulturzentrum** (Gasteig Culture Center). Sitting high above the Isar River, this striking postmodern, brick cultural complex for music, theater, and film has an open-plan interior and a maze of courtyards and plazas. The center has two theaters, where plays in English are occasionally staged. ✉ *Rosenheimerstr. 5, Haidhausen* ☎ *089/480–980* Ⓤ *Rosenheimerplatz (S-bahn).*

1 **Hauptbahnhof** (Main Train Station). Traveling is not all you come here for. A host of rather fancy sandwich bars attracts people for a quick meal or snack at all times of the day and well into the night. On the underground level you'll find all sorts of shops that remain open even on Sunday and holidays. The city tourist office here has maps and helpful information on events around town. ✉ *Bahnhofpl., Leopoldvorstadt* ☎ *089/2333–0256 or 089/2333–0257* Ⓤ *Hauptbahnhof (U-bahn and S-bahn).*

2 **Karlsplatz.** In 1755 Eustachius Föderl opened an inn and beer garden here, which became known as the Stachus. The beer garden is long gone, but the name has remained—locals still refer to this busy intersection as the Stachus. One of Munich's most popular fountains is here, a circle of water jets that acts as a magnet on hot summer days when city shoppers and office workers seek a cool place to relax. In winter it makes way for an ice-skating rink. A semicircle of yellow buildings with tall windows and delicate, cast-iron balconies backs the fountain. Ⓤ *Karlsplatz (U-bahn and S-bahn).*

★ 6 **Marienplatz.** Bordered by the Neues Rathaus, shops, and cafés, this square is named after the gilded statue of the Virgin Mary that has watched over it for more than three centuries. It was erected in 1638 at the behest of Elector Maximilian I as an act of thanksgiving for the city's survival of the Thirty Years' War, the cataclysmic religious struggle that devastated vast regions of Germany. When the statue was taken down from its marble column for cleaning in 1960, workmen found a small casket in the base containing a splinter of wood said to be from the cross of Christ. ✉ *Bounded by Kaufingerstr., Rosenstr., Weinstr., and Dienerstr., City Center* Ⓤ *Marienplatz (U-bahn and S-bahn).*

3 **Michaelskirche** (St. Michael's Church). A curious story explains why this sturdy Renaissance church has no tower. Seven years after the start of construction the principal tower collapsed. Its patron, pious Duke Wilhelm V, regarded the disaster as a heavenly sign that the church wasn't big enough, so he ordered a change in the plans—this time without a tower. Completed seven years later, the Michaelskirche was the first Renaissance church of this size in southern Germany. The duke is buried

in the crypt, along with 40 other Wittelsbachs, including the eccentric King Ludwig II. A severe neoclassical monument in the north transept contains the tomb of Napoléon's stepson, Eugene de Beauharnais, who married one of the daughters of King Maximilian I and died in Munich in 1824. The church is the venue for free performances of church music. A poster to the right of the front portal gives the dates. ✉ *Neuhauserstr. 52, City Center* ☎ *089/231–7060* 🎫 *€1* ⏲ *Daily 8–7, except during services* Ⓤ *Karlsplatz (U-bahn and S-bahn).*

⓾ **Münchner Stadtmuseum** (City Museum). Wedged in by Oberanger, Rosental, and St.-Jakobsplatz (site of a Jewish community center to be completed in 2007, including a synagogue, museum, and cultural center), this museum is as eclectic within as the architecture is without. Though the entire complex was rebuilt in several stages after World War II, the original building fronting St.-Jakobsplatz dates to 1491. Inside are instrument collections, international cultural exhibits, a film museum showing rarely screened movies, notably German silents, a photo and fashion museum, a puppet theater, and one of the liveliest cafés in town. ✉ *St.-Jakobspl. 1, City Center* ☎ *089/2332–2370* 🌐 *www.stadtmuseum-online.de* 🎫 *€2.50, free Sun.; special exhibitions €4* ⏲ *Tues.–Sun. 10–6* Ⓤ *Marienplatz (U-bahn and S-bahn).*

⓮ **Münze** (Mint). Originally the royal stables, the Münze was created by court architect Wilhelm Egkl between 1563 and 1567 and now serves as an office building. A stern neoclassical facade emblazoned with gold was added in 1809; the interior courtyard has Renaissance-style arches. ✉ *Pfisterstr. 4, City Center* 🎫 *Free* ⏲ *Mon.–Thurs. 8–4, Fri. 8–2* Ⓤ *Marienplatz (U-bahn and S-bahn).*

❼ **Neues Rathaus** (New Town Hall). Munich's present town hall was built between 1867 and 1908 in the fussy, turreted, neo-Gothic style so beloved by King Ludwig II. Architectural historians are divided over its merits, though its dramatic scale and lavish detailing are impressive. Perhaps the most serious criticism is that the Dutch and Flemish styles of the building seem out of place amid the baroque and rococo styles of so much of the rest of the city. The tower's 1904 Glockenspiel (a chiming clock with mechanical figures) plays daily at 11 AM, noon, and 9 PM, with an additional performance at 5 PM June–October. As chimes peal out over the square, the clock's doors flip open and brightly colored dancers and jousting knights go through their paces. They act out two events from Munich's past: a tournament held in Marienplatz in 1568 and the *Schäfflertanz* (Dance of the Coopers), which commemorated the end of the plague of 1517. When Munich was in ruins after World War II, an American soldier contributed some paint to restore the battered figures, and he was rewarded with a ride on one of the jousters' horses, high above the cheering crowds. You, too, can travel up there, by elevator, to an observation point near the top of one of the towers. On a clear day the view is spectacular. ✉ *Marienpl., City Center* 🎫 *Tower €1.50* ⏲ *Mon.–Thurs. 9–4, Fri. 9–1* Ⓤ *Marienplatz (U-bahn and S-bahn).*

⓬ **Peterskirche** (St. Peter's Church). Munich's oldest and smallest parish church traces its origins to the 11th century and has been restored in various architectural styles. The rich baroque interior has a magnificent late-Gothic high altar and aisle pillars decorated with exquisite 18th-century figures of the apostles. In clear weather it's well worth the climb up the 300-foot tower—the view includes glimpses of the Alps. The Peterskirche has a Scottish priest who is glad to show English-speaking visitors around. ✉ *Rindermarkt, City Center* ☎ *089/260–4828* 🎫 *Tower €1.50* ⏲ *Mon.–Sat. 9–6, Sun. 10–6* Ⓤ *Marienplatz (U-bahn and S-bahn).*

off the beaten path

THERESIENWIESE – The site of Munich's annual beer festival—the notorious Oktoberfest—and of the very hip Christmas market (the Tollwood) is only a 10-minute walk from the Hauptbahnhof or a single stop away by subway (U-4 or U-5). The enormous exhibition ground is named after Princess Therese von Sachsen-Hildburghausen, who celebrated her marriage to the Bavarian crown prince Ludwig—later Ludwig I—here in 1810. The accompanying agricultural fair was such a success that it became an annual event. Beer was served then as now, but what began as a night out for the locals has become a 16-day international bonanza at the end of September and the beginning of October, attracting more than 6 million people each year (it qualifies as an *Oktober* fest by ending the first Sunday in October).

Overlooking the Theresienwiese is a 19th-century hall of fame featuring busts of numerous popular figures of the time—one of the last works of Ludwig I—and a monumental bronze statue of the maiden **Bavaria**, more than 100 feet high. The statue is hollow, and 130 steps take you up into the braided head for a view of Munich through Bavaria's eyes. 🎫 *€2.50* ⏲ *Dec.–Oct., Tues.–Sun. 10–noon and 2–4.* Ⓤ *Theresienhöhe (U-bahn).*

★ ❾ **Viktualienmarkt** (Victuals Market). The city's open-air food market has a wide range of produce, German and international foodstuffs, and tables and counters for eating and drinking, which make the area a feast for the eyes as well as the stomach. All kinds of people come here for a quick snack at any number of stands, from well-heeled businesspeople and casual tourists to mortar- and paint-spangled workers. It's also the realm of the garrulous, sturdy market women who run the stalls with dictatorial authority. Whether here, or at a bakery, *do not* try to select your pickings by hand; ask for help. Ⓤ *Marienplatz (U-bahn and S-bahn).*

off the beaten path

ZAM – Nestled in a passageway just off the Isartor, the ZAM (which stands for the German equivalent of Center for Unusual Museums) consists of the private collections belonging to the late Manfred Klauda, a Munich lawyer. There's no specific guiding theme, except perhaps the obsession of a single individual. Exhibitions include collections of chamber pots, *bourdalous* (a convenience for women in 17th- and 18th-century clothing), corkscrews, locks, Easter bunnies, pedal cars, perfume bottles, and ephemera relating to Empress Elisabeth of Austria (known as Sissi, the cousin of Ludwig II). ✉ *Westenriederstr. 41, City Center* ☎ *089/290–4121* 🌐 *www.zam-museum.de* 🎫 *€4* ⏲ *Daily 10–6* Ⓤ *Isartor (S-bahn).*

Royal Munich

From the relatively modest palace of the Alter Hof, the Wittelsbachs expanded their quarters northward, away from the jumble of narrow streets in the old quarter. Three splendid avenues radiated outward from their new palace and garden grounds, and fine homes arose along them. One of them—Prinzregentenstrasse—marks the southern end of Munich's huge public park, the Englischer Garten, also the creation of a Wittelsbach ruler. Lehel is an upmarket residential neighborhood that also serves as Munich's museum quarter.

a good walk

A good way to start this very long walk is with a Bavarian breakfast of Weisswurst, pretzels, and beer at the **Hofbräuhaus** 17, perhaps Munich's best-known beer hall, on Am Platzl. Turn right from the Hofbräuhaus for the short walk along Orlandostrasse to **Maximilianstrasse** 18, Munich's most elegant shopping street. Opposite you is a handsome city landmark: the Hotel Vier Jahreszeiten, a historic host to traveling princes, millionaires, and the expense-account jet set. Maximilianstrasse was named after King Maximilian II, whose statue you'll see far down on the right. This wide boulevard has many grand buildings, which contain government offices and the city's ethnological museum, the **Staatliches Museum für Völkerkunde** 19. The Maximilianeum, on a rise beyond the Isar River, is an impressive mid-19th-century palace where the Bavarian state parliament now meets.

Turn left on Maximilianstrasse and you'll arrive at Max-Joseph-Platz, a square dominated by the pillared portico of the 19th-century **Nationaltheater** 20, home of the Bavarian State Opera Company. The statue in the square's center is of Bavaria's first king, Max Joseph. Along the north side is the lofty and austere south wall of the **Residenz** 21, the royal palace of Wittelsbach rulers for more than six centuries.

Directly north of the Residenz, on Hofgartenstrasse, lies the former royal garden, the **Hofgarten** 22, which was started in the 16th century and eventually achieved its Italian Renaissance look. The plaza in front of the Hofgarten is Odeonsplatz. The monument on the southern end is the 19th-century **Feldherrnhalle** 23, modeled after the familiar Loggia dei Lanzi in Florence. Looking north up Ludwigstrasse, the arrow-straight avenue that begins at the Feldherrnhalle, you'll see the **Siegestor** 24, or victory arch, which marks the beginning of Leopoldstrasse. Completing this impressively Italianate panorama is the great yellow bulk of the former royal church of St. Kajetan, the **Theatinerkirche** 25, an imposing baroque structure across from the Feldherrnhalle. A few steps down Theatinerstrasse is the **Kunsthalle der Hypo-Kulturstiftung** 26. A left on Briennerstrasse and a right on Oskar-von-Miller-Ring will take you to the **SiemensForum** 27, which explores the long history of one of Germany's number-one companies.

Now head north up Ludwigstrasse. Court architect Leo von Klenze designed this first stretch of the generous avenue to give the road to the village of Schwabing a look befitting what had become a kingdom after the Napoleonic wars. In much the same way that Baron Haussmann would

BAVARIA: A COUNTRY WITHIN A COUNTRY

For most visitors, Bavaria, with its traditional Gemütlichkeit, beer gardens, quaint little villages, and culturally rich cities, is often seen as the quintessence of Germany. In fact, nothing could be farther from the truth. Of the 16 German Länder, as the German federal states are called, none is more fiercely independent than Bavaria. In fact, it was an autonomous dukedom and later kingdom until 1871, when it was incorporated into the German empire.

For Bavarians, anything beyond the state's borders remains foreign territory. The state has its own anthem and its own flag, part of which, the blue-and-white lozenges in the center, has virtually become a regional trademark symbolizing quality and tradition. Bavarian politicians discussing the issue of Europe in speeches will often refer to Bavaria almost as if it were a national state. And they will inevitably call it by its full official name: Freistaat Bayern, or simply der Freistaat, meaning "the Free State." The term was coined by Kurt Eisner, Minister President of the socialist government who rid the land of the Wittelsbach dynasty in 1918. It is simply a German way of saying republic—a land governed by the people. And it has an honorable place in the first line of the separate Bavarian constitution that was signed under the aegis of the American occupational forces in 1946.

Bavaria is not the only Freistaat in Germany, a fact not too many Germans are aware of. Thuringia and Saxony also sport that title. But the Bavarians are the only ones who make such a public point of it. As they say, clocks in Bavaria run differently. Now you know why . . .

— Marton Radkai

later demolish many of the old streets and buildings in Paris, replacing them with stately boulevards, von Klenze swept aside the small dwellings and alleys that stood here and replaced them with severe neoclassical structures such as the Bayerische Staatsbibliothek (Bavarian State Library), the Universität (University), and the peculiarly Byzantine Ludwigskirche. Müncheners either love or hate the architect's formal buildings, which end just before Ludwigstrasse becomes Leopoldstrasse. Another leading architect, Friedrich von Gärtner, took over construction here with more delicate structures that are a pleasant backdrop to the busy street life in summer. Once the hub of the legendary artists' district of Schwabing, Leopoldstrasse still throbs with life from spring to fall, exuding the atmosphere of a Mediterranean boulevard, with cafés, wine terraces, and artists' stalls. In comparison, Ludwigstrasse is inhabited by ghosts of the past.

At the south end of Leopoldstrasse lies the great open quadrangle of the university. A circular area divides into two piazzas named after anti-Nazi resistance leaders: Geschwister-Scholl-Platz and Professor-Huber-Platz. From the university, Leopoldstrasse then continues into Schwabing itself, once Munich's bohemian quarter but now distinctly upscale and chic to the point of being monotonous. Explore the streets of old

Schwabing around Wedekindplatz to get the feel of the place. Or enjoy the shops and cafés in the student quarter parallel to Leopoldstrasse. (Those in search of the bohemian mood that once animated Schwabing should head to Haidhausen, on the other side of the Isar River, though it is about to end there, too, owing to gentrification and high rents.)

Bordering the east side of Schwabing is the **Englischer Garten** (28). Five kilometers (3 mi) long and 1½ km (about 1 mi) wide, it's Germany's largest city park, stretching from Prinzregentenstrasse, the broad avenue laid out by Prince Regent Luitpold at the end of the 19th century, to the city's northern boundary, where the lush parkland is taken over by the rough embrace of open countryside. Dominating the park's southern border is one of the few examples of Hitler-era architecture still standing in Munich: the colonnaded **Haus der Kunst** (29), a leading art gallery and home to Munich's most fashionable nightclub, the P 1.

A few hundred yards farther along Prinzregentenstrasse are two other leading museums, the **Bayerisches Nationalmuseum** (30) and the **Schack-Galerie** (31), and around the first left-hand corner, on Lerchenfeldstrasse, is a museum of prehistory, the **Archäologische Staatssammlung** (32), in a modern concrete building appropriately covered with rusting steel Cor-Ten plates.

On a hill at the eastern end of Prinzregentenstrasse, just across the Isar River from the Schack-Galerie, is Munich's well-loved Friedensengel (Angel of Peace), a gilt angel crowning a marble column. Beyond the Friedensengel is another historic home that became a major Munich art gallery—the **Museum Villa Stuck** (33), an art-nouveau fantasy wrapped in a sober, neoclassical shell.

TIMING You'll need a day (and good walking shoes) for this stroll. Set aside at least two hours for a tour of the Residenz. If the weather is good, return to the southern end of the Englischer Garten at dusk—you'll be treated to an unforgettable silhouette of the Munich skyline, black against the retreating light.

What to See

(32) **Archäologische Staatssammlung** (State Archaeological Collection). This is Bavaria's principal record of its prehistoric, Roman, and Celtic past. The perfectly preserved body of a ritually sacrificed young girl, recovered from a Bavarian peat moor, is among the more spine-chilling exhibits. Head down to the basement to see the fine Roman mosaic floor. ✉ *Lerchenfeldstr. 2, Lehel* ☎ *089/211–2402* 🎫 *€4.50, free Sun.* ⏲ *Tues.–Sun. 9–4:30* Ⓤ *Lehel (U-bahn).*

(30) **Bayerisches Nationalmuseum** (Bavarian National Museum). Although the museum places emphasis on Bavarian cultural history, it has art and artifacts of international importance and regular exhibitions that attract worldwide attention. The highlight for some will be the medieval and Renaissance wood carvings, with many works by the great Renaissance sculptor Tilman Riemenschneider. Tapestries, arms and armor, a unique collection of Christmas crèches (the *Krippenschau*), and Bavarian and German folk art compete for your attention. ✉ *Prinzregentenstr. 3, Lehel* ☎ *089/211–*

2401 🌐 www.bayerisches-nationalmuseum.de 🎫 €3, free Sun., special exhibitions €5 ⏲ Tues.–Sun. 10–5, Thurs. 10–8 Ⓤ Lehel (U-bahn).

★ 28 **Englischer Garten** (English Garden). This virtually endless park, which melds into the open countryside at Munich's northern city limits, was designed for the Bavarian prince Karl Theodor by Benjamin Thompson, later Count Rumford, from Massachusetts, who fled America after having taken the wrong side during the War of Independence. The open, informal nature of the park—reminiscent of the rolling parklands with which English aristocrats of the 18th century liked to surround their country homes—gave the park its name. It has a boating lake, four beer gardens, and a series of curious decorative and monumental constructions, including the Monopteros, a Greek temple designed by Leo von Klenze for King Ludwig I and built on an artificial hill in the southern section of the park. In the center of the park's most popular beer garden is a Chinese pagoda erected in 1789. It was destroyed during the war and then reconstructed. The Chinese Tower beer garden is world famous, but the park has prettier places for sipping a beer: the Aumeister, for example, along the northern perimeter. The Aumeister's restaurant is in an early-19th-century hunting lodge. At the Seehaus, on the shore of the Kleinhesseloher *See* (lake), choose between a smart restaurant or a cozy *Bierstube* (beer tavern).

The Englischer Garten is a paradise for joggers, cyclists, musicians, soccer players, sunbathers, dog owners, and, in winter, cross-country skiers. The Munich Cricket Club grounds are in the southern section—and spectators are welcome. The park has designated areas for nude sunbathing—the Germans have a positively pagan attitude toward the sun—so don't be surprised to see naked bodies bordering the flower beds and paths. ✉ *Main entrances at Prinzregentenstr. and Koniginstr., Schwabing and Lehel.*

need a break?

For lunch, wander across the Ludwigstrasse to the heart of the student quarter. Light vegetarian food with a definite Asian touch is served to those on the fly at **S. M. Vegetarisch** (✉ Amalienstr. 45 ☎ 089/281–882). The prices are perfect for those on a budget.

23 **Feldherrnhalle** (Generals' Hall). This open-sided, pavilion-like building was modeled after the 14th-century Loggia dei Lanzi in Florence and honors three centuries' worth of Bavarian generals. Two huge Bavarian lions are flanked by the larger-than-life statues of Count Johann Tserclaes Tilly, who led Catholic forces in the Thirty Years' War, and Prince Karl Philipp Wrede, hero of the 19th-century Napoleonic Wars. The imposing structure was turned into a militaristic shrine in the 1930s and '40s by the Nazis, who found it significant because it marked the site of Hitler's abortive coup, or putsch, which took place in 1923. All who passed it had to give the Nazi salute. Viscardigasse, a tiny alley behind the Feldherrnhalle linking Residenzstrasse and Theatinerstrasse and now lined with exclusive boutiques, was used by those who wanted to dodge the tedious routine, hence its nickname Heil Hitler Street. ✉ *South end of Odeonspl., City Center* Ⓤ *Odeonsplatz (U-bahn).*

29 **Haus der Kunst** (House of Art). This colonnaded, classical-style building is one of Munich's few remaining examples of Hitler-era architecture and was officially opened by the führer himself. In the Hitler years it showed only work deemed to reflect the Nazi aesthetic. One of its most successful postwar exhibitions was devoted to works banned by the Nazis. It hosts exhibitions of art, photography, and sculpture, as well as theatrical and musical happenings. The survival-of-the-chicest disco, P 1, is in the building's west wing. ✉ *Prinzregentenstr. 1, Lehel* ☎ *089/211–270* 🌐 *www.hausderkunst.de* 🎫 *Varies* ⏲ *Fri.–Wed. 10–8, Thurs. 10–10* Ⓤ *Odeonsplatz (U-bahn).*

17 **Hofbräuhaus.** Duke Wilhelm V founded Munich's most famous brewery in 1589. Hofbräu means "court brewery," and the golden beer is poured in king-size liter mugs. If the cavernous downstairs hall is too noisy for you, try the quiet restaurant upstairs. Americans, Australians, and Italians far outnumber Germans, and the brass band that performs here most days adds modern pop and American folk music to the traditional German numbers. ✉ *Am Platzl 9, City Center* ☎ *089/290–136* ⏲ *Daily 11–11* Ⓤ *Marienplatz (U-bahn and S-bahn).*

22 **Hofgarten** (Royal Garden). The formal garden was once part of the royal palace grounds. It's bordered on two sides by arcades designed in the 19th century by the royal architect Leo von Klenze. On the east side of the garden stands the new state chancellery, built around the ruins of the 19th-century Army Museum and incorporating the remains of a Renaissance arcade. Its most prominent feature is a large copper dome. Bombed during World War II air raids, the museum stood untouched for almost 40 years as a grim reminder of the war. It's now known as Palazzo Prozzi, an untranslatable joke referring to the huge sums that went into rebuilding it and its ostentatious look.

In front of the chancellery stands one of Europe's most unusual—some say most effective—war memorials. Instead of looking up at a monument, you are led down to a **sunken crypt** covered by a massive granite block. In the crypt lies a German soldier from World War I. The crypt is a stark contrast to the **memorial** that stands unobtrusively in front of the northern wing of the chancellery: a simple cube of black marble bearing facsimiles of handwritten wartime manifestos by anti-Nazi leaders, including members of the White Rose movement. ✉ *Hofgartenstr., north of Residenz, City Center* Ⓤ *Odeonsplatz (U-bahn).*

26 **Kunsthalle der Hypo-Kulturstiftung** (Hall of the Hypobank's Cultural Foundation). Chagall, Giacometti, Picasso, and Gauguin were among the artists featured in the past at this exhibition hall in the midst of the commercial pedestrian zone. Other exhibits have included art ranging from antiquity to the most modern studios. The foundation's success over the years has led to its expansion, designed by the Swiss architect team Herzog and de Meuron, who also designed London's Tate Modern. ✉ *Theatinerstr. 8, City Center* ☎ *089/224–412* 🌐 *www.hypo-kunsthalle.de* 🎫 *€7* ⏲ *Daily 10–8* Ⓤ *Odeonsplatz (U-bahn).*

Ludwigskirche (Ludwig's Church). Planted halfway along the severe, neoclassical Ludwigstrasse is this curious neo-Byzantine–early-Renaissance–style church, built at the behest of Ludwig I to provide his newly completed suburb with a parish church. It's worth a stop to see the fresco of the *Last Judgment* in the choir. At 60 feet by 37 feet, it's one of the world's largest. ✉ *Ludwigstr. 22, Maxvorstadt* ☎ *089/288–334* ⏲ *Daily 7–7* Ⓤ *Universität (U-bahn).*

18 **Maximilianstrasse.** Munich's sophisticated shopping street was named after King Maximilian II, who wanted to break away from the Greek-influenced classical style of city architecture favored by his father, Ludwig I. With the cabinet's approval, he created this broad boulevard and lined its central stretch with majestic buildings. It culminates on a rise beyond the Isar River in the stately outlines of the **Maximilianeum,** a lavish 19th-century arcaded palace built for Maximilian II and now home to the Bavarian state parliament. Only the terrace can be visited.

33 **Museum Villa Stuck.** This neoclassical villa is the former home of one of Munich's leading turn-of-the-20th-century artists, Franz von Stuck (1863–1928). His work, which is at times haunting, at times erotic, and occasionally humorous, covers the walls of the ground-floor rooms, along with various special exhibitions. Renovation of the upstairs rooms, the artist's former quarters, was completed in 2005. ✉ *Prinzregentenstr. 60, Haidhausen* ☎ *089/455–5510* 🌐 *www.villastuck.de* 🎫 *Free* ⏲ *Wed.–Sun. 11–6* Ⓤ *Prinzregentenplatz (U-bahn).*

20 **Nationaltheater** (National Theater). Built in the late 19th century as a royal opera house with a pillared portico, this large theater was bombed during the war but is now restored to its original splendor and has some of the world's most advanced stage technology. ✉ *Max-Joseph-Pl., City Center* ☎ *089/2185–1920* Ⓤ *Odeonsplatz (U-bahn).*

★ 21 **Residenz** (Royal Palace). Munich's royal palace began as a small castle in the 14th century. The Wittelsbach dukes moved here when the tenements of an expanding Munich encroached upon their Alter Hof. In succeeding centuries the royal residence developed according to the importance, requirements, and interests of its occupants. It came to include the Königsbau (on Max-Joseph-Platz) and then (clockwise) the Alte Residenz; the Festsaal (Banquet Hall); the Altes Residenztheater/Cuvilliés-Theater; the newly restored Allerheiligenhofkirche (All Souls' Church), a venue for cultural events; the Residenztheater; and the Nationaltheater.

Building began in 1385 with the **Neuveste** (New Fortress), which comprised the northeast section. Most of it burned to the ground in 1750, but one of its finest rooms survived: the 16th-century **Antiquarium,** which was built for Duke Albrecht V's collection of antique statues (today it's used chiefly for state receptions). The throne room of King Ludwig I, the **Neuer Herkulessaal,** is now a concert hall. The accumulated Wittelsbach treasures are on view in several palace museums. The **Schatzkammer** (Treasury; 🎫 €6, combined ticket with Residenzmuseum €9 ⏲ Apr.–Oct. 15, daily 9–6; Oct. 16–Mar., daily 10–6) has a rather rich centerpiece—a small Renaissance statue of St. George, studded with 2,291 diamonds, 209 pearls, and 406 rubies. Paintings, tapestries, furniture, and porcelain are housed in the **Residenzmuseum** (🎫 €4 ⏲ Apr.–Oct. 15, daily 9–6; Oct. 16–Mar., daily 10–6). Antique coins glint in the

Staatliche Münzsammlung (€2, free Sun. Wed.–Sun. 10–5). Egyptian works of art make up the **Staatliche Sammlung Ägyptischer Kunst** (✉ Hofgarten entrance ☎ 089/298–546 €5, Sun. €1 Tues. 9–5 and 7–9 PM, Wed.–Fri. 9–5, weekends 10–5).

In summer, chamber-music concerts take place in the inner courtyard. Also in the center of the complex is the small, rococo **Altes Residenztheater/Cuvilliés-Theater** (✉ Residenzstr. €3 Apr.–Oct. 15, daily 9–6; Oct. 16–Mar., daily 10–4; closed during rehearsals). It was built by François Cuvilliés between 1751 and 1755, and performances are still held here. The French-born Cuvilliés was a dwarf who was admitted to the Bavarian court as a decorative "bauble." Prince Max Emanuel recognized his innate artistic ability and had him trained as an architect. The prince's eye for talent gave Germany some of its richest rococo treasures. ✉ *Max-Joseph-Pl. 3, entrance through archway at Residenzstr. 1, City Center* ☎ *089/290–671* *Closed a few days in early Jan.* U *Odeonsplatz (U-bahn).*

31 **Schack-Galerie.** Those with a taste for florid and romantic 19th-century German paintings will appreciate the collections of the Schack-Galerie, originally the private collection of Count Schack. Others may find the gallery dull, filled with plodding and repetitive works by painters who now repose in well-deserved obscurity. ✉ *Prinzregentenstr. 9, Lehel* ☎ *089/2380–5224* *€2.50, free Sun.* *Wed.–Mon. 10–5* U *Lehel (U-bahn).*

24 **Siegestor** (Victory Arch). Marking the beginning of Leopoldstrasse, the Siegestor has Italian origins—it was modeled after the Arch of Constantine in Rome—and was built to honor the achievements of the Bavarian army during the Wars of Liberation (1813–15). The writing on the gable facing the inner city reads: DEDICATED TO VICTORY, DESTROYED BY WAR, ADMONISHING PEACE. ✉ *Leopoldstr., Schwabing* U *Unversität (U-bahn).*

27 **SiemensForum.** Siemens corporation has been one of Germany's major employers and technological innovators for more than 150 years. This company museum, housed in a spaceship-like building, shows visitors the many areas in which Siemens has been active, from old-fashioned telegraph systems to hypermodern dentist chairs and fuel cells. Hands-on displays such as video telephones spice up the experience. ✉ *Oskar-von-Miller-Ring* ☎ *089/6363–3210* *www.siemensforum.de* *Free* *Sun.–Fri. 9–5, 1st Tues. in month 9–9* U *Odeonsplatz (U-bahn).*

19 **Staatliches Museum für Völkerkunde** (State Museum of Ethnology). Arts and crafts from around the world are displayed in this extensive museum. There are also regular special exhibits. ✉ *Maximilianstr. 42, Lehel* ☎ *089/2101–3610* *www.voelkerkundemuseum-muenchen.de* *€3, Sun €1* *Tues.–Sun. 9:30–5:15* U *Lehel (U-bahn).*

25 **Theatinerkirche** (Theatine Church). This mighty baroque church owes its Italian appearance to its founder, Princess Henriette Adelaide, who commissioned it in gratitude for the birth of her son and heir, Max Emanuel, in 1663. A native of Turin, the princess distrusted Bavarian architects and builders and thus summoned a master builder from

Bologna, Agostino Barelli, to construct her church. Barelli worked on the building for 11 years but was dismissed before the project was completed. It was another 100 years before the Theatinerkirche was finished. Its lofty towers frame a restrained facade capped by a massive dome. The superb stucco work on the inside has a remarkably light feeling owing to its brilliant white color. The gaping space before the Feldherrnhalle and Theatinerkirche is often used for outdoor stage events. ✉ *Theatinerstr. 22, City Center* Ⓤ *Odeonsplatz (U-bahn).*

need a break?

Munich's oldest café, **Tambosi** (✉ Odeonspl., Maxvorstadt ☎ 089/224–768), borders the street across from the Theatinerkirche. Watch the hustle and bustle from an outdoor table or retreat through a gate in the Hofgarten's western wall to the café's tree-shaded beer garden. If the weather is cool or rainy, find a corner in the cozy, eclectically furnished interior.

DenkStätte Weisse Rose (Memorial to the Weisse Rose Resistance Group). Siblings Hans and Sophie Scholl, fellow students Alexander Schmorell and Christian Probst, and Kurt Huber, Professor of Philosophy, founded the short-lived resistance movement against the Nazis in 1942–43 known as the Weisse Rose (White Rose). All were executed. A small exhibition about their work is in the inner quad of the university, where the Scholls were caught distributing leaflets and denounced by the janitor. ✉ *Geschwister-Scholl-Pl. 1, Maxvorstadt* ☎ *089/2180–3053* 🎫 *Free* 🕓 *Mon.–Thurs. 10–4, Fri. 10–3* Ⓤ *Unversität (U-bahn).*

Schwabing & Maxvorstadt

Most of the city's leading art galleries and museums are congregated in Schwabing and neighboring Maxvorstadt, making this area the artistic center of Munich. Schwabing, the old artists' quarter, is no longer the bohemian area where such diverse residents as Lenin and Kandinsky were once neighbors, but the solid cultural foundations of the Maxvorstadt, where you'll find Munich's largest and most important museums, are immutable. Where the two areas meet (in the streets behind the university), life hums with a creative vibrancy that is difficult to detect elsewhere in Munich.

a good walk

Begin with a stroll through the city's old botanical garden, the **Alter Botanischer Garten** 34 ▸. The grand-looking building opposite the garden's entrance is the Palace of Justice, law courts built in 1897 in suitably awe-inspiring dimensions. On one corner of busy Lenbachplatz, you can't fail to notice one of Munich's most impressive fountains: the monumental late-19th-century Wittelsbacher Brunnen, designed by Franz von Stuck. Beyond the fountain, in Pacellistrasse, is the baroque **Dreifaltigkeitskirche** 35.

Leave the garden at its Meiserstrasse exit. On the right-hand side you'll pass two solemn neoclassical buildings closely associated with the Third Reich. The first served as the administrative offices of the Nazi Party in Munich. The neighboring building is the Music Academy, where, in 1938, Hitler, Mussolini, Chamberlain, and Daladier signed the prewar pact that carved up Czechoslovakia.

At the junction of Meiserstrasse and Briennerstrasse, look right to see the obelisk dominating the circular **Karolinenplatz** 36. To your left will be the expansive **Königsplatz** 37, bordered by two museums, the **Glyptothek** 38 and the **Antikensammlungen** 39, and closed off by the Propyläen, a colonnade framed by two Egyptian pylons.

After walking by the museums, turn right onto Luisenstrasse and you'll arrive at a Florentine-style villa, the **Städtische Galerie im Lenbachhaus** 40, which has an outstanding painting collection. Continue down Luisenstrasse, turning right on Theresienstrasse to reach Munich's three leading art galleries, the **Alte Pinakothek** 41; the **Neue Pinakothek** 42, opposite it; and the **Pinakothek der Moderne** 43. They are as complementary as their buildings are contrasting: the Alte Pinakothek, severe and serious in style; the Neue Pinakothek, almost frivolously Florentine; and the Pinakothek der Moderne, glass-and-concrete new.

After a few hours immersed in culture, end your walk with a leisurely stroll through the neighboring streets of Schwabing, which are lined with boutiques, bars, and restaurants. If it's a nice day, head for the **Elisabethmarkt,** Schwabing's permanent market.

TIMING This walk may take an entire day, depending on how long you linger at the major museums en route. Avoid the museum crowds by visiting as early in the day as possible. All of Munich seems to discover an interest in art on Sunday, when admission to most municipal and state-funded museums is free; you might want to take this day off from culture and join the late-breakfast and brunch crowd at the Elisabethmarkt, a beer garden, or at any of the many bars and Gaststätten. Some have Sunday-morning jazz concerts. Many Schwabing bars have happy hours between 6 and 8—a relaxing way to end your day.

What to See

41 Fodor's Choice ★ **Alte Pinakothek** (Old Picture Gallery). The long, massive brick Alte Pinakothek was constructed by Leo von Klenze between 1826 and 1836 to exhibit the collection of old masters begun by Duke Wilhelm IV in the 16th century. It's now judged one of the world's great picture galleries. Among its many famous works are paintings by Dürer, Titian, Rembrandt, Rubens (the museum has one of the world's largest collections of works by Rubens), and two celebrated Murillos. ✉ *Barerstr. 27, Maxvorstadt* ☎ *089/2380–5216* 🌐 *www.alte-pinakothek.de* 🎫 *€5, combined day ticket with Neue Pinakothek and Pinakothek der Moderne €11; €1 Sun.* ⏲ *Wed.–Sun. 10–5, Tues. 10–8* Ⓤ *Königsplatz (U-bahn).*

34 **Alter Botanischer Garten** (Old Botanical Garden). Munich's first botanical garden began as the site of a huge glass palace, built in 1853 for Germany's first industrial exhibition. In 1931 it shared the fate of a similarly palatial glass exhibition hall, London's Crystal Palace, when its garden burned to the ground; six years later it was redesigned as a public park. Two features from the 1930s remain: a small, square **exhibition hall,** still used for art shows, and the 1933 **Neptune Fountain,** an enormous work in the heavy, monumental style of the prewar years. At the international electricity exhibition of 1882, the world's first high-tension electrical cable was run from the park to a Bavarian village 48

km (30 mi) away. ✉ *Entrance at Lenbachpl., Maxvorstadt* Ⓤ *Karlsplatz (U-bahn and S-bahn).*

need a break?

Ideal for a quick lunch with either German, French, or Italian flair is the art deco **Brasserie Tresznjewski** (✉ Theresienstrasse 72, at Barerstrasse, Maxvorstadt ☎ 089/282–349). It's a good spot especially if visiting the neighboring Pinakotheks . . . and it serves food well into the wee hours.

39 **Antikensammlungen** (Antiquities Collection). This museum has a collection of small sculptures, Etruscan art, Greek vases, gold, and glass. ✉ *Königspl. 1, Maxvorstadt* ☎ *089/5998–8830* 🌐 *www.antike-am-koenigsplatz.mwn.de* 🎫 *€3, combined ticket to Antikensammlungen and Glyptothek €5; Sun. €1* ⏲ *Tues. and Thurs.–Sun. 10–5, Wed. 10–8* Ⓤ *Königsplatz (U-bahn).*

35 **Dreifaltigkeitskirche** (Church of the Holy Trinity). After a local woman prophesied doom for the city unless a new church was erected, this striking baroque exterior was promptly built between 1711 and 1718. It has frescoes by Cosmas Damian Asam depicting various heroic scenes. ✉ *Pacellistr. 10, City Center* ☎ *089/290–0820* ⏲ *Daily 7–7, except during services* Ⓤ *Karlsplatz (U-bahn and S-bahn).*

Elisabethmarkt (Elisabeth Market). Schwabing's permanent market is smaller than the popular Viktualienmarkt, but hardly less colorful. It has a pocket-size beer garden, where a jazz band performs every Saturday from spring to autumn. ✉ *Arcistr. and Elisabethstr., Schwabing* Ⓤ *Giselastrasse (U-bahn).*

★ 38 **Glyptothek.** These Greek and Roman sculptures are among the finest collections in Munich. The small café that expands into the quiet courtyard is a favorite for visitors, which include budding artists practicing their drawing skills. ✉ *Königspl. 3, Maxvorstadt* ☎ *089/286–100* 🌐 *www.antike-am-koenigsplatz.mwn.de* 🎫 *€3, combined ticket to Glyptothek and Antikensammlungen €5; Sun. €1* ⏲ *Tues., Wed., and Fri.–Sun. 10–5, and Thurs. 10–8* Ⓤ *Königsplatz (U-bahn).*

36 **Karolinenplatz** (Caroline Square). At the junction of Barerstrasse and Brienerstrasse, this circular area is dominated by an obelisk unveiled in 1812 as a memorial to Bavarians killed fighting Napoléon. **Amerika-haus** (America House) faces Karolinenplatz. It has an extensive library with many magazines to flip through and a year-round program of cultural events. ✉ *Karolinenpl. 3, Maxvorstadt* ☎ *089/552–5370* Ⓤ *Königsplatz (U-bahn).*

37 **Königsplatz** (King's Square). This expansive square is lined on three sides with the monumental Grecian-style buildings by Leo von Klenze that gave Munich the nickname Athens on the Isar. The two templelike structures are now the Antikensammlungen and the Glyptothek museums. Although a busy road passes through it, the square has maintained the dignified appearance intended by Ludwig I thanks to the broad green lawns sprawling in front of the museums. In summertime, concerts and outdoor cinema take place on this grand square. Ⓤ *Königsplatz (U-bahn).*

42 **Neue Pinakothek** (New Picture Gallery). This exhibition space opened in 1981 to house the royal collection of modern art left homeless and scattered after its building was destroyed in the war. The exterior of the modern building mimics an older one with Italianate influences. The interior offers a magnificent environment for picture gazing, at least partly owing to the natural light flooding in from skylights. French impressionists—Monet, Degas, Manet—are all well represented. The 19th-century German and Scandinavian paintings—misty landscapes predominate—are only now coming to be recognized as admirable products of their time. ✉ *Barerstr. 29, Maxvorstadt* ☎ *089/2380–5195* 🌐 *www.neue-pinakothek.de* 🎫 *€5, combined day ticket with Alte Pinakothek and Pinakothek der Moderne €11; €1 Sun.* ⏲ *Mon. and Thurs.–Sun. 10–5, Wed. 10–8* Ⓤ *Königsplatz (U-bahn).*

43 **Pinakothek der Moderne.** Munich's latest cultural addition is also Germany's largest museum for modern art, architecture, and design. The striking glass-and-concrete complex holds four outstanding art and architectural collections, including modern art, industrial and graphic design, the Bavarian State collection of graphic art, and the Technical University's architectural museum. ✉ *Barerstr. 40, Maxvorstadt* ☎ *089/2380–5360* 🌐 *www.pinakothek-der-moderne.de* 🎫 *€9, combined day ticket with Neue Pinakothek and Pinakothek der Moderne €11; €1 Sun.* ⏲ *Tues., Wed., weekends 10–5, Thurs. and Fri. 10–8* Ⓤ *Königsplatz (U-bahn).*

40 **Städtische Galerie im Lenbachhaus** (Municipal Gallery). This delightful late-19th-century Florentine-style villa is the former home and studio of the artist Franz von Lenbach (1836–1904). Inside you'll find renowned works from the Gothic period to the present, including an exciting assemblage of art from the early-20th-century *Blaue Reiter* (Blue Rider) group: Kandinsky, Klee, Jawlensky, Macke, Marc, and Münter. The chambers of Lenbach are on view as well. The adjoining **Kunstbau** (art building), a former subway platform of the Königsplatz station, hosts changing exhibitions of modern art. ✉ *Luisenstr. 33, Maxvorstadt* ☎ *089/233–32000* 🌐 *www.lenbachhaus.de* 🎫 *€4–€6* ⏲ *Tues.–Sun. 10–6* Ⓤ *Königsplatz (U-bahn).*

Outside the Center

Bavaria Filmstadt. Munich is Germany's leading moviemaking center, and the local Hollywood-like neighborhood, Geiselgasteig, is on the southern outskirts of the city. The Filmexpress transports you on a 1½-hour tour of the sets of *Das Boot* (*The Boat*), *Die Unendliche Geschichte* (*The Neverending Story*), and other productions. Stunt shows are held at 11:30, 1, and 2:30, and action movies are screened in Showscan, the super-wide-screen cinema. The *Erlebniskino* (experience cinema) is a computer-animated thriller where you sit in a chair that moves with five-channel audio to really get you into the picture. Take U-bahn 1 or 2 from the city center to Silberhornstrasse and then change to Tram 25 to Bavariafilmplatz. The Munich transit authority (MVV) offers its own combined ticket for two adults plus three other people under 18 for €29.50, including travel. ✉ *Bavariafilmpl. 7, Geiselgasteig* ☎ *089/64990* 🌐 *www.filmstadt.*

de 🎫 *€10, stunt show €8, 4-D cinema €4, combined ticket €19* ⏲ *Early Nov.–Feb., daily 10–3, tours only on the hr; Mar.–early Nov., daily 9–4, tours every 10 min.*

BMW Museum Zeithorizonte. Munich is the home of the famous BMW car firm. Its museum, a circular tower that looks as if it served as a set for *Star Wars,* contains not only a dazzling collection of BMWs old and new but also items and exhibitions relating to the company's social history and its technical developments. It adjoins the **BMW factory** (☎ 089/3895–3308 ⏲ weekdays 10–1) on the eastern edge of the Olympiapark. You can see the factory as well, but only with a tour that begins at the museum's box office. Call ahead of time to reserve a spot. ✉ *Petuelring 130, Milbertshofen* ☎ *089/3822–5652* 🌐 *www.bmwmobiletradition.de* 🎫 *€3* ⏲ *Apr.–Oct., daily 10–10; Nov.–Mar., daily 10–8* Ⓤ *Petuelring (U-bahn).*

Deutsches Museum–"Flugwerft Schleissheim." Connoisseurs of fine airplanes and of the art of flying in general will appreciate this magnificent offshoot of the Deutsches Museum, some 20 km (12 mi) north of the city center off A–9. Old flying machines from the earliest days to a Soviet MiG fighter jet share the space with countless other exhibits that tell the fascinating tale of how humans have taken to the air over the past 100 years. It's an ideal complement to a visit to Schloss Schleissheim. Take S-bahn 1 to Oberschleissheim, and then Bus 292 (which doesn't run on weekends). If you're planning to visit the Deutsches Museum as well, ask for a combination ticket. ✉ *Effnerstr. 7, Oberschleissheim* ☎ *089/315–7140* 🌐 *www.deutsches-museum.de* 🎫 *€3.50, combined ticket with the Deutsches Museum €10* ⏲ *Daily 9–5* Ⓤ *Oberschleissheim (S-bahn) and Bus No. 292.*

Hellabrunn Zoo. There are many parklike enclosures but a minimum of cages at this attractive zoo. Some of the older buildings are in typical art nouveau style. Care has been taken to group animals according to their natural and geographical habitats. One of the latest additions is the **Urwaldhaus** (Rain-Forest house), which offers guided tours at night (call ahead of time). The 170 acres include restaurants and children's areas. Take Bus 52 from Marienplatz or U-bahn 3 to Thalkirchen, at the southern edge of the city. ✉ *Tierparkstr. 30, Harlaching* ☎ *089/625–080* 🌐 *www.zoo-munich.de* 🎫 *€9* ⏲ *Late Mar.–Sept., daily 8–6; Oct.–late Mar., daily 9–5* Ⓤ *Thalkirchen (U-bahn).*

Olympiapark (Olympic Park). On the northern edge of Schwabing, undulating circus-tent-like roofs cover the stadiums built for the 1972 Olympic Games. The roofs are made of translucent tiles that glisten in the sun and act as amplifiers for the rock concerts held here. A €25 fee lets you climb the roofs with rubber-sole shoes in good weather. Tours of the park are conducted on a Disneyland-style train throughout the day. An elevator will speed you up the 960-foot **Olympia Tower** (€4) for a view of the city and the Alps; there's also a revolving restaurant near the top. Take U-bahn 3 to the park. ☎ *089/3067–2414, 089/3066–8585 restaurant* 🌐 *www.olympiapark-muenchen.de* 🎫 *Adventure tour €7, stadium tour €5* ⏲ *Tour schedules vary, call ahead for departure times* Ⓤ *Olympiazentrum (U-bahn).*

★ **Schloss Nymphenburg.** This glorious baroque and rococo palace is the largest of its kind in Germany, stretching more than 1 km (½ mi) from one wing to the other. The palace grew in size and scope over a period of more than 200 years, beginning as a summer residence built on land given by Prince Ferdinand Maria to his beloved wife, Henriette Adelaide, on the occasion of the birth of their son and heir, Max Emanuel, in 1663. The princess hired the Italian architect Agostino Barelli to build both the Theatinerkirche and the palace, which was completed in 1675 by his successor, Enrico Zuccalli. Within the original building, now the central axis of the palace complex, is a magnificent hall, the **Steinerner Saal,** extending over two floors and richly decorated with stucco and grandiose frescoes. In summer, chamber-music concerts are given here. One of the surrounding royal chambers houses the famous **Schönheitsgalerie** (Gallery of Beauties). The walls are hung from floor to ceiling with portraits of women who caught the roving eye of Ludwig I, among them a butcher's daughter and an English duchess. The most famous portrait is of Lola Montez, a sultry beauty and high-class courtesan who, after a time as the mistress of Franz Liszt and later Alexandre Dumas, so enchanted King Ludwig I that he almost bankrupted the state for her sake and was ultimately forced to abdicate.

The palace is in a park laid out in formal French style, with low hedges and gravel walks extending into woodland. Among the ancient tree stands are three fascinating structures. The **Amalienburg** hunting lodge is a rococo gem built by François Cuvilliés, architect of the Altes Residenztheater. The silver-and-blue stucco of the little Amalienburg creates an atmosphere of courtly high life, making clear that the pleasures of the chase did not always take place outdoors. In the lavishly appointed kennels you'll see that even the dogs lived in luxury. The **Pagodenburg** was built for royal tea parties. Its elegant French exterior disguises a suitably Asian interior in which exotic teas from India and China were served. Swimming parties were held in the **Badenburg,** Europe's first post-Roman heated pool.

Nymphenburg contains so much of interest that a day hardly provides enough time. Don't leave without visiting the former royal stables, now the **Marstallmuseum** (Museum of Royal Carriages; 🎫 €2.50). It houses a fleet of vehicles, including an elaborately decorated sleigh in which King Ludwig II once glided through the Bavarian twilight, postilion torches lighting the way. On the walls hang portraits of the royal horses. Also exhibited are examples of Nymphenburg porcelain, produced here between 1747 and the 1920s.

A popular museum in the north wing of the palace has nothing to do with the Wittelsbachs but is one of Nymphenburg's major attractions. The **Museum Mensch und Natur** (Museum of Man and Nature; ☎ 089/179–589120 🎫 €1.50, free Sun. ⏲ Tues.–Sun. 9–5) concentrates on three areas of interest: the variety of life on Earth, the history of humankind, and our place in the environment. Main exhibits include a huge representation of the human brain and a chunk of Alpine crystal weighing half a ton. Take Tram 17 or Bus 41 from the city center to the Schloss Nymphenburg stop. ✉ *Notburgastr. at bridge crossing Nymphenburg*

Canal, Nymphenburg ☎ *089/179–080* 🎟 *Schloss Nymphenburg complex, combined ticket, including Marstall Museum but not Museum Mensch und Natur, €7.50, €6.50 in winter, when parts of complex are closed* ⏲ *Apr.–Oct. 15, daily 9–6; Oct. 16–Mar., daily 10–4; all except Amalienburg and gardens closed Mon.*

Schloss Schleissheim (Schleissheim Palace). In 1597 Duke Wilhelm V decided to look for a peaceful retreat outside Munich and found what he wanted at this palace, then far beyond the city walls but now only a short ride on a train and a bus. The large ballroom where concerts are sometimes held is quite a sight. A later ruler, Prince Max Emanuel, added a second, smaller palace, the **Lustheim.** Separated from Schleissheim by a formal garden and a decorative canal, the Lustheim houses Germany's largest collection of Meissen porcelain. To reach the palace, take the suburban S-bahn 1 line to Oberschleissheim station and then walk about 15 minutes to the palace, or take Bus 292 (which doesn't run on weekends). ✉ *Maximilianshof 1, Oberschleissheim* ☎ *089/315–5272* 🎟 *Combined ticket for palaces and porcelain collection €2.50* ⏲ *Tues.–Sun. 10–5.*

WHERE TO EAT

Munich claims to be Germany's gourmet capital. It certainly has an inordinate number of very fine restaurants, some with chef-owners who honed their skills under such Gallic masters as Paul Bocuse. For connoisseurs, wining and dining at Tantris or the Königshof could well turn into the equivalent of a religious experience; culinary creations are accorded the status of works of art on a par with a Bach fugue or a Dürer painting, with tabs equal to a king's ransom. Epicureans are convinced that one can dine as well in Munich as in any other city on the continent.

Many Munich restaurants serve sophisticated cuisine, and they require their patrons to dress for the occasion. Less expensive restaurants will serve you regardless of what you wear.

WHAT IT COSTS In Euros

	$$$$	$$$	$$	$	¢
AT DINNER	over €25	€21–€25	€16–€20	€9–€15	under €9

Restaurant prices are per person for a main course at dinner.

City Center

$$$$ ✕ **Königshof.** This reliable old hotel restaurant is among Munich's finest and most traditional dining rooms. The outstanding menus created by chef Götz Rothacker are French influenced, the surroundings elegant—and if you book a window table, you'll have a view of Munich's busiest square, the Stachus, an incandescent experience at night. ✉ *Karlspl. 25, City Center* ☎ *089/5513–6142* ✍ *Reservations essential* 👔 *Jacket and tie* 💳 *AE, DC, MC, V* ⏲ *Closed Sun. No lunch in Aug.* Ⓤ *Karlsplatz (U-bahn and S-bahn).*

ALL ABOUT GERMAN BEER

HOWEVER MANY FINGERS *you want to hold up, just remember the easy-to-pronounce* Bier *(beer)* Bit-te *(please) when ordering a beer. The tricky part is, Germans don't just produce one beverage called beer; they brew more than 5,000 varieties. Germany has about 1,300 breweries, 40% of the world's total. The hallmark of the country's dedication to beer is the purity law,* das Reinheitsgebot, *unchanged since Duke Wilhelm IV introduced it in Bavaria in 1516. The law decrees that only malted barley, hops, yeast, and water may be used to make beer, except for specialty Weiss- or Weizenbier (wheat beers, which are a carbonated, somewhat spicy, and sour brew, often with floating yeast particles).*

Most taverns have several drafts in addition to bottled beers. The type available depends upon the region you're in, and in southern Germany the choice can also depend on the time of year. The alcohol content of German beers also varies. At the weaker end of the scale is the light Munich Helles (a lager, from 3.7% to 4.8% alcohol by volume); stronger brews are the bitter-flavored Pilsner (around 5%) and the dark Doppelbock (more than 7%).

Germany's biggest breweries are in the city of Dortmund, which feeds the industrial Ruhr region. Popular northern beers are Export Lagers or the paler, more pungent Pilsners. Köln and Düsseldorf breweries in the Rhine region produce "old-fashioned" beers similar to English ales. But Bavaria is where the majority of breweries—and beer traditions—are found. The Bavarians and the Saarlanders consume more beer per person than any other group in the country.

In Munich you'll find the most famous breweries, the largest beer halls and beer gardens, the biggest and most indulgent beer festival, and the widest selection of brews. Even the beer glasses are bigger: a Mass *is a 1-liter (almost 2-pint) serving; a* Halbe *is half liter and the standard size. The Hofbräuhaus is Munich's most well-known beer hall, but its oompah band's selections are geared more to Americans and Australians than to your average Münchener. You'll find locals in one of the English Garden's four beer gardens or in the local* Wirtshaus *(tavern).*

Not even the widest Bavarians can be held wholly responsible for the staggering consumption of beer and food at the annual Oktoberfest, which starts at the end of September and ends in early October (it is always 3 weekends long, ending on the first weekend in October). On average, around 5 million liters (1,183,000 gallons) of beer, as well as 750,000 roasted chickens and 650,000 sausages, are put away by revelers of many nationalities in the two-week period. To partake, book lodging by April, and if you're traveling with a group, also reserve bench space within one of the 14 tents. See Munich's Web site, www.muenchen-tourist.de, for beer tent contacts. The best time to arrive at the grounds is lunchtime, when it's easier to find a seat—by 4 PM it's packed and they'll just close the doors. The beer tents are actually huge pavilions, heaving and pulsating with thousands of beer-swilling, table-pounding "serious" drinkers, animated by brass bands pounding out their music on boxing-ring-style stages. The grounds close by 11:30 PM. Take advantage of an hour or two of sobriety to tour the fairground rides, which are also an integral part of Oktoberfest. Under no circumstances attempt any of these rides—all of which claim to be the world's most dangerous—after a liter or two of the Oktoberfest beer. The disgrace of throwing up on the figure eight is truly Germanic in scale.

— Robert Tilley

$$$ ✕ **Halali.** The Halali is an old-style Munich restaurant—polished wood paneling and antlers on the walls—which is *the* place to try traditional dishes of venison and other game. Save room for the homemade vanilla ice cream. ✉ *Schönfeldstr. 22, City Center* ☎ *089/285–909* *Jacket and tie* ▭ *AE, MC, V* ⊙ *Closed Sun. No lunch Sat.* Ⓤ *Odeonsplatz (U-bahn and S-bahn).*

$$–$$$ ✕ **Hunsinger's Pacific.** Werner Hunsinger, one of Germany's top restaurateurs, has brought Munich a reasonably priced restaurant serving eclectic cuisine, borrowing from the Pacific Rim of East Asia, Australia, and North and South America. The restaurant's clam chowder is the best in the city, while another praised specialty is the Chilean-style steak fillet, wrapped in a mantle of onion and eggplant-flavor maize. The many "small dishes" will give you a good panoramic taste of the place. At lunch, two-course meals cost around €12. ✉ *Maximiliansplatz 5, City Center* ☎ *089/5502–9741* ▭ *AE, DC, MC, V* ⊙ *No lunch weekends* Ⓤ *Karlsplatz (U-bahn and S-bahn).*

★ **$–$$$** ✕ **Buffet Kull.** This simple yet charming international bistro delivers a high-quality dining experience accompanied by a wonderful variety of wines and friendly service. Dishes range from Bohemian pheasant soup to venison medallions and New York steaks. The daily specials are creative, portions are generous, and the prices are reasonable for the quality. Reservations are recommended, or at least get there early (they start dinner service at 6 PM). ✉ *Marienstr. 4, City Center* ☎ *089/221–509* ▭ *No credit cards* Ⓤ *Marienplatz (U-bahn).*

★ **$–$$$** ✕ **Dukatz.** A literary and business crowd mixes at this smart bar and restaurant in the Literaturhaus, a converted city mansion where regular book readings are presented. Food includes German nouvelle cuisine, but there's a strong Gallic touch with dishes such as calves' head and lamb tripe. Note the verbal art, some of it by New York artist Jennifer Holzer, such as the statement at the bottom of your cup saying: MORE EROTICISM, GENTLEMEN! ✉ *Salvatorpl. 1, City Center* ☎ *089/291–9600* ▭ *No credit cards* Ⓤ *Odeonsplatz (U-bahn).*

$–$$$ ✕ **Hackerhaus.** The cozy, upscale restaurant belonging to the Hacker brewery (founded in the 15th century) has three floors of wood-panel rooms. In summer you can order a cheese plate and beer in the cool, flower-bedecked inner courtyard; in winter you can snuggle in a corner of the Ratsstube and warm up on thick homemade potato broth, followed by schnitzel and *Bratkartoffeln* (pan-fried potatoes), or take a table in the Bürgerstube and admire its proud centerpiece, the world's largest beer mug. ✉ *Sendlingerstr. 14, City Center* ☎ *089/260–5026* ▭ *AE, DC, MC, V* Ⓤ *Sendlinger Tor (U-bahn).*

★ **$–$$$** ✕ **Spatenhaus.** A view of the opera house and the royal palace complements the Bavarian mood of the wood-panel and beamed Spatenhaus. The menu is international, with everything from artichokes to *zuppa Romana* (alcohol-soaked, fruity Italian cake-pudding). But since you're in Bavaria, try the Bavarian plate, an enormous mixture of local meats and sausages. Make reservations if you want to go after a concert or opera. ✉ *Residenzstr. 12, City Center* ☎ *089/290–7060* ▭ *AE, MC, V* Ⓤ *Odeonsplatz (U-bahn).*

$–$$ ✕ **Ganga.** The upholstery is becoming worn at the Ganga, but this, and the friendly service, only contributes to the warm atmosphere. So do

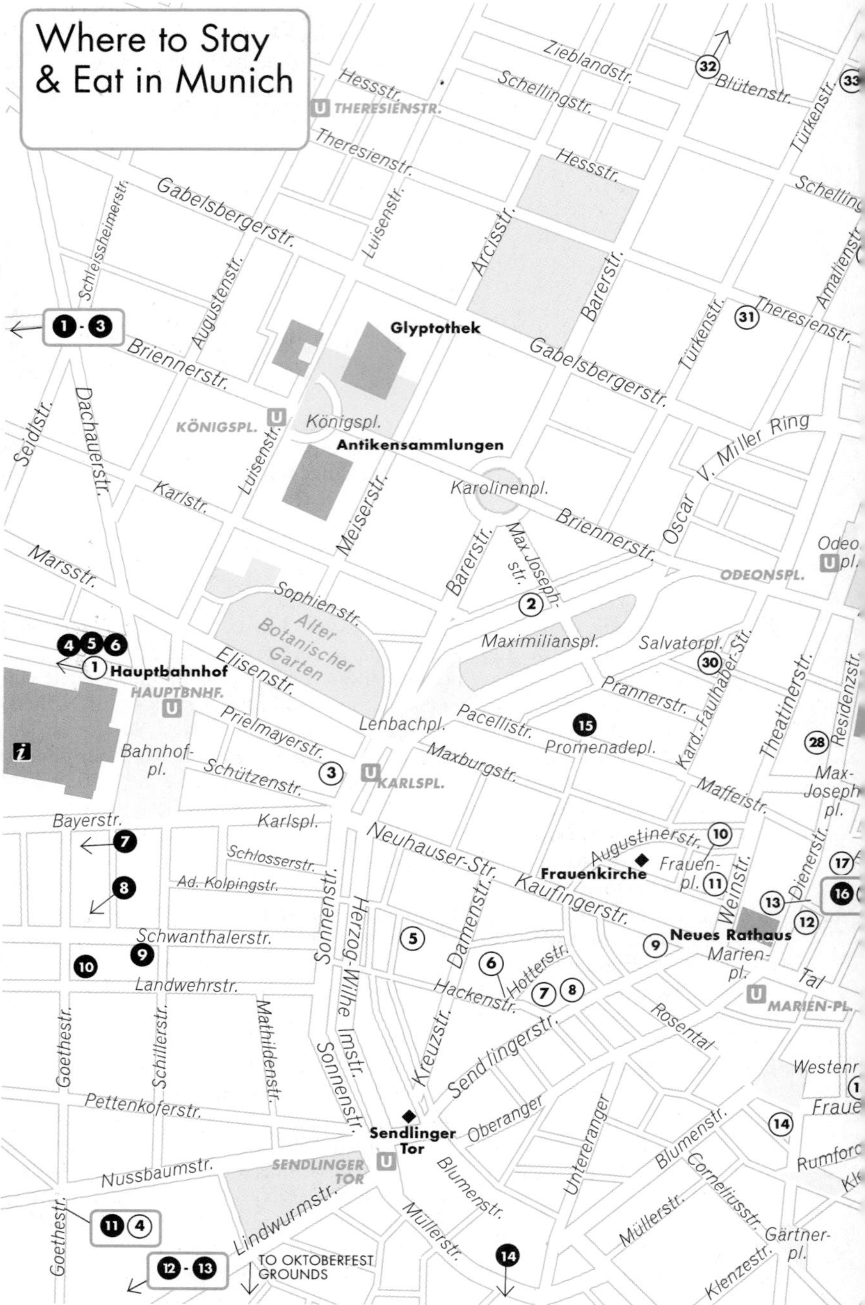
Where to Stay & Eat in Munich
Zieblandstr.
Hessstr.
Schellingstr.
Blütenstr.
Türkenstr.
THERESIENSTR.
Theresienstr.
Gabelsbergerstr.
Schleissheimerstr.
Luisenstr.
Arcisstr.
Barerstr.
Augustenstr.
Glyptothek
Briennerstr.
Königspl.
KÖNIGSPL.
Antikensammlungen
Seidlstr.
Dachauerstr.
Karlstr.
Meiserstr.
Karolinenpl.
Oscar V. Miller Ring
Marsstr.
Sophienstr.
Max-Joseph-str.
ODEONSPL.
Odeonspl.
Alter Botanischer Garten
Maximilianspl.
Salvatorpl.
Hauptbahnhof
HAUPTBNHF.
Elisenstr.
Prannerstr.
Kard.-Faulhaber-Str.
Theatinerstr.
Residenzstr.
Prielmayerstr.
Lenbachpl.
Pacellistr.
Promenadepl.
Bahnhofpl.
Schützenstr.
Maxburgstr.
KARLSPL.
Maffeistr.
Max-Joseph pl.
Bayerstr.
Karlspl.
Neuhauser-Str.
Augustinerstr.
Schlosserstr.
Frauenkirche
Frauenpl.
Ad. Kolpingstr.
Kaufingerstr.
Weinstr.
Dienerstr.
Sonnenstr.
Herzog-Wilhelmstr.
Damenstr.
Neues Rathaus
Schwanthalerstr.
Marienpl.
Hotterstr.
Tal
Landwehrstr.
Hackenstr.
MARIEN-PL.
Rosental
Goethestr.
Schillerstr.
Mathildenstr.
Kreuzstr.
Sendlingerstr.
Westenr
Pettenkoferstr.
Frauen
Oberanger
Unteranger
Sendlinger Tor
SENDLINGER TOR
Blumenstr.
Corneliusstr.
Rumford
Nussbaumstr.
Lindwurmstr.
Müllerstr.
Gärtnerpl.
Klenzestr.
TO OKTOBERFEST GROUNDS

Restaurants

Am Marstall **20**
Andescher am Dom **10**
Augustiner Keller **1**
Bistro Cezanne **32**
Buffet Kull **22**
Buxs, City Center **15**
Buxs, Maxvorstadt **35**
Café am Beethovenplatz **4**
Cohen's **31**
Due passi **18**
Dukatz **30**
Dürnbräu **23**
Gandl **27**
Ganga **25**
Gasthaus Isarthor **26**
Hackerhaus **8**
Halali **36**
Hofbräuhaus **21**
Hofer **12**
Hundskugel **6**
Hunsinger's Pacific **2**
Jodlerwirt **13**
Königshof **3**
Max-Emanuel-Brauerei **33**
Monaco **14**
Nürnberger Bratwurst Glöckl am Dom **11**
Orlandohaus **19**
Pfälzer Weinprobierstube **29**
Prinz Myshkin **7**
Riva Pizzeria **24**
Spatenhaus **28**
Spöckmeier **9**
Tantris **34**
Vinorant Alter Hof **17**
Weinhaus Neuner **5**
Weisses Bräuhaus **16**

Hotels

Admiral **19**
Adria **25**
Advokat **20**
ArabellaSheraton Grand Hotel **26**
Bayerischer Hof **15**
Biederstein **28**
Brack **12**
Cortiina **17**
Creatif Hotel Elephant . . . **5**
Eden-Hotel Wolff **4**
Erzgiesserei Europe **3**
Gästehaus am Englischen Garten **27**
Hotel Amba **6**
Hotel Concorde **22**
Hotel Mirabell **10**
Hotel Pension Am Siegestor **29**
Hotel-Pension Beck **21**
Hotel-Pension Mariandl **11**
Hotel-Pension Schmellergarten **13**
Jagdschloss **7**
Kempinski Hotel Vier Jahreszeiten München **23**
Kriemhild **1**
Kurpfalz **9**
Olympic **14**
Opera **24**
Park-Hotel Theresienhöhe **8**
Platzl **16**
Rotkreuzplatz **2**
Torbräu **18**

the curry and tandoori dishes, which are among the best in Munich, and the price is right. Remember that what is mild for an Indian may send you through the roof! ✉ *Baaderstr. 11* ☎ *089/201–6465* ▭ *AE, MC, V* ⊗ *No lunch weekends* Ⓤ *Isartor (U-bahn).*

★ $–$$ ✕ **Hundskugel.** This is Munich's oldest tavern and also one of the city's smallest. You'll be asked to squeeze together and make room for latecomers looking for a spot at one of the few tables that clutter the handkerchief-size dining room. The tavern dates from 1440 and in many ways doesn't appear to have changed much over the centuries. Even the menu is medievally basic and a bit hit-and-miss, although any combination of pork and potatoes or sauerkraut can be recommended. ✉ *Hotterstr. 18, City Center* ☎ *089/264–272* ▭ *No credit cards* Ⓤ *Sendlinger Tor (U-bahn).*

$–$$ ✕ **Monaco.** One of the nicest additions to the Italian scene, the Monaco makes its guests feel at home right away, ensuring returning customers. The decor is simple and unpretentious. Excellent wines on the menu are backed by a serendipitous selection; ask your waiter for recommendations. ✉ *Reichenbachstr. 10, City Center* ☎ *089/268–141* ▭ *MC, V* Ⓤ *Sendlinger Tor (U-bahn).*

$–$$ ✕ **Nürnberger Bratwurst Glöckl am Dom.** Munich's most original beer tavern is dedicated to the delicious *Nürnberger Bratwürste* (finger-size sausages), a specialty from the rival city of Nürnberg. They're served by a busy team of friendly waitresses dressed in Bavarian dirndls, who flit between the crowded tables with remarkable agility. In summer, tables are placed outside under a bright awning and in the shade of the nearby Frauenkirche. In winter the mellow dark-panel dining rooms provide relief from the cold. ✉ *Frauenpl. 9, City Center* ☎ *089/220–385* ▭ *DC, MC, V* Ⓤ *Marienplatz (U-bahn and S-bahn).*

$–$$ ✕ **Spöckmeier.** This rambling Bavarian beer restaurant spread over three floors, including a snug *Keller* (cellar), is famous for its homemade Weisswurst. If you've just stopped in for a snack and don't fancy the boiled breakfast sausage, order coffee and pretzels or, in the afternoon, a wedge of cheesecake. The menu changes daily and offers more than two dozen hearty main-course dishes and a choice of four draft beers. The house *Eintopf* (a rich broth of noodles and pork) is a meal in itself. The Spöckmeier is 50 yards from Marienplatz; on sunny summer days tables are set outside in the car-free street. ✉ *Rosenstr. 9, City Center* ☎ *089/268–088* ▭ *AE, DC, MC, V* Ⓤ *Marienplatz (U-bahn and S-bahn).*

$–$$ ✕ **Weinhaus Neuner.** Munich's oldest wine tavern serves good food as well as superior wines in its three nooks: the wood-panel restaurant, the Weinstübe, and the small bistro. The choice of food is remarkable, from nouvelle German to old-fashioned country. Specialties include home-smoked beef and salmon. ✉ *Herzogspitalstr. 8, City Center* ☎ *089/260–3954* ▭ *AE, MC, V* ⊗ *Closed Sun.* Ⓤ *Marienplatz (U-bahn and S-bahn).*

¢–$$ ✕ **Andechser am Dom.** The vaulted frescoed ceiling and the old stone floor recall the Andechs monastery. The boldly Bavarian food—blood sausage with potatoes, Weisswurst in champagne—and fine selection of Andechs beers will quickly put you at ease. The covered terrace with a view of the Frauenkirche is a favorite meeting place, rain or shine, for shoppers, local businesspeople, and even the occasional VIP. ✉ *Weinstr. 7a* ☎ *089/298–481* ▭ *AE, MC, V* Ⓤ *Marienplatz (U-bahn and S-bahn).*

¢–$$ ✕ **Buxs.** This self-service vegetarian place has a full range of salads, excellent entrées, freshly pressed juices and smoothies, and desserts that are worth the caloric splurge. On warm days you can sit outside and watch the Viktualienmarkt activities. It closes daily at 8 PM. ✉ *Frauenstr. 9, City Center* ☎ *089/291–9195* ▭ *No credit cards* ⊙ *Closed Sun. No dinner Sat.* Ⓤ *Marienplatz (U-bahn and S-bahn).*

¢–$$ ✕ **Dürnbräu.** A fountain plays outside this picturesque old Bavarian inn. Inside, it's crowded and noisy, and you should expect to share a table (the 21-foot table in the middle of the place is a favorite). Your fellow diners will range from businesspeople to students. The food is resolutely traditional—try the cream of spinach soup and the boiled beef. ✉ *Dürnbräug. 2, City Center* ☎ *089/222–195* ▭ *AE, DC, MC, V* Ⓤ *Isartor (S-bahn).*

¢–$$ ✕ **Jodlerwirt.** This cozy little restaurant is a splendid treat for those craving an old-world tavern feel combined with a bit of live entertainment. As its name suggests, yodlers perform nightly, telling jokes and poking fun at their adoring guests in unintelligible Bavarian slang. The food is traditional, including Käsespatzle (a hearty German version of macaroni and cheese), goulasch soup, and meal-size salads. The tasty beer is from the Ayinger brewery. The place is small and fills up fast. ✉ *Altenhof 4 City Center* ☎ *089/221–249* ▭ *No credit cards* ⊙ *Closed Sun. No lunch* Ⓤ *Marienplatz (U-bahn and S-bahn).*

¢–$$ ✕ **Riva Pizzeria.** This stylish but casual Italian joint serves brick-oven pizzas, a variety of pastas, and the city's best beer, Augustiner. Its chic status is reflected in slightly higher prices, the food is quite tasty, and the lively staff make it an enjoyable experience. Get there early as it fills up fast after 7 PM. ✉ *Tal 44 City Center* ☎ *089/220–240* ▭ *No credit cards* Ⓤ *Marienplatz (U-bahn and S-bahn).*

$ ✕ **Vinorant Alter Hof.** If you don't make it to Franconia, then you can at least get a taste of the region's food and wine in this simply decorated restaurant nestled in the old vaulted cellar and first floor of Munich's castle. The wine bar in the cellar serves hearty Franconian snacks along with Franconian wines, which can be ordered in small amounts, allowing you to let your taste buds travel among Franconia's vineyards. It's the perfect place to recover after a concert at the nearby national theater or the Residenz. ✉ *Alter Hof 3, City Center* ☎ *089/2424–3733* ⊙ *Closed Sun.* ▭ *AE, DC, V* Ⓤ *Marienplatz (U-bahn and S-bahn).*

¢–$ ✕ **Due passi.** This former dairy shop, now an Italian specialty shop, offers excellent Italian meals for a quick, stand-up lunch. There's a small but fine selection of fresh antipasti, pasta, and desserts such as the white chocolate mousse. You can eat at the high marble tables and counters, or take your food to go. Menus change daily. ✉ *Ledererstr. 11* ☎ *089/224–271* ▭ *No credit cards* ⊙ *Closed Sat. afternoon and Sun.* Ⓤ *Isartor (S-bahn).*

¢–$ ✕ **Hofbräuhaus.** The pounding oompah band draws the curious into this father of all beer halls, where singing and shouting drinkers contribute to the earsplitting din. This is no place for the fainthearted, although a trip to Munich would be incomplete without a look. Upstairs is a quieter restaurant. In March, May, and September ask for one of the special, extra-strong seasonal beers (Starkbier, Maibock, Märzen), which complement the heavy, traditional Bavarian fare. ✉ *Am Platzl 9, City Center* ☎ *089/221–676 or 089/290–1360* ✍ *Reservations not accepted* ▭ *V* Ⓤ *Isartor (S-bahn).*

¢–$$ ✕ **Hofer.** In the old scribe's house (Schreiberhaus), oak-plank floors and a red color scheme recall old Munich without the heaviness. The cuisine is influenced by Austrian home cooking with such dishes as fried potatoes with spinach and fried eggs, dumpling specialties, *Schweinsbraten* (roast pork), or irresistible apricot dumplings for dessert. A small selection of so-called retrofood is also available: restoration sandwich, for example, is typical 1960s Germany with thick buttered bread, cheese, roast pork, and smoked bacon. The inner courtyard is perfect for a meal on a hot summer day, and the vaulted cellar hosts live music on Friday and Saturday evenings. ✉ *Burgstr. 5, City Center* ☎ *089/2421–0445* ▭ *AE, DC, MC* Ⓤ *Marienplatz (U-bahn and S-bahn).*

¢–$ ✕ **Orlandohaus.** The Orlandohaus is located next to the famous Hofbräuhaus on the bustling Platzl square. This large, airy establishment with richly gilded walls, vaulted ceilings, and a cozy beer cellar in the evening was named after composer Orlando di Lasso (1532–94), who once lived here. The specialty of the house is all-you-can-eat buffets, offering a large number of dishes, usually with a theme: Bavarian, international, brunch, and so on. Prices are moderate: lunch €13, afternoon coffee and cakes €3.10, Sunday brunch €15.95. ✉ *Platzl 4, City Center* ☎ *089/2423–8030* ▭ *AE, MC, V* Ⓤ *Isartor (S-bahn).*

¢–$ ✕ **Pfälzer Weinprobierstube.** A maze of stone-vaulted rooms, wooden tables, flickering candles, dirndl-clad waitresses, and a long list of wines add up to a storybook image of a timeless Germany. The wines are mostly from the *Pfalz* (Palatinate), as are many of the specialties on the limited menu. You'll find former chancellor Kohl's favorite dish, *Saumagen* (meat loaf, spiced with herbs and cooked in a pig's stomach). Beer drinkers, take note—beer is not served here. ✉ *Residenzstr. 1, City Center* ☎ *089/225–628* ✍ *Reservations not accepted* ▭ *No credit cards* Ⓤ *Odeonsplatz (U-bahn).*

¢–$ ✕ **Prinz Myshkin.** This sophisticated vegetarian restaurant spices up predictable cuisine by mixing Italian and Asian influences. You have a choice of antipasti, homemade gnocchi, tofu, stir-fried dishes, and excellent wines. If you're not very hungry, you can request half portions. The airy room has a majestically vaulted ceiling, and there's always some art exhibited to feed the eye and mind. ✉ *Hackenstr. 2, City Center* ☎ *089/265–596* ▭ *MC, V* Ⓤ *Sendlinger Tor (U-bahn).*

Fodor's Choice ★

¢–$ ✕ **Weisses Bräuhaus.** If you have developed a taste for Munich's Weissbier, this is the place to enjoy it. The flavorful Weisse (from the Schneider brewery) is served with hearty Bavarian dishes, mostly variations of pork and dumplings or cabbage. Some of Munich's friendlier waitresses work here—good-humored women in crisp black dresses, who appear to match the art-nouveau style of the restaurant's beautifully restored interior. ✉ *Tal 7, City Center* ☎ *089/299–875* ▭ *No credit cards* Ⓤ *Isartor (S-bahn).*

ON THE MENU

Snacks

It seems that Munich loves to snack, and a tempting array of food is available almost anytime, save in the wee hours when absolutely nothing is open in the city center. The generic term for snacks is Imbiss, *and thanks to growing internationalism you'll find all types of them, from the generic* Wiener *(hot dogs) to the Turkish* Döner Kebap *sandwich (pressed and roasted lamb, beef, or chicken). Almost all butcher shops and bakeries offer some sort of* Brotzeit *snack, which can range from a modest sandwich to a steaming plate of goulash with potatoes and salad.*

Some edibles come with social etiquette attached. The Weisswurst, *a tender minced-veal sausage—made fresh daily, steamed, and served with sweet mustard and a crisp roll or a pretzel—is a Munich institution and is served before noon with a* Weissbier *(wheat beer), supposedly to counteract the effects of a hangover. Legend has it that this white sausage was invented in 1857 by a butcher who had a hangover and mixed the wrong ingredients. A plaque on a wall on Marienplatz marks where the "mistake" was made. Some people use a knife and fork to remove the edible part from the skin; the rougher crowd might indulge in* auszuzeln, *sucking the sausage out of the Weisswurst.*

Another favorite Bavarian specialty is Leberkäs*—literally "liver cheese"—although neither liver nor cheese is among its ingredients. It's a sort of meat loaf baked to a crusty turn each morning and served in succulent slabs throughout the day. A* Leberkäs Semmel*—a wedge of the meat loaf between two halves of a crispy bread roll slathered with a slightly spicy mustard—is the favorite Munich on-the-go snack.*

Good Home Cooking

Old Munich inns feature solid regional specialties and gutbürgerliche Küche, *loosely translated as good home cooking. The settings for such victuals include boisterous brewery restaurants, beer halls, beer gardens, rustic cellars, and* Kneipen, *restaurant-pubs serving any manner of food depending on the owner's fancy. The crowd here is generally a mix of students, white-collar workers, and chic artist-types.*

A Real Meal

Typical, more substantial dishes in Munich include Tellerfleisch, *boiled beef with freshly grated horseradish and boiled potatoes on the side, served on wooden plates (there is a similar dish called* Tafelspitz*). Among roasts, sauerbraten (beef) and* Schweinebraten *(roast pork) are accompanied by dumplings and sauerkraut.* Hax'n *(ham hocks) are roasted until they're crisp on the outside and juicy on the inside. They are served with sauerkraut and potato puree. Game in season (venison or boar, for instance) and duck are served with potato dumplings and red cabbage. As for fish, the region has not only excellent trout, served either smoked as an hors d'oeuvre or fried or boiled as an entrée, but also the perch-like* Rencke *from Lake Starnberg.*

You'll also find soups, salads, casseroles, hearty stews, and what may well be the greatest variety and the highest quality of baked goods in Europe, including pretzels. And for dessert, indulge in a bowl of Bavarian cream, apple strudel, or Dampfnudel, *a fluffy leavened-dough dumpling usually served with vanilla sauce.*

Maxvorstadt

¢–$$ ✕ **Buxs.** A smaller version of the Buxs on Vitualienmarkt, this branch offers self-service of the same fare: salads, warm dishes, and excellent cakes. It's a good place to watch Munich's chic student crowd while taking a break from the nearby art museums. ✉ *Amalienstr. 38, Maxvorstadt* ☎ *089/2802–9940* ▭ *No credit cards* ⏲ *Closed Sat. afternoon and Sun.* Ⓤ *Theresienstrasse (U-bahn).*

$ ✕ **Cohen's.** Reviving the old Jewish Central European tradition of good, healthy cooking together with hospitality and good cheer seems to be the underlying principle at Cohen's. Dig into a few hearty latkes, a steaming plate of Chulend stew, or a standard gefilte fish doused with excellent Golan wine from Israel. The kitchen is open from 12:30 PM to about 10:30 PM, and if the atmosphere is good, patrons may hang out chattering until the wee hours. Klezmer singers perform on Friday evenings. ✉ *Theresienstr. 31, Maxvorstadt* ☎ *089/280–9545* ▭ *AE, MC, V* Ⓤ *Theresienstrasse (U-bahn).*

Lehel

$–$$ ✕ **Gandl.** This Italian specialty shop, where you can buy various staples from vinegar to coffee, doubles as a very comfortable, relaxed restaurant during the day. Seating is a little crowded inside, but chairs and tables have a homelike feel and the service is excellent. It's just the place for a quick pastry or excellent antipasto misto before proceeding with the day's adventures. ✉ *St.-Anna-Pl. 1, Lehel* ☎ *089/2916–2525* ▭ *V* ⏲ *Closed Sun. No dinner.* Ⓤ *Lehel (U-bahn).*

¢–$ ✕ **Gasthaus Isarthor.** The old-fashioned *Wirtshaus,* where the innkeeper keeps his patrons in sight and the mood going, lives on in this old, wedge-shape dining room. For Rainer Menne, who comes from Salzburg, Austria, having a social mix at his simple wooden tables is the secret of a good establishment—actors, government officials, apprentice craftspersons, journalists, and retirees sit side by side. Besides pork roasts, roast beef with onions, boiled beef, and the like, the house specialty is the Augustiner beer from a wooden barrel, tapped once a day around 6 PM. When the barrel is empty, that's it for the day. ✉ *Kanalstr. 2, Lehel* ☎ *089/227–753* ▭ *No credit cards* Ⓤ *Isartor (S-bahn).*

Schwabing

★ $$$$ ✕ **Tantris.** Chef Hans Haas, named the country's best chef by Germany's premier food critics in the past, has kept this restaurant among the top-five dining establishments in Munich. You, too, will be impressed by the exotic nouvelle cuisine on the menu, including such specialties as shellfish and creamed-potato soup, or roasted wood pigeon with scented rice. But you may wish to ignore the bare concrete surroundings and the garish orange-and-yellow decor. ✉ *Johann-Fichte-Str. 7, Schwabing* ☎ *089/361–9590* ✍ *Reservations essential* 👔 *Jacket and tie* ▭ *AE, DC, MC, V* ⏲ *Closed Sun.* Ⓤ *Münchener Freiheit (U-bahn).*

$$ ✕ **Bistro Cezanne.** You're in for French-Provençal dining at this truly Gallic bistro-restaurant in the heart of Munich's former bohemian quarter.

Owner-chef Patrick Geay learned his craft from some of Europe's best teachers. His regularly changing blackboard menu offers the freshest market products, with vegetables prepared as only the French can do. Among the fish dishes, the scallops melt in the mouth, while the coq au vin will conquer the greatest hungers. Reservations are advised. ✉ *Konradstr. 1, Schwabing* ☎ *089/391–805* ▭ *No credit cards* Ⓤ *Giselastrasse (U-bahn).*

¢–$ ✕ **Max-Emanuel-Brauerei.** This historic old brewery tavern is a great value, with Bavarian dishes rarely costing more than €10; at lunchtime that amount will easily cover the cost of an all-you-can-eat buffet including a couple of beers. The main dining room has a stage, and there's often a cabaret or jazz concert during dinner. In summer take a table outside in the secluded little beer garden tucked amid the apartment blocks. ✉ *Adalbertstr. 33, Schwabing* ☎ *089/271–5158* ▭ *AE, MC* Ⓤ *Josephsplatz (U-bahn).*

Leopoldvorstadt

¢–$ ✕ **Augustiner Keller.** This 19th-century establishment is the flagship beer restaurant of one of Munich's oldest breweries. The menu changes daily and offers Bavarian specialties, but try to order *Tellerfleisch* (boiled beef with horseradish), served on a big wooden board. Follow that with a *Dampfnudel* (yeast dumpling served with custard), and you probably won't feel hungry again for the next 24 hours. ✉ *Arnulfstr. 52, Leopoldvorstadt* ☎ *089/594–393* ▭ *AE, MC* Ⓤ *Hauptbahnhof (U-bahn and S-bahn).*

¢–$ ✕ **Café am Beethovenplatz.** Live music accompanies excellent fare every evening. An international breakfast menu is served daily (on Sunday with live classical music), followed by suitably creative lunch and dinner menus. The pork is supplied by a farm where the free-range pigs are fed only the best natural fodder—so the *Schweinsbraten* (roast pig) is recommended. Reservations are advised as a young and intellectual crowd fills the tables quickly. ✉ *Goethestr. 51 (at Beethovenpl.), Leopoldvorstadt* ☎ *089/5440–4348* ▭ *AE, MC, V* Ⓤ *Goetheplatz (U-bahn).*

WHERE TO STAY

Though Munich has a vast number of hotels in all price ranges, many are fully booked year-round; this is a major trade and convention city as well as a prime tourist destination. If you're visiting during any of the major trade fairs such as the ispo (sports, fashion) in February, the IHM (crafts) in mid-March, or Oktoberfest at the end of September, make reservations at least six months in advance.

Some of the large, very expensive hotels that cater to expense-account business travelers have very attractive weekend discount rates—sometimes as much as 50% below normal prices. Conversely, regular rates can go up during big trade fairs.

Munich's two tourist information offices—at the main railway station and in the city center (Marienplatz, in the Rathaus)—make hotel bookings. Telephone lines are often busy, so your best bet is to visit one of the offices in person.

WHAT IT COSTS In Euros					
	$$$$	$$$	$$	$	¢
FOR 2 PEOPLE	over €225	€175–€225	€100–€175	€50–€100	under €50

Hotel prices are for two people in a standard double room, including tax and service.

City Center

$$$$ **Bayerischer Hof.** Germany's most respected family-owned hotel, the Bayerischer Hof began its rich history by hosting Ludwig I's guests. To this day, it still plays host to VIPs and international political confabs. Public rooms are grandly laid out with marble, antiques, and oil paintings. Laura Ashley–decorated rooms look out to the city's skyline of towers. Nightlife is built into the hotel, with Trader Vic's bar, and dancing at the Night Club. ✉ *Promenadepl. 2–6, City Center, D–80333* ☎ *089/21200* 🖷 *089/212–0906* 🌐 *www.bayerischerhof.de* *395 rooms, 58 suites* *3 restaurants, cable TV with movies and video games, in-room broadband, data ports, Wi-Fi, Internet room, pool, spa, hair salon, massage, sauna, bar, nightclub, meeting rooms, parking (fee), some pets allowed (fee), no-smoking rooms* *AE, DC, MC, V* *BP* *Karlsplatz (U-bahn and S-bahn).*

★ **$$$$** **Kempinski Hotel Vier Jahreszeiten München.** The Kempinski has been playing host to the world's wealthy and titled for more than a century. It has an unbeatable location on Maximilianstrasse, Munich's premier shopping street, only a few minutes' walk from the heart of the city. Elegance and luxury set the tone throughout; many rooms have handsome antique pieces. The Vier Jahreszeiten Eck restaurant is on the main floor. The afternoon tea in the poshly decorated foyer is a special treat. ✉ *Maximilianstr. 17, City Center, D–80539* ☎ *089/21250, 516/794–2670 Kempinski Reservation Service* 🖷 *089/2125–2000* 🌐 *www.Kempinski-Vierjahreszeiten.de* *268 rooms, 48 suites* *Restaurant, cable TV with movies, in-room broadband, data ports, Wi-Fi, Internet room, pool, health club, massage, sauna, piano bar, meeting rooms, car rental, parking (fee), some pets allowed (fee), no-smoking rooms* *AE, DC, MC, V* *BP* *Odeonsplatz (U-bahn).*

$$–$$$$ **Platzl.** The Platzl, a privately owned enterprise, has won awards and wide recognition for its ecologically aware management, which uses heat recyclers in the kitchen, environmentally friendly detergents, recyclable materials, waste separation, and other ecofriendly practices. It stands in the historic heart of Munich, near the famous Hofbräuhaus beer hall and a couple of minutes' walk from Marienplatz and many other landmarks. Its Pfistermühle restaurant, with 16th-century vaulting, is one of the area's oldest and most historic establishments. ✉ *Sparkassenstr. 10, City Center, D–80331* ☎ *089/237–030, 800/448–8355 in U.S.* 🖷 *089/2370–3800* 🌐 *www.platzl.de* *167 rooms* *Restaurant, cable TV with movies, in-room broadband, in-room data ports, Wi-Fi,* *gym, sauna, steam room, bar, parking (fee), some pets allowed (fee), no-smoking rooms; no a/c in some rooms* ▭ *AE, DC, MC, V* 🍴 *BP* Ⓤ *Marienplatz (U-bahn and S-bahn).*

$$–$$$$ **Torbräu.** In this snug hotel you'll sleep under the shadow of one of Munich's ancient city gates—the 14th-century Isartor. The location is excellent, as it's midway between the Marienplatz and the Deutsches Museum (and around the corner from the Hofbräuhaus). The hotel has been run by the same family for more than a century. Comfortable rooms are decorated in a plush and ornate Italian style. Its Italian restaurant, La Famiglia, is one of the best in the area. ✉ *Tal 41, City Center, D–80331* ☎ *089/242–340* 📠 *089/2423–4235* 🌐 *www.torbraeu.de* *89 rooms, 3 suites* *Restaurant, café, cable TV, in-room broadband, in-room data ports, Wi-Fi, Internet room, business services, meeting rooms, some pets allowed (fee), no-smoking rooms* ▭ *AE, MC, V* 🍴 *BP* Ⓤ *Isartor (S-bahn).*

$$$ **Cortiina.** Munich's latest designer hotel, built and run by Rudi Krull, Munich's top design guru, and Albert Weinzierl, follows the minimalist gospel. The reception is in sleek gray stone, with indirect green-tinted lighting. Along one wall a high-tech gas fireplace can be switched on and off like a TV. For guests, the emphasis is on subtle luxury—fresh flowers, mattresses made from natural rubber, sheets made of untreated cotton. The rooms are paneled in dark moor oak and come with all the amenities. The hotel has no fitness center, but the Elixir, 15 minutes on foot to Lenbachplatz, gives special discounts for hotel guests. ✉ *Ledererstr. 8, City Center, D–80331* ☎ *089/242–2490* 📠 *089/2422–49100* 🌐 *www.cortiina.com* *54 rooms* *Cable TV, in-room broadband, in-room data ports, Wi-Fi, bar, parking (fee), some pets allowed (fee), no-smoking rooms* ▭ *AE, DC, MC, V* 🍴 *BP* Ⓤ *Isartor (S-bahn).*

Isarvorstadt

$$$–$$$$ Fodor's Choice ★ **Admiral.** The small, privately owned Admiral enjoys a quiet side-street location and its own garden, close to the Isar River and Deutsches Museum. Many of the simply furnished and warmly decorated bedrooms have a balcony overlooking the garden. Bowls of fresh fruit are part of the friendly welcome awaiting guests. The breakfast buffet is a dream, complete with homemade jams, fresh bread, and Italian and French delicacies. ✉ *Kohlstr. 9, Isarvorstadt, D–80469* ☎ *089/216–350* 📠 *089/293–674* 🌐 *www.hotel-admiral.de* *33 rooms* *Cable TV, in-room broadband, Wi-Fi, bar, Internet room, parking (fee), some pets allowed, no-smoking rooms; no a/c* ▭ *AE, DC, MC, V* 🍴 *BP* Ⓤ *Isartor (S-bahn).*

$$–$$$$ **Advokat.** If you value the clean lines of modern taste over plush luxury, this is the hotel for you. It's within a residential neighborhood that's an easy walk from the Marienplatz and a shorter one from the subway. Between outings you can snack on the fruit plate that welcomes you upon arrival. ✉ *Baaderstr. 1, Isarvorstadt, D–80469* ☎ *089/216–310* 📠 *089/216–3190* 🌐 *www.hotel-advokat.de* *50 rooms* *Cable TV, in-room broadband, Wi-Fi, Internet room, parking (fee), some pets*

allowed, no-smoking rooms; no a/c ☰ *AE, DC, MC, V* 🍽 *BP* Ⓤ *Isartor (S-bahn).*

$$ **Olympic.** The English-style lobby, with its leather easy chairs and mahogany fittings, is an attractive introduction to this friendly small hotel, a beautifully converted turn-of-the-20th-century mansion, amid the bars and boutiques of the colorful district between Sendlinger Tor and Isartor. Most of the rooms look out over a quiet interior courtyard. Do not expect constant and fawning care: the style of the hotel is casual; the idea is to make the guest feel really at home. ✉ *Hans-Sachs-Str. 4, Isarvorstadt, D–80469* ☎ *089/231–890* 📠 *089/2318–9199* 🌐 *www.olympic.de* *38 rooms, 3 apartments* *Cable TV, in-room broadband, Internet room, parking (fee), some pets allowed (fee); no a/c* ☰ *AE, DC, MC, V* 🍽 *BP* Ⓤ *Sendlinger Tor (U-bahn).*

Maxvorstadt

$$–$$$ **Erzgiesserei Europe.** Though this hotel is in a residential section of the city, the nearby subway whisks you in five minutes to Karlsplatz, convenient to the pedestrian shopping area and the main railway station. Rooms in this attractive, modern hotel are particularly bright, decorated in soft pastels with good reproductions on the walls. The cobblestone garden café is a haven of peace. ✉ *Erzgiessereistr. 15, Maxvorstadt, D–80335* ☎ *089/126–820* 📠 *089/123–6198* 🌐 *www.topinternational.com* *105 rooms, 1 suite* *Restaurant, café, cable TV with movies, in-room data ports, Wi-Fi, bar, parking (fee), some pets allowed (fee), no-smoking rooms; no a/c* ☰ *AE, DC, MC, V* 🍽 *BP* Ⓤ *Stiglmaierplatz (U-bahn).*

$$–$$$ **Hotel Amba.** The Amba, which is right next to the train station, has clean, bright rooms, good service, no expensive frills, and everything you need to plug and play. The lobby, with a small bar, invites you to relax in a Mediterranean atmosphere of wicker sofas with bright-color upholstery. No sooner have you enjoyed a solid breakfast at the buffet (with sparkling wine) on the first floor overlooking the station than you'll be out on the town visiting the nearby sights on foot. Budget travelers should ask for rooms without bathrooms. ✉ *Arnulfstr. 20, Maxvorstadt, D–80335* ☎ *089/545–140* 📠 *089/5451–1555* 🌐 *www.hotel-amba.de* *86 rooms* *Cable TV with movies, Wi-Fi, Internet room, some pets allowed (fee), no-smoking rooms; no a/c* ☰ *AE, DC, MC, V* 🍽 *BP* Ⓤ *Hauptbahnhof (U-bahn and S-bahn).*

★ **$** **Hotel Pension Am Siegestor.** This modest but very appealing pension is a great deal in a fairly expensive city. It takes up three floors of a fin-de-siècle mansion between the Siegestor monument, on Leopoldstrasse, and the university. An ancient elevator with a glass door brings you to the fourth-floor reception desk. Most of the simply furnished rooms face the impressive Arts Academy across the street. Rooms on the fifth floor are particularly cozy, tucked up under the eaves. ✉ *Akademiestr. 5, Maxvorstadt, D–80799* ☎ *089/399–550 or 089/399–551* 📠 *089/343–050* 🌐 *www.siegestor.com* *20 rooms* *No a/c, no room phones, no TV in some rooms* ☰ *No credit cards* 🍽 *CP* Ⓤ *Universität (U-bahn).*

Schwabing

$$–$$$ **Biederstein.** This hotel is not the prettiest from the outside—a modern, uninspired block—but it seems to want to fit into its old Schwabing surroundings. At the rim of the Englischer Garten, the Biederstein has many advantages: peace and quiet; excellent service; and comfortable, well-appointed rooms that were carefully renovated. Guests are requested to smoke on the balconies, not inside. *Keferstr. 18, Schwabing, D–80335* *089/389–9970* *089/3899–97389* *34 rooms, 7 suites* *Cable TV, bar, free parking, some pets allowed (fee); no a/c* *AE, DC, MC, V* *BP* *Münchner Freiheit (U-bahn).*

★ **$–$$** **Gästehaus am Englischen Garten.** Reserve well in advance for a room at this popular converted water mill, more than 200 years old, adjoining the Englischer Garten. The hotel is only a five-minute walk from the bars, shops, and restaurants of Schwabing. Be sure to ask for one of the 12 nostalgically old-fashioned rooms in the main building, which has a garden on an island in the old millrace; a modern annex down the road has 13 apartments, all with cooking facilities. In summer, breakfast is served on the terrace of the main house. *Liebergesellstr. 8, Schwabing, D–80802* *089/383–9410* *089/3839–4133* *www.hotelenglischergarten.de* *12 rooms, 6 with bath or shower; 13 apartments* *Cable TV, in-room data ports, free parking, some pets allowed (fee); no a/c* *AE, DC, MC, V* *BP* *Münchner Freiheit (U-bahn).*

Leopoldvorstadt

$$–$$$$ **Creatif Hotel Elephant.** Tucked away on a quiet street near the train station and a 10-minute walk to the city center, this hotel appeals to a wide range of travelers, from businesspeople on the fly to tourists on a budget. The rooms are simple, clean, and quiet. A bright color scheme in the reception and breakfast room creates a cheery atmosphere. Note that prices skyrocket during Octoberfest. *Lämmerstr. 6, Leopoldvorstadt, D–80335* *089/555–785* *089/550–1746* *40 rooms* *Cable TV, in-room data ports, some pets allowed; no a/c* *AE, MC, V* *BP* *Hauptbahnhof (U-bahn and S-bahn).*

$$–$$$$ **Eden-Hotel Wolff.** Chandeliers and dark-wood paneling in the public rooms contribute to the old-fashioned elegance of this downtown favorite. It's directly across the street from the train station and near the Theresienwiese fairgrounds. The rooms are well furnished with large comfortable beds, and the colors are relaxing pastels. You can dine on excellent Bavarian specialties in the intimate wood-panel Zirbelstube restaurant. *Arnulfstr. 4, Leopoldvorstadt, D–80335* *089/551–150* *089/5511–5555* *www.ehw.de* *209 rooms, 7 suites* *Restaurant, café, cable TV with movies, Wi-Fi, in-room broadband, in-room data ports, gym, bar, meeting rooms, parking (fee), some pets allowed (fee); no a/c in some rooms* *AE, DC, MC, V* *BP* *Hauptbahnhof (U-bahn and S-bahn).*

$–$$$ **Brack.** Oktoberfest revelers value the Brack's proximity to the beer-festival grounds, and its location—on a busy, tree-lined thoroughfare just south of the city center—is handy for city attractions. Rooms are furnished in light, friendly veneers and are soundproof (a useful feature during Oktoberfest) and have amenities such as hair dryers. The buffet breakfast will set you up for the day. ✉ *Lindwurmstr. 153, Leopoldvorstadt, D–80337* ☎ *089/747–2550* 🖷 *089/7472–5599* 🌐 *www.hotel-brack.de* *50 rooms* *Cable TV with movies, in-room data ports, in-room broadband, Wi-Fi, free parking, some pets allowed; no a/c* 💳 *AE, DC, MC, V* 🍴 *BP* Ⓤ *Poccistrasse (U-bahn).*

★ $–$$ **Hotel Mirabell.** This family-run hotel is used to American tourists who appreciate the friendly service, central location (between the main railway station and the Oktoberfest fairgrounds), and reasonable room rates. Three apartments are for small groups or families. Rooms are furnished in modern light woods and bright prints. Breakfast is the only meal served, but snacks can be ordered at the bar. Prices are much higher during trade fairs and Oktoberfest. ✉ *Landwehrstr. 42, entrance on Goethestr., Leopoldvorstadt, D–80336* ☎ *089/549–1740* 🖷 *089/550–3701* 🌐 *www.hotelmirabell.de* *65 rooms, 3 apartments* *Cable TV with movies, in-room data ports, bar, some pets allowed (fee), no-smoking rooms* 💳 *AE, MC, V* 🍴 *BP* Ⓤ *Hauptbahnhof (U-bahn and S-bahn).*

$–$$ **Hotel-Pension Mariandl.** The American armed forces commandeered this turn-of-the-20th-century neo-Gothic mansion in May 1945 and established Munich's first postwar nightclub, the Femina, on the ground floor (now the charming café-restaurant Café am Beethovenplatz, which also has computers for Internet use). Most rooms are mansion size, with high ceilings and large windows overlooking a leafy avenue. The Oktoberfest grounds and the main railway station are both a 10-minute walk away. ✉ *Goethestr. 51, Leopoldvorstadt, D–80336* ☎ *089/534–108* 🖷 *089/5440–4396* 🌐 *www.hotelmariandl.com* *28 rooms* *Restaurant, Wi-Fi, some pets allowed; no a/c, no room phones, no room TVs* 💳 *AE, DC, MC, V* 🍴 *BP* Ⓤ *Hauptbahnhof (U-bahn and S-bahn).*

$ **Kurpfalz.** Visitors have praised the friendly welcome and service they receive at this centrally placed and affordable lodging. Rooms are comfortable, if furnished in a manner only slightly better than functional, and all are equipped with satellite TV. Breakfast is included. The main train station and Oktoberfest grounds are both within a 10-minute walk, and the area is rich in restaurants, bars, and movie theaters. ✉ *Schwantalerstr. 121, Leopoldvorstadt, D–80339* ☎ *089/540–9860* 🖷 *089/5409–8811* 🌐 *www.kurpfalz-hotel.de* *44 rooms with shower* *Cable TV, in-room data ports, in-room broadband, bar, some pets allowed, no-smoking rooms; no a/c* 💳 *AE, MC, V* 🍴 *BP* Ⓤ *Hackerbrücke (S-bahn).*

Isarvorstadt

★ $ **Hotel-Pension Schmellergarten.** This genuine family business will make you feel right at home and is very popular with young budget travelers. The little place is on a quiet street just off Lindwurmstrasse, a few minutes' walk from the Theresienwiese. The Poccistrasse subway station is around the corner to take you into the center of town. ✉ *Schmellerstr. 20, Isarvorstadt, D–80337* ☎ *089/773–157* 🖷 *089/725–6886* ✉ *milankuhn@web.de* *14 rooms* *Some pets allowed; no a/c* 💳 *No credit cards* 🍴 *CP* Ⓤ *Poccistrasse (U-bahn).*

Lehel

$$–$$$ **Adria.** This modern, comfortable hotel is ideally set in the middle of Munich's museum quarter. Rooms are large and tastefully decorated, with old prints on the pale-pink walls, Oriental rugs on the floors, and flowers beside the double beds. A spectacular breakfast buffet (including a glass of sparkling wine) is included in the room rate. There's no hotel restaurant, but there's free coffee and tea in the lobby and the area is rich in good restaurants, bistros, and bars. ✉ *Liebigstr. 8a, Lehel, D–80538* ☎ *089/242–1170* 🖷 *089/2421–17999* 🌐 *www.adria-muenchen.de* *43 rooms* *Cable TV, in-room data ports, Wi-Fi, Internet room, some pets allowed (fee), no-smoking rooms; no a/c* ▭ *AE, MC, V* 🍴 *BP* Ⓤ *Lehel (U-bahn).*

$$–$$$ **Opera.** In the quiet residential district of Lehel (St.-Anna-Strasse is a cul-de-sac accessed through the neo-Renaissance arcades of the Ethnographic Museum), the Opera offers rooms decorated in an elegant style—lots of Empire, some art deco. Some rooms have glassed-in balconies. The service is perhaps the best in Munich. Instead of having minibars, guests can order room service round the clock. Enjoy summer breakfast in the little back courtyard decorated with orange and lemon trees. ✉ *St. Anna-Strasse 10, Lehel, D–80331* ☎ *089/210–4940* 🖷 *089/2104–9477* 🌐 *www.hotel-opera.de* *25 rooms* *Cable TV, in-room data ports, Wi-Fi, bar, some pets allowed, no-smoking rooms; no a/c* ▭ *AE, DC, MC, V* 🍴 *BP* Ⓤ *Lehel (U-bahn).*

Fodor's Choice ★

$$ **Hotel Concorde.** The privately owned Concorde is right in the middle of Munich and yet very peaceful owing to its location on a narrow sidestreet. The nearest S-bahn station (Isartor) is only a two-minute walk away. Rooms in one tract are done in pastel tones and light woods; in the other tract they tend to be somewhat darker and more rustic. Fresh flowers and bright prints add a colorful touch. A large breakfast buffet is served in a stylish, mirrored dining room. ✉ *Herrnstr. 38, Lehel, D–80539* ☎ *089/224–515* 🖷 *089/228–3282* 🌐 *www.concorde-muenchen.de* *67 rooms, 4 suites* *Cable TV, in-room data ports, Wi-Fi, Internet room, parking (fee), some pets allowed (fee), no-smoking rooms; no a/c* ▭ *AE, DC, MC, V* 🍴 *BP* Ⓤ *Isartor (S-bahn).*

★ **$** **Hotel-Pension Beck.** American and British visitors receive a particularly warm welcome from the Anglophile owner of the rambling, friendly Beck (she and her pet canary are a regular presence). Bright carpeting, with matching pinewood furniture, gives rooms a cheerful touch. The pension has no elevator but does have a prime location convenient to the museums on Prinzregentenstrasse and to the Englischer Garten. ✉ *Thierschstr. 36, Lehel, D–80538* ☎ *089/220–708 or 089/225–768* 🖷 *089/220–925* 🌐 *www.pension-beck.de* *44 rooms, 7 with shower* *Cable TV, some in-room data ports, some pets allowed; no a/c* ▭ *MC, V* 🍴 *CP* Ⓤ *Lehel (U-bahn).*

Nymphenburg

$–$$ **Kriemhild.** If you're traveling with children, you'll appreciate this welcoming, family-run pension in a quiet western suburb near parks and gardens. It's a 10-minute walk from Schloss Nymphenburg and around the corner from the Hirschgarten Park, site of one of the city's best beer gardens. The tram ride (No. 16 or 17 to Kriemhildenstrasse stop) from the train station is 10 minutes. The buffet breakfast is included in the rate. ✉ *Guntherstr. 16, Nymphenburg, D–80639* ☎ *089/171–1170* 🖷 *089/1711–1755* 🌐 *www.kriemhild.de* *18 rooms* *Cable TV, in-room data ports, bar, free parking, some pets allowed; no a/c* 💳 *AE, MC, V* *BP* Ⓤ *Kriemhildstrasse (Tram-bahn 16/17).*

Outer Munich

$$–$$$$ **ArabellaSheraton Grand Hotel.** The building itself may raise a few eyebrows. It stands on a slight elevation and is not the most shapely on the Munich skyline. What goes on inside, however, is sheer five-star luxury. Guests are greeted with a glass of champagne, and snacks and drinks are available round the clock in the Towers Lounge. The excellent restaurant Ente vom Lehel has come to roost here as well. And if you'd like to add a special Bavarian flavor to your stay, book one of the 60 "Bavarian rooms." ✉ *Arabellastr. 5, Bogenhausen, D–81925* ☎ *089/92640* 🖷 *089/9264–8699* 🌐 *www.arabellasheraton.de* *644 rooms, 31 suites* *2 restaurants, cable TV with movies, pool, hair salon, sauna, steam room, bars, in-room data ports, Wi-Fi, Internet room, meeting rooms, free parking, some pets allowed (fee), no-smoking rooms* 💳 *AE, DC, MC, V* *BP* Ⓤ *Richard-Strauss-Strasse (U-bahn).*

$$–$$$ **Park-Hotel Theresienhöhe.** The Park-Hotel claims that none of its rooms are less than 400 square feet. Suites are larger than many luxury apartments, and some of them come with small kitchens. The sleek, modern rooms are mostly decorated with light woods and pastel-color fabrics and carpeting; larger rooms and suites get a lot of light, thanks to the floor-to-ceiling windows. Families are particularly welcome, and a baby-sitting service is provided. There's no in-house restaurant, but you can order in. ✉ *Parkstr. 31, Westend, D–80339* ☎ *089/519–950* 🖷 *089/5199–5420* *35 rooms* *Cable TV, some in-room data ports, Wi-Fi, bar, baby-sitting, some pets allowed, no-smoking rooms; no a/c* 💳 *AE, DC, MC, V* *BP* Ⓤ *Theresienwiese (U-bahn).*

$$–$$$ **Rotkreuzplatz.** This small, family-run business on lively Rotkreuzplatz is five minutes by subway (U-1 and U-7) from the main train station. Breakfast in the neighboring café is included in the price. There are no grand amenities, but a pleasant stay is guaranteed. The café and many rooms look out over one of Munich's most original squares, Rotkreuzplatz, where people from all walks of life meet around a modern fountain. ✉ *Rotkreuzpl. 2, Neuhausen, D–80634* ☎ *089/139–9080* 🖷 *089/166–469* 🌐 *www.hotel-rotkreuzplatz.de* *56 rooms* *Cable TV, in-room data ports, in-room broadband, Wi-Fi, free parking, some pets allowed, no-smoking rooms; no a/c* 💳 *AE, DC, MC, V* *BP* Ⓤ *Rotkreuzplatz (U-bahn).*

$–$$ **Jagdschloss.** This century-old hunting lodge in Munich's leafy Obermenzing suburb is a delightful hotel. The rustic look has been retained with lots of original woodwork and white stucco. Many of the comfortable pastel-tone bedrooms have wooden balconies with flower boxes bursting with color. In the beamed restaurant or sheltered beer garden you'll be served Bavarian specialties by a staff dressed in traditional lederhosen (shorts in summer, breeches in winter). ✉ *Alte Allee 21, D–81245 München-Obermenzing ☎ 089/820–820 📠 089/8208–2100 🌐 www.weber-gastronomie.de* *22 rooms, 1 suite* *Restaurant, cable TV, in-room broadband, in-room data ports, sauna, hot tub, beer garden, playground, free parking, some pets allowed; no a/c* *MC, V* *BP.*

NIGHTLIFE & THE ARTS

The Arts

Bavaria's capital has an enviable reputation as an artistic hot spot. Details of concerts and theater performances are listed in *Vorschau* and *Monatsprogramm,* booklets available at most hotel reception desks, newsstands, and tourist offices. The English-language magazine *Munich Found* is also a good source. Otherwise, just keep your eye open for advertising pillars and posters especially on church walls. Some hotels will make ticket reservations, or you can book through ticket agencies in the city center, such as **Max Hieber Konzertkasse** (✉ Liebfrauenstr. 1, City Center ☎ 089/2900–8014). Two **Zentraler Kartenverkauf** (✉ City Center ☎ 089/264–620) ticket kiosks are in the underground concourse at Marienplatz. The **Abendzeitung Schalterhalle** (✉ Sendlingerstr. 10, City Center ☎ 089/267–024) is a ticket service offered by one of Munich's two rags, the *Abendzeitung*. It's open weekdays 8:30–7, Saturday 10–4. The **Residenz Bücherstube** (✉ Residenzstr. 1, City Center ☎ 089/220–868) sells only concert tickets. Tickets for performances at the Altes Residenztheater/Cuvilliés-Theater, Bavarian State Theater–New Residence Theater, Nationaltheater, Prinzregententheater, and Staatheater am Gartnerplatz are sold at the **central box office** (✉ Maximilianstr. 11, City Center ☎ 089/2185–1920). It's open weekdays 10–6, Saturday 10–1, and one hour before curtain time. One ticket agency, **München Ticket** (☎ 089/5481–8181 🌐 www.muenchenticket.de), has a German-language Web site where tickets for most Munich theaters can be booked.

Concerts

Munich and music go together. The first Saturday in May, the **Long Night of Music** (☎ 089/5481–8181 €10) is devoted to live performances through the night by untold numbers of groups, from heavy-metal bands to medieval choirs, at more than 100 locations throughout the city. One ticket covers everything, including transportation on special buses between locations.

Munich's world-class concert hall, the **Gasteig Culture Center** (✉ Rosenheimerstr. 5, Haidhausen ☎ 089/480–980 🌐 www.muenchenticket.de), is a lavish brick complex standing high above the Isar River, east of downtown. Its Philharmonic Hall is the permanent home of the Munich Philharmonic Orchestra. The city has three other principal orchestras, and the leading choral ensembles are the Munich Bach Choir, the Munich Motettenchor, and Musica Viva, the last specializing in contemporary music. The choirs perform mostly in city churches.

The Bavarian Radio Symphony Orchestra performs at the **Bayerischer Rundfunk** (✉ Rundfunkpl. 1, Maxvorstadt ☎ 089/558–080 🌐 www.br-online.de) and also at other city venues. The box office is open Monday–Thursday 9–noon and 2–4, Friday 9–noon.

The Bavarian State Orchestra is based at the **Nationaltheater** (also called the Bayerische Staatsoper; ✉ Opernpl., City Center ☎ 089/2185–1920 🌐 www.staatstheater-am-gaertnerplatz.de). The Kurt Graunke Symphony Orchestra performs at the romantic art nouveau **Staatstheater am Gärtnerplatz** (✉ Gärtnerpl. 3, Isarvorstadt ☎ 089/2185–1960).

Herkulessaal in der Residenz (✉ Hofgarten, City Center ☎ 089/2906–7263) is a leading orchestral and recital venue. Free concerts featuring conservatory students are given at the **Hochschule für Musik** (✉ Arcisstr. 12, Maxvorstadt ☎ 089/128–901).

Munich's major pop-rock concert venue is the **Olympiahalle** (✉ U-3 Olympiazentrum stop, Georg-Brauchle-Ring ☎ 089/3061–3577 🌐 www.olympiapark-muenchen.de). The box office, at the ice stadium, is open weekdays 10–6 and Saturday 10–3. You can also book by calling **München Ticket** (☎ 089/5481–8181).

Opera, Ballet & Musicals

Munich's Bavarian State Opera Company and its ballet ensemble perform at the **Nationaltheater** (✉ Opernpl., City Center ☎ 089/2185–1920). The **Staatstheater am Gärtnerplatz** (✉ Gärtnerpl. 3, Isarvorstadt ☎ 089/2185–1960 🌐 www.staatstheater-am-gaertnerplatz.de) presents a less ambitious but nevertheless high-quality program of opera, ballet, operetta, and musicals.

Theater

Munich has scores of theaters and variety-show venues, although most productions will be largely impenetrable if your German is shaky. Listed here are all the better-known theaters, as well as some of the smaller and more progressive spots. Note that most theaters are closed during July and August.

English Comedy Club (✉ Rupertstr. 28 Leopoldvorstadt Ⓤ Poccistr. [U6 or U3 U-bahn] ☎ 089/721–2749 🌐 www.englishcomedyclub.de). With the Substanz Live Club & Bar, this evening on the first Sunday of each month has gotten rave reviews. Entry is €14.

Altes Residenztheater/Cuvilliés-Theater (✉ Max-Joseph-Pl., entrance on Residenzstr., City Center ☎ 089/2185–1940). This is an intimate stage for compact opera productions such as Mozart's *Singspiele* and classic and contemporary plays (Arthur Miller met with great success here).

Amerika Haus (America House; ✉ Karolinenpl. 3, Maxvorstadt ☎ 089/343–803 🌐 www.amerikahaus.de). A very active American company, the American Drama Group Europe, presents regular English-language productions here.

Bayerisches Staatsschauspiel/Neues Residenztheater (Bavarian State Theater–New Residence Theater; ✉ Max-Joseph-Pl., City Center ☎ 089/2185–1940 🌐 www.bayerischesstaatsschauspiel.de). This is Munich's leading stage for classic playwrights such as Goethe, Schiller, Lessing, Shakespeare, and Chekhov.

Deutsches Theater (✉ Schwanthalerstr. 13, Leopoldvorstadt ☎ 089/5523–4444 🌐 www.deutsches-theater.de). Musicals, revues, balls, and big-band shows take place here. The box office is open weekdays noon–6 and Saturday 10–1:30.

Feierwerk (✉ Hansastr. 39, Westend ☎ 089/743–1340 🌐 www.feierwerk.de) has four venues that present a wide range of musical fare, cabaret, and experimental art shows.

The Carl-Orff Saal and the Black Box theaters, in the **Gasteig Culture Center,** occasionally present English-language plays. The box office is open weekdays 10:30–6 and Saturday 10–2.

Münchner Kammerspiele-Schauspielhaus (✉ Maximilianstr. 26, City Center ☎ 089/2333–7000 🌐 www.muenchner-kammerspiele.de). A city-funded rival to the nearby state-backed Staatliches Schauspiel, this theater of international renown presents the classics as well as new works by contemporary playwrights.

For a spectrum of good jazz, chansons, and café theater, check out the **Pasinger Fabrik** (✉ August-Exter-Str. 1, Pasing ☎ 089/8292–9079 🌐 www.pasinger-fabrik.com), which also offers live music with breakfast, lunch, dinner ($–$$), or late-night drinks. To get there, take any S-bahn out to Pasing (exit the station to the north). The box office is open Thursday–Saturday 4:30–8:30 PM.

Prinzregententheater (✉ Prinzregentenpl. 12, City Center ☎ 089/2185–2899 🌐 www.prinzregententheater.de). Munich's art-nouveau theater, an audience favorite, presents not only opera but musicals and musical gala events.

CHILDREN'S THEATER

Munich has several theaters for children. Because pantomime plays such a strong part in the repertoire, the language problem tends to disappear. Munich is the winter quarters of the big-top **Circus Krone** (✉ Zirkus-Krone-Str. 1–6, Leopoldvorstadt ☎ 089/545–8000), which performs from Christmas until the end of March. The **Münchner Marionettentheater** (✉ Blumenstr. 32, City Center ☎ 089/265–712 🌐 www.muenchner-marionettentheater.de) lets its puppets chew on highbrow material, notably works of Carl Orff. The **Münchner Theater für Kinder** (✉ Dachauerstr. 46, Neuhausen ☎ 089/595–454 🌐 www.kindertheater-muenchen.de) will keep the young ones happy with fairy-tales and traditional pieces such as *Pinocchio*. The puppet shows at **Otto Bille's Marionettenbühne** (✉ Bereiterangerstr. 15, Au ☎ 089/150–2168) are for young children.

Nightlife

Munich's nocturnal attractions vary with the seasons. The year starts with the abandon of Fasching, the Bavarian carnival time, which begins quietly in mid-November with the crowning of the King and Queen of Fools, expands with fancy-dress balls, and ends with a great street party on Fasching Dienstag (Shrove Tuesday), which can take place between early February and late March. Men should forget wearing neckties on Fasching Dienstag: women posing as witches make a point of cutting them off. From spring until late fall the beer garden dictates the style and pace of Munich's nightlife. When it rains, the indoor beer halls and taverns absorb the thirsty like blotting paper.

The beer gardens and most beer halls close at midnight, but there's no need to go home: some bars and nightclubs are open until 6 AM. A word of caution about bars: most are run honestly, but a few may intentionally overcharge, especially the seedier ones near the main train station. Stick to beer or wine if you can, and pay as you go.

Clubs, discos, and the like can be a bit of a problem in Munich: the bouncers outside are primarily there to add to the often specious exclusivity of the inside. Bouncers are usually rude, crude, and somewhat thick and as such have achieved dubious notoriety throughout Germany. They are in charge of picking who is "in" and who is "out," and there's no use trying to warm up to them.

Bars

Alter Simpl (✉ Turkenstr. 57, Schwabing ☎ 089/272–3083) turned 100 in 2002. Media types drink Guinness and Kilkenny at its square bar and German pub food is served throughout the day and night. **Bar Centrale** (✉ Ledererstr. 23, City Center ☎ 089/223–762) has a retro-looking back room with leather sofas and is very Italian—the waiters don't seem to speak any other language. The coffee is excellent; small fine meals are served as well.

The Bayerischer Hof's **Night Club** (✉ Promenadepl. 2–6, City Center ☎ 089/212–00) has live music, from jazz to reggae to hip-hop; a small dance floor; and a very lively bar. Just behind the Frauenkirche, **Kilian's Irish Pub and Ned Kelly's Australian Bar** (✉ Frauenpl.11, City Center ☎ 089/2421–9899), offer an escape from the German tavern scene. Naturally, they have Guinness and Foster's, but they also serve Munich's best lager, Augustiner, and regularly televise English soccer, rugby, and sports in general. At the English, nautical-style **Pusser's New York Bar** (✉ Falkenturmstr. 9, City Center ☎ 089/220–500), great cocktails and Irish-German black and tans (Guinness and strong German beer) are made to the sounds of live jazz. The pricey sandwiches are about the only "New York" in Pusser's.

The bartenders are busy shaking cocktails at **Schumann's** (✉ Odeonspl. 6–7, City Center ☎ 089/229–060) after the curtain comes down at the nearby opera house (the bar is closed on Saturday). Exotic cocktails are the specialty at **Trader Vic's** (✉ Promenadenpl. 4, City Center ☎ 089/226–192), a smart cellar bar in the Hotel Bayerischer Hof that's popular among out-of-town visitors. The **Kempinski Vier Jahreszeiten** (✉ Maximilianstr. 17, City Center ☎ 089/21250) offers piano music until 9 and then dancing to recorded music or a small combo.

Eisbach (✉ Marstallstr. 3, Lehel ☎ 089/2280–1680) occupies a corner of the Max Planck Institute building opposite the Bavarian Parliament.

The bar is among Munich's longest and is overlooked by a mezzanine restaurant area where you can choose from a limited but ambitious menu. Outdoor tables nestle in the expansive shade of huge parasols. The nearby Eisbach Brook, which gives the bar its name, tinkles away like ice in a glass. The incredibly modern **Scalar** (✉ Seitzstr. 12, Lehel ☎ 089/2157–9636) attracts a fairly mixed crowd of fashionable people. Its cellar is home to the Blue Oyster Club, where dancing is encouraged.

Beer Gardens

Everybody in Munich has at least one favorite beer garden, so you're in good hands if you ask someone to point you in the right direction. You do not need to reserve. No need to phone either: if the weather says yes, then go. Note, however, that Munich has very strict noise laws, so beer gardens tend to close around 11. The famous **Biergarten am Chinesischen Turm** (☎ 089/383–8730) is at the five-story Chinese Tower in the Englischer Garten. The Englischer Garten's smaller beer garden, **Hirschau** (☎ 089/369–945), has minigolf to test your skills after a few beers. It's about 10 minutes north of the Kleinhesselohersee. The **Seehaus im Englischen Garten** (☎ 089/381–6130) is on the banks of the artificial lake Kleinhesselohersee, where all of Munich converges on hot summer days (bus line 44, exit at Osterwaldstrasse; you can't miss it).

Surprisingly large and green for a place so centrally located is the **Hofbräukeller** (✉ Innere Wiener Str. 19, tramway 18 to Wiener-Pl. or U-bahn 4 or 5 to Max-Weber-Pl., Haidhausen ☎ 089/459–9250), which is a beer relative of the Hofbräuhaus. Some evenings you can move into the spacious cellar for live jazz. The **Augustiner Beer Garden** (☎ 089/594–393) is one of the more authentic of the beer gardens, with excellent food, beautiful chestnut shade trees, a mixed local crowd, and Munich's legendary Augustiner beer. From the north exit of the main train station, go left on Arnulfstrasse and walk about 10 minutes. It's on the right.

Out in the district of Laim is the huge **Königlicher Hirschgarten** (☎ 089/172–591), where the crowd is somewhat more blue-collar and foreign. To get there, take any S-bahn toward Pasing, exit at Laim, walk down Wotanstrasse, take a right on Winifriedstrasse and then a left into De-la-Paz-Strasse. The crowd at the **Taxisgarten** (☎ 089/156–827) in the Gern district (U-bahn Gern, Line 1 toward "Westfriedhof") is more white-collar and tame, hence less chance of communicating with the natives, but the food is excellent, and while parents refresh themselves, children exhaust themselves on the playground.

Dance Clubs

Schwabing claims more than a dozen dance clubs and live-music venues between its central boulevard, Leopoldstrasse, and the area around its central square, the Münchner-Freiheit. Two streets—Feilitzstrasse and Occamstrasse—are lined with clubs, discos, and pubs. Haidhausen is Munich's other "in" area. A former factory hosts the city's largest rave scene: the **Kultfabrik** (✉ Grafingerstr. 6, Haidhausen Ⓤ Ostbahnhof [S-bahn] ☎ 089/4900–9070), has no fewer than 17 "entertainment areas," including a Latin dance club among others, bars, and a huge slot-machine and computer-game hall. The once famous Kunstpark Ost—in the same area as Kultfabrik—is now the Optimolwerke, still with many clubs. **Muffathalle** (✉ Rosenheimerstr. 1, behind the Müllersche Volksbad, Haidhausen ☎ 089/4587–5010) usually posts orange-and-purple schedules on advertising pillars. Hodgepodge is the only way to describe the events, but the people here are relaxed, young, and nonchalant. The **Backstage** (✉ Friedenheimerbrücke 7, Laim Ⓤ Friedenheimerbrücke [S-bahn] ☎ 089/126–6100) is very relaxed, with several areas for either dancing or enjoying drinks. Old Bavarian thrillers are screened in summer as a backdrop to the nocturnal beer garden. The crowd ranges from 18-year-olds to thirtysomethings. The **Skyline** (✉ Münchner-Freiheit, Schwabing ☎ 089/333–131) is at the top of the Hertie department store and focuses mainly on Latin American sounds and salsa. Bordering the Englischer Garten, **P 1** (✉ Prinzregentenstr., on the west side of Haus der Kunst, Lehel ☎ 089/294–252) is allegedly the trendiest club in town; find out for yourself, if you can make it past the bouncer. The **Parkcafé** (✉ Sophienstr. 7, Maxvorstadt ☎ 089/598–313) is one of those fashionable places where you'll have to talk your way past the doorman to join the chic crowd inside.

The **Feierwerk** (✉ Hansastr. 39, Westend ☎ 089/7248–8109) has that ramshackle old factory look to it, but it's a genuine institution in the musical scene. Many local bands were launched to fame—and back—here. The big FEST festival in July is one of the city's best in the music scene. **Nachtwerk** (✉ Landsbergerstr. 185, Westend ☎ 089/570–7390), in a converted factory, blasts the sounds of punk and avant-garde nightly between 8 PM and 4 AM. Live bands perform regularly. Just a few buildings down the street from the Nachtwerk is the industrial-size dance palace **4004** (✉ Landsbergerstr. 169, Westend ☎ 0171/154–8038), with four different clubs on two floors, three bars, and so forth. The real ravers ride the S-bahn to Munich's Franz-Josef-Strauss Airport, alighting at the Besucherpark station for techno and other beats until dawn at **Nightflight** (☎ 089/9759–7999). The **Nachtgalerie** (✉ Arnulfstr. 17, Leopoldvorstadt ☎ 089/3245–5595) offers nights with solid disco for plain old fun dancing. The **Schlachthof** (✉ Zenettistr. 8, Thalhausen ☎ 089/765–448) is, as the name suggests, at the slaughterhouse. The mixed crowd is not overly hip, and the music usually includes excellent jazz and soul.

Gay & Lesbian Bars

Munich's growing gay scene stretches between Sendlingertorplatz and Isartorplatz. For an overview check 🌐 www.munich-cruising.de. The **Nil** (✉ Hans-Sachs-Str. 2, Isarvorstadt ☎ 089/265–545) is famous for its decent prices and its schnitzel. The **Fortuna** (✉ Maximilianstr. 5, Isarvorstadt ☎ 089/554–070) is more than just a bar and disco for women; it's also an events venue and organizer (skiing excursions, rafting on the Isar, for example). **Fred's Pub** (✉ Reisingerstr. 15, Isarvorstadt ☎ 089/2602–2809) shows gay movies on a large screen. The upscale **Morizz** (✉ Klenzestr. 43, Isarvorstadt ☎ 089/201–6776) fills with a somewhat moneyed crowd. The **Ochsengarten** (✉ Müllerstr. 47, Isarvorstadt ☎ 089/266–446) is Munich's leather bar. **Old Mrs. Hen-**

derson (✉ Rumfordstr. 2, Isarvorstadt ☎ 089/263–469) puts on the city's best transvestite cabaret for a mixed crowd and has various other events. You can dance here, too.

Jazz

Munich likes to think it's Germany's jazz capital, and some beer gardens have taken to replacing their brass bands with funky combos. Jazz musicians sometimes accompany Sunday brunch at pubs, too. One top club is the tiny **Mr. B's** (✉ Herzog-Heinrich-Str. 38, Isarvorstadt ☎ 089/534–901), run by New Yorker Alex Best, who also mixes great cocktails and, unlike so many barkeeps, usually sports a welcoming smile. At tiny **Alfonso's** (✉ Franzstr. 5, Schwabing ☎ 089/338–835), the nightly live music redefines the concept of intimacy. **Coccodrillo** (✉ Hohenzollernstr. 11, Schwabing ☎ 089/336–639) claims the city's longest bar and is accessed through the Caffè Florian (where you can eat as well). From September to May the old brick vaulting resounds to the sounds of live jazz and rock three times a week. The **Unterfahrt** (✉ Einsteinstr. 42, Haidhausen ☎ 089/448–2794) is the place for the serious jazzologist, though hip-hop is making heavy inroads into the scene. A haunt with nondescript furnishings rather than chic dilapidation is **Nachtcafé** (✉ Maximilianpl. 5, City Center ☎ 089/595–900). Food (costly) is served all night, and there's no dancing. Sunday is set aside for jazz at **Waldwirtschaft Grosshesselohe** (✉ Georg-Kalb-Str. 3, Grosshesselohe ☎ 089/795–088) in a southern suburb. If it's a nice day, the excursion is worth it.

SPORTS & THE OUTDOORS

The **Olympiapark** (Ⓤ Olympiazentrum [U-bahn]), built for the 1972 Olympics, is one of the largest sports and recreation centers in Europe. For general information about sports in and around Munich contact the sports emporium **Sport Scheck** (✉ Sendlingerstr. 6, City Center ☎ 089/21660). The big store not only sells every kind of equipment but is very handy with advice.

Bicycling

A bike allows you to cover more ground and is a really excellent way to experience this flat, pedal-friendly city that has lots of bike lanes and paths that wind through its parks and along the Isar River. Bike-rental shops will give you maps and tips, or you can get a map at any city tourist office. Bikes are also allowed on the S-bahn (except during rush hours from 6 AM to 9 AM and from 4 PM to 6 PM), which take you out to the many lakes and attractions outside town. Bicycles on public transportation cost either one strip on a multiple ticket, or €2.50 for a day ticket, €0.90 for a single ticket.

Two companies lead English-language bike tours and rent bikes as well. The tours are non-strenuous, very informative, often quite funny, and cost between €12 and €30. **Rad City Bike Tours** (✉ Senefelderstr. 1, City Center ☎ 172/168–9333 🌐 www.radcitybiketours.com), across from the main train station, offers great value for their various services and prides itself on the humorous guides who lead tours through the city, around Dachau, and to the Neuschwanstein castle in Füssen. Near the Hofbräuhaus, **Mike's Bike Tours** (✉ Bräuhausstr. 10, City Center ☎ 089/2554–3988 or 172/852–0660 🌐 www.mikesbiketours.com) is an American-owned institution in Munich and offers rentals and similar tours as Rad City Bike. The tours start daily at the Old Town Hall (the Altes Rathaus) at 11:20 and 3:50. They cost €22, including bike rental. Mike also organizes walking tours for €9.

There are many **bike-rental outlets**: **Aktiv-Rad** (✉ Hans-Sachs-Str. 7, Isarvorstadt ☎ 089/266–506); **the bike and walk company GmbH** (✉ Tal 31, City Center ☎ 089/5895–8930); **Hauptbahnhof** (✉ Radius Touristik, opposite platform 31, Leopoldvorstadt ☎ 089/596–113); **Spurwechsel** (✉ Steinstr. 3, Haidhausen ☎ 089/692–4699); **Will Fahrradverleih** (✉ Kleinhesselohe 4, at Kleinhesselohe Lake in Englischer Garten, Schwabing ☎ 089/338–353).

Ice-Skating

In winter, depending on weather conditions, there's outdoor skating on the lake in the Englischer Garten and on the Nymphenburger Canal, where you can also go curling (*Eisstockschiessen*). Rental equipment is available at the little wooden huts, which also sell hot drinks. Players rent sections of machine-smoothed ice on the canal. Watch out for signs reading GEFAHR (danger), warning you of thin ice. Additional information is available from **Bayerischer Eissportverband** (✉ Georg-Brauchle-Ring 93, Moosach ☎ 089/157–9920). In winter the fountain on **Karlsplatz** is turned into a public rink with lots of music, an outdoor bar for drinks, and a rowdy crowd. For outdoor rinks use the **Prinzregentenstadion** (✉ Prinzregentenstr. 80, Haidhausen ☎ 0180/179–6223).

Jogging

The best place to jog is the **Englischer Garten** (Ⓤ Münchner-Freiheit or Universität [U-bahn]), which is 11 km (7 mi) around and has dirt and asphalt paths amid its lakes. You can also jog through **Olympiapark** (Ⓤ Olympiazentrum [U-bahn]). The 500-acre park of **Schloss Nymphenburg** (✣ Take Tramway 12 to Romanplatz) is ideal for running. The banks of the **Isar River** are a favorite route. For a longer jog along the river, take the S-bahn to Unterföhring and pace yourself back to Münchner-Freiheit—a distance of 6½ km (4 mi).

Swimming & Spas

You can try swimming outdoors in the Isar River at Maria-Einsiedel, but because the water comes from the Alps, it's frigid even in summer. Warmer lakes near Munich are the **Ammersee** and the **Starnbergersee.** A very relaxing experience is swimming at one of the metropolitan spas. There are pools at the **Cosima Bad** (✉ Englschalkingerstr. and Cosimastr., Bogenhausen), with man-made waves. The **Dantebad** (✉ Dantestr. 6, Gern) has a huge lawn and is very popular in summer. It also has a heated, outdoor Olympic-size pool and a fun pool available in winter, which is usually not too crowded and provides a nice respite in the frigid months. The **Müllersche Volksbad** (✉ Rosenheimerstr. 1, Haidhausen ☎ 089/2361–3434) is in a grand art-nouveau building right on the Isar. Tuesday and Thursday are reserved for women only in the wellness section. And remember: if you use the saunas and steam baths in these spas, the rules say it's in your birthday suit. The **Nordbad** (✉ Schleissheimerstr. 142, Schwabing) has a small, pleasant wellness center. The **Olympia-Schwimmhalle** (✉ Olympiapark, Schwabing) has not only an Olympic-size pool but also a sauna area with a "steam cavern" as an extra delight.

SHOPPING

Shopping Districts

Munich has an immense central shopping area, a 2-km (1-mi) *Fussgängerzone* (pedestrian zone) stretching from the train station to Marienplatz and north to Odeonsplatz. The two main streets here are Neuhauserstrasse and Kaufingerstrasse, the sites of most major department stores. For upscale shopping, Maximilianstrasse, Residenzstrasse, and Theatinerstrasse are unbeatable and contain classy and tempting stores that are the equal of any in Europe. Schwabing, north of the university, has several of the city's most intriguing and offbeat shopping streets—Schellingstrasse and Hohenzollernstrasse are two to try.

Antiques

Bavarian antiques—from a chipped pottery beer mug to a massive farmhouse dresser—are found in the many small shops around the Viktualienmarkt, including on Westenriederstrasse, just south of the market. Number 8 Westenriederstrasse houses three antiques shops packed from floor to ceiling with curios, including a great collection of ancient dolls and toys. Also try the area north of the university—Türkenstrasse, Theresienstrasse, and Barerstrasse are all filled with antiques stores.

Strictly for window-shopping—unless you're looking for something really rare and special and money's no object—are the exclusive shops lining Prannerstrasse, at the rear of the Hotel Bayerischer Hof. Interesting and inexpensive antiques and assorted junk from all over eastern Europe are laid out at the weekend flea markets beneath the Donnersberger railway bridge on Arnulfstrasse (along the northern side of the Hauptbahnhof).

In **Antike Uhren Eder** (✉ Hotel Bayerischer Hof, Prannerstr. 4, City Center ☎ 089/220–305), the silence is broken only by the ticking of dozens of highly valuable German antique clocks and by discreet negotiation over the high prices. Old, beautiful beer steins are the specialty of **Ulrich Schneider** (✉ Am Radlsteg 2, City Center ☎ 089/292–477). Nautical items or antiquated sports equipment fill the **Captain's Saloon** (✉ Westenriederstr. 31, City Center ☎ 089/221–015). German antique silver and porcelain are the specialty of **Roman Odesser** (✉ Westenriederstr. 16, City Center ☎ 089/226–388). For Munich's largest selection of dolls and marionettes, head to **Die Puppenstube** (✉ Luisenstr. 68, Maxvorstadt ☎ 089/272–3267).

Bookstores

The monthly English-language magazine *Munich Found* is sold at most newspaper stands and in many hotels. It contains excellent list-

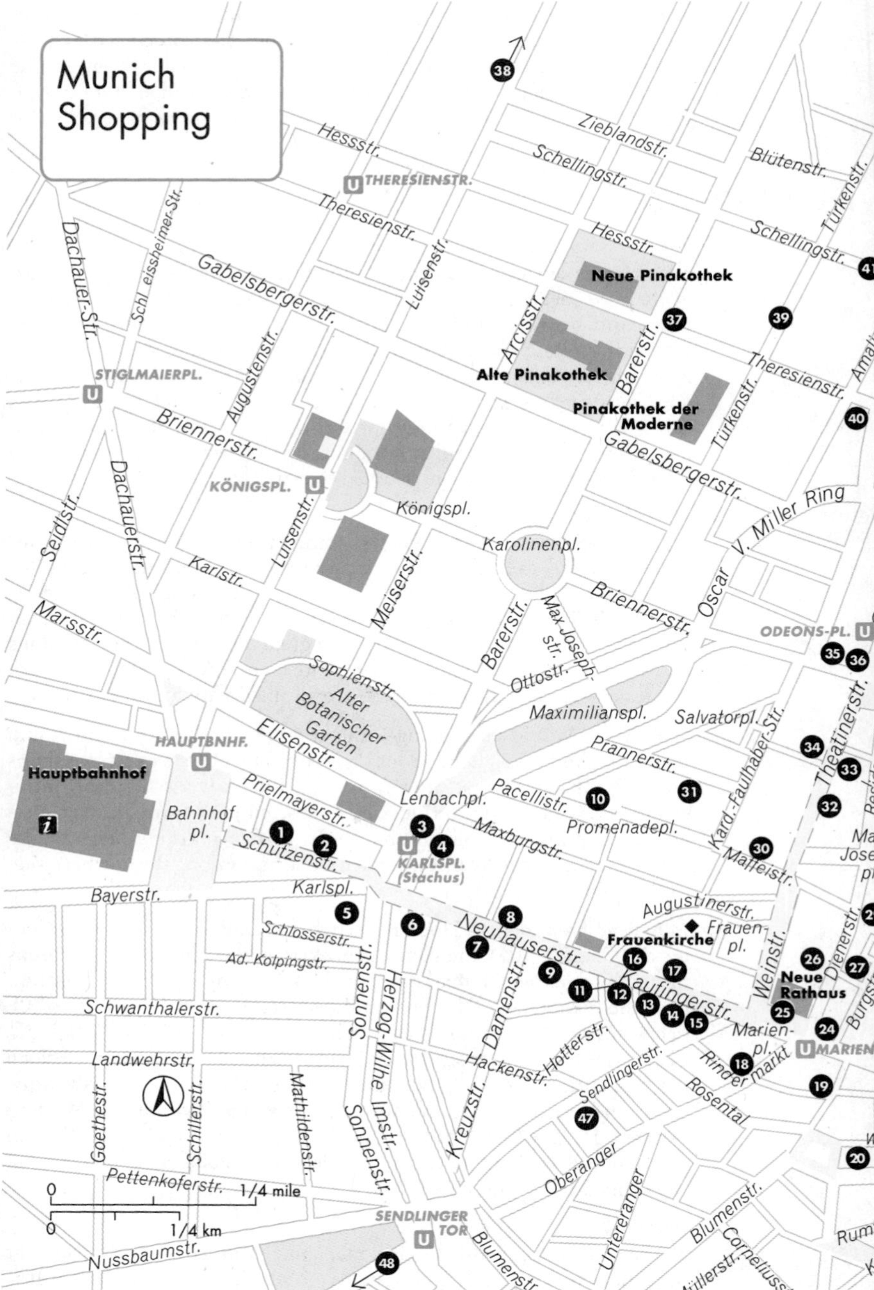
Munich
Shopping
Hessstr.
THERESIENSTR.
Theresienstr.
Zieblandstr.
Schellingstr.
Blütenstr.
Türkenstr.
Schellingstr.
Hessstr.
Neue Pinakothek
Luisenstr.
Gabelsbergerstr.
Schl. eissheimer-Str.
Dachauer-Str.
Arcisstr.
Barerstr.
Alte Pinakothek
Pinakothek der Moderne
Theresienstr.
Türkenstr.
Amalienstr.
STIGLMAIERPL.
Augustenstr.
Briennerstr.
Gabelsbergerstr.
KÖNIGSPL.
Königspl.
Oscar V. Miller Ring
Dachauerstr.
Seidlstr.
Luisenstr.
Karlstr.
Karolinenpl.
Meiserstr.
Marsstr.
Briennerstr.
Barerstr.
Max-Joseph-str.
Oscar
ODEONS-PL.
Ottostr.
Sophienstr.
Alter Botanischer Garten
Maximilianspl.
Salvatorpl.
Elisenstr.
HAUPTBNHF.
Prannerstr.
Kard.-Faulhaber-Str.
Theatinerstr.
Hauptbahnhof
Priemayerstr.
Lenbachpl.
Pacellistr.
Bahnhof pl.
Schützenstr.
KARLSPL. (Stachus)
Maxburgstr.
Promenadepl.
Maffeistr.
Karlspl.
Bayerstr.
Augustinerstr.
Frauen-pl.
Frauenkirche
Schlosserstr.
Neuhauserstr.
Ad. Kolpingstr.
Weinstr.
Neue Rathaus
Dienerstr.
Burgstr.
Kaufingerstr.
Sonnenstr.
Herzog-Wilhelmstr.
Damenstr.
Schwanthalerstr.
Marien-pl.
MARIENPL.
Hotterstr.
Rindermarkt
Landwehrstr.
Hackenstr.
Sendlingerstr.
Rosental
Mathildenstr.
Sonnenstr.
Kreuzstr.
Goethestr.
Schillerstr.
Oberanger
Pettenkoferstr.
0 1/4 mile
0 1/4 km
Unteranger
Blumenstr.
SENDLINGER TOR
Blumenstr.
Corneliusstr.
Müllerstr.
Nussbaumstr.
Rumfordstr.
1 2 3 4 5 6 7 8 9 10 11 12 13 14 15 16 17 18 19 20 24 25 26 27 30 31 32 33 34 35 36 37 38 39 40 41 47 48

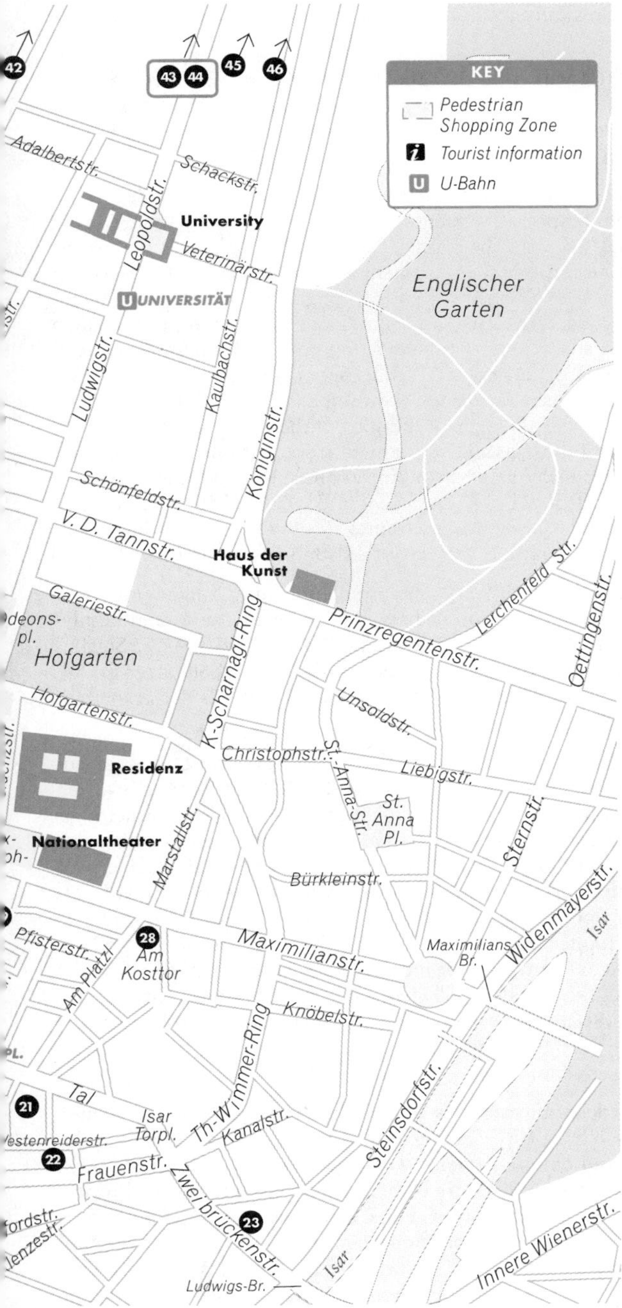
KEY
Pedestrian Shopping Zone
Tourist information
U-Bahn
42
43
44
45
46
Adalbertstr.
Schackstr.
University
Leopoldstr.
Veterinärstr.
UNIVERSITÄT
Englischer Garten
Ludwigstr.
Kaulbachstr.
Königinstr.
Schönfeldstr.
V. D. Tannstr.
Haus der Kunst
Galeriestr.
Odeons-pl.
Hofgarten
Hofgartenstr.
K-Scharnagl-Ring
Prinzregentenstr.
Lerchenfeld Str.
Oettingenstr.
Unsoldstr.
Christophstr.
St.-Anna-Str.
Liebigstr.
St. Anna Pl.
Residenz
Nationaltheater
Marstallstr.
Sternstr.
Bürkleinstr.
Widenmayerstr.
Isar
Pfisterstr.
28
Am Kosttor
Am Platzl
Maximilianstr.
Maximilians Br.
Knöbelstr.
Th-Wimmer-Ring
Tal
21
Isar Torpl.
Kanalstr.
Steinsdorfstr.
Frauenstr.
22
Zweibrückenstr.
23
Innere Wienerstr.
Ludwigs-Br.

ings, reviews restaurants and shows, and generally gives an idea of life in the city.

Hugendubel (✉ Marienpl. 22, 2nd fl., City Center ☎ 089/23890 or 01803/484–484 ✉ Karlspl. 3, City Center ☎ 089/552–2530) has a good selection of novels in English. The **Internationale Presse** (☎ 089/13080) in the main train station has magazines and novels.

Department Stores & Malls

★ **Hertie** (✉ Bahnhofpl. 7, City Center ☎ 089/55120), commanding an entire city block between the train station and Karlsplatz, is the largest and, some claim, the best department store in the city. The basement has a high-class delicatessen with a champagne bar and stand-up bistro that offers a menu that changes daily and puts many high-price Munich restaurants to shame. Hertie's Schwabing branch is a high-gloss steel-and-glass building. **Karstadt** (✉ Neuhauserstr. 18, City Center ☎ 089/290–230 ✉ Schleissheimerstr. 93, Schwabing ☎ 089/13020), in the 100-year-old Haus Oberpollinger, at the start of the Kaufingerstrasse shopping mall, is another upscale department store, with Bavarian arts and crafts. Karstadt also has a Schwabing branch, **Karstadt am Nordbad. Kaufhof** (✉ Karlspl. 21–24, City Center ☎ 089/51250 ✉ Corner of Kaufingerstr. and Marienpl., City Center ☎ 089/231–851) offers goods in the middle price range. The end-of-season sales are bargains.

For a classic selection of German clothing, including some with a folk touch, and a large collection of hats, try Munich's traditional family-run **Breiter** (✉ Kaufingerstr. 23, City Center ☎ 089/599–8840 ✉ Stachus underground mall City Center ☎ 089/599–8840 ✉ Schützenstr. 14, Maxvorstadt ☎ 089/599–8840 ✉ Zweibrückenstr. 5–7, Isarvorstadt ☎ 089/599–8840).

Ludwig Beck (✉ Marienpl. 11, City Center ☎ 089/236–910) is considered a step above other department stores by Müncheners. It's packed from top to bottom with highly original wares—from fine feather boas to roughly finished Bavarian pottery. In December a series of booths, each delicately and lovingly decorated, are occupied by craftspeople, who turn out traditional German toys and decorations. The collection of CDs on the upper floor is one of the finest in the city. **Hirmer** (✉ Kaufingerstr. 28, City Center ☎ 089/236–830) has Munich's most comprehensive collection of German-made men's clothes, with a markedly friendly and knowledgeable staff. **Hallhuber** (✉ Kaufingerstr. 9, City Center ☎ 089/260–4862) dresses men and women in toned-down elegance and at good value for the quality. Hallhuber has a branch farther down the road on Marienplatz.

The main pedestrian area has two malls. The aptly named **Arcade** (✉ Neuhauserstr. 5, City Center) is where the young find the best designer jeans and chunky jewelry. **Kaufinger Tor** (✉ Kaufingerstr. 117, City Center) has several floors of boutiques and cafés packed neatly together under a high glass roof. For a more upscale-shopping experience, visit the many stores, boutiques, galleries, and cafés of the **Fünf Höfe**, a modern arcade carved into the block of houses between Theatinerstrasse and Kardinal-Faulhaber-Strasse. The architecture of the passages and courtyards is cool and elegant, in sharp contrast to the facades of the buildings.

Folk Costumes

If you want to deck yourself out in lederhosen or a dirndl, or acquire a green loden coat and little pointed hat with feathers, you have a wide choice in the Bavarian capital. Much of the fine loden clothing on sale at **Lodenfrey** (✉ Maffeistr. 7–9, City Center ☎ 089/210–390) is made at the company's own factory, on the edge of the Englischer Garten. **Wallach** (✉ Residenzstr. 3, City Center ☎ 089/220–8710) has souvenirs downstairs and shoes and clothing upstairs (though no children's wear). The tiny **Lederhosen Wagner** (✉ Tal 2, City Center ☎ 089/225–697), right up against the Heiliggeist Church, carries lederhosen, woolen sweaters called *Walk* (not loden), and children's clothing. For a more affordable option, the department store **C&A** (✉ Kaufingerstr. 13, City Center ☎ 089/231930), in the pedestrian zone, carries all the gear you'll need to immerse yourself in the Oktoberfest spirit.

Gift Ideas

Munich is a city of beer, and items related to its consumption are obvious choices for souvenirs and gifts. Munich is also the home of the famous Nymphenburg Porcelain factory. **Dallmayr** (✉ Dienerstr. 014–15, City Center ☎ 089/21350) is an elegant gourmet-food store, with delights ranging from the most exotic fruits to English jams, served by efficient Munich matrons in smart blue-and-white-linen costumes. The store's famous specialty is coffee, with more than 50 varieties to blend as you wish. There's also an enormous number of breads and a temperature-controlled cigar room. Visit **Ludwig Mory** (✉ Marienpl. 8, City Center ☎ 089/224–542) for items relating to beer, from mugs of all shapes and sizes and in all sorts of materials, to warmers for those who don't like their beer too cold. Check out **Sebastian Wesely** (✉ Rindermarkt 1, at Peterspl., City Center ☎ 089/264–519) for beer-related vessels and schnapps glasses (*Stampferl*), walking sticks, scarves, and napkins with the famous Bavarian blue-and-white lozenges. If you've been to the Black Forest and forgot to equip yourself with a clock, or if you need a good Bavarian souvenir, try **Max Krug** (✉ Neuhauserstr. 2, City Center ☎ 089/224–501) in the pedestrian zone.

The **Nymphenburg store** (✉ at Odeonspl. and Briennerstr., Maxvorstadt ☎ 089/282–428) resembles a drawing room of the Munich palace, with soft dove-gray furnishings and delicate, expensive porcelain safely locked away in bowfront cabinets. You can buy directly from the factory on the grounds of Schloss Nymphenburg (✉ Nördliches Schlossrondell 8, Nymphenburg ☎ 089/1791–9710). For Dresden and Meissen ware, go to **Kunstring Meissen** (✉ Briennerstr. 4, Maxvorstadt ☎ 089/281–532).

Bavarian craftspeople have a showplace of their own, the **Bayerischer Kunstgewerbe–Verein** (✉ Pacellistr. 6–8, City Center ☎ 089/290–1470); here you'll find every kind of handicraft, from glass and pottery to textiles. **Kunst und Spiel** (✉ Leopoldstr. 49, Schwabing ☎ 089/381–6270) has a fine selection of toys and clothing for children and various other handcrafted items. Germany is known for its work ethic, so you are bound to find excellent work clothing, shirts, aprons, boots, jackets, and even dishrags made to last at **Berufsbekleidung Neubert** (✉ Sendlingerstr. 11, City Center ☎ 089/260–9076).

Lehmkuhl (✉ Leopoldstr. 45, Schwabing ☎ 089/3801–5013), one of Munich's finest bookshops, also sells beautiful cards. In an arcade of the Neues Rathaus is tiny **Johanna Daimer Filze aller Art** (✉ Dienerstr., City Center ☎ 089/776–984), a shop selling every kind and color of felt imaginable. For an unusual gift of genuine art made of "alternative materials," try **Galerie Biro** (✉ Zieblandstr. 19, Schwabing ☎ 089/273–0686). The works are by no means inexpensive, but they are crafted by top artists working with unusual materials, from Bakelite to plywood. The gallery is closed from Sunday through Tuesday.

A little way outside the center to the south is **tragbar** (✉ Zenettistr. 33, Thalkirchen ☎ 089/7670–3974 Ⓤ Poccisstrasse [U-bahn]), where you can find handcrafted jewelry and homemade noodles, chocolates, and other edibles.

All sorts of lighters, little statues, fine Bavarian snuff boxes, and many other quality gifts to bring home are available at the **Münchner Feuerzeugzentrale** (✉ Karlspl. 3, City Center ☎ 089/591–885). **Otto Kellnberger's Holzhandlung** (✉ Heiliggeiststr. 7–8, City Center ☎ 089/226–479) specializes in wooden crafts. **Obletter's** (✉ Karlspl. 11–12, City Center ☎ 089/5508–9510) has two extensive floors of toys, many of them handmade playthings of great charm and quality. From the end of November until December 24, the open-air stalls of the **Christkindlmarkt** (✉ Marienpl., City Center) are a great place to find gifts and warm up with mulled wine. Two other perennial Christmas-market favorites are those in Schwabing (Münchner-Freiheit Square) and at the Chinese Tower, in the middle of the Englischer Garten.

Markets

Munich's **Viktualienmarkt** is *the* place to shop and to eat. Just south of Marienplatz, it's home to an array of colorful stands that sell everything from cheese to sausages, from flowers to wine. A visit here is more than just collecting picnic makings; it's central to an understanding of the Müncheners' easy-come-easy-go nature. If you're in the Schwabing area, the daily market at **Elisabethplatz** is worth a visit—it's much, much smaller than the Viktualienmarkt, but the range and quality of produce are comparable.

SIDE TRIPS FROM MUNICH

Munich's excellent suburban railway network, the S-bahn, brings several quaint towns and attractive rural areas within easy reach for a day's excursion. The two nearest lakes, the Starnbergersee and the Ammersee, are popular year-round. Dachau attracts overseas visitors, mostly because of its concentration-camp memorial site, but it's a picturesque and historic town in its own right. Landshut, north of Munich, is way off the tourist track, but if it were the same distance south of Munich, this jewel of a Bavarian market town would be overrun.

All these destinations have a wide selection of restaurants and hotels, and you can bring a bike on any S-bahn train. German railways, DB, often has weekend specials that allow a family or group of five to travel for as little as €17.50 during certain times. (Inquire at the main train station for the *Wochenendticket*).

Keep in mind that there are quite a few options for day trips to the famous castles built by King Ludwig, which are only a couple hours away. Mike's Bike Tours or Rad City Bike Tours organize trips, or ask at your hotel for bus-tour excursions. A train out to Schloss Neuschwanstein in Schwangau takes 2 ½ hours. For more information on this fairy-tale castle and others, *see* Chapter 3, The Romantic Road.

Starnbergersee

20 km (12 mi) southwest of Munich.

The Starnbergersee was one of Europe's first pleasure grounds. Royal coaches were already trundling out from Munich to the lake's wooded shores in the 17th century. In 1663 Elector Ferdinand Maria threw a shipboard party at which 500 guests wined and dined as 100 oarsmen propelled them around the lake. Today, pleasure steamers provide a taste of such luxury for the masses. The lake is still lined with the small baroque palaces of Bavaria's aristocracy, but their owners now share the lakeside with public parks, beaches, and boatyards. The Starnbergersee is one of Bavaria's largest lakes—20 km (12 mi) long, 5 km (3 mi) wide, and 406 feet at its deepest point—so there's plenty of room for swimmers, sailors, and windsurfers. The water is of drinking quality (as with most other Bavarian lakes), a testimony to stringent environmental laws and the very limited number of motor boats allowed.

The Starnbergersee is named after its chief resort, **Starnberg,** the largest town on the lake and the nearest to Munich. Pleasure boats set off from the jetty for trips around the lake. The resort has a tree-lined lakeside promenade and some fine turn-of-the-20th-century villas, some of which are now hotels. There are abundant restaurants, taverns, and chestnut-tree-shaded beer gardens.

On the lake's eastern shore, at the village of Berg, you'll find the **King Ludwig II Memorial Chapel.** A well-marked path leads through thick woods to the chapel, built near the point in the lake where the drowned king's body was found on June 13, 1886. He had been confined in nearby Berg Castle after the Bavarian government took action against his withdrawal from reality and his bankrupting castle-building fantasies. A cross in the lake marks the point where his body was recovered.

The castle of **Possenhofen,** home of Ludwig's favorite cousin, Sisi, stands on the western shore, practically opposite Berg. Local lore says they used to send affectionate messages across the lake to each other. Sisi married the Austrian emperor Franz Joseph I but spent more than 20 summers in the lakeside castle, now a luxury hotel, the **Kaiserin Elisabeth.** ✉ *Tutzingerstr. 2–6, Feldafing* ☎ *08157/93090* 🌐 *www.kaiserin-elisabeth.de.*

Buchheim Museum. The Buchheim Collection is one of the finest private collections of German expressionist art in the form of paintings, drawings, watercolors, and prints. Among the artists represented are Otto Dix, Max Beckmann, Ernst Ludwig Kirchner, Karl Schmitt-Rotluff, and other painters of the so-called Brücke movement (1905–13). The museum is housed in an impressive modern building on the lakeside. Some areas of the museum are reserved for African cultic items and Bavarian folk art. The nicest way to get to the museum from Starnberg is by ship. Ask for a combined ticket (€16). ✉ *Am Hirschgarten 1* ☎ *08158/997–060* 🌐 *www.buchheimmuseum.de* 🎫 *€7.80* ⏲ *Apr.–Oct., Tues.–Sun. and holidays 10–6; Nov.–Mar., Tues.–Sun. and holidays 10–6.*

Just offshore is the tiny **Roseninsel** (Rose Island), where King Maximilian II built a summer villa. You can swim to its tree-fringed shores or sail across in a dinghy or on a Windsurfer (rentals are available at Possenhofen's boatyard and at many other rental points along the lake).

Where to Stay & Eat

$–$$ ✕ **Seerestaurant Undosa.** This restaurant is only a short walk from the Starnberg railroad station and boat pier. Most tables command a view of the lake, which provides some of the best fish specials on the international menu. This is the place to try the mild-tasting *Renke,* a perch-type fish. The Undosa also has jazz evenings and a large café, the Oberdeck, also overlooking the lake. ✉ *Seepromenade 1* ☎ *08151/998–930* ✍ *Reservations not accepted* 💳 *AE, MC, V* ⏲ *Closed last 2 wks Feb. In winter, no dinner and closed Mon. and Tues.*

¢–$ ✕ **Königswasser.** A large, airy atrium welcomes you to this comfortable spot. You can enjoy coffee and cakes or a meal ranging from fresh salad to an Argentinean steak drowned in pepper sauce. The Königswasser has a shelf full of photography books and travel guides that invite you to just sit, relax, and enjoy some time off your feet. It's open past midnight from Wednesday through Saturday, and until 6 PM the rest of the week. ✉ *Maximilianstr. 2b, Starnberg* ☎ *08151/444–086* 💳 *MC, V.*

$–$$ ✕🏨 **Hotel Seehof.** This small hotel right next to the train station has several rooms with a view of the lake. Rooms are simply done, with light colors and flower prints hanging on the walls. The Italian restaurant attached, Al Gallo Nero ($–$$$), has dishes ranging from low-price pizzas to high-price fish items that will satisfy any palate. ✉ *Bahnhofpl. 6, D–82319 Starnberg* ☎ *08151/908–500* 📠 *08151/28136* 🌐 *www.hotel-seehof-starnberg.de* 🛏 *38 rooms* 👍 *Restaurant, cable TV, in-room data ports, some pets allowed (fee); no a/c* 💳 *AE, DC, MC, V* 🍽 *BP.*

$$–$$$ ✕🏨 **Forsthaus am See.** The handsome, geranium-covered Forsthaus faces the lake, and so do most of the large, pinewood-furnished rooms. The excellent restaurant ($$$) has a daily changing international menu, with lake fish a specialty. The hotel has its own lake access and boat pier, with a chestnut-shaded beer garden nearby. ✉ *Am See 1, D–82343 Possenhofen* ☎ *08157/93010* 📠 *08157/4292* 🌐 *www.forsthaus-am-see.de* 🛏 *21 rooms, 1 suite* 👍 *Restaurant, beer garden, Internet, some pets allowed (fee); no a/c* 💳 *AE, MC, V* 🍽 *BP.*

Starnbergersee A to Z

TRANSPORTATION TO & FROM STARNBERGERSEE

Starnberg and the north end of the lake are a 25-minute drive from Munich on the A–95 autobahn. Follow the signs to Garmisch and take the Starnberg exit. Country roads then skirt the west and east banks of the lake, but most are closed to the public.

The S-bahn 6 suburban line runs from Munich's central Marienplatz to Starnberg and three other towns on the lake's west bank: Possenhofen, Feldafing, and Tutzing. The journey from Marienplatz to Starnberg takes 35 minutes. The east bank of the lake can be reached by bus from the town of Wolfratshausen, the end of the S-bahn 7 suburban line.

VISITOR INFORMATION

The quickest way to visit the Starnbergersee area is by ship. On Saturday evenings, the good ship *Seeshaupt* has dancing and dinner.

Tourist-Information **Seeshaupt** ☎ 08151/12023. **Tourismusverband Starnberger Fünf-Seen-Land** ✉ Wittelsbacher Str. 2c, D–82319 Starnberg ☎ 08151/90600 📠 08151/906–090 🌐 www.starnberg.de.

Ammersee

40 km (25 mi) southwest of Munich.

The Ammersee, the "peasant lake," is the country cousin of the better-known, more cosmopolitan Starnbergersee ("the prince lake"), and, accordingly, many Bavarians (and tourists, too) like it all the more. Munich cosmopolites of centuries past thought it too distant for an excursion, not to mention too rustic, so the shores remained relatively free of villas and parks. Though some upscale holiday homes claim some stretches of the eastern shore, the Ammersee still offers more open areas for bathing and boating than the larger lake to the east. Bicyclists circle the 19-km-long (12-mi-long) lake (it's nearly 6 km [4 mi] across at its widest point) on a path that rarely loses sight of the water. Hikers can spread out the tour for two or three days, staying overnight in any of the comfortable inns along the way. Dinghy sailors and windsurfers zip across in minutes with the help of the Alpine winds that swoop down from the mountains. A ferry cruises the lake at regular intervals during summer, stopping at several piers. Board it at Herrsching.

Herrsching has a delightful promenade, part of which winds through the resort's park. The 100-year-old villa that sits so comfortably there seems as if it were built by Ludwig II; such is the romantic and fanciful mixture of medieval turrets and Renaissance-style facades. It was actually built for the artist Ludwig Scheuermann in the late 19th century and became a favorite meeting place for Munich and Bavarian artists. It's now a municipal cultural center and the scene of chamber-music concerts on some summer weekends.

The Benedictine monastery of **Andechs,** one of southern Bavaria's most famous pilgrimage sites, lies 5 km (3 mi) south of Herrsching. You can reach it on Bus 951 from the S-bahn station (the bus also connects Ammersee and Starnbergersee). This extraordinary ensemble, surmounted by an octagonal tower and onion dome with a pointed helmet, has a busy history going back more than 1,000 years. The church, originally built in the 15th century, was entirely redone in baroque style in the early 18th century. The **Heilige Kapelle** contains the remains of the old treasure of the Benedictines in Andechs, including Charlemagne's "Victory Cross," and a monstrance containing the three sacred hosts brought back from the crusades by the original rulers of the area, the Counts of Diessen-Andechs. One of the attached chapels contains the remains of composer Carl Orff, and one of the buildings on the grounds has been refurbished as a concert stage for the performance of his works. The church is being renovated completely in preparation for the 550th anniversary of the monastery in 2005. Crowds of pilgrims are drawn not only by the beauty of the hilltop monastery but also by the beer brewed here (600,000 liters [159,000 gallons] annually). The monastery makes its own cheese as well, and it's an excellent accompaniment to the rich, almost black beer. You can enjoy both at large wooden tables in the monastery tavern or on the terrace outside. 🌐 *www.andechs.de* ⏲ *Daily 7–7.*

The little town of **Diessen** at the southwest corner of the lake has one of the most magnificent religious buildings of the whole region: the **Augustine abbey church of St. Mary.** No lesser figure than the great Munich architect Johann Michael Fischer designed this airy, early rococo structure. François Cuvillié the Elder, whose work can be seen all over Munich, did the sumptuous gilt-and-marble high altar. Visit in late afternoon, when the light falls sharply on its crisp gray, white, and gold facade, etching the pencil-like tower and spire against the darkening sky over the lake. Don't leave without at least peeping into neighboring St. Stephen's courtyard, its cloisters smothered in wild roses. But Diessen is not all church. It has attracted artists and craftspeople since the early 20th century. Among the most famous who made their home here was the composer Carl Orff, author of numerous works inspired by medieval material, including the famous *Carmina Burana.* His life and work—notably the pedagogical Schulwerk instruments—are exhibited in the **Carl-Orff-Museum** (✉ Hofmark 3, Diessen ☎ 08807/91981 ⏲ Weekends 2–5).

Where to Stay & Eat

$$ ✕🏨 **Ammersee Hotel.** This very comfortable, modern resort hotel has views from an unrivaled position on the lakeside promenade. Rooms overlooking the lake are more expensive and in demand. The Artis restaurant ($–$$) has an international menu with an emphasis on fish. You can enjoy a spicy bouillabaisse or catfish from the Danube. ✉ *Summerstr. 32, D–82211 Herrsching* ☎ *08152/96870, 08152/399–440 restaurant* 📠 *08152/5374* 🌐 *www.ammersee-hotel.de* *40 rooms* *Restaurant, cable TV, in-room data ports, gym, hot tub, sauna, some pets allowed (fee); no a/c* 💳 *AE, DC, MC, V* *BP.*

$ 🏨 **Hotel Garni Zur Post.** Families feel particularly at home here where children can amuse themselves at the playground and small deer park. Rooms are Bavarian country style, with solid-pine furnishings, and are clean and functional. A delicious breakfast buffet will prepare you for a long day of touring. ✉ *Starnberger Str. 2, D–82346 Andechs* ☎ *08152/3433* 🖷 *08152/2303* 🌐 *www.hotelzurpost-andechs.de* 17 *rooms* *Cable TV, playground, Internet, some pets allowed (fee); no a/c* 💳 *MC* 🍽 *CP.*

Ammersee A to Z

TRANSPORTATION TO & FROM AMMERSEE

Take A–96, follow the signs to Lindau, and 20 km (12 mi) west of Munich take the exit for Herrsching, the lake's principal town.

Herrsching is also the end of the S-bahn 5 suburban line, a 47-minute ride from Munich's Marienplatz. From the Herrsching train station, Bus 952 runs north along the lake, and Bus 951 runs south and continues on to Starnberg in a 40-minute journey.

Getting around on a boat is the best way to visit. Each town on the lake has an *Anlegestelle* (pier).

VISITOR INFORMATION

Tourist-Information **Verkehrsbüro** ✉ Bahnhofspl. 2, Herrsching ☎ 08152/5227 ⏲ Weekdays 8:30–noon.

Dachau

20 km (12 mi) northwest of Munich.

Dachau predates Munich, with records going back to the time of Charlemagne. It's a handsome town, too, built on a hilltop with views of Munich and the Alps. A guided tour of the town, including the castle and church, leaves from the Rathaus on Saturday at 10:30, from May through mid-October. Dachau is better known worldwide as the site of the first Nazi concentration camp, which was built just outside it. Dachau preserves the memory of the camp and the horrors perpetrated there with deep contrition while trying, with commendable discretion, to signal that the town has other points of interest.

To get a history of the town, drop in on the **Bezirksmuseum,** the district museum, which displays historical items, furniture, and traditional costumes from Dachau and its surroundings ✉ *Augsburgerstr. 3* ☎ *08131/567–511* 🎟 *€2* ⏲ *Wed.–Fri. 11–5, weekends 1–5.*

The site of the infamous camp, now the **KZ-Gedenkstätte Dachau** (Dachau Concentration Camp Memorial), is just outside town. Photographs, contemporary documents, the few remaining cell blocks, and the grim crematorium create a somber and moving picture of the camp, where more than 30,000 of the 200,000-plus prisoners lost their lives. A documentary film in English is shown daily at 11:30 and 3:30. The former camp has become more than just a grisly memorial: it's now a place where people of all nations meet, to reflect upon the past and on the present. Several religious shrines and memorials have been built to honor the dead, who came from Germany and all occupied nations. To reach the memorial by car, leave the center of the town along Schleissheimerstrasse and turn left into Alte Römerstrasse; the site is on the left. By public transport take Bus 724 or 726 from the Dachau S-bahn train station or the town center. Both stop within a two-minute walk from the site (ask the driver to let you out there). If you are driving from Munich, turn right on the first country road (marked B) before entering Dachau and follow the signs. ✉ *Alte Römerstr. 75* ☎ *08131/669–970* 🌐 *www.kz-gedenkstaette-dachau.de* 🎫 *Free* ⏲ *Tues.–Sun. 9–5. Guided English tour June–Aug., Tues.–Sun. at 12:30; Sept.–May, weekends at 12:30.*

Schloss Dachau, the hilltop castle, dominates the town. What you'll see is the one remaining wing of a palace built by the Munich architect Josef Effner for the Wittelsbach ruler Max Emanuel in 1715. During the Napoleonic Wars the palace served as a field hospital and then was partially destroyed. King Max Joseph lacked the money to rebuild it, so all that's left is a handsome cream-and-white building, with an elegant pillared and lantern-hung café on the ground floor and a former ballroom above. About once a month the grand Renaissance hall, with a richly decorated and carved ceiling, covered with painted panels depicting figures from ancient mythology, is used for chamber concerts. The east terrace affords panoramic views of Munich and, on fine days, the distant Alps. There's also a 250-year-old *Schlossbrauerei* (castle brewery), which hosts the town's beer and music festival each year in the first two weeks of August. ✉ *Schlosspl.* ☎ *08131/87923* 🎫 *€1, tour €2.50* ⏲ *Apr.–Sept., Tues.–Sun. 9–6; Oct.–Mar., Tues.–Sun. 10–4; tour of town and Schloss May–mid-Oct., Sat. at 10:30.*

St. Jacob, Dachau's parish church, was built in the early 16th century in late-Renaissance style on the foundations of a 14th-century Gothic structure. Baroque features and a characteristic onion dome were added in the late 17th century. On the south wall you can admire a very fine 17th-century sundial. A visit to the church is included in the guided tour of the town. ✉ *Konrad-Adenauer-Str. 7* ⏲ *Daily 7–7.*

An artists' colony formed here during the 19th century, and the tradition lives on. Picturesque houses line Hermann-Stockmann-Strasse and part of Münchner Strasse, and many of them are still the homes of successful artists. The **Gemäldegalerie** displays the works of many of the town's 19th-century artists. ✉ *Konrad-Adenauer-Str. 3* ☎ *08131/567–516* 🎫 *€2* ⏲ *Wed.–Fri. 11–5, weekends 1–5.*

Where to Eat

$–$$ Fodor's Choice ★ ✕ **Weilachmühle.** You have to drive a ways for this absolute gem of a restaurant–cum–beer garden–cum–stage and exhibition room in the little village of Thalhausen. It's in a farmhouse that was restored the way it should be, the old dark wooden door opening onto a generous dining area paneled in simple light pine. The food is faultless, beginning with the benchmark Schweinsbraten. To get to the Weilachmüle, drive 26 km (16 mi) north of Dachau toward Aichach; when you reach the village of Wollomoos, take a right toward Thalhausen. (Thalhausen is 2 km [1 mi] from Wollomoos.) ✉ *Am Mühlberg 5, Thalhausen* ☎ *08254/1711* 🌐 *www.weilachmuehle.de* 💳 *No credit cards* ⏲ *Closed Mon.–Thurs.*

¢–$ ✕ **Gasthof drei Rosen.** In a 19th-century building at the foot of Dachau's old town, this little inn caters primarily to locals. Among the inexpensive and filling Bavarian specialties on the menu is *Hendl à la Parkvilla,* chicken marinated in milk and deep fried. You can order it to go as well. ✉ *Schlossstr. 8* ☎ *08131/354–515* ▭ *No credit cards* ⊙ *Closed Mon. and Tues.*

¢–$ ✕ **Zieglerbräu.** Dachau's leading beer tavern, once a 17th-century brewer's home, is a warren of cozy wood-panel rooms where you'll probably share a table with a party of locals on a boys' night out. The food consists of pork, potato, and sausages prepared in various ways. In summer the tables spill out onto the street for a very Italian feeling. The restaurant runs the neighboring nightclub. ✉ *Konrad-Adenauer-Str. 8* ☎ *08131/454–396* ▭ *No credit cards.*

1

Dachau A to Z

TRANSPORTATION TO & FROM DACHAU

Take the B–12 country road or the Stuttgart autobahn to the Dachau exit from Munich. Dachau is also on the S-bahn 2 suburban line, a 20-minute ride from Munich's Marienplatz.

VISITOR INFORMATION

Tourist-Information **Verkehrsverein Dachau** ✉ Konrad-Adenauer-Str. 1 ☎ 08131/75286 🖷 08131/84529 🌐 www.dachau.info.

Landshut

64 km (40 mi) north of Munich.

If fortune had placed Landshut south of Munich, in the protective folds of the Alpine foothills, instead of the same distance north, in the subdued flatlands of Lower Bavaria—of which it is the capital—the historic town would be teeming with tourists. Landshut's geographical misfortune is the discerning visitor's good luck, for the town is never overcrowded, with the possible exception of the three summer weeks when the *Landshuter Hochzeit* (Landshut Wedding) is celebrated (it takes place every four years, the next occasion being in 2009). The festival commemorates the marriage in 1475 of Prince George of Bavaria-Landshut, son of the expressively named Ludwig the Rich, to Princess Hedwig, daughter of the king of Poland. Within its ancient walls, the entire town is swept away in a colorful reconstruction of the event. The wedding procession, with the "bride" and "groom" on horseback accompanied by pipes and drums and the hurly-burly of a medieval pageant, is held on three consecutive weekends while a medieval-style fair fills the central streets throughout the three weeks.

Landshut has two magnificent cobblestone market streets. The one in **Altstadt** (Old Town) is one of the most beautiful city streets in Germany; the other is in **Neustadt** (New Town). The two streets run parallel to each other, tracing a course between the Isar River and the heights overlooking the town. A steep path from Altstadt takes you up to **Burg Trausnitz.** This castle was begun in 1204 and accommodated the Wittelsbach dukes of Bavaria-Landshut until 1503. ☎ *0871/924–110* 🌐 *www.*

burgtrausnitz.de 🎫 *€2.50, including guided tour* ⏲ *Apr.–Sept., daily 9–6; Oct.–Mar., daily 10–4.*

The **Stadtresidenz** in Altstadt was the first Italian Renaissance building of its kind north of the Alps. It was built from 1536 to 1537 but was given a baroque facade at the end of the 19th century. The Wittelsbachs lived here during the 16th century. The facade of the palace forms an almost modest part of the architectural splendor and integrity of the Altstadt, where even the ubiquitous McDonald's has to serve its hamburgers behind a baroque exterior. The Stadtresidenz includes exhibitions on the history of Landshut. ✉ *Altstadt 79, Altstadt* ☎ *0871/22638* 🎫 *€2.50* ⏲ *Apr.–Sept., daily 9–6; Oct.–Mar., daily 10–4.*

The **Rathaus** (Town Hall) stands opposite the Stadtresidenz, an elegant, light-color building with a typical neo-Gothic roof design. It was originally a set of 13th-century burgher houses, taken over by the town in the late 1300s. The famous bride and groom allegedly danced in the grand ceremonial hall during their much-celebrated wedding in 1475. The frescos here date to 1880, however. The tourist information bureau is on the ground floor. ✉ *Altstadt 315* ☎ *0871/922–050* 🎫 *Free* ⏲ *Weekdays 2–3, and on official tours.*

The **Martinskirche** (St. Martin's Church), with the tallest brick church tower (436 feet) in the world, soars above the other buildings with its bristling spire. The church, which was elevated to the rank of *basilica minor* in 2002, contains some magnificent late-Gothic stone and wood carvings, notably a 1518 Madonna by the artist Martin Leinberger. It's surely the only church in the world to contain an image of Hitler, albeit in a devilish pose. The führer and other Nazi leaders are portrayed as executioners in a 1946 stained-glass window showing the martyrdom of St. Kastulus. In the nave of the church is a clear and helpful description of its history and treasures in English. Every first Sunday of the month, a tour is conducted between 11:30 and 12:30 that will take you up the tower and to the **Schatzkammer**, the church's treasure chamber. ✉ *At Altstadt and Kirchg.* ☎ *0871/922–1780* ⏲ *Apr.–Sept., Tues.–Sun. 7–6:30; Oct.–Mar., Tues.–Sun. 7–5.*

Built into a steep slope of the hill crowned by Burg Trausnitz is an unusual art museum, the **Skulpturenmuseum im Hofberg,** containing the entire collection of the Landshut sculptor Fritz Koenig. His own work forms the permanent central section of the labyrinthine gallery. ✉ *Kolpingstr. 481* ☎ *0871/89021* 🎫 *€3* ⏲ *Tues.–Sun. 10:30–1 and 2–5.*

off the beaten path

FREISING – This ancient episcopal seat, 35 km (22 mi) southwest of Landshut, houses a cathedral and Old Town well worth visiting. The town is also accessible from Munich (at the end of the S-bahn 1 line, a 45-minute ride from central Munich).

Where to Stay & Eat

There are several attractive Bavarian-style restaurants in Altstadt and Neustadt, most of them with beer gardens. Although Landshut brews a fine beer, look for a *Gaststätte* offering a *Weihenstephaner*, from the world's oldest brewery, in Freising. Helles (light) is the most popular beer variety.

$$ **Hotel Goldene Sonne.** The steeply gabled Renaissance exterior of the "Golden Sun" fronts a hotel of great charm and comfort. It stands in the center of town, near all the sights. Its dining options are a paneled, beamed restaurant ($–$$); a vaulted cellar; and a courtyard beer garden, where the service is friendly and helpful. The menu follows the seasons and tows the "quintessential Bavarian" line, with pork roast, steamed or smoked trout with horseradish, asparagus in the spring (usually accompanied by potatoes or ham), and venison in the fall. *Neustadt 520, D–84028 0871/92530 0871/925–3350 www.goldenesonne.de 53 rooms Restaurant, cable TV, in-room data ports, beer garden, pub, some pets allowed (fee), no-smoking rooms; no a/c AE, DC, MC, V BP.*

$$ **Romantik Hotel Fürstenhof.** This handsome Landshut city mansion, located a few minutes on foot from the center of town, had no difficulty qualifying for inclusion in the Romantik group of hotels—it just breathes romance, from its plush gourmet restaurant ($$$), covered in wood paneling, to the cozy bedrooms. A vine-covered terrace shadowed by a chestnut tree adds charm. *Stethaimerstr. 3, D–84034 0871/92550 0871/925–544 www.romantikhotels.com/landshut 24 rooms Restaurant, cable TV, sauna, Internet, no-smoking rooms; no a/c in some rooms AE, DC, MC, V BP Restaurant closed Sun.*

$–$$ **Schloss Schönbrunn.** This country mansion is now a luxurious hotel, with many of its original features intact. Rooms in the most historic part of the building are particularly attractive, with huge double beds, and represent excellent value. The handsome house stands in the Schönbrunn district of Landshut, about 2 km (1 mi) from the center. The journey is worthwhile even for the excellent restaurant ($$–$$$), where the menu includes fish from the hotel's own pond, or for a romantic evening at the beer garden. *Schönbrunn 1, D–84036 0871/95220 0871/952–2222 www.hotel-schoenbrunn.de 33 rooms Restaurant, café, cable TV, in-room data ports, bar, beer garden, some pets allowed (fee), no-smoking rooms; no a/c AE, DC, MC, V BP.*

Landshut A to Z

TRANSPORTATION TO & FROM LANDSHUT

Landshut is a 45-minute drive northwest of Munich on either the A–92 autobahn—follow the signs to Deggendorf—or the B–11 highway. The Plattling–Regensburg–Passau train line brings you from Munich in about 50 minutes. A round-trip costs about €20.

VISITOR INFORMATION

Tourist-Information Verkehrsverein Altstadt 315 0871/922–050 www.landshut.de.

MUNICH A TO Z

To research prices, get advice from other travelers, and book travel arrangements, visit www.fodors.com.

AIRPORTS

Munich's International Airport is 28 km (17 mi) northeast of the city center, between the small towns of Freising and Erding. When departing from Munich for home, you can claim your V.A.T. refund (for purchases made during your stay) at a counter either between areas B and C, or between C and D.

Flughafen München ☎ 089/97500 🌐 www.munich-airport.de.

AIRPORT TRANSFERS An excellent train service links the airport with Munich's main train station. The S-1 and S-8 lines operate from a terminal directly beneath the airport's arrival and departure halls. Trains leave every 10 minutes, and the journey takes around 40 minutes. Several intermediate stops are made, including the Ostbahnhof (convenient for lodgings east of the Isar River) and such city-center stations as Marienplatz. A one-way ticket costs €8, or €7.20 if you purchase a multiple-use "strip" ticket (you will have two strips left at the end). A family of up to five (two adults and three children under 15) can make the trip for €15 by buying a *Tageskarte* (which allows travel until 6 AM the next morning). The bus service is slower than the S-bahn link (€9 one-way, €14.50 round-trip). A taxi from the airport costs around €50. During rush hours (7 AM–10 AM and 4 PM–7 PM), allow up to an hour of traveling time. If you're driving from the airport to the city, take route A–9 and follow the signs for MÜNCHEN STADTMITTE (downtown). If you're driving from the city center, head north through Schwabing, join the A–9 autobahn at the Frankfurter Ring intersection, and follow the signs for the airport (FLUGHAFEN).

BUS TRAVEL TO & FROM MUNICH

Long-distance buses arrive at and depart from an area to the west of the main train station. The actual office of the bus company, Touring GmbH, is in the northern section of the train station itself, an area referred to as the Starnberger Bahnhof.

Zentraler Busbahnhof ✉ Arnulfstr., Leopoldvorstadt ☎ 089/545–8700.

CAR TRAVEL

From the north (Nürnberg or Frankfurt), leave the autobahn at the Schwabing exit. From Stuttgart and the west, the autobahn ends at Obermenzing, Munich's most westerly suburb. The autobahns from Salzburg and the east, Garmisch and the south, and Lindau and the southwest all join the Mittlerer Ring (city beltway). When leaving any autobahn, follow the signs reading STADTMITTE for downtown Munich.

PARKING Parking in Munich is nerve-racking and not cheap. There are several parking garages throughout the center, but your best bet is to use public transportation, which is exemplary.

CONSULATES

Canada **Canadian Consulate** ✉ Tal 29, City Center ☎ 089/219-9570.
United Kingdom **British Consulate General** ✉ Bürkleinstr. 10, Lehel ☎ 089/211-090.
United States **U.S. Consulate General** ✉ Königinstr. 5, Maxvorstadt ☎ 089/28880.

EMERGENCIES

Police (☎ 110).

Fire department, ambulance, and medical emergencies (☎ 112).

PHARMACIES

Internationale Ludwigs-Apotheke and Europa-Apotheke, both open weekdays 8–6 and Saturday 8–1, stock over-the-counter medications. Munich pharmacies stay open late on a rotating basis, and every pharmacy has a schedule in its window.

Europa-Apotheke ✉ Schützenstr. 12, near the Hauptbahnhof, Leopoldvorstadt ☎ 089/595-423. **Internationale Ludwigs-Apotheke** ✉ Neuhauserstr. 11, City Center ☎ 089/260-3021.

TAXIS

Munich's cream-color taxis are numerous. Hail them in the street or phone for one (there's an extra charge of €1 if you call). Rates start at €2.40. Expect to pay €8–€10 for a short trip within the city. There's a €0.50 charge for each piece of luggage.

Taxi ☎ 089/21610 or 089/19410.

TOURS

For the cheapest sightseeing tour of the city center on wheels, board Streetcar 19 outside the Hauptbahnhof on Bahnhofplatz and make the 15-minute journey to Max Weber Platz. Explore the streets around the square, part of the old Bohemian residential area of Haidhausen (with some of the city's best bars and restaurants, many on the villagelike Kirchenstrasse), and then return by a different route on Streetcar 18 to Karlsplatz. A novel way of seeing the city is to hop on one of the bike-rickshaws. The bike-powered two-seater cabs operate between Marienplatz and the Chinesischer Turm in the Englischer Garten. Just hail one—or book ahead by calling Rikscha-Mobil. Cost is €37 per hour.

The tourist office offers individual guided tours for fees ranging between €100 and €250. Bookings must be made at least 10 days in advance. Taxi tours with specially trained drivers are offered by IsarFunk Taxizentrale GmbH. These are a good alternative for groups of up to four people. Cost is €68 per trip for the first hour and €18 for each subsequent half-hour. *See* the Sports & the Outdoors section for information on bike tours.

IsarFunk Taxizentrale GmbH ☎ 089/450-540. **Munich Tourist Office** ☎ 089/2333-0234. **Riksha-Mobil** ☎ 089/129-4808.

BUS TOURS Bus excursions to the Alps, to Austria, to the royal palaces and castles of Bavaria, or along the Romantic Road can be booked through DER. Next to the main train station, Panorama Tours operates numerous trips, including the Royal Castles Tour (Schlösserfahrt) of "Mad" King Ludwig's dream palaces; the cost is €41, excluding entrance fees to the palaces. Bookings for both companies can also be made through all major hotels in the city. The tours depart from the front of the Hauptbahnhof outside the Hertie department store.

City bus tours are offered by Panorama Tours. The blue buses operate year-round, departing from the Hertie department store on Bahnhofplatz. A one-hour tour of Munich highlights leaves daily at 10, 11, 11:30, noon, 1, 2:30, 3, and 4. The cost is €11. A 2½-hour city tour departs daily at 10 AM and includes brief visits to the Alte Pinakothek, the Peterskirche, and Marienplatz for the Glockenspiel. An afternoon tour, also 2½ hours and starting at 2:30 PM, includes a tour of Schloss Nymphenburg. The cost of each tour is €19. Another 2½-hour tour, departing Saturday, Sunday, and Monday at 10 AM, includes a visit to the Bavaria film studios. The cost is €23. A four-hour tour, starting daily at 10 AM and 2:30 PM, includes a visit to the Olympic Park. The cost is €19. The München bei Nacht tour provides 4½ hours of Munich by night and includes dinner and a show at the Hofbräuhaus, a trip up the Olympic Tower to admire the lights of the city, and a final drink in a nightclub. It departs April through November, Friday and Saturday at 7:30 PM; the cost is €60.

Yellow Cab Stadtrundfahrten has a fleet of yellow double-decker buses, in which tours are offered simultaneously in eight languages. They leave hourly between 10 AM and 4 PM from the front of the Elisenhof shopping complex on Bahnhofplatz. Tours cost €9.

DER ✉ Hauptbahnhofpl. 2, in main train-station bldg., Leopoldvorstadt ☎ 089/5514-0100. **Panorama Tours** ✉ Arnulfstr. 8, Leopoldvorstadt ☎ 089/323-040. **Yellow Cab Stadtrundfahrten** ✉ Sendlinger-Tor-Pl. 2, Isarvorstadt ☎ 089/303-631.

WALKING TOURS

Downtown Munich is only a mile square and is easily explored on foot. Almost all the major attractions in the city center are on the interlinking web of pedestrian streets that run from Karlsplatz, by the main train station, to Marienplatz and the Viktualienmarkt and extend north around the Frauenkirche and up to Odeonsplatz. The two tourist information offices issue a free map with suggested walking tours.

Two-hour tours of the Old City center are given daily in summer (March–October) and on Friday and Saturday in winter (November–February). Tours organized by the visitor center start at 10:30 and 1 in the center of Marienplatz. The cost is €8. The theme walks of Radius Tours & Bikes includes Munich highlights, Third Reich Munich, Jewish Munich, and the Dachau concentration camp. The cost is €10 (€19 for the Dachau tour). Tours depart daily from the Hauptbahnhof, outside the EurAide office by Track 11, and also meet 15 minutes later at the New Town Hall's Glockenspiel on Marienplatz.

Radius Tours & Bikes ☎ 089/5502-9374 🌐 www.radiusmunich.com.

TRAIN TRAVEL

All long-distance rail services arrive at and depart from the Hauptbahnhof; trains to and from some destinations in Bavaria use the adjoining Starnbergerbahnhof, which is under the same roof. The high-speed

InterCity Express (ICE) trains connect Munich, Augsburg, Frankfurt, and Hamburg on one line; Munich, Nürnberg, Würzburg, and Hamburg on another. Regensburg can be reached from Munich on Regio trains. For tickets and travel information at the main train station, go to the DB counters or the EurAide office at track 11 that serves English-speaking train travelers. You can also try the ABR-DER travel agency, right by the station on Bahnhofplatz.

ABR-DER ✉ Bahnhofpl., Leopoldvorstadt ☎ 089/5514-0200. **Hauptbahnhof** ✉ Bahnhofpl., Leopoldvorstadt ☎ 089/2333-0256, 089/2333-0257, 01805/996-633 train schedules.

TRANSPORTATION AROUND MUNICH

Munich has an efficient and well-integrated public-transportation system, consisting of the U-bahn (subway), the S-bahn (suburban railway), the Strassenbahn (streetcars), and buses. Marienplatz forms the heart of the U-bahn and S-bahn network, which operates from around 5 AM to 1 AM. An all-night tram and bus service operates on main routes within the city. For a clear explanation in English of how the system works, pick up a copy of *Rendezvous mit München,* free at all tourist offices.

Fares are uniform for the entire system. As long as you are traveling in the same direction, you can transfer from one mode of transportation to another on the same ticket. You can also interrupt your journey as often as you like, and time-punched tickets are valid for up to four hours, depending on the number of zones you travel through. Fares are constantly creeping upward, but a basic *Einzelfahrkarte* (one-way ticket) costs €2 for a ride in the inner zone and €1 for a short journey of up to four stops. If you're taking a number of trips around the city, save money by buying a *Mehrfahrtenkarte,* or multiple-strip ticket. Red-strip tickets are valid for children under 15 only. Blue strips cover adults—€9 buys a 10-strip ticket. All but the shortest inner-area journeys (up to four stops) cost two strips (one for young people between 15 and 21), which must be validated at one of the many time-punching machines at stations or on buses and trams. For two to five people on a short stay the best option is the *Partner-Tageskarte,* which provides unlimited travel for one day (maximum of two adults, plus three children under 15). It's valid anytime except 6 AM to 9 AM on weekdays. The costs are €7.50 for an inner-zone ticket and €15 for the entire network. The day card exists in single version for €4.50 for the inner city, €9 for the whole network. A three-day card is also available, costing €11 for a single and €17.50 in the partner version.

The *Welcome Card* covers transport within the city boundaries and includes up to 50% reductions in admission to many museums and attractions in Munich and in Bavaria (lifts up to the Zugspitze in Garmisch-Partenkirchen, for example). The card, obtainable from visitor information offices, costs €6.50 for one day and €15.50 for three days. A three-day card for two people costs €22.50. You can also get a partner card that includes airport transport fare for €38.

All tickets are sold at the blue dispensers at U- and S-bahn stations and at some bus and streetcar stops. Bus drivers have single tickets (the most expensive kind). There are ticket-vending machines in trams, but they don't offer the strip cards. Otherwise tourist offices and Mehrfahrtenkarten booths (which display a white K on a green background) also sell tickets. Spot checks are common and carry an automatic fine of €30 if you're caught without a valid ticket. Holders of a EurailPass, a Youth Pass, or an Inter-Rail card can travel free on all suburban railway trains (S-bahn).

TRAVEL AGENCIES

DER, the official German travel agency, has outlets all over Munich. The two most central ones are in the main train-station building and at the Münchner-Freiheit Square, in Schwabing.

American Express ✉ Promenadenpl. 6, City Center ☎ 089/290-900. **DER** ✉ Bahnhofpl. 2, Leopoldvorstadt ☎ 089/5514-0100 ✉ Münchner-Freiheit 6, Schwabing ☎ 089/336-033.

VISITOR INFORMATION

The Hauptbahnhof tourist office is open Monday–Saturday 9–8 and Sunday 10–6; the Info-Service in the Rathaus is open weekdays 10–8 and Saturday 10–4.

For information on the Bavarian mountain region south of Munich, contact the Tourismusverband München-Oberbayern.

Hauptbahnhof ✉ Bahnhofpl. 2, next to DER travel agency, Leopoldvorstadt ☎ 089/2333-0123 🌐 www.munich-tourist.de. **Info-Service** ✉ Marienpl., City Center ☎ 089/2332-8242. **Tourismusverband München-Oberbayern** (Upper Bavarian Regional Tourist Office) ✉ Bodenseestr. 113, Pasing D-81243 ☎ 089/829-2180.

The Bavarian Alps

2

WORD OF MOUTH

"If you stay in Garmisch-Partenkirchen, you really ought to visit King Ludwig II's Schloss Linderhof. It is very interesting, especially the artificial blue grotto he had built. "

—Eye Spy

"If you want to see the most elegant Ludwig palace of all, take the train to Prien and then the ferry over to Schloss Herrenchiemsee . . . [it's] more elaborately appointed than Neuschwanstein, and more like a miniature Versailles than Linderhof."

—JonJon

www.fodors.com/forums

Updated by
Kevin White

OBERBAYERN, OR UPPER BAVARIA, a region of fir-clad mountains, comes closest to what most of us envision as "Germany." Quaint towns full of half-timber houses—fronted by flowers in summer and snowdrifts in winter—pop up among the mountain peaks, as do the creations of "Mad" King Ludwig II. Shimmering Alpine lakes abound, and the whole area has sporting opportunities galore, making this Germany's favorite year-round vacationland.

This part of Bavaria fans south from Munich to the Austrian border, and as you follow this direction, you'll soon find yourself on a gently rolling plain leading to lakes fed by rivers and streams and surrounded by ancient forests. In time the plain merges into foothills, which suddenly give way to jagged Alpine peaks. In places such as Königsee, near Berchtesgaden, snowcapped mountains seem to rise straight up from the gemlike lakes.

Continuing south, you'll encounter cheerful villages with richly frescoed houses, churches and monasteries filled with the especially voluble and sensuous Bavarian baroque and rococo styles, and several minor spas where you can "take the waters" and tune up your system. Sports possibilities are legion: downhill and cross-country skiing, snowboarding, and ice-skating in winter; tennis, swimming, sailing, golf, and, above all (sometimes literally), hiking, paragliding, and ballooning in summer.

EXPLORING THE BAVARIAN ALPS

The Bavarian Alps comprise a fairly small region. You can easily stay in one spot and make day trips to specific sights. The A–8 autobahn is the region's great traffic artery.

About the Restaurants

You can still find many old *Gasthöfe* with geraniums gushing off balconies and a wood-panel dining area with simple tables and benches, or beer gardens in the region. The mood at these spots is casual; you may even be asked to share a table with strangers. The more upscale places also try to maintain a feeling of familiarity, although you may feel more comfortable at the truly gourmet restaurants if you dress up a bit. Note that many restaurants take a break between 2:30 PM and 6 PM. If you want to eat during these hours, look for the magic words *Durchgehend warme Küche,* meaning warm food served throughout the day, possibly snacks during the off-hours.

About the Hotels

With few exceptions, a hotel or *Gasthof* in the Bavarian Alps and lower Alpine regions has high standards and is traditionally styled, with balconies, pine woodwork, and gently angled roofs upon which the snow sits and insulates. Check out the seven-day packages in the larger resort towns. Private homes all through the region offer Germany's own version of bed-and-breakfasts, indicated by signs reading ZIMMER FREI (rooms available). Their rates may be less than €25 per person. As a general rule, the farther from the popular and sophisticated Alpine resorts you go, the lower the rates. Note, too, that many places

Numbers in the text correspond to numbers in the margin and on the Bavarian Alps map.

If you have 3 days

Consider basing yourself in one spot and exploring the immediate area—you'll still experience just about everything the Bavarian Alps have to offer. Choose between the western (Garmisch-Partenkirchen) area and the eastern (Berchtesgaden) corner. If busy little **Garmisch-Partenkirchen** 1 is your base, devote a couple of days to exploring the magnificent countryside. Wait for good weather to take the cable car or cog railway to the summit of Germany's highest mountain, the Zugspitze. A comfortable day trip takes in the monastery at **Ettal** 2 and **Schloss Linderhof** 3. Also worth a visit is **Oberammergau** 4, where villagers stage the famous Passion Play every 10 years (the next performance is in 2010). Allow a third day to visit **Mittenwald** 5 and its violin museum, taking in the village of Klais (with Germany's highest-altitude railroad station) on the way. If you devote your three days to **Berchtesgaden** 15, allow one of them for **Obersalzberg** 16, site of Hitler's retreat, called Eagle's Nest, and a second for a boat outing on Königsee, deep in the mountains' embrace. On the third day choose between a trip down into Berchtesgaden's salt mine, the Salzbergwerk, or a cross-border run into the Austrian city of Salzburg.

If you have 5 days

Spend a day or two in **Garmisch-Partenkirchen** 1, and then head for Bavaria's largest lake, **Chiemsee** 12 (about a two-hour trip via the autobahn). Spend the night in one of the several villages on its western shore (Prien has a main-line railway station and a boat harbor) and take boat trips to **Schloss Herrenchiemsee** island and to the smaller and utterly enchanting **Fraueninsel.** Round off the journey with two days in **Berchtesgaden** 15 and the **Berchtesgaden National Park** 17.

If you have 7 days

Begin with a day or two based in **Garmisch-Partenkirchen** 1 for excursions to **Schloss Linderhof** 3 and **Oberammergau** 4. Next, strike out east along the well-signposted Deutsche Alpenstrasse. Leave the route after 20 km (12 mi), at Wallgau, to relax for an hour or two on the southern shore of picturesque Walchensee. Then dodge in and out of Austria on a highland road that snakes through the tree-lined Aachen Pass to **Tegernsee** 7, where hills dip from all sides into the lake. Book two or three nights at one of the nearby, moderately priced Gasthöfe, or spoil yourself at one of the luxurious hotels in upscale Rottach-Egern. A day's walk (or a 20-minute drive) takes you to Tegernsee's neighboring lake, the shimmering **Schliersee** 8. From there the road becomes a switchback (one stretch is a privately maintained toll road), climbing from narrow valleys to mountain ski resorts and finally plunging to the Inn River valley. Consider leaving the Alpine route here for a stay on the shores of the **Chiemsee** 12, where King Ludwig's Schloss Herrenchiemsee stands on one of the three islands. Back on the Alpine route, you'll inevitably head back into the mountains, dropping down again into elegant **Bad Reichenhall** 14, another overnight stop. From here it's only 20 km (13 mi) to **Berchtesgaden** 15, where you conclude your stay in the Alps viewing the town, its castle museum, Hitler's mountaintop retreat, and the beautiful Königsee in the **Berchtesgaden National Park** 17.

offer a small discount if you stay more than one night. By the same token, at some places you will harvest a frown if you are staying only one night, especially during the high seasons, in summer, at Christmas, and on winter weekends. In spas and many mountain resorts a "spa tax" is added to the hotel bill. It amounts to no more than €3 per person per day and allows free use of spa facilities and entry to local attractions and concerts.

WHAT IT COSTS In Euros

	$$$$	$$$	$$	$	¢
RESTAURANTS	over €25	€21–€25	€16–€20	€9–€15	under €9
HOTELS	over €225	€175–€225	€100–€175	€50–€100	under €50

Restaurant prices are per person for a main course at dinner. Hotel prices are for two people in a standard double room, including tax and service.

Timing

This mountainous region is a year-round holiday destination. Snow is promised by most resorts from December through March, although there's year-round skiing on the glacier slopes at the top of the Zugspitze. Spring and autumn are ideal times for mountain walking. November is a between-seasons time, when many hotels and restaurants close down or attend to renovations. Note, too, that many locals take a vacation after January 6, and businesses may be closed for anywhere up to a month.

Garmisch-Partenkirchen

1 *90 km (55 mi) southwest of Munich.*

Garmisch, as it's more commonly known, is the undisputed capital of Alpine Bavaria, a bustling, year-round resort and spa. Once two separate communities, Garmisch and Partenkirchen fused in 1936 to accommodate the Winter Olympics. Today, with a population of 28,000, the area is large enough to offer every facility expected from a major Alpine resort without being overwhelming. Garmisch is walkable but spread out, and the narrow streets and buildings of smaller Partenkirchen hold snugly together. In both parts of town pastel frescoes of biblical and bucolic scenes decorate facades.

Partenkirchen was founded by the Romans, and you can still follow the road they built between Partenkirchen and neighboring Mittenwald, which was part of a major route between Rome and Germany well into the 17th century. In the early 18th century the region experienced an economic boom thanks to the discovery of iron ore.

Winter sports rank high on the agenda here. There are more than 99 km (62 mi) of downhill ski runs, 40 ski lifts and cable cars, and 180 km (112 mi) of *Loipen* (cross-country ski trails). One of the principal stops on the international winter-sports circuit, the area hosts a week of races every January. You can usually count on good skiing from December through April (and into May on the Zugspitze).

Biking & Hiking With its lakeside and mountain trails, this region is a mountain biker's paradise. Sports shops rent mountain bikes for around €15 a day. Well-marked and well-groomed hiking trails lead from the glorious countryside, along rivers and lakes, through woods, and high into the Alps. If you just want an afternoon stroll, head for the lower slopes. If you're a serious hiker, make for the mountain trails of the Zugspitze, in Garmisch-Partenkirchen; the heights above Oberammergau, Berchtesgaden, or Bad Reichenhall; or the lovely Walchensee. Well-marked trails near the Schliersee or Tegernsee (lakes) lead steadily uphill and to mountaintop inns. A special treat is a hike to the Tatzelwurm Gorge near Bayrischzell.

Boating & Sailing All the Bavarian Alpine lakes have sailing schools that rent sailboards as well as various other types of boats. At Tegernsee you can hire motorboats at the pier in front of the Schloss Cafe, in the Tergensee town center. Chiemsee, with its wide stretch of water whipped by Alpine winds, is a favorite for both sailing enthusiasts and windsurfers. There are boatyards all around the lake and a very good windsurfing school at Bernau.

On the Menu Designed to pack in the calories after a day's walking or skiing, the food in Bavaria's mountainous areas is understandably hearty and filling. Portions are usually huge, whether they're great wedges of roast pork, dumplings big enough to fire from a cannon, or homemade *Apfelstrudel* (apple-filled pastry), which is a meal in itself. In lakeside inns and restaurants the day's catch might be plump perch (*Renke*) or freshwater trout (*Forelle, Lachsforelle,* or *Bachsaibling*). Many inns have pools where the trout grow even fatter, although they lack the mountain-water tang. Most districts in the Alps distill their own brand of schnapps from mountain herbs, and you can quaff what is arguably the region's best beer on the banks of the Tegernsee.

Skiing & Snowboarding Garmisch-Partenkirchen was the site of the 1936 Winter Olympics and remains Germany's premier winter-sports resort. The upper slopes of the Zugspitze and surrounding mountains challenge the best ski buffs and snowboarders, and there are also plenty of runs for intermediate skiers and families.

Garmisch-Partenkirchen isn't all sporty, however. In Garmisch, beautiful examples of Upper Bavarian houses line Frühlingstrasse, and a pedestrian zone begins at Richard-Strauss-Platz. Off Marienplatz, at one end of the car-free zone, is the 18th-century parish church of **St. Martin.** It contains some significant stucco work by the Wessobrunn artists Schmutzer, Schmidt, and Bader. The chancel is by another fine 18th-century artist from Austria, Franz Hosp. Across the Loisach River, on Pfarrerhausweg, stands another **St. Martin** church, dating from 1280, whose Gothic wall paintings include a larger-than-life-size figure of St. Christopher.

The Bavarian Alps
München
A99
A96
Kirchseeon
Unterhaching
Ottobrunn
Pullach
Grünwald
Taufkirchen
Hohenbrunn
Stegen
Inning
Oberhaching
Starnberg
Herrsching
Berg
Ammersee
Andechs
Feldkirchen
Westerham
Diessen
Wolfratshausen
Tutzing
Holzkirchen
Isar
Geretsried
Starnberger See
Miesbach
472
Bad Tölz
Gmund
Schliersee
A95
Blomberg
Tegernsee
Tegernsee
Rottach-Egern
Benediktbeuren
Bad Wiessee
Murnau
Wallberg
Spitzingsee
Lenggries
Staffelsee
Kochel
Kochelsee
Oberammergau
Walchensee
Sylvenstein Stausee
Schloss Linderhof
Vorderiss
Wallgau
Ettal
Garmisch-Partenkirchen
Zugspitze
Klais
Mittenwald
Jenbach
Schwaz
KEY
Deutsche Alpenstrasse
Start of itinerary

GERMANY
AUSTRIA
Salzach
20
Trostberg
Wasserburg
Alz
304
Laufen
Traunreut
Seebruck
15
Amerang
Inn
Chiemsee
12
Fraueninsel
Teisendorf
Freilassing
Bad Endorf
Traunstein
Prien
Schloss Herrenchiemsee
Ainring
11
Rosenheim
Wals
Bernau
Rottau
Ruhpolding
305
Bad Reichenhall
A8
14
Grassau
A12
13
Aschau
Marquartstein
Rossholzen
Unterwössen
Obersalzberg
Oberwössen
16
305
Reit im Winkl
15
Berchtesgaden
Tatzelwurm
10
Bayrischzell
17
Berchtesgaden National Park
Obersee
Kufstein
St. Johann
Königssee
Saalfelden
Kitzbühel
Wörgl
AUSTRIA
Zell am See
0
20 miles
0
30 km

Objects and exhibitions on the region's history can be found in the excellent **Werdenfelser Museum,** which is itself housed in a building dating back to around 1200. The museum is spread over five floors and explores every aspect of life in the Werdenfels region, which was an independent county for more than 700 years (until 1802). ✉ *Ludwigstr. 47, Partenkirchen* ☎ *08821/2134* 🎫 *€1.50* ⏲ *Tues.–Fri. 10–1 and 3–6, Sat. 10–1.*

On the eastern edge of Garmisch, at the end of Zöppritzstrasse, stands the **villa of composer Richard Strauss,** who lived here until his death in 1949. It's the center of activity during the *Richard-Strauss-Tage,* an annual music festival held in mid-June that features concerts and lectures on the town's most famous son.

The number-one attraction in Garmisch is the **Zugspitze,** the highest mountain (9,731 feet) in Germany. There are two ways up the mountain: a leisurely 75-minute ride on a cog railway from the train station in the town center, combined with a cable-car ride up the last stretch; or a 10-minute hoist by cable car, which begins its giddy ascent from the Eibsee, 10 km (6 mi) outside town on the road to Austria. There are two restaurants with sunny terraces at the summit and another at the top of the cog railway. A round-trip combination ticket allows you to mix your mode of travel up and down the mountain. Prices are lower in winter than in summer, even though they include use of all the ski lifts on the mountain. You can rent skis at the top. ✉ *Cog railway leaves from Olympiastr. 27* ☎ *08821/7970* 🌐 *www.zugspitze.de* 🎫 *Funicular or cable car €44 in summer, €35 in winter, round-trip; parking €3.*

A four-seat cable car goes to the top of one of the lesser peaks: the **Wank** or the **Alpspitze,** some 2,000 feet lower than the Zugspitze. You can tackle both mountains on foot, provided you're properly shod and physically fit.

Where to Stay & Eat

For information about accommodation packages with ski passes, call the **Zugspitze** (☎ 08821/7970 📠 08821/797–901 🌐 www.zugspitze.de) or get in touch with the tourist office in Garmisch.

$–$$$$ ✕ **Riessersee.** On the shores of a small, green tranquil lake—a 3-km (2-mi) walk from town—this café-restaurant is an ideal spot for lunch or afternoon tea (on weekends there's live zither music from 3 to 5). House specialties are fresh trout and local game (which fetches the higher prices on the menu). ✉ *Riess 5* ☎ *08821/95440* 💳 *AE, MC, V* ⏲ *Closed Mon. and Dec. 1–15.*

★ **$$–$$$$** ✕🏨 **Reindl's Partenkirchner Hof.** Owner Karl Reindl ranks among the world's top hoteliers. His award-winning hotel is a real family concern, with daughter Marianne in charge of the kitchen, which cooks up excellent Bavarian specialties and international gastronomical goodies. The light-filled bistro annex serves meals, coffee, and cake in an atmosphere that contrasts sharply with the heavier, wood-and-velvet main building. Each guest room has pinewood furniture and a balcony or patio. Some of the double rooms are huge. If you're planning to stay for several days, ask about specials. ✉ *Bahnhofstr. 15, D–82467*

08821/943–870 08821/9438–7250 www.reindls.de 65 rooms, 23 suites Restaurant, cable TV with movies, Wi-Fi in suites, pool, gym, sauna, bicycles, bar, no-smoking rooms; no a/c in some rooms AE, DC, MC, V BP.

$–$$ **Post-Hotel Partenkirchen.** What makes the Post-Hotel a delight to the eye and a unique spot in the region is the original old furnishings, beginning with the reception area's 20-foot oak refectory table. The rooms continue in the same style, with wood paneling, heavy drapes, and comfortable chairs. The elegant, 500-year-old vaulted cellar tavern offers Italian specialties with hand-picked wines and a daily changing menu, with dishes such as leg of lamb in rosemary sauce. The café boasts opulently carved paneling and delicious cakes. *Ludwigstr. 49, D–82467 08821/93630 08821/9363–2222 56 rooms Restaurant, café, cable TV, Internet room, some pets allowed (fee); no a/c AE, DC, MC, V BP.*

$ **Gasthof Fraundorfer.** You can sled your way to dreamland in this beautiful old Bavarian Gasthof—some of the beds are carved like old-fashioned sleighs; others take the form of antique automobiles. The colorfully painted facade is covered with geraniums most of the year. The tavern-restaurant, its walls covered with pictures and other ephemera, presents "Bavarian evenings" of folk entertainment. *Ludwigstr. 24, D–82467 08821/9270 08821/92799 www.gasthof-fraundorfer.de 20 rooms, 7 suites Restaurant, cable TV, in-room data ports, sauna, steam room, some pets allowed (fee); no a/c AE, MC, V Closed late Nov.–early Dec. BP.*

$ **Hotel-Gasthof Drei Mohren.** In the Partenkirchen village you'll find all the simple, homey comforts you'd expect of a 150-year-old Bavarian inn. All rooms have mountain views, and most are furnished with farmhouse-style painted beds and cupboards. A free bus to Garmisch and the cable-car stations will pick you up right outside the house. The restaurant ($–$$) serves solid fare, including a series of *Pfanderl*, large portions of meat and potatoes in various guises: fried, roasted, or in sauce. *Ludwigstr. 65, D–82467 08821/9130 08821/18974 www.dreimohren.de 21 rooms, 2 apartments Restaurant, cable TV, bar, Internet room, some pets allowed (fee); no a/c AE, MC, V BP.*

★ $$ **Wittelsbacher Hof.** Dramatic mountain vistas from bedroom balconies and a spacious garden terrace make this hotel especially attractive. Public rooms are elegantly Bavarian, and the restaurant has graceful art-nouveau features. The bedrooms are spacious, with corner lounge areas and mahogany or cherrywood furniture. Ask for a room facing south for Zugspitze views. *Von-Brug-Str. 24, D–82467 08821/53096 08821/57312 www.wittelsbacher-hof.com 60 rooms, 2 suites Restaurant, cable TV, pool, sauna, spa, piano bar, Internet room, some pets allowed (fee), no-smoking rooms; no a/c AE, DC, MC, V BP.*

$–$$ **Edelweiss.** Like its namesake, the "eternally white" Alpine flower of *Sound of Music* fame, this small downtown hotel has plenty of mountain charm. Inlaid with warm pinewood, it has Bavarian furnishings and individually decorated rooms. *Martinswinkelstr. 15–17, D–82467 08821/2454 09621/4849 www.hoteledelweiss.de 31 rooms Cable TV, some pets allowed (fee), no-smoking rooms; no a/c V BP.*

Sports & the Outdoors

HIKING & WALKING There are innumerable spectacular walks on 300 km (186 mi) of marked trails through the lower slopes' pinewoods and upland meadows. If you have the time and good walking shoes, try one of the two trails that lead to striking gorges. The **Höllentalklamm** route starts at the **Zugspitze Mountain railway terminal** (✉ Olympiastr. 27) in town and ends at the mountaintop (you'll want to turn back before reaching the summit unless you have mountaineering experience). The **Partnachklamm** route is quite challenging and takes you through a spectacular, tunneled water gorge (entrance fee), past a pretty little mountain lake, and far up the Zugspitze; to do all of it, you'll have to stay overnight in one of the huts along the way. Ride part of the way up in the **Eckbauer cable car** (€7.50 one-way, €10 round-trip), which sets out from the Skistadion off Mittenwalderstrasse. The second cable car, the **Graseckbahn,** takes you right over the dramatic gorges (€3.50 one-way, €5 round-trip). There's a handy inn at the top, where you can gather strength for the hour-long walk back down to the Graseckbahn station. Horse-drawn carriages also cover the first section of the route in summer; in winter you can skim along it in a sleigh. The carriages wait near the Skistadion. Or you can call the local coaching society, the **Lohnkutschevereinigung** (☎ 08821/942–920), for information. Contact **Deutscher Alpenverein** (German Alpine Association; ✉ Von-Kahr-Str. 2–4, D–80997 Munich ☎ 089/140–030 🌐 www.alpenverein.de) for details on hiking and on staying in mountain huts.

SKIING & SNOWBOARDING Garmisch-Partenkirchen's principal draw in winter is skiing. The local mountains are crisscrossed with slopes for all skill levels. The area is divided into two basic regions. The **Riffelriss** with the **Zugspitzplatt** is Germany's highest skiing area, with snow guaranteed from November to May. Access is with the **Zugspitzbahn** funicular. Cost for a day pass is €34, for a 2½-day pass €68 (valid from noon on the first day). The **CLASSIC-Gebiet,** or classical area, has 17 lifts in the **Alpspitz, Kreuzeck** and **Hausberg** region. Day passes cost €28, a two-day pass €48. The town has a number of ski schools and tour organizers. The best place for information for all your snow-sports needs is the Alpine office at the tourist information office, **Alpine Auskunftstelle** (✉ Richard-Strauss-Pl. 2, Garmisch ☎ 08821/180–744 ⏲ Mon.–Thurs. 4–6). Skiers looking for instruction can try the **Skischuke Alpin** (✉ Reintalstr. 8, Garmisch ☎ 08821/945–676). Cross-country skiers should check with the **Erste Skilanglaufschule Garmisch-Partenkirchen** (☎ 08821/1516) at the eastern entrance of the Olympic stadium in Garmisch. For snowboarders, there's the **Snowboardschule Erwin Gruber** (✉ Mittenwalderstr. 47d, Garmisch ☎ 08821/76490). Telemark skiing is also popular in these rugged mountains. For information, contact the **Telemark Schule Leismüller** (✉ Waldeckstr. 7, Garmisch ☎ 08821/752–696).

Nightlife & the Arts

In season there's a busy **après-ski scene.** Many hotels have dance floors, and some have basement discos that pound away until the early hours. Bavarian folk dancing and zither music are regular features of nightlife. In summer there's entertainment every Saturday evening at the **Bayern-**

halle (✉ Brauhausstr. 19). Wednesday through Monday the cozy tavern-restaurant **Gasthof Fraundorfer** (✉ Ludwigstr. 24 ☎ 08821/9270) hosts lots of yodeling and folk dancing. Concerts are presented from Saturday to Thursday, mid-May through September, in the park bandstand in Garmisch, and on Friday in the Partenkirchen park. Tickets are available at **Garmisch-Partenkirchen-Ticket** (✉ Richard-Strauss-Pl. 2 ☎ 08821/752–545 📠 08821/752–547 ⏲ Weekdays 9–1 and 2–7, Sat. 9–1).

The **casino** (✉ Am Kurpark 10 ☎ 08821/95990) is open daily 3 PM–2 AM and Saturday 3 PM–3 AM, with more than 100 slot machines, roulette, blackjack, and poker tables.

Ettal

★ ❷ *16 km (10 mi) north of Garmisch-Partenkirchen, 85 km (53 mi) south of Munich.*

The village of Ettal is presided over by the massive bulk of **Kloster Ettal,** the great monastery founded in 1330 by Holy Roman Emperor Ludwig the Bavarian for a group of knights and a community of Benedictine monks. The abbey was replaced with new buildings in the 18th century and now serves as a school. The original 10-sided church was brilliantly redecorated in 1744–53, becoming one of the foremost examples of Bavarian rococo. The church's chief treasure is its enormous dome fresco (83 feet wide), painted by Jacob Zeiller, circa 1751–52. The mass of swirling clouds and the pink-and-blue vision of heaven are typical of the rococo fondness for elaborate and glowing illusionistic ceiling painting.

Ettaler, a liqueur made from a centuries-old recipe, is still distilled at the monastery. It's made with more than 70 mountain herbs and has legendary health-giving properties. The ad tells it best: "Two monks know how it's made, 2 million Germans know how it tastes." You can buy bottles of the libation from the gift shop and bookstore outside the monastery. This is the largest Benedictine monastery in Germany; approximately 55 monks live here, including one from Compton, Los Angeles. ☎ *08822/740 for guided tour of church* 🎫 *Free* ⏲ *Daily 8–6.*

Where to Stay & Eat

¢–$ ✕ **Edelweiss.** This friendly café and restaurant next to the monastery is an ideal spot for a light lunch or coffee and homemade cakes. ✉ *Kaiser-Ludwig-Pl. 3* ☎ *08822/4509* 💳 *No credit cards.*

$ ✕🏨 **Hotel Ludwig der Bayer.** Backed by mountains, this fine old hotel is run by the Benedictine order. There's nothing monastic about it, except for the exquisite religious carvings and motifs that adorn the walls. Most come from the monastery's own carpentry shop, which also made much of the sturdy furniture in the comfortable bedrooms. The hotel has two excellent restaurants ($–$$) with rustic, Bavarian atmosphere and a vaulted tavern that serves sturdy fare and beer brewed at the monastery. The extensive wellness area includes a Finnish sauna, herbal steam bath, pool, solarium, and massage. ✉ *Kaiser-Ludwig-Pl. 10, D–82488* ☎ *08822/9150* 📠 *08822/74480* *70 rooms, 32 apartments* *2 restaurants, cable TV, tennis court, pool, gym, sauna, steam bath, massage, bicycles, bowling, 2 bars, some pets allowed (fee); no a/c* 💳 *MC, V.*

$ ✕ **Posthotel.** Families are warmly welcomed at this traditional Gasthof in the center of town. There's a playground in the shady garden, and the Bavarian restaurant ($–$$), which is covered in warm wood paneling, has a children's menu. ✉ *Kaiser-Ludwig-Pl. 18, D–82488* ☎ *08822/3596* 🖷 *08822/6971* 🌐 *www.posthotel-ettal.de* *21 rooms, 4 apartments* *Restaurant, cable TV, Wi-Fi, Internet room, gym, sauna, steam room, playground, some pets allowed (fee), no-smoking rooms; no a/c, no room phones* 💳 *MC, V* ⏲ *Closed Oct. 26–Dec. 18* 🍽 *BP.*

Schloss Linderhof

❸ *10 km (6 mi) west of Ettal on B–23, 95 km (59 mi) south of Munich.*

Built between 1870 and 1879 on the grounds of his father's hunting lodge, Schloss Linderhof was the only one of Ludwig II's royal residences to have been completed during the monarch's short life and in which he spent much time. Linderhof was the smallest of this ill-fated king's castles and his favorite country retreat. Set in sylvan seclusion, between a reflecting pool and the green slopes of a gentle mountain, the charming, French-style, rococo confection is said to have been inspired by the Petit Trianon at Versailles. From an architectural standpoint it's a whimsical combination of conflicting styles, lavish on the outside, somewhat overdecorated on the inside. But the main inspiration came from the Sun King of France, Louis XIV, who is referred to in numerous reliefs, mosaics, paintings, and stucco pieces. Ludwig's bedroom is filled with brilliantly colored and gilded ornaments, the Hall of Mirrors is a shimmering dream world, and the dining room has a clever piece of 19th-century engineering—a table that rises from and descends to the kitchens below.

The formal gardens contain still more whimsical touches. There's a Moorish pavilion—bought wholesale from the 1867 Paris Universal Exposition—and a huge artificial grotto in which Ludwig had scenes from Wagner operas performed, with full lighting effects. It took the BASF chemical company much research to develop the proper glass for the blue lighting Ludwig desired. The gilded Neptune in front of the castle spouts a 100-foot water jet. According to hearsay, while staying at Linderhof the eccentric king would dress up as the legendary knight Lohengrin to be rowed in a swan boat on the grotto pond; in winter he took off on midnight sleigh rides behind six plumed horses and a platoon of outriders holding flaring torches (in winter be prepared for an approach road as snowbound as in Ludwig's day—careful driving is called for). ☎ *08822/92030* *Summer €6, winter €4.50; grounds alone in summer €3* ⏲ *Fri.–Wed. 9–6, Thurs. 9–8; pavilion and grotto closed Nov.–Mar.*

Oberammergau

❹ *20 km (12 mi) northwest of Garmisch-Partenkirchen, 4 km (2½ mi) northwest of Ettal, 90 km (56 mi) south of Munich.*

Its location alone, in an Alpine valley beneath a sentinel-like peak, makes this small town a major attraction (allow a half hour for the drive from Garmisch). Its main streets are lined with frescoed houses (such as the 1784 Pilatushaus on Ludwig-Thoma-Strasse), and in summer the village bursts with color as geraniums pour from every window box. Many of these lovely houses are occupied by families whose men are highly skilled in the art of wood-carving, a craft that has flourished here since the early 12th century.

Oberammergau, however, is best known for its **Passion Play,** first presented in 1634 as an offering of thanks after the Black Death stopped just short of the village. In faithful accordance with a solemn vow, it will next be performed in the year 2010 as it has every 10 years since 1680. Its 16 acts, which take 5½ hours, depict the final days of Christ, from the Last Supper through the Crucifixion and Resurrection. It's presented daily on a partly open-air stage against a mountain backdrop from late May to late September. The entire village is swept up in the production, with some 1,500 residents directly involved in its preparation and presentation. Men grow beards in the hope of capturing a key role; young women have been known to put off their weddings—the role of Mary went only to unmarried girls until 1990, when, amid much local controversy, a 31-year-old mother of two was given the part.

You'll find many wood-carvers at work in town, and shop windows are crammed with their creations. From June through October a workshop is open free to the public at the **Pilatushaus** (✉ Ludwig-Thoma-Str. 10 ☎ 08822/92310 tourist office); working potters and painters can also be seen. Pilatushaus was completed in 1775, and the frescoes—considered among the most beautiful in town—were done by Franz Seraph Zwinck, one of the greatest *Lüftlmalerei* painters. The house is named for the fresco over the front door depicting Christ before Pilate. Contact the tourist office to sign up for a weeklong course in wood carving (classes are in German), which costs between €330 and €460, depending on whether you stay in a B&B or a hotel.

The **Heimatmuseum** (Natural History Museum) has historic examples of the wood craftsman's art and an outstanding collection of Christmas crèches, which date from the mid-18th century. Numerous exhibits also document the wax and wax-embossing art, which also flourishes in Oberammergau. ✉ *Dorfstr. 8* ☎ *08822/94136* 🎟 *€2.50* ⏲ *Mid-May–Oct., Tues.–Sun. 2–6; Nov.–mid-May, Sat. 2–6.*

The immense theater, the **Oberammergau Passionsspielhaus,** in which the Passion Play is performed every 10 years, can be toured. Visitors are given a glimpse of the costumes, the sceneries, the stage, and even the auditorium. ✉ *Passionstheater, Passionswiese* ☎ *08822/32278* 🎟 *€2.50* ⏲ *Summer daily 9:30–5, winter daily 10–4.*

The 18th-century **St. Peter and St. Paul Church** is regarded as the finest work of rococo architect Josef Schmutzer and has striking frescoes by Matthäus Günther and Franz Seraph Zwinck (in the organ loft). Schmutzer's son, Franz Xaver Schmutzer, did a lot of the stucco work. ✉ *Pfarrpl. 1* ☎ *08824/553* ⏲ *Daily 9 AM–dusk.*

Where to Stay & Eat

¢–$ ✕ **Ammergauer Stubn.** A homey restaurant with pink tablecloths and a lot of wood, the Stubn has a comprehensive menu that serves both Bavarian specialties and international dishes. You can expect nice roasts and some Swabian dishes, such as *Maultaschen,* a large meat-filled ravioli. ✉ *Wittelsbach Hotel, Dorfstr. 21* ☎ *08822/92800* 💳 *AE, DC, MC* ⏲ *Closed Tues. and Nov.–mid-Dec. No lunch.*

$ **Alte Post.** You can enjoy carefully prepared local cuisine (¢–$) on the original pine tables in this 350-year-old inn. There's a special children's menu, and in summer, meals are also served in the beer garden. If it weren't for the steady automobile traffic groaning through Oberammergau, the front terrace of this delightful old building would be something close to paradise. The rooms are simply appointed, with tasteful rustic furniture. ✉ *Dorfstr. 19 D–82487* ☎ *08822/9100* 📠 *08822/910–100* 🌐 *www.altepost.ogau.de* *31 rooms* *Restaurant, cable TV, Internet room, some pets allowed (fee), no-smoking rooms; no a/c* 💳 *DC, V* ⏲ *Closed Nov.–mid-Dec.* *BP.*

$ **Gasthaus zum Stern.** This is a traditional old place (around 500 years old), with coffered ceilings, thick walls, an old Kachelofen that heats the dining room beyond endurance on cold winter days, and smiling waitresses in dirndls. The food ($–$$) is hearty, traditional Bavarian. For a quieter dinner or lunch, reserve a space in the Bäckerstube. ✉ *Dorfstr. 33, D–82487* ☎ *08822/867* 📠 *08822/7027* *12 rooms* *Some pets allowed; no a/c, no room phones* 💳 *AE, DC, MC, V* ⏲ *Restaurant closed Wed.* *BP.*

$ **Hotel Landhaus Feldmeier.** This quiet family-run hotel, idyllically set just outside the village, has mostly spacious rooms with modern pinewood furniture. All have geranium-bedecked balconies, with views of the village and mountains. The rustic restaurant ($$–$$$) is one of the region's best. You can dine on the sunny, covered terrace in summer. Only hotel guests can use credit cards in the restaurant. ✉ *Ettalerstr. 29, D–82487* ☎ *08822/3011* 📠 *08822/6631* 🌐 *www.hotel-feldmeier.de* *22 rooms, 4 apartments* *Cable TV, gym, hot tub, sauna, steam room, Internet room, some pets allowed (fee), no-smoking rooms; no a/c* 💳 *MC, V* ⏲ *Closed mid-Nov.–mid-Dec.* *BP.*

★ $ **Hotel Turmwirt.** Rich wood paneling reaches from floor to ceiling in this transformed 18th-century inn, set in the shadow of Oberammergau's mountain, the Kofel. The hotel's own band presents regular folk evenings in the restaurant ($–$$). The *Ammergauer Pfanne,* a combination of meats and sauces, will take care of even industrial-size hunger. Rooms have corner lounge areas, and most come with balconies and sweeping mountain views. ✉ *Ettalerstr. 2, D–82487* ☎ *08822/92600* 📠 *08822/1437* 🌐 *www.turmwirt.de* *44 rooms* *Restaurant, cable TV, recreation room, Internet room, some pets allowed (fee), no-smoking rooms; no a/c* 💳 *AE, DC, MC, V* ⏲ *Closed Jan. 7–Jan. 21* *BP.*

$$ **Parkhotel Sonnenhof.** Away from the sometimes crowded town center, the modern Sonnenhof provides a balcony with every guest room, so you can sun yourself and soak up the Alpine view. There's also a children's playroom. ✉ *König-Ludwig-Str. 12, D–82487* ☎ *08822/9130* 📠 *08822/3047* 🌐 *www.parkhotellerie-sonnenhof.de* *51 rooms, 10 suites* *Restaurant, cable TV, Internet room, some in-room data ports, pool, sauna, billiards, bowling, bar, some pets allowed (fee); no a/c* 💳 *AE, DC, MC, V* *BP.*

The Arts

Though the Passion Play theater was traditionally not used for anything other than the Passion Play (the next Passion Play will be done in 2010), Oberammergauers decided that using it for opera during the 10-year pause between the religious performances might be a good idea. The first stagings of Verdi's *Nabucco* and Mozart's *Magic Flute* in 2002 established a new tradition. Ticket prices are between €34 and €69. For reservations, call 08822/923–158.

Mittenwald

5 *20 km (12 mi) southeast of Garmisch, 105 km (66 mi) south of Munich.*

Many regard Mittenwald as the most beautiful town in the Bavarian Alps. It has somehow avoided the architectural sins found in other Alpine villages by maintaining a balance between conservation and the needs of tourism. Its medieval prosperity is reflected on its main street, which has splendid houses with ornately carved gables and brilliantly painted facades. Goethe, Germany's greatest author and thinker, called it "a picture book come alive," and it still is. The town has even re-created the stream that once flowed through the market square, and the main road was detoured around Mittenwald, markedly raising the quality of life in town.

In the Middle Ages, Mittenwald was the staging point for goods shipped from the wealthy city-state of Venice by way of the Brenner Pass and Innsbruck. From Mittenwald, goods were transferred to rafts, which carried them down the Isar River to Munich. In the mid-17th century, however, the international trade route was moved to a different pass, and the fortunes of Mittenwald declined.

In 1684 Matthias Klotz, a farmer's son turned master violin maker, returned from a 20-year stay in Cremona, Italy. There, along with Antonio Stradivari, he had studied under Nicolo Amati, who gave the violin its present form. Klotz taught the art of violin making to his brothers and friends; before long, half the men in the village were crafting the instruments using woods from neighboring forests. Mittenwald became known as the Village of a Thousand Violins, and stringed instruments—violins, violas, and cellos—were shipped around the world. In the right weather—sunny, dry—you may even catch the odd sight of laundry lines hung with new violins out to receive their natural dark hue. The violin has made Mittenwald a small cultural oasis in the middle of the Alps. Not only is there an annual violin- (and viola-, cello-, and bow-) building contest each year in June, with concerts and lectures, but also an organ festival in the church of St. Peter and St. Paul held from the end of July to the end of September. The town also boasts a violin-making school.

The **Geigenbau und Heimatmuseum** (Violin and Local Museum) describes in fascinating detail the history of violin making in Mittenwald. Ask the museum curator to direct you to the nearest of several violin makers—they'll be happy to demonstrate the skills handed down to them. ✉ *Bal-*

lenhausg. 3 ☎ 08823/2511 €2.50 ⊙ Mid-Dec.–Oct., Tues.–Fri. 10–1 and 3–6, weekends 10–1.

On the back of the altar in the 18th-century **St. Peter and St. Paul Church** (as in Oberammergau, built by Josef Schmutzer and decorated by Matthäus Günther), you'll find Matthias Klotz's name, carved there by the violin maker himself. Note that on some of the ceiling frescoes, the angels are playing violins, violas da gamba, and lutes. In front of the church, Klotz is memorialized as an artist at work in a vivid bronze sculpted by Ferdinand von Miller (1813–79), creator of the mighty Bavaria monument in Munich. The church, with its elaborate and joyful stuccowork coiling and curling its way around the interior, is one of the most important rococo structures in Bavaria. Note its Gothic choir loft, added in the 18th century. The bold frescoes on its exterior are characteristic of *Lüftlmalerei,* a style that reached its height in Mittenwald. Images, usually religious motifs, were painted on the wet stucco exteriors of houses and churches. On nearby streets you can see other fine examples on the facades of three famous houses: the Goethehaus, the Pilgerhaus, and the Pichlerhaus. Among the artists working here was the great Franz Seraph Zwinck. ✉ *Ballenhausg., next to Geigenbau und Heimatmuseum.*

Where to Stay & Eat

★ **$$–$$$$** ✕ **Arnspitze.** Get a table at the large picture window and soak in the towering Karwendel Mountain range as you ponder a menu that combines the best traditional ingredients with international touches. Chef and owner Herbert Wipfelder looks beyond the edge of his plate all the way to Asia, if need be, to find inspiration. The fish pot-au-feu has a Mediterranean flare; the jugged hare in red wine is truly Bavarian. The restaurant also offers accommodations in a separate house. ✉ *Innsbrucker Str. 68* ☎ *08823/2425* ▭ *AE* ⊙ *Closed Nov.–mid-Dec. No lunch Tues. and Wed.*

$–$$ ✕ **Post.** Stagecoaches carrying travelers and mail across the Alps stopped here as far back as the 17th century. The hotel has changed a lot since then, but it still retains much of its historic charm. The elegant rooms come in various styles, from modern to art nouveau to Bavarian rustic. The lounge-bar, with its dark woods and green velvet upholstered armchairs, lightens up when the open fire is crackling and live music gets you on the dance floor. You can have dinner here, in the wine tavern or at the low-beam Postklause ($–$$). The food in each is excellent, with an emphasis on Bavarian fare such as roasts and great *Semmelknödel* (bread dumplings). ✉ *Obermarkt 9, D–82481* ☎ *08823/938–2333* *08823/938–2999* 🌐 *www.posthotel-mittenwald.de* *74 rooms, 7 suites* *2 restaurants, cable TV, in-room data ports, pool, sauna, Ping-Pong, bar, some pets allowed (fee), no-smoking rooms; no a/c* ▭ *MC, V* *BP.*

$ ✕ **Alpenrose.** Once part of a monastery and later given one of the town's most beautiful painted baroque facades, the Alpenrose is one of the area's handsomest hotels. The typical Bavarian bedrooms and public rooms have lots of wood paneling, farmhouse cupboards, and finely woven fabrics. The restaurant ($–$$) devotes the entire month of October to veni-

BETWEEN MITTENWALD AND MUNICH

For a beautiful drive, take the B–11 20 km (12 mi) north of Mittenwald to Walchensee, an Alpine lake wedged between the twin fir-clad peaks of the Benediktenwand and the Herzogstand. Trails leading off from the town Walchensee allow you to stretch your legs, or you can hop the chairlift to the summit of the 5,539-foot-high Herzogstand (€12 round-trip; open daily 9–4:15, longer in summer if the weather is good). From here, the B–11 becomes a serpentine mountain road on its way to Kochelsee (15 km [10 mi] north). This famous Alpine lake provided inspiration to the Blaue Reiters, a group of painters including Paul Klee and Franz Marc. The Museum Franz Marc, in a house south of Kochel, has a collection of more than 150 of his works. Further north, the road goes through the village of Benediktbeuren. Its great mid-8th-century monastery is thought to be the oldest Benedictine institution north of the Alps. The monastery has a delightful beer garden that fills with day-trippers in summer.

son dishes, for which it has become renowned. In winter the hotel organizes sleigh rides for its guests. A zither player strums away most evenings in the Josefi wine cellar. ✉ *Obermarkt 1, D–82481* ☎ *08823/92700* 📠 *08823/3720* *16 rooms, 2 apartments* *Restaurant, cable TV, sauna, bar, Internet room, some pets allowed (fee); no a/c* 💳 *AE, DC, MC, V* 🍽 *BP.*

$ **Gasthof Stern.** This white house with brilliant blue shutters is right in the middle of Mittenwald. The painted furniture is not antique but reminiscent of old peasant Bavaria, and the featherbeds are incredibly soft. Locals meet in the dining room for loud conversation, folk music dribbles quietly from the speakers, and the beer garden is a pleasant, familial place to while away the hours with a *Bauernschmaus,* a plate of sausage with sauerkraut and homemade liver dumplings. ✉ *Fritz-Plössl-Pl. 2, D–82481* ☎ *08823/8358* 🌐 *www.stern-mittenwald.de* 📠 *08823/94322* *5 rooms* *Restaurant, beer garden, some pets allowed; no a/c, no room phones* 💳 *No credit cards* 🍽 *BP.*

$ **Bichlerhof.** Carved oak furniture gives the rooms of this Alpine-style hotel a solid German feel. A breakfast buffet is served until 11 AM and will keep the hardiest hiker going all day. Although the restaurant serves only breakfast, there's no shortage of taverns in the area. Most guest rooms have mountain views. ✉ *Adolf-Baader-Str. 5, D–82481* ☎ *08823/9190* 📠 *08823/4584* 🌐 *www.bichlerhof-mittenwald.de* *30 rooms* *Cable TV, in-room data ports, pool, gym, sauna, steam room, some pets allowed (fee), no-smoking rooms; no a/c* 💳 *AE, DC, MC, V* 🍽 *BP.*

Sports & the Outdoors

Mittenwald lies literally in the shadow of the mighty **Karwendel** Alpine range, which rises to a height of nearly 8,000 feet. The **Dammkar** run is nearly 5 mi long and offers some of the best free-riding skiing, telemarking, or snowboarding in the German Alps. A **cable car** (☎ 08823/8480 €12.50 one-way, €20 round-trip, day pass €25 ⏲ Dec.–Oct., daily

8:30–5) carries hikers and skiers to a height of 7,180 feet, the beginning of numerous trails down, or farther up into the Karwendel range. You can book a guide with **Bergerlebnis und Wanderschule Oberes Isartal** (☎ 08651/5835). Skiers, cross-country and downhill, and snowboarders can find all they need including equipment and instruction at the **Erste Schischule Mittenwald** (✉ Bahnhofsparkplatz, parking next to train station ☎ 08823/3582 or 08823/8548).

Shopping

It's not the kind of gift every visitor wants to take home, but if you'd like a violin, a cello, or even a double bass, the Alpine resort of Mittenwald can oblige. There are more than 30 craftsmen whose work is coveted by musicians throughout the world. If you're buying or even just curious, call on **Anton Maller** (✉ Professor-Schreyögg-Pl. ☎ 08823/5865). He's been making violins and other stringed instruments for more than 25 years. The **Geigenbau Leonhardt** (✉ Mühlenweg 53a ☎ 08823/8010) is another good place to purchase one of the town's famous stringed instruments. For traditional Bavarian costumes—dirndls, embroidered shirts and blouses, and lederhosen—try **Trachten Werner** (✉ Hochstr. 1 ☎ 08823/3785). **Trachten Werner-Leichtl** (✉ Dekan-Karl-Pl. 1 ☎ 08823/8282) has a large selection of dirndls and other traditional wear for women.

en route

One of the most beautiful stretches of the Deutsche Alpenstrasse follows the course of the fast-flowing Isar River and is lined with fir tree forests and rocky peaks. A toll road (€2) runs from Wallgau (7 km [4½ mi] north of Mittenwald at the junction of the road north to Benediktbeuren) 15 km (9 mi) to Vorderiss, but the booths are not always manned. Vorderiss is at the western end of the Sylvenstein dam-lake, whose mysterious waters cover a submerged village. Halfway along the lake the road divides and you can either drive east to the Achen Pass, which cuts through Austria (there is no official border, but make sure you have your passport just in case) and on to Tegernsee, or north to the Alpine resort of Lenggries and on to the beautiful spa town of Bad Tölz.

Bad Tölz

❻ *14 km (8 mi) north of Sylvenstein Lake, 48 km (30 mi) south of Munich.*

If you can, visit Bad Tölz on a Wednesday morning—market day—when stalls stretch along the main street to the Isar River, the dividing line between the old and new towns. The latter, dating from the mid-19th century, sprang up with the discovery of iodine-laden springs, which allowed the locals to call their town *Bad* (bath or spa) Tölz. You can take the waters, either by drinking a cupful from the local springs or going all the way with a full course of health treatments at a specially equipped hotel.

Bad Tölz clings to its ancient customs more tightly than does any other Bavarian community. It is not uncommon to see people wearing traditional clothing as their daily dress. The town is also famous for its painted furniture, particularly farmhouse cupboards and chests. Several local shops specialize in this type of *Bauernmöbel* (farmhouse furniture, usually hand-carved from pine) and will usually handle export formalities.

If you're in Bad Tölz on November 6, you'll witness one of the most colorful traditions of the Bavarian Alpine area: the Leonhardiritt equestrian procession, which marks the anniversary of the death in 559 of St. Leonhard, the patron saint of animals, specifically horses. The procession ends north of town at an 18th-century chapel on the Kalvarienberg, above the Isar River.

★ The **Alpamare,** Bad Tölz's very attractive spa complex, pumps spa water into its pools, one of which is disguised as a South Sea beach complete with surf. Its five water slides include a 1,082-foot-long adventure run. Another—the Alpa-Canyon—has 90 degree drops, and only the hardiest swimmers are advised to try it. A nightmarish dark tunnel is aptly named the Thriller. ✉ *Ludwigstr. 13* ☎ *08041/509–999* 🌐 *www.alpamare.de* 🎫 *4-hr ticket €23; €15 for 4 hrs on weekdays from 9 AM–11 AM; €17 after 5 PM* 🕓 *Mon.–Thurs. 9–9, Fri.–Sun. 9 AM–10 PM.*

2

The **Heimatmuseum,** in the Altes Rathaus (Old Town Hall), has many fine examples of Bauernmöbel, as well as a fascinating exhibit on the history of the town and its environs. ✉ *Marktstr. 48* ☎ *08041/504–688* 🎫 *€2.50* 🕓 *Tues.–Sun. 10–4.*

Bad Tölz's local mountain, the **Blomberg,** 3 km (2 mi) west of town, has moderately difficult ski runs and can also be tackled on a toboggan in winter and in summer. The winter run of 5 km (3 mi) is the longest in Bavaria, although the artificial concrete channel used in summer snakes only 3,938 feet down the mountain. A ski-lift ride to the start of the run and toboggan rental are included in the price. ☎ *08041/3726* 🎫 *€7 per toboggan ride* 🕓 *Jan.–Oct., daily 9–4; Nov.–Dec., hrs depend on weather conditions.*

Where to Stay & Eat

★ **$$–$$$$** **Hotel Jodquellenhof-Alpamare.** The *Jodquellen* are the iodine springs that have made Bad Tölz wealthy. You can take advantage of these revitalizing waters at this luxurious spa, where the emphasis is on fitness. Vegetarian and low-calorie entrées are served in the restaurant ($$$–$$$$). The imposing 19th-century building, with private access to the Alpamare Lido, contains stylish rooms, with granite and marble bathrooms. The room price includes full use of the spa facilities. There are discounts for children. ✉ *Ludwigstr. 13–15, D–83646* ☎ *08041/5090* 📠 *08041/509–441* 🌐 *www.jodquellenhof.com* *71 rooms* *Restaurant, cable TV, in-room data ports, pool, hot tubs, sauna, spa, steam room; no a/c* 💳 *AE, DC, MC, V* *BP.*

$–$$ **Hotel Kolbergarten.** Located right near the old town and surrounded by a quiet garden with old trees, this hotel offers comfortable rooms, each carefully done in a particular style such as baroque or biedermeier. The restaurant ($$) offers gourmet food at affordable prices and a wine list that will take you around the world. ✉ *Fröhlichgasse 5, D–83646* ☎ *08041/78920* 📠 *08041/9069* 🌐 *www.hotel-kolbergarten.de* *13* *rooms, 2 suites* ♿ *Cable TV, in-room data ports, Internet room, some pets allowed, no-smoking rooms; no a/c* 💳 *AE, DC, MC, V* 🍽 *BP.*

Nightlife & the Arts

Bad Tölz is world renowned for its outstanding **boys' choir** (☎ 08041/78670 for program details from Städtische Kurverwaltung). When it's not on tour, the choir gives regular concerts in the Kurhaus.

The town has four discos; **Arena** (✉ Demmeljochstr. 42) is considered the best.

Shopping

Looking for a typical piece of Bavarian farmhouse furniture to ship home? Bad Tölz and the surrounding villages provide a rich hunting ground. Try the **Scheune** (✉ Miesbacherstr. 33 ☎ 09041/83240), an old barn stacked high with pine and oaken cupboards, tables, chairs, and carved bedsteads.

Tegernsee

★ 7 *16 km (10 mi) east of Bad Tölz, 50 km (31 mi) south of Munich.*

The beautiful shores of the Tegernsee are among the most expensive property in all of Germany. The interest in the region shown by King Maximilian I of Bavaria at the beginning of the 19th century attracted VIPs and artists, leading to a boom that has never really faded. Most hotels have sensible rates. Tegernsee's wooded shores, rising gently to scalable mountain peaks of no more than 6,300 feet, invite hikers, walkers, and picnicking families (the tourist office in the town of Tegernsee has hiking maps). The lake itself draws swimmers and yachters. In fall the russet-clad trees provide a colorful contrast to the snowcapped mountains.

On the eastern shore of the lake, the town of Tegernsee is home to a large **Benedictine monastery** (✉ Schlosspl.). Founded in the 8th century, this was one of the most productive cultural centers in southern Germany; the Minnesänger (musician and poet), Walther von der Vogelweide (1170–1230), was a welcome guest. Not so welcome were Hungarian invaders who laid waste to the monastery in the 10th century. During the Middle Ages the monastery made a lively business producing stained-glass windows thanks to a nearby quartz quarry, and in the 16th century it became a major center of printing. It was secularization that sealed its fate at the beginning of the 19th century: almost half of the buildings were torn down. Maximilian I bought the surviving ones and had Leo von Klenze redo them for use as a summer retreat.

The late-Gothic **church** was refurbished in Italian baroque style in the 18th century. The frescoes are by Hans Georg Asam, whose work also graces the Benediktbeuren monastery. The property houses a beer tavern, a brewery, a restaurant, and a high school. Students in what was the monastery write their exams beneath inspiring baroque frescoes.

Olaf Gulbransson Museum. This museum is housed in a discreet modern building set back from the main lakeside road of Tegernsee. It's devoted to the Norwegian painter Olaf Gulbrannson, who went to Munich in

1902 and worked as a caricaturist for the satirical magazine *Simplicissimus*. His light, almost transparent works depict noisy politicians and snooty social upper-crusters as well as other subjects. ✉ *Im Kurgarten, Tegernsee* ☎ *08022/3338* 🌐 *www.olaf-gulbransson-museum.de* 🎟 €4 ⏲ *Tues.–Sun. 11–5.*

Maximilian showed off this corner of his kingdom to Czar Alexander I of Russia and Emperor Franz I of Austria during their journey to the Congress of Verona in October 1821. You can follow their steps through the woods to one of the loveliest lookout points in Bavaria, the **Grosses Paraplui.** A plaque marks the spot where they admired the open expanse of the Tegernsee and the mountains beyond. The path starts opposite Schlossplatz and is well marked.

Rottach-Egern is the fashionable and upscale resort at the southern end of the lake. Its classy shops, chic restaurants, and expensive boutiques are as well stocked and interesting as many in Munich; its leading hotels are world-class. Rottach-Egern's church, **St. Laurentius,** is worth seeing for its baroque influences.

While at the Rottach-Egern tourist office (*Kuramt*), have a look at the collection of horse-drawn vehicles at the adjoining **Kutschen-, Wagen- und Schlittenmuseum.** It contains beautifully restored coaches, sleds, oxcarts, and all the implements of the wagondriver's trade. ✉ *Nördliche Hauptstrasse 9* ☎ *08022/671–341* 🎟 €2 ⏲ *Tues.–Sun. 2–5.*

Where to Stay & Eat

$$–$$$$ ✕ **Freihaus Brenner.** Proprietor Josef Brenner has brought a taste of nouvelle cuisine to the Tegernsee. His attractive restaurant commands fine views from high above Bad Wiessee. Try any of his suggested dishes, ranging from roast pheasant in wine sauce to fresh lake fish. ✉ *Freihaushöhe 4, Bad Wiessee* ☎ *08022/82004* 🌐 *www.freihaus-brenner.de* 💳 *MC, V* ⏲ *Closed Tues. and Wed.*

$–$$ ✕ **Weinhaus Moschner.** You're pretty much expected to drink wine in this dark, old tavern on the edge of ritzy Rottach-Egern, though beer from the monastery brewery is also served. The menu has a wide range of options, from sturdy smoked pork to homemade ravioli filled with grilled salmon. But nobody comes here just to eat. You are welcome to join the locals at a rough wooden table in the log-wall tavern taproom, order a glass of ale or Franconian wine, and leave the fine dining until tomorrow. ✉ *Kisslingerstr. 2, Rottach-Egern* ☎ *08022/5522* 💳 *AE, DC, MC, V* ⏲ *Closed Mon. and Tues.*

¢–$ ✕ **Herzogliches Bräustüberl.** Once part of Tegernsee's Benedictine monastery, then a royal retreat, the Bräustüberl is now an immensely popular beer hall and brewery. Only basic Bavarian snacks (sausages, pretzels, all the way up to steak tartare) are served in this crowded place, but hearty meals can be had in the adjoining **Schlossgaststätte** ($–$$). In summer, quaff your beer beneath the huge chestnuts and admire the delightful view of the lake and mountains. ✉ *Schlosspl. 1, Tegernsee* ☎ *08022/4141* ✍ *Reservations not accepted* 💳 *No credit cards* ⏲ *Closed Nov.*

$$–$$$ Fodor'sChoice ★ ✕🏨 **Bischoff am See.** Owners Petra and Markus Bischoff have their heart in their hotel, and it shows in every detail. Each room is individually designed in understated yet warm style with an Asian touch. The bar, breakfast room, restaurant, and terrace have a splendid view of the lake. This top-of-the-line hideaway has four suites, two of which have their own sauna, and the others have whirlpool tubs. The restaurant ($$$–$$$$; closed Mon. and Tues.) prepares international specialties and has 950 wines on its wine list. Every fourth Thursday in the month is sushi night. ✉ *Schweighofstr. 53, D–83684* ☎ *08022/3966* 📠 *08022/1720* 🌐 *www.bischoff-am-see.de* *7 rooms, 5 suites* *Restaurant, cable TV with movies, bar, some pets allowed (fee), no-smoking rooms; no a/c* ▭ *MC, V* 🍽 *BP.*

$$ ✕🏨 **Hotel Bayern.** The elegant, turreted Bayern and its two spacious annexes sit high above the Tegernsee, backed by the wooded slopes of Neureuth Mountain. Rooms overlooking the lake are in big demand despite their relatively high cost, so book early. All guests can enjoy panoramic views of the lake and mountains from the extensive terrace fronting the main building. You can dine in the hotel's stylish little restaurant ($$$–$$$$) or the cozy tavern. The extensive Bayern spa includes a heavenly musical tub and a colored light and aroma solarium. ✉ *Neureuthstr. 23, D–83684* ☎ *08022/1820* 📠 *08022/3775* 🌐 *www.hotel-bayern.de* *63 rooms, 10 suites* *2 restaurants, cable TV, in-room data ports, pool, hair salon, spa, bowling, bar, some pets allowed (fee), no-smoking rooms; no a/c* ▭ *AE, MC, V* 🍽 *BP.*

$$ ✕🏨 **Seegarten.** This lakeside hotel, with pinewood paneling and matching furniture, has cheerful rooms in the bright primary colors typical of Bavarian country-farmhouse style. Ask for a room with a balcony overlooking the Tegernsee. The Seegarten's kitchen ($–$$) is famous for its cakes, made by the in-house pastry chef. In winter a log fire and hot, spiced wine welcome you in the cozy vestibule. ✉ *Adrian-Stoop-Str. 4, D–83707 Bad Wiessee* ☎ *08022/98490* 📠 *08022/85087* *18 rooms* *Restaurant, cable TV, Internet room, some pets allowed; no a/c* ▭ *AE, MC, V* 🍽 *BP.*

$ ✕🏨 **Seehotel Zur Post.** The lake views from most rooms are somewhat compromised by the main road outside, but a central location and a winter garden and terrace are pluses. The restaurant (¢–$), with a panoramic view of the mountains and the lake, serves fresh fish, and there are also special venison weeks worthy of a long detour. ✉ *Seestr. 3, D–83684* ☎ *08022/66550* 📠 *08022/1699* 🌐 *www.seehotel-zur-post.de* *43 rooms, 39 with bath or shower* *Restaurant, cable TV, some pets allowed (fee), no-smoking rooms; no a/c* ▭ *DC, MC, V* 🍽 *BP.*

Nightlife & the Arts

Every resort has its **spa orchestra**—in the summer they play daily in the music-box-style bandstands that dot the lakeside promenades. A strong Tegernsee tradition is the summerlong program of **festivals,** some set deep in the forest. Tegernsee's lake festival in August, when sailing clubs deck their boats with garlands and lanterns, is an unforgettable experience.

Bad Wiessee has a lakeside **casino** (☎ 08022/82028) that's open daily 3 PM–2 AM and sets the tone for a surprisingly lively after-dark scene.

The **Bischoff am See** (✉ Schweighoferstr. 53 ☎ 08022/3966), on the lake shore in Tegernsee, has a sensational terrace bar with prices to match one of Bavaria's finest views.

Shopping

In Bad Tölz, **Schöttl** (✉ 61a Marktstr.) offers a wide assortment of traditional regional items, from trinkets to clothing. To get there, follow the lovely Marktstrasse up from the river and watch for the oversize top hat at the corner of Hindenburgstrasse. **Greif** (✉ Nördliche Hauptstr. 24, Rottach-Egern ☎ 08022/5540) has a fine selection of tastefully modern Bavarian fashions and a large stock of handwoven fabrics that you can either buy or have a costume fitted from. At her workshop just outside Gmund, **Marianne Winter-Andres** (✉ Miesbacherstr. 88, Gmund ☎ 08022/74643) creates a wide and attractive range of high-quality pottery at sensible prices.

Sports & the Outdoors

GOLF Besides swimming, hiking, and skiing, the Tegernsee area has become a fine place for golfing. The **Tegernseer GOLFCLUB e. V** (✉ 83707 Bad Wiessee ☎ 08022/8769), has an 18-hole course overlooking the lake with a clubhouse and excellent restaurant. It also has fine apartments for rent.

off the beaten path

WALLBERG – For the best vista in the area, climb this 5,700-foot mountain at the south end of the Tegernsee. It's a hard four-hour hike, though anyone in good shape should be able to make it since it involves no rock climbing. A cable car makes the ascent in just 15 minutes and costs €8 one-way, €13 round-trip. At the summit are a restaurant and sun terrace and several trailheads; in winter the skiing is excellent.

Schliersee

8 *20 km (12 mi) east of Tegernsee, 55 km (34 mi) southeast of Munich.*

Schliersee is smaller, quieter, and less fashionable than Tegernsee, but hardly less beautiful. The different histories of the two lakes are made clear in the names local people have long given them: the Tegernsee is *Herrensee* (Masters' Lake), while the Schliersee is *Bauernsee* (Peasants' Lake), although today Schliersee is more for the well-heeled. There are walking and ski trails on the mountain slopes that ring its placid waters. The lake is shallow and often freezes over in winter, when the tiny island in its center is a favorite hiking destination.

Schliersee was the site of a monastery, built in the 8th century by a group of noblemen. It subsequently became a choral academy, which eventually moved to Munich. Today only the restored 17th-century **Schliersee church,** in the middle of town, recalls this piece of local history. The church has some frescoes and stucco work by Johann Baptist Zimmermann.

Where to Stay & Eat

¢–$ ✕ **Zum Hofhaus am See.** What better place to enjoy a meal than in a small beer garden on the shore? The Hofhaus radiates a kind of friendly intimacy—even if the waitress doesn't crack a smile. Down-to-earth food, such as hocks or fresh forest mushrooms in cream with an herbed dumpling, is the order of the day. In winter the Hofhaus offers fondue as a specialty. ✉ *Mesnerg. 2* ☎ *08026/94499* ▭ *No credit cards.*

$ **Gästehaus Franke am See.** Light, clean rooms with simple no-nonsense furniture can be very pleasant as a change from all the heavy dark beams and wood paneling you may have seen on your journey. The house's garden is a few steps from the lake. The Franke is small, giving it a nice family feel. ✉ *Seestr. 8, D–83727* ☎ *08026/4097* 📠 *08026/4098* 🌐 *www.gaestehaus-franke-schliersee.de* *7 rooms, 2 suites* *Cable TV, some pets allowed; no a/c* ▭ *No credit cards* *CP.*

Shopping

If, at the end of your Upper Bavarian tour, you're still looking for *something,* stop at the busy market town of Miesbach (north of Schliersee) and climb the stairs to **Cilly's Gschirrladn** (✉ Stadtpl. 10, Miesbach ☎ 08025/1705). A warren of rooms is stocked ceiling high with every variety of item for the home, from embroidered tablecloths to fine German porcelain.

Spitzingsee

9 *10 km (6 mi) south of Schliersee, 65 km (40 mi) southeast of Munich.*

Arguably the most beautiful of this group of Bavarian lakes, the Spitzingsee is cradled 3,500 feet up between the Taubenstein, Rosskopf, and Stumpfling peaks, and the drive here is spectacular. The lake is usually frozen over in winter and almost buried in snow. In summer it's warm enough for a swim. Walking in this area is breathtaking in every season and in every sense. The skiing is very good, too. The only downside is the overrun town of Spitzingsee, whose modern architecture violates almost every rule of aesthetics.

Where to Stay & Eat

¢–$ ✕ **Alte Wurzhütte.** If you can't sit outside on the terrace and enjoy a dreamy view of the lake, then you'll have to make due with the cozy, Bavarian log-cabin atmosphere inside. Dishes here, such as Bavarian duck with red cabbage and a monster potato dumpling, are nice and heavy and come at excellent prices. ✉ *Rosskopfweg 1* ☎ *08026/60680* ▭ *No credit cards.*

$$–$$$ ✕ **Arabella Sheraton Alpenhotel.** For an out-of-the-way break in the mountains, head for this luxurious hotel on the shore of the Spitzingsee—even though its architecture is an eyesore. Rooms meet the high standards of comfort expected from the hotel chain that runs the establishment. If you can't stay overnight, come for a leisurely lunch ($$–$$$) at the **König Ludwig Stuben,** or for a fondue night or theme buffet. Try the lake fish or the venison, in-season. For lighter Italian fare, you can enjoy **Osteria L'Oliva** with a menu of pasta, salads, and dishes from the grill. ✉ *Seeweg 7, D–83727* ☎ *08026/7980* 📠 *08026/798–879* 🌐 *www.arabellasheraton.de* *120 rooms, 13 suites* *2 restaurants, cable TV, some in-room data ports, 2 tennis courts, pool, gym,*

sauna, steam room, boating, bowling, bar, library, some pets allowed (fee), no-smoking rooms; no a/c ⊟ *AE, DC, MC, V* 🍽 *BP.*

Bayrischzell

⑩ *10 km (6 mi) east of Schliersee, 65 km (40 mi) southeast of Munich.*

Bayrischzell is in an attractive family-resort area, where many a Bavarian first learned to ski. The wide-open slopes of the Sudelfeld Mountain are ideal for undemanding skiing; in summer and fall you can explore countless upland walking trails. Access to the Sudelfeld area costs €1.50 per car.

The town sits at the end of a wide valley overlooked by the 6,000-foot **Wendelstein** Mountain, which draws expert skiers. At its summit is a tiny stone-and-slate-roof chapel that's much in demand for wedding ceremonies. The cross above the entrance was carried up the mountain by Max Kleiber, who designed the 19th-century church. An instructive **geopark,** laid out beneath the summit, explains the 250-million-year geological history of the area on 36 graphic signboards. You can reach the summit from two directions: The cable car sets out from Osterhofen on the Bayrischzell-Munich road and costs €17 round-trip, €10 one-way (its last descent is at 4 PM). The historic cog railway leaves from Brannenburg, on the north side of the mountain, between Bayrischzell and the Inn Valley autobahn. A round-trip costs €23.50, a single trip €14.50; it's closed November and the first three weeks of December. The cable car closes for two weeks in mid-April.

Where to Stay & Eat

$–$$ ✕🏨 **Hotel Feuriger Tatzelwurm.** This archetypal old Bavarian inn (with a modern wing) is named after the nearby Tatzelwurm Gorge and is ideally placed for hikes or ski trips. The inn sits in isolated splendor above a forest pond, some 980 feet from the main Oberaudorf-Bayrischzell road. Bavarian dishes (also vegetarian) are served in the warren of paneled dining rooms (¢–$$$$), one of which is dominated by a historic tile stove. The two-person *Jadgherrenplatte Brünnstein* will let you sample the game of the area (both people need to be ravenous to finish off this plate). The spa area has everything anyone could desire. ✉ *Am Tatzelwurm, D–82080 Oberaudorf/Bayrischzell* ☎ *08034/30080* 📠 *08034/7170* 🛏 *45 rooms* 👍 *Restaurant, cable TV, in-room data ports, spa, bicycles, Ping-Pong, some pets allowed (fee), no-smoking rooms; no a/c* ⊟ *DC, MC, V* 🍽 *BP.*

$ ✕🏨 **Wendelstein.** This large restaurant ($) in the middle of Bayrischzell fills up quickly on winter evenings. On warm summer days, there's always the beer garden, shaded by old chestnut trees. The generous portions come at reasonable prices. If you are not into slabs of meat, you can try some of the vegetarian dishes such as a schnitzel of celery. Rooms here are simple but comfortable. ✉ *Ursprungstr. 1* ☎ *08023/80890* 📠 *08023/808–969* 🛏 *18 rooms* 👍 *Restaurant, cable TV, beer garden, Internet room, some pets allowed (fee), no-smoking rooms; no a/c* ⊟ *AE, MC, V* ⏲ *Restaurant closed Nov.–mid-Dec. and Mon.* 🍽 *BP.*

en route

A few miles east of Bayrischzell on the Sudelfeld Road is the **Tatzelwurm** gorge and waterfall, named for a winged dragon that supposedly inhabits these parts. Dragon or not, this can be an eerie place to drive at dusk. A hiking trail is signposted. From the gorge, the road drops sharply to the valley of the Inn River, leading to the busy ski resort of Oberaudorf.

The Inn River valley, an ancient trade route, is the most important road link between Germany and Italy. The wide, green Inn gushes here, and in the parish church of St. Bartholomew, at **Rossholzen** (16 km [10 mi] north of Oberaudorf), you can see memorials and naively painted tributes to the local people who have lost their lives in its chilly waters. The church has a baroque altar incorporating vivid Gothic elements. A simple tavern adjacent to the church offers an ideal opportunity for a break on the Alpine Road.

Rosenheim

⓫ *34 km (21 mi) north of Bayrischzell, 55 km (34 mi) east of Munich.*

Bustling Rosenheim is a medieval market town that has kept much of its character despite the onslaught of industrial development. The arcaded streets of low-eaved houses are characteristic of Inn Valley towns. Lake Chiemsee is nearby, and the area has a handful of rural lakes of its own (Simssee, Hofstättersee, and Rinssee). Leisure activities and culture at lower prices than in Munich have made the area very popular.

The old restored locomotive shed, the **Lokschuppen** (✉ Rathausstr. 24 ☎ 08031/365–9036), attracts crowds from as far away as Salzburg and Munich to its special exhibitions (mostly of art).

The Inn River was a major trade artery that bestowed a fair amount of wealth onto Rosenheim, especially in the Middle Ages. It not only served the purpose of transportation but also created jobs thanks to fishing, shipping, bridge-building, shipbuilding, and the like. The **Inn Museum** tells the story of the river, from geology to business. ✉ *Innstr. 74* ☎ *08031/31511* 🎫 *€2* ⏲ *Apr.–Oct., Fri. 9–noon, weekends 10–4.*

Wood is another traditional big business around Rosenheim. **Das Holztechnische Museum** documents how it's grown and how it's used, for example in interior decoration, transportation, architecture, and art. ✉ *Max-Josephs-Pl. 4* ☎ *08031/16900* 🎫 *€2* ⏲ *Tues.–Sat. 10–5.*

need a break?

The **aran coffeehouse** (✉ Kaiserstr. 16 ☎ 08031/357–673 ⏲ closed weekend afternoons), on the main square, makes the best coffee and tea in the region, as well as sandwiches made of freshly home-baked bread, and sweets. You can also purchase coffee beans to go, or other gifts, such as books and large candles.

Where to Stay & Eat

$ ✕🏨 **Fortuna.** This modern hotel at the entrance of Rosenheim (when arriving from the autobahn) has its focus on comfort and good value.

Rooms are done in minimalist style, in contrast perhaps to the restaurant (¢–$). A large Italian menu with everything from simple pizza to grilled fish is a nice change in the Pork-Roast Belt of Germany. ✉ *Hochplattenstr. 42, D–83026* ☎ *08031/616–363* 📠 *08031/6163–6400* 🌐 *www.hotel-fortuna.de* 18 *rooms* *Restaurant, cable TV, in-room data ports, some pets allowed (fee)* 💳 *MC, V* 🍽 *BP.*

$$ **Panorama Cityhotel.** The Panorama is a modern, convenient hotel in the middle of town offering comfortable rooms. It even has two nicely furnished apartments at reasonable rates. Note that prices are lower on weekends, but rise during Oktoberfest (Rosenheim is 45 minutes by train from Munich) and the big trade fairs in Munich. ✉ *Brixstr. 3, D–83022* ☎ *08031/3060* 📠 *08031/306–415* 🌐 *www.panoramacityhotel.de* *89 rooms* *Minibars, cable TV with movies, in-room data ports, bar, parking (fee), some pets allowed, no-smoking rooms; no a/c* 💳 *AE, DC, MC, V* 🍽 *BP.*

Chiemsee

⓬ *20 km (12 mi) east of Rosenheim, 80 km (50 mi) east of Munich.*

Chiemsee is north of the Deutsche Alpenstrasse, but it demands a detour, if only to visit King Ludwig's huge palace on one of its idyllic islands. It's the largest Bavarian lake, and although it's surrounded by reedy flatlands, the nearby mountains provide a majestic backdrop. The town of **Prien** is the lake's principal resort. The tourist offices of Prien and Aschau offer an €18 transportation package covering a boat trip, a round-trip rail ticket between the two resorts, and a round-trip ride by cable car to the top of Kampen Mountain, above Aschau.

Despite its distance from Munich, the beautiful Chiemsee drew Bavarian royalty to its shores. Its dreamlike, melancholy air caught the imagination of King Ludwig II, and it was on one of the lake's three islands that he built his third and last castle, sumptuous **Schloss Herrenchiemsee.** The palace was modeled after Louis XIV's Versailles, but this was due to more than simple admiration: Ludwig, whose name was the German equivalent of Louis, was keen to establish that he, too, possessed the absolute authority of his namesake, the Sun King. As with most of Ludwig's projects, the building was never completed, and Ludwig only spent nine days in the castle. Moreover, Herrenchiemsee broke the state coffers and Ludwig's private ones as well. The gold leaf that seems to cover more than half of the rooms is especially thin. Nonetheless, what remains is impressive—and ostentatious. Regular ferries out to the island depart from Stock, Prien's harbor. If you want to make the journey in style, board the original 1887 steam train from Prien to Stock to pick up the ferry. A horse-drawn carriage takes you to the palace itself.

Fodor's Choice ★

Most spectacular is the Hall of Mirrors, a dazzling gallery where candlelighted concerts are held in summer. Also of interest are the ornate bedrooms Ludwig planned, the "self-rising" table that ascended from the kitchen quarters, the elaborately painted bathroom with a small pool for a tub, and the formal gardens. The south wing houses a **museum** containing Ludwig's christening robe and death mask, as well as other artifacts of his life. While the palace was being built, Ludwig stayed in a royal suite of apartments in a former monastery building on the island, the Alten Schloss. Germany's postwar constitution was drawn up here in 1948, and this episode of the country's history is the centerpiece of the museum housed in the ancient building, the **Museum im Alten Schloss** (€3) *08051/68870 palace Palace, including Museum im Alten Schloss €7 Mid-Mar.–late Oct., daily 9–6; late Oct.–mid-Mar., daily 10–4:45; English-language palace tours daily at 11:45 and 2:25.*

Boats going between Stock and Herrenchiemsee Island also call at the small retreat of **Fraueninsel** (Ladies' Island). The **Benedictine convent** there, founded 1,200 years ago, now serves as a school. One of its earliest abbesses, Irmengard, daughter of King Ludwig der Deutsche, died here in the 9th century. Her grave in the convent chapel was discovered in 1961, the same year that early frescoes there were brought to light. The chapel is open daily from dawn to dusk. Otherwise, the island has just a few private houses, a couple of shops, and a hotel.

off the beaten path

AMERANG – There are two interesting museums in this town, northwest of Chiemsee. In the **Museum für Deutsche Automobilgeschichte** (Museum of German Automobile History), 220 automobiles begin with an 1886 Benz and culminate in contemporary models. The world's largest small-gauge model-railway panorama is spread out over nearly 6,000 square feet. *Wasserburger Str. 38 08075/8141 www.efa-automuseum.de €6.50 Late Mar.–Oct., Tues.–Sun. 10–6; last entry at 5.*

The **Bauernhausmuseum** (Farmhouse Museum) consists of four beautiful farmhouses with a bakery, beehives, sawmill, and blacksmith's workshop. It's worth seeing to find out more about everyday life in the Chiemgau. Every Sunday afternoon an 85-year-old roper shows off his craft, as does a lace maker. On alternate Sundays, spinning, feltmaking, and blacksmithing are demonstrated. You can take in the idyllic surroundings from the beer garden. *Im Hopfgarten 08075/915–090 €3 Mid-Mar.–mid-Nov., Tues.–Sun. 9–6; last entry at 5.*

Where to Stay & Eat

★ ¢–$$ **Wirth von Amerang.** Theme restaurants are an up-and-coming business in Bavaria, and the Wirth is the spearhead. The interior design comes very close to medieval, with brick stoves of handmade bricks, dripping candles, and a floor resembling packed clay. The food is definitely Bavarian, with *Knödels* (dumplings) and pork roast, hocks, and a top-notch potato soup. Reservations are recommended. You may want to purchase the pumpkinseed oil or a homemade schnapps. *Postweg 4, Amerang 08075/185–918 No credit cards No lunch Nov.–Mar.*

$$ **Inselhotel zur Linde.** Catch a boat to this enchanting inn on the car-free Fraueninsel: but remember, if you miss the last connection to the mainland (at 9 PM), you'll have to stay the night. The island is by and large a credit-card-free zone, so be sure to bring cash. Rooms are simply furnished and decorated with brightly colored fabrics. The Linde is

one of Bavaria's oldest hotels, founded in 1396 as a refuge for pilgrims. Artists have favored the inn for years, and one of the tables in the small Fischerstüberl dining room ($–$$) is reserved for them. ✉ *Faueninsel im Chiemsee 1, D–83256* ☎ *08054/90366* 🖷 *08054/7299* 🌐 *www.inselhotel-zurlinde.de* *14 rooms* *Restaurant, bar, Internet room, no a/c* 💳 *MC, V* ⏲ *Closed mid-Jan.–mid-Mar.* *BP.*

$–$$ **Hotel Luitpold am See.** Boats to the Chiemsee islands tie up right outside your window at this handsome old Prien hotel, which organizes shipboard disco evenings as part of its entertainment program. Rooms have traditional pinewood furniture, including carved cupboards and bedsteads. Fish from the lake is served at the pleasant restaurant ($–$$). ✉ *Seestr. 110, D–83209 Prien am Chiemsee* ☎ *08051/609–100* 🖷 *08051/609–175* 🌐 *www.luitpold-am-see.de* *51 rooms* *Restaurant, café, cable TV, Internet room, some pets allowed (fee), no-smoking rooms; no a/c* 💳 *AE, DC, MC, V* *BP.*

$ **Schlosshotel Herrenchiemsee.** This handsome mansion on the island of Herrenchiemsee predates King Ludwig's palace, which is a 15-minute walk through the woods. The rooms aren't palatial but are comfortable. A big plus is the pavilionlike restaurant ($–$$), which serves fresh fish. If you're just here to eat, make sure to catch the last boat to the mainland (9 PM)—otherwise you'll be sleeping on this traffic-free island. ✉ *Herrenchiemsee, D–83209* ☎ *08051/1509* 🖷 *08051/1509* *12 rooms, 6 with bath or shower* *Restaurant, some pets allowed; no a/c, no room phones* 💳 *AE, DC, MC, V* ⏲ *Hotel closed Oct.–Easter* *CP.*

Sports & the Outdoors

There are boatyards all around the lake and several windsurfing schools. The **Mistral-Windsurfing-Center** (✉ Waldstr. 20 ☎ 08054/909–906), at Gdstadt, has been in operation for decades. From its boatyard the average windsurfer can make it with ease to the next island. The gentle hills of the region are ideal for golf. **Chiemsee Golf-Club Prien e.V** (☎ 08051/62215), in Prien, has a year-round, 9-hole course. **SportLukas** (✉ Hauptstr. 3, D–83259 Schkeching ☎ 08649/243) provides equipment for any kind of sport imaginable, from skiing to kayaking, climbing to curling, and it organizes tours.

Aschau

13 *10 km (6 mi) south of Chiemsee, 75 km (46 mi) east of Munich.*

Aschau is an enchanting red-roof village nestled in a wide valley of the Chiemgauer Alps. Its **Schloss Hohenaschau** is one of the few medieval castles in southern Germany to have been restored in the 17th century in baroque style. Chamber-music concerts are presented regularly in the Rittersaal (Knights Hall) during the summer. Parts of the castle can be visited—the rest of the rooms are used as a vacation home for Germany's federal tax officials. The **Prientalmuseum** (Museum of the Prien Valley), with historical documents on the region, is in the former deacon's house. Exhibitions by contemporary international artists are also on display. ☎ *08052/904–937* *Castle €2.50* ⏲ *May–Sept., Tues.–Fri. tours at 9:30, 10:30, and 11:30; Apr. and Oct., Thurs. at 9:30, 10:30, and 11:30; museum during tour times and Sun. 1:30–5.*

Where to Stay & Eat

$$–$$$$ Fodor'sChoice ★ **Residenz Heinz Winkler.** Star chef Heinz Winkler has turned a sturdy village inn into one of Germany's most extraordinary hotel-restaurant complexes. Rooms in the main house are noble in proportions and furnishings, and the maisonette-style suites in the annexes are cozy and romantic. All have views of the mountains. The restaurant ($$$$) has kept with ease the awards that Winkler won when in charge of Munich's Tantris. A grand piano and a harp add harmony to this deliciously sophisticated scene. *Kirchpl. 1, D–83229 08052/17990 08052/179–966 www.residenz-heinz-winkler.de 19 rooms, 13 suites Restaurant, cable TV, in-room data ports, pool, sauna, spa, steam room, bar, some pets allowed (fee); no a/c AE, DC, MC, V BP.*

$–$$ **Hotel Bonnschlössl.** This turreted country palace is set in its own park studded with centuries-old trees. In good weather breakfast is served on the balustraded terrace. The hotel is 6 km (4 mi) north of Aschau and has a similarly enchanting sister property in the nearby village of Bernau, the Gasthof Alter Wirt. Both the Schloss and the Gasthof are protected by preservation orders. Emperor Maximilian I stayed overnight at the Gasthof in 1503 on his way to besiege the castle of Marquartstein. *Kirchpl. 9, D–83233 Bernau 08051/89011 08051/89103 www.alter-wirt-bernau.de 22 rooms Restaurant, cable TV, sauna, spa, beer garden, Weinstube, some pets allowed, no-smoking rooms; no a/c MC, V Closed Mon. BP.*

Bad Reichenhall

14 *50 km (30 mi) east of Aschau, 20 km (12 mi) west of Salzburg.*

Bad Reichenhall is remarkably well located, near the mountains for those who want to hike and ski, and near Salzburg in Austria for visitors who wish to enjoy a lively cultural scene. The town shares a remote corner of Bavaria with another prominent resort, Berchtesgaden. Although the latter is more famous, Bad Reichenhall is older, with saline springs that made the town rich. Salt is so much a part of the town that you can practically taste it in the air. Europe's largest source of brine was first tapped here in pre-Christian times; salt mining during the Middle Ages supported the economies of cities as far away as Munich and Passau. Tourism gave the local economy an additional boost and another use for the salt, namely for its healing properties, starting in the early 20th century.

In the early 19th century, King Ludwig I built an elaborate saltworks and spa house—the **Alte Saline und Quellenhaus**—in vaulted, pseudomedieval style. Their pump installations, which still run, are astonishing examples of 19th-century engineering. A "saline" **chapel** is part of the spa's facilities and was built in exotic Byzantine style. An interesting museum in the same complex looks at the history of the salt trade. The Alte Saline also houses a small **glass foundry** (08651/69738 www.riedl-glaskunst.de free weekdays 9–1 and 2–6, Sat. 9–1), run by the famous company Riedl, makers of fine tableware. Glassblowers and engravers display their art in a small self-service restaurant, and children can try their mouths, so to speak, at glassblowing. The showroom has many articles for sale, notably glass globes used to ensure your potted plants are being slowly watered while you are away. There are tours through the whole salt complex, including visits to the museum. ✉ *Salinen Str.* ☎ *08651/700–2146* 🌐 *www.suedsalz.de* 🎫 *€5.20, combined ticket with Berchtesgaden salt mine €14.50* ⏲ *May–Oct., daily 10–1:30 and 2–4; Nov.–Apr., Tues. and Thurs. 2–4.*

The pride and joy of the Reichenhallers is the steep, craggy mountain appropriately named the **Predigtstuhl** (Preaching Pulpit), which stands at 5,164 feet, southeast of town. A ride to the top offers a splendid view of the area. You can hike, ski in winter, or just enjoy a meal at the **Berhotel Predigtdstuhl** ($–$$). The cable-car ride costs €9.50 one-way up, €8 one-way down, and €15 round-trip. Departures begin at 9:30 AM and continue (as needed) until the last person is off the mountain. ✉ *Südtiroler Platz 1* ☎ *08651/1719* 🌐 *www.predigtstuhl-bahn.de.*

2

Hotels here base spa treatments on the health-giving properties of the saline springs and the black mud from the area's waterlogged moors. The waters can also be taken in the elegant, pillared **Wandelhalle** pavilion of the attractive spa gardens throughout the year. Breathing salt-laden air is a remedy for various lung conditions. All you need to do is walk along the 540-foot Gradierwerk, a massive wood-and-concrete construction that produces a fine salty mist by trickling brine down a 40-foot wall of dense blackthorn bundles. ✉ *Salzburgerstr.* ⏲ *Mon.–Sat. 8–12:30 and 3–5, Sun. 10–12:30.*

The ancient church **St. Zeno** is dedicated to the patron saint of those imperiled by floods and the dangers of the deep, an ironic note in a town that flourishes on the riches of its underground springs. This 12th-century basilica, one of the largest in Bavaria, was remodeled in the 16th and 17th centuries, but some of the original Romanesque cloisters remain, although these can be seen only during services and from 11 to noon on Sunday and holidays. ✉ *Kirchpl. 1* ☎ *08651/4889.*

Where to Stay & Eat

$$$–$$$$ ✕🏨 **Steigenberger-Hotel Axelmannstein.** Ludwig would have enjoyed the palatial air that pervades this hotel—and he would have been able to afford the price, which rivals that of top hotels in Germany's most expensive cities but does include a meal. Luxurious comfort is found in rooms ranging in style from rustic to demure. The fine restaurant ($$–$$$$) always has a range of interesting creations, from goosefish and angler to delicate lamb roasts. There is a new "beauty farm" with 6 rooms and products from Babor. ✉ *Salzburgerstr. 2–6, D–83435* ☎ *08651/7770* 📠 *08651/5932* 🌐 *www.bad-reichenhall.steigenberger.de* *143 rooms, 8 suites* *2 restaurants, cable TV with movies, Wi-Fi, Internet room, tennis court, pool, gym, hair salon, sauna, spa, bowling, bar, babysitting, some pets allowed (fee), no-smoking rooms; no a/c* 💳 *AE, DC, MC, V* 🍽 *BP.*

$$ ✕🏨 **Parkhotel Luisenbad.** If you fancy spoiling yourself in a typical German fin-de-siècle spa hotel, this is *the* place—a fine porticoed and pillared building whose imposing pastel-pink facade promises luxury within. Rooms are large, furnished in deep-cushioned, dark-wood com-

Fodor's Choice ★

fort, most with flower-filled balconies or loggias. The elegant restaurant ($–$$) serves international and traditional Bavarian cuisines with an emphasis on seafood (lobster Thermidor, for example), and a pine-panel tavern, Die Holzstubn'n, pours excellent local brew. ✉ *Ludwigstr. 33, D–83435* ☎ *08651/6040* 🖷 *08651/62928* 🌐 *www.parkhotel.de* *70 rooms, 8 suites* *Restaurant, cable TV, pool, gym, hot tub, sauna, bicycles, bar, beer garden, recreation room, Wi-Fi, Internet room, some pets allowed (fee); no a/c* 💳 *DC, MC, V* *BP.*

$ **Bürgerbräu.** Each dining area in this old brewery inn reflects the social class that once met here: politicos, peasants, burghers, and salt miners. Reichenhallers from all walks of life still meet here to enjoy good conversation, hearty beer, and excellent food. Rooms at the inn are simple but airy and modern, and best of all, you're in the middle of town. ✉ *Am Rathausplatz, D–83435* ☎ *08651/6089* 🖷 *08651/608–504* 🌐 *www.brauereigasthof-buergerbraeu.de* *32 rooms* *Restaurant, cable TV, Wi-Fi, some pets allowed (fee); no a/c* 💳 *AE, DC, MC, V* *BP.*

$ **Hotel-Pension Erika.** This four-story villa, painted a staid red, has been family-run since 1898, and it shows in the best sense. Everything radiates comfort, from the light-filled dining room to the generous garden, which supplies the kitchen with herbs. Owner Anton Oberarzbacher cooks the dinner options ($) himself, tapping a repertoire that includes French and Italian cuisines. The pedestrian zone in town is a minute away. ✉ *Adolf-Schmid-Str. 3, D–83435* ☎ *08651/95360* 🖷 *08651/953–6200* 🌐 *www.hotel-pension-erika.de* *32 rooms, 1 suite* *Restaurant, cable TV, in-room data ports, some pets allowed; no a/c* 💳 *AE, MC, V* *Closed Nov.–Feb. Restaurant closed Sun.* *BP.*

★ ¢–$ **Pension Hubertus.** This delightfully traditional family-run lodging stands on the shore of the tiny Thumsee, 5 km (3 mi) from the town center. The Hubertus's private grounds lead down to the lake, where guests can swim or boat (the water is bracingly cool). Rooms, some with balconies overlooking the lake, are furnished with hand-carved beds and cupboards. Excellent meals or coffee can be taken at the neighboring rustic **Madlbauer** ($–$$). There are special rates in the off-season (October–April). ✉ *Am Thumsee 5, D–83435* ☎ *08651/2252* 🖷 *08651/63845* *18 rooms* *Cable TV, gym, boating, paddle tennis, some pets allowed (fee), no-smoking rooms; no a/c, no phones in some rooms* 💳 *AE, DC, MC, V* *CP.*

Nightlife & the Arts

Bad Reichenhall is proud of its long musical tradition and of its orchestra, founded more than a century ago. It performs six days a week throughout the year in the chandelier-hung Kurgastzentrum Theater or, when weather permits, in the open-air pavilion, and at a special Mozart Week in March. Call the **Orchesterbüro** (☎ 08651/8661 🖷 08651/710–551) for program details. As a spa town and winter resort, Bad Reichenhall is a natural for night haunts. The big draw is the elegant **casino** (✉ Wittelsbacherstr. 17 ☎ 08651/95800 €2.50, free with a Kurkarte; ask for one at your hotel Jacket and tie), open daily 3 PM–1 or 2 AM depending on business.

Sports & the Outdoors

The tourist-information office on Wittelsbacherstrasse, just a couple hundred yards from the train station, has all of the necessary information regarding the numerous sporting activities possible in Bad Reichenhall and its surrounding area. You can do everything from skiing and hiking to mountain biking and rock climbing.

Shopping

Using flowers and herbs grown in the Bavarian Alps, the **Josef Mack Company** (✉ Ludwigstr. 36 ☎ 08651/78280) has made medicinal herbal preparations since 1856. **Leuthenmayr** (✉ Ludwigstr. 27 ☎ 08651/2869) is a youngster in the business, selling its "cure-all" dwarf-pine oil since 1908. Your sweet tooth will be fully satisfied at the confection emporium of **Paul Reber** (✉ Ludwigstr. 10–12 ☎ 08651/60030), makers of the famous chocolate and marzipan *Mozartkugel,* and many other dietary bombs. Candle-making is a local specialty, and **Kerzenwelt Donabauer** (✉ Reichenhaller Str. 15, Piding ☎ 08651/8143), just outside Bad Reichenhall, has a selection of more than 1,000 decorative items in wax. It also has a free wax museum depicting fairy-tale characters.

2

Berchtesgaden

15 *18 km (11 mi) south of Bad Reichenhall, 20 km (12 mi) south of Salzburg.*

Berchtesgaden's reputation is unjustly rooted in its brief association with Adolf Hitler, who dreamed besottedly of his "1,000-year Reich" from the mountaintop where millions of tourists before and after him drank in only the superb beauty of the Alpine panorama. Below those giddy heights of his retreat is a historic old market town and mountain resort of great charm. In winter it's a fine place for skiing and snowboarding; in summer it becomes one of the region's most popular (and crowded) resorts. An ornate palace and working salt mine make up some of the diversions in this heavenly setting.

Salt—or "white gold," as it was known in medieval times—was once the basis of Berchtesgaden's wealth. In the 12th century Emperor Barbarossa gave mining rights to a Benedictine abbey that had been founded here a century earlier. The abbey was secularized early in the 19th century, when it was taken over by the Wittelsbach rulers. Salt is still important today because of all the local wellness centers. The entire area has been declared a "health resort region" (*Kurgebiet*) and was put on the UNESCO biosphere list. Not surprisingly, salt is celebrated in the *Salzsaga* (the Salt Saga), a musical by Klaus Ammann based on a story by the Bavarian author Ludwig Ganghofer. This love story full of romance, passion, betrayal, and politics is performed at the Königsee Lake at the **Theater am Königsee** (✉ Seestr. 3 ☎ 01805/588–775).

The last royal resident of the Berchtesgaden abbey, Crown Prince Rupprecht (who died here in 1955), furnished it with rare family treasures that now form the basis of a permanent collection—the **Königliches Schloss Berchtesgaden Museum.** Fine Renaissance rooms exhibit the prince's sacred art, which is particularly rich in wood sculptures by such great late-Gothic artists as Tilman Riemenschneider and Veit Stoss. You can also visit the abbey's original, cavernous 13th-century dormitory and cool cloisters. ✉ *Schlosspl. 2* ☎ *08652/947–980* 🌐 *www.haus-bayern.com* 🎫 *€7 with tour* ⏲ *Mid-May–mid-Oct., Sun.–Fri. 10–noon and 2–4; mid-Oct–mid-May, weekdays 11–2; last entry and tour at 2.*

The **Heimatmuseum,** in the Schloss Adelsheim, displays examples of wood carving and other local crafts. Wood carving in Berchtesgaden dates to long before Oberammergau established itself as the premier wood-carving center of the Alps. ✉ *Schroffenbergallee 6* ☎ *08652/4410* 🎫 *€2* ⏲ *Dec.–Oct., Tues.–Sun. 10–4, guided tours at 3.*

★ The **Salzbergwerk** (salt mine) is one of the chief attractions of the region. In the days when the mine was owned by Berchtesgaden's princely rulers, only select guests were allowed to see how the source of the city's wealth was extracted from the earth. Today, during a 90-minute tour, you can sit astride a miniature train that transports you nearly 1 km (½ mi) into the mountain to an enormous chamber where the salt is mined. Included in the tour are rides down the wooden chutes used by miners to get from one level to another and a boat ride on an underground saline lake the size of a football field. You may wish to partake in the special four-hour **brine dinners** down in the mines (€65). ✉ *2 km (1 mi) from center of Berchtesgaden on B–305 Salzburg Rd.* ☎ *08652/600–220* 🌐 *www.salzbergwerk-berchtesgaden.de* 🎫 *€12.90, combined ticket with Bad Reichenhall's saline museum €14.90* ⏲ *May–mid-Oct., daily 9–5; mid-Oct.–Apr., Mon.–Sat. 11:30–3.*

16 The **Obersalzberg,** site of Hitler's luxurious mountain retreat, is part of the north slope of the Hoher Goll, high above Berchtesgaden. It was a remote mountain community of farmers and foresters before Hitler's deputy, Martin Bormann, selected the site for a complex of Alpine homes for top Nazi leaders. Hitler's chalet, the Berghof, and all the others were destroyed in 1945, with the exception of a hotel that had been taken over by the Nazis, the Hotel zum Türken. Beneath the hotel is a section of the labyrinth of tunnels built as a last retreat for Hitler and his cronies; the macabre, murky **bunkers** (🎫 €2.50 ⏲ May–Oct., Tues.–Sun. 9–5; Nov.–Apr., daily 10–3) can be visited. Nearby, the **Dokumentation Obersalzbergmuseum** (✉ Salzbergstr. 41 ☎ 08652/947–960 🌐 www.obersalzberg.de 🎫 €2.50 ⏲ Apr.–Oct., Tues.–Sun. 9–5; Nov.–Mar., Tues.–Sun. 10–3; last entry at 2) documents the Third Reich's history in the region.

Beyond Obersalzberg, the hairpin bends of Germany's highest road come to the base of the 6,000-foot peak on which sits the **Kehlsteinhaus** (☎ 08652/2969), also known as the Adlerhorst (Eagle's Nest), Hitler's personal retreat and his official guesthouse. It was Martin Bormann's gift to the führer on Hitler's 50th birthday. The road leading to it, built in 1937–39, climbs more than 2,000 dizzying feet in less than 6 km (4 mi). A tunnel in the mountain will bring you to an elevator that whisks you up to what appears to be the top of the world (you can walk up in about a half hour). There are refreshment rooms and a restaurant.

The round-trip from Berchtesgaden's post office by bus and elevator costs €16.20 per person. The bus runs mid-May through September, daily from 9 to 4:50. By car you can travel only as far as the Obersalzberg bus station. From there the round-trip fare is €12.50. The full round-trip takes one hour. From July through September the tourist office organizes Eagle's Nest by Night tours, including a cocktail and three-course dinner accompanied by live Bavarian music.

Where to Stay & Eat

$ **Alpenhotel Denninglehen.** Nonsmokers appreciate the special dining room set aside just for them in this mountain hotel's restaurant. The house was built in 1981 in Alpine style, with lots of wood paneling, heavy beams, and wide balconies with cascades of geraniums in summer. Skiers enjoy the fact that the slopes are about 200 yards away. The restaurant's menu is regional (the usual schnitzels and roasts) with a few items from the French repertoire (a fine steak in pepper sauce, for example). *Am Priesterstein 7, D–83471 Berchtesgaden-Oberau 08652/97890 08652/64710 www.denninglehen.de Restaurant, pool, sauna, some pets allowed (fee), no-smoking rooms; no a/c MC Closed last 2 wks in Jan. BP.*

$ **Hotel Grünberger.** Only a few strides from the train station in the town center, the Grünberger overlooks the River Ache—it even has a private terrace beside the river you can relax on. The cozy rooms have farmhouse-style furnishings and some antiques. The wellness area has in-house acupuncture and traditional Chinese medicine treatments. The hotel restaurant focuses on German fare with some international dishes to lighten the load. Those who need to check e-mail head to the Internet café nearby. *Hansererweg 1, D–83471 08652/4560 08652/62254 www.hotel-gruenberger.de 65 rooms Restaurant, cable TV, pool, sauna, beer garden; no-smoking rooms, no a/c, no room phones, no TV in some rooms MC, V Closed Nov.–mid-Dec. BP.*

$ **Hotel Post.** This central and reliable hostelry offers fine Bavarian food (¢–$), with some lighter Italian fare—pastas, salmon, flounder—for anyone needing a break from hocks and pork roast. If trout from the nearby Königsee is available, order it. In summer you can eat in the beer garden. The rooms are basic but clean and pleasant. *Maximilianstr. 2a, D–83471 08652/5067 08652/64801 www.hotel-post-bgd.de Restaurant, cable TV, some pets allowed (fee); no a/c MC, V BP.*

$–$$ **Hotel zum Türken.** The view alone is worth the 10-minute journey from Berchtesgaden to this hotel. Confiscated during World War II by the Nazis, the hotel is at the foot of the road to Hitler's mountaintop retreat. Beneath it are remains of Nazi wartime bunkers. The decor, though fittingly rustic, is a bit dated. There's no restaurant, although evening meals can be ordered in advance. *Hintereck 2, D–83471 Obersalzberg-Berchtesgaden 08652/2428 08652/4710 www.hotel-zum-tuerken.de 17 rooms, 12 with bath or shower Some pets allowed, no-smoking rooms; no a/c, no phones in some rooms AE, DC, MC, V Closed Nov.–Dec. 20 BP.*

$–$$ **Stoll's Hotel Alpina.** Set above the Königsee in the delightful little village of Schönau, the Alpina offers rural solitude and easy access to Berchtesgaden. Families are catered to with apartments, a resident doctor, and a playroom. ✉ *Ulmenweg 14, D–83471 Schönau* ☎ *08652/65090* 🖷 *08652/61608* 🌐 *www.stolls-hotel-alpina.de* *52 rooms, 8 apartments* *Restaurant, cable TV, some in-room data ports, pool, hair salon, sauna, some pets allowed (fee); no a/c* 💳 *AE, DC, MC, V* ⏲ *Closed early Nov.–mid-Dec.* *BP.*

$ **Hotel Wittelsbach.** This is one of the oldest (built in 1892) and most traditional lodgings in the area. The small rooms have dark pinewood furnishings and deep red and green drapes and carpets. Ask for one with a balcony. The breakfast room has a mountain view. If you have to send thoughts back home, there's an Internet terminal available. ✉ *Maximilianstr. 16, D–83471* ☎ *08652/96380* 🖷 *08652/66304* 🌐 *www.hotel-wittelsbach.com* *26 rooms, 3 apartments* *Cable TV, Internet room, some pets allowed; no a/c* 💳 *AE, DC, MC, V* *BP.*

off the beaten path

SCHELLENBERG EISHÖHLEN – Germany's largest ice caves lie 10 km (6 mi) north of Berchtesgaden. By car take B–305, or take the bus (€4) from the Berchtesgaden post office to the village of Marktschellenberg. From there you can reach the caves on foot by walking 2½ hours along the clearly marked route. A guided tour of the caves takes one hour. On the way to Marktschellenberg watch for the **Almbachklamm**, a narrow valley good for hikes. At its entrance is an old (1683) mill for making and polishing marble balls. *€4* ☎ *08650/352* ⏲ *Mid-June–mid-Oct., daily 10–5.*

Shopping

The **Berchtesgadener Handwerkskunst** (✉ Schlosspl. 1½, D–83471 ☎ 08652/979–790 ⏲ Mon.–Sat. 9–noon, weekdays 2–6) offers handicrafts—such as wooden boxes, woven tablecloths, woodcarvings, and Christmas-tree decorations—from Berchtesgaden, the surrounding region, and other parts of Bavaria.

Sports & the Outdoors

Germany's highest course, the **Berchtesgaden Golf Club** (✉ Salzbergstr. 33 ☎ 08652/2100), is on a 3,300-foot plateau of the Obersalzberg. Only fit players should attempt the demanding 9-hole course. Seven Berchtesgaden hotels offer their guests a 30% reduction on the €25 greens fee—contact the tourist office or the club for details.

Whatever your mountain-related needs, whether it's climbing and hiking in summer or cross-country tours in winter, you'll find it at the **Erste Bergschule Berchtesgadenerland** (✉ Silbergstr. 25, Strub ☎ 08652/2420 May–Oct., 08652/5371 Nov.–Apr. 🖷 08652/2420).

At the sleek and classy **Watzmann Therme** you'll find fragrant steam rooms, saunas with infrared cabins for sore muscles, an elegant pool, whirlpools, and more. If you happen to be staying a few days, you might catch a tai chi course, enjoy a bio-release facial massage, or partake in an evening of relaxing underwater exercises. ✉ *Bergwerkstr.* ☎ *08652/94640* *4 hrs €12.80, day including sauna €14.30* ⏲ *Daily 10–10.*

Berchtesgaden National Park

17 *5 km (3 mi) south of Berchtesgaden.*

The deep, mysterious, and fabled Königsee is the most photographed panorama in Germany. Together with its much smaller sister, the Obersee, it's nestled within the Berchtesgaden National Park, 210 square km (82 square mi) of wild mountain country where flora and fauna have been left to develop as nature intended. No roads penetrate the area, and even the mountain paths are difficult to follow. The park administration organizes guided tours of the area from June through September. *Nationalparkhaus ✉ Franziskanerpl. 7, D–83471 Berchtesgaden ☎ 08652/64343 🌐 www.nationalpark-berchtesgaden.de.*

One less strenuous way into the Berchtesgaden National Park is by boat. A fleet of 21 excursion boats, electrically driven so that no noise disturbs the peace, operates on the **Königsee** (King Lake). Only the skipper of the boat is allowed to shatter the silence—his trumpet fanfare demonstrates a remarkable echo as notes reverberate between the almost vertical cliffs that plunge into the dark green water. A cross on a rocky promontory marks the spot where a boatload of pilgrims hit the cliffs and sank more than 100 years ago. The voyagers were on their way to the tiny, twin-tower baroque chapel of St. Bartholomä, built in the 17th century on a peninsula where an early Gothic church once stood. The princely rulers of Berchtesgaden built a hunting lodge at the side of the chapel; a tavern and restaurant now occupy its rooms.

Smaller than the Königsee but equally beautiful, the **Obersee** can be reached by a 15-minute walk from the second stop (Salet) on the boat tour. The lake's backdrop of jagged mountains and precipitous cliffs is broken by a waterfall, the Rothbachfall, that plunges more than 1,000 feet to the valley floor.

Boat service (☎ 08652/9636–18 🌐 www.bayerische-seenschifffahrt.de) on the Königsee runs year-round, except when the lake freezes. A round-trip to St. Bartholomä and Salet, the landing stage for the Obersee, lasts almost two hours, without stops, and costs €14. A round-trip to St. Bartholomä lasts a little over an hour and costs €11. In summer, the Berchtesgaden tourist office organizes evening cruises on the Königsee, which includes a concert in St. Bartholomä Church and a four-course dinner in the neighboring hunting lodge.

THE BAVARIAN ALPS A TO Z

To research prices, get advice from other travelers, and book travel arrangements, visit www.fodors.com.

AIRPORTS

Munich, 95 km (59 mi) northwest of Garmisch-Partenkirchen, is the gateway to the Bavarian Alps. If you're staying in Berchtesgaden, consider the closer airport in Salzburg, Austria, although it has fewer international flights.

BOAT TRAVEL

Passenger boats operate on all the major Bavarian lakes. They're mostly excursion boats, and many run only in summer. However, there's year-round service on the Chiemsee. Eight boats operate year-round on the Tegernsee, connecting the towns of Tegernsee, Rottach-Egern, Bad Wiessee, and Gmund.

BUS TRAVEL

The Alpine region is not well served by long-distance buses. There's a fairly good network of local buses, but they tend to run at commuter times. Inquire at any local train station, travel agent, or at your hotel, or log onto the German railways' itinerary-planning site, 🌐 www.bahn.de. Larger resorts operate buses to outlying areas. The Wendelstein region, for example, is serviced by the Wendelstein Ringlinie, offering fares from a simple €7 per day to more complex ones involving skiing tickets. It connects the skiing areas of Sudelfeld with Bayrischzell, the Tatzelwurm Gorge, Bad Aibling near Rosenheim, and other towns and areas. Garmisch-Partenkirchen runs night buses to and from Murnau, Oberammergau, Mittenwald, and Krün. Night buses also run between Murnau and Oberammergau. The cost is €2.50.

CAR TRAVEL

Three autobahns reach into the Bavarian Alps: A–7 comes in from the northwest (Frankfurt, Stuttgart, Ulm) and ends near Füssen in the western Bavarian Alps; A–95 runs from Munich to Garmisch-Partenkirchen; take A–8 from Munich for Tegernsee, Schliersee, and Chiemsee and for Berchtesgaden. All provide speedy access to a network of well-paved country roads that penetrate high into the mountains. (Germany's highest road runs above Berchtesgaden at more than 5,000 feet.) Note that on weekends and at the start and end of national holidays, A–8 can become a long parking lot heading toward Austria or Munich. The two major climbs around the Irschenberg and Bernau are particularly affected. Weekend traffic also jams up the end of A–95 near Garmisch-Partenkirchen.

EMERGENCIES

Police and ambulance ☎ 110. **Fire and emergency medical aid** ☎ 112.

TOURS

BERCHTESGADEN In Berchtesgaden, the Schwaiger bus company runs tours of the area and across the Austrian border as far as Salzburg. An American couple runs Berchtesgaden Mini-bus Tours out of the local tourist office, opposite the railroad station.

Schwaiger ☎ 08652/2525. **Berchtesgaden Mini-bus Tours** ☎ 08652/64971.

GARMISCH-PARTENKIRCHEN Bus tours to King Ludwig II's castles at Neuschwanstein and Linderhof and to the Ettal Monastery, near Oberammergau, are offered by DER travel agencies. Local agencies in Garmisch also run tours to Neuschwanstein, Linderhof, Ettal, and into the neighboring Austrian Tyrol.

The Garmisch mountain railway company, the Bayerische Zugspitzbahn, offers special excursions to the top of the Zugspitze, Germany's highest mountain, by cog rail and/or cable car.

Bayerische Zugspitzbahn ☎ 08821/7970. **DER** ✉ Garmisch-Partenkirchen ☎ 08821/55125. **Dominikus Kümmerle** ☎ 08821/4955. **Hans Biersack** ☎ 08821/4920. **Hilmar Röser** ☎ 08821/2926. **Weiss-Blau-Reisen** ☎ 08821/3766.

TRAIN TRAVEL

Most Alpine resorts are connected with Munich by regular express and slower services. Trains to Garmisch-Partenkirchen depart hourly from Munich's Hauptbahnhof. Garmisch-Partenkirchen and Mittenwald are on the InterCity Express network, which has regular direct service to all regions of the country. (Klais, just outside Garmisch, is Germany's highest-altitude InterCity train station.) A train from Munich also connects to Gmund on Tegernsee. Bad Reichenhall, Berchtesgaden, Prien, and Rosenheim are linked directly to north German cities by long-distance express service. If you're making a day trip to the Zugspitze from Munich, Augsburg, or any other southern Bavarian center, take advantage of an unbeatable deal offered by Deutsche Bahn that includes rail fare and a day pass to all the Garmisch-Partenkirchen mountains, including the Zugspitze.

VISITOR INFORMATION

The Bavarian regional tourist office in Munich, Tourismusverband München Oberbayern, provides general information about Upper Bavaria and the Bavarian Alps.

Aschau ✉ Verkehrsamt, Kampenwandstr. 38, D-83229 ☎ 08052/904-937 🌐 www.aschau.de. **Bad Reichenhall** ✉ Kur-und-Verkehrsverein, im Kurgastzentrum, Wittelsbacherstr. 15, D-83424 ☎ 08651/606-303 🌐 www.bad-reichenhall.de. **Bad Tölz** ✉ Kurverwaltung, Ludwigstr. 11, D-83646 ☎ 08041/78670 🌐 www.bad-toelz.de. **Bad Wiessee** ✉ Kuramt, Adrian-Stoop-Str. 20, D-837004 ☎ 08022/86030 🌐 www.bad-wiessee.de. **Bayrischzell** ✉ Kirchpl. 2, Kurverwaltung 📫 Postfach 2, Kurverwaltung D-83735 ☎ 08023/1034 🌐 www.bayrischzell.de. **Berchtesgaden** ✉ Kurdirektion, D-83471 ☎ 08652/9670 🌐 www.berchtesgadener-land.com. **Chiemsee** ✉ Tourismusverband Chiemsee, Kurverwaltung, Alte Rathausstr. 11, D-83209 Prien ☎ 08051/69050 🌐 www.chiemsee.de. **Ettal** ✉ Verkehrsamt, Kaiser-Ludwig-Pl., D-82488 ☎ 08822/3534. **Garmisch-Partenkirchen** ✉ Verkehrsamt der Kurverwaltung, Richard-Strauss-Pl. 2, D-82467 ☎ 08821/180-420 🌐 www.garmisch-partenkirchen.de. **Mittenwald** ✉ Kurverwaltung, Dammkarstr. 3, D-82481 ☎ 08823/33981 🌐 www.mittenwald.de. **Oberammergau** ✉ Verkehrsamt, Eugen-Papst-Str. 9a, D-82487 ☎ 08822/92310 📠 08822/923-190 🌐 www.oberammergau.de. **Prien am Chiemsee** ✉ Alter Rathausstr. 11, D-83209 ☎ 08051/69050 🌐 www.prien.chiemsee.de. **Rottach-Egern/Tegernsee** ✉ Kuramt, Nördliche Hauptstr. 2, D-83684 ☎ 08022/180-149 🌐 www.tegernsee.de. **Tourismusverband München Oberbayern** ✉ Bodenseestr. 113, D-81243 Munich ☎ 089/829-2180.

3 The Romantic Road

WORD OF MOUTH

". . . the highlight [of Würzburg] must certainly be the Residenz, a baroque castle built by Balthasar Newman, which I found to be more beautiful than even Versailles. . . . If you want a high energy, lots of activity kind of holiday, I don't think Würzburg is for you. It's quite laid back, the kind of place for leisurely strolls around the old town."

—Mariannah

"We recently spent the night in Rothenburg ob der Tauber and loved it. Arrive in the evening, but before sunset. Dusk there is absolutely breathtaking. . . . It gets very, and I do mean VERY, crowded during the day. So take a walk around the city . . . and then try and get out of there before noon."

—JAGIRL

www.fodors.com/forums

Updated by Uli Ehrhardt

OF ALL THE TOURIST ROUTES that crisscross Germany, none rivals the aptly named Romantische Strasse, or Romantic Road. The scenery is more pastoral than spectacular, but the route is memorable for the medieval towns, villages, castles, and churches that anchor its 355-km (220-mi) length. Many of these are tucked away beyond low hills, their spires and towers just visible through the greenery.

The road runs south from Würzburg, in northern Bavaria, to Füssen, on the border of Austria. You can, of course, follow it in the opposite direction, as a number of bus tours do. Either way, among the major sights you'll see are one of Europe's most scintillating baroque palaces, in Würzburg, and perhaps the best-preserved medieval town on the continent, Rothenburg-ob-der-Tauber. Then there's the handsome Renaissance city of Augsburg. Finally the fantastical highlight will be Ludwig II's castle, Neuschwanstein.

The Romantic Road concept developed as West Germany rebuilt its tourist industry after World War II. A public-relations wizard coined the catchy title for a historic passage through Bavaria and Baden-Württemberg that could be advertised as a unit. In 1950 the Romantic Road was born. The name itself isn't meant to attract lovebirds but, rather, uses the word *romance* as meaning wonderful, fabulous, and imaginative. And, of course, the Romantic Road started as a road on which the Romans traveled.

Along the way, the road crosses centuries-old battlefields. The most cataclysmic conflict, the Thirty Years' War, destroyed the region's economic base in the 17th century. The depletion of resources prevented improvements that would have modernized the area—thereby assuring the survival of the historic towns' now charmingly quaint infrastructures.

As you travel the Romantic Road, two names crop up repeatedly: Walther von der Vogelweide and Tilman Riemenschneider. Walther von der Vogelweide, who died in Würzburg in 1230, was the most famous of the German *Minnesänger*, poet-musicians who wrote and sang of courtly love in the age of chivalry. Knights and other nobles would hire them to help win the favors of fair ladies. Von der Vogelweide broke with this tradition by writing love songs to maidens of less-than-noble rank. He also accepted commissions of a political nature, producing what amounted to medieval political manifestos. His work was romantic, lyrical, witty, and filled with a sighing wistfulness and philosophical questioning. Medieval sculptor Tilman Riemenschneider spent his most creative and esteemed years in Würzburg. Owing to his support of farmers and guildsmen during the 1524–25 Peasants' War, he also ended his life in Würzburg as a pauper and outcast.

Exploring the Romantic Road

The Romantic Road runs from the vineyard-hung slopes of the Main River valley at Würzburg to the snow-covered mountains overlooking Füssen in the Allgäuer Alps. For much of its route it follows two enchanting rivers, the Tauber and the Lech, and at one point crosses the great Danube, still a surprisingly narrow river this far from the end of its journey in the Black Sea. The city of Augsburg marks the natural halfway point of the Romantic Road. South of Augsburg, the road climbs gradually into the Alpine foothills, and the landscape changes from the lush green of Franconian river valleys to mountain-backed meadows and forests.

About the Restaurants

During peak season, restaurants along the Romantic Road tend to be crowded, especially in the larger towns. You may want to plan your mealtimes around visits to smaller villages, where there are fewer people and the restaurants are pleasant. The food will be more basic Franconian or Swabian, but it will also be generally less expensive than in the well-known towns. You may find that some of the small, family-run restaurants close around 2 PM, or whenever the last lunch guests have left, and open again at 5 or 5:30 PM. Some serve cold cuts or coffee and cake during that time, but no hot food.

About the Hotels

With a few exceptions, the Romantic Road hotels are quiet and rustic, and you'll find high standards of comfort and cleanliness. Make reservations as far in advance as possible if you plan to visit in summer. Hotels in Würzburg, Rothenburg, and Füssen are often full year-round. Augsburg hotels are in great demand during trade fairs in nearby Munich. Tourist information offices can usually help with accommodations, especially if you arrive early in the day.

WHAT IT COSTS In Euros

	$$$$	$$$	$$	$	¢
RESTAURANTS	over €25	€21–€25	€16–€20	€9–€15	under €9
HOTELS	over €225	€175–€225	€100–€175	€50–€100	under €50

Restaurant prices are per person for a main course at dinner. Hotel prices are for two people in a standard double room, including tax and service.

Timing

Late summer and early autumn are the best times to travel the Romantic Road, when the grapes ripen on the vines around Würzburg and the geraniums run riot on the medieval walls of towns such as Rothenburg and Dinkelsbühl. You'll also miss the high-season summer crush of tourists. Otherwise, consider visiting the region in the depths of December, when Christmas markets pack the ancient squares of the Romantic Road towns and snow gives turreted Schloss Neuschwanstein a final magic touch.

NORTHERN ROMANTIC ROAD

The northern section of the Romantic Road skirts the wild, open countryside of the Spessart uplands before heading south through the plains of Swabia and along the lovely Tauber and Lech rivers.

Although a long-distance bus covers the Romantic Road daily during summer in less than 12 hours, it's difficult to resist an overnight stay. Würzburg and Augsburg are each worth two or three days of exploration, and such attractions as the minster of Ulm are time-consuming but rewarding diversions from the recognized Romantic Road.

Numbers in the text correspond to numbers in the margin and on the maps in this chapter.

3

If you have 3 days

Spend the first day in **Würzburg** 1–16, where you can stroll through the streets and enjoy the splendor of the city. The next morning, head south and stop in **Bad Mergentheim** 17, once the home of the Teutonic Knights. Next, head east for a few miles to visit the castle of the counts of Hohenlohe in **Weikersheim** 18. Continue east to **Creglingen** 19, where you can admire the Tilman Riemenschneider altar in the **Herrgottskirche** 20. Continue toward Rothenburg but do not drive into the town; rather follow the signs to Ansbach. You'll pass under the autobahn and continue for 18 km (11 mi) toward **Castle Colmberg,** where you can stay for the night and dine like a duke in medieval settings. The next morning, venture into **Rothenburg-ob-der-Tauber** 21–28 before the crowds arrive. In the afternoon drive back to Würzburg.

If you have 5 days

Tackle the entire length of the Romantic Road by just hitting the highlights: Spend a night and day in **Würzburg** 1–16, with all its baroque splendor. The next afternoon, head south toward **Bad Mergentheim** 17, making a short stop before continuing on to **Rothenburg-ob-der-Tauber** 21–28. Try to arrive in the early evening, when the tourist buses have left. Spend the evening roaming the streets, and the next morning—before the daily crowds arrive—look at the highlights. Spend the rest of the day exploring the towns of **Dinkelsbühl** 29, **Nördlingen** 30, and **Augsburg** 33–45. The next morning, continue south toward **Füssen** 47, first taking a detour at the small town of Steingaden, which has signs leading to the rococco Wieskirche, which stands in a heavenly Alpine meadow (*Wiese*). Spend your last nights in Füssen while you explore **Neuschwanstein and Hohenschwangau** 46 during the day.

If you have 7 days

Devote two days to **Würzburg** 1–16 before heading south. Take Day 3 to investigate **Bad Mergentheim** 17 and **Rothenburg-ob-der-Tauber** 21–28, overnighting in **Castle Colmberg** 18 km (11 mi) east of Rothenburg. Spend the fourth day visiting two other exquisitely preserved medieval towns, **Dinkelsbühl** 29 and **Nördlingen** 30. Continue on to **Ulm** 32 to look at the mighty cathedral and the old city. The next day, head back to the Romantic Road to **Augsburg** 33–45, where you can explore and shop. On the sixth day continue south to the lovely Wieskirche. Spend the night in **Füssen** 47, and use your last day for a day trip to **Schloss Neuschwanstein and Schloss Hohenschwangau** 46.

Würzburg

115 km (71 mi) east of Frankfurt.

The baroque city of Würzburg, the pearl of the Romantic Road, is a heady example of what happens when great genius teams up with great wealth. Beginning in the 10th century, Würzburg was ruled by powerful (and rich) prince-bishops, who created the city with all the remarkable attributes you see today.

The city is at the junction of two age-old trade routes in a calm valley backed by vineyard-covered hills. Festung Marienberg, a fortified castle on the steep hill across the Main River, overlooks the town. Constructed between 1200 and 1600, the fortress was the residence of the prince-bishops for 450 years.

Present-day Würzburg is by no means completely original. On March 16, 1945, seven weeks before Germany capitulated, Würzburg was all but obliterated by Allied saturation bombing. The 20-minute raid destroyed 87% of the city and killed at least 4,000 people. Reconstruction has returned most of the city's famous sights to their former splendor. Except for some buildings with modern shops, it remains a largely authentic restoration.

a good walk

No two sights are more than 2 km (1 mi) from each other. Begin your tour on Marktplatz (Market Square) at the city tourist office, in the mansion **Haus zum Falken** 1. Collect the handy English-language tour map with a route marked out. Red signs throughout the city point the way between major sights. Next door to the Haus zum Falken is one of the city's loveliest churches, the delicate **Marienkapelle** 2. Leave the square at its eastern exit and you'll find yourself on Würzburg's traffic-free shopping street, **Schönbornstrasse** 3, named after the city's greatest patron, the prince-bishop Johann Philipp Franz von Schönborn. Head north, passing the **Augustinerkirche** 4, a former Dominican church, and you'll arrive within a few minutes at the broad Juliuspromenade, dominated by the impressive baroque **Juliusspital** 5, an infirmary. Follow Juliuspromenade eastward; it will become Heinestrasse, and you'll come to the first baroque church built in Franconia, the **Stift Haug** 6. Next, retrace your steps along Heinestrasse and make a left on Theaterstrasse. After one block, you'll pass the Gothic **Bürgerspital** 7, another charitable institution. At the end of Theaterstrasse stands the mighty **Residenz** 8 of the Würzburg prince-bishops, built for Schönborn by the great baroque-era architect Balthasar Neumann.

From the Residenz, walk down Domerschulstrasse and turn left onto Schönthalstrasse for the **Alte Universität** 9. The southern section of the building is taken up by the Neubaukirche, a fine Renaissance church. Next, head north on Schönthalstrasse to Plattnerstrasse; where this street becomes Schönbornstrasse, you'll find Würzburg's cathedral, the **Dom St. Kilian** 10, and the nearby **Neumünster** 11 church. From the cathedral take Domstrasse westward, and you'll see the high tower of the 14th-century **Rathaus** 12; beyond this the **Alte Mainbrücke** 13 crosses the Main River. Before you cross the bridge, stroll north along the riverbank to

Bicycling One of the most interesting ways to get to know the Romantic Road is by bicycle, especially because the route, which mostly follows rivers, is relatively flat. Even if you pedal all the way from Würzburg to Füssen, you won't have to climb any mountains. In the Alpine foothills you'll have a few longer inclines, but even those can be managed by an average cyclist. Of course, if you'd rather avoid inclines altogether, start in Füssen and then roll back down in the opposite direction, following the River Lech.

There are three ways to explore the Romantic Road by bicycle. One is to venture out with as little baggage as possible, finding places to stay along the way. Another possibility is to have a tour operator book rooms for you and your group and transport your luggage. Or, you can do day trips. Most tourist offices and good hotels along the Romantic Road will supply bicycles, maps, and information for local and regional bike trips.

The Romantic Road office in Dinkelsbühl has a booklet with detailed maps for cycling, and signs mark the Romantic Road bicycle path (all 420 km [260 mi] of it) from beginning to end. In any town on the Romantic Road you can board the Deutsche Touring bus (with a trailer for bicycles), which travels the length of the Romantic Road daily.

On the Menu The best Franconian and Swabian food combines hearty regional specialties with nouvelle elements. Various forms of pasta are common. *Schupfnudeln* (little potato dumplings) are eaten either with a sweet or savory accompaniment, and spaetzle (small tagliatellelike ribbons of rolled dough) is often served with *Rinderbraten* (roast beef), the traditional Sunday lunchtime dish. One of the best regional dishes is *Maultaschen,* a Swabian version of ravioli, usually served floating in broth strewn with chives. Würzburg is one of the leading wine-producing areas of Germany, and the many Franconian beers range from *Räucherbier* (literally, "smoked beer") to the lighter ales of Augsburg.

---

one of Würzburg's familiar landmarks, the **Alter Kranen** 14, a wharf crane. To conclude your walk, retrace your steps, cross the Alte Mainbrücke to the other side of the river, and climb the vineyard-covered hill to the great brooding fortress, the **Festung Marienberg** 15. Within its massive walls are two very interesting museums. You can ride back into central Würzburg on the bus that stops in front of the main entrance.

TIMING You need two days to do full justice to Würzburg. The Residenz alone demands several hours of attention. If time is short, head for the Residenz as the doors open in the morning, before the first crowds assemble, and aim to complete your tour by lunchtime. Then continue to the nearby Juliusspital Weinstuben or one of the many traditional taverns in the area for lunch. In the afternoon explore central Würzburg and

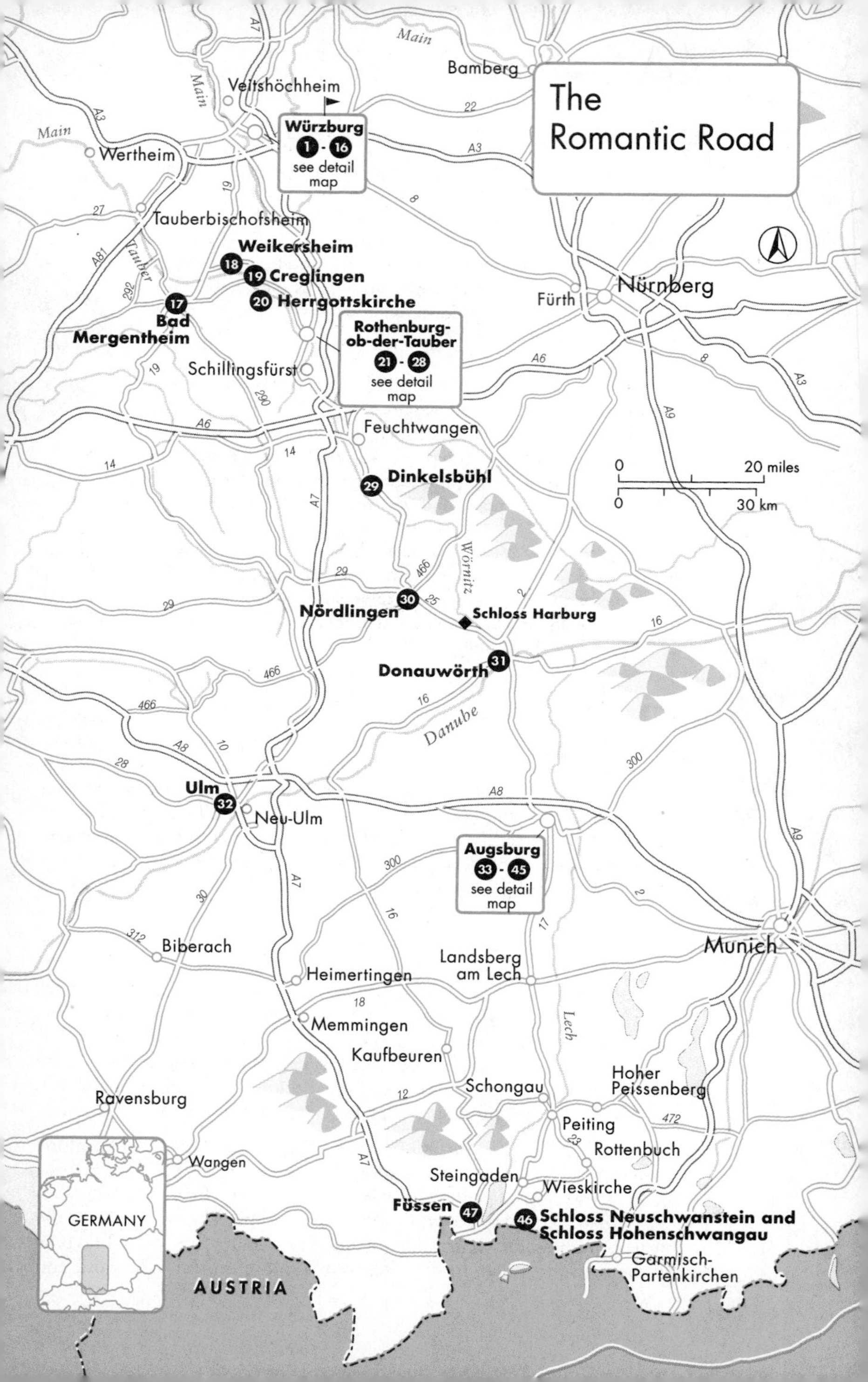

The Romantic Road
Würzburg
1 - 16
see detail map
Rothenburg-ob-der-Tauber
21 - 28
see detail map
Augsburg
33 - 45
see detail map
Main
Bamberg
Veitshöchheim
Wertheim
Tauberbischofsheim
Tauber
Weikersheim
18
19 Creglingen
20 Herrgottskirche
17
Bad Mergentheim
Schillingsfürst
Fürth
Nürnberg
Feuchtwangen
29 Dinkelsbühl
0
20 miles
0
30 km
Wörnitz
30
Nördlingen
Schloss Harburg
31
Donauwörth
Danube
Ulm
32
Neu-Ulm
Biberach
Heimertingen
Memmingen
Landsberg am Lech
Lech
Munich
Kaufbeuren
Schongau
Hoher Peissenberg
Ravensburg
Peiting
Rottenbuch
Wangen
Steingaden
Wieskirche
Füssen
47
46
Schloss Neuschwanstein and Schloss Hohenschwangau
Garmisch-Partenkirchen
GERMANY
AUSTRIA
A7
A3
A81
A6
A8
A9
22
8
27
19
292
290
14
29
466
25
2
16
10
28
300
30
312
18
17
12
472
23

cross the Main River to visit the Festung Marienberg and the Mainfränkisches Museum.

What to See

13 **Alte Mainbrücke** (Old Main Bridge). Construction on this ancient structure, which crosses the Main River, began in 1473. Twin rows of infinitely graceful statues of saints line the bridge. They were placed here in 1730, at the height of Würzburg's baroque period. Note the *Patronna Franconiae* (commonly known as the Weeping Madonna). There's a beautiful view of the Marienberg Fortress from the bridge.

9 **Alte Universität** (Old University). Founded by Prince-Bishop Julius Echter and built in 1582, this rambling institution is one of Würzburg's most interesting Renaissance structures. ✉ *Neubaustr. 1–9.*

14 **Alter Kranen** (Old Crane). Near the Main River and north of the Old Main Bridge, the crane was erected in 1772–73 by Balthasar Neumann's son, Franz Ignaz Michael. It was used to unload boats; beside it is the old customs building.

4 **Augustinerkirche** (Church of St. Augustine). This baroque church, a work by Balthasar Neumann, was a 13th-century Dominican chapel. Neumann retained the soaring, graceful choir and commissioned Antonio Bossi to add colorful stuccowork to the rest of the church. ✉ *Dominikanerpl. 2* ☎ *0931/30970* ⏲ *Daily 7–6.*

7 **Bürgerspital** (Almshouse). Wealthy burghers founded this refuge for the city's poor and needy in 1319; it now sells wine. The arcade courtyard is baroque in style. From mid-March through October there's a weekly tour (Saturday at 2), which includes a glass of wine. ✉ *Theaterstr. 19* ☎ *0931/35030* 🌐 *www.buergerspital.de* 🎫 *Tour €5.*

10 **Dom St. Kilian** (St. Kilian Basilica). Würzburg's Romanesque cathedral, the fourth largest of its kind in Germany, was begun in 1045. Step inside and you'll find yourself, somewhat disconcertingly, in a shimmering rococo treasure house. Prince-Bishop von Schönborn is buried here. His tomb is the work of his architect and builder Balthasar Neumann. Tilman Riemenschneider carved the tombstones of two other bishops at the cathedral. ✉ *Paradepl., south end of Schönbornstr.* ☎ *0931/321–1830* 🎫 *Tour €2* ⏲ *Easter–Oct., daily 8–6; Nov.–Easter, daily 8–noon and 2–6; guided tours May–Oct., Mon.–Sat. at 12:20, Sun. at 12:30.*

15 **Festung Marienberg** (Marienberg Fortress). This complex was the original home of the prince-bishops, beginning in the 13th century. The oldest buildings—note especially the **Marienkirche** (Church of the Virgin Mary)—date from around 700, although excavations have disclosed evidence that there was a settlement here in the Iron Age, 3,000 years ago. In addition to the rough-hewn medieval fortifications, there are a number of Renaissance and baroque apartments. To reach the hilltop Marienberg, you can make the fairly stiff climb on foot through vineyards or take the bus from the Residenz. It runs every 40 minutes from February to October, starting at 9:45 AM.

Alte Mainbrücke . . 13
Alte Universität 9
Alter Kranen . 14
Augustinerkirche 4
Bürgerspital . . 7
Dom St. Kilian 10
Festung Marienburg . . 15
Haus zum Falken 1
Juliusspital 5
Marienkapelle 2
Neumünster . . . 11
Rathaus 12
Residenz 8
Schönbornstrasse 3
Stift Haug 6

★ The highlight is the remarkable collection of art treasures in the **Mainfränkisches Museum** (Main-Franconian Museum; ☎ 0931/205–940 🌐 www.mainfraenkisches-museum.de 🎫 €3 ⏱ Apr.–Oct., Tues.–Sun. 10–5; Nov.–Mar., Tues.–Sun. 10–4), which traces the city's rich and varied history. Be sure to visit the gallery devoted to Würzburg-born sculptor Tilman Riemenschneider, who lived from the late 15th to the early 16th century. Also on view are paintings by Tiepolo and Cranach the Elder, as well as exhibits of porcelain, firearms, antique toys, and ancient Greek and Roman art. Other exhibits include enormous old winepresses and exhibits about the history of Franconian wine making. From April through October, tours around the fortress are offered for €2 per person, starting from the Scherenberg Tor.

The Marienberg collections are so vast that they spill over into another outstanding museum that is part of the fortress, the **Fürstenbaumuseum** (Princes' Quarters Museum), which traces 1,200 years of Würzburg's history. The holdings include breathtaking exhibits of local goldsmiths' art. 🎫 *Combined ticket for Mainfränkisches and Fürstenbau museums €4* ⏱ *Apr.–Sept., Tues.–Sun. 9–5; Oct.–Mar., Tues.–Sun. 10–4.*

⚑ ❶ **Haus zum Falken.** The city's most splendid baroque mansion, formerly a humble inn, now houses the city tourist office. Its colorful rococo facade was added in 1751. ✉ *Am Marktpl. 9* ☎ *0931/372–398* ⏲ *Jan.–Mar., weekdays 10–6, Sat. 10–1; Apr.–Oct., weekdays 10–6, weekends 10–2.*

5 **Juliusspital.** Founded in 1576 by Prince-Bishop Julius Echter as a home for the poor, the elderly, and the sick, this enormous edifice now houses an impressive restaurant serving wine from the institution's own vineyards. It also sells wineglasses. All profits from the restaurant are used to run the adjacent home for the elderly. A glass of wine is included in a weekly tour of the wine cellars. ✉ *Juliuspromenade 19* ☎ *0931/393–1400* 🎫 *Tour €5* ⏲ *Daily 10 AM–midnight; tours Apr.–Oct., Fri. at 3.*

2 **Marienkapelle** (St. Mary's Chapel). This tranquil Gothic church (1377–1480) tucked modestly away at one end of Würzburg's market square is almost lost amid the historic old facades. Balthasar Neumann lies buried in the church. ✉ *Marktpl.* ☎ *0931/321–1830* ⏲ *Daily 8–6:30.*

11 **Neumünster** (New Minster). Next to the Dom St. Kilian, this 11th-century Romanesque basilica was completed in 1716. The original church was built above the grave of the early Irish martyr St. Kilian, who brought Christianity to Würzburg and, with two companions, was put to death here in 689. Their missionary zeal bore fruit, however—17 years after their death a church was consecrated in their memory. By 742 Würzburg had become a diocese, and over the following centuries 39 flourishing churches were established throughout the city. ✉ *Schönbornstr.* ☎ *0931/321–1830* ⏲ *Daily 7–6.*

12 **Rathaus.** The Gothic town hall, once headquarters of the bishop's administrator, has been the center of municipal government since 1316. A permanent exhibition in the tower documents Würzburg's destruction by Allied bombs, some examples of which are on display. ✉ *Marktpl.* ☎ *0931/370* 🎫 *Free* ⏲ *Weekdays 9–5; tours May–Oct., Sat. at 11.*

★ 8 **Residenz** (Residence). The line of Würzburg's prince-bishops lived in this glorious baroque palace after moving down from the hilltop Festung Marienberg. Construction started in 1719 under the brilliant direction of Balthasar Neumann. Most of the interior decoration was entrusted to the Italian stuccoist Antonio Bossi and the Venetian painter Giovanni Battista Tiepolo. It's the spirit of the pleasure-loving prince-bishop Johann Philipp Franz von Schönborn, however, that infuses the Residenz. Now considered one of Europe's most sumptuous palaces, this dazzling structure is a 10-minute walk from the railway station, along pedestrians-only Kaiserstrasse and then Theaterstrasse.

As you enter the building, the largest baroque staircase in the country, the **Treppenhaus,** greets you. Halfway up, the stairway splits and peels away 180 degrees to the left and to the right. Soaring above on the vaulting is Tiepolo's giant fresco *The Four Continents,* a gorgeous exercise in blue and pink, with allegorical figures at the corners representing the four continents known at the time (take a careful look at the elephant's trunk). Tiepolo immortalized himself and Balthasar Neumann as two of the figures—they're not too difficult to spot. The fresco, which survived a devastating wartime bombing raid, is being restored bit by bit, so don't be surprised to find a small section covered by scaffolding.

CloseUp

GERMANY'S MASTER SCULPTOR

*T***ILMAN RIEMENSCHNEIDER,** *Germany's master of late-Gothic sculpture (1460–1531), lived an extraordinary life. His skill with wood and stone was recognized at an early age, and he soon presided over a major Würzburg workshop. Riemenschneider worked alone, however, on the life-size figures that dominate his sculptures. Details such as the folds of a robe or wrinkles upon a face highlight his grace and harmony of line.*

At the height of his career Riemenschneider was appointed city counselor; later he became mayor of Würzburg. In 1523, however, he made the fateful error of siding with the small farmers and guild members in the Peasants' War. He was arrested and held for eight weeks in the dungeons of the Marienberg Fortress, above Würzburg, where he was frequently tortured. Most of his wealth was confiscated, and he returned home a broken man. He died in 1531.

For nearly three centuries he and his sculptures were all but forgotten. Only in 1822, when ditchdiggers uncovered the site of his grave, was Riemenschneider once again included among Germany's greatest artists. Today Riemenschneider is recognized as the giant of German sculpture. The richest collection of his works is in Würzburg, although other masterpieces are on view in churches and museums along the Romantic Road as well as in other parts of Germany; for example, the renowned Windsheim Altar of the Twelve Apostles *is in the Palatine Museum in Heidelberg.*

Next, make your way to the **Weissersaal** (White Room) and then beyond to the grandest of the state rooms, the **Kaisersaal** (Throne Room). Tiepolo's frescoes show the 12th-century visit of Emperor Frederick Barbarossa, when he came to Würzburg to claim his bride. If you take part in the guided tour, you'll also see private chambers of the various former residents (guided tours in English are given daily at 11 and 3).

The **Hofkirche** (chapel; ⏲ Apr.–Oct., daily 9–noon and 1–5; Nov.–Mar., daily 9–noon and 1–4) demonstrates the prince-bishops' love of ostentation. Among the lavish marble, rich gilding, and delicate stuccowork, note the Tiepolo altarpieces, ethereal visions of *The Fall of the Angels* and *The Assumption of the Virgin.* Finally, tour the **Hofgarten**; the entrance is next to the chapel. The 18th-century formal garden has stately gushing fountains and trim ankle-high shrubs outlining geometric flower beds and gravel walks. ✉ *Residenzpl.* ☎ *0931/355–170* 🎫 *€4.50, including guided tour* ⏲ *Apr.–Oct., daily 9–5:30; Nov.–Mar., daily 10–4.*

Schloss Veitshöchheim. This first summer palace of the prince-bishops is 8 km (5 mi) north of Würzburg, at Veitshöchheim. The palace cannot be visited because of renovations, but the gardens remain open. A bus service to the palace runs from Würzburg's Kirchplatz. From mid-April to mid-October a boat service operates between Würzburg and the palace daily 10–4. The 40-minute trip costs €8 round-trip. ☎ *0931/355–170* *Gardens free* ⊙ *Gardens daily 7–dusk.*

❸ **Schönbornstrasse.** Würzburg's main pedestrian mall is filled with shops, cafés, and affordable eateries.

❻ **Stift Haug.** Franconia's first baroque church, designed by the Italian architect Antonio Petrini, was built between 1670 and 1691. Its elegant twin spires and central cupola make an impressive exterior. The altarpiece is a 1583 Crucifixion scene by Tintoretto. ✉ *Bahnhofstr. at Heinestr.* ☎ *0931/54102* ⊙ *Daily 8–6:30.*

3

Where to Stay & Eat

$–$$$ ✕ **Ratskeller.** The vaulted cellars of Würzburg's Rathaus shelter one of the city's most popular restaurants. Beer is served, but Franconian wine is what the regulars drink. The food is staunch Franconian fare. ✉ *Beim Grafeneckart, Langg. 1* ☎ *0931/13021* ▭ *AE, DC, MC, V.*

★ $–$$$ ✕ **Wein- und Speisehaus zum Stachel.** On a warm spring or summer day take a bench in the ancient courtyard of the Stachel, which is shaded by a canopy of vine leaves and enclosed by tall ivy-covered walls. The entrées are satisfyingly Franconian, from lightly baked onion cake in season to hearty roast pork. Excellent fish from their own pond is a specialty. ✉ *Gresseng. 1* ☎ *0931/52770* 🌐 *www.weinhaus-stachel.de* ▭ *No credit cards.*

★ ¢–$$ ✕ **Backöfele.** More than 400 years of tradition are sustained by this old tavern. Hidden away behind huge wooden doors in a back street, the Backöfele's cavelike interior is a popular meeting and eating place for regulars and newcomers alike. The menu includes local favorites such as suckling pig and marinated pot roast as well as some good fish dishes. ✉ *Ursulinerg. 2* ☎ *0931/59059* 🌐 *www.backoefele.de* ▭ *AE, MC, V.*

¢–$$ ✕ **Juliusspital Weinstuben.** This tavern serves wine from its own vineyard and good portions of basic Franconian fare. In summer you can enjoy your food and drinks on a quiet terrace in the courtyard. ✉ *Juliuspromenade 19* ☎ *0931/54080* ▭ *MC, V.*

$$ ✕🏨 **Hotel Greifensteiner Hof.** The modern Greifensteiner offers comfortable, individually furnished rooms in a quiet corner of the city, just off the market square. The cheaper doubles are small but lack no comforts or facilities. The hotel restaurant, the Fränkische Stuben ($–$$), has excellent cuisine—mostly Franconian specialties. ✉ *Dettelbacherg. 2, D–97070* ☎ *0931/35170* 📠 *0931/57057* 🌐 *www.greifensteiner-hof.de* *42 rooms* *Restaurant, cable TV, Wi-Fi, meeting room; no a/c* ▭ *AE, DC, MC, V.*

$$ ✕🏨 **Hotel Walfisch.** Guest rooms are furnished in solid Franconian style with farmhouse cupboards, bright fabrics, and heavy drapes. You'll breakfast in a dining room on the banks of the Main with views of the vineyard-covered Marienberg. For lunch and dinner try the hotel's cozy Walfisch-Stube restaurant ($$–$$$). ✉ *Am Pleidenturm 5, D–97070* ☎ *0931/35200* 📠 *0931/352–0500* 🌐 *www.hotel-walfisch.com* *40 rooms* *Restaurant, cable TV, meeting room; no a/c* ▭ *AE, DC, MC, V* 🍽 *CP.*

$–$$ **Hotel Zur Stadt Mainz.** This traditional Franconian inn dates from the early 15th century. The cuisine ($–$$$) is based on its own historic recipe book. Eel from the Main River and locally caught carp and pike are specialties. Homemade apple strudel is served with afternoon coffee; the breakfast buffet is enormous. Rooms are comfortably furnished, with old-fashioned touches such as gilt mirrors and heavy drapes. *Semmelstr. 39, D–97070 0931/53155 0931/58510 www.hotel-stadtmainz.de 15 rooms Restaurant, shops; no a/c AE, MC, V Closed 2 wks in Jan. Restaurant closed Sun. evening CP.*

$–$$ **Ringhotel Wittelsbacher Höh.** Most of the cozy rooms in this historic redbrick mansion offer views of Würzburg and the vineyards. The restaurant's wine list embraces most of the leading local vintages, and Franconian and Italian dishes ($$–$$$) pack the menu. In summer take a table on the terrace and soak up the view. *Hexenbruchweg 10, D–97082 0931/453–040 0931/415–458 www.ringhotels.de 73 rooms, 1 suite Restaurant, cable TV, sauna; no a/c AE, DC, MC, V CP.*

★ $$–$$$ **Hotel Rebstock zu Würzburg.** This hotel's rococo facade has welcomed guests for centuries. The spacious lobby, with its open fireplace and beckoning bar, sets the tone, and there's an attractive winter garden where you can enjoy a cup of coffee. All rooms are individually decorated and furnished in English country-house style. *Neubaustr. 7, D–97070 0931/30930 0931/309–3100 www.rebstock.com 63 rooms, 9 suites Restaurant, cable TV, Wi-Fi, bar, meeting rooms, no-smoking rooms; no a/c in some rooms AE, DC, MC, V CP.*

$ **Spehnkuch.** What was once a large apartment with high-ceiling rooms is today a small, spotlessly clean, very price-worthy pension. It's just opposite the main railway station. The only possible drawback is that the shower and toilet are located down the hall. *Röntgenstr. 7, D–97070 0931/54752 0931/54760 www.pension-spehnkuch.de 7 rooms No a/c, no room phones, no room TVs No credit cards CP.*

$ **Strauss.** Close to the river and the pedestrians-only center, the pink-stucco Strauss has been in the same family for more than 100 years. Rooms are simply furnished in light woods. The beamed restaurant Würtzburg serves Franconian cuisine, as well as international dishes, complemented by excellent Franconian wines. *Juliuspromenade 5, D–97070 0931/30570 0931/305–7555 www.hotel-strauss.de 75 rooms, 3 suites Restaurant, cable TV, bicycles; no a/c AE, DC, MC, V Restaurant closed late Dec.–Feb.*

Festivals

Würzburg's cultural year starts with the International Film Weekend in January and ends with a Johann Sebastian Bach Festival in November. Its annual Mozart Festival, between May and June, attracts visitors from all over the world. Most concerts are held in the magnificent setting of the Residenz. The annual jazz festival is in November. The town hosts a series of wine festivals from May to August.

Sports & the Outdoors

If you're interested in bicycling, turn left as you leave the main railway station and walk 100 feet to **Fahrradstation** (Bahnhofplatz 4 0931/57445), a bicycle shop that rents bikes for €10 a day or €45 a week.

You can also get professional advice here on the best places to cycle along the Romantic Road.

Shopping

Würzburg is the true wine center of the Romantic Road. Visit any of the vineyards that rise from the Main River and choose a *Bocksbeutel*, the distinctive green, flagon-shape wine bottle of Franconia. It's claimed that the shape came about because wine-guzzling monks found it the easiest to hide under their robes. The **Haus des Frankenweins** (House of Franconian Wine; ✉ Kranenkai 1 ☎ 0931/390–110) has wine tastings for individual visitors. Some 100 Franconian wines and a wide range of wine accessories are sold.

Die Murmel (✉ Augustinerstr. 7 ☎ 0931/59349) is the place to go if you're looking for a special toy. **Ebinger** (✉ Karmelitenstr. 23 ☎ 0937/59449) sells fine antique jewelry, clocks, watches, and silver. At the **Eckhaus** (✉ Langgasse 8, off the Marktpl. ☎ 0931/12001) you'll find high-quality gifts. In summer the selection consists mostly of garden and terrace decorations; from October through December the store is filled with delightful Christmas ornaments and candles.

en route

From Würzburg, follow the Romantic Road through Bavarian Franconia and Swabia and into the mountains of Upper Bavaria. For the first stretch, to Bad Mergentheim, B–19 takes you through the open countryside of the Hohenloher Plain.

Bad Mergentheim

17 *38 km (23 mi) south of Würzburg.*

Between 1525 and 1809 Bad Mergentheim was the home of the Teutonic Knights, one of the most successful medieval orders of chivalry. In 1809 Napoléon expelled them as he marched toward his ultimately disastrous Russian campaign. The expulsion seemed to sound the death knell of the little town, but in 1826 a shepherd discovered mineral springs on the north bank of the river. They proved to be the strongest sodium sulfate and bitter saltwaters in Europe, with health-giving properties that ensured the town's future prosperity.

The **Deutschordensschloss,** the Teutonic Knights' former castle, at the eastern end of the town, has a museum that follows the history of the order. ✉ *Schloss 16* ☎ *07931/52212* *€3.50, guided tour €1.50* *Tues.–Sun. 10–5; tours Thurs. and Sun. at 3.*

The **Wildpark Bad Mergentheim,** just outside Bad Mergentheim, is a wildlife park with Europe's largest selection of European species, including wolves and bears. ✉ *B–290* ☎ *07931/41344* *www.wildtierpark.de* *€8* *Mid-Mar.–Oct., daily 9–6; Nov.–mid-Mar., weekends 10:30–4.*

off the beaten path

STUPPACH – This village, 11 km (7 mi) southeast of Bad Mergentheim, has a **chapel** guarding one of the great Renaissance German paintings, the *Stuppacher Madonna*, by Matthias Grünewald (circa 1475–1528). It was only in 1908 that experts finally recognized it as the work of Grünewald; repainting in the 17th century had turned it into an unexceptional work. Though Grünewald was familiar with the developments in perspective and natural lighting of Italian Renaissance painting, his work remained resolutely anti-Renaissance in spirit: tortured, emotional, dark. *Chapel Mar. and Apr., daily 10–5; May–Oct., daily 9–5:30; Nov.–Feb., daily 11–4.*

Where to Stay & Eat

¢–$ **Klotzbücher.** You can order 10 different kinds of beer—4 from the tap—at the long wooden bar in this renovated Franconian brewery tavern. In the other room, paneled with dark wood, you can have the obligatory bratwurst on heavy wooden tables, but why not try the trout on sauerkraut or a good steak? In summer, head for the beer garden. *Boxbergerstr. 6 07931/562–928 www.victoria-hotel.de No credit cards No lunch.*

$$–$$$ **Hotel Victoria.** As you enter this hotel, you'll find yourself in an elegant lounge, with a library and open fireplace. The bedrooms are large and luxurious, and most have both a bath and shower. The restaurant Zirbelstube ($$$$) is open only for dinner but is known as one of the best in the region. In the Vinothek ($$), open all day, you can eat at the bar and watch the chefs prepare your next dish behind a huge glass partition. The hotel very conveniently has its own wine shop. *Poststr. 2–4, D–97980 07931/5930 07931/593–500 www.victoria-hotel.de 75 rooms, 3 suites Restaurant, cable TV, hair salon, massage, sauna, steam room, bar, pub; no a/c AE, DC, MC, V Restaurant Zirbelstube closed Jan. and Sun. CP.*

Weikersheim

18 *10 km (6 mi) east of Bad Mergentheim, 40 km (25 mi) south of Würzburg.*

The Tauber River town of Weikersheim is dominated by the **castle** of the counts of Hohenlohe. Its great hall is the scene each summer of an international youth music festival. The **Rittersaal** (Knights' Hall) contains life-size stucco wall sculptures of animals, reflecting the counts' love of hunting. In the cellars you can drink a glass of wine drawn from the huge casks that seem to prop up the building. Outside, stroll through the gardens and enjoy the view of the Tauber River. *07934/8364 €4, gardens only €1.50 Apr.–Oct., daily 9–6; Nov.–Mar., daily 10–noon and 1:30–4:30.*

Where to Stay & Eat

$ **Flair Hotel Laurentius.** This traditional hotel on Weikersheim's market square is a good stopover on the Romantic Road. You can avoid the crowds and the relatively high prices of nearby Rothenburg and visit that town the next morning. Rooms are comfortable and individually furnished, some with German antiques. The vaulted ground floor has a wine tavern as well as a good restaurant ($$–$$$; dinner only). The brasserie ($–$$), served by the same excellent kitchen, is open all day. *Marktpl. 5, D–97990 07934/91080 07934/910–818 www.*

hotel-laurentius.de 13 rooms Restaurant, café, cable TV, Weinstube; no a/c AE, DC, MC, V CP.

Creglingen

19 *20 km (12 mi) east of Weikersheim, 40 km (25 mi) south of Würzburg.*

The village of Creglingen has been an important pilgrimage site since the 14th century, when a farmer had a vision of a heavenly host plowing his field. The **Herrgottskirche** (Chapel of Our Lord) is in the Herrgottstal (Valley of the Lord), 3 km (2 mi) south of Creglingen; the way there is well signposted. The chapel was built by the counts of Hohenlohe, and in the early 16th century Tilman Riemenschneider carved an altarpiece for it. This enormous work, 33 feet high, depicts in minute detail the life and ascension of the Virgin Mary. Riemenschneider entrusted much of the background detail to the craftsmen of his Würzburg workshop, but he allowed no one but himself to attempt its life-size figures. Its intricate detail and attenuated figures are a high point of late-Gothic sculpture. *07933/508 €1.50 Apr.–Oct., daily 9:15–5:30; Nov.–early Jan. and Mar., Tues.–Sun. 10–noon and 1–4.*

★ 20

The **Fingerhutmuseum** is opposite the Herrgottskirche. *Fingerhut* is German for "thimble," and this delightful, privately run museum has thousands of them, some dating from Roman times. *07933/370 €1.50 Apr.–Oct., daily 9–6; Nov.–Mar., daily 1–4.*

The fascinating **Feuerwehrmuseum** (Firefighting Museum), with an impressive collection of old fire engines, lies 8 km (5 mi) north of Creglingen, within the stout castle walls of Schloss Waldmannshofen. *Waldmannshofen 09335/674 €2.50 Daily 10–noon and 2–5.*

Where to Stay

¢ **Heuhotel Ferienbauernhof.** For a truly off-the-beaten-track experience, book a space in the hayloft of the Stahl family's farm at Creglingen. Guests bed down in freshly turned hay in the farmhouse granary. Bed linen and blankets are provided. The overnight rate of €16 includes a cold supper and breakfast. For €21 you can swap the granary for one of three double rooms or even an apartment. Children are particularly well catered to, with tours of the farmyard and their own playground. *Frauental-Weidenhof 1, D–97993 07933/378 07933/7515 www.ferienpension-heuhotel.de Bicycles; no a/c, no room TVs No credit cards CP.*

Rothenburg-ob-der-Tauber

Fodor'sChoice ★ *20 km (12 mi) southeast of Creglingen, 75 km (47 mi) west of Nürnberg.*

Rothenburg-ob-der-Tauber (literally, "red castle on the Tauber") is the kind of medieval town that even Walt Disney might have thought too picturesque to be true, with half-timber architecture galore and a wealth of fountains and flowers against a backdrop of towers and turrets. As late as the 17th century it was a small but thriving market town that had grown up around the ruins of two 12th-century churches destroyed by an earthquake. Then it was laid low economically by the havoc of the Thirty Years' War, and with its economic base devastated, the town slumbered until modern tourism rediscovered it. It's undoubtedly something of a tourist trap but genuine enough for all the hype. There really is no place quite like it. Whether Rothenburg is at its most appealing in summer, when the balconies of its ancient houses are festooned with flowers, or in winter, when snow lies on its steep gables, is a matter of taste. Few people are likely to find this extraordinary little survivor from another age anything short of remarkable.

a good walk

Sights are dotted around town, and the streets don't lend themselves to a particular route. However, the **Rathaus** 21 ⚑, on Rathausplatz, is a logical place to begin a tour. The **Herterichbrunnen** 22 is just steps away, on Marktplatz. Continue walking south on Schmiedgasse until you come to the **Plönlein,** a small square that is an excellent spot for taking pictures of a small half-timber house in the foreground and a city gate on each side. Go back along Schmiedgasse and turn left on Burggasse to visit the **Mittelalterliches Kriminalmuseum** 23. Opposite the museum walk up the Hofbronnengasse, to the **Puppen und Spielzeugmuseum** 24 on your left. Continue back to the Marktplatz. Turn left along Herrengasse and right into the small Kirchgasse, which leads you to the **Stadtpfarrkirche St. Jakob** 25, where you'll find a magnificent Riemenschneider altar. From the church, follow Klingengasse north to the church of **St. Wolfgang** 26, built into the defenses of the town. On the outside it blends into the forbidding **Stadtmauer** 27 (city wall). If you stay inside the city wall and turn left, you'll reach the **Reichsstadtmuseum** 28. If you turn right, you can continue along the wall for nearly a mile.

TIMING Crowds will affect the pace at which you can tour the town. Early morning is the only time to appreciate the place in relative calm. The best times to see the mechanical figures on the Rathaus wall are in the evening, at 8, 9, or 10.

What to See

22 **Herterichbrunnen** (Herterich Fountain). A *Schäfertanz* (Shepherds' Dance) was performed around the ornate Renaissance fountain on the central Marktplatz whenever Rothenburg celebrated a major event. The dance is still done, though it's now for the benefit of tourists. It takes place in front of the Rathaus several times a year, chiefly at Easter, on Whitsunday, and in September. ✉ *Marktpl.*

23 **Mittelalterliches Kriminalmuseum** (Medieval Criminal Museum). The gruesome medieval implements of torture on display here are not for the fainthearted. The museum, the largest of its kind in Europe, also soberly documents the history of German legal processes in the Middle Ages. ✉ *Burgg. 3* ☎ *09861/5359* 🎫 *€3.20* ⏲ *Apr.–Oct., daily 9:30–6; Nov. and Jan.–Mar., daily 2–4; Dec., daily 10–4.*

24 **Puppen und Spielzeugmuseum** (Doll and Toy Museum). This complex of medieval and baroque buildings houses more than 1,000 dolls, the oldest dating from 1780, the newest from 1940, as well as a collection of dollhouses, model shops, and theaters guaranteed to charm every young-

Herterich-brunnen **22**
Mittelalter-liches Kriminal-museum **23**
Puppen und Spielzeug-museum **24**
Rathaus..... **21**
Reichsstadt-museum **28**
St. Wolfgang ... **26**
Stadtmauer .. **27**
Stadtpfarr-kirche St. Jakob **25**

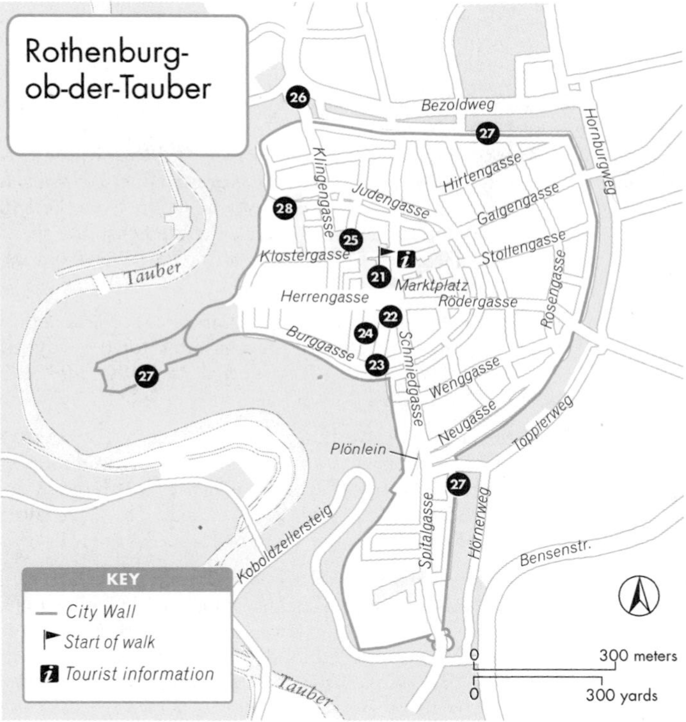

ster. ✉ *Hofbronneng. 13* ☎ *09861/7330* €4 *Jan. and Feb., daily 11–5; Mar.–Dec., daily 9:30–6.*

⚑ 21 **Rathaus.** Half of the town hall is Gothic, begun in 1240; the other half is neoclassic, started in 1572. Below the building are the **Historiengewölbe** (Historic Vaults; €2 Apr.–Oct., daily 9:30–5:30; Christmas market season, daily 1–4), housing a museum that concentrates on the Thirty Years' War.

Great prominence is given to an account of the *Meistertrunk* (Master Drink), an event that will follow you around Rothenburg. It came about when the Protestant town was captured by Catholic forces. During the victory celebrations, the conquering general was embarrassed to find himself unable to drink a great tankard of wine in one go, as his manhood demanded. He volunteered to spare the town further destruction if any of the city councillors could drain the mighty 6-pint draft. The mayor took up the challenge and succeeded, and Rothenburg was preserved. The tankard itself is on display at the Reichsstadtmuseum. On the north side of the main square is a fine clock, placed there 50 years after the mayor's feat. A mechanical figure acts out the epic Master Drink daily on the hour from 11 to 3 and in the evening at 8, 9, and 10. The feat is also celebrated at two annual pageants, when townsfolk parade through the streets in 17th-century garb. The Rathaus tower offers a good view of the town. ✉ *Rathauspl.*

28 **Reichsstadtmuseum** (Imperial City Museum). This city museum is two attractions in one. Its artifacts illustrate Rothenburg and its history. Among them is the great tankard, or *Pokal,* of the Meistertrunk. The setting of the museum is the other attraction; it's in a former Dominican convent, the oldest parts of which date from the 13th century. Tour the building to see the cloisters, the kitchens, and the dormitory; then see the collections. ✉ *Klosterhof 5* ☎ *09861/939–043* 🎫 *€3* ⏲ *Apr.–Oct., daily 10–5; Nov.–Mar., daily 1–4.*

26 **St. Wolfgang.** A historic parish church of Gothic origins with a baroque interior, St. Wolfgang's is most notable for the way it blends into the forbidding city wall. ✉ *Klingeng.* ☎ *09861/40492* 🎫 *€1* ⏲ *Mid-Mar.–Oct., daily 10–1 and 2–5.*

27 **Stadtmauer** (City Wall). Rothenburg's city walls are more than 2 km (1 mi) long and provide an excellent way of circumnavigating the town from above. The walls' wooden walkway is covered by eaves. Stairs every 200 or 300 yards provide ready access. There are superb views of the tangle of pointed and tiled red roofs and of the rolling country beyond.

25 **Stadtpfarrkirche St. Jakob** (Parish Church of St. James). The church has some notable Riemenschneider sculptures, including the famous *Heiliges Blut* (Holy Blood) altar. Above the altar a crystal capsule is said to contain drops of Christ's blood. There are three 14th- and 15th-century stained-glass windows in the choir, and the Herlin-Altar is famous for its 15th-century painted panels. ✉ *Klosterg. 15* ☎ *09861/700–620* 🎫 *€1.50* ⏲ *Jan.–Mar. and Nov., daily 10–noon and 2–4; Apr.–Oct., daily 9–5:30; Dec., daily 10–5. English tour Sat. at 3.*

Where to Stay & Eat

$$–$$$ Fodor'sChoice ★ **Hotel Eisenhut.** It's fitting that the prettiest small town in Germany should have one of the prettiest small hotels. Every one of the 79 rooms is different—each with its own charming color scheme, most with antique furniture. Try for one on the top floor toward the back overlooking the old town and the Tauber River valley. The restaurant ($$$–$$$$), one of the region's best, offers impeccable service along with delicious food and a lovely view of the garden. In summer you'll want to eat on the terrace, surrounded by flowers. ✉ *Herrng. 3–5, D–91541* ☎ *09861/7050* 📠 *09861/70545* 🌐 *www.eisenhut.com* *77 rooms, 2 suites* *Restaurant, café, cable TV, in-room data ports, Wi-Fi, piano bar; no a/c* 💳 *AE, DC, MC, V* ⏲ *Closed early Jan.–early Mar.*

★ $–$$ **Hotel-Restaurant Burg Colmberg.** East of Rothenburg in Colmberg, this castle turned hotel maintains a high standard of comfort within its original medieval walls. As you enter the hotel, logs are burning in the fireplace of the entrance hall, illuminating an original Tin Lizzy from 1917. The restaurant Zur Remise ($–$$$) serves venison from the castle's own hunting grounds. ✉ *Burg 1–3, D–91598 Colmberg, 18 km (11 mi) east of Rothenburg* ☎ *09803/91920* 📠 *09803/262* 🌐 *www.burg-colmberg.de* *24 rooms, 2 suites* *Restaurant, cable TV, 9-hole golf* *course, bicycles, Weinstube, playground, no-smoking rooms; no a/c* 💳 *AE, MC, V* ⏲ *Closed Feb.* 🍽 *CP.*

★ $$ **Burg-Hotel.** This exquisite little hotel abuts the town wall and was once part of a Rothenburg monastery. Most rooms have a view of the Tauber Valley. All have plush furnishings, with antiques or fine reproductions. Ask for a room with a four-poster bed. The music room holds both a grand piano and a computer with a high-speed Internet connection. Breakfast is served in good weather on the terrace on top of the town wall that has an even more stunning wide-angle view into the Tauber valley and to the hills beyond. The owner and staff are gracious hosts. ✉ *Klosterg. 1–3, D–91541* ☎ *09861/94890* 📠 *09861/948–940* 🌐 *www.burghotel.rothenburg.de* *17 rooms* *Cable TV, Wi-Fi, Internet room, laundry service, no a/c* 💳 *AE, DC, MC, V* 🍽 *CP.*

$$ **Romantik-Hotel Markusturm.** The Markusturm began as a 13th-century custom house, an integral part of the city defense wall, and has since developed over the centuries into an inn and staging post and finally into a luxurious small hotel. Some rooms are beamed, others have Laura Ashley decor or gaily painted bedsteads, and some have valuable antiques from the Middle Ages. In the beamed, elegant restaurant you can order three kinds of home-brewed beer. ✉ *Röderg. 1, D–91541* ☎ *09861/94280* 📠 *09861/113* 🌐 *www.markusturm.de* *23 rooms, 2 suites* *Restaurant, cable TV, no-smoking rooms; no a/c* 💳 *AE, DC, MC, V* 🍽 *CP.*

$–$$ **Hotel-Gasthof Zum Rappen.** Close to the Würzburger Tor (a town gate) and first mentioned in town records in 1603, this tavern offers a surprisingly high standard of comfort. Guest rooms have a colorful, airy touch, with light woods and floral fabrics. Those in the more modern Hotel Zum Rappen just beside the Gasthof Zum Rappen have balconies overlooking a quiet courtyard and are a bit higher priced. ✉ *Würzburger Tor 6 and 10, D–91541* ☎ *09861/95710* 📠 *09861/6076* 🌐 *www.hotel-rappen.com* *35 rooms* *Restaurant, beer garden, Weinstube; no a/c* 💳 *AE, DC, MC, V* 🍽 *CP.*

$–$$ **Hotel Reichs-Küchenmeister.** Master chefs in the service of the Holy Roman Emperor were the inspiration for the name of this historic hotel-restaurant, one of the oldest trader's houses in Rothenburg. For five generations it's been run by the same energetic family. Rooms are furnished in a stylish mixture of old and new; light veneer pieces share space with heavy oak bedsteads and painted cupboards. ✉ *Kirchpl. 8–10, D–91541* ☎ *09861/9700* 📠 *09861/970–409* 🌐 *www.reichskuechenmeister.com* *45 rooms, 2 suites, 3 apartments* *Restaurant, cable TV, hot tub, sauna, pub, no-smoking rooms; no a/c* 💳 *AE, MC, V* 🍽 *CP.*

$ **Hotel-Gasthof Post.** This small family-run hotel, two minutes on foot from the eastern city gate, must be one of the friendliest in town. The rooms are simple but clean, and all have shower or bath. ✉ *Ansbacherstr. 27, D–91541* ☎ *09861/6058* 📠 *09861/7896* 🌐 *www.post-rothenburg.com* *18 rooms* *Restaurant, cable TV; no a/c* 💳 *DC, MC, V* 🍽 *CP.*

¢–$ **Gasthof Klingentor.** This sturdy old staging post is outside the city walls but still within a 10-minute walk of Rothenburg's historic center. Rooms are spacious and furnished in the local rustic style. Its inexpensive restaurant serves substantial Franconian fare. A well-marked path for hiking or biking starts outside the front door. ✉ *Mergentheimerstr. 14,*

D–91541 ☎ 09861/3468 🖷 09861/3492 🌐 www.hotel-klingentor.de ⇨ 20 rooms, 16 with bath ♨ Restaurant, cable TV, beer garden, no-smoking rooms; no a/c, no TV in some rooms ▭ MC, V ‖◎‖ CP.

Festivals

Highlights of Rothenburg's annual calendar are the **Meistertrunk Festival,** over the Whitsun weekend, celebrating the famous wager said to have saved the town from destruction in the Thirty Years' War, and the **Reichstadt-Festtage,** on the first weekend of September, commemorating Rothenburg's attainment of Free Imperial City status in 1274. Both are spectacular festivals, when thousands of townspeople and local horsemen reenact the events in period costume.

Shopping

On the old and atmospheric premises of the **Kunstwerke Friese** (✉ Grüner Markt 7–8, near the Rathaus ☎ 09861/7166) you'll find everything from cuckoo clocks and beer tankards to porcelain and glassware. If you are looking specifically for Hummel articles, try **Haus der Tausend Geschenke** (✉ Obere Schmiedeg. 13 ☎ 09861/4801).

Käthe Wohlfahrt (✉ Herrng. 1 ☎ 09861/4090) carries children's toys and seasonal decorations. The Christmas Village part of the store is a wonderland of mostly German-made toys and decorations. **Teddyland** (✉ Herrng. 10 ☎ 09861/8904 🌐 www.teddyland.de) has Germany's largest teddy bear population. More than 5,000 of them pack this extraordinary store. Children adore the place, but be prepared: these are pedigree teddies, and they don't come cheap.

en route

Schloss Schillingsfürst (✉ Schlossplatz 1 ☎ 09868/201), a baroque castle of the Princes of Hohenlohe-Schillingsfürst, is 20 km (12 mi) south of Rothenburg-ob-der-Tauber. Standing on an outcrop, it can be seen from miles away. If you visit the castle, try to arrive in time for one of the demonstrations of Bavarian falconry, held in the courtyard. You can watch eagles and falcons, on a single command, shoot down from the sky to catch their prey. The castle is open Tuesday–Sunday 10–6; the falconry show and guided tour of the castle (€7 for both) are March–October, daily at 11 and 3.

Dinkelsbühl

★ 29 *26 km (16 mi) south of Schillingsfürst.*

Within the walls of Dinkelsbühl, a beautifully preserved medieval town, the rush of traffic seems a lifetime away. There's less to see here than in Rothenburg, and the mood is much less tourist-oriented. Like Rothenburg, Dinkelsbühl was caught up in the Thirty Years' War, and it also preserves a fanciful episode from those bloody times. Local lore says that when Dinkelsbühl was under siege by Swedish forces and in imminent danger of destruction, a young girl led the children of the town to the enemy commander and implored him in their name for mercy. The commander of the Swedish army is said to have been so moved by the plea that he spared the town. Whether or not it's true, the story is retold every year during the Kinderzech Festival, a pageant by the children of Dinkelsbühl during a 10-day festival in July. An annual open-air-theater festival takes place from mid-June until mid-August.

The **Münster St. Georg** (Minster St. George) is the standout sight in town. At 235 feet in length it's large enough to be a cathedral, and it's among the best examples in Bavaria of the late-Gothic style. Note the complex fan vaulting that spreads sinuously across the ceiling. If you can face the climb, head up the 200-foot tower for amazing views over the jumble of rooftops. ✉ *Marktpl.* ☎ *09851/2245* *Tower €1.50* ⏱ *Church daily 9–noon and 2–6; tower May–Sept., Sat. 10–6, Sun. 1–6.*

Where to Stay & Eat

$$ **Hotel Deutsches Haus.** This medieval inn, with a facade of half-timber gables and flower boxes, has many rooms fitted with antique furniture. One of them has a romantic four-poster bed. Dine beneath heavy oak beams in the restaurant (¢–$$), where you can try the local specialty, a type of grain called Dinkel. It's very nutritious and often served roasted with potatoes and salmon. ✉ *Weinmarkt 3, D–91550* ☎ *09851/6058 or 09851/6059* 📠 *09851/7911* 🌐 *www.deutsches-haus-dkb.de* *8 rooms, 2 suites* *Restaurant, cable TV, Internet, meeting rooms, no-smoking rooms; no a/c* 💳 *AE, DC, MC, V* ⏱ *Closed 3 wks in Jan.* *CP.*

$–$$ **Goldene Rose.** Since 1450 the inhabitants of Dinkelsbühl and their guests—among them Queen Victoria in 1891—have enjoyed good food and refreshing drinks in this half-timber house. Dark paneling in the restaurant creates the cozy atmosphere in which you can enjoy good regional cuisine, especially fish and game. Even in some of the modern bedrooms you will find half-timber walls. ✉ *Marktplatz 4, D–91550* ☎ *09851/57750* 📠 *09851/577–575* 🌐 *www.hotel-goldene-rose.com* *31 rooms* *Restaurant, cable TV, Internet; no a/c* 💳 *AE, DC, MC* *CP.*

$ **Hotel Goldene Kanne.** This central hotel was built in 1690. Rooms are furnished with solid German oak; many have sitting-room corners with desks. It's particularly recommended for families (seven of the rooms have children's beds), although couples are also catered to with a special honeymoon suite. The cozy restaurant ($$–$$$) serves both local and international cuisine. ✉ *Segringerstr. 8, D–91550* ☎ *09851/57290* 📠 *09851/572–929* *22 rooms, 2 suites* *Restaurant, cable TV, Internet; no a/c* 💳 *AE, DC, MC, V* *CP.*

Shopping

Deleika (✉ Waldeck 33 ☎ 09857/97990) makes barrel organs to order, although it won't deliver the monkey! The firm also has a museum of barrel organs and other mechanical instruments. It's just outside Dinkelsbühl. Call ahead. At **Dinkelsbüler Kunst-Stuben** (✉ Segringer Str. 52 ☎ 08951/6750), the owner, Mr. Appelberg, sells his own drawings, paintings, and etchings of the town. **Jürgen Pleikies** (✉ Segringerstr. 53–55 ☎ 09851/7596) is doing his part to restore his town's former reputation for fine earthenware; he also offers courses at the potter's wheel. At **Weschcke und Ries** (✉ Segringerstr. 20 ☎ 09851/9439), Hummel porcelain figures share window space with other German porcelain and glassware.

Nördlingen

30 *32 km (20 mi) southeast of Dinkelsbühl, 70 km (43 mi) northwest of Augsburg.*

In Nördlingen the cry of "*So G'sell so*"—"All's well"—still rings out every night across the ancient walls and turrets. Sentries sound out the traditional message from the 300-foot tower of the central parish church of **St. Georg** at half-hour intervals between 10 PM and midnight. The tradition goes back to an incident during the Thirty Years' War, when an enemy attempted to slip into the town and was detected by a resident. You can climb the 365 steps up the tower—known locally as the Daniel—for an unsurpassed view of the town and countryside, including, on clear days, 99 villages. The ground plan of the town is two concentric circles. The inner circle of streets, whose central point is St. Georg, marks the earliest medieval boundary. A few hundred yards beyond it is the outer boundary, a wall built to accommodate expansion. Fortified with 11 towers and punctuated by five massive gates, it's one of the best-preserved town walls in Germany. ✉ *Marktpl.* 🎫 *Tower €1.50* ⏲ *Daily 9–dusk.*

Nördlingen lies in the center of a huge, basinlike depression, the **Ries,** that until the beginning of this century was believed to be the remains of an extinct volcano. In 1960 it was proven by two Americans that the 24-km-wide (15-mi-wide) crater was caused by a meteorite at least 1 km (½ mi) in diameter. The compressed rock, or *Suevit,* formed by the explosive impact of the meteorite was used to construct many of the town's buildings, including St. Georg's tower.

Nördlingen possesses one of Germany's largest steam railway–engine museums, the **Bayerisches Eisenbahnmuseum,** adjacent to the railroad station. About a dozen times a year some of the old locomotives puff away on outings to Harburg. Call for a timetable. ✉ *Am Hohen Weg 6* ☎ *09081/9808* 🌐 *www.bayerisches-eisenbahnmuseum.de* 🎫 *€4* ⏲ *Mar.–June, Sept., and Oct., Sun. 10–5; July and Aug., Tues.–Sat. noon–4, Sun. 10–5.*

Where to Stay & Eat

$–$$ 🏨 **Kaiserhof-Hotel-Sonne.** The great German poet Goethe stayed here, only one in a long line of distinguished guests starting with Emperor Friedrich III in 1487. The vaulted-cellar wine tavern is a reminder of those days. The three honeymoon suites are furnished in 18th-century style, with hand-painted four-poster beds. ✉ *Marktpl. 3, D–86720* ☎ *09081/5067* 📠 *09081/29290* 🌐 *www.kaiserhof-hotel-sonne.de* 🛏 *40 rooms* 👍 *Restaurant, cable TV, Weinstube; no a/c* 💳 *AE, MC, V* 🍽 *CP.*

$ 🏨 **Braunes Ross.** This Gasthaus in the central square, directly opposite the city tower, was first mentioned in city archives in 1481 as "a place to eat and drink." The Haubner family bought the house 517 years later, in 1998, and renovated it from top to bottom. It now features modern rooms with cable TV, phones, and private baths; and a cozy, Bavarian-style restaurant. ✉ *Marktplatz 12, D–86720* ☎ *09081/290–120* 📠 *0981/290–1228* 🛏 *14 rooms* 👍 *Restaurant, cable TV; no a/c* 💳 *MC, V* 🍽 *CP.*

$ **Hotel Goldene Rose.** This small, modern hotel is in the heart of town and is ideal for those who wish to explore Nördlingen on foot. The in-house restaurant serves wholesome, inexpensive dishes. ✉ *Baldingerstr. 42, D–86720* ☎ *09081/86019* 📠 *09081/24591* 🌐 *www.goldene-rose-noerdlingen.de* *17 rooms, 1 apartment* *Restaurant, cable TV, no-smoking rooms; no a/c* 💳 *MC, V* *CP.*

Festivals

From the end of June through July, an annual open-air **theater festival** takes place in front of the ancient walls of Nördlingen's Alter Bastei (Old Bastion).

3

Sports & the Outdoors

Ever cycled around a huge meteor crater? You can do just that in the **Nördlingen Ries,** the basinlike depression left by a meteor that hit the area in prehistoric times. The **Nördlingen tourist office** (☎ 09081/84116) has a list of 10 recommended bike routes, including one 47-km (29-mi) trail around the northern part of the meteor crater. **Radsport Boeckle** (✉ Reimlingerstr. 19 ☎ 09081/801–040) rents bikes. For a spectacular view of the town and Ries crater, contact the local flying club, the **Rieser Flugsportverein** (☎ 09081/28963), for a ride in a light aircraft.

A traditional **horse race,** the Scharlachrennen, with medieval origins, is held annually in August. It's the central focus of an international show-jumping festival.

Shopping

Nördlingen has a **market** in the pedestrian shopping zone on Wednesday and Saturday. **Otto Wolf** (✉ Marktpl. ☎ 09081/4606) stocks a wide selection of Hummel figures at competitive prices.

en route

At the point where the little Wörnitz River breaks through the Franconian Jura Mountains, 20 km (12 mi) southeast of Nördlingen, you'll find one of southern Germany's best-preserved medieval castles. **Schloss Harburg** was already old when it passed into the possession of the counts of Oettingen in 1295; before that time it belonged to the Hohenstaufen emperors. The ancient and noble house of Oettingen still owns the castle, and inside you can view treasures collected by the family. Among them are works by Tilman Riemenschneider, along with illuminated manuscripts dating as far back as the 8th century, and an exquisite 12th-century ivory crucifix. The castle is literally on B–25, which runs under it through a tunnel in the rock. ✉ *Harburg* ☎ *09080/96990* 🌐 *www.fuerst-wallerstein.de* *€4, including guided tour* *Apr.–Oct., Tues.–Sun. 10–5; Nov.–Mar., Tues.–Sun. 10–4.*

Donauwörth

31 *11 km (7 mi) south of Harburg, 41 km (25 mi) north of Augsburg.*

At the old walled town of Donauwörth, the Wörnitz River meets the Danube. If you're driving, pull off into the clearly marked lot on B–25, just north of town. Below you sprawls a striking natural relief map of

Donauwörth and its two rivers. The oldest part of town is on an island. A wood bridge connects it to the north bank and the single surviving town gate, the Riederstor. North of the gate is one of the finest avenues of the Romantic Road: Reichsstrasse (Empire Street), so named because it was once a vital link in the Road of the Holy Roman Empire between Nürnberg and Augsburg. The Fuggers, a famous family of traders and bankers from Augsburg, acquired a palatial home here in the 16th century; its fine Renaissance-style facade, under a steeply gabled roof, stands proudly at the upper end of Reichsstrasse.

Donauwörth is the home of the famous Käthe Kruse dolls, beloved for their sweet looks and frilly, floral outfits. You can buy them at several outlets in town, and they have their own museum, where more than 130 examples dating from 1912 are displayed in a specially renovated monastery building, the **Käthe-Kruse-Puppen-Museum.** ✉ *Pflegstr. 21a* ☎ *0906/789–185* 🎫 *€2* ⏲ *May–Sept., Tues.–Sun. 11–5; Apr. and Oct., Tues.–Sun. 2–5; Nov.–Mar., Wed. and weekends 2–5.*

Where to Stay & Eat

$–$$ **Parkhotel.** Members of the Landidyll chain of hotels have one feature in common: an idyllic location. This one qualifies with its position high above Donauwörth. Most rooms have floor-to-ceiling windows with panoramic views. All are decorated in bright pastel tones and have wicker chairs and sofas. ✉ *Sternschanzenstr. 1, D–86609* ☎ *0906/706–510* 📠 *0906/706–5180* 🌐 *www.parkhotel-donauwoerth.de* *45 rooms* *Cable TV, in-room data ports, Wi-Fi, pool, Weinstube, no-smoking rooms; no a/c* 💳 *AE, DC, MC, V* *CP.*

Sports & the Outdoors

There's challenging canoeing on the four rivers (including the Danube) in and around Donauwörth. The **Kanu-Laden in Donauwörth** (✉ Alte Augsburger Str. 12 ☎ 0906/8086) rents canoes and can provide professional advice and suggested routes.

Ulm

32 *60 km (40 mi) west of Augsburg.*

Ulm isn't considered part of the Romantic Road, but it's definitely worth visiting, if only for one reason: its mighty Münster, which has the world's tallest church tower (536 feet). To get to Ulm from Donauwörth, take Highway B–16 west, connecting with B–28. Or, from Augsburg, take a 40-minute ride on one of the superfast ICE (Intercity Express) trains that run to Ulm every hour.

Ulm grew as a medieval trading city thanks to its location on the Danube River. Today the proximity of the Old Town to the river adds to Ulm's charm. In the Fisherman and Tanner quarters the cobblestone alleys and stone-and-wood bridges over the Blau (a small Danube tributary) are especially picturesque.

★ Ulm's **Münster,** the largest church in southern Germany, was unscathed by wartime bombing. It stands over the huddled medieval gables of Old Ulm, visible long before you hit the ugly suburbs encroaching on the

Swabian countryside. Its single, filigree tower challenges the physically fit to plod 536 feet up the 768 steps of a giddily twisting spiral stone staircase to a spectacular observation point below the spire. On clear days the highest steeple in the world will reward you with views of the Swiss and Bavarian Alps, 160 km (100 mi) to the south. The Münster was begun in the late-Gothic age (1377) and took five centuries to build, with completion in the neo-Gothic years of the late 19th century. It contains some notable treasures, including late-Gothic choir stalls and a Renaissance altar. ✉ *Münsterpl.* 🎫 *Tower €3, organ recitals €1.50* ⏲ *Daily 9–5; organ recitals May–Oct., daily at 11:30.*

The central **Marktplatz** is bordered by medieval houses with stepped gables. Every Wednesday and Saturday there's a market here. Summer or winter, farmers from the surrounding area arrive by 6 AM to erect their stands and unload their produce. Potatoes, vegetables, apples, pears, berries, honey, fresh eggs, poultry, homemade bread, and all kinds of other edible things are carefully displayed. Flowers of every color and variety are also available. If you plan to come, be sure to get here early; the market packs up around noon.

A reproduction of local tailor Ludwig Berblinger's flying machine hangs inside the elaborately painted **Rathaus.** In 1811 Berblinger, a tailor and local eccentric, cobbled together a pair of wings and made a big splash by trying to fly across the river. He didn't make it, but he grabbed a place in German history books for his efforts. ✉ *Marktpl. 1.*

The **Ulmer Museum** (Ulm Museum), on the south side of Marktplatz, is an excellent natural history and art museum. Exhibits illustrate centuries of development in this part of the Danube Valley, and a modern art section has works by Kandinsky, Klee, Léger, and Lichtenstein. ✉ *Marktpl. 9* ☎ *0731/161–4330* 🎫 *€2.50* ⏲ *Tues., Wed., and Fri.–Sun. 11–5, Thurs. 11–8; guided tour Thurs. at 6.*

Einstein's home was a casualty of an Allied raid and was never rebuilt. The **Einstein Denkmal** (Einstein Monument; ✉ Friedrich-Ebert-Str.), erected in 1979, marks the site opposite the main railway station.

German bread is world renowned, so it's not surprising that a national museum is devoted to bread making. The **Deutsches Brotmuseum** (German Bread Museum) is housed in a former salt warehouse, just north of the Münster. It's by no means as crusty or dry as some might fear, with some often-amusing tableaux illustrating how bread has been baked over the centuries. ✉ *Salzstadelg. 10* ☎ *0731/69955* 🌐 *www.brotmuseum-ulm.de* 🎫 *€2.50* ⏲ *Thurs.–Tues. 10–5, Wed. 10–8:30; guided tour Wed. at 7.*

Complete your visit to Ulm with a walk down to the banks of the Danube, where you'll find long sections of the **old city wall** and fortifications intact.

Where to Stay & Eat

★ **$–$$$** ✕ **Zur Forelle.** For more than 350 years, the aptly named Forelle, which means "trout," has stood over the small River Blau which flows through a large trout basin right under the restaurant. If you're not a trout fan, there are 10 other fish dishes available, as well as excellent venison, in season. On a nice summer evening try to get a table on the small terrace. You'll literally sit over the small river, with a weeping willow on one side, half-timber houses all around you, and the towering cathedral in the background. ✉ *Fischerg. 25* ☎ *0731/63924* 🌐 *www.zurforelle.com* 💳 *DC, MC, V.*

¢–$$ ✕ **Zunfthaus der Schiffleute.** The sturdy half-timber Zunfthaus (Guildhall) has stood here for more than 500 years, first as a fishermen's pub and now as a charming tavern-restaurant. Ulm's fishermen had their guild headquarters here, and when the nearby Danube flooded, the fish swam right up to the door. Today they land on the menu. One of the "foreign" intruders on the menu is Bavarian white sausage, *Weisswurst.* The local beer is an excellent accompaniment. The minimum amount for credit cards is €25. ✉ *Fischerg. 31* ☎ *0731/64411* 🌐 *www.zunfthaus-ulm.de* 💳 *AE, DC, MC, V.*

$$ ✕🏨 **Maritim.** Whether you come here to eat or stay, be prepared for incredible views. The elegant rooms and restaurants all offer breathtaking panoramas. In the main restaurant on the 16th floor, the international dishes are good and the view is amazing. Huge floor-to-ceiling windows reveal the Old Town of Ulm with the cathedral, the Danube, and the Swabian Alb all at your fingertips. The large, luxurious bar with cozy corners and live piano music every night has become a favorite with hotel and restaurant guests. Ask for weekend rates. ✉ *Basteistr. 40, D–89073* ☎ *0731/9230* 📠 *0731/923–1000* 🌐 *www.maritim.de* *287 rooms* *2 restaurants, cable TV with movies, in-room data ports, Wi-Fi, pool, gym, massage, sauna, steam room, bar, meeting rooms, parking (fee), no-smoking rooms; no a/c* 💳 *AE, DC, MC, V.*

$ 🏨 **Hotel am Rathaus/Reblaus.** The owner's love for antique paintings, furniture, and dolls is evident throughout this hotel. Some of the rooms have antique furniture. In the annex, the half-timber Reblaus, most rooms have hand-painted cupboards. If you take a room toward the front, look up from your window and you'll see the cathedral with its huge spire a few hundred feet away. The hotel is behind the old historic Rathaus, on the fringe of the Old City, where you'll find more than a dozen restaurants and taverns. ✉ *Kronengasse 10, D–89073* ☎ *0731/968–490* 📠 *0731/968–4949* 🌐 *www.rathausulm.de* *34 rooms* *Cable TV, no-smoking rooms; no a/c* 💳 *AE, DC* 🍽 *CP.*

¢–$ 🏨 **Zum Bäumle.** Hidden away in the little street just north of the mighty cathedral is this small half-timber hotel. The rooms are nice, but simply furnished. Some have a private shower and toilet; others share. The cozy wood-panel Weinstube, where you'll get solid Swabian food, is a favorite with locals. ✉ *Kohlgasse 6, D–89073* ☎ *0731/62287* 📠 *0731/602–2604* *baeumle.ulm@t-online.de* *21 rooms* *Restaurant; no a/c, no room phones, no room TVs* 💳 *MC* ⏲ *Restaurant closed weekends* 🍽 *CP.*

Nightlife & the Arts

The mighty organ of the **Münster** can be heard in special recitals every Sunday at 11:15 from Easter until November.

Ulm has a lively after-hours scene. The piano bar in the **Hotel Maritim** (✉ Basteistr. 40 ☎ 0731/9230) has nightly music. Jazz fans make for the **Jazzkeller** (✉ Prittwitzstr. 10 ☎ 0731/601–210).

Augsburg

41 km (25 mi) south of Donauwörth, 60 km (37 mi) west of Munich.

Augsburg is Bavaria's third-largest city, after Munich and Nürnberg. It dates to 15 years before the birth of Christ, when a son of the Roman emperor Augustus set up a military camp here on the banks of the Lech River. The settlement that grew up around it was known as Augusta, a name Italian visitors to the city still call it. It was granted city rights in 1156, and 200 years later was first mentioned in municipal records of the Fugger family, who were to Augsburg what the Medici family was to Florence.

a good walk

A walking tour of Augsburg is easy because signs on almost every street corner point the way to the chief sights. The signs are integrated into three color-charted tours devised by the tourist office. There's an office at Bahnhofstrasse 7, near the Hauptbahnhof, and on the south side of the central Rathausplatz. Pick up tour maps and begin your walk at Rathausplatz; the walk described below covers several of the sights described in the "green" tour.

On the eastern side of Rathausplatz rises the impressive bulk of the city's 17th-century town hall, the **Rathaus** 33. Even taller than the two onion domes of the Rathaus is the nearby **Perlachturm** 34. Follow the green signs north along Schlachthausgasse to the **Brecht Haus** 35, where the playwright Bertolt Brecht was born; it's now a museum. Cross the nearby brook via the small bridge leading to Auf dem Rain and turn left into Barfüsserstrasse, leading to Jakoberstrasse. After 300 feet you'll find on the right the **Fuggerei** 36, a 16th-century housing project. Following the green signs, recross the brook (which follows the route of a Roman-built canal), pass the small alley Hinterer Lech, and turn left down Mittlerer Lech. This will lead you to the **Holbein Haus** 37, the home of painter Hans Holbein the Elder (at Vorderer Lech).

Continue farther south, recrossing the brook onto Oberer Graben, and head south through the Vogeltor, a Gothic city gate, to the southern extremities of the medieval defense wall. The gate here, the **Rotes Tor** 38, was the main entrance to Augsburg in earlier centuries. Now follow the green route north through a small park enclosed by the remains of the ancient bastion. Continue north and you'll soon see the soaring tower of the Gothic church of **Sts. Ulrich and Afra** 39, on Ulrichsplatz. Ulrichsplatz leads directly north into **Maximilianstrasse,** Augsburg's main thoroughfare. At No. 46 stands the **Schaezler Palais** 40, home of two impressive art collections. The Herkulesbrunnen, the fountain in the center of the street outside the palace, is a symbolic work by the Renaissance sculptor Adrian de Vries. You can see a second de Vries fountain farther north on the same street. Just steps away, at Maximilianstrasse 36, is the sturdy **Fuggerhäuser** 41, former home of Jakob Fugger, founder of the Fuggerei.

Wend your way across Zeugplatz, Bürgermeister-Fischer-Strasse, and Martin-Luther-Platz to Anna-Strasse. If you have time and energy, stop at the **Maximilian-Museum** 42, on Phillipine-Welser-Strasse. The exquisite **St.**

Brecht Haus 35
Dom St. Maria 44
Fuggerei 36
Fuggerhäuser 41
Holbein Haus 37
Maximilian-Museum 42
Mozart-Haus 45
Perlachturm 34
Rathaus 33
Rotes Tor 38
St. Annakirche . . 43
Sts. Ulrich and Afra 39
Schaezler Palais 40

Annakirche 43 is on Anna-Strasse. Head north from here, cross busy Karlstrasse, and go through the Kesselmarkt and across Johannisgasse to the gardens of the city cathedral, **Dom St. Maria** 44. A short walk north along Frauentorstrasse takes you to the **Mozart-Haus** 45, birthplace of Mozart's father, Leopold. By retracing your steps to the cathedral, into Hoher Weg and then Karolinenstrasse, you'll arrive within a few minutes back at Rathausplatz.

TIMING You'll need a complete day if you linger in any of the museums. Set aside at least two hours for the Schaezler Palais and a half hour each for the churches of Sts. Ulrich and Afra and the Dom St. Maria. There are plenty of opportunities en route for lunch or a coffee break.

What to See

35 **Brecht Haus.** This modest artisan's house was the birthplace of the renowned playwright Bertolt Brecht (1898–1956), author of *Mother Courage* and *The Threepenny Opera.* ✉ *Auf dem Rain 7* 🎫 *€1.50* ⏲ *Tues.–Sun. 10–5.*

44 **Dom St. Maria** (Cathedral of St. Mary). Augsburg's cathedral stands out within the city's panorama because of its square Gothic towers, which were built in the 9th century. A 10th-century Romanesque crypt, built

in the time of Bishop Ulrich, also remains from the cathedral's early years. The 11th-century windows on the south side of the nave, depicting the prophets Jonah, Daniel, Hosea, Moses, and David, form the oldest cycle of stained glass in central Europe. Five important paintings by Hans Holbein the Elder adorn the altar.

The cathedral's treasures are on display at the **Diözesan Museum St. Afra** (✉ Kornhausg. 3–5 🎫 €2.50 ⏲ Tues.–Sat. 10–5, Sun. 2–5). A short walk from the cathedral will take you to the quiet courtyards and small raised garden of the former episcopal residence, a series of 18th-century buildings in baroque and rococo styles that now serve as the Swabian regional government offices ✉ *Dompl.* ⏲ *Daily 9–dusk.*

36 **Fuggerei.** This neat little settlement is the world's oldest social housing project, established by the Fugger family in 1516 to accommodate the city's deserving poor. The 104 homes still serve the same purpose; the annual rent of "one Rhenish guilder" (€1) hasn't changed, either. Residents must be Augsburg citizens, Catholic, and destitute through no fault of their own—and they must pray daily for their original benefactors, the Fugger family. ✉ *Jacoberstr.*

41 **Fuggerhäuser.** The 16th-century former home and business quarters of the Fugger family now houses a restaurant in its cellar and offices on the upper floors. In the ground-floor entrance are busts of two of Augsburg's most industrious Fuggers, Raymund and Anton. Beyond a modern glass door is a quiet courtyard with colonnades, the Damenhof (Ladies' Courtyard), originally reserved for the Fugger women. ✉ *Maximilianstr. 36–38.*

37 **Holbein Haus.** The rebuilt 16th-century home of painter Hans Holbein the Elder, one of Augsburg's most famous residents, is now a city art gallery, with changing exhibitions. ✉ *Vorderer Lech 20* 🎫 *Varies* ⏲ *May–Oct., Tues., Wed., and Fri.–Sun. 10–5, Thurs. 10–8; Nov.–Apr., Tues., Wed., and Fri.–Sun. 10–4, Thurs. 10–8.*

42 **Maximilian-Museum.** Augsburg's main museum houses a permanent exhibition of Augsburg arts and crafts in a 16th-century merchant's mansion. ✉ *Philippine-Welser-Str. 24* 🎫 *€4* ⏲ *Tues.–Sun. 10–5.*

Maximilianstrasse. This main shopping street was once a medieval wine market. Most of the city's sights are on this thoroughfare or a short walk away. Two monumental and elaborate fountains punctuate the long street. At the north end is the **Merkur,** designed in 1599 by the Dutch master Adrian de Vries (after a Florentine sculpture by Giovanni da Bologna), which shows winged Mercury in his classic pose. Farther up Maximilianstrasse is another de Vries fountain: a bronze **Hercules** struggling to subdue the many-headed Hydra.

45 **Mozart-Haus** (Mozart House). Leopold Mozart, the father of Wolfgang Amadeus Mozart, was born in this bourgeois 17th-century residence; he was an accomplished composer and musician in his own right. The house now serves as a Mozart memorial and museum, with some fascinating contemporary documents on the Mozart family. ✉ *Frauentorstr. 30* ☎ *0821/324–3894* 🎫 *€1.50* ⏲ *Tues.–Sun. 10–5.*

34 **Perlachturm** (Perlach Tower). This 258-foot-high plastered brick bell tower has foundations dating to the 11th century. Although it's a long climb to the top of the tower, the view over Augsburg and the countryside is worth the effort. ✉ *Rathauspl.* ☎ *No phone* 🎫 *€1* ⏲ *May–mid-Oct., daily 10–6; Dec., weekends noon–7.*

33 **Rathaus.** Augsburg's city hall was Germany's largest when it was built in the early 17th century; it's now regarded as the finest Renaissance secular structure north of the Alps. Its **Goldenener Saal** (Golden Hall) was given its name because of its rich decoration—a gold-based harmony of wall frescoes, carved pillars, and coffered ceiling. ✉ *Rathauspl.* ☎ *0821/502–0724* 🎫 *€1.50* ⏲ *10–6 on days when no official functions take place.*

38 **Rotes Tor** (Red Gate). The city's most important medieval entrance gate once straddled the main trading road to Italy. It provides the backdrop to an open-air opera and operetta festival in June and July. ✉ *Eserwallstr.*

43 **St. Annakirche** (St. Anna's Church). This site was formerly part of a Carmelite monastery, where Martin Luther stayed in 1518 during his meetings with Cardinal Cajetanus, the papal legate sent from Rome to persuade the reformer to renounce his heretical views. Luther refused, and the place where he publicly declared his rejection of papal pressure is marked with a plaque on Maximilianstrasse. You can wander through the quiet cloisters, dating from the 14th century, and view the chapel used by the Fugger family until the Reformation. ✉ *Anna-Str., west of Rathauspl.* ⏲ *Tues.–Sat. 10–12:30 and 3–6, Sun. noon–6.*

39 **Sts. Ulrich and Afra.** Standing at the highest point of the city, this basilica was built on the site of a Roman cemetery where St. Afra was martyred in AD 304. The original structure was begun in the late-Gothic style in 1467; a baroque preaching hall was added in 1710 as the Protestant church of St. Ulrich. St. Afra is buried in the crypt, near the tomb of St. Ulrich, a 10th-century bishop who helped stop a Hungarian army at the gates of Augsburg in the Battle of the Lech River. The remains of a third patron of the church, St. Simpert, are preserved in one of the church's most elaborate side chapels. From the steps of the magnificent altar, look back along the high nave to the finely carved baroque wrought-iron and wood railing that borders the entrance. As you leave, look into the separate but adjacent church of St. Ulrich, the former chapter house that was reconstructed by the Lutherans after the Reformation. ✉ *Ulrichspl.* ⏲ *Daily 9–dusk.*

40 **Schaezler Palais.** This elegant 18th-century city palace was built by the von Liebenhofens, a family of wealthy bankers. Schaezler was the name of a baron who married into the family. Today the palace rooms contain the **Deutsche Barockgalerie** (German Baroque Gallery), a major art collection that features works of the 17th and 18th centuries. The palace adjoins the former church of a Dominican monastery. A steel door behind the palace's banquet hall leads into another world of high-vaulted ceilings, where the **Staatsgalerie Altdeutsche Meister,** a Bavarian state collection, highlights old-master paintings, among them a Dürer portrait of one of the Fuggers. ✉ *Maximilianstr. 46* 🎫 *€2* ⏲ *Tues.–Sun. 10–5.*

Where to Stay & Eat

$$–$$$$ Fodor'sChoice ★ **Die Ecke.** Situated on an *Ecke* (corner) of the small square right behind Augsburg's city hall, the Ecke is valued for the imaginative variety of its cuisine and the scope of its wine list. In season, the venison dishes are among Bavaria's best. The fish, in particular the *Zander* (green pike) or the trout sautéed in butter and lightly dressed with herbs and lemon, is magnificent and complemented nicely by the Riesling Gimmeldinger Meersspinne, the house wine for 40 years. ✉ *Elias-Holl-Pl. 2* ☎ *0821/510–600* 🌐 *www.restaurantdieecke.de* *Reservations essential* 💳 *AE, DC, MC, V.*

★ **$$** **Steigenberger Drei Mohren Hotel.** Kings and princes, Napoléon and the Duke of Wellington, have all slept here. Except the modern fourth- and fifth-floor rooms, all the rooms maintain a luxurious, traditional style. Ask for weekend rates. Dining options include the elegant, Mediterranean-style restaurant Maximilian's ($$$) and Bistro 3M ($$). The Sunday Jazz Brunch at Maximilian's has been a town favorite since the late '90s. If ever you loved Paris in the springtime, you'll enjoy Bistro 3M; the atmosphere is thoroughly French, the food is excellent, and the service is very efficient. ✉ *Maximilianstr. 40, D–86150* ☎ *0821/50360* *0821/157–864* 🌐 *www.steigenberger.com* *106 rooms, 5 suites* *2 restaurants, cable TV, Wi-Fi, bar, meeting rooms, no-smoking rooms; no a/c in some rooms* 💳 *AE, DC, MC, V.*

$–$$ **Privat Hotel Riegele.** The hotel is just opposite the main railway station. The tavern-restaurant ($$–$$$), the Bräustüble, is a local favorite. The food is good German cooking and the service is efficient and friendly. Public rooms and some bedrooms have plush armchairs, deep-pile rugs, and heavy drapes. ✉ *Viktoriastr. 4, D–86150* ☎ *0821/509–000* *0821/517–746* 🌐 *www.hotel-riegele.de* *27 rooms, 1 apartment* *Restaurant, cable TV, Wi-Fi, Internet room, meeting rooms; no a/c* 💳 *AE, DC, MC, V* *Restaurant closed Sun. evening* *CP.*

$–$$ **Romantikhotel Augsburger Hof.** A preservation order protects the beautiful Renaissance facade of this charming old Augsburg mansion, but rather than remake an old-world atmosphere inside, the owners opted for a cheerful but classic look with natural wood finishes and flowered curtains. The restaurant ($–$$$) serves excellent Maultaschen and other Swabian dishes. In season, try the duck. The cathedral is around the corner; the town center is a five-minute stroll. ✉ *Auf dem Kreuz 2, D–86152* ☎ *0821/343–050* *0821/343–0555* 🌐 *www.augsburger-hof.de* *36 rooms* *Restaurant, cable TV, Wi-Fi, sauna, no-smoking rooms; no a/c* 💳 *AE, DC, MC, V* *CP.*

$–$$ **Dom Hotel.** Just around the corner from Augsburg's cathedral, this snug establishment has personality. Ask for one of the attic rooms, where you'll sleep under beam ceilings and wake to a rooftop view of the city. Or try for one of the rooms on the top floor that have a small terrace facing the cathedral. Even if you have to settle for a room in the apartment-house extension, you'll lack no comforts. A garden terrace borders the old city walls, and there's also an indoor pool, sauna, and solarium. ✉ *Frauentorstr. 8, D–86152* ☎ *0821/343–930* *0821/3439–3200* 🌐 *www.domhotel-augsburg.de* *44 rooms, 8 suites* *Cable TV, pool, sauna; no a/c* 💳 *AE, DC, MC, V* *CP.*

$ **Hotel-Garni Schlössle.** From the main railroad station, a 10-minute ride on tram number 3 to the end of the line at Stadtbergem brings you to this friendly, family-run hotel. Soccer fans will enjoy the cozy Bavarian restaurant *Lamm* on the ground floor. Rooms under the steep eaves are particularly cozy. The location offers fresh country air, walks, and sporting facilities (a golf course is within a good tee-shot's range). ✉ *Bauernstr. 37, Stadtbergen D–86391* ☎ *0821/243–930* 📠 *0821/437–451* *14 rooms* *Cable TV; no a/c, no smoking* *MC, V* *Restaurant closed Sat.* *CP.*

The Arts

Augsburg has chamber and symphony orchestras, as well as ballet and opera companies. The city stages a Mozart Festival of international stature in September. The **Kongresshalle** (✉ Göggingerstr. 10 ☎ 0821/324–2348) presents music and dance performances from September through July.

Augsburg's annual open-air **opera and operetta** (☎ 0821/502–070 city tourist office) season takes place in June and July. Productions move to the romantic inner courtyard of the **Fugger Palace** for part of July and August. Phone the city tourist office for details.

Children love the city's excellent **Augsburger Puppenkiste** (Puppet theater; ✉ Spitalg. 15, next to Rotes Tor ☎ 0821/4503–4540).

en route

Leaving Augsburg southward on B–17—the southern stretch of the Romantic Road—you'll drive across the Lech battlefield, where Hungarian invaders were stopped in 955. Rich Bavarian pastures extend as far as the Lech River, which the Romantic Road meets at the historic town of Landsberg.

TOWARD THE ALPS

South of Augsburg, the Romantic Road climbs gradually into the foothills of the Bavarian Alps, which burst into view between Landsberg and Schongau. The route ends dramatically at the northern wall of the Alps at Füssen, on the Austrian border. Landsberg was founded by the Bavarian ruler Heinrich der Löwe (Henry the Lion) in the 12th century and grew wealthy from the salt trade. Solid old houses are packed within its turreted walls; the early-18th-century Rathaus is one of the finest in the region.

Schongau has virtually intact wall fortifications, complete with towers and gates. In medieval and Renaissance times, the town was an important trading post on the route from Italy to Augsburg. The steeply gabled 16th-century Ballenhaus was a warehouse before it was elevated to the rank of Rathaus. A popular Märchenwald ("fairy-tale forest") lies 1½ km (1 mi) outside Schongau, suitably set in a clearing in the woods. It comes complete with mechanical models of fairy-tale scenes, deer enclosures, and an old-time miniature railway.

Neuschwanstein & Hohenschwangau

46 *18 km (11 mi) south of Steingaden, 93 km (60 mi) south of Augsburg, 105 km (65 mi) southwest of Munich.*

These two famous castles belonging to the Wittelbachs, one historic and the other nearly "make-believe," are 1 km (½ mi) across a valley from each other, near the town of Schwangau. Bavaria's King Ludwig II (1845–86) spent much of his youth at Schloss Hohenschwangau (Hohenschwangau Castle). It's said that its neo-Gothic atmosphere provided the primary influences that shaped his wildly romantic Schloss Neuschwanstein (Neuschwanstein Castle), the fairy-tale castle he built after he became king, and which has since become one of Germany's most recognized sights.

From Schwangau, follow the road signs marked KONIGSCHLÖSSER (King's castles). After 2 mi you come to Hohenschwangau, a small village consisting of a few houses, some good hotels, and five spacious parking lots (parking fee €4). You have to park in one of them and then walk to the ticket center serving both castles.

Bear in mind that more than 1 million people pass through one or both castles every year. If you visit in summer, get there early. The best time to see either castle without waiting a long time is a weekday between January and April. The prettiest time, however, is in fall. Tickets are for timed entry and the average wait to enter Neuschwanstein is one hour. With a deposit or credit-card number you can book your tickets in advance for either castle through **Verwaltung Hohenschwangau** (✉ Alpseestr. 12, D–87645 Hohenschwangau ☎ 08362/930–830 📠 08362/930–8320 🌐 www.hohenschwangau.de). You can change entrance times or cancel up to two hours before the confirmed entrance time.

Fodor'sChoice ★ **Neuschwanstein** was conceived by a set designer instead of an architect, thanks to King Ludwig II's deep love of the theater. The castle soars from its mountainside like a stage creation—it should hardly come as a surprise that Walt Disney took it as the model for his castle in the movie *Sleeping Beauty* and later for the Disneyland castle itself.

The life of this spectacular castle's king reads like one of the great Gothic mysteries of the 19th century, and the castle symbolizes that life. Yet during the 17 years from the start of Schloss Neuschwanstein's construction until King Ludwig's death, the king spent less than six months in the country residence, and the interior was never finished. The Byzantine-style throne room is without a throne; Ludwig died before one could be installed. However, the walls of the rooms leading to Ludwig's bedroom are painted with murals depicting characters from Wagner's operas—Siegfried and the Nibelungen, Lohengrin, Tristan, and others. Ludwig's bed and its canopy are made of intricately carved oak. A small corridor behind the bedroom was made as a ghostly grotto, reminiscent of Wagner's *Tannhäuser.* **Chamber concerts** (☎ 08362/81980) are held in September in the gaily decorated minstrels' hall—one room, at least, that was completed as Ludwig conceived it. On the walls outside the castle's gift shop are plans and photos of the castle's construction. There are some spectacular walks around the castle. The delicate **Marienbrücke** (Mary's Bridge) is spun like a medieval maiden's hair across a deep, narrow gorge. From this vantage point there are giddy views of the castle and the great Upper Bavarian Plain beyond.

To reach Neuschwanstein from the ticket center below, take one of the clearly marked paths (about a 25-minute uphill walk) or one of the horse-drawn carriages that leave from Hotel Müller (uphill €5, downhill €2.50). A small bus also leaves from the Hotel Lisl (uphill €1.80, downhill €1), and takes you halfway up the hill to an outlook called Aussichtspunkt Jugend. From there it's a 10-minute walk to the castle. ✉ *Neuschwansteinstr. 20* ☎ *08362/930–830* 🌐 *www.neuschwanstein.de* 🎫 *€9, including guided tour* ⏲ *Apr.–Sept., daily 9–6; Oct.–Mar., daily 10–4.*

★ **Hohenschwangau** was built by the knights of Schwangau in the 12th century. It was remodeled later by King Ludwig II's father, the Bavarian crown prince (and later king) Maximilian, between 1832 and 1836. Unlike Ludwig's more famous castle across the valley, Neuschwanstein, the somewhat garishly yellow Schloss Hohenschwangau has the feeling of a noble home, where comforts would be valued as much as outward splendor. It was here that the young Ludwig met the composer Richard Wagner. Their friendship shaped and deepened the future king's interest in theater, music, and German mythology—the mythology Wagner drew upon for his *Ring* cycle of operas.

After obtaining your ticket at the ticket center in the village, you can take a 15-minute walk up either of two clearly marked paths to the castle, or, board one of the horse-drawn carriages that leave from Hotel Müller (uphill €3.50, downhill €1.50). 🎫 *€9, including guided tour* ☎ *08362/930–830* 🌐 *www.hohenschwangau.de* ⏲ *Apr.–Sept., daily 9–6; Oct.–Mar., daily 10–4.*

off the beaten path

Fodor'sChoice ★

WIESKIRCHE – This church—a glorious example of German rococo architecture—stands in an Alpine meadow just off the Romantic Road. In the village of Steingaden (22 km [14 mi] north of Füssen on the B–17 or, if you come from the north, 74 km [46 mi] south of Augsburg), turn east and follow the signs to Wieskirche. Its yellow-and-white walls and steep red roof are set off by the dark backdrop of the Trauchgauer Mountains. The architect Dominicus Zimmermann, former mayor of Landsberg and creator of much of that town's rococo architecture, built the church in 1745 on the spot where six years earlier a local woman claimed to have seen tears running down the face of a picture of Christ. Although the church was dedicated as the Pilgrimage Church of the Scourged Christ, it's now known simply as the Wieskirche (Church of the Meadow). Visit it on a bright day if you can, when light streaming through its high windows displays the full glory of the glittering interior. A complex oval plan is animated by brilliantly colored stuccowork, statues, and gilt. A luminous ceiling fresco completes the decoration. Concerts are presented in the church from the end of June through the beginning of August. Contact the **Pfarramt Wieskirche** (☎ *Pastor's*

THE FAIRY-TALE KING

KING LUDWIG II (1845–86), the enigmatic presence indelibly associated with Bavaria, was one of the last rulers of the Wittelsbach dynasty, which ruled Bavaria from 1180 to 1918. Though his family had created grandiose architecture in Munich, Ludwig II disliked the city and preferred isolation in the countryside, where he constructed monumental edifices born of fanciful imagination and spent most of the royal purse on his endeavors. Although he was also a great lover of literature, theater, and opera (he was Richard Wagner's great patron), it is his fairy-tale-like castles that are his legacy.

Ludwig II reigned from 1864 to 1886, all the while avoiding political duties whenever possible. By 1878 he had completed his Schloss Linderhof retreat and immediately began Schloss Herrenchiemsee, a tribute to Versailles and Louis XIV (⇨ Chapter 2). The grandest of his extravagant projects is Neuschwanstein, one of Germany's top attractions and concrete proof of the king's eccentricity. In 1886, before Neuschwanstein was finished, members of the government became convinced that Ludwig had taken leave of his senses. A medical commission declared the king insane and forced him to abdicate. Within two days of incarceration in the Berg Castle, on Starnbergersee (⇨ Side Trips from Munich in Chapter 1), Ludwig and his doctor were found drowned in the lake's shallow waters. Their deaths are still a mystery.

3

office, 08862/932–930 🌐 www.wieskirche.de) for details. 🎫 Free ⏲ Daily 8–dusk.

Where to Stay & Eat

$$–$$$ ✕🏨 **Schlosshotel Lisl und Jägerhaus.** These jointly run 19th-century properties are across the street from one another, and both share views of the nearby castles. The intimate Jägerhaus has five suites and six double rooms, all decorated with floral wallpaper and drapery. The bathrooms have swan-motif golden fixtures. The Lisl's rooms have bright blue carpeting and fabrics. Lisl's restaurant, Salon Wittelsbacher ($–$$$), provides a view of Neuschwanstein as well as a tasty dish of *Tafelspitz* (boiled beef with horseradish). ✉ *Neuschwansteinstr. 1–3, D–87643* ☎ *08362/8870* 📠 *08362/81107* 🌐 *www.lisl.de* 🛏 *42 rooms, 5 suites* 👍 *2 restaurants, cable TV, bar, lobby lounge; no a/c* 💳 *AE, MC, V.*

$$ ✕🏨 **Hotel Müller.** Between the two Schwangau castles, the Müller fits beautifully into the stunning landscape, its creamy Bavarian baroque facade complemented by the green mountain forest. Inside, the baroque influence is everywhere, from the finely furnished bedrooms to the chandelier-hung public rooms and restaurant ($). The mahogany-paneled, glazed veranda (with open fireplace) provides a magnificent view of Hohenschwangau Castle. Round your day off with a local specialty such as the *Allgäuer Lendentopf* (sirloin) served with spaetzle. ✉ *Alpseestr. 16, Hohenschwangau D–87643* ☎ *08362/81990* 📠 *08362/819–913* 🌐 *www.hotel-mueller.de* 🛏 *39 rooms, 4 suites* 🛎 *2 restaurants, cable TV, bar; no a/c* 💳 *AE, DC, MC, V* ⏲ *Closed Jan. and Feb.* 🍽 *CP.*

Füssen

47 *5 km (3 mi) southwest of Schwangau, 110 km (68 mi) south of Munich.*

Füssen is beautifully located at the foot of the mountains that separate Bavaria from the Austrian Tyrol. The Lech River, which accompanies much of the final section of the Romantic Road, embraces the town as it rushes northward. The town's **Hohes Schloss** (High Castle) is one of the best-preserved late-Gothic castles in Germany. It was built on the site of the Roman fortress that once guarded this Alpine section of the Via Claudia, the trade route from Rome to the Danube. Evidence of Roman occupation of the area has been uncovered at the foot of the nearby Tegelberg Mountain, and the **excavations** next to the Tegelberg cable-car station are open for visits daily. The Hohes Schloss was the seat of Bavarian rulers before Emperor Heinrich VII mortgaged it and the rest of the town to the bishop of Augsburg for 400 pieces of silver. The mortgage was never redeemed, and Füssen remained the property of the Augsburg episcopate until secularization in the early 19th century. The bishops of Augsburg used the castle as their summer Alpine residence. It has a spectacular 16th-century **Rittersaal** (Knights' Hall) with a carved ceiling, and a princes' chamber with a Gothic tile stove. ✉ *Magnuspl. 10* ☎ *08362/940–162* 🎫 *€2.50* ⏲ *Apr.–Oct., Tues.–Sun. 11–4; Nov.–Mar., Tues.–Sun. 2–4.*

The summer presence of the bishops of Augsburg ensured that Füssen received an impressive number of baroque and rococo churches. Füssen's **Rathaus** (✉ Lechalde 3) was once a Benedictine abbey, built in the 9th century at the site of the grave of St. Magnus, who spent most of his life ministering in the area. A Romanesque crypt beneath the baroque abbey church has a partially preserved 10th-century fresco, the oldest in Bavaria. In summer, chamber concerts are held in the high-ceiling baroque splendor of the former abbey's **Fürstensaal** (Princes' Hall). Program details are available from the tourist office.

Füssen's main shopping street, called **Reichenstrasse,** was, like Augsburg's Maximilianstrasse, once part of the Roman Via Claudia. This cobblestone walkway is lined with high-gabled medieval houses and backed by the bulwarks of the castle and the easternmost buttresses of the Allgäu Alps.

Where to Stay & Eat

¢ ✕ **Markthalle.** This is a farmers' market where you can grab a quick bite and drink at very reasonable prices. Try the fish soup. There are even a few tables. The building started in 1483 as the *Kornhaus* (grain storage) and then became the *Feuerhaus* (fire station). ✉ *Schrannenplatz 1* 💳 *No credit cards* ⏲ *Weekdays 8–6, Sat. 8–noon.*

$ ✕ **Altstadthotel Zum Hechten.** Geraniums flower most of the year on this comfortable inn's balconies. It's one of the town's oldest lodgings and is directly below the castle. In one of the two restaurants ($), which have sturdy, round tables and colorfully frescoed walls, vegetarian meals are served. ✉ *Ritterstr. 6, D–87629* ☎ *08362/91600* 📠 *08362/916–099* 🌐 *www.hotel-hechten.com* *36 rooms, 30 with bath or shower* *2 restaurants, cable TV, gym, sauna, bowling; no a/c* 💳 *AE, MC* *CP.*

Sports & the Outdoors

Pleasure boats cruise Forggensee lake mid-June–early October. Alpine winds ensure good sailing and windsurfing. The **Forgensee-Yachtschule** (✉ Seestr. 10, Dietringen ☎ 08367/471 🌐 www.segeln-info.de) offers sailing courses of up to two weeks' duration, with hotel or apartment accommodations. There are also boatyards and jetties with craft for rent at Waltenhofen.

There's good downhill skiing in the mountains above Füssen. Cross-country enthusiasts are catered to with more than 20 km (12 mi) of trails. Füssen's highest peak, the Tegelberg, has a ski school, **Skischule Tegelberg A. Geiger** (☎ 08362/8455).

THE ROMANTIC ROAD A TO Z

To research prices, get advice from other travelers, and book travel arrangements, visit www.fodors.com.

AIRPORTS

The major international airports serving the Romantic Road are Frankfurt and Munich. Regional airports include Nürnberg and Augsburg.

BICYCLE TOURS

From April through September, Velotours offers a five-day trip from Würzburg to Rothenburg for €320 per person and a five-day trip from Rothenburg to Donauwörth for €320 per person. These two trips can be combined for a nine-day tour for €640. The tour operator Alpenland-Touristik offers several guided six- to eight-day bike tours starting from Landsberg am Lech into the Alpine foothills. Please call for exact dates.

Velotours ✉ Ernst-Sachsstr. 1, D–78467 Konstanz ☎ 07531/98280 📠 07531/982-898 🌐 www.velotours.de. **Alpenland-Tourisitk** Box 10-13-13, D-86899 Landsberg ☎ 08191/308-620 📠 08191/4913 🌐 www.alpenlandtouristik.de.

BUS TRAVEL

From April through October daily bus service covers the northern stretch of the Romantic Road, leaving Frankfurt at 8 AM and arriving in Munich at 8 PM; daily buses in the opposite direction leave Munich at 9 AM and arrive in Frankfurt at 8:30 PM. A second bus covers the section of the route between Dinkelsbühl and Füssen. Buses leave Dinkelsbühl daily at 4:15 PM and arrive in Füssen at 8 PM. In the other direction, buses leave Füssen daily at 8 AM, arriving in Dinkelsbühl at 12:45 PM. All buses stop at the major sights along the road. A Frankfurt–Füssen ticket costs €69 (€137 round-trip). Deutsche Touring also operates six more extensive tours along the Romantic Road and along the region's other major holiday route, the Burgenstrasse (Castle Road), which ends at Rothenburg. The tours range from two to five days and cost from €256 to €770. Reservations are essential; contact Deutsche Touring. Local buses cover much of the route but are infrequent and slow.

Deutsche Touring ✉ Am Römerhof 17, D-60486 Frankfurt am Main ☎ 069/790-350 🌐 www.touring-germany.com.

CAR TRAVEL

Würzburg is the northernmost city of the Romantic Road and the natural starting point for a tour. It's on the Frankfurt–Nürnberg autobahn, A–3, and is 115 km (71 mi) from Frankfurt. If you're using Munich as a gateway, Augsburg is 60 km (37 mi) from Munich via A–8.

The Romantic Road is most easily traveled by car, starting from Würzburg as outlined above and following country highway B–27 south to meet Roads B–290, B–19, B–292, and B–25 along the Wörnitz River.

The roads are busy and have only two lanes, so figure on covering no more than 70 km (40 mi) each hour, particularly in summer. The 40-km (24-mi) section of the route that's the least "romantic," the A–2 between Augsburg and Donauwörth, is also heavily used by trucks and other large vehicles traveling to northern Bavaria, so expect delays. For route maps, with roads and sights highlighted, contact the Tourist-Information Land an der Romantischen Strasse or Touristik-Arbeitsgemeinschaft Romantische Strasse (⇨ Visitor Information).

TOURS

Many of the cities and towns on the Romantic Road offer guided tours, either on foot or by bus. Details are available from local tourist information offices. Following are a few of the most interesting guided tours.

AUGSBURG Augsburg has self-guided walking tours, with routes posted on color-coded signs throughout the downtown area. From mid-May to mid-October a bus tour (€9.50) starts from the Rathaus at 10, from Thursday through Sunday, and walking tours (€7) set out from the Rathaus daily at 2. From November 'til April this walking tour takes place only on Saturday. All tours are conducted in German and English.

DINKELSBÜHL In Dinkelsbühl you can join guided tours from Easter through October at 2:30 PM or at 8:30 PM for €2.50, or you can patrol the illuminated old town with the night watchman at 9 PM free of charge. Weather permitting you can drive around the old town in horse-drawn carriages (April–October) for €5. Tours in English are by reservation only and cost €41. All tours start from the tourist office.

ROTHENBURG-OB-DER-TAUBER The costumed night watchman conducts a nightly tour of the town, leading the way with a lantern. From Easter to December a one-hour tour in English begins at 8 PM and costs €4 (a 90-minute daytime tour begins at 2 PM). All tours start at the Marktplatz (Market square) and, though you don't have to be a group yourself, at least 10 people are required for the tour. Private group tours with the night watchman can be arranged through www.nightwatchman.de. Art, patrician houses, and church theme tours for groups (€53) can be arranged by the tourist office.

ULM The tourist office's 90-minute tour includes a visit to the Münster, the Old Town Hall, the Fischerviertel (Fishermen's Quarter), and the Danube riverbank. From May through October there are tours at 10 and 2:30 Monday–Saturday, 11:30 and 2:30 Sunday; from November through April tours are at 10 on Saturday and 11:30 on Sunday. The departure point is the tourist office on Münsterplatz; the cost is €5. From May to mid-October you can view Ulm from on-board the motor cruiser *Ulmer Spatz*. There are up to five 50-minute cruises daily (€6.50). The boats tie up at the Metzgerturm, a two-minute walk from the city hall.

WÜRZBURG One-hour guided strolls through the old town in English start at the Haus zum Falken tourist office and take place from early June to late September, daily at 6:30 PM. Tickets (€5) can be bought from the guide. German speaking guided walking tours start at the Haus zum Falken tourist office from April through October, daily at 10:30 AM. The 90-minute tours cost €5. If you'd rather guide yourself, pick up a map from the same tourist office and follow the extremely helpful directions marked throughout the city by distinctive signposts. Two-hour bus tours of the city start at the main railway station from April through October, Monday–Saturday at 2 and Sunday and holidays at 10:30. The fare is €8.50. Look for the sign STADTRUNDFAHRTEN (guided city tours).

Two cruise companies ply the Main River from Würzburg. The Fränkische Personenschiffahrt (FPS) and the Würzburger Personenschiffahrt Kurth & Schiebe operate excursions to vineyards; wine tasting is included in the price. Fränkische Personenschiffahrt also offers cruises of up to two weeks on the Main, Neckar, and Danube rivers and on the Main–Danube Canal. Kurth & Schiebe and Veitshöchheimer Personenschiffahrt offer daily service to Veitshöchheim, once the summer residence of the bishops of Augsburg.

Fränkische Personenschiffahrt (FPS) ✉ Unterer Fuchsgraben 18, D-97318 Kitzingen ☎ 09321/91810. **Veitshöchheimer Personenschiffahrt** ✉ Obere Maing. 8, D-97209 Veitshöchheim ☎ 0931/55633. **Würzburger Personenschiffahrt Kurth & Schiebe** ✉ St.-Norbert-Str. 9, D-97299 Zell ☎ 0931/58573.

TRAIN TRAVEL

Infrequent trains link most major towns of the Romantic Road, but both Würzburg and Augsburg are on the InterCity and high-speed InterCity Express routes and have fast, frequent service to and from Berlin, Frankfurt, Munich, Stuttgart, and Hamburg. Deutsche Bahn offers special weekend excursion rates covering travel from most German railroad stations to Würzburg and hotel accommodations for up to four nights. Details are available at any train station.

VISITOR INFORMATION

A central tourist office based in Dinkelsbühl covers the entire Romantic Road: Touristik-Arbeitsgemeinschaft Romantische Strasse. Its brochure describes all the attractions along the Romantic Road.

Touristik-Arbeitsgemeinschaft Romantische Strasse (Central Tourist Information Romantic Road) ✉ Marktpl., D-91550 Dinkelsbühl ☎ 09851/90271 ☎ 09851/90281 🌐 www.romantischestrasse.de. **Augsburg** ✉ Tourist-Information, Bahnhofstr. 7,

D-86150 ☎ 0821/502-070 🌐 www.regio-augsburg.de. **Bad Mergentheim** ✉ Städtisches Kultur-und Verkehrsamt, Marktpl. 3, D-96980 ☎ 07931/57135 🌐 www.bad-mergentheim.de. **Dinkelsbühl** ✉ Tourist-Information, Marktpl., D-91550 ☎ 09851/90240 🌐 www.dinkelsbuehl.de. **Donauwörth** ✉ Städtisches Verkehrs-und Kulturamt, Rathausg. 1, D-86609 ☎ 0906/789-151 🌐 www.donauwoerth.de. **Füssen** ✉ Kurverwaltung, Kaiser-Maximilian-Pl. 1 D-87629 ☎ 08362/93850 🌐 www.fuessen.de. **Harburg** ✉ Fremdenverkehrsverein, Schlossstr. 1, D-86655 ☎ 09080/96990. **Nördlingen** ✉ Städtisches Verkehrsamt, Marktpl. 2, D-86720 ☎ 09081/84116. **Rothenburg-ob-der-Tauber** ✉ Tourist-Information, Rathaus, Marktpl. 2, D-91541 ☎ 09861/40492 🌐 www.rothenburg.com. **Ulm** ✉ Tourist-Information, Münsterpl. 50 (Stadthaus), D-89073 ☎ 0731/161-2830 🌐 www.tourismus.ulm.de. **Weikersheim** ✉ Städtisches Kultur-und Verkehrsamt, Marktpl. 12, D-97990 ☎ 07934/10255 📠 07934/10558. **Würzburg** ✉ Fremdenverkehrsamt, Am Congress-Centrum, D-97070 ☎ 0931/372-335 🌐 www.wuerzburg.de.

Franconia & the German Danube

4

WORD OF MOUTH

"[Franconia] is a delightful area to explore . . . there are endless little treasures of landscape and architecture . . . not to mention the gorgeous wines and regional delicacies in what is, by the way, the least expensive part of the country for the visitor."

—harzer

"Bamberg: fantastic and underrated. I've never understood what foreigners like so much about Heidelberg; Bamberg is much prettier."

—Christian

"Regensburg is vastly overlooked, and if you make it that far, drive another hour and visit Passau on the Austrian border at the confluence of three rivers. It was postcard pretty and a surprise on our way by auto to the Czech Republic."

—cstepane

www.fodors.com/forums

Updated by Uli Ehrhardt

ALL THAT IS LEFT OF THE HUGE, ANCIENT kingdom of the Franks is the region known today as Franken (Franconia), stretching from the Bohemian Forest on the Czech border to the outskirts of Frankfurt. The Franks were not only tough warriors but also hard workers, sharp tradespeople, and burghers with a good political nose. The name *frank* means bold, wild, and courageous in the old Frankish tongue. It was only in the early 19th century, following Napoléon's conquest of what is now southern Germany, that the area was incorporated into northern Bavaria.

The east-west border between the Germanies once isolated this area, but since Germany's reunification it has experienced a minor economic revolution. Its rural appearance belies a solid economic backbone that is buttressed by a solid infrastructure of new businesses, electronics firms, call centers, and software. Franconia is hardly an overrun tourist destination, yet its long and rich history, its landscapes and leisure activities (including skiing, golfing, hiking, and cycling), and its gastronomic specialties place it high on the enjoyment scale.

Franconia's northern border is marked by the Main River, which is seen as the dividing line between northern and southern Germany. Its southern border ends at the Danube, where Lower Bavaria (Niederbayern) begins. Traveling along this eastern part of the German Danube you'll come to two cities that are well worth visiting, Regensburg and Passau.

Exploring Franconia & the German Danube

Although many proud Franconians would dispute it, this historic homeland of the Franks, one of the oldest Germanic peoples, is unmistakably part of Bavaria. Franconian towns such as Bayreuth, Coburg, and Bamberg are practically places of cultural pilgrimage and an easy day trip from one another. Rebuilt Nürnberg (Nuremberg in English) is the epitome of German medieval beauty, though its name recalls both the Third Reich's huge rallies at the Zeppelinfeld and its henchmen's trials held in the city between 1945 and 1950.

About the Restaurants & Hotels

Many restaurants in the rural parts of this region serve hot meals only between 11:30 AM and 2 PM, and 6 PM and 9 PM. *Durchgehend warme Küche* means that hot meals are also served between lunch and dinner.

Make reservations well in advance for hotels in all the larger towns and cities if you plan to visit anytime between June and September. During the Nürnberg Toy Fair at the beginning of February rooms are rare and at a premium. If you're visiting Bayreuth during the annual Wagner Festival, in July and August, consider making reservations up to a year in advance. Remember, too, that during the festival, prices can be double the normal rates.

Numbers in the text correspond to numbers in the margin and on the Franconia and Nürnberg, Regensburg and Passau maps.

If you have 3 days

Make **Nürnberg** 6–19 your base and take day trips on each of the three days to **Bayreuth** 4 (an imperative visit whether or not it's Wagner Festival season); **Bamberg** 5, once the seat of the most powerful ruling families in the country; and **Coburg** 1, home of the Saxe-Coburg duchy. Each town is only a 50- to 70-minute drive away.

If you have 5 days

Spend three days in **Nürnberg** 6–19, taking day trips to **Bamberg** 5, a city not touched by war, and to **Bayreuth** 4, a city worth visiting especially if it is not crowded with Festival guests. For days 4 and 5, travel to **Regensburg** 20–32, another city that has retained its original splendor. From here you can take a day trip to **Passau** 33–40. Make sure that you leave enough time to take a boat trip to view these cities from the waters of the Danube.

WHAT IT COSTS In Euros

	$$$$	$$$	$$	$	¢
RESTAURANTS	over €25	€21–€25	€16–€20	€9–€15	under €9
HOTELS	over €225	€175–€225	€100–€175	€50–€100	under €50

Restaurant prices are per person for a main course at dinner. Hotel prices are for two people in a standard double room, including tax and service.

Timing

Summer is the best time to explore Franconia, though spring and fall are also fine when the weather cooperates. Avoid the cold and wet months of November, January, and February; many hotels and restaurants close, and no matter how pretty, many towns do seem quite dreary. If you're in Nürnberg in December, you're in time for one of Germany's largest and loveliest Christmas markets.

NORTHERN FRANCONIA

Three major German cultural centers lie within easy reach of one another: Coburg, a town with blood links to royal dynasties throughout Europe; Bamberg, with its own claim to German royal history and an Old Town area designated as a UNESCO World Heritage site; and Bayreuth, where composer Richard Wagner finally settled, making it a place of musical pilgrimage for Wagner fans from all over the world.

Coburg

❶ *105 km (65 mi) north of Nürnberg.*

Coburg is a surprisingly little-known treasure that was founded in the 11th century and remained in the possession of the dukes of Saxe-Coburg-Gotha until 1918; the present duke still lives here. The remarkable Saxe-Coburg dynasty established itself as something of a royal stud farm, providing a seemingly inexhaustible supply of blue-blood marriage partners to ruling houses the length and breadth of Europe. The most famous of these royal mates was Prince Albert (1819–1861), who married the English Queen Victoria, after which she gained special renown in Coburg. Their numerous children, married off to other kings, queens, and emperors, helped to spread the tried-and-tested Saxe-Coburg stock even farther afield. Despite all the history that sweats from each sandstone ashlar, Coburg is a modern and bustling town.

Coburg's **Marktplatz** (Market Square) has a statue of Prince Albert, the high-minded consort, standing proudly surrounded by gracious Renaissance and baroque buildings. The **Stadhaus,** former seat of the local dukes, begun in 1500, is the most imposing structure here. A forest of ornate gables and spires projects from its well-proportioned facade. Opposite is the **Rathaus** (Town Hall). Look for the statue of the **Bratwurstmännla** on the building's tympanum (it's actually St. Mauritius in armor); the staff he carries is said to be the official length against which the town's famous bratwursts are measured. These tasty sausages, roasted on pinecone fires, are available on the market square.

Prince Albert spent much of his childhood in **Schloss Ehrenburg,** the ducal palace. Built in the mid-16th century, it has been greatly altered over the years, principally following a fire in the early 19th century. Duke Ernst I invited Karl Friedrich Schinkel from Berlin to redo the palace in the then-popular Gothic style. Some of the original Renaissance features were kept. The rooms of the castle are quite special, especially those upstairs, where the ceilings are heavily decorated with stucco and the floors have wonderful patterns of various woods. The Hall of Giants is named for the larger-than-life caryatids that support the ceiling; the favorite sight downstairs is Queen Victoria's flush toilet, which was the first one installed in Germany. Here, too, the ceiling is worth noting for its playful, gentle stuccowork. The baroque chapel attached to Ehrenburg is often used for weddings. ✉ *Schlosspl.* ☎ *09561/80880* 🌐 *www.sgvcoburg.de* 🎫 *€3, combined ticket with Schloss Rosenau €4.50* 🕓 *Tour Tues.–Sun. 10–5 on the hr; additional 4:30 tour Apr.–Sept.*

Near Schloss Ehrenburg, the **Puppenmuseum** (Doll Museum) contains a collection of more than 900 antique dolls and art dolls, and around 50 carefully furnished dollhouses arranged chronologically to represent lifestyles from the period between 1810 and 1950. The building was once home to the poet and orientalist Friedrich Rückert. The museum includes a doll and toy shop. ✉ *Rückertstr. 2–3* ☎ *09561/74047* 🎫 *€2* 🕓 *Apr.–Oct., daily 9–5; Nov.–Mar., Tues.–Sun. 10–5.*

On the Menu Franconia is known for its good and filling food and for its simple and atmospheric *Gasthäuser.* Pork is a staple, served either as *Schweinsbraten* (a plain roast) or sauerbraten (marinated). Nürnberg has a unique shoulder cut called *Schäfele* (literally "little shovel"), served with *Knödel* (dumplings made from either bread or potatoes). Short sausages are also a specialty in Nürnberg, where they are eaten either grilled or heated in a stock of onions and wine (*saurer Zipfel*).

Vineyards & Breweries Not to be missed are Franconia's liquid refreshments from both the grape and the grain. Franconian wines, usually white and sold in distinctive flagons called *Bocksbeutel,* are renowned for their special bouquet (Silvaner is the traditional grape). The region has the largest concentration of local breweries in the world (Bamberg alone has 10, Bayreuth 7), producing a wide range of brews, the most distinctive of which is the dark, smoky *Rauchbier.*

The **Veste Coburg** fortress, one of the largest and most impressive in the country, is Coburg's main attraction. The brooding bulk of the castle guards the town from a 1,484-foot hill. Construction began around 1055, but with progressive rebuilding and remodeling, today's predominantly late Gothic–early-Renaissance edifice bears little resemblance to the original crude fortress. One part of the castle harbors the **Kunstsammlungen,** a grand set of collections including art, with works by Dürer, Cranach, and Hans Holbein, among others; sculpture from the school of the great Tilman Riemenschneider (1460–1531); furniture and textiles; magnificent weapons, armor, and tournament garb spanning four centuries (in the so-called **Herzoginbau,** or Duchess's Building); carriages and ornate sleighs; and more. The room where Martin Luther lived for six months in 1530 while he observed the goings-on of the Augsburg Diet has an especially dignified atmosphere. The **Jagdintarsien-Zimmer** (Hunting Marquetry Room), an elaborately decorated room that dates back to the early 17th century, has some of the finest woodwork in southern Germany. Inquire at the ticket office for tours and reduced family tickets. Finally, there's the **Carl-Eduard-Bau** (Carl-Eduard Building), which contains a valuable antique glass collection, mostly from the baroque age. Inquire at the ticket office for tours and reduced family tickets. ☎ *09561/8790* 🌐 *www.kunstsammlungen-coburg.de* 🎫 *€3* 🕒 *Museums Apr.–Oct., daily 10–5; Nov.–Mar., Tues.–Sun. 1–4; castle Apr.–Oct., Tues.–Sun. 10–5; Nov.–Mar., Tues.–Sun. 2–5; castle grounds daily 6:30–6.*

need a break?

The **Burgschänke** (✉ Veste Coburg ☎ 09561/80980), Veste Coburg's own tavern, allows you to relax and soak up centuries of history while sampling a Coburg beer and one of the traditional dishes from the basic menu. The tavern is closed Monday and January–mid-February.

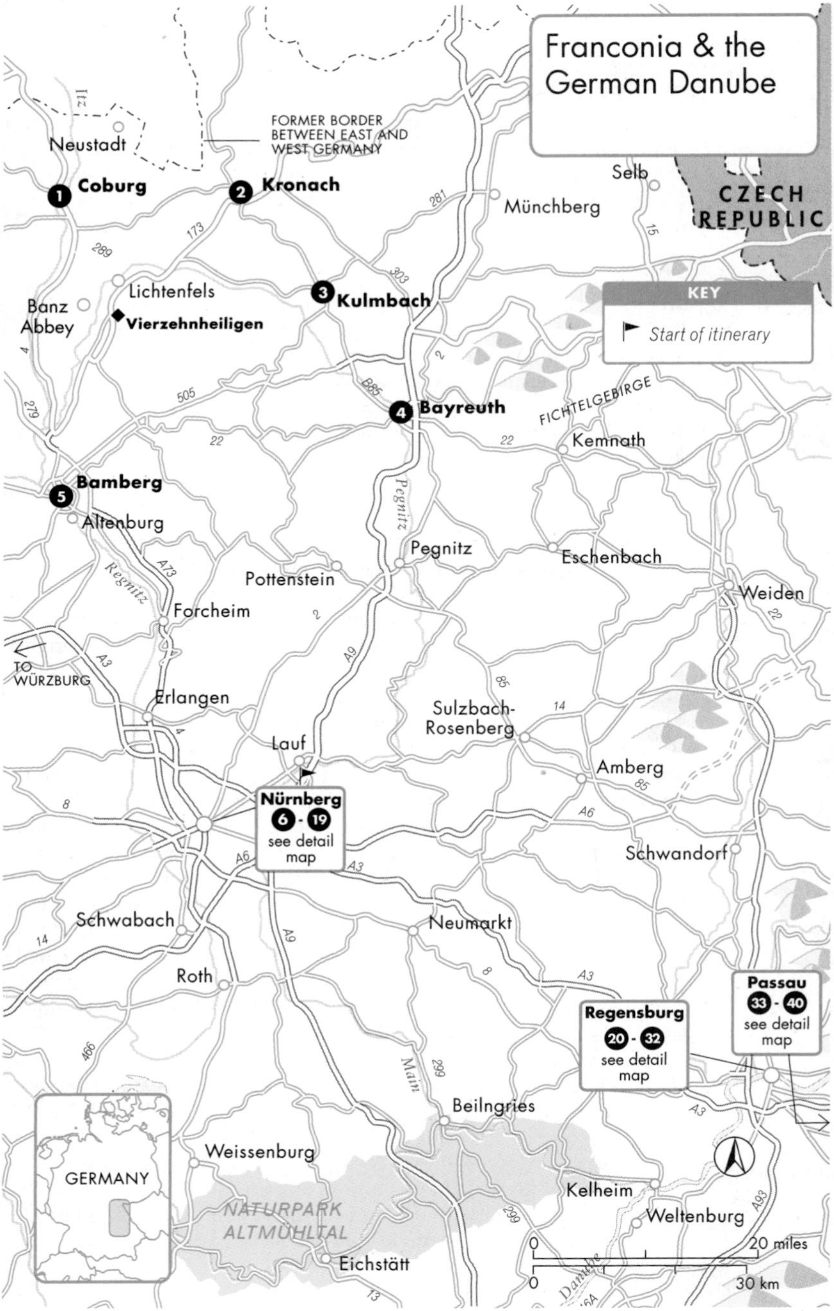

Franconia & the German Danube
KEY
Start of itinerary
FORMER BORDER BETWEEN EAST AND WEST GERMANY
Itz
Neustadt
1 Coburg
2 Kronach
3 Kulmbach
4 Bayreuth
5 Bamberg
Selb
CZECH REPUBLIC
Münchberg
Lichtenfels
Banz Abbey
Vierzehnheiligen
FICHTELGEBIRGE
Kemnath
Altenburg
Regnitz
Pegnitz
Pegnitz
Pottenstein
Eschenbach
Weiden
Forcheim
TO WÜRZBURG
Erlangen
Sulzbach-Rosenberg
Lauf
Amberg
Nürnberg
6 - 19
see detail map
Schwandorf
Schwabach
Neumarkt
Roth
Regensburg
20 - 32
see detail map
Passau
33 - 40
see detail map
Main
Beilngries
Weissenburg
GERMANY
Kelheim
Weltenburg
NATURPARK ALTMÜHLTAL
Eichstätt
Danube
0
20 miles
0
30 km
281
173
289
303
2
B85
505
22
22
4
279
A73
2
A9
A3
85
14
4
8
A6
A6
A3
85
22
15
14
A9
8
A3
466
299
299
A3
A93
13
16A

The **Naturkundemuseum** (Natural History Museum) is in the castle's former palace garden, the Hofgarten. This is the country's leading museum of its kind, with more than 8,000 exhibits of flora and fauna, geology, human history, and mineralogy. The museum is being revamped, a process that will still take a few years, but it can be visited nonetheless. ✉ *Veste Coburg* ☎ *09561/808–120* 🎫 *€1.50* 🕒 *Daily 9–5.*

Perched on a hill 5 km (3 mi) to the west of Coburg is **Schloss Callenberg,** until 1231 the main castle of the Knights of Callenberg. In the 16th century it was taken over by the Coburgs. From 1842 on it served as the summer residence of the hereditary Coburg prince and later Duke Ernst II. It holds a number of important collections, including that of the Windsor gallery; arts and crafts from Holland, Germany, and Italy from the Renaissance to the 19th century; precious baroque, empire, and Biedermeier furniture; table and standing clocks from three centuries; a selection of weapons; and various handicrafts. The best way to reach the castle is by car via Baiersdorf or by Bus 5 from the Marktplatz. ✉ *Callenberg* ☎ *09561/55150* 🌐 *www.schloss-callenberg.de* 🎫 *€4* 🕒 *Daily 1–5.*

4

off the beaten path ★

The **MUSEUM DER DEUTSCHEN SPIELZEUGINDUSTRIE** (Museum of the German Toymaking Industry) – in Neustadt (15 km [10 mi] northeast of Coburg) is a must. All manner of toys and dolls, from wooden to plasticine, are included. Dolls model traditional German costumes in one room, and in another the craft of doll- and toy-making is revealed. A bevy of very sooty-looking teddy bears makes up part of the antiques collection, which stands in contrast to modern action figures, various ethnic dolls, and, of course, Barbie. Christmas decorations are also on display. In short, everything you ever wanted to know about toys is right here in a modern, barnlike building. ✉ *Hindenburgpl. 1* ☎ *09568/5600* 🌐 *www.spielzeugmuseum-neustadt.de* 🎫 *€3* 🕒 *Daily 10–5; last entry at 4:15.*

Where to Stay & Eat

¢–$$ ✕ **Künstlerklause.** This little maze of rooms with dark-wood paneling, a fireplace, old photos, and comfortable leather seats welcomes a mixed crowd, from businesspeople to artists. The upscale cuisine gets the occasional exotic touch through spices. You might find a standard turkey schnitzel with dumplings, or venison in aspic with diced and fried sweet potato, celery, and carrots in juniper sauce. The Sunday specialty is Omas Braten (Grandma's Roasts), traditional home cooking. ✉ *Theaterpl. 4a* ☎ *09561/90705* ✍ *Reservations advised* 💳 *No credit cards* 🕒 *Closed Mon. No lunch Tues.–Sat.*

¢–$ ✕ **Ratskeller.** The local specialties taste better here beneath the old vaults and within earshot of the Coburg marketplace. Try the sauerbraten, along with a glass of crisp Franconian white wine. The prices become a little higher in the evening, and the menu adds a few more dishes. ✉ *Markt 1* ☎ *09561/92400* 💳 *No credit cards.*

¢–$ ✕🏨 **Goldene Rose.** One of the region's oldest, this agreeable inn is located about 5 km (3 mi) southeast of Coburg. The rustic interior carries its age well, with simple wooden paneling and floors. On a warm summer evening, however, the beer garden is the best place to enjoy traditional Franconian dishes, or a plate of homemade sausages, and meet some of the locals. Rooms are well appointed and comfortable—the wooden theme is continued but the style is definitely modern. ✉ *Coburgerstr. 31, D–96271* ☎ *09560/92250* 📠 *09560/1423* 🌐 *www.goldene-rose.de* *14 rooms* *Restaurant, cable TV, Wi-Fi, beer garden; no a/c* 💳 *MC, V* 🍽 *BP* ⏲ *Restaurant closed Mon.*

$$ **Romantic Hotel Goldene Traube.** The first guests were welcomed to this hotel in 1756. Rooms are individually decorated, and for dining you can choose between the elegant restaurant "Meer und mehr" (The Sea and More) or the cozy Weinstüble. After a day of sighteeing, relax in the sauna complex with solarium or with one of the vintages from the small wine boutique just opposite the reception. 1 ✉ *Am Viktoriabrunnen 2, D–96450* ☎ *09561/8760* 📠 *09561/876–22* 🌐 *www.goldenetraube.com* *72 rooms, 1 suite* *Restaurant, cable TV, Wi-Fi, miniature golf, gym, sauna, steam room, bicycles, bar, some pets allowed (fee), no-smoking rooms; no a/c* 💳 *AE, DC, MC, V* 🍽 *BP.*

$–$$ **Hotel Festungshof.** Duke Carl Eduard had this guest mansion built right outside the Veste in Coburg. This turn-of-the-20th-century building has comfortably (if not very imaginatively) furnished rooms. The café has a generous terrace and the beer garden seats 300. A bus will take you to the town center, or you can take a 20-minute walk through the castle garden and the wooded landscape to reach the market square. ✉ *Rosenauerstr. 30, D–96450* ☎ *09561/80290* 📠 *09561/802–933* 🌐 *www.hotel-festungshof.de* *14 rooms* *Restaurant, café, cable TV, beer garden, some pets allowed (fee); no a/c* 💳 *MC, V* 🍽 *BP* ⏲ *No dinner Sun. Closed Mon.*

$–$$ **Hotel Mercure Coburg.** You can expect modern, clean, well-designed rooms that are airy and functional at the Mercure, which is about 15 minutes, on foot, south of Coburg's center. ✉ *Ketschendorfer Str. 86, D–96450* ☎ *09561/8210* 📠 *09561/821–444* 🌐 *www.mercure.com* *123 rooms* *Cable TV with movies, in-room data ports, some pets allowed, no-smoking rooms; no a/c* 💳 *AE, DC, MC, V* 🍽 *BP.*

Nightlife & the Arts

Coburg's **Brazilian Samba Festival** is a three-day bacchanal held in mid-July. Check the Coburg tourist office's Web site for this and other events.

Coburg's **Landestheater** (✉ Schlosspl. 6 ☎ 09561/99447) opera season runs from October through mid-July.

Shopping

Coburg is full of culinary delights; its *Schmätzen* (gingerbread) and *Elizenkuchen* (almond cake) are famous. You'll find home-baked versions in any of the many excellent **patisseries** or at a Grossman store (there are three in Coburg). Rödental, northeast of Coburg, is the home of the world-famous M. I. Hummel figurines, made by the Göbel porcelain manufacturer. There's a **Hummel Museum** (✉ Coburgerstr. 7, Rödental ☎ 09563/92303 🌐 www.goebel.de) devoted to them, and 18th- and 19th-century porcelain from other manufacturers. The museum is open weekdays 9–5 and Saturday 9–12. Besides the museum's store, there are several retail outlets in the village.

en route

Near the village of Rödental, 9 km (5½ mi) northeast of Coburg, the 550-year-old **Schloss Rosenau** sits in all its neo-Gothic glory in the midst of an English-style park. Prince Albert was born here in 1819, and one room is devoted entirely to Albert and his queen, Victoria. Much of the castle furniture was made especially for the Saxe-Coburg family by noted Viennese craftsmen. In the garden's Orangerie is the **Museum für Modernes Glas** (Museum for Modern Glass), which displays nearly 40 years' worth of glass sculptures (dating from 1950–90) that contrast sharply with the venerable architecture of the castle itself. ☎ *09563/1606* 🌐 *www.kunstsammlungen-coburg.de* *Castle €4, museum €1* ⏲ *Tours Apr.–Oct., daily at 10, 11, noon, 2, 3, and 4; Nov.–Mar., Tues.–Sun. at 3 and 4; and by appointment. Closed last 3 wks of Jan.*

4

Kronach

2 *23 km (15 mi) east of Coburg, 120 km (74 mi) north of Nürnberg.*

Kronach is a charming little gateway to the natural splendor of the Frankenwald region. In its old medieval section, the **Obere Stadt** (Upper Town), harmonious sandstone houses are surrounded by old walls and surmounted by a majestic fortress. Kronach is best known as the birthplace of Renaissance painter Lucas Cranach the Elder (1472–1553), but there's a running argument as to which house he was born in—Am Marktplatz 1 or in the house called Am Scharfen Eck, at Lucas-Cranach-Strasse 38. The latter is now a meeting place for locals, where you can enjoy a good, inexpensive Franconian meal. A good time to be in Kronach is the last weekend in June, when the town celebrates its past with a medieval festival featuring authentic garb, food, troubadours, and more.

Fodor'sChoice ★ **Festung Rosenberg** (Rosenberg Fortress) is a few minutes' walk from the town center. As you stand below its mighty walls, it's easy to see why it was never taken by enemy forces. During World War I it served as a POW camp with no less a figure than Charles de Gaulle as a "guest." Today Rosenberg houses a youth hostel and, more importantly, the **Fränkische Galerie** (the Franconian Gallery), an extension of the Bavarian National Museum in Munich, featuring paintings and sculpted works from the Middle Ages and the Renaissance. Lucas Cranach the Elder and Tilman Riemenschneider are represented, as well as artists from the Dürer School and the Bamberg School. In July and August the central courtyard is an atmospheric backdrop for performances of Goethe's *Faust*. The grounds of the fortress are also used by wood sculptors in the summer. ☎ *09261/60410* 🌐 *www.kronach.de* *€3.50* ⏲ *Fortress tours Apr.–Oct., Tues.–Sun. 9:30–5:30; Nov.–Mar., Tues.–Sun. 11–2.*

Kulmbach

3 *19 km (12 mi) southeast of Kronach*

Kulmbach has a claim to fame that belies its size. In a country where brewing and beer drinking break all records, this town produces more beer per capita than anywhere else: 9,000 pints for each man, woman, and child. A quarter of Kulmbachers earn their living directly or indirectly from beer. A special local brew only available in winter and during the Lenten season is *Eisbock*, a dark beer that is frozen as part of the brewing process to make it stronger. The locals claim it's the sparkling-clear springwater from the nearby Fichtelgebirge hills that makes their beer so special.

Kulmbach celebrates its beer every year in a nine-day festival that starts on the last Saturday in July. The main festival site, a mammoth tent, is called the *Festspulhaus*—literally, "festival swill house"—a none-too-subtle dig at nearby Bayreuth and its tony *Festspielhaus*, where Wagner's operas are performed.

The **Kulmbacher Brewery** (✉ Lichtenfelserstr. ☎ 09221/705–113), a merger of four Kulmbach breweries, produces among others the strongest beer in the world—the *Doppelbock* Kulminator 28—which takes nine months to brew and has an alcohol content of more than 11%. The brewery runs the **Bayerisches Brauereimuseum Kulmbach** (Kulmbach Brewery Museum) jointly with the nearby Mönchshof-Bräu brewery and inn. *✉ Hoferstr. 20 ☎ 09221/4264 Tour €3.50 ⏲ Tues.–Sun. 10–5.*

The **Plassenburg**, the town's castle and symbol, is the most important Renaissance castle in the country. It stands on a rise overlooking Kulmbach, a 20-minute hike from the Old Town. The first building here, begun in the mid-12th century, was torched by marauding Bavarians who were eager to put a stop to the ambitions of Duke Albrecht Alcibiades—a man who spent several years murdering, plundering, and pillaging his way through Franconia. His successors built today's castle, starting in about 1560. Externally there's little to suggest the graceful Renaissance interior, but as you enter the main courtyard, the scene changes abruptly. The tiered space of the courtyard is covered with precisely carved figures, medallions, and other intricate ornaments, the whole comprising one of the most remarkable and delicate architectural ensembles in Europe. Inside, the **Deutsches Zinnfigurenmuseum** (Tin Figures Museum), with more than 300,000 miniature statuettes and tin soldiers, holds the largest collection of its kind in the world. The figures are arranged in scenes from all periods of history. From April to October, casting of the tin figures is demonstrated daily from 2 to 5. *☎ 09221/947–505 €4 ⏲ Daily 10–5.*

off the beaten path

NEUENMARKT – In this "railway village" near Kulmbach, more than 25 beautifully preserved gleaming locomotives huff and puff in a living railroad museum. Every now and then a nostalgic train will take you to the Brewery Museum in Kulmbach. Or you can enjoy a round trip to Marktschorgast that takes you up the very steep "schiefe Ebene" stretch (literally, slanting level). The museum also has model trains set up in incredibly detailed replicas of landscapes. *✉ Birkenstr. 5 ☎ 09227/5700 🌐 www.dampflokmuseum.de €4.50 ⏲ Tues.–Sun. 10–5.*

Where to Stay & Eat

$ **Hotel zur Gondel.** It's well worth driving the few miles to Altenkunstadt, between Kulmbach and Lichtenfels, for a few nights at these two elaborate half-timber houses right on the main square. The restaurant serves an excellent candlelit meal of Franconian and international specialties in a stylized rustic setting or in the delightful inner courtyard. The Jahn family has made sure that well-appointed rooms welcome you for a well-deserved rest. ✉ *Marktpl. 7, D–96264 Altenkunstadt* ☎ *09572/3661* 📠 *09572/4596* *36 rooms* *Restaurant, cable TV, some pets allowed; no a/c* 💳 *MC, V* *BP* *No lunch Sat.*

$$ **Hotel Kronprinz.** This old hotel tucked away in the middle of Kulmbach's old town, right in the shadow of Plassenburg Castle, covers all basic needs, though the furnishings are somewhat bland. The café serves snacks and cakes. ✉ *Fischerg. 4–6, D–95326* ☎ *09221/92180* 📠 *09221/921–836* 🌐 *www.kronprinz-kulmbach.de* *19 rooms* *Café, cable TV, in-room data ports, bar; no a/c* 💳 *AE, DC, MC, V* *BP.*

4

Bayreuth

❹ *24 km (15 mi) south of Kulmbach, 80 km (50 mi) northeast of Nürnberg.*

The small town of Bayreuth, pronounced Bye-*roit,* owes its fame to the music giant, Richard Wagner (1813–83). The 19th-century composer and musical revolutionary finally settled here after a lifetime of rootless shifting through Europe. He built his great theater here, the Festspielhaus, as a suitable setting for his grand operas on mythological Germanic themes. The annual Wagner Festival dates to 1876 and brings droves of Wagner fans who push prices sky-high, fill hotels to bursting, and earn themselves much-sought-after social kudos in the process. The festival is held from late July until late August, so unless you plan to visit the town specifically for it, this is the time to stay away. But Wagner is not all there is to the town. You'll find street musicians of all kinds playing in the sun-drenched streets, rock concerts, the occasional sports event, and museums and galleries. The Bayreuth tourist office on Luitpoldplatz offers the Bayreuth Card for €9, giving you unlimited use of the bus system, a tour of the town, entrance to nine museums, and a daily paper, the *Nordbayrischer Kurier.*

"Wahnfried," built by Wagner in 1874 and the only house he ever owned is now the **Richard-Wagner-Museum.** It's a simple, austere neoclassic building whose name, "peace from madness," was well earned. Wagner lived here with his wife, Cosima, daughter of pianist Franz Liszt, and they were both laid to rest here. King Ludwig II of Bavaria, the young and impressionable "Fairy-Tale King," who gave Wagner so much financial support, is remembered in a bust before the entrance. The exhibits, arranged along a well-marked tour through the house, require a great deal of German-language reading. The thrill is in seeing Wagner's handwriting and the original scores of such masterpieces as *Parsifal, Tristan und Isolde, Lohengrin, Der Fliegende Holländer,* and *Götterdämmerung.* You can also see designs for productions of his operas, as well as his piano and huge library. A multimedia display lets you watch and listen to various productions of his operas. The little house where Franz Liszt lived and died is right next door and can be visited on the Wagner ticket, but be sure to express your interest in advance. It, too, is heavy on the paper, but the last rooms—with pictures, photos, and silhouettes of the master, his students, acolytes, and friends—is well worth the detour. ✉ *Richard-Wagner-Str. 48* ☎ *0921/757–2816* 🌐 *www.wagnermuseum.de* 🎫 *€4, during festival €4.50* ⏲ *Apr.–Oct, Fri.–Mon. and Wed. 9–6, Tues. and Thurs. 9–8; Nov.–Mar., daily 10–5.*

The **Festspielhaus** (Festival Theater) is by no means beautiful. In fact, this high temple of the Wagner cult is surprisingly plain. The spartan look is explained partly by Wagner's desire to achieve perfect acoustics. The wood seats have no upholstering, for example, and the walls are bare. The stage is enormous, capable of holding the huge casts required for Wagner's largest operas. Performances take place only during the annual Wagner Festival, still masterminded by descendants of the composer. ✉ *Festspielhügel 1* ☎ *0921/78780* 🎫 *€2.50* ⏲ *Tour Tues.–Sun. at 10, 10:45, 2:15, and 3; closed Nov., during rehearsals, and afternoons during festival.*

The **Neues Schloss** (New Palace) is a glamorous 18th-century palace built by the Margravine Wilhelmine, sister of Frederick the Great of Prussia and a woman of enormous energy and decided tastes. Though Wagner is the man most closely associated with Bayreuth, his choice of this setting is largely due to the work of this woman, who lived 100 years before him. Wilhelmine devoured books, wrote plays and operas (which she directed and, of course, acted in), and had buildings constructed, transforming much of the town and bringing it near bankruptcy. Her distinctive touch is evident at the palace, built when a mysterious fire conveniently destroyed parts of the original palace. Anyone with a taste for the wilder flights of rococo decoration will love it. Some rooms have been given over to one of Europe's finest collections of faience. ✉ *Ludwigstr. 21* ☎ *0921/759–6921* 🎫 *€4* ⏲ *Apr.–Sept., daily 9–6; Oct.–Mar., daily 10–4.*

Another great architectural legacy of Wilhelmine is the **Markgräfliches Opernhaus** (Margravial Opera House). Built between 1745 and 1748, it is a rococo jewel, sumptuously decorated in red, gold, and blue. Apollo and the nine Muses cavort across the frescoed ceiling. It was this delicate 500-seat theater that originally drew Wagner to Bayreuth; he felt that it might prove a suitable setting for his own operas. It's a wonderful setting for the concerts and operas of Bayreuth's "other" musical festivals, which in fact go on virtually throughout the year. Visitors are treated to a sound-and-light show. ✉ *Opernstr.* ☎ *0921/759–6922* 🎫 *€5* ⏲ *Apr.–Sept., daily 9–6, Oct.–Mar., daily 10–4. Sound-and-light shows daily in the opera house every hour starting at 9:15 in summer and 10:15 in winter. Closed during performances, and on rehearsal days.*

Bayreuth is an industrious town and there's a lot more to it than opera and Wagner. Visiting the **Historisches Museum Bayreuth** (Bayreuth Historical Museum) is like poking around a miraculous attic with 34 rooms. A wonderfully eclectic collection includes items from the life of the town, be they royal remnants, faience items from the 18th century, clothes, or odd sports equipment. ✉ *Kirchpl. 6* ☎ *0921/764–010* 🎫 *€1.60* ⏲ *Tues.–Sun. 10–5.*

Bayreuth's small but high-quality **Kunstmuseum** (Art Museum) houses several permanent collections donated or lent by private collectors. Works by Lyonel Feininger, Max Beckmann (lithographs from his *Berlin Journeys*), and woodcuts by Emil Schuhmacher are highlights. An unusual collection donated by the British American Tobacco company features paintings, sculptures, and ephemera relating to all aspects of tobacco, from cultivation to smoking. The museum lies within the generous rooms of the old Town Hall and shares space with an upscale restaurant called Oskar. ✉ *Maximilianstr. 33* ☎ *0921/764–5310* 🌐 *www.kunstmuseum-bayreuth.de* 🎟 *€1.60* ⏲ *Tues.–Sun. 10–5.*

Near the center of town in the 1887 Maisel Brewery building, the **Brauerei und Büttnerei-Museum** (Brewery and Coopers Museum) reveals the tradition of the brewing trade over the past two centuries with a focus on the Maisel's trade, of course. The brewery operated until 1981, when its much bigger home was completed next door. After the 90-minute tour, you can quaff a cool, freshly tapped beer in the museum's pub, which has traditional Bavarian Weissbier (wheat beer). ✉ *Kulmbacherstr. 40* ☎ *0921/401–234* 🌐 *www.maisel.com* 🎟 *€3.60* ⏲ *Tour Mon.–Thurs. at 10 AM; individual tours by prior arrangement.*

The **Altes Schloss Eremitage,** 5 km (3 mi) north of Bayreuth on B–85, makes an appealing departure from the sonorous and austere Wagnerian mood of much of the town. It's an early-18th-century palace, built as a summer palace and remodeled in 1740 by the Margravine Wilhelmine. Although her taste is not much in evidence in the drab exterior, the interior, alive with light and color, displays her guiding hand in every elegant line. The extraordinary **Japanischer Saal** (Japanese Room), filled with Asian treasures and chinoiserie furniture, is the finest room. The park and gardens, partly formal, partly natural, are enjoyable for idle strolling. Fountain displays take place at the two fake grottoes at the top of the hour, 10–5 daily. ☎ *0921/759–6937* 🎟 *Schloss €3, park free* ⏲ *Schloss Apr.–Sept., daily 9–6.*

Where to Stay & Eat

★ ¢–$ ✕ **Oskar.** A huge glass ceiling gives the large dining room a light atmosphere even in winter. In summer, try for a table in the beer garden to enjoy fine Franconian specialties and continental dishes. The kitchen uses the freshest produce and service is friendly. The room fills up at night and during Sunday brunch, especially if a jazz band is playing in one of the alcoves. ✉ *Maximilianstr. 33* ☎ *0921/516–0553* 💳 *No credit cards.*

¢–$ ✕ **Wolffenzacher.** This self-described "nostalgic inn" harks back to the days when the local *Wirtshaus* (inn–pub) was the meeting place for everyone from the mayor's scribes to the local carpenters. Beer and hearty food are shared at wooden tables either in the rustic interior or out in the shady beer-garden (in the middle of town!), weather permitting. The hearty Franconian specialties are counterbalanced by a few lighter French and Italian dishes. ✉ *Sternenpl. 5* ☎ *0921/64552* 💳 *MC, V.*

$$–$$$ ✕🏨 **Schlosshotel Thiergarten.** Staying at this 250-year-old former hunting lodge is like being at your favorite aunt's, if she were an elderly millionaire. Rooms are individually furnished and have a plush, lived-in feel. The intimate Kaminhalle, with an ornate fireplace, and the Venezian-

ischer Salon, dominated by a glittering 300-year-old Venetian chandelier, offer regional and nouvelle cuisine ($$–$$$$). The hotel is 8 km (5 mi) from Bayreuth in the Thiergarten suburb. ✉ *Oberthiergärtenerstr. 36, D–95448* ☎ *09209/9840* 🖷 *09209/98429* 🌐 *www.schlosshotel-thiergarten.de* *8 rooms, 1 suite* *2 restaurants, cable TV, pool, sauna, bar, some pets allowed (fee); no a/c* 💳 *AE, DC, MC, V* *BP.*

★ $–$$$ **Goldener Anker.** No question about it, this is *the* place to stay in Bayreuth. The hotel is right next to the Markgräfliches Opernhaus and has been entertaining composers, singers, conductors, and players for more than 100 years. The establishment has been run by the same family since 1753. Some rooms are small, others have a royal splendor. One huge suite has a spiral staircase leading up to the bedroom. All are individually decorated and many have antique pieces. The restaurant ($$–$$$$) is justly popular. Book your room far in advance. ✉ *Opernstr. 6, D–95444* ☎ *0921/65051* 🖷 *0921/65500* 🌐 *www.anker-bayreuth.de* *38 rooms, 2 suites* *Restaurant, cable TV, some in-room data ports, some pets allowed; no a/c* 💳 *AE, DC, MC, V* *Restaurant closed Mon., Tues., and Dec. 20–Jan. 10* *BP.*

$–$$ **Hotel Lohmühle.** The old part of this hotel is in Bayreuth's only half-timber house, a former saw mill by a stream. It's just a two-minute walk to the town center. The rooms are rustic with visible beams; the newer, neighboring building has correspondingly modern rooms. Between the two is a gallery with a bar where you can enjoy a small aperitif before trying some of the restaurant's traditional, hearty cooking ($$–$$$), such as Schaüfele or carp. ✉ *Badstr. 37, D–95445* ☎ *0921/53060* 🖷 *0921/530–6469* 🌐 *www.hotel-lohmuehle.de* *42 rooms* *Restaurant, cable TV, bar, some pets allowed (fee), no-smoking rooms; no a/c* 💳 *AE, DC, MC, V* *No dinner Sun.* *BP.*

Nightlife & the Arts

Opera lovers swear that there are few more intense operatic experiences than that of the annual **Wagner Festival** in Bayreuth, held July and August. For tickets write to the **Bayreuther Festspiele Kartenbüro** (Postfach 100262, D–95402 Bayreuth ☎ 0921/78780), but be warned: the waiting list is years long. You'll do best if you plan your visit a couple of years in advance. Rooms can be nearly impossible to find during the festival, too. If you don't get Wagner tickets, console yourself with visits to the exquisite 18th-century **Markgräfliches Opernhaus** (✉ Opernstr. ☎ 0921/759–6922).

Shopping

The **Hofgarten Passage,** off Richard-Wagner-Strasse, is one of the fanciest shopping arcades in the region; it's full of smart boutiques selling anything from high German fashion to simple local craftwork.

en route

The B–22 highway cuts through the Fränkische Schweiz—or Franconian Switzerland—which got its name from its fir-clad upland landscape. Just north of Hollfeld, 23 km (14 mi) west of Bayreuth, the Jurassic rock of the region breaks through the surface in a bizarre, craggy formation known as the Felsgarten (Rock Garden).

Bamberg

5 *65 km (40 mi) west of Bayreuth, 80 km (50 mi) north of Nürnberg.*

Few towns in Germany survived the war with as little damage as Bamberg, which is on the Regnitz River. This former residence of one of Germany's most powerful imperial dynasties is on UNESCO's World Heritage Site list. Bamberg, originally nothing more than a fortress in the hands of the Babenberg dynasty (later contracted to Bamberg), rose to prominence in the 11th century thanks to the political and economic drive of its most famous offspring, Holy Roman Emperor Heinrich II. He transformed the imperial residence into a flourishing episcopal city. His cathedral, consecrated in 1237, still dominates the historic area. For a short period Heinrich II proclaimed Bamberg the capital of the Holy Roman Empire of the German nation. Moreover, Bamberg earned fame as the second city to introduce book printing, in 1460.

Bamberg's historic core, the **Altes Rathaus** (Old Town Hall), is tucked snugly on a small island in the Regnitz. To the west of the river is the so-called Bishops' Town; to the east, Burghers' Town. This rickety, extravagantly decorated building was built in this unusual place so that the burghers of Bamberg could avoid paying real-estate taxes to their bishops and archbishops. The excellent collection of porcelain here is a vast sampling of 18th-century styles, from almost sober Meissens with bucolic Watteau scenes to simple but rare Haguenau pieces from Alsace and faience from Strasbourg. ✉ *Obere Brücke 1* ☎ *0951/871–871* 🎫 *€4* ⏲ *Tues.–Sun. 9:30–4:30.*

need a break?

Before heading up the hill to the main sights in the Bishops' Town, take a break with coffee, cake, small meals, or cocktails in the half-timber **Rathaus-Schänke** (✉ Obere Brücke 3 ☎ 0951/208–0890). It overlooks the river on the Burghers' Town side of the Town Hall.

The **Neue Residenz** (New Residence) is a glittering baroque palace that was once the home of the prince-electors. Their plans to extend the immense palace even further is evident at the corner on Obere Karolinenstrasse, where the ashlar bonding was left open to accept another wing. The most memorable room in the palace is the **Kaisersaal** (Throne Room), complete with impressive ceiling frescoes and elaborate stuccowork. Among the thousands of books and illuminated manuscripts in the **Staatsbibliothek** (State Library) are the original prayer books belonging to Heinrich II& and his wife, a 5th-century codex of the Roman historian Livy, and manuscripts by the 16th-century painters Dürer and Cranach. The rose garden behind the Neue Residenz offers an aromatic and romantic space to stroll with a view of Bamberg's roof landscape. ✉ *Dompl. 8* ☎ *0951/519–390 Staatsbibliothek* 🎫 *€4,* ⏲ *Neue Residenz by tour only, Apr.–Sept., daily 9–6; Oct.–Mar., daily 10–4; Staatsbibliothek Sept.–July, weekdays 9–5, Sat. 9–noon; Aug., weekdays 9–noon.*

★ Bamberg's great **Dom** (Cathedral) is one of the country's most important, a building that tells not only the town's story but that of Germany as well. The first building here was begun by Heinrich II in 1003, and it was in this partially completed cathedral that he was crowned Holy Roman Emperor in 1012. In 1237 it was destroyed by fire, and the present late-Romanesque–early-Gothic building was begun. The dominant features are the massive towers at each corner. Heading into the dark interior, you'll find one of the most striking collections of monuments and art treasures of any European church The most famous piece is the **Bamberger Reiter** (Bamberg Rider), an equestrian statue carved—no one knows by whom—around 1230 and thought to be an allegory of chivalrous virtue or a representation of King Stephen of Hungary. Compare it with the mass of carved figures huddled in the tympana above the church portals. In the center of the nave you'll find another masterpiece, the massive tomb of Heinrich and his wife, Kunigunde. It's the work of Tilman Riemenschneider. Pope Clement II is also buried in the cathedral, in an imposing tomb beneath the high altar; he's the only pope to be buried north of the Alps. ✉ *Dompl.* ☎ *0951/502–330* ⏲ *Nov.–Mar., daily 8–5, Apr.–Oct. 8–6, no visits during services.*

The **Diözesanmuseum** (Cathedral Museum), directly next to the cathedral, contains one of many nails and splinters of wood reputed to be from the cross of Jesus. The "star-spangled" cloak stitched with gold that was given to Emperor Heinrich II by an Italian prince is among the finest items displayed. More macabre exhibits in this rich ecclesiastical collection are the elaborately mounted skulls of Heinrich and Kunigunde. The building itself was designed by Balthasar Neumann (1687–1753), the architect of Vierzehnheiligen, and constructed between 1730 and 1733. ✉ *Dompl. 5* ☎ *0951/502–325* 🎫 *€3* ⏲ *Tues.–Sun. 10–5; tour in English by prior arrangement.*

Bamberg's wealthy burghers built no fewer than 50 churches. Among the very special ones is the Church of Our Lady, known simply as **Obere Pfarre** (Upper Parish), whose history goes back to around 1325. It's unusual because it's still entirely Gothic from the outside. Also, the grand choir, which was added at a later period, is lacking windows. And then there's the odd, squarish box perched atop the tower. This watchman's abode served to cut the tower short before it grew taller than the neighboring cathedral, thereby avoiding a great scandal. The interior is heavily baroque. Note the slanted floor, which allowed crowds of pilgrims to see the object of their veneration, a 14th-century Madonna. Don't miss the *Ascension of Mary* by Tintoretto at the rear of the church. Around Christmas, the Obere Pfarre is the site of the city's greatest Nativity scene. Avoid the church during services, unless you're worshipping. ✉ *Untere Seelgasse* ⏲ *Daily 7–7.*

St. Michael, a former Benedictine monastery, has been gazing over Bamberg since about 1015. After being overwhelmed by so much baroque elsewhere, entering this haven of simplicity is quite an experience. The entire choir is intricately carved, but the ceiling is gently decorated with very exact depictions of 578 flowers and healing herbs. The tomb of St. Otto is in a little chapel off the transept, and the stained-glass windows hold symbols of death and transfiguration. The monastery is now used as a home for the aged. One tract, however, was taken over by the **Franconian Brewery Museum,** which exhibits everything that has to do with beer, from the making of malt to recipes. ✉ *Michelsberg 10f* ☎ *0951/53016* 🎟 *Museum €2* ⏲ *Apr.–Oct., Wed.–Sun. 1–5.*

Laser technology, art, and photography meet at the **Naturkunde Museum** (Museum of Natural History). Located in a unique 18th-century university building, the museum covers a wide range of subjects, from fossils to volcanoes. The pride of the place is the collection of 800 stuffed birds in a magnificent room that also has a whale's jawbone casually lying on the floor. ✉ *Fleischstr. 2* ☎ *0951/863–1248* 🌐 *www.uni-bamberg.de/NatMus* 🎟 *€ 2* ⏲ *Apr.–Sept., Tues.–Sun. 9–5; Oct.–Mar., Tues.–Sun. 10–4.*

off the beaten path

Fodor's Choice ★

North of Bamberg are two religious gems, a church and an abbey, each proudly crowning the heights along the banks of the Main River. On the east side of the Main is **VIERZEHNHEILIGEN** – a tall, elegant yellow-sandstone edifice whose interior represents one of the great examples of rococo decoration. The church was built by Balthasar Neumann (architect of the Residenz at Würzburg) between 1743 and 1772 to commemorate a vision of Christ and 14 saints—*vierzehn Heiligen*—that appeared to a shepherd in 1445. The interior, known as "God's ballroom," is supported by 14 columns. In the middle of the church is the Gnadenaltar (Mercy Altar) featuring the 14 saints. Thanks to clever play with light, light colors, and fanciful gold-and-blue trimmings, the interior seems to be in perpetual motion. Guided tours of the church are given on request; a donation is expected. ✥ *36 km (22 mi) north of Bamberg via B–173* ☎ *09571/95080* 🌐 *www.vierzehnheiligen.de* ⏲ *Oct.–May, daily 8–4; June–Sept., daily 7–7.*

On the west bank of the Main is **KLOSTER BANZ** (Banz Abbey) – standing on what some call the "holy mountain of Bavaria." There had been a monastery here since 1069, but the present buildings—now a political-seminar center and think tank—date from the end of the 17th century. The highlight of the complex is the **Klosterkirche** (Abbey Church), the work of architect Leonard Dientzenhofer and his brother, the stuccoist Johann Dientzenhofer (1663–1726). Balthasar Neumann later contributed a good deal of work. Concerts are occasionally held in the church, including some by members of the renowned "Bamberger Symphoniker." To get to Banz from Vierzehnheiligen, drive south to Unnersdorf, where you can cross the river. ☎ *09573/7311* ⏲ *May–Oct., daily 9–noon and 2–4; Nov.–Apr., daily 9–noon; call to request a tour.*

Where to Stay & Eat

¢–$ ✕ **Bischohsmühle.** It doesn't always have to be beer in Bamberg. The old mill, its grinding wheel providing a sonorous backdrop for patrons, specializes in wines from Franconia and elsewhere. The menu offers Franconian specialties such as the French-derived *Böfflamott,* or beef stew. ✉ *Geyerswörthstr. 4* ☎ *0951/27570* 💳 *No credit cards* ⏲ *Closed Wed.*

¢–$ ✕ **Klosterbräu.** This massive old stone–and–half-timber house has been standing since 1533. Regulars nurse their dark, smoky beer called "Schwärzla" near the big stove. If you like the brew, you can buy a 5-liter bottle as well as other bottled beers and the corresponding beer steins at the counter. The cuisine is basic, robust, filling, and tasty, with such items as a bowl of beans with a slab of smoked pork, or marinated pork kidneys with boiled potatoes. ✉ *Obere Mühlbrücke* ☎ *0951/52265* 💳 *No credit cards.*

$$ Fodor'sChoice ★ ✕🏨 **Hotel-Restaurant St. Nepomuk.** This half-timber house seems to float over the Regnitz. Sitting in the dining room, with its podium fireplace, discreet lights, serene atmosphere, and direct view of the river, you get the feeling of being on board a ship. The Grüner family makes a special effort to bring not only high-quality food to the restaurant ($$$) but a world of excellent wines as well. The rooms are comfortable, and many have quite a view of the river and the old town hall on the island. Each is furnished individually in elegant style. ✉ *Obere Mühlbrücke 9, D–96049* ☎ *0951/98420* 📠 *0951/984–2100* 🌐 *www.hotel-nepomuk.de* 🛏 *47 rooms* 🖒 *Restaurant, cable TV, Wi-Fi, some pets allowed (fee), no-smoking rooms; no a/c* 💳 *DC, MC, V* 🍽 *BP.*

★ $$ ✕🏨 **Romantik Hotel Weinhaus Messerschmitt.** Willy Messerschmitt of aviation fame grew up in this beautiful late-baroque house with a steep-eaved, green-shutter stucco exterior. The very comfortable hotel has spacious and luxurious rooms, some with exposed beams and many of them lighted by chandeliers. You'll dine under beams and a coffered ceiling in the excellent Messerschmitt restaurant ($$–$$$), one of Bamberg's most popular culinary havens for Franconian specialties in gourmet cloak. ✉ *Langestr. 41, D–96047* ☎ *0951/297–800* 📠 *0951/297–8029* 🌐 *www.hotel-messerschmitt.de* 🛏 *19 rooms* 🖒 *Restaurant, cable TV, bar, no-smoking rooms; no a/c* 💳 *AE, DC, MC, V* 🍽 *BP.*

The Arts

The **Sinfonie an der Regnitz** (✉ Muss-Str. 20 ☎ 0951/964–7200), a fine riverside concert hall, is home to Bamberg's world-class resident symphony orchestra. The **Hoffmann Theater** (✉ Schillerpl. 5 ☎ 0951/871–433) has opera and operetta from September through July. The city's first-class choir, **Capella Antiqua Bambergensis,** concentrates on ancient music. Throughout the summer organ concerts are given in the **Dom.** For program details and tickets to all cultural events, call ☎ 0951/297–6200.

Shopping

Of the many shops in Bamberg, the **AGIL** (✉ Schranne 14 ☎ 0951/519–0389) may be the one you'll want to visit for an unusual souvenir. Jost Lohmann sells replicas of medieval household utensils and other peculiar items. If you happen to be traveling around Christmastime, make sure you keep an eye out for crèches, a Bamberg specialty.

en route

From Bamberg you can either take the fast autobahn (A–73) south to Nürnberg, or the parallel country road (B–4) that follows the Main-Donau Canal (running parallel to the Regnitz River at this point) and joins A–73 just under 25 km (15 mi) later at Forchheim-Nord. The canal, a mighty feat of engineering first envisioned by Charlemagne but only completed in the 1990s, connects the North Sea and the Black Sea by linking the Rhine and the Danube rivers via the Main River. There's no tangible division between northern and southern Franconia. You do, however, leave the thickly wooded heights of the Fichtelgebirge and the Fränkische Schweiz behind, and the countryside opens up as if to announce the imminent arrival of a more populated region.

Eighteen kilometers (11 mi) south of Bamberg in the village of Buttenheim is a little blue-and-white half-timber house where Löb Strauss was born—in egregious poverty—in 1826. Take the tape-recorded tour of the **Levi-Strauss Museum** (✉ Marktstr. 33 ☎ 09545/442–602 🎫 €2.60 ⏲ Tues.–Thurs. 2–6, weekends 11–5 and by appointment) and learn how Löb emigrated to the United States, changed his name to Levi, and became the first name in denim. One of the special exhibits is a pair of jeans dating to 1880 discovered in the Nevada desert (the jeans on display are actually a replica). The stone-washed color of the house's beams, by the way, is the original 17th-century color. The museum also hosts special exhibitions and other events, all revolving around jeans, of course.

NÜRNBERG

Nürnberg (Nuremberg) is the principal city of Franconia and the second-largest city in Bavaria. With a recorded history stretching back to 1050, it's among the most historic of Germany's cities; the core of the Old Town, through which the Pegnitz River flows, is still surrounded by its original medieval walls. Nürnberg has always taken a leading role in German affairs. It was here, for example, that the Holy Roman Emperors traditionally held the first Diet, or convention of the estates, of their incumbency. And it was here, too, that Hitler staged the most grandiose Nazi rallies; later, this was the site of the Allies' war trials, where top-ranking Nazis were charged with—and almost without exception convicted of—crimes against humanity. The rebuilding of Nürnberg after the war was virtually a miracle considering the 90% destruction of the Old Town. As if putting an end to its difficult, violent history, Nürnberg, in 2001, became the world's first city to receive the UNESCO prize for Human Rights Education.

As a major intersection on the medieval trade routes, Nürnberg became a wealthy town where the arts and sciences flowered. Albrecht Dürer (1471–1528), the first indisputable genius of the Renaissance in Germany, was born here in 1471. He married in 1509 and bought a house in the city where he lived and worked for the rest of his life. Other leading Nürnberg artists of the Renaissance include painter Michael Wolgemut (a teacher of Dürer), stonecutter Adam Kraft, and the brass founder Peter Vischer. The tradition of the Meistersinger also flourished here in the 16th century, thanks to the high standard set by the local cobbler Hans Sachs (1494–1576). The Meistersinger were poets and musicians who turned songwriting into a special craft with a wealth of rules and regulations. They were celebrated three centuries later by Wagner in his *Meistersinger von Nürnberg.*

The Thirty Years' War and the shift to sea routes for transportation led to the city's long decline, which ended only in the early 19th century when the first railroad opened in Nürnberg. Among a great host of inventions associated with the city, the most significant are the pocket watch, gun casting, the clarinet, and the geographic globe (the first of which was made before Columbus discovered the Americas). Among Nürnberg's famous products are *Lebkuchen* (gingerbread of sorts) and Faber-Castell pencils.

Exploring

Nürnberg is 63 km (39 mi) south of Bamberg and rich in special events and celebrations. By far the most famous is the **Christkindlesmarkt** (Christ-Child Market), an enormous pre-Christmas fair that runs from the Friday before Advent to Christmas Eve. One of the highlights is the candle procession, held every second Thursday of the market season, during which thousands of children parade through the city streets.

a good walk

Start your walk at the **Hauptbahnhof** ⚑, the main train station, whose tourist office offers maps and brochures. Enter the Old Town through the **Königstor,** the old King's Gate. The Old Town walls, finished in 1452, come complete with moats, sturdy gateways, and watchtowers. Year-round floodlighting adds to their brooding romance. Take a left on Luitpoldstrasse and note, on your left, the **Neues Museum** 6, Nürnberg's museum for contemporary art. Take a left on Vordere Sterngasse and then a right when you reach the old wall again. Take your second right onto Strasse der Menschenrechte (Street of Human Rights), which has an installation of 30 columns inscribed with the articles from the Declaration of Human Rights. On the right is one of Germany's most extraordinary museums, the **Germanisches Nationalmuseum** 7. A few hours spent here examining the sections devoted to the city will prepare you for the step back in time you'll make during the rest of your walk through Nürnberg. Follow Kornmarkt east and turn left on Pfannenschmiedsgasse to reach the beautiful **St. Lorenz Kirche** 8.

Continue north on Königstrasse and cross the bridge over the Pegnitz River at its most photogenic point, where the former hospital **Heilig-Geist-Spital** broods over the waters, and soon you'll reach the city's central market square, the **Hauptmarkt** 9, with the delicate late-Gothic **Frauenkirche** 10 standing modestly on the east side and the handsome **Schöner Brunnen** 11 (fountain) in the northwestern corner. Just north of the Hauptmarkt is Rathausplatz, site of another Gothic masterpiece of church architecture, **St. Sebaldus Kirche** 12. The **Altes Rathaus** 13 faces the church; behind the town hall is another pretty fountain, the **Gänsemännchenbrunnen** 14. To the north of the Altes Rathaus on Burgstrasse stands the fine Renaissance Fembohaus, which contains the **Stadtmuseum** 15. Save some energy for the climb up Burgstrasse to the great **Kaiserburg** 16, whose shadow falls on the **Albrecht-Dürer-Haus** 17, at the top of Albrecht-Dürer-Strasse, just below the castle. Follow this street southward and you'll

Albrecht-Dürer-Haus 17
Altes Rathaus 13
Frauenkirche 10
Gänsemännchenbrunnen 14
Germanisches Nationalmuseum 7
Hauptmarkt . . . 9
Kaiserburg . . . 16
Museum für Kommunikation 19
Neues Museum 6
St. Lorenz Kirche 8
St. Sebaldus Kirche 12
Schöner Brunnen 11
Spielzeugmuseum 18
Stadtmuseum 15

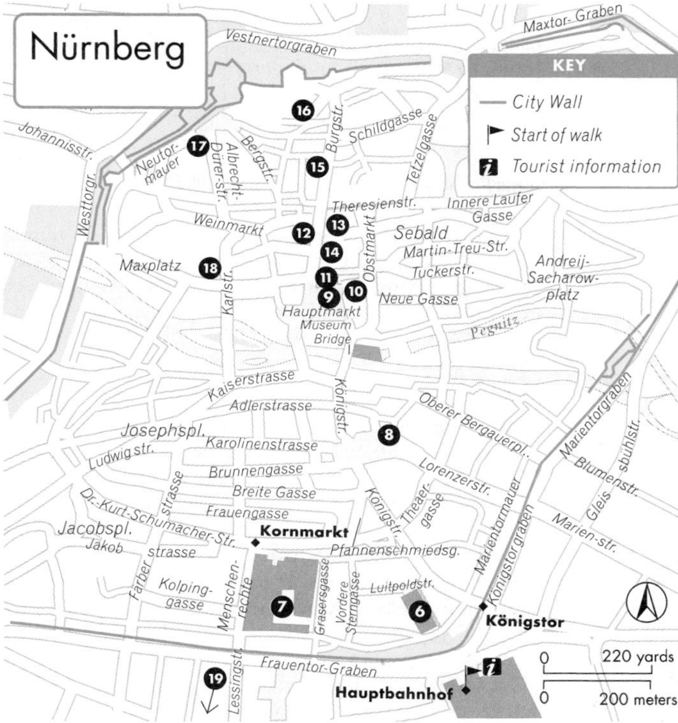

come to a delightful toy museum, the **Spielzeugmuseum** ⑱, on Karlstrasse. If you still have time or energy, it's about a 15-minute walk to the trains and stamps of the **Museum für Kommunikation** ⑲, on Lessingstrasse, just south of the Germanisches Nationalmuseum. You can then return to your starting point for that much-needed refreshment. The train station has an extensive mall of restaurants and bars.

TIMING You'll need a full day to walk around Nürnberg, two if you wish to take more time at its fascinating museums. Most of the major sights are within a few minutes' walk of each other. Begin or end your day at the Kaiserburg, whose ramparts offer a spectacular view over this medieval gem of a town.

What to See

★ ⑰ **Albrecht-Dürer-Haus** (Albrecht Dürer House). The great painter Albrecht Dürer lived here from 1509 until his death in 1528. This beautifully preserved late-medieval house is typical of the prosperous merchants' homes that once filled Nürnberg. Dürer, who enriched German art with Italianate elements, was more than a painter. He raised the woodcut, a notoriously difficult medium, to new heights of technical sophistication, combining great skill with a haunting, immensely detailed drawing style and complex, allegorical subject matter while earning a good living at the same time. A number of original prints adorn the walls, and printing techniques using the old press are demonstrated in the studio. An excellent opportunity to find out about life in the house is the Saturday 2 PM tour with a guide role-playing Agnes Dürer, Dürer's wife. ✉ *Albrecht-Dürer-Str. 39* ☎ *0911/231–2568* 🎫 *€5, with tour €7.50* ⏲ *Tues., Wed., and Fri.–Sun. 10–5, Thurs. 10–8; guided tour in English Sat. at 2.*

13 **Altes Rathaus** (Old Town Hall). This ancient building on Rathausplatz abuts the rear of St. Sebaldus Kirche; it was erected in 1332, destroyed in World War II, and subsequently restored. Its intact medieval dungeons, consisting of 12 small rooms and one large torture chamber called the **Lochgefängnis** (or the Chapel, owing to the vaulted ceilings), provide insight into the gruesome applications of medieval law. ✉ *Rathauspl. 2* ☎ *0911/231–2690* 🎫 *€3, tours only beginning with 5 people* ⏲ *Tues.–Sun. 10–5:30; during Christkindlesmarkt daily 10–4.*

10 **Frauenkirche** (Church of Our Lady). The fine late-Gothic Frauenkirche was built in 1350, with the approval of Holy Roman Emperor Charles IV, on the site of a synagogue that was burned down during a 1349 pogrom. The modern tabernacle beneath the main altar was designed to look like a Torah scroll as a kind of memorial to that despicable act. The church's real attraction is the **Männleinlaufen,** a clock dating from 1509, which is set in its facade. It's one of those colorful mechanical marvels at which Germans have long excelled. Every day at noon the seven electors of the Holy Roman Empire glide out of the clock to bow to Emperor Charles IV before sliding back under cover. It's worth scheduling your morning to catch the display. ✉ *Hauptmarkt* ⏲ *Mon.–Sat. 9–6, Sun. 12:30–6.*

14 **Gänsemännchenbrunnen** (Gooseman's Fountain). A work of rare elegance and great technical sophistication, this lovely Renaissance bronze fountain facing the Altes Rathaus was cast in 1550. ✉ *Rathauspl.*

★ 7 **Germanisches Nationalmuseum** (German National Museum). You could spend days visiting this vast museum, which showcases the country's cultural and scientific achievements, ethnic background, and history. It's the largest of its kind in Germany and perhaps the best arranged. The museum is in what was once a Carthusian monastery, complete with cloisters and monastic outbuildings. The extensions, however, are modern and sleek. The exhibition begins outside, with the tall, sleek pillars of the Way of Human Rights designed by Israeli artist Dani Karavan. There are few aspects of German culture, from the Stone Age to the 19th century, that are not covered by the museum, and quantity and quality are evenly matched. One highlight is the superb collection of Renaissance German paintings (with Dürer, Cranach, and Altdorfer well represented). Others may prefer the exquisite medieval ecclesiastical exhibits—manuscripts, altarpieces, statuary, stained glass, jewel-encrusted reliquaries—the collections of arms and armor, the scientific instruments, or the toys. Few will be disappointed. ✉ *Kartäuserg. 1* ☎ *0911/13310* 🌐 *www.gnm.de* 🎫 *€5* ⏲ *Tues. and Thurs.–Sun. 10–6, Wed. 10–9.*

need a break?

Opposite the Germanisches Nationalmuseum is a minimalist, Italian restaurant named **Vivere** (✉ Kartäuserg. 12 ☎ 0911/133–1286 ⏲ closed Mon.). Al dente pasta or meat and fish dishes will bring you back to earth after the long hours spent in the museum.

9 **Hauptmarkt** (Main Market). Nürnberg's central market square was at one time the city's Jewish Quarter. When the people of Nürnberg petitioned their emperor, Charles IV, for a big central market, the emperor happened to be in desperate need of money and, above all, political support. The Jewish Quarter was the preferred site, but as the official protector of the Jewish people, the emperor could not just openly take away their property. Instead, he instigated a pogrom that left the Jewish Quarter in flames and more than 500 dead. The next step of razing the ruins and resettling the remaining Jews thus appeared perfectly logical.

A market still operates here. Its colorful stands are piled high with produce, fruit, bread, homemade cheeses and sausages, sweets, and anything else you might need for a snack or picnic. It's here that the Christkindlesmarkt is held.

16 **Kaiserburg** (Imperial Castle). The city's main attraction is a grand yet playful collection of buildings standing just inside the city walls; it was once the residence of the Holy Roman Emperors. The complex comprises three separate groups. The oldest, dating from around 1050, is the **Burggrafenburg** (Castellan's Castle), with a craggy old pentagonal tower and the bailiff's house. It stands in the center of the complex. To the east is the **Kaiserstallung** (Imperial Stables), built in the 15th century as a granary and now serving as a youth hostel. The real interest of this vast complex of ancient buildings, however, centers on the westernmost part of the fortress, which begins at the **Sinwell Turm** (Sinwell Tower). The **Kaiserburg Museum** is here, a subsidiary of the Germanisches Nationalmuseum that displays ancient armors and has exhibits relating to horsemanship in the imperial era and to the history of the fortress. This section of the castle also has a wonderful Romanesque **Doppelkappelle** (Double Chapel). The upper part—richer, larger, and more ornate than the lower chapel—was where the emperor and his family worshipped. Also visit the **Rittersaal** (Knights' Hall) and the **Kaisersaal** (Throne Room). Their heavy oak beams, painted ceilings, and sparse interiors have changed little since they were built in the 15th century. ✉ *Burgstr.* ☎ *0911/24465–9115* 🎫 €6 ⏲ *Apr.–Sept., daily 9–6; Oct.–Mar., daily 10–4.*

19 **Museum für Kommunikation** (Communication Museum). Two museums have been amalgamated under a single roof here, the German Railway Museum and the Museum of Communication, in short, museums about how people get in touch. The first train to run in Germany did so on December 7, 1835, from Nürnberg to nearby Fürth. A model of the epochal train is here, along with a series of original 19th- and early-20th-century trains and stagecoaches. Philatelists will want to check out some of the 40,000-odd stamps in the extensive exhibits on the German postal system. You can also find out about the history of sending messages—from old coaches to optical fiber networks. ✉ *Lessingstr. 6* ☎ *0911/219–2428* 🎫 €3 ⏲ *Tues.–Sun. 9–5.*

❻ **Neues Museum** (New Museum). Anything but medieval, this museum opened in mid-2000 and is devoted to international design since 1945. The remarkable collection, supplemented by changing exhibitions, is in a slick, modern edifice that achieves the perfect synthesis between old and new. It's mostly built of traditional pink-sandstone ashlars, while the facade is a flowing, transparent composition of glass. The interior is a work of art in itself—cool stone, with a ramp that slowly spirals up to the gallery. Extraordinary things await, including a Joseph Beuys installation (*Ausfegen,* or Sweep-out) and *Avalanche* by François Morellet, a striking collection of violet, argon gas–filled fluorescent tubes. The café-restaurant adjoining the museum contains modern art, silver-wrapped candies, and video projections. ✉ *Luitpoldstr. 5* ☎ *0911/240–200* 🎫 *€3.50* ⏲ *Tues.–Fri. 10–8, weekends 10–6.*

Fodor'sChoice ★

❽ **St. Lorenz Kirche** (St. Laurence Church). In a city with several striking churches, St. Lorenz is considered by many to be the most beautiful. It was begun around 1250 and completed in about 1477; it later became a Lutheran church. Two towers flank the main entrance of the sizable church, which is covered with a forest of carvings. In the lofty interior, note the works by sculptors Adam Kraft and Veit Stoss: Kraft's great stone tabernacle, to the left of the altar, and Stoss's *Annunciation,* at the east end of the nave, are their finest works. There are many other carvings throughout the building, testimony to the artistic wealth of late-medieval Nürnberg. ✉ *Lorenzer Pl.* ⏲ *Mon.–Sat. 9–5, Sun. noon–4.*

⓬ **St. Sebaldus Kirche** (St. Sebaldus Church). Although St. Sebaldus lacks the quantity of art treasures found in its rival St. Lorenz, its nave and choir are among the purest examples of Gothic ecclesiastical architecture in Germany: elegant, tall, and airy. Veit Stoss carved the crucifixion group at the east end of the nave, while the elaborate bronze shrine, containing the remains of St. Sebaldus himself, was cast by Peter Vischer and his five sons around 1520. Not to be missed is the **Sebaldus Chörlein,** an ornate Gothic oriel that was added to the Sebaldus parish house in 1361 (the original is in the Germanisches Nationalmuseum). ✉ *Albrecht-Dürer-Pl. 1* ☎ *0911/214–2500* ⏲ *Jan.–Mar., daily 9:30–4, Apr., May, and Oct.–Dec., daily 9:30–6, June–Sept., daily 9:30–8.*

⓫ **Schöner Brunnen** (Beautiful Fountain). The elegant 60-foot-high Gothic fountain, carved around the year 1400, looks as though it should be on the summit of some lofty Gothic cathedral. It's adorned with 40 figures arranged in tiers—prophets, saints, local noblemen, sundry electors of the Holy Roman Empire, and one or two strays such as Julius Caesar and Alexander the Great. A gold ring is set into the railing surrounding the fountain, reportedly placed there by an apprentice carver. Stroking it is said to bring good luck. ✉ *Hauptmarkt.*

⓲ **Spielzeugmuseum** (Toy Museum). Young and old are captivated by this playful museum, which has a few exhibits dating from the Renaissance; most, however, are from the 19th century. Simple dolls vie with mechanical toys of extraordinary complexity, such as a wooden Ferris wheel from the Erz Mountains adorned with little colored lights. The top floor displays Barbies and intricate Lego constructions. ✉ *Karlstr. 13–15* ☎ *0911/231–3164* 🎫 *€5* ⏲ *Tues.–Sun. 10–5.*

need a break?

Honoring Nürnberg's partnership with the French city of Nice, the **D'Azur** (✉ Burgstr. 11 ☎ 0911/235–5355) has baguette sandwiches and other snacks with a Provençal touch. You can also purchase all sorts of delicacies here, such as ratatouille and fish soup in jars.

15 **Stadtmuseum** (City Museum). This city history museum is in the Fembohaus, a dignified patrician dwelling completed in 1598. It's one of the finest Renaissance mansions in Nürnberg. Each room explores another aspect of Nürnberg history, from crafts to gastronomy. The 50-minute multivision show provides a comprehensive look at the long history of the city. ✉ *Burgstr. 15* ☎ *0911/231–2595* *€7* *Tues.–Sun. 10–5.*

4

off the beaten path

DOCUMENTATION CENTRE NAZI PARTY RALLY GROUNDS – On the eastern outskirts of the city, the **Ausstellung Faszination und Gewalt** (Fascination and Terror exhibition) documents the political, social, and architectural history of the Nazi Party. The 19-room exhibition is within a horseshoe-shape Congressional Hall that was intended to harbor a crowd of 50,000; the Nazis never completed it. Austrian architect Günther Domenig added a courageous glass corridor that adds light to the overwhelmingly solid construction. The Nazis did make famous use of the nearby Zeppelin Field, the enormous parade grounds where Hitler addressed his largest Nazi rallies. Today it sometimes shakes to the amplified beat of pop concerts. Tours of the grounds are offered by a private association called Geschichte für Alle (History for All). ☎ *0911/231–5666, 0911/332–735 for tour* *www.museen.nuernberg.de* *€5; tour of Zeppelin Field €5* *Museum daily 9–6, weekends 10–6. Tours Dec.–Mar., Sun. at 2; Apr.–Nov., weekends at 2. Meet at Luitpoldhain tram terminus (No. 9).*

JÜDISCHES MUSEUM FRANKEN – The everyday life of the Jewish community in Franconia and Fürth are examined in this Jewish museum: books, Seder plates, coat hangers, old statutes concerning Jews, and children's toys are among the exhibits. Among the most famous members of the Fürth community was Henry Kissinger, born here in 1923. Changing exhibitions relate to contemporary Jewish life in Germany, and in the basement is the Mikwe, the ritual bath, which was used by the family who lived here centuries ago. A subsidiary to the museum, which houses special exhibitions, has been opened in the former synagogue in nearby Schnaittach. To get to the museum from Nürnberg, you can take the U1 U-bahn to the Rathaus stop. ✉ *Königstr. 89, Fürth, 10 km (6 mi) west of Nürnberg* ☎ *0911/770–577* *www.juedisches-museum.org* *€3* *Wed.–Sun. 10–5, Tues. 10–8.*

THE NÜRNBERG TRIALS – Nazi leaders and German organizations were put on trial here in 1945 and 1946 during the first international war-crimes trials, conducted by the Allied victors of World War II. The trials were held in the Landgericht (Regional Court) in courtroom No.

600 and resulted in 11 death sentences, among other convictions. The guided tours are in German, but English-language material is available. Take the U1 subway line to Bärenschanze. ✉ *Bärenschanzstr. 72* ☎ *0911/231–8411* 🌐 *www.museen.nuernberg.de* 🎟 *€2.50* ⏲ *Weekend guided tours at 1, 2, 3, and 4* PM.

★ **TIERGARTEN NÜRNBERG** – The well-stocked Nürnberg Zoo has a dolphinarium where dolphins perform to the delight of children; it's worth the extra admission fee. The zoo is on the northwest edge of town; reach it by taking the No. 5 streetcar from the city center. ✉ *Am Tiergarten 30* ☎ *0911/54546* 🌐 *www.tiergarten.nuernberg.de* 🎟 *€7, dolphinarium €4.50* ⏲ *Zoo and dolphinarium Apr.–Sept., daily 8–7:30; Mar. and Oct., daily 8–5:30; Nov.–Feb., daily 9–5; dolphin show daily at 11, 2, and 4.*

Where to Stay & Eat

$$–$$$$ Fodor'sChoice ★ ✕ **Essigbrätlein.** It ranks as the top restaurant in the city, and among the best in Germany. As the oldest restaurant in Nürnberg, built in 1550 and originally used as a meeting place for wine merchants, it's unquestionably one of the most atmospheric. Today its tiny but elegant period interior caters to the distinguishing gourmet with a taste for special spice mixes (owner Andrée Köthe's hobby). The menu changes daily. ✉ *Weinmarkt 3* ☎ *0911/225–131* ✍ *Reservations essential* 💳 *AE, DC, MC, V* ⏲ *Closed Sun. and Mon.*

★ **$–$$$** ✕ **Heilig-Geist-Spital.** Heavy wood furnishings and a choice of more than 100 wines make this huge, 650-year-old wine tavern—built as the refectory of the city hospital—a popular spot. Try for a table in one of the alcoves, where you can see the river below you as you eat your fish. The menu also includes grilled pork chops, pan-fried potatoes, and other Franconian dishes. ✉ *Spitalg. 16* ☎ *0911/221–761* 💳 *AE, DC, MC, V.*

★ **¢–$** ✕ **Historische Bratwurst-Küche Zum Gulden Stern.** This house, built in 1375, survived the last war and holds the oldest bratwurst restaurant in the world. The famous Nürnberg bratwursts are always freshly roasted on a beechwood fire; the boiled variation is prepared in a tasty stock of Franconian wine and onions. This is where the city council meets occasionally to decide upon the official size and weight of the Nürnberg bratwurst. ✉ *Zirkelschmiedg. 26* ☎ *0911/205–9288* 💳 *DC, MC, V.*

★ **$$$–$$$$** ✕🏨 **Le Meridien Grand Hotel.** Across the square from the central railway station is this stately building with the calling card of GRAND HOTEL arching over its entranceway. The spacious and imposing lobby with marble pillars feels grand and welcoming. Since 1896 kings, politicians, and celebrities have soaked up the luxury of large rooms and tubs in marble bathrooms. On Sunday, the locals of Nuremberg arrive for the exquisite brunch or candlelight dinner ($$–$$$) with live piano music in the restaurant of glittering glass and marble. ✉ *Bahnhofstr. 1, 90402* ☎ *0911/23220* 📠 *0911/232–2444* 🌐 *www.nuremberg.lemeridien.com* 🛏 *180 rooms, 5 suites* 👍 *Restaurant, bar, cable TV, Wi-Fi, in room broadband, fitness studio, sauna, Internet room, business services, no-smoking rooms, valet parking (fee)* 💳 *AE, DC, MC, V.*

$–$$ **Hotel-Weinhaus Steichele.** This skillfully converted former 18th-century bakery has been managed by the same family for four generations. It's handily close to the main train station, on a quiet street of the old walled town. The cozy rooms are decorated in rustic Bavarian style. Two wood-paneled, traditionally furnished taverns ($–$$$) serve Franconian fare with an excellent fish menu. *Knorrstr. 2–8, D–90402 0911/202–280 0911/221–914 www.steichele.de 56 rooms Restaurant, cable TV, Wi-Fi, Weinstube, some pets allowed; no a/c AE, DC, MC, V BP.*

$$–$$$ **Agneshof.** This comfortable hotel is sandwiched north of the Old Town between the fortress and St. Sebaldus Church. Interiors are very modern and tastefully done. The hotel also has a small wellness section and even some lounges for sunning in the small garden. *Agnesg. 10, D–90403 0911/214–440 0911/2144–4144 www.agneshof-nuernberg.de 72 rooms Cable TV with movies, in-room safe, some in-room data ports, Wi-Fi, hot tub, sauna, some pets allowed (fee), no-smoking rooms; no a/c AE, DC, MC, V BP.*

★ $$ **Hotel Drei Raben.** Legends and tales of Nürnberg form the leitmotiv running through the designer rooms at this hotel. One room celebrates the local soccer team with a table-soccer game; in another room sandstone friezes recall sights in the city. There are also standard rooms in the lower price category. The reception, with its pods, is modeled after *2001: A Space Odyssey* yet doesn't seem overbearingly modern. You are three minutes from the train station, just within the Old Town walls. *Königstr. 63, D–90402 0911/274–380 0911/232–611 www.hotel-drei-raben.de 25 rooms In-room fax, cable TV, Wi-Fi, bar, some pets allowed (fee); no a/c, no smoking AE, DC, MC, V BP.*

$–$$ **Burghotel Stammhaus.** This little family-run hotel does all it can to make you feel at home. Accommodations are small but cozy, and the service is familial and friendly. If you need more space, ask about the wedding suite. The breakfast room with its balcony overlooking the houses of the Old Town has a charm all its own. A pool is in the basement. *Schildg. 14, D–90403 0911/203–040 0911/226–503 www.burghotel-stamm.de 22 rooms Cable TV, indoor pool, some pets allowed; no a/c AE, DC, MC, V BP.*

$–$$ **Hotel Fackelmann.** This compact, convenient hotel near the Old Town is designed for giving quiet comfort to either the leisure or the business traveler. Clean and light rooms, a breakfast buffet, and a fitness area are all included. *Essenweinstr. 10, D–90443 0911/206–840 0911/2068–460 www.hotel-fackelmann.de 34 rooms Cable TV, in-room data ports, gym, sauna, some pets allowed (fee), no-smoking rooms; no a/c AE, MC, V Closed Dec. 24–Jan. 6 BP.*

Nightlife & the Arts

Nürnberg has an annual summer festival, **Sommer in Nürnberg,** from May through September, with more than 200 events. Its international organ festival in June and July is regarded as Europe's finest. From May through August classical music concerts are given in the Rittersaal of the **Kaiserburg,** while regular pop and rock shows are staged in the dry moat of the castle. In June and July open-air concerts are given in the Kaiserburg's Serenadenhof. For details, call ☎ 0911/244–6590.

Shopping

Step into the **Handwerkerhof,** in the tower at the Old Town gate (Am Königstor) opposite the main railway station, and you'll think you're back in the Middle Ages. Craftspeople are busy at work in a "medieval mall," turning out the kind of handiwork that has been produced in Nürnberg for centuries: pewter; glassware; basketwork; wood carvings; and, of course, toys. The Lebkuchen specialist **Lebkuchen-Schmidt** has a shop here as well. The mall is open mid-March–December 24, weekdays 10–6:30, Saturday 10–4. December 1–24 the mall is also open Sunday 10–6:30.

The **Scherenschnittstudio** (✉ Albrecht-Dürer-Str. 13 ☎ 0911/244–7483 ⏲ Tues.–Fri. 1–6 or by appointment) specializes in scissor-cut silhouettes. You can come and pose for owner Karin Dütz, send a picture (profile, do not smile), or just browse to pick up some items of this old and skilled craft.

THE GERMAN DANUBE

For many people, the sound of the Danube River is the melody of the waltz written by Austrian Johann Strauss, *The Blue Danube.* The famous 1,800-mi-long river flows through ten countries and originates in Germany's Black Forest. In Germany, the river is called the Donau, and it's mostly a rather unremarkable stream as it passes through cities such as Ulm on its southeastern route. However, that changes at Kelheim, just west of Regensburg, where the Main-Donau Canal (completed in 1992) brings big river barges all the way from the North Sea. The river becomes sizeable in Regensburg, where the ancient Steinerne Brücke (stone bridge) needs 15 spans of 30 to 48 feet each to bridge the water. Here, everything from small pleasure boats to cruise liners join the commercial traffic. In the university town of Passau, two more rivers join the waters of the Danube before Europe's longest river continues into Austria.

Regensburg

85 km (52 mi) southeast of Nuremberg, 120 km (74 mi) northwest of Munich.

Few visitors to Bavaria venture this far off the well-trod tourist trails, and even Germans are surprised when they discover medieval Regensburg. Because it escaped World War II with no major damage, it is one of the best-preserved medieval cities in Germany.

Regensburg's story begins with the Celts around 500 BC. In AD 179, as an original marble inscription in the Historisches Museum proclaims, it became a Roman military post called Castra Regina. The Porta Praetoria, or gateway, built by the Romans, remains in the Old Town, and whenever you see huge ashlars incorporated into buildings, you are looking at bits of the old Roman settlement. When Bavarian tribes migrated to the area in the 6th century, they occupied what remained of the Roman town and, apparently on the basis of its Latin name, called it Regensburg. Anglo-Saxon missionaries led by St. Boniface in 739 made the town a bishopric before heading down the Danube to convert the heathen in even more far-flung lands. Charlemagne, first of the Holy Roman Emperors, arrived at the end of the 8th century and incorporated Regensburg into his burgeoning domain. Regensburg benefited from the fact that the Danube wasn't navigable to the west of it, and thus it was able to control trade as goods traveled between Germany and central Europe.

By the Middle Ages Regensburg had become a political, economic, and intellectual center. For many centuries it was the most important city in southeast Germany, serving as the seat of the Perpetual Imperial Diet from 1663 until 1806, when Napoléon ordered the dismantlement of the Holy Roman Empire.

Today, the ancient and hallowed walls of Regensburg continue to buzz with life. Students from the university fill the restaurants and pubs, and locals do their daily shopping and errand-running in the inner city, where small shops and stores have managed to keep international consumer chains out. Any serious tour of Regensburg includes an unusually large number of places of worship. If your spirits wilt at the thought of inspecting them all, you should at least see the Dom (cathedral), famous for its Domspatzen (boys' choir—the literal translation is "cathedral sparrows").

a good walk

Begin your walk in the very center of Regensburg, on medieval Rathausplatz. At the tourist office you can book a tour of the adjacent **Altes Rathaus** (Old Town Hall) 20 ⚑ and pick up maps and brochures. Head east along Goliathstrasse; turn left on Bruckstrasse to take a short detour down to the bank of the Danube and the **Steinerne Brücke** (Stone Bridge) 21, which was key to the city's rise to medieval trading power. Walk to the bridge's center for an unforgettable view of Regensburg's Old Town center, with the ancient tower, now the **Brückturm Museum** (Bridge Tower Museum) 22, acting as a gate leading to the jumble of cobblestone streets and steeply eaved houses. From the tower follow Residenzstrasse south, and within a few minutes you'll reach Domplatz, dominated by Regensburg's soaring cathedral, **Dom St. Peter** 23. Behind the cathedral square is the quieter Alter Kornmarkt, bordered on three sides by historic churches: the **Alte Kapelle** 24, the adjoining **Karmelitenkirche** 25, and the **Niedermünster** 26. At the northern exit of Alter Kornmarkt is a reminder of Regensburg's Roman past, the **Porta Praetoria** 27, a former gateway to the Roman camp. Other Roman remains can be viewed in Regensburg's city museum, the **Historisches Museum** 28, on Dachauplatz, just south of the Alter Kornmarkt. Regensburg's oldest church, **St. Kassian** 29, is 200 yards west of Dachauplatz and Alter Kornmarkt, at the southern edge of another ancient city square, **Neupfarrplatz** 30, where you'll also find the city's first Protestant church, the Neupfarrkirche. Leave Neupfarrplatz at its southern edge and a short stroll brings you to the great bulk of Regensburg's extraordinary palace,

Schloss Emmeram ㉛. Across from the palace is the church of **St. Emmeram** ㉜. To complete your walk, continue westward along Obermünsterstrasse, turning right into Obere Bachgasse. This street becomes Untere Bachgasse and will take you back within minutes to your starting point, Rathausplatz.

TIMING Regensburg is compact; its Old Town center is about 1 square mi. All of its attractions lie on the south side of the Danube, so you won't have to cross it more than once—and then only to admire the city from the north bank. Try to time your tour so that you arrive at lunchtime at the ancient Historische Wurstküche, a tavern nestling between the river and the bridge. You'll need about two hours or more to explore Schloss Emmeram and St. Emmeram Church. Schedule at least another hour to visit the cathedral.

What to See

㉔ **Alte Kapelle** (Old Chapel). The Carolingian structure was erected in the 9th century. Its dowdy exterior gives little hint of the joyous rococo treasures within—extravagant concoctions of sinuous gilt stucco, rich marble, and giddy frescoes, the whole illuminated by light pouring in from the upper windows. ✉ *Alter Kornmarkt 8* ☎ *No phone* ⊙ *Daily 9–dusk.*

⚑ ⑳ **Altes Rathaus** (Old Town Hall). The picture-book complex of medieval, half-timber buildings, with windows large and small, and flowers in tubs, is one of the best preserved town halls in the country, as well as one of the most historically important. It was here, in the imposing Gothic **Reichssaal** (Imperial Hall), that the Perpetual Imperial Diet met from 1663 to 1806. This parliament of sorts consisted of the emperor, the electors (seven or eight), the princes (about 50), and the burghers, who assembled to discuss and determine the affairs of the far-reaching German lands. The hall is sumptuously appointed with tapestries, flags, and heraldic designs. Note the wood ceiling, built in 1408, and the different elevations for the various estates. The Reichssaal is occasionally used for concerts. The neighboring **Ratsaal** (Council Room) is where the electors met for their consultations. The cellar holds the actual torture chamber of the city; the **Fragstatt** (Questioning Room); and the execution room, called the **Armesünderstübchen** (Poor Sinners' Room). Any prisoner who withstood three degrees of questioning without confessing was considered innocent and released—which tells you something about medieval notions of justice. ✉ *Rathauspl.* ☎ *0941/507–4411* 🎫 *€2.50* ⊙ *Daily 9–4; tours in English May–Sept., Mon.–Sat. at 3:15.*

need a break? Just across the square from the Altes Rathaus is the **Prinzess Confiserie Café** (✉ Rathauspl. 2 ☎ 0941/595–310), Germany's oldest coffeehouse, which first opened its doors to the general public in 1686. The homemade chocolates are highly recommended, as are the rich cakes.

㉒ **Brückturm Museum** (Bridge Tower Museum). With its tiny windows, weathered tiles, and pink plaster, this 17th-century tower stands at the south end of the Steinerne Brücke. The tower displays a host of items relating to the construction and history of the old bridge. It also offers

a gorgeous view of the Regensburg roof landscape. The brooding building, with a massive roof to the left of the Brückturm, is an old salt warehouse that now houses the Salzstadel Wirtshaus, where you can try your first Regensburger sausage. ✉ *Steinerne Brücke* ☎ *0941/565–746* €2 ⏲ *Apr.–Oct., daily 10–5; call ahead to ask about English tours.*

★ 23 **Dom St. Peter** (St. Peter's Cathedral). Regensburg's transcendent cathedral, modeled on the airy, vertical lines of French Gothic architecture, is something of a rarity this far south in Germany. Begun in the 13th century, it stands on the site of a much earlier Carolingian church. Remarkably, the cathedral can hold 6,000 people, three times the population of Regensburg when building began. Construction dragged on for almost 600 years until Ludwig I of Bavaria, then ruler of Regensburg, finally had the towers built. These had to be replaced in the mid-1950s. Behind the Dom is a little workshop where a team of 15 stonecutters is busy full-time during the summer recutting and restoring parts of the cathedral.

Before heading into the Dom, take time to admire the intricate and frothy carvings of its facade. Inside, the glowing 14th-century stained glass in the choir and the exquisitely detailed statues of the archangel Gabriel and the Virgin in the crossing (the intersection of the nave and the transepts) are among the church's outstanding features. ✉ *Dompl.*

☎ 0941/597–1002 🎟 Tour, only in German (for tours in English call ahead), €2.50 ⏲ Cathedral tour May–Oct., weekdays at 10, 11, and 2, Sun. at noon and 2; Nov.–Apr., weekdays at 11, Sun. at noon.

Be sure to visit the **Kreuzgang** (Cloisters), reached via the garden. There you'll find a small octagonal chapel, the Allerheiligenkapelle (All Saint's Chapel), a Romanesque building that is all sturdy grace and massive walls, a work by Italian masons from the mid-12th century. You can barely make out the faded remains of stylized 11th-century frescoes on its ancient walls. The equally ancient shell of St. Stephan's Church, the Alter Dom (Old Cathedral), can also be visited. The cloisters, chapel, and Alter Dom can be seen only on a guided one-hour tour. *🎟 €2.50 ⏲ Tour mid-May–Oct., daily at 10, 11, and 2; Nov.–Mar., weekdays at 11, Sun. at noon; Apr.–mid-May, daily at 11 and 2.*

The **Domschatzmuseum** (Cathedral Museum) contains valuable treasures going back to the 11th century. Some of the vestments and the monstrances, which are fine examples of eight centuries' worth of the goldsmith's trade, are still used during special services. The entrance is in the nave. *✉ Dompl. ☎ 0941/57645 🎟 €1.50 ⏲ Apr.–Oct., Tues.–Sat. 10–5, Sun. noon–5; Dec.–Mar., Fri. and Sat. 10–4, Sun. noon–4.*

need a break?

The restaurant **Haus Heuport** (✉ Dompl. 7 ☎ 0941/599–9297), opposite the entrance of the Dom, is in one of the old and grand private ballrooms of the city. The service is excellent, all dishes taste good, and the tables at the windows have a wonderful view of the Dom. For snack fare, such as sandwiches and salads, head for the bistro area.

★ 28 **Historisches Museum** (Historical Museum). The municipal museum vividly relates the cultural history of Regensburg. It's one of the highlights of the city, both for its unusual and beautiful setting—a former Gothic monastery—and for its wide-ranging collections, from Roman artifacts to Renaissance tapestries and remains from Regensburg's 16th-century Jewish ghetto. The most significant exhibits are the paintings by Albrecht Altdorfer (1480–1538), a native of Regensburg and, along with Cranach, Grünewald, and Dürer, one of the leading painters of the German Renaissance. His work has the same sense of heightened reality found in that of his contemporaries, in which the lessons of Italian painting are used to produce an emotional rather than a rational effect. His paintings would not have seemed out of place among those of 19th-century Romantics. Far from seeing the world around him as essentially hostile, or at least alien, he saw it as something intrinsically beautiful, whether wild or domesticated. Altdorfer made two drawings of the old synagogue of Regensburg, priceless documents that are on exhibit here. *✉ Dachaupl. 2–4 ☎ 0941/507–2448 🎟 €2.20 ⏲ Tues.–Sun. 10–4.*

25 **Karmelitenkirche** (Church of the Carmelites). This lovely church, in the baroque style from crypt to cupola, stands next to the Alte Kapelle. It has a finely decorated facade designed by the 17th-century Italian master Carlo Lurago. *✉ Alter Kornmarkt.*

(30) **Neupfarrplatz.** This oversize open square was once a Jewish ghetto. The Regensburg Jews had lived in fair harmony with the town's citizens, but hard economic times and superstition led to their eviction by decree in 1519. While the synagogue was being torn down, one worker survived a very bad fall. A church was promptly built to celebrate the miracle and before long a pilgrimage began. The **Neupfarrkirche** (New Parish Church) was built as well to accommodate the flow of pilgrims. During the Reformation, the Parish Church was given to the Protestants, hence its bare-bones interior. In the late 1990s, excavation work (for the power company) on the square uncovered well-kept cellars, and to the west of the church, the old synagogue, including the foundations of its Romanesque predecessor. Archaeologists salvaged the few items they could from the old stones (including a stash of 684 gold coins) and, not knowing what to do with the sea of foundations, ultimately carefully reburied them. Recovered items were carefully restored and are on exhibit in the Historisches Museum. Only one small underground area to the south of the church, the **Documen,** accommodates viewing of the foundations. In a former cellar, surrounded by the original walls, visitors can watch a short video reconstructing life in the old Jewish ghetto. Over the old synagogue, the Israeli artist Dani Karavan designed a stylized plaza where people can sit and meet. Call the educational institution VHS for a tour of the Document (reservations are requested). For spontaneous visits, tickets are available at Tabak Götz on the western side of the square, at Neupfarrplatz 3. ✉ *Neupfarrpl.* ☎ *0941/507–2433 for tours led by VHS* 🌐 *www.vhs-regensburg.de* 🎫 *Document €2.50* 🕓 *Church daily 9–dusk, document tour Thurs.–Sat. at 2:30.*

need a break?

Dampfnudel is a kind of sweet yeast-dough dumpling that is tasty and filling. The best in Bavaria can be had at **Dampfnudel Uli** (✉ Watmarkt 4 🕓 Tues.–Fri. 10–6 and Sat. 10–3), a little establishment in a former chapel. The decoration is incredibly eclectic, from Bavarian crafts to a portrait of Ronald Reagan inscribed "To Uli Deutzer, with best wishes, Ronald Reagan."

(26) **Niedermünster.** This 12th-century building with a baroque interior was originally the church of a community of nuns, all of them from noble families. For a quarter hour beginning at 12:05 PM daily, concerts are given by students of the church music school. ✉ *Alter Kornmarkt 5* ☎ *0941/597–1002.*

(27) **Porta Praetoria.** The rough-hewn former gate to the old Roman camp, built in AD 179, is one of the most interesting relics of Roman times in Regensburg. Look through the grille on its east side to see a section of the original Roman street, about 10 feet below today's street level. ✉ *North side of Alter Kornmarkt.*

(32) **St. Emmeram.** The family church of the princely Thurn und Taxis family stands across from their ancestral palace, the Schloss Emmeram. The foundations of the church date to the 7th and 8th centuries. A richly decorated baroque interior was added in 1730 by the Asam brothers. St. Emmeram contains the graves of the 7th-century martyred Regensburg

bishop Emmeram and the 10th-century saint Wolfgang. ✉ *Emmeramspl. 3* ☎ *0941/51030* ⏲ *Mon.–Thurs. and Sat. 10–4:30, Fri. 1–4:30, Sun. noon–4:30.*

29 **St. Kassian.** Regensburg's oldest church was founded in the 8th century. Don't be fooled by its dour exterior; inside, it's filled with delicate rococo decoration. ✉ *St. Kassianpl. 1* ☎ *No phone* ⏲ *Daily 9–5:30.*

31 **Schloss Emmeram** (Emmeram Palace). Formerly a Benedictine monastery, this is the ancestral home of the princely Thurn und Taxis family, who made their fame and fortune after being granted the right to carry official and private mail throughout the empire and Spain by Emperor Maximilian I (1493–1519) and by Philip I, king of Spain, who ruled during the same period. Their business extended over the centuries into the Low Countries (Holland, Belgium, and Luxembourg), Hungary, and Italy. The little horn that still symbolizes the post office in several European countries comes from the Thurn und Taxis coat of arms. For a while Schloss Emmeram was heavily featured in the gossip columns thanks to the wild parties and somewhat extravagant lifestyle of the young dowager Princess Gloria von Thurn und Taxis. After the death of her husband, Prince Johannes, in 1990, she had to auction off belongings in order to pay inheritance taxes. Ultimately a deal was cut, allowing her to keep many of the palace's treasures as long they were put on display.

The **Thurn und Taxis Palace,** with its splendid ballroom and throne room, allows you to witness the eloquent setting of courtly life in the 19th century. A visit usually includes the fine **Kreuzgang** (cloister) of the former Benedictine abbey of St. Emmeram. The items in the **Thurn und Taxis Museum,** which is part of the Bavarian National Museum in Munich, have been carefully selected for their fine craftsmanship—be it dueling pistols, a plain marshal's staff, a boudoir, or a snuffbox. The palace's **Marstallmuseum** (former royal stables) holds the family's coaches and carriages as well as related items. ☎ *0941/504–8133* 🎫 *Palace and cloisters €8; Marstallmuseum €4.50; Marstall plus Thurn und Taxis Museum €4.50; Thurn und Taxis Museum alone €3.50* ⏲ *Weekdays 11–5, weekends 10–5; Marstallmuseum closed Nov.–Mar.*

★ 21 **Steinerne Brücke** (Stone Bridge). This impressive old bridge resting on massive pontoons is Regensburg's most celebrated sight. It was completed in 1146 and was rightfully considered a miraculous piece of engineering at the time. As the only crossing point over the Danube for miles, it effectively cemented Regensburg's control over trade. The significance of the little statue on the bridge is a mystery, but the figure seems to be a witness to the legendary rivalry between the master builders of the bridge and those of the Dom.

Where to Stay & Eat

¢–$ ✕ **Café Felix.** A modern bi-level café and bar, Felix offers everything from sandwiches to steaks and buzzes with activity from breakfast until the early hours. Light from an arty chandelier and torch-like fixtures bounces off the many large framed mirrors. The crowd tends to be young. ✉ *Fröhliche-Türkenstr. 6* ☎ *0941/59059* 💳 *No credit cards.*

¢–$ ✕ **Leerer Beutel.** Excellent international cuisine—from antipasti to solid pork roast—is served in a pleasant vaulted room supported by massive rough-hewn beams. The restaurant is in a huge warehouse that's also a venue for concerts, exhibitions, and film screenings, making it a good place to start or end an evening. ✉ *Bertoldstr. 9* ☎ *0941/58997* ▭ *AE, DC, MC, V.*

¢–$ ✕ **Lokanta.** With a mixed crowd at the tables and a pastel-orange color scheme, this lively restaurant serves simple and excellent Kurdish-Turkish dishes. A few plates of the *amuse-gueules* (cocktail snacks) will be just the thing before or after a concert. ✉ *Wollwirkerg.* ☎ *0941/53321* ▭ *No credit cards.*

¢ ✕ **Historische Wurstküche.** Succulent Regensburger sausages—the best in town—are prepared right before your eyes on an open beech-wood charcoal grill in this tiny kitchen. If you eat them inside in the tiny dining room, you'll have to squeeze past the cook to get there. Inside are plaques recording the levels the river reached in the various floods that have doused the restaurant's kitchen in the past 100 years. ✉ *Thundorferstr. 3* ☎ *0941/466–210* ▭ *No credit cards.*

$$ ✕ **Hotel-Restaurant Bischofshof am Dom.** This is one of Germany's most historic hostelries, a former bishop's palace where you can sleep in an apartment that includes part of a Roman gateway. Other chambers are only slightly less historic, and some have seen emperors and princes as guests. The hotel's restaurant (¢–$) serves fine regional cuisine (including the famous Regensburger sausages) at reasonable prices. The beer comes from a brewery founded in 1649. ✉ *Krauterermarkt 3, D–93047* ☎ *0941/58460* 🖷 *0941/584–6146* 🌐 *www.bischofshof-am-dom.de* *55 rooms, 3 suites* *Restaurant, cable TV, bar, beer garden, some pets allowed (fee), parking (fee); no a/c* ▭ *AE, DC, MC, V.*

$–$$ ✕ **Hôtel Orphée.** This protected monument hotel offers a special experience with theme rooms. The first floor is devoted to the upcoming bourgeoisie of the 19th century (the Sigmund Freud room, for example); the second floor gives you a feel for how the aristocracy lived. The reception and breakfast room are in the dark wood-panel Orphée Restaurant on the next street. The menu is mostly French ($$–$$$), with a selection of crepes, salads, and heavier meat dishes. ✉ *Untere Bachgasse, D–93047* ☎ *0941/596–020* 🖷 *0941/5960–2222* 🌐 *www.hotel-orphee.de* *15 rooms* *Restaurant, bar, some pets allowed (fee); no a/c, no TV in some rooms* ▭ *MC, V.*

$$ **Parkhotel Maximilian.** This handsome 18th-century palace hotel is between the railway station and the Old Town. Rooms are well-appointed, generous in size, and luxurious. Breakfast, meals, or drinks can be had on a pretty terrace in the back of the hotel. ✉ *Maximilianstr. 28, D–93047* ☎ *0941/56850* 🖷 *0941/52942* 🌐 *www.maximilian-hotel.de* *52 rooms, 5 suites* *Café, cable TV with movies, Wi-Fi, 2 bars, recreation room, some pets allowed (fee), parking (fee), no-smoking rooms; no a/c* ▭ *AE, DC, MC, V.*

$–$$ **Held.** The Held hotel offers a range of facilities at reasonable prices in the small village of Irl. To get here, follow Route 8 east from Regensburg for a few miles and, before the Autobahn overpass, turn right to the village. The rooms are basic. Enjoy regional or international cuisine in the cozy restaurant or on the patio. The meats comes from their own butchery. ✉ *Irl 11, D–93055* ☎ *09401/9420* 📠 *09401/7682* 🌐 *www.hotel-held.de* *80 rooms* *Restaurant, minibars, cable TV, Wi-Fi, indoor pool, sauna, steam room, bowling, bar, parking (fee), no smoking rooms, some pets allowed (fee)* 💳 *AE, MC, V* *BP.*

$–$$ **Kaiserhof am Dom.** Renaissance windows punctuate the green facade of this historic city mansion. The rooms are 20th-century modern, with perks such as under-floor heating and cable TV. Try for one with a view of the cathedral, which stands directly across the street. Breakfast is served beneath the high-vaulted ceiling of the former 14th-century chapel. ✉ *Kramgasse 10–12, D–93047* ☎ *0941/585–350* 📠 *0941/585–3595* 🌐 *www.kaiserhof-am-dom.de* *30 rooms* *Café, cable TV, some pets allowed (fee); no a/c* 💳 *AE, DC, MC, V.*

$ **Hotel Münchner Hof.** In this little hotel, in a block near the Neupfarrkirche, the rooms are big and tastefully decorated. In some, the original arches of the ancient building are visible. The restaurant is quiet and comfortable, serving Bavarian specialties and good Munich beer. The bottom line: you get top service at a good price, and Regensburg is at your feet. ✉ *Tändlergasse 9, D–93047* ☎ *0941/58440* 📠 *0941/561–709* 🌐 *www.muenchner-hof.de* *53 rooms* *Restaurant, cable TV, Wi-Fi, some pets allowed (fee), no-smoking rooms; no a/c* 💳 *AE, DC, MC, V.*

¢ **Am Peterstor.** The clean and basic rooms of this popular hotel in the heart of the Old Town represent unbeatable value. The many local eateries, including the excellent Café Felix a few doors away, more than compensate for the lack of an in-house restaurant. ✉ *Fröhliche-Türken-Str. 12, D–93047* ☎ *0941/54545* 📠 *0941/54542* 🌐 *www.hotel-am-peterstor.de* *36 rooms* *No a/c, no room phones* 💳 *MC, V.*

Shopping

Regensburg is a shopper's paradise. The winding alleyways of the Altstadt are packed with small boutiques, ateliers, jewelers, and other small shops offering a vast array of arts and crafts. You may also want to visit the daily market (Monday through Saturday, 9–4) at the Neupfarrplatz, where you can buy regional specialities such as *Radi* (juicy radish roots), which local people love to wash down with a glass of wheat beer.

Nightlife & the Arts

Regensburg offers a range of musical experiences, though none so moving as a performance by the famous boys' choir, the Regensburger Domspatzen, at the cathedral. The best-sung mass is held on Sunday at 9 AM. It can be a remarkable experience, and it's worth scheduling your visit to the city to hear the choir. If you're around in summer, look out for the Citizens Festival (Bürgerfest) and the Bavarian Jazz Festival (Bayreisches Jazzfest) (www.bayernjazz.de) in July, both in the Old Town.

The kind of friendly, mixed nightlife that has become hard to find in some cities is alive and well in this small university city in the many *Kneipen,* bar-cum-pub-cum-bistros or -restaurants, such as the Leerer Beutel. It's good to ask around for what happens to be hopping at any given time. The club **Scala** (✉ Gesandtenstr. 6 ☎ 0941/52293) has three bars and some of the best dance music in town.

off the beaten path

★ **WALHALLA** – Walhalla (11 km [7 mi] east of Regensburg) is an excursion from Regensburg you won't want to miss, especially if you have an interest in the wilder expressions of 19th-century German nationalism. Danube River cruises (*see* details on river cruises in the A to Z section at the end of this chapter) stop here for the town's incongruous Greek-style Doric temple. To get to the temple from the river, you'll have to climb 358 marble steps. There is, however, a parking lot near the top. To drive to it, take the Danube Valley country road (unnumbered) east from Regensburg 8 km (5 mi) to Donaustauf. The Walhalla temple is 1 km (½ mi) outside the village and well signposted. Walhalla—a name resonant with Nordic mythology—was where the god Odin received the souls of dead heroes. This monumental temple was erected in 1840 for Ludwig I to honor important German personages through the ages. In the neoclassic style then prevailing, it's actually a copy of the Parthenon, in Athens. Even if you consider the building more a monument to kitsch, it remains a supremely well-built structure, and its expanses of costly marble are evidence of both the financial resources and the craftsmanship at Ludwig's command. If you're around in late October, look out for the free spectacular classical music firework display held between the Walhalla and the Danube.

4

STIFTSKIRCHE STS. GEORG UND MARTIN – In Weltenburg (25 km [15 mi] southwest of Regensburg) you'll find the great Stiftskirche Sts. Georg und Martin (Abbey Church of Sts. George and Martin), on the bank of the Danube River. The most dramatic approach to the abbey is by boat from Kelheim, 10 km (6 mi) downstream. On the stunning ride the boat winds between towering limestone cliffs that rise straight up from the tree-lined riverbanks. The abbey, constructed between 1716 and 1718, is commonly regarded as the masterpiece of the brothers Cosmas Damian and Egid Quirin Asam, two leading baroque architects and decorators of Bavaria. Their extraordinary composition of painted figures whirling on the ceiling, lavish and brilliantly polished marble, highly wrought statuary, and stucco figures dancing in rhythmic arabesques across the curving walls is the epitome of Bavarian baroque. Note especially the bronze equestrian statue of St. George above the high altar, reaching down imperiously with his flamelike, twisted gilt sword to dispatch the winged dragon at his feet. ⏲ *Daily 9–dusk.*

en route

Halfway between Regensburg and Passau are the village of Metten and the town of Deggendorf. Metten's **Benedictine monastery,** founded in the 9th century by Charlemagne, is an outstanding example of baroque art. The 18th-century library has a collection of 160,000 books whose gilt leather spines are complemented by the heroic splendor of their surroundings—Herculean figures support the frescoed, vaulted ceiling, and allegorical paintings and fine stuccowork identify different categories of books. In the church is Cosmas Damian Asam's altarpiece *Lucifer Destroyed by St. Michael*; created around 1720, it has vivid coloring and a swirling composition that are typical of the time. ✉ *7 km (4 ½ mi) west of Deggendorf* ☎ *0991/91080* 🎫 *€2* ⏲ *Guided tours daily at 10 and 3.*

Deggendorf was once on the banks of the Danube, but flooding forced its inhabitants to higher ground in the 13th century. You can ★ still see a 30-yard stretch of protective wall. The **Heilig Grabkirche** (Church of the Holy Sepulchre; ✉ Michael-Fischer-Pl.) was originally built as a Gothic basilica in the 14th century. Its lofty tower—regarded as the finest baroque church tower in southern Germany—was added 400 years later.

Exhibits at the **Handwerksmuseum** (Museum of Trades and Crafts; ✉ *Maria-Ward-Pl. 1* ☎ *0991/296–0555* 🎫 *€2* ⏲ *Tues.–Sat. 10–4, Sun. 10–5) focus on typical regional handicrafts such as glassmaking and wood carving.*

Passau

137 km (86 mi) southeast of Regensburg, 179 km (111 mi) northeast of Munich.

Flanking the borders of Austria and the Czech Republic, Passau boasts a history dating back over 2,500 years. Originally settled by the Celts, then by the Romans, Passau later passed into the possession of prince-bishops whose domains stretched into present-day Hungary. At its height, the Passau episcopate was the largest in the entire Holy Roman Empire.

Passau's location is truly unique. Nowhere else in the world do three rivers—the Ilz from the north, the Danube from the west, and the Inn from the south—meet. Wedged between the Inn and the Danube, the Old Town is a maze of narrow cobble-stone streets lined with beautifully preserved burgher and patrician houses and riddled with churches. Many streets have been closed to traffic, giving the town an almost Venetian feel and making it a pedestrian's paradise.

For 45 post-war years Passau was a backwater in a "lost" corner of West Germany. The collapse of the Iron Curtain opened nearby frontiers, putting the historic city back on the central European map. Despite its small size, Passau has a stately, grande-dame atmosphere.

a good walk

Begin your walk at the tourist office on the west side of Rathausplatz, where you can pick up brochures and maps. Passau's 14th-century **Rathaus** 33 ⚑ forms one side of the square and faces the Danube and its landing stages. Before leaving the square in the direction of the city center, stop by the **Glasmuseum** 34, in the Hotel Wilder Mann. Next, turn right at the end of the short street, Schrottgasse, and you're on Residenzplatz, dominated by the baroque bulk of the Neue Bischöfliche Residenz, where religious treasures from the city's illustrious episcopal past are housed in the **Domschatz- und Diözesanmuseum** 35. A flight of steps leading up from the Domschatz- und Diözesan Museum brings you to the **Domplatz** 36 and Passau's towering **Dom** 37. Descend the steps in the square's southwest corner and you'll arrive at the Inn River. A 15-minute stroll east will take you to the gardens of the **Dreiflusseck** 38, the confluence of the Danube, Inn, and Ilz rivers. Continue along the southern bank of the Danube upstream to the Luitpoldbrücke; cross this bridge to reach the northern bank, where a steep path leads you to the **Veste Oberhaus** 39; you can also catch a bus to this fortress from Rathausplatz. Now make your way back to Rathausplatz to explore Passau's attractive pedestrian shopping zone (an area of eight streets). If time permits and you're in museum mode, walk south along the Heilig Geist Gasse and cross the Inn River by its pedestrian bridge to the outstanding **Römermuseum Kastell Boiotro** 40, which holds remnants of Passau's Roman past.

TIMING Passau can be toured leisurely in the course of one day. Try to visit the Dom at noon to hear a recital on its great organ, the world's largest. Early morning is the best time to catch the light falling from the east on the old town walls and the confluence of the three rivers. Passau shrouded in the dank river fogs of winter rivals even Venice for its brooding atmosphere.

What to See

37 **Dom** (St. Stephan's Cathedral). Passau's mighty cathedral rises majestically on the highest point of the earliest-settled part of the city. A baptismal church stood here in the 6th century. Two hundred years later, when Passau became a bishop's seat, the first basilica was built. It was dedicated to St. Stephan and became the original mother church of St. Stephan's Cathedral in Vienna. A fire reduced the medieval basilica to smoking ruins in 1662; it was then rebuilt by Italian master architect Carlo Lurago. What you see today is the largest baroque basilica north of the Alps, complete with an octagonal dome and flanking towers. Little in its marble- and stucco-encrusted interior reminds you of Germany, and much proclaims the exuberance of Rome. Beneath the dome is the largest church organ assembly in the world. Built between 1924 and 1928 and enlarged in 1979–80, it claims no fewer than 17,774 pipes and 233 stops. The church also houses the most powerful bell chimes in southern Germany. ✉ *Dompl.* 🎫 *Free; concerts midday €3, evening €5* ⏲ *May–Oct., daily 8–11 and 12:30–6; Nov.–Apr., daily 8–dusk. Tours May–Oct. weekdays 12:30, assemble at cathedral's front right-hand aisle; Nov.–Apr., Mon.–Sat. noon, assemble under the cathedral organ; concerts May–Oct. and Dec. 20–25, Mon.–Wed. and Fri. noon, Thurs. noon and 7:30 PM.*

36 **Domplatz** (Cathedral Square). This large square in front of the Dom is bordered by sturdy 17th- and 18th-century buildings, including the **Alte Residenz,** the former bishop's palace and now a courthouse. The fine statue depicts Bavarian king Maximilian Joseph I.

35 **Domschatz- und Diözesanmuseum** (Cathedral Treasury and Diocesan Museum). The cathedral museum houses one of Bavaria's largest collections of religious treasures, the legacy of Passau's rich episcopal history. The museum is part of the **Neue Residenz,** which has a stately baroque

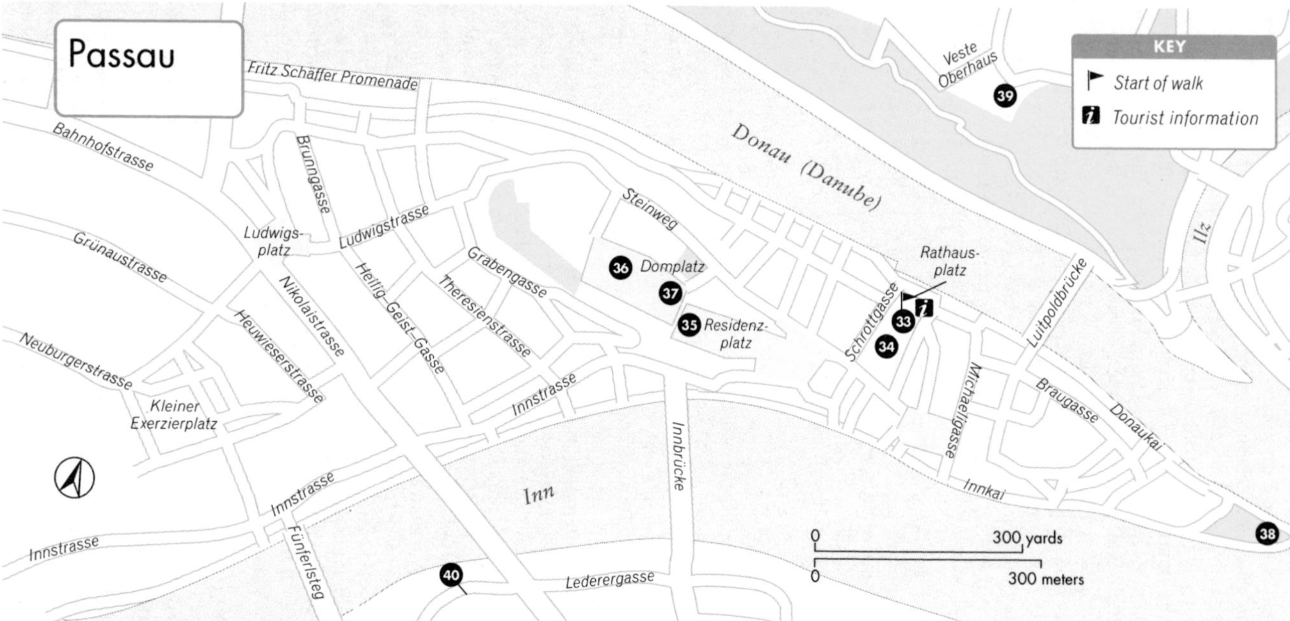
Passau
KEY
Start of walk
Tourist information
Fritz Schäffer Promenade
Bahnhofstrasse
Brunngasse
Ludwigs-platz
Ludwigstrasse
Grünaustrasse
Nikolaistrasse
Heilig-Geist-Gasse
Heuwieserstrasse
Neuburgerstrasse
Kleiner Exerzierplatz
Grabengasse
Theresienstrasse
Innstrasse
Steinweg
Domplatz
Residenz-platz
Donau (Danube)
Veste Oberhaus
Ilz
Rathaus-platz
Schrottgasse
Luitpoldbrücke
Michaeligasse
Braugasse
Donaukai
Innkai
Innbrücke
Inn
Fünferlsteg
Lederergasse
0
300 yards
300 meters
33
34
35
36
37
38
39
40

entrance opening onto a magnificent staircase—a scintillating study in marble, fresco, and stucco. ✉ *Residenzpl.* 🎫 *€1.50* ⏲ *Apr.–Oct., Mon.–Sat. 10–4.*

38 **Dreiflusseck** (Junction of the Three Rivers). At this tongue of land at the eastern extremity of Passau, the Danube, Inn, and tiny Ilz rivers join together in an embrace that, thanks to a phenomenon of nature, leaves each of them with a distinct identity until they all flow out of Passau's grip and into Austria, where their waters merge into the Danube, bound for the Black Sea. For the best perspective, climb to the Veste Oberhaus to see how the Inn's chalky green water, typical of a mountain river, slowly gives way to the darker hues of the Danube, more brown than blue, and how the almost black Ilz adds its small contribution. It's the end of the journey for the Inn—which flows here from the mountains of Switzerland—and the much shorter Ilz, which rises in the Bavarian Forest.

34 **Glasmuseum** (Glass Museum). The world's most comprehensive collection of Bohemian glass is housed in the lovely Hotel Wilder Mann. The history of central Europe's glassmaking is captured in 30,000 items, from baroque to art deco, spread over 35 rooms. ✉ *Am Rathauspl.* ☎ *0851/35071* 🎫 *€5* ⏲ *Daily 1–5.*

33 **Rathaus.** Passau's 14th-century city hall sits like a Venetian merchant's house on a small square fronting the Danube. It was the home of a wealthy German merchant before being declared the seat of city government after a 1298 uprising. Two assembly rooms have wall paintings depicting scenes from local history and lore, including the (fictional) arrival in the city of Siegfried's fair Kriemhild, from the Nibelungen fable. The Rathaus tower has Bavaria's largest glockenspiel, which plays daily at 10:30, 2, and 7:25, with an additional performance at 3:30 on Saturday. ✉ *Rathauspl.* ☎ *0851/3960* 🎫 *€1.50* ⏲ *Apr.–Oct. and late Dec.–early Jan., daily 10–4.*

40 **Römermuseum Kastell Boiotro** (Roman Museum). A stout fortress with five defense towers and walls more than 12 feet thick came to light as archaeologists excavated the site of a 17th-century pilgrimage church on a hill known as Mariahilfberg, on the south bank of the Inn. The Roman citadel Boiotro was discovered along with a Roman well, its water still plentiful and fresh. Pottery, lead figures, and other artifacts from the area are housed in this museum at the edge of the site. ✉ *Ledererg. 43* ☎ *0851/34769* 🎫 *€2* ⏲ *Mar.–May and Sept.–Nov., Tues.–Sun. 10–noon and 2–4; June–Aug., Tues.–Sun. 10–noon and 1–4.*

39 **Veste Oberhaus** (Upper House Stronghold). The powerful fortress and summer castle commissioned by Bishop Ulrich II in 1219 looks over Passau from an impregnable site on the other side of the river, opposite the Rathaus. Today the Veste Oberhaus is Passau's most important museum, containing exhibits that illustrate the city's 2,000-year history. From the terrace of its café-restaurant (open Easter–October), there's a magnificent view of Passau and the convergence of the three rivers. ✉ *Oberhausleitenstiege* ☎ *0851/493–3512* 🎫 *Museum €5* ⏲ *Mar.–Oct., weekdays 9–5, weekends 10–6* ☞ *Bus from Rathauspl. to museum Apr.–Oct. every ½ hr 10:30–5.*

Where to Stay & Eat

$–$$ ✕ **Gasthaus zur blauen Donau.** In 2004 Passau's esteemed chef Richard Kerscher turned this old house with thick walls and recessed windows into a simple but stylish restaurant. The dining room has a commanding view of the Danube. His delicacies are all based on traditional German recipes, and from a perch at the bar you can watch the kitchen crew at work. ✉ *Höllgasse 14* ☎ *0851/490–8660* ▭ *MC, V.*

¢–$$ ✕ **Blauer Bock.** This is one of Passau's oldest houses (first mentioned in city records in 1257) and has been welcoming travelers since 1875. The Danube flows by the tavern windows, and in summer you can watch the river traffic from a beer garden. The food is traditional; you'll find pork and potatoes in every variety. The tavern also offers accommodation in tastefully fitted rooms. ✉ *Höllg. 20* ☎ *0851/34637* ▭ *MC, V.*

¢–$$ ✕ **Peschl Terrasse.** The beer you sip on the high, sunny terrace overlooking the Danube is brought fresh from the Old Town brewery below, which, along with this traditional Bavarian restaurant, has been in the same family since 1855. ✉ *Rossstränke 4* ☎ *0851/2489* ▭ *DC, MC, V.*

$$ **Hotel König.** Though built in 1984, the König blends successfully with the graceful Italian-style buildings alongside the elegant Danube waterfront. Rooms are large and airy; most have a fine view of the river. ✉ *Untere Donaulände 1, D–94032* ☎ *0851/3850* 🖷 *0851/385–460* 🌐 *www.hotel-koenig.de* *61 rooms* *Cable TV, Wi-Fi, sauna, steam room, bar, meeting room; no a/c* ▭ *AE, DC, MC, V.*

★ $–$$ **Hotel Wilder Mann.** Passau's most historic hotel dates from the 11th century and shares prominence with the ancient city hall on the waterfront market square. Empress Elizabeth of Austria and American astronaut Neil Armstrong have been among its guests. On beds of carved oak you'll sleep beneath chandeliers and richly stuccoed ceilings. For sheer indulgence, ask for either the King Ludwig or Sissi (Empress Elisabeth) suite. The esteemed Glasmuseum is within the hotel. ✉ *Am Rathauspl. 1, D–94032* ☎ *0851/35071* 🖷 *0851/31712* 🌐 *www.rotel-tours.de,* *48 rooms, 5 suites* *Restaurant, cable TV; no a/c* ▭ *AE, DC, MC, V.*

$–$$ **Schloss Ort.** This 13th-century castle's large rooms have views of the Inn River, which flows beneath the hotel's stout walls. The rooms are decorated in a variety of styles with old-fashioned four-poster beds or modern wrought-iron details. The restaurant is closed in winter and Monday, but the kitchen will always oblige hungry hotel guests. In summer the garden terrace is a delightful place to eat and watch the river. ✉ *Ort 11, D–94032* ☎ *0851/34072* 🖷 *0851/31817* 🌐 *www.schlosshotel-passau.de* *18 rooms* *Restaurant, cable TV; no a/c* ▭ *D, MC, V.*

¢ **Rotel Inn.** "Rotels" are usually hotels on wheels, an idea developed by a local entrepreneur to accommodate tour groups in North Africa and Asia. The first permanent Rotel Inn is on the banks of the Danube in central Passau and resembles an ocean liner. Its rooms are truly shipshape—hardly any wider than the bed inside—but they're clean, decorated in a pop-art style, and amazingly cheap. The building's unique design—a red, white, and blue facade with flowing roof lines—has actually been patented. It's definitely for young travelers but also fun for families. ✉ *Am Hauptbahnhof/Donauufer, D–94032* ☎ *0851/95160*

0851/951–610 www.rotel-tours.de 100 rooms No a/c No credit cards Closed Oct.–late Apr.

Sports & the Outdoors

If you're looking for sports equipment, **Big Point** (Neuburgerstr. 108, 94032 Passau 0851/720–2450) is a well-stocked chain store, which sells and rents a wide selection of sports clothes and equipment, including ski gear.

CYCLING Cyclists can choose between eight long-distance paths along the rivers Danube (as far as Vienna) and Inn (tracing the river to its source in the Swiss Engadine). Bikes are permitted on most Danube boats and local trains, so you can cover part of the journey by river or rail. **Fahrrad-Laden Passau** (Rosstränke 12, 94032 Passau 0851/722–26) is the best address in Passau for renting and repairing bicycles.

4

Nightlife & the Arts

Passau is the cultural center of Lower Bavaria. Its **Europäische Wochen** (European Weeks) festival—featuring everything from opera to pantomime—is a major event on the European music calendar. Now into its 53rd year, the festival runs from June to July. For program details and reservations, write the **Kartenzentrale der Europäischen Wochen Passau** (Dr.-Hans-Kapfinger-Str. 22, D–94032 Passau 0851/560–960 www.europaeische-wochen-passau.de).

off the beaten path

MT. DREISESSEL – You can't get much more off the beaten track than in the remote corner of the country north of Passau, where the German frontier bobs and weaves along the Czech Republic and Austria. It's possible to walk in and out of a virtually forgotten corner of the Czech Republic—a feat that was possible even when the border was guarded everywhere else by heavily armed soldiers—in the area where the border cuts across the summit of Mt. Dreisessel, west of Altreichenau. *Dreisessel* means "three armchairs," an apt description of the summit and its boulders, which are shaped like the furniture of a giant's castle. If you're driving to the Dreisessel, take B–12 to Philippsreut, just before the frontier, and then follow the well-marked country road. The mountain is about 67 km (42 mi) from Passau. Several bus operators in Passau and surrounding villages offer tours. There are no visitor facilities within the forest.

FRANCONIA & THE GERMAN DANUBE A TO Z

To research prices, get advice from other travelers, and book travel arrangements, visit www.fodors.com.

AIRPORTS

The international airports near Franconia are at Frankfurt and Munich. Nürnberg and Bayreuth have regional airports; there are frequent flights between Frankfurt and Nürnberg. If there's fog in Munich, the Nürnberg airport serves as backup.

BIKE TRAVEL

Cycling along the Danube is a popular activity, and there are usually paths on both sides of it. Ships let you take a bicycle along for a small fee (usually €2), so you can enjoy the scenery one-way and get exercise on the other.

BOAT TRAVEL

There are about 15 different lines that operate cruises on the Main River and the Main-Donau Canal in summer. In Bamberg, Personenschiffahrt Kropf boats leave daily from March through October beginning at 11 AM for short cruises on the Regnitz River and the Main-Donau Canal; the cost is €6.50.

In Regensburg all boats depart from the Steinerne Brücke. The most popular excursions are boat trips to Ludwig I's imposing Greek-style Doric temple of Walhalla. There are daily sailings to Walhalla from Easter through October. The round-trip costs €8 and takes three hours. Another very popular trip is to the monastery of Weltenburg, which involves a boat change at Kelheim. The trip takes about three hours one way.

In Passau cruises on the three rivers begin and end at the Danube jetties on Fritz-Schäffer Promenade. Ludwig Wurm has a range of small cruise-ship services upriver between Passau and Regensburg, taking in Deggendorf, Metten, Straubing, and Walhalla. A two-hour Danube cruise aboard the *Sissi* costs €9; cruises run daily at 11:15 and 2:45 from early May to the end of October. DDSG offers two-day cruises from Passau to Vienna for around €130 per person one-way, as well as Danube cruise connections via Budapest all the way to the Black Sea.

Personenschiffahrt Kropf ✉ Kapuzinerstr. 5, Bamberg ☎ 0951/26679. **Personenschiffahrt Klinger** ✉ Thundorfstr. 1, D–93047 Regensburg ☎ 0941/55359. **DDSG** ✉ Im Ort 14a, D–94032 Passau ☎ 0851/33035 🌐 www.ddsg-blue-danube.at. **Ludwig Wurm** ✉ Donaustr. 71, D–94342 Irlbach ☎ 09424/1341.

CAR TRAVEL

Franconia is served by five main autobahns: A–7 from Hamburg, A–3 from Köln and Frankfurt, A–81 from Stuttgart, A–6 from Heilbronn, and A–9 from Munich. Nürnberg is 167 km (104 mi) north of Munich and 222 km (138 mi) southeast of Frankfurt. Regensburg and Passau are reached on the A–3 from Nürnberg.

Some nearby scenic driving includes the eastern section of the Burgenstrasse (Castle Road), running from Heidelberg to Nürnberg; the Bocksbeutel Strasse (Franconian Wine Road), which follows the course of the Main River from Zeil am Main along the wine-growing slopes of the valley to Aschaffenburg; and the Strasse der Kaiser und Könige (Emperors' and Kings' Road), leading from Frankfurt to Vienna through Franconia via Aschaffenburg, Würzburg, and Nürnberg.

EMERGENCIES

Police & Ambulance ☎ 110. **Fire and emergency medical aid** ☎ 112.

TOURS

In Bamberg, guided walking tours set out from the tourist- information office April–October, Monday–Saturday at 10:30 and 2 and Sunday at 11; November and December, Monday–Saturday at 2 and Sunday at 11; and January–March, Monday–Saturday at 2. The cost is €5. Bayreuth also offers walking tours beginning at Leopoldplatz at 10:30 daily from May to October. They cost €4.50.

In Nürnberg, English-language bus tours of the city are conducted April–October and December, daily at 9:30, starting at the Mauthalle, Hallplatz 2. The 2½-hour tour costs €11. For more information, call ☎ 0911/202–2910. An English-language tour on foot through the Old Town is conducted daily May–October at 2:30; it departs from the tourist-information office on Hauptmarkt. The tour costs €7.50 (plus entrance to the Kaiserburg €4.50). City tours are also conducted in brightly painted trolley buses April–October, daily at 45-minute intervals beginning at 10 at the Schöner Brunnen; November–March, they run weekends only. Tours are in German unless at least five participants request English. The cost is €5. For more information call the Nuremberg tourist office.

In Regensburg English-language guided walking tours are conducted May–September, Wednesday and Saturday at 1:30. They cost €6 and begin at the tourist office.

The Passau tourist office leads tours from April through October. There are two tours (at 10:30 and 2:30) on weekdays and one (at 2:30) on weekends. Tours start at the Maximilian Joseph statue in the Domplatz (Cathedral Square) and last one hour.

TRAIN TRAVEL

Regular InterCity services connect Nürnberg and Regensburg with Frankfurt and other major German cities. Trains run hourly from Frankfurt to Munich, with a stop at Nürnberg. The trip takes about three hours to Munich, two hours to Nürnberg. There are hourly trains from Munich direct to Regensburg.

Nürnberg is a stop on the high-speed InterCity Express north–south routes, and there are hourly trains from Munich direct to Nürnberg. Some InterCity trains stop in Bamberg, which is most speedily reached from Munich. Local trains from Nürnberg connect with Bayreuth and areas of southern Franconia. Regensburg and Passau are on the EC line from Nürnberg to Vienna.

VISITOR INFORMATION

The principal regional tourist office for Franconia is Fremdenverkehrsverband Franken e.V. For information on resorts and snow conditions, call the Tourist-Information Fichtelgebirge.

Franconia Tourist Board ✉ Tourismusverband Franken e.V., Fürtherstr. 21, D-90429 Nürnberg ☎ 0911/941-510. **Bamberg** ✉ Fremdenverkehrsamt, Geyerswörthstr. 3, D-96047 ☎ 0951/297-6200 ⊕ www.bamberg.de/tourismus. **Bayreuth** ✉ Fremdenverkehrsverein, Luitpoldpl. 9, D-95444 ☎ 0921/88588 🖷 0921/88555 ⊕ www.bayreuth.

de. **Coburg** ✉ Fremdenverkehrs- und Kongressbetrieb, Herrng. 4, D-96450 ☎ 09561/74180 🌐 www.coburg-tourist.de. **Kronach** ✉ Marktpl., D-96317 ☎ 09261/97236 🌐 www.kronach.de. **Kulmbach** ✉ Fremdenverkehrsbüro, Stadthalle, Sutte 2, D-95326 ☎ 09221/95880. **Nürnberg** ✉ Congress- und Tourismus-Zentrale Frauentorgraben 3, D-90443 ☎ 0911/23360 🌐 www.nuernberg.de. **Passau** ✉ Tourist-Information Passau, Rathauspl. 3, D-94032 ☎ 0851/955-980 🌐 www.passau.de. **Regensburg** ✉ Altes Rathaus, D-93047 ☎ 0941/507-4410 🌐 www.regensburg.de.

The Bodensee

5

WORD OF MOUTH

"Though I stayed in Überlingen, I thought Lindau was a delightful small city. Staying there overnight will give you time to wander without the rest of us day trippers."

—jmw

"We were in Meersburg and Friedrichshafen last summer and we preferred Meersburg as a place to stay. . . . The atmosphere was quaint and quiet in Meersburg, particularly after the tourists left in the afternoon. The ferries will take you to Mainau Island (which is a must) and bus service around the lake to other towns is also good."

—kitty

"Mainau Island is an awesome place to visit. I have never seen 30-foot roses before!"

—Anne

www.fodors.com/forums

Updated by Marton Radkai

LAPPING THE SHORES of Germany, Switzerland, and Austria, the Bodensee (Lake Constance), at 65 km (40 mi) long and 15 km (9 mi) wide, is the largest lake in the German-speaking world. Though called a lake, it's actually a vast swelling of the Rhine, gouged out by a massive glacier in the Ice Age and flooded by the river as the ice receded. The Rhine flows into its southeast corner, where Switzerland and Austria meet, and flows out at its west end. On the German side, the Bodensee is bordered almost entirely by the state of Baden-Württemberg (a small portion of the eastern tip, from Lindau to Nonnenhorn, belongs to Bavaria).

A natural summer playground, the Bodensee is ringed with little towns and busy resorts. It's one of the warmest areas of the country, not just because of its southern latitude but also owing to the warming influence of the water, which gathers heat in the summer and releases it in the winter. The lake itself practically never freezes over—it has done so only once during the last two centuries. The climate is excellent for growing fruit, and along the roads you'll find stands and shops selling apples, peaches, strawberries, jams, juices, wines, and schnapps, much of it homemade.

The lake's natural attractions—including its abundance of fresh fish and its fertile soil—were as compelling several thousand years ago as they are today, making this one of the oldest continually inhabited areas of Germany. Highlights include the medieval island town of Lindau; Friedrichshafen, birthplace of the zeppelin; the rococo pilgrimage church in Birnau; and the town of Konstanz on the Swiss-German border. A day trip to Austria and Switzerland (and to little Liechtenstein) is easy to make, and border formalities are few.

Exploring the Bodensee

You can travel the entire length of the German shore of the Bodensee easily in a day—by car, train, or boat—but the enchanting towns along the way will deter any plan to rush through. Lindau is a pretty and unusual resort, close to Austria, Liechtenstein, and the mountains of the German Allgäu. Friedrichshafen is busier and sits at the head of a road inland to Ravensburg, Weingarten, and the extraordinary churches of the Baroque Road. Meersburg, built on a slope that slides down to the lakeside, is arguably the loveliest Bodensee town and is just a short ferry ride from the area's largest city, Konstanz, the regional gateway to Switzerland.

About the Restaurants & Hotels

In this area, international dishes are not only on the menu but on the map—you only have to drive a few miles to try the Swiss or Austrian dish you're craving in its own land. *Seeweine* (lake wines) from vineyards in the area include Müller-Thurgau, Spätburgunder, Ruländer, and Kerner.

The towns and resorts around the lake have a wide range of hotels, from venerable wedding-cake-style, fin-de-siècle palaces to more modest *Gasthöfe*. If you're visiting in July and August, make reservations in advance. For lower rates and a more rural atmosphere, consider staying a few miles away from the lake.

Numbers in the text correspond to numbers in the margin and on the Bodensee (Lake Constance) map.

If you have 3 days

Stroll around **Lindau** 1. Reserve a couple of hours for the Zeppelin Museum in **Friedrichshafen** 2, which celebrates the airships once built there. Stay overnight in lovely **Meersburg** 3, rising early to catch the sunrise over the lake and the ferry to **Konstanz** 8, on the opposite shore. From here, there's a difficult choice—a day trip either to the Swiss Alps or to two Bodensee islands, **Mainau** 9 and **Reichenau** 10. After an overnight stay in Konstanz, rent a bike and explore the **Höri** 11 peninsula.

If you have 5 days

Start your itinerary at **Lindau** 1, stopping in Wasserburg and Langenargen, before continuing on to **Friedrichshafen** 2; then head inland via B–30 to medieval **Ravensburg** 5, where you can find a number of historic hostelries. Although the great baroque pilgrimage church of **Weingarten** 6 is only 5 km (3 mi) north of Ravensburg, allow a morning or an afternoon to do the magnificent structure justice. Return south to the lake for an overnight stay in **Meersburg** 3. Catch the ferry to **Konstanz** 8, on the opposite shore, and allow a full day and night to get to know this fascinating city. Devote the next day to the islands of **Mainau** 9 and eat at one of the ancient taverns of **Reichenau** 10; then head for **Überlingen** 4, where you can easily relax in its balmy clime. A visit to the nearby pilgrimage church of Birnau—a rococo masterpiece—is a marvelous finale to any Bodensee tour.

WHAT IT COSTS In Euros

	$$$$	$$$	$$	$	¢
RESTAURANTS	over €25	€21–€25	€16–€20	€9–€15	under €9
HOTELS	over €225	€175–€225	€100–€175	€50–€100	under €50

Restaurant prices are per person for a main course at dinner. Hotel prices are for two people in a standard double room, including tax and service.

Timing

The Bodensee's temperate climate makes for pleasant weather from April to October. In spring, orchard blossoms explode everywhere, and on Mainau, the "island of flowers," more than a million tulips, hyacinths, and narcissi burst into bloom. Holiday crowds come in summer, and autumn can be warm and mellow. Some hotels and restaurants in the smaller resort towns close for the winter.

THE NORTHERN SHORE

There's a feeling here, in the midst of a peaceful Alpine landscape, that the Bodensee is part of Germany and yet separated from it—which is literally the case in towns such as Lindau, which sits in the lake tethered to land by a causeway. At the northwestern finger of the lake, Überlingen, a beautiful resort beached on a small inlet of water, attracts many vacationers and spa goers. Clear days reveal the snowcapped mountains of Switzerland to the south and the peaks of the Austrian Vorarlberg to the east.

Lindau

❶ *180 km (112 mi) southwest of Munich.*

If not for the narrow causeway linking it with the mainland, ancient Lindau would be an island. On a hazy summer's day, the walls and roofs of Old Lindau seem to float on the shimmering lake. Lindau was made a Free Imperial City within the Holy Roman Empire in 1275. It had developed as a fishing settlement and then spent hundreds of years as a trading center along the route between the rich lands of Swabia and Italy. The Lindauer Bote, an important stagecoach service between Germany and Italy in the 18th and 19th centuries, was based here; Goethe traveled via this service on his first visit to Italy in 1786. The stagecoach was revived a few years ago, and every June it sets off on its 10-day journey to Italy. You can book a seat through the Lindau tourist office.

As the German empire crumbled toward the end of the 18th century, battered by Napoléon's revolutionary armies, Lindau fell victim to competing political groups. It was ruled by the Austrian Empire before passing into Bavarian control in 1805. Lindau's harbor was rebuilt in 1856. Its most striking landmark is a **seated lion,** the proud symbol of Bavaria. Carved from Bavarian marble and standing 20 feet high, the lion stares out across the lake from a massive plinth. Standing sentinel with the seated lion is the **Neuer Leuchtturm** (New Lighthouse), across the inner harbor's passageway. At the harbor's edge is the **Alter Leuchtturm** (Old Lighthouse), firmly based on the weathered remains of the 13th-century city walls. The third tower watching over the harbor is the old **Mangturm,** which was once the seat of the clothiers' guild.

A maze of ancient streets leading from the harbor makes up the **Altstadt.** Half-timber and gable houses line its main street, pedestrians-only Maximilianstrasse. The **Altes Rathaus** (Old Town Hall; ✉ Maximilianstr.) is the finest of Lindau's handsome historical buildings. It was constructed between 1422 and 1436 in the midst of a vineyard and given a Renaissance face-lift 150 years later, though the original stepped gables remain. Emperor Maximilian I held an imperial diet here in 1496; a fresco on the south facade depicts the scene. A part of the building that served as the town prison is identified by an ancient inscription enjoining the townsfolk "to turn away from evil and learn to do good."

The **Barfüsserkirche** (Church of the Barefoot Pilgrims; ✉ Fischerg.), built from 1241 to 1270, is now Lindau's principal theater, and the Gothic choir is a memorable setting for concerts. Ludwigstrasse and Fischergasse lead to a watchtower, once part of the original city walls. Pause in the little park behind it, the **Stadtgarten** (City Park). If it's early evening, you'll see the first gamblers of the night making for the neighboring casino.

Bicycling From spring through autumn, Germans pack their wheels and head for the scenic bike path that circles the entire lake. You can rent a bike as a guest at many hotels, at some tourist offices, from sports shops, and from bicycle tour operators. You can always save yourself some pumping by cutting across the lake on a ferry. Biking maps are available from newspaper stands, bookshops, and tourist offices, and you can leave your baggage in the long-term storage available at the train stations in Konstanz, Überlingen, Friedrichshafen, and Lindau.

On the Menu Fish specialties predominate around the Bodensee. There are 35 types of fish in the lake, with *Felchen* (a meaty whitefish) the most highly prized. Felchen belongs to the salmon family and is best eaten *blau* (poached in a mixture of water and vinegar with spices called *Essigsud*) or *Müllerin* (baked in almonds). Wash it down with a top-quality Meersburg white wine. If you venture north to Upper Swabia, *Pfannkuchen* and *spätzle,* both flour-and-egg dishes, are the most common specialties. Pfannkuchen (pancakes) are generally filled with meat, cheese, jam, or sultanas or chopped into fine strips and scattered in a clear consommé known as *Flädlesuppe*. Spätzle are roughly chopped, golden-color fried egg noodles that are the usual accompaniment to the Swabian Sunday roast-beef lunch of *Rinderbraten.* One of the best-known Swabian dishes is *Maultaschen,* a kind of ravioli, usually served floating in a broth strewn with chives.

Shopping The Bodensee is artists' territory, and shopping means combing the many small galleries for watercolors, engravings, and prints. Local potters sell their wares directly from their shops. International goods are available in abundance. In Konstanz, if you must have Swiss chocolate or a Swiss watch, walk a few feet across the border into Kreuzlingen, the Swiss part of the twin-city. To do some serious shopping there are two cities within an hour's drive—St. Gallen, known for its textiles and embroidery, and Zurich, with its famous Bahnhofstrasse, Switzerland's most elegant and expensive shopping street. Across the bay from Lindau is the Austrian city of Bregenz, with some reputable Loden shops that carry fashionable alpine apparel.

The **Peterskirche** (St. Peter's Church; ✉ Schrannenpl.) is a solid Romanesque building, constructed in the 10th century and reputedly the oldest church in the Bodensee region. Step inside to see the frescoes by Hans Holbein the Elder (1465–1524) on the northern wall, some of which depict scenes from the life of St. Peter, the patron saint of fishermen. Attached to the church is the old 16th-century bell foundry, now housing a pottery, where you can pick up plates, bowls, candleholders, and other household objects. Also worthy of note is the adjacent Unterer Schrannenplatz, where the bell-makers used to live. A 1989 fountain depicts five of the *Narren* (Fools) that make up the VIPs of the Alemannic Mardi Gras celebrations.

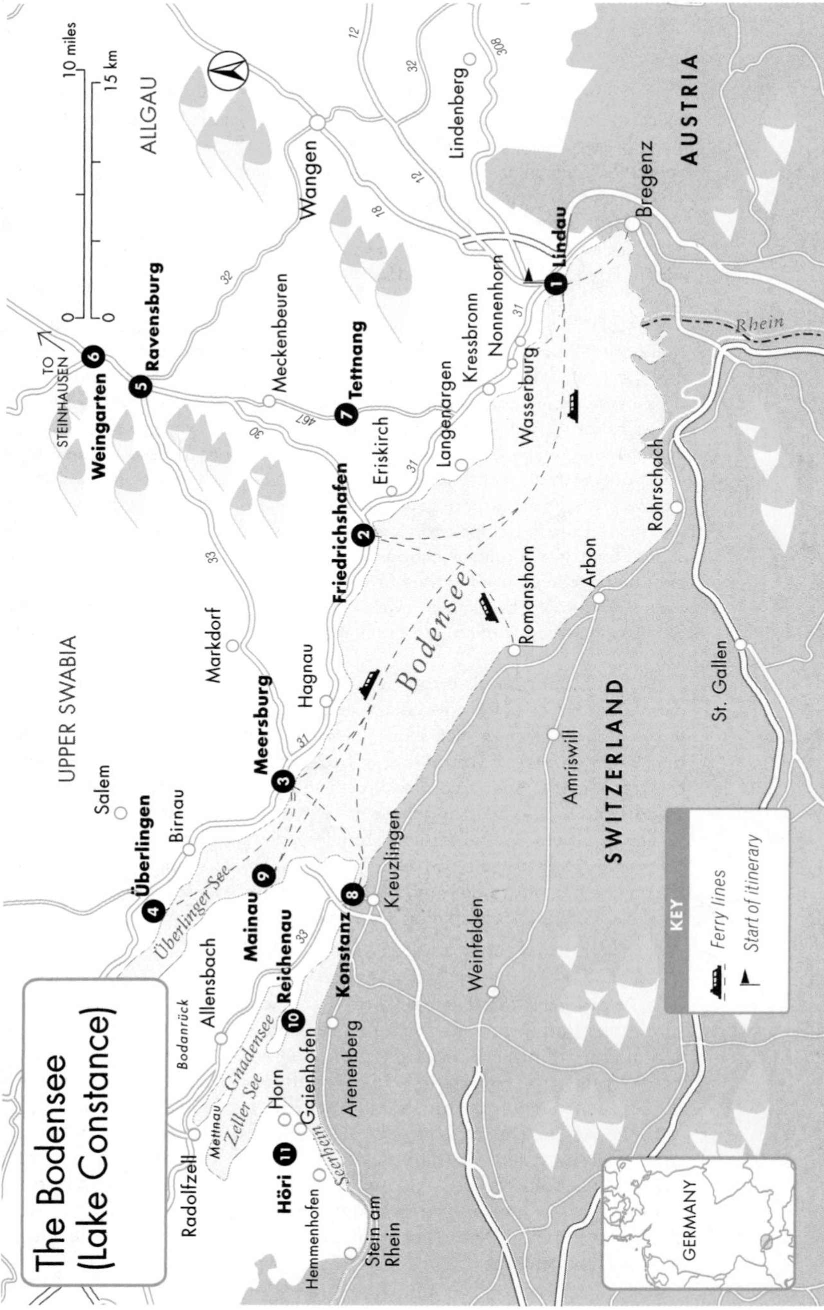
The Bodensee (Lake Constance)
ALLGAU
UPPER SWABIA
SWITZERLAND
AUSTRIA
GERMANY
Bodensee
Überlinger See
Gnadensee
Zeller See
Seerhein
Rhein
Bodanrück
Mettnau
1 Lindau
2 Friedrichshafen
3 Meersburg
4 Überlingen
5 Weingarten
6 Ravensburg
7 Tettnang
8 Konstanz
9 Mainau
10 Reichenau
11 Höri
TO STEINHAUSEN
Wangen
Lindenberg
Meckenbeuren
Nonnenhorn
Kressbronn
Langenargen
Wasserburg
Eriskirch
Markdorf
Hagnau
Salem
Birnau
Allensbach
Radolfzell
Horn
Gaienhofen
Hemmenhofen
Arenenberg
Stein am Rhein
Kreuzlingen
Weinfelden
Amriswill
Romanshorn
Arbon
Rohrschach
St. Gallen
Bregenz
0 10 miles
0 15 km
KEY
Ferry lines
Start of itinerary

Lindau's **Marktplatz** (market square) is an almost austere place. It's lined by a series of sturdy and attractive old buildings. The Gothic **Stephanskirche** (St. Stephen's Church) is simple and sparsely decorated, as befits a Lutheran place of worship. It dates to the late 12th century but went through numerous transformations. One of its special features is the green-hue stucco ornamentation on the ceiling, which immediately attracts the eye toward the heavens. In contrast, the Catholic **Marienkirche** (St. Mary's Church), which stands right next to the Stephanskirche, is exuberantly baroque.

The **Haus zum Cavazzen** home dates to 1728. It belonged to a wealthy merchant and is now considered one of the most beautiful houses in the Bodensee region, owing to its rich decor of frescoes. Today it serves as a local history museum, with collections of glass and pewter items, paintings, and furniture from the last five centuries. ✉ *Am Marktpl. 6* ☎ *08382/944–073* *€2.50* ⏲ *Apr.–Oct., Tues.–Fri. and Sun. 11–5, Sat. 2–5.*

Where to Stay & Eat

★ **$$$–$$$$** ✕ **Restaurant Hoyerberg Schlössle.** A commanding terrace view across the lake to Bregenz and the Alps combined with excellent nouvelle cuisine makes this one of the best dining experiences in Lindau. The specialties are fish and game, which change seasonally, and there are prix-fixe menus of four and six courses (€80); one offers tuna carpaccio, monkfish medalion, and Thai coconut soup with scampi. Brick-trim arched windows, fresh flowers, and elegant high-back chairs complete the experience. ✉ *Hoyerbergstr. 64* ☎ *08382/25295* *Reservations essential* ▭ *AE, DC, MC, V* ⏲ *Closed Mon. and Feb. No lunch Tues.*

¢–$$ ✕ **Gasthaus zum Sünfzen.** This ancient inn was serving warm meals to the patricians, officials, merchants, and other good burghers of Lindau back in the 14th century. The chef insists on using fresh ingredients preferably from the region, such as fish from the lake, venison from the mountains, and apples—pressed to juice or distilled to schnapps—from his own orchard. The evening menu features specialties from the times of yore. Try either the herb-flavored *Maultaschen* (large raviolis), the excellent *Felchen* (whitefish) fillet in wine sauce, or the peppery Schübling sausage from the inn's butchershop. ✉ *Maximilianstr. 1* ☎ *08382/5865* ▭ *AE, MC, V* ⏲ *Closed Feb.*

$$–$$$$ ✕ **Hotel Bayerischer Hof/Hotel Reutemann.** This is *the* address in town, a stately hotel directly on the edge of the lake, its terrace lush with semitropical, long-flowering plants, trees, and shrubs. Most of the luxuriously appointed rooms have views of the lake and the Austrian and Swiss mountains beyond. Freshly caught pike perch is a highlight of the extensive menus in the stylish restaurants ($$–$$$$). Rooms at the Reutemann are a little cheaper than those at the Bayerischer next door. ✉ *Seepromenade, D–88131* ☎ *08382/9150* *08382/915–591* 🌐 *www.bayerischerhof-lindau.de* *98 rooms, 2 suites* *Restaurant, café, cable TV, in-room data ports, pool, massage, sauna, boating, bicycles, bar, meeting rooms; no a/c* ▭ *DC, MC, V* *BP.*

$ ✕ **Gasthof Engel.** The Engel traces its pedigree back to 1390. Tucked into one of the Old Town's ancient, narrow streets, the property creaks with history. Twisted oak beams are exposed inside and outside the terraced house. The bedrooms are simply furnished but comfortable. The restaurant (¢–$) serves Swabian specialties with a few Swiss potato dishes (*Rösti*) for good measure. ✉ *Schafg. 4, D–88131* ☎ *08382/5240* 🖷 *08382/5644* *9 rooms, 7 with shower* *Restaurant; no a/c, no room TVs* *No credit cards* ⏲ *Closed Nov.* *CP.*

¢–$$ **Insel-Hotel.** What better place to wake up than in the middle of the pedestrian zone of Lindau? Rooms at this family-run enterprise are perhaps not the most modern, but the atmosphere is friendly. In good weather, breakfast can be taken on the sidewalk, where you can watch the town come alive. ✉ *Maximilianstr. 42, D–88131* ☎ *08382/5017* 🖷 *08382/6756* 🌐 *www.insel-hotel-lindau.de* *24 rooms* *Restaurant, cable TV, some pets allowed (fee); no a/c* *AE, MC, V* *BP.*

$ **Landhotel Martinsmühle.** The old converted mill about 11 km (7 mi) northeast of Lindau stands in a quiet setting amid woods and fields and orchards. It's the ideal place to come back to after a day's sightseeing. Taste homemade jams at breakfast; put your day to bed with a shot of fragrant homemade schnapps. Rooms are in rustic style; some have traditional painted furniture. A meal is served if you request one (there's no menu); otherwise you can have hearty snacks, sandwiches, plates of wurst and cheese. ✉ *Bechtersweiler 25, D–88131* ☎ *08382/5849* 🖷 *08382/6355* 🌐 *www.landhotel-martinsmuehle.de* *98 rooms, 2 suites* *Café, cable TV; no a/c* *MC, V* *BP.*

¢ **Jugendherberge.** This well-run youth hostel is open to travelers up to 26 years old and families with at least one child under 18. Rooms have one to six beds and a shower and toilet. There are also special family rooms. ✉ *Herbergsweg 11, D–88131* ☎ *08382/96710* 🖷 *08382/967–150* 🌐 *www.jugendherberge.de/jh/lindau* *65 rooms* *Café, cafeteria, recreation room, laundry facilities; no a/c, no room phones, no room TVs* *No credit cards* *CP.*

Nightlife & the Arts

You can play roulette, blackjack, poker, and slot machines at Lindau's modern and elegant **casino** (✉ Chelles Alle 1 ☎ 08382/27740). It's open weekdays 3 PM–2 AM, weekends 3 PM–3 AM; the one-arm bandit room is open at noon. You can enjoy opera in the intimate setting at the **Lindauer Marionettentheater,** where puppets do the singing. Tickets are available at the **Stadttheater** (✉ Fischerg. 37 ☎ 08382/944–650 🌐 www.lindauer-mt.de ⏲ weekdays 10–1:30). A dramatic floating stage supports orchestras and opera stars during the famous **Bregenzer Festspiele** (Bregenz Music Festival; ✉ Bregenz ☎ 0043/5574–4076 🌐 www.bregenzerfestspiele.com) from mid-July to the end of August. Make reservations well in advance. Bregenz is 13 km (8 mi) from Lindau, on the other side of the bay.

Sports & the Outdoors

BIKING You can rent bikes and accessories such as child trailers at **Fahrradstation** (✉ Im Hauptbahnhof ☎ 08382/21261). Bikes cost €8 to €30 per day depending on the bike. The shop offers discounts for longer rentals.

BOATING & WINDSURFING The best way to see Lindau is from the lake. Take one of the pleasure boats of the **Weisse Flotte** that leave Lindau's harbor five or six times a day for the 20-minute ride to Bregenz in Austria. These large boats carry up to 800 people on three decks. The round-trip costs €7.

The **Bodensee Yachtschule** (✉ Christoph Eychmüller Schiffswerfte 3 ☎ 08382/944–588 🌐 www.bodensee-yachtschule.de), in Lindau, charters yachts and has one-week camp sessions for children. You can rent windsurfing boards at **Windsurfschule Kreitmeir** (✉ Strandbad Eichwald ☎ 08382/23346 🌐 www.hermanno.de).

Shopping

Biedermann (✉ Maximilianstr. 2 ☎ 08382/944–913) carries the expensive Collections Femmes et Hommes from Italy, as well as custom-made clothing, cashmere sweaters, and Italian shoes. A find for interior decorators, **Böhm** (✉ Maximilianstr. 21 and Krummg. 6 ☎ 08382/94880) consists of three old houses full of lamps, mirrors, precious porcelain, and elegant furniture. Böhm will deliver worldwide. Michael Zeller's reputable shop, the **Colony** (✉ Binderg. 7 ☎ 08382/93020 🌐 www.zeller.de), sells watercolors, engravings, prints, silver, and furniture. Michael Zeller also organizes the celebrated, twice-yearly Internationale Bodensee-Kunstauktion (art auction) in May and October. Smaller auctions are held during the Christmas season and in February and June.

en route

Six kilometers (4 mi) west of Lindau lies **Wasserburg**, whose name means "water castle," an exact description of what this enchanting island town once was—a fortress. Built by the St. Gallen Monastery in 924, the owners, the counts of Montfort zu Tettnang, sold the fortress to the Fugger family of Augsburg. The Fuggers couldn't afford to maintain the drawbridge that connected the castle with the shore and instead built a causeway. In the 18th century the castle passed into the hands of the Habsburgs, and in 1805 the Bavarian government took it over. Wasserburg has some of the most photographed sights of the Bodensee: the yellow, stair-gabled presbytery; the fishermen's St. Georg Kirche, with its onion dome; and the little Malhaus museum, with the castle, Schloss Wasserburg, in the background.

Another 8 kilometers (5 mi) west of Wasserburg is the small, pretty town of Langenargen, famous for the region's most unusual castle, **Schloss Montfort** (Montfort Castle). Named for the original owners, the counts of Montfort-Werdenberg—this structure was a conventional medieval fortification until the 19th century, when it was rebuilt in pseudo-Moorish style by its new owner, King Wilhelm I of Württemberg. If you can, see it from a passenger ship on the lake; the castle is especially memorable in the early morning or late afternoon, when the softened, watery light gives additional mystery to its outline. These days the castle houses a café, restaurant, disco, and small concert hall that hosts classical chamber music concerts every Friday at 8 PM. Its tower is open to visitors. ✉ *Untere Seestr. 5* 🎫 *Tower €1* ⏲ *Mar.–Oct. 19, Mon.–Thurs. and Sat. 2–5, Fri. and Sun. 10–5.*

Friedrichshafen

❷ *24 km (15 mi) west of Lindau.*

Named for its founder, King Friedrich I of Württemberg, Friedrichshafen is a young town (dating to 1811). In an area otherwise given over to resort towns and agriculture, Friedrichshafen played a central role in Germany's aeronautics tradition, which saw the development of the zeppelin airship before World War I and the Dornier seaplanes in the 1920s and '30s. The zeppelins were once launched from a floating hangar on the lake, and the Dornier water planes were tested here. The World War II raids on its factories virtually wiped the city off the map. The current layout of the streets is the same, but the buildings are all new and not necessarily pretty. The atmosphere, however, is good and lively, and occasionally you'll find a plaque with a picture of the old building that stood at the respective spot. The factories are back, too. Friedrichshafen is home to such international firms as EADS (airplanes, rockets, and helicopters) and ZF (gear wheels).

Graf Zeppelin (Ferdinand Graf von Zeppelin) was born across the lake in Konstanz, but Friedrichshafen was where, on July 2, 1900, his first "airship"—the LZ 1—was launched. The fascinating story of the zeppelin airships is told in the ★ **Zeppelin Museum,** which holds the world's most significant collection of artifacts pertaining to airship history in its 43,000 square feet of exhibition space. In a wing of the restored Bauhaus **Friedrichshafen Hafenbahnhof** (harbor railway station), the main attraction is the reconstruction of a 108-foot-long section of the legendary *Hindenburg,* the LZ 129, which exploded at its berth in Lakehurst, New Jersey, on May 6, 1937. (The airships were filled with hydrogen, because the United States refused to sell the Germans helium, for political reasons.) Climb aboard the airship via a retractable stairway and stroll past the authentically furnished passenger room, the original lounges, and the dining room. The illusion of traveling in a zeppelin is followed by exhibits on the history and technology of airship aviation: propellers, engines, dining-room menus, and films of the airships traveling or at war. Car fans will appreciate the great Maybach standing on the ground floor; passengers once enjoyed being transported to the zeppelins in it. The museum's restaurant is a good place to take a break and enjoy lunch or dinner. ✉ *Seestr. 22* ☎ *07541/38010* 🌐 *www.zeppelin-museum.de* 🎫 *€7.50* ⏲ *May–Oct., Tues.–Sun. 10–5 (last entry at 4:30); July–Sept., Mon. 9–5 as well; Nov.–Apr., Tues.–Sun. 10–5.*

The **Deutsche Zeppelin Reederei GmbH** operates zeppelins in Friedrichshafen. You can board the *Zeppelin NT* (New Technology) for either an air journey or a tour of the zeppelin itself on its mooring mast at the airport. ✉ *Allmannsweilerstr. 132* ☎ *0700/9377–2001* 📠 *07541/590–0499* 🌐 *www.zeppelinflug.de.*

Schloss Hofen (Hofen Castle), a short walk from town along the lakeside promenade, is a small palace that served as the summer residence of Württemberg kings until 1918. Today Duke Friedrich von Württemberg lives here with his family. The palace was formerly a priory—its foundations date from the 11th century. You can visit the adjoining priory **church,** a splendid example of regional baroque architecture. The swirling white stucco of the interior was executed by the Schmuzer family from Wessobrunn whose master craftsman, Franz Schmuzer, also created the priory church's magnificent marble altar. The church is open from 9 AM to 6 PM daily, from Easter to the end of October; otherwise only on Sunday.

off the beaten path

SIDE TRIP TO SWITZERLAND – From Friedrichshafen you can go directly to Romanshorn in Switzerland on a car ferry that leaves every hour from the harbor. The 40-minute trip offers an impressive view from the upper passenger deck: Swiss mountains ahead; Austrian mountains on your left; and the rolling green hills of Germany behind you. If you take your car, go one way by boat, and then return by driving from Romanshorn to Bregenz in Austria, then past Lindau, and back to Friedrichshafen. (If you take the highway in Austria, you will need a *Vignette* (available at most gas stations €7.60); avoid the Swiss autobahn, which also requires a toll sticker that costs €27. Car and driver one-way on the ferry costs between €14 and €20 depending on the length of the car; an extra person costs €6.20.

5

Where to Stay & Eat

$–$$ ✕ **Zeppelin-Museumrestaurant.** The grand view of the harbor and the lake is only one of the attractions of this café and restaurant, in the Zeppelin Museum. You can enjoy cakes and drinks, or a wide range of Swabian specialties (such as lentils) or more Italianate dishes. ✉ *Seestr. 22* ☎ *07541/33306* ▭ *No credit cards.*

¢–$$ ✕ **Lukullum.** Students, businesspeople, and guests from the nearby top hotels rub elbows at this lively, novel restaurant. The friendly service keeps up with the pace of the socializing. Partitioned areas named after tourist regions allow privacy for groups or families. Other sitting arrangements are theme oriented: you sit in a beer barrel, in a bedroom, next to a waterwheel, etc. The dishes are good and basic, with surprising international touches, everything from a Balkan kebab to jambalaya. ✉ *Friedrichstr. 21* ☎ *07541/6818* ▭ *AE, DC, MC, V.*

$–$$$ ✕ **Ringhotel Buchhorner Hof.** This traditional hotel near the train station, now part of the Ring group, has been run by the same family since it opened in 1870. Hunting trophies on the walls, leather armchairs, and Turkish rugs decorate the public areas; bedrooms are large and comfortable. One floor is reserved fo the business traveler, with fax machines, modem and extra large desks in the rooms. The restaurant ($–$$$) is plush and subdued, with delicately carved chairs and mahogany-panel walls. It offers a choice of menus with dishes such as pork medallions, perch fillet, and lamb chops. ✉ *Friedrichstr. 33, D–88045* ☎ *07541/2050* 🖷 *07541/32663* 🌐 *www.buchhorn.de* *90 rooms, 4 suites, 2 apartments* *Restaurant, some in-room faxes, cable TV, in-room data ports, miniature golf, gym, massage, sauna, bicycles, bar, meeting rooms, some pets allowed; no a/c in some rooms* ▭ *AE, DC, MC, V* *BP.*

$$ ✕🏨 **Ringhotel Krone.** This Bavarian-theme hotel, made up of four buildings, is in the Schnetzenhausen district's semirural surroundings, 6 km (4 mi) from the center of town. You can roam the area on a bike rented from the hotel. All rooms have balconies. The restaurant ($–$$$) specializes in game dishes and fish. ✉ *Untere Mühlbachstr. 1, D–88045* ☎ *07541/4080* 📠 *07541/43601* 🌐 *www.ringhotel-krone.de* *115 rooms* *Restaurant, some in-room data ports, 4 tennis courts, pool, gym, hot tub, sauna, bicycles, bowling, bar, meeting rooms, some pets allowed; no a/c in some rooms* 💳 *AE, DC, MC, V* 🍽 *BP.*

$ ✕🏨 **Hotel Wohlwender.** If a hotel is simply a place for you to sleep, choose this small, clean, inexpensive one. You get the basics here. The restaurant serves Chinese and Vietnamese specialties. ✉ *Olgastr. 64, D–88045* ☎ *07541/32818* 📠 *07540/707–828* 🌐 *www.hotel-wohlwender.de* *14 rooms* *Restaurant, Wi-Fi, some pets allowed; no a/c* 💳 *AE, DC, MC, V* 🍽 *CP.*

Nightlife & the Arts

College students and a mostly young crowd raise their glasses and voices above the din at **Cafebar Belushi** (✉ Montfortstr. 3 ☎ 07541/32531). A more mature crowd meets for music, food, dancing, and drinks at the **Halbhuber** (✉ Flughafen, P2 parking ☎ 07541/953–350), which is in the airport to the west of town.

Friedrichshafen's **Graf-Zeppelin-Haus** (✉ Olgastr. 20 ☎ 07541/72071) is a modern convention center on the lakeside promenade, a seven-minute walk from the train station. It's also a cultural center, where musicals, light opera, and classical as well as pop-rock concerts take place several times a week.

Shopping

Most of the town's shops line the pedestrian zone near the harbor. **Christina Teske** (✉ Seestr. 1 ☎ 07541/75356) carries women's and men's clothing. The gift shop **Ebe** (✉ Buchhornpl. ☎ 07541/26036) sells handmade candles, dolls, and postcards. Excellent chocolates, including a specialty in the shape of a zeppelin airship, are sold at **Weber & Weiss** (✉ Charlottenstr. 11 ☎ 07541/21771).

Meersburg

❸ *18 km (11 mi) west of Friedrichshafen.*

Meersburg is one of the most romantic old towns on the German shore of the lake. Seen from the water on a summer afternoon with the sun slanting low, the steeply terraced town looks like a stage set, with its bold castles, severe patrician dwellings, and a gaggle of half-timber houses arranged around narrow streets. It's no wonder that cars have been banned from the center: the crowds of people who come to visit the sights on weekends fill up the streets. The town is divided into the Unterstadt (Lower Town), which is joined by several steep streets and stairs to the Obere Stadt (Upper Town).

★ Majestically guarding the town is the **Altes Schloss** (Old Castle), the original Meersburg ("sea castle"). It's Germany's oldest inhabited castle, having been founded in 628 by Dagobert, king of the Franks. The massive central tower, with walls 10 feet thick, is named after him. The bishops of Konstanz used it as a summer residence until 1526, at which point they moved in permanently. They remained until the mid-18th century, when they built themselves what they felt to be a more suitable residence—the baroque Neues Schloss. Plans to tear down the Altes Schloss in the early 19th century were shelved when it was taken over by Baron Joseph von Lassberg, a man much intrigued by the castle's medieval romance. He turned it into a home for like-minded poets and artists, among them the Grimm brothers and his sister-in-law, Annette von Droste-Hülshoff (1797–1848), one of Germany's most famous poets. The Altes Schloss is still private property, but much of it can be visited, including the richly furnished rooms where Droste-Hülshoff lived and the chamber where she died, as well as the imposing knights' hall, the minstrels' gallery, and the sinister dungeons. The **Altes Schloss Museum** (Old Castle Museum) contains a fascinating collection of weapons and armor, including a rare set of medieval jousting equipment. ☎ *07532/80000* 🎫 *€5.50* ⏲ *Mar.–Oct., daily 9–6:30; Nov.–Feb., daily 10–6:30.*

The spacious and elegant **Neues Schloss** (New Castle) is directly across from its predecessor. Designed by Christoph Gessinger at the beginning of the 18th century, it took nearly 50 years to complete. The grand double staircase, with its intricate grillwork and heroic statues, was the work of Balthasar Neumann. The interior's other standout is the glittering **Spiegelsaal** (Hall of Mirrors). In an unlikely combination of 18th-century grace and 20th-century technology, the first floor of the palace houses the **Dornier Museum.** Three rooms are devoted to Claude Dornier, the pioneer airplane builder, and his flying machines, which are exhibited in model form and pictures. Several videos are shown on request. ☎ *07532/440–4900* 🎫 *€4, combined ticket that includes Weinbau Museum, Droste Museum and City Museum; available at the Tourist Information Office, €5* ⏲ *Apr.–Oct., daily 10–1 and 2–6.*

Sunbathed, south-facing Meersburg and the neighboring towns have been the center of the Bodensee wine trade for centuries. You can pay your respects to the noble profession in the **Weinbau Museum** (Vineyard Museum). A barrel capable of holding 50,000 liters (about the same number of quarts) and an immense wine press dating from 1607 are highlights of the collection. ✉ *Vorburg. 11* ☎ *07532/431–110* 🎫 *€2* ⏲ *Apr.–Oct., Tues., Fri., and Sun. 2–6.*

An idyllic retreat almost hidden among the vineyards, the Fürstenhäusle was built in 1640 by a local vintner and later used as a holiday home by poet Annette von Droste-Hülshoff. It's now the **Droste Museum,** containing many of her personal possessions and giving a vivid sense of Meersburg in her time. ✉ *Stettenerstr. 9, east of Obertor, town's north gate* ☎ *07532/6088* 🎫 *€3* ⏲ *Apr.–mid-Oct., weekdays 10–12:30 and 2–5, Sun. 2–5.*

Right next to the Meersburg Tourist Office is the **Stadtmuseum,** or City Museum, in a former Dominican priory. You can see an overview of the town's history that celebrates some of its famous residents, such as Franz Anton Mesmer, who developed the theory of "animal magnetism."

(His name gave rise to the verb "to mesmerize.") ✉ *Kirchstr. 4* ☎ *07532/431–125* €2 ⏲ *Apr.–Oct., Wed., Thurs., and Sat. 2–6.*

Where to Stay & Eat

★ **$–$$$** ✕ **Winzerstube zum Becher.** This traditional restaurant near the New Castle has been in the Benz family for three generations. If you want to try regional dishes and especially fresh fish from the lake, this is the place. A popular meat entrée is *badische Ente,* duck with bacon and apples in a wine-kirsch sauce. Do try the white wine from the restaurant's own vineyard. Reservations are recommended. ✉ *Höllg. 4* ☎ *07532/9009* *AE, DC, MC, V* ⏲ *Closed Jan. and Mon.*

$$–$$$ ✕ **Romantik Hotel Residenz am See.** This tastefully modern hotel is one of the finest in town. Most of the elegant rooms face the lake, but the quieter ones look out onto a vineyard. The restaurant ($$$$) has earthy, terra-cotta-tone walls and floor-to-ceiling windows. Fish is the specialty—try the pike perch in season. The vegetarian menu is a pleasant surprise. Any guilt you feel at disturbing the form of your artfully composed dessert will quickly dissipate once you taste it. ✉ *Uferpromenade 11, D–88709* ☎ *07532/80040* *07532/800–470* *www.romantikhotels.com* *23 rooms* *Restaurant, cable TV, bar, meeting rooms; no a/c* *AE, MC, V* *BP.*

$–$$ ✕ **Löwen.** This centuries-old, ivy-clad tavern on Meersburg's market square is a local landmark. Its welcoming restaurant ($$–$$$), with pine paneling, serves regional and seasonal specialties, notably a tasty stew of local fish. Guest rooms are cozily furnished and have their own sitting corners, and some have genuine Biedermeier furniture. ✉ *Marktpl. 2, D–88709* ☎ *07532/43040* *07532/430–410* *www.hotel-loewen-meersburg.de* *21 rooms* *Restaurant, cable TV, bicycles, Weinstube, meeting rooms, some pets allowed, no-smoking rooms; no a/c* *AE, DC, MC, V* *BP.*

★ **$–$$** ✕ **See Hotel Off.** Colors, lots of glass, and a fantastic lakeside location make this a place you will not want to leave. Owner Elisabeth Off has added little personal touches to the rooms that make you feel completely at home. Twelve rooms have been designed according to the laws of feng shui. In the restaurant, her husband, chef Michael Off, transforms local ingredients into gustatory adventures with a nod to nouvelle cuisine. The wellness area includes all sorts of alternative healing measures, from Reiki to aromatherapy. And you are only a few steps away from the lake if you feel like a swim. ✉ *Uferpromenade 51, D–88709* ☎ *07532/44740* *07532/447–444* *www.hotel.off.mbo.de* *19 rooms* *Restaurant, cable TV, spa, some pets allowed; no a/c* *AE, MC, V* *BP.*

$ ✕ **Zum Bären.** Built in 1605 and incorporating 13th-century Gothic foundations, the Bären was an important staging point for Germany's first postal service. The ivy-smothered facade, with its characteristic steeple, hasn't changed much over the centuries, but interior comforts certainly have. The restaurant ($–$$) is rustic in an uncluttered way; people will travel from afar to enjoy the rack of lamb. Some rooms are furnished with Bodensee antiques and brightly painted rustic wardrobes. If you have the chance, book Room 23 or 13. Both have semicircular alcoves with two overstuffed armchairs and six windows overlooking the marketplace. ✉ *Marktpl. 11, D–88709* ☎ *07532/43220* *07532/432–244* *www.baeren-meersburg.de* *17 rooms* *Restaurant, cable TV, some pets allowed; no a/c* *No credit cards* *Closed Dec.–Feb.* *BP.*

$ **Gästehaus am Hafen.** This family-run, half-timber pension is in the middle of the Old Town, near the harbor. The rooms are small but have refrigerators and room for a child's bed, if needed. There's a place to store bikes as well. *Spitalg. 3* *07532/7069* *07532/7789* *7 rooms* *Refrigerators; no a/c, no room phones* *No credit cards* *CP.*

Sports & the Outdoors

You can rent rowboats and paddle boats in the harbor, and just west of town are rocky beaches for swimming and sunbathing. The new, heavenly **Meersburg Thermen** (outdoor pool fed by hot springs) east of the harbor has lots of grass, a little sand, three pools, a thermal bath (33°C [91.4°F]), a sauna, minigolf, and a volleyball court. *Uferpromenade* *07532/4460–2850* *€9.50 for the indoor pool and sauna (3 hours), €16 for the whole day; the lido costs € 3.50 extra* *Weekdays 10–10, Sat. 10–8, Sun. 9–9.*

Shopping

Just at the entrance to Schlossplatz—the square in front of the Neues Schloss—are a few nice shops. **Ulmer** (Schlosspl. 3 07532/5788) has interesting gifts. Its specialty is children's clothes, including charming lederhosen for kids. If you can't find something at the incredible gift shop (toys, enamelware, books, dolls, model cars, and much more) called **Omas Kaufhaus** (Marktpl. at Steigstr. 2 07532/5788 daily 10–6:30), then at least you should see the exhibition of toy trains and tin boats on the first floor, the latter in a long canal filled with real water. **Benz** (Höllg. 2 07532/9965) sells handmade pottery.

en route

As you proceed northwest along the lake's shore, a settlement of **Pfahlbauten** ("pile dwellings")—a reconstructed village of Stone Age and Bronze Age dwellings built on stilts—sticks out of the lake. This is how the original lake dwellers lived, surviving off the fish that swam outside their humble huts. Real dwellers in authentic garb give you an accurate picture of prehistoric lifestyles. The nearby **Pfahlbauten Freilichtmuseum** (Open-Air Museum of German Prehistory) contains actual finds excavated in the area. *Strandpromenade 6, Unteruhldingen* *07556/8543* *www.pfahlbauten.de* *€6* *Apr.–Oct., daily 8–6; Nov.–Mar., daily 9–5.*

Just northwest of Unteruhldingen the **Wallfahrtskirche Birnau** (Pilgrimage Church) overlooks the lake from a small hill. The church was built by the master architect Peter Thumb between 1746 and 1750. Its simple exterior consists of plain gray-and-white plaster and a tapering clock-tower spire above the main entrance. The interior, by contrast, is overwhelmingly rich, full of movement, light, and color. It's hard to single out highlights from such a profusion of ornament, but seek out the *Honigschlecker* ("honey sucker"), a gold-and-white cherub beside the altar, dedicated to St. Bernard of Clairvaux, "whose words are sweet as honey" (it's the last altar on the right as you face the high altar). The cherub is sucking honey from his finger, which he's just pulled out of a beehive. The fanciful spirit of this dainty pun is continued in the small squares of glass set into the pink screen that rises high above the main altar; the gilt dripping from the walls; the swaying, swooning statues; and the swooping figures on the ceiling. ✉ *Birnau* ⏲ *Daily 7–7.*

Überlingen

❹ *13 km (8 mi) west of Meersburg, 24 km (15 mi) west of Friedrichshafen.*

This Bodensee resort has an attractive waterfront and an almost Mediterranean flair. It's midway along the north shore of the Überlingersee, a narrow finger of the Bodensee that points to the northwest. Überlingen is ancient—it's first mentioned in records dating back to 770. In the 13th century it earned the title of Free Imperial City and was known for its wines. No fewer than seven of its original city gates and towers remain from those grand days, as well as substantial portions of the old city walls. What was once the moat is now a grassy walkway, with the walls of the Old Town towering on one side and the Stadtpark stretching away on the other. The **Stadtgarten** (city garden), which opened in 1875, cultivates exotic plants, has a famous collection of cacti, a fuchsia garden and a small deer corral. The heart of the city is the Münsterplatz.

★ The huge **Münster St. Nikolaus** (Church of St. Nicholas) was built between 1512 and 1563 on the site of at least two previous churches. The interior is all Gothic solemnity and massiveness, with a lofty stone-vaulted ceiling and high, pointed arches lining the nave. The single-most remarkable feature is not Gothic at all but opulently Renaissance—the massive high altar, carved by Jörg Zürn from lime wood that almost looks like ivory. The focus of the altar is the Christmas story. ✉ *Münsterpl.*

Inside the late-Gothic **Altes Rathaus** (Old Town Hall) is a high point of Gothic decoration, the **Rathaussaal,** or council chamber, which is still in use today. Its most striking feature amid the riot of carving is the series of figures, created between 1492 and 1494, representing the states of the Holy Roman Empire. There's a naïveté to the figures—their beautifully carved heads are all just a little too large, their legs a little too spindly—that makes them easy to love. ✉ *Münsterpl.* 🎟 *Free* ⏲ *Apr.–mid-Oct., weekdays 9–noon and 2:30–5, Sat. 9–noon.*

The **Städtisches Museum** (City Museum) is in the Reichlin-von-Meldegg house, 1462, one of the earliest Renaissance dwellings in Germany. It displays exhibits tracing Bodensee history and a vast collection of antique dollhouses. ✉ *Krummebergstr. 30* ☎ *07531/991–079* 🎟 *€2* ⏲ *Apr.–Oct., Tues.–Sat. 9–12:30 and 2–5, Sun. 10–3.*

off the beaten path

Fodor's Choice ★

SCHLOSS SALEM (Salem Castle) – This huge castle, located in the tiny village of Salem (10 km [6 mi] north of Überlingen), began its existence as a convent and large church. After many architectural permutations, it was transformed into a palace for the Baden princes, though traces of its religious past can still be seen. You can view the royally furnished rooms of the abbots and princes, a library, stables, and the church. The castle also houses an interesting array of museums, workshops, and activities, including a museum of firefighting, a potter, a musical instrument builder, a goldsmith shop, a glassblowing shop, pony farms, a golf driving range, and a fantasy garden for children. ✉ *88682 Salem* ☎ *07553/81437* 🌐 *www.salem.de* 🎫 *€5.50* ⏲ *Apr.–Oct., Mon.–Sat. 9:30–6, Sun. 10:30–6.*

AFFENBERG (Monkey Mountain) – On the road between Überlingen and Salem, the Affenberg is a 50-plus-acre park with an old farm that serves as home to more than 200 Barbary apes, as well as aquatic birds, grey herons, coots, and ducks. There's also a gallery that explores some of the artistic views of monkeys. ✉ *On road between Überlingen and Salem* ☎ *07583/381* 🌐 *www.affenberg-salem.de* 🎫 *€7* ⏲ *Mar. 15–Oct., daily 9–6; last entry at 5:30.*

5

Where to Stay & Eat

$–$$ **Bad Hotel mit Villa Seeburg.** This stately hotel has the double advantage of being both on the lake and in the center of town. The spare, modern rooms are done in crisp whites and creams. Try to get a room looking toward the park and the lake, though they are a bit more expensive. The restaurant ($–$$) is furnished in the same airy Mediterranean style, and the food is a lighter, healthier version of local Swabian cuisine. ✉ *Christophstr. 2, D–88662* ☎ *07551/8370* 📠 *07551/837–100* 🌐 *www.bad-hotel-ueberlingen.de* *65 rooms* *Restaurant, cable TV, Wi-Fi, bar, meeting rooms; no a/c* 💳 *AE, MC, V* ⏲ *Restaurant closed Jan.–Mar. 14* *BP.*

★ $$ **Romantik Hotel Johanniter Kreuz.** The setting is a small village 3 km (2 mi) to the north of Überlingen. The old part of the hotel dates from the 17th century and is truly romantic—half-timber, with a huge fireplace in the center of the restaurant ($–$$$). In the modern annex you can relax on your room's balcony. An 18-hole golf course overlooking the lake is just 1½ km (1 mi) away. ✉ *Johanniterweg 11, D–88662 Andelshofen* ☎ *07551/61091* 📠 *07551/67336* 🌐 *www.romantikhotels.com/ueberlingen* *25 rooms* *Restaurant, cable TV, some in-room data ports, hot tub, massage, sauna, bar, meeting rooms; no a/c* 💳 *DC, MC, V* *BP.*

$ **Landgasthof zum Adler.** You'll appreciate the unpretentiousness of this rustic country inn in a small village a few miles north of Überlingen. It has a blue-and-white half-timber facade, scrubbed wooden floors, maplewood tables, and thick down comforters on the beds. The Adler also keeps 10 apartments in a separate house for families at very affordable rates. The food ($–$$) is simple and delicious; trout is a specialty, as are several vegetarian dishes, such as potato gratin with fennel. ✉ *Hauptstr. 44, D–88662 Üb–Lippertsreute* ☎ *07553/82550* 📠 *07553/825–570* 🌐 *www.landgasthofadler.de* *17 rooms* *Restaurant, cable TV, meeting rooms, some pets allowed; no a/c* 💳 *No credit cards* ⏲ *Closed 2 wks in Nov.* *BP.*

$ **Schäpfle.** This ivy-covered hotel is in the center of town. The charm of the old house has been preserved and supplemented through time. In the hallways you'll find quaint furniture and even an old Singer sewing machine painted with flowers. The rooms are done with light, wooden

Scandinavian farm furniture. Guests and Überlingen residents congregate in the comfortable taproom, where the regional and international dishes are reasonably priced ($–$$). The chef prides himself on his homemade noodles. If you need a lake view, the hotel has a second building a few steps away right on the lake. ✉ *Jakob-Kessenringstr. 14, D–88662* ☎ *07551/63494* 🖷 *07551/67695* *32 rooms in 2 houses* *Restaurant, cable TV, some pets allowed, no-smoking floor; no a/c* 💳 *No credit cards* *BP.*

Shopping

The beauty and charm of Überlingen must attract artists to come, work, and live here, as there are more than 20 ateliers and artist shops in town (the tourist office has a brochure that lists them). **Galerie Tschirschky** (✉ Turmg. 9 ☎ 07551/308–797) has a fine selection of exquisite chinaware, all hand-painted by the proprietor and at reasonable prices. **Holzer** (✉ Turmg. 8 ☎ 07551/61525) is the studio of a master craftsman of gold jewelry.

THE UPPER SWABIAN BAROQUE ROAD

From Friedrichshafen, B–30 leads north along the valley of the little River Schussen and links up with one of Germany's less-known but most attractive scenic routes. The Oberschwäbische Barockstrasse (Upper Swabian Baroque Road) follows a rich series of baroque churches and abbeys, including Germany's largest baroque church, the basilica in Weingarten.

Ravensburg

❺ *20 km (12 mi) north of Friedrichshafen.*

The Free Imperial City of Ravensburg once competed with Augsburg and Nürnberg for economic supremacy in southern Germany. The Thirty Years' War put an end to the city's hopes by reducing it to little more than a medieval backwater. The city's loss proved fortuitous only in that many of its original features have remained much as they were built (in the 19th century, medieval towns usually tore down their medieval walls and towers, which were considered ungainly and constraining). Fourteen of Ravensburg's town gates and towers survive, and the Altstadt is among the best-preserved in Germany. The area around Marktstrasse, known as *Humpis,* is being developed into a museum with exhibitions showing 600 years of life and work in Ravensburg. An official **tour** of the city lets you climb some of those towers for a splendid view of Ravensburg and the surrounding countryside. Tours are available at the tourist office. ✉ *Kirchstrasse 16* ☎ *0751/82324* ⏲ *Weekdays 9–5:30, Sat. 10–1.*

That ecclesiastical and commercial life were never entirely separate in medieval towns is evident in the former **Karmeliterklosterkirche** (Carmelite Monastery Church), once part of a 14th-century monastery. The stairs on the west side of the church's chancel lead to the meeting room of the Ravensburger Gesellschaft (Ravensburg Society), an organization of linen merchants established in 1400. After the Reformation, Catholics and Protestants shared the church, but in 1810 the Protestants were given the entire building. The neo-Gothic stained-glass windows on the west side, depicting important figures of the Reformation such as Martin Luther and Huldreich Zwingli, were sponsored by wealthy burghers.

Many of Ravensburg's monuments that recall the town's wealthy past are concentrated on **Marienplatz.** To the west is the 14th-century **Kornhaus** (Granary); once the corn exchange for all of Upper Swabia, it now houses the public library. The late-Gothic **Rathaus** is a staid, red building with a Renaissance bay window and imposing late-Gothic rooms inside. Next to it stands the 15th-century **Waaghaus** (Weighing House), the town's weighing station and central warehouse. Its tower, the **Blaserturm,** which served as the watchman's abode, was rebuilt in 1556 after a fire and now bears a pretty Renaissance helmet. It can be climbed for a delightful view of the town (weekdays 2–5, Saturday noon–4, €2). Finally there's the colorfully frescoed **Lederhaus,** once the headquarters of the city's leather workers, now home to a café. On Saturday morning the square comes alive with a large market.

One of Ravensburg's **defensive towers** is visible from Marienplatz: the **Grüner Turm** (Green Tower), so called for its green tiles, many of which are 14th-century originals. Another stout defense tower is the massive **Obertor** (Upper Tower), the oldest gate in the city walls. One of the city's most curious towers, the **Mehlsack,** or Flour Sack Tower (so called because of its rounded shape and whitewash exterior), stands 170 feet high and sits upon the highest point of the city. The Tourist-Information Office offers tours of the Mehlsack on Saturday from 10 to 1 for €2. ☎ *0751/82324, 0751/82326 Tourist-Information Office.*

Ravensburg's true parish church, the **Liebfrauenkirche** (Church of Our Lady), is a 14th-century structure, elegantly simple on the outside but almost entirely rebuilt inside. Among the church's finest treasures are the 15th-century stained-glass windows in the choir and the heavily gilted altar. In a side altar is a copy of a carved Madonna, the *Schutzmantelfrau*; the late-14th-century original is in Berlin's Dahlem Museum. ✉ *Kirchstr. 18* ⏲ *Daily 7–7.*

Ravensburg is a familiar name to all jigsaw-puzzle fans, because its eponymous Ravensburg publishing house produces the world's largest selection of puzzles, in addition to many other children's games. The company was founded in 1883 by Otto Robert Maier. You can explore its history and have a closer look at its games and puzzles at the **Verlagsmuseum.** Note the neatly cut-out keyhole on the portal. ✉ *Markstr. 26* ☎ *0751/860* 🎟 *Free* ⏲ *Apr.–Oct., Thurs. 2–6, Sat. 10–1.*

Just to the west of town in the village of Weissenau stands the **Kirche St. Peter und St. Paul.** It was part of a 12th-century Prémontré monastery and now boasts a high baroque facade. The interior is a stupendous baroque masterpiece, with ceiling paintings by Joseph Hafner that create the illusion of cupolas, and vivacious stucco work by Johannes Schmuzer, one of the famous stucco artists from Wessobrunn. ✉ *Weissenau* ⏲ *Daily 9–6.*

Ravensburger Spieleland is an amusement park designed for small children, located 10 km (6 mi) from Ravensburg, in the direction of Lindau. Entrance is free to children on their birthday. ✉ *Liebenau–Am Hangenwald 1, Meckenbeuren* ☎ *07542/4000* 🌐 *www.spieleland.com* 🎟 *€17* ⏲ *Apr.–May and Sept.–early Nov., daily 10–5; June–Aug., daily 10–6.*

Where to Stay & Eat

★ ¢–$$ ✕ **Humpis.** When you first walk in, you may think you've been time-warped to the Middle Ages, but the dark-wood panels are lightened up with children's paintings. The restaurant attracts people from all walks of life with its Swabian specialties—some given a vivacious Italian touch. Portions are designed to satisfy big appetites. You may want to reserve a seat if you're coming after 7:30 PM. ✉ *Marktstr. 47* ☎ *0751/25698* 💳 *No credit cards.*

¢–$ ✕ **Café-Restaurant Central.** This popular place, with two floors and a large terrace on Marienplatz, has an international range of dishes, from kebabs and curries to pastas and local specialties. You can also enjoy coffee, cakes, or an aperitif. ✉ *Marienpl. 48* ☎ *0751/32533* 💳 *MC, V.*

★ $–$$$ ✕🏨 **Romantikhotel Waldhorn.** This historic hostelry has been in the Dressel-Bouley family for more than 150 years. Suites and rooms in the main building overlook the square. Rooms in the annex have views into the gardens or a quiet street. The menu ($$$$) is prepared by Albert Bouley, fifth-generation proprietor and chef. In the dark-wood-panel dining room you can enjoy the seven-course Waldhorn menu. Albert Bouley also minds the kitchen of the Rebleute, around the corner at Schulgasse 15. The setting, an old guild hall with a beautiful *Tonnendecke* (barrel ceiling), serves more regional (and less expensive) specialties. ✉ *Marienpl. 15, D–88212* ☎ *0751/36120* 📠 *0751/361–2100* 🌐 *www.waldhorn.de* ⇆ *30 rooms, 3 suites, 7 apartments* 👍 *Restaurant, cable TV, in-room data ports, bar, meeting rooms, some pets allowed; no a/c* 💳 *AE, DC, MC, V* ⏲ *Restaurant closed Sun. and Mon.* 🍽 *BP.*

$ ✕🏨 **Gasthof Ochsen.** The Ochsen is a typical, family-owned Swabian inn, and the personable Kimpfler family extends a warm welcome. If you have a choice, choose Room 2, which has three windows overlooking the lively scene (in summer, especially) of the Marktplatz. When checking in, reserve a table for dinner, as the restaurant (¢–$$) can often book up. This is the place to try Maultaschen and *Zwiebelrostbraten* (roast beef with lots of onions). ✉ *Eichelstr. 17, just off Marienpl., D–88212* ☎ *0751/25480* 📠 *0751/352–5350* 🌐 *www.ochsen-rv.de* ⇆ *15 rooms* 👍 *Restaurant, cable TV, Wi-Fi, meeting rooms, some pets allowed; no a/c* 💳 *MC* 🍽 *BP.*

Weingarten

❻ *5 km (3 mi) north of Ravensburg.*

Weingarten is famous Germany-wide for its huge and hugely impressive pilgrimage church, which you can see up on a hill from miles away, long before you get to the town.

At 220 feet high and more than 300 feet long, **Weingarten Basilica** is the largest baroque church in Germany. It was built as the basilica of one of the oldest and most venerable convents in the country, founded in 1056 by the wife of Guelph IV. The Guelph dynasty ruled large areas of Upper Swabia, and generations of family members lie buried in the church. The majestic edifice was renowned because of the little vial it possesses, said to contain drops of Christ's blood. First mentioned by Charlemagne, the vial passed to the convent in 1094, entrusted to its safekeeping by the Guelph queen Juditha, sister-in-law of William the Conqueror. At a stroke Weingarten became one of Germany's foremost pilgrimage sites. To this day, on the day after Ascension Thursday, the anniversary of the day the relic was entrusted to the convent, a huge procession of pilgrims headed by 2,000 horsemen—many local farmers breed horses just for this occasion—wends its way to the basilica. (This is well worth seeing if you happen to be visiting at the time.) The basilica was decorated by leading early-18th-century German and Austrian artists: stuccowork by Franz Schmuzer, ceiling frescoes by Cosmas Damian Asam, and a Donato Frisoni altar—one of the most breathtakingly ornate in Europe, with nearly 80-foot-high towers on either side. The organ, installed by Josef Gabler between 1737 and 1750, is among the largest in the country. ⏲ *Daily 8–6.*

If you want to learn about early Germans—residents from the 6th, 7th, and 8th centuries whose graves are just outside town—visit the **Alemannenmuseum** in the Kornhaus, at one time a granary. Archaeologists discovered the hundreds of Alemannic graves in the 1950s. ✉ *Karlstr. 28* 🎫 *Free* ⏲ *Mar.–Oct., Dec., and Jan., Tues.–Sun. 3–5, Thurs. 3–6.*

off the beaten path

★ **PILGRIMAGE CHURCH –** Thirty-five kilometers (21 mi) northeast of Weingarten on B–30, in the village of Steinhausen, is one of the finest examples of late-baroque religious architecture, the Pilgrimage Church. Built between 1728 and 1733, this harmonious white construction dwarfs the houses of the village around it. Architect Dominikus Zimmermann designed the interior on an oval ground plan. Ten powerful pillars topped with elaborate stuccowork support the roof. The transparent, almost pastel-hue ceiling painting, glorifying the life of the Virgin, is the work of Zimmermann's older brother Johann Baptist and his two sons. The stuccowork integrated into the edge of this masterpiece was done by a dozen Wessobrunn stucco artists. ✉ *Dorfstr. 3* ☎ *07583/942710* ⏲ *May–Oct., daily 7:30–7:30; Nov.–Apr., daily 7:30–dusk.*

Tettnang

❼ *13 km (8 mi) south of Ravensburg on B–467.*

Looking at Tettnang from the south, you see almost nothing of the small town but the Neues Schloss, former ancestral home of the counts of Montfort zu Tettnang. By 1780 the dynasty had fallen on such hard times that it ceded the town to the Habsburgs for hard cash, and 25 years later it passed to the Bavarian Wittelsbachs. Today, Tettnang is known for its beer and electronics industry. It's even referred to as "Little Silicon Valley."

The **Neues Schloss** (New Castle) is an extravagant baroque palace that was built in the early 18th century, burned down in 1753, and then partially rebuilt before the Montfort finances ran dry. Enough remains, however, to give some idea of the rulers' former wealth and ostentatious lifestyle. The palace is open only for tours. Call ahead to arrange for an English-speaking guide. ☎ *07542/953–839* €2.50 ⏲ *Tours in German Apr.–Oct., daily at 10:30, 2:30, and 4.*

off the beaten path

HOPFENMUSEUM TETTNANG (Tettnang Hops Museum) – If you're a beer drinker, you've probably already tasted a product of the Tettnang area. Tettnang is the second-largest hops-growing area in Germany and exports most of its so-called "green gold" to the United States. This museum, dedicated to brewing, is in the tiny village of Siggenweiler, 3 km (2 mi) northwest of Tettnang. ✉ *Siggenweiler* ☎ *07542/952–206* 🌐 *www.tettnanger-hopfenmuseum.de* ⏲ *May–Oct., Tues.–Sun. 2–5.*

AROUND THE BODANRÜCK PENINSULA

The immense Bodensee owes its name to a small, insignificant town, Bodman, on the Bodanrück Peninsula, at the northwestern edge of the lake. The area's most popular destinations, Konstanz and Mainau, are reachable by ferry from Meersburg. That's by far the most romantic way to cross the lake, though a main road (B–31, then B–34, and finally B–33) skirts the eastern side of the Bodensee and ends its German journey at Konstanz.

Konstanz

8 *A ½-hr ferry ride from Meersburg.*

The university town of Konstanz is the largest on the Bodensee; it straddles the Rhine as it flows out of the lake, placing itself both on the Bodanrück Peninsula and the Swiss side of the lake. Konstanz is among the best-preserved medieval towns in Germany; during the war the Allies were unwilling to risk inadvertently bombing neutral Switzerland. On the peninsula side of the town, east of the main bridge connecting Konstanz's two halves, runs **Seestrasse,** a stately promenade of neoclassical mansions with views of the Bodensee. The old town center is a labyrinth of narrow streets lined with restored half-timber houses and dignified merchant dwellings. This is where you'll find eateries, hotels, pubs, and much of the nightlife.

It's claimed that Konstanz was founded in the 3rd century by Emperor Constantine Chlorus, father of Constantine the Great. The story is probably untrue, though it's certain there was a Roman garrison here. In the late 6th century, Konstanz was made a bishopric; in 1192 it became a Free Imperial City. What put it on the map was the Council of Constance, held between 1414 and 1418 to settle the Great Schism

(1378–1417), the rift in the church caused by two separate lines of popes, one leading from Rome, the other from Avignon. The Council resolved the problem in 1417 by electing Martin V as the true, and only, pope. The church had also agreed to restore the German Holy Roman Emperor's (Sigismund's) role in electing the pope, but only if Sigismund silenced the rebel theologian Jan Hus of Bohemia. Even though Sigismund had allowed Hus safe passage to Konstanz for the Council, he won the church's favor by having Hus burned at the stake in July 1415.

In a historic satire, French author Honoré de Balzac created a character called Imperia, a courtesan of great beauty and cleverness, who raised the blood pressure of both religious and secular VIPs during the Council. No one visiting the harbor today can miss the 28-foot statue of **Imperia** standing out on the breakwater. Dressed in a revealing and alluring style, in her hands she holds two dejected figures: the Emperor and the Pope. This hallmark of Konstanz, created by Peter Lenk, caused controversy when it was unveiled in April 1993.

Most people enjoy Konstanz for its worldly pleasures—the elegant Altstadt, trips on the lake, walks along the promenade, the classy shops, the restaurants, the views. The heart of the city is the **Marktstätte** (Marketplace), near the harbor, with the simple bulk of the Konzilgebäude looming behind it. Erected in 1388 as a warehouse, the **Konzilgebäude** (Council Hall) is now a concert hall. Beside the Konzilgebäude are statues of Jan Hus and native son Count Ferdinand von Zeppelin (1838–1917). The Dominican monastery where Hus was held before his execution is still here, doing duty as a luxurious hotel, the Steigenberger Insel-Hotel.

The huge aquarium **Sealife** has gathered all the fish species that inhabit the Rhine and Lake Constance, from the river's beginnings in the Swiss Alps to its end in Rotterdam and the North Sea. If you're pressed for time, or the aquarium is crowded with schoolchildren, visit the **Bodensee Naturmuseum** at the side entrance, which gives a comprehensive overview of the geological history of the Bodensee and its fauna and flora right down to the microscopic creatures of the region. ✉ *Hafenstr. 9* ☎ *07531/128–270* 🌐 *www.sealife.de* 🎫 *€10* 🕙 *July and Aug., daily 10–7; May, June, and Sept., daily 10–6; Nov.–Apr., daily 10–5.*

The **Altes Rathaus** (Old Town Hall) was built during the Renaissance and painted with vivid frescoes—swags of flowers and fruits, shields, and sturdy knights wielding immense swords. Walk into the courtyard to admire its Renaissance restraint. Within the medieval guild house of the city's butchers, the **Rosgartenmuseum** (Rose Garden Museum) has a rich collection of art and artifacts from the Bodensee region. Highlights include exhibits of the life and work of the people around the Bodensee, from the Bronze Age through the Middle Ages and beyond. There's also a collection of sculpture and altar paintings from the Middle Ages. ✉ *Rosgartenstr. 3–5* ☎ *07531/900–246* 🎫 *€1.50* 🕙 *Tues.–Fri. 10–6, Fri.–Sun. 10–5.*

Konstanz's cathedral, the **Münster,** was the center of one of Germany's largest bishoprics until 1827, when the seat was moved to Freiburg. Construction on the cathedral continued from the 10th through the 19th centuries, resulting in an interesting coexistence of architectural styles: the twin-tower facade is sturdily Romanesque; the elegant and airy chapels along the aisles are full-blown 15th-century Gothic; the complex nave vaulting is Renaissance; and the choir is severely neoclassic. The Mauritius Chapel behind the altar is a 13th-century Gothic structure, 12 feet high, with some of its original vivid coloring and gilding. It's studded with statues of the Apostles and figures depicting the childhood of Jesus. ✉ *Münsterpl.*

The **Niederburg,** the oldest part of Konstanz, is a tangle of twisting streets leading to the Rhine. From the river take a look at the two city towers: the Rheintor (Rhine Tower), the one nearer the lake, and the aptly named Pulverturm (Powder Tower), the former city arsenal.

Where to Stay & Eat

¢–$$$ ✕ **Latinos.** Every university town needs one of these places where you can either snack, have coffee, enjoy a cocktail, or eat a full meal. Mexican cuisine is supplemented by various vegetarian dishes. The crowd that meets within these adobe walls in the middle of Konstanz is young and dynamic. ✉ *Fischmarkt* ☎ *07531/17399* ▭ *AE, MC, V.*

$–$$ ✕ **Hafenhalle.** You don't have to cross the Swiss border for Swiss *Rösti*—pan-fried potatoes and onions mixed with chopped smoked ham—and Bauernbratwurst; you can just take a seat at this warm-weather spot on the harbor. Sit outside on the terrace and watch the busy harbor traffic. The beer garden has a sandbox for children and a screen to watch sports events, and Sunday brunch is served to live Dixieland jazz. ✉ *Hafenstr. 10* ☎ *07531/21126* ▭ *MC.*

¢–$ ✕ **Brauhaus J. Albrecht.** This small brewery with shiny copper cauldrons has a large dining room serving simple dishes such as fried eggs with home fries, and *Kassler* (smoked pork chops) with potato salad. If you're in a hurry, there are stand-up tables. ✉ *Konradig. 2* ☎ *07531/25045* ▭ *No credit cards.*

¢ ✕ **Sedir.** This little establishment in the house of the "Virgin of the silver moon" looks like an antiques store turned restaurant, with worn-out (but clean) tables, motionless old clocks hanging on the wall, 1970s upholstery on the benches, and an industrial woodstove for heat in winter. But it has charm, a good crowd, and above all, excellent Turkish food including kebabs, noodles, and vegetarian dishes. ✉ *Hofhalde 11* ☎ *07531/29352* ▭ *No credit cards* ⊙ *No lunch Sun.*

$$$–$$$$ Fodor's Choice ★ ✕▣ **Steigenberger Insel-Hotel.** This former 16th-century monastery, with its original cloisters, offers the most luxurious lodging in town. Jan Hus was held prisoner here, and centuries later, Graf Zeppelin was born here. Bedrooms are spacious and stylish, more like those of a private home than a hotel, and many have lake views. The formal terrace restaurant has superb views of the lake. The Dominikanerstube is a smaller, more intimate restaurant. Both restaurants ($$$–$$$$) feature regional specialties, and there's the clubby, relaxed Zeppelin Bar. ✉ *Auf der Insel 1, D–78462* ☎ *07531/125–444* 📠 *07531/26402* 🌐 *www.steigenberger.com* ⇨ *100 rooms, 2 suites* ♨ *2 restaurants, cable TV, Wi-Fi, beach, bar, recreation room, babysitting, meeting rooms, some pets allowed; no a/c* ▭ *AE, DC, MC, V* 🍽 *BP.*

$–$$ ✕🏨 **Barbarossa.** This stately old town house has been modernized inside, but historic elements such as the huge wooden support beams are still visible. Rooms are comfortably furnished; several have been given special themes, such as Romeo and Juliet or Complete Harmony. The stained-glass windows and dark-wood paneling give the restaurant ($–$$$) a cozy, warm atmosphere. Fish and game in season are the specialties. ✉ *Obermarkt 8* ☎ *07531/128–990* 🖷 *07531/1289–9700* 🌐 *www.barbarossa-hotel.com* *55 rooms* *Restaurant, cable TV, in-room data ports, some pets allowed, no-smoking rooms; no a/c* 💳 *AE, D, MC, V* 🍽 *BP.*

$–$$ ✕🏨 **Stadthotel.** This friendly hotel is a five-minute walk from the lake. Some rooms have a bath, others just a shower, but all have a TV. The Poseidon restaurant ($) draws locals and guests with its Greek cuisine. ✉ *Bruderturmg. 12, D–78462* ☎ *07531/90460* 🖷 *07531/904–646* 🌐 *www.stadthotel-konstanz.com* *24 rooms* *Restaurant, cable TV, in-room data ports, some pets allowed; no a/c* 💳 *AE, DC, MC, V* 🍽 *CP.*

$–$$ 🏨 **ABC Hotel.** This sturdy building about 15 minutes on foot or 5 minutes by bus from the center of Konstanz was once upon a time a barracks and casino. Rooms here are large, comfortable, and individually furnished. ✉ *Steinstr. 19, 78467* ☎ *07531/8900* 🖷 *07531/890–299* 🌐 *www.abc-hotel.de* *29* *Cable TV, in-room data ports, no a/c, pets allowed* 💳 *AE, D, MC, V* 🍽 *BP.*

Nightlife & the Arts

The season of the **Bodensee Symphony Orchestra,** based in Konstanz, runs from October through April. Konstanz's international **summer music festival** (☎ 07531/133–030) runs from mid-June to mid-July, including celebrated organ concerts in the cathedral. Performances are held in the picturesque *Renaissancehof* (courtyard) of the town hall. The **Zeltfestival Konstanz** (Tent Festival; ☎ 07531/908–844) at the harbor draws international pop stars to Konstanz on weekends throughout the summer, concluding with the **Rock am See** event at the beginning of September. And if you're in Konstanz around August 9, you will experience the one-day city festival Konstanz shares with neighboring Kreuzlingen in Switzerland called **Seenachtfest** (Lake Night Festival), with street events, music, clowns, and magicians and ending with fireworks over the lake.

The **Stadttheater** (✉ Konzilstr. 11, D–78462 ☎ 07531/130–050 for festival office, 07531/20070 for program details, 07532/82383 for Meersburg program), Germany's oldest active theater, has staged plays since 1609 and has its own repertory company. The local season runs from September through June. From July through August the company moves to its summer theater in Meersburg.

The Bodensee nightlife scene is concentrated in Konstanz. The **casino** (✉ Seestr. 2 ☎ 07531/81570 €3) is open 3 PM–3 AM. **K 9** (✉ Obere Laube 71 ☎ 07531/16713) draws all ages with its dance club, theater, and cabaret in the former Church of St. Paul. Concerts and variously themed DJ nights are held at **Kulturladen** (✉ Joseph Belli Weg 5 ☎ 07531/52954).

An absolute must is the cozy and crowded **Seekuh** (✉ Konzilstr. 1 ☎ 07531/27232), which features the occasional live jazz night. The very popular **Theatercafé** (✉ Konzilstr. 3 ☎ 07531/20243) draws a stylish crowd that's not too hip to dance when the mood strikes.

Shopping

It's worthwhile to roam the streets of the old part of town where there are several gold- and silversmiths and jewelers. Elegant **Modehaus Jacqueline** (✉ Hussenstr. 29 ☎ 07531/22990) has enough style for a city 10 times the size of Konstanz. The store gets most of its business from wealthy Swiss who come to Konstanz for what they consider bargain prices. Jacqueline deals in well-known names such as Rena Lange and Celine and has some unusual Italian lines such as Cavalli. Accessories from Moschino include handbags and exquisite shoes. **Oexle–China and Glassware** (✉ Marktstätte 26 ☎ 07531/21307) carries not only famous china brands such as Meissen, Rosenthal, and Arzberg but also beautiful china and glass of lesser-known names such as Theresienthal and Royal Copenhagen. Among their quality gift items are Hummel figures, Kristallglass, and Swiss army knives.

The small but fine and not too expensive **pierre-moden** (✉ Hussenstr. 3 ☎ 07531/22150) carries bold but stylish men's fashions. You'll find well-known Carlo Colucci's imaginative knitwear, Signum shirts, Joker jeans, and items from Lacoste.

Sports & the Outdoors

BIKING Bike rentals generally cost €10 per day. You can book bicycle tours and rent bikes at **velotours** (✉ Fritz Arnold-Str. 2d ☎ 07531/98280 🌐 www.velotours.de). **Kultur-Rädle** (✉ Hauptbahnhof ☎ 07531/27310) rents bikes at the main train station. The longer you rent the bike, the cheaper the daily rate.

BOATING Sail and motor yachts are available at **Engert Yachtcharter** (✉ Hafenstr. 8 ☎ 07531/26075 🌐 www.bodensee-yachtzentrum.de). Small sailboats can be chartered from **Bodensee Segelschule Konstanz/Wallhausen** (✉ Zum Wittmoosstr. 10, Wallhausen ☎ 07533/4780).

Mainau

9 *7 km (4½ mi) north of Konstanz by road; by ferry, 50 min from Konstanz, 20 min from Meersburg.*

One of the most unusual sights in Germany, Mainau is a tiny island given over to the cultivation of rare plants and splashy displays of more than a million tulips, hyacinths, and narcissi. Rhododendrons and roses bloom from May to July; dahlias dominate the late summer. A greenhouse nurtures palms and tropical plants.

The island was originally the property of the Teutonic Knights, who settled here during the 13th century. In the 19th century Mainau passed to Grand Duke Friedrich I of Baden, a man with a passion for botany. He laid out most of the gardens and introduced many of the island's more exotic specimens. His daughter Victoria, later queen of Sweden, gave the island to her son, Prince Wilhelm, and it has remained Swedish ever since. Today it's owned by Prince Wilhelm's son, Count Lennart

Bernadotte, who lives in the castle. In the former main reception hall are changing art exhibitions.

Beyond the flora, the island's other colorful extravagance is **Das Schmetterlinghaus,** Germany's largest butterfly conservatory. On a circular walk through a semitropical landscape with water cascading through rare vegetation, you'll see hundreds of butterflies flying, feeding, and mating. The exhibition in the foyer explains the butterflies' life-cycle, habitats, and ecological connections. Like the park, this oasis is open year-round.

At the island's information center, **Nature and Culture on Lake Constance,** you can view a multimedia show in which 14 projectors create a three-dimensional effect, capturing the beauty of the countryside around Lake Constance. The show also addresses environmental issues and ways to observe ecologically sound behavior on vacation and at home.

Ferries to the island from Meersburg and Konstanz depart approximately every 1½ hours between 9 and 5. The entrance fee to the island is €11.

Where to Eat

There are three restaurants on the island but no lodgings.

$$–$$$ ✕ **Schwedenschenke.** The lunchtime crowd gets what it needs here—fast and good service. At dinnertime candlelight adds some extra style. The resident Bernadotte family is Swedish, and so are the specialties of the chef. Have your hotel reserve a table for you. In the evening your reservation will be checked at the gate, and you can drive onto the island without having to pay the admission fee. ✉ *Insel Mainau* ☎ *07531/3030* ⏲ *Mar.–Apr. and Oct., Wed.–Sun 10 AM–11 PM; Mon. and Tues. 10 AM–6 PM* ✍ *Reservations essential* 💳 *AE, D, MC, V.*

Reichenau

❿ *10 km (6 mi) northwest of Konstanz, 50 min by ferry from Konstanz.*

Reichenau is an island rich in vegetation, but unlike Mainau, vegetables, not flowers, prevail here. In fact, 15% of its area (the island is 5 km [3 mi long and 1½ km [1 mi wide) is covered by greenhouses and crops of one kind or another. Though it seems unlikely amid the cabbage, cauliflower, lettuce, and potatoes, Reichenau has three of Europe's most beautiful Romanesque churches. This, and the warm microclimate, has earned the island a place on UNESCO's World and Nature Heritage list. Connected to the Bodanrück Peninsula by just a narrow causeway, Reichenau was a great monastic center of the early Middle Ages. Secure from marauding tribesmen on its fertile island, the monastic community blossomed from the 8th through the 12th century, in the process developing into a major center of learning and the arts. The churches are in each of the island's villages—**Oberzell, Mittelzell, and Niederzell,** which are separated only by 1 km (½ mi). Along the shore are pleasant pathways for walking or biking.

The **Stiftskirche St. Georg** (Collegiate Church of St. George), in Oberzell, was built around 900; now cabbages grow in ranks up to its rough plaster walls. Small round-head windows, a simple square tower, and massive buttresses signal the church's Romanesque origin from the outside. The interior is covered with frescoes painted by the monks around 1000. They depict the eight miracles of Christ. Above the entrance is a depiction of the Resurrection.

Begun in 816, the **Münster of St. Maria and St. Markus,** the monastery's church, is the largest and most important of the island's trio of Romanesque churches. Perhaps its most striking architectural feature is the roof, whose beams and ties are open for all to see. The monastery was founded in 725 by St. Pirmin and became one of the most important cultural centers of the Carolingian Empire. It reached its zenith around 1000, when 700 monks lived here. It was then probably the most important center of book illumination in Germany. The building is simple but by no means crude. Visit the **Schatzkammer** (Treasury) to see some of its more important holdings. They include a 5th-century ivory goblet with two carefully incised scenes of Christ's miracles and some priceless stained glass that is almost 1,000 years old. ✉ *Münsterpl. 3, Mittelzell* ☎ *07534/999–5999 for guided tours* ⏲ *May–Sept., daily 11–noon and 3–4.*

Museum Reichenau, a museum of local history, in the Old Town Hall of Mittelzell lends interesting insights into life on the island over the centuries. ✉ *Mittelzell* 🎫 *€1* ⏲ *May–Sept., Tues.–Sun. 3–5.*

The **Stiftskirche St. Peter und St. Paul** (St. Peter and Paul Parish Church), at Niederzell, was revamped around 1750. The faded, Romanesque frescoes in the apse are now contrasted with strong rococo paintings on the ceiling and flowery stucco.

off the beaten path

WOLLMATINGER RIED – Just north of Konstanz on the Bodanrück Peninsula is the 1,000-acre Wollmatinger Ried, a moorland bird sanctuary. There are three-hour guided tours of the moor April through mid-October (Wednesday and Saturday at 4 PM) as well as other nature walks. Native breeding birds include the marsh harrier, hobby falcon, black kite, great reed warbler, and black-necked grebe. There are also remains of prehistoric pile houses. Bring sturdy, comfortable shoes and mosquito repellent. Binoculars can be rented. ✉ *Kindlebildstr. 87* ☎ *07531/78870* 🎫 *Donation requested* ⏲ *Apr.–Sept., weekdays 9–noon and 2–5, weekends 1–5; Oct.–Mar., weekdays 9–noon and 2–5.*

Where to Stay & Eat

$$ **Strandhotel Löchnerhaus.** The Strandhotel (Beach Hotel) stands commandingly on the water's edge, and about 80 yards from its own boat pier. Fresh lake fish figures prominently on the menu of the restaurant ($–$$), as do the island's famous vegetables. Most rooms have lake views; those that don't look out over a quiet, shady garden. ✉ *An der Schiffslände 12, D–78479* ☎ *07534/8030* 📠 *07534/582* *44 rooms* *Restaurant, cable TV, beach, boating, meeting rooms, some pets allowed; no a/c* 💳 *MC, V* *BP.*

Höri

⓫ *Due west across the Bodsensee from Konstanz (follow signs to Radolfzell), about 30 km (19 mi) by road.*

Höri is a rural peninsula, settled with small villages, between the Zeller See and Seerhein portions of Bodensee. In the village of Horn, the beautiful setting of the church **St. Johannes und Veit of Horn** inspired a king of Württemberg to admit, "If I weren't king, I'd like to be the priest of Horn." From here you have a view of the reedy landscape; the Zeller See and the island of Reichenau; the silhouette of Konstanz; and, on a clear day, the snowcapped Alps.

In the early 1900s members of Dresden's artist group Die Brücke discovered the area. The most expressive paintings of the Bodensee landscape were created by Erich Heckel (1883–1970) and Otto Dix (1891–1969). Dix lived in the village of Hemmenhofen from 1936 until his death. You can see some of his landscapes in the **Otto Dix Haus.** ✉ *Hemmenhofen* ☎ *07735/3151* 🎟 *€2.50* ⏲ *Apr.–Oct., Wed.–Sat. 2–5, Sun. 11–4.*

Two handsome half-timber houses in Gaienhofen, one a former schoolhouse, the other a farmhouse, have been turned into a multifunctional museum, the **Herrmann-Hesse-Höri Museum.** The Nobel laureate novelist and poet Hermann Hesse (1877–1962) lived in the farmhouse with his family from 1904 to 1908. His desk, his books, hundreds of pictures, and one of his typewriters are on exhibit. A few rooms are devoted to his friend the writer Ludwig Finck. A typical old Höri living room has been installed, while other rooms are used for special exhibitions and tableaux by local painters. ✉ *Gaienhofen* ☎ *07735/81832* 🎟 *€2.50* ⏲ *Apr.–Oct., Tues.–Sat. 2–5, Sun. 11–5.*

Where to Eat

¢–$ ✕ **Schlössli.** After visiting the museums, this Renaissance castle turned restaurant and beer garden in Horn is an ideal place to muse about life and art while gazing out over the lake. Local dishes are served in the restaurant (fish in lemon sauce, for example), and typical beer-garden food is available out on the lawn: sausages, spare ribs, giant pretzels. ✉ *Hornstaaderstr.* ☎ *07735/2041* 💳 *No credit cards.*

THE BODENSEE A TO Z

To research prices, get advice from other travelers, and book travel arrangements, visit www.fodors.com.

AIRPORTS

The closest international airport to the Bodensee is in Zurich, Switzerland, 60 km (37 mi) from Konstanz, connected by the autobahn. There are also direct trains from the Zurich airport to Konstanz. There are several flights from Berlin, Düsseldorf, Frankfurt, London, and other destinations to the regional airport at Friedrichshafen.

BOAT & FERRY TRAVEL

Note that the English pronunciation of "ferry" sounds a lot like the German word *fähre,* which means car ferry. *Schiffe* is the term used for passenger ferries, which have different docking points from the car ferries in the various towns. The car ferries run all year; in summer you may have to wait in line. The passenger routes, especially the small ones, often do not run in winter, from November to March.

The Weisse Flotte line of boats, which is run by the BSB, or Bodensee-Schiffsbetriebe, links most of the larger towns and resorts. One of the nicest trips is from Konstanz to Meersburg and then on to the island of Mainau. The round-trip cost is €8.80. Excursions around the lake last from one hour to a full day. Many cross to Austria and Switzerland; some head west along the Rhine to the Schaffhausen Falls, the largest waterfall in Europe. Information on lake excursions is available from all local tourist offices and travel agencies.

The best deal for ferry travel is with the *BodenseeErlebniskarte* (Bodensee Card), available at all tourist offices, which gives the holder free use of passenger ships on the Bodensee (not car ferries!) and free access to 190 sights in Germany, Austria, Switzerland, and Liechtenstein, including the island of Mainau, the Zeppelin Museum in Friedrichshafen, the old castle of Meersburg, and the Sealife center in Konstanz. A 3-day card costs €54, a 7-day card €69, and a 14-day card €98. The Bodensee info line gives more information (☎ 07531/90940).

Bodensee-Schiffsbetriebe ✉ Hafenstr. 6, D-78462 Konstanz ☎ 07531/281-389 🌐 www.bsb-online.com ✉ Friedrichshafen ☎ 07541/923-8389 ✉ Lindau ☎ 08382/944-416. In Überlingen, the BSB runs through **Schiffsbetriebe Alfons Heidegger** ✉ Im Guggenbül 3 ☎ 07551/66463. In Konstanz, it's **Ewald Giess** ✉ Seehorn 2 ☎ 07531/5261 who runs tours from the city, notably tours of the harbor.

BUS TRAVEL

Buses serve most smaller communities that have no train links, but service is infrequent. Along the shore there are buses that run every half hour during the day from Überlingen to Friedrichshafen, stopping in towns such as Meersburg, Hagnau, and Immenstaad (which have no train connections).

CAR TRAVEL

Construction on the A–96 autobahn that runs from Munich to Lindau is ongoing. For a more scenic route, take B–12 via Landsberg and Kempten. For a scenic but slower route from Frankfurt, take B–311 at Ulm and follow the Oberschwäbische Barockstrasse (Upper Swabian Baroque Road) to Friedrichshafen. Lindau is also a terminus of the Deutsche Alpenstrasse (German Alpine Road). It runs east–west from Salzburg to Lindau.

Lakeside roads in the Bodensee area boast wonderful vistas but experience occasional heavy traffic in summer. Stick to the speed limits in spite of the aggressive tailgaters: speed traps are frequent, especially in built-up areas. Formalities at border-crossing points are few. However, in addition to your passport you'll need insurance and registration papers for your car. For rental cars check with the rental company to make sure you are allowed to take the car into another country. Car ferries link Romanshorn, in Switzerland, with Friedrichshafen, as well as Konstanz with Meersburg. Taking either ferry saves substantial mileage. The fare depends on the size of the car; a one-way fare for a medium-size car including the driver costs €7.

TOURS

Most of the larger tourist centers have city tours with English-speaking guides, but call ahead to confirm availability.

AIRPLANE TOURS A fascinating way to view the lake is from a three-passenger Cessna operated by Slansky/Dussmann from Friedrichshafen's airport. They will also take you into the Alps, if you wish.

Slansky/Dussmann ☎ 07532/808–866 or 08388/1269.

BIKING TOURS The Bodensee is a paradise for bike travelers, with hundreds of miles of well-signposted paths that keep riders safe from cars. You can go on your own or enjoy the comfort of a customized tour with accommodations and baggage transport around the Bodensee (including a bike, if need be).

Bodensee-Radweg-Service GmbH ✉ Mainaustr. 34, Konstanz ☎ 07531/942–3640 🌐 www.bodensee-radweg.com. **Velotours** ✉ Fritz-Arnold-Str. 2d, Konstanz ☎ 07531/98280 🌐 www.velotours.de.

WINE TOURS Wine-tasting tours are available in Überlingen, in the atmospheric Spitalweingut zum Heiligen Geist, as well as in Konstanz and Meersburg. Call the local tourist offices for information.

Spitalweingut zum Heiligen Geist ✉ Mühlbachstr. 115 ☎ 07551/65855.

ZEPPELIN TOURS Zeppelin tours operated by the DZR (*Deutsche Zeppelin Reederei)* are not cheap (a one-hour sightseeing trip costs €335–€375), but they do offer a special feel and a reminder of the grand old days of flight. The zeppelins depart from the airport in Friedrichshafen.

DRZ ☎ 07541/59000 🌐 www.zeppelinflug.de.

TRAIN TRAVEL

From Frankfurt to Friedrichshafen and Lindau, take the ICE (InterCity Express) to Ulm and then transfer (total time 3½ hours). There are direct trains to Konstanz from Frankfurt every two hours (travel takes 4½ hours), which pass through the beautiful scenery of the Black Forest. From Munich to Lindau, the EC (Europe Express) train takes 2½ hours. From Zurich to Konstanz, the trip lasts 1½ hours. Local trains encircle the Bodensee, stopping at most towns and villages.

VISITOR INFORMATION

Information on the entire Bodensee region is available from the Internationaler Bodensee Tourismus.

Friedrichshafen ✉ Tourist-Information, Bahnhofpl. 2, D–88045 ☎ 07541/30010 🌐 www.friedrichshafen.de. **Internationaler Bodensee Tourismus** ✉ Insel Mainau, D–78465 Konstanz ☎ 07531/90940 📠 07531/909–494 🌐 www.bodensee-tourismus.com. **Konstanz** ✉ Tourist-Information, Konstanz, Fischmarkt 2, D–78462 ☎ 07531/133–030 🌐 www.konstanz.de. **Lindau** ✉ Verkehrsverein Lindau, Stadtpl., D–88103 ☎ 08381/

80328 🌐 www.lindau.de. **Meersburg** ✉ Verkehrsverwaltung, Kirchstr. 4, D-88709 ☎ 07532/431-110 🌐 www.meersburg.de. **Ravensburg** ✉ Städtisches Verkehrsamt, Kirchstr. 16, D-88212 ☎ 0751/82324 🌐 www.ravensburg.de. **Reichenau** ✉ Verkehrsbüro, Pirminstr. 145, D-78479 ☎ 07534/92070 🌐 www.reichenau.de. **Tettnang** ✉ Verkehrsamt, Montfortpl. 1, D-88069 ☎ 07542/953-839 🌐 www.tettnang.de. **Überlingen** ✉ Kur und Touristik Überlingen, Am Landungspl. 14, D-88662 ☎ 07551/991-122 🌐 www.ueberlingen.de. **Weingarten** ✉ Kultur- und Verkehrsamt, Münsterpl. 1, D-88250 ☎ 0751/405-125 🌐 www.weingarten-online.de.

The Black Forest

6

WORD OF MOUTH

"If you want some forest with your Black Forest, you need to go deeper than Freiburg or Tübingen. Triberg's all right, but Titisee . . . enjoys a dramatic lakeside setting with wonderful mountain scenery and has no lack of cuckoo clocks or 'Kaffee und Kuchen' spots."

—Russ

"Gengenbach is very, very pretty, with lots of half-timbered houses, old towers, walls, etc. In the days leading up to Christmas, they dress up the town hall as a giant advent calendar, the windows being the days, and each day they open one."

—chtiet

www.fodors.com/forums

Updated by
Ted Shoemaker

THE NAME CONJURES UP IMAGES OF A WILD, isolated place where time passes slowly. The dense woodland of the Black Forest—Schwarzwald in German—stretches away to the horizon, but this southwest corner of Baden-Württemberg (in the larger region known as Swabia) is neither inaccessible nor dull. Its distinctive characteristics include the cuckoo clock, the women's native costume with big red or black pom-poms on the hat, and the weird, almost pagan way the Carnival season is celebrated. The first travelers checked in here 19 centuries ago, when the Roman emperor Caracalla and his army rested and soothed their battle wounds in the natural-spring waters at what later became Baden-Baden.

Europe's upper-crust society discovered Baden-Baden when it convened nearby for the Congress of Rastatt from 1797 to 1799, which attempted to end the wars of the French Revolution. In the 19th century, kings, queens, emperors, princes, princesses, members of Napoléon's family, and the Russian nobility, along with actors, writers, and composers, flocked to the little spa town. Turgenev, Dostoyevsky, and Tolstoy were among the Russian contingent. Victor Hugo was a frequent visitor. Brahms composed lilting melodies in this calm setting. Queen Victoria spent her vacations here, and Mark Twain waxed poetic on the forest's beauty in his 1880 book *A Tramp Abroad,* putting the Black Forest on the map for Americans.

Today it's a favorite getaway for movie stars and millionaires, and you, too, can "take the waters," as the Romans first did, at thermal resorts large or small. The Black Forest sporting scene caters particularly to the German enthusiasm for hiking. The Schwarzwald-Verein, an outdoors association in the region, maintains no fewer than 30,000 km (18,000 mi) of hiking trails. In winter the terrain is ideally suited for cross-country skiing.

The Black Forest's enviable great outdoors is blessed with dependable snow in winter and sun in summer. Freudenstadt, at the center of the Black Forest, claims the greatest number of annual hours of sunshine of any town in Germany. The summer's warmth also benefits the vineyards of the Badische Weinstrasse (Baden Wine Road), which parallels, mainly to the east, the A–5 autobahn and the Rhine, using secondary roads to link up such places as Baden-Baden, Offenburg, Lahr, and Schliengen. Baden cooperatives produce mostly dry wines that go well with the region's fine traditional food.

The Black Forest also happens to be the home of the cuckoo clock. It's still made (and sold) here, as it has been for centuries, along with handcarved wood items and exquisite examples of glassblowing. Clockmaking gave rise to a precision-mechanics industry that is a guarantor of prosperity and employment throughout the region.

Despite its fame and the wealth of some of its visitors, the Black Forest doesn't have to be an expensive place to visit. It's possible to stay at a modest family-run country inn or farmhouse where the enormous breakfast will keep you going for the better part of the day—all for not much more than the price of a meal in a city restaurant.

Many first-time visitors to the Black Forest literally can't see the forest for the trees. Take time to stray from the beaten path and inhale the cool air of the darker recesses. Walk or ride through its shadowy corridors; paddle a canoe down the rippling currents of the Nagold and Wolf rivers. Then take time out to relax in a spa, order a dry Baden wine, and seek out the nearest restaurant for local specialties.

Numbers in the text correspond to numbers in the margin and on the Black Forest map.

If you have
3 days

Start at the confluence of three rivers in **Pforzheim** 1. Envy the glittering jewelry collection at the famous Schmuckmuseum, and then visit nearby Maulbronn's beautiful 12th-century Cistercian abbey. Spend a night in **Calw** 2, and, after a visit to the nearby ruined abbey in **Hirsau,** head south to **Triberg** 11, site of Germany's highest waterfall and the lore of the cuckoo clock. Spend the night in Triberg and on the last day go north to look at the farmhouses at the Open-Air Museum Vogtsbauernhof, near **Gutach** 10, before driving along the Schwarzwald-Hochstrasse (Black Forest Highway) from Mummelsee (with a stop at the lake) to **Baden-Baden** 5, the best spot for a special evening out.

If you have
5 days

Begin your trip by following the first two days of the three-day itinerary described above. On the third day continue directly south of Triberg to **Furtwangen** 12 to survey Germany's largest clock museum. The **Titisee** 13, the jewel of the Black Forest lakes, is a good place to spend the third night. After taking some time to enjoy the water, head up the winding road northwest through the **Höllental.** End your day in **Freiburg** 15; its Münster (cathedral) has the most perfect spire of any German Gothic church. On your fourth day, drive north from Freiburg on B–3 through the Baden vineyards to elegant **Baden-Baden** 5, where you can soak away your fifth day in thermal waters.

If you have
10
days

After visiting the attractions near **Pforzheim** 1, spend the first two nights in **Calw** 2, from which, on the second day, you can visit Hirsau and Weil der Stadt. **Freudenstadt** 3 is a good base for the next two days; from here make excursions to the Schwarzwälder Freilichtmuseum Vogtsbauernhof in **Gutach** 10; **Baiersbronn** 4; and Glaswaldsee (Glasswald Lake), near Schapbach. On the fifth day continue on to **Triberg** 11 to explore its waterfall and cuckoo-clock museum and then to **Furtwangen** 12. Spend the fifth and sixth nights near the shores of the **Titisee** 13. From the lake, visit the Feldberg, the Black Forest's highest mountain, and the Schluchsee. Spend the following two days and nights in **Freiburg** 15, allowing time for the town of **Staufen** 16, where the legendary Dr. Faustus made his pact with the devil; the vineyards on the slopes of the **Kaiserstuhl** 17; and Germany's biggest amusement park, **Europa Park** 18. Finally, drive north through the Rhine Valley for two nights in **Baden-Baden** 5. Indulge in the city's attractions and take a trip to nearby Merkur Mountain.

Exploring the Black Forest

The northern Black Forest is known for its broad ridges and thickly forested slopes; it contains the largest number of spas in the region. The central Black Forest, Triberg in particular, is especially popular for its associations with folklore, cuckoo clocks, and the Schwarzwaldbahn (Black Forest Railway). The southern Black Forest has the most dramatic scenery and the most-frequented recreation areas. Two main attractions are the Titisee and the Schluchsee, two beautiful lakes created by glaciers.

About the Restaurants & Hotels

Restaurants in the Black Forest range from the well-upholstered luxury of Baden-Baden's chic eating spots to simple country inns. Old *Kachelöfen* (tile-heating stoves) are still in use in many area restaurants; try to sit by one if it's cold outside.

Accommodations in the Black Forest are varied and numerous, from simple rooms in farmhouses to five-star luxury. Some properties have been passed down in the same family for generations. *Gasthöfe* offer low prices and as much local color as you'll ever want.

WHAT IT COSTS In Euros

	$$$$	$$$	$$	$	¢
RESTAURANTS	over €25	€21–€25	€16–€20	€9–€15	under €9
HOTELS	over €225	€175–€225	€100–€175	€50–€100	under €50

Restaurant prices are per person for a main course at dinner. Hotel prices are for two people in a standard double room, including tax and service.

Timing

The Black Forest is one of the most heavily visited mountain regions in Europe, so make reservations well in advance for the better-known spas and hotels. In summer the areas around Schluchsee and Titisee are particularly crowded. In early fall and late spring, the Black Forest scenery is less crowded (except during the Easter holidays) but just as beautiful. Some spa hotels close for the winter.

THE NORTHERN BLACK FOREST

This region is crossed by broad ridges that are densely wooded, with little lakes such as the Mummelsee and the Wildsee. The Black Forest Spa Route (270 km [167 mi]) links many of the spas in the region, from Baden-Baden (the best known) to Bad Wildbad. Other regional treasures are the lovely Nagold River; ancient towns such as Bad Herrenalb and Hirsau; and the magnificent abbey at Maulbronn, near Pforzheim.

Bicycling Bicycles can be rented in nearly all towns and many villages. The Deutsche Bahn, Germany's national railway, has excellent deals on bicycle rentals at train stations. Several regional tourist offices sponsor tours on which the biker's luggage is transported separately from one overnight stop to the next. Six- to 10-day tours are available at reasonable rates, including bed-and-breakfast and bike rental.

On the Menu Don't pass up the chance to try *Schwarzwälder Schinken* (pinecone-smoked ham) and *Schwarzwälder Kirschtorte* (kirsch-soaked layers of chocolate cake with sour cherry and whipped-cream filling). *Kirschwasser,* locally called *Chriesewässerle* (from the French *cerise,* meaning "cherry"), is cherry brandy, the most famous of the region's excellent schnapps varieties. If traveling in May or June, keep an eye out for white asparagus, the "king of vegetables."

Hiking & Walking The Black Forest is ideal for walkers. The principal trails are well marked and cross the region from north to south, the longest stretching from Pforzheim to the Swiss city of Basel, 280 km (174 mi) away. Walks vary in length from a few hours to a week. As in many other German regions, the tourist office has gotten together with local inns to create *Wandern ohne Gepäck* (Hike without Luggage) tours along the old clock carriers' route. Your bags are transported ahead by car to meet you each evening at that day's destination.

Spas & Health Resorts There's an amazing variety of places to have a relaxing soak, from expensive spa towns to rustic places deep in the woods—any town that begins with "Bad" is home to either natural thermal or mineral springs that are pumped into modern spa facilities. Many Germans come here for two- to three-week health treatments; others use the same healing waters as a weekend refresher. Baden-Baden is the most stately and expensive of the spa towns. Hinterzarten also provides opportunities to hike. Many of the spas offer special rates for longer stays.

Winter Sports Despite Swiss claims to the contrary, the Black Forest is the true home of downhill skiing. In 1891 a French diplomat was sighted sliding down the slopes of the Feldberg, the Black Forest's highest mountain, on what are thought to be the world's first downhill skis. The idea caught on among the locals, and a few months later Germany's first ski club was formed. The world's first ski lift opened at Schollach in 1907. There are now more than 200 ski lifts in the Black Forest, but the slopes of the Feldberg are still the top ski area.

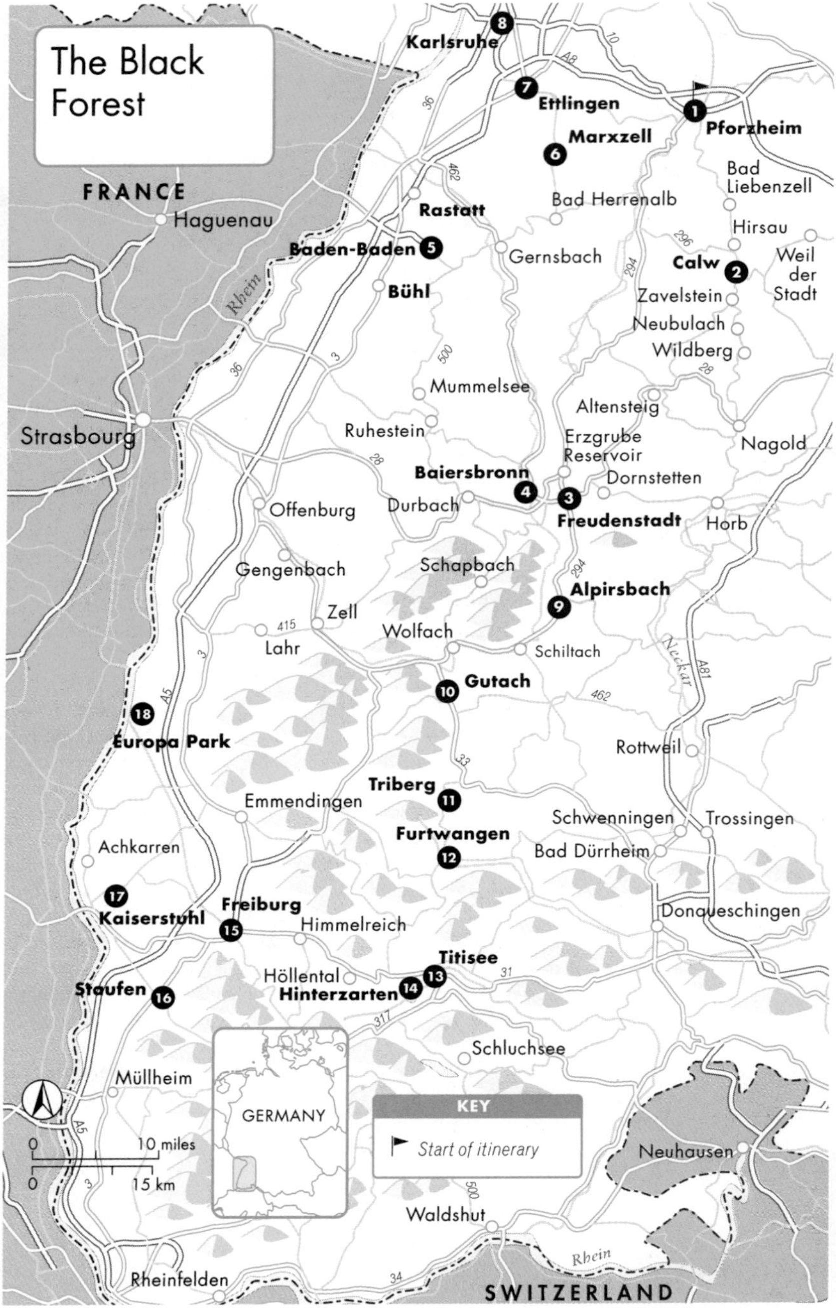
The Black Forest
FRANCE
Haguenau
Strasbourg
Rhein
Karlsruhe
Ettlingen
Pforzheim
Marxzell
Bad Liebenzell
Bad Herrenalb
Rastatt
Hirsau
Baden-Baden
Gernsbach
Calw
Weil der Stadt
Bühl
Zavelstein
Neubulach
Wildberg
Mummelsee
Altensteig
Ruhestein
Erzgrube Reservoir
Nagold
Baiersbronn
Dornstetten
Durbach
Freudenstadt
Horb
Offenburg
Gengenbach
Schapbach
Alpirsbach
Zell
Lahr
Wolfach
Schiltach
Neckar
Gutach
Europa Park
Rottweil
Triberg
Emmendingen
Schwenningen
Trossingen
Furtwangen
Bad Dürrheim
Achkarren
Kaiserstuhl
Freiburg
Himmelreich
Donaueschingen
Titisee
Höllental
Hinterzarten
Staufen
Schluchsee
Müllheim
GERMANY
KEY
Start of itinerary
0 10 miles
0 15 km
Neuhausen
Waldshut
Rheinfelden
SWITZERLAND

Pforzheim

1 *35 km (22 mi) southeast of Karlsruhe, just off A–8 autobahn, the main Munich–Karlsruhe route.*

The Romans founded Pforzheim at the meeting place of three rivers, the Nagold, the Enz, and the Würm, and it's known today as the "gateway to the Black Forest." The city was almost totally destroyed in World War II, which accounts for its not-so-attractive blocky postwar architectural style. Pforzheim owes its prosperity to its role in Europe's jewelry trade and its wristwatch industry. To get a sense of the "Gold City," explore the jewelry shops on streets around Leopoldplatz and the pedestrian area. The restored church of **St. Michael** (✉ Schlossberg 10), near the train station, is the final resting place of the Baden princes. The original mixture of 13th- and 15th-century styles has been faithfully reproduced; compare the airy Gothic choir with the church's sturdy Romanesque entrance.

The Reuchlinhaus, the city cultural center, houses the **Schmuckmuseum** (Jewelry Museum). Its collection of jewelry from five millennia is one of the finest in the world. The museum nearly doubled in size in 2005, adding pocket watches and ethnographic jewelry to its objects of envy. ✉ *Jahnstr. 42* ☎ *07231/392–126* 🌐 *www.schmuckmuseum-pforzheim.de* 🎫 *Free* ⏲ *Tues.–Sun. 10–5.*

Pforzheim has long been known as a center of the German clock-making industry. In the **Technisches Museum** (Technical Museum), one of the country's leading museums devoted to the craft, you can see makers of watches and clocks at work; there's also a reconstructed 18th-century clock factory. ✉ *Bleichstr. 81* ☎ *07231/392–869* 🎫 *Free* ⏲ *Wed. 9–noon and 3–6, 2nd and 4th Sun. of month 10–5.*

★ **Kloster Maulbronn** (Maulbronn Monastery), in the little town of Maulbronn, 18 km (11 mi) northeast of Pforzheim, is the best-preserved medieval monastery north of the Alps, with an entire complex of 30 buildings on UNESCO's World Heritage List. The main buildings were constructed between the 12th and 14th centuries. The name Maulbronn (Mule Fountain) derives from a legend. Monks seeking a suitably watered site for their monastery considered it a sign from God when one of their mules discovered and drank at a spring. The monastery's fortified walls still stand, and its medieval water-management system, with its network of drains, irrigation canals, and reservoirs, remains intact. ✉ *Off B–35* ☎ *07043/926–610* 🌐 *www.maulbronn.de* 🎫 *€4.50* ⏲ *Mar.–Oct., daily 9–5:30; Nov.–Feb., Tues.–Sun. 9:30–5; guided tour at 11:15 and 3.*

Where to Eat

$$–$$$ ✕ **Silberburg.** The Alsatian owners of this cozy restaurant serve classic French cuisine. Try the duck with one of chef Gilbert Noesser's exquisite sauces. ✉ *Altstädter Kirchenweg 3* ☎ *07231/441–159* 💳 *AE, DC, MC, V* ⏲ *Closed June and Aug. No lunch Sat. and Mon.*

en route

The road south of Pforzheim, B–463, follows the twists and turns of the pretty little Nagold River. Gardening enthusiasts should follow the signs to the **Alpine Garden** (on the left as you leave the city limits). The garden, on the banks of the Würm River, stocks more than 100,000 varieties of plants, including the rarest Alpine flowers. It has a pleasant café and florist shop. ☎ *07231/70590* 🌐 *www.alpengarten-pforzheim.de* 🎫 *€2.50* ⏲ *Apr.–Oct., daily 8–7.*

Weil der Stadt, a former imperial city, is in the hills 17 km (10 mi) southeast of Pforzheim. This small, sleepy town of turrets and gables has only its well-preserved city walls and fortifications to remind you of its onetime importance. The astronomer Johannes Kepler, born here in 1571, was the first man to track and accurately explain the orbits of the planets. And, appropriately, the town now has a planetarium to graphically show you what he learned. The little half-timber house in which he was born is now the **Kepler Museum** (✉ Keplerg. 2 ☎ 07033/6586 🌐 www.kepler-museum.de 🎫 €2, tour €10 ⏲ Tues.–Fri. 10–noon and 2–4, Sat. 11–noon and 2–4, Sun. 11–noon and 2–5) in the town center. It's devoted to his writings and discoveries.

Calw

❷ *24 km (14 mi) south of Pforzheim on B–463.*

Calw, one of the Black Forest's prettiest towns, was the birthplace of Nobel prize–winning novelist Hermann Hesse (1877–1962). He was born at Marktplatz 6, now a private home. The town's market square, with its two sparkling fountains surrounded by 18th-century half-timber houses whose sharp gables pierce the sky, is an ideal spot for relaxing, picnicking, or people-watching, especially when it's market time.

The **Hermann Hesse Museum** recounts the life of the Nobel Prize–winning philosopher, author of *Steppenwolf* and *The Glass Bead Game,* who rebelled against his middle-class German upbringing to become a pacifist and the darling of the beat generation. The story of his life is told in personal belongings, photographs, manuscripts, and documents. (You can rent a recorder with earphones to guide you in English.) ✉ *Marktpl. 30* ☎ *07051/7522* 🌐 *www.hermann-hesse.com* 🎫 *€5* ⏲ *Tues.–Wed. and Fri.–Sun. 11–5, Thurs. 11–7.*

Hirsau, 3 km (2 mi) north of Calw, has ruins of a 9th-century monastery, now the setting for the Klosterspiele Hirsau (open-air theater performances) in July and August. Buy advance tickets at the **Calw tourist office** (✉ Marktbrücke 1 ☎ 07051/968–810).

Where to Stay & Eat

★ $–$$ ✕🏨 **Hotel Kloster Hirsau.** This hotel, a model of comfort and gracious hospitality, is just outside Calw in Hirsau, near the ruins of the monastery. The Klosterschenke restaurant ($–$$) serves such regional specialties as *Flädelsuppe* (containing pieces of a special, very thin pancake) and *Schwäbischer Rostbraten* (panfried beefsteak topped with sautéed onions). ✉ *Wildbaderstr. 2, D–75365* ☎ *07051/96740* 🖷 *07051/967–469* 🌐 *www.hotel-kloster-hirsau.de* *42 rooms* *Restaurant, cable TV, in-room broadband, in-room data ports, Wi-Fi, 2 tennis courts, indoor pool, sauna, bowling, some pets allowed (fee), no-smoking rooms; no a/c* *AE, MC, V* *BP.*

¢ **Ratsstube.** Most of the original features, including 16th-century beams and brickwork, are preserved at this historic house in the center of Calw. Rooms are small but half-timber like the exterior. The restaurant (¢–$) serves a selection of sturdy German and Greek dishes. A salad buffet will take care of smaller appetites, and lunchtime always has a special dish. ✉ *Marktpl. 12, D–75365* ☎ *07051/92050* 🖷 *07051/70826* 🌐 *www.hotel-ratsstube.de* *13 rooms* *Restaurant, some pets allowed; no a/c, no TV in some rooms* *MC, V* *BP.*

Freudenstadt

3 *65 km (35 mi) south of Calw, 22 km (14 mi) southwest of Altensteig.*

At an altitude of 2,415 feet, Freudenstadt claims to be the sunniest German resort. The town was flattened by the French in April 1945, and it has since been rebuilt with painstaking care. It was founded in 1599 to house both silver miners and refugees from religious persecution in what is now the Austrian province of Carinthia (*Freudenstadt* means "city of joy").

The vast central square, more than 650 feet long and edged with arcaded shops, is Germany's largest marketplace, though it's difficult to admire its vastness. A busy, four-lane street cuts it in two. The square still awaits the palace that was supposed to be built here for the city's founder, Prince Frederick I of Württemberg, who died before work could begin. When the fountains all spout on this vast expanse, it can be quite a sight, and a refreshing one as well. Don't miss Freudenstadt's Protestant **stadtkirche,** just off the square. Its lofty nave is L-shape, a rare architectural liberty in the early 17th century. It was constructed in this way so the sexes would be separated and unable to see each other during services.

off the beaten path

SCHAPBACH – This town lies 22 km (14 mi) southwest of Freudenstadt, in the enchanting Wolfach River valley. From here, head up into the hills to **Glaswaldsee** (Glasswald Lake). You will probably find yourself alone with the tree-fringed lake. Parts of the neighboring Poppel Valley are so wild that carnivorous flowers number among the rare plants carpeting the countryside. In July and August the bug-eating *Sonnentau* is in full bloom in the **Hohlohsee** (Hohloh Lake) nature reserve, near Enzklösterle. Farther north, just off B–500 near Hornisgrinde Mountain, a path to the remote **Wildsee** passes through a nature reserve where rare wildflowers bloom in spring.

Where to Stay & Eat

★ $$–$$$$ **Warteck.** The lead-pane windows with stained-glass work, flowers, and beautifully upholstered banquettes create a bright setting in the two dining rooms. Proprietor and chef Werner Glässel uses only natural products and spotlights individual ingredients. A popular dish is the squab in a dough jacket. In season the *Spargel* (asparagus) is dressed in an aromatic hazelnut vinaigrette. ✉ *Stuttgarterstr. 14* ☎ *07441/91920* 💳 *AE, DC, MC, V* ⊙ *Closed Tues.*

¢–$ ✕ **Ratskeller.** Though there's a cellar, this restaurant with pine furnishings is more a modern bistro than traditional Ratskeller. Meatless Black Forest dishes, served in frying pans, are huge and filling. Also offered are such Swabian dishes as Zwiebelrostbraten, served with sauerkraut, and pork fillet with mushroom gravy. A special menu for seniors has smaller portions. ✉ *Marktpl. 8* ☎ *07441/952–805* 💳 *AE, MC, V* ⊙ *Closed Tues. Nov.–Mar.*

$ ✕🏨 **Bären.** The Montigels have owned the sturdy old Gasthof Bären since 1878, and they strive to maintain tradition and personal service. In the beamed restaurant ($–$$$) the wine is served in a *viertele* glass with a handle and a grape pattern; game comes from the family's own preserve; they have their own *schnaps* distillery, and the trout is caught locally. Sauerkraut, that typical German dish, is imported from *France,* and is soaked in champagne. Rooms are modern. ✉ *Langestr. 33, D–72250* ☎ *07441/2729* 📠 *07441/2887* 🌐 *www.hotel-baeren-freudenstadt.de* *33 rooms* *Restaurant, cable TV, no-smoking rooms; no a/c* 💳 *DC, MC, V* ⊙ *Restaurant closed Fri. No lunch except Sun.* 🍽 *BP.*

¢–$ ✕🏨 **Hotel Adler.** This is a simple hotel between the main square and the train station. Some of the very affordable rooms even have balconies so you can enjoy a view of behind-the-scenes Freudenstadt. The restaurant ($) provides a square meal with local dishes. There are four Flammkuchen evenings a week. Flammkuchen is a specialty of neighboring Alsace, similar to a pizza but thinner, and with toppings such as sour cream, bacon, and onions. ✉ *Forststr. 15–17, D–72250* ☎ *07441/91520* 📠 *07441/915–252* 🌐 *www.adler-fds.de* *13 rooms* *Restaurant, cable TV, in-room broadband, in-room data ports, Internet room; no a/c* 💳 *MC, V* ⊙ *Restaurant closed Wed.* 🍽 *BP.*

$ ✕🏨 **Zum Schwanen.** This bright, white building just a few steps from the main square has a guest room with a water bed for those with allergies. Many locals come to the restaurant ($) to enjoy fine regional specialties, not to mention giant pancakes. The pancakes, big as a platter, are topped with everything from salmon and mushrooms to applesauce and plums. ✉ *Forststr. 6, D–72250* ☎ *07441/91550* 📠 *07441/915–544* 🌐 *www.schwanen-freudenstadt.de* *17 rooms, 1 apartment* *Restaurant, cable TV, in-room data ports, some pets allowed (fee), no-smoking rooms; no a/c* 💳 *MC, V* 🍽 *BP.*

Shopping

Germans prize Black Forest ham as an aromatic souvenir. You can buy one at any butcher shop in the region, but it's more fun to visit a *Schinkenräucherei* (smokehouse), where the ham is actually cured in a stone chamber. **Hermann Wein's** (✉ Dornstetterstr. 29, 72250 Musbach ☎ 07443/2450 🌐 www.schinken-wein.de) Schinkenräucherei, in the village of Musbach, near Freudenstadt, is one of the leading smokehouses in the area. If you have a group of people, call ahead to find out if the staff can show you around.

Baiersbronn

4 *7 km (4½ mi) northwest of Freudenstadt.*

The mountain resort of Baiersbronn has an incredible collection of hotels and bed-and-breakfasts providing rest and relaxation in beautiful surroundings. Most people come here to walk, ski, golf, and ride horseback. You may want to walk through the streets to preview the many restaurants. Near the town hall and church in the upper part of town is the little **Hauff's Märchenmuseum** (Fairy-Tale Museum), devoted to the crafts and life around Baiersbronn and the fairy-tale author Wilhelm Hauff (1802–27), who once lived here. ✉ *Rosenpl. 3* ☎ *07442/841–414* 🎫 *€1.50* ⏲ *Wed. and weekends 2–5.*

Where to Stay & Eat

★ $$$$ ✕🏨 **Bareiss.** This modern resort resembles a cruise ship moored on a hilltop above Baiersbronn. Inside, some guest rooms have dark-wood furniture and tapestry-papered walls, whereas others have a light and airy look. Its three restaurants range from the elegant Bareiss ($$$$), where you'll find 30 brands of champagne, to the Kaminstube ($$$–$$$$), which offers dining near the fireplace. There's also the rustic Dorfstube ($$). The hotel itself is among the most lavish and best equipped in the Black Forest. Suites start at €470 and one has its own sauna, solarium, and whirlpool bath. ✉ *Gärtenbühlweg 14, D–72270 Mitteltal/Baiersbronn* ☎ *07442/470* 📠 *07442/47320* 🌐 *www.bareiss.com* *69 rooms, 39 apartments, 11 suites* *3 restaurants, cable TV, some in-room data ports, tennis court, 9 pools (8 indoor), hair salon, sauna, bicycles, bowling, bar, some pets allowed (fee), no-smoking rooms; no a/c in some rooms* 💳 *AE, DC, MC, V in restaurants only; no credit cards in hotel* 🍽 *MAP.*

$$$$ Fodor'sChoice ★ ✕🏨 **Traube Tonbach.** The luxurious Traube Tonbach hotel has three restaurants. If the classic French cuisine of the Schwarzwaldstube (menus begin at €74) is too expensive, try either the international fare of the Köhlerstube or the Bauernstube, renowned for its Swabian dishes. In the latter two you'll dine beneath beam ceilings at tables bright with fine silver and glassware. The hotel is a harmonious blend of old and new, and each room presents sweeping views of the Black Forest. A small army of extremely helpful and friendly staff nearly outnumbers the guests. ✉ *Tonbachstr. 237, D–72270 Tonbach/Baiersbronn* ☎ *07442/4920* 📠 *07442/492–692* 🌐 *www.traube-tonbach.de* *108 rooms, 55 apartments, 12 suites* *3 restaurants, cafeteria, cable TV, tennis court, 3 pools (2 indoor), gym, hair salon, sauna, bowling, bar, Internet room; no a/c in some rooms* 💳 *AE, DC, MC, V in restaurants only; no credit cards in hotel* 🍽 *BP.*

$$ ✕🏨 **Hotel Lamm.** The steep-roofed exterior of this 200-year-old typical Black Forest building presents a clear picture of the traditional hotel within. Rooms are furnished with heavy oak fittings and some fine antiques. In winter the lounge's fireplace is a welcome sight when returning from the slopes (the ski lift is nearby). In its beamed restaurant ($–$$) you can order fish fresh from the hotel's trout pools. ✉ *Ellbacherstr. 4, D–72270 Mitteltal/Baiersbronn* ☎ *07442/4980* 📠 *07442/49878* 🌐 *www.lamm-*

mitteltal.de 🛏 *33 rooms, 13 apartments* ⚐ *Restaurant, cable TV, Wi-Fi, pool, sauna, some pets allowed (fee); no a/c* 💳 *DC, MC, V* 🍽 *BP.*

en route

The back road from Baiersbronn, via Mitteltal and Obertal, enables you to join the Schwarzwald Hochstrasse at the little village of Ruhestein. From this little village, there's a well-marked back road to the west that leads to the **Allerheiligen** (All Saints) ruins. This 12th-century monastery was secularized in 1803, when plans were drawn up to turn it into a prison. Two days later lightning started a fire that burned the monastery to the ground. The locals claim it was divine intervention.

Bühl

17 km (11 mi) north of Ruhestein, 16 km (10 mi) south of Baden-Baden.

Several of the finest hotels and restaurants in the Black Forest are on Bühlerhöhe, the thickly wooded heights above the town of Bühl. The Bühl Valley and the surrounding area have spas, ruins, quaint villages, and a legendary velvety red wine called *Affenthaler.*

Where to Stay & Eat

★ $$$$ **Schlosshotel Bühlerhöhe.** This premier "castle-hotel" stands majestically on its own extensive grounds 15 km (9 mi) above Baden-Baden, with spectacular views over the heights of the Black Forest. Walking trails start virtually at the hotel door. Its restaurant, the Imperial ($$$$; closed Monday and Tuesday and January–mid-February), features French fare with international touches, such as lamb in feta cheese crust with ratatouille and gnocchi. In its Schlossrestaurant, overlooking the Rhine Valley, regional and international dishes are offered. ✉ *Schwarzwaldhochstr. 1, D–77815 Bühl/Baden-Baden* ☎ *07226/550* 📠 *07226/55777* 🌐 *www.buehlerhoehe.de* 🛏 *64 rooms, 16 suites* ⚐ *2 restaurants, in-room safes, minibars, cable TV, in-room broadband, in-room data ports, Wi-Fi, tennis court, pool, health club, sauna, bar, Internet room, some pets allowed (fee), no-smoking rooms; no a/c in some rooms* 💳 *AE, DC, MC, V.*

$ **Cafe-Pension Jägersteig.** Magnificent views of the wide Rhine Valley as far as the French Vosges Mountains are included in the room rate at this spectacularly situated pension, high above the town of Bühl and its vineyards. ✉ *Kappelwindeckstr. 95a, D–77815 Bühl/Baden-Baden* ☎ *07223/98590* 📠 *07223/985–998* 🌐 *www.jaegersteig.de* 🛏 *14 rooms* ⚐ *Restaurant, cable TV, in-room data ports, some pets allowed (fee); no a/c* 💳 *MC, V* 🍽 *BP.*

Baden-Baden

★ 5 *51 km (32 mi) north of Freudenstadt, 24 km (15 mi) north of Mummelsee.*

Baden-Baden, the famous and fashionable spa, is downhill all the way north on B–500 from the Mummelsee. The town rests in a wooded valley and is atop the extensive underground hot springs that gave the city its name. Roman legions of the emperor Caracalla discovered the springs and named the area Aquae. The leisure classes of the 19th century rediscovered the bubbling waters, establishing Baden-Baden as the unofficial summer residence of many European royal families. The town's fortunes also rose and fell with gaming: gambling began in the mid-18th century and was banned between 1872 and 1933. Palatial homes and stately villas grace the tree-lined avenues and the spa tradition continues at the ornate casino and two thermal baths, one historic and luxurious, the other modern and well-used by families.

The small city offers a good life to the many millionaires who retire here. Though some Germans come here for doctor-prescribed treatments, the spa concept also embraces "wellness" for those just looking for pampering. Shops line several pedestrian streets that eventually climb up towards the old marketplace. Two theaters present frequent ballet performances, plays, and concerts (by the excellent Southwest German Radio Symphony Orchestra).

6

Bordering the slender Oos River that runs through town, the **Lichtentaler Allee** is a groomed park with two museums and an extensive rose garden, the **Gönneranlage,** which contains more than 300 types of roses. Close by is the **Russian church** (€.50 Feb.–Nov. 10–6), identifiable by its golden onion dome.

In 2004 the museum **Sammlung Frieder Burda** opened within a modern structure by acclaimed New York architect Richard Meier. The private collection focuses on classic modern and contemporary art. Highlights are works of Picasso, German expressionists, the New York School, and American abstract expressionists. *Lichtentaler Allee 8 07221/398–980 www.sammlung-frieder-burda.de €8 Tues. and Thurs.–Sun. 11–6, Wed. 11–8.*

The Lichtentaler Allee ends at **Kloster Lichtenthal,** a medieval Cistercian abbey surrounded by defensive walls. The small royal chapel next to the church was built in 1288 and was used from the late 14th century onward as a final resting place for the Baden dynasty princes. You must call ahead if your group wants a tour. *Hauptstr. 40 07221/504–910 Tours in groups of 7 or more €2 Tours Tues.–Sun. at 3.*

Baden-Baden is quite proud of its **casino,** Germany's oldest, opened in 1855 after Parisian interior decorators and artists had polished the last chandelier. Its concession to the times is that you may wear your jeans amidst all the frescoes, stucco, and porcelain (but why would you?). Gentlemen must wear a jacket and tie with their jeans, and whatever you do leave your sneakers at the hotel. It was in 1853 that a Parisian, Jacques Bénazet, persuaded the sleepy little Black Forest spa to build gambling rooms to enliven its evenings. The result was a series of richly decorated gaming rooms in which even an emperor could feel at home—and did. Kaiser Wilhelm I was a regular visitor, as was his chancellor, Bismarck. The Russian novelist Dostoyevsky, the Aga Khan, and Marlene Dietrich all patronized the place. The minimum stake is €2; maximum €7,000. Passports are necessary as proof of identity. Guided tours (30 minutes) are offered. *Kaiserallee 1 07221/30242 www.casino-*

baden-baden.de *€3, tour €4 Sun.–Thurs. 2 PM–2 AM, Fri. and Sat. 2 PM–3 AM. Tours Apr.–Sept., daily 9:30–11:45 AM; Oct.–Mar., daily 10–11:45 AM.*

The region's wines, especially the dry Baden whites and delicate reds, are highly valued in Germany. Buy them directly from any vintner on the Baden Wine Road. At Yburg, outside Baden-Baden, the 400-year-old **Nägelsförster Hof vineyard** (✉ Nägelsförsterstr. 1 ☎ 07221/35550) has a shop where you can buy the product and sample what you buy (weekdays 9–6, Saturday 10–4).

Where to Stay & Eat

$$$–$$$$ ✕ **Le Jardin de France.** This clean, crisp little French restaurant, whose owners are actually French, emphasizes elegant, imaginative dining in an elegant Victorian setting. The duck might be roasted with raisins, figs, and nuts at Christmastime; the Breton lobster is prepared with bouillon and ginger. ✉ *Lichtentalerstr. 13* ☎ *07221/300–7860* *AE, DC, MC, V* *Closed Mon. No lunch Tues.*

$–$$ ✕ **Klosterschänke.** This rustic restaurant is a 10-minute drive from the center of Baden-Baden, and the food is well worth the trip, particularly on a summer evening, when you can dine outside on a tree-covered terrace. You'll probably share a rough oak table with locals; the Baden wine and locally brewed beer ensure conviviality. The menu is surprisingly imaginative, and it's the best place for venison when it's in season in fall and winter. ✉ *Landstr. 84* ☎ *07221/25854* *MC, V* *Closed Mon. and 2 wks in Aug. No lunch Tues.*

¢–$ ✕ **Weinstube Zum Engel.** The Frölich family has been in charge of the Angel (in the suburb of Neuweier) for four generations. Eduard Frölich is responsible for the wine, Gerti Frölich for the kitchen. It's an ideal place for traditional German food such as sauerbraten or Wiener schnitzel. The selection of wines, served by the glass, does supreme justice to the fine local vintages. ✉ *Mauerbergstr. 62* ☎ *07223/57243* *No credit cards* *Closed Mon. and Tues.*

★ **$$$–$$$$** ✕ **Der Kleine Prinz.** Antoine de Saint-Exupéry's illustrations for his 1943 French children's classic, *Le Petit Prince,* are everywhere, from a multistoried mural in the courtyard to the plates in the posh restaurant ($$$–$$$$). Owners Norbert Rademacher, a veteran of the New York Hilton and Waldorf Astoria, and his interior-designer wife, Edeltraud, have skillfully combined two elegant city mansions into a unique, antiques-filled lodging. ✉ *Lichtentalerstr. 36, D–76530* ☎ *07221/346–600* *07221/346–6059* *www.derkleineprinz.de* *25 rooms, 15 suites* *Restaurant, minibars, cable TV with movies, in-room data ports, bar, laundry service, Internet room, parking (fee), some pets allowed (fee)* *AE, MC, V* *BP.*

$$$$ FodorsChoice ★ **Brenner's Park Hotel & Spa.** With some justification, this stately hotel set in a private park claims to be one of the best in the world. Behind it passes leafy Lichtentaler Allee, where Queen Victoria and Czar Alexander II, among others, strolled in their day. Luxury abounds in the hotel, and all the rooms and suites (the latter costing up to €680 a day) are sumptuously furnished and appointed. An extensive beauty and fitness program is offered. ✉ *Schillerstr. 6, D–76530* ☎ *07221/9000* *07221/*

38772 🌐 www.brenners-park.de ⇨ 68 rooms, 30 suites ♖ 2 restaurants, cable TV, in-room data ports, indoor pool, gym, hair salon, 4 saunas, spa, bar, Internet room, some pets allowed (fee); no a/c in some rooms ▭ AE, DC, MC, V.

$$$–$$$$ **Belle Époque.** The heyday of Baden-Baden was during the decades prior to World War I, which the French refer to as the *belle époque* (beautiful era). This spacious two-story 1870s house, in its own garden behind wrought-iron gates, captures the gracious spirit of this period. The entire building, a sister hotel to Der Kleine Prinz, is under monument protection. Each of its suites and rooms, many with whirlpool baths, is furnished in a separate style, ranging from Henri II to art nouveau, and afternoon tea is included in the room price along with breakfast. Under the eaves are the Brahms or Mozart rooms, garrets of sheer luxury. In the garden is Baden-Baden's only California redwood. ✉ *Maria-Victoria-Str. 2c, D–76530 ☎ 07221/300–660 📠 07221/300–666 🌐 www.hotelbelleepoque.de ⇨ 5 rooms, 9 suites ♖ Cable TV, in-room data ports, Wi-Fi ▭ AE, MC, V 🍴 BP.*

$$ **Deutscher Kaiser.** This central, established hotel provides homey and individually styled rooms at comfortable prices. All the double rooms have balconies on a quiet street. The hotel is around the corner from the casino. ✉ *Merkurstr. 9, D–76530 ☎ 07221/2700 📠 07221/270–270 🌐 www.deutscher-kaiser-baden-baden.de ⇨ 28 rooms ♖ Cable TV, in-room broadband, in-room data ports, some pets allowed (fee); no a/c ▭ AE, DC, MC, V 🍴 BP.*

$$ **Merkur.** The Merkur's large, comfortable rooms typify the high standards of German hospitality. A solid breakfast is served in the pleasant breakfast room. In the middle of Baden-Baden, the hotel's setting is quiet. If you stay for three, five, or seven days, ask for the special package, which includes cheaper rates, free admission to the casino and the Caracalla-Therme, a sumptuous meal, free parking, a glass of champagne, and a special cocktail at the bar. ✉ *Merkurstr. 8 ☎ 07221/3030 📠 07221/303–333 🌐 www.hotel-merkur.com ⇨ 44 rooms ♖ Restaurant, cable TV with movies, in-room data ports, Wi-Fi, bar, Internet room, no-smoking rooms; no a/c ▭ AE, DC, MC, V 🍴 BP.*

$ **Am Markt.** This 250-plus-year-old building houses a modest inn run (for more than 50 years) by the Bogner family. In the oldest part of town—a traffic-free zone, reached by pedestrians through an uphill climb—it's close to such major attractions as the Roman baths. Some rooms overlook the city. ✉ *Marktpl. 17–18, D–76530 ☎ 07221/27040 📠 07221/270–444 🌐 www.hotel-am-markt-baden.de ⇨ 25 rooms, 14 with bath ♖ Internet room, some pets allowed; no a/c, no TV in some rooms ▭ AE, DC, MC, V 🍴 BP.*

Nightlife & the Arts

Nightlife revolves around Baden-Baden's elegant **casino,** but there are more cultural attractions as well. Baden-Baden has one of Germany's most beautiful performance halls, the **Theater** (✉ Am Goethepl. ☎ 07221/932–700), a late-baroque jewel built in 1860–62 in the style of the Paris Opéra. It opened with the world premiere of Berlioz's opera *Beatrice et Benedict.* Today the theater presents a regular series of dramas, operas, and ballets.

The **Festspielhaus** (✉ Beim Alten Bahnhof 2 ☎ 07221/301–3101) is a state-of-the-art concert hall superbly fitted onto the old train station. Each summer Baden-Baden holds a two-week **Philharmonischer Sommer Festival** (✉ Schloss Solms, Solmsstr. 9 ☎ 07221/932–791). Venues include the Kurhaus, the Kurgarten, Marktplatz, and the Brenner's Park Hotel. The **Kurhaus** (✉ Kaiserallee 1 ☎ 07221/353202) adjoining the casino hosts concerts year-round.

Baden-Baden attracts a mature crowd, but the deep leather seats of the **Trinkhalle** (✉ Kaiserallee 3) make a hip lounge for those under 40. At night, this daytime bistro also takes over the portion of the hall where the tourist office has a counter, turning it into a dance floor. The Hotel Merkur has a small nightclub called the **Living Room** (✉ Merkurstr. 8 ☎ 07221/303–366). For a subdued evening stop by the **Oleander Bar** (✉ Schillerstr. 6 ☎ 07221/9000), in Baden-Baden's top hotel, the Brenner's Park.

Sports & the Outdoors

GOLF The 18-hole Baden-Baden course is considered one of Europe's finest. Contact the **Golf Club** (✉ Fremersbergstr. 127 ☎ 07221/23579).

HORSEBACK RIDING The racetrack at nearby **Iffezheim** (☎ 07229/1870) still shows signs of Baden-Baden's elegant past. Its tradition dates back to 1858, and annual international meets take place in late May, late August, early September, and October. Those wishing to ride can rent horses and get instruction at the **Reitzentrum Baden-Baden** (✉ Buchenweg 42 ☎ 07221/55920).

SWIMMING The **Caracalla Therme** is the most lavish thermal swimming-pool complex in the Black Forest region. Built in the 1980s, it has one indoor and two outdoor pools, six saunas, a solarium, Jacuzzis, and several state-of-the-art fitness areas. ✉ *Römerpl. 1* ☎ *07221/275–940* 🌐 *www.carasana.de* 🎫 *2 hrs €12, 3 hrs €14, 4 hrs €16* ⏲ *Daily 8 AM–10 PM.*

The **Friedrichsbad** is a 19th-century bathing paradise of steam baths and thermal pools, to be taken in a particular sequence. The sexes have different entrances but meet in the middle, so to speak, after dipping into various hot (and cold) bathing areas. Visit on Monday or Thursday, or use the Caracalla-Therme if you're not comfortable with the mixed nude bathing on other days. You must be 14 or older to enter the Friedrichsbad. ✉ *Römerpl. 1* ☎ *07221/275–920* 🌐 *www.carasana.de* 🎫 *3 hrs €21; 3½ hrs, including brush massage, €29* ⏲ *Mon.–Sat. 9 AM–10 PM, Sun. noon–8.*

en route

The road to Gernsbach, a couple of miles east of Baden-Baden, skirts the 2,000-foot-high mountain peak **Merkur,** named after a Roman monument to the god Mercury, which still stands just below the mountain summit. You can take the cable car to the summit, but it's not a trip for the fainthearted—the incline of close to 50% is one of Europe's steepest. 🎫 *Round-trip €4* ⏲ *Daily 10–10.*

Rastatt

12 km (7½ mi) north of Baden-Baden.

The pink-sandstone, three-wing **Schloss,** the centerpiece of Rastatt, was built at the end of the 17th century by Margrave Ludwig Wilhelm of Baden (known as Ludwig the Turk for his exploits in the Turkish wars). It was the first baroque palace of such enormous proportions to be built in Germany. Its highlights include the chapel, gardens, and a pagoda. Inside the palace itself are museums of German history. Guided tours are possible if you call ahead. ✉ *Herrenstr. 8, D–76437* ☎ *07222/34244* 🎫 *€3* ⏲ *Nov.–Mar., Fri.–Sun. 9:30–5; Apr.–Oct., Tues.–Sun. 9:30–5.*

Five kilometers (3 mi) south of Rastatt, in Förch, Ludwig the Turk's Bohemian-born wife, Sibylle Augusta, constructed her own charming little summer palace, **Schloss Favorite,** after his death. Inside, in an exotic, imaginative baroque interior of mirrors, tiles, and marble, her collection of miniatures, mosaics, and porcelain is strikingly displayed. ✉ *Am Schloss Favorite 5* ☎ *07222/41207* 🎫 *€6* ⏲ *Mid-Mar.–Sept., Tues.–Sun. 10–5; Oct.–mid-Nov., Tues.–Sun. 10–4.*

Marxzell

❻ *36 km (22 mi) northeast of Baden-Baden.*

In the village of Marxzell a group of ancient locomotives and other old machines at the side of the road lure you into the **Fahrzeugmuseum** (Vehicle Museum). It looks more like a junkyard, with geese and ducks waddling freely about, but every kind of early engine is represented in this museum dedicated to the German automobile pioneer Karl Benz (1844–1929). Germans say it was he who built the first practical automobile, in 1888, a claim hotly disputed by the French. They assert a Frenchman constructed a steam-powered tricycle in 1769 that seated four and traveled for 20 minutes at 3.6 kph (2.25 mph). Items on display, many of them French, include motorcycles, Rolls-Royces, Mercedes, Alfa Romeos, Jaguars, and a vintage fire engine. ✉ *Albtalstr. 2* ☎ *07248/6262* 🌐 *www.fahrzeugmuseum-marxzell.de* 🎫 *€3* ⏲ *Daily 2–5.*

Ettlingen

❼ *12 km (7 mi) north of Marxzell.*

Ettlingen is a 1,200-year-old town that is now practically a suburb of its newer and much larger neighbor, Karlsruhe, just a streetcar ride away. Bordered by the Alb River, Ettlingen's ancient center is a maze of auto-free cobblestone streets. Come in summer for the annual Schlossberg theater and music festival in the beautiful baroque **Schloss.** The palace was built in the mid-18th century, and its striking domed chapel has been converted into a concert hall. Its ornate, swirling ceiling fresco is typical of the heroic, large-scale, illusionistic decoration of the period. ✉ *Schlosspl. 3* ☎ *07243/101–273* 🎫 *Free* ⏲ *Wed.–Sun. 10–5; tour weekends at 2.*

Where to Stay & Eat

$–$$$ **Ratsstuben.** Originally used to store salt, these 16th-century cellars by the fast-flowing Alb River now welcome diners who come to enjoy international fare. There's also a pleasant terrace for summer dining on the marketplace. *Kirchenpl. 1–3* *07243/76130* *AE, DC, MC, V.*

★ $$$ **Hotel-Restaurant Erbprinz.** For many, the real reason for staying at this historic hotel is the top-rated restaurant's magnificent nouvelle German cuisine ($$$$)—though the rooms are also very comfortable. In summer dine in the charming garden, hidden away behind the hotel's green-and-gilt fencing. You might want to try apple pancakes flambéed with calvados for dessert. *Rheinstr. 1, D–76275* *07243/3220* *07243/322–322* *www.hotel-erbprinz.de* *83 rooms, 8 suites* *Restaurant, minibars, cable TV, in-room broadband, in-room data ports, gym, 3 saunas, some pets allowed (fee); no a/c in some rooms* *AE, DC, MC, V* *BP.*

Karlsruhe

8 *10 km (6 mi) north of Ettlingen.*

Karlsruhe, founded at the beginning of the 18th century, is a young upstart, but what it lacks in years it makes up for in industrial and administrative importance, sitting as it does astride a vital autobahn and railroad crossroads. It's best known as the seat of the German Supreme Court and has a high concentration of legal practitioners.

The town quite literally grew up around the former **Schloss** of the Margrave Karl Wilhelm, which was begun in 1715. Thirty-two avenues radiate from the palace, 23 leading into the extensive grounds, and the remaining nine forming the grid of the Old Town. The **Badisches Landesmuseum** (Baden State Museum), in the palace, has a large number of Greek and Roman antiquities and trophies that Ludwig the Turk brought back from campaigns in Turkey in the 17th century. Most of the other exhibits are devoted to local history. *Schloss* *0721/926–6514* *www.landesmuseum.de* *€4* *Tues.–Thurs. 10–5, Fri.–Sun. 10–6.*

★ One of the most important collections of paintings in the Black Forest region hangs in the **Staatliche Kunsthalle** (State Art Gallery). Look for masterpieces by Grünewald, Holbein, Rembrandt, and Monet and also for work by the Black Forest painter Hans Thoma. In the **Kunsthalle Orangerie,** next door, is work by such modern artists as Braque and Beckmann. *Hans-Thoma-Str. 2* *0721/926–3355* *www.kunsthalle-karlsruhe.de* *Both museums €4* *Tues.–Fri. 10–5, weekends 10–6.*

★ In a former munitions factory, the vast **Zentrum für Kunst und Medientechnologie** (Center for Art and Media Technology), or simply ZKM, is an all-day adventure consisting of two separate museums. At the **Medienmuseum** (Media Museum) you can watch movies, listen to music, try out video games, flirt with a virtual partner, or sit on a real bicycle and pedal through a virtual New York City. The **Museum für Neue Kunst** (Museum of Modern Art; 0721/8100–1325) is a top-notch collection of media art in all genres from the end of the 20th century. Take

Bus 55 to Brauerstrasse to get here. ✉ *Lorenzstr. 19* ☎ *0721/8100–1200* 🌐 *www.zkm.de* *Either museum €5, combined ticket €8* ⏲ *Both museums Wed.–Fri. 10–6, weekends 11–6.*

Where to Stay & Eat

$$–$$$$ ✕ **Buchmanns.** Elke and Günter Buchmann run a "linen tablecloth and real silver" establishment, with a beer garden and a bar. The various suggested courses are grouped in fancy handwriting on the menu, along with the fancy price of each dish. You can, of course, just order one of the courses, but be prepared for a disapproving look. The proprietors are Austrian, and the specialties of their country, such as *Tafelspitze* (boiled beef with chive sauce) and *Kaiserschmarrn* (egg pancakes with apples, raisins, cinnamon and jam) are especially recommended. ✉ *Mathystr. 22–24* ☎ *0721/820–3730* 💳 *AE, V* ⏲ *Closed Sun.*

$$$$ ✕ **Schlosshotel.** A few steps from the main station and adjacent to the zoo you'll find this "Palace Hotel," so called because it looks, and sometimes behaves, like a palace. It's proud of its marble bathrooms and an elevator dating from 1914 with mirrors and a menu from 1943, but the guest rooms are similar to that of modern hotels. The restaurant Zum Grossherzog ($$–$$$) serves international haute cuisine and the very *gemütlich* Schwarzwaldstube ($$–$$$) has Baden specialties. ✉ *Bahnhofpl. 2, D–76137* ☎ *07/213–8320* 📠 *0721/383–2333* 🌐 *www.schlosshotel-karlsruhe.de* *96 rooms, 3 suites* *2 restaurants, snack bar, in-room broadband, in-room data ports, minibars, gym, sauna, steam room, bar, Weinstube, library, some free parking, Internet room; some pets allowed (fee), no-smoking rooms, a/c in some rooms* 💳 *AE, DC, MC, V* ⏲ *Zum Grossherzog closed Sun.*

The Arts

One of the best opera houses in the region is Karlsruhe's **Badisches Staatstheater** (✉ Baumeisterstr. 11 ☎ 0721/35570).

THE CENTRAL BLACK FOREST

The Central Black Forest takes in the Simonswald, Elz, and Glotter valleys as well as Triberg and Furtwangen, with their clock museums. The area around the Triberg Falls—the highest falls in Germany—is also renowned for pom-pom hats, thatch-roof farmhouses, and mountain railways. The Schwarzwaldbahn (Black Forest Railway; Offenburg–Villingen line), which passes through Triberg, is one of the most scenic in all of Europe.

Alpirsbach

9 *16 km (10 mi) south of Freudenstadt.*

The Kloster Alpirsbach monastery was built in flamboyant Gothic style and has had several restorations. The **Brauerei** (brewery) was once part of the monastery and has brewed beer since the Middle Ages. The unusually soft water gives the beer a flavor that is widely acclaimed. The brewery has a museum and souvenir shop. The museum can only be visited weekends at 3 PM from April through October, when a tour is offered. The charge for it is €4, which includes two glasses of beer. At other times, call ahead to arrange a visit. ✉ *Marktpl. 1* ☎ *01805/001–862* 🌐 *www.alpirsbacher.de* 🎟 *€4 for tour on Sat. at 3* PM.

Where to Stay & Eat

¢–$ ✕ **Zwickel & Kaps.** That name is a highly sophisticated brewing term, describing the means by which the brewmaster samples the fermenting product. Sit down at one of the massive wooden tables—next to the porcelain-tile stove if it's a cold day—and order a bowl of *Flädelsuppe* (broth with pancake strips) and beef stewed in local wine. ✉ *Marktstr. 3* ☎ *07444/51727* 💳 *AE, MC, V* ⏲ *Closed Mon., 2 wks after Carnival, and 2 wks late Aug.–early Sept.*

Gutach

10 *17 km (11 mi) north of Triberg.*

Gutach lies in Gutachtal, a valley famous for the traditional costume, complete with pom-pom hats, worn by women on feast days and holidays. Married women wear black ones, unmarried women red ones. The village is one of the few places in the Black Forest where you can still see thatch roofs. However, escalating costs caused by a decline in skilled thatchers, and soaring fire insurance premiums, make for fewer thatch roofs than there were 20 years ago.

Near Gutach is one of the most appealing museums in the Black Forest, the **Schwarzwälder Freilichtmuseum Vogtsbauernhof** (Black Forest Open-Air Museum). Farmhouses and other rural buildings from all parts of the region have been transported here from their original locations and reassembled, complete with traditional furniture, to create a living museum of Black Forest building types through the centuries. Demonstrations ranging from traditional dances to woodworking capture life as it was in centuries past. ✉ *B–33* ☎ *07831/93560* 🌐 *www.vogtsbauernhof.org* 🎟 *€5* ⏲ *Apr.–Oct., daily 9–6.*

off the beaten path

SCHWARZWALDER TRACHTENMUSEUM – Regional traditional costumes can be seen at this museum in a former Capuchin monastery in the village of Haslach, 10 km (6 mi) northwest of Gutach. Pom-pom-topped straw hats, bejeweled headdresses, embroidered velvet vests, and *Fasnet* (Carnival) regalia of all parts of the forest are on display. The town, which is somewhat secluded, still has an original and unpolished look and feel to it. ✉ *Klosterstr. 1* ☎ *07832/706–172* 🌐 *www.trachtenmuseum-haslach.de.vu* 🎟 *€2* ⏲ *Apr.–Oct., Tues.–Sat. 9–5, Sun. 10–5; Nov.–Dec. and Feb.–Mar., Tues.–Fri. 9–noon and 1–5; Jan. by appointment.*

Triberg

★ 11 *16 km (10 mi) south of Gutach.*

The cuckoo clock, that symbol of the Black Forest, is at home in the Triberg area. It was invented here, it's made and sold here, it's featured in two museums, and the town has "the world's largest cuckoo clock."

At the head of the Gutach Valley, the Gutach River plunges nearly 500 feet over seven huge granite steps at Triberg's **waterfall,** Germany's highest. The pleasant 45-minute walk from the center of town to the top of the spectacular falls is well signposted. You can also take a longer walk that goes by a small pilgrimage church and the old Mesnerhäschen, the sacristan's house. *Waterfall €1.50. €1.30 in winter.*

Black Forest culture is the focus of Triberg's famous **Schwarzwaldmuseum** (Black Forest Museum), with its impressive collection of cuckoo clocks and other items deriving from the woodworking tradition. ✉ *Wallfahrtstr. 4* ☎ *07722/4434* *www.schwarzwaldmuseum.de* *€4* *Daily 10–5.*

6

You can buy a cuckoo clock, or just about any other souvenir, at the huge **Eble Uhren-Park,** which is also the location of the giant, house-sized cuckoo clock. ✉ *On Hwy. B–33 between Triberg and Hornberg* ☎ *07722/96220* *www.eble-uhren-park.de* *Apr.–Oct., Mon.–Sat. 9–6, Sun. 10–6; Nov.–Mar., Mon.–Sat. 9–6, Sun. 11–4.*

The **Haus der 1000 Uhren** (House of 1,000 Clocks) occupies two old houses right at the waterfall. A second store, just off B–33 toward Offenburg, in the suburb of Gremmelsbach, boasts a giant cuckoo clock. ✉ *Hauptstr. 79–81* ☎ *07722/96300* *www.houseof1000clocks.de* *Apr.–Oct., Mon.–Sat. 9–5, Sun. 10–4; Nov.–Mar., Mon.–Sat. 10–5, Sun. 10–4.*

Hubert Herr is the only factory that continues to make nearly all their own components for their cuckoo clocks. You can examine the various types and models in the exhibition room and, if you wish, buy your own Hubert Herr original. ✉ *Hauptstr. 8* ☎ *07722/4268* *www.huberthherr.de.*

The Horberg–Triberg–St. Georgen segment of the **Schwarzwaldbahn** (Black Forest Railway) is one of Germany's most scenic train rides. The 149-km (93-mi) Schwarzwaldbahn, built from 1866 to 1873, runs from Offenburg to Lake Constance via Freudenstadt and Triberg. It has no fewer than 39 tunnels and at one point climbs 600 meters (656 yards) in just 11 km (6½ mi). It's now part of the German Railway, and you can make inquiries at any station.

Where to Stay & Eat

$$–$$$$ **Romantik Parkhotel Wehrle.** The steep-eaved, wisteria-covered facade of this large mansion dominates the town center. Rooms are individually furnished in a variety of woods with such pleasant touches as fresh flowers. The main restaurant ($$–$$$$) has international haute cuisine; the Ochsenstube ($–$$) tends toward specialties from Baden, such as trout done a dozen different ways, all delicious. ✉ *Gartenstr. 24, Triberg im Schwarzwald D–78098* ☎ *07722/86020* *07722/860–290* *www.parkhotel-wehrle.de* *50 rooms, 1 apartment, 1 suite* *3 restaurants, cable TV, in-room broadband, in-room data ports, Wi-Fi, 2 pools (1 indoor), gym, massage, sauna, parking, some pets allowed (fee), no-smoking rooms; no a/c* *AE, DC, MC, V* *BP.*

★ **$** **Hotel-Restaurant-Pfaff.** This old post-and-beam restaurant ($–$$$$), with its blue-tile Kachelofen, attracts people of all types with affordable regional specialties. Try the fresh *Forelle* (trout), either steamed or

CUCKOO! FOR CUCKOO CLOCKS

"**SWITZERLAND HAD BROTHERLY LOVE** *and 500 years of democracy and peace. And what did they produce? The cuckoo clock."*

So said Orson Welles in the classic 1949 film The Third Man. *He misspoke in two ways. First, the Swiss are an industrious, technologically advanced people. And second, they didn't invent the cuckoo clock. That was the work of the Germans living in the adjacent Black Forest.*

The first cuckoo clock was designed and built in 1750 by Franz Anton Ketterer in Schönwald near Triberg. He cleverly produced the cuckoo sound with a pair of wooden whistles, each attached to a bellows activated by the clock's mechanism.

Over the following years the making of carved wooden clocks developed rapidly in the Black Forest. The people on the farms needed ways to profitably occupy their time during the long snowbound winters, and the carving of clocks was the answer. Wood was abundant, and the early clocks were entirely of wood, even the works.

Come spring one of the sons would don a traditional smock and hat, mount the family's winter output on a big rack, hoist it to his back, and set off into the world to sell the clocks. In 1808 there were 688 clock-makers and 582 clock peddlers in the districts of Triberg and Neustadt.

The Uhrentrager *(clock carrier) is an important part of the Black Forest tradition. Guides often wear his costume and a Triberg travel bureau arranges for hikers to travel the trails he knew.*

The traditional cuckoo clock is made with brown stained wood with a gabled roof and some sort of woodland motif carved into it, such as a deer's head or a cluster of leaves. The works are usually activated by cast-iron weights, in the form of pinecones, on chains.

Today's clocks can be much more elaborate. Dancing couples in traditional dress automatically move to the sound of a music box, a mill wheel turns on the hour, a farmer chops wood on the hour, the Uhrentrager *even makes his rounds. The cuckoo itself moves its wings and beak and rocks back and forth when calling.*

The day is long past when the clocks were made entirely of wood. The works are of metal, and therefore more reliable and accurate. Other parts of the clock, such as the whistles, the face, and the hands, are usually of plastic now, but hand-carved wood is still the rule for the case.

The industry is still centered around Triberg. There are two museums in the area with sections dedicated to it, and clocks are sold everywhere, even in the kiosks. In Triberg itself, you can visit the "House of 1000 Clocks," located right at Germany's highest waterfall, or the firm of Hubert Herr, the only factory that continues to make cuckoo clocks practically from scratch.

The regional tourist office offers Wandern ohne Gepäck *(Hike without Luggage) tours along the old clock carriers' route. The participating hotels are connected by one-day hikes in a circular route, each section ranging from 16 km to 27 km (10 mi to 17 mi). Your bags are transported ahead by car to meet you each evening at that day's destination. Prices are reasonable: three nights with hotel and breakfast start at €185. For reservations and information contact* **Wandern Ohne Gepäck** *(Uhrenträgergemeinschaft ✉ Gartenstr. 24, D–78098 Triberg ☎ 07722/860–236 📠 07722/860–290 🌐 www.uhrentraeger.de).*

— Ted Shoemaker

Gasthof (in the pan), garnished with mushrooms. The Pfaff family has owned the inn since 1882, and some rooms have balconies overlooking the famous waterfall. ✉ *Hauptstr. 85, D–78098* ☎ *07722/4479* 📠 *07722/7897* 🌐 *www.hotel-pfaff.com* *10 rooms* *Restaurant, cable TV, some pets allowed (fee), no-smoking rooms; no a/c* 💳 *AE, DC, MC, V* 🍽 *BP.*

Rottweil

26 km (16 mi) east of Triberg.

Rottweil has the best of the Black Forest's Fasnet celebrations. Outside the Black Forest, the celebrations are good-natured and sophisticated, but here and in adjacent areas of Switzerland they're pagan and fierce. In the days just before Ash Wednesday, usually in February, witches and devils roam the streets wearing ugly wooden masks and making fantastic gyrations as they crack whips and ring bells. If you can't make it to Rottweil during the Carnival season, you can still catch the spirit of Fasnet. There's an exhibit on it at the **Stadtmuseum,** and tours are organized to the shops where they carve the masks and make the costumes and bells. The name *Rottweil* may be more familiar to you as the name for a breed of dog. The area used to be a center of meat production, and the Rottweiler was bred to herd the cattle.

Furtwangen

12 *16 km (10 mi) south of Triberg.*

The somewhat nondescript Furtwangen is on a tourist route dubbed the German Clock Road. You don't have to be a clock enthusiast, however, to drop in on the **Uhren Museum** (Clock Museum), the largest such museum in Germany. In a huge, ingeniously designed space, the museum charts the development of Black Forest clocks and exhibits all types of timepieces, from cuckoo clocks, church clock mechanisms, kinetic wristwatches, and old decorative desktop clocks to punch clocks and digital blinking objects. The oddest piece is the "art clock" by local artisan August Noll, which was built from 1880 to 1885 and features the time in Calcutta, New York, Melbourne, and London, among other places. It emits the sound of a crowing rooster in the morning, and other chimes mark yearly events. It's occasionally demonstrated during tours. You can set your own watch to the sun dial built into the concrete of the square in front of the museum. This remarkable creation nearly ticks off the seconds. ✉ *Robert-Gerwig-Pl. 1* ☎ *07723/920–2800* 🌐 *www.deutsches-uhrenmuseum.de* *€3* *Apr.–Oct., daily 9–6; Nov.–Mar., daily 10–5.*

off the beaten path

NATURPARK SUDSCHWARZWALD – Traveling 7 km (4 mi) northeast of Furtwangen, first along the Katzensteig and then along the Neuweg, gets you into the heart of the Naturpark Sudschwarzwald. There you'll find a little spring with an adjacent mountain guest house called the Kolmenhof. A plaque smugly proclaims this little trickle of water to be the source of one of Europe's longest and mightiest rivers, the Danube. Locals won't admit it, but this fact is disputed. Donaueschingen, a little to the east, also claims this honor for one of its little springs. One thing of which there can be no argument: the Danube isn't "blue," here or anyplace else. Muddy yellow is more like it.

THE SOUTHERN BLACK FOREST

In the south you'll find the most spectacular mountain scenery in the area, culminating in the Feldberg—at 4,899 feet the highest mountain in the Black Forest. The region also has two large lakes, the Titisee and the Schluchsee. Freiburg is a romantic university city with vineyards and a superb Gothic cathedral.

Titisee

13 *37 km (23 mi) south of Furtwangen.*

The Titisee, carved by a glacier in the last ice age, is the most scenic lake in the Black Forest. The landscape is heavily wooded and ideal for long bike tours, which can be organized through the Titisee tourist office. The lake measures 2½ km (1½ mi) long and is invariably crowded in summer. Boats and Windsurfers can be rented at several points along the shore.

Where to Stay & Eat

$ **Hotel Adler Post.** This solid old building is in the middle of Neustadt, a township to the east of Titisee, about 5 km (3 mi) from the lake. All the rooms are comfortable and traditionally furnished, some with hand-painted furniture and exposed beams. The reception room is full of Biedermeier antiques. The restaurant (¢–$$) cooks up excellent local specialties. ✉ *Hauptstr. 16, Titisee/Neustadt, D–79822* ☎ *07651/939–390* 🖷 *07651/93939–33* 🌐 *www.adler-post-titisee.de* *28 rooms* *Restaurant, cable TV, in-room broadband, Wi-Fi, pool, gym, massage, sauna, bar, some pets allowed (fee), no-smoking rooms; no a/c* *MC, V* *BP.*

Hinterzarten

14 *5 km (3 mi) west of Titisee, 32 km (20 mi) east of Freiburg.*

The lovely 800-year-old town of Hinterzarten is the most important resort in the southern Black Forest. Some buildings date from the 12th century, among them St. Oswaldskirche, a church built in 1146. Hinterzarten's oldest inn, the Weisses Rossle, has been in business since 1347. The Park Hotel Adler was established in 1446, although the original building was burned down during the Thirty Years' War. Hinterzarten is known throughout Germany for its summer ski jump, the **Adlerschanze** (✉ off Winterhaldenweg, to the south of town), which is used for competitions and for training purposes. Several smaller jumps for "beginners" are currently being built. The town's small **Schwarzwälder Skimuseum** recounts in photographs, paintings, costumes, and equipment the history of Black Forest skiing, which began in the 1890s on the nearby Feldberg. ✉ *Im Hugenhof* ☎ *07652/982–192* 🌐 *www.schwarzwaelder-skimuseum.de* 🎫 *€2.50* ⏲ *Tues., Wed., and Fri. 3–6, weekends noon–6.*

Where to Stay & Eat

★ $$$–$$$$ ✕🏨 **Park Hotel Adler.** The proprietress of this 560-year-old hotel was named Germany's "Hotelier of the Year" for 2004. At a gala ceremony in Munich, Katja Trescher was lauded for rescuing the once threatened hotel through such things as a beautiful private park, an extensive wellness facility, top gastronomy, and superb service. Many of the rooms have marble baths and balconies overlooking the park. The rustic Wirtshaus-Stube ($$–$$$$), with its wood paneling and tile stove, serves Black Forest specialties. ✉ *Adlerpl. 3, D–79856* ☎ *07652/1270* 📠 *07652/127–717* 🌐 *www.parkhoteladler.de* *46 rooms, 32 suites* *2 restaurants, cable TV, in-room data ports, driving range, indoor pool, sauna, spa, massage, Ping-Pong, bar, some pets allowed (fee), no-smoking rooms; no a/c* 💳 *AE, DC, MC, V* *BP.*

$–$$ 🏨 **Sassenhof.** Traditional Black Forest style reigns supreme here, from the steep-eaved wood exterior, with window boxes everywhere, to the elegant sitting areas and guest rooms furnished with rustic, brightly painted pieces, many of them decoratively carved. Afternoon tea, like breakfast, is included in the price. ✉ *Adlerweg 17, D–79856* ☎ *07652/1515* 📠 *07652/484* 🌐 *www.hotel-sassenhof.de* *17 rooms, 6 suites* *Cable TV, Wi-Fi, pool, massage, sauna, bicycles, some pets allowed (fee); no a/c* 💳 *AE, MC, V* ⏲ *Closed Nov.* *BP.*

Sports & the Outdoors

Hinterzarten is at the highest point along the Freiburg–Donaueschingen road; from it a network of far-ranging trails fans out into the forest, making it one of Germany's most popular centers for *Langlauf* (cross-country skiing) in winter and hiking in summer. Cycling is another favorite sport up in these hills and dales. The topography offers something for everyone, gentle excursions or tough mountain-bike expeditions.

The best Alpine skiing in the Black Forest is on the slopes of the Feldberg. The Seebuck, Grafenmatt, and Fahl Alpin area offers 12 lifts and 25 km (15 mi) of slopes (all accessible with a single lift ticket). For more information contact Feldberg's tourist office (☎ 07655/8019). The largest of the Black Forest lakes, mountain-enclosed Schluchsee, is near the Feldberg. Schluchsee is a diverse resort, where sports enthusiasts swim, windsurf, fish, and, in winter, ski.

en route

To get to Freiburg, the largest city in the southern Black Forest, you have to brave the curves of the winding road through the **Höllental** (Hell Valley). In 1770 Empress Maria Theresa's 15-year-old daughter—the future queen Marie Antoinette—made her way along what was then a coach road on her way from Vienna to Paris. She traveled with an entourage of 250 officials and servants in some 50 horse-drawn carriages. The first stop at the end of the valley is a little village called **Himmelreich,** or Kingdom of Heaven. Railroad engineers are said to have given the village its name in the 19th century, grateful as they were to finally have laid a line through Hell Valley. At the entrance to Höllental is a deep gorge, the **Ravennaschlucht.** It's worth scrambling through to reach the tiny 12th-century chapel of **St. Oswald,** the oldest parish church in the Black Forest (there are parking spots off the road). Look for a bronze statue of a deer high on a roadside cliff, 5 km (3 mi) farther on. It commemorates the legend of a deer that amazed hunters by leaping the deep gorge at this point. Another 16 km (10 mi) will bring you to Freiburg.

Freiburg

15 *25 km (15 ½ mi) northwest of Hinterzarten.*

Freiburg, or Freiburg im Breisgau (to distinguish it from the Freiberg in Saxony), was founded in the 12th century. After extensive wartime bomb damage, skillful restoration has helped re-create the original and compelling medieval atmosphere of one of the loveliest historic towns in Germany. The 16th-century geographer Martin Waldseemüller was born here; in 1507 he was the first to put the name *America* on a map.

For an intimate view of Freiburg, wander through the car-free streets around the Münster or follow the main shopping artery of Kaiser-Joseph-Strasse. After you pass the city gate (Martinstor), follow Gerberau off to the left. You'll come to quaint shops along the bank of one of the city's larger canals, which continues past the former Augustinian cloister to the equally picturesque area around the *Insel* (island). This canal is a larger version of the *Bächle* (brooklets) running through many streets in Freiburg's Old Town. The Bächle, so narrow you can step across them, were created in the 13th century to bring fresh water into the town. The tourist office sponsors English walking tours April through October, Monday to Saturday at 10:30, Friday and Saturday also at 2:30. The two-hour tour costs €7.

The **Münster unserer Lieben Frau** (Cathedral of Our Dear Lady), Freiburg's most famous landmark, towers over the medieval streets. The pioneering 19th-century Swiss art historian Jacob Burckhardt described its delicately perforated 380-foot spire as the finest in Europe. The cathedral took three centuries to build, from around 1200 to 1515. You can easily trace the progress of generations of builders through the changing architectural styles, from the fat columns and solid, rounded arches of the Romanesque period to the lofty Gothic windows and airy interior of the choir. Of particular interest are the luminous 13th-century stained-glass windows. Masterpieces include a 16th-century triptych by Hans Baldung Grien and paintings by Holbein the Younger and Lucas Cranach the Elder. If you can summon the energy, climb the tower. In addition to a magnificent view of the city and the Black Forest beyond, you'll get a closer look at the 16 Minster bells including the 3-ton-plus 1258 "Hosanna," one of Germany's oldest functioning bells. ✉ *Münsterpl.* ☎ *0761/388–101* 🎫 *Bell tower €1.50* ⏲ *Mon.–Sat. 9:30–5, Sun. 1–5.*

The **Münsterplatz,** the square around Freiburg's cathedral, which once served as a cemetery, holds a market (Monday–Saturday) in front of the

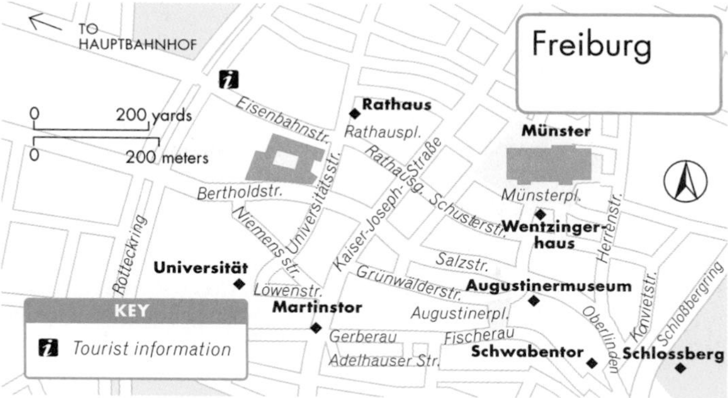

Renaissance **Kaufhaus** (Market House). You can stock up on local specialties, from wood-oven baked bread to hams, wines, vinegars, fruits, and Kirschwasser. The square is also lined with traditional taverns. The big iron door at No. 12 houses the **Foltermuseum** (Torture Museum), whose texts do not fail to point out the gruesomeness and often sheer stupidity of jurisprudence in history. ✉ *Münsterpl. 12* ☎ *0761/292–1900* 🌐 *www.folterkabinett.de* 🎟 *€4.10* ⏲ *Apr.–Oct., Mon.–Sat. 10–6, Sun. 10–7; Nov.–Mar., Mon.–Sat. 11–5, Sun. 10–5.*

Freiburg's famous **Rathaus** is constructed from two 16th-century patrician houses joined together. Among its attractive Renaissance features is an oriel, or bay window, clinging to a corner and bearing a bas-relief of the romantic medieval legend of the Maiden and the Unicorn. ✉ *Rathauspl. 2–4* ⏲ *Weekdays 8–noon.*

The former house of painter, sculptor, and architect Johann Christian Wentzinger (1710–97), the **Wentzingerhaus,** contains fascinating exhibits on the history of the city, including a 1:50 scale model of the Minster as a construction site, and the poignant remains of a typewriter recovered from a bombed-out bank. The ceiling fresco in the stairway, painted by Wentzinger himself, is the museum's pride and joy. ✉ *Münsterpl. 30* ☎ *0761/201–2515* 🌐 *www.msg-freiburg.de* 🎟 *€ 2* ⏲ *Tues.–Sun. 10–5.*

A visit to Freiburg's cathedral is not really complete without also exploring the **Augustinermuseum,** at the former Augustinian cloister. Original sculpture from the cathedral is on display, as well as gold and silver reliquaries. The collection of stained-glass windows, dating from the Middle Ages to today, is one of the most important in Germany. ✉ *Am Augustinerpl.* ☎ *0761/201–2531* 🌐 *www.augustinermuseum.de* 🎟 *€2* ⏲ *Tues.–Sun. 10–5.*

Where to Stay & Eat

$$$$ Fodor's Choice ★ ✕ **Hans Thoma Stube.** Within Freiburg's most luxurious hotel, the Colombi, this restaurant has outfitted itself with venerable tables, chairs, and wood paneling from some older establishments. Old tile stoves pro-

vide a deeply satisfying warmth in winter, and black-tied waiters serve local dishes such as lentil soup and venison. The menu in the Zirbelstube and the Falkenstube pairs innovative sauces with traditional meat and fish dishes. ✉ *Am Colombi Park/Rotteckring 16, D–79098* ☎ *0761/21060* 🖷 *0761/31410* ✍ *Reservations essential* ▭ *AE, DC, MC, V.*

$–$$$ ✕ **Kühler Krug.** Wild game and goose liver terrine are among the specialties at this restaurant, which has even given its name to a distinctive saddle-of-venison dish. Those who prefer fish shouldn't despair—there's an imaginative range of freshwater varieties available. ✉ *Torpl. 1, Günterstal* ☎ *0761/29103* ▭ *MC, V* ⏲ *Closed Wed.*

★ $–$$ ✕ **Markgräfler Hof.** The imaginative Baden cuisine in this restaurant ranges from braised tomatoes and artichokes with lukewarm vegetables to fricasseed calves' liver with fresh herbs and *brägele* (pan-fried potatoes). It's hard to go wrong with the wide variety of choices. A small but fine wine list complements the menu. ✉ *Gerberau 22* ☎ *0761/32540* ▭ *AE, DC, MC, V.*

★ $$$$ ✕🏨 **Colombi.** Freiburg's most luxurious hotel dates to the 1950s and is one of the few still operated on-site by its owners. Its tastefully furnished rooms have floor-to-ceiling windows overlooking the romantic old city. Despite its central location, the hotel basks in near-countryside quiet. ✉ *Am Colombi Park/Rotteckring 16, D–79098* ☎ *0761/21060* 🖷 *0761/31410* 🌐 *www.colombi.de* 🛏 *58 rooms, 59 suites* 👍 *Restaurant, patisserie, room service, cable TV, in-room data ports, Wi-Fi, indoor pool, gym, sauna, steam room, piano bar, baby-sitting, parking (fee), Internet room, some pets allowed (fee), no-smoking rooms* ▭ *AE, DC, MC, V.*

★ $$–$$$ ✕🏨 **Zum Roten Bären.** Like several other hotels, the "Red Bear" claims to be the "oldest in Germany" but its documentation looks best. The inn dates from 1311 and retains its individual character, with very comfortable lodgings and excellent dining in a warren of dining rooms and bars ($$–$$$). Take a tour of the two basement floors, where you'll find cellars dating from the 12th century that are now well stocked with fine wines. ✉ *Oberlinden 12, D–79098* ☎ *0761/387–870* 🖷 *0761/387–8717* 🌐 *www.roter-baeren.de* 🛏 *22 rooms, 3 apartments* 👍 *Restaurant, cable TV, some in-room broadband, some in-room data ports, sauna, parking (fee), some pets allowed (fee), no-smoking rooms; no a/c* ▭ *AE, DC, MC, V* ⏲ *Restaurant closed Sun.* 🍽 *BP.*

$$ ✕🏨 **Oberkirch.** Across from the cathedral, this wine cellar, restaurant, and hotel is a bastion of tradition and Gemütlichkeit (comfort and conviviality). The proprietor personally bags some of the game that ends up on the menu ($–$$$). Fresh trout is another specialty. In summer the dark-oak dining tables spill onto a garden terrace. Approximately 20 Baden wines are served by the glass, many supplied from the restaurant's own vineyards. Twenty-six charming guest rooms are in the Weinstuben and in a neighboring centuries-old house. ✉ *Münsterpl. 22, D–79098* ☎ *0761/202–6868* 🛏 *26 rooms* 👍 *Restaurant, cable TV, some pets allowed (fee); no a/c* ▭ *AE, MC, V* ⏲ *Restaurant closed Sun. and 2 wks in Jan.* 🍽 *BP.*

$–$$ ✕🏨 **Rappen.** This hotel's brightly painted rooms are on the sunny side of the cobblestoned cathedral square and marketplace. Tables are set out amid the lively chatter in summer. Three rooms are designated as "anti-allergy." The restaurant ($–$$) serves fresh vegetables, game, and fish, and hosts the market people and locals who come in for a glass of wine in the morning (there are about 40 wines available, German and French). ✉ *Münsterpl. 13, D–79098* ☎ *0761/31353* 📠 *0761/382–252* 🌐 *www.hotelrappen.de* *24 rooms* *Restaurant, cable TV, in-room data ports, Wi-Fi, some pets allowed (fee); no a/c* 💳 *AE, DC, MC, V* 🍽 *BP.*

$ ✕🏨 **Hotel Schwarzwälder Hof.** Part of this hotel occupies a former mint, complete with graceful cast-iron railings on the spiral staircase and, unfortunately, paper-thin walls. Despite the low prices it's in the downtown pedestrian zone and is very handy to both a parking garage and public transportation. The Badische Winzerstube (¢–$$) provides all you could want in local atmosphere, wine, and food. ✉ *Herrenstr. 43, D–79098* ☎ *0761/38030* 📠 *0761/380–3135* *45 rooms* *Restaurant, in-room data ports, cable TV, some pets allowed; no a/c* 💳 *MC, V* 🍽 *BP.*

¢–$ ✕🏨 **Gasthaus zur Sonne.** The downside: the bathroom is down the hall, there are no eggs at breakfast, the bedside lamps may or may not work, and it's a long way from the center of town. The upside: the hotel is spotlessly clean, the food in the restaurant (¢–$) sticks to your ribs, a bus at the door gets you downtown with ease, it's just minutes from the Freiburg Nord autobahn exit, and you'll find a piece of chocolate on your bedside table each night. Not a bad choice for travelers on a budget. ✉ *Hochdorfstr. 1, D–79108* ☎ *07665/2650* 📠 *07665/1288* *15 rooms without bath* *Restaurant, cable TV, bar, free parking, some pets allowed; no a/c, no room phones* 💳 *No credit cards* 🍽 *BP.*

$$ 🏨 **Park Hotel Post Meier.** This century-old building, near the train station, has a copper dome and stone balconies overlooking a park. You'll be greeted with a drink upon your arrival, find fruit in your room, and can plug in the phone at the bed, at the desk, or even in the bathroom. ✉ *Eisenbahnstr. 35–37, D–79098* ☎ *0761/385–480* 📠 *0761/31680* *43 rooms, 2 apartments* *Cable TV, in-room data ports, no-smoking rooms; no a/c* 💳 *AE, MC, V* 🍽 *BP.*

$–$$ 🏨 **Best Western Premier Hotel Victoria.** Though this 1870s hotel has changed hands, its reputation as an ecofriendly place carries on. Black Forest sawdust has replaced oil for heating, solar panels provide some of the electricity and hot water, other electricity comes from a wind farm, windows have thermal panes, bathtubs are ergonomically designed to use less hot water, packaged food and throwaway cans and bottles are avoided, and everything from the stationery to the toilet tissue is of recycled paper. ✉ *Eisenbahnstr. 54, D–79098* ☎ *0761/207–340* 📠 *0761/2073–4444* 🌐 *www.victoria.bestwestern.de* *63 rooms* *Cable TV, in-room broadband, in-room data ports, Wi-Fi, bar, parking (fee), some pets allowed (fee), no-smoking rooms; no a/c* 💳 *AE, DC, MC, V.*

Nightlife & the Arts

Nightlife in Freiburg takes place in the city's *Kneipen* (pubs), wine bars, and wine cellars, which are plentiful on the streets around the cathedral. For student pubs, wander around **Stühlinger,** the neighborhood immediately south of the train station. Plenty of people take their night-cap at the **Cocktailbar Hemingway** (✉ Eisenbahnstr. 54 ☎ 0761/207–340), which stays open until 2 AM on weekends. **Funpark** (✉ Hans-Bunte-Str. 16, near the autobahn access road for the Freiburg Nord exit ☎ 0761/556–5757), the large-scale, cool nightclub for the young, is in the northern industrial zone of Freiburg. The wild decor includes an airplane. **Jazzhaus** (✉ Schnewlinstr. 1 ☎ 0761/34973) sometimes has live music and draws big acts and serious up-and-coming artists to its brick cellar. A very mixed crowd meets daily and nightly at **Kagan café bar club lounge** (✉ Bismarckallee 9 ☎ 0761/767–2766 🎟 €6) on the 18th floor of the skyscraper over the train station, with an incomparable view of the Old Town. The club is open Wed.–Sat from 10 PM until the wee hours. There's a café one floor down that is open both before and during club hours.

Staufen

⓰ *20 km (12 mi) south of Freiburg via B–31.*

Once you've braved Hell Valley to get to Freiburg, a visit to the nearby town of Staufen, where Dr. Faustus is reputed to have made his pact with the devil, should hold no horrors. The Faustus legend is remembered today chiefly because of Goethe's *Faust,* perhaps, the most famous account of a man who sells his soul to the devil in return for eternal youth and knowledge. The original Faustus was a 16th-century alchemist and scientist. His pact was not with the devil but with a local baron who was convinced that Faustus could make his fortune by converting base metal into gold. While attempting to do so, Dr. Faustus caused an explosion that produced such noise and such a sulfurous stink that the townspeople were convinced the devil had carried him off. In fact, he was killed in the accident. You can visit the ancient **Gasthaus zum Löwen** (✉ Hauptstr. 47), where Faustus lived, allegedly in room number 5, and died. The inn is right on the central square of Staufen, a town with a visible inclination toward modern art in ancient settings.

Where to Stay & Eat

$$–$$$$ ✕🏨 **Romantik Hotel Spielweg.** A half-hour's drive from Freiburg, this family-run inn has everything for an indulgent holiday, with pools, tennis courts, Karl-Josef Fuchs's regional cooking ($$–$$$), and its own cheese factory, which you can visit. ✉ *Spielweg 61, D–79244 Obermünstertal, 12 km (7 mi) southeast of Staufen* ☎ *07636/7090* 📠 *07636/70966* 🌐 *www.spielweg.com* 🛏 *43 rooms, 3 suites* 🛎 *2 restaurants, cable TV, 2 pools (1 indoor), massage, sauna, bicycles, some pets allowed (fee), no-smoking rooms; no a/c* 💳 *AE, DC, MC, V* 🍽 *BP.*

$–$$ ✕🏨 **Landgasthaus zur Linde.** Guests have been welcomed here for 350 years, but the comforts inside the inn's old walls are contemporary. The kitchen ($–$$) creates wholesome sustenance out of local ingredients and plays up seasonal specialties, such as asparagus in May and June, and mushrooms from the valley in autumn. The terrace is a favorite for hikers passing through, as are the various snacks. ✉ *Krumlinden 13, D–79244 Münstertal, 14 km (9 mi) southeast of Staufen* ☎ *07636/447* 📠 *07636/1632* 🌐 *www.landgasthaus.de* 🛏 *10 rooms, 2 suites* 🛎 *Restau-*

rant, cable TV, some pets allowed (fee); no a/c ▭ *V* ⏲ *Restaurant closed Mon.* 🍽 *BP.*

Kaiserstuhl

17 *20 km (12 mi) northwest of Freiburg on B–31.*

One of the incredible sights of the Black Forest is the **Kaiserstuhl** (Emperor's Chair), a volcanic outcrop clothed in vineyards that produce some of Baden's best wines—reds from the Spätburgunder grape and whites that have an uncanny depth. A third of Baden's wines are produced in this single area, which has the warmest climate in Germany. The especially dry and warm microclimate has given rise to tropical vegetation, including sequoias and a wide variety of orchids.

Sample high-quality wines—the Weissherbst, in particular—in one of the taverns of Achkarren or take a short hike along a vineyard path.

The fine little **Weinmuseum** (Wine Museum) is in a renovated barn in the village center. A small vineyard out front displays the various types of grapes used to make wine in the Kaiserstuhl region. ✉ *Schlossstr. Vogtsburg-Achkarren* ☎ *07662/81263* 🎟 *€1.50* ⏲ *Apr.–Oct., Tues.–Fri. 2–5, weekends 11–5.*

Where to Eat & Stay

$ ✕🏨 **Hotel Krone.** You could spend an entire afternoon and evening here, either on the terrace or in the dining room ($–$$$), trying the wines and enjoying, say, a fillet of wild salmon in a horseradish crust, a boar's roast, or some lighter asparagus creation. The house dates to 1561 and the Höfflin-Schüssler family, now in its fourth generation as hoteliers, knows how to make visitors feel welcome. ✉ *Schlossbergstr. 15, D–79235 Vogtsburg-Achkarren* ☎ *07662/93130* 📠 *07662/931–350* 🌐 *www.Hotel-Krone-Achkarren.de* *23 rooms* *Restaurant, cable TV, in-room broadband, in-room data ports, tennis court, some pets allowed (fee); no a/c* ▭ *MC, V* ⏲ *Restaurant closed Wed.* 🍽 *BP.*

Europa Park

18 *35 km (22 mi) north of Freiburg*

The town of Rust, on the Rhine almost halfway from Freiburg to Strasbourg, boasts a castle dating from 1577 and painstakingly restored half-timber houses. But its big claim to fame is Germany's biggest amusement park, with its own autobahn exit.

Fodor'sChoice ★ On an area of 160 acres, **Europa Park** draws more than 3 million visitors a year with its variety of shows, rides, dining, and shops. Among many other things, it has the "Eurosat" to take you on a virtual journey past clusters of meteors and falling stars; the "Silver Star," Europe's highest roller coaster (80 mph, 240 feet); a Spanish jousting tournament; and a 4-D movie. Four lodgings provide a nearby place for families to rest up after the excitement of the day. ✉ *Europa-Park-Str. 2, D–77977* ☎ *01805/776–688* 🌐 *www.europapark.de* 🎟 *€27* ⏲ *Mid-Mar.–mid-Nov., daily 9–6; later July–mid-Sept.*

THE BLACK FOREST A TO Z

To research prices, get advice from other travelers, and book travel arrangements, visit www.fodors.com.

AIRPORTS

The closest international airports in Germany are Stuttgart and Frankfurt. Strasbourg, in neighboring French Alsace, and the Swiss border city of Basel, the latter just 70 km (43 mi) from Freiburg, are also reasonably close.

BUS TRAVEL

The bus system works closely together with the German railways to reach every corner of the Black Forest. Bus stations are usually at or near the train station. For more information, contact the Regionalbusverkehr Südwest (Regional Bus Lines) in Karlsruhe.

Regionalbusverkehr Südwest (Regional Bus Lines) ☎ 0721/84060 in Karlsruhe.

CAR TRAVEL

The main autobahns are A–5 (Frankfurt–Karlsruhe–Basel), which runs through the Rhine Valley along the western length of the Black Forest; A–81 (Stuttgart–Bodensee), in the east; and A–8 (Karlsruhe–Stuttgart), in the north. Good two-lane highways crisscross the entire region. B–3 runs parallel to A–5 and follows the Baden Wine Road. Traffic jams on weekends and holidays are not uncommon. Taking the side roads might not save time, but they are a lot more interesting. The Schwarzwald-Hochstrasse is one of the area's most scenic (but also most trafficked) routes, running from Freudenstadt to Baden-Baden. The region's tourist office has mapped out thematic driving routes: the Valley Road, the Spa Road, the Baden Wine Road, the Asparagus Road, and the Clock Road. Most points along these routes can also be reached by train or bus.

Freiburg, the region's major city, is 275 km (170 mi) south of Frankfurt and 410 km (254 mi) west of Munich.

SPORTS & THE OUTDOORS

BIKING Much of the Black Forest is a biker's paradise (provided the rider is stalwart, since there are so many ups and downs). There are many bike-rental shops throughout the region, and cycling maps are available at most tourist offices. For information on biking in Germany, contact the National German Cycling Association. To facilitate your bike traveling, you may want to cover certain distances by train. Call the Deutsche Bahn's special line for bicyclists. Deutsche Bahn also rents bikes.

Deutsche Bahn ☎ 01805/151–415 bike hotline. **Baden-Württemberg Regional Cycling Association** ✉ Augustenstr. 99, D–70197 Stuttgart ☎ 0711/628–999.

TRAIN TRAVEL

The main rail route through the Black Forest runs north–south, following the Rhine Valley from Karlsruhe to Basel. There are fast and frequent trains to Freiburg and Baden-Baden from most major German cities (you generally have to change at Karlsruhe).

Local lines connect most of the smaller towns. Two east–west routes—the Schwarzwaldbahn (Black Forest Railway) and the Höllental Railway—are among the most spectacular in the country. Details are available from Deutsche Bahn.

VISITOR INFORMATION

For information on the northern Black Forest, contact Touristik Nördlicher Schwarzwald. For the central area, contact Mittlere Schwarzwald Tourismus GmbH. For the southern area, contact Tourismus Südlicher Schwarzwald.

Baden-Baden ✉ Baden-Baden Kur- und Tourismus GmbH, Solmsstrasse 1, D-76530 ☎ 07221/275-2001 🌐 www.baden-baden.de. **Calw** ✉ Stadtinformation Calw, Marktbrücke 1, D-75365 ☎ 07051/968-810 🌐 www.calw.de. **Feldberg** ✉ Tourist-Information, Kirchgasse 1, D-79868 ☎ 07655/8019 🌐 www.feldberg-das-hoechste-im-schwarzwald.de. **Freiburg** ✉ Tourist-Information, Rotteckring 14, D-79098 ☎ 0761/388-1880 🌐 www.freiburg.de. **Freudenstadt** ✉ Kongresse-Touristik-Kur, Marktpl. 64, D-72250 ☎ 07441/8640 🌐 www.freudenstadt.de. **Hinterzarten** ✉ Hinterzarten-Breitnau Tourismus GmbH, Freiburgerstr. 1, D-75896 ☎ 07652/12060 🌐 www.hinterzarten.de. **Karlsruhe** ✉ Tourist-Information, Bahnhofpl. 6, D-76137 ☎ 0721/19433 🌐 www.karlsruhe.de/tourismus. **Mittlere Schwarzwald Tourismus GmbH** ✉ Gerberstr. 8, D-77652 Offenburg ☎ 0781/923-7777 🖷 0781/923-7770 🌐 www.schwarzwald-tourismus.com. **Pforzheim** ✉ Tourist-Information, Marktpl. 1, D-75175 ☎ 07231/145-4560 🌐 www.pforzheim.de. **Schluchsee** ✉ Tourist-Information, Fischbacherstr. 7, D-79859 ☎ 07656/7732 🌐 www.schluchsee.de. **Titisee-Neustadt** ✉ Tourist-Information, Strandbadstr. 4, D-79822 ☎ 07651/98040 🌐 www.titisee.de. **Tourismus Südlicher Schwarzwald** ✉ Ludwigstr. 23, D-79104 Freiburg ☎ 0761/296-2271 🖷 0761/296-2270 🌐 www.schwarzwald-sued.de. **Touristik Nördlicher Schwarzwald** ✉ Am Weisenhauspl. 26, D-75172 Pforzheim ☎ 07231/147-380 🖷 07231/147-3820 🌐 www.noerdlicher.schwarzwald-tourismus.info. **Triberg** ✉ Tourist-Information, Wahlfahrtstr. 4, D-78098 ☎ 07722/866-490 🖷 07722/866-499 🌐 www.triberg.de.

Heidelberg & the Neckar Valley

7

WORD OF MOUTH

"Heidelberg is well worth a visit, especially if you enjoy walking. The Hauptstrasse boasts a number of interesting shops and restaurants; the Schloss is a fun hike and a very interesting visit, and Philosophers' Way—a hiking path across the Neckar River from the main town—is worth a visit."

—lynn

"Don't skip Tübingen! It is the second oldest University in Germany and the most prestigious in Europe for the study of medicine, philosophy, etc. It is far more charming than Heidelberg."

—liz

www.fodors.com/forums

Updated by
Heather Phibbs

THE NECKAR RIVER UNITES BEAUTY and historic resonance as it flows toward the Rhine through the state of Baden-Württemberg, eventually reaching Heidelberg's graceful baroque towers and the majestic ruins of its red sandstone castle. Much of this route follows the west–east course of the Burgenstrasse (Castle Road), which stretches nearly 1,000 km (621 mi) from Mannheim to Prague, taking in some 70 castles and palaces along the way. Every town or bend in the river seems to have its guardian castle, sometimes in ruins but often revived as a museum or hotel. Off the main road, quiet side valleys and little towns slumber in leafy peace.

Exploring Heidelberg & the Neckar Valley

Heidelberg is a destination unto itself, but it can also be seen as the major stop on the Burgenstrasse, which makes its way through the narrower parts of the Neckar Valley. The route in this chapter follows the Neckar River upstream (east, then south) from Heidelberg. The road snakes between the river and the wooded slopes of the Odenwald forest before reaching the rolling, vine-covered countryside around Heilbronn. From there it's a 50-km (31-mi) drive, partly along the Neckar, to Stuttgart. About 40 km (25 mi) farther you rejoin the river at the charming university town of Tübingen.

About the Restaurants

Mittagessen (lunch) in this region is generally served from noon until 2 or 2:30, *Abendessen* (dinner) from 6 until 9:30 or 10. *Durchgehend warme Küche* means that hot meals are also served between lunch and dinner. Slowly but surely, credit cards have gained acceptance, but this is by no means universal, and many restaurants will only accept cash or debit cards issued by a German bank. Casual attire is typically acceptable at restaurants here, and reservations are generally not needed. "Gourmet temples" that require reservations and coat-and-tie are noted as such in this chapter.

About the Hotels

This area is full of castle-hotels and charming country inns that range in comfort from upscale rustic to luxurious. For a riverside view, ask for a *Zimmer* (room) or *Tisch* (table) *mit Neckarblick* (with a view of the Neckar). The Neckar Valley offers idyllic alternatives to the cost and crowds of Heidelberg. Driving time from Eberbach, for example, is a half hour; from Bad Wimpfen, about an hour.

WHAT IT COSTS In Euros

	$$$$	$$$	$$	$	¢
RESTAURANTS	over €25	€21–€25	€16–€20	€9–€15	under €9
HOTELS	over €225	€175–€225	€100–€175	€50–€100	under €50

Restaurant prices are per person for a main course at dinner. Hotel prices are for two people in a standard double room, including tax and service.

Timing

If you plan to visit Heidelberg in summer, make reservations well in advance and expect to pay top rates. To get away from the crowds, consider staying out of town and driving or taking the bus into the city. Hotels and restaurants are much cheaper just a little upriver. A visit in late fall, when the vines turn a faded gold, or early spring, with the first green shoots of the year, can be captivating. In the depths of winter, river mists creep through the narrow streets of Heidelberg's Old Town and awaken the ghosts of a romantic past.

THE NECKAR-RHINE TRIANGLE

The natural beauty of Heidelberg is created by the embrace of mountains, forests, vineyards, and the Neckar River—all crowned by the famous ruined castle. The Neckar and the Rhine meet at nearby Mannheim, a major industrial center and the second-largest river port in Europe. Schwetzingen, known as Germany's asparagus capital, lies in the triangle's center.

Heidelberg

57 km (35 mi) northeast of Karlsruhe.

If any city in Germany encapsulates the spirit of the country, it is Heidelberg. Scores of poets and composers—virtually the entire 19th-century German Romantic movement—have sung its praises. Goethe and Mark Twain both fell in love here: the German writer with a beautiful young woman, the American author with the city itself. Sigmund Romberg set his operetta *The Student Prince* in the city; Carl Maria von Weber wrote his lushly Romantic opera *Der Freischütz* here. Composer Robert Schumann was a student at the university. The campaign these artists waged on behalf of the town has been astoundingly successful. Heidelberg's fame is out of all proportion to its size (population 140,000); more than 3½ million visitors crowd its streets every year.

Heidelberg was the political center of the Rhineland Palatinate. At the end of the Thirty Years' War (1618–48), the elector Carl Ludwig married his daughter to the brother of Louis XIV in the hope of bringing peace to the Rhineland. But when the elector's son died without an heir, Louis XIV used the marriage alliance as an excuse to claim Heidelberg, and in 1689 the town was sacked and laid to waste. Four years later he sacked the town again. From its ashes arose what you see today: a baroque town built on Gothic foundations, with narrow, twisting streets and alleyways. Modern Heidelberg changed under the influence of U.S. army barracks and industrial development stretching into the suburbs, but the old heart of the city remains intact, exuding the spirit of romantic Germany.

a good walk

Begin a tour of Heidelberg at the **Königstuhl Bergbahn** (funicular) ❶, which will take you up to the famous **Schloss** ❷, one of Germany's most memorable sights. It was already in ruins when 19th-century Romantics fell under its spell, drawn by the mystery of its Gothic turrets, Renaissance walls, and abandoned gardens. (You can also choose to hike up the winding Burgweg [castle walk] to the complex.) The fascinating

Numbers in the text correspond to numbers in the margin and on the Neckar Valley and Heidelberg maps.

If you have 3 days

Spend a full day and night exploring the university town of **Heidelberg** 1–17. On the second day take a trip up the Neckar to the castles of **Hirschhorn** 19 and **Burg Hornberg** 22 (both have hotels for an overnight stay, with excellent restaurants). On the third day visit the **Staatsgalerie** (State Gallery) in **Stuttgart** 26.

If you have 5 days

Spend your first two days and nights in **Heidelberg** 1–17. On the third day continue up the Neckar to **Burg Guttenberg** (with its aviary of birds of prey) and the castles of **Hirschhorn** 19 and **Burg Hornberg** 22. Stay overnight at one of the many castle hotels in the area. Investigate the remains of the imperial palace and other sights in **Bad Wimpfen** 23 on the fourth day, and end the trip in the medieval streets of **Tübingen** 28.

If you have 7 days

Spend your first two days and nights in **Heidelberg** 1–17. On the third day head up the Neckar to **Burg Guttenberg** and the **Hirschhorn** 19 castle, staying there or in **Eberbach** 20 for two nights. Continue on to explore **Mosbach** 21 and the castle at **Burg Hornberg** 22, with time out for a river cruise. Spend the fifth day and night in **Bad Wimpfen** 23, with a possible side trip to the museum of bicycle and motorcycle technology at **Neckarsulm** 24. On the sixth day and night visit the sights and enjoy the nightlife of **Stuttgart** 26. On Day 7 stop in **Bebenhausen** 27 en route to **Tübingen** 28, where you can spend your final day.

Deutsches Apotheken–Museum (German Apothecary Museum) is within the castle walls. The funicular can take you higher from the Schloss to **Molkenkur** 3, the site of another castle ruin, and **Königstuhl** 4, a high hill with fine views.

From the Schloss ramparts, take the Burgweg down to the city's Altstadt (Old Town), sandwiched between the Neckar River and the surrounding hills. The steep path from the castle ends abruptly near the **Kornmarkt** (Grain Market). Cross the square north to Hauptstrasse, an elegant pedestrian street that runs straight through the city. Bear right, and you will immediately enter Karlsplatz; on the far side are two traditional pubs, Zum Sepp'l and Zum Roten Ochsen, where fraternity students have engaged in beer-drinking contests for the last 200-some years. As you go left from Kornmarkt, it's only a few steps to the **Marktplatz,** the city's main square. The **Rathaus** (Town Hall) 5 is a stately baroque building dating from 1701 that fronts the market square. From the center of the square, the late-Gothic **Heiliggeistkirche** 6 towers over the city. Just as in medieval times, there are shopping stalls between its buttresses. **Hotel zum Ritter** 7, with an elaborate Renaissance facade of curlicues, columns, and gables, stands opposite Heiliggeistkirche. Walking farther down Hauptstrasse west of Marktplatz, you reach Universitätsplatz and the **Alte Univer-**

sität 8, which was founded in 1386 and rebuilt in the early 18th century. It's one of four separate university complexes in the town. Go behind the Old University and down tiny Augustinerstrasse to find the **Studentenkarzer** 9, or Student Prison. Tradition once dictated that the university rather than the police should deal with unruly students. To the south, the **Neue Universität** 10 is on the southeast corner of Universitätsplatz. Just off Universitätsplatz, on the street called Plöck, stands the **Universitätsbibliothek** 11 (University Library). The Gothic **Peterskirche** 12, the city's oldest parish church, is opposite the library.

Next, return to Hauptstrasse and walk west a couple of blocks to visit the **Kurpfälzisches Museum** 13, Heidelberg's leading museum, housed in a former baroque palace. Six blocks west of the Kurpfälzisches Museum, on the south side of Hauptstrasse, is an alley leading to a courtyard and the entrance to Europe's only museum devoted to the history of industrial packaging, the **Deutsches Verpackungs-Museum** 14. Walk back toward Marktplatz and turn left at Dreikönigstrasse; a short block brings you to Untere Strasse, where you go right, then immediately left at the first street, called Pfaffengasse. Halfway down the street on the left-hand side (No. 18) is the **Friedrich-Ebert-Gedenkstätte** 15, the birthplace of the president of the ill-fated Weimar Republic. Continue on to the end of the street and turn right along the river to reach the twin turrets of the **Alte Brücke** 16. From the bridge you'll have views of the Old Town and the castle above. For the most inspiring view of Heidelberg, climb up the steep, winding **Schlangenweg** 17 through the vineyards to the Philosophenweg (Philosophers' Path); then go right and continue through the woods above the river to the Hölderlin Memorial, a grove traditionally frequented by poets and scholars. Try to arrive there as the sun sets and watch the red sandstone castle turn to gold.

TIMING Allow at least two hours to tour the Schloss—and expect long lines in summer (up to 30 minutes). For the rest of the tour, add another two hours, four if you plan on seeing the collection of the Kurpfälzisches Museum, the manuscript exhibition at the University Library, and the inside of the Student Prison.

What to See

16 **Alte Brücke** (Old Bridge). Walk onto the bridge from the Old Town under a portcullis spanned by two *Spitzhelm* towers (so called for their resemblance to old German helmets). The twin towers were part of medieval Heidelberg's fortifications. In the west tower are three dank dungeons that once held common criminals. Between the towers, above the gate, are more salubrious lockups, with views of the river and the castle; these were reserved for debtors. Above the portcullis you'll see a memorial plaque that pays warm tribute to the Austrian forces who helped Heidelberg beat back a French attempt to capture the bridge in 1799. The bridge itself is the ninth to be built on this spot; ice floes and floods destroyed its predecessors. The elector Carl Theodor, who built it in 1786–88, must have been confident this one would last: he had a statue of himself erected on it, upon a plinth decorated with river gods and goddesses (symbolic of the Rhine, Danube, Neckar, and Mosel rivers). Just to be safe, he also put up a statue of the saint John Nepomuk. As

Festivals Important cultural festivals for music, opera, and theater include the **Schlossfestspiele** on castle grounds in Schwetzingen (May), Heidelberg (July and August), Zwingenberg (late August), and Ludwigsburg (June to mid-September). Since 1818 thousands have flocked to the Stuttgart suburb of Cannstatt in early October for the annual **Volksfest** (folk festival), which kicks off with a colorful parade of folk-dance groups and horse-drawn brewery wagons. Two wine festivals of particular note are the **Stuttgarter Weindorf,** from late August to early September, and the **Heilbronner Weindorf** in mid-September. Last but not least are the fabulous fireworks and castle illuminations in Heidelberg (with an arts-and-crafts market on the riverbank) on the first Saturday of June and September and the second Saturday of July.

Food & Wine Fish and *Wild* (game) from the streams and woods lining the Neckar Valley, as well as seasonal favorites—*Spargel* (asparagus), *Pilze* (mushrooms), *Morcheln* (morels), *Pfifferlinge* (chanterelles), and *Steinpilze* (crèpes)—are regulars on menus in this area. Pfälzer specialties are also common, but the penchant for potatoes yields to *Knödel* (dumplings) and pasta farther south. The latter includes the Swabian and Baden staples, *Maultaschen* (stuffed "pockets" of pasta) and *spätzle* (roundish egg noodles), as well as *Schupfnudeln* (finger-size noodles of potato dough), also called *Bube-* or *Buwespitzle.* Look for *Linsen* (lentils) and sauerkraut in soups or as sides. *Schwäbischer Rostbraten* (beefsteaks topped with fried onions) and *Schäufele* (pickled and slightly smoked pork shoulder) are popular meat dishes.

Considerable quantities of red wine are produced along the Neckar Valley. Crisp, light Trollinger is often served in the traditional *Viertele,* a round, quarter-liter (8-ounce) glass with a handle. Deeper-color, more substantial reds include Spatburgunder (Pinot Noir) and its mutation Schwarzriesling (Pinot Meunier), Lemberger, and Dornfelder. Riesling, Kerner, and Müller-Thurgau (synonymous with Rivaner), as well as Grauburgunder (Pinot Gris) and Weissburgunder (Pinot Blanc) are the typical white wines. A birch broom or wreath over the doorway of a vintner's home signifies a *Besenwirtschaft* ("broomstick inn"), a rustic pub where you can enjoy wines with snacks and simple fare. Many vintners offer economical B&Bs.

---

you enter the bridge from Old Town, you'll also notice a statue of an animal that appears somewhat catlike. It's actually a monkey holding a mirror. Legend has it that the statue was erected to symbolize the need for both city-dwellers and those who live on the other side of the bridge to take a look over their shoulders as they cross—that neither group is more elite than the other. From the center of the bridge you'll have some of the finest views of the Old Town and the castle above.

8 **Alte Universität** (Old University). The three-story baroque structure was built between 1712 and 1718 at the behest of the elector Johann Wilhelm on the site of an earlier university building. It houses the impres-

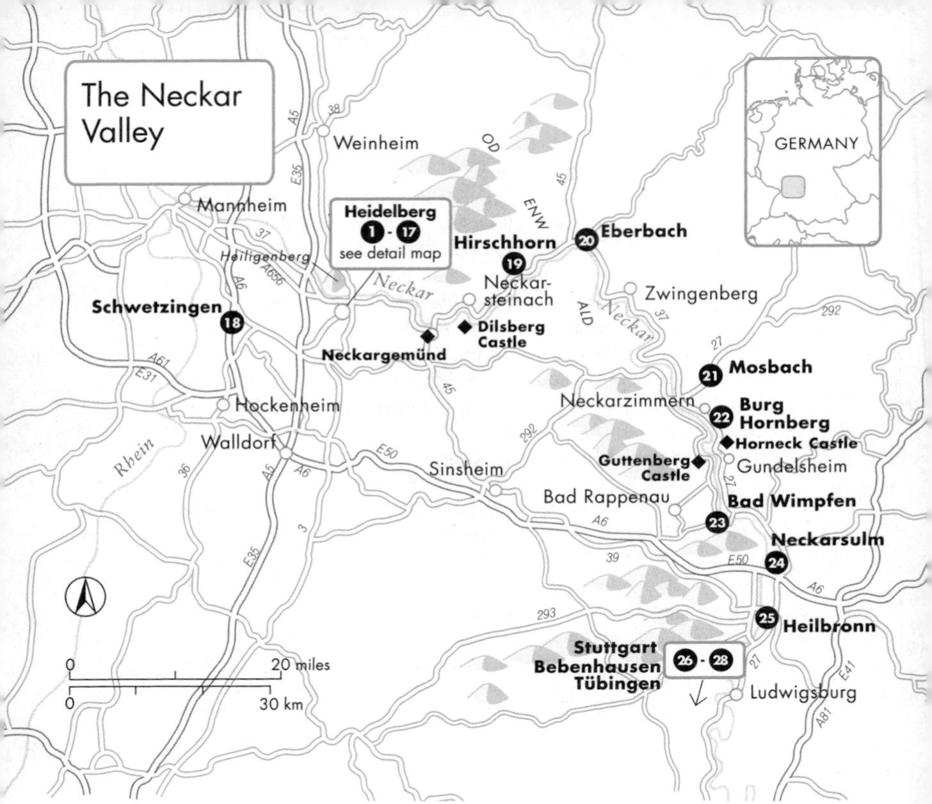

sive *Alta Aula* (Old Auditorium) and the University Museum, with exhibits that chronicle the history of Germany's oldest university. The present-day *Universitätsplatz* (University Square) was built over the remains of an Augustinian monastery that was destroyed by the French in 1693. ✉ *Grabeng. 1–3* ☎ *06221/542–152* 🎟 *€2.50* ⏲ *Apr.–Oct., Tues.–Sun. 10–4; Nov.–Mar., Tues.–Sat. 10–4.*

14 **Deutsches Verpackungs-Museum** (German Packaging Museum). A former church was innovatively converted to house this fascinating documentation of packaging and package design of brand-name products. Representing the years 1800 to the present, historic logos and slogans are a trip down memory lane. The entrance is not on Hauptstrasse but in the courtyard behind the street, reached via an alley. ✉ *Hauptstr. 22* ☎ *06221/21361* 🌐 *www.verpackungsmuseum.de* 🎟 *€3.50* ⏲ *Wed.–Fri. 1–6, weekends 11–6.*

15 **Friedrich-Ebert-Gedenkstätte** (Friedrich Ebert Memorial). The humble rooms of a tiny back-street apartment were the birthplace of Friedrich Ebert, Germany's first democratically elected president (in 1920) and leader of the ill-fated Weimar Republic. Display cases have documents that tell the story of the tailor's son who took charge of a nation accustomed to being ruled by a kaiser. ✉ *Pfaffeng. 18* ☎ *06221/91070*

🌐 *www.ebert-gedenkstaette.de* 🎫 *Free* ⏲ *Tues., Wed., and Fri.–Sun. 10–6, Thurs. 10–8.*

❻ **Heiliggeistkirche** (Church of the Holy Ghost). The foundation stone of the building was laid in 1398, but it was not actually finished until 1544. Unlike that of most other Gothic churches, the facade of the Heiliggeistkirche is uniform—you cannot discern the choir or naves from the outside. The gargoyles looking down on the south side (where Hauptstrasse crosses Marktplatz) are remarkable for their sheer ugliness. The church fell victim to the plundering General Tilly, leader of the Catholic League during the Thirty Years' War. Tilly loaded the church's greatest treasure—the *Bibliotheca Palatina,* at the time the largest library in Germany—onto 500 carts and trundled it off to Rome, where he presented it to the pope. Few volumes found their way back to Heidelberg. At the end of the 17th century, French troops plundered the church again, destroying the family tombs of the Palatinate electors; only the 15th-century tomb of Elector Ruprecht III and his wife, Elisabeth von Hohenzollern, remains today. ✉ *Marktpl.* ☎ *06221/21117* 🌐 *www.heiliggeistkirche.de* ⏲ *Late Mar.–Oct., Mon.–Sat. 11–5, Sun. 12:30–5; Nov.–late Mar., Fri. and Sat. 11–3, Sun. 12:30–3.*

❼ **Hotel zum Ritter.** The hotel's name refers to the statue of a Roman knight ("Ritter") atop one of the many gables. Its French builder, Charles Bélier, had the Latin inscription PERSTA INVICTA VENUS added to the facade in gold letters—"Venus, Remain Unconquerable." It appears this injunction was effective, as this was the city's only Renaissance building to be spared the attentions of the invading French in 1689 and 1693. Between 1695 and 1705 it was used as Heidelberg's town hall; later it became an inn, and it's still a hotel today. ✉ *Hauptstr. 178* ☎ *06221/1350.*

❹ **Königstuhl** (King's Throne). The second-highest hill in the Odenwald range—1,700 feet above Heidelberg—is only a hop, skip, and funicular ride from Heidelberg. On a clear day you can see south as far as the Black Forest and west to the Vosges Mountains of France. The hill is at the center of a close-knit network of hiking trails. Signs and colored arrows from the top lead hikers through the woods of the Odenwald.

❶ **Königstuhl Bergbahn** (funicular). The funicular hoists visitors in 17 minutes to the summit of Königstuhl. On the way it stops at the ruined Heidelberg Schloss and Molkenkur. The funicular usually leaves every 10 minutes in summer and every 20 minutes in winter. However, renovation work may be under way. During this time buses will run from the funicular station to Königstuhl (weekdays every half hour, weekends every 20 minutes), and Bus 21 from Bismarckplatz to Königstuhl runs the same route (every hour). Both stop at the castle and Molkenkur. ✉ *Kornmarkt* 🎫 *Round-trip to Schloss, Molkenkur, or Königstuhl €3.50.*

Kornmarkt (Grain Market). A baroque statue of the Virgin Mary is in the center of this old Heidelberg square, which has a view of the castle ruins.

⓭ **Kurpfälzisches Museum** (Palatinate Museum). The baroque palace that houses the museum was built as a residence for a university professor in 1712. It's a pleasure just to wander around, which is more or less un-

Alte Brücke 16
Alte Universität 8
Deutches Verpackungs-Museum 14
Friedrich-Ebert-Gedenkstätte . 15
Heiliggeist-kirche 6
Hotel zum Ritter 7
Königstuhl 4
Königstuhl Bergbahn 1
Kurpfälzisches Museum 13
Molkenkur 3
Neue Universität . . . 10
Peters-kirche 12
Rathaus 5
Schlangen-weg 17
Schloss 2
Studenten-karzer 9
Universitäts-bibliothek . . . 11

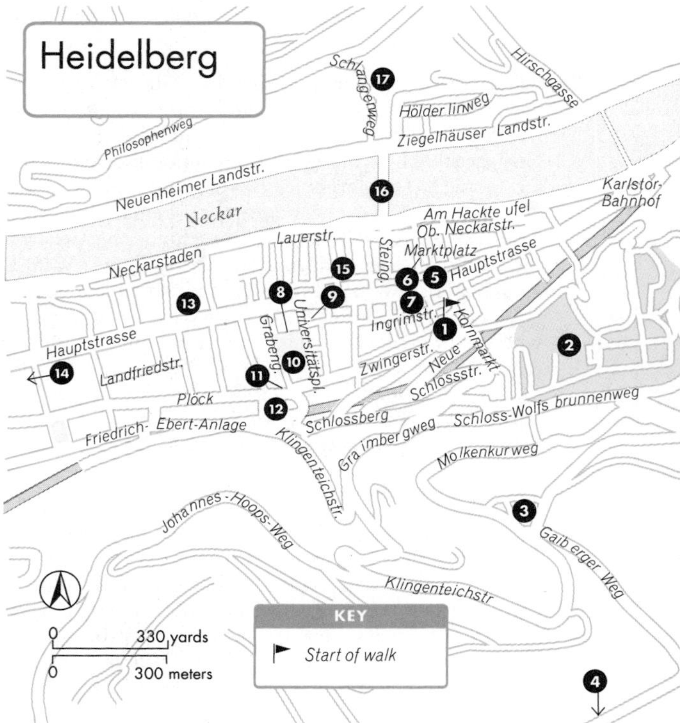

avoidable, since the museum's layout is so confusing. The collections chart the history of the city and its region. Among the exhibits are two standouts. One is a replica of the jaw of Heidelberg Man, a key link in the evolutionary chain thought to date from a half-million years ago; the original was unearthed near the city in 1907. The larger attraction is the ***Windsheimer Zwölfbotenaltar** (Twelve Apostles Altarpiece)*, one of the largest and finest works of early Renaissance sculptor Tilman Riemenschneider. Its exquisite detailing and technical sophistication are evident in the simple faith that radiates from the faces of the Apostles. On the top floor of the museum there's a rich range of 19th-century German paintings and drawings, many depicting Heidelberg. The restaurant in the museum's quiet, shady courtyard is a good place for a break. ✉ *Hauptstr. 97* ☎ *06221/583–402* 🎫 *€2.50* ⏲ *Tues.–Sun. 10–6.*

Marktplatz (Market Square). Heidelberg's main square, with the Rathaus on one side and the Heiliggeistkirche on the other, has been its focal point since the Middle Ages. Public courts of justice were held here in earlier centuries, and people accused of witchcraft and heresy were burned at the stake. The baroque fountain in the middle, the *Herkulesbrunnen* (Hercules Fountain), is the work of 18th-century artist H. Charrasky. Until 1740 a rotating, hanging cage stood next to it. For minor crimes, people were imprisoned in it and exposed to the laughter, insults, and abuse of their fellow citizens. The square is surrounded by narrow side streets that should be explored.

9 **Molkenkur.** The next stop after the castle on the Königstuhl funicular, Molkenkur was the site of Heidelberg's second castle. Lightning struck it in 1527, and it was never rebuilt. Today it's occupied by a restaurant with magnificent views of the Odenwald and the Rhine plain.

10 **Neue Universität** (New University). The plain building on the south side of Universitätsplatz was erected between 1930 and 1932 through funds raised by the U.S. ambassador to Germany, J. G. Schurman, who had been a student at the university. The only decoration on the building's three wings is a statue of Athena, the Greek goddess of wisdom, above the entrance. The inner courtyard contains a medieval tower from 1380, the ***Hexenturm*** (Witches Tower). The tower is all that's left of the old city walls and has been incorporated into the newer building. Suspected witches were locked up there in the Middle Ages. It later became a memorial to former students killed in World War I. ✉ *Grabeng.*

off the beaten path

NEUENHEIM – To escape the crowds of Heidelberg, walk across the Theodor Heuss Bridge to the suburb of Neuenheim. At the turn of the 20th century this old fishing village developed into a residential area full of posh art-nouveau villas. North of the Brückenkopf (bridgehead) you'll find antiques and designer shops, boutiques, and cafés on Brückenstrasse, Bergstrasse (one block east), and Ladenburger Strasse (parallel to the river). To savor the neighborhood spirit, visit the charming farmers' market on Wednesday or Saturday morning at the corner of Ladenburger and Luther streets. The beer pubs Vetter's and o'reilly's (once voted best Irish pub in Germany) draw a young crowd; the chic bistros Le Coq and Bar d'Aix cater to a more mature set; and Marktstübel and Dorfschänke serve good food in a casual, cozy atmosphere. All are within a five-minute walk from one another on the streets named above.

12 **Peterskirche** (St. Peter's Church). Many famous Heidelberg citizens' tombstones, some more than 500 years old, line the outer walls of the city's oldest parish church (1485–1500). The church itself is not open for visits. ✉ *Plöck 62.*

5 **Rathaus** (Town Hall). Work began on the town hall in 1701, a few years after the French destroyed the city. The massive coat of arms above the balcony is the work of sculptor Heinrich Charrasky, who also created the statue of Hercules atop the fountain in the middle of the square. ✉ *Marktpl.*

17 **Schlangenweg** (Snake Path). This walkway starts just above the Alte Brücke opposite the Old Town and cuts steeply through terraced vineyards until it reaches the woods, where it crosses the Philosophenweg (Philosophers' Path).

2 **Schloss** (Castle). What's most striking is the architectural variety of this great complex. The oldest parts still standing date from the 15th century, though most of the castle was built in the Renaissance and baroque

Fodor's Choice ★

styles of the 16th and 17th centuries, when the castle was the seat of the Palatinate electors. There's even an "English wing," built in 1612 by the elector Friedrich V for his teenage Scottish bride, Elizabeth Stuart; its plain, square-window facade is positively foreign compared to the more opulent styles of the castle. (The enamored Friedrich also had a charming garden laid out for his young bride; its imposing arched entryway, the Elisabethentor, was put up overnight as a surprise for her 19th birthday.) The architectural highlight remains the Renaissance courtyard—harmonious, graceful, and ornate.

The castle includes the ***Deutsches Apotheken–Museum*** (German Apothecary Museum; ☎ 06221/25880 ⏲ daily 10–5:30). This museum, on the lower floor of the Ottheinrichsbau (Otto Heinrich Building), is filled with ancient carboys and other flagons and receptacles (each with a carefully painted enamel label), beautifully made scales, little drawers, shelves, a marvelous reconstruction of an 18th-century apothecary shop, dried beetles and toads, and a mummy with a full head of hair.

Even if you have to wait, you should make a point of seeing the ***Grosses Fass*** (Great Cask), an enormous wine barrel in the cellar, made from 130 oak trees and capable of holding 58,500 gallons. It was used to hold wines paid as taxes by wine growers in the Palatinate. During the rule of the elector Carl Philip, the barrel was guarded by the court jester, a Tyrolean dwarf called Perkeo—when offered wine, he always answered, "*Perche no?*" ("Why not?"), hence his nickname. Legend has it that he could consume frighteningly large quantities of wine and that he died when he drank a glass of water by mistake. A statue of Perkeo stands next to the two-story-high barrel.

The castle may be reached by taking the Königstuhl Bergbahn. Generations of earlier visitors hiked up to it on the Burgweg, a winding road. Of course, it's easier to walk down. In summer there are fireworks displays from the castle terrace (on the first Saturday in June and September and the second Saturday in July). In July and August the castle hosts an open-air theater festival. Performances of *The Student Prince* often figure prominently. ☎ *06221/538–421 castle* 🌐 *www.heidelberg-schloss.de/index.html* 🎟 *Courtyard, Great Cask, and Apotheken–Museum €2.50; tours of interior an additional €3.50* ⏲ *Mar.–Nov., daily 9:30–6, Dec.–Feb., daily 10–5; tours in English daily, when demand is sufficient.*

9 **Studentenkarzer** (Student Prison). University officials locked students up here from 1778 to 1914—mostly for minor offenses. They could be held for up to 14 days and were left to subsist on bread and water for the first three days; thereafter, they were allowed to attend lectures, receive guests, and have food brought in from the outside. A stay in the jail became as coveted as a scar inflicted in the university's fencing clubs. There's bravado, even poetic flair, to be deciphered from two centuries of graffiti that cover the walls and ceilings of the narrow cells. ✉ *Augustinerg.* ☎ *06221/543–554* 🎟 *€2.50* ⏲ *Apr.–Sept., Tues.–Sun. 10–6; Oct., Tues.–Sun. 10–4; Nov.–Mar., Tues.–Sat. 10–4.*

11 **Universitätsbibliothek** (University Library). Its 2½ million volumes include the 14th-century *Manesse Codex,* a unique collection of medieval songs and poetry once performed in the courts of Germany by the *Minnesänger* (singers). The original is too fragile to be exhibited, so a copy is on display. ✉ *Plöck 107–109* ☎ *06221/542–380* 🌐 *www.ub.uni-heidelberg.de* 🎟 *Free* ⏲ *Mon.–Sat. 10–6.*

Where to Stay & Eat

★ $$$$ ✕ **Schlossweinstube.** This spacious baroque dining room specializes in *Ente von Heidelberg* (roast duck) and offers refuge from the castle crowds. The menu changes seasonally and offers an extensive selection of international wines. Adjacent to the dining room is the Bistro Backhaus ($; open Apr.–Sept., daily; Mar.–Oct., Fri.–Sun.), which has rustic furnishings and a nearly 50-foot-high *Backkamin* (baking oven). Light fare as well as coffee and cake are served indoors and on the shaded terrace. You can sample rare wines (Eiswein, Beerenauslese) by the glass in the shared wine cellar, or pick up a bottle with a designer label depicting Heidelberg. Reservations are essential for terrace seating at either restaurant in the summer. ✉ *Schlosshof, on castle grounds* ☎ *06221/97970* 🌐 *www.schoenmehl.de* 💳 *AE, DC, MC, V* ⏲ *Schlossweinstube closed Jan. and Wed. No lunch.*

$$$$ ✕ **schwarz Das Restaurant.** Sleek, contemporary furnishings, soft lighting, stunning panoramic views, and Manfred Schwarz's creative cuisine make for unforgettable dining in this new 12th-floor restaurant, complete with an apéritif bar and cigar lounge. The gourmet and regional menus (three to seven courses) change every month, but Mediterranean accents are a constant, as are dishes flavored with caviar or truffles, such as sautéed goose liver on "truffled" polenta with raspberry vinegar sauce or gratinated scallops with chive sauce and caviar. ✉ *Print Media Academy, Kurfürsten-Anlage 60, opposite the train station* ☎ *06221/757–030* 🌐 *www.schwarzdasrestaurant.com* 💳 *AE, DC, MC, V* ⏲ *Closed Sun., Mon., and 3 wks in Aug. No lunch.*

★ $$$ ✕ **Simplicissimus.** Olive oil and herbs of Provence accentuate many of chef Johann Lummer's culinary delights. Saddle of lamb and sautéeed liver in honey-pepper sauce are specialties; the *Dessertteller,* a sampler, is a crowning finish to any meal here. The wine list focuses on old-world estates, particularly clarets. The elegant art-nouveau interior is done in shades of red with dark-wood accents. In summer dine alfresco in the courtyard. ✉ *Ingrimstr. 16* ☎ *06221/183–336* 🌐 *www.restaurant-simplicissimus.de* 💳 *AE, MC, V* ⏲ *Closed Tues., 2 wks in Jan. and Feb., and 2 wks in Aug. and Sept. No lunch.*

★ $–$$$ ✕ **Zur Herrenmühle.** "Spontaneität" (spontaneity) is the new motto of Ursula and Günter Ueberle's fresh, light cuisine. It's served in a 17th-century grain mill that's been transformed into a romantic, cozy restaurant with an idyllic courtyard. Fish, lamb, homemade pasta, and a delicious Wiener schnitzel are specialties. The prix-fixe menus offer good value. ✉ *Hauptstr. 239, near Karlstor* ☎ *06221/602–909* 🌐 *www.zur-herrenmuehle.de* 💳 *AE, DC, MC, V* ⏲ *Closed Sun. and Mon. and 1st half of Jan. No lunch.*

$–$$ ✕ **Schnitzelbank.** A hole-in-the-wall where tourists rarely venture, this former cooper's workshop is now a candlelit pub filled with locals seated at long wooden tables. It's hard not to fall into conversation with the people at your elbow. The menu features wines and specialties from Baden and the Pfalz, such as *Schäufele* (pickled and slightly smoked pork shoulder); or a hearty *Pfälzer Teller,* a platter of bratwurst, *Leberknödel* (liver dumplings), and slices of *Saumagen* (a spicy meat-and-potato mixture encased in a sow's stomach). ✉ *Bauamtsg. 7* ☎ *06221/21189* 💳 *MC, V* ⏲ *No lunch weekdays.*

$–$$ ✕ **Trattoria Toscana.** You can choose from antipasti, pasta, salads, pizzas, and special daily offerings all in generous portions at this authentic Italian eatery. The partly rustic, partly modern interior is accented by ornamental ironwork. Though the atmosphere inside is quite comfortable, the best seats are those outside, from which you may view the castle, Old Bridge and other Old Town sites. Wait staff here are very friendly and accommodating. ✉ *Marktplatz 1* ☎ *062/212–8619* 💳 *AE, V.*

¢–$$ ✕ **Zum Roten Ochsen.** Many of the rough-hewn oak tables here have initials carved into them, a legacy of the thousands who have visited Heidelberg's most famous old tavern. Mark Twain, Marilyn Monroe, and John Wayne may have left their mark—they all ate here. You can wash down simple fare, such as goulash soup and bratwurst, or heartier dishes, such as *Tellerfleisch* (boiled beef) and sauerbraten, with German wines or Heidelberg beer. The "Red Ox" has been run by the Spengel family for 165 years. ✉ *Hauptstr. 217* ☎ *06221/20977* 🌐 *www.roterochsen.de* ✍ *Reservations essential* 💳 *No credit cards* ⏲ *Closed Sun. and mid-Dec.–mid-Jan. No lunch Nov.–Mar.*

¢–$ ✕ **Havana Cocktailbar–Restaurant.** Palm trees and salsa music add Latin zest to the handsome interior of the neoclassical *Kongresshaus* (convention center) and its broad terrace. It's a perfect backdrop for sipping one of the more than 100 cocktails or the hearty house wine (a Spanish red) with the freshly prepared tapas, *Rollos* (stuffed tortillas), or pasta and vegetarian dishes. There's live piano music some evenings, and on Friday and Saturday 8–10 PM beginners can take a salsa class. ✉ *Neckarstaden 24* ☎ *06221/389–3430* 🌐 *www.heidelberg.havana-restaurants.de* 💳 *MC, V* ⏲ *No lunch.*

¢ ✕ **Café Knösel.** Heidelberg's oldest (1863) coffeehouse has always been a popular meeting place for students and professors. It's still producing café founder Fridolin Knösel's *Heidelberger Studentenkuss* ("student kiss," a chocolate wrapped in paper showing two students touching lips), an acceptable way for 19th-century students to "exchange kisses" in public. ✉ *Haspelg. 20* ☎ *06221/22345* 💳 *No credit cards* ⏲ *Closed Mon.*

★ $$$–$$$$ ✕🏨 **Der Europäische Hof–Hotel Europa.** This is the most luxurious of Heidelberg's hotels, centrally located and offering a wide range of facilities. Public rooms are sumptuously furnished, and bedrooms are spacious and tasteful; all suites have whirlpools. In the elegant restaurant, Kurfürstenstube ($$$–$$$$), rich shades of yellow and blue are offset by the original woodwork of 1865. In summer, meals are served on the fountain-lined terrace. There are great views of the castle from the glass-lined fitness and wellness centers. ✉ *Friedrich-Ebert-Anlage 1, D–69117* ☎ *06221/5150* 📠 *06221/515–506* 🌐 *www.europaeischerhof.com* 🛏 *102 rooms, 13 suites, 3 apartments* 👍 *Restaurant, cafeteria, minibars, cable TV, in-room data ports, Wi-Fi, indoor pool, gym, hair salon, sauna, steam room, bar, lobby lounge, babysitting, dry cleaning, laun-*

dry service, Internet room, business services, some pets allowed, no-smoking rooms; no a/c in some rooms ▭ *AE, DC, MC, V* 🍽 *BP.*

$$–$$$$ Fodor's Choice ★ **Hotel Die Hirschgasse.** A stunning castle view marks this historical inn (1472), located across the river opposite Karlstor (15-minute walk to Old Town). Convivial Ernest Kraft and his British wife, Allison, serve upscale regional specialties (and wines from the vineyard next door) in the Mensurstube ($–$$), once a tavern where university students indulged in fencing duels, as mentioned in Mark Twain's *A Tramp Abroad.* Beamed ceilings, stone walls, and deep red fabrics make for romantic dining in the elegant Le Gourmet ($$$$). The hotel's decor is also romantic, filled with floral prints, artwork, and deep shades of red. The suites are quite large, comfortable, and elegantly appointed. ✉ *Hirschg. 3, D–69120* ☎ *06221/4540* 📠 *06221/454–111* 🌐 *www.hirschgasse.de* *20 suites* *2 restaurants, minibars, cable TV, in-room data ports, lobby lounge, babysitting, laundry service, business services, some pets allowed (fee); no a/c, no smoking* ▭ *AE, DC, MC, V* ⏲ *Le Gourmet closed 2 wks in early Jan., 2 wks in early Aug., and Sun. and Mon.; Mensurstube closed Sun. No lunch at either restaurant.*

★ **$$–$$$** **Romantik Hotel zum Ritter St. Georg.** If this is your first visit to Germany, try to stay here. It's the only Renaissance building in Heidelberg (1592) and has a top location opposite the market square in the heart of Old Town. The staff is exceptionally helpful and friendly. Some rooms are more modern and spacious than others, but all are comfortable. You can enjoy German and international favorites in the restaurants Belier or Ritterstube ($–$$$). Both are wood paneled and have old-world charm. ✉ *Hauptstr. 178, D–69117* ☎ *06221/1350* 📠 *06221/135–230* 🌐 *www.ritter-heidelberg.de* *39 rooms, 36 with bath; 1 suite* *2 restaurants, minibars, cable TV, in-room data ports, Wi-Fi, Internet room, babysitting, dry cleaning, laundry service, some pets allowed, no-smoking rooms; no a/c* ▭ *AE, DC, MC, V.*

$$ **KulturBrauerei Heidelberg.** Rooms with warm, sunny colors and modern decor are brilliantly incorporated into this old malt factory in the heart of Old Town. The restaurant ($–$$; no credit cards) is lively until well past midnight. House-brewed Scheffel's beer is the beverage of choice (although there are two wines from the excellent Baden estate Dr. Heger). Try the *Kohlrouladen* (homemade stuffed cabbage rolls) or *Spannferkel* (roast suckling pig). The cellar houses the brewery (tours and tasting possible) and a weekend jazz club; in the courtyard is a huge beer garden. ✉ *Leyerg. 6, D–69117* ☎ *06221/502–980* 📠 *06221/502–9879* 🌐 *www.heidelberger-kulturbrauerei.de* *20 rooms, 1 suite* *Restaurant, minibars, cable TV, business services, some pets allowed (fee), no-smoking rooms; no a/c* ▭ *MC, V* 🍽 *BP.*

$$ **Weisser Bock.** Exposed beams and stucco ceilings are part of this hotel's charm. Rooms are individually decorated with warm wood furnishings and offer modern comfort. Art-deco fans will be charmed by the restaurant ($–$$$; no credit cards) decor and pretty table settings. Fresh fish is a highlight of the creative cuisine. The homemade smoked salmon and an unusual cream-of-Jerusalem-artichoke soup with crayfish are recommended. The proprietor is a great wine fan, and the extensive wine list reflects it. Smoking is permitted only in the restaurant.

✉ *Grosse Mantelg. 24, D–69117* ☎ *06221/90000* 📠 *06221/900–099* 🌐 *www.weisserbock.de* *21 rooms, 2 suites* *Restaurant, minibars, cable TV, bar, business services; no a/c, no smoking* 💳 *MC, V.*

$–$$ **Gasthaus Backmulde.** This traditional tavern in the heart of Heidelberg has a surprising range of items on its menu ($–$$), from delicately marinated fresh vegetables that accompany the excellent meat dishes to imaginative soups that add modern twists to ancient recipes (a Franconian potato broth, for instance, rich with garden herbs). Guest rooms are small but comfortable. ✉ *Schiffg. 11, D–69117* ☎ *06221/53660* 📠 *06221/536–660* 🌐 *www.gasthaus-backmulde.de* *19 rooms, 12 with bath* *Restaurant, cable TV, lobby lounge, Internet room, some pets allowed (fee); no a/c* 💳 *AE, MC, V* *Restaurant closed Sun. No lunch Mon.* *BP.*

$ **Schnookeloch.** This lively old tavern ($–$$$) dates from 1703 and is inextricably linked with Heidelberg's history and university. Young and old alike crowd around the wooden tables in the wood-panel room, and piano music adds to the din Thursday through Sunday nights. From salads and pasta to hearty roasts and steaks, there's a broad selection of food, including many fish dishes. Upstairs there are modern, pleasantly furnished guest rooms. ✉ *Haspelg. 8, D–69117* ☎ *06221/138–080* 🌐 *www.schnookeloch.de* 📠 *06221/138–0813* *11 rooms* *Restaurant, refrigerators, cable TV, beer garden, some pets allowed; no a/c* 💳 *AE, MC, V* *BP.*

$$–$$$$ **Crowne Plaza Heidelberg.** Located just a few blocks from the Old Town, the Crowne Plaza is a top-choice for business travelers and tourists alike. It's not quite as luxurious as some of this well-known hotel chain's properties, but it offers very nice accommodations and a full range of amenities. What many do consider luxurious is the indoor swimming pool and spa in the hotel's lower level—it includes a sauna, steam bath, Jacuzzi, massage parlor, and poolside bar. On weekends, a wonderful North-American style brunch buffet is offered at an additional cost of €16. ✉ *Kurfürstenanlage 1, D–69115* ☎ *06221/9170* 📠 *06221/21007* 🌐 *www.crowneplaza.com* *232 rooms, 4 suites* *2 restaurants, room service, minibars, cable TV with movies, in-room data ports, pool, gym, bar, Internet room, business services, meeting rooms, parking (fee)* 💳 *AE, MC, V.*

$–$$ **Holländer Hof.** The pink-and-white-painted facade of this ornate 19th-century building opposite the Alte Brücke stands out in its row fronting the Neckar River. Many of its rooms overlook the busy waterway and the forested hillside of the opposite shore. The rooms are modern and pleasant, and the staff is very friendly. ✉ *Neckarstaden 66, D–69117* ☎ *06221/60500* 📠 *06221/605–060* 🌐 *www.hollaender-hof.de* *38 rooms, 1 suite* *Minibars, cable TV, in-room data ports, Wi-Fi, dry cleaning, laundry service, Internet room, business services, some pets allowed (fee), no-smoking floor; no a/c* 💳 *AE, DC, MC, V.*

$–$$ **Nh Heidelberg.** This modern hotel, housed in a former brewery, is located just far enough from Old Town that it offers reasonable room rates, but it's still within walking distance of Heidelberg's major sites (about 1 km [½ mi] from Old Town). You can dine at one of three on-site restaurants, including the Raustubert, which specializes in regional German fare. Rooms are colorful and cozy, and a wide range of amenities are included. ✉ *Bergheimerstr 91, D–69115* ☎ *06221/13270* 📠 *06221/132–7100* *174 rooms* *3 restaurants, room service, minibars, cable TV, in-room data ports, Wi-Fi, gym, bar, babysitting, meeting rooms, parking (fee)* 💳 *AE, MC, V.*

¢ **Jugendherberge Tiergartenstrasse.** For youth-hostel cardholders (cards cost €20), these are clean, inexpensive accommodations near miniature golf, a large pool, stables, and the zoo. Check on the curfew and get a key if you plan to stay out late. To and from the Hauptbahnhof, take Bus 33 (10-minute ride)—ask the reception desk for precise times. Reception is open 7:30 AM–9 AM and 1 PM–11:30 PM. ✉ *Tiergartenstr. 5 D–69120* ☎ *06221/412–066 or 06221/651–190* 📠 *06221/651–1928* 🌐 *www.djh.de* *500 beds* *Cafeteria, Wi-Fi, boccie, Ping-Pong, volleyball, lounge, recreation room, laundry facilities, no-smoking rooms; no a/c, no room phones, no room TVs* 💳 *MC, V* 🍽 *BP.*

Nightlife & the Arts

Information on all upcoming events is given in the monthly *Heidelberg aktuell,* free and available from the tourist office or on the Internet (🌐 www.heidelberg-aktuell.de). Theater tickets may be purchased at **heidelbergTicket** (✉ Theaterstr. 4 ☎ 06221/582–000).

THE ARTS Heidelberg has a thriving theater scene. The **Kulturzentrum Karlstorbahnhof** (✉ Am Karlstor 1 ☎ 06221/978–911) is a 19th-century train station reincarnated as a theater, cinema, and café. The **Theater der Stadt** (✉ Theaterstr. 8 ☎ 06221/583–520) is the best-known theater in town. Avant-garde productions take place at the **Zimmertheater** (✉ Hauptstr. 118 ☎ 06221/21069). Performances are held at the castle during the annual **Schlossfestspiele** (☎ 06221/582–000).

NIGHTLIFE Heidelberg nightlife is concentrated in the area around the Heiliggeistkirche (Church of the Holy Ghost), in the Old Town. Don't miss a visit to one of the old student taverns that have been in business for ages and have the atmosphere to prove it. Today's students, however, are more likely to hang out in one of the dozen or more bars on **Untere Strasse,** which runs parallel to and between Hauptstrasse and the Neckar River, starting from the market square. Begin at one end of the street and work your way down; you'll find bars that specialize in all sorts of tastes. The fanciest bars and yuppie cafés are along **Hauptstrasse.** One of these is **Pepper Bar** (✉ Heugasse 1 ☎ 06221/168617), located on a side street just off the Hauptstrasse. This trendy nightspot, frequented by a young professional crowd, is highly regarded for its tasty cocktails.

Mark Twain rubbed elbows with students at **Zum Roten Ochsen** (✉ Hauptstr. 217 ☎ 06221/20977). **Zum Sepp'l** (✉ Hauptstr. 213 ☎ 06221/23085) is another traditional, always-packed pub. **Schnookeloch** (✉ Haspelg. 8 ☎ 06221/138–080) has long been patronized by dueling frats.

Billy Blues (im Ziegler) (✉ Bergheimer Str. 1b ☎ 06221/25333) is a restaurant, bar, and disco, with live music Monday and Thursday. The hot sounds of salsa fill the cellar of the **Havana Club** (✉ Neckarstaden 24 ☎ 06221/389–3430) Friday and Saturday after 9 PM, with salsa classes 8–10 PM. The cover charge includes a drink voucher. **Nachtschicht** (Night

Shift; ✉ Bergheimer Str. 147 ☎ 06221/438–550), in the Landfried factory, is a popular meeting point for drinks and disco Wednesday through Saturday after 10 PM.

Facing the main train station and futuristic equestrian statue is the chic, modern **print media lounge** (✉ Kurfürsten–Anlage 60 ☎ 06221/653–949), where you can dine inexpensively (breakfast, lunch, dinner, and late-night menu), dance, or simply enjoy delicious cocktails. It's open daily, with DJs Friday and Saturday after 10 PM and soul, funk, and jazz Sunday after 7 PM. Smoky, loud, and always crowded after 10 PM, the old beer hall **Reichsapfel/Lager** (✉ Untere Str. 35 ☎ 06221/485–542) has taken on a sleek, contemporary look after renovations. Seated, or standing around high tables, you can enjoy drinks and light fare, often with live music and/or DJs. Check out the reduced drink prices during the Lounge Hour (nightly, 7–9 PM) or Midnight Express (Friday and Saturday, midnight–1 AM).

The **Schwimmbad Musik Club** (Swimming Pool Music Club; ✉ Tiergartenstr. 13, near the zoo ☎ 06221/470–201) is a multicultural fixture of Heidelberg nightlife with its ambitious concert program (Nirvana used to play here), DJs, disco, videos, and movies. This club fills the former grounds of a swimming pool and park (hence the name). Theme evenings and parties round out the offerings. It's closed Sunday through Tuesday. For a terrific view of the town and castle, delicious drinks, and relaxing music, head for the glass-lined **Turm Lounge** (✉ Alte Glockengiesserei 9 ☎ 06221/653–949). Choose between trendy sofas and dark-red walls on the seventh floor or an atmosphere shaded in deep blue on the eighth floor. It's worth elbowing your way into **Vetters Alt-Heidelberger Brauhaus** (✉ Steing. 9 ☎ 06221/165–850) for the brewed-on-the-premises beer. There's also a branch in Neuenheim (across the river) with a butcher shop, where the homemade sausage is produced for both pubs.

Shopping

Heidelberg's **Hauptstrasse,** or Main Street, is a pedestrian zone lined with shops, sights, and restaurants that stretches more than 1 km (½ mi) through the heart of town. But don't spend your money before exploring the shops on such side streets as **Plöck, Ingrimstrasse,** and **Untere Strasse,** where there are candy stores, bookstores, and antiques shops on the ground floors of baroque buildings. If your budget allows, the city can be a good place to find reasonably priced German antiques, and the Neckar Valley region produces fine glass and crystal. Heidelberg has open-air **farmers' markets** on Wednesday and Saturday mornings on Marktplatz, and Tuesday and Friday mornings on Friedrich-Ebert-Platz. A ***Flohmarkt*** (flea market) takes place on Messplatz am Kirchheimer Weg several times each month. From the train station take Bus 41 or 42 toward Kirchheim.

In **Aurum & Argentum** (✉ Brückenstr. 22 ☎ 06221/473–453) you'll find a local gold- and silversmith with impeccable craftsmanship; the finely executed pieces start at €150. Its hours are Tuesday through Friday 2:30 to 6:30 and Saturday 10 to 2.

The old glass display cases at **Heidelberger Zuckerladen** (✉ Plöck 52 ☎ 06221/24365) are full of lollipops and "penny" candy. If you're looking for an unusual gift, the shop fashions colorful, unique items out of sugary ingredients such as marshmallow and sweetened gum. Drop in weekdays noon–7 and Saturday 11–3.

Buy your cutlery and tableware at **Unholtz** (✉ Hauptstr. 160 ☎ 06221/20964) and keep it for life—it's made by famous German manufacturers of some of the world's best knives.

Sports & the Outdoors

JOGGING/BICYCLING The riverside path is an ideal route for walking, jogging, and bicycling, since it's traffic-free and offers excellent views of the area. If you access the paved pathway in the center of town, you can follow it for many kilometers in either direction.

SWIMMING & SPAS Just a short drive or S-bahn ride from the city is **Miramar Therma** (Spa) (✉ Waidallee 100, Weineim ☎ 06201/60000). Their motto is "Jeden tag ein kleiner urlaub" (Every day's a small vacation). The huge complex houses several saunas, Jacuzzis, an outdoor pool (heated in winter), massage center, restaurant, and more. Be warned, however, that it's not a place for the bashful—a large portion of the premises is strolled by people wearing only towels or nothing at all.

Schwetzingen

18 *10 km (6 mi) west of Heidelberg.*

A rare pleasure awaits you if you're in Schwetzingen in April, May, or June: the town is Germany's asparagus center, and nearly every local restaurant has a *Spargelkarte* (a special menu featuring fresh asparagus dishes).

Schwetzingen is famous for its **Schloss**, a formal 18th-century palace constructed as a summer residence by the Palatinate electors. It's a noble, rose-color building, imposing and harmonious; a highlight is the rococo theater in one wing. The extensive park blends formal French and informal English styles, with neatly bordered gravel walks trailing off into the dark woodland. The 18th-century planners of this delightful oasis had fun adding such touches as an exotic mosque, complete with minarets and a shimmering pool (although they got a little confused and gave the building a very baroque portal), and the "classical ruin" that was de rigueur in this period. ☎ *06202/128–828* 🌐 *www.schloesser-und-gaerten.de* *Palace, including tour and gardens, Apr.–Oct. €6.50, Nov.–Mar. €5; gardens only, Apr.–Oct. €4, Nov.–Mar. €2.50* ⏲ *Palace tours, on the hr, Apr.–Oct., Tues.–Fri. 11–4, weekends 11–5; Nov.–Mar., Fri. tour 2 PM, weekends at 11, 2, and 3. Gardens Apr.–Sept., daily 8–8; Nov.–Feb., daily 9–5; Mar. and Oct., daily 9–6.*

The Arts

The annual **Schwetzinger Festspiele,** from late April to early June, features operas and concerts by international artists in the ornate rococo theater of Schwetzingen Palace. The period rooms of the palace are also the venue for the **Mozartfest** (☎ 06202/945–875 tourist office) during the last half of September. The local tourist office has details on both performing-arts festivals.

THE BURGENSTRASSE (CASTLE ROAD)

Upstream from Heidelberg, the Neckar Valley narrows, presenting a landscape of orchards, vineyards, and wooded hills crowned with castles rising above the gently flowing stream. It's one of the most impressive stretches of the Burgenstrasse. The small valleys along the Neckar Valley road (B–37)—the locals call them *Klingen*—that cut north into the Odenwald are off-the-beaten-track territory. One of the most atmospheric is the Wolfsschlucht, which starts below the castle at Zwingenberg. The dank, shadowy little gorge inspired Carl Maria von Weber's opera *Der Freischütz* (The Marksman).

Hirschhorn

19 *23 km (14 mi) east of Heidelberg.*

Hirsch (stag) and *Horn* (antlers) make up the name of the Knights of Hirschhorn, the medieval ruling family that gave its name to both its 12th-century castle complex and the village it presided over. The town's coat of arms depicts a leaping stag. Ensconced into the hillside halfway between the castle and the river is a former Carmelite monastery and its beautiful 15th-century Gothic church with remarkable frescoes (open for visits). Hirschhorn's position on a hairpin loop of the Neckar can best be savored from the castle terrace, over a glass of wine, coffee and cake, or a fine meal.

The past comes to life the first weekend of September at the annual, two-day **Ritterfest**, a colorful "Knights' Festival" complete with a medieval arts-and-crafts market.

Where to Stay & Eat

★ $–$$ **Schlosshotel auf der Burg Hirschhorn.** This very pleasant hotel and restaurant is set in historic Hirschhorn Castle, perched high over the medieval village and the Neckar. The terrace offers splendid views (ask for Table 30 in the corner). The rooms are modern and well furnished. Eight are in the castle and 17 in the old stables. *Wildschwein* (wild boar), *Hirsch* (venison), and fresh fish are the house specialties ($–$$$). The friendly proprietors, the Oberrauners, bake a delicious, warm Apfelstrudel based on a recipe from their home in Vienna. A good selection of wines is available. ✉ *D–69434 Hirschhorn/Neckar* ☎ *06272/92090* 📠 *06272/3267* 🌐 *www.castle-hotel.de* *21 rooms, 4 suites* *Restaurant, café, minibars, in-room data ports, some pets allowed (fee); no a/c* 💳 *AE, MC, V* ⏲ *Hotel and restaurant closed Dec. 15–Jan. Restaurant closed Mon. Feb.–Easter and Nov.–mid-Dec.* *BP.*

Eberbach

20 *11 km (7 mi) east of Hirschhorn.*

The Neckar makes a wide bend to the south here. The landscape around romantic Eberbach is punctuated by four square towers from the medieval town fortifications and three castle ruins. The meadows and beechwood forests here provide ideal growing conditions for a regional specialty, *Bärlauch* (wild garlic or ramson). During the "Bärlauch Days" from mid-March to mid-April, restaurants have special Bärlauch menus, and there are guided hikes to gather the greens and learn about their healthful benefits. Historic houses abound, and on **Alter Markt** (old market square) there's a particularly fine graffito facade to admire at the **Hotel Karpfen.** Stop by the **Naturpark-Informationszentrum** (Natural Park Information Center) for details about the extensive hiking trails through the Odenwald forest.

Where to Stay & Eat

$–$$ ✕ **Pleutersbacher Weinstube.** Jürgen and Martina Klier's cozy wine restaurant in Pleutersbach (on the south side of the Neckar, opposite Eberbach proper) is a favorite with locals. Amid exposed beams and rustic furnishings you can enjoy tasty regional fare, such as *Käs'Spätzle* (a cheese-gratin version of these wonderful noodles), as well as daily specials and theme menus based on seasonal ingredients, such as matjes herring, kale, or Bärlauch. A good selection of by-the-glass, half bottles, and older-vintage German and international wines is served. ✉ *Eberbacherstr. 5* ☎ *06271/5705* 🌐 *www.pleutersbacher-weinstube.de* ▭ *No credit cards* ⏲ *Closed Mon. No lunch Mon.–Sat.*

$ ✕🏨 **Hotel Karpfen.** Behind the beautiful painted facade of this traditional hotel and restaurant a warm welcome from the Rohrlapper and Jung families awaits you. The wooden furnishings and floors lend the rooms warmth and a rustic charm. The restaurant ($–$$$) has wallpapered walls and antique-rose accents, a nice setting for fresh *Forelle* (trout) from the streams of the Odenwald forest, rabbit and game, and regional specialties, including local wines. ✉ *Am Alten Markt 1, D–69412* ☎ *06271/71015* 📠 *06271/71010* 🌐 *www.hotel-karpfen.com* *47 rooms, 2 suites, 1 apartment* *Restaurant, cable TV, some in-room data ports, some pets allowed (fee); no a/c* ▭ *AE, MC, V* ⏲ *Restaurant closed Tues. and 4 wks in Jan. and Feb.* 🍽 *BP.*

en route

Eight kilometers (5 mi) beyond Eberbach, a castle stands above the village of **Zwingenberg,** its medieval towers thrusting through the dark woodland. Some say it's the most romantic of all the castles along the Neckar (the one at Heidelberg excepted). The annual **Schlossfestspiele** (☎ 06271/71286 🌐 www.schlossfestspiele-zwingenberg.de), with performances of *Der Freischutz,* takes place within its ancient walls in August. Park at the train station (15-minute walk to the castle, or take the shuttle bus departing from the station 30 minutes before the performance).

Mosbach

21 *25 km (16 mi) southeast of Eberbach.*

The little town of Mosbach is one of the most charming towns on the Neckar. Its ancient market square contains one of Germany's most exquisite half-timber buildings—the early-17th-century **Palm'sches Haus** (Palm House), its upper stories laced with intricate timbering. The **Rathaus,** built 50 years earlier, is a modest affair by comparison.

Where to Stay & Eat

★ $–$$$ **Zum Ochsen.** Chef Achim Münch and his vivacious American wife, Heyley, run this country inn in Nüstenbach, a suburb north of Mosbach. The decor is stylish—one room elegant, the other more rustic. The interesting display of antique silver is for sale. Fresh, seasonal cuisine and fish are always featured, as well as such creative dishes as baked fondue or venison in a pistachio crust. There's a good selection of wines at very fair prices. You can spend the night in the antique-filled cottage next door ($, sleeps four, no smoking). *Im Weiler 6 06261/15428 06261/893–645 www.restaurant-zum-ochsen.de MC Closed 2 wks in Feb. or Mar., 2 wks in Aug. or Sept., and Tues. No lunch Mon.–Sat.*

$ **Zum Lamm.** The half-timber "Lamb" on Mosbach's main street is one of the town's prettiest houses. Its cozy rooms are individually furnished, with flowers filling the window boxes. The restaurant (¢–$$), complete with requisite exposed beams, serves local and international dishes, incorporating meat from the hotel's own butcher shop. *Hauptstr. 59, D–74821 06261/89020 06261/890–291 50 rooms, 1 suite Restaurant, some minibars, cable TV, lounge, laundry service, some pets allowed, no-smoking rooms; no a/c AE, MC, V BP.*

Neckarzimmern

5 km (3 mi) south of Mosbach.

★ 22 The massive, circular bulk of **Burg Hornberg** rises above the woods that drop to the riverbank and the town of Neckarzimmern. The road to the castle leads through vineyards that have been providing dry white wines for centuries. Today the castle is part hotel-restaurant and part museum. In the 16th century it was home to the larger-than-life knight Götz von Berlichingen (1480–1562). When he lost his right arm fighting in a petty dynastic squabble, he had a blacksmith fashion an iron replacement for him. The original designs for this fearsome artificial limb are on view in the castle, as is a suit of armor that belonged to him. Scenes from his life are also represented. For most Germans, the rambunctious knight is best remembered for a remark he delivered to the Palatinate elector that was faithfully reproduced in Goethe's play *Götz von Berlichingen.* Responding to a reprimand, von Berlichingen told the elector, more or less, to "kiss my ass" (the original German is substantially more earthy). To this day the polite version of this insult is known as a *Götz von Berlichingen.* Inquire at the hotel reception for details about visiting the castle ruins. *€3.*

Where to Stay & Eat

★ $$ **Burg Hornberg.** Your host is the present baron of the castle. From the heights of the terrace and glassed-in restaurant ($–$$$)—housed in the former *Marstall,* or royal stables—there are stunning views. Fresh fish and game are specialties, as are the estate-bottled wines. There are good Riesling wines and the rarities Traminer and Muskateller—also sold in the wineshops in the courtyard and at the foot of the hill. The hotel's rooms are comfortable and modern in style. *D–74865 06261/92460 06261/924–644 www.castle-hotel-hornberg.com 22 rooms, 2 suites Restaurant, some minibars, cable TV, in-room* *data ports, some pets allowed (fee), no-smoking rooms; no a/c* ▭ *MC, V* ⊙ *Closed late Dec.–late Jan.* 🍽 *BP.*

Shopping

The factory **Franz Kaspar** (✉ Hauptstr. 11, in the courtyard ☎ 06261/92400 for tour reservations), known for its fine crystal, gives free tours (weekdays 9–4, Saturday 10–6, Sunday 10:30–6) that demonstrate the manufacturing process. Its outlet shop is open daily.

At the hand of master pastry chef and chocolatier Eberhard Schell of **Café Schell,** an unlikely duo—*essig* (vinegar), made from Spätlese and Auslese wines, and chocolate—is handcrafted into a scrumptious, not-too-sweet delicacy known as *Essig Schleckerle.* The unusual *Pralinen* (chocolates) filled with wine vinegar were the first chocolates to be patented and listed in the *Guinness Book of Records.* Since their debut in 1995, innovative Schell has created a range of exquisite chocolates filled with wine and wine-based products from several of Germany's leading wine estates. ✉ *Schloss-Str. 31, D–74831 Gundelsheim* ☎ *06269/350* 🌐 *www.weinpralinen.de* ⊙ *Closed Mon. afternoon and Tues.*

en route

One of the best preserved of the Neckar castles is the 15th-century **Burg Guttenberg.** Within its stout stone walls are a museum and a restaurant (closed January, February, and Monday) with views of the river valley. The castle is also home to Europe's leading center for the study and protection of birds of prey, and some are released on demonstration flights (€8) from the castle walls from April through October, daily at 11 and 3, and in March and November, daily at 3. ✉ *Neckarmühlbach, 6 km (4 mi) west of Gundelsheim* ☎ *06266/388* 🌐 *www.burg-guttenberg.de* 🎫 *Castle €4, castle and flight demonstration €11* ⊙ *Apr.–Oct., daily 10–6.*

Bad Wimpfen

23 *8 km (5 mi) south of Neckarzimmern.*

Fodor's Choice ★

At the confluence of the Neckar and Jagst rivers, Bad Wimpfen is one of the most stunning towns of the Neckar Valley. The Romans built a fortress and a bridge here, on the riverbank site of an ancient Celtic settlement, in the 1st century AD. Wimpfen im Tal (Wimpfen in the Valley), the oldest part of town, is home to the Benedictine monastery Gruessau and its church, **Ritterstiftskirche St. Peter** (✉ Lindenpl.), which dates from the 10th and 13th centuries. The cloisters are delightful, an example of German Gothic at its most uncluttered.

On the hilltop, Wimpfen am Berg, the Staufen emperor Barbarossa built his largest **Pfalz** (residence) in 1182. The town not only thrived thereafter but also enjoyed the status of a Free Imperial City from 1300 to 1803. Since then, its fortune has been tied to the local saltworks that enabled it to develop medicinal saline baths and its reputation as a spa—hence the town was renamed Bad Wimpfen in 1930.

A walking tour marked by signs bearing the town arms begins at the Rathaus on the market square, adjacent to the Burgviertel (palace quarter) and the buildings of the former imperial residence. These are nestled along the town wall between the turreted **Blauer Turm** (Blue Tower) and the massive stone **Roter Turm** (Red Tower), the western and eastern strongholds of the palace, respectively. Ascend either for a grand view. The **Steinhaus,** Germany's largest Romanesque living quarters and once the imperial apartments reserved for women, is now a history museum (closed Monday). Next to the Steinhaus are the remains of the northern facade of the palace, an arcade of superbly carved Romanesque pillars that flanked the imperial hall in its heyday. The imperial chapel, next to the Red Tower, holds a collection of ecclesiastical artworks (closed Monday). Other historical houses in the quarter are on Schwibbogengasse (Nos. 5 and 16). ✉ *Kaiserpl.* ☎ *07063/97200* ⏲ *Palace tours daily by advance reservation.*

Among Bad Wimpfen's finest 15- and 16th-century half-timber houses are those on Badgasse (Nos. 8 and 10), Hauptstrasse (Nos. 69 and 83), and Klostergasse (Nos. 4, 6, 8, and 9). The 13th-century stained glass, wall paintings, medieval altars, and the stone pietà in the Gothic **Stadtkirche** (city church) are worth seeing, as are the Crucifixion sculptures (1515) by the Rhenish master Hans Backoffen on Kirchplatz, behind the church.

In late August the Old Town's medieval past comes alive during the **Zunftmarkt,** a historical market dedicated to the *Zünfte* (guilds). "Artisans" in period costumes demonstrate the old trades and open the festivities with a colorful parade on horseback.

In Germany, pigs are a symbol of good luck. At the **Schweine-Museum** (Pig Museum), you'll see them in every form imaginable—depicted on posters and porcelain, modeled into household items, and as toys, including Porky Pig. In all, it's a mixture of historically valuable items and kitsch. ✉ *Kronengässchen 2* ☎ *07063/6689* 🌐 *www.schweinemuseum.de* 🎫 *€2.60* ⏲ *Daily 10–5.*

Where to Stay & Eat

$–$$ ✕ **Tafelhaus Perkeo.** The interior and decor of this lovingly restored historical house are warm and inviting. Alfresco dining is also possible. Beate Stiefel oversees service, and Heiko Habelt is in the kitchen, preparing well-made regional dishes, seasonal cuisine (the menu changes frequently), and fresh fish. The ambience, food, and wine offered here set this restaurant well apart from the town's many group-oriented eateries. ✉ *Hauptstr. 82* ☎ *07063/932–354* 💳 *MC, V* ⏲ *Closed Wed.*

★ $–$$ ✕ **Hotel Schloss Heinsheim.** This baroque castle is in a beautiful park. The rooms are individually furnished—some with antiques, others more rustic in style. You can dine on the terrace or in the country manor-like restaurant ($–$$$$). Start with a Swabian *Hochzeitssuppe* (wedding soup), followed by breast of duck with pink peppercorns or Dover sole in champagne sauce. Most wines on the list are French or German. ✉ *Gundelsheimer Str. 36, D–74906 Bad Rappenau–Heinsheim* ☎ *07264/95030* 📠 *07264/4208* 🌐 *www.schloss-heinsheim.de* *40 rooms, 1 suite* *Restaurant, minibars, cable TV, some in-room data ports, 18-hole golf course, pool, bicycles, bar, lobby lounge, babysitting, laundry ser-*

vice, business services, some pets allowed (fee); no a/c ▭ *AE, DC, MC, V* ⏲ *Closed Jan. Restaurant also closed Mon. and Tues.* 🍽 *BP.*

$ **Hotel Sonne und Weinstube Feyerabend.** Just before Christmas 2003, the Schachtsiek family's hotel-restaurant in the center of town burned down. Their second house (in a medieval half-timber building) and traditional café–Weinstube Feyerabend (¢; no credit cards) are still in operation and worth a stay or visit. ✉ *Langg. 3, D–74206* ☎ *07063/245* 📠 *07063/6591* 🌐 *www.sonne-wimpfen.de* *10 rooms* *Café, cable TV, some in-room data ports, Weinstube, some pets allowed (fee); no a/c* ▭ *MC, V* ⏲ *Closed late Dec.–mid-Jan. Café and Weinstube closed Mon.* 🍽 *BP.*

$ **Hotel Neckarblick.** The Sailer family extends the warmest of welcomes to its guests. There's a peaceful terrace, where you can sit and contemplate the Neckar River. Many rooms have a view and flower boxes in the windows. The furniture is comfortable and modern, like the hotel building. For medieval atmosphere, the heart of Bad Wimpfen is only a few blocks away. Although there is no restaurant, the Sailers serve platters of cold cuts and cheese upon request and offer free shuttle service to and from the train station. ✉ *Erich-Sailer-Str. 48, D–74206* ☎ *07063/961–620* 📠 *07063/8548* 🌐 *www.neckarblick.de* *14 rooms* *Minibars, cable TV, in-room data ports, bicycles, lounge, dry cleaning, laundry service, some pets allowed (fee), no-smoking rooms; no a/c* ▭ *AE, MC, V* 🍽 *BP.*

Neckarsulm

24 *10 km (6 mi) south of Bad Wimpfen.*

Motorbike fans won't want to miss the town of Neckarsulm. It's a busy industrial center, home of the German automobile manufacturer Audi and the **Deutsches Zweirad–Museum** (German Motorcycle Museum). It's close to the factory where motorbikes were first manufactured in Germany. Among its 300 exhibits are the world's first mass-produced motorcycles (the Hildebrand and Wolfmüller); a number of famous racing machines; and a rare Daimler machine, the first made by that legendary name. The museum also has an exhibit of early bicycles, dating from 1816, as well as early automobiles. All are arranged over five floors in a handsome 400-year-old castle that belonged to the Teutonic Knights until 1806. ✉ *Urbanstr. 11* ☎ *07132/35271* 🌐 *www.zweirad-museum.de* *€4* ⏲ *Tues., Wed., and Fri.–Sun. 9–5, Thurs. 9–7.*

SWABIAN CITIES

Heilbronn, Stuttgart, and Tübingen are all part of the ancient province of Swabia, a region strongly influenced by Protestantism and Calvinism. The inhabitants speak the Swabian dialect of German. Heilbronn lies on both sides of the Neckar. Stuttgart, the capital of the state of Baden-Würtemberg and one of Germany's leading industrial cities, is surrounded by hills on three sides, with the fourth side opening up toward its river harbor. The medieval town of Tübingen clings to steep slopes and hilltops above the Neckar.

Heilbronn

25 *6 km (4 mi) south of Neckarsulm, 50 km (31 mi) north of Stuttgart.*

Most of the leading sights in Heilbronn are grouped in and around the Marktplatz. The sturdy **Rathaus,** built in the Gothic style in 1417 and remodeled during the Renaissance, dominates the square. Set into the Rathaus's clean-lined facade and beneath the steep red roof is a magnificently ornate 16th-century **clock.** It's divided into four distinct parts. The lowest is an astronomical clock, showing the day of the week, the month, and the year. Above it is the main clock—note how its hour hand is larger than the minute hand, a convention common in the 16th century. Above this there's a smaller dial that shows the phases of the sun and the moon. The final clock is a bell at the topmost level. Suspended from a delicate stone surround, it's struck alternately by the two angels on either side. The entire elaborate mechanism swings into action at noon. As the hour strikes, an angel at the base of the clock sounds a trumpet; another turns an hourglass and counts the hours with a scepter. Simultaneously, the twin golden rams between them charge each other and lock horns while a cockerel spreads its wings and crows. Behind the market square is the **Kilianskirche** (Church of St. Kilian), Heilbronn's most famous church, dedicated to the Irish monk who brought Christianity to the Rhineland in the Dark Ages and who lies buried in Würzburg. Its lofty Gothic tower was capped in the early 16th century with a fussy, lanternlike structure that ranks as the first major Renaissance work north of the Alps. At its summit there's a soldier carrying a banner decorated with the city arms. Walk around the church to the south side (the side opposite the main entrance) to see the well that gave the city its name.

Where to Stay & Eat

$–$$ ✕ **Ratskeller.** Both the handsome table settings in the vaulted cellar and the seats on the spacious terrace in front of the town hall are pleasant settings for the Mosthaf brothers' tasty food, excellent wines, and cheerful service. Try the braised rabbit in mustard sauce or a salmon trout fillet in a whipped lemon sauce. The *Tagesessen* (daily special) is a good value. ✉ *Marktpl. 7* ☎ *07131/84628* ▭ *AE* ⏲ *Closed Sun.*

$ ✕ **Vinum.** Whether you want coffee and a croissant, fresh tapas, or a beefsteak with onions, it's all available here from 10 AM 'til midnight, six days of the week. As the name implies, Vinum is also a wine bar—with 140 German and international wines to choose from. ✉ *Marktplatz 1* ☎ *07131/642–7220* ▭ *AE* ⏲ *Closed Sun.*

¢–$ ✕ **Restaurant-Café Am Stadtgarten Harmonie.** Eat on the terrace in summer to enjoy the view of the city park. Inside, the decor is traditional with a modern twist, as is the menu. Traditional German dishes and Swabian specialties, such as Rostbraten and *sauere Kutteln* (tripe), are served, and there are two inexpensive specials (€5 and €7) daily. ✉ *Allee 28* ☎ *07131/87954* ▭ *AE, DC, MC, V* ⏲ *Closed Tues. and Aug. No dinner Sun.*

$$ ✕🏨 **Hotel und Gutsgaststätte Rappenhof.** This cheerful country inn is on a hill in the midst of the vineyards of Weinsberg (6 km [4 mi] northeast of Heilbronn). You can take in the fresh air and panoramic views from the terrace or on a scenic walk along the signposted Wine Panorama Path. The restaurant ($–$$) features hearty country cooking, such as sauerbraten with *Semmelknödel* (bread dumplings), and regional wines. *✉ D–74189 Weinsberg ☎ 07134/5190 📠 07134/51955 🌐 www.rappenhof.de 🛏 39 rooms ♁ Restaurant, minibars, cable TV, some in-room data ports, bicycles, lobby lounge, Internet room, some pets allowed (fee), no-smoking rooms; no a/c 💳 MC, V ⊙ Closed mid-Dec.–mid-Jan. 🍽 BP.*

$$ **Insel-Hotel.** *Insel* means "island," and that's where the luxurious Insel-Hotel is—on a river island tethered to the city by the busy Friedrich Ebert Bridge. The Mayer family combines a personal touch with polished service and facilities, including 24-hour beverage room service. Enjoy alfresco dining in summer, when chefs fire up the charcoal grill on the Mediterranean-like terrace of the Schwäbisches Restaurant ($$–$$$$). The roof garden affords great views. *✉ Friedrich-Ebert-Brücke, D–74072 ☎ 07131/6300 📠 07131/626–060 🌐 www.insel-hotel.de 🛏 122 rooms, 5 suites, 1 apartment ♁ Restaurant, cable TV, in-room data ports, Wi-Fi, pool, gym, massage, sauna, bar, business services, free parking, some pets allowed, no-smoking rooms; no a/c 💳 AE, DC, MC, V 🍽 BP.*

★ $$ **Schlosshotel Liebenstein.** Nestled in the hills above the village of Neckarwestheim, south of Heilbronn, is one of the area's most beautiful castles, Schloss Liebenstein. Within the 3-foot-thick, whitewashed castle walls, the peaceful hush of centuries reigns over a setting of comfort and noble elegance. Guest rooms have views of forests, vineyards, and a golf course. The restaurant Lazuli ($$$$) has gourmet cuisine (three- to seven-course menus only); Kurfürst ($–$$) serves regional fare; and light meals are available in the beer garden. *✉ Schloss Liebenstein, D–74382 Neckarwestheim ☎ 07133/98990 📠 07133/6045 🌐 www.liebenstein.com 🛏 22 rooms, 2 suites ♁ 3 restaurants, cable TV, in-room data ports, 2 golf courses, bicycles, bar, beer garden, lounge, babysitting, dry cleaning, laundry service, business services, meeting rooms, some pets allowed, no-smoking rooms; no a/c 💳 AE, MC, V ⊙ Hotel and restaurants closed late Dec.–early Jan. No lunch at Lazuli; no lunch weekdays at Kurfürst. 🍽 BP.*

Nightlife & the Arts

The Konzert- und Kongresszentrum Harmonie, Theaterschiff, and Stadttheater are the major (but not the only) venues for theater, dance, opera, musicals, and concerts. The city has two resident orchestras: **Württemberg Chamber Orchestra** and **Heilbronn Symphony Orchestra.** The **Heilbronn tourist office** (☎ 07131/562–270) distributes a bi-monthly *Veranstaltungskalender* (calendar of events) and also sells tickets to cultural events.

Shopping

The city's internationally renowned **Weindorf** wine festival, in mid-September, showcases nearly 300 wines and sparkling wines from the Heilbronn region alone. Most of the year you'll find numerous shops stocking wine along Heilbronn's central pedestrian shopping zone, and you can also sample and purchase directly from private wine estates or a *Weingärtner genossenschaft* (vintners' cooperative winery). One of Württemberg's finest producers, the **Staatsweingut Weinsberg** (State Wine Domain; ✉ Traubenpl. 5, Weinsberg ☎ 07134/504–167), has an architecturally striking wineshop with 70 wines and 30 other products of the grape on offer. It's open weekdays 9–5.

en route

Ludwigsburg, a scant 15 km (9 mi) north of Stuttgart, merits a stop to visit Germany's largest baroque palace, **Residenzschloss Ludwigsburg.** It celebrated its 300th anniversary in 2004, after 15 years of renovation at a cost of 92 million euros.

The "Versailles of Swabia" is surrounded by the fragrant, colorful 74-acre park **Blühendes Barock** (Blooming Baroque; €7 www.blueba.de Mid-Mar.–Oct., daily 7:30 AM–8:30 PM; winter hrs shorter), replete with splendid gardens, fountains, aviaries, a Märchengarten (fairy-tale garden), and a "water playground" that delights visitors of all ages. The palace is also home to the **Porzellan-Manufaktur Ludwigsburg** (store weekdays 9:30–12:30 and 1:30–5:30, Sat. 10–1 www.ludwigsburger-porzellan.de), where a film, shown daily, presents the artists who hand-paint the manufactory's exquisite porcelain. A five-minute walk north of the palace (across Marbacher Strasse) brings you to the **Jagdschloss Favorite,** a "small" summer residence and hunting lodge of the dukes of Württemberg.

Additional highlights are the annual **Schlossfestspiele,** with concerts, theater, opera, dance, and exhibitions in the palace and the surrounding park (June–mid-September) and the three new museums that opened in the palace in 2004: the **Barockgalerie,** a collection of German and Italian baroque paintings from the 17th and 18th centuries; the **Keramikmuseum,** a collection of historical treasures from the porcelain manufactories in Meissen, Nymphenburg, Berlin, Vienna, and Ludwigsburg, supplemented by a section devoted to contemporary ceramics; and the **Modemuseum,** showcasing three centuries of fashion, particularly royal clothing of the 18th century. ✉ *Schloss Str. 30, Ludwigsburg* ☎ *07141/182–004 for information* *www.schloesser-und-gaerten.de* *Residenzschloss €5; Favorite €2.50; museums only €5; Barocke Erlebniskarte (park, 2 palaces, 3 museums) €13* *Palaces and museums daily 10–5.*

Stuttgart

26 *50 km (31 mi) south on B–27 from Heilbronn.*

Stuttgart is a place of fairly extreme contradictions. It has been called, among other things, "Germany's biggest small town" and "the city where work is a pleasure." For centuries Stuttgart, whose name derives from *Stutengarten,* or "stud farm," remained a pastoral backwater along the Neckar. Then the Industrial Revolution propelled the city into the machine age, after which it was leveled in World War II. Since then Stuttgart has regained its position as one of Germany's top industrial centers.

Here, *Schaffen*—"doing, achieving"—is an inherent feature of the modus operandi. This is Germany's can-do city, whose natives have turned out Mercedes-Benz and Porsche cars, Bosch electrical equipment, and a host of other products exported worldwide. Yet Stuttgart is also a city of culture and the arts, with world-class museums, opera, and a ballet company. Moreover, it's the domain of fine local wines; the vineyards actually approach the city center in a rim of green hills. Forests, vineyards, meadows, and orchards compose more than half the city, which is enclosed on three sides by woods.

An ideal introduction to the contrasts of Stuttgart is a guided city bus tour. Included is a visit to the needle-nose TV tower, high on a mountaintop above the city, affording stupendous views. Built in 1956, it was the first of its kind in the world. The tourist office also offers superb walking tours. On your own, the best place to begin exploring Stuttgart is the Hauptbahnhof (main train station, opposite the tourist office); from there walk down the pedestrian street Königstrasse to Schillerplatz, a small, charming square named after the 18th-century poet and playwright Friedrich Schiller, who was born in nearby Marbach. It's surrounded by historic buildings, many of them rebuilt after the war.

Just off Schillerplatz, the **Stiftskirche** (Collegiate Church of the Holy Cross; ✉ Stiftstr. 12, Mitte) is Stuttgart's most familiar sight, with its two oddly matched towers. Built in the 12th century and then substantially rebuilt in a late-Gothic style (1433–1531), the church became Protestant in 1534. It was reconsecrated in 1958 after being badly damaged in a 1944 bombing raid. The choir has a famous series of Renaissance figures of the counts of Württemberg sculpted by Simon Schlör (1576–1608).

Schlossplatz (Palace Square) is a huge area enclosed by royal palaces, with elegant arcades branching off to other stately plazas. The magnificent baroque **Neues Schloss** (New Castle), now occupied by Baden-Württemberg state government offices, dominates the square. The **Kunstgebäude** (House of Art), the building with a golden stag on its cupola, houses the **Württembergischer Kunstverein** (Württemberg Art Society) and has changing shows of contemporary German artists' works. ✉ *Schlosspl., Mitte* ☎ *0711/216–2188.*

Kunstmuseum Stuttgart (Stuttgart Art Museum). In autumn 2004 the collection of the former Galerie der Stadt Stuttgart (Stuttgart City Art Gallery) was renamed and moved across the square from the Kunstgebäude to its new home—a sleek structure encased in a glass facade and a work of art in its own right. It features artwork of the 19th and 20th centuries and the world's largest Otto Dix collection (including the *Grossstadt* [*Metropolis*] triptych, which distills the essence of 1920s Germany on canvas). The bistro-café on the rooftop terrace affords great views; the foyer houses a café and the museum shop. ✉ *Kleiner Schlosspl.* ⏲ *Tues.–Sun. 10–6; Thurs. 10–9.*

The **Schlossgarten** (Palace Garden) borders the Schlossplatz and extends northeast across Schillerstrasse all the way to Bad Cannstatt on the Neckar River. The park is graced by an exhibition hall, planetarium, lakes, sculptures, and the hot spring–mineral baths Leuze and Berg.

Adjacent to the Schlossgarten is Rosenstein Park, with the city's two natural-history museums and the **Wilhelma** zoological and botanical gardens. From here it's but a brief walk along the riverbank to the pier for Neckar-Käpt'n boat trips on the Neckar. ✉ *Neckartalstr., Wilhelma* ☎ *0711/54020* 🌐 *www.wilhelma.de* *€9.40; Nov.–Feb. and in summer after 4 PM €6.40* ⏲ *May–Aug., daily 8:15–6; Sept.–Apr., daily 8:15–4. Greenhouses and animal halls open 30 min and 45 min longer, respectively, than box office.*

Across the street from the Neues Schloss stands the **Altes Schloss** (Old Castle). This former residence of the counts and dukes of Württemberg was originally built as a moated castle around 1320. Wings were added in the mid-15th century, creating a Renaissance palace. The palace now houses the **Württembergisches Landesmuseum** (Württemberg State Museum), with imaginative exhibits tracing the development of the area from the Stone Age to modern times. The displays of medieval life are especially noteworthy. International design and applied arts during the 20th century are shown in the *Ritterhalle* (knights' hall). ✉ *Schillerpl. 6, Mitte* ☎ *0711/279–3400* *€2.60* ⏲ *Tues. 10–1, Wed.–Sun. 10–5.*

Fodor'sChoice ★

The **Staatsgalerie** (State Gallery) possesses one of the finest art collections in Germany. The old part of the complex, dating from 1843, has paintings from the Middle Ages through the 19th century, including works by Cranach, Holbein, Hals, Memling, Rubens, Rembrandt, Cézanne, Courbet, and Manet. Connected to the original building is the **Neue Staatsgalerie** (New State Gallery), designed by British architect James Stirling in 1984 as a melding of classical and modern, sometimes jarring, elements (such as chartreuse window mullions). Considered one of the most successful postmodern buildings, it houses works by such 20th-century artists as Braque, Chagall, de Chirico, Dalí, Kandinsky, Klee, Mondrian, and Picasso. ✉ *Konrad-Adenauer-Str. 30–32, Mitte* ☎ *0711/470–400* 🌐 *www.staatsgalerie.de* *€4.50, free Wed.* ⏲ *Tues., Wed., and Fri.–Sun. 10–6, Thurs. 10–9, 1st Sat. of month 10 AM–midnight.*

In late 2002, Stuttgart's "cultural mile" was enriched with yet another postmodern architectural masterpiece by James Stirling, the **Haus der Geschichte Baden-Württemberg** (Museum of the History of Baden-Württemberg). It chronicles the state's history during the 19th and 20th centuries. Theme parks and multimedia presentations enable you to interact with the thousands of fascinating objects on display. ✉ *Konrad-Adenauer-Str. 16, Mitte* ☎ *0711/212–3989* 🌐 *www.hdgbw.de* *€3* ⏲ *Tues., Wed., and Fri.–Sun. 10–6, Thurs. 10–9.*

An extraordinary urban-planning project under way is "Stuttgart 21." An area comprising about 250 acres—now covered with train tracks north of the main station—is being converted into a new neighborhood, and the tracks are being moved underground. The **Bahnhofsturm** (train-station tower), crowned by the Mercedes star, has an information center with three floors of exhibitions on the project as well as a great viewing platform. ✉ *Arnulf-Klett-Pl., Mitte* ☎ *0711/2092–2920* *Free* ⏲ *Tues.–Sun. 10–6, Thurs. 10–9.*

off the beaten path

GOTTLIEB-DAIMLER-GEDÄCHTNISSTÄTTE (Gottlieb Daimler Memorial Workshop) – The first successful internal-combustion engine was perfected here in 1883, and you can see the tools, blueprints, and models of early cars that helped pave the way for the Mercedes line. ✉ *Taubenheimstr. 13, Stuttgart-Bad Cannstatt* ☎ *0711/569–399* 🎫 *Free* ⏲ *Tues.–Sun. 10–4.*

MERCEDES-BENZ MUSEUM – The oldest car factory in the world shows off a collection of about 100 historic racing and luxury cars. Follow signs to the soccer stadium. New quarters are being built and scheduled to open in spring 2006. ✉ *Mercedesstr. 137, Stuttgart-Untertürkheim* ☎ *0711/172–2578* 🎫 *Free* ⏲ *Tues.–Sun. 9–5.*

PORSCHE MUSEUM – This Porsche factory in the northern suburb of Zuffenhausen has a small but significant collection of legendary Porsche racing cars. ✉ *Porschepl. 1, Stuttgart-Zuffenhausen* ☎ *0711/911–5685* 🎫 *Free* ⏲ *Weekdays 9–4, weekends 9–5.*

WEISSENHOFSIEDLUNG – The Weissenhof Colony was a minicity created for a 1927 exhibition of the "New Home." Sixteen leading architects from five countries—among them Mies van der Rohe, Le Corbusier, and Walter Gropius—created residences that offered optimal living conditions at affordable prices. The still-functioning colony is on a hillside overlooking Friedrich-Ebert-Strasse. To get there from the city center, take Bus 43 toward Killesberg/Messe to the Kunstakadamie stop or subway U7 to the Messe. The i-Punkt Weissenhof issues a brochure indicating which architects designed the various homes and is the meeting point for guided tours (Saturday 11 AM). ✉ *Am Weissenhof 20, Stuttgart-Killesberg* ☎ *0711/854–641 or 0711/257–9187.*

Where to Stay & Eat

★ $$$$ ✕ **Wielandshöhe.** One of Germany's top chefs, Vincent Klink, and his wife, Elisabeth, are very down-to-earth, cordial hosts. Her floral arrangements add a baroque touch to the otherwise quiet decor, but your vision—and palate—will ultimately focus on the artfully presented cuisine. To the extent possible, all products are sourced locally or are homemade. House specialties, such as saddle of lamb with a potato terrine and ratatouille or the gratinated Breton lobster with basil potato salad, are recommended. The wine list is exemplary. ✉ *Alte Weinsteige 71, Degerloch* ☎ *0711/640–8848* 🌐 *www.wielandshoehe.com* ✍ *Reservations essential* 💳 *AE, DC, MC, V* ⏲ *Closed Sun. and Mon.*

★ $$$$ ✕🏨 **Am Schlossgarten.** Stuttgart's top accommodation is a modern structure set in spacious gardens, a stone's throw from sights, shops, and the train station. Pretty floral prints and plush chairs add a homey feeling to the elegant rooms. Luxurious baths and business amenities add to the overall comfort. In addition to receiving first-class service, you can wine and dine in the French restaurant Zirbelstube ($$$$); the less-expensive Schlossgarten restaurant ($$–$$$$); the bistro Vinothek ($$); or the café (¢) overlooking the garden. ✉ *Schillerstr. 23, Mitte, D–70173*

☎ 0711/20260 📠 0711/202–6888 🌐 www.hotelschlossgarten.com 🛏 106 rooms, 10 suites 👍 3 restaurants, café, minibars, cable TV, in-room data ports, bicycles, bar, lobby lounge, babysitting, dry cleaning, laundry service, concierge, Internet room, business services, some pets allowed (fee), no-smoking rooms 💳 AE, DC, MC, V ⏲ Zirbelstube closed 4 wks Aug. and Sept., Sun. and Mon. Schlossgarten closed Fri. and Sat. Vinothek closed Sun. and Mon.

★ **$$–$$$$** ✕🏨 **Der Zauberlehrling.** The "Sorcerer's Apprentice" is aptly named. In addition to their popular restaurant, Z-Bistro ($$$–$$$$; no credit cards)—with magical entertainment on *Tischzauberei* evenings (*Tisch* means "table"; *Zauberei* means "magic")—Karen and Axel Heldmann have conjured up a small luxury hotel. Each room's decor is based on a theme (Asian, Mediterranean, Country Manor), and four have a private whirlpool. Innovative dishes, a three-course menu of organic products, and regional favorites are all part of the culinary lineup, enhanced by a very good wine list. Enjoy the terrace in summer and end the evening with cigars and single malts. ✉ *Rosenstr. 38, Bohnenviertel, D–70182 ☎ 0711/237–7770 📠 0711/237–7775 🌐 www.zauberlehrling.de 🛏 9 rooms 👍 Restaurant, fans, minibars, cable TV, in-room data ports, lobby lounge, dry cleaning, laundry service, business services, no-smoking rooms; no a/c 💳 AE, MC, V ⏲ No lunch weekends 🍽 BP.*

★ **$–$$** ✕🏨 **Alter Fritz.** Katrin Fritsche describes her small country mansion as a "hotel for individualists." With only 10 rooms, she is able to cater to guests with a personal touch. The picturesque house with its steep eaves and shuttered windows, high up on the wooded Killesberg Hill, is ideally located for visitors attending trade fairs and is a 15-minute bus ride from the main railway station. Der kleine Fritz serves good food at reasonable prices ($–$$$). House guests can opt to dine in the pretty breakfast room and select from a smaller menu ($). ✉ *Feuerbacher Weg 101, Killesberg, D–70192 ☎ 0711/135–650 📠 0711/135–6565 🌐 www.alter-fritz-am-killesberg.de 🛏 10 rooms 👍 Restaurant, minibars, some in-room data ports, free parking; no a/c 💳 No credit cards ⏲ Closed 2 wks in Aug. and 2 wks in Dec. Restaurant closed Mon. No lunch 🍽 BP.*

$–$$ 🏨 **Hotel Mercure Stuttgart Airport.** This hotel has a light and airy design, with large windows throughout the spacious lobby, restaurant, public rooms, and comfortable bedrooms. Everything is decorated in tasteful, pastel colors. Shuttle service is available to the airport (3 km [2 mi]), and downtown Stuttgart (11 km [7 mi]) can be reached by public transportation or by car in less than a half hour. It's a three-minute drive to the shops, casino, and musical productions at the SI-Erlebnis-Centrum. ✉ *Eichwiesenring 1, Fasanenhof, D–70567 ☎ 0711/72660 📠 0711/726–6444 🌐 www.mercure.de 🛏 148 rooms 👍 2 restaurants, minibars, cable TV, in-room data ports, gym, sauna, bicycles, bar, dry cleaning, laundry service, airport shuttle, free parking, some pets allowed (fee), no-smoking rooms 💳 AE, DC, MC, V 🍽 BP.*

Nightlife & the Arts

The **i-Punkt tourist office** (✉ Königstr. 1A, Mitte ☎ 0711/222–8243) keeps a current calendar of events and sells tickets via phone weekdays

9–8 and Saturday 9–4; or in the office weekdays 9–8, Saturday 9–6, and Sunday 11–6 (May–October) or 1–6 (November–April).

THE ARTS Stuttgart's internationally renowned ballet company performs in the **Staatstheater** (✉ Oberer Schlossgarten 6, Mitte ☎ 0711/202–090). The ballet season runs from September through June and alternates with the highly respected State Opera. For program details contact the Stuttgart tourist office. The box office is open weekdays 10–6, Saturday 10–2.

The **SI-Erlebnis-Centrum** is an entire entertainment complex (hotels, bars, restaurants, gambling casino, wellness center, cinemas, shops, theaters) built in 1994 to showcase musicalssuch as *42nd Street* and *Mamma Mia!*. ✉ *Plieninger Str. 100, Stuttgart-Möhringen* 🌐 *www.si-centrum.de.*

NIGHTLIFE There's no shortage of rustic beer gardens, wine pubs, or sophisticated cocktail bars in and around Stuttgart. Night owls should head for the **Schwabenzentrum** on Eberhardstrasse; the **Bohnenviertel,** or "Bean Quarter" (Charlotten-, Olga-, and Pfarrstrasse); the "party-mile" along Theodor-Heuss-Strasse; **Calwer Strasse;** and **Wilhelmsplatz.**

If you enjoy live music, you may want to visit the **Classic Rock Cafe** (✉ Eberhardstr. 22 [city center] ☎ 0711/234–8858) on a Thursday night. To choose from an enormous selection of cocktails, head to **Adulis I** (✉ Holzstr. 17 ☎ 0711/243–259), a popular bar near Charlottenplatz.

Sports & the Outdoors

BOAT TRIPS From the pier opposite the zoo entrance, **Neckar-Käpt'n** (☎ 0711/5499–7060 🌐 www.neckar-kaeptn.de) offers a wide range of boat trips, as far north as scenic Besigheim and Lauffen.

HIKING Stuttgart has a 53-km (33-mi) network of marked hiking trails in the nearby hills; follow the signs with the city's emblem: a horse set in a yellow ring.

SWIMMING & SPAS Bad Cannstatt's mineral springs are more than 2,000 years old and, with a daily output of about 22 million liters (5.8 million gallons), the second most productive (after Budapest) in Europe. The **MineralBad Cannstatt** (✉ Sulzerrainstr. 2 ☎ 0711/216–9240) has indoor and outdoor mineral pools, hot tubs, sauna, steam room, and spa facilities. On the banks of the Neckar near the König-Karl bridge is the **Mineralbad Leuze** (✉ Am Leuzebad 2–6 ☎ 0711/216–4210), with eight pools indoor and out and an open-air mineral-water sauna. **Mineralbad Berg** (✉ Am Schwanenpl. 9 ☎ 0711/923–6516) has indoor and outdoor pools and sauna and offers therapeutic water treatments.

Shopping

Stuttgart is a shopper's paradise, from the department stores on the Königstrasse, to the boutiques in the Old Town's elegant passages, and the factory outlet stores. Calwer Strasse is home to the glitzy chrome-and-glass arcade **Calwer Passage.** Shops here carry everything from local women's fashion (Beate Mössinger) to furniture. Don't miss the beautiful art-nouveau **Markthalle** on Dorotheenstrasse. One of Germany's finest market halls, it's an architectural gem brimming with exotic fruits and spices, meats, and flowers.

Two of Germany's top men's fashion designers—Hugo Boss and Ulli Knecht—are based in Stuttgart. **Holy's** (✉ Königstr. 54/A, Mitte ☎ 0711/222–9444) is an exclusive boutique that carries clothes (for men and women) by the most sought-after designers.

Günter Krauss (✉ Kronprinzstr. 21, Mitte ☎ 0711/297–395) specializes in designer jewelry. The shop itself—walls of white Italian marble with gilt fixtures and mirrors—has won many design awards.

Breuninger (✉ Marktstr. 1–3, Mitte ☎ 0711/2110), a leading regional department-store chain, has glass elevators that rise and fall under the dome of the central arcade.

Some of Stuttgart's more unique shops are found in the older **Bohnenviertel** ("Bean Quarter"). A stroll through the neighborhood's smaller streets reveals many tucked-away shops specializing in fashion, jewelry, artwork, and gifts.

Bebenhausen

27 *6 km (4 mi) north of Tübingen, on west side of B–27/464.*

If you blink, you'll miss the turnoff for the little settlement of Bebenhausen, and that would be a shame, because it's really worth a visit.

Fodor'sChoice ★

The **Zisterzienzerkloster** (Cistercian Monastery) is a rare example of an almost perfectly preserved medieval monastery dating from the late 12th century. Owing to the secularization of 1806, the abbot's abode was rebuilt as a hunting castle for King Frederick of Württemberg. Expansion and restoration continued as long as the castle and monastery continued to be a royal residence. Even after the monarchy was dissolved in 1918, the last Württembergs were given lifetime rights here; this came to an end in 1946 with the death of Charlotte, wife of Wilhelm II. For a few years after World War II the state senate convened in the castle; today both castle and monastery are open to the public, although the castle is open for guided tours only. ☎ *07071/602–802* 🎫 *Monastery €3, castle €3, both €5.50* ⏲ *Monastery Apr.–Oct., Mon. 9–noon and 1–6, Tues.–Sun. 9–6; Nov.–Mar., Tues.–Sun. 9–noon and 1–5. Castle tours on the hr Apr.–Oct., Tues.–Fri. 9–noon and 2–5, weekends 10–noon and 2–5; Nov.–Mar., Tues.–Fri. 9–noon and 2–4, weekends 10–noon and 2–4.*

Where to Eat

$$–$$$$ Fodor'sChoice ★

✕ **Waldhorn.** Dorothea Schulz-Schilling and her husband, Helmut Schulz, operate this exceptional restaurant. Old favorites, such as foie gras and fish, the *Vorspeisenvariation* (medley of appetizers), and iced cappuchino are recommended. The wine list features a well-chosen selection of international and top Baden and Württemberg wines. Garden tables have a castle view. A meal here is a perfect start or finale to the concerts held on the monastery-castle grounds in the summer. ✉ *Schönbuchstr. 49, on B–27/464* ☎ *07071/61270* 🌐 *www.waldhorn-bebenhausen.de* ✍ *Reservations essential* 💳 *No credit cards* ⏲ *Closed Tues. and 10 days in Aug. No lunch Mon.*

Tübingen

28 *40 km (25 mi) south of Stuttgart on B–27 on the Neckar River.*

With its half-timber houses, winding alleyways, and hilltop setting overlooking the Neckar, Tübingen provides the quintessential German experience. The medieval flavor is quite authentic, as the town was untouched by wartime bombings. Dating to the 11th century, Tübingen flourished as a trade center; its weights and measures and currency were the standard through much of the area. The town declined in importance after the 14th century, when it was taken over by the counts of Württemberg. Between the 14th and the 19th centuries, its size hardly changed as it became a university and residential town, its castle the only symbol of ruling power.

Yet Tübingen hasn't been sheltered from the world. It resonates with a youthful air. Even more than Heidelberg, Tübingen is virtually synonymous with its university, a leading center of learning since it was founded in 1477. Illustrious students of yesteryear include the astronomer Johannes Kepler and the philosopher G. W. F. Hegel. The latter studied at the Protestant theological seminary, still a cornerstone of the university's international reputation. One of Hegel's roommates was Friedrich Hölderlin, a visionary poet who succumbed to madness in his early thirties. Tübingen's population is around 83,000, of which at least 20,000 are students. During term time it can be hard to find a seat in pubs and cafés; during vacations the town sometimes seems deserted. The best way to see and appreciate Tübingen is simply to stroll around, soaking up its age-old atmosphere of quiet erudition.

a good walk

Tübingen's modest size makes it ideal for a walk. Begin at the Eberhards-Brücke, which crosses an island with a magnificent planting of trees—most of them at least 200 years old—known as the Platanenallee. If time permits, stroll up and down the island. If not, go to the north end of the bridge, take a sharp left down a steep staircase to reach the shore of the Neckar, and follow it to a yellow tower, the **Hölderlinturm.** The poet Friedrich Hölderlin was housed in the tower after he lost his sanity, and it's now a small museum commemorating his life and work. Next, walk away from the river up the steps of Hölderlinsteg and continue left up the Bursagasse to pass by the **Bursa,** a former student dormitory that dates from the Middle Ages. Facing the Bursa, turn left up the street called Klosterberg and then turn left again into the courtyard of the **Evangelisches Stift.** Richer in history than in immediate visual interest, this site was a center of European intellectual thought for centuries. Proceed up Klosterberg to the narrow steps and cobblestones of Burgsteige, one of the oldest thoroughfares in the town and lined with houses dating from the Middle Ages. You might be a little breathless when you finally arrive at the top and enter the portal of the **Schloss Hohentübingen.** The portal is fitted as a Roman-style triumphal arch in true Renaissance spirit.

Cross the Schloss's courtyard and enter the tunnel-like passage directly in front of you; it leads to the other side of the castle. Take a moment to enjoy the view of the river from the ruined ramparts and then descend to your right through tree-shaded Kapitansweg—looking at the remains of the original city walls on your way—to Haaggasse and then left into the narrow Judengasse (Jewish Alley). Jewish citizens lived in this neighborhood until 1477, when they were driven out of the city. Next, stop at the intersection of Judengasse and Ammergasse; all around you are old half-timber buildings. The little stream that runs through Ammergasse was part of the medieval sewage system.

Across the square, Jakobsgasse leads to Jakobuskirche (St. James Church), in medieval times a station on the famous pilgrims' route to Santiago di Compostella in Spain. Go to the other side of the church, make a right into Madergasse, and then turn left at Schmiedtorstrasse, where you will find the Fruchtschranne on the right-hand side—a massive half-timber house built to store fruit and grain in the 15th century. Continue down the street to Bachgasse; turn right, then right again onto the street called Bei der Fruchtschranne and follow it a short distance to a courtyard on the left just before the intersection with Kornhausstrasse. The courtyard leads to the entrance of the 15th-century **Kornhaus,** now a city museum. Continue to Kornstrasse and go left and immediately right into Marktgasse, which takes you uphill to the **Marktplatz,** a sloping, uneven cobblestone parallelogram that dominates the heart of Tübingen's Altstadt (Old City). Its **Neptune Fountain** is graced with a statue of the sea god. The square is bounded on one side by the amazing **Rathaus.**

From the square turn into Wienergasse and then left into Münzgasse; No. 20 is the site of the former **Studentenkarzer.** The large yellow baroque building just beyond is the **Alte Aula,** for many centuries the university's most important building. The well-preserved late-Gothic **Stiftskirche** now rises before you. Climbing the hundred-odd steps up the bell tower will allow you to take a second, faraway look at almost everything you've seen en route.

TIMING The walk around town takes about 1½ hours. If you go inside the Hölderlinturm, Stadtsmuseum, or Stiftskirche, add a half hour for each.

What to See

Alte Aula (Old Auditorium). Erected in 1547, the half-timber university building was significantly altered in 1777, when it acquired an Italian roof, a symmetrical facade, and a balcony decorated with two crossed scepters, symbolizing the town's center of learning. In earlier times grain was stored under the roof as part of the professors' salaries. The libraries and lecture halls were on the lower floors. ⊠ *Münzg.*

Bursa (Student Dormitory). The word *bursa* meant "purse" in the Middle Ages and later came to refer to student lodgings such as this former student dormitory. Despite its classical facade, which it acquired in the early 19th century, the building actually dates back to 1477. Medieval students had to master a broad curriculum that included the *septem artes liberales* (seven liberal arts) of Grammar, Dialectic, Rhetoric, Arithmetic, Geometry, Astronomy, and Music, in addition to praying several times a day, fasting regularly, and speaking only Latin within the confines of the building. ⊠ *Bursag. 4.*

Evangelisches Stift (Protestant Seminary). From the outside you can't tell that this site has served for centuries as a center of European intellectual thought. It was founded in 1534, partly as a political move during the Reformation; the Protestant duke of Württemberg, Ulrich, wanted facilities to train Protestant clerics so that Protestantism could retain its foothold in the region (he would have been disappointed to know a major Catholic seminary arrived near here in 1817). Since that time philosophical rather than political considerations have prevailed within these walls. Hegel, Hölderlin, and the philosopher Schelling all lived and studied here, as have students of Protestant theology ever since. ✉ *Klosterg.*

Hölderlinturm (Hölderlin's Tower). "Mad" Friedrich Hölderlin lived here for 36 years, until his death in 1843, in the care of the master cabinetmaker Zimmer and his daughter. If you don't speak German, the Web site's English version provides good background to help you get the most out of your visit. ✉ *Bursag. 6* ☎ *07071/22040* 🌐 *www.hoelderlin-gesellschaft.de* 🎟 *€1.50, with tour €2.50* ⏲ *Tues.–Fri. 10–noon and 3–5, weekends 2–5. Tours weekends at 5 PM; English-language tours available by arrangement.*

Kornhaus (Grain House). During the Middle Ages, townspeople stored and sold grain on the first floor of this structure (built in 1453); social events took place on the second floor. Among the Kornhaus's occupants through the centuries were duelists, medieval apprentices, traveling players, 18th-century schoolchildren, an academy for young ladies, the Nazi Women's League, a driving school, and the city's restoration department. It now houses the City Museum. ✉ *Kornhausstr. 10* ☎ *07071/945–460* 🌐 *www.tuebingen.de* 🎟 *€2.50* ⏲ *Tues.–Fri. 3–6, weekends 11–6.*

off the beaten path

KUNSTHALLE (Art Gallery) – North of the Neckar, the art gallery has become a leading exhibition venue and generates a special kind of "art tourism," making it difficult to find lodging if a popular show is on. ✉ *Philosophenweg 76* ☎ *07071/96910* 🌐 *www.kunsthalle-tuebingen.de* 🎟 *€6–€8, depending on exhibit* ⏲ *Tues.–Sun. 10–6.*

★ **Marktplatz** (Market Square). Houses of prominent burghers of centuries gone by surround the square. At the open-air market on Monday, Wednesday, and Friday, you can buy flowers, bread, pastries, poultry, sausage, and cheese.

★ **Rathaus** (Town Hall). Begun in 1433, the Rathaus slowly expanded over the next 150 years or so. Its ornate Renaissance facade is bright with colorful murals and a marvelous astronomical clock dating from 1511. The halls and reception rooms are adorned with half-timber and paintings from the late 19th century. ✉ *Marktpl.*

Schloss Hohentübingen. The original castle of the counts of Tübingen (1078) was significantly enlarged and altered by Duke Ulrich during the 16th century. Particularly noteworthy is the elaborate Renaissance portal patterned after a Roman triumphal arch. The coat of arms of the Duchy of Württemberg depicted in the center is framed by the emblems of various orders, including the Order of the Garter. Today the castle houses several university departments, the university's archaeological and ethnological collections, and reproductions of Greek and Roman sculptures. The castle's main attraction, however, is its magnificent view over the river and town.

★ **Stiftskirche** (Collegiate Church). The late-Gothic church has been well preserved; its original features include the stained-glass windows, the choir stalls, the ornate baptismal font, and the elaborate stone pulpit. The windows are famous for their colors and were much admired by Goethe. The dukes of Württemberg, from the 15th through the 17th centuries, are interred in the choir. ✉ *Holzmarkt.* 🎟 *Bell tower €1* ⏲ *Church Feb.–Oct., daily 9–5; Nov.–Jan., daily 9–4; bell tower Fri.–Sun. 11:30–5.*

Studentenkarzer (Student Prison). The oldest surviving university prison in Germany consists of just two small rooms. For more than three centuries (1515–1845) students were locked up here for such offenses as swearing, failing to attend sermons, wearing clothing considered lewd, or playing dice. The figures on the walls are not graffiti but scenes from biblical history that were supposed to contribute to the moral improvement of the incarcerated students. You can enter the prison only on a guided tour organized by the Tübingen Tourist Board. ✉ *Münzg. 20* ☎ *07071/91360 for tour* 🎟 *€1* ⏲ *Tour weekends at 2.*

Where to Stay & Eat

$–$$ ✕ **Forelle.** Beautiful ceilings painted with vine motifs, exposed beams, and an old tile oven make for a Gemütlich atmosphere. This small restaurant fills up fast, not least because the Swabian cooking is excellent. All products (and the wines) are sourced locally, including the inn's namesake, trout. Splurge on the saddle of venison in *Wacholdersahnesosse* (juniper-berry cream sauce) with mushroom-filled Maultauschen. ✉ *Kronenstr. 8* ☎ *07071/24094* 🌐 *www.weinstube-forelle.de* 💳 *MC, V.*

¢–$ ✕ **Gasthausbrauerei Neckarmüller.** This shady, riverside beer garden and restaurant near the Eberhards-Brücke serves house-brewed beer with snacks, salads, and Swabian specialties (Maultaschen, spätzle, sauerkraut, and beefsteaks in cream sauce). Don't wait to be served. The sign that reads SELBSTABHOLUNG means you fetch it yourself. ✉ *Gartenstr. 4* ☎ *07071/27848* 🌐 *www.neckarmueller.de* 💳 *DC, MC, V.*

¢ ✕ **Neckarbistro.** The café has light and airy 1960s decor and a beautiful view up and down the Neckar. Hölderlin's Tower is just a few houses upriver. The eclectic menu includes vegetarian dishes, pasta, schnitzel, and Swabian fare, or drop in for coffee and delicious pastry. Sunday brunch ($) is a feast (reservations advised). ✉ *Neckarg. 22* ☎ *07071/22122* 🌐 *www.neckarbistro.de* 💳 *No credit cards.*

★ **$–$$** ✕🏨 **Hotel Am Schloss.** The climb is steep from the Altstadt to this hotel, next to the castle that towers over the town, but the reward is a lovely view from the windows and terrace. Proprietor Herbert Rösch is an expert on Maultaschen. In his restaurant ($–$$), 28 versions of "Swabian tortellini" are on the menu, together with other regional dishes and wines from Württemberg. The hotel can help you with parking, or with a ride to the airport. ✉ *Burgsteige 18, D–72070* ☎ *07071/92940* 📠 *07071/*

929–410 ⊕ www.hotelamschloss.de 37 rooms Restaurant, some minibars, cable TV, bicycles, laundry service, Internet room, business services, some pets allowed (fee), no-smoking rooms; no a/c AE, MC, V Restaurant closed Tues. Oct.–Mar. BP.

$–$$ **Hotel Hospiz.** This modern, family-run hotel provides friendly service, comfort, and a convenient Altstadt location near the castle. Several rooms are small. If you're unhappy about the size of your room, please let the front desk know and they will try to move you into larger quarters. Parking is difficult, so take advantage of the hotel's offer to park the car for you. ✉ *Neckarhalde 2, at Burgsteige, D–72070 ☎ 07071/9240 07071/924–200 ⊕ www.hotel-hospiz.de 50 rooms, 45 with bath or shower Minibars, cable TV, in-room data ports, lobby lounge, business services, some pets allowed, no-smoking rooms; no a/c AE, MC, V BP.*

Nightlife & the Arts

Tübingen has an active small theater scene. Check with the tourist office for a listing of what is going on—the more eclectic offerings are likely to be the better ones. In addition to dozens of Old Town student pubs, there's a lively crowd after 9 at the **Jazzkeller** (✉ Haagg. 15/2 ☎ 07071/550–906). **Die Kelter** (✉ Schmiedtorstr. 17 ☎ 07071/254–675) is good for jazz, music, and light fare, and it has a wineshop. The upstairs cocktail bar at **Café Nass** (✉ Kirchg. 19 ☎ 07071/551–250) opens at 7 PM. From 9 AM until well past midnight there's action at **Tangente-Jour** (✉ Münzg. 17 ☎ 07071/24572), a bistro next to the Stiftskirche. **Zentrum Zoo** (✉ Schleifmühleweg 86 ☎ 07071/94480) has live music, a dance club, and a huge beer garden that is immensely popular with all ages. It's about a 20-minute walk from the town center.

Sports & the Outdoors

The Tübingen tourist office has maps with hiking routes around the town, including historical and geological *Lehrpfade,* or **educational walks.** A classic Tübingen walk goes from the castle down to the little chapel called the **Wurmlinger Kapelle,** taking about two hours. On the way you can stop off at the restaurant Schwärzlocher Hof (closed Monday and Tuesday) for a glass of *Most* (apple wine), bread, and sausages—all are homemade.

off the beaten path

BURG HOHENZOLLERN – The Hohenzollern House of Prussia was the most powerful family in German history. It lost its throne when Kaiser William II abdicated after Germany's defeat in World War I. The Swabian branch of the family owns one-third of the castle, the Prussian branch two-thirds. Today's neo-Gothic structure, perched high on a conical wooded hill, is a successor of a castle dating from the 11th century. Its majestic silhouette is visible from miles away. On the fascinating castle tour you'll see the Prussian royal crown and beautiful period rooms—splendid from floor to ceiling, with playful details, such as door handles carved to resemble peacocks and dogs. The royal tombs, once housed in the Christ Chapel, were returned to Potsdam in 1991 after German reunification. The restaurant on the castle grounds, Burgschänke (closed January and Monday in February

and March), is catered by the talented chefs of Hotel Brielhof (which is at the foot of the hill where the ascent from the B–27 begins). You can enjoy a first-class meal at the Brielhof, then make the one-hour hike up to the castle. From the castle parking lot it's a 20-minute walk to the entrance, or take the shuttle bus (€2.55 round-trip).
✉ Hechingen, 25 km (15 mi) south of Tübingen on B–27 ☎ 07471/2428 🌐 www.burg-hohenzollern.com 🎫 €5 ⏲ Mid-Mar.–Oct., daily 9–5:30; Nov.–mid-Mar., daily 10–4:30.

HEIDELBERG & THE NECKAR VALLEY A TO Z

To research prices, get advice from other travelers, and book travel arrangements, visit www.fodors.com.

AIRPORTS

From the Frankfurt and Stuttgart airports, there's fast and easy access, by car and train, to all major centers along the Neckar.

With advance reservations you can get to Heidelberg from the Frankfurt airport via the shuttle service TLS. The trip takes about an hour and costs €29 per person; with four people, €22.25 each. No reservations are needed for the Lufthansa Airport Bus (not restricted to Lufthansa passengers). Service is daily, on the hour, 8–1, 3–7, and 10 or 11 PM. Confirm the schedule by phone or on the Internet. It departs from Frankfurt airport, Terminal One, Hall B, arrivals level. Exit at B–4, close to the *Treffpunkt* (Meeting Point) to reach the bus stop. The trip ends at the Crowne Plaza Hotel in Heidelberg and costs €19 per person.
TLS ☎ 06221/770–077 📠 06221/770–070 🌐 www.tls-heidelberg.de. **Lufthansa Airport Bus** ☎ 06221/653–256 in Heidelberg 🌐 www.lufthansa-airportbus.com.

BUS TRAVEL

Europabus 189 runs the length of the Burgenstrasse daily from May through September, making stops all along the Neckar. For information, contact Deutsche Touring (⇨ Bus Travel *in* Smart Travel Tips). Local buses run from Mannheim, Heidelberg, Heilbronn, and Stuttgart to most places along the river.

CAR TRAVEL

Heidelberg is a 15-minute drive (10 km [6 mi]) on A–656 from Mannheim, a major junction of the autobahn system. Heilbronn is near the east–west A–6 and the north–south A–81. The route followed in this chapter, the Burgenstrasse (Route B–37), follows the north bank of the Neckar River from Heidelberg to Mosbach, from which it continues south to Heilbronn as B–27, the road parallel to and predating the autobahn (A–81). B–27 still leads to Stuttgart and Tübingen.

CITYTOURS

Medieval Bad Wimpfen offers a town walk year-round, Sunday at 2 (€1.80), departing from the Alter Bahnhof (old train station), and free guided tours in English for visitors who spend at least one night. Upon arrival, ask the hotel to arrange a town tour and ask for the free pass

Bad Wimpfen à la card for reduced or free admission to historic sights and museums.

From April through October there are daily walking tours of Heidelberg in German (Friday and Saturday in English) at 10:30 AM; from November through March, tours are in German only, Saturday at 10:30; the cost is €6. They depart from the Lion's Fountain on Universitätsplatz. Bilingual bus tours run April–October on Thursday and Friday at 2:30, and on Saturday at 10:30 and 2:30. From November through March bus tours depart Saturday at 2:30. They cost €12 and depart from Universitätsplatz. The *HeidelbergCard* costs €12 (two days) or €20 (four days) and includes free or reduced admission to most tourist attractions as well as free use of all public transportation (including the Bergbahn to the castle) and other extras, such as free guided walking tours, discounts on bus tours, and a city guidebook. It can be purchased at the Tourist-Information office at the main train station, and at many local hotels.

Walking tours (in German) of Heilbronn and Mosbach depart from their respective tourist offices. Heilbronn's year-round tours are Saturday at 11:30, for €2.10. There's also a tour April–September, Tuesday evening at 6:15 (€4.50), that concludes with a Viertele glass of wine in a Heilbronn wine restaurant. Free tours of Mosbach take place May–September, Wednesday at 2:30. June–September there are free (German) tours of Hirschhorn on Saturday at 10.

The visitor-friendly (three-day) STUTTCARD PLUS (€17) and STUTTCARD (€11.50), with or without access to free public transportation, are available from the Stuttgart tourist office opposite the main train station. This is also the place to book tours and the meeting point for city walking tours in German (year-round, Saturday at 10) for €7.50. There are daily bilingual walks April–October at 11 AM and an extra tour Friday at 5 PM for €6. Bilingual bus tours depart from the bus stop around the corner from the tourist office, in front of Hotel am Schlossgarten (April–October, daily at 1:30; November–March, Friday–Sunday at 1:30) for €17. All tours last from 1½ to 2½ hours. A bilingual Saturday-evening walking tour (7 PM–after midnight) includes a visit to a nightclub (with a show), a pub crawl, and dinner for €60.

The Tübingen tourist office runs guided city tours year-round, weekends at 2:30. From February through October there are also tours on Wednesday at 10 AM and Tuesday, Thursday, and Friday at 2:30 for €3.10. Tours start at the Rathaus on the market square. Overnight guests receive a free *Tourist-Regio-Card* from their hotel (ask for it) for reduced admission fees to museums, concerts, theaters, and sports facilities.

TRAIN TRAVEL

Western Germany's most important rail junction is in nearby Mannheim, with hourly InterCity trains from all major German cities. Heidelberg is equally easy to get to. The super-high-speed InterCity Express service, which reaches 280 kph (174 mph), is Germany's fastest. Travel time between Frankfurt and Stuttgart is less than 1½ hours; between Heidelberg and Stuttgart, 26 minutes. There are express trains to Heilbronn from Heidelberg and Stuttgart and direct trains from Stuttgart to Tübingen. Local services link many of the smaller towns.

VISITOR INFORMATION

For information on the entire Burgenstrasse, contact Die Burgenstrasse. For information on the hilly area south of Stuttgart and Tübingen, contact the Schwäbische Alb Tourismusverband.

Regional Tourist Offices **Die Burgenstrasse** ✉ Allee 28, D-74072 Heilbronn ☎ 07131/564-028 📠 07131/564-029 🌐 www.burgenstrasse.de. **Schwäbische Alb Tourismusverband** ✉ Marktpl. 1, D-72574 Bad Urach ☎ 07125/948-106 📠 07125/948-108 🌐 www.schwaebischealb.de.

Tourist Offices **Bad Wimpfen** ✉ Tourist-Information Bad Wimpfen-Gundelsheim, Carl-Ulrich-Str. 1, D-74206 ☎ 07063/97200 📠 07063/972-020 🌐 www.badwimpfen.de. **Heidelberg** ✉ Tourist-Information am Hauptbahnhof, Willy-Brandt-Pl. 1, D-69115 ☎ 06221/19433 📠 06221/138-8111 🌐 www.cvb-heidelberg.de. **Heilbronn** ✉ Tourist-Information, Kaiserstr. 17, D-74072 ☎ 07131/562-270 📠 07131/563-349 🌐 www.heilbronn-marketing.de. **Hirschhorn** ✉ Tourist-Information, Alleeweg 2, D-69434 ☎ 06272/1742 📠 06272/912-351 🌐 www.hirschhorn.de. **Mosbach** ✉ Tourist-Information, Am Marktplatz 4, D-74821 ☎ 06261/91880 📠 06261/918-815 🌐 www.mosbach.de. **Schwetzingen** ✉ Stadtinformation, Dreikönigstr. 3, D-68723 ☎ 06202/945-875 📠 06202/945-877 🌐 www.schwetzingen.de. **Stuttgart** ✉ Touristik-Information i-Punkt, Königstr. 1A, D-70173 ☎ 0711/222-8246 📠 0711/222-8253 🌐 www.stuttgart-tourist.de. **Tübingen** ✉ Verkehrsverein Tübingen, An der Neckarbrücke, D-72072 ☎ 07071/91360 📠 07071/35070 🌐 www.tuebingen-info.de.

WINE INFORMATION

The regional wine-promotion boards can provide information on the local wines and where to sample them. Ask for details about wine growers who also run economical bed-and-breakfasts. In Baden, which includes Heidelberg, contact Weinwerbezentrale badischer Winzergenossenschaften. The vineyards of Württemberg line the Neckar Valley; contact Werbegemeinschaft Württembergischer Weingärtnergenossenschaften.

Weinwerbezentrale badischer Winzergenossenschaften ✉ Kesslerstr. 5, D-76185 Karlsruhe ☎ 0721/557-028 📠 0721/557-020 🌐 www.sonnenmaennchen.de. **Werbegemeinschaft Württembergischer Weingärtnergenossenschaften** ✉ Raiffeisenstr. 6, D-71696 Möglingen ☎ 07141/24460 📠 07141/244-620 🌐 www.wwg.de.

Frankfurt

8

WORD OF MOUTH

"It [Frankfurt] doesn't compare to somewhere like London or Paris or Barcelona, but I enjoyed myself there nonetheless. I spent most of my time outside (the old town is easy to walk), and I found the contrast between the modern skyscrapers and the centuries-old buildings both beautiful and sad."

—Julie

"Everyone always gives Frankfurt such a bad rap, but I found it to be a nice place to go. I shopped in the main area and found the prices slightly cheaper than in Munich. Oddly enough, I found the people much more laid-back than in the stressed-out tourist centers like Munich."

—MelissaHI

www.fodors.com/forums

Updated by
Heather Phibbs

STANDING IN THE CENTER of the Römerberg (medieval town square), visitors to Frankfurt at once notice the city's striking contrasts. Re-creations of 15th-, 16th-, 17th-, and 18th-century houses and government buildings line the square while modern skyscrapers tower overhead. Unlike German cities that reclaimed much of their prewar appearance after World War II, Frankfurt looked to the future and focused on erecting skyscrapers to house its many banking institutions (though the city did meticulously restore selected historic buildings in amazing, accurate detail). The city cheekily nicknamed itself Mainhattan, using the name of the Main River that flows through it to suggest that other famous metropolis across the Atlantic. Although modest in size (fifth among German cities, with a population of 652,000), Frankfurt is Germany's financial powerhouse. Not only is the German Central Bank (Bundesbank) here but also the European Central Bank (ECB), which manages the euro. Some 370 credit institutions (more than half of them foreign banks) have offices in Frankfurt, including the headquarters of five of Germany's largest banks.

According to legend, a deer is said to have revealed the ford in the Main River to the Frankish emperor Charlemagne. A stone ridge, now blasted away, made the shallow river a great conduit for trade, and by the early 13th century Frankfurt (*furt* means "ford") had emerged as a major trading center. Frankfurt's first international Autumn Fair was held in 1240; in 1330 it added a Spring Fair. Today these and other trade shows showcase the latest in books, cars, consumer goods, and technology. The city's stock exchange, one of the half dozen most important in the world, was established in 1585, and the Rothschild family opened their first bank here in 1798. The long history of trade might help explain the temperament of many Frankfurters—competitive but open-minded. It's also one of the reasons Frankfurt has become Germany's most international city. Almost 30% of its residents are foreign, including a large number of Turks, Italians, Eastern Europeans, and others who relocated here for business.

So why come to Frankfurt if not on business? Partly for its history, which spans more than 1,200 years. It was one of the joint capitals of Charlemagne's empire; the city where Holy Roman emperors were elected and crowned; the site of Gutenberg's print shop; the birthplace of Goethe (1749–1832), Germany's greatest poet; and the city where the first German parliament met.

Because of its commercialism, Frankfurt has a reputation for being crass, cold, and boring. But people who know the city think this characterization is unfair. The district of Sachsenhausen is as *gemütlich* (fun, friendly, and cozy) as you will find anywhere. The city has world-class ballet, opera, theater, and art exhibitions; an important piece of Germany's publishing industry; a large university (38,000 students); and two of the three most important daily newspapers in Germany. In Frankfurt you find yourself in the heart of a powerful, sophisticated, and cosmopolitan nation. There may not be that much here to remind you of the Old World, but there's a great deal that explains the success story of postwar Germany.

If you have **1 day**

Begin at the Goethehaus und Goethemuseum, the home of Germany's greatest poet. The house is within a 5- to 10-minute walk of either the Hauptwache or Willy Brandt Platz subway station. Next, follow Bethmannstrasse as it turns into Braubachstrasse to reach the Museum für Moderne Kunst, one of Frankfurt's modern architectural monuments. Walk a few blocks and several centuries back in time south to the Kaiserdom. The cathedral is next to the heart of the city, the Römerberg. The medieval square holds the Römer, or city hall. After lunch, cross over the Main on the Eiserner Steg to reach the Städelsches Kunstinstitut und Städtische Galerie, with its important collection of old master and impressionist paintings, and the Städtische Galerie Liebieghaus, which contains sculpture from the third millennium BC up to the modern age. In the evening, relax in one of Sachsenhausen's apple-cider taverns.

If you have **2 days**

Spend your first morning at the Goethehaus und Goethemuseum and Römerberg Square, with the Römer, Nikolaikirche, Historisches Museum, Paulskirche, and the Kaiserdom all nearby. After viewing the cathedral, continue up Domstrasse to the Museum für Moderne Kunst. Take a midday break before continuing north to Germany's shop-'til-you-drop Zeil district and the Zoologischer Garten, one of Europe's best zoos. End the evening listening to music in the Frankfurter Jazzkeller. The entire second day can be devoted to the Sachsenhausen museums, starting with the Städelsches Kunstinstitut und Städtische Galerie and the Städtische Galerie Liebieghaus. Finally, explore Sachsenhausen's nightlife.

If you have **3 days**

Spend your first two days following the itinerary outlined above. On the morning of the third day, see the Naturkundemuseum Senckenberg; it has a famous collection of dinosaurs and giant whales. Afterward visit the nearby Palmengarten und Botanischer Garten, which have climatic zones from tropical to sub-Antarctic and a dazzling range of orchids. Take the U-bahn to Opernplatz, and emerge before the 19th-century splendor of the Alte Oper; lunch on Fressgasse is not far away. In the afternoon, go to the visitors' gallery of the Börse to feel the pulse of Europe's banking capital. Then continue on to the less-worldly Karmeliterkloster. Secularized in 1803, the monastery and buildings house the Museum für Vor- und Frühgeschichte. Just around the corner on the bank of the Main, in the former Rothschild Palais, the Jüdisches Museum tells the 1,000-year story of Frankfurt's Jewish quarter and its end in the Holocaust.

EXPLORING FRANKFURT

The Hauptbahnhof (main train station) area and adjoining Westend district are mostly devoted to business, as evidenced by the banks towering overhead. You'll find the department stores of the Hauptwache and Zeil just a short walk east of the station, but avoid the drug-ridden red-light district southwest of the station. The city's past can be found in the Old Town's restored medieval quarter and in Sachsenhausen, across the river, where pubs and museums greatly outnumber banks.

Numbers in the text correspond to numbers in the margin and on the Frankfurt map.

City Center & Westend

Frankfurt was rebuilt after World War II with little attention paid to the past. Nevertheless, important historical monuments can still be found among the modern architecture. The city is very walkable; its growth hasn't encroached on its parks, gardens, pedestrian arcades, or outdoor cafés.

a good tour

Römerberg 1 ⚑, the historic heart of Frankfurt, has been the center of civic life for centuries. Taking up most of the west side of the square is the city hall, called the **Römer** 2, a modest-looking building compared with many of Germany's other city halls. In the center of the square stands the fine 16th-century Fountain of Justitia.

On the south side of the Römerberg is the red sandstone **Nikolaikirche** 3. Beside it stands the **Historisches Museum** 4, where you can see a perfect scale model of historic Frankfurt. On the east side of the square is a row of painstakingly restored half-timber houses called the Ostzeile, dating from the 15th and 16th centuries.

From the Römerberg, walk up the pedestrian street called Neue Kräme. Looming up on the left is the circular bulk of the **Paulskirche** 5, a mostly 18th-century church, more interesting for its political than its religious significance. It was here that the short-lived German parliament met for the first time in May 1848. From the Paulskirche keep heading along the Neue Kräme, which becomes Liebfrauenstrasse, and you'll reach the **Liebfrauenkirche** 6, a late-Gothic church dating from the end of the 14th century.

Liebfrauenstrasse ends at the **Hauptwache** 7, a square that is the hub of the city's transportation network and is named after the 18th-century building that stands on it. The café in the Hauptwache building can attend to your appetite if you need a break. A vast shopping mall lies below the square. To the south of the Hauptwache is the **Katharinenkirche** 8, the most important Protestant church in the city. North of the Hauptwache, Schillerstrasse leads to the Börsenplatz and Germany's leading stock exchange, the **Börse** 9.

To the east of the Hauptwache lies the **Zeil,** Frankfurt's largest pedestrian zone and main shopping street. Its department stores sell every conceivable type of consumer goods and can get very crowded. A 15- to 20-minute walk down the Zeil brings you to Alfred-Brehm-Platz and the entrance to the **Zoologischer Garten** 10. This is one of Frankfurt's chief attractions, ranking among the best zoos in Europe. If you don't want to walk the Zeil's full length, turn right at the square Konstabler Wache onto Fahrgasse. Follow the signs reading AN DER STAUFENMAUER to the **Staufenmauer** 11, which is one of the few surviving stretches of the old city wall.

Continue down Fahrgasse, and turn right onto Battonstrasse. At the corner of Battonstrasse and Domstrasse you'll see the striking wedge-shape outline of the **Museum für Moderne Kunst** 12. Walk south down Domstrasse

On the Menu Many international cuisines are represented in the financial hub of Europe. For vegetarians there's usually at least one meatless dish on a German menu, and substantial salads are popular, too (though often served with bacon). Frankfurt's local cuisine comes from the region's farm tradition. Pork ribs and chops, stewed beef, blood sausage, potato soup, and pancakes with bacon fulfill such proverbs as "Better once full than twice hungry" and "You work the way you eat." The city's most famous contribution to the world's diet is the *Frankfurter Würstchen*—a thin smoked pork sausage—better known to Americans as the hot dog. *Grüne Sosse* is a thin cream sauce of herbs served with potatoes and hard-boiled eggs. The oddly named *Handkäs mit Musik* (hand cheese with music) consists of slices of cheese covered with raw onions, oil, and vinegar, served with bread and butter (an acquired taste for many). All these things are served in *Apfelwein* (apple-wine, or hard cider) taverns in the Sachsenhausen area. Apfelwein is poured from a distinctive gray stoneware pitcher, called a *Bembel,* into an equally distinctive, ribbed tumbler.

Jazz & Techno Frankfurt was a real pioneer in the German jazz scene and also has done much for the development of techno music. Jazz musicians make the rounds from smoky backstreet cafés all the way to the Old Opera House, and the local broadcaster Hessischer Rundfunk sponsors the German Jazz Festival in the fall. The Frankfurter Jazzkeller has been the most noted venue for German jazz fans for decades.

Museums Frankfurt is full of museums, and 13 of them were newly built or renovated during the 1980s. Interesting for their architecture as well as for their content, the exhibition halls are Frankfurt's tourist draw. The Sachsenhausen area is home to seven of these museums. They line the side of the Main, on Schaumainkai, known locally as the Museumsufer (Museum Riverbank).

---

a few steps and another silhouette appears, that of the grand Gothic cathedral, **Kaiserdom** 13. There is an archaeological site next to the cathedral containing remains of Roman baths; from there walk through the pedestrian zone alongside the modern edifice of the **Schirn Kunsthalle** 14, a major venue for art exhibitions.

Continue back to the Römerberg and turn left to get to the Mainkai, the busy street that runs parallel to the tree-lined Main River. On your left you will see the Rententurm, one of the city's medieval gates, with its pinnacled towers at the base of the main spire extending out over the walls. To your right and in front is the **Eiserner Steg** 15, an iron footbridge connecting central Frankfurt with the old district of Sachsenhausen. River trips, boat excursions, and the old steam train leave from here.

Past the Eiserner Steg is the **Leonhardskirche** 16, which has one of the few 15th-century stained-glass windows to have survived World War II. Continue down the river, just past the Untermainbrücke to the **Jüdisches**

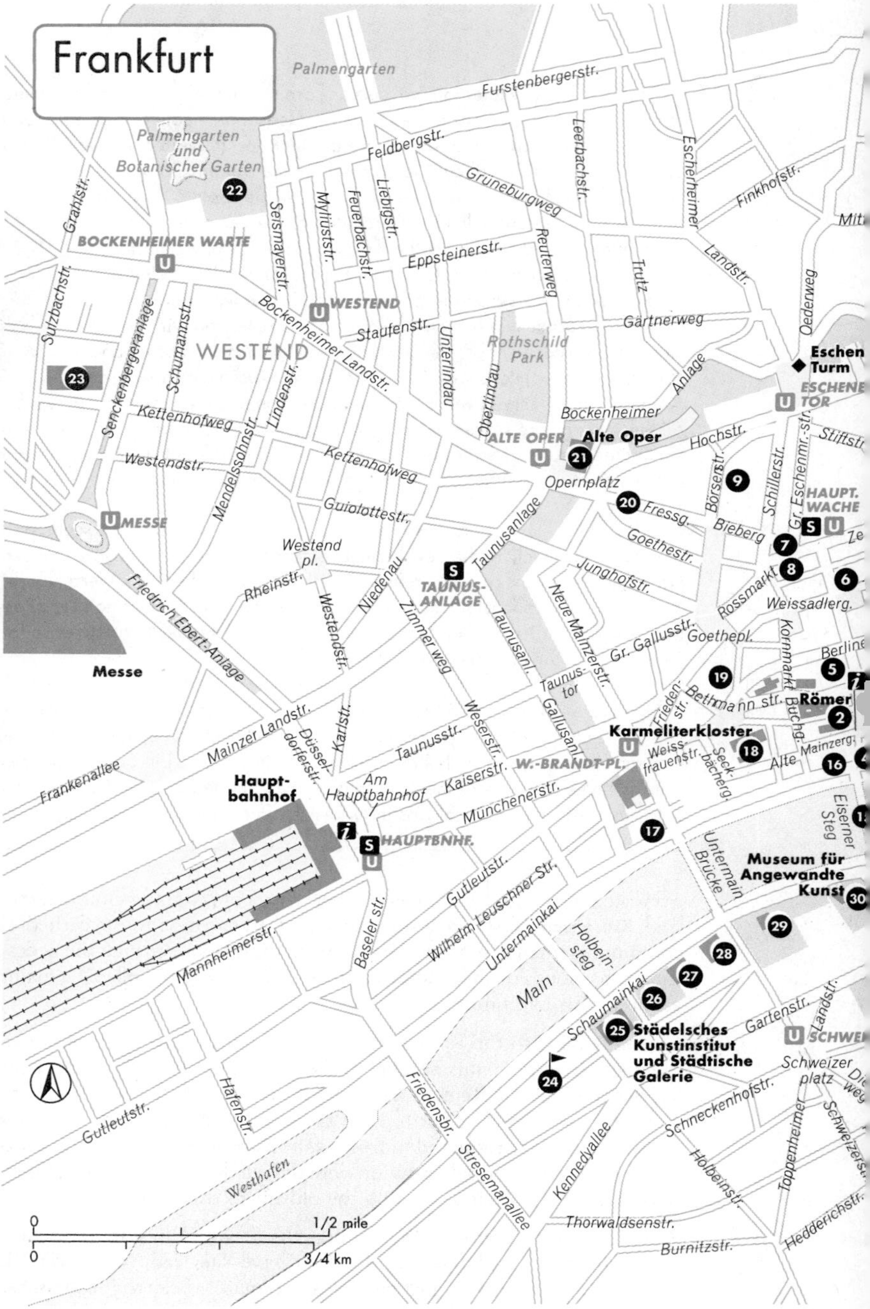
Frankfurt
Palmengarten
Palmengarten und Botanischer Garten
22
Furstenbergerstr.
Feldbergstr.
Grüneburgweg
Leerbachstr.
Eschenheimer Landstr.
Finkhofstr.
Grahstr.
BOCKENHEIMER WARTE
U
Seismayerstr.
Myliusstr.
Feuerbachstr.
Liebigstr.
Eppsteinerstr.
Reuterweg
Trutz
Oederweg
Sulzbachstr.
Senckenberganlage
Schumannstr.
WESTEND
Bockenheimer Landstr.
Staufenstr.
Unterlindau
Rothschild Park
Oberlindau
Gärtnerweg
Anlage
Eschenheimer Turm
ESCHENHEIMER TOR
23
Kettenhofweg
Lindenstr.
Mendelssohnstr.
Bockenheimer
ALTE OPER
Alte Oper
21
Hochstr.
Stiftstr.
Westendstr.
Kettenhofweg
Opernplatz
Börsenstr.
9
Schillerstr.
Gr. Eschenheimer str.
HAUPTWACHE
MESSE
Guiolottestr.
20
Fressg.
Bieberg
Goethestr.
7
8
6
Westend pl.
Taunusanlage
Junghofstr.
Rossmarkt
Weissadlerg.
Rheinstr.
Westendstr.
Niedenau
TAUNUS-ANLAGE
Neue Mainzerstr.
Friedrich-Ebert-Anlage
Zimmerweg
Taunusanl.
Gr. Gallusstr.
Goethepl.
Kornmarkt
Berliner
Messe
19
5
Taunustor
Frieden-str.
Bethmann str.
Römer
2
Gallusanl.
Karmeliterkloster
Mainzer Landstr.
Düsseldorferstr.
Karlstr.
Weserstr.
Taunusstr.
18
Buchg.
Mainzerg.
Alte
16
W.-BRANDT-PL.
Weissfrauenstr.
Seckbächerg.
Frankenallee
Hauptbahnhof
Am Hauptbahnhof
Kaiserstr.
Münchenerstr.
Eiserner Steg
HAUPTBNHF.
17
Untermain Brücke
Museum für Angewandte Kunst
30
Gutleutstr.
Wilhelm Leuschner Str.
Baseler str.
29
Holbeinsteg
Untermainkai
28
Mannheimerstr.
27
Main
26
Schaumainkai
25
Städelsches Kunstinstitut und Städtische Galerie
Gartenstr.
Landstr.
SCHWEIZER
Schweizer platz
24
Hafenstr.
Gutleutstr.
Friedensbr.
Schneckenhofstr.
Dreieichweg
Schweizerstr.
Westhafen
Stresemanallee
Kennedyallee
Holbeinstr.
Toppenheimer
Heddericher.
0
1/2 mile
0
3/4 km
Thorwaldsenstr.
Burnitzstr.

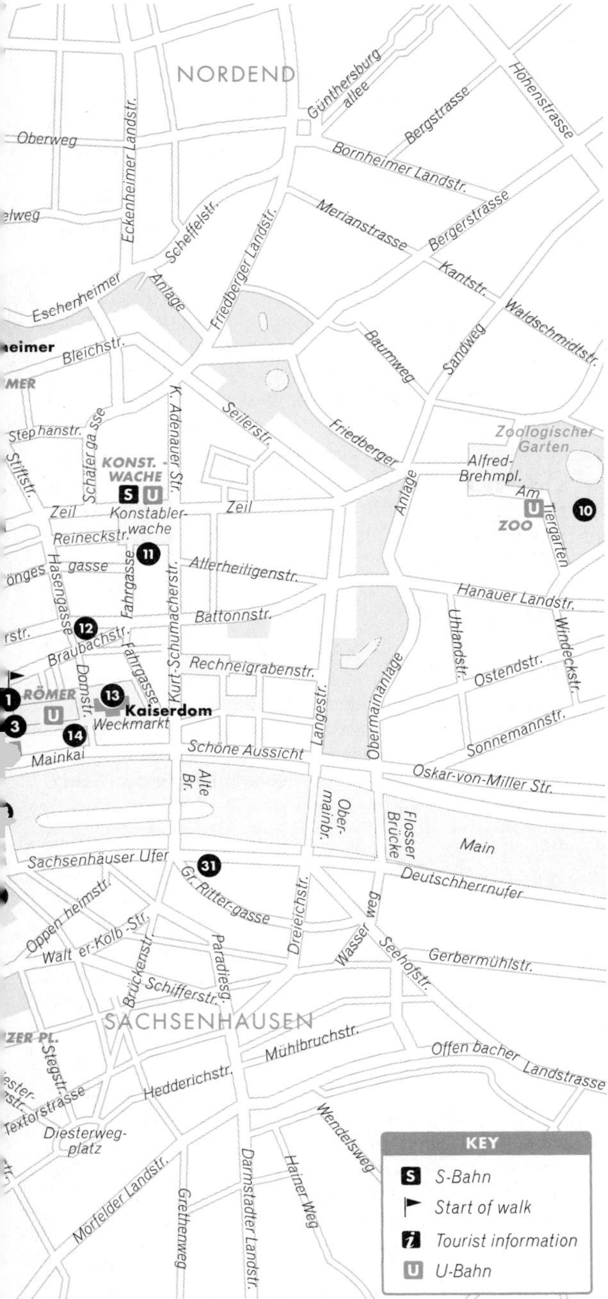

City Center & Westend

- Alte Oper 21
- Börse 9
- Eiserner Steg 15
- Fressgasse 20
- Goethehaus und Goethemuseum 19
- Hauptwache 7
- Historisches Museum 4
- Jüdisches Museum 17
- Kaiserdom 13
- Karmeliterkloster 18
- Katharinenkirche 8
- Leonhardskirche 16
- Liebfrauenkirche 6
- Museum für Moderne Kunst 12
- Naturkundemuseum Senckenberg 23
- Nikolaikirche 3
- Palmengarten und Botanischer Garten 22
- Paulskirche 5
- Römer 2
- Römerberg 1
- Schirn Kunsthalle 14
- Staufenmauer 11
- Zoologischer Garten 10

Sachsenhausen

- Deutsches Architekturmuseum 27
- Deutsches Filmmuseum 28
- Kuhhirtenturm 31
- Museum für Kommunication 26
- Museum für Angewandte Kunst 30
- Museum für Volkerkunde 29
- Städelsches Kunstinstitut und Städtische Galerie 25
- Städtische Galerie Liebieghaus 24

Museum 17. At No. 14–15 in the former Rothschild Palais, this museum focuses on the history of Frankfurt's Jewish community.

Backtrack a short way, and turn left into the narrow Karmelitergasse, which will take you to the **Karmeliterkloster** 18. The monastery and its buildings house an early history museum and the largest religious fresco north of the Alps. Exit onto Münzgasse, turn left, and go to the junction of Bethmannstrasse and Berlinerstrasse. Use the pedestrian walkway and cross over to the north side of Berlinerstrasse; then turn left again onto Grosser Hirschgraben. At No. 23 there will probably be a small crowd outside the **Goethehaus und Goethemuseum** 19, where writer Johann Wolfgang von Goethe was born in 1749.

On leaving the Goethehaus, go to Goetheplatz and continue past the Gutenberg Memorial into the pedestrian zone to Rathenau-Platz. At the end of the square turn left again, this time onto Grosse Bockenheimer Strasse, known locally as **Fressgasse** 20 because of its many delicatessens, bakeries, and cafés.

Fressgasse ends at Opernplatz and the **Alte Oper** 21, a prime venue for classical concerts as well as conferences and, every now and then, an opera. You can get a good look at Frankfurt's skyline from the opera house steps, or from the street Taunusanlage, opposite. Looking down Taunusanlage, you'll see the twin towers of the Deutsche Bank (the two towers are known as *zoll und haben,* or "debit and credit"). The very tall building to the left, topped by an antenna, is the 849-foot Commerzbank, the tallest building in Europe. Between them is the Maintower, headquarters of the Hessischer Landesbank.

Take the U-bahn two stops from Alte Oper to Bockenheimer Warte, walk down Bockenheimer Landstrasse, and turn left on Palmengartenstrasse to reach the delightful **Palmengarten und Botanischer Garten** 22. Also close to the Bockenheimer Warte stop is the **Naturkundemuseum Senckenberg** 23, with fun, hands-on exhibits.

TIMING Count on spending a full day on this tour. It's impossible to see all the museums in one trip. You should block out 45 minutes for the Goethehaus und Goethemuseum, an hour and 15 minutes for the Städelsches Kunstinstitut und Städtische Galerie, and an hour for the Städtische Galerie Liebieghaus. For the remaining museums it's a question of time and preference. Pick the one or two that interest you most and allow at least 45 minutes for each. If you intend to visit the Zoologischer Garten, expect to spend 1½ hours there.

What to See

21 **Alte Oper** (Old Opera House). Kaiser Wilhelm I traveled from Berlin for the gala opening of the opera house in 1880. Gutted in World War II, the house remained a hollow shell for 40 years while controversy raged over its reconstruction. The exterior and lobby are faithful to the original, though the remainder of the building is more like a modern multipurpose hall. Even if you don't go to a performance, it's worth having a look at the ornate lobby, an example of 19th-century neoclassicism at its most confident. ✉ *Opernpl., City Center* ☎ *069/134–0400* 🌐 *www.alte-oper-frankfurt.de* Ⓤ *Alte Oper (U-bahn).*

off the beaten path

ALTER JÜDISCHER FRIEDHOF (Old Jewish Cemetery) – The old Jewish quarter is east of Börneplatz, a short walk south of the Konstablerwache, or east of the Römer U-bahn station. Partly vandalized in the Nazi era, the cemetery was in use between the 13th and 19th centuries and is one of the few reminders of prewar Jewish life in Frankfurt. A newer Jewish cemetery is part of the cemetery at Eckenheimer Landstrasse 238 (about 1½ mi north). ✉ *Kurt-Schumacher-Str. and Battonstr., City Center* ☎ *069/561–826* 🎫 *Free* ⏲ *Daily 8:30–4:30* Ⓤ *Konstablerwache (U-bahn and S-bahn).*

9 **Börse** (Stock Exchange). This is the center of Germany's stock and money market. The Börse was founded by Frankfurt merchants in 1585 to establish some order in their often chaotic dealings, but the present building dates from the 1870s. These days computerized networks and international telephone systems have removed some of the drama from the dealers' floor, but it's still an exciting scene to watch from the visitor gallery. ✉ *Börsepl., City Center* ☎ *069/21010* 🌐 *www.deutsche-boerse.com* 🎫 *Free* ⏲ *Visitor gallery weekdays 10:30–6* Ⓤ *Hauptwache (U-bahn and S-bahn).*

15 **Eiserner Steg** (Iron Bridge). A pedestrian walkway and the first suspension bridge in Europe, the Eiserner Steg connects the city center with Sachsenhausen.

Eschenheimer Turm (Eschenheim Tower). Built in the early 15th century, this tower, a block north of the Hauptwache, remains the finest example of the city's original 42 towers. ✉ *Eschenheimer Tor, City Center* Ⓤ *Eschenheimer Tor (U-bahn).*

20 **Fressgasse** ("Pig-Out Alley"). Grosse Bockenheimer Strasse is the proper name of this pedestrian street, one of the city's liveliest thoroughfares, but Frankfurters have given it this sobriquet because of its amazing choice of delicatessens, wine merchants, cafés, and restaurants. Food shops offer fresh or smoked fish, cheeses, delicious soups, and a wide range of local specialties, including frankfurters. In the summer you can dine alfresco. Ⓤ *Hauptwache (U-bahn and S-bahn), Alte Oper (U-bahn).*

★ 19 **Goethehaus und Goethemuseum** (Goethe's House and Museum). The house where Germany's most famous poet was born in 1749 is furnished with many original pieces that belonged to his family, including manuscripts in his own hand. Though Goethe is associated with Weimar, where he lived most of his life, Frankfurters are proud to claim him as a native son. The original house was destroyed by Allied bombing and has been carefully rebuilt and restored in every detail.

Johann Wolfgang von Goethe studied law and became a member of the bar in Frankfurt. He was quickly drawn to writing, however, and eventually wrote the first version of his masterpiece, *Faust,* here. The adjoining museum contains works of art that inspired Goethe (he was an amateur painter) and works associated with his literary contemporaries. ✉ *Grosser Hirschgraben 23–25, Altstadt* ☎ *069/138–800* 🌐 *www.goethehaus-frankfurt.de* 🎫 *€5* ⏲ *Weekdays and Sun. 10–5:30, Sat. 10–6* Ⓤ *Hauptwache (U-bahn and S-bahn).*

7 **Hauptwache.** This square is where Grosse Bockenheimer Strasse (Fressgasse) runs into the Zeil, a main shopping street. The attractive baroque building with a steeply sloping roof is the actual Hauptwache (Main Guardhouse), from which the square takes its name. Built in 1729, the building had been tastelessly added to over the years and was demolished to permit excavation for a vast underground shopping mall and subway station, which you'll find beneath the square. The building was then restored to its original appearance. Today it houses a café. Ⓤ *Hauptwache (U-bahn and S-bahn).*

4 **Historisches Museum** (Historical Museum). This fascinating museum encompasses all aspects of the city's history over the past eight centuries. It contains a scale model of historic Frankfurt, complete with every street, house, and church. There's also an astonishing display of silver, a children's museum, and a permanent exhibit on Apfelwein. The museum's restaurant, Historix, serves Apfelwein and all the typical food and accoutrements of the hard-cider business. ✉ *Saalg. 19, Altstadt* ☎ *069/2123–5599* 🌐 *www.historisches-museum.frankfurt.de* 🎫 *€4* ⏲ *Tues., Thurs., Fri., and Sun. 10–5; Sat. 1–5; Wed. 10–8* Ⓤ *Römer (U-bahn).*

17 **Jüdisches Museum** (Jewish Museum). The story of Frankfurt's Jewish quarter is told in the former Rothschild Palais. Prior to the Holocaust, the community was the second largest in Germany. The museum contains extensive archives of Jewish history and culture, including a library of 5,000 books, a large photographic collection, and a documentation center. A branch of the museum, **Museum Judengasse** (✉ Kurt-Schumacher-Str. 10, City Center ☎ 069/297–7419 🎫 €1.50 ⏲ Tues. and Thurs.–Sun. 10–5, Wed. 10–8 Ⓤ Römer [U-bahn]), is built around the foundations of mostly 18th-century buildings, which once made up the ghetto. The branch is also near the Old Jewish Cemetery (Alter Jüdischer Friedhof). ✉ *Untermainkai 14–15, Altstadt* ☎ *069/2123–5000* 🌐 *www.juedischesmuseum.de* 🎫 *€2.60* ⏲ *Tues. and Thurs.–Sun. 10–5, Wed. 10–8.*

13 **Kaiserdom.** Because the Holy Roman emperors were chosen and crowned here from the 16th to the 18th century, the church is known as the Kaiserdom (Imperial Cathedral), even though it isn't the seat of a bishop. Officially the Church of St. Bartholomew, it was built largely between the 13th and 15th centuries and survived World War II with most of its treasures intact. Its many magnificent, original Gothic carvings include a life-size Crucifixion group and the fine 15th-century *Maria-Schlaf* (Altar of Mary Sleeping). The most impressive exterior feature is the tall, red sandstone tower (almost 300 feet high), which was added between 1415 and 1514. It was the tallest structure in Frankfurt before the skyscrapers, and the view from the top remains an exciting panorama. In 1953 excavations in front of the main entrance revealed the remains of a Roman settlement and the foundations of a Carolingian imperial palace. The **Dommuseum** (Cathedral Museum) occupies the former Gothic cloister. ✉ *Dompl. 1, Altstadt* ☎ *069/1337–6184* 🌐 *www.dom-frankfurt.de* 🎫 *Dommuseum €2* ⏲ *Church Apr.–Oct., Mon.–Thurs. and Sat. 9–noon and 2:30–6, Fri. and Sun. 2:30–6; Nov.–Mar., Mon.–Thurs. and Sat. 9–noon and 2:30–5, Fri. and Sun. 2:30–5. Dommuseum Tues.–Fri. 10–5, weekends 11–5* Ⓤ *Römer (U-bahn).*

Fodor's Choice ★

18 **Karmeliterkloster** (Carmelite Monastery). Secularized in 1803, the church and adjacent buildings contain the **Museum für Vor- und Frühgeschichte** (Museum of Prehistory and Early History). The **main cloister** (Free) displays the largest religious fresco north of the Alps, a 16th-century representation of Christ's birth and death by Jörg Ratgeb. *Karmeliterg. 1, Altstadt 069/2123–5896 Museum €4, free Wed. Museum and cloister Tues. and Thurs.–Sun. 10–5, Wed. 10–8 U Römer (U-bahn).*

8 **Katharinenkirche** (St. Catherine's Church). This house of worship, the first independent Protestant church in Gothic style, was originally built between 1678 and 1681. The church it replaced, dating from 1343, was the setting of the first Protestant sermon preached in Frankfurt, in 1522. Goethe was confirmed here. *An der Hauptwache, City Center Weekdays 2–6 U Hauptwache (U-bahn and S-bahn).*

16 **Leonhardskirche** (St. Leonard's Church). Begun in the Romanesque style and continued in the late-Gothic style, this beautifully preserved Catholic church contains five naves, two 13th-century Romanesque arches, and 15th-century stained glass. The "pendant," or hanging vaulting, was already a major Frankfurt tourist attraction in the 17th century. Masses are held in English on Saturday at 5 and Sunday at 10. *Am Leonhardstor and Untermainkai, Altstadt Tues.–Sun. 10–noon and 3–6 U Römer (U-bahn).*

6 **Liebfrauenkirche** (Church of Our Lady). The peaceful, concealed courtyard of this Catholic church makes it hard to believe you're in the swirl of the shopping district. Dating from the 14th century, the late-Gothic church still has a fine tympanum relief over the south door and ornate rococo wood carvings inside. *Liebfrauenberg 3, City Center Daily 7–7, except during services U Hauptwache (U-bahn and S-bahn).*

Messegelände (Fairgrounds). Also called the congress center, this huge complex is Europe's busiest trade-show center. Important international trade fairs showcase the latest books, cars, fashion, medical and high technology, and consumer goods. *Ludwig-Erhard-Anlage 1, Messe 069/75750 www.messe-frankfurt.de U Festhalle/Messe (U-bahn).*

12 **Museum für Moderne Kunst** (Museum of Modern Art). Austrian architect Hans Hollein designed this distinctive triangular building, shaped like a wedge of cake. The collection features American pop art and works by such German artists as Gerhard Richter and Joseph Beuys. *Domstr. 10, City Center 069/2123–0447 www.mmk-frankfurt.de €5 Tues. and Thurs.–Sun. 10–5, Wed. 10–8 U Römer (U-bahn).*

Fodor's Choice ★

23 **Naturkundemuseum Senckenberg** (Natural History Museum). An important collection of fossils, animals, plants, and geological exhibits is upstaged by the famous diplodocus dinosaur, imported from New York—the only complete specimen of its kind in Europe. Many of the exhibits of prehistoric animals have been designed with children in mind, including a series of dioramas featuring stuffed animals. *Senckenberganlage 25, Bockenheim 069/75420 www.senckenberg.uni-frankfurt.de €5 Mon., Tues., Thurs., and Fri. 9–5, Wed. 9–8, weekends 9–6 U Bockenheimer Warte (U-bahn).*

❸ **Nikolaikirche** (St. Nicholas Church). This small red sandstone church was built in the late 13th century as the court chapel for emperors of the Holy Roman Empire. Try to time your visit to coincide with the chimes of the carillon, which rings three times a day, at 9, noon, and 5. ✉ *South side of Römerberg, Altstadt* ⏲ *Oct.–Mar., daily 10–6; Apr.–Sept., daily 10–8* Ⓤ *Römer (U-bahn).*

❷❷ **Palmengarten und Botanischer Garten** (Tropical Garden and Botanical Gardens). A splendid cluster of tropical and semitropical greenhouses contains a wide variety of flora, including cacti, orchids, and palms. The surrounding park, which can be surveyed from a miniature train, has many recreational facilities including a small lake where you can rent rowboats, a play area for children, and a wading pool. Between the Palmengarten and the adjoining Grüneburgpark, the botanical gardens have a wide assortment of wild, ornamental, and rare plants from around the world. Special collections include a 2½-acre rock garden as well as rose and rhododendron gardens. In summer, concerts are held in an outdoor music pavilion. ✉ *Siesmayerstr. 63, Westend* ☎ *069/2123–3939* 🌐 *www.palmengarten-frankfurt.de* 🎫 *€3.50* ⏲ *Feb.–Oct., daily 9–6; Nov.–Jan., daily 9–4* Ⓤ *Westend (U-bahn).*

❺ **Paulskirche** (St. Paul's Church). The first all-German parliament was held here in 1848. The parliament lasted only a year, having achieved little more than offering the Prussian king the crown of Germany. Today the church, which has been secularized and not very tastefully restored, remains a symbol of German democracy and is used mainly for ceremonies. The German Book Dealers' annual Peace Prize is awarded in the hall, as is the Goethe Prize. ✉ *Paulspl., Altstadt* ⏲ *Daily 10–5* Ⓤ *Römer (U-bahn).*

❷ **Römer** (City Hall). Three individual patrician buildings make up the Römer. From left to right, they are the Alt-Limpurg, the Zum Römer (from which the entire structure takes its name), and the Löwenstein. The mercantile-minded Frankfurt burghers used the complex not only for political and ceremonial purposes but also for trade fairs and other commercial ventures. Its gabled Gothic facade with an ornate balcony is widely known as the city's official emblem.

The most important events to take place in the Römer were the festivities celebrating the coronations of the Holy Roman emperors. The first was in 1562 in the glittering **Kaisersaal** (Imperial Hall), which was last used in 1792 to celebrate the election of the emperor Francis II, who would later be forced to abdicate by Napoléon. When no official business is being conducted, you can see the impressive, full-length 19th-century portraits of the 52 emperors of the Holy Roman Empire, which line the walls of the reconstructed banquet hall. ✉ *West side of Römerberg, Altstadt* ☎ *069/2123–4814* 🎫 *€1.50* ⏲ *Daily 10–1 and 2–5; closed during official functions* Ⓤ *Römer (U-bahn).*

❶ **Römerberg.** This square north of the Main River, lovingly restored after wartime bomb damage, is the historical focal point of the city. The Römer, the Nikolaikirche, the Historiches Museum, and the half-timber Ostzeile houses are all found here. The 16th-century Fountain of Justitia (Justice) stands in the center of the Römerberg. At the coronation of Emperor Matthias in 1612, wine flowed from the fountain instead of water. This practice has been revived by the city fathers on special occasions. The square is also the site of many public festivals throughout the year, including the Christmas markets in December. ✉ *Between Braubachstr. and Main River, Altstadt* Ⓤ *Römer (U-bahn).*

⓮ **Schirn Kunsthalle** (Schirn Art Gallery). One of Frankfurt's most modern museums is devoted exclusively to changing exhibits of modern art and photography. Past shows have included "Audio-Visual Spaces," "Shopping," Henri Matisse drawings, Mercedes posters, and Polish landscapes of the 19th and 20th centuries. It stands opposite the Kaiserdom. ✉ *Am Römerberg 6a, Altstadt* ☎ *069/299–8820* 🌐 *www.schirn-kunsthalle.de* 🎫 *€ 8* ⏲ *Tues. and Fri.–Sun., 10–7, Wed., Thurs., 10–10* Ⓤ *Römer (U-bahn).*

⓫ **Staufenmauer** (Staufen Wall). The Staufenmauer is one of the few remaining sections of the old city's fortifications and dates from the 12th century. ✉ *Fahrg., Altstadt* Ⓤ *Römer (U-bahn).*

Struwwelpeter-Museum (Slovenly Peter Museum). This museum contains a collection of letters, sketches, and manuscripts by Dr. Heinrich Hoffmann, a Frankfurt physician and creator of the children's-book hero Struwwelpeter, or Slovenly Peter, the character you see as a puppet or doll in Frankfurt's shops. ✉ *Benderg. 1, Altstadt* ☎ *069/281–333* 🎫 *Free* ⏲ *Tues. and Thurs.–Sun. 11–5, Wed. 11–8* Ⓤ *Römer (U-bahn).*

Zeil. The heart of Frankfurt's shopping district is this bustling pedestrian street, running east from Hauptwache Square. You'll find almost every type of store here, including department stores, boutiques, drugstores, electronics shops, fast-food eateries, restaurants, and more. City officials claim it's the country's busiest shopping street. Ⓤ *Hauptwache, Konstablerwache (U-bahn and S-bahn).*

★ ❿ **Zoologischer Garten** (Zoo). Founded in 1858, this is one of the most important and attractive zoos in Europe. Its remarkable collection includes some 5,000 animals of 600 different species, a bears' castle, an exotarium (aquarium plus reptiles), and an aviary, reputedly the largest in Europe. Nocturnal creatures move about in a special section. The zoo has a restaurant and a café, along with afternoon concerts in summer. ✉ *Alfred-Brehm Pl. 16, Ostend* ☎ *069/2123–3735* 🌐 *www.zoo-frankfurt.de* 🎫 *€8* ⏲ *Nov.–Mar., daily 9–5; Apr.–Oct., daily 9–7* Ⓤ *Zoo (U-bahn).*

Sachsenhausen

★ The old quarter of Sachsenhausen, on the south bank of the Main River, has been sensitively preserved, and its cobblestone streets, half-timber houses, and beer gardens make it a very popular area to stroll. Sachsenhausen's two big attractions are the Museumufer (Museum Riverbank), which has seven museums almost next door to one another, and the famous *Apfelwein* (apple-wine or cider) taverns around the Rittergasse pedestrian area. A green pine wreath above a tavern's entrance tells passersby that a freshly pressed—and alcoholic—apple cider is on tap. You can eat well in these small establishments, too. Formerly a separate village, Sachsenhausen is said to have been established by Charlemagne, who settled the Main's banks with a group of Saxon families in the 8th century. It was an important bridgehead for the crusader Knights of the Teutonic Order and in 1318 officially became part of Frankfurt.

a good walk

The best place to begin is at the charming 17th-century villa housing the **Städtische Galerie Liebieghaus** 24 ⚑, the westernmost of the museums. It has an internationally famous collection of classical, medieval, and Renaissance sculpture. From it you need only turn to your right and follow the riverside road, Schaumainkai, for about 2 km (1 mi), passing all of the museums and winding up around the Rittergasse.

The **Städelsches Kunstinstitut und Städtische Galerie** 25 houses one of the most significant art collections in Germany, and the **Museum für Kommunikation** 26 displays postal coaches, ancient telephones that work, and a huge stamp collection. The **Deutsches Architekturmuseum** 27 traces man's structures from Stone Age huts to high-rises. Film artifacts and classic film videos are featured at the **Deutsches Filmmuseum** 28. After this museum, you could take a break at an Apfelwein tavern on Schweizer Strasse. The next museum, past the Untermain Brucke (Bridge), is the **Museum für Völkerkunde** 29, which holds ethnological artifacts from the Pacific, Indonesia, Africa, and America. A stunning collection of European and Asian applied art in the **Museum für Angewandte Kunst** 30 comes next. Continue down the river road (the name changes from Schaumainkai to Sachsenhäuser Ufer). Just beyond the first bridge carrying car traffic, follow Grosse Rittergasse to the right. A bit down this street, on your left, is the **Kuhhirtenturm** 31, the only remaining part of Sachsenhausen's original fortifications.

A few steps farther and you will be in the heart of the Apfelwein district, which is especially lively on summer evenings when it becomes one big outdoor festival. Some of the apple-wine taverns and other watering places are also open weekday afternoons. The area has a distinctly medieval air, with narrow back alleys, quaint little inns, and quiet squares that escaped the modern developer, yet it's also full of shops, cafés, and bars thronging with people. This is a great spot to relax and sample some apple-wine at the end of the day.

TIMING Allow an hour and 15 minutes for the Städelsches Kunstinstitut und Städtische Galerie, and an hour for the Städtische Galerie Liebieghaus. You could spend at least 45 minutes in each of the other museums along the walk.

What to See

27 **Deutsches Architekturmuseum** (German Architecture Museum). Created by German architect Oswald Mathias Ungers, this 19th-century villa contains an entirely modern interior. There are five floors of drawings, models, and audiovisual displays that chart the progress of architecture through the ages. ✉ *Schaumainkai 43, Sachsenhausen* ☎ *069/2123–8844* 🌐 *www.dam-online.de* 🎫 *€4* ⏲ *Tues. and Thurs.–Sun. 11–6, Wed. 11–8* Ⓤ *SchweizerPlatz (U-bahn).*

28 **Deutsches Filmmuseum** (German Film Museum). Germany's first museum of cinematography houses an exciting collection of film artifacts. Visitors can view its collection of classic film videos, and a theater in the basement has regular evening screenings of films ranging from avant-garde to Hungarian to silent-era flicks. ✉ *Schaumainkai 41, Sachsenhausen* ☎ *069/2123–8830* 🌐 *www.deutsches-filmmuseum.de* 🎫 *€2.50* 🕒 *Tues., Thurs.–Fri., and Sun. 10–5, Wed. 10–8, Sat. 2–8* Ⓤ *SchweizerPlatz (U-bahn).*

need a break?

Two of Sachsenhausen's liveliest Apfelwein taverns are well removed from the Rittergasse and handy to the Museumufer. You'll find them adjacent to one another if you turn south down Schweizer Strasse, next to the Deutsches Filmmuseum, and walk five minutes. **Zum Gemalten Haus** (✉ Schweizerstr. 67, Sachsenhausen ☎ 069/614–559) will provide all the hard cider and *gemütlichkeit* you could want. **Zum Wagner** (✉ Schweizerstr. 71, Sachsenhausen ☎ 069/612–565) reeks so with "old Sachsenhausen" schmaltz that it's downright corny.

31 **Kuhhirtenturm** (Shepherd's Tower). This is the last of nine towers, built in the 15th century, that formed part of Sachsenhausen's fortifications. The composer Paul Hindemith lived in the tower from 1923 to 1927 while working at the Frankfurt Opera. ✉ *Grosser Ritterg., Sachsenhausen* Ⓤ *SchweizerPlatz (U-bahn).*

26 **Museum für Kommunikation** (Museum for Communication). This is the place for getting in on the electronic age. You can surf the Internet, talk to one another on picture telephones, and learn of glass-fiber technology. Exhibitions on historic communication methods include mail coaches, stamps, ancient dial telephones with their clunky switching equipment, and a reconstructed 19th-century post office. ✉ *Schaumainkai 53, Sachsenhausen* ☎ *069/60600* 🌐 *www.museumsstiftung.de/frankfurt* 🎫 *€2* 🕒 *Tues.–Fri. 9–5, weekends 11–7* Ⓤ *SchweizerPlatz (U-bahn).*

30 **Museum für Angewandte Kunst** (Museum of Applied Arts). More than 30,000 objects representing European and Asian decorative arts are exhibited in this museum designed by American architect Richard Meier. The collection of furniture, glassware, and porcelain has expanded to include Web sites, computers, and graphic design. ✉ *Schaumainkai 17, Sachsenhausen* ☎ *069/2123–4037* 🌐 *www.museumfuerangewandtekunst.frankfurt.de* 🎫 *€5* 🕒 *Tues. and Thurs.–Sun. 10–5, Wed. 10–9* Ⓤ *SchweizerPlatz (U-bahn).*

29 **Museum für Völkerkunde** (Ethnological Museum). The lifestyles and customs of aboriginal societies from around the world are examined through items such as masks, ritual objects, and jewelry. ✉ *Schaumainkai 29, Sachsenhausen* ☎ *069/2123–1510* 🎫 *€3.50; free Wed.* 🕒 *Tues. and Thurs.–Sun. 10–5, Wed. 10–8* Ⓤ *SchweizerPlatz (U-bahn).*

★ 25 **Städelsches Kunstinstitut und Städtische Galerie** (Städel Art Institute and Municipal Gallery). You'll find one of Germany's most important art collections at this museum, with paintings by Dürer, Vermeer, Rembrandt,

Rubens, Monet, Renoir, and other masters. The section on German expressionism is particularly strong, with representative works by Frankfurt artist Max Beckmann. ✉ *Schaumainkai 63, Sachsenhausen* ☎ *069/605–0980* 🌐 *www.staedelmuseum.de* 🎫 *€8* ⏲ *Tues. and Fri.–Sun. 10–7, Wed.–Thurs. 10–9* Ⓤ *SchweizerPlatz (U-bahn).*

⚑ ★ 24 **Städtische Galerie Liebieghaus** (Liebieg Municipal Museum of Sculpture). The sculpture collection here, from 5,000 years of civilizations and epochs, is considered one of the most important in Europe. From antiquity the collection includes a statue of a Sumarian functionary and a relief from the temple of Egyptian king Sahure (2455–2443 BC). From the Middle Ages there's an 11th-century throned Madonna with child from Trier and from the Renaissance an altar relief by the noted Florentine sculptor Lucca della Robbia (1399–1482). Works such as the *Immaculata,* by Matthias Steinl (1688), represent the baroque era. Some pieces are exhibited in the lovely gardens surrounding the house. ✉ *Schaumainkai 71, Sachsenhausen* ☎ *069/2123–8617* 🌐 *www.liebieghaus.de* 🎫 *€4, free last Sat. of month* ⏲ *Tues. and Thurs.–Sun. 10–5, Wed. 10–8* Ⓤ *SchweizerPlatz (U-bahn).*

WHERE TO EAT

Business travelers keep the nicer restaurants busy, so be sure to make advance reservations for lunch or dinner whenever possible. Several upscale restaurants serve discounted lunch menus. For example, Erno's Bistro and Gargantua have midday menus for €25. At the apple-wine taverns there's always room for a few more people at the long tables, and patrons are very accommodating when it comes to squeezing together.

WHAT IT COSTS In Euros

	$$$$	$$$	$$	$	¢
AT DINNER	over €25	€21–€25	€16–€20	€9–€15	under €9

Restaurant prices are per person for a main course at dinner.

City Center

$–$$$ ✕ **Central Park.** From Thursday to Saturday, the bar here is just as popular as the restaurant, making this a prime spot for people-watching. The menu has a bit of everything: pasta, salads, seafood, vegetarian dishes, and German fare. Located near the Alte Oper (Old Opera), this is an excellent choice for post-concert dining and business entertaining. ✉ *Kaiserhofstr. 12* ☎ *069/9139–6146* 🌐 *www.central-park.com* 💳 *MC, V* ⏲ *Closed Sun.* Ⓤ *Alte Oper (U-bahn).*

★ $–$$$ ✕ **Maintower.** Atop the skyscraper that houses Hessischer Landesbank, this popular restaurant-cum-café-cum-bar captures an unbeatable view. Through 25-foot floor-to-ceiling windows, all of "Mainhattan" is at your feet. Prices are surprisingly reasonable, though you will have to pay €4.50 per person just to take the elevator up. The cuisine is part global, part regional. It's hard to get a table for supper, though it's less of a problem for afternoon coffee or an evening at the bar. ✉ *Neue*

Mainzerstr. 52–58, City Center ☎ *069/3650–4770* 💳 *AE, V* Ⓤ *Alte Oper (U-bahn).*

$–$$ ✕ **Embassy.** Its location near many of the city's largest banks makes it a venue for business lunches, but it's also a popular spot for socializing. This modern restaurant, bar, and lounge attracts many young professionals for dinner and evening drinks. The moderately priced menu offers contemporary dishes, including pizzas, pastas, salads, steaks, duck, and a long list of appetizers. Terrace seating is available in summer. ✉ *Zimmerweg 1 (corner of Mainzer Landstr.) City Center* ☎ *069/7409–0844* 💳 *AE, MC, V* ⏲ *Closed Sun.* Ⓤ *Taunusanlage (S-bahn).*

$–$$ ✕ **Garibaldi.** The fresh pasta and fun atmosphere are equally appealing at this Italian restaurant between the Alte Oper and Hauptwache. In response to its overwhelming popularity, the size of the dining room has been doubled. Selections of antipasti, seafood, pizzas, and pasta dishes are extensive, and the signature pasta is topped with freshly shaved truffles. Waiters are energetic and friendly, as is the chef, who occasionally mingles with diners. Reservations are highly recommended. ✉ *Klein Hochstr. 4, City Center* ☎ *069/2199–7644* 💳 *V* ⏲ *Closed Sun.* Ⓤ *Alte Oper (U-bahn).*

$–$$ ✕ **Steinernes Haus.** Diners share long wooden tables beneath prints of old Frankfurt and traditional clothing mounted on the walls. The house specialty is a rump steak brought to the table uncooked with a heated rock tablet on which it is prepared. The beef broth is the perfect antidote to cold weather. The menu has other old German standards along with daily specials. Traditional fare popular with locals includes *Rippchen* (smoked pork) and *Zigeunerhackbraten* (spicy meat loaf). If you don't specify a *Kleines,* or small glass of beer, you'll automatically get a liter mug. ✉ *Braubachstr. 35, Altstadt* ☎ *069/283–491* ✍ *Reservations essential* 💳 *MC, V* Ⓤ *Römer (U-bahn).*

$ ✕ **Café Karin.** An understated café that attracts an interesting cross section of patrons, this is a great place to breakfast (only a few euros), to recover from a shopping spree, or to eat something healthy in preparation for a night out. Sample the goat cheese salad or wholegrain ratatouille crepes. Cakes and baked goods come from a wholegrain bakery. There's a no-smoking section. ✉ *Grosser Hirschgraben 28, Altstadt* ☎ *069/295–217* 💳 *No credit cards* Ⓤ *Hauptwache (U-bahn and S-bahn).*

$ ✕ **Zwölf Apostel.** There are few inner-city restaurants who brew their own beer, and the "12 Apostles" is one of the pleasant exceptions. Enjoy homemade pilsners in the dimly-lit, cavernous cellar, and sample traditional German and Croatian dishes. It's a cozy place to relax, but not necessarily a great pick for those in a hurry—service tends to be slow. Servings are large and prices quite reasonable. ✉ *Rosenbergerstr. 1* ☎ *069/288–668* 💳 *MC, V* Ⓤ *Konstablerwache (U-bahn, S-bahn).*

¢–$ ✕ **Metropol.** Brunch is the main attraction at this café near the Römerberg and Dom. The dining room is large, and in the warmer months it's extended to include outdoor seating on a garden patio. In addition to the daily selection of tantalizing cakes and pastries, the menu features eggs, salads, pasta, and a few traditional German dishes. Take a quick break from sightseeing or relax for several hours with a good book.

Metropol is open daily until 1 AM. ✉ *Weckmarkt 13–15, City Center* ☎ *069/288–287* ▭ *V* Ⓤ *Römer (U-bahn).*

¢ ✕ **Altes Cafe Schneider.** Though it's not striking from the outside, this family-owned establishment has a warm and inviting interior. You can lounge on couches and armchairs while enjoying coffee and a variety of freshly baked treats. The main appeal here is a long list of cakes, pies, and other desserts, but the café also offers light fare such as quiche, soups, and salads. ✉ *Kaiserstr. 12* ☎ *069/281–447* ▭ *No credit cards* Ⓤ *Willy-Brandt-Platz (U-bahn).*

¢ ✕ **Souper.** Germans are among the world's best soup-makers, and one of Frankfurt's best varieties of hearty soups is found here. This small place, a favorite of locals in wintertime, sits on a small street between Hauptwache and the Römer. A selection of six to eight soups is offered daily, including such creations as Thai-coconut chicken and tomato soup with mozzarella. Eat at the counter or take your soup to go. They also serve sandwiches. ✉ *Weissadlerg. 3* ☎ *069/2972–4545* 📠 *069/2972–4544* 🌐 *www.souper.de* ▭ *No credit cards* ⏲ *Closed Sun.* Ⓤ *Hauptwache (U-bahn and S-bahn).*

Nordend/Bornheim

$–$$ ✕ **Harvey's.** This restaurant first achieved notoriety as a gay and lesbian hangout, deriving its name from San Francisco's martyred gay supervisor Harvey Milk. But the straight community has been coming here more and more to enjoy the imaginative menu, good music, friendly atmosphere, and chameleonlike changes in design, several times a year. Breakfast is served until 4 PM. ✉ *Bornheimer Landstr. 64, Nordend* ☎ *069/497–3032* ▭ *No credit cards* Ⓤ *Merianplatz (U-bahn).*

¢–$$ ✕ **El Pacifico.** Some of Frankfurt's best Mexican cuisine is found two blocks from Bergerstrasse, in this festive little place that appeals to patrons of all ages. Warm and colorful, this restaurant serves a variety of fruit-flavor margaritas, and is well known for its hearty chicken-wings appetizer. El Pacifico also offers a full menu of traditional Mexican fare, including burritos, enchiladas, and fajitas. The dimly lit dining room is fairly small; reservations are recommended on weekends. ✉ *Sandweg 79, Bornheim* ☎ *069/446–988* ▭ *AE* Ⓤ *Bornheim Mitte (U-bahn).*

¢–$$ ✕ **Grossenwahn.** The Nordend is noted for its "scene" establishments, and this corner locale is one of the best. The name translates as "megalomania," which says it all. One whiff of the air tells you that smoking is tolerated without restriction, and the menu is esoteric with German, Greek, Italian, and French elements. ✉ *Lenaustr. 97, Nordend* ☎ *069/599–356* ▭ *AE, MC, V* Ⓤ *Glauburgstr. (U-bahn).*

¢–$ ✕ **Weisse Lilie.** Come to this Bornheim favorite for the fresh garlic aioli and the paella, not to mention the reasonably priced red wines. The dark interior has wooden tables brightened by fresh-cut flowers and candles, making it a good spot for an intimate dinner or a large gathering. A variety of moderately priced tapas is always available. In summer you can dine outside, German style, at long tables. Reservations are recommended on weekends. ✉ *Bergerstr. 275* ☎ *069/453–860* ▭ *No credit cards* Ⓤ *Bornheim Mitte (U-bahn).*

Westend

★ $$$$ ✕ **Erno's Bistro.** This tiny, unpretentious looking place in a quiet Westend neighborhood seems like an unlikely candidate for "the best restaurant in Germany." Yet that's what one French critic called it. The bistro's specialty, fish, is often flown in daily from France. It's closed weekends, during the Christmas and Easter seasons, and during much of the summer—in other words, when its clientele, the well-heeled elite of the business community, are unlikely to be in town. ✉ *Liebigstr. 15, Westend* ☎ *069/721–997* ✍ *Reservations essential* ▭ *AE, DC, MC, V* ⏲ *Closed weekends and July–early Aug.* Ⓤ *Westend (U-bahn).*

$$$ Fodor'sChoice ★ ✕ **Gargantua.** One of Frankfurt's most creative chefs, Klaus Trebes, who doubles as a food columnist, serves up modern versions of German classics and French-accented dishes in a laid-back dining room decorated with contemporary art. His menu features dishes such as artichoke risotto with goose liver, lentil salad with stewed beef, and grilled dorado served on pureed white beans and pesto. One corner of the restaurant is reserved for those who want only to sample the outstanding wine list. ✉ *Liebigstr. 47, Westend* ☎ *069/720–718* ▭ *AE, MC, V* ⏲ *Closed Sun. No lunch Sat.* Ⓤ *Westend (U-bahn).*

$$–$$$ ✕ **Omonia.** This cozy cellar locale offers the best Greek cuisine in town. If you have a good appetite, try the Omonia Platter, with lamb in several forms and Greek-style pasta. Vegetarians go for the *mestos sestos,* a plate of lightly breaded, grilled vegetables served in a rich tomato-feta cheese sauce. The family-owned and -operated place is popular and the tables few, so make a reservation. ✉ *Vogtstr. 43, Westend* ☎ *069/593–314* ✍ *Reservations essential* ▭ *AE, DC, MC, V* ⏲ *No lunch weekends* Ⓤ *Holzhausenstr (U-bahn).*

$–$$$ ✕ **La Boveda.** This quaint but somewhat expensive restaurant is tucked inside the dimly lit basement of a Westend residential building. (La Boveda is Spanish for "wine cellar.") In addition to the smaller plates of tapas, the menu features a long list of larger dinner entrées. Especially interesting are the creative seafood combinations. And true to its name, La Boveda offers an extensive wine menu. Patio dining is available May through September. Reservations are recommended on weekends. ✉ *Feldbergstr 10, Westend* ☎ *069/723–220* 🌐 *www.la-boveda.de* ▭ *AE, MC, V* ⏲ *Closed Sun.* Ⓤ *Westend (U-bahn).*

¢–$ ✕ **Café Laumer.** The ambience of an old-time Viennese café is well preserved at this popular spot. It owes its literary tradition to Theodor Adorno, a philosopher and sociologist of the "Frankfurt School," who drank his daily coffee here. For fear of attracting more patrons than the often crowded café can handle, it isn't listed in the phone book. The café is open for breakfast, lunch, and afternoon coffee but closes at 7 PM. ✉ *Bockenheimer Landstr. 67, Westend* ☎ *069/727–912* ▭ *DC, MC, V* ⏲ *No dinner* Ⓤ *Westend (U-bahn).*

Sachsenhausen

★ $$$$ ✕ **Maingau Stuben.** Chef Werner Döpfner himself greets you and lights your candle at this excellent restaurant. A polished clientele is drawn by the linen tablecloths, subdued lighting, and such nearly forgotten prac-

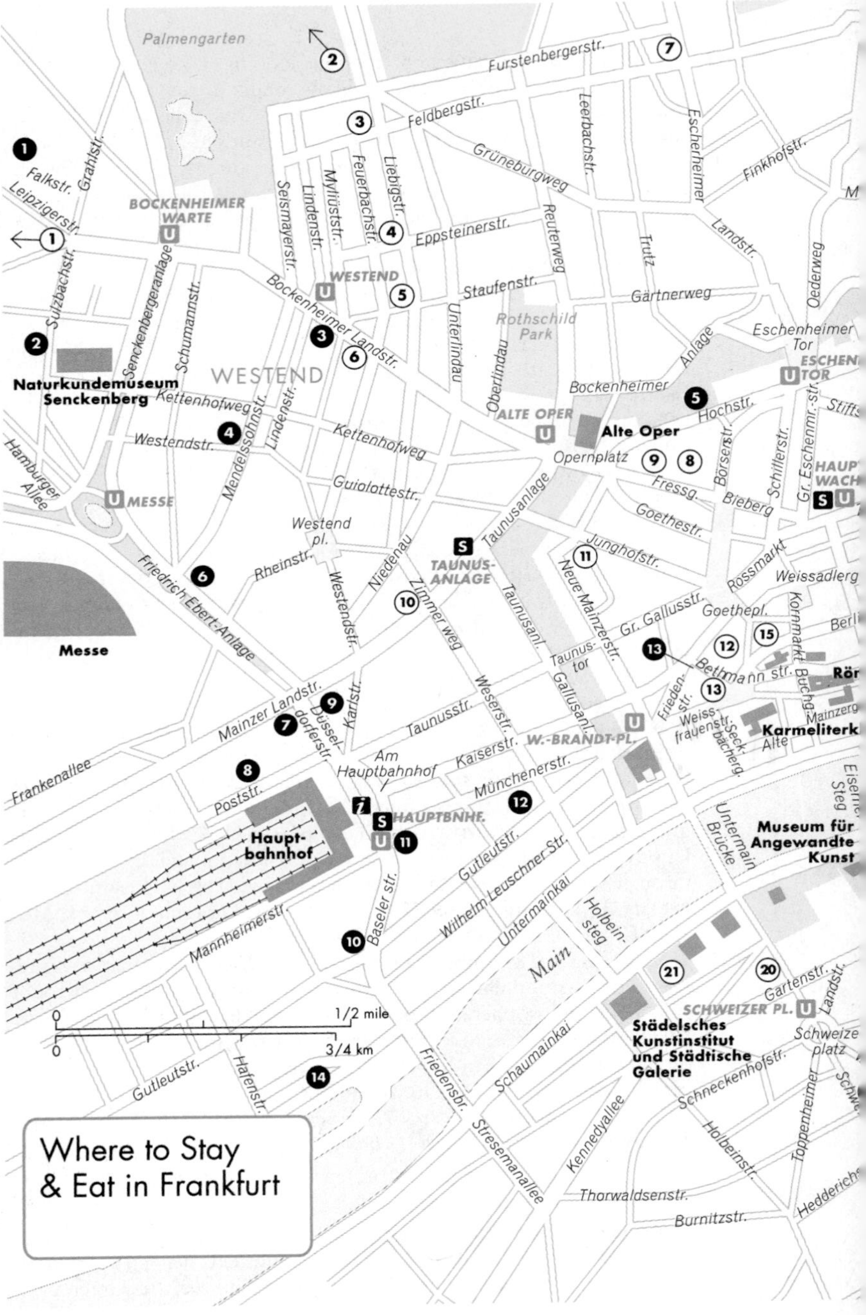
Palmengarten
Fürstenbergerstr.
Feldbergstr.
Grüneburgweg
Leerbachstr.
Eschenheimer Landstr.
Finkhofstr.
Falkstr.
Grahtstr.
Leipzigerstr.
BOCKENHEIMER WARTE
Seismayerstr.
Lindenstr.
Myliusstr.
Feuerbachstr.
Liebigstr.
Eppsteinerstr.
Reuterweg
Trutz
Sulzbachstr.
WESTEND
Staufenstr.
Gärtnerweg
Oederweg
Senckenbergeranlage
Schumannstr.
Bockenheimer Landstr.
Unterlindau
Oberlindau
Rothschild Park
Eschenheimer Tor
ESCHENHEIMER TOR
Naturkundemuseum Senckenberg
WESTEND
Bockenheimer Anlage
Kettenhofweg
Hochstr.
ALTE OPER
Alte Oper
Westendstr.
Mendelssohnstr.
Opernplatz
Fressg.
Börsenstr.
Schillerstr.
Gr. Eschenheimerstr.
HAUPTWACHE
Hamburger Allee
MESSE
Guiolottestr.
Bieberg
Goethestr.
Westend pl.
TAUNUSANLAGE
Taunusanlage
Junghofstr.
Rheinstr.
Niedenau
Westendstr.
Neue Mainzerstr.
Rossmarkt
Weissadlerg.
Friedrich-Ebert-Anlage
Zimmerweg
Taunusanl.
Goethepl.
Kornmarkt
Messe
Gr. Gallusstr.
Taunustor
Bethmannstr.
Buchg.
Weserstr.
Gallusanl.
Friedenstr.
Mainzer Landstr.
Düsseldorferstr.
Karlstr.
Taunusstr.
Weissfrauenstr.
Seckbächerg.
Karmeliterkloster
Alte Mainzerg.
W.-BRANDT-PL.
Frankenallee
Am Hauptbahnhof
Kaiserstr.
Münchenerstr.
Poststr.
HAUPTBNHF.
Hauptbahnhof
Gutleutstr.
Wilhelm Leuschner Str.
Untermainbrücke
Museum für Angewandte Kunst
Eiserner Steg
Baseler str.
Untermainkai
Holbeinsteg
Mannheimerstr.
Main
Gartenstr.
SCHWEIZER PL.
Landstr.
0
1/2 mile
0
3/4 km
Schaumainkai
Städelsches Kunstinstitut und Städtische Galerie
Schweizer platz
Schneckenhofstr.
Gutleutstr.
Hafenstr.
Friedensbr.
Stresemanallee
Kennedyallee
Holbeinstr.
Toppenheimer
Thorwaldsenstr.
Burnitzstr.
Heddericher
Where to Stay & Eat in Frankfurt

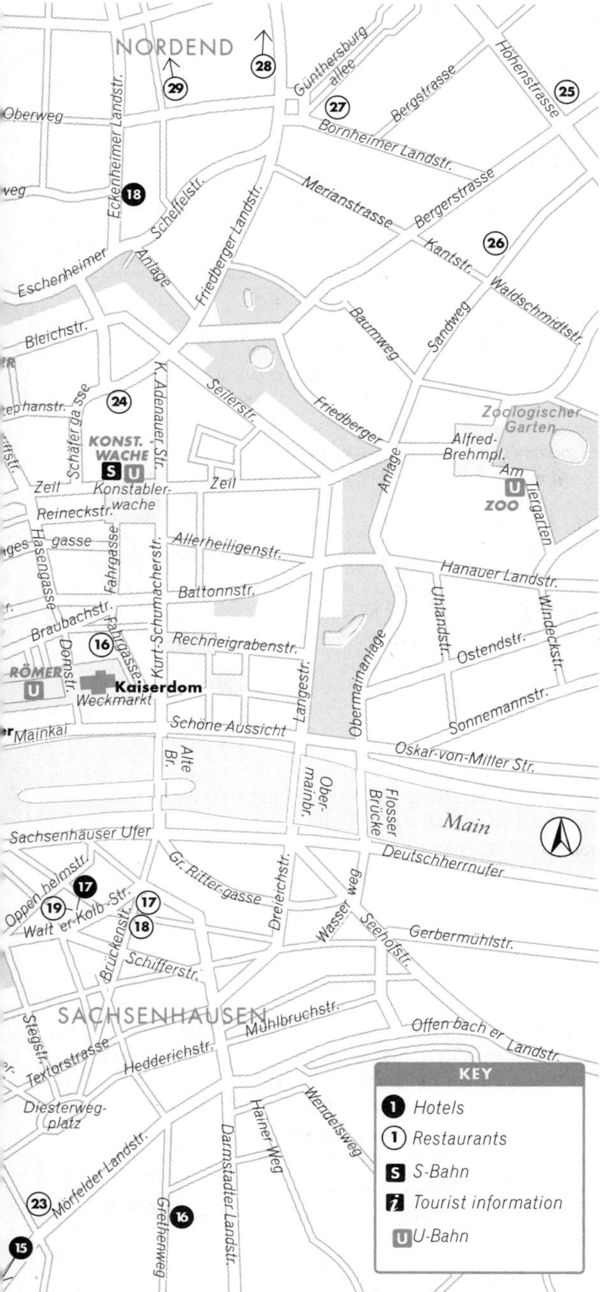

Restaurants

Altes Cafe Schneider 12
Altes Zollhaus 28
Amalfi 23
Arche Nova 1
Café Karin 13
Café Laumer 6
Central Park 8
El Pacifico 26
Embassy 10
Erno's Bistro 5
Fichtekränzi 18
Gargantua 4
Garibaldi 9
Grossenwahn 29
Harvey's 27
Holbeins 21
La Boveda 3
Lobster 17
Maingau Stuben 19
Maintower 11
Metropol 16
Omonia 7
Souper 15
Steinernes Haus 14
Taj Mahal 20
Wäldches 2
Weisse Lilie 25
Zum Wagner 22
Zwölf Apostle 24

Hotels

Am Berg 16
Art Hotel Robert Mayer 2
Bristol 7
Falk Hotel 1
Hessischer Hof 6
Hilton Frankfurt 5
Hotel Nizza 12
Hotel Westend 4
Ibis Friedensbrücke 14
InterCity Hotel 8
Maingau 17
Manhattan 9
Palmenhof 3
Pension Aller 10
Sheraton Frankfurt 15
Steigenberger Hotel Frankfurter Hof 13
Terminus 11
Villa Orange 18

CloseUp

APFELWEIN: SWEET, SOUR, OR STRAIGHT-UP?

***DON'T EXCEPT ANY WINE** from the vine at the city's better Apfelwein taverns. A restaurant that makes its own Apfelwein, or hard apple cider, will probably not offer anything of the grape variety. In fact, some don't even sell beer (aren't we in Germany?).*

Apfelwein, sometimes called ebbelwoi *by locals, is truly unique to Frankfurt and the surrounding state of Hessen. The drink was being made here as early as 794, when Charlemagne visited the city. To produce Apfelwein, juice from pressed apples is fermented for approximately eight weeks. Some restaurants make their own; others purchase it from farms outside the city. You may find that Apfelwein tastes like cider, or vinegar. Because it's rather sour, many people choose to mix it with sparkling water (called "sauergespritzt," or sour) or with lemonade (called "süssgespritzt," or sweet). Locals will be impressed, and may even tell you so, if they see you try it straight. Be careful, though: consuming large quantities of Apfelwein will make most stomachs unhappy.*

Most Apfelwein bars and restaurants serve the drink in bembels, gray-and-blue clay pitchers, which come in a variety of sizes. The drink is an especially nice accompaniment to the many pork dishes served in restaurants. You will notice that Germans, and especially Frankfurters, use apples heavily in their cooking—not just in Apfelwein. You might want to try some warm apple strudel (usually served with heavy cream or vanilla ice cream) or apple cakes (Apfel Kuchen) during your visit.

The largest concentration of Frankfurt Apfelwein establishments is in the old neighborhood of Sachsenhausen. If you want to visit a bar or restaurant that sells its own homemade Apfelwein, look for a pine wreath hanging over the door.

tices as carving the meat tableside. The menu includes contemporary dishes such as seafood salad with scallops and lobster mousse and rack of venison in a walnut crust. Dopfner also has a cellar full of rare German wines. ✉ *Schifferstr. 38–40, Sachsenhausen* ☎ *069/610–752* ▭ *AE, MC, V* ⏲ *Closed Mon. No lunch Sat., no dinner Sun.* Ⓤ *SchweizerPlatz (U-bahn).*

$–$$$ ✕ **Holbeins.** Portions are not large here, but selections on the international menu are creative. The elegantly modern dining room was built in the space between two museums on the Main River. Choose from a variety of pasta creations, fish, steak, and even a few traditional German dishes. Live piano (and sometimes jazz) is performed most evenings. ✉ *Holbeinstr. 1, Sachsenhausen* ☎ *069/6605–6666* ✍ *Reservations essential* ▭ *V* ⏲ *Closed Mon.* Ⓤ *SchweizerPlatz (U-bahn).*

$–$$$ ✕ **Taj Mahal.** Not only is this restaurant often referred to as the best place for Indian food in Frankfurt, but its staff are among the city's most attentive. The menu, a bit pricey, features authentic, delicious tandoori and marsala dishes. ✉ *Schweizerstr. 28, Sachsenhausen* ☎ *069/620–240* 🌐 *www.tajmahal-restaurant.de* ✍ *Reservations essential* ▭ *V* Ⓤ *SchweizerPlatz (U-bahn).*

$–$$ ✕ **Lobster.** This small Old Sachsenhausen restaurant is a favorite of locals and visitors alike. The menu, dramatically different from those of neighboring apple-wine taverns, offers mostly seafood. Fish and shellfish are prepared in a variety of international styles, but the strongest influence is French. Contrary to the restaurant's name, lobster does not appear on the regular menu, but it's occasionally offered as a daily special. This cozy restaurant also has a large collection of European wines. Reservations are strongly recommended on weekends. ✉ *Wallstr. 21, Sachsenhausen* ☎ *069/612–920* ▭ *V* Ⓤ *SchweizerPlatz (U-bahn).*

¢–$ ✕ **Amalfi.** Many locals say Amalfi turns out the best pizza in town, making it a popular lunch spot. In addition to pizza (both personal and larger sizes), pasta, antipasti, and salads are on the menu. Eat in or take it out. This is a great choice if you're dining on a budget, grabbing a quick meal, or simply craving tasty pizza. ✉ *Morfelder Landstr. 82, Sachsenhausen* ☎ *069/618–319* ▭ *No credit cards* Ⓤ *SchweizerPlatz (U-bahn).*

¢–$ ✕ **Fichtekränzi.** This is the real thing—a traditional apple-cider tavern in the heart of Sachsenhausen. In summer the courtyard is the place to be; in winter you sit in the noisy tavern at long tables with benches. It's often crowded, so if there isn't room when you arrive, order a glass of apple cider and hang around until someone leaves. Traditional cider-tavern dishes include Rippchen (smoked pork). ✉ *Wallstr. 5, Sachsenhausen* ☎ *069/612–778* ▭ *No credit cards* ⊙ *No lunch* Ⓤ *Lokalbahnhof (S-bahn).*

★ ¢–$ ✕ **Zum Wagner.** The kitchen produces the same hearty German dishes as other apple-wine taverns, only better. Try the schnitzel or *Tafelspitz mit Frankfurter Grüner Sosse* (stewed beef with a sauce of green herbs), or come on Friday for fresh fish. Beer and cider are served in large quantity in the often crowded, noisy dining room. This Sachsenhausen classic, with sepia-tone murals of merrymaking, succeeds in being touristy and traditional all at once. ✉ *Schweizerstr. 71, Sachsenhausen* ☎ *069/612–565* ▭ *No credit cards* Ⓤ *SchweizerPlatz (U-bahn).*

Outer Frankfurt

$–$$ ✕ **Altes Zollhaus.** Excellent versions of traditional German specialties are served in this beautiful, 200-year-old half-timber house on the edge of town. Try a game dish. In summer you can eat in the beautiful garden. To get here, take Bus 30 from Konstablerwache to Heiligenstock, or drive out on Bundestrasse 521 in the direction of Bad Vilbel. ✉ *Friedberger Landstr. 531, Seckbach* ☎ *069/472–707* ▭ *AE, DC, MC, V* ⊙ *Closed Mon. No lunch Mon.–Sat.*

¢–$$ ✕ **Arche Nova.** This sunny establishment is a feature of Frankfurt's Ökohaus, which was built according to environmental principles (solar panels, catching rainwater, etc.). It's more or less vegetarian, with such dishes as a vegetable platter with feta cheese or curry soup with grated coconut and banana. Much of what's served, even some of the beer, is organic. ✉ *Kasselerstr. 1a, Bockenheim* ☎ *069/707–5859* ▭ *No credit cards* Ⓤ *Bockenheimer Warte (U-bahn).*

★ ¢–$ ✕ **Wäldches.** This is Frankfurt's busiest brewpub. Though outside of town, it's a 10-minute walk from the Ginnheim U-bahn station and is a favorite stop for bikers and hikers. By noon on pleasant summer Sundays, the big beer garden is standing room only. The home-brewed light and dark beers go nicely with the largely German cuisine, which is substantial but not stodgy. If you like the beer, you can take some of it with you in an old-fashioned bottle with a wired porcelain stopper. ✉ *Am Ginnheimer Wäldchen 8, Ginnheim* ☎ *069/520–522* ▭ *No credit cards* ⊗ *No lunch Oct.–Mar.* Ⓤ *Ginnheim (U-bahn).*

WHERE TO STAY

Businesspeople descend on Frankfurt year-round, so most hotels in the city are expensive (though many offer significant reductions on weekends) and are frequently booked up well in advance. Many hotels add as much as a 50% surcharge during trade fairs (*Messen*), of which there are about 30 a year. You can contact the German National Tourist Office for the trade-fair schedule. The majority of the larger hotels are close to the main train station, fairgrounds, and business district (Bankenviertel) and are a 20-minute walk from the Old Town. Lower prices and—for some, anyway—more atmosphere are found at smaller hotels and pensions in the suburbs; the efficient public transportation network makes them easy to reach.

WHAT IT COSTS In Euros

	$$$$	$$$	$$	$	¢
FOR 2 PEOPLE	over €225	€175–€225	€100–€175	€50–€100	under €50

Hotel prices are for two people in a standard double room, including tax and service.

City Center

★ $$$$ **Hilton Frankfurt.** This respected chain's downtown Frankfurt location has all the perks the business traveler wants, from fax and modem lines to voice mail and video on command. Its Pacific Colors Restaurant has a large terrace overlooking a park. The Vista Bar & Lounge is just below the hotel's airy and transparent atrium. ✉ *Hochstr. 4, City Center, D–60313* ☎ *069/133–8000* 🖷 *069/1338–1338* 🌐 *www.frankfurt.hilton.com* *342 rooms* *Restaurant, room service, in-room safes, minibars, cable TV with movies and video games, in-room data ports, Web TV, Wi-Fi, indoor pool, health club, hair salon, hot tub, massage, sauna, steam room, 2 bars, meeting room, parking (fee), some pets allowed, no-smoking floors* ▭ *AE, DC, MC, V* Ⓤ *Eschenheimer Tor (U-bahn).*

$$$–$$$$ **Bristol.** You'll notice that great attention is paid to making you comfortable at the Bristol, one of the nicest hotels in the neighborhood around the main train station. The modern hotel features minimalistic decor in soothing earth tones. The brunch buffet, included in room rates, is impressive—offering a wide variety of warm and cold dishes—and can be enjoyed on the beautiful garden patio during warmer months. ✉ *Ludwigstr. 15 City Center, D–60327* ☎ *069/242–390* 🖷 *069/251–539* 🌐 *www.bristol-hotel.de* *145 rooms* *Restaurant, minibars, room service, cable TV with movies, in-room data ports, Wi-Fi, in-room safes, bar, meeting rooms, parking (fee)* ▭ *MC, V* Ⓤ *Hauptbahnhof (U-bahn and S-bahn).*

$$$–$$$$ **Hessischer Hof.** This is the choice of many businesspeople, not just for its proximity to the fairgrounds but also for the air of class that pervades its handsome interior (the exterior is nondescript). Many of the public room furnishings are antiques owned by the family of the Princes of Hessen. Rooms are done in either a British or a Biedermeyer style. The Sèvres Restaurant, so called for the fine display of that porcelain arranged along the walls, features excellent contemporary cuisine. Jimmy's is one of the cult bars in town. ✉ *Friedrich-Ebert-Anlage 40, Messe, D–60325* ☎ *069/75400* 🖷 *069/7540–2924* 🌐 *www.hessischer-hof.de* *106 rooms, 11 suites* *Restaurant, room service, minibars, cable TV, in-room data ports, bar, meeting rooms, parking (fee), some pets allowed, no-smoking rooms* 💳 *AE, DC, MC, V* Ⓤ *Messe (S-bahn).*

8

$$–$$$$ Fodor'sChoice ★ **Steigenberger Hotel Frankfurter Hof.** The neo-Gothic Frankfurter Hof is one of the city's oldest hotels, but its modern services earn it kudos from business publications around the world. The atmosphere is one of old-fashioned, formal elegance, with burnished woods, fresh flowers, and thick carpet. Kaiser Wilhelm once slept here, and so have modern heads of state. The hotel has rooms and suites, as well as five restaurants. Although it fronts on a courtyard, you must enter it through a modest side entrance. ✉ *Am Kaiserpl., City Center, D–60311* ☎ *069/21502* 🖷 *069/215–900* 🌐 *www.frankfurter-hof.steigenberger.com* *286 rooms, 46 suites* *5 restaurants, room service, minibars, cable TV with movies, in-room data ports, Wi-Fi, sauna, bar, concierge, Internet room, meeting rooms, parking (fee), some pets allowed (fee)* 💳 *AE, DC, MC, V* Ⓤ *Willy-Brandt-Platz (U-bahn).*

$$–$$$$ **Villa Orange.** This bright, charming hotel is centrally located, but tucked away from the bustle on a residential street. The moderately priced rooms include country-style furnishings and spacious bathrooms. The high-ceiling lobby and breakfast room are decorated with modern art, and there's a small library with a selection of English books. Hotel staff are friendly and accommodating. ✉ *Hebelstr. 1, Nordend, D–60318* ☎ *069/405–840* 🖷 *069/4058–4100* 🌐 *www.villa-orange.de* *38 rooms* *Minibars, cable TV, in-room data ports, Wi-Fi, bar, Internet room, meeting room, parking (fee), no-smoking rooms* 💳 *AE, MC, V* *BP* Ⓤ *Musterschule (U-bahn).*

★ **$–$$** **Hotel Nizza.** This beautiful Victorian building is furnished with antiques, and the proprietor added a modern touch in some bathrooms with her own artistic murals. There's a pleasant roof garden with lots of potted shrubbery where you can have breakfast with views of rooftops and the skyline. ✉ *Elbestr. 10, City Center, D–60329* ☎ *069/242–5380* 🖷 *069/2425–3830* *24 rooms, 21 with bath* *Cable TV, Web TV, bar, some pets allowed; no a/c* 💳 *MC, V* *CP* Ⓤ *Hauptbahnhof (U-bahn and S-bahn).*

$–$$ Fodor'sChoice ★ **InterCity Hotel.** InterCity hotels were set up by the Steigenberger chain with the business traveler in mind, and if there ever was a hotel at the vortex of arrivals and departures, it's this centrally located hostelry in an elegant old-world building. It's right across the street from the main train station, and guests get a pass good for unlimited travel on local public transportation. The station's underground garage is also at your disposal. ✉ *Poststr. 8, Bahnhof, D–60329* ☎ *069/273–910*

069/2739–1999 www.intercityhotel.de 384 rooms, 3 suites Restaurant, minibars, cable TV with movies, in-room data ports, Wi-Fi, bar, Internet room, business services, meeting rooms, some pets allowed (fee), no-smoking floor AE, DC, MC, V Hauptbahnhof (U-bahn and S-bahn).

$–$$ Manhattan. Get to all parts of town quickly from this modern hotel opposite the Hauptbahnhof. Rooms are fairly spacious, and you can connect to the Internet at one of the terminals in the lobby. There's no restaurant, but the hotel's bar is open around the clock. *Düsseldorferstr. 10, City Center, D–60329 069/269–5970 069/2695–97777 www.manhattan-hotel.com 60 rooms Cable TV, Wi-Fi, bar, Internet room, meeting room, no-smoking rooms; no a/c AE, MC, V Musterschule (U-bahn).*

$ Ibis Friedensbrücke. The Ibis is a reliable budget hotel offering simple, clean rooms. A short walk from both the main train station and the museums of Sachsenhausen, the hotel sits on a quiet street near the river. Breakfast may be purchased at an additional cost. *Speicherstr. 3–5, City Center, D–60327 069/273–030 069/237–024 www.accorhotels.com 233 rooms Cable TV, in-room data ports, Wi-Fi, bar, meeting room, parking (fee), no-smoking rooms MC, V Hauptbahnhof (U-bahn and S-bahn).*

$ Pension Aller. Quiet, solid comforts come for a modest price and with a friendly welcome at this pension near the main train station and river. The third floor of a sociologist's private home offers cozy, well-lighted rooms. Frau Kraus, the resident-owner, was born in this house nearly 60 years ago and is always eager to share city history and sightseeing recommendations with you. Reserve in advance, because it gets a lot of return guests. *Gutleutstr. 94, City Center, D–60329 069/252–596 069/232–330 www.pension-aller.de 10 rooms Meeting room, some pets allowed; no a/c, no phones in some rooms, no TV in some rooms, data ports in some rooms No credit cards Hauptbahnhof (U-bahn and S-bahn).*

$ Terminus. Across the street from the main train station, this modern, sparkling-clean hotel has its own underground garage. It somehow also manages to keep a quiet summer garden despite its location. The rooms are some of the least expensive in town and include a bath, TV, and phone. *Münchenerstr. 59, City Center, D–60329 069/242–320 069/237–411 107 rooms Restaurant, cable TV with movies, bar, Internet room, meeting rooms, parking (fee), some pets allowed; no a/c AE, DC, MC, V Hauptbahnhof (U-bahn and S-bahn).*

Westend

$$–$$$ Hotel Westend. "*Klein aber fein*" ("small but nice") is what Germans say about a place like this. Everywhere you turn in the stylish, family-run establishment, you'll trip over antiques. The hotel has no restaurant, but the classy neighborhood has plenty—some of which offer delivery service. *Westendstr. 15, Westend, D–60325 069/7898–8180 069/745–396 www.hotelwestend.com 20 rooms, 5 without bath Cable TV, in-room data ports, meeting rooms, some pets allowed; no a/c AE, DC, MC, V Westend (U-bahn).*

★ $$–$$$ **Palmenhof.** Near the botanical garden, this luxuriously modern hotel occupies a renovated art-nouveau building. The high-ceiling rooms have up-to-date comfort but retain the elegance of the old building. In the basement is a cozy restaurant, L'Artechoc, with a Mediterranean menu. ✉ *Bockenheimer Landstr. 89–91, Westend, D–60325* ☎ *069/753–0060* 🖷 *069/7530–0666* 🌐 *www.palmenhof.com* *46 rooms, 37 apartments, 2 suites* *Restaurant, some microwaves, cable TV with movies, in-room data ports, some pets allowed; no a/c* 💳 *AE, DC, MC* Ⓤ *Westend (U-bahn).*

Sachsenhausen

★ $–$$ **Maingau.** You'll find this pleasant hotel-restaurant in the middle of the lively Sachsenhausen quarter. Rooms are modest but spotless, comfortable, and equipped with TVs; the room rate includes a substantial breakfast buffet. Chef Werner Döpfner has made the restaurant, Maingau-Stuben, one of Frankfurt's best. (Caution: though the hotel is inexpensive, the restaurant is anything but!) ✉ *Schifferstr. 38–40, Sachsenhausen, D–60594* ☎ *069/609–140* 🖷 *069/620–790* 🌐 *www.maingau.de* *100 rooms* *Restaurant, room service, minibars, cable TV with video games, Wi-Fi, meeting rooms, some pets allowed; no a/c* 💳 *AE, MC, V* Ⓤ *SchweizerPlatz (U-bahn).*

¢–$ **Am Berg.** A colorful, romantic inn, the Am Berg is not so much a hotel as a nice guesthouse. Because of its location, hidden away in a residential area near the Sudbahnhof (south train station), many locals aren't even aware it exists. The Mock-Tudor–style hotel was built in the late 1800s and has a quiet backyard garden where guests may relax. Each room has its own unique decor. A stay here is worth much more than the price. Breakfast is an extra €9. ✉ *Grethenweg 23, Sachsenhausen, D–60598* ☎ *069/612–021* 🖷 *069/615–109* 🌐 *www.hotel-am-berg-ffm.de* *21 rooms* *No-smoking rooms* 💳 *MC, V* Ⓤ *Sudbahnhof (U-bahn).*

Outer Frankfurt

$$–$$$$ **Sheraton Frankfurt.** This huge hotel is immediately accessible to one of Frankfurt Airport's terminals. It, like the airport, is also adjacent to the Frankfurter Kreuz, the major autobahn intersection, with superhighway connections to all of Europe. No need to worry about noise, though—the rooms are all soundproof. In addition to the usual comforts, each room includes an answering machine and a modem. Forty-four of the rooms have ISDN connections that permit fax machines and printers; a few rooms are equipped with fax machines. ✉ *Hugo-Eckener-Ring 15, Flughafen Terminal 1, Airport, D–60549* ☎ *069/69770* 🖷 *069/6977–2209* 🌐 *www.sheraton.com/frankfurt* *1,006 rooms, 28 suites* *2 restaurants, minibars, cable TV with movies, in-room data ports, Wi-Fi, gym, massage, sauna, steam room, 2 bars, concierge, meeting rooms, parking (fee), some pets allowed, no-smoking rooms* 💳 *AE, DC, MC, V* Ⓤ *Flughafen (S-bahn).*

★ $$ **Art Hotel Robert Mayer.** For creative types who shun the sterile decor of hotel chains, this elegant villa dating from 1905 offers an alternative: 11 rooms, each decorated by a different Frankfurt artist, with furniture designs by the likes of Rietveld and Frank Lloyd Wright. The art tradition is stressed in a special weekend arrangement that includes an individual guided tour of an art museum. It has no restaurant, but a large breakfast buffet is included in the price of the room. ✉ *Robert-Mayer-Str. 44, Bockenheim, D–60486* ☎ *069/970–9100* 📠 *069/9709–1010* 🌐 *www.art-hotel-robert-mayer.de* *11 rooms, 1 suite* *Cable TV, in-room data ports, some pets allowed (fee); no a/c* 💳 *AE, DC, MC, V* *BP* Ⓤ *Bockenheimer Warte (U-bahn).*

$–$$ **Falk Hotel.** Although it's removed from Frankfurt's city center, this hotel is within walking distance of two U-bahn (subway) stations, and is a relatively inexpensive alternative for those on a budget. The location is especially interesting to younger travelers—two blocks from Leipzigerstrasse, it stands in the heart of the Bockenheim neighborhood, home of Goethe University and numerous ethnic cafés, bars, and shops. Rooms are simple yet comfortable. The staff is friendly and quick to offer help or advice. The room rate includes a full breakfast and discounted rates at a nearby fitness studio. ✉ *Falkstr. 38 A, Bockenheim, D–60487* ☎ *069/7191–8870* 📠 *069/7191–88777* 🌐 *www.hotel-falk.de* *29 rooms* *Restaurant, cable TV, in-room data ports, meeting room, no-smoking rooms; no a/c* 💳 *AE, MC, V* *CP* Ⓤ *Leipzigerstr., Bockenheimer Warte (U-bahn).*

NIGHTLIFE & THE ARTS

The Arts

Frankfurt has the largest budget for cultural affairs of any city in the country. The Städtische Bühnen—municipal theaters, including the city's opera company—are the prime venues. Frankfurt has what is probably the most lavish theater in the country, the Alte Oper, a magnificently ornate 19th-century opera house. The building is no longer used for opera but as a multipurpose hall for pop and classical concerts and dances.

Theater tickets can be purchased from the tourist office at Römerberg 27 and from theater box offices. **Best Tickets GmbH** (✉ Zeil 112–114, City Center ☎ 069/9139–7621) is downtown in the Zeilgalerie. **Frankfurt Ticket GmbH** (✉ Hauptwache Passage, City Center ☎ 069/134–0400) is one of the best ticket agencies. The **Karstadt department store** (✉ Zeil 90, City Center ☎ 069/294–848) doubles as a ticket office.

Ballet, Concerts & Opera

Telephone ticket sales for the Alte Oper, Frankfurt Opera, and Frankfurt Ballet are all handled through **Frankfurt Ticket** (☎ 069/134–0400). The most glamorous venue for classical-music concerts is the **Alte Oper** (✉ Opernpl., City Center); tickets to performances can range from €10 to nearly €150. The **Frankfurt Opera** (✉ Städtische Bühnen, Untermainanlage 11, City Center) has made a name for itself as a company for dramatic artistry. Sharing the same venue as the Frankfurt Opera is the **Frankfurt Ballet** (✉ Städtische Bühnen, Untermainanlage 11, City Center), world-renowned for its modern choreography.

The **Festhalle** (✉ Ludwig-Erhard-Anlage 1, Messe ☎ 069/7575–6404), on the fairgrounds, is the scene of many rock concerts, horse shows, ice shows, sporting events, and other large-scale spectaculars.

The city is also the home of the Radio-Sinfonie-Orchester Frankfurt, part of Hessischer Rundfunk. It performs regularly in the 850-seat **Kammermusiksaal** (✉ Bertramstr. 8, Dornbusch ☎ 069/550–123), part of that broadcasting operation's campuslike facilities.

Theater

Theatrical productions in Frankfurt are nearly always in German. For English-language productions, try the **English Theater** (✉ Kaiserstr. 52, City Center ☎ 069/2423–1620), which offers an array of musicals, thrillers, dramas, and comedy with British or American casts. The **Künstlerhaus Mouson Turm** (✉ Waldschmidtstr. 4, Nordend ☎ 069/4058–9520) is a cultural center that hosts a regular series of concerts of all kinds, as well as plays and exhibits. The municipally owned **Schauspielhaus** (✉ Willy-Brandt-Pl., City Center ☎ 069/134–0400) has a repertoire including works by Sophocles, Goethe, Shakespeare, Brecht, and Beckett. For a zany theatrical experience, try **Die Schmiere** (✉ Seckbächerg. 2, City Center ☎ 069/281–066), which offers trenchant satire and also disarmingly calls itself "the worst theater in the world." Renowned for international experimental productions, including dance theater and other forms of nonverbal drama, is **Theater am Turm** (TAT; ✉ Bockenheimer Warte, Bockenheim ☎ 069/134–0400), in the Bockenheimer Depot, a former trolley barn.

Nightlife

Frankfurt at night is a city of stark contrasts. Old hippies and sharply dressed bankers, Turkish and Greek guest workers, people on pensions, chess players, exhibitionists, and loners all have their piece of the action. People from the banking world seek different amusements than the city's 38,000 students, but their paths cross in such places as the cider taverns in Sachsenhausen and the gay bars of the Nordend. Sachsenhausen (Frankfurt's "Left Bank") is a good place to start for bars, clubs, and Apfelwein taverns. The ever-more-fashionable Nordend has an almost equal number of bars and clubs but fewer tourists. Frankfurt is one of Europe's leading cities for techno, the computer-generated music of ultrafast beats that's the anthem of German youth culture. Please note that most dance and nightclubs charge entrance fees ranging from €5 to €20. In addition, some trendy nightclubs, such as the Living and King Kamehameha, enforce dress codes—usually no jeans, tennis shoes, or khaki pants admitted. Most bars close between 2 AM and 4 AM.

Bars & Live Music Venues

A major trend in the night spots is the "After Work" or "After Hours" happy hour with half-price drinks, lasting usually from 5 or 6 PM to 9 or 10 PM one weekday per week. You can go to Jimmy's every weeknight, EuroDeli on Tuesday, the Studio Bar on Wednesday, and King Kamehameha on Thursday.

The tiny, cozy **Balalaika** (✉ Dreikönigstr. 30, Sachsenhausen ☎ 069/612–226) provides intimacy and live music without charging the high prices you'd expect. The secret is proprietress Anita Honis, a professional American singer from Harlem, who usually gets out her acoustic guitar several times during an evening.

Like much of the Marriott Hotel it's in, the **Champion's Bar** (✉ Hamburger Allee 2–10, Messe ☎ 069/7955–2540) is designed to make Americans feel at home. The wall is lined with jerseys, and autographed helmets and photographs of American athletes. The TV is tuned to baseball, football, and basketball broadcasts, and the food leans to buffalo wings, potato skins, and hamburgers. Parties take place on American holidays like Halloween, Thanksgiving, and Valentine's Day.

On Tuesday night, avoid waiting in line by arriving early at **EuroDeli** (✉ Neue Mainzerstr. 60–66 ☎ 069/2980–1950). Because it's near many of the city's major banks, it's a popular after-work hangout. A mix of popular music is played by a DJ most nights. Order cocktails and food at the bar.

Frankfurt teems with Irish pubs, but **Fox and Hound** (✉ Niedenau 2, Westend ☎ 069/9720–2009) is the only *English* pub in town. The patrons, mainly British, come to watch constant satellite transmissions of the latest football (soccer to Americans), rugby, and cricket matches. Enjoy the authentic pub grub (try the basket of chips), and participate in the Sunday-night quiz for free drinks and cash prizes. It's a noisy bunch.

★ **Jimmy's Bar** (✉ Friedrich-Ebert-Anlage 40, Messe ☎ 069/7540–2961) is classy and expensive—like the Hessischer Hof Hotel in which it's located. It's been the meeting place of the business elite since 1951, and what every other bar in town would like to be. The ladies are more chic; the gentlemen more charming; the pianist, who plays from 10 PM onward, more winning. The bar stools and lounge chairs are red leather, the bar of mahogany. There's hot food from the hotel kitchen until 3 AM. You must ring the doorbell to get in, although regulars have a key.

The **Luna Bar** (✉ Stiftstr. 6, City Center ☎ 069/294–774) is a cocktail lover's paradise, with good drinks at reasonable prices by Frankfurt standards. Dress is smart but casual, and there is live music twice a month.

Though it's also a restaurant, **Coconut Groove** (✉ Kaiserstr. 53 ☎ 069/2710–7999) is more popular as a drinking destination. A red bar runs half the length of its modern interior. "New-world" cuisine, such as Caribbean chicken rolls, pepper-encrusted tuna, and pumpkin soup are served late into the night.

University students and young professionals frequent the **Stereo Bar** (✉ Abstgässchen 7, Sachsenhausen ☎ 069/617–116), which has cheaper drinks than many other popular bars in town. You'll find it in a former wine cellar beneath a narrow Sachsenhausen alleyway. The carpeted walls are bright red, and there's an aquarium and tiny dance floor. DJs usually spin the music, though there are occasional live acts.

★ The soothing interior attracts many to **Unity** (✉ Hanauer Landstr. 2, Ostend) lounge in Frankfurt's east end (Ostend). Large couches line the walls of this dimly lit, three-room bar. A mix of rock, funk, and soul is played by a DJ in the center room, where small groups of people sometimes dance.

Caipirinhas and Long Island ice teas are specialties of the house at **Wega** (✉ Schweizerstr. 73, Sachsenhausen ☎ 069/617–564). This bar is especially popular with women who enjoy watching the buff male waiters and bartenders. Many come for dinner—the food is good—then stay late for drinking and mingling. Directly across the street is **Keepers Lounge** (✉ Schweizerstr. 78, Sachsenhausen ☎ 069/6060–7210), a modern bar that's constantly flooded with young professionals. The cocktail menu looks like a short novel.

Dance & Nightclubs

One of Germany's most revered DJ's, Sven Väth, spins regularly at **Cocoon Club** (✉ Carl-Benz-Str. 21 ☎ 069/5069–6948 🌐 www.cocoonclub.net). This ultra-modern nightclub has a spacious dance floor, three bars, and two restaurants serving Asian–European cuisine. Comfort is a priority throughout the expansive club filled with reclining chairs and couches, some of which are built into the walls. Techno is the presiding music genre. A night out here will take a toll on your wallet: a taxi is required to reach its location on the eastern edge of town, cover charges average €15, and cocktails are pricey. It's open Friday and Saturday only.

Beneath the heating pipes of a former brewery, **King Kamehameha** (✉ Hanauer Landstr. 192, Ostend ☎ 069/4800–3701) is designed to suit every type of night owl. You can relax in the quiet cocktail bar, dance to a house band, or see one of the many live concerts, cabarets, comedy acts, or fashion shows that take place on stage. Young professionals flock to the club's Thursday night after-work parties for the live music and special cocktail prices. It's closed Monday.

Trendy **Living XXL** (✉ Kaiserstr. 29, City Center ☎ 069/242–9370) is one of the biggest bar-restaurants in Germany and is as hyped as the Eurotower in which it's located, the headquarters of the European Central Bank. On Friday and Saturday it offers a "subdued" disco, geared to the easy-listening preferences of the banking community, but it's not so prudish as to exclude regular gay entertainment. Its spacious, terraced interior has drawn architectural praise.

The type of crowd at **Odeon** (✉ Seilerstr. 34 City Center ☎ 069/285–055 🌐 www.theodeon.de) depends on the night. The large club hosts student nights on Thursday, a "27 up Club" on Friday (party exclusively for guests 27 or older), disco nights on Saturday, as well as "black Mondays"—a night of soul, hip-hop and R&B music. It's housed in a beautiful white building that looks more like a museum.

There's not much that doesn't take place at the **Tigerpalast** (✉ Heiligkreuzg. 16–20, City Center ☎ 069/9200–2250). The best variety shows and circus performances entertain guests, who dine elegantly and get some dancing in themselves. Shows often sell out, so book tickets as far in advance as possible. Closed Monday.

In 2003, a former police headquarters was transformed into **Praesidium** (✉ Friedrich-Ebert-Anlage 11, Ostend ☎ 069/7474–3978), a huge nightclub on Frankfurt's west side. High ceilings, chandeliers, columns, and a grand staircase fill its stunning interior. Bars and sofas are scattered throughout the club; several DJs will often perform on a single night. Drinks are reasonably priced—compared to those of other Frankfurt dance clubs.

Jazz

The oldest jazz cellar in Germany, **Der Frankfurter Jazzkeller** (✉ Kleine Bockenheimerstr. 18a, City Center ☎ 069/288–537) was founded by legendary trumpeter Carlo Bohländer and has hosted such luminaries as Louis Armstrong. It offers hot, modern jazz, often free (otherwise the cover is around €20). It's closed Monday.

Anything can happen at **Dreikönigskeller** (✉ Färberstr. 71, Sachsenhausen ☎ 069/629–273): you might hear 1940s or '50s jazz, blues, funk, or indie-punk. It's patronized mostly by students, as well as a sprinkling of older hipsters, all smoking as voraciously as the musicians.

Sinkkasten (✉ Brönnerstr. 5–9, City Center ☎ 069/280–385), a Frankfurt musical institution, is a class act—a great place for jazz, rock, pop, and African music, often by unknown or hardly known groups. It's sometimes hard to get in but worth the effort. There's live music Monday through Wednesday and Saturday.

SPORTS & THE OUTDOORS

Despite the ever-present smog in summer, Frankfurt is full of parks and other green oases where you can breathe easier. South of the city, the huge, 4,000-acre **Stadtwald** makes Frankfurt one of Germany's most forested metropolises. The forest has innumerable paths and trails, bird sanctuaries, impressive sports stadiums, and a number of good restaurants. The Waldlehrpfad trail there leads past a series of rare trees, each identified by a small sign. The Oberschweinstiege stop on streetcar line 14 is right in the middle of the park. Alternately, you can take Bus 36 from Konstablerwache to Hainerweg.

The **Taunus Hills** are also a great getaway for Frankfurters. Take U-bahn 3 to Hohemark. In the Seckbach district, northeast of the city, Frankfurters hike the 590-foot **Lohrberg Hill.** The climb yields a fabulous view of the town and the Taunus, Spessart, and Odenwald hills. Along the way you'll also see the last remaining vineyard within the Frankfurt city limits, the Seckbach Vineyard. Take the U-4 subway to Seckbacher Landstrasse, then Bus 43 to Draisbornstrasse.

Biking

There are numerous biking paths within the city limits. The Stadtwald in the southern part of the city is crisscrossed with well-tended paths that are nice and flat. The city's riverbanks are, for the most part, lined with paths bikers can use. There are not only on both sides of the Main but also on the banks of the little Nidda River, which flows through Heddernheim, Eschersheim, Hausen, and Rödelheim before joining the

Main at Höchst. Some bikers also like the Taunus Hills, but note that word *Hills*.

Theo Intra's shop (✉ Westerbachstr. 273, Sossenheim ☎ 069/342–780) has a large selection of bikes, from tandems to racing models. It's located on the city's northern edge, convenient to the inviting trails of the Taunus. Take the U-6 or U-7 to Bockenheimer Warte, then Bus 50 to Carl-Sonnenschein-Strasse. Also on the edge of the city is **Fahrradverlieh Werkstatt** (✉ Am Burghof 55, Bonames ☎ 069/9504–1716), reachable by taking the U-2 suburban train from the Hauptwache to Kalbach. Bike rentals will cost you €6–€9 per day.

8

Fitness Centers

Near the central Hauptwache, the **Fitness Company** (✉ Zeil 109, City Center ☎ 069/9637–3100) has everything needed to work out. There are more than 60 aerobics and other classes and 150 different fitness machines, from Nautilus to StairMaster. English is spoken. A day's training costs €18. **CityFitness** (✉ Trakehnerstr. 5, Hausen ☎ 069/703–788) has an extensive program of bodybuilding, aerobics, and stretching, mainly in the evening and on weekends. An hour's course costs €10.

Ice-Skating

Home to the Lions, Frankfurt's ice-hockey team, the **Eissporthalle** (✉ Bornheimer Hang 4, Ostend ☎ 069/2123–0825, 069/941–4111 Lions schedule and tickets) is open to the public for ice-skating. The indoor and outdoor rinks are open daily 9 AM–10 PM during winter months. Cost is €5.

Jogging

The banks of the Main River are a good place to jog, and to avoid retracing your steps, you can always cross a bridge and return down the opposite side. In the Westend, **Grüneberg Park** is 2 km (1 mi) around, with a *Trimm Dich* (literally, "get fit") exercise facility in the northeast corner. The **Anlagenring,** a park following the line of the old city walls around the city, is also a popular route. For a vigorous forest run, go to the Stadtwald or the Taunus Hills.

Rollerblading

For sports enthusiasts who travel with Rollerblades, the Main riverbanks and Stadtwald are great locations for skating. And Tuesday nights (March through October) give visitors the chance to tour Frankfurt on wheels—join the weekly **In-line Skating Night** at 8 PM in Sachsenhausen. Starting outside the Zwischendurch bar (Dreieichstr. 34), you will cross the river and loop around the city, from west to east. The group returns to Zwischendurch two hours later for post-blading beers. Skates may be rented at **Sport Grācmann** (✉ Frankfurterstr. 57, Offenbach ☎ 069/800–3931) for €6–€12 per day.

Swimming

Incredible as it may seem, people used to swim along the banks of the Main. Pictures from the 1930s show happy crowds splashing in a roped-off area. Those days are long gone (you'd probably dissolve), but there are a number of indoor and outdoor pools. The often-crowded

Brentanobad (✉ Rödelheimer Parkweg, Rödelheim ☎ 069/2123–9020) is an outdoor pool surrounded by lawns and old trees. The **Stadionbad** (✉ Morfelder Landstr. 362, Niederrad ☎ 069/678–041) has an outdoor pool, a giant water chute, and exercise lawns. For everything from "adventure pools" and bowling to a sauna and fitness center, head to the **Titus Therme** (✉ Walter-Möller-Pl. 2, Nordweststadt ☎ 069/958–050) pool complex.

SHOPPING

Shopping Districts

The tree-shaded pedestrian zone of the **Zeil** is said to be the richest shop-'til-you-drop mile in Germany. Other cities ask where Frankfurt gets the figures to prove the boast, but there's no doubt that the Zeil, between Hauptwache and Konstablerwache, is incredible for its variety of department and specialty stores. The area abounds in arcades. The moderately priced **Zeilgallerie** (✉ Zeil 112–114, City Center ☎ 069/9207–3414) has 56 shops and an IMAX theater. The **Schillerpassage** (✉ Rahmhofstr. 2, City Center) is strong on men's and women's fashion boutiques.

The Zeil is only the centerpiece of the downtown shopping area. The subway station below the Hauptwache also doubles as a vast underground mall. West of the Hauptwache are two parallel streets highly regarded by shoppers. One is the luxurious **Goethestrasse,** lined with boutiques, art galleries, jewelry stores, and antiques shops. The other is **Grosse Bockenheimer Strasse,** better known as the Fressgasse ("Pig-Out Alley"). Cafés, restaurants, a shopping arcade, and pricey food stores line the street, tempting gourmands with everything from crumbly cheeses and smoked fish to vintage wines and chocolate creams. Heading south toward the cathedral and the river, you'll find an area of art and antiques shops on **Braubachstrasse, Fahrgasse,** and **Weckmarkt.** In addition to these major shopping areas, **Schweizerstrasse** in Sachsenhausen is home to many clothing boutiques, shops, galleries, and cafés. This street runs south through Sachsenhausen, starting from the Main riverbank.

Clothing Stores

Bailly Diehl (✉ Schweizerstr. 41, Sachsenhausen ☎ 069/9620–0018) is an upscale clothier offering a variety of fashions for both men and women. Most labels in this two-story collection are European.

All of the top women's labels are represented in Inge Winterberg's collection at **Class-X** (✉ Börsenstr. 7–11, City Center ☎ 069/131–0853). There are bags from Coccinelle, shoes from Free Lance, jewelry from Rio Berlin. Tailors can provide an item in another color or fabric if you like, but the styles can't be altered.

★ **Peek & Cloppenburg** (✉ Zeil 71–75, City Center ☎ 069/298–950) is a huge, nicely departmentalized clothing store where men and women can find what they need for the office, gym, and nightclub. Clothes range from easily affordable items to pricey labels.

Pfüller Modehaus (✉ Goethestr. 15–17, City Center ☎ 069/1337–8070) offers a wide range of choices on three floors for women, from classic to trendy, from lingerie to overcoats, from hats to stockings. Gavinci and Hugo Boss are just a few of the many labels sold.

Department Stores

There are two department stores on the Zeil, offering much in the way of clothing, furnishings, electronics, food, and other items. The **Galerie Kaufhof** (✉ Zeil 116–126, City Center ☎ 060/21910) has an array of up-to-date retailing practices including touch screens that describe products. (One tells you what wines at what temperature go with what food.) The Dinea Restaurant on the top floor has a striking view. The **Karstadt** (✉ Zeil 90, City Center ☎ 069/929–050) is similar to Galerie Kaufhof in variety, with the best gourmet-food department in town.

Flea Markets

Sachsenhausen's weekend flea market takes place on Saturday from 8 to 2 on the riverbank, between **Dürerstrasse** and the **Eiserner Steg.** Purveyors of the cheap have taken over. Get there early for the bargains, as the better-quality stuff gets snapped up quickly. Shopping success or no, the market can be fun for browsing.

Gift Ideas

Cold, hard cash is what springs to mind when in the financial capital of Germany, not souvenirs. Frankfurt does produce fine porcelain, though, and it can be bought at the **Höchster Porzellan Manufaktur,** in the suburb of Höchst.

One thing typical of Frankfurt is the Apfelwein (apple-wine). You can get a bottle of it at any grocery store, but more enduring souvenirs would be Bembel pitchers and glasses that are equally a part of the Apfelwein tradition. The blue-stoneware Bembels have a fat belly, and the glasses, usually with a crest, are ribbed to give them "traction" (in the old days this was good for preventing the glass from slipping from greasy hands). You can get the Bembels and glasses at just about any gift shop, but **Frankfurter Dippemarkt** (✉ Fahrg. 80, Altstadt ☎ 069/282–559) has a selection that will overwhelm you.

A famous children's book in Germany, *Struwwelpeter* (*Slovenly Peter*), was the work of a Frankfurt doctor, Heinrich Hoffmann. He wrote the poems and drew the rather amateurish pictures in 1844 just to warn his own children of the dire consequences of being naughty. The book has several English translations, one by Mark Twain no less. The **Struwwelpeter-Museum** (✉ Benderg. 1, Altstadt ☎ 069/281–333) has copies of some of them, including one with the German version on one page and the Mark Twain version facing.

An edible gift you can take home is the Frankfurter sausage. The hot dog, on a long roll, made its first appearance at Chicago's World's Columbian Exhibition in 1893, and this sausage, sent over in cans from ★ Frankfurt, was the basic ingredient. It's still available in cans. Try **Plöger** (✉ Grosse Bockenheimerstr. 30, City Center ☎ 069/138–7110) on the Fressgasse. One taste of this high-quality smoked sausage will convince you that American imitations resemble the true frankfurter only in size and shape.

Food & Drink

The pastry shop **Konditorei Lochner** (✉ Kalbächerg. 10, City Center ☎ 069/920–7320) has local delicacies such as *Bethmännchen und Brenten* (marzipan cookies) and *Frankfurter Kranz* (a kind of creamy cake). All types of sweets and pastries are found at the café **Laumer** (✉ Bockenheimer Landstr. 67, Westend ☎ 069/727–912).

Weinhandlung Dr. Teufel (✉ Kleiner Hirschgraben 4, City Center ☎ 069/283–236) is as good a place as any for the popular wines, and the best place in town for diversity. There's also a complete line of glasses, carafes, corkscrews and other accessories, and books on all aspects of viticulture.

SIDE TRIPS FROM FRANKFURT

Frankfurt is so centrally located in Germany that the list of possible excursions—day trips and longer treks—is nearly endless. It's the ideal starting point for journeys to the Rhineland, to the west; Heidelberg and the Neckar Valley, to the south; and Würzburg and Franconia, to the southeast.

Destinations reachable by the local transportation system include Höchst, Neu-Isenburg, and the Taunus Hills, which includes Bad Homburg and Kronberg. Just to the northwest and west of Frankfurt, the Taunus Hills are an area of mixed pine and hardwood forest, medieval castles, and photogenic towns that many Frankfurters regard as their own backyard. It's home to Frankfurt's wealthy bankers and businesspeople, and on weekends you can see them enjoying their playground: hiking through the hills, climbing the Grosse Feldberg, taking the waters at Bad Homburg's health-enhancing mineral springs, or just lazing in elegant stretches of parkland.

Bad Homburg

The Taunus Hills area has many royal associations. Emperor Wilhelm II, the infamous "kaiser" of World War I, spent a month each year at Bad Homburg, the area's principal city. And it was the kaiser's mother, the daughter of Britain's Queen Victoria, who built the magnificent palace, now a luxurious hotel, in the Taunus town of Kronberg. Another frequent visitor to Bad Homburg was Britain's Prince of Wales, later King Edward VII, who made the name *Homburg* world famous by attaching it to a hat.

Bad Homburg's greatest attraction has been the **Kurpark** (spa), in the heart of the Old Town, with more than 31 fountains. Romans first used the springs, which were rediscovered and made famous in the 19th century. In the park you'll find not only the popular, highly saline Elisabethenbrunnen Spring but also a Siamese temple and a Russian chapel, mementos left by more royal guests—King Chulalongkorn of Siam and Czar Nicholas II. The Kurpark is a good place to begin a walking tour of the town; Bad Homburg's **tourist office** (✉ Louisenstr. 58 ☎ 06172/1780) is in the nearby Kurhaus. ✉ *Between Paul-Ehrlich-Weg and Kaiser-Friedrich-Promenade.*

Adjacent to the Kurpark, the **casino** boasts with some justice that it is the "Mother of Monte Carlo." The first casino in Bad Homburg, and one of the first in the world, was established in 1841 but closed down in 1866 because Prussian law forbade gambling. The proprietor, François Blanc, then moved his operation to the French Riviera, and the Bad Homburg casino wasn't reopened until 1949. A bus runs between the casino and Frankfurt's Hauptbahnhof (south side). It leaves Frankfurt every hour on the hour between 2 PM and 10 PM and then hourly from 10:25 PM to 1:25 AM. Buses back to Frankfurt run every hour on the hour, from 4 PM to the casino's closing. The €6 fare will be refunded after the casino's full entry fee has been deducted. ✉ *Im Kurpark* ☎ *06172/17010* 🎫 *Full gaming area €2.50, slot machines only €1* ⏲ *Slot machines 2 PM–1:30 AM, remainder 3 PM–3 AM.*

The most historically noteworthy sight in Bad Homburg is the 17th-century **Schloss,** where the kaiser stayed when he was in residence. The 172-foot Weisser Turm (White Tower) is all that remains of the medieval castle that once stood here. The Schloss was built between 1680 and 1685 by Friedrich II of Hesse-Homburg, and a few alterations were made during the 19th century. The state apartments are exquisitely furnished, and the Spiegelkabinett (Hall of Mirrors) is especially worthy of a visit. In the surrounding park look for two venerable cedars from Lebanon, both now about 200 years old. ✉ *Herrng.* ☎ *06172/926–2147* 🎫 *€3.50* ⏲ *Mar.–Oct., Tues.–Sun. 10–5; Nov.–Feb., Tues.–Sun. 10–4.*

The **Hutmuseum** (Hat Museum), a part of the Museum im Gotisches Haus, is a shrine to headgear. Its collection includes everything from 18th-century three-corner hats to silk toppers, from simple bonnets to the massive, feathered creations of 19th-century milliners. But mainly it's a shrine to the distinguished hat that was developed in Bad Homburg and bears its name. The Homburg hat was made around the turn of the 20th century for Britain's Prince of Wales, later King Edward VII, a frequent visitor. He liked the shape of the Tyrolean hunting hat but found its green color and decorative feather a bit undignified. So, for him, the Homburg hatters removed the feather, turned the felt gray, and established a fashion item once worn by diplomats, state dignitaries, and other distinguished gentlemen worldwide. ✉ *Tannenwaldweg 102* ☎ *06172/37618* ⏲ *Tues. and Thurs.–Sat. 2–5, Wed. 2–7, Sun. noon–6.*

Just a short, convenient bus ride from Bad Homburg is the highest mountain in the Taunus, the 2,850-foot, eminently hikable **Grosse Feldberg.**

Only 6½ km (4 mi) from Bad Homburg, and accessible by direct bus service, is the **Römerkastell-Saalburg** (Saalburg Roman Fort). Built in AD 120, the fort could accommodate a cohort (500 men) and was part of the fortifications along the Limes Wall, which ran from the Danube River to the Rhine River and was meant to protect the Roman Empire from barbarian invasion. On the initiative of Kaiser Wilhelm II, the fort was rebuilt as the Romans originally left it—with wells, armories, parade grounds, and catapults, as well as shops, houses, baths, and temples. All of these are for viewing only. You can't take a bath or buy a souvenir in the shops, though there is a contemporary restaurant on the grounds. There is also a **museum** with Roman exhibits. The Saalburg is north of Bad Homburg on Route 456 in the direction of Usingen. ✉ *Saalburg-Kastell* ☎ *06175/93740* 🎟 *€2.50* ⏲ *Fort and museum Mar.–Oct., daily 9–6; Nov.–Feb., daily 9–4.*

About a 45-minute walk through the woods along a well-marked path from the Römerkastell-Saalburg is an open-air museum at **Hessenpark,** near Neu Anspach. The museum presents a clear picture of the world in which 18th- and 19th-century Hessians lived, using 135 acres of rebuilt villages with houses, schools, and farms typical of the time. The park, 15 km (9 mi) outside Bad Homburg in the direction of Usingen, can also be reached by public transportation. Take the Taunusbahn from the Frankfurt main station to Wehrheim; then transfer to Bus 514. ✉ *Laubweg, Neu-Anspach* ☎ *06081/5880* 🎟 *€4* ⏲ *Mar., Apr., Sept., and Oct., daily 9–6; May–Aug., daily 9–8.*

Where to Stay & Eat

Although most of the well-known spas in Bad Homburg have expensive restaurants, there are still enough affordable places to eat.

★ **$–$$$** ✕ **Zum Wasserweibchen.** Chef Inge Kuper is a local culinary legend. Although prices are high for some items on the menu, the portions are large. The clientele sometimes includes celebrities, and the service is friendly and unpretentious. You can't go wrong with the potato cakes with salmon mousse, the brisket of beef, or any of the desserts. ✉ *Am Mühlberg 57* ☎ *06172/29878* 💳 *AE, MC, V* ⏲ *Closed Sat.*

¢–$ ✕ **Kartoffelküche.** This simple restaurant serves traditional dishes accompanied by potatoes cooked every way imaginable. The potato and broccoli gratin and the potato pizza are excellent, and for dessert try potato strudel with vanilla sauce. ✉ *Audenstr. 4* ☎ *06172/21500* 💳 *AE, DC, MC, V.*

$$–$$$ ✕🏨 **Maritim Kurhaus Hotel.** Standing in a quiet location on the edge of the spa park but near the city center, the hotel offers large, richly furnished rooms with king-size beds and deep armchairs. Some rooms have balconies. The cozy Bürgerstube ($$) serves both solid German cuisine and international dishes. For late-night gamblers and those with early planes to catch, the hotel offers "early-bird breakfasts" from 11 PM to 6:30 AM. ✉ *Ludwigstr. 3, D–61348* ☎ *06172/6600* 📠 *06172/660–100* 🌐 *www.maritim.de* *148 rooms, 10 suites* *Restaurant, café, bar, cable TV with movies, in-room data ports, Wi-Fi, meeting rooms, some pets allowed (fee), no-smoking rooms; no a/c* 💳 *AE, DC, MC, V.*

★ **$$–$$$** 🏨 **Steigenberger Bad Homburg.** Renowned for catering to Europe's royalty in its pre–World War I heyday, this hotel began as the Ritters Parkhotel in 1883 after Conrad Ritter combined a row of villas opposite Kurpark. Though the Steigenberger group has since dropped the historic and prominent name, it knows how to cater to the still well-heeled clientele. Rooms are furnished in art-deco style, and Charley's Bistro evokes the spirit of *gaie Paris* with literary dinners and jazz brunches. The nearby park is ideal for jogging. ✉ *Kaiser-Friedrich-Promenade*

69–75, D–61348 ☎ 06172/1810 📠 06172/181–630 🌐 www.bad-homburg.steigenberger.com 152 rooms, 17 suites Restaurant, room service, in-room safes, minibars, cable TV, in-room data ports, gym, sauna, steam room, bar, laundry service, concierge, meeting rooms, no-smoking floor ▭ AE, DC, MC, V.

Kronberg

The Taunus town of Kronberg, 15 km (9 mi) northwest of Frankfurt, has a magnificent castle-hotel originally built by the daughter of Queen Victoria, and an open-air zoo. Kronberg's half-timber houses and crooked, winding streets, all on a steep hillside, were so picturesque that a whole 19th-century art movement, the Kronberger Malerkolonie, was inspired by them.

★ Established by a wealthy heir of the man who created the Opel automobile, the large **Opel Zoo** has more than 1,000 native and exotic animals, plus a petting zoo and an "adventure" playground with more than 100 rides and amusements. There's also a nature path, a geological garden, and a picnic area with grills that can be reserved. Camel and pony rides are offered in summer. ✉ *Königsteinerstr. 35* ☎ *06173/79749* €6 *Apr.–Sept., daily 8:30–6; Oct.–Mar., daily 9–5.*

Where to Stay

$$$$ **Schlosshotel Kronberg.** This magnificent palace was built for Kaiserin Victoria, daughter of the British queen of the same name and mother of Wilhelm II, the infamous kaiser of World War I. It's richly endowed with furnishings and works of art and is surrounded by a park with old trees, a grotto, a rose garden, and an 18-hole golf course. It's one of the few hotels left where you can leave your shoes outside your door for cleaning. Jimmy's Bar, with pianist, is a local rendezvous. Hotel guests receive complimentary visits to a nearby fitness center. ✉ *Hainstr. 25, D–61476 Kronberg im Taunus ☎ 06173/70101 📠 06173/701–267 🌐 www.schlosshotel-kronberg.de 51 rooms, 7 suites Restaurant, room service, minibars, cable TV with movies, bar, concierge, meeting rooms, some pets allowed (fee), no-smoking rooms; no a/c ▭ AE, DC, MC, V.*

Bad Homburg & Kronberg A to Z

BUS & TRAIN TRAVEL

Bad Homburg and Kronberg are easily reached by the S-bahn from Hauptwache, the main station, and other points in downtown Frankfurt. S-5 goes to Bad Homburg, S-4 to Kronberg. There's also a Taunusbahn (from the main station only) that stops in Bad Homburg and then continues into the far Taunus, including the Römerkastell-Saalburg and Wehrheim, with bus connections to Hessenpark.

CAR TRAVEL

Bad Homburg is about a 30- to 45-minute drive north of Frankfurt on A–5. You can get to Kronberg in about the same time by taking A–66 (Frankfurt–Wiesbaden) to the Nordwestkreuz interchange and following the signs to Eschborn and Kronberg.

VISITOR INFORMATION

The Bad Homburg tourist office is open until 6:30 PM weekdays, 2 PM Saturday, and is closed on Sunday. Kronberg's office closes at noon on weekdays and is closed the entire weekend.

Kur- und Kongress GmbH Bad Homburg ✉ Louisenstr. 58, D-61348 Bad Homburg ☎ 06172/1780 🌐 www.bad-homburg.de. **Verkehrs- und Kulturamt Kronberg** ✉ Katharinenstr. 7, D-61476 Kronberg ☎ 06173/703-220 🌐 www.kronberg.de.

Höchst

Take S-1 or S-2 suburban train from Frankfurt's main train station, Hauptwache, or Konstablerwache.

Höchst, a town with a castle and an Altstadt (Old Town) right out of a picture book, was not devastated by wartime bombing, so its castle and the market square, with its half-timber houses, are well preserved. The name *Höchst* is synonymous with chemicals because of the huge firm that has been here for more than a century. The historic part of town is well removed from the industrial area, and, indeed, the company Höchst has made major contributions to the Altstadt's fine state of repair. For a week in July the whole Alstadt is hung with lanterns for the Schlossfest, one of Frankfurt's more popular outdoor festivals.

The **Höchster Schloss,** first built in 1360, houses two **museums,** one about company history and one about Höchst history, the latter with an excellent collection of porcelain. (The castle and a nearby villa were used for decades following the war by the American military broadcaster AFN.) ✉ *Am Burggraben 3* ☎ *069/305–6988* *Free* *Daily 10–4.*

Höchst was once a porcelain-manufacturing town to rival Dresden and Vienna. Production ceased in the late 18th century but was revived by an enterprising businessman in 1965. Of special interest in town is the **Höchster Porzellan Manufaktur,** where you can watch the whole porcelain manufacturing process in the attractive "Porzellanhof." The store sells everything from figurines to dinner services, as well as a selection of glassware and silver. ✉ *Palleskestr. 32* ☎ *069/300–9020* *€10; €5 off any purchase* *Weekdays 9–6, Sat. 9–1.*

Not far from the Höchster Schloss, you can also see a fine exhibit of porcelain at the **Bolongaropalast** (Bolongaro Palace), a magnificent residence facing the river. It was built in the late 18th century by an Italian snuff manufacturer. Its facade—almost the length of a football field—is nothing to sneeze at. ✉ *Bolongarostr. at Königsteinerstr.* ☎ *069/3106–5520* *Free* *Daily 9–4.*

Höchst's most interesting attraction is the **Justiniuskirche** (Justinius Church), Frankfurt's oldest building. Dating from the 7th century, the church is part early Romanesque and part 15th-century Gothic. The view from the top of the hill is well worth the walk. ✉ *Justiniuspl. at Bolongarostr.*

Where to Stay

$ **Hotel-Schiff *Peter Schlott*.** The hotel ship is moored on the Main River, a 15-minute train or tram ride from the city center. Guest cabins are on the small side, but the river views more than compensate, and there's a common room with a television. It's not for you if you're subject to seasickness but ideal if you like to be rocked to sleep. ✉ *Bolongarostr. 25, D–65929* ☎ *069/300–4643* 🖷 *069/307–671* 🌐 *www.hotel-schiff-schlott.de* 🛏 *19 rooms, 10 with bath* ⚐ *Restaurant, some pets allowed; no a/c, no room phones, no room TVs* 💳 *AE, MC, V.*

FRANKFURT A TO Z

8

To research prices, get advice from other travelers, and book travel arrangements, visit www.fodors.com.

AIRPORTS & TRANSFERS

Flughafen Frankfurt Main is the biggest airport on the continent, second in Europe only to London's Heathrow. There are direct flights to Frankfurt from many U.S. cities and from all major European cities.

The airport is 10 km (6 mi) southwest of the downtown area by the A–5 autobahn, and has its own railway station for the high-speed InterCity (IC) and InterCity Express (ICE) trains. Getting into Frankfurt from the airport is easy. The S-bahn 8 (suburban train) runs from the airport to downtown. Most travelers get off at the Hauptbahnhof (main train station) or at Hauptwache, in the heart of Frankfurt. Trains run at least every 15 minutes, and the trip takes about 15 minutes. The one-way fare is €3.05. A taxi from the airport into the city center normally takes around 20 minutes; allow double that during rush hours. The fare is around €15. If driving a rental car from the airport, take the main road out of the airport and follow the signs reading STADTMITTE (downtown).

ℹ **Flughafen Frankfurt Main** ☎ 01805/372–4636 🌐 www.frankfurt-airport.de.

BUS TRAVEL TO & FROM FRANKFURT

Some 100 European cities have bus links with Frankfurt. Buses arrive at and depart from the south side of the Hauptbahnhof.

ℹ **Deutsche Touring** ✉ Am Römerhof 17, Rebstock ☎ 069/79030.

CAR TRAVEL

Frankfurt is the meeting point of a number of major autobahns. The most important are A–3, running south from Köln and then west on to Würzburg and Nürnberg, and A–5, running south from Giessen and then on toward Mannheim and Heidelberg. A complex series of beltways surrounds the city. If you're driving to Frankfurt on A–5 from either north or south, exit at Nordwestkreuz and follow A–66 to the Nordend district, just north of downtown. Driving south on A–3, exit onto A–66 and follow the signs to Frankfurt-Höchst and then the Nordwestkreuz. Driving west on A–3, exit at the Offenbacher Kreuz onto A–661 and follow the signs for Frankfurt-Stadtmitte.

Traffic, accidents, and construction can make driving in Frankfurt irritating. Speeders are caught with hidden cameras, and tow trucks cruise the streets in search of illegal parkers. On the positive side, there are many reasonably priced parking garages around the downtown area and a well-developed "park and ride" system with the suburban train lines.

The transit map shows nearly a hundred outlying stations with a "P" symbol beside them, meaning there is convenient parking there.

CONSULATES

Australia ✉ Grüneburgweg 58-62, Westend, D-60322 ☎ 069/905-580.

United Kingdom ✉ Bockenheimer Landstr. 42, Westend, D-60323 ☎ 069/170-0020.

United States ✉ Siesmayerstr. 21, Westend, D-60323 ☎ 069/75350.

EMERGENCIES

Ambulance & Fire Services ☎ 112.

Dentists ☎ 069/660-7271.

Doctors ☎ 069/19292.

Police ☎ 110.

ENGLISH-LANGUAGE MEDIA

British Bookshop ✉ Börsenstr. 17, City Center ☎ 069/280-492.

TELEVISION & RADIO Though the U.S. military has moved out of Frankfurt, the news, sports, and music of the American Forces Network, the celebrated soldier radio station, is still easy to receive. Its AM broadcast (primarily talk) is at 87.3; the FM signal (primarily music) is at 98.7.

TAXIS

Cabs are not always easy to hail from the sidewalk; some stop, whereas others will pick up only from the city's numerous taxi stands or outside hotels or the train station. You can always order a cab. Fares start at €2.05 (€2.55 in the evening) and increase by a per-kilometer (½ mi) charge of €1.48 for the first 3, €1.33 thereafter. Count on paying €6.50 for a short city ride.

Taxi Companies ☎ 069/250-001, 069/230-001, or 069/230-033.

TOURS

BOAT TOURS Day trips on the Main River and Rhine excursions run from March through October and leave from the Frankfurt Mainkai am Eiserner Steg, just south of the Römer complex.

Frankfurt Personenschiffahrt GmbH ✉ Mainkai 36, Altstadt ☎ 069/281-884.

BUS TOURS Two-and-a-half-hour city bus tours with English-speaking guides are offered throughout the year. From April through October tours leave from outside the main tourist information office at Römerberg 27 daily at 10 AM and 2 PM; you can also pick up these tours 15 minutes later from the south side of the train station. The tour includes the price of admission to the Goethehaus and the top of the Maintower. November through March, tours leave daily at 2, stopping at 2:15 at the south side of the train station. The cost is €22.50. Gray Line offers two-hour city tours by bus four times a day for €28.50. They leave from the line's office at Wiesenhüttenplatz 39, or they will pick you up at an inner-city hotel.

APPLEWINE EXPRESS TOUR You can easily find time for the one-hour Applewine Express (Ebbelwoi Express) tram tour. Offered daily, including many holidays, this tour gives you a quick look at the city's neighborhoods, a bit of Frankfurt history, and a chance to sample Apfelwein (a bottle, along with pretzels, is included in the €5 fare). You can't miss the brightly painted blue-and-red streetcar around town. Departures are from the Heide Strasse tram stop, near the Bornheim Mitte U-bahn station—the route takes you past the zoo, around the city center, across the bridge to Sachsenhausen, and then returns. Timetables change with the season, so it's best to call ahead (☎ 069/2132–2425).

Gray Line ✉ Wiesenhüttenpl. 39, City Center ☎ 069/230-492. **Tourist Office** ✉ Römerberg 27, Altstadt ☎ 069/2123-8708. **Verkehrsgesellschaft Frankfurt am Main** ☎ 069/2132-2425 City Transit Authority.

EXCURSION TOURS The Historische Eisenbahn Frankfurt runs a vintage steam train with a buffet car along the banks of the Main River on weekends. The train runs from the Eiserner Steg bridge west to Frankfurt-Griesham and east to Frankfurt-Mainkur. The fare is €4.

Deutsche Touring will take you to Rothenburg, Heidelberg, and the Black Forest. Gray Line has trips to the Rhine, the Black Forest, and the Romantic Road.

Deutsche Touring ✉ Am Römerhof 17, Rebstock ☎ 069/79030. **Gray Line** ✉ Wiesenhüttenpl. 39, City Center ☎ 069/230-492. **Historische Eisenbahn Frankfurt** ✉ Eisener Steg, Altstadt ☎ 069/436-093.

WALKING TOURS The tourist office's walking tours cover a variety of topics, including Goethe, Jewish history, literature, transportation, architecture, and business. Tours can also be tailored to your interests. For an English-speaking guide, the cost is €119 for up to two hours, and €59 per hour after that.

Tourist office ✉ Römerberg 27, Altstadt ☎ 069/2123-8800.

TRAIN TRAVEL

EuroCity, InterCity, and InterCity Express trains connect Frankfurt with all German cities and many major European ones. The InterCity Express line links Frankfurt with Berlin, Hamburg, Munich, and a number of other major hubs. All long-distance trains arrive at and depart from the Hauptbahnhof, and many also stop at the long-distance train station at the airport. Be aware that the red-light district is just northeast of the train station.

Deutsche Bahn (German Railways) ☎ 01805/996-633.

TRANSPORTATION AROUND FRANKFURT

Frankfurt's smooth-running, well-integrated public transportation system (called RMV) consists of the U-bahn (subway), S-bahn (suburban railway), Strassenbahn (streetcars), and buses. Fares for the entire system, which includes a very extensive surrounding area, are uniform, though they are based on a complex zone system. Within the time that your ticket is valid (one hour for most inner-city destinations), you can transfer from one part of the system to another.

A basic one-way ticket for a ride in the inner zone costs €1.90 during the peak hours of 6 AM–9 AM and 4 PM–6:30 PM weekdays (€1.60 the rest of the time). There's also a reduced *Kurzstrecke* ("short stretch") fare of €1.50 (€1.05 off-peak). A day ticket for unlimited travel in the inner zones costs €4.35.

DISCOUNT FARES The Frankfurt tourist office offers a one- or two-day ticket—the Frankfurt Card—allowing unlimited travel in the inner zone (and to the airport) and a 50% reduction on admission to 15 museums (€6.15 for one day, €9.75 for two days). If you're attending a conference in Frankfurt, go to the tourist office and ask for a Congress Ticket (€2.60), a one-day ticket valid for unlimited travel in the city and to the airport.

PAYING Tickets may be purchased from automatic vending machines, which are at all U-bahn and S-bahn stations. Each station has a list of short-stretch destinations that can be reached from it, and if you're going to one of them, press the *Kurzstrecke* button on the vending machine. There's a second vertical row of buttons for the lower children's fares. Vending machines also have an extensive list of what might be called "long-stretch" destinations, those beyond the city limits. Each has a number beside it. Press the appropriate buttons for this destination, and then for either the adult or child fare, and the proper fare will appear. If your destination isn't on either list, it's a standard fare. Machines accept coins and notes and make change. If you're caught without a ticket, there's a fine of €30.

Bus drivers also sell tickets, but only if you boarded at a stop that does not have a vending machine. Weekly and monthly tickets are sold at central ticket offices and newsstands.

TRAVEL AGENCIES

American Express International ✉ Theodor Heuss Allee 112, Bockenheim ☎ 069/97970. **Hapag-Lloyd Reisebüro** ✉ Kaiserstr. 14, City Center ☎ 069/216-216.

VISITOR INFORMATION

For advance information, write to the Tourismus und Congress GmbH Frankfurt–Main. The main tourist office is at Römerberg 27 in the heart of the Old Town. It's open weekdays 9:30–5:30 and weekends 10–4. There are two other information offices. One is in the main hall of the railroad station. The other, at Zeil 94a, is open weekdays 10–6 and Saturday 10–4. All three offices can help you find accommodations.

Two airport information offices can also help with accommodations. The airport's Flughafen-Information, on the first floor of Arrivals Hall B, is open daily 6 AM–10 PM. The DER Deutsches Reisebüro, in Terminal 1 Arrivals Hall B, is open weekdays 6 AM–8 PM and weekends 7 AM–1 PM. **Tourismus und Congress GmbH Frankfurt/Main** ✉ Kaiserstr. 56, City Center, D-60329 Frankfurt am Main ☎ 069/2123-8800 🌐 www.frankfurt.de. **Main tourist office** ✉ Römerberg 27, Altstadt ☎ 069/2123-8708.

The Pfalz & Rhine Terrace

9

WORD OF MOUTH

"The Pfalz is an area I recommend heartily . . . the wine—the wine!! . . . There are so many wonderful small towns along the Weinstrasse. I loved Deidesheim (the town just smells good). I look for Deidesheimer wine all the time but can seldom find it in the States. They keep the good stuff at home."

—Shanna

"[In Bad Dürkheim] be prepared for fun and LOTS of wine—they serve it up in LARGE glasses. Make sure you get one of the toy hammers that they sell—they have squeakers in them and everyone starts hitting one another over the head with them in time with the music. Have to be there. I think this particular festival was the second weekend of September."

—anissa

www.fodors.com/forums

Updated by
Kerry Brady

THE ROMANS PLANTED THE FIRST RHINELAND VINEYARDS 2,000 years ago. By the Middle Ages viticulture was flourishing at the hands of the church and the state, and a bustling wine trade had developed. This ancient vineyard area is now the state of Rheinland-Pfalz (Rhineland Palatinate), home to 6 of Germany's 13 wine-growing regions, including the 2 largest, Rheinhessen and the Pfalz. Bordered on the east by the Rhine and stretching from the French border north to Mainz, these two regions were the "wine cellar of the Holy Roman Empire." Thriving viticulture and splendid Romanesque cathedrals are the legacies of the bishops and emperors of Speyer, Worms, and Mainz. Two routes parallel to the Rhine link dozens of wine villages. In the Pfalz follow the Deutsche Weinstrasse (German Wine Road); in the eastern Rheinhessen (Rhine Terrace), the home of the mild wine Liebfraumilch, the Liebfrauenstrasse guides you from Worms to Mainz.

The Pfalz has a mild, sunny climate and an ambience to match. Vines carpet the foothills of the thickly forested Haardt Mountains, an extension of the Alsatian Vosges. The Pfälzerwald (Palatinate Forest) with its pine and chestnut trees is the region's other natural attraction. Hiking and cycling trails lead through the vineyards, the woods, and up to castles on the heights. As the Wine Road winds its way north from the French border, idyllic wine villages beckon with flower-draped facades and courtyards full of palms, oleanders, and fig trees. WEINVERKAUF (wine for sale) or WEINPROBE (wine-tasting) signs are posted everywhere, each one an invitation to stop in to sample the wines.

The border between the Pfalz and Rheinhessen is invisible. Yet a few miles into the hinterland, a profile takes shape. Rheinhessen is a region of gentle, rolling hills and expansive farmland, where grapes are but one of many crops; vineyards are often scattered miles apart. The slopes overlooking the Rhine between Worms and Mainz—the so-called Rhine Terrace—are a notable exception. This is a nearly uninterrupted ribbon of vines culminating with the famous vineyards of Oppenheim, Nierstein, and Nackenheim on the outskirts of Mainz.

Exploring the Pfalz & Rhine Terrace

The Pfalz and Rheinhessen wine regions lie west of the Rhine in the central and southern part of the state of Rheinland-Pfalz. The area between Schweigen-Rechtenbach, on the French border, and Neustadt is known as the Südliche Weinstrasse (Southern Wine Road, abbreviated SÜW) and is the most romantic and serpentine part of the Wine Road. The scene farther north is more spacious, and the vineyards fan out onto the vast Rhine Plain. The 45-km (28-mi) stretch between Worms and Mainz along the Rhine takes in Rheinhessen's most prestigious vineyards. From here you are poised to explore the northern portion of the Rhineland.

About the Restaurants

Lunch in this region is generally served from noon until 2 or 2:30, dinner from 6 until 9:30 or 10. Credit cards have gained acceptance, but many restaurants will only accept cash, or debit cards issued by a German bank. Casual attire is typically acceptable at restaurants here and

If time is short, it's best to explore the Pfalz and Rheinhessen by car. There are, however, many scenic paths for hikers and cyclists, and public transportation is excellent.

Numbers in the text correspond to numbers in the margin and on the Pfalz and the Rhine Terrace and Worms maps.

If you have 3 days

Start at the French border in **Schweigen-Rechtenbach** 1, and then visit two sites west of the Wine Road: enchanting Dörrenbach and the legendary **Burg Trifels,** near **Annweiler** 4. For a contrast, tour the Pompeian-style palace **Schloss Villa Ludwigshöhe,** overlooking Edenkoben on the Wine Road; then continue uphill via chairlift to the vantage point at the **Rietburg castle.** Stay overnight in **St. Martin** 5. The next day travel via **Neustadt** 6 to **Speyer** 7 to see the Romanesque imperial cathedral, the **Kaiserdom,** and the world's oldest bottle of wine, in the **Historisches Museum der Pfalz.** Backtrack to the Wine Road to overnight in either **Deidesheim** 8 or **Bad Dürkheim** 9. Begin your third day with a visit to the magnificent **Limburg Monastery** ruins above Bad Dürkheim. Continue north on the Wine Road, with detours to the romantic medieval towns of **Freinsheim** 10 and Neuleiningen. Your journey and the Wine Road end in **Bockenheim.**

If you have 5 days

From **Schweigen-Rechtenbach** 1 visit **Dörrenbach** before exploring the cliffs and castles of the **Wasgau** area west of **Bad Bergzabern** 2. Overnight in **Gleiszellen** or **Herxheim-Hayna.** Devote the second day to the sights between **Klingenmünster** and **Edenkoben,** with an excursion to **Burg Trifels.** After staying in **St. Martin** 5, see the **Kalmit,** the region's highest peak, before heading for **Speyer** 7. Back on the Wine Road, visit **Deidesheim** 8 en route to **Bad Dürkheim** 9, home base for two nights. In the morning visit **Limburg Monastery** or **Hardenburg Fortress**; then relax at the spa, hike or bike through the Palatinate Forest, or tour a wine estate. The final day take in the northern end of the Wine Road via **Freinsheim** 10 and Neuleiningen, before turning east to **Worms** 11–19 for a look at the amazing **Wormser Dom** and the **Judenfriedhof,** Europe's oldest and largest Jewish cemetery.

If you have 7 days

Follow the five-day itinerary above, overnighting in **Worms** 11–19 the fifth night. Proceed north on B–9 to see Rheinhessen's most famous wine villages. In **Oppenheim** 20 visit the **Katharinenkirche,** a beautiful Gothic church, and in **Nierstein** 21 enjoy a Rhine panorama. Spend a peaceful night in **Nackenheim** 22 or end the day in **Mainz** 23 with a pub crawl. On the seventh day see the **Mainzer Dom** and the **Gutenberg Museum,** devoted to the history of printing. Visit the **Kupferberg Sekt Cellars** for a sparkling finale to your trip.

reservations are generally not needed. "Gourmet temples" that require reservations and jacket and tie are noted as such in this chapter.

About the Hotels

Accommodations in all price categories are plentiful, but book in advance if your visit coincides with a large festival. Bed-and-breakfasts abound. Look for signs reading FREMDENZIMMER or ZIMMER FREI (rooms available). A *Ferienwohnung* (holiday apartment), abbreviated FeWo in tourist brochures, is an economical alternative if you plan to stay in one location for several nights. Given the region's proximity to Kaiserslautern, one of the 2006 FIFA World Cup venues, advance booking for all types of accommodation from mid-June through early July is strongly recommended.

WHAT IT COSTS In Euros

	$$$$	$$$	$$	$	¢
RESTAURANTS	over €25	€21–€25	€16–€20	€9–€15	under €9
HOTELS	over €225	€175–€225	€100–€175	€50–€100	under €50

Restaurant prices are per person for a main course at dinner. Hotel prices are for two people in a standard double room, including tax and service.

Timing

The wine-festival season begins in March with the *Mandelblüten* (blossoming of the almond trees) along the Wine Road and continues through October. By May the vines' tender shoots and leaves appear. As the wine harvest progresses in September and October, foliage takes on reddish-golden hues.

THE GERMAN WINE ROAD

The Wine Road spans the length of the Pfalz wine region. You can travel from north to south or vice versa. Given its central location, the Pfalz is convenient to visit before or after a trip to the Black Forest, Heidelberg, or the northern Rhineland.

Schweigen-Rechtenbach

1 *21 km (13 mi) southwest of Landau on B–38.*

The southernmost wine village of the Pfalz lies on the French border. During the economically depressed 1930s, local vintners established a route through the vineyards to promote tourism. The German Wine Road was inaugurated in 1935; a year later the massive stone **Deutsches Weintor** (German Wine Gate) was erected to add visual impact to the marketing concept. Halfway up the gateway is a platform that offers a fine view of the vineyards—to the south, French; to the north, German. Schweigen's 1-km (½-mi) **Weinlehrpfad** (educational wine path) wanders through the vineyards and, with signs and exhibits, explains the history of viticulture from Roman times to the present.

Biking, Hiking & Walking Country roads and traffic-free vineyard paths are a cyclist's paradise. There are also well-marked cycling trails, such as the *Radwanderweg Deutsche Weinstrasse,* which runs parallel to its namesake from the French border to Bockenheim, and the *Radweg* (cycling trail) along the Rhine between Worms and Mainz. The Palatinate Forest, Germany's largest single tract of woods, has more than 10,000 km (6,200 mi) of paths.

The Wanderweg Deutsche Weinstrasse, a walking route that traverses vineyards, woods, and wine villages, covers the length of the Pfalz. It connects with many trails in the Palatinate Forest that lead to Celtic and Roman landmarks and dozens of castles dating primarily from the 11th to 13th centuries. In Rheinhessen you can hike along two marked trails parallel to the Rhine: the Rheinterrassenwanderweg and the Rheinhöhenweg along the heights.

Festivals Wine and *Sekt* (sparkling wine) flow freely from March through October at festivals that include parades, fireworks, and rides. The Pfalz is home to the world's largest wine festival in mid-September, the Dürkheimer Wurstmarkt ("sausage market," so named because of the 400,000 pounds of sausage consumed during eight days of merrymaking). In Neustadt, the German Wine Queen is crowned during the 10-day Deutsches Weinlesefest (German wine harvest festival) in October. The Mainzer Johannisnacht (in honor of Johannes Gutenberg) in late June, the Wormser Backfischfest (fried-fish festival) in late August, and the Brezelfest (pretzel festival) in Speyer on the second weekend in July are the major wine and folk festivals along this part of the Rhine.

On the Menu The best introduction to regional country cooking is the *Pfälzer Teller,* a platter of bratwurst (grilled sausage), *Leberknödel* (liver dumplings), and slices of *Saumagen* (a spicy meat-and-potato mixture encased in a sow's stomach), with *Weinkraut* (sauerkraut braised in wine) and *Kartoffelpüree* (mashed potatoes) on the side. Rheinhessen is known for the hearty casseroles *Dippe-Has* (hare and pork baked in red wine) and *Backes Grumbeere* (scalloped potatoes cooked with bacon, sour cream, white wine, and a layer of pork). *Spargel* (asparagus); *Wild* (game); chestnuts; and mushrooms, particularly *Pfifferlinge* (chanterelles), are seasonal favorites. During the grape harvest, from September through November, try *Federweisser* (fermenting grape juice) and *Zwiebelkuchen* (onion quiche)—specialties unique to the wine country.

Local Wine Savor the local wines. Those from Rheinhessen are often sleeker and less voluminous than their Pfälzer counterparts. Many are sold as *offene Weine* (wines by the glass) and are *trocken* (dry) or *halbtrocken* (semidry). The classic white varieties are Riesling, Silvaner, Müller-Thurgau (also called Rivaner), Grauburgunder (Pinot Gris), and Weissburgunder (Pinot Blanc); Spätburgunder (Pinot Noir), Dornfelder, and Portugieser are the most popular red wines. The word *Weissherbst,* after the grape variety, signals a rosé wine.

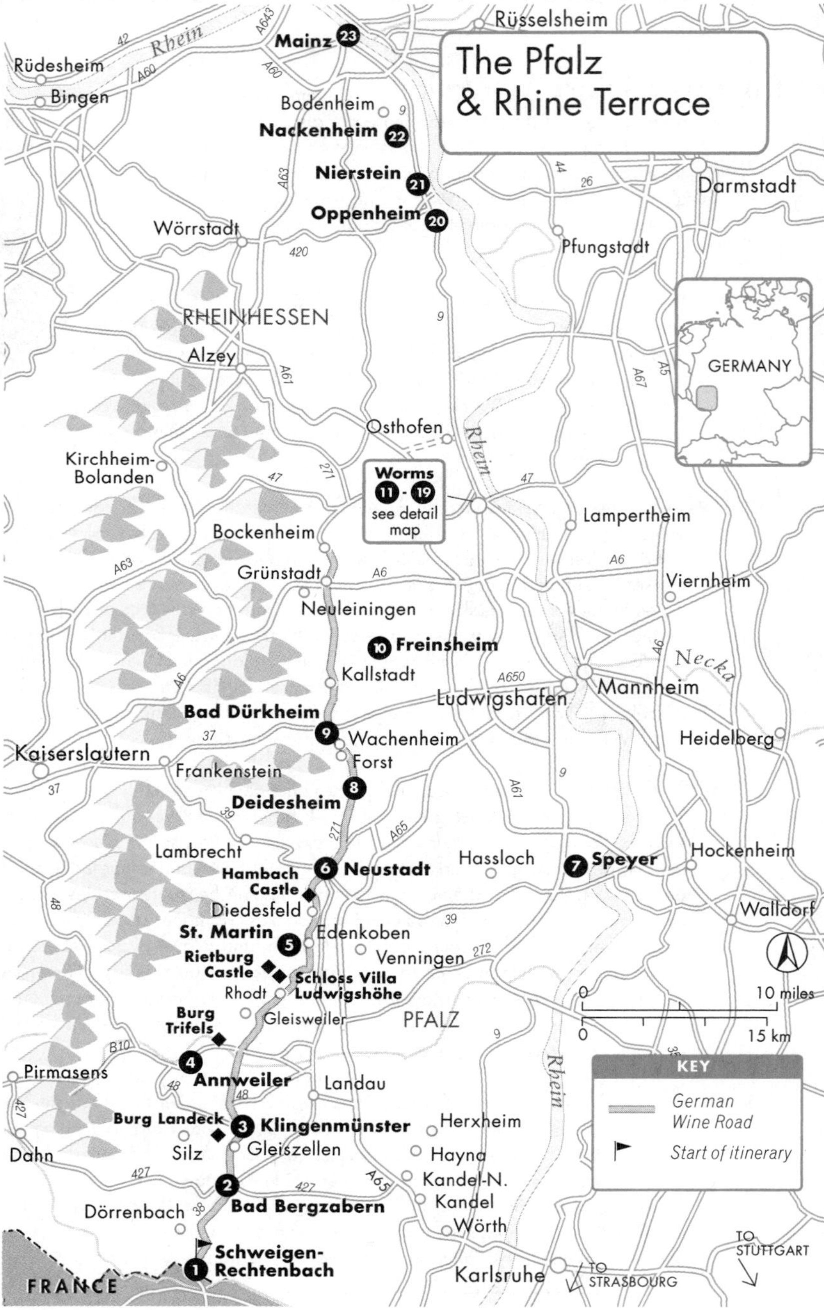
The Pfalz
& Rhine Terrace
Rüdesheim
Bingen
Rhein
Mainz 23
Rüsselsheim
Bodenheim
Nackenheim 22
Nierstein 21
Oppenheim 20
Darmstadt
Wörrstadt
Pfungstadt
RHEINHESSEN
Alzey
GERMANY
Osthofen
Kirchheim-
Bolanden
Worms
11 - 19
see detail
map
Lampertheim
Bockenheim
Grünstadt
Viernheim
Neuleiningen
10 Freinsheim
Kallstadt
Necka
Mannheim
Ludwigshafen
Bad Dürkheim
9 Wachenheim
Kaiserslautern
Forst
Frankenstein
Heidelberg
8
Deidesheim
Lambrecht
6 Neustadt
Hassloch
7 Speyer
Hockenheim
Hambach
Castle
Diedesfeld
Walldorf
St. Martin
5 Edenkoben
Venningen
Rietburg
Castle
Schloss Villa
Ludwigshöhe
Rhodt
Gleisweiler
Burg
Trifels
PFALZ
0 10 miles
0 15 km
4
Annweiler
Pirmasens
Landau
KEY
German
Wine Road
Start of itinerary
Burg Landeck
3 Klingenmünster
Herxheim
Silz
Gleiszellen
Dahn
Hayna
2
Kandel-N.
Bad Bergzabern
Kandel
Dörrenbach
Wörth
Schweigen-
1 Rechtenbach
FRANCE
Karlsruhe
TO
STRASBOURG
TO
STUTTGART

en route

Drive north on B–38 toward Bad Bergzabern. Two kilometers (1 mi) before you reach the town, turn left to see the enchanting village of **Dörrenbach.** It has an uncommon Gothic *Wehrkirche* (fortified church) that overlooks the Renaissance town hall, considered the most beautiful half-timber building in the Pfalz.

Bad Bergzabern

2 *10 km (6 mi) north of Schweigen-Rechtenbach on B–38.*

The landmark of this little spa town is the baroque **Schloss** (palace) of the dukes of Zweibrücken. Walk into the courtyard to see the elaborate portals of earlier residences on the site. The town's other gem is an impressive stone building with scrolled gables and decorative oriels. Built about 1600, it houses the wine restaurant **Zum Engel.** There are many historic facades to admire along Marktstrasse. Stop at No. 48, **Café Herzog,** to sample *Weinperlen* (wine pearls), unusual wine-filled chocolates, or the ice-cream version, *Weinperleneis.* Other scrumptious homemade treats here include "Adam and Eve" (sweet, peppery chocolates) as well as ice cream in almond blossom, rose, fig, or Dornfelder red-wine flavors. "Duchess Karoline" chocolates, cake, and ice cream (based on bitter orange) debuted in 2005. The café is closed Wednesday morning and Monday.

Where to Stay & Eat

$–$$ ✕ **Zum Engel.** Enjoy Palatinate specialties or *Käs'Spätzle mit Rostzwiebeln* (a cheese-gratin pasta dish topped with fried onions) in the prettiest Renaissance house of the Pfalz. Despite the name, a *kleine Portion* (small serving) of tender, juicy *Tafelspitz mit Meerrettich* (boiled beef with horseradish) is quite generous and as reasonably priced as Willi Egger's selection of local wines. ✉ *Königstr. 45, Bad Bergzabern* ☎ *06343/989–300* ▭ *MC, V* ⊙ *Closed Wed. and 2 wks Feb.–Mar.*

$$ Fodor'sChoice ★ ✕▦ **Hotel–Restaurant Zur Krone.** The simple facade belies this upscale inn that offers modern facilities, tasteful decor, and above all, a warm welcome from the Kuntz family. Reservations are essential at the main restaurant ($$$$). Start with chef Karl-Emil Kuntz's *Gruss aus der Küche* ("greetings from the kitchen"). This medley of appetizers was served at a luncheon in Mainz in April 2005 for President George W. Bush, who commented: "It was wonderful." Terrines and parfaits are specialties, as is the homemade goat cheese. The same kitchen team cooks for the Pfälzer Stube ($$–$$$; no lunch Tuesday). The wine list is excellent. Hayna, an idyllic suburb of Herxheim, lies between the Rhine and the Wine Road, 20 km (12 mi) east of Bad Bergzabern via B–427. ✉ *Hauptstr. 62–64, D–76863 Herxheim-Hayna* ☎ *07276/5080* 📠 *07276/50814* 🌐 *www.hotelkrone.de* *50 rooms, 3 suites* *2 restaurants, minibars, cable TV, in-room broadband, Wi-Fi, 2 tennis courts, indoor pool, massage, sauna, steam room, bicycles, bar, lobby lounge, pub, babysitting, dry cleaning, laundry service, Internet room, business services, some pets allowed (fee), no-smoking rooms; no a/c* ▭ *AE, MC, V* ⊙ *Restaurant Zur Krone closed Mon. and Tues., 1st 2 wks in Jan., and 2 wks July and Aug. No lunch* *BP.*

$ **Gasthof Zum Lam.** Flowers cascade from the windowsills of this half-timber inn in the heart of Gleiszellen (to the north of Bad Bergzabern). Exposed beams add rustic charm to the airy rooms; the bathrooms are bright and very modern. Eleven of the rooms are in the main house, three are close by. The restaurant (¢–$$) is inviting with its dome-shape tile stove and natural stone walls. In summer you can dine in front of the house, in the courtyard, or on a vine-shaded terrace. *Winzerg. 37, D–76889 Gleiszellen 06343/939–212 06343/939–213 www.zum-lam.de 14 rooms Restaurant, cable TV, beer garden, some pets allowed (fee); no a/c, no phones in some rooms No credit cards Hotel closed 3 wks Jan. Restaurant closed Wed. No lunch Nov.–Apr. BP.*

en route

Continue north on the Wine Road—now B–48 (B–38 leads to Landau)—toward Klingenmünster. Four kilometers (2½ mi) north of Bad Bergzabern turn left and drive to **Gleiszellen** to see the Winzergasse (Vintners' Lane). This little vine-canopied street is lined with a beautiful ensemble of half-timber houses. Try a glass of the town's specialty: spicy, aromatic Muskateller wine, a rarity seldom found elsewhere in Germany.

Klingenmünster

3 *8 km (5 mi) north of Bad Bergzabern on B–48.*

The village grew out of the **Benedictine monastery** founded here by the Merovingian king Dagobert in the 7th century. The monastery church is still in use. Despite its baroque appearance, parts of it date from the 12th century, as do the remains of the cloister. On the hillside are ruins of **Burg Landeck,** built around 1200 to protect the monastery. The keep and inner walls are accessible via a drawbridge that spans a 33-foot-deep moat. A walk through the chestnut forest from the monastery to the castle takes a half hour. Your reward will be a magnificent view over the Rhine Valley and south as far as the Black Forest.

Annweiler

4 *11 km (7 mi) northwest of Klingenmünster at junction of B–48 and B–10.*

In 1219 Annweiler was declared a Free Imperial City by Emperor Friedrich II. Stroll along Wassergasse, Gerbergasse (Tanners' Lane), and Quodgasse to see the half-timber houses and the waterwheels on the Queich River, which is more like a creek. Annweiler is a gateway to the **Wasgau,** the romantic southern portion of the Palatinate Forest, marked by sandstone cliffs and ancient castles. Festivities at the Triftfest in late June focus on the history of the once-important timber industry and the work of lumberjacks a century ago. The fruits of the forest are celebrated in early October, when local chefs present chestnut-theme menus during the *Käschdefescht* (chestnut festival).

★ **Burg Trifels,** one of Germany's most imposing castles, is perched on the highest of three sandstone bluffs overlooking Annweiler. Celts, Romans, and Salians all had settlements on this site, but it was under the Hohenstaufen emperors (12th and 13th centuries) that Trifels was built on a grand scale. It housed the crown jewels from 1125 to 1274 (replicas are on display today). It was also an imperial prison, perhaps where Richard the Lion-Hearted was held captive in 1193–94.

Although it was never conquered, the fortress was severely damaged by lightning in 1602. Reconstruction began in 1938, shaped by visions of grandeur to create a national shrine of the imperial past. Accordingly, the monumental proportions of some parts of today's castle bear no resemblance to those of the original Romanesque structure. The imperial hall is a grand setting for the *Serenaden* (concerts) held in summer. You can experience the ambience of the Middle Ages at the Burgfest, held on the first weekend in August. ☎ *06346/8470* 🌐 *www.burgen-rlp.de* 🎫 *€2.60* ⏲ *Easter–Oct., daily 9–6; Nov. and Jan.–Mar., daily 9–5.*

Museum unterm Trifels. A historic mill, tanners' houses, and a tannery "beneath Trifels" showcase diverse artifacts and models that chronicle the development of Burg Trifels, Annweiler, and the natural surroundings. The museum ticket entitles reduced admission at Burg Trifels and the Shoe Factory Museum in Hauenstein. ✉ *Am Schipkapass 4* ☎ *06346/1682* 🎫 *€2.60* ⏲ *Mid-Mar.–Oct., Tues.–Sun. 10–5; Nov.–mid-Mar., weekends 1–5.*

off the beaten path

MUSEUM "DIE SCHUHFABRIK" (Shoe Factory Museum) – In this former shoe factory in Hauenstein, 12 km (7½ mi) west of Annweiler on B–10, you can learn about the history of shoemaking, once an important industry in this part of Germany. Demonstrations on historical machinery and 15 nearby factory outlet stores (open April to October, Sunday 1 to 6, in addition to regular opening hours) make this a worthwhile excursion. ✉ *Turnstr. 5* ☎ *06392/915–165* 🌐 *www.deutsches-schuhmuseum.de* 🎫 *€3.20* ⏲ *Mid-Dec.–Feb., weekdays 1–4, weekends 10–4; Mar.–mid-Dec., daily 10–5.*

DIE GLÄSERNE SCHUHFABRIK – You can watch workers produce handmade footwear during working hours and on tours at the Seibel family's glass-lined shoe factory—home of The European Comfort Shoe™. ✉ *Waldenburgerstr. 1* ☎ *06392/922–1371* 🌐 *www.glaeserne-schuhfabrik.de* 🎫 *Free* ⏲ *Apr.–Oct., weekdays 10–5, weekends 1–5; Nov.–Mar., weekdays 10–noon and 12:45–4. Year-round, weekday tours 10:30 and 2:30; Apr.–Oct., weekends 2:30.*

Where to Stay & Eat

¢–$ ✕ **Restaurant s'Reiwerle.** Enjoy Pfälzer cuisine and chestnut-based dishes, such as *Keschtebrieh* (chestnut soup), in this 300-year-old half-timber house. Braised lamb with a creamy cranberry sauce is the house specialty. *Reiwerle* (RYE vair leh) is dialect for a spigot to tap wine from a cask. ✉ *Flitschberg 7* ☎ *06346/929–362* 💳 *No credit cards* ⏲ *Closed Jan., Feb., and 2 wks in Aug.*

★ ¢–$ ✕ **Zur alten Gerberei.** An open fireplace, exposed beams, and sandstone walls give this old *Gerberei* (tannery) a cozy feel. The Queich flows right past the outdoor seats. In addition to Pfälzer specialties and vegetarian dishes, you can try Alsatian *Flammkuchen,* similar to pizza but baked on a wafer-thin crust. There are 15 Pfälzer wines available by the glass. ✉ *Am Prangertshof 11, at Gerberg.* ☎ *06346/3566* 🌐 *www.gerberei.de* ▭ *No credit cards* ⏲ *Closed Mon. and 4 wks Jan. and Feb. No lunch Tues.–Sat.*

$–$$ ✕🏨 **Landhaus Herrenberg.** A flower-filled courtyard welcomes guests to this country inn. The rooms are modern and spacious (there's a whirlpool in the suite), with blond-wood furnishings. The Lergenmüllers are vintners known for excellent red wines. In the restaurant ($–$$), Chef Cuscuna Pasquale showcases their wines with fresh, seasonal dishes using local ingredients, and a Mediterranean touch. ✉ *Lindenbergstr. 72, D–76829 Landau-Nussdorf* ☎ *06341/60205* 📠 *06341/60709* 🌐 *www.landhaus-herrenberg.de* *8 rooms, 1 suite* *Restaurant, minibars, cable TV, Weinstube, some pets allowed (fee), no-smoking rooms; no a/c, no room phones* ▭ *MC, V (hotel); no credit cards (restaurant)* ⏲ *Restaurant closed Thurs. No lunch Mon.–Sat.* 🍽 *BP.*

Sports & the Outdoors

BIKING & HIKING Dozens of marked trails guide you to the Wasgau's striking geological formations and castles carved into the sandstone cliffs. From Annweiler you can access many of these trails via a circular tour by car (55½ km [35 mi]). Proceed west on B–10 to Hinterweidenthal (16½ km [10 mi]), then south on B–427 to Dahn (7 km [4 mi]), and continue southeast to Erlenbach (9 km [5½ mi]). Return to Annweiler via Vorderweidenthal (1 km [½ mi]) and Silz (7 km [4 mi]). Each town is a good starting point for a scenic ride, climb, or hike.

Shopping

The **süw Shop** (✉ An der Kreuzmühle 2 ☎ 06341/940–407), in Landau's Südliche Weinstrasse regional tourist office, sells gift items, grape products, wine-related accessories, and detailed maps of cycling and hiking trails. The shop is closed Friday afternoon and weekends.

Schloss Villa Ludwigshöhe

★ *24 km (15 mi) north of Annweiler, slightly west of Edenkoben on the Wine Rd.*

Bavaria's King Ludwig I built a summer residence on the slopes overlooking Edenkoben, in what he called "the most beautiful square mile of my realm." You can reach the neoclassical Schloss Villa Ludwigshöhe by car or bus from Edenkoben or take a scenic 45-minute walk through the vineyards along the Weinlehrpfad. Historical wine presses and vintners' tools are displayed at intervals along the path. It starts at the corner of Landauer Strasse and Villa Strasse in Edenkoben.

The layout and decor—Pompeian-style murals, splendid parquet floors, and Biedermeier and Empire furnishings—of the palace provide quite a contrast to medieval castles elsewhere in the Pfalz. An extensive collection of paintings and prints by the leading German impressionist Max Slevogt (1868–1932) is on display. Tours begin on the hour and are included in the admission fee. ☎ *06323/93016* 🌐 *www.burgen-rlp.de*

€2.60 *Apr.–Sept., Tues.–Sun. 9–6; Oct., Nov., and Jan.–Mar., Tues.–Sun. 9–5.*

From Schloss Villa Ludwigshöhe you can hike (30 minutes) or ride the Rietburgbahn chairlift (10 minutes) up to the **Rietburg** castle ruins for a sweeping view of the Pfalz. A restaurant, game park, and playground are on the grounds. *Chairlift €5 round-trip, €3.50 one-way Mar., Sun. 9–5; Apr.–Oct., weekdays 9–5, weekends 9–6.*

Where to Stay & Eat

$$ **Alte Rebschule.** Sonja Hafen's modern, beautifully appointed hotel on the edge of the forest was once an old *Rebschule* (vine nursery). Fireside seating in the lobby lounge, elegant table settings, and spacious rooms (all with balcony) make for a pleasant, peaceful stay. Light, seasonal cuisine with Asian and Mediterranean accents is served à la carte ($–$$) and in very reasonably priced prix-fixe menus. Sign up for a themed excursion (wine, culture, nature) and ask about health and wellness treatments. Rhodt proper is a 15-minute walk from the hotel. Be sure to take a stroll along Theresienstrasse with its venerable old chestnut trees. It's one of the most picturesque lanes of the Pfalz. *3 km (2 mi) west of Schloss Villa Ludwigshöhe, Theresienstr. 200 D–76835 Rhodt u. Rietburg 06323/70440 06323/704–470 www.alte-rebschule.de 29 rooms, 1 suite Restaurant, minibars, cable TV, in-room broadband, in-room data ports, sauna, spa, steam room, bar, lobby lounge, babysitting, dry cleaning, laundry service, Internet room, business services, some pets allowed (fee); no a/c, no smoking MC, V BP.*

St. Martin

5 *26 km (16 mi) north of Annweiler, slightly west of the Wine Rd. Turn left at the northern edge of Edenkoben.*

This is one of the most charming wine villages of the Pfalz. The entire **Altstadt** (Old Town) is under historical preservation protection. For 350 years the Knights of Dalberg lived in the castle **Kropsburg,** the romantic ruins of which overlook the town. The Renaissance tombstones are among the many artworks in the late-Gothic Church of **St. Martin.** The town's namesake is honored with a parade and wine festival on November 11.

Where to Stay & Eat

$ **Landhaus Christmann.** This bright, modern house in the midst of the vineyards has stylish rooms decorated with both antiques and modern furnishings. Some rooms have balconies with a view of the Hambacher Schloss. Vintners and distillers, the Christmanns offer 20 wines by the glass in their restaurant, Gutsausschank Kabinett (¢–$), as well as culinary wine tastings. In addition to their wines and spirits, they sell antiques. *Riedweg 1, D–67487 06323/94270 06323/942–727 www.landhaus-christmann.de 6 rooms, 3 apartments Restaurant, cable TV, Internet room, some pets allowed (fee); no a/c, no room phones, no smoking MC, V Hotel and restaurant closed 2 wks Jan. and Feb. and 2 wks July and Aug. Restaurant closed Mon.–Wed. No lunch BP.*

★ $ **St. Martiner Castell.** The Mücke family transformed a simple vintner's house into a fine hotel and restaurant, retaining many of the original features, such as exposed beams and an old wine press. Though it's in the heart of town, the hotel is an oasis of peace, particularly the rooms with balconies overlooking the garden. A native of the Loire Valley, Frau Mücke adds French flair to the menu ($–$$$), including a six-course *Schlemmer-Menü* (gourmet menu). The wine list offers a good selection of bottles from a neighboring wine estate. ✉ *Maikammerer Str. 2, D–67487* ☎ *06323/9510* 🖷 *06323/951–200* 🌐 *www.hotelcastell.de* *26 rooms* *Restaurant, cable TV, in-room data ports, sauna, babysitting, laundry service, some pets allowed (fee), no-smoking rooms; no a/c* *MC, V* *Hotel and restaurant closed Feb. Restaurant closed Tues.* *BP.*

The Arts

Schloss Villa Ludwigshöhe, Kloster Heilsbruck (a former Cistercian convent near Edenkoben), and **Schloss Edesheim** are backdrops for concerts and theater in summer. For a calendar of events contact the Südliche Weinstrasse regional tourist office in Landau.

Shopping

Artist Georg Wiedemann is responsible for both content and design of the exquisite products of Germany's premier wine-vinegar estate, **Doktorenhof** (✉ Raiffeisenstr. 5 ☎ 06323/5505 🌐 www.doktorenhof.de) in Venningen, 2 km (1 mi) east of Edenkoben. Make an appointment for a unique vinegar tasting and tour of the cellars or pick up a gift at his shop. He's open weekdays 8–4, Wednesday until 6, and Saturday 9–2 (no credit cards).

en route

Depart St. Martin via the Totenkopf-Höhenstrasse, a scenic road through the forest. Turn right at the intersection with Kalmitstrasse and proceed to the vantage point atop the **Kalmit,** the region's highest peak (2,200 feet). The view is second to none. Return to the Kalmitstrasse, drive toward Maikammer, and stop at **Mariä-Schmerzen-Kapelle** (Our Lady of Sorrows Chapel) in Alsterweiler. It houses the work of an unknown master, a remarkable Gothic triptych depicting the Crucifixion. Maikammer has half-timber houses, patrician manors, and a baroque church and is the last (or first) wine village in the Südliche Weinstrasse district.

Back on the Wine Road it's a brief drive to the Neustadt suburb of Hambach. The sturdy block of **Hambacher Schloss** is considered the "cradle of German democracy." It was here, on May 27, 1832, that 30,000 patriots demonstrated for German unity, raising the German colors for the first time. Inside there are exhibits about the uprising and the history of the castle. The French destroyed the 11th-century imperial fortress in 1688. Reconstruction finally began after the Second World War, in neo-Gothic style, and the castle is now an impressive setting for theater and concerts. On a clear day you can see the spire of Strasbourg Cathedral and the northern fringe of the Black Forest from the terrace restaurant. ✉ *Hambach* ☎ *06321/30881* 🌐 *www.hambacher-schloss.de* *€4.50* *Mar.–Nov., daily 10–6.*

Neustadt

6 *8 km (5 mi) north of St. Martin, 5 km (3 mi) north of Hambach on the Wine Rd.*

Neustadt and its nine wine suburbs are at the midpoint of the Wine Road and the edge of the district known as Deutsche Weinstrasse–Mittelhaardt. With around 5,000 acres of vines, they jointly compose Germany's largest wine-growing community. The **Deutsches Weinlesefest** (German Wine Harvest Festival) culminates every October with the coronation of the German Wine Queen and a parade with more than 100 floats. You can sample some 30 of the 100 Neustadt wines sold at the **Haus des Weines** (House of Wine), which is opposite the town hall. The Gothic house from 1276 is bordered by a splendid Renaissance courtyard, the Kuby'scher Hof. ✉ *Rathausstr. 6* ☎ *06321/355–871* ⏲ *Closed Sun. and Mon.*

The **Marktplatz** (market square) is the focal point of the Old Town and a beehive of activity on Tuesday, Thursday, and Saturday, when farmers come to sell their wares. The square itself is ringed by baroque and Renaissance buildings (Nos. 1, 4, 8, and 11) and the Gothic **Stiftskirche** (Collegiate Church), built as a burial church for the Palatinate counts. In summer, concerts take place in the church (Saturday 11:30–noon). Afterward, you can ascend the southern tower (187 feet) for a bird's-eye view of the town (the tower is only open after concerts). The world's largest cast-iron bell—weighing more than 17 tons—hangs in the northern tower. Indoors, see the elaborate tombstones near the choir and the fanciful grotesque figures carved into the baldachins and corbels.

The Pfalz is home to the legendary, elusive *Elwetritschen*, part bird and part human, said to roam the forest and vineyards at night. "Hunting Elwetritschen" is both a sport and an alibi. Local sculptor Gernot ★ Rumpf has immortalized these creatures by depicting them in a **fountain** on Marstallplatz. No two are alike. Near the market square, hunt for the one that "escaped" from its misty home. End a walking tour of the Old Town on the medieval lanes Metzgergasse, Mittelgasse, and Hintergasse to see beautifully restored half-timber houses, many of which are now pubs, cafés, and boutiques.

Otto Dill Museum. The late impressionist painter Otto Dill (1884–1957), a native of Neustadt, is known for powerful animal portraits (especially lions, tigers, horses) and vivid landscapes. Some 100 oil paintings and 50 drawings and watercolors of the Manfred Vetter collection are on display. ✉ *Rathausstr. 12, at Bachgängel 8* ☎ *06321/398–321* 🌐 *www.otto-dill-museum.de* 🎫 *€2.50* ⏲ *Wed. and Fri. 2–5, weekends 11–5.*

Thirty historical train engines and railway cars are on display at the **Eisenbahn Museum,** behind the main train station. Take a ride through the Palatinate Forest on one of the museum's historical steam trains, the *Kuckucksbähnel* (€12), which departs from track 5 around 10:30 AM every other Sunday between Easter and mid-October. It takes a good hour to cover the 13-km (8-mi) stretch from Neustadt to Elmstein. ✉ *Neustadt train station, Schillerstr. entrance* ☎ *06321/30390* 🌐 *www.eisenbahnmuseum-neustadt.de* 🎫 *€3* ⏲ *Tues.–Fri. 10–1, weekends 10–4.*

Where to Stay & Eat

$$–$$$ ✕ **Brezel.** The gilded *Brezel* (pretzel) hanging in front of the 17th-century half-timber house (once a bakery) is the namesake of Helga and Stefan Braun's classy yet comfortable wine restaurant. White walls, softened by light wooden floors and beams, are hung with paintings by the late impressionist Otto Dill. In the back, dine beneath the vaulted ceiling of a former wine cellar. Fish is the specialty, but the entire menu is based on fresh, seasonal ingredients. The luncheon special is a good value, and the excellent wines are reasonably priced. ✉ *Rathausstr. 32, between Ludwigstr. and Sauter Str.* ☎ *06321/481–971* 🌐 *www.brezel-restaurant.de* 💳 *MC, V* ⏲ *Closed 1 wk in Jan., 2 wks in late July, and Tues. and Wed.*

$–$$$ ✕ **Altstadtkeller bei Jürgen.** Tucked behind a wooden portal, this vaulted sandstone "cellar" (it's actually on the ground floor) is a cozy setting for very tasty food. Equally inviting is the terrace, with its citrus, olive, palm, and fig trees. The regular menu includes a number of salads and a good selection of fish and steaks, and the daily specials are geared to what's in season. Owner Jürgen Reis is a wine enthusiast, and his well-chosen list shows it. ✉ *Kunigundenstr. 2* ☎ *06321/32320* 🌐 *www.altstadtkeller-neustadt.de* 💳 *DC, MC, V* ⏲ *Closed 10 days in early Aug., 2 wks in Feb., and Mon. No dinner Sun.*

¢–$ ✕ **Weinstube Eselsburg.** The *Esel* (donkey) lends its name to Mussbach's best-known vineyard, Eselshaut (donkey's hide); this wine pub; and one of its specialties, *Eselssuppe,* a hearty soup of pork, beef, and vegetables. Always packed with regulars, the Eselsburg is decorated with original artwork by the owner, Peter Wiedemann, and his late father, Fritz, the pub's founder. Enjoy top Pfälzer wines in the flower-filled courtyard in summer or in the warmth of an open hearth in winter. From October to May, try the *Schlachtfest* (meat and sausages from freshly slaughtered pigs) the first Tuesday of the month. ✉ *Kurpfalzstr. 62, Neustadt-Mussbach* ☎ *06321/66984* 🌐 *www.eselsburg.de* 💳 *MC, V* ⏲ *Closed Sun.–Tues., 2 wks in Aug., and mid-Dec.–mid-Jan. No lunch.*

★ $ ✕🏨 **Mithras-Stuben/Weinstube Kommerzienrat.** Convivial proprietor and wine devotee Bernd Hagedorn named his four spacious apartments after Mithras, the ancient Persian god of light and deity of a religious cult embraced by Roman legionnaires. The contemporary furnishings, Oriental rugs, and modern baths are a far cry from what the Romans had in the Pfalz 2,000 years ago. Upon request, cell phones are available for the two apartments with no in-room phones. In the restaurant ($), an incredible 300 Pfälzer wines can be sampled by the glass (and 250 imported wines by the bottle). *Rumpsteak* (beef steak), served with tasty *Bratkartoffeln* (home-fried potatoes) or *Rösti* (potato pancakes), and Pfälzer Gyros (a unique meat-and-cheese dish) are favorites. ✉ *Kurpfalzstr. 161/Loblocherstr. 34, D–67435 Neustadt-Gimmeldingen* ☎ *06321/679–0335 or 06321/68200* 📠 *06321/679–0331* 🌐 *www.weinstube-kommerzienrat.de* *4 apartments* *Restaurant, kitchenettes, cable TV, some in-room data ports, some pets allowed (fee), no-smoking rooms; no a/c, no phones in some rooms* 💳 *No credit cards* ⏲ *Restaurant closed Thurs. No lunch.*

$ ✕🏨 **Rebstöckel/Weinstube Schönhof.** Enjoy vintner's hospitality in Hannelore and Stephan Hafen's 17th-century stone guesthouse at the Weingut

Schönhof estate. All rooms have blond-wood furnishings; some have kitchenettes. A common refrigerator is stocked with the estate's wines (and other drinks), or try them in the Weinstube with a hearty *Schönhof Pfännchen* (ham gratin in a brandy cream sauce). Wine tastings and vineyard hikes can be arranged and cycling fans can rent bikes at a shop around the corner. Neustadt proper is 5 km (3 mi) north. ✉ *Weinstr. 600, D–67434 Neustadt-Diedesfeld* ☎ *06321/86198* 📠 *06321/86823* 🌐 *www.weingut-schoenhof.de* *1 room, 4 apartments* *Restaurant, refrigerators; no a/c, no smoking* *No credit cards* *Restaurant closed Jan. and Tues.–Thurs. No lunch* *BP.*

$ **Steinhäuser Hof.** The 14th-century Kuby'scher Hof is an architectural gem in the heart of the Old Town. The former stables have been converted into modern rooms with light wood furnishings and a cozy restaurant ($–$$$) run by cheerful Ilona Jochim. She serves regional, seasonal, and vegetarian specialties beneath a 16th-century vaulted brick ceiling and in the beautiful courtyard. There's fresh fish on Friday and *Pfälzer Dampfnudeln* (tasty yeast dumplings with wine or vanilla sauce) on Tuesday. ✉ *Turmsstr. 11, D–67433 Neustadt* ☎ *06321/480–706* 📠 *06321/480–712* *6 rooms* *Restaurant, cable TV, some pets allowed (fee), no-smoking rooms; no a/c, no room phones* *No credit cards* *Closed 4 wks in Jan. and Feb. Restaurant closed Wed. No dinner Sun.* *BP.*

Nightlife & the Arts

The **Saalbau** (✉ Bahnhofstr. 1 ☎ 06321/926–812), opposite the train station, is Neustadt's convention center and main venue for concerts, theater, and events. In summer there's open-air theater at **Villa Böhm** (✉ Maximilianstr. 25), which also houses the city's history museum. Concerts, art exhibits, and wine festivals are held at the **Herrenhof** (✉ An der Eselshaut 18) in the suburb of Mussbach. Owned by the Johanniter-Orden (Order of the Knights of St. John) from the 13th to 18th century, it's the oldest wine estate of the Pfalz. Contact the Neustadt tourist office for program details and tickets.

Shopping

After seeing the water-spewing Elwetritschen in action, you might want to take one home. The pottery store, **Keramik-Atelier Ingrid Zinkgraf** (✉ Badstubeng. 5, Am Klemmhof ☎ 06321/30162 🌐 www.keramikatelier-zinkgraf.de), has amusing ceramic renditions of the mythical birds, as well as modern and traditional pottery and sculptures.

Sports & the Outdoors

The Neustadt tourist office has brochures and maps that outline circular biking and hiking routes, including the educational wine paths in Gimmeldingen and Haardt.

en route

The **Holiday Park,** in Hassloch, 10 km (6 mi) east of Neustadt, is one of Europe's largest amusement parks. The admission fee (free on your birthday) covers all attractions, from shows to giant-screen cinema, and special activities for children. The free-fall tower, hell barrels, and Thunder River rafting are standing favorites, and

Expedition GeForce, has the steepest drop (82 degrees) of any roller coaster in Europe. ☎ *06324/599–3318* 🌐 *www.holidaypark.de* 🎫 *€22.50* ⏲ *Early Apr.–Oct., daily 10–6.*

Speyer

❼ *25 km (15 mi) east of Neustadt via B–39, 22 km (14) mi south of Mannheim via B–9 and B–44.*

Speyer was one of the great cities of the Holy Roman Empire, founded in pre-Celtic times, taken over by the Romans, and expanded in the 11th century by the Salian emperors. Between 1294, when it was declared a Free Imperial City, and 1570, no fewer than 50 imperial diets were convened here. The term "Protestant" derives from the diet of 1529, referring to those who protested when the religious freedom granted to evangelicals at the diet of 1526 was revoked and a return to Catholicism was decreed. The neo-Gothic **Gedächtniskirche** on Bartolomäus-Weltz-Platz commemorates those 16th-century Protestants. Ascend the **Altpörtel,** the impressive town gate, for a grand view of Maximilianstrasse, the street that led kings and emperors straight to the cathedral. 🎫 *€1* ⏲ *Apr.–Oct., weekdays 10–noon and 2–4, weekends 10–5.*

Fodor'sChoice ★ The **Kaiserdom** (Imperial Cathedral), one of the finest Romanesque cathedrals in the world and a UNESCO World Heritage site, conveys the pomp and majesty of the early Holy Roman Emperors. It was built between 1030 and 1061, by the emperors Konrad II, Henry III, and Henry IV. The last replaced the flat ceiling with groined vaults in the late 11th century, an innovative feat in its day. A restoration program in the 1950s returned the building to almost exactly its original condition.

See the exterior before venturing inside. You can walk most of the way around it, and there's a fine view of the east end from the park by the Rhine. Much of the architectural detail, including the dwarf galleries and ornamental capitals, was inspired and executed by stone masons from Lombardy, which belonged to the German Empire at the time. The four towers symbolize the four seasons and the idea that the power of the empire extends in all four directions. Look up as you enter the nearly 100-foot-high portal. It's richly carved with mythical creatures. In contrast to Gothic cathedrals, whose walls are supported externally by flying buttresses, allowing for a minimum of masonry and a maximum of light, at Speyer the columns supporting the roof are massive. The **Krypta** (crypt) lies beneath the chancel. It's the largest crypt in Germany and is strikingly beautiful in its simplicity. Four emperors, four kings, and three empresses are buried here. ✉ *Dompl.* 🎫 *Donation requested* ⏲ *Apr.–Oct., daily 9–7; Nov.–Mar., daily 9–5; closed during services.*

★ Opposite the cathedral, the **Historisches Museum der Pfalz** (Palatinate Historical Museum) houses the **Domschatz** (Cathedral Treasury). Other collections chronicle the art and cultural history of Speyer and the Pfalz from the Stone Age to modern times. Don't miss the precious "Golden Hat of Schifferstadt," a golden, cone-shape object used for religious purposes during the Bronze Age. The **Wine Museum** exhibits artifacts from

Roman times to the present, including the world's oldest bottle of wine, from circa AD 300. A major exhibition, "The Jews of Europe in the Middle Ages," runs from mid-November 2004 to mid-March 2005. ✉ *Dompl. 4* ☎ *06232/13250* 📠 *06232/132–540* 🌐 *www.museum.speyer.de* 🎫 *€7, combination ticket with Sea Life €14* ⏲ *Tues.–Sun. 10–6.*

Speyer was an important medieval Jewish cultural center. In the **Jewish quarter,** behind the Palatinate Historical Museum, you can see synagogue remains from 1104 and Germany's oldest (pre-1128) ritual baths, the 33-foot-deep ***Mikwe.*** ✉ *Judeng.* ☎ *06232/291–971* 🎫 *€1* ⏲ *Apr.–Oct., daily 10–5.*

9

A turn-of-the-20th-century factory hall houses the **Technik-Museum** (Technology Museum), a large collection of locomotives, aircraft, old automobiles, and fire engines. Automatic musical instruments, historical dolls and toys, and 19th-century fashion are displayed in the Wilhelmsbau. Highlights of the complex are the 420-ton U-boat (you can go inside) and the massive 3-D IMAX cinemas. ✉ *Am Technik Museum 1* ☎ *06232/67080* 🌐 *www.technik-museum.de* 🎫 *Museum €11, IMAX €7.50, combined ticket €15.50* ⏲ *Weekdays 9–6, weekends 9–7.*

Sea Life, in the old harbor of Speyer, enables you to travel the length of the Rhine from the Alps to the North Sea via a walk through a 33-foot-long tunnel. All types of marine life native to this region glide through 105,600 gallons of water. ✉ *Hafenstr. 2/Im Hafenbecken, 15-min walk from large parking lot on Festpl.* ☎ *06232/69780* 🌐 *www.sealife.de* 🎫 *€11, combination ticket with historical museum €14* ⏲ *Daily 10–5.*

Where to Stay & Eat

★ **$$–$$$$** ✕ **Backmulde.** Bread is still baked daily in this historic bakery, now a comfortable, upscale wine restaurant. Homemade bread, homegrown produce, and local products are all part of chef and proprietor Gunter Schmidt's requirement for freshness. The aromas and flavors of his fare often have a Mediterranean accent, and the menu changes according to season. The wine list features an array of champagnes, and more than 850 wines—half from the Pfalz and a well-chosen selection from abroad—spanning decades of vintages. Schmidt's own wines are from the Heiligenstein vineyard on the outskirts of Speyer. ✉ *Karmeliterstr. 11–13* ☎ *06232/71577* 🌐 *www.backmulde.de* 💳 *AE, DC, MC, V* ⏲ *Closed Sun. and Mon. and mid-Aug.–early Sept.*

$–$$ ✕ **Wirtschaft Zum Alten Engel.** This 200-year-old vaulted brick cellar, with its rustic wood furnishings and cozy niches, is an intimate setting for a hearty meal. Winter luncheon specials are a good value. Seasonal dishes supplement the large selection of Pfälzer and Alsatian specialties, such as *Ochsenfetzen* (slices of beef), coq au vin, or *Choucroute* (similar to a Pfälzer Teller). The wine list features about 180 Pfälzer, European, and New World wines. ✉ *Mühlturmstr. 7* ☎ *06232/70914* 🌐 *www.zumaltenengel.de* 💳 *V* ⏲ *Closed 3 wks in Aug. No lunch May–Aug., and no lunch Sun., Sept.–Apr.*

$ ✕ **Ratskeller.** Friendly service and Gunter Braun's fresh seasonal dishes make for an enjoyable dining experience in the town hall's vaulted cellar (1578). The menu changes frequently and offers more than standard fare: creative soups (pretzel soup, Tuscan bread soup) and entrées, such as *Kalbsnieren* (veal kidneys), or *Bachsaibling* (brook char on a red-wine-butter sauce). Wines from the Pfalz predominate, with 18 available by the glass. Small fare and drinks are served in the idyllic courtyard, May through September. ✉ *Maximilianstr. 12* ☎ *06232/78612* ▭ *AE, MC, V* ⏲ *Closed 2 wks in late Feb., 1 wk in late Oct., and Mon. No dinner Sun.*

$ ✕ **Kutscherhaus.** Charming rustic decor and a profusion of flowers have replaced the *Kutschen* (coaches) in this turn-of-the-20th-century coachman's house. The menu (¢–$$) offers Flammkuchen and Pfälzer specialties as well as creative fish, vegetarian, and pasta dishes. In summer you can sit beneath the old plane trees in the beer garden and select from a sumptuous buffet. Three modern, comfortable suites can sleep up to four persons each. ✉ *Fischmarkt 5a, D–67346* ☎ *06232/70592* 🖷 *06232/620–922* 🌐 *www.kutscherhaus-speyer.de* *3 suites* *Restaurant, minibars, cable TV, bicycles, beer garden, some pets allowed; no a/c* ▭ *MC, V* ⏲ *Restaurant closed Wed., Thurs., and 4 wks in July–Aug. (Note: Beer garden open all summer)* 🍴 *BP.*

$ **Hotel Goldener Engel.** A scant two blocks west of the Altpörtel is the "Golden Angel," a friendly, family-run hotel furnished with antiques and innovative metal-and-wood designer furniture. Paintings by contemporary artists and striking photos of Namibia and the Yukon line the walls—the photos are a tribute to proprietor Paul Schaefer's wanderlust. The restaurant Wirtschaft Zum Alten Engel is in the cellar. ✉ *Mühlturmstr. 5–7, D–67346* ☎ *06232/13260* 🖷 *06232/132–695* 🌐 *www.goldener-engel-speyer.de* *44 rooms, 2 suites* *Restaurant, cable TV, in-room data ports, some pets allowed (fee); no a/c in some rooms* ▭ *MC, V* ⏲ *Closed 2 wks late Dec.–early Jan.* 🍴 *BP.*

Nightlife & the Arts

Highlights for music lovers are **Orgelfrühling,** the organ concerts in the Gedächtniskirche (Memorial Church) in spring, the jazz festival in mid-August, and the concerts in the cathedral during September's **Internationale Musiktage.** Call the Speyer tourist office for program details and tickets. Walk into the town-hall courtyard to enter the **Kulturhof Flachsgasse,** home of the city's art collection and special exhibitions. ✉ *Flachsg.* ☎ *06232/142–399* *Free* ⏲ *Tues.–Sun. 11–6.*

Deidesheim

❽ *8 km (5 mi) north of Neustadt via the Wine Rd., now B–271.*

Deidesheim is the first of a trio of villages on the Wine Road renowned for their vineyards and the wine estates known as the Three Bs of the Pfalz—Bassermann, Buhl, and Bürklin.

The half-timber houses and historical facades framing Deidesheim's **Marktplatz** form a picturesque group, including the Church of St. Ulrich, a Gothic gem inside and out, and the old **Rathaus** (Town Hall), whose doorway is crowned by a baldachin and baroque dome. The attractive open staircase leading up to the entrance is the site of the festive *Geissbock-Versteigerung* (billy-goat auction) every Pentecost Tuesday, followed by a parade and folk dancing. The goat is the tribute neighboring Lambrecht has paid Deidesheim since 1404 for grazing rights. Inside see the richly appointed **Ratssaal** (council chamber) and the museum of wine culture. ✉ *Marktpl.* 🎟 €2 ⏲ *Mar.–Dec., Wed.–Sun. 4–6.*

Vines, flowers, and *Feigen* (fig trees) cloak the houses behind St. Ulrich on Heumarktstrasse and its extension, Deichelgasse (nicknamed Feigengasse). To see the workshops and ateliers of about a dozen local artists, follow the *Künstler-Rundweg,* a signposted trail (black "K" on yellow signs). The tourist office has a list of their opening hours. Cross the Wine Road to reach the grounds of **Schloss Deidesheim,** now a wine estate and pub (closed Wednesday and Thursday; lunch on Sunday only). The bishops of Speyer built a moated castle on the site in the 13th century. Twice destroyed and rebuilt, the present castle dates from 1817 and the moats have been converted into gardens.

Where to Stay & Eat

$$ ✕ **Weinschmecker.** The restaurant and Vinothek of Herbert Nikola, an expert on Pfälzer wines and festivals, is on the eastern edge of town. Italian tiles and whitewashed walls give it a light, airy Mediterranean look—the menu reflects the same. The focus, however, is on top-quality Pfälzer wines, 200 of which (from about 40 estates) are featured; 120 are available by the glass. ✉ *Steing. 2* ☎ *06326/980–460* 💳 *No credit cards* ⏲ *Closed Mon. No lunch Tues.–Sat. No dinner Sun.*

$–$$ ✕ **Gallino.** The Hotel Deidesheimer Hof's outdoor restaurant sits in a quiet little courtyard and embodies the Pfalz's nickname, the "Tuscany of Germany." Lots of fresh herbs and tomatoes are featured in pasta dishes such as porcini-filled ravioli with a salad dressed in tomato vinaigrette, or basil-spiced spaghetti salad with shrimp kebabs. Open only if weather permits. ✉ *Am Marktpl. 1* ☎ *06326/96870* 💳 *AE, DC, MC, V* ⏲ *May–Aug., Wed.–Sun. No lunch.*

$–$$ ✕ **Weinstube St. Urban.** Named after St. Urban, the vintners' patron saint, this is not a "typical" Weinstube but rather an upscale wine restaurant offering excellent regional cuisine and wines in beautiful rooms. Try the homemade *Entenbratwurst* (duck sausage) with potato salad. The restaurant is in (and on the front patio of) the Hotel Deidesheimer Hof. ✉ *Am Marktpl. 1* ☎ *06326/96870* 💳 *AE, DC, MC, V.*

$$–$$$ ✕🏨 **Hotel Deidesheimer Hof.** If your timing's right, you could rub elbows with the heads of state, entertainers, or sports stars who frequent this house. Despite the aura of the guest book, the hotel retains its country charm and friendly service. Rooms are luxurious, and several have baths with round tubs or whirlpools. The restaurant Schwarzer Hahn ($$–$$$$) is for serious wining and dining. Chef Stefan Neugebauer's set menus are an excellent choice. À la carte you can sample Pfälzer specialties, including sophisticated renditions of the region's famous dish, Saumagen, with foie gras and truffles. More than 600 wines grace the wine list. ✉ *Am Marktpl. 1, D–67146* ☎ *06326/96870* 📠 *06326/7685* 🌐 *www.deidesheimerhof.de* 🛏 *24 rooms, 4 suites* 👍 *3 restaurants, minibars, cable TV, some in-room data ports, Wi-Fi, bicycles, bar, lobby lounge, lounge, Weinstube, library, babysitting, dry cleaning, laundry service, Internet room, business services, some pets allowed (fee), no-*

Fodor'sChoice ★

smoking rooms; no a/c in some rooms ▭ *AE, DC, MC, V* ⊙ *Restaurant closed Sun. and Mon., early Jan., and 6 wks July and Aug. No lunch.*

$$ ✕ **Hatterer's Hotel-Restaurant Le Jardin d'Hiver.** Clément Hatterer, the hospitable Alsatian owner and chef, has anticipated all the comforts you could ask for in his stylish hotel. Whether you dine in the winter garden, decorated in soothing shades of lilac, or in the sunny courtyard garden filled with exotic plants, the food and wine are exceptional. Like the menu ($$–$$$), the wine list features Pfälzer and Alsatian specialties. First-floor guest rooms have a contemporary look; those on the second floor are more spacious and are outfitted in a country style with wood furniture. ✉ *Weinstr. 12, D–67146* ☎ *06326/6011* 🖷 *06326/7539* 🌐 *www.hotel-hatterer.com* *57 rooms* *Restaurant, minibars, cable TV, Wi-Fi, bicycles, bar, lobby lounge, dry cleaning, laundry service, some pets allowed, no-smoking rooms; no a/c* ▭ *AE, DC, MC, V* ⊙ *Restaurant closed 2 wks in Jan.* *BP.*

$ **Landhotel Lucashof.** Klaus and Christine Lucas are well known for their wines and hospitality. Their beautifully decorated, modern guest rooms are named after famous vineyards in Forst, and four have balconies—the room called Pechstein is particularly nice. You can enjoy their excellent wines in the tasting room, beneath a shady pergola in the courtyard, or in the privacy of your room (the refrigerator in the breakfast room is stocked for guests). Delicious food and wine at pubs in Forst's Old Town are a three-minute walk away. ✉ *Wiesenweg 1a, D–67147 Forst* ☎ *06326/336* 🖷 *06326/5794* 🌐 *www.lucashof.de* *7 rooms* *Cable TV, some pets allowed (fee), no-smoking rooms; no a/c* ▭ *No credit cards* ⊙ *Closed mid-Dec.–Jan.*

Shopping

The Biffar family not only runs a first-class **wine estate** but also manufactures very exclusive candied fruits and ginger (delicious souvenirs). ✉ *Niederkircher Str. 13* ☎ *06326/96760* 🌐 *www.biffar.com* ▭ *No credit cards* ⊙ *Weekdays 9–noon and 1–5:30, Sat. 10–noon and 1:30–4.*

en route

Forst and **Wachenheim,** both a few minutes' drive north of Deidesheim, complete the trio of famous wine villages. As you approach Forst, depart briefly from B–271 (take the left fork in the road) to see the Old Town with its vine- and ivy-clad sandstone and half-timber vintners' mansions. Peek through the large portals to see the lush courtyards. Many estates on this lane have pubs, as does the town's *Winzerverein* (cooperative winery). Wachenheim is another 2 km (1 mi) down the road. Its cooperative, Wachtenburg Winzer (with a good restaurant), is on the left at the entrance to town. Head for the Wachtenburg (castle) ruins up on the hill for a glass of wine. The Burgschänke (castle pub) is open if the flag is flying.

Bad Dürkheim

9 *6 km (4 mi) north of Deidesheim on B–271.*

This pretty spa is nestled into the hills at the edge of the Palatinate Forest and ringed by vineyards. The saline springs discovered here in

1338 are the source of today's drinking and bathing cures, and at harvesttime there's also a detoxifying *Traubenkur* (grape-juice cure). A trip to the neoclassical **Kurhaus** and its beautiful gardens might be just the ticket if you've overindulged at the Dürkheimer Wurstmarkt, the world's largest wine festival, held in mid-September. Legendary quantities of *Weck, Worscht, un Woi* (dialect for rolls, sausage, and wine) are consumed at the fair, including half a million *Schoppen,* the region's traditional pint-size glasses of wine. The festival grounds are also the site of the world's largest wine cask, the **Dürkheimer Riesenfass,** with a capacity of 1.7 million liters (450,000 gallons). Built in 1934 by an ambitious cooper, the cask is now a restaurant that can seat well over 450 people.

Northwest of town is the **Heidenmauer** (heathen wall), the remains of an ancient Celtic ring wall more than 2 km (1 mi) in circumference and up to 20 feet thick in parts, and nearby are the rock drawings at **Kriemhildenstuhl,** an old Roman quarry where the legionnaires of Mainz excavated sandstone.

Overlooking the suburb of Grethen are the ruins of **Kloster Limburg** (Limburg Monastery). Emperor Konrad II laid the cornerstone in 1030, supposedly on the same day that he laid the cornerstone of the Kaiserdom in Speyer. The monastery was never completely rebuilt after a fire in 1504, but it's a majestic backdrop for open-air performances in summer. From the tree-shaded terrace of the Klosterschänke restaurant ($–$$), adjacent to the ruins, you can combine good food and wine with a great view of the ruins (closed Tuesday, September to March).

The massive ruins of 13th-century **Burgruine Hardenburg** (Hardenburg Fortress) lie 3 km (2 mi) west (via B–37) of the Kloster Limburg. In its heyday it was inhabited by more than 200 people. It succumbed to fire in 1794. ✉ *B–37* 🎫 *€2.10* ⏲ *Apr.–Sept., Tues.–Sun. 10–6; Jan.–Mar., Oct., and Nov., Tues.–Sun. 10–5.*

Where to Stay & Eat

$–$$ ✕ **Dürkheimer Riesenfass.** The two-story "giant cask" is divided into various rooms and niches with rustic wood furnishings. Ask to see the impressive *Festsaal mit Empore* (banquet hall with gallery) upstairs. Regional wines, Pfälzer specialties, and international dishes are served year-round. ✉ *St. Michael Allee 1* ☎ *06322/2143* 🌐 *www.duerkheimer-fass.de* 💳 *MC, V.*

★ **$$** ✕🏨 **Kurparkhotel.** Part of the Kurhaus complex, the Kurparkhotel is the place to be pampered from head to toe. Haus A has the most elegant rooms, several with balconies. Haus B, also modern and comfortable, is less exclusive. This is a typical, elegant spa hotel, with extensive health and beauty facilities, thermal baths, a casino, and concerts in the garden. The flower-lined terrace at the restaurant Graf zu Leiningen ($–$$$) is a beautiful setting for coffee or tea with delicious homemade pastries in the afternoon or an elegant *Feinschmecker-Menü* (five-course gourmet menu) in the evening. ✉ *Schlosspl. 1–4, D–67098* ☎ *06322/7970* 📠 *06322/797–158* 🌐 *www.kurpark-hotel.de* 🛏 *113 rooms* 👍 *Restaurant, minibars, cable TV, in-room data ports,*

Wi-Fi, pool, sauna, spa, steam room, bicycles, bowling, bar, lobby lounge, casino, dry cleaning, laundry service, Internet room, business services, some pets allowed (fee), no-smoking floors; no a/c ▭ *AE, DC, MC, V* 🍽 *BP.*

$ **Weingut und Gästehaus Ernst Karst und Sohn.** This cheerful guesthouse is adjacent to the Karst family's wine estate, in the midst of the vineyards. Rooms are light and airy, furnished mostly in pine; all of them have splendid views of the countryside—which you are invited to explore on the bikes the Karsts loan. Tastings and cellar tours are possible, or sample the wines with regional dishes at the nearby restaurant, Weinrefugium ($–$$), located at Schlachthausstrasse 1a (via B–37). (Restaurant days and hours vary; call ahead.) ✉ *In den Almen 15, D–67098* ☎ *06322/2862 for guesthouse, 06322/791–0980 for restaurant* 🖷 *06322/65965* 🌐 *www.weingut-karst.de* *3 rooms, 6 apartments* *Restaurant, minibars, Wi-Fi, bicycles, no-smoking rooms; no a/c* ▭ *No credit cards (hotel); AE, MC, V (restaurant)* ⏲ *Closed Nov.–Jan.* 🍽 *BP.*

★ $$ **Weingut Fitz-Ritter.** Konrad Fitz and his American wife, Alice, have a centuries-old stone cottage that sleeps up to four people on the park-like grounds of their 221-year-old wine estate. You'll have a pool all to yourself, and there are concerts and festivals in the garden, courtyard, and vaulted cellars (request a calendar of events). Tastings and tours of the cellars, vineyards, and garden are possible. The minimum stay is seven nights. ✉ *Weinstr. Nord 51, D–67098* ☎ *06322/5389* 🖷 *06322/66005* 🌐 *www.fitz-ritter.de* *1 cottage* *Kitchen, cable TV, pool, some pets allowed; no a/c, no smoking* ▭ *MC, V.*

Shopping

Several hundred wines from Bad Dürkheim and vicinity can be sampled and purchased daily (10–5) at the **WEINDOM** next to the "giant cask" on St. Michael Allee. The shop also sells other grape products and accessories. To learn how grapes are cultivated and wines are made, take the Saturday afternoon (4 PM) tour that begins at the WEINDOM with a glass of sparkling wine and is followed by a vineyard and cellar tour and tasting at Weingut Fitz-Ritter. "Piccolo" tours last 75 minutes (€6); "Magnum" tours last 2.5 hours (€12.50).

Nightlife & the Arts

The **Spielbank** (Casino; €2.50), in the Kurparkhotel, is a daily diversion after 2 PM; jacket and tie are no longer required, but no sports shoes or tee shirts are allowed. Free introductory tours are offered every other Thursday at 1 PM. Concerts and theater take place at the **Limburg Monastery.** Contact the local tourist office for program details.

en route

When the vineyards of Ungstein, a suburb north of Bad Dürkheim, were modernized in 1981, a **Roman wine estate** was discovered. Among the finds was an ancient *Kelterhaus* (pressing house). A romantic wine festival is held on this historic site every year, in late June. Watch for signs to Villa Weilberg, to the left of the Wine Road (B–271).

Around Freinsheim

10 *7 km (4½ mi) northeast of Bad Dürkheim, via Kallstadt, right turn to Freinsheim is signposted midway through Kallstadt.*

The next village on the Wine Road north of Bad Dürkheim is **Kallstadt,** where you can enjoy Saumagen in your glass and on your plate—for this is the home of the excellent **Saumagen Vineyard.** Both its wine and the specialty dish are served with pride everywhere in town, not just at the *Saumagenkerwe* (wine festival) the first weekend in September.

Off the Wine Road to the east, **Freinsheim's** *Stadtmauer* (town wall), probably built between 1400 and 1540, is one of the best-preserved fortifications in the Pfalz. Walk along it to see the massive town gates (Eisentor and Haintor) and the numerous towers, two of which can be rented as holiday apartments. Many of the town's historical houses are baroque, including the **Rathaus** (1737), with its covered stairway and sandstone balustrade. Next to it is a **Protestant church,** a Gothic structure to which Renaissance and baroque elements were added over the years. No fewer than five large festivals are celebrated here between April and September—quite a showing for a town this small.

Drive 5 km (3 mi) west to Weisenheim am Berg (you'll cross over the Wine Road at Herxheim) and watch for signs toward Bobenheim and Kleinkarlbach. This road, which runs parallel to the Wine Road and along the vineyard heights, affords a wonderful panorama of the expansive vineyards stretching onto the Rhine Plain. Follow the signs to **Neuleiningen,** and then wind your way uphill to reach the romantic Old Town, ringed by a medieval wall. The ruins of the 13th-century castle are a good start for a town walk.

Where to Stay & Eat

★ $–$$ ✕ **Alt Freinsheim.** Chef Axel Steffl's domain is tucked away on a narrow lane between Hauptstrasse and Freinsheim's town wall (northern edge). Old stone walls, exposed beams, and the tiny size of the restaurant make for a cozy dining experience. Whether you opt for his country cooking, or a refined entrée with one of his creative sauces (lamb filet in red wine-thyme sauce or crayfish tails in Pernod cream sauce), everything is homemade. The good selection of local wines is as reasonably priced as the food. ✉ *Korngasse 5, Freinsheim* ☎ *06353/2582* 🌐 *www.restaurant-alt-freinsheim.de* 💳 *No credit cards* ⏲ *Closed Wed. and 3 wks in July and Aug. No lunch.*

$–$$ ✕ **Weinhaus Henninger.** Walter Henninger numbers among the elite of Pfälzer vintners, but there's nothing pretentious about the atmosphere or cooking at his wood-panel wine pub. It's a jovial place, frequented by locals who come for the delicious, hearty fare and excellent wines. The soups, *Eintopf* dishes (stews), rumpsteak with sautéed onions, and daily specials are recommended. ✉ *Weinstr. 93, Kallstadt* ☎ *06322/2277* 🌐 *www.weinhaus-henninger.de* 💳 *No credit cards* ⏲ *No lunch Mon.*

★ $–$$ ✕🏨 **Hotel–Restaurant Alte Pfarrey.** Once a rectory, this hotel-restaurant is on the hilltop above the Old Town of Neuleiningen. The comfortable inn with modern facilities is made up of several Gothic houses. Rooms are distinctive for their antique furnishings. Susanne and Utz Ueberschaer believe in personal service and first-rate culinary delights ($$–$$$$). The menu focuses on light international favorites prepared with fresh, local ingredients. The wine list is very good, with offerings from the New and Old World. Jewelry fans: don't miss son Tobias's designer jewelry. ✉ *Unterg. 54, D–67271 Neuleiningen* ☎ *06359/86066* 📠 *06359/86060* 🌐 *www.altepfarrey.de* *9 rooms* *Restaurant, some pets allowed (fee); no a/c, no room TVs* 💳 *MC, V* ⊙ *Restaurant closed Mon. and Tues.* 🍽 *BP.*

$–$$ Fodor'sChoice ★ **Hotel–Restaurant Luther.** This elegant country inn is set in a baroque manor next to Freinsheim's town wall. The rooms provide modern comfort amid refined decor, with fresh flowers throughout the house. Gisela Luther's handsome table settings and Dieter Luther's artistic food presentations make dining here ($$$–$$$$) a joy for all the senses. One of Germany's leading chefs, Dieter is known for his imaginative combinations, such as lobster with fennel or venison with kumquats. Save room for a chocolate creation or the crème brûlée quintet. Spanish, Bordeaux, and top Pfälzer wines are focal points of the wine list. ✉ *Hauptstr. 29, D–67251 Freinsheim* ☎ *06353/93480* 📠 *06353/934–845* 🌐 *www.luther-freinsheim.de* *23 rooms* *Restaurant, minibars, cable TV, in-room data ports, no-smoking rooms; no a/c* 💳 *AE, MC, V* ⊙ *Hotel closed Feb. Restaurant closed Sun. and Feb. No lunch* 🍽 *BP.*

★ $–$$ **Hotel–Restaurant Weinkastell Zum Weissen Ross.** Behind the cheerful facade of this half-timber house, with its wrought-iron sign depicting a *weisser Ross* (white stallion), you can experience Pfälzer hospitality at its best. Rooms have warm colors, solid oak furnishings, and modern baths, and several have romantic alcoves or four-poster beds. Jutta and Norbert Kohnke offer service and cuisine ($$$–$$$$) that are top-notch. Most of the superb wines come from her brother's wine estate next door, Weingut Koehler-Ruprecht (tours and tastings are possible), as well as red wines from his affiliated estates in Portugal and South Africa. This is the best place in the Pfalz to sample "Saumagen twice." ✉ *Weinstr. 80–82, D–67169 Kallstadt* ☎ *06322/5033* 📠 *06322/66091* 🌐 *www.weinkastell-kohnke.de* *13 rooms, 1 apartment* *Restaurant, in-room broadband, bicycles, business services, some pets allowed; no a/c* 💳 *AE, MC, V* ⊙ *Hotel closed Jan.–mid-Feb. Restaurant closed Mon. and Tues., Jan.–mid-Feb., and 1 wk late July–early Aug.* 🍽 *BP.*

$ **Town Wall Tower.** For a room with a view in a highly original setting, stay overnight in a medieval *Turm* (tower). The Hahnenturm sleeps two; the Herzogturm can accommodate a family. Contact the Freinsheim tourist office for reservations. ✉ *Hauptstr. 2, D–67251 Freinsheim* ☎ *06353/989–294* 📠 *06353/989–904* *2 rooms* *Kitchenettes; no a/c, no room phones, no room TVs* 💳 *No credit cards.*

en route

Neuleiningen is 4 km (2½ mi) west of the Wine Road town Kirchheim. **Bockenheim,** 10 km (6 mi) north, is dominated by an imposing gateway. There's a panoramic view of the Pfalz's "sea of vineyards" from the viewing platform. Like its counterpart in Schweigen-Rechtenbach, the **Haus der Deutschen Weinstrasse** marks the end (or start) of its namesake, the German Wine Road.

THE RHINE TERRACE

Like Speyer, the cities of Worms and Mainz were Free Imperial Cities and major centers of Christian and Jewish culture in the Middle Ages. Germany's first synagogue and Europe's oldest surviving Jewish cemetery, both from the 11th century, are in Worms. The imperial diets of Worms and Speyer in 1521 and 1529 stormed around Martin Luther (1483–1546) and the rise of Protestantism. In 1455 Johannes Gutenberg (1400–68), the inventor of movable type, printed the Gutenberg Bible in Mainz.

9

Worms

15 km (9 mi) east of Bockenheim via B–47 from Monsheim, 45 km (28 mi) south of Mainz on B–9.

Although devastated in World War II, Worms (pronounced *vawrms*) is among the most ancient cities of Germany, with a history going back some 6,000 years. Once settled by the Romans, Worms later became one of the imperial cities of the Holy Roman Empire. More than 100 imperial diets were held here, including the 1521 meeting where Martin Luther pleaded his cause. In addition to having a great Romanesque cathedral, Worms is a center of the wine trade.

Worms developed into an important garrison town under the Romans, but it's better known for its greatest legend, the *Nibelungenlied,* derived from the short-lived kingdom established by Gunther and his Burgundian tribe in the early 5th century. The complex and sprawling story was given its final shape in the 12th century and tells of love, betrayal, greed, war, and death. It ends when Attila the Hun defeats the Nibelungen (Burgundians), who find their court destroyed, their treasure lost, and their heroes dead. One of the most famous incidents tells how Hagen, treacherous and scheming, hurls the court riches into the Rhine. Near the Nibelungen Bridge there's a bronze statue of him caught in the act. The *Nibelungenlied* may be legend, but the story is based on fact. A Queen Brunhilda, for example, is said to have lived here. It's also known that a Burgundian tribe was defeated in 436 by Attila the Hun in what is present-day Hungary.

Not until Charlemagne resettled Worms almost 400 years later, making it one of the major cities of his empire, did the city prosper again. Worms was more than an administrative and commercial center; it was a great ecclesiastical city as well. The first expression of this religious importance was the original cathedral, consecrated in 1018. Between 1130 and 1181 it was rebuilt in three phases into the church you see today.

★ 11 The *Nibelungenlied* comes to life in the **Nibelungen Museum,** a stunning sight-and-sound exhibition cleverly installed in two medieval towers and the portion of the Old Town wall between them. The structure itself is architecturally fascinating inside and out, and the rampart affords a wonderful view of the town. Language is no problem: the tour script (via headphones and printed matter) is offered in English. Allow 1½ hours for a thorough visit. ✉ *Fischerpförtchen 10* ☎ *06241/202–120* 🌐 *www.nibelungen-museum.de* 🎫 *€5.50* ⏲ *Tues.–Thurs. and weekends 10–5, Fri. 10 AM–10 PM.*

★ ⓬ If you've seen Speyer Cathedral, you'll quickly realize that the **Wormser Dom St. Peter** (Cathedral of St. Peter), by contrast, contains many Gothic elements. In part this is simply a matter of chronology. Speyer Cathedral was completed nearly 70 years before the one in Worms was even begun, long before the lighter, more vertical lines of the Gothic style evolved. Furthermore, once built, Speyer Cathedral was left largely untouched in later periods; the Worms Cathedral was remodeled frequently as new architectural styles and new values developed. The Gothic influence can be seen both inside and out, from the elaborate tympanum with biblical scenes over the southern portal (today's entrance) to the great rose window in the west choir to the five sculptures in the north aisle recounting the life of Christ. The cathedral was completely gutted by fire in 1689 in the War of the Palatinate Succession. For this reason many of the furnishings are baroque, including the magnificent gilt high altar from 1742, designed by the master architect Balthasar Neumann (1687–1753). The choir stalls are no less decorative. They were built between 1755 and 1759 in rococo style. Walk around the building to see the artistic detail of the exterior. ✉ *Dompl.* ☎ *06241/6115* 🎫 *Donation requested* ⏲ *Apr.–Oct., daily 9–6; Nov.–Mar., daily 9–5; closed during services.*

An imperial palace once stood in what is now the **Heylshofgarten,** a park just north of the cathedral. This was the site of the fateful meeting between Luther and Emperor Charles V in April 1521 that ultimately led to the Reformation. Luther refused to recant his theses demanding Church reforms and went into exile in Eisenach, where he translated the New Testament in 1521 and 1522.

★ ⓭ The **Kunsthaus Heylshof** (Heylshof Art Gallery) in the Heylshofgarten is one of the leading art museums of the region. It has an exquisite collection of German, Dutch, and French paintings as well as stained glass, glassware, porcelain, and ceramics from the 15th to the 19th centuries. ✉ *Stephansg. 9* ☎ *06241/22000* 🌐 *www.museum-heylshof.de* 🎫 *€2.50* ⏲ *May–Sept., Tues.–Sun. 11–5; Oct.–Dec. and mid-Feb.–Apr., Tues.–Sat. 2–5, Sun. 11–5.*

⓮ The Lutheran **Dreifaltigkeitskirche** (Church of the Holy Trinity) is just across the square from the Heylshofgarten. Remodeling during the 19th and 20th centuries produced today's austere interior, although the facade and tower are still joyfully baroque. ✉ *Marktpl.* ⏲ *Apr.–Sept., daily 9–5; Oct.–Mar., daily 9–4.*

⓯ The **Lutherdenkmal** (Luther Monument) commemorates Luther's appearance at the Diet of Worms. He ended his speech with the words: "Here I stand. I have no choice. God help me. Amen." The 19th-century monument includes a large statue of Luther ringed by other figures from the Reformation. It's set in a small park on the street named Lutherring.

Dreifaltigkeitskirche 14
Judenfriedhof Heiliger Sand 17
Kunsthaus Heylshof 13
Liebfrauenkirche 19
Lutherdenkmal 15
Nibelungen Museum 11
Städtisches Museum 18
Synagoge . . . 16
Wormser Dom St. Peter 12

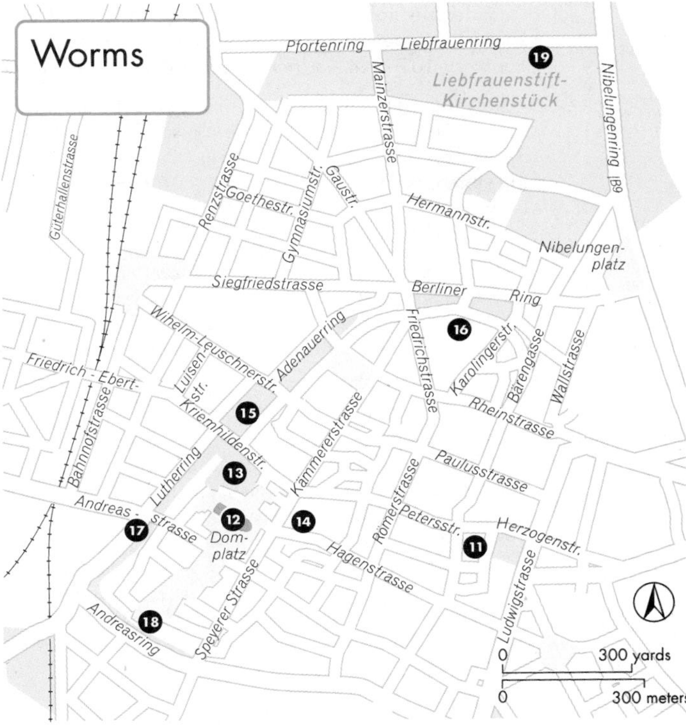

The Jewish quarter is along the town wall between Martinspforte and Friesenspitze and between Judengasse and Hintere Judengasse. The first ★ 16 **Synagoge** (synagogue) was built in 1034, rebuilt in 1175, and expanded in 1212 with a building for women. Destroyed in 1938, it was rebuilt in 1961 using as much of the original masonry as had survived. ✉ *Hintere Judeng.* ⏲ *Apr.–Oct., daily 10–12:30 and 1:30–5; Nov.–Mar., daily 10–noon and 2–4; closed during services.*

The **Raschi-Haus,** the former study hall, dance hall, and Jewish home for the elderly, is next door to the synagogue. It houses the city archives and the **Jewish Museum.** The well-written, illustrated booklet *Jewish Worms* chronicles a millennium of Jewish history in Worms. A bilingual exhibition about the life and work of Rashi (Rabbi Solomon ben Isaac of Troyes [1040-1105]), who studied at the Worms Talmud academy in circa 1060, will run from April to October 2005. Bilingual walking tours of Jewish Worms and concerts are also planned. For more details contact: gerold.boennen@worms.de. ✉ *Hintere Judeng. 6* ☎ *06241/853–4701* 🎫 *€1.50* ⏲ *Apr.–Oct., Tues.–Sun. 10–12:30 and 1:30–5; Nov.–Mar., Tues.–Sun. 10–12:30 and 1:30–4:30.*

17 The **Judenfriedhof Heiliger Sand** (Holy Sand Jewish Cemetery) is the oldest Jewish cemetery in Europe. The oldest of some 2,000 tombstones date from 1076. ✉ *Andreasstr. and Willy-Brandt-Ring* ⏲ *Daily.*

18 To bone up on the history of Worms, visit the **Städtisches Museum** (Municipal Museum), housed in the cloisters of a Romanesque church in the Andreasstift. ✉ *Weckerlingpl. 7* ☎ *06241/946–3911* 🎟 *€2* ⏲ *Tues.–Sun. 10–5.*

19 On the northern outskirts of Worms, the twin-tower Gothic **Liebfrauenkirche** (Church of Our Lady) is set amid vineyards. The church is the namesake of the mild white wine named Liebfraumilch, literally, the "Milk of Our Lady." Today this popular wine can be made from grapes grown throughout Rheinhessen, the Pfalz, the Nahe, and the Rheingau wine regions, since the original, small vineyard surrounding the church could not possibly meet demand.

Where to Stay & Eat

★ **$$$–$$$$** ✕ **Rôtisserie Dubs.** A pioneer of the Rheinhessen restaurant scene, Wolfgang Dubs focused on creative regional cuisine and seasonal specialties long before it was in vogue. Fish, fowl, meat, and game are all expertly prepared and garnished. For a more casual meal, try his cozy Gasthaus Zum Schiff (¢–$$), next door. The daily specials are a very good value. A wine enthusiast, Dubs offers his own wines, top German and French estates, and a few New World wines, such as Opus One. Rheindürkheim is 9 km (5½ mi) north of Worms via B–9. The restaurant is near the *Kirche* (church), not far from the riverbank. ✉ *Kirchstr. 6 Worms-Rheindürkheim* ☎ *06242/2023* 🌐 *www.dubs.de* 💳 *AE, MC, V* ⏲ *Closed Tues. and 2 wks in Jan. No lunch Sat.*

$–$$ ✕🏨 **Landhotel Zum Schwanen.** Bärbel Berkes runs this lovingly restored country inn in Osthofen (10 km [6 mi] northwest of Worms). You can linger over a meal or a glass of wine in its pretty courtyard, the hub of the 18th-century estate. Like the rooms, the restaurant ($$) is light, airy, and furnished with sleek, contemporary furniture. Regional favorites are served as well as dishes with a Mediterranean touch. The lineup of fine, local wines is exemplary. The beer garden is also inviting. ✉ *Friedrich-Ebert-Str. 40, D–67574 Osthofen, West of B–9* ☎ *06242/9140* 📠 *06242/914–299* 🌐 *www.zum-schwanen-osthofen.de* 🛏 *30 rooms* 🖒 *Restaurant, minibars, cable TV, some in-room data ports, bicycles, beer garden, Internet room, business services, some pets allowed (fee), no-smoking rooms; no a/c* 💳 *AE, MC, V* ⏲ *No lunch Sat., no dinner Sun.* 🍽 *BP.*

$ ✕🏨 **Hotel and Weinstube Römischer Kaiser.** Housed in an 18th-century baroque patrician manor, the Lehr family's "Roman Emperor" is a down-to-earth, friendly little hotel and wine pub (¢) that quickly fills up with regulars in the evening. The nearly two dozen wines-by-the-glass are as moderately priced as the simple, hearty fare, such as Flammkuchen, Saumagen, or the daily specials. The Bratwurst is truly excellent. ✉ *Römerstr. 72* ☎ *06241/93370* 📠 *06241/970–168* 🌐 *www.roemischer-kaiser-worms.de* 🛏 *11 rooms* 🖒 *Restaurant, cable TV; no a/c* 💳 *AE, MC, V* ⏲ *Closed 1 wk in Jan., 1 wk July and Aug. No lunch* 🍽 *BP.*

¢–$ **Land- und Winzerhotel Bechtel.** The friendly Bechtel family, winegrowers and proud parents of a former German Wine Queen, offer very pleasant accommodations on the grounds of their wine estate in the suburb of Heppenheim, about 10 km (6 mi) west of Worms (depart Worms on Speyerer Strasse, an extension of Valckenbergstrasse, which runs parallel to the east side of the Dom). The rooms are modern, and all have balconies. You can enjoy country cooking (daily specials) as well as more refined fare in the restaurant ($) or on its terrace with the estate's wines. Wine tastings in the vaulted cellars are also possible. ✉ *Pfälzer Waldstr. 100, D–67551 Worms-Heppenheim* ☎ *06241/36536* 📠 *06241/34745* 🌐 *www.landhotel-bechtel.de* *15 rooms, 1 apartment* *Restaurant, minibars, cable TV, in-room broadband, in-room data ports, gym, sauna, bicycles, lounge, some pets allowed (fee), no-smoking rooms; no a/c* ▭ *AE, MC, V* 🍽 *BP.*

$ **Dom-Hotel.** The appeal of this hotel with modern, comfortable rooms lies in its friendly staff and its terrific location in the heart of the pedestrian zone (a parking garage is available). ✉ *Obermarkt 10, D–67547* ☎ *06241/9070* 📠 *06241/23515* 🌐 *www.dom-hotel.de* *60 rooms, 2 apartments* *Minibars, cable TV, in-room data ports, bicycles, babysitting, dry cleaning, laundry service, business services, some pets allowed (fee), no-smoking rooms; no a/c* ▭ *AE, DC, MC, V* 🍽 *BP.*

$ **Haus Kalisch am Dom.** For more than 30 years the Kalisch family has welcomed guests to its little inn opposite the cathedral. There are no frills, but the rooms are comfortable and have private baths and TVs. ✉ *Neumarkt 9, D–67547* ☎ *06241/27666* 📠 *06241/25073* *13 rooms* *Cable TV, some pets allowed; no a/c, no room phones* ▭ *No credit cards* ⏲ *Closed 3 wks Dec. and Jan.* 🍽 *BP.*

Nightlife & the Arts

Worms's nine-day wine and folk festival, the **Backfischfest** (Fried-Fish Festival), begins the last weekend of August. It evolved from the thanksgiving celebrations held by the once-powerful fishers' guild. There are rides, entertainment, a parade, fireworks, and *Fischerstechen* (jousting) in the harbor.

The **Städtisches Spiel- und Festhaus** (✉ Rathenaustr. ☎ 06241/22525) is the cultural hub of Worms, presenting theater, concerts, ballet, and special events. Concerts are also held in the Municipal Museum, in the Andreasstift, and at the 19th-century palace Schloss Herrnsheim, in the northern suburb of Herrnsheim. The annual **jazz festival** (mid-July) is staged primarily around Weckerlingplatz and the cathedral. Contact the tourist office for program details.

Shopping

For tasteful wine accessories and excellent wines, drop by P. J. Valckenberg's wine shop, **Der Weinladen** (✉ Weckerlingpl. 1 ☎ 06241/911–180), near the Municipal Museum. The winery owns nearly all of the Liebfrauenstift-Kirchenstuck vineyard surrounding the Liebfrauenkirche. The store is closed Sunday and Monday and does not accept credit cards.

Oppenheim

20 *26 km (16 mi) north of Worms, 23 km (16 mi) south of Mainz on B–9.*

En route to Oppenheim, the vine-covered hills parallel to the Rhine gradually steepen. Then, unexpectedly, the spires of Oppenheim's Gothic ★ **Katharinenkirche** (St. Katharine's Church) come into view. The contrast of its pink sandstone facade against a bright blue sky is striking. Built between 1220 and 1439, it's the most important Gothic church between Strasbourg and Köln. The interior affords a rare opportunity to admire original 14th-century stained-glass windows and two magnificent rose windows, the Lily Window and the Rose of Oppenheim. The church houses masterfully carved tombstones, while the chapel behind it has a *Beinhaus* (charnel house) that contains the bones of 20,000 citizens and soldiers from the 15th to 18th century. ✉ *Katharinenstr. at Merianstr., just north of market sq.* ⏲ *Apr.–Oct., daily 8–6; Nov.–Mar., daily 9–5.*

Oppenheim and its neighbors to the north, Nierstein and Nackenheim, are home to Rheinhessen's finest vineyards. The **Deutsches Weinbaumuseum** (German Viticultural Museum) has wine-related artifacts that chronicle the region's 2,000-year-old wine-making tradition and the world's largest collection of mousetraps. ✉ *Wormser Str. 49* ☎ *06133/2544* 🎫 *€3.50* ⏲ *Apr.–Oct., Tues.–Fri. 2–5, weekends 10–5.*

Nightlife & the Arts

Concerts are held in St. Katharine's, and open-air theater takes place in the **Burgruine Landskrone,** the 12th-century imperial fortress ruins a few minutes' walk northwest of the church. From here there's a wonderful view of the town and the vineyards, extending all the way to Worms on a clear day. For more jovial entertainment, accompanied by *Blasmusik* (brass-band oompah music), attend the **wine festival** in mid-August on the market square, which is ringed by half-timber houses and the 16th-century Rathaus.

Nierstein

21 *3 km (2 mi) north of Oppenheim on B–9.*

Surrounded by 2,700 acres of vines, Nierstein is the largest wine-growing community on the Rhine and boasts Germany's oldest documented **vineyard** (AD 742), the Glöck, surrounding St. Kilian's Church. You can sample wines at the **Winzergenossenschaft** (Cooperative winery; ✉ Karolingerstr. 6), which is the starting point of an easy hike or drive to the vineyard heights and the vantage point at the *Wartturm* (watchtower). Tasting stands are set up along the route, providing delightful wine presentations in the vineyards *am roten Hang* (referring to the steep sites of red soils of slate, clay, and sand) in mid-June. Early August brings the wine festival, with stands throughout the town and a festive parade in medieval costumes.

Where to Stay & Eat

★ $$ **Best Western Wein & Parkhotel.** Quiet elegance and Mediterranean flair mark this country inn. Spacious, light rooms decorated in warm shades of ocher, chic bathrooms, and an inviting lounge and terrace make for comfortable, relaxing quarters. Cuisine at the restaurant Am Heyl'schen Garten ($–$$$) ranges from barbecue on the terrace to Sunday brunch to well-prepared regional specialties and dishes with an Asian touch; the Irish pub serves light fare. The staff is exceptionally cheerful and competent. ✉ *An der Kaiserlinde 1, D–55283* ☎ *06133/5080* 🖷 *06133/508–333* 🌐 *www.weinhotel.bestwestern.de* *47 rooms, 8 suites* *Restaurant, minibars, cable TV, in-room data ports, indoor pool, gym, hot tub, sauna, bicycles, bar, lobby lounge, pub, babysitting, Internet room, business services, some pets allowed (fee), no-smoking rooms* 💳 *AE, MC, V* *BP.*

9

Nackenheim

22 *5 km (3 mi) north of Nierstein on B–9.*

This wine village lies slightly to the west of B–9; from the south, turn left and cross the railroad tracks (opposite the tip of the island in the Rhine) to reach the town center, 2 km (1 mi) down the country road. The writer Carl Zuckmayer (1896–1977) was born here and immortalized the town in his farce *Der fröhliche Weinberg* (*The Merry Vineyard*) in 1925. He described Rheinhessen wine as "the wine of laughter . . . charming and appealing." You can put his words to the test the last weekend of July, when wine-festival booths are set up between the half-timber town hall on Carl-Zuckmayer-Platz and the baroque **Church of St. Gereon.** The church's scrolled gables, belfry, and elaborate altars are worth seeing.

Where to Stay & Eat

$–$$ ✕ **Zum alten Zollhaus.** Walk through the arched gateway to reach the beautiful garden and entrance to this historical house. Cozy niches, fresh flowers, and handsome antiques provide a pleasant setting for good food and wine. Ilse Hees, the friendly proprietor, offers daily specials as well as standards such as roast breast of duck. The *Trilogie vom Lachs* (cold salmon) served with a mustard sauce is excellent. The wine list focuses on Rheinhessen wines, and a good number are available by the glass. ✉ *Wormser Str. 7, at Carl-Gunderloch-Pl.* ☎ *06135/8726* 🌐 *www.zum-alten-zollhaus.de* 💳 *No credit cards* ⏲ *Closed Sun. and Mon., 2 wks in late Feb., and 2 wks in late Sept. No lunch.*

★ $ ✕ **Jordan's Landhotel und Restaurant St. Gereon.** The Jordan family's charming half-timber country inn has modern rooms that feature blond-wood floors and light-color furnishings. Stone walls and light pine furniture on terra-cotta tiles give the restaurant ($$) a warm, rustic look, too. Ask if the hearty regional specialties *Dippe-Has* or *Backes Grumbeere* are available, or try the unique *Handkäs'carpaccio* in Zuckmeyer's Weingewölbe in the cellar (open September through April, evenings). All 20 wines served come from Rheinhessen. ✉ *Carl-Zuckmayer-Pl. 3, D–55299* ☎ *06135/92990* 🖷 *06135/929–992* 🌐 *www.landhotel-st-gereon.de* *15 rooms* *Restaurant, cable TV, in-room data ports, bicycles, Weinstube, laundry service, some pets allowed (fee), no-smoking rooms; no a/c* 💳 *DC, MC, V* ⏲ *Restaurant closed Tues. and Wed.* *BP.*

¢–$ **Gästehaus im Karthäserhof.** Michaela Schmidt runs this smart little guest house in the wine village of Bodenheim, 9 km (5½ mi) south of Mainz. The historic house has rooms with modern amenities. Its location within walking distance of many local vintners' pubs and the personal service offered make it an attractive overnight option. ✉ *Gaustr. 21, D–55294 Bodenheim* ☎ *06135/702–880* 🖷 *06135/7028–8288* *11 rooms* *Cable TV, in-room data ports, some pets allowed (fee), no-smoking rooms; no a/c* *MC, V* *BP.*

Sports & the Outdoors

BIKING The old towpath along the riverbank is an ideal cycling trail to Mainz or Worms, and the vineyard paths are well suited for exploring the countryside.

HIKING Enjoy the views from the vineyard heights on the **Rheinhöhenweg** trail. Allow three hours to hike the 10-km (6-mi) stretch between Nackenheim, Nierstein, and Oppenheim. Start at the corner of Weinbergstrasse and Johann-Winkler-Strasse. The educational wine path through the St. Alban vineyard is a pleasant walk in Bodenheim (4 km [2½ mi] northwest of Nackenheim).

Mainz

23 *14 km (9 mi) north of Nackenheim, 45 km (28 mi) north of Worms on B–9, and 42 km (26 mi) west of Frankfurt on A–3.*

Mainz is the capital of the state of Rheinland-Pfalz. Today's city was built on the site of a Roman citadel from 38 BC, though some of the local artifacts in its Landesmuseum date from 300,000 BC. Given its central location at the confluence of the Main and Rhine rivers, it's not surprising that Mainz has always been an important trading center, rebuilt time and time again in the wake of wars. The city's fine museums and historical buildings bear witness to a splendid past.

To see the sights, head for the Touristik Centrale (tourist office) to pick up a *Mainz Card,* a terrific one-day pass for €6 that includes a basic walking tour, unlimited use of public transportation, and free entry to museums and the casino, as well as a reduction in price on some hotel rooms, KD cruises, and theater tickets.

The **Marktplatz** and *Höfchen* (little courtyard) around the cathedral, the focal points of the town, are especially colorful on Tuesday, Friday, and Saturday, when farmers set up their stands to sell produce and flowers. This is also the site of the *Sektfest* (sparkling wine festival) in late May or early June and *Johannisnacht,* a huge wine festival with fireworks, a few weeks later.

★ The entrance to the **Dom** (Cathedral of St. Martin and St. Stephan) is on the south side of the market square, midway between the eastern and western chancels, which symbolize the worldly empire and the priestly realm, respectively. Emperor Otto II began building the oldest of the Rhineland's trio of grand Romanesque cathedrals in 975, the year in which he named Willigis archbishop and chancellor of the empire. Henry II, the last Saxon emperor of the Holy Roman Empire, was crowned here in 1002, as was his successor, Konrad II, the first Salian emperor, in 1024. In 1009, on the very day of its consecration, the cathedral burned to the ground. It was the first of seven fires the Dom has endured in the course of its millennium. Today's cathedral dates mostly from the 11th to 13th century. During the Gothic period, remodeling diluted the Romanesque identity of the original; an imposing baroque spire was added in the 18th century. Nevertheless, the building remains essentially Romanesque, and its floor plan demonstrates a clear link to the cathedrals in Speyer and Worms. The interior is a virtual sculpture gallery of elaborate monuments and tombstones of archbishops, bishops, and canons, many of which are significant artworks from the 13th to 19th century. ✉ *Domstr. 3 (Markt)* ☎ *06131/253–412* 🎫 *Donations requested* 🕓 *Mar.–Oct., weekdays 9–6:30, Sat. 9–4, Sun. 1–2:45 and 4–6:30; Nov.–Feb., weekdays 9–5, Sat. 9–4, Sun. 1–2:45 and 4–5; closed during services.*

From the Middle Ages until secularization in the early 19th century, the archbishops of Mainz, who numbered among the imperial electors, were extremely influential politicians and property owners. The wealth of religious art treasures they left behind can be viewed in the **Dom und Diözesanmuseum,** in the cathedral cloisters. ✉ *Domstr. 3* ☎ *06131/253–344* 🌐 *www.bistum-mainz.de* 🎫 *Free, Schatzkammer (treasure chamber) €3* 🕓 *Tues.–Sun. 10–5.*

★ Opposite the east end of the cathedral (closest to the Rhine) is the **Gutenberg Museum,** devoted to the history of writing and printing from Babylonian and Egyptian times to the present. Exhibits include historical printing presses, incunabula, and medieval manuscripts with illuminated letters, as well as two precious 42-line Gutenberg Bibles printed circa 1455. A replica workshop demonstrates how Gutenberg implemented his invention of movable type. ✉ *Liebfrauenpl. 5* ☎ *06131/122–640* 🌐 *www.gutenberg-museum.de* 🎫 *€5* 🕓 *Tues.–Sat. 9–5, Sun. 11–3.*

★ The Kurfürstliches Schloss (Electoral Palace) houses the **Römisch-Germanisches Zentralmuseum,** a wonderful collection of original artifacts and copies of items that chronicle cultural developments in the area up to the early Middle Ages. ✉ *Ernst-Ludwig-Pl. on Grosse Bleiche* ☎ *06131/91240* 🌐 *www.rgzm.de* 🎫 *Free* 🕓 *Tues.–Sun. 10–6.*

The remains of five 4th-century wooden Roman warships and two full-size replicas are on display at the **Museum für Antike Schiffahrt** (Museum of Ancient Navigation). These were unearthed in 1981 when the foundation for the Hilton's wing was dug. For more than a decade the wood was injected with a water-and-paraffin mixture to restore hardness. ✉ *Neutorstr. 2b* ☎ *06131/286–630* 🎫 *Free* 🕓 *Tues.–Sun. 10–6.*

The various collections of the **Landesmuseum** (Museum of the State of Rheinland-Pfalz) are in the former electors' stables, easily recognized by the statue of a golden stallion over the entrance. Exhibits range from the Stone Age to the 20th century. Among the highlights are a tiny Celtic glass dog from the 1st or 2nd century BC, Roman masonry, paintings by Dutch masters, artworks from the baroque to art-nouveau period,

CloseUp

THE FATHER OF MODERN PRINTING

HIS INVENTION—*printing with movable type—transformed the art of communication, yet much about the life and work of Johannes Gutenberg is undocumented, starting with his year of birth. It's estimated that he was born in Mainz circa 1400 into a patrician family that supplied the city mint with metal to be coined. Gutenberg's later accomplishments attest to his own skill in working with metals. Details about his education are unclear, but he probably helped finance his studies by copying manuscripts in a monastic scriptorium. He moved to Strasbourg circa 1434, where he was a goldsmith by day and an inventor by night. It was here that he worked—in great secrecy—to create movable type and develop a press suitable for printing by adapting the conventional screw press used for winemaking. By 1448 Gutenberg had returned to Mainz. Loans from a wealthy businessman enabled him to set up a printer's workshop and print the famous 42-line Bible. The lines of text are in black ink, yet each of the original 180 Bibles printed from 1452 to 1455 is unique, thanks to the artistry of the handpainted illuminated letters.*

Despite its significance, Gutenberg's invention was not a financial success. His quest for perfection rather than profit led to a legal battle during which his creditor was awarded the workshop and the Bible type. Gutenberg's attempts to set up another print shop in Mainz failed, but from 1465 until his death in 1468, he received an allowance for service to the archbishop of Mainz, which spared the "father of modern printing" from dying in poverty.

and collections of porcelain and faience. ✉ *Grosse Bleiche 49–51* ☎ *06131/28570* 🌐 *www.landesmuseum-mainz.de* 🎫 *€2, free Sat.* ⏲ *Tues. 10–8, Wed.–Sun. 10–5.*

The animals in Mainz's **Naturhistorisches Museum** (Natural History Museum) may all be stuffed and mounted, but these lifelike groups can demonstrate the relationships among various families of fauna better than any zoo. Fossils and geological exhibits show the evolution of the region's plants, animals, and soils. ✉ *Reichklarastr. 10* ☎ *06131/122–646* 🎫 *€1.50, free Sun.* ⏲ *Tues. 10–8, Wed. 10–2, Thurs.–Sun. 10–5.*

Schillerplatz, ringed by beautiful baroque palaces, is the site of the ebullient **Fastnachtsbrunnen** (Carnival Fountain), with 200 figures related to Mainz's "fifth season" of the year.

★ From Shillerplatz it's but a short walk up Gaustrasse to **St. Stephanskirche** (St. Stephen's Church), which affords a hilltop view of the city. In 990 Willigis built a basilica on the site; today's Gothic church dates from the late 13th and early 14th centuries. Postwar restoration included the installation of six vividly blue stained-glass windows depicting scenes from the Bible, designed in the 1970s by the Russian-born painter Marc

Chagall. ✉ *Kleine Weissg. 12, via Gaustr.* ☎ *06131/231–640* ⏲ *Feb.–Nov., Mon.–Sat. 10–noon and 2–5, Sun. 2–5; Dec. and Jan., Mon.–Sat. 10–noon and 2–4:30, Sun. 2–4:30.*

The hillside **Kupferberg Sektkellerei** (sparkling wine cellars) were built in 1850 on a site where the Romans cultivated vines and built cellars. The Kupferberg family expanded the cellars into 60 seven-story-deep vaulted cellars—the deepest in the world. The winery has a splendid collection of glassware; posters from the Belle Epoque period (1898–1914); richly carved casks from the 18th and 19th centuries; and the **Traubensaal** (Grape Hall), a tremendous example of the art-nouveau style. Two-hour tours include a tasting of five sparkling wines; 1½-hour tours include three sparkling wines; one-hour tours include one glass of Sekt. Reservations are required. ✉ *Kupferbergterrasse 17–19* ☎ *06131/9230* 🌐 *www.kupferberg.de* 🎫 *2-hr tours €12, 1½-hr tours € 9.50, 1-hr tours €6.50* ⏲ *Shop Mon.–Sat. 10–6* 💳 *MC, V.*

Where to Stay & Eat

★ $–$$$ ✕ **Gebert's Weinstuben.** Gebert's traditional wine restaurant serves refined versions of regional favorites in a very personal atmosphere. Try the *Handkäs-Suppe* (cheese soup) or Saumagen made not of pork but *Wildschwein* (wild boar). *Gans mit Schmoräpfel und Klöse* (goose with braised apples and dumplings) is served from November 11 until Christmas. The seasonal specialties, homemade noodles and handmade chocolate pralines, are always delicious. German wines (especially Rheinhessen) dominate the excellent wine list. Summer dining alfresco is possible in the smartly renovated courtyard. ✉ *Frauenlobstr. 94, near Rhine* ☎ *06131/611–619* 🌐 *www.geberts-weinstuben.de* 💳 *AE, DC, MC, V* ⏲ *Closed Sat. and 3 wks in July or Aug. No lunch Sun.*

★ $–$$ ✕ **Haus des Weines.** In addition to the pleasant ambience, tasty food, and a great selection of wines, the late hours are customer-friendly. The luncheon specials (€5.20) and huge salads are a very good value, and the menu covers a broad range, from snacks to full-course meals. Game is a specialty and available year-round. Enjoy a glass of wine with the Mainz specialties *Spundekäs* (cheese whipped with cream and onions) or *Handkäse mit Musik* (pungent, semihard cheese served with diced onions in vinaigrette). ✉ *Gutenbergpl. 3–5* ☎ *06131/221–300* 🌐 *www.hdw-mainz.de* 💳 *AE, MC, V.*

$–$$ ✕ **Mollers im Staatstheater.** For a fabulous view of Mainz, head for the terrace (fourth floor) or glass-lined restaurant atop the state theater (6th floor). Walk through the bistro (open daily 9–9) to reach the elevator. Sumptuous buffets, traditional favorites, and creative dishes, such as monkfish wrapped in ham with coconut risotto or couscous-coated rabbit, offer something for every taste. Brunch is served (11–2:30) Sunday. ✉ *Gutenbergplatz 7* ☎ *06131/627–9211* 🌐 *www.mollers.de* 💳 *AE, MC, V* ⏲ *Closed Wed.*

¢–$$ ✕ **Fischrestaurant Jackob.** Gernot Grundmann's fish shop supplies his restaurant with an array of absolutely fresh fish and, when in season, *Muscheln* (mussels). Half portions and the daily special are especially good values. Other specialties worth asking about: fish lasagne and homemade tortelloni stuffed with salmon. ✉ *Fischtor 7* ☎ *06131/229–299* *www.fischjackob.de* *No credit cards* *Closed Sun. No dinner except Fri., Oct.–Apr.*

¢–$$ **Heiliggeist.** Meals are served until midnight at this lively café-bistro-bar. Modern, minimal decor provides an interesting contrast to the historic vaulted ceilings, and in summer the beer garden is always packed. The compact menu includes elaborate salad platters as well as creatively spiced and sauced fish and meat dishes. One house specialty worth trying is the *Croustarte,* an upscale version of pizza. There's an extensive drink list. *Mailandsg. 11* *06131/225–757* *www.heiliggeist-online.de* *No credit cards* *No lunch Mon.–Thurs.*

¢–$ **Eisgrub-Bräu.** It's loud, it's lively, and the beer is brewed in the vaulted cellars on-site. An Eisgrub brew is just the ticket to wash down a hearty plate of *Haxen* (pork hocks) or *Meterwurst* (yard-long, rolled bratwurst), *Bratkartoffeln* (home fries), and sauerkraut. Breakfast (daily) and a buffet lunch (weekdays) are also served. Brewery tours are free, but make a reservation in advance. It's open daily 9 AM–1 AM. *Weisslilieng. 1a* *06131/221–104* *www.eisgrub.de* *MC, V.*

$$ **FAVORITE parkhotel.** Mainz's city park is a lush setting for the Barth family's hotel, restaurants, and beer garden with a Rhine view. After indulging in the superb breakfast buffet, it's but a 10-minute, downhill walk through the park to the Old Town. The hotel's original rooms are quite comfortable. In June 2005, expanded wellness facilities, a rooftop sundeck with a Jacuzzi, and 80 luxurious rooms/suites were added. The Stadtpark ($$–$$$) serves international cuisine (lobster is a specialty); casual dining is available in the hotel's other three restaurants ($–$$). *Karl-Weiser-Str. 1, D–55131* *06131/80150* *06131/801–5420* *www.favorite-mainz.de* *113 rooms, 9 suites* *4 restaurants, room service, minibars, cable TV, in-room data ports, Wi-Fi, indoor pool, gym, hot tubs (indoor and outdoor), massage, sauna, steam room, bicycles, bar, beer garden, lobby lounge, babysitting, dry cleaning, laundry service, concierge, Internet room, business services, some pets allowed (fee); no-smoking rooms, no a/c in some rooms* *AE, MC, V* *Stadtpark closed Sun. evening and Mon.* *BP.*

$$$–$$$$ **Hyatt Regency Mainz.** The blend of contemporary art and architecture with the old stone walls of historical Fort Malakoff on the Rhine is a visually stunning success. From the spacious atrium lobby to the luxurious rooms, everything is sleek, modern, and designed for comfort. The M-Lounge & Bar in the lobby serves light fare from 10 to midnight (drinks until 1 AM), and tables in the garden courtyard are always at a premium in the summer. The boutiques and pubs of the Old Town are only a 5- to 10-minute walk away. *Malakoff-Terrasse 1, D–55116* *06131/731–234* *06131/731–235* *www.mainz.regency.hyatt.com* *265 rooms, 3 suites* *Restaurant, room service, minibars, cable TV, in-room broadband, indoor pool, gym, massage, sauna, steam room, bicycles, bar, lobby lounge, babysitting, dry cleaning, laundry service, concierge, Internet room, business services, no-smoking rooms* *AE, DC, MC, V.*

$ **Hotel Ibis.** Modern, functional rooms and a great location on the edge of the Old Town are what the Ibis offers. Ask about the various discount rates that are available (except during trade fairs and major events). *Holzhofstr. 2, at Rheinstr., D–55116* *06131/2470* *06131/*

234–126 🌐 www.ibishotel.com 144 rooms Cable TV, in-room data ports, some Wi-Fi, bar, laundry service, Internet room, business services, some pets allowed (fee), no-smoking rooms AE, DC, MC, V.

Nightlife & the Arts

Mainz supports a broad spectrum of cultural events—music (from classical to avant-garde), dance, opera, and theater performances—at many venues throughout the city. Music lovers can attend concerts in venues ranging from the cathedral, the Kurfürstliches Schloss, and the Kupferberg sparkling wine cellars to the Rathaus, market square, and historic churches. The home stage of the Staatstheater Mainz is the **Grosses Haus** (✉ Gutenbergpl. ☎ 06131/28510 or 06131/285–1222). A smaller stage, the Kleines Haus, is also on the premises. **TiC** (✉ Spritzeng. 2 ☎ 06131/28510) is a sister stage of the Grosses Haus that features works of contemporary artists. **Mainzer Kammerspiele** (✉ Rheinstr. 4, Fort Malakoff Park ☎ 06131/225–002) is a multi-arts venue. The Mainzer Forum-Theater (cabaret) performs in the **Unterhaus** (✉ Münsterstr. 7 ☎ 06131/232–121).

Musicals and large-scale concerts are held in the high-tech **Phönix Halle** (✉ Hauptstr. 17–19 ☎ 06131/962–830) in the suburb of Mombach. **KUZ** (✉ Dagobertstr. 20b ☎ 06131/286–860) and its beer garden attract young and old for international rock, jazz, and pop concerts. The **Frankfurter Hof** (✉ Augustinerstr. 55) hosts many (often contemporary) musical events and lively dance parties. A traditional setting for concerts is the **Villa Musica** (✉ Auf der Bastei 3), with a repertoire ranging from classical to modern.

Nightlife is centered in the numerous wine pubs. Rustic and cozy, they're packed with locals who come to enjoy a meal or snack with a glass (or more) of local wine. Most are on the Old Town's main street, **Augustinerstrasse,** and its side streets (Grebenstrasse, Kirschgarten, Kartäuserstrasse, Jakobsbergstrasse) and around the Gutenberg Museum, on Liebfrauenplatz. The wood-panel pub **Wilhelmi** (✉ Rheinstr. 51 ☎ 06131/224–949) is a favorite with the post-student crowd. **Schreiner** (✉ Rheinstr. 38 ☎ 06131/225–720) attracts a mixed, jovial clientele and is an old, traditional Mainz favorite.

Carnival season runs from November 11 at 11:11 AM to Ash Wednesday. There are dozens of costume balls, parties, and political cabaret sessions that culminate in a huge parade of colorful floats and marching bands through downtown on the Monday before Lent.

Shopping

The Old Town is full of boutiques, and the major department stores (Karstadt and Kaufhof-Galeria) sell everything imaginable, including gourmet foods in their lower levels. The shopping district lies basically between the Grosse Bleiche and the Old Town and includes the **Am Brand** Zentrum, an ancient marketplace that is now a pedestrian zone brimming with shops. At the shopping mall **Römerpassage** (Lotharstrasse, near Grosse Bleiche), head for the cellar to see the remains of a Roman temple (AD 1) dedicated to the goddesses Isis and Mater Magna. The discovery was made in 1999 during construction of the mall.

The **Gutenberg-Shop** (✉ Markt 17 🌐 www.gutenberg-shop.de ⏲ closed Sun.) on the first floor of the *AZ* (local newspaper) customer center has a better selection of splendid souvenirs and gifts—including pages from the Bible, books, posters, stationery, pens, and games—than the shop in the Gutenberg Museum. The excellent **Weincabinet** (✉ Leichhofstr. 10, behind cathedral ☎ 06131/228–858) sells an array of the region's best wines and accessories. The flea market **Krempelmarkt** is on the banks of the Rhine between the Hilton hotel and Kaiserstrasse. It takes place from 7 to 1 the first and third Saturday of the month from April to October and the first Saturday from November to March.

THE PFALZ & RHINE TERRACE A TO Z

To research prices, get advice from other travelers, and book travel arrangements, visit www.fodors.com.

AIRPORTS

Frankfurt is the closest major international airport for the entire Rhineland. International airports in Stuttgart and France's Strasbourg are closer to the southern end of the German Wine Road.

BIKE TRAVEL

There's no charge for transporting bicycles on local trains throughout Rheinland-Pfalz weekdays after 9 AM and anytime weekends and holidays. The train stations in the towns of this chapter, however, do not rent bicycles. For maps, suggested routes, bike-rental locations, and details on *Pauschal-Angebote* (package deals) or *Gepäcktransport* (luggage-forwarding service), contact Pfalz-Touristik or Rheinhessen-Information.

CAR TRAVEL

It's 162 km (100 mi) between Schweigen-Rechtenbach and Mainz, the southernmost and northernmost points of this itinerary. The main route is the Deutsche Weinstrasse, which is a *Bundesstrasse* (two-lane highway), abbreviated "B," as in B–38, B–48, and B–271. The route from Worms to Mainz is B–9. The autobahn, abbreviated "A," parallel to the Wine Road in the Pfalz is A–65 from Kandel to Kreuz Mutterstadt (the junction with A–61, south of Ludwigshafen), and in Rheinhessen, A–61 to Alzey, and, finally, A–63 to Mainz. The A–6 runs west to east through the Pfalz from Kaiserslautern to Kreuz Frankenthal (the junction with A–61, north of Ludwigshafen).

Autobahn access to Mainz, the northernmost point of the itinerary, is fast and easy. A–63, A–61, and A–65 run through the area roughly north–south, and A–8 approaches the southern part of the German Wine Road via Karlsruhe.

TOURS

Town walking tours usually begin at the tourist-information office. Annweiler tours are at 10 AM on Wednesday from May to October, free of charge. Bad Dürkheim has tours (€2) March to mid-November, departing Monday at 10:30 at the sign marked TREFFPUNKT FÜHRUNGEN, near the entrance of the train station. Deidesheim conducts tours from May to October on Saturday at 10 (€3). Mainz has year-round tours departing Saturday at 2 (€5) from the Touristik Centrale. The office is one story above street level on the footbridge over Rheinstrasse. There are additional tours from May to October, Wednesday and Friday at 2.

Neustadt tours cost €3 and take place April through October, Wednesday and Saturday at 10:30. Speyer tours are at 11 on weekends between April and November; the cost is €3.50. Worms begins its tours at the southern portal (main entrance) of the cathedral on Saturday at 10:30 and Sunday at 2, between March and October. The cost is €4.

TRAIN TRAVEL

Mainz and Mannheim are hubs for IC (InterCity) and ICE (InterCity Express) trains.

TRANSPORTATION AROUND THE PFALZ & RHINE TERRACE

An excellent network of public transportation called *Rheinland-Pfalz-Takt* operates throughout the region with well-coordinated *RegioLinie* (buses) and *Nahverkehrszüge* (local trains). The travel service of the Deutsche Bahn (German Railway) provides schedules, connections, prices, and so on, 24 hours daily from anywhere in Germany.

VISITOR INFORMATION

The *KulturCard* (€5) entitles you to a 50% discount at many cultural events, museums, and sights in Rheinland-Pfalz. The card is sold by mail through the regional broadcaster SWR and at the newspaper *RZ* (RheinZeitung) shops. For discounts in Mainz, buy the *MainzCard* (€6) at the tourist office or at a hotel.

The regional and local tourist- and wine-information offices in the southern Pfalz, the northern Pfalz, and Rheinhessen can help make the most of your visit. The German Wine Information Bureau (⇨ Wine, Beer & Spirits *in* Smart Travel Tips) promotes the wines of all the regions.

KulturCard **SWR** ✉ Stichwort KulturCard, D-55114 Mainz. ***RZ* shop** ✉ Grosse Bleiche 17-23, Mainz.

Pfalz Region **Pfalz.Touristik** ✉ Martin-Luther-Str. 69, D-67433 Neustadt a.d. Weinstrasse ☎ 06321/39160 📠 06321/391-619 🌐 www.pfalz-touristik.de. **Pfalzwein** ✉ Martin-Luther-Str. 69, D-67433 Neustadt a.d. Weinstrasse ☎ 06321/912-328 📠 06321/12881 🌐 www.pfalzwein.de.

Northern Pfalz **Deutsche Weinstrasse** ✉ Martin-Luther-Str. 69, D-67433 Neustadt a.d. Weinstrasse ☎ 06321/912-333 📠 06321/912-330 🌐 www.deutsche-weinstrasse.de.

Southern Pfalz **Südliche Weinstrasse** ✉ An der Kreuzmühle 2, D-76829 Landau ☎ 06341/940-407 📠 06341/940-502 🌐 www.suedlicheweinstrasse.de.

Rheinhessen Area **Rheinhessen-Information** ✉ Wilhelm-Leuschner-Str. 44, D-55218 Ingelheim ☎ 06132/44170 📠 06132/441-744 🌐 www.rheinhessen-info.de. **Rheinhessenwein** ✉ Otto-Lilienthal-Str. 4, D-55232 Alzey ☎ 06731/951-0740 📠 06731/9510-7499 🌐 www.rheinhessenwein.de.

ℹ **Annweiler** ✉ Büro für Tourismus, Messplatz 1, D-76855 ☎ 06346/2200 📠 06346/7917 🌐 www.trifelsland.de. **Bad Dürkheim** ✉ Tourist-Information, Kurbrunnenstr. 14, D-67098 ☎ 06322/956-6250 📠 06322/956-6259 🌐 www.bad-duerkheim.de. **Deidesheim** ✉ Tourist Service, Bahnhofstr. 5, D-67146 ☎ 06326/96770 📠 06326/967-718 🌐 www.deidesheim.de. **Landau** ✉ Büro für Tourismus, Marktstr. 50, D-76829 ☎ 06341/13182 📠 06341/13195 🌐 www.landau.de. **Mainz** ✉ Touristik Centrale, Brückenturm am Rathaus, D-55116 ☎ 06131/286-210 📠 06131/286-2155 🌐 www.info-mainz.de/tourist. **Neustadt-an-der-Weinstrasse** ✉ Tourist-Information, Hetzelpl. 1, D-67433 ☎ 06321/926-892 📠 06321/926-891 🌐 www.neustadt.pfalz.com. **Speyer** ✉ Tourist-Information, Maximilianstr. 13, D-67346 ☎ 06232/142-392 📠 06232/142-332 🌐 www.speyer.de. **Wachenheim** ✉ Tourist-Information, Weinstr. 15, D-67157 ☎ 06322/958-032 📠 06322/958-011 🌐 www.wachenheim.de. **Worms** ✉ Tourist-Information, Neumarkt 14, D-67547 ☎ 06241/25045 📠 06241/26328 🌐 www.worms.de.

The Rhineland

10

WORD OF MOUTH

"I'd suggest going to St. Goar. . . . Take a short, steep hike up the trail behind the train station to the top of the cliffs. From the lookout hut up top, you can see the gorge, some vineyards, and three different castles that keep watch over the Rhine. If you walk south along the trail . . . you'll reach another lookout where you can spy the Loreley Cliffside across the river. . . . The views here are super."

—Russ

"Don't miss Burg Eltz! The hills on the way up to the castle are green and winding. . . . You're twisting your way up thinking this is 'the middle of nowhere,' when all of a sudden you come upon this 800-year-old castle."

—aggiemom

www.fodors.com/forums

Updated by
Kerry Brady

VATER RHEIN, OR "FATHER RHINE," is Germany's historic lifeline, and the region from Mainz to Koblenz is its heart. Its banks are crowned by magnificent castle after castle and by breathtaking, vine-terraced hills that provide the livelihood for many of the villages hugging the shores. In the words of French poet Victor Hugo, "The Rhine combines everything. The Rhine is swift as the Rhône, wide as the Loire, winding as the Seine . . . royal as the Danube and covered with fables and phantoms like a river in Asia. . . ."

The importance of the Rhine can hardly be overestimated. Although not the longest river in Europe (the Danube is more than twice its length), the Rhine has been the main river-trade artery between the heart of the continent and the North Sea (and Atlantic Ocean) throughout recorded history. The Rhine runs 1,320 km (820 mi) from the Bodensee (Lake Constance) west to Basel, then north through Germany, and, finally, west through the Netherlands to Rotterdam.

Vineyards, a legacy of the Romans, are an inherent part of the Rhine landscape from Wiesbaden to Bonn. The Rhine tempers the climate sufficiently for grapes to ripen this far north. Indeed, the wine regions along the Rhine, such as the Rheingau, and its most important tributary, the Mosel, are synonymous with the world's finest Riesling wines. Thanks to the river, these wines were shipped far beyond the borders of Germany, which in turn gave rise to the wine trade that shaped the fortune of many riverside towns. Rüdesheim, Bingen, Koblenz, and Köln (Cologne) remain important commercial wine centers to this day.

The Rhine became Germany's top tourist site more than 200 years ago. Around 1790 a spearhead of adventurous travelers from throughout Europe arrived by horse-drawn carriages to explore the stretch of the river between Bingen and Koblenz, now known as the Rhine gorge, or Mittelrhein (Middle Rhine)—and declared a UNESCO World Heritage site in June 2002. The Prussian-Rhine Steamship Co. (forerunner of the Köln-Düsseldorfer) started passenger service between Mainz and Köln in 1827. Shortly thereafter, the railroad opened the region to an early form of mass tourism.

The river is steeped in legend and myth. The Loreley, a jutting sheer slate cliff, was once believed to be the home of a beautiful and bewitching maiden who lured boatmen to a watery end in the swift currents. Heinrich Heine's poem *Song of Loreley* (1827), inspired by Clemens Brentano's *Legend of Loreley* (1812) and set to music in 1837 by Friedrich Silcher, has been the theme song of the landmark ever since. The Nibelungen, a Burgundian race said to have lived on the banks of the Rhine, serve as subjects for Wagner's epic-opera cycle *Der Ring des Nibelungen* (1852–72).

William Turner captured misty Rhine sunsets on canvas. Famous literary works, such as Goethe's *Sanct Rochus-Fest zu Bingen* (The Feast of St. Roch; 1814), Lord Byron's *Childe Harold's Pilgrimage* (1816), and Mark Twain's *A Tramp Abroad* (1880), captured the spirit of Rhine Romanticism on paper, encouraging others to follow in their footsteps.

Driving is the ideal way to travel—up one side of the Rhine and down the other—with time out for a cruise. But even the train route between Wiesbaden and Koblenz offers thrilling views.

If you have 3 days

Travel down the Rhine toward Rüdesheim, stopping near **Eltville** 2 to visit the historical monastery **Kloster Eberbach,** the cultural wine center of the Rheingau. Take in the beauty of the Rhine Gorge, with its steep vineyards, legendary castles, and the **Loreley** rock, on a Rhine steamer cruise from **Rüdesheim** 4 to **St. Goarshausen** 10. Return by train and stay overnight in a Rheingau wine village between Eltville and Rüdesheim. The second day, ferry from Rüdesheim to **Bingen** 5 for a closer look at the romantic Mittelrhein. The period rooms in Rheinstein, Reichenstein, and Sooneck castles evoke the region's medieval past, as do the town walls, towers, and historic buildings in the wine villages of **Bacharach** 6, **Oberwesel** 8, **St. Goar** 9, and **Boppard** 11. The last also has significant relics from Roman times. From there drive about 20 km (12 mi) to the Mosel Valley (toward Brodenbach) to spend the night in a wine village such as Dieblich, **Alken** 23, or **Treis-Karden** 24. Start the third day with a visit to the fairy-tale castle **Burg Eltz.** Follow the Mosel downstream to its confluence with the Rhine at **Koblenz** 12–21, spending the rest of the day exploring the sights of the city or the nearby castles **Stolzenfels, Marksburg,** and **Ehrenbreitstein.**

10

If you have 5 days

Spend an afternoon and night in **Wiesbaden** 1 to enjoy the thermal springs, elegant shops, and nightlife. The next morning visit **Kloster Eberbach** and a wine estate, or proceed to **Rüdesheim** 4 for a Rhine steamer cruise to **St. Goarshausen** 10. Return by train and take the cable car to the Niederwald-Denkmal (monument) overlooking Rüdesheim for an outstanding panoramic view of the Rhine Valley. The third morning continue downstream to **Kaub** 7 to visit the **Pfalz,** a medieval fortress. Ferry across the Rhine to **Bacharach** 6. See the medieval towns of **Oberwesel** 8, **St. Goar** 9, and **Boppard** 11. Overnight in **Koblenz** 12–21. The fourth day travel along the Mosel River to **Burg Eltz,** followed by stops in **Cochem** 25 and a few of the charming wine villages upstream. Stay overnight in or near **Bernkastel-Kues** 28, with its picturesque market square, wine museum, and wine-tasting centers. On Day 5 enjoy the natural beauty of the Mosel during an hour-long boat excursion from Bernkastel before following the river upstream to **Trier** 29–42, the former capital of the western Roman Empire.

If you have 7 days

Follow the five-day itinerary above. Travel from **Trier** 29–42 to **Köln** 53–67 via the autobahn. Spend the sixth day and night in Köln, visiting the Dom, a masterpiece of Gothic architecture, and one or more of the Romanesque churches and excellent museums. Devote the last day to **Aachen,** an elegant spa and the single-greatest storehouse of Carolingian architecture in Europe.

No less romantic is the dreamy landscape of the Mosel Valley. Vines and forests still carpet the steep slate slopes lining the river from Trier, the former capital of the western Roman Empire, to its confluence with the Rhine at Koblenz. En route there's a wealth of Roman artifacts, medieval churches, and castle ruins to admire.

About the Restaurants

Although Düsseldorf, Köln, and Wiesbaden are home to many talented chefs, some of Germany's most creative classic and contemporary cooking is found in smaller towns or country inns.

About the Hotels

The most romantic places to lay your head are the old riverside inns and castle hotels. Ask for a *Rheinblick* (Rhine view) room. Hotels are often booked well in advance, especially for festivals and when there are trade fairs in Köln, Düsseldorf, or Frankfurt, making rooms in Wiesbaden and the Rheingau scarce and expensive. Many hotels close for the winter.

WHAT IT COSTS In Euros

	$$$$	$$$	$$	$	¢
RESTAURANTS	over €25	€21–€25	€16–€20	€9–€15	under €9
HOTELS	over €225	€175–€225	€100–€175	€50–€100	under €50

Restaurant prices are per person for a main course at dinner. Hotel prices are for two people in a standard double room, including tax and service.

Timing

The peak season for cultural, food, and wine festivals is March–mid-November, followed by colorful Christmas markets in December. The season for many hotels, restaurants, riverboats, cable cars, and sights is from Easter through October, particularly in smaller towns. Opening hours at castles, churches, and small museums are shorter during winter. Orchards blossom in March, and the vineyards are verdant from May until mid-September, when the vines turn a shimmering gold.

THE RHEINGAU

The heart of the region begins in Wiesbaden, where the Rhine makes a sharp bend and flows east to west for some 30 km (19 mi) before resuming its south–north course at Rüdesheim. Wiesbaden is a good starting point to follow any of the well-marked cycling, hiking, and driving routes through the Rheingau's villages and vineyards. The cycling and hiking trails extend to Kaub in the Mittelrhein. Nearly every Rheingau village has an outdoor *Weinprobierstand* (wine-tasting stand), usually near the riverbank. They are staffed and stocked by a different wine estate every weekend in summer.

Festivals

The Rhineland is a stronghold of Germany's Fastnacht (Carnival festivities), which takes place from 11:11 AM on November 11 to Ash Wednesday, culminating with huge parades in Düsseldorf, Köln, and Mainz on the Monday before Lent. Some attractions close for the five days leading up to Ash Wednesday.

Festivals lasting well over a week at venues throughout the Rheingau are the Gourmet Festival (mid-March) and Glorreiche Tage (mid-November); the Rheingau Musik Festival (mid-June through August), with more than 100 concerts, often held at Kloster Eberbach, Schloss Johannisberg, or Wiesbaden's Kurhaus; and theater and concerts during the Burghof Spiele in and near Eltville (late June to late August). Wiesbaden hosts the region's largest wine festival, the Rheingauer Weinwoche (mid-August), and the Internationale Maifestspiele (throughout May), featuring performances by world-renowned artists. Bonn is home to the International Beethoven Festival (mid-September).

The spectacular fireworks display Rhein in Flammen (Rhine in Flames) takes place the first Saturday evening in May (Linz–Bonn), July (Bingen–Rüdesheim), and August (Andernach); the second Saturday evening in August (Koblenz) and September (Oberwesel); and the third Saturday evening in September (St. Goar).

Throughout the Mosel, Saar, and Ruwer valleys top chefs and winemakers present fine wine and food at 100 events, often with musical entertainment, during the International Wein & Gourmet Festival (mid-April to mid-May). From late May to early October some 60 indoor and open-air concerts (classical to contemporary) are held throughout the region during the Moselfestwochen Musikfestival.

On the Menu

Regional cuisine features fresh fish and *Wild* (game), as well as sauces and soups based on the local Riesling and Spätburgunder (Pinot noir) wines. *Tafelspitz* (boiled beef) and *Rheinischer Sauerbraten* (Rhenish marinated pot roast in a sweet-and-sour raisin gravy) are traditional favorites. The *Kartoffel* (potato) is prominent in soups, *Reibekuchen* and *Rösti* (potato pancakes), and *Dibbe- or Dippekuchen* (dialect: *Döppekoche*), a casserole baked in a cast-iron pot and served with apple compote. *Himmel und Erde,* literally "heaven and earth," is a mixture of mashed potatoes and chunky applesauce, topped with pan-fried slices of blood sausage and onions.

Classical Music

Few regions in Europe rival the quality of classical music performances and venues on the Rhine. Beethoven was born in Bonn, and the city hosts a Beethoven festival every year in mid- to late September. Düsseldorf, once home to Mendelssohn, Schumann, and Brahms, has the finest concert hall in Germany after Berlin's Philharmonie: the Tonhalle, in a former planetarium. Köln also has one of Germany's best concert halls, and its opera company is known for exciting classical and contemporary productions. The cathedrals of Aachen, Köln, and Trier are magnificent settings for concerts and organ recitals.

Wine Regions Riesling is the predominant white grape, and Spätburgunder (Pinot noir) the most important red variety in the Rheingau, Mittelrhein, and Mosel wine regions covered in this chapter. Three abutting wine regions—Rheinhessen and the Nahe, near Bingen, and the Ahr, southwest of Bonn—add to the variety of wines available along the route.

Wiesbaden

❶ *40 km (25 mi) west of Frankfurt via A–66.*

Wiesbaden, the capital of the state of Hesse, is a small city of tree-lined avenues with elegant shops and handsome facades. Its hot mineral springs have been a drawing card since the days when it was known as Aquis Mattiacis ("the waters of the Mattiaci")—the words boldly inscribed on the portal of the Kurhaus—and Wisibada ("the bath in the meadow"). In the first century AD the Romans built thermal baths here, a site then inhabited by a Germanic tribe, the Mattiaci. Modern Wiesbaden dates from the 19th century, when the dukes of Nassau and, later, the Prussian aristocracy commissioned the grand public buildings and parks that shape the city's profile today. Wiesbaden developed into a fashionable spa that attracted the rich and the famous. Their ornate villas on the Neroberg and turn-of-the-20th-century town houses are part of the city's flair.

The tourist-information office sells the two-day pass *Wiesbaden Tourist Card* (€9.50), which provides free public transportation in the city, to the main train station in Mainz, and to Frankfurt airport, as well as many discounts in museums and shops.

For a one-hour ride through the city, board the little train **THermine** (April to October). The one-day ticket (€5.40) enables you to get on and off as often as you'd like to explore the sights. It departs six times daily (10:30–5) from Café Lumen (behind the Marktkirche), and stops at the Rhein-Main-Halle (opposite the museum), Dorint Hotel, Staatstheater, Greek chapel, and Neroberg railway station.

★ Built in 1907, the neoclassical **Kurhaus** (✉ Kurhauspl.) is the social-cultural center of town. It houses the casino and the Thiersch-Saal, a splendid setting for concerts. The Staatstheater (1894), opulently appointed in baroque and rococo revival styles, and two beautifully landscaped parks flank the Kurhaus. Today you can "take the waters" in an ambience reminiscent of Roman times in the **Irisch-Römisches Bad** (Irish-Roman Bath; ✉ Langg. 38–40) at the Kaiser-Friedrich-Therme, a superb art-nouveau bathhouse from 1913. On Kranzplatz, 15 of Wiesbaden's 26 springs converge at the steaming **Kochbrunnen Fountain,** where the healthful waters are there for the tasting.

Historical buildings ring the Schlossplatz (Palace Square) and the adjoining **Marktplatz** (Market Square), site of the farmers' market (Wednesday and Saturday). Behind the neo-Gothic brick Marktkirche (Market Church), food and wine vendors ply their wares in the vaulted cellars of the Marktkeller. The **Altstadt** (Old Town) is just behind the Schloss (now the seat of parliament, the Hessischer Landtag) on Grabenstrasse, Wagemannstrasse, and Goldgasse. The **Museum Wiesbaden** is known for its collection of expressionist paintings, particularly the works of Russian artist Alexej Jawlensky. Renovations are underway; during this time the entrance is on the back side of the building (August-Viktoria-Str.). ✉ *Friedrich-Ebert-Allee 2* ☎ *0611/335–2250* 🌐 *www.museum-wiesbaden.de* 🎟 *€2.50, free Tues. 4–8* ⏲ *Tues. 10–8, Wed.–Sun. 10–5.*

Where to Stay & Eat

$$–$$$$ ✕ **Käfer's.** This popular Kurhaus bistro with striking art-nouveau decor, a grand piano (live music nightly), and a good-size bar attracts an upscale clientele. Ambience is the main attraction here. Book a table for two in one of the window alcoves (Nos. 7, 12, 25, and 29) for some privacy among the otherwise close-set tables. *Lachstatar* (salmon tartare) and *Bauernente* (farmer's duck) are standard favorites. A few Champagnes are available by the glass, and a bottle of Veuve Clicquot Brut Champagne at €45.60 is an excellent value. Käfer's also caters the beer garden behind the Kurhaus. ✉ *Kurhauspl. 1* ☎ *0611/536–200* 🌐 *www.kurhaus-gastronomie.de* 💳 *AE, MC, V.*

$–$$$ ✕ **M Restaurant.** Behind the historical facade (1880) of house No. 49 is an upscale culinary gem that attracts a sophisticated crowd. Despite its cozy size, "M" is light and spacious. Changing modern-art exhibitions and a large African kudu trophy line the walls. Native Austrians Markus Seegert and Bernhard Weber have added a "touch of home" to the excellent wine list and serve a few classic German/Austrian dishes. Their creative cooking, often with Mediterranean and Asian accents, and desserts are top notch. Try the sour cream ice cream or orange-chocolate cake with Valrhona chocolate mousse. ✉ *Taunusstr. 49* ☎ *0611/204–8765* 🌐 *www.mrestaurant.de* 💳 *AE* ⏲ *Closed Mon. No lunch Sun.*

$–$$ ✕ **Prinz von Oranien.** Nina and "Fips" Geilfuss run a chic little restaurant near Rheinstrasse and the pedestrian zone. The homemade soups, generous salads, and seasonal specialties are recommended, as are traditional favorites, such as breast of duck in a honey-ginger sauce or Charolais steak with potato gratin. With its sleek, modern furnishings, fresh flowers, and soft lighting, this dining spot is classy, comfortable, and friendly. ✉ *Oranienstr. 2* ☎ *0611/724–3200* 🌐 *www.prinz-von-oranien.com* 💳 *AE, MC, V* ⏲ *Closed Sun. No lunch Wed. or Sat.*

¢–$ ✕ **Sherry & Port.** Gerd Royko's friendly neighborhood bistro-pub hosts live music on Friday from October through March. During warm months, dine at outdoor tables surrounding a huge fountain on tree-lined Adolfsallee. In addition to the fantastic number of sherries (30), ports (17), and malt whiskeys (18) by the glass, there's a good selection of beers (Guinness on tap) and wines to accompany everything from tapas and salads to steaks and popularly priced daily specials (€5.55). ✉ *Adolfsallee 11* ☎ *0611/373–632* 🌐 *www.sherry-und-port.de* 💳 *No credit cards.*

$$$$ ✕🏨 **Nassauer Hof.** Wiesbaden's premier address for well over a century, this elegant hotel opposite the Kurhaus lies on the site of a Roman fortress that was converted into a spa and, ultimately, a guesthouse. It's internationally renowned for its luxuriously appointed rooms, topflight ser-

Fodor's Choice ★

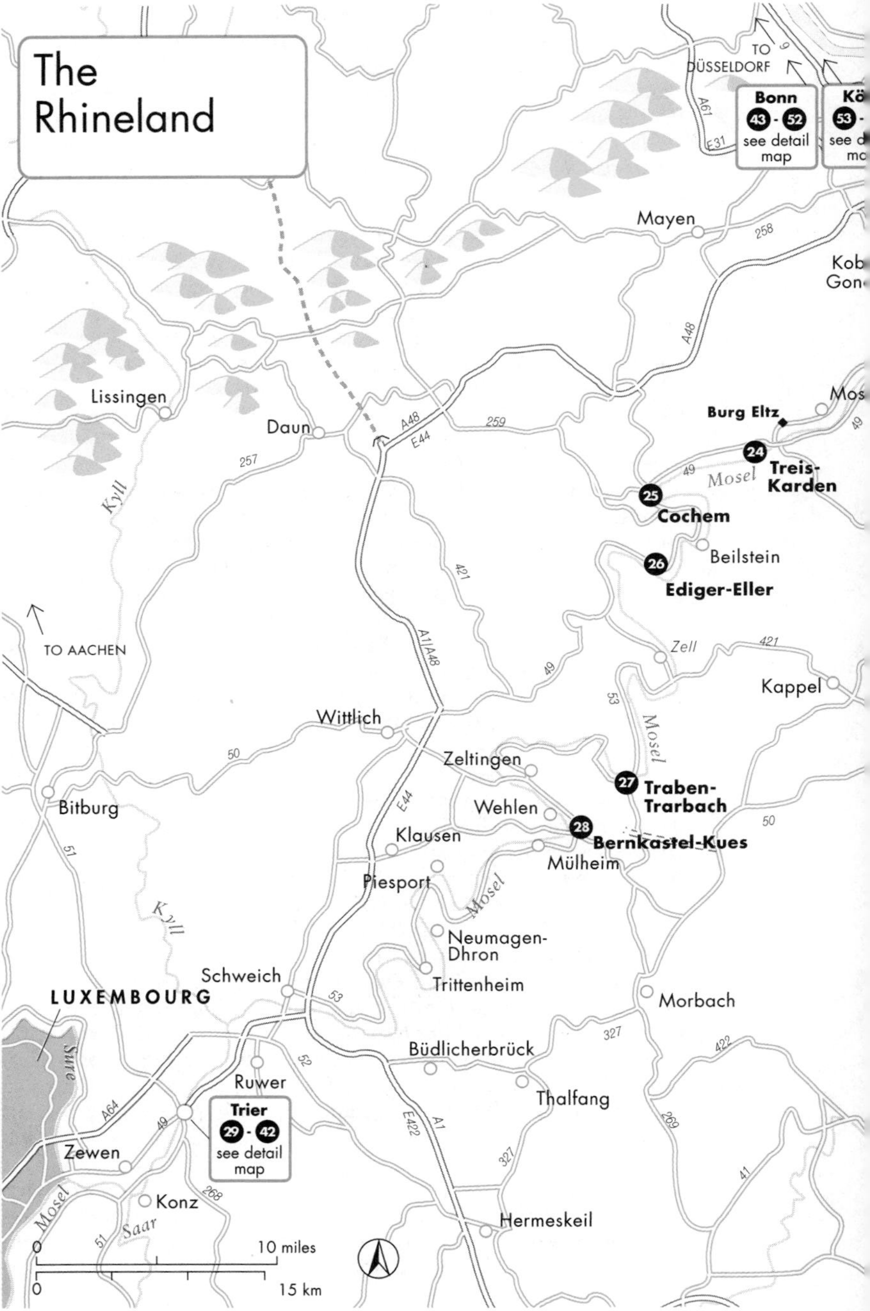
The Rhineland
TO DÜSSELDORF
Bonn
43 - 52
see detail map
Mayen
Lissingen
Daun
Burg Eltz
24 Treis-Karden
25 Cochem
Beilstein
26 Ediger-Eller
Mosel
Kyll
TO AACHEN
Zell
Kappel
Wittlich
Zeltingen
27 Traben-Trarbach
Bitburg
Wehlen
28 Bernkastel-Kues
Klausen
Mülheim
Piesport
Neumagen-Dhron
Trittenheim
Schweich
LUXEMBOURG
Morbach
Büdlicherbrück
Ruwer
Thalfang
Trier
29 - 42
see detail map
Zewen
Konz
Saar
Sure
Hermeskeil
0
10 miles
0
15 km

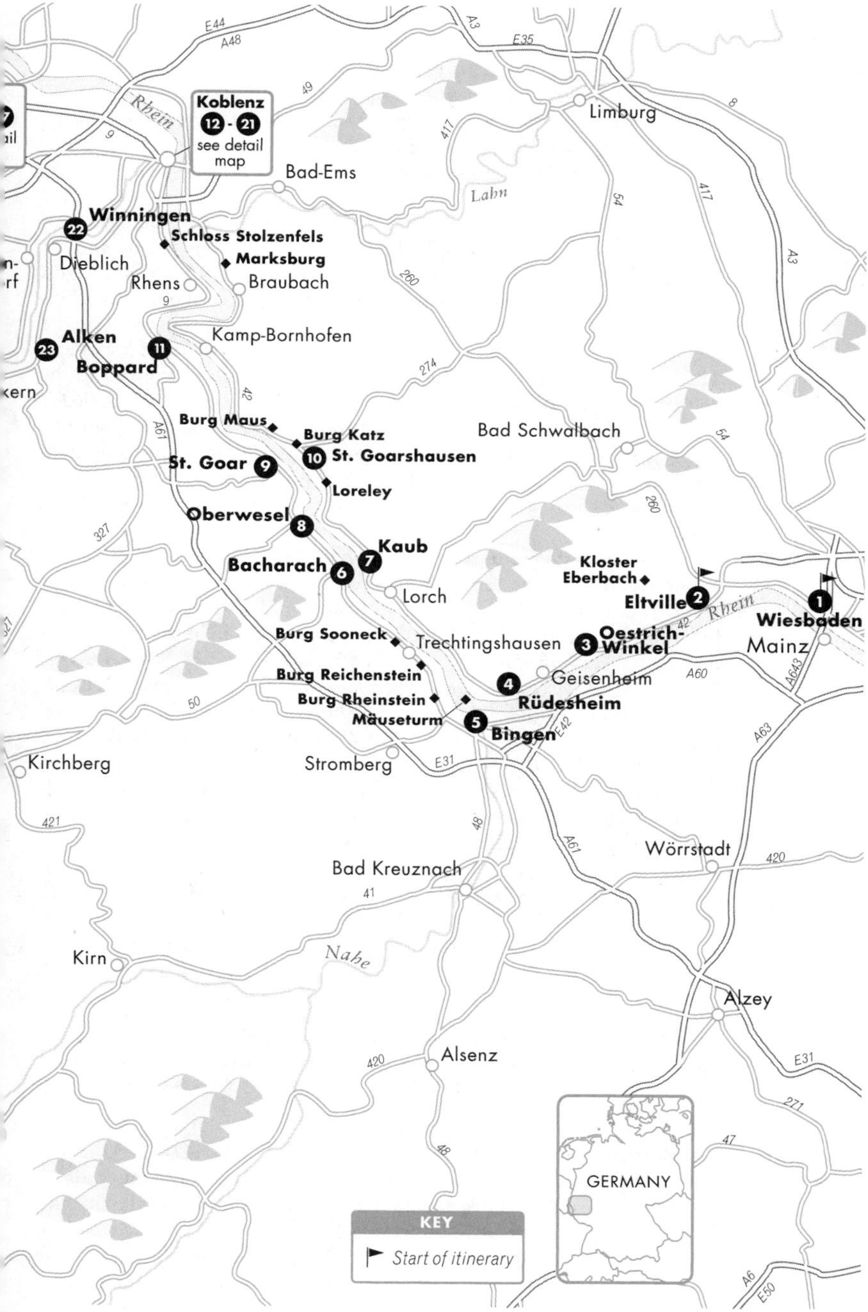
Koblenz
12 - 21
see detail map
Limburg
Bad-Ems
Lahn
Rhein
Winningen
22
Schloss Stolzenfels
Marksburg
Dieblich
Rhens
Braubach
Kamp-Bornhofen
Alken
23
Boppard
11
Burg Maus
Burg Katz
St. Goarshausen
10
St. Goar
9
Loreley
Bad Schwalbach
Oberwesel
8
Kaub
7
Bacharach
6
Lorch
Kloster Eberbach
Eltville
2
Wiesbaden
1
Mainz
Oestrich-Winkel
3
Burg Sooneck
Trechtingshausen
Burg Reichenstein
Geisenheim
4
Burg Rheinstein
Mäuseturm
Rüdesheim
5
Bingen
Kirchberg
Stromberg
Wörrstadt
Bad Kreuznach
Kirn
Nahe
Alzey
Alsenz
GERMANY
KEY
Start of itinerary

vice, and restaurants—Ente ($$$$, closed one week in January, 2 weeks in August, and Sunday) and Orangerie ($–$$$$), both open for lunch and dinner. ✉ *Kaiser-Friedrich-Pl. 3–4, D–65183* ☎ *0611/1330* 📠 *0611/133–632* 🌐 *www.nassauer-hof.de* ⇆ *139 rooms, 30 suites* ♁ *2 restaurants, minibars, cable TV, in-room data ports, indoor pool, gym, sauna, spa, bicycles, lobby lounge, piano bar, babysitting, dry cleaning, laundry service, concierge, Internet room, business services, no-smoking rooms* ▭ *AE, DC, MC, V.*

★ **$$–$$$** **Trüffel.** For years truffle lovers have indulged in the "diamonds of the kitchen"—or the sumptuous chocolate versions—at Cristina and Dr. Manuel Stirn's first-rate delicatessen and bistro. A classy hotel and restaurant round out operations. Personal service, stylish decor, and luxury baths make for a very pleasant stay. Trüffel (truffles) are still on the menu at the bistro ($) and at the restaurant Trüffel First Floor ($$–$$$). The chocolates (and superb foods and beverages) merit a detour to the delicatessen. ✉ *Weberg. 6–8, D–65183* ☎ *0611/990–550* 📠 *0611/990–5511* 🌐 *www.trueffel.net* ⇆ *24 rooms, 4 suites* ♁ *2 restaurants, café, patisserie, minibars, cable TV, in-room broadband, in-room data ports, Wi-Fi, 2 bars, shop, babysitting, dry cleaning, laundry service, some pets allowed (fee); no smoking* ▭ *AE, DC, MC, V* ⊙ *Restaurant closed Sun.* 🍽 *BP.*

$$–$$$ **Best Western Hotel Hansa.** This very comfortable, modern hotel in an art-nouveau house is centrally located and only a brief walk to the main train station, the Kurhaus, and the Old Town. Enjoy the hearty breakfast buffet on the ground floor, or head for one of the many cafés nearby. ✉ *Bahnhofstr. 23, D–65185* ☎ *0611/901–240* 📠 *0611/9012–4666* 🌐 *www.hansa.bestwestern.de* ⇆ *80 rooms, 1 suite* ♁ *Cable TV, in-room broadband, in-room data ports, some Wi-Fi, dry cleaning, laundry service, some pets allowed (fee), no-smoking floors; no a/c* ▭ *AE, DC, MC, V.*

$ **Ibis.** This modern hotel opposite the Kochbrunnen on Kranzplatz offers excellent value and a location within walking distance of the shop-filled pedestrian zone, the Old Town, and all sights. The well-kept rooms have contemporary furnishings and are functional. ✉ *Georg-August-Zinn-Str. 2, D–65183* ☎ *0611/36140* 📠 *0611/361–4499* 🌐 *www.ibishotel.com* ⇆ *131 rooms* ♁ *Cable TV, in-room data ports, Wi-Fi, bar, lobby lounge, some pets allowed (fee), no-smoking rooms* ▭ *AE, DC, MC, V.*

Nightlife & the Arts

In addition to the casino, restaurants, bars, and beer garden at the Kurhaus, nightlife is centered in the many bistros and pubs on Taunusstrasse and in the Old Town. The tourist office provides schedules and sells tickets for most venues listed below.

The **Hessisches Staatstheater** (✉ Chr.-Zais-Str. 3 ☎ 0611/132–325) presents classical and contemporary opera, theater, ballet, and musicals on three stages: Grosses Haus, Kleines Haus, and Studio. Great classics and avant-garde films, as well as dance and small theatrical productions, are specialties of the **Caligari Filmbühne** (✉ Marktpl. 9, behind Marktkirche ☎ 0611/313–779). Smaller dramatic productions and cabaret are performed at the intimate **Pariser Hoftheater** (✉ Spiegelg. 9 ☎ 0611/300–607). **Thalhaus** (✉ Nerotal 18 ☎ 0611/185–1267) is a lively, multiarts venue. Live concerts (jazz, blues, rock, and pop), often accompanied by readings or theater, are held at the **Walhalla Studio Theater** (✉ Mauritiusstr. 1a [use entrance of movie theater Bambi Kino] ☎ 0611/910–3743 🌐 www.walhalla-studio.de).

The Hessian State Orchestra performs in the **Kurhaus** (✉ Kurhauspl. 1 ☎ 0611/17290). Concerts and musicals are staged at the **Rhein-Main-Hallen** (✉ Rheinstr. 20 ☎ 0611/1440). The **Villa Clementine** (✉ Frankfurter Str. 1 ☎ 0611/313–642) is a regular concert venue. The sparkling-wine cellars of **Henkell & Söhnlein** (✉ Biebricher Allee 142 ☎ 0611/630) host a series of concerts in their splendid foyer. Many churches offer concerts, including the free organ concerts Saturday at 11:30 in the **Marktkirche.**

At the **Spielbank** (casino), the Grosses Spiel (roulette, blackjack) in the Kurhaus is lively from 3 PM to 3 AM, while the Kleines Spiel (slots) in the neighboring Kolonnade, is hopping from 1 PM to 4 AM. The former is one of Europe's grand casinos, where jacket and tie are required. Minimum age is 18 (bring your passport). ✉ *Kurhauspl. 1* ☎ *0611/536–100* 🌐 *www.spielbank-wiesbaden.de* 🎟 *Grosses Spiel €2.50, Kleines Spiel €1.*

Thermal Springs, Spas & Pools

Pamper yourself with the **Kaiser-Friedrich-Therme**'s thermal spring and cold-water pools, various steam baths and saunas, two solaria, and a score of health and wellness treatments in elegant art-nouveau surroundings. Towels and robes can be rented on-site, but come prepared for "textile-free" bathing. Children under 16 are not admitted. ✉ *Langg. 38–40, entrance faces Weberg.* ☎ *0611/172–9660* 🎟 *4 hrs in pools, steam baths, and saunas €17.50* ⏲ *Sat.–Thurs. 10–10, Fri. 10 AM–midnight; Tues. women only; massage and treatments by appointment.*

Another art-nouveau spa with its own thermal spring is the **Badhaus** in the Radisson SAS Schwarzer Bock Hotel opposite the Kochbrunnen. The very professional, personalized service for massage and individual therapeutic and beauty baths is excellent. ✉ *Kranzplatz 12* ☎ *0611/1550 or 0611/155–630* 🎟 *Pool, sauna, fitness room, no time limit €13* ⏲ *Weekdays 7 AM–9 PM, weekends 9 AM–5 PM; massage and treatments by appointment.*

There's year-round swimming indoors and out thanks to the thermal springs (32°C [90°F]) that feed the pools at the **Thermalbad Aukammtal.** The facility includes eight saunas, a whirlpool, massage, and balneological treatments. ✉ *Leibnizstr. 7, bus No. 18 from Wilhelmstr. to Aukamm Valley* ☎ *0611/172–9880* 🎟 *Pools €8.50; saunas €15 combination €20. Ticket valid for one day* ⏲ *Sun.–Thurs. 8 AM–10 PM, Fri. and Sat. 8 AM–midnight.*

The **Opelbad,** a large, outdoor swimming pool on the Neroberg, is idyllically set on the edge of the city forest, overlooking Wiesbaden and the Rheingau. To get there, you can drive, walk, or take the **Nerobergbahn,** a historical railway dating from 1888. ✉ *Neroberg* ☎ *0611/172–9885* 🎫 €6 ⏲ *May–Sept., daily 7 AM–8 PM.*

Shopping

Broad, tree-lined Wilhelmstrasse, with designer boutiques housed in its fin-de-siècle buildings, is one of Germany's most elegant shopping streets. Wiesbaden is also known as one of the best places in the country to find antiques; Taunusstrasse has excellent antiques shops. The Altstadt is full of upscale boutiques; Kirchgasse and its extension, Langgasse, are the heart of the shop-filled pedestrian zone.

Eltville

2 *14 km (9 mi) west of Wiesbaden via A–66 and B–42.*

Eltville, Alta Villa in Roman times, was first in the Rheingau to receive town rights (1332). Eltville flourished as a favorite residence of the archbishops of Mainz in the 14th and 15th centuries, and it was during this time that the **Kurfürstliche Burg** (Electors' Castle) was built. The castle has an exhibition commemorating Johannes Gutenberg (1400–68), the inventor of movable type. He lived in Eltville on and off, and it was here that he was named a courtier by elector Adolf II of Nassau in 1465. More than 300 varities of **roses** can be admired in the castle's courtyard garden, on the wall, and along the Rhine promenade. During "Rose Days" (the first weekend in June) the flower is celebrated in shops and restaurants (as an ingredient in recipes) throughout town. ✉ *Burgstr. 1* ☎ *06123/90980* 🎫 *Tower €1.50, rose garden free* ⏲ *Tower open Apr.–mid-Oct., Fri. 2–6 and weekends 11–6; exhibition Sun. 3–5; rose garden Easter–mid-Oct., daily 9:30–7 and mid-Oct.–Easter, daily 10:30–5.*

The parish church of **Sts. Peter und Paul** has late-Gothic frescoes, Renaissance tombstones, and a carved baptismal by the Rhenish sculptor Hans Backoffen (or his studio). Worth seeing are Burg Crass (Crass Castle) on the riverbank and the half-timber houses and aristocratic **manors** on the lanes between the river and Rheingauer Strasse (B–42), notably the Bechtermünzer Hof (Kirchgasse 6), Stockheimer Hof (Ellenbogengasse 6), and Eltzer Hof (at the Martinstor gateway).

Sekt (sparkling-wine) production in the Rheingau is concentrated in Eltville, Wiesbaden, and Rüdesheim. The tree-lined Rhine promenade here hosts the annual Sekt festival during the first weekend of July. The administrative headquarters and main cellars of the **Hessian State Wine Domains,** Germany's largest wine estate, are in town. The estate owns nearly 500 acres of vineyards throughout the Rheingau and in the Hessische Bergstrasse wine region south of Frankfurt. Its shops—in the art nouveau–press house built in 1911 and at nearby Kloster Eberbach—offer a comprehensive regional selection. ✉ *Schwalbacher Str. 56–62* ☎ *06123/92300* 🌐 *www.weingut-kloster-eberbach.de* 💳 *AE, MC, V* ⏲ *Weekdays 10–6, Sat. 10–4.*

For a good look at the central Rheingau, make a brief circular tour from Eltville. Drive 3 km (2 mi) north via the Kiedricher Strasse to the Gothic village of **Kiedrich.** In the distance you can see the tower of Scharfenstein castle (1215) and the spires of **St. Valentine's Church** and St. Michael's Chapel, both from the 15th century. If you attend the church's 9:30 AM mass on Sunday, you can admire the splendid Gothic furnishings and star vaulting amid the sounds of Gregorian chants and one of Germany's oldest organs. The chapel next door, once a charnel house, has a unique chandelier sculpted around a nearly life-size, two-sided Madonna.

These Gothic gems have survived intact thanks to 19th-century restorations patronized by the English baronet John Sutton. Today Sutton's beautiful villa south of the church is home to one of Germany's leading wine estates, **Weingut Robert Weil.** Its famed Kiedricher Gräfenberg Riesling wines can be sampled in the ultramodern wein*galerie* (tasting room and wineshop). ✉ *Mühlberg 5* ☎ *06123/2308* 🌐 *www.weingut-robert-weil.com* ⏲ *Weekdays 8–5:30, Sat. 10–4, Sun. 11–5.*

Fodor'sChoice ★ The former Cistercian monastery **Kloster Eberbach** is idyllically set in a secluded forest clearing 3 km (2 mi) west of Kiedrich. Its Romanesque and Gothic buildings (12th–14th centuries) look untouched by time—one reason why the film of Umberto Eco's medieval murder mystery *The Name of the Rose,* starring Sean Connery, was partially filmed here. The monastery's impressive collection of old wine presses and the historic Cabinet Cellar, once reserved for the best barrels, bear witness to a viticultural tradition that spans nearly nine centuries. The wines can be sampled year-round in the **wineshop** or restaurants on the grounds. The church, with its excellent acoustics, and the large medieval dormitories are the settings for concerts, wine auctions, and festive wine events. *Stiftung Kloster Eberbach* ✉ *Postfach 1453, D–65334 Eltville* ☎ *06723/91780* 🌐 *www.klostereberbach.de* 🎫 *€3.50* ⏲ *Easter–Oct., daily 10–6; Nov.–Easter, daily 11–5.*

From Eberbach take the road toward Hattenheim, stopping at the first right-hand turnoff to admire the monastery's premier vineyard, **Steinberg.** It's encircled by a 3-km-long (2-mi-long) stone wall (13th–18th centuries). The vineyard has an **outdoor pub,** Brot und Wein ("bread and wine"). ⏲ *May–Sept., weekends 11–7.*

The *Brunnen* (springs) beneath the vineyards of Hattenheim and Erbach, both on the Rhine, lend their name to three excellent **vineyards**: Nussbrunnen, Wisselbrunnen, and Marcobrunnen—on the boundary between the two towns. As you return to Eltville (2 km [1 mi] east of Erbach on B–42), you will pass the elegant 19th-century palace Schloss Reinhartshausen (now a hotel and wine estate).

Where to Stay & Eat

$ ✕ **Gutsausschank im Baiken.** Andrea and Stefan Seyffardt's cozy wine restaurant is set on a hilltop amid the famed Rauenthaler Baiken vineyard. The magnificent panorama from the vine-canopied terrace, the fresh country cooking, and superb wines—from the Hessian State Wine Domains—make for a "Rheingau Riesling" experience par excellence. Riesling cream soup and Riesling lasagne (with ground meat and leeks) are house specialties. ✉ *Wiesweg 86, via Eltville* ☎ *06123/900–345* 🌐 *www.baiken.de* 💳 *MC, V* ⊗ *Closed Mon. and Nov.–mid-Apr. No lunch.*

$$$$ **Fodor's Choice** ★ ✕🏨 **Schloss Reinhartshausen.** A palace in every sense of the word, this hotel and wine estate overlooks the Rhine and beautifully landscaped gardens. Antiques and artworks fill the house, and some rooms have fireplaces and whirlpools. From morning until night you can dine in the airy, glass-lined Wintergarten ($$$–$$$$) or on its terrace. Upscale contemporary cuisine and dishes with a Mediterranean accent are served in the elegant Balzerís Schlosskeller ($$–$$$$; no lunch). The casual Schloss Schänke (¢; no credit cards; no lunch weekdays) in the old press house offers light fare and hearty snacks. The estate's wines are also sold daily in the Vinothek (AE, MC, V). ✉ *Hauptstr. 43, D–65346 Eltville-Erbach* ☎ *06123/6760* 🖷 *06123/676–400* 🌐 *www.schloss-hotel.de* *39 rooms, 15 suites* *3 restaurants, room service, minibars, cable TV, in-room data ports, Wi-Fi, indoor pool, hot tub, sauna, spa, bicycles, bar, lobby lounge, Weinstube, babysitting, dry cleaning, laundry service, concierge, business services, some pets allowed (fee), no-smoking rooms* 💳 *AE, DC, MC, V.*

$$ ✕🏨 **Klosterschänke und Gästehaus Kloster Eberbach.** The monks never had it this good: the Marschollek family's modern and comfortable rooms are a far cry from the unheated stone dormitories of the past. Beneath the vaulted ceiling of the Klosterschänke ($–$$) you can sample the wines of the Hessian State Wine Domains with regional cuisine. Try the *Weinfleisch* (pork goulash in Riesling sauce) or *Zisterzienser Brot,* which translates to "Cistercian bread" (minced meat in a plum-and-bacon dressing with boiled potatoes). The Pfortenhaus (¢), next to the western gateway entrance of the wall, serves snacks and a few warm dishes (Thurs.–Sun.). ✉ *Kloster Eberbach, D–65346 Eltville, Via Kiedrich or Hattenheim* ☎ *06723/9930* 🖷 *06723/993–100* 🌐 *www.klostereberbach.com* *28 rooms* *Restaurant, snack bar, cable TV, in-room data ports, sauna, some pets allowed, no-smoking rooms; no a/c* 💳 *AE, MC, V* 🍽 *BP.*

$$ **Fodor's Choice** ★ ✕🏨 **Kronenschlösschen.** The atmosphere of this stylish art-nouveau house (1894) is intimate, and the individually designed rooms have antique furnishings and marble baths. Chef Patrik Kimpel oversees both the gourmet restaurant Kronenschlösschen ($$$$) and the more casual Bistro ($$–$$$). Fish is a house specialty (try the scallops in a sesame-vanilla crust), but all dishes are beautifully presented with very flavorful sauces. You can also dine in the parklike garden. The wine list focuses on the finest Rheingau estates for whites and Old and New World estates for reds. ✉ *Rheinallee, D–65347 Eltville-Hattenheim* ☎ *06723/640* 🖷 *06723/7663* 🌐 *www.kronenschloesschen.de* *8 rooms, 10 suites* *2 restaurants, minibars, cable TV, in-room data ports, Wi-Fi, bar, lobby lounge, babysitting, dry cleaning, laundry service, business services, some pets allowed (fee), no-smoking rooms; no a/c* 💳 *AE, MC, V.*

★ $$ ✕🏨 **Zum Krug.** Winegrower Josef Laufer more than lives up to the hospitality promised by the wreath and *Krug* (earthenware pitcher) hanging above the front door. The rooms have modern baths and dark-wood furnishings. Equally cozy is the wood-panel restaurant ($$–$$$), with its old tiled oven. The German fare includes wild duck, goose, game, or sauerbraten served in rich, flavorful gravies. The three-course lunch specials (€10) are a great value. The wine list is legendary for its scope (600 Rheingau wines) and large selection of older vintages. ✉ *Hauptstr. 34, D–65347 Eltville-Hattenheim* ☎ *06723/99680* 📠 *06723/996–825* 🌐 *www.hotel-zum-krug.de* 🛏 *8 rooms* 👍 *Restaurant, minibars, cable TV, laundry service, Internet room, business services, some pets allowed; no a/c, no smoking* 💳 *DC, MC, V* ⏲ *Closed 1st half of Jan. and 2nd half of July. Restaurant also closed Mon. No dinner Sun., no lunch Tues.* 🍽 *BP.*

$ ✕🏨 **Maximilianshof.** For generations the von Oetinger family has shared its home, its wines, and its simple, hearty cooking (¢–$) with guests from near and far. In winter the warm art-nouveau parlor beckons with its plush sofas; in summer, tables are set out on the pretty terrace. Across the courtyard, there's a cheerful, modern guesthouse with nine rooms, each named after a local vineyard. Honigberg has a private sauna; Hohenrain has a nifty little kitchen and can be booked as a holiday flat for up to five people. ✉ *Rheinallee 2, D–65346 Eltville-Erbach* ☎ *06123/92240* 📠 *06123/922–425* 🌐 *www.maximilianshof.de* 🛏 *9 rooms* 👍 *Restaurant, cable TV, in-room broadband, in-room data ports, dry cleaning, laundry service, business services, some pets allowed; no a/c* 💳 *DC, MC, V* ⏲ *Restaurant closed Mon. and mid-Jan.–mid-Feb. No lunch weekdays Apr.–Oct. or Mon.–Sat. Nov.–Mar.* 🍽 *BP.*

Oestrich-Winkel

❸ *21 km (13 mi) west of Wiesbaden, 7 km (4½ mi) west of Eltville on B–42.*

Oestrich's vineyard area is the largest in the Rheingau. Lenchen and Doosberg are the most important vineyards. You can sample the wines at the outdoor wine-tasting stand, opposite the 18th-century crane.

The village of Winkel (pronounced *vin*-kle) lies west of Oestrich. A Winkeler Hasensprung wine from the fabulous 1811 vintage was Goethe's wine of choice during his stay here with the Brentano family in 1814. The Goethe Zimmer (Goethe Room) in the **Brentano Haus,** with mementos and furnishings from Goethe's time, may be visited by appointment only. ✉ *Am Lindenpl. 2 65375 Oestrich-Winkel* ☎ *06723/2068* 🌐 *www.brentanohaus.de.*

★ The oldest (1211) of Germany's great private wine estates, **Schloss Vollrads,** lies 3 km (2 mi) north of town. The moated tower (1330) was the Greiffenclau residence for 350 years until the present palace was built in the 17th century. The period rooms are open during concerts, festivals, and wine tastings. ✉ *North on Schillerstr., turn right on Greiffenclaustr.* ☎ *06723/660* 🌐 *www.schlossvollrads.com* 💳 *MC, V* ⏲ *Vinothek Easter–Oct., weekdays 9–6, weekends 11–7; Nov.–Easter, weekdays 9–5, weekends noon–5. Outdoor tasting stand Easter–late Oct., weekends 11–7.*

★ The origins of the grand wine estate, **Schloss Johannisberg,** date from 1100, when Benedictine monks built a monastery and planted vines on the slopes below. The palace and remarkable cellars (visits by appointment only) were built in the early 18th century by the prince-abbots of Fulda. Every autumn a courier was sent from Johannisberg to Fulda to obtain permission to harvest the grapes. In 1775 the courier returned after considerable delay. The harvest was late and the grapes were far riper than usual; the resulting wines were exceptionally rich and fruity. *Spätlese* (literally, "late harvest," pronounced *shpate*-lay-zeh) wines have been highly esteemed ever since. A statue in the courtyard commemorates the "late rider." There are tastings at the Vinothek and the Gutsauschank (estate's restaurant). To get here from Winkel's main street, drive north on Schillerstrasse and proceed all the way uphill (there's a fine view at the top). After the road curves to the left, watch for the left turn to the castle. ✉ *Weinbaudomäne Schloss Johannisberg, Geisenheim-Johannisberg* ☎ *06722/70090 or 06722/700–935* 🌐 *www.schloss-johannisberg.de* ⏲ *Vinothek Mar.–Oct., weekdays 10–1 and 2–6, weekends 11–6; Nov.–Feb., weekdays 10–1 and 2–6, weekends 11–5.*

Where to Stay & Eat

$–$$ ✕ **Die Wirtschaft.** Beate and Florian Kreller's warm welcome and refined, seasonal country cooking have moved from Brentano Haus to historical quarters on Winkel's *Hauptstrasse* (main street). Indoors, fresh flowers and candles top the tables in a labyrinth of cozy niches with exposed beams and old stone walls (1602). No less inviting is the pretty courtyard. Tuesday, in winter, it's "steak night" (€12); in summer, BBQs in the courtyard (€16). Top-quality German specialties, such as *Heidschnuke* (lamb from the Lüneburger heath) and *hällisches Landschwein* (Swabian pork), are also served. ✉ *Hauptstr. 70, Winkel* ☎ *06723/7426* 💳 *No credit cards* ⏲ *Closed Mon. and 2 wks in July–Aug. No dinner Sun.*

$–$$ ✕ **Gutsausschank Schloss Johannisberg.** The glassed-in terrace affords a spectacular view of the Rhine and the vineyards from which the wine in your glass originated. Rheingau Riesling soup and *Bauernente* (farmer's duck) are house specialties. The lunch specials (€10) are a good value. ✉ *Schloss Johannisberg* ☎ *06722/96090* 🌐 *www.schloss-johannisberg.de* 💳 *AE, MC, V.*

$–$$ ✕ **Gutsrestaurant Schloss Vollrads.** Chef Matthias Böhler's "farmers' specialties" and creative seasonal menus are served with the estate's wines in the cavalier house (1650) or on the flower-lined terrace facing the garden. Check the Schloss Vollrads Web site (www.schlossvollrads.com) for a calendar of the many food-and-wine events throughout the year. ✉ *Schloss Vollrads, north of Winkel* ☎ *06723/5270* 💳 *MC, V* ⏲ *Closed Wed. Apr.–Oct.; Tues.–Thurs. Nov.–Mar.; and Jan.*

$$ 🏨 **Hotel Schwan.** This green-and-white half-timber inn has been in the Wenckstern family since it was built in 1628. All rooms offer modern comfort; the decor in the guesthouse is simpler than in the historic main building. Many rooms afford a Rhine view (103 [a junior suite] is especially nice), as does the beautiful terrace. The staff is friendly and helpful, and you can sample the family's wines in the historic wine cellar and purchase them on site. ✉ *Rheinallee 5, in Oestrich, D–65375*

Oestrich-Winkel ☎ 06723/8090 📠 06723/7820 🌐 www.hotel-schwan.de 52 rooms, 3 suites Restaurant, cable TV, in-room data ports, bar, lobby lounge, babysitting, dry cleaning, laundry service, business services, some pets allowed, no-smoking rooms; no a/c ▭ AE, DC, MC, V BP.

Rüdesheim

4 *30 km (19 mi) west of Wiesbaden, 9 km (5½ mi) west of Oestrich-Winkel on B–42.*

10

Tourism and wine are the heart and soul of Rüdesheim and best epitomized by the **Drosselgasse** (Thrush Alley). Less than 500 feet long, this narrow, pub-lined lane is abuzz with music and merrymaking from noon until well past midnight every day from Easter through October.

The **Asbach Weinbrennerei** (wine distillery) has produced Asbach, one of Germany's most popular brands of *Weinbrand* (wine brandy, the equivalent of cognac) here since 1892. It's a key ingredient in its brandy-filled *Pralinen* (chocolates) and in the local version of Irish coffee, Rüdesheimer Kaffee. A tour of the distillery operations concludes with a tasting. ✉ *Asbach Besucher Center, Ingelheimer Str. 4, on eastern edge of town* ☎ *06722/497–345* 🌐 *www.asbach.de* *€5* *Jan.–Mar. and Nov., Mon.–Thurs. 9–6, Fri. 9–1; Apr.–Oct. and Dec., Mon.–Thurs. 9–6, Fri. 9–1, Sat. 9–6; Sun. on request.*

The **Weinmuseum Brömserburg** (Brömserburg Wine Museum), housed in one of the oldest castles on the Rhine (circa AD 1000), displays wine-related artifacts and drinking vessels dating from Roman times. There are great views from the roof and the terrace, where you can sample local wines on weekends from mid-March to October. ✉ *Rheinstr. 2* ☎ *06722/2348* 🌐 *www.rheingauer-weinmuseum.de* *€3* *Mid-Mar.–Oct., daily 9–6.*

The 15th-century **Brömserhof** (Brömser Manor) holds Germany's largest collection of mechanical music instruments. Tours are educational and entertaining. ✉ *Siegfried's Mechanisches Musikkabinett, Oberstr. 29* ☎ *06722/49217* *€5.50* *Mar.–Dec., daily 10–6.*

High above Rüdesheim and visible for miles stands *Germania*, a colossal female statue crowning the **Niederwald-Denkmal** (Niederwald Monument). It was built between 1877 and 1883 to commemorate the rebirth of the German Empire after the Franco-Prussian War (1870–71). There are splendid panoramic views from the monument and from other vantage points on the edge of the forested plateau. You can reach the monument on foot, by car (via Grabenstrasse), or over the vineyards in the *Seilbahn* (cable car). There's also a *Sessellift* (chairlift) to and from Assmannshausen, a red-wine enclave, on the other side of the hill. ✉ *Oberstr. 37* ☎ *06722/2402* 🌐 *www.seilbahn-ruedesheim.de* *One-way €5, round-trip or combined ticket for cable car and chairlift €7. Ring-Ticket €10 for cable car, chairlift, and Rhine cruise* *Mid-Mar.–Apr. and Oct., daily 9:30–4:30; May–Sept., daily 9:30–6.*

With the wings of a glider you can silently soar over the Rhine Valley. At the **Luftsport-Club Rheingau** you can catch a 30- to 60-minute *Segelflug* (glider flight) on a glider plane between Rüdesheim and the Loreley; allow 1½ hours for pre- and postflight preparations. During the club's annual festival in mid-August, there are one-hour hot-air balloon flights early mornings/late evenings (€150–€200) by advance reservation only. ✉ *3 km (2 mi) north of Niederwald-Denkmal and Landgut Ebenthal* ☎ *06722/2979* 🌐 *www.lcr.rheingau-media.com* 🎫 *1st 5 min €12, each additional min €0.50; €1.50 per min in glider with motor* ⏲ *Apr.–Oct., weekends 10–7.*

Where to Stay & Eat

$–$$ ✕ **Rüdesheimer Schloss.** In a tithe house built in 1729, this wine tavern specializes in Hessian cuisine and Rheingauer Riesling and Spätburgunder wines from the Breuer family's own estate and those of its illustrious neighbors. The selection of older vintages is remarkable. Start with the delectable *Riesling-Käse-Suppe* (Riesling cheese soup). *Ente* (duck), *geräucherte Forelle* (smoked trout), and *Wildschweinwurst* (wild boar sausage) are all excellent. The daily lunch special (€9) includes a glass of wine. Typical Drosselgasse music and dancing are an entertaining backdrop indoors and in the tree-shaded courtyard. ✉ *Drosselg.* ☎ *06722/90500* 💳 *AE, DC, MC, V* ⏲ *Closed Jan. and Feb., except on request.*

$$–$$$ **Fodor'sChoice ★** ✕🏨 **Hotel Krone Assmannshausen.** This elegant, antiques-filled hotel and restaurant ($$$–$$$$) offers first-class service and fine wining and dining. Classic cuisine prepared by chef Willi Mittler and a superb collection of wines, including the famed Spätburgunder red wines of Assmannshausen, make for very memorable meals indoors or on the terrace overlooking the Rhine. Two of the suites have their own sauna. ✉ *Rheinuferstr. 10, D–65385 Rüdesheim-Assmannshausen* ☎ *06722/4030* 📠 *06722/3049* 🌐 *www.hotel-krone.com* 🛏 *52 rooms, 13 suites, 1 apartment* 👍 *Restaurant, minibars, cable TV, in-room data ports, Wi-Fi, pool, bar, babysitting, dry cleaning, laundry service, Internet room, business services, some pets allowed (fee), no-smoking rooms; no a/c* 💳 *AE, DC, MC, V.*

★ $$ 🏨 **Breuer's Rüdesheimer Schloss.** Gracious hosts Susanne and Heinrich Breuer have beautifully integrated modern designer decor into the historic walls of this stylish hotel. The Constantinescu Suite (No. 20) and the Rhine Suite (No. 14), with its large terrace, are popular; most rooms offer a vineyard view. Cellar or vineyard tours and wine tastings can be arranged. Wines from the family's Rheingau estate, Weingut Georg Breuer, and tasteful wine accessories are available at the Vinothek (on Grabenstr. 8). ✉ *Steing. 10, D–65385 Rüdesheim* ☎ *06722/90500* 📠 *06722/905–050* 🌐 *www.ruedesheimer-schloss.com* 🛏 *23 rooms, 3 suites* 👍 *Restaurant, minibars, cable TV, in-room data ports, Wi-Fi, bicycles, Ping-Pong, bar, lobby lounge, babysitting, dry cleaning, laundry service, business services, some pets allowed, no-smoking rooms; no a/c* 💳 *AE, DC, MC, V* ⏲ *Closed Christmas–early Jan.* 🍽 *BP.*

THE MITTELRHEIN

Updated by Kerry Brady

Bingen, like Rüdesheim, is a gateway to the Mittelrhein. From here to Koblenz lies the greatest concentration of Rhine castles. Most date from the 12th and 13th centuries but were destroyed in 1689 when French troops systematically blew them up and burned them down during the war of Palatinate succession. It's primarily thanks to the Prussian royal family and its penchant for historical preservation that numerous Rhine castles were rebuilt or restored in the 19th and early 20th centuries.

Two roads run parallel to the Rhine: B–42 (east side) and B–9 (west side). The spectacular views from the heights can best be enjoyed via the routes known as the Loreley-Burgenstrasse (east side), from Kaub to the Loreley to Kamp-Bornhofen; or the Rheingoldstrasse (west side), from Rheindiebach to Rhens. The Rheinhöhenweg (Rhine Heights Path) affords hikers the same splendid views, including descents into the villages en route. These marked trails run between Oppenheim on the Rhine Terrace and Bonn for 240 km (149 mi) and between Wiesbaden and Bonn-Beuel for 272 km (169 mi). The traffic-free paths through the vineyards and along the riverbanks are wonderful routes for hikers and cyclists alike.

Bingen

5 *35 km (22 mi) west of Wiesbaden via Mainz and A–60; ferry from wharf opposite Rüdesheim's train station.*

Bingen overlooks the Nahe-Rhine conflux near a treacherous stretch of shallows and rapids known as the Binger Loch (Bingen Hole). Early on, Bingen developed into an important commercial center, for it was here—as in Rüdesheim on the opposite shore—that goods were moved from ship to shore to circumvent the unnavigable waters. Bingen was also the crossroad of Roman trade routes between Mainz, Koblenz, and Trier. Thanks to this central location, it grew into a major center of the wine trade and remains so today. Wine is celebrated during 11 days of merrymaking in early September at the annual **Winzerfest.**

Bingen was destroyed repeatedly by wars and fires; thus there are many ancient foundations but few visible architectural remains of the past. Since Celtic times the Kloppberg (Klopp Hill), in the center of town, has been the site of a succession of citadels, all named **Burg Klopp** since 1282. The existing terrace has good views of the Rhine, the Nahe, and the surrounding hills.

Not far from the thousand-year-old Drususbrücke, a stone bridge over the Nahe, is the late Gothic **Basilika St. Martin.** It was originally built in 793 on the site of a Roman temple. The 11th-century crypt and Gothic and baroque furnishings merit a visit.

★ The **Historisches Museum am Strom** (History Museum) is housed in a former power station (1898) on the riverbank. Here you can see an intact set of Roman surgical tools (2nd century), period rooms from the Rhine

Romantic era, and displays about the Abbess St. Hildegard von Bingen (1098–1179), one of the most remarkable women of the Middle Ages. An outspoken critic of papal and imperial machinations, she was a highly respected scholar, naturopath, and artist whose mystic writings and music are much in vogue today. An excellent illustrated booklet in English on Rhine Romanticism, *The Romantic Rhine,* is sold at the museum shop. ✉ *Museumsstr. 3* ☎ *06721/990–654 or 06721/991–531* 🌐 *www.bingen.de* 🎟 *€3* ⏲ *Tues.–Sun. 10–5.*

The forested plateau of the Rochusberg (St. Roch Hill) is the pretty setting of the **Rochuskapelle** (St. Roch Chapel). Originally built in 1666 to celebrate the end of the plague, it has been rebuilt twice. On August 16, 1814, Goethe attended the consecration festivities, the forerunner of today's Rochusfest, a weeklong folk festival in mid-August. The chapel (open during Sunday services at 8 and 10) contains an altar dedicated to St. Hildegard and relics and furnishings from the convents she founded on the Ruppertsberg (in the suburb of Bingerbrück) and in Eibingen (east of Rüdesheim). The **Hildegard Forum** (☎ 06721/181–000 🌐 www.hildegard-forum.de ⏲ Tues.–Sun. 11–6), near the chapel, has exhibits related to St. Hildegard, a medieval herb garden, and a restaurant serving tasty, wholesome foods (*Dinkel,* or spelt, is a main ingredient) based on Hildegard's nutritional teachings. The lunch specials (Tues.–Sat. €8, Sun. €15) are a good value.

Where to Stay & Eat

$ ✕ **Schlösschen am Mäuseturm.** Dining on the terrace of this Schlösschen (little castle) with its view of the Mäuseturm and the Rhine makes for a very pleasant evening. The Steiningers serve fresh, seasonal cuisine as well as Pfälzer specialties. The wine list offers 24 wines by the glass, including *Trockenbeerenauslese,* a rare, liqueurlike wine. ✉ *Stromberger Str. 28A, in suburb of Bingerbrück* ☎ *06721/36699* 💳 *MC* ⏲ *Closed Sun. No lunch.*

★ $ ✕ **Weinstube Kruger-Rumpf.** It's well worth the 10-minute drive from Bingen (just across the Nahe River) to enjoy Cornelia Rumpf's refined country cooking with Stefan Rumpf's exquisite Nahe wines (Riesling, Weissburgunder [Pinot Blanc], and Silvaner are especially fine). House specialties are *geschmorte Schweinebacken* (braised pork jowls) with kohlrabi, boiled beef with green herb sauce, and *Winzerschmaus* (casserole of potatoes, sauerkraut, bacon, cheese, and herbs). The house dates from 1790; the wisteria-draped garden beckons in summer. ✉ *Rheinstr. 47, Münster-Sarmsheim, 4 km (2½ mi) southwest of Bingen* ☎ *06721/43859* ✍ *Reservations essential* 💳 *MC* ⏲ *Closed Mon. and 3 wks late Dec.–early Jan. No lunch.*

$$–$$$$ ✕🏨 **Johann Lafer's Stromburg.** It's a pretty 15-minute drive through the Binger Wald (Bingen Forest) to this luxurious castle hotel and restaurant overlooking Stromberg. Johann Lafer is a prolific chef who pioneered cooking shows in Germany. In the elegant Le Val d'Or ($$$$, reservations essential), the *Variationen* (medley) of foie gras and the *Dessert–Impressionen* are classics. He prepared crème brûlée for President Bush's lunch in Mainz in 2005. The less formal Turmstube ($$–$$$) offers tasty regional dishes. The wine list features 200 top Nahe wines

Fodor's Choice ★

and several hundred Old- and New-World wines, with a particularly fine collection from Bordeaux and Burgundy. ✉ *Am Schlossberg 1, D–55442 Stromberg, 12 km (7½ mi) west of Bingerbrück via Weiler and Waldalgesheim* ☎ *06724/93100* 📠 *06724/931–090* 🌐 *www.johannlafer.de* *13 rooms, 1 suite* *2 restaurants, minibars, cable TV, in-room broadband, in-room data ports, bar, lobby lounge, shop, babysitting, dry cleaning, laundry service, some pets allowed (fee); no a/c* 💳 *AE, DC, MC, V* ⏲ *Le Val d'Or closed Mon. No lunch weekdays.*

en route

On the 5-km (3-mi) drive on B–9 to Trechtingshausen, you will pass by Bingen's landmark, the **Mäuseturm** (Mice Tower), perched on a rocky island near the Binger Loch. The name derives from a gruesome legend. One version tells that during a famine in 969, the miserly Archbishop Hatto hoarded grain and sought refuge in the tower to escape the peasants' pleas for food. The stockpile attracted scads of mice to the tower, where they devoured everything in sight, including Hatto. In fact, the tower was built by the archbishops of Mainz in the 13th and 14th centuries as a *Mautturm* (watch tower and toll station) for their fortress, Ehrenfels, on the opposite shore (now a ruin). It was restored in neo-Gothic style by the king of Prussia in 1855, who also rebuilt Burg Sooneck.

The three castles open for visits near Trechtingshausen (turnoffs are signposted on B–9) will fascinate lovers of history and art. As you enter each castle's gateway, consider what a feat of engineering it was to have built such a massive *Burg* (fortress or castle) on the stony cliffs overlooking the Rhine. They have all lain in ruin once or more during their turbulent histories. Their outer walls and period rooms still evoke memories of Germany's medieval past as well as the 19th-century era of Rhine Romanticism. You can enjoy superb Rhine vistas from the castles' terraces, where coffee, cake, and local wines are served (except Monday). Reichenstein also serves meals.

Burg Rheinstein was the home of Rudolf von Habsburg from 1282 to 1286. To establish law and order on the Rhine, he destroyed the neighboring castles of Burg Reichenstein and Burg Sooneck and hanged their notorious robber barons from the oak trees around the Clemens Church, a late-Romanesque basilica near Trechtingshausen. The Gobelin tapestries, 15th-century stained glass, wall and ceiling frescoes, and antique furniture—including a rare "giraffe spinet" upon which Kaiser Wilhelm I is said to have tickled the ivories—are well worth seeing. In 2004 a new floor of royal apartments, featuring additional period rooms, was opened. Rheinstein was the first of many a Rhine ruin to be rebuilt by a royal Prussian family in the 19th century. ☎ *06721/6348* 🌐 *www.burg-rheinstein.de* *€4* ⏲ *Mid-Mar.–mid-Nov., daily 9:30–5:30; mid-Nov.–mid-Mar., Mon.–Thurs. 2–5, Sun. 10–5. Terrace café closed Mon.*

Burg Reichenstein has collections of decorative cast-iron slabs (from ovens and historical room-heating devices), hunting weapons and armor, period rooms, and paintings. ☎ *06721/6117* 🌐 *www.burg-reichenstein.de* 🎫 *€3.40* ⏲ *Mar.–mid-Nov., Tues.–Sun. 10–6.*

Burg Sooneck, on the edge of the Soon (pronounced *zone*) Forest, houses a valuable collection of Empire, Biedermeier, and neo-Gothic furnishings, medieval weapons, and paintings from the Rhine Romantic era. ✉ *Niederheimbach* ☎ *06743/6064* 🌐 *www.burgen-rlp.de* 🎫 *€2.60* ⏲ *Apr.–Sept., Tues.–Sun. 10–6; Oct., Nov., and Jan.–Mar., Tues.–Sun. 10–5.*

Bacharach

❻ *16 km (10 mi) north of Bingen; ferry 3 km (2 mi) north of town, to Kaub.*

Bacharach, a derivative of the Latin *Bacchi ara* (altar of Bacchus), has long been associated with wine. Like Rüdesheim, Bingen, and Kaub, it was a shipping station where barrels would interrupt their Rhine journey for land transport. Riesling wine from the town's most famous vineyard, the Bacharacher Hahn, is served on the KD Rhine steamers, and Riesling ice cream is sold at Eis Café Italia 76 (Oberstrasse 48). In late June you can sample wines at the Weinblütenfest (vine blossom festival) in the side valley suburb of Steeg and, in late August, at Kulinarische Sommernacht in Bacharach proper. Numerous events are planned from May to October 2006 to celebrate 650 years of town rights.

Park on the riverbank and enter the town through one of its medieval gateways. You can ascend the 14th-century town wall for a walk along the ramparts facing the Rhine, then stroll along the main street (one street, but three names: Koblenzer Strasse, Oberstrasse, and Mainzer Strasse) for a look at patrician manors, typically built around a *Hof* (courtyard), and half-timber houses. Haus Sickingen, Posthof, Zollhof, Rathaus (Town Hall), and Altes Haus are fine examples. The massive tower in the center of town belongs to the parish church of **St. Peter.** A good example of the transition from Romanesque to Gothic styles, it has an impressive four-story nave. From the parish church a set of stone steps (signposted) leads to Bacharach's landmark, the sandstone ruins of the Gothic **Werner Kapelle,** highly admired for its filigree tracery. The chapel's roof succumbed to falling rocks in 1689, when the French blew up Burg Stahleck. Originally a Staufen fortress (11th century), the castle lay dormant until 1925, when a youth hostel was built on the foundations. The sweeping views it affords are worth the 10-minute walk.

Where to Stay & Eat

★ $–$$ ✕ **Weinhaus Altes Haus.** Charming inside and out, this medieval half-timber house is a favorite setting for films and photos. The cheerful proprietor, Reni Weber, uses the freshest ingredients possible and buys her meat and game from local butchers and hunters. *Rieslingrahmsuppe* (Riesling cream soup), *Reibekuchen* (potato pancakes), and the hearty *Hunsrücker Tellerfleisch* (boiled beef with horseradish sauce) are favorites, in addition to the seasonal specialties. She offers a good selection of local wines. ✉ *Oberstr. 61* ☎ *06743/1209* ▭ *MC, V* ⏲ *Closed Wed. and Dec.–Easter.*

¢ ✕ **Gutsausschank Zum Grünen Baum.** Winegrower Fritz Bastian runs this cozy tavern in a half-timber house (1579). He is the sole owner of the vineyard Insel Heyles'en Werth, on the island opposite Bacharach. The "wine carousel" is a great way to sample a full range of flavors and styles (15 wines) under the tutelage of the congenial host. Snacks are served (from 1 PM), including delicious *Wildsülze* (game in aspic) with home fries, sausages, and cheese. ✉ *Oberstr. 63* ☎ *06743/1208* ▭ *No credit cards* ⏲ *Closed Thurs. and Feb.*

$ ✕ **RheinHotel Andreas Stüber.** This friendly, family operation offers modern rooms (each named after a vineyard) with Rhine or castle views. The restaurant ($–$$) has an excellent selection of Bacharacher wines to help wash down hearty regional specialties, such as *Hinkelsdreck* (chicken liver pâté), *Rieslingbraten* (beef marinated in wine), or *Wildschwein Sauerbraten* (wild boar sauerbraten). ✉ *Langstr. 50, on town wall, D–55422* ☎ *06743/1243* 🖷 *06743/1413* 🌐 *www.rhein-hotel-bacharach.de* *14 rooms, 1 apartment* *Restaurant, fans, minibars, cable TV, Wi-Fi, bicycles, lounge, Weinstube, laundry service, business services, some pets allowed (fee); no smoking* ▭ *AE, MC, V* ⏲ *Hotel and restaurant closed mid-Dec.–mid-Mar.* *BP.*

$–$$ **Altkölnischer Hof.** Flowers line the windows of the Scherschlicht family's pretty, half-timber hotel near market square. The rooms are simply but attractively furnished in country style, and some have balconies. ✉ *Blücherstr. 2, D–55422* ☎ *06743/1339* 🖷 *06743/2793* 🌐 *www.hotel-bacharach-rhein.de* *20 rooms, 2 suites, 4 apartments* *Restaurant, some minibars, cable TV, bicycles, bar, Weinstube, Internet room, business services, some pets allowed (fee), no-smoking rooms; no a/c* ▭ *MC, V* ⏲ *Closed Nov.–Mar.* *BP.*

Kaub

❼ *19 km (12 mi) north of Rüdesheim; ferry from Bacharach.*

The village of Kaub (pronounced *cowp*), once a major customs post, has profited from its slate quarries and wine for centuries. On New Year's Eve 1813–14, General Blücher led his troops from here across the Rhine on a pontoon bridge of barges to expel Napoleon's troops from the Rhineland. The small **Blüchermuseum** with furnishings and militaria from that time is housed in his former headquarters. ✉ *Metzgerg. 6* ☎ *06774/400* *€3* ⏲ *Apr.–Oct., Tues.–Sun. 11–4; Nov.–Mar., Tues.–Sun. 2–5.*

★ **Pfalzgrafenstein** castle—known locally as the Pfalz—is built on a rock in the middle of the Rhine. Originally a five-sided tower, it was later enclosed by a six-sided defense wall that makes it look like a stone ship anchored in the Rhine. It was never destroyed. Unlike the elaborate period rooms of many Rhine castles, the Pfalz provides a good look at sparse medieval living quarters and has an interesting collection of ordinary household goods. ☎ *0172/262–2800* 🌐 *www.burgen-rlp.de* *€4.10, including boat ride to and from Kaub* ⏲ *Apr.–Sept., Tues.–Sun. 10–1 and 2–6; Oct., Nov., and Jan.–Mar., Tues.–Sun. 10–1 and 2–5.*

Where to Stay & Eat

$ **Zum Turm.** Set next to a medieval *Turm* (tower) near the Rhine, this little inn offers spacious, comfortable guest rooms on the floors above its cozy restaurant ($–$$$$) and terrace. Any fish, game, and produce chef Harald Kutsche can't find at local farms are imported from the market stalls of Paris. For a starter try the home-smoked salmon or splurge on anglerfish served over lobster ragout. The daily set menus are excellent options. The Mittelrhein and Rheingau are the focus of the wine list. ✉ *Zollstr. 50, D–56349* ☎ *06774/92200* 📠 *06774/922–011* 🌐 *www.rhein-hotel-turm.com* *6 rooms* *Restaurant, minibars, cable TV, in-room data ports, Wi-Fi, bicycles, laundry service, business services, some pets allowed (fee), no-smoking rooms* 💳 *AE, DC, MC, V* ⏲ *Hotel and restaurant closed 1 wk in Jan., 1 wk in Aug., and 1st half Nov. Restaurant closed Tues.; lunch weekdays on request only Nov.–Mar.* *BP.*

Oberwesel

8 *8 km (5 mi) north of Bacharach.*

Oberwesel retains its medieval silhouette. Sixteen of the original 21 towers and much of the town wall still stand in the shadow of Schönburg Castle. The "town of towers" is also renowned for its Riesling wines, celebrated at a lively wine festival, the Weinmarkt, during the first half of September. Both Gothic churches on opposite ends of town are worth visiting. The **Liebfrauenkirche** (Church of Our Lady), popularly known as the "red church" because of its brightly colored exterior, has a superb rood screen, masterful sculptures, tombstones and paintings, and one of Germany's oldest altars (1331). Set on a hill, **St. Martin**—the so-called white church—with a fortresslike tower, has beautifully painted vaulting and a magnificent baroque altar.

Where to Stay & Eat

$ **Historische Weinwirtschaft.** Tables in the flower-laden garden in front of this lovingly restored stone house are at a premium in summer, yet seats in the nooks and crannies indoors are just as inviting. Dark beams, exposed stone walls, and antique furniture set the mood on the ground and first floors, and the vaulted cellar houses contemporary-art exhibitions. Ask Iris Marx, the ebullient proprietor, to translate the menu (it's in local dialect) of regional dishes. She offers country cooking at its best. The wine list is excellent and features 32 wines by the glass. ✉ *Liebfrauenstr. 17* ☎ *06744/8186* 🌐 *www.historische-weinwirtschaft.de* 💳 *AE, MC, V* ⏲ *Closed Tues. and Jan. No lunch except Sun. May–Sept.*

$$–$$$ Fodor's Choice ★ **Burghotel Auf Schönburg.** Part of the Schönburg Castle complex (12th century) has been lovingly restored as a romantic hotel and restaurant ($$–$$$; closed Monday except for hotel guests), with terraces in the courtyard and overlooking the Rhine. Antique furnishings and historical rooms (library, chapel, prison tower) make for an unforgettable stay, enhanced by the extraordinarily friendly, personal service of your hosts, the Hüttls, and staff. If you have only a night or two in the area, go for this hotel's first-rate lodging, food, and wine. The route to the hotel is signposted. ✉ *Oberwesel, D–55430* ☎ *06744/93930* 🖷 *06744/1613* 🌐 *www.hotel-schoenburg.com* *20 rooms, 2 suites* *Restaurant, minibars, cable TV, some in-room data ports, lounge, library, Internet room, some pets allowed (fee), no-smoking rooms; no a/c* ▭ *MC, V* ⏲ *Hotel and restaurant closed Jan.–mid-Mar.* *BP.*

$–$$ **Römerkrug.** Rooms with exposed beams, pretty floral prints, and historic furnishings are tucked within the half-timber facade (1458) of Elke Matzner's small inn on the market square. Fish (fresh trout from the Wisper Valley) and game are house specialties ($–$$), but there's also light cuisine with Asian accents as well as Rhine specialties, such as Himmel und Erde. There's a well-chosen selection of Mittelrhein wines. ✉ *Marktpl. 1, D–55430* ☎ *06744/7091* 🖷 *06744/1677* 🌐 *www.roemerkrug.de* *6 rooms, 1 suite* *Restaurant, cable TV, Wi-Fi, bicycles, business services, some pets allowed; no a/c* ▭ *MC, V* ⏲ *Restaurant closed Wed. and Jan.* *BP.*

St. Goar

9 *7 km (4½ mi) north of Oberwesel; ferry to St. Goarshausen.*

St. Goar and its counterpoint on the opposite shore, St. Goarshausen, are named after a Celtic missionary who settled here in the 6th century. He became the patron saint of innkeepers—an auspicious sign for both towns, which now live off tourism and wine. September is especially busy, with Weinforum Mittelrhein (a major wine-and-food presentation in Burg Rheinfels) on the first weekend, and wine festivals and the splendid fireworks display "Rhine in Flames" on the third weekend.

St. Goar's tomb once rested in the 15th-century collegiate church, the **Stiftskirche,** built over a Romanesque crypt reminiscent of those of churches in Speyer and Köln. ✉ *Kirchpl.* ⏲ *Apr.–Oct., daily 11–5.*

The castle ruins of **Burg Rheinfels,** overlooking the town, bear witness to the fact that St. Goar was once the best-fortified town in the Mittelrhein. From its beginnings in 1245, it was repeatedly enlarged by the counts of Katzenelnbogen, a powerful local dynasty, and their successors, the landgraves of Hesse. Although it repelled Louis IV's troops in 1689, Rheinfels was blasted by the French in 1797. Take time for a walk through the impressive ruins and the museum, which has an exquisite model of how the fortress looked in its heyday. To avoid the steep ascent on foot, buy a round-trip ticket (€3) for the *Burgexpress,* which departs from the bus stop on Heerstrasse, opposite the riverside parking lot for tour buses. ✉ *Off Schlossberg Str.* ☎ *06741/383* 🌐 *www.burg-rheinfels.com* *€4* ⏲ *Mid-Mar.–Oct., daily 9–6; Nov.–mid-Mar., weekends, weather permitting, 10–4.*

Where to Stay & Eat

★ **$$–$$$** **SchlossRheinfels & Villa Rheinfels.** Directly opposite Burg Rheinfels, this hotel offers modern comfort and expansive views from the terrace of its restaurant, Auf Scharfeneck ($–$$$; try to book a window alcove—Nos. 51, 52, 61, or 62), and the snack bar (¢–$). Game from the Hunsrück Hills or the *Wispertal Forelle* (trout from the Wisper Valley) are recommended, as are the seasonal specialties. The excellent wine list showcases the region's finest producers. The rooms are tastefully furnished in country manor style. ✉ *Schlossberg 47, D–56329* ☎ *06741/8020* 🖷 *06741/802–802* 🌐 *www.schloss-rheinfels.de* *56 rooms, 4 suites* *2 restaurants, snack bar, minibars, cable TV, in-room data ports, Wi-Fi, 2 tennis courts, indoor pool, sauna, spa, steam room, Turkish bath, bicycles, bar, lobby lounge, shop, babysitting, dry cleaning, laundry service, Internet room, business services, some pets allowed (fee), no-smoking rooms; no a/c* 💳 *AE, DC, MC, V* *BP.*

$–$$ **Hotel Landsknecht.** The Nickenig family makes everyone feel at home in its riverside restaurant ($–$$) and hotel north of St. Goar. Daughter Martina, a former wine queen, and her winemaker husband, Joachim Lorenz, operate the Vinothek, where you can sample his delicious Bopparder Hamm wines. These go well with the restaurant's hearty local dishes, such as Rhine-style sauerbraten or seasonal specialties (asparagus, game). Rooms are individually furnished and quite comfortable; some offer a Rhine view (Nos. 4, 5, and 8 are especially nice). ✉ *Rheinuferstr. (B–9), D–56329 St. Goar–Fellen* ☎ *06741/2011* 🖷 *06741/7499* 🌐 *www.hotel-landsknecht.de* *15 rooms, 1 suite, 2 apartments* *Restaurant, minibars, cable TV, in-room broadband, in-room data ports, Wi-Fi, bicycles, laundry service, Internet room, some pets allowed (fee); no a/c, no smoking* 💳 *AE, DC, MC, V* ⏲ *Hotel and restaurant closed Jan.* *BP.*

Shopping

The two **Montag shops** (✉ Heerstr. 128 ☎ 06741/2488 ✉ Schlossberg 2 ☎ 06741/93093) sell highly esteemed "made in Germany" collectibles: 12 dozen different beer steins; elaborate pewter drinking vessels; superb German cutlery; and a zoo of Steiff stuffed animals and teddy bears (in the Schlossberg location). Videos, CDs, and cassettes highlighting the region's landscape and folk music are also for sale. They issue tax-free documents and ship worldwide.

St. Goarshausen

❿ *29 km (18 mi) north of Rüdesheim, ferry from St. Goar.*

St. Goarshausen lies at the foot of two 14th-century castles whose names, Katz (cat) and Maus (mouse), reflect but one of the many power plays on the Rhine in the Middle Ages. Territorial supremacy and the concomitant privilege of collecting tolls fueled the fires of rivalry. In response to the construction of Burg Rheinfels, the archbishop of Trier erected a small castle north of St. Goarshausen to protect his interests. In turn the masters of Rheinfels, the counts of Katzenelnbogen, built a bigger castle directly above the town. Its name was shortened to Katz, and its smaller neighbor was scornfully referred to as Maus. Katz is not open to the public. **Maus** has a terrace café (great views) and demonstrations featuring eagles and falcons in flight. ☎ *06771/7669* 🌐 *www.burg-maus.de* *€6.50* ⏲ *Mid-Mar.–mid-Oct., Tues.–Sat. at 11 and 2:30, Sun. at 11, 2:30, and 4:30.*

Some 10 km (6 mi) north of the Maus castle, near Kamp-Bornhofen, is a castle duo separated by a "quarrel wall": **Liebenstein and Sterrenberg,** known as the *Feindliche Brüder* (rival brothers). Both impressive ruins have terrace cafés that afford good views.

One of the Rhineland's main attractions lies 4 km (2½ mi) south of St. Goarshausen: the steep (430-foot-high) slate cliff named after the beautiful blond nymph **Loreley.** Here she sat, singing songs so lovely that sailors and fishermen were lured to the treacherous rapids—and their demise. The legend stems from a tale by Clemens Brentano, retold as a ballad by Heinrich Heine and set to music by Friedrich Silcher at the height of Rhine Romanticism in the 19th century. The summit is a great vantage point.

off the beaten path

BESUCHERZENTRUM LORELEY – The 10-minute film and hands-on exhibits at this visitor center are entertaining ways to learn about the region's flora and fauna, geology, wine, shipping, and, above all, the myth of the Loreley. You can stock up on souvenirs in the shop and have a snack at the bistro before heading for the nearby vantage point at the cliff's summit. Hiking trails are signposted in the landscaped park. ✉ *Auf der Loreley* ☎ *06771/599–093* 🌐 *www.besucherzentrum-loreley.de* 🎫 *€2.50* ⏲ *Apr.–Oct., Tues.–Sun. 10–5.*

Boppard

⓫ *17 km (11 mi) north of St. Goar; ferry to Filsen.*

Boppard is a pleasant little resort that evolved from a Celtic settlement into a Roman fortress, Frankish royal court, and Free Imperial City. The Roman garrison Bodobrica, established here in the 4th century, was enclosed by a 26-foot-high rectangular wall (1,010 by 505 feet) with 28 defense towers. You can see portions of these in the fascinating open-air **archaeological park** (✉ Angertstr. near B–9 and the railroad tracks). The **Stadtmuseum** (town museum), housed in the 14th-century Kurfürstliche Burg (elector's castle) built by the archbishop of Trier, has exhibits on Boppard's Roman and medieval past, as well as an extensive collection of bentwood furniture designed by the town's favorite son, Michael Thonet (1796–1871). The cane-bottom *Stuhl Nr. 14* (Chair No. 14) is the famous classic found in coffeehouses around the world since 1859. ✉ *Burgstr.near ferry dock* ☎ *06742/10369* 🎫 *Free* ⏲ *Apr.–Oct., Tues.–Sun. 10–12:30 and 1:30–5.*

Excavations in the 1960s revealed ancient Roman baths beneath the twin-tower, Romanesque **Severuskirche** (Church of St. Severus; 1236) on the market square. The large triumphal crucifix over the main altar and a lovely statue of a smiling Madonna date from the 13th century. Two baroque altars dominate the interior of the Gothic **Karmeliterkirche** (Carmelite Church) on Karmeliterstrasse, near the Rhine. It houses intricately carved choir stalls and tombstones and several beautiful Madonnas. Winegrowers still observe the old custom of laying the first-picked

Trauben (grapes) at the foot of the Traubenmadonna (1330) to ensure a good harvest. The annual wine festival takes place in late September, just before the Riesling harvest.

On the northern edge of Boppard, the Rhine makes its largest loop, skirting the majestic hillside vineyard known as the **Bopparder Hamm.** From the Mühltal station, let the *Sessellift* (chairlift) whisk you 1,300 feet uphill to the **Vierseenblick** (four-lake vista), a vantage point from which the Rhine looks like a chain of lakes. *Round-trip €6.20, one-way €4.20 Apr.–Oct., daily 10–5.*

Where to Stay & Eat

$$ **Best Western Hotel Bellevue.** You can enjoy a Rhine view from many of the rooms in this traditional hotel or from the terrace next to the pretty Rhine promenade. Afternoon tea, dinner, and Sunday lunch are served in the gourmet restaurant Le Chopin ($$$$). Le Bristol ($$–$$$) serves regional and traditional German cuisine. Both restaurants use local products, such as Hunsrück beef, or lamb from the meadows of Bacharach. *Rheinallee 41, D–56154 06742/1020 06742/102–602 www.bellevue-boppard.de 92 rooms, 1 suite 2 restaurants, minibars, cable TV, in-room data ports, Wi-Fi, indoor pool, gym, sauna, spa, steam room, bar, recreation room, shop, babysitting, laundry service, Internet room, business services, some pets allowed (fee), no-smoking rooms; no a/c in some rooms AE, DC, MC, V Le Chopin closed Mon. No lunch Mon.–Sat.*

¢–$ **Weinhaus Heilig Grab.** This wine estate's tavern (¢), Boppard's oldest, is full of smiling faces: the wines are excellent, the fare is simple but hearty, and the welcome is warm. Old chestnut trees shade tables in the courtyard. Rooms are furnished with rustic pine furniture. If you'd like to visit the cellars or vineyards, ask your friendly hosts, Rudolf and Susanne Schoeneberger. They also arrange wine tastings. *Zelkesg. 12, D–56154 06742/2371 06742/81220 www.heiliggrab.de 5 rooms Restaurant, cable TV, no-smoking rooms; no a/c, no room phones MC, V Hotel closed Nov.–Easter. Restaurant closed Tues. and 3 wks late Dec.–early Jan. No lunch BP.*

Sports & the Outdoors

HIKING The 10-km (6-mi) **Weinwanderweg** (Wine Hiking Trail) through the Bopparder Hamm, from Boppard to Spay, begins north of town on Peternacher Weg. Many other marked trails in the vicinity are outlined on maps and in brochures available from the tourist office.

en route

On the outskirts of Koblenz, the neo-Gothic towers of **Schloss Stolzenfels** come into view. The castle's origins date from the mid-13th century, when the archbishop of Trier sought to counter the influence (and toll rights) of the archbishop of Mainz, who had just built Burg Lahneck, a castle at the confluence of the Lahn and Rhine rivers. Its superbly furnished period rooms and beautiful gardens are well worth a visit. It's a wonderful setting for concerts. From B–9 (curbside parking) it's about a 15-minute walk to the castle entrance. *0261/51656 www.burgen-rlp.de €2.60 Apr.–Sept., Tues.–Sun. 10–6; Oct., Nov., and Jan.–Mar., Tues.–Sun. 10–5.*

On the eastern shore overlooking the town of Braubach is the **Marksburg.** Built in the 12th century to protect the silver and lead mines in the area, it's the only land-based castle on the Rhine to have survived the centuries intact. Within its massive walls are a collection of weapons and manuscripts, a medieval botanical garden, and a snack bar. *02627/206 www.deutsche-burgen.org €4.50 Easter–Oct., daily 10–5; Nov.–late Dec. and Jan.–Easter, daily 11–4; snack bar open daily.*

Koblenz

20 km (12 mi) north of Boppard.

The ancient city of Koblenz is at a geographic nexus known as the **Deutsches Eck** (German Corner) in the heart of the Mittelrhein region. Rivers and mountains converge here: the Mosel flows into the Rhine on one side; the Lahn flows in on the other a few miles south; and three mountain ridges intersect. Koblenz is one of the Rhineland-Palatinate's cultural, administrative, and business centers.

Founded by the Romans in AD 9, the city was first called Castrum ad Confluentes (Fort at the Confluence). It became a powerful city in the Middle Ages, when it controlled trade on both the Rhine and the Mosel. Air raids during World War II destroyed 85% of the city, but extensive restoration has done much to re-create its former atmosphere. English-speaking walking tours of the Old Town can be arranged by the tourist office on request.

Koblenz is centered on the west bank of the Rhine. On the east bank
12 stands Europe's largest fortress, **Festung Ehrenbreitstein,** offering a commanding view from 400 feet above the river. The earliest buildings date from about 1100, but the bulk of the fortress was constructed in the 16th century. In 1801 it was partially destroyed by Napoléon, and the French occupied Koblenz for the next 18 years. As for the fortress's 16th-century Vogel Greif cannon, the French absconded with it in 1794, the Germans took it back in 1940, and the French commandeered it again in 1945. The 15-ton cannon was peaceably returned by French president François Mitterrand in 1984 and is now part of the exhibit on the history of local technologies, from wine growing to industry, in the fortress's **Landesmuseum** (State Museum; 0261/66750 €3.10, including fortress grounds Mid-Mar.–mid-Nov., daily 9:30–5).

To reach the fortress on the east bank of the Rhine, take Bus No. 9 from the train station or the **ferry** (0261/76673 €2.40 round-trip Mar.–Apr. and Nov., daily 8–6; May–Oct., daily 7 AM–7 PM) from the Pegelhaus on the Koblenz riverbank (near Rheinstrasse). Take the **Sesselbahn** (Cable car; €6.90 round-trip, including fortress grounds Apr., May, and Oct., daily 10–4:50; June–Aug., daily 9–5:50; Sept., daily 10–5:50) to ascend to the fortress. For the best value, purchase the combination ticket that includes the grounds, museum, and a 45-minute tour. *0261/6675–4000 Grounds €1.10, combined ticket and tour €4.20 Mid-Mar.–mid-Nov., daily 9–5.*

Deutsches Eck 18
Festung Ehrenbreitstein 12
Kurfürstliches Schloss 16
Liebfrauenkirche 21
Ludwig Museum 19
Pfaffendorfer Brücke 13
Rheinanlagen 15
Rheinkran . . . 17
St. Kastor Kirche 20
Weindorf 14

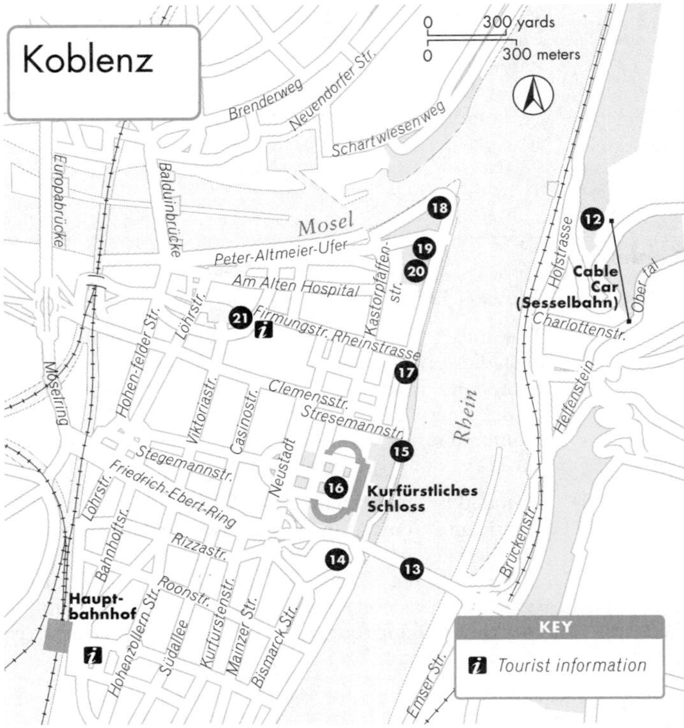

13 The **Pfaffendorfer Brücke** (Pfaffendorf Bridge) marks the beginning of the Old Town. Just off the Pfaffendorf Bridge, between the modern blocks 14 of the Rhein-Mosel-Halle and the Hotel Mercure, is the **Weindorf** (🌐 www.weindorf-koblenz.de), a wine "village" constructed for a mammoth exhibition of German wines in 1925, which is now a restaurant.

15 The **Rheinanlagen** (Rhine Gardens), a 10-km (6-mi) promenade, runs along the riverbank past the Weindorf. Strolling along the promenade toward 16 town, you'll pass the gracious **Kurfürstliches Schloss,** the prince-elector's palace. It was built in 1786 by Prince-Elector Clemens Wenzeslaus as an elegant escape from the grim Ehrenbreitstein fortress. He lived here for only three years, however; in 1791 he was forced to flee to Augsburg when the French stormed the city. The palace is used for city offices and is closed to visitors. It's open to the public the first Sunday in May for *Wein im Schloss,* a large presentation of Lower Mosel, Nahe, Mittelrhein, and Ahr wines. In the garden behind the palace, don't miss the handsome statue of "Father Rhine & Mother Mosel."

17 The squat form of the **Rheinkran** (Rhine Crane), built in 1611, is one of Koblenz's landmarks. Marks on the side of the building indicate the heights reached by floodwaters of bygone years. In the mid-19th century a pontoon bridge consisting of a row of barges spanned the Rhine here; when

ships approached, two or three barges were simply towed out of the way to let them through.

18 The **Deutsches Eck** (German Corner) is at the sharp intersection of the Rhine and Mosel, a pointed bit of land jutting into the river like the prow of some early ironclad warship. One of the more effusive manifestations of German nationalism—an 1897 statue of Kaiser Wilhelm I, first emperor of the newly united Germany—was erected here. It was destroyed at the end of World War II and replaced in 1953 with a ponderous, altarlike monument to Germany's unity. After German reunification a new statue of Wilhelm was placed atop this monument in 1993. Pieces of the Berlin Wall stand on the Mosel side—a memorial to those who died as a result of the partitioning of the country.

From the Deutsches Eck, the Moselanlagen (Mosel Promenade) leads to Koblenz's oldest restaurant, the Deutscher Kaiser, which marks the start of the Old Town.

19 The **Ludwig Museum** stands just behind the Deutsches Eck, housed in the spick-and-span Deutschherrenhaus, a restored 13th-century building. Industrialist Peter Ludwig, one of Germany's leading contemporary-art collectors, has filled this museum with part of his huge collection. Two special exhibitions are scheduled in 2006: the "blue paintings" of French contemporary artists Marie Raymond and Yves Klein (April–May) and a show devoted to Chagall and Mozart (autumn). ✉ *Danziger Freiheit 1* ☎ *0261/304–040* 🌐 *www.ludwigmuseum.org* 🎫 *€2.50, combined ticket with Mittelrhein Museum €3.50* ⏲ *Tues.–Sat. 10:30–5, Sun. 11–6.*

★ 20 The **St. Kastor Kirche** (St. Castor Church) is a sturdy Romanesque basilica consecrated in 836. It was here in 842 that plans were drawn for the Treaty of Verdun, formalizing the division of Charlemagne's great empire and leading to the creation of Germany and France as separate states. Inside, compare the squat Romanesque columns in the nave with the intricate fan vaulting of the Gothic sections. **The St. Kastor Fountain** outside the church is an intriguing piece of historical one-upmanship. It was built by the occupying French to mark the beginning of Napoléon's ultimately disastrous Russian campaign of 1812. ✉ *Kastorhof* ⏲ *Daily 9–6 except during services.*

The **Mittelrhein Museum** houses the city's art collection in a lovely 16th-century building near the Old Town's central square, Am Plan. ✉ *Florinsmarkt 15* ☎ *0261/129–2520* 🌐 *www.mittelrhein-museum.de* 🎫 *€2.50, combined ticket with Ludwig Museum €3.50* ⏲ *Tues.–Sat. 10:30–5, Sun. 11–6.*

War damage is evidenced by the blend of old buildings and modern store
21 blocks on and around Am Plan. The **Liebfrauenkirche** (Church of Our Lady) stands on Roman foundations at the Old Town's highest point. The bulk of the church is of Romanesque design, but its choir is one of the Rhineland's finest examples of 15th-century Gothic architecture, and the west front is graced with two 17th-century baroque towers. ✉ *Am Plan* ⏲ *Mon.–Sat. 8–6, Sun. 9–8 except during services.*

Where to Stay & Eat

$$–$$$ ✕ **Da Vinci.** Noble and creative are the decor and fare at this smart restaurant in the heart of the Old Town. Da Vinci reproductions, including an original-sized rendition of *The Last Supper,* adorn the walls. Leather upholstery, an elegant bar, and soft lighting round out the ambience. Specialties include suckling pig from the Swabian Alb, Charolais and Angus beef, fresh fish, homemade pasta, and truffles. The wine list focuses on fine Italian wines. ✉ *Firmunstr. 32b* ☎ *0261/921–5444* 🌐 *www.davinci-koblenz.de* ▭ *AE, DC, MC, V.*

$–$$ ✕ **Café Einstein.** Portraits of Einstein line the walls of this lively café-restaurant-bar just off Görresplatz. The friendly Tayhus family serves tasty fare daily, from a hearty breakfast buffet (brunch on Sunday—reservations recommended) to late-night finger food. Fish is a specialty in summer. This place fills up quickly on nights with live music—jazz on Wednesday and Thursday, contemporary music on Friday and Saturday. ✉ *Firmungstr. 30* ☎ *0261/914–4999* 🌐 *www.einstein-koblenz.de* ▭ *AE, DC, MC, V.*

¢–$$ ✕ **Grand Café.** The multistory atrium of a historic house (once a furniture store) has been turned into a very classy yet comfortable meeting point. From early morning until late at night, food and drinks are served amid fabulous art-nouveau decor, complete with huge palm trees. Thursday through Saturday, the lower level is a disco. Thursday evening (5–9) there's a cigar club on the upper level. The huge terrace on Görres Square is a perfect spot for people-watching and soaking up the sun. ✉ *Firmungstr. 2, Am Görrespl.* ☎ *0261/100–5833* 🌐 *www.grand-cafe.biz* ▭ *AE, MC, V.*

$ ✕ **Weinhaus Hubertus.** Hunting scenes and trophies line the wood-panel walls of this cozy wine restaurant named after the patron saint of hunters. Karin and Dieter Spahl serve hearty portions of traditional fare, such as Himmel und Erde, and local wines. Try their dessert specials, *Feigenmus* (fig puree) and *Tête de Moine* cheese, served with a glass of the rare dessert wine Beerenauslese. ✉ *Florinsmarkt 6* ☎ *0261/31177* 🌐 *www.weinhaus-hubertus.de* ▭ *AE, DC, MC, V* ⊙ *Closed Tues. No lunch.*

¢–$ ✕ **Circus Maximus.** Here's a laid-back setting for breakfast, lunch, dinner, or drinks with live music and theme parties from Wednesday to Saturday evening. Jason Wright ("The Wright Thing") plays the first Wednesday of the month. Weekdays, the *Mittagstisch* (lunch special) at €4.80 is an excellent value. The menu offers everything from sandwiches, salads, and baked potatoes to potato gratins, steaks, and pizza. Try the tasty couscous with chicken and hummus. ✉ *Stegemannstr. 30, at Viktoriastr.* ☎ *0261/300–2357* 🌐 *www.circus-maximus.org* ▭ *No credit cards* ⊙ *No lunch weekends.*

¢–$ ✕ **Weindorf–Koblenz.** The Bastian family has upgraded the food and wine selection at this reconstructed "wine village" of half-timber houses grouped around a tree-shaded courtyard. Fresh renditions of traditional Rhine and Mosel specialties, a good selection of local wines, and a fabulous Sunday brunch—wine, beer and nonalcoholic beverages are included in the price (€20)—make this a popular spot. ✉ *Julius-Wegeler-Str. 2-4* ☎ *0261/133–7190* 🌐 *www.weindorf-koblenz.de* ▭ *AE, DC, MC, V* ⊙ *No lunch Nov.–Apr.*

★ $ **Zum weissen Schwanen.** Guests have found a warm welcome in this half-timber inn and mill since 1693, a tradition carried on by the Kunz family. Located next to a 13th-century town gateway, this is a charming place to overnight or enjoy well-prepared, contemporary German cuisine ($–$$$) and excellent local wines. Brasserie Brentano ($) serves lighter fare and Sunday brunch. Rooms are individually decorated with period furniture ranging from Biedermeier to Belle Epoque. *Brunnenstr. 4, D–56338 Braubach, 12 km (7½ mi) south of Koblenz via B–42 02627/9820 02627/8802 www.zum-weissen-schwanen.de 19 rooms, 1 suite 2 restaurants, cable TV, in-room data ports, bicycles, bar, babysitting, dry cleaning, laundry service, Internet room, business services, some pets allowed, no-smoking rooms; no a/c AE, DC, MC, V Restaurant closed Wed. and Jan. No lunch Mon.–Sat. Brasserie closed Sun. evening and Feb.–Mar. BP.*

$$–$$$$ **Hotel Mercure.** This modern high-rise on the Rhine is next to the city's conference and events center, the Rhein-Mosel-Halle, and within a short walk of all major sights. Rooms are modern and well appointed; those on the fifth floor and above have fabulous Rhine views. *Julius-Wegeler-Str. 6, D–56068 0261/1360 0261/136–1199 www.mercure.com 167 rooms, 1 suite 2 restaurants, minibars, cable TV, in-room data ports, some Wi-Fi, gym, hot tub, sauna, bicycles, bar, lobby lounge, babysitting, dry cleaning, laundry service, Internet room, business services, some pets allowed (fee), no-smoking rooms AE, DC, MC, V BP.*

Nightlife & the Arts

The **Staatsorchester Rheinische Philharmonie** (Rhenish Philharmonic Orchestra; Julius-Wegeler-Str. 0261/301–2272) plays regularly in the Rhein-Mosel-Halle. The gracious neoclassic **Theater der Stadt Koblenz** (Clemensstr. 1–5 0261/129–2840), built in 1787, is still in regular use.

Night owls frequent the bar and Abaco Club (a disco Thursday–Saturday) at **Grand Café** (Firmungstr. 2, Am Görrespl. 0261/100–5833). **Café Einstein** (Firmungstr. 30, near Görresplatz 0261/914–4999) usually has live music Wednesday to Saturday nights. **Circus Maximus** (Stegemannstr. 30, at Viktoriastr. 0261/300–2357) offers disco sounds, live music, and theme parties from Thursday to Saturday. For Latin American music and good cocktails, head for **Enchilada** (Gerichtsstr. 2 0261/100–4666). There are also many pubs and bars on or near Florinsmarkt. **Café Hahn** (Neustr. 15 0261/42302), in the suburb of Güls, features everything from cabaret and stand-up comedians to popular musicians and bands.

Shopping

Koblenz's most pleasant shopping is in the Old City streets around the market square Am Plan. **Löhr Center** (Hohenfelder Str., at Am Wöllershof), a modern, American-style, windowless mall, has some 130 shops and restaurants.

en route

Take a fascinating walk through the **Garten der Schmetterlinge Schloss Sayn** (Garden of Butterflies), where butterflies from South America, Asia, and Africa flit back and forth over your head between the branches of banana trees and palms. The palace proper houses a small museum of decorative cast-iron objects, a restaurant, and a café. It's 15 km (9 mi) north of Koblenz (Bendorf exit off B–42). *Im Fürstlichen Schlosspark, D–56170 Bendorf-Sayn 02622/15478 www.sayn.de Butterfly garden and museum €6 Mar.–Sept., daily 9–6; Oct., daily 10–5; Nov., daily 10–4.*

THE MOSEL VALLEY

Updated by Kerry Brady

The Mosel is one of the most hauntingly beautiful river valleys on earth. Here, as in the Rhine Valley, forests and vines carpet steep hillsides; castles and church spires dot the landscape; and medieval wine villages line the riverbanks. The Mosel landscape is no less majestic, but it's less narrow and more peaceful than that of the Rhine Gorge; the river's countless bends and loops slow its pace and lend the region a special charm.

From Koblenz to Treis-Karden, two roads run parallel to the Mosel: B–416 (west side) and B–49 (east side). Thereafter, only one road continues upstream, occasionally traversing the river as it winds toward Trier: until Alf, it's B–49; afterward, B–53.

The signposted routes between Koblenz and Trier include the Mosel Weinstrasse (Mosel Wine Road) along the riverbank and, on the heights, the hiking trails on both sides of the river known as the Moselhöhenweg. The latter extends 224 km (140 mi) on the Hunsrück (eastern) side and 164 km (102 mi) on the Eifel (western) side of the river. Driving time for the river route is at least three hours. On the autobahn (A–1) the distance between Koblenz and Trier can be covered in about an hour.

Winningen

22 *11 km (7 mi) southwest of Koblenz on B–416.*

Winningen is a gateway to the Terrassenmosel (Terraced Mosel), the portion of the river characterized by steep, terraced vineyards. Monorails and winches help winegrowers and their tools make the ascent, but tending and harvesting the vines are all done by hand. For a bird's-eye view of the valley, drive up Fährstrasse to Am Rosenhang, the start of a pleasant walk along the Weinlehrpfad (Educational Wine Path).

As you head upstream toward Kobern-Gondorf, you'll pass the renowned vineyard site Uhlen. In Kobern the Oberburg (upper castle) and the St. Matthias Kapelle, a 12th-century chapel, are good vantage points. Near the market square in the village below, you can see an old half-timber house (1321), now quarters for Kobern's tourist office.

Where to Stay & Eat

★ $$–$$$ **Höreth im Wald/Alte Mühle Höreth.** At Thomas and Gudrun Höreth's country inn and restaurant ($$–$$$$), a labyrinth of little rooms and cellars is grouped around romantic oleander-lined courtyards. The menu offers something for every taste, but the absolute hits are the homemade cheeses, terrines, pâtés, and *Entensülze* (goose in aspic), served with the Höreths' own wines as well as mature Bordeaux selections. ✉ *Mühlental 17, via B–416, D–56330 Kobern* ☎ *02607/6474* 📠 *0261/6848* 🌐 *www.thomas-hoereth.de* *10 rooms, 2 apartments nearby* *Restaurant, cable TV, in-room broadband, in-room data ports, Wi-Fi, bicycles, Weinstube, babysitting, dry cleaning, laundry service, Internet room, business services, some pets allowed (fee), no-smoking rooms; no a/c* 💳 *DC, MC, V* ⏲ *No lunch weekdays* *BP.*

$ **Halferschenke.** This *Schenke* (inn) was once an overnight stop for *Halfer*, who, with their horses, towed cargo-laden boats upstream. Today the stone-house inn (1832) is run by a friendly young couple, Thomas and Eva Balmes. Light walls, dark wood, and lots of candles and flowers are a lovely setting for his artfully prepared food ($$–$$$). An excellent selection of Terrassenmosel wines is available. The rooms, each named after an artist, are modern, airy, and bright. ✉ *Hauptstr. 63, D–56332 Dieblich, Via B–49, opposite Kobern* ☎ *02607/1008* 📠 *02607/960–294* 🌐 *www.halferschenke.de* *4 rooms* *Restaurant, some pets allowed; no a/c, no room phones, no TV in some rooms* 💳 *AE, MC, V* ⏲ *Restaurant closed Mon. No lunch Tues.–Sat.* *BP.*

Alken

23 *22 km (13½ mi) southwest of Koblenz.*

The 12th-century castle **Burg Thurant** towers over the village and the Burgberg (castle hill) vineyard. Wine and snacks are served in the courtyard; castle tours take in the chapel, cellar, tower, and a weapons display. Allow a good half hour for the climb from the riverbank. ☎ *02605/2004* 🌐 *www.thurant.de* *€3* ⏲ *Mar.–Nov., daily 10–5; Dec.–Feb., weekends 10–4.*

Where to Stay & Eat

$ **Burg Thurant.** The Kopowskis' stylish restaurant ($–$$) and guesthouse lie at the foot of the castle, next to a venerable stone tower on the riverbank (B–49). They serve tasty renditions of *Mosel Aal* (Mosel eel), *Bachforelle* (fresh stream trout) in almond butter, and *Entenbrust an Brombeerjus* (breast of duck in blackberry sauce), accompanied by wines from the region's finest producers. The guest rooms are outfitted with a mixture of antiques and country-style furnishings. ✉ *Moselstr. 16, D–56332* ☎ *02605/3581* 📠 *02605/2152* 🌐 *www.kopowski.de* *3 rooms* *Restaurant, bicycles, Weinstube, dry cleaning, laundry service, some pets allowed (fee), no-smoking rooms; no a/c, no room TVs* 💳 *MC* ⏲ *Hotel and restaurant closed Mon. and Feb. No lunch Mon.–Sat. Nov.–late May* *BP.*

en route

Burg Eltz (Eltz Castle) is one of Germany's most picturesque, genuinely medieval castles (12th–16th centuries) and merits as much attention as King Ludwig's trio of castles in Bavaria. The 40-minute tour, with excellent commentary on the castle's history and furnishings, guides you through the period rooms and massive kitchen but does not include the treasure chamber, a collection of fascinating artworks displayed in five historical rooms. In summer the lines are long, so bring some water, particularly if you're traveling with children. To get here, exit B–416 at Hatzenport (opposite and southwest of Alken), proceed to Münstermaifeld, and follow signs to the parking lot near the Antoniuskapelle. From here it's a 15-minute walk, or take the shuttle bus (€1.50). Hikers can reach the castle from Moselkern in 40 minutes. ✉ *Burg Eltz/Münstermaifeld* ☎ *02672/950–500* 🌐 *www.burg-eltz.de* 🎫 *Castle tour €6, treasure chamber €2.50* ⏲ *Apr.–Oct., daily 9:30–5:30.*

Treis-Karden

24 *39 km (24 mi) southwest of Koblenz; Karden is on B–416; Treis is on B–49.*

Treis-Karden consists of two towns joined for administrative purposes. You can visit the richly furnished Romanesque and Gothic **Stiftskirche St. Castor** (Church of St. Castor), named after the saint who introduced Christianity to the area in the middle of the 4th century, as well as is the **Stiftsmuseum** (Foundation Museum) in the historical tithe house (1238) behind the church. Exhibits illustrate Karden's history as a religious center, starting with the Celtic and Roman eras. The two stars on the weather vane symbolize the star of Bethlehem and allude to the church's precious "altar of the three kings," Europe's only remaining terra-cotta-altar shrine (1420). Attend Sunday service to hear the magnificent baroque organ (1728) built by Johann Michael Stumm, founder of one of the world's greatest organ-building dynasties. ✉ *St.-Castor-Str. 1, Karden* ☎ *02672/6137* 🎫 *Museum €3* ⏲ *Easter and May–Oct., Wed.–Fri. 2–5, weekends 10–noon and 2–5.*

Where to Stay & Eat

$–$$ ✕🏨 **Schloss-Hotel Petry.** From a simple guesthouse a century ago, this family-run hotel has developed into a complex of buildings with very attractive, comfortably furnished rooms and modern facilities. House specialties at the two restaurants (Schloss Stube $$$, Weinstube $–$$) are *Mosel Aal*, eel cooked and served cold with a green-herb sauce, and rib roast of lamb. The wine list has a good selection of Mosel wines. ✉ *St.-Castor-Str. 80 (B–416), D–56253* ☎ *02672/9340* 📠 *02672/934–440* 🌐 *www.schloss-hotel-petry.de* *55 rooms, 19 suites* *2 restaurants, some minibars, cable TV, in-room data ports, Wi-Fi, gym, hot tub, sauna, billiards, bowling, Ping-Pong, bar, lounge, shop, babysitting, dry cleaning, laundry service, business services, some pets allowed (fee), no-smoking rooms; no a/c* 💳 *AE, DC, MC, V restaurant only* ⏲ *Schloss Stube closed Tues. and Wed.* 🍽 *BP.*

Cochem

25 *51 km (31½ mi) southwest of Koblenz on B–49, approximately 93 km (58 mi) from Trier.*

Cochem is one of the most attractive towns of the Mosel Valley, with a riverside promenade to rival any along the Rhine. It's especially lively during the wine festivals in June and late August. If time permits, savor the landscape from the deck of a boat—many excursions are available, lasting from one hour to an entire day. The tourist office on Endertplatz has an excellent English-language outline for a walking tour of the town. From the **Enderttor** (Endert Town Gate) you can see the entrance to Germany's longest railway tunnel, the Kaiser-Wilhelm, an astonishing example of 19th-century engineering. The 4-km-long (2½-mi-long) tunnel saves travelers a 21-km (13-mi) detour along one of the Mosel's great loops.

The 15-minute walk to the **Reichsburg** (Imperial Fortress), the 1,000-year-old castle overlooking the town, will reward you with great views of the area. Flight demonstrations (eagles and falcons) take place Tuesday through Sunday at 11, 1, 2:30, and 4. With advance reservations, you can get a taste of the Middle Ages at a medieval banquet, complete with costumes, music, and entertainment. Banquets take place on Friday (7 PM) and Saturday (6 PM), and last four hours; the price (€39) includes a castle tour. During the *Burgfest* (castle festival) the first weekend of August, there's a medieval market and colorful tournaments. ☎ *02671/255* 🌐 *www.reichsburg-cochem.de* *€4, including 40-min tour; flight demonstration €3* ⏲ *Mid-Mar.–early Nov., daily 9–5.*

Historische Senfmühle. On tours of his 200-year-old mustard mill (daily at 11, 2, 3, and 4), Wolfgang Steffens shows how he produces his gourmet mustard. Garlic, cayenne, honey, curry, and even Riesling wine are among the types you can sample and purchase in the shop. From the Old Town, walk across the bridge toward Cond. The mill is to the left of the bridgehead. ✉ *Stadionstr. 1* ☎ *02671/607–665* 🌐 *www.senfmuehle.net* *Tours €2.50* ⏲ *Daily 10–6.*

A ride on the **chairlift** to the Pinner Kreuz provides great vistas. ✉ *Endertstr.* ☎ *02671/989–063* *Round-trip €5.50* ⏲ *Late Mar.–mid-Nov., daily 10–6.*

Where to Stay & Eat

$–$$ ✕ **Alte Thorschenke.** Next to the Enderttor, near the river, this inn dates from 1332. Winding staircases, ancient wooden beams, and historic decor set the mood. Many of the rooms have period furniture (some with four-poster beds). Hunting trophies and portraits of prince electors adorn the wood-panel walls of the restaurant ($$–$$$). There's also a cozy Weinstube and a patio for alfresco dining. Highly recommended are the fresh trout and the *Wildplatte* (game platter). The parent firm, Weingut Freiherr von Landenberg, supplies the excellent Mosel wine and welcomes visitors to tour the estate. ✉ *Brückenstr. 3, D–56812* ☎ *02671/7059* *02671/4202* 🌐 *www.castle-thorschenke.com* *31 rooms, 3 suites, 1 apartment* *Restaurant, minibars, cable TV, bicycles, Weinstube, dry cleaning, laundry service, business services, some pets allowed (fee), no-smoking rooms; no a/c* *AE, DC, MC, V* *BP.*

$–$$ ✕ **Weissmühle.** This lovely inn is set amid the forested hills of the Enderttal (Endert Valley) on the site of a historic mill. Lined with photos and memorabilia from the original mill, it's an oasis from traffic and crowds yet only 2½ km (1½ mi) from Cochem. The rooms are individually decorated—some in an elegant country-manor style, others with rustic farmhouse furnishings. Beneath the exposed beams and painted ceiling of the restaurant ($$–$$$), food from the hotel's own bakery, butcher shop, and trout farm will grace your table. German and French wines are served. ✉ *Im Enderttal, via Endertstr., toward Greimersburg; from A–48 exit Kaisersesch, D–56812* ☎ *02671/8955* 🖷 *02671/8207* 🌐 *www.weissmuehle.de* *36 rooms* *Restaurant, minibars, cable TV, in-room broadband, some in-room data ports, sauna, spa, steam room, bowling, bar, lounge, some pets allowed (fee); no a/c* 💳 *DC, MC, V* *BP.*

$ **Lohspeicher–l'Auberge du Vin.** In times past, oak bark for leather tanners was dried and stored in this house (1834) near the market square. Today it's a charming inn with a pretty terrace, run by a vivacious young couple, Ingo and Birgit Beth. His delicacies ($$–$$$) are a pleasure for the palate and the eye. At least one saltwater and one freshwater fish are featured daily. Some 20 French and Italian wines supplement the family's own estate-bottled wines. The rooms are pleasant and modern. ✉ *Oberg. 1, at Marktpl., D–56812* ☎ *02671/3976* 🌐 *www.lohspeicher.de* 🖷 *02671/1772* *9 rooms* *Restaurant, cable TV, some pets allowed (fee), no-smoking rooms; no a/c* 💳 *MC, V* *Restaurant closed Wed. Hotel and restaurant closed Feb.* *BP.*

en route

Ten kilometers (6 mi) south of Cochem, on the opposite shore, the ruins of Metternich Castle crown the Schlossberg (Castle Hill) vineyard next to the romantic village of **Beilstein.** Take in the stunning Mosel loop panorama from the castle's terrace café before heading for the market square below. Then ascend the *Klostertreppe* (monastery steps) leading to the baroque monastery church for views of the winding streets lined with half-timber houses.

Ediger-Eller

26 *61 km (38 mi) southwest of Koblenz on B–49.*

Ediger is another photogenic wine village with well-preserved houses and remnants of a medieval town wall. The **Martinskirche** (St. Martin's Church; ✉ Kirchstr.) is a remarkable amalgamation of art and architectural styles, inside and out. Take a moment to admire the 117 carved bosses in the star-vaulted ceiling of the nave. Among the many fine sculptures throughout the church and the chapel is the town's treasure: a Renaissance stone relief, *Christ in the Wine Press.*

Where to Stay & Eat

$ **Zum Löwen.** This hotel and wine estate, run by the Saffenreuther family, boasts friendly service and excellent wine and cuisine ($–$$$$). The house specialties are game (from their own preserve) and fine, fruity Rieslings (a mature Riesling with a balance of acidity and naturally ripe sweetness is superb with venison and boar). The rooms have simple decor; some have a balcony facing the Mosel. In addition to wine tastings and hikes in Calmont, Europe's steepest vineyard site, fishing or hunting trips can be arranged. ✉ *Moselweinstr. 23, D–56814 Ediger-Eller* ☎ *02675/208* 🖷 *02675/214* 🌐 *www.mosel-hotel-loewen.de*

21 rooms Restaurant, cable TV, Wi-Fi, bicycles, Weinstube, dry cleaning, laundry service, some pets allowed (fee), no-smoking rooms; no a/c, no room phones AE, MC, V Hotel and restaurant closed Jan.–mid-Mar. Restaurant closed Tues. and Wed. mid-Mar.–Apr. BP.

en route

As you continue along the winding course of the Mosel, you'll pass Europe's steepest vineyard site, **Calmont,** opposite the romantic ruins of a 12th-century Augustinian convent and before the loop at Bremm. **Zell** is a popular village full of pubs and wineshops plying the crowds with Zeller Schwarze Katz, "Black Cat" wine, a commercially successful product and the focal point of a large wine festival in late June. Some 6 million vines hug the slopes around Zell, making it one of Germany's largest wine-growing communities. The area between Zell and Schweich (near Trier), known as the Middle Mosel, is home to some of the world's finest Riesling wines.

10

Traben-Trarbach

27 *30 km (19 mi) south of Cochem.*

The Mosel divides Traben-Trarbach, which has pleasant promenades on both sides of the river. Its wine festivals are held the second and last weekends in July. Traben's art-nouveau buildings are worth seeing (Hotel Bellevue, the gateway on the Mosel bridge, the post office, the train station, and town hall). For a look at fine period rooms and exhibits on the historical development of the area, visit the **Mittelmosel Museum,** in the Haus Böcking (1750). *Casino Str. 2 06541/9480 www.mittelmosel-museum.de €2.50 Mid-Apr.–Oct., Tues.–Sun. 10–5.*

en route

During the next 24 km (15 mi) you'll pass by world-famous vineyards, such as Erdener Treppchen, Ürziger Würzgarten, the *Sonnenuhr* (sundial) sites of Zeltingen and Wehlen, and Graacher Himmelreich, before reaching Bernkastel-Kues.

Bernkastel-Kues

28 *22 km (14 mi) southwest of Traben-Trarbach, 100 km (62 mi) southwest of Koblenz on B–53.*

Bernkastel and Kues straddle the Mosel, on the east and west banks, respectively. Elaborately carved half-timber houses (16th–17th centuries) and a Renaissance town hall (1608) frame St. Michael's Fountain (1606), on Bernkastel's photogenic **market square.** In early September the square and riverbank are lined with wine stands for one of the region's largest wine festivals, the Weinfest der Mittelmosel. From the hilltop ruins of the 13th-century castle, **Burg Landshut,** there are splendid views. It was here that Trier's Archbishop Boemund II is said to have recovered from an illness after drinking the local wine. This legendary vineyard, still known as the "Doctor," soars up from Hinterm Graben street near the town gate, Graacher Tor. You can purchase these exquisite wines from Weingut J. Lauerburg (one of the three original owners of the tiny site) at the estate's tasteful wineshop. ✉ *Am Markt 27* ☎ *06531/2481* ⏲ *Apr.–Oct., weekdays 10–5, Sat. 11–5.*

The philosopher and theologian Nikolaus Cusanus (1401–64) was born in Kues. The **St.-Nikolaus-Hospital** is a charitable *Stiftung* (foundation) he established in 1458, and it still operates a home for the elderly and a wine estate. Within it is the **Mosel-Weinmuseum** (Wine museum; 🎫 €2 ⏲ mid-Apr.–Oct., daily 10–5; Nov.–mid-Apr., daily 2–5), as well as a bistro and a wineshop. You can sample more than 100 wines from the entire Mosel-Saar-Ruwer region in the **Vinothek** (🎫 €12 ⏲ mid-Apr.–Oct., daily 10–5; Nov.–mid-Apr., daily 2–5) in the vaulted cellar. The hospital's famous library, with precious manuscripts, cloister, and Gothic chapel, may be visited only on tours. ✉ *Cusanus-Str. 2* ☎ *06531/4141* 🎫 *Historic room tours €4* ⏲ *Mid-Apr.–Oct., Tues. at 10:30, Fri. at 3, or by appointment.*

Some 2,800 winegrowers throughout the region deliver their grapes to the **Moselland Winzergenossenschaft** (Cooperative Winery), where wines are produced, bottled, and marketed. It's an impressive operation, and the large wineshop is excellent. ✉ *Bornwiese 6, in industrial park* ☎ *06531/570* 🎫 *Tours with wine tasting €3.50* ⏲ *Tours with wine tasting Tues. and Thurs. at 2 or by appointment. Wineshop Jan.–Mar., weekdays 9–noon and 1–5, Sat. 9–12:30; Apr.–Dec., weekdays 9–noon and 1–6, Sat. 9–12:30.*

Where to Stay & Eat

$$–$$$$ Fodor'sChoice ★ ✕🏨 **Waldhotel Sonnora.** Helmut and Ulrike Thieltges offer guests one of Germany's absolute finest dining ($$$$, reservations essential) and wining experiences in their elegant country inn set within the forested Eifel Hills. Mr. Thieltges is an extraordinary chef, renowned for transforming exclusive ingredients (foie gras, truffles, Persian caviar) into culinary masterpieces. The wine list is equally superb. The dining room, with gilded and white-wood furnishings and plush red carpets, has a Parisian look. Attractive guest rooms and pretty gardens add to a memorable visit. ✉ *Auf dem Eichelfeld, D–54518 Dreis, 8 km (5 mi) southwest of Wittlich, which is 18 km (11 mi) west of Kues via B–50; from A–1, exit Salmtal* ☎ *06578/98220* 📠 *06578/1402* 🌐 *www.hotel-sonnora.de* *20 rooms* *Restaurant, minibars, babysitting; no a/c* 💳 *AE, MC, V* ⏲ *Restaurant closed Mon. and Tues. Hotel and restaurant closed Jan. and 1st 2 wks in July* 🍽 *BP.*

$$ ✕🏨 **Weinromantikhotel Richtershof.** Very comfortable, individually furnished rooms and first-class friendly service make for a pleasant stay in this 17th-century manor house set in a shady park. Relax over breakfast or a glass of wine on the garden terrace, or take advantage of the 24-hour room service. Culinarium R ($$$–$$$$) serves innovative regional cuisine, including a local version of Riesling soup, in handsome surroundings. The Richtershof wine estate is open for cellar and vineyard tours as well as tastings. ✉ *Hauptstr. 81–83, D–54486 Bernkastel-Kues/Mülheim, 6 km (4 mi) south of Bernkastel via B–53* ☎ *06534/9480* 📠 *06534/948–100* 🌐 *www.weinromantikhotel.de* *40 rooms,*

4 suites ♂ *Restaurant, cable TV, in-room broadband, in-room data ports, gym, sauna, spa, steam room, bicycles, bar, lobby lounge, babysitting, dry cleaning, laundry service, Internet room, business services, some pets allowed (fee), no-smoking rooms; no a/c* ▭ *MC, V* ⊙ *No lunch Mon.–Sat.* 🍴 *BP.*

$ **Zur Post.** The Rössling family will make you feel welcome in their house (1827) with its comfortable guest rooms and cozy restaurant, Poststube ($–$$), and Weinstube. It's near the riverbank, and the market square is just around the corner. Try the Mosel trout *nach Müllerin Art* (dredged in flour and fried). The wine list is devoted exclusively to Mosel Rieslings. ✉ *Gestade 17, D–54470 Bernkastel-Kues* ☎ *06531/96700* 📠 *06531/967–050* 🌐 *www.hotel-zur-post-bernkastel.de* ⇨ *42 rooms, 1 suite* ♂ *Restaurant, minibars, cable TV, Weinstube, some pets allowed (fee), no-smoking rooms; no a/c* ▭ *DC, MC, V* ⊙ *Hotel and restaurant closed Jan. Restaurant closed Tues. and Feb.–Apr.* 🍴 *BP.*

$ **Gästehaus Erika Prüm.** The traditional wine estate S. A. Prüm has state-of-the-art cellars, a tastefully designed Vinothek, and a beautiful guesthouse with an idyllic patio facing the Mosel. The spacious rooms and baths are individually decorated in a winning mixture of contemporary and antique furnishings. Erika Prüm is a charming hostess, and her husband, Raimund (the redhead), is an excellent winemaker who offers tastings and cellar tours. ✉ *Uferallee 25, D–54470 Bernkastel-Wehlen, North of Kues* ☎ *06531/3110* 📠 *06531/8555* 🌐 *www.sapruem.com* ⇨ *8 rooms* ♂ *Cable TV, in-room data ports, some pets allowed (fee); no a/c* ▭ *AE, MC, V* ⊙ *Closed Dec.–mid-Feb.* 🍴 *BP.*

en route

The 55-km (34-mi) drive from Bernkastel to Trier takes in another series of outstanding hillside vineyards, including those 10 km (6 mi) upstream at **Brauneberg** (✉ Paulinsstr. 14, Kesten ☎ 06535/544 🌐 www.paulinshof.de ⊙ weekdays 8–6, Sat. 9–6), where Thomas Jefferson was enchanted by a 1783 Brauneberger Kammer Auslese during his visit here in 1788. Today, the vineyard is solely owned by Weingut Paulinshof. You can sample contemporary vintages of this wine in the beautiful chapel on the estate grounds. On a magnificent loop 12 km (7½ mi) southwest of Brauneberg is the famous village of **Piesport,** whose steep, slate cliff is known as the "Loreley of the Mosel." The village puts on the Mosel in Flammen (Mosel in Flames) fireworks display and festival the first weekend in July. Wines from its 35 vineyards are collectively known as Piesporter Michelsberg; however, the finest individual vineyard site, and one of Germany's very best, is the Goldtröpfchen ("little droplets of gold"). On the western edge of the town, the largest Roman press house (4th century) north of the Alps is on display.

Dhrontal

If the heat of the Mosel's slate slopes becomes oppressive in summer, revitalize body and soul with a scenic drive through the cool, fragrant forest of the Dhrontal (Dhron Valley), south of Trittenheim, and make a stop at this oasis for food-and-wine lovers.

Where to Stay & Eat

★ $–$$$ **Landhaus St. Urban.** Talented chef Harald Rüssel, his charming wife, Ruth, and their friendly staff see to it that guests enjoy excellent food, wine, and service in comfortable surroundings ($$$$). Aromatic, visually stunning food presentations are served with wines from Germany's leading producers, including the family's Weingut St. Urbans-Hof in Leiwen, where visitors are welcome for tours and tastings. The house decor is stylish, and like the food, it reflects Mediterranean flair. *Büdlicherbrück 1, D–54426 Naurath/Wald, 8 km (5 mi) south of Trittenheim, toward Hermeskeil; from A–1, exit Mehring 06509/91400 06509/914–040 www.landhaus-st-urban.de 13 rooms, 3 suites Restaurant, minibars, cable TV, some in-room data ports, laundry service, Internet room, business services, some pets allowed (fee); no a/c, no smoking. AE, MC, V Hotel and restaurant closed 2 wks in Jan. Restaurant also closed Tues. and Wed. BP.*

Trier

55 km (34 mi) southwest of Bernkastel-Kues via B–53, 150 km (93 mi) southwest of Koblenz; 30 min by car to Luxemburg airport.

By 400 BC a Celtic tribe, the Treveri, had settled the Trier Valley. Eventually Julius Caesar's legions arrived at this strategic point on the river, and Augusta Treverorum (the town of Emperor Augustus in the land of the Treveri) was founded in 16 BC. It was described as a most opulent city, as beautiful as any outside Rome.

Around AD 275 an Alemannic tribe stormed Augusta Treverorum and reduced it to rubble. But it was rebuilt in even grander style and renamed Treveris. Eventually it evolved into one of the leading cities of the empire and was promoted to "Roma secunda" (a second Rome) north of the Alps. As a powerful administrative capital it was adorned with all the noble civic buildings of a major Roman settlement, as well as public baths, palaces, barracks, an amphitheater, and temples. The Roman emperors Diocletian (who made it one of the four joint capitals of the empire) and Constantine both lived in Trier for years at a time.

Trier survived the collapse of Rome and became an important center of Christianity and, ultimately, one of the most powerful archbishops in the Holy Roman Empire. The city thrived throughout the Renaissance and baroque periods, taking full advantage of its location at the meeting point of major east–west and north–south trade routes and growing fat on the commerce that passed through. It also became one of Germany's most important wine-exporting centers. A later claim to fame is the city's status as the birthplace of Karl Marx. Trier is a city of wine as well as history, and beneath its streets are cellars capable of storing nearly 8 million gallons. To do justice to Trier, consider staying for at least two full days. The **Trier Card** entitles the holder to free public transportation and discounts on tours and admission fees to Roman sights, museums, and sports and cultural venues. It costs €9 and is valid for three days. There's also a ticket good for all the Roman sights for €6.20.

a good walk

Nearly all of Trier's main sights are close together. Begin your walk where Simeonstrasse passes around the city gate of the Roman city—the **Porta Nigra** 29 —one of the grandest Roman buildings still standing. Climb up inside for a good view of Trier from the tower gallery. **Tourist-Information Trier** 30, next to the Porta Nigra, sells various tours, the discount *Trier Card*, wines, and souvenirs. In a courtyard off the Porta Nigra, the **Städtisches Museum Simeonstift** 31 holds remains of the Romanesque church honoring the early medieval hermit Simeon. (Closed for renovation during 2006.) From here follow Simeonstrasse to the **Hauptmarkt** 32, in the center of the Old Town. You'll find yourself surrounded by old gabled houses, with facades from several ages—medieval, baroque, and 19th century. Turn left onto Domstrasse and come almost immediately face-to-face with Trier's **Dom** 33, the oldest Christian church north of the Alps. The 13-century Gothic **Liebfrauenkirche** 34 stands next door. Just behind the Dom, the **Bischöfliches Museum** 35 houses many antiquities unearthed in excavations around the cathedral.

Next, walk south of the cathedral on Liebfrauenstrasse, curving left through a short street (An-der-Meer-Katz) to Konstantinplatz for a look at the **Römische Palastaula** 36, the largest surviving single-hall structure of the ancient world. The **Rheinisches Landesmuseum** 37, with an extensive collection of Roman antiquities, stands south of the Palastaula, facing the grounds of the prince-elector's palace. The ruins of the **Kaiserthermen** 38, or Imperial Baths, are just 200 yards from the museum. The smaller **Barbarathermen** 39 lies west of the Kaiserthermen on Südallee, while the remains of the **Amphitheater** 40 are just east of the Kaiserthermen. Continue from the Barbarathermen toward the town center along Lorenz-Kellner-Strasse to Brückenstrasse to visit the **Karl-Marx-Haus** 41. Then proceed to Viehmarkt, east of St. Antonius Church, to visit the **Viehmarktthermen** 42, and an excavated Roman bath. From here Brotstrasse will lead you back to the main market square.

TIMING The walk will take a good two hours. It takes extra time to climb the tower of the Porta Nigra, walk through the vast interior of the Dom and its treasury, visit the underground passageways of the Kaiserthermen, and examine the cellars of the Amphitheater. Allow at least another half hour each for the Städtisches Museum Simeonstift, the Bischöfliches Museum, and Viehmarktthermen, as well as an additional hour for the Rheinisches Landesmuseum.

What to See

★ 40 **Amphitheater.** The sheer size of Trier's oldest Roman structure (circa AD 100) is impressive. In its heyday it seated 20,000 spectators; today it's a stage for the Antiquity Festival. You can climb down to the cellars beneath the arena—animals were kept in cells here before being unleashed to do battle with gladiators. During *Brot & Spiele* (Bread &Circus) in mid–August, there are live gladiator games in the arena, complete with horses (but not lions). ✉ *Olewiger Str. 25* *€2.10, Brot Spiele €9.60* *Apr.–Sept., daily 10–6; Oct. and Mar., daily 10–5; Nov.–Feb., daily 10–4.*

Amphitheater 40
Barbarathermen 39
Bischöfliches Museum 35
Dom 33
Hauptmarkt . . 32
Kaiserthermen 38
Karl-Marx-Haus 41
Liebfrauenkirche 34
Porta Nigra 29
Rheinisches Landesmuseum 37
Römische Palastaula . . . 36
Städtisches Museum Simeonstift . . 31
Tourist-Information Trier 30
Viehmarktthermen 42

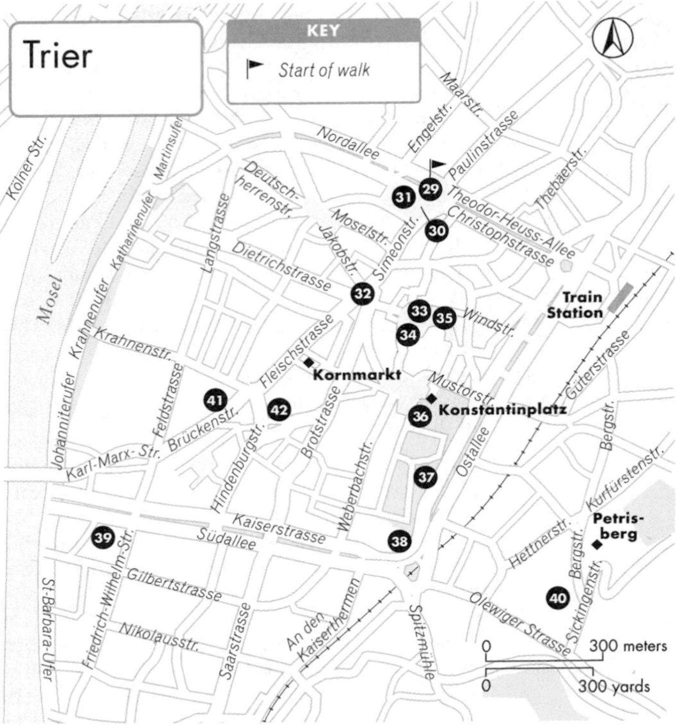

39 **Barbarathermen** (Barbara Baths). These Roman baths are much smaller and two centuries older than the Kaiserthermen. ✉ *Südallee 48, near Friedrich-Wilhelm-Str. and river* 🎫 *€2.10* ⏲ *Apr.–Sept., daily 10–6; Oct. and Mar., daily 10–5; Nov.–Feb., daily 10–4.*

35 **Bischöfliches Museum** (Episcopal Museum). The collection here focuses on medieval sacred art, but there are also fascinating models of the cathedral as it existed in Roman times and 15 Roman frescoes (AD 326), discovered in 1946, that may have adorned the emperor Constantine's palace. ✉ *Windstr. 6* ☎ *0651/710–5255* 🎫 *€2; combination ticket with Domschatzkammer €3* ⏲ *Apr.–Oct., Mon.–Sat. 9–5, Sun. 1–5; Nov.–Mar., Tues.–Sat. 9–5, Sun. 1–5.*

★ **33** **Dom** (Cathedral). Practically every period of Trier's past is represented here. The Dom stands on the site of the Palace of Helen, named for the mother of the emperor Constantine, who tore the palace down in AD 330 and put up a large church in its place. The church burned down in 336, and a second, even larger one was built. Parts of the foundations of this third building can be seen in the east end of the present structure (begun in about 1035). The cathedral you see today is a weighty and sturdy edifice with small round-head windows, rough stonework, and asymmetrical towers, as much a fortress as a church. Inside, Gothic styles predominate—the result of remodeling in the 13th century—although there are also many baroque tombs, altars, and confessionals. ✉ *Domfreihof* ☎ *0651/979–0790* 🌐 *www.dominformation.de* 🎫 *Tours €3* ⏲ *Apr.–Oct., daily 6:30–6; Nov.–Mar., daily 6:30–5:30; tours Apr.–Oct., daily at 2* PM.

The **Domschatzkammer** (Cathedral Treasure Chamber; 🎫 €1.50; combination ticket with Bischöfliches Museum €3 ⏲ Apr.–Oct. and Dec., Mon.–Sat. 9:30–5:30, Sun. noon–5:30; Nov. and Jan.–Mar., weekdays 9:30–5:30, Sat. 9:30–2) houses many extraordinary objects. The highlight is the 10th-century Andreas Tragaltar (St. Andrew's Portable Altar), constructed of oak and covered with gold leaf, enamel, and ivory by local craftsmen. It's a reliquary for the soles of St. Andrew's sandals, symbolized by the gilded, life-size foot on the top of the altar.

32 **Hauptmarkt.** The main market square of Old Trier is easily reached via Simeonstrasse. The market cross (958) and richly ornate St. Peter's Fountain (1595), dedicated to the town's patron saint, stand in the square. The farmers' market is open weekdays 7–6 and Saturday 7–1.

38 **Kaiserthermen** (Imperial Baths). This enormous 4th-century bathing palace once housed cold- and hot-water baths and a sports field. Although only the masonry of the **Calderium** (hot baths) and the vast basements remain, they are enough to give a fair idea of the original splendor and size of the complex—it covered an area 270 yards long and 164 yards wide. Originally 98 feet high, the walls you see today are 62 feet high. During *Brot & Spiele* (Bread & Circus) in mid–August, there is a reconstucted Roman village on the sports field, with Roman arts-and-crafts workshops, and a sound-and-light show in the basements. ✉ *At Weimarer-Allee and Kaiserstr.* 🎫 *€2.10, Brot Spiele €5.20* ⏲ *Apr.–Sept., daily 10–6; Oct. and Mar., daily 10–5; Nov.–Feb., daily, 10–4.*

41 **Karl-Marx-Haus.** Marx was born on May 5, 1818, in this bourgeois house built in 1727. Visitors with a serious interest in social history will be fascinated by its small museum. A signed first edition of *Das Kapital,* the study in which Marx sought to prove the inevitable decline of capitalism, has a place of honor. ✉ *Brückenstr. 10* ☎ *0651/970–680* 🎫 *€2* ⏲ *Apr.–Oct., Mon. 1–6, Tues.–Sun. 10–6; Nov.–Mar., Mon. 2–5, Tues.–Sun. 10–1 and 2–5.*

34 **Liebfrauenkirche** (Church of Our Lady). This is the first Gothic church in Germany, built in the 13th century on the site of a Roman basilica. The original statues from the portal (those that have survived) are in the **Bischöfliches Museum.** Inside, the decoration is austere except for Karl von Metternich's 17th-century tomb. ✉ *Liebfrauenstr.* ⏲ *Apr.–Oct., daily 7:30–6; Nov.–Mar., daily 7:30–5:30.*

★ 29 **Porta Nigra** (Black Gate). The best-preserved Roman structure in Trier was originally a city gate, built in the 2nd century (look for holes left by the iron clamps that held the structure together). Its name is misleading, however; the sandstone gate is not black but dark gray. The gate also served as part of Trier's defenses and was proof of the sophistication of Roman military might and its ruthlessness. Attackers were often lured into the two innocent-looking arches of the Porta Nigra, only to find themselves enclosed in a courtyard. In the 11th century the upper stories were converted into two churches, in use until the 18th century. The tourist office is next door. ✉ *Porta-Nigra-Pl.* 🎫 *€2.10* ⏲ *Apr.–Sept., daily 10–6; Oct. and Mar., daily 10–5; Nov.–Feb., daily 10–4.*

★ 37 **Rheinisches Landesmuseum** (Rhenish State Museum). The largest collection of Roman antiquities in Germany is housed here. The highlight is the 4th-century stone relief of a Roman ship transporting barrels of wine up the river. This tombstone of a Roman wine merchant was discovered in 1874 when Constantine's citadel in Neumagen was excavated. Have a look at the 108-square-foot model of the city as it looked in the 4th century—it provides a sense of perspective to many of the sights you can still visit today. ✉ *Weimarer-Allee 1* ☎ *0651/97740* 🌐 *www.landesmuseum-trier.de* 🎫 *€5.50* ⏲ *May–Oct., weekdays 9:30–5, weekends 10:30–5; Nov.–Apr., Tues.–Fri. 9:30–5, weekends 10:30–5.*

★ 36 **Römische Palastaula** (Roman Basilica). An impressive reminder of Trier's Roman past, this edifice is now Trier's major Protestant church. When first built by the emperor Constantine around AD 310, it was the imperial throne room of the palace. At 239 feet long, 93 feet wide, and 108 feet high, it demonstrates the astounding ambition of its Roman builders and the sophistication of their building techniques. The basilica is one of the two largest Roman interiors in existence (the other is the Pantheon in Rome). Look up at the deeply coffered ceiling; more than any other part of the building, it conveys the opulence of the original structure. ✉ *Konstantinpl.* ☎ *0651/72468 or 0651/42570* ⏲ *Apr.–Oct., Mon.–Sat. 10–6, Sun. noon–6; Nov.–Mar., Tues.–Sat. 11–noon and 3–4, Sun. noon–1.*

31 **Städtisches Museum Simeonstift** (Simeon Foundation City Museum). Built around the remains of the Romanesque Simeonskirche, this church is now a museum. It was constructed in the 11th century by Archbishop Poppo in honor of the early medieval hermit Simeon, who for seven years shut himself up in the east tower of the Porta Nigra. Collections include art and artifacts produced in Trier from the Middle Ages to the 19th century. ✉ *An der Porta Nigra* ☎ *0651/718–1454* 🎫 *€2.60* ⏲ *Apr.–Oct., daily 9–5; Nov.–Mar., Tues.–Fri. 9–5, weekends 9–3. At this writing, closed for renovation until 2007.*

30 **Tourist-Information Trier.** In addition to dispensing city information, this tourist office sells regional wines and souvenirs, from Trier mousepads and replicas of Roman artifacts to Porta Nigra pasta. ✉ *An der Porta Nigra* ☎ *0651/978–080* ⏲ *Jan. and Feb., Mon.–Sat. 10–5, Sun. 10–1; Mar., Apr., and Oct.–Dec., Mon.–Sat. 9–6, Sun. 10–3; May–Sept., Mon.–Sat. 9–7, Sun. 10–5* 💳 *AE, MC, V.*

42 **Viehmarktthermen.** Trier's third Roman bath (early 1st century) was discovered beneath Viehmarktplatz when ground was broken for a parking garage. Finds of the excavations from 1987 to 1994 are now beneath a protective glass structure. You can visit the baths and see the cellar of a baroque Capuchin monastery. ✉ *Viehmarktpl.* ☎ *0651/994–1057* 🎫 *€2.10* ⏲ *Tues.–Sun. 10–5.*

off the beaten path

★ **ROSCHEIDER HOF –** For a look at 19th- and 20th-century rural life in the Mosel-Saar area, visit the hilltop open-air Freilichtmuseum near Konz–Saar (10 km [6 mi] southwest of Trier via B–51). Numerous farmhouses and typical village buildings in the region were saved from the wrecking ball by being dismantled and brought to the Roscheider Hof, where they were rebuilt and refurnished as they were decades ago. Old school rooms, a barbershop and beauty salon, a tavern, a shoemaker's workshop, a pharmacy, a grocery, and a dentist's office have been set up in the rooms of the museum proper, along with period rooms and exhibitions on local trades and household work, such as the history of laundry. In 2005, a large collection of tin figures was added. A Biedermeier rose garden, museum shop, and restaurant with a beer garden (closed Monday, no credit cards) are also on the grounds. ✉ *Konz* ☎ *06501/92710* 🌐 *www.roscheiderhof.de* *€3* *Tues.–Fri. 9–6, weekends 10–6.*

10

Where to Stay & Eat

$$$–$$$$ ✕ **Pfeffermühle.** For nearly three decades chef Siegbert Walde has offered guests classic cuisine in elegant surroundings. The 18th-century house on the northern edge of town has two stories of cozy niches, with beautiful table settings in shades of pink; the terrace directly overlooks the Mosel. Foie gras is a favorite ingredient, served in a terrine or sautéed and served in *Ahorn-jus* (maple-flavor juices). White wines from the Mosel's finest producers and top red Bordeaux wines make up a good part of the excellent wine list. ✉ *Zurlaubener Ufer 76* ☎ *0651/26133* *Reservations essential* *MC, V* *Closed Sun. No lunch Mon.*

$$–$$$ ✕ **Palais Kesselstatt.** This baroque palace opposite the Liebfrauenkirche is a wonderful setting for fine dining—elegant but not pretentious. There's also seating in the beautiful courtyard in the summer. Specialties include rack of lamb or lamb medallions as well as fish. End a meal with an unusual, but tasty, red pepper-vanilla parfait. Wines from the Reichsgraf von Kesselstatt estate dominate the wine list, supplemented by Old- and New-World reds. ✉ *Liebfrauenstr. 10* ☎ *0651/40204* 🌐 *www.restaurant-kesselstatt.de* *AE, DC, MC, V* *Closed Sun., Mon., and Jan.*

★ $–$$$ ✕ **Schlemmereule.** The name literally means "gourmet owl," and, indeed, chef Peter Schmalen caters to gourmets within the 19th-century Palais Walderdorff complex opposite the cathedral. Lots of windows lend a light, airy look, and a replica of one of Michelangelo's Sistine Chapel paintings graces the ceiling. There's courtyard seating in summer. The fish is always excellent, or try the *Gänsestopfleber* (foie gras) with port-wine aspic. The daily specials at lunch ($) include a glass of wine. The wine list features 10 wines by the glass and 180 by the bottle, with an emphasis on Mosel wines. ✉ *Palais Walderdorff, Domfreihof 1B* ☎ *0651/73616* 🌐 *www.schlemmereule.de* *Reservations essential* *AE, DC, MC, V* *Closed Tues.*

★ $–$$ ✕ **Zum Domstein.** Whether you dine inside or out, don't miss the collection of Roman artifacts displayed in the cellar. In addition to the German dishes on the regular menu, you can order à la carte or prix-fixe menus (€9.50–€30) based on the recipes of Roman gourmet Marcus Gavius Apicius in the evening. Proprietor Rose-Marie Gracher is an expert on the subject. It's a unique experience and highly recommended. ✉ *Am Hauptmarkt 5* ☎ *0651/74490* 🌐 *www.domstein.de* 💳 *MC, V.*

¢–$ ✕ **Walderdorff's Vinothek-Café-Club.** This trio has added a lively note to the 19th-century palace opposite Trier cathedral. The café-bistro offers breakfast, sandwiches, salads, pasta, and light fare—prepared by the Schlemmereule team. Some 250 local and Old- and New-World wines are sold in the Vinothek, where tastings are offered. The club offers music and dancing in the baroque cellars. ✉ *Palais Walderdorff, Domfreihof 1* ☎ *0651/9946–9210* 🌐 *www.walderdorffs.de* 💳 *DC, MC, V.*

¢–$ ✕ **Weinstube Kesselstatt.** The Hilgers family runs this casual offshoot of Palais Kesselstatt. The interior has exposed beams and polished wood tables; the shady terrace is popular in summer. Two soups daily, light fare, and fresh, regional cuisine are served with wines from the Reichsgraf von Kesselstatt estate. With the sampler "Das Beste aus der Region" you can taste several local specialties (such as fish, sausage, and cheese). ✉ *Liebfrauenstr. 10* ☎ *0651/41178* 🌐 *www.weinstube-kesselstatt.de* 💳 *MC, V* ⊙ *Closed Jan.*

$ ✕🏨 **Ambiente.** Modern flair marks the style and decor that Markus and Monika Stemper—a passionate cook and a gracious hostess—offer in their country inn. Their legendary garden (with palms, ponds, and flowers galore), comfortable rooms, and personal service are remarkable. Both Restaurant Jardin ($$–$$$) and Stempers Brasserie ($–$$) serve dishes with Mediterranean accents, enhanced by an extensive wine list. ✉ *In der Acht 1–2, D–54294 Trier-Zewen, 7 km (4½ mi) southwest of Trier via B–49* ☎ *0651/827–280* 📠 *0651/827–2844* 🌐 *www.hotel-ambiente-trier.de* *11 rooms* *2 restaurants, minibars, cable TV, in-room data ports, Wi-Fi, bicycles, bar, babysitting, dry cleaning, laundry service, Internet room, business services, no-smoking rooms; no a/c* 💳 *AE, DC, MC, V* ⊙ *Restaurants closed Thurs.* 🍽 *BP.*

★ $ ✕🏨 **Weinhaus Becker.** This family-run hotel, gourmet restaurant ($$$$), and wine estate is in the peaceful suburb of Olewig, near the amphitheater. The rooms are individually decorated with light-wood furnishings; some have balconies. You can dine in the restaurant's romantic, candlelighted niches or on the terrace. The three-course menu for hotel guests ($$$) offers very good value. Bordeaux and Burgundy wines are available in addition to the estate's own wines—and wine tastings, cellar visits, and guided tours on the wine path can be arranged. ✉ *Olewiger Str. 206, D–54295 Trier-Olewig* ☎ *0651/938–080* 📠 *0651/938–0888* 🌐 *www.weinhaus-becker.de* *19 rooms* *Restaurant, cable TV, bicycles, babysitting, some pets allowed (fee); no a/c* 💳 *AE, DC, MC, V* ⊙ *Restaurant closed Mon., 3 wks Jan. and Feb., and 1 wk late July. No lunch Tues., no dinner Sun.* 🍽 *BP.*

$–$$ 🏨 **Römischer Kaiser.** Centrally located near the Porta Nigra, this handsome patrician manor from 1895 offers well-appointed, attractive, modern rooms. The staff is friendly and helpful, and while some of Trier's other restaurants offer more flair, the food here is tasty, as is the hearty breakfast buffet. ✉ *Am Porta-Nigra-Pl. 6, D–54292* ☎ *0651/97700* 🖷 *0651/977–099* 🌐 *www.hotels-trier.de* ⇒ *43 rooms* ♁ *Restaurant, minibars, cable TV, some in-room data ports, Wi-Fi, bar, laundry service, business services, some pets allowed (fee), no smoking floor; no a/c* ▭ *AE, DC, MC, V* 🍽 *BP.*

$ **Hotel Petrisberg.** The Pantenburgs' friendly, family-run hotel is high on Petrisberg hill overlooking Trier, not far from the amphitheater. You can walk to the Old Town in 20 minutes. The individually decorated rooms have solid-pine furnishings; all have balconies—some with a fabulous view of the city. All rooms are no smoking. In the evenings, you can enjoy snacks and good local wines in the wine pub. ✉ *Sickingenstr. 11–13, D–54296* ☎ *0651/4640* 🖷 *0651/46450* 🌐 *www.hotelpetrisberg.de* ⇒ *26 rooms, 4 apartments* ♁ *Cable TV, some in-room data ports, bicycles, Weinstube, laundry service, Internet room, business services; no a/c, no smoking* ▭ *MC, V* 🍽 *BP.*

Festivals

The **Europa-Volksfest** (European Folk Festival), in May or early June, features wine and food specialties from several European countries, in addition to rides and entertainment. In late June the entire Old Town is the scene of the **Altstadtfest.** The amphitheater is an impressive setting for the theatrical performances of the **Antikenfestspiele** (Antiquity Festival) from late June to mid-July. The **Moselfest,** with wine, sparkling wine, beer, and fireworks, takes place in July along the riverbank in Zurlauben, followed by a large **Weinfest** (Wine Festival) in Olewig in early August, and Germany's largest Roman festival, **Brot &Spiel** (Bread & Circus), in mid-August. From late November until December 22, the annual **Weihnachtsmarkt** (Christmas market) takes place on the market square and in front of the cathedral.

Nightlife & the Arts

For absolutely up-to-the-minute information on performances, concerts, and events all over town, visit the Web site **www.trier-today.de.** Pop-up maps show exactly where everything is located.

Theater Trier (✉ Am Augustinerhof ☎ 0651/718–1818 for box office) offers opera, theater, ballet, and concerts.

Concerts, theater, and cultural events are staged at **TUFA–Tuchfabrik** (✉ Wechselstr. 4, at Weberstr. ☎ 0651/718–2412).

Pubs and cafés are centered on Viehmarktplatz and Stockplatz in the Old Town. **Walderdorff's** (✉ Domfreihof 1 ☎ 0651/9946–9210) in the Palais Walderdorff has trendy DJ nights, early after-work parties, and occasional live bands.

The restaurant-lounge-café **FORUM** (✉ Hindenburgstr. 4 ☎ 0651/170–4363) features international DJs, theme parties, and live music. There's music and dancing at **Riverside** (✉ Zurmaiener Str. 173, near traffic circle on northern edge of town ☎ 0651/21006), a large entertainment center.

BONN & THE COLOGNE LOWLANDS

Updated by Jürgen Scheunemann

Bonn, the former capital of Germany, is the next major stop after Koblenz on the Rhine. It's close to the legendary Siebengebirge (Seven Hills), a national park and site of Germany's northernmost vineyards. According to German mythology, Siegfried (hero of the Nibelungen saga) killed a dragon here and bathed in its blood to make himself invincible. The lowland, a region of gently rolling hills north of Bonn, lacks the drama of the Rhine gorge upstream but offers the urban pleasures of Köln (Cologne), an ancient cathedral town, and Düsseldorf, an elegant city of art and fashion. Although not geographically in the Rhineland proper, Aachen is an important side trip for anyone visiting the region. Its stunning cathedral and treasury are the greatest storehouses of Carolingian art and architecture in Europe.

Bonn

44 km (27 mi) north of Koblenz, 28 km (17 mi) south of Köln.

Bonn was the postwar seat of the federal government and parliament until the capital returned to Berlin in 1999. Aptly described by the title of John le Carré's spy novel *A Small Town in Germany,* the quiet university town was chosen as a stopgap measure to prevent such weightier contenders as Frankfurt from becoming the capital, a move that would have lessened Berlin's chances of regaining its former status. With the exodus of the government from Bonn, the city has lost some of its international flair. Still, other organizations and industries have moved to Bonn to fill the gap, and its status as a U.N. city has been strengthened. The fine museums and other cultural institutions that once served the diplomatic elite are still here to be enjoyed.

Although Bonn seems to have sprung into existence only after the war, the Romans settled this part of the Rhineland 2,000 years ago, calling it Castra Bonnensia. Life in Bonn's old markets, pedestrian malls, and handsome Sudstadt residential area is unhurried. The town center is a car-free zone; an inner-ring road circles it with parking garages on the perimeter. A convenient parking lot is just across from the railway station and within 50 yards of the tourist office. Check with the tourism office for *RegioBonnCard* packages, which offer free or reduced entry into museums, low-cost transportation, and more.

a good tour

After picking up what you need at the tourist office at Windeckstrasse 2, continue to the cathedral **Münster** 43 ⚑, the site where two Roman soldiers were executed in AD 253 for holding Christian beliefs. Across from the cathedral are the **Kurfürstliches Residenz** 44, now the main Friedrich-Wilhelm University building, and its gardens (Hofgarten). Walk away from the river and down chestnut-tree-lined Poppelsdorfer Allee to the **Poppelsdorfer Schloss** 45, which has a tropical garden. Return toward the Kurfürstliches Residenz along Am Hof, and turn left onto the Marktplatz to arrive at the lavish, rococo **Rathaus** 46. Off the square, Bonngasse leads to the modest **Beethoven-Haus** 47, the residence of the great composer until he was 22. Backtrack to the Markt, and take

Stockenstrasse past the palace gardens to Adenauerallee. Walk south along Adenauerallee and turn right onto Am Hofgarten. At the corner of Lennéstrasse is the glassed-in building of the offbeat **Arithmeum** 48. Return via Am Hofgarten to Adenauerallee. About 1½ km (1 mi) southeast along the Rhine is the Museum Mile. There you'll find the **Haus der Geschichte** 49, the **Kunst- und Ausstellungshalle der Bundesrepublik Deutschland** 50, and the **Kunstmuseum Bonn** 51, among others. To save yourself the walk, catch Bus No. 610 or take U-bahn 16 at the Juridicum subway on Adenauerallee, between Am Hofgarten and Weberstrasse. Get off at the Heussallee–Museumsmeile stop. Finally, take a casual walk through the **Bundesviertel** 52, West Germany's government district for half a century. Most of the sights can be toured by walking down Adenauerallee to Willy-Brandt-Allee (you can also take the U-bahn to the Museum Koenig station).

If you'd like to spend more time inside Bonn's museums, follow the above route, but skip the long walk to the Poppelsdorfer Schloss.

TIMING Allow a little more than 2 hours for the first walk and 1½ for the shorter version, not including time spent in museums or shopping.

What to See

48 **Arithmeum.** Technophiles and technophobes alike enjoy this university-run museum, where even the abstract theme of discrete mathematics is made comprehensible. Its stated aim is to show "the interface of art and technology," and the core of the exhibit is a 1,200-piece collection of historical mechanical-calculating machines, which became obsolete with the advent of computers. The art comes in the form of a collection of constructivist paintings that resemble enlarged, colorful computer-chip designs. ✉ *Lennéstr. 2* ☎ *0228/738–790* 🌐 *www.arithmeum.uni-bonn.de* 🎫 *€3* ⏲ *Tues.–Sun. 11–6.*

off the beaten path

ALTER FRIEDHOF (Old Cemetery) – This ornate, leafy cemetery is the resting place of many of the country's most celebrated sons and daughters. Look for the tomb of composer Robert Schumann (1810–56) and his wife, Clara, also a composer and accomplished pianist. To reach the cemetery from the main train station, follow Quantiusstrasse north until it becomes Herwarthstrasse; before the street curves, turning into Endenlicherstrasse, take the underpass below the railroad line. You'll then be on Thomastrasse, which borders the cemetery. ✉ *Am Alten Friedhof* ⏲ *Jan., daily 9–5; Feb., daily 8–6; Mar.–Aug., daily 7:15 AM–8 PM; Sept., daily 8–8; Oct., daily 8–7; Nov. and Dec., daily 8–5.*

47 **Beethoven-Haus** (Beethoven House). Beethoven was born in Bonn in 1770 and, except for a short stay in Vienna, lived here until the age of 22. The house where he grew up is a museum celebrating his career. You'll find scores, paintings, a grand piano (his last, in fact), and an ear trumpet or two. Perhaps most impressive is the room in which Beethoven was born—empty save for a bust of the composer. The attached museum shop carries everything from kitsch to elegant Beethoven memorabilia. ✉ *Bongasse 20* ☎ *0228/981–7525* 🌐 *www.beethoven-haus-bonn.de* 🎫 *€4*

Arithmeum . . 48
Beethoven-Haus 47
Bundes-viertel 52
Haus der Geschichte . . . 49
Kunst- und Ausstellungs-halle der Bundesrepublik Deutsch-land 50
Kunstmuseum Bonn 51
Kurfürstliches Residenz 44
Münster 43
Poppelsdorfer Schloss 45
Rathaus 46

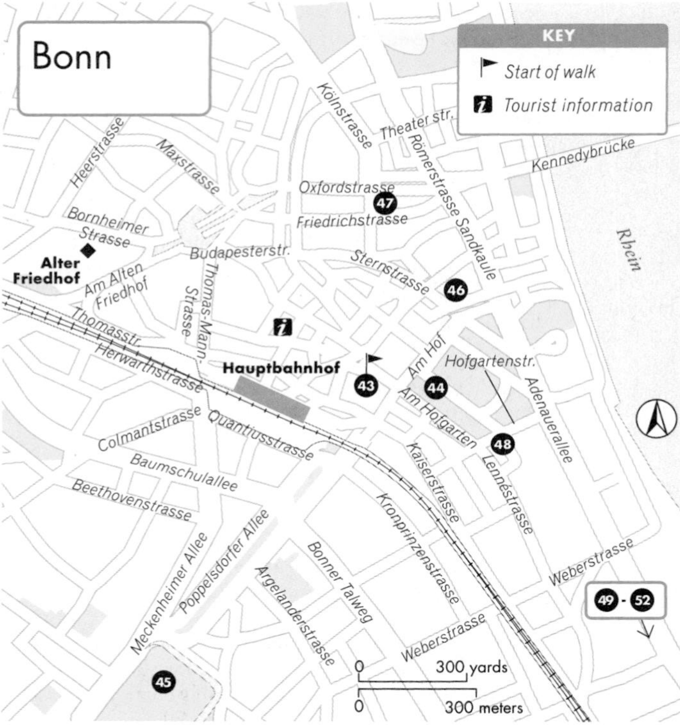

Apr.–Oct., Mon.–Sat. 10–6, Sun. 11–6; Nov.–Mar., Mon.–Sat. 10–5, Sun. 11–5.

52 **Bundesviertel** (Federal Government District). Walking through the amiable, former government district is like taking a trip back in time to an era when Bonn was still the sleepy capital of West Germany. Bordered by Adenauerallee, Willy-Brandt-Allee, Friedrich-Ebert-Allee, and the Rhine, the quarter boasts sights such as the **Bundeshaus** with the Plenarsaal. This building, designed to serve as the new Federal Parliament, was completed only six years before the capital was relocated to Berlin in 1999. A few steps away, you'll find the historic **Villa Hammerschmidt,** the German equivalent of the White House. This stylish classicist mansion began serving as the Federal president's permanent residence in 1950 and is still his home when he stays in Bonn. Equally impressive is the **Palais Schaumburg,** another fine example of the Rhein Riveria estates that once housed the Federal Chancellery (1949–76). It became the center of Cold War politics during the Adenauer administration. Tours of the quarter, including a visit to the Villa Hammerschmidt, are offered by the Bonn Tourist Office. ✉ *Adenauerallee.*

★ 49 **Haus der Geschichte** (House of History). German history since World War II is the subject of this museum, which begins with "hour zero," as the

Germans call the unconditional surrender of 1945. The museum displays an overwhelming amount of documentary material organized on five levels and engages various types of media. It's not all heavy either—temporary exhibits have featured political cartoonists, "Miss Germany" pageants, and an in-depth examination of the song *Lili Marleen,* sung by troops of every nation during World War II. Take a look at the historical reconstructions of typical German backyards, behind the museum. ✉ *Willy-Brandt-Allee 14* ☎ *0228/91650* 🌐 *www.hdg.de* 🎫 *Free* ⏲ *Tues.–Sun. 9–7.*

★ 50 **Kunst- und Ausstellungshalle der Bundesrepublik Deutschland** (Art and Exhibition Hall of the German Federal Republic). This is one of the Rhineland's most important venues for major exhibitions about culture and science. Recent exhibits included treasures from Venetian palaces, mythical representations and reality of Troy, and art from the Iranian national museum. Its modern design, by Viennese architect Gustave Peichl, is as interesting as anything on exhibit in the museum. It employs three enormous blue cones situated on a lawnlike rooftop garden. ✉ *Friedrich-Ebert-Allee 4* ☎ *0228/917–1200* 🌐 *www.bundeskunsthalle.de* 🎫 *€7* ⏲ *Tues. and Wed. 10–9, Thurs.–Sun. 10–7.*

51 **Kunstmuseum Bonn** (Art Museum). Devoted to contemporary art, this large museum is renowned for the high standard of its collection. The two main focuses are on Rheinish Expressionists and German art since 1945 (Beuys, Baselitz, and Kiefer, for example). Changing exhibits are generally excellent and help maintain a link to the international art scene. The museum's airy and inexpensive café is preferable to the stuffier version across the plaza at the Kunst- und Ausstellungshalle. ✉ *Friedrich-Ebert-Allee 2* ☎ *0228/776–260* 🌐 *www.bonn.de/kunstmuseum* 🎫 *€5* ⏲ *Tues. and Thurs.–Sun. 11–6, Wed. 11–9.*

44 **Kurfürstliche Residenz** (Prince-Electors' Residence). Built in the 18th century by the prince-electors of Köln, this grand palace now houses a university. If the weather is good, stroll through the Hofgarten (Palace Gardens). ✉ *Am Hofgarten.*

43 **Münster** (Cathedral). The 900-year-old cathedral is vintage late Romanesque, with a massive octagonal main tower and a soaring spire. It saw the coronations of two Holy Roman Emperors (in 1314 and 1346) and was one of the Rhineland's most important ecclesiastical centers in the Middle Ages. The 17th-century bronze figure of St. Helen and the ornate rococo pulpit are highlights of the interior. ✉ *Münsterpl.* ☎ *0228/985–880* 🎫 *Free* ⏲ *Daily 9–7.*

45 **Poppelsdorfer Schloss** (Poppelsdorf Palace). This former electors' palace was built in the baroque style between 1715 and 1753 and now houses the university's mineralogical collection. Its botanical gardens are open to the public and have an impressive display of tropical plants. The best exhibit is the mammoth Amazon water lilies, which can support up to 175 pounds. ✉ *Meckenheimer Allee 171* ☎ *0228/732–764* 🎫 *Free* ⏲ *Apr.–Sept., weekdays 9–6, weekends 9–1; Oct.–Mar., weekdays 9–4.*

46 **Rathaus** (Town Hall). Not very austere, this 18th-century town hall looks somewhat like a pink dollhouse. Its elegant steps and perron have seen a great many historic figures, including French president Charles de Gaulle and U.S. president John F. Kennedy. ✉ *Am Markt* ☎ *0228/774–288* *Free* *By tour only: May–Oct., 1st Sat. of month, noon–4.*

Where to Stay & Eat

$–$$$ ✕ **Sassella.** When the Bundestag was still in town, this Bonn institution used to be cited in the press as frequently for its backroom political dealings as for its Lombardi-influenced food. But locals, prominent and otherwise, still flock to the restaurant, in an 18th-century house outside the town center. The style is pure Italian farmhouse, with stone walls and exposed beams, but the handmade pastas often stray from the typical—note the salmon-filled black-and-white pasta pockets in shrimp sauce. ✉ *Karthäuserpl. 21* ☎ *0228/5308–1512* *AE, MC, V* *Closed Mon.*

$–$$ ✕ **Amadeo.** The popularity of this neighborhood restaurant is due in part to the German affinity for all things Spanish but also because its food—40 different tapas (€2–€6), inventive salads, and main dishes—rarely misses the mark. The seafood kebabs with Spanish potatoes and spicy tomato sauce are recommended, and the mixed-tapas plate is excellent. ✉ *Mozartstr. 1* ☎ *0228/635–534* *No credit cards* *No lunch.*

$–$$ ✕ **Pirandello.** This trattoria with its frescoed brick walls is so cozy that it borders on kitsch. But the decor is redeemed by the quality of chef-owner Fausto Langui's Italian regional dishes and the wines he recommends to go with them. The seasonally changing menu features pizzas, pastas, fish, and meats—all, as a rule, excellently prepared. ✉ *Brüderg. 22* ☎ *0228/656–606* *No credit cards* *Closed Sun.*

¢–$ ✕ **Em Höttche.** Travelers and Bonn residents (Beethoven was a regular) have taken sustenance at this tavern since the late 14th century, and today it offers one of the best-value lunches in town. The interior is rustic; the food stout and hearty. ✉ *Markt 4* ☎ *0228/690–009* *No credit cards.*

$$$ **Best Western Domicil.** A group of buildings around a quiet, central courtyard has been converted into a charming and comfortable hotel. The rooms are individually furnished and decorated—in styles ranging from fin-de-siècle romantic to Italian modern. Huge windows give the public rooms a spacious airiness. ✉ *Thomas-Mann-Str. 24–26, D–53111* ☎ *0228/729–090* *0228/691–207* *www.bestwestern.de* *43 rooms, 1 apartment* *Restaurant, room service, cable TV, in-room data ports, Wi-Fi, sauna, some free parking, some pets allowed (fee), no-smoking rooms; no a/c* *AE, DC, MC, V* *BP.*

$–$$ **Sternhotel.** For solid comfort and a central location in the Old Town, the Stern is tops. About 80% of the rooms have been renovated in a Danish modern style; the rest are more old-fashioned. Weekend rates are a bargain. ✉ *Markt 8, D–53111* ☎ *0228/72670* *0228/726–7125* *www.sternhotel-bonn.de* *80 rooms* *Cable TV, in-room data ports, some pets allowed (fee), no-smoking rooms; no a/c* *DC, MC, V* *CP.*

$ **Mozart.** Elegant on the outside and simple on the inside, this small, attractive hotel is often recommended to friends by Bonn residents. Part of its appeal is its location amid traditional town houses in the romantic, residential "musician's quarter," just a four-minute walk from the main train station and the city center. ✉ *Mozartstr. 1, D–53115* ☎ *0228/659–071* 🖷 *0228/659–075* 🌐 *www.hotel-mozart-bonn.de* *39 rooms* *Cable TV, parking (fee); no a/c* *AE, DC, MC, V* *CP.*

The Arts

MUSIC The Bonn Symphony Orchestra opens its season in grand style every September with a concert on the market square, in front of city hall. Otherwise, concerts are held in the **Beethovenhalle** (✉ Wachsbleiche 16 ☎ 0228/72220). Indoor and outdoor concerts are held at numerous venues during September's **Beethoven-Festival** (☎ 0228/201–0345 🌐 www.beethovenfest-bonn.de). In the **Beethoven-Haus** (✉ Bonngasse 20 ☎ 0228/981–750), intimate recitals are sometimes given on an 18th-century grand piano.

Operas are staged regularly at the **Oper der Stadt Bonn** (✉ Am Boeselagerhof 1 ☎ 0228/778–000 🌐 www.theater.bonn.de), popularly known as La Scala of the Rhineland. The **Pantheontheater** (✉ Bundeskanzlerpl. ☎ 0228/212–521) is a prime venue for all manner of pop concerts and cabaret. Chamber-music concerts are given regularly at the **Schuman** (✉ Sebastianstr. 182 ☎ 0228/773–656).

THEATER & DANCE Musicals and ballet are performed at the **Oper der Stadt Bonn.** From May through October, the **Bonner Sommer** (✉ Tourist office, Windeckstr. 1 ☎ 0228/775–000) festival offers folklore, music, and street theater, much of it outdoors and most of it free. Information is available at the tourist office.

Shopping

There are plenty of department stores and boutiques in the pedestrian shopping zone around the Markt and the Münster. Bonn's **Wochenmarkt** (Weekly Market) is open daily except Sunday, filling the Markt with vendors of produce and various edibles. Bargain hunters search for secondhand goods and knickknacks at the city's renowned—and huge—**Flohmarkt** (Flea Market; ✉ Ludwig-Erhard-Allee), held in Rheinaue park under the Konrad-Adenauer-Brücke on the third Saturday of each month from April through October. **Pützchens Markt,** a huge country fair, takes place in the Bonn area the second weekend of September.

Königswinter

12 km (7 mi) southeast of Bonn.

The town of Königswinter has one of the most visited castles on the Rhine, the **Drachenfels.** Its ruins crown one of the highest hills in the Siebengebirge, Germany's oldest nature reserve, with a spectacular view of the Rhine. The reserve has more than 100 km (62 mi) of hiking trails. The castle was built in the 12th century by the archbishop of Köln. Its name commemorates a dragon said to have lived in a nearby cave. As legend has it, the dragon was slain by Siegfried, hero of the epic *Nibelungenlied.* You can reach the castle ruins by taking the **Drachenfelsbahn** (✉ Drachenfelsstr. 53 ☎ 02223/92090 🌐 www.drachenfelsbahnkoenigswinter.de), a steep, narrow-gauge train that makes trips to the summit every hour or occasionally every half hour. The trip costs €6.50 one-way, €8 round-trip. The train runs daily in March and October, from 10 to 6; in April it runs daily from 10 to 7; from May through September, it runs daily from 9 to 7; from November through February, it runs weekdays from noon to 5 and weekends from 11 to 6.

Where to Eat

$–$$$ ✕ **Gasthaus Sutorius.** Across from the church of St. Margaretha, this wine tavern serves refined variations on German cuisine with a nice selection of local wines. In summer, food is served outdoors beneath the linden trees. ✉ *Oelinghovener Str. 7* ☎ *02244/912–240* 💳 *MC, V* ⏲ *No dinner Sun. and Mon. No lunch Tues.–Sat.*

Brühl

20 km (12 mi) southwest of Bonn.

In the heart of Brühl you'll discover the Rhineland's most important baroque palace. **Schloss Augustusburg** and the magnificent pleasure park that surrounds it were created in the time of Prince Clemens August, between 1725 and 1768. The palace contains one of the most famous achievements of rococo architecture, a staircase by Balthasar Neumann. The castle can be visited only on guided tours, which leave the reception area every hour or so. An English cassette guide is available. **Concerts** (☎ 02232/792–640) are held here in summer. ✉ *Schlossstr. 6* ☎ *02232/44000* 🌐 *www.schlossbruehl.de* 🎟 *€4* ⏲ *Feb.–Nov., Tues.–Fri. 9–noon and 1:30–4, weekends 10–5.*

The smaller **Jagdschloss Falkenlust,** at the end of an avenue leading straight through Schloss Augustusburg's grounds, was built as a getaway where the prince could indulge his passion for falconry. ✉ *Schlossstr. 6* ☎ *02232/12111* 🎟 *€3* ⏲ *Feb.–Nov., Tues.–Sat. 10–noon and 1:30–4; Sun. 10–5.*

Köln

28 km (17 mi) north of Bonn, 47 km (29 mi) south of Düsseldorf, 70 km (43 mi) southeast of Aachen.

Köln is the largest city on the Rhine (the fourth largest in Germany) and one of the most interesting. Although not as old as Trier, it has been a dominant power in the Rhineland since Roman times. Known throughout the world for its "scented water," eau de cologne (first produced here in 1705 from an Italian formula), Köln is today a major commercial, intellectual, and ecclesiastical center. The city is vibrant and bustling, with a light and jolly flair that is typical of the Rhineland. At its heart is tradition, manifested in the abundance of bars and brew houses serving the local Kölsch beer and old Rhine cuisine. These meeting places are a good place to start a night on the town. Köln also puts on Germany's most exciting carnival every February, when the whole city follows the famous motto of *Kölle alaaf!* ("Cologne is alive") in an orgiastic revelry with bands, parades, and parties that last all night. Tradition, however, is mixed with the contemporary, found in a host of elegant shops, sophisticated restaurants, modern bars and dance clubs, and an important modern-art scene.

Köln was first settled by the Romans in 38 BC. For nearly a century it grew slowly, in the shadow of imperial Trier, until a locally born noblewoman, Julia Agrippina, daughter of the Roman general Germanicus, married the Roman emperor Claudius. Her hometown was elevated to the rank of a Roman city and given the name Colonia Claudia Ara Agrippinensium. For the next 300 years Colonia (hence Cologne, or Köln) flourished. Evidence of the Roman city's wealth resides in the Römisch-Germanisches Museum. In the 9th century, Charlemagne, the towering figure who united the sprawling German lands (and ruled much of present-day France) as the first Holy Roman Emperor, restored Köln's fortunes and elevated it to its preeminent role in the Rhineland. Charlemagne also appointed the first archbishop of Köln. The city's ecclesiastical heritage is one of its most striking features; it has a full dozen Romanesque churches and one of the world's largest and finest Gothic cathedrals. In the Middle Ages it was a member of the powerful Hanseatic League, occupying a position of greater importance in European commerce than either London or Paris.

Köln was a thriving modern city until World War II, when bombings destroyed 90% of it. Only the cathedral remained relatively unscathed. But like many German cities that rebounded during the "Economic Miracle" of the 1950s, Köln is a mishmash of old and new, sometimes awkwardly juxtaposed. A good part of the former Old Town along the Hohe Strasse (old Roman High Road) was turned into a remarkably charmless pedestrian shopping mall. The ensemble is framed by six-lane expressways winding along the rim of the city center—barely yards from the cathedral—perfectly illustrating the problems of postwar reconstruction. However, much of the Altstadt (Old Town), ringed by streets that follow the line of the medieval city walls, is closed to traffic. Most major sights are within this area and are easily reached on foot. Here, too, you'll find the best shops.

Modern Cologne is proud to be one of Europe's media capitals, with RTL and WDR, two of the continent's biggest private and public TV companies, based here. The arrival of a new business elite has also ended decades of the infamous rule of *Klüngel* in the city, a legendary system of old boys' political and economic networks, which has been uprooted after a series of cover-ups and political scandals.

At the tourist office, ask about the KölnTourismus card, which offers free or reduced entry into museums and other attractions, combined with free transit in and around the city.

a good walk

Any tour of the city should start beneath the towers of the extraordinary Gothic cathedral, the **Dom** 53, comparable to the great French cathedrals and a highlight of a trip to Germany. Spend some time admiring the outside of the building (you can walk almost all the way around it). Notice how there are practically no major horizontal lines—all the accents of the building are vertical. The cathedral's treasures are kept in the **Domschatzkammer**, the cathedral treasury. Behind the Dom toward the river is the **Museum Ludwig** 54, which holds artworks from the early 20th century onward. Sharing the Roncalliplatz plaza with the Museum Ludwig is the **Römisch-Germanisches Museum** 55, which has a large, well-preserved floor mosaic dating from Roman times. From the museum, walk away from the cathedral across Roncalliplatz, go down the steps, and turn left on Am Hof Strasse. Walk one block and turn right onto Unter Taschenmacher, which, after crossing Kleine Budengasse, becomes Burgerstrasse. Continue down Burgerstrasse to the **Altes Rathaus** 56. To your right as you face the Rathaus, on the other side of Obenmarspforten, is the basalt-and-glass building housing the **Wallraf-Richartz-Museum** 57 and its fine and massive collection of 13th- to 19th-century art. Just south of the museum on Martinstrasse is the 15th-century hall, **Gürzenich** 58. Crossing back to the Rathaus, enter the small alley beneath the Rathaus tower (to the left as you face it) and walk down a flight of steps to the **Alter Markt** 59. Cross the square and enter Lintgasse; after taking a few steps, you will be in the shadow of the outstanding **Gross St. Martin** 60, one of Köln's 12 Romanesque churches. You are also near the bank of the Rhine. Turn left and walk north through the Rhein Garten park for a view of the river. Soon you'll reach Heinrich-Böll-Platz, named after the native son who was Germany's greatest postwar novelist. (Five blocks north, along the Rhine, stands **St. Kunibert** 61, the last of Köln's famous Romanesque churches to be built.) Continuing from Heinrich-Böll-Platz, go up the steps and walk past the cathedral again, continuing beyond the Dom Hotel and across Hohe Strasse, an ugly pedestrian shopping street, into Burgmauer Strasse. Follow the waist-high, block-long remnant of the old city walls to Mohrenstrasse. Go right two blocks, then left to a square. On the other side of the square stands **St. Gereon** 62, the jewel of the city's Romanesque churches.

From the church, just walk back on Zeughausstrasse toward the cathedral, and you'll pass the **Kölnisches Stadtmuseum** 63, the city's history museum, on your right. Sights to the south can easily be reached on foot. Head down Mohrenstrasse, which becomes Auf dem Berlich and then Richmodstrasse. Here, on the top floor of a shopping center, is the **Käthe Kollwitz Museum** 64, one of two collections in the country. Cut diagonally across the Neumarkt to Cäcilienstrasse, and continue walking east to the **Museum Schnütgen** 65, which holds a fine collection of medieval art. Farther east on Cäcilienstrasse is the somber 11th-century **St. Maria im Kapitol** 66. Need a sugar boost? On the Rhine, about four blocks south of the Deutzer Bridge, is the impressive building—part postmodern ship, part medieval castle—housing the **Imhoff-Stollwerck-Museum** 67.

TIMING Allow two hours just for the walk. To see the interior of the cathedral and the cathedral treasury and to climb the cathedral tower will add almost an hour. The museum collections could take several hours depending on your interests. Visits to the Wallraf-Richartz Museum and the Römisch-Germanisches Museum require at least 45 minutes each.

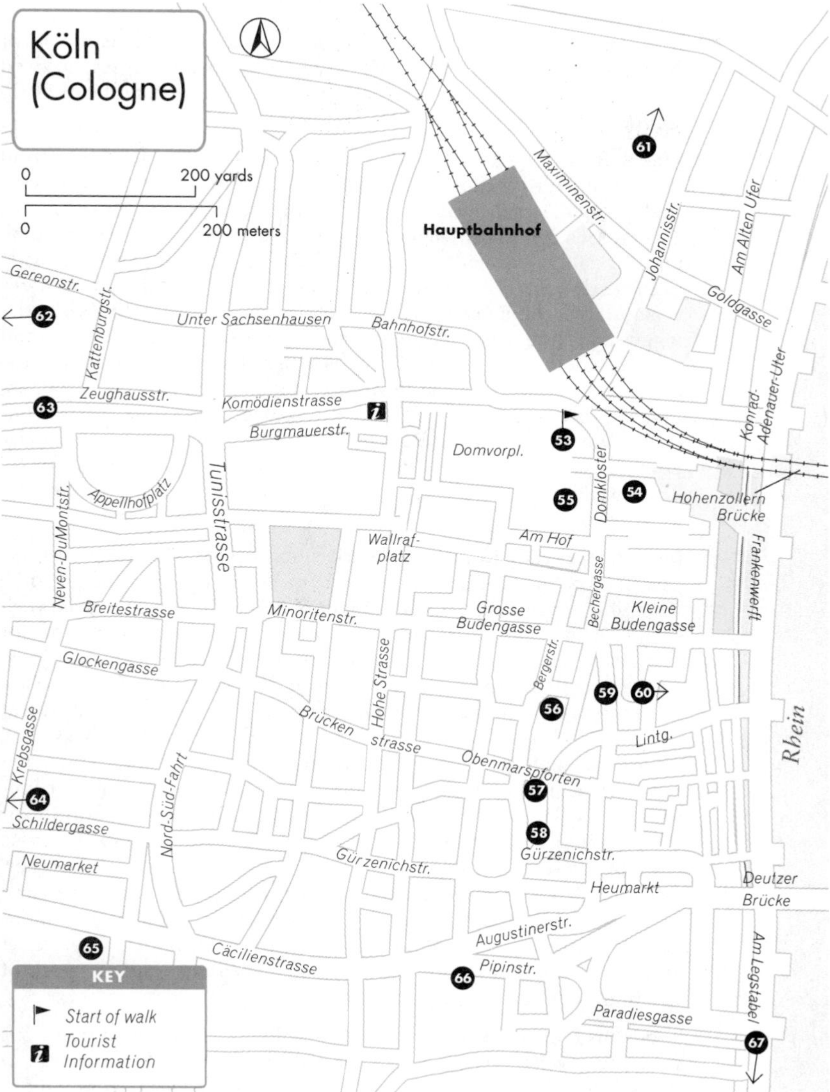
Köln (Cologne)
0 200 yards
0 200 meters
Hauptbahnhof
Maximinenstr.
Johannisstr.
Am Alten Ufer
Goldgasse
Konrad-Adenauer-Ufer
Gereonstr.
Kattenburgstr.
Unter Sachsenhausen
Bahnhofstr.
Zeughausstr.
Komödienstrasse
Burgmauerstr.
Domvorpl.
Domkloster
Hohenzollern Brücke
Appellhofplatz
Neven-DuMontstr.
Tunisstrasse
Wallraf-platz
Am Hof
Frankenwerft
Breitestrasse
Minoritenstr.
Grosse Budengasse
Bechergasse
Kleine Budengasse
Glockengasse
Bergerstr.
Hohe Strasse
Brücken strasse
Obenmarspforten
Lintg.
Rhein
Krebsgasse
Nord-Süd-Fahrt
Schildergasse
Neumarket
Gürzenichstr.
Gürzenichstr.
Heumarkt
Deutzer Brücke
Augustinerstr.
Cäcilienstrasse
Pipinstr.
Am Legstabel
Paradiesgasse
53
54
55
56
57
58
59
60
61
62
63
64
65
66
67
KEY
Start of walk
Tourist Information

What to See

59 **Alter Markt** (Old Market). The square has an eclectic assembly of buildings, most of them postwar; two 16th-century houses survived the war intact—Nos. 20 and 22. The oldest structure dates from 1135. ✉ *Altstadt.*

56 **Altes Rathaus** (Old Town Hall). The Rathaus is worth a look even from the outside, for it's the oldest town hall in Germany, even if it was entirely rebuilt after the war (it was originally erected in the 14th century). The famous bell tower rings its bells daily at noon and 5 PM. Standing on pedestals at one end of the town hall are figures of prophets, made in the early 15th century. Ranging along the south wall are nine additional statues, the so-called *Nine Good Heroes,* carved in 1360. Charlemagne and King Arthur are among them. Beneath a small glass pyramid near the south corner of the Rathaus is the **Mikwe,** a 12th-century ritual bath from the medieval Jewish quarter. When the Rathaus is open, you can request a key from the guard and descend to the Mikwe's interior. Directly below the Rathaus are the remains of the Roman city governor's headquarters, the Praetorium. ✉ *Rathauspl., Altstadt* ☎ *0221/2212–3332* ⏲ *Mon.–Thurs. 7:30–4:45, Fri. 7:30–2; call for tour info. as hours vary.*

Fodor's Choice ★

53 **Dom** (Cathedral). Köln's landmark embodies one of the purest expressions of the Gothic spirit in Europe. The cathedral, meant to be a tangible expression of God's kingdom on Earth, was conceived with such immense dimensions that construction, begun in 1248, was not completed until 1880, though builders adhered to the original plans. At 515 feet high, the two west towers of the cathedral were by far the tallest structures in the world when they were finished. The cathedral was built to house what are believed to be the relics of the Magi, the three kings who paid homage to the infant Jesus (the trade in holy mementos was big business in the Middle Ages—and not always scrupulous). The size of the building was not simply an example of self-aggrandizement on the part of the people of Köln, however; it was a response to the vast numbers of pilgrims who arrived to see the relics. The ambulatory, the passage that curves around the back of the altar, is unusually large, allowing cathedral authorities to funnel large numbers of visitors up to the crossing (where the nave and transepts meet and where the relics were originally displayed), around the back of the altar, and out again.

Today the relics are kept just behind the altar, in the original enormous gold-and-silver **reliquary.** The other great treasure of the cathedral, in the last chapel on the left as you face the altar, is the **Gero Cross,** a monumental oak crucifix dating from 971. The *Adoration of the Kings* (1440), a triptych by Stephan Lochner, Köln's most famous medieval painter, is to the right. The **Domschatzkammer** (Cathedral Treasury; 🎫 €4 ⏲ daily 10–6) includes the silver shrine of Archbishop Engelbert, who was stabbed to death in 1225. Other highlights are the stained-glass windows, some dating from the 13th century; the 15th-century altarpiece; and the early-14th-century high altar with its glistening white figures and intricate choir screens. Climb to the top of the bell tower to get the complete vertical experience. ✉ *Dompl., Altstadt* ☎ *0221/9258–4730* 🌐 *www.koelner-dom.de* 🎫 *Tower € 2; tour of tower and cathedral treasury €5* ⏲ *Daily 6 AM–7 PM; tower and stairwell Nov.–Feb., daily 9–4; Mar. and Apr., daily 9–5; May–Sept., daily 9–6; Oct., daily 9–5; guided tours in English Mon.–Sat. at 10:30 and 2:30, Sun. at 2:30.*

60 **Gross St. Martin** (Big St. Martin). This remarkable Romanesque parish church was rebuilt after being flattened in World War II. Its massive 13th-century tower, with distinctive corner turrets and an imposing central spire, is another landmark of Köln. The church was built on the site of a Roman granary. ✉ *An Gross St. Martin 9, Altstadt* ☎ *0221/1642–5650* ⏲ *Weekdays 10:15–6, Sat. 10–12:30 and 1:30–6; Sun. 2–4.*

10

58 **Gürzenich.** This Gothic structure, located at the south end of Martinsviertel, was all but demolished in World War II but carefully reconstructed afterward. It's named after a medieval knight from whom the city acquired valuable real estate in 1437. The official reception and festival hall here has played a central role in civic life through the centuries. At one end of the complex are the remains of the 10th-century Gothic church of **St. Alban,** which were left ruined after the war as a memorial. On what's left of the church floor, you can see a sculpture of a couple kneeling in prayer, *Mourning Parents,* by Käthe Kollwitz, a fitting memorial to the ravages of war. ✉ *Gürzenichstr., Altstadt.*

67 **Imhoff-Stollwerck-Museum.** This riverside museum recounts 3,000 years of civilization's production and delectation of chocolate, from the Central American Maya to the colonizing and industrializing Europeans. It's also a real factory with lava flows of chocolate and a conveyer belt jostling thousands of truffles. Visitors get a free tasting. The museum shop, with candy bars stacked to the ceiling, is a great place to pick up interestingly packaged edible gifts. ✉ *Rheinauhafen 1a, Rheinufer* ☎ *0221/931–8880* 🌐 *www.schokoladenmuseum.de* 🎫 *€6* ⏲ *Tues.–Fri. 10–6, weekends 11–7; closed 1 wk mid-Feb.*

64 **Käthe Kollwitz Museum.** The works of Käthe Kollwitz (1867–1945), the most important German female artist of the 20th century, focus on social themes like the plight of the poor and the atrocities of war. This is the larger of the country's two Kollwitz collections and comprises all of her woodcuts, as well as paintings, etchings, lithographs, and sculptures. There are also changing exhibits of other modern artists. ✉ *Neumarkt 18–24, in Neumarkt Galerie, Innenstadt* ☎ *0221/227–2363* 🌐 *www.kollwitz.de* 🎫 *€3* ⏲ *Tues.–Fri. 10–6, weekends 11–6.*

63 **Kölnisches Stadtmuseum** (Cologne City History Museum). The triumphs and tragedies of Cologne's rich past are packed into this museum at the historic *Zeughaus,* the city's former arsenal. Here, you'll find an in-depth chronicle of Cologne's history—including information about the lives of ordinary people and high-profile politicians, the industrial revolution (car manufacturer Henry Ford's influence on the city is also retraced), and the destruction incurred during World War II. For those who've always wanted to be privy to the inside stories surrounding local words such as *Klüngel, Kölsch,* and *Karneval,* the answers are waiting to be discovered within the museum's walls. ✉ *Zeughausstr. 1–3, Altstadt*

☎ 0221/2212–5790 🌐 www.museenkoeln.de 🎫 €4.20 ⏲ Mon.–Sun. 10–5, Tues. 10–8; closed 1 wk mid-Feb.

54 **Museum Ludwig.** This museum is dedicated to art from the beginning of the 20th century to the present day. Its American pop-art collection (including Andy Warhol, Jasper Johns, Robert Rauschenberg, Claes Oldenburg, and Roy Lichtenstein) rivals that of New York's Guggenheim Museum. Within the building and at no extra cost is the **Agfa Foto-Historama** (Agfa Photography Museum), which has one of the world's largest collections of historic photographs and cameras. *✉ Bischofsgartenstr. 1, Innenstadt ☎ 0221/2212–6165 🌐 www.museum-ludwig.de 🎫 €7.50 ⏲ Tues.–Sun. 10–6; 1st Fri. of every month 10–11 PM; closed 1 wk mid-Feb.*

65 **Museum Schnütgen.** A treasure house of medieval art from the Rhine region, the museum has an ideal setting in a 12th-century basilica. Don't miss the crucifix from the St. Georg Kirche or the original stained-glass windows and carved figures from the Dom. Many of the exhibits—intricately carved ivory book covers, rock crystal reliquaries, illuminated manuscripts—require intense concentration to be fully appreciated. *✉ Cäcilienstr. 29, Innenstadt ☎ 0221/2212–3620 🌐 www.museenkoeln.de 🎫 €3.20 ⏲ Tues.–Fri. 10–5, weekends 11–5; closed Feb. 19–24, Dec. 24, 25, 31, and Jan. 1.*

need a break?

Cologne's main pedestrian shopping street is practical but utterly uninspiring—some even say ugly. An airy, artsy oasis is **Café Stanton, The Fine Art of Leisure** (✉ Schilderg. 57, behind Antoniterkirche ☎ 0221/271–0710), with outdoor terrace seating and a view of the Antoniter church's late-Gothic walls. The food is international with an emphasis on the Mediterranean; the selection of cakes is divinely German. Three enormous, surprisingly delicate chandeliers, made entirely of plastic waste, provide lighting.

★ 55 **Römisch-Germanisches Museum** (Roman-Germanic Museum). This cultural landmark was built in the early 1970s around the famous Dionysius mosaic discovered here during the construction of an air-raid shelter in 1941. The huge mosaic, more than 100 yards square, once formed the dining-room floor of a wealthy Roman trader's villa. Its millions of tiny earthenware and glass tiles depict some of the adventures of Dionysius, the Greek god of wine and, to the Romans, the object of a widespread and sinister religious cult. The pillared 1st-century tomb of Lucius Publicius (a prominent Roman officer), some stone Roman coffins, and everyday objects of Roman life are among the museum's other exhibits. Bordering the museum on the south is a restored 90-yard stretch of the old Roman harbor road. *✉ Roncallipl. 4, Altstadt ☎ 0221/2212–4438 🌐 www.museenkoeln.de 🎫 €4.30 ⏲ Tues.–Sun. 10–5. Closed Feb. 19–24, Dec. 24, 25, 31, and Jan. 1.*

62 **St. Gereon.** Experts regard St. Gereon as one of the most noteworthy medieval structures in existence. This exquisite Romanesque church stands on the site of an old Roman burial ground six blocks west of the train station. An enormous dome rests on walls that were once clad in gold

mosaics. Roman masonry forms part of the structure, which is believed to have been built over the grave of its namesake, the 4th-century martyr and patron saint of Köln. ✉ *Gereonsdriesch 2–4, Ringe* ☎ *0221/134–922* 🎫 *Free* ⏲ *Mon.–Sat. 9–12:30 and 1:30–6, Sun. 1:30–6.*

61 **St. Kunibert.** The most lavish of the churches from the late Romanesque period is by the Rhine, three blocks north of the train station. Its precious stained-glass windows have filtered light for more than 750 years. Consecrated in 1247, the church contains an unusual room, concealed under the altar, which gives access to a pre-Christian well once believed to promote fertility in women. ✉ *Kunibertsklosterg. 2, Altstadt-Nord* ☎ *0221/121–214* 🎫 *Free* ⏲ *Daily 9–noon and 3–6.*

10

66 **St. Maria im Kapitol.** Built in the 11th and 12th centuries on the site of a Roman temple, St. Maria is best known for its two beautifully carved 16-foot-high doors and its enormous crypt, the second largest in Germany after the one in Speyer's cathedral. ✉ *Marienpl. 19, Altstadt* ☎ *0221/214–615* 🎫 *Free* ⏲ *Mon.–Sat. 9–6; Sun. 11:30–5; closed during services.*

57 **Wallraf-Richartz-Museum.** The Wallraf-Richartz-Museum contains paintings spanning the years 1300 to 1900. The Dutch and Flemish schools are particularly well represented, as is the 15th- to 16th-century Cologne school of German painting. Its two most famous artists are the Master of the St. Veronica (whose actual name is unknown) and Stefan Lochner, represented by two luminous works, *The Last Judgment* and *The Madonna in the Rose Bower.* Large canvases by Rubens, who spent his youth in Köln, hang prominently on the second floor. There are also outstanding works by Rembrandt, Van Dyck, and Frans Hals. Among the other old masters are Tiepolo, Canaletto, and Boucher. ✉ *Martinstr. 39, Altstadt* ☎ *0221/2212–2393* 🌐 *www.museenkoeln.de* 🎫 *€5.80* ⏲ *Tues. 10–8, Wed.–Fri. 10–6, weekends 11–6. Closed Feb. 19–24, Dec. 24, 25, 31, and Jan. 1.*

Where to Stay & Eat

The tourist office, across from the cathedral, can make hotel bookings for you for the same night, at a cost of €10 per room. If you plan to be in town for the Karneval, be sure to reserve a room well in advance.

$$$$ **Fodor's Choice** ★ ✕ **Capricorn i Aries.** This hip, fine-dining establishment houses but four tables, each covered with crisp, white linens and enhanced by surrounding dark wood and sophisticated lighting. You'll be personally waited on by the owners, Judith Werner (Capricorn) and Klaus Jaquemod (Aries), as you indulge in truly heavenly French cuisine with a Rhineland twist. Just opposite this intimate little restaurant, a new and somewhat larger Brasserie serves the staples in French rural cuisine. ✉ *Alteburger Str. 34, Neustadt* ☎ *0221/397–5710 or 0221/323–182* ✍ *Reservations essential* 💳 *AE, DC, MC, V* ⏲ *No lunch.*

$$$–$$$$ ✕ **Le Moissonnier.** Part of the charm of this restaurant—arguably one of the best in the city—is its lack of pretension. The turn-of-the-20th-century bistro decor radiates warmth from its mirrors, Tiffany lamps, and painted flowers. Owners Vincent and Liliane Moissonnier greet their guests in person, seating them at one of 20 tables. The cuisine is French at its base but intertwines an array of global influences. ✉ *Krefelder Str. 25, Neustadt-Nord* ☎ *0221/729–479* ✍ *Reservations essential* ▭ *No credit cards* ⊙ *Closed Sun. and Mon.*

$$$ ✕ **Bizim.** The extraordinary chef Enis Akisik has made his Bizim one of the best Turkish restaurants in Germany. Forget shish kebab and prepare yourself for a leisurely gourmet experience that might include scampi with tarragon sauce, eggplant-coated lamb fillets with a garlic yogurt sauce, or quail grilled on a rosemary spit and served in its own juices. There are four-course tasting menus for lunch (€28) and dinner (€50). ✉ *Weideng. 47–49, Nordstadt* ☎ *0221/131–581* ✍ *Reservations essential* ▭ *MC, V* ⊙ *Closed Sun. and Mon. No lunch Sat.*

$$$ ✕ **Fischers Weingenuss und Tafelfreuden.** If someone were to create a shrine to wine, it would look a lot like this restaurant. Run by one of Germany's star sommeliers (who happens to be a woman), the restaurant offers 800 wines, 40 of which can be bought by the glass. The kitchen experiments with regional cuisine, with influences from France, the Mediterranean, and even Southeast Asia. The dining experience is always elegant, and an expert staff will help you pick the perfect wine for each dish. ✉ *Hohenstaufenring 53, Ringe* ☎ *0221/310–8470* ▭ *DC, MC, V* ⊙ *Closed Sun. No lunch Sat.*

$$–$$$ ✕ **Casa di Biase.** This romantic eatery serves sophisticated Italian cuisine in a warm, elegant setting. The seasonally changing menu focuses on fish and game, and the wine list is interesting and extensive—although sometimes pricey. Just next door is the Casa's smaller and more casual sister, the Teca di Biasi. This cozy, wood-panel wine bar serves antipasti, salads, and main dishes for €13 or less. ✉ *Eifelpl. 4, Südstadt* ☎ *0221/322–433* ▭ *AE, MC, V* ⊙ *Closed Sun. No lunch Sat.*

★ **$$–$$$** ✕ **Heising & Adelmann.** At this cheerful counterpart to the old-style Kölsche Kneipe, young locals do what people along the Rhine have done for centuries—talk, drink, and enjoy good company. Heising & Adelmann, consistently voted one of the best deals in town, offers good German beer, tangy cocktails (even a proper Long Island Ice Tea), and a creative mixture of German and French food. On the menu, a solid German burger served with fried potatoes is found next to exquisite French goose liver with fried beef jowl on spinach and au gratin potatoes. ✉ *Friesenstr. 58–60, Neustadt-Nord* ☎ *0221/1309–424* ▭ *AE, MC, V* ⊙ *No lunch. Closed Sun.*

¢–$$$ ✕ **Früh am Dom.** For real down-home Köln food, there are few places that compare with this time-honored former brewery. Bold frescoes on the vaulted ceilings establish the mood, and the authentically Teutonic experience is completed by such dishes as *Hämmchen* (pork knuckle). The beer garden is delightful for summer dining. ✉ *Am Hof 12–14, Altstadt* ☎ *0221/26130* ▭ *MC, V.*

¢–$ Fodor'sChoice ★ ✕ **Paeffgen.** There's no better *Brauhaus* in Köln in which to imbibe Kölsch, the city's home brew. You won't sit long in front of an empty glass before a blue-aproned waiter sweeps by and places a full one before you. With its worn wooden decor, colorful clientele, and typical German fare (sauerbraten, Hämmchen, and Reibekuchen), Paeffgen sums up tradition—especially when compared to the trendy nightspots that surround it. ✉ *Friesenstr. 64–66, Friesenviertel* ☎ *0221/135–461* ▭ *No credit cards.*

$$$$ **Excelsior Hotel Ernst.** The Empire-style lobby in this 1863 hotel is striking in sumptuous royal blue, bright yellow, and gold. Old-master paintings (including a Van Dyck) grace the lobby walls; Gobelins tapestries hang in the ballroom of the same name. Breakfast is served either in the "petit palais" ballroom or in the two-story atrium. The Hansestube restaurant ($$–$$$$) attracts a business crowd with its lunch specials and has a more hushed ambience in the evening, when it serves French haute cuisine. A sleek, hip restaurant, Taku ($$–$$$$), serves pan-Asian cuisine at slightly less-elevated prices. ✉ *Trankg. 1, Altstadt, D–50667* ☎ *0221/2701* 🖷 *0221/270–3333* 🌐 *www.excelsiorhotelernst.de* *140 rooms, 20 suites* *2 restaurants, room service, minibars, cable TV with movies, in-room data ports, Wi-Fi, gym, massage, sauna, bar, babysitting, dry cleaning, laundry service, concierge, Internet room, business services, meeting rooms, parking (fee), some pets allowed (fee), no-smoking rooms; no a/c in some rooms* ▭ *AE, DC, MC, V* *BP.*

★ **$$$–$$$$** **Hotel im Wasserturm.** What used to be Europe's tallest water tower is now an 11-story luxury hotel-in-the-round. The neoclassic look of the brick exterior remains, and few modern architects could create a more unusual setting. The ultramodern interior was the work of the French designer Andrée Putman, known for her minimalist work on Morgans, a stylish hotel in New York City. The 11th-floor restaurant-in-the-round ($$$$) has a stunning view of the city. The menu, which changes daily, offers continental haute cuisine. ✉ *Kayg. 2, Altstadt, D–50676* ☎ *0221/20080* 🖷 *0221/200–8888* 🌐 *www.hotel-im-wasserturm.de* *48 rooms, 40 suites* *Restaurant, room service, in-room safes, minibars, cable TV, in-room data ports, Wi-Fi, gym, sauna, bar, dry cleaning, laundry service, concierge, business services, meeting rooms, parking (fee), some pets allowed* ▭ *AE, DC, MC, V* *BP.*

$$$–$$$$ **Hyatt Regency Köln.** This sleek glass-and-steel building, sitting like a huge futuristic cube on the right bank of the Rhine, relies on high-tech, luxurious comfort and excellent service to compensate for what it lacks in atmosphere. It's favored by business travelers for its quiet and spacious rooms, but all will relish the hotel's spectacular views of Cologne's skyline, particularly at night. All this, along with a world-class spa and pool, and two superb restaurants (the Glashaus restaurant offers the better view) may indeed make the Hyatt the region's finest hotel. ✉ *Kennedy-Ufer 2a, Deutz, D–50679* ☎ *0221/828–1234* 🖷 *0221/828–1370* 🌐 *www.cologne.hyatt.com* *289 rooms, 16 suites* *2 restaurants, room service, minibars, cable TV with movies, in-room broadband, indoor pool, health club, hair salon, massage, sauna, bar, babysitting, dry cleaning, laundry service, concierge, Internet room, business services, meeting rooms, parking (fee), some pets allowed (fee), no-smoking rooms* ▭ *AE, DC, MC, V* *CP.*

$$ **Hopper Hotel et cetera.** The rooms in this chicly renovated monastery are spare but not spartan, although a startlingly realistic sculpture of a bishop, sitting in the reception area, serves as a constant reminder of the building's ecclesiastic origins. The rooms are decorated with modern works by Cologne artists. The courtyard Hopper Restaurant et cetera ($–$$) serves upscale Mediterranean cuisine and has delightful garden seating. ✉ *Brüsselerstr. 26, Belgisches Viertel, D–50674* ☎ *0221/924–400* 🖷 *0221/924–406* 🌐 *www.hopper.de* 🛏 *48 rooms, 1 suite* 👍 *Restaurant, café, cable TV, in-room data ports, gym, sauna, Internet room, business services, parking (fee), some pets allowed (fee), no-smoking rooms; no a/c* 💳 *AE, DC, MC, V* 🍽 *BP.*

$–$$ **Chelsea.** This designer hotel has a very strong following among artists and art dealers, as well as the musicians who come to play in the nearby Stadtgarten jazz club. Breakfast is served until noon for these late-risers. The best features of the rooms are the luxuriously large bathrooms and bathtubs. The restaurant-café ($–$$) is great for informal gatherings and for people-watching. It's 20 minutes to the city center on foot, 10 by subway or tram. ✉ *Jülicherstr. 1, Belgisches Viertel, D–50674* ☎ *0221/207–150* 🖷 *0221/239–137* 🌐 *www.hotel-chelsea.de* 🛏 *36 rooms, 2 suites, 1 apartment* 👍 *Restaurant, cable TV, Wi-Fi, parking (fee), some pets allowed; no a/c* 💳 *AE, DC, MC, V.*

$ **Das Kleine Stapelhäuschen.** One of the few houses along the riverbank that survived World War II bombings, this is among the oldest buildings in Köln. You can't beat the location, overlooking the river and right by Gross St. Martin; yet the rooms are reasonably priced, making up in age and quaintness for what they lack in luxury. The restaurant ($$–$$$$) is in a slightly higher price bracket and does a respectable enough job with spruced-up versions of German specialties. ✉ *Fischmarkt 1–3, Altstadt, D–50667* ☎ *0221/257–7862* 🖷 *0221/257–4232* 🌐 *www.koeln-altstadt.de/stapelhaeuschen* 🛏 *31 rooms* 👍 *Restaurant, cable TV, in-room data ports, parking (fee), some pets allowed, no-smoking rooms; no a/c* 💳 *AE, MC, V* 🍽 *BP.*

$ **Hotel Good Sleep.** What it lacks in personality this hotel makes up for in price and location. A favorite with students and backpackers, Hotel Good Sleep is just steps from the Dom. The small rooms are bland but bright and clean. Cheaper rooms, with a shower in the hallway, are also available. ✉ *Komödienstr. 19–21, Altstadt, D–50667* ☎ *0221/257–2257* 🖷 *0221/257–2259* 🌐 *www.goodsleep.de* 🛏 *33 rooms* 👍 *Cable TV, some pets allowed; no a/c* 💳 *AE, D, MC, V* 🍽 *CP.*

¢–$ **Hotel Im Kupferkessel.** The best things about this small, unassuming hotel are the location (in the shadow of St. Gereon church and a 15-minute walk from the Dom) and the price (single rooms with shared bath can be had for as low as €30). The slightly shabby lobby and breakfast room look like they might have been decorated by someone's grandmother, circa 1950, but the rooms are clean and functional. Be prepared to deal with stairs here, as most of the rooms are on the third and fourth floors. ✉ *Probsteig. 6, Ringe, D–50670* ☎ *0221/270–7960* 🌐 *www.im-kupferkessel.de* 🖷 *0221/2707–9629* 🛏 *13 rooms* 👍 *Cable TV, Web TV, parking (fee); no a/c* 💳 *AE, MC, V* 🍽 *CP.*

Nightlife & the Arts

THE ARTS Köln's Westdeutsche Rundfunk Orchestra performs regularly in the city's excellent concert hall, the **Philharmonie** (✉ Bischofsgartenstr. 1, Altstadt ☎ 0221/280–280 🌐 www.koelnticket.de). The Gürzenich Orchestra gives regular concerts in the Philharmonie, but the primary setting for its music is the restored **Gürzenich** (✉ Martinstr. 29/37, Altstadt ☎ 0221/925–8990), medieval Köln's official reception mansion. Köln's opera company, the **Oper der Stadt Köln** (✉ Offenbachpl. 1, Innenstadt ☎ 0221/2212–8400), is known for exciting classical and contemporary productions. Year-round organ recitals in Köln's cathedral are supplemented from June through August with a summer season of organ music. Organ recitals and chamber concerts are also presented in many of the Romanesque churches and in **Antoniterkirche** (✉ Schilderg. 57, Innenstadt ☎ 0221/660–5720).

Köln's principal theater is the **Schauspielhaus** (✉ Offenbachpl. 1, Innenstadt ☎ 0221/2212–8400), home to the 20 or so private theater companies in the city.

NIGHTLIFE Köln's nightlife is centered in three distinct areas: between the Alter Markt and Neumarkt in the Old Town; on Zulpicherstrasse; and around the Friesenplatz S-bahn station. Many streets off the Hohenzollernring and Hohenstaufenring, particularly Roonstrasse, also provide a broad range of nightlife.

In summer head straight for the **Stadtgarten** (✉ Venloerstr. 40, Friesenviertel ☎ 0221/9529–9410) and sit in the Bier Garten for some good outdoor Gemütlichkeit. At other times of the year it's still worth a visit for its excellent jazz club. In summer, the Martinsviertel, a part of the Altstadt around the Gross St. Martin church, which is full of restaurants, brew houses, and *Kneipen* (pubs), is a good place to go around sunset. One particular spot to check out there is **Papa Joe's Biersalon** (✉ Alter Markt 50–52, Altstadt ☎ 0221/258–2132), which is kind of kitschy but often has classic and Dixieland jazz.

Das Ding (✉ Hohenstaufenring 30–34, Ringe ☎ 0221/246–348), literally "The Thing," is a student club that is never empty, even on weeknights. For a true disco experience, make for the **Alter Wartesaal** (✉ Am Hauptbahnhof, Johannisstr. 11, Altstadt ☎ 0221/912–8850) in the Hauptbahnhof on Friday or Saturday night. The old train-station waiting room has been turned into a concert hall and disco, where dancers swivel on ancient polished parquet and check their style in original mahogany-frame mirrors. The new star of Köln's nightlife, the sleek **Triple A** (✉ An der Hahnepooz 8/Rudolfpl., Altstadt ☎ 0221/2775–68080), attracts a fabulously stylish mid-thirties crowd. Its disco-lounge and bar hosts music and different theme parties every night.

Shopping

A good shopping loop begins at the **Neumarkt Galerie** (✉ Richmodstr. 8, Innenstadt), a bright, modern indoor shopping arcade with a web of shops and cafés surrounding an airy atrium. From there, head down the charmless but practical pedestrian shopping zone of the Schildergasse. The big department store **Kaufhof** (✉ Hohestr. 41–53, Innenstadt ☎ 0221/2230) is off the mall and central to city life. Its offerings are rich in quantity and quality.

From Schildergasse, go north on Herzogstrasse to arrive at **Glockengasse** (✉ No. 4711, Innenstadt ☎ 0221/925–0450), where Köln's most celebrated product, eau de cologne No. 4711, was first concocted by the

18th-century Italian chemist Giovanni-Maria Farina. The shop has extended its selection to include other scents, but the original product remains the centerpiece, available in all sizes from a purse-size bottle to a container that holds a quart or so.

On Breite Strasse, another pedestrian shopping street, **Heubel** (✉ Breite Str. 118, Innenstadt ☎ 0221/257–6013) carries unusual, beautiful, and often inexpensive imported antiques, housewares, and jewelry. At the end of Breite Strasse is Eherenstrasse, where the young and young-at-heart can shop for hip fashions and trendy housewares. After a poke around here, explore the small boutiques on Benesisstrasse, which will lead you to Mittelstrasse, best known for high-tone German fashions and luxury goods. Follow Mittelstrasse to the end to return to the Neumarkt.

Because train stations are exempt from restrictive German laws on store-opening hours, the shopping arcade in the **Hauptbahnhof** (main train station) offers the rare opportunity to shop in Germany on Sunday, and on weekdays until as late as 10 PM.

Aachen

70 km (43 mi) west of Köln.

At the center of Aachen, the characteristic *drei-Fenster* facades, three windows wide, give way to buildings dating from the days when Charlemagne made Aix-la-Chapelle (as it was then called) the great center of the Holy Roman Empire. Thirty-two German emperors were crowned here, gracing Aachen with the proud nickname Kaiserstadt (Emperors' City). Roman legions had been drawn here for the healing properties of the sulfur springs emanating from the nearby Eifel Mountains. Charlemagne's father, Pepin the Short, also settled here to enjoy the waters that gave Bad Aachen—as the town is also known—its name; the waters continue to attract visitors today. But it was certainly Charlemagne who was responsible for the town's architectural wealth. After his coronation in Rome in 800, he spent more and more time in Aachen, building his spectacular palace and ruling his vast empire from within its walls. Aachen is now home to almost 30,000 students, keeping this beautiful old town a bustling center of activity. One-and-a-half-hour walking tours depart from the tourist-information office weekends at 11, year-round, and weekdays at 2, from April through October. **English-language tours** can be set up by prior arrangement. ☎ *0241/180–2960.*

★ The stunning **Dom** (Cathedral) in Aachen, the "Chapelle" of the town's earlier name, remains the single greatest storehouse of Carolingian architecture in Europe. Though it was built over the course of 1,000 years and reflects architectural styles from the Middle Ages to the 19th century, its commanding image is the magnificent octagonal royal chapel, rising up two arched stories to end in the cap of the dome. It was this section, the heart of the church, that Charlemagne saw completed in AD 800. His bones now lie in the Gothic choir, in a golden shrine surrounded by wonderful carvings of saints. Another treasure is his marble throne. Charlemagne had to journey all the way to Rome for his coronation, but the next 32 Holy Roman emperors were crowned here in Aachen, and each marked the occasion by presenting a lavish gift to the cathedral. In the 12th century Barbarossa donated the great chandelier now hanging in the center of the imperial chapel; his grandson, Friedrich II, donated Charlemagne's shrine. Emperor Karl IV journeyed from Prague in the late 14th century for the sole purpose of commissioning a bust of Charlemagne for the cathedral; now on view in the treasury, the bust incorporates a piece of Charlemagne's skull. ✉ *Münsterpl.* ☎ *0241/477–090* 🎫 *Free* 🌐 *www.aachendom.de* 🕒 *Mar.–Oct., daily 7–7; Nov.–Apr., 7–6.*

The **Domschatzkammer** (Cathedral Treasury) houses sacred art from late antiquity and the Carolingian, Ottonian, and Hohenstaufen eras; highlights include the Cross of Lothair, the Bust of Charlemagne, and the Persephone Sarcophagus. ✉ *Am Domhof, entrance via Klosterg.* ☎ *0241/4770–9127* 🎫 *€2.50* 🕒 *Mon. 10–1; Tues., Wed., and Fri.–Sun. 10–6; Thurs. 10–9.*

The back of the **Rathaus** (Town Hall) is opposite the Dom, across Katschhof Square. It was built in the early 14th century on the site of the *Aula,* or "great hall," of Charlemagne's palace. Its first major official function was the coronation banquet of Emperor Karl IV in 1349, held in the great Gothic hall you can still see today (though this was largely rebuilt after the war). On the north wall of the building are statues of 50 emperors of the Holy Roman Empire. The greatest of them all, Charlemagne, stands in bronze atop the Kaiserbrunnen (Imperial Fountain) in the center of the market square. ✉ *Marktpl.* ☎ *0241/432–7310* 🎫 *€2* 🕒 *Daily 10–1 and 2–5.*

An old Aachen tradition that continues today is "taking the waters." The arcaded, neoclassical **Elisenbrunnen** (Elisa Fountain), built in 1822, is south of the cathedral and contains two fountains with thermal drinking water. Experts agree that the spa waters here—the hottest north of the Alps—are effective in helping to cure a wide range of ailments. Drinking the sulfurous water in the approved manner can be unpleasant, but as you hold your nose and gulp away, you're emulating the likes of Dürer, Frederick the Great, and Charlemagne.

You can try sitting in the spa waters at **Carolus-Thermen Bad Aachen,** a high-tech sauna-spa facility. In Dürer's time there were regular crackdowns on the orgiastic goings-on at the baths. Today taking the waters is done with a bathing suit on, but be aware—the casual German attitude toward nudity takes over in the sauna area, which is declared a "textile-free zone." ✉ *Passstr. 79* ☎ *0241/182–740* 🌐 *www.carolus-thermen.de* 🎫 *€9.50–€28* 🕒 *Daily 9 AM–11 PM.*

Like many other German spa towns, Aachen has its **Spielbank** (casino). It's housed in the porticoed former Kurhaus, on the parklike grounds fronting Monheimsallee and facing the Kurbad Quellenhof. Jacket and tie are required. Bring your passport for identification. ✉ *Monheimsallee 44* ☎ *0241/18080* 🎫 *€5* 🕒 *Sun.–Fri. 3 PM–3 AM, Sat. 3 PM–4 AM.*

Aachen has a modern side as well—one of the world's most important art collectors, Peter Ludwig, has endowed two museums in his hometown. The **Ludwig Forum für Internationale Kunst** holds a portion of Ludwig's truly enormous collection of contemporary art and hosts traveling exhibits. ✉ *Jülicher Str. 97–109* ☎ *0241/180–7103 or 0241/180–7104* 🌐 *www.heimat.de/ludwigsforum* 🎫 *€3* ⏲ *Tues.–Sun. noon–6.*

The **Suermondt-Ludwig Museum** is devoted to classical painting up to the beginning of the 20th century. ✉ *Wilhelmstr. 18* ☎ *0241/479–800* 🌐 *www.suermondt-ludwig-museum.de* 🎫 *€3* ⏲ *Tues. and Thurs.–Sun. noon–6, Wed. noon–9.*

Where to Stay & Eat

$$$–$$$$ ✕ **La Becasse.** Sophisticated French nouvelle cuisine is offered in this modern restaurant just outside the Old Town by the Westpark. Try the distinctively light calves' liver. ✉ *Hanbrucherstr. 1* ☎ *0241/74444* ✍ *Reservations essential* ▭ *MC, V* ⏲ *Closed Sun. No lunch Sat. and Mon.*

$–$$ ✕ **Der Postwagen.** This annex of the more upscale Ratskeller is worth a stop for the building alone, a half-timber medieval edifice at one corner of the old Rathaus. Sitting at one of the low wooden tables, surveying the marketplace through the wavy old glass, you can dine very respectably on solid German fare. If you really want to go local, try *Himmel und Erde* ("Heaven and Earth"), a hearty Westphalian specialty made of potatoes, apples, and blood sausage. ✉ *Am Markt* ☎ *0241/35001* ▭ *AE, DC, MC, V.*

¢–$$ ✕ **Am Knipp.** At this historic old Aachen Bierstube, guests dig into their German dishes at low wooden tables next to the tile stove. Pewter pots and beer mugs hang from the rafters. ✉ *Bergdriesch 3* ☎ *0241/33168* ▭ *No credit cards* ⏲ *Closed Tues., Dec. 24–Jan. 2, and 2 wks in Oct.*

$ ✕ **Magellan.** Nestling against part of Aachen's ancient 13th-century city wall, this historic and upscale establishment, true to the city's international heritage and the restaurant's namesake, serves up a varied selection of Mediterranean cuisine under an imposing Greek-Orthodox chandelier. Despite the elegant background, the atmosphere is very lively and relaxed. ✉ *Pontstr. 78* ☎ *0241/401–6440* ▭ *DC, MC, V.*

$$$–$$$$ ✕🏨 **Dorint Quellenhof Aachen.** Built during World War I as a country home for the kaiser, this is one of Europe's grande dames: spacious, elegant, and formal. Rooms have high ceilings, a mix of conservative-style furniture, a walk-in closet, and huge, modern bathrooms. Flowers fill the bistro La Brasserie ($$), where light German and Mediterranean cuisine is offered. ✉ *Monheimsallee 52, D–52062* ☎ *0241/91320* 📠 *0241/91100* 🌐 *www.dorint.de* 🛏 *185 rooms, 2 suites* 👍 *1 restaurant, room service, minibars, cable TV with movies, in-room data ports, Wi-Fi, health club, hair salon, massage, sauna, bar, babysitting, dry cleaning, laundry service, concierge, Internet room, business services, meeting rooms, parking (fee), some pets allowed (fee), no-smoking rooms* ▭ *AE, DC, MC, V* 🍽 *BP.*

$$ 🏨 **Hotel Brülls am Dom.** In the historic heart of the city, this family-run hotel offers tradition, convenience, and considerable comfort. It's a short walk to nearly all the major attractions. ✉ *Hühnermarkt 2–3, D–52062* ☎ *0241/31704* 📠 *0241/404–326* 🛏 *12 rooms* 👍 *Cable TV, parking (fee); no a/c* ▭ *No credit cards* 🍽 *CP.*

$ **Hotel Dura.** This small, family-run hotel, one block from the train station, on a noisy street, is one of the few low-budget options in the city. There's no restaurant, but you can buy snacks in the kiosk downstairs. ✉ *Lagerhausstr. 5, D–52064* ☎ *0241/403–135* 📠 *0241/401–8450* *8 rooms, 1 apartment* *Cable TV, bar; no a/c* *MC, V* *CP.*

Nightlife & the Arts

Most activity in town is concentrated around the market square and Pontstrasse, a pedestrian street that radiates off the square. Start out at Aachen's most popular bar, the **Dom Keller** (✉ Hof 1 ☎ 0241/34265), to mingle with locals of all ages at old wooden tables. The Irish pub **Wild Rover** (✉ Hirschgraben 13 ☎ 0241/35453) serves Guinness on tap to live music every night starting at 9:30. The municipal orchestra gives regular concerts in the **Kongresszentrum Eurogress** (✉ Monheimsallee 48 ☎ 0241/91310).

Shopping

Don't leave Aachen without stocking up on the traditional local gingerbread, *Aachener Printen*. Most bakeries in town offer assortments. Some of the best are at the **Alte Aachener Kaffeestuben** (✉ Büchel 18 ☎ 0241/35724), also known as the *Konditorei van den Daele*. The store-café is worth a visit for its atmosphere and tempting aromas, whether or not you intend to buy anything. It also ships goods.

Düsseldorf

47 km (29 mi) north of Köln.

Düsseldorf, the state capital of North Rhine–Westphalia, may suffer by comparison to Köln's remarkable skyline, but the elegant city has more than enough charm—and money—to boost its confidence. It has a reputation for being one of the richest cities in Germany, with an extravagant lifestyle that epitomizes the economic success of postwar Germany. Since 80% of Düsseldorf was destroyed in World War II, the city has since been more or less rebuilt from the ground up—in part re-creating landmarks of long ago and restoring a medieval riverside quarter.

At the confluence of the Rivers Rhine and Düssel, this dynamic city started as a small fishing town. The name means "village on the Düssel," but obviously this Dorf is a village no more. Raised expressways speed traffic past towering glass-and-steel structures; within them, glass-enclosed shopping malls showcase the finest clothes, furs, jewelry, and other goods that money can buy.

An inexpensive way to explore the city is with the new Düsseldorf WelcomeCard. Good for up to six days, the card allows free public transportation and reduced entrance fees to museums, theaters, and even boat tours on the Rhine River.

The **Königsallee,** the main shopping avenue, is the epitome of Düsseldorf affluence; it's lined with the crème de la crème of designer boutiques and stores. Known as the Kö, this wide, double boulevard is divided by an ornamental waterway that is actually a part of the River Düssel. Rows of chestnut trees line the Kö, shading a string of sidewalk cafés. Beyond the Triton Fountain, at the street's north end, begins a series of parks and gardens. In these patches of green you can sense a joie de vivre hardly expected in a city devoted to big business.

The lovely **Hofgarten Park,** once the garden of the elector's palace, is reached by heading north to Corneliusplatz. Laid out in 1770 and completed 30 years later, the Hofgarten is an oasis of greenery at the heart of downtown and a focal point for Düsseldorf culture.

The baroque **Schloss Jägerhof,** at the far-east edge of the Hofgarten, is more a combination town house and country lodge than a castle. It houses the **Goethe Museum,** featuring original manuscripts, first editions, personal correspondence, and other memorabilia of Germany's greatest writer. There's also a museum housing a collection of **Meissner porcelain.** ✉ *Jacobistr. 2* ☎ *0211/899–6262* 🌐 *www.goethe-museum.com* 🎟 *€2* ⏲ *Tues.–Fri. and Sun. 11–5, Sat. 1–5.*

The **museum kunst palast** (art museum foundation) lies at the northern extremity of the Hofgarten, close to the Rhine. The collection of paintings runs the gamut from Rubens, Goya, Tintoretto, and Cranach the Elder to the romantic Düsseldorf school and such modern German expressionists as Beckmann, Kirchner, Nolde, Macke, and Kandinsky. The collection also includes works from Asia and Africa. ✉ *Ehrenhof 4–5* ☎ *0211/899–2460* 🌐 *www.museum-kunst-palast.de* 🎟 *€6* ⏲ *Tues.–Sun. 11–6.*

The **Kunstsammlung Nordrhein-Westfalen** (Art Collection of North Rhine–Westphalia) displays a dazzling array of 20th-century classic modern paintings, including works by Bonnard, Braque, Matisse, Léger, Johns, and Pollock; there are also many by Paul Klee, the Swiss painter who lived in Düsseldorf for a time and taught at the National Academy of Art. The collection is across the street from the city opera house. ✉ *Grabbepl. 5* ☎ *0211/83810* 🌐 *www.kunstsammlung.de* 🎟 *€7.50* ⏲ *Tues.–Fri. 10–6, weekends 11–6, 1st. Wed. of each month 10–10.*

The restored **Altstadt** (Old Town) faces the Rhine. Narrow alleys thread their way to some 200 restaurants and taverns offering a wide range of cuisines, all crowded into the 1-square-km (½-square-mi) area between the Rhine and Heine Allee. Traffic is routed away from the river and underneath the **Rhine Promenade,** which is lined by chic shopping arcades and cafés. Joggers, rollerbladers, and folks out for a stroll make much use of the promenade as well. Occasionally you can still see the *Radschläger,* young boys who demonstrate their cartwheeling abilities, a Düsseldorf tradition, for the admiration (and tips) of visitors.

A plaque at **Bolkerstrasse 53** indicates where poet Heinrich Heine was born in 1797. The **Heinrich Heine Institute** has a museum and an archive of significant manuscripts. Part of the complex was once the residence of the composer Robert Schumann. ✉ *Bilkerstr. 12–14* ☎ *0211/899–2902* 🌐 *www.duesseldorf.de/kultur/heineinstitut* 🎟 *€ 2* ⏲ *Tues.–Fri. and Sun. 11–5, Sat. 1–5.*

The stylish **MedienHafen** is an eclectic mixture of late-19th-century warehouses and ultramodern new businesses, shopping, and entertainment amenities. The fashionable and hip neighborhood is one of Europe's masterpieces in urban redevelopment. Surrounding the historic, commercial harbor, now occupied by yachts and leisure boats, at the foot of the Rhine Tower, many media companies have made this area their new home. International star architects including David Chipperfield, Fumihiko Maki, Claude Vasconi, and Frank O. Gehry have left their mark. On the riverbank, you'll find Gehry's **Neuer Zollhof,** a particularly striking ensemble of three organic-looking high-rises. The best way to tackle the buzzing architecture is to take a stroll down the promenade Am Handelshafen from the Rhine Tower toward Franziusstrasse, and then back along the opposite side on Speditionsstrasse.

The traffic-free cobblestone streets of the Old Town lead to **Burgplatz** (Castle Square). The 13th-century **Schlossturm** (Castle Tower) is all that remains of the castle built by the de Berg family, which founded Düsseldorf. The tower also houses the **Schifffahrtsmuseum,** which charts 2,000 years of Rhine boatbuilding and navigation. ✉ *Burgpl. 30* ☎ *0211/899–4195* 🎟 *€3* ⏲ *Tues.–Sun. 11–6.*

The Gothic **St. Lambertus** (St. Lambertus Church; ✉ Stiftspl.) is near the castle tower on Burgplatz. Its spire became distorted because unseasoned wood was used in its construction. The Vatican elevated the 14th-century brick church to a basilica minor (small cathedral) in 1974 in recognition of its role in church history. Built in the 13th century, with additions from 1394, St. Lambertus contains the tomb of William the Rich and a graceful late-Gothic tabernacle.

Where to Stay & Eat

$$$$ ✕ **Im Schiffchen.** Although it's a bit out of the way, dining in one of Germany's best restaurants makes it worth a trip. This is grande luxe, with cooking that's a fine art. A typical dish might be fried saddle of French milk calf in vervain sauce. The restaurant Aalschokker, on the ground floor, features local specialties created by the same chef but at lower prices. There are 900 wines on the menu. ✉ *Kaiserswerther Markt 9* ☎ *0211/401–050* *Reservations essential* *Jacket and tie* ▭ *AE, DC, MC, V* ⏲ *Closed Sun. and Mon. No lunch.*

★ **$$–$$$$** ✕ **Berens am Kai.** This sleek restaurant is the gourmet playing ground for the young business elite of this affluent city. Set in the once derelict but now modernized Düsseldorf harbor, the glass-and-steel building with its ceiling-to-floor windows looks more like a modern office complex than a restaurant. The steep prices are warranted by the exquisite cuisine, the refined service, and the great setting with magnificent views of the harbor and Düsseldorf, particularly stunning at night. Dishes include creative French–German recipes, a wine list with vintages from around the world, and tempting desserts—a must-see if you are tired of old-style German cooking. ✉ *Kaistr. 16* ☎ *0211/300–6750* ▭ *AE, MC, V* ⏲ *Closed Sun. No lunch Sat.*

$$–$$$ ✕ **Weinhaus Tante Anna.** This charming restaurant is furnished with antiques. The cuisine presents modern versions of German classics, demonstrating that there's a lot more to the country's cooking than wurst and sauerkraut—a specialty is the hearty roast beef with mustard. ✉ *Andreasstr. 2* ☎ *0211/131–163* ▭ *AE, DC, MC, V* ⏲ *Closed Sun. No lunch.*

$–$$$ ✕ **Malkasten.** If artists seem to live in restaurants and pubs, then the Malkasten ("paint box") shines as a most favored haven. The stylish bar and restaurant is a designer's dream come true. Chef Aldo Villani serves a wild mix of German–Italian and French cooking as colorful as his restaurant's name suggests. ✉ *Jacobistr. 6* ☎ *0211/173–040* ▭ *AE, MC, V* ⏲ *No lunch Sat.*

¢–$ ✕ **Brauerei Zur Uel.** A nontraditional brew house, the Uel is the popular hangout for Düsseldorf's students. The basic menu consists of soups, salads, and pastas; the ingredients are fresh and the portions are generous. Every cultural and political event in the city is advertised in the entry hall. ✉ *Ratingerstr. 16* ☎ *0211/325–369* ▭ *MC, V.*

¢–$ ✕ **Zum Uerige.** Among beer buffs, Düsseldorf is famous for its *Altbier,* so called because of the old-fashioned brewing method. The mellow and malty copper-color brew is produced by eight breweries in town. This tavern provides the perfect atmosphere for drinking it. The beer is poured straight out of polished oak barrels and served with hearty local food by busy waiters in long blue aprons. ✉ *Bergerstr. 1* ☎ *0211/866–990* ▭ *No credit cards.*

$$$$ **Steigenberger Parkhotel.** Miraculously quiet despite its central location on the edge of the Hofgarten and at the beginning of the Königsallee, this old hotel is anything but stodgy. The soaring ceilings add to the spaciousness of the guest rooms, each individually decorated in a restrained, elegant style. The pampering continues at the breakfast buffet, served in the Menuette restaurant, where champagne and smoked salmon are appropriate starters for a shopping expedition on the Kö. ✉ *Corneliuspl. 1, D–40213* ☎ *0211/13810* 🖷 *0211/138–1592* 🌐 *www.steigenberger.de* *122 rooms, 11 suites* *Restaurant, café, in-room safes, minibars, cable TV, some in-room data ports, Wi-Fi, 2 bars, dry cleaning, laundry service, concierge, Internet room, business services, meeting rooms, free parking, some pets allowed (fee), no-smoking rooms; no a/c in some rooms* ▭ *AE, DC, MC, V* 🍽 *BP.*

$$$–$$$$ **Günnewig Hotel Esplanade.** This small, modern hotel has an exceptionally quiet, leafy location still close to the action. From the inviting lobby to the attractive rooms, the ambience here is one of intimacy. Room rates vary depending on the view. ✉ *Fürstenpl. 17, D–40215* ☎ *0211/386–850* 🖷 *0211/3868–5555* 🌐 *www.guennewig.de* *80 rooms, 2 suites* *Cable TV, in-room data ports, Wi-Fi, pool, sauna, bar, Internet room, business services, parking (fee), some pets allowed (fee), no-smoking floors; no a/c* ▭ *AE, DC, MC, V* 🍽 *BP.*

$$ **Carathotel.** Besides bright, well-sized rooms, the true strength of this modern hotel is its location, at the southern edge of the Altstadt. After a generous buffet breakfast you can quickly reach either the Rhine or the Kö with a three-block walk. ✉ *Benratherstr. 7a, D–40213* ☎ *0211/13050* 🖷 *0211/322–214* 🌐 *www.horega.de* *72 rooms, 1 suite* *Cable TV, in-room data ports, Wi-Fi, sauna, Internet room, business services, meeting room, parking (fee), some pets allowed (fee), no-smoking floors; no a/c in some rooms* ▭ *AE, DC, MC, V* 🍽 *BP.*

$ **Diana.** If a trade fair hasn't filled this place, it's one of the best bets for a low-price stay in this high-price town. The small rooms with adjoining bathrooms are comfortable, if somberly furnished. The Altstadt is a 15-minute walk away. ✉ *Jahnstr. 31, D–40215* ☎ *0211/375–071*

0211/385–0070 20 rooms Cable TV, Wi-Fi, some pets allowed (fee); no a/c AE, DC, MC, V BP.

Nightlife & the Arts

The **Altstadt** is a landscape of pubs, dance clubs, ancient brewery houses, and jazz clubs in the vicinity of the Marktplatz and along cobblestone streets named Bolker, Kurze, Flinger, and Mühlen. These places may be crowded, but some are very atmospheric. The local favorite for nightlife is the **Hafen** neighborhood. Its restaurants and bars cater to the hip thirtysomething crowd that works and parties there. **Front Page** (Mannesman Ufer 9 0211/323–264) is a slick watering hole. The most popular dance club is **Sam's West** (Königsallee 52 0211/328–171).

Düsseldorf, once home to Mendelssohn, Schumann, and Brahms, has the finest concert hall in Germany after Berlin's Philharmonie, the **Tonhalle** (Ehrenhof 1 0211/899–6123), a former planetarium on the edge of the Hofgarten. It's the home of the Düsseldorfer Symphoniker, which plays from September to mid-June. **Deutsche Oper am Rhein** (Heinrich Heine Allee 16a 0211/890–8211) showcases the city's highly regarded opera company and ballet troupe. The **Robert Schumann Saal** (Ehrenhof 4 0211/899–6211 www.museum-kunst-palast.de) has classic and pop concerts, symposia, film, and international theater. One of Germany's finest variety and artistic shows is presented nightly at the **Roncalli's Apollo Varieté** (Apollopl./Haroldstr. 1 0211/828–9090 www.apollo-variete.com).

A 30-minute ride outside Düsseldorf by car, train, or S-bahn (from the Hauptbahnhof) will get you to the industrial city of Wuppertal, whose main claim to fame is its transit system of suspended trains, the *Schwebebahn*. It is also home to the **Tanztheater Wuppertal** (Spinnstr. 4 0202/569–4444 www.pina-bausch.de), the dance-theater company of world-famous choreographer Pina Bausch.

Shopping

For antiques, go to the area around Hohe Strasse. The east side of the **Königsallee** is lined with some of Germany's trendiest boutiques, grandest jewelers, and most extravagant furriers. The shopping arcade **Kö Center** (Königsallee 30) features the most famous names in fashion, from Chanel to Louis Vuitton. **Kö Galerie** (Königsallee 60) has trendy boutiques and includes a Mövenpick restaurant on its luxurious two-story premises. **Schadow Arcade** (Off Schadowpl., at end of Kö Galerie) caters to normal budgets, with such stores as Hennes & Mauritz (H&M) and Habitat.

THE RHINELAND A TO Z

To research prices, get advice from other travelers, and book travel arrangements, visit www.fodors.com.

AIRPORTS

The Rhineland is served by three international airports: Frankfurt, Düsseldorf, and Köln-Bonn. Bus and rail lines connect each airport with its respective downtown area and provide rapid access to the rest of the region. No-frills carriers that fly within Europe are based at Frankfurt-Hahn Airport in Lautzenhausen, between the Rhine and Mosel valleys (a 45-minute drive from Wiesbaden; a 1½-hour bus ride from Frankfurt Airport). The Luxembourg Findel International Airport (a 30-minute drive from Trier) is close to the upper Mosel River Valley.

Flughafen Düsseldorf ☎ 0211/421-2223.**Flughafen Frankfurt** ☎ 01805/372-4636 🌐 www.frankfurt-airport.de.**Luxembourg Findel International Airport** ☎ 352/2456-5050 🌐 www.lux-airport.lu. **Flughafen Hahn** ☎ 06543/509-200 🌐 www.hahn-airport.de. **Flughafen Köln/Bonn** ✉ Waldstr. 247, Köln ☎ 02203/404-001.

BIKE TRAVEL

The Mosel Valley, with its small hamlets lining the riverbanks, is an excellent area for biking. The train station in Trier rents bikes; call the Deutsche Bahn bicycle hotline to reserve. Cyclists can follow the marked route of the *Radroute Nahe-Hunsrück-Mosel* from Trier to Bingen, which partially overlaps with the *Moselradwanderweg* from Koblenz to Trier. Both Bonn and Köln have extensive bike paths downtown; these are designated, red-painted or red-brick paths on the edges of roads or sidewalks. (Pedestrians, beware: anyone walking on a bike path risks getting mowed down.) Bicyclists are expected to follow the same traffic rules as cars. In Bonn, the Radstation, at the main train station, not only will rent you a bike and provide maps, but will fill your water bottle and check the pressure in your tires for free. In Köln, Rent-a-Bike offers bike rental by the day from April through October as well as a daily three-hour bike tour of the city.

Deutsche Bahn bicycle hotline ☎ 01805/151-415. **Radstation** ✉ Quantiusstr. 26, Bonn ☎ 0228/981-4636. **Rent-a-Bike** ✉ Markmannsg. under Deutzer Brücke, Köln ☎ 0171/629-8796.

CAR TRAVEL

The autobahns and other highways of the Rhineland are busy, so allow plenty of time for driving. Frankfurt is 126 km (78 mi) from Koblenz, 175 km (109 mi) from Bonn, 190 km (118 mi) from Köln, and 230 km (143 mi) from Düsseldorf (the A–3 links Frankfurt with Köln and Düsseldorf and passes near Koblenz and Bonn). The most spectacular stretch of the Rhineland is along the Middle Rhine, between Mainz and Koblenz, which takes in the awesome castles and vineyards of the Rhine gorge. Highways hug the river on each bank (B–42 on the north and eastern sides, and B–9 on the south and western sides), and car ferries crisscross the Rhine at many points.

CONSULATES

Canada **Canadian Consulate** ✉ Benratherstr. 8, D-40213 Düsseldorf ☎ 0211/172-170.

United Kingdom **British General Consulate** ✉ Yorckstr. 19, D-40476 Düsseldorf ☎ 0211/94480.

United States **US Consulate General** ✉ Willi-Becker-Allee 10, D-40227 Düsseldorf ☎ 0211/788-8927.

TOURS

BOAT TOURS No visit to the Rhineland is complete without at least one river cruise, and there are many options from which to choose. Even rowboats and canoes can be rented at most Rhine and Mosel river resorts.

Trips along the Rhine and Mosel range in length from a few hours to days or even a week or more (⇨ *see* Cruise Travel *in* Smart Travel Tips). Viking River Cruises offers various multiday cruises on cabin ships. A major day-trip line is Köln-Düsseldorfer Deutsche Rheinschiffahrt (KD Rhine Line). Its fleet travels the Rhine between Köln and Mainz, daily from Easter to late October, and the Mosel from Koblenz to Cochem, daily from June to September (and reduced service during the spring and fall). There are many special offers, such as free travel on your birthday (bring your passport as proof); half-price for senior citizens on Monday and Friday; two cyclists for the price of one on Tuesday, with no charge for the bikes; family day on Wednesday (three children travel free per paying adult); and economical fares for time-saving round-trip travel—one way by train, return by boat.

Many smaller, family-operated boat companies offer daytime trips and, often, nighttime dinner-dance cruises. The Koblenz operator Rhein- und Moselschiffahrt Hölzenbein travels between Koblenz and Winningen on the Mosel and between Bonn and Rüdesheim on the Rhine. From Koblenz, Personenschiffahrt Merkelbach makes round-trip "castle cruises" to Schloss Stolzenfels (one hour) or the Marksburg (two hours), passing by six castles en route. The Hebel-Linie has Loreley Valley trips from Boppard. Another important Mittelrhein specialist traveling to the Loreley is the Bingen-Rüdesheimer Fahrgastschiffahrt. The Frankfurt-based Primus-Linie cruises between Frankfurt and the Loreley via Wiesbaden and, occasionally, between Wiesbaden and Heidelberg. The spacious, luxurious boat *Princesse Marie-Astrid,* headquartered in Grevenmacher, Luxembourg, offers gourmet dining, and occasionally evening shows or live music, during Mosel cruises along the German–Luxembourgian border from Trier or Grevenmacher to Schengen. Costs range from €14 to €19, excluding food; entertainment cruises vary in price. Cruises depart from Trier from July through mid-September; and from Grevenmacher from Easter through mid-November.

Three shipping companies in Köln leave from the Rhine landing stages near the Hohenzollern Brücke, a short walk from the cathedral.

For Rhine Trips **Bingen-Rüdesheimer Fahrgastschiffahrt** ✉ Bingen ☎ 06721/14140 🖷 06721/17398 🌐 www.bingen-ruedesheimer.com/rhine-cruise. **Dampfschiffahrt Colonia** ✉ Köln ☎ 0221/257–4225. **Hebel-Linie** ✉ Boppard ☎ 06742/2420 🖷 06742/4727 🌐 www.hebel-linie.de. **KD Rhine Line** ✉ Köln ☎ 0221/208–8318, 800/346–6525 in U.S. 🌐 www.k-d.com. **Kölntourist Personenschiffahrt am Dom** ✉ Köln ☎ 0221/121–714. **Personenschiffahrt Merkelbach** ✉ Koblenz ☎ 0261/76810 🖷 0261/973–3264 🌐 www.merkelbach.personenschiffe.de. **Primus-Linie** ✉ Frankfurt ☎ 069/133–8370 🌐 www.primus-linie.de. **Rhein- und Moselschiffahrt Hölzenbein** ✉ Koblenz ☎ 0261/37744 🖷 0261/16640 🌐 www.hoelzenbein.de. **Viking River Cruises** ✉ Köln ☎ 0221/25860, 877/668–4546 in U.S. 🌐 www.vikingkd.com.

For Mosel Trips **Personenschifffahrt Hans Michels** ✉ Bernkastel-Kues ☎ 06531/8222 🖷 06531/7603 🌐 www.mosel-personenschifffahrt.de. **Personenschiffahrt Kolb** ☎ 02673/1515 🖷 02673/1510 🌐 www.moselfahrplan.de. **Princesse Marie-Astrid** ✉ Grevenmacher, Luxembourg ☎ 758–275 (country code for Luxembourg is 352) 🌐 www.moselle-tourist.lu. **Rhein- und Moselschiffahrt Hölzenbein** ☎ 0261/37744 🖷 0261/16640 🌐 www.hoelzenbein.de.

BUS TOURS Limousine Travel Service has a daily bus trip from Frankfurt to Rhine wine country. From Rüdesheim, travel continues by boat to St. Goarhausen; return to Frankfurt is by bus. The €69 fee includes lunch and a wine tasting. Tours depart Frankfurt at 11:15. Guests in Wiesbaden can be brought to Frankfurt for an additional €10.

Bus trips into the Köln countryside (to the Eifel Hills, the Ahr Valley, and the Westerwald) are organized by several city travel agencies. Reisebüro Knipper sells tours to individuals looking for trips outside the city.

Limousine Travel Service ✉ Wiesenhüttenpl. 39, Frankfurt/Main ☎ 069/230–492 🌐 www.ets-frankfurt.de. **FTI Ferienwelt Reisebüro Kimmel** ✉ Hahnenstr. 41, near Neumarkt ☎ 0221/205–0820.

CITY TOURS Tours of Bonn start from the tourist office and are conducted April–October, Tuesday–Sunday, and November–March, Saturday only. Call the tourist office ahead to check times for tours in English.

Bus tours of Düsseldorf leave year-round at 11 daily and also at 2:30 on Saturday, from the corner of Steinstrasse and Königsallee. From April to October, the 2:30 tour is daily as well. Tickets (€17.50 in summer, and €15 in winter) can be purchased on the bus, at the information center, or through Adorf Reisebüro.

The Koblenz tourist office has guided tours on Saturday at 2:30, in April, and on Friday, Saturday, and Sunday at 2:30, May through October, departing from the Historisches Rathaus on Jesuitenplatz (€3). English-language tours are available upon request.

Bus tours of Köln leave from outside the tourist office, opposite the main entrance to the cathedral, at the Köln Tourismus Office, hourly 10–3, April–October (more frequently on weekends), and at 11 and 2, November–March. The tour lasts two hours and costs €10; it's conducted in English and German. A two-hour Köln walking tour is available by prior arrangement with the tourist office.

In Trier you can circumnavigate the town with the narrated tours of the Römer-Express trolley, the CityTour double-decker bus, or a tourist office bus; all cost €6 and normally depart from Porta Nigra, near the tourist office. Due to renovation of the Simeonstift throughout 2006, the bus stops will be moved (inquire at the tourist office).

There are also tours Friday, Saturday, and Sunday April through October, in which actors dressed in Roman costume bring the history of three sights to life. In the amphitheater cellars, the slave Valerius explains how he trained to become a gladiator to win his freedom. The tribune Mallobaudes tells about his secret mission to Trier toward the end of Roman rule to infiltrate a Franconian military camp in the Kaiserthermen. During "The Secret of the Porta Nigra," a centurion shares details about the illustrious—and sinister—past of the old town gate. Each tour lasts an hour and costs €8.50. Reservations are essential. If you don't speak German, speak up! The tour guide and/or someone in the group probably speaks some English and will translate the basic points. The tourist office sells tickets for all tours and also leads various walks. A tour in English (€6) departs Saturday, May through October, at 1:30.

Bilingual walking (€6) and bus (€10) tours of Wiesbaden depart from the bus stop in front of the Staatstheater on Kurhausplatz. The walking tour is conducted April–October, Saturday at 10 (November–March, the first and third Saturday). The bus tour is offered year-round, Saturday at 2.

Adorf Reisebüro Mündelheimer Weg 10, Düsseldorf 0211/418-970.

TRAIN TRAVEL

InterCity and EuroCity expresses connect all the cities and towns of the area. Hourly InterCity routes run between Düsseldorf, Köln, Bonn, and Mainz, with most services extending as far south as Munich and as far north as Hamburg. The Mainz–Bonn route runs beside the Rhine, providing spectacular views all the way. The city transportation networks of Bonn, Köln, and Düsseldorf are linked by S-bahn (for information contact the KVB).

Deutsche Bahn 0180/11861. **Kölner Verkehrs-Betriebe** (KVB) 0221/547-3333.

TRAVEL AGENCIES

American Express Immamannstr. 65b, D-40215 Düsseldorf 0211/385-0069 Burgmauer 14, D-50667 Köln 0221/257-5186.

VISITOR INFORMATION

The Rhineland regional tourist office, Rheinland-Pfalz Tourismus, provides general information on the entire region. The events calendar *Veranstaltungskalender Rheinland-Pfalz* gives a comprehensive overview of the wine, regional, and folk festivals, as well as concerts, theater, and art exhibitions taking place in many parts of this area.

Mosellandtouristik's illustrated booklets *Discover and Enjoy the Moselle Countryside* and *Moselle: Cities, Wine and Culture* are an excellent introduction to the Mosel Valley and include information on events, package deals, and additional sources of information.

Many cultural events and museums in the state of Rhineland-Pfalz accept the *KulturCard* (€5), which grants up to 50% discounts. The card is sold by mail through the regional broadcaster SWR and in person at the newspaper *RZ* (RheinZeitung) shops. The *Mittelrhein Burgen-Ticket,* sold at 10 participating castles in the Mittelrhein area between Rüdesheim and Koblenz, offers a tremendous savings on admission fees to 10 castles. The cost is €14 for adults and allows free admission to the castles.

Bonn's tourism office sells the *RegioBonnCard* package, which offers an array of reductions, plus free entry into most museums, in combination with low- or no-cost transportation for €12.25 per day or €23.50 for two days.

In Köln, most central hotels sell the *KölnTourismus Card* (€15.50), which entitles you to a sightseeing tour, admission to all the city's museums, free city bus and tram travel, and other reductions.

Discount Tickets **KulturCard** SWR, Stichwort KulturCard, D-55114 Mainz. **Mittelrhein Burgen-Ticket** www.burgen-am-rhein.de.

Tourist-Information **Aachen** ✉ Aachen Tourist Service, Friedrich-Wilhelm-Pl., Postfach 2007, D-52022 ☎ 0241/180-2960 🌐 www.aachen-tourist.de. **Bacharach** ✉ Tourist-Information, Oberstr. 45, D-55422 ☎ 06743/919-303 📠 06743/919-304 🌐 www.rhein-nahe-touristik.de. **Bernkastel-Kues** ✉ Tourist-Information, Gestade 6, D-54470 ☎ 06531/4023 📠 06531/7953 🌐 www.bernkastel.de. **Bingen** ✉ Tourist-Information; Rheinkai 21, D-55411 ☎ 06721/184-205 📠 06721/184-214 🌐 www.bingen.de. **Bonn** ✉ Bonn Information, Windeckstr. 2 am Münsterpl., D-53111 ☎ 0228/775-000 🌐 www.bonn.de. **Boppard** ✉ Tourist-Information, Marktpl., D-56154 ☎ 06742/3888 📠 06742/81402 🌐 www.boppard.de. **Cochem** ✉ Tourist-Information, Endertpl. 1, D-56812 ☎ 02671/60040 📠 02671/600-444 🌐 www.cochem.de. **Düsseldorf** ✉ Tourismus & Marketing GmbH Konrad Adenauer Pl. 12, D-40210 ☎ 0211/172-020 🌐 www.duesseldorf-tourismus.de. **Koblenz** ✉ Tourist-Information, Jesuitenplatz 2-4, D-56068 ☎ 0261/129-1610 📠 0261/130-9211 🌐 www.koblenz.de. **Köln** ✉ Köln Tourismus Office, Unter Fettenhenen 19, D-50667 ☎ 0221/2213-0400 🌐 www.koeln.de. **Mosellandtouristik** ✉ Kordelweg 1, D-54470 Bernkastel-Kues/Andel ☎ 06531/97330 📠 06531/973-333 🌐 www.mosellandtouristik.de. **Rheingau-Taunus Kultur & Tourismus** ✉ An der Basilika 11a, D-65375 Oestrich-Winkel ☎ 06723/99550 📠 06723/995-555 🌐 www.rheingau-taunus-info.de. **Rheinland-PfalzTourismus** ✉ Löhrstr. 103-105, D-56068 Koblenz ☎ 0261/915-200 📠 0261/915-2040 🌐 www.rlp-info.de. **Rüdesheim** ✉ Tourist-Information, Geisenheimer Str. 22, D-65385 ☎ 06722/19433 📠 06722/3485 🌐 www.ruedesheim.de. **Trier** ✉ Tourist-Information, An der Porta Nigra, D-54290 ☎ 0651/978-080 📠 0651/44759 🌐 www.trier.de/tourismus. **Wiesbaden** ✉ Tourist-Information, Marktstr. 6, D-65183 ☎ 0611/17290 📠 0611/172-9798 🌐 www.wiesbaden.de.

WINE INFORMATION

Wines of Germany provides background information and brochures about all German wine-growing regions. Tips on wine-related events and package offers are available from regional wine-information offices.

The Ahr River Valley near Bonn is a red-wine region that is also known for its spas (hot mineral springs) and sparkling water (Apollinaris springs). Mosel-Saar-Ruwer Wein supplies wine information about the Mosel, Saar, and Ruwer River valleys. Between the Mosel and Rhine valleys lies the Nahe region.

Wines of Germany ✉ 950 Third Ave., 7th fl., New York, NY 10022 ☎ 212/994-7523 📠 212/994-7598 🌐 www.germanwineusa.org. **Gesellschaft für Rheingauer Weinkultur** ✉ Adam-von-Itzstein-Str. 20, D-65375 Oestrich-Winkel ☎ 06723/91757 📠 06723/917-591 🌐 www.rheingauer-wbv.de. **Mittelrhein-Wein** ✉ Am Hafen 2, D-56329 St. Goar ☎ 06741/7712 📠 06741/7723 🌐 www.mittelrhein-wein.com. **Mosel-Saar-Ruwer Wein** ✉ Gartenfeldstr. 12a, D-54295 Trier ☎ 0651/710-280 📠 0651/45443 🌐 www.msr-wein.de. **Tourisismus & Service Ahr Rhein Eifel** ✉ Klosterstr. 13, D-53507 Marienthal ☎ 02641/97730 📠 02641/977-373 🌐 www.wohlsein365.de. **Weinland Nahe** ✉ Burgenlandstr. 7, D-55543 Bad Kreuznach ☎ 0671/834-050 📠 0671/834-0525 🌐 www.weinland-nahe.de.

The Fairy-Tale Road

11

WORD OF MOUTH

"Marburg is marvelous—a real gem. Not only does it have a well-preserved medieval old town, but a spectacular castle overlooking the city. In addition it is the home of a fabled University so there are tons of things to do (nightlife, restaurants, concerts and exhibitions). . . . It is one of my favorite towns in Germany—far more intriguing and 'real' than any of the towns along the Romantic Road."

—CharlieB

"Kassel was well worth the journey. Wilhelmshohe park and the schloss are beautiful. . . . Go in the morning, and watch the mist rise from the city below and the forest surrounding!"

—jedi_kitty

www.fodors.com/forums

Updated by Ted Shoemaker

IF YOU'RE IN SEARCH OF SLEEPING BEAUTY, the Pied Piper, or Rumpelstiltskin, the Fairy-Tale Road, or Märchenstrasse, is the place to look. One of Germany's special tour routes, which celebrated its 30th anniversary in 2005, the Märchenstrasse leads deep into the heart of the country through the landscapes that inspired the Brothers Grimm. It begins 20 minutes east of Frankfurt in the city of Hanau and from there wends its way north 600 km (about 370 mi), mainly through the states of Hesse and Lower Saxony, following the Fulda and Weser rivers and traversing a countryside as beguiling as any other in Europe.

This designated tour route doesn't have the glamour of the Romantic Road, but it also doesn't have the crowds and commercialism. It's a route perhaps even more in tune with romantics. Fairy tales come to life in forgotten villages, ancient castles, and misty valleys where the silence of centuries is broken only by the splash of a ferryman's oar. The meandering, progressive path seems to travel back in time, into the reaches of childhood, imagination, and the German folk consciousness. These Old-World settings are steeped in legend and fantasy.

This part of Germany shaped the lives and imaginations of the two most famous chroniclers of German folk history and tradition, the Brothers Grimm. They sought out the region's best storytellers to bring us such unforgettable characters as Cinderella, Hansel and Gretel, Little Red Riding Hood, Rapunzel, Rumpelstiltskin, Sleeping Beauty, and Snow White.

The zigzag course detailed in this chapter follows the spine of the Fairy-Tale Road and includes a number of side trips and detours. The route is best explored by car, though train service is available to the larger cities.

Exploring the Fairy-Tale Road

This isn't a route for travelers in a hurry. The road extends about half the length of Germany, from the banks of the Main River, which marks the border between northern and southern Germany, to the North Sea ports of Bremen and Bremerhaven. The diverse regions have been linked together to highlight the region's connection with the Grimm brothers and their stories, and to create a meandering tour route for travelers seeking a quieter, more intimate view of Germany's many charms. Some towns on the journey—Bremerhaven and Hanau, for example—are modern, while others, such as Steinau an der Strasse, Hannoversch-Münden, and Hameln, might have stepped right out of a Grimm story.

About the Restaurants

Old restaurant habits persist to some extent on the Fairy-Tale Road. In urban areas you can find restaurants that serve hot meals around the clock, even at breakfast time. But don't count on that in this largely rural area. Many restaurants serve hot meals only between 11:30 AM and 2 PM, and 6 PM and 9 PM. You rarely need a reservation here and casual clothing is generally acceptable.

The itineraries below assume you'll be starting off from Frankfurt, Germany's transportation hub. You could also approach the Fairy-Tale Road from Hamburg in the north.

Numbers in the text correspond to numbers in the margin and on the Fairy-Tale Road map.

If you have
3 days

You won't get much farther than the first stretch of the route, but that's enough for an introduction to the region. Skip **Hanau** 1 altogether and stop off in **Gelnhausen** 2 for a visit of the remains of Barbarossa's greatest castle. Then explore **Steinau an der Strasse** 3, where the Grimm brothers spent much of their childhood. Spend the night in Steinau or perhaps return to Gelnhausen for an overnight stay and dinner at the **Romantisches Hotel Burg Mühle.** On your second day, continue on to **Fulda** 4, to see its impressive palace and cathedral. After lunch, proceed north, calling at the medieval towns of **Alsfeld** and **Marburg** 5, both perfect settings for Grimm tales. On the third day continue on to **Kassel** 6 for your last night. Try to catch the sunset from the heights of the Wilhelmshöhe.

If you have
5 days

Follow the itinerary described above but include a short stop in **Hanau** 1 on your first day. On the fourth day, traverse the valley of the Fulda River to where it meets the Werra to form the Weser at **Hannoversch-Münden** 7, which claimed a place on geographer Alexander von Humboldt's list of the world's most beautiful towns. Follow the lazily winding Weser northward now, making a short detour to **Göttingen** 8 for lunch in one of the student taverns in this busy university city. Try to fit in an overnight stay at Sleeping Beauty's Castle in **Sababurg** 9, half hidden in the depths of the densely wooded Reinhardswald. On the fifth day return to the Weser River valley road and take time for stops at **Bad Karlshafen** 10, **Höxter** 11, and **Bodenwerder** 12 to explore their streets of half-timber houses. End your trip at **Hameln** 13, the Pied Piper's town.

If you have
7 days

After the five-day itinerary described above, leave the Fairy-Tale Road at Hameln for a detour to **Hannover** 14–19, which has a magnificent royal park. An overnight stay in Hannover will give you the opportunity to enjoy some nightlife after the tranquility of the Weser Valley route. The next day head for **Bremen** 22, 110 km (68 mi) northwest. Bremen is the northernmost point on the Fairy-Tale Road, famous for the fable about the donkey, dog, cat, and rooster of the Bremen Town Musicians. If you have time, venture the final 66 km (40 mi) to the seaport of **Bremerhaven,** where you'll find Germany's largest maritime museum.

About the Hotels

Make advance reservations if you plan to visit in summer. Though it's one of the less-traveled tourist routes in Germany, the main points of the Fairy-Tale Road are popular. Hannover is particularly busy during trade-fair times.

WHAT IT COSTS In Euros					
	$$$$	$$$	$$	$	¢
RESTAURANTS	over €25	€21–€25	€16–€20	€9–€15	under €9
HOTELS	over €225	€175–€225	€100–€175	€50–€100	under €50

Restaurant prices are per person for a main course at dinner. Hotel prices are for two people in a standard double room, including tax and service.

Timing

Summer is the ideal time to travel through this varied landscape, although in spring you'll find the river valleys carpeted in the season's first flowers and in fall the sleepy current of the Weser is often blanketed in mist. Keep in mind that retail stores and shops in the smaller towns in this area often close for two to three hours at lunchtime.

HESSE

The first portion of the Fairy-Tale Road, from Hanau to Kassel, lies within the state of Hesse. Frankfurt, the gateway to the state, is less than a half hour west of the road's starting point in Hanau.

Hanau

1 *16 km (10 mi) east of Frankfurt.*

The Fairy-Tale Road begins in once-upon-a-time fashion at Hanau, the town where the Brothers Grimm were born. Although Grimm fans will want to start their pilgrimage here, Hanau is now a traffic-congested suburb of Frankfurt, with post–World War II buildings that are not particularly attractive. Hanau was almost completely obliterated by wartime bombing raids, and there's little of the Altstadt (Old Town) that the Grimm brothers would recognize now.

Hanau's main attraction can be reached only on foot—the **Nationaldenkmal Brüder Grimm** (Brothers Grimm Memorial) in the Marktplatz. The bronze memorial, erected in 1898, is a larger-than-life-size statue of the brothers, one seated, the other leaning on his chair, the two of them pondering an open book—a fitting pose for these scholars who unearthed so many medieval myths and legends, earning their reputation as the fathers of the fairy tale. There is also a small Grimm exhibit, featuring clothing, artifacts, and writings, at **Schloss Phillipsruhe** (✉ Phillipsruher Allee 45 ☎ 06181/20209 🌐 www.museen-hanau.de), on the banks of the Main in the suburb of Kesselstadt (Bus 1 will take you there in 10 minutes). Historical Hanau treasures, including a priceless collection of faience, are also on display in the palace museum.

On the Menu

A specialty of northern Hesse is sausages with *Beulches,* made from potato balls, leeks, and black pudding. *Weck,* which is local dialect for "heavily spiced pork," appears either as *Musterweck,* served on a roll, or as *Weckewerk,* a frying-pan concoction with white bread. Heading north into Lower Saxony, you'll encounter the ever-popular *Speckkuchen,* a heavy and filling onion tart. Another favorite main course is *Pfefferpothast,* a sort of heavily browned goulash with lots of pepper. Trout and eels are common in the rivers and streams around Hameln, and by the time you reach Bremen, north German cuisine has taken over the menu. *Aalsuppe grün,* eel soup seasoned with dozens of herbs, is a must in summer, and the hearty *Grünkohl mit Pinkel,* a cabbage dish with sausage, bacon, and cured pork, appears in winter. Be sure to try the coffee. Fifty percent of the coffee served in Germany comes from beans roasted in Bremen. The city has been producing the stuff since 1673 and knows just how to serve it in pleasantly cozy or, as locals say, *gemütlich* surroundings.

Golf Courses

There are golf courses in or near Bremen, Göttingen, Hanau, Kassel, Hameln, Hannover, and Celle; visiting golfers are welcome, preferably Monday to Thursday, at most locations (provided they can produce a handicap from their local clubs). The courses at Hanau (on the former hunting grounds at Wilhelmsbad) and Kassel (high above the city on the edge of Wilhelmshöhe Park) are particularly attractive. At Schloss Schwöbber, near Hameln, golfers tee off on the extensive castle grounds.

Hiking & Walking

Two protected nature parks—the Weserergland and the Lüneburg Heath—are in or near the Fairy-Tale Road. You can hike the banks of the Weser, stopping at ancient waterside inns, from Hannoversch-Münden, in the south, to Porta-Westfalica, where the Weser River breaks through the last range of north German hills and into the plain of Lower Saxony. The Lüneburg Heath is flat, and hiking is particularly pleasant in late summer, when the heather is in bloom. The tourist offices in the area can give you good tips on where to find nearby trails. A book entitled *Weserbergland: Rother Wanderführer,* by Ulrich Tubbesing, describes 50 selected walks in the area, several of them lasting two or more days. It's available at area bookstores in German only, but the many maps may be useful to non–German speakers as well.

The solid bulk of Hanau's 18th-century **Rathaus** (Town Hall) stands behind the Grimm brothers statue. Every day at noon, 4, and 6 its bells play tribute to another of the city's famous sons, the composer Paul Hindemith (1895–1963), by chiming out one of his canons. On Wednesday and Saturday mornings the Rathaus is the backdrop for the largest street market in the state of Hesse. ✉ *Marktpl. 14.*

The **Altes Rathaus** (Old Town Hall), behind the Rathaus, dominates a corner that has been faithfully reconstructed. This handsome 16th-century

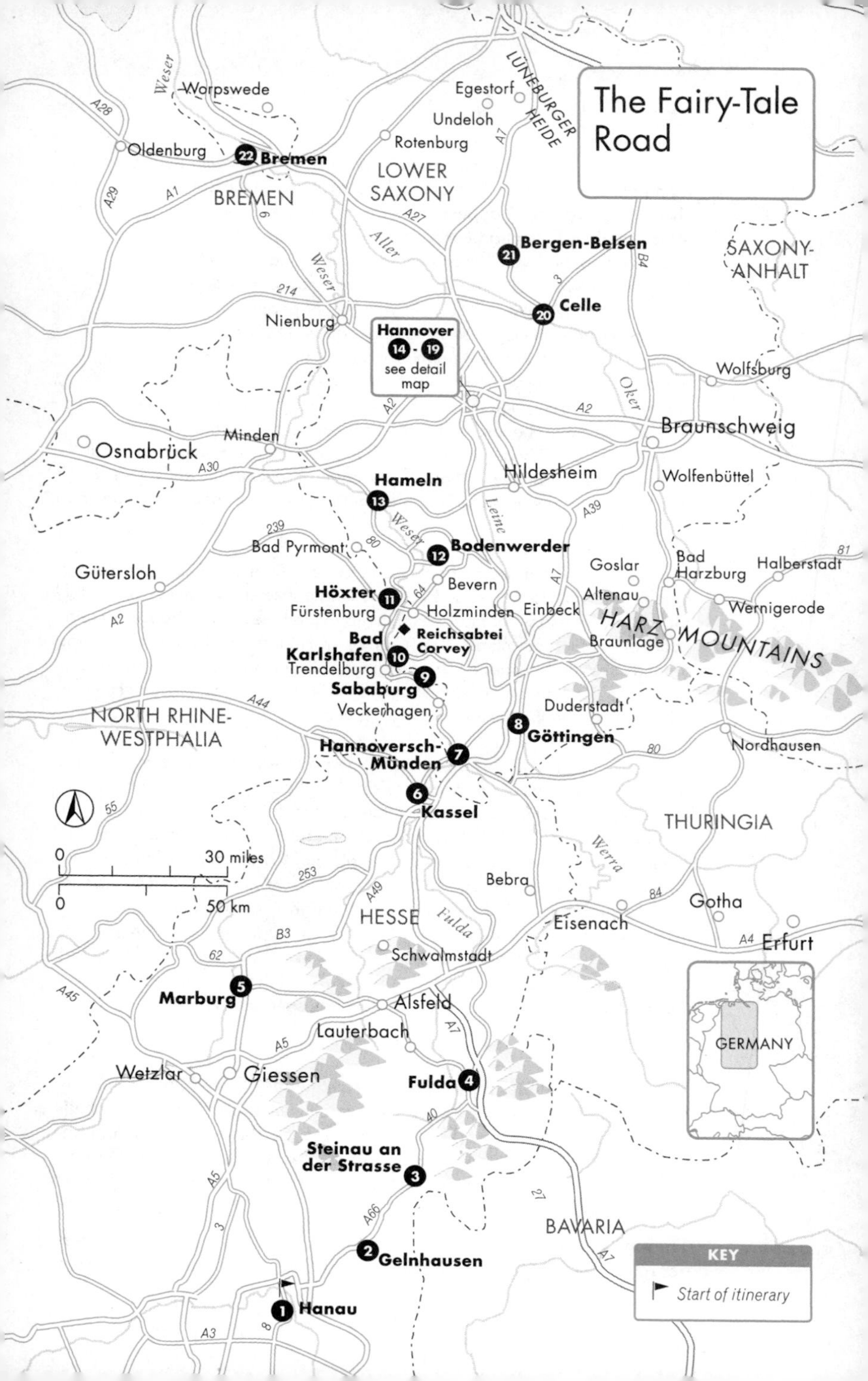
The Fairy-Tale Road
Worpswede
Egestorf
Undeloh
Rotenburg
LÜNEBURGER HEIDE
Oldenburg
22 Bremen
BREMEN
LOWER SAXONY
Aller
Weser
21 Bergen-Belsen
SAXONY-ANHALT
20 Celle
Nienburg
Hannover 14 - 19 see detail map
Wolfsburg
Oker
Braunschweig
Osnabrück
Minden
Hildesheim
Wolfenbüttel
13 Hameln
Leine
Bad Pymont
12 Bodenwerder
Goslar
Bad Harzburg
Halberstadt
Gütersloh
Bevern
11 Höxter
Altenau
Fürstenburg
Holzminden
Einbeck
Wernigerode
HARZ MOUNTAINS
Reichsabtei Corvey
Braunlage
10 Bad Karlshafen
Trendelburg
9 Sababurg
Veckerhagen
Duderstadt
NORTH RHINE-WESTPHALIA
8 Göttingen
7 Hannoversch-Münden
Nordhausen
6 Kassel
THURINGIA
Werra
0 30 miles
0 50 km
Bebra
HESSE
Fulda
Gotha
Eisenach
Erfurt
Schwalmstadt
5 Marburg
Alsfeld
GERMANY
Lauterbach
Wetzlar
Giessen
4 Fulda
3 Steinau an der Strasse
BAVARIA
2 Gelnhausen
KEY
Start of itinerary
1 Hanau
A28
A29
A1
A27
A7
B4
214
A2
A30
239
A39
A44
A49
253
B3
62
A45
A5
A66
A3
A4
55
80
81
84
64
40
27
9
3
8

Renaissance building has two half-timber upper stories weighted down by a steep slate roof. Today it's a museum. Known as the **Deutsches Goldschmiedehaus** (German Goldsmiths' House), it has exhibitions about the craft, contemporary and historical, of the goldsmith and silversmith. ✉ *Altstädter Markt 6* ☎ *06181/428–8888* *€2* ⏲ *Tues.–Sun. 10–noon and 2–5.*

Gelnhausen

❷ *20 km (12 mi) northeast of Hanau, 35 km (21 mi) northeast of Frankfurt.*

If you're flying into Frankfurt, Gelnhausen is an ideal spot for your first night on the Fairy-Tale Road. It's smaller and more charming than Hanau and is still less than an hour's drive from Frankurt's main airport. The town's picturesque *Altstadt* (old town) will give you a first taste of the half-timber architecture and cobblestone streets that await you in abundance further north.

On an island in the sleepy little Kinzig River you'll find the remains of **Burg Barbarossa.** Emperor Friedrich I—known as Barbarossa, or Red Beard—built the castle in this idyllic spot in the 12th century; in 1180 it was the scene of the first all-German Imperial Diet, a gathering of princes and ecclesiastical leaders. Today only parts of the russet walls and colonnaded entrance remain. Still, stroll beneath the castle's ruined ramparts on its water site, and you'll get a tangible impression of the medieval importance of the court of Barbarossa. Enter through the museum, an unmarked building to your left as you face the castle. ✉ *Burgstr. 14* ☎ *06051/3805* *€1.80* ⏲ *Mar.–Oct., Sun. and Tues.–Fri. 10–5, Sat. 1–5; Nov.–Dec., Sun. and Tues.–Fri. 10–4, Sat. 1–4.*

The **Hexenturm** (Witches Tower), a grim prison, remains from the time when Gelnhausen was the center of a paranoiac witch hunt in the late 16th century; dozens of women were burned at the stake or thrown—bound hand and foot—into the Kinzig River. Suspects were held in the Hexenturm of the town battlements. Today it houses a bloodcurdling collection of medieval torture instruments. Tours of the tower, in German only, are offered on Sunday afternoons from May through October. English-language tours for groups of up to 30 persons can be booked in advance for €52. ✉ *Am Fretzenstein* ☎ *06051/380–300* ⏲ *May–Oct., tour Sun., except 1st Sun. of month, at 2:30.*

Where to Stay & Eat

$ **Romantisches Hotel Burg Mühle.** *Mühle* means "mill," and this hotel was once the mill of the neighboring castle, delivering flour to the community until 1958. In the restaurant ($–$$) the mill wheel churns away as you eat. The furniture and carpeting in the hotel is showing a little wear, but the rooms are large (many with small balconies), and spotlessly clean. There is no elevator; reserve a room on the ground floor if this is a problem. ✉ *Burgstr. 2, D–63571* ☎ *06051/82050* *06051/820–554* *www.burgmuehle.de* *42 rooms* *Restaurant, minibars, cable TV, gym, massage, sauna, bar, no-smoking rooms; no a/c* *DC, MC, V* *BP.*

Steinau an der Strasse

❸ *30 km (18 mi) northeast of Gelnhausen, 65 km (40 mi) northeast of Frankfurt.*

You need only travel to the little town of Steinau—full name Steinau an der Strasse (Steinau "on the road," referring to an old trade route between Frankfurt and Leipzig)—for clear evidence of its formative influence on the Brothers Grimm. They were preschoolers on arrival and under 12 when they left after their father's untimely death.

Steinau dates from the 13th century and is typical of villages in the region. Marvelously preserved half-timber houses are set along cobblestone streets; an imposing castle bristles with towers and turrets. In its woodsy surroundings you can well imagine encountering Little Red Riding Hood, Snow White, or Hansel and Gretel. A major street is named after the brothers; the building where they lived is now known as the Brothers Grimm House.

★ **Schloss Steinau** (Steinau Castle) is straight out of a Grimm fairy tale. It stands at the top of the town, with a "Fairy-tale Fountain" in front of it. Originally an early medieval fortress, it was rebuilt in Renaissance style between 1525 and 1558 and first used by the counts of Hanau as their summer residence. Later, it was used to guard the increasingly important trade route between Frankfurt and Leipzig. It's not difficult to imagine the young Grimm boys playing in the shadow of its great gray walls or venturing into the encircling dry moat.

The castle houses a **Grimm Museum,** one of two in Steinau, as well as an exhibition of marionettes from the marionette theater. The Grimm Museum exhibits the family's personal effects, including portraits of the Grimm relatives, the family Bible, an original copy of the Grimms' dictionary (the first in the German language), and all sorts of mundane things such as spoons and drinking glasses. Climb the tower for a breathtaking view of Steinau and the countryside. ☎ *06663/6843* 🎫 *Museum €2, tower €1, tour of castle and museum €3.20* ⏲ *Mar.–Sept., Tues.–Thurs. and weekends 10–5; Oct.–mid-Dec., Tues.–Thurs. and weekends 10–4.*

The **Steinauer Marionettentheater** (Steinau Marionette Theater) is in the castle's former stables and portrays Grimm fairy tales and other children's classics. Performances are held most weekends at 3. ✉ *Am Kumpen 4* ☎ *06663/245* 🎫 *€6.50.*

★ The carefully restored **Brüder-Grimm-Haus,** where the brothers lived as children and where their father had his office, is the only Grimm residence that's still extant. Other Grimm houses, in Hanau and Kassel, were destroyed during World War II. The house is a few hundred yards from the castle and contains a museum devoted to the brothers. Among the exhibits are books and pictures, some dating from their time, plus reminders of their work as lexicographers. ✉ *Brüder-Grimm-Str. 80* ☎ *06663/7605* 🎫 *€2* ⏲ *Mar.–Dec., daily 2–5; Jan. and Feb., weekends 2–5.*

THE BROTHERS GRIMM

THE TWO ESSENTIAL FEATURES of a Grimm's fairy tale are generally deep, gloomy forests (Hansel and Gretel, Snow White), and castles (Cinderella, The Sleeping Beauty). It would seem logical that the region where the stories originated would be abundantly endowed with both. And, as you will see if you explore the Fairy-Tale Road, it is indeed.

This area, mainly in the state of Hesse, was the home region of the brothers Jacob (1785–1863) and Wilhelm (1786–1859) Grimm. They didn't originate the stories for which they are famous. Their feat was to mine the great folklore tradition that was already deeply ingrained in local culture.

For generations eager children had been gathering at dusk around the village storyteller to hear wondrous tales of fairies, witches, and gnomes; tales passed down from storytellers who had gone before. The Grimms sought out these storytellers and recorded their tales.

The result was the two volumes of their work Kinder und Hausmärchen *(Children and Household Tales), published in 1812 and 1814, and revised and expanded six times during their lifetimes. The last edition, published in 1857, is the basis for the stories we know today. Earlier versions contained more violence and cruelty than deemed suitable for children.*

That is how the world got the stories of Cinderella, Sleeping Beauty, Hansel and Gretel, Little Red Riding Hood, Snow White and the Seven Dwarfs, Rumpelstiltskin, Puss-in-Boots, Mother Holle, Rapunzel, and some 200 others, most perhaps unfamiliar.

Both Jacob and Wilhelm Grimm had distinguished careers as librarians and scholars, and probably would be unhappy to know that they are best remembered for the fairy tales. Among other things, they compiled the first dictionary of the German language and an analysis of German grammar.

The brothers were born in Hanau, near Frankfurt, which has a statue memorializing them and a Grimm exhibit at Schloss Phillipsruhe. They spent their childhood in Steinau, 30 km (18 mi) to the north, where their father was magistrate. There are two Grimm museums there, one in their home. On their father's untimely death they moved to their mother's home city of Kassel, which also has an important Grimm museum. They attended the university at Marburg from 1802 to 1805, then worked as librarians in Kassel. It was in the Kassel area that they found the best of their stories. They later worked as librarians and professors in the university town of Göttingen and spent their last years as academics in Berlin.

Where to Stay & Eat

$ **Brathähnchenfarm.** This cheery hotel-restaurant ($$–$$$) is a long, long way from the center of Steinau, uphill all the way. But it's worth it. As your nose will tell you immediately, just about everything on the menu is charcoal-grilled. The name, *Brathähnchenfarm* (Roast Chicken Farm) sets the theme, though other grilled meats are available. *Im Ohl, D–36396 06663/228 06663/1579 www.brathaehnchenfarm.de 14 rooms Restaurant, cable TV, bowling, bar, meeting rooms, some pets allowed; no a/c AE, DC, MC, V Closed mid-Dec.–mid-Feb. Restaurant closed Mon.*

$ **Weisses Ross.** This may be a simple inn, but you can sleep within its gnarled walls in the knowledge that the Grimm brothers dined and imbibed in its tavern almost 200 years ago. (There's a sketch of them doing just that, done by their brother Ludwig Emil, on display at the Brüder-Grimm-Haus.) Rooms facing the street have views of ancient buildings but suffer from traffic noise. *Brüder-Grimm-Str. 48, D–36396 06663/5804 7 rooms, 5 with shower Meeting room; no a/c, no room phones, no room TVs No credit cards BP.*

Fulda

4 *32 km (20 mi) northeast of Steinau an der Strasse, 100 km (62 mi) northeast of Frankfurt.*

The episcopal city of Fulda is well worth a detour off the Fairy-Tale Road. There are two distinct parts to its downtown area. One is a stunning display of baroque architecture, replete with cathedral, Orangerie, and formal garden, that grew up around the palace. The other is the Old Town, where the incredibly narrow and twisty streets are lined with boutiques, bistros, and a medieval tower.

The city's grandest example of baroque design is the immense **Stadtschloss** (City Palace), formerly the residence of the prince bishops. Much of the palace is used as municipal offices, but there are a few public areas. The **Fürstensaal** (Princes' Hall), on the second floor, provides a breathtaking display of baroque decorative artistry, with ceiling paintings by the 18th-century Bavarian artist Melchior Steidl, and fabric-clad walls. The palace also has permanent displays of the faience for which Fulda was once famous, as well as some fine Fulda porcelain.

Also worth seeing is the **Spiegelsaal,** with its many tastefully arranged mirrors. Pause at the windows of the Grünes Zimmer (Green Chamber) to take in the view across the palace park to the **Orangerie,** a large garden with summer-flowering shrubs and plants. If you have time after your palace tour, stroll over for a visit. *Schlossstr. 1 0661/102–1813 €3 Sat.–Thurs. 10–6, Fri. 2–6.*

The **Dom** (cathedral), Fulda's 18th-century cathedral with tall twin spires, stands on the other side of the broad boulevard that borders the palace park. The basilica accommodated the ever-growing number of pilgrims who converged on Fulda to pray at the grave of the martyred St. Boniface, the "Apostle of the Germans." A black alabaster bas-relief depicting his death marks the martyr's grave in the crypt. The **Cathe-**

dral Museum (☎ 0661/87207 €2.10 ⏲ Apr.–Oct., Tues.–Sat. 10–5:30, Sun. 12:30–5:30; Nov.–Mar., Tues.–Sat. 10–12:30 and 1:30–4, Sun. 12:30–4 ⏲ closed Jan. 15–Mar. 1) contains a document bearing St. Boniface's writing, along with several other treasures, including Lucas Cranach the Elder's fine 16th-century painting of Christ and the Adulteress. ✉ *Dompl.* ⏲ *Apr.–Oct., 6–6; Nov.–Mar., 6–5.*

Directly across from the Dom is the two-towered **Michaelskirche** (Church of St. Michael), one of Germany's oldest churches. Built in the 9th century, its Carolingian and Romanesque architecture contrasts strikingly with the neighboring Baroque cathedral. A brochure is available in English for a small fee. ✉ *Michaelsberg. 1* ⏲ *Apr.–Oct., daily 10–6; Nov.–Mar., daily 2–4* ⏲ *Closed Jan.*

The **Vonderau Museum** is housed in a former Jesuit seminary. Its exhibits chart the cultural and natural history of Fulda and eastern Hesse. A popular section of the museum is its **planetarium,** with a variety of shows, including one for children. Since it has only 35 seats, an early reservation is advisable. Shows take place Thursday at 7, Friday at 5 and 8, Saturday at 3 and 8, and Sunday at 10:30 and 3. ✉ *Jesuitenpl. 2* ☎ *0661/928–3510* *Museum €3, planetarium €3.50* ⏲ *Tues.–Sun. 10–6.*

The **Rathaus** (Town Hall) is possibly the finest in this part of the country. The particularly delicate half-timber separates the arcaded first floor from the steep roof and its incongruous but charming battery of small steeples. It can be viewed only from the outside. ✉ *Schlossstr. 1.*

If you need a break from cultural pursuits, head to the **Gokart Bahn** (Go-Cart Track) on the southern outskirts of Fulda. Hop into one of the 5.5 HP Honda machines and navigate the 11 curves of a 1,320-foot-long indoor track. A special "top grip" surface keeps you safely on the piste. It's expensive fun, but where else can you play at being a top Formula One driver? ✉ *Frankfurter Str. 142* ☎ *0661/402–053* *€9.50 per ride* ⏲ *Mon.–Thurs. 3 PM–11 PM, Fri. 3 PM–midnight, Sat. 1 PM–midnight, Sun. 10 AM–11 PM.*

Where to Stay & Eat

$–$$ ✕ **Zum Stiftskämmerer.** This former episcopal treasurer's home is now a charming tavern-restaurant, its menu packed with local fare prepared with imagination. A four-course menu priced around €30 is an excellent value, although à la carte dishes can be ordered for as little as €5. Try the *Schlemmertöpfchen,* a delicious (and very filling) combination of pork, chicken breast, and venison steak. ✉ *Kämmerzeller Str. 10* ☎ *0661/52369* *DC, MC, V* ⏲ *Closed Tues.*

$$$ ✕ **Maritim Hotel am Schlossgarten.** This is the luxurious showpiece of the Maritim chain. The large breakfast room and conference rooms are housed in a stunning 18th-century orangerie overlooking Fulda Palace Park. Guest rooms are in a modern wing with a large central atrium. The historic atmosphere of the grand old building extends to the basement foundations, where you can dine beneath centuries-old vaulted arches in the Dianakeller restaurant ($–$$$). The rooms are large and comfortable; many have balconies with views over the park. ✉ *Paulus-promenade 2, D–36037* ☎ *0661/2820* *0661/282–499* *www.*

maritim.de *111 rooms, 1 suite* *Restaurant, café, cable TV, in-room broadband, indoor pool, sauna, bar, some pets allowed (fee); no a/c* *AE, DC, MC, V* *BP.*

★ $$–$$$$ **Romantik Hotel Goldener Karpfen.** Fulda is famous for its baroque buildings, and this hotel is a short walk from the finest of them. The hotel, too, dates from the baroque era (circa. 1750), though the facade was redone around 1900. Inside it's been renovated to a high standard of comfort. Afternoon coffee in the tapestry-upholstered chairs of the hotel's lounge is one of Fulda's delights, while dining in the elegant restaurant, with linen tablecloths, Persian rugs, and subdued lighting, is another. *Simpliciusbrunnen 1, D–36037* *0661/86800* *0661/868–0100* *www.hotel-goldener-karpfen.com* *50 rooms* *Restaurant, cable TV, in-room broadband, Wi-Fi, sauna, Weinstube, meeting rooms, some pets allowed (fee), no-smoking rooms; no a/c in some rooms* *AE, DC, MC, V* *BP.*

¢–$ **Zum Kronhof.** This homey hotel vies for "funkiest decor" around. There's an array of clashing colors in every room, but it's clean and friendly. You're right behind the Dom, so you won't need an alarm clock. A room is usually available, but call ahead just to be safe. *Am Kronhof 2, D–36037* *0661/74147* *0661/74147* *14 rooms* *Restaurant, cable TV, meeting rooms, free parking, some pets allowed, no-smoking rooms; no a/c, no room phones* *No credit cards* *BP.*

en route

Marburg is the next major stop on the road. Take B–254 to Alsfeld (34 km [21 mi] northwest of Fulda), where you can make a short stop, then take B–62 into Marburg.

Alsfeld is notable for its beautifully preserved half-timber houses on narrow, winding cobbled streets. The numerous cafés and restaurants make this an ideal place to stop for lunch. The jewel of Alsfeld—and one of Germany's showpieces—is the **Altes Rathaus** (Old Town Hall), built in 1512. Its facade—combining a ground floor of stone arcades; half-timber upper reaches; and a dizzyingly steep, top-heavy slate roof punctuated by two pointed towers shaped like witches' hats—would look right at home in Walt Disney World. To get an unobstructed snapshot of this remarkable building (which is closed to the public), avoid the Marktplatz on Tuesday and Friday, when market stalls clutter the square. Information and a self-guided walking tour of the town are available in English at the tourist office, located across from the Altes Rathaus.

Marburg

5 *60 km (35 mi) northwest of Fulda.*

"I think there are more steps in the streets than in the houses." That is how Jacob Grimm described the half-timber hillside town of Marburg. He and his brother Wilhelm studied at the town's famous university from 1802 to 1805.

Marburg rises steeply from the Lahn River to the spectacular castle that crowns the hill. Many of the winding, crooked "streets" are indeed stone staircases; a free elevator near the tourist-information office on Pilgrimstein can transport you from the level of the river to the marketplace. Several of the hillside houses have a back door five stories above the front door.

A great deal of money went into restoring the buildings to their original appearance (half-timbering went out of fashion after the 1600s, and the building facades had been stuccoed over). Much of the old city is closed to automobile traffic, which is just as well, because the cobblestone streets are slippery when wet, especially on a steep hillside. One of the main streets of the old city is named Barfüsserstrasse (Barefoot Street) because it led to a Franciscan monastery, the residents of which were sworn to humility and poverty.

The university and its students are the main influence on the town's social life, which pulses through the many cafés, restaurants, and student hangouts around the marketplace. It is said that the leaning tower of the Pfarrkirche will become straight if ever a female student leaves the university a virgin. Because so many of the streets are traffic-free, the whole area is filled with outdoor tables when the weather cooperates.

Marburg's most important building is the **Elisabethkirche** (St. Elizabeth Church; ✉ Elisabethstr. 3), which marks the burial site of St. Elizabeth (1207–31), the town's favorite daughter. She was a Hungarian princess, betrothed at 4 and married at 12 to a member of the nobility, Ludwig IV of Thuringia. She was widowed in 1228 when her husband fell in one of the Crusades and thereafter gave up all worldly pursuits. She moved to Marburg, founded a hospital, gave her wealth to the poor, and spent the rest of her very short life (she died at the age of 24) in poverty, caring for the sick and the aged. She is largely responsible for what Marburg became. Because of her selflessness she was made a saint only four years after her death. The Teutonic Knights built the Elisabethkirche, which quickly became the goal of pilgrimages, enabling the city to prosper. You can visit the shrine in the sacristy that once contained her bones, a masterpiece of the goldsmith's art. The church is a veritable museum of religious art, full of statues and frescoes.

Where to Stay & Eat

¢ ✕ **Cafe Vetter.** This café has the most spectacular view in town—and Marburg is famous for its panoramas. The outdoor terrace is pleasant in good weather, but there's also a glassed-in terrace and two floors of dining rooms with plush chairs and windows facing the valley. The homemade cakes are hard to resist. The café offers piano music Sunday afternoon and jazz Friday evening. ✉ *Reitg. 4* ☎ *06421/25888* ▭ *No credit cards* ⌚ *No dinner.*

$$ ✕▣ **Sorat Hotel Marburg.** This rather unconventional luxury hotel is at the river level, just across the street from the elevator to the marketplace. The color scheme is orange, apricot, and yellow, contrasted with fiery-red tables and upholstered furniture. Its Tartagua Restaurant ($–$$), with bar, terrace, and beer cellar, has become a hip meeting place for those who can afford it. In addition to the usual rolls, eggs, and sausages, the breakfast buffet includes smoked salmon and champagne. ✉ *Pil-*

grimstein 29, D–35037 ☎ 06421/9180 🖷 06421/918–444 🌐 www.sorat-hotels.com/marburg 143 rooms, 3 suites Restaurant, minibars, cable TV, in-room broadband, Wi-Fi, gym, sauna, bar, meeting room, parking (fee), some pets allowed (fee), no-smoking rooms ▭ AE, DC, MC, V BP.

Kassel

❻ *100 km (62 mi) northeast of Marburg.*

The Brothers Grimm lived in Kassel, their mother's hometown, as teenagers, and also worked there as librarians at the court of the king of Westphalia, Jerome Bonaparte (Napoléon's youngest brother), and for the elector of Kassel. In researching stories and legends, their best source was not books but storyteller Dorothea Viehmann, who was born in the Knallhütte tavern, which is still in business in nearby Baunatal.

Much of Kassel was destroyed in World War II and the city was rebuilt with little regard for its architectural history. The city's museums and the beautiful Schloss Wilhelmshöhe and Schlosspark, however, are well worth a day or two of exploration. When you arrive, you may want to purchase a ServiceCard. This entitles you to a city bus tour, free travel on the local transportation system, and reduced admission to the museums and the casino. It's available at the **tourist office** (✉ Tourist GmbH, Obere Königstr. 15 ☎ 0561/707–707) for €7 per day.

The **Brüder Grimm Museum,** in the center of Kassel, occupies five rooms of the Palais Bellevue, where the brothers once lived and worked. Exhibits include furniture, memorabilia, letters, manuscripts, and editions of their books, as well as paintings, watercolors, etchings, and drawings by Ludwig Emil Grimm, a third brother and a graphic artist of note. *✉ Palais Bellevue, Schöne Aussicht 2 ☎ 0561/770–550 €1.50 ⏲ Daily 10–5.*

The **Deutsches Tapeten Museum** (German Wallpaper Museum), the world's most comprehensive museum of wallpaper, has more than 600 exhibits tracing the art through the centuries. *✉ Brüder-Grimm-Pl. 5 ☎ 0561/3168–0300 🌐 www.museum-kassel.de €3.50 ⏲ Tues.–Sun. 10–5.*

The magnificent grounds of the 18th-century **Schloss und Schlosspark Wilhelmshöhe** (Wilhelmshöhe Palace and Palace Park), at the western edge of Kassel, are said to be Europe's largest hill park. If you have time, plan to spend an entire day here exploring the various gardens, museums, and wooded pathways. Wear good walking shoes and bring some water if you want to hike all the way up to the giant statue of Hercules that crowns the hilltop. Tramline 1 runs from the city to the bottom of the palace grounds. Bus 43 runs from the city to the base of the Hercules statue.

The Wilhelmshöher Park was laid out as a baroque park in the early 18th century, its elegant lawns separating the city from the thick woods of the Habichtswald (Hawk Forest). Schloss Wilhelmshöhe was added between 1786 and 1798. It served as a royal residence from 1807 to 1813, when Jerome was king of Westphalia. Later it became the summer residence of the German emperor Wilhelm II. The great palace stands at the end of the 5-km-long (3-mi-long) Wilhelmshöher Allee, an avenue that runs straight as an arrow from one side of the city to the other.

Kassel's leading art gallery and the state art collection lie within Schloss Wilhelmshöhe as part of the **Staatliche Museen.** Its esteemed collection includes 11 Rembrandts as well as outstanding works by Rubens, Hals, Jordaens, Van Dyck, Dürer, Altdorfer, Cranach, and Baldung Grien. ✉ *Schloss Wilhelmshöhe* ☎ *0561/316–800* 🌐 *www.museum-kassel.de* 🎫 *€3.50, free Fri.* ⏲ *Tues.–Sun. 10–5.*

Amidst the thick trees of the Wilhelmshöher Park, it comes as something of a surprise to see the turrets of a romantic medieval castle, the **Löwenburg** (Lion Fortress), breaking the harmony. There are more surprises, for this is no true medieval castle but a fanciful, stylized copy of a Scottish castle, built 70 years after the Hercules statue that towers above it. The architect was a Kassel ruler who displayed an early touch of the mania later seen in the castle-building excesses of Bavaria's eccentric Ludwig II. The Löwenburg contains a collection of medieval armor and weapons, tapestries, and furniture. ✉ *Schloss Wilhelmshöhe* ☎ *0561/3168–0244* 🎫 *€3.50 including tour* ⏲ *Tues.–Sun. 10–5.*

The giant 18th-century **statue of Hercules** that crowns the Wilhelmshöhe Heights is an astonishing sight. You can climb the stairs of the statue's castlelike base—and the statue itself—for a rewarding look over the entire city. At 2:30 PM on Sunday and Wednesday from mid-May through September, water gushes from a fountain beneath the statue, rushes down a series of cascades to the foot of the hill, and ends its precipitous journey in a 175-foot-high jet of water. An open-air concert follows this *wasserspiel* at 4:30. It takes so long to accumulate enough water that the sight can be experienced only on those two days, on holidays, and on the first Saturday evening of June, July, August, and September. On these evenings the cascade is also floodlighted. A favorite souvenir of Kassel is a Hercules miniature available in everything from bronze to chocolate. A café lies a short walk from the statue. ✉ *Schlosspark 3* ☎ *0561/312–456* 🎫 *€2* ⏲ *Mar.–Oct., Tues.–Sun. 10–5; Nov.–Feb., Tues.–Sun. 10–3.*

Where to Stay & Eat

¢–$$ ✕ **Autobahnraststätte Knallhütte.** This brewery-cum-inn, established in 1752, was the home of village storyteller Dorothea Viehmann. The Grimms got the best of their stories from her, including *Little Red Riding Hood, Hansel and Gretel,* and *Rumpelstiltskin.* The Knallhütte was once a wayside inn on the road to Frankfurt. That road is now the autobahn, making the tavern a superhighway rest stop. You'll find it on autobahn A–49 between the Baunatal Nord and Baunatal Mitte exits. You can dine at the restaurant at any time. With prior notice, you can tour the brewery and sample the beer and food for €12.80. ✉ *Knallhüttestr. 1, D–34255 Baunatal* ☎ *0561/492–076* 💳 *MC, V.*

$$ ✕🏨 **Hotel Gude.** This modern hotel is 10 minutes by public transportation from the city center. Rooms are spacious and come with marble bathrooms. The Pfeffermühle ($–$$$$) is one of the region's finest restaurants, with an inventive international menu that includes German fare. The hotel is ideal for conferences and has its own underground garage. ✉ *Frankfurter Str. 299, D–34134* ☎ *0561/48050* 🖷 *0561/480–5101* 🌐 *www.hotel-gude.de* ↩ *85 rooms* ♁ *Restaurant, in-room safes, minibars, cable TV, in-room data ports, Wi-Fi, indoor pool, gym, massage, sauna, bicycles, bar, meeting room, free parking, some pets allowed, no-smoking rooms; no a/c in some rooms* ▭ *AE, DC, MC, V* 🍽 *BP.*

$–$$ **Mövenpick Hotel Kassel.** Located in the heart of the city, this modern hotel is all about convenience. The rooms may lack charm, but they are large and comfortable and include amenities such as a kettle with teabags and coffee (a rarity in this region). The hotel is attached to a shopping mall, which has a large food court in the lower level. A 32,000-square-foot fitness center and spa opened in the hotel in 2004 and is accessible to hotel guests for €5 per day. Discount room rates are available on weekends. ✉ *In der Kurfürsten Galerie, Spohrstr. 4, 34117* ☎ *0561/72850* 🖷 *0561/728–5118* 🌐 *www.movenpick-kassel.com* ↩ *110 rooms, 18 suites* ♁ *Restaurant, room service, in-room safes, minibars, cable TV, in-room broadband, Wi-Fi, bar, dry cleaning, laundry service, meeting rooms, parking (fee), some pets allowed* ▭ *AE, DC, MC, V.*

$–$$ **Schlosshotel Wilhelmshöhe.** Set in the beautiful baroque Wilhelmshöhe Park, 5 km (3 mi) from town, this is no ancient palace but a contemporary hotel with a sleek gambling casino. Secure a window table in the elegant restaurant for a view of the park grounds. Sports facilities in the immediate vicinity include an 18-hole golf course, tennis courts, pool, and horse stables. The park's palace is a two-minute walk away. ✉ *Am Schlosspark 8, D–34131* ☎ *0561/30880* 🖷 *0561/308–8428* ↩ *96 rooms, 5 suites* ♁ *Restaurant, cable TV, bar, casino, meeting rooms, some pets allowed (fee), no-smoking rooms; no a/c* ▭ *AE, DC, MC, V* 🍽 *BP.*

$ **Hotel Lenz.** All rooms have a bath or shower in this clean and quiet hotel, which is somewhat out of the way. To get here take Tram 5 or 9 to Bahnhof Niederzwehren, and then walk down Frankfurter Strasse. ✉ *Frankfurter Str. 176, D–34134* ☎ *0561/43373* 🖷 *0561/41188* 🌐 *www.hotel-lenz-kassel.de* ↩ *13 rooms* ♁ *Restaurant, cable TV, bar, free parking, some pets allowed; no a/c, no phones in some rooms* ▭ *AE, DC, MC, V* 🍽 *BP.*

Nightlife & the Arts

THE ARTS The Kasseler Musiktage (Kassel Music Days) is held at the end of October and has the motto "New forms of the concert, with music of the classic and the modern." The municipal orchestra gives classical concerts in the **Stadttheater** (✉ Friedrichspl. 15). Kassel has no fewer than 35 theater companies. The principal venues are the Schauspielhaus, the Stadthalle, and the Stadttheater. Call ☎ 0561/109–4222 for program details and tickets for all.

NIGHTLIFE Kassel's pulsating nightlife is concentrated in the bars and discos of Friedrich-Ebert-Strasse. The **casino** (✉ Schlosspark 8 ☎ 0561/930–850) in the Schlosshotel Wilhelmshöhe provides a note of elegance with its gray-blue-silver decor and windows that afford a spectacular view of the city below. It's open daily 3 PM–3 AM. Admission is €1 for roulette, card games, and slot machines.

Shopping

Königstrasse, Kassel's pedestrian-only shopping street, offers numerous department stores, shops, and cafés. The **Königsgalerie** (✉ Obere Königstr. 39), is a chic, glass-roof atrium that's packed with boutiques, restaurants, and bars.

In the village of Immenhausen, just north of Kassel, a local glass museum, **Glasmuseum Immenhausen,** exhibits work by German glassblowers; many of the pieces are for sale. The museum has an extensive collection of modern glass, but its centerpiece is work by the celebrated but now-closed Immenhausen glass foundry, the Glashütte Süssmuth. ✉ *Am Bahnhof 3* ☎ *05673/2060* *€2.50* ⏲ *May–Sept., Tues.–Thurs. 10–5, Fri.–Sun. 1–5; Oct.—Apr., Tues.–Thurs. 10–5, Fri.–Sat. 1–5, and Sun. 1–5.*

11

LOWER SAXONY

Lower Saxony (Niedersachsen), Germany's second-largest state after Bavaria, was formed from an amalgamation of smaller states in 1946. Its landscape is quite diverse, but the focus here is on the Weser River's course from Hannoversch-Münden, in the south, to its end in the North Sea at Bremerhaven. Between Hannoversch-Münden and Hameln is one of Germany's most haunting river roads (B–80 to Bad Karlshafen, B–83 the rest of the way), where the fast-flowing Weser snakes between green banks that hardly show where land ends and water begins. Standing sentinel along the banks are superb little towns, whose half-timber architecture has given rise to the expression "Weser Renaissance."

The states of Lower Saxony and Saxony-Anhalt share the Harz Mountains; (⇨ *see* Saxony-Anhalt *in* Chapter 15 for more coverage of the region).

Hannoversch-Münden

★ ❼ *24 km (15 mi) north of Kassel, 150 km (93 mi) south of Hannover.*

This delightful town, known as Hann. Münden and seemingly untouched by the modern age, shouldn't be missed. You'll have to travel a long way through Germany to find a grouping of half-timber houses (700 of them) as harmonious as these. The town is surrounded by forests and the Fulda and Werra rivers, which join and flow northward as the Weser River.

Much is made of the fact that the quack doctor to end all quacks died here. Dr. Johann Andreas Eisenbart (1663–1727) would be forgotten today if a ribald 19th-century drinking song (*"Ich bin der Doktor Eisenbart, widda, widda, wit, boom! boom!"*) hadn't had him shooting out aching teeth with a pistol, anesthetizing with a sledgehammer, and removing boulders from the kidneys. He was, as the song has it, a man who could make "the blind walk and the lame see." This is terribly exaggerated, of course, but the town takes advantage of it. It stages Eisenbart plays Sunday at 11:15 AM in summer; the doctor has "office hours" in the city hall at 1:30 on Saturday from mid-May through September;

and a glockenspiel on the city hall depicts Eisenbart's feats, to the tune of the 19th-century drinking song, daily throughout the year at noon, 3 PM, and 5 PM. There's a statue of the doctor in front of his home at Langestrasse 79, and his grave is outside the St. Ägidien Church. For information on the Dr. Eisenbart plays, contact the **Touristik Naturpark Münden** (✉ Lotzestr. 2 ☎ 05541/75313 📠 05541/75404 🌐 www.hann.muenden.de).

Göttingen

❽ *30 km (19 mi) northeast of Hannoversch-Münden, 110 km (68 mi) south of Hannover.*

Although Göttingen is not strictly on the Fairy-Tale Road, it's closely associated with the Brothers Grimm because they served as professors and librarians at the city's university from 1830 to 1837. The university dominates life in Göttingen, and most houses more than a century old bear plaques that link them to a famous student or professor.

Among the delights of Göttingen are the **ancient taverns** where generations of students have lifted their steins. Among the best known are the **Kleine Ratskeller** (✉ Judenstr. 30) and **Mutter Jütte** (✉ Heiligstädterstr. 4, in nearby Bremke). Don't be shy about stepping into either of these taverns or any of the others that catch your eye; the food and drink are inexpensive, and the welcome is invariably warm and friendly.

The statue of **Gänseliesel,** the little Goose Girl of German folklore, stands in the central market square, symbolizing the strong link between the students and their university city. The girl, according to the story, was a princess who was forced to trade places with a peasant, and the statue shows her carrying her geese and smiling shyly into the waters of a fountain. Above her pretty head is a charming wrought-iron art-nouveau bower of entwined vines. The students of Göttingen contributed money toward the bronze statue and fountain in 1901 and gave it a ceremonial role: traditionally, graduates who earn a doctorate bestow a kiss of thanks upon Gänseliesel. Göttingen's citizens say she's the most-kissed girl in the world.

Behind the Gänseliesel statue is the **Altes Rathaus** (Old Town Hall), begun in the 13th century but basically a part-medieval, part-Renaissance building. The bronze lion's-head knocker on the main door dates from the early 13th century. Inside, the lobby's striking murals tell the city's story. Beneath the heavily beamed ceiling of the medieval council chamber, the council met, courts sat in judgment, visiting dignitaries were officially received, receptions and festivities were held, and traveling theater groups performed. The Tourist-Information office is located on the first floor. ✉ *Markt. 9* ☎ *0551/499–800* 🎫 *Free* ⏲ *Apr.–Oct., weekdays 9:30–6, weekends 10–4; Nov.–Mar., weekdays 9:30–6, Sat. 10–4.*

In the streets around the Rathaus you'll find magnificent examples of Renaissance architecture. Many of these half-timber, low-gable buildings house businesses that have been here for centuries. The **Ratsapotheke** (pharmacy) across from the Rathaus is one of the town's oldest buildings; medicines have been doled out here since 1322. ✉ *Weenderstr. 30* ☎ *0551/57128.*

The 16th-century **Schrödersches Haus** (Schröder House), a short stroll from the Altes Rathaus up Weenderstrasse, is possibly the most appealing storefront—with an ornate, half-timber front—in all Germany. ✉ *Weenderstr. 62.*

The **Städtisches Museum** (City Museum) is in Göttingen's only noble home, a 16th-century palace. It charts the history of Göttingen and its university with exhibits of church art, glass objects, and Judaica and has a valuable collection of antique toys and a reconstructed apothecary's shop. ✉ *Ritterplan 7–8* ☎ *0551/400–2843* *€1.50* *Tues.–Fri. 10–5, weekends 11–5.*

Just to the east of Göttingen is the **Wilhelm Busch Mühle,** a rustic mill and museum honoring a man who could justifiably be called "the godfather of the comic strip." The mill, with a wheel that still turns, belonged to Busch's uncle, and Busch lived there for five years. The admission price includes a tour of the mill, in English if desired. There is a more extensive Busch Museum in Hannover. ✉ *Mühleng. 8, 37136 Ebergötzen* ☎ *05507/7181* *€3.50* *Mar.–Dec., Tues.–Sat. 9–1 and 2–5, Sun. 10–1 and 2–5.*

Where to Stay & Eat

¢–$ ✕ **Historischer Rathskeller.** Dine in the vaulted underground chambers of Göttingen's Altes Rathaus and choose from a traditional menu. If you're tired of cream sauces (which are abundant on menus in this region), try the *Altdeutscher Bauernschmaus,* which includes a small portion of grilled chicken, pork, and sausage—with no cream sauce—as well as fried potatoes and a side salad. ✉ *Altes Rathaus, Markt 9* ☎ *0551/56433* *AE, DC, MC, V.*

★ ¢–$ ✕ **Zum Schwarzen Bären.** The Black Bear is one of Göttingen's oldest tavern-restaurants, a 16th-century half-timber house that breathes history and hospitality. Its specialties are *Bärenpfanne,* a generous mixture of beef, pork, and lamb (but no bear meat), and its wide selection of fried potato dishes. ✉ *Kurzestr. 12* ☎ *0551/58284* *AE, DC, MC, V* *Closed Mon. No dinner Sun.*

$$–$$$$ **Romantik Hotel Gebhards.** Though just across a busy road from the train station, this family-run hotel stands aloof and unflurried on its own grounds, a modernized 18th-century building that's something of a local landmark. Rooms are furnished in dark woods and floral prints highlighted by bowls of fresh flowers. The suites are particularly spacious, with completely separate bedrooms. ✉ *Goethe-Allee 22–23, D–37073* ☎ *0551/49680* *0551/496–8110* *www.romantikhotels.com/goettingen* *53 rooms, 7 suites* *Restaurant, in-room safes, minibars, cable TV, sauna, meeting rooms, parking (fee), some pets allowed (fee), no-smoking rooms; no a/c* *AE, DC, MC, V* *BP.*

$–$$ **Hotel Stadt Hannover.** The Netke family has run this charming hotel, an 18th-century town house in the historic Altstadt, for four generations. The somewhat spacious rooms are simply decorated in pastel colors with wooden furnishings. The location, two minutes from the train station and just down the street from the pedestrian zone, is ideal. ✉ *Goethe-Allee 21, 37073* ☎ *0551/547–960* 📠 *0551/45470* 🌐 *www.hotelstadthannover.de* 👍 *In-room safe, cable TV, laundry service, Wi-Fi, Internet room, meeting room, parking (fee); no a/c* 💳 *AE, DC, MC, V* 🍽 *BP.*

¢–$ 🏨 **Landgasthaus Lockemann.** If you like to walk and hike, consider this half-timber lodge at the edge of the Stadtwald (city forest). Locals descend on the friendly, country-style restaurant for hearty German cooking. Take Bus 10 from the Busbahnhof, direction Herbershausen, to the last stop then walk left on Im Beeke. The trip will take 20 minutes. ✉ *Im Beeke 1, D–37075* ☎ *0551/209–020* 📠 *0551/209–0250* 🛏 *18 rooms, 8 with bath* 👍 *Restaurant, cable TV, beer garden, some pets allowed; no a/c, no phones in some rooms* 💳 *No credit cards* 🍽 *BP.*

Nightlife & the Arts

Göttingen's symphony orchestra presents about 20 concerts a year. In addition, the city has a nationally known boys' choir and an annual Handel music festival in May and June. Call the tourist office for program details and tickets for all three.

Göttingen's elegant **Deutsches Theater** (✉ Theaterpl. 11 ☎ 0551/496–911), built in 1890, is known throughout Germany. It has four performing areas, including the large Grösse Bühne, with its two tiers of horseshoe-shape balconies, where much experimental theater is performed, and the intimate Keller, with its cabaretlike performances.

en route To pick up the Fairy-Tale Road where it joins the scenic Weser Valley Road, return to Hannoversch-Münden and head north on B–80. In the village of Veckerhagen take a left turn to the signposted Sababurg.

Sababurg

★ 9 *60 km (36 mi) west of Göttingen, 100 km (62 mi) south of Hannover.*

Sababurg is home to the **Dornröschenschloss** (Sleeping Beauty's Castle). It stands just as the Grimm fairy tale tells us it did, in the depths of the densely wooded Reinhardswald, still inhabited by deer and wild boar. Today it's a fairly fancy hotel. Even if you don't stay the night, a drive to the castle is scenic. There's a nominal fee to tour the grounds, which include a rose garden and ruins.

The **Tierpark Sababurg** is one of Europe's oldest wildlife refuges. Bison, red deer, wild horses, and all sorts of waterfowl populate the park. There's also a petting zoo for children. ✉ *Kasinoweg 22* ☎ *05671/8001–2251* 🎟 *Apr.–Nov. €4, Dec.–Mar. €3.50* 🕐 *Apr.–Sept., daily 8–7; Oct., daily 9–6; Nov.–Feb., daily 10–4; Mar., daily 9–5.*

Where to Stay & Eat

★ $$–$$$ ✕🏨 **Dornröschenschloss Sababurg.** The medieval fortress thought to have inspired *The Sleeping Beauty* is now a small luxury hotel, surrounded by a forest of oaks, a bit to the northeast of Hofgeismar. It's a popular place for weddings, and on request, a "prince" and "princess" will present a version of the Sleeping Beauty story. The restaurant ($$–$$$)

serves fine venison in the autumn, and fresh trout with a Riesling-based sauce in the spring. ✉ *Im Reinhardswald, D–34369 Hofgeismar* ☎ *05671/8080* 📠 *05671/808–200* 🌐 *www.sababurg.de/dornroeschenschloss* *18 rooms* *Restaurant, bicycles, meeting rooms, some pets allowed (fee); no a/c* 💳 *AE, DC, MC, V* *BP.*

en route

A short distance away is another hilltop castle hotel, **Trendelburg.** It's near the town of the same name on Route 83 between Hofgeismar and Bad Karlshafen. Legend has it that its tower is the one in which a wicked witch imprisoned Rapunzel. Since it had neither a door nor stairs, the witch, and eventually a handsome prince, could get to Rapunzel only by climbing her long, golden tresses. From Trendelburg follow Route 83 north to Bad Karlshafen.

11

Bad Karlshafen

10 *42 km (26 mi) north of Hannoversch-Münden, 55 km (34 mi) northwest of Göttingen, 125 km (77 mi) south of Hannover.*

From the inland harbor of the pretty little spa of Bad Karlshafen, German troops of the state of Waldeck embarked to join the English forces in the American War of Independence. Flat barges took the troops down the Weser to Bremen, where they were shipped across the North Sea for the long voyage west. Many American families can trace their heritage to this small spa and the surrounding countryside.

Viewed from one of the benches overlooking the harbor, there's scarcely a building that's not in the imposing baroque style—grand and starkly white. The **Rathaus** (✉ Hafenpl. 8) behind you is the best example. Bad Karlshafen stands in surprising contrast to the abundance of half-timber architecture of other riverside towns.

Where to Stay & Eat

$$ **Hotel Menzhausen.** The half-timber exterior of this 16th-century establishment in the small town of Uslar, 12 km (7 mi) east of the Weser River, is complemented by the elegant interior of its restaurant ($–$$), which serves traditional German fare. Ask for a guest room in the Mauerschlösschen, a luxurious extension that incorporates traditional Weser Renaissance design, such as half-timber and carved beams. ✉ *Langestr. 12, D–37170 Uslar* ☎ *05571/92230* 📠 *05571/922–330* *40 rooms* *Restaurant, cable TV, indoor pool, sauna, meeting room, some pets allowed (fee); no a/c* 💳 *V* *BP.*

$ **Gaststätte-Hotel Weserdampfschiff.** You can step right from the deck of a Weser pleasure boat into the welcoming garden of this popular hotel-tavern. Fish from the river go straight into the tavern's frying pan. The rooms are snug; ask for one with a river view. The restaurant (¢–$$$) is closed Monday. ✉ *Weserstr. 25, D–34385* ☎ *05672/2425* 📠 *05672/8119* *14 rooms* *Restaurant, some pets allowed (fee); no a/c* 💳 *No credit cards* *BP.*

$ **Hessischer Hof.** In the heart of town, this inn started as a tavern for the locals and now includes several comfortably furnished bedrooms, plus an apartment suitable for larger families and the numerous cycling groups that visit. The restaurant ($–$$) serves good, hearty German fare. Breakfast is included in the room price, or you may request half-pension. ✉ *Carlstr. 13–15, D–34385* ☎ *05672/1059* 📠 *05672/2515* 🌐 *www.hess-hof.de* *17 rooms* *Restaurant, in-room safes, cable TV, bar, meeting rooms, some pets allowed; no a/c* 💳 *AE, DC, MC, V.*

en route

Germany's oldest **porcelain factory** is at Fürstenberg, 8 km (5 mi) south of Höxter, in a baroque castle high above the Weser River. The crowned Gothic letter *F*, which serves as its trademark, is world famous. You'll find Fürstenberg porcelain in Bad Karlshafen and Höxter, but it's more fun to journey to the 18th-century castle, where production first began in 1747, and buy directly from the manufacturer. Fürstenberg and most dealers will take care of shipping arrangements and any tax refunds. Tours of the factory in English are possible with advance notice. There's also a sales outlet, museum, and café. ✉ *Schloss Fürstenberg* ☎ *05271/401–161* *Museum €3.50* *Museum Apr.–Oct., Tues.–Sun. 10–5; Nov.–Mar., weekends 10–5. Shop Apr.–Oct., Tues.–Sun. 10–6; Nov.–Mar., Tues.–Sat. 10–6.*

Höxter

11 *24 km (14 mi) north of Bad Karlshafen, 100 km (62 mi) south of Hannover.*

Stop at Höxter to admire its **Rathaus,** a perfect example of the Weser Renaissance style, combining three half-timber stories with a romantically crooked tower. Though it has no better claim than any other town to the story of Hansel and Gretel, Höxter presents a free performance of the story on the first Saturday of each month, from May to September.

The **Reichsabtei Corvey** (Imperial Abbey of Corvey), or Schloss Corvey, is idyllically set between the wooded heights of the Solling region and the Weser River. During its 1,200-year history it has provided lodging for several Holy Roman emperors. Heinrich Hoffmann von Fallersleben (1798–1874), author of the poem "Deutschland, Deutschland über Alles," worked as librarian here in the 1820s. The poem, set to music by Joseph Haydn, became the German national anthem in 1922. A music festival is held in the church and great hall, the Kaisersaal, in May and June. Corvey, also the name of the village, is reached on an unnumbered road heading east from Höxter (3 km [2 mi]) toward the Weser. There are signposts to "Schloss Corvey." ☎ *05271/694–010* *€4.20, abbey church €0.60* *Apr.–Oct., daily 9–6.*

off the beaten path

EINBECK – Bock beer originated in this storybook town 20 km (12 mi) east of Höxter. The good burghers started brewing beer in their houses in 1341; the name *Bockbier* is a corruption of the original Einbecker Bier. The town tourist office (✉ Altes Rathaus, Marktpl. 6, D–37574 Einbeck ☎ 05561/916–121 📠 05561/916–300) will, with advance notice, organize a visit that includes beer tastings, the awarding of a "beer diploma," and a tour of a brewery that still makes the strong stuff.

Where to Stay & Eat

★ ¢–$$ **Schlossrestaurant Corvey.** In summer you can dine under centuries-old trees at the Reichsabtei Corvey's excellent restaurant. With advance notice, a *Fürstenbankett,* or princely banquet, can be arranged for groups in the vaulted cellars. *Reichsabtei Corvey 05271/8323 MC, V Closed Jan.–Mar. No dinner Apr.–Oct. No lunch Nov. and Dec.*

$–$$ **Niedersachsen Ringhotel.** Behind the three-story half-timber facade of this fine old Höxter house is a hotel with modern comfort and amenities, a member of the respected Ring group. Rooms are spacious, and equipped with everything you'd expect in a luxury hotel, including voice mail and turn-down service. The restaurant ($–$$) has a garden terrace and features fresh river fish. *Grubestr. 3–7, D–37671 05271/6880 05271/688–444 www.hotelniedersachsen.de 80 rooms 2 restaurants, cable TV with movies, indoor pool, sauna, bar, some pets allowed (fee); no a/c AE, DC, MC, V BP.*

Sports & the Outdoors

Busch Freizeitservice (Postweg Nord 7 05271/921–363) organizes canoe trips on the Fulda, Weser, and Werra rivers, as well as bicycle tours in the surrounding countryside.

Bodenwerder

12 *34 km (21 mi) north of Höxter, 70 km (43 mi) south of Hannover.*

The charming Weser town of Bodenwerder plays a central role in German popular literature. It's the home of the Lügenbaron (Lying Baron) von Münchhausen (1720–97), who was known as a teller of whoppers. His reputation was not without foundation, but it was mainly created by a book based in part on the baron's stories and published anonymously by an acquaintance. According to one tale, the baron rode a cannonball toward an enemy fortress but then, having second thoughts, returned to where he started by leaping onto a cannonball heading the other way.

The **Münchhausen-Erinnerungszimmer** (Münchhausen Memorial Room), in the imposing family home in which Baron von Münchhausen grew up (now the Rathaus), is crammed with mementos of his adventurous life, including his cannonball. A fountain in front of the house represents another story. The baron, it seems, was puzzled when his horse kept drinking insatiably at a trough. Investigating, he discovered that the horse had been cut in two by a closing castle gate and that the water ran out as fast as the horse drank. The water in the fountain, of course, flows from the rear of a half-horse. Other statues in the town show the other half of the horse and the baron mounted on his cannonball. On the first Sunday of the month from May through October, townspeople retell von Münchhausen's life story with performances in front of the Rathaus. *Münchhausenpl. 1 05533/409–147 Museum €2 Apr.–Oct., daily 10–noon and 2–5.*

Where to Stay & Eat

$ **Hotel Goldener Anker.** The Weser boats tie up outside this half-timber tavern and hotel, and the sleepy river flows right past your bedroom window. The restaurant ($–$$) prepares hearty German fare and sometimes fresh Weser fish; in summer a beer garden right on the river beckons. ✉ *Brückenstr. 5, D–37619* ☎ *05533/400–730* 📠 *05533/400–733* 🌐 *www.goldeneranker.com* *11 rooms* *Restaurant, cable TV, bicycles, meeting room, some pets allowed, no-smoking rooms; no a/c* 💳 *MC, V* *BP.*

$ **Parkhotel Deutsches Haus.** The fine half-timber facade of this comfortable country hotel vies for attention with the nearby home of Baron von Münchhausen, now Bodenwerder's town hall. Original wood beams and oak paneling add to the rural feel inside. The hotel's own extensive grounds adjoin the own park, and the Weser River is a short walk away. The restaurant's terrace ($) adjoins the Münchhausen house. A specialty is Münchhausen *Kugeln* (Cannonballs), a dish with turkey, pork, vegetables, and croquettes. ✉ *Münchhausenpl. 4, D–37619* ☎ *05533/3925* 📠 *05533/4113* 🌐 *www.hotel-deutsches-haus-bodenwerder.de* *42 rooms* *2 restaurants, cable TV, in-room broadband, Wi-Fi, bowling, beer garden, some pets allowed (fee), no-smoking rooms; no a/c* 💳 *AE, MC, V* *BP.*

Hameln

★ 13 *24 km (15 mi) north of Bodenwerder, 47 km (29 mi) southwest of Hannover.*

Hameln (or Hamelin, in English) is home to the story of the gaudily attired Pied Piper, who rid the town of rats by playing seductive melodies on his flute. The rodents followed him willingly, waltzing their way right into the Weser. When the town defaulted on its contract and refused to pay the piper, he settled the score by playing his merry tune to lead Hameln's children on the same route. As the children reached the river, the Grimms wrote, "they disappeared forever." The tale is included in the Grimms' book *German Legends*. The origin of the story is lost in the mists of time, but the best guess is that it is associated with the forced resettlement of young people to the sparsely populated eastern territories. Also, during the 13th century, an inordinate number of Hameln's young men were conscripted to fight in an unpopular war in Bohemia and Moravia.

The Pied Piper tale is immortalized in an ultramodern sculpture set above a reflecting pool in the town's pedestrian zone. And there are rat-shape pastries in the windows of Hameln's bakeries. On central Osterstrasse you'll see several beautiful half-timber houses, including the Rattenfängerhaus (Rat-Catcher's House) and the **Hochzeitshaus** (Wedding House), a 17th-century Weser Renaissance building now containing city offices. Between mid-May and mid-September the Hochzeithaus terrace is the scene of two free open-air events commemorating the legend. Local actors and children present a half-hour reenactment each Sunday at noon, and there is now also a 40-minute musical, *Rats,* each Wednesday at 4:30. Get there early to ensure a good seat. The carillon of the Hochzeitshaus plays tunes every day at 9:35 and 11:35, and mechanical figures enact the piper story on the west gable of the building at 1:05, 3:35, and 5:35.

In 2005, Hameln and several nearby communities introduced the "Renaissance Live" program. It's similar to the audio guides often available for rent at museums, only here you rent a small computer which hangs around your neck. The computer senses what you're looking at and tells you all about it. Historical pictures are displayed on a small TV screen, and stereo earphones allow you to listen to a description in your language, with appropriate music—and perhaps the shout of a Renaissance tradesman—in the background. Ask at the **Hameln tourist office** (✉ Deisterallee 1, D–31785 ☎ 05151/202–617 🌐 www.hameln.de) for more information.

11

Where to Stay & Eat

★ ¢–$$ ✕ **Rattenfängerhaus.** This brilliant example of Weser Renaissance architecture is Hameln's most famous building, reputedly where the Pied Piper stayed during his rat-extermination assignment (actually, it wasn't built until centuries after his supposed exploits). A plaque in front of it fixes the date of the incident at June 26, 1284. Rats are all over the menu, from the "rat-killer cocktail" to a "rat-tail flambé." But don't be put off: the traditional dishes are excellent, and the restaurant is guaranteed rodent free. ✉ *Osterstr. 28* ☎ *05151/3888* 💳 *AE, DC, MC, V.*

$ 🏨 **Hotel zur Börse.** This upscale hotel is in the pedestrian zone in the heart of the old city. It offers comfortable accommodations and friendly service, and its Börsenbistro serves Mediterranean food. ✉ *Osterstr. 41a, entrance on Kopmanshof, D–31785* ☎ *05151/7080* 📠 *05151/25485* 🛏 *31 rooms* 👍 *Restaurant, minibars, cable TV with movies, bar, meeting rooms, some pets allowed (fee); no a/c* 💳 *AE, DC, MC, V* 🍽 *BP.*

★ $ 🏨 **Hotel zur Krone.** If you fancy a splurge, ask for one of the hotel's elegant suites, with prices starting at €128 a night. It's an expensive but delightful comfort. The building dates from 1645 and is a half-timber marvel. Avoid the modern annex, however; it lacks all charm. ✉ *Osterstr. 30, D–31785* ☎ *05151/9070* 📠 *05151/907–217* 🌐 *www.hotelzurkrone.de* 🛏 *27 rooms, 5 suites* 👍 *Restaurant, minibars, cable TV, meeting rooms, some pets allowed (fee), no-smoking rooms; no a/c* 💳 *AE, MC, V* 🍽 *BP.*

$ 🏨 **Pension Ragazzi.** Don't be fooled by the inappropriate Italian name. This very reasonable little hostelry, with simple but modern rooms, is pure Fairy-Tale Road, situated in the pedestrian zone in the old part of town. There used to be a pizzeria on the ground floor, but it's now a café. A continental breakfast is included in the rate. ✉ *Fischpfortenstr. 25, D–31785* ☎ *05151/21513* 📠 *05151/923–667* 🛏 *8 rooms* 👍 *Café, cable TV, some pets allowed; no a/c* 💳 *No credit cards* 🍽 *BP.*

Hannover

47 km (29 mi) northeast of Hameln.

Hannover is somewhat off the Fairy-Tale Road, yet its culture and commerce influence the quieter surrounding towns. As a trade-fair center, Hannover competes with such cities as Munich and Leipzig. It's also an exemplary arts center, with leading museums, an opera house of international repute, and the finest baroque park in the country. Its patronage of the arts is evident in unexpected places. For example, in an international competition, architects and designers created nine unique bus stops for the city.

A Hannover Card entitles you to free travel on local transportation, reduced admission to five museums, and discounts on certain sightseeing events and performances. It's available through the **tourist office** (✉ Hannover Tourismus Service, Ernst-August-Pl. 2, D–30159 ☎ 0511/1684–9700 🌐 www.hannover.de), for €8 per day (€12 for three days).

The major sights of Hannover are strung together on an easy-to-follow tourist trail known as the "Red Thread." The trail begins at the tourism office next to the main train station. Just follow the red line (that is literally painted on the sidewalks and streets) to 35 points of interest. A map and information booklet explaining the various sites is available at the tourism office for a nominal fee. The route takes about two hours and follows a loop that brings you back to where you started.

What to See

19 **Altes Rathaus.** It took nearly 100 years, starting in 1410, to build this gabled-brick edifice, which once contained a merchants hall and an apothecary. In 1844 it was restored to the style of about 1500. The facade's fired-clay frieze depicts coats of arms and representations of princes, and a medieval game somewhat comparable to arm wrestling. Inside is a modern interior with boutiques and a restaurant. ✉ *Köbelingerstr. 2.*

Herrenhausen. The gardens of the former Hannoverian royal summer residence are the city's showpiece (the 17th-century palace was never rebuilt after wartime bombing). The baroque park is unmatched in Germany for its formal precision, with patterned walks, gardens, hedges, and chestnut trees framed by a placid moat. There is a "fig garden" with a collapsible shelter to protect it in the winter and a gastronomy pavilion behind a grotto. From Easter until October, fountains play for a few hours daily (weekdays 11–noon and 3–5, weekends 11–noon and 2–5). Herrenhausen is outside the city, a short ride on Tramline 4 or 5. ✉ *Herrenhauserstr.* ☎ *0511/1684–7576* 🎫 *€4* ⏲ *Mar. and Oct., daily 9–6; Apr. and Sept., daily 9–7; May–Aug., daily 9–8; Nov.–Jan., daily 9–4:30; Feb., daily 9–5:30.*

18 **Leineschloss.** The former Hannoverian royal palace stands above the River Leine and is now the seat of the Lower Saxony State Parliament. From 1714 until 1837, rulers of the house of Hannover sat on the British throne as Kings George I–IV. The first of them, George I, spoke no English. George III presided over the loss of the American colonies in the Revolutionary War but sent no Hannoverian troops to help fight, even though he hired troops from other German states for this purpose. The period of joint rule came to an end when Queen Victoria ascended the throne (Hannover didn't allow female monarchs). Tours are conducted weekdays. Brochures in English are available. ✉ *Hinrich-Wilhelm-Kopf-Pl. 1* ☎ *0511/3030–2042* 🎫 *Free* ⏲ *Tours Mon.–Thurs. at 10:30 and 1:30, Fri. at 10:30.*

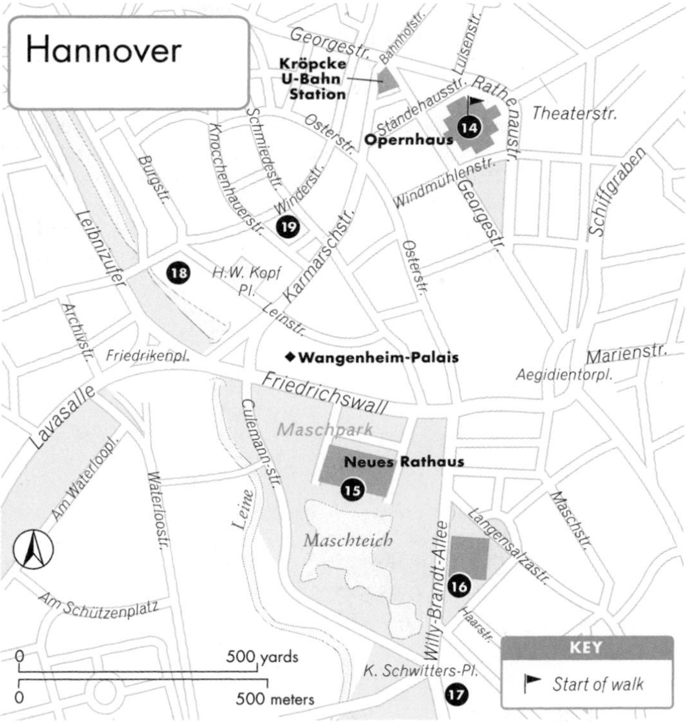

15 Neues Rathaus. The new town hall was built at the start of the 20th century in Wilhelmine style (for Kaiser Wilhelm), at a time when pomp and circumstance were important ingredients of heavy German bureaucracy. Four scale models on the ground floor depict Hannover in various stages of development and destruction: as a medieval walled city, in the years before World War II, immediately following World War II, and in its present-day form. An elevator rises diagonally to the dome for a splendid view. ✉ *Trammpl. 2* ☎ *0511/1684–5333* 🎫 *Dome €2.50* ⏲ *Mar.–Oct., daily 9:30–6:30.*

16 Niedersächsisches Landesmuseum (Lower Saxony State Museum). The priceless art collection of this prestigious museum includes works by Tilman Riemenschneider, Veit Stoss, Hans Holbein the Younger, and Lucas Cranach. There are also historical and natural history sections. ✉ *Willy-Brandt-Allee 5* ☎ *0511/98075* 🌐 *www.nlmh.de* 🎫 *€4* ⏲ *Tues., Wed., and Fri.–Sun. 10–5, Thurs. 10–7.*

14 Opernhaus. Hannover's late classical opera house, completed in 1852, has two large wings and a covered, colonnaded portico adorned with statues of great composers and poets. This enabled the finely attired operagoers to disembark from their coaches with dry feet, a function now taken over by an underground garage. The building originally served as the court theater but now is used almost exclusively for opera. It was gutted by fire in a 1943 air raid and restored in 1948. Unless you have tickets to a performance, the only part of the interior you can visit is the foyer with ticket windows. ✉ *Opernpl. 1* ☎ *0511/9999–1298.*

⓱ **Sprengel Museum.** An important museum of modern art, the Sprengel holds major works by Max Beckmann, Max Ernst, Paul Klee, Emil Nolde, and Pablo Picasso. The street where it's located is named after Kurt Schwitters, a native son and prominent dadaist, whose works are also exhibited. ✉ *Kurt-Schwitters-Pl. 1* ☎ *0511/1684–3875* 🌐 *www.sprengel-museum.de* €7 ⏲ *Tues. 10–8, Wed.–Sun. 10–6.*

off the beaten path

WILHELM BUSCH MUSEUM – This section of the Georgenpalais, near Herrenhausen, is devoted to the works of cartoonists and caricaturists through the centuries. Emphasis is on Wilhelm Busch, the "godfather of the comic strip," whose original drawings and effects are on display. More than a century ago, Busch (1832–1908) wrote and illustrated a very popular children's book, still in print, called *Max und Moritz.* The story tells of two boys who mixed gunpowder in the village tailor's pipe tobacco and, with fishing lines down the chimney, filched roasting chickens off the fire. The first American comic strip, *The Katzenjammer Kids* (1897), drew not only on Busch's naughty boys (they even spoke with a German accent) but also on his loose cartoon style. ✉ *Georgengarten 1* ☎ *0511/1699–9911* 🌐 *www.wilhelm-busch-museum.de* €4.50 ⏲ *Tues.–Fri. 11–5, weekends 11–6.*

Where to Stay & Eat

$–$$ ✕ **Basil.** Constructed in 1867 as a riding hall for the Royal Prussian military, this hip restaurant's home is as striking as the menu. Cast-iron pillars support the vaulted brick ceiling, and two-story drapes hang in the huge windows. The menu changes every three weeks and includes eclectic dishes from the Mediterranean to Asia. Game and white *Spargel* (asparagus) are served in season. ✉ *Dragonerstr. 30* ☎ *0511/622–636* 💳 *AE, MC, V* ⏲ *Closed Sun.*

¢–$$ ✕ **Brauhaus Ernst August.** This brewery has so much artificial greenery that you could imagine yourself in a beer garden. Hannoverian pilsner is brewed on the premises, and regional specialties are the menu's focus. There's a souvenir shop where, besides beer paraphernalia such as mugs and coasters, you can purchase, empty or full, a huge old-fashioned beer bottle with a wired porcelain stopper. The pub's own potent schnapps is also sold in a miniature version of this bottle. There's live music at least five evenings a week. ✉ *Schmiedstr. 13* ☎ *0511/365–950* 💳 *AE, MC, V.*

¢–$ ✕ **Grapenkieker.** An ancient pot steams in the aromatic, farmhouse-style kitchen, and simple, hearty fare prevails. Proprietors Gabriele and Karl-Heinz Wolf are locally famous for their culinary prowess and the warm welcome they give their guests. The half-timber restaurant is 5 km (3 mi) from the city center, in the Isernhagen District, but it's well worth seeking out. ✉ *Hauptstr. 56, Isernhagen* ☎ *05139/88068* 💳 *AE, DC, MC, V* ⏲ *Closed Sun. and Mon.*

$$ ✕▣ **Kastens Hotel Luisenhof.** This very traditional hotel, both in appearance and service, is a few steps from the main train station. Antiques are everywhere: tapestries on the lobby walls, oil paintings in the foyer, copper engravings in the bar, and an elegant wardrobe on every floor. In-room facilities don't include pay-per-view movies, as most mass-market films wouldn't appeal to the taste of the clientele here. The restaurant ($$$–$$$$) is international with French touches. ✉ *Luisenstr.1–3, D–30159* ☎ *0511/30440* 🖷 *0511/304–4807* 🌐 *www.kastens-luisenhof.de* *124 rooms, 7 suites* *Restaurant, in-room safes, minibars, cable TV, in-room broadband, Wi-Fi, bar, meeting rooms, some pets allowed (fee), no-smoking rooms; no a/c in some rooms* 💳 *AE, DC, MC, V* *BP.*

$$ ▣ **Hotel Körner.** The modern Körner has an old-fashioned feel, probably created by the friendly and personal service. Rooms are comfortably furnished in light veneers and pastel shades. The small courtyard terrace has a fountain; breakfast is served here in summer. ✉ *Körnerstr. 24–25, D–30159* ☎ *0511/16360* 🖷 *0511/18048* 🌐 *www.hotelkoerner.de* *77 rooms* *Minibars, cable TV, in-room broadband, Wi-Fi, indoor pool, gym; no a/c* 💳 *AE, DC, MC, V* *BP.*

Nightlife & the Arts

Hannover's nightlife is centered on the Bahnhof and the Steintor red-light district. The **opera company** of Hannover is internationally known, with productions staged in one of Germany's finest 19th-century classical opera houses. Call 0511/9999–1298 for program details and tickets. Hannover's elegant **casino** (✉ Osterstr. 40 ☎ 0511/980–660) is open from 3 PM to 3 AM.

Shopping

Hannover is one of northern Germany's most fashionable cities, and its central pedestrian zone has international shops and boutiques, as well as the very best of German-made articles, from stylish clothes to handmade jewelry. In the glassed-over **Galerie Luise** (✉ Luisenstr. 5) you can spend a couple of hours browsing, with a leisurely lunch or afternoon tea at one of the several restaurants and cafés.

Hannover has what it claims is Germany's oldest **Flohmarkt** (flea market; ✉ Am Hohen Ufer)—it's certainly one of the largest and most interesting. It's held every Saturday on the bank of the River Leine from 7 to 4.

en route

The Fairy-Tale Road continues north of Hannover as far as Bremen, though any connection to the Grimm brothers is faint here. You can reach Bremen in less than an hour by taking autobahn A–7 to the Walsrode interchange and then continuing on autobahn A–27. An alternative is to return to Hameln and follow the Weser as it breaks free of the Wesergebirge uplands at Porta Westfalica. The meandering route runs through the German plains to the sea and Bremen. Another alternative is a quick side trip to the northeast, to Celle and the Lüneburg Heath.

Celle

20 *60 km (35 mi) northeast of Hannover.*

The main street of Celle's Old Town is quite different from the narrow, twisting streets you'd expect to find in a half-timber town. The **Stechbahn** is very broad and was once used for jousting tournaments. A horseshoe sunk in the pavement in front of the Löwenapotheke supposedly marks where the man who established Celle's present location, Duke Otto the Severe, died in such a tournament.

This charming city, with more than 500 half-timber buildings, is also the southern gateway to the **Lüneburg Heath**, one of Germany's most pleasant pastoral areas. It's a landscape of bizarrely shaped juniper bushes, heather that flowers in pinkish purple in the late summer, and grazing flocks of the heath's own breed of sheep, the cuddly Heidschnucken.

Thanks to a bend in the Aller River and a small tributary, Celle was protected on three sides by streams. To guard the fourth side from invasion by robber barons, Duke Otto built a fortified castle. This became the city's present palace, set in a lush park with the oldest baroque theater in Germany still used for performances. The castle chapel is an important example of north German Renaissance. The town hall (Rathaus) also traces its origins back to Duke Otto's time. It was extended and elaborately decorated in the 14th and 16th centuries.

The **Bomann Museum**, which concentrates on the local history and culture, is a must for anyone charmed by old furnishings. Its aim is to depict the folk culture of the area along with the history of Celle and of the Kingdom of Hannover. You can see a completely furnished reconstruction of a farmhouse and numerous reconstructed interiors, including a wagon maker's shop and a smithy. ✉ *Schlosspl. 7* ☎ *05141/12372* 🌐 *www.bomann-museum.de* 🎟 *€3* ⏲ *Tues.–Sun. 10–5.*

Where to Stay & Eat

$$$$ Fodor'sChoice ★ ✕ **Endtenfang.** Chef Hans Sobotka, a master of French cuisine, has turned this elegant restaurant, part of the Hotel Fürstenhof, into one of the culinary magnets of northern Germany. In his popular dish *le canard du duc,* the duck breast is served with a pepper sauce and potatoes au gratin, and the legs, after a sorbet to clear the palate, with a port-wine sauce and mushrooms. The menu otherwise leans toward seafood, and there's an imaginative dessert menu that sometimes includes crepes flambée and cheese from the cart. ✉ *Hannoverische Str. 55* ☎ *05141/201–177* ▭ *AE, DC, MC, V* ⏲ *Closed Sun. and Mon.*

¢–$$ ✕ **Ratskeller Celle.** This subterranean establishment with a vaulted stone ceiling lays claim to being the oldest restaurant in Lower Saxony. If you can stand slow service, it's a good place to try the regional specialties, notably dishes from the Heidschnucken lamb. Boar is also a regional specialty, as are seasonal tender white asparagus and chanterelle mushrooms, served with an endless variety of accompaniments. ✉ *Markt 14* ☎ *05141/29099* ▭ *AE, MC, V.*

$$$ ✕ **Hotel Fürstenhof.** This baroque hunting château, surrounded by huge chestnut trees in the center of town, proudly displays its patrician past. The grand salon, with its groupings of overstuffed chairs, has a mirror ceiling supported by Grecian columns; the oak-panel library has a fireplace; and conferences can be held in an ornate room hung with tapestries. Its restaurant, the Endtenfang ($$$$), is famous throughout the region. Try to book one of the four rooms with antique furnishings in the original lodge. The other rooms are in a modern wing with less character. ✉ *Hannoverische Str. 55, D–29221* ☎ *05141/201–140* 📠 *05141/201–120* 🌐 *www.fuerstenhof.de* *73 rooms* *3 restaurants, minibars, cable TV, in-room broadband, Wi-Fi, indoor pool, gym, sauna, bar, meeting rooms, some pets allowed (fee); no a/c* 💳 *AE, DC, MC, V* 🍽 *BP.*

$ **Best Western Celler Hof.** This moderately priced hotel is right in the heart of the half-timber old city, just steps from the Rathaus, palace, and Bomann Museum. Guests are welcome to use the indoor pool and solarium at the nearby Fürstenhof. ✉ *Stechbahn 11, D–29221* ☎ *05141/911–960* 📠 *05141/911–9644* 🌐 *www.cellerhof.bestwestern.de* *47 rooms* *Minibars, cable TV, in-room broadband, bar, some pets allowed (fee); no a/c* 💳 *AE, DC, MC, V* 🍽 *BP.*

Bergen-Belsen

㉑ *25 km (15 mi) north of Celle.*

Just outside Celle is a sobering contrast to the charm of half-timber and heather. At the site of the infamous concentration camp on the Lüneburg Heath, the **Gedenkstätte Bergen-Belsen** (Bergen-Belsen Memorial) pays tribute to the victims of the Holocaust. Diarist Anne Frank was among the more than 80,000 persons who died here.

Only the gruesome photographs on display will tell what the camp looked like. There's nothing left of it. The British liberators found thousands and thousands of unburied corpses all over the camp, so as a precaution against disease, all structures were burned to the ground. Volunteer youth groups have unearthed the foundations of the barracks.

Those who venture onto the site of the camp may be surprised at its pleasant, parklike appearance. Reminders of the horrors that once happened here include numerous burial mounds, mostly overgrown with heather and with stones with such inscriptions as HERE LIE 1,000 DEAD. Anne Frank probably lies in one of them. The SS officers had hoped to have the dead buried and out of sight before the British forces arrived, but the starving prisoners were too weak for the job. Under the direction of the British, the graves you see were dug and filled by the SS officers themselves. The British tried and executed the camp's SS commandant, Josef Kramer, the "Beast of Belsen."

Monuments and shrines include a Jewish memorial dating to 1946, with a commemorative stone dedicated by the Israeli president in 1987; an obelisk and memorial wall erected by the British; a wooden cross dating to only weeks after the liberation; and a commemorative stone from the German government. The main feature of the memorial is a permanent exhibition on the history of the camp and the Nazi persecution system. Though all signs are in German, there are supplementary guides (€2.50) in English and eight other languages. There are also regular showings of a movie on the camp in English, German, and French. Children under 12 are not admitted to the showings, and it's said that one of the British photographers who made the footage couldn't bear to look at his work in later years. ✉ *Just off the unnumbered hwy. connecting Bergen and Winsen* ☎ *05051/6011* 🌐 *www.bergenbelsen.de* 🎫 *Free* ⏲ *Daily 9–6.*

Where to Stay

$ **Hof Averbeck.** This typical heath farm doubling as a bed-and-breakfast proves the Lüneburg Heath is an ideal place for a farm vacation. Well off the main highway, it's great for children, with ponies to ride, animals to feed, and a playground. The farm, which is close to the Bergen-Belsen Memorial and central for day trips to Hamburg and Hannover, also has cattle, with boar and deer in the surrounding forest and meadows. ✉ *Hassel 3, D–29303 Bergen* ☎ *05054/249* 🖷 *05054/269* 🌐 *www.hofaverbeck.de* *14 rooms, 2 apartments* *Cable TV, some pets allowed (fee); no a/c, no room phones* 💳 *MC, V* *BP.*

Bremen

22 *110 km (68 mi) northwest of Hannover.*

Germany's smallest city-state, Bremen, is also Germany's oldest and second largest port (only Hamburg is larger). Together with Hamburg and Lübeck, Bremen was an early member of the merchant-run Hanseatic League, and its rivalry with the larger port on the Elbe River is still tangible. Though Hamburg may still claim its title as Germany's "door to the world," Bremen likes to boast: "But we have the key." Bremen's symbol is, in fact, a golden key, which you will see displayed on flags and signs throughout the city.

Bremen is also central to the fable of the Bremer Stadtmusikanten, or Bremen Town Musicians—a rooster, cat, dog, and donkey quartet that came to Bremen to seek its fortune. (Their music and singing were so awful that they caused a band of robbers to flee in terror.) You'll find statues of this group in various parts of the city.

There are numerous sights to see in Bremen's charming Altstadt. The **Marktplatz** is one of Europe's most impressive market squares. It's bordered by the St. Petri Dom, an imposing 900-year-old Gothic cathedral; an ancient Rathaus; a 16th-century guildhall; and a modern glass-and-steel state parliament building, with gabled town houses finishing the panorama. Alongside the northwest corner of the Rathaus is the famous bronze statue of the four **Bremen Town Musicians,** one atop the other in a sort of pyramid. Their feats are reenacted in a free, open-air play in the courtyard of the Liebfrauenkirche, near the Marktplatz, at noon each Sunday, from May to October. Another well-known figure on the square is the stone statue of the knight in service to Charlemagne, **Roland,** erected in 1404. Three times larger than life, the statue serves as Bremen's good-luck piece and a symbol of freedom and independence. It is said that as long as Roland stands, Bremen will remain a free and independent state.

Construction of the **St. Petri Dom** (St. Peter's Cathedral) began in the mid-11th century. Its two prominent towers are Gothic, but in the late 1800s the cathedral was restored in the Romanesque style. It served as the seat of an archbishop until the Reformation turned the cathedral Protestant. ✉ *Marktpl.* *Free* *Weekdays 10–5, Sat. 10–2, Sun. 2–5.*

Charlemagne had established a diocese here in the 9th century, and a 15th-century statue of him, together with seven princes, adorns the Gothic **Rathaus,** which acquired a Weser Renaissance facade during the early 17th century. Tours are given in German. ✉ *Marktpl.* *Tour €4* *Tours Mon.–Sat. at 11, noon, 3, and 4; Sun. at 11 and noon, unless an official function is in progress.*

Don't leave Bremen's Altstadt without strolling down **Böttcherstrasse** (Barrel Maker's Street), at one time inhabited by coopers. Between 1924 and 1931 their houses were torn down and reconstructed, in a style at once historically sensitive and modern, by Bremen coffee millionaire Ludwig Roselius. (He was the inventor of decaffeinated coffee and held the patent for many years; Sanka was its brand name in the United States.) Many of the restored houses are used as galleries for local artists.

At one end of Böttcherstrasse is the **Roselius-Haus,** a 14th-century building that is now a museum, established on the initiative of the coffee baron. It showcases German and Dutch paintings, as well as wood carvings, furniture, textiles, and decorative arts from the 12th through the 18th centuries. Notice also the arch of Meissen bells at the rooftop. Except when freezing weather makes them dangerously brittle, these chime daily on the hour from noon to 6 (only at noon, 3, and 6, January–April). ✉ *Böttcherstr. 6–10* ☎ *0421/336–5077* *€5* *Tues.–Sun. 11–6.*

Also take a walk through the nearby narrow streets of the idyllic ★ **Schnoorviertel** (Schnoor District), a jumble of houses, taverns, and shops once occupied or frequented by fishermen and tradespeople. This is Bremen's oldest district, dating back to the 15th and 16th centuries. The neighborhood is fashionable among artists and craftspeople, who have restored the tiny cottages to serve as galleries and workshops. Other buildings have been converted into popular antiques shops, small cafés, and pubs.

At the **Universum Science Center,** you can study the Earth and cosmos through interactive exhibits, videos, and simulations. ✉ *Wiener Str. 2* ☎ *0421/334–6333* *€11* *Weekdays 9–6, weekends 10–7.*

The **Übersee Museum** (Overseas Museum) has unusual displays on the histories and cultures of the many peoples with whom Bremen traders came into contact. One section is devoted to North America. ✉ *Bahnhofspl. 13* ☎ *0421/1603–8101* *www.uebersee-museum.de* *€6* *Tues.–Fri. 9–6, weekends 10–6.*

off the beaten path

BREMERHAVEN – This busy port city belongs to Bremen and is 66 km (41 mi) upriver, where the Weser empties into the North Sea. You can take in the enormity of the port from a promenade or from a platform in the North Harbor. The country's largest and most fascinating maritime museum, the **Deutsches Schifffahrtsmuseum** (German Maritime Museum), is a fun place to explore. Part of the museum consists of a harbor, open from April through October, with seven old trading ships. A train to Bremerhaven from Bremen takes about one hour. ✉ *Hans-Scharoun-Pl. 1, from Bremen take A–27 to exit for Bremerhaven-Mitte* ☎ *0471/482–070* 🌐 *www.dsm.de* 🎫 *€5* ⏲ *Apr.–Oct., daily 10–6; Nov.–Mar., Tues.–Sun. 10–6.*

In August 2005, the **Deutsches Auswandererhaus** (German Emigration Center) opened in Bremerhaven. The center is dedicated to understanding the experience of the more than 7 million men, women, and children who left Germany via Bremerhaven, between 1830 and 1974, to embark on a transatlantic passage to the New World. ✉ *Columbusstr. 65* ☎ *0471/902–200* 🌐 *www.dah-bremerhaven.de* 🎫 *€8.50* ⏲ *Apr.–Oct., Sun.–Fri. 10–6, Sat. 10–7; Nov.–Mar., daily 10–5.*

Where to Stay & Eat

★ **$$$–$$$$** ✕ **Grashoffs Bistro.** An enthusiastic crowd, willing to put up with incredibly cramped conditions, descends at lunchtime on this gourmet restaurant-cum-deli. The room is so small that there's no room between the square tables; a table has to be pulled out for anyone who has a seat next to the wall. The menu has a French touch, with an emphasis on fresh fish from the Bremerhaven market. The deli has a whole wall of teas, another of cheeses, and a huge assortment of wines. ✉ *Contrescarpe 80* ☎ *0421/14740* 💳 *AE, DC, MC, V* ⏲ *Closed Sun. No dinner.*

★ **$$–$$$$** ✕ **Park Restaurant.** The stunning dining room, within the Park Hotel Bremen, is decorated in yellow and cream, with shimmering crystal chandeliers, classical moldings, marble urns, Louis XVI chairs, floor-to-ceiling windows, and a lacquered ceiling. Chef Henri Precht includes a dash of fantasy in his classic French and German dishes. Fish is filleted at the table and specialties include a three-soup starter and a four-course dessert meal. The latter sounds caloric but actually includes kumquats, almonds, passion fruit, buttermilk, a Granny Smith–apple sorbet, and other healthy-sounding things in addition to the chocolate and pudding. ✉ *Im Bürgerpark* ☎ *0421/340–8633* 💳 *AE, DC, MC, V.*

★ **¢–$** ✕ **Ratskeller.** This cavernous cellar, with a three-story-high vaulted ceiling, is said to be Germany's oldest and most renowned town-hall restaurant—it's been here for 600 years. The waiters and waitresses wear medieval costumes and serve solid, typical north German fare. The walls are lined with wine casks, and there are intimate alcoves with closable doors, once used by merchants as they closed their deals. It was long a tradition that only German wines were served here. This is no longer true, but there are still 650 of them on the menu along with the non-German selections. ✉ *Am Markt 1* ☎ *0421/321–676* 💳 *AE, DC, MC, V.*

$$$$ Fodor'sChoice ★ **Park Hotel Bremen.** This palatial hotel, with a lake on one side and an extensive area of park and forest on the other sides, is only minutes from the central station. In winter, guests can swim in a heated outdoor pool or sit cozily beside a fireplace in the lobby. In summer they can dine on a lakeside terrace. Waiters wear white ties and bellhops wear flat caps and brass buttons right out of an old movie. The bathrooms are exquisite marble affairs, and the Park Restaurant is the best fine dining around. ✉ *Im Bürgerpark, D–28209* ☎ *0421/34080* 📠 *0421/340–8602* 🌐 *www.parkhotel-bremen.de* *150 rooms, 12 suites* *2 restaurants, café, some cable TV with movies and video games, Wi-Fi, pool, hair salon, massage, bicycles, bar, meeting rooms, some pets allowed (fee), no-smoking rooms; no a/c in some rooms* *AE, DC, MC, V* *BP.*

★ $ **Hotel Landhaus Louisenthal.** This charming complex of buildings, all under the hotel's management, consists of two half-timber restaurants and a 150-year-old hotel. Across the street is a windmill. It's all about as far from downtown as you can get and still be in Bremen, but the price is right, the service and food are fine, a streetcar at the door takes you downtown in minutes, it's near the Hohe-Lehe Autobahn exit, and there's plenty of parking. ✉ *Leher Heerstr. 105, D–28359* ☎ *0421/232–076* 📠 *0421/236–716* 🌐 *www.landhaus-louisenthal.de* *61 rooms* *2 restaurants, cable TV, sauna, meeting rooms, some pets allowed (fee), no-smoking rooms; no a/c* *AE, DC, MC, V* *BP.*

Nightlife & the Arts

Bremen may be Germany's oldest seaport, but it can't match Hamburg for racy nightlife. Nevertheless, the streets around the central Marktplatz and in the historic Schnoor District are filled with all sorts of taverns and bars.

Try your luck at American or French roulette and blackjack at the **Bremen casino** (✉ Böttcherstr. 3–5 ☎ 0421/329–000), open daily 5 PM–3 AM. The **Bremerhaven casino** (✉ Theodor-Heuss-Pl. 3 ☎ 0471/413–641), open daily 11 AM until midnight, is strictly for one-arm bandits and machine players.

Music and theater lovers have much to choose from. The **Theater am Goetheplatz** (✉ Goethepl. 1–3) presents operas, operettas, music, and dance programs. The **Concordia** (✉ Schwachhäuser Heerstr. 1) is a multipurpose theater whose stage and audience area can be adjusted to suit the needs of the mostly experimental programs it presents. The **Schauspielhaus** (✉ Goethepl. 1–3) presents theater, everything from Goethe to Brecht to Woody Allen, but nearly always in German. Program and ticket information for the Theater am Goetheplatz, Concordia, and Schauspielhaus is available through a single **box office** (☎ 0421/365–300). The **philharmonic orchestra,** which plays regularly at the city's concert hall, Die Glocke (✉ Domsheide 4–5 ☎ 0421/336–699), is of national stature. Bremen's **Shakespeare Company** (✉ Schulstr. 26 ☎ 0421/500–333) presents the works of the Bard and other plays in German.

Shopping

Bremen's **Schnoorviertel** is the place to go for souvenirs. Its stores are incredibly specialized, selling porcelain dolls, teddy bears, African jewelry, and smoking pipes among many other things. One of the most whimsical shops in town is **Atelier GAG** (✉ Auf den Häfen 12-15 ☎ 0421/701–137). The tiny shop is overflowing with paper models of lighthouses, famous buildings, spaceships, and other fun creations. All of the models are for sale as flat sheets of paper, ready to be cut and pasted into their various forms.

THE FAIRY-TALE ROAD A TO Z

To research prices, get advice from other travelers, and book travel arrangements, visit www.fodors.com.

AIRPORTS

Frankfurt, Hannover, and Hamburg have the closest international airports to the area. Frankfurt is less than a half hour from Hanau, and Hamburg is less than an hour from Bremen.

Langenhagen Airport ✉ Petzelstr. 84, Hannover ☎ 0511/9770.

BIKE & MOPED TRAVEL

The Fulda and Werra rivers have 190 km (118 mi) of cycle paths, and you can cycle the whole length of the Weser River from Hannoversch-Münden to the outskirts of Bremen without making too many detours from the river valley. Five- and seven-day cycle tours of the Fulda and Werra river valleys are possible, including bike rentals, overnight accommodations, and luggage transport between stops.

SRJ Gasteservice ✉ Gneisenaustr. 4, D-32423 Minden ☎ 0571/889-1900.

BUS TRAVEL

Bremen, Kassel, Göttingen, Fulda, and Hanau are all reachable via Europabus (⇨ Deutsche Touring under Bus Travel *in* Smart Travel Tips). Frankfurt, Kassel, Göttingen, and Bremen all have city bus services that extend into the countryside along the Fairy-Tale Road. A local bus serves the scenic Weser Valley Road stretch.

CAR TRAVEL

The Fairy-Tale Road incorporates one of Germany's loveliest scenic drives, the Wesertalstrasse, or Weser Valley Road (B–80 and B–83), between Hannoversch-Münden and Hameln; total mileage is approximately 103 km (64 mi). The autobahn network penetrates deep into the area, serving Hanau, Fulda, Kassel, Göttingen, and Bremen directly. Bremen is 60 km (35 mi) northwest of Hannover and 100 km (60 mi) northwest of Celle.

TOURS

BOAT TOURS

Reederei Warrings offers a one-hour trip around the Bremerhaven harbor for €7. Förde Reederei Seetouristik of Flensburg has a full-day round-trip from Bremerhaven to the North Sea island of Helgoland for €32.50. Book through the Bremerhaven tourist office, Reederei Warrings, or Förde Reederei Seetouristik. (If you're in a hurry to see the stark, red-cliff island Helgoland, there's a daily round-trip flight for €145 per person with OLT Airlines.)

The seven boats of Flotte Weser operate short summer excursions along a considerable stretch of the Weser River between Bremen and Bad Karlshafen. The trip between Corvey and Bad Karlshafen, for example, takes slightly under three hours and costs €23.75.

Rehbein-Linie Kassel operates a service from Kassel to Bad Karlshafen. It also prides itself on the only "three-river tour" in the area. In a single trip you travel on the Fulda and Werra rivers and also on the river formed when these two meet at the tour's starting point of Hannoversch-Münden, the Weser. One of the company's three boats, the *Deutschland*, has a bowling alley aboard. Personenschifffahrt K. & K. Söllner has two excursion boats plying between Kassel and Hannoversch-Münden.

Flotte Weser ✉ Deisterallee 1, D-31785 Hameln ☎ 05151/939-999. **Förde Reederei Seetouristik** ✉ Norderhofenden 19-20 D-24937 Flensburg ☎ 0180/320-2025. **OLT Airlines** ✉ Flughafen, Am Luneort 15, D-27572 Bremerhaven ☎ 0471/77-188. **Personenschifffahrt K. & K. Söllner** ✉ Die Schlagd, D-34125 Kassel ☎ 0561/774-670. **Reederei Warrings** ✉ Neuestr. 9, D-26409 Wittmund/Carolinensiel ☎ 04464/94950. **Rehbein-Linie Kassel** ✉ Ostpreusenstr. 8, D-34233 Fuldatal ☎ 0561/18505.

BUS TOURS

Year-round tours of the region are offered by Herter-Reisen. Guided bus tours of Kassel set off from the Stadttheater on Saturday at 2 PM from Easter through October, and at 11 AM in November and December. Tours are free if you buy a ServiceCard at the tourist office. Some local authorities—those in Bad Karlshafen, for example—also organize bus tours. Contact individual tourist offices for details.

Herter-Reisen ✉ Am Klei 26, D-31863 Coppenbrügge ☎ 05159/969-244.

WALKING TOURS

Many of the communities on the Fairy-Tale Road conduct scheduled walking tours, though most of them are offered in German only. Of the ones we list below, only Bremen offers its scheduled tours in both English and German. All of the others will provide tours in English only if requested in advance for a large group. Bremen's tours depart daily at 10:30 from the central bus station on Breiteweg. Fulda has tours of the Old Town, starting at the tourist office on Bonifatiusplatz, April–October, daily at 11:30 and 3; November–March, weekends and holidays at 11:30. Göttingen shows visitors around April–October, Friday, Saturday, and Sunday at 11:30 (starting from the Old Town Hall).

Hameln offers tours April–October, Monday–Saturday at 2:30 and Sunday at 10:15 and 2:30, leaving from the tourist office. The tourist office of Steinau an der Strasse conducts tours at 11:15 on the first Sunday of each month, April–October, departing from the Märchenbrunnen. Contact the respective tourist offices for details.

TRAIN TRAVEL

Hanau, Fulda, Kassel, and Göttingen are on both the InterCity Express (ICE) Frankfurt–Hamburg line and the Frankfurt–Berlin line (not all of these trains stop at Hanau). The Frankfurt-Hamburg line also stops in Hannover, and there's additional ICE service to Hannover and Bremen from Frankfurt and other major cities.

Rail service, but not ICE service, is available to Hannoversch-Münden, Marburg, Hameln, and Celle.

VISITOR INFORMATION

Information on the entire Fairy-Tale Road can be obtained from the **Deutsche Märchenstrasse** (✉ Obere Königstr. 15, D–34117 Kassel ☎ 0561/707–707 🌐 www.deutsche-maerchenstrasse.de).

Alsfeld ✉ Verkehrsbüro Touristcenter, Am Markt 12, D-36304 ☎ 06631/182-165 🌐 www.tca-alsfeld.de. **Bad Karlshafen** ✉ Kur- und Tourist-Information, Hafenplatz 8, D-34385 ☎ 05672/999-922 🌐 www.hessennet.de/badkarlshafen. **Bodenwerder** ✉ Tourist Information, Münchausenplatz 3, D-37619 ☎ 05533/40542 🌐 www.bodenwerder.de. **Bremen** ✉ Touristik-Zentrale, Findorffstr. 105, D-28215 ☎ 01805/101-030 🌐 www.bremen-tourism.de. **Bremerhaven** ✉ Bremerhaven Touristik, H.-H.-Meierstr. 6, D-27568 ☎ 0471/946-4610 🌐 www.seestadt-bremerhaven.de. **Celle** ✉ Tourismus Region Celle, Markt 14-16, D-29221 ☎ 05141/1212 🌐 www.region-celle.de. **Fulda** ✉ Tourismus- und Kongressmanagement, Bonifatiuspl. 1, D-36037 ☎ 0661/102-1813 🌐 www.fulda.de. **Gelnhausen** ✉ Tourist Information, Obermarkt 7, D-63571 ☎ 06051/830-300 🌐 www.gelnhausen.de. **Göttingen** ✉ Tourist-Information, Altes Rathaus, Markt 9, D-37073 ☎ 0551/499-800 🌐 www.goettingen.de. **Hameln** ✉ Hameln Marketing und Tourismus, Deisterallee 1, D-31785 ☎ 05151/202-617 🌐 www.hameln.de. **Hanau** ✉ Tourist-Information Hanau, Am Markt 14-18, D-63450 ☎ 06181/295-950 🌐 www.hanau.de. **Hannover** ✉ Hannover Tourismus Service, Ernst-August-Pl. 2, D-30159 ☎ 0511/1684-9700 🌐 www.hannover.de. **Hannoversch-Münden** ✉ Touristik Naturpark Münden, Lotzestr. 2, D-34346 ☎ 05541/75313 🌐 www.hann.muenden.de. **Höxter** ✉ Touristik- und Kulturinformation, Historisches Rathaus, Weserstr. 11, D-37671 ☎ 05271/963-431 🌐 www.hoexter.de. **Kassel** ✉ Tourist GmbH, Obere Königstr. 15, D-34117 ☎ 0561/707-707 🌐 www.kassel.de. **Marburg** ✉ Tourismus und Marketing, Pilgrimstein 26, D-35037 ☎ 06421/99120 🌐 www.marburg.de. **Steinau an der Strasse** ✉ Verkehrsbüro, Bruder-Grimm-Str. 70, D-36396 ☎ 06663/96310 🌐 www.steinau.de.

Hamburg

12

WORD OF MOUTH

"Hamburg is fantastic and the nightlife is amazing. I always need a holiday when I get back to recover."

—xx

"If you go, take a guided tour of the port, or a ferry to Finkenwerder and just take in the skyline from the water. It's simply beautiful!"

—hsv

"I don't think Hamburg is so much about must-sees, but more about enjoying a comfortable city by the water, nice restaurants, and various neighborhoods. . . . My kids were impressed by the best looking Burger King on earth on Mönckebergstrasse. "

—DAX

www.fodors.com/forums

Updated by Jürgen Scheunemann

WATER—IN THE FORM OF THE ALSTER LAKES AND THE ELBE RIVER—is Hamburg's defining feature and the key to the city's success. A harbor city with an international past, Hamburg is the most tolerant and open-minded of German cities. The media have made Hamburg their capital by planting some of the leading newspapers, magazines, and television stations here. Add to that the slick world of advertising, show business, and modeling agencies, and you have a populace of worldly and fashionable professionals. Not surprisingly, the city of movers and shakers is also the city with most of Germany's millionaires.

But for most Europeans, the port city invariably triggers thoughts of the gaudy Reeperbahn underworld, that sleazy strip of clip joints, sex shows, and wholesale prostitution that helped earn Hamburg its reputation as "Sin City." Today the infamous red-light district is just as much a hip meeting place for young Hamburgers and tourist crowds, who flirt with the bright lights and chic haunts of the not-so-sinful Reeperbahn, especially on warm summer nights.

Hamburg, or "Hammaburg," was founded in 810 by Charlemagne. For centuries it was a walled city, its gigantic outer fortifications providing a tight little world relatively impervious to outside influences. The city is at the mouth of the Elbe, one of Europe's great rivers and the 97-km (60-mi) umbilical cord that ties the harbor to the North Sea. Its role as a port gained it world renown. It was a powerful member of the Hanseatic League, the medieval union of northern German merchant cities that dominated shipping in the Baltic and North seas.

The Thirty Years' War left Hamburg unscathed, and Napoléon's domination of much of the continent in the early 19th century also failed to affect it. Indeed, it was during the 19th century that Hamburg reached the crest of its power, when the largest shipping fleets on the seas with some of the fastest ships afloat were based here. Its merchants traded with the far corners of the globe. During the four decades leading up to World War I, Hamburg became one of the world's richest cities. Its aura of wealth and power continued right up to the outbreak of World War II. These days, about 15,000 ships sail up the lower Elbe each year, carrying more than 50 million tons of cargo—from petroleum and locomotives to grain and bananas.

What you see today is the "new" Hamburg. The Great Fire of 1842 all but obliterated the original city; a century later World War II bombing raids destroyed port facilities and leveled more than half of the city proper. In spite of the 1940–44 raids, Hamburg now stands as a remarkably faithful replica of that glittering prewar city—a place of enormous style, verve, and elegance, with considerable architectural diversity, including turn-of-the-20th-century art-nouveau buildings.

The comparison that Germans like to draw between Hamburg and Venice is somewhat exaggerated. But the city *is* threaded with countless canals and waterways spanned by about 1,000 bridges, even more than you'll find in Venice. Swans glide on the canals. Arcaded passageways run along the waterways. In front of the Renaissance-style Rathaus (Town Hall) is a square that resembles the Piazza San Marco.

If you have 2 days

Start at the Alster Lakes and head toward the main shopping boulevards of Jungfernstieg and Mönckebergstrasse. A short walk south of Mönckebergstrasse takes you to the majestic Rathaus Square, while a brief walk north on the same street leads to the equally impressive Hauptbahnhof. To the southeast, the Kontorhausviertel is one of the nicest parts of town, a collection of old brick warehouses dating back to the 1920s. On your second day, take a quick tour of the Freihafen Hamburg, Hamburg's port. Compare the port's modern warehouses with their antique counterparts on photogenic Deichstrasse in the Altstadt (Old City). You may want to inspect at least one of the city's great churches; a good choice is the city's premier baroque landmark, St. Michaeliskirche. Finally, head over to the Landungsbrücken, the starting point for boat rides in the harbor and along the Elbe River. And don't leave Hamburg without a jaunt down St. Pauli's Reeperbahn.

If you have 3 days

Begin watching wild animals roam free at Hagenbecks Tierpark. Equally green are the two parks, Planten un Blomen and the Alter Botanischer Garten, in the business district. After exploring the downtown's other attractions, from the Alster to the Hauptbahnhof, detour to the Kunsthalle and the Museum für Kunst und Gewerbe, both showcasing some of the best art in Germany. Devote your second day to historic Hamburg and the harbor. Take in the docks and don't miss the Speicherstadt's 19th-century warehouses. After a walk among the charming houses on Deichstrasse, continue on to the meticulously restored Krameramtswohnungen, the late-medieval Shopkeepers' Guild Houses. Next, visit the Museum für Hamburgische Geschichte for an excellent overview of the city's dramatic past. Save your third day for St. Pauli. Board one of the boats at the Landungsbrücken for a sightseeing tour through the harbor. One evening should be spent along the Reeperbahn, perhaps including the Erotic Art Museum, one of the few tasteful displays of eroticism on the strip.

If you have 4 days

To get a glimpse of Hamburg's playful art-nouveau architecture, start the first day west of the lakes at the Dammtorbahnhof and make quick trips to Hagenbecks Tierpark and the Planten un Blomen and Alter Botanischer Garten parks. The inner-city district has many highlights, from the Alster to the Kontorhausviertel, including the Chilehaus and St. Jacobikirche, a medieval church with Gothic altars. On the second day, explore Hamburg's past at the harbor and in other old parts of town. Begin with the St. Katharinenkirche, the city's perfectly restored baroque church. Then spend the afternoon at Hamburg's harbor and its historic attractions, from the Freihafen Hamburg to Krameramtswohnungen, including the Alte St. Nikolaikirche, a church ruin now preserved as a memorial. End the day by viewing the city from the giant Bismarck-Denkmal. Spend a third day in St. Pauli. On the fourth day, return to the Landungsbrücken and embark on a boat ride to the village of Blankenese and the historic ships at the Museumshafen Övelgönne.

The distinguishing feature of downtown Hamburg is the Alster (Alster Lakes). Once an insignificant waterway, it was dammed in the 18th century to form an artificial lake. Divided at its south end, it's known as the Binnenalster (Inner Alster) and the Aussenalster (Outer Alster)—the two separated by a pair of graceful bridges, the Lombard Brücke and the John F. Kennedy Brücke. The Inner Alster is lined with stately hotels, department stores, fine shops, and cafés; the Outer Alster is framed by parks and gardens against a backdrop of private mansions. From late spring into fall, sailboats and windsurfers skim across the surface of the Outer Alster and white excursion steamers ferry back and forth. The view from these vessels (or from the shore of the Outer Alster) is of the stunning skyline of six spiny spires (five churches and the Rathaus) that is Hamburg's identifying feature. It all creates one of the most distinctive downtown areas of any European city.

EXPLORING HAMBURG

Hamburg's most important attractions stretch between the Alster Lakes to the north, and the harbor and Elbe River to the south. This area consists of four distinct quarters. St. Georg is the business district around the Hauptbahnhof (main train station). The historic Altstadt (Old City) clusters near the harbor and surrounds the Rathaus (Town Hall). West of Altstadt is Neustadt (New City). The shabby but thrilling district of St. Pauli includes the Reeperbahn, a strip of sex clubs and bars.

Downtown Hamburg

The city's heart (and shops) is centered on two long boulevards, the Jungfernstieg and the Mönckebergstrasse. The area was heavily bombarded during World War II, so most of the buildings here were constructed after the war; they now house banks, insurance companies, and other big businesses. Downtown may not be the most beautiful part of town, but its atmosphere is invigorating.

Numbers in the text correspond to numbers in the margin and on the Hamburg map.

a good walk

Begin at **Dammtorbahnhof** 1, a fine example of Hamburg's art-nouveau architecture. Departing from the south exit, you can easily take a detour to Hamburg's zoo, **Hagenbecks Tierpark** 2, one of Germany's oldest and most popular urban animal habitats. It has its own subway stop on the U-2 line. After visiting the zoo, return to the south exit of the Dammtor station; on your right you'll see the SAS Plaza Hotel and the Congress Centrum Hamburg (CCH), a vast, modern conference-and-entertainment complex. Continue past the Congress Centrum and bear left in a sweeping arc through the ornamental park **Planten un Blomen** 3. Leave the park at Marseillerstrasse and cross over into the less formal **Alter Botanischer Garten** 4. Both the park and the gardens are in the larger Wallringpark, which encompasses four parks in all. At the garden's southeast exit at Stephansplatz, cross over the Esplanade and walk down Colonnaden to reach the **Alster Lakes** 5 and the **Jungfernstieg** 6, the most elegant boulevard in downtown Hamburg.

12

On the Menu Hamburg is undoubtedly one of the best places in the country to enjoy fresh seafood. The flotilla of fishing boats brings a wide variety of fish to the city—to sophisticated upscale restaurants as well as simple harborside taverns. One of the most celebrated dishes among the robust local specialties is *Aalsuppe* (eel soup), a tangy concoction not entirely unlike Marseilles's famous bouillabaisse. A must in summer is *Aalsuppe grün* (eel soup seasoned with dozens of herbs); *Räucheraal* (smoked eel) is equally good. In the fall, try *Bunte oder Gepflückte Finten,* a dish of green and white beans, carrots, and apples. Available any time of year is *Küken* ragout, a concoction of sweetbreads, spring chicken, tiny veal meatballs, asparagus, clams, and fresh peas cooked in a white sauce. Other northern German specialties include *Stubenküken* (young, male oven-fried chicken); *Vierländer Mastente* (duck stuffed with apples, onions, and raisins); *Birnen, Bohnen, und Speck* (pears, beans, and bacon); and the sailors' favorite, *Labskaus*—a stew made from pickled meat, potatoes, and (sometimes) herring, garnished with a fried egg, sour pickles, and lots of beets.

The Harbor A cruise of Germany's gateway to the world is a must. The energy from the continuous ebb and flow of huge cargo vessels and container ships, the harbor's prosperity, and its international flavor best symbolize the city's spirit. The surrounding older parts of town, with their narrow cobblestone streets and late-medieval warehouses, testify to Hamburg's powerful Hanseatic past. Bars and nightclubs have transformed some of the harbor area into a hot spot for eyebrow-raising entertainment.

Shopping Although not as rich or sumptuous on first sight as Düsseldorf or Munich, Hamburg is nevertheless expensive and ranks first among Germany's shopping experiences. Chic boutiques sell primarily distinguished and somewhat conservative fashion; understatement is the style here. Some of the country's premier designers, such as Karl Lagerfeld, Jil Sander, and Wolfgang Joop, are native Hamburgers or at least worked here for quite some time. Hamburg has the greatest number of shopping malls in the country, mostly small but elegant downtown arcades offering entertainment, fashion, and fine food.

Turn right off the Jungfernstieg onto Reesendamm and make your way to the **Rathaus** 7 and its square. Leave by its east side, perhaps pausing to join those relaxing on the steps of the memorial to the poet Heinrich Heine, a great fan of the city.

Beyond the memorial lies **Mönckebergstrasse** 8, Hamburg's not-so-elegant but always-bustling shopping boulevard. At its end you'll meet the busy main road of Steintorwall, which was the easternmost link of the defense wall encircling the Old Town in the 17th century. Take the pedestrian underpass to the **Hauptbahnhof** 9, Hamburg's impressive central train station. Leave the Hauptbahnhof the way you entered and turn

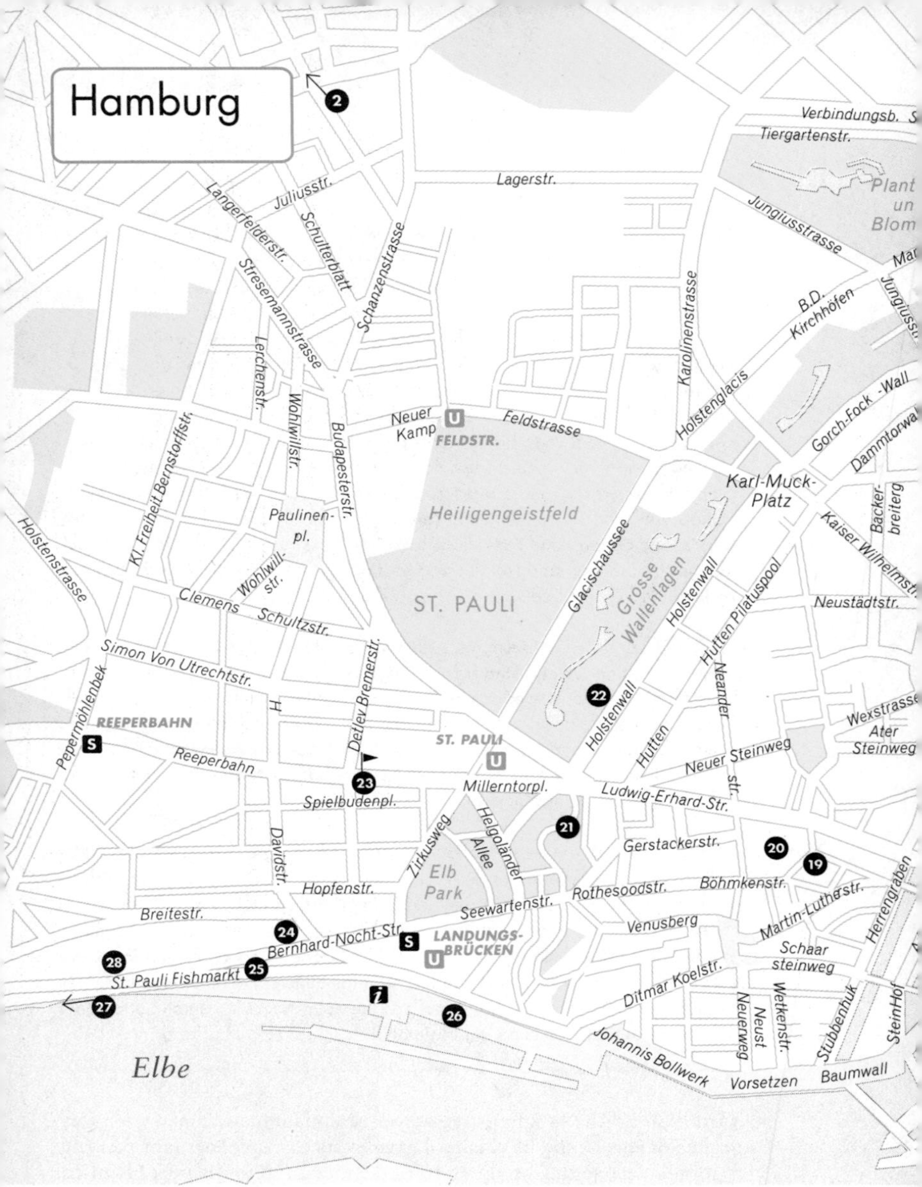
Hamburg
2
Verbindungsb.
Tiergartenstr.
Lagerstr.
Plant un Blom
Juliusstr.
Langerfelderstr.
Schulterblatt
Schanzenstrasse
Jungiusstrasse
Stresemannstrasse
Karolinenstrasse
B.D. Kirchhöfen
Lerchenstr.
Wohlwillstr.
Holstenglacis
Gorch-Fock-Wall
Dammtorwall
Neuer Kamp
FELDSTR.
Feldstrasse
Budapesterstr.
Kl. Freiheit Bernstorffstr.
Karl-Muck-Platz
Paulinenpl.
Heiligengeistfeld
Backerbreiterg
Kaiser Wilhelmstr.
Holstenstrasse
Glacischaussee
Wohlwillstr.
Grosse Wallenlagen
ST. PAULI
Clemens Schultzstr.
Holstenwall
Hutten Pilatuspool
Neustädtstr.
Simon Von Utrechtstr.
Detlev Bremerstr.
22
Holstenwall
Neanderstr.
Wexstrasse
Ater Steinweg
Pepermöhlenbek
REEPERBAHN
Reeperbahn
ST. PAULI
Hutten
Neuer Steinweg
23
Millerntorpl.
Ludwig-Erhard-Str.
Spielbudenpl.
Zirkusweg
Helgoländer Allee
21
Gerstackerstr.
20
19
Davidstr.
Elb Park
Hopfenstr.
Rothesoodstr.
Böhmkenstr.
Martin-Lutherstr.
Herrengraben
Breitestr.
Seewartenstr.
Venusberg
24
Bernhard-Nocht-Str.
LANDUNGSBRÜCKEN
Schaar steinweg
28
25
St. Pauli Fishmarkt
Ditmar Koelstr.
27
26
Neuerweg
Neust
Wetkenstr.
Stubbenhuk
SteinHöft
Elbe
Johannis Bollwerk
Vorsetzen
Baumwall

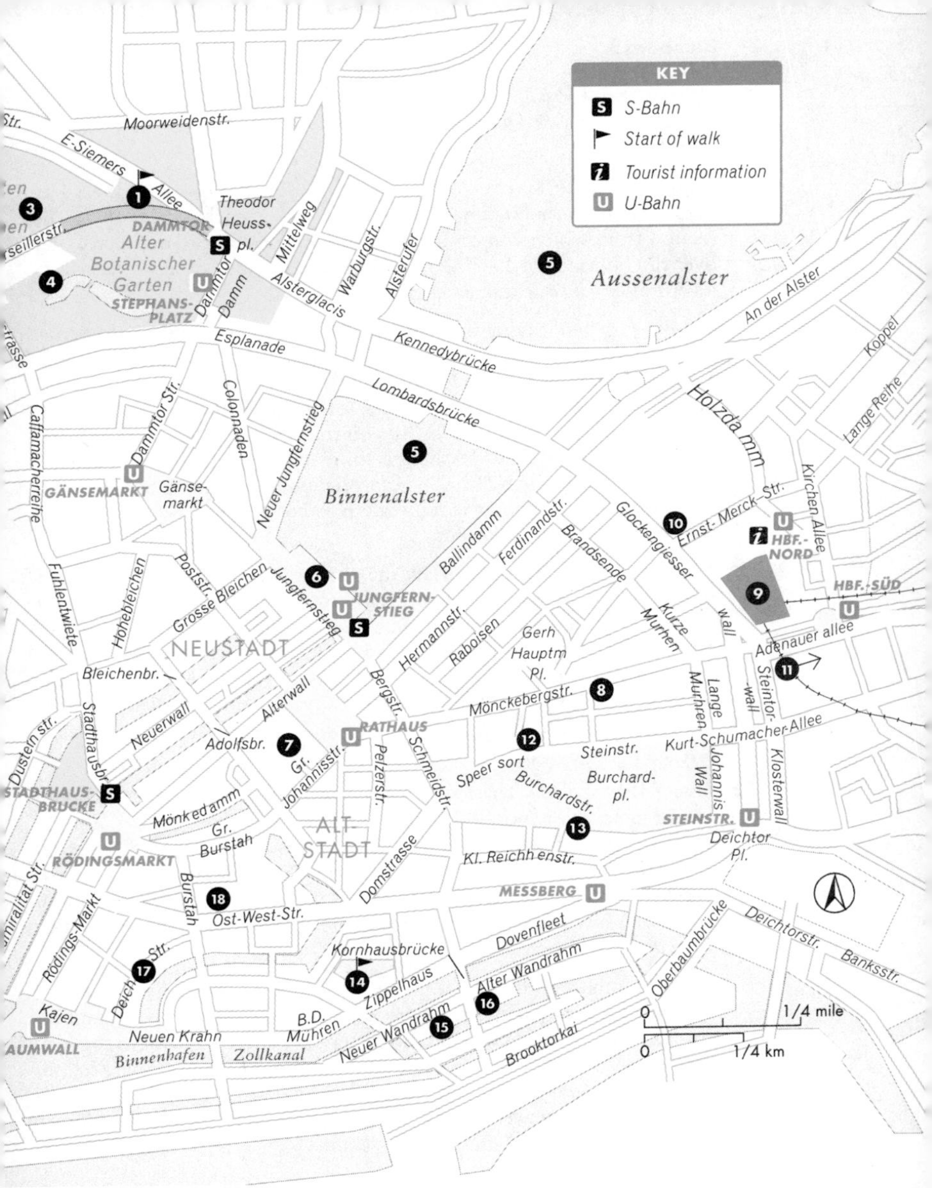
KEY
S-Bahn
Start of walk
Tourist information
U-Bahn
Moorweidenstr.
E-Siemers Allee
Theodor Heuss-pl.
DAMMTOR
Alter Botanischer Garten
STEPHANS-PLATZ
Dammtor Damm
Mittelweg
Warburgstr.
Alsterufer
Alsterglacis
Aussenalster
An der Alster
Esplanade
Kennedybrücke
Lombardsbrücke
Holzdamm
Koppel
Lange Reihe
Colonnaden
Dammtor Str.
Caffamacherreihe
GÄNSEMARKT
Gänsemarkt
Neuer Jungfernstieg
Binnenalster
Ballindamm
Ferdinandstr.
Brandsende
Glockengiesser
Ernst-Merck-Str.
Kirchen Allee
HBF.-NORD
HBF.-SÜD
Fuhlentwiete
Hohebleichen
Poststr.
Grosse Bleichen
Jungfernstieg
JUNGFERN-STIEG
NEUSTADT
Hermannstr.
Raboisen
Gerh Hauptm Pl.
Kurze Murhen
Wall
Adenauer allee
Bleichenbr.
Alterwall
Bergstr.
Mönckebergstr.
Lange Murhen
Steintor-wall
Stadthausbr.
Neuerwall
Adolfsbr.
RATHAUS
Gr. Johannisstr.
Pelzerstr.
Schmeidstr.
Speer sort
Steinstr.
Burchardstr.
Burchard-pl.
Kurt-Schumacher-Allee
Johannis Wall
Klosterwall
Dusteín str.
STADTHAUS-BRÜCKE
Mönkedamm
Gr. Burstah
ALT-STADT
Domstrasse
Kl. Reichhenstr.
STEINSTR.
Deichtor Pl.
RÖDINGSMARKT
Admiralitat Str.
Burstah
MESSBERG
Ost-West-Str.
Rödings-Markt
Deich Str.
Kornhausbrücke
Dovenfleet
Oberbaumbrücke
Deichtorstr.
Banksstr.
Zippelhaus
Alter Wandrahm
Kajen
B.D. Mühren
Neuer Wandrahm
Brooktorkai
BAUMWALL
Neuen Krahn
Binnenhafen
Zollkanal
0
1/4 mile
1/4 km

right on Steintorwall, which continues as Glockengiesserwall, until you come to the major art museum, **Kunsthalle** ⑩, on the corner of Ernst-Merck-Strasse.

A quite different but equally fascinating perspective on art is offered at the nearby **Museum für Kunst und Gewerbe** ⑪. To reach it, head in the direction from which you came and turn left on Steintordamm, crossing over the railroad tracks. The large, yellow museum is across the street, its entrance on Brockestrasse.

Turn right when leaving the museum, then right again onto Kurt-Schumacher-Allee. Cross over Steintorwall near the subway and continue west along Steinstrasse to the **St. Jacobikirche** ⑫—you'll recognize it by its needle spire. Cross over Steinstrasse when leaving the church and head down Burchardstrasse, which will bring you to Burchardplatz. This area between Steinstrasse and Messberg is known as the Kontorhausviertel, a restored quarter with redbrick commercial buildings dating to the 1920s. The most famous building is at the south end of Burchardplatz—the **Chilehaus** ⑬ resembles a huge ship.

TIMING You need half a day just to walk the proposed tour, depending on how much time you devote to the parks, the zoo (both are crowded but most enjoyable on summer weekends), and to shopping (which isn't advisable on Saturday morning because of the crowds). If you add two hours for visits to the museums and the Rathaus and two more hours for the delightful boat tour on the Alster Lakes, you'll end up spending more than a full day downtown.

What to See

❺ **Alster** (Alster Lakes). These twin lakes provide downtown Hamburg with one of its most memorable vistas. The two lakes meet at the Lombard and Kennedy bridges. In summer the boat landing at the Jungfernstieg, below the Alsterpavillion, is the starting point for the *Alsterdampfer,* the flat-bottom passenger boats that traverse the lakes. Small sailboats and rowboats, hired from yards on the shores of the Alster, are very much a part of the summer scene.

Every Hamburger dreams of living within sight of the Alster, but only the wealthiest can afford it. Some lucky millionaires own the magnificent garden properties around the Alster's perimeter, known as the Millionaire's Coast. But you don't have to be a guest on one of these estates to enjoy the waterfront—the Alster shoreline has 6 km (4 mi) of tree-lined public pathways. Popular among joggers, these trails are a lovely place for a stroll. Ⓤ *Jungfernstieg (U-bahn).*

❹ **Alter Botanischer Garten** (Old Botanical Gardens). This green and open park within Wallringpark cultivates rare and exotic plants. Tropical and subtropical species grow under glass in five hothouses, including the large Schaugewächshaus (Show Greenhouse). Specialty gardens, including herbal and medicinal plantings, are clustered around the moat. ✉ *Stephanspl., Neustadt* ☎ *040/4283–82327* 💳 *Free* ⏲ *Schaugewächshaus Mar.–Oct., weekdays 9–4:15, weekends 10–5:15; Nov.–Feb., weekdays 9–3:15, weekends 10–3:15* Ⓤ *Stefanspl. (U-bahn).*

13 **Chilehaus** (Chile House). This fantastical 10-story structure, which looks like a vast landlocked ship, is the standout of the **Kontorhausviertel,** a series of imaginative clinker-brick buildings designed in the New Objectivity style of 1920s civic architect Fritz Schumacher. The building was commissioned by businessman Henry Sloman, who traded in saltpeter from Chile, and now houses modern offices. ✉ *Buchardspl., Altstadt* 🌐 *www.chilehaus.de* U *Messberg (U-bahn).*

1 **Dammtorbahnhof** (Dammtor Train Station). Built in 1903, this elevated steel-and-glass art-nouveau structure is among Hamburg's finest train stations. It's one of many art-nouveau buildings you'll see in the city. You can buy a city map at the newsstand in the station. ✉ *Ernst-Siemers-Allee, Altstadt* U *Dammtor (U-bahn).*

Deichtorhallen. This complex of warehouses built in 1911–12 is near the Kontorhausviertel and is now one of the country's largest exhibition halls for modern art. Its interior resembles an oversize loft, and its changing exhibits have presented the works of such artists as Andy Warhol, Roy Lichtenstein, and Miró. ✉ *Deichtorstr. 1–2, Altstadt* ☎ *040/321–0307* 🌐 *www.deichtorhallen.de* *Varies depending on exhibit* ⏲ *Tues.–Sun. 11–6* U *Steinstrasse (U-bahn).*

2 **Hagenbecks Tierpark** (Hagenbecks Zoo). One of the country's oldest and most popular zoos is family-owned. Founded in 1848, it was the world's first city park to let wild animals such as lions, elephants, chimpanzees, and others roam freely in vast, open-air corrals. Weather permitting, you can ride one of the elephants. In the Troparium, an artificial habitat creates a rain forest, an African desert, and a tropical sea. ✉ *Lokstedter Str. at Hamburg-Stellingen, Niendorf* ☎ *040/540–0010* 🌐 *www.hagenbeck.de* *€14.50* ⏲ *Mid-Mar.–Oct., daily 9–6; Nov.–mid-Mar., daily 9–4:30; last admission at 3:30* U *Hagenbecks Tierpark (U-bahn).*

9 **Hauptbahnhof** (Main Train Station). This central train station's cast-iron-and-glass architecture evokes the grandiose self-confidence of imperial Germany. The chief feature of the enormous 394-foot-long structure is its 460-foot-wide glazed roof supported only by pillars at each end. The largest structure of its kind in Europe, it's remarkably spacious and light inside. Though built in 1906 and having gone through many modernizations, it continues to have tremendous architectural impact. Today it sees a heavy volume of international, national, and suburban rail traffic. ✉ *Steintorpl., St. Georg* U *Hauptbahnhof (U-bahn).*

6 **Jungfernstieg.** This wide promenade looking out over the Alster Lakes is the city's premier shopping boulevard. Laid out in 1665, it used to be part of a muddy millrace that channeled water into the Elbe. Hidden from view behind the sedate facade of Jungfernstieg is a network of nine covered arcades that together account for almost a mile of shops selling everything from souvenirs to haute couture. Many of these air-conditioned passages have sprung up in the past two decades, but some have been here since the 19th century; the first glass-covered arcade, called Sillem's Bazaar, was built in 1845. ✉ *Neustadt* U *Jungfernstieg (U-bahn).*

need a break?

Hamburg's best-known and oldest café, the **Alex im Alsterpavillon** (✉ Jungfernstieg 54, Neustadt ☎ 040/350–1870) is a sleek 1950s retro café with an ideal vantage point from which to observe the constant activity on the Binnenalster.

★ 10 **Kunsthalle** (Art Gallery). One of the most important art museums in Germany, the Kunsthalle has 3,000 paintings, 400 sculptures, and a coin and medal collection that dates from the 14th century. In the postmodern, cube-shape building designed by Berlin architect O. M. Ungers, the **Galerie der Gegenwart** has housed a collection of international modern art since 1960, including works by Andy Warhol, Joseph Beuys, Georg Baselitz, and David Hockney. Graphic art is well represented, with a special collection of works by Pablo Picasso and the late Hamburg artist Horst Janssen, famous for his satirical worldview. In the old wing, you can view works by local artists dating from the 16th century. The outstanding collection of German Romantic paintings includes works by Runge, Friedrich, and Spitzweg. Paintings by Holbein, Rembrandt, Van Dyck, Tiepolo, and Canaletto are also on view, while late-19th-century impressionism is represented by works by Leibl, Liebermann, Manet, Monet, and Renoir. ✉ *Glockengiesserwall, Altstadt* ☎ *040/4281–31200* 🌐 *www.hamburger-kunsthalle.de* 🎫 *€8.50* ⏲ *Tues., Wed., and Fri.–Sun. 10–6, Thurs. 10–9* Ⓤ *Hauptbahnhof (U-bahn).*

8 **Mönckebergstrasse.** This broad, bustling street of shops—Hamburg's major thoroughfare—cuts through both the historic and the new downtown areas. It was laid out in 1908 when this part of the Old Town was redeveloped. The shops here are not as exclusive as those on Jungfernstieg; the stores and shopping precincts on both sides of the street provide a wide selection of goods at more affordable prices. ✉ *Altstadt* Ⓤ *Jungfernstieg (U-bahn).*

11 **Museum für Kunst und Gewerbe** (Arts and Crafts Museum). The museum houses a wide range of exhibits, from 15th- to 18th-century scientific instruments to an art-nouveau interior complete with ornaments and furnishings. It was built in 1876 as a combination museum and school. Its founder, Justus Brinckmann, intended it to be a bastion of the applied arts that would counter what he saw as a decline in taste owing to industrial mass production. A keen collector, Brinckmann amassed a wealth of unusual objects, including a collection of ceramics from around the world. ✉ *Steintorpl. 1, Altstadt* ☎ *040/42813–42732* 🌐 *www.mkg-hamburg.de* 🎫 *€7.20 or €8.20 depending on exhibit, Thurs. after 5 €4.10* ⏲ *Tues., Wed., and Fri.–Sun. 10–6, Thurs. 10–9* Ⓤ *Hauptbahnhof (U-bahn).*

3 **Planten un Blomen** (Plants and Flowers Park). Opened in 1935, this huge, tranquil park is renowned in Germany for its well-kept gardens. The park lies within the remains of the 17th-century fortified wall that guarded the city during the Thirty Years' War. If you visit on a summer evening, you'll see the Wasserballet, the play of an illuminated fountain set to organ music. Make sure you get to the lake in good time for the show—it begins at 10 PM each evening during the summer (at 9 PM in September). Also in summer, traditional tea ceremonies are presented

in the Japanese Garden, the largest of its kind in Europe. ✉ *Stephanspl., Neustadt* ☎ *040/4285–44723* 🎫 *Free* ⏲ *Mar.–Oct., daily 6 AM–10 PM; Nov.–Feb., daily 7 AM–8 PM* Ⓤ *Stephansplatz (U-bahn).*

7 Fodor's Choice ★ **Rathaus** (Town Hall). To most Hamburgers this large building is the symbolic heart of the city. As a city-state—an independent city and simultaneously one of the 16 federal states of Germany—Hamburg has a city council and a state government, both of which have their administrative headquarters in the Rathaus. A pompous neo-Renaissance affair, the building dictates political decorum in the city. To this day, the mayor of Hamburg never welcomes VIPs at the foot of its staircase but always awaits them at the very top—whether it's a president or the queen of England.

12

Both the Rathaus and the **Rathausmarkt** (Town Hall Market) lie on marshy land, a fact vividly brought to mind in 1962, when the entire area was severely flooded. The large square, with its surrounding arcades, was laid out after Hamburg's Great Fire of 1842. The architects set out to create a square with the grandeur of Venice's Piazza San Marco. The Rathaus was begun in 1866, when 4,000 piles were sunk into the moist soil to support the structure. It was completed in 1892, the year a cholera epidemic claimed the lives of 8,605 people in 71 days. A fountain and monument to that unhappy chapter in Hamburg's history are in a rear courtyard of the Rathaus.

The immense building, with its 647 rooms (6 more than Buckingham Palace) and imposing central clock tower, is not the most graceful structure in the city, but the sheer opulence of its interior is astonishing. A 45-minute tour begins in the ground-floor Rathausdiele, a vast pillared hall. Although you can only view the state rooms, their tapestries, huge staircases, glittering chandeliers, coffered ceilings, and grand portraits give you a sense of the city's great wealth in the 19th century and its understandable civic pride. ✉ *Rathausmarkt, Altstadt* ☎ *040/428–310* 🌐 *www.hamburg.de* 🎫 *English-language tour €1.50* ⏲ *Tours Mon.–Thurs., hourly 10:15–3:15, Fri.–Sun., hourly 10:15–1:15* Ⓤ *Mönckebergstr. (U-bahn).*

12 **St. Jacobikirche** (St. James's Church). This 13th-century church was almost completely destroyed during World War II. Only the furnishings survived, and reconstruction was completed in 1962. The interior is not to be missed—it houses such treasures as the vast baroque organ on which Bach played in 1720 and three Gothic altars from the 15th and 16th centuries. ✉ *Jacobikirchhof 22, at Steinstr., Altstadt* ☎ *040/303–7370* ⏲ *Apr.–Sept., Mon.–Sat. 10–5, Sun. 10–noon; Oct.–Mar., Mon.–Sat. 11–5* Ⓤ *Mönckebergstr. (U-bahn).*

The Harbor & Historic Hamburg

Hamburg's historic sections are a fascinating patchwork of time periods where buildings restored to their medieval splendor hold ground next to sleek high-rises. Along the waterfront, late-medieval and 19th-century warehouses contrast with the high-tech harbor installations nearby. Narrow cobblestone streets with richly decorated mansions lead to churches of various faiths, reflecting the diverse origins of the sailors and merchants drawn to the city. Small museums and old restaurants occupy buildings that once served as sailor taverns.

a good walk

This tour takes you south to the picturesque quarters around the harbor area (bring your passport, as there's a customs point on the walk). Start with a visit to the restored **St. Katharinenkirche** 14 ⚑. To get there from the Messberg U-bahn station, cross the busy Ost-West-Strasse and continue down Dovenfleet, which runs alongside the Zollkanal (Customs Canal). On your way, you will pass the Kornhausbrücke, a bridge with a sign on it announcing your entrance to the **Freihafen Hamburg** 15 (Free Port) and the **Speicherstadt** 16, a complex of 19th-century warehouses. Continue until Dovenfleet turns into Bei den Mühren, and you'll see the church's distinctive green-copper spire.

As you leave the Free Port over the Brooksbrücke (two bridges down from the Kornhausbrücke), you'll pass through a customs control point, at which you may be required to make a customs declaration. Turn left after the bridge, where Bei den Mühren becomes Bei dem Neuen Krahn. Take your second right onto **Deichstrasse** 17, the city's 18th-century business district, which runs alongside Nikolaifleet, a former channel of the Alster and one of Hamburg's oldest canals. After exploring this lovely area, take the Cremon Bridge, at the north end of Deichstrasse. This angled pedestrian bridge spans Ost-West-Strasse. You may wish to make a small detour down one of the narrow alleys (Fleetgänge) between the houses to see the fronts of the houses facing the Nikolaifleet.

The Cremon Bridge will take you to Hopfenmarkt Square, just a stone's throw from the ruins of the **Alte St. Nikolaikirche** 18. From here head west on Ost-West-Strasse and cross to the other side at the Rödingsmarkt U-bahn station. Continue along Ost-West-Strasse, which turns into Ludwig-Erhard-Strasse, until you reach Krayenkamp, a side street to your left that will take you to the historic **Krameramtswohnungen** 19 (Shopkeepers' Guild Houses). The distance from the Nikolaikirche to Krayenkamp is about 1 km (½ mi). Hamburg's best-loved and most famous landmark, the **St. Michaeliskirche** 20, is on the other side of the alley Krayenkamp.

From St. Michaeliskirche, walk west on Bömkenstrasse until you reach a park and the enormous **Bismarck-Denkmal** 21, rising high above the greenery. From the monument's northeast exit cross Ludwig-Erhard-Strasse and continue on Holstenwall to the **Museum für Hamburgische Geschichte** 22, with exhibits depicting the city's past.

TIMING This can be a rather short walk, manageable in a half day if you stroll only through the historic harbor quarters. You may wish to spend another 1½ hours at the Museum of Hamburg History and still another hour taking a closer look inside the churches.

What to See

18 **Alte St. Nikolaikirche** (Old St. Nicholas's Church). The tower and outside walls of this 19th-century neo-Gothic church are all that survived World War II. Today these ruins serve as a monument to those killed

and persecuted during the war. Next to the tower, which offers a magnificent view of the surrounding historic streets, is a center documenting the church. It's run by a citizens' organization that is also spearheading private efforts to partially rebuild the church and redesign the surrounding area. A cellar wine store is open for browsing and wine tasting. ✉ *Ost-West-Str. at Hopfenmarkt, Altstadt* ☎ *040/371–125* €2 ⏲ *Daily 11–5* Ⓤ *Rödingsmarkt (U-bahn).*

㉑ **Bismarck-Denkmal** (Bismarck Memorial). The colossal 111-foot granite monument, erected between 1903 and 1906, is an equestrian statue of Otto von Bismarck, Prussia's Iron Chancellor, who was the force behind the unification of Germany. The plinth features bas-reliefs of various German tribes. Created by sculptor Hugo Lederer, the statue calls to mind Roland, the famous warrior from the Middle Ages, and symbolizes the German Reich's protection of Hamburg's international trade. ✉ *St. Pauli* Ⓤ *St. Pauli (U-bahn).*

★ ⑰ **Deichstrasse.** The oldest residential area in the Old Town of Hamburg, which dates from the 14th century, now consists of lavishly restored houses from the 17th through the 19th centuries. Many of the original houses on Deichstrasse were destroyed in the Great Fire of 1842, which broke out in No. 42 and left approximately 20,000 people homeless; only a few of the early dwellings escaped its ravages. Today Deichstrasse and neighboring **Peterstrasse** (just south of Ost-West-Strasse) are of great historical interest. At No. 39 Peterstrasse, for example, is the baroque facade of the Beylingstift complex, built in 1700. Farther along, No. 27, constructed as a warehouse in 1780, is the oldest of its kind in Hamburg. All the buildings in the area have been painstakingly restored, thanks largely to the efforts of individuals. ✉ *Altstadt* Ⓤ *Rödingsmarkt (U-bahn).*

need a break?

There are two good basement restaurants in this area. The **Alt-Hamburger Aalspeicher** (✉ Deichstr. 43, Altstadt ☎ 040/362–990) serves fresh fish dishes, including Hamburg's famous eel soup with dried fruits. **Das Kontor** (✉ Deichstr. 32, Altstadt ☎ 040/371–471), an upscale historic Hamburg tavern, offers some of the city's best fried potatoes and delicious, traditional desserts.

★ ⑮ **Freihafen Hamburg.** Hamburg's Free Port, the city's major attraction, dates to the 12th century, when the city was granted special privileges by Holy Roman Emperor Frederick I (Barbarossa). One of these was freedom from paying duties on goods transported on the Elbe River. The original Free Port was where the Alster meets the Elbe, near Deichstrasse, but it was moved farther south as Hamburg's trade expanded. When Hamburg joined the German Empire's Customs Union in the late 1800s, the Free Port underwent major restructuring to make way for additional storage facilities. An entire residential area was torn down (including many Renaissance and baroque buildings), and the **Speicherstadt** warehouses, the world's largest block of continuous storage space, came into being between 1885 and 1927. Ⓤ *St. Pauli Landungsbrücken (U-bahn).*

19 **Krameramtswohnungen** (Shopkeepers' Guild Houses). The shopkeepers' guild built this tightly packed group of courtyard houses between 1620 and 1626 for members' widows. The houses became homes for the elderly after 1866. The half-timber, two-story dwellings, with unusual twisted chimneys and decorative brick facades, were restored in the 1970s and are now protected. The house marked "C" is open to the public. A visit inside gives you a sense of what life was like in these 17th-century dwellings. ✉ *Historic House "C," Krayenkamp 10, Speicherstadt* ☎ *040/365–800* *€1, Fri. €.50* ⏲ *Tues.–Sun. 10–5* Ⓤ *Rödingsmarkt (U-bahn).*

need a break?

Krameramtsstuben (✉ Krayenkamp 10, Speicherstadt ☎ 040/365–800) is a rustic bar-cum-restaurant, in the heart of the historic harbor, where you can sample hearty local dishes, mostly made with fish. It's open daily 10 AM–midnight.

22 **Museum für Hamburgische Geschichte** (Museum of Hamburg History). The museum's vast and comprehensive collection of artifacts gives you an excellent overview of Hamburg's development, from its origins in the 9th century to the present. Pictures and models portray the history of the port and shipping between 1650 and 1860. One exhibit chronicles pirates in the North Sea during the late Middle Ages. ✉ *Holstenwall 24, Neustadt* ☎ *040/42813–22380* 🌐 *www.hamburgmuseum.de* *€7.50* ⏲ *Tues.–Sat. 10–5, Sun. 10–6* Ⓤ *St. Pauli (U-bahn).*

14 **St. Katharinenkirche** (St. Catherine's Church). Completed in 1660, this house of worship was severely damaged during World War II but has since been carefully reconstructed. Only two 17th-century epitaphs (to Moller and to von der Feehte) remain from the original interior. ✉ *Katharinenkirchhof 1, near Speicherstadt, Altstadt* ☎ *040/3037–4730* ⏲ *May–Sept., Mon.–Sat. 9–5, Sun. noon–5; Oct.–Apr., Sat. 9–4, Sun. noon–4* Ⓤ *Messberg (U-bahn).*

20 Fodor's Choice ★ **St. Michaeliskirche** (St. Michael's Church). The Michel, as it's called locally, is Hamburg's principal church and northern Germany's finest baroque-style ecclesiastical building. Constructed between 1649 and 1661 (the tower followed in 1669), it was razed after lightning struck almost a century later. It was rebuilt between 1750 and 1786 in the decorative Nordic baroque style but was gutted by a terrible fire in 1906. The replica, completed in 1912, was demolished during World War II. The present church is a reconstruction.

The distinctive 433-foot brick-and-iron tower bears the largest tower clock in Germany, 26 feet in diameter. Just above the clock is a viewing platform (accessible by elevator or stairs) that affords a magnificent panorama of the city, the Elbe River, and the Alster Lakes. Twice a day, at 10 AM and 9 PM (Sunday at noon), a watchman plays a trumpet solo from the tower platform, and during festivals an entire wind ensemble crowds onto the platform to perform. The **Multivisionsshow** (slide and audio show), located one floor beneath the viewing platform, recounts Hamburg's history on a 16.4-foot screen and a refined audio system. ✉ *St. Michaeliskirche, Altstadt* ☎ *040/376–780* 🌐 *www.st-michaelis.*

de 🎫 *Tower €2.50; crypt €1.25; tower and show €4; crypt and show €2.75; show, tower, and crypt €4.50* ⏲ *May–Oct., Mon.–Sat. 9–6, Sun. 11:30–5:30; Nov.–Apr., Mon.–Sat. 10–5, Sun. 11:30–4:30; multimedia screening Thurs. and weekends on the half hr, 12:30–3:30* Ⓤ *Landungsbrücken, Rödingsmarkt (U-bahn).*

need a break?

Just opposite St. Michaeliskirche is one of Hamburg's most traditional restaurants, the **Old Commercial Room** (✉ Englische Planke 10, Speicherstadt ☎ 040/366–319). Try one of the local specialties, such as Labskaus or Aalsuppe. If you don't make it to the restaurant, you can buy its dishes (precooked and canned) in department stores in both Hamburg and Berlin.

12

⑯ **Speicherstadt** (Warehouse District). These imposing warehouses in the Freihafen Hamburg reveal yet another aspect of Hamburg's extraordinary architectural diversity. A Gothic influence is apparent here, with a rich overlay of gables, turrets, and decorative outlines. These massive rust-brown buildings are still used to store and process every conceivable commodity, from coffee and spices to raw silks and handwoven Oriental carpets.

Hamburg's proud past as Europe's gateway to the world comes to life at the tiny but fascinating **Spicy's Gewürzmuseum,** where you can smell, touch, and feel close to 50 spices. More than 700 objects chronicle five centuries of the once-prosperous spice trade in Hamburg. ✉ *Am Sandtorkai 32, Speicherstadt* ☎ *040/367–989* 🌐 *www.spicys.de* 🎫 *€3* ⏲ *Tues.–Sun. 10–5* Ⓤ *Messberg (U-bahn).*

Although you won't be able to enter the buildings, the nonstop comings and goings will give you a good sense of a port at work. If you want to learn about the history and architecture of the old warehouses, detour to the **Speicherstadtmuseum.** ✉ *St. Annenufer 2, Block R, Speicherstadt* ☎ *040/321–191* 🌐 *www.speicherstadtmuseum.de* 🎫 *€2.80* ⏲ *Tues.–Sun. 10–5* Ⓤ *Messberg (U-bahn).*

Opposite the historic Speicherstadt, one of Europe's largest urban-development projects, the **HafenCity,** continues to be under construction. This new city district with business and living areas encompasses 387 acres. You can see a model of the project, slated for final completion in 2025, in the Speicherstadt's old power plant, along with an exhibition of the architectural and economic aspects of the new harbor district. ✉ *Am Sandtorkai 30, Speicherstadt* ☎ *040/3690–1799* 🌐 *www.hafencity.com* 🎫 *Free* ⏲ *Tues.–Sun. 10–6* Ⓤ *Messberg (U-bahn).*

St. Pauli & the Reeperbahn

The run-down maritime district of St. Pauli is sometimes described as a "Babel of sin," but that's not entirely fair. The Reeperbahn, its major thoroughfare as well as a neighborhood moniker, offers a broad menu of entertainment in addition to the striptease and sex shows. Beyond this strip of pleasure, St. Pauli and Altona are defined by their Elbe waterfront.

a good walk

At the St. Pauli U-bahn station, you'll find yourself at the beginning of a long, neon-lit street stretching nearly 1 km (½ mi). This is the red-light **Reeperbahn** 23 ⚑, full of nightlife entertainment and sex clubs. The best areas to check out are the Grosse Freiheit, Hans-Albers-Platz, and Davidstrasse. Walk down Davidstrasse to reach the not-to-be-missed **Erotic Art Museum** 24, exhibiting all aspects of human sexuality. From the museum, walk west on Hafenstrasse until you see the first market booths of the **Fischmarkt** 25, a shopper's paradise stocked with fresh fish, meat, and produce (open Sunday only).

From the market you can head back on Hafenstrasse to the nearby piers at **Landungsbrücken** 26, where ferries depart for short round-trips. Walk through the long limestone building with two towers to reach the ticket booths.

Try to make the trip to the riverside village of **Blankenese** 27, 14½ km (9 mi) west of Hamburg. You can get there by ferry, S-bahn, or on foot. The celebrated Elbe River walk is long, but it's one of Hamburg's prettiest. On the way to Blankenese (or on the return trip), stop by **Museumshafen Övelgönne** 28, a quaint little fishing town and harbor filled with historic vessels.

TIMING This tour can last a full day and a long night, including a very enjoyable boat trip through the harbor, and a few hours in the theaters and bars along the Reeperbahn. However, you can walk down the red-light strip and check out the Erotic Art Museum and the Landungsbrücken in less than three hours. You have to be either a night owl or an early riser to catch the Fischmarkt on Sunday.

What to See

27 **Blankenese.** Blankenese is one of Hamburg's surprises—a suburb west of the city with the character of a quaint 19th-century fishing village. Some Germans like to compare it to the French and Italian rivieras; many consider it the most beautiful part of Hamburg. The most picturesque part of town is the steeply graded hillside, where paths and stairs barely separate closely placed homes. The town has a lively fruit and vegetable market, open Tuesday 8–2, Friday 8–6, and Saturday 8–1. Weekday ferries to Blankenese leave from Pier 3 every 10 to 15 minutes and involve two transfers. ⌚ *Nonstop HADAG ferries depart from Pier 2 for Blankenese late Mar.–Oct., weekends at 10:30 and 2:30* Ⓤ *Blankenese (S-bahn).*

need a break?

A fine view and well-prepared fish await you at one of Hamburg's most traditional fish restaurants, the **Sagebiel's Fährhaus** (✉ Blankeneser Hauptstr. 107, Blankenese ☎ 040/861–514), a former farmhouse where Kaiser Wilhelm once celebrated his birthday.

24 **Erotic Art Museum.** Sexually provocative art from 1520 to the present—1,800 original works (mostly photographs) in all—is showcased here. The collection is presented with such great taste and decorum that it has won the respect of many who doubted the museum's seriousness. Special exhibits of modern erotic photography and events are staged in

a building on Bernhard-Nocht-Strasse. ✉ *Bernhard-Nocht-Str. 69, St. Pauli* ☎ *040/3178–4126* 🌐 *www.eroticartmuseum.de* ☞ *Minimum age 16* 🎫 *€8* ⏲ *Sun.–Thurs. 10 AM–midnight, Fri. and Sat. 10 AM–2 AM* Ⓤ *St. Pauli (U-bahn).*

25 **Fischmarkt** (Fish Market). The open-air Altona Fischmarkt is worth getting out of bed early for (or staying up all night). The pitch of fervent deal making is unmatched in Germany. Offering real bargains, the market's barkers are famous for their sometimes rude but usually successful bids to shoppers. Sunday fish markets became a tradition in the 18th century, when fishermen sold their catch before church services. Today, freshly caught fish are only a part of the scene. You can find almost anything here—from live parrots and palm trees to armloads of flowers and bananas, valuable antiques, and fourth-hand junk. ✉ *Between Grosse Elbestr. and St. Pauli Landungsbrücken, St. Pauli* ⏲ *Sun. 5:30 AM–10:30 AM* Ⓤ *Landungsbrücken (U-bahn).*

26 **Landungsbrücken** (Piers). A visit to the port is not complete without a tour of one of the most modern and efficient harbors in the world. Hamburg is Germany's largest seaport, with 33 individual docks and 500 berths lying within its 78 square km (30 square mi). Barge tours of the harbor leave from the main passenger terminal, along with a whole range of ferries and barges heading to other destinations in the North Sea. There's usually a breeze, so dress warmly. ***Rickmer Rickmers,*** an 1896 sailing ship that once traveled as far as the West Indies, is open to visitors and is docked at Pier 1. ✉ *St. Pauli Landungsbrücken 1, St. Pauli* ☎ *040/319–5959* 🌐 *www.rickmer-rickmers.de* 🎫 *Rickmer Rickmers €3* ⏲ *Daily 10–6* Ⓤ *Landungsbrücken (U-bahn).*

28 **Museumshafen Övelgönne** (Museum Harbor Övelgönne). The glorious days of *Windjammern,* Hamburg's commercial fleet, come alive in this small harbor museum on the Elbe River. Eighteen antique steam and sailing vessels from the late 19th century can be inspected from the pier, or boarded on weekends if a crew is around. Behind the harbor, along the quay, are charming little cottages with tidy gardens. ✉ *Anleger Neumühlen, Ottensen* ☎ *040/4191–2761* 🌐 *www.museumshafen-oevelgoenne.de* 🎫 *Free* ⏲ *Daily.*

need a break?

No Hanseatic Sunday would be complete without a visit to the **Strandperle** (✉ Am Schulberg, Ottensen ☎ 040/880–1112), a small but stylish kiosk on the riverbanks near Övelgönne. Join the Hamburg locals and watch the cargo ships pass while downing your beer with lemonade (an *Alsterwasser*) and munching on a bratwurst.

23 **Reeperbahn.** The hottest spots in town are concentrated in the St. Pauli Harbor area on the Reeperbahn thoroughfare and on a little side street known as the Grosse Freiheit (Great Liberty—and that's putting it mildly). In the early '60s, a then obscure band called the Beatles had their first live acts at the now demolished Star Club. The striptease shows are expensive and explicit, but a walk through this area is an experience in itself and costs nothing. Saturday night finds St. Pauli pulsating with people determined to have a good time. It's *not* advisable,

however, to travel through this part of the city alone in the wee hours of the morning.

Although some of the sex clubs may be relatively tame, a good many others are pornographic in the extreme. They all get going around 10 PM and will accommodate you until the early hours. Order your own drinks rather than letting the hostess do it, and pay for them as soon as they arrive, double-checking the price list again before handing over the money.

Among the attractions in the St. Pauli area are theaters, clubs, music pubs, discos, and a bowling alley. Ⓤ *St. Pauli (U-bahn).*

WHERE TO EAT

Hamburg has plenty of chic restaurants to satisfy the fashion-conscious local professionals, as well as the authentic salty taverns typical of a harbor town.

WHAT IT COSTS In Euros

	$$$$	$$$	$$	$	¢
AT DINNER	over €25	€21–€25	€16–€20	€9–€15	under €9

Restaurant prices are per person for a main course at dinner.

Downtown & Historic Hamburg

$–$$$$ ✕ **Ratsweinkeller.** For atmosphere and robust local specialties, there are few more-compelling restaurants than this cavernous, late-19th-century haunt under the city hall. The simple tables are wooden, and ship models hang from the high stone-and-brick arches. You can order surprisingly fancy or no-nonsense meals. Fish specialties predominate, but there's a wide range of choices. ✉ *Grosse Johannisstr. 2, Altstadt* ☎ *040/364–153* ▭ *AE, DC, MC, V* ⏲ *No dinner Sun.* Ⓤ *Rathaus (U-Bahn).*

$$–$$$ ✕ **Deichgraf.** This small and elegant fish restaurant in the heart of the old harbor warehouse district is a Hamburg classic. It's one of the best places to get traditional dishes such as *Hamburger Pannfisch* (fried pieces of the day's catch prepared in a wine and mustard sauce) at a very reasonable price of €17.40. The restaurant is in an old merchant house, and historic oil paintings in the dining room depict the hardships of the fisherman of the late 19th century. Reservations are essential on weekends. ✉ *Deichstr. 23, Altstadt* ☎ *040/364–208* ▭ *AE, MC, V* ⏲ *Closed Sun. No lunch Sat.* Ⓤ *Rödingsmarkt (U-bahn).*

$–$$ ✕ **Das Feuerschiff.** This bright-red lightship served in the English Channel before it retired to the city harbor in 1989 and became a landmark restaurant and pub. Fresh and tasty fish dishes are on the menu, as well as traditional seafood entrées from Scandinavia, Poland, and other seafaring nations. On Monday, local bands jam, and once a month a cabaret show is staged. ✉ *Vorsetzen, Hamburg City Sporthafen, Speicherstadt* ☎ *040/362–553* ▭ *AE, DC, MC, V* Ⓤ *Baumwall (U-bahn).*

St. Pauli & Altona

$$$$ ✕ **Darling Harbour.** True to its name, the Darling Harbour, named after the world-famous Sydney attraction, has become everybody's darling—at least that of Hamburg's bold and beautiful. Familiar faces from the media world come to this fine yet understated restaurant to see and be seen. Though some may find the menu lacking, the chef pulls out every stop to create an innovative and daring cuisine. The stunning view from the bay windows is worth a visit in itself. ✉ *Neumühlen 17, Altona* ☎ *040/380–8900* ▭ *AE, MC, V* ⏲ *No lunch Sat., closed Sun.* Ⓤ *Altona (U-bahn).*

$$–$$$$ ✕ **Fischereihafen-Restaurant Hamburg.** For the best fish in Hamburg, book a table at this big, upscale restaurant in Altona, just west of the downtown area, along the Elbe. The menu changes daily according to what's available in the fish market that morning. The restaurant and its oyster bar are a favorite with the city's beau monde. In summer, try to get a table on the sun terrace for a great view of the Elbe. ✉ *Grosse Elbstr. 143, Altona* ☎ *040/381–816* ✍ *Reservations essential* ▭ *AE, DC, MC, V* Ⓤ *Altona (S-bahn).*

★ $–$$$$ ✕ **Au Quai.** The Au Quai is the hippest addition to a row of upscale, romantic restaurants nestled on the harbor's waterfront. The terrace, situated directly over the water, makes the elegant yet stylishly modern Au Quai a summer must. Indulge in French-Asian fusion cuisine, while taking in chugging tugboats, container ships, and sightseeing boats. The staff, dressed in blue-and-white-stripe scoop-neck sailor sweaters, enriches the maritime flair, and the menu offers a tasty selection of fish. ✉ *Grosse Elbstr. 145, Altona* ☎ *040/3803–7730* ▭ *AE, DC, MC, V* ⏲ *No lunch Sat., no dinner Sun.* Ⓤ *Königstrasse (S-bahn).*

$–$$$$ ✕ **Rive.** This harborside oyster bar is a Hamburg establishment, known for both its German nouvelle cuisine and its classic local dishes. Choose between dishes such as hearty *Matjes mit drei Saucen* (herring with three sauces), or *Dorade in der Salzkruste* (dorado fried in salt crust). Media types come to this shiplike building for the fresh oysters, clams, and the spectacular view. ✉ *Van der Smissen Str. 1, Kreuzfahrt-Center, Altona* ☎ *040/380–5919* ✍ *Reservations essential* ▭ *AE* Ⓤ *Königstrasse (S-bahn).*

$$–$$$ ✕ **Stocker.** *Nordlichter,* as northern Germans are affectionately called, love Austrian cuisine, and for delicacies including Viennese classics such as schnitzel or boiled beef brisket, they come to Stocker, the city's expert. The restaurant is casual and full of charm. A good choice is the *Schmankerlteller,* a hearty sampler with Austrian favorites, or the three-course lunch menu for just €18. In summer request a table in the quaint garden. ✉ *Max-Brauer-Allee 80, Altona* ☎ *040/3861–5056* ▭ *AE, DC, MC, V* ⏲ *Closed Mon.* Ⓤ *Altona (U-Bahn).*

★ $–$$$ ✕ **Fischerhaus.** The family-owned fish restaurant may look mediocre, but the food, prepared from family recipes, is outstanding. Most dishes focus on North Sea fish and Hamburg classics such as Labskaus or a plaice (a kind of flounder) dish. A favorite is the *Scholle Finkenwerder Art* (pan-fried plaice with smoked ham and potato salad). When making a reservation, ask for a table upstairs to get a harbor view. ✉ *Fischmarkt 14, St. Pauli* ☎ *040/314–053* ▭ *MC, V* Ⓤ *Landungsbrücken (U-Bahn).*

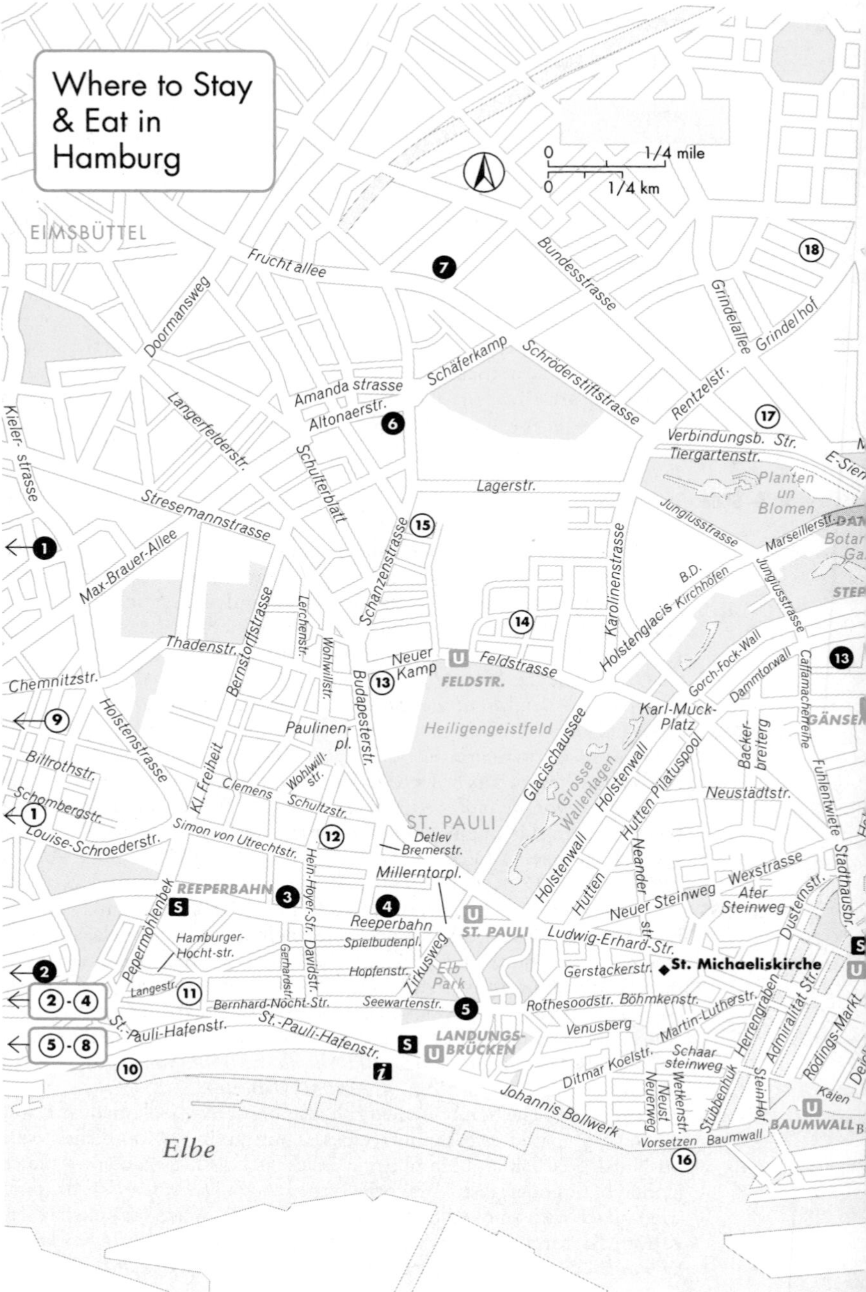
Where to Stay & Eat in Hamburg
0 1/4 mile
0 1/4 km
EIMSBÜTTEL
Frucht allee
Bundesstrasse
Doormansweg
Grindelallee
Grindelhof
Schäferkamp
Schröderstiftstrasse
Amanda strasse
Altonaerstr.
Rentzelstr.
Langerfelderstr.
Kieler- strasse
Schulterblatt
Verbindungsb. Str.
Tiergartenstr.
Lagerstr.
Planten un Blomen
Stresemannstrasse
Jungiusstrasse
Schanzenstrasse
Karolinenstrasse
Marseillerstr.
Max-Brauer-Allee
B.D. Kirchhöfen
Holstenglacis
Bernstorffstrasse
Lerchenstr.
Thadenstr.
Wohlwillstr.
Neuer Kamp
Feldstrasse
FELDSTR.
Gorch-Fock-Wall
Dammtorwall
Caffamacherreihe
Chemnitzstr.
Budapesterstr.
Karl-Muck-Platz
Holstenstrasse
Paulinenpl.
Heiligengeistfeld
Glacischaussee
Backerbreiterg
Billrothstr.
Kl. Freiheit
Grosse Wallenlagen
Holstenwall
Pilatuspool
Schombergstr.
Clemens
Wohlwillstr.
Schultzstr.
Neustädtstr.
Fuhlentwiete
Louise-Schroederstr.
Simon von Utrechtstr.
ST. PAULI
Detlev Bremerstr.
Hutten
Neander str.
Stadthausbr.
Hein-Hoyer-Str.
Millerntorpl.
Wexstrasse
Ater Steinweg
Neuer Steinweg
REEPERBAHN
Reeperbahn
Duesternstr.
Pepermöhlenbek
Hamburger-Hocht-str.
Spielbudenpl.
ST. PAULI
Ludwig-Erhard-Str.
Gerhardstr.
Davidstr.
Zirkusweg
Gerstackerstr.
St. Michaeliskirche
Hopfenstr.
Elb Park
Langestr.
Bernhard-Nocht-Str.
Seewartenstr.
Rothesoodstr.
Böhmkenstr.
Martin-Lutherstr.
Herrengraben
Admiralität Str.
Rödings-Markt
St.-Pauli-Hafenstr.
St.-Pauli-Hafenstr.
LANDUNGSBRÜCKEN
Venusberg
Schaar steinweg
Ditmar Koelstr.
Johannis Bollwerk
Neuerweg
Neust
Wetkenstr.
Stubbenhuk
SteinHof
Kajen
BAUMWALL
Vorsetzen
Baumwall
Elbe

Restaurants

- Abendmahl 11
- Artisan 15
- Au Quai 6
- Balutschi 17
- Cox 22
- Darling Harbour 5
- Das Feuerschiff 16
- Deichgraf 19
- Eisenstein 1
- Fischereihafen-Restaurant Hamburg 8
- Fischerhaus 10
- Genno's 21
- La Mer 23
- Landhaus Scherrer 2
- Le Canard 3
- Mess 14
- Nil 13
- Phuket 24
- Poletto 25
- Ratsweinkeller 20
- Rive 7
- Seven Seas 4
- Shalimar 18
- Stocker 9
- Weite Welt 12

Hotels

- Aussen Alster 24
- Baseler Hof 12
- Dorint am Alten Wall 15
- Fritzhotel 6
- Garden Hotels Hamburg 11
- Gastwerk Hotel Hamburg 1
- Hotel Abtei 9
- Hotel-Garni Mittelweg 10
- Hotel Hafen Hamburg Classic and Hotel Residenz Hafen Hamburg 5
- Hotel Louis C. Jacob 2
- Hotel Monopol 4
- Hotel Prem 25
- Hotel Stern 3
- Hotel Terminus Garni 19
- Hotel Village 17
- Kempinski Atlantic Hotel Hamburg 22
- Kronprinz 18
- Mellingburger Schleuse 8
- Nippon Hotel 20
- Park Hyatt Hamburg 16
- Raffles Vier Jahreszeiten 14
- Side 13
- Steen's Hotel 21
- Wedina 23
- Yoho 7

¢–$$$ ✕ **Weite Welt.** Weite Welt is an absolute must if you are visiting St. Pauli. The restaurant's name recalls the longing of Hamburg's seafaring folk to see the "great wide world." In an old fish smokehouse on the Reeperbahn's notorious Grosse Freiheit (the live sex shows are just a few steps away), regulars feel right at home thanks to owner Nikolaus Bornhofen's hospitality. The fish dishes cross the continents of Europe and Asia and the theme dishes (such as the "Last Supper of the *Titanic*") are a good value. Reservations are essential on weekends. ✉ *Grosse Freiheit 70, St. Pauli* ☎ *040/319–1214* ▭ *No credit cards* ⊙ *No lunch* Ⓤ *Reeperbahn (U-bahn).*

$$ ✕ **Nil.** Media types—the intellectual and cultural elite of Hamburg—gather at this trendy venue for business dinners and prepartying on weekends. The Nil is worth a visit for its interior alone: it's in an old 1950s-style, three-floor shoe shop. The kitchen serves seafood and modern German cuisine, including four different three- to six-course menus, offering fare such as *Entenkeule Hamburger Art* (roasted duck joint in spicy sauce) in winter or lighter Italian-oriented fare in summer. Reservations are essential for dinner. ✉ *Neuer Pferdemarkt 5, St. Pauli* ☎ *040/439–7823* ▭ *No credit cards* ⊙ *No lunch. Closed Tues.* Ⓤ *Feldstrasse (U-bahn).*

$–$$ ✕ **Mess.** The Mess is one of the most popular restaurants in the hip and upcoming Karolinenviertel (called "Karo-Viertel" by Hamburgers). True to its worldy, young patrons, it dares to offer a wild mixture of old German standards like *Königsberger Klopse* (meatballs in a thick butter-and-caper sauce served with potatoes) along with more exotic fare such as ostrich steak. For lunch, order the three-course menu (€19) or the daily pasta special for just €6. In summer, try to get a table in the small garden under the pergola and sample vintages from the restaurant's own specialty wine store. ✉ *Turnerstr. 9, St. Pauli* ☎ *040/4325–0152* ▭ *AE* ⊙ *No lunch Sat. and Sun.* Ⓤ *Messehallen (U-bahn).*

★ ¢–$$ ✕ **Artisan.** Don't be surprised to see the words I HATE PEOPLE WHO ARE NOT SERIOUS ABOUT THEIR MEALS scribbled on the slate, where one would normally find the specials. Artisan chef Thorsten Gillert has adopted this Oscar Wilde quote as his personal credo. This subdued, minimalist restaurant—Hamburg's newcomer of recent years—is the perfect place to acquaint yourself with the revolutionary fusion cuisine of international and local culinary favorites. The ever-changing selection of the three- and seven-course prix-fixe meals go for €28 and €55, respectively. ✉ *Kampstr. 27, Altona* ☎ *040/4210–2915* ▭ *No credit cards* ⊙ *Closed Mon.* Ⓤ *Sternschanze (U-bahn).*

$ ✕ **Abendmahl.** Off the Reeperbahn, the small Abendmahl is a launching point for crowds getting ready for bars and clubs. The fresh dishes on the small menu change daily and focus on French and Italian recipes. But the food plays second fiddle to the inexpensive and inventive drinks and the flirtatious atmosphere. The three-course dinner meal for just €24 is a great deal. ✉ *Hein-Köllisch-Pl. 6, St. Pauli* ☎ *040/312–758* ▭ *No credit cards* ⊙ *No lunch* Ⓤ *St. Pauli (U-bahn).*

St. Georg

$$–$$$ ✕ **La Mer.** The old-fashioned dining room of the Hotel Prem is perhaps the best hotel restaurant in the city, beautifully set on the Aussenalster, a 10-minute ride from downtown. A host of specialties changes daily, including *Zanderfilet auf Pefferkraut mit gefüllten Waffelkartoffeln* (pike-perch fillet on pepper sauerkraut with stuffed waffle potatoes) or *Brust und Keule vom Perlhuhn auf Schwarzwurzeln mit Kartoffelgratin* (breast and leg of guinea fowl on black salsify with potato gratin). ✉ *An der Alster 9, St. Georg* ☎ *040/2483–4040* *Jacket and tie* ▭ *AE, DC, MC, V* ⏲ *Closed Sun. No lunch Mon.* Ⓤ *Hauptbahnhof (U- or S-bahn).*

★ $$ ✕ **Cox.** The Cox has been a reliably stylish restaurant for several years. It remains one of the hippest places around, with waitstaff (and patrons, for that matter) who won't give you any attitude. The dishes, mostly German nouvelle cuisine, are known for the careful use of fresh produce and spices from around the globe. The simple and cool interior with red-leather banquettes is reminiscent of a French brasserie. ✉ *Lange Reihe 68, at Greifswalder Str. 43, St. Georg* ☎ *040/249–422* ▭ *AE* ⏲ *No lunch weekends* Ⓤ *Hauptbahnhof (U-bahn and S-Bahn).*

Rotherbaum

¢–$ ✕ **Balutschi.** A favorite among neighborhood students, Balutschi serves affordable and tasty Pakistani food, prepared with organic products. The richly decorated restaurant always seems to be crowded, and the smell of fresh spices and meat dishes, mostly lamb, hangs thick in the air. On weekend nights, a reservation is a must. ✉ *Grindelallee 33, Rotherbaum* ☎ *040/452–479* ▭ *AE, MC, V* Ⓤ *Dammtor (S-bahn).*

Ottensen, Uhlenhorst & Elsewhere

$$$$ ✕ **Landhaus Scherrer.** Though this establishment is a 10-minute drive from downtown, its parklike setting seems worlds away from the high-rise bustle of the city. Wood-panel walls and soft lighting create a low-key mood in the building, which was originally a brewery. The food fuses sophisticated specialties with more down-to-earth local dishes. The wine list is exceptional. ✉ *Elbchaussee 130, Ottensen* ☎ *040/880–1325* ▭ *AE, DC, MC, V* ⏲ *Closed Sun.* Ⓤ *Altona (S-bahn).*

★ $$$$ ✕ **Poletto.** Cornelia Poletto is one of Germany's few female chefs with a Michelin star. Also ranked as one of the country's best ethnic restaurants, the Poletto offers straightforward but top-quality Italian cooking. Dishes are prepared without the somewhat affected creativity of other award-winning restaurants, and probably even more tasty. This family-style approach—Mr. Poletto will personally explain the food and wine menues to guests placed around huge round tables—makes the little restaurant even more inviting. ✉ *Eppendorfer Landstrasse 154, Eppendorf* ☎ *040/480–2159* ▭ *No credit cards* ⏲ *No lunch Sat. Closed Sun. and Mon.* Ⓤ *Lattenkamp (U-bahn).*

$$$$ ✕ **Seven Seas.** Süllberg, a small hill in the countryside along the River Elbe, boasts one of northern Germany's most traditional "getaway restaurants." The Seven Seas is run by one of Europe's premier chefs, Karlheinz Hauser, and features international and French fish specialties in four- to six-course dinners only. If you don't want all the frills, try the Bistro dining room or come on a Sunday, when you can enjoy a bountiful Sunday brunch (€45 per person). ✉ *Süllbergsterrasse 12, Blanke-*

nese ☎ *040/866–2520* ▭ *AE, MC, V* ⊙ *Closed Mon. and Tues. No lunch* Ⓤ *Blankenese (S-bahn).*

$$ ✕ **Eisenstein.** The food is fantastic considering the low prices, and the crowd bubbly and mostly stylish. A sure bet are the daily menus or the Italian-Mediterranean dishes, including pastas and some excellent pizzas. The Pizza Helsinki (made with sour cream, onions, and fresh gravlax) is truly delicious. The setting, a 19th-century industrial complex with high ceilings and dark redbrick walls, is very rustic. Reservations are essential for dinner. ✉ *Friedensallee 9, Ottensen* ☎ *040/390–4606* ▭ *No credit cards* Ⓤ *Altona (S-bahn).*

★ $$ ✕ **Shalimar.** The spices and exotic fare the locals have come to know at Freihafen Hamburg are commonplace at Shalimar, *the* Indian restaurant that has been dazzling Hamburg for 22 years strong. Its refined atmosphere, compliments of the gentle sitar sounds and swift, silent waiters, beguiles its guests as much as its prices. Neither, however, can hold a candle to the food itself. A mixed crowd of students, hipsters, bankers, and Indian businessmen make for an exciting evening. And be sure to try the mango ice cream—no meal is complete without it. ✉ *Dillstr. 16, Harvestehude* ☎ *040/442–484* ▭ *AE, DC, MC, V* ⊙ *No lunch* Ⓤ *Hallerstrasse (U-bahn).*

★ $–$$ ✕ **Phuket.** Though it has an unimaginative name and dull facade, Phuket is by far the best Thai, or Asian for that matter, restaurant in town. The place is often jammed with Hamburgers from all districts who come to sample the truly hot fish dishes or the famous chicken in red-wine sauce. ✉ *Adolph-Schönfelder-Str. 33–35, Uhlenhorst* ☎ *040/2982–3380* ▭ *AE, V* Ⓤ *Hamburger Strasse (U-bahn).*

★ $ ✕ **Genno's.** Genno's is far from the downtown district, in Hamburg-Ham—a run-down residential area where you would hardly expect to find such a gem of high-quality dining. Owner Eugen Albrecht makes you feel at home with warm service and equally tasty dishes. The cuisine is a mixture of his personal preferences, including dishes such as *Lammfilet mit Senfsauce* (fillet of lamb with mustard sauce). ✉ *Hammer Steindamm 123, Hamm* ☎ *040/202–567* ▭ *No credit cards* ⊙ *Closed Sun. No lunch* Ⓤ *Hasselbrook (S-bahn).*

WHERE TO STAY

Hamburg has a full range of hotels, from five-star, grande-dame luxury enterprises to simple pensions. Nearly year-round conference and convention business keeps most rooms booked well in advance, and the rates are high. But many of the more expensive hotels lower their rates on weekends, when businesspeople have gone home. The tourist office can help with reservations if you arrive with nowhere to stay; ask about the many Happy Hamburg special-accommodation packages.

WHAT IT COSTS In Euros

	$$$$	$$$	$$	$	¢
FOR 2 PEOPLE	over €225	€175–€225	€100–€175	€50–€100	under €50

Hotel prices are for two people in a standard double room, including tax and service.

Downtown & Historic Hamburg

$$$$ **Raffles Vier Jahreszeiten.** Some claim that this 19th-century town house on the edge of the Binnenalster is the best hotel in Germany. Antiques—the hotel has a set of near-priceless Gobelin tapestries—fill the public rooms and accentuate the stylish bedrooms; fresh flowers overflow from massive vases; rare oil paintings adorn the walls; and all rooms are individually decorated with superb taste. One of the three restaurants, the Jahreszeiten-Grill, has been restored to its 1920s art-deco look with dark woods, making it worth a visit. ✉ *Neuer Jungfernstieg 9–14, Neustadt, D–20354* ☎ *040/34940* 📠 *040/3494–2600* 🌐 *www.hvj.de* *156 rooms, 23 suites* *3 restaurants, room service, in-room safes, minibars, cable TV with movies, in-room broadband, in-room data ports, Web TV, Wi-Fi, health club, hair salon, massage, sauna, bar, wineshop, baby-sitting, dry cleaning, laundry service, concierge, business services, meeting room, parking (fee), some pets allowed (fee), no-smoking rooms* ▭ *AE, DC, MC, V* Ⓤ *Jungfernstieg (U-bahn).*

Fodor's Choice ★

★ **$$$–$$$$** **Park Hyatt Hamburg.** This ultramodern hotel is built within the historic walls of the Levantehaus, an old warehouse, not far from the train station. Guest rooms have bright and modern furnishings, somewhat minimalist and Asian in style. Original artwork by local painters adorns the suites. The Club Olympus pool and fitness area is breathtaking, both for its streamlined design and the variety of activities. ✉ *Bugenhagenstr. 8, Neustadt, D–20095* ☎ *040/3332–1234* 📠 *040/3332–1235* 🌐 *www.hamburg.hyatt.com* *252 rooms, 30 apartments* *2 restaurants, room service, minibars, cable TV with movies, in-room broadband, in-room data ports, Web TV, Wi-Fi, indoor pool, health club, hair salon, massage, sauna, bar, baby-sitting, dry cleaning, laundry service, concierge, business services, meeting room, parking (fee), some pets allowed (fee), no-smoking room* ▭ *AE, DC, MC, V* *BP* Ⓤ *Steinstrasse (U-bahn).*

$$ **Baseler Hof.** It's hard to find a fault in this central hotel near the Binnenalster and the opera house. Service is friendly and efficient, all rooms are neatly furnished, and prices are quite reasonable for this expensive city. The hotel caters to both individuals and convention groups, so the lounge area can be crowded at times. ✉ *Esplanade 11, Neustadt, D–20354* ☎ *040/359–060* 📠 *040/3590–6918* 🌐 *www.baselerhof.de* *151 rooms, 4 suites* *Restaurant, room service, Wi-Fi, bar, baby-sitting, dry cleaning, laundry service, concierge, meeting room, parking (fee), some pets allowed (fee), no-smoking rooms; no a/c* ▭ *AE, DC, MC, V* *CP* Ⓤ *Stephansplatz (U-bahn).*

$$ **Dorint am Alten Wall.** The flagship hotel of the German hotel chain, the Dorint is one of the city's finest. Behind the facade of Hamburg's 19th-century Postsparkassenamt, the German mail service's customer bank, is a sleek decor dominated by gray, white, and dark-brown hues. All rooms are furnished with timelessly stylish furniture, huge beds (by German standards), and even bigger marble bathrooms. ✉ *Alter Wall 38–46, Altstadt, D–20457* ☎ *040/369–500* 📠 *040/3695–01000* 🌐 *www.dorint.de* *224 rooms, 18 suites* *Restaurant, room service, in-room safes, minibars, cable TV with movies, in-room broadband, Web*

TV, Wi-Fi, pool, health club, massage, sauna, bar, baby-sitting, dry cleaning, laundry service, business services, meeting rooms, parking (fee), some pets allowed (fee), no-smoking rooms 💳 *AE, DC, MC, V* 🍽 *BP* Ⓤ *Rödingsmarkt (U-bahn).*

★ **$$** **Side.** Deeming itself to be "the luxury hotel of the 21st century," this ambitious newcomer is one of Germany's most architecturally sophisticated hotels. Premier Milanese designer Matteo Thun served as the driving force behind the five-star resort in the heart of the city. His vision provided for the stunning lighting arrangement as well as the interior design. Whether soothed by the eggshell-white accents in your room or wowed by the lobby's soaring and stark atrium, you won't ever want to leave. ✉ *Drehbahn 49, Altstadt, D–20304* ☎ *040/309–990* 🖷 *040/3099–9399* 🌐 *www.side-hamburg.de* 🛏 *158 rooms, 10 suites* 👍 *Restaurant, room service, in-room safes, minibars, cable TV with movies, in-room broadband, Web TV, Wi-Fi, health club, sauna, spa, bar, dry cleaning, laundry service, meeting rooms, parking (fee), some pets allowed (fee), no-smoking rooms* 💳 *AE, DC, MC, V* Ⓤ *Gänsemarkt (U-bahn).*

$ **Hotel Terminus Garni.** Unlike its famous namesake in Paris, the Hamburg Hotel Terminus is a simple and inexpensive hotel near the central train station. It's popular among British and American budget travelers who appreciate its relaxed atmosphere and reliable service (the hotel is part of the Garni hotel chain). Double rooms share either a bath or a shower. ✉ *Steindamm 5, Altstadt, D–20999* ☎ *040/280–3144* 🖷 *040/241–518* 🌐 *www.hotel-terminus-hamburg.de* 🛏 *20 rooms, 4 with shared bath; 1 apartment* 👍 *Cable TV; no a/c, no room phones* 💳 *AE, DC, MC, V* 🍽 *CP* Ⓤ *Hauptbahnhof-Süd (U-bahn, S-bahn).*

★ **$** **Hotel Village.** The small and charming Hotel Village was once a thriving brothel near the central train station. Red-and-black carpets and glossy wallpaper in the rooms are a nod to the hotel's past. Some rooms even have their old large beds, replete with canopy and a revolving mirror. The service (including a 24-hour coffee bar) is extremely friendly and casual. ✉ *Steindamm 4, Altstadt, D–20099* ☎ *040/246–137* 🖷 *040/486–4949* 🌐 *www.hotel-village.de* 🛏 *20 rooms* 👍 *Cable TV, parking (fee), some pets allowed (fee); no a/c* 💳 *AE, MC, V* 🍽 *CP* Ⓤ *Hauptbahnhof (U-bahn and S-bahn).*

$ **Kronprinz.** For its humble position (on a busy street opposite the railway station) and its moderate price, the Kronprinz is a surprisingly attractive hotel, with a whiff of four-star flair. Rooms are individually styled, modern but homey. ✉ *Kirchenallee 46, Altstadt, D–20099* ☎ *040/243–258* 🖷 *040/280–1097* 🛏 *73 rooms* 👍 *Restaurant, minibars, cable TV, baby-sitting, parking (fee), some pets allowed (fee), no-smoking rooms; no a/c* 💳 *AE, DC, MC, V* 🍽 *CP* Ⓤ *Hauptbahnhof (U-bahn and S-bahn).*

St. Pauli & Altona

$$–$$$ **Gastwerk Hotel Hamburg.** Proudly dubbing itself Hamburg's first design hotel, the Gastwerk, in a century-old, redbrick gas plant, certainly is the most stylish accommodation in town. The simple but incredibly chic furnishings reflect the building's industrial design but are warmed by the use of natural materials, various woods, and thick carpets. The loft rooms with large windows, bare walls, and a lot of space are probably the most exciting hotel rooms in Hamburg. ✉ *Beim alten Gaswerk 3, at Daimlerstr. 67, Altona, D–22761* ☎ *040/890–620* 🖷 *040/890–6220* 🌐 *www.gastwerk-hotel.de* *122 rooms, 13 suites* *Restaurant, room service, in-room safes, minibars, cable TV, in-room broadband, in-room data ports, Wi-Fi, health club, massage, sauna, bar, dry cleaning, laundry service, meeting rooms, free parking, some pets allowed (fee), no-smoking rooms* 💳 *AE, DC, MC, V* Ⓤ *Bahrenfeld (S-bahn).*

12

$$ **Hotel Hafen Hamburg Classic and Hotel Residenz Hafen Hamburg.** Located in one building complex just across from the famous St. Pauli Landungsbrücken, both hotels are good value considering their three- and four-star status, respectively. The older Hotel Hafen Hamburg, with its small but nicely renovated rooms, offers a great view of the harbor, while the larger, ultramodern and upscale Hotel Residenz Hafen annex has less flair but more comfort. The location makes this hotel a perfect starting point for exploring St. Pauli and the Reeperbahn. ✉ *Seewartenstr. 7–9, St. Pauli, D–20459* ☎ *040/3111–3600* 🖷 *040/3111–3751* 🌐 *www.hotel-hamburg.de* *Hotel Hafen: 230 rooms; Hotel Residenz: 125 rooms* *Restaurant, in-room safes, minibars, cable TV with movies, Wi-Fi, sauna, 3 bars, baby-sitting, dry cleaning, laundry service, meeting room, parking (fee), some pets allowed (fee), no-smoking floor; no a/c in some rooms* 💳 *AE, MC, V* Ⓤ *Landungsbrücken (U-bahn).*

$ **Fritzhotel.** This intimate yet stylish hotel, squeezed into an old city apartment complex, has small but bright designer rooms complete with amenities such as TV and Internet access. The hotel does not offer breakfast but it shares the relatively quiet street with many bistros and breakfast cafés. ✉ *Schanzenstr. 101–103, St. Pauli, D–20357* ☎ *040/8222–2830* 🖷 *040/8222–28322* 🌐 *www.fritzhotel.com* *17 rooms* *Cable TV; no a/c* 💳 *No credit cards* Ⓤ *Sternschanze (U-bahn).*

$ **Hotel Monopol.** There's no other hotel in the Reeperbahn neighborhood where budget travelers can enjoy a safe and clean stay in the heart of Europe's most bizarre red-light district. Despite a makeover in 2002, the small rooms are mostly old-fashioned, and some look like an odd mixture of 1950s and '80s designs, but the service is warm and has a touch of Hamburger Kiez. You might run into an artist performing in a Hamburg musical—or in the live sex shows on Reeperbahn. ✉ *Reeperbahn 48, St. Pauli, D–20359* ☎ *040/311–770* 🖷 *040/3117–7151* 🌐 *www.monopol-hamburg.de* *82 rooms* *Restaurant, room service, cable TV, in-room data ports, bar, dry cleaning, laundry service, meeting room, free parking, some pets allowed (fee); no a/c* 💳 *AE, MC, V* *BP* Ⓤ *St. Pauli (U-bahn).*

¢ **Hotel Stern.** One of the best deals in town, the huge Hotel Stern is located in the heart of St. Pauli and primarily attracts students and young backpacker tourists from around the world. The modern rooms are sparsely furnished but well-kept. A great plus are the Stern's many partner restaurants where you can dine and wine for just a few euros. ✉ *Reeperbahn 154, St. Pauli, D–20359* ☎ *040/3176–9990* 🖷 *040/3176–9999* 🌐 *www.stern-hamburg.de* *308 rooms* *Restaurant, cable TV, in-room data ports, free parking, some pets allowed (fee); no a/c* 💳 *AE, MC, V* *BP* Ⓤ *St. Pauli (U-bahn).*

St. Georg

$$$–$$$$ Fodor's Choice ★ **Kempinski Atlantic Hotel Hamburg.** There are few hotels in Germany more sumptuous than this gracious Edwardian palace facing the Aussenalster. The stylish mood is achieved with thick carpet, marble-inlaid floors and walls, sophisticated lighting, and a newly refurbished lobby that is positively baronial. Some rooms are traditionally furnished while others are more modern, but all are typical of Hamburg in their understated luxury. Each room has a spacious sitting area and large bathroom. Guests can lounge in the formal outdoor courtyard, where only the gurgling fountain disturbs the peace. ✉ *An der Alster 72–79, St. Georg, D–20099* ☎ *040/28880* 📠 *040/247–129* 🌐 *www.kempinski.atlantic.de* *241 rooms, 13 suites* *2 restaurants, café, room service, in-room safes, minibars, cable TV with movies, in-room data ports, Wi-Fi, pool, health club, massage, sauna, boating, bicycles, bar, shops, baby-sitting, dry cleaning, laundry service, concierge, business services, meeting room, parking (fee), some pets allowed (fee), no-smoking rooms* 💳 *AE, DC, MC, V* Ⓤ *Hauptbahnhof (U-bahn, S-bahn).*

$$–$$$ **Hotel Prem.** Facing the Aussenalster, this extremely personable, quiet hotel is Hamburg's gem. Most guests are regulars and have favorite rooms; no two rooms are the same. The Adenauer Suite (named after the chancellor, who stayed here) is traditionally furnished, including an antique chaise longue and a period writing desk in an alcove with a lake view. Room 102, across the hall, has contemporary furnishings and a platform bed. Suite 2 has two rooms with modern furnishings and a terrace overlooking the lake. The bar is intimate, and the dining at La Mer is superb. ✉ *An der Alster 9, St. Georg, D–20099* ☎ *040/2483–4040* 📠 *040/280–3851* 🌐 *www.hotel-prem.de* *51 rooms, 3 suites* *Restaurant, room service, in-room safes, minibars, cable TV, in-room data ports, bar, baby-sitting, dry cleaning, laundry service, concierge, business services, meeting room, free parking, some pets allowed (fee); no a/c* 💳 *AE, DC, MC, V* 🍽 *BP* Ⓤ *Hauptbahnhof (U-bahn and S-bahn).*

$$ **Aussen Alster.** Crisp and contemporary in design, this boutique hotel prides itself on the personal attention it gives its guests. Rooms are compact; most have a full bathroom, but three have a shower only, no bathtub. Stark white walls, white bedspreads, and light-hue carpets create a bright, fresh ambience. A small bar is open in the evening, and there's a tiny garden for summer cocktails. The restaurant serves Italian fare for lunch and dinner. The Aussenalster, where the hotel keeps a sailboat for guests to use, is at the end of the street. ✉ *Schmilinskystr. 11, St. Georg, D–20099* ☎ *040/241–557* 📠 *040/280–3231* 🌐 *www.aussen-alster.de* *27 rooms* *Restaurant, room service, in-room safes, cable TV, Wi-Fi, sauna, boating, bicycles, bar, baby-sitting, dry cleaning, laundry service, meeting room, parking (fee), some pets allowed (fee); no a/c* 💳 *AE, DC, MC, V* 🍽 *BP* Ⓤ *Hauptbahnhof (U-bahn and S-bahn).*

$$ **Wedina.** Rooms at this small hotel are neat and compact. When you make a reservation, either ask for a room in the Italian-style Yellow House, with its elegant parquet floor, or check out the rooms in the new, minimalist-style Green House. In the main building, the bar and breakfast area face the veranda and a small garden and pool that bring Tuscany to mind. All lodgings are a half block from the Aussenalster and a brisk 10-minute walk from the train station. ✉ *Gurlittstr. 23, St. Georg, D–20099* ☎ *040/280–8900* 🖷 *040/280–3894* 🌐 *www.wedina.de* ⇨ *48 rooms, 11 apartments* 👍 *In-room safes, cable TV, in-room broadband, in-room data ports, bicycles, bar, concierge, business services, parking (fee), some pets allowed (fee), no-smoking rooms; no a/c* 💳 *DC, MC, V* 🍴 *CP* Ⓤ *Hauptbahnhof (U-bahn and S-bahn).*

$ **Steen's Hotel.** This small, family-run hotel in a narrow, four-story town house near the central train station provides modest but congenial service. The rooms are spacious and clean but lack atmosphere. Bathrooms are tiny. A great plus are the comfortable beds with reclining head and foot rests. The breakfasts amply make up for the uninspired rooms, and the hotel's garage is a blessing, since there's never a parking space in this neighborhood. ✉ *Holzdamm 43, St. Georg, D–20099* ☎ *040/244–642* 🖷 *040/280–3593* 🌐 *www.steens-hotel.com* ⇨ *11 rooms* 👍 *Minibars, cable TV, parking (fee); no a/c* 💳 *AE, DC, MC, V* 🍴 *CP* Ⓤ *Hauptbahnhof (U-bahn and S-bahn).*

Elsewhere

★ $$$$ **Hotel Louis C. Jacob.** Would-be Hanseats frequent this small yet luxurious hotel nestled amid the older wharf dwellings along the banks of the Elbe. Far from the hustle-bustle of the city, the intimate Louis C. Jacob, named after the French landscape gardener who founded it in 1791, makes a point of meticulously pampering its guests. Artist Max Liebermann stayed here and painted the terrace with its linden trees. One of the classically furnished suites even bears his name. From a riverview room, you'll be able to watch passing ships and listen as their foghorns bid Hamburg farewell. ✉ *Elbchaussee 401–403, Blankenese, D–22609* ☎ *040/822–550* 🖷 *040/8225–5555* 🌐 *www.hotel-jacob.de* ⇨ *66 rooms, 19 suites* 👍 *2 restaurants, room service, in-room safes, minibars, cable TV with movies, in-room broadband, in-room data ports, Wi-Fi, hot tub, massage, sauna, bar, dry cleaning, laundry service, meeting rooms, parking (fee), some pets allowed (fee), no-smoking rooms* 💳 *AE, DC, MC, V* Ⓤ *Hochkamp (S-bahn).*

$$$–$$$$ **Hotel Abtei.** On a quiet, tree-lined street about 2 km (1 mi) north of the downtown area, in Harvestehude, this elegant period hotel offers understated luxury and friendly, personal service. If you want a room with a four-poster bed, ask when making a reservation. One of the nicest rooms in the small hotel is No. 7 with its antique 19th-century washing tables. All guest rooms have English antique cherrywood and mahogany furniture. ✉ *Abteistr. 14, Harvestehude, D–20149* ☎ *040/442–905* 🖷 *040/449–820* 🌐 *www.abtei-hotel.de* ⇨ *8 rooms, 3 suites* 👍 *Restaurant, room service, in-room safes, minibars, cable TV, dry cleaning, laundry service, free parking, some pets allowed (fee); no a/c* 💳 *AE, MC, V* 🍴 *BP* Ⓤ *Klosterstern (U-bahn).*

$$–$$$ **Garden Hotels Hamburg.** The location in chic Pöseldorf, 2 km (1 mi) from the downtown area, may discourage those who want to be in the thick of things, but this is one of the most appealing hotels in Hamburg,

offering outstanding personal service and classy accommodations in three attractive mansions. ✉ *Magdalenenstr. 60, Pöseldorf, D–20148* ☎ *040/414–040* 📠 *040/414–0420* 🌐 *www.garden-hotels.de* *57 rooms, 3 suites* *Room service, minibars, cable TV, in-room data ports, bicycles, bar, baby-sitting, dry cleaning, laundry service, concierge, business services, meeting room, free parking, some pets allowed (fee); no a/c* *AE, MC, V* Ⓤ *Hallerstrasse (U-bahn).*

$$ **Hotel-Garni Mittelweg.** With chintz curtains, flowered wallpaper, old-fashioned dressing tables, and a country-house-style breakfast room, this hotel exudes small-town charm in big-business Hamburg. The converted mansion is in upmarket Pöseldorf, a short walk from the Aussenalster and a quick bus ride from the city center. ✉ *Mittelweg 59, Pöseldorf, D–20149* ☎ *040/414–1010* 📠 *040/4141–0120* 🌐 *www.hotel-mittelweg.de* *30 rooms, 1 apartment* *Room service, in-room safes, minibars, cable TV, in-room broadband, Wi-Fi, baby-sitting, parking (fee), some pets allowed (fee), no-smoking rooms; no a/c* *AE, DC, MC, V* *CP* Ⓤ *Klosterstern (U-bahn).*

$$ **Nippon Hotel.** You'll be asked to remove your shoes before entering your room at the Nippon. Tatami mats line the floor, futon mattresses are on the beds, and an attentive Japanese staff is at your service. The authenticity might make things a bit *too* spartan and efficient for some, but by cutting some Western-style comforts, the hotel offers a good value in the attractive Uhlenhorst District. The Nippon has a Japanese restaurant and sushi bar. ✉ *Hofweg 75, Uhlenhorst, D–22085* ☎ *040/227–1140* 📠 *040/2271–1490* 🌐 *www.nippon-hotel-hh.de* *41 rooms, 1 suite* *Restaurant, in-room safes, minibars, cable TV, Wi-Fi, bicycles, dry cleaning, laundry service, concierge, business services, meeting room, parking (fee), no-smoking rooms; no a/c* *AE, DC, MC, V* *BP* Ⓤ *Mundsburg (U-bahn).*

$–$$ **Mellingburger Schleuse.** If you prefer off-the-beaten-track lodgings, this member of the Ringhotel-Association is a 20-minute drive from the downtown area, idyllically set in a forest. The Alsterwanderweg hiking trail passes right by the doorstep. The hotel is more than 200 years old, with a thatch roof, peasant-style furnishings, and a restaurant that serves traditional northern German dishes. ✉ *Mellingburgredder 1, Sasel, D–22395* ☎ *040/6024–00103* 📠 *040/602–7912* *40 rooms* *2 restaurants, cable TV, billiards, bowling, bar, concierge, meeting room, free parking, some pets allowed (fee), no-smoking rooms; no a/c* *AE, DC, MC, V* *BP* Ⓤ *Poppenbüttel (U-bahn).*

★ $ **Yoho.** Centrally located between the hip Schanzenviertel and the downtown area, the new Yoho is the upscale youth hostel of the 21st century. Housed in an historic, imposing villa with contemporary interior design, it offers simple yet elegant rooms with modern amenities otherwise not found in a hostel. Guests under 26 receive a special rate of €67 for a single or €87 for a double room, including breakfast. This is the perfect place for the international backpacker with an edge. ✉ *Moorkamp 5, Eimsbüttel, D–20357* ☎ *040/284–1910* 📠 *040/2841–9141* 🌐 *www.yoho-hamburg.de* *30 rooms* *Restaurant, cable TV, in-room data ports, free parking, some pets allowed; no a/c* *AE, DC, MC, V* *CP* Ⓤ *Schlump (U-bahn).*

NIGHTLIFE & THE ARTS

The Arts

The arts flourish in this cosmopolitan metropolis. The city's ballet company is one of the finest in Europe, and the Ballet Festival in July is a cultural high point. Information on events is available in the magazines *Hamburger Vorschau*—pick it up for free in tourist offices and most hotels—and *Szene Hamburg,* sold at newsstands for €2.50.

12

The best way to order tickets for all major Hamburg theaters, musicals, and most cultural events is the central phone **Hamburg-Hotline** (☎ 040/3005–1300). A number of travel agencies also sell tickets for plays, concerts, and the ballet. The tourist office at the **Landungsbrücken** (✉ between Piers 4 and 5, St. Pauli ☎ 040/3005–1200 or 040/3005–1203) has a ticket office. One of the large downtown ticket agencies is the **Theaterkasse im Alsterhaus** (✉ Jungfernstieg 16, Neustadt ☎ 040/353–555). The downtown **Theaterkasse Central** (✉ Gerhart-Hauptmann-Pl. 48, Neustadt ☎ 040/337–124) is at the Landesbank-Galerie.

Ballet & Opera

One of the most beautiful theaters in the country, **Hamburgische Staatsoper** (✉ Grosse Theaterstr. 35, Altstadt ☎ 040/356–868) is the leading northern German venue for opera and ballet. The Hamburg Ballet is directed by American John Neumeier.

The **Operettenhaus Hamburg** (✉ Spielbudenpl. 1, St. Pauli ☎ 01805/114–113) is currently running *Mamma Mia,* a fun and popular musical about the pop band Abba.

Concerts

Both the Hamburg Philharmonic and the Hamburg Symphony Orchestra appear regularly at the **Laeiszhalle** (✉ Johannes-Brahms-Pl., Neustadt ☎ 040/346–920). Visiting orchestras from overseas are also presented.

Film

Independent and mainstream English-language movies are shown at the **Metropolis** (✉ Dammtorstr. 30a, Neustadt ☎ 040/342–353) and are often subtitled in German. Students often show up at the **Grindel Kino** (✉ Grindelberg 7a, Harvestehude ☎ 040/449–333) for blockbuster English-language movies.

Theater

Deutsches Schauspielhaus (✉ Kirchenallee 39, St. Georg ☎ 040/248–713), one of Germany's leading drama stages, is lavishly restored to its full 19th-century opulence and is the most important Hamburg venue for classical and modern theater.

English Theater (✉ Lerchenfeld 14, Uhlenhorst ☎ 040/227–7089) is the city's only theater presenting English-language drama.

Musicaltheater am Hamburger Hafen (✉ Norderelbstr. 6, at Hamburger Hafen, follow signs to Schuppen 70, St. Pauli ☎ 040/3005–1150) is currently staging a German version of the Broadway musical hit *The Lion King*.

Hamburg is by far Germany's capital for musicals, and the **Neue Flora Theater** (✉ Stresemannstr. 159a, at Alsenstr., Altona ☎ 01805–4444 or 040/4316–5490) offers the best deal.

Nightlife

The Reeperbahn

Whether you think it sordid or sexy, the Reeperbahn, in the St. Pauli District, is as central to the Hamburg scene as the classy shops along Jungfernstieg. A walk down **Herbertstrasse** (men only, no women or children permitted), just two blocks south of the Reeperbahn, can be quite an eye-opener. Here, prostitutes sit displayed in windows as they await customers. On nearby **Grosse Freiheit,** you'll find a number of the better-known sex-show or table-dance clubs: **Colibri,** at No. 30; **Safari,** at No. 24; and **Dollhouse,** at No. 11. They cater to the package-tour trade as well as those on the prowl by themselves. Prices are high. If you order a drink, ask for the price list, which must be displayed by law, and pay as soon as you're served. Not much happens here before 10 PM.

Schmidts Tivoli (✉ Spielbudenpl. 27–28, St. Pauli ☎ 040/3177–8899 or 040/3005–1400) has become Germany's most popular variety theater, presenting a classy repertoire of live music, vaudeville, chansons, and cabaret.

Bars

The Hansestadt has a buzzing and upscale bar scene, with many spots that feature live music or DJs and dancing. A nightlife institution still going strong is the fashionable but cozy **Bar Hamburg** (✉ Rautenbergstr. 6–8, St. Georg ☎ 040/2805–4880). The **Bereuther** (✉ Klosterallee 100, Hoheluft ☎ 040/4140–6789) is a sleek bar and bistro for thirtysomethings. **Christiansen's** (✉ Pinnasberg 60, St. Pauli ☎ 040/317–2863), near the Fischmarkt, is said to mix the best cocktails in town.

Dance Clubs

One of the most appealing and entertaining new clubs in Hamburg, **Stage Club** (✉ Stresenabbstr, 159a, Altona ☎ 040/4316–5460), on the first floor of the Neue Flora theater, welcomes a mixed crowd to live and soul, funk, or jazz music every night, followed by a DJ. The new **China Lounge** (✉ Nobistor 14, St. Pauli ☎ 040/3197–6622), in a former Chinese restaurant, is Hamburg's coolest lounge and bar, mostly attracting hip and beautiful twentysomethings. The stylish **Funky Pussy Club** (✉ Grosse Freiheit 34, St. Pauli ☎ 040/314–236) is a small dance club with '70s retro design, where a young crowd dances to techno, hip-hop, and Latin music. The more mature business crowd meets at Hamburg's smallest dance club, **Top of Town** (✉ Marseillerstr. 2, Rotherbaum ☎ 040/3502–3432), on the 26th floor of the SAS Radisson Hotel. It's both elegant and expensive, as most Hamburg clubs are.

Jazz & Live Music Clubs

Birdland (✉ Gärtnerstr. 122, Hoheluft ☎ 040/405–277) is one of the leading clubs among Hamburg's more than 100 venues, offering everything from traditional New Orleans sounds to avant-garde electronic noise. The **Cotton Club** (✉ Alter Steinweg 10, Neustadt ☎ 040/343–878), Hamburg's oldest jazz club, books classic New Orleans jazz as well as swing. **Docks** (✉ Spielbudenplatz 19, St. Pauli ☎ 040/317–8830) has a stylish bar and is Hamburg's largest venue for live music. It also puts on disco nights.

SPORTS & THE OUTDOORS

Biking

Most major streets in Hamburg have bicycle lanes. Some of the major hotels will lend their guests bikes. The most central location for renting bikes is at the **Hauptbahnhof** (✉ entrance on Kirchenallee, St. Georg ☎ 040/3918–50475). Bikes rent for €8 a day (7 AM–9 PM). A wide selection of bikes, including racing, mountain, and children's bikes, are rented at Mr. Petersen's **Hamburg anders erfahren** (✉ Insterburger Str. 15, Bramfeld ☎ 040/640–1800). The bikes cost between €7.50 and €20 a day. There's a discount on multiday rentals. A complete list of bike rentals in Hamburg and the surrounding countryside can be obtained from the **ADFC Hamburg** (✉ Markstr. 18, D–22041 ☎ 040/393–933 or 040/390–7050).

Jogging

The best places for jogging are the Planten un Blomen and Alter Botanischer Garten parks and along the leafy promenade around the Alster. The latter route is about 6 km (4 mi) long.

Sailing

You can rent rowboats and sailboats on the Alster in summer between 10 AM and 9 PM. Rowboats cost around €12 an hour, sailboats around €16 an hour. The largest selection of boats is at the Gurlittinsel pier off An der Alster (on the east bank of the Aussenalster). Another rental outlet is at the very tip of the Alster, at the street Fernsicht.

SHOPPING

Shopping Districts

Hamburg's shopping districts are among the most elegant on the continent, and the city has Europe's largest expanse of covered shopping arcades, most of them packed with small, exclusive boutiques. The streets **Grosse Bleichen** and **Neuer Wall,** which lead off Jungfernstieg, are a high-price-tag zone. The Grosse Bleichen leads to six of the city's most important covered (or indoor) malls, many of which are connected. The marble-clad **Galleria** is modeled after London's Burlington Arcade. Daylight streams through the immense glass ceilings of the **Hanse-Viertel,** an otherwise ordinary reddish-brown brick building. The **Kaufmannshaus,** also known as the Commercie, and the upscale (and former first-class hotel) **Hamburger Hof** are two of the oldest and most fashionable indoor malls. There are also the **Alte Post** and the **Bleichenhof.**

Hamburg's premier shopping street, **Jungfernstieg,** is just about the most expensive in the country. It's lined with jewelers' shops—Wempe, Brahmfeld & Guttruf, and Hintze are the top names—and chic clothing boutiques such as Linette, Ursula Aust, Selbach, Windmöller, and Jäger & Koch.

In the fashionable **Pöseldorf** district north of downtown, take a look at Milchstrasse and Mittelweg. Both are filled with small boutiques, restaurants, and cafés.

Running from the main train station to Gerhard-Hauptmann-Platz, the boulevard **Spitalerstrasse** is a pedestrians-only street lined with stores. Prices here are noticeably lower than those on Jungfernstieg.

Antiques

Take a look at the shops in the **St. Georg** district behind the train station, especially those between Lange Reihe and Koppel. You'll find a mixture of genuine antiques (*Antiquitäten*) and junk (*Trödel*). You won't find many bargains, however. ABC-Strasse is another happy hunting ground for antiques lovers.

The **Antik-Center** (✉ Klosterwall 9–21, Altstadt ☎ 040/335–065) is an assortment of 39 shops in the old market hall, close to the main train station. It features a wide variety of antiques from all periods.

Department Stores

Alsterhaus (✉ Jungfernstieg 16–20, Neustadt ☎ 040/359–010) is Hamburg's most famous department store. It's large and elegant, and a favorite with locals.

GaleriaKaufhof (✉ Mönckebergstr. 3, Altstadt ☎ 040/333–070) offers far more bargains than most other department stores.

Karstadt (✉ Mönckebergstr. 16, Altstadt ☎ 040/30940) is Germany's leading department-store chain and offers the same goods as the Alsterhaus at similar prices. Hamburg's downtown Karstadt is the city's best place to shop for sports clothing.

Stilwerk (✉ Grosse Elbstr. 68, Altona ☎ 040/306–210), Hamburg's most fashionable shopping mall, resembles a department store and primarily houses furniture and home-accessory shops.

Flea & Food Markets

A lively fruit-and-vegetable market in the heart of **Blankenese** manages to preserve the charm of a small village. ✉ *Bahnhofstr., Blankenese* ⏲ *Tues. 8–2, Fri. 8–6, Sat. 8–1* Ⓤ *Blankenese (S-bahn).*

Fischmarkt (⇨ St. Pauli and the Reeperbahn *in* Exploring Hamburg).

Gift Ideas

Binikowski (✉ Lokstedter Weg 68, Eppendorf ☎ 040/462–852 or 040/4607–1848) sells the most famous must-buy *Buddelschiffe* (ships in bottles). There are few better places to shop for one, or for a blue-and-white-stripe sailor's shirt, a sea captain's hat, ship models, or even ships' charts.

Captain's Cabin (✉ St. Pauli Landungsbrücken, St. Pauli ☎ 040/316–373), a Hamburg institution, is an experience not to be missed. It's the best place for all of the city's specialty maritime goods.

Harry's Hafenbasar (✉ Balduinstr. 18, St. Pauli ☎ 040/312–482) is full of dusty goods traders and seamen have brought back from the corners of the globe. This eerie, bazaarlike store is jam-packed and is a bargain-hunter's paradise for anything maritime.

Seifarth and Company (✉ Robert-Koch-Str. 19, Norderstedt ☎ 040/524–0027) is one of the best places to buy tea in Hamburg, and Hamburg is one of the best places to buy tea in Europe. Smoked salmon and caviar are terrific buys here as well.

Jewelry

Wempe (✉ Jungfernstieg 8, Neustadt ☎ 040/3344–8824) is Germany's largest and most exclusive jeweler. This is its flagship store (one of three Hamburg locations); the selection of watches here is particularly outstanding.

Men's Clothing

The stylish store **Doubleeight. Another Level** (✉ Jungfernstieg 52, Neustadt ☎ 040/3571–5510) carries both designer and less-expensive everyday fashions. A Hamburg classic and a must for the fashion-conscious traveler, **Thomas I-Punkt** (✉ Mönckebergstr. 21, Altstadt ☎ 040/327–172) sells hip designer clothes and suits of its own label.

Women's Clothing

Among the increasing number of intimate, upscale shopping complexes with a wide variety of designer clothing, jewelry, and gift stores, the historic **Hamburger Hof** (✉ Jungfernstieg/Grosse Bleichen, Neustadt ☎ 040/350–1680) is one of the most beautiful, primarily catering to women. The upscale shopping complex **Kaufrausch** (✉ Isestr. 74, Eppendorf ☎ 040/480–8313) has mostly clothing and accessories stores for women. **Kleidermacher** (✉ Michaelisbrücke 1–3, Neustadt ☎ 040/3751–8787) carries several young local designers' labels. A small but elegant and very personal store, **Linette** (✉ Eppendorfer Baum 19, Eppendorf ☎ 040/460–4963), stocks only top designers.

SIDE TRIPS FROM HAMBURG

Hamburg is surrounded by the fertile green marshlands of the neighboring states of Schleswig-Holstein and Lower Saxony (Niedersachsen). Two popular side trips are described here.

Altes Land

23 km (14 mi) west of downtown Hamburg (on Finkenwerder Str. and Cranzer Hauptdeich).

The marshy Altes Land extends 30 km (19 mi) west from Hamburg along the south bank of the Elbe River to the town of Stade. This fruit-growing region is dotted with huge half-timber farmhouses and crisscrossed by canals. Hikers come out for walks, especially in spring, when the apple and cherry trees are in blossom. Some of the prettiest trails take you along the dikes running next to the Este and Lühe rivers. Much of the territory is best covered on foot, so wear walking shoes. You may want to bring a picnic lunch as well and spend a long (summer) day here.

From the dock at Cranz, walk south into the suburb of **Neuenfelde.** Visit the **St. Pancratius Kirche** (Church of St. Pancratius), a baroque church with an unusual painted barrel roof, worth a visit for its northern German baroque-style altar. It was built in 1688, and the organ, dating from the same period, was designed by Arp Schnitger, an organ builder and local farmer. ✉ *Am Organistenweg, Altes Land* ☎ *040/745–9296* ⏲ *Daily 9–5.*

The 18th-century church and decorative farmhouses of the village of **Jork** lie some 9 km (5½ mi) on foot to the west of Neuenfelde, just beyond the confluence of the Este and Elbe rivers (Bus No. 257 travels to and from Neuenfelde as well). The windmill in **Borstel,** a 10-minute walk from Jork, is worth a short detour.

Stade

60 km (37 mi) west of Hamburg on B–73.

The medieval town of Stade is skirted by marshland, rivers, and small lakes on the western edge of the Altes Land. Founded sometime before AD 994, and once a thriving member of the Hanseatic League, Stade was later conquered by the Swedes, who controlled the city for 70 years: and their heritage is still visible.

Close to the **Alter Hafen** (Old Harbor), which looks rather like a narrow canal, is Stade's most beautiful (and lively) square, the tiny Fischmarkt. Nearby streets, particularly **Wasser West,** have many cafés and restaurants as well as some of the best-preserved Renaissance and baroque merchants' mansions. The **Schwedenspeicher-Museum** (Swedish Warehouse Museum) once stored food for the Swedish garrison and now traces the city's history from the Stone Age to the present. ✉ *Wasser West 39, Stade* ☎ *04141/3222* 🎫 *€1* ⏲ *Tues.–Fri. 10–5, weekends 10–6.*

A walk through the **Altstadt** (Old Town), which is set on a little island in the River Elbe, gives you a vivid impression of what a northern German city looked like 300 years ago. Many of the buildings are built in the half-timber or redbrick style typical of the region. The heart of the Old City is the **Altes Rathaus** (Old Town Hall), built in 1667, a redbrick blend of Dutch Renaissance and early baroque recalling the city's proud mercantile days. Exhibitions are sometimes held in the historic main hall. ✉ *Hökerstr. 22, Stade* ☎ *04141/4010* ⏲ *Mon.–Wed. 7:30–4:30, Thurs. 7:30–6, Fri. 7:30–1.*

HAMBURG A TO Z

To research prices, get advice from other travelers, and book travel arrangements, visit www.fodors.com.

AIR TRAVEL

Hamburg's international airport, Fuhlsbüttel, is 11 km (7 mi) northwest of the city. The Airport-City-Bus (the private Jasper Airport-Shuttle) runs nonstop between the airport and Hamburg's main train station daily at 30-minute intervals between 5 AM and 10:30 PM. Tickets are €5 (one-way). The (public) Airport-Express (Bus 110) runs every 10 minutes between the airport and the Ohlsdorf U- and S-bahn stations, a 15-minute ride from the main train station. The fare is €1.95. A taxi to the downtown area will cost about €20. If you're driving a rental car from the airport, follow the signs to STADTZENTRUM (downtown).

Fuhlsbüttel ☎ 040/50750 🌐 www.ham.airport.de.

BOAT & FERRY TRAVEL

HADAG ferries to Altes Land and Lühe depart from the Landungsbrücken (⇨ Tours) twice daily during the week and four times daily on the weekends from mid-April through August and on weekends only in September. Get off at the stop in Lünhe. To reach Neunfelde, take the ferry from Blankenese.

A more exciting way to reach Altes Land or Stade is via a 45-minute ride on a high-speed boat. Elbe-city-jets depart four times a day for Stade from the St. Pauli Landungsbrücken, between 10:30 AM and 7:30 PM, and cost €16 (round-trip). You can also reach the Cranz dock in Altes Land by Elbe-city-jet.

HADAG ☎ 040/311-7070. **SAL Schiffahrtskontor** ☎ 04142/81170, 040/317-7170 Elbe-city-jet 🌐 www.elbe-city-jet.de.

BUS TRAVEL

Hamburg's bus station, the Zentral-Omnibus-Bahnhof, is directly behind the main train station.

Zentral-Omnibus-Bahnhof (ZOB) ✉ Adenauerallee 78, St. Georg ☎ 040/247-575.

CAR TRAVEL

Hamburg is easier to handle by car than many other German cities, and traffic is relatively uncongested. During rush hour, however, there can be gridlock. Several autobahns (A–1, A–7, A–23, A–24, and A–250) connect with Hamburg's three beltways, which then easily take you to the downtown area. Follow the STADTZENTRUM signs. To reach Altes Land and Stade from Hamburg, take B–73 west.

CONSULATES

Ireland ✉ Feldbrunnenstr. 43, Winterhude ☎ 040/4418-6213. **New Zealand** ✉ Domstr. 19, Neustadt ☎ 040/442-5550. **U.K** ✉ Harvestehuder Weg 8a, Harvestehude ☎ 040/448-0320. **U.S** ✉ Alsterufer 27, Neustadt ☎ 040/4117-1100.

EMERGENCIES

For medical emergencies: 112 is a direct line to the ambulance service operated by the fire department; 110 is the general ambulance service; 040/228–022 is a special city ambulance service providing doctors in an ambulance. The kind of service provided does not differ, only the institution behind it.

Pharmacies offer late-night service on a rotating basis. Every pharmacy displays a notice indicating the schedule. For emergency pharmaceutical assistance, inquire at the nearest police station or call 112.

Ambulance & Police ☎ 110. **Central Poison Center** ☎ 0551/19240 or 030/19240. **Dentist** ☎ 040/11500. **Emergency medical aid and Fire** ☎ 112. **Medical emergencies** ☎ 040/228-022. **Pharmacies** ☎ 112.

ENGLISH-LANGUAGE BOOKSTORE

Frensche International ✉ Spitalerstr. 26c, Altstadt ☎ 040/327-585.

TOURS

BOAT TOURS There are few better ways to get to know the city than by taking a trip around the massive harbor. The HADAG line and other companies organize round-trips in the port, lasting about one hour (€8.50–€9). Between April and October, excursion boats and barges leave every half hour from the Landungsbrücken—Piers 1, 2, 3, and 7—between 10 AM and 5:30 PM. From early November through March, departures are at 11, 12:30, 2, and 3:30 on weekends. From March through November, an English-language tour leaves at noon daily from Pier 1.

From April through October, Alster Touristik operates boat trips around the Alster Lakes and through the canals. There are two tour options; both leave from the Jungfernstieg promenade in the city center. The Aussenalster 50-minute lake tour ("Alster-Rundfahrt") costs €9 and leaves every half hour, April–October 3, daily 10–6. A two-hour-long *Fleet-Fahrt* costs €14 and explores the canals of the historic Speicherstadt (late March–November, daily at 10:45, 1:45, and 4:45). From May through September there's also the romantic twilight tour, called Dämmertour, every evening (Wednesday–Saturday in September) at 8 (€14).

Alster Touristik ☎ 040/357-4240. **Bordparty-Service** ✉ Landungsbrücken, Pier 9, St. Pauli ☎ 040/313-687. **HADAG** ☎ 040/311-7070, 040/313-130, 040/313-959, 040/3178-2231 for English-language tour.

ORIENTATION TOURS Sightseeing bus tours of the city, all with guides who rapidly narrate in both English and German, leave from Kirchenallee by the main train station. A bus tour lasting 1¾ hours sets off at varying times daily and costs €13. For €20, one of the bus tours can be combined with two one-hour boat trips on the Alster Lake and the Elbe River. Departure times for tours vary, according to season. City tours aboard the nostalgic *Hummelbahn* (a converted railroad wagon pulled by a tractor) start from the Kirchenallee stop. They run daily April–October. The fare is €13 for 1¾ hours.

Hummelbahn ☎ 040/792-8979.

WALKING TOURS Tours of downtown, the harbor district, and St. Pauli are offered from April through November, weekdays at 2:30 by the Hamburg Tourismus GmbH. All guided walking tours (€6) are conducted in German and start at different locations. Downtown tours by Stattreisen Hamburg are held on Saturday (February–November) and are conducted in German only. Tours of the historic Speicherstadt district are conducted by the Speicherstadtmuseum (Sunday at 11, €7).

Speicherstadtmuseum ✉ St. Annenufer 2, Block R, Speicherstadt ☎ 040/321-191 🌐 www.speicherstadtmuseum.de. **Stattreisen Hamburg** ☎ 040/430-3481. **Hamburg Tourismus GmbH** ✉ Steinstr. 7, Altstadt, D-20015 ☎ 040/3005-1144.

TAXIS

Taxi meters start at €2, and the fare is €1.30–€1.50 per km or ½ mi. You can hail taxis on the street or at stands, or order one by phone.

Taxi Information ☎ 040/441-011, 040/686-868, or 040/666-666.

TRAIN TRAVEL

There are two principal stations: the central Hauptbahnhof (main train station) and Hamburg-Altona, west of the downtown area. EuroCity and InterCity trains connect Hamburg with all German cities and many major European ones. Two InterCity Express "supertrain" lines link Hamburg with Berlin, Frankfurt, and Munich, and with Würzburg and Munich. Trains to Stade depart from the Hauptbahnhof.

Hauptbahnhof ✉ Steintorpl., Altstadt ☎ 11861.

TRANSPORTATION AROUND HAMBURG

The HVV, Hamburg's public transportation system, includes the U-bahn (subway), the S-bahn (suburban train), and buses. A one-way fare starts at €1.05; €1.85 covers one unlimited ride in the Hamburg city area. Tickets are available on all buses and at automatic machines in all stations and at most bus stops. A *Ganztageskarte* (all-day ticket), valid until 1 AM on the day of purchase, costs €5.50. A *9 Uhr-Tageskarte* for just €4.65 is valid between 9 AM and 1 AM on the day of purchase. If you're traveling with family or friends, a *Gruppen-* or *Familienkarte* (group or family ticket) is a good value—a group of up to five can travel for the entire day for only €7.75–€18.60 (depending on the number of fare zones the ticket covers).

Available from all Hamburg tourist offices, the Hamburg CARD allows unlimited travel on all public transportation within the city and admission to state museums. The Hamburg CARD is valid for 24 hours (beginning at 6 PM through 6 PM the following day) and costs €7.30 for one adult and up to three children under the age of 12. The Hamburg CARD for three days (valid starting at noon the first day) costs €15. The Hamburg CARD *Gruppenkarte* costs €23.90 for any group of five and is valid for three days; a *Gruppenkarte* for just one day is available for €13.50.

You must validate your ticket at a machine at the start of your journey. If you are found without a validated ticket, the fine is €40.

In the north of Hamburg, the HVV system connects with the A-bahn (Alsternordbahn), a suburban train system that extends into Schleswig-Holstein. Night buses (Nos. 600–640) serve the downtown area all night, leaving the Rathausmarkt and Hauptbahnhof every hour.

Hamburg Passenger Transport Board (Hamburger Verkehrsverbund) ✉ Steinstr. 7, Altstadt ☎ 040/19449 🌐 www.hvv.de ⏲ Daily 24/7.

TRAVEL AGENCIES

Agencies **Reiseland American Express** ✉ Grosse Bäckerstr. 3, Neustadt ☎ 040/309-080. **Hapag-Lloyd** ✉ Verkehrspavillon Jungfernstieg, Neustadt ☎ 040/325-8560.

VISITOR INFORMATION

Hamburg has tourist offices around the city. The main office is in the Hauptbahnhof (main train station) and is open daily 7 AM–11 PM. At the harbor there's an office at the St. Pauli Landungsbrücken, between Piers 4 and 5, open November–February, daily 10–7, and March–October, daily 10–5:30.

In addition to its comprehensive hotel guide, the tourist office also copublishes *Hamburger Vorschau,* a free monthly program of events in the city. The free magazine *Hamburg Tips* is issued quarterly and details major seasonal events.

All tourist offices can help with accommodations, and there's a central call-in booking office for hotel and ticket reservations and general information, the Hamburg-Hotline. A €4 fee is charged for every room reserved.

Hamburg-Hotline ☎ 040/3005–1300 🌐 www.hamburg-tourism.de. **Hamburg Tourismus GmbH** ✉ Hauptbahnhof, Altstadt ☎ 040/3005–1200 ✉ St. Pauli Landungsbrücken, St. Pauli ☎ 040/3005–1200 or 040/3005–1203 ✉ Steinstr. 7, Altstadt D–20015 ☎ 040/3005–1144. **Stade Tourismus GmbH** ✉ Schiffertorstr. 6, D–21682 Stade Stade ☎ 04141/4091–7074 📠 04141/409–110 🌐 www.stade.de.

Schleswig-Holstein & the Baltic Coast

13

WORD OF MOUTH

"Lübeck is definitely worth a day's visit. Have lunch at Schiffergesellschaft, a rustic restaurant . . . one of the oldest and most popular places in town."

—Budman

"Sylt is one of the most expensive places to vacation in Germany. . . . Rügen is developing more slowly. As part of former East Germany [Rügen] still has a lot of affordable condos and hotels, but prices are already picking up. The beaches must be among the most gorgeous and unspoiled in Europe."

—Miriam

www.fodors.com/forums

By Jürgen Scheunemann

GERMANY'S TRUE NORTH IS A QUIET AND PEACEFUL REGION that belies its past status as one of the most powerful trading centers in Europe. The salty air and lush, green landscape of marshlands, endless beaches, fishing villages, and lakes are the main pleasures here, not sightseeing. On foggy November evenings, or during the hard winter storms that sometimes strand islanders from the mainland, you can well imagine the fairy tales spun by the Vikings who lived here.

The Danish-German heritage in Schleswig-Holstein, Germany's northernmost state, is the result of centuries of land disputes between the two nations—you could call this area southern Scandinavia. Since the early 20th century, its shores and islands have become popular weekend and summer retreats for the well-to-do from Hamburg and Berlin. The island of Sylt, in particular, is known throughout Germany for its rich and beautiful sunbathers.

The rest of Schleswig-Holstein, though equally appealing in its green and mostly serene landscape, is far from rich and worldly. Most people farm or fish and often speak Plattdütsch, or low German, which is difficult for outsiders to understand. Cities such as Flensburg, Husum, Schleswig, Kiel (the state capital), and even Lübeck all exude a laid-back, small-town charm.

The neighboring state of Mecklenburg-Vorpommern includes the Baltic Coast and is even more rural. On the resort islands of Hiddensee and Usedom, the clock appears to have stopped before World War II; the architecture, the pace of life, even the old-fashioned trains seem like products of a magical time warp. Though it has long been a popular summer destination for families, few foreign tourists venture here.

This area was not always a restful retreat. Between the 12th and 16th centuries the sea was crucial to the rise of the Hanseatic League, a consortium of merchants who monopolized trade across the Baltic. You'll see their wealth invested in some of the finest examples of northern German Gothic and Renaissance redbrick architecture, with buildings topped by tall, stepped gables. The shipbuilding industry in Schleswig-Holstein closed down more than 20 years ago, however, and the mid-1990s bankruptcy of the industry in Rostock and Stralsund further depressed the economy. The unemployment rate in Mecklenburg-Vorpommern is among the highest in Germany, and a dramatic, westward migration is further depleting this sparsely populated region.

Exploring Schleswig-Holstein & the Baltic Coast

This chapter follows a route through five main ports of the medieval Hanseatic League—Flensburg, Lübeck, Wismar, Rostock, and Stralsund. Except for these main cities, both states are essentially rural, with a countryside of lakes, meadows, fertile fields, and tree-lined roads. The three major areas of interest are the western coastline of Schleswig-Holstein—primarily Sylt island, eastern Mecklenburg, and Vorpommern's secluded, tundralike landscape of sandy heath and dunes. In Mecklenburg-Vorpommern any interesting roads that head off to the north are likely to lead to the coast. Vorpommern ends at the Polish

Numbers in the text correspond to numbers in the margin and on the Schleswig-Holstein and Baltic Coast maps.

If you have 3 days

Start your trip in **Lübeck** 5, western Germany's most historic Hanseatic town, just 1 ½ hours away from Hamburg. On the following day visit **Wismar's** 6 delightful market square and grand churches and make a side trip south to **Schwerin** 7, known for its lakes and magnificent castle. The next morning head to **Rostock** 9, once the center of eastern Germany's shipbuilding industry, before touring **Stralsund** 11, a charming medieval town. It serves as a gateway to the most remote part of the Baltic Coast: the island of **Rügen** 12 with its pristine beaches and dramatic cliffs.

If you have 5 days

Devote a morning to the cities of **Husum** 1, a quaint fishing village, and **Schleswig** 3, with its Viking museums and archaeological sites. Continue to medieval **Lübeck** 5 to overnight. After seeing Lübeck, visit **Wismar** 6 before spending the night in **Schwerin** 7. On the third day, after a tour of the Schweriner lakes and the Schweriner Schloss, continue east to **Bad Doberan** 8 and Kühlungsborn, a top beach resort. The little Molli train pulled by a steam locomotive connects the resort and Bad Doberan. Spend the late afternoon and night in **Rostock** 9. Once you have finished your tour of Rostock on the fourth day, relax at the beach resort of **Warnemünde** 10. On the fifth day explore the medieval port of **Stralsund** 11 and the island of **Rügen** 12.

If you have 8 days

Spend your first day and night in the romantic fishing town of **Husum** 1. On the next morning take the train to the island of **Sylt** 2 and enjoy its beaches and nature for a full day. You may find it more economical to leave your car at the Niebüll train embarkment and use bikes, buses, or a rental car on the island. On your third day visit **Schleswig** 3 and the state capital **Kiel** 4 on your way to **Lübeck** 5. Spend another full day in the medieval Hanseatic town and then head east to **Wismar** 6 and **Schwerin** 7 for a day of sight-seeing. The sixth day you can sightsee around **Bad Doberan** 8 and **Rostock** 9, as well as **Warnemünde** 10. Spend the following night in **Stralsund** 11 and your next two days on the island of **Rügen** 12.

---

border. Barring summer traffic jams, you could easily drive through the whole region from west to east in less than two days, but that would be the surest way to miss all the hidden treasures in the villages and medieval cities along the way. Instead, try to do it like the locals—at a slow pace.

About the Restaurants & Hotels

Don't count on eating a meal at odd hours in this largely rural area. Many restaurants serve hot meals only between 11:30 AM and 2 PM, and 6 PM and 9 PM. You rarely need a reservation here and casual clothing is generally acceptable.

In northern Germany you'll find both small *Hotelpensionen* and fully equipped large hotels; along the eastern Baltic Coast, some hotels are renovated high-rises dating from GDR (German Democratic Republic) times. Many of the small hotels and pensions in towns such as Kühlungsborn and Binz have been restored to the romantic, quaint splendor of German *Bäderarchitektur* (spa architecture) from the early 20th century. In high season all accommodations, especially on the islands, are in great demand. If you can't book well in advance, inquire at the local tourist office, which will also have information on the 150 campsites along the Baltic coast and on the islands.

WHAT IT COSTS In Euros

	$$$$	$$$	$$	$	¢
RESTAURANTS	over €25	€21–€25	€16–€20	€9–€15	under €9
HOTELS	over €225	€175–€225	€100–€175	€50–€100	under €50

Restaurant prices are per person for a main course at dinner. Hotel prices are for two people in a standard double room, including tax and service.

Timing

The region's climate is at its best when the two states are most crowded with vacationers—in July and August. Winter is extremely harsh in this area, and even spring and fall are rather windy, chilly, and rainy. To avoid the crowds, schedule your trip for June or September. But don't expect tolerable water temperatures or hot days on the beach.

SCHLESWIG-HOLSTEIN

This region once thrived, thanks to the Hanseatic League and the Salzstrasse (Salt Route), a merchant route connecting northern Germany's cities. The kings of Denmark warred with the dukes of Schleswig and, later, the German Empire over the prized northern territory of Schleswig-Holstein. The northernmost strip of land surrounding Flensburg became German in 1864. The quiet, contemplative spirit of the region's people, the marshland's special light, and the ever-changing face of the sea are inspiring. Today the world-famous Schleswig-Holstein-Musikfestival ushers in classical concerts to farmhouses, palaces, and churches.

Husum

❶ *158 km (98 mi) northwest of Hamburg.*

The town of Husum is the epitome of northern German lifestyle and culture. Immortalized in a poem as the "gray city upon the sea" by its famous son, Theodor Storm, Husum is in fact a popular vacation spot in summer. Its wonderful, deserted beaches and proximity to Sylt and the Danish border make it a perfect place to relax.

The central **Marktplatz** (market square) is bordered by 17th- and 18th-century buildings, including the historic Rathaus (Town Hall), which houses the tourist-information office. The best impression of Husum's

Beaches Beaches stretch all along the coast of the North Sea and the Baltic. Virtually all these sandy beaches are clean and safe, sloping gently into the water, which is equally gentle and calm. Vacationers pack the seaside resorts during the high season (July and August). Be aware that water temperatures even in August rarely exceed 20°C (65°F). The busiest beaches are at Westerland (Sylt island), Binz (Rügen Island), Ostseebad Kühlungsborn, and Warnemünde. The most beautiful beaches are at Timmendorf on Poel Island (you can drive there from Wismar or take a White Fleet boat); Kap Arkona (reachable only on foot); and Hiddensee Island, off Rügen. The more remote coves can be found at Kampen on Sylt, at the Ahrenshoop Weststrand, on the Darss Peninsula; at Nienhagen (near Warnemünde); and the Grosser Jasmunder Bodden, on Rügen Island to the west of Lietzow.

There's a *Kurtaxe* (entrance fee) of €1.50–€5 for most beaches; the fees on Sylt average €3 per entry. Some beaches allow nude bathing. In German it's known as *Freikörperkultur* (literally "free body culture"), or FKK for short. The most popular of these bare-all beaches are on Sylt island, at Nienhagen, and Prerow (on Darss).

Churches Throughout the region medieval churches with red-and-white facades are prime examples of the German redbrick Gothic style. In Mecklenburg-Vorpommern even the smallest village proudly boasts a redbrick church, and the cathedrals in cities such as Wismar and Stralsund testify to the region's prosperous past as Hanseatic seaports. Note how many churches are named after the sailors' patron saint, St. Nikolai.

On the Menu The restaurants in both coastal states serve mostly seafood such as *Scholle* (flounder) or North Sea *Krabben* (shrimp), often with fried potatoes, eggs, and bacon. Mecklenburg specialties to look for are *Mecklenburger Griebenroller,* a custardy casserole of grated potatoes, eggs, herbs, and chopped bacon; *Mecklenburger Fischsuppe,* a hearty fish soup with vegetables, tomatoes, and sour cream; *Gefüllte Ente* (duck with bread stuffing); and *Pannfisch* (fish patty). A favorite local nightcap since the 17th century is *Grog,* a strong blend of rum, hot water, and local fruits.

---

beginnings in the mid-13th century is found south of the Marktplatz, along **Krämerstrasse;** the **Wasserreihe,** a narrow and tortuous alley; and **Hafenstrasse,** right next to the narrow **Binnenhafen** (city harbor).

The most famous house on Wasserreihe is the **Theodor-Storm-Haus,** where writer Theodor Storm (1817–88) lived between 1866 and 1880. It's a must if you're interested in German literature or if you want to gain insight into the life of the few well-to-do people in this region during the 19th century. The small museum includes the poet's living room and a small *Poetenstübchen* (poets' parlor), where he wrote many of his nov-

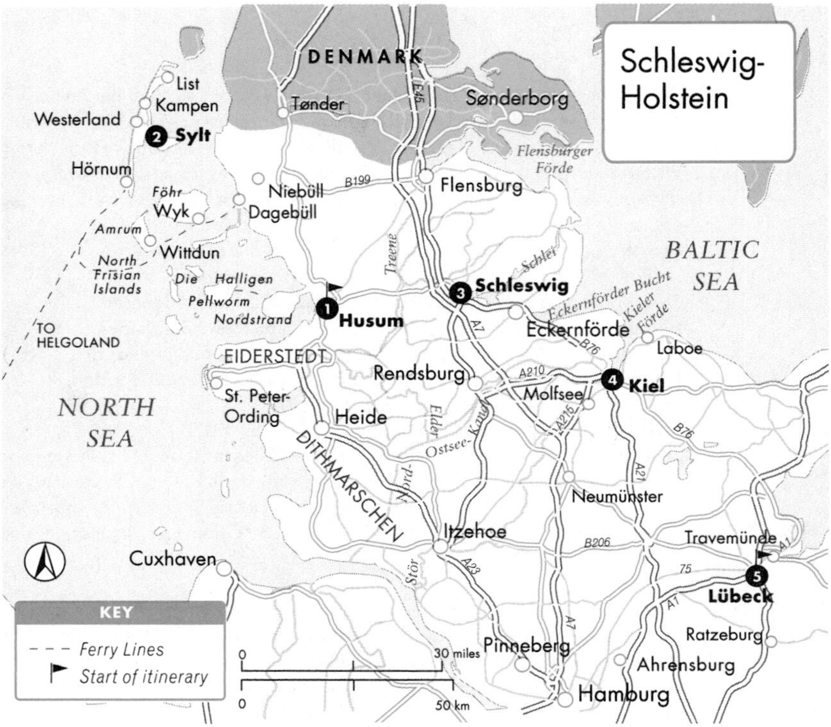

els, including the famous *Schimmelreiter* (*The Rider on the Gray Horse*). All of the rooms, the furniture, and many of the writer's belongings are original. ✉ *Wasserreihe 31* ☎ *04841/666–270* 🌐 *www.storm-gesellschaft.de* 🎫 *€2.50* ⏲ *Apr.–Oct., Tues.–Fri. 10–5, Mon. and Sun. 2–5, Sat. 11–5; Nov.–Mar., Tues., Thurs., and Sat. 2–5.*

Despite Husum's remoteness amid the stormy sea, wide marshes, and dunes, the city used to be a major seaport and administrative center. The **Schloss vor Husum** (Palace of Husum), originally built as a Renaissance castle in the late 16th century, was transformed in 1752 by the dukes of Gottorf into a redbrick baroque country palace. ✉ *Professor-Ferdinand-Tönnies-Allee* ☎ *04841/897–3130* 🎫 *€2.50* ⏲ *Mid-Jan.–Oct., Tues.–Sun. 11–5.*

Where to Stay & Eat

★ $$ **Romantik-Hotel Altes Gymnasium.** In a former redbrick high school behind an orchard of pear trees, you'll find a surprisingly elegant country-style hotel. The rooms are spacious, with wood-panel floors and modern office amenities. The restaurant Eucken ($$) serves game (from its own hunter) and German country cooking such as *Rücken vom Salzwiesenlamm mit Kartoffel-Zucchini-Rösti* (salted lamb back with potato and zucchini hash browns). The hotel's huge health and indoor pool area helps you forget the often bad weather in this region. ✉ *Süderstr. 6, D–25813* ☎ *04841/8330* 🖷 *04841/83312* 🌐 *www.altes-gymnasium.de* 🛏 *66 rooms, 6 suites* 🛎 *2 restaurants, room service, in-room safes, minibars, cable TV, Wi-Fi, indoor pool, gym, health club, massage, sauna, bicycles, bar, baby-sitting, dry cleaning, laundry service, free parking, some pets allowed (fee), no-smoking rooms; no a/c* 💳 *AE, DC, MC, V* 🍽 *BP.*

Sylt

❷ *44 km (27 mi) northwest of Husum, 196 km (122 mi) northwest of Hamburg.*

Fodor'sChoice ★

Sylt is a long, narrow island (38 km [24 mi] by as little as 220 yards) of unspoiled beaches and marshland off the western coast of Schleswig-Holstein and Denmark. Famous for its clean air and white beaches, Sylt is the hideaway for the jet set of Germany. They come for the secluded beaches and the exclusiveness provided by the island's inaccessibility. The island is a mecca for windsurfers, who rely on constant strong winds.

A popular activity here is *Wattwanderungen* (walking in the Watt, the shoreline tidelands), whether on self-guided or guided tours. The small villages with their thatch-roof houses, the beaches, and the nature conservation areas make Sylt the most enchanting German island, rivaled only by Rügen.

The island's major town is **Westerland,** which is not quite as expensive as Kampen but more crowded. An ugly assortment of modern hotels lines an undeniably clean and broad beach. Each September windsurfers meet for the Surf Cup competition off the **Brandenburger Strand,** the best surfing spot.

If you are looking for privacy, detour to the village of **List,** on the northern tip of Sylt, or to **Archsum** or **Hörnum.** The last is on the southernmost point of the island and, like List, has a little harbor and a lighthouse.

Kampen

9 km (6 mi) northeast of Westerland.

The island's unofficial capital is Kampen, which is the main destination for the wealthier crowd. Redbrick buildings or shining white thatch-roof houses spread along the coastline. The real draw—apart from the fancy restaurants and chic nightclubs—are the beaches.

One of the island's best-known features is the **Rotes Kliff** (Red Cliff), a dune cliff on the northern end of the Kampen beaches, which turns an eerie dark red when the sun sets.

The **Naturschutzgebiet Kampener Vogelkoje** (Birds' Nest Nature Conservation Area) was built in the mid-17th century and once served as a mass trap for wild geese. Today it serves as a nature preserve for wild birds. ✉ *Lister Str., Kampen* ☎ *04651/871–077* 🎫 *€1.70* ⏲ *Apr.–Oct., Tues.–Sun. 10–4.*

For a glimpse of the rugged lives of 19th-century fishermen, visit the small village of **Keitum** to the south and drop in on the **Altfriesisches Haus** (Old Frisian House), which preserves an old-world peacefulness in a lush garden setting. The house also documents a time when most seamen thrived on extensive whale hunting. ✉ *Am Kliff 13, Keitum* ☎ *04651/31101* 🎫 *€2.50* ⌚ *Apr.–Oct., daily 10–5; Nov.–Mar., Tues.–Fri. 1–4.*

The 800-year-old church of **St. Severin** was built on the highest elevation in the region. Its tower once served the island's fishermen as a beacon. Strangely enough, the tower also served as a prison until 1806. Today the church is a popular site for weddings. ✉ *Keitum* ☎ *04651/31713* 🎫 *Free* ⌚ *Apr.–Oct., tour Thurs. at 5; Nov.–Mar. at 4.*

The small **Sylter Heimatmuseum** (Sylt Island Museum) tells the centuries-long history of the island's seafaring people. It presents traditional costumes, tools, and other gear from fishing boats and tells the stories of prominent islanders such as Uwe Jens Lornsen, who fought for Sylt's independence. ✉ *Am Kliff 19, Keitum* ☎ *04651/31669* 🎫 *€2.20* ⌚ *Apr.–Oct., weekdays 10–5, weekends 11–5; Nov.–Mar., Tues.–Fri. 1–4.*

Where to Stay & Eat

★ $$–$$$$ ✕ **Sansibar.** Sansibar is one of the island's most popular restaurants. The cuisine includes seafood and fondue with fish or scampi, served with any one of more than 800 wines. To get a table even in the afternoon, you must reserve well in advance. ✉ *Strand, Rantum-Süd, Rantum* ☎ *04651/964–646* *Reservations essential* 💳 *AE, V.*

$–$$ ✕ **Dorfkrug Rotes Kliff.** The Dorfkrug has fed the island's seafaring inhabitants since 1876. Enjoy meals such as *Steinbuttfilet* (halibut fillet) or *Gebratener Zander* (fried perch fillet) in a homey setting where the walls are covered in traditional blue-white Frisian tiles. ✉ *Braderuper Weg 3, Kampen* ☎ *04651/43500* 💳 *AE, MC* ⌚ *Closed Mon.*

★ $$$$ ✕🏨 **Dorint Söl'ring Hof.** The latest newcomer to the upscale hotel scene of Sylt is this luxurious resort set in a white, thatch-roof country house *on* the dunes: the view from most of the rooms is magnificent—with some luck you may even spot frolicking harbor porpoises. The brightly furnished rooms are spacious, covering two floors, and equipped with a fire place. The real attraction here, however, is the restaurant ($$$$), where renowned chef Johannes King creates delicious German-Mediterranean fish dishes. The hotel is in quiet Rantum, at the southeast end of the island. ✉ *Am Sandwall 1, D–25980 Sylt-Rantum* ☎ *04651/836–200* 📠 *04651/836–2020* 🌐 *www.dorint.de* *11 rooms, 4 suites* *Restaurant, room service, in-room safes, minibars, cable TV with movies, Web TV, health club, massage, sauna, spa, steam room, beach, bar, lounge, baby-sitting, dry cleaning, laundry service, concierge, meeting room, free parking, no-smoking rooms; no a/c* 💳 *AE, DC, MC, V* *BP.*

$$$ Fodor'sChoice ★ ✕🏨 **Hotelrestaurant Jörg Müller.** The old thatch-roof farmhouse hotel has a handful of lovely rooms combining Frisian-style designs with classical elegance. A wing added three years ago has modern rooms that lack the intimate interior of the historic house but have luxurious bathrooms, and each has a balcony or terrace. The restaurant Pesel ($$$$)

serves local fish dishes, whereas the upscale main restaurant offers a high-quality blend of international and Mediterranean cuisine. ✉ *Süderstr. 8, D–25980 Westerland* ☎ *04651/27788* 📠 *04651/201–471* 🌐 *www.hotel-joerg-mueller.de* *19 rooms, 4 suites* *2 restaurants, room service, in-room safes, minibars, cable TV, Wi-Fi, hot tub, sauna, steam room, bar, dry cleaning, laundry service, free parking, some pets allowed (fee), no-smoking rooms; no a/c* ▭ *AE, DC, MC, V* 🍽 *BP.*

$$–$$$ **Ulenhof Wenningstedt.** The Ulenhof, one of Sylt's loveliest old thatch-roof apartment houses, is a quiet alternative to the busier main resorts in Kampen and Westerland. The Ulenhof has two buildings 750 yards away from the beach in Wenningstedt. The larger apartments, for up to three persons, are a good deal. A separate bathing facility offers a huge wellness area with two saunas, a pool, and a *Tecaldarium,* a Roman bathhouse. ✉ *Sachsenring 14, D–25996 Wenningstedt* ☎ *04651/94540* 📠 *04651/945–431* 🌐 *www.ulenhof.de* *35 apartments* *Cable TV, Wi-Fi, indoor pool, health club, hot tub, massage, sauna, steam room, free parking, no-smoking rooms; no a/c* ▭ *No credit cards* 🍽 *BP.*

$$–$$$ **Witthüs-Apparthotel.** The tiny hotel in a historic thatched-roof house is a very reasonably priced alternative to similar hotels on the island. It offers suites with fully equipped kitchens, and separate living and bedrooms. Most of the rooms have been carefully furnished in bright yellows and reds, creating a homely Scandinavian ambiance. When making a reservation, try for the maisonette suite just beneath the roof: There's nothing more romantic than being lulled to sleep by the soothing whistles of the North Sea winds. ✉ *Alte Dorfstr. 9, D–25996 Wenningstedt* ☎ *04651/98910* 📠 *04651/985–633* 🌐 *www.witthues-sylt.de* *8 rooms, 10 suites* *Cable TV, sauna, free parking, some pets allowed (fee), no-smoking rooms; no a/c* ▭ *No credit cards* 🍽 *BP.*

Nightlife & the Arts

The nightspots in Kampen are generally more upscale and quite expensive compared to the pubs and clubs of Westerland. One of the most classic clubs on Sylt is the **Club Rotes Kliff** (✉ Braderuper Weg 3, Kampen ☎ 04651/43400), a bar and dance club that attracts a hip crowd of all ages. The **Compass** (✉ Friedrichstr. 42, Westerland ☎ 04651/23513) is not as trendy as the typical Sylt nightclub. The mostly young patrons, however, create a cheerful party atmosphere on weekend nights.

Schleswig

❸ *82 km (51 mi) southeast of Sylt, 114 km (71 mi) north of Hamburg.*

Schleswig-Holstein's oldest city is also one of its best-preserved examples of a typical North German town. Once the seat of the dukes of Schleswig-Holstein, it has not only their palace but also ruins left by the area's first rulers, the Vikings. Those legendary and fierce warriors from Scandinavia brought terror (but also commerce) to northern Germany between 800 and 1100. Under a wide sky, Schleswig lies on the Schlei River in a landscape of freshwater marshland and lakes, making it a good departure point for bike or canoe tours.

The fishing village comes alive along the **Holm,** an old settlement with tiny and colorful houses. The windblown buildings give a good impression of what villages in northern Germany looked like 150 years ago. Relax in one of the cafés or further inspect the city's history at the **Städtisches Museum** (Municipal Museum). In this typical noble country palace of the late 17th century, you can explore Schleswig's history from the Stone Age onward. ✉ *Günderothscher Hof, Friedrichstr. 9–11* ☎ *04621/936–820* 🎫 *€3* ⏲ *Tues.–Sun. 10–5.*

The impressive baroque **Schloss Gottorf,** dating from 1703, is the state's largest secular building and once housed the ruling family. It has been transformed into the **Schleswig-Holsteinisches Landesmuseum** (State Museum of Schleswig-Holstein) and holds a collection of art and handicrafts of northern Germany from the Middle Ages to the present, including paintings by Lucas Cranach the Elder. Among the museum's archaeological exhibits are ancient mummified corpses retrieved from nearby swamps. ✉ *Schloss Gottorf* ☎ *04621/8130* 🌐 *www.schloss-gottorf.de* 🎫 *€6* ⏲ *Apr.–Oct., daily 10–6; Nov.–Mar., Tues.–Fri. 10–4, weekends 10–5.*

The most thrilling museum in Schleswig, the **Wikinger-Museum Haithabu** (Haithabu Viking Museum), is at the site of a Viking settlement. This was the Vikings' most important German port, and the boats, gold jewelry, and graves they left behind are displayed in the museum. ✉ *Haddeby* ☎ *04621/8130* 🌐 *www.schloss-gottorf.de* 🎫 *€4* ⏲ *Apr.–Oct., daily 9–5; Nov.–Mar., Tues.–Sun. 10–4.*

Where to Stay & Eat

$–$$ ✕ **Stadt Flensburg.** This small restaurant in a city mansion that dates back to 1699 serves mostly fish from the Schlei River. Fishermen living on the Holm will have caught your dinner. The food is solid regional fare such as *Zanderfilet* (perch fillets) or *Gebratene Ente* (baked duck). The familial, warm atmosphere and the local dark tap beers more than make up for the simplicity of the setting. Reservations are advised. ✉ *Lollfuss 102* ☎ *04621/23984* 💳 *AE, DC, MC, V* ⏲ *Closed Wed.*

$–$$ 🏨 **Ringhotel Strandhalle Schleswig.** A modern hotel overlooking the small yacht harbor and the Schlei, this establishment has surprisingly low rates and a good value for its many services. The rooms are furnished in timeless dark furniture, and all have cable television. If you plan to stay a couple of days, ask about the special weekend packages that include nightly four-course meals and other extras. ✉ *Strandweg 2, D–24837* ☎ *04621/9090* 📠 *04621/909–100* 🌐 *www.hotel-strandhalle.de* 🛏 *25 rooms* ♨ *Restaurant, in-room safes, minibars, cable TV, in-room broadband, pool, boating, bicycles, meeting room, free parking, some pets allowed (fee), no-smoking rooms; no a/c* 💳 *AE, MC, V* 🍽 *BP.*

Shopping

The tiny **Keramik-Stube** (✉ Rathausmarkt ☎ 04621/24757) offers craft work and beautiful handmade pottery. It's the ideal place to buy a gift. The best place to buy tea is **Teekontor Hansen** (✉ Kornmarkt 3 ☎ 04621/23385). Try the *Schliekieker,* a very strong blend of different teas.

Kiel

4 *53 km (33 mi) southeast of Schleswig, 130 km (81 mi) north of Hamburg.*

The state capital Kiel has 250,000 inhabitants and is known throughout Europe for its annual *Kieler Woche,* a festival and regatta that attracts hundreds of sailing boats from around the world. Despite the many wharves and industries concentrated in Kiel, the **Kieler Föhrde** (Bay of Kiel) has remained mostly unspoiled. Unfortunately, this cannot be said about the city itself. Because of Kiel's strategic significance during World War II—it served as the main German submarine base—the historic city, founded more than 750 years ago, was completely destroyed. Kiel's buildings are mostly modern, and its attraction lies in its outlying beaches, parks, and small towns.

At the **Kieler Hafen** (Kiel Harbor), Germany's largest passenger shipping harbor, you can always catch a glimpse of one of the many ferries leaving for Scandinavia from the **Oslokai** (Oslo Quay). In the background you can spot some of the shipbuilding wharves and—in the Kiel Bay—sometimes even a German submarine charting its way home.

The **Schifffahrtsmuseum** (Maritime Museum) , housed in a hall of the old fish market, includes two antique fishing boats. In the past, fishing was Kiel's primary industry. ✉ *Wall 65* ☎ *0431/901–3428* 🌐 *www.kiel.de* 🎫 *€2* ⏲ *Mid-Apr.–mid-Oct., daily 10–6; mid-Oct.–mid-Apr., Tues.–Sun. 10–5.*

A grim reminder of a different marine past is exhibited at the **U-Boot-Museum** (Submarine Museum) in Kiel-Laboe. The vessels of the much-feared German submarine fleet in World War I were mostly built and stationed in Kiel, before leaving for the Atlantic where they attacked American and British supply convoys. Today the submarine U995 serves as a public-viewing model of a typical German submarine. The 280-foot-high **Marineehrenmal** (Marine Honor Memorial), in Laboe, was built in 1927–36. All German submarine personnel are required to salute when passing the memorial. You can reach Laboe via ferry from the Kiel harbor or take B–502 north. ✉ *Strandstr. 92, Kiel-Laboe* ☎ *04343/42700* 🎫 *Memorial €3, museum €2.50* ⏲ *Mid-Apr.–mid-Oct., daily 9:30–6; mid-Oct.–mid-Apr., daily 9:30–4.*

One of northern Germany's best (though small) collections of modern art can be found at the **Kunsthalle zu Kiel** (Kiel Art Gallery), which specializes in Russian art of the 19th and early 20th centuries, German expressionism, and contemporary international art. The collections include paintings, prints, and sculptures. ✉ *Düsternbrooker Weg 1* ☎ *0431/880–5756* 🌐 *www.kunsthalle-kiel.de* 🎫 *€5* ⏲ *Tues. and Thurs.–Sun. 10–6, Wed. 10–8.*

Two attractive beach towns close to Kiel, **Laboe** and **Strande,** are crowded with sun-loving Kielers on summer weekends. Both retain their fishing-village appeal, and you can buy fresh fish directly from the boats in the harbor. Most fishermen here still smoke the fish on board, preparing, for example, the famous *Kieler Sprotten,* a small, salty fish somewhat like sardines. Though you can get to Laboe and Strande by car, it's more fun to catch a ferry leaving from Kiel.

Where to Stay & Eat

★ $–$$$$ **Quam.** Locals who dine out aren't looking for old-fashioned fish dishes (that's why there isn't a good, traditional fish restaurant in town); they prefer international preparations of fish from all over the world. The stylish Quam, its yellow walls and dimmed lights paying homage to Tuscany, serves international cuisine, including fish specialties from Germany, Italy, France, and Japan, to a mostly young, very chic crowd. The menu changes frequently. ✉ *Düppelstr. 60* ☎ *0431/85195* *Reservations essential* ▭ *AE* ⊙ *Closed Sun. No lunch.*

★ ¢–$ **Kieler Brauerei.** The only historic brewery in town has produced beer since the Middle Ages and offers its very own *Naturtrübes Kieler* to this day. You can try this and other North German beers in pitchers, or order a small barrel for your table and tap it yourself (other patrons will cheer you). The hearty food—mostly fish, pork, and potato dishes—does not earn gourmet awards, but certainly helps get down just one more beer. ✉ *Alter Markt 9* ☎ *0431/906–290* ▭ *MC, V.*

$$ **Hotel Kieler Yachtclub.** This traditional hotel provides standard yet elegant, newly refurbished rooms in the main building and completely new, bright accommodations in the Villentrakt. The restaurant ($$$) serves mostly fish dishes; in summer try to get a table on the terrace. The club overlooks the Kieler Föhrde. ✉ *Hindenburgufer 70, D–24105* ☎ *0431/88130* *0431/881–3444* *www.hotelkieleryachtclub.de* *57 rooms, 4 suites* *Restaurant, room service, minibars, cable TV, in-room broadband, Web TV, bar, dry cleaning, laundry service, meeting room, free parking, some pets allowed (fee), no-smoking rooms; no a/c* ▭ *AE, DC, MC, V* *BP.*

Nightlife & the Arts

This city may be relatively sleepy, but maybe because it has a thriving nightlife. One of the many chic and hip bars is the **Hemingway** (✉ Alter Markt ☎ 0431/96812). A college crowd goes to **Traumfabrik** (✉ Grasweg 19 ☎ 0431/544–450) to eat pizza, watch a movie, or dance (Friday is best for dancing). The popular bar Nachtcafé has a basement disco, **Velvet** (✉ Eggerstedtstr. 14 ☎ 0431/800–1919).

Lübeck

5 *60 km (37 mi) southeast of Kiel, 56 km (35 mi) northeast of Hamburg.*

Fodor's Choice ★

The ancient core of Lübeck, one of Europe's largest Old Towns dating from the 12th century, was a chief stronghold of the Hanseatic merchant princes. But it was the roving Heinrich der Löwe (King Henry the Lion) who established the town and, in 1173, laid the foundation stone of the redbrick Gothic cathedral. The town's famous landmark gate, the **Holstentor,** built between 1464 and 1478, is flanked by two round, squat towers and serves as a solid symbol of Lübeck's prosperity as a trading center.

In the **Altstadt** (Old Town), proof of Lübeck's former position as the golden queen of the Hanseatic League is found at every step. More 13th- to

15th-century buildings stand in Lübeck than in all other large northern German cities combined, which has earned the Altstadt a place on UNESCO's register of the world's greatest cultural and natural treasures. The **Rathaus,** dating from 1240, is among the buildings lining the arcaded Marktplatz, one of Europe's most striking medieval-market squares. It has been subjected to several architectural face-lifts that have added Romanesque arches, Gothic windows, and a Renaissance roof. ✉ *Breitestr. 64* ☎ *0451/122–1005* 🎫 *Guided tour in German €3* ⏲ *Tour weekdays at 11, noon, and 3.*

The impressive redbrick Gothic **Marienkirche** (St. Mary's Church), which has the highest brick nave in the world, looms behind the Rathaus. ✉ *Marienkirchhof* ☎ *0451/397–700* ⏲ *Nov.–Feb., daily 10–4; Mar. and Oct., daily 10–5; Apr.–Sept., daily 10–6.*

The **Buddenbrookhaus–Günter Grass-Haus,** two highly respectable-looking mansions, are devoted to two of Germany's most prominent writers, Thomas Mann (1875–1955) and Günter Grass (born 1927). The older mansion is named after Mann's saga *Buddenbrooks.* Mann's family once lived here, and it's now home to the **Heinrich und Thomas Mann Zentrum** (Heinrich and Thomas Mann Center). This museum documents the lives and works of two of the most important German writers of the 20th century. A tour and video in English are offered.

Near the museum is the second mansion, which houses the **Günter Grass-Haus** (Günter Grass House), devoted to Germany's most famous living writer and winner of the Nobel prize for literature (1999). His most famous novel translated into English is *The Tin Drum* (1959). Changing cultural and literary exhibits are also shown here. ✉ *Mengstr. 4 and Glockengiesserstr. 21* ☎ *0451/122–4190* 🌐 *www.buddenbrookhaus.de* 🎫 *Both museums: €7; Grass-Haus: € 5; Buddenbrookhaus: € 4* ⏲ *Apr.–Oct., daily 10–6; Nov. and Dec., daily 10–6; Jan.–Mar., daily 11–5.*

Take a look inside the entrance hall of the Gothic **Heiligen-Geist-Hospital** (Hospital of the Holy Ghost). It was built in the 14th century by the town's rich merchants and is still caring for the infirm. ✉ *Am Koberg* ☎ *0451/7907–841* 🎫 *Free* ⏲ *Apr.–Sept., Tues.–Sun. 10–5; Oct.–Mar., Tues.–Sun. 10–4.*

Construction of the **Lübecker Dom** (Lübeck Cathedral), the city's oldest building, began in 1173. Both the Dom and the Marienkirche present frequent organ concerts, a real treat in these magnificent redbrick Gothic churches. ✉ *Domkirchhof* ☎ *0451/74704* ⏲ *Apr.–Oct., daily 10–6; Nov.–Feb., daily 10–4.*

Where to Stay & Eat

$$$–$$$$ ✕ **Wullenwever.** Culinary critics say this restaurant has set a new standard of dining sophistication for Lübeck. Committed to the city's maritime heritage, the Wullenwever primarily serves fish such as bass, halibut, plaice, pike, and trout, that is fried or sautéed according to local country cooking. It's certainly one of the most attractive establishments in town, with dark furniture, chandeliers, and oil paintings on pale pastel walls. In summer tables fill a quiet flower-strewn courtyard. ✉ *Beckergrube 71* ☎ *0451/704–333* *Reservations essential* 💳 *AE, DC, V* ⊙ *Closed Sun. and Mon. No lunch.*

★ $–$$$ ✕ **Schiffergesellschaft.** Women weren't allowed in the Schiffergesellschaft (Mariners' Society) from its opening in 1535 until 1870. Today mixed company sits in church-style pews at long 400-year-old oak tables. At each end of the pew is a sculpted coat of arms of a particular city. Shipowners had their set trading routes, and they each had their own pew and table. A good meal here is the *Ostseescholle* (plaice), fried with bacon and served with potatoes and cucumber salad. ✉ *Breitestr. 2* ☎ *0451/76776* 💳 *AE, V.*

★ $$ **SAS Radisson Senator Hotel Lübeck.** Close to the famous Holstentor, this ultramodern hotel, with its daring architecture, still reveals a North German heritage: the redbrick building, with its oversize windows and generous, open lobby, mimics an old Lübeck warehouse. When making a reservation, ask for a (larger) Business Class room, whose price includes a breakfast. A big plus are the very comfortable beds, which are large by German standards. The Nautilo restaurant ($–$$) serves light Mediterranean cuisine. ✉ *Willy-Brandt-Allee 6, D–23554* ☎ *0451/1420* 📠 *0451/142–2222* 🌐 *www.senatorhotel.de* *217 rooms, 7 suites* *2 restaurants, room service, minibars, cable TV with movies, Web TV, Wi-Fi, pool, health club, hair salon, massage, sauna, spa, bar, baby-sitting, dry cleaning, laundry service, concierge, meeting room, parking (fee), some pets allowed (fee), no-smoking rooms* 💳 *AE, DC, MC, V.*

$$ **Kaiserhof.** The most comfortable hotel in Lübeck consists of two early 19th-century merchants' houses linked together, retaining many of the original architectural elements. It's a five-minute walk from the cathedral. The spacious bedrooms all have a restful, homey ambience, and the quietest of them overlook the garden at the back. A marvelous breakfast is included in the room cost. ✉ *Kronsforder Allee 11–13, D–23560* ☎ *0451/703–301* 📠 *0451/795–083* 🌐 *www.kaiserhof-luebeck.de* *58 rooms, 6 suites* *Room service, in-room safes, minibars, cable TV, Web TV, pool, sauna, bar, free parking, some pets allowed (fee); no a/c* 💳 *AE, DC, MC, V* 🍽 *BP.*

★ $ **Hotel zur Alten Stadtmauer.** This historic town house in the heart of the city has been converted into a family-operated hotel hideaway. Two floors house small, modest, well-kept guest rooms. Comfortable beds, bright birchwood furniture, a quiet setting, and a great (not to mention nutritious) German breakfast buffet make this a perfect choice for budget travelers yearning for romance. ✉ *An der Mauer 57, D–23552* ☎ *0451/73702* 📠 *0451/73239* 🌐 *www.hotelstadtmauer.de* *24 rooms, some with bath* *Parking (fee), no-smoking rooms; no a/c* 💳 *AE, DC, MC, V* 🍽 *BP.*

$ **Ringhotel Jensen.** Only a stone's throw from the Holstentor, this hotel is close to all the main attractions and faces the moat surrounding the Old Town. It's family run and very comfortable, with modern rooms, mostly decorated with bright cherrywood furniture. Though small, the guest rooms are big enough for two twin beds and a coffee table and come with either a shower or a bath. ✉ *An der Obertrave 4–5, D–23552* ☎ *0451/71646* 📠 *0451/73386* 🌐 *www.hotel-jensen.de* *41 rooms,*

1 suite ♿ *Restaurant, cable TV, Web TV, Internet room, parking (fee), some pets allowed (fee); no a/c* 💳 *AE, DC, MC, V* 🍽 *BP.*

The Arts

Contact the **Musik und Kongresshallen Lübeck** (✉ Willy-Brandt-Allee 10, D–23554 ☎ 0451/790–400) for schedules of the myriad concerts, operas, and theater performances in Lübeck.

In summer try to catch a few performances of the **Schleswig-Holstein Music Festival** (mid-July–late August), which features orchestras composed of young musicians from more than 25 countries. Some concerts are held in the Dom or the Marienkirche; some are staged in barns in small towns and villages. Each year between 1986 and 1989, Leonard Bernstein conducted the festival orchestra on a site where cows and chickens are normally fed. For exact dates and tickets, contact **Schleswig-Holstein Konzertorganisation** (✉ Kartenzentrale Kiel, Postfach 3840, D–24037 Kiel ☎ 0431/570–470 📠 0431/570–4747).

13

Shopping

Local legend has it that marzipan was invented in Lübeck during the great medieval famine. According to the story, a local baker ran out of grain for bread and, in his desperation, began experimenting with the only four ingredients he had: almonds, sugar, rose water, and eggs. The result was a sweet almond paste known today as marzipan. Though the story is more fiction than fact (it is generally agreed that marzipan's true origins lie in the Middle East), Lübecker Marzipan, a designation that has been trademarked, is now considered among the best in the world. Lübeck's most famous marzipan maker, **Konditorei-Café Niederegger** (✉ Breitestr. 89 ☎ 0451/530–1126), sells the delicacy molded into a multitude of imaginative forms. The Niederegger shop, located across from the Rathaus, has a cozy café at the back and a small, free marzipan museum upstairs.

The city's largest downtown mall, **Holstentor-Passage** (✉ An der Untertrave 111 ☎ 0451/704–425), is next to the Holstentor and is filled with stores selling clothing or home accessories.

WESTERN MECKLENBURG

This long-forgotten Baltic Coast region, pinned between two sprawling urban areas—the state capital of Schwerin, in the west, and Rostock, in the east—is thriving again. Despite its perennial economic woes, this part of Germany, and Schwerin in particular, has attracted many businesses, which suggests a light at the end of the tunnel. Though the region is close to the sea, it's made up largely of seemingly endless fields of wheat and yellow rape and a dozen or so wonderful lakes. "When the Lord made the Earth, He started with Mecklenburg," wrote native novelist Fritz Reuter.

Wismar

★ 6 *60 km (37 mi) east of Lübeck on Route 105.*

The old city of Wismar was one of the original three sea-trading towns, along with Lübeck and Rostock, that banded together in 1259 to com-

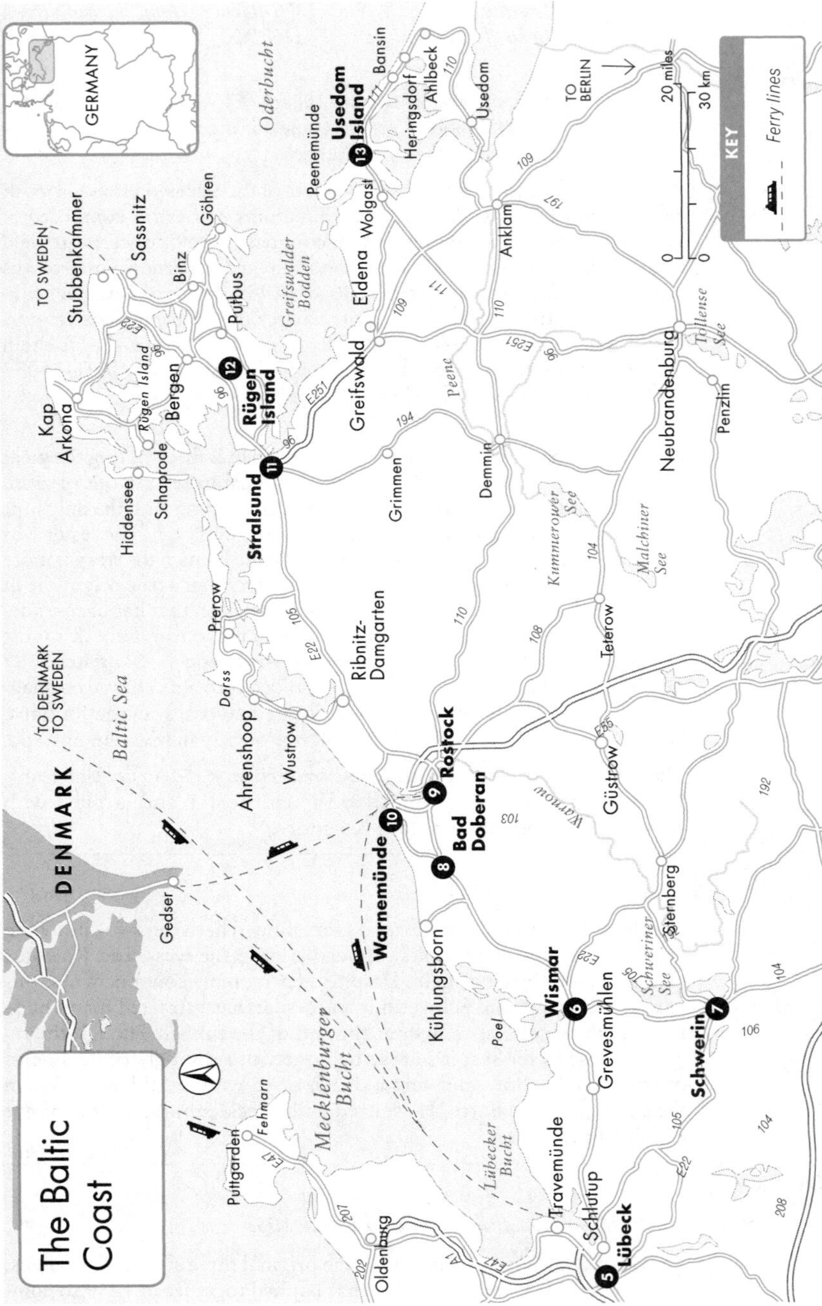
The Baltic Coast
GERMANY
DENMARK
TO DENMARK
TO SWEDEN
TO SWEDEN
TO BERLIN
Baltic Sea
Mecklenburger Bucht
Lübecker Bucht
Oderbucht
Greifswalder Bodden
Kummerower See
Malchiner See
Tollense See
Schweriner See
Peene
Warnow
Gedser
Puttgarden
Fehmarn
Oldenburg
Lübeck
Schlutup
Travemünde
Grevesmühlen
Poel
Wismar
Schwerin
Kühlungsborn
Sternberg
Bad Doberan
Warnemünde
Rostock
Güstrow
Ahrenshoop
Wustrow
Darss
Prerow
Ribnitz-Damgarten
Teterow
Stralsund
Hiddensee
Schaprode
Kap Arkona
Rügen Island
Bergen
Putbus
Binz
Göhren
Sassnitz
Stubbenkammer
Grimmen
Demmin
Greifswald
Eldena
Wolgast
Peenemünde
Usedom Island
Heringsdorf
Ahlbeck
Bansin
Usedom
Anklam
Neubrandenburg
Penzlin
5
6
7
8
9
10
11
12
13
KEY
Ferry lines
0 20 miles
0 30 km

bat Baltic pirates. From this mutual defense pact grew the great and powerful private-trading bloc, the Hanseatic League, which dominated the Baltic for centuries. The wealth generated by the Hanseatic merchants can still be seen in Wismar's ornate architecture.

★ The **Marktplatz** (Market Square), one of the largest and best preserved in Germany, is framed by patrician gabled houses. Their style ranges from redbrick late Gothic through Dutch Renaissance to 19th-century neoclassical. In 1922 filmmaker Friedrich Wilhelm Murnau used the tortuous streets of Wismar's Old Town in his expressionist horror-film classic, *Nosferatu*. The square's **Wasserkunst,** the ornate pumping station done in Dutch Renaissance style, was built between 1580 and 1602 by the Dutch Master Philipp Brandin. Not only was it a work of art, it supplied the town with water until the mid-19th century.

The **Alter Schwede** (Old Swede), a seamen's tavern since 1878, has entertained guests ranging from sailors to the Swedish royal family. Dating from 1380, it's the oldest building on the Marktplatz and is easily identified by its stepped gables and redbrick facade. ✉ *Am Markt 19–22* ☎ *03841/283–552.*

The ruins of the **Marienkirche** (St. Mary's Church) with its 250-foot tower, bombed in World War II, lie just behind the Marktplatz; the church is still undergoing restoration. At noon, 3, and 5, listen for one of 14 hymns played on its carillon.

The **Fürstenhof** (Princes' Court), home of the former dukes of Mecklenburg, stands next to the Marienkirche. It's an early-16th-century Italian Renaissance structure with touches of late Gothic. The facade is a series of fussy friezes depicting scenes from the Trojan War. The **St. Georgen zu Wismar** (St. George's Church), another victim of the war, is next to the Fürstenhof. One of Northern Germany's biggest Gothic churches, built between 1315 and 1404, it has been almost completely restored to its former glory. Though the simple interior is not particularly intriguing, the spiral towers and many architectural details on the facade are an intriguing sight.

The city's turbulent history is chronicled at the **Stadtgeschichtliches Museum Wismar Schabbellhaus** (Museum for City History), located in one of North Germany's oldest Renaissance buildings, the Schabbellhaus (1569–71). Exhibits present the medieval past of the city and focus on the Swedish occupation during the Thirty Years' War. Included are fine paintings, scrimshaw art, and paintings, whose origins (Australia and New Zealand) testify to the extensive trade links Wismar once had. ✉ *Schweinsbrücke 8* ☎ *03841/282–350* 🌐 *www.schabbellhaus.de* 🎫 €2 ⏲ *May–Oct., Tues.–Sun. 10–8; Nov.–Apr., Tues.–Sun. 10–5.*

The late-Gothic **St. Nikolaikirche** (St. Nicholas's Church), with a 120-foot-high nave, was built between 1381 and 1487. A remnant of the town's long domination by Sweden is the additional altar built for Swedish sailors. ✉ *Marktpl.* ☎ *03841/210–143* ⏲ *May–Sept., daily 8–8; Apr. and Oct., daily 10–6; Nov.–Mar., daily 11–4.*

If you have an hour to spare, wander among the jetties and quays of the port, a mix of the medieval and the modern. **To'n Zägenkrog,** a seamen's haven decorated with sharks' teeth, stuffed seagulls, and maritime gear, is a good pit stop along the harbor. ✉ *Ziegenmarkt 10* ☎ *03841/282–716.*

Where to Stay & Eat

★ $–$$$ ✕ **Alter Schwede.** Regarded as one of the most attractive, authentic taverns on the Baltic—and correspondingly busy—this eatery focuses not only on Mecklenburg's game and poultry dishes, such as the traditional *Mecklenburger Ente* (Mecklenburg duck), filled with baked plums, apples, raisins, and served with red cabbage and potatoes, but also on new North German cuisine such as *Lachsfilet im Bierteig gebacken auf Hummersauce, mit Brokkoli und Kartoffelgratin* (salmon baked in beer dough, served with lobster sauce, broccoli, and potato gratin). ✉ *Am Markt 19–22* ☎ *03841/283–552* ▭ *AE, MC, V.*

★ $$ ✕ **Seehotel Neuklostersee.** Set at the dreamy Naun Lake, this country hotel is a hidden gem just 15 km (9 mi) east of Wismar. The redbrick farmhouse and old thatch-roof barn comprise an upscale yet casual hotel. Each room has a different design (the owners are acclaimed Berlin interior designers), with white walls and terra-cotta tiles. There's a fine restaurant ($) serving German-Italian seafood on a terrace. A sauna at the lake and a beach invite you to relax; a health club was added in 2004. ✉ *Seestr. 1, D–23992 Nakenstorf* ☎ *038422/4570* 🖷 *038422/45717* 🌐 *www.seehotel-neuklostersee.de* *11 rooms, 1 suite, 1 apartment* *Restaurant, cable TV, Web TV, sauna, beach, boating, bicycles, hiking, horseback riding, free parking, some pets allowed (fee), no-smoking rooms; no a/c* ▭ *MC* *BP.*

$–$$ ✕ **Citypartner Hotel Alter Speicher.** This small and very personal family-owned hotel is behind the facade of an old merchant house in the downtown area. Some of the rooms may be tiny, but their size contributes to the warm and cozy atmosphere. The lobby and restaurants are decorated with wooden beams and panels. The main restaurant ($$–$$$$) primarily serves game, but it also prepares regional dishes. ✉ *Bohrstr. 12–12a, D–23966* ☎ *03841/211–746* 🖷 *03841/211–747* 🌐 *www.hotel-alter-speicher.de* *70 rooms, 3 suites, 2 apartments* *Restaurant, café, in-room safes, minibars, cable TV, Web TV, Internet room, gym, sauna, bar, meeting room, parking (fee), some pets allowed (fee), no-smoking rooms; no a/c* ▭ *DC, MC, V* *BP.*

$ **Steigenberger–Hotel Stadt Hamburg.** This first-class hotel hides behind a rigid gray facade dating back to the early 19th century. The interior is surprisingly open and airy, with skylights and a posh lobby. The rooms have elegant cherrywood art deco–style furnishings. Downstairs, the Bierkeller, a cavernous 17th-century room with vaulted ceilings, is a trendy nightspot. Ask for special package deals such as the *Joker-Wochenende,* which includes two nights, a four-course dinner, a sightseeing tour or boat trip on the Baltic Sea, and a bottle of champagne—all for €178 per person. ✉ *Am Markt 24, D–23966* ☎ *03841/2390* 🖷 *03841/239–239* 🌐 *www.wismar.steigenberger.de* *104 rooms, 2 suites* *Restaurant, café, minibars, cable TV, Internet room, sauna, meeting room, some pets allowed (fee), no-smoking floor; no a/c* ▭ *AE, DC, MC, V* *BP.*

The Arts

At the **Niederdeutsche Bühne** (✉ Philipp-Müllerstr. 5 ☎ 03841/705–501), plays in German and operas are performed regularly; concerts occasionally take place.

Schwerin

★ 7 *32 km (20 mi) south of Wismar on Route 106.*

Schwerin, the second-largest town in the region after Rostock and the capital of the state of Mecklenburg-Vorpommern, is worth a trip just to visit its giant island palace. On the edge of Lake Schwerin, the **Schweriner Schloss** once housed the Mecklenburg royal family. The original palace dates from 1018 but was enlarged by Henry the Lion when he founded Schwerin in 1160. Portions of it were later modeled on Chambord, in the Loire Valley. As it stands now, the palace is surmounted by 15 turrets, large and small, and is reminiscent of a French château. The part of it that's neo-Renaissance in style are its many ducal staterooms, which date from between 1845 and 1857.

North of the main tower is the **Neue Lange Haus** (New Long House), built between 1553 and 1555 and now used as the **Schlossmuseum.** The Communist government restored and maintained the fantastic opulence of this rambling, 80-room reminder of an absolutist monarchy—and then used it to board kindergarten teachers in training. A fifth of the rooms are now used for state-government offices. Antique furniture, objets d'art, silk tapestries, and paintings are sprinkled throughout the salons (the throne room is particularly extravagant), but of special interest are the ornately patterned and highly burnished inlaid wooden floors and wall panels. The parkland contains many beautiful and rare species of trees. Sandstone replicas of Permoser sculptures adorn the boulevards. ✉ *Lennéstr. 1* ☎ *0385/525–2927* 🌐 *www.museum-schwerin.de* 🎫 *€4* ⏲ *Mid-Apr.–mid-Oct., daily 10–6; mid-Oct.–mid-Apr., Tues.–Sun. 10–5.*

The **Alte Garten** (Old Garden), the town's showpiece square, was the setting of military parades during the years of Communist rule. It's dominated by two buildings: the ornate neo-Renaissance state theater, constructed in 1883–86; and the **Staatliches Museum** (State Museum), which houses an interesting collection of paintings by Max Liebermann and Lovis Corinth, plus an exhibition of Meissen porcelain. ✉ *Alter Garten 3* ☎ *0385/59580* 🌐 *www.museum-schwerin.de* 🎫 *€3* ⏲ *Mid-Apr.–mid-Oct., Mon. and Wed.–Sun. 10–6, Tues. 10–8; mid-Oct.–mid-Apr., Wed.–Sun. 10–5, Tues. 10–8.*

The **Dom,** a Gothic cathedral, is the oldest building (built 1222–48) in the city. The bronze baptismal font is from the 14th century; the altar was built in 1440. Religious scenes painted on its walls date from the Middle Ages. Sweeping views of the Old Town and lake await those with the energy to climb the 219 steps to the top of the 320-foot-high cathedral tower. ✉ *Am Dom 4* ☎ *0385/565–014* ⏲ *Tower and nave May–mid-Oct., Mon.–Sat. 10–3, Sun. noon–4; mid-Oct.–Apr., weekdays 11–2, Sat. 11–4, Sun. noon–3.*

The **Mecklenburgisches Volkskundemuseum** (Mecklenburg Ethnology Museum) is a living-history museum representing traditional work and farm life in Germany. Children and history buffs in particular will enjoy wandering through the 17 preserved buildings, which include a blacksmith's shop dating from 1736, a village school from the 19th century, and a traditional fire station. You can watch demonstrations of the tools. *Alte Crivitzer Landstr. 13, 6 km (4 mi) south of Schwerin 0385/208–410 €2.50 May–Oct., Tues.–Sun. 10–6.*

The quintessential experience in Schwerin is one of the **Weisse Flotte** boat tours of the lakes—there are seven in the area. A trip to the island of Kaninchenwerder, a small sanctuary for more than 100 species of water birds, is an unforgettable experience. Boats for this 1½-hour standard tour depart from the pier adjacent to the Schweriner Schloss. *Anlegestelle Schlosspier 0385/557–770 www.weisse-flotte-schwerin.de €9.50 Apr.–Oct., daily 10–5:30.*

Where to Stay & Eat

★ $–$$ **Weinhaus Uhle.** One of the most traditional and popular eateries in Schwerin, this restaurant is named after the wine merchant who opened the restaurant back in 1740. The newer *Weinbistro* (wine bistro) offers primarily German wine tasting and a small menu (mostly cheese plates or soups such as lobster cream soup). In the restaurant, regional specialties and international mixed grills are served in a rustic setting, accompanied by a piano player on Friday and Saturday nights. *Schusterstr. 13–15 0385/562–956 AE, MC, V.*

★ $ **Alt-Schweriner Schankstuben.** A small family-owned restaurant and hotel, the Schankstuben extends standard but very personal service with emphasis on Mecklenburg tradition. The hotel is within three old houses in the historic downtown district. Its restaurant ($–$$) serves local dishes. The guest rooms are small but bright and furnished with simple pine furniture. *Schlachtermarkt 9–13, D–19055 0385/592–530 0385/557–4109 www.alt-schweriner-schankstuben.de 16 rooms Restaurant, café, cable TV, Web TV, meeting room, free parking, some pets allowed (fee), no-smoking rooms; no a/c AE, DC, MC, V BP.*

★ $$ **Hotel Niederländischer Hof.** The city's most elegant hotel has a 4½-star rating as a result of its luxurious interior, decorated in a classicist style; its romantic, airy rooms; the impeccable service; and, of course, the fine nouvelle cuisine à la Mecklenburg (mostly seafood dishes). All this is tucked inside a late-19th-century historic mansion located on old Schwerin's Pfaffenteich. *Karl-Marx-Str. 12–13, D–19055 0385/591–100 0385/5911–0999 www.niederlaendischer-hof.de 27 rooms, 6 suites Restaurant, room service, in-room safes, minibars, cable TV, Wi-Fi, dry cleaning, laundry service, meeting room, free parking, some pets allowed (fee), no-smoking rooms; no a/c AE, MC, V BP.*

$$ **Sorat-Hotel Speicher am Ziegelsee.** Towering seven stories above the old harbor, the Speicher am Ziegelsee was built within a redbrick wheat warehouse dating to 1939. The hotel's spacious rooms and apartments are decorated with natural materials and earthy tones and have all the amenities of a modern, first-class hotel. A choice spot for sitting is the

wooden terrace bordering the lake. ✉ *Speicherstr. 11, D–19055* ☎ *0385/50030* 📠 *0385/500–3111* 🌐 *www.speicher-hotel.com* *59 rooms, 20 apartments* *Restaurant, lounge, room service, kitchenettes, cable TV, Wi-Fi, gym, hot tub, massage, sauna, steam room, bar, dry cleaning, laundry service, meeting room, free parking, some pets allowed (fee), no-smoking floor; no a/c* 💳 *AE, DC, MC, V* 🍽 *BP.*

Nightlife & the Arts

The **Mecklenburgisches Staatstheater** (✉ Am Alten Garten ☎ 0385/53000) stages German drama and opera. In June check out the **Schlossfestspiele** for open-air drama or comedy performances.

The **Mexxclub** (✉ Klöresgang 2 ☎ no phone) is the city's hottest dance club, featuring house and soul DJs who attract a stylish young crowd every Saturday night.

Shopping

Antiques and bric-a-brac that have languished in cellars and attics since World War II are still surfacing throughout eastern Germany, and the occasional bargain can be found. The best places to look in Schwerin are on and around **Schmiedestrasse, Schlossstrasse,** and **Mecklenburgstrasse.**

Bad Doberan

❽ *60 km (37 mi) east of Wismar on Route 105, 90 km (56 mi) northeast of Schwerin.*

★ Bad Doberan is home to the meticulously restored redbrick **Doberaner Münster** (monastery church), one of the finest of its kind in Germany. It was built by Cistercian monks between 1294 and 1368 in the northern German Gothic style, with a central nave and transept. The main altar dates from the early 14th century; its highlight is a 45-foot-tall cross. ✉ *Klosterstr. 2* ☎ *038203/16439* 🌐 *www.doberanermuenster.de* *€2* ⏲ *May–Sept., Mon.–Sat. 9–6, Sun. noon–6; Mar., Apr., and Oct., Mon.–Sat. 9–5, Sun. 11–5; Nov.–Feb., Mon.–Sat. 10–4, Sun. 11–4. Tours Apr.–Sept., Mon.–Sat. at 11, 2, and 3; Oct.–Mar., Mon.–Sat. at 2 and 3.*

No visit to this part of the country would be complete without a ride on ***Molli,*** a quaint steam train that has been chugging up and down a 16-km (10-mi) narrow-gauge track between Bad Doberan and the nearby beach resorts of **Heiligendamm** and **Kühlungsborn** since 1886. The train was nicknamed after a little local dog that barked its approval every time the smoking iron horse passed by. At the start of the 45-minute journey the engine and its old wooden carriages make their way through the center of Bad Doberan's cobble streets. In summer *Molli* runs 13 times daily between Bad Doberan and Kühlungsborn. ✉ *Mecklenburgische Bäderbahn Molli, Küstenbus GmbH* ☎ *038203/4150* 🌐 *www.molli-bahn.de* *Same-day round-trip €5.40–9.60* ⏲ *From Bad Doberan: May–Sept., daily 8:35–6:45; Oct.–Apr., daily 8:35–4:40.*

Where to Stay & Eat

¢–$ ✕ **Weisser Pavillon.** Here's a mixed setting for you: a 19th-century Chinese pagoda–type structure in an English-style park. Come for lunch or high tea; regional specialties are featured. In summer the café closes at 10 PM. ✉ *Auf dem Kamp* ☎ *038203/62326* ▭ *No credit cards.*

★ $$ ✕🏨 **Hotel Friedrich-Franz-Palais.** Built in 1793 for a Mecklenburg duke, this whitewashed hotel has accommodated guests for more than 200 years. Completely restored and renovated, each room exudes old-world elegance with modern comforts. The small restaurant ($–$$$) mostly serves fresh fish and game in a setting ideal for a candlelight dinner. ✉ *Am Kamp, D–18209* ☎ *038203/63036* 📠 *038203/62126* 🌐 *www.friedrich-franz-palais.de* *40 rooms, 2 suites, 3 apartments* *Restaurant, café, room service, minibars, cable TV, sauna, bicycles, Internet room, free parking, some pets allowed (fee), no-smoking rooms; no a/c* ▭ *AE, DC, MC, V* *BP.*

$$$$ Fodor'sChoice ★ 🏨 **Kempinski Grand Hotel.** The small beach resort of Heiligendamm has regained its prewar reputation as a getaway for Berlin's up-and-coming crowd–and the Kempinski Grand Hotel, the finest first-class hotel on the German coastline, is where to find the well-to-do. In 2007, attendees of the G8 Summit will overnight here. Nestled in five meticulously restored, gleaming white structures on a secluded beach, the Kempinski offers timelessly furnished rooms decorated in soft colors, and exudes an almost Californian Bel Air charm. There are endless activities offered, and the spa area is breathtaking. ✉ *Grand Hotel at Heiligendamm, D–18209 Heiligendamm* ☎ *038203/7400* 📠 *038203/740–7474* 🌐 *www.kempinski.com* *225 rooms, 119 suites* *Restaurant, room service, in-room safes, minibars, cable TV with movies, in-room broadband, Web TV, Wi-Fi, Internet room, indoor-outdoor pool, health club, massage, sauna, spa, beach, bar, baby-sitting, dry cleaning, laundry service, concierge, meeting rooms, parking (fee), some pets allowed (fee), no-smoking floor* ▭ *AE, DC, MC, V* *BP.*

Rostock

❾ *14 km (9 mi) east of Bad Doberan on Route 105.*

Rostock, the biggest port and shipbuilding center of the former East Germany, was founded around 1200. Of all the Hanseatic cities, the once-thriving Rostock suffered the most from the dissolution of the League in 1669. The GDR (German Democratic Republic) reestablished Rostock as a major port, but since reunification, port work has been cut in half and, though ferries come from Gedser (Denmark) and Trelleborg (Sweden), there's little traffic. The biggest local annual attraction is Hanse Sail, a week of yacht racing held in August.

Because it was home to wartime armament factories, the city suffered severe bombings, but much of the Old Town's core has been rebuilt. The main street, the pedestrians-only **Kröpelinerstrasse,** begins at the old western gate, the Kröpeliner Tor. Here you'll find the finest examples of the late-Gothic and Renaissance houses of rich Hanse merchants. The triangular **Universitätsplatz** (University Square), commemorating the founding of northern Europe's first university here in 1419, is home to Rostock University's Italian Renaissance–style main building, finished in 1867.

At the **Neuer Markt** (Town Square) you'll immediately notice the architectural potpourri of the **Rathaus.** Basically 13th-century Gothic with a baroque facade, the town hall spouts seven slender, decorative towers that look like candles on a peculiar birthday cake. Historic gabled houses surround the rest of the square.

Four-century-old **St. Marienkirche** (St. Mary's Church), the Gothic architectural prize of Rostock, boasts a bronze baptismal font from 1290 and some interesting baroque features, notably the oak altar (1720) and organ (1770). Unique is the huge astronomical clock dating from 1472; it has a calendar extending to the year 2017. ✉ *Am Ziegenmarkt* ☎ *0381/492–3396* ⏲ *Nov.–May, Mon.–Sat. 10–12:30 and 2–4, Sun. 11–noon; June–Oct., Mon.–Sat. 10–6, Sun. 11–5.*

13

The **Schifffahrtsmuseum** (Maritime Museum) traces the history of shipping on the Baltic and displays models of ships, which especially intrigue children. It's just beyond the city wall, at the old city gateway, Steintor. ✉ *August-Bebel-Str. 1* ☎ *0381/252–060* *€3* ⏲ *Tues.–Sun. 11–5.*

The **Zoologischer Garten** (Zoological Garden) has one of the largest collections of exotic animals and birds in northern Germany. This zoo is particularly noted for its polar bears, some of which were bred in Rostock. If you're traveling with children, a visit is a must. ✉ *Rennbahnallee 21* ☎ *0381/20820* *www.zoo-rostock.de* *€8* ⏲ *Nov.–Mar., daily 9–4; Apr.–Oct., daily 9–7.*

Where to Stay & Eat

★ $–$$ ✕ **Restaurant & Bar Silo 4.** Rostock's latest culinary venture is proof that eastern Germany can do sleek and modern. At the top of a waterfront office tower, this innovative restaurant offers spectacular views of the river and a fun and interesting approach to Asian-fusion cuisine. The menu consists of a list of ingredients and seasonings. Guests choose what they like and then leave it to the experts in the show kitchen to work their magic. Don't leave without taking a peek at the designer bathrooms and the funky upstairs bar. ✉ *Am Strande 3d* ☎ *0381/458–5800* *www.silo4.de* *AE, DC, MC, V* ⏲ *Closed Mon. No lunch.*

¢–$ ✕ **Petrikeller.** Once you've crossed the threshold to the Petrikeller, you'll be in the medieval world of the Hanseatic merchants, seamen, and wild pirates such as Klaus Störtebecker. The restaurant's motto, "*Wer nicht liebt Wein, Weib und Gesang bleibt ein Narr sein Leben lang*" (He who doth not love wine, woman and song will be a fool his whole life long), a quote from Martin Luther no less, sets the tone for the giddy atmosphere, hearty food, and live music on weekend nights. ✉ *Harte Str. 27* ☎ *0381/455–855* *www.petrikeller.de* *No credit cards* ⏲ *Closed Mon. No lunch.*

★ ¢–$ ✕ **Zur Kogge.** Looking like the cabin of some ancient sailing vessel, the oldest sailors' beer tavern in town serves mostly fish. Order the *Mecklenburger Fischsuppe* (fish soup) if it's on the menu. *Grosser Fischteller,* consisting of three kinds of fish—depending on the day's catch—served with vegetables, lobster and shrimp sauce, and potatoes is also a popular choice. ✉ *Wokrenterstr. 27* ☎ *0381/493–4493* *Reservations essential* *DC, MC, V.*

$$ **Courtyard by Marriott.** A 19th-century mansion, this hotel is a genuine part of Rostock's historic Old Town. It provides smooth service, and the modern rooms are tastefully decorated. Despite its downtown location, it's a quiet place to stay. A breakfast buffet is included in the room rate. *Schwaansche/Kröpeliner Str., D–18055 0381/49700 0381/497–0700 www.marriott.com 150 rooms, 2 suites Restaurant, room service, minibars, cable TV with movies, Web TV, gym, sauna, bar, dry cleaning, laundry service, meeting room, parking (fee), some pets allowed (fee), no-smoking floor; no a/c AE, DC, MC, V BP.*

★ **$$** **Steigenberger–Hotel zur Sonne Rostock.** With more than 200 years of history behind it, the "zur Sonne," located within the Old Town, is one of the nicest hotels in Rostock. Guests here relax and enjoy the Hanseatic mansion's maritime atmosphere, impeccable service, and modern rooms. When making a reservation, ask for one of the weekend offers and a top-floor room, cozily fitted under the eaves. *Neuer Markt 2, D–18055 0381/49730 0381/497–3351 www.rostock.steigenberger.de 103 rooms, 21 suites Restaurant, café, cable TV, Web TV, massage, sauna, bar, meeting room, parking (fee), some pets allowed (fee), no-smoking rooms; no a/c AE, DC, MC, V BP.*

Nightlife & the Arts

The summer season brings with it a plethora of special concerts, sailing regattas, and parties on the beach. The **Volkstheater** (Patriotischer Weg 33 0381/381–4600) presents plays and concerts. **Farellis** (Grubenstr. 6 0381/490–7100) is a disco that appeals to all ages.

Shopping

Echter Rostocker Doppel-Kümmel und -Korn, a kind of schnapps made from various grains, is a traditional liquor of the area around Rostock. Fishermen have numbed themselves to the cold for centuries with this 80-proof beverage; a bottle costs €8–€11.

Warnemünde

❿ *14 km (9 mi) north of Rostock on Route 103.*

Warnemünde is a quaint seaside resort town with the best hotels and restaurants in the area, as well as 20 km (12 mi) of beautiful white beach. It's been a popular summer getaway for families in eastern Germany for years. Children enjoy climbing to the top of the town landmark, a 115-foot-high **Leuchtturm** (lighthouse), dating from 1898; on clear days it offers views of the coast and Rostock Harbor. Inland from the lighthouse is the yacht marina known as **Alter Strom** (Old Stream). Once the entry into the port of Warnemünde, it now has bars, cozy restaurants, and specialty shops.

Where to Stay & Eat

¢–$ **Fischerklause.** Sailors have stopped in at this restaurant's bar since the turn of the 20th century. The smoked fish sampler, served on a lazy Susan, is delicious, and the house specialty of fish soup is best washed down with some Rostocker Doppel-Kümmel schnapps. An accordionist entertains the crowd on Friday and Saturday evenings. *Am Strom 123 0381/52516 Reservations essential AE, DC, MC, V.*

$–$$ **Hotel Neptun.** The 19-story concrete-and-glass Neptun is an eyesore on the outside, but inside it has the redeeming qualities of an upscale hotel. Every one of the neatly decorated rooms has a sea view and a balcony. The hotel's Spa Arkona is one of eastern Germany's finest fitness and sauna clubs. ✉ *Seestr. 19, D–18119* ☎ *0381/7770* 🖷 *0381/54023* 🌐 *www.hotel-neptun.de* *340 rooms, 5 suites* *4 restaurants, café, room service, in-room safes, minibars, cable TV, Web TV, saltwater pool, health club, hair salon, sauna, spa, boating, bicycles, 2 bars, dance club, baby-sitting, dry cleaning, laundry service, Internet room, meeting room, parking (fee), some pets allowed (fee), no-smoking rooms; no a/c* *AE, DC, MC, V* *BP.*

$ **Hotel Germania.** At the harbor entrance and only one block from the beach and the Alter Strom promenade, this small hotel's location alone makes it a good choice. All rooms are tastefully decorated and include a TV. With so many good eateries nearby you won't mind that there's no hotel restaurant. ✉ *Am Strom 110–111, D–18119* ☎ *0381/519–850* 🖷 *0381/519–8510* 🌐 *www.germania-warnemuende.de* *18 rooms* *Minibars, cable TV, bar, parking (fee), some pets allowed (fee); no a/c* *AE, DC, MC, V* *BP.*

$ **Landhotel Ostseetraum.** This family-owned hotel, in a thatched-roof farmhouse outside Warnemünde, expertly blends modern style with rural architecture. The recently refurbished apartments all feature a kitchenette, and separate sitting or living areas. The standard rooms are smaller—some have a maritime flair with dark, heavy but modern furniture and large beds; others, which are even smaller, have a country feel with bright pinewood furnishings. The hotel is 500 yards from the beach. ✉ *Stolteraerweg 34b, D–18119 Warnemünde-Diedrichshagen* ☎🖷 *0381/51719* 🌐 *www.ostseetraum.de* *18 rooms* *Restaurant, cable TV, free parking, some pets allowed (fee); no a/c* *AE, MC, V* *BP.*

Sports & the Outdoors

FISHING Every port along the coast has small boats for rent, and some boatmen will lead fishers to the shoals. For information on equipment, contact the **Rostock tourist office** (☎ 0381/403–0500) for **Warnemünder Hafen** (Warnemünde Harbor).

Nightlife

In Warnemünde nearly all the seaside hotels and resorts, down to the smallest, have dances almost nightly during the summer months. The pubs in marina **Alter Strom** are fun gathering places. The **Skybar** (✉ Seestr. 19, 19th fl. of Neptun Hotel ☎ 0381/7770) is open until 3 AM. Roof access gives you the chance to sit under the stars and watch ship lights twinkle on the sea.

en route

Ribnitz-Damgarten, 30 km (19 mi) northeast of Warnemünde, is the center of the amber (in German, *Bernstein*) business, unique to the Baltic Coast. Amber is a yellow-brown fossil formed from the sap of ancient conifers and is millions of years old. Head for a beach and join the locals in the perennial quest for amber stones washed up among the seaweed.

In the **Deutsches Bernsteinmuseum** (German Amber Museum), which adjoins the main factory, you can see a fascinating exhibit of how this precious "Baltic gold" is collected from the sea and refined to make jewelry. The museum has pieces of amber that are between 35 and 50 million years old. ✉ *Im Kloster 1–2 Ribnitz-Damgarten* ☎ *03821/2931* 🌐 *www.bernsteinmuseum.info* €4.50 ⏲ *Apr.–Oct., daily 9:30–6; Nov.–Mar., Wed.–Sun. 9:30–5; last entry 45 min before closing.*

VORPOMMERN

The best description of this region is found in its name, which simply means "before Pomerania." This area, indeed, seems trapped between Mecklenburg and the authentic, old Pomerania farther east, now part of Poland. Although Vorpommern is not the dull, monotonous backwater it's made out to be, its tundralike appearance, pine barrens, heaths, and dunes are not typical tourist draws, either. Its very remoteness ensures an unforgettable view of unspoiled nature, primarily attracting families and young travelers.

Stralsund

11 *68 km (42 mi) east of Rostock on Route 105.*

This jewel of the Baltic has retained its historic city center and parts of its 13th-century defensive wall. The wall was built following an attack by the Lübeck fleet in 1249. In 1815 the Congress of Vienna awarded the city, which had been under Swedish control, to the Prussians.

The **Alter Markt** (Old Market Square) has the best local architecture, ranging from redbrick Gothic through Renaissance to baroque. Most buildings were rich merchants' homes, notably the late-Gothic **Wulflamhaus,** with 17 ornate, steeply stepped gables. Stralsund's architectural masterpiece, however, is the 14th-century **Rathaus,** considered by many to be the finest secular example of redbrick Gothic. Its open corridors reduced wind pressure on the tall facade.

The treasures of the 13th-century Gothic **St. Nikolaikirche** (St. Nicholas's Church) include a 15-foot-high crucifix from the 14th century, an astronomical clock from 1394, and a famous baroque altar. ✉ *Alter Markt* ☎ *03831/297–199* ⏲ *Apr.–Sept., weekdays 10–5, Sat. 10–4, Sun. 11–noon and 2–4; Oct.–Mar., Mon.–Sat. 10–noon and 2–4, Sun. 11–noon and 2–4.*

The **Katherinenkloster** (St. Catherine's Monastery) is a former cloister; 40 of its rooms now house two museums: the famed Deutsches Meeresmuseum, and the Kulturhistorisches Museum.

The **Kulturhistorisches Museum** (Cultural History Museum), exhibits diverse artifacts from more than 10,000 years of this coastal region's history. Highlights include a toy collection and 10th-century Viking gold jewelry found on Hiddensee. You'll reach the museums by walking along Ossenreyerstrasse through the Apollonienmarkt on Mönchstrasse.

Kulturhistorisches Museum, Mönchstr. 25–27 03831/28790 €3 Tues.–Sun. 10–5.

The Stralsund aquarium of Baltic Sea life is part of the three-floor **Deutsches Meeresmuseum** (German Sea Museum), which also displays the skeletons of a giant whale and a hammerhead shark, and a 25-foot-high chunk of coral. The museum is partly set within an early Gothic church. *Katharinenberg 14–20, entrance on Mönchstr. 03831/26500 www.meeresmuseum.de €5.50 Oct.–Mar., daily 10–5; June–Sept., daily 10–6.*

The monstrous **St. Marienkirche** (St. Mary's Church) is the largest of Stralsund's three redbrick Gothic churches. With 4,000 pipes and intricate decorative figures, the magnificent 17th-century Stellwagen organ (played only during Sunday services) is a delight to see and hear. The view from the church tower of Stralsund's old city center is well worth climbing the 349 steps to the top. *Neuer Markt, entrance at Bleistr. 03831/293–529 Tour of church tower €2 May–Oct., weekdays 9–6, weekends 10–noon; Nov.–Apr., weekdays 10–noon, 2–6, weekends 10–noon.*

Where to Stay & Eat

¢–$ **Wulflamstuben.** This restaurant is on the ground floor of Wulflamhaus, a 14th-century gabled house on the old market square. Steaks and fish are the specialty; in late spring or early summer, get the light and tasty *Ostseeflunder* (grilled plaice), fresh from the North Sea. In winter, the hearty *Stralsunder Aalsuppe* (Stralsund eel soup) is a must. *Alter Markt 5 03831/291–533 Reservations essential AE, DC, MC, V.*

¢–$ **Zum Alten Fritz.** It's worth the trip here just to see the rustic interior and copper brewing equipment. Good, old German beer and ale of all shades are the main focus. In summer the beer garden gets somewhat rambunctious. *Greifswalder Chaussee 84–85, at B–96a 03831/255–500 MC, V.*

★ $$ **Dorint im HanseDom.** This ultramodern hotel, part of Germany's Dorint chain, makes up for a lack of historic ambience with winning amenities and great hospitality at an unbeatable price. The high-rise hotel doesn't look very appealing at first glance, but the spacious rooms (featuring many extras such as a baby bed, satellite TV, and a work desk) are furnished in bright colors and ensure a most pleasant stay. The biggest attraction, the hotel's Vital Spa, is a huge wellness facility and one of the best complexes to be found in northern Germany. *Grünhofer Bogen, D–18437 03831/37730 03831/377–3100 www.dorint.de 106 rooms, 8 suites Restaurant, room service, in-room safes, minibars, cable TV, Wi-Fi, Internet room, 5 pools (4 indoor), sauna, spa, bar, dry cleaning, laundry service, meeting rooms, parking (fee), some pets allowed (fee), no-smoking rooms AE, DC, MC, V BP.*

$$ **Hotel zur Post.** This redbrick hotel is a great deal for travelers who want to enjoy a homey yet first-class ambience. It's on the market square near the Old Town. The hotel's interior is a thoughtful mix of traditional North German furnishings and modern design. *Am Neuen Markt, Tribseerstr. 22, D–18439 03831/200–500 03831/200–510 www.hotel-zur-post-stralsund.de 104 rooms, 2 suites, 8 apartments Restaurant, room service, in-room safes, minibars, cable*

TV, Web TV, Wi-Fi, sauna, bar, dry cleaning, laundry service, meeting room, parking (fee), some pets allowed (fee), no-smoking rooms; no a/c ▭ *AE, V* 🍽 *BP.*

$ ▦ **Norddeutscher Hof.** Don't let the weathered facade fool you; this hotel is in good shape, even if the lobby and restaurant were not as tastefully redecorated as the guest rooms. Still, you get the basics at a fair price. ✉ *Neuer Markt 22, D–18439* ☎ *03831/293–161* 🖷 *03831/287–939* 🌐 *www.nd-hof.de* *13 rooms* *Restaurant, cable TV, Internet room, free parking, some pets allowed (fee); no a/c* ▭ *AE, MC, V* 🍽 *BP.*

Nightlife

Bar Hemingway (✉ Tribseerstr. 22 ☎ 03831/200–500) lures a thirtysomething clientele with the best cocktails in town. A young crowd dances at **Fun und Lollipop** (✉ Grünhofer Bogen 11–14 ☎ 03834/3410). For a genuine old harbor *Kneipe* (tavern), head to the **Kuttel Daddeldu** (✉ Hafenstr. on Hafeninsel ☎ 03831/299–526).

Shopping

Buddelschiffe (ships in a bottle) are a symbol of the magnificent sailing history of this region. They look easy to build, but they aren't, and they're quite delicate. Expect to pay more than €70 for a 1-liter bottle. Also look for ***Fischerteppiche*** (fisherman's carpets). Eleven square feet of these traditional carpets take 150 hours to create, which explains why they're meant only to be hung on the wall—and why they cost from €260 to €1,200. They're decorated with traditional symbols of the region, such as the mythical griffin.

Rügen Island

⓬ *4 km (2½ mi) northeast of Stralsund on Route 96.*

Fodor's Choice ★

Rügen's diverse and breathtaking landscapes have inspired poets and painters for more than a century. Railways in the mid-19th century brought the first vacationers, and many of the grand mansions and villas on the island date from this period. The island's main route runs between the **Grosser Jasmunder Bodden** (Big Jasmund Inlet), a giant sea inlet, and a smaller expanse of water, the **Kleiner Jasmunder Bodden** (Little Jasmund Inlet Lake), to the port of Sassnitz. You're best off staying at any of the island's four main vacation centers—Sassnitz, Binz, Sellin, and Göhren.

Equipment for windsurfing, sailing, surfing (although the waves here are modest), and pedal-boat riding is available for hire at the beach resorts. If you have difficulty locating what you want, contact the local tourist offices. The best-protected area along the coast for sailing is Grosser Jasmunder Bodden; boats for the bay can be hired at Lietzow and Ralswiek (if you have a German or International sailing license).

The small town of **Bergen,** the island's administrative capital, was founded as a Slavic settlement some 900 years ago. The **Marienkirche** (St. Mary's Church) has geometric murals dating back to the late 1100s and painted brick octagonal pillars. The pulpit and altar are baroque. Outside the front door and built into the church facade is a grave from the 1200s.

off the beaten path

HIDDENSEE – Off the northwest corner of Rügen is a smaller island called Hiddensee. The undisturbed solitude of this sticklike island has attracted such visitors as Albert Einstein, Thomas Mann, Rainer Maria Rilke, and Sigmund Freud. As Hiddensee is an auto-free zone, leave your car in Schaprode, 21 km (13 mi) west of Bergen, and take a ferry. Vacation cottages and restaurants are on the island.

Marking the northernmost point in eastern Germany is the lighthouse at **Kap Arkona,** a nature lover's paradise filled with blustery sand dunes. The redbrick lighthouse was designed by Karl Friedrich Schinkel, the architect responsible for so many of today's landmarks in Berlin. You can see the Danish island of Moen from a restored watchtower next to the lighthouse.

The small fishing town **Sassnitz** is the island's harbor for ferries to Sweden. Sassnitz is surrounded by some of the most pristine nature to be found along the Baltic Coast. From Sassnitz, walk to **Jasmund Nationalpark** (🌐 www.nationalpark-jasmund.de) to explore the marshes, lush pine forests, and towering chalk cliffs. For information about the park, contact the Sassnitz tourist office.

Ten kilometers (6 mi) north of Sassnitz are the twin chalk cliffs of Rügen's main attraction, the **Stubbenkammer** headland. From here you can best see the much-photographed white-chalk cliffs called the**Königstuhl,** rising 350 feet from the sea. A steep trail leads down to a beach.

South of Sassnitz, **Binz** is the largest resort town on Rügen's east coast, with white villas and a beach promenade. Standing on the highest point of East Rügen is the **Jagdschloss Granitz,** a hunting lodge built in 1836. It offers a splendid view in all directions from its lookout tower and has an excellent hunting exhibit. ✥ *2 km (1 mi) south of Binz,* ☎ *038393/2263* 🎫 *€3* ⏲ *May–Sept., daily 9–6; Oct.–Apr., Tues.–Sun. 10–4.*

Four km (2.5 mi) north of Binz are five concrete quarters of **Bad Prora,** where the Nazis once planned to provide vacation quarters for up to 20,000 German workers. The complex was never used, except by the East German army. Museums and galleries here today include one that documents the history of the site. Hostel guests at **World Camp Prora** (☎ 038393/330–000 🌐 www.oneworldcamp.de) get beach-view rooms. Reception is open daily from 2 to 4.

The heart of the town **Putbus,** 28 km (17 mi) southwest of Binz, is the Circus, a round central plaza dating back to the early 19th century. The immaculate white buildings surrounding the Circus give the city its nickname, Weisse Stadt (White City). In summer the blooming roses in front of the houses (once a requirement by the ruling noble family of Putbus) are truly spectacular.

Lovers of old watches and clocks should not miss the tiny **Uhrenmuseum Putbus,** where watchmaker Franz Sklorz showcases a historic collection of more than 600 clocks, watches, musical gadgets, and more. You might catch him at work. ✉ *Alleestr. 13* ☎ *038301/60988* 🎫 *€3* ⏲ *Apr.–Nov., daily 10–6; Dec.–Mar., daily 11–4.*

From Putbus you can take a ride on the 90-year-old miniature steam train, the **Rasender Roland** (Racing Roland), which runs 24 km (16 mi) to Göhren, at the southeast corner of the Rügen. Trains leave hourly; the ride takes 70 minutes one way. ✉ *Binzer Str. 12* ☎ *038301/8010* 🌐 *www.rasender-roland.de* 🎟 *€8* ⏲ *Apr.–Oct., daily 5:30 AM–10:15 PM from Putbus. Nov.–Mar., same hrs but trains depart only every 2 hrs.*

Where to Stay & Eat

★ $–$$ ✕ **Panoramahotel Lohme.** Dinner at this restaurant dubbed "Rügen's balcony" offers the most beautiful view on the island, just outside the National Park Jasmund. While enjoying fresh fish from local waters, prepared with a light Italian touch, you can watch the sunset over the cliffs of Kap Arkona. Chef Michael Raatz uses fresh produce from local farmers and the superb vintages are from small private wineries. Make a reservation, and insist on a table in the *Fontane-Veranda* (in winter) or the *Arkonablick-Terrasse* (in summer). ✉ *Dorfstr. 35 Lohme* ☎ *038302/9221* 🌐 *www.lohme.com* 💳 *No credit cards* ⏲ *Closed Mon.*

$$$ ✕🏨 **Hotel Kurhaus Binz.** The grand old lady of the Baltic Sea, the neoclassicist 19th-century Kurhaus Binz, is reviving the splendor of times past, when Binz was called the Nice of the North. The five-star Kurhaus is right on the beach, with a breathtaking sea view in most of the spacious and elegantly furnished rooms. The huge Egyptian-theme spa and wellness area is a real treat. Of the two restaurants, the Kurhaus-Restaurant ($–$$$) is the better choice—it serves traditional seafood but adds exotic touches with special fusion-cuisine events. ✉ *Strandpromenade 27, D–18609 Binz-Rügen* ☎ *038393/6650* 📠 *038393/665–555* 🌐 *www.tc-hotels.de* 🛏 *106 rooms, 20 suites* ♨ *2 restaurants, room service, minibars, cable TV with movies, Web TV, Wi-Fi, indoor-outdoor pool, health club, massage, sauna, spa, beach, bar, cabaret, babysitting, dry cleaning, laundry service, concierge, meeting rooms, parking (fee), some pets allowed (fee), no-smoking floor* 💳 *AE, DC, MC, V* 🍽 *BP.*

$–$$ ✕🏨 **Hotel Godewind.** Two hundred yards from the beaches of Hiddensee that have so inspired writers, this small hotel offers food and lodging at very reasonable prices. In addition, the hotel rents small cottages and apartments around the island, which are a good value if you intend to stay for more than a few days. Godewind's restaurant ($) is known on the island for its regional dishes. ✉ *Süderende 53, D–18565 Vitte-Hiddensee* ☎ *038300/6600* 📠 *038300/660–222* 🌐 *www.hotelgodewind.de* 🛏 *23 rooms, 19 cottages* ♨ *Restaurant, some pets allowed (fee); no a/c, no room TVs* 💳 *No credit cards* 🍽 *BP.*

★ $ ✕🏨 **Villa Seestern.** This cozy yet stately mansion is just a stone's throw from the beach. Many of the simply but contemporarily furnished rooms are a true bargain, on account of both the low rates and the terrific views from the private balconies. Equally inviting is the Fisch-Brasserie Seestern ($), with a pierlike extension leading to the water. ✉ *Mühlenstr. 5, D–18546 Sassnitz* ☎ *038392/33257* 📠 *038392/36765* ✉ *villa.seestern@arcormail.de* 🛏 *14 rooms* ♨ *Restaurant, cable TV, free parking, some pets allowed (fee), no-smoking rooms; no a/c* 💳 *MC* 🍽 *BP.*

★ $$ **Vier Jahreszeiten.** This first-class beach resort in Binz is a sophisticated blend of historic seaside architecture and modern elegance. Behind the ornamental white facade, the hotel boasts spacious rooms, decorated with 19th-century reproduction furniture, as well as more-secluded apartments. A great plus is the nearly 6,000-square-foot spa and wellness center, one of the best in Mecklenburg-Pomerania. ✉ *Zeppelinstr. 8, D–18609 Binz-Rügen* ☎ *038393/500* 🖷 *038393/50430* 🌐 *www.jahreszeiten-hotels.de* *69 rooms, 7 suites, 77 apartments* *3 restaurants, room service, minibars, cable TV with movies, in-room data ports, indoor-outdoor pool, health club, massage, sauna, spa, bar, baby-sitting, dry cleaning, laundry service, concierge, meeting rooms, parking (fee), some pets allowed (fee), no-smoking floor* 💳 *AE, MC, V* 🍽 *BP.*

$ **Hotel Loev.** The Loev, set in a great white building at the promenade in Binz, looks very much like a Victorian seaside resort. The spacious rooms are quite modern, with dark-wood furniture, thick carpets, and a wonderful view of the sea. ✉ *Hauptstr. 20–22, D–18609 Binz-Rügen* ☎ *038393/390* 🖷 *038393/39444* 🌐 *www.loev.de* *74 rooms, 4 apartments* *2 restaurants, in-room safes, minibars, cable TV, Wi-Fi, Internet room, gym, sauna, bar, parking (fee), some pets allowed (fee); no a/c* 💳 *AE, MC, V* 🍽 *BP.*

★ $ **Hotel Villa Granitz.** The little town of Baabe claims to have Rügen's most beautiful beach. This mostly wooden mansion is a small and quiet retreat for those who want to avoid the masses in the island's other resorts. All rooms are spacious and have a large terrace or balcony; pastel colors (a soft white and yellow) add to the tidy, fairy-tale look of the building. The apartments have small kitchenettes. ✉ *Birkenallee 17, D–18586 Baabe* ☎ *038303/1410* 🖷 *038303/14144* 🌐 *www.villa-granitz.de* *44 rooms, 8 suites, 12 apartments* *Refrigerators, cable TV, dry cleaning, laundry service, free parking, some pets allowed (fee), no-smoking rooms; no a/c* 💳 *No credit cards* 🍽 *BP.*

Shopping

At the end of the 19th century, 16 pieces of 10th-century Viking jewelry were discovered on the Baltic coastline (presently housed in the Kulturhistorisches Museum in Stralsund). Gold and silver replicas of the **Hiddensee Golden Jewelry** are a great souvenir, and their distinctive patterns are found in shops on Rügen Island and on Hiddensee Island.

Usedom Island

⓭ *67 km (42 mi) to Wolgast bridge from Stralsund.*

Usedom Island has almost 32 km (20 mi) of sandy shoreline and a string of resorts. Much of the island's untouched landscape is a nature preserve that provides refuge for a number of rare birds, including the giant sea eagle, which has a wingspan of up to 8 feet. Even in the summer this island is more or less deserted and is ready to be explored by bicycle. From the west, Usedom is accessed via the causeway at **Wolgast.** The bridge closes to traffic at times to allow boats to pass through.

At the northwest tip of Usedom, 16 km (10 mi) from landside Wolgast, is **Peenemünde,** the launch site of the world's first jet rockets, the V1 and V2, developed by Germany toward the end of World War II and mostly fired at London. You can view these rockets as well as models of early airplanes and ships at the extensive **Historisch-Technisches informationszentrum** (Historical-Technical Information Center) housed in a former army power plant. The ethics of scientific research are also examined. One exhibit covers the secret underground plants where most of the rocket parts were assembled and where thousands of slave laborers died. Explanation of the exhibits in English are available. ✉ *Im Kraftwerk* ☎ *038371/5050* 🎫 *€5* ⏲ *Apr.–Oct., Tues.–Sun. 9–6; Nov.–Mar., Tues.–Sun. 10–4.*

SCHLESWIG-HOLSTEIN & THE BALTIC COAST A TO Z

To research prices, get advice from other travelers, and book travel arrangements, visit www.fodors.com.

AIR TRAVEL

The international airport closest to Schleswig-Holstein is in Hamburg. For an eastern approach to the Baltic Coast tour, use Berlin's Tegel Airport.

BOAT & FERRY TRAVEL

The Weisse Flotte (White Fleet) line operates ferries linking the Baltic ports, as well as short harbor and coastal cruises. Boats depart from Warnemünde, Zingst (to Hiddensee), Sassnitz, and Stralsund. In addition, ferries run from Stralsund and Sassnitz to destinations in Sweden, Denmark, Poland, and Finland.

Scandlines operates ferries between Sassnitz and the Danish island of Bornholm as well as Sweden.

Scandlines ☎ 01805/72263–54637 🌐 www.scandlines.de. **Weisse Flotte** ☎ 0180/321–2120 central phone, 03831/519–860 for Warnemünde, 03831/26810 for Stralsund, 0385/557–770 for Schwerin.

BUS TRAVEL

Local buses link the main train stations with outlying towns and villages, especially the coastal resorts. Buses operate throughout Sylt, Rügen, and Usedom islands.

CAR TRAVEL

The two-lane roads (Bundesstrassen) along the coast can be full of traffic during June, July, and August. The ones leading to Usedom Island can be extremely log-jammed, as the causeway bridges have scheduled closings to let ships pass. Using the Bundesstrassen takes more time, but these often tree-lined roads are by far more scenic than the autobahn.

Sylt island is 196 km (122 mi) from Hamburg via autobahn A–7 and Bundesstrasse 199 and is ultimately reached via train. B–199 cuts through some nice countryside, and instead of A–7 or B–76 between

Schleswig and Kiel, you could take the slow route through the coastal hinterland (B–199, 203, 503). Lübeck, the gateway to Mecklenburg-Vorpommern, is 56 km (35 mi) from Hamburg via A–1. B–105 leads to all sightseeing spots in Mecklenburg-Vorpommern. A faster route is the new autobahn A–20, connecting Lübeck and Rostock. From Stralsund, Route 96 cuts straight across Rügen Island, a distance of 51 km (32 mi). From Berlin take A–11 and head toward Prenzlau for B–109 all the way to Usedom Island, a distance of 162 km (100 mi). A causeway connects the mainland town of Anklam to the town of Peenemünde, on Usedom Island; coming from the west, use the causeway at Wolgast.

TOURS

Although tourist offices and museums have worked to improve the quality and amount of English-language literature about this area, English-speaking tours are infrequent and must be requested ahead of time through the local tourist office. Because most tours are designed for groups, there's usually a flat fee of €20–€30. Towns currently offering tours are Lübeck, Stralsund, and Rostock. Schwerin has two-hour boat tours of its lakes.

Tours of Old Lübeck depart daily from the tourist offices on the Alter Markt between mid-April and mid-October and on weekends only from mid-October to mid-April. Harbor and coastal cruises also operate from Lübeck; contact the Lübeck tourist office for details.

Many of the former fishermen in these towns give sunset tours of the harbors or shuttle visitors between neighboring towns. This is a unique opportunity to ride on an authentic fishing boat. In Kiel, Rostock, and on Sylt, cruise lines make short trips through the respective bays and/or islands off the coast, sailing even as far as Denmark and Sweden. Inquire at the local tourist office about companies and times, as well as about fishing-boat tours.

TRAIN TRAVEL

Train travel is much more convenient than bus travel in this area. Sylt, Kiel, Lübeck, Schwerin, and Rostock have InterCity train connections to either Hamburg, Berlin, or both.

A north–south train line links Schwerin and Rostock. An east–west route connects Kiel, Hamburg, Lübeck, and Rostock, and some trains continue through to Stralsund and Sassnitz, on Rügen Island. Train service between the smaller cities of former East Germany is generally much slower than in the west.

Trains are the *only* way to access Sylt, which is connected to the mainland via the train causeway Hindenburgdamm. Deutsche Bahn will transport you and your car from central train stations at Dortmund, Düsseldorf, Hamburg, Stuttgart, and Frankfurt directly onto the island. In addition, a daily-shuttle car train leaves Niebüll roughly every 30 minutes from 5:20 AM to 8:45 PM (Friday and Sunday until 9:35 PM). There are no reservations on this train.

VISITOR INFORMATION

The regional tourism board for the Baltic Coast is the TOURBU-Zentrale, Landesfremdenverkehrsverband Mecklenburg-Vorpommern. When writing to any information office, address your letter to "Touristeninformation" and then add the city's name.

Baltic Coast Information **Bad Doberan** ✉ Goethestr. 1, D-18209 ☎ 038203/91530 🖷 038203/62154 🌐 www.m-vp.de. **Lübeck** ✉ Breite Str. 62 📫 Beckergrube 95, D-23552 ☎ 01805/882-233 🖷 0451/122-5419 🌐 www.luebeck.de. **Rostock-Warnemünde** ✉ Neuer Markt 3, D-18055 ☎ 0381/548-000 🖷 0381/381-2601 🌐 www.rostock.de. **Rügen Island** ✉ Tourismusverband Rügen, Am Markt 4, D-18528 Bergen ☎ 03838/80770 🖷 03838/254-440 🌐 www.ruegen.de. **Sassnitz** ✉ Seestr. 1, D-18546 ☎ 038392/5160 🖷 038392/51616 🌐 www.sassnitz.de. **Schwerin** ✉ Am Markt 10, D-19055 ☎ 0385/592-5212 🖷 0385/555-094 🌐 www.schwerin.de. **Stralsund** ✉ Alter Markt 9, D-18439 ☎ 03831/24690 🖷 03831/246-949 🌐 www.stralsund.de. **TOURBU-Zentrale, Landesfremdenverkehrsverband Mecklenburg-Vorpommern** ✉ Pl. der Freundschaft 1, D-18059 Rostock ☎ 0381/403-0500 🖷 0381/403-0555 🌐 www.tmv.de. **Usedom Island** ✉ Tourismusverband Insel Usedom e.V., Bäderstr. 4, D-17459 Seebad Ückeritz ☎ 038375/23410 🖷 038375/23429 🌐 www.usedom.de. **Wismar** ✉ Stadthaus, Am Markt 11, D-23966 ☎ 03841/19433 🖷 03841/251-3090 🌐 www.wismar.de.

Schleswig-Holstein Information **Husum** ✉ Grossstr. 27, D-25813 ☎ 04841/89870 🖷 04841/898-790 🌐 www.husum.de. **Kampen** ✉ Kurverwaltung, Hauptstr. 12, D-25999 ☎ 04651/46980 🖷 04651/469-860 🌐 www.kampen.de. **Kiel** ✉ Andreas-Gayk-Str. 31, D-24103 ☎ 01805/656-700, 0.12¢ per min. 🖷 0431/679-1099 🌐 www.kiel.de. **Westerland** ✉ Strandstr. 33 📫 Stephanstr. 6, Postfach 1260, D-25969 ☎ 04651/9980 🖷 04651/998-6000 🌐 www.westerland.de.

Berlin

14

WORD OF MOUTH

"Berlin is fabulous. It is the only city in Europe without fixed closing hours, which means the nightlife makes New York City look like a church social."

—JP

"I finally made it to Berlin last year and really loved it. . . . On the other hand, lots of friends really hated it. You can't go expecting quaint and charming. . . . But if you like vibrant and modern cities, Berlin should please."

—Patrick

www.fodors.com/forums

Updated by Christina Knight

SINCE THE FALL OF THE IRON CURTAIN, no city in Europe has seen more development and change. Two Berlins that had been separated for 40 years struggled to meld into one, and in the scar of barren borderland between them sprang government and commercial centers that have become the glossy spreads of travel guides and architecture journals. After successfully uniting its own east and west, Berlin will play a pivotal role in a European Union that has undertaken the same task.

But even as the capital thinks and moves forward, history is always tugging at its sleeve. Between the wealth of neoclassical and 21st-century buildings, there are constant reminders, both subtle and stark, of the events of the 20th century. For every new embassy and relocated corporate headquarters, a church stands half-ruined, a synagogue is under 24-hour guard, and an empty lot remains where a building either crumbled in World War II or went up in dynamite as East Germany cleared a path for its Wall. In the chillier months, the scent of coal wafts through the trendy neighborhoods of Prenzlauer Berg and Friedrichshain, where young residents who fuel the cultural scene heat their unrenovated apartments with coal ovens.

Much of what's new in Berlin is firmly rooted to history. A popular city view is from the stunning glass cupola atop the Reichstag, a 1999 crown upon an 1894 parliament building. One block south of the Brandenburg Gate, the unusual sculptural landscape that opened in May 2005 is the Memorial to the Murdered Jews of Europe, dedicated to those killed in the Holocaust.

Compared to other German cities, Berlin is quite young and, ironically, began as two separate entities more than 760 years ago. The Spree River divided the slightly older Cölln on Museum Island from the fishing village Berlin. By the 1300s, Berlin was prospering thanks to its location at the intersection of important trade routes. After the ravages of the Thirty Years' War, Berlin rose to power as the seat of the Hohenzollern dynasty. The Great Elector Friedrich Wilhelm, in the almost 50 years of his reign (1640–88), touched off a renaissance by supporting such institutions as the Academy of Arts and the Academy of Sciences. Later, Frederick the Great (1712–1786) made Berlin and Potsdam his glorious centers of the enlightened yet autocratic Prussian monarchy.

In 1871, Prussia, ruled by the "Iron Chancellor" Count Otto von Bismarck, unified the many independent German states into the German Empire. Berlin maintained its status as capital for the duration of the German Empire (1871–1918), through the post–World War I Weimar Republic (1919–33), and also through Hitler's so-called Third Reich (1933–45). The city's golden years were the Roaring '20s, when Berlin, the energetic, modern, and sinful counterpart to Paris, became a center for the cultural avant-garde. World-famous writers, painters, and artists met here while the impoverished bulk of its 4 million inhabitants lived in heavily overpopulated quarters. This "dance on the volcano," as those years of political and economic upheaval have been called, came to a grisly and bloody end after January 1933, when Adolf Hitler became

If you have 2 days

Start in western, downtown Berlin by visiting the stark shell of the Kaiser-Wilhelm-Gedächtniskirche. Catch the double-decker public Bus 100 (in front of the Zoo railway station) and get a seat on top. The entire scenic ride through the park Tiergarten, past the Reichstag, along Unter den Linden, and around Alexanderplatz shows you the prime attractions in Berlin before doubling back again. Save a good amount of time and energy for the museums on Museum Island and the German History Museum. You can take a break with German cakes and coffee in the Opernpalais on Unter den Linden. On your second day visit the dome of the Reichstag (to avoid long lines, arrive at 8 AM) and Potsdamer Platz, a study in urban renewal and modern architecture. Whatever order you do it in, walk along Ebertstrasse between the sights, as it takes you past the Brandenburg Gate and the Memorial to the Murdered Jews of Europe. Behind the showy corporate buildings of Potsdamer Platz is the Gemäldegalerie and Neue Nationalgalerie, two outstanding fine-arts museums. From Potsdamer Platz it's a 10-minute walk to the Topography of Terror, a free, open-air exhibit on the organizations of the SS and the Gestapo, their crimes, and their victims. The site is bordered by a remaining stretch of the Berlin Wall and Checkpoint Charlie lies another 250 yards further east. Spend one evening or some shopping hours meandering the smaller streets around Hackescher Markt in Mitte.

If you have 3 days

Follow the two-day itinerary above. After viewing the Topography of Terror, continue on to the Mauermusuem Haus am Checkpoint Charlie, which is open until 10 PM. On your third day, round out the sights and eras of history you've seen by visiting the royals' apartments in Schloss Charlottenburg and the lovely gardens behind it. After touring the palace, hop the U-7 subway from Richard-Wagner-Platz to Adenauerplatz. Head east and browse the most elegant of the Kurfürstendamm boutiques within old city mansions. Turn left on Bleibtreustrasse to reach the cafés and restaurants in the fashionable, but casual Savignyplatz area. Spend one evening at a show, perhaps at Chämeleon Varieté or Bar Jeder Vernunft.

If you have 5 days

A five-day visit allows you to spread the sights out at your leisure, linger at cafés, and dip into shops that catch your eye. Follow the three-day itinerary above, then begin your fourth day in the district of Kreuzberg. See if the current exhibits at the Martin-Gropius-Bau interest you, or visit the Jüdisches Museum, where the architecture by Daniel Libeskind is a main draw. Before sunset, ride up to the observatory floor of Berlin's highest structure, the Berliner Fernsehturm (Television Tower). Spend your last day either visiting Potsdam, particularly the summer-palace grounds of Schloss Sanssouci, or cruising the Spree River and its canals on a three-hour boat tour. Narrations by the captains are in German, but you do get amazing views of the city and can quaff beer or coffee and snack as you go.

chancellor. The Nazis made Berlin their capital but ultimately failed to remodel the city into a silent monument to their power. By World War II's end, 70% of the city lay in ruins, with more rubble than in all other German cities combined.

Along with the division of Germany after World War II, Berlin was partitioned into American, British, and French zones in the west and a Soviet zone in the east. By 1947 Berlin had become one of the Cold War's first testing grounds. The three western-occupied zones gradually merged, becoming West Berlin, while the Soviet-controlled eastern zone defiantly remained separate. Peace conferences repeatedly failed to resolve the question of Germany's division, and in 1949 the Soviet Union established East Berlin as the capital of its new puppet state, the German Democratic Republic (GDR). The division of the city was cruelly finalized in concrete in August 1961, when the East German government erected the Berlin Wall, the only border fortification in history built to keep a people from leaving, rather than to protect them.

For nearly 30 years Berlin suffered under one of the greatest geographic and political anomalies of all time, a city split in two by a concrete wall—its larger western half an island of capitalist democracy surrounded by an East Germany run by hard-line Communists. With the Wall relegated to the souvenir pile of history (most of it was recycled but it's still being sold off chip by chip to tourists), visitors can now appreciate the qualities that mark the city as a whole. Its particular charm has always lain in its spaciousness, its trees and greenery, and its anything-goes atmosphere. Moreover, the really stunning parts of the prewar capital are in the historic eastern part of town, which has grand avenues, monumental architecture, and museums that house world treasures. Berlin's further progress has been delayed by the city's bankruptcy. In 2001, the city-owned state bank nearly went bankrupt and forced the city government to resign. A staggering US$3 billion bank debt incurred by risky real-estate deals in East Germany now has to be paid by the state. Unemployment in 2004 and 2005 remained at 19%, a level not seen since the 1930s.

Berlin is known for having the most international residents in Germany, and its bristly natives are just as famous. Berliners' brash, witty, and often plain grumpy attitudes come across well with their piquant dialects. Whatever the bad press their bad moods might earn them, Berliners consider themselves a city of "*Herz mit Schnauze*" (a big heart hidden behind every big mouth).

EXPLORING BERLIN

Berlin is laid out on an epic scale—western Berlin alone is four times the size of the city of Paris. When the city-state of Berlin was incorporated in 1920, it swallowed towns and villages far beyond the downtown area. Of its 12 boroughs, the five of most interest to visitors are Charlottenburg-Wilmersdorf in the west; Tiergarten (a district of the Mitte borough) and Kreuzberg in the center; Mitte, the historic core of the city in the eastern part of town; and Prenzlauer Berg in the northeast.

Eat Like a Local Top-end restaurants can easily import fresh ingredients from other European countries, but some rely on the farmers close to home. Surrounding this city is the rural state of Brandenburg, whose name often comes before *Ente* (duck) on a menu. In spring, *Spargel,* white asparagus from Beelitz, is all the rage, showing up in soups and side dishes. Berlin's most traditional four-part meal is *Eisbein* (pork knuckle), always served with sauerkraut, puréed peas, and boiled potatoes. Other old-fashioned Berlin dishes include *Rouladen* (rolled stuffed beef), *Spanferkel* (suckling pig), *Berliner Schüsselsülze* (potted meat in aspic) and *Hackepeter* (ground beef). Since Berlin became the capital again in 1999, restaurants have increasingly offered other regional German cuisine to feed those who followed the federal government here from their home state.

Stands near subway stations sell spicy *Currywurst,* a chubby frankfurter served with tomato sauce made with curry and pepper. Turkish food is an integral part of the Berlin diet. On almost every street you'll find narrow storefronts selling *Döner kebab* (grilled lamb or chicken served with salad in a flat-bread pocket).

Museums Visiting museums is a bargain in Berlin. At the world-class state museums, children under 16 receive free admission and a €6–€8 entrance fee for adults includes a free audio guide. All state museums are free during the four hours before closing on Thursday. With the moving of the Egyptian Museum from Charlottenburg to Museum Island in April 2005, the famous bust of Queen Nefertiti and other parts of the Egyptian collection joins the island's Greek and Roman antiquities, as well as superb monuments of Greek, Persian, and Roman architecture. The private Flick Collection, the most important and largest collection of contemporary art in the world, has begun a seven-year residency at the state museum Hamburger Bahnhof, which has doubled in size as a result. Berlin's other new collection is the Helmut Newton Stiftung, located just behind the central Zoo Station. The late fashion photographer Helmut Newton donated his works to the city of his birth shortly before his death in 2004.

Culture & Cocktails Berlin is the only European city without official closing hours, so you can stretch your drinks until the wee hours of the morning without fear of a last call. Eastern districts Mitte, Prenzlauer Berg, and Friedrichshain have unusual, impromptu venues for parties and bars. The posher scenes tend to be in the west. Dance clubs don't get going until about 12:30 AM, but parties labeled "after-work" start as early as 8 PM for professionals looking to socialize during the week. Culture abounds between three opera houses, one of the world's leading philharmonic orchestras, innovative German theaters, and cabaret and variety shows.

Southwest Berlin has lovely escapes in the secluded forests and lakes of the Grunewald area.

Many of the 17 Staatliche Museen zu Berlin (national museums of Berlin) are world-renowned and offer several ticket options (children under 17 are welcomed free of charge). A single ticket ranges €4–€8. An all-day pass (*Tageskarte*) to all state museums costs €10. The SchauLust Museen ticket (€12) allows entrance to all state museums plus many others for three consecutive days. State museums tend to cluster near one another and usually a single entrance ticket grants admission to all museums in that area. These areas include Charlottenburg (€6), Dahlem (€4), the Kulturforum (including the out-of-the-way Hamburger Bahnhof, €6), and Museum Island (€8). All these entrance tickets are for the permanent exhibitions and include an audio guide; special exhibits cost extra. State museums are free on Thursday for the last four open hours (there is a fee for the audio guide during free hours).

Numbers in the text correspond to numbers in the margin and on the Berlin map.

Kurfürstendamm & Western Downtown Berlin

Ku'damm is the easy-to-pronounce nickname for Kurfürstendamm, a broad, tree-lined boulevard that stretches for 3 km (2 mi) through the heart of western downtown. It developed in the late 19th century as wealthy Berliners moved out to the "New West." Shoppers are the lifeforce of the boulevard, with enough energy and euros to support the local boutiques on the quieter side streets, too. Out-of-towners take it easy at Ku'damm's sidewalk tables as Berliners bustle by with a purpose.

a good walk

Many bus lines serve the boulevard **Kurfürstendamm** 1 and the U-bahn station Uhlandstrasse is a good starting point. The multimedia museum **Story of Berlin** 2 lies within the mall Ku-damm-Karree near the corner of Uhlandstrasse. You can't miss it for the airplane wing exhibited outside. This was once part of a "Raisen bomber," a U.S. air force DC-3 that supplied Berlin during the Berlin Airlift in 1948 and '49. Two blocks west is Bleibtreustrasse, a street peppered with local stores and eateries north of Ku'damm. After passing under the S-bahn tracks that cross Bleibtreustrasse, turn right into a pedestrian alley. Gift shops, eateries, and bookstores nest within the S-bahn's redbrick viaduct. To the left is Savignyplatz, a green square surrounded by cafés. Grolmanstrasse leads off in a diagonal to the right and will return you to the intersection of Ku'damm and Uhlandstrasse. Walk east on Ku'damm four long blocks toward the jagged steeple of the **Kaiser-Wilhelm-Gedächtniskirche** 3 on Breitscheidplatz. Its ruined bell tower stands as a reminder of World War II. The steps around this symbol of war's destructiveness was once a prime hangout in West Berlin.

Breitscheidplatz separates the church from the dowdy Europa Center mall. At the mall's Budapester Strasse entrance on the left, you'll find the **Tourist Info-Center** 4. Opposite the tourist office is the Asian-style Elefantentor (Elephant Gate), the main entrance to the **Zoologischer Garten** 5, western Berlin's zoo and aquarium. Walk back along Budapester Strasse, passing the ruined bell tower and the bus and taxi stands at Zoo Station. After walking under the train trestle, turn right onto quiet Jebenstrasse. On the left side is the **Museum für Fotographie Helmut Newton Stiftung** 6, which exhibits the photography of native Berliner Helmut Newton.

TIMING Ambling in this area, browsing the stores, and stopping for a coffee will take at least an hour and a half, without visiting sights. The Story of Berlin deserves at least two hours, and the selection of Helmut Newton photos can be seen in an hour. Set aside three hours for the admirable zoo and aquarium—it has the most species in Europe. The Ku'damm is most crowded on Saturday; stores are not open on Sunday.

14

What to See

6 **Museum für Fotographie Helmut Newton Stiftung.** In 2004 Berlin received the permanent loan of 1,000 photographs from native son Helmut Newton (1920–2004), who had pledged the collection to the city months before his unexpected death. The man who defined fashion photography in the 1960s through 1980s was an apprentice to Yva, a Jewish fashion photographer in Berlin in the 1930s. Newton fled Berlin with his family in 1938 and his mentor was killed in a concentration camp. The photographs, now part of the state museum collection, are shown on a rotating basis in the former art library behind the train station Zoologischer Garten. ✉ *Jebenstr. 2, Western Downtown* ☎ *030/266–2951* 🌐 *www.smb.museum* 🎫 *€6* 🕒 *Tues., Wed., and Fri.–Sun. 10–6, Thurs. 10–10* Ⓤ *Zoologischer Garten (U-bahn and S-bahn).*

3 **Kaiser-Wilhelm-Gedächtniskirche** (Kaiser Wilhelm Memorial Church). A dramatic reminder of World War II's destruction, the ruined bell tower is all that remains of the once massive church, which was completed in 1895 and dedicated to the emperor, Kaiser Wilhelm I. The Hohenzollern dynasty is depicted inside in a gilded mosaic, whose damage, like that of the building, will not be repaired. The exhibition revisits World War II's devastation throughout Europe. On the hour, the tower chimes out a melody composed by the last emperor's great-grandson, the late Prince Louis Ferdinand von Hohenzollern.

In stark contrast to the old bell tower (dubbed the Hollow Tooth), are the adjoining Memorial Church and Tower, designed by the noted German architect Egon Eiermann in 1959–61. These ultramodern octagonal structures, with their myriad honeycomb windows, have nicknames as well: the Lipstick and the Powder Box. Brilliant, blue stained glass from Chartres dominates the interiors. Church music and organ concerts are presented in the church regularly. ✉ *Breitscheidpl., Western Downtown* ☎ *030/218–5023* 🌐 *www.gedaechtniskirche.com* 🎫 *Free* 🕒 *Old Tower Mon.–Sat. 10–4, Memorial Church daily 9–7* Ⓤ *Zoologischer Garten (U-bahn and S-bahn).*

need a break?

Forget the fast-food options at Zoo Station. Instead, follow the train tracks to the back of the taxi and bus queues, where you'll enter Tiergarten and within 100 meters come upon the best hideaway in the area: **Schleusen Krug** (✉ Tiergarten, Western Downtown

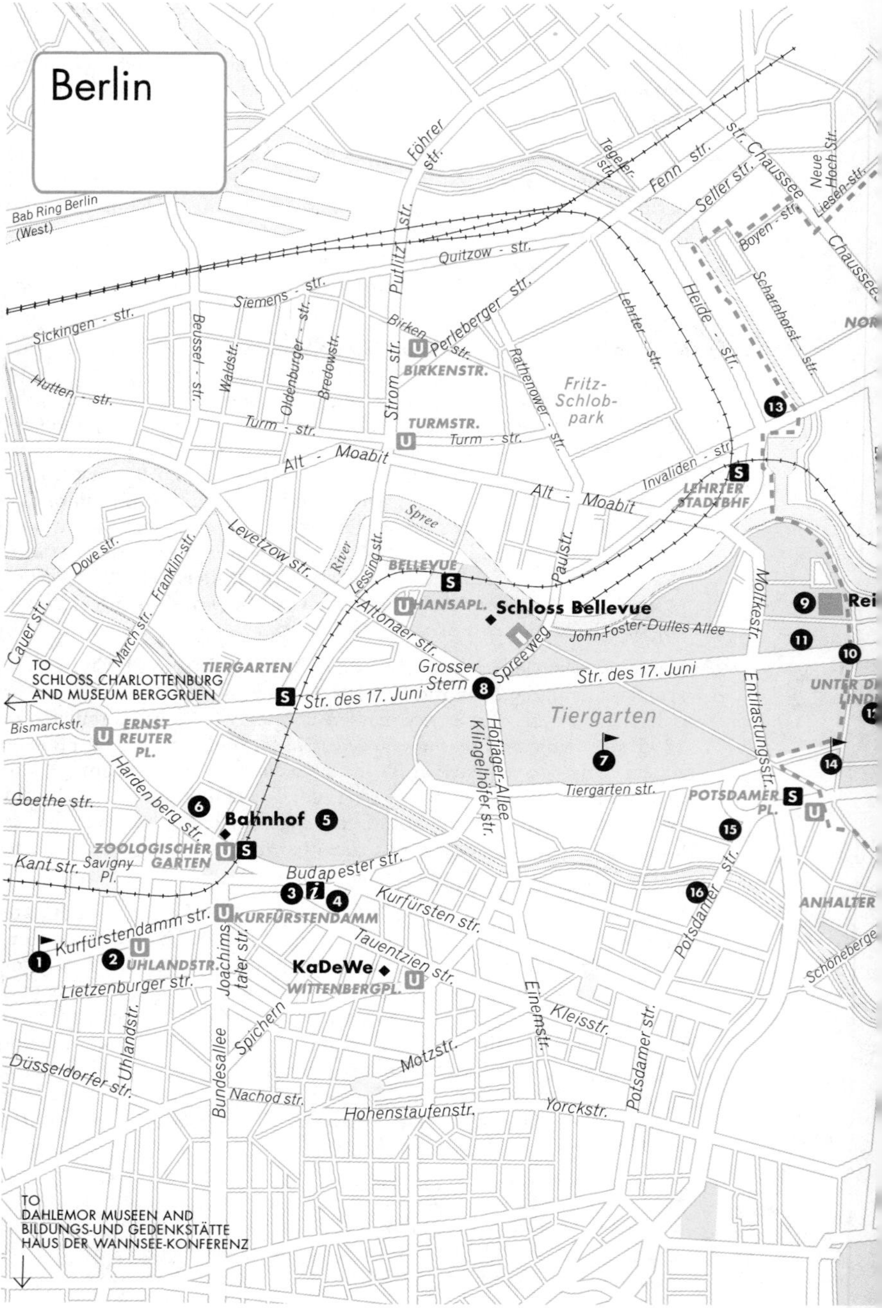
Berlin
Bab Ring Berlin (West)
Föhrer str.
Tegeler str.
Fenn str.
Chaussee str.
Seller str.
Neue Hoch Str.
Liesen-str.
Boyen-str.
Chaussee
Quitzow - str.
Siemens - str.
Sickingen - str.
Putlitz str.
Perleberger str.
Birken str.
BIRKENSTR.
Lehrter - str.
Heide - str.
Scharnhorst - str.
NOR
Hutten - str.
Beussel - str.
Waldstr.
Oldenburger - str.
Bredowstr.
Strom str.
Rathenower - str.
Fritz-Schloß-park
13
Turm - str.
TURMSTR.
Alt - Moabit
Invaliden - str.
LEHRTER STADTBHF
Spree
River
Levetzow str.
Dove str.
Franklin-str.
Lessing str.
BELLEVUE
Paulstr.
Moltkestr.
Cauer str.
March str.
HANSAPL.
Schloss Bellevue
Altonaer str.
John-Foster-Dulles Allee
9
Rei
11
10
TO SCHLOSS CHARLOTTENBURG AND MUSEUM BERGGRUEN
TIERGARTEN
Grosser Stern
8
Spreeweg
Str. des 17. Juni
Str. des 17. Juni
Entlastungsstr.
UNTER DEN LINDEN
Bismarckstr.
ERNST REUTER PL.
Hofjäger-Allee
Klingelhöfer str.
Tiergarten
7
14
Harden berg str.
Goethe str.
6
Bahnhof
5
Tiergarten str.
POTSDAMER PL.
15
ZOOLOGISCHER GARTEN
Kant str.
Savigny Pl.
Budapester str.
3
4
Kurfürsten str.
16
Potsdamer str.
ANHALTER
KURFÜRSTENDAMM
Kurfürstendamm str.
1
2
UHLANDSTR.
Joachims taler str.
Tauentzien str.
KaDeWe
WITTENBERGPL.
Schöneberger
Lietzenburger str.
Uhlandstr.
Spichern
Einemstr.
Kleisstr.
Potsdamer str.
Düsseldorfer str.
Bundesallee
Motzstr.
Nachod str.
Hohenstaufenstr.
Yorckstr.
TO DAHLEMOR MUSEEN AND BILDUNGS-UND GEDENKSTÄTTE HAUS DER WANNSEE-KONFERENZ

Kurfürstendamm & Western Downtown Berlin

- Kaiser-Wilhelm-Gedächtniskirche **3**
- Kurfürstendamm **1**
- Museum für Fotographie Helmut Newton Stiftung **6**
- The Story of Berlin **2**
- Tourist Info-Center **4**
- Zoologischer Garten . . . **5**

Tiergarten & the Government District

- Brandenburger Tor . . . **10**
- Denkmal für die Ermordeten Juden Europas **12**
- Hamburger Bahnhof, Museum für Gegenwart-Berlin **13**
- Reichstag **9**
- Siegessäule **8**
- Sowjetisches Ehrenmal **11**
- Tiergarten **7**

Potsdamer Platz & Kreuzberg

- Berlinische Galerie . . . **21**
- Jüdisches Museum **20**
- Kulturforum **15**
- Martin-Gropius-Bau . . **17**
- Mauermuseum-Museum Haus am Checkpoint Charlie **19**
- Neue Nationalgalerie . . **16**
- Sony Center **14**
- Topographie des Terrors **18**

Mitte: Unter den Linden to Alexanderplatz

- Alexanderplatz **35**
- AquaDom & Sea Life Berlin **30**
- Bebelplatz **24**
- Berliner Dom **29**
- Berliner Fernsehturm . **34**
- Berliner Rathaus **32**
- Deutsches Historisches Museum **26**
- Friedrichstrasse **22**
- Gendarmenmarkt **23**
- Märkisches Museum **36**
- Museumsinsel **27**
- Neue Wache **25**
- Nikolaiviertel **33**
- Schlossplatz **28**
- St. Marienkirche **31**

Mitte's Scheunenviertel & Prenzlauer Berg

- Dokumentationszentrum Berliner Mauer **37**
- Hackesche Höfe **39**
- Kulturbrauerei **40**
- Neue Synagoge **38**

☎ 030/313–9909). In warmer weather you can order at the window and sit in the beer garden or on the back patio, watching pleasure ships go through the lock. Inside is a casual restaurant with a changing daily menu. Between October and mid-March, the Krug closes at 6 PM.

❶ **Kurfürstendamm.** This busy thoroughfare began as a riding path in the 16th century. The elector Joachim II of Brandenburg used it to travel between his palace on the Spree River and his hunting lodge in the Grunewald. The Kurfürstendamm (Elector's Causeway) was transformed into a major route in the late 19th century, thanks to the initiative of Bismarck, Prussia's Iron Chancellor.

Even in the 1920s, the Ku'damm was still relatively new and by no means elegant; it was fairly far removed from the old heart of the city, which was Unter den Linden in Mitte. The Ku'damm's prewar fame was due mainly to its rowdy bars and dance halls, as well as the cafés where the cultural avant-garde of Europe gathered. Almost half of its 245 late-19th-century buildings were completely destroyed in the 1940s, and the remaining buildings were damaged in varying degrees. As in most of western Berlin, what you see today is either restored or newly constructed. Some of the 1950s buildings have been replaced by high-rises, in particular at the corner of Kurfürstendamm and Joachimstaler Strasse.

❷ **The Story of Berlin.** Eight hundred years of the city's history, from the first settlers casting their fishing poles to Berliners heaving sledgehammers at the Wall, are conveyed through hands-on exhibits, film footage, and multimedia devices in this unusual venue. The sound of footsteps over broken glass follows your path through the exhibit on the "*Kristallnacht*" pogrom, and to pass through the section on the Nazis' book-burning on Bebelplatz, you must walk over book bindings. Many original artifacts are on display, such as the stretch Volvo that served as Erich Honnecker's state carriage in East Germany. The eeriest relic is the 1974 nuclear shelter, which you can visit by guided tour on the hour. Museum placards are also in English. ✉ *Ku'damm Karree, Kurfürstendamm 207–208, Western Downtown* ☎ *030/8872–0100* 🌐 *www.story-of-berlin.de* €9.30 ⏲ *Daily 10–8; last entry at 6* Ⓤ *Uhlandstrasse (U-bahn).*

❹ **Tourist Info-Center.** Berlin Tourismus Marketing's main tourist office is hidden at the back of the Europa Center, a neon-lit shopping and business complex. This is the largest of the three Info-Centers, and staff can book tickets to performances and hotel rooms for you. There's a large selection of free leaflets and a larger section of souvenirs to buy. ✉ *Budapester Str., Western Downtown* ☎ *030/250–025* 🌐 *www.berlin-tourist-information.de* ⏲ *Mon.–Sat. 10–7, Sun. 10–6; longer hours Apr.–Oct.* Ⓤ *Zoologischer Garten (U-bahn and S-bahn).*

★ ❺ **Zoologischer Garten** (Zoological Gardens). Germany's oldest zoo opened in 1844 and today holds more species than any other zoo in Europe. Home to more than 14,000 animals belonging to 1,500 different species, the zoo has been successful at breeding rare and endangered species. A baby gorilla, rhinocerous, camel, hippo, and kiwi bird arrived in early 2004. Check the feeding times posted to watch creatures such as seals, apes, hippos, crocodiles, and pelicans during their favorite time of day. The animals' enclosures are designed to resemble their natural habitats, though some structures are ornate, such as the 1910 Arabian-style Zebra house. Pythons, frogs, turtles, invertebrates, and Komodo Dragons are part of the three-floor aquarium. ✉ *Hardenbergpl. 8 and Budapester Str. 34, Western Downtown* ☎ *030/254–010* 🌐 *www.zoo-berlin.de* 🎫 *Zoo or aquarium €10, combined ticket €15* ⏲ *Zoo: mid-Oct.–mid-Mar., daily 9–5; mid-Mar.–mid-Oct., daily 9–6:30. Aquarium: daily 9–6* Ⓤ *Zoologischer Garten (U-bahn and S-bahn).*

14

Tiergarten & the Government District

The Tiergarten, a bucolic 630-acre park with lakes, meadows, and wide paths, is the "green lung" of Berlin. In the 17th century it served as the hunting grounds of the Great Elector. Now it's Berliners' backyard for sunbathing and barbecuing. Berlin's most fertile grounds for modern architecture—the government district, Potsdamer Platz, and the embassy district—ring the park from its eastern to southern edges. Many of the embassies have exhibitions open to the public, and Germany's parliament convenes beneath one of the city's most popular attractions: the glass dome of the Reichstag. Bordering Tiergarten and the government district is the meticulously restored Brandenburger Tor, the unofficial symbol of the city, and the Memorial to the Murdered Jews of Europe, whose design and scope engendered many debates during its long preparation.

a good walk

Berlin's peaceful **Tiergarten** 7 ⚑ begins within 150 meters of the train station, Zoologischer Garten. Keep the elevated train tracks to your left, passing the zoo on your right. The path bends at the beer garden and café Schleusen Krug, and is bordered on one side by the grass-banked Landwehr canal, and on the other by the zoo's aviaries. Take the footbridge onto Lichtensteinallee, passing the larger beer garden, Café am Neuen See, on your left and the Spanish embassy on the right. The tree-lined path continues straight to the park's traffic circle Grosser Stern (Big Star), where five roads meet. The **Siegessäule** 8 column provides a lookout from the center of the rotary.

Save yourself a half-hour walk by hopping onto Bus 100 (in the direction of Alexanderplatz). The bus passes Schloss Bellevue, the residence of Germany's president, on the left before turning east onto John-Foster-Dulles Allee. Exit the bus at the **Reichstag** 9. The parliament building of the German Empire and Weimar Republic has housed the federal parliament since the government returned to Berlin in 1999. The short walk from the Reichstag to the pristinely restored **Brandenburger Tor** 10 passes a simple fence hung with white, wooden crosses. These are in memory of East Germans who were killed while trying to cross the Wall, whose course ran between the Reichstag and the Brandenburg Gate. The cobblestones embedded in the roadway mark the Wall's path. In front of the Brandenburger Tor is Pariser Platz. On its north side is the Dresdner Bank, the French embassy, and a Starbucks. To the south is the DZ bank designed by Frank O. Gehry. Step in the foyer to see the monstrous, fishlike construction thrusting forth from the back of its atrium. On one side of the bank is the glass front of the prestigious Akademie der Künste (Academy of Arts). On the other side, the U.S. embassy is being rebuilt on its pre-World War II location. On the southeast side of the square, the historic Hotel Adlon hosts well-heeled travelers, as it did when it opened in 1907.

Walk back through the Brandenburger Tor and you'll see the Siegessäule in the distance. The wide street bisecting the park is Strasse des 17. Juni. Follow this 200 meters to the **Sowjetisches Ehrenmal** 11 on the right hand of the street. The Soviet tanks at this war memorial were two that helped defeat the Nazis during the Battle of Berlin. That West Berliners renamed the street in front of it Strasse des 17. Juni was rather controversial. The name honors the uprising of East Berlin workers in 1953 that was quashed by Soviet tanks.

Return to the the Brandenburger Tor and take Eberstrasse south one block to the expansive Holocaust memorial, **Denkmal für die Ermordeten Juden Europas** 12. The undulating gridlike landscape is filled with over 2,700 rectangular pillars. From here, you can use public transport to reach the **Hamburger Bahnhof, Museum für Gegenwart–Berlin** 13, one of Europe's largest museums of contemporary art. Take Bus 248 (marked "Richtung U Leopoldplatz) from Ebertstrasse, close to the Holocaust memorial. The ride to the Heidestrasse/Invalidenstrasse stop takes 10 minutes. The museum is on Invalidenstrasse, a short walk from the corner of Heidestrasse.

TIMING A leisurely walk from Zoo Station through the Tiergarten to the Brandenburger Tor and the Reichstag will take 90 minutes, two hours if you want to spend more time photographing and visiting the Holocaust memorial. The line to visit the dome of the Reichstag varies in length with tourist seasons and school vacations. If the line is down the Reichstag's steps and bending around its driveway, expect a 45-minute wait. The Hamburger Bahnof, Museum für Gegenwart–Berlin isn't ideally located, but Bus 248 does reach it quickly from the Holocaust memorial or the Reichstag. A quick way to get roughly the same city impressions is by taking a ride on Bus 100. It starts in the bus queue outside Zoo Station and makes several stops in the western downtown and Tiergarten areas.

What to See

★ 10 **Brandenburger Tor** (Brandenburg Gate). Once the pride of imperial Berlin and the city's premier landmark, the Brandenburger Tor was left in a desolate no-man's-land when the Wall was built. Since the Wall's dismantling, the sandstone gateway has become the scene of the city's Unification Day and New Year's Eve parties. This is the sole remaining gate of 14 built by Carl Langhans in 1788–91, designed as a triumphal arch for King Frederick Wilhelm II. Its virile classical style pays tribute to Athens's Acropolis. The quadriga, a chariot drawn by four horses and driven by the Goddess of Victory, was added in 1794. Troops paraded through the gate after successful campaigns—the last time in 1945, when victorious Red Army troops took Berlin. The upper part of the gate, together with its chariot and Goddess of Peace, was destroyed in the war. In 1957 the original molds were discovered in West Berlin, and a new quadriga was cast in copper and presented as a gift to the people of East Berlin. A tourist-information center is on the south side of the gate. ✉ *Pariser Pl., Mitte* Ⓤ *Unter den Linden (S-bahn).*

⓬ **Denkmal für die Ermordeten Juden Europas** (Memorial to the Murdered Jews of Europe). This expansive and unusual memorial dedicated to the 6 million Jews who were killed in the Holocaust was completed in May 2005. Designed by American architect Peter Eisenman, the place of remembrance is a grid of more than 2,700 concrete stelae of varying heights, planted into undulating ground. The abstract memorial can be entered from all sides, and offers no prescribed path. An Information Center that goes into specifics about the Holocaust lies underground at the southeast corner. ✉ *At Ebertstr. and Behrenstr., Mitte* ☎ *030/7407–2929* 🌐 *www.holocaust-mahnmal.de* 🎫 *Free* ⏲ *Daily 24 hours. Information Center daily 10–8* Ⓤ *Unter den Linden (S-bahn).*

⓭ **Hamburger Bahnhof, Museum für Gegenwart–Berlin** (Museum of Contemporary Art). This light-filled, remodeled train station is home to a rich survey of post-1960 Western art. In 2004 the museum doubled its exhibition space to accommodate a seven-year loan of the Flick Collection, the largest and most valuable collection of contemporary art in the world. The 2,000 works will rotate, but you're bound to see some by Bruce Naumann, Rodney Graham, and Pipilotti Rist. The permanent collection includes installations by German artists Joseph Beuys and Anselm Kiefer as well as paintings by Andy Warhol, Cy Twombly, Robert Rauschenberg, and Robert Morris. Works of Marcel Duchamp and Marcel Broodthaers are exhibited on the second floor. ✉ *Invalidenstr. 50–51, Tiergarten* ☎ *030/3978–3412* 🌐 *www.smb.museum* 🎫 *€6* ⏲ *Tues.–Fri. 10–6, weekends 11–6* Ⓤ *Zinnowitzer Str. (U-bahn), Lehrter Bahnhof (S-bahn).*

★ ❾ **Reichstag** (Parliament Building). After last meeting here in 1933, the Bundestag, Germany's federal parliament, returned to its traditional seat in the spring of 1999. British architect Sir Norman Foster lightened up the gray monolith with a glass dome, which quickly became one of the city's main attractions: you can circle up a gently rising ramp while taking in the rooftops of Berlin and the parliamentary chamber below. At the base of the dome is an exhibit on the Reichstag's history, in German and English. The best way to visit the Reichstag dome without waiting in line is to arrive at 8 AM, or to make a reservation for the pricey rooftop **Käfer restaurant** (☎ 030/2262–9933). Those with reservations can use the doorway to the right of the Reichstag's main staircase.

Completed in 1894, the Reichstag housed the imperial German parliament and later served a similar function during the ill-fated Weimar Republic. On the night of February 27, 1933, the Reichstag burned down in an act of arson, a pivotal event in Third Reich history. The fire led to state protection laws which gave the Nazis a pretext to arrest their political opponents. The Reichstag was rebuilt but again badly damaged in 1945. The graffiti of the victorious Russian soldiers can still be seen on some of the walls in the hallways. The building is surrounded by ultramodern new federal government offices, such as the boxy, concrete **Bundeskanzleramt** (German Federal Chancellery). Built by Axel Schultes, it's one of the few new buildings in the government district by a Berlin architect. A riverwalk with great views of the government buildings lies behind the Reichstag. ✉ *Pl. der Republik 1, Tiergarten* ☎ *030/2273–2152 or 030/2273–5908* 📠 *030/2273–0027* 🌐 *www.bundestag.de* 🎫 *Free* ⏲ *Daily 8 AM–midnight; last admission 10 PM. Reichstag dome closes for 1 wk 4 times a yr* Ⓤ *Unter den Linden (S-bahn).*

❽ **Siegessäule** (Victory Column). The 227-foot granite, sandstone, and bronze column is topped by a winged, golden goddess and has a splendid view of Berlin. It was erected in front of the Reichstag in 1873 to commemorate Prussia's military successes and then moved to the Tiergarten in 1938–39. You have to climb 285 steps up through the column to reach the observation platform, but the view is rewarding. The gold-tipped canons striping the column are those the Prussians captured from the French in the Franco-Prussian War. ✉ *Am Grossen Stern, Tiergarten* ☎ *no phone* 🎫 *€2.20* ⏲ *Nov.–Mar., daily 10–5:30; Apr.–Oct., weekdays 10–6, weekends 10–7:30; last admission ½ hr before closing* Ⓤ *Tiergarten (S-bahn), Bellevue (S-bahn).*

⓫ **Sowjetisches Ehrenmal** (Soviet Memorial). Built immediately after World War II, this monument stands as a reminder of the Soviet victory over the shattered German army in Berlin in May 1945. The Battle of Berlin was one of the deadliest on the European front. A hulking bronze statue of a soldier stands atop a marble plinth taken from Hitler's former Reichkanzlei (headquarters). The memorial is flanked by what are said to be the first two T-34 tanks to have fought their way into the city. ✉ *Str. des 17. Juni, Tiergarten* Ⓤ *Unter den Linden (S-bahn).*

⚑ ❼ **Tiergarten** (Animal Garden). The quiet greenery of the 630-acre Tiergarten is a beloved oasis, with some 23 km (14 mi) of footpaths, meadows, and two beer gardens. The inner park's 6½ acres of lakes and ponds were landscaped by garden architect Joseph Peter Lenné in the mid-1800s. On the shores of the lake in the southwest part, you can relax at the **Café am Neuen See** (✉ Lichtensteinallee), a café and beer garden. Off the Spree River and bordering the Kanzleramt (Chancellory) is the **Haus der Kulturen der Welt** (✉ House of the World Cultures, John-Foster-Dulles Allee 10 ☎ 030/397–870 🌐 www.hkw.de), referred to as the "pregnant oyster" for its design. Thematic exhibits and festivals take place here and it's also a boarding point for Spree River cruises.

Potsdamer Platz & Kreuzberg

The once-divided capital is rejoined on this square, which was Berlin's inner-city center and Europe's busiest plaza before World War II. Bombings and the wall system left this area a sprawling, desolate lot, where tourists in West Berlin could climb a wooden platform to peek into East Berlin's deathstrip. After the Wall fell, Sony, the former Daimler-Benz, Asea Brown Boveri, and other companies made a rush to build their headquarters on this prime real estate. In the mid-1990s Potsdamer Platz became Europe's largest construction site. Today's modern complexes of red sandstone, terra-cotta tiles, steel, and glass have made it a city within a city. The subtle reminder that this was an empty plot for nearly 50 years is a line of cobblestones that traces the path of the Wall on the west side of Stresemannstrasse.

A few narrow streets cut between the hulking modern architecture, which includes two high-rise towers that are part of the headquarters of debis, the software subsidiary of DaimlerChrysler. The debis center was designed by star architect Renzo Piano. The round atrium of the Sony Center is the closest rendering of a traditional square in terms of being used as a public meeting point. You'll notice more shoppers and moviegoers than businesspeople. Farther down Potsdamer Strasse are the state museums and cultural institutes of the Kuturforum.

Not far from modern Berlin is the hot spot of the Cold War, Checkpoint Charlie. This border crossing manned by the Soviets and Americans lay between West Berlin's Kreuzberg district and East Berlin's Mitte district. It was reserved for non-Germans. All that remains where Soviet and American tanks had a tense stand-off in October 1961 are a replica guardhouse and signage, plus the cobblestones marking the old border.

Kreuzberg is one of the liveliest districts in Berlin. A largely Turkish population lives cheek-by-jowl with a variegated assortment of political radicals and bohemians of all nationalities. There are few attractions here, but it's a great place to people-watch.

a good walk

The Potsdamer Platz U- and S-bahn stations drop you at the edge of the area; follow Potsdamer Strasse to the **Sony Center** 14, one of the city's most striking new buildings. It's surrounded by an entertainment complex with plenty of eateries. Follow Potsdamer Strasse westward; in 10 minutes you'll reach the **Kulturforum** 15, a complex that includes the Philharmonic, state museums, and state library. A short walk futher brings you to the **Neue Nationalgalerie** 16. Head back toward the S-bahn station, and turn right on Stresemannstrasse. The Wall ran along the current street and you'll see where it turned at Niederkirchnerstrasse. Cobblestones in the pavement mark the Wall's path. Follow it.

Niederkirchnerstrasse is yet another strip of German history with one sight after another: the old Preussischer Landtag, the seat of Berlin's parliament, faces the museum **Martin-Gropius-Bau** 17, which is next to the barren landscape where the Nazi's SS headquarters stood, now an exhibit called the **Topographie des Terrors** 18. Bordering the cellar remains is one of the few sections of the Wall that still stands. Opposite the wall is the enormous former Luftwaffeministerium—the Air Force Ministry of the Third Reich. Today it's home to the federal finance ministry. Cross Wilhelmstrasse and continue east on Zimmerstrasse until you reach Friedrichstrasse. The border-crossing Checkpoint Charlie was here, and oversize photographs of a young Soviet and American soldier still face their opposing super-power's sector. A half-block further south on Friedrichstrasse, gripping stories of the Wall, refugees, and spies are told in the **Mauermuseum-Museum Haus am Checkpoint Charlie** 19. From here, round the corner to continue east on Kochstrasse, the newspaper district of the early 20th century. Turn right on Markgrafenstrasse, which ends across from the **Jüdisches Museum** 20. The art museum **Berlinische Galerie** 21 can be reached by taking the street to the left of the Jewish Museum's entrance, and taking the next left onto Alte Jakobstrasse.

TIMING The sights on this tour are close to one another until you set off for the Jüdisches Museum. In 30 minutes you can take in the architecture at Potsdamer Platz and reach the Kulturforum complex for a look from the outside. To retrace your steps and reach the Topographie des Terrors will take 20 minutes. Owing to its small size and popularity, you may experience a wait or slow line at "the Checkpoint Charlie museum." Monday is a popular day for both it and the Jüdisches Museum since the state museums are closed that day.

What to See

21 **Berlinische Galerie.** Talk about site-specific art: all the modern art, photography, and architecture models and plans here, created between 1870 and the present, were made in Berlin (or in the case of architecture competition models, intended for the city). Russians, secessionists, dadaists, and expressionists all had their day in Berlin and individual works by Otto Dix, George Grosz, and Georg Baselitz, as well as artist archives such as the Dadaist Hannah Höch's, are highlights. The entire collection was homeless for years and finally settled here in 2004. Bus M29 to Lindenstrasse is the closest transportation stop. ✉ *Alte Jakobstr. 124-128* ☎ *030/7890–2600* 🌐 *www.berlinischegalerie.de* 🎫 *€5* ⏲ *Mon.–Sat. noon–8, Sun. 10–6* U *Kochstrasse (U-bahn).*

20 **Jüdisches Museum** (Jewish Museum). The history of Germany's Jews from the Middle Ages through today are chronicled here, from explanations of religious traditions to exhibits on prominent historical figures and the evolution of laws regarding Jews' participation in civil society. An attraction in itself is the highly conceptual building, which was designed by Daniel Libeskind (the architect now redeveloping the World Trade Center site). Various physical "voids" represent the loss German society faces because of the Holocaust, and a portion of the exhibits document the Holocaust as well. Reserve at least 3 hours for the museum and devote more time to the second floor if you're already familiar with basic aspects of Judaica, which are the focus of the third floor. ✉ *Lindenstr. 9–14, Kreuzberg* ☎ *030/2599–3300* 🌐 *www.jmberlin.de* 🎫 *€5* ⏲ *Mon. 10–10, Tues.–Sun. 10–8* U *Hallesches Tor (U-bahn).*

15 **Kulturforum** (Cultural Forum). This unique ensemble of museums, galleries, and the Philharmonic Hall was long in the making. The first designs were submitted in the 1960s and the last building completed in ★ 1998. The **Gemäldegalerie** (Picture Gallery) reunites formerly separated collections from East and West Berlin. It's one of Germany's finest art galleries and has an extensive selection of European paintings from the 13th to the 18th century. Seven rooms are reserved for paintings by German masters, among them Dürer, Cranach the Elder, and Holbein. A special collection has works of the Italian masters—Botticelli, Titian, Giotto, Lippi, and Raphael—as well as paintings by Dutch and Flemish masters of the 15th and 16th centuries: Van Eyck, Bosch, Brueghel

the Elder, and van der Weyden. The museum also holds the world's second-largest Rembrandt collection. ✉ *Matthäikirchpl. 4, Tiergarten* ☎ *030/266–2951* 🌐 *www.smb.museum* 🎫 *€6* ⏲ *Tues., Wed., and Fri.–Sun. 10–6, Thurs. 10–10* Ⓤ *Potsdamer Pl. (U-bahn and S-bahn).*

Steps away from the Gemäldegalerie are two examples of ultramodern architecture. The **Kunstbibliothek** (Art Library; ✉ Matthäikirchpl. 4, Tiergarten ☎ 030/266–2951 🌐 www.smb.museum 🎫 €6 ⏲ Tues.–Fri. 10–6, weekends 11–6; reading room Mon. 2–8, Tues.–Fri. 9–4) contains art posters, a costume library, ornamental engravings, and a commercial-art collection. The **Kupferstichkabinett** (Drawings and Prints Collection; ✉ Matthäikirchpl. 4, Tiergarten ☎ 030/266–2951 🌐 www.smb.museum 🎫 €6 ⏲ Tues.–Fri. 10–6, weekends 11–6) has occasional exhibits, which include European woodcuts, engravings, and illustrated books from the 15th century to the present (highlights of its holdings are pen-and-ink drawings by Dürer and drawings by Rembrandt). You can request to see one or two drawings in the study room. Another building displays paintings dating from the late Middle Ages to 1800.

Inside the **Kunstgewerbemuseum** (Museum of Decorative Arts) are European arts and crafts from the Middle Ages to the present. Among the notable exhibits are the Welfenschatz (Welfen Treasure), a collection of 16th-century gold and silver plates from Nürnberg, as well as ceramics and porcelains. ✉ *Matthäikirchpl. 4, Tiergarten* ☎ *030/266–2902* 🌐 *www.smb.museum* 🎫 *€6* ⏲ *Tues.–Fri. 10–6, weekends 11–6.*

The mustard-yellow complex that resembles a great tent belongs to the **Philharmonie** (☎ 030/2548–8156), home to the renowned Berlin Philharmonic Orchestra since 1963. The Philharmonie and the smaller Chamber Music Hall adjoining it were designed by Hans Scharoun. There's a free tour of the Philharmonie daily at 1 PM. Across the parking lot from the Philharmonie, the **Musikinstrumenten-Museum** (Musical Instruments Museum) has a fascinating collection of keyboard, string, wind, and percussion instruments. These are demonstrated during an 11 AM tour on Saturday, which closes with a 20-minute Wurlitzer organ concert. *Museum* ✉ *Tiergartenstr. 1, Tiergarten* ☎ *030/2548–1129* 🎫 *€3, tour €2* ⏲ *Tues.–Fri. 9–5, weekends 10–5.*

The **Staatsbibliothek** (National Library; ✉ Postdamer Str. 33 ☎ 030/2660 🎫 €.50 ⏲ weekdays 9–9, Sat. 9–7) is one of the largest libraries in Europe and was one of the Berlin settings in Wim Wender's 1987 film, *Wings of Desire*.

⑰ **Martin-Gropius-Bau.** This magnificent exhibition hall dates back to 1877 and once housed Berlin's Arts and Crafts Museum. Its architect, Martin Gropius, was the uncle of Walter Gropius, the Bauhaus architect who also worked in Berlin. Since 1980, the international, changing exhibits on art and culture have been among Berlin's most attention-grabbing. The Berlin Wall once stood between the museum and the Preussischer Landtag (now the Berlin Senate) across the street. ✉ *Niederkirchnerstr. 7, Kreuzberg* ☎ *030/2548–6112* 🌐 *www.gropiusbau.de* 🎫 *Varies with exhibit* ⏲ *Wed.–Mon. 10–8* Ⓤ *Kochstr. (U-bahn), Potsdamer Pl. (U-bahn and S-bahn).*

★ 19 **Mauermuseum-Museum Haus am Checkpoint Charlie.** Just steps from the famous crossing point between the two Berlins, the Wall Museum—House at Checkpoint Charlie tells the story of the Wall, and even more riveting, the stories of those who escaped through, under, and over it. The homespun museum reviews the events leading up to the Wall's construction and with original tools and devices, plus recordings and photographs, shows how East Germans escaped to the West (one of the most ingenious contraptions was a miniature submarine). Exhibits about human rights and paintings interpreting the Wall round out the experience. Come early or late in the day to avoid the multitudes dropped off by tour buses. Monday can be particularly crowded. ✉ *Friedrichstr. 43–45, Kreuzberg* ☎ *030/253–7250* 🌐 *www.mauermuseum.com* 🎫 *€9.50* 🕒 *Daily 9 AM–10 PM* Ⓤ *Kochstr. (U-bahn).*

need a break?

Try your best to conjure up an image of the Wall from a window seat at **Café Adler** (✉ Friedrichstr. 206, Kreuzberg ☎ 030/251–8965), which once bumped right up against it. The quality fare is inexpensive and the soups are particularly delicious. Breakfast is served until 5 PM.

★ 16 **Neue Nationalgalerie** (New National Gallery). Bauhaus member Mies van der Rohe originally designed this glass-box structure for Bacardi Rum in Cuba, but Berlin became the site of its realization in 1968. The main exhibitions are below ground. Highlights of the 20th-century collection of paintings, sculptures, and drawings include works by Otto Dix, Ernst Ludwig Kirchner, and Georg Grotz. Special exhibits often take precedence over the permanent collection however, such as the wildly successful "MoMA in New York" exhibit in 2004. The man who negotiated that exhibit was voted "Berliner of the Year" in a daily newspaper poll. ✉ *Potsdamer Str. 50, Tiergarten* ☎ *030/266–2951* 🌐 *www.smb.museum* 🎫 *€6* 🕒 *Tues., Wed., and Fri. 10–6, Thurs. 10–10, weekends 11–8.*

off the beaten path

ORANIENSTRASSE – The spine of life in the Kreuzberg district has mellowed from hard-core to funky since reunification. When Kreuzberg literally had its back against the Wall, West German social outcasts, punks, and the radical left made this old working-class street their territory. Since the 1970s the population has become largely Turkish, and many of yesterday's outsiders have turned into successful owners of shops and simple eateries. The vibrant stretch is between Skalitzer Strasse and Oranienplatz. Ⓤ *Görlitzer Bahnhof (U-bahn), Kottbusser Tor (U-bahn).*

⚑ 14 **Sony Center.** This light glass-and-steel construction wraps around a spectacular circular forum. Topping it off is a tentlike structure meant to emulate Mount Fuji. The architectural jewel, designed by German-American architect Helmut Jahn, is one of the most stunning public spaces of Berlin's new center, filled with restaurants, cafés, movie theaters, apartments, and the European headquarters of Sony. A faint reminder of glorious days gone by is the old **Kaisersaal** (Emperor's Hall), held within a very modern glass enclosure, and today a pricey restaurant. The hall originally stood 50 yards away in the Grand Hotel Esplanade (built in 1907) but was moved here lock, stock, and barrel.

Within the center the **Filmmuseum Berlin** (✉ Potsdamer Str. 2, Tiergarten ☎ 030/300–9030 🌐 www.filmmuseum-berlin.de 🎫 €6 ⏲ Tues.–Sun. 10–6, Thurs. 10–8) presents the ground-breaking history of German moviemaking with eye-catching displays. The texts are also in English and there's an audioguide as well. Memorabilia includes personal belongings of Marlene Dietrich and plans and costumes for fantasy and science-fiction films.

★ 18 **Topographie des Terrors** (Topography of Terror). Within the cellar remains of the Nazis' Reich Security Main Office (which was comprised of the SS, SD, and Gestapo), photos and documents explain the secret state police and intelligence organizations that planned and executed Nazi crimes against humanity. The fates of both perpetrators and victims are included in the free, open-air exhibit. Within a humble trailer, you can leaf through books and copies of official documents. Pick up a free audio guide here before viewing the exhibit. ✉ *Niederkirchnerstr. 8, Kreuzberg* ☎ *030/2548–6703* 🌐 *www.topographie.de* 🎫 *Free* ⏲ *Oct.–Apr., daily 10–5; May–Sept., daily 10–8.*

off the beaten path

TÜRKENMARKT (Turkish Market) – On Tuesday and Friday from noon to 6:30 you can find the country's best selection of Arab and Turkish foods on the Maybachufer lining the southern bank of the Landwehrkanal. The bohemian café on the Kottbusser bridge, Ankerklause, or those on Paul-Lincke-Ufer, on the opposite bank, are great places for a coffee break and local color. ✉ *Maybachufer Neukölln* Ⓤ *Kottbusser Tor (U-bahn), Schönlein Str. (U-bahn).*

Mitte: Unter den Linden to Alexanderplatz

The Mitte (Middle) district is where Berlin first began as two fishing villages separated by the Spree River. Throughout its 760-year-plus history it has served as a seat of government for Prussian kings, German emperors, the Weimar Republic, Hitler's Third Reich, the communist German Democratic Republic, and since 1999, for reunited Germany. Treasures once split between East and West Berlin museums are also reunited on Museum Island, a UNESCO World Heritage site.

The historic boulevard Unter den Linden proudly rolls out Prussian architecture and world-class museums. Its major cross-street is Friedrichstrasse, which was revitalized in the mid-1990s with car showrooms (including Bentley, Bugatti, and Volkswagen) and upscale malls. At its eastern end, Unter den Linden turns into Karl-Liebknecht-Strasse, which leads to vast Alexanderplatz, where eastern Berlin's handful of skyscrapers are dwarfed beneath the city's most visible landmark, the Berlin TV tower.

SYMBOLS & SHIFTS IN EAST & WEST

IN 1989 TELEVISED IMAGES *of jubilant Berliners cheering atop the Wall stunned the world. Both West and East Berliners were euphoric, embracing one another with mutual bewilderment and curiosity. The two city administrations managed to successfully integrate, but in the years since, West Berlin—once a refuge for alternative lifestyles—lost its edgy reputation to the East thanks to a burgeoning art and nightlife scene that attracts young people, and tourists' ever-growing interest in historic Mitte.*

Prenzlauer Berg and Mitte, two proud East Berlin districts, are now flooded by transplanted yuppies and dinks (double-income, no-kids couples). The new arrivals are mostly West Germans and young European and English-speaking expatriates. Until the early 1990s Prenzlauer Berg had been a poor area where East German punks eked out an existence and phone service was rare. Now it's one of the trendiest districts.

The days of Ostalgie *(nostalgia for the East) have passed, but East Germany's iconography has reemerged as trendy. An East Berlin design that was first discontinued after unification but then won wide appreciation is the figure that appears on the crosswalk traffic lights. The stocky* Ampelmann *("street-light man") wears a wide-brim hat and walks with an animated gait. He has regained his ground in most of East Berlin and, since 2004, has even inched his way into West Berlin neighborhoods. Now one of the most distinctive Berlin souvenir icons, the Ampelmann adorns coffee cups and t-shirts and there's even candy made in his image. Entire gift shops are dedicated to him, such as in the Hackesche Höfe in Mitte and the Arkaden mall at Potsdamer Platz.*

The 18th-century, Prussian Brandenburg Gate may be the city symbol for Berlin tourism, but the East German soaring television tower, the Berliner Fernsehturm, is an enormously popular silhouette for Berlin-based companies' logos, nightclubs' flyers, and advertisements of all sorts. The fate of another symbol of the East German regime, the Palace of the Republic that housed the East German parliament, remains undecided. The building is a near-ruin on Schlossplatz. Though slated for demolition after unification, it couldn't be blown up because of the asbestos discovered inside. The now fully gutted building serves as a venue for the occasional performance or event. Its position on the riverbed makes it difficult and expensive to remove, and while one organization is lobbying for the building's preservation, another continues to raise funds to rebuild the historic Hohenzollern Palace that once stood in the same spot.

The latest icon to receive a jolt from the city's march of progress is the west's Bahnhof Zoo, which has done double duty as a local hub and long-distance train station since the days of the Berlin Wall. Now that Lehrter Bahnhof near the government district has been transformed into "Hauptbahnhof" (the central station), Zoo is bound to lose significance, and the surrounding businesses, money. However, "Zoo" has a grungy reputation, and perhaps transportation's eastward shift will make room for a postive regeneration.

a good walk

Layers of history seem to be laid out for your convenience on this walk. Leading away from the Brandenburger Tor and Pariser Platz is Unter den Linden, the grand eastern counterpart to Kurfürstendamm. On the boulevard's long procession, you'll pass several government offices and consulates, among them the Russian embassy on the right. Turn right at **Friedrichstrasse** 22, passing Volkswagen's Automobile Forum and other fancy storefronts. After two blocks, turn left at Französische Strasse to reach **Gendarmenmarkt** 23, considered Berlin's most impressive square.

Bordering the east side of the square, Markgrafenstrasse leads north to Behrenstrasse, where **Bebelplatz** 24 is just steps away to the right. Surrounding it is an architectural ensemble begun in the mid-18th century under Frederick the Great. The square opens onto Unter den Linden, which you should cross to reach the temple-like **Neue Wache** 25 and the pale pink **Deutsches Historisches Museum** 26. Looking back across the street, you'll have a better view of the sculpture-topped Crown Prince's Palace, a baroque-style building originally constructed in 1732 for Crown Prince Friedrich (later Frederick the Great). The Deutsches Historisches Museum borders the Spree River, which splits around **Museumsinsel** 27, the island of museums where one of Berlin's two medieval settlements began. Several bridges connect to the island; the grandest is Schinkel's Schloss Brücke, completed in 1824 and lined with statues depicting young heroes guided by the godesses Nike, Athena, and Iris. The vast lot on the right is **Schlossplatz** 28, the site of the Hohenzollern city palace that the East German government detonated in 1950. More attention-grabbing is the dilapidated former parliament building of the German Democratic Republic on its eastern edge, and opposite it, the enormous **Berliner Dom** 29.

After the Schloss Bruke, Unter den Linden becomes Karl-Liebknecht-Strasse. Past the Berliner Dom and Marx-Engels-Forum, the next cross street is Spandauer Strasse. To the left behind a small entranceway is the aquarium, **AquaDom & Sea Life Berlin** 30; to the right is a square that holds the 13th-century **St. Marienkirche** 31, the Neptune Fountain, and the redbrick **Berliner Rathaus** 32. The city hall is at the border of the **Nikolaiviertel** 33, Berlin's small medieval quarter out of which rises the twin spires of the St. Nikolaikirche. Soaring considerably higher is the **Berliner Fernsehturm** 34, the TV tower planted at the east end of the square and opposite a transportation hub and perennial demonstration ground, the scruffy and clearly socialist-era **Alexanderplatz** 35. Give your feet a break and hop the U-2 line to reach the city's history museum, **Märkisches Museum** 36 (the subway stop is named for it). To reach the redbrick building, walk back along Wallstrasse in the direction the train came from.

TIMING If you don't look closely at any museums or highlights, you could ramble this route in two hours. To speed your way down Unter den Linden, you can hop one of the three bus lines that make stops between Wilhelmstrasse and Alexanderplatz. The state museums in this area are closed on Monday.

What to See

35 **Alexanderplatz.** This bleak square, bordered by the train station, the Galeria Kaufhof department store, and the 40-story Park Inn hotel, once formed the hub of East Berlin and was originally named in 1805 for czar Alexander I. German writer Alfred Döblin dubbed it the "heart of a world metropolis" (text from his 1929 novel *Berlin Alexanderplatz* is written on a building across the northeastern side of the square). Today, it's a basic center of commerce and the occasional demonstration. The unattractive modern buildings are a reminder not just of the results of Allied bombing but also of the ruthlessness practiced by East Germans when they demolished what remained. A famous meeting point in the south corner is the World Time Clock (1969), which even keeps tabs on Tijuana.

off the beaten path

EAST SIDE GALLERY – This 1-km (½-mi) stretch of concrete went from guarded border to open-air gallery within three months. East Berliners breached the wall on November 9, 1989, and between February and June of 1990, 118 artists from around the globe created unique works of art on the longest remaining section of the Berlin Wall. Much of the paint is now peeling and many panels have been vandalized by graffiti. One of the best-known works, by Russian artist Dmitri Vrubel, depicts Brezhnev and Honnecker (the former East German leader) kissing, with the caption "My God. Help me survive this deadly love." The stretch along the Spree Canal runs between the Warschauer Strasse S- and U-bahn station and Ostbahnhof. The redbrick Oberbaumbrücke (an 1896 bridge) at Warschauer Strasse makes that end more scenic. ✉ *Mühlenstr., Friedrichshain* Ⓤ *Warschauer Str. (U-bahn and S-bahn), Ostbahnhof (S-bahn).*

30 **AquaDom & Sea Life Berlin.** The SeaLife group has aquariums Europe-wide, each with a focus on local marine life. In Berlin, the tanks begin with the Spree River, move on to Berlin's lakes, and then take you on a course from fresh- to saltwater. Waterfront city scenes are part of the decor, which gradually gives way to starfish-petting beds, overhead tanks, and a submarinelike room. The last darkened environment emulating a rocky coastline gets dramatic when rains come down and thunder and lightning crashes. Don't come looking for sharks or colorful tropical fish: the most exotic creatures here are perhaps the tiny sea horses and spotted rays. The aquarium's finale is a state-of-the-art glass elevator that brings you through a silo-shape fish tank to the exit. Young children love this place, but the timed wait for the elevator can be frustrating for all ages. Be prepared for a line at the entrance, too. ✉ *Spandauer Str. 3, Mitte* ☎ *030/992–800* 🌐 *www.sealife.de* 🎫 *€13.50* ⏲ *Sept.–Mar., daily 10–6; Apr.–Aug., daily 10–7* Ⓤ *Hackescher Markt (S-bahn).*

24 **Bebelplatz.** After he became ruler in 1740, Frederick the Great personally planned the buildings surrounding this square. The area received the nickname *Forum Fridericianum,* or Frederick's Forum. A music lover, Frederick's first priority was the **Staatsoper Unter den Linden** (State

Opera). Berlin's lavish opera house was completed in 1743 by the same architect that built Sanssouci in Potsdam, Georg Wenzeslaus von Knobelsdorff. Daniel Barenboim is maestro of the house. ✉ *Unter den Linden 7, Mitte* ☎ *030/2035–4555* 🌐 *www.staatsoper-berlin.de* ⏲ *Box office weekdays 11–8, weekends 2–8; last hour for tickets to that night's performance only; reservations by phone Mon.–Sat. 10–8, Sun. 2–8* Ⓤ *Französische Str. (U-bahn).*

The green patina dome belongs to **St. Hedwigskathedrale** (St. Hedwig's Cathedral). Begun in 1747, it was modeled after the Pantheon in Rome and was the first Catholic church built in resolutely Protestant Berlin since the 16th-century Reformation. It was Frederick the Great's effort to appease Prussia's Catholic population after his invasion of Catholic Silesia (then Poland). A treasury lies inside. ✉ *Bebelpl., Mitte* ☎ *030/203–4810* 🎫 *Free* 🌐 *www.hedwigs-kathedrale.de* ⏲ *Weekdays 10–5, Sun. 1–5* ☞ *Tours (€1.50) available in English, call ahead* Ⓤ *Französische Str. (U-bahn).*

Running the length of the west side of Bebelplatz, the former royal library is now part of **Humboldt-Universität** (✉ Unter den Linden 6, Mitte), whose main campus is across the street on Unter den Linden. The university building was built in 1766 as a palace for Prince Heinrich, the brother of Frederick the Great. With its founding in 1810, the university moved in. The fairy-tale collecting Grimm brothers studied here, as did political philosophers Karl Marx and Friedrich Engels. Albert Einstein taught physics from 1914 to 1932, when he left Berlin for the United States. On May 10, 1933, Joseph Goebbels, the Nazi minister for propaganda and "public enlightenment," organized one of the nationwide book-burnings on Bebelplatz. The books, thrown on a pyre by Nazi officials and students, included works by Jews, pacifists, and Communists. In the center of Bebelplatz, a modern and subtle memorial marks where 20,000 books went up in flames.

29 **Berliner Dom** (Berlin Cathedral). A church has stood here since 1536, but this enormous version dates from 1905, making it the largest 20th-century Protestant church in Germany. The royal Hohenzollerns worshiped here until 1918, when Kaiser Wilhelm II abdicated and left Berlin for Holland. The massive dome wasn't restored from World War II damage until 1982; the interior was completed in 1993. The climb to the dome's outer balcony is made easier by a wide stairwell, plenty of landings with historic photos and models, and even a couple of chairs. The more than 80 sarcophagi of Prussian royals in the crypt are significant, but to less-trained eyes, can seem uniformly dull. All morning services include communion. ✉ *Am Lustgarten 1, Mitte* ☎ *030/2026–9136* 🌐 *www.berlinerdom.de* 🎫 *€5* ⏲ *Apr.–Oct., Mon.–Sat., 9–8, Sun. noon–8; Nov.–Mar., Mon.–Sat. 9–7, Sun. noon–7* Ⓤ *Hackescher Markt (S-bahn).*

34 **Berliner Fernsehturm** (Berlin TV Tower). Finding Alexanderplatz is no problem: just head toward the 1,198-foot-high tower piercing the sky. It was completed in 1969 and is not accidentally 710 feet higher than western Berlin's broadcasting tower and 98 feet higher than the Eiffel Tower.

You can get the best view of Berlin from within the tower's disco ball-like observation level; on a clear day you can see for 40 km (25 mi). One floor above, the city's highest restaurant rotates for your panoramic pleasure. Make reservations in advance and stick to the German dishes. ✉ *Panoramastr. 1a, Mitte* ☎ *030/242–3333* 🌐 *www.berlinerfernsehturm.de* 🎫 *€7.50* ⏲ *Nov.–Feb., daily 10 AM–midnight; Mar.–Oct., daily 9 AM–midnight; last admission ½ hr before closing* Ⓤ *Alexanderpl. (S-bahn and U-bahn).*

32 **Berliner Rathaus** (Berlin Town Hall). Nicknamed the Rotes Rathaus (red town hall) for its redbrick design, the town hall was completed in 1869. Its most distinguishing features are its neo-Renaissance clock tower and frieze that depicts Berlin's history up to 1879 in 36 terra-cotta plaques, each 6 meters long. Climb the grand stairwell to view the coat of arms hall and a few exhibits. ✉ *Jüdenstr. 1 at Rathausstr. 15, Mitte* ☎ *030/90260* 🎫 *Free* ⏲ *Weekdays 9–6* Ⓤ *Alexanderpl. (S-bahn and U-bahn).*

26 **Deutsches Historisches Museum** (German History Museum). The museum is composed of two buildings. The magnificent pink, baroque Prussian arsenal (Zeughaus) was constructed between 1695 and 1730 and is the oldest building on Unter den Linden. After reunification its exhibits were closed for years as curators from East and West debated how to articulate a history that encompasses empires and two postwar Germanys. The exhibits will be ready at last in early 2006. Behind the arsenal, the granite and glass Pei-Bau building by I. M. Pei holds changing exhibits. ✉ *Unter den Linden 2, Mitte* ☎ *030/203–040* 🌐 *www.dhm.de* 🎫 *€6* ⏲ *Daily 10–6.*

22 **Friedrichstrasse.** The once-bustling street of cafés and theaters of prewar Berlin has risen from the rubble of war and Communist neglect to reclaim the crowds with shopping emporiums.

Heading south from the train station Friedrichstrasse, you'll pass hotels, bookstores, and south of Unter den Linden, the car showrooms of the **Lindencorso** and several upscale clothing stores. Standing at the corner of Französische Strasse ("French Street") is the the French department store **Galeries Lafayette** (✉ Französische Str. 23 ☎ 030/209–480). French architect Jean Nouvel included an impressive steel-and-glass funnel at its center which is surrounded by four floors of expensive clothing and luxuries.

23 **Gendarmenmarkt.** Anchoring this large square are the beautifully reconstructed 1818 **Konzerthaus** and the **Deutscher Dom** and **Französischer Dom** (German and French cathedrals). The Französischer Dom contains the **Hugenottenmuseum** (✉ Gendarmenmarkt 5, Mitte ☎ 030/229–1760 🎫 €2 ⏲ Tues.–Sat. noon–5, Sun. 11–5), with exhibits charting the history and art of the French Protestant refugees who settled in Berlin. These Huguenots were expelled from France at the end of the 17th century by King Louis XIV. Their energy and commercial expertise did much to help boost Berlin during the 18th century.

The **Deutscher Dom** (✉ Gendarmenmarkt 1, Mitte ☎ 030/2273–0431 🌐 www.deutscherdom.de 🎫 free ⏲ Sept.–May, Wed.–Sun. 10–6, Tues.

10–10; June–Aug., Wed.–Sun. 10–7, Tues. 10–10) holds an extensive exhibition on the emergence of the democratic parliamentary system in Germany since the late 1800s. The free museum is sponsored by the German parliament. Leadership and opposition in East Germany are also documented. An English-language audio guide covers a portion of the exhibits on the first three floors. Floors four and five have temporary exhibitions with no English text or audio.

36 **Märkisches Museum** (Brandenburg Museum). This redbrick attic includes exhibits on the city's theatrical past, its guilds, its newspapers, and the March 1848 revolution. Paintings capture the look of the city before it crumbled in World War II. The fascinating collection of mechanical musical instruments is demonstrated on Sunday at 3 PM. ✉ *Am Köllnischen Park 5, Mitte* ☎ *030/240–020* 🌐 *www.stadtmuseum.de* 🎫 *€4, instrument demonstration €2* ⏲ *Tues., Thurs.–Sun. 10–6; Wed. 12–8* Ⓤ *Märkisches Museum (U-bahn).*

27 Fodor'sChoice ★ **Museumsinsel** (Museum Island). On the site of one of Berlin's two original settlements, this unique complex of four state museums is an absolute must. The **Alte Nationalgalerie** (Old National Gallery, entrance on Bodestrasse) houses an outstanding collection of 18th-, 19th-, and early-20th-century paintings and sculptures. Works by Cézanne, Rodin, Degas, and one of Germany's most famous portrait artists, Max Liebermann, are part of the permanent exhibition. Its **Galerie der Romantik** (Gallery of Romanticism) collection has masterpieces from such 19th-century German painters as Karl Friedrich Schinkel and Caspar David Friedrich, the leading members of the German Romantic school.

The **Altes Museum** (Old Museum), a red marble, neoclassical building abutting the green Lustgarten, was Prussia's first building purpose-built to serve as a museum. Designed by Karl Friedrich Schinkel, it was completed in 1830. In 2005 it became the temporary home of the **Egyptian collection,** which traces Egypt's history from 4000 BC and whose prize piece is the exquisite 3,300-year-old bust of Queen Nefertiti (the beauty portrayed on film by Halle Berry). The Egyptian works will relocate to the Neue Museum in 2009. The permanent collection of the Altes Museum consists of everyday utensils from ancient Greece as well as vases and sculptures from the 6th to 4th century BC. Etruscan art is its highlight, and there are a few examples of Roman art. Antique sculptures, clay figurines, and bronze art of the **Antikensammlung** (Antiquities Collection) are also housed here; the other part of the collection is in the Pergamonmuseum.

Even if you think you aren't interested in the ancient world, make an exception for the **Pergamonmuseum** (entrance on Am Kupfergraben), one of the world's greatest museums. The museum's name is derived from its principal display, the Pergamon Altar, a monumental Greek temple discovered in what is now Turkey and dating from 180 BC. The altar was shipped to Berlin in the late 19th century. Equally impressive is the gateway to the Roman town of Miletus and the Babylonian processional way. ✉ *Entrance to Museumsinsel: Am Kupfergraben, Mitte* ☎ *030/209–5577 Museumsinsel, 030/2090–5560* 🌐 *www.smb.museum* 🎫 *€8* *for all Museum Island museums* ⊙ *Pergamonmuseum Tues., Wed., and Fri.–Sun. 10–6, Thurs. 10–10; Alte Nationalgalerie Tues., Wed., and Fri.–Sun. 10–6, Thurs. 10–10; Altes Museum Tues.–Sun. 10–6* Ⓤ *Hackescher Markt. (S-bahn).*

25 **Neue Wache** (New Guardhouse). One of many Berlin constructions by the early-19th-century architect Karl Friedrich Schinkel, this building served as both the Royal Prussian War Memorial (honoring the dead of the Napoleonic Wars) and the royal guardhouse until the Kaiser abdicated in 1918. In 1931 it became a memorial to those who fell in World War I. Badly damaged in World War II, it was restored in 1960 by the East German state and rededicated as a memorial for the victims of militarism and fascism. After unification it regained its Weimar Republic appearance and was inaugurated as Germany's central war memorial. Inside is a copy of Berlin sculptor Käthe Kollwitz's *Pietà,* showing a mother mourning over her dead son. The inscription in front of it reads, TO THE VICTIMS OF WAR AND TYRANNY. ✉ *Unter den Linden, Mitte* ⊙ *Daily 10–6.*

33 **Nikolaiviertel** (Nicholas Quarter). Renovated in the 1980s and a tad concrete-heavy, this tiny quarter grew up around Berlin's oldest parish church, the medieval, twin-spire **St. Nikolaikirche** (St. Nicholas's Church), dating from 1230. The adjacent Fischerinsel (Fisherman's Island) area was the heart of Berlin 750 years ago and retains a bit of its medieval character. At Breite Strasse you'll find two of Berlin's oldest buildings: No. 35 is the **Ribbeckhaus,** the city's only surviving Renaissance structure, dating from 1624, and No. 36 is the early baroque **Marstall,** built by Michael Matthais between 1666 and 1669. The area feels rather artificial, but draws tourists to its gift stores, cafés, and restaurants. ✉ *Church: Nikolaikirchpl., Mitte* ☎ *030/240–020* 🌐 *www.stadtmuseum.de* 🎫 *€1.50* ⊙ *Tues., and Thurs.–Sun. 10–6; Wed. 12–8* Ⓤ *Alexanderpl. (S-bahn and U-bahn).*

28 **Schlossplatz** (Palace Square). One of the biggest cultural debates in Berlin is whether to rebuild a portion of the Hohenzollern palace that stood here from the 15th century, or save the country and city some 6.7 million euros. The East German government detonated the war-damaged palace for ideological reasons in 1950. Some 60 plaques describe the history of the palace, and you can also see some tiled cellar remains.

The question of reconstructing even the facade of the glorious palace that had 1,200 rooms has pitted Prussian fans against those nostalgic for the German Democratic Republic, whose gutted former parliament building, the **Palast der Republik** (Palace of the Republic) wastes away on this empty lot's edge. The building (built 1976) had to be cleared of asbestos, and its intended demolition has been stalled by costs and questions of cultural significance.

At Schlossplatz's south end is the brick-and-glass **Staatsrat** (State Senate) where East German dictator Eric Honnecker worked. The stone portal to this building was one of the few parts of the palace that the East German government preserved. It's believed that it was from this portral that Karl Liebknecht attempted to declare a Soviet-style republic after the Kaiser abdicated in November 1918. Irony upon irony, this former Communist building is home to Germany's first private business university. ✉ *Unter den Linden, Mitte* Ⓤ *Hackescher Markt (S-bahn).*

31 **St. Marienkirche** (St. Mary's Church). This medieval church, one of the finest in Berlin, is best known for its late-Gothic, macabre fresco *Der Totentanz* (*Dance of Death*), which is in need of restoration. Tours on Monday and Tuesday at 1 PM highlight the fresco. ✉ *Karl-Liebknecht-Str. 8, Mitte* ☎ *030/242–4467* *Free* ⏲ *Apr.–Oct., daily 10–6; Nov.–Mar., daily 10–4. Organ recital Sat. 4:30* Ⓤ *Alexanderplatz, Hackescher Markt (S-bahn).*

14

need a break?

The **Opernpalais** (✉ Unter den Linden 5, Mitte ☎ 030/202–683), next to the opera house and within the former Crown Princesses Palace, is home to a café famous for its selection of 40 cakes and pies, plus other sweet treats.

Unter den Linden. The name of this historic Berlin thoroughfare, between the Brandenburg Gate and Schlossplatz, means "under the linden trees"—and as Marlene Dietrich once sang, "As long as the old linden trees still bloom, Berlin is still Berlin." Imagine Berliners' shock when Hitler decided to fell the trees in order to make Unter den Linden more parade-friendly. The grand boulevard began as a riding path that the royals used to get from their palace to their hunting grounds (now Tiergarten). Lining it now are linden trees planted after World War II, embassies and consulates, cafés and shops, a university, museums, and an opera house.

Mitte's Scheunenviertel & Prenzlauer Berg

The hip scene of Mitte, the historic core of Berlin, is best experienced in the narrow streets and courtyard mazes of the Scheunenviertel (Barn Quarter), which also encompasses the former Spandauer Vorstadt (Jewish Quarter)—the streets around Oranienburger Strasse. Some streets are lined with hip shops, bars, and eateries while others look empty and forlorn. During the second half of the 17th century, artisans, small businessmen, and Jews moved into this area at the encouragement of the Great Elector, who sought to improve his financial situation through their skills. As industrialization intensified, the quarter became poorer, and in the 1880s many East European Jews escaping pogroms settled here.

Northeast of Mitte, the old working-class district of Prenzlauer Berg used to be one of the poorest sections of Berlin. In socialist East Germany, the old (and mostly run-down) tenement houses attracted the artistic avant-garde, who transformed the area into a refuge for alternative lifestyles. The renovated 19th-century buildings with balconies and stucco work still tend to feature unwanted graffiti, but Prenzlauer Berg is now a trendy area full of young couples with baby in tow.

a good tour

From the Bernauer Strasse U-bahn station, turn left on Bernauer Strasse, and when you reach Strelitzer Strasse, cut to the path that runs parallel to the sidewalk. This path through the former border zone behind the Wall will lead you to a modern chapel. This replaced the church that the East Germans detonated in order to have clear sightlines in the death-strip. The path continues to the memorial and museum **Dokumentationszentrum Berliner Mauer** 37 ⚑. Follow the Wall that still stands to Gartenstrasse, and hop on a southbound S-bahn at Nordbahnhof. Exit one stop later at Oranienburger Strasse, the center of the old Jewish Quarter (Spandauer Vorstadt) and today full of restaurants and bars. You can't miss the gilded cupola of the **Neue Synagoge** 38, which is a museum open to the public and always guarded by police officers. Before reaching it, peek into the shops of the courtyard Heckmann Höfe on the left. After the synagogue, take Krausnickstrasse to Grosse Hamburger Strasse, once the hub of life in Jewish Berlin. In 1941–42 at the home at Nos. 25–26, Nazis assembled Berlin's last 50,000 Jews to be transported to concentration camps. Of the oldest Jewish cemetery in the city, which dated to 1672, only the green lawn and a few gravestones mark what the Nazis destroyed. The Sophienkirche nearby was the first Protestant church built in the Spandauer Vorstadt (1712).

Grosse Hamburger Strasse leads back to Oranienburger Strasse. Turn left on Oranienburger Strasse, following it as it curves into Rosenthaler Strasse and the entrance to the **Hackesche Höfe** 39, an art nouveau–warehouse complex dating to 1907. To reach the trendy part of Prenzlauer Berg, follow Rosenthaler Strasse to its end at Tor Strasse, cross it, and take Tram M1 heading uphill (the stop is outside the Circus Hostel). Alight at Eberswalder Strasse in Prenzlauer Berg. Walk back in the direction you came from on Kastanienallee (which is now derisively nicknamed "Casting Allee" for all the fashionable café-sitters). After one block, turn left on Oberberger Strasse and cross Schönhauser Allee to reach the fringe-arts and culture center **Kulturbrauerei** 40. This old brewery complex is a typical example of late-19th-century industrial architecture. You're now in a good neighborhood in which to scout drinks or a meal. For local flavor, follow Sredzkistrasse to the east, or Knaackstrasse in either direction.

TIMING If you want to indulge in the small art galleries and boutiques or relax at any of the many cafés along the way, reserve a full day for Mitte and Prenzlauer Berg. It's also possible to take in all spots along the tour within four hours.

What to See

37 **Dokumentationszentrum Berliner Mauer** (Berlin Wall Memorial Site). This site combines memorials and a museum and research center on the Berlin Wall. The division of Berlin was particularly heart-wrenching on Bernauer Strasse, where neighbors and families on opposite sides of the street were separated overnight. The Reconciliation Chapel, completed in 2000, replaced the community church dynamited by the Communists in 1985. The church had been walled into the "death strip" and was seen as a hindrance to patrolling it. A portion of the Wall remains on Bernauer Strasse and an installation meant to serve as a memorial

unfortunately only confuses those wondering what the border once looked like. For a wealth of images and information, head into the museum, where German-speakers can even hear radio broadcasts from the time the Wall was erected. ✉ *Bernauer Str. 111, Wedding* ☎ *030/464–1030* 🌐 *www.berliner-mauer-dokumentationszentrum.de* 🎫 *Free* ⏲ *Apr.–Oct., Tues.–Sun. 10–6; Nov.–Mar., Tues.–Sun. 10–5* Ⓤ *Bernauer Strasse (U-bahn).*

★ 39 **Hackesche Höfe** (Hacke Warehouses). Built in 1905–07, this series of eight connected courtyards is the finest example of art nouveau–industrial architecture in Berlin. Most buildings are covered with glazed white tiles, and additional Moorish mosaic designs decorate the main courtyard off Rosenthaler Strasse. Shops (including one dedicated to Berlin's beloved street crossing signal, the "Ampelmann"), restaurants, the variety theater Chamäleon Varieté, a klezmer music venue, and a movie theater populate the spaces once occupied by ballrooms, a poets society, and a Jewish girls' club. ✉ *Rosenthaler Str. 40–41 and Sophienstr. 6, Mitte* ☎ *No phone* 🌐 *www.hackesche-hoefe.com* Ⓤ *Hackescher Markt (S-bahn).*

need a break?

Within the first courtyard of Hackesche Höfe **Anatre Feinkost** (✉ Rosenthaler Str. 40–41, Mitte ☎ 030/2838–9915) uses top-quality ingredients for its Mediterranean sandwiches and pastas. You can also just sit with a coffee or glass of wine.

off the beaten path

JÜDISCHER FRIEDHOF (Jewish Cemetery) – More than 150,000 graves make this peaceful retreat in Berlin's Weissensee district Europe's largest Jewish cemetery. The grounds and tombstones are in excellent condition—a seeming impossibility, given its location in the heart of the Third Reich. To reach the cemetery, take Tram 2, 3, 4, 23, or 24 from Hackescher Markt to Albertinenstrasse and head south on Herbert-Baum-Strasse. At the gate you can get a plan from the attendant. The guidebook is in German only. ☎ *030/925–3330* ⏲ *Apr.–Oct., Sun.–Thurs. 8–5, Fri. 8–3; Nov.–Mar., Sun.–Thurs. 8–4, Fri. 8–3.*

40 **Kulturbrauerei** (Culture Brewery). The redbrick buildings of the old Schultheiss brewery are now occupied by a multicinema, pubs, clubs, and a concert venue that together make up a fringe-arts and entertainment nexus. The Prezlauer Berg tourist-information center is also here. Parts of the brewery were built in 1842 and at the turn of the 20th century the complex was expanded to include the main brewery of Berlin's famous Schultheiss beer, then the world's largest brewery. The buildings are completely restored, though no one makes beer here. The **Sammlung Industrielle Gestaltung** (✉ Knaackstr. 97, Aufgang B ☎ 030/4431–7868 ⏲ Wed.–Sun. 1–8) is a museum that features design and everyday products of the former East Germany. Come Christmastime, a market includes children's rides. ✉ *Schönhauser Allee 36–39 and Knaackstr. 97, Prenzlauer Berg* 🌐 *www.kulturbrauerei-berlin.de* Ⓤ *Eberswalder Str. (U-bahn).*

need a break? For coffee and cake or Berliner Kindl, Potsdamer Rex, or Paulaner Hefeweizen on tap, stop by **Restauration 1900** (✉ Husemannstr. 1, Prenzlauer Berg ☎ 030/442–2494). It's one of the few popular cafés and restaurants from socialist times still in business today. It sits on the now prime real estate of Kollwitzplatz.

38 **Neue Synagoge** (New Synagogue). This meticulously restored landmark, built between 1859 and 1866, is an exotic amalgam of styles, the whole faintly Middle Eastern. Its bulbous, gilded cupola stands out in the skyline. When its doors opened, it was the largest synagogue in Europe, with 3,200 seats. The synagogue was damaged on November 9, 1938 (*Kristallnacht*—Night of the Broken Glass), when Nazi looters rampaged across Germany, burning synagogues and smashing the few Jewish shops and homes left in the country. Destroyed by Allied bombing in 1943, it wasn't until the mid-1980s that the East German government restored it. The effective exhibit on the history of the building and its congregants includes fragments of the original architecture and furnishings. Sabbath services are held in a modern addition. ✉ *Oranienburger Str. 28–30, Mitte* ☎ *030/8802–8316* 🌐 *www.cjudaicum.de* *€3, €4.60 including special exhibits; tour €1.50, German only* ⏲ *Sept.–Apr., Sun.–Thurs. 10–6, Fri. 10–2; May–Aug., Tues.–Thurs. 10–6, Mon. and Sun. 10–8, Fri. 10–5. Tours Wed. at 4, Sun. at 2 and 4. Cupola Apr.–Sept.* U *Oranienburger Str. (U-bahn), Oranienburger Tor (S-bahn).*

Palaces, Museums & Nature in Outer Berlin

The city's outlying areas abound with palaces, lakes, and museums set in lush greenery. Central to the former West Berlin but now a western district of the united city, Charlottenburg was once an independent and wealthy city that only became part of Berlin in 1920. It holds the baroque Charlottenburg Palace and, across the street, a collection of Picassos in the Museum Berggruen. The southwest part of Berlin holds the vast Grunewald (forest) that borders the Havel River and lake Wannsee. In good weather Berliners come out in force, swimming, sailing their boats, tramping through the woods, and riding horseback. A starting point for cruises plying the water is opposite the Wannsee stop on the S-Bahn. The Wannsee station is also the transfer point for buses to the Wannsee beach to the north; Bus 216 to Pfaueninsel (Peacock Island); and Bus 114 to the lakeside villa where the Holocaust was first planned. From Wannsee, Potsdam, the city of summer palaces, is just another three stops on the S-Bahn.

Sights to See

Bildungs- und Gedenkstätte Haus der Wannsee-Konferenz (Wannsee Conference Memorial Site). The lovely lakeside setting of this Berlin villa belies the unimaginable Holocaust atrocities planned here. This elegant edifice hosted the fateful conference held on January 20, 1942, at which Nazi leaders and German bureaucrats, under SS leader Reinhard Heydrich, planned the systematic deportation and mass extinction of Europe's Jewish population. Today this so-called *Endlösung der Judenfrage* ("final solution of the Jewish question") is illustrated with an exhibition that documents the conference, and more extensively, the escalation of persecution against Jews, and the Holocaust itself. A reference library offers source materials in English. Allow at least two hours for a visit. ✉ *Am Grossen Wannsee 56–58, Zehlendorf, from the Wannsee S-bahn station take Bus 114* ☎ *030/805–0010* 🌐 *www.ghwk.de* 🎫 *Free* ⏲ *Daily 10–6. Library closed weekends* Ⓤ *Wannsee (S-bahn).*

Dahlemer Museen (Dahlem Museums). This complex of four museums includes the **Ethnologisches Museum** (Ethnographic Museum) as well as museums for Indian, East Asian, and early European art. It's internationally known for its art and artifacts from Africa, Asia, the South Seas, and the Americas. The large collection of Mayan, Aztec, and Incan ceramics and stone sculptures should not be missed. ✉ *Lansstr. 8, Zehlendorf* ☎ *030/830–1438* 🌐 *www.smb.museum* 🎫 *€4* ⏲ *Tues.–Fri. 10–6, weekends 11–6* Ⓤ *Dahlem-Dorf (U-bahn).*

★ **Museum Berggruen.** This small modern art museum holds works by Matisse, Klee, Giacometti, and Picasso, who is particularly well represented with more than 100 works. Heinz Berggruen, a businessman who left Berlin in the 1930s, collected the excellent paintings. He narrates portions of the free audio guide, sharing anecdotes about how he came to acquire pieces directly from the artists, as well as his opinions of the women portrayed in Picasso's portraits. ✉ *Schlossstr. 1, Charlottenburg* ☎ *030/3269–5815* 🌐 *www.smb.museum* 🎫 *€6* ⏲ *Tues.–Sun. 10–6* Ⓤ *Sophie-Charlotte-Pl. (U-bahn), Richard-Wagner-Pl. (U-bahn).*

Pfaueninsel (Peacock Island). Prussian king Friedrich Wilhelm II whisked his mistresses away to this small island oasis on the Great Wannsee. **Schloss Pfaueninsel,** the small white palace, erected in 1794 according to the ruler's plans—and in accordance with the taste of the era—was built as a fake ruin. The simple building looks strangely cartoonlike; you can see the interior on half-hour tours. In the early 19th century, garden architect Joseph Peter Lenné designed an English garden on the island, which ultimately became western Berlin's favorite summer getaway. ✣ *from the Wannsee S-bahn station, take Bus 216 (leaving every 20 minutes) and then a ferry* ✉ *Pfaueninselchaussee, Zehlendorf* ☎ *030/8058–6830* 🌐 *www.spsg.de* 🎫 *€3, ferry service €2* ⏲ *Palace Apr.–Oct., Tues.–Sun. 10–5; ferry to Pfaueninsel year-round* Ⓤ *Wannsee (S-bahn).*

off the beaten path

★ **SACHSENHAUSEN GEDENKSTÄTTE** (Sachsenhausen Memorial) – This concentration camp near the Third Reich capital was established in 1936. It held prisoners from every nation in Europe, including British officers, Joseph Stalin's son, and 12,000 Soviet prisoners of war who were systematically murdered. The work camp had held approximately 200,000 prisoners and it's estimated that 50,000 died here. Between 1945 and 1950 the Soviets used the site as a prison, where malnutrition and disease claimed the lives of 20% of the inmates. The East German government made the site a concentration camp memorial in April 1961. A few original facilities remain; the barracks, which hold exhibits, are reconstructions. To reach Sachsenhausen, take the S-bahn 1 to Oranienburg, the last stop. The ride from the Friedrichstrasse station will take 50 minutes. From the Oranienburg station it's a 25-minute walk (follow signs), or you can take a taxi or Bus 804 (a 7-minute ride) in the direction of Malz. Allow three hours at the memorial. Oranienburg is 35 km (22 mi) north of Berlin. ✉ *Str. der Nationen 22, Oranienburg* ☎ *03301/200–200* 🌐 *www.gedenkstaette-sachsenhausen.de* 🎫 *Free, audio guide €3* ⏲ *Mid-Mar.–mid-Oct., Tues.–Sun. 8:30–6; mid-Oct.–mid-Mar., Tues.–Sun. 8:30–4:30; last admission ½ hr before closing* Ⓤ *Oranienburg (S-bahn).*

Schloss Charlottenburg (Charlottenburg Palace). A grand reminder of imperial days, this showplace served as a city residence for the Prussian rulers. The gorgeous palace started as a modest royal summer residence in 1695, built on the orders of King Friedrich I for his wife, Sophie-Charlotte. In the 18th century Frederick the Great made a number of additions, such as the dome and several wings designed in the rococo style. By 1790 the complex had evolved into a massive royal domain that could take a whole day to explore. Behind heavy iron gates, the Court of Honor—the front courtyard—is dominated by a baroque statue of the Great Elector on horseback. ✉ *Luisenpl., Charlottenburg* ☎ *030/320–911* 🌐 *www.spsg.de* 🎫 *A Tageskarte (day card) for €7 covers admission for all bldgs., excluding tour of Altes Schloss baroque apartments; a two-day €12 card covers all palace sights in Berlin area, except Sanssouci* Ⓤ *Richard-Wagner-Pl. or Sophie-Charlotten-Pl. (U-Bahn).*

The **Altes Schloss** (Nering-Eosander-Bau; ☎ 030/3209–1440 🎫 €8 with tour; €2 for upper floor only ⏲ Tues.–Fri. 9–5) is the main building with the ground-floor suites of Friedrich I and Sophie-Charlotte. Paintings include royal portraits by Antoine Pesne, a noted court painter of the 18th century. A guided tour visits the Oak Gallery, the early-18th-century palace chapel, and the suites of Friedrich Wilhelm II and Friedrich Wilhelm III, furnished in the Biedermeier style. Tours leave every hour on the hour from 9 to 5. The upper floor has the apartments of Friedrich Wilhelm IV, a silver treasury, and Berlin and Meissen porcelain. It can be seen on its own.

The **Neuer Flügel** (New Wing; ☎ 030/3209–1454 🎫 €5 ⏲ late Mar.–Oct., Tues.–Sun. 10–6; Nov.–late Mar., Tues.–Sun. 11–5), where Frederick the Great once lived, was designed by Knobbelsdorff, who also built Sanssouci. The 138-foot-long Goldene Galerie (Golden Gallery) was the palace's ballroom. West of the staircase are Frederick's rooms, in which his extravagant collection of works by Watteau, Chardin, and Pesne is displayed. An audio guide is included in the admission.

The park behind the palace was laid out in the French baroque style beginning in 1697 and was transformed into an English garden in the early 19th century. In it stand the **Neuer Pavillon** by Karl Friedrich Schinkel and Carl Langhan's **Belvedere teahouse** (☎ 030/3209–1412 🎫 €2 ⏲ late Mar.–Oct., Tues.–Fri. noon–5, weekends 10–5; Nov.–late Mar., Tues.–Sun. noon–4), which overlooks the lake and the Spree River and holds a collection of Berlin porcelain.

The **Museum für Vor- und Frühgeschichte** (Museum of Pre- and Early History; ☎ 030/326–7480 €6 ⏲ Tues.–Fri. 9–5, weekends 10–5) traces the evolution of mankind from 1 million BC to AD 1,000. It's opposite Klausener Platz (to the left as you face the palace).

need a break?

Between visits to the museums clustering around Schloss Charlottenburg, give your feet a rest in the country-kitchen room of the **Kleine Orangerie** (✉ Spandauer Damm 20, Charlottenburg ☎ 030/322–2021 ⏲ Easter–Oct., daily 9 AM–9:30 PM; Nov.–Easter, Tues.–Sun. 9–8), next door to the palace. The breakfast is a good deal. There's also atrium and outdoor seating.

WHERE TO EAT

Neighborhood stalwarts serve residents from morning to night with a mix of German and international cuisine. Berlin is known for curt or slow service, except at very high-end restaurants. Note that many of the top restaurants are closed on Sunday.

The most common food for meals on-the-go are *Wursts* (sausages). Currywurst, a pork sausage served with a mildly curried ketchup, is local to Berlin. Even more popular are Turkish *Döner* shops that sell pressed lamb or chicken in flatbread pockets.

WHAT IT COSTS In Euros

	$$$$	$$$	$$	$	¢
AT DINNER	over €25	€21–€25	€16–€20	€9–€15	under €9

Restaurant prices are per person for a main course at dinner.

Charlottenburg

$$$$ ✕ **Alt Luxemburg.** This popular restaurant creates an intimate setting with 19th-century-style furniture, wrought-iron lamps, and wonderfully attentive service. Working behind the stove since 1982, owner and chef Karl Wannemacher uses only the freshest ingredients for his modern German dishes, which change monthly. Lobster is always on the menu in some form, be it in a salad or the divine lobster lasagna. Entrée options might include rolled saddle of rabbit in coffee sauce. You can order à la carte or opt for a four-course meal for €65. ✉ *Windscheidstr. 31, Charlottenburg* ☎ *030/323–8730* 💳 *AE, DC, MC, V* ⏲ *Closed Sun. No lunch* Ⓤ *Charlottenburg (S-bahn), Wilmersdorfer Str. (U-bahn).*

★ **$$$$** ✕ **Ana e Bruno.** Most of the guests here are making an evening out of the four- and eight-course meals. This Berlin classic is expensive but exudes a warm and homey atmosphere thanks to the hospitality of the owners, Bruno and Ana. Don't expect hearty home cooking, though: the chef favors a low-calorie interpretation of Mediterranean cuisine and prefers fresh vegetables and salads over pasta. The four-course meals are €67;

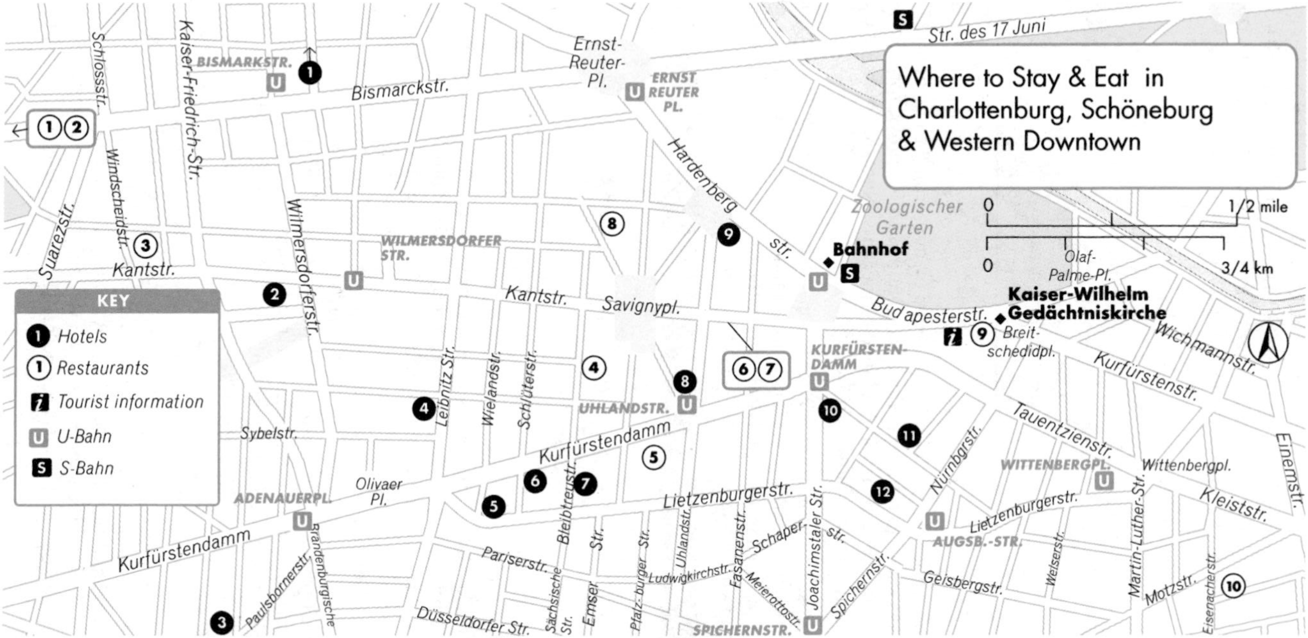

Restaurants ▼

Alt Luxemburg 3
Ana e Bruno 1
April 10
Dressler Kurfürstendamm 5
Engelbecken 2
First Floor 9
Florian 8
Ottenthal 6
Paris Bar 7
Die Zwölf Apostel 4

Hotels ▼

Art Nouveau Hotel 4
Blibtreu Berlin 7
Charlottenburger Hof . . . 2
Econtel 1
Hotel Astoria 9
Hotel Bogota 6
Hotel Brandenburger Hof 12
Hotel-Pension Dittberner 5
Kempinski Hotel Bristol Berlin 8
Propeller Island City Lodge 3
Steigenberger Berlin 11
Swissôtel Berlin 10

the eight-course, €99. ✉ *Sophie-Charlotten-Str. 101, Charlottenburg* ☎ *030/325–7110* ✍ *Reservations essential* ▭ *AE, V* ⏲ *Closed Sun. and Mon. No lunch* Ⓤ *Westend (S-bahn).*

★ ¢–$ ✕ **Engelbecken.** The beer coasters are trading cards of the Wittelsbach dynasty in this relaxed, but high-quality restaurant serving dishes from Bavaria and the Alps. Classics like Wienerschnitzel, goulasch, or grilled saddle steak are made of "bio" meat and vegetable products, meaning that even the veal, lamb, and beef are the tasty results of organic and humane upbringing. The room is like a dine-in art gallery, but in warm weather, reserve a sidewalk table. With its corner position facing a park bordering Lake Lietzensee, Engelbecken is one of the loveliest open-air dining spots in town. ✉ *Witzlebenstr. 31, Charlottenburg* ☎ *030/615–2810* ▭ *MC, V* ⏲ *No lunch Mon.–Sat.* Ⓤ *Sophie-Charlotte-Pl. (U-bahn).*

14

Western Downtown

$$$$ ✕ **First Floor.** Few hotel-restaurants become a sensation, but this award-winning one is outstanding, even if it doesn't shake the hotel-restaurant look with its carpeting and heavy drapes. Chef Matthias Buchholz prepares French cuisine like a native. Occasionally the menu turns to German roots, with *Müritzlammrücken in Olivenkruste mit Bohnenmelange* (Müritz lamb back in olive crust, served with green beans). The four-course menu costs €66.50. If you're a wine connoisseur, ask sommelier Herr Tietz for a look at the caveau that holds more than 800 red wines. ✉ *Hotel Palace, Budapester Str. 42, Western Downtown* ☎ *030/2502–1020* ✍ *Reservations essential* ▭ *AE, DC, MC, V* ⏲ *No lunch Sat.* Ⓤ *Kurfürstendamm or Wittenbergpl (U-bahn).*

$$–$$$ ✕ **Paris Bar.** Just off the Ku'damm, this trendy restaurant attracts a polyglot clientele of film stars, artists, entrepreneurs, and executives to whom food plays second fiddle to socializing. Meals can be ordered until 1 AM; snacks at the bar are served until 2 AM (but cash only at the bar!). The cuisine, including such delights as Jacques oysters and lamb chops with Provençal herbs, is reliably French. ✉ *Kantstr. 152, Western Downtown* ☎ *030/313–8052* ▭ *AE.*

$–$$$ ✕ **Dressler.** Both in its cuisine and in its service, Dressler is a mixture of French brasserie culture and German down-to-earth reliability. Accordingly, the dishes are conceived for a wide range of palates: oysters on the half-shell, duck with red cabbage, or cod with Pommery mustard sauce, for example. The menu changes according to season. Of the two (very similar) Dressler establishments, the one on Kurfürstendamm is livelier, with a genuinely French atmosphere. Reservations are advised. ✉ *Kurfürstendamm 207/208, Western Downtown* ☎ *030/883–3530* ✉ *Unter den Linden 39, Mitte* ☎ *030/204–4422* ▭ *AE, DC, MC, V.*

$$ ✕ **Ottenthal.** This intimate restaurant with white tablecloths and a
Fodor'sChoice ★ checkerboard floor is the city cousin of the Austrian village of Ottenthal, which delivers up the wines, pumpkinseed oil, and organic ingredients on the menu. Curious combinations on the menu might include pike-perch with lobster sauce and pepper–pine nut risotto, or venison medallions with vegetable-potato-strudel, red cabbage, and rowanberry

sauce. The huge Wienerschnitzel extends past the plate's rim and the pastas and strudel are homemade. One of the best meals for your money in Berlin, Ottenthal is a particularly good choice on Sunday evening, when most of Berlin's finer restaurants are closed. ✉ *Kantstr. 153, Charlottenburg* ☎ *030/313–3162* ▭ *AE, DC, MC, V* ⊙ *No lunch* Ⓤ *Zoologischer Garten (S-bahn and U-bahn).*

★ $–$$ ✕ **Florian.** The handwritten menu is just one page, but there's always a changing variety of fish, fowl, and meat dishes in this well-established restaurant. *Steinbeisser,* a white, flaky fish, might be served with an exciting salsa of rhubarb, chile, coriander, and ginger, or you can opt for some Franconian comfort cuisine such as *Kirchweihbraten* (marinated pork with baked apples and plums) or the *Nürnberger Rostbratwurst* (small pork sausages) served as late-night snacks. The kitchen is open until 1 AM, and smaller dishes are available until 2 AM. Reservations are advised. ✉ *Grolmanstr. 52, Western Downtown* ☎ *030/313–9184* ▭ *MC, V* ⊙ *No lunch* Ⓤ *Savignyplatz (S-bahn).*

¢–$$ ✕ **Die Zwölf Apostel.** Both of the "Twelve Apostles" are known for their stimulating settings and their great stone-oven pizzas named for Jesus's disciples. The Savignyplatz location in Charlottenburg is open around the clock, has a lunch special for €4.95, and offers a winter garden and outdoor dining. In Mitte, eyes are often riveted to the frescoed, vaulted ceilings that rumble as trains pass overhead. In each, garlands of garlic are hung along the wall and fish and meat dishes round out the menu. Pizzas are discounted to €6 weekdays noon–4. ✉ *Bleibtreustr. 49, Charlottenburg* ☎ *030/312–1433* Ⓤ *Savignypl. (S-bahn)* ✉ *Georgenstr. 2, Mitte* ☎ *030/201–0222* Ⓤ *Friedrichstr. (S-bahn and U-bahn)* ▭ *No credit cards.*

Schöneberg

¢–$ ✕ **April.** The back room is dressed with white tablecloths, but most regulars pick a place in the front where there are art-nouveau light fixtures, stuccowork, and a street view. This is a relaxed bistro, meaning the service can be sluggish, but the consistently delicious meals are very reasonably priced. The menu has a mix of Italian, French, and German cooking and a kids' section. The only lackluster items are the thin-crust Alsatian pizzas (*Pfannkuchen*). The generous *Vorspeisenteller* (selection of five appetizers) might include bresaola over arugula, grilled vegetables, and shrimp tempura. The restaurant is near Winterfeld Platz. ✉ *Winterfeldstr. 56, Schöneberg* ☎ *030/216–8869* ▭ *No credit cards* Ⓤ *Nollendorfpl (U-bahn).*

Kreuzberg

$–$$ ✕ **Abendmahl.** The exquisite vegetarian and fish preparations here prove that an inexpensive meal doesn't have to leave you hungry. Hearty creations have playful names such as *Flammendes Inferno* (Flaming Inferno), a fish curry whose spiciness means business. The campy desserts are particularly over the top, like *Whatever Happened to Simone de Beauvoir?* (part of the Deadly Ice Creams series). Healthy eaters such as Wim Wenders and Nina Hagen are among the artsy crowd frequenting the small

Restaurants

Abendmahl . . 17
Borchardt 9
Diekmann im Weihaus Huth 14
Dressler Unter den Linden . . . 6
Grossbeeren-keller 16
Kaiserstuben . . 4
Lindenbräu . . 13
Lutter & Wegner . . 1,7,15
Monsieur Vuong 2
Reinhard's . . . 10
Treffpunkt Berlin 5
VAU 8
Weihen-stephaner 3
Zur Letzten Instanz 12
Zur Rippe . . . 11

Hotels

Alexander Plaza 5
Die Fabrik 17
Dorint Sofitel am Gendarmen-markt 12
Eastern Comfort 13
Grand Hyatt Berlin 15
Hilton Berlin . . 14
Hotel Adlon Berlin 9
Hotel Hackescher Markt 4
Hotel Künstlerheim Luise 3
Hotel-Pension Kastanienhof . . 2
Hotel Unter den Linden 7
Houseboat-Berlin 8
Mitte's Backpacker Hostel 1
Park Inn 6
The Regent Berlin 11
Riehmers Hofgarten . . . 16
Westin Grand Hotel 10

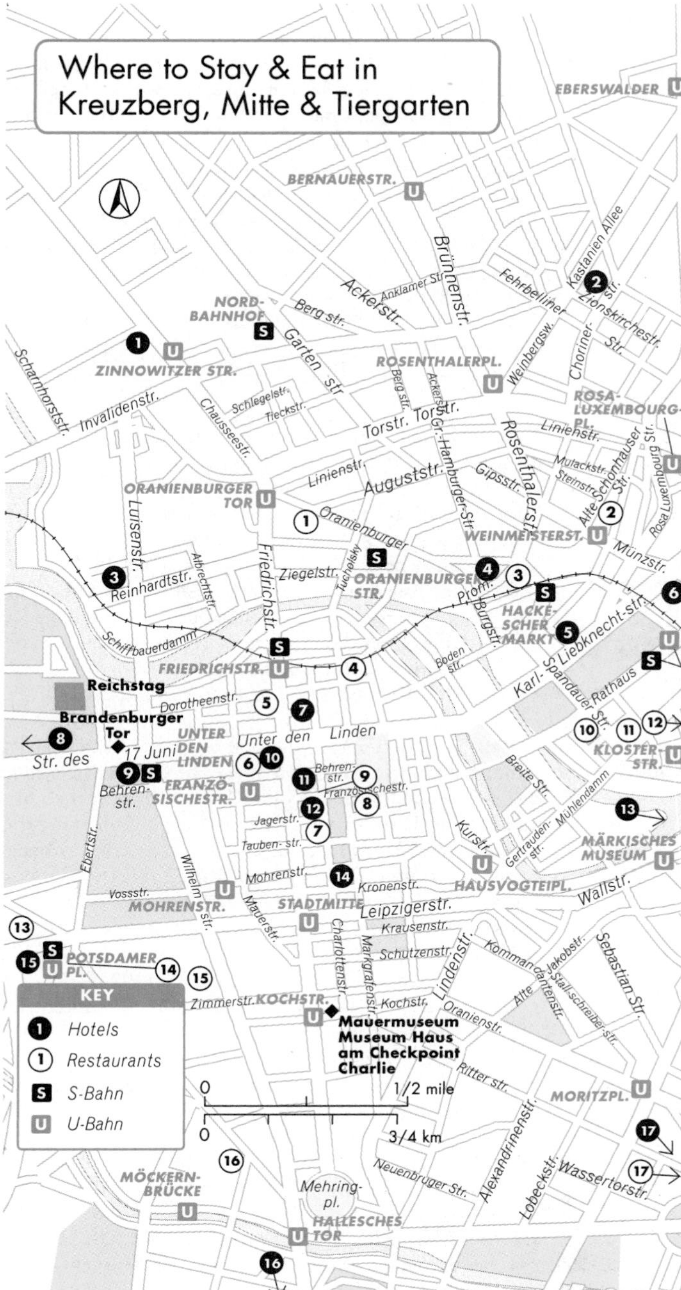

restaurant. ✉ *Muskauer Str. 9, Kreuzberg* ☎ *030/612–5170* ▭ *No credit cards* ⏲ *No lunch* Ⓤ *Görlitzer Bahnhof (U-bahn).*

¢–$ ✕ **Grossbeerenkeller.** With dark paneling, old photos of Berlin, and worn furnishings, this basement restaurant is where Berliners bring visitors to experience something "German." If there were such a thing as a German road movie, proprietor Ingeborg Zinn-Baier would be well cast as the diner hostess. Ask for an English menu and succumb to the cholesterol and saltiness of dishes like *Hoppel-Poppel* (an omelettelike dish of smoked and pickeled pork, eggs, home fries, onions, and herbs) or *Kasseler Nacken mit Grünkohl* (boiled salt-pork meat with green cabbage). The restaurant opens at 4 PM weekdays and in summer you can sup in the simple courtyard. ✉ *Grossbeerenstr. 90, Kreuzberg* ☎ *030/251–3064* ▭ *No credit cards* ⏲ *Closed Sun. No lunch* Ⓤ *Möckernbrücke (U-bahn).*

Mitte

$$$$ ✕ **Kaiserstuben.** This 16-seat room is secreted on the second floor of a palace dating to 1753. In this quiet nook, the only sounds you'll hear are soft conversation and music—the kitchen is on another part of the floor. The cuisine balances regional heritage with French influences. Entrées on the small à la carte menu might include roasted turbot with rice noodles and coconut-ginger sauce or poached veal saddle with truffle risotto. The four-course meal costs €49. After your dinner, move to the Tadjikistan tea room on the other side of the "palace." Once you've removed your shoes, you're free to recline on pillows while sipping tea from a samovar. ✉ *Am Festungsgraben 1, Mitte* ☎ *030/2061–0548* ▭ *AE, MC, V* ⏲ *Closed Sun. and Mon. No lunch* Ⓤ *Friedrichstr. (S-bahn and U-bahn).*

$$$$ Fodor's Choice ★ ✕ **VAU.** Trendsetter VAU defined hip in the Mitte district years ago, and remains a favorite even as it ages. The excellent German fish and game dishes prepared by chef Kolja Kleeberg have earned him endless praise and awards. Daring combinations include *Ente mit gezupftem Rotkohl, Quitten, und Maronen* (duck with selected red cabbage, quinces, and sweet chestnuts) and *Steinbutt mit Kalbbries auf Rotweinschalotten* (turbot with veal sweetbread on shallots in red wine). A four-course menu costs €78; a six-course, €115. A lunch entrée is a bargain at €12. The cool interior was designed by one of Germany's leading industrial architects. ✉ *Jägerstr. 54/55, Mitte* ☎ *030/202–9730* ✍ *Reservations essential* ▭ *AE, DC, MC, V* ⏲ *Closed Sun.* Ⓤ *Französische Str. (U-bahn) or Stadmitte (U-bahn).*

★ $$–$$$$ ✕ **Borchardt.** The menu changes daily at this fashionable celebrity meeting place. The high ceiling, plush maroon benches, art-nouveau mosaic (discovered during renovations), and marble columns create the impression of a 1920s café. The cuisine is high-quality French-German, including several dishes with fresh fish, veal, and some of Berlin's best (and most tender) beef classics. A three-course €50 prix-fixe menu is available. ✉ *Französische Str. 47, Mitte* ☎ *030/8188–6262* ✍ *Reservations essential* ▭ *AE, MC, V* Ⓤ *Französische Str. (U-bahn).*

★ $$–$$$ ✕ **Lutter & Wegner.** One of the city's oldest vintners (*Sekt,* German champagne, was first conceived here in 1811 by actor Ludwig Devrient), Lutter & Wegner has returned to its historic location on Charlottenstrasse off Gendarmenmarkt. The dark wood-panel walls, parquet floor, and multitude of rooms takes you back to 19th-century Vienna. The cuisine is mostly Austrian with superb game dishes in winter and, of course, a Wiener schnitzel with lukewarm potato salad. The *Sauerbraten* (marinated pot roast) with red cabbage has been a national prize-winner. In the Weinstube, meat and cheese plates are served until 3 AM. The high prices for the relatively small portions include the great setting, which is similar in all locations. ✉ *Charlottenstr. 56, Mitte* ☎ *030/2029–5417* ▭ *AE, MC, V* Ⓤ *Französische Str. and Stadtmitte (U-Bahn)* ✉ *Alte Potsdamer Str. 5, Potsdamer Platz* ☎ *030/2529–4350* ▭ *AE, MC, V* Ⓤ *Potsdamer Platz (S-bahn and U-bahn)* ✉ *Oranienburger Str. 52-53, Mitte* ☎ *030/2478–1078* ▭ *AE, MC, V* Ⓤ *Oranienburger Tor.*

$–$$ ✕ **Reinhard's.** Friends meet here in the Nikolaiviertel to enjoy the carefully prepared entrées and to sample spirits from the amply stocked bar, all served by friendly, tie-wearing waiters. The honey-glazed breast of duck, *Adlon,* is one of its specialties. There's a nice outdoor area for dining. ✉ *Poststr. 28, Mitte* ☎ *030/242–5295* ✍ *Reservations essential* ▭ *AE, DC, MC, V* Ⓤ *Alexanderpl. (U-Bahn).*

$–$$ **Weihenstephaner.** Home-baked pretzels, *Weisswurst* (white veal sausages), and other Bavarian fare make for a very German experience on this ample square opposite the Hackescher Markt station. Though a youthful nightlife area, the traditional zyther musician and dirndl-wearing waitresses don't stick out at all in the restaurant's 18th-century building or around the outdoor tables covered in checkered cloth. The beers originate from Weihenstephaner, Germany's oldest brewery. The menu offers more appetizers than entrées; daily specials might include roast lamb cutlets, stuffed spring chicken, or pork roasted in dark beer. ✉ *Neue Promenade 5, north side of Hackescher Markt S-Bahn station, Mitte* ☎ *030/25762871* ▭ *AE, DC, MC, V* Ⓤ *Hackescher Markt (S-Bahn).*

¢–$ ✕ **Treffpunkt Berlin.** This smoky, side-street "meeting point" is easily overlooked, but down-to-earth Berliners fill its bar stools and cluster of tables. The servers are gracious to non–German speakers and can coach you in eating the *Sol Ei* (hard-boiled egg), a dying breed of Berlin snack, in the correct manner: scoop out the yolk, fill the crevice with the condiments delivered, and replace the yolk. Aside from the Berlin specialities, the kitchen cooks up a spicy goulash. This is one of the few inexpensive restaurants with local character near Friedrichstrasse and the attractions of Unter den Linden. ✉ *Mittelstr. 55, Mitte* ☎ *030/204–1819* ▭ *No credit cards* Ⓤ *Friedrichstr. (S-bahn and U-bahn).*

★ **¢–$** ✕ **Zur Letzten Instanz.** Established in 1621, Berlin's oldest restaurant resides in a forgotten nest of medieval streets, but German tourists do find it and then disperse among the warren of rooms. The small menu points to Berlin's most traditional dish and the specialty: *Eisbein* (pork knuckle). Napoléon is said to have sat alongside the tile stove, Mikhail Gorbachev sipped a beer here in 1989, and Chancellor Gerhard Schröder treated French president Jacques Chirac to a meal here in 2003. Actor Jack Nicholson took in its humble atmosphere while attending the Berlinale festival in 2004. Service can be erratic, though always friendly.

✉ *Waisenstr. 14–16, Mitte* ☎ *030/242–5528* ✍ *Reservations essential* ▭ *AE, DC, MC, V* Ⓤ *Klosterstr. (U-bahn).*

¢–$ ✕ **Zur Rippe.** This popular place in the Nikolaiviertel serves wholesome food in an intimate setting of oak paneling and ceramic tiles. Specialties include the platter of *Kasseler, Ribbchen, und Eisbein* (cured pork, ribs, and pig knuckle), and a herring casserole. ✉ *Poststr. 17, Mitte* ☎ *030/242–4248* ▭ *AE, DC, MC, V* Ⓤ *Alexanderplatz (S-bahn).*

¢ ✕ **Monsieur Vuong.** Filling this hip eatery are people who share a love for Vietnamese cuisine from Saigon and the Mekong Delta. It's also a convenient place to meet before hitting Mitte's nightlife, or for slipping in just a few calories before wiggling into the wares of neighboring boutiques. Inevitably, the same steamy dishes and soups, such as *goi bo* (spicy beef salad), land on each low table, as there's only five items and two specials on offer. The menu changes every two days but you can always finish with an artichoke or jasmine tea. ✉ *Alte Schönhauser Str. 46, Mitte* ☎ *030/3087–2643* ✍ *Reservations not accepted* ▭ *No credit cards* ⊗ *No lunch Sun.* Ⓤ *Rosenthaler Str. (U-bahn).*

Potsdamer Platz

$–$$ ✕ **Diekmann im Weinhaus Huth.** Berlin restaurateur Diekmann was one of the first to bring affordable, quality French cuisine to the city in the 1980s. His second restaurant resides in this historic house, the only one in Potsdamer Platz that survived the war and the Wall. The dining room of white-tableclothed tables in arrow-straight rows also has a patio overlooking a whimsical Robert Rauschenberg sculpture. The menu changes, but regularly has coq au vin, half-duck, and crepes Suzette. The raw oysters are a good deal, as is the lunch menu. ✉ *Alte Potsdamer Str. 5, Tiergarten* ☎ *030/2529–7524* ▭ *AE, MC, V.*

$–$$ ✕ **Lindenbräu.** It's hardly a typical Bavarian brew-house, but its rooftop and outdoor seating within the quasi open-air Sony Center provides a place to gape at the glass and steel construction. This is also the only spot in Berlin where you can get wheat beer brewed on the premises. The long tables with high stools are often occupied with business people enjoying the social part of their Berlin trip. The Bavarian meals are really secondary to the setting and beer. ✉ *Sony Center, Bellvuestr. 3–5, Tiergarten* ☎ *030/2575–1280* ▭ *AE, MC, V.*

WHERE TO STAY

Tourism is on the upswing in Berlin. A row of new hotels filling nearly a whole block opened in late 2004, and prices in mid-range to luxury hotels have dropped on average. Compared to old European cities such as Paris or London, most hotel rooms in Berlin are large, though many are part of chains that allow for less individual character. Ibis and Mercure are reliable European chains with several central locations. Perhaps the only downside to Berlin lodging is the late check-in time at most; an inconvenience for those arriving at any hour prior to 2 PM.

The least expensive accommodations are in local pensions, mostly in western districts such as Charlottenburg, Schöneberg, and Wilmersdorf;

hostels with attractive double rooms, mostly in the former East Berlin; or through private room agencies. Internet services like Expedia can sometimes book a room at a five-star hotel in Berlin for half the normal price, even in summer. Hotels listed here as often come down to a level on weekends or when there is low demand. You usually have the option to decline the inclusion of breakfast, which can save you anywhere from €8 to €18 per person per day.

Year-round business conventions and tourism peaks during Christmas and summer (especially from mid-June—early July this year, due to the 2006 World Cup–soccer championships), meaning you should make reservations well in advance. If you arrive without reservations, consult hotel boards at airports and train stations, which show hotels with vacancies; or go to the tourist office in the Europa Center for help with reservations.

WHAT IT COSTS In Euros					
	$$$$	**$$$**	**$$**	**$**	**¢**
FOR 2 PEOPLE	over €200	€160–€200	€120–€160	€60–€120	under €60

Hotel prices are for two people in a standard double room, including tax and service.

Charlottenburg

★ **$$** **Art Nouveau Hotel.** The owners' discerning taste in antiques, color combinations, and even televisions (designed by Philip Starke) make this B&B-like pension a pleasure to live in. Each room has a prize piece, such as a handcarved 18th-century Chinese dresser or a chandelier from the Komische Opera's set of *Don Carlos*. Several rooms are hung with a large black-and-white photo by Sabine Kačunko. The apartment building shows its age only in the antique wood elevator, high stucco ceilings, and an occasionally creaky floor. You can serve yourself tea or coffee in the breakfast room throughout the day and mix your own drinks at the honor bar. Your English-speaking hosts are Mr. and Mrs. Schlenzka. ✉ *Leibnitzstr. 59, Charlottenburg, D–10629* ☎ *030/327–7440* 🖷 *030/3277–4440* 🌐 *www.hotelartnouveau.de* *19 rooms, 3 suites* *Cable TV, Wi-Fi, bar, lounge, dry cleaning, laundry service, meeting rooms; no a/c, no smoking* 💳 *AE, MC, V* *CP* Ⓤ *Adenauerpl. (U-bahn).*

$–$$ **Econtel.** Within walking distance of the Spree River and Charlottenburg Palace, the hotel is also just two stops on Bus X9 from Zoo Station. Families fit in well, most imaginatively in the Mickey Mouse rooms with bunk beds. A crib and children's toilet are available free of charge. Those in the business and comfort rooms have wireless Lan. All the rooms are spotless and have a homey feel. The 70-foot breakfast-buffet spread (€13) could delay your sightseeing. Keep an eye on the Web site for special two- and three-night rates. ✉ *Sömmeringstr. 24–26, Charlottenburg, D–10589* ☎ *030/346–810* 🖷 *030/3468–1163* 🌐 *www.econtel.de* *205 rooms* *Restaurant, in-room safes, some* *in-room data ports, Wi-Fi in some rooms, cable TV, bar, babysitting, dry cleaning, laundry service, meeting room, parking (fee), some pets allowed (fee), no-smoking rooms; no a/c* ▭ *AE, MC, V* Ⓤ *Mierendorffpl. (U-bahn).*

$–$$ **Propeller Island City Lodge.** Make like Alice and fall down the rabbit hole, but in this wildly eccentric accommodation you can choose from 32 Wonderlands (read the Web site carefully before picking which pill to pop). Multitalented artist Lars Stroschen is responsible for each one-of-a-kind, handcrafted furnishing. Theatrical settings such as the Upside Down and Flying Bed rooms predominate, but there are tamer abodes, like the monastic Orange and Temple rooms. Only children get to inhabit the Gnome Room, which keeps out anyone over 4′8″. This creative getaway serves breakfast (€7) but is not service-oriented; reception is open 8 AM–noon only. ✉ *Albrecht-Achilles-Str. 58, Charlottenburg, D–10709* ☎ *030/891–9016 8 AM–noon, 0163/256–5909 noon–8 PM* 🖷 *030/8928–721* 🌐 *www.propeller-island.de* *30 rooms, 26 with bath; 1 suite* *Some kitchenettes, Wi-Fi, some pets allowed, no-smoking rooms; no a/c, no room phones, no TV in some rooms* ▭ *MC, V* Ⓤ *Adenauerpl. (U-bahn).*

$ **Charlottenburger Hof.** Fodor's Choice ★ No-fuss travelers will find great value in this low-key hotel. The variety of rooms, all brightened by sunlight and primary-color schemes with prints by Kandinsky, Miró, and Mondrian, can accommodate travelers whether they be friends, couples, or families. All rooms have computers with free Internet access, and amenities include hair dryers. The 24-hour restaurant serves healthy dishes and draws locals, too. The Ku'damm is a 10-minute walk away and the bus to and from Tegel Airport stops on the next block. ✉ *Stuttgarter Pl. 14, Charlottenburg, D–10627* ☎ *030/329–070* 🖷 *030/323–3723* 🌐 *www.charlottenburger-hof.de* *46 rooms* *Restaurant, in-room safes, cable TV, in-room broadband, lounge, laundry facilities, laundry service, meeting rooms, parking (fee), some pets allowed (fee), no-smoking rooms; no a/c* ▭ *AE, MC, V* Ⓤ *Charlottenburg (S-bahn).*

Western Downtown

$$$$ **Hotel Brandenburger Hof.** Fodor's Choice ★ The foyer of this turn-of-the-20th-century mansion is breathtaking with its soaring white Doric columns, but once past these you'll find luxurious minimalism. You can breakfast and sip afternoon tea at the sun-soaked tables in the atrium courtyard, or in the evening, sit and listen to the tinkling of ivories. Between courses of French cuisine in the restaurant Quadriga, diners lean back in cherrywood chairs by Frank Lloyd Wright. Guest rooms' furnishings include pieces by Corbusier and Mies van der Rohe. Complementing the timeless Bauhaus style are ikebana floral arrangements. The spa features Asian silk cosmetic treatments. ✉ *Eislebener Str. 14, Western Downtown, D–10789* ☎ *030/214–050* 🖷 *030/2140–5100* 🌐 *www.brandenburger-hof.de* *58 rooms, 14 suites* *Restaurant, minibars, cable TV, in-room broadband, Wi-Fi, massage, spa, steam room, piano bar, library, Internet room, meeting rooms, parking (fee), no-smoking rooms; no a/c in some rooms* ▭ *AE, DC, MC, V* Ⓤ *Augsburger Str. (U-bahn).*

$$$$ **Kempinski Hotel Bristol Berlin.** Destroyed in the war and rebuilt in 1952, the "Kempi" is a historic Berlin classic with a great view of the Ku'damm scene from its restaurant. Tradition is personified in repeat guests and longtime employees. All rooms and suites are luxuriously decorated and have marble bathrooms. Use of the steam room and dry sauna is complimentary, but watch out for the breakfast charges. Children under 12 stay for free if they share their parents' room. The best shopping is at the hotel's doorstep, and it has some fine boutiques of its own. ✉ *Kurfürstendamm 27, Western Downtown, D–10719* ☎ *030/884–340* 🖷 *030/883–6075* 🌐 *www.kempinskiberlin.de* *249 rooms, 52 suites* *2 restaurants, room service, minibars, cable TV with movies and video games, in-room broadband, Wi-Fi, indoor pool, gym, hair salon, massage, sauna, steam room, bar, lobby lounge, shops, babysitting, dry cleaning, laundry service, concierge, business services, Internet room, meeting rooms, parking (fee), some pets allowed (fee), no-smoking floors* 💳 *AE, DC, MC, V* Ⓤ *Uhlandstr. (U-bahn).*

$$$–$$$$ **Steigenberger Berlin.** This exemplary hotel is very central, only steps from the Ku'damm, but remarkably quiet. Little things that can make your day are the umbrella on loan, extra-large towels, double sinks, and 24-hour room service. Bathrobes and a keyboard to access the Internet through the TV are available upon request; there's also wireless LAN. The sixth-floor Executive Club rooms include late check-out, ironing and shoe-shine service, and a lounge where complimentary breakfast and afternoon tea are served. Louis, the hotel's esteemed restaurant, is probably the only one in town fusing Japanese and Italian cuisine. ✉ *Los-Angeles-Pl. 1, Western Downtown, D–10789* ☎ *030/21270* 🖷 *030/212–7799* 🌐 *www.berlin.steigenberger.de* *386 rooms, 11 suites* *2 restaurants, room service, in-room safes, Wi-Fi, minibars, cable TV with movies and video games, pool, massage, sauna, piano bar, babysitting, dry cleaning, laundry service, concierge, Internet room, business services, meeting room, parking (fee), some pets allowed, no-smoking floor* 💳 *AE, DC, MC, V* Ⓤ *Augsburgerstr. (U-bahn), Kurfürstendamm (U-bahn).*

★ **$$$–$$$$** **Swissôtel Berlin.** At the bustling corner of Ku'damm and Joachimsthaler Strasse, this hotel excels with its reputable Swiss hospitality—from accompanying guests to their floor after check-in to equipping each room with an iron, an umbrella, and a Lavazza espresso machine that preheats the cups. Beds are specially designed to avoid allergens and provide maximum comfort. After using the wireless LAN, you can store and recharge your laptop in the room safe (the safe also charges cell phones). The unusual, rounded building has a sleek interior with a respected restaurant and original artwork by Marcus Lupertz. Your room's sound-proof windows give you a fantastic view of the city lights. ✉ *Augsburger Str. 44, Western Downtown, D–10789* ☎ *030/220–100* 🖷 *030/2201–02222* 🌐 *www.swissotel.com* *291 rooms, 25 suites* *Restaurant, room service, in-room safes, minibars, cable TV with movies and video games, in-room data ports, Wi-Fi, health club, hot tub, massage, sauna, steam room, bar, babysitting, dry cleaning, laundry service, concierge, Internet room, business services, meeting rooms, parking (fee), some pets allowed (fee), no-smoking floors* 💳 *AE, DC, MC, V.*

★ $$–$$$$ **Bleibtreu Berlin.** Opened in 1995, Berlin's first design hotel is as fresh as ever. Rooms are simple and serene, with untreated oak, polished stone, and neutral shades. The eye candy lies in the terra-cotta–tile courtyard that is secreted from the street, but still in front of the hotel. You can sip drinks at its 7-meter-long table, which is covered in shiny blue ceramic shards and rests on a bed of glass pebbles. A tall chestnut tree lends shade. To reinvigorate after shopping at the nearby boutiques, help yourself to the free items in your minifridge or slip into the herbal steam bath. ✉ *Bleibtreustr. 31, Western Downtown, D–10707* ☎ *030/884–740* 🖷 *030/8847–4444* 🌐 *www.bleibtreu.com* *60 rooms* *Restaurant, snack bar, room service, in-room fax, in-room safes, minibars, cable TV, in-room data ports, massage, steam room, bar, dry cleaning, laundry service, meeting room, no-smoking floor; no a/c* 💳 *AE, DC, MC, V* Ⓤ *Uhlandstr. (U-bahn).*

$–$$ **Hotel Astoria.** Each simple room in this small building dating to 1898 is different and the family owners are diligent about making renovations every year. When making a reservation, state whether you'd like a bathtub or shower and ask about weekend specials or package deals for longer stays. The fifth- and sixth-floor rooms have air-conditioning for an extra charge. Two terraces allow you to sun yourself and a stroll down the charming street leads to the shops along Ku'damm. Internet use is free in the lobby and wireless LAN is planned for the near future. ✉ *Fasanenstr. 2, Western Downtown, D–10623* ☎ *030/312–4067* 🖷 *030/312–5027* 🌐 *www.hotelastoria.de* *31 rooms, 1 suite* *Room service, in-room safes, minibars, cable TV with movies, bar, dry cleaning, laundry service, Internet room, parking (fee), some pets allowed; no a/c in some rooms* 💳 *AE, DC, MC, V* Ⓤ *Uhlandstr. (U-bahn), Zoologsicher Garten (U-bahn and S-bahn).*

★ $ **Hotel Bogota.** Fashion photography and hall lamps remind guests of the artists and designers who lived in this apartment house beginning in 1911. Each basic room is different, but they all share dated elements such as olive rotary phones, or sherbert combinations of bright red carpeting and mango-color walls. Triples and quads can be set up in these mostly high-ceiling rooms, children stay for free, and a warm breakfast is included. Doubles that have a shower but share a toilet with a second room range from €64–€84. Ask for a fourth-floor room. Special offers may be available in winter and for stays beginning on a Sunday night. ✉ *Schlüterstr. 45, Western Downtown, D–10707* ☎ *030/881–5001* 🖷 *030/883–5887* 🌐 *www.hotelbogota.de* *120 rooms, 60 with bath* *Lounge, Wi-Fi, no-smoking rooms; no a/c, no TV in some rooms* 💳 *AE, DC* 🍽 *BP* Ⓤ *Uhlandstr. (U-bahn).*

★ $ **Hotel-Pension Dittberner.** For traditional Berlin accommodations, this third-floor pension (with wooden elevator) run by Frau Lange since 1958 is the place to go. Close to Olivaer Platz and next to the Ku'damm, the turn-of-the-20th-century house shows its age, but the huge rooms are wonderfully furnished with antiques, plush stuffed sofas, and artwork selected by Frau Lange's husband, a gallery owner. The high ceilings have stucco work, and some rooms have balconies. Wi-Fi Internet access is available in the foyer. The pension received Berlin's "Most Friendly Hotel" award in 2002. ✉ *Wielandstr. 26, Western Downtown, D–10707*

☎ 030/884–6950 🖷 030/885–4046 🌐 *www.hotel-dittberner.de* *21 rooms, 1 suite* *Cable TV, Wi-Fi, laundry service, concierge, some pets allowed; no a/c* *CP* *No credit cards* *Adenauerpl. (U-bahn).*

Kreuzberg

$$ **Riehmers Hofgarten.** The appeal of this late-19th-century apartment house with a leafy courtyard is its location in a lively neighborhood marked by the streets Mehringdamm and Bergmannstrasse. The richly decorated facade hints that 100 years ago the aristocratic officers of Germany's imperial army lived here. Rooms with low-lying beds are spartanly modern, quiet, and functional. Downstairs is a light-filled lounge and restaurant. In less than five minutes you can reach the subway that speeds you to Mitte and the Friedrichstrasse train station. ✉ *Yorckstr. 83, Kreuzberg, D–10965* ☎ *030/7809–8800* 🖷 *030/7809–8808* 🌐 *www.riehmers-hofgarten.de* *22 rooms* *Restaurant, room service, cable TV, in-room broadband, Wi-Fi, bar, laundry service, parking (fee), some pets allowed (fee), no-smoking rooms; no a/c* *AE, MC, V* *CP* *Mehringdamm (U-bahn).*

¢–$ **Die Fabrik.** Near Kreuzberg's and Friedrichshain's alternative nightlife scene and a five-minute walk from the subway, this former factory building—solar powered—is perfect for those who place a priority on mixing with the local scene. Though this is a backpacker stop, basic double rooms and suites with carpeting and metal lockers are also available. To connect to the Internet, insert a euro into the computer at reception. Downside: there are no private bathrooms. Upside: there's a small courtyard with plants and the café is decent. Five doubles have a washbasin and double prices drop between November and February. ✉ *Schlesische Str. 18, Kreuzberg, D–10997* ☎ *030/611–7116* 🖷 *030/618–2974* 🌐 *www.diefabrik.com* *48 rooms without bath* *Café, Internet room; no a/c, no room phones, no room TVs* *No credit cards* *Schlesisches Tor (U-bahn).*

¢–$ **Eastern Comfort.** The Spree River is one of Berlin's best assets, and you'll wake up on it in this moored, three-level ship with simple cabins. First-class cabins for one or two people are on the middle deck, and the lower deck rooms can accommodate one to four guests; some cabins have a private bath. Your view is of either the river or the stretch of the Berlin Wall called the East Side Gallery. Within sight of the wraparound deck is the turreted Oberbaum bridge. The setting is great for watching the sunset, and is close to plenty of nightlife. The crew minds the reception desk 24 hours. ✉ *Mühlenstr. 73–77, Kreuzberg, D–10243* ☎ *030/6676–3806* 🖷 *030/6676–3805* 🌐 *www.eastern-comfort.com* *24 cabins* *Café, microwave, bar, lounge, some room TVs, Internet room, bicycles, laundry service; no a/c, no room phones, no smoking* *No credit cards* *Warschauer Str. (S- and U-bahn).*

Mitte

★ $$$$ **Grand Hyatt Berlin.** Europe's first Grand Hyatt is *the* address for entourages attending the Berlinale Film Festival in February. Stylish guests feel at home with a minimalist, Feng Shui–approved design that combines Japanese and Bauhaus elements. The large rooms (they start at 406 square feet) have cherrywood furniture and bathrooms that include tubs from which water can safely overflow onto the marble floor. The Premiere channel on your TV allows you to pick free movies and wireless Lan is available in public areas. You'll get a wonderful view of Potsdamer Platz from the top-floor pool. The restaurant and bar, Vox, whets guests' appetites for its international and Asian cuisine with a "show kitchen"; there's live jazz Monday–Saturday. ✉ *Marlene-Dietrich-Pl. 2, Mitte, D–10785* ☎ *030/2553–1234* 🖷 *030/2553–1235* 🌐 *www.berlin.grand.hyatt.com* *326 rooms, 16 suites* *2 restaurants, café, room service, in-room safes, minibars, room TVs with movies and video games, in-room broadband, pool, gym, massage, sauna, spa, bar, babysitting, dry cleaning, laundry service, concierge, business services, meeting room, parking (fee), some pets allowed (fee), no-smoking floor* 💳 *AE, DC, MC, V* Ⓤ *Potsdamer Pl. (U-bahn and S-bahn).*

$$$$ **Hotel Adlon Berlin.** Aside from its prime setting on Pariser Platz, the allure of the government's unofficial guesthouse is its almost mythical predecessor. Until its destruction during the war, the Hotel Adlon was considered Europe's ultimate luxury resort. Rebuilt in 1997, the hotel's elegant rooms are furnished in 1920s style with cherrywood trim, myrtle-wood furnishings, and brocade silk bedspreads. The large bathrooms are done in black marble. Book a suite for a Brandenburger Tor view. Sipping coffee in the lobby of creamy marble and limestone makes for good people-watching. Meetings at the nearby Reichstag or Chancellory sometimes continue with a meal at Lorenz Adlon. ✉ *Unter den Linden 77, Mitte, D–10117* ☎ *030/22610* 🖷 *030/2261–2222* 🌐 *www.hotel-adlon.de* *264 rooms, 121 suites* *3 restaurants, room service, in-room safes, minibars, cable TV with movies and video games, Wi-Fi, pool, health club, hair salon, massage, sauna, spa, bar, lobby lounge, shops, babysitting, dry cleaning, laundry service, concierge, business services, meeting room, parking (fee), some pets allowed (fee), no-smoking floor* 💳 *AE, DC, MC, V.*

★ **$$$$** **The Regent Berlin.** One of Germany's most esteemed hotels, the Regent pairs the opulence of gilt furniture, thick carpets, marble floors, tasseled settees, and crystal chandeliers with such modern conveniences as cell-phone rentals and flatscreen TVs. You'll be escorted to your large guest room, where you'll find first-class amenities, such as a DVD player. Twice-daily housekeeping, overnight dry cleaning, and valet parking are other services. The intimate feel of the property is a sign of its exclusiveness, and the privacy of the often famous guests is well guarded. ✉ *Charlottenstr. 49, Mitte, D–10117* ☎ *030/20338* 🖷 *030/2033–6119* 🌐 *www.regenthotels.com* *162 rooms, 42 suites* *Restaurant, room service, minibars, cable TV with movies and video games, in-room broadband, Web TV, gym, massage, sauna, bar, baby-sitting, dry cleaning, laundry service, concierge, business services, meeting room, parking (fee), some pets allowed (fee); no-smoking floors* 💳 *AE, DC, MC, V.*

$$–$$$$ **Hilton Berlin.** Old-fashioned elegance reigns in rooms with light colors, gold-frame watercolor paintings, and large art-deco desks. If you can't open your window to a view of Gendarmentmarkt, you can at least see the square from the breakfast room, where the rather pricey spread (€21) is delectable. Executive-floor guests enjoy a private lounge for breakfast and drinks, as well as late check-out privileges. Wireless LAN is available throughout the hotel. The state-of-the-art spa offers Ayurvedic massage and hot stone treatments. Another place to relax is the moodily lit Trader Vic's & Mai Tai Bar. ✉ *Mohrenstr. 30, Mitte, D–10117* ☎ *030/20230* 📠 *030/2023–4324* 🌐 *www.hilton.com* *589 rooms, 16 suites* *3 restaurants, 2 cafés, room service, minibars, cable TV with movies and video games, in-room data ports, Wi-Fi, pool, gym, hair salon, massage, sauna, spa, 2 bars, shops, babysitting, dry cleaning, laundry service, concierge, Internet room, business services, meeting room, parking (fee), some pets allowed (fee), no-smoking floors* 💳 *AE, DC, MC, V.*

$$$–$$$$ **Westin Grand Hotel.** This large hotel has a great location at the corner of Friedrichstrasse and Unter den Linden. Rooms have mustard-color, floral wallpaper, easy chairs, and the trademark Heavenly Bed found at all Westin hotels. The inner courtyard view is of an attractive garden area with an unusual Dragon House conference pagoda. Soundproof bay windows make for a good night's sleep in any room. The marble and brass lobby is light-filled and enlivened with a piano player and guests taking a coffee break at the sofas. ✉ *Friedrichstr. 158–164, Mitte, D–10117* ☎ *030/20270* 📠 *030/2027–3362* 🌐 *www.westin.com/berlin* *323 rooms, 35 suites* *2 restaurants, room service, in-room safes, minibars, room TVs with movies and video games, in-room broadband, Wi-Fi, pool, hair salon, hot tub, sauna, bar, lobby lounge, shops, babysitting, laundry service, concierge, business services, convention center, meeting room, parking (fee), some pets allowed (fee), no-smoking floor* 💳 *AE, DC, MC, V.*

★ **$$$** **Dorint Sofitel am Gendarmenmarkt.** Built before the Wall came tumbling down, this luxurious lodging has maximized that era's minimalist look. In the formerly austere conference room, the designers added an illuminated glass floor that made it a masterpiece. The spa tucked under the mansard roof is suffused with light, thanks to the new angled windows. Request a room facing Gendarmenmarkt, one of the city's most impressive squares. Decorative motifs are inspired by plant photographer Karl Blossfeldt, whose models inspired wrought-iron craftsmen. Toy-like bedside pull chains set off a short tinkling tune to send you off to sleep with. ✉ *Charlottenstr. 50–52, Mitte, D–10117* ☎ *030/203–750* 📠 *030/2037–5100* 🌐 *www.sofitel.com* *70 rooms, 22 suites* *Restaurant, room service, in-room safes, minibars, cable TV with movies and video games, in-room data ports, Wi-Fi, health club, massage, sauna, spa, steam room, laundry service, Internet room, business services, meeting room, no-smoking floors* 💳 *AE, DC, MC, V* U *Französische Str. (U-bahn).*

$$–$$$ **Alexander Plaza.** A modern refitting of this mercantile building compliments the original mosaic floor, tiled walls, and stairwells of stone, iron, and stuccowork. The hotel welcomes a mostly European, trendy clientele. The business center offers Internet access, and for €160–€200, you can get one of the suites in the turret. The hotel's entranceway has an exhibit on the significant Jewish history of the area. Automatic glass doors to the street reveal nearby landmarks including the late-20th-century Hackescher Markt train station, the TV tower (1969), and the 13th-century St. Marienkirche. ✉ *Rosenstr. 1, Mitte, D–10178* ☎ *030/240–010* 🖷 *030/2400–1777* 🌐 *www.hotel-alexander-plaza.de* *83 rooms, 9 suites* *Restaurant, room service, some kitchenettes, minibars, cable TV, Wi-Fi, gym, massage, sauna, steam bath, bar, babysitting, dry cleaning, laundry service, concierge, Internet room, business services, meeting rooms, parking (fee), some pets allowed (fee), no-smoking floors* 💳 *AE, DC, MC, V.*

$$–$$$ **Hotel Hackescher Markt.** Amid the nightlife around the Hackescher Markt, this hotel provides discreet and inexpensive first-class services. Unlike those of many older hotels in eastern Berlin, rooms here are spacious and light and furnished with wicker chairs and floral patterns in an English cottage style. In winter, you'll appreciate the under-floor heating in your bathroom, and in summer, you can enjoy a coffee in the small courtyard. The staff is friendly and attentive. Guests can use the gym of the Alexander Plaza hotel nearby. Wireless LAN is available in the bar area. ✉ *Grosse Präsidentenstr. 8, Mitte, D–10178* ☎ *030/280–030* 🖷 *030/2800–3111* 🌐 *www.hotel-hackescher-markt.de* *28 rooms, 3 suites* *Room service, in-room safes, minibars, cable TV, in-room data ports, bar, babysitting, dry cleaning, laundry service, parking (fee), some pets allowed (fee), no-smoking floor; no a/c* 💳 *DC, MC, V* Ⓤ *Hackescher Markt (S-bahn).*

$–$$$ **Park Inn.** A bird's-eye view of Berlin and a location above a main transportation hub are the draws of this 40-story high-rise with plenty of room for tour groups. Rooms have a cabinlike feel with low furnishings and narrow desks. The frosted glass walls in the bathrooms are a nice touch; not-so-usual amenities include a coffeemaker and an ironing board. Alexanderplatz is safe, but not scenic, and convenient to the museums along Unter den Linden and the neighborhoodlike streets of Mitte and Prenzlauer Berg. The casino on the 37th floor is open until 3 AM. ✉ *Alexanderpl., Mitte, D–10178* ☎ *030/23890* 🖷 *030/2389–4305* 🌐 *www.parkinn.com* *994 rooms, 12 suites* *2 restaurants, room service, snack bar, minibars, cable TV with movies, in-room data ports, Wi-Fi, gym, massage, sauna, bar, casino, babysitting, dry cleaning, laundry service, concierge, business services, meeting rooms, parking (fee), some pets allowed (fee), no-smoking floor; no a/c in some rooms* 💳 *AE, DC, MC, V.*

★ **$$** **Hotel Künstlerheim Luise.** This hotel's name, which means "home for artists," suggests a bohemian commune, but all the residents are paying guests. The Künstlerheim is one of Berlin's most original boutique hotels, with each fantastically creative room in the 1825 house or new wing—facing the Reichstag—styled by a different artist. Memorable furnishings range from a suspended bed and airplane seats to a gigantic sleigh bed and a free-standing, podlike shower with multiple nozzles. A lavish breakfast buffet in the neighboring restaurant costs €7. The hotel is a stretch from the Friedrichstrasse train station, but a convenient bus line stops outside the hotel. ✉ *Luisenstr. 19 Mitte, D–10117* ☎ *030/284–480* 🖷 *030/2844–8448* 🌐 *www.kuenstlerheim-luise.de* *44 rooms, 40 with bath, 2 suites* *Restaurant, cable TV, in-*

room data ports, dry cleaning, laundry service, some pets allowed, no-smoking rooms; no a/c in some rooms, no TV in some rooms ☰ *AE, DC, MC, V.*

$–$$ **Hotel Unter den Linden.** Within walking distance of Berlin's best attractions, this hotel's inexpensive room and parking rates are jaw-dropping. The well-kept rooms are somewhat small, but you'll have plenty of opportunity to stretch your legs at the nearby Friedrichstrasse shops and Unter den Linden's grand landmarks. You can also hop on the sightseeing bus that stops outside. For the best view of this central corner, join the mostly middle-age and older clientele in the restaurant. Drink machines on each floor replace minibars, and there's the quaint novelty of an ironing room. Wireless LAN is available on the ground floor. ✉ *Unter den Linden 14, Mitte, D–10017* ☎ *030/238–110* 🖷 *030/2381–1100* 🌐 *www.hotel-unter-den-linden.de* *331 rooms* *Restaurant, room service, cable TV, in-room data ports, bar, dry cleaning, laundry service, meeting rooms, parking (fee), no-smoking rooms* 🍽 *CP* ☰ *AE, DC, MC, V* Ⓤ *Friedrichstr. (S-bahn and U-bahn).*

$ **Hotel-Pension Kastanienhof.** The rooms in this small hotel in a 19th-century tenement house are simply furnished but spacious. An elevator serves the four floors and there are separate breakfast rooms for smokers and nonsmokers. You can dial up the Internet on an analog line in your room, or use the lobby's laptop for checking the Internet (€2 per 15 minutes). The Kastanienhof is well located for those bent on exploring the nightlife in Prenzlauer Berg and Mitte; note that reception and the tiny bar close at 10 PM, so don't misplace your key. ✉ *Kastanienallee 65, Prenzlauer Berg, D–10119* ☎ *030/443–050* 🖷 *030/4430–5111* 🌐 *www.hotel-kastanienhof-berlin.de* *32 rooms, 2 apartments, 1 suite* *In-room safes, minibar, cable TV, in-room data ports, bicycles, bar, meeting room, parking (fee), no-smoking rooms; no a/c* ☰ *AE, MC, V.*

¢ **Mitte's Backpacker Hostel.** Accommodations are simple but creative in this orange-painted hostel, and service goes the extra mile, with cheap bike rentals, free city maps, ticket services, and ride-sharing arrangements. Rooms—from doubles to girls-only sleepaways—are individually decorated. The location is convenient for both sightseeing and nightlife—in the evening you can opt to stay in for happy hour or a film. ✉ *Chausseestr. 102, Mitte, D–10115* ☎ *030/2839–0965* 🖷 *030/2839–0935* 🌐 *www.backpacker.de* *4 double rooms, 2 with bath; 2 singles, 4 quads, 1 triple, 9 dorm rooms* *Kitchen, bicycles, bar, lounge, laundry facilities, Internet room, travel services; no a/c, no room phones, no room TVs* ☰ *AE, MC, V.*

Tiergarten

¢ **Houseboat-Berlin.** It's rare to wake up in a city and watch water gently flowing one foot beneath your floor-to-ceiling window. Tiny as the bare-bone cabins are, being near the great outdoors of Tiergarten is the point. This houseboat community is also near civilization: an S-bahn stop and fun weekend flea market are a minute's walk away, and shops and restaurants 10 minutes farther. Two can snuggle on the small beds, and you can stretch out on the common-room couch or at its long wooden table. Bedding costs €7 during your stay; drinking water is included. Make reservations by e-mail and be advised that the boat is not always available for bookings; in that case, ⇨ see Eastern Comfort, their "botel" in Mitte. ✉ *Strasse des 17. Juni, houseboat 5, Tiergarten, D–10623* ☎ *No phone or fax* 🌐 *www.houseboat-berlin.com* 5 *rooms* *Kitchenette, lounge; no a/c, no room phones, no room TVs, no kids, no smoking* 💳 *No credit cards* ⏲ *Closed late Oct.–mid-Mar.* Ⓤ *Tiegarten (S-bahn).*

NIGHTLIFE & THE ARTS

The Arts

Today's Berlin has a tough time living up to the reputation it gained from the film *Cabaret*. In the 1920s it was said that in Berlin, if you wanted to make a scandal in the theater, you had to have a mother committing incest with *two* sons; one wasn't enough. Political gaffes are now the prime comic material for Berlin's cabarets. Even if nightlife has toned down since the 1920s and '30s, the arts and the avant-garde still flourish. Detailed information about events is covered in the *Berlin Programm,* a monthly tourist guide to Berlin arts, museums, and theaters. The magazines *Tip* and *Zitty,* which appear every two weeks, provide full arts listings (in German). For listings in English, consult the monthly *Ex-Berliner.*

The **Berlin Festival Weeks** (Kartenbüro ✉ Schaperstr. 24, D–10719 Berlin ☎ 030/254–890 📠 030/2548–9111 🌐 www.berlinerfestspiele.de), held annually from late August through September or early October, include concerts, operas, ballet, theater, and art exhibitions. For information and reservations, write **Berliner Festspiele.**

If your hotel can't book a seat for you or you can't make it to a box office directly, go to a ticket agency. Surcharges are 18–23 percent of the ticket. **Showtime Konzert- und Theaterkassen** (✉ KaDeWe, Tauentzienstr. 21, Western Downtown ☎ 030/217–7754 ✉ Wertheim, Kurfürstendamm 181, Western Downtown ☎ 030/882–2500) has offices within the major department stores. The **Theaterkasse Centrum** (✉ Meinekestr. 25, Western Downtown ☎ 030/882–7611) is a small agency but employs a very informed and helpful staff. The **Hekticket offices** (✉ Karl-Liebknecht-Str. 12, off Alexanderpl., Mitte ☎ 030/2431–2431 ✉ At Zoo-Palast, Hardenbergstr. 29d, Western Downtown ☎ 030/230–9930) offers discounted and last-minute tickets.

Concerts

Among the major symphony orchestras and orchestral ensembles in Berlin is one of the world's best, the Berlin Philharmonic Orchestra, which resides at the **Philharmonie mit Kammermusiksaal** (✉ Herbert-von-Karajan-Str. 1, Tiergarten ☎ 030/2548–8999). The Kammermusiksaal is dedicated to chamber music. Tickets sell out in advance for the nights when Sir Simon Rattle conducts the Berlin Philharmonic, but other orchestras and artists appear here as well. Free guided tours take place daily at 1 PM.

The beautifully restored hall at **Konzerthaus Berlin** (✉ Schauspielhaus, Gendarmenmarkt, Mitte ☎ 030/2030–92101 or 030/2030–92102) is a prime venue for classical music concerts. Its box office is open from noon to curtain time. A wide range of performances take the stage at the **Universität der Künste** (University of Arts; ✉ Hardenbergstr. at Fasanenstr., Charlottenburg ☎ 030/3185–2374). The box office is open Tuesday–Friday 3–6:30, and Saturday 11–2.

Dance, Musicals & Opera

Berlin's three opera houses also host guest productions and companies from around the world. Vladimir Malakhov, a principal guest dancer with New York's American Ballet Theatre, is a principal in the Staatsballett Berlin as well as its director. The company jetés their classic and modern productions between the Deutsche Oper in the west and the Staatsoper in the east. Of the 17 composers represented in the repertoire of **Deutsche Oper Berlin** (✉ Bismarckstr. 35, Charlottenburg ☎ 030/343–8401), Verdi is the most presented. Most of the operas are sung in German at the **Komische Oper** (✉ Behrenstr. 55–57, Mitte ☎ 030/4799–7400 or 01805/304–168). On the day of the performance, discount tickets are sold at the box office on Unter den Linden 41. Though renovated twice after bombings, the **Staatsoper Unter den Linden** (✉ Unter den Linden 7, Mitte ☎ 030/2035–4555 🌐 www.staatsoper-berlin.de) dates to 1743, when Frederick the Great oversaw productions. Maestro Daniel Barenboim oversees a diverse repertoire. Tickets can be as inexpensive as €7.

Sasha Waltz (born 1963) is the heir apparent to the still cutting-edge dance-theater choreographer Pina Bausch. Waltz's modern-dance troupe performs on the enormous stage of the **Schaubühne am Lehniner Platz** (✉ Kurfürstendamm 153, Western Downtown ☎ 030/890–023).

Musicals and dance extravaganzas are occasionally staged at the **Schiller-Theater** (✉ Bismarckstr. 110, Charlottenburg ☎ 0800/248–9842). The late-19th-century **Theater des Westens** (✉ Kantstr. 12, Western Downtown ☎ 030/882–2888), one of Germany's best musical theaters, features musicals such as *The Three Musketeers*.

In a white tentlike home beyond the ruined facade of Anhalter Bahnhof, the future of bankrupt **Tempodrom** (✉ Askanischer Pl. 4, Kreuzberg ☎ 030/6110–1313) is uncertain. It normally features international pop and rock stars. The **Tanzfabrik** (✉ Möckernstr. 68, Kreuzberg ☎ 030/786–5861) is still Berlin's best venue for young dance talents and the latest from Europe's avant-garde. **Hebbel am Ufer** (✉ Stresemann Str. 29, Kreuzberg ☎ 030/2590–0427) consists of three houses (Haus Eins, Zwei, Drei) within a five-minute walk of one another. Fringe theater, international modern dance, and solo performers share its stages.

Film

International and German movies are shown in the big theaters on Potsdamer Platz, and around the Ku'damm. If a film isn't marked "OF" or "OV" (*Originalfassung*, or original version) or "OmU" (original with subtitles), it's dubbed. Previews often run for 25 minutes, so don't worry if you're late. In February, theaters around Berlin host the **Internationale Filmfestspiele** (🌐 www.berlinale.de) , or Berlinale, a 10-day international festival at which the Golden Bear award is bestowed on the best films, directors, and actors. Individual tickets are first sold three days prior to a film's screening. Film buffs should purchase the season pass or accept shut-outs and third-choice films after hour-long waits at ticket outlets.

On a hard-to-find dead-end street, **Babylon** (✉ Dresdnerstr. 126, Kreuzberg ☎ 030/6160–9693) shows English-language films with German subtitles. You can reach Bablyon by cutting through a building overpass off Adalbertstrasse, near the Kottbusser Tor U-bahn station. Mainstream U.S., British, and other foreign productions are screened in their original versions at the sleek **CineStar im Sony Center** (✉ Potsdamer Str. 4, Tiergarten ☎ 030/2606–6400). Tuesday and Thursday are discount evenings.

Documentary films, international films in their original language, and German arthouse films are shown at **Hackesche Höfe** (✉ Rosenthaler Str. 40–41, Mitte ☎ 030/283–4603). There's no elevator to this top-floor moviehouse, but you can recover on the wide banquettes in the lounge.

Theater

Theater in Berlin is outstanding, but performances are usually in German. The exceptions are operettas and the (nonliterary) cabarets. The theater most renowned for both its modern and classical productions is the **Deutsches Theater** (✉ Schumannstr. 13a, Mitte ☎ 030/2844–1221 or 030/2844–1225). It has an excellent studio theater next door, the **Kammerspiele,** which has evolved as a thrilling playground for the country's most promising young directors, writers, and actors. The rebellious actors at the **Schaubühne am Lehniner Platz** (✉ Kurfürstendamm 153, Western Downtown ☎ 030/890–023), once the city's most experimental stage, have somewhat mellowed but are still up to great performances.

The excellent **Berliner Ensemble** (✉ Bertolt Brecht-Pl. 1, off Friedrichstrasse, just north of the train station, Mitte ☎ 030/2840–8155) is dedicated to Brecht and works of other international playwrights. The **Hebbel Theater** (✉ Stresemannstr. 29, Kreuzberg ☎ 030/2590–0427) showcases international theater and modern-dance troupes in three venues (HAU 1, 2, and 3). The **Renaissance-Theater** (✉ Hardenbergstr. 6, Charlottenburg ☎ 030/312–4202) shows German productions of international-hit dramatic plays. The **Volksbühne am Rosa-Luxemburg-Platz** (✉ Rosa-Luxemburg-Pl., Mitte ☎ 030/247–6772 or 030/247–7694) is unsurpassed for its aggressively experimental style, and Berliners often fill its 750 seats. The unusual building was reconstructed in the 1950s using the original 1914 plans. The program changes daily, and the name of the day's play is posted on a large banner outside the theater.

For children's theater head for the world-famous **Grips Theater** (✉ Altonaer Str. 22, Tiergarten ☎ 030/3974–7477), whose musical hit *Linie 1,* about life in Berlin viewed through the subway, is just as appealing for adults.

In a blackbox theater, the **Friends of Italian Opera** (✉ Fidicinstr. 40, Kreuzberg ☎ 030/691–1211 🌐 www.thefriends.de) presents dramas and comedies in English.

Variety Shows, Comedy & Cabaret

Berlin's variety shows can include magicians, circus performers, musicians, and classic cabaret stand-ups. A popular Berlin comedian and singer is American Gayle Tufts, famous for her mixing of the English and German language. Be aware that in order to understand and enjoy traditional cabaret, which involves a lot of political humor, your German has to be up to snuff. The intimate **Bar Jeder Vernunft** (✉ Schaperstr. 24, Wilmersdorf ☎ 030/883–1582) is housed within a glamorous tent and features solo entertainers and recently, the musical *Cabaret*. Within the Hackesche Höfe, the **Chamäleon Varieté** (✉ Rosenthaler Str. 40–41, Mitte ☎ 030/282–7118) is the most affordable and offbeat variety venue in town. German isn't required to enjoy most of the productions. Europe's largest variety show takes place at the **Friedrichstadtpalast** (✉ Friedrichstr. 107, Mitte ☎ 030/2326–2326), a glossy showcase for revues, famous for its leggy female dancers. Most of the guests seem to arrive via bus tours and package hotel deals. **Tipi das Zelt** (✉ Grosse Querallee, Tiergarten ☎ 0180/327–9358) is a tent venue between the Kanzleramt (Chancellor's Office) and Haus der Kulturen der Welt. Artists featured are well suited for an international audience and you can opt to dine here before the show. Even the back row seats are good. The **Wintergarten Varieté** (✉ Potsdamer Str. 96, Tiergarten ☎ 030/2500–8888) pays romantic homage to the old days of Berlin's original variety theater in the 1920s.

Social and political satire has a long tradition in cabaret theaters. The **BKA–Berliner Kabarett Anstalt** (✉ Mehringdamm 34, Kreuzberg ☎ 030/202–2007) features not only guest performances by Germany's leading young comedy talents but also *Chanson* vocalists.

Nightlife

Berlin's nightspots are open to the wee hours of the morning, but if you stay out after 12:45 Monday–Thursday or Sunday, you'll have to find a night bus line or the last S-bahn to get you home. On Friday and Saturday, most subway lines run every 15 to 20 minutes throughout the night. Clubs often switch the music they play nightly, so their crowds and popularity can vary widely. Though club nights are driven by the DJ name, the music genres are written in English in listing magazines.

The happening places in western Berlin are around Savignyplatz in Charlottenburg, Nollendorfplatz and Winterfeldplatz in Schöneberg, Ludwigkirchplatz in Wilmersdorf, and along Oranienstrasse and Wienerstrasse in Kreuzberg, as well as Lützowplatz in Tiergarten. In Mitte most of the action radiates off Rosenthaler Platz and the Hackesche Höfe. Kastanienallee and Helmholzplatz are the hubs in Prenzlauer Berg.

Clubs and bars in downtown western Berlin tend to be dressier and more conservative; the scene in Kreuzberg, Prenzlauer Berg, Mitte, and Friedrichshain is laid-back, alternative, grungy, and only occasionally stylish. For the latest information on Berlin's bustling house, electro, and hip-hop club scene, pick up *(030)*, a free weekly.

Bars

In Germany the term *Kneipen* is used for down-to-earth bars that are comparable to English pubs. These places are pretty simple and laid-back; you probably shouldn't try to order a three-ingredient cocktail at one unless you spot a lengthy drink menu.

The most elegant bars and lounges are in western downtown Berlin, and though not frequented by Berliners, Berlin's four-star hotels provide stylish, seductive settings. The cocktail menu is the size of a small guidebook at **Bar am Lützowplatz** (✉ Am Lützowpl. 7, Tiergarten ☎ 030/262–6807), where an attractive, professional crowd lines the long blond-wood bar. The Grand Hotel Esplanade's **Harry's New-York Bar** (✉ Am Lützowufer 15, Tiergarten ☎ 030/2547–88633) is the best hotel bar in town. In good weather, you can sit outside and watch moneyed guests make their entrance into the hotel. A pianist entertains Monday–Saturday. Old-World **E. & M. Leydicke** (✉ Mansteinstr. 4, Schöneberg ☎ 030/216–2973) is a must for out-of-towners. The proprietors operate their own distillery and have a superb selection of sweet wines and liqueurs. Shabby **Kumpelnest 3000** (✉ Lützowstr. 23, Tiergarten ☎ 030/261–6918) has a reputation as wild as its carpeted walls. It's the traditional last stop of the evening, and both gays and heteros mingle on the tiny dance floor. There's no tap beer.

A mature crowd who wants to concentrate on conversation and appreciating outstanding cocktails heads to **Green Door** (✉ Winterfeldstr. 50, Schöneberg ☎ 030/215–2515), a Schöneberg classic with touches of kitsch that lighten the mood. Now the oldest posh bar in Mitte, marble-lined **Newton** (✉ Charlottenstr. 57, Mitte ☎ 030/2029–5421) flaunts Helmut Newton's larger-than-life photos of nude women across its walls. Upstairs is a cigar lounge. Subterranean **Lola Lounge** (✉ Rosa-Luxemburg-Str. 17, Mitte ☎ 030/2759–4430) discreetly heralds the arrival of the "see and be seen set" in the former East. Make a reservation to avoid a wait for a seat. The low stools at center stage are circled by a canvas top like a sultan's tent. The overall design is seductive down to the sink the men's and women's bathroom share. The lounge is closed Sunday through Tuesday.

Groups of friends fill the tables, battle at foozball tables, and dance in the small back room at **August Fengler** (✉ Lychner Str. 11, Prenzlauer Berg ☎ 030/4435–6640). On weekends the place is packed. If there's no room, head further up the street to the bars around Hemholtzplatz. Sitting canalside on a deckchair at **Freischwimmer** (✉ Vor dem Schlesischen Tor 2a, Kreuzberg ☎ 030/6107–4309) is perfect for warm nights, but heat lamps and an enclosed section make a cozy setting on cool ones, too. To get here, walk five minutes south of the Schlesisches Tor subway station and turn left down a path after the gas station. It opens at 6 PM during the week in winter; and at noon in warmer months. Year-round, weekends begin at 11 AM. There's another bar with a floating dock across the way.

Casinos

On Potsdamer Platz, **Spielbank Berlin** (✉ Marlene-Dietrich-Pl. 1, Tiergarten ☎ 030/255–990 🌐 www.spielbank-berlin.de) is Berlin's posher casino. You can try your luck at roulette tables, three blackjack tables, and slot machines from 2 PM to 3 AM. The **Casino Berlin** (✉ Alexanderpl., Mitte ☎ 030/2389–4113 🌐 www.casino-berlin.de) is located on the 37th floor of the Park Inn. It's worth blowing a few euros for the view.

Clubs

Perhaps the only nonmainstream club in western Berlin, **Big Eden** (✉ Kurfürstendamm 202, Western Downtown ☎ 030/882–6120) points the way with a huge, flashing red-and-white sign. Curving booths and huge cushions are perfect for taking in the bands or revues that sometimes usher in the evening. Many nights are gay parties, and others feature rhythm and bass or electro-trash. The decor is an eyeful of mirrors and tube lighting.

14

More like a lounge than a club, **Delicious Doughnuts** (✉ Rosenthaler Str. 9, Mitte ☎ 030/283–3021) has a small dance floor and its layout is fairly conducive for mingling.

Thursday through Saturday, the docked boat **Hoppetosse** (✉ Eichenstr. 4, Treptow ☎ 030/4171–5437) rocks steady to reggae and dancehall, house, techno, or hip-hop. Just south of Kreuzberg, it's a bit out of the way, but you get a fantastic Spree Canal view from either the lower-level dance floor or the top deck.

The tiered, white chill-out area is much larger than the dance floor at **90 Grad** (✉ Dennewitzstr. 37, Tiergarten ☎ 030/2300–5954), but the resident DJ could pack more dancers onto the floor if only the doormen weren't so particular. German MTV has held DJ battles here and Hollywood stars tend to drop by. The place really gets going around 2 AM. **Bastard** (✉ Kastanienallee 7–9, Prenzlauer Berg ☎ 030/448–5688), the club next to the beer garden Prater, presents bands before dancers work off their energy with indie music and Brit pop. **Sage-Club** (✉ Köpenicker Str. 78, Mitte ☎ 030/278–9830) is the most popular of Berlin's venues for young professionals who dance to hip-hop, house, and some techno. On some nights it can be tough getting past the man with the "by invitation only" list.

Gay & Lesbian Bars

Berlin is unmistakably Germany's gay capital, and many Europeans come to partake in the diverse scene, which is concentrated in Schöneberg (around Nollendorfplatz) and Kreuzberg. Check out the magazines *Siegessäule, (030),* and *Sergej* (free and available at the places listed below as well as at many other locations around town).

Close to Wittenbergplatz, the dance club **Connection** (✉ Fuggerstr. 33, Schöneberg ☎ 030/218–1432) provides heavy house music and lots of dark corners. The decor and the energetic crowd at **Hafen** (✉ Motzstr. 18, Schöneberg ☎ 030/211–4118) make it ceaselessly popular and a favorite singles mixer. At 4 AM people move next door to Tom's Bar, open until 6 AM. A gay thirtysomething crowd frequents the upscale **Lenz** (✉ Eisenacher Str. 3, Schöneberg ☎ 030/217–7820).

You can get extensive information on gay life, groups, and events at **Mann-O-Meter** (✉ Bülowstr. 106, Schöneberg ☎ 030/216–8008). Talks are held in the café, which has a variety of books and magazines. It's open weekdays 3–11, Saturday 3–10. If you don't bump up against any eye candy at tiny **Roses** (✉ Oranienstr. 187, Kreuzberg ☎ 030/615–6570) there's always the furry red walls and kitschy paraphernalia to admire. It opens at 10 PM. **Schwuz** (✉ Mehringdamm 61, Kreuzberg ☎ 030/693–7025) consists of two dance floors underneath the laid-back café Melitta Sundström. Eighties music and house are the normal fare.

Jazz Clubs

A-Trane Jazzclub (✉ Bleibtreustr. 1, Charlottenburg ☎ 030/313–2550 🌐 www.a-trane.de), on the corner of Pestalozzistrasse, also has nights for electronic jazz, Afro-Cuban music, and "the art of duo." With no columns to obstruct your view, you can see young German artists almost every night at **B-Flat** (✉ Rosenthaler Str. 13, Mitte ☎ 030/280–6349). The Wednesday jam sessions focus on free and experimental jazz. On Sunday, dancers come for tango night. Snacks are available. **Quasimodo** (✉ Kantstr. 12a, Charlottenburg ☎ 030/312–8086 🌐 www.quasimodo.de), the most established and popular jazz venue in the city, has a college-town pub feel in its basement. Seats are few.

SPORTS & THE OUTDOORS

Berlin's famous sports attraction is the 1936 **Olympic Stadium** that received a thorough modernization in 2004. American sprinter Jesse Owens won the gold medals in 1936; lately it's the Berlin Thunder, a mixed nationality team playing American football in the European league, who are the champions of the stadium. Local soccer team Hertha BSC doesn't do quite as well. In June and July 2006 the stadium hosts World Cup–soccer matches, including the final. These sure to be sold-out games take place on June 15, 16, 20, 23, 30; the final is July 7. Various tours are offered throughout the year; one option is touring on your own with an audioguide (€6). ✉ *Olympischer Platz 3 Charlottenburg* ☎ *030/2500–2322* 🎫 *€2, tours €6–€10* 🕓 *Daily general tour at 11, 1, 3, and 5, but open times vary, so call ahead* 🌐 *www.olympiastadion-berlin.de* Ⓤ *Olympiastadion (U-bahn).*

Biking

Bike paths are generally marked by red pavement or white markings on the sidewalks. Be careful when walking on bike paths or crossing them. Many stores that rent or sell bikes carry the Berlin biker's atlas. **Fahrradstation** (✉ Friedrichstrasse train station, Mitte ☎ 030/2045–4500 ✉ Hackesche Höfe, Rosenthaler Str. 40–41, Mitte ☎ 030/2838–4848 🌐 www.fahrradstation.de) rents bikes for €10–€25 per day (12 hours), or €25 for three days. Bring ID and call for its other locations. **Fahrrad Vermietung Berlin** (✉ Kurfürstendamm 236, Western Downtown ☎ 030/261–2094) rents black bikes with baskets that it keeps in front of the

Marmorhaus movie theater, opposite the Gedächtniskirche. Rates are €10 a day, and you must leave either a €50 deposit or ID as security.

Jogging

The Tiergarten is the best place for jogging in the downtown area. Run down the paths parallel to Strasse des 17. Juni and back, and you'll have covered 8 km (5 mi). Joggers can also take advantage of the grounds of Charlottenburg Palace, 3 km (2 mi) around. For longer runs, make for the forest Grunewald.

Soccer

The **2006 FIFA World Cup** (✉ Olympic Stadium, Olympischer Platz 3 Charlottenburg ☎ 1805/262–006 ⊕ www.fifaworldcup.com Ⓤ Olympiastadion [U-bahn], the world s soccer championship, is being held in 10 cities in Germany, including 6 matches in Berlin s Olympic Stadium between June 12 and the final on July 9. Get online as soon as possible to apply for tickets, which began distribution in lottery form in April 2005.

Swimming

Public pools throughout the city cost €4 for a day pass. For full listings ask at the tourist office or navigate (in German) www.berlinerbaederbetriebe.de. The lakes Wannsee, Halensee, Müggelsee, and Plötzensee all have beaches. The huge **Strandbad Wannsee** (✉ Wannseebad-weg 25, Zehlendorf ☎ 030/803–5612) attracts as many as 40,000 Berliners to its fine, sandy beach on summer weekends. The **Sommerbad Olympiastadion** (✉ Olympischer Pl. 1, Charlottenburg ☎ 030/6663–1142 Ⓤ Olympiastadion [U-bahn and S-bahn]) was made for the 1936 Olympic games and includes a separate area with three diving platforms. It's open late May to late August, daily 7–8. The **Blub Badeparadies lido** (✉ Buschkrugallee 64, Neuköulln ☎ 030/606–6060 Ⓤ Grenzallee [U-bahn]) has indoor and outdoor pools, a sauna garden, hot whirlpools, and a solarium. A 1½-hour card costs €8.20–€9.20; to include the sauna landscape costs extra.

SHOPPING

What's fashionable in Berlin is creative, bohemian style, so designer labels have less appeal here than in Hamburg, Düsseldorf, or Munich. Young people seem to spend more money on cell-phone cards than clothing.

Shopping Districts

Charlottenburg

Although Ku'damm is still touted as the shopping mile of Berlin, many shops are ho-hum retailers. The best stretch for exclusive fashions, such as Bruno Magli, Hermès, and Jil Sander, are the three blocks between Leibniz Strasse and Bleibtreustrasse. For home furnishings, gift items, and unusual clothing boutiques, follow this route off Ku'damm: Leibniz Strasse to Mommsenstrasse to Bleibtreustrasse, then on to the ring around Savignyplatz. Fasanenstrasse, Knesebeckstrasse, Schlüterstrasse, and Uhlandstrasse are also fun places to browse.

Ku'damm ends at Breitscheidplatz but the door-to-door shopping continues along Tauentzienstrasse, which, in addition to international retail stores, offers Europe's largest department store, the upscale Kaufhaus des Westens, or KaDeWe.

Mitte

The finest shops in historic Berlin are along Friedrichstrasse, including the French department store, Galeries Lafayette. Nearby, Unter den Linden has just a few souvenir shops and a Meissen ceramic showroom. Smaller clothing and specialty stores populate the Scheunenviertel. The area between Hackescher Markt, Weinmeister Strasse, and Rosa-Luxemburg-Platz alternates pricey independent designers with groovy secondhand shops. Neue Schönhauser Strasse curves into Alte Schönhauser Strasse and both streets are full of stylish casual wear. Galleries along Gipsstrasse and Sophienstrasse round out the mix.

Department Stores & Arcades

The smallest and most luxurious department store in town, **Department Store Quartier 206** (✉ Friedrichstr. 71, Mitte ☎ 030/2094–6240) offers primarily French women's and men's designer clothes, perfumes, and home accessories. Intimate and elegant, **Galeries Lafayette** (✉ Französische Str. 23, Mitte ☎ 030/209–480) carries almost exclusively French products, including designer clothes, perfume, and all the produce you might need for preparing haute cuisine at home. Anchoring Alexanderplatz, **Galeria Kaufhof** (✉ Alexanderpl. 9, Mitte ☎ 030/247–430 🌐 www.kaufhof.de) is the most successful branch of the German chain, though the wares are fairly basic.

The largest department store in Europe, classy **Kaufhaus des Westens** (KaDeWe; ✉ Tauentzienstr. 21, Western Downtown ☎ 030/21210 🌐 www.kadewe.de) surpasses even London's Harrods. It has a grand selection of goods on seven floors, as well as food and deli counters, champagne bars, beer bars, and a winter garden on its two upper floors. Its wealth of services includes fixing umbrellas and repairing leather and furs.

Similar to an American mall, the three-tiered **Potsdamer Platz Arkaden** (✉ Alte Potsdamer Str. 7, Tiergarten ☎ 030/255–9270) has shops such as Benetton, H & M, Esprit, Eddie Bauer, an Ampelmann gift store and reputedly the best gelato café in Berlin. All the upscale shops on the four floors of **Stilwerk** (✉ Kantstr. 17, Charlottenburg ☎ 030/315–150 🌐 www.stilwerk.de/berlin) cater to stylish home furnishings and accessories. **Wertheim** (✉ Kurfürstendamm 181, Western Downtown ☎ 030/883–8152) is neither as big nor as attractive as KaDeWe but offers a large selection of fine wares.

Gift Ideas

All the books, maps, and souvenirs focus on the city at **Berlin Story** (✉ Unter den Linden 40, Mitte ☎ 030/2045–3842), which is even open on Sunday. Fine porcelain is still produced by **Königliche Porzellan Manufaktur** (✉ Kurfürstendamm 27, Western Downtown ☎ 030/886–7210

⊠ Unter den Linden 35, Mitte ☎ 030/206–4150 ⊠ Factory salesroom, Str. des.17 Juni, Tiergarten ☎ 030/3900–9215), the former Royal Prussian Porcelain Factory, also called KPM. You can buy this delicate handmade, hand-painted china at KPM's two stores, but it may be more fun to visit the factory salesroom, which also sells seconds at reduced prices. Kitschy props, costumes, and imitation antiques from the Komische Oper and other theaters are on sale at **Kunstsalon** (⊠ Unter den Linden 41, Mitte ☎ 030/2045–0203).

Puppenstube im Nikolaiviertel (⊠ Propststr. 4, Mitte ☎ 030/242–3967) is the ultimate shop for any kind of (mostly handmade) dolls, including designer models as well as old-fashioned German dolls. It's for collectors, not kids. Tucked under the elevated train tracks, **Scenario** (⊠ Savignypassage, Bogen 602, Western Downtown ☎ 030/312–9199) sells stationery articles, gifts of any kind, and a lot of leather wares and jewelry. The designs here are modern. In the homey setting of **Wohnart Berlin** (⊠ Uhlandstr. 179–180, Western Downtown ☎ 030/882–5252) you can imagine how the stylish European furnishings, lamps, housewares, or stationery items might suit your own pad.

Specialty Stores

Antiques

Not far from Wittenbergplatz lies Keithstrasse, a street full of antiques stores. Eisenacher Strasse, Fuggerstrasse, Kalckreuthstrasse, Motzstrasse, and Nollendorfstrasse—all close to Nollendorfplatz—have many antiques stores of varying quality. Another good street for antiques is Suarezstrasse, between Kantstrasse and Bismarckstrasse. Other antiques stores are found under the tracks from Friedrichstrasse station east to Universitätsstrasse, open Monday and Wednesday–Sunday 11–6.

On weekends from 10 to 5, the lively **Berliner Trödelmarkt und Kunstmarkt** (Berlin Flea and Art Market) on Strasse des 17. Juni swings into action. The flea-market stands are nearer the Tiergarten S-bahn station; the handicrafts begin past the Charlottenburg gates. **Villa Grisebach** (⊠ Fasanenstr. 25, Western Downtown ☎ 030/885–9150 🌐 www.villa-grisebach.de), one of the city's most classic arts and antiques auction houses, also hosts exhibitions and special events at which you can buy paintings.

Jewelry

Bucherer (⊠ Kurfürstendamm 26a, Western Downtown ☎ 030/880–4030 🌐 www.bucherer.de) carries fine handcrafted jewelry, watches, and other stylish designer accessories. German designers featured at **Klaus Kaufhold** (⊠ Kurfürstendamm 197, Western Downtown ☎ 030/8847–1790) share a philosophy of sleek minimalism. Rubber and diamond rings and matte platinum and diamond pieces are conscious understatements.

Men's Clothing

For guys who envy the diversity of wares offered to gals, **Boyz 'R' Us** (⊠ Maassenstr. 8, Schöneberg ☎ 030/2363–0640) is your chance to grab a pink-gingham shirt or spangled turquoise top. Patterned jeans and loud tartan pants make this store a magnet for gay and straight clubbers. The

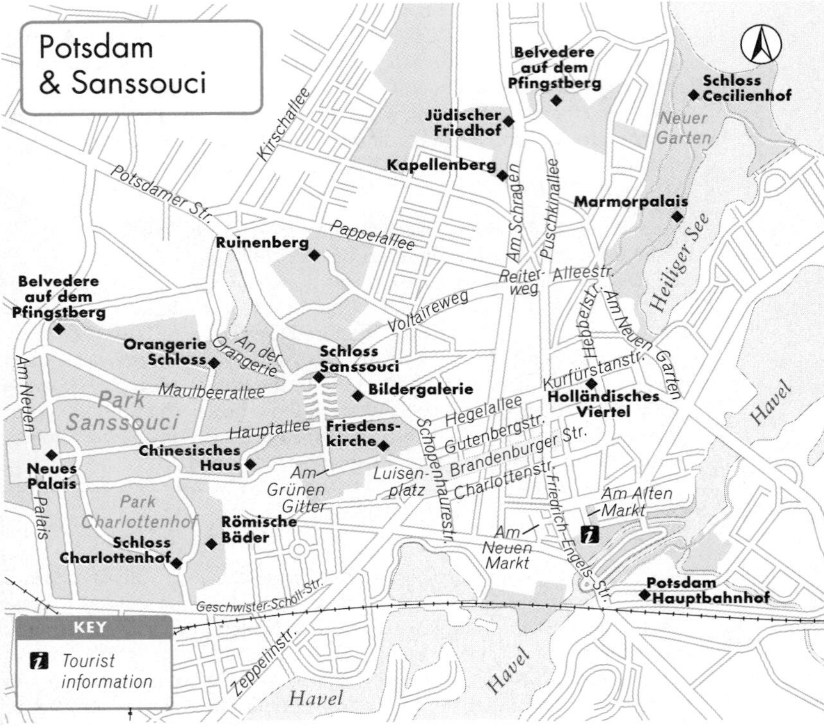

most sought-after German label here is Kresse Hamburg. Handmade and timeless shoes and brogues, mostly from England, Austria, and Hungary, are sold at **Budapester Schuhe** (✉ Kurfürstendamm 199, Western Downtown ☎ 030/881–1707 ✉ Friedrichstr. 81, Mitte ☎ 030/2038–8110). The gentlemen's outfitter **Mientus** (✉ Wilmersdorfer Str. 73, Western Downtown ☎ 030/323–9077 ✉ Kurfürstendamm 52, Western Downtown ☎ 030/323–9077) stocks Armani, Versace Classic, and Boss and has an in-house tailor. The Wilmersdorfer Strasse location offers free parking for customers.

Women's Clothing

The designs of **Anette Petermann** (✉ Bleibtreustr. 49, Western Downtown ☎ 030/323–2556) are a delight of Berlin haute couture. Roses are her trademark; you'll find fabric buds sewn into pinstripe jackets or taffeta stoles. Crushed organza evening wear or functional wool and fur are popular with local celebrities. The creations of Berlin's top avant-garde designer, **Claudia Skoda** (✉ Alte Schönhauser Str. 35, Mitte ☎ 030/280–7211), are mostly for women, but there's also men's knitwear. The flagship store of German designer **Jil Sander** (✉ Kurfürstendamm 185, Western Downtown ☎ 030/886–7020) carries her complete line of understated clothing. **Peek und Cloppenburg**

(✉ Tauentzienstr. 19, Western Downtown ☎ 030/212–900), or "P and C," stocks women's, men's, and children's clothes on five floors. Don't miss the Joop! designer store on the top floor and the international designer department in the basement.

SIDE TRIP FROM BERLIN

A trip to Berlin wouldn't be complete without paying a visit to Potsdam and its park, which surrounds the Prussian palaces Neue Palais and Sanssouci. This separate city, which was in East Germany, can be reached within a half hour from Berlin's Zoo Station.

Potsdam

Potsdam still retains the imperial character it earned during the many years it served as a royal residence and garrison quarters. The Alter Markt and Neuer Markt show off stately Prussian architecture, and both are easily reached from the main train station by any tram heading into the town center. Karl Friedrich Schinkel designed the Alter Markt's domed **Nikolaikirche.** In front of it stands an Egyptian obelisk erected by Schloss Sanssouci architect von Knobelsdorff. A gilded figure of Atlas tops the tower of the old **Rathaus,** built in 1755. The region's history museum, the **Haus der Brandenburg-Preussischen Geschichte,** is in the royal stables in the square opposite the Nikolaikirche. ✉ *Am Neuen Markt* ☎ *0331/620–8549* 🌐 *www.hbpg.de* 🎫 *€4, €7.50 combined with special exhibits* ⏲ *Tues. and Thurs.–Sun. 11–6, Wed. 11–8.*

The center of the small **Holländisches Viertel** (Dutch Quarter) is an easy walk north along Friedrich-Ebert-Strasse to Mittelstrasse. Friedrich Wilhelm I built the settlement in 1732 to entice Dutch artisans who could support the city's rapid growth. Few Dutch came, and the gabled, mansard-roof brick houses were largely used to house staff. Stores and restaurants inhabit the buildings now, and the area is Potsdam's most visited.

need a break?

Fine coffee blends and rich cakes are offered at the **Wiener Restaurant-Café** (✉ Luisenpl. 4 ☎ 0331/967–8314), an old-style European coffeehouse on the way to the Grünes Gitter entrance to Sanssouci. A favorite cake here is the *Sanssouci-Torte.*

Prussia's most famous king, Friedrich II—Frederick the Great—spent more time at his summer residence, **Schloss Sanssouci,** than in the capital of Berlin. Its name means "without a care" in French, the language Frederick cultivated in his own private circle and within the court. Some experts believe Frederick actually named the palace "Sans, Souci," which they translate as "with and without a care," a more apt name; its construction caused him a lot of trouble and expense and sparked furious rows with his master builder, Georg Wenzeslaus von Knobelsdorff. His creation nevertheless became one of Germany's greatest tourist attractions. The palace lies on the edge of Park Sanssouci, which includes various buildings and palaces with separate admissions and hours.

Be advised that during peak tourism times, timed tickets for Schloss Sanssouci tours can sell out before noon.

Executed according to Frederick's impeccable French-influenced taste, the palace, built between 1745 and 1747, is extravagantly rococo, with scarcely a patch of wall left unadorned. Leading up to the building is an unusual formal terrace where wine was once cultivated. To the west of the palace are the **Neue Kammern** (New Chambers; ☎ 0331/969–4206 🎟 €2, guided tour €3 ⏲ late Mar.–mid-May, weekends 10–5; mid-May–Oct., Tues.–Sun. 10–5), which housed guests of the king's family after its beginnings as a greenhouse. Just east of Sanssouci Palace is the **Bildergalerie** (Picture Gallery; ☎ 0331/969–4181 🎟 €2 ⏲ mid-May–mid-Oct., Tues.–Sun. 10–5), with expensive marble from Siena in the main cupola. The gallery displays Frederick's collection of 17th-century Italian and Dutch paintings, including works by Caravaggio, Rubens, and Van Dyck. ✉ *Park Sanssouci* ☎ *0331/969–4202 or 0331/969–4190* 🌐 *www.spsg.de* 🎟 *Guided tour €8; park free. Two-day card for all Berlin area palaces €15 (only available here)* ⏲ *Late Mar.–Oct., Tues.–Sun. 9–5; Nov.–late Mar., Tues.–Sun. 9–4.*

★ The **Neues Palais** (New Palace), a much larger and grander palace than Sanssouci, stands at the end of the long avenue that runs through Sanssouci Park. It was built after the Seven Years' War (1756–63), when Frederick loosened the purse strings. It's said he wanted to demonstrate that the state coffers hadn't been depleted too severely by the long conflict. Interiors that impress include the grotto hall with walls and columns set with shells, coral, and other aquatic decor. The royals' upper apartments have paintings by 17th-century Italian masters. Even if the tour is German, you can borrow a good English guide to follow along with. You can opt to tour the palace yourself only on weekends between late March and mid-May. ✉ *Strasse am Neuen Palais, Sanssouci* ☎ *0331/969–4255* 🌐 *www.spsg.de* 🎟 *Late Mar.–Oct., €5, €6 with tour; Nov.–late Mar., €5 with tour* ⏲ *Late Mar.–Oct., Sat.–Thurs. 10–5; Nov.–late Mar., Sat.–Thurs. 9–4.*

Schloss Charlottenhof (☎ 0331/969–4228 🎟 €4 with tour ⏲ Easter week and mid-May–mid-Oct., Tues.–Sun. 10–5) is in the southern part of Sanssouci Park. After Frederick the Great died in 1786, the ambitious Sanssouci building program ground to a halt, and the park fell into neglect. It was 50 years before another Prussian king, Friedrich Wilhelm IV, restored Sanssouci's earlier glory. He engaged the great Berlin architect Karl Friedrich Schinkel to build this small palace for the crown prince. Schinkel's demure interiors are preserved and the most fanciful room is the bedroom, decorated like a Roman tent, with its walls and ceiling draped in striped canvas.

Between the Sanssouci palaces are later additions to the park. In 1836 Friedrich Wilhelm IV built the **Römische Bäder** (Roman Baths; 🎟 €2, €3 with exhibit ⏲ mid-May–mid-Oct., Tues.–Sun. 10–5). The **Orangerieschloss und Turm** (🎟 guided tour €3, tower only €1 ⏲ palace and tower open mid-May–mid-Oct., Tues.–Sun. 10–5; tower only open late Mar.–mid-May, weekends 10–5) was completed in 1860; its two massive towers linked by a colonnade evoke an Italian Renaissance palace. Today it houses 47 copies of paintings by Raphael. The **Chinesisches Teehaus** (Chinese Teahouse; €1 mid-May–mid-Oct., Tues.–Sun. 10–5) was erected in 1757 in the Chinese style, which was all the rage at the time, and houses porcelain from Meissen and Asia. Completed in 1848, the Italianate **Friedenskirche** (Peace Church; 0331/969–4228 Free late Mar.–Apr. and first 2 wks in Oct., Mon.–Sat. 11–5, Sun. noon–5; May–Sept., Mon.–Sat. 10–6, Sun. noon–6) houses a 12th-century Byzantine mosaic taken from an island near Venice.

need a break?

Halfway up the park's Drachenberg Hill, above the Orangerie, stands the curious **Drachenhaus** (Dragon House), modeled in 1770 after the Pagoda at London's Kew Gardens and named for the gargoyles ornamenting the roof corners. It now houses a popular café.

14

Resembling a rambling, Tudor manor house, **Schloss Cecilienhof** (Cecilienhof Palace) was built for Crown Prince Wilhelm in 1913, on a newly laid-out stretch of park called the New Garden, which borders the Heiliger See. It was in this last palace built by the Hohenzollerns that the Allied leaders Truman, Attlee, and Stalin hammered out the fate of postwar Germany at the 1945 Potsdam Conference. From Potsdam's main train station, take a tram to Reiterweg/Alleestrasse, and then transfer to Bus 692 to Am Neuer Garten. *0331/969–4244 www.spsg.de €4, € 5 with tour; tour of prince's private rooms €3 Late Mar.–Oct., Tues.–Sun. 9–5; Nov.–late Mar., Tues.–Sun. 9–4. Tours of prince's rooms at 11, 1, and 3.*

On a hill near Schloss Cecilienhof, the colonnaded **Belvedere auf dem Pfingstberg** was a lofty observation platform for the royals. Farther down the hill is the simple **Pomonatempel** (Apr.–Oct., weekends 3–6), the first building built by Karl Friedrich Schinkel (1801). *Am Pfingstberg 0331/2701972 www.spsg.de €3.50 Apr., May, Sept., daily 10–6; June–Aug, daily 10–8; Oct., daily 10–4; Mar. and Nov., weekends 10–4.*

Where to Stay & Eat

$$–$$$ **Juliette.** In a city proud of its past French influences, the highly praised French cuisine here is delivered to your table by French waiters, no less. The intimate restaurant at the edge of the Dutch Quarter has old-fashioned brick walls and a fireplace. The menu offers small portions of dishes such as rack of lamb, wild hare pie with hot peppered cherries, and a starter plate of four foie gras preparations. Its wine list of 120 French vintages is unique in the Berlin area. Potsdam's proximity to the Babelsberg film studios assures regular appearances by those shooting there. *Jägerstr. 39 0331/270–1791 AE, DC, MC, V.*

$$ **Hotel am Luisenplatz.** Behind a somber-looking facade, this intimate hotel conceals a warm, upscale elegance and friendly, personal service. The large rooms are decorated in dark blue, red, or turquoise—and all have bathtubs. There's free Internet use for those who don't have a laptop, and a spa area with sauna and solarium was added in 2005. The

biggest draw, however, is the hotel's location, which offers a spectacular view of historic Luisenplatz and its restored Prussian city mansions. ✉ *Luisenpl. 5, D–14471* ☎ *0331/971–900* 📠 *0331/971–9019* 🌐 *www.hotel-luisenplatz.de* *22 rooms, 3 suites* *Restaurant, in-room safes, minibars, cable TV, Wi-Fi, spa, sauna, dry cleaning, laundry service, Internet room, meeting room, parking (fee), some pets allowed, no-smoking rooms; no a/c* *AE, DC, MC, V* *CP.*

$$ **Steigenberger Maxx Hotel Sanssouci Potsdam.** The terrace of this fine hotel overlooks the palace and park of Sanssouci. The Maxx, a slimmed-down and casual version of the luxurious Steigenberger chain, offers spacious, movie-theme rooms (complete with Hollywood and Babelsberg vintage photos and memorabilia) with terra-cotta floors and rattan furniture. A nice plus is the free transportation card for Berlin and Potsdam for the duration of your stay. The hotel restaurant serves international dishes, including those of the Brandenburg region. ✉ *Allee nach Sanssouci 1, D–14471* ☎ *0331/90910* 📠 *0331/909–1909* 🌐 *www.steigenberger.de* *133 rooms, 4 suites* *Restaurant, minibars, cable TV, in-room data ports, massage, sauna, steam room, bicycles, bar, shops, babysitting, dry cleaning, laundry service, meeting room, parking (fee), some pets allowed (fee), no-smoking floor; no a/c* *AE, DC, MC, V.*

Potsdam A to Z

Potsdam is 20 km (12 mi) southwest of Berlin's center and a half-hour journey by car or bus. From Zoo Station to Potsdam's main train station, the regional train RE 1 takes 17 minutes, the S-7 line of the S-bahn takes about 40 minutes; use an ABC zone ticket for either service. City traffic is heavy, so a train journey is recommended. Several Berlin tour operators have Potsdam trips.

BOAT TRAVEL There are several tours that include Potsdam (most are two or six hours). They leave from the landing across from Berlin's Wannsee S-bahn station between late March and early October. A round-trip ticket costs €9.50–14.

Stern- und Kreisschiffahrt ☎ 030/536–3600 🌐 www.sternundkreis.de.

BUS TRAVEL From Berlin there's regular service to Potsdam from the bus station at the Funkturm on Messedamm 8 (U-1 U-bahn: Kaiserdamm). From Spandau (U-7 U-bahn: Rathaus Spandau), take Bus 638 to Potsdam. From Potsdam's train station, Bus 695 goes to Sanssouci and makes stops all around its park.

CAR TRAVEL From central Berlin take Potsdamer Strasse south until it becomes Route 1 and then follow the signs to Potsdam. A faster way is taking the highway from Funkturm through Zehlendorf to Potsdam.

TOURS All major sightseeing companies (⇨ *see* Tours *in* Berlin A to Z) offer three- to four-hour tours of Potsdam and Sanssouci for €28. April through October the Potsdam Tourist Office offers a 3½-hour bus tour including a walk through Sanssouci for €26; a 1½-hour bus tour of the city alone is €15. Both tours are offered in English and German.

TRAIN TRAVEL From Berlin, take the S-bahn 7 or 1 line, or the RE 1 train to Potsdam Hauptbahnhof. From the Potsdam train station, take Tram 90, 92, or 95 into the city, or Bus 695 to Sanssouci. You could also transfer to the RE 21 train (marked "Wustermark") to reach the station Park Sanssouci, which is close to the Neues Palais.

VISITOR INFORMATION The Potsdam tourist office has information on tours, attractions, and events and also reserves hotel rooms for tourists. It's open weekdays 10–6. Between November and March it closes at 2 on weekends, between April and October at 4.

Potsdam Tourist Office ✉ Touristenzentrum am Alten Markt, Friedrich-Ebert-Str. 5 D-14467 Potsdam ☎ 0331/275-580 📠 0331/275-5829 🌐 www.potsdam.de.

14

BERLIN A TO Z

To research prices, get advice from other travelers, and book travel arrangements, visit www.fodors.com.

AIR TRAVEL TO & FROM BERLIN

Major airlines serve western Berlin's Tegel Airport after a first stop at a major European hub (such as Frankfurt). Massive Tempelhof Airport is an example of fascist architecture and is used by smaller airlines for flights within Europe. Eastern Berlin's Schönefeld Airport is about 24 km (15 mi) outside the downtown area and is used principally by charter and low-budget airlines. The three airports share a central phone number.

Central airport service ☎ 0180/500-0186 🌐 www.berlin-airport.de.

AIRPORTS & TRANSFERS

Tegel Airport is 6 km (4 mi) from the downtown area. The express X9 airport bus runs at 10-minute intervals between Tegel and Bahnhof Zoologischer Garten (Zoo Station), the center of western Berlin. From here you can connect to bus, train, or subway. The trip takes 25 minutes; the fare is €3.10, or an additional €1 if you already have a regular metro or bus ticket. Alternatively, you can take Bus 128 to Kurt Schumacher Platz or Bus 109 to Jakob Kaiser Platz and change to the subway, where your bus ticket is also valid. Expect to pay about €14 for a taxi from the airport to the western downtown area. If you rent a car at the airport, follow the signs for the Stadtautobahn into Berlin. The Halensee exit leads to Kurfürstendamm.

Tempelhof Airport is linked directly to the city center by the U-6 subway line. From Schönefeld Airport a free express shuttle bus leaves every 10–15 minutes for the S-bahn station (a 10-minute walk). The system is a bit clumsy here. Look carefully for the DB office, which is up stairs to your right after you initially descend into the station. Buy an Einzelfahrt €2 ticket (AB zone) from here or from an S-bahn platform vending machine (no credit cards) to get you into town. This ticket is good for both the S-Bahn and the Airport Express train, which runs about every half hour from a track that has no vending machine. To take the Airport Express, look for a small dark-blue sign at the foot of the stairs leading to its platform. Bus 171 also leaves Schönefeld every 20 minutes for the Rudow subway station. A taxi ride from the Schönefeld Airport takes about 40 minutes and will cost around €28. By car, follow the signs for Stadtzentrum Berlin.

BUS TRAVEL TO & FROM BERLIN

BerlinLinien Bus is the only intra-Germany company serving Berlin. Gullivers Reisen serves foreign destinations. Make reservations for either through ZOB-Reisebüro, or buy your ticket at its office at the central bus terminal, the Omnibusbahnhof. Public buses are the best way to reach the bus terminal, served by the lines X34, X49, 104, 139, 149, 218, and 349. A more central place to buy bus tickets is Mitfahrzentrale, a tiny, busy office that also arranges car-ride shares. Only EC credit cards and cash are accepted.

Mitfahrzentrale ✉ U-2 Pankow-bound platform, Zoologischer Garten subway station Western Downtown ☎ 030/19440 ⏲ Weekdays 9–8, weekends 10–6 🌐 www.mfzoo.de. **ZOB-Reisebüro** ✉ Zentrale Omnibusbahnhof, Masurenallee 4–6 at Messedamm, Charlottenburg ☎ 030/301–0380 for reservations ⏲ Weekdays 6 AM–9 PM, weekends 6 AM–3 PM 🌐 www.berlinlinienbus.de.

CAR TRAVEL

Rush hour is relatively mild in Berlin, but the public transit system is so efficient here, it's best to leave your car at the hotel. Daily parking fees at hotels can run up to €18 per day. Vending machines in the city center dispense timed tickets to display on your dashboard. Thirty minutes cost €.50.

DISABILITIES & ACCESSIBILITY

All major S- and U-bahn stations have elevators, and most buses have hydraulic lifts. Check the public transportation maps or call the Berliner Verkehrsbetriebe. The Service-Ring-Berlin e.V. runs a special bus service for travelers with physical disabilities. Though hotels can often make the arrangement, you can call the Verband Geburts- und anderer Behinderter e.V. to borrow a wheelchair (donations are accepted).

Berliner Verkehrsbetriebe ☎ 030/19449 🌐 www.bvg.de. **Service-Ring-Berlin e. V** ☎ 030/859–4010. **Verband Geburts- und anderer Behinderter e.V** ☎ 030/341–1797.

EMBASSIES

⇨ *See* Embassies *in* Smart Travel Tips.

EMERGENCIES

Pharmacies in Berlin offer late-night service on a rotating basis and display a schedule with shop addresses on their doors. The American Hotline is a private service that serves English-speakers in need of medical, legal, or counseling referrals.

Police ☎ 030/110. **Ambulance** ☎ 030/112. **Pharmacy** ☎ 030/11880. **Emergency poison assistance** ☎ 030/19240. **American Hotline** ☎ 0177/814–1510.

ENGLISH-LANGUAGE MEDIA

The Ex-Berliner (€2) is an English-language monthly that includes cultural, arts, and nightlife listings. The weekly *New Berlin* is a summary of restaurants, sights, club nights, and hostels and is free at many hotels and some chain coffee shops.

LODGING

PRIVATE ROOMS & APARTMENTS German and European travelers often use rooming agents, and Americans on a budget should consider this as well (apartments start at €200 per month). In Berlin, double rooms with shared bathrooms in private apartments begin around €36. Wohn-Agentur Freiraum is an English-speaking agency that has its own guesthouse with rooms and apartments. All of its private room listings are in the Kreuzberg district.

Wohn-Agentur Freiraum ✉ Wiener Str., Kreuzberg ☎ 030/618-2008 📠 030/618-2006 🌐 www.freiraum-berlin.com.

14

TAXIS

The base rate is €2.50, after which prices vary according to a complex tariff system. Figure on paying around €8 for a ride the length of the Ku'damm. If you've hailed a cab on the street and are taking a short ride of less than 2 km (1 mi), ask the driver as soon as you start off for a special fare (€3) called *Kurzstreckentarif*. There's no additional fee if you call a cab by phone. You can also get cabs at taxi stands or order one by calling. U-bahn employees will call a taxi for passengers after 8 PM.

Velotaxis, rickshaw-like bicycle taxis, pedal along Kurfürstendamm, Friedrichstrasse, and Unter den Linden; and in Tiergarten. Just hail one of the cabs on the street or look for the VELOTAXI-STAND signs along the boulevards mentioned. The fare is €2.50 for up to 1 km (½ mi), €2.50 for a tour between sightseeing landmarks (for example, Europa Center to the Brandenburger Tor), and €7.50 for 30 minutes of travel. Velotaxis operate April–October, daily 1–8.

Taxis ☎ 030/210-101, 030/210-202, 030/443-322, or 030/261-026.

TOURS

The easiest and most inexpensive way to orient yourself within West and East Berlin's downtown areas is a ride on public bus lines No. 100 or 200, which run between Zoo Station and Alexanderplatz (No. 100) and between Zoo Station, Potsdamer Platz, Alexanderplatz, and Prenzlauer Allee (No. 200), stopping at almost all major sightseeing spots on the way.

BOAT TOURS Tours of central Berlin's Spree and Landwehr canals give you up-close and unusual views of sights such as Charlottenburg Palace, the Reichstag, and the Berliner Dom—bring plenty of film. Tours usually depart twice a day from several bridges and piers in Berlin, such as Schlossbrücke in Charlottenburg; Hansabrücke and Haus der Kulturen der Welt in Tiergarten; Friedrichstrasse, Museum Island, and Nikolaiviertel in Mitte; and near the Jannowitzbrücke S- and U-bahn station. Drinks, snacks, and wursts are available during the narrated trips. Reederei Riedel offers three inner-city trips that range from €6 to €14.

A tour of the Havel Lakes (which include Tegeler See and Wannsee) begins at the Greenwich Promenade in Tegel (U-bahn: Tegel). From

Tegel, you can sail on either the whale-shape vessel *Moby Dick* or the *Havel Queen*, a Mississippi-style boat, and cruise 28 km (17 mi) through the lakes and past forests (Stern- und Kreisschiffahrt). Tours can last from one to seven hours and cost between €8 and €14. There are 20 operators.

Reederei Bruno Winkler ☎ 030/349-9595. **Reederei Riedel** ☎ 030/693-4646. **Stern- und Kreisschiffahrt** ☎ 030/536-3600 🌐 www.sternundkreis.de.

BUS TOURS Four companies (Berliner Bären, Berolina Berlin-Service, Bus Verkehr Berlin, and Severin & Kühn) jointly offer city tours on yellow, double-decker City Circle buses, which run every 15 or 30 minutes, depending on the season. The full-circuit takes two hours as does the recorded narration listened to through headphones. For €18 you can jump on and off at the 14 stops. The bus driver sells tickets. During the warmer months, the last circuit leaves at 4 PM from the corner of Rankestrasse and Kurfürstendamm. Most companies have tours to Potsdam. Severin & Kühn also runs all-day tours to Dresden and Meissen.

The Stadtrundfahrtbüro Berlin offers a 2½-hour tour (€15) and 1¾-hour tour (€12) at 11, 2, and 3:45. A guide narrates in both German and English. The bus departs from Kurfürstendamm 236, at the corner of Rankestrasse.

Berliner Bären Stadtrundfahrten (BBS) ✉ Seeburgerstr. 19b, Charlottenburg ☎ 030/3519-5270 🌐 www.sightseeing.de. **Berolina Berlin-Service** ✉ Kurfürstendamm 220, at Meinekestr., Western Downtown ☎ 030/8856-8030 🌐 www.berolina-berlin.com. **Bus Verkehr Berlin** (BVB) ✉ Kurfürstendamm 225, Western Downtown ☎ 030/683-8910 🌐 www.bvb.net. **Severin & Kühn** ✉ Kurfürstendamm 216, Western Downtown ☎ 030/880-4190 🌐 www.severin-kuehn-berlin.de. **Stadtrundfahrtbüro Berlin** ✉ Kurfürstendamm 236, Western Downtown ☎ 030/2612-001 🌐 www.stadtrundfahrtbuero-berlin.de.

WALKING & BIKE TOURS Getting oriented through a walking tour is a great way to start a Berlin visit. In additon to daily city highlight tours, companies have theme tours such as Third Reich Berlin, Potsdam, and pub crawls. Berlin Walks offers a Monday "Jewish Life" tour, a Potsdam tour on Sunday, and visits to the Sachsenhausen concentration camp. Insider Tours has a "Red Star" Berlin tour about the Soviet-era and a bike tour as well. Brit Terry Brewer's firsthand accounts of divided and reunified Berlin are a highlight of the all-day "Brewer's Best of Berlin" tour. Tours cost from €9 to €15. Printable discount coupons may be available on the tour operators' Web sites; some companies grant discounts to WelcomeCard holders. Fat Tire Bike Tours rides through Berlin daily, early March–November and has a Berlin Wall tour. The 4½-hour city tour costs €20, bike rental included.

Berlin Walks ☎ 030/301-9194 🌐 www.berlinwalks.com. **Insider Tours** ☎ 030/692-3149 🌐 www.insidertour.com. **"Brewer's Best of Berlin"** ☎ 030/2900-0081 🌐 www.brewersberlin.com. **Fat Tire Bike Tours Berlin** ✉ Panoramastr. 1a, base of TV Tower ☎ 030/2404-7991 🌐 www.fattirebiketoursberlin.com.

TRANSPORTATION AROUND BERLIN

The city has one of the most efficient public-transportation systems in Europe, a smoothly integrated network of subway (U-bahn) and suburban (S-bahn) train lines, buses, and trams (in eastern Berlin only). Get a map from any information booth. Don't be afraid to try to figure out the posted schedules of buses and trams—they often cut the most direct path to your destination. From Sunday through Thursday, U-bahn trains stop around 12:45 AM and S-bahn trains stop by 1:30 AM. All-night bus and tram service operates seven nights a week (indicated by the letter *N* next to route numbers). On Friday and Saturday night, most S- and U-bahn lines run all night.

Most visitor destinations are in the broad reach of the fare zones A and B. Both the €2 ticket (fare zones A and B) and the €2.60 ticket (fare zones A, B, and C) allow you to make a one-way trip with an unlimited number of changes between trains, buses, and trams. There are reduced rates for children ages 6–13

Buy a *Kurzstreckentarif* ticket (€1.20) for short rides of up to six bus or tram stops or three U-bahn or S-bahn stops. The best deal if you plan to travel around the city extensively is the *Tageskarte* (day card for zones A and B), for €5.60, good on all transportation until 3 AM. (It's €6 for A, B, C zones.) A *7-Tage-Karte* (seven-day ticket) costs €23.40 and allows unlimited travel for fare zones A and B; €30 buys all three fare zones.

The Berlin WelcomeCard (sold by EurAid, BVG offices, the tourist office, and some hotels) entitles one adult and three children under the age of 14 to either two or three days of unlimited travel in the ABC zones for €16 or €22, respectively and includes admission and tour discounts detailed in a booklet. The CityTourCard, good for two or three days of unlimited travel in the AB zones costs €14.50 and €18.90, respectively, and details 50 discounts on a leaflet; up to three children under 6 can accompany an adult.

Tickets are available from vending machines at U-bahn and S-bahn stations. Look for rib-high red or yellow machines that time-validate tickets. If you're caught without a ticket or with an unvalidated one, the fine is €40. Some stations have intercom stands through which you can ask for travel advice. The Berliner Verkehrsbetriebe also answers calls day and night. There's a BVG-information office on Hardenbergplatz, directly in front of the Zoo train station. Questions about S-bahn connections can be answered by S-bahn Berlin GmbH.

Information about all transportation methods within and between Berlin and the outlying state of Brandenburg is provided by the region's central transit authority, the VBB.

Berliner Verkehrsbetriebe ☎ 030/19449 🌐 www.bvg.de. **S-Bahn Berlin GmbH** ☎ 030/297-4333 🌐 www.s-bahn-berlin.de. **VBB** ✉ Hardenbergpl. 2, Western Downtown ☎ 030/254-140, lost property 030/19449 🌐 www.vbbonline.de.

TRAIN TRAVEL

Berlin has had two "main" train stations for years: Bahnhof Zoo (in the West) and Ostbahnhof (in the East). Regional trains also stop at the central eastern stations Friedrichstrasse and Alexanderplatz. By the time the World Cup games are held in Berlin in June 2006, the city hopes to have long-distance trains stopping at the new central station, Hauptbahnhof, which lies at the north edge of the government district in former West Berlin. Note that Bahnhof Zoo has the most connecting lines to buses and subways.

TRAVEL AGENCIES

Sharing the same space as Deutsche Bahn in the Zoologischer Garten train station is EurAide, which serves English-speaking travelers. It can book your long-distance train tickets and inform you about local Berlin tours. It's closed on weekends and the entire month of January.

EurAide ✉ Hardenbergpl., Western Downtown 🌐 www.euraide.com ⏲ June–Oct., weekdays 8–noon and 1–6; Nov., Dec., and Feb.–May, weekdays 8–noon and 1–4:45.

VISITOR INFORMATION

The main information office of Berlin Tourismus Marketing is in the Europa Center, a short walk from Zoo Station. There are branches in the south wing of the Brandenburg Gate and at the base of the Fernsehn Turm (TV tower) at Alexanderplatz that are open daily 10–6. The tourist-information centers have longer hours April–October. To request materials before your trip, write Berlin Tourismus Marketing GmbH.

The tourist office publishes the *Berlin Kalender* (€1.60) six times a year and *Berlin Buchbar* (free) two times a year. Both are written in German and English. The office and Berlin's larger transportation offices (BVG) sell the WelcomeCard (€21) that grants three days of free transportation and 25%–50% discounts at museums and theaters (it does not included the state museums).

Staatliche (state) museums are closed on Monday and free on Thursday during the last four hours of operation. A free audio guide is included at all state museums, though you must pay for it during free admission times. The MD Infoline provides comprehensive information about all of Berlin's museums, exhibits, and theme tours.

Berlin Tourist Info Center ✉ Budapester Str. 45, Western Downtown ☎ 030/250-025 ⏲ Mon.–Sat. 10–7, Sun. 10–6 🌐 www.berlin-tourist-information.de. **MD Infoline** ☎ 030/9026-99444 ⏲ Weekdays 9–4, weekends 9–1. **Staatliche Museen zu Berlin** ☎ 030/266-2951 operator 🌐 www.smb.museum. **Tourist Information Center in Prenzlauer Berg** ✉ Kuturbrauerei entrances on Schönhauser Allee 36-37, Knaackstr. 97, Sredzkistr. 1 ☎ 030/4431-5151 🌐 www.tic-prenzlauerberg.de.

Saxony, Saxony-Anhalt & Thuringia

15

WORD OF MOUTH

"The Opera House [in Dresden] was breathtaking. I highly recommend taking the time well in advance of your trip to secure tickets. . . . Make sure you visit the upstairs during one of the intermissions. (Side note: People in Dresden dress for the opera.)"

—apseals

"I love the Wartburg castle—it is really a medieval fairy-tale castle (and unlike Neuschwanstein it HAS history)."

—Ingo

www.fodors.com/forums

Updated by Jürgen Scheunemann

THE EASTERN STATES of Saxony, Saxony-Anhalt, and Thuringia have a great many secrets in store and some gems of German culture. An Old World state of mind exists here, the likes of which you will never find in West Germany. Communism never penetrated the culture here as deeply as the American influence did in West Germany. The German Democratic Republic (GDR, commonly referred to by its German acronym—DDR) clung to its German heritage, proudly preserving connections with such national heroes as Luther, Goethe, Schiller, Bach, Handel, Wagner, and the Hungarian-born Liszt. Towns in the regions of the Thüringer Wald (Thuringian Forest) or the Harz Mountains—long considered the haunt of witches—are drenched in history and medieval legend.

East Germans rebuilt extensively after bombings devastated most of their cities during World War II. Though you will see eyesores of industrialization and stupendously bland housing projects, most historic centers were restored to their old glamour. Some of Europe's most famous palaces and cultural wonders—the Zwinger and Semperoper in Dresden, the Wartburg at Eisenach, the Schiller and Goethe houses in Weimar and Jena, as well as Luther's Wittenberg—await the traveler here.

Traditional tourist sights aside, East Germany is also worth visiting precisely because it is *still* in transition. In 1989 the resolute people of Leipzig, with their now legendary *Montagsdemonstrationen* (Monday demonstrations) through the streets of their proud city, startled the East German regime and triggered the peaceful revolution. A year later the initiative for unification came as much from the West as it did from the East, and the "Wall" finally came down. This is not the end of the story, however. Both the East and West are still struggling with problems caused by the sudden unification of their country. In the former East Germany, the closing of factories and a shrunken welfare system have left many jobless; in the former West, people are burdened by additional taxes imposed to help rebuild the East.

Though economic woes still haunt parts of the eastern region, a class of young entrepreneurs has transformed such cities as Leipzig and Dresden with a wave of start-up businesses. This is particularly impressive when you consider this upswing in light of the past. When the GDR was communism's "Western Front," it was largely isolated from Western ideas. Saxony's Dresden area, in particular, was nicknamed *Tal der Ahnungslosen* (Valley of the Know-Nothings), as residents there couldn't receive Western television or radio signals.

The three states described here survived under a harsh political regime and have now embarked on a mostly promising future. Eastern Germany used to move very slowly, but today, the pace of cities such as Leipzig and Dresden has overtaken that of their West German counterparts.

Exploring Saxony, Saxony-Anhalt & Thuringia

These three states cover the southeastern part of the former East Germany, and some of the old and now run-down industrial towns will remind you of its communist past. But Germany's most historically important cities are here, and reconstruction programs are slowly restor-

Numbers in the text correspond to numbers in the margin and on the Saxony, Saxony-Anhalt, and Thuringia, Leipzig, and Dresden maps.

If you have **3 days**

Spend your first day and night in **Dresden** 1–14, with its impressive Zwinger complex and fine museums. Set out the next afternoon for **Meissen** 17, to see how its famous porcelain is produced. Continue northwest to spend the next two nights in **Leipzig** 19–33, where Bach once resided.

If you have **5 days**

Spend your first day and night in **Dresden** 1–14. Finish taking in its splendors in the morning and continue to **Meissen** 17, stopping long enough for a visit to the porcelain factory, before ending the day in **Leipzig** 19–33. On the third day, head north to the birthplace of Martin Luther and the Reformation, **Wittenberg** 34. An indirect route then takes you to the old Harz Mountain towns of **Quedlinburg** 37, **Wernigerode,** and **Goslar** 38, the unofficial capital of the Harz region. Drive south to **Eisenach** 39, and prowl through the Wartburg Castle, where Luther translated the Bible in hiding. The final stops are **Erfurt** 40, a city of towers that mostly managed to escape wartime bombing, and **Weimar** 41, where you might want to peek into its most famous hotel, the charming and luxurious Elephant.

If you have **7 days**

Your first day and night should be fully devoted to the various sights in **Dresden** 1–14. The next day, explore the **Sächsische Schweiz** 15, a mountainous region south of the city. Depending on how long you hiked through the mountains, you should still have enough time to drive to the Polish-border town of **Görlitz** 16. Spend the night there and travel to **Meissen** 17, and then follow a northern route on A–14 autobahn to **Leipzig** 19–33, spending the rest of the day there. Leave enough time in Leipzig for visits to its outstanding museums, including the Grassimuseum complex and the Museum der Bildenden Künste. On your fourth and fifth days, from Leipzig drive back to the sights at **Halle** 36 before touring the old towns of **Wittenberg** 34 and **Quedlinburg** 37. You can spend the nights in any of the Harz towns and venture into the mountains for some fresh air. The sixth day is best spent at the Wartburg in **Eisenach** 39, which can be reached by following either the country roads or the autobahn from the Harz Mountains toward the south. From there, proceed to **Erfurt** 40 and **Weimar** 41. Spend your last day either in both cities or concentrate fully on the culture and museums in Weimar. If time permits, also detour to **Jena** 42.

---

ing them. Dresden is promoting its reputation as the "Florence on the River Elbe," and just downstream, Meissen has undergone an impressive face-lift. Weimar, one of the continent's old cultural centers, and Leipzig, in particular, have washed off their grime and almost completely restored their historic city centers.

About the Restaurants

Enterprising young managers and chefs are beginning to establish themselves in the East, so look for new and mostly small restaurants along the way. Some successfully blend nouvelle German cuisine with such regional specialties as *Thüringer Sauerbraten mit Klössen* (roast corned beef with dumplings), spicy *Thüringer Wurst* (sausage), *Bärenschinken* (cured ham), *Harzer Köhlerteller mit Röstkartoffeln* (charcoal-grilled meat with fried potatoes), *Harze Käse* (a strong-smelling cheese), and *Moskigauer Bauerngulasch mit Klump* (goulash with dumplings).

About the Hotels

All major hotel chains are present in the larger cities, most of them within beautifully restored mansions. Smaller and family-run hotels often combine a good restaurant with fairly good accommodations. In an effort to further improve tourism, most big hotels offer special (weekend) or activity-oriented packages that aren't found in the western part of the country.

During the trade fairs and shows of the **Leipziger Messe,** particularly in March and April, most Leipzig hotels increase their prices.

WHAT IT COSTS In Euros

	$$$$	**$$$**	**$$**	**$**	**¢**
RESTAURANTS	over €25	€21–€25	€16–€20	€9–€15	under €9
HOTELS	over €225	€175–€225	€100–€175	€50–€100	under €50

Restaurant prices are per person for a main course at dinner. Hotel prices are for two people in a standard double room, including tax and service.

Timing

Winters in this part of Germany can be cold, wet, and dismal, so unless you plan to ski in the Harz Mountains or the Thüringer Wald, visit in late spring, summer, or early autumn. Avoid Leipzig at trade-fair times, particularly in March and April.

SAXONY

The people of Saxony, a once almost-forgotten corner of Germany near the Czech and Polish borders, identify themselves more as Saxon than German, and their somewhat indecipherable dialect is the target of endless jokes and puns. However, Saxon pride is rebuilding three cities magnificently: Dresden and Leipzig—the showcase cities of eastern Germany—and the smaller town of Görlitz, on the Neisse River. If you make your way from Dresden to the West, you can cut north to the Elbe River and the enchanting little city of Meissen.

Dresden

205 km (127 mi) south of Berlin.

Saxony's capital city sits in baroque splendor on a wide sweep of the Elbe River, and its proponents are working with German thoroughness to recapture the city's old reputation as the "Florence on the River Elbe." Its yellow and pale-green facades are enormously appealing, and their mere presence is even more overwhelming when you compare what you

Trains & Steamers Eastern Germany is a treasure house of old steam-driven tractors, factory engines, train engines, and riverboats, many lovingly restored by enthusiasts. Deutsche Bahn (German Railways) regularly runs trains from the years 1899–1930 on a small-gauge line that penetrates deep into the Saxon countryside and the Fichtelberg Mountains. In Saxony-Anhalt you can ride the steam-powered narrow-gauge Brockenbahn to the Harz Mountains' highest point. The world's largest and oldest fleet of paddle steamers (Weisse Flotte) plies the Elbe. Eight old steamers (all of them under historic preservation orders) and two reconstructed ships cruise the Elbe, following the Saxon Wine Route as far as the Czech Republic.

Sports & the Outdoors You can canoe on the Elbe and Saale rivers and seldom see another paddler. Contact the tourist office in Dresden, or Halle for rental information.

Hiking is good in the Harz Mountains, particularly around Thale and Wittenberg. Maps and guides to bicycle and walking trails are available in most hotels and bookstores. The Thale and Wernigerode tourist offices and the Wittenberg District Rural Information Office have great resources. Goslar, in the Harz, offers good family skiing.

The elevated, dense Thuringian Forest is a popular holiday destination in summer and winter. Its center is Suhl, the administrative heart of an area where every 10th town and village is a spa or mountain resort. The region south of Erfurt, centering on Oberhof, has comfortable hotels and full sports facilities.

Wine & Vineyards Saxony has cultivated vineyards for more than 800 years and is known for its dry red and white wines, among them Müller-Thurgau, Weissburgunder, Ruländer, and the spicy Traminer. The Sächsische Weinstrasse (Saxon Wine Route) follows the course of the Elbe River from Diesbar-Seusslitz (north of Meissen) to Pirna (southeast of Dresden). Meissen, Radebeul, and Dresden have upscale wine restaurants, and wherever you see a green seal with the letter *S* and grapes depicted, good local wine is being served. Most of the hotels and restaurants reviewed in this chapter have their own wine cellars.

---

see today with photographs of Dresden from February 1945, after an Allied bombing raid destroyed the city overnight. Dresden was the capital of Saxony as early as the 15th century, although most of its architectural masterpieces date from the 18th century and the reigns of Augustus the Strong and his son, Frederick Augustus II.

Though some parts of the city center still look as if they're stuck halfway between demolition and construction, the present city is an enormous tribute to Dresdeners' skills and dedication. The resemblance of today's

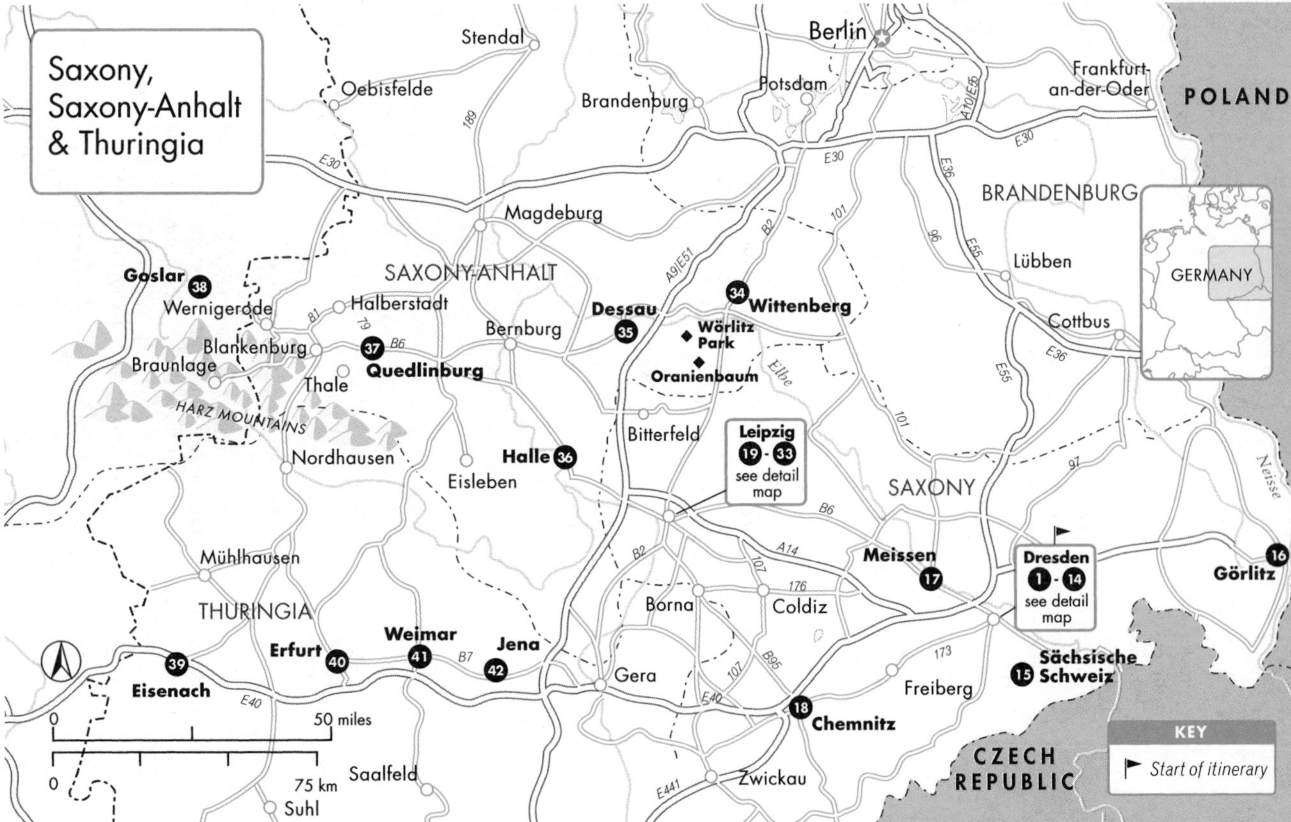
Saxony,
Saxony-Anhalt
& Thuringia
POLAND
GERMANY
BRANDENBURG
SAXONY-ANHALT
SAXONY
THURINGIA
CZECH REPUBLIC
HARZ MOUNTAINS
Berlin
Potsdam
Frankfurt-an-der-Oder
Stendal
Oebisfelde
Brandenburg
Magdeburg
Lübben
Cottbus
Goslar 38
Wernigerode
Halberstadt
Blankenburg
Braunlage
Thale
37 Quedlinburg
Bernburg
Dessau 35
34 Wittenberg
Wörlitz Park
Oranienbaum
Elbe
Bitterfeld
Leipzig 19 - 33 see detail map
Nordhausen
Eisleben
Halle 36
Mühlhausen
Dresden 1 - 14 see detail map
Meissen 17
Görlitz 16
Neisse
Borna
Coldiz
Sächsische Schweiz 15
Eisenach 39
Erfurt 40
Weimar 41
Jena 42
Gera
Freiberg
18 Chemnitz
Zwickau
Saalfeld
Suhl
E30
E36
E55
E40
E441
A9/E51
A10/E55
A14
B2
B6
B7
B95
79
81
96
97
101
107
173
176
189
0
50 miles
0
75 km
KEY
Start of itinerary

riverside to Dresden cityscapes painted by Canaletto in the mid-1700s is remarkable. Unfortunately, the war-inflicted gaps in the urban landscape in other parts of the city are too big to be closed anytime soon.

a good walk

It's easy to cover the downtown area of Dresden on foot. From the main railway station (which has adequate parking), you'll first have to cross a featureless expanse surrounded by postwar high-rises to reach the old part of the city. Pick up any materials you like at the tourist-information office on pedestrians-only Pragerstrasse (No. 8).

Buildings representing several centuries of architecture border the **Altmarkt** 1. At the square's southeast side, take a look at the **Kreuzkirche** 2 before heading east on Wilsdruffer Strasse to the **Stadtmuseum Dresden im Landhaus** 3 with its historic exhibits. Continue east toward Pirnaischer Platz, and make a sharp left turn onto Landhausstrasse, which connects to Dresden's historic heart, the Neumarkt (New Market). On your left is the baroque, almost completely restored **Frauenkirche** 4. On the other side of the Neumarkt behind the church, off Brühlsche Gasse, stands the impressive **Albertinum** 5, which has one of the world's leading art galleries. If you leave the Albertinum by the Brühlsche Terrasse exit, you'll find yourself on what was once known as the Balcony of Europe, a terrace high above the Elbe, carved from a 16th-century stretch of the city fortifications. From the terrace, a breathtaking vista of the Elbe River and the Dresden skyline opens up. From here, you can detour to **Schloss Pillnitz** and its museum. Back at the Neumarkt, you'll see the **Johanneum** 6 on its northwestern corner. The historic building is part of the former palace that now houses a transportation museum. The outside wall of the Johanneum has a unique porcelain-tile painting of a royal procession; walk along the wall, and at the end of the street you'll reach the restored **Residenzschloss** 7 with some of Europe's most outstanding art exhibits.

Next, walk a short distance north on any of the small paths from the Neumarkt, crossing Augustusstrasse in the direction of Terrassenufer. Cross Schlossplatz and then turn left, where you'll encounter Sophienstrasse. If you turn left, you can't miss Saxony's largest church, the **Katholische Hofkirche** 8. Just opposite the church on the Theaterplatz is the architecturally wondrous **Semperoper** 9, one of Europe's finest opera houses. Theaterplatz has as its centerpiece a proud equestrian statue of King Johann, who ruled Saxony when Gottfried Semper was at work. Don't be misled by Johann's confident pose in the saddle—he was terrified of horses and never learned to ride. Five minutes south of the Semperoper is the world-famous **Zwinger** 10, a richly decorated baroque palace with an entrance off Ostra-Allee. From the Zwinger, walk north, crossing the Elbe River on the **Augustusbrücke** 11, and then turn left on Grosse Meissner Strasse. You'll pass the **Japanisches Palais** 12, a baroque-classicist palace, on your left before crossing Albertplatz to reach **Königstrasse** 13, one of Dresden's most beautiful, historic little streets. To get a further glimpse of Dresden's magnificent past, cross Albertplatz and continue down Bautzener Strasse to **Pfund's Molkerei** 14, an old dairy specialty shop.

Albertinum . . . **5**
Altmarkt **1**
Augustus-brücke **11**
Frauenkirche . . **4**
Japanisches Palais **12**
Johanneum . . . **6**
Katholische Hofkirche **8**
König-strasse **13**
Kreuzkirche **2**
Pfund's Molkerei **14**
Residenz-schloss **7**
Semperoper . . . **9**
Stadtmuseum Dresden im Landhaus **3**
Zwinger **10**

TIMING A full day is sufficient for a quick tour of historic Dresden, but if you plan to explore any of the museums, such as the Zwinger, or take a guided tour of the Semperoper, you'll need more than a day. Allow at least two hours each for the Zwinger, the Johanneum, and the Albertinum. In summer, schedule some time to relax in one of the cafés along the Elbe River. Take note that in winter and early spring, it can get quite windy on the wide, open squares.

What to See

5 **Albertinum.** This massive, imperial-style building houses Dresden's leading art museum, one of the world's great galleries. The Albertinum is named after Saxony's King Albert, who between 1884 and 1887 converted a royal arsenal into a suitable setting for the treasures he and his forebears had collected. The upper story of the Albertinum, accessible from the Brühlsche Terrasse, houses 19th- and 20th-century paintings and sculptures in the **Gemäldegalerie Neue Meister** (Gallery of Modern Masters). Permanent exhibits include outstanding works by German masters of the 19th and 20th centuries (Caspar David Friedrich's haunting *Das Kreuz im Gebirge* is here) and French impressionists and postimpressionists.

Next door is the **Skulpturensammlung** (Sculpture Collection), which includes ancient Egyptian and classical works and examples by Giovanni da Bologna and Adriaen de Vries. ✉ *Am Neumarkt, Brühlsche Terrasse* ☎ *0351/491–4714* 🌐 *www.skd-dresden.de* 🎫 *€6, including Gemäldegalerie Neue Meister, Grünes Gewölbe, Münzkabinett (coin collection), and Skulpturensammlung* ⏲ *Wed.–Mon. 10–6.*

1 **Altmarkt** (Old Market Square). Although dominated by the nearby unappealing Kulturpalast (Palace of Culture), a concrete leftover from the 1970s, the broad square and its surrounding streets are the true center of Dresden. The square's colonnaded beauty (from the Stalinist-era architecture of the early 1950s) survived the disfiguring efforts of city planners to turn it into a huge outdoor parking lot. The rebuilt **Rathaus** (Town Hall) is here, as well as the yellow-stucco, 18th-century Landhaus, which contains the Stadtmuseum Dresden im Landhaus.

11 **Augustusbrücke** (Augustus Bridge). This bridge, which spans the river in front of the Katholische Hofkirche, is the reconstruction of a 17th-century baroque bridge blown up by the SS shortly before the end of World War II. The bridge was restored and renamed for Georgi Dimitroff, the Bulgarian Communist accused by the Nazis of instigating the Reichstag fire; after the fall of communism the original name, honoring Augustus the Strong, was reinstated.

off the beaten path

DEUTSCHES HYGIENE-MUSEUM DRESDEN – This unique museum (even in a country with a national tendency for excessive cleanliness) relates the history of public health and often features special art exhibits. ✉ *Lingnerpl. 1* ☎ *0351/48460* 🌐 *www.dhmd.de* 🎫 *€6* ⏲ *Tues.–Sun. 10–6.*

4 **Frauenkirche** (Church of Our Lady). With the completion of the sandstone facade and the reconstruction of its cupola, the baroque Frauenkirche, one of Europe's greatest churches, is once again shining in its historic splendor. Germany's greatest Protestant church was reduced to jagged ruins after the infamous February 1945 Allied bombing raid during World War II. The painstaking reconstruction of the Frauenkirche will be completed by the year 2006, the 800th anniversary of the founding of Dresden. The church has also evolved as a symbol of German–British reconciliation. The golden church cross (worth US$400,000) was donated to the building by a British foundation. The new cupola's viewing platform now offers magnificent views of the city and the surrounding countryside—it is only recommended for fit visitors, the cupola's entrance is at entrance gate G. Daily tours of the church's completed sections and the construction site start at entrance F of the church (northern facade). Try to avoid the always-crowded weekend tours. ✉ *An der Frauenkirche* ☎ *0351/498–1131* 🌐 *www.frauenkirche-dresden.org* 🎫 *Tours: free; cupola and tower: € 8* ⏲ *Tours daily 10–4 on the hour. Cupola and tower: daily 10–1 and 2–6 tour tours on the hour. Call for dates and times of English-language tours.*

Fodor's Choice ★

12 **Japanisches Palais** (Japanese Palace). This baroque palace was built in 1715–1733 to hold Augustus the Strong's collection of fine china. One

of the city's most magnificent buildings, it features Asian architectural elements such as porticos and courtyard statues as well as a roof reminiscent of a pagoda. Today, the palace houses the **Museum für Völkerkunde** (Museum of Ethnology; ☎ 0351/814–4860) and the **Museum für Vorgeschichte** (Prehistoric Museum; ☎ 0351/814–450). Those who have already visited similar museums in Berlin may wish to skip these, though special exhibits may make them worth your while. ✉ *Palaispl. 11* 🌐 *www.archsax.sachsen.de* 🎫 *Prehistoric Museum €2, Museum of Ethnology €6* ⏲ *Prehistoric Museum Mon.–Sun. 10–6; Museum of Ethnology Tues.–Sun. 10–6.*

6 **Johanneum.** At one time the royal stables, this 16th-century building now houses the **Verkehrsmuseum** (Transportation Museum), a collection of historical conveyances, including vintage automobiles and engines. The former **stable exercise yard,** behind the Johanneum and enclosed by elegant Renaissance arcades, was used during the 16th century as an open-air festival ground. A ramp leading up from the courtyard made it possible for royalty to reach the upper story to view the jousting below without having to dismount. More popular even than jousting in those days was *Ringelstechen,* a risky pursuit in which riders at full gallop had to catch small rings on their lances. Horses and riders often came to grief in the narrow confines of the stable yard.

On the outside wall of the Johanneum is a remarkable example of **Meissen porcelain art**: a Meissen tile mural of a royal procession, 336 feet long. More than 100 members of the royal Saxon house of Wettin, half of them on horseback, are represented on the giant mosaic of 25,000 porcelain tiles, painted in 1904–07 after a design by Wilhelm Walther. The Johanneum is reached by steps leading down from the Brühlsche Terrasse. ✉ *Am Neumarkt at Augustusstr. 1* ☎ *0351/86440* 🌐 *www.verkehrsmuseum.sachsen.de* 🎫 *€3* ⏲ *Tues.–Sun. 10–5.*

8 **Katholische Hofkirche** (Catholic Court Church). The largest church in Saxony is also known as the Cathedral of St. Trinitatis. Frederick Augustus II (reigned 1733–63) brought architects and builders from Italy to construct a Catholic church in a city that had been the first large center of Lutheran Protestantism (like his father, Frederick Augustus II had to convert to Catholicism to be eligible to wear the Polish crown). Inside, the treasures include a beautiful stone pulpit by the royal sculptor Balthasar Permoser and a painstakingly restored 250-year-old organ said to be one of the finest ever to come from the mountain workshops of the famous Silbermann family. In the cathedral's crypt are the tombs of 49 Saxon rulers and a relic containing the heart of Augustus the Strong. Owing to restoration work, the cathedral's opening hours may vary. ✉ *Schlosspl.* ☎ *0351/484–4712* 🎫 *Free* ⏲ *Mon.–Thurs. 9–5, Fri. 1–5, Sat. 10–5, Sun. noon–4:30.*

13 **Königstrasse** (King Street). The grand estates lining this historic boulevard attest to Dresden's bygone wealth. The street itself was once an important thoroughfare of a residential quarter founded by Augustus the Strong in the mid-18th century. Some of the meticulously restored buildings house restaurants, shops, and art galleries in their lovely open courtyards. ✉ *Between Grosse Meissner Str. and Albertpl.*

2 **Kreuzkirche** (Cross Church). Soaring high above the Altmarkt, the richly decorated tower of the baroque Kreuzkirche dates back to 1792. The city's main Protestant church is still undergoing postwar restoration, but the tower and church hall are open to the public. A famous boys' choir, the Kreuzchor, performs here regularly (check Web site or call for scheduled concerts). ✉ *Altmarkt* ☎ *0351/439–390* 🌐 *www.dresdner-kreuzkirche.de* 🎟 *Tower €1* ⏲ *Nov.–Feb., weekdays 10–4, Sun. noon–4; Mar.–Oct., daily 10–5.*

14 **Pfund's Molkerei** (Pfund's Dairy Shop). This decorative 19th-century shop has been a Dresden institution since 1880 and offers a wide assortment of cheese and other goods. The shop is renowned for its intricate tile mosaics on the floor and walls. Pfund's is also famous for introducing pasteurized milk to the industry; it invented milk soap and specially treated milk for infants as early as 1900. ✉ *Bautzener Str. 79* ☎ *0351/808–080* 🌐 *www.pfunds.de* ⏲ *Mon.–Sat. 10–6, Sun. 10–3.*

off the beaten path

RADEBEUL – Follow the road along the north bank of the Elbe to Meissen. The small town of Radebeul, on the way, is a mecca for fans of westerns. Radebeul is the birthplace of Germany's well-loved novelist Karl May, who wrote popular, convincing westerns without once visiting America. A museum here explains just how he did it. ✉ *Karl-May-Str. 5* ☎ *0351/837–300* 🌐 *www.karl-may-museum.de* 🎟 *€5* ⏲ *Mar.–Oct., Tues.–Sun. 9–5:30; Nov.–Feb., Tues.–Sun. 10–3:30.*

SCHLOSS PILLNITZ (Pillnitz Palace) – This romantic baroque palace, once a summer retreat for King Augustus the Strong, was built in 1720–22 and is surrounded by a landscaped garden and two smaller palaces, the Wasserpalais and the Bergpalais. Both buildings were designed in Germany's late baroque faux-Chinese pagoda style. Today, they house the **Kunstgewerbemuseum,** which showcases baroque furniture and crafts as well as modern design. To get to Schloss Pillnitz, take Tram 10 from the central train station toward Striesen, exit there and continue with Tram 12 (to Schillerplatz), change there again, and take Bus 83 to Pillnitz. ✉ *Kleinzschachwitz* ☎ *0351/261–3201* 🌐 *www.skd-dresden.de* 🎟 *€3* ⏲ *Bergpalais May–Oct., Tues.–Sun. 10–6; Wasserpalais, May–Oct., Wed.–Mon. 10–6.*

7 **Residenzschloss** (Dresden City Royal Palace). Restoration work is still under way (scheduled for completion in 2006) behind the Renaissance facade of this former royal palace, much of which was built between 1709 and 1722. Some of the finished rooms in the **Georgenbau** host historical exhibitions, among them an excellent one on the reconstruction of the palace itself. The palace's main gateway, the Georgentor, has an enormous statue of the fully armed Saxon count George. From April through October, the palace's old **Hausmannsturm** (Hausmann Tower) offers a wonderful view of the city and the Elbe River.

But the main attraction is the world-famous **Grünes Gewölbe** (Green Vault) that was returned to the palace, its original location, in 2004 (prior to that, it had been housed in the Albertinum). Named after a green room in the palace of Augustus the Strong, it contains an exquisite collection of unique objets d'art fashioned from gold, silver, ivory, amber, and other precious and semiprecious materials. Among the crown jewels is the world's largest "green" diamond, 41 carats in weight, and a dazzling group of tiny gem-studded figures called *Hofstaat zu Delhi am Geburtstag des Grossmoguls Aureng-Zeb* (the Court at Delhi during the Birthday of the Great Mogul Aureng-Zeb). The unwieldy name gives a false idea of the size of the work, dating from 1708; some parts of the tableau are so small they can be admired only through a magnifying glass. Somewhat larger and less delicate is the drinking bowl of Ivan the Terrible, perhaps the most sensational artifact in this extraordinary museum.

The palace also houses the **Kupferstichkabinett** (Museum of Prints and Drawings) with more than 500,000 pieces of art spanning several centuries. Changing exhibits present masterworks by Albrecht Dürer, Peter Paul Rubens, and Jan van Eyck, but also 20th-century art by Otto Dix, Edvard Munch, and Ernst Ludwig Kirchner as well as East European art and some Southeast Asian prints.

Two equally impressive collections, the **Münzkabinett** (Coin Museum), and the **Rüstkammer** (Armory), will be moving back to the palace sometime in 2006. ✉ *Schlosspl.* ☎ *0351/491–4619* 🎫 *€6, for all museums and collections at palace* ⏲ *Wed.–Mon. 10–6.*

★ ❾ **Semperoper** (Semper Opera House). One of Germany's best-known and most popular theaters, this magnificent opera house saw the premieres of Richard Wagner's *Rienzi, Der Fliegende Holländer,* and *Tannhäuser,* and Richard Strauss's *Salome, Elektra,* and *Der Rosenkavalier.* The Dresden architect Gottfried Semper built the house in 1838–41 in Italian Renaissance style, then saw his work destroyed in a fire caused by a careless lamplighter. Semper had to flee Dresden after participating in a democratic uprising, so his son Manfred rebuilt the theater in the neo-Renaissance style you see today. Even Manfred Semper's version had to be rebuilt after the devastating bombing raid of February 1945. On the 40th anniversary of that raid—February 13, 1985—the Semperoper reopened with a performance of *Der Freischütz,* by Carl Maria von Weber, another artist who did much to make Dresden a leading center of German music and culture. Even if you're no opera buff, the Semper's lavish interior can't fail to impress. Velvet, brocade, and well-crafted imitation marble create an atmosphere of intimate luxury (it seats 1,323). Guided tours of the building are offered throughout the day, depending on the opera's rehearsal schedule. Tours begin at the entrance to your right as you face the Elbe River. ✉ *Theaterpl. 2* ☎ *0351/491–1496* 🌐 *www.semperoper.de* 🎫 *Tour €6* ⏲ *Tours usually weekdays at 1:30, 2, and 3; weekends at 10.*

❸ **Stadtmuseum Dresden im Landhaus** (Dresden City Museum at the Country Mansion). The city's small but fascinating municipal museum tells the ups and downs of Dresden's turbulent past—from the dark Middle Ages to the bombing of Dresden in February 1945. There are many peculiar exhibits on display, such as an American 250-kg bomb and a stove made from Allied bomb casing. ✉ *Wilsdruffer Str. 2* ☎ *0351/656–480* 🌐 *http://stadtmuseum.dresden.de* 🎫 *€2.50* ⏲ *Tues.–Sun. 10–6.*

10 **Zwinger** (Bailey). Dresden's magnificent baroque showpiece is entered by way of the mighty Kronentor (Crown Gate), off Ostra-Allee. Augustus the Strong hired a small army of artists and artisans to create a "pleasure ground" worthy of the Saxon court on the site of the former bailey, part of the city fortifications. The artisans worked under the direction of the architect Matthäus Daniel Pöppelmann, who came reluctantly out of retirement to design what would be his greatest work, begun in 1707 and completed in 1728. Completely enclosing a central courtyard filled with lawns, pools, and fountains, the complex is made up of six linked pavilions, one of which boasts a carillon of Meissen bells, hence its name: Glockenspielpavillon.

Fodor's Choice ★

The Zwinger is quite a scene—a riot of garlands, nymphs, and other baroque ornamentation and sculpture. Wide staircases beckon to galleried walks and to the romantic Nymphenbad, a coyly hidden courtyard where statues of nude women perch in alcoves to protect them from a fountain that spits unexpectedly. The Zwinger once had an open view of the riverbank, but the Semper Opera House now closes in that side. Stand in the center of this quiet oasis, where the city's roar is kept at bay by the outer wings of the structure, and imagine the court festivities held here.

The **Sempergalerie** (Semper Gallery), in the northwestern corner of the complex, was built to house portions of the royal art collections. It contains the world-renowned Gemäldegalerie Alte Meister (Old Masters Gallery). The Zwinger Palace complex also contains a porcelain collection, a zoological museum, and the Staatlicher Mathematisch-Physikalischer Salon, which displays old scientific instruments.

Among the priceless paintings in the Sempergalerie collection are works by Dürer, Holbein, Jan van Eyck, Rembrandt, Rubens, van Dyck, Hals, Vermeer, Raphael (*The Sistine Madonna*), Titian, Giorgione, Veronese, Velázquez, Murillo, Canaletto, and Watteau. On the wall of the entrance archway you'll see an inscription in Russian, one of the few amusing reminders of World War II in Dresden. It reads, in rhyme: MUSEUM CHECKED. NO MINES. CHANUTIN DID THE CHECKING. Chanutin, presumably, was the Russian soldier responsible for checking one of Germany's greatest art galleries for anything more explosive than a Rubens nude. ☎ *0351/491–4619* 🌐 *www.staatl-kunstsammlungen-dresden.de* 🎫 *€6* ⏲ *Tues.–Sun. 10–6.*

The Zwinger's **Porzellansammlung** (Porcelain Collection; ☎ 0351/491–4619 🎫 €5 ⏲ Tues.–Sun. 10–6), stretching from the curved gallery that adjoins the Glockenspielpavillon to the long gallery on the east side, is considered one of the best of its kind in the world. The focus, naturally, is on Dresden and Meissen china, but there are also outstanding examples of Japanese, Chinese, and Korean porcelain. The **Rüstkammer** (Armory; ☎ 0351/491–4619 🎫 €3 ⏲ Tues.–Sun. 10–6) holds medieval and Renaissance suits of armor and weapons. The **Naturhistorische Sammlung** (Natural History Collection; ☎ 0351/495–2503 🎫 €3 ⏲ Tues.–Sun.

10–6) has a small but very interesting collection of natural-history exhibits, including skeletons of wild animals that once roamed the Elbe Valley. The **Staatlicher Mathematisch-Physikalischer Salon** (State Mathematics and Physics Salon; ☎ 0351/491–4660 €3 ⏲ Tues.–Sun. 10–6) is packed with rare and historic scientific instruments. ✉ *Zwinger entrance, Ostra–Allee.*

Where to Stay & Eat

★ $$–$$$ ✕ **Alte Meister.** Set in the historic mansion of the architect who rebuilt the Zwinger and named after the school of medieval German painters that includes Dürer, Holbein, and Rembrandt, the Alte Meister has a sophisticated Old World flair that charms locals and tourists alike. The food, however, is very current, and the light German nouvelle cuisine with careful touches of Asian spices and ingredients has earned chef Dirk Wende praise by Michelin gourmet critics. In summer, this is one of the city's premier dining spots, offering a grand view of the Semperoper from a shaded terrace. ✉ *Braun'sches Atelier Theaterpl. 1a* ☎ *0351/481–0426* ▭ *AE, MC, V.*

★ $ ✕ **Sophienkeller.** One of the liveliest restaurants in town re-creates an 18th-century beer cellar in the basement of the Taschenberg Palace. Waitresses wear period costumes, and the furniture and porcelain are as rustic as the food is traditional, including the typically Saxon *Gesindeessen* (rye bread, pan-fried with mustard, slices of pork, and mushrooms, baked with cheese). The Sophienkeller is popular with larger groups; you might have to wait if you're a party of three or fewer. ✉ *Taschenbergpalais, Taschenberg 3* ☎ *0351/497–260* ▭ *AE, DC, MC, V.*

¢–$ ✕ **Ballhaus Watzke.** One of the city's oldest microbreweries, the Ballhaus Watzke offers a great panorama view of Dresden from outside the historic downtown area. Several different beers are on tap (you can even help brew one). The extensive menu is made up of mostly hearty local dishes and also has a great variety of Saxon desserts. In summer, the beer garden is open for seating. ✉ *Koetzschenbroderstr. 1* ☎ *0351/852–920* ▭ *AE, MC, V.*

¢–$ ✕ **Ristorante Bellotto im Italienischen Dörfchen.** The name of the restaurant refers to the fact that this historic building on the bank of the Elbe once housed Italian craftsmen. They were brought to Dresden to work on the Hofkirche. Today the lavishly restored, colorful rooms offer a warm welcome. Choose between the beer tavern, café, or shady garden for a mostly Saxon menu. The Bellotto restaurant upstairs serves upscale Italian cuisine. ✉ *Theaterpl. 3* ☎ *0351/498–160* ▭ *AE, DC, MC, V.*

★ $$$$ **Kempinski Hotel Taschenbergpalais Dresden.** Destroyed in wartime bombing but now rebuilt, the historic Taschenberg Palace—the work of the Zwinger architect Matthäus Daniel Pöppelmann—is Dresden's premier address and the last word in luxury, as befits the former residence of the Saxon crown princes. Rooms are as big as city apartments, although suites earn the adjective *palatial;* they are all furnished with bright elm-wood furniture and have several phone lines, as well as fax machines and data ports. ✉ *Taschenberg 3, D–01067* ☎ *0351/49120* *0351/491–2812* 🌐 *www.kempinski-dresden.de* *188 rooms, 25 suites* *4 restaurants, room service, in-room safes, minibars, cable TV with movies, in-room broadband, in-room data ports, pool, hair salon, mas-*

sage, sauna, bar, shops, babysitting, dry cleaning, laundry service, concierge, business services, meeting room, parking (fee), some pets allowed (fee), no-smoking rooms ▭ *AE, DC, MC, V.*

$$$–$$$$ **Hotel Bülow-Residenz.** One of the most intimate first-class hotels in East Germany, the Bülow-Residenz is in a baroque palace built in 1730 by a wealthy Dresden city official. Each spacious room is tastefully decorated with thick carpets and mostly dark, warm cherrywood furniture and has individual accents and modern amenities. In summer the verdant courtyard is a romantic setting for dinner. The Caroussel restaurant ($$$–$$$$) holds Saxony's sole Michelin star and serves a large variety of sophisticated fish and game dishes. ✉ *Rähnitzg. 19, D–01097* ☎ *0351/80030* 📠 *0351/800–3100* 🌐 *www.buelow-residenz.de* *25 rooms, 5 suites* *Restaurant, room service, in-room safes, minibars, cable TV with movies, Wi-Fi, bar, babysitting, dry cleaning, laundry service, concierge, meeting room, parking (fee), some pets allowed (fee), no-smoking floor; no a/c in some rooms* ▭ *AE, DC, MC, V.*

$$ **artotel Dresden.** The artotel keeps the promise of its rather unusual name. It's all modern, designed by Italian interior-architect Denis Santachiara and decorated with more than 600 works of art by Dresden-born painter and sculptor A. R. Penck. It's definitely a place for the artsy crowd; you might find the heavily styled rooms a bit much. The Kunsthalle Dresden and its exhibits of modern art are right next door. Apart from offering art, the hotel's rooms and service have genuine first-class appeal at slightly better prices. ✉ *Ostra-Allee 33, D–01067* ☎ *0351/49220* 📠 *0351/492–2777* 🌐 *www.artotels.de* *155 rooms, 19 suites* *2 restaurants, room service, minibars, cable TV, in-room data ports, gym, massage, sauna, bar, babysitting, dry cleaning, laundry service, concierge, business services, meeting room, parking (fee), some pets allowed (fee), no-smoking rooms* ▭ *AE, DC, MC, V* 🍽 *BP.*

$$ **Hotel Elbflorenz.** This centrally located hotel lives up to Dresden's somewhat presumptuous nickname *Elbflorenz,* or Florence on the River Elbe, thanks to its first-class service and stylish ambience. The Italian-designed rooms are bathed in red and yellow tones and sit alongside a garden courtyard. There's a fine sauna and relaxation area, and the hotel's restaurant, Quattro Cani della Citta, serves delicious Italian seafood and other specialties. ✉ *Rosenstr. 36, D–01067* ☎ *0351/86400* 📠 *0351/864–0100* 🌐 *www.hotel-elbflorenz.de* *212 rooms, 15 suites* *Restaurant, café, in-room safes, minibars, cable TV, in-room data ports, gym, sauna, bar, children's programs (from infancy to age 14), concierge, meeting room, parking (fee), some pets allowed (fee), no-smoking rooms* ▭ *AE, DC, MC, V* 🍽 *BP.*

$$ **Rothenburger Hof.** One of Dresden's smallest and oldest luxury hotels, the historic Rothenburger Hof opened in 1865 and is only a few steps away from the city's sightseeing spots. A highlight is the dining room, which gives you some insight as to how Dresden's wealthy wined and dined 150 years ago. The rooms are not very large, but they're comfortable and nicely decorated with furniture that looks antique but, in fact, is reproduction. ✉ *Rothenburger Str. 15–17, D–01099* ☎ *0351/81260* 📠 *0351/812–6222* 🌐 *www.dresden-hotel.de* *26 rooms, 13 apartments* *Room service, minibars, cable TV, in-room broadband,*

Wi-Fi, pool, health club, sauna, bar, dry cleaning, laundry service, meeting room, parking (fee), no-smoking rooms; no a/c ▭ *AE, MC, V* 🍽 *BP.*

$$ 🏨 **Schlosshotel Dresden-Pillnitz.** On the grounds of Schloss Pillnitz (Pillnitz Palace), this small hotel allows you to enjoy the countryside without getting too far from the city. The beautifully restored mansion is run by the Zepp family, who extend extremely personal service. The airy rooms are decorated with bright colors and timeless, elegant country furniture. Just a few hundred yards from the hotel is a pier where Elbe River cruises depart. The spa Vitalzentrum zum goldenen Apfel is a short walk away. ✉ *August-Böckstiegel-Str. 10, D–01326* ☎ *0351/26140* 📠 *0351/261–4400* 🌐 *www.schlosshotel-pillnitz.de* *42 rooms, 3 suites* *Restaurant, minibars, cable TV, in-room broadband, in-room data ports, bar, dry cleaning, laundry service, meeting rooms, free parking, some pets allowed (fee), no-smoking floor; no a/c* ▭ *AE, MC, V* 🍽 *BP.*

Nightlife & the Arts

Dresdeners are known for their industriousness and very efficient way of doing business, but they also know how to spend a night out. Most of Dresden's pubs, bars, and *Kneipen* are in the **Äussere Neustadt** district and along the buzzing **Münzgasse** (between Frauenkirche and Brühlsche Terrasse). Folk and rock music are regularly featured at **Bärenzwinger** (✉ Brühlscher Garten ☎ 0351/495–1409). One of the best bars in town is the groovy and hip **Aqualounge** (✉ Louisenstr. 56 ☎ 0351/810–6116). The name of the **Planwirtschaft** (✉ Louisenstr. 20 ☎ 0351/801–3187) ironically refers to the Socialist economic system and attracts an alternative crowd. The hip dance club **Dance Factory** (✉ Bautzner Str. 118 ☎ 0351/802–0066) is in an old Stasi garrison. The **Motown Club** (✉ St. Petersburger Str. 9 ☎ 0351/487–4150) attracts a young and stylish crowd.

The opera in Dresden regained its international reputation when the **Semper Opera House** (Sächsische Staatsoper Dresden; ✉ Theaterpl. ✉ Evening box office, Abendkasse, left of main entrance ☎ 0351/491–1705) reopened in 1985 following an eight-year reconstruction. Tickets are reasonably priced but also hard to come by; they're often included in package tours. Try your luck at the evening box office about a half-hour before the performance. If that doesn't work, take one of the opera-house tours.

Dresden's fine **Philharmonie Dresden** (Philharmonic Orchestra Dresden; ✉ Kulturpalast am Altmarkt ☎ 0351/486–6286) takes center stage in the city's annual music festival, from mid-May to early June. In addition to the annual film festival in April, open-air **Filmnächte am Elbufer** (Elbe Riverside Film Nights; ✉ Am Königsufer, next to the State Ministry of Finance ☎ 0351/899–320) take place on the bank of the Elbe from late June to late August.

May brings an annual international Dixieland **jazz** festival, and the Jazz Autumn festival follows in October. Jazz musicians perform most nights of the week at the friendly, laid-back **Tonne Jazz Club** (✉ Waldschlösschen, Am Brauhaus 3 ☎ 0351/802–6017).

Shopping

Dresden is almost as famous as Meissen for its porcelain. It's manufactured outside the city in **Freital,** where there's a showroom and shop, **Sächsische Prozellan-Manufaktur Dresden** (✉ Carl-Thieme-Str. 16, Freital ☎ 0351/647–130), open Monday through Saturday 9 to 5. Within Dresden you'll find exquisite Meissen and Freital porcelain at the department store **Karstadt** (✉ Prager Str. 12 ☎ 0351/490–6833). The **Kunststube am Zwinger** (✉ Hertha-Lindner-Str. 10–12 ☎ 0351/490–4082) sells wooden toys and the famous Saxon *Rächermännchen* (Smoking Men) and *Weihnachtspyramiden* (Christmas Lights Pyramids) manufactured by hand in the Erzbirge Mountains.

15

Sächsische Schweiz

⓯ *42 km (26 mi) southeast of Dresden.*

True mountain climbers may smile at the name of the Sächsische Schweiz (Saxon Switzerland), the mountainous region southeast of Dresden. The highest summit is a mere 182 feet, but the scenery in this region, a mixture of cliffs, gorges, and small canyons, certainly has drama. The stone formations are at least 100 million years old and are leftovers from the Elbe River's sandstone deposits. In time, the soft stone was sculpted by wind and water into grim but fantastic looking tall columns of stone.

The **Nationalpark** covers 97 square km (37 square mi) of the region. Thanks to its inaccessibility, Saxon Switzerland is home to game and many other wild animals (such as the lynx), which are otherwise extinct in Germany. The park is divided into two parts, which can be explored by foot, either following marked routes or by registering with the park rangers for guided tours. To reach the park from Dresden, drive southeast on B–172 toward Pirna, or take the S-bahn from the central train station to Königsstein or Bad Schandau; both towns are served by buses and minitrains. The train ride itself takes close to an hour. ✉ *Nationalpark- und Forstamt Sächsische Schweiz, An der Elbe 4, D–01814 Bad Schandau* ☎ *035022/900–600* 🌐 *www.nationalpark-saechsische-schweiz.de* 🎫 *Free* ⏲ *Free guided walking tours mid-Apr.–Oct., Mon. at 10 AM at Bad Schandau; Tues. at 10 AM at Kurort Rathen; Wed. at 10:20 AM at Hinterhermsdorf; Thurs. at 10 AM at Wehlen. Call for exact meeting points.*

Görlitz

⓰ *60 km (38 mi) northeast of Dresden, 265 km (165 mi) southeast of Berlin.*

Quiet, narrow cobblestone alleys and late-medieval and Renaissance structures make Görlitz one of the most charming finds in eastern Germany. Once a major commercial hub between Dresden and Wroclaw, Germany's easternmost city fell into small-town oblivion after World War II, which left the city almost completely intact.

A vivid reminder of the city's wealthy past is the richly decorated Renaissance homes and warehouses on the **Obermarkt** (Upper Market). During the late Middle Ages the most common merchandise here was cloth, which was bought and sold from covered wagons and the first floors of many buildings. On **Verrätergasse** (Traitors' Alley), off the Obermarkt, is the **Peter-Liebig-Haus,** where the city's cloth makers secretly met in 1527 to plan a rebellion against the city council. Their plans were uncovered, and the plotters were hanged. The initials of the first four words of their meeting place, *Der verräterischen Rotte Tor* (t&he treacherous gang's gate), are inscribed above the door.

The **Städtische Kunstsammlung** (Municipal Art Collection) has two locations. The massive **Kaisertrutz** (Emperor's Fortress) once protected the western city gates and now houses late-Gothic and Renaissance art from the area around Görlitz. The **Barockhaus Neissestrasse** mostly displays 17th- to 19th-century furniture and art. ✉ *Kaisertrutz, Am Obermarkt* ✉ *Barockhaus Neissestrasse, Neissestr. 30* ☎ *03581/671–351* 🎫 *€3.50* ⏲ *Tues.–Thurs., and weekends 10–5, Fri. 10–8; Kaisertrutz closed Nov.–Apr.*

The city's oldest section surrounds the **Untermarkt** (Lower Market), whose most prominent building is the **Rathaus.** Its winding staircase is as peculiar as the statue of the goddess of justice, whose eyes—contrary to European tradition—are not covered. The corner house on the square, the **Alte Ratsapotheke** (Old Council Pharmacy), has a sundial on the facade (painted in 1550) based on the 12 signs of the zodiac.

The **Schlesisches Museum** (Silesian Museum) is housed in the magnificent Schönhof building, one of Germany's oldest *Patrizierhäuser* (grand mansion of the city's ruling business and political elite, the Patricians). The museum showcases the history—primarily 17th–19th century—and art of formerly German Silesia. ✉ *Untermarkt 4* ☎ *03581/87910* 🌐 *www.schlesisches-museum.de* 🎫 *€1* ⏲ *Tues.–Sun. 10–5.*

The **Karstadt** department store, off busy Marienplatz, dates to 1912–13 and is Germany's only original art nouveau–department store. The main hall has a colorful glass cupola and several stunning freestanding staircases. ✉ *An der Frauenkirche 5–7* ☎ *03581/4600.*

Perched high above the river is the **Kirche St. Peter und Paul** (St. Peter and Paul Church), one of Saxony's largest late-Gothic churches, dating to 1423. The real draw of the church is its famous organ, built in 1703 by Eugenio Casparini. Its full and deep sound can be heard during guided tours (which must be prearranged by phone). ✉ *Bei der Peterkirche 5* ☎ *03581/409–590* 🎫 *Free* ⏲ *Mon.–Sat. 10:30–4, Sun. 11:30–4; guided tours Thurs. and Sun. at noon.*

off the beaten path

KULTURINSEL EINSIEDEL – This handcrafted amusement park is a delightful wonderland of ships, forts, games, and mazes. Kids descend into tunnels and can choose between various routes that lead to surprising places. This topsy-turvy world is mirrored in the expressionist-like design of the outdoor stage, restaurant, and covered buildings. A family entry price includes a credit toward snacks. ✉ *Zentdendorfer Str., Zentendorf, 17 km (11 mi) north of Görlitz* ☎ *035891/4910* 🌐 *www.kulturinsel.de* 🎫 *€4.50* ⏲ *Mar.–Oct., daily 10–6.*

Where to Stay & Eat

$ **Le Trou Normand.** Behind the thick walls of a historic baroque building, this charming little restaurant serves the cuisine of northern France. The wine list is impressive, the atmosphere is friendly and familial, and the menu changes monthly. *Untermarkt 13 03581/417–037 MC, V No lunch Mon.*

★ $$ **Romantik-Hotel Tuchmacher.** The city's best hotel is also its most modern accommodation in antique disguise. In a mansion dating to 1528, guest rooms with wooden floors and thick ceiling beams are sparsely furnished with modern dark-cherrywood furniture. The colorful ceilings may remind you of Jackson Pollock paintings, but they are original ornaments from the Renaissance. The Schneider-Stube ($–$$$) serves traditional Saxon dishes. All room prices include a luxurious breakfast buffet. *Peterstr. 8, D–02826 03581/47310 03581/473–179 www.tuchmacher.de 42 rooms, 1 suite Restaurant, room service, minibars, cable TV, in-room data ports, gym, sauna, bar, dry cleaning, laundry service, meeting room, free parking, some pets allowed (fee), no-smoking rooms; no a/c AE, DC, MC, V BP.*

Meissen

17 *25 km (16 mi) northwest of Dresden.*

This romantic city on the Elbe River is known the world over for its porcelain, bearing the trademark crossed blue swords. The first European porcelain was made in this area in 1708, and in 1710 the Royal Porcelain Workshop was established in Meissen, close to the local raw materials.

The story of how porcelain came to be produced in Meissen reads like a German fairy tale: The Saxon elector Augustus the Strong, who ruled from 1694 to 1733, urged his court alchemists to find the secret of making gold, something he badly needed to refill a state treasury depleted by his extravagant lifestyle. The alchemists failed to produce gold, but one of them, Johann Friedrich Böttger, discovered a method for making something almost as precious: fine hard-paste porcelain. Already a rapacious collector of Oriental porcelains, Prince August put Böttger and a team of craftsmen up in a hilltop castle—Albrechtsburg—and set them to work.

The **Albrechtsburg,** where the story of Meissen porcelain began, sits high above Old Meissen, towering over the Elbe River far below. The 15th-century castle is Germany's first truly residential one, a complete break with the earlier style of fortified bastions. In the central *Schutzhof,* a typical Gothic courtyard protected on three sides by high rough-stone walls, is an exterior spiral staircase, the **Wendelstein,** a masterpiece of early masonry hewn in 1525 from a single massive stone block. The ceilings of the castle halls are richly decorated, although many date only from a restoration in 1870. Adjacent to the castle is an early Gothic cathedral. It's a bit of a climb up Burgstrasse and Amtsstrasse to the castle, but a bus runs regularly up the hill from the Marktplatz. *03521/47070 www.albrechtsburg-meissen.de €3.50, €5 with tour Mar.–Oct., daily 10–6; Nov.–Feb., daily 10–5.*

A set of porcelain bells at the late-Gothic **Frauenkirche** (Church of Our Lady), on the central Marktplatz, was the first of its kind anywhere when installed in 1929. Nearby the Frauenkirche is the **Alte Brauerei** (Old Brewery), which dates to 1569 and is graced by a Renaissance gable. It now houses city offices.

The city's medieval past is recounted in the museum of the **Franziskanerkirche** (St. Francis Church), a former monastery. ✉ *Heinrichspl. 3* ☎ *03521/458–857* 🎫 *€3* ⏲ *Daily 11–5.*

The **Staatliche Porzellan–Manufaktur Meissen** (Meissen Porcelain Works) outgrew its castle workshop in the mid-19th century and today is on the southern outskirts of town. One of its buildings has a demonstration workshop and a museum whose Meissen collection rivals that of the Porcelain Museum in Dresden. ✉ *Talstr. 9* ☎ *03521/468–700* 🌐 *www.meissen.de* 🎫 *Museum €4.50; workshop €3, including guided tour; combined ticket €5* ⏲ *May–Oct., daily 9–6; Nov.–Apr., daily 9–5.*

Near the porcelain works is the **Nikolaikirche** (St. Nicholas Church; ✉ Neumarkt 29), which holds the largest set of porcelain figures ever crafted (8¼ feet) and also has remains of early Gothic frescoes.

Where to Stay & Eat

★ **$–$$** ✕ **Restaurant Vincenz Richter.** Tucked away in a yellow wooden-beam house, this historic restaurant has been painstakingly maintained by the Richter family since 1873. The dining room is adorned with rare antiques, documents, and medieval weapons, as well as copper and tin tableware. Guests can savor the exquisite dishes on the Saxon-German menu, while sampling the restaurant's own personally produced white wine; a bottle of the Riesling is a real pleasure. *Meissener Kapitelberg.* ✉ *An der Frauenkirche 12* ☎ *03521/453–285* 💳 *AE, DC, MC, V* ⏲ *Closed Mon. No lunch, no dinner Sun.*

$ ✕ **Domkeller.** Part of the centuries-old complex of buildings ringing the town castle, this ancient and popular hostelry is the best place to enjoy fine wines and hearty German dishes in Meissen. It's also worth a visit for the sensational view of the Elbe River valley from its large dining room and tree-shaded terrace. ✉ *Dompl. 9* ☎ *03521/457–676* 💳 *AE, DC, MC, V.*

$$ ✕🏨 **Mercure Parkhotel Meissen.** This art-nouveau villa on the bank of the Elbe sits across from the hilltop castle. Although most of the luxuriously furnished and appointed rooms are in the newly built annexes, try for one in the villa—and for an unforgettable experience book the *Hochzeitssuite* (wedding suite), on the top floor (€203 a night), for its stunning view. The restaurant serves nouvelle cuisine in a dining room ($$) with original stained glass and elegantly framed doors. ✉ *Hafenstr. 27–31, D–01662* ☎ *03521/72250* 📠 *03521/722–904* 🌐 *www.mercure.de* 🛏 *92 rooms, 5 suites* 🛎 *Restaurant, room service, minibars, cable TV, in-room broadband, in-room data ports, gym, hot tub, massage, sauna, bar, babysitting, dry cleaning, laundry service, meeting room, parking (fee), some pets allowed (fee), no-smoking rooms; no a/c* 💳 *AE, DC, MC, V* 🍽 *BP.*

The Arts

Meissen's cathedral, the **Dom** (✉ Dompl. 7 ☎ 03521/452–490), has a year-long music program, with organ and choral concerts every Saturday during the summer. Regular **concerts** (☎ 03521/47070) are held at the Albrechtsburg castle, and in early September the *Burgfestspiele*—open-air evening performances—are staged in the castle's romantic courtyard.

Shopping

Meissen porcelain can be bought directly from the **Staatliche Porzellan–Manufaktur Meissen** (✉Talstr. 9 ☎03521/468–700) and in every china and gift shop in town. To wine connoisseurs, the name *Meissen* is associated with vineyards producing top-quality wines much in demand throughout Germany—try a bottle of Müller-Thurgau, Weissburgunder, or Goldriesling. They can be bought from the producer **Sächsische Winzergenossenschaft Meissen** (✉ Bennoweg 9 ☎ 03521/780–970).

Chemnitz

18 *75 km (47 mi) southwest of Meissen, 80 km (50 mi) southeast of Leipzig.*

On older maps Chemnitz may appear as Karl-Marx-Stadt, an appellation imposed on the city in 1953 to remind the East German working community of the man who really started it all. In 1990 the inhabitants, free to express a choice, overwhelmingly voted to restore the original name. Badly damaged during World War II, Chemnitz has been revived as a center of industry and culture.

Chemnitz's main visual attraction is its 12th-century **Rote Turm** (Red Tower; ✉ off Strasse der Nationen) in the center of the city. The **Altes Rathaus** (Old Town Hall; ✉ Marktpl.), dating from 1496–98, incorporates a variety of styles from many reconstructions. Outside the city museum (which is not particularly interesting) on Theaterplatz is a group of 250-million-year-old **petrified tree trunks,** unique in Europe and oddly resembling a modern work of sculpture.

The **Kunstsammlungen Chemnitz im König-Albert-Museum** (Chemnitz Art Collection at the King Albert Museum) boasts some 80,000 paintings and sculptures, spanning centuries of European art, from Romanticism to French impressionism and the German 20th-century expressionist movement known as *Die Brücke* (The Bridge). One of the most famous members of this lattermost movement, Karl Schmidt-Rotluff (1884–1976), was born in the neighboring vicinity, and the museum houses the world's second-largest collection of his paintings. ✉ *Theaterpl.1* ☎ *0371/488–4424* 🎫 *€6* ⏲ *Tues.–Fri. noon–7, weekends 11–7.*

Where to Stay & Eat

$$ ✕🏨 **Günnewig Hotel Chemnitzer Hof.** This city-center hotel was built in 1930 in early Bauhaus style, in which ornamentation was discarded in favor of abstract design (it's now on the National Historic Register). The spacious rooms are furnished with fine veneers and attractive shades of blue. The restaurant Opera ($–$$) serves international dishes and has an extensive menu of local fish. ✉ *Theaterpl. 4, D–09111* ☎ *0371/6840* 🖷 *0371/676–2587* 🌐 *www.guennewig.de* *98 rooms, 3 apartments* *Restaurant, room service, in-room safes, minibars, cable TV, in-room broadband, sauna, bar, dry cleaning, laundry service, meeting room, parking (fee), some pets allowed (fee), no-smoking rooms; no a/c* 💳 *AE, DC, MC, V* 🍽 *BP.*

$ ✕ **Adelsberger Parkhotel Hoyer.** The first hotel built in Chemnitz after reunification has a modern, graceful exterior and elegant, comfortable guest rooms. The apartments under the steeply sloping eaves are particularly attractive, especially where sunlight streams through large dormer windows. The restaurant's (¢–$) royal-blue-and-white furnishings are flooded with light from floor-to-ceiling bay windows. The imaginative menu includes hearty Saxon specialties. ✉ *Wilhelm-Busch-Str. 61, D–09127* ☎ *0371/774–200* 🖷 *0371/773–377* 🌐 *www.adelsberger-parkhotel.de* *23 rooms, 3 suites* *Restaurant, room service, minibars, cable TV, Wi-Fi, gym, sauna, dry cleaning, laundry service, meeting room, free parking, some pets allowed (fee); no a/c* 💳 *AE, DC, MC, V* 🍽 *CP.*

en route

B–95 leads to Leipzig, but for a scene out of World War II, detour at Borna, taking 176 to **Colditz.** A pretty river valley holds the town whose name still sends a chill through Allied veterans. During the war the Germans converted the town's massive, somber castle into what they believed would be an escape-proof prison for prisoners regarded as security risks. But many managed to flee, employing a catalog of ruses that have since been the stuff of films and books. The castle is now a home for the elderly, but the courtyards and some of the installations used during the war can be visited. You can continue to Leipzig via 107 to the autobahn.

Leipzig

80 km (50 mi) northwest of Chemnitz, 32 km (20 mi) southeast of Halle.

With a population of about 500,000, Leipzig is the second-largest city in East Germany (after Berlin) and has long been a center of printing and bookselling. Astride major trade routes, it was an important market town in the Middle Ages, and it continues to be a trading center, thanks to the *Leipziger Messe* (trade and fair shows) throughout the year that bring together buyers from East and West.

Those familiar with music history associate Leipzig with the great composer Johann Sebastian Bach (1685–1750), who was organist and choir director at the Thomaskirche, and the 19th-century composer Richard Wagner, who was born here in 1813.

World War II left little of old Leipzig intact. Restoration conveys touches of the city's Renaissance character and art-nouveau flair, although some of the newer buildings (notably the university's skyscraper tower) distort the perspective and proportions of the old city.

a good walk

Start your tour of downtown Leipzig at the gigantic **Hauptbahnhof** 19, the city's main train station and premier shopping mall. Cross the broad expanse of Willy-Brandt-Platz to walk south on Goethestrasse. On your left you'll see the modern **Opernhaus** 20, whose socialist facade is a sad contrast to the magnificent old architecture of the Hauptbahnhof. Turn right onto Grimmaischestrasse and after a short walk turn right onto Nikolaistrasse, where you can visit the **Nikolaikirche** 21. As you return south, Nikolaistrasse turns into Universitätstrasse, where the rather unappealing **Leipziger Universitätsturm** 22 looms above every other building in the city center. On its east side, the tower faces the vast Augustusplatz; across this square stands the **Neues Gewandhaus** 23, home of the city's renowned orchestra. Return north to Grimmaischestrasse and walk west; on your left you'll pass by the **Mädlerpassage** 24, one of the city's finest shopping arcades, which dates to the turn of the 20th century. Continue a bit farther west, and just off the street on your right is the market square, the **Markt** 25, with the old town hall and its museum devoted to Leipzig's past. Not far away, off the narrow Barfussgässchen, is the **Museum zum Arabischen Kaffeebaum** 26, a coffeehouse and museum devoted to the bitter bean. From here it's just a five-minute walk northeast to the Sachsenplatz with the newly built, ultramodern **Museum der Bildenden Künste** 27, the city's leading art gallery. Continue west on to the **Museum in der Runden Ecke** 28, a special exhibition about East Germany's secret police, the Stasi. Take the Dittrichring to **Thomaskirche** 29, where Johann Sebastian Bach once worked as choirmaster. Opposite the church is the **Bach-Museum im Bach-Archiv Leipzig** 30. Following Thomasgasse eastwards, the street name will change to Grimmaischestrasse, you'll reach the **Grassimuseum** 31, Leipzig's grand historic museum center, in about 10 minutes.

After a stop here you can take a streetcar (No. 15 to Meusdorf) from Johannisplatz to the **Völkerschlachtdenkmal** 32, a huge memorial to the battle that marked the beginning of Napoléon's final defeat in 1815. For another side trip, take streetcar No. 6 to the **Schillerhaus** 33, once the home of German poet and playwright Friedrich Schiller.

TIMING It's possible to walk around the downtown area in just about three hours and still stop at some of the sights mentioned above. The churches can be inspected in less than 20 minutes each. But if you're interested in German history and art, you'll need perhaps two full days so you can spend a whole day just visiting the museums. The Völkerschlachtdenkmal is perfect for a half-day side trip.

What to See

off the beaten path

BOTANISCHER GARTEN (Botanical Garden) – This set of splendid open-air gardens and greenhouses incorporates Germany's oldest university botanical garden, which dates from 1542. The journey to the Botanischer Garten stop takes about 15 minutes on Tram 2 or 21 (get off at the Johannisallee stop). ✉ *Lennéstr. 1* ☎ *0341/97108* *Gardens free, greenhouses €3* ⏲ *Gardens Nov.–Feb., daily 9–4; Mar, Apr., and Oct., daily 9–6; May–Sept., daily 9–8. Greenhouses Nov.–Feb., daily 9–4; Mar., Apr., and Oct., daily 9–6; May–Sept.,*

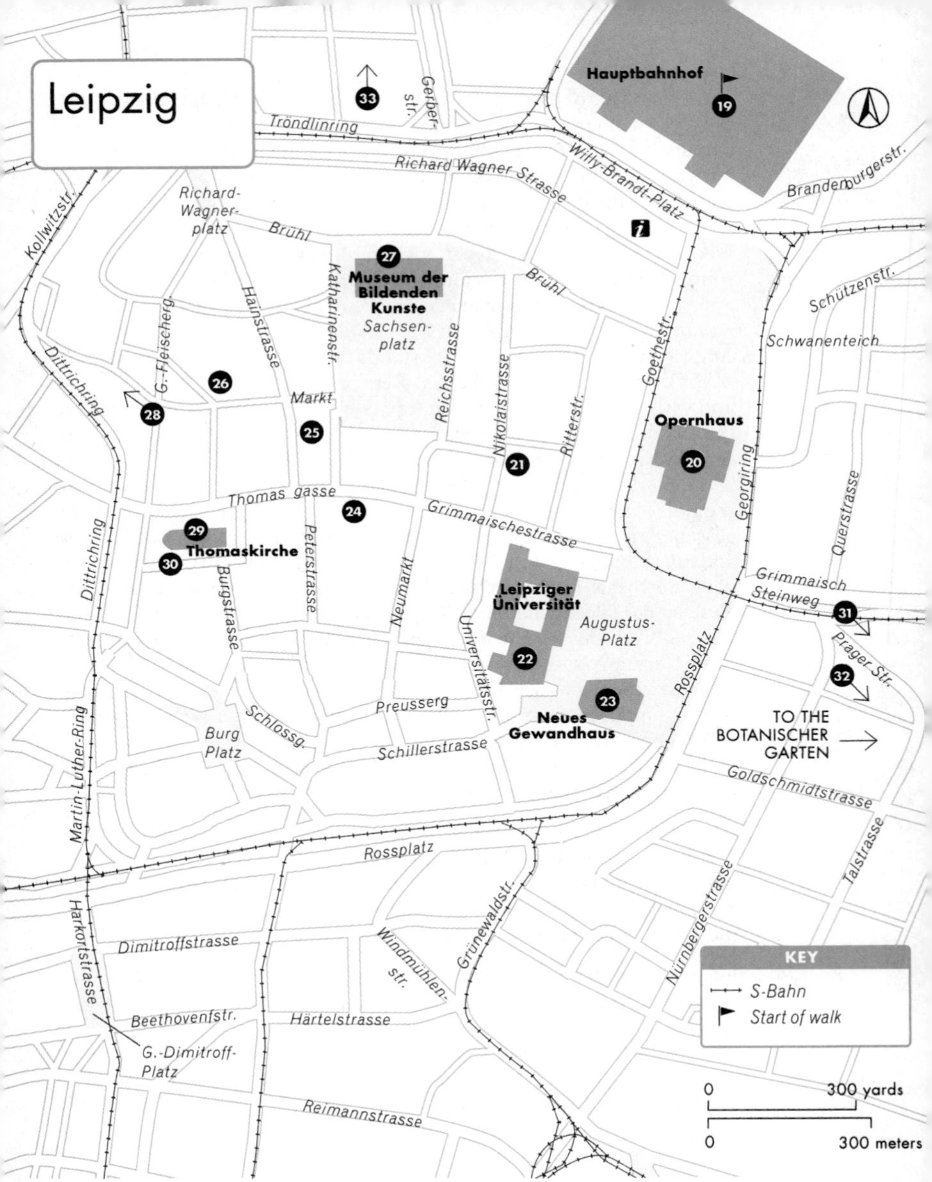

Bach-Museum im Bach-Archiv Leipzig **30**
Grassimuseum **31**
Hauptbahnhof **19**
Leipziger Universitätsturm ... **22**
Mädlerpassage **24**
Markt **25**
Museum der Bildenden Künste .. **27**
Museum in der Runden Ecke **28**
Museum zum Arabischen Kaffeebaum **26**
Neues Gewandhaus **23**
Nikolaikirche **21**
Opernhaus **20**
Schillerhaus **33**
Thomaskirche **29**
Völkerschlachtdenkmal **32**

daily 9–8, greenhouse hrs can vary according to events. Butterfly house May–Oct., daily 10–6.

30 **Bach-Museum im Bach-Archiv Leipzig** (Bach Museum at the Bach Archives Leipzig). The Bach family home, the old Bosehaus, stands opposite the Thomaskirche and is now a museum devoted to the composer's life and work. Musical instruments on display date to Bach's time. The exhibits are in German only; an English-language guide can be purchased in the shop. ✉ *Thomaskirchhof 16* ☎ *0341/91370* 🎫 *€3, €4.50 with guided tour* ⏲ *Daily 10–5.*

31 **Grassimuseum.** This major cultural venue is a fine example of German art deco and was restored and modernized by British star architect David Chipperfield in 2003–05. The building, dating to 1925–29, houses three important museums, which will be gradually reopened in 2006. The **Museum für Kunsthandwerk** (Museum of Arts and Crafts; ☎ 0341/213–3719 🌐 www.grassimuseum.de 🎫 €4 ⏲ Tues. and Thurs.–Sun. 10–6, Wed. 10–8) showcases works from Leipzig's and East Germany's proud tradition of handicrafts such as exquisite porcelain, fine tapestry art, and modern Bauhaus design.

The **Museum für Völkerkunde** (Ethnological Museum; ☎ 0341/213–3719 🌐 www.grassimuseum.de 🎫 €2 ⏲ Tues.–Fri. 10–6, weekends 10–5) presents arts and crafts from all continents and various era, including a thrilling collection of Southeast Asian antique art. The **Musikinstrumentenmuseum** (Musical Instruments Museum; ☎ 0341/973–0750 🌐 www.uni-leipzig.de/museum/musik 🎫 €3 ⏲ Tues.–Sun. 11–5) showcases musical instruments, mostly from the Renaissance, including the world's oldest clavichord, constructed in 1543 in Italy. There are also spinets, flutes, and lutes. Sample sounds of these instruments can be heard while looking at them. ✉ *Johannispl. 5–11.*

19 **Hauptbahnhof.** With 26 platforms, Leipzig's main train station is Europe's largest. It was built in 1915, and while a protected monument, modern commerce rules its bi-level shopping mall (the Promenaden). Many of the shops and eateries stay open until 10 PM. ✉ *Willy-Brandt-Pl.* ☎ *0341/141–270 for mall, 0341/9968–3275 for train station.*

22 **Leipziger Universitätsturm** (Leipzig University Tower). Towering over Leipzig's city center is this 470-foot-high structure, which houses administrative offices and lecture rooms. Some of the University of Leipzig students have dubbed it the Jagged Tooth. Students were also largely responsible for changing the university's name, replacing its postwar title, Karl Marx University, with the original one. The **Augustusplatz** spreads out below the university tower like a space-age campus.

24 **Mädlerpassage** (Mädler Mall). This shopper's paradise is Leipzig's finest arcade, where the ghost of Goethe's Faust lurks in every marble corner. Goethe set one of the scenes of *Faust* in the famous Auerbachs Keller restaurant, at No. 2. A bronze group of characters from the play, sculpted in 1913, beckons you down the stone staircase to the restaurant. A few yards away is a delightful art-nouveau bar called Mephisto, done in devilish reds and blacks. ✉ *Grimmaische Str.*

25 **Markt.** Leipzig's showpiece is its huge, old market square. One side is occupied completely by the Renaissance town hall, the **Altes Rathaus,** which houses the **Stadtgeschichtliches Museum,** where Leipzig's past is well documented. ✉ *Markt 1* ☎ *0341/965–130* 🎫 *€3* ⏲ *Tues.–Sun. 10–6.*

★ 27 **Museum der Bildenden Künste** (Museum of Fine Arts). The city's leading art gallery is set in a new, ultramodern, cubelike complex at the exact location of the original, historic museum which was destroyed by Allied bombing. The museum has more than 2,700 paintings representing everything from the German Middle Ages to contemporary American art; one of its finest collections focuses on Cranach the Elder. ✉ *Sachsenpl.* ☎ *0341/216–990* 🌐 *www.mdbk.de* 🎫 *€5, free 2nd Sun. of month* ⏲ *Tues. and Thurs.–Sun. 10–6, Wed. noon–8.*

★ 28 **Museum in der Runden Ecke** (Museum in the Round Corner). This building once served as the headquarters of the city's secret police, the dreaded *Staatssicherheitsdient.* The exhibition, *Stasi—Macht und Banalität* (Stasi—Power and Banality), not only presents the offices and surveillance work of the Stasi but also shows hundreds of documents revealing the magnitude of its interests in citizens' private lives. The material is written in German, but the items and the atmosphere still give an impression of how life under such a regime might have felt. ✉ *Dittrichring 24* ☎ *0341/961–2443* 🌐 *www.runde-ecke-leipzig.de* 🎫 *Free, €3 with tour in English, by appointment only* ⏲ *Daily 10–6.*

26 **Museum zum Arabischen Kaffeebaum** (Arabic Coffee Tree Museum). This museum and café–restaurant tells the fascinating history of coffee culture in Europe, particularly in Saxony. The café is one of the oldest on the continent and once proudly served coffee to such luminaries as Lessing, Schumann, Goethe, and Liszt. The museum features many paintings, Arabian coffee vessels, and coffeehouse games. It also explains the basic principles of roasting coffee. ✉ *Kleine Fleischerg. 4* ☎ *0341/9602–632* 🎫 *Free* ⏲ *Tues.–Sun. 11–5.*

23 **Neues Gewandhaus** (New Orchestra Hall). In the shadow of the Leipziger Universitätsturm is the glass-and-concrete home of the city orchestra, one of Germany's greatest. Kurt Masur is a former director and Herbert Blomstedt is currently at the helm. Owing to the world-renowned acoustics of the concert hall, a tone resonates here for a full two seconds. ✉ *Augustuspl. 8* ☎ *0341/127–0280.*

★ 21 **Nikolaikirche** (St. Nicholas Church). This church with its undistinguished facade was center stage during the demonstrations that helped bring down the Communist regime. Every Monday for months before the government collapsed, thousands of citizens gathered in front of the church chanting, "*Wir sind das Volk*" ("We are the people"). Inside is a soaring Gothic choir and nave. Note the unusual patterned ceiling supported by classical pillars that end in palm tree–like flourishes. Luther is said to have preached from the ornate 16th-century pulpit. ✉ *Nikolaikirchhof* ☎ *0341/960–5270* 🎫 *Free* ⏲ *Mon.–Sat. 10–6; Sun. services at 9:30, 11:15, and 5.*

20 **Opernhaus** (Opera House). Leipzig's stage for operas was the first postwar theater to be built in Communist East Germany. Its solid, boxy style is the subject of ongoing local controversy. ✉ *Opposite Gewandhaus, on north side of Augustuspl.*

33 **Schillerhaus** (Schiller House). This small country residence was, for a time, the home of the German poet and dramatist Friedrich Schiller. While staying here in 1785, Schiller wrote parts of his *Don Carlos* and the first draft of his world-famous *Ode an die Freude* (Ode to Joy). Documenting the 18th-century country lifestyle, the small museum contains period furniture, personal items, and other objects. To reach the Schillerhaus, take streetcar Line 6, 20, or 24 to Menckestrasse or Fritz-Seger-Strasse. ✉ *Menckestr. 42* ☎ *0341/566–2170* 🎟 *€2* ⏲ *Apr.–Oct., Tues.–Sun. 10–6; Nov.–Mar., Wed.–Sun. 10–4.*

29 **Thomaskirche** (St. Thomas's Church). Bach was choirmaster at this Gothic church for 27 years, and Martin Luther preached here on Whitsunday 1539, signaling the arrival of Protestantism in Leipzig. Originally the center of a 13th-century monastery, the tall church (rebuilt in the 15th century) now stands by itself. Bach wrote most of his cantatas for the church's famous boys' choir, the *Thomanerchor,* which was founded in the 13th century; the church continues as the choir's home as well as a center of Bach tradition.

Fodor'sChoice ★

The great music Bach wrote during his Leipzig years commanded little attention in his lifetime, and when he died, he was given a simple grave, without a headstone, in the city's Johannisfriedhof (St. John Cemetery). It wasn't until 1894 that an effort was made to find where the great composer lay buried, and after a thorough, macabre search his coffin was removed to the Johanniskirche. That church was destroyed by Allied bombs in December 1943, and Bach subsequently found his final resting place in the church he would have selected: the Thomaskirche. You can listen to the famous boys' choir during the *Motette,* a service with a special emphasis on choral music.

Bach's 12 children and the infant Richard Wagner were baptized in the early-17th-century font; Karl Marx and Friedrich Engels also stood before this same font, godfathers to Karl Liebknecht, who grew up to be a revolutionary as well. ✉ *Thomaskirchhof, off Grimmaischestr.* ☎ *0341/960–2855* 🌐 *www.thomaskirche.org* 🎟 *Free, Motette €1* ⏲ *Daily 9–6; Motette, Fri. at 6 PM, Sat. at 3.*

32 **Völkerschlachtdenkmal** (Memorial to the Battle of the Nations). On the city's outskirts, Prussian, Austrian, Russian, and Swedish forces stood ground against Napoléon's troops in the Battle of the Nations of 1813, a prelude to the French general's defeat two years later at Waterloo. An enormous, 300-foot-high monument erected on the site in 1913 commemorates the battle. Despite its ugliness, the site is well worth a visit, if only to wonder at the lengths—and heights—to which the Prussians went to celebrate their military victories and to take in the view from a windy platform (provided you can climb the 500 steps to get there). The Prussians did make one concession to Napoléon in designing the monument: a stone marks the spot where he stood during the three-day bat-

tle. An exhibition hall explains the history of the memorial. The memorial can be reached via Streetcar 15 or 21 (leave the tram at the Probstheida station). ✉ *Prager Str.* ☎ *0341/878–0471* 🎫 *€3* ⏲ *Nov.–Apr., daily 10–4; May–Oct., daily 10–6; tour daily at 10:30, 1:30, and 2:30.*

Where to Stay & Eat

¢–$$$ ✕ **Auerbachs Keller.** The most famous of Leipzig's restaurants consists of an upscale, international gourmet restaurant and another restaurant specializing in hearty Saxon fare. It has been around since 1530, and Goethe immortalized one of the several vaulted historic rooms in his *Faust.* The menu features regional dishes from Saxony, mostly hearty, roasted meat recipes. There's also a good wine list. ✉ *Mädlerpassage, Grimmaische Str. 2–4* ☎ *0341/216–100* ✍ *Reservations essential* 💳 *AE, DC, MC, V* ⏲ *Closed Mon.*

Fodor's Choice ★

$–$$ ✕ **Barthels Hof.** The English-language menu at this restaurant explains not only the cuisine but the history of Leipzig as well. Waitresses wear traditional *Trachten* dresses, but the rooms are quite modern. The restaurant is popular with locals, especially for breakfast. ✉ *Hainstr. 1* ☎ *0341/141–310* 💳 *AE, DC, MC, V.*

★ **$–$$** ✕ **Kaiser Maximilian.** Leipzig's best Mediterranean restaurant serves inventive Italian and French dishes in a setting dominated by high, undecorated walls and black, leather seats. The Maximilian is known for its pasta and fish dishes such as *Schwarze Lachstortelloni im Safransud* (black salmon tortelloni cooked in saffron juice). ✉ *Neumarkt 9–19* ☎ *0341/998–6900* 🌐 *www.kaiser-maximilian.de* ✍ *Reservations essential* 💳 *AE, MC, V.*

$ ✕ **Thüringer Hof.** One of Germany's oldest restaurants and pubs (dating back to 1454) served its hearty Thuringian and Saxon fare to Martin Luther and the likes—who certainly had more than a mere pint of the beers on tap here. The menu in the reconstructed, cavernous and always buzzing dining hall doesn't exactly offer gourmet cuisine but rather an impressively enormous variety of game, fish, and bratwurst dishes. The Thuringian sausages (served with either sauerkraut and potatoes or onions and mashed potatoes) and the famous Thuringian *Sauerbraten* (beef marinated in a sour essence) are a must. ✉ *Burgstr. 19* ☎ *0341/994–4999* 💳 *AE, MC, V.*

¢–$ ✕ **Apels Garten.** This elegant little restaurant in the city center pays homage to nature with landscape paintings on the wall, floral arrangements on the tables, and fresh produce on the imaginative menu. In winter the wild-duck soup with homemade noodles is an obligatory starter; in summer try the *Räucherfischsuppe* (smoked fish soup)—you won't find another soup like it in Leipzig. ✉ *Kolonnadenstr. 2* ☎ *0341/960–7777* 💳 *AE, MC, V* ⏲ *No dinner Sun.*

¢–$ ✕ **Paulaner Restaurant Hutter Culinaria.** Munich's Paulaner Brewery returned to its Leipzig subsidiary of prewar times and transformed the building into a vast complex, with restaurants, a banquet hall, a café, and a beer garden. There's something here for everyone, from intimate dining to noisy, Bavarian-style tavern-table conviviality. The food, such as *Schweinshaxen mit Sauerkraut* (salty pork with sauerkraut), is a mix of Bavarian and Saxon. The Paulaner beer is a perfect accompaniment. ✉ *Klosterg. 3–5* ☎ *0341/211–3115* 💳 *AE, DC, MC, V.*

¢–$ Zill's Tunnel. The "tunnel" refers to the barrel-ceiling ground-floor restaurant, where foaming glasses of excellent local beer are served with a smile. The friendly staff will also help you decipher the Old Saxon descriptions of the menu's traditional dishes. Upstairs there's a larger wine restaurant with an open fireplace. *Barfussgässchen 9* *0341/960–2078* *AE, DC, MC, V.*

$$–$$$ Fodor'sChoice ★ **Hotel Fürstenhof Leipzig.** The city's grandest hotel is inside the renowned Löhr-Haus, a revered old mansion. The stunning banquet section is the epitome of 19th-century grandeur, with red wallpaper and black serpentine stone; the bar is a lofty meeting area under a bright glass cupola. Rooms are spacious and decorated with cherrywood designer furniture. *Tröndlinring 8, D–04105* *0341/1400* *0341/140–3700* *www.luxurycollection.com* *80 rooms, 12 suites* *Restaurant, room service, in-room safes, minibars, cable TV with movies, in-room data ports, Wi-Fi, pool, gym, massage, sauna, spa, bar, piano bar, babysitting, dry cleaning, laundry service, concierge, business services, meeting room, parking (fee), some pets allowed (fee), no-smoking floors* *AE, DC, MC, V.*

$$–$$$ **Westin Leipzig.** Although the hotel's service is outstanding, the high-rise edifice and its accommodations lack true atmosphere. Rooms, however, offer every luxury, including bathrooms with marble floors and walls and full air-conditioning. The owners have included a Japanese restaurant and garden. The hotel is convenient to the main train station. *Gerberstr. 15, D–04105* *0341/9880* *0341/988–1229* *www.westin-leipzig.com* *447 rooms, 27 suites* *3 restaurants, room service, in-room safes, minibars, cable TV with movies, in-room data ports, pool, gym, hair salon, massage, sauna, spa, bar, babysitting, dry cleaning, laundry service, concierge, business services, meeting room, parking (fee), some pets allowed (fee), no-smoking rooms* *AE, MC, V* *BP.*

$$ **Park Hotel-Seaside Hotel Leipzig.** A few steps from the central train station, the Park Hotel is primarily geared to the business traveler. The modern rooms may lack some individuality and are definitely not designed for romantic weekends, but the warm service and exceptional bathrooms and swimming-pool area make for a pleasant stay. The Orient Express restaurant, a reconstruction of the famous 19th-century train, is another plus. *Richard-Wagner-Str. 7, D–04109* *0341/98520* *0341/985–2750* *www.seaside-hotels.de* *281 rooms, 9 suites* *Restaurant, room service, in-room safes, minibars, cable TV, in-room broadband, Wi-Fi, health club, hot tub, sauna, bar, babysitting, dry cleaning, laundry service, concierge, meeting room, parking (fee), some pets allowed (fee), no-smoking floor; no a/c* *AE, DC, MC, V* *BP.*

$$ **Renaissance Leipzig Hotel.** One of the largest hotels in the city, the Renaissance Leipzig is popular with business travelers because of its quiet atmosphere. It has large, elegant rooms—with fashionable bathrooms in dark marble. When making a reservation, ask for a room on the Club Floor: for about €12 a day you get access to the Club Lounge. The hotel's restaurant serves light nouvelle German cuisine. The Renaissance is in the heart of old Leipzig, a perfect spot from which to explore the city

on foot. ✉ *Grosser Brockhaus 3, D–04103* ☎ *0341/12920* 🖷 *0341/129–2800* 🌐 *www.renaissancehotels.com* 295 *rooms, 61 suites* *Restaurant, room service, minibars, cable TV, in-room data ports, Wi-Fi, pool, gym, massage, sauna, bar, dry cleaning, laundry service, concierge, business services, meeting room, parking (fee), some pets allowed (fee), no-smoking floor* *AE, DC, MC, V* *BP.*

$ **Ringhotel Adagio Leipzig.** The quiet Adagio, tucked away behind the facade of a 19th-century city mansion, is centrally located between the Grassimuseum and the Neues Gewandhaus. All rooms are individually furnished; when making a reservation, ask for a "1920s room," which features the style of the Roaring '20s and bathtubs almost as large as a whirlpool. ✉ *Seeburgstr. 96, D–04103* ☎ *0341/216–699* 🖷 *0341/960–3078* 🌐 *www.hotel-adagio.de* *30 rooms, 2 suites, 1 apartment* *Cable TV, in-room data ports, dry cleaning, laundry service, meeting room, parking (fee), some pets allowed (fee), no-smoking rooms; no a/c* *AE, DC, MC, V* *CP.*

Nightlife & the Arts

The *Kneipenszene* (pub scene) of Leipzig is centered on the **Drallewatsch** (a Saxon slang word for "going out"), the small streets and alleys around Grosse and Kleine Fleischergasse. A magnet for young people is the **Moritzbastei** (✉ Universitätsstr. 9 ☎ 0341/702–590), reputedly Europe's largest student club, with bars, a disco, a café, a theater, and a cinema. Nonstudents are welcome. One of the city's top dance clubs is the hip **Spizz Keller** (✉ Markt 9 ☎ 0341/960–8043). The **Tanzpalast** (✉ Dittrichring ☎ 0341/960–0596), in the august setting of the *Schauspielhaus* (city theater), attracts a thirtysomething crowd. The upscale bar, pub, and restaurant **Weinstock** (✉ Markt 7 ☎ 0341/1406–0606) is in a Renaissance building and offers a huge selection of good wines. A favorite hangout among the city's business elite is the **Schauhaus** (✉ Bosestr. 1 ☎ 0341/960–0596), a stylish bar serving great cocktails.

The **Neues Gewandhaus** (✉ Augustuspl. 8, D–04109 ☎ 0341/127–0280 🌐 www.gewandhaus.de), a controversial piece of architecture, is home to an undeniably splendid orchestra. Tickets to concerts are very difficult to obtain unless you reserve well in advance and in writing only. Sometimes spare tickets are available at the box office a half hour before the evening performance. Leipzig's annual music festival, **Music Days,** is in June.

One of Germany's most famous cabarets, the **Leipziger Pfeffermühle** (✉ Thomaskirchhof 16 ☎ 0341/960–3196), has a lively bar off a courtyard opposite the Thomaskirche. On pleasant evenings the courtyard fills with benches and tables, and the scene rivals the indoor performance for entertainment. The variety theater **Krystallpalast** (✉ Magazingasse. 4 ☎ 0341/140–660 🌐 www.krystallpalast.de) features a blend of circus, vaudeville, and comedy not to be missed.

The **Gohliser Schlösschen** (✉ Menckestr. 23 ☎ 0341/589–690), a small rococo palace outside Leipzig's center, frequently holds concerts. It's easily reached by public transportation: take streetcar No. 20 or No. 24 and then walk left up Poetenweg; or take streetcar No. 6 to Menckestrasse. Daytime tours can be arranged for groups.

Shopping

Small streets leading off the Markt attest to Leipzig's rich trading past. Tucked in among them are glass-roof arcades of surprising beauty and elegance, including the wonderfully restored **Specks Hof, Barthels Hof, Jägerhof,** and the **Passage zum Sachsenplatz.** Invent a headache and step into the *Apotheke* (pharmacy) at Hainstrasse 9—it is spectacularly art nouveau, with finely etched and stained glass and rich mahogany. For more glimpses into the past, check out the antiquarian bookstores of the nearby **Neumarkt Passage.**

The **Hauptbahnhof** (✉ Willy-Brandt-Pl.) offers more than 150 shops, restaurants, and cafés. All shops are open Monday through Saturday 9:30 AM–10 PM, and many shops are also open on Sunday, with the same hours. Thanks to the historic backdrop, it's one of the most beautiful and fun shopping experiences in East Germany.

15

SAXONY-ANHALT

The central state of Saxony-Anhalt is a region rich in natural attractions. In the Altmark, on the edge of the Harz Mountains, fields of grain and sugar beets stretch to the horizon. In the mountains themselves are the deep gorge of the Bode River and the stalactite-filled caves of Rubeland. The songbirds of the Harz are renowned, and though pollution has taken its toll, both the flora and the fauna of the Harz National Park (which encompasses much of the region) are coming back. Atop the Brocken, the Harz's highest point, legend has it that witches convene on Walpurgis Night (the night between April 30th and May 1st).

Saxony-Anhalt's Letzlinger Heide (Letzling Heath), another home to rare birds and animals, is one of Germany's largest tracts of uninhabited land. The Dübener Heide (Düben Heath), south of Wittenberg, has endless woods of oaks, beeches, and evergreens that are wonderful to explore by bike or on foot. In and around Dessau are magnificent parks and gardens.

Architecturally, Saxony-Anhalt abounds in half-timber towns and Romanesque churches. Quedlinburg has both the oldest half-timber house in Germany and the tomb of Germany's first king, 10th-century Henry I. In Dessau, the Bauhaus School pointed the world to modern architecture and design just before the start of World War II. Music has thrived in Saxony-Anhalt as well. Among its favorite sons are the composers Georg Philipp Telemann, of Magdeburg; Georg Friedrich Handel, of Halle; and in modern times Kurt Weill, of Dessau. And it was in Wittenberg that Martin Luther nailed his 95 Theses to a church door.

Wittenberg

34 *107 km (62 mi) southwest of Berlin, 67 km (40 mi) north of Leipzig.*

Protestantism was born in the little town of Wittenberg (officially called Lutherstadt-Wittenberg). In 1508 the fervent, idealistic young Martin Luther, who had become a priest only a year earlier, arrived to study and teach at the new university founded by Elector Frederick the Wise.

Nine years later, enraged that the Roman Catholic Church was pardoning sins through the sale of indulgences, Luther posted his 95 Theses attacking the policy on the door of the Castle Church.

Martin Luther is still the center of attention in Wittenberg, and sites associated with him are marked with plaques and signs. You can see virtually all of historic Wittenberg on a 2-km (1-mi) stretch of Collegienstrasse and Schlossstrasse that begins at the railroad tracks and ends at the Schlosskirche (Castle Church).

In a small park where Weserstrasse meets Collegienstrasse, the **Luthereiche** (Luther Oak) marks the spot where in 1520 Luther burned the papal bull excommunicating him for his criticism of the Church. The present oak was planted in the 19th century.

Fodor'sChoice ★ Within **Lutherhalle** (Luther Hall) is the Augustinian monastery where Martin Luther lived both as a teacher-monk and later, after the monastery was dissolved, as a married man. Today it's a museum dedicated to Luther and the Reformation. Visitors enter Lutherhalle through a garden and an elegant door with a carved stone frame; it was a gift to Luther from his wife, Katharina von Bora. Inside the much-restored structure is the monks' refectory, where works of Luther's contemporary, the painter Lucas Cranach the Elder, are displayed. The room that remains closest to the original is the dark, wood-panel Lutherstube. The Luthers and their six children used it as a living room, study, and meeting place for friends and students. Prints, engravings, paintings, manuscripts, coins, and medals relating to the Reformation and Luther's translation of the Bible into the German vernacular are displayed throughout the house. ✉ *Collegienstr. 54* ☎ *03491/42030* 🌐 *www.martinluther.de* 🎫 €5 ⏲ *Apr.–Oct., daily 9–6; Nov.–Mar., Tues.–Sun. 10–5.*

In the elegantly gabled Renaissance **Melanchthonhaus** (Melanchthon House), the humanist teacher and scholar Philipp Melanchthon corrected Luther's translation of the New Testament from Greek into German. Luther was hiding in the Wartburg in Eisenach at the time, and as each section of his manuscript was completed it was sent to Melanchthon for approval. (Melanchthon is a Greek translation of the man's real name, Schwarzerdt, which means "black earth"; humanists routinely adopted such classical pseudonyms.) The second-floor furnishings have been painstakingly re-created after period etchings. ✉ *Collegienstr. 60* ☎ *03491/403–279* 🌐 *www.martinluther.de* 🎫 €2.50 ⏲ *Apr.–Oct., daily 10–6; Nov.–Mar., Tues.–Sun. 10–5.*

From 1514 until his death in 1546, Martin Luther preached two sermons a week in the twin-tower **Stadtkirche St. Marien** (Parish Church of St. Mary). He and Katharina von Bora were married here (Luther broke with monasticism in 1525 and married the former nun). The altar triptych by Lucas Cranach the Elder includes a self-portrait, as well as portraits of Luther wearing the knight's disguise he adopted when hidden away at the Wartburg; Luther preaching; Luther's wife and one of his sons; Melanchthon; and Lucas Cranach the Younger. Also notable is the 1457 bronze baptismal font by Herman Vischer the Elder. On the church's southeast corner you'll find a discomforting juxtaposition of two Jewish-related **monuments**: a 1304 mocking caricature called the Jewish Pig, erected at the time of the expulsion of the town's Jews, and, on the cobblestone pavement, a contemporary memorial to the Jews who died at Auschwitz. ✉ *Kirchpl.* ☎ *03491/404–415* 🎫 *€1.50, including tour* ⏲ *May–Oct., daily 10–5; Nov.–Apr., daily 10–4.*

Two statues are the centerpiece of the **Marktplatz** (market square): an 1821 statue of Luther by Johann Gottfried Schadow, designer of the quadriga and Victory goddess atop Berlin's Brandenburg Gate, and an 1866 statue of Melanchthon by Frederick Drake. Their backdrop is the handsome white high Renaissance **Rathaus** (Town Hall). Gabled Renaissance houses containing shops line part of the square. ✉ *Markt 26* ☎ *03491/421–720* 🎫 *€3* ⏲ *Daily 10–5.*

15

The **Cranachhaus** is believed to have been the first home, in town, of Lucas Cranach the Elder, the court painter, printer, mayor, pharmacist, and friend of Luther's. His son, the painter Lucas Cranach the Younger, was born here. Some of the interior has been restored to its 17th-century condition. It's now a gallery showing an exhibition about the life and work of Cranach. ✉ *Markt 4* ☎ *03491/420–190* 🎫 *€3* ⏲ *Mon.–Sat. 10–5, Sun. 1–5.*

Renaissance-man Lucas Cranach the Elder, probably the wealthiest man in Wittenberg in his day, lived in two different houses during his years in town. In a second **Cranachhaus,** near the Schlosskirche (Castle Church), he not only lived and painted but also operated a print shop, which has been restored, and an apothecary. The courtyard, where it's thought he did much of his painting, remains much as it was in his day. Children attend the **Malschule** (drawing school) here. ✉ *Schlossstr. 1* ☎ *03491/410–912* 🎫 *Free* ⏲ *Mon.–Thurs. 8–4, Fri. 8–3.*

Fodor'sChoice ★

In 1517 the indignant Martin Luther affixed to the doors of the **Schlosskirche** (Castle Church) his 95 Theses attacking the Roman Catholic Church's policy of selling indulgences. Written in Latin, the theses might have gone unnoticed had not someone—without Luther's knowledge—translated them into German and distributed them. In 1521 the Holy Roman Emperor Charles V summoned Luther to Worms when Luther refused to retract his position. It was on the way home from his confrontation with the emperor that Luther was "captured" by his protector, Elector Frederick the Wise, and hidden from papal authorities in Eisenach for the better part of a year. Inside the church, simple bronze plaques mark the burial places of Luther and Melanchthon. ✉ *Schlosspl.* ☎ *03491/402–585* 🎫 *€1.50* ⏲ *May–Oct., Mon.–Sat. 10–5, Sun. 11:30–5; Nov.–Apr., Mon.–Sat. 10–4, Sun. 11:30–4.*

Where to Stay & Eat

★ ¢–$$ ✕ **Brauhaus Wittenberg.** This historic brewery cum restaurant is the perfect stop for a cold beer after a long day of sightseeing. Set in the Old Town's magnificent Beyerhof, the Brauhaus still produces local beer such as *Wittenberger Kuckucksbier.* In the medieval restaurant with its huge beer kettles, you can sample local and South German cuisine; a specialty is the smoked fish such as eel, trout, and halibut from the Brauhaus smokery. In summer, try to get a table in the nice and cool courtyard. ✉ *Markt 6* ☎ *03491/433–130* 💳 *AE, MC, V.*

¢–$ ✕ **Schlosskeller.** At the back of the Schlosskirche, this restaurant's four dining rooms are tucked away in a basement with 16th-century stone walls and barrel-vaulted ceilings. The kitchen specializes in German dishes, such as *Schlosskellerpfanne* (pork fillets with fried potatoes, tomatoes, and pepper bells). ✉ *Schlosspl. 1* ☎ *03491/480–805* 💳 *AE, MC, V.*

$$ **Best Western Stadtpalais Wittenberg.** In an old city mansion just a few steps from the Lutherhaus, this hotel offers modern style and high-quality service. The elegant lobby and upscale rooms may suggest high prices, but the rates are more than reasonable. The best deals are the special executive double rooms, which are 330 square feet and have many extras. The rooms lack creativity, but their shiny new look and the quality furniture make up for the blandness. ✉ *Collegienstr. 56–57, D–06886* ☎ *03491/4250* 📠 *03491/425–100* 🌐 *www.bestwestern.com* *78 rooms* *Restaurant, minibars, cable TV, Wi-Fi, sauna, steam room, bar, babysitting, dry cleaning, laundry service, meeting room, parking (fee), some pets allowed (fee), no-smoking rooms; no a/c in some rooms* 💳 *AE, DC, MC, V* *BP.*

$ **Hotel Grüne Tanne.** Four hundred years ago a knight's estate stood on the land occupied today by this cozy country hotel. A hostelry since 1871, the Grüne Tanne is a starting place for walks and bicycle and horseback rides into the countryside. Rooms are fairly basic and somewhat outdated but very clean and comfortable. The two suites with a separate living-room area make for a romantic stay. A shuttle service goes to the Wittenberg train station. ✉ *Am Teich 1, D–06896 Wittenberg/Reinsdorf* ☎ *03491/6290* 📠 *03491/629–250* 🌐 *www.gruenetanne.de* *40 rooms, 1 apartment, 2 suites* *Restaurant, cable TV, free parking, some pets allowed (fee); no a/c* 💳 *AE, DC, MC, V* *BP.*

en route

From Wittenberg take B–187 west for 13 km (8 mi); then turn onto B–107 south for 8 km (5 mi) to Wörlitz. Leopold III Friedrich Franz of Anhalt-Dessau loved gardens and sought to create a garden kingdom in his lands. He had **Wörlitz Park** laid out between 1765 and 1802, largely in the naturalistic English style. It was the first such garden created in central Europe, with meadowlands, a lake, canals, woods, rocks, and grottoes. You can walk or bicycle the 42 km (26 mi) to Dessau through the park.

From Wörlitz continue another 5 km (3 mi) on B–107 to the **Oranienbaum-Park.** Leopold enlarged his garden kingdom by incorporating Oranienbaum—a 17th-century baroque palace—and adding an English–Chinese garden with a tea house as well as a pagoda inspired by the one in England's Kew Gardens. After visiting Oranienbaum, go west on the road that becomes B–185 in Dessau.

On B–185, 9 km (5½ mi) outside Dessau, you'll come to Mosigkau and its 18th-century late-baroque **Schloss Mosigkau** (Mosigkau Palace). Prince Leopold of Anhalt-Dessau commissioned the palace for his favorite daughter, Anna Wilhelmine. When she died, she left the property to an order of nuns. They immediately tore up the formal grounds to make an English-style park, and after a post–World War II attempt to restore the original baroque appearance, money and enthusiasm ran out. The palace itself, however, was always well maintained. Only a quarter of the rooms can be visited, but they include one of Germany's very few baroque picture galleries. Its stucco ceiling is a marvel of rococo decoration, a swirling composition of pastel-color motifs. ✉ *Knobelsdorffallee 3, Dessau* ☎ *0340/521–139* *Palace €4.50, including tour; gardens free* ⏲ *Apr. and Oct., Tues.–Sun. 10–5; May–Sept., Tues.–Sun. 10–6.*

15

Dessau

35 *35 km (22 mi) southwest of Wittenberg.*

The name *Dessau* is known to every student of modern architecture. In 1925–26 architect Walter Gropius set up his highly influential Bauhaus school of design here. Gropius hoped to replace the dark and inhumane tenement architecture of the 1800s with standardized yet spacious and bright apartments. His ideas and methods were used in building 316 villas in the city's Törten section in the 1920s.

For a contrast to the no-nonsense Bauhaus architecture, look at downtown Dessau's older buildings, including the Dutch baroque **Georgkirche** (St. George's Church; ✉ Georgenstr. 15), built in 1712.

★ Architectural styles that would influence the appearance of such cities as New York, Chicago, and San Francisco were conceived in the **Bauhaus Building.** The architecture school is still operating, and the building can be visited. Other structures designed by Gropius and the Bauhaus architects, among them the Meisterhäuser, are open for inspection off Ebertallee and Elballee. ✉ *Gropiusallee 38* ☎ *0340/650–8251* 🌐 *www.bauhaus-dessau.de* *€4* ⏲ *Daily 10–6. Meisterhäuser Nov.–mid-Feb., Tues.–Sun. 10–5; mid-Feb.–Oct., Tues.–Sun. 10–6.*

Halle

36 *52 km (32 mi) south of Dessau.*

This 1,000-year-old city, built on the salt trade, has suffered from the shortfalls of Communist urban planning; the hastily built residential area, Halle-Neustadt, was cynically nicknamed Hanoi. Yet the Old City has an unusual beauty, particularly its spacious central marketplace, the **Markt,** and its five distinctive sharp-steepled towers.

Of the four towers belonging to the late-Gothic **Marienkirche** (St. Mary's Church), two are connected by a vertiginous catwalk bridge. Martin Luther preached in the church, and George Friedrich Handel (Händel in German), born in Halle in 1685, was baptized at its font. He went on to learn to play the organ beneath its high, vaulted ceiling. The Markt's fifth tower is Halle's celebrated **Roter Turm** (Red Tower; ✉ Markt), built between 1418 and 1506 as an expression of the city's power and wealth. It houses a carillon and the local tourist office.

The **Marktschlösschen** (Market Palace), a late-Renaissance structure just off the market square, has an interesting collection of historical musical instruments, some of which could have been played by Handel and his contemporaries. ✉ *Marktpl. 13* ☎ *0345/202–9141* 🎫 *Free* 🕐 *Tues.–Fri. 10–7, weekends 10–6.*

Handel's birthplace, the **Händelhaus,** is now a museum devoted to the composer. The entrance hall displays glass harmonicas and curious musical instruments perfected by Benjamin Franklin in the 1760s. ✉ *Grosse Nikolaistr. 5* ☎ *0345/500–900* 🎫 *Free* 🕐 *Tues.–Sun. 9:30–5:30, Thurs. 9:30–7.*

The **Moritzburg** (Moritz Castle) was built in the late 15th century by the archbishop of Magdeburg after he claimed the city for his archdiocese. The typical late-Gothic fortress, with a dry moat and a sturdy round tower at each of its four corners, was a testament to Halle's early might, which vanished with the Thirty Years' War. Prior to World War II the castle contained a leading gallery of German expressionist paintings, which were ripped from the walls by the Nazis and condemned as "degenerate." Some of the works are back in place at the **Staatliche Galerie Moritzburg,** together with some outstanding late-19th- and early-20th-century art. You'll find Rodin's famous sculpture *The Kiss* here. ✉ *Friedemann-Bach-Pl. 5* ☎ *0345/212–590* 🌐 *www.moritzburg.halle.de* 🎫 *€4* 🕐 *Tues. 11–8:30, Wed.–Sun. 10–6.*

Halle's only early Gothic church, the **Dom** (cathedral) stands about 200 yards southeast of the Moritzburg. Its nave and side aisles are of equal height, a common characteristic of Gothic church design in this part of Germany. ✉ *Dompl. 3* ☎ *0345/202–1379* 🎫 *Free* 🕐 *June–Oct., Mon.–Sat. 2–4.*

The former archbishop's home, the 16th-century **Neue Residenz** (New Residence), houses the **Geiseltalmuseum** and its world-famous collection of fossils dug from brown coal deposits in the Geisel Valley near Halle. ✉ *Dornstr. 5* ☎ *0345/552–6135* 🎫 *Free* 🕐 *Weekdays 9–noon and 1–5; every 2nd and 4th weekend 9–1.*

The salt trade on which Halle built its prosperity is documented in the **Technisches Halloren- und Salinemuseum** (Technical Mine Museum). A replica salt mine shows the salt-mining process, and the exquisite silver goblet collection of the Salt Workers' Guild is on display. The old method of evaporating brine from local springs is sometimes demonstrated. The museum is on the south side of the Saale River (cross the Schiefer Bridge to get there). ✉ *Mansfelderstr. 52* ☎ *0345/202–5034* 🎫 *€2.10* 🕐 *Tues.–Sun. 10–5.*

Where to Stay & Eat

$–$$ ✕ **Restaurant Mönchshof.** Hearty German fare in hearty portions is served in high-ceiling, dark-wood surroundings. Lamb from Saxony-Anhalt's Wettin region and venison are specialties in season, but there are always fish and crisp roast pork on the menu. The wine list is extensive, with international vintages. ✉ *Talamtstr. 6* ☎ *0345/202–1726* 💳 *AE, MC, V.*

$ **Ankerhof Hotel.** A tollhouse once stood here beside the saltworks, and some of the hotel's unique features are reminiscent of this past. All rooms are decorated individually, and most have wooden beams under the ceiling, naked stone walls, and heavy furniture made from exquisite wood. The hotel's Saalkahn restaurant ($–$$) serves both regional and international dishes, such as *Anhaltinischer Krustenbraten mit Sauerkraut und Klössen* (Anhaltine roasted pork with crust, served with sauerkraut and potato dumplings). *Ankerstr. 2a, D–06108 0345/232–3200 0345/232–3219 www.ankerhofhotel.de 49 rooms, 1 suite Restaurant, in-room safes, minibars, cable TV, in-room broadband, Web TV, health club, sauna, bowling, free parking, some pets allowed (fee), no-smoking rooms; no a/c AE, DC, MC, V BP.*

$$ **Kempinski Hotel Rotes Ross.** Behind a 265-year-old facade in the city center, this friendly, well-equipped modern hotel has a certain old-fashioned elegance. There's a modern wing, however, that lacks the Old World atmosphere of the original main building. *Leipziger Str. 76, D–06108 0345/233–430 0345/2334–3699 www.kempinski.com 89 rooms, 1 suite Restaurant, room service, in-room safes, minibars, cable TV with movies, health club, hot tub, sauna, Weinstube, dry cleaning, laundry service, concierge, convention center, meeting room, parking (fee), some pets allowed (fee), no-smoking rooms AE, DC, MC, V.*

The Arts

The city of Händel's birth is of course an important music center. Halle is famous for its opera productions, its orchestral concerts, and particularly its choirs. For schedules, prices, and reservations of opera performances staged at the city's renowned **Opernhaus,** call 0345/5110–0355. The city's main orchestra, the **Philharmonisches Staatsorchester Halle** (State Philharmonic Orchestra; Grosse Gosenstr. 12 0345/523–3141 for concert information and tickets), performs at the Konzerthalle. The annual **Händel Festival** (0345/5009–0222) takes place in the first half of June, and two youth-choir festivals occur in May and October.

en route

To reach Quedlinburg in the Harz, you can take E–49 directly, or take a somewhat longer route via E–80 to **Eisleben** first. Martin Luther came into and out of this world here. Both the square Franconian house with the high-pitched roof that was his birthplace and the Gothic patrician house where he died are open to the public as are, on request, the Petri-Pauli Kirche (Church of Sts. Peter and Paul), where he was baptized, and the Andreaskirche (St. Andrew's Church), where his funeral was held. From Eisleben take B–180 north to join with E–49 to Quedlinburg.

Quedlinburg

37 *79 km (49 mi) northwest of Halle.*

This medieval Harz town has more half-timber houses than any other town in Germany: More than 1,600 of them line the narrow cobblestone streets and squares. The town escaped World War II unscathed, and was treasured in GDR days, though not very well preserved. Today, the nicely restored town is a UNESCO World Heritage Site.

For nearly 200 years Quedlinburg was a favorite imperial residence and site of imperial diets, beginning with the election in 919 of Henry the Fowler (Henry I), as the first Saxon king of Germany. It became a major trading city and a member of the Hanseatic League, equal in stature to Köln.

The Altstadt (Old Town) is full of richly decorated half-timber houses, particularly along Mühlgraben, Schuhof, the Hölle, Breitestrasse, and Schmalstrasse. Notable on the **Marktplatz** are the Renaissance **Rathaus** (Town Hall), with a 14th-century statue of Roland signifying the town's independence, and the baroque 1701 Haus Grünhagen. Street and hiking maps and guidebooks (almost all in German) are available in the information office at the Rathaus. ✉ *Markt 2* ☎ *03946/90550* 🎟 *Free* 🕒 *Mon.–Sat. 9–3.*

The oldest half-timber house in Quedlinburg, built about 1310, is the **Ständerbau Fachwerkmuseum,** a museum of half-timber construction. ✉ *Wordg. 3* ☎ *03946/3828* 🎟 *€2.50* 🕒 *Nov.–Mar., Fri.–Wed. 10–4; Apr.–Oct., Fri.–Wed. 10–5.*

Placed behind half-timber houses so as not to affect the town's medieval feel is the sophisticated, modern **Lyonel Feininger Gallery.** When the art of American-born painter Lyonel Feininger, a Bauhaus teacher in both Weimar and Dessau, was declared "decadent" by the Hitler regime in 1938, the artist returned to America. Left behind with a friend were engravings, lithographs, etchings, and paintings. The most comprehensive Feininger print collection in the world is displayed here. ✉ *Finkenherd 5a* ☎ *03946/2238* 🌐 *www.feininger-galerie.de* 🎟 *€6* 🕒 *Apr.–Oct., Tues.–Sun. 10–6; Nov.–Mar., Tues.–Sun. 10–5.*

Quedlinburg's largely Renaissance castle buildings perch on top of the Schlossberg (Castle Hill), with a terrace overlooking woods and valley. The grounds include the **Schlossmuseum** (Castle Museum), which has exhibits on the history of the town and castle, artifacts of the Bronze Age, and the wooden cage in which a captured 14th-century robber baron was put on public view. Restored 17th- and 18th-century rooms give an impression of castle life at that time. ✉ *Schlossberg 1* ☎ *03946/2730* 🎟 *€3.50* 🕒 *Mar.–Oct., daily 10–6; Nov.–Feb., Sat.–Thurs. 10–4.*

The simple, graceful **Stiftskirche St. Servatius** (Collegiate Church of St. Servatius) is one of the most important and best-preserved 12th-century Romanesque structures in Germany. Henry I and his wife, Mathilde, are buried in its crypt. The renowned Quedlinburg Treasure of 10th-, 11th-, and 12th-century gold and silver and bejeweled manuscripts are also kept here (what's left of it). In Nazi days SS leader Heinrich Himmler made the church into a shrine dedicated to the SS, insisting that it was only appropriate, since Henry I was the founder of the first German Reich. ✉ *Schlossberg 1* ☎ *03946/709–900* 🎟 *€4* 🕒 *May–Oct., Tues.–Fri. 10–6, Sat. 10–5, Sun. noon–6; Nov.–Apr., Tues.–Sat. 10–4, Sun. noon–4.*

Where to Stay & Eat

$$ **Romantik Hotel Theophano.** This 1668 baroque half-timber merchant's house was the seat of the tanners' guild in the 18th century, a restaurant-coffeehouse in the early 20th century, and a domestic linen store until the Communists "deprivatized" the business. Now restored with care, its elegant rooms have country antiques. The vault-ceiling restaurant ($–$$$) serves such dishes as Harz trout and local wild boar. *Markt 13–14, D–06484 03946/96300 03946/963–036 www.hoteltheophano.de 22 rooms Restaurant, cable TV, free parking, some pets allowed (fee), no-smoking rooms; no a/c AE, DC, MC, V BP.*

$ **Hotel Zum Bär.** There are stuffed bears in the hall and a bear motif in the maroon stair carpet of this 250-year-old half-timber hostelry, which has views out onto the marketplace. The French provincial furniture is painted white and gold. Careful detail has gone into the interior decorating, and no two rooms are alike. The restaurant ($–$$) is known for its filling local dishes. *Markt 8–9, D–06484 03946/7770 03496/700–268 www.hotelzumbaer.de 50 rooms, 1 suite Restaurant, minibars, free parking, some pets allowed (fee); no a/c MC, V BP.*

★ $ **Hotel Zur Goldenen Sonne.** Rooms in this baroque half-timber inn are furnished in a pleasing, rustic fashion. The cozy restaurant ($–$$) offers such Harz fare as venison stew with plum sauce and potato dumplings as well as smoked ham in apricot sauce. *Steinweg 11, D–06484 03946/96250 03946/962–530 www.hotelzurgoldenensonne.de 27 rooms Restaurant, minibars, cable TV, free parking, some pets allowed (fee), no-smoking rooms; no a/c AE, MC, V BP.*

en route

The most scenic way to go from Quedlinburg to Goslar is via Blankenburg, with its hilltop castle, and Wernigerode, 28 km (20 mi) away. Half-timber **Wernigerode** has a colorful twin-tower Rathaus on the marketplace, and the neo-Gothic castle above it is a starting point for walks in the Harz. Also departing from this town is the steam-power narrow-gauge **Harzquerbahn,** which takes passengers to the heights (3,745 feet) of the Brocken. From Wernigerode take B–6 west 30 km (19 mi) along mountain roads through spruce forests to Goslar.

Goslar

38 *48 km (30 mi) northwest of Quedlinburg.*

Goslar, the lovely, unofficial capital of the Harz region, is one of Germany's oldest cities and is known for the medieval glamour expressed in the fine Romanesque architecture of the Kaiserpfalz, an imperial palace of the German Empire. Thanks to the deposits of ore close to the town, Goslar was one of the country's most wealthy hubs of trade during the Middle Ages. In this town of 46,000 today, time seems to have stood still among the hundreds of well-preserved (mostly typical northern German half-timber) houses that were built during the course of seven centuries. The town has been declared a UNESCO World Heritage site.

Despite Goslar's rapid decline after the breakup of the medieval German empire, the city—thanks to its ore deposits—maintained all the luxury and worldliness born of economic success. The **Rathaus** with its magnificent **Huldigungssaal** (Hall of Honor) dates to 1450 and testifies to the wealth of Goslar's merchants. ✉ *Markt 7* ☎ *05321/78060* 🎫 *€2* 🕒 *Daily 11–4.*

★ The impressive **Kaiserpfalz,** set high above the historic downtown area, dates to the early Middle Ages. It once was the center of German imperial glory, when emperors held their regular diets here. Among the rulers who frequented Goslar were Heinrich III (1039–1056) and his successor, Heinrich IV (1056–1106), who was also born in Goslar. You can visit an exhibit about the German medieval kaisers who stayed here, inspect the small chapel where the heart of Heinrich III is buried (the body is in Speyer), or view the beautiful ceiling murals in the Reichssaal (Imperial Hall). ✉ *Kaiserbleek 6* ☎ *05321/311–9693* 🎫 *€4.50* 🕒 *Apr.–Oct., daily 10–5; Nov.–Mar., daily 10–4.*

The source of the town's riches is outside the city in the **Erzbergwerk Rammelsberg,** the world's only silver mine that was in continuous operation for more than 1,000 years. It stopped operating in 1988, but you can inspect the many tunnels and shafts of the old mine. ✉ *Bergtal 19* ☎ *05321/7500* 🌐 *www.rammelsberg.de* 🎫 *€10, including tour* 🕒 *Daily 9–6; tours given as needed 9:30–4:30.*

Where to Stay & Eat

$$ ✕🏨 **Kaiserworth-Hotel und Restaurant.** Hidden behind the reddish-brown walls of a 500-year-old house, the seat of medieval tailors and merchants, this hotel offers small but bright, pleasantly furnished rooms. The front rooms have windows on the medieval city market. The restaurant ($–$$$) offers reliable German food. ✉ *Markt 3, D–38640* ☎ *05321/7090* 📠 *03521/709–345* 🌐 *www.kaiserworth.de* 🛏 *66 rooms* 👍 *Restaurant, room service, cable TV, in-room data ports, babysitting, dry cleaning, laundry service, meeting room, parking (fee), some pets allowed (fee), no-smoking rooms; no a/c* 💳 *AE, DC, MC, V* 🍽 *BP.*

Sports & the Outdoors

SKIING Many cross-country trails (lighted at night for after-dark skiing) wind their way through the evergreen forests of Goslar and surrounding towns. Alpine skiers have five ski slopes and a ski jump. The jump was closed until the Wall fell—because the bottom of it was in the GDR. For Alpine skiing, a cable car rises to the top of the 3,237-foot-high Wurmberg. It has three ski lifts. There are also toboggan runs, horse-drawn sleigh rides, ski instruction, and equipment rentals. Contact the tourist office for more information.

THURINGIA

The tiny state of Thuringia is one of Germany's most historic regions, with a rich cultural past still present in small villages, medieval cities, and country palaces throughout the hilly countryside. In the 14th century traders used the 168-km (104-mi) Rennsteig ("fast trail") through the dark depths of the Thuringian Forest, and cities such as Erfurt and Eisenach evolved as major commercial hubs. Today the forests and the Erzgebirge Mountains are a remote paradise for hiking and fishing. The city of Weimar is one of Europe's old cultural centers, and the short-lived German democracy, the Weimar Republic, was established here in 1918. Already a prime vacation spot during Communist times, Thuringia boomed when it attracted investors after reunification.

Eisenach

39 *160 km (100 mi) south of Goslar, 95 km (59 mi) northeast of Fulda (nearest ICE rail station).*

When you stand in Eisenach's ancient market square, it's difficult to imagine this half-timber town as an important center of the East German automobile industry. Yet this is where trabis and wartburgs (very tiny, noisy, and cheaply produced cars, which are now collector's items) were made. The cars were named after the famous castle that broods over Eisenach, atop one of the foothills of the Thuringian Forest, the Wartburg. Today, West German automaker Opel is continuing the automobile tradition. The GM company built one of Europe's most modern car-assembly lines on the outskirts of Eisenach.

Fodor'sChoice ★ 1067 (and expanded through the centuries), the mighty **Wartburg** has hosted a parade of German historical celebrities. Hermann I (1156–1217), count of Thuringia and count palatine of Saxony, was a patron of the poets Walther von der Vogelweide (1170–1230) and Wolfram von Eschenbach (1170–1220). Legend has it that this is where Walther von der Vogelweide, the greatest lyric poet of medieval Germany, prevailed in the celebrated *Minnesängerstreit* (minnesinger contest), which is featured in Richard Wagner's *Tannhäuser.*

Within the castle's stout walls, Frederick the Wise (1486–1525) shielded Martin Luther from papal proscription from May 1521 until March 1522, even though he did not share the reformer's beliefs. Luther completed the first translation of the New Testament from Greek into German while in hiding, an act that paved the way for the Protestant Reformation. You can peek into the simple study in which Luther worked.

Frederick was also a patron of the arts. Lucas Cranach the Elder's portraits of Luther and his wife are on view in the castle, as is a very moving sculpture, the *Leuchterengelpaar* (Candlestick Angel Group), by the great 15th-century artist Tilman Riemenschneider. The 13th-century great hall is breathtaking; it's here that the minstrels sang for courtly favors. Don't leave without climbing the belvedere for a panoramic view of the Harz Mountains and the Thuringian Forest. ☎ *03691/77073* 🌐 *www.wartburg-eisenach.de* 🎫 *€6.50, including guided tour* ⏲ *Nov.–Feb., daily 9–3:30; Mar.–Oct., daily 8:30–5.*

The **Lutherhaus,** in downtown Eisenach, has many fascinating exhibits illustrating the life of Luther, who lived here as a student. ✉ *Lutherpl. 8* ☎ *03691/29830* 🎫 *€3* ⏲ *Daily 10–5.*

Johann Sebastian Bach was born in Eisenach in 1685. The **Bachhaus** has exhibits devoted to the entire lineage of the musical Bach family and includes a collection of historical musical instruments. ✉ *Frauenplan 21* ☎ *03691/79340* 🌐 *www.bachhaus.de* 🎫 *€4* ⏲ *Daily 10–6.*

Composer Richard Wagner gets his due at the **Reuter-Wagner-Museum,** which has the most comprehensive exhibition on Wagner's life and work outside Bayreuth. Monthly concerts take place in the old **Teezimmer** (tearoom), a hall with wonderfully restored French wallpaper. The Erard piano, dating from the late 19th century, is occasionally rolled out. ✉ *Reuterweg 2* ☎ *03691/743–293* 🎫 *€3* ⏲ *Tues.–Sun. 11–5, Thurs. 3–8.*

At Johannesplatz 9, look for what is said to be the **narrowest house** in East Germany, built in 1890; its width is just over 6 feet, 8 inches; its height, 24½ feet; and its depth, 34 feet.

Where to Stay & Eat

$ **Hotel Glockenhof.** At the base of Wartburg Castle, this former church-run hostel has blossomed into a handsome hotel, cleverly incorporating the original half-timber city mansion into a modern extension. The excellent restaurant ($–$$) has been joined by a brasserie. ✉ *Grimmelg. 4, D–99817* ☎ *03691/2340* 📠 *03691/234–131* 🌐 *www.glockenhof.de* *38 rooms, 2 suites* *2 restaurants, room service, cable TV, in-room data ports, meeting room, parking (fee), some pets allowed (fee), no-smoking rooms; no a/c* 💳 *AE, DC, MC, V* 🍽 *BP.*

★ $ **Steigenberger Hotel Thüringer Hof.** Enter the lobby of this historic 16th-century mansion, admire its huge chandelier and wooden stairways, set foot on the luxurious carpets, and you'll be instantly transported to the Middle Ages. Traditional Thuringian hospitality and the professional service one has grown to expect of the Steigenberger hotels make this establishment the town's hotel gem, while the upscale Galerie restaurant ($–$$), serving international and local dishes with an accent on fish recipes, is one of the better restaurants to be found in Eisenach. ✉ *Karlspl. 11, D–99817* ☎ *03691/280* 📠 *03691/28190* 🌐 *www.eisenach.steigenberger.de* *127 rooms, 1 suite* *Restaurant, room service, minibars, cable TV, Wi-Fi, gym, massage, sauna, bar, dry cleaning, laundry service, concierge, business services, meeting room, parking (fee), some pets allowed (fee), no-smoking floor* 💳 *AE, DC, MC, V* 🍽 *BP.*

★ $$$$ **Hotel auf der Wartburg.** In this castle hotel, where Martin Luther, Johann Sebastian Bach, and Richard Wagner were guests, you'll get a splendid view over the town and the countryside. The standard of comfort is above average, and antiques and Oriental rugs mix with modern furnishings. The hotel runs a shuttle bus to the rail station and parking lot of the Wartburg. ✉ *Wartburg, D–99817* ☎ *03691/7970* 📠 *03691/797–100* 🌐 *www.wartburghotel.de* *35 rooms* *2 restaurants, room service, in-room safes, minibars, cable TV, Wi-Fi, dry cleaning, laundry service, meeting room, free parking, some pets allowed (fee), no-smoking rooms; no a/c* 💳 *AE, DC, MC, V* 🍽 *BP.*

Erfurt

40 *55 km (34 mi) east of Eisenach.*

The city of Erfurt emerged from World War II relatively unscathed, and with most of its innumerable towers intact. The city's highly decorative and colorful facades are easy to admire on a walking tour. Downtown Erfurt is a photographer's delight, with narrow, busy ancient streets dominated by a magnificent 14th-century Gothic cathedral, the Mariendom. The **Domplatz** (Cathedral Square) is bordered by houses dating from the 16th century. The pedestrian-zone **Anger** is also lined with restored Renaissance houses. The **Bartholomäusturm** (Bartholomew Tower), the base of a 12th-century tower, holds a 60-bell carillon.

On weekends, you can take an old-fashioned horse-drawn open-carriage **tour** of Erfurt's Old Town center. Tours leave from the Tourist-Information office. ✉ *Tourist-Information, Benediktsplatz 1* ⏲ *Apr.–Dec., weekdays at 1, weekends 11 and 1; Jan.–Mar., weekends 11 and 1.*

★ The **Mariendom** (St. Mary's Cathedral) is reached by a broad staircase from the expansive Cathedral Square. Its Romanesque origins (foundations can be seen in the crypt) are best preserved in the choir's glorious stained-glass windows and beautifully carved stalls. The cathedral's biggest bell, the Gloriosa, is the largest free-swinging bell in the world. Cast in 1497, it took three years to install in the tallest of the three sharply pointed towers, painstakingly lifted inch by inch with wooden wedges. No chances are taken with this 2-ton treasure; its deep boom resonates only on special occasions, such as Christmas and New Year's. ✉ *Dompl.* ☎ *0361/646–1265* 🎫 *Tour €2.50* ⏲ *May–Oct., Mon.–Sat. 9–5, Sun. 1–4; Nov.–Apr., Mon.–Sat. 10–11:30 and 12:30–4, Sun. 1–4.*

The Gothic church of **St. Severus** has an extraordinary font, a masterpiece of intricately carved sandstone that reaches practically to the ceiling. It's linked to the cathedral by a 70-step open staircase.

Behind the predominantly neo-Gothic Rathaus you'll find Erfurt's most outstanding attraction spanning the Gera River, the **Krämerbrücke** (Shopkeepers' Bridge). This Renaissance bridge, similar to the one in Florence, incorporates shops and homes. Built in 1325 and restored in 1967–73, the bridge served for centuries as an important trading center. Today, antiques shops fill the majority of the timber-frame houses built into the bridge, some dating from the 16th century. The area around the bridge, crisscrossed with old streets lined with picturesque and often crumbling homes, is known as **Klein Venedig** (Little Venice) because of the recurrent flooding it endures.

The young Martin Luther spent his formative years in the **St. Augustin Kloster** (St. Augustine Monastery; ✉ Gotthardstr.), which is now a seminary. Erfurt's interesting local-history museum is in a late-Renaissance house, **Zum Stockfisch.** ✉ *Johannesstr. 169* ☎ *0361/655–5644* 🎫 *Museum €3* ⏲ *Tues.–Sun. 10–6.*

Where to Stay & Eat

★ $–$$$ ✕ **Alboth's.** This restaurant in the historic, elegant Kaisersaal edifice is the new star in Erfurt's very small gourmet sky. Chef Claus Alboth has worked in various top restaurants in Berlin and now develops his own style and vision of a gourmet restaurant: a cozy, service-oriented oasis to enjoy delicious international dishes with a Thuringian accent. If offered, order the *Thüringenmenü,* a set four-course dinner with local specialties such as ravioli filled with Thuringian blood sausage. The wine list is one of the best in East Germany, offering more than 300 vintages from around the world. ✉ *Futterstr.1, 15–16* 🌐 *www.alboths.de* ☎ *0361/568–8207* ▭ *AE, MC, V* ⏲ *No lunch. Closed Sun. and Mon.*

¢–$$$ ✕ **Paganini im Gildehaus.** This Italian restaurant in one of the city's oldest (and most beautiful) historic mansions serves a wide variety of both basic country cooking and complex fish dishes. In summer the restaurant opens its beer garden, where Thuringian specialties are served, but the focus is on Italian cooking, whose quality is far better than that of the German dishes. The chef, after all, is Italian. ✉ *Fischmarkt 13–16* ☎ *0361/643–0692* ▭ *AE, DC, MC, V.*

$ ✕ **Faustus Restaurant.** In the heart of historic Erfurt the stylish Faustus defines fine Thuringian dining. This restaurant is in an old mansion, with both an inviting summer terrace and a bright, airy dining room. An after-dinner drink at the superb bar is an absolute must. ✉ *Wenigermarkt 5* ☎ *0361/540–0954* ▭ *AE, DC, MC, V.*

$$ ✕🏨 **Radisson SAS Hotel Erfurt.** Since the SAS group gave the ugly high-rise Kosmos a face-lift, the socialist-realist look of the GDR years no longer intrudes on Hotel Erfurt. The hotel underwent several renovations, and the rooms now have bright, modern colors and fabrics (including leather-upholstered furniture). The Classico restaurant ($–$$) serves mostly local dishes and is one of Erfurt's best. ✉ *Juri-Gagarin-Ring 127, D–99084* ☎ *0361/55100* 🖷 *0361/551–0210* 🌐 *www.radissonsas.com* *282 rooms, 3 suites* *Restaurant, room service, minibars, cable TV, Wi-Fi, gym, sauna, spa, bar, babysitting, dry cleaning, laundry service, meeting room, car rental, parking (fee), some pets allowed (fee), no-smoking floor* ▭ *AE, DC, MC, V* *BP.*

Weimar

41 *21 km (13 mi) east of Erfurt.*

Sitting prettily on the Ilm River between the Ettersberg and Vogtland hills, Weimar occupies a place in German political and cultural history completely disproportionate to its size (population 63,000). It's not even particularly old by German standards, with a civic history that started as late as 1410. By the early 19th century the city had become one of Europe's most important cultural centers, where poets Goethe and Schiller wrote, Johann Sebastian Bach played the organ for his Saxon patrons, Carl Maria von Weber composed some of his best music, and Franz Liszt was director of music, presenting the first performance of *Lohengrin* here. In 1919 Walter Gropius founded his Staatliches Bauhaus here, and behind the classical pillars of the National Theater, the German National Assembly drew up the constitution of the Weimar Republic, the first German democracy. After the collapse of the Weimar government, Hitler chose the little city as the site for the first national congress of his Nazi party. On the outskirts of Weimar the Nazis built—or forced prisoners to build for them—the infamous Buchenwald concentration camp.

Much of Weimar's greatness is owed to the widowed countess Anna Amalia, whose home, the **Wittumspalais** (Wittum Mansion), is surprisingly modest. In the late 18th century the countess went talent hunting for cultural figures to decorate the glittering court her Saxon forebears had established. Goethe was one of her finds, and he served the countess as a counselor, advising her on financial matters and town design. Schiller followed, and he and Goethe became valued visitors to the countess's home. Within this exquisite baroque house you can see the drawing room in which she held soirées, complete with the original cherrywood table at which the company sat. The east wing of the house contains a small museum that's a fascinating memorial to those cultural gatherings. ✉ *Am Theaterpl.* ☎ *03643/545–377* 🎫 *€3.50* ⏲ *Nov.–Mar., Tues.–Sun. 10–4; Apr.–Oct., Tues.–Sun. 9–6.*

15

A statue on **Theaterplatz,** in front of the National Theater, shows Goethe placing a paternal-like hand on the shoulder of the younger Schiller. Goethe spent 57 years in Weimar, 47 of them in a house two blocks south of Theaterplatz that has since become a shrine for millions of visitors. The **Goethe Nationalmuseum** (Goethe National Museum) consists of several houses, including the **Goethehaus,** where Goethe lived. It shows an exhibit about life in Weimar around 1750 and contains writings that illustrate not only the great man's literary might but his interest in the sciences, particularly medicine, and his administrative skills (and frustrations) as minister of state and Weimar's exchequer. You'll see the desk at which Goethe stood to write (he liked to work standing up) and the modest bed in which he died. The rooms are dark and often cramped, but an almost palpable intellectual intensity seems to illuminate them. ✉ *Frauenplan 1* ☎ *03643/545–320* 🌐 *www.weimar-klassik.de/english* 🎫 *€6* ⏲ *Nov.–Mar., Tues.–Fri., Sun. 9–4, Sat. 9–9; Apr.–Oct., Tues.–Sun. 9–6.*

Fodor's Choice ★

The **Schillerhaus,** a green-shutter residence and part of the Goethe National Museum, is on a tree-shaded square not far from Goethe's house. Schiller and his family spent a happy, all-too-brief three years here (he died here in 1805). Schiller's study is tucked underneath the mansard roof, a cozy room dominated by his desk, where he probably completed *Wilhelm Tell.* Much of the remaining furniture and the collection of books were added later, although they all date from around Schiller's time. ✉ *Schillerstr. 17* ☎ *03643/545–350* 🌐 *www.weimar-klassik.de/english* 🎫 *€3.50* ⏲ *Nov.–Mar., Wed.–Mon. 9–4; Apr.–Oct., Wed.–Mon. 9–6.*

Goethe's beloved **Gartenhaus** (Garden House) is a modest country cottage where he spent many happy hours, wrote much poetry and began his masterly classical drama *Iphigenie.* It's set amid meadowlike parkland on the bank of the River Ilm. Goethe is said to have felt very close to nature here, and you can soak up the same rural atmosphere on footpaths along the peaceful little river. ✉ *Goethepark* ☎ *03643/545–375* 🌐 *www.weimar-klassik.de/english* 🎫 *Cottage €3* ⏲ *Nov.–Mar., daily 10–4; Apr.–Oct., daily 9–6.*

Goethe and Schiller are buried in the **Historischer Friedhof** (Historic Cemetery), a leafy cemetery where virtually every gravestone commemorates a famous citizen of Weimar. Their tombs are in the vault of the classical-style chapel. The cemetery is a short walk past Goethehaus and Wieland Platz. 🎫 *Goethe-Schiller vault €2* ⏲ *Nov.–Mar., Wed.–Mon. 10–1 and 2–4; Apr.–Oct., Wed.–Mon. 9–1 and 2–6.*

On the central town square, at the **Herderkirche** (two blocks east of Theaterplatz), you'll find the home of Lucas Cranach the Elder. Cranach lived here during his last years, 1552–53. Its wide, imposing facade is richly decorated and bears the coat of arms of the Cranach family. It now houses a modern art gallery. The Marktplatz's late-Gothic **Herderkirche** (Herder Church) has a large winged altar started by Lucas Cranach the Elder and finished by his son in 1555.

★ Weimar's 16th-century **Stadtschloss,** the city castle, is around the corner from the Herderkirche. It has a finely restored classical staircase, a festival hall, and a falcon gallery. The tower on the southwest projection dates from the Middle Ages but received its baroque overlay circa 1730. The **Kunstsammlung** (art collection) here includes several works by Cranach the Elder and many early-20th-century pieces by such artists as Böcklin, Liebermann, and Beckmann. ✉ *Burgpl. 4* ☎ *03643/545–930* 🌐 *www.kunstfreunde-weimar.de* 🎫 *€4.50* ⏲ *Apr.–Oct., Tues.–Sun. 10–6; Nov.–Mar., Tues.–Sun. 10–4.*

The city is proud of the **Neues Museum Weimar** (New Museum Weimar), eastern Germany's first museum exclusively devoted to contemporary art. The building, dating from 1869, was carefully restored and converted to hold collections of American minimalist and conceptual art and works by German installation-artist Anselm Kiefer and American painter Keith Haring. In addition, it regularly presents international modern-art exhibitions. ✉ *Weimarpl. 5* ☎ *03643/545–930* 🌐 *www.kunstsammlungen-weimar.de* 🎫 *€3* ⏲ *Apr.–Oct., Tues.–Sun. 11–6; Nov.–Mar., Tues.–Sun. 11–4.*

off the beaten path

SCHLOSS BELVEDERE (Belvedere Palace) – Just 8 km (5 mi) south of Weimar is the lovely 18th-century, yellow-stucco Belvedere Palace, which once served as a hunting and pleasure castle; today you'll find a baroque museum and an interesting collection of coaches and other historic vehicles inside. The formal gardens were in part laid out according to Goethe's concepts. ✉ *Belvedere Allee* ☎ *03643/545–962* 🌐 *www.kunstfreunde-weimar.de* 🎫 *€3.50* ⏲ *Apr.–mid-Oct., Tues.–Sun. 10–6.*

GEDENKSTÄTTE BUCHENWALD – In the Ettersberg Hills just north of Weimar is a blighted patch of land that contrasts cruelly with the verdant countryside that so inspired Goethe: Buchenwald, one of the most infamous Nazi concentration camps. Sixty-five thousand men, women, and children from 35 countries met their deaths here through forced labor, starvation, disease, and gruesome medical experiments. Each is commemorated by a small stone placed on the outlines of the barracks, which have long since disappeared from the site, and by a massive memorial tower. Besides exhibits, tours are available. To reach Buchenwald, you can take the public bus (No. 6), which leaves every 10 minutes from Goetheplatz in downtown Weimar. The one-way fare is €1.25. ☎ *03643/4300* 🌐 *www.buchenwald.de* *Free* ⏲ *May–Sept., Tues.–Sun. 10–5:30; Oct.–Apr., Tues.–Sun. 9–4:30.*

15

Where to Stay & Eat

¢–$ ✕ **Ratskeller.** This is one of the region's most authentic town hall–cellar restaurants. Its whitewashed, barrel-vaulted ceiling has witnessed centuries of tradition. At the side is a cozy bar, where you can enjoy a preprandial drink beneath a spectacular art-nouveau skylight. The delicious sauerbraten and the famous bratwurst (with sauerkraut and mashed potatoes) are the highlights of the Thuringian menu. If venison is in season, try it—likewise the wild duck or wild boar in red-wine sauce. ✉ *Am Markt 10* ☎ *03643/850–573* 💳 *MC, V.*

¢–$ ✕ **Scharfe Ecke.** Thuringia's traditional *Knödel* (dumplings) are at their best here, but be patient—they're made to order and take 20 minutes. The *Klösse* are salty and less dense than the Knödel and come with just about every dish, from roast pork to venison stew, and the wait is well worth it. The ideal accompaniment to anything on the menu is one of the three locally brewed beers on tap. ✉ *Eisfeld 2* ☎ *03643/202–430* 💳 *AE, DC, MC, V* ⏲ *Closed Mon.*

¢–$ ✕ **Sommer's Weinstuben und Restaurant.** The city's oldest pub and restaurant, a 130-year-old landmark in the center of Weimar, is still going strong. The authentic Thuringian specialties and huge *Kartoffelpfannen* (potato pans) with fried potatoes and various kinds of meat are prepared by the 5th generation of the Sommer family and are as tasty as ever. Add to that the superb wine list with some rare vintages from local vineyards and the romantic courtyard, and your Weimar experience will be perfect. ✉ *Humboldtstr. 2* ☎ *03643/400–691* 💳 *No credit cards* ⏲ *Closed Sun. No lunch.*

$$–$$$ ✕🏨 **Grand Hotel Russischer Hof.** This historic, classicist hotel, once a hallmark of the European nobility and intellectual society, continues to be a luxurious gem in the heart of Weimar—it's one of eastern Germany's finest hotels. Tolstoy, Liszt, Schumann, Turgenev, and others once stayed at this former Russian city palace, whose (partly historic) rooms are decorated today with antique French tapestries, linens, and furniture. The service is impeccable. The atmosphere is casual yet serene and elegant. The restaurant Anastasia ($$) serves fine Austrian-Thuringian cuisine. ✉ *Goethepl. 2, D–99423* ☎ *03643/7740* 📠 *03643/774–840* 🌐 *www.russischerhof.com* *119 rooms, 6 suites* *Restaurant, room service, in-room safes, minibars, cable TV with movies, in-room data ports, Wi-Fi, bar, babysitting, dry cleaning, laundry service,*

Fodor's Choice ★

concierge, meeting room, parking (fee), some pets allowed (fee), no-smoking floor ▭ *AE, DC, MC, V.*

$$–$$$ Fodor'sChoice ★ **Hotel Elephant.** The historic Elephant, dating from 1696, is famous for its charm—even through the Communist years. Book here (well in advance), and you'll follow the choice of Goethe, Schiller, Herder, Liszt (after whom the hotel bar is named)—and Hitler—all of whom were guests. Behind the sparkling white facade are comfortable modern rooms decorated in beige, white, and yellow in a timeless blend of art deco and Bauhaus styles. A sense of the past is ever present. ✉ *Markt 19, D–99423* ☎ *03643/8020* 🖷 *03643/802–610* 🌐 *www.luxurycollection.com* *94 rooms, 5 suites* *2 restaurants, room service, in-room safes, minibars, cable TV, in-room broadband, Wi-Fi, piano bar, dry cleaning, laundry service, meeting room, parking (fee), some pets allowed (fee), no-smoking rooms; no a/c* ▭ *AE, DC, MC, V* *BP.*

$ **Amalienhof VCH Hotel.** Book far ahead to secure a room at this friendly little hotel central to Weimar's attractions. The building opened in 1826 as a church hostel. Double rooms are furnished with first-rate antique reproductions; public rooms have the real thing. ✉ *Amalienstr. 2, D–99423* ☎ *03643/5490* 🖷 *03643/549–110* 🌐 *www.vch.de* *23 rooms, 9 apartments* *Cable TV, Wi-Fi, free parking, some pets allowed (fee), no-smoking rooms; no a/c* ▭ *AE, MC, V* *CP.*

Nightlife

Weimar's lively after-dark scene is focused on piano bars and nightclubs around the Marktplatz such as **Shakespeares** (✉ Windischenstr. 4–6 ☎ 03643/901–285), a Bauhaus-style bar and restaurant.

Jena

42 *26 km (16 mi) east of Weimar.*

This charming 800-year-old valley town is overlooked by barnacle cliffs and lies right on the River Saale. Blessed with a fair share of sunshine, it's one of Thuringia's cheeriest towns and home to one of Germany's oldest and most renowned universities. The academic institution dates back to 1558 and, in the 19th century, attracted some of the nation's greatest minds, including Schiller, Goethe, and Fichte. Jena has also thrived as an industrial hub thanks to Zeiss Optikwerke, one of the world's premier high-tech glass and optics manufacturers.

It was in Jena that Germany's two most prominent writers, the romantic Friedrich Schiller, and the less flowery Johann Wolfgang von Goethe, met and became friends. You can educate yourself on the great thinker's most varied interests at the **Goethe-Gedenkstätte.** Goethe lived and worked here as a writer, scientist, and Prussian minister. ✉ *Fürstengraben 26* ☎ *03641/949–009* *€1* *Apr.–Oct., Wed.–Sun. 11–3.*

The lovely **Schiller's Gartenhaus** (Schiller's Garden house) is Schiller's last remaining residence, where he lived while working as a Jena university professor. The tiny *Gartenzinne,* an annex to the main building, served as the writer's study. It's here that he penned some of Germany's most celebrated plays such as *Wallenstein, Maria Stuart,* and *The Maid of Orleans.* ✉ *Schillergäschen 2* ☎ *03641/931–188* 🎫 *€2.50* ⏲ *Apr.–Oct., Tues.–Sun. 11–5; Nov.–Mar., Tues.–Sat. 11–5.*

For those wanting to see history a bit more in focus, there's the Zeiss Corporation's **Optisches Museum** (Optical Museum). Exhibits include microscopes, binoculars, telescopes, and spectacles from throughout the ages. The informative facility also houses a more futuristic-looking holographic art collection. Zeiss's latest breakthroughs and inventions can be seen in action at the **Zeiss Planetarium** (✉ Am Planetarium 5 ☎ 03641/885–488). The mind-boggling, artificial night sky jeweled by thousands of stars is not to be missed. Call for program times and details. ✉ *Carl-Zeiss-Pl. 12* ☎ *03641/443–165* 🎫 *€5 museum; €6 planetarium; €9 combined ticket* ⏲ *Tues.–Fri. 10–4:30, Sat. 11–5.*

15

SAXONY-ANHALT & THURINGIA A TO Z

To research prices, get advice from other travelers, and book travel arrangements, visit www.fodors.com.

AIR TRAVEL

It's easiest, and usually cheapest, to fly into Berlin and rent a car from there. However, Dresden Flughafen is about 10 km (6 mi) north of Dresden, and Leipzig's Flughafen Leipzig-Halle is 12 km (8 mi) northwest of the city.

Dresden Flughafen ☎ 0351/881–3360 🌐 www.dresden-airport.de. **Flughafen Leipzig-Halle** ☎ 0341/224–1155 🌐 www.leipzig-halle-airport.de.

BUS TRAVEL

Long-distance buses travel to Dresden and Leipzig. Bus service within the area is infrequent and mainly connects with rail lines. Check schedules carefully at central train stations or call the service phone number of Deutsche Bahn at local railway stations.

CAR TRAVEL

Expressways connect Berlin with Dresden (A–13) and Leipzig (A–9). Both journeys take about two hours. A–4 stretches east–west across the southern portion of Thuringia and Saxony.

A road-construction program in eastern Germany is ongoing, and you should expect traffic delays on any journey of more than 300 km (186 mi). The Bundesstrassen throughout eastern Germany are narrow, tree-lined country roads, often jammed with traffic. Roads in the western part of the Harz Mountains are better and wider.

TRAIN TRAVEL

The fastest and most inexpensive way to explore the region is by train. All cities are connected by a network of trains and some—Dresden and Meissen, for example—by commuter trains. Slower D- and E-class or InterRegio trains link smaller towns. From Dresden a round-trip ticket to Chemnitz costs about €21 (a 1½-hour journey one-way); to Görlitz,

€31 (a 1½-hour ride). Trains connect Leipzig and Halle or Erfurt and Eisenach within 40 minutes, and tickets cost around €10 each way. The train ride between Chemnitz and Eisenach, for example, (3½ hours) costs €42 one-way.

TOURS

BOAT TOURS Viking K–D has two luxury cruise ships on the Elbe River. It operates a full program of cruises of up to eight days in length, from mid-April until late October, that go from Hamburg as far as Prague. All the historic cities of Saxony and Thuringia are ports of call—including Dresden, Meissen, Wittenberg, and Dessau. For details *see* Cruise Travel *in* Smart Travel Tips.

Weisse Flotte's historic paddle-steam tours depart from and stop in Dresden, Meissen, Pirna, Pillnitz, Königsstein, and Bad Schandau. Besides tours in the Dresden area, boats also go into the Czech Republic. For more information contact the Sächsische Dampfschiffahrt.

Sächsische Dampfschiffahrt ✉ Hertha-Lindner-Str. 10, D-01067 Dresden ☎ 0351/866-090 🌐 www.saechsische-dampfschiffahrt.de.

BUS TOURS Dresden bus tours (in German and English, run by the Dresdner Verkehrsbetriebe) leave from Postplatz (daily at 10, 11:30, and 3); the Stadtrundfahrt Dresden bus tours (also in German and English), leaving from Theaterplatz/Augustusbrücke (April–October, daily 9:30–5 every 30 minutes; November–March, daily 10–3, every hour), stop at most sights.

Guided bus tours of Leipzig (in English and German) run April–October, daily 1:30; November and March, Monday–Thursday 10:30, Friday–Sunday 1:30; December–February, Friday and Sunday 10:30 and Saturday 1:30. Tours leave opposite the Tourist-Information office on Richard-Wagner-Strasse 1.

Dresdner Verkehrsbetriebe AG ☎ 0351/857-2201 🌐 www.dvbag.de. **Stadtrundfahrt Dresden** ☎ 0351/899-5650 🌐 www.stadtrundfahrt.com.

CANOE & PADDLE TOURS Tour operators and boat-rental companies can be found throughout the region. One of the largest operators is Saale-Unstrut-Tours, which runs canoe tours on the Rivers Saale and Unstrut. In Dresden, contact the Kanuverein Laubegast e.V., an association that offers canoe rentals and guided tours on the Elbe River. For canoe rental and tours on the Elbe River starting near Meissen, try Sachsenboote Marlies Trepte.

Kanuverein Laubegast e.V ✉ Laubegaster Ufer 35, Dresden ☎ 0351/252-5613. **Saale-Unstrut-Tours** ✉ Campingplatz Blütengrund, D-06618 Naumburg ☎ 03445/202-711. **Sachsenboote Marlies Trepte** ✉ Niedermuschützer Str. 20, D-01665 Zehren ☎ 035247/51215.

TRAIN TOURS In Saxony, two historic narrow-gauge trains still operate on a regular schedule. Both the *Lössnitzgrundbahn,* which connects Ost-Radebeul-Ost and Radeburg, as well as the *Weisseritzelbahn,* which operates between Freital-Hainsberg and Kurort Kipsdorf, are perfect for taking in some of Saxony's romantic countryside and Fichtelberg Mountains. A two-way ticket is between €6.60 and €10.70, depending on the length of the ride. For schedule and information contact Deutsche Bahn's regional Dresden office.

The famous steam locomotive *Harzquerbahn* connects Nordhausen-Nord with Wernigerode and Gernerode in the Harz Mountains. The most popular track of this line is the *Brockenbahn,* a special narrow-gauge train transporting tourists to the top of northern Germany's highest mountain. For schedule and further information contact the Harzer Schmalspurbahnen GmbH.

Lössnitzgrundbahn ☎ 0351/46165-63684. **Harzer Schmalspurbahnen GmbH** ✉ Bahnhof Westerntor, Friedrichstr. 151, Wernigerode ☎ 03943/5580 🌐 www.hsb-wr.de.

WALKING TOURS A walking tour of Leipzig (in English) sets off from the tourist office May–September, daily 1:30; October–April, Saturday 1:30 and Sunday 10:30.

TRAVEL AGENCIES

Information on travel and tours to and around East Germany is available from most travel agents. Most Berlin tourist offices carry brochures about travel in East Germany.

Berolina Berlin-Service ✉ Meinekestr. 3, D-10719 Berlin ☎ 030/8856-8030. **Reiseland** ✉ Lindenaumarkt 80, D-04177 Leipzig ☎ 0341/961-7373 ✉ Dohnaer Str. 246, D-01239 Dresden ☎ 0351/288-1109 🌐 www.reiseland.de.

VISITOR INFORMATION

Most of the region's larger cities offer special tourist (exploring) cards such as the Dresdencard, Hallecard, Leipzigcard, and Weimarcard, which include discounts at museums, concerts, hotels, and restaurants or special sightseeing packages for up to three days. For details, call the cities' Tourist-Information offices. State tourism offices may have more English-language resources than the tourist offices of smaller towns.

State Tourist Offices **Saxony-Anhalt** (Sachsen-Anhalt) ✉ Am Alten Theater 6, D-39104 Magdeburg ☎ 0391/567-7080 🖷 0391/567-7081 🌐 www.sachsen-anhalt.de. **Thuringia** (Thüringen) ✉ Weimarische Str. 45, D-99099 Erfurt ☎ 0361/37420 🖷 0361/374-2299 🌐 www.thueringen-tourismus.de.

Lower Saxony Tourist Offices **Goslar** ✉ Tourist-Information, Markt 7, D-38640 ☎ 05321/78060 🖷 05321/780-644 🌐 www.goslarinfo.de.

Saxony Tourist Offices **Chemnitz** ✉ Tourist-Information Chemnitz, Markt 1, D-09111 ☎ 0371/19433 🖷 0371/690-6830 🌐 www.chemnitz-tourismus.de. **Dresden** ✉ Dresden Werbung und Tourismus GmbH, Ostraallee 11, D-01067 ☎ 0351/491-920 🖷 0351/4919-2244 🌐 www.dresden-tourist.de. **Görlitz** ✉ Tourist-Information, Bruderstr. 1, D-02826 ☎ 03581/47570 🖷 03581/475-727 🌐 www.goerlitz.de. **Leipzig** ✉ Leipzig Tourist Service e.V., Richard-Wagner-Str. 1, D-04109 ☎ 0341/710-4260 🖷 0341/710-4301 🌐 www.leipzig.de. **Meissen** ✉ Tourist-Information Meissen, Markt 3, D-01662 ☎ 03521/41940 🖷 03521/419-419 🌐 www.touristinfo-meissen.de.

Saxony-Anhalt Tourist Offices **Dessau** ✉ Tourist-Information Dessau, Zerbster Str. 2c, D-06844 ☎ 0340/204-1442 🖷 0340/220-3003 🌐 www.dessau.de. **Halle** ✉ Stadtmarketing Halle, Grosse Ullrichstr. 60 D-06108 ☎ 0345/472-330 🖷 0345/472-3363 🌐 www.halle-tourist.de. **Quedlinburg** ✉ Tourismus-Marketing GmbH, Markt 2, D-06484 ☎ 03946/905-624 🖷 03946/905-629 🌐 www.quedlinburg.de. **Thale** ✉ Tourist-Information, Rathaustr. 1, D-06502 ☎ 03947/2597 🖷 03947/2277 🌐 www.thale.de. **Wernigerode** ✉ Tourist-Information, Nikolaipl. 1, D-38855 ☎ 03943/633-035 🖷 03943/632-040 🌐 www.wernigerode.de. **Wittenberg** ✉ Tourist-Information, Schlosspl. 2,

D-06886 Wittenberg ☏ 03491/498-610 🖷 03491/498-611 🌐 www.wittenberg.de. **Wittenberg District Rural Information Office** ✉ Neustr. 13, D-06886 ☏ 03491/402-610 🖷 03491/405-857. **Wörlitz** ✉ Wörlitz-Information, Förstergasse 26, D-06786 ☏ 034905/20216 🖷 034905/31010 🌐 www.woerlitz-information.de.

Thuringia Tourist Offices **Eisenach** ✉ Eisenach-Information, Markt 2, D-99817 ☏ 03691/79230 🖷 03691/792-320 🌐 www.eisenach-tourist.de. **Erfurt** ✉ Tourist-Information, Benediktspl. 1, D-99084 ☏ 0361/66400 🖷 0361/664-0290 🌐 www.erfurt-tourist-info.de. **Suhl** ✉ Tourist-Information Suhl, Kongresszentrum, Friedrich-König-Str. 7, D-98527 ☏ 03681/720-052 🖷 03681/720-052 🌐 www.suhl.com. **Weimar** ✉ Tourist-Information Weimar, Markt 10, D-99421 ☏ 03643/7450 🖷 03643/745-420 🌐 www.weimar.de.

UNDERSTANDING GERMANY

GERMANY AT A GLANCE

Fast Facts

Name in local language: Deutschland
Capital: Berlin
National anthem: *Das Lied der Deutschen (The Song of the Germans)*
Type of government: Federal republic
Administrative divisions: 16 states
Independence: January 18, 1871 (German Empire unification); U.K., U.S., U.S.S.R., and France formally relinquished rights to post-WWII zones on March 15, 1991
Constitution: October 3, 1990
Legal system: Civil law system with indigenous concepts; judicial review of legislative acts in the Federal Constitutional Court
Suffrage: 18 years of age; universal
Legislature: Bicameral parliament consists of the Federal Assembly (603 seats; elected by popular vote under a system combining direct and proportional representation; a party must win 5% of the national vote or three direct mandates to gain representation; members serve four-year terms) and the Federal Council (69 votes; state governments are directly represented by votes; each has 3 to 6 votes depending on population and are required to vote as a block)
Population: 82.4 million
Population density: 611 people per square mi
Median age: Female 42.8, male 39.9
Life expectancy: Female 81.6, male 75.5
Infant mortality rate: 4.2 deaths per 1,000 live births
Literacy: 99%
Language: German (official)
Ethnic groups: German 91.5%; other 6.1%; Turkish 2.4%
Religion: Protestant 34%; Roman Catholic 34%; unaffiliated and other 28.3%; Muslim 3.7%
Discoveries & inventions: Printing press with moveable type, aka "Gutenberg Press" (1440), globe (1492), Bunsen burner (1855), contact lenses (1887), diesel engine (1892), X-ray (1895), Geiger counter (1912), electron microscope (1931), ballistic missile (1944)

German diligence is actually endurance.

—Franz Grillparzer

Geography & Environment

Land area: 349,223 square km (134,836 square mi), slightly smaller than Montana
Coastline: 2,389 km (1,484 mi) along North Sea, Baltic Sea
Terrain: Lowlands in north, uplands in center, Bavarian Alps in south; highest point: Zugspitze 9,721 feet
Natural resources: Arable land, coal, copper, iron ore, lignite, natural gas, nickel, potash, salt, timber, uranium
Natural hazards: Flooding
Environmental issues: Emissions from coal-burning utilities and industries contribute to air pollution; acid rain, resulting from sulfur-dioxide emissions, is damaging forests; pollution in the Baltic Sea from raw sewage and industrial effluents from rivers in eastern Germany; hazardous waste disposal

Economy

Currency: Euro
Exchange rate: €.81 = $1
GDP: €1.8 trillion ($2.16 trillion)
Per capita income: €18,529 ($22,670)
Inflation: 1.2%
Unemployment: 11.6%
Work force: 41.9 million; services 63.8%; industry 33.4%; agriculture 2.8%
Major industries: Cement, chemicals, coal, electronics, food and beverages, iron, machine tools, machinery, shipbuilding, steel, textiles, vehicles
Agricultural products: Barley, cattle, cabbages, fruit, pigs, potatoes, poultry, sugar beets, wheat
Exports: $608 billion
Major export products: Chemicals, foodstuffs, machinery, metals, textiles, vehicles
Export partners: France 10.7%; U.S. 10.3%; U.K. 8.4%; Italy 7.3%; Netherlands 6.1%; Austria 5.1%; Belgium 4.8%; Spain 4.6%; Switzerland 4.2%
Imports: $487.3 billion
Major import products: Chemicals, foodstuffs, machinery, metals, textiles, vehicles
Import partners: France 9.5%; Netherlands 8.2%; U.S. 7.7%; U.K. 6.5%; Italy 6.4%; Belgium 5.2%; Austria 4%; China 4%

Political Climate

Germany's entrance into the European Union was not smooth, leaving political fallout that has been difficult to overcome. Unemployment rose to its highest postwar levels and cutbacks in benefits, which were necessary to meet requirements for the euro, were met with strikes and protests. In 2001, Chancellor Gerhard Schröderís support for the United States invasion of Afghanistan strained his coalition. Schröder opposed the U.S.-led war in Iraq in 2003, but disagreement between the Social Democrats and the Greens continued to slow the political agenda.

Did You Know?

- Germany is the world's largest recycler of paper. Almost 80% gets reused, compared to about 35% in the U.S.
- Germany routinely submits more patent applications than any other European country.
- Between the world wars, Germany's inflation was so high that $1 equaled more than 4,000,000,000,000 German Marks.
- There are 13 breeds of dogs that people are not allowed to breed or sell in Germany because they are labeled "attack dogs." Twenty-nine other breeds are considered potential attack dogs and must be muzzled when walked.
- In 1916, Germany became the first country to institute Daylight Savings Time.
- Munich's Oktoberfest was officially named the world's largest beer festival in 1999, when 7 million people consumed a record 1.5 million gallons of beer in 11 beer tents standing on a site as large as 50 football fields.
- German citizens are required to pay special taxes on their dogs.
- Many holiday customs originated in Germany, including the Christmas Tree and the Easter Bunny.

CHRONOLOGY

ca. 5000 BC Indo-Germanic tribes settle in the Rhine and Danube valleys

ca. 2000–800 BC Distinctive German Bronze Age culture emerges, with settlements ranging from coastal farms to lakeside villages

ca. 450–50 BC Salzkammergut people, whose prosperity is based on abundant salt deposits (in the area of upper Austria), trade with Greeks and Etruscans; Salzkammerguts spread as far as Belgium and have first contact with the Romans

9 BC–AD 9 Roman attempts to conquer the "Germans"—the tribes of the Cibri, the Franks, the Goths, and the Vandals—and are only partly successful; the Rhine becomes the northeastern border of the Roman Empire (and remains so for 300 years)

212 Roman citizenship is granted to all free inhabitants of the empire

ca. 400 Pressed forward by Huns from Asia, such German tribes as the Franks, the Vandals, and the Lombards migrate to Gaul (France), Spain, Italy, and North Africa, scattering the empire's populace and eventually leading to the disintegration of central Roman authority

486 The Frankish kingdom is founded by Clovis; his court is in Paris

497 The Franks convert to Christianity

Early Middle Ages

776 Charlemagne becomes king of the Franks

800 Charlemagne is declared Holy Roman Emperor; he makes Aachen capital of his realm, which stretches from the Bay of Biscay to the Adriatic and from the Mediterranean to the Baltic. Under his enlightened patronage there is an upsurge in art and architecture—the Carolingian renaissance

843 The Treaty of Verdun divides Charlemagne's empire among his three sons: West Francia becomes France; Lotharingia becomes Lorraine (territory to be disputed by France and Germany into the 20th century); and East Francia takes on, roughly, the shape of modern Germany

911 Five powerful German dukes (of Bavaria, Lorraine, Franconia, Saxony, and Swabia) establish the first German monarchy by electing King Conrad I; Henry I (the Fowler) succeeds Conrad in 919

962 Otto I is crowned Holy Roman Emperor by the pope; he establishes Austria—the East Mark. The Ottonian renaissance is marked especially by the development of Romanesque architecture

Middle Ages

1024–1125 The Salian dynasty is characterized by a struggle between emperors and the Church that leaves the empire weak and disorganized; the great Romanesque cathedrals of Speyer, Trier, and Mainz are built

1138–1254 Frederick Barbarossa leads the Hohenstaufen dynasty; there is temporary recentralization of power, underpinned by strong trade and Church relations

1158 Munich, capital of Bavaria, is founded by Duke Henry the Lion; Henry is deposed by Emperor Barbarossa, and Munich is presented to the House of Wittelsbach, which rules it until 1918

1241 The Hanseatic League is founded to protect trade; Bremen, Hamburg, Köln, and Lübeck are early members. Agencies are soon established in London, Antwerp, Venice, and along the Baltic and North seas; a complex banking and finance system results

mid-1200s The Gothic style, exemplified by the grand Köln Cathedral, flourishes

1349 The Black Death plague kills one-quarter of the German population

Renaissance & Reformation

1456 Johannes Gutenberg (1400–68) prints the first book in Europe

1471–1553 Renaissance flowers under influence of painter and engraver Albrecht Dürer (1471–1528); Dutch-born philosopher and scholar Erasmus (1466–1536); Lucas Cranach the Elder (1472–1553), who originates Protestant religious painting; portrait and historical painter Hans Holbein the Younger (1497–1543); and landscape-painting pioneer Albrecht Altdorfer (1480–1538). Increasing wealth among the merchant classes leads to strong patronage of the revived arts

1517 The Protestant Reformation begins in Germany when Martin Luther (1483–1546) nails his 95 Theses to a church door in Wittenberg, contending that the Roman Church has forfeited divine authority through its corrupt sale of indulgences. Luther is outlawed, and his revolutionary doctrine splits the Church; much of north Germany embraces Protestantism

1524–30 The (Catholic) Habsburgs rise to power; their empire spreads throughout Europe (and as far as North Africa, the Americas, and the Philippines). Erasmus breaks with Luther and supports reform within the Roman Catholic Church. In 1530 Charles V (a Habsburg) is crowned Holy Roman Emperor; he brutally crushes the Peasants' War, one in a series of populist uprisings in Europe

1545 The Council of Trent marks the beginning of the Counter-Reformation. Through diplomacy and coercion, most Austrians, Bavarians, and Bohemians are won back to Catholicism, but the majority of Germans remain Lutheran; persecution of religious minorities grows

Thirty Years' War

1618–48 Germany is the main theater for the Thirty Years' War. The powerful Catholic Habsburgs are defeated by Protestant forces, swelled by disgruntled Habsburg subjects and the armies of King Gustav Adolphus of Sweden. The bloody conflict ends with the Peace of

Westphalia (1648); Habsburg and papal authority are severely diminished

Absolutism & Enlightenment

1689 Louis XIV of France invades the Rhineland Palatinate and sacks Heidelberg. At the end of the 17th century, Germany consolidates its role as a center of scientific thought

1708 Johann Sebastian Bach (1685–1750) becomes court organist at Weimar and launches his career; he and Georg Friederic Handel (1685–1759) fortify the great tradition of German music. Baroque and, later, rococo art and architecture flourish

1740–86 Reign of Frederick the Great of Prussia; his rule sees both the expansion of Prussia (it becomes the dominant military force in Germany) and the spread of Enlightenment thought

ca. 1790 The great age of European orchestral music is raised to new heights with the works of Joseph Haydn (1732–1809), Wolfgang Amadeus Mozart (1756–91), and Ludwig van Beethoven (1770–1827)

early 1800s Johann Wolfgang von Goethe (1749–1832) is part of the Sturm und Drang movement, which leads to Romanticism. Painter Caspar David Friedrich (1774–1840) leads early German Romanticism. Other luminary cultural figures include writers Friedrich Schiller (1759–1805) and Heinrich von Kleist (1777–1811); and composers Robert Schumann (1810–56), Hungarian-born Franz Liszt (1811–86), Richard Wagner (1813–83), and Johannes Brahms (1833–97). In architecture, the severe lines of neoclassicism become popular

Road to Nationhood

1806 Napoléon's armies invade Prussia; it briefly becomes part of the French Empire

1807 The Prussian prime minister Baron vom und zum Stein frees the serfs, creating a new spirit of patriotism; the Prussian army is rebuilt

1813 The Prussians defeat Napoléon at Leipzig

1815 Britain and Prussia defeat Napoléon at Waterloo. At the Congress of Vienna, the German Confederation is created as a loose union of 39 independent states, reduced from more than 300 principalities. The Bundestag (national assembly) is established at Frankfurt. Already powerful Prussia increases its territory, gaining the Rhineland, Westphalia, and most of Saxony

1848 The "Year of the Revolutions" is marked by uprisings across the fragmented German Confederation; Prussia expands. A national parliament is elected, taking the power of the Bundestag to prepare a constitution for a united Germany

1862 Otto von Bismarck (1815–98) becomes prime minister of Prussia; he is determined to wrest German-populated provinces from Austro-Hungarian (Habsburg) control

1866 Austria-Hungary is defeated by the Prussians at Sadowa; Bismarck sets up the Northern German Confederation in 1867. A key figure in Bismarck's plans is Ludwig II of Bavaria. Ludwig—a political simpleton—lacks successors, making it easy for Prussia to seize his lands

1867 Karl Marx (1818–83) publishes *Das Kapital*

1870–71 The Franco-Prussian War: Prussia lays siege to Paris. Victorious Prussia seizes Alsace-Lorraine but eventually withdraws from all other occupied French territories

1871 The four south German states agree to join the Northern Confederation; Wilhelm I is proclaimed first kaiser of the united Empire

Modernism

1882 The Triple Alliance is forged between Germany, Austria-Hungary, and Italy. Germany's industrial revolution blossoms, enabling it to catch up with the other great powers of Europe. Germany establishes colonies in Africa and the Pacific

ca. 1885 Daimler and Benz pioneer the automobile

1890 Kaiser Wilhelm II (rules 1888–1918) dismisses Bismarck and begins a new, more aggressive course of foreign policy; he oversees the expansion of the navy

1890s A new school of writers, including Rainer Maria Rilke (1875–1926), emerges. Rilke's *Sonnets to Orpheus* give German poetry new lyricism

1905 Albert Einstein (1879–1955) announces his theory of relativity

1906 Painter Ernst Ludwig Kirchner (1880–1938) helps organize *Die Brücke,* a group of artists who, along with *Der Blaue Reiter,* create the avant-garde art movement expressionism

1907 Great Britain, Russia, and France form the Triple Entente, which, set against the Triple Alliance, divides Europe into two armed camps

1914–18 Austrian archduke Franz-Ferdinand is assassinated in Sarajevo. The attempted German invasion of France sparks World War I; Italy and Russia join the Allies, and four years of pitched battle ensue. By 1918 the Central Powers are encircled and must capitulate

Weimar Republic

1918 Germany is compelled by the Versailles Treaty to give up its overseas colonies and much European territory (including Alsace-Lorraine to France) and to pay huge reparations to the Allies; Kaiser Wilhelm II repudiates the throne and goes into exile in Holland. The tough terms leave the new democracy (the Weimar Republic) shaky

1919 The Bauhaus school of art and design, the brainchild of Walter Gropius (1883–1969), is born. Thomas Mann (1875–1955) and Hermann Hesse (1877–1962) forge a new style of visionary intellectual writing

1923 Germany suffers runaway inflation. Adolf Hitler's Beer Hall Putsch, a rightist revolt, fails; leftist revolts are frequent

1925 Hitler publishes *Mein Kampf* (My Struggle)

1932 The Nazi party gains the majority in the Reichstag (parliament)

1933 Hitler becomes chancellor; the Nazi "revolution" begins. In Berlin, Nazi students stage the burning of more than 25,000 books by Jewish and other politically undesirable authors

Nazi Germany

1934 President Paul von Hindenburg dies; Hitler declares himself Führer (leader) of the Third Reich. Nazification of all German social institutions begins, spreading a policy that is virulently racist and anticommunist. Germany recovers industrial might and rearms

1936 Germany signs anticommunist agreements with Italy and Japan, forming the Axis; Hitler reoccupies the Rhineland

1938 The *Anschluss* (annexation): Hitler occupies Austria. Germany occupies the Sudetenland in Czechoslovakia. *Kristallnacht* (Night of Broken Glass), in November, marks the Nazis' first open and direct terrorism against German Jews. Synagogues and Jewish-owned businesses are burned, looted, and destroyed in a night of violence

1939–40 In August Hitler signs a pact with the Soviet Union; in September he invades Poland; war is declared by the Allies. Over the next three years, there are Nazi invasions of Denmark, Norway, the Low Countries, France, Yugoslavia, and Greece. Alliances form between Germany and the Baltic states

1941–45 Hitler launches his anticommunist crusade against the Soviet Union, reaching Leningrad in the north and Stalingrad and the Caucasus in the south. In 1944 the Allies land in France; their combined might brings the Axis to its knees. In addition to the millions killed in the fighting, more than 6 million Jews and other victims die in Hitler's concentration camps. Germany is again in ruins. Hitler kills himself in April 1945. East Berlin and what becomes East Germany are occupied by the Soviet Union

The Cold War

1945 At the Yalta Conference, France, the United States, Britain, and the Soviet Union divide Germany into four zones; each country occupies a sector of Berlin. The Potsdam Agreement expresses the determination to rebuild Germany as a democracy

1946 East Germany's Social Democratic Party merges with the Communist Party, forming the SED, which would rule East Germany for the next 40 years

1948 The Soviet Union tears up the Potsdam Agreement and attempts, by blockade, to exclude the three other Allies from their agreed zones in Berlin. Stalin is frustrated by a massive airlift of supplies to West Berlin

1949 The three Western zones are combined to form the Federal Republic of Germany; the new West German parliament elects Konrad Adenauer as chancellor (a post he held until his retirement in 1963). Soviet-held East Germany becomes the Communist German Democratic Republic (GDR)

1950s West Germany, aided by the financial impetus provided by the Marshall Plan, rebuilds its devastated cities and economy—the *Wirtschaftswunder* (economic miracle) gathers speed. The writers Heinrich Böll, Wolfgang Koeppen, and Günter Grass emerge

1957 The Treaty of Rome heralds the formation of the European Economic Community (EEC); West Germany is a founding member

1961 Communists build the Berlin Wall to stem the outward tide of refugees

1969–74 The vigorous chancellorship of Willy Brandt pursues *Ostpolitik*, improving relations with Eastern Europe and the Soviet Union and acknowledging East Germany's sovereignty

mid-1980s The powerful German Green Party emerges as the leading environmentalist voice in Europe

Reunification

1989 Discontent in East Germany leads to a flood of refugees westward and to mass demonstrations; Communist power collapses across Eastern Europe; the Berlin Wall falls

1990 In March the first free elections in East Germany bring a center-right government to power. The Communists, faced with corruption scandals, suffer a big defeat but are represented (as Democratic Socialists) in the new, democratic parliament. The World War II victors hold talks with the two German governments, and the Soviet Union gives its support for reunification. Economic union takes place on July 1, with full political unity on October 3. In December, in the first democratic national German elections in 58 years, Chancellor Helmut Kohl's three-party coalition is reelected

1991 Nine months of emotional debate end on June 20, when parliamentary representatives vote to move the capital from Bonn—seat of the West German government since 1949—to Berlin, the capital of Germany until the end of World War II

1998 Helmut Kohl's record 16-year-long chancellorship of Germany ends with the election of Gerhard Schröder. Schröder's Social Democratic Party (SPD) pursues a coalition with the Greens in order to replace the three-party coalition of the Christian Democratic Union, Christian Social Union, and Free Democratic Party

1999 The Bundestag, the German parliament, returns to the restored Reichstag in Berlin on April 19. The German federal government also leaves Bonn for Berlin, making Berlin capital of Germany again

1999–2003 For the first time since 1945, the German army (the Bundeswehr) is deployed in combat missions in the former Yugoslavia and Afghanistan

2000 Hannover hosts Germany's first world's exposition, EXPO 2000, the largest ever staged in the 150-year history of the event

2006 Germany hosts the 2006 FIFA World Cup, the world's soccer championship

VOCABULARY

	English	German	Pronunciation
Basics			
	Yes/no	Ja/nein	yah/nine
	Please	Bitte	**bit**-uh
	Thank you (very much)	Danke (vielen Dank)	**dahn**-kuh (**fee**-lun-dahnk)
	Excuse me	Entschuldigen Sie	ent-**shool**-de-gen zee
	I'm sorry.	Es tut mir leid.	es toot meer lite
	Good day	Guten Tag	**goo**-ten tahk
	Good bye	Auf Wiedersehen	auf **vee**-der-zane
	Mr./Mrs.	Herr/Frau	hair/frau
	Miss	Fräulein	**froy**-line
Numbers			
	1	ein(s)	eint(s)
	2	zwei	tsvai
	3	drei	dry
	4	vier	fear
	5	fünf	fumph
	6	sechs	zex
	7	sieben	**zee**-ben
	8	acht	ahkt
	9	neun	noyn
	10	zehn	tsane
Days of the Week			
	Sunday	Sonntag	**zone**-tahk
	Monday	Montag	**moan**-tahk
	Tuesday	Dienstag	**deens**-tahk
	Wednesday	Mittwoch	**mit**-voah
	Thursday	Donnerstag	**doe**-ners-tahk
	Friday	Freitag	**fry**-tahk
	Saturday	Samstag/ Sonnabend	**zahm**-stakh/ **zonn**-a-bent
Useful Phrases			
	Do you speak English?	Sprechen Sie Englisch?	**shprek**-hun zee **eng**-glish?
	I don't speak German.	Ich spreche kein Deutsch.	ich **shprek**-uh kine doych

Please speak slowly.	Bitte sprechen Sie langsam.	**bit**-uh **shprek**-en-zee **lahng**-zahm
I am American/ British	Ich bin Amerikaner(in)/ Engländer(in)	ich bin a-mer-i-**kahn**-er(in)/ **eng**-glan-der(in)
My name is . . .	Ich heiße . . .	ich **hi**-suh
Where are the restrooms?	Wo ist die Toilette?	vo ist dee twah-**let**-uh
Left/right	links/rechts	links/rechts
Open/closed	offen/geschlossen	O-fen/geh-**shloss**-en
Where is . . . the train station? the bus stop? the subway station? the airport? the post office? the bank? the police station? the Hospital? the telephone	Wo ist . . . der Bahnhof? die Bushaltestelle? die U-Bahn-Station? der Flugplatz? die Post? die Bank? die Polizeistation? das Krankenhaus? das Telefon	**vo** ist **dare bahn-hof** **dee booss-hahlt-uh**-shtel-uh dee oo-bahn-**staht**-sion dare **floog**-plats dee **post** dee **banhk** dee po-lee-tsai-**staht**-sion dahs **krahnk**-en-house **dahs te-le-fone**
I'd like . . . a room the key a map a ticket	Ich hätte gerne . . . ein Zimmer den Schlüssel eine Stadtplan eine Karte	ich **het**-uh gairn . . . ein **tsim**-er den **shluh**-sul **I**-nuh **staht**-plahn **I**-nuh cart-uh
How much is it?	Wieviel kostet das?	**vee-feel cost**-et dahs?
I am ill/sick	Ich bin krank	ich bin krahnk
I need . . . a doctor the police help	Ich brauche . . . einen Arzt die Polizei Hilfe	ich **brow**-khuh **I-nen** artst dee po-li-**tsai** **hilf-uh**
Stop!	Halt!	**hahlt**
Fire!	Feuer!	**foy**-er
Look out/Caution!	Achtung!/Vorsicht!	**ahk**-tung/for-zicht

Dining Out

A bottle of . . .	eine Flasche . . .	I-nuh **flash**-uh
A cup of . . .	eine Tasse . . .	I-nuh **tahs**-uh
A glass of . . .	ein Glas . . .	ein glahss
Ashtray	der Aschenbecher	dare **Ahsh**-en-bekh-er
Bill/check	die Rechnung	dee **rekh**-nung

Do you have . . .?	Haben Sie . . .?	**hah**-ben zee
I am a vegetarian.	Ich bin Vegetarier(in)	ich bin ve-guh-**tah**-re-er
I'd like to order . . .	Ich möchte . . . bestellen	ich **mohr**-shtuh . . . buh-**shtel**-en
Menu	die Speisekarte	dee **shpie**-zeh-car-tuh
Napkin	die Serviette	dee zair-vee-**eh**-tuh

MENU GUIDE

English	German
General Dining	
Side dishes	Beilagen
Extra charge	Extraaufschlag
When available	Falls verfügbar
Entrées	Hauptspeisen
(not) included	. . .(nicht) inbegriffen
Depending on the season	je nach Saison
Lunch menu	Mittagskarte
Desserts	Nachspeisen
at your choice	. . . nach Wahl
at your request	. . . nach Wunsch
Prices are . . .	Preise sind . . .
Service included	*inklusive Bedienung*
Value added tax included	*inklusive Mehrwertsteuer (Mwst.)*
Specialty of the house	Spezialität des Hauses
Soup of the day	Tagessuppe
Appetizers	Vorspeisen
Is served from . . . to . . .	Wird von . . . bis . . . serviert
Breakfast	
Bread	Brot
Roll(s)	Brötchen
Eggs	Eier
Hot	heiß
Cold	kalt
Jam	Konfitüre
Milk	Milch
Orange juice	Orangensaft
Scrambled eggs	Rühreier
Bacon	Speck
Fried eggs	Spiegeleier
Lemon	Zitrone
Sugar	Zucker
Soups	
Stew	Eintopf
Chicken soup	Hühnersuppe
Potato soup	Kartoffelsuppe
Liver dumpling soup	Leberknödelsuppe
Onion soup	Zwiebelsuppe

Methods of Preparation

Blue (boiled in salt and vinegar)	Blau
Baked	Gebacken
Fried	Gebraten
Steamed	Gedämpft
Grilled (broiled)	Gegrillt
Boiled	Gekocht
Sauteed	In Butter geschwenkt
Breaded	Paniert
Raw	Roh

When ordering steak, the English words "rare, medium, (well) done" are used and understood in German.

Fish and Seafood

Eel	Aal
Oysters	Austern
Trout	Forelle
Flounder	Flunder
Prawns	Garnelen
Halibut	Heilbutt
Herring	Hering
Lobster	Hummer
Scallops	Jakobsmuscheln
Cod	Kabeljau
Crab	Krabbe
Salmon	Lachs
Mackerel	Makrele
Mussels	Muscheln
Squid	Tintenfisch
Tuna	Thunfisch

Meats

Veal	Kalb(s)
Lamb	Lamm
Beef	Rind(er)
Pork	Schwein(e)

Cuts of Meat

Example: For "Lammkeule" see "Lamm" (above) + ". . . keule" (below)

breast	. . . brust
leg	. . . keule
liver	. . . leber
tenderloin	. . . lende
kidney	. . . niere

rib	. . . rippe
Meat patty	Frikadelle
Meat loaf	Hackbraten
Ham	Schinken

Game and Poultry

Duck	Ente
Pheasant	Fasan
Chicken	Hähnchen (Huhn)
Deer	Hirsch
Rabbit	Kaninchen
Venison	Reh
Pigeon	Taube
Turkey	Truthahn
Quail	Wachtel

Vegetables

Eggplant	Aubergine
Cauliflower	Blumenkohl
Beans	Bohnen
green	*grüne*
white	*weiße*
Peas	Erbsen
Cucumber	Gurke
Cabbage	Kohl
Lettuce	Kopfsalat
Asparagus, peas and carrots	Leipziger Allerlei
Corn	Mais
Carrots	Mohrrüben
Peppers	Paprika
Mushrooms	Pilze
Celery	Sellerie
Asparagus (tips)	Spargel(spitzen)
Tomatoes	Tomaten
Onions	Zwiebeln

Condiments

Vinegar	Essig
Garlic	Knoblauch
Horseradish	Meerettich
Oil	Öl
Mustard	Senf
Artificial sweetener	Süßstoff
Cinnamon	Zimt
Sugar	Zucker
Salt	Salz

Cheese

Mild	Allgäuer Käse, Altenburger (goat cheese), Appenzeller, Greyerzer, Hüttenkäse (cottage cheese), Quark, Räucherkäse (smoked cheese), Sahnekäse (creamy), Tilsiter, Ziegekäse (goat cheese).
Sharp	Handkäse, Harzer Käse, Limburger.
curd	frisch
hard	hart
mild	mild

Fruits

Apple	Apfel
Orange	Apfelsine
Apricot	Aprikose
Blueberry	Blaubeere
Strawberry	Erdbeere
Raspberry	Himbeere
Cherry	Kirsche
Grapefruit	Pampelmuse
Raisin	Rosine
Grape	Weintraube
Banana	Banane
Pear	Birne

Drinks

with/without ice	mit/ohne Eis
with/without water	mit/ohne Wasser
straight	pur
brandy	. . . geist
liqueur	. . . likör
Mulled claret	Glühwein
Caraway-flavored liquor	Kümmel
Fruit brandy	Obstler

When ordering a Martini, you have to specify "gin (vodka) and vermouth," otherwise you will be given a vermouth (Martini & Rossi).

Beer and Wine

non-alcoholic	Alkoholfrei
A dark beer	Ein Dunkles
A light beer	Ein Helles
A mug (one quart)	Eine Maß
Draught	Vom Faß
Dark, bitter, high hops content	Altbier
Strong, high alcohol content	Bockbier (Doppelbock, Märzen)

Wheat beer with yeast	Hefeweizen
Light beer, strong hops aroma	Pils(ener)
Wheat beer	Weizen(bier)
Light beer and lemonade	Radlermaß
Wines	Wein
Rosé wine	Rosëwein
Red wine	Rotwein
White wine and mineral water	Schorle
Sparkling wine	Sekt
White wine	Weißwein
dry	herb
light	leicht
sweet	süß
dry	trocken
full-bodied	vollmundig

Non-alcoholic Drinks

Coffee	Kaffee
decaffeinated	*koffeinfrei*
with cream/sugar	*mit Milch/Zucker*
black	*schwarz*
Mineral water	Mineralwasser
carbonated/non-carbonated	*mit/ohne Kohlensäure*
juice	. . . saft
(hot) Chocolate	(heiße) Schokolade
Tea	Tee
iced tea	*Eistee*
herb tea	*Kräutertee*
with cream/lemon	*mit Milch/Zitrone*

INDEX

A

B

C

H

I

J

N

O

S

V

W

Y

Z

PHOTO CREDITS

Cover Photo (Dinkelsbuhl Annual Children's Festival): Robert Harding World Imagery. F8, *Frank Lukasseck/age fotostock*. F9 (left), *Corbis*. F9 (right), *Walter Bibikow/viestiphoto.com*. F10, *Atlantide S.N.C./age fotostock*. F11 (left), *Corbis*. F11 (right), *Corbis*. F12, *Martin Siepmann/age fotostock*. F13 (left), *Alan Copson/age fotostock*. F13 (right), *Martin Rugner/age fotostock*. F16, *Martin Siepmann/age fotostock*. F17, *Kaczmarcz/viestiphoto.com*. F18, *Joe Viesti/viestiphoto.com*. F20, *G. Schiffmann/ASA*. F21 (left), *Walter Bibikow/viestiphoto.com*. F21 (right), *Picture Finders/age fotostock*. F26, *Martin Siepmann/age fotostock*. F27 (left), *Kunst & Scheidulin/age fotostock*. F27 (right), *Martin Siepmann/age fotostock*. F28, *Joe Viesti/viestiphoto.com*.

NOTES

ABOUT OUR WRITERS

Kerry Brady was born in St. Louis, Missouri, and now lives in Wiesbaden. After working at the German Wine Information Bureau in New York, she moved to Germany in 1981 to coordinate the activities of the European and overseas press services of the German Wine Institute, Mainz. Today she runs Fine Lines, a public relations agency specializing in wine, food, and travel. Her latest books are *The Hungry Traveler: Germany,* and *A Traveller's Wine Guide to Germany.*

Uli Ehrhardt, a native German, has had a long career in the travel and tourism fields. He began as an interpreter and travel consultant in the United States and then for 20 years served as director of the State Tourist Board Bodensee–Oberschwaben (Lake Constance–Upper Swabia). He now makes his home in the city of Ulm as a tourism consultant, writer, and teacher at a state college for tourism.

Christina Knight, a former Fodor's editor, spent years editing guides to Germany before gathering up her notes and moving to Berlin. She currently writes for the city's English-language monthly, the *Ex-Berliner,* and other publications.

Heather Phibbs moved to Frankfurt in early 2002, pursuing a long-held desire to live in Europe. A native of Richmond, Virginia, she studied journalism at the University of North Carolina. She has also lived in Washington, D.C., South Carolina, New York City, and Sydney, Australia. Heather works as an advertising copywriter and freelance travel writer.

Marton Radkai is a native New Yorker of Bavarian-Hungarian descent and lives in Munich. Since 1985 he has worked as a travel photographer, translator, editor, and writer for radio and print media in Germany and Austria.

Jürgen Scheunemann grew up in Hamburg and fell in love with Berlin 15 years ago. He has written, published, and translated several history and travel books on U.S. and German cities, including *Fodor's Berlin,* First Edition (2002), and has been an editor at Berlin's leading daily, *Der Tagesspiegel,* and an associate producer for BBC Television. Today his award-winning articles are also published in U.S. magazines such as *Hemispheres.*

Ted Shoemaker settled in Germany more than 40 years ago when, as a U.S. Army officer, he married a German. He has been editor of three English-language magazines in Germany and a correspondent for many American publications. He lives in Frankfurt.

Kevin White is a native of California who has spent much of the last ten years working overseas, finally settling in Munich in 1999 as a freelance translator, writer and editor for a variety of publications and agencies.